PENGUIN REFERENCE BOOKS

## THE PENGUIN
# FRENCH DICTIONARY

Raymond Escoffey was born in 1923 in Neuchâtel, Switzerland. He was educated at Haberdasher's Aske's Hampstead School and at Cambridge University, where he gained a First Class Honours degree in Modern and Medieval Languages. He also has a Diploma in Education. He taught modern languages at Dulwich College from 1945 to 1954. Following this he was modern languages programme producer in the Schools Broadcasting Department of the BBC and subsequently executive producer. In 1982 he retired from the BBC to become a freelance writer. He writes scripts for radio and television schools language programmes in French and English in Great Britain and the German Federal Republic, where he also directs programmes. He is an awarder and examiner in French for Oxford and Cambridge Schools Examination Board.

Merlin Thomas was born in 1920 and educated at Taunton School, Somerset, and New College, Oxford. Following a brief period in the army from 1943 to 1945 he returned to New College, first as lecturer and, from 1953, as Fellow and Tutor in French. His publications include editions of Anouilh's *L'Alouette* and Giraudoux's *Électre* (both in collaboration with Simon Lee) and *Louis-Ferdinand Céline* (1979); and he is co-editor (with Professor W.D. Howarth) of *Molière: Stage and Study*. He has also published articles on Rabelais, Molière and Anouilh. He is engaged at present on a general book on the French novel from Laclos to Proust. Dr Thomas is a senior member of the Oxford University Dramatic Society and he has directed at the Oxford Playhouse plays by Shakespeare and, in French, works by Corneille, Molière, Racine and Beaumarchais.

# THE PENGUIN
# FRENCH DICTIONARY

## COMPILED BY MERLIN THOMAS
## AND RAYMOND ESCOFFEY

PENGUIN BOOKS

Penguin Books Ltd, Harmondsworth, Middlesex, England
Viking Penguin Inc., 40 West 23rd Street, New York, New York 10010, U.S.A.
Penguin Books Australia Ltd, Ringwood, Victoria, Australia
Penguin Books Canada Limited, 2801 John Street, Markham, Ontario, Canada L3R 1B4
Penguin Books (N.Z.) Ltd, 182–190 Wairau Road, Auckland 10, New Zealand

First published 1985
Reprinted 1986, 1987

Printed and bound in Great Britain by
Cox & Wyman Ltd, Reading

# CONTENTS

# CONTENTS

# INTRODUCTION

All dictionaries, since those early miracles in the sixteenth century, rely greatly on their predecessors. We have taken as ultimate arbiters the various Oxford dictionaries on the English side, the *Grand* and *Petit Robert* dictionaries on the French side, with occasional reference to *Littré*, and only very rarely indeed have we challenged their authority. We have also used, as a guide for the selection of words in a dictionary of this size, G.N. Garmonsway's *Penguin English Dictionary*.

The *Penguin French Dictionary* sets out to provide a useful and manageable guide to the present state of the vocabulary of French and English languages, and also to that of the literary languages from about 1800. This means that many slang and colloquial words are included, as are also a number of so-called 'obscene' words – preceded by the indication *vulg* – which are now to be found in the written as well as in the spoken languages. In a dictionary of this size there clearly have to be limits when it comes to technical vocabularies, but we have sought to provide as large as possible a range of useful terms in domains such as natural history, the sciences, the law, sport, motoring, seafaring, politics etc. Words common in American are also given (though, to save space, words spelt slightly differently in American – e.g. *theater* instead of *theatre* – are not normally separately included), preceded by the indication *US*. However, many American words have passed firmly into at least the *spoken* English language: conservative English readers may be surprised in some cases that these are *not* noted as *US*.

Again in order to save space in what is essentially a reading/translating dictionary, no indications about pronunciation are given. (No one, we feel, except perhaps the occasional trained phonetician, ever acquired a convincing accent in a foreign language from a dictionary.)

## Introduction

A brief summary of certain points of *French* grammar follows this Introduction. There is no parallel summary of *English* grammar, but, apart from this, the dictionary is also designed to help French students of the English language.

## *Layout and conventions*

Words are listed in alphabetical order. Inside each entry, alternative synonymous translations are separated by *commas*, whereas *semi-colons* separate different meanings. Where phrases are given within an entry (and we have tried to give as many as possible), the head-word is represented by a tilde ( ~ ). The order in which phrases are given is as follows. First come phrases which begin with the head-word. The alphabetical order of these phrases depends on the letter immediately following the head-word: e.g. in the entry (English–French) **party** the order of such phrases is ' ~ **line** ligne partagée; ~ **politics** politique *f* de partis; ~ **wall** mur mitoyen'. Then come phrases which do *not* begin with the head-word. They follow obvious alphabetical order (examples again taken from the English–French entry **party**) thus: 'a third ~ un tiers; **be a small** ~ être peu nombreux; **be no** ~ **to sth** ne pas s'associer à qch.' Homonyms with major semantic differences are indicated by separate head-words preceded by a numeral 1, 2, etc:

    [1]**vice** *n* vice *m*; (trait) défaut *m*
    [2]**vice** *n* (tool) étau *m*
    [3]**vice** *prep* à la place de

Adverbs formed *regularly* (see the grammatical summary below) in either French or English are usually omitted, unless there is some special reason for their inclusion. Genders are shown for nouns in French – *nm*, *nf* – but if *no* gender indication is given it means that the word can be both masculine and feminine – e.g. '**dactylo(graphe)** *n* typist'. If it differs from the masculine form the feminine form of a noun is shown as part of the head-word, thus – '**défendeur -eresse** *n leg* defendant'. Plurals of nouns and compound nouns which do not conform to the 'regular' pattern indicated below in the grammatical summary are shown. Adjectives which in the feminine and the plural do not conform to the 'regular' pattern indicated below in the grammatical section are also shown.

As far as possible we have of course sought to give *translations* of both French and English words and phrases rather than *descriptions*. From time to time, however, descriptive entries are unavoidable, e.g. '**barrière de dégel** barrier on road to protect surface during thaw'. Sometimes an *equivalent* is provided, preceded by an equals sign, e.g. '**arpent** *nm ar* = (nearly) acre'.

Both languages are of course changing fast, especially in spoken usage. This is most clearly seen in the use of abbreviations such as *vulg, sl* and *coll*. Only a few years ago, most of the words we list as *vulg* would not have been printed in ordinary dictionaries in either language. A number of these now seem in some usages no more than *sl*, e.g. '**con** *nm* . . . fool', or '**ball** *n* . . . *sl* ~**s!** conneries!'. The distinction between *sl* and *coll* is often very hard to draw: our decisions on this have been along the following lines: *sl* indicates a term certainly unacceptable in the formal written languages, and also in formal speech, whereas *coll* suggests a term not really acceptable in the formal written languages, but already very common in the spoken languages.

Two other abbreviations need brief comment – *ar* and *obs*. Our principle has been to use *ar* for words that have an out-dated flavour – e.g. '**forsooth** *adv ar+joc* en vérité' – and *obs* for words likely in time to disappear from current usage – e.g. '**shilling** *n obs* shilling *m*'. We know this to be a dangerous area: the French word **sou** is still very alive, and we have not yet heard of anyone threatening to cut off his heir with 5 p. . . .

Bracketed Roman numerals after certain *verb* head-words in the French–English section refer to the verb section of the grammatical summary – e.g. '**déjeter** *vt* (5)'.

---

Where the only necessary translation of a French word is an English word of identical spelling (except for accents) – e.g. **déformation** (French), **deformation** (English) – the word is *omitted* from the French–English section, allowing space for further entries. Accents and genders, where appropriate, are given in the English–French section.

# LIST OF ABBREVIATIONS

| | | | | | |
|---|---|---|---|---|---|
| *abbr* | abbreviation | *econ* | economics | *log* | logic |
| *adj* | adjective | *eg* | for example | | |
| *adv* | adverb | *elect* | electricity | *m* | masculine |
| *aer* | aeronautics | *eng* | engineering | *magn* | magnetism |
| *agr* | agriculture | *ent* | entomology | *math* | mathematics |
| *anat* | anatomical | *esp* | especially | *mech* | mechanics |
| *anthrop* | anthropology | *euph* | euphemistic | *med* | medical |
| *antiq* | antiquity | | | *met* | metaphysics |
| *ar* | archaic | *f* | feminine | *metal* | metallurgy |
| *arch* | archaeology | *fig* | figurative(ly) | *meteor* | meteorology |
| *archi* | architecture | *Fr* | French | *mil* | military |
| *art* | article | *fut* | future | *min* | mineralogy |
| *arts* | in the arts | | | *mot* | motoring |
| *astrol* | astrology | *geneal* | genealogy | *mus* | music |
| *astron* | astronomy | *geog* | geography | *myth* | mythology |
| *aux* | auxiliary | *geol* | geology | | |
| | | *geom* | geometry | *n* | noun |
| *bibl* | biblical | *gramm* | grammar | *naut* | nautical |
| *bioch* | biochemistry | | | *neg* | negative |
| *biol* | biology | *her* | heraldry | *neut* | neuter |
| *bot* | botany | *hist* | history, his- | *nom* | nominative |
| *bui* | building | | torical | *num* | numeral |
| | | *hort* | horticulture | | |
| *cap* | capital letter | | | *obs* | obsolete |
| *carp* | carpentry | *ie* | that is | *opp* | opposite |
| *cer* | ceramics | *imper* | imperative | *opt* | optics |
| *chem* | chemistry | *impers* | impersonal | *orig* | originally |
| *cin* | cinema | *incl* | including | *orni* | ornithology |
| *coll* | colloquial | *ind* | indicative | | |
| *collect* | collective | *indef* | indefinite | *path* | pathology |
| *comm* | commerce | *infin* | infinitive | *pej* | pejorative |
| *comp* | comparative | *inter* | interrogative | *pers* | person |
| *conj* | conjunction | *interj* | interjection | *phil* | philology |
| *cont* | contemptuous | *invar* | invariable | *philos* | philosophy |
| *cul* | culinary | *iron* | ironical | *phon* | phonetics |
| | | | | *phot* | photography |
| *def* | definite | *joc* | jocular | *phr* | phrase |
| *dem* | demonstrative | | | *phys* | physics |
| *dial* | dialect | *lang* | language | *physiol* | physiology |
| *dim* | diminutive | *leg* | legal | *pl* | plural |
| | | *lit* | literary | *poet* | poetic(al) |
| *eccles* | ecclesiastical | *liturg* | liturgical | *pol* | politics |

# List of Abbreviations

| | | | | | |
|---|---|---|---|---|---|
| *p part* | past participle | *Rom* | Roman | *typ* | typography |
| *pref* | prefix | | | | |
| *prep* | preposition | *sci* | science | *US* | United States |
| *pres* | present | *Scots* | Scots, Scottish | *usu* | usually |
| *pres part* | present participle | *sing* | singular | | |
| | | *sl* | slang | *v aux* | auxiliary verb |
| *print* | printing | *sp* | sport | *vi* | intransitive verb |
| *pron* | pronoun | *subj* | subjunctive | | |
| *pros* | prosody | *superl* | superlative | *v refl* | reflexive verb |
| *psych* | psychology | *surg* | surgery | *vt* | transitive verb |
| | | | | *vet* | veterinary |
| *rad* | radio | *tel* | telegraphy | *vulg* | vulgar |
| *refl* | reflexive | *theat* | of the theatre | | |
| *rel* | relative | *theol* | theology | *zool* | zoology |
| *rhet* | rhetoric(al) | *TV* | television | | |
| *RC* | Roman Catholic | | | | |

# LISTE DES ABRÉVIATIONS

Dans la plupart des cas le lecteur français comprendra tout de suite pourquoi les abréviations – calquées sur l'anglais – sont établies comme elles le sont. Dans les cas où une abréviation est liée uniquement à un mot ou à une phrase anglais, le mot ou la phrase anglais est donné en parenthèse.

| | | | | | |
|---|---|---|---|---|---|
| *abbr* | abréviation | *comm* | commerce | *her* | héraldique |
| *adj* | adjectif | *comp* | comparatif | *hist* | historique, |
| *adv* | adverbe | *conj* | conjonction | | histoire |
| *aer* | aéronautique | *cont* | méprisant | *hort* | horticulture |
| *agr* | agriculture | | [con- | | |
| *anat* | anatomique | | temptuous] | *ie* | c'est à dire [id |
| *anthrop* | anthropologie | *cul* | culinaire | | est] |
| *antiq* | antiquité | | | *imper* | impératif |
| *ar* | archaïque | *def* | défini | *impers* | impersonnel |
| *arch* | archéologie | *dem* | démonstratif | *ind* | indicatif |
| *archi* | architecture | *dial* | dialecte | *indef* | indéfini |
| *art* | article | *dim* | diminutif | *infin* | infinitif |
| *arts* | langage des | | | *inter* | interrogatif |
| | arts | *eccles* | ecclésiastique | *interj* | interjection |
| *astrol* | astrologie | *econ* | économie | *invar* | invariable |
| *astrom* | astronomie | *eg* | par exemple | *iron* | ironique |
| *aux* | auxiliaire | | [exempli | | |
| | | | gratia] | *joc* | facétieux |
| *bibl* | biblique | *elect* | électricité | | [jocular] |
| *bioch* | biochimie | *eng* | ingénierie [en- | | |
| *biol* | biologie | | gineering] | *lang* | langage |
| *bot* | botanique | *ent* | entomologie | *leg* | droit [legal] |
| *bui* | construction | *esp* | spécialement | *lit* | littéraire |
| | (bâtiments) | | [especially] | *liturg* | liturgique |
| | [building] | *euph* | euphémique | *log* | logique |
| *cap* | majuscule | *f* | féminin | *m* | masculin |
| | [capital] | *fig* | figuré | *magn* | magnétique |
| *carp* | menuiserie | *Fr* | français | *math* | mathématique |
| | [carpentry] | *fut* | futur | *mech* | mécanique |
| *cer* | céramique | | | *med* | médical |
| *chem* | chimie | *geneal* | généalogie | *met* | métaphysique |
| *cin* | cinéma | *geog* | géographie | *metal* | métallurgie |
| *coll* | familier [col- | *geol* | géologie | *meteor* | météorologie |
| | loquial] | *geom* | géométrie | *mil* | militaire |
| *collect* | collectif | *gramm* | grammaire | *min* | minéralogie |

xii

| | | | |
|---|---|---|---|
| *mot* | automobile [motoring] | *physiol* | physiologie |
| *mus* | musique | *pl* | pluriel |
| *myth* | mythologie | *poet* | poétique |
| *n* | nom | *pol* | politique |
| *naut* | nautique | *p part* | participe passé |
| *neg* | négatif | *pref* | préfixe |
| *neut* | neutre | *prep* | préposition |
| *nom* | nominatif | *pres* | présent |
| *num* | nombre [numeral] | *pres part* | participe présent |
| *obs* | vieux, vieilli [obsolete] | *print* | imprimerie [printing] |
| *opp* | opposé | *pron* | pronom |
| *opt* | optique | *pros* | prosodie |
| *orig* | originalement | *psych* | psychologie |
| *orni* | ornithologie | *rad* | radio |
| *path* | pathologie | *refl* | réfléchi |
| *pej* | péjoratif | *rel* | relatif |
| *pers* | personne | *rhet* | rhétorique |
| *phil* | philologie | *RC* | Catholique [Roman Catholic] |
| *philos* | philosophie | *Rom* | romain |
| *phon* | phonétique | *sci* | scientifique |
| *phot* | photographie | *sing* | singulier |
| *phr* | phrase | *sl* | argot [slang] |
| *phys* | physique | *sp* | sport |

| | |
|---|---|
| *subj* | subjonctif |
| *superl* | superlatif |
| *surg* | chirurgie [surgery] |
| *tel* | télégraphie |
| *theat* | théâtre |
| *theol* | théologie |
| *TV* | télévision |
| *typ* | typographie |
| *US* | américain [United States] |
| *usu* | normalement [usually] |
| *v aux* | verbe auxiliaire |
| *vi* | verbe intransitif |
| *v refl* | verbe réfléchi |
| *vt* | verbe transitif |
| *vet* | vétérinaire |
| *vulg* | indécent [vulgar] |
| *zool* | zoologie |

# MAIN POINTS OF FRENCH GRAMMAR

## The Article

### Definite article (the)

**le** *m*, **la** *f*, **l'** (before vowel and **h** mute), **les** *mfpl*

(of the) **du** *m*, **de la** *f*, **de l'** (before vowel and **h** mute), **des** *mfpl*

(to the) **au** *m*, **à la** *f*, **à l'** (before vowel and **h** mute), **aux** *mfpl*

Note: the definite article, in addition to its meaning of 'the', is used with nouns in a general sense e.g. **l'alcool est mauvais pour la santé, les salades sont vertes.**

### Indefinite article (a)

**un** *m*, **une** *f*, **des** *mfpl*, **de** (**d'**) after negative and often before adjective preceding a plural noun.

### Partitive article (some, any)

As for definite article (of the): all forms become **de** or **d'** after a negative, and these latter forms are also used after expressions denoting quantity (e.g. **un kilo de pommes, un verre d'eau**).

## Nouns

### Gender

Nouns are either masculine or feminine. As a rough guide, it may be said that those ending in **-e** are feminine (with the notable exception of those ending in **-isme** and nearly all in **-age**), and that most others are masculine (with the notable exception of those ending in **-ion** and **-té**).

Masculine nouns which can also have a feminine meaning normally add **-e**, e.g. **ami**, **amie**. Exceptions to this are masculine nouns in **-iste**, which remain unaltered, in **-er**, which change to **-ère**, **-on**, **-ien**, **-eur**, and **-ateur**, which change to **-onne**, **-ienne**, **-euse** and **-atrice**. Some conform to none of these patterns, e.g. **acteur**, **actrice**; **maître**, **maîtresse**; **mari**, **femme**; **neveu**, **nièce**; **roi**, **reine**; and **cheval**, **jument**.

### Plural

The plural is normally formed by adding **-s** to the singular form. Nouns ending in **-s**, **-x** and **-z** do not change.

Nouns ending in **-au** and **-eu** add **-x** (except **bleu** *m*), as do **bijou**, **chou**, **caillou**, **genou**, **hibou**, and **pou**. Those ending in **-al** change to **-aux**. Those ending in **-ail** take **-s**, sometimes **-aux**, e.g. **détails**, **détails**; **travail**, **travaux**. There are a few totally irregular ones, e.g. **ciel**, **cieux**; **œil**, **yeux**; **bal**, **bals**.

### Compound nouns

When written as one word, compound nouns normally take **-s**. Note the exceptions **bonhomme**, **bonshommes**; **gentilhomme**, **gentilshommes**.

Hyphened compound nouns vary. The plural of any which take anything other than -s at the end (or already end in -s, -x or -z in the singular), e.g. **avant-poste**, **avant-postes**, will be indicated in the body of the dictionary, e.g. **chou-fleur** *nm* (*pl* **choux-fleurs**).

## *Adjectives*

### Pcsition

Adjectives normally follow the noun, although meaning and considerations of style or emphasis can require them to precede. A few common adjectives normally precede the noun, e.g. **bon, meilleur, beau, grand, petit, mauvais, vieux**.

### Agreement

Adjectives agree with the noun they qualify in number and gender. The feminine is normally formed by adding **-e** to the masculine form, e.g. **grand, grande**, unless this already ends in **-e**.

The following are important variations:

| | |
|---|---|
| **-if -ive** | e.g. **vif, vive** |
| **-eux -euse** | e.g. **peureux, peureuse** |
| **-er -ère** | e.g. **amer, amère** |
| **-as -asse** | e.g. **bas, basse** |
| **-el -elle** | e.g. **formel, formelle** |
| **-eil -eille** | e.g. **pareil, pareille** |
| **-en -enne** | e.g. **ancien, ancienne** |
| **-on -onne** | e.g. **bon, bonne** |
| **-et -ète** or **-ette** | e.g. **complet, complète aigrelet, aigrelette** |
| **-ic -ique** | e.g. **public, publique** |
| **-eur -euse** | e.g. **moqueur, moqueuse** |

Some are totally irregular, e.g. **doux, douce; vieux, vieille; grec, grecque; meilleur, meilleure; favori, favorite; blanc, blanche; sec, sèche; fou, folle**.

A few adjectives have two masculine forms, as follows (the second form being used before a vowel or **h** mute): **vieux, vieil; beau, bel; nouveau, nouvel; fou, fol; mou, mol**.

A very few have no feminine form, e.g. **chic**, and nouns used as adjectives, especially of colour.

### Plural

The general rule, as for nouns, is to add -s to the singular form.

Adjectives ending in -s, -x and -z are unchanged.

Those ending in **-al** form their plural in **-aux** (exceptions **banal, fatal, final, glacial, natal, naval**, which all take -s), e.g. **loyal, loyaux**.

**Tout** becomes **tous** in the plural.

### Comparative

The comparative is formed by using **plus** (more) before the adjective, e.g. **grand, plus grand**. The following are exceptions: **bon, meilleur; mauvais, pire** (or **plus mauvais**); **petit, moindre** (only when not denoting size).

The following words are used in comparisons: **plus** (more), **aussi** (as, so), **si** (so), **moins** (less) and the second part of the comparison is introduced by **que** (as, than).

**Aussi . . . que** renders as . . . as,
**pas si . . . que** not so . . . as.

In comparisons of quantity **plus, moins, autant** etc., are followed by **de** or **d'**.

### Superlative

The appropriate form of the article is used with the comparative form, e.g. **la plus belle voiture, le film le plus intéressant**.

# Main Points of French Grammar

Note that after a superlative 'in' is normally rendered by **de**, e.g. **le plus grand du monde**, the biggest in the world.

## Numeral adjectives (cardinal)

**Un, deux, trois, quatre, cinq, six, sept, huit, neuf, dix, onze, douze, treize, quatorze, quinze, seize, dix-sept, dix-huit, dix-neuf, vingt, vingt et un, vingt-deux, trente, quarante, cinquante, soixante, soixante-dix, soixante et onze, quatre-vingts, quatre-vingt-dix, quatre-vingt-onze, cent, cent un, deux cents, mille, deux mille, deux mille un, un million.**

Nearly all numerals are invariable.

The **un** of **vingt et un**, etc., agrees in the feminine, e.g. **vingt et une maisons**.

**Quatre-vingts** drops the **-s** in compounds, e.g. **quatre-vingt-onze**. Similarly **cents**, when followed by another number, drops its plural **-s**.

**Mille** is invariable (the form **mil** is used in dates).

**Un million**, a million, is a noun, not an adjective.

## Numeral adjective (ordinal)

Ordinal numeral adjectives are formed by adding **-ième** to the cardinal number (note the spellings **cinquième** and **neuvième**).

The exception is **premier, première** (first) and **second** (second), which is less used than the form **deuxième**.

## Fractions

$\frac{1}{2}$ **une moitié**, $\frac{1}{3}$ **un tiers**, $\frac{1}{4}$ **un quart**.

For other fractions, the ordinal is used, e.g. $\frac{3}{11}$ **trois onzièmes**, $\frac{1}{50}$ **un cinquantième**.

Note: Cardinal numbers are used instead of ordinals, with the exception of **premier**, in:

(a) Titles of sovereigns, e.g. **Élisabeth II (Deux)**.

(b) Dates, e.g. **le 3 (trois) mars**.

## Demonstrative adjectives

The equivalent of 'this' and 'that' is normally **ce** $m$ **cet** $m$ (before a vowel or **h** mute), **cette** $f$, **ces** $mfpl$. Differentiation between 'this' and 'that' is conveyed by the addition of **-ci** or **-là** after the noun, e.g. **ce crayon-ci, cette lampe-là**.

## Possessive adjectives

| | |
|---|---|
| My | **mon** $m$, **ma** $f$, **mon** $f$ (before vowel or **h** mute), **mes** $mfpl$ |
| Your | (familiar form) **ton** $m$, **ta** $f$, **ton** $f$ (before vowel or **h** mute), **tes** $mfpl$ <br> **votre, vos** $pl$ |
| His, its | **son** $m$, **sa** $f$, **son** $f$ (before vowel or **h** mute), **ses** $pl$ |
| Our | **notre, nos** $pl$ |
| Their | **leur** $mf$, **leurs** $pl$ |

Examples: **mon frère, mon amie, sa jupe, tes livres, son toit, leurs amies.**

## Interrogative adjective

Which: **quel** $m$, **quelle** $f$, **quels** $mpl$, **quelles** $fpl$

Note: **quel** is also used to convey the exclamatory what a . . .!, e.g. **Quel beau paysage!**

---

# Pronouns

## Personal subject pronouns

**Je, tu, il, elle, nous, vous, ils, elles.**

Note: **tu** and its related words and forms are used when addressing relatives, close friends and children and also normally among young people.

## Personal object pronouns

Direct (accusative): **me, te, le, la, nous, vous, les**

Indirect (dative): **me, te, lui, y** (referring to anything but persons), **nous, vous, leur, y** (referring to anything but persons)

**En** (of it or of them) is not used to refer to persons. Meaning some or any, it can refer to both persons and things. The following table indicates the order of object pronouns before the verb.

| me | | | | |
| te | le | lui | | |
| nous | la | leur | y | en |
| vous | les | | | |

e.g. **Elle nous en offre.**

**Je vous y ai vu.**

But note that object pronouns follow the imperative affirmative, e.g. **mangez-les**. **Moi** is used instead of **me**, e.g. **regardez-moi**, but note **donnez-m'en**.

When two pronouns follow an imperative the order is as in English, e.g. **donnez-le-moi, passe-le-lui**.

Reflexive pronouns (accusative and dative)

**me, te, se, nous, vous, se.**

Stressed pronouns

**moi, toi, lui, elle, nous, vous, eux, elles** and the third person singular reflexive **soi.**

These forms are mainly used:

(a) after prepositions, e.g. **avec moi**

(b) for emphasis, e.g. **toi, tu ne fais rien**

(c) in double subjects, e.g. **eux et leur mère**

(d) to indicate possession, after **être**, e.g. **cette voiture est à lui**

(e) when the pronoun stands alone, e.g. **Qui est-ce? – Moi.**

The form **soi** is used with reference to the indefinite subjects **on** and **il** (impersonal), e.g. **il faut penser à soi, on s'occupe de soi**

(f) with **c'est** and **ce sont**, e.g. **c'est lui, ce sont eux**

Demonstrative pronouns

This one: **celui-ci** *m*, **celle-ci** *f*; that one: **celui-là** *m*, **celle-là** *f*; these: **ceux-ci** *mpl*, **celles-ci** *fpl*; those: **ceux-là** *mpl*, **celles-là** *fpl*.

**Ceci** and **cela (ça)** (this and that) are invariable and refer to things, facts etc.

The unstressed form **ce** is used as subject to the verb **être**, e.g. **c'est possible**. Where **être** has as its complement a pronoun in the third person plural it often becomes plural, e.g. **c'est lui, ce sont eux**.

**Ce** also frequently occurs as antecedent to a relative pronoun, e.g. **Ce que vous me dites n'a aucun sens**.

**Celui** *m* (the one, he, him), **celle** *f* (the one, she, her) and the plural forms **ceux**, **celles** (those) are followed:

(a) by a relative clause, e.g. **J'ai vu celui que vous m'avez décrit**.

(b) by **de**, e.g. **Donnez-moi celle de votre frère**.

Possessive pronouns

**Le mien, la mienne, les miens, les miennes** – mine

**Le tien, la tienne, les tiens, les tiennes** – yours (thine)

**Le sien, la sienne, les siens, les siennes** – his, hers

**Le nôtre, la nôtre, les nôtres** – ours

**Le vôtre, la vôtre, les vôtres** – yours

**Le leur, la leur, les leurs** – theirs

The predicative mine, his, etc. is normally expressed by **à moi, à lui**, etc., e.g. **ce livre est à moi, cette serviette est à lui**.

Interrogative pronouns

| | |
| --- | --- |
| Who, whom | **qui**, e.g. **Qui vous l'a dit? Qui avez-vous vu?** The compound forms **qui est-ce qui** (who) and **qui est-ce que** (whom) are also used, generally in conversation. |
| What | **qu'est-ce qui** (subject), e.g. **Qu'est-ce qui se passe?** **que** or **qu'est-ce que** (object), e.g. **Que faites-vous là?** **quoi** (after a preposition, alone and before |

partitive **de**), e.g.
**À quoi rêves-tu?,
Quoi? Que dis-tu?,
Quoi de neuf?**

To whom     **à qui**, e.g. **l'enfant
à qui j'ai donné
cela**

Whose, of whom,     **dont**, e.g. **la chose**
of which     **dont je parle, le
garçon dont j'ai vu
les devoirs**

Relative pronouns

Who, which (subject)     **qui**, e.g. **la table qui
se trouve dans le
salon**

Note: which, after a preposition, is
normally translated by **lequel** (except
where **dont** is appropriate), e.g. **la table
sur laquelle j'ai posé le livre, les maisons
derrière lesquelles passe le train.**

Whom, which (object)     **que**, e.g. **le monsieur que nous
avons vu**

## Adverbs

Adverbs are formed in most cases by
adding **-ment** to the feminine singular
form of the adjective, e.g. **heureusement**.

Adjectives in **-ant** and **-ent** form their
adverbs with the endings **-amment** and
**-emment**, e.g. **indépendamment,
patiemment**.

In a few cases the **-e** of the feminine
becomes **-é**, e.g. **profondément**.

In cases where the masculine ends in a
vowel, the feminine **-e** is dropped, e.g.
**hardiment**.

Certain irregularities to the above
rules do occur, e.g. **bon, bien; meilleur,
mieux; mauvais, mal; pire, pis; petit,
peu; moindre, moins; assidu,
assidûment; gentil, gentiment; gai,
gaîment (gaiement); lent, lentement;
présent, présentement**.

## Negation

A negation which accompanies a verb
has two components, the first, **ne**,
coming before the verb, the latter after,
e.g. **je ne vois rien, il ne dort jamais**.

In the case of compound tenses the
second component comes immediately
after the auxiliary, e.g. **nous n'avons
rien vu**. The exception is **ne . . . personne**, e.g. **ils n'ont rencontré personne**.

Where a negation stands on its own
without a verb, the **ne** is not used, e.g.
**Vient-il quelquefois chez vous? –
Jamais**.

## Verbs

There are four regular conjugations.

Compound tenses are formed with
**avoir** or **être** and the past
participle. **Avoir** is used in all cases
except for reflexive verbs and a number
of common verbs, mostly indicating

movement or change of state: **aller,
arriver, décéder, devenir, échoir, éclore,
entrer, mourir, naître, partir,
re-partir, rentrer, rester, retourner,
sortir, tomber, venir**.

The past participle appears mostly in

the masculine singular form. In cases of verbs conjugated with **être** in compound tenses it agrees with the subject. In reflexive verbs it agrees with the reflexive pronoun in all cases where the latter is the direct object of the verb. In verbs whose compound tenses are conjugated with **avoir** it agrees with the direct object whenever this precedes it (e.g. **nous les avons vus**). As an adjective or when used to form the passive, it agrees with the noun or pronoun to which it refers (e.g. **elle a été achetée, ils sont cassés**).

Below is set out the conjugation of regular verbs followed by a list of irregular verbs with their particular irregularities. The latter are each given a number. These numbers are given in the body of the dictionary and refer users to the verb in the table to whose type it conforms.

### Regular conjugation in -er

#### PORTER, carry

INDICATIVE

| Present | Future | Imperfect | Past definite |
|---|---|---|---|
| je porte | je porterai | je portais | je portai |
| tu portes | tu porteras | tu portais | tu portas |
| il porte | il portera | il portait | il porta |
| nous portons | nous porterons | nous portions | nous portâmes |
| vous portez | vous porterez | vous portiez | vous portâtes |
| ils portent | ils porteront | ils portaient | ils portèrent |

| Perfect | Pluperfect | Future perfect | Past anterior |
|---|---|---|---|
| j'ai porté | j'avais porté | j'aurai porté | j'eus porté |
| tu as porté | tu avais porté | tu auras porté | tu eus porté |
| il a porté | il avait porté | il aura porté | il eut porté |
| nous avons porté | nous avions porté | nous aurons porté | nous eûmes porté |
| vous avez porté | vous aviez porté | vous aurez porté | vous eûtes porté |
| ils ont porté | ils avaient porté | ils auront porté | ils eurent porté |

CONDITIONAL

| Present | Past |
|---|---|
| je porterais | j'aurais porté |
| tu porterais | tu aurais porté |
| il porterait | il aurait porté |
| nous porterions | nous aurions porté |
| vous porteriez | vous auriez porté |
| ils porteraient | ils auraient porté |

# Main Points of French Grammar

| Present | Imperfect | Perfect | Pluperfect |
|---------|-----------|---------|------------|
| je porte | je portasse | j'aie porté | j'eusse porté |
| tu portes | tu portasses | tu aies porté | tu eusses porté |
| il porte | il portât | il ait porté | il eût porté |
| nous portions | nous portassions | nous ayons porté | nous eussions porté |
| vous portiez | vous portassiez | vous ayez porté | vous eussiez porté |
| ils portent | ils portassent | ils aient porté | ils eussent porté |

### INFINITIVE

| Present | Past |
|---------|------|
| porter | avoir porté |

### IMPERATIVE

| Present | Past |
|---------|------|
| porte | aie porté |
| portons | ayons porté |
| portez | ayez porté |

### PARTICIPLE

| Present | Past |
|---------|------|
| portant | porté (passive) |
| | ayant porté (active) |

## Regular conjugation in -ir
## PUNIR, punish

### INDICATIVE

| Present | Future | Imperfect | Past definite |
|---------|--------|-----------|---------------|
| je punis | je punirai | je punissais | je punis |
| tu punis | tu puniras | tu punissais | tu punis |
| il punit | il punira | il punissait | il punit |
| nous punissons | nous punirons | nous punissions | nous punîmes |
| vous punissez | vous punirez | vous punissiez | vous punîtes |
| ils punissent | ils puniront | ils punissaient | ils punirent |

# Main Points of French Grammar

| *Perfect* | *Pluperfect* | *Future perfect* | *Past anterior* |
|---|---|---|---|
| j'ai puni | j'avais puni | j'aurai puni | j'eus puni |
| tu as puni | tu avais puni | tu auras puni | tu eus puni |
| il a puni | il avait puni | il aura puni | il eut puni |
| nous avons puni | nous avions puni | nous aurons puni | nous eûmes puni |
| vous avez puni | vous aviez puni | vous aurez puni | vous eûtes puni |
| ils ont puni | ils avaient puni | ils auront puni | ils eurent puni |

CONDITIONAL

| *Present* | *Past* |
|---|---|
| je punirais | j'aurais puni |
| tu punirais | tu aurais puni |
| il punirait | il aurait puni |
| nous punirions | nous aurions puni |
| vous puniriez | vous auriez puni |
| ils puniraient | ils auraient puni |

SUBJUNCTIVE

| *Present* | *Imperfect* | *Perfect* | *Pluperfect* |
|---|---|---|---|
| je punisse | je punisse | j'aie puni | j'eusse puni |
| tu punisses | tu punisses | tu aies puni | tu eusses puni |
| il punisse | il punît | il ait puni | il eût puni |
| nous punissions | nous punissions | nous ayons puni | nous eussions puni |
| vous punissiez | vous punissiez | vous ayez puni | vous eussiez puni |
| ils punissent | ils punissent | ils aient puni | ils eussent puni |

INFINITIVE

| *Present* | *Past* |
|---|---|
| punir | avoir puni |

IMPERATIVE

| *Present* | *Past* |
|---|---|
| punis | aie puni |
| punissons | ayons puni |
| punissez | ayez puni |

# Main Points of French Grammar

| Present | Past |
|---------|------|
| **punissant** | **puni** (passive) |
|  | **ayant puni** (active) |

## Regular conjugation in -re
### RENDRE, give back

INDICATIVE

| Present | Future | Imperfect | Past definite |
|---------|--------|-----------|---------------|
| **je rends** | **je rendrai** | **je rendais** | **je rendis** |
| **tu rends** | **tu rendras** | **tu rendais** | **tu rendis** |
| **il rend** | **il rendra** | **il rendait** | **il rendit** |
| **nous rendons** | **nous rendrons** | **nous rendions** | **nous rendîmes** |
| **vous rendez** | **vous rendrez** | **vous rendiez** | **vous rendîtes** |
| **ils rendent** | **ils rendront** | **ils rendaient** | **ils rendirent** |

| Perfect | Pluperfect | Future perfect | Past anterior |
|---------|------------|----------------|---------------|
| **j'ai rendu** | **j'avais rendu** | **j'aurai rendu** | **j'eus rendu** |
| **tu as rendu** | **tu avais rendu** | **tu auras rendu** | **tu eus rendu** |
| **il a rendu** | **il avait rendu** | **il aura rendu** | **il eut rendu** |
| **nous avons rendu** | **nous avions rendu** | **nous aurons rendu** | **nous eûmes rendu** |
| **vous avez rendu** | **vous aviez rendu** | **vous aurez rendu** | **vous eûtes rendu** |
| **ils ont rendu** | **ils avaient rendu** | **ils auront rendu** | **ils eurent rendu** |

CONDITIONAL

| Present | Past |
|---------|------|
| **je rendrais** | **j'aurais rendu** |
| **tu rendrais** | **tu aurais rendu** |
| **il rendrait** | **il aurait rendu** |
| **nous rendrions** | **nous aurions rendu** |
| **vous rendriez** | **vous auriez rendu** |
| **ils rendraient** | **ils auraient rendu** |

SUBJUNCTIVE

| Present | Imperfect | Perfect | Pluperfect |
|---------|-----------|---------|------------|
| **je rende** | **je rendisse** | **j'aie rendu** | **j'eusse rendu** |
| **tu rendes** | **tu rendisses** | **tu aies rendu** | **tu eusses rendu** |
| **il rende** | **il rendît** | **il ait rendu** | **il eût rendu** |

| | | | |
|---|---|---|---|
| nous rendions | nous rendissions | nous ayons rendu | nous eussions rendu |
| vous rendiez | vous rendissiez | vous ayez rendu | vous eussiez rendu |
| ils rendent | ils rendissent | ils aient rendu | ils eussent rendu |

### INFINITIVE

| Present | Past |
|---|---|
| rendre | avoir rendu |

### IMPERATIVE

| Present | Past |
|---|---|
| rends | aie rendu |
| rendons | ayons rendu |
| rendez | ayez rendu |

### PARTICIPLE

| Present | Past |
|---|---|
| rendant | rendu (passive) |
| | ayant rendu (active) |

## Regular conjugation in -oir

### RECEVOIR, receive

#### INDICATIVE

| Present | Future | Imperfect | Past definite |
|---|---|---|---|
| je reçois | je recevrai | je recevais | je reçus |
| tu reçois | tu recevras | tu recevais | tu reçus |
| il reçoit | il recevra | il recevait | il reçut |
| nous recevons | nous recevrons | nous recevions | nous reçûmes |
| vous recevez | vous recevrez | vous receviez | vous reçûtes |
| ils reçoivent | ils recevront | ils recevaient | ils reçurent |

| Perfect | Pluperfect | Future perfect | Past anterior |
|---|---|---|---|
| j'ai reçu | j'avais reçu | j'aurai reçu | j'eus reçu |
| tu as reçu | tu avais reçu | tu auras reçu | tu eus reçu |
| il a reçu | il avait reçu | il aura reçu | il eut reçu |
| nous avons reçu | nous avions reçu | nous aurons reçu | nous eûmes reçu |
| vous avez reçu | vous aviez reçu | vous aurez reçu | vous eûtes reçu |
| ils ont reçu | ils avaient reçu | ils auront reçu | ils eurent reçu |

# Main Points of French Grammar

| *Present* | *Past* |
|---|---|
| je recevrais | j'aurais reçu |
| tu recevrais | tu aurais reçu |
| il recevrait | il aurait reçu |
| nous recevrions | nous aurions reçu |
| vous recevriez | vous auriez reçu |
| ils recevraient | ils auraient reçu |

SUBJUNCTIVE

| *Present* | *Imperfect* | *Perfect* | *Pluperfect* |
|---|---|---|---|
| je reçoive | je reçusse | j'aie reçu | j'eusse reçu |
| tu reçoives | tu reçusses | tu aies reçu | tu eusses reçu |
| il reçoive | il reçût | il ait reçu | il eût reçu |
| nous recevions | nous reçussions | nous ayons reçu | nous eussions reçu |
| vous receviez | vous reçussiez | vous ayez reçu | vous eussiez reçu |
| ils reçoivent | ils reçussent | ils aient reçu | ils eussent reçu |

INFINITIVE

| *Present* | *Past* |
|---|---|
| recevoir | avoir reçu |

IMPERATIVE

| *Present* | *Past* |
|---|---|
| reçois | aie reçu |
| recevons | ayons reçu |
| recevez | ayez reçu |

PARTICIPLE

| *Present* | *Past* |
|---|---|
| recevant | reçu (passive) |
| | ayant reçu (active) |

Irregular Verbs

1   AVOIR, have

INDICATIVE

| *Present* | *Future* | *Imperfect* | *Past definite* |
|---|---|---|---|
| j'ai | j'aurai | j'avais | j'eus |
| tu as | tu auras | tu avais | tu eus |
| il a | il aura | il avait | il eut |
| nous avons | nous aurons | nous avions | nous eûmes |
| vous avez | vous aurez | vous aviez | vous eûtes |
| ils ont | ils auront | ils avaient | ils eurent |

| *Perfect* | *Pluperfect* | *Future perfect* | *Past anterior* |
|---|---|---|---|
| j'ai eu | j'avais eu | j'aurai eu | j'eus eu |
| tu as eu | tu avais eu | tu auras eu | tu eus eu |
| il a eu | il avait eu | il aura eu | il eut eu |
| nous avons eu | nous avions eu | nous aurons eu | nous eûmes eu |
| vous avez eu | vous aviez eu | vous aurez eu | vous eûtes eu |
| ils ont eu | ils avaient eu | ils auront eu | ils eurent eu |

CONDITIONAL

| *Present* | *Past* |
|---|---|
| j'aurais | j'aurais eu |
| tu aurais | tu aurais eu |
| il aurait | il aurait eu |
| nous aurions | nous aurions eu |
| vous auriez | vous auriez eu |
| ils auraient | ils auraient eu |

SUBJUNCTIVE

| *Present* | *Imperfect* | *Perfect* | *Pluperfect* |
|---|---|---|---|
| j'aie | j'eusse | j'aie eu | j'eusse eu |
| tu aies | tu eusses | tu aies eu | tu eusses eu |
| il ait | il eût | il ait eu | il eût eu |
| nous ayons | nous eussions | nous ayons eu | nous eussions eu |
| vous ayez | vous eussiez | vous ayez eu | vous eussiez eu |
| ils aient | ils eussent | ils aient eu | ils eussent eu |

INFINITIVE

| Present | Past |
|---|---|
| **avoir** | **avoir eu** |

IMPERATIVE

Present

**aie**
**ayons**
**ayez**

PARTICIPLE

| Present | Past |
|---|---|
| **ayant** | **eu** (passive) |
| | **ayant eu** (active) |

## 2  ÊTRE, be

INDICATIVE

| Present | Future | Imperfect | Past definite |
|---|---|---|---|
| **je suis** | **je serai** | **j'étais** | **je fus** |
| **tu es** | **tu seras** | **tu étais** | **tu fus** |
| **il est** | **il sera** | **il était** | **il fut** |
| **nous sommes** | **nous serons** | **nous étions** | **nous fûmes** |
| **vous êtes** | **vous serez** | **vous étiez** | **vous fûtes** |
| **ils sont** | **ils seront** | **ils étaient** | **ils furent** |

| Present | Pluperfect | Future perfect | Past anterior |
|---|---|---|---|
| **j'ai été** | **j'avais été** | **j'aurai été** | **j'eus été** |
| **tu as été** | **tu avais été** | **tu auras été** | **tu eus été** |
| **il a été** | **il avait été** | **il aura été** | **il eut été** |
| **nous avons été** | **nous avions été** | **nous aurons été** | **nous eûmes été** |
| **vous avez été** | **vous aviez été** | **vous aurez été** | **vous eûtes été** |
| **ils ont été** | **ils avaient été** | **ils auront été** | **ils eurent été** |

## CONDITIONAL

| Present | Past |
|---|---|
| je serais | j'aurais été |
| tu serais | tu aurais été |
| il serait | il aurait été |
| nous serions | nous aurions été |
| vous seriez | vous auriez été |
| ils seraient | ils auraient été |

## SUBJUNCTIVE

| Present | Imperfect | Perfect | Pluperfect |
|---|---|---|---|
| je sois | je fusse | j'aie été | j'eusse été |
| tu sois | tu fusses | tu aies été | tu eusses été |
| il soit | il fût | il ait été | il eût été |
| nous soyons | nous fussions | nous ayons été | nous eussions été |
| vous soyez | vous fussiez | vous ayez été | vous eussiez été |
| ils soient | ils fussent | ils aient été | ils eussent été |

## INFINITIVE

| Present | Past |
|---|---|
| être | avoir été |

## IMPERATIVE

Present

sois
soyons
soyez

## PARTICIPLE

| Present | Past |
|---|---|
| étant | été |
|  | ayant été |

# Main Points of French Grammar

3 Verbs in -ger add e before endings in a and o, e.g. **manger, mangeais, mangeons**

4 Verbs in -cer change c to ç before endings in a and o, e.g. **menacer, menaçais, menaçons**

5 Verbs in -eler and -eter double l or t before e mute, e.g. **appeler, appelle, jeter, jette**. The following verbs are exceptions, the e before l or t changing to è: **acheter, agneler, becqueter, cacheter, celer, ciseler, congeler, corseter, déceler, dégeler, démanteler, écarteler, fureter, geler, haleter, harceler, marteler, modeler, peler, racheter, receler, regeler**, e.g. **acheter, achète**

6 Verbs having mute e or é in the penultimate syllable of the infinitive change these to è before a mute syllable (except in the future and conditional), e.g. **espérer, espère**

7 Verbs in -yer: Those ending in -oyer and -uyer change the y to i before e mute, e.g. **essuyer, essuie**. Those ending in -ayer may either keep the y or change to i before e mute. Those ending in -eyer keep the y throughout

8 **absoudre** *Pres ind* **absous, absous, absout, absolvons, absolvez, absolvent.** *Imperf* **absolvais.** *Fut* **absoudrai.** *Condit* **absoudrais.** *Imp* **absous, absolvons, absolvez.** *Pres subj* **absolve, absolvions.** *Pres part* **absolvant.** *P part* **absous, absoute.** No *p def*, no *imperf subj*

9 **abstraire** *Pres ind* **abstrais, abstrayons.** *Imperf* **abstrayais.** *Fut* **abstrairai.** *Condit* **abstrairais.** *Imp* **abstrais, abstrayons, abstrayez.** *Pres subj* **abstraie, abstrayions.** *Pres part* **abstrayant.** *P part* **abstrait.** No *p def*, no *imperf subj*

10 **accroire** Used only in *infin*, and always after **faire**

11 **advenir** Used only in third pers. Conjugated like **venir**

12 **aller** *Pres indic* **vais, vas, va, vont.** *Imperf* **allais.** *Fut* **irai.** *Condit* **irais.** *Imp* **va (vas-y), allons, allez.** *Pres subj* **aille, ailles, aille, allions, alliez, aillent.** *Pres part* **allant.** *P part* **allé**

13 **apparoir** *Pres indic third pers* only **appert**

14 **assaillir** *Pres indic* **assaille, assaillons.** *Imperf* **assaillais.** *Imp* **assaille, assaillons, assaillez.** *Pres subj* **assaille, assaillions.** *Pres part* **assaillant**

15 **asseoir** *Pres indic* **assieds, assieds, assied, asseyons, asseyez, asseyent (assois, assoyons, assoient).** *Imperf* **asseyais (assoyais).** *P def* **assis.** *Fut* **assiérai (assoirai).** *Condit* **assiérais (assoirais).** *Imper* **assieds, asseyons, asseyez (assois, assoyons).** *Pres subj* **asseye, asseyions (assoie, assoyions, assoient).** *Pres part* **asseyant (assoyant).** *P part* **assis**

16 **battre** *Pres indic* **bats, battons.** *Imperf* **battais.** *Imper* **bats, battons, battez.** *Pres subj* **batte, battions.** *Pres part* **battant**

17 **boire** *Pres indic* **bois, bois, boit, buvons, buvez, boivent.** *Imperf* **buvais.** *P def* **bus.** *Fut* **boirai.** *Condit* **boirais.** *Imper* **bois, buvons, buvez.** *Pres subj* **boive, buvions.** *Pres part* **buvant.** *P part* **bu**

18 **bouillir** *Pres indic* **bous, bous, bout, bouillons, bouillez, bouillent.** *Imperf*
**bouillais.** *P def* **bouillis** . *Fut* **bouillirai.** *Imper* **bous, bouillons, bouillez.** *Pres*
*subj* **bouille, bouillions.** *Pres part* **bouillant.** *P part* **bouilli**

19 **braire** *Third pers* only. *Pres indic* **brait, braient.** *Fut* **braira, brairont**

20 **bruire** *Third pers* only. *Pres indic* **bruit, bruissent.** *Imperf* **bruissait, bruissaient.**
*Pres part* **bruissant**

21 **choir** Only in: *Pres indic* **chois, chois, choit.** *P def* **chus, chûmes.** *Fut*
**choirai.** *P part* **chu**

22 **circoncire** *Pres indic* **circoncis, circoncisons.** *Imperf* **circoncisais, circoncisions.**
*P def* **circoncis.** *Fut* **circoncirai.** *Imper* **circoncis, circoncisons, circoncisez.**
*Pres subj* **circoncisse.** *Pres part* **circoncisant.** *P part* **circoncis**

23 **clore** Only in: *Pres indic* **clos, clos, clôt.** *Fut* **clorai, clorons.** *Condit* **clorais,**
**clorions.** *Pres subj* **close, closions.** *P part* **clos**

24 **comparoir** Only in *infin* and *pres part* **comparant**

25 **conclure** *Pres indic* **conclus, conclus, conclut, concluons, concluez, concluent.**
*Imperf* **concluais, concluions.** *P def* **conclus.** *Fut* **conclurai.** *Imper* **conclus,**
**concluons, concluez.** *Pres subj* **conclue, concluions.** *Pres part* **concluant.** *P part*
**conclu**

26 **confire** *Pres indic* **confis, confisons.** *Imperf* **confisais.** *P def* **confis.** *Fut* **confirai,**
**confirons.** *Imper* **confis, confisons, confisez.** *Pres subj* **confise, confisions.** *Pres*
*part* **confisant.** *P part* **confit**

27 **conquérir** *Pres indic* **conquiers, conquiers, conquiert, conquérons, conquérez,**
**conquièrent.** *Imperf* **conquérais.** *P def* **conquis.** *Fut* **conquerrai.** *Pres subj*
**conquière, conquières, conquière, conquérions, conquériez, conquièrent.** *Pres*
*part* **conquérant.** *P part* **conquis**

28 **coudre** *Pres indic* **couds, couds, coud, cousons, cousez, cousent.** *Imperf* **cousais.**
*P def* **cousis.** *Fut* **coudrai.** *Imper* **couds, cousons, cousez.** *Pres subj* **couse.** *Pres*
*part* **cousant.** *P part* **cousu**

29 **courir** *Pres indic* **cours, cours, court, courons, courez, courent.** *Imperf* **courais.**
*P def* **courus.** *Fut* **courrai.** *Imper* **cours, courons, courez.** *Pres subj* **coure.** *Pres*
*part* **courant.** *P part* **couru**

30 **couvrir** *Pres indic* **couvre, couvres, couvre, couvrons, couvrez, couvrent.** *Imperf*
**couvrais.** *P def* **couvris.** *Fut* **couvrirai.** *Imper* **couvre, couvrons, couvrez.** *Pres*
*subj* **couvre.** *Pres part* **couvrant.** *P part* **couvert**

31 **croire** *Pres indic* **crois, crois, croit, croyons, croyez, croient.** *Imperf* **croyais.** *P*
*def* **crus.** *Fut* **croirai.** *Imper* **crois, croyons, croyez.** *Pres subj* **croie, croyions.**
*Pres part* **croyant.** *P part* **cru**

32 **croître** *Pres indic* **croîs, croîs, croît, croissons, croissez, croissent.** *Imperf*
**croissais.** *P def* **crûs.** *Fut* **croîtrai.** *Imper* **croîs, croissons, croissez.** *Pres subj*
**croisse.** *Pres part* **croissant.** *P part* **crû**

# Main Points of French Grammar

33 **cueillir** *Pres indic* cueille, cueilles, cueille, cueillons, cueillez, cueillent. *Imperf* cueillais, cueillions. *P def* cueillis. *Fut* cueillerai. *Imper* cueille, cueillons, cueillez. *Pres subj* cueille, cueillions. *Pres part* cueillant. *P part* cueilli

34 **déchoir** *Pres indic* déchois, déchois, déchoit, déchoient. *P def* déchus. *Pres subj* déchoie, déchoyions. *P part* déchu

35 **déconfire** Only in *infin* and *p part* déconfit

36 **défaillir** *Pres indic* défaille, défailles, défaille (défaut), défaillons, défaillez, défaillent. *Imperf* défaillais. *P def* défaillis. *Fut* défaillerai (défaillirai). *Pres subj* défaille. *Pres part* défaillant

37 **devoir** *Pres indic* dois, dois, doit, devons, devez, doivent. *Imperf* devais. *P def* dus. *Fut* devrai. *Imper* dois, devons, devez. *Pres subj* doive, devions. *Pres part* devant. *P part* dû (*f* due)

38 **dire** *Pres indic* dis, dis, dit, disons, dites, disent. *Imperf* disais. *P def* dis. *Fut* dirai. *Imper* dis, disons, dites. *Pres subj* dise. *Pres part* disant. *P part* dit

39 **dormir** *Pres indic* dors, dors, dort, dormons, dormez, dorment. *Imperf* dormais. *P def* dormis. *Fut* dormirai. *Imper* dors, dormons, dormez. *Pres subj* dorme. *Pres part* dormant. *P part* dormi

40 **échoir** *Third pers sing* only. *Pres indic* échoit. *P def* échut. *Fut* il échoira (écherra). *Pres part* échéant. *P part* échu

41 **éclore** *Third pers* only. *Pres indic* éclôt, éclosent. *Fut* éclora, écloront. *Pres subj* éclose, éclosent. *P part* éclos

42 **écrire** *Pres indic* écris, écris, écrit, écrivons, écrivez, écrivent. *Imperf* écrivais. *P def* écrivis. *Fut* écrirai. *Imper* écris, écrivons, écrivez. *Pres subj* écrive. *Pres part* écrivant. *P part* écrit

43 **ensuivre (s')** *Third pers* only. *Pres indic* s'ensuit, s'ensuivent. *Imperf* s'ensuivait, s'ensuivaient. *P def* s'ensuivit, s'ensuivirent. *Fut* s'ensuivra, s'ensuivront. *Pres subj* s'ensuive, s'ensuivent. *Pres part* s'ensuivant. *P part* ensuivi

44 **envoyer** *Pres indic* envoie, envoies, envoie, envoyons, envoyez, envoient. *Imperf* envoyais. *Fut* enverrai. *Pres subj* envoie, envoyions. *Pres part* envoyant. *P part* envoyé

45 **faillir** Only in: *P def* faillis. *Fut* faudrai (faillirai). *Condit* faudrais (faillirais). *Pres part* faillant. *P part* failli

46 **faire** *Pres indic* fais, fais, fait, faisons, faites, font. *Imperf* faisais. *P def* fis. *Fut* ferai. *Imper* fais, faisons, faites. *Pres subj* fasse. *Pres part* faisant. *P part* fait

47 **falloir** *Third pers* only. *Pres indic* faut. *Imperf* fallait. *P def* fallut. *Fut* faudra. *Pres subj* faille. *P part* fallu

48 **férir** *Infin* only (in expression sans coup férir)

49 **fleurir** Following irregularities when in sense of prosper: *Imperf* **florissais**. *Pres part* **florissant**

50 **forfaire** Only used in *infin*, *pres indic* and compound tenses

51 **frire** Only used in *pres indic* **fris, fris, frit**. *Fut* **frirai**

52 **fuir** *Pres indic* **fuis, fuis, fuit, fuyons, fuyez, fuient**. *Imperf* **fuyais, fuyions**. *P def* **fuis**. *Fut* **fuirai**. *Imper* **fuis, fuyons, fuyez**. *Pres subj* **fuie, fuyions**. *Pres part* **fuyant**. *P part* **fui**

53 **gésir** Only in: *Pres indic* **gît, gisons, gisez, gisent**. *Imperf* **gisais, gisions**. *Pres part* **gisant**

54 **haïr** *Pres indic* **hais, hais, hait, haïssons, haïssez, haïssent**. *Imperf* **haïssais**. *P def* **haïs**. *Fut* **haïrai**. *Pres part* **haïssant**. *P part* **haï**

55 **joindre** *Pres indic* **joins, joins, joint, joignons, joignez, joignent**. *Imperf* **joignais**. *P def* **joignis**. *Fut* **joindrai**. *Imper* **joins, joignons, joignez**. *Pres subj* **joigne**. *Pres part* **joignant**. *P part* **joint**

56 **lire** *Pres indic* **lis, lis, lit, lisons, lisez, lisent**. *Imperf* **lisais**. *P def* **lus**. *Fut* **lirai**. *Imper* **lis, lisons, lisez**. *Pres subj* **lise**. *Pres part* **lisant**. *P part* **lu**

57 **luire** *Pres indic* **luis, luis, luit, luisons, luisez, luisent**. *Imperf* **luisais**. *P def* **luis** or **luisis** (but very rare). *Fut* **luirai**. *Imper* **luis, luisons, luisez**. *Pres subj* **luise**. *Pres part* **luisant**. *P part* **lui**

58 **maudire** *Pres indic* **maudis, maudis, maudit, maudissons, maudissez, maudissent**. *Imperf* **maudissais**. *P def* **maudis**. *Fut* **maudirai**. *Imper* **maudis, maudissons, maudissez**. *Pres subj* **maudisse**. *Pres part* **maudissant**. *P part* **maudit**

59 **mentir** *Pres indic* **mens, mens, ment, mentons, mentez, mentent**. *Imperf* **mentais**. *P def* **mentis**. *Fut* **mentirai**. *Imper* **mens, mentons, mentez**. *Pres subj* **mente**. *Pres part* **mentant**. *P part* **menti**

60 **mettre** *Pres indic* **mets, mets, met, mettons, mettez, mettent**. *Imperf* **mettais**. *P def* **mis**. *Fut* **mettrai**. *Imper* **mets, mettons, mettez**. *Pres subj* **mette**. *Pres part* **mettant**. *P part* **mis**

61 **moudre** *Pres indic* **mouds, mouds, moud, moulons, moulez, moulent**. *Imperf* **moulais**. *P def* **moulus**. *Fut* **moudrai**. *Imper* **mouds, moulons, moulez**. *Pres subj* **moule**. *Pres part* **moulant**. *P part* **moulu**

62 **mourir** *Pres indic* **meurs, meurs, meurt, mourons, mourez, meurent**. *Imperf* **mourais**. *P def* **mourus**. *Fut* **mourrai**. *Imper* **meurs, mourons, mourez**. *Pres subj* **meure, mourions, meurent**. *Pres part* **mourant**. *P part* **mort**

63 **mouvoir** *Pres indic* **meus, meus, meut, mouvons, mouvez, meuvent**. *Imperf* **mouvais**. *P def* **mus**. *Fut* **mouvrai**. *Imper* **meus, mouvons, mouvez**. *Pres subj* **meuve, mouvions, meuvent**. *Pres part* **mouvant**. *P part* **mû** (*f* **mue**)

# Main Points of French Grammar

64 **naître** *Pres indic* **nais, nais, naît, naissons, naissez, naissent.** *Imperf* **naissais.** *P def* **naquis.** *Fut* **naîtrai.** *Imper* **nais, naissons, naissez.** *Pres subj* **naisse.** *Pres part* **naissant.** *P part* **né**

65 **nuire** *P def* **nuisis.** Otherwise like **luire**

66 **ouïr** Used only in *infin, imper* **oyez,** *p part* **ouï** and compound tenses

67 **paître** *Pres indic* **pais, pais, paît, paissons, paissez, paissent.** *Imperf* **paissais.** *P def* none. *Fut* **paîtrai.** *Imper* **pais, paissons, paissez.** *Pres subj* **paisse.** *Pres part* **paissant.** *P part* none

68 **paraître** *Pres indic* **parais, parais, paraît, paraissons, paraissez, paraissent.** *Imperf* **paraissais.** *P def* **parus.** *Fut* **paraîtrai.** *Imper* **parais, paraissons, paraissez.** *Pres subj* **paraisse.** *Pres part* **paraissant.** *P part* **paru**

69 **plaire** *Pres indic* **plais, plais, plaît, plaisons, plaisez, plaisent.** *Imperf* **plaisais.** *P def* **plus.** *Fut* **plairai.** *Imper* **plais, plaisons, plaisez.** *Pres subj* **plaise.** *Pres part* **plaisant.** *P part* **plu**

70 **pleuvoir** *Third pers sing* only. *Pres indic* **pleut.** *Imperf* **pleuvait.** *P def* **plut.** *Fut* **pleuvra.** *Pres subj* **pleuve.** *Pres part* **pleuvant.** *P part* **plu**

71 **poindre** Only in: *Pres indic* **point.** *Imperf* **poignait.** *P def* **poignit.** *Fut* **poindra.** *Pres subj* **poigne.** *Pres part* **poignant.** *P part* **point**

72 **pourvoir** *Pres indic* **pourvois, pourvois, pourvoit, pourvoyons, pourvoyez, pourvoient.** *Imperf* **pourvoyais.** *Fut* **pourvoirai.** *Imper* **pourvois, pourvoyons, pourvoyez.** *Pres subj* **pourvoie, pourvoyions.** *Pres part* **pourvoyant.** *P part* **pourvu**

73 **pouvoir** *Pres indic* **peux (puis), peux, peut, pouvons, pouvez, peuvent.** *Imperf* **pouvais.** *P def* **pus.** *Fut* **pourrai.** *Imper* none. *Pres subj* **puisse.** *Pres part* **pouvant.** *P part* **pu**

74 **prédire** As **dire,** except for *pres indic* and *imper* **prédisez**

75 **prendre** *Pres indic* **prends, prends, prend, prenons, prenez, prennent.** *Imperf* **prenais.** *P def* **pris.** *Fut* **prendrai.** *Imper* **prends, prenons, prenez.** *Pres subj* **prenne, prenions, prennent.** *Pres part* **prenant.** *P part* **pris**

76 **prévaloir** As **valoir,** except for *pres subj* **prévale**

77 **prévoir** As **voir,** except for *fut* **prévoirai** and *condit* **prévoirais**

78 **promouvoir** As **mouvoir,** but used only in *infin*, compound tenses and *passive*

79 **quérir** Used only in *infin* after verbs **aller, envoyer, faire, venir**

80 **réduire** *Pres indic* **réduis, réduis, réduit, réduisons, réduisez, réduisent.** *Imperf* **réduisais.** *P def* **réduisis.** *Fut* **réduirai.** *Imper* **réduis, réduisons, réduisez.** *Pres subj* **réduise.** *Pres part* **réduisant.** *P part* **réduit**

81 **repaître** As **paître,** but also has *p def* **repus,** *imperf subj* **repusse,** *p part* **repu**

82 **résoudre** *Pres indic* **résous, résous, résout, résolvons, résolvez, résolvent.**
*Imperf* **résolvais.** *P def* **résolus.** *Fut* **résoudrai.** *Imper* **résous, résolvons,**
**résolvez.** *Pres subj* **résolve.** *Pres part* **résolvant.** *P part* **résolu**

83 **ressortir** As **sortir** in meaning 'go out again'. As **finir** in *leg* sense

84 **rire** *Pres indic* **ris, ris, rit, rions, riez, rient.** *Imperf* **riais, riions.** *P def* **ris.** *Fut*
**rirai.** *Imper* **ris, rions, riez.** *Pres subj* **rie, riions.** *Pres part* **riant.** *P part* **ri**

85 **rompre** As **rendre,** but *third pers pres indic* **rompt**

86 **saillir** (in sense of jut out) Only in: *Third pers pres indic* **saille.** *Imperf* **saillait.** *Fut*
**saillera (saillira).** *Condit* **saillerait.** *Pres subj* **saille.** *Pres part* **saillant.** *P part* **sailli**

87 **savoir** *Pres indic* **sais, sais, sait, savons, savez, savent.** *Imperf* **savais.** *P def* **sus.**
*Fut* **saurai.** *Imper* **sache, sachons, sachez.** *Pres subj* **sache.** *Pres part* **sachant.** *P*
*part* **su**

88 **seoir** Only in: *Pres indic* **sied, siéent.** *Imperf* **seyait, seyaient.** *Fut* **siéra, siéront.**
*Condit* **siérait, siéraient.** *Pres subj* **siée, siéent.** *Pres part* **seyant.** *P part* **sis**

89 **servir** *Pres indic* **sers, sers, sert, servons, servez, servent.** *Imperf* **servais.** *P def*
**servis.** *Fut* **servirai.** *Imper* **sers, servons, servez.** *Pres subj* **serve.** *Pres part*
**servant.** *P part* **servi**

90 **sourdre** Used only in *infin* and *pres indic third pers* **sourd, sourdent**

91 **suffire** *Pres indic* **suffis, suffis, suffit, suffisons, suffisez, suffisent.** *Imperf*
**suffisais.** *P def* **suffis.** *Fut* **suffirai.** *Imper* **suffis, suffisons, suffisez.** *Pres subj*
**suffise.** *Pres part* **suffisant.** *P part* **suffi**

92 **suivre** *Pres indic* **suis, suis, suit, suivons, suivez, suivent.** *Imperf* **suivais.** *P def*
**suivis.** *Fut* **suivrai.** *Imper* **suis, suivons, suivez.** *Pres subj* **suive.** *Pres part*
**suivant.** *P part* **suivi**

93 **surseoir** *Pres indic* **sursois, sursois, sursoit, sursoyons, sursoyez, sursoient.**
*Imperf* **sursoyais.** *P def* **sursis.** *Fut* **sursoirai.** *Imper* **sursois, sursoyons, sursoyez.**
*Pres subj* **sursoie, sursoyions.** *Pres part* **sursoyant.** *P part* **sursis**

94 **vaincre** *Pres indic* **vaincs, vaincs, vainc, vainquons, vainquez, vainquent.** *Imperf*
**vainquais.** *P def* **vainquis.** *Fut* **vaincrai.** *Imper* **vaincs, vainquons, vainquez.**
*Pres subj* **vainque.** *Pres part* **vainquant.** *P part* **vaincu**

95 **valoir** *Pres indic* **vaux, vaux, vaut, valons, valez, valent.** *Imperf* **valais.** *P def*
**valus.** *Fut* **vaudrai.** *Imper* not used. *Pres subj* **vaille, valions, vaillent.** *Pres part*
**valant.** *P part* **valu**

96 **venir** *Pres indic* **viens, viens, vient, venons, venez, viennent.** *Imperf* **venais.** *P def*
**vins.** *Fut* **viendrai.** *Imper* **viens, venons, venez.** *Pres subj* **vienne, venions,**
**viennent.** *Pres part* **venant.** *P part* **venu**

97 **vêtir** *Pres indic* **vêts, vêts, vêt, vêtons, vêtez, vêtent.** *Imperf* **vêtais.** *P def* **vêtis.** *Fut* **vêtirai.** *Imper* **vêts, vêtons, vêtez.** *Pres subj* **vête.** *Pres part* **vêtant.** *P part* **vêtu**

98 **vivre** *Pres indic* **vis, vis, vit, vivons, vivez, vivent.** *Imperf* **vivais.** *P def* **vécus.** *Fut* **vivrai.** *Imper* **vis, vivons, vivez.** *Pres subj* **vive.** *Pres part* **vivant.** *P part* **vécu**

99 **voir** *Pres indic* **vois, vois, voit, voyons, voyez, voient.** *Imperf* **voyais.** *P def* **vis.** *Fut* **verrai.** *Imper* **vois, voyons, voyez.** *Pres subj* **voie, voyions.** *Pres part* **voyant.** *P part* **vu**

100 **vouloir** *Pres indic* **veux, veux, veut, voulons, voulez, veulent.** *Imperf* **voulais.** *P def* **voulus.** *Fut* **voudrai.** *Imper* **veuille, veuillons, veuillez.** *Pres part* **voulant.** *P part* **voulu**

# FRENCH–ENGLISH

# A

**à** *prep* at, in; to, into; by, for, from, of, on with; ~ **deux (trois)** both (all three) together; ~ **dix kilomètres** ten kilometres away; ~ **l'anglaise** in the English style; **un homme** ~ **lunettes** a man with glasses

**abaissable** *adj* lowerable

**abaissement** *nm* lowering, fall (price, temperature)

**abaisser** *vt* lower; bring down, pull down; humiliate, humble; **s'** ~ fall away, sink; humble oneself; condescend, stoop

**abandon** *nm* abandonment, surrender; neglect; abandon, freedom from restraint

**abandonner** *vt* forsake, leave, desert, abandon; renounce, surrender; give up; **s'** ~ neglect oneself; let oneself go; succumb, become addicted

**abasourdir** *vt* stun, daze; amaze, dumbfound

**abasourdissement** *nm* bewilderment, stupefaction

**abâtardir** *vt* bastardize, degrade, debase

**abâtardissement** *nm* degeneracy; debasement

**abat-jour** *nm invar* lamp-shade; skylight

**abats** *nmpl* offal, giblets

**abattage** *nm* felling; slaughtering; *coll* reprimand, blowing up

**abattant** *nm* leaf (of table), flap (of counter); **siège** ~ tilting seat

**abattement** *nm* deduction, reduction (in tax, price); prostration, depression, dejection

**abattis** *nm* heap, pile; *pl* giblets, offal

**abattre** *vt* fell; slaughter, shoot down; lay (dust); enfeeble; get through (a lot of work); **s'** ~ fall suddenly, come down; swoop

**abattu** *adj* discouraged; enfeebled; brought down

**abat-vent** *nm* louvre-boards; chimney-cowl; wind-screen

**abat-voix** *nm* sounding-board (over pulpit)

**abbatial** *adj* **église** ~ **e** minster

**abbaye** *nf* abbey, monastery

**abbé** *nm* abbot; priest

**abbesse** *nf* abbess

**abcès** *nm* abscess, gathering

**abdiquer** *vt* + *vi* abdicate, renounce

**abdominal -aux** *adj* abdominal

**abécédaire** *nm* A B C, spelling-book; *adj* elementary

**abeille** *nf* bee

**aberrant** *adj* aberrant, abnormal, irregular; *coll* absurd, crazy

**abêtir** *vt* stupefy, besot, make s/o stupid; **s'** ~ become stupid

**abêtissant** *adj* besotting, stupefying

**abêtissement** *nm* stupefaction, stupidity

**abhorrer** *vt* abhor, have a horror of; detest

**abîme** *nm* bottomless gulf, abyss, chasm

**abîmer** *vt* damage, spoil; *coll* ~ **le portrait à qn** smash s/o's face in; **s'** ~ be swallowed up, sink

**abjurer** *vt* abjure, recant, retract

**ablatif** *nm* ablative

**ablation** *nf* ablation, removal; excision

**ablette** *nf* bleak, ablet

**aboiement** *nm* bark, barking

**abois** *nmpl* **être aux** ~ be at bay, in a desperate situation

**abolir** *vt* abolish, suppress

**abominer** *vt* abominate

**abondamment** *adv* abundantly, copiously

**abondance** *nf* abundance, plenty; **parler avec (d')** ~ improvise

**abondant** *adj* abundant, rich

**abonder** *vi* abound, be plentiful; ~ **dans le sens de qn** support s/o's opinion to an exaggerated degree

**abonné -e** *n* subscriber

**abonnement** *nm* subscription; season-ticket

**abonner** *vt* take out a subscription for (s/o); **s'** ~ take out a subscription, subscribe

**abord** *nm* approach, landing; bearing; **d'** ~ at first; **dès l'** ~ from the outset; **d'un** ~ **facile** (person) easy to approach; **au premier** ~ at first sight; **aux abords de** on the outskirts of; **de prime** ~ at first sight, offhand

**abordable** *adj* approachable, accessible

**abordage** *nm* boarding, coming alongside, berthing

**aborder** *vt* board, come alongside; run into; approach

**aborigène** *n* + *adj* aboriginal, native

**abortif -ive** *adj* abortive

**aboutir** *vi* come to an end; lead, end; *med* come to a head, burst; **ne pas** ~ fizzle out

**aboutissement** *nm* outcome, end-product; *med* coming to a head

I

**aboyer** *vi* (7) bark, bay, yelp

**aboyeur** *nm* (fairground) barker

**abracadabrant** *adj* extraordinary and incoherent

**abrasif -ive** *adj* abrasive

**abrégé** *nm* précis, summary, abstract

**abrègement** *nm* abridgement

**abréger** *vt* (6,3) shorten, abridge, cut short, abbreviate

**abreuver** *vt* water (animals); give generously; s' ~ drink copiously

**abreuvoir** *nm* watering-place, drinking-trough; *sl* bar, pub

**abréviation** *nf* abbreviation

**abri** *nm* shelter, refuge, dug-out; **les sans-** ~ the homeless

**abricot** *nm* apricot, *vulg* cunt

**abricotier** *nm* apricot-tree

**abriter** *vt* shelter, protect; lodge, put up

**abroger** *vt* (3) abrogate, repeal, rescind, annul

**abruti -e** *n* dullard, fool, idiot; *adj* dull-witted, besotted; tired-out

**abrutir** *vt* make stupid; besot, stupefy; exhaust, stun

**abrutissant** *adj* dulling, stupefying

**abrutissement** *nm* stupefaction, besottedness; exhaustion

**absentéisme** *nm* absenteeism, truancy

**absentéiste** *n* absentee; supporter of absenteeism

**absenter (s')** *v refl* absent oneself, quit; be away

**abside** *nf archi* apse

**absidial** *adj archi* apsidal

**absinthe** *nf bot* wormwood; absinth(e)

**absolu** *nm* + *adj* absolute

**absolument** *adv* absolutely, really, utterly

**absorber** *vt* drink, consume; absorb; swallow up

**absorption** *nf* absorption; drinking, eating, swallowing

**absoudre** *vt* (8) absolve, pardon

**absoute** *nf* absolution

**abstenir (s')** *v refl* abstain

**abstentionniste** *n* one who abstains from voting

**abstraction** *nf* abstraction; **faire** ~ **de** set aside; not to take account of

**abstraire** *vt* (9) abstract, dissociate; s' ~ become absorbed in thought

**abstrait** *adj* abstract

**abstrus** *adj* abstruse

**absurde** *nm* + *adj* absurd

**absurdité** *nf* absurdity

**abus** *nm* abuse, misuse, violation; *coll* **il y a de l'** ~ it's a bit thick, that's going too far

**abuser** *vt* abuse, deceive; *vi* ~ **de** misuse, deceive, take advantage of; s' ~ deceive oneself, be mistaken

**abusif -ive** *adj* excessive, unauthorized; *gramm* improper

**abusivement** *adv* in an unauthorized manner; *gramm* improperly

**abyssal -aux** *adj* abyssal; unfathomable

**abysse** *nm* unfathomable (ocean); depths, abyss

**acabit** *nm* **de cet** ~ , **du même** ~ *pej* of the same kind, birds of a feather

**académie** *nf* learned society; specialized school; (educational) zone centred on a university; *arts* painting (or drawing) from the nude; *sl* figure; **elle a une belle (une superbe)** ~ she's got a fantastic figure

**académique** *adj* academic; strictly according to convention

**acajou** *nm* mahogany; **noix d'acajou** cashew-nut; *adj* dark auburn (hair)

**acanthe** *nf bot* + *archi* acanthus

**acariâtre** *adj* difficult, disagreeable (character)

**accablant** *adj* overwhelming

**accablement** *nm* overwhelming prostration

**accabler** *vt* oppress, overwhelm

**accalmie** *nf* calm, repose

**accaparement** *nm* keeping for oneself, cornering, monopolizing

**accaparer** *vt* hoard, monopolize, buttonhole

**accapareur -euse** *n* hoarder, monopolizer; *adj* possessive

**accéder** *vi* (6) have access; accede

**accélérateur** *nm* accelerator

**accéléré** *nm cin* quick motion

**accélérer** *vt* + *vi* (6) accelerate

**accentué** *adj* accentuated; stressed, marked

**accentuer** *vt* accentuate; stress; intensify

**acceptation** *nf* acceptance

**accepter** *vt* accept, agree to, consent to

**accès** *nm* access, way-in; *med* attack, fit, bout

**accessoire** *nm* accessory; ~ s accessories; *theat* props; **magasin des** ~ s property room; *adj* accessory, secondary

**accessoirement** *adv* secondarily

**accessoiriste** *n theat* property master (mistress); *mot* dealer in accessories

**accident** *nm* accident; ~ s **de terrain** unevenness of the ground

**¹accidenté** *nm* casualty, victim (of accident)

**²accidenté** *adj* uneven, rough; eventful; injured

**accidentel -elle** *adj* accidental

**acclamer** *vt* acclaim

**acclimatation** *nf* acclimatization; **jardin d'** ~ zoological garden

**acclimatement** *nm* adaptation to an alien environment

**acclimater** *vt* acclimatize; **s'** ~ become acclimatized

**accointance** *nf* acquaintance; relationship

**accolade** *nf* accolade; hug, embrace; *mus* + *print* brace

**accoler** *vt* juxtapose, couple; *mus* + *print* bracket

**accommodant** *adj* accommodating, easygoing

**accommodement** *nm* (friendly) agreement; compromise

**accommoder** *vt* accommodate, adapt; focus; prepare, season a dish

**accompagnateur -trice** *n* accompanist; guide

**accompagnement** *nm* accompaniment, consequence; *cul* garnishing

**accompagner** *vt* accompany, go with; **s'** ~ de result in

**accompli** *adj* accomplished, perfect; completed

**accomplir** *vt* accomplish; carry out, execute; perform; **s'** ~ happen, occur; be fulfilled

**accomplissement** *nm* accomplishment; fulfilment

**accord** *nm* agreement, consent; concord, harmony; *mus* chord; tuning; **d'** ~ agreed; in agreement; **en** ~ harmoniously; **mettre d'** ~ reconcile

**accordéon** *nm* accordion; **en** ~ rumpled, pleated

**accordéoniste** *n* accordionist

**accorder** *vt* reconcile; harmonize; *mus* tune; concede, admit; grant, bestow; *gramm* make agree; **s'** ~ be in agreement, get on well; *gramm* agree

**accordeur** *nm mus* tuner

**accordoir** *nm mus* tuning-hammer

**accort** *adj* lively, sprightly; attractive

**accostage** *nm naut* coming alongside; accosting

**accoster** *vt* accost, go up to; *naut* come alongside

**accotement** *nm* verge; ~ **non stabilisé** soft shoulder

**accoter** *vt* lean, prop; **s'** ~ lean

**accouchée** *nf* woman who has given birth

**accouchement** *nm* childbirth, parturition

**accoucher** *vt* deliver; *vi* give birth; ~ **de** give birth to; *sl* explain; cough up

**accoucheur -euse** *n* obstetrician, *f* midwife

**accoudement** *nm* leaning on the elbows

**accouder (s')** *vt refl* lean on one's elbows

**accoudoir** *nm* arm-rest

**accoupler** *vt* couple; **s'** ~ copulate

**accourir** *vi* run up

**accoutrement** *nm* accoutrement; *coll* absurd get-up

**accoutrer** *vt obs* dress; dress absurdly

**accoutumance** *nf* habit, use; *med* tolerance

**accoutumé** *adj* accustomed, normal

**accoutumer** *vt* accustom, acquire the habit; **s'** ~ à get used to

**accréditer** *vt* accredit; sanction; **s'** ~ gain acceptance

**accroc** *nm* tear; snag

**accrochage** *nm* hanging up, attaching; squabble; *mot* slight accident; *mil* encounter, brush

**accroche-cœur** *nm* kiss-curl

**accrocher** *vt* hang up; hook up; take hold of, grip; collide with; attract; *mil* engage; **s'** ~ hang on; **s'** ~ à hang on to

**accrocheur -euse** *adj* that catches the eye

**accroire** *vt* (10) **faire** ~ make believe; **en faire** ~ delude

**accroissement** *nm* growth, increase; accretion

**accroître** *vt* (32) make bigger, augment, increase; add to, heighten; *leg* accrue

**accroupir (s')** *v refl* squat, crouch

**accroupissement** *nm* squatting, crouching

**accu** *nm coll* accumulator; *coll fig* **recharger ses** ~ **s** regain one's energies

**accueil** *nm* welcome; reception, reaction; **centre d'** ~ reception centre; information bureau; **faire bon** ~ **à** welcome

**accueillant** *adj* welcoming, friendly

**accueillir** *vt* (33) receive; welcome; greet

**acculer** *vt* corner, bring to bay; ~ **à** force to; bring close to

**accumulateur** *nm* accumulator

**accumuler** *vt* accumulate; **s'** ~ accumulate

**accusateur -trice** *n* accuser; *adj* accusing

**accusatif** *nm gramm* accusative

**accusé -e** *n* defendant

**accuser** *vt* accuse; blame; indicate; *coll* ~ **le coup** take the point; ~ **réception** acknowledge receipt

**acerbe** *adj* sour, bitter

**acéré** *adj* sharp; biting

**acérer** *vt* (6) sharpen

**acétique** *adj* acetic; vinegary

**acétylène** *nm* acetylene

**achalandage** *nm* customers, clientèle

**achalandé** *adj* well patronized; *coll* well stocked

**acharné** *adj* fierce; inveterate

**acharnement** *nm* fury; obstinacy

**acharner (s')** *v refl* persevere, persist

**achat** *nm* purchase, acquisition; **pouvoir d'** ~ purchasing power

**acheminement** *nm* progress; transmission

3

**acheminer** vt progress; transmit, forward; s' ~ advance

**acheter** vt (5) buy, purchase; bribe

**acheteur -euse** n purchaser, buyer

**achevé** adj perfect; complete; ended

**achèvement** nm completion; perfection

**achever** vt (6) complete, finish; round off; finish off; s' ~ end

**achoppement** nm lit obstacle; difficulty; **pierre d'** ~ obstacle, snag

**acide** nm acid; coll L.S.D.; adj acid

**acidifier** vt acidify; s' ~ become acid

**acidité** nf acidity

**acidose** nf med acidosis

**aciduler** vt acidulate; **bonbon acidulé** acid drop

**acier** nm steel

**aciérie** nf steelworks

**acmé** nf acme; culminating point

**acné** nf acne

**acompte** nm instalment; down-payment; coll something to be going on with

**aconit** nm aconite

**acoquiner (s')** v refl lower oneself, have an undesirable liaison

**à-côté** nm side-issue; ~ s perks

**à-coup** nm jerk; **par** ~ s jerkily, intermittently

**acoustique** nf acoustics; adj acoustic

**acquéreur** nm purchaser

**acquérir** vt (27) acquire, obtain; purchase, buy; s' ~ obtain

**acquiescement** nm acquiescence

**acquiescer** vi (4) acquiesce

**acquis** nm experience gained; adj acquired; bought; ~ à belonging to; strongly in favour of

**acquit** nm receipt; **pour** ~ received with compliments

**acquit-à-caution** nm (pl **acquits-à-caution**) document accepting liability for payment of tax, excise, etc

**acquittement** nm discharge, payment; leg acquittal

**acquitter** vt discharge, pay; leg acquit; s' ~ free oneself; perform; repay

**âcre** adj acrid, bitter

**âcreté** nf acridness, bitterness

**acrimonie** nf acrimony

**acrimonieux -ieuse** adj acrimonious

**acrobate** n acrobat

**acrobatie** nf acrobatics

**acrobatique** adj acrobatic

**acrostiche** nm acrostic

**¹acte** nm action, deed; document, certificate; ~ s records, proceedings; bibl Acts; **demander** ~ **de** request official confirmation of; **donner** ~ **de** give official confirmation of; **étant** ~ duly noted; **faire** ~ **de présence** put in an appearance; **prendre** ~ **de** take due note of

**²acte** nm theat act

**acteur** nm actor

**actif** nm assets; credit; gramm active voice; **avoir à son** ~ have to one's credit; adj (f **-ive**) active; lively, dynamic; **armée active** regular army; **population active** working population

**¹action** nf action, deed; activity; lawsuit; theat plot; **entrer en** ~ become operative

**²action** nf fin share; **compagnie par** ~ s joint-stock company

**actionnaire** n share-holder

**actionnement** nm setting in motion

**actionner** vt set in motion, work, start; leg prosecute

**activer** vt activate; s' ~ be busy; bustle about

**activisme** nm activism

**activiste** n activist

**activité** nf activity; energy, vivacity; active employment, active service

**actrice** nf actress

**actuaire** n actuary

**actualiser** vt actualize

**actualité** nf actuality; relevance; current affairs; ~ s news

**actuel -uelle** adj actual; present, contemporary

**acuité** nf acuteness, intensity

**acutangle** adj acute-angled

**adamantin** adj adamantine

**adaptateur -trice** n adapter

**adapter** vt adapt; s' ~ adapt oneself

**additif** nm supplement; additive; adj (f **-ive**) additive; math to be added

**addition** nf addition; bill in restaurant

**additionnel -elle** adj additional

**additionner** vt add up; ~ **de** mix into, enrich

**adducteur** nm physiol adductor; water-supply channel; adj physiol adducent; carrying water supply

**adduction** nf physiol adduction; carrying of water supply

**adénoïde** adj adenoid, adenoidal

**adepte** n adept; initiate

**adéquat** adj adequate, sufficient

**adhérence** nf adherence; med adhesion

**adhérent -e** n + adj adherent

**adhérer** vi (6) adhere, stick; subscribe; join

**adhésif** nm adhesive; adj (f **-ive**) adhesive; **ruban** ~ adhesive tape

**adhésion** nf adhesion; agreement

**adieu** nm + interj farewell, goodbye

**adipeux -euse** adj adipose

**adjectif** nm adjective; adj (f **-ive**) adjectival

**adjoindre** vt (55) appoint, allocate; associate; s' ~ take on, engage

**adjoint -e** *n* deputy, assistant

**adjudant** *nm mil* warrant-officer, sergeant major; ~ **chef** regimental sergeant major; ~ **major** adjutant

**adjudicateur -trice** *n* adjudicator

**adjudication** *nf* auction; knocking down at auction; acceptance of tender

**adjuger** *vt* award; knock down; **une fois, deux fois, trois fois, adjugé!** going! going! gone!

**adjurant** *nm* additive; stimulant; stimulus

**adjurer** *vt* adjure, entreat

**admettre** *vt* (60) admit, accept; authorize, permit; allow in

**administrateur -trice** *n* administrator; (company) director

**administratif -ive** *adj* administrative

**administration** *nf* administration, management; public service, civil service; **conseil d' ~** board of directors; board of governors

**administré -e** *n* s/o subject to an authority

**administrer** *vt* administer, manage; rule; *leg* adduce; *coll* give, deal out

**admirateur -trice** *n* admirer

**admiratif -ive** *adj* admiring

**admirer** *vt* admire, wonder at

**admissibilité** *nf* admissibility; (in French examination system) qualification to sit second part of an examination

**admissible** *adj* admissible; tolerable; qualified; admitted to second part of an examination

**admonestation** *nf* reprimand

**admonester** *vt* admonish, reprimand

**adolescent -e** *n* + *adj* adolescent

**adonner (s')** *v refl* devote oneself; ~ **à** go in for; indulge in; **adonné à** given to

**adopter** *vt* adopt; choose, follow

**adoptif -ive** *adj* adoptive

**adorable** *adj* adorable; delightful, charming, marvellous

**adorateur -trice** *n* worshipper; devoted admirer; *adj* adoring

**adorer** *vt* adore; worship; *coll* be terribly fond of, dote on

**adosser** *vt* back on, build against; **s' ~** lean one's back

**adouber** *vt* dub; try out a move (chess, draughts)

**adoucir** *vt* soften; **s' ~** become soft

**adoucissement** *nm* softening; attenuation

**adrénaline** *nf* adrenalin

**¹adresse** *nf* address; **à l' ~ de** directed at

**²adresse** *nf* dexterity, skill; finesse

**adresser** *vt* address; send, direct; **s' ~ à** speak to; go and find; have recourse to

**adroit** *adj* adroit; skilful

**adulateur -trice** *n* adulator, sycophant;

*adj* adulatory, sycophantic

**aduler.** *vt* adulate, flatter grossly

**adulte** *n* + *adj* adult

**adultère** *n* adulterer, adulteress; *nm* adultery; *adj* adulterous

**adultérer** *vt* (6) adulterate, falsify

**advenir** *vi* (11) occur, happen; **advienne que pourra** come what may

**adventice** *adj* adventitious

**adverbe** *nm* adverb

**adversaire** *n* adversary

**adversité** *nf* adversity

**aérateur** *nm* ventilator

**aération** *nf* airing, ventilation

**aérer** *vt* (6) air, ventilate; thin, lighten

**aérien -ienne** *adj* aerial; air; airy

**aérodrome** *nm* aerodrome

**aérodynamique** *nf* aerodynamics; *adj* aerodynamic, streamlined

**aérogare** *nf* air-terminal

**aéroglisseur** *nm* hovercraft

**aéronaute** *n* aeronaut

**aéronautique** *nf* aeronautics; *adj* aeronautical

**aéroplane** *nm ar* aeroplane

**aéroport** *nm* airport

**aéroporté** *adj* airborne

**aérospatial** *adj* interplanetary

**affabilité** *nf* affability

**affabulation** *nf* organization of the plot of a narrative

**affadir** *vt* make insipid; make dull; **s' ~** become insipid; become dull

**affadissement** *nm* insipidity

**affaiblir** *vt* enfeeble, weaken; attenuate; **s' ~** become weak; become weakened

**affaiblissement** *nm* weakening, diminution, enfeebling

**affaire** *nf* affair, matter; lawsuit; trial; *mil* engagement; business, business proposition; ~**s** affairs, public business; *comm* business; possessions, belongings; ~ **de cœur** love-affair; **avoir ~ à** deal with; **avoir ~ avec** do business with; **ça fait l' ~** that will do; **ce n'est pas une ~** there's nothing in it; **ce n'est pas une ~ d'État** it's not a matter of great importance; **c'est toute une ~!** it's very complicated!; **faire son ~ à qn** settle s/o's hash; **homme d' ~s** business man; **la belle ~!** what a damned nuisance!; so what!; **se tirer d' ~** get oneself out of trouble

**affairé** *adj* busy

**affairement** *nm* fuss; *coll* flap

**affairer (s')** *v refl* bustle about, fuss; be busy

**affairiste** *nm* profiteer, shark

**affaissement** *nm* subsidence, sinking; collapsing; prostration

**affaisser** *vt* cause to sink; weight down; **s' ~** subside, sink; collapse; decline,

5

become weak

**affaler** vt naut haul down; cause to run aground; s' ~ naut run aground; slide down; fig slump, sink

**affamé -e** n starving person; adj hungry, starving; ~ **de** eager for, avid for

**affamer** vt starve

¹**affectation** nf allotment, designation, allocation

²**affectation** nf affectation, show; putting on

**affecté** adj affected; false; put on; mannered

¹**affecter** vt allot, designate

²**affecter** vt affect; simulate; put on; assume

³**affecter** vt affect, touch, move; s' ~ be upset, be concerned

**affectif -ive** adj affective; emotional

**affectionné -e** adj affectionate

**affectionner** vt be fond of, be attached to

**affectivité** nf sensibility

**affectueux -ueuse** adj affectionate

**afférent** adj pertaining, leg accruing; physiol afferent

**affermage** nm renting of a farm; renting advertisement space (hoardings, newspapers)

**affermer** vt let (farm)

**affermir** vt strengthen; harden; consolidate, reinforce; s' ~ become more stable, become firmer

**afféterie** nf affectation, preciosity

**affichage** nm bill-posting; display; sp **tableau d'** ~ score-board

**affiche** nf poster; **une pièce qui tient (reste à) l'** ~ a play that is still running

**afficher** vt post up; announce by posters; display, parade, make no secret of; **défense d'** ~ stick no bills; s' ~ **avec** display oneself with, be seen everywhere with

**afficheur** nm bill-poster

**affichiste** n poster-artist, poster-designer

**affilage** nm whetting, sharpening

**affilée (d')** adv phr uninterruptedly, without stopping

**affiler** vt whet, sharpen; bore; **avoir la langue bien affilée** be very talkative

**affilier** vt affiliate; s' ~ join, belong

**affiloir** nm hone, whetstone; knife-sharpener

**affinage** nm refining, purification; ripening (cheese)

**affinement** nm refinement

**affiner** vt purify (metal, glass, etc); ripen (cheese); refine; s' ~ become sophisticated, become refined

**affinité** nf affinity; relationship; mutual understanding

**affirmatif -ive** adj affirmative; positive, emphatic, assertive

**affirmation** nf affirmation, proposition, assertion, statement; manifestation

**affirmative** nf **répondre par l'** ~ say yes

**affirmer** vt affirm, maintain, assert; swear; s' ~ assert oneself, assert itself

**affleurement** nm levelling; geol outcropping; emergence

**affleurer** vt level off; vi emerge, be manifested

**affligeant** adj afflicting, distressing

**affliger** vt (3) afflict, cause to suffer, sadden

**affluence** nf crowd; affluence; **heures d'** ~ rush hour

**affluer** vi flow; crowd; flood

**afflux** nm influx; crowd; rush (of flood)

**affolant** adj disturbing, frightening; coll awful, terrible

**affolé** adj terrified; excited; bewildered; swinging (compass)

**affolement** nm panic; anxiety; swinging (compass)

**affoler** vt bewilder; terrify; s' ~ panic

**affranchi -e** n freed slave; adj open, free, unprejudiced

**affranchir** vt free; grant freedom; pay postage on; exempt (from tax); sl put in the know; s' ~ become free

**affranchissement** nm freeing; grant of freedom; payment of postage

**affres** nfpl lit torment, torture

**affrètement** nm naut chartering

**affréter** vt (6) naut charter

**affréteur** nm naut charterer

**affreux** nm coll white mercenary; adj (f -euse) horrible, monstrous, hideous; very disagreeable

**affriolant** adj exciting, alluring

**affront** nm insult, affront

**affrontement** nm confrontation; levelling of two edges

**affronter** vt confront, face; level two edges

**affubler** vt pej rig out, dress absurdly; s' ~ rig oneself out

**affût** nm ambush; hide; gun carriage; **être à l'** ~ **de** be on the look-out for

**affûter** vt sharpen

**affûtiaux** nmpl coll trinkets; sl tools

**afin de** prep phr in order to

**afin que** conj phr in order that

**Africain -e** n African

**africain** adj African

**afro-asiatique** adj Afro-asian

**agaçant** adj irritating, annoying; provocative

**agacement** nm irritation, impatience

**agacer** vt (4) irritate, annoy; provoke

**agacerie** nf flirtatious words; flirtatious behaviour

**agape** nf obs banquet; ~ s joc feast

**âge** nm age; epoch; old age; **deuxième** ~

youth; ~ **critique** change of life; ~ **ingrat** awkward age; **d'un certain** ~ getting on, elderly; **premier** ~ childhood; **troisième** ~ old age

**âgé** *adj* old; aged

**agence** *nf* agency; branch-office of bank

**agencement** *nm* arrangement, disposition, ordering

**agencer** *vt* (4) arrange, dispose, order

**agenda** *nm* diary, engagement-book

**agenouillement** *nm* kneeling

**agenouiller (s')** *v refl* kneel; submit, humble oneself

**agent** *nm* agent, cause, factor; representative; member of staff; policeman; ~ **comptable** accountant; ~ **de change** stockbroker; ~ **public** civil servant

**agglomération** *nf* agglomeration; built-up area; urban area

**aggloméré** *nm* briquette; breeze-block

**agglomérer** *vt* (6) agglomerate

**agglutiner** *vt* agglutinate

**aggravant** *adj* aggravating, making worse

**aggravation** *nf* aggravation, worsening; *leg* increase (in sentence)

**aggraver** *vt* aggravate, worsen; augment

**agilité** *nf* agility

**agir** *vi* act, do; behave; take effect, operate; influence; act on; *v impers* s' ~ **de** be a question of; **de quoi s'agit-il?** what is the matter?, what's up?; **il ne s'agit pas de ça** that's not the point

**agissant** *adj* effective, active, efficacious

**agissements** *nmpl pej* dealings, machinations

**agitateur -trice** *n* agitator

**agitation** *nf* agitation; restlessness; turbulence, unrest; commotion

**agité** *adj* agitated; restless; turbulent; rough (sea); *med* disturbed

**agiter** *vt* move; wave, stir, flap; trouble, agitate, worry; discuss; s' ~ move about, go to and fro; become excited; bustle about; fidget

**agneau** *nm* lamb

**agneler** *vi* (5) lamb

**agnelet** *nm* little lamb

**agnosticisme** *nm* agnosticism

**agnostique** *n* + *adj* agnostic

**agonie** *nf* death agony; **entrer en** ~, **être à l'** ~ be on the point of death

**agonisant -e** *n* dying person; *adj* dying

**agoniser** *vi* be dying

**agoraphobie** *nf* agoraphobia

**agrafage** *nm* pinning together; buckling up; clamping

**agrafe** *nf* clasp; buckle; clip; hook; clamp, staple

**agrafer** *vt* attach; clip together; hook; buckle; *sl* nab, arrest

**agraire** *adj* agrarian

**agrandir** *vt* enlarge; make more important; s' ~ grow, expand

**agrandissement** *nm* enlargement, expansion; development

**agrandisseur** *nm phot* enlarger

**agrarien -ienne** *n* + *adj hist* + *pol* agrarian

**agréable** *adj* agreeable, pleasant, charming, delightful; *obs* **avoir pour** ~ approve

**agréer** *vt* accept; agree to; **veuillez** ~ **l'assurance de mes sentiments distingués** yours faithfully; *vi* please, suit

**agrégat** *nm* agglomerate; aggregate

**agrégatif -ive** *n* student preparing the **agrégation**

**agrégation** *nf* competitive graduate examination in France, giving entitlement to posts in lycées and (in certain faculties) in universities; aggregation, binding

**agrégé -e** *n* successful candidate at the **agrégation**

**agréger** *vt* (6) aggregate; incorporate; s' ~ join

**agrément** *nm* approval; pleasantness; pleasure, delight; *mus* grace-note

**agrémenter** *vt* ornament, embellish

**agrès** *nmpl naut* rigging, tackle; gymnasium equipment

**agresser** *vt* assault

**agresseur** *nm* aggressor

**agressif -ive** *adj* aggressive, violent

**agression** *nf* aggression

**agressivité** *nf* aggressiveness

**agreste** *adj* rustic

**agricole** *adj* agricultural

**agriculteur** *nm* farmer

**agripper** *vt* clutch; s' ~ seize, clutch at

**agronome** *n* agronomist

**agronomie** *nf* agronomy

**agrumes** *nmpl* citrus fruit

**aguerrir** *vt* train for war; inure; s' ~ harden

**aguets** *nmpl* **aux** ~ on the alert

**aguichant** *adj* alluring, enticing

**aguicher** *vt* excite, entice, arouse

**aguicheur -euse** *n* enticer; *adj* seductive

**ah** *interj* ah!, oh!

**ahuri** *adj* bewildered, amazed, flabbergasted

**ahurir** *vt* bewilder, amaze, flabbergast

**ahurissant** *adj* bewildering, amazing; unbelievable

**ahurissement** *nm* bewilderment, amazement, stupefaction

**aide** *n* aide, assistant, helper; *nf* aid, help, assistance; support, collaboration; **à l'** ~ ! help!; **à l'** ~ **de** with, by means of

**aide-mémoire** *nm* handbook; digest

**aider** *vt* aid, help, assist; support, contribute to; *vi* contribute; s' ~ **de** make use of

**aïe** *interj* ow!

**aïeul -e** *n* (*pl* aïeuls, aïeules) grandfather, grandmother; (*pl* aïeux) ancestors

**aigle** *nm* eagle; lectern; *coll* ce n'est pas un ~ he's not very bright; *nf* female eagle; eagle as military emblem; ~ impériale Napoleonic eagle; ~ romaine Roman eagle

**aiglefin** *nm* haddock

**aiglon -onne** *n* eaglet

**aigre** *nm* sour taste, bitterness; acrimony; **tourner à l'** ~ (argument) become heated; *adj* sour, tart; shrill, piercing; bitter; sharp, acrimonious

**aigre-doux** (*f* aigre-douce) *adj* bittersweet

**aigrefin** *nm* shark, crook

**aigrelet -ette** *adj* slightly sour; slightly sharp

**aigrette** *nf orni* egret; plume, aigrette; spray

**aigreur** *nf* sour taste, bitterness; acrimony, ill-humour; ~s *med* heartburn

**aigri** *adj* embittered

**aigrir** *vt* sour, embitter; *vi* turn sour; s' ~ become embittered

**aigu -uë** *adj* pointed; sharp; *geom* + *gramm* acute; shrill; intense, violent, penetrating, subtle

**aiguière** *nf* ewer

**aiguillage** *nm* operation of points (railway); points, switches; *fig* direction

**aiguille** *nf* needle; pointer; hand (clock); spire; sharp rock peak; pine cone; **de fil en** ~ little by little

**aiguiller** *vt* direct (train) onto one track or another; direct, orientate; *sl* have sex with

**aiguillette** *nf* aglet; shoulder-knot; cut of beef (part of rump); slice of duck

**aiguilleur** *nm* pointsman (railway); *coll* ~ **du ciel** air-traffic controller

**aiguillier** *nm* needle-case

**aiguillon** *nm* goad; sting; prickle, thorn; stimulus, spur

**aiguillonner** *vt* goad, prod; stimulate, animate

**aiguiser** *vt* sharpen, point; stimulate, -sharpen

**aiguiseur** *nm* knife-grinder

**aiguisoir** *nm* sharpener

**ail** *nm* garlic

**aile** *nf* wing; **avoir du plomb dans l'** ~ compromised, be about to fail; *sl* **avoir un coup dans l'** ~ be drunk; **battre d'une** ~ be in a bad way; **voler de ses propres** ~s cope by oneself, be independent

**ailé** *adj* winged

**aileron** *nm* pinion, wing-tip; fin; aileron; *archi* ornamental scroll

**ailette** *nf* vane, fin, blade

**ailier** *nm sp* winger

**aillade** *nf* vinegar and garlic sauce

**ailleurs** *adv* elsewhere, somewhere else; **d'** ~ moreover, besides; **par** ~ in other respects

**ailloli** *nm* garlic mayonnaise

**aimable** *adj* pleasing, agreeable; amiable, pleasant, nice

**aimant** *nm* magnet; magnetic force

**aimantation** *nf* magnetization

**aimanter** *vt* magnetize

**aimer** *vt* love; like, be fond of; be interested in, enjoy; *vi* be in love; **s'** ~ be in love with oneself; love one another; make love; ~ **autant** like just as well; ~ **mieux** prefer; **j'aime autant vous dire** I may as well tell you

**aine** *nf* groin

**aîné -e** *n* older brother (sister); older person; first-born; *lit* ~s ancestors, predecessors; *adj* older; oldest

**ainsi** *adv* so, thus, in this way; in the same way; ~ **que** just as; ~ **soit-il** so be it

**¹air** *nm* air; atmosphere; **armée de l'** ~ air force; **au grand** ~ in the open air; **courant d'** ~ draught; **en l'** ~ úg unfounded; not serious; **en plein** ~ in the open air; *coll* **fiche(r) en l'** ~ throw overboard, give up; **prendre l'** ~ go for a breath of fresh air; **regarder en l'** ~ look upwards; **vivre de l'** ~ **du temps** live on next to nothing

**²air** *nm* air, appearance; manner; expression; **avoir l'** ~ seem, look, appear; **il en a tout l'** ~ it looks very much like it; *lit* **le bel** ~ aristocratic manners; **n'avoir l'** ~ **de rien** seem insignificant, look unimportant

**³air** *nm mus* air, aria

**airain** *nm obs* bronze; *fig* **d'** ~ implacable, unrelenting

**air-air** *adj invar* air-to-air

**aire** *nf* area, site; flat surface; zone; eyrie; *aer* apron, tarmac; *bui* substructure; *geol* shelf; (motorway) service area

**air-sol, air-terre** *adj invar* air-to-ground

**aisance** *nf* ease, effortlessness, grace; comfortable financial state, sufficiency; ~s de voirie easements, rights of access; **cabinets d'** ~, **lieux d'** ~ lavatory

**aise** *nf* ease, comfort; *lit* joy; ~s comforts; **à l'** ~ at ease, well-off; **à votre** ~ as you will; **en prendre à son** ~ **avec** be cavalier with; *adj* pleased

**aisé** *adj* easy, effortless; comfortably off

**aisselle** *nf* armpit

**ajiste** *n* youth hosteller

**ajonc** *nm* furze, gorse

**ajour** *nm* aperture; open-work

**ajourer** *vt* pierce holes in; hemstitch

**ajournement** *nm leg* summons; adjournment, postponement; referring (examination candidate); *mil* deferment

**ajourner** *vt leg* summons; adjourn, postpone; refer (examination candidate); *mil* defer

**ajouter** *vt* add; say further; ~ **foi à** give credence to; **s'** ~ be added

**ajustement** *nm* adjustment

**ajuster** *vt* adjust; settle; make fit; **s'** ~ be adjusted; fit

**ajusteur** *nm mech* fitter

**alacrité** *nf* alacrity

**alambic** *nm* alembic

**alambiqué** *adj* tortuous, over-complicated

**alanguir** *vt* weaken, enfeeble, make languid; **s'** ~ become languid

**alanguissement** *nm* languor; decline

**alarme** *nf* alarm, alert; state of alarm

**alarmer** *vt* alarm, disquiet, frighten; **s'** ~ be alarmed, be frightened

**alarmiste** *n* alarmist

**Albanais -e** *n* Albanian

**albanais** *nm* Albanian (language); *adj* Albanian

**albâtre** *nm* alabaster

**albinos** *n* albino

**albumine** *nf* albumin

**alcalescent** *adj* alkalescent

**alcali** *nm* alkali

**alcalin** *adj* alkaline

**alcaloïde** *nm* alkaloid

**alchimie** *nf* alchemy

**alchimiste** *nm* alchemist

**alcool** *nm* alcohol; *coll* spirits; ~ **à brûler** methylated spirits; ~ **à 90°** surgical spirit

**alcoolique** *n + adj* alcoholic

**alcooliser** *vt* alcoholize; fortify (wine, etc); **s'** ~ *coll* drink too much

**alcoolisme** *nm* alcoholism

**alcooltest, alcool-test, alcootest** *nm* breathalyser

**alcôve** *nf* alcove; *esp* place for making love; **secrets d'** ~ amorous secrets

**aléa** *nm* hazard, chance; unforseeable occurrence

**aléatoire** *adj* aleatory, chancy, risky, problematical

**alémanique** *nm* Swiss-German (language); *adj* Swiss-German, German-Swiss

**alène** *nf* awl

**alentour** *adv* around; *obs* ~ **de** around

**alentours** *nmpl* surroundings

¹**alerte** *nf* alert; alarm; **fin d'** ~ all clear

²**alerte** *adj* alert, lively, brisk

**alerter** *vt* alert, warn

**alésage** *nm mech* boring; cylinder bore

**aleviner** *vt* stock with fish

**alexandrin** *nm pros* alexandrine; *adj* Alexandrine

**alezan** *adj* reddish-brown, chestnut (of horse, mule)

**algarade** *nf* furious verbal attack, tirade; storm of abuse

**algèbre** *nf* algebra; **c'est de l'** ~ **pour moi** it's double-Dutch to me

**algébrique** *adj* algebraic

**Algérien -ienne** *n* Algerian

**algérien -ienne** *adj* Algerian

**Algérois -e** *n* inhabitant of Algiers

**algorithme** *nm* algorithm

**algue** *nf* seaweed

**aliénable** *adj leg* alienable

**aliénation** *nf leg* alienation, conveyance; insanity, madness; aversion; surrender

**aliéné -e** *n* mental patient

**aliéner** *vt* (6) *leg* alienate, convey; give up; alienate, estrange

**aliéniste** *n med* alienist

**alignement** *nm* alignment; building-line; *mil* dressing; *pol* falling into line; row, linc; ~ **monétaire** adjustment of currency exchange rate; **frapper d'** ~ instruct to conform to the building-line

**aligner** *vt* align; conform; adjust (currency); *mil* dress; set out; **s'** ~ get into line, toe the line

**aligoté** *nm* type of white Burgundy grape

**aliment** *nm* food, aliment, nourishment; ~ **s** *leg* subsistance

**alimentaire** *adj* alimentary, nutritious; **pâtes** ~ **s** pasta; **pension** ~ alimony; allowance

**alimentation** *nf* alimentation, nourishment; feeding, providing; **carte d'** ~ ration card; **magasin d'** ~ grocer's shop

**alimenter** *vt* nourish; feed, supply; **s'** ~ feed oneself

**alinéa** *nm typ* indented line; paragraph

**aliquante** *adj math* aliquant

**aliquote** *adj math* aliquot

**aliter** *vt* confine to bed; **s'** ~ take to one's bed

**alizé** *nm* trade-wind; *adj* **vent** ~ trade-wind

**allaitement** *nm* suckling; ~ **artificiel** bottle-feeding; ~ **maternel** breast-feeding

**allaiter** *vt* suckle

**allant** *nm* dash, liveliness; ~ **s et venants** people coming and going; *adj* active, lively

**alléchant** *adj* attractive, alluring

**allécher** *vt* (6) attract, allure

**allée** *nf* tree-lined avenue, tree-lined walk; ~ **(s) et venue(s)** coming(s) and going(s)

**allégation** *nf* allegation
**allège** *nf naut* tender, lighter; *bui* window-breast
**allégeance** *nf* allegiance
**allégement** *nm* lightening, alleviation
**alléger** *vt* (6, 3) lighten
**allégorie** *nf* allegory
**allégorique** *adj* allegorical
**allègre** *adj* lively, spry, gay
**allégresse** *nf* joy, cheerfulness
**alléguer** *vt* (6) cite, produce as evidence, adduce, bring forward; allege
**Allemand -e** *n* German
**allemand** *nm* German (language); *adj* German
**aller** *nm* outward journey; single ticket; ~ **simple** single ticket; ~ **et retour** return ticket; *vi* (12) go; suit, fit; ~+*infin* be about to, be going to; **allez!** go!; come on!; come off it!; **allez donc savoir** find out if you can; **allez-y!** go on!;**allons!** let's go!; come come!; **allons bon!** well!; confound it!; **allons donc!** come off it!; **ça ira** that will be all right; it will work; **ça me va** all right by me, that suits me; **ça va comme ça** that'll do; **cela va de soi** that's obvious; **cela va tout seul** it's working nicely; **comment ça va?** how are you?; **comme vous y allez!** you're really getting on with it!; **il n'en va pas de même** that's a different matter; **il y va de la vie** it's a matter of life or death; **je vais bien** I am well; **les prix vont croissant** prices go on rising; *fig* **où allons-nous?** what are things coming to?; **rien ne va plus** no more bets taken; **va pour quatre francs** four francs – agreed; **s'en** ~ go away, leave, disappear; *euph* die; **je m'en vais vous dire qch** I am going to tell you sth
**allergie** *nf* allergy
**allergique** *adj* allergic
**aller-retour** *nm* return ticket; return journey
**alliage** *nm* alloy
**alliance** *nf* alliance; agreement, union; marriage; relationship by marriage; wedding-ring
**allié -e** *n* ally; *leg* relative; *adj* allied; related
**allier** *vt* ally; alloy; **s'** ~ ally oneself; marry; become connected by marriage; combine, blend
**allô** *interj* hullo!
**allocation** *nf* allocation; allotment; allowance
**allocution** *nf* short speech
**allonger** *vt* (3) lengthen, extend; stretch, stretch out; *cul* thin; *sl* fork out (money); knock down; *coll* ~ **une gifle** slap; *vi* become longer; **s'** ~ become

longer; lie down, stretch oneself out; *coll* fall down flat; *sl* **s'** ~ **qch** treat oneself to sth
**allopathie** *nf med* allopathy
**allotropie** *nf chem* allotropy
**allouer** *vt* allocate; allot; grant
**allumage** *nm* lighting; setting alight; *mot* ignition
**allume-cigares** *nm mot* cigar-lighter
**allume-gaz** *nm invar* gas-lighter
**allumer** *vt* light; set light to; switch on; arouse, excite; **s'** ~ light up
**allumette** *nf* match; *cul* straw, stick; ~ **suédoise** safety match
**allumeur -euse** *n ar* lamp-lighter; *nm mot* distributor; *nf coll* vamp; *vulg* prickteaser
**allure** *nf* speed, pace; gait; air, behaviour; distinction in bearing; appearance; **à toute** ~ at full speed; **avoir de l'** ~ have style; **avoir une drôle** ~ look odd, look strange
**allusif -ive** *adj* allusive
**alluvion** *nf geol* alluvion; alluvium; ~ **s** alluvion, alluvium
**alluvionnement** *nm* alluvium
**almanach** *nm* almanac; ~ **de Gotha** = European Debrett
**aloès** *nm* aloe
**aloi** *nm obs* alloy; official status of coinage; hallmark; *fig* **de bon** ~ of high quality; **de mauvais** ~ of base quality
**alors** *adv* then; in that case; so; therefore; ~ **que** when, whereas; **d'** ~ of that time; **et** ~ so what?; *coll* **non, mais** ~? come off it
**alouette** *nf* lark; *cul* ~ **sans tête** veal olive
**alourdir** *vt* make heavy, weigh down; make dull; **s'** ~ become heavy
**alourdissement** *nm* heaviness; growing heaviness
**aloyau** *nm cul* sirloin
**alpaga** *nm* alpaca
**alpe** *nf* high mountain pasture
**Alpes** *nfpl* Alps
**alpestre** *adj* Alpine
**alphabétique** *adj* alphabetical
**alpin** *adj* Alpine
**alpinisme** *nm* mountaineering
**alpiniste** *n* mountaineer, climber
**Alsacien -ienne** *n* Alsatian
**alsacien** *nm* Alsatian dialect; *adj* (*f* -ienne) Alsatian
**altérable** *adj* liable to deterioration
**altérant** *adj* thirst-provoking; causing deterioration
**altération** *nf* change, modification; deterioration, change for the worse; falsification; *mus* sign for altering pitch (sharp, flat, natural)
**altérer** *vt* (6) change, modify; deterio-

rate, change for the worse; falsify; make thirsty; make desirous

**alternance** *nf* alternation

**alternant** *adj* alternating; **cultures ~ es** rotating crops

**alternateur** *nm elect* alternator

**alternatif -ive** *adj* alternative; *elect* alternating

**alternative** *nf obs* alternation; alternative

**alterné** *adj* in alternation, alternate

**alterner** *vt* rotate (crops); *vi* alternate

**altesse** *nf* Highness

**altier -ière** *adj* haughty, noble

**altimètre** *nm* altimeter

**altiport** *nm* airport at mountain resort

**alto** *nm* viola; counter-tenor; *nf* contralto

**altruisme** *nm* altruism

**altruiste** *n + adj* altruist

**alumine** *nf* alumina

**alun** *nm* alum

**alunir** *vi* land on the moon

**alunissage** *nm* moon landing

**alvéolaire** *adj* alveolar

**alvéole** *nf* alveolus; honeycomb

**amabilité** *nf* amiability; kindness, affability; **veuillez avoir l' ~ de** please be so kind as to

**amadou** *nm* tinder

**amadouer** *vt* soften, wheedle, coax

**amaigrir** *vt* emaciate, make thin; **s' ~** lose weight

**amaigrissant** *adj* slimming, reducing

**amaigrissement** *nm* loss of weight

**amalgame** *nm* alloy of mercury; amalgam, mixture

**amalgamer** *vt* amalgamate, mix

**amande** *nf* almond

**amandier** *nm* almond-tree

**amant -e** *n obs* someone in love; *nm* lover; *nf* mistress; **~ s** lovers

**amarante** *nf bot* amaranth; *adj invar* deep purple

**amariner** *vt naut* put a prize crew on board; make a seaman of

**amarrage** *nm* mooring

**amarre** *nf naut* hawser, mooring-rope

**amarrer** *vt naut* moor; lash

**amas** *nm* heap, pile, store; *astron* nebula

**amasser** *vt* amass, pile up, gather together; **s' ~** pile up, gather together

**amateur** *nm* enthusiast, lover; amateur

**amateurisme** *nm* amateurishness; *sp* amateur status

**amazone** *nf* amazon; horse-woman; **monter en ~** ride side-saddle

**ambages** *nfpl* **sans ~** without circumlocutions, plainly

**ambassade** *nf* embassy; delicate mission; embassy staff

**ambassadeur** *nm* ambassador

**ambassadrice** *nf* woman ambassador; wife of an ambassador

**ambiance** *nf* atmosphere, mood; milieu, environment; *coll* **il y a de l' ~ ici** it's very lively here

**ambiant** *adj* ambient

**ambidextre** *adj* ambidextrous

**ambigu -uë** *adj* ambiguous; equivocal; ambivalent

**ambiguïté** *nf* ambiguity; ambivalence

**ambitieux -ieuse** *n* ambitious person; go-getter; *adj* ambitious; *pej* presumptuous, pretentious

**ambitionner** *vt* aspire to, strongly desire

**ambre** *nm* amber; **~ gris** ambergris; *adj* amber-coloured; smelling of ambergris

**ambroisie** *nf* ambrosia

**ambulance** *nf* ambulance; *mil* field-hospital

**âme** *nf* soul; spirit; living person; guiding spirit; core; bore (rifle, gun); *coll* **~ damnée de s/o** totally devoted to; **~ sœur** kindred spirit; **avoir charge d' ~ s** have care of souls; **état d' ~** state of mind; **être comme une ~ en peine** be inconsolable; *coll* **like a lost soul; ma chère ~** dearest, darling; **rendre l' ~** die

**amélioration** *nf* improvement, betterment, amelioration

**améliorer** *vt* improve, ameliorate; revise, correct; **s' ~** improve

**aménagement** *nm* arranging, fitting out; organization; **~ du territoire** regional economic and social development

**aménager** *vt* (3) arrange, fit out, dispose

**amende** *nf* fine, penalty; **faire ~ honorable** admit one's faults; ask forgiveness; **sous peine d' ~** on pain of a fine

**amendement** *nm* amendment; amelioration of soil; fertilizer

**amender** *vt* improve; correct; amend; improve (soil); **s' ~** mend one's ways

**amène** *adj lit* agreeable, amiable

**amener** *vt* (6) bring; lead; convey; bring about; pull in; **s' ~** *sl* come, turn up

**aménité** *nf* pleasantness, amenity; charm, niceness; *iron* **~ s** disagreeable words

**amenuiser** *vt* diminish; make thinner

**amer** *nm* bitters; *adj* (*f* **-ère**) bitter; sharp, painful; biting

**Américain -e** *n* American

**américain** *nm* American (language); *adj* American

**américaniser** *vt* americanize

**américanisme** *nm* americanism; American studies

**amérindien -ienne** *adj* American Indian

**Amerlo(t), Amerloque** *n sl* Yank

**amerrir** *vi* come down on the sea

**amertume** *nf* bitterness, disquiet,

melancholy

**améthyste** *nf* amethyst

**ameublement** *nm* furniture, furnishings; **tissu d'** ~ furnishing fabric

**ameuter** *vt* muster a crowd; rouse up a crowd; form a pack of hounds; **s'** ~ assemble with hostile intent, band together

**ami -e** *n* friend; *euph* lover, mistress; supporter, fan; **en** ~ as a friend, as friends; **mon** ~ my dear fellow; **petit** ~ boy-friend; **petite** ~**e** girl-friend; *adj* friendly; kindly; favourable

**amiable** *adj* amicable; **à l'** ~ by agreement

**amiante** *nm* amianthus, asbestos

**amibe** *nf* amoeba

**amical** *adj* friendly

**amicale** *nf* club, association

**amidon** *nm* starch

**amidonner** *vt* starch

**amincir** *vt* make thinner; make look thin; **s'** ~ grow thinner

**amino-acide** *nm* amino-acid

**amiral** *nm* admiral; *adj* **vaisseau** ~ flagship

**amirauté** *nf* naval high command

**amitié** *nf* friendship; friendly gesture, understanding; ~ **particulière** homosexual friendship

**ammoniac -iaque** *adj* ammoniac; **gaz** ~ ammonia

**ammoniaque** *nf* solution ammonia

**amnésie** *nf* amnesia

**amnésique** *adj* amnesic

**amnistie** *nf* amnesty

**amnistier** *vt* amnesty

**amocher** *vt sl* damage, spoil; bash; **s'** ~ get damaged

**amoindrir** *vt* diminish, reduce; **s'** ~ decrease, diminish

**amoindrissement** *nm* diminution, reduction

**amollir** *vt* soften; weaken; **s'** ~ soften

**amonceler** *vt* (5) pile up, accumulate; **s'** ~ increase, pile up

**amoncellement** *nm* piling up, accumulation

**amont** *nm* head waters; **en** ~ **de** upstream; **vent d'** ~ off-shore wind

**amoralisme** *nm* amoralism

**amorçage** *nm* priming; setting off

**amorce** *nf* bait, lure; attraction; detonator; commencement, first step

**amorcer** *vt* (4) bait; attract; commence, begin; prime, inveigle

**amorphe** *adj* amorphous; soft; inconsistent

**amortir** *vt* attenuate, deaden; soften; amortize

**amortissement** *nm* amortization; diminution; deadening; writing off; depre-

ciation

**amortisseur** *nm mot* shock-absorber

**amour** *nm* love; liking; sexual attraction; love-making; person loved; darling; passion; love-affair; ~**s** love-affairs; *poet nf* feelings of love; **Amour** Cupid; **avec** ~ lovingly; **faire l'** ~ make love, have sex; **filer le parfait** ~ be happily in love; **un** ~ **de robe** a sweet little dress; **vous seriez un** ~ **si** it would be sweet of you to

**amouracher (s')** *v refl pej* fall in love

**amourette** *nf* passing infatuation; calf-love

**amoureux -euse** *n* someone in love; *adj* in love, amorous; avid for

**amour-propre** *nm* self-esteem; self-pride

**amovible** *adj* removable, detachable

**ampère-heure** *nm* ampere-hour

**amphi** *nm coll* lecture-hall

**amphibie** *adj* amphibious

**amphigourique** *adj* (style) rambling, involved

**amphore** *nf* amphora

**ampleur** *nf* spaciousness; fullness, amplitude

**ampli** *nm coll* amplifier

**ampliation** *nf leg* true copy; **pour** ~ certified true copy

**amplificateur** *nm* amplifier

**amplifier** *vt* amplify

**ampoule** *nf* ampoule, phial; *elect* bulb; blister

**ampoulé** *adj* bombastic, inflated

**amputé -e** *n* person with amputated limb

**amputer** *vt* amputate

**amulette** *nf* amulet

**amure** *nf naut* tack (of sail)

**amurer** *vt naut* board, tack

**amusant** *adj* amusing

**amuse-gueule** *nm invar* cocktail snack

**amuser** *vt* amuse, please, entertain; distract; **s'** ~ enjoy oneself; waste one's time; *pej* live it up; **s'** ~ **de** toy with

**amusette** *nf* plaything

**amuseur -euse** *n* entertainer

**amygdale** *nf* tonsil

**amygdalite** *nf* tonsilitis

**an** *nm* year; **bon** ~ **mal** ~ year in year out; **il a vingt** ~**s** he is twenty years old; **l'** ~ **prochain** next year; **le jour de l'** ~ New Year's Day; **par** ~ per year

**anabaptiste** *n* anabaptist

**anachorète** *nm* hermit

**anachronique** *adj* anachronistic

**anachronisme** *nm* anachronism

**anacoluthe** *nf* anacoluthon

**anagramme** *nf* anagram

**analgésie** *nf* analgesia

**analgésique** *adj* analgesic

**analogie** *nf* analogy
**analogique** *adj* analogous
**analogue** *nm* analogue; *adj* analogous
**analphabète** *n + adj* illiterate
**analphabétisme** *nm* illiteracy
**analyse** *nf* analysis; summary, résumé; **esprit d' ~** analytical mind
**analyser** *vt* analyse; give an abstract of
**analyste** *n* analyst; computer programmer
**analytique** *adj* analytic, analytical
**ananas** *nm* pineapple
**anarchie** *nf* anarchy
**anarchique** *adj* anarchical, anarchic
**anarchisme** *nm* anarchism
**anarchiste** *n* anarchist
**anathématiser** *vt* anathematize; denounce
**anathème** *nm* anathema; curse
**anatomie** *nf* anatomy
**anatomique** *adj* anatomical
**anatomiste** *n* anatomist
**ancêtre** *n* ancestor
**anche** *nf mus* reed
**anchois** *nm* anchovy
**ancien** *nm* senior; ~ s ancients, peoples of antiquity; *adj* (*f* -**ienne**) ancient, old; antique; former; ~ **maire** ex-mayor
**ancienneté** *nf* ancientness; seniority (in post, rank)
**ancrage** *nm* anchorage; anchoring
**ancre** *nf* anchor; *bui* brace; **jeter l' ~** anchor; **lever l' ~** weigh anchor
**ancrer** *vt* fix firmly; *naut ar* anchor; **s' ~** *fig* be rooted in; *naut ar* anchor
**andalou -ouse** *n + adj* Andalusian
**andouille** *nf* chitterlings; *fig sl* idiot, fool
**androgyne** *nm* hermaphrodite; *adj* androgynous
**âne** *nm* ass, donkey; *fig* ass, idiot; **à dos d' ~** humpbacked; **bonnet d' ~** dunce's cap
**anéantir** *vt* annihilate, exterminate, destroy completely; stun, depress; **s' ~** disappear completely; come to nothing
**anéantissement** *nm* annihilation, complete destruction; prostration, depression
**anecdotique** *adj* anecdotal
**anémie** *nf* anaemia
**anémier** *vt* make anaemic, debilitate
**anémique** *adj* anaemic
**anémomètre** *nm* anemometer, wind-gauge
**ânerie** *nf* stupidity, gross ignorance; silly remark; tomfoolery
**anéroïde** *adj* aneroid
**ânesse** *nf* female donkey, she-ass
**anesthésie** *nf* anaesthesia; *fig* insensibility
**anesthésier** *vt* anaesthetize

**anesthésique** *nm + adj* anaesthetic
**anesthésiste** *n* anaesthetist
**anévrisme** *nm* aneurism
**anfractuosité** *nf* hollow, crack
**ange** *nm* angel; angel fish; ~ **gardien** guardian angel; *coll* bodyguard; **être aux ~ s** be delighted; *coll* **faiseuse d' ~ s** abortionist; **un ~ passe** that was an embarrassing silence
¹**angélique** *nf* angelica
²**angélique** *adj* angelic
**angine** *nf* severe sore throat; tonsilitis; quinsy; ~ **(de poitrine)** angina (pectoris)
**Anglais -e** *n* Englishman, Englishwoman
**anglais** *nm* English (language); *adj* English; *coll* **capote ~ e** French letter; **filer à l' ~** take French leave
**anglaises** *nfpl* ringlets
**angle** *nm* corner; *geom* angle; *fig* angle, point of view
**anglicanisme** *nm* Anglicanism
**angliciser** *vt* anglicize
**anglicisme** *nm* anglicism
**angliciste** *n* specialist in English studies
**anglomanie** *nf* anglomania
**anglo-normand** *nm* Anglo-Norman (dialect); *adj* Anglo-Norman; **les îles ~ es** the Channel Islands
**anglophobie** *nf* anglophobia
**anglophone** *adj* English-speaking
**angoissant** *adj* agonizing, very painful
**angoisse** *nf* anguish
**angoissé** *adj* anguished, distressed
**anguille** *nf* eel; ~ **de mer** conger eel; **il y a ~ sous roche** there's more to this than meets the eye, there's something fishy about this
**angulaire** *adj* angular
**anguleux -euse** *adj* angular; long; difficult.
**anicroche** *nf* snag
**animal** *nm* animal; *pej* idiot, fool; *adj* animal
**animalité** *nf* animality
**animateur -trice** *n* animator; organizer, leader; compère
**animé** *adj* animated
**animer** *vt* animate, give life to; enliven, excite; incite; **s' ~** become alive, become animated; warm up (discussion)
**animisme** *nm* animism
**animosité** *nf* animosity
**anis** *nm* aniseed
**anisette** *nf* (alcoholic) drink made with aniseed
**ankylose** *nf med* anchylosis
**ankyloser** *vt med* stiffen, paralyse; **s' ~** *med* become anchylotic, stiffen; *fig* become paralysed

**annales** *nfpl* annals

**annaliste** *nm* chronicler; annalist

**anneau** *nm* ring; link (chain); coil (spoke); ringlet

**année** *nf* year; **bonne ~!** Happy New Year!; **d' ~ en ~** from year to year

**année-lumière** *nf* (*pl* **années-lumières**) light-year

**annelé** *adj* ringed

**annexe** *nf* annex; *anat + biol* process; *adj* annexed, subsidiary

**annexer** *vt* annex, incorporate; **s' ~** *coll* take for oneself

**annexion** *nf* annexation

**annihiler** *vt* annihilate

**anniversaire** *nm* anniversary; birthday; *adj* anniversary

**annonce** *nf* announcement; advertisement; presage; call (cards); **petites ~ s** small ads

**annoncer** *vt* announce; proclaim; indicate, show; predict; usher in; call (cards); **s' ~** seem likely to happen; promise

**annonceur** *nm* advertiser

**annonciateur -trice** *adj* heralding, presaging

**Annonciation** *nf* Annunciation

**annotateur -trice** *n* commentator (text)

**annoter** *vt* annotate

**annuaire** *nm* (annual) directory, year-book

**annuel -elle** *adj* annual

**annuité** *nf* annuity

**annulaire** *nm* ring finger; *adj* annular

**annulation** *nf* quashing; cancellation; annulment (marriage)

**annuler** *vt* annul; quash; cancel; **s' ~** cancel out

**anoblir** *vt* ennoble

**anoblissement** *nm* ennoblement

**anodin** *adj* anodyne

**anomalie** *nf* anomaly

**ânon** *nm* little donkey

**ânonnement** *nm* hesitant reading, hesitant speech

**ânonner** *vi* read hesitantly; speak hesitantly; stumble (reading, speaking)

**anonymat** *nm* anonymity

**anonyme** *adj* anonymous; *fig* impersonal

**anorexie** *nf med* anorexia

**anormal** *adj* abnormal; exceptional

**anse** *nf* handle; *geog* cove; **faire danser l' ~ du panier** make a bit on the side (servant when shopping)

**antagonique** *adj* antagonistic

**antagonisme** *nm* antagonism

**antagoniste** *n* antagonist

**antan** *nm lit* **d' ~** of time past, of bygone days

**Antarctique** *nf* Antarctica

**antarctique** *adj* antarctic

**antédiluvien -ienne** *adj* antediluvian

**antenne** *nf* antenna; aerial; **avoir des ~ s** be very perceptive; **passer sur les ~ s** be broadcast; **temps d' ~** duration (broadcast)

**antépénultième** *adj* antepenultimate

**antérieur** *adj* anterior; former

**anthologie** *nf* anthology

**anthropoïde** *nm + adj* anthropoid

**anthropologie** *nf* anthropology

**anthropologiste, anthropologue** *n* anthropologist

**anthropométrie** *nf* anthropometry

**anthropomorphique** *adj* anthropomorphic

**anthropomorphisme** *nm* anthropomorphism

**anthropophage** *nm + adj* cannibal

**anthropophagie** *nf* cannibalism

**antiaérien -ienne** *adj* anti-aircraft

**antibiotique** *nm + adj* antibiotic

**antibrouillard** *nm mot* fog-lamp; *adj mot* **phare ~** fog-lamp

**antibuée** *nm + adj* demister

**antichambre** *nf* antechamber; **faire ~** dance attendance

**antichar** *adj* anti-tank

**anticipé** *adj* early, premature

**anticiper** *vt* anticipate; foresee; *vi* anticipate; **~ sur** encroach on

**anticléricalisme** *nm* anticlericalism

**anticommunisme** *nm* anticommunism

**anticommuniste** *adj* anticommunist

**anticonceptionnel -elle** *adj* contraceptive

**anticorps** *nm* antibody

**antidater** *vt* antedate

**antidémocratique** *adj* antidemocratic

**antidérapant** *adj mot* non-skid

**antienne** *nf eccles* antiphon; *fig* same old tune

**antifasciste** *adj* antifascist

**antigel** *nm mot* antifreeze

**antigène** *nm physiol* antigen

**antigivrant** *nm mot* de-icer

**antihistaminique** *nm + adj* antihistamine

**antilope** *nf* antelope

**antimoine** *nm chem* antimony

**antimonarchique** *adj* antimonarchical

**antinomie** *nf* antinomy, contradiction

**antiparasite** *adj rad* **dispositif ~** suppressor

**antipathie** *nf* antipathy

**antipathique** *adj* antipathetic

**antiphrase** *nf* antiphrasis

**antipode** *nm* exact opposite; **~ s** antipodes; **aux ~ s** far away; poles apart

**antiquaille** *nf pej* junk, valueless antique

**antiquaire** *n* antique dealer

**antique** *nm* art of antiquity; *nf obs* antique (object); *adj* antique, of antiquity; old-fashioned

**antiquité** *nf* antiquity; ~ **s** antiquities; antiques

**antisémitisme** *nm* antisemitism

**antisepsie** *nf* antisepsis

**antiseptique** *nm + adj* antiseptic

**antithèse** *nf* antithesis; sharp contrast

**antithétique** *adj* antithetical

**antitoxine** *nf* antitoxin

**antitoxique** *adj* antitoxic

**antivol** *nm mot* anti-theft device

**antonyme** *nm* antonym

**antre** *nm* den, lair; cavern; *physiol* antrum

**anxiété** *nf* anxiety

**anxieux -ieuse** *adj* anxious, worried; eager, impatient

**aorte** *nf anat* aorta

**août** *nm* August

**aoûtat** *nm dial* harvest-bug

**aoûtien -ienne** *n* August holiday-maker; one who remains in a big city in August

**apaisement** *nm* appeasement, pacification; calming down, assuagement; ~ **s** reassurances

**apaiser** *vt* appease, pacify; calm, assuage; (hunger) satisfy; (thirst) quench; **s' ~** become calm, be pacified

**aparté** *nm theat* aside; side conversation

**apathie** *nf* apathy, indolence

**apathique** *adj* apathetic, indolent

**apatride** *n* stateless person

**apercevoir** *vt* see, perceive, discern; **laisser ~** show; **s' ~ de** perceive, become aware of, notice

**aperçu** *nm* glimpse; first idea, notion; outline, summary; remark, observation

**apéritif** *nm* aperitif, cocktail; *adj (f -ive)* which stimulates the appetite

**apesanteur** *nf* weightlessness

**à-peu-près, à peu près** *nm* approximation; imperfection

**apeurer** *vt* frighten

**aphasie** *nf med* aphasia

**aphasique** *adj med* aphasic

**aphone** *adj med* aphonic, voiceless

**aphonie** *nf med* aphonia

**aphorisme** *nm* aphorism

**aphrodisiaque** *nm + adj* aphrodisiac

**aphte** *nm med* aphtha

**aphteux -euse** *adj* covered with aphthae; *vet* **fièvre aphteuse** foot-and-mouth disease

**apiculteur -trice** *n* bee-keeper

**apiculture** *nf* bee-keeping

**apitoiement** *nm* pity, compassion

**apitoyer** *vt* touch; **s' ~** pity

**aplanir** *vt* level, flatten, smooth; *fig* smooth out, resolve

**aplatir** *vt* flatten, level; (hair) plaster down; **s' ~** become flattened; *coll* fall

flat on the ground; *fig* grovel

**aplomb** *nm* verticality; balance; equilibrium; *fig* aplomb, self-possession; *pej* nerve; **d' ~** vertical, plumb; in balance; *fig* in good form

**apocalyptique** *adj* apocalyptic

**apocryphe** *nm bibl* apocrypha; *adj* apocryphal

**apogée** *nm astron* apogee; *fig* summit, highest point

**apolitique** *adj* apolitical

**apologétique** *nf eccles* apologetics

**apologie** *nf* apology; justification

**apologiste** *n* apologist

**apophtègme** *nm* apophthegm, maxim

**apoplectique** *adj* apoplectic

**apoplexie** *nf* apoplexy

**apostasie** *nf* apostasy

**apostat** *nm* apostate

**apostille** *nf* marginal note; recommendation

**apostolique** *adj* apostolic

**apostropher** *vt* apostrophize; address rudely; **s' ~** exchange insults

**apothéose** *nf* apotheosis

**apothicaire** *nm* apothecary

**apôtre** *nm eccles* apostle; advocate; **faire le bon ~** sham virtue in order to deceive

**apparaître** *vi* (68) appear, become visible; seem, be apparent

**apparat** *nm* pomp, display; ~ **critique** critical apparatus; **costume d' ~** ceremonial dress; **discours d' ~** formal speech

**appareil** *nm ar = ***apparat*** qv*; apparatus, machinery, instrument; mechanism; appliance; (telephone) receiver; aircraft; brace (teeth); ~ **digestif** digestive system; ~ **électrique** electrical appliance; ~ **photo(graphique)** camera; **dans le plus simple ~** naked; **qui est à l' ~?** who is speaking? (telephone)

**appareillage** *nm naut* leaving port, getting under way; equipment; installation

¹**appareiller** *vt* prepare; install; *naut* (ship) make ready for sea; (fishing-net) prepare; *bui* (stone) dress; *vi naut* set sail; depart

²**appareiller** *vt* match

**apparence** *nf* appearance, aspect, form; trace; verisimilitude; **en ~** apparently; **il y a toute ~** it would seem that; **sauver les ~ s** save face

**apparent** *adj* apparent; ostensible; obvious, evident; illusory, false

**apparenté** *adj* related, allied

**apparentement** *nm pol* alliance for electoral purposes

**apparenter (s')** *v refl* **s' ~ à** marry into;

resemble; *pol* enter into an electoral alliance

**apparier** *vt* mate, couple

**appariteur** *nm* beadle, usher

**apparition** *nf* appearance; apparition; vision; ghost

**apparoir** *vi* (13) *leg* be apparent

**appartement** *nm* flat, *US* apartment

**appartenance** *nf* membership, belonging

**appartenir** *vi* (96) ~ à belong to; (sexually) be possessed by; **il m'appartient de** I am responsible for; **s' ~** be free, be independent

**appât** *nm* bait; *fig* attraction; ~s *obs* or *joc* (sexual) charms

**appâter** *vt* entice; fatten (poultry)

**appauvrir** *vt* impoverish, exhaust; **s' ~** become impoverished

**appauvrissement** *nm* impoverishment, exhaustion

**appeau** *nm* decoy

**appel** *nm* call, summons; roll-call; *mil* call up; appeal, exhortation; *leg* appeal; **cour d' ~** court of appeal; **faire ~** ask, appeal; **faire l' ~** call the roll; **sans ~** irrevocably

**appelant-e** *n* + *adj leg* appellant

**appelé** *nm mil* conscript; *adj* called; **être ~ à** be obliged to

**appeler** *vt* (5) call, summon; call for, require; appoint, designate; name; invoke; *mil* call up; **~ au téléphone** ring up; **~ le médecin** send for the doctor; *leg* **en ~** appeal against sentence; **en ~ à** appeal to; **s' ~** be called, be named; *coll* **voilà ce qui s'appelle chanter** that's what real singing is like

**appellation** *nf* appellation, designation; *comm* **~ d'origine** designation of a product's place of origin; **vin d' ~ contrôlée** wine certified to come from a designated place

**appendice** *nm* appendage, addition; *anat* appendix; appendix (book)

**appendicite** *nf* appendicitis

**appentis** *nm* lean-to roof; lean-to, outhouse

**appesantir** *vt* weigh down; press down; **s' ~** become heavy; *fig* insist; talk too much; **~ sur** weigh upon; dwell on

**appesantissement** *nm* heaviness, dullness

**appétissant** *adj* appetizing; pleasing, attractive

**appétit** *nm* appetite; desire, inclination; **~ de** strong desire for; **~ de loup** large appetite; *fig* **l' ~ vient en mangeant** the more one has the more one wants

**applaudir** *vt* + *vi* applaud, clap; **s' ~ de** be glad about

**applaudissement** *nm* applause, clapping; *fig* approval, satisfaction

**application** *nf* application, applying; employment, use; covering; (mind) concentration; (law) enforcement

**applique** *nf* (sewing) appliqué; *elect* wall-light, sconce

**appliquer** *vt* apply, put; employ, use; (mind) concentrate; (law) enforce; (blow) deal; **s' ~** apply; apply oneself, concentrate

**appoint** *nm* complement, addition; sum in small change; **d' ~** supplementary; **faire l' ~** pay the exact amount; top up

**appointements** *nmpl* emoluments

¹**appointer** *vt* pay emoluments to

²**appointer** *vt* sharpen

**appontement** *nm naut* pier

**apponter** *vi* (aircraft) land on deck of aircraft-carrier

**apport** *nm* contribution; bringing; *leg* ~s assets

**apporter** *vt* bring, carry; provide, furnish; display; produce, cause

**apposer** *vt* place on, put on; affix; (poster) stick up; *leg* **les scellés** put under seals; **~ sa signature** sign, set one's hand

**appréciable** *adj* appreciable; considerable, notable

**appréciatif -ive** *adj* appreciative

**appréciation** *nf* appreciation; evaluation; judgement, opinion

**apprécier** *vt* appreciate, enjoy, like; evaluate; estimate, judge

**appréhender** *vt leg* arrest; apprehend

**appréhensif -ive** *adj* apprehensive

**apprendre** *vt* (75) learn; hear (of), discover; inform, teach; **~ à** learn how to; **~ à qn à** teach s/o how to; **~ qch à qn** teach s/o sth; **cela lui apprendra à vivre** that will teach him a lesson

**apprenti -e** *n* apprentice; novice

**apprentissage** *nm* apprenticeship; beginning, first experience

**apprêt** *nm* preparation, making ready; *fig* affectation; **sans ~(s)** naturally, unaffectedly

**apprêté** *adj* affected

**apprêter** *vt* prepare, arrange, make ready; prepare (food); **s' ~** be being prepared; prepare oneself; dress oneself up

**apprivoisement** *nm* taming

**apprivoiser** *vt* tame, train; soften; **s' ~** (animal) become tame; become sociable; become accustomed

**approbateur -trice** *n* one who agrees; *adj* approving

**approbatif -ive** *adj* approving

**approchable** *adj* approachable

**approchant** *adj* approaching; approximate; **qch d'** ~ something like

**approche** *nf* approach, drawing near; access, surround; point of view; approach; **lunette d'** ~ magnifying glass; *mil* **travaux d'** ~ defence works; *fig* subtle manoeuvres

**approcher** *vt* bring near, draw near; come close to; frequent; *vi* approach; be near; be close to; **s'** ~ **de** approach; come close to, be near to

**approfondir** *vt* deepen; examine closely; **s'** ~ become deeper

**approfondissement** *nm* deepening; study, examination

**approprié** *adj* appropriate, pertinent

**approprier** *vt* adapt, make appropriate; **s'** ~ appropriate, seize; usurp

**approuvé** *adj* agreed

**approuver** *vt* approve, agree, accept; recognize

**approvisionnement** *nm* provisioning, stocking; provisions

**approvisionner** *vt* stock, provide, furnish; **s'** ~ stock up

**approximatif -ive** *adj* approximate

**appui** *nm* support; prop, protection; **à l'** ~ **de** in support of; **mur d'** ~ supporting wall; **point d'** ~ fulcrum; key point; **prendre** ~ **sur** rely on

**appui-bras, appuie-bras** *nm* (*pl* **appuis-bras, appuie-bras**) arm rest

**appui-tête, appuie-tête** *nm* (*pl* **appuis-tête, appuie-tête**) head rest; antimacassar

**appuyer** *vt* (7) support; place; maintain, confirm; help, push; press; *vi* ~ **sur** be held up by; weigh upon; emphasize; insist upon; ~ **sur la d**. **oite (gauche)** go right (left); **s'** ~ **sur** support oneself on; rely on; lean on, rest on

**âpre** *adj* rough, harsh; biting (wind); bitter, rough (taste); hard (struggle); avid, tough (person)

**après** *adv* after; behind; **et** ~ **?** and so what?; what then?; *prep* after; **d'** ~ according to

**après-demain** *adv* the day after tomorrow

**après-dîner** *nm* after dinner

**après-guerre** *nm* post-war period

**après-midi** *nm* afternoon

**après-ski** *nm* soft boot (for use after skiing); activities after skiing

**après-vente** *adj* service ~ after-sales service

**âpreté** *nf* roughness, hardness; bitterness (taste)

**à-propos** *nm* appropriateness, suitability

**apte** *adj* apt, capable

**aquaplaning** *nm mot* skid on wet surface

**aquatique** *adj* aquatic

**aqueduc** *nm* aqueduct

**aquilin** *adj* aquiline

**aquilon** *nm lit* north wind

**Arabe** *n* Arab

**arabe** *nm* Arabic; *adj* Arab

**arabisant -e** *n* specialist in Arabic

**arachide** *nf* peanut, ground-nut

**arachnides** *nmpl zool* arachnids

**araignée** *nf* spider; ~ **de mer** kind of crab; *coll* **avoir une** ~ **au plafond** have a screw loose; **toile d'** ~ spider's web

**araser** *vt* level (wall); plane (plank)

**arbalète** *nf ar* cross-bow

**arbitrage** *nm* arbitration; *sp* refereeing; *comm* arbitrage

**arbitraire** *nf* arbitrary nature; arbitrary action; *adj* arbitrary

**arbitre** *nm* arbitrator, conciliator; arbiter; *sp* referee, umpire; *philos* **libre** ~ free will

**arbitrer** *vt* arbitrate; settle; *sp* referee, umpire

**arborer** *vt* hoist (flag, banner); wear (medal); display; ~ **un sourire** wear a set smile

**arbre** *nm* tree; *mech eng* shaft, axle; ~ **de Noël** Christmas tree; ~ **fruitier** fruit-tree

**arbrisseau** *nm* bush, shrub

**arbuste** *nm* small bush

**arc** *nm* bow; *geom* arc; arch

**arcane** *nm* arcanum, mystery; elixir; ~ **s** secrets

**arc-boutant** *nm* (*pl* **arcs-boutants**) *archi* flying buttress

**arc-bouter** *vt archi* support with a flying buttress; prop up; **s'** ~ *fig* brace oneself

**arceau** *nm* small archway; arch (vault); hoop (croquet)

**arc-en-ciel** *nm* (*pl* **arcs-en-ciel**) *nm* rainbow

**archaïque** *adj* archaic

**archaïsme** *nm* archaism

**archange** *nm* archangel

¹**arche** *nf* ark; ~ **d'alliance** ark of the covenant

²**arche** *nf* arch

**archéologie** *nf* archaeology

**archéologique** *adj* archaeological

**archéologue** *n* archaeologist

**archet** *nm* bow (violin, etc)

**archevêché** *nm* archbishopric; archbishop's palace

**archevêque** *nm* archbishop

**archi-** *pref* very, extremely, super

**archidiacre** *nm* archdeacon

**archidiocèse** *nm* archdiocese

**archiduc** *nm* archduke

**archiduchesse** *nf* archduchess

**archipel** *nm* archipelago

**architecte** *nm* architect

**architectonique** *adj* architectonic
**archiviste** *n* archivist
**arçon** *nm* pommel, saddle-bow; **cheval d' ~ s** vaulting horse
**Arctique** *nm* Arctic
**arctique** *adj* arctic
**ardent** *adj* ardent, keen, passionate; burning, scorching; **être sur des charbons ~ s** be like a cat on hot bricks
**ardeur** *nf* heat; ardour
**ardoise** *nf* slate; debt; slate grey; **avoir des ~ s** be in debt
**ardu** *adj* arduous
**arène** *nf* arena; **~ s** bull-ring
**arête** *nf* fish-bone; ridge; **~ du nez** bridge of nose
**argent** *nm* silver; silver coin; money; **~ de poche** pocket money; **en avoir pour son ~** have one's money's worth; **être cousu d' ~** be rolling in money
**argentan, argenton** *nm* nickel-silver, German silver
**argenté** *adj* silvery; *coll* rich
**argenter** *vt* silver, plate with silver
**argenterie** *nf* silverware, silver-plate
**Argentin -e** *n* Argentinian
¹**argentin** *adj* Argentinian
²**argentin** *adj* clear-sounding, silvery
**argile** *nf* clay
**argileux -euse** *adj* clayey
**argot** *nm* slang; thieves' jargon
**argotique** *adj* slangy
**argotisme** *nm* slang term
**arguer** *vt* deduce, infer; **~ de** put forward as argument, allege
**argument** *nm* argument; proof, reason; summary
**argumenter** *vi* argue
**argus** *nm* *lit* vigilant observer, vigilant spy; spy; paper giving specialized information; **Argus de l'automobile** second-hand car price guide
**argutie** *nf* cavil, quibble
**aride** *adj* arid, sterile; *fig* dry, tedious
**aridité** *nf* aridity, sterility; *fig* dryness, tediousness
**aristocrate** *n* aristocrat, noble
**aristocratie** *nf* aristocracy, nobility; élite
**aristocratique** *adj* aristocratic
**arithmétique** *nf* arithmetic; arithmetic book; *adj* arithmetical
**arlequin -e** *n* harlequin; **habit d' ~** motley
**armateur** *nm* ship-owner
**armature** *nf* structure, framework; basis; *mus* key-signature
**arme** *nf* arm, weapon; **~ absolue** ultimate weapon; **~ à double tranchant** two-edged weapon; **~ à feu** firearm; **être sous les ~ s** be under arms; **faire ses premières ~ s** make one's début; **les ~ s** fencing; **maître d' ~ s** fencing-master; **passer par les ~ s** execute, shoot; **porter**

les ~ s bear arms; **portez ~ s!** slope arms!; **présentez ~ s!** present arms!; **rendre les ~ s** surrender; **salle d' ~ s** fencing school
**armé** *adj* armed; provided with; **vol à main ~ e** armed robbery
**armée** *nf* army; vast number, host; **~ active** regular army; **~ de l'air** airforce; **~ de mer** navy; **~ du Salut** Salvation Army
**armement** *nm* arming; armament; *naut* commissioning, fitting out; shipowning
**Arménien -ienne** *n* Armenian
**arménien** *nm* Armenian (language); *adj* (*f* -ienne) Armenian
**armer** *vt* arm; cock (gun, rifle); fortify; *naut* commission, equip; **s' ~** arm oneself; protect oneself; **s' ~ de** provide oneself with
**armoire** *nf* cupboard
**armoiries** *nf pl* *her* arms
**armorial** *adj* armorial
**armure** *nf* armour
**armurerie** *nf* profession of armourer; *elect* armature; gunsmith's trade
**armurier** *nm* armourer, gunsmith
**aromate** *nm* aromatic
**aromatique** *adj* aromatic
**aromatiser** *vt* aromatize, flavour
**arôme, arome** *nm* aroma
**aronde** *nf* *ar* *orni* swallow; *carp* **queue d' ~** dovetail
**arpège** *nm* *mus* arpeggio
**arpent** *nm* *ar* = (nearly) acre
**arpenter** *vt* walk up and down
**arpenteur** *nm* surveyor
**arpion** *nm* *sl* foot
**arqué** *adj* arched
**arquebuse** *nf* *hist* (h)arquebus
**arquer** *vt* arch, bend, curve; *vi* bend; *sl* walk; **s' ~** arch, curve
**arrachage** *nm* uprooting, pulling out; extraction (tooth)
**arrache-clou** *nm* wrench (nail)
**arrachement** *nm* removal; extraction; *fig* wrench
**arrache-pied (d')** *adv phr* steadily, ceaselessly
**arracher** *vt* uproot; lift (potatoes); pull out, remove; tear off; extract (tooth); seize, take; save from (danger); obtain, extort; **s' ~ à, s' ~ de** detach oneself from, tear oneself away from; **s' ~ les cheveux** tear one's hair, be desperate; **s' ~ les yeux** have a violent quarrel with s/o; **s' ~ qn** compete for s/o's company
**arracheur -euse** *n* **mentir comme un ~ de dents** lie like a trooper
**arraisonner** *vt* inspect (ship)
**arrangeable** *adj* repairable; arrangeable
**arrangeant** *adj* conciliatory, accommodating

**arrangement** *nm* arrangement, ordering, disposition; classification; agreement, accommodation; ~ s preparations, measures; terms

**arranger** *vt* (3) arrange, order, dispose; classify; repair; suit; please; *coll* ~ qn **de la belle manière** sort s/o out; s' ~ manage; become ordered, improve; tidy oneself; be mended; take steps; come to an agreement; s' ~ **de** put up with

**arrérages** *nmpl* arrears

**arrestation** *nf* arrest

**arrêt** *nm* stop; arrest; halt; *leg* decision, judgement; *mil* ~ s arrest; *mil* ~ s **de rigueur** close arrest; *mil* ~ s **simples** open arrest; **sans** ~ without pause; **temps d'** ~ pause

**arrêté** *nm* decision; decree; *adj* decided, fixed

**arrêter** *vt* stop, halt; arrest; interrupt; choose, determine; *vi* stop; s' ~ stop, halt; pay attention

**arrhes** *nfpl comm* deposit, down payment

**arriération** *nf* backwardness

**arrière** *nm* rear; *sp* back; *adj* rear; *adv* behind, back; **en** ~ backwards, behind; **en** ~ **de** behind; *mot* **marche** ~ reverse

**arriéré** *nm* arrears; *adj* owing, overdue; *pej* out of date, old-fashioned; backward, retarded

**arrière-ban** *nm hist* rear-vassals; **ban et** ~ **the** whole lot of them

**arrière-boutique** *nf* room behind shop

**arrière-cour** *nf* back-yard

**arrière-garde** *nf mil* rearguard

**arrière-goût** *nm* after-taste

**arrière-grand-mère** *nf* great-grand-mother

**arrière-grand-père** *nm* (*pl* **arrière-grands-pères**) great-grandfather

**arrière-grands-parents** *nmpl* great-grandparents

**arrière-neveu** *nm* grand-nephew; *lit* remote descendant

**arrière-pays** *nm invar* hinterland; places near a large town

**arrière-pensée** *nf* after-thought

**arrière-petite-fille** *nf* (*pl* **arrière-petites-filles**) great-granddaughter

**arrière-petit-fils** *nm* (*pl* **arrière-petits-fils**) great-grandson

**arrière-petits-enfants** *nmpl* great grand-children

**arrière-plan** *nm* background

**arriérer** *vt* (6) postpone, delay

**arrière-saison** *nf* autumn; *fig* near to old age

**arrière-train** *nm* rear; *coll* backside

**arrimage** *nm naut* loading, stowing

**arrimer** *vt naut* load, stow

**arrivage** *nm* arrival (of goods)

**arrivé -e** *n* arrival (person)

**arrivée** *nf* arrival; arrival platforms (railway); *fig* **à l'** ~ in the end, in the final instance; **ligne d'** ~ finishing post

**arriver** *vi* arrive; attain, reach; succeed; happen, occur; **en** ~ **à** reach a point where; **en** ~ **là** end up there; **j'arrive!** coming!; **n'** ~ **à rien** come to nothing; **quoi qu'il arrive** come what may

**arrivisme** *nm* place-seeking

**arriviste** *n* place-seeker, climber

**arroger (s')** *v refl* (3) arrogate to oneself; claim

**arrondi** *nm* roundness; *adj* rounded

**arrondir** *vt* round, make round; complete, round off; s' ~ become round

**arrondissement** *nm* rounding off; = district (in France), part of large town

**arrosage** *nm* watering; **tuyau d'** ~ hose

**arroser** *vt* water; irrigate; wash down (meal with wine); celebrate (with a drink); *cul* baste; *coll* give money to; ~ **son café** add alcohol to one's coffee; **se faire** ~ *coll* get soaked with rain

**arroseur** *nm* sprinkler

**arroseuse** *nf* watering-cart

**arrosoir** *nm* watering-can

**arsenal** *nm* arsenal; store of weapons and munitions; *fig* storehouse; stock; ~ **de la marine** naval dockyard

**arsouille** *n* rogue, blackguard

**art** *nm* art; skill, craft, knack; ~ **de faire qch** way to do sth; ~ s **ménagers** domestic arts; **avoir l'** ~ **de** know how to; **beaux** ~ s fine arts; **l'** ~ **pour l'** ~ art for art's sake

**artère** *nf* anat artery; *fig* main road; (town) main street

**artériel -ielle** *adj anat* arterial

**artériosclérose** *nf* arteriosclerosis

**artésien -ienne** *adj* artesian

**arthrite** *nf* arthritis

**arthritique** *adj* arthritic

**artichaut** *nm* artichoke; *coll* **avoir un cœur d'** ~ be fickle-hearted; **fond d'** ~ artichoke heart

**article** *nm* clause, section (text); point, topic; article; ~ s **de Paris** fancy goods; **à l'** ~ **de la mort** on the point of death; **faire l'** ~ boost a product, plug

**articulaire** *adj* articular

**articulation** *nf anat* articulation, joint; knuckle; *mech* joint; articulation (speech); pronouncing; *leg* enumeration, enunciation

**articulé** *adj anat* articulated, jointed; articulated (speech)

**articuler** *vt* (speech) articulate, pronounce; *leg* enumerate, enounce; s' ~

*anat* be articulated, be jointed; *mech* be jointed

**artifice** *nm* clever device; trick, ruse, artifice; **feux d'** ~ fireworks

**artificiel -ielle** *adj* artificial; false; arbitrary; synthetic

**artificieux -ieuse** *adj* cunning, wily

**artillerie** *nf* artillery, ordnance; **tir d'** ~ artillery fire

**artilleur** *nm* artilleryman

**artimon** *nm naut* mizzen-mast

**artisan -e** *n* artisan, craftsman; *fig* author, architect

**artisanal** *adj* relating to craft

**artisanat** *nm* craftsman's trade; craftsman

**artiste** *n* artist; actor, actress, performer; ~ **peintre** painter; **entrée des** ~ s stagedoor

**artistique** *adj* artistic

**arythmie** *nf* irregular heart-beat

**as** *nm* ace; *sp* champion; *coll* **être ficelé comme l'** ~ **de pique** be badly dressed; *sl* **être plein aux** ~ have packets of money

**asbeste** *nm* asbestos

**ascendance** *nf astron* rising; ancestry, lineage

**ascendant** *nm astron* rising; *astrol* ascendant; *fig* influence, ascendancy; charm; *leg* ~ s parents; *adj* rising, progressing upwards; *astrol* **astre** ~ ascendant

**ascenseur** *nm* lift

**ascension** *nf* ascension; ascent (mountain); *fig* rise, progress; *eccles* **l'Ascension** Ascension

**ascèse** *nf* asceticism

**ascète** *n* ascetic

**ascétique** *adj* ascetic

**ascétisme** *nm* asceticism, austerity

**asepsie** *nf* asepsis

**aseptique** *adj* aseptic

**asexué** *adj biol* asexual; without sexual urges

**Asiate** *n see* **Asiatique**

**Asiatique** *n* Asiatic, Asian

**asiatique** *adj* Asiatic

**asile** *nm* asylum, refuge; sanctuary; *fig* haven; old people's home; mental hospital; *obs* nursery-school; ~ **d'aliénés** mental hospital, psychiatric hospital; ~ **de nuit** night-shelter, doss house; ~ **de vieillards** old people's home; ~ **des morts** tomb

**asocial** *adj* antisocial

**asparagus** *nm bot* asparagus fern

**aspect** *nm* aspect; view, angle; sight, view; **à l'** ~ **de** at the sight of; **au premier** ~ at first sight; **sous cet** ~ from this point of view

**asperge** *nf* asparagus; *coll* tall thin person

**asperger** *vt* (3) sprinkle, spray; splash

**aspérité** *nf* asperity; roughness; harshness

**aspersion** *nf eccles* aspersion, sprinkling

**aspersoir** *nm eccles* aspergillum; rose (watering-can)

**asphalte** *nm* asphalt

**asphalter** *vt* asphalt

**asphodèle** *nm bot* asphodel

**asphyxiant** *adj* asphyxiating

**asphyxie** *nf* asphyxiation

**asphyxier** *vt* asphyxiate, gas; *fig* suppress

**¹aspic** *nm zool* asp; **avoir une langue d'** ~ have a serpent's tongue

**²aspic** *nm cul* aspic

**¹aspirant -e** *n* candidate, aspirant

**²aspirant** *nm mil* officer-cadet; *naut* = midshipman; *adj* sucking; **pompe** ~ **e** suction-pump

**aspirateur** *nm* vacuum-cleaner; aspirator

**aspiration** *nf* aspiration; ideal, desire; breathing in

**aspirer** *vt* breathe in, inhale; suck in, draw up; *phon* aspirate; *vi* breathe in; aspire, desire

**aspirine** *nf* aspirin

**assagir** *vt* make wiser; make calmer, moderate; smooth down (hair); **s'** ~ become wiser; sober down

**assagissement** *nm* calming down, settling down

**assaillant -e** *n* assailant; *adj* attacking

**assaillir** *vt* (14) assail, attack; assault; *fig* harass, set upon

**assainir** *vt* make healthier; disinfect, decontaminate; drain (marsh); *econ* balance, stabilize; *fig* purify

**assainissement** *nm* disinfection, decontamination; draining (marsh); drainage; *econ* stabilization; *fig* purification

**assaisonnement** *nm cul* seasoning, flavouring; condiment, spice, salad dressing

**assaisonner** *vt cul* season, flavour; dress (salad); *fig* give spice to, season; enliven; *coll* reprimand, tear a strip off

**assassin** *nm* assassin, murderer; *adj* murderous; *lit* killing; seductive, provocative (glance)

**assassinat** *nm* assassination, murder

**assassiner** *vt* assassinate, murder; *coll* overcharge

**assaut** *nm* attack, charge, assault; *sp* bout; **faire** ~ **de vie** in; **prendre d'** ~ take by storm

**assèchement** *nm* drying; draining

**assécher** *vt* (6) dry; drain

**assemblage** *nm mech* assembling, assemblage; putting together; collection; assortment, mixture

**assemblée** *nf* assembly; gathering, audience; meeting (company, society); *pol* national legislative body; **l'Assemblée nationale** national assembly ( = House of Commons, U.S. House of Representatives)

**assembler** *vt* assemble, gather, collect; bring together; *mech* assemble, join, couple; *obs* bring together, summon; **s'** ~ come together, meet

**assener, asséner** *vt* (6) hit, strike

**assentiment** *nm* agreement, consent, assent

**asseoir** *vt* (15) seat, install; establish, base; ~ **un impôt** make an assessment of tax; **s'** ~ sit down

**assermenté** *adj leg* sworn-in, on oath

**asservir** *vt* enslave, subjugate; conquer, master; **s'** ~ submit oneself, become enslaved

**asservissement** *nm* bondage, enslavement; subjection

**assesseur** *nm* assessor; *leg* deputy

**assez** *adv* enough, sufficiently; quite, rather, fairly; ~ **!** that's enough!, that will do!; ~ **de** enough; ~ **de personnes imaginent** plenty of people suppose; ~ **grand** large enough; quite large; ~ **longtemps** long enough; for quite a time; ~ **pour** enough to; **c'en est** ~, **en voilà** ~ that's enough; **en avoir** ~ be bored, be fed up; **j'ai** ~ **de ça** I have had enough of that

**assidu** *adj* assiduous, regular; diligent; constant

**assiduité** *nf* assiduity, assiduousness; frequent presence; ~ **s** (unwelcome) attentions to a woman

**assiéger** *vt* (6,3) besiege, lay siege to; surround, encircle; *fig* harass, assail

**assiette** *nf* plate; plateful; balance; basis; *fig* state of mind, condition; situation, position; *naut* trim; *leg* basis of tax; ~ **anglaise** dish of assorted cold meats; *coll* ~ **au beurre** cushy job; **avoir une bonne** ~ have a good seat (horserider); **ne pas être dans son** ~ not feel well, not feel up to the mark

**assiettée** *nf* plateful

**assignation** *nf leg* assignment, allotment, dividing out; *leg* sub-poena

**assigner** *leg* assign, allot; designate; determine, fix; *leg* sub-poena

**assimiler** *vt* assimilate; integrate, incorporate; compare; **s'** ~ become assimilated; become similar; *fig* absorb

**assis** *adj* seated; assured; firm, stable; **magistrature** ~ **e** judiciary, bench; **place** ~ **e** seat

**assise** *nf* basis, foundation; *bui* course; *geol* stratum

**assises** *nfpl leg* assizes; *pol* congress; formal meeting

**assistance** *nf* audience; assistance, help; ~ **judiciaire** legal aid; ~ **médicale** medical services; ~ **sociale** social services

**assistant -e** *n* assistant, helper; lecturer (university); ~ **e sociale** social welfare worker; ~ **s** audience; persons present

**assisté -e** *n* person receiving aid; *adj* in receipt of aid

**assister** *vt* help, aid; succour, minister to; *vi* ~ **à** be present at

**association** *nf* association; society; *comm* company; *sp* club; analogy, similitude

**associé -e** *n* associate; *comm* partner

**associer** *vt* associate; join, unite, bring together, link; ~ **qn à qch** make s/o a party to sth; **s'** ~ group together; combine; **s'** ~ **à** adhere to, associate oneself with; **s'** ~ **à (avec) qn** join with s/o, enter into partnership with s/o

**assoiffé** *adj* thirsty; arid; eager for

**assolement** *nm* rotation of crops

**assombrir** *vt* darken; sadden; make anxious; **s'** ~ become dark; become sad; become anxious

**assombrissement** *nm* darkening; gloom, gloominess

**assommant** *adj coll* boring, tedious; tiresome, maddening

**assommer** *vt* kill by a blow on the head, fell; knock (s/o) out; *fig* stun, affect deeply; inconvenience; bore, fatigue

**Assomption** *nf eccles* Assumption

**assorti** *adj* matched, suited, going well together; ~ **s** varied, assorted; **bien** ~ well stocked

**assortiment** *nm* arrangement, disposition, matching; collection; service, set; *comm* stock

**assortir** *vt* arrange, match, harmonize; (people) bring together, unite; **s'** ~ match, go together; **s'** ~ **de** stock up with

**assoupi** *adj* half-asleep, somnolent; assuaged

**assoupir** *vt* make sleepy; calm, attenuate, assuage

**assoupissement** *nm* somnolence, torpor; calming; attenuation

**assouplir** *vt* make supple; soften, attenuate; **s'** ~ become supple; become softer, supple

**assouplissement** *nm* making supple; softening

**assourdir** *vt* deafen; muffle, deaden; **s'** ~ *phon* become unvoiced

**assourdissant** *adj* deafening

**assourdissement** *nm* making deaf, deafening; deadening, softening

**assouvir** *vt* satisfy, satiate; quench; gratify; s' ~ be gratified, be assuaged

**assouvissement** *nm* satisfaction, satiation; satiety

**assujetti** -e *n* tax-payer; *adj* subject, liable; fixed

**assujettir** *vt* subjugate, enslave; fix, fasten; ~ à subject to, make liable to; s'~ submit

**assujettissant** *adj* exacting, demanding

**assujettissement** *nm* subjugation, conquest; submission; constraint, subjection

**assumer** *vt* assume, take upon oneself

**assurance** *nf* assurance, certainty; self-confidence; insurance; *coll* insurance company; *mot* ~ **au tiers** third-party insurance; *mot* ~ **tous risques** comprehensive insurance; ~**s sociales** social security; ~ -**vie** life insurance

**assuré** -e *adj* insured person, policy-holder; *adj* certain, clear, without doubt; confident, sure

**assurer** *vt* assure, affirm; defend, preserve; guarantee; fix, make firm, strengthen, wedge; insure; ~ **qn de qch** certify sth to s/o; ~ **à qn que** assure s/o that; s'~ check, verify; s'~ **contre** insure oneself against; s'~ **de** guarantee, make sure of

**assureur** *nm* insurance agent; ~ **vie** life-insurance agent

**assyrien** -**ienne** *adj* Assyrian

**astérie** *nf* starfish

**astérisque** *nm* asterisk

**astéroïde** *nm* asteroid

**asthmatique** *n* + *adj* asthmatic

**asthme** *nm* asthma

**asticot** *nm* maggot; *coll* chap; *sl* **engraisser les** ~**s** be pushing up the daisies

**asticoter** *vt coll* nag, worry

**astigmate** *adj* astigmatic

**astigmatisme** *nm* astigmatism

**astiquer** *vt* polish, polish up

**astragale** *nm* astragal

**astrakan** *nm* astrakhan

**astre** *nm* star

**astreindre** *vt* (55) compel, oblige; s'~ force oneself

**astreinte** *nf* constraint; *leg* delay in payment of debt

**astrologie** *nf* astrology

**astronaute** *n* astronaut

**astronautique** *nf* astronautics

**astronef** *nm* space ship

**astronome** *n* astronomer

**astronomie** *nf* astronomy

**astronomique** *adj* astronomic, astronomical

**astrophysique** *nf* astrophysics

**astuce** *nf* ingenious idea, device; joke; *obs pej* trick

**astucieux** -**ieuse** *adj* ingenious; *obs pej* cunning

**asymétrie** *nf* asymmetry

**asymétrique** *adj* asymmetrical

**ataraxie** *nf phil* ataraxy

**atavique** *adj* atavistic

**atavisme** *nm* atavism

**ataxie** *nf* ataxia

**ataxique** *adj* ataxic

**atelier** *nm* workshop; studio (painter, sculptor); *arts* school

**atermoiement** *nm leg* stay; postponement, delay

**atermoyer** *vi* (7) delay, defer

**athée** *n* atheist; *adj* atheistic

**athéisme** *nm* atheism

**athlétique** *adj* athletic

**athlétisme** *nm* athleticism

**Atlantique** *nm* Atlantic

**atlantique** *adj* Atlantic

**atlantisme** *nm pol* approval of N.A.T.O. policy

**atmosphérique** *adj* atmospheric

**atome** *nm* atom

**atomique** *adj* atomic

**atomiser** *vt* vaporize; pulverize; destroy by atomic weapons

**atomiseur** *nm* atomizer, aerosol, spray

**atonalité** *nf mus* atonality

**atone** *adj path* atonic; inert; dull, lacking in energy; *phon* unaccentuated

**atonie** *nf path* lack of muscular tone; inertia, feebleness

**atour** *nm* finery; ~**s** *obs* or *joc* ornaments

**atout** *nm* trump, winning card; **trois sans** ~ **s** three no-trumps

**atrabilaire** *adj* atrabilious, surly; misanthropic

**âtre** *nm* hearth

**atroce** *adj* atrocious, appalling

**atrocité** *nf* atrocity, cruelty; crime

**atrophie** *nf* atrophy

**atrophier** *vt* atrophy; s'~ atrophy, waste away

**attabler (s')** *v refl* sit down to table

**attachant** *adj* attractive, fascinating; interesting

**attache** *nf* fastening; tying up; clip, paper-clip, pin, cord, button, lace, knot; *bot* sucker; *anat* joint; *fig* attachment; ~**s** *anat* wrist and ankle; *fig* links, bonds

**attachement** *nm* attachment, affection; fidelity

**attacher** *vt* attach, fasten, do up; tie; chain; pin together; clip; buckle; button; lace; join; *fig* link, unite; take on, engage; (gaze) fix; (idea) associate; (value) attribute, grant; *vi cul* stick (in pan); s' ~ be attached, be fixed; s' ~ à be joined to; *fig* be attached to, be connected with; be devoted to; apply oneself to

**attaquant -e** *n* attacker, assailant; *sp* forward

**attaque** *nf* attack; *coll* d' ~ in good form

**attaquer** *vt* attack; destroy, corrode, eat away; begin, get down to; *coll* start eating; s' ~ à attack, criticize; seek to resolve (problem)

**attardé -e** *n* someone mentally retarded; *adj* delayed; old-fashioned; retarded

**attarder** *vt* delay; s' ~ delay; remain, hang about; remain behind; proceed slowly

**atteindre** *vt* (55) reach, attain, arrive at; equal; strike, wound; affect (illness); *fig* upset, trouble; ~ à reach

**atteinte** *nf* injury, blow, attack; *med* symptom; *med* attack; **hors d'** ~ out of reach; **porter** ~ à cast a slur on; attack

**attelage** *nm* (animals) harnessing; coupling (railway waggons); harness; yoke

**atteler** *vt* (5) harness, yoke; put between shafts; *fig* put to work; s' ~ à harness oneself to, apply oneself to

**attelle** *nf* splint

**attenant** *adj* adjacent

**attendre** *vt* await, wait for; expect, foresee; ~ **après qch** need sth; ~ **son heure** bide one's time; **attendez! (attends!)** wait!, hang on!; **en attendant** in the meantime; **en attendant de** while waiting to; **en attendant que** until; **faire** ~ **qn** keep s/o waiting; **se faire** ~ be late, be slow in coming; s' ~ à expect; s' ~ **que**, s' ~ **à ce que** expect; *vi* wait, pause

**attendrir** *vt* touch, move; *cul* make tender; s' ~ have pity, feel sympathy

**attendrissement** *nm* compassion, pity, feeling

**attendu** *adj* awaited, expected; *prep* given, in view of; ~ **que** given that; *leg* whereas

**attendus** *nmpl leg* reasons

**attentat** *nm* murder attempt; outrage; bomb attack; crime, offence; *leg* ~ **à la pudeur** indecent exposure

**attente** *nf* waiting, wait; desire, expectation; **contre toute** ~ contrary to all expectations; **être dans l'** ~ **de** be waiting for; **salle d'** ~ waiting-room

**attenter** *vi* ~ à make an attempt against; ~ **à la vie de qn** make an attempt on s/o's life; ~ **à ses jours** attempt to commit suicide

**attentif -ive** *adj* attentive; mindful; thoughtful; considerate; ~ à desirous of; scrupulous

**attention** *nf* attention, notice, heed; care, thoughtfulness; ~! be careful!; ~ s solicitude, attentions; ~ **à la marche** mind the step; **faire** ~ à take notice of; **faire** ~ **que** take notice that; **faire** ~ **que, faire** ~ **à ce que** take care that

**attentionné** *adj* considerate, attentive

**attentisme** *nm pol* temporization; policy of wait and see

**atténuant** *adj* attenuating

**atténuer** *vt* attenuate; moderate

**atterrer** *vt* astound, stun

**atterrir** *vi* land; *fig* end up

**atterrissage** *nm* landing

**attester** *vt* attest, affirm; show, bear witness

**attiédir** *vt* make tepid (by cooking or by warming); *fig* temper, tone down, cool

**attifer** *vt coll* deck out absurdly

**Attique** *nm geog* Attica

**attique** *nm bui* attic; *adj* Attic

**attirail** *nm* equipment; *coll* paraphernalia, gear, apparatus

**attirant** *adj* attractive, seductive

**attirer** *vt* draw, attract; entice; attract, please, charm; s' ~ bring upon oneself

**attiser** *vt* stir up, poke (fire); excite, arouse, revive

**attitré** *adj* appointed; **fournisseur** ~ supplier by appointment

**attouchement** *nm* touching with the hand; ~ s (impurs) self-abuse

**attractif -ive** *adj phys* attractive; enticing, captivating

**attraction** *nf phys* attraction; fascination; ~ s cabaret, floor-show

**attrait** *nm* attraction, charm, fascination; taste, desire; *lit* ~ s (female) charms

**attrape** *nf* trick, device; joke, hoax; *obs* trap

**attrape-nigaud** *nm coll* device to deceive the simple-minded

**attraper** *vt* catch; snare; dupe, catch out, have on; scold; catch (illness); hit off (style, likeness); s' ~ be catching; *sl* **attrape!** take that!

**attrayant** *adj* attractive, pleasant, agreeable

**attribuable** *adj* attributable

**attribuer** *vt* attribute, assign; grant; confer; allot

**attribut** *nm* attribute, characteristic, quality

**attribution** *nf* attribution, allocation; *gramm* attributive; ~ s powers, authority

**attristant** *adj* saddening; deplorable

**attrister** *vt* sadden, pain, afflict; depress

**attroupement** *nm* crowd; *esp* riotous assembly, mob

**attrouper** vt gather together; **s'** ~ form into a mob

**atypique** adj atypical

**au, aux** see **à + le**

**aubaine** nf windfall, stroke of luck

¹**aube** nf dawn; beginning; **dès l'** ~ very early in the morning

²**aube** nf eccles alb

³**aube** nf mech vane, blade; **navire à** ~ **s** paddle-steamer

**aubépine** nf hawthorn

**auberge** nf ar inn, tavern; country restaurant; ~ **de (la) jeunesse** youth hostel

**aubergine** nf aubergine, egg-plant; coll traffic warden

**aubergiste** n innkeeper

**aucun** adj any; **il n'y a** ~ **espoir** there is no hope; **ne ...** ~ not any; **y a-t-il** ~ **espoir?** is there any hope?; pron any; no one, nobody

**aucunement** adv not at all; US no way; in any way

**audace** nf daring, courage, audacity; innovation; pej arrogance, cheek; insolence; nerve

**audacieux -ieuse** n audacious person; adj audacious, daring

**au-deçà** adv obs on this side; prep phr ~ **de** on this side of

**au-dedans** adv inside; prep phr ~ **de** inside

**au-dehors** adv outside; prep phr ~ **de** outside

**au-delà** nm the beyond; adv beyond, further than; prep phr ~ **de** beyond

**au-dessous** adv below, underneath; prep phr ~ **de** beneath

**au-dessus** adv above, over; prep phr ~ **de** above

**au-devant de** prep phr **aller** ~ go to meet; anticipate

**audibilité** nf audibility

**audience** nf hearing; conversation; audience

**audiophone** nm deaf-aid

**audio-visuel** nm audio-visual methods; audio-visual equipment; adj (f **-uelle**) audio-visual

**auditeur -trice** n listener; ~ **s** audience, public

**auditif -ive** adj auditory

**audition** nf audition; hearing; mus performance

**auditionner** vt audition; vi give an audition

**auditoire** nm audience; readership

**auge** nf drinking trough; feeding trough

**augmentation** nf augmentation, increase; lengthening; rise (cost, salary); US raise

**augmenter** vt augment, increase; enlarge; lengthen; intensify; ~ **qn** give s/o a rise; vi grow, increase, become larger; **s'** ~ become larger

**augure** nm augur, prophet; augury, omen, prediction

**augurer** vt augur, predict

**auguste** adj august, venerable

**aujourd'hui** nm the present day; adv today; nowadays, at the present time

**aulne, aune** nm bot alder

**aulx** nmpl obs see **ail**

**aumône** nf alms; favour

**aumônier** nm eccles chaplain

**aune** nf ell

**auparavant** adv before, first

**auprès** adv near, nearly; prep phr ~ **de** near to; attached to (diplomat); according to; compared with

**auquel** see **lequel**

**auréole** nf aureola, aureole, halo; ~ **de martyr** martyr's crown

**auréoler** vt halo

**auréomycine** nf med aureomycin

**auriculaire** nm little finger; adj auricular; **témoin** ~ witness testifying to words actually heard

**auricule** nf anat auricle

**aurifère** adj auriferous

**aurore** nf day-break, dawn; origin, commencement

**ausculter** vt med examine, sound (esp with stethoscope)

**auspice** nm antiq auspice; ~ **s** auspices, protection, patronage

**aussi** adv as, so; also, as well, equally, too; however; therefore; ~ **belle qu'elle soit** however pretty she is; ~ **bien** equally well; ~ **bien que** as well as; just as much as; ~ **vite que possible** as fast as possible; **est-ce qu'il est** ~ **stupide?** is he so stupid?; **mais** ~ moreover; **tout** ~ **bien** just as well

**aussitôt** adv at once, immediately; ~ **dit** ~ **fait** no sooner said than done; conj phr ~ **que** as soon as

**austérité** nf austerity; severity, rigour; ~ **s** eccles mortification, penance

**autan** nm south wind

**autant** adv as many, as much; ~ **...** ~ **as ... as;** ~ **que** as much as, as many as; in so far as; ~ **(vaut)** one may as well; **d'** ~ a great deal; in proportion; **d'** ~ **plus** all the more; conj phr **d'** ~ **mieux que** even better because; **d'** ~ **moins que** even less because; **d'** ~ **plus que** even more because, all the more so as; **d'** ~ **que** especially since

**autel** nm altar; **aller à l'** ~ get married; **maître** ~ high altar; **s'approcher de l'** ~ take communion

**auteur** nm author; mus composer; founder, inventor; first cause; **droit d'** ~

copyright; **droits d'~** royalties; **femme ~** female writer
**authenticité** nf authenticity, truth, veracity
**authentifier** vt authenticate
**authentique** adj authentic, genuine; authoritative
**autisme** nm autism
**auto** nf car; **~ tamponneuse** dodgem
**auto-accusation** nf self-accusation
**autobiographie** nf autobiography
**autobiographique** adj autobiographical
**autobus** nm bus
**autocar** nm coach
**autocensure** nf self-censoring
**autochtone** n autochthon; adj autochthonic, autochthonous
**autoclave** nm autoclave; pressure-cooker; adj self-sealing
**autocollant** adj self-sealing (envelope)
**autocopie** nf duplicating
**auto-couchettes** adj invar **train ~** car-sleeper train
**autocrate** nm autocrat
**autocratie** nf autocracy
**autocratique** adj autocratic
**autocritique** nf self-criticism
**autocuiseur** nm pressure-cooker
**autodéfense** nf self-defence
**autodégivrage** nm automatic defrosting (refrigerator)
**autodestruction** nf self-destruction
**autodétermination** nf self-determination
**autodidacte** n self-taught person; adj self-taught
**autodrome** nm motor-racing track
**auto-école** nf driving school
**autogestion** nf workers' control (factory)
**autographe** nm autograph; adj written by hand
**autoguidé** adj self-directional
**automate** nm robot, automaton
**¹automatique** nm automatic pistol; adj automatic; involuntary, instructive; coll inevitable, bound to happen; **distributeur ~** slot-machine
**²automatique** nf science of automation
**automatisation** nf automation
**automatiser** vt automate
**automatisme** nf automatism
**automitrailleuse** nf machine-gun carrier
**automnal** adj autumnal
**automne** nm autumn
**automobile** nf car, automobile; adj concerning cars; **assurances ~s** car insurance; **industrie ~** car industry
**automobiliste** n motorist
**automoteur -trice** adj self-propelling
**automotrice** nf rail-car

**autonome** adj autonomous; independent
**autonomie** nf autonomy; independence; range (vehicle)
**autonomiste** n autonomist, separatist
**autopompe** nf fire-engine
**autoportrait** nm self-portrait
**autopropulsé** adj self-propelled
**autopropulsion** nf self-propulsion
**autopsie** nf autopsy, post-mortem
**autopsier** vt do a post-mortem on
**autoradio** nm car radio
**autorail** nm (diesel) railcar
**auto-réglable** adj self-adjustable
**autorégulation** nf automatic regulation
**autorisation** nf authorization; permission; permit, pass
**autorisé** adj authorized; official; approved
**autoriser** vt authorize; entitle, permit; **s'~ de** rely upon, base upon
**autoritaire** adj authoritarian; authoritative, peremptory
**autoritarisme** nm authoritarianism
**autorité** nf authority; influence, prestige; **d'~** without argument, without discussion; **faire ~** be an authority; **faire acte d'~** bring one's authority to bear
**autoroute** nf motorway; **~ de dégagement** toll-free motorway for first few miles outside large city; **~ de liaison** long-distance motorway (with toll)
**auto-stop** nm hitch-hiking; **faire de l'~** hitch-hike
**auto-stoppeur -euse** n hitch-hiker
**autour** adv around, round; prep phr **~ de** around, round; near; about
**autre** adj other; different; quite another; **c'est ~ chose** that's quite different; **l'~ fois** recently; **une ~ fois** on another occasion; adv phr **~ part** elsewhere; **d'~ part** moreover; pron another; **à d'~s!** tell that to the marines!; **comme dirait l'~** as they say; **de temps à ~** from time to time; **d'un bout à l'~** from start to finish; **d'un moment à l'~** any minute; **en avoir vu d'~s** have seen more surprising things; **entre ~s** among others; **l'un et l'~** both of them; **l'un l'~** (**les uns les ~s**) each other, one another; **l'un ou l'~** one or other
**autrefois** adv formerly, in the past, of old
**autrement** adv otherwise, differently; very; **pas ~** not very, not particularly
**Autriche** nf Austria
**autrichien -ienne** adj Austrian
**autruche** nf ostrich; **la politique de l'~** burying one's head in the sand
**autrui** pron another; other people

25

**auvent** *nm* lean-to roof, projecting roof

**auxiliaire** *n* auxiliary, assistant, helper; *adj* auxiliary, complementary; *mil* ser-vices ~s non-combatant troops

**avachi** *adj* (shoes) shapeless; flabby, soft

**avachir** *vt* soften, make flabby; s' ~ become soft, become flabby; *coll* become fat; be slipping

**avachissement** *nm* flabbiness

¹**aval** *nm* lower reaches of river; **en ~** downstream

²**aval** *nm* (*pl* ~s) *comm* endorsement

**avaler** *vt* swallow; put up with; conceal; ~ **la pilule (le morceau)** accept without protest; ~ **sa rage** conceal one's anger; ~ **sa salive** keep a hold on one's tongue; ~ **un livre** devour a book

**avaliser** *vt comm* endorse; support, back

**à-valoir** *nm invar* instalment

**avance** *nf* advance; lead, start; loan; **à l' ~** before, in advance; **d' ~** in advance; **en ~** early, in advance; **la belle ~!** that's a fat lot of good!; **par ~** in advance; **prendre de l' ~** go into the lead, increase one's lead

**avancé** *adj* advanced; *mil* forward; late, far gone; precocious; nearing completion; **n'être pas plus ~** be no further ahead; *iron* **vous voilà bien ~!** that's helped a lot!

**avancement** *nm* advance; progress; improvement; promotion; ~ **à l'ancienneté** promotion by seniority

**avancer** *vt* (4) push forward, hold out; advance; propose, affirm; put forward, bring forward (time); make progress; (money) lend; put forward (watch, clock); **ça ne m'avance pas** that doesn't help me; *vi* advance, project; progress, get on; be promoted; be fast (watch, clock); s' ~ come forward, approach; make progress; jut out; pass by (time); s' ~ **trop** expose oneself to risk

**avanie** *nf* affront, humiliation

**avant** *nm* front; *naut* prow; *sp* forward; *adv* before; first; in front; **bien ~** far in; **en ~** in front, forward, forwards; towards the future; **en ~ de** in front of; **trop ~** too far forward, too far in; *prep* before, earlier; ~ **de** before; *conj phr* ~ **que** before

**avantage** *nm* advantage, profit, benefit; superiority; *sp* (tennis) advantage; ~ **pécuniaire** profit; **avoir ~ à** be well-advised to

**avantager** *vt* (3) favour, benefit

**avantageux -euse** *adj* advantageous, favourable; *pej* conceited, self-satisfied

**avant-bras** *nm invar* forearm

**avant-centre** *nm sp* centre-forward

**avant-coureur** *nm* forerunner, precursor; *adj* precursory, announcing, premonitory

**avant-dernier -ière** *adj* penultimate

**avant-garde** *nf* advance-guard; avant-garde

**avant-goût** *nm* foretaste; anticipation

**avant-guerre** *nm or nf invar* pre-war period

**avant-hier** *adv* two days ago, on the day before yesterday

**avant-poste** *nm mil* forward position

**avant-première** *nf* preview; private showing; advance notice (journalism); **en ~** before public presentation

**avant-propos** *nm* preface, foreword

**avant-scène** *nf* stage-box; proscenium

**avant-toit** *nm* projecting roof; ~s eaves

**avare** *n* miser; *adj* avaricious, miserly; ~ **de** sparing of

**avaricieux -ieuse** *adj* miserly

**avarie** *nf naut* damage; breakdown

**avarié** *adj* damaged; rotten; *coll obs* poxed

**avarier** *vt* deteriorate

**avec** *adv* with; *coll* **tu viens ~?** are you coming along?; *prep* with; at the same time as; in the company of; in the same way as; in addition; by means of; thanks to; **et ~ cela, Madame?** will there be anything else, Madam?; **être bien (mal) ~** be on good (bad) terms with; **marié ~** married to

¹**avenant** *nm* new clause in insurance policy, endorsement

²**avenant** *adj* pleasant, agreeable, charming

³**avenant (à l')** *adv phr* in accordance, in keeping; ~ **de** in keeping with

**avènement** *nm eccles* advent of Christ; *pol* accession

**avenir** *nm* future; destiny; posterity; **à l' ~** from now on, in the future; **d' ~** with a future

**Avent** *nm eccles* Advent

**aventure** *nf* adventure; occurrence, incident; love-affair; *obs* future, destiny; **à l' ~** at random; **d' ~**, **par ~** by chance; **dire la bonne ~ à qn** tell s/o's fortune; **diseuse de bonne ~** fortune-teller

**aventurer** *vt* venture, risk, hazard; s' ~ venture

**aventureux -euse** *adj* adventurous; hazardous, risky

**aventurier** *nm ar* soldier of fortune, mercenary; pirate; *n (f* -ière) adventurer, adventuress

**aventurisme** *nm pol* recklessness

**avenu** *adj leg* **nul et non ~** non-existent, null and void

**avenue** nf avenue; tree-lined drive

**avéré** adj attested, authenticated

**avérer** vt (6) obs attest; s' ~ be confirmed, be shown to be true

**averse** nf shower; fig flood, stream

**averti** adj informed, experienced; **un homme ~ en vaut deux** forewarned is forearmed

**avertir** vt warn, caution; inform, notify

**avertissement** nm warning, caution; premonition; advice, recommendation; foreword; notice; demand (tax); reprimand

**avertisseur** nm alarm, warning signal; mot horn; adj (f -euse) warning

**aveu** nm confession, avowal; acknowledgement; declaration (love); lit consent, agreement; **de l' ~ de** in the opinion of; **sans ~** of no fixed abode

**aveuglant** adj blinding, dazzling

**aveugle** n blind person; **en ~** without thought, blindly; adj blind; fig blind, unreasoning; implicit, unquestioning

**aveuglement** nm fig blindness, unreason, folly; obs blindness

**aveuglément** adv blindly

**aveugler** vt make blind, blind; dazzle; fig confuse; stop (leak); s' ~ blind oneself, refuse to see the truth

**aveuglette (à l')** adv phr blindly

**aveulir** vt enfeeble, make limp; s' ~ become feeble, become limp

**aveulissement** nm enfeeblement, limpness

**aviateur -trice** n aviator; pilot; member of aircrew

**aviculteur -trice** n bird-farmer, aviculturalist

**avide** adj very hungry, voracious; greedy, rapacious; avid, eager; passionate

**avidité** nf voracity; avidity

**avili** adj degraded

**avilir** vt degrade; discredit, dishonour; comm depreciate; s' ~ degrade oneself, become debased; comm be depreciated, lose value

**avilissant** adj degrading, debasing

**avilissement** nm degradation, debasement; dishonour; comm depreciation

**aviné** adj drunk

**avion** nm aircraft, plane; ~ **à réaction** jet; ~ **de ligne** air-liner; **défense contre** ~ s anti-aircraft defence; **en ~** by air; **l' ~** aviation, flying; **par ~** by air, air-mail

**avionique** nf avionics

**aviron** nm oar; sp rowing; **faire de l' ~** row

**avis** nm view, judgement, opinion; vote; advice; announcement, notification; lit warning; ~ **au lecteur** foreword; à

**mon ~** in my opinion; **de l' ~ de tous** in everyone's opinion; **être de l' ~ de qn** agree with s/o; **jusqu'à nouvel ~** until further notice; obs **m'est ~ que** it seems to me that; **sauf ~ contraire** unless I (you, we) hear to the contrary

**avisé** adj prudent, sensible

¹**aviser** vt notice, spot; vi ~ **à** reflect on, think about, consider; s' ~ realize, discover; have the idea; s' ~ **de** dare to

²**aviser** vt notify, advise

**aviver** vt stir up, revive; freshen (colour); increase, arouse

¹**avocat -e** n leg barrister, counsel; defender, champion (cause); ~ **du diable** devil's advocate

²**avocat** nm avocado (pear)

**avoine** nf oat, oats; **farine d' ~** oatmeal; **flocons d' ~** porridge

**avoir** nm possession(s), wealth; comm credit side (of accounts); v aux (1) have; vt have, possess; be, feel; have on, wear; obtain, buy, get; ~ **beau faire qch** do sth in vain; ~ **faim, soif, chaud, froid** be hungry, thirsty, hot, cold; ~ **lieu** take place; ~ **qn** trick s/o, dupe s/o; coll have s/o, make love with s/o; ~ **vingt ans** be twenty years old; sl **en ~** have guts; coll **en ~ à, contre, après** have it in for; **en ~ assez** have enough of; **en ~ pour son argent** get one's money's worth; **j'en ai pour cinq minutes** it will take me five minutes; **qu'est-ce qu'il a?** what's the matter with him?; (telephone) **vous avez Paris** you've got Paris on the line; **y ~** impers **il y a** there is, there are; **il n'y a pas de quoi** it doesn't matter; not at all, don't mention it; **il n'y a pas que lui** he's not the only one; **il n'y a qu'à** it is only necessary to; **il y a deux jours que** it is two days since; **qu'est-ce qu'il y a?** what's the matter?

**avoisinant** adj neighbouring, adjacent

**avoisiner** vt be near to, be close to

**avortement** nm abortion, miscarriage; fig failure

**avorter** vi abort, miscarry; fail, come to nothing

**avorteur -euse** n abortionist

**avorton** nm stunted tree, stunted plant; child or animal of arrested development; pej squirt, abortion

**avouable** adj that can be avowed

**avoué** nm leg solicitor; adj acknowledged

**avouer** vt recognize; approve; avow, admit, confess

**avril** nm April; **poisson d' ~** April fool

**avunculaire** adj avuncular

**axe** nm axis; axle; spindle; direction, line; pol axis, alliance; mot main road

**axer** vt orientate, direct; ~ **sur centre** upon

**axillaire** adj anat axillary

**axiome** nm axiom

**ayant** pres part avoir

**ayant-cause** nm (pl **ayants-cause**) leg assignee, assign

**ayant-droit** nm (pl **ayants-droit**) leg rightful owner

**azalée** nf bot azalea

**azimut** nm azimuth; **dans tous les** ~ **s** in all directions; **tous** ~ **s** in all directions, right, left and centre; of every kind, in every domain

**azote** nm chem nitrogen

**Aztèque** n Aztec

**aztèque** adj Aztec

**azur** nm azure, blue; poet sky; infinite; **Côte d'Azur** French Riviera

**azuré** adj azure, sky-blue

**azuréen -éenne** n inhabitant of French Riviera

**azyme** nm unleavened bread; adj unleavened

# B

**¹baba** nm sponge cake steeped in rum

**²baba** adj invar coll staggered; **en rester** ~ be speechless with surprise

**babeurre** nm buttermilk

**babil** nm chattering, babbling; twittering (of birds)

**babillage** nm see babil

**babillard -e** n chatterbox; adj garrulous, talkative

**babiller** vi prattle, chatter, babble

**babines** nfpl lips, chops (of animal); sl **se lécher les** ~ lick one's lips

**babiole** nf bauble, trifle, knick-knack

**bâbord** nm naut port (side)

**babouche** nf Turkish slipper

**babouin** nm baboon; little monkey (child)

**baby-foot** nm table football

**¹bac** nm ferry(-boat)

**²bac** nm tank, vat

**³bac** nm coll ( = baccalauréat)

**baccalauréat** nm advanced school-leaving certificate

**baccara** nm baccara (card-game)

**baccarat** nm Baccarat glass

**bacchanale** nf uproarious dance; drunken revel, orgy

**bâche** nf canvas covering, tarpaulin; garden-frame; tank, cistern

**bachelier -ière** n one who has passed the baccalauréat examination

**¹bachot** nm wherry, punt

**²bachot** nm ( = baccalauréat); **boîte à** ~ cramming shop

**bachotage** nm cramming

**bachoter** vi cram, swot

**bacillaire** adj bacillary

**bacille** nm bacillus

**bâclage** nm coll botching, scamping

**bâcle** nf bar (of door)

**bâcler** vt coll botch, scamp; bar (door); **travail bâclé** slap-dash job

**bactérie** nf bacterium

**bactériologique** adj bacteriological; **guerre** ~ germ warfare

**badaud -e** n lounger, idler, gaper (in street)

**baderne** nf naut fender; coll **vieille** ~ old fogey

**badigeon** nm whitewash, distemper

**badigeonnage** nm whitewashing, distempering

**badigeonner** vt whitewash, distemper; med paint

**badigeonneur** nm whitewasher; coll poor painter

**badin** adj playful, waggish

**badinage** nm banter, fun, trifling

**badine** nf cane, switch

**badiner** vi trifle, jest

**baffe** nf sl blow, cuff

**bafouer** vt make fun of, flout, make ridiculous

**bafouillage** nm unintelligible speech; coll nonsense

**bafouiller** vt + vi splutter, blurt out; coll talk nonsense

**bâfrer** vt + vi sl stuff, guzzle; **se** ~ guzzle, feed one's face

**bagage** nm baggage; stock of knowledge; ~ **s** luggage; **faire enregistrer ses** ~ **s** register one's luggage; **plier** ~ coll clear out

**bagagiste** nm luggage porter (at hotel)

**bagarre** *nf* scuffle, brawl, fight

**bagarrer** *vi coll* fight, struggle; **se ~** fight, quarrel

**bagatelle** *nf* trifle; vet nothing

**bagne** *nm* convict prison; penal servitude; *coll* place where one has to work hard

**bagnole** *nf coll* car

**bagou** *nm coll* gift of the gab

**bague** *nf* ring

**baguenauder** *vi* fool around

¹**baguer** *vt* ring (bird)

²**baguer** *vt archi* tack (in needlework)

**baguette** *nf* wand, stick, rod; long thin loaf of bread; **faire marcher qn à la ~** be very strict with s/o

**bah** *interj* nonsense!; who cares!

**bahut** *nm* round-topped wooden chest; *sl* school

**bai** *nm* bay (horse)

¹**baie** *nf geog* bay

²**baie** *nf archi* bay, opening

³**baie** *nf bot* berry

**baignade** *nf* bathe; bathing-place

**baigner** *vt* give a bath to, soak, dip; *vi* soak; **se ~** have a bathe; take a bath

**baigneur -euse** *n* bather; bathing attendant; *nm* small celluloid or plastic doll

**baignoire** *nf* bath, bath tub; *theat* box at stalls level

**bail** *nm* (*pl* baux) lease

**bâillement** *nm* yawn; gaping

**bâiller** *vi* yawn; fit badly (door or window); be ajar

**bailli** *nm* bailiff

**bâillon** *nm* gag

**bâillonner** *vt* gag

**bain** *nm* bath; **~s** baths, spa; *coll* **être dans le ~** be well up in; **prendre un ~ de foule** *US* press the flesh

**bain-marie** *nm* (*pl* bains-marie) double saucepan; *chem* water bath

**baïonnette** *nf* bayonet; **~ au canon!** fix bayonets!; *elect* **douille à ~** bayonet socket

**baise-en-ville** *nm invar* small hold-all

**baisemain** *nm* hand-kissing

**baiser** *nm* kiss; *vt obs + lit* kiss; *vulg* have sex with, fuck; **~ la main à qn** kiss s/o's hand

**baisse** *nf* fall, drop (prices); going down (water); failing (eyesight); **être en ~** be falling (temperature, shares)

**baisser** *vt* lower, let down; hang (head); cast down (eyes); *vi* go, come down, sink (sun); fail (sight, strength); ebb (tide); **se ~** bend down, stoop

**bajoue** *nf* chap, cheek (animal); *coll* falling cheek (person)

**bal** *nm* (*pl* **~s**) ball, dance; dance-hall

**balade** *nf coll* stroll, ramble

**balader** *vt* take for a walk; **se ~** stroll

**baladeur -euse** *n* stroller

**baladeuse** *nf* barrow; inspection lamp; trailer (vehicle)

**baladin** *nm* mountebank, showman (circus), buffoon

**balafre** *nf* gash, cut, scar

**balafrer** *vt* gash, slash, scar

**balai** *nm* broom; *aer coll* joystick; *sl* last bus; *elect* brush; *mot* blade (windscreen wiper); **manche à ~** broomstick

**balance** *nf* balance, scales; equilibrium; *comm* balance; dipping-net; **faire pencher la ~** turn the scale

**balancé** *adj sl* **bien ~** well stacked

**balancement** *nm* swinging; rocking (boat)

**balancer** *vt* swing, rock, balance; *sl* chuck away, get rid of; *vi* hesitate, be uncertain; **se ~** swing, sway, rock; *sl* **je m'en balance** I couldn't care less

**balancier** *nm* pendulum (clock); balancing-pole

**balançoire** *nf* swing; seesaw

**balayage** *nm* sweeping, sweeping up

**balayer** *vt* (7) sweep, sweep out, sweep up; scour

**balayette** *nf* dusting brush, small broom

**balayeur -euse** *n* sweeper

**balayeuse** *nf* sweeping machine

**balayures** *nfpl* sweepings

**balbutiement** *nm* stammering, stuttering

**balbutier** *vt + vi* stammer, mumble

**balcon** *nm* balcony; *theat* dress-circle; *sl* **il y a du monde au ~!** she's got a bosom!

**baldaquin** *nm* canopy

**Bâle** *nf* Basel, Basle

**baleine** *nf* whale; whalebone (corset); rib (umbrella)

**baleinier** *nm* whaling-ship, whaler

**balise** *nf naut* buoy, beacon, sea-mark; *aer* runway-light

**baliser** *vt naut + aer* mark out (channel, runway)

**balistique** *nf* ballistics, gunnery; *adj* ballistic

**baliverne** *nf* piece of nonsense

**balkanique** *adj* Balkan

**ballade** *nf* ballad

**ballant** *adj* swinging, dangling (arms, legs)

¹**balle** *nf* ball; bullet; **~ perdue** stray shot; **~ traçante** tracer bullet

²**balle** *nf* bale (cotton, etc)

³**balle** *nf* chaff, husk

⁴**balle** *nf sl* franc

**ballerine** *nf* ballerina, ballet-dancer

**ballon** *nm* balloon; large ball, football; **~ d'essai** pilot balloon; *fig* feeler

29

# ballonnement

**ballonnement** *nm* swelling, distending (stomach), flatulence
**ballonner** *vt + vi* swell, distend; balloon out (skirt)
**¹ballottage** *nm* shaking, jolting
**²ballottage** *nm* indecisive election result
**ballottement** *nm* tossing (of ship); shaking
**ballotter** *vt* toss, shake about; *vi* shake, wobble, rattle (door)
**ballottine** *nf cul* chicken galantine
**ball-trap** *nm* clay-pigeon shoot
**balnéaire** *adj* bathing; **station ~** spa, seaside resort
**balourd -e** *n* awkward person, idiot; *adj* awkward, stupid
**balourdise** *nf* awkwardness; stupid blunder; **raconter des ~ s** talk rot
**balsamine** *nf bot* balsam
**baluchon** *nm coll* bundle (clothes)
**balustrade** *nf* balustrade, hand-rail
**bambin -e** *n coll* little child, kid
**bamboche** *nf* puppet, marionette; *sl* spree, lark; **faire ~** paint the town red
**bambou** *nm* bamboo
**bamboula** *nm* bamboo drum; *sl* negro
**ban** *nm* proclamation; banns (marriage); ban, exile; **mettre au ~** banish, send to Coventry
**banal** (*pl* ~ s) *adj* commonplace, hackneyed, banal
**banalité** *nf* triteness, banality; commonplace
**banane** *nf* banana; *mot* over-rider; *coll* medal
**bananier** *nm* banana-tree; banana-boat
**banc** *nm* bench, seat, form, pew; ~ **de glace** ice-field; ~ **de poissons** shoal of fish; ~ **de sable** sandbank; ~ **des accusés** dock, bar; ~ **d'essai** testing bench; ~ **du jury** jury box
**bancaire** *adj* relating to banking
**bancal** *adj* (*pl* ~s) bandy-legged; rickety
**bandage** *nm* bandaging, bandage; *med* truss; solid tyre
**¹bande** *nf* band, strip; wrapper; reel of film; ~ **dessinée** comic strip; ~ **magnétique** recording tape
**²bande** *nf* band, gang, party; flight, flock, pack; **faire ~ à part** keep to oneself
**³bande** *nf naut* list; **donner de la ~** list
**bandeau** *nm* head-band; bandage (over eyes)
**bander** *vt* bandage, bind up; tighten; ~ **les yeux à qn** blindfold someone; *vi vulg* have an erection
**banderole** *nf* streamer
**bandit** *nm* bandit, brigand; *coll* rascal
**bandoulière** *nf* shoulder-strap; **en ~** slung over one's shoulder

**bang** *nm* sonic boom
**banlieue** *nf* outskirts (of town), outer suburbs
**banlieusard -e** *n coll* inhabitant of suburbia
**banni -e** *n* exile, outlaw
**bannière** *nf* banner, flag, standard; **en ~** in one's shirt-tails
**bannir** *vt* banish, exile
**bannissement** *nm* exile, banishment
**banque** *nf* bank; banking
**banqueroute** *nf* bankruptcy
**banqueroutier -ière** *n* bankrupt
**banquette** *nf* bench, seat, form; bunker (golf)
**banquier** *nm* banker
**banquise** *nf* ice-floe, ice-pack
**baptême** *nm* baptism, christening; **nom de ~** Christian name
**baptiser** *vt* baptize, christen; *coll* call, nickname; *coll* ~ **du vin** add water to wine
**baquet** *nm* tub, bucket
**bar** *nm* sea-perch
**baragouin** *nm coll* gibberish
**baragouiner** *vt + vi coll* jabber, talk gibberish
**baraque** *nf* hut, shanty; booth (at fair); *sl* house, hovel
**baraquement** *nm* hutting; ~s huts, hutments
**baratin** *nm* chatting up, patter
**baratte** *nf* churn (for making butter)
**barbacane** *nf* barbican
**barbant** *adj sl* boring
**¹barbare** *nm* barbarian
**²barbare** *adj* barbaric, uncouth, barbarous
**barbarie** *nf* barbarity; barbarousness
**barbe** *nf* beard; *sl* bore; ~ **à papa** candy-floss; **quelle ~!** what a nuisance!; **rire dans sa ~** laugh up one's sleeve
**barbelé** *adj* barbed; **les ~s** barbed-wire entanglements
**barber** *vt sl* bore; **se ~** be bored
**barbiche** *nf* goatee, short beard
**barbier** *nm* barber
**barboter** *vt* paddle, splash about; *sl* steal, pinch
**barboteuse** *nf* child's rompers
**barbouiller** *vt* daub, scrawl, smear; **barbouillé de larmes** tear-stained; **se ~** get one's face dirty
**barbouze** *nm* unofficial secret agent
**barbu** *adj* bearded
**barde** *nm* bard, poet
**¹barder** *vi coll* ça va ~ things are hotting up
**²barder** *vt cul* cover with slices of bacon; *mil* encase in armour
**barème** *nm* ready-reckoner; scale

30

(marks, etc); printed table

**baril** *nm* barrel, cask, keg

**barillet** *nm* small barrel; chamber (revolver)

**bariolé** *adj* motley, many-coloured

**barioler** *vt* paint in many colours, variegate

**baromètre** *nm* barometer

**baronne** *nf* baroness

**baroque** *nm* baroque style; *adj* odd, quaint, baroque

**baroud** *nm* *mil sl* fight, scrap

**baroudeur** *nm* fighter, scrapper

**barque** *nf* boat; **bien mener sa ~** manage one's affairs well

**barrage** *nm* barring, closing, blocking; barrier, block, dam, weir; *mil* (**tir de**) **~ barrage**; **match de ~** replay

**barre** *nf* bar, rod; **~ fixe** horizontal bar; tiller; stroke (writing); stripe; **avoir ~ sur qn** have a hold over s/o

**barrer** *vt* bar, obstruct, dam; cross out, cross (cheque); *naut* steer; *sl* **se ~** clear off

¹**barrette** *nf* hair-slide; ankle strap; brooch

²**barrette** *nf* biretta; cardinal's cap

**barreur -euse** *n* helmsman

**barrière** *nf* barrier, obstacle; fence; gate; **~ de dégel** barrier on road to protect surface during thaw

**barrique** *nf* large barrel, cask

**barrir** *vi* trumpet (elephant)

**baryton** *nm + adj invar* baritone

¹**bas** *nm* lower part, bottom; **les hauts et les ~** the ups and downs; *adj* (*f* **basse**) low; base, mean; **au ~ mot** at the lowest estimate; **avoir la vue ~** se short-sighted; **faire main ~** se sur lay hands on; *adv* low, low down; **à ~** down with; **en ~** down, downwards; **mettre ~** bring forth (young); lay down (arms); **parler ~** speak softly

²**bas** *nm* stocking

**basané** *adj* sunburnt, tanned, swarthy

**bas-bleu** *nm* blue-stocking

**bas-côté** *nm* aisle (church)

**bascule** *nf* rocker; see-saw; weighing-machine; **chaise à ~** rocking-chair

**basculer** *vt + vi* rock, swing, tip up, lose balance; *fig* **~ dans** tend towards, finish up as

**base** *nf* base, foundation, basis; grass roots, rank and file

**baser** *vt* base, ground, found; **se ~ sur** take as a basis

**bas-fond** *nm* low ground, shallows; **les ~ s** slums; lowest classes of society

**basilique** *nf* basilica

**basquais** *adj* Basque

**basque** *nf* skirt, (coat-)tail, flap

**basse** *nf* bass (voice, instrument)

**basse-cour** *nf* farm-yard, poultry-yard

**bassement** *adv* basely, meanly, scurvily

**bassesse** *nf* baseness, lowness; ignoble action

**bassin** *nm* basin, bowl; dock; ornamental pond; pelvis; **~ houiller** coal field; **entrer au ~** dock

**bassinant** *adj sl* boring, tiresome

**bassine** *nf* pan

**bassinoire** *nf* warming pan

**bastingage** *nm naut* bulwark

**bastringue** *nm* *sl* low dance-hall; din; paraphernalia

**bas-ventre** *nm* lower part of abdomen

**bât** *nm* pack-saddle; *coll* **c'est là que le ~ le blesse** that's where the shoe pinches

**bataclan** *nm sl* paraphernalia

**bataille** *nf* battle, fight; **cheveux en ~** ruffled hair

**batailler** *vi* battle, struggle, fight

**batailleur -euse** *adj* pugnacious, quarrelsome

**bataillon** *nm* battalion

**bâtard -e** *n + adj* bastard; **chien ~** mongrel

**bâtarde** *nf* slanting writing (intermediate between round hand and running hand)

**batavia** *nf* kind of lettuce

¹**bateau** *nm* boat, ship

²**bateau** *nm* part of pavement in front of entrance

³**bateau** *nm* hoax; **monter un ~ à qn** hoax s/o

**bateau-citerne** *nm* (*pl* **bateaux-citernes**) tanker

**bateau-mouche** *nm* (*pl* **bateaux-mouches**) passenger-boat on the Seine in Paris

**bateau-pêcheur** *nm* (*pl* **bateaux-pêcheurs**) fishing-boat

**batelier -ière** *n* boatman, boatwoman

**batellerie** *nf* inland waterway transport; canal and river craft (in collective sense)

**bath** *adj invar sl* first-rate, fine, bang on

**bâti** *nm* structure, frame(work); tacking (needlework)

**batifoler** *vi coll* romp, frolic, play about

**bâtiment** *nm* building, building-trade; large ship

¹**bâtir** *vt* build, construct; **terrain à ~** building land

²**bâtir** *vt* baste, tack (needlework)

**bâtisse** *nf* bricks and mortar; masonry; ramshackle building

**batiste** *nf* batiste, cambric

**bâton** *nm* stick, rod, staff; stroke (writing); **~ de rouge** lipstick; **à ~ s rompus** by fits and starts, irregularly; *sl* **mener une vie de ~ de chaise** lead a gay life, sleep around; **mettre les ~ s dans les roues** put a spoke in the wheels

**bâtonner** *vt* beat, cudgel

**bâtonnier** *nm leg* president of the Bar

**battage** *nm* threshing (corn); churning (butter)

¹**battant** *nm* clapper (bell); flap (table); **porte à deux ~ s** double doors

²**battant** *adj* beating; **pluie ~ e** driving rain; **porte ~ e** swing door; **tambour ~** with drums beating; hastily, roughly; **tout ~ neuf** brand-new

**battement** *nm* beating, clapping, fluttering, throbbing (heart), banging (door)

**batterie** *nf mil+elect* battery; wait, pause; percussion instruments of the orchestra; **~ de cuisine** set of kitchen utensils; **dresser ses ~ s** lay one's plans

¹**batteur** *nm* whisk, beater (machine)

²**batteur -euse** *n* beater (of gold); thresher; drummer

**batteuse** *nf* threshing-machine; harvester

**battoir** *nm* beater (instrument); *sl* large hand

**battre** *vt* (16) beat, strike, thrash; defeat; whisk (eggs); shuffle (cards); coin (money); churn (butter); scour (countryside); **~ la mesure** beat time; **~ le pavé** loaf around the streets; **'~ son plein** be in full swing; **~ un pavillon** fly the flag; *vi* beat; **~ des mains** clap; **en retraite** beat a retreat; **se ~** fight

**battu** *adj* beaten; **avoir les yeux ~ s** have rings round one's eyes; **chemin ~** beaten track

**battue** *nf* battue; (police) round-up

**baudet** *nm* ass, donkey; trestle

**baudrier** *nm* shoulder-belt

**baume** *nm* balm, balsam

**bavard -e** *n* chatterbox; indiscreet person; *adj* talkative

**bavardage** *nm* chattering, gossip

**bavarder** *vi* chatter, gossip

**bavarois** *adj* Bavarian

**bavaroise** *nf cul* cold flavoured cream (sweet)

**bave** *nf* spittle, slaver, foam

**baver** *vi* dribble, slaver, slobber; run (pen); *coll* **en ~** be staggered; have a rough time

**bavette** *nf* bib; skirt (beef)

**baveux -euse** *adj* dribbling, slavering; moist (omelette)

**Bavière** *nf* Bavaria

**bavoir** *nm* bib

**bavure** *nf eng* burr; smudge; *coll fig* error; **sans ~** perfect

**bayer** *vi obs* gape; **~ aux corneilles** stand gaping

**bazar** *nm* bazaar, general store; *coll* **tout le ~** the whole lot

**béant** *adj* gaping (wound); yawning (chasm)

**béat** *adj* blissful, smug

**béatitude** *nf* beatitude, bliss; complacency

**beau** *nm* beauty; beau; **faire le ~** show off; beg (dog); **le plus ~ de l'histoire, c'est...** the best of it is ...; **le temps est au ~ fixe** the weather is set fair; *adj* (**bel**) (*f* **belle**, *mpl* **beaux**) beautiful, handsome, fair; fine, noble; **à la belle étoile** in the open air; **avoir ~ faire qch** do sth in vain; **bel et bien** quite, entirely; **ce n'est pas ~ de votre part** that's not nice of you; **de plus belle** more than ever; **il est ~ joueur** he is a good loser; **il fait ~** the weather is fine; **le ~ côté** the bright side; **le ~ monde** high society; **l'échapper belle** have a narrow escape; **tout ~ !** gently!; **un bel âge** a ripe old age; **une belle fortune** a large fortune; **une belle occasion** a marvellous opportunity; **voir les choses en ~** see things in a good light; **belle** *nf* beautiful woman, belle; **faire la ~** play the deciding game; **la Belle et la Bête** Beauty and the Beast

**beaucoup** *adv* much, very much; **~ de** a lot of, many; **c'est déjà ~ qu'il ne dise pas non** it's something to be thankful for that he does not refuse; **de ~** by far

**beau-fils** *nm* (*pl* **beaux-fils**) son-in-law; step-son

**beau-frère** *nm* (*pl* **beaux-frères**) brother-in-law; step-brother

**beau-père** *nm* (*pl* **beaux-pères**) father-in-law; step-father

**beaupré** *nm* bowsprit

**beauté** *nf* beauty; beautiful woman; **~ du diable** bloom of youth; **de toute ~** very beautiful; **être en ~** be looking one's best; **perdre en ~** lose in fine style; **se faire une ~** make up

**beaux-arts** *nmpl* fine arts

**beaux-parents** *nmpl* parents-in-law

**bébé** *nm* baby

**bébé-éprouvette** *nm* (*pl* **bébés-éprouvette**) *coll* test-tube baby

**bébête** *adj coll* childish, silly

**bec** *nm* beak; nib; spout (jug); burner (stove, lamp); mouth-piece (musical instrument); *coll* mouth; **~ de lièvre** hare-lip; **avoir bon ~** have the gift of the gab; **clouer le ~ à qn** shut s/o up; **fin ~** gourmet; **prise de ~** squabble

**bécane** *nf coll* bicycle, bike

**bécasse** *nf* woodcock; *fig+coll* ninny, goose

**bécassine** *nf* snipe; *fig+coll* ninny, goose

**bec-de-cane** *nm* lever-handle (door)

**béchamel** *nf* **sauce (à la) ~** white cream sauce

**bêche** *nf* spade

**bêcher** *vt* dig; *fig* + *coll* criticize, run down

**bécoter** *vt coll* give little kisses to

**becquée** *nf* beakful; **donner la ~ à** feed (young birds)

**becqueter** *vt* (5) peck up; *sl* eat

**bedaine** *nf sl* paunch, belly

**bedeau** *nm* beadle; verger

**bedon** *nm coll* paunch, belly

**bedonnant** *adj* pot-bellied

**bée** *adj f* open, gaping; **bouche ~** open-mouthed

**beffroi** *nm* belfry

**bégaiement** *nm* stammering, stuttering

**bégayer** *vt* + *vi* (7) stammer (out), stutter

**bègue** *n* stutterer; *adj* stammering, stuttering

**bégueule** *nf* prude; *adj* prudish, strait-laced

**béguin** *nm* hood (of Beguine nun); baby's bonnet; *fig* + *coll* infatuation

**béguinage** *nm* (Beguine) convent

**beige** *adj* beige; natural, raw (wood)

**beignet** *nm* fritter

**bel** *adj see* **beau**

**bêler** *vi* bleat; *fig* + *coll* complain, grouse

**belette** *nf* weasel

**belge** *adj* Belgian

**bélier** *nm* ram; battering ram

**belladone** *nf* belladonna, deadly nightshade

**bellâtre** *nm* fop; *adj* vulgarly handsome

**belle-famille** *nf* (*pl* **belles-familles**) in-laws

**belle-fille** *nf* (*pl* **belles-filles**) daughter-in-law; step-daughter

**belle-mère** *nf* (*pl* **belles-mères**) mother-in-law; step-mother

**belles-lettres** *nfpl* belles-lettres, humanities

**belle-sœur** *nf* (*pl* **belles-sœurs**) sister-in-law; step-sister

**belligérant** *adj* belligerent

**belliqueux -euse** *adj* warlike, bellicose

**belvédère** *nm* belvedere, view-point

**bémol** *nm mus* flat

**bénédicité** *nm* grace (before meal)

**bénédictin** *nm* Benedictine monk; **~e** *nf* Benedictine nun; Benedictine (liqueur)

**bénédiction** *nf* benediction, blessing; godsend

**bénéfice** *nm* profit, gain, benefit; *eccles* living; **au ~ de** in aid of; **sous ~ d'inventaire** subject to satisfaction

**bénéficiaire** *n* beneficiary

**bénéficier** *vi* benefit, derive advantage

**benêt** *nm* clot; *adj* silly, stupid

**bénévole** *adj* gratuitous, without charge; voluntary

**bénin** (*f* **bénigne**) *adj* benign, kind; mild; **maladie bénigne** slight illness

**béni-oui-oui** *nm coll* yes-man

**bénir** *vt* bless, consecrate; **~ un mariage** solemnize a marriage; **je bénis la voiture** (I say) thank God for the car

**bénit** *adj* consecrated, blessed; **eau ~e** holy water; **pain ~** holy bread

**bénitier** *nm* font, holy water vessel, stoup

**benne** *nf* dredger-bucket, cable-car, little truck

**benzine** *nf* benzine; (in Switzerland) petrol

**béquille** *nf* crutch

**bercail** *nm* sheepfold; *fig* fold (Church), bosom (family)

**berceau** *nm* cradle, cot; arbour; **dès le ~** from earliest childhood

**bercer** *vt* (4) rock, lull; **~ qn de promesses** delude s/o with promises

**berceuse** *nf* lullaby; rocking-chair

**berge** *nf* steep bank

**berger** *nm* shepherd; **(chien) ~** sheep-dog

**¹bergère** *nf* shepherdess

**²bergère** *nf* easy-chair

**bergerie** *nf* sheepfold

**berlue** *nf fig* blindness; **avoir la ~** see things wrong

**berne** *nf* **en ~** at half-mast

**berner** *vt* make fun of, hoax

**bernique** *interj coll* nothing doing, no use

**besace** *nf* beggar's bag, scrip

**besicles** *nfpl coll* goggles, specs

**besogne** *nf* task, job, piece of work; **abattre de la ~** get through a lot of work

**besogner** *vi* work hard

**besogneux -euse** *adj* hard-up, needy

**besoin** *nm* need, want, poverty; **au ~** if necessary; **avoir ~ de** need; **faire ses ~s** relieve oneself

**bestial** *adj* bestial, brutish

**bestiaux** *nmpl* cattle, livestock

**bestiole** *nf* tiny beast (*usu* insect)

**bêta** (*f* **bêtasse**) *n sl* stupid person, silly ass

**bétail** *nm* cattle, livestock

**bête** *nf* beast, animal; stupid person; **~ à bon Dieu** ladybird; **~ de somme** beast of burden; **~ noire** bugbear; *coll* **chercher la petite ~** split hairs

**bêtise** *nf* stupidity; foolish act, blunder; trifle

**béton** *nm* concrete; **~ armé** reinforced concrete

**bette** *nf* beet; Swiss chard

**betterave** *nf* beet(root); **~ à salade** beetroot

**beugler** *vi* low, bellow; *coll* bawl

**beurre** *nm* butter; **œil au ~ noir** black eye

**beurrer** *vt* butter

**beurrier** *nm* butter-dish

**beuverie** *nf* drinking bout

**bévue** *nf* blunder, slip, howler

**biais** *nm* skew, slant; bias (of bowl); expedient; **de ~** aslant, askew

**biaiser** *vi* be on the slant; be evasive

**bibelot** *nm* curio, knick-knack

¹**biberon** *nm* baby's feeding-bottle

²**biberon** *nm* tippler, drunkard

**bibi** *nm sl* number one, myself; woman's hat

**bibliobus** *nm* mobile library, *US* bookmobile

**bibliographie** *nf* bibliography

**bibliothécaire** *n* librarian

**bibliothèque** *nf* library; bookcase

**biblique** *adj* biblical

**bic** *nm* ball-point pen; *adj* **pointe ~** ball-point pen

**biche** *nf* hind, doe

**bicher** *vi sl* **ça biche?** everything going well?

**bichonner** *vt* smarten up; **se ~** titivate

**bicoque** *nf* shanty, hovel; *coll* little house

**bicyclette** *nf* bicycle

**bidet** *nm* nag, small horse; bidet

**bidon** *nm* can, drum

**bidonville** *nm* shanty town

**bidule** *nm coll* thingummy, thing

**bielle** *nf* connecting-rod; **mot j'ai coulé une ~** my big end has gone

**bien** *nm* good; benefit, advantage; property; **~s** property, belongings; **mener à ~** bring to a successful conclusion; **prendre la chose en ~** take sth in good part; *adv* well, good; right, proper; much, very; **~ des** plenty of; **~ entendu** of course; **c'est ~ fait** it serves you (him, her, etc) right; **elle est ~** she is nice-looking; **il y en avait ~ mille** there were at least a thousand; **il va (se porte) ~** he is well; **je suis ~ avec lui** I'm on good terms with him; **nous sommes très ~ ici** we're quite comfortable here; **tant ~ que mal** somehow or other; **vous faites ~ de partir** you are wise to leave; *conj* **~ que** although

**bien-aimé** *adj* beloved, favourite

**bien-être** *nm* well-being, welfare

**bienfaisance** *nf* charity, beneficence

**bienfaisant** *adj* beneficent, charitable, salutary

**bienfait** *nm* kindness, favour; blessing, boon

**bienfaiteur -trice** *n* benefactor, benefactress

**bien-fondé** *nm* justice, merits (of a case)

**bienheureux -euse** *adj* blissful, happy; blessed

**biennal** *adj* biennial, two-yearly

**bienséance** *nf* propriety, decorum, decency

**bienséant** *adj* becoming, seemly, proper

**bientôt** *adv* soon, very soon, shortly, before long; quickly; **à ~** see you soon

**bienveillance** *nf* benevolence, kindness, good-will

**bienveillant** *adj* kind, benevolent, kindly

**bienvenu** *adj* welcome; **soyez le ~!** welcome!

**bienvenue** *nf* welcome; **souhaiter la ~ à qn** welcome s/o

¹**bière** *nf* beer; **~ blonde** light ale; **~ brune** brown ale

²**bière** *nf* coffin

**biffer** *vt* cross out, strike out

**bifteck** *nm* steak, beefsteak; **~ pommes frites** steak and chips

**bifurcation** *nf* fork, bifurcation

**bifurquer** *vi* fork

**bigame** *adj* bigamous

**bigamie** *nf* bigamy

**bigarreau** *nm* white-heart cherry

**bigarrer** *vt* variegate, mottle

**bigorneau** *nm coll* winkle

**bigot -e** *n* bigot; *adj* bigoted

**bigoudi** *nm* hair-curler

**bigre** *interj obs* + *coll* by jove!

**bigrement** *adv* jolly (well)

**bijou** *nm* gem; sweet thing, sweet person

**bijouterie** *nf* jewellery; jeweller's shop; jeweller's trade

**bijoutier -ière** *n* jeweller

**bilan** *nm* balance-sheet; **déposer son ~** file one's petition (in bankruptcy)

**bile** *nf* bile, gall; bad temper; **s'échauffer la ~** get worked up; *sl* **se faire de la ~** worry

**bileux -euse** *adj coll* easily worried

**biliaire** *adj* biliary; **la vésicule ~** gall bladder

**bilieux -ieuse** *adj* bilious; irascible, irritable

**bilingue** *adj* bilingual

**billard** *nm* billiards; billiard table; billiard saloon; *coll* operating table; *coll* bald head; *coll* **c'est du ~** it's easy

**bille** *nf* billiard ball; marble; **roulement à ~s** ball-bearing; **stylo à ~** ball-point pen

**billet** *nm* note, short letter; ticket; **~ d'aller et retour** return ticket; **~ (de banque)** (bank-)note; **~ simple** single ticket

**billion** *nm* one thousand million

**billot** *nm* block (wood); executioner's block

**bimensuel -uelle** *adj* fortnightly, twice monthly
**bimoteur** *nm* twin-engined plane; *adj invar* twin-engined
**binaire** *adj* binary
**biner** *vt* dig, hoe
¹**binette** *nf sl* face
²**binette** *nf* hoe
**biniou** *nm* Breton bagpipes
**binocle** *nm* pince-nez, eye-glasses
**biochimie** *nf* biochemistry
**biographe** *nm* biographer
**biographie** *nf* biography
**biologie** *nf* biology
**bique** *nf* she-goat; *sl* hag
¹**bis** *adj* brown (bread)
²**bis** *adv* twice; encore!
**bisaïeul** *nm* (*pl* **bisaïeux**) great-grand-father
**bisaïeule** *nf* great-grandmother
**bisannuel -elle** *adj* biannual
**bisbille** *nf coll* petty quarrel
**biscornu** *adj* mis-shapen; queer (ideas)
**biscotte** *nf* rusk
**biscuit** *nm* plain cake; biscuit
¹**bise** *nf* north wind
²**bise** *nf coll* kiss
**biseau** *nm* bevel
**biseauter** *vt* bevel, chamfer
**bisque** *nf cul* shell-fish soup, bisque
**bisser** *vt* encore (performance)
**bissextile** *adj* **année** ~ leap year
**bistouri** *nm med* lancet
**bistre** *nm* bistre (colour); *adj* blackish-brown
**bistré** *adj* swarthy
**bistrot** *nm coll* small restaurant; pub
**bitte** *nf naut* bitt; *vulg* prick
**bitume** *nm* bitumen; asphalt
**bivouaquer** *vi* bivouac, camp
**bizarre** *adj* queer, odd, peculiar; eccentric
**blackbouler** *vt* blackball; *coll* reject (candidate)
**blafard** *adj* pale, wan, pallid, dim
**blague** *nf* tobacco-pouch; *coll* tall story, leg-pull; **sans** ~ ? no joking?, really?
**blaguer** *vt* chaff, make fun of; *vi coll* joke
**blagueur -euse** *n* humbug, joker; *adj* mocking, bantering
**blaireau** *nm* badger; shaving-brush
**blâme** *nm* blame, censure; reprimand
**blâmer** *vt* blame; reprimand
**blanc** *nm* white, whiteness; whitening liquid; blank space (on page); white man; (white) linen; *cul* breast (chicken); **chauffer à** ~ make white hot; **chèque en** ~ blank cheque; **saigner qn à** ~ bleed s/o white; **tirer à** ~ fire blanks; *adj* (*f* **blanche**) white; light-coloured; clean, pure; blank; **donner**

**carte blanche** give unlimited powers; **mariage** ~ unconsummated marriage; **nuit blanche** sleepless night; **voix blanche** expressionless voice
**blanc-bec** *nm coll* (*pl* **blancs-becs**) greenhorn, youngster
**blanchaille** *nf* whitebait
**blanchâtre** *adj* whitish
**blanche** *nf* white woman; *mus* minim; **traite des** ~ s white slave traffic
**blancheur** *nf* whiteness; purity
**blanchir** *vt* make white, whiten, bleach; ~ **du linge** wash clothes; ~ (**à la chaux**) whitewash; *vi* turn white
**blanchissage** *nm* washing, laundering; whitewashing
**blanchisserie** *nf* laundry, wash-house
**blanchisseur** *nm* laundryman
**blanchisseuse** *nf* laundress
**blanc-seing** *nm* (*pl* **blancs-seings**) signed document with blank space above
¹**blanquette** *nf* blanquette (stew of white meat)
²**blanquette** *nf* kind of white wine
**blasé** *adj* indifferent
**blaser** *vt* blunt, cloy, make indifferent
**blason** *nm* coat of arms; heraldry; **redorer son** ~ make a rich marriage (poor nobleman)
**blasphémateur -trice** *n* blasphemer; *adj* blasphemous
**blasphématoire** *adj* blasphemous
**blasphème** *nm* blasphemy
**blatte** *nf* cockroach, black beetle
**blé** *nm* corn, wheat; **manger son** ~ **en herbe** spend one's income before one gets it
**bled** *nm* the interior (in N. Africa); *sl* hole, one-horse town
**blême** *adj* livid, deathly pale
**blêmir** *vi* turn deathly pale, blanch
**blennorragie** *nf* gonorrhoea
**blessé** *adj* + *n* wounded, injured (man or woman)
**blesser** *vt* wound, injure; wrong
**blessure** *nf* wound, injury
**blet** (*f* **blette**) *adj* overripe (fruit)
¹**bleu** *nm* blue; blue dye; bruise; blue dungarees, overalls; ~ **marine** navy blue; *sl* recruit
²**bleu** *adj* blue; **peur** ~ **e** blue funk
**bleuâtre** *adj* bluish
**bleuet** *nm* cornflower
**bleuir** *vt* make blue; *vi* turn blue
**bleuter** *vt* make slightly blue
**blindage** *nm* armour-plating; metal casing; timbering
**blindé** *nm* armoured vehicle; *adj* armour-plated; **division** ~ **e** armoured division
**blinder** *vt* armour-plate; case; timber
**bloc** *nm* block, lump; writing pad; *pol*

coalition; *sl* prison; **à ~** fully, right home; **en ~** in a lump

**blocage** *nm* freeze (prices, etc); *bui* hardcore

**bloc-cuisine** *nm* (*pl* **blocs-cuisines**) kitchen equipment

**blockhaus** *nm* blockhouse; *naut* conning-tower

**bloc-moteur** *nm* (*pl* **blocs-moteurs**) *eng* engine unit

**blocus** *nm* blockade, siege; **forcer le ~** run the blockade

**blond** *nm* blond colour; *adj* fair (-haired), blond

**blondeur** *nf* blondness, fairness

**blondin** *nm* fop; fair-haired person; *adj* fair-haired

**blondir** *vt* bleach, dye blond; *vi* turn yellow

**bloquer** *vt* block up, fill up; lock, clamp; blockade, invest; obstruct; freeze (prices); **~ les freins** brake hard; **~ un chèque** stop a cheque

**blottir (se)** *v refl* hide, huddle, nestle

**¹blouse** *nf* overall, smock, pinafore, blouse

**²blouse** *nf* pocket (billiards)

**¹blouser** *vi* puff out (dress)

**²blouser** *vt* pocket (billiard ball); *coll* take in, deceive

**blouson** *nm* jerkin (windcheater); **~ noir** rocker, leather boy

**blue-jean** *nm* jeans

**bluet** *nm* cornflower

**bluffer** *vt + vi* bluff; boast

**bobard** *nm coll* tall story

**bobèche** *nf* sconce, socket (candlestick)

**bobine** *nf* spool, reel, bobbin; *sl* face

**bobiner** *vt* wind, spool, reel

**bobo** *nm coll* (talking to children) sore, bump; **faire ~** hurt

**bocage** *nm* copse, grove; wooded area

**bocal** *nm* jar, bowl

**Boche** *n sl + pej* German, Hun

**boche** *adj sl + pej* German

**bock** *nm* beer-glass; glass of beer

**bof** *interj* oh well (scorn, resignation, etc)

**boggie** *nm* bogie (railway carriage)

**bohème** *nm + adj* Bohemian; **(vie de) ~** easy, carefree life

**bohémien -ienne** *n* gipsy

**boire** *vt* (17) drink; soak up, absorb; drink in; **~ un affront** swallow an insult; *coll* **~ un coup** have a drink; *sl* **ce n'est pas la mer à ~** it's not as bad as all that

**bois** *nm* wood, timber; *pl* antlers; *mus* wood instruments; **~ blanc** deal, white wood; **~ de lit** bedstead; **le Bois de Boulogne** the Bois de Boulogne

**boisé** *adj* wooded

**boiser** *vt* wainscot; timber; afforest

**boiserie** *nf* woodwork, panelling

**boisson** *nf* drink, beverage; **pris de ~** drunk

**boîte** *nf* box, tin; *sl* poky little room, school, place of work; **~ crânienne** brain pan; **~ (de nuit)** night-club; *sl* **mettre en ~** make fun of

**boiter** *vi* limp, hobble

**boiteux -euse** *adj* lame; rickety; **projet ~** poor plan

**boîtier** *nm* case, watch-case

**bol** *nm* bowl, basin

**bolide** *nm* meteor, meteorite; fast-moving car

**bombance** *nf sl* feasting; **faire ~** feast

**bombardement** *nm* bombardment, bombing

**bombarder** *vt* bombard, shell, bomb; pelt; *iron* appoint suddenly

**bombardier** *nm* bomber

**bombe** *nf* bomb; atomizer; aerosol; **~ glacée** ice-cream pudding; **faire la ~** go on the binge

**bomber** *vt* make bulge, swell, arch, camber; **~ la poitrine** throw out one's chest; *vi* bulge out

**bon** *nm* good, goodness; voucher, order, ticket; bond; *adj* (*f* **bonne**) good, virtuous; nice, kind, good-natured; capable, clever; right, correct; fit; profitable, advantageous; **~ à savoir** worth knowing; **~ marché** cheap; **à la ~ne heure!** fine!; **à quoi ~?** what's the use?; **de ~ne heure** early; **si ~ vous semble** if you think fit; **souhaiter la ~ne année** wish a happy New Year; **trouver ~** de think it advisable to; *adv* agreed!, right!; **c'est ~!** that'll do!; **il fait ~ ici** it's nice here; **pour de ~** for good; seriously speaking; **sentir ~** smell nice; **tenir ~** stand firm

**bonasse** *adj* simple-minded

**bonbon** *nm* sweet(meat)

**bonbonne** *nf* demijohn

**bonbonnière** *nf* sweetmeat box

**bond** *nm* jump, leap, bound; **faire faux ~ à** let down

**bondé** *adj* packed, full

**bondir** *vi* leap, spring up; **cela m'a fait ~** that made me furious

**bonheur** *nm* good fortune, luck; happiness, pleasure; **au petit ~** in a haphazard fashion; *sl* **par ~** fortunately; **porter ~ à qn** bring s/o luck; **quel ~!** what a blessing!

**bonhomie** *nf* good nature

**bonhomme** *nm* (*pl* **bonshommes**) (*f* **bonne femme**) good-natured simple fellow (woman); *sl* man, fellow (woman); **aller son petit ~ de chemin** jog quietly along; **conte de bonne**

**femme** old wives' tale; **petit ~** little boy

**boni** *nm* bonus; surplus

**bonification** *nf* improvement; bonus

**bonifier** *vt* improve, make good (shortage)

**boniment** *nm* patter; *coll* spiel

**bonjour** *nm* good morning, good day; **simple comme ~** simple as A B C

**bonne** *nf* maid(-servant)

**bonne-maman** *nf* (*pl* **bonnes-mamans**) *coll* grandma

**bonnement** *adv* **tout ~** simply

**bonnet** *nm* cap; *sl* **gros ~** bigwig; **jeter son ~ par-dessus les moulins** throw propriety to the winds; **prendre sous son ~** invent; act on one's own responsibility; **triste comme un ~ de nuit** dull as ditchwater

**bonneterie** *nf* hosiery

**bon(n)iche** *nf sl* young maid(-servant)

**bon-papa** *nm coll* grandpa

**bonsoir** *nm* good evening, good night

**bonté** *nf* goodness, kindness; **~s** kind actions

**bord** *nm* edge, border, rim; side (ship); shore; **à ~ de** on board; **au ~ de la mer** at the seaside; *coll* **sur les ~s** slightly

**bordeaux** *nm* Bordeaux wine, claret

**bordée** *nf* broadside, volley; **~ d'injures** string of insults

**bordel** *nm* brothel; *sl* **quel ~!** what a shambles!

**bordelais** *adj* of Bordeaux

**border** *vt* border, edge, hem; tuck in; ship (oars)

**bordereau** *nm* memorandum, statement (account, etc)

**bordure** *nf* border, edging, fringe

**borgne** *adj* one-eyed, blind in one eye; *coll* low, disreputable

**borne** *nf* boundary-stone or mark; corner-post, bollard; **~ kilométrique** kilometre marker; **~s** boundaries, limits; **cela dépasse les ~s** that's going too far

**borné** *adj* restricted; narrow-minded

**borner** *vt* limit, restrict

**bosquet** *nm* thicket, grove

**bosse** *nf* bump, bruise, dent, hump; *coll* **avoir la ~ du calcul** be good at figures; *sl* **rouler sa ~** knock about the world

**bosseler** *vt* (5) dent; emboss

**bosser** *vi sl* work hard, slave

**bossu-e** *n + adj* hunch-backed (person)

**bot** *adj invar* **pied-~** club-footed, clubfooted person

**botanique** *adj* botanical

¹**botte** *nf* bunch, bundle

²**botte** *nf* high boot, wellington

³**botte** *nf* thrust, lunge

**botter** *vt* put boots or shoes on; kick; **le Chat Botté** Puss in Boots

**bottier** *nm* bootmaker, shoemaker

**Bottin** *nm* street directory (in France)

**bottine** *nf* ankle-boot, bootee

**bouc** *nm* male goat; goatee; **~ émissaire** scapegoat

**boucan** *nm sl* din, row, uproar

**boucanier** *nm* buccaneer, pirate

**bouche** *nf* mouth; muzzle; opening, aperture; **~ d'eau** hydrant; **~ de chaleur** hot-air vent; **~ d'incendie** hydrant; **bonne ~** titbit; **le ~ à ~** the kiss of life

**bouché** *adj* corked, bunged up; *sl* stupid, dense

**bouchée** *nf* mouthful; **~ à la reine** small chicken vol-au-vent; **mettre les ~s doubles** gobble up; **ne faire qu'une ~ de** overcome easily

¹**boucher** *nm* butcher

²**boucher** *vt* stop up, plug, cork

**bouchère** *nf* butcher's wife

**boucherie** *nf* butcher's shop; butcher's trade; slaughter

**bouche-trou** *nm* stop-gap, substitute

**bouchon** *nm* cork, plug, stopper; float (fishing); wisp (straw); **~ de circulation** traffic block, traffic jam

**bouclage** *nm mil* encirclement

**boucle** *nf* buckle; loop (river, road); curl; ring; **~ d'oreille** ear-ring

**bouclé** *adj* curly

**boucler** *vt* buckle, fasten; *coll* lock up, imprison; *mil* encircle; **~ le budget** make both ends meet; *sl* **la ~** shut up

**bouclier** *nm* shield, buckler

**bouddhiste** *n + adj* Buddhist

**bouder** *vt* **~ qch** stay away from sth, not patronize sth; **~ qn** be sulky with s/o; *vi* sulk

**bouderie** *nf* sulkiness, sulks

**boudeur -euse** *n + adj* sulky (person)

**boudin** *nm* black pudding

**boudoir** *nm* boudoir

**boue** *nf* mud, mire, dirt; **traîner qn dans la ~** drag s/o's name in the mud

**bouée** *nf naut* buoy; **~ de sauvetage** life-buoy

**boueur** *nm* dustman

**boueux -euse** *adj* muddy

**bouffant** *adj* puffed, baggy

**bouffe** *adj* **opéra ~** comic opera

**bouffée** *nf* puff, whiff; fit (anger, pride); **~ de chaleur** sudden flush

**bouffer** *vt sl* eat; *vi* puff out (dress)

**bouffi** *adj* puffed, swollen, bloated

**bouffir** *vt* blow out, swell; *vi* become swollen

**bouffissure** *nf* puffiness, swelling

**bouffon** *nm* clown, fool, jester

**bouffonnerie** *nf* buffoonery

**bouge** *nm* hovel, den; low place; bilge (barrel)

**bougeoir** *nm* candlestick

**bougeotte** *nf coll* **avoir la ~** be fidgety

**bouger** *vt* (3) move, displace; *vi* move, budge, stir

**bougie** *nf* (wax) candle, taper; *mot* sparking plug

**bougnat** *nm coll* coal-merchant

**bougon -onne** *n + adj coll* grumpy (person)

**bougonner** *vi coll* grumble, grouse

**bougran** *nm* buckram

**bougre** *nm sl* chap; **~ d'idiot!** idiot!; **un bon ~** a good type; **bougresse** *nf sl* woman

**bougrement** *adv sl* very

**bouillabaisse** *nf* Provençal fish soup

**bouillant** *adj* boiling(-hot); hot-headed

**bouille** *nf sl* face, dial, mug

**bouilleur** *nm* distiller; **~ de cru** home distiller

**bouilli** *nm* boiled beef

**bouillie** *nf* pap; gruel, porridge

**bouillir** *vi* (18) boil; **faire ~ de l'eau** boil water

**bouilloire** *nf* kettle

**bouillon** *nm* stock, broth; cheap restaurant; bubbling, bubble; *comm* remainders

**bouillonnement** *nm* bubbling, seething

**bouillonner** *vi* bubble, boil, seethe

**bouillotte** *nf* hot-water bottle

**boulanger** *nm* baker

**boulangère** *nf* baker's wife

**boulangerie** *nf* baker's shop; bakery

**boule** *nf* ball, globe; **avoir les nerfs en ~** be all tensed up; **partie de ~s** game of bowls; *sl* **perdre la ~** go mad; **se mettre en ~** curl up

**bouleau** *nm* birch-tree

**bouledogue** *nm* bulldog

**bouler** *vt coll* muff; *vi* swell (dough); *coll* **envoyer ~ qn** send s/o to blazes

**boulet** *nm* cannon-ball; *coll* dead-weight (person); (coal) ovoid

**boulette** *nf* meat-ball, bread-ball; *sl* blunder

**boulevard** *nm* boulevard

**boulevardier** *nm* man about town

**bouleversant** *adj* staggering, upsetting

**bouleversement** *nm* upheaval, confusion

**bouleverser** *vt* upset; turn topsy-turvy

**Boul' Mich'** *nm coll* Boulevard Saint-Michel

**boulon** *nm* bolt, pin

**boulonner** *vt* bolt, pin; *vi sl* work hard

**¹boulot** *nm sl* work

**²boulot -otte** *adj* dumpy, fat

**boulotter** *vt sl* eat

**bouquet** *nm* bunch; cluster of trees; tuft; aroma, bouquet; prawn; finishing-piece (firework-display); **ça, c'est le ~!** that's the end!

**bouquin** *nm coll* book; old book

**bouquiner** *vi* browse, pore over books; hunt for old books

**bouquiniste** *nm* second-hand bookseller

**bourbe** *nf* mire, mud

**bourbeux -euse** *adj* muddy

**bourbier** *nm* mire, slough; *fig* mess

**bourdaine** *nf bot* black alder

**bourde** *nf coll* blunder, bloomer

**bourdon** *nm mus* drone; great bell; bumble-bee

**bourdonnement** *nm* buzz, hum

**bourdonner** *vi* buzz, hum

**bourg** *nm* small market town

**bourgade** *nf* large village

**bourgeois -e** *n* member of middle class; citizen, townsman (townswoman); *nm sl* boss; *nf sl* wife, missus; **les petits ~** the lower middle classes; *adj* middle-class; ordinary, unrefined; homely, plain; **cuisine ~e** plain cooking

**bourgeoisie** *nf* the middle class; **la haute ~** the upper middle class

**bourgeon** *nm* bud; *sl* pimple

**bourgeonner** *vi* bud; *coll* break out in pimples

**bourgmestre** *nm* burgomaster

**bourgogne** *nm* Burgundy (wine)

**bourguignon** *nm* beef cooked with onions and wine; *adj* (*f* -**onne**) Burgundian

**bourlinguer** *vi* toil (ship); *coll* travel around

**bourrade** *nf* blow; dig in the ribs

**bourrage** *nm* stuffing, padding; **~ de crâne** eye-wash

**bourrasque** *nf* squall

**bourre** *nf* padding, flock (wool); wad (gun)

**bourreau** *nm* executioner, hangman; inhuman person; **~ d'enfants** cruel parent

**bourrée** *nf* bundle of fire-wood; bourrée (dance)

**bourreler** *vt* (5) to torment, rack (mentally)

**bourrelet** *nm* pad, cushion; rim (tyre); *coll* roll (fat)

**bourrelier** *nm* saddler

**bourrer** *vt* stuff, pad, fill (pipe); **~ qn de coups** rain blows on s/o

**bourriche** *nf* hamper

**bourricot** *nm coll* little donkey

**bourrique** *nf* female donkey; *sl* idiot, ignorant person

**bourru** *adj* surly, boorish

**bourse** *nf* purse; scholarship (for studies); pouch (animals); **Bourse** Stock Exchange; **Bourse du Travail**

Labour Exchange; **sans ~ délier** without forking out a penny

**boursette** *nf* lamb's lettuce, corn salad

**boursicoter** *vi* buy and sell shares in a small way

**boursier -ière** *n* holder of a bursary; speculator

**boursouflé** *adj* bloated; turgid (style)

**boursoufler** *vt* puff out (flesh), bloat

**boursouflure** *nf* swelling, puffiness; turgidity (style)

**bousculade** *nf* jostling, scuffle

**bousculer** *vt* knock over, turn upside down, jostle

**bouse** *nf* cow-pat

**bousiller** *vt coll* botch, scamp; *sl* damage badly; kill

**boussole** *nf* compass; *sl* head, conk

**boustifaille** *nf sl* food; tuck-in

**bout** *nm* end, extremity, tip; bit, piece, scrap; **à ~ portant** at point blank range; **au ~ du compte** after all; **être à ~ (de forces)** be exhausted; **pousser qn à ~** drive s/o to extremes; *coll* **un ~ d'homme** a little chap; **venir à ~ de** overcome

**boutade** *nf* flash of wit, joke; whim

**boute-en-train** *nm coll* life and soul of the party

**bouteille** *nf* bottle, bottleful; cylinder (gas); **~ isolante** vacuum flask

**boutique** *nf* shop; boutique; craftsman's workshop

**boutiquier -ière** *n* shopkeeper

**bouton** *nm* bud; button; knob; handle (door); switch; pimple; **~ de col** collar stud; **~ d'or** buttercup

**boutonner** *vt* button up; *vi* bud

**boutonnière** *nf* button-hole

**bouton-poussoir** *nm* (*pl* **boutons-poussoirs**) knob, switch-button

**bouton-pression** *nm* (*pl* **boutons-pression**) snap-fastener

**bouture** *nf hort* cutting

**bouvier** *nm* cowman

**bouvreuil** *nm* bullfinch

**bovin** *adj* bovine

**box** *nm* (*pl* **~**, **~es**) lock-up garage; horse-box; cubicle (dormitory)

**boxe** *nf* boxing

**boxer** *vi* + *vt* box

**boxeur** *nm* boxer

**boy** *nm* native servant

**boyau** *nm* intestine (animal), gut; hosepipe; narrow street

**boycotter** *vt* boycot

**bracelet** *nm* bracelet, bangle

**bracelet-montre** *nm* (*pl* **bracelets-montres**) wrist-watch

**braconnage** *nm* poaching

**braconner** *vt* + *vi* poach

**braconnier** *nm* poacher

**brader** *vt* sell off cheap

**braderie** *nf* sale of old stock

**braguette** *nf* flies (trousers)

**brahmane** *nm* Brahmin

**braillard** *adj* bawling, noisy

**brailler** *vt* + *vi* bawl out, shout, yell

**braillerie** *nf* shouting, bawling

**brailleur -euse** *adj* bawling, noisy

**braire** *vi* (19) bray

**braise** *nf* embers

**braiser** *vt cul* braise

**bramer** *vi* bell (stag); *sl* bawl

**brancard** *nm* stretcher; shaft (carriage)

**brancardier** *nm* stretcher-bearer

**branchage** *nm* branches

**branche** *nf* branch; side (spectacles); leg (compasses); blade (propeller); **vieille ~** old chap

**branchement** *nm* branching

**brancher** *vt* plug in, connect; *coll* **être branché** know all about it, understand; *vi* perch, roost

**branchies** *nfpl* gills

**brandade** *nf cul* cod cooked with cream, oil and garlic

**brande** *nf* heather; heath

**brandir** *vt* flourish, brandish

**brandon** *nm* fire-brand

**branlant** *adj* shaky, rickety, loose (tooth)

**branle** *nm* swinging motion; impulse; **mettre en ~** start, set in motion

**branle-bas** *nm coll* bustle, upset

**branler** *vt* swing, shake (leg), wag (head); *vi* be loose, move; *vulg* **se ~** masturbate, toss oneself off

**braquage** *nm* turning (steering-wheel); aiming

**braquer** *vt* point (gun), train (telescope); fix (eyes); turn (steering-wheel); irritate

**bras** *nm* arm; hand (manual labourer); lever; **~ dessus ~ dessous** arm in arm; **à ~ le corps** round the waist; **à plein ~** in armfuls; **à tour de ~** with all one's might; **avoir le ~ long** have great influence; **avoir qn sur les ~** be left with the responsibility for s/o; **en ~ de chemise** in one's shirt sleeves

**braser** *vt* braze

**brasero** *nm* brazier

**brasier** *nm* blazing fire, furnace; fire of live coals; fierce fire

**brasiller** *vt* broil; *vi* sizzle

**brassard** *nm* armlet, arm-band

**brasse** *nf* arm-span; breast-stroke; fathom

**brassée** *nf* armful

**brasser** *vt* brew (beer); mix, stir; **~ des affaires** handle a lot of business

**brasserie** *nf* brewery, brewing; brasserie

39

**brasseur -euse** n brewer; breast-stroke swimmer; ~ **d'affaires** big-business man

**brassière** nf baby's vest; ~s shoulder straps (rucksack)

**bravache** adj blustering, swaggering

**bravade** nf bravado

**brave** adj brave, bold; worthy, honest; **mon ~** my good man; coll **un ~ type** a decent chap

**braver** vt brave, defy, face up to

**bravoure** nf gallantry, bravery

**break** nm estate car, shooting-brake

**brebis** nf ewe; sheep; ~ **galeuse** black sheep

**brèche** nf breach, gap, opening, notch (blade); **battre en ~** batter in, make a violent attack on

**bredouille** adj empty-handed

**bredouiller** vt + vi stammer out, mumble

**bref** (f **brève**) adj brief, short; adv briefly, in a word

**breloque** nf charm, trinket; sl **battre la ~** be barmy, go haywire

**Brésil** nm Brazil

**bretelle** nf strap, brace, sling; spur (motorway); ~s braces

**breton -onne** adj Breton

**breuvage** nm beverage, drink

**brevet** nm patent, certificate, warrant; ~ **élémentaire** lower certificate of education; **prendre un ~** take out a patent

**breveté -e** n patentee; adj patented, qualified, licensed

**breveter** vt (5) grant a patent; patent

**bréviaire** nm breviary

**bribes** nfpl scraps, fragments

**bric-à-brac** nm curios, bric-à-brac; odds and ends; curiosity shop

**brick** nm naut brig

**bricole** nf strap, breast-strap (harness); coll odd job; trifle

**bricoler** vi do odd jobs; vt arrange (piece of business)

**bricoleur** nm handy-man

**bride** nf bridle, rein; string (bonnet); **à ~ abattue** full tilt; **tenir en ~** keep a tight rein on

**bridé** adj constricted; **yeux ~s** slit eyes

**brider** vt bridle, curb, tie up; be tight on (clothes); cul truss

**bridgeur -euse** n bridge-player

**brièvement** adv briefly, succinctly

**brièveté** nf brevity; conciseness

**brigade** nf brigade; detachment; gang (workmen)

**brigadier** nm corporal (cavalry); sergeant (police); brigadier; ganger

**brigand** nm robber; brigand

**brigue** nf intrigue

**briguer** vt intrigue for, solicit

**brillamment** adv brilliantly

**brillance** nf brilliance

**brillant** nm brilliancy, lustre, brightness; adj brilliant, sparkling, shining

**briller** vi shine, sparkle; be conspicuous, be successful

**brimade** nf practical joke (on newcomers), rag; annoying petty regulation or measure

**brimbaler** vt cart about; vi swing to and fro

**brimer** vt rag

**brin** nm shoot (tree); blade (grass); strand (rope); coll bit, piece; coll **un beau ~ de fille** a good-looking girl

**brindille** nf sprig, tiny branch

**bringue** nf sl binge, spree; sl **grande ~** large, gawky woman

**brio** nm dash, vigour

**brioche** nf cul brioche; coll blunder

**brique** nf brick; cake (soap); sl one million (old) francs

**briquet** nm lighter; flint and steel

**brisant** nm reef, shoal; breaker

**brise** nf breeze

**brisées** nfpl broken branches; **aller sur les ~ de qn** compete with s/o

**brise-glace** nm invar ice-breaker

**brise-jet** nm invar anti-splash

**brise-lames** nm breakwater

**briser** vt smash, shatter, break; wear out, exhaust; interrupt; se ~ break

**brise-tout** nm invar destructive child or person

**brise-vent** nm invar wind-break, windscreen (trees)

**britannique** adj British

**broc** nm pitcher, large jug; pitcherful

**brocanter** vt coll buy and sell; vi deal in curios or second-hand goods

**brocanteur -euse** n second-hand dealer

**brocart** nm brocade

**broche** nf cul spit; brooch; peg, pin

**brocher** vt brocade; **livre broché** paperback

**brochet** nm pike

**brochette** nf skewer; kebab

**brochure** nf booklet, pamphlet, brochure

**brodequin** nm laced boot

**broder** vt embroider

**broderie** nf embroidery, piece of embroidery

**bromure** nm bromide

**broncher** vi stumble (horse); shy; coll falter

**bronches** nfpl bronchial tubes

**bronchite** nf bronchitis

**broncho-pneumonie** nf bronchial pneumonia

**bronzer** vt + vi bronze; brown; tan; se ~ go brown

**broquette** nf tack, tin-tack

**brosse** nf brush; sl moustache; **cheveux (taillés) en ~** crew-cut; **coup de ~** brushing, brush-up

**brosser** vt brush, scrub; paint sketchily; coll go without, miss; coll beat up

**brou** nm husk; **~ de noix** walnut stain

**brouet** nm gruel

**brouette** nf wheelbarrow

**brouettée** nf barrowful

**brouhaha** nm coll hubbub, din

**brouillage** nm rad jamming

**brouillard** nm fog, mist, haze

**brouille** nf discord, falling out

**brouiller** vt mix up, confuse, entangle; rad jam; scramble (eggs); set at loggerheads; **se ~** become confused, grow dim; quarrel, fall out

¹**brouillon** nm rough copy

²**brouillon -onne** adj muddle-headed

**broussaille** nf brushwood, undergrowth; **cheveux en ~** tousled hair

**brousse** nf the bush (in Australia and other remote areas); coll the country

**brouter** vt browse, graze

**broyer** vt (7) crush, pound, pulverize; destroy; **~ du noir** be depressed

**bru** nf daughter-in-law

**brucelles** nfpl tweezers

**brugnon** nm nectarine

**bruine** nf drizzle

**bruiner** vi drizzle

**bruire** vi (20) rustle, murmur

**bruissement** nm rustling, rustle, murmur

**bruit** nm noise, sound; rumour, report; fuss

**brûlant** adj burning, scorching, boiling-hot

**brûle-gueule** nm invar short clay pipe

**brûle-pourpoint (à)** adv phr point-blank

**brûler** vt burn; scorch; dry up (sun); pass without stopping; coll crack (ring, gang); **~ du café** roast coffee; **~ le pavé** tear along; **être brûlé** be ruined, be done for; **odeur de brûlé** smell of burning; **se ~ la cervelle** blow one's brains out; **tête brûlée** dare-devil; vi burn, be on fire; get warm (in games); **~ d'envie** long to

**brûleur -euse** n burner; brandy distiller; nm gas-jet, burner

**brûlure** nf burn, scald

**brumaire** nm hist second month of the French Republican calendar (October to November)

**brume** nf thick fog, (sea-)mist; **~ artificielle** smoke-screen

**brumeux -euse** adj foggy, misty

**brun** nm brown; adj brown; **à la ~ e** at dusk

**brunâtre** adj brownish

**brune** nf brunette

**brunir** vt brown, tan; burnish; vi turn brown, darken

**brusque** adj rough, abrupt, blunt; sudden; sharp (bend)

**brusquer** vt be sharp with; rush (business)

**brusquerie** nf abruptness, bluntness

**brut** adj rough, brute, raw; crude, unrefined, uncut (diamond); gross (weight, profit); **champagne ~** natural (very dry) champagne

**brutal** adj brutal, brutish, savage; rough

**brutaliser** vt ill-treat, use roughly, bully

**brutalité** nf brutality, savagery; roughness; act of cruelty

**brute** nf brute, beast; coarse or cruel person

**Bruxelles** nf Brussels

**bruyamment** adv noisily

**bruyant** adj noisy; loud, boisterous

**bruyère** nf heather; heathland; briar

**buanderie** nf wash-house

**bubonique** adj bubonic

**buccal** adj buccal; **par voie ~ e** by the mouth, orally

**bûche** nf fire-log; **~ de Noël** log-shaped Christmas cake; coll dolt; **ramasser une ~** come a cropper

¹**bûcher** nm wood-shed; wood-pile; pyre

²**bûcher** vt + vi work hard (at), swot (up)

**bûcheron** nm woodcutter

**bucolique** adj bucolic, pastoral

**budgétaire** adj budgetary

**buée** nf steam, vapour, mist

**buffet** nm sideboard; buffet

**buffle** nm buffalo

**building** nm large building

**buis** nm box-tree, boxwood

**buisson** nm bush, thicket

**buissonnier -ière** adj that lives in the bushes; **faire l'école buissonnière** play truant

**bulbe** nm bot + anat bulb

**bulbeux -euse** adj bulbous

**bulle** nf bubble; blister; (papal) bull

**bulletin** nm bulletin, report (school, weather, etc); receipt, certificate; **~ de commande** order form; **~ de vote** voting paper

**buraliste** n clerk (in post-office or tax-office); tobacconist

**bure** nf homespun

**bureau** nm office; board; writing-desk; **~ de placement** employment agency; **~ de tabac** tobacconist's shop; **le deuxième ~** military intelligence

**bureaucrate** n bureaucrat

**bureaucratie** nf bureaucracy

**burette** nf cruet; oil-can

**burin** nm graver, graving-tool

**buriner** vt engrave (copperplate)

**burnous** *nm* Arab cloak, burnous
**buse** *nf* buzzard; *coll* dolt
**busqué** *adj* hooked (nose), aquiline
**buste** *nm* bust
**but** *nm* target, aim, objective; goal; purpose, design; **de ~ en blanc** point-blank, on the spur of the moment; **marquer un ~** score a goal
**buté** *adj* pig-headed, obstinate
**buter** *vt* prop up, support; *vi* strike, knock; stumble; **~ sur une difficulté** come up against a difficulty; **se ~** be obstinately set on
**butin** *nm* booty, plunder; *coll* junk
**butiner** *vt + vi* gather honey (bees)
**butoir** *nm* buffer-stop
**butor** *nm* bittern; *coll* lout, coarse person
**butte** *nf* hillock, knoll; butts (shooting); **être en ~ à** be exposed to
**butter** *vt* earth up (plants)
**buvable** *adj* drinkable; *coll fig* bearable
**buvard** *nm* blotting-paper, blotting-pad
**buvette** *nf* refreshment room
**buveur -euse** *n* drinker, drunkard

# C

**ça** *pron abbr for* cela; *coll* **~ alors!** well I'll be damned!; **~ oui!** yes indeed!; *coll* **~ y est!** got it!; **comme ci comme ~** so-so
**çà** *adv* hither; **~ et là** here and there; **ah ~ !** look here!
**cabale** *nf* cabal; intrigue; clique
**cabalistique** *adj* cabalistic
**cabane** *nf* hut, cabin, shanty; hutch (rabbits); *sl* prison, jug
**cabanon** *nm* little hut; tiny house in the country (particularly Provence); padded cell
**cabaret** *nm* tavern, little restaurant; night-club
**cabas** *nm* basket, bag
**cabestan** *nm* capstan, windlass
**cabillaud** *nm* fresh cod
**cabine** *nf* cabin; call-box (telephone); cab (locomotive)
**cabinet** *nm* small room, closet; **~ de toilette** dressing-room, lavatory; **~ de travail** study; consulting-room (doctor); cabinet
**câble** *nm* cable, line, rope; cablegram
**câbler** *vt* cable; twist into a cable
**caboche** *nf sl* head; hobnail
**cabosse** *nf coll* dent, bruise, bump
**cabosser** *vt* dent, bruise, bump
**cabot** *nm coll* dog; bull-head (fish); *sl* corporal
**cabotage** *nm* coasting trade
**cabotin -e** *n* strolling player; *coll* ham actor
**caboulot** *nm* low café, cheap bar
**cabrer (se)** *v refl* rear (horse)

**cabri** *nm* kid (goat)
**cabriole** *nf* caper, leap
**cabriolet** *nm* cabriolet; convertible (car)
**caca** *nm coll* excrement
**cacahouète, cacahuète** *nf* peanut
**cacao** *nm* cocoa
**cacatoès** *nm* cockatoo
**cachalot** *nm* sperm whale
**cache** *nf* hiding-place; cache
**cache-cache** *nm* hide-and-seek
**cache-col** *nm* scarf
**cachemire** *nm* cashmere
**cache-nez** *nm invar* muffler
**cache-pot** *nm* flower-pot case, pot-holder
**cacher** *vt* hide, conceal, keep hidden; **se ~** hide, shun; **je ne m'en cache pas** I make no secret of it
**cache-sexe** *nm* G-string, briefs
**cachet** *nm* seal, stamp, signet; mark, sign; fee (artiste); *med* tablet; **avoir du ~** look distinguished, have character; **lettre de ~** sealed royal order
**cacheter** *vt* (5) seal; **vin cacheté** vintage wine
**cachette** *nf* hiding-place; **en ~** in secret
**cachot** *nm* cell, dungeon; *coll* prison
**cachotterie** *nf* secrecy over trifling matters
**cachottier -ière** *adj* close, secretive
**cacophonie** *nf* cacophony
**cadastre** *nm* cadastral survey
**cadavérique** *adj* cadaverous
**cadavre** *nm* corpse, dead body; carcase; *coll* emptied bottle, 'dead man'
**caddy** *nm* trolley (supermarket)

**cadeau** *nm* present, gift

**cadenas** *nm* padlock

**cadenasser** *vt* padlock

**cadence** *nf* rhythm, cadence; **en ~** rhythmically

**cadencé** *adj* rhythmical, measured

**cadencer** *vt* impart rhythm to

**cadet -ette** *n+adj* younger (child), junior; cadet; young player; **le ~ de mes soucis** the least of my worries

**cadran** *nm* dial

**cadre** *nm* frame, framework; border; surroundings; senior rank, senior member of staff

**cadrer** *vi* tally, square with, fit

**caduc -uque** *adj* decrepit, decaying; deciduous; null and void, lapsed

**¹cafard** *nm* cockroach; *coll* **avoir le ~** be fed up

**²cafard** *adj* hypocritical, sanctimonious

**cafarder** *vi* sneak, tell tales

**café** *nm* coffee; café; **~ arrosé** laced coffee; **~ complet** coffee and hot milk with rolls and butter; **~ crème** white coffee; **~ nature (noir)** black coffee; *adj invar* coffee-coloured

**cafetier -ière** *n* café-owner; *nf* coffee-pot

**cafouiller** *vi coll* get into a mess; miss (engine)

**cage** *nf* cage, coop; well (staircase); shaft (lift); **~ thoracique** thorax

**cagneux -euse** *adj* knock-kneed

**cagnotte** *nf* kitty, pool

**cagot -e** *n+adj* hypocritical (person)

**cagoule** *nf* cowl

**cahier** *nm* exercise-book

**cahin-caha** *adv* so-so, middling

**cahot** *nm* jolt (vehicle)

**cahoter** *vt+vi* jolt, bump, shake

**cahoteux -euse** *adj* bumpy (road), rough

**cahute** *nf* hut, hovel

**caïd** *nm* Arab leader; *sl* boss, gang-leader; *sl* super chap, ace

**caille** *nf* quail

**caillé** *nm* curdled milk, curds

**cailler** *vt+vi* curdle

**caillot** *nm* clot (blood)

**caillou** *nm* pebble

**caillouter** *vt* pave with pebbles

**caillouteux -euse** *adj* pebbly, stony, shingly

**caïman** *nm* alligator, cayman

**Caire (le)** *nm* Cairo

**caisse** *nf* case, packing-case, chest; cash-box, till, cashier's desk; fund; body (vehicle); drum; **~ d'épargne** savings bank; **grosse ~** bass drum

**caissier -ière** *n* cashier

**caisson** *nm* large box; locker; *eng* coffer-dam

**cajoler** *vt* coax, cajole

**cajolerie** *nf* coaxing, wheedling

**cake** *nm* fruit-cake

**calamine** *nf* calamine; carbon (deposit in cylinders)

**calamité** *nf* calamity

**calamiteux -euse** *adj* calamitous

**calandre** *nf* mangle, roller (paper, materials); (car-)radiator grille

**calcaire** *adj* chalky, calcareous

**calcéolaire** *nf bot* calceolaria

**calciner** *vt* burn to ashes

**calcul** *nm* reckoning, arithmetic; calculation, plan; *med* stone

**calculateur -trice** *n* computer, reckoner, calculator; *adj* wily

**calculé** *adj* premeditated, intentional, deliberate

**calculer** *vt* calculate, reckon up, compute

**cale** *nf* hold (ship); wedge, chock; **~ sèche** dry dock; **être à fond de ~** be down and out

**calé** *adj coll* knowledgeable, well up

**calèche** *nf* light open four-wheeled carriage

**caleçon** *nm* men's pants; **~ de bain** bathing trunks

**calembour** *nm* pun

**calendes** *nfpl* Kalends; **renvoyer aux ~ grecques** put off indefinitely

**calendrier** *nm* calendar

**calepin** *nm* notebook

**caler** *vt* wedge, scotch, clamp, prop up; *vt+vi* stall (engine); *vi sl* give way, funk

**calfeutrer** *vt* plug, stop up, pad (against draughts); **se ~** make oneself nice and warm

**calibre** *nm* calibre, bore, size; gauge; quality (character)

**calibrer** *vt* gauge, calibrate

**calice** *nm* chalice; *bot* calyx; **boire le ~ jusqu'à la lie** put up with every humiliation

**calicot** *nm* calico; *coll* assistant in draper's shop

**calife** *nm* caliph

**califourchon (à)** *adv phr* astride

**câlin** *adj* coaxing, wheedling, caressing

**calleux -euse** *adj* horny (hands), hard

**calligraphie** *nf* calligraphy, penmanship

**callosité** *nf* callosity, hardness (skin)

**calmant** *nm* sedative, tranquillizer; *adj* soothing

**calme** *nm* calm, stillness, calmness; *adj* calm, quiet, still; unruffled (manner)

**calmer** *vt* calm, still, allay, soothe; **se ~** calm down; die down, abate

**calomniateur -trice** *n* calumniator, slanderer; *adj* slanderous

**calomnie** *nf* calumny, slander

**calomnier** *vt* calumniate, slander

**calorifère** *nm* (slow-burning) stove, heating installation; *adj* heat-conveying

**calorifuge** *adj* non-conducting, insulating; heat-proof

**calot** *nm* forage-cap

**calotte** *nf* skull-cap; crown (hat); priesthood; *coll* box on the ears; canopy (heavens)

**calque** *nm* tracing; slavish imitation

**calquer** *vt* trace; copy closely

**calvados** *nm* apple-brandy

**calvaire** *nm* Calvary; stations of the Cross; moral suffering

**calviniste** *n* + *adj* calvinist

**calvitie** *nf* baldness

**camarade** *n* comrade, companion, friend, chum

**camaraderie** *nf* comradeship, friendship; clan, set

**camard** *adj* flat-nosed; **la Camarde** Death

**cambouis** *nm* dirty grease or oil (from engine)

**cambrer** *vt* arch, bend, camber; **se ~** throw out one's chest, draw oneself up to full height

**cambriolage** *nm* housebreaking, burgling, burglary

**cambrioler** *vt* burgle, break into

**cambrioleur -euse** *n* housebreaker, burglar

**cambrure** *nf* camber, arching, arch (foot)

**cambuse** *nf naut* steward's room; *sl* dump

**came** *nf* cam; *sl* dope (*esp* cocaine); **arbre à ~ s** camshaft

**camée** *nm* cameo

**camélia** *nm* camellia

**camelot** *nm* street-hawker; news-vendor

**camelote** *nf sl* junk, shoddy piece of work

**camembert** *nm* Camembert cheese

**caméra** *nf* cine-camera

**camion** *nm* lorry, wagon; *US* truck

**camionnette** *nf* van

**camionneur** *nm* haulier, carrier

**camisole** *nf* camisole; **~ de force** strait-jacket

**camomille** *nf* camomile

**camoufler** *vt* camouflage; disguise

**camouflet** *nm coll* insult, snub

**camp** *nm* camp; side, party; *sl* **ficher (foutre) le ~** clear off (out)

**campagnard -e** *n* countryman (woman); *adj* of the country, rustic

**campagne** *nf* countryside, open country; campaign; **battre la ~** scour the countryside; be delirious; **en pleine ~** right out in the open country; **faire une ~** take part in a campaign; **partie de ~** picnic, country outing; *coll* **se**

**mettre en ~** get down to work

**campanule** *nf bot* bellflower

**campé** *adj* **bien ~** well set-up

**camper** *vi* camp; put up; *coll* put; *coll* **se ~** plant oneself

**camphre** *nm* camphor

**camus** *adj* snub-nosed, pug-nosed

**Canadien -ienne** *n* Canadian

**canadien -ienne** *adj* Canadian

**canadienne** *nf* fur-lined (man's) jacket; estate car

**canaille** *nf* rabble, riff-raff; scoundrel; *adj* rascally

**canal** *nm* canal; channel; duct; means

**canalisation** *nf* canalization; mains, pipes; wiring

**canaliser** *vt* canalize; lay down mains

**canapé** *nm* couch, sofa; *cul* canapé

**canard** *nm* (male) duck; *coll* false piece of news; *coll* newspaper, rag; *coll* lump of sugar dipped in liqueur or coffee; *mus* false note; **froid de ~** biting cold

**canari** *nm* canary

**canasson** *nm sl* nag (horse)

**cancan** *nm coll* tittle-tattle, piece of scandal; cancan

**cancaner** *vi coll* talk scandal

**cancanier -ière** *adj coll* fond of spreading scandal

**cancéreux -euse** *n* cancer patient; *adj* cancerous

**cancérigène** *adj* carcinogenic

**cancre** *nm coll* crab; *coll* dunce

**candélabre** *nm* branched candelabra; lamp-post (with branches)

**candeur** *nf* artlessness, ingenuousness

**candi** *adj m* candied; **sucre ~** sugar candy

**candidat -e** *n* applicant, candidate

**candidature** *nf* candidature; **poser sa ~** apply (for post)

**candide** *adj* artless, ingenuous

**cane** *nf* (female) duck

**caner** *vi sl* funk

**caneton** *nm* duckling

**can(n)ette** *nf* (beer) bottle

**canevas** *nm* canvas; outline, sketch

**caniche** *nm* poodle

**caniculaire** *adj* sultry

**canicule** *nf* dog-days; heatwave

**canif** *nm* penknife

**canin** *adj* canine

**canine** *nf* canine tooth

**caniveau** *nm* gutter; conduit

**canne** *nf* cane, reed; walking stick; **~ à pêche** fishing rod; **~ à sucre** sugar cane

**canneler** *vt* (5) flute; corrugate

**cannelle** *nf* cinnamon

**canner** *vt* cane (chair)

**cannette** *nf see* can(n)ette

**cannibale** *n* cannibal

**canoë** *nm* canoe
**canon** *nm* cannon; barrel (rifle); glass of wine; *eccles* canon; *mus* canon, round
**canonique** *adj* canonical; *coll* respectable (age)
**canoniser** *vt* canonize
**canonnade** *nf* cannonade
**canonnière** *nf* gun-slit; gun-boat
**canot** *nm* dinghy, boat; **~ de sauvetage** lifeboat
**canotage** *nm* boating, rowing
**canotier** *nm* straw-hat; oarsman
**cantate** *nf* cantata
**cantatrice** *nf* (professional) singer
**cantine** *nf* canteen
**cantique** *nm* hymn, canticle; **Cantique des ~ s** Song of Songs
**canton** *nm* district; canton
**cantonade** *nf theat* wings; **parler à la ~** speak to s/o off-stage
**cantonnement** *nm* billeting, cantonment
**cantonner** *vt* billet; confine; **se ~** shut oneself up, isolate oneself
**cantonnier** *nm* roadmender; platelayer
**canule** *nf* nozzle (syringe); *sl* bore
**canuler** *vt sl* bore
**caoutchouc** *nm* rubber; *pl* galoshes
**caoutchouter** *vt* treat or coat with rubber
**cap** *nm* cape, headland; head (ship); **de pied en ~** from head to foot; **doubler un ~** round a cape; **mettre le ~ sur** set course for
**capable** *adj* capable; able
**capacité** *nf* capacity; ability, competence
**caparaçonner** *vt* caparison
**cape** *nf* cape, cloak; **rire sous ~** laugh up one's sleeve
**capillaire** *adj* capillary
**capitaine** *nm* captain, master (ship), leader
**capital** *nm* capital, assets; *adj* capital, principal, chief; deadly (sin)
**capitale** *nf* chief town, capital
**capitaliser** *vt* capitalize
**capitalisme** *nm* capitalism
**capitaliste** *n* capitalist
**capiteux -euse** *adj* heady
**capitonner** *vt* pad, upholster
**capitulation** *nf* surrender, capitulation
**capituler** *vi* surrender, capitulate
**caporal** *nm* corporal; cheap tobacco
**capot** *nm* hood, casing; *mot* bonnet, US hood; hatch
**capote** *nf* hooded cloak; great-coat; hood (car); cowl (chimney); *sl* **~ anglaise** French letter
**capoter** *vi* turn turtle, capsize, overturn
**câpre** *nf bot* caper
**caprice** *nm* caprice, whim
**capricieux -ieuse** *adj* capricious, whimsical

**capsule** *nf* capsule; bottle-top
**capter** *vt* obtain (cunningly); pick up (radio programme, message); catch (water)
**captieux -ieuse** *adj* specious, fallacious
**captif -ive** *n + adj* captive, prisoner
**captivant** *adj* captivating, fascinating
**captiver** *vt* captivate, charm
**captivité** *nf* captivity
**capture** *nf* capture, seizure, prize
**capturer** *vt* capture (ship), catch (large animal)
**capuchon** *nm* hood, cowl, cap (fountain-pen)
**capucin** *nm* Capuchin friar
**capucine** *nf* nasturtium; Capuchin nun
**caque** *nf* keg, barrel (herrings); **la ~ sent toujours le hareng** what's bred in the bone will out in the flesh
**caquet** *nm* cackling, cackle, chatter; **rabattre le ~ à qn** shut s/o up
**caqueter** *vi* (5) cackle; chatter, gossip
**¹car** *nm* (motor-)coach; **~ de police** police van
**²car** *conj* for, because
**carabine** *nf* carbine, rifle
**carabiné** *adj coll* violent, strong; **rhume ~** stinking cold
**caraco** *nm* working jacket (woman)
**caractère** *nm* character, nature, disposition; characteristic; handwriting
**caractériser** *vt* characterize; **se ~** be distinguished
**caractéristique** *nf* characteristic, trait; *adj* characteristic, typical
**carafe** *nf* carafe, decanter
**carafon** *nm* small carafe
**carambolage** *nm* cannon (billiards); collision
**caramel** *nm* caramel, burnt sugar; toffee
**carapace** *nf* carapace, shell (crab, etc)
**caravane** *nf* caravan
**caravansérail** *nm* caravanserai
**caravelle** *nf* caravel
**carbone** *nm* carbon
**carbonique** *adj* carbonic
**carboniser** *vt* carbonize, burn to a cinder
**carburant** *nm* motor-fuel
**carbure** *nm* carbide
**carcan** *nm* iron collar, pillory; *sl* jade (horse)
**carcasse** *nf* carcass; framework; *coll* body
**carcinome** *nm* carcinoma
**carde** *nf bot* chard
**carder** *vt* card (wool)
**cardiaque** *nf* heart-case; *adj* cardiac
**cardon** *nm bot* cardoon
**carême** *nm* Lent; **faire (son) ~** fast, observe Lent

45

**carénage** *nm* streamlining; careening (ship)

**carence** *nf* insolvency; *med* deficiency; shortcoming, default

**carène** *nf* hull (ship)

**caresse** *nf* caress, pat

**caresser** *vt* caress, stroke, fondle; cherish (a hope)

**cargaison** *nf* cargo, load, freight

**cargo** *nm* cargo-boat

**carie** *nf* decay (teeth); blight (trees)

**carier** *vt* decay, rot; **se** ~ decay, rot

**carillon** *nm* carillon, chimes

**carillonner** *vt* announce by ringing; *coll fig* broadcast; *vi* ring the bells, chime; jingle

**carlingue** *nf naut* ke(e)lson; cockpit, cabin

**carmagnole** *nf* carmagnole; short jacket (worn by 1789 Revolutionaries)

**carmélite** *nf* Carmelite nun

**carmin** *nm* carmine

**carnage** *nm* carnage, slaughter

**carnassier -ière** *adj* carnivorous (animals)

**carnassière** *nf* game-bag

**carnet** *nm* notebook; ~ **de bal** dance card; ~ **de chèques** cheque-book; ~ **de tickets** book of tickets (bus, métro)

**carnier** *nm* game-bag

**carnivore** *adj* carnivorous

**carotte** *nf* carrot; plug (tobacco); *coll* trick; **poil de** ~ ginger (hair)

**carotter** *vt coll* wangle; ~ **qch à qn** diddle s/o out of sth

**carpe** *nf* carp; **muet comme une** ~ dumb as an oyster

**carpette** *nf* rug

**carquois** *nm* quiver

**carré** *nm* square; landing (staircase); *naut* mess-room; bed, patch (garden); four similar cards in one hand; *adj* square; frank, plain; **partie** ~ **e** party of two men and two women

**carreau** *nm* small square, check; tile (floor), floor; window-pane; diamond (cards); *sl* monocle; ~ **des Halles** fruit and vegetable section of the Halles; *coll* **rester sur le** ~ be left dead

**carrefour** *nm* crossroads; intersection

**carrelage** *nm* tile floor; tiling

**carreler** *vt* (5) lay tiles, pave with tiles

**carrelet** *nm* plaice; square fishing net

**carrément** *adv* frankly, bluntly; squarely

**carrer** *vt* square; **se** ~ make oneself comfortable

**¹carrière** *nf* career, profession; scope; **donner (libre)** ~ **à son imagination** give free rein to one's imagination

**²carrière** *nf* quarry

**carriole** *nf* light cart; ramshackle car

**carrossable** *adj* suitable for vehicles (road)

**carrosse** *nm* carriage, coach; **rouler** ~ own a carriage, be well off

**carrosser** *vt* fit coach-work to, put the body on (car)

**carrosserie** *nf* coach-work, body (car); car-body manufacture, coach-building

**carrossier** *nm* coach-builder, car-body builder

**carrousel** *nm* roundabout; tournament

**carrure** *nf* breadth (shoulders, chest)

**cartable** *nm* satchel

**carte** *nf* card; map; playing-card; bill of fare; ~ **d'entrée** ticket of admission; ~ **grise** car licence; **battre les** ~ **s** shuffle the cards; **brouiller les** ~ **s** embroil matters; **connaître le dessous des** ~ **s** be in the know; **donner** ~ **blanche à qn** give s/o a free hand; **tirer les** ~ **s** tell fortunes

**cartel** *nm* challenge; wall-clock; dial-case; cartel, trust

**carte-lettre** *nf* ( *pl* **cartes-lettres**) letter-card

**carter** *nm* crank-case, gear-case; **fond de** ~ sump

**cartographe** *n* map-maker

**cartomancien -ienne** *n* fortune-teller (by means of cards)

**carton** *nm* cardboard; cardboard box, carton; target (shooting-range)

**cartonner** *vt* bind in boards, case

**cartonnier** *nm* file, file-case

**carton-pâte** *nm* papier-mâché

**¹cartouche** *nf* cartridge; cartridge-shaped packing, packet

**²cartouche** *nm* scroll (round title, etc)

**cartouchière** *nf* cartridge pouch

**cas** *nm* case, instance, matter; **au (dans le)** ~ **où** in case; **dans le** ~ **de** in a position to; **en tout** ~ in any case; **le** ~ **échéant** should the occasion arise; **faire** ~ **de** value

**casanier -ière** *adj* stay-at-home

**casaque** *nf obs* coat, jacket; **tourner** ~ be a turn-coat

**cascade** *nf* waterfall, cascade

**cascadeur** *nm* stunt-man

**case** *nf* hut, cabin; compartment (drawer); space (on form); square (chess-board)

**caser** *vt* put away, put in order; find a job for, settle (one's daughter); **se** ~ settle down

**caserne** *nf* barracks

**casier** *nm* set of pigeon-holes; rack; ~ **judiciaire** criminal record

**casque** *nm* helmet; head-phones

**casquer** *vi sl* fork out, pay up

**casquette** *nf* peaked cap

**cassant** *adj* brittle, crisp; abrupt (tone)

**cassation** *nf* quashing; reduction to the ranks; **Cour de** ~ Supreme Court of Appeal

**casse** *nf* breakage; **il va y avoir de la ~** there's going to be trouble; *coll* **payer la ~** pay for the damage

**cassé** *adj* broken, worn out

**casse-cou** *nm invar* death-trap; *n* daredevil

**casse-croûte** *nm invar* snack, light meal

**casse-noisettes** *nm* nutcracker

**casse-pieds** *nm coll* bore, pain in the neck

**casser** *vt* break, snap; quash; reduce to the ranks; **~ la tête à qn** deafen s/o; importune s/o; **les pieds à qn** get on s/o's nerves; **à tout ~** violently; *sl* **ça ne casse rien** it's not up to much; **se ~ la tête** rack one's brains; **se ~ le nez** find the door closed; fail; *vi* break; **se ~ crack up (person)

**casserole** *nf* saucepan; *sl* informer, squealer

**casse-tête** *nm invar* club, cosh; task fraught with problems; din

**cassette** *nf* casket; cassette

**casseur** *nm* breaker, smasher; vandal (demonstration, etc)

¹**cassis** *nm* blackcurrant; blackcurrant liqueur

²**cassis** *nm* cross-drain

**cassonade** *nf* brown sugar

**cassure** *nf* break, fracture

**castel** *nm* castle (in S. France)

**castor** *nm* beaver

¹**casuel** *nm* fees

²**casuel -uelle** *adj* accidental, fortuitous

**casuiste** *nm* casuist

**casuistique** *nf* casuistry

**cataclysme** *nm* disaster, cataclysm

**catacombes** *nfpl* catacombs

**catalan** *adj* Catalan, Catalonian

**catalogue** *nm* catalogue, list

**catalyse** *nf* catalysis

**cataplasme** *nm* poultice

**cataracte** *nf* cataract, falls; *med* cataract

**catarrhe** *nm* catarrh

**catastrophe** *nf* catastrophe, disaster

**catastropher** *vt coll* astound; depress

**catéchiser** *vt* catechize; lecture, try to persuade

**catéchisme** *nm* catechism

**catégorie** *nf* category

**catégorique** *adj* categorical; explicit

**cathédrale** *nf* cathedral

**Catherine** *nf* **coiffer Sainte ~** reach one's twenty-fifth birthday without marrying

**catherinette** *nf coll* unmarried girl who celebrates her twenty-fifth birthday

**cathode** *nm elect* cathode

**catholicisme** *nm* Roman Catholicism

**catholique** *n* Catholic; *adj* Roman Catholic; *coll* normal, orthodox

**catimini (en)** *adv phr* stealthily

**catin** *nf coll* whore, tart

**cauchemar** *nm* nightmare

**causant** *adj* talkative, chatty

**cause** *nf* cause, reason; action, suit; **à ~ de** because of; **avoir gain de ~** win, get the better of an argument; **en connaissance de ~** with full knowledge; **en tout état de ~** in any case; **et pour ~** and for a very good reason; **hors de ~** irrelevant; **mettre en ~** implicate

¹**causer** *vt* cause

²**causer** *vi* chat, talk; say too much

**causerie** *nf* talk, chat

**causette** *nf* little chat

**causeur -euse** *n* talker; *nf* small settee; *adj* talkative, chatty

**caustique** *adj* caustic; biting, cutting

**cauteleux -euse** *adj pej* cunning, sly

**cautériser** *vt* cauterize

**caution** *nf* security, guarantee, surety; **en liberté sous ~** out on bail; **se porter ~ pour qn** go bail for someone; **sujet à ~** unconfirmed, suspect

**cautionnement** *nm* security, caution-money

**cautionner** *vt* go bail for

**cavalcade** *nf* cavalcade, procession

**cavaler** *vt sl* bore; *sl* **se ~** run, hop it

**cavalerie** *nf* cavalry

¹**cavalier** *nm* horseman, rider; cavalier; escort, dancing-partner; knight (chess); **~ seul** lone wolf

²**cavalier -ière** *adj* cavalier, off-hand

**cavalière** *nf* horsewoman; dancing-partner

¹**cave** *nf* cellar

²**cave** *nf* stake (cards); *nm sl* dupe

³**cave** *adj* hollow, sunken

**caveau** *nm* little cellar, vault; burial vault

**caver** *vt* hollow out, excavate

**caverne** *nf* cave, cavern, den

**caverneux -euse** *adj* cavernous, hollow, sepulchral

**caviar** *nm* caviare

**cavité** *nf* cavity, hollow

¹**ce, c'** *dem pron* (used mainly with être) it, this, that; **~ faisant** doing which; **~ que** what, that which; **~ que vous voulez** what you like; *coll* **~ qu'il peut être embêtant!** what a nuisance he can be!; **~ sont eux** it is they; **c'est ici** this is; **c'est là** that is; **pour ~ faire** in order to do this; **sur ~** thereupon; **tout ~ qu'il voudra** everything he wants

²**ce, cet** (*f* **cette**, *pl* **ces**) *dem adj* this, that, these, those; **~ garçon-ci** this boy; **~ garçon-là** that boy

**céans** *adv* in here; **le maître de ~** the master of this place

**ceci** *dem pron* this

**cécité** nf blindness

**céder** vt (6) give up, surrender, make over; **le ~ à qn** be inferior to s/o; vi yield, give way

**cédille** nf cedilla

**cèdre** nm cedar

**cégétiste** n + adj (member) of C.G.T. (French trade union)

**ceindre** vt (55) gird, encircle, encompass

**ceinture** nf belt, girdle, sash; circle (railway or bus); **~ de sauvetage** lifebelt

**ceinturer** vt girdle; tackle

**ceinturon** nm mil belt

**cela (ça)** dem pron that; **c'est ~** that's right; **comment ~?** how so?; **et avec ~, Madame?** anything else, madam?; **sans ~** but for that

**célèbre** adj famous, celebrated

**célébrer** vt (6) celebrate, solemnize

**célébrité** nf fame, celebrity

**celer** vt (5) conceal, hide, keep secret

**céleri** nm celery

**célérité** nf speed, swiftness, dispatch

**céleste** adj celestial, heavenly

**célibat** nm celibacy

**célibataire** n bachelor, bachelor-girl, spinster; adj single, unmarried

**celle** pron see celui

**cellier** nm store-room (wine, provisions)

**cellulaire** adj cellular; **voiture ~** prison van, Black Maria

**cellule** nf cell

**cellulite** nf cellulitis

**Celte** n Celt

**celte** adj Celtic

**celtique** adj Celtic

**celui** (f celle, pl ceux, celles) pron the one(s); he, she, it, they; **~ -ci** this one; the latter; **~ -là** that one; the former

**cénacle** nm coterie, group

**cendre** nf ash, ashes, cinders

**cendré** adj ash-coloured, ash-grey

**cendrer** vt colour ash-grey; cinder

**cendreux -euse** adj ashy; full of ashes, gritty

**cendrier** nm ash-tray; ash-pan; eng ash-pit

**cène** nf **la Sainte Cène** the Last Supper; Holy Communion (in Protestant Church)

**cénotaphe** nm cenotaph

**censé** adj supposed

**censément** adv supposedly; practically

**censeur** nm censor; critic; vice-principal (in charge of school discipline)

**censure** nf censorship; blame

**censurer** vt censor; censure, find fault with

**cent** nm a hundred; **pour ~** per cent; adj a hundred; **être aux ~ coups** be in despair; **faire les ~ pas** walk up and down; **faire les quatre ~s coups** kick up a shindy

**centaine** nf about a hundred

**centenaire** nm centenary, centenarian; adj a hundred years old

**centennal** adj centennial

**centième** nm + adj hundredth

**centimètre** nm centimetre; tape-measure

**central** nm **~ téléphonique** telephone exchange; adj central; **maison ~e** prison

**centrale** nf elect power-station

**centralisation** nf centralization

**centraliser** vt centralize

**centre** nm centre, middle; centre party

**centrer** vt centre

**centrifuge** adj centrifugal

**centripète** adj centripetal

**centuple** nm + adj centuple, hundredfold

**cep** nm vine-plant

**cépage** nm vine-plant

**cèpe** nm kind of mushroom

**cependant** adv meanwhile; conj yet, however, nevertheless

**céramique** nf ceramics, pottery; adj ceramic

**cerceau** nm hoop

**cercle** nm circle, ring, hoop; club

**cercler** vt ring, encircle, hoop

**cercueil** nm coffin

**céréale** nf + adj cereal

**cérémonie** nf ceremony; **faire des ~s** be excessively polite

**cérémonieux -ieuse** adj ceremonious

**cerf** nm stag

**cerfeuil** nm chervil

**cerf-volant** nm (pl cerfs-volants) kite (toy); stag-beetle

**cerisaie** nf cherry-orchard

**cerise** nf cherry; adj invar cherry-coloured

**cerne** nm ring, circle (under eyes)

**cerner** vt surround (town), encircle (army); shell (nuts); **avoir les yeux cernés** have rings under the eyes

**certain** adj certain, sure; fixed; **~s** adj + pron some, certain (people)

**certes** adv indeed, to be sure

**certificat** nm certificate, testimonial; **~ d'aptitude professionnelle (C.A.P.)** trade qualification or certificate

**certification** nf certification, authentication

**certifier** vt certify, vouch for

**certitude** nf certainty

**céruse** nf white lead

**cerveau** nm brain; mind, intelligence; **rhume de ~** cold in the head

**cervelas** nm saveloy

**cervelet** nm cerebellum

**cervelle** nf brains (brain-matter); **se brûler la ~** blow out one's brains; **se creuser la ~** rack one's brains

**ces** *dem pron see* **ce**

**cessation** *nf* cessation, ceasing, stopping

**cesse** *nf* ceasing; **sans ~** unceasingly

**cesser** *vt + vi* stop, cease, leave off; **faire ~ qch** put a stop to sth

**cessez-le-feu** *nm invar* cease-fire

**cessible** *adj* transferable, assignable

**cession** *nf* transfer, assignment

**c'est-à-dire** *conj phr* that is to say

**césure** *nf* caesura

**cet** *dem pron see* **ce**

**cette** *dem pron see* **ce**

**ceux** *pron see* **celui**

**chabot** *nm* chub

**chacal** *nm* (*pl* ~s) jackal

**chacun** *pron* each (one), every one; everybody

**chafouin -e** *n + adj* sly-looking (person)

**chagrin** *nm* grief, sorrow, affliction; annoyance; shagreen; *adj* sad, distressed; fretful

**chagriner** *vt* distress, grieve; vex

**chah** *nm* Shah

**chahut** *nm coll* din, noise, shindy; rag

**chahutage** *nm coll* rowdyism, ragging

**chahuter** *vt coll* rag (teacher); *vi* make a' row

**chahuteur -euse** *n + adj coll* rowdy

**chaîne** *nf* chain; range (mountains); channel, network (radio and TV); **travail à la ~** work on conveyor belt

**chaînette** *nf* small chain

**chaînon** *nm* link (chain)

**chair** *nf* flesh; meat; **~ à canon** cannon-fodder; *coll* **~ de poule** goose-flesh; **bien en ~** nice and plump; **en ~ et en os** in the flesh

**chaire** *nf* chair, throne; pulpit; rostrum; professorship

**chaise** *nf* chair, seat; **~ de chœur** choir stall (church); **~ longue** deck-chair; settee; **~ percée** night-commode; **~ roulante** bath chair

**chaisier -ière** *n* chair-attendant (park, church)

**chaland** *nm* lighter, barge

**châle** *nm* shawl

**chalet** *nm* chalet; **~ de nécessité** public convenience

**chaleur** *nf* heat, warmth; ardour; **craint la ~** keep in a cool place

**chaleureux -euse** *adj* warm; ardent; cordial

**chaloupe** *nf* launch

**chalumeau** *nm* straw; *mus* pipe; blow-pipe

**chalut** *nm* drag-net, trawl

**chalutier** *nm* trawler

**chamailler (se)** *v refl coll* squabble, bicker

**chamarrer** *vt* bedeck, trim (with lace)

**chambard** *nm sl* row, upheaval, shindy

**chambarder** *vt* upset, turn upside down

**chambellan** *nm* chamberlain

**chambouler** *vt sl* turn topsy-turvy

**chambranle** *nm* frame (door, window); mantelpiece

**chambre** *nf* (bed-)room, chamber; house (government); **~ à air** inner tube; **Chambre des Députés** Chamber of Deputies; **garder la ~** be confined to one's room (through illness)

**chambrée** *nf* roomful (of people); barrack-room

**chambrer** *vt* bring up to room temperature

**chambrette** *nf* little room

**chambrière** *nf* long whip; prop (cart); *obs* chambermaid

**chameau** *nm* camel; *sl* swine (of man), scoundrel

**chamelier** *nm* camel-driver

**chamois** *nm* chamois; **peau de ~** shammy-leather

**champ** *nm* field; scope, range, extent; **~ de courses** race-course; **~ de foire** fair-ground; **à tout bout de ~** at every turn; **à travers ~s** across country; **le ~ est libre** the coast is clear; **prendre la clef des ~s** abscond, clear off; **sur le ~** immediately

**Champagne** *nf* Champagne; **(vin de) ~** *nm* champagne (wine); **fine ~** brandy

**champenois** *adj* from Champagne, of Champagne

**champêtre** *adj* rural, country, rustic; **garde ~** kind of village policeman

**champignon** *nm* mushroom; (milliner's) hatstand; *sl* accelerator (pedal)

**champion -ionne** *n* champion

**championnat** *nm* championship

**chançard** *adj coll* lucky

**chance** *nf* chance; luck, fortune; **~s** likelihood, probability; **avoir de la ~** be lucky

**chanceler** *vi* (5) totter, stagger; **santé chancelante** precarious health

**chancelier** *nm* chancellor

**chancelière** *nf* foot-muff

**chancellerie** *nf* chancellery; secretary-ship of a legation

**chanceux -euse** *adj coll* lucky; risky, chancy

**chancir** *vi* (4) go mouldy

**chancre** *nm* canker; ulcer

**chandail** *nm* sweater, jumper

**Chandeleur (la)** *nf* Candlemas

**chandelier** *nm* candlestick

**chandelle** *nf* (tallow) candle; support (construction); *coll* drop (on the end of s/o's nose); **devoir une fière (belle) ~ à qn** owe a great deal to s/o; *coll* **économies de bouts de ~** cheeseparing economies; **le jeu n'en vaut pas la ~**

the game is not worth the candle; **voir trente-six** ~ **s** see stars

**chanfreiner** *vt* chamfer, bevel

**change** *nm* exchange; **bureau de** ~ foreign exchange office; **cours du** ~ rate of exchange; **donner le** ~ **à qn** take s/o in; **lettre de** ~ bill of exchange

**changeable** *adj* changeable; exchangeable

**changeant** *adj* changing, changeable, fickle

**changement** *nm* change, alteration; ~ **de vitesse** gear change

**changer** *vt* (3) change, exchange, alter, modify; *coll* **ça me changera** it will be a change for me; *coll* **change de disque** give it a rest; *vi* change; ~ **d'avis** change one's mind; **se** ~ change one's clothes; change

**changeur** *nm* money-changer

**chanoine** *nm eccles* canon

**chanson** *nf* song; ~ **à boire** drinking-song; ~**s!** nonsense!; **c'est toujours la même** ~ it's the same old story

**chansonnette** *nf* ditty, popular song

**chansonnier -ière** *n* writer of satirical songs

**chant** *nm* song, singing; crowing (cock); canto

**chantage** *nm* blackmail

**chantant** *adj* sing-song; tuneful

**chantepleure** *nf* wine-funnel; tap; spout

**chanter** *vt* + *vi* sing; crow (cock); ~ **la gloire** sing the praises; **faire** ~ blackmail; **qu'est-ce que vous me chantez?** what's this tale you're telling me?; **si ça vous chante** if this appeals to you

**chanterelle** *nf* kind of mushroom

**chanteur -euse** *n* singer; blackmailer

**chantier** *nm* yard (timber, building, shipping); site (building, road-works); stand (barrels); **fin de** ~ road clear

**chantonner** *vt* + *vi* sing softly, hum

**chantre** *nm* bard, singer

**chanvre** *nm* hemp

**chaos** *nm* chaos, disorder; mass (rocks)

**chaotique** *adj* chaotic, confused

**chaparder** *vt sl* pinch, pilfer, steal

**chape** *nf eccles* cope; covering; tread (tyre)

**chapeau** *nm* hat; cap; cowl (chimney); short introduction; ~ **de roue** hub-cap; ~ **haut de forme** top-hat; ~ **melon** bowler-hat; ~ **mou** felt hat; **donner un coup de** ~ raise one's hat; **( je lui tire mon)** ~ **!** I take my hat off to him

**chapelet** *nm* rosary; string (onions, insults); stick (bombs); **dire (égrener) son** ~ tell one's beads

**chapelier** *nm* hatter

**chapelle** *nf* chapel

**chapelure** *nf cul* dried bread-crumbs

**chaperon** *nm* hood; chaperon; coping (wall); **le petit** ~ **rouge** Little Red Riding Hood

**chaperonner** *vt* hood; chaperon

**chapiteau** *nm* capital (column); circus tent, big top

**chapitre** *nm* chapter; matter, subject; **avoir voix au** ~ have a say in the matter

**chapon** *nm* capon

**chaque** *adj* each, every

**char** *nm* chariot; wagon; ~ **d'assaut** tank

**charabia** *nm* gibberish

**charançon** *nm* weevil

**charbon** *nm* coal; blight; anthrax; ~ **(de bois)** charcoal; **être sur des** ~ **s ardents** be on tenterhooks

**charbonnage** *nm* coalmining; colliery

**charbonner** *vt* carbonize, char; blacken with charcoal

**charbonnier -ière** *n* coal-merchant; ~ **est maître chez lui** a man is master in his own house; *nm* coal-ship, collier

**charcuter** *vt* cut (meat) badly; *coll* butcher (patient)

**charcuterie** *nf* pork butcher's shop; pork-butcher's wares

**charcutier -ière** *n* pork-butcher

**chardon** *nm* thistle

**chardonneret** *nm* goldfinch

**charge** *nf* load, burden; responsibility, charge; duty, office; expense; charge (shell, bomb); caricature; ~ **s sociales** social insurance expenses; **être à la** ~ **de qn** be dependent on s/o; be chargeable to s/o; **témoin à** ~ witness for the prosecution

**chargement** *nm* loading, lading; shipment, cargo; charging (accumulator); registration (letter)

**chargé-e** *n* **d'affaires** chargé d'affaires; ~ **de cours** part-time lecturer

**charger** *vt* (3) load; charge, instruct; *coll* take a fare (taxi); exaggerate; overact; **se** ~ become overcast; **se** ~ **de** undertake

**chariot** *nm* wagon, truck, cart; carriage (typewriter); undercarriage (plane)

**charité** *nf* charity, love; act of charity; **faire la** ~ give alms

**charivari** *nm* din; discordant music

**charlatan -e** *n* charlatan, quack

**charmant** *adj* charming

**charme** *nm* charm, spell; attractiveness; **faire du** ~ lay on the charm; **se porter comme un** ~ be as fit as a fiddle

**charmer** *vt* charm, delight

**charmille** *nf* arbour, bower

**charnel -elle** *adj* carnal, sensual, of the flesh

50

**charnier** *nm* charnel-house; heap of bodies

**charnière** *nf* hinge

**charnu** *adj* plump, fleshy

**charogne** *nf* carrion, carcass; *sl* swine, scoundrel

**charpente** *nf* frame(work)

**charpenter** *vt* shape, hew (wood); frame; **bien charpenté** well-built (man)

**charpenterie** *nf* carpentry

**charpentier** *nm* carpenter

**charpie** *nf* lint; **mettre en ~** cut to shreds

**charretée** *nf* cartful

**charretier -ière** *n* carter, carrier; **jurer comme un ~** swear like a trooper

**charrette** *nf* (two-wheeled) cart; **~ à bras** barrow

**charrier** *vt* cart, transport, carry down; *sl* make fun of; *vi sl* exaggerate, come it strong

**charron** *nm* wheelwright, cartwright

**charrue** *nf* plough; **mettre la ~ devant les bœufs** put the cart before the horse

**charte** *nf* charter; deed

**chartreuse** *nf* Carthusian monastery; chartreuse (liqueur)

**chartreux -euse** *n+adj* Carthusian (monk, nun)

**chas** *nm* eye (needle)

**chasse** *nf* hunting; hunt, hunting-ground; **~ à courre** hunting with hounds; **~ d'eau** flush (lavatory); **~ gardée** private hunting-ground; **avion de ~** fighter-plane

**châsse** *nf* shrine; frame (spectacles), mounting

**chassé-croisé** *nm* (*pl* chassés-croisés) chassé-croisé (dance-step); fruitless running around

**chasse-mouches** *nm invar* fly-swatter

**chasse-neige** *nm invar* snow-plough; **descendre en ~** (ski-ing) come down braking

**chasser** *vt* hunt, chase; drive away; sack, dismiss, expel; dispel; drive (wind); knock in (nail); *vi* hunt, shoot; blow (wind); skid; drag (anchor)

**chasseresse** *nf poet* huntress

**chasseur -euse** *n* hunter, huntsman, huntress; *nm* page-boy, commissionaire; bellhop; rifleman; fighter-plane; *naut* chaser; *adj cul* with mushroom and tomato sauce

**chassie** *nf* rheum

**chassieux -ieuse** *adj* rheumy

**châssis** *nm* frame (door, window); chassis; *phot* slide; garden-frame; **~ d'atterrissage** landing-gear

**chasteté** *nf* chastity

**chasuble** *nf* chasuble

**chat** (*f* **chatte**) *n* cat; **à bon ~ bon rat** tit

for tat; **avoir d'autres ~s à fouetter** have other fish to fry; **avoir un ~ dans la gorge** be hoarse; **donner sa langue au ~** give up; **le Chat Botté** Puss-in-Boots; **ma petite ~te** darling, *US* honey; **pas un ~!** not a soul anywhere!

**châtaigne** *nf* chestnut

**châtaignier** *nm* chestnut-tree

**châtain** *adj invar* chestnut brown; **~ clair** auburn

**château** *nm* castle; large country house; royal palace; **~ d'eau** water-tower; **~ fort** fortress; **~x en Espagne** castles in the air

**châteaubriant** *nm* grilled fillet steak (with potatoes)

**châtelain -e** *n* lord (lady) of the manor

**châtelaine** *nf* chain (for keys or jewels)

**chat-huant** *nm* (*pl* chats-huants) tawny owl

**châtié** *adj* polished (style)

**châtier** *vt* chastise, punish

**châtiment** *nm* punishment, chastisement

**chatoiement** *nm* sheen; glistening

**chaton -onne** *n* kitten; *nm* catkin

**chatouillement** *nm* tickling

**chatouiller** *vt* tickle; **~ l'amour-propre de qn** flatter s/o's ego

**chatouilleux -euse** *adj* ticklish; touchy; delicate (matter)

**chatoyer** *vi* (7) shimmer; glisten

**châtrer** *vt* castrate

**chattemitte** *nf* flattering hypocrite, toady

**chatterie** *nf* coaxing

**chat-tigre** *nm* (*pl* chats-tigres) tiger-cat

**chaud** *nm* warmth, heat; **avoir ~** be warm (person); **être au ~** be warm; **cela ne me fait ni ~ ni froid** it's all the same to me; *adj* warm, hot; lively; ardent; **il fait ~** it's hot; **pleurer à ~es larmes** weep bitterly

**chaudière** *nf* boiler; copper (for washing)

**chaudron** *nm* cauldron

**chaudronnerie** *nf* boiler-making; copper-smith's workshop

**chaudronnier -ière** *n* boiler-maker; copper-smith

**chauffage** *nm* heating, warming; stoking

**chauffard** *nm coll* road-hog

**chauffe** *nf* heating; stoking

**chauffe-assiettes** *nm invar* plate-warmer

**chauffe-bain** *nm* bath-heater

**chauffe-eau** *nm invar* water-heater

**chauffe-pieds** *nm invar* foot-warmer

**chauffe-plats** *nm invar* hot-plate

**chauffer** *vt* warm, heat; *coll* cram (exam-candidate); **~ une affaire** expedite a matter; *vi* become warm, hot; overheat (bearings); **ça chauffe** things are warming up

**chaufferette** *nf* foot-warmer

**chauffeur -euse** *n* stoker, fireman (steam-engine); driver, chauffeur

**chaume** *nm* straw; thatch

**chaumière** *nf* thatched cottage

**chaussée** *nf* causeway; roadway

**chausse-pied** *nm* shoe-horn

**chausser** *vt* put shoes on; supply shoes to; ~ **du 44** take size 44 in shoes; *coll* ~ **ses lunettes** put on one's glasses; **se** ~ put on one's shoes

**chausses** *nfpl* hose, breeches

**chaussette** *nf* sock

**chausson** *nm* slipper; dancing-shoe; *cul* turnover

**chaussure** *nf* shoe; footwear; shoe-industry

**chauve** *adj* bald; denuded (mountain)

**chauve-souris** *nf* (*pl* **chauves-souris**) *zool* bat

**chauvin** *adj* jingoistic, chauvinistic

**chauvinisme** *nm* jingoism, chauvinism

**chaux** *nf* lime; **blanchir à la** ~ whitewash

**chavirer** *vt* turn upside down; *vi* capsize, overturn

**chef** *nm* chief, principal, leader; heading; *ar* head; ~ **de cabinet** principal private secretary; ~ **de cuisine** chef; ~ **de gare** station-master; ~ **d'orchestre** conductor of an orchestra; ~ **de rayon** floor-walker, *US* floor-walker; ~ **de service** head of department; ~ **de train** guard, *US* conductor; **de son propre** ~ on one's own responsibility

**chef-d'œuvre** *nm* (*pl* **chefs-d'œuvre**) masterpiece

**chef-lieu** *nm* (*pl* **chefs-lieux**) chief town

**cheik** *nm* sheik

**chemin** *nm* way, road, path; ~ **battu** beaten track; ~ **de croix** stations of the Cross; ~ **de fer** railway, *US* railroad; ~ **faisant** on the way; **faire son** ~ get on; **ne pas y aller par quatre (trente-six)** ~ **s** not beat about the bush

**chemineau** *nm* tramp, *US* hobo

**cheminée** *nf* chimney, funnel; fireplace, mantelpiece

**cheminer** *vi* make one's way, proceed

**cheminot** *nm* railwayman, *US* railroad man

**chemise** *nf* (man's) shirt; chemise; folder; dust-jacket (book); casing; ~ **de nuit** nightshirt (-dress); **en bras de** ~ in one's shirt-sleeves

**chemiserie** *nf* shirt shop or factory

**chenal** *nm* channel; mill-race

**chenapan** *nm* rogue, scoundrel

**chêne** *nm* oak

**chéneau** *nm* gutter

**chenet** *nm* fire-dog, andiron

**chenil** *nm* kennels

**chenille** *nf* caterpillar; caterpillar-track

**chenillette** *nf* military tracked vehicle

**chenu** *adj* bleached (hair); hoary

**cheptel** *nm* livestock

**chèque** *nm* cheque, *US* check; ~ **barré** crossed cheque; ~ **de voyage** traveller's cheque; ~ **sans provision** dud cheque; **toucher un** ~ cash a cheque

**cher** (*f* **chère**) *n* **mon** ~ my dear fellow; **ma chère** my dear, darling; *adj* dear, beloved; expensive, costly; *adv* **coûter** ~ cost a lot; **il l'a payé** ~ he paid dearly (or a lot of money) for it

**chercher** *vt* look for, seek; try; ~ **la petite bête** be over-critical; ~ **midi à quatorze heures** look for difficulties where there aren't any; **aller** ~ fetch; *coll* **cela va** ~ **dans les mille francs** it fetches about a thousand francs; **envoyer** ~ send for; *coll* **tu l'as cherché!** you asked for it!

**chercheur -euse** *n* seeker, investigator; research-worker

**chère** *nf* fare, food, cheer; **faire bonne** ~ live well

**chéri -e** *n + adj* darling, beloved

**chérir** *vt* cherish, hold dear

**cherté** *nf* dearness, high price

**chérubin** *nm* cherub

**chétif -ive** *adj* weak, puny; wretched

**cheval** *nm* horse; ~ **de bataille** pet subject; **à** ~ on horseback; **à** ~ **sur** astride, overlapping; a stickler for; **chevaux de bois** merry-go-round; **fièvre de** ~ raging fever; **monter à** ~ go in for riding; **monter sur ses grands chevaux** ride one's high horse; **une deux chevaux** a two-horse-power car (French rating)

**chevaleresque** *adj* chivalrous

**chevalerie** *nf* knighthood; chivalry

**chevalet** *nm* support, trestle; easel; clothes-horse; bridge (violin)

**chevalier** *nm* knight; *zool* sandpiper; ~ **d'industrie** crook, swindler

**chevalière** *nf* signet-ring

**chevalin** *adj* equine; **boucherie** ~ **e** horse-butcher's

**cheval-vapeur** *nm* (*pl* **chevaux-vapeur**) horse-power

**chevauchée** *nf* ride on horseback; cavalcade

**chevaucher** *vt* sit astride; **se** ~ overlap; *vi* ride on horseback; overlap

**chevelu** *adj* hairy, long-haired; **cuir** ~ scalp

**chevelure** *nf* head of hair; tail (of comet)

**chevet** *nm* bedhead; bolster; **lampe de** ~ bedside lamp; **livre de** ~ favourite book

**cheveu** *nm* (single) hair; ~x hair; **comme un ~ sur la soupe** very inappropriate; **couper les ~x en quatre** split hairs; **en ~x** (woman) hatless; **s'arracher les ~x** tear one's hair; *coll* **se faire des ~x** worry; **tenir à un ~** be touch and go; **tiré par les ~x** far-fetched

**cheville** *nf* peg, pin, bolt; ankle; plug; padding (verse); ~ **ouvrière** king-pin; mainspring; **il ne vous arrive (vient) pas à la ~** he can't hold a candle to you

**cheviller** *vt* pin, peg, bolt; **avoir l'âme chevillée au corps** be very difficult to kill

**chèvre** *nf* (she-)goat; derrick; **ménager la ~ et le chou** run with the hare and hunt with the hounds

**chevreau** *nm* kid

**chèvrefeuille** *nm* honeysuckle

**chevrette** *nf* kid-goat, roe-deer; tripod; *coll* shrimp or prawn

**chevreuil** *nm* roe-buck; roe-deer; venison

**chevrier -ière** *n* goatherd, goatgirl

**chevron** *nm* rafter; *mil* stripe; chevron

**chevroter** *vi* speak or sing in a quavering voice

**chevrotine** *nf* buckshot

**chez** *prep* at the home or house of; among; with; ~ **Dupont** care of Dupont; ~ **l'épicier** at the grocer's; ~ **Racine** in Racine('s works); **faites comme ~ vous** make yourself at home; **un ~-soi** a home

**chiader** *vt + vi coll* swot (for)

**chialer** *vi sl* cry, blubber

**chic** *nm* knack, skill; smartness, chic; **avoir du ~** be smart; **avoir le ~ pour** have the knack of; *adj invar* elegant, smart, stylish; pleasant, nice, first-rate; **elle a été très ~** she behaved very generously; *coll* **un ~ type** a smashing fellow

**chicane** *nf* chicanery, quibbling, wrangling

**chicaner** *vt* quibble, wrangle with; *vi* quibble, carp

**chicanerie** *nf* chicanery, quibbling

**chicaneur -euse** *n + adj* quibbling, argumentative (person)

¹**chiche** *nm* **pois ~** chick pea

²**chiche** *adj* poor, scanty; stingy

³**chiche** *interj coll* I dare you, bet you I will (can)

**chichi** *nm coll* affectation; **faire du ~ (des ~s)** put on airs

**chicorée** *nf* endive; chicory

**chicot** *nm* stump (tree or tooth)

**chien** (*f* **chienne**) *n* dog, bitch; hammer (gun); *coll* charm, sex-appeal; ~ **de**

(**chienne de**) ... wretched ...; ~ **d'arrêt** pointer; ~ **de berger** sheep-dog; ~ **de garde** watch-dog; **couché en ~ de fusil** lying curled up; **entre ~ et loup** at dusk; **être ~** be mean; **être coiffé à la ~** ne wear a fringe; **se regarder en ~s de faïence** glare at each other; **temps de ~** filthy weather; **un mal de ~** a lot of trouble; **vie de ~** rotten life; **vivre comme ~ et chat** get on badly

**chiendent** *nm* couch-grass; *coll* difficulty, snag

**chienlit** *nf* mess, chaos; *obs* carnival mask

**chier** *vi vulg* shit

**chiffon** *nm* rag; scrap (paper); *coll* **parler ~s** talk about dress (women)

**chiffonner** *vt* rumple, crumple; vex

**chiffonnier -ière** *n* rag-and-bone man, rag-picker; *nm* chiffonier

**chiffre** *nm* figure, numeral, code, cipher; monogram; ~ **d'affaires** turnover; **un zéro en ~** a nonentity, a poor fish

**chiffrer** *vt* number; work out; write in code; mark; *vi* calculate, reckon; mount up (cost, expenses)

**chignon** *nm* coil of hair, bun

**chimère** *nf* chimera, idle dream

**chimérique** *adj* chimerical

**chimie** *nf* chemistry

**chimique** *adj* chemical; **produit ~** chemical

**chimiste** *n* chemist

**chimpanzé** *nm* chimpanzee

**Chine** *nf* China; **encre de ~** Indian ink

**chine** *nm* (**papier de**) rice-paper

**chiner** *vt* cloud, mottle (fabrics); run down, mock at; *vi sl* work hard

**Chinois -e** *n* Chinese (man or woman)

**chinois** *nm* Chinese (language); *adj* Chinese

**chinoiserie** *nf* Chinese curio; *coll* nonsense, futile measure; ~s **administratives** red tape

**chiot** *nm* pup, puppy

**chiottes** *nfpl vulg* bog, shit-house, *US* can

**chiourme** *nf* gang of convicts or galleyslaves

**chiper** *vt coll* pinch, swipe

**chipie** *nf coll* shrew, old bitch

**chipoter** *vt + vi* nibble (at one's food); *vi* quibble; waste time

**chips** *nmpl* potato crisps; *US* potato chips; game chips

**chique** *nf* quid (tobacco)

**chiqué** *nm coll* affectation, sham; **faire du ~** put it on

**chiquement** *adv* smartly, stylishly

**chiquenaude** *nf* flick of the finger

**chiquer** *vi* chew tobacco

**chiromancie** *nf* chiromancy, palmistry

**chiropracteur** *nm* bone-setter

**chirurgical** *adj* surgical; *med* **ventre ~** acute abdomen

**chirurgie** *nf* surgery

**chirurgien** *nm* surgeon

**chlore** *nm* chlorine

**chlorer** *vt* chlorinate

**chloroforme** *nm* chloroform

**chlorophylle** *nf* chlorophyll

**chlorure** *nm* chloride

**chnouf** *nm sl* heroin, snow

**choc** *nm* impact, collision; *med* shock; *adj invar or pl* **~ s** staggering, amazing

**chocolat** *nm* chocolate; *adj* chocolate-coloured

**chocolatier -ière** *n* chocolate-maker

**chœur** *nm* chorus; choir (singers); *archi* choir; **en ~** unanimously; in chorus

**choir** *vi* (21) *obs* fall

**choisir** *vt* choose, select; **~ ses mots** pick one's words; **société choisie** select company

**choix** *nm* choice, selection; **au ~** all at the same price; **avoir l'embarras du ~** have plenty to choose from; **de ~** choice; **de premier ~** best quality; **je n'ai pas le ~** I have no option, alternative

**chômage** *nm* unemployment; ceasing of work; *coll* dole; **en ~** out of work

**chômer** *vi* stop work; be out of work, be unemployed

**chômeur -euse** *n* unemployed worker

**chope** *nf* beer-mug, tankard; mugful of beer

**choper** *vt coll* catch

**chopine** *nf* half-litre mug

**choquant** *adj* offensive, unpleasant

**choquer** *vt* knock, collide with; clink (glasses); offend; scandalize; **se ~** collide; take offence

**chorale** *nf* choral society

**chorégraphie** *nf* choreography

**choriste** *n* chorus-singer

**chorus** *nm* faire **~** repeat in chorus; join in agreement

**¹chose** *nf* thing, affair, matter; chattel; slave; **le cours des ~ s** the course of events; **Monsieur Chose** Mr So-and-so; **pas grand-~** not much; **porté sur la ~** highly sexed; *nm coll* thingumajig

**²chose** *adj invar coll* **être tout ~** feel queer

**chou** *nm* cabbage; **~ à la crème** cream bun; **~ pommé** garden cabbage; **~ x de Bruxelles** Brussels sprouts; **aller planter ses ~ x** go and retire into the country; **être (finir) dans les ~ x** be among the last in the race; **faire ses ~ x gras** feather one's nest; **feuille de ~** rag (newspaper); **mon petit ~** darling,

*US* honey; **oreilles en feuilles de ~** saucer-ears

**chouan** *nm* insurgent Breton royalist

**choucas** *nm* jackdaw

**chouchouter** *vt coll* pet, fondle

**choucroute** *nf cul* sauerkraut

**¹chouette** *nf* owl

**²chouette** *adj coll* fine, *US* swell

**chou-fleur** *nm* ( *pl* **choux-fleurs**) cauliflower

**chou-rave** *nm* ( *pl* **choux-raves**) kohlrabi

**choyer** *vt* (7) pet, coddle; **~ une idée** entertain an idea

**chrétien -ienne** *n* + *adj* Christian

**chrétienté** *nf* Christendom

**chris-craft** *nm* small motor-boat

**Christ** *nm* Christ; crucifix

**christianiser** *vt* christianize

**christianisme** *nm* Christianity

**chromage** *nm* chromium plating

**chrome** *nm* chromium

**chromé** *adj* chromium-plated; chrome-tanned

**chromer** *vt* chrome

**¹chronique** *nf* chronicle; news, newspaper report; **défrayer la ~** be in the news

**²chronique** *adj* chronic

**chroniqueur** *nm* chronicler; writer of newspaper articles

**chronologie** *nf* chronology

**chronologique** *adj* chronological

**chronomètre** *nm* chronometer

**chronométrer** *vt* (6) time, keep the time

**chrysalide** *nf* chrysalis, pupa

**chrysanthème** *nm* chrysanthemum

**chu** *p part* choir

**chuchotement** *nm* whispering

**chuchoter** *vt + vi* whisper

**chuinter** *vi* hoot (owl); pronounce 's' as 'j' or 'sh'

**chut** *interj* hush!, quiet!

**chute** *nf* fall; **~ d'eau** waterfall; **~ des reins** small of the back; **~ du jour** nightfall; **faire une ~** fall down; **point de ~** place to settle; situation

**chuter** *vi coll* fall, come a cropper

**Chypre** *nf* Cyprus

**¹ci** *adv* here; **de-~, de-là** on every side; **par-~, par-là** here and there; *see* **ce** *and* **celui**

**²ci** *pron* **~ et ça** this and that; **comme ~, comme ça** so-so

**ci-après** *adv* hereafter; further on (in book)

**ci-bas** *adv* here below

**cible** *nf* target

**ciboire** *nm* pyx

**ciboule** *nf* small onion

**ciboulette** *nf* chive(s)

**cicatrice** *nf* scar

**cicatriser** vt heal up; scar; **se ~** (wound) heal up

**cicérone** nm guide, cicerone

**ci-contre** adv on the page opposite

**ci-dessous** adv below, undermentioned

**ci-dessus** adv above, above-mentioned

**ci-devant** n hist aristocrat of the Ancien Régime; adv formerly

**cidre** nm cider

**ciel** nm (pl **cieux**, **~s**) sky, heaven; climate; Heaven; pl **~s** canopy, skies (in painting); **à ~ ouvert** out of doors; **aide-toi, le ~ t'aidera** God helps those who help themselves; **au ~, aux cieux** in Heaven; coll **tomber du ~** come as a godsend; arrive unexpectedly

**cierge** nm eccles wax candle, taper

**cigale** nf cicada

**cigare** nm cigar

**ci-gît, ci-gisant** see **gésir**

**cigogne** nf stork

**ciguë** nf hemlock

**ci-inclus** adj (invar before n) enclosed, herewith

**ci-joint** adj (invar before n) enclosed, herewith

**cil** nm eyelash

**cilice** nm hair-shirt

**ciller** vi blink

**cime** nf summit, peak; top (tree)

**ciment** nm cement; **~ armé** reinforced concrete

**cimenter** vt cement; consolidate

**cimeterre** nm scimitar

**cimetière** nm cemetery; graveyard

**cimier** nm crest (helmet)

**ciné** nm coll cinema

**ciné-actualités** nm news-theatre

**cinéaste** n member of film-making team

**cinéma** nm cinema; cinema industry; coll **c'est du ~** it's all a farce, it's very unlikely; **faire du ~** act in films

**cinématographe** nm cinematograph

**cinématographie** nf cinematography

**cinématographique** adj cinematographic

**cinéraire** adj cinerary (urn)

**cinglant** adj lashing (wind, rain), bitter, biting; scathing

**cinglé** adj sl daft, barmy, nuts

¹**cingler** vi sail before the wind

²**cingler** vt lash, cut (wind, rain)

**cinq** nm + adj five; fifth; **en ~ sec** in a jiffy; **il était moins ~** it was a near thing; **les ~ lettres** the four letter-word (euphemism for **merde**)

**cinquantaine** nf about fifty; the fifties (age)

**cinquante** nm + adj fifty

**cinquantenaire** nm fiftieth anniversary

**cinquantième** nm + adj fiftieth (part)

**cinquième** nm fifth (part); **être en ~** be in the second year class at the lycée; adj fifth

**cintre** nm interior concave surface (arch or vault); arch; coathanger; bend (handle-bar); **voûte en plein ~** semicircular arch

**cintrer** vt curve, arch, bend

**cirage** nm waxing, polishing; waxpolish; shoe-polish

**circoncire** vt (22) circumcize

**circoncision** nf circumcision

**circonférence** nf circumference; perimeter (town)

**circonflexe** adj circumflex (accent)

**circonlocution** nf circumlocution

**circonscription** nf circumscription; district; electoral district, ward

**circonscrire** vt (42) circumscribe; encircle; limit

**circonspect** adj circumspect, cautious

**circonspection** nf circumspection, caution

**circonstance** nf circumstance, event; **agir en raison des ~s** act in keeping with the circumstances; **à la hauteur des ~s** equal to the occasion; **de ~** improvised for the occasion

**circonstancié** adj detailed

**circonstanciel -ielle** adj circumstantial; gramm adverbial

**circonvenir** vt (96) circumvent; thwart

**circuit** nm circuit; circumference (town); course, lap (race); trip; detour; **~ imprimé** printed circuit; **court ~** short circuit; **mettre en ~** switch on

**circulaire** nf circular (letter); adj circular

**circulation** nf circulation; traffic; **~ interdite** no thoroughfare

**circuler** vi circulate, flow; move about, move along

**cire** nf wax

**cirer** vt wax; polish (shoes); **toile cirée** oilcloth

**cireur -euse** n polisher; shoeblack

**cireux -euse** adj wax-like

**cirque** nm circus; amphitheatre (mountains)

**cisaille** nf parings, shavings (metal); **~s** metal-shears

**cisailler** vt shear (metal)

**cisalpin** adj cisalpine

**ciseau** nm chisel; **~x** scissors

**ciseler** vt (5) engrave; chisel; emboss; shear

**ciselure** nf chiselling; embossing

**citadelle** nf citadel

**citadin -e** n townsman, townswoman

**citation** nf quoting; quotation; summons (to court); subpoena; citation

**cité** nf city; large town; housing estate

**citer** vt quote, cite; **~ qn à l'ordre du**

**jour** mention s/o in despatches

**citerne** *nf* cistern, tank; **camion-~** tanker (lorry)

**cithare** *nf* zither

**citoyen -enne** *n* citizen

**citrique** *adj* citric

**citron** *nm* lemon; *adj invar* lemon-coloured

**citronnade** *nf* lemonade

**citronnier** *nm* lemon-tree

**citrouille** *nf* pumpkin

**civet** *nm* stew (game); **~ de lièvre** jugged hare

**civette** *nf* civet-cat; chives

**civière** *nf* stretcher; handbarrow

**civil** *nm* civilian; **dans le ~** in private life; **en ~** in plain clothes; *adj* civil; civic; secular; civilian; polite

**civilisateur -trice** *n* civilizer; *adj* civilizing

**civilisation** *nf* civilization

**civiliser** *vt* civilize

**civilité** *nf* civility, courtesy

**civique** *adj* civic; civil (rights)

**clabauder** *vi* babble (hound); backbite

**claie** *nf* wattle; hurdle

**clair** *nm* light, shine; **en ~** not in cipher; **tirer une affaire au ~** clear up a matter; *adj* clear; bright; light (colour); obvious; thin (soup); **voilà qui est ~!** that's obvious enough; *adv* clearly, plainly; **voir ~** see clearly; **y voir ~** see properly

**clairement** *adv* distinctly, clearly

**clairet -ette** *adj* light red (wine); thin (voice)

**claire-voie** *nf* (*pl* **claires-voies**) open-work, lattice-work; clerestory; **porte à ~** gate

**clairière** *nf* glade, clearing

**clair-obscur** *nm* (*pl* **clairs-obscurs**) chiaroscuro

**clairon** *nm* bugle; bugler

**claironner** *vt* trumpet; noise abroad, broadcast

**clairsemé** *adj* scattered, sparse; thinly sown (corn); thin (hair)

**clairvoyance** *nf* perspicacity; clairvoyance

**clairvoyant** *adj* clear-sighted, shrewd; clairvoyant

**clamer** *vt* cry out

**clameur** *nf* clamour, outcry

**clan** *nm* clan; clique

**clandestin** *adj* clandestine, secret; **passager ~** stowaway

**clapier** *nm* rabbit-warren; rabbit-hutch

**clapotement** *nm* lapping, plashing

**clapoter** *vi* lap, plash

**clapotis** *nm* plashing, lapping

**claque** *nf* smack, slap; *theat* hired clappers; *nm* opera-hat

**claquement** *nm* smacking; chattering (teeth); slamming; crack (whip)

**claquemurer** *vt* shut up, immure

**claquer** *vt* + *vi* slap, smack; clap; bang (door); crack (whip); snap (fingers); click (heels); *sl* die; fail; *sl* exhaust; *sl* **se ~** wear oneself out

**clarifier** *vt* clarify, purify

**clarinette** *nf* clarinet; clarinettist

**clarté** *nf* clearness; brightness, light

**classe** *nf* class; division; rank; **aller en ~** go to school; **faire la ~** teach; **la ~ 1952** the contingent of conscripts born in 1952

**classement** *nm* classification; filing (papers); *sp* placing

**classer** *vt* classify; rate; sort out; file (papers); **~ une affaire** shelve a matter

**classeur** *nm* filing-cabinet; file; sorter

**classification** *nf* classification; classifying, sorting out

**classifier** *vt* classify; rate; sort out

**classique** *adj* classic(al); for school use; **les ~s** the classics

**claustral** *adj* claustral, monastic

**claustration** *nf* cloistering

**clavecin** *nm* harpsichord

**clavicule** *nf* collar-bone, clavicle

**clavier** *nm* keyboard (piano, typewriter); range (voice, instrument); key-ring or charm

**clé** *nf* see **clef**

**clef** *nf* key; spanner; *mus* clef; **~ (à bascule)** switch-key; **~ anglaise** adjustable spanner; **~ de voûte** keystone; **fausse ~** skeleton key; **fermer à ~** lock

**clématite** *nf* clematis

**clémence** *nf* clemency, mercy; mildness (weather)

**clément** *adj* clement, merciful; mild

**cleptomane** *n* see **kleptomane**

**cleptomanie** *nf* see **kleptomanie**

**clerc** *nm* cleric; scholar; clerk (lawyer's office); **pas de ~** blunder

**clergé** *nm* clergy

**clic-clac** *nm* clatter (shoes); crack (whip)

**cliché** *nm typ* slate, block; *phot* negative; cliché

**client -e** *n* customer; client; patient; guest (hotel)

**clientèle** *nf* customers; goodwill; practice (doctor)

**clignement** *nm* winking, blinking

**cligner** *vt* + *vi* wink, blink; **~ de l'œil** wink

**clignotant** *nm mot* winker, direction indicator; *econ* warning sign

**clignotement** *nm* winking; flickering

**clignoter** *vi* wink; flicker

**climat** *nm* climate; region

**climatique** *adj* climatic

**climatisation** nf air-conditioning
**climatiser** vt air-condition; adapt to a climate
**climatiseur** nm air-conditioning apparatus
**clin** nm ~ d'œil wink
**clinfoc** nm flying jib
**clinique** nf clinic; medical teaching; adj clinical
**clinquant** nm tinsel; cheap imitation jewellery; adj flashy
**clip** nm brooch
**clique** nf coll+pej gang
**cliqueter** vi (5) click; jingle; rattle; clink; mot pink
**cliquetis** nm clank(ing), rattling; jingle; clink(ing); mot pinking
**cliquette** nf castanets
**clivage** nm cleavage
**cloaque** nm cesspool, sink
**clochard -e** n coll tramp, US hobo
**cloche** nf bell; bell-jar; dish-cover; sl clot, dope; sl être de la ~ be a tramp, hobo; sonner les ~ s à qn tell s/o off
**cloche-pied (à)** adv phr hopping, on one foot
¹**clocher** nm belfry, steeple; esprit de ~ parochial mentality
²**clocher** vi limp; coll be wrong, go wrong
**clocheton** nm bell-turret
**clochette** nf little bell; bell-shaped flower
**cloison** nf partition, division; ~ étanche watertight bulkhead
**cloisonné** adj cloisonné (enamel)
**cloisonner** vt divide into compartments
**cloître** nm cloister; monastery; convent
**cloîtrer** vt cloister
**clopin-clopant** adv with a limp
**clopiner** vi limp, hobble
**cloporte** nm woodlouse
**cloque** nf swelling, blister
**cloquer** vi+v refl blister
**clore** vt (23) close, shut; conclude
**clos** nm enclosure (particularly of vineyard); adj closed, shut; à huis ~ in camera, in secret session; maison ~ e brothel
**clôture** nf fence, enclosure; closing; conclusion (meeting)
**clôturer** vt fence in, enclose; shut down; conclude (meeting); wind up
**clou** nm nail; boil; coll old car or bicycle; coll pawn-shop, US hock shop; stud; coll star turn; ~ de girofle clove; traverser aux ~ s (dans les ~ s) cross at the pedestrian crossing (US crosswalk)
**clouer** vt nail; fix, hold fast; ~ le bec à qn shut s/o up; être cloué au lit be bedridden
**clouter** vt stud; passage clouté pedestrian crossing, US crosswalk

**club** nm club; golf-club
**coadjuteur** nm coadjutor
**coagulation** nf coagulation
**coaguler** vt coagulate; se ~ clot
**coaliser (se)** v refl form a coalition, unite
**coassement** nm croaking
**coasser** vi croak
**cobalt** nm cobalt
**cobaye** nm guinea-pig
**cobra** nm cobra
**cocagne** nf mât de ~ greasy pole; pays de ~ land of plenty
**cocaïne** nf cocaine
**cocarde** nf rosette, cockade
**cocasse** adj laughable, ludicrous, comical
**coccinelle** nf ladybird
¹**coche** nm stagecoach; mouche du ~ busybody
²**coche** nf notch, nick, score
**cochère** adj f porte ~ main entrance, carriage entrance
**cochon** nm pig, hog; swine; ~ de lait sucking pig; coll ~ de payant mug, US sucker; ~ d'Inde guinea-pig; tour de ~ swinish trick; adj (f -onne) swinish, beastly; dirty, smutty
**cochonnaille** nf sl pork meats
**cochonnerie** nf sl filthiness; rubbish; filthy trick; smut
**cochonnet** nm young pig; jack (bowls); twelve-sided dice
¹**coco** nm mon petit ~ my little darling; noix de ~ coconut; sl fellow; un drôle de ~ a queer character
²**coco** nf sl cocaine, snow
**cocon** nm cocoon
**cocorico** nm cock-a-doodle-doo
**cocotier** nm coconut palm
**cocotte** nf stew-pan; high-class tart, floozy; hen (child language); sty (eyelid); coll darling
**cocu** nm+adj cuckold
**code** nm code, law; rules; ~ de la route highway code; mot se mettre en ~ dip one's lights
**codicille** nm codicil
**codification** nf codification; coding
**codifier** vt codify; code
**coéquipier -ière** n team-mate
**cœur** nm heart; mind, feelings; courage; hearts (cards); midst, core; à ~ joie to one's heart's content; à contre ~ against one's will; avoir le ~ gros be very sad; avoir mal au ~ feel sick; avoir sur le ~ resent; cela lui tient à ~ he's keen on that; de bon ~ willingly; de tout ~ whole-heartedly; en avoir le ~ net get to the bottom of a matter; si le ~ vous en dit if you feel like it
**coexister** vi co-exist

**coffrage** *nm* lining (mine-shaft); *bui* framework

**coffre** *nm* chest, bin, coffer; *mot* boot, *US* trunk; mooring buoy; *coll* chest

**coffre-fort** *nm* (*pl* **coffres-forts**) safe

**coffrer** *vt* line (shaft); *sl* put in prison

**coffret** *nm* small chest; casket

**cogérer** *vt* (6) manage in common

**cognac** *nm* cognac, brandy

**cognassier** *nm* quince-tree

**cognée** *nf* axe, hatchet

**cogner** *vt* + *vi* knock, beat, hammer

**cohorte** *nf* cohort

**cohue** *nf* mob, crowd

**coi** (*f* **coite**) *adj obs* quiet, still; **se tenir ~** keep quiet

**coiffe** *nf* headdress; *med* caul

**coiffer** *vt* cover (head); beat, overtake; **~ Sainte Catherine** be twenty-five and unmarried; **être coiffé de qn** be keen on s/o; **se ~** put on one's hat; do one's hair

**coiffeur -euse** *n* hairdresser; *nf* dressing-table

**coiffure** *nf* headdress; hair-style; hair-dressing

**coin** *nm* corner, angle; wedge; place; stamp, die; **au ~ du feu** by the fireside; **jouer aux quatre ~s** play puss in the corner

**coincer** *vt* (4) wedge, jam; trap

**coïncider** *vi* coincide

**coing** *nm* quince

**coït** *nm* coitus, copulation

**col** *nm* neck; collar; pass (mountains); **faux ~** separate collar; *coll* froth on glass of beer

**coléoptère** *nm* beetle, coleopter

**colère** *nf* anger, fit of anger; **être en ~** be in a temper; **se mettre en ~** get angry; *adj* angry; irascible

**coléreux -euse** *adj* irascible, quick-tempered

**colérique** *adj* choleric

**colibri** *nm* humming-bird

**colifichet** *nm* bauble, trinket

**colimaçon** *nm* snail; **escalier en ~** spiral staircase

**colin-maillard** *nm* blind-man's buff

**colique** *nf* colic; belly-ache

**colis** *nm* parcel, package; article of luggage

**colite** *nf* colitis

**collaborateur -trice** *n* collaborator; associate

**collaborer** *vi* collaborate

**collage** *nm* gluing, sticking; *arts* collage; *sl* cohabitation

**collant** *nm* tights; *adj* sticky; close-fitting; clinging (person)

**collation** *nf* conferment; collation; light meal

**collationner** *vt* collate, compare; *vi* have a snack

**colle** *nf* paste, gum; poser; *coll* detention; **~ à empois** size; **~ forte** glue; **poser une ~** ask a sticky question

**collecte** *nf* (church) collection

**collecteur -trice** *n* collector

**collectif** *nm* block (of flats); *adj* (*f* **-ive**) collective

**collection** *nf* collecting; collection

**collectionner** *vt* collect

**collectionneur -euse** *n* collector

**collectivité** *nf* collectivity; community

**collège** *nm* college; school

**collégien -ienne** *n* schoolboy, school-girl

**collègue** *n* colleague, fellow worker

**coller** *vt* paste, stick, glue; *coll* place; *coll* give; *coll* floor (s/o); *coll* punish (pupil); *coll* fail, plough, *US* flunk; *vi* stick, adhere; *sl* suit, work out (well); **se ~** stick, cling; *coll* **se ~ avec** live with

**collerette** *nf* little collar

**collet** *nm* collar (coat, etc); cape; flange; snare; **~ monté** prim and proper; **prendre au ~** seize by the scruff of the neck; arrest

**colleter** *vt* (5) collar; grapple; **se ~** come to blows

**collier** *nm* necklace; collar; (type of) beard; *coll* **donner un coup de ~** make a big effort

**colline** *nf* hill

**colloque** *nm* colloquy; conference (scholars, specialists)

**colmater** *vt* warp (land); fill in (holes, etc)

**colombe** *nf* dove, pigeon

**colombier** *nm* dovecot

**colon** *nm* farmer; settler

**colonie** *nf* colony, settlement; **~ de vacances** holiday camp (for children)

**colonisateur -trice** *n* colonizer

**colonisation** *nf* colonization

**coloniser** *vt* colonize

**colonne** *nf* column, pillar; **~ vertébrale** spine

**colorant** *nm* colouring (matter)

**coloration** *nf* colouring; colour

**colorer** *vt* colour, stain

**colorier** *vt* apply colour(s)

**coloris** *nm* colouring, hue

**colosse** *nm* colossus, giant

**colportage** *nm* hawking; spreading of news or rumours

**colporter** *vt* hawk, peddle; propagate, spread (news)

**colporteur -euse** *n* pedlar, hawker

**coltiner** *vt* carry, lug

**colza** *nm* colza, rape

**comateux -euse** *adj* comatose

**combat** *nm* combat, fight; **engager le ~** go into action; **hors de ~** out of action, disabled

**combatif -ive** *adj* aggressive, pugnacious

**combattant -e** *n* combatant; **ancien ~** ex-serviceman

**combattre** *vt + vi* combat, struggle

**combe** *nf* dale, valley, combe

**combien** *adv exclam* how; *adv inter* how much (many)?; **c'est ~?** how much is it?; **le ~ sommes-nous?** what is the date?; **tous les ~?** at what intervals?

**combinaison** *nf* combination, arrangement; *coll* scheme; overalls

**combinard** *nm sl* trickster

**combine** *nf* scheme, racket

**combiner** *vt* combine; arrange; devise

**comble** *nm* full measure; roofing; summit, height; **c'est le ~!** that beats everything!; **de fond en ~** from top to bottom; **pour ~ de malheur** worst of all; **sous les ~s** in the attic; *adj* very full; crowded out; **faire salle ~** attract a full house

**combler** *vt* fill, fill up; make up, satisfy fully; **~ qn de bienfaits** heap kindnesses on s/o; **~ un déficit** make up a deficit

**combustible** *nm* fuel; *adj* combustible

**comédie** *nf* comedy; play; **faire la ~** sham

**comédien -ienne** *n* actor, actress; shammer

**comestible** *adj* edible; **~s** provisions, victuals

**comète** *nf* comet

**comices** *nmpl* **~ agricoles** agricultural show

**comique** *nm* comedy; comic actor; comedian; **le ~, c'est** the funny part is; *adj* comic; funny

**comité** *nm* committee; **~ de lecture** (literary) selection committee; **~ d'entreprise** workers' or staff council; **petit ~** small informal gathering

**commandant** *nm* commandant; commanding officer; major; squadron-leader; (naval) captain

**commande** *nf comm* order; *mech* control; **~ ferme** firm order; **de ~** forced, artificial; **levier de ~** control lever; **passer une ~** place an order; **sur ~** to order

**commandement** *nm* command, order; authority

**commander** *vt* command; order; be in command; overlook, dominate; compel (respect); control; **~ à ses passions** control one's passions; **se ~** control oneself

**commanditaire** *nm comm* sleeping partner, *US* silent partner; *theat* backer

**commanditer** *vt* finance

**comme** *adv* as, like, how; as though; **~ de juste** of course; *coll* **c'est tout ~** it comes to the same thing; **qu'est-ce que vous avez ~ fruits?** what have you in the way of fruit?; *conj* as, just as

**commémoratif -ive** *adj* commemorative

**commémorer** *vt* commemorate

**commencement** *nm* beginning

**commencer** *vt + vi* (4) begin, start; **pour ~** to begin with

**comment** *adv inter* how?; what did you say?; *interj* what!; why!; **mais ~ donc!** by all means!

**commentaire** *nm* commentary; comment

**commentateur -trice** *n* commentator

**commenter** *vt* comment, annotate; make remarks on

**commérage** *nm* gossip

**commerçant -e** *n* tradesman, shopkeeper; *adj* commercial; **peu ~** not keen on or good at doing business

**commerce** *nm* commerce; trade; business; dealings; **dans le ~** in the business world; **d'un ~ agréable** pleasant to deal with; **faire le ~ de** deal in; **maison de ~** firm

**commercer** *vi* (4) trade; have dealings

**commercialiser** *vt* commercialize

**commère** *nf* gossip, crony

**commérer** *vi* (6) gossip

**commettre** *vt* (60) commit, perpetrate; **~ une erreur** make a mistake; **se ~** commit oneself

**comminatoire** *adj* comminatory, threatening

**commis** *nm* clerk, shop-assistant; **~ voyageur** (commercial) traveller

**commissaire** *nm* member of commission, commissioner; steward; police superintendent

**commissaire-priseur** *nm* auctioneer

**commissariat** *nm* office of commissioner; **~ (de police)** police station

**commission** *nf* commission; brokerage; errand, message; committee

**commissionnaire** *nm* messenger, commission-agent

**commode** *nf* chest-of-drawers; *adj* suitable, convenient, handy; comfortable; accommodating, good-natured

**commodité** *nf* convenience, comfort

**commotion** *nf* commotion, upheaval; concussion; shell-shock

**commotionné** *adj* suffering from concussion

**commuer** *vt leg* commute

**commun** *nm* common run; generality;

~s outbuildings; **hors du** ~ above average; **le** ~ **des mortels** the common herd; *adj* common, general, usual, widespread; vulgar, commonplace; **d'un** ~ **accord** with one accord; **lieu** ~ truism

**communal** *adj* common (land); communal; **école** ~ **e** primary school

**communauté** *nf* community; society; ~ **de biens** joint ownership (marriage)

**commune** *nf* borough, parish; commune; **la Chambre des Communes** the House of Commons

**communément** *adv* commonly, generally

**communiant -e** *n* communicant

**communicant** *adj* communicating (room)

**communicateur -trice** *adj* connecting (wire)

**communicatif -ive** *adj* communicative, talkative; infectious (laughter)

**communication** *nf* communication, (telephone) call; message; **fausse** ~ wrong number; **obtenir la** ~ get through (telephone); **se mettre en** ~ **avec** get in touch with

**communier** *vi* attend communion; be in communion

**communion** *nf* communion; Holy Communion

**communiquer** *vt* communicate, convey; transmit; *vi* lead into (door); **se** ~ be communicative; spread (fire)

**communisme** *nm* communism

**communiste** *n + adj* communist

**commutateur** *nm* elect switch, commutator

**compact** *adj* compact, dense

**compagne** *n see* **compagnon**

**compagnie** *nf* company; party; firm; **fausser** ~ **à qn** give s/o the slip; **tenir** ~ **à qn** keep s/o company

**compagnon** (*f* **compagne**) *n* companion, comrade; ~ journeyman

**comparaison** *nf* comparison; **en** ~ **de** compared with

**comparaître** *vi* (68) appear before a court

**comparatif -ive** *adj* comparative

**comparer** *vt* compare; **littérature comparée** comparative literature

**comparse** *n theat* actor or actress in walk-on part; confederate

**compartiment** *nm* compartment; division

**compas** *nm* pair of compasses; mariner's compass

**compassé** *adj* formal, stiff

**compasser** *vt* measure with compasses; regulate; weigh (words)

**compassion** *nf* compassion, pity

**compatibilité** *nf* compatibility

**compatir** *vi* sympathize

**compatissant** *adj* compassionate

**compatriote** *n* compatriot

**compensateur -trice** *adj* compensating, equalizing

**compensation** *nf* compensation; **chambre de** ~ clearing house

**compenser** *vt* compensate, make up for; make good; *naut* adjust (compass)

**compère** *nm* accomplice, crony; compère, announcer; godfather

**compère-loriot** *nm* (*pl* **compères-loriots**) sty (eyelid)

**compétence** *nf* leg competence, jurisdiction; ability, skill; **ce n'est pas de ma** ~ that's outside my province

**compétent** *adj* competent (authority)

**compétitif -ive** *adj* competitive

**compilateur -trice** *n* compiler

**compilation** *nf* compiling, compilation

**compiler** *vt* compile

**complainte** *nf* lament

**complaire** *vi* (69) please, humour; **se** ~ **à** take a delight in

**complaisance** *nf* complaisance, obligingness; self-satisfaction; **ayez la** ~ **de** please be so kind as to; **par** ~ out of kindness

**complaisant** *adj* obliging, complaisant; self-satisfied

**complément** *nm* complement; *gramm* object

**complémentaire** *adj* complementary

**complet** *nm* suit; *adj* (*f* -**ète**) complete, entire; full (bus, theatre); **au** ~ full up

**compléter** *vt* (6) complete, finish off; make up

**complexe** *nm* complex; *coll* hang-up; *adj* complex; complicated; intricate

**complexion** *nf* constitution, temperament

**complexité** *nf* complexity

**complication** *nf* complication, intricacy

**complice** *n + adj* accessory, accomplice

**complicité** *nf* complicity

**complies** *nfpl eccles* compline

**compliment** *nm* compliment; **mes** ~s **à** give my kind regards to

**complimenter** *vt* compliment, congratulate

**compliqué** *adj* complicated, involved

**compliquer** *vt* complicate; **se** ~ **la vie** make life (unnecessarily) difficult for oneself

**complot** *nm* plot, conspiracy

**comploter** *vt + vi* plot, scheme

**componction** *nf* compunction

**comporter** *vt* admit, allow of; require; comprise, entail; **se** ~ behave

**composant** *adj* composing, component

**composé** *nm* compound

**composer** *vt* compose, form, make up; set (type); **temps composé** compound tense; *vi* come to terms

**composition** *nf* composition; arrangement; compromise; type-setting; **de bonne** ~ easy to get on with; **entrer en** ~ **avec qn** come to terms with s/o

**composter** *vt* date-stamp, validate (ticket)

**compote** *nf* stewed fruit, compote

**compotier** *nm* fruit-dish

**compréhensif -ive** *adj* comprehensive; understanding, tolerant

**compréhension** *nf* comprehension; indulgence, understanding

**comprendre** *vt* (75) understand; comprise, include; **cela se comprend** naturally; **faire** ~ **à qn** give s/o to understand; **je n'y comprends rien** I can't make it out; **se faire** ~ make oneself understood; **tout compris** inclusive; **y compris** including, inclusive of

**compresse** *nf med* compress

**compresseur** *nm* compressor; *eng* supercharger; **rouleau** ~ steam roller

**compression** *nf* compression; reduction; repression

**comprimable** *adj* compressible

**comprimé** *nm med* tablet

**comprimer** *vt* compress; squeeze; restrain (feelings)

**compris** *p part* **comprendre**

**compromettre** *vt* (60) compromise; endanger, jeopardize; *vi* compromise

**compromis** *nm* compromise

**comptabilité** *nf* book-keeping, accounts; accounts department; ~ **en partie simple (double)** single-(double-) entry book-keeping; **tenir la** ~ keep the books

**comptable** *n* accountant; *adj* accountable; responsible; **machine** ~ calculating machine

**comptant** *adj* **argent** ~ ready cash; *adv* **payer** ~ pay in cash

**compte** *nm* account, reckoning; amount, score; due; **à rebours** count-down; ~ **rendu** report, review; **à bon** ~ cheap; *sl* **avoir son** ~ be drunk; **en fin de** ~ all things considered; **le** ~ **y est** that's the right amount; **pour mon** ~ for my part; **régler son** ~ **à qn** settle s/o's hash; **se rendre** ~ **de qch** realize; **son** ~ **est bon** I'll settle him; **tenir** ~ **de qch** take sth into consideration

**compte-gouttes** *nm invar* dropper, pipette

**compter** *vt* count, number; reckon, value; pay out; charge for; **à pas**

**comptés** with measured tread; **sans** ~ ... not to mention ..., without counting ...; *vi* reckon, rely; be of consequence; **j'y compte bien** I'm banking on it

**compte-tours** *nm invar* rev counter

**compteur** *nm* counter, meter; speedometer; mileage indicator; parking meter

**comptine** *nf* children's song

**comptoir** *nm* counter; warehouse

**compulser** *vt* examine; go through (documents)

**computer** *vt* compute

**comte** *nm* count

**comté** *nm* county; cheese (from Franche-Comté district)

**comtesse** *nf* countess

**con** *nm vulg* cunt; *sl* fool, clot, dope; *adj* (*f* **conne**) *sl* stupid, dumb

**concasser** *vt* pound, crush

**concéder** *vt* (6) grant, concede, admit

**concentration** *nf* concentration; application

**concentré** *nm* extract, concentrate

**concentrer** *vt* concentrate; focus; contain (feelings); **lait concentré** condensed milk; **se** ~ concentrate

**concentrique** *adj* concentric

**conception** *nf* conception, idea; conceiving

**concernant** *prep* about, concerning, regarding

**concerner** *vt* concern, relate to, affect

**concert** *nm* concert; agreement, harmony; **agir de** ~ **avec qn** act in concert with s/o

**concerter** *vt* concert, plan; **se** ~ act in concert

**concessif -ive** *adj* concessive

**concession** *nf* concession; grant; conceding

**concessionnaire** *n* authorized agent; holder of a concession

**concevable** *adj* conceivable

**concevoir** *vt* conceive; understand, imagine; **ainsi conçu** worded as follows

**concierge** *n* caretaker, (hall-)porter

**concile** *nm eccles* council

**conciliabule** *nm* secret meeting

**conciliant** *adj* conciliatory

**concilier** *vt* conciliate, reconcile; win over

**concis** *adj* concise, terse

**concision** *nf* conciseness, brevity

**concitoyen -enne** *n* fellow-citizen; fellow-countryman (-countrywoman)

**concluant** *adj* conclusive; **peu** ~ inconclusive

**conclure** *vt* (25) conclude, end, finish; ~ **un marché** strike a bargain; *vi* come to a conclusion, infer

**conclusif**

**conclusif -ive** *adj* conclusive
**conclusion** *nf* conclusion; concluding; end; inference
**concombre** *nm* cucumber
**concomitant** *adj* concomitant, attendant
**concordance** *nf* concordance; agreement
**concordat** *nm eccles* concordat; bankrupt's certificate
**concorde** *nf* harmony, concord
**concorder** *vi* tally, agree
**concourant** *adj* concurrent
**concourir** *vi* (29) converge, concur; combine; compete
**concours** *nm* concourse, gathering; help, assistance; competition, competitive examination; **hors-~** not competing; **se présenter à un ~** go in for an examination (competition)
**concret -ète** *adj* concrete
**concrétion** *nf* coagulation; concretion
**conçu** *p part* **concevoir**
**concupiscence** *nf* lust
**concurrence** *nf* concurrence; competition
**concurrencer** *vt* (4) be in competition with
**concurrent -e** *n* competitor
**concussion** *nf* misappropriation; extortion
**condamnable** *adj* blameworthy, reprehensible
**condamnation** *nf* condemnation; conviction, sentence; censure
**condamné -e** *n* condemned man (woman)
**condamner** *vt* condemn; sentence, convict; censure; **~ un malade** give up hope for a sick person; **~ sa porte** refuse to see anyone; **~ une porte** block up a door
**condensateur** *nm* condenser
**condenser** *vt* condense
**condescendance** *nf* condescension
**condescendre** *vi* condescend
**condiment** *nm* seasoning, condiment
**condisciple** *nm* fellow-student, schoolfellow
**condition** *nf* condition; state; rank; **~s** conditions, circumstances; terms; **acheter sous ~** buy on approval; **à ~ de** providing; **dans ces ~s** under these circumstances; **être en ~** be in service; **être en ~ de faire qch** be in a fit state to do sth; **gens de ~** people of fashion, quality
**conditionnel -elle** *adj* conditional
**conditionner** *vt* condition; season
**condoléance** *nf* condolence
**conducteur -trice** *n* leader, guide, driver; conductor (heat, electricity)

**conductibilité** *nf* conductibility
**conductible** *adj* conductive
**conductivité** *nf* conductivity
**conduire** *vt* (80) conduct, lead, escort, accompany; drive (car, etc), steer; induce; manage; **se ~** behave
**conduit** *nm* conduit, duct, pipe
**conduite** *nf* conducting; driving; behaviour; management; piping, conduit; **~ intérieure** saloon car, *US* sedan; **changer de ~** mend one's ways; **faire un bout de ~ à qn** walk a little way with s/o
**confection** *nf* making, manufacture; ready-made clothes; **s'habiller en ~** get one's clothes off the peg
**confédéré** *adj* confederate
**confédérer** *vt* (6) confederate, unite
**conférence** *nf* conference; lecture; **maître de ~s** university lecturer
**conférencier -ière** *n* lecturer
**conférer** *vt* (6) confer, award; *vi* confer, talk
**confesse** *nf eccles* confession; **aller à ~** go to confession
**confesser** *vt* confess, own up; *eccles* hear confession of; **se ~** confess one's sins
**confesseur** *nm* confessor
**confession** *nf* confession; religious denomination
**confessionnel -elle** *adj* confessional; denominational
**confiance** *nf* trust, confidence; assurance; **abus de ~** breach of trust; **avoir ~ en qn** trust s/o; **crise de ~** credibility gap; **de (toute) ~** reliable; confidently
**confiant -e** *adj* trustful; confident; assured
**confidence** *nf* confidence (secret); **faire une ~ à qn** tell s/o a secret
**confident -e** *n* confidant
**confidentiel -ielle** *adj* confidential; **à titre ~** confidentially
**confier** *vt* trust, entrust, commit; disclose, confide; **~ qch à qn** entrust s/o with sth; tell s/o sth in confidence; **se ~ à qn** put one's trust in s/o; take s/o into one's confidence
**confiner** *vt* confine, shut up; *vi* border on
**confins** *nmpl* borders, confines
**confire** *vt* (26) preserve; pickle
**confirmatif -ive** *adj* confirmative
**confirmer** *vt* confirm, corroborate
**confiscation** *nf* confiscation, seizure
**confiserie** *nf* confectioner's shop; confectionery; preserving (in sugar)
**confiseur -euse** *n* confectioner; sweetmaker
**confisquer** *vt* confiscate
**confit** *adj* preserved, candied; pickled; **~ en dévotion** steeped in piety
**confiture** *nf* jam
**confiturier** *nm* jam-maker; jam-dish

**conflit** nm conflict, struggle; clash
**confluent** nm junction (rivers)
**confluer** vi meet (rivers)
**confondre** vt confound; confuse, mistake; mingle; embarrass; **se ~** blend; be identical; **se ~ en excuses** be profusely apologetic
**confondu** adj confounded; confused; dumbfounded
**conforme** adj conformable; consistent, corresponding
**conformément** adv according, in conformity
**conformer** vi shape; conform; **se ~** conform, comply
**conformité** nf conformity
**confort** nm comfort
**confortable** adj comfortable, cosy
**confrère** nm (professional) colleague; fellow-member
**confrérie** nf brotherhood; confraternity
**confrontation** nf confrontation; comparison
**confronter** vt confront (witnesses); collate
**confus** adj confused, mixed; indistinct, blurred; abashed; obscure
**confusément** adv confusedly; indistinctly; obscurely
**confusion** nf confusion; disorder; embarrassment
**congé** nm leave of absence, holiday; dismissal; discharge; permission; **donner ~** give notice; **donner ~ à qn** dismiss s/o, give s/o notice; **en ~** on leave; **prendre ~ de qn** take leave of s/o
**congédier** vt dismiss; discharge
**congélateur** nm freezer
**congélation** nf congelation, freezing
**congeler** vt (5) freeze; congeal
**congestion** nf med congestion; **~ cérébrale** stroke; **~ pulmonaire** pneumonia
**congestionné** adj congested; flushed
**congestionner** vt congest
**conglomérer** vt (6) conglomerate
**congratuler** vt congratulate, compliment
**congre** nm conger-eel
**congrès** nm congress
**congru** adj adequate, suitable; **portion ~e** barely adequate portion
**conifère** nm conifer; adj coniferous
**conique** adj conical
**conjecture** nf conjecture, surmise
**conjecturer** vt conjecture, surmise
**conjoindre** vt (55) join in marriage
**conjoint -e** n marriage partner, spouse
**conjoncteur** nm elect switch
**conjonctif -ive** adj conjunctive; connective (tissue)

**conjonction** nf connection; conjunction
**conjonctivite** nf conjunctivitis
**conjoncture** nf conjuncture, contingency; (economic) prospect
**conjugaison** nf conjugation
**conjugal** adj conjugal; **vie ~e** married life
**conjuguer** vt conjugate
**conjuration** nf plot, conspiracy; spell; **~s** entreaties
**conjuré -e** n conspirator
**conjurer** vt plot; conjure up; avert (danger); beseech; **se ~** plot together
**connaissance** nf knowledge; acquaintance; consciousness; **~s** learning; **en ~ de cause** with full knowledge of the facts; **en pays de ~** in familiar surroundings, among friends; **faire ~ avec qn, faire la ~ de qn** make s/o's acquaintance
**connaisseur -euse** n connoisseur, expert
**connaître** vt (68) know; be aware of; be acquainted with; coll **ça me connaît** I know all there is to know about that; **faire ~ qch** make sth known; **ne plus se ~** be beside oneself with rage; **on lui connaissait cette qualité-là** people knew he had that quality; **se (s'y) ~ (à) qch** be an expert in, know all about sth; **se faire ~** introduce oneself by name; become well-known
**connard** nm sl see con
**connecter** vt elect connect
**connerie** nf sl nonsense, absurdity; stupid behaviour
**connétable** nm hist High Constable
**connexion** nf connection
**connexité** nf kinship (ideas)
**connivence** nf connivance, complicity; **de ~ avec** in collusion with
**connu** adj (well-)known; certain
**conque** nf conch
**conquérant -e** n conqueror
**conquérir** vt (27) conquer; win over
**conquête** nf conquest; conquered territory
**consacrer** vt consecrate; ordain; dedicate; devote, assign; sanction; sanctify; **expression consacrée** stock phrase
**consanguin** adj consanguineous; **frère ~** half-brother on father's side
**consciemment** adv conscientiously
**conscience** nf consciousness; conscience; conscientiousness; **~ large** accommodating conscience; **avoir la ~ nette** have a clear conscience; **en ~** conscientiously; **sans ~** unscrupulous
**conscient** adj conscious
**conscrit** nm conscript
**consécration** nf consecration; dedication; ratification
**consécutif -ive** adj consecutive

**conseil** *nm* advice, counsel; council, committee; adviser; ~ **d'administration** board of directors; ~ **de guerre** council of war; court-martial; **homme de bon** ~ wise man; **la nuit porte** ~ better sleep on it; **prendre** ~ **de qn** ask s/o's advice; **tenir** ~ hold a council

**conseillable** *adj* advisable

¹**conseiller -ère** *n* adviser; councillor

²**conseiller** *vt* advise

**consentement** *nm* consent, assent

**consentir** *vt* (59) grant; *vi* consent, agree; **qui ne dit mot consent** silence means consent

**conséquence** *nf* consequence, outcome, result; **de** ~ important; **en** ~ accordingly; **sans** ~ unimportant; **tirer à** ~ be of importance

**conséquent** *adj* consistent; following; *coll* important; **par** ~ consequently

**conservateur -trice** *n* conservator, keeper; curator; conservative

**conservation** *nf* conserving, preserving; preservation; care; state of preservation

**conservatoire** *nm* academy (music, etc)

**conserve** *nf* preserved food; **naviguer de** ~ sail in convoy

**conserver** *vt* preserve; take care of; keep, maintain, keep up; **bien conservé** well preserved; **se** ~ keep

**considérable** *adj* considerable, large; eminent, important

**considération** *nf* consideration; thought; esteem, respect; **prendre en** ~ take into account

**considéré** *adj* circumspect

**considérer** *vt* (6) consider; gaze on; regard

**consignataire** *nm* consignee

**consignateur** *nm* consignor

**consignation** *nf* consignation, deposit; consignment

**consigne** *nf* *mil* order; confinement to barracks; (school) detention; left-luggage office, *US* check-room; deposit

**consigner** *vt* deposit; consign (goods); confine to barracks; detain; record, write down; put out of bounds

**consistance** *nf* consistency; firmness; **sans** ~ unfounded

**consistant** *adj* firm, solid

**consister** *vi* consist

**consistoire** *nm* *eccles* consistory

**consolateur -trice** *adj* comforting, consoling

**consolation** *nf* consolation, comfort

**consoler** *vt* console, comfort

**consolidation** *nf* consolidation; healing (fracture); funding

**consolider** *vt* consolidate, strengthen; fund; **se** ~ grow firm; heal (fracture)

**consommable** *adj* consumable

**consommateur -trice** *n* consumer; customer (in café)

**consommation** *nf* consumption; drink (in café); consummation

¹**consommé** *nm* clear soup; stock

²**consommé** *adj* consummate

**consommer** *vt* consume; consummate

**consomption** *nf* wasting, decline

**consonne** *nf* consonant

**consort -e** *n* consort; ~s associates

**consortium** *nm* consortium, trust

**conspirateur -trice** *n* conspirator

**conspiration** *nf* plot, conspiracy

**conspirer** *vt* plot; *vi* plot, conspire; tend

**conspuer** *vt* boo; decry

**constance** *nf* constancy; invariability

**constant** *adj* constant; firm

**constat** *nm* (official) report, affidavit

**constatation** *nf* verification, establishment (fact)

**constater** *vt* establish, ascertain, notice; find out; record

**consteller** *vt* constellate

**consterner** *vt* dismay

**constiper** *vt* constipate

**constituer** *vt* constitute, make up; institute, set up, settle (money); **se** ~ become, make oneself

**constitution** *nf* constitution; constituting; composition; settlement

**constitutionnel -elle** *adj* constitutional

**constricteur** *nm* constrictor

**constructeur -trice** *n* constructor, builder

**constructif -ive** *adj* constructive

**construction** *nf* construction, building; erection; edifice

**construire** *vt* (80) construct, build; put together; construe

**consulaire** *adj* consular

**consulat** *nm* consulate; consulship

**consultatif -ive** *adj* consultative; advisory

**consultation** *nf* consultation; (medical) advice; (legal) opinion; **heures de** ~ surgery hours

**consulter** *vt* consult; take advice

**consumer** *vt* consume; wear out

**contact** *nm* contact, touch; *elect* connection; **clef de** ~ ignition key; **couper le** ~ switch off; **perdre le** ~ lose touch

**contagieux -ieuse** *adj* contagious; infectious

**contagionner** *vt* infect

**contamination** *nf* contamination, infection

**contaminer** *vt* contaminate; infect

**conte** *nm* tale, story; fib

**contemplateur -trice** *n* contemplator

**contempler** *vt* contemplate; behold; reflect

**contemporain -e** *n* contemporary; *adj*

contemporary; contemporaneous

**contenance** nf capacity; bearing; **faire bonne ~** put on a good face

**conteneur** nm container

**contenir** vt (96) contain; restrain; control

**content** nm fill, sufficiency; adj content, satisfied; pleased; joyful

**contentement** nm contentment, satisfaction

**contenter** vt content, satisfy; **~ un créancier** pay a creditor; **se ~ de peu** be satisfied with little

**contentieux** nm disputed matter; **service du ~** legal department; adj (f -ieuse) contentious

**contenu** nm contents

**conter** vt tell, relate; **en ~ de belles** say absurd things; **s'en laisser ~** let oneself be fooled

**contestable** adj questionable, debatable

**contestataire** n protester; adj protesting

**contestation** nf contestation, dispute, objection

**conteste** nf **sans ~** unquestionably

**contester** vt contest, dispute; vi dispute

**conteur -euse** n story-teller; story-writer

**contexte** nm context

**contigu -uë** adj adjoining, contiguous

**contiguïté** nf contiguity

**continent** nm continent; mainland

**contingent** nm contingent; share; mil (conscript) intake

**contingentement** nm limiting; allocation, quota

**contingenter** vt fix a quota for; ration out

**continu** adj continuous; **courant ~** direct current

**continuel -elle** adj continual, unceasing

**continuer** vt continue, carry on

**continuité** nf continuity

**contorsion** nf contortion

**contour** nm outline, contour; winding, bend

**contournement** nm outlining; skirting, by-passing

**contourner** vt shape; by-pass, skirt; warp; **~ la loi** get round the law

**contraceptif** nm contraceptive; adj (f -ive) contraceptive

**contracter** vt contract; incur; acquire (habit); catch (illness); **traits contractés** drawn features

**contraction** nf contraction, shrinking; narrowing

**contractuel -uelle** n contractual; **(agent) ~** unestablished public servant, esp traffic-warden; adj contractual

**contradicteur** nm contradictor

**contradiction** nf contradiction; discrepancy; **esprit de ~** cussedness

**contradictoire** adj contradictory; inconsistent; conflicting

**contraindre** vt (55) constrain; restrain; compel, force

**contraint** adj constrained; forced, awkward, stiff

**contrainte** nf constraint; restraint; compulsion; **sans ~** freely

**contraire** nm opposite; **au ~** on the contrary; adj contrary, opposite; adverse; harmful

**contrarier** vt oppose, cross; annoy; contrast (colours)

**contrariété** nf annoyance, vexation; contrariety

**contraste** nm contrast; **faire ~ avec** contrast with

**contrat** nm contract; deed; agreement; **passer un ~ avec** enter into an agreement with

**contravention** nf contravention, infringement, breach; summary conviction; **dresser une ~ à qn** give s/o a ticket

**contre** nm opposite; **le pour et le ~** the pros and cons; **par ~** on the other hand; prep + adv against; contrary to; in exchange for; up against

**contre-amiral** nm rear-admiral

**contre-attaque** nf counter-attack

**contre-attaquer** vt counter-attack

**contre-balancer** vt (4) counter-balance, offset

**contrebande** nf contraband, smuggling

**contrebandier** nm smuggler

**contre-bas (en)** adv phr down, below; downwards

**contrebasse** nf mus double-bass

**contrebasson** nm double-bassoon

**contrecarrer** vt thwart, cross

**contrecœur (à)** adv phr grudgingly, against one's will

**contre-coup** nm rebound, recoil; repercussion; consequence

**contre-courant** nm counter-current; **à ~** against the stream

**contre-danse** nf quadrille; sl police ticket

**contredire** vt (74) contradict; be inconsistent with

**contredit (sans)** adv phr unquestionably

**contrée** nf region; country, district

**contre-écrou** nm lock-nut

**contre-espionnage** nm counter-espionage

**contrefaçon** nf counterfeiting; forgery; infringement (copyright)

**contrefaire** vt (46) imitate, mimic; counterfeit; forge; pirate

**contrefait** adj feigned; forged; pirated; deformed (person)

**contre-fil** nm opposite direction

**contre-filet** *nm* sirloin
**contrefort** *nm* buttress; ~ s foothills
**contre-haut (en)** *adv phr* higher up
**contre-indication** *nf med* contra-indication
**contre-indiquer** *vt* counter-indicate
**contre-interrogatoire** *nm* cross-examination
**contre-jour** *nm* light from behind; **à ~** against the light
**contremaître** *nm* foreman
**contremander** *vt* countermand, cancel, revoke
**contre-manifestation** *nf* counter-demonstration
**contremarche** *nf* countermarch
**contremarque** *nf* counter-mark (gold, etc); pass-out check; voucher
**contre-offensive** *nf* counter-offensive
**contre-ordre** *nm* counter-order, countermand
**contrepartie** *nf* counterpart; duplicate; cross-entry; opposite view; *sp* return match; **en ~** in exchange, as against this
**contre-passer** *vt* endorse back; reverse (entry in book-keeping)
**contrepèterie** *nf* spoonerism
**contre-pied** *nm* opposite; **prendre le ~** take the opposite view or course
**contre-plaqué** *nm* plywood; *adj* laminated
**contrepoids** *nm* counterweight; counterpoise
**contre-poil (à)** *adv phr* against the way of the hair (fur); **prendre qn à ~** rub s/o up the wrong way
**contrepoint** *nm mus* counterpoint
**contrepoison** *nm* antidote
**contre-proposition** *nf* counter-proposal, counter-suggestion
**contrer** *vt* counter (boxing); double (cards); oppose
**contre-révolution** *nf* counter-revolution
**contre-saison** *nf* off-season period
**contrescarpe** *nf* counterscarp
**contre-sceau** *nm* counterseal
**contresens** *nm* wrong way; wrong sense; false interpretation; **à ~** in the wrong direction or sense
**contresigner** *vt* countersign
**contretemps** *nm* mishap, hitch; inconvenience; *mus* note played against the beat; **à ~** inopportunely
**contre-torpilleur** *nm* destroyer
**contrevenant -e** *n* infringer; delinquent
**contrevenir** *vi* (96) contravene, infringe
**contrevent** *nm* shutter (window)
**contre-voie (à)** *adv phr* (train) on the wrong side, in the wrong direction
**contribuable** *n* taxpayer, ratepayer

**contribuer** *vt* contribute; *vi* conduce
**contributif -ive** *adj* contributive
**contribution** *nf* contribution; tax, rate; **mettre qn à ~** make s/o contribute
**contrister** *vt* sadden
**contrit** *adj* contrite, penitent
**contrition** *nf* contrition, penitence
**contrôle** *nm* roll, register; checking, testing, control, verification; auditing; hall-mark; check-point; box-office
**contrôler** *vt* control; check, inspect; stamp; audit; examine (passport); hold in check
**contrôleur -euse** *n* controller; ticket-inspector, ticket-collector; tax-inspector; auditor; supervisor; *nm* checking apparatus
**controuvé** *adj* fabricated, made up
**controverse** *nf* controversy
**controverser** *vt* question, dispute
**contumace** *nf* contumacy, non-appearance; **par ~** by default, in absentia
**contusion** *nf* bruise, contusion
**contusionner** *vt* bruise
**convaincre** *vt* (94) convince; prove
**convenable** *adj* appropriate, suitable, fitting; decent
**convenance** *nf* fitness, suitability, propriety; conformity; convenience; **observer (respecter) les ~s** act with propriety
**convenir** *vi* (96) suit, fit; agree; admit; **il convient de** the right thing to do is
**convention** *nf* convention; agreement; **de ~** conventional
**conventionné** *adj* bound by agreement; **médecin ~** = doctor in national health service
**conventionnel -elle** *adj* conventional
**convenu** *adj* agreed, appointed
**converger** *vi* (3) converge
**conversation** *nf* conversation, talk; **lier ~** enter into conversation
**converser** *vi* converse, talk
**conversion** *nf* conversion, change; *mil* wheeling; altering of interest rate
**converti -e** *n* convert
**convertir** *vt* convert
**convexe** *adj* convex
**conviction** *nf* conviction; *leg* **pièce à ~** exhibit
**convier** *vt* invite; urge
**convive** *n* guest, table-companion
**convocation** *nf* summons, convocation; convening; calling up
**convoi** *nm* convoy; train, group of vehicles; escort; ~ **funèbre** funeral procession
**convoiter** *vt* covet, desire; lust after
**convoitise** *nf* covetousness, greed, cupidity
**convoler** *vi* marry, quit the single state

**convoquer** *vt* summon, convoke; convene; invite

**convoyer** *vt* (7) convoy, escort

**convulser** *vt* convulse

**convulsif -ive** *adj* convulsive

**convulsionner** *vt* convulse

**coopérateur -trice** *n* co-operator

**coopératif -ive** *adj* co-operative stores; co-operative (producers, etc)

**coopérer** *vi* (6) co-operate, work together

**coopter** *vt* co-opt

**coordonnées** *nfpl coll* personal details

**coordonner** *vt* co-ordinate

**copain** *nm coll* pal, mate, *US* buddy

**copeau** *nm* (wood) shaving; chip (metal)

**copie** *nf* copy, reproduction; paper, script (examination); imitation; **pour ~ conforme** certified true copy

**copier** *vt* copy, transcribe; reproduce; imitate

**copieux -ieuse** *adj* copious

**copilote** *n* co-pilot

**copine** *nf* girl friend

**copiste** *n* copier, copyist; imitator

**copropriétaire** *n* co-proprietor, joint owner

**copropriété** *nf* co-proprietorship, joint ownership

**copte** *n + adj* Copt, coptic

**coq** *nm* cock; weather-cock; **~ de bruyère** grouse; **au chant du ~** at cockcrow; **comme un ~ en pâte** in clover; **le ~ du village** cock of the walk

**coq-à-l'âne** *nm invar* string of non-sequiturs

**coque** *nf* shell; husk; hull; bow (ribbon); **œuf à la ~** soft-boiled egg

**coquelicot** *nm* (field) poppy

**coqueluche** *nf* whooping-cough; *coll* popular person

**coquerico** *nm* cock-a-doodle-doo

**coquerie** *nf* ship's galley

**coquet -ette** *adj* coquettish; smart, attractive, trim

**coqueter** *vi* (5) flirt, act the coquette

**coquetier** *nm* egg-cup; egg-seller

**coquette** *nf* flirt, coquette

**coquetterie** *nf* coquetry, coquettishness; fastidiousness; smartness

**coquillage** *nm* shell-fish, sea-shell

**coquille** *nf* shell (snail, etc); misprint; casing (motor); **~ Saint-Jacques** scallop; **escalier en ~** spiral staircase

**coquin -e** *n* rascal, rogue; *adj* rascally, roguish

**coquinerie** *nf* roguery; knavery

**cor** *nm* horn; horn-player; corn (foot); tine (antler); **~ anglais** tenor oboe; **à ~ et à cri** vociferously; **sonner du ~** sound the horn

**corail** *nm* (*pl* **coraux**) coral

**corallin** *adj* coral-red

**Coran (le)** *nm* Koran

**corbeau** *nm* crow; *archi* corbel

**corbeille** *nf* basket; (round) flower-bed; *archi* bell; *theat* dress-circle; **~ d'argent** shepherd's purse; **~ de mariage, de noces** wedding presents

**corbillard** *nm* hearse

**cordage** *nm* rope; roping; **~s** ropes, cordage

**corde** *nf* rope, cord, line; string; **~ à linge** clothes line; **~ à sauter** skipping rope; **~ de boyau** catgut; **avoir plusieurs ~s à son arc** have more than one string to one's bow; **ce n'est pas dans mes ~s** that's not in my line; **tenir la ~** be on the inside; have the advantage; **usé jusqu'à la ~** threadbare

**cordeau** *nm* line, tracing line

**cordée** *nf* party of mountaineers roped together

**cordelette** *nf* small cord; plait

**cordelier -ière** *n* Franciscan friar (nun)

**cordelière** *nf* friar's girdle; pyjama-cord

**cordelle** *nf* tow-line

**corder** *vt* twist into rope, cord; string

**corderie** *nf* rope-making; rope-trade; rope-walk

**cordial** *nm* cordial, restorative; *adj* cordial, hearty; stimulating

**cordialité** *nf* cordiality, heartiness

**cordier** *nm* rope-maker; tail-piece (violin)

**cordon** *nm* cord, string, strand, thread; lace; ribbon (decoration); cordon (troops); **~ de sonnette** bell-pull; **~ souple** flex

**cordon-bleu** *nm* (*pl* **cordons-bleus**) *coll* first-rate cook

**cordonner** *vt* twist, twine

**cordonnerie** *nf* shoemaking; cobbler's workshop

**cordonnet** *nm* braid, cord

**cordonnier** *nm* shoemaker, cobbler

**Corée** *nf* Korea

**coreligionnaire** *n* person of the same religion

**coriace** *adj* tough, hard; *coll* obstinate

**Corinthe** *nf* **raisin de ~** currant

**cormoran** *nm* cormorant

**cornac** *nm* mahout

**corne** *nf* horn, horny matter; feeler, antenna; motor-horn; **~ d'abondance** cornucopia; **~ d'une page** dog's ear; **chapeau à ~s** cocked hat; *coll* **faire les ~s à** jeer at; **porter des ~s** be a cuckold

**corné** *adj* horny; dog-eared

**cornée** *nf* cornea

**corneille** *nf* crow, rook

**cornemuse** *nf* bagpipes

**corner** *vt* proclaim; turn down (corner

cornet

of a page); *vi* trumpet, blow the horn, hoot

**cornet** *nm* small horn; dice-box; cornet; cream horn; **à pistons** cornet

**cornette** *nf* nun's cornet; *naut* burgee

**corniaud** *nm sl* fool, clot

**corniche** *nf* cornice; ledge (rock); cliff road

**cornichon** *nm* gherkin; *coll* fool, clot

**Cornouailles** *nf* Cornwall

**cornu** *adj* horned

**cornue** *nf* retort

**corollaire** *nm* corollary

**corolle** *nf bot* corolla

**coron** *nm dial* mining village

**corporatif -ive** *adj* corporate

**corporation** *nf* corporation; guild

**corporel -elle** *adj* corporal, bodily; corporeal

**corps** *nm* body; substance, main part; corps; trunk (tree, body); frame (bicycle); **à** hand to hand; **composé** compound; **de garde** guard-room; **simple** element; **à bras le** round the waist; **à perdu** headlong; **avoir le diable au** be bursting with devilment; **faire avec** be an integral part of; **garde du** body-guard; **périr et biens** go down with all hands; **prendre** take shape; **se donner et âme** give oneself heart and soul

**corpulence** *nf* corpulence, stoutness

**corpulent** *adj* stout, fat, corpulent

**corpus** *nm* body (work, vocabulary)

**corpuscule** *nm* corpuscle

**correct** *adj* correct, accurate; proper (behaviour, etc)

**correcteur -trice** *n* corrector; proof-reader

**correctif -ive** *adj* corrective

**correction** *nf* correction, correcting; proof-reading; punishment; correctness; **maison de** reformatory

**correctionnel -elle** *adj* tribunal magistrate's court, police court

**correctionnelle** *nf* magistrate's court, police court

**corrélatif -ive** *adj* correlative

**correspondance** *nf* correspondence; agreement; connection (train, etc); communication (places)

**correspondant** *nm* correspondent; person in loco parentis; *adj* corresponding; connecting (train, etc)

**correspondre** *vi* correspond; agree, tally; communicate (rooms); run in connection (train, etc)

**corrida** *nf* bull-fight; *coll* free-for-all; complicated business

**corridor** *nm* corridor, passage

**corrigé** *nm* fair copy (exercise)

**corriger** *vt* (3) correct, read (proofs);

sub-edit; rectify; amend; punish, chastise; **se d'un défaut** cure a fault

**corroborer** *vt* corroborate

**corroder** *vt* corrode, eat away

**corrompre** *vt* (85) corrupt, pervert, deprave; bribe; taint (meat)

**corrosif -ive** *adj* corrosive

**corrupteur -trice** *n* corrupter; briber; *adj* corrupting, depraving

**corruptible** *adj* corruptible; bribable

**corruption** *nf* corruption; bribing; tainting; decay; corruptness, depravity

**corsage** *nm* bodice

**corsaire** *nm* privateer; pirate, corsaire; **pantalon** calf-length trousers, breeches

**Corse** *nf* Corsica

**corse** *adj* Corsican

**corsé** *adj* full-bodied; stout (cloth); spicy (story)

**corser** *vt* give body to; strengthen; **se** become serious, complex (affair)

**corso** *nm* **fleuri** floral procession

**cortège** *nm* procession; train, retinue

**corvée** *nf* forced labour; *mil* fatigue; *coll* chore, piece of drudgery

**cosaque** *nm* Cossack

**cosinus** *nm* cosine

**cosmétique** *nm* + *adj* cosmetic

**cosmique** *adj* cosmic

**cosmographie** *nf* cosmography

**cosmonaute** *n* cosmonaut, astronaut, spaceman (-woman)

**cosmopolite** *adj* cosmopolitan

**cosse** *nf* husk, shell, pod; *elect* spade terminal; *sl* **avoir la** feel like doing nothing

**cossu** *adj* rich, well-to-do; rich-looking, grand

**costaud** *nm* tough guy, strong man; *adj* tough, hefty

**costume** *nm* costume dress; suit; (~) **tailleur** lady's tailor-made costume

**costumer** *vt* dress; **bal costumé** fancy-dress ball

**costumier -ière** *n* costumier; wardrobe-keeper

**cote** *nf* mark, number (classification); quota, share; quotation (stock-exchange); odds (race); assessment; marks (school exercise); **d'alerte** danger point; **mal taillée** compromise; **avoir une bonne** be highly thought of

**côte** *nf* coast, shore; rib; slope, hill; **à** side by side; **à mi-** half-way up the hill; **être à la** be on one's beam-ends; **la Côte d'Azur** the French riviera

**côté** *nm* side; **faible** weak spot; **à** to one side; near; **à de** next to; **de** on one side; sideways; **de et**

68

**d'autre** in all directions; **de mon** ~ for my part; **du** ~ **de** towards; **mettre de** ~ save, put by

**coteau** *nm* slope, hillside; hill

**côtelé** *adj* ribbed; **velours** ~ corduroy

**côtelette** *nf* chop, cutlet

**coter** *vt* number, classify; assess; quote (shares); award (marks)

**coterie** *nf* set, coterie

**côtier -ière** *adj* coasting; coastal; inshore

**cotillon** *nm* cotillon; *ar* petticoat

**cotisation** *nf* clubbing together; quota, share; contribution; assessment

**cotiser (se)** *v refl* club together, subscribe

**coton** *nm* cotton; *coll* **filer un mauvais** ~ be in a bad way

**cotonnade** *nf* cotton fabric

**cotonner (se)** *v refl* become fluffy; become sleepy (fruit)

**cotonneux -euse** *adj* cottony, downy; sleepy (fruit)

**cotonnier** *nm* cotton plant

**coton-poudre** *nm* gun cotton

**côtoyer** *vt* (7) hug (shore), keep close to, skirt; border

**cotte** *nf* skirt, petticoat, tunic; ~ **de mailles** coat of mail

**cou** *nm* neck; **prendre ses jambes à son** ~ take to one's heels

**couac** *nm* goose-note

**couard -e** *n* coward

**couardise** *nf* cowardice

**couchage** *nm* bedding; **sac de** ~ sleeping-bag

**couchant** *nm* sunset; west; *adj* **soleil** ~ setting sun

**couche** *nf* layer, bed, nappy, *US* diaper; social stratum; *lit* bed; ~**s** confinement; **fausse** ~ miscarriage; *sl* **il en a (tient) une** ~! he's a prize idiot!

**coucher** *nm* bedtime; sunset; *vt* put to bed; put up, accommodate; lay down; ~ **par écrit** put down in writing; ~ **qn sur son testament** mention s/o in one's will; **être couché** be in bed; be lying down; *vi* sleep, spend the night; **se** ~ lie down; go to bed; set (sun)

**coucherie** *nf coll* sleeping around

**couchette** *nf* bunk, berth, couchette; cot

**coucheur -euse** *nm sl* bedfellow; *nm sl* womanizer; **mauvais** ~ difficult person to get on with

**couci-couça** *adv coll* so-so

**coude** *nm* elbow; bend (road); knee (pipe); ~ **à** ~ side by side; **jouer des** ~**s** elbow one's way; *sl* **lever le** ~ drink a lot

**coudée** *nf* cubit; **avoir ses** ~**s franches** have a free hand; have elbow-room

**cou-de-pied** *nm* (*pl* **cous-de-pied**) instep

**couder** *vt* bend (pipe); crank (shaft)

**coudoyer** *vt* (7) jostle; elbow

**coudre** *vt* (28) sew, stitch; **cousu de fil blanc** easily seen through; **machine à** ~ sewing-machine

**coudrier** *nm* hazel-tree

**couenne** *nf* skin (pig), rind; membrane (diphtheria)

**couic** *nm* chirp, cheep, squeak

**couille** *nf vulg* ball, testicle

**couillon** *nm sl* fool, clot, dope; *vulg* ball

**coulage** *nm* pouring (metal); casting; leaking; scuttling; waste

**coulant** *adj* flowing, running; easy-going; **nœud** ~ slip-knot

**coulée** *nf* running, flow; outflow (lava); casting

**couler** *vt* pour; sink; scuttle; slip; cast; ruin (person); *coll* slip (coin, note); *sl* **se la** ~ **douce** take things easy; *vi* flow, run; leak; sink; trickle; pass by (time); ~ **de source** happen effortlessly; be self-evident

**couleur** *nf* colour, hue, colouring; paint; appearance; complexion; paint; **boîte de** ~**s** paint-box; **changer de** ~ turn pale; **il m'en fait voir de toutes les** ~**s** he's a real trial to me; **marchand de** ~**s** ironmonger; **sous** ~ **de** under the guise of

**couleuvre** *nf* grass-snake; **avaler des** ~ swallow insults

**coulis** *nm* broth; (plaster) filling

**coulissant** *adj* sliding (*esp* door)

**coulisse** *nf* groove, slide; hem; ~ **s** wings (theatre); **dans les** ~**s** back-stage; in the background; **trombone à** ~ slide trombone

**couloir** *nm* corridor, passage-way; gully; lane (traffic)

**coup** *nm* blow, knock, stroke; shot; attempt; threat; influence; ~ **de coude** nudge; ~ **de couteau** stab; ~ **de crayon** pencil-stroke; ~ **de dents** bite; ~ **d'essai** first attempt; *coll* ~ **de fil** phone call; ~ **de foudre** love at first sight; ~ **d'œil** glance; ~ **de poing** punch; ~ **de sang** apoplectic fit; ~ **de téléphone** telephone call; ~ **de tête** impulsive act; ~ **sur** ~ repeatedly; **à** ~ **s de** with (by means of) blows from; **à** ~ **sûr** certainly; **après** ~ too late; **boire un** ~ have a drink; **donner un** ~ **de main à qn** give s/o a helping hand; *coll* **du** ~ as a result; **du premier** ~ from the very first; **entrer en** ~ **de vent** burst in; **être aux cent** ~**s** be at one's wits' end; *coll* **être dans le** ~ be with it; **faire d'une pierre deux** ~**s** kill two birds with one stone; **faire les quatre cents** ~**s** get up to all sorts of tricks; **il m'a fait un sale** ~ he played me a dirty trick; **manquer (rater) son** ~ fail; **monter le** ~ deceive, fool; **porter un**

~ deal a blow; **pour le** ~ for once; **sous le** ~ de under the threat of, as a result of; **sur le** ~ immediately; **tenir le** ~ resist; **valoir le** ~ be worth it

**coupable** *adj* guilty; sinful

**coupage** *nm* watering (wine)

**coup-de-poing** *nm* (*pl* **coups-de-poing**) ~ **américain** knuckle duster

**coupe** *nf* (wine-)cup; fruit-bowl; cutting; cut (coat, etc); division (verse); section; cut (cards); *coll* **être sous la** ~ **de qn** be under s/o's thumb

**coupé** *nm* brougham

**coupe-cigares** *nm invar* cigar-cutter

**coupe-circuit** *nm invar elect* cut-out

**coupe-file** *nm invar* pass, police permit

**coupe-gorge** *nm invar* cut-throat alley, death trap

**coupe-jarret** *nm* ruffian, cut-throat

**coupe-ongles** *nm invar* nail-clippers

**coupe-papier** *nm invar* paper-knife

**couper** *vt* cut; intersect, cross; interrupt, cut off; water (wine); mix, blend; cut (cards); trump; switch off; geld; ~ **la parole à qn** cut s/o short; ~ **l'appétit à qn** take s/o's appetite away; *vi* cut; be sharp; **se** ~ cut oneself; crack (skin); intersect; contradict oneself

**couperet** *nm* cleaver, chopper; knife

**couperosé** *adj* blotchy

**coupeur -euse** *n* cutter

**couple** *nm* couple, pair; coupling; *nf* brace, couple; leash

**couplet** *nm* verse (song)

**coupoir** *nm* cutter

**coupole** *nf* cupola; *coll* **sous la Coupole** in the French Academy

**coupon** *nm* cutting, piece (of material), remnant; coupon; counterfoil

**coupure** *nf* cut, gash; cutting; section or piece cut out; note of small denomination

**cour** *nf* court; court of law; yard; courtyard; playground (school); **être bien en** ~ be in favour; **faire la** ~ **à qn** pay court to s/o; court s/o

**courage** *nm* courage, bravery

**courageux -euse** *adj* brave, courageous; spirited, hard-working

**couramment** *adv* fluently; readily; generally, usually

**courant** *nm* current, stream; forward movement; ~ **d'air** draught; **dans le** ~ **du mois** during the course of the month; **être au** ~ **de** know all about; **mettre qn au** ~ inform s/o; *adj* running, flowing; current; **écriture** ~ **e** cursive handwriting; **fin** ~ at the end of this month; **le 5** ~ the fifth inst.

**courbatu** *adj* stiff, aching

**courbature** *nf* stiffness

**courbaturer** *vt* tire out, wear out;

founder (horse)

**courbe** *nf* curve, bend; *adj* curved

**courber** *vt* + *vi* bend, curve; **se** ~ stoop, bend; bow

**courbette** *nf* **faire des** ~ s bow and scrape

**courbure** *nf* curvature

**courette** *nf* little yard, small courtyard

**coureur -euse** *n* runner; racer; frequenter; *coll* wolf, tart

**courge** *nf* gourd, marrow

**courgette** *nf* young marrow, courgette

**courir** *vt* (29) hunt, pursue; run (risk); wander over; frequent; **l'argent ne court pas les rues** money doesn't grow on trees; *vi* run; race; sail (ship); **le bruit court** rumour has it; **par le temps qui court** nowadays

**courlis** *nm* curlew

**couronne** *nf* crown, coronet; wreath; crown (coin, tooth)

**couronnement** *nm* crowning, coronation; capping, coping (wall); summit, perfection

**couronner** *vt* crown; honour, award a prize; cap, cope

**courre** *vt ar* **chasse à** ~ hunting (with hounds)

**courrier** *nm* courier, messenger; mail, correspondence, post; column (newspaper); **par retour de** ~ by return (of post)

**courroie** *nf* strop, thong; *mech* belt

**courroucer** *vt* (4) *lit* anger

**courroux** *nm lit* anger

**cours** *nm* course; flow, current; lesson, course of study; text book; currency, circulation; rate; price (commodities); ~ **d'eau** stream; **avoir** ~ be legal tender; be generally accepted; **donner libre** ~ **à** give free rein to

**course** *nf* running, run; race; excursion, trip; errand; course; ~ s (horse) races; **champ de** ~ race-course; **faire ses** ~ s do one's shopping; **n'être plus dans la** ~ be left behind, be out of the running

**coursier** *nm lit* warhorse, charger

¹**court** *nm* tennis-court

²**court** *adj* short, brief; **à** ~ **de** short of; **avoir la vue** ~ **e** be short-sighted, lack foresight; **de** ~ **e durée** short-lived; **pris de** ~ taken unawares; *adv* short; **rester** (**demeurer**) ~ stop short (speech); **tout** ~ simply

**courtage** *nm* brokerage

**courtaud** *adj* thickset, squat, short and stocky

**court-bouillon** *nm* (*pl* **courts-bouillons**) stock for cooking fish (with wine, butter, spices)

**court-circuit** *nm* (*pl* **courts-circuits**) short circuit

**courtepointe** *nf* counterpane
**courtier** *nm* broker
**courtisan** *nm* courtier
**courtisane** *nf* courtesan
**courtiser** *vt* court, pay court to; fawn on; woo
**courtois** *adj* courteous, polite; courtly
**courtoisie** *nf* courtesy, politeness
**court-vêtue** *adj f* short-skirted
**couru** *adj* popular, in demand; *coll* c'est ~ it's a cert
**couseuse** *nf* seamstress
¹**cousin -e** *n* cousin; ~ **germain** first cousin
²**cousin** *nm* gnat, daddy-long-legs
**cousinage** *nm* cousinship
**cousiner** *vi* live on good terms
**coussin** *nm* cushion
**coussinet** *nm* small cushion; *mech* bearing, bush; chair (rail)
**cousu** *p part* **coudre**
**coût** *nm* cost
**couteau** *nm* knife; ~ **à découper** carving-knife; **à ~x tirés** at daggers drawn
**coutelas** *nm* cutlass
**coutelier** *nm* cutler
**coutellerie** *nf* cutlery; cutler's shop
**coûter** *vi* cost; be hard, difficult; ~ **les yeux de la tête** cost a fortune; **coûte que coûte** at all costs; **prix coûtant** cost price
**coûteux -euse** *adj* costly, expensive; **peu** ~ inexpensive
**coutil** *nm* twill, drill
**coutume** *nf* custom, habit, practice; **de** ~ usually; **une fois n'est pas** ~ one swallow doesn't make a summer
**coutumier -ière** *adj* in the habit of; customary; ~ **du fait** in the habit of doing it; **droit** ~ common law
**couture** *nf* needlework, sewing; seam; scar; *coll* **battre à plate** ~ beat hollow, lick; **examiner sous toutes les** ~**s** inspect thoroughly; **haute** ~ high-class fashion-trade
**couturer** *vt* scar; seam
**couturier -ière** *n* dress-designer; dressmaker
**couvage** *nm* incubation
**couvaison** *nf* brooding time
**couvée** *nf* clutch, sitting (eggs); brood
**couvent** *nm* convent
**couver** *vt* sit on (eggs); brood; sicken for; lavish attention on; ~ **qn des yeux** gaze fondly on s/o; *vi* smoulder; be brewing
**couvercle** *nm* lid, cap, top
**couvert** *nm* shelter, cover; knife, fork and spoon; place (at table); cover charge; **à** ~ under cover; **mettre le** ~ lay the table; **sous le** ~ **de** under cover

of
**couverture** *nf* cover, covering; blanket, rug; roofing; ~ **de lit** bedspread; **tirer la** ~ **à soi** take the lion's share
**couveuse** *nf* sitting-hen; incubator
**couvre-chef** *nm* headdress, hat
**couvre-feu** *nm* curfew
**couvre-lit** *nm* bedspread, counterpane
**couvre-livre** *nm* dust-jacket
**couvre-pied(s)** *nm* coverlet; bedspread
**couvre-plat** *nm* dish-cover
**couvreur** *nm* roofer; tiler, slater, thatcher
**couvrir** *vt* (30) cover; roof; clothe; shield, protect, safeguard; drown (noise); **se** ~ put on clothes; put on a hat; become overcast
**crabe** *nm* crab
**crac** *nm* + *interj* crack, snap
**crachat** *nm* spittle, spit; *coll* **se noyer dans un** ~ make a mountain out of a molehill
**crachement** *nm* spitting, spit
**cracher** *vt* spit out; *sl* cough up (money); *coll* **tout craché** the spitting image of; *vi* spit
**crachin** *nm* mist, fine drizzle
**crachoir** *nm* spittoon; *sl* **tenir le** ~ hold forth
**crack** *nm coll* ace, champion
**crackage**, **craquage** *nm* cracking (oil)
**craie** *nf* chalk
**craindre** *vt* (55) fear, dread; be unable to stand (something)
**crainte** *nf* fear, dread; **de (dans la)** ~ **de** for fear of
**craintif -ive** *adj* timid, fearful
**cramoisi** *adj* crimson
**crampe** *nf* cramp
**crampon** *nm* cramp-iron; hook-nail, stud; *coll* bore; ~**s** crampons
**cramponner** *vt* clamp together; *coll* pester, button-hole, stick to; **se** ~ **à** hang on to
**cran** *nm* notch; cog; *coll* nerve; ~ **de sûreté** safety-catch; **couteau à** ~ **d'arrêt** flick knife; **être à** ~ be exasperated
¹**crâne** *nm* skull
²**crâne** *adj* plucky, jaunty
**crâner** *vi coll* show off
**crânien -ienne** *adj* cranial; **boîte** ~ **ne** skull
**crapaud** *nm* toad; low easy chair; baby grand piano; *coll* kid
**crapouillot** *nm coll* (trench) mortar; mortar-bomb
**crapule** *nf* debauchery; riff-raff; scoundrel
**crapuleux -euse** *adj* dissolute, crapulous
**craque** *nf coll* tall story
**craqueler** *vt* (5) *cer* crackle

**craquelure** nf crack
**craquer** vi crack, crackle; crunch; creak
¹**crasse** nf dirt, filth; dross; mire; avarice; sl **faire une ~ à qn** play a dirty trick on s/o
²**crasse** adj ignorance **~** gross ignorance
**crasser** vt clog, foul
**crasseux -euse** adj dirty, filthy; sl stingy
**crassier** nm slag-heap
**cratère** nm crater, shell-hole
**cravache** nf riding-whip
**cravacher** vt flog (horse); horsewhip
**cravate** nf tie; cravat, scarf; coll **~ de chanvre** hangman's rope
**crayère** nf chalk-pit
**crayeux -euse** adj chalky
**crayon** nm pencil, crayon
**crayonnage** nm pencilling
**crayonner** vt pencil; jot down; make a pencil sketch of
**créance** nf credit; belief; **lettres de ~** credentials
**créancier -ière** n creditor
**créateur -trice** n creator; adj creative
**création** nf creation; founding
**crécelle** nf rattle; **voix de ~** rasping voice
**crécerelle** nf kestrel
**crèche** nf manger; crib, day-nursery
**crédence** nf sideboard, buffet
**crédibilité** nf credibility
**crédit** nm credit; repute; influence; **à ~** on credit; **faire ~ à qn** give s/o credit
**créditer** vt credit
**créditeur -trice** n creditor
**credo** nm creed
**crédule** adj credulous
**crédulité** nf credulity
**créer** vt create; found, establish
**crémaillère** nf pot-hanger; mech toothed rack; **chemin de fer à ~** cog-wheel railway; **pendre la ~** give a house-warming party
**crémation** nf cremation
**crématoire** adj crematory; **four ~** crematorium
**crème** nf cream; **un (café) ~** a white coffee
**crémer** vt (6) cream
**crémerie** nf dairy (shop), creamery; small restaurant
**crémeux -euse** adj creamy
**crémier -ière** n dairyman, dairywoman
**créneau** nm crenel, battlement; space, interval
**créneler** vt (5) crenelate; notch (wheel); mill (coin)
**crénelure** nf crenellation
**créosoter** vt creosote
¹**crêpe** nf pancake
²**crêpe** nm crepe; mourning band
**crêpelé** adj fuzzy

**crêper** vt frizz; crimp; coll **se ~ le chignon** fly at one another (women)
**crépir** vt rough-cast (wall); grain (leather)
**crépitement** nm crackling
**crépiter** vi crackle; patter; sputter
**crépu** adj fuzzy, frizzy
**crépusculaire** adj twilight, crepuscular
**crépuscule** nm twilight, dusk
**cresson** nm cress; **~ de fontaine** water-cress
**cressonnière** nf water-cress bed
**crête** nf comb (bird); crest; ridge, top
**crête-de-coq** nf ( pl **crêtes-de-coq**) cocks-comb
**crétin -e** n cretin, idiot; coll fool
**crétinisme** nm cretinism
**cretonne** nf cretonne
**creuser** vt dig, excavate; hollow out; bore; **~ un sujet** go deeply into a subject; **se ~ la tête** rack one's brains
**creuset** nm crucible, melting-pot
**creux** nm hollow, cavity; hole; trough (wave); **~ de l'estomac** pit of the stomach; adj (f -euse) hollow; **chemin ~** sunken road; **période creuse** slack period; **ventre ~** empty stomach
**crevaison** nf puncture (tyre)
**crevant** adj coll exhausting; coll funny
**crevasse** nf crevasse; crevice; crack (skin)
**crevasser** vt crack; chap
**crève** nf sl death
**crève-cœur** nm invar bitter disappointment; heartbreak
**crève-la-faim** nm invar sl starving wretch
**crever** vt (6) burst; puncture; **~ le cœur** break the heart; coll **~ les yeux** be perfectly obvious; coll **~ un cheval** exhaust a horse; vi burst; split; sl die; get a puncture; **~ de rire** split one's sides with laughter
**crevette** nf shrimp
**cri** nm cry, shout; chirp; squeak, squeal; **à grands ~s** loudly; **dernier ~** latest fashion; **pousser les hauts ~s** complain bitterly
**criailler** vi bawl, cry out; complain
**criaillerie** nf coll crying, shouting; complaining
**criant** adj flagrant, gross, crying
**criard** adj crying, noisy, shrill; gaudy
**crible** nm sieve, riddle; **passer au ~** sift
**cribler** vt sift, riddle; **~ de balles** riddle with bullets; **criblé de dettes** up to one's ears in debt
¹**cric** nm lifting-jack
²**cric** interj snap!, crack!
**cri-cri** nm invar coll cricket
**criée** nf auction
**crier** vt + vi shout, cry out; call, call out;

squeal; creak; proclaim; hawk
**crieur -ieuse** *n* shouter, crier; **~ public** town-crier
**crime** *nm* crime
**criminel -elle** *n + adj* criminal
**crin** *nm* horsehair
**crinière** *nf* mane
**crique** *nf* creek
**criquet** *nm* locust
**crise** *nf* crisis; slump; attack, fit (illness); shortage
**crispant** *adj coll* aggravating
**crispation** *nf* crispation, shrivelling up; nervous twitching
**crisper** *vt* contract, clench; *coll* irritate
**crissement** *nm* grating, grinding (teeth)
**crisser** *vi* grate; rasp; grind (teeth); crunch (gravel)
**cristal** *nm* crystal; **~ taillé** cut glass
**cristalline** *adj* crystalline; clear as crystal
**cristallisation** *nf* crystallization
**cristalliser** *vt* crystallize; **sucre cristallisé** granulated sugar
**critère** *nm* criterion, test
**critérium** *nm sp* competition
**critiquable** *adj* open to criticism
**critique** *n* critic, reviewer; *nf* criticism; censure; review; *adj* critical, crucial
**croassement** *nm* cawing
**croasser** *vi* caw
**croc** *nm* hook; fang, tusk
**croc-en-jambe** *nm* (*pl* **crocs-en-jambe**) **faire un ~ à qn** trip s/o up
**croche** *nf mus* quaver, *US* eighth note
**crocher** *vt* hook
**crochet** *nm* hook; fang (snake); sudden turn, swerve; square bracket; *coll* **vivre aux ~s de qn** live at s/o's expense
**crocheter** *vt* (5) pick (lock); crochet
**crocheteur** *nm* porter; lock-picker, thief
**crochu** *adj* hooked; crooked; **avoir les doigts ~s** be light-fingered; be greedy
**croire** *vt + vi* (31) believe, think; have faith, trust; **à l'en ~** if one is to believe him; **c'est à ne pas y ~** it's beyond all belief; **je (le) crois bien** I should think so; **je lui croyais du courage** I thought he was brave; **n'en croyez rien** don't believe a word of it; **se ~** fancy oneself
**croisade** *nf* crusade
**croisé** *nm* crusader
**croisée** *nf* crossing; casement window
**croisement** *nm* crossing, intersection; cross-breeding, cross(-breed)
**croiser** *vt* cross; fold over; pass, meet (traffic or person coming from opposite direction); meet (eyes); **mots croisés** crossword puzzle(s); **rester les bras croisés** remain arms folded; stay idle; **veston croisé** double-breasted jacket
**croiseur** *nm* cruiser

**croisière** *nf* cruise; **vitesse de ~** cruising speed
**croisillon** *nm* cross-piece, transom
**croissance** *nf* growth
¹**croissant** *nm* crescent; croissant; bill-hook
²**croissant** *pres part* **croître**
**croître** *vi* (32) grow, increase
**croix** *nf* cross; (print) dagger; **en ~** crosswise
¹**croquant** *nm* rustic, wretch
²**croquant** *adj* crisp, crunchy
**croque-mitaine** *nm* bogy-man
**croque-monsieur** *nm invar* fried cheese and ham sandwich
**croque-mort** *nm* (undertaker's) mute
**croquer** *vt* crunch, munch; sketch; **~ le marmot** wait a long time; **belle à ~** perfectly lovely; *vi* crunch
**croquet** *nm* croquet; *cul* almond biscuit
**croquignole** *nf* flick; kind of biscuit
**croquis** *nm* sketch
**cross** *nm* cross-country
**crosse** *nf* bishop's crook; rifle-butt; hockey-stick
**crotale** *nm* rattlesnake
**crotte** *nf* dung; mud, dirt; **~ de chocolat** chocolate (drop); *interj sl* blast!
**crotter** *vt* dirty, make muddy
**crottin** *nm* dung (*esp* horses)
**croulant** *nm sl* old fogey; *adj* tumble-down, tottering
**croulement** *nm* collapse, falling-in
**crouler** *vi* collapse; totter
**croupe** *nf* rump, croup, crupper; little hill; **monter en ~** ride behind, ride pillion
**croupetons (à)** *adv phr* crouching
**croupi** *adj* stagnant, foul
**croupier** *nm* croupier
**croupière** *nf* crupper
**croupion** *nm* rump (bird); parson's nose
**croupir** *vi* wallow (in filth); stagnate
**croustillant** *adj* crisp, crusty; *coll* spicy
**croustiller** *vi* crunch
**croûte** *nf* crust, rind; scab; *coll* daub (painting); *coll* **casser la ~** eat, have a meal
**croûton** *nm* piece of crust; sippet
**croyable** *adj* believable
**croyance** *nf* belief
**croyant -e** *n* believer
¹**cru** *nm* vineyard; place of growth; **de son ~** of one's own invention; **grand ~** great wine
²**cru** *adj* raw; crude, harsh; **à ~** next to the skin; directly
**cruauté** *nf* cruelty; act of cruelty
**cruche** *nf* jug, pitcher; *coll* fool
**cruchon** *nm* small jug
**crucifier** *vt* crucify
**cruciforme** *adj* cruciform

**cruciverbiste** *n* crossword puzzle enthusiast

**crudité** *nf* crudity, crudeness; coarseness; ~s raw vegetables (*esp* as hors d'œuvres)

**crue** *nf* rising (river), spate, flood

**cruel -elle** *adj* cruel

**crûment** *adv* crudely, roughly

**crustacés** *nmpl* shell-fish, crustacea

**crypte** *nf* crypt

**cryptogame** *nm* mushroom

**cryptogramme** *nm* cipher, cryptogram

**cubage** *nm* cubic content

**cubain** *adj* Cuban

**cube** *nm* cube; **jeu de ~s** set of building blocks; *adj* cubic

**cuber** *vt* cube; have a cubic content of

**cubique** *adj* cubical

**cubisme** *nm* cubism

**cueillage** *nm* gathering, picking, plucking

**cueillette** *nf* gathering, picking

**cueillir** *vt* (33) gather, pick, pluck; *coll* nab, pinch, arrest

**cuiller, cuillère** *nf* spoon

**cuillerée** *nf* spoonful

**cuir** *nm* hide, leather; error in liaison

**cuirasse** *nf* cuirass, breast-plate; armour-plate

**cuirassé** *nm* battleship

**cuirasser** *vt* armour-plate

**cuire** *vt+vi* (80) cook; *vt* fire, bake (pottery, etc); ~ **à l'eau** boil; **il vous en cuira** you will regret it

**cuisant** *adj* smarting, burning, acute

**cuisine** *nf* kitchen; art of cookery, cooking; *coll* jiggery-pokery; **faire la ~** do the cooking

**cuisiner** *vt+vi* cook; *vt coll* cook (books); *coll* grill (prisoner)

**cuisinier -ière** *n* cook

**cuisinière** *nf* cooker

**cuissard** *adj* **bottes ~es** waders, thigh-boots

**cuisse** *nf* thigh

**cuisson** *nf* cooking; firing (pottery, etc); smarting

**cuistre** *nm* pedant

**cuite** *nf sl* **prendre une ~** get drunk

**cuivre** *nm* copper; ~s brass (instruments); ~ **jaune** brass

**cuivrer** *vt* copper; **teint cuivré** bronzed complexion

**cul** *nm sl* bottom, arse, *US* ass; haunches

**culasse** *nf* breech (firearm); cylinder-head

**culbute** *nf* somersault, tumble

**culbuter** *vt* upset, knock over, tip over; *vi* fall head over heels

**culbuteur** *nm eng* tipper; rocker-arm

**cul-de-jatte** *nm* (*pl* **culs-de-jatte**) legless cripple

**cul-de-sac** *nm* (*pl* **culs-de-sac**) blind alley; dead end

**culinaire** *adj* culinary

**culminant** *adj* **point ~** highest point

**culot** *nm* bottom (church lamp); *coll* cheek, nerve

**culotte** *nf* shorts, knickerbockers; rump (beef); **c'est elle qui porte la ~** she's the one who wears the trousers

**culotté** *adj* cocky, cheeky

**culotter** *vt* put breeches on; season (pipe)

**culpabilité** *nf* culpability, guilt

**culte** *nm* worship; religious service

**cul-terreux** *nm* (*pl* **culs-terreux**) *coll* peasant

**cultivable** *adj* arable

**cultivateur** *nm* farmer

**cultivé** *adj* cultivated; cultured

**cultiver** *vt* cultivate, farm, grow (plants)

**cultuel -uelle** *adj* pertaining to worship

**culture** *nf* cultivation; breeding; culture; ~s land under cultivation

**cumul** *nm* cumulation (offices)

**cumuler** *vt* cumulate (offices)

**cunéiforme** *adj* wedge-shaped

**cupide** *adj* greedy, covetous

**cupidité** *nf* cupidity, greed

**Cupidon** *nm* Cupid

**curateur -trice** *n* trustee, guardian

**curatif -ive** *adj* curative

**cure** *nf* care; cure (souls); treatment; curé's residence

**curé** *nm* parish priest

**cure-dents** *nm invar* toothpick

**curée** *nf* quarry (hunting); kill; **âpre à la ~** eager for gain

**cure-pipe** *nm* pipe-cleaner

**curer** *vt* pick (teeth); clean (nails); clean out

**curetage** *nm* curetting, curettage

**curieux -ieuse** *nm* curious part; *n* (*f* **-ieuse**) sightseer; *adj* (*f* **-ieuse**) curious, inquisitive; inquiring (mind); quaint, odd

**curiosité** *nf* curiosity, inquisitiveness; peculiarity

**cursif -ive** *adj* cursive, running (handwriting); cursory

**cutané** *adj* cutaneous

**cuve** *nf* vat

**cuvée** *nf* vatful; wine produced from vineyard

**cuver** *vt* ~ **son vin** sleep it off

**cuvette** *nf* wash-basin; shallow dish; depression (land)

**cuvier** *nm* wash-tub

**cyanose** *nf med* cyanosis

**cyanure** *nm* cyanide

**cyclable** *adj* reserved for bicycles; **piste ~** cycle path

**cyclique** *adj* cyclic

**cyclisme** *nm* cycling

cycliste *n* cyclist
cyclomoteur *nm* autocycle
cyclope *nm* Cyclops
cygne *nm* swan
cylindre *nm* cylinder
cylindrée *nf* cylinder-capacity
cylindrer *vt* roll (lawn, road); mangle
cylindrique *adj* cylindrical
cymbale *nf* cymbal

cymbalier *nm* cymbalist
cynique *adj* cynical; shameless, impudent
cynisme *nm* cynicism; effrontery, shamelessness
cynodrome *nm* greyhound-racing track
cyprès *nm* cypress-tree
cypriote *adj* Cypriot
cystite *nf* cystitis
cytise *nm* laburnum; cytisus

# D

D *nm coll* le système D resourcefulness
d'abord *adv phr* at first; tout ~ first of
all
dac, d'acc *adv phr+interj coll* =
d'accord
dactyle *nm* dactyl
dactylo(graphe) *n* typist
dactylographie *nf* typing
dactylographier *vt* type
dada *nm* gee-gee; *coll* hobby, pet subject; *arts* dada
dadais *nm* booby
dague *nf* dagger
daigner *vi* condescend, deign
daim *nm* fallow-deer, buck; buckskin;
suède
dais *nm* canopy
dallage *nm* paving; pavement; tiled floor
dalle *nf* flagstone; floor-tile; slab; *sl* se
rincer la ~ wet one's whistle
daller *vt* pave; tile (floor)
daltonien -ienne *adj* colour-blind
daltonisme *nm* colour-blindness
Damas *nm* Damascus
damas *nm* damask; damson (plum)
damasser *vt* damask
¹dame *nf* lady; *sl* missus, good lady;
queen (cards, chess); king (draughts);
jeu de ~ s draughts
²dame *interj* (*usu* with oui) indeed
damer *vt* crown (draughts)
damier *nm* draught-board; en ~ che-
quered
damnable *adj* damnable; detestable
damner *vt* damn; âme damnée slave of
s/o; se ~ incur damnation
damoiseau *nm* young beau
dandiner (se) *v refl* waddle
Danemark *nm* Denmark

danger *nm* danger, peril; mettre en ~
endanger; pas de ~! no fear of that!
dangereux -euse *adj* dangerous
Danois -e *n* Dane
danois *nm* Danish (language); *adj*
Danish
dans *prep* in; within; during; ~ le temps
formerly; boire ~ un verre drink out
of a glass; cela coûte ~ les cent francs
that costs about a hundred francs; il
arrivera ~ les dix jours he will arrive
during the next ten days
dansant *adj* dancing; thé ~ tea-dance
danse *nf* dance, dancing; ~ de Saint-
Guy St Vitus's dance; *coll* entrer en ~
join in; mener la ~ be the ringleader
danser *vi* dance; ne savoir sur quel pied
~ not know what to do
danseur -euse *n* dancer; ballet-dancer;
dancing partner; *sp* pédaler en
danseuse stand up on one's pedals
dard *nm* sting (insect); forked tongue
(snake); *ar* dart, spear
darder *vt* shoot forth, dart; flash
(glance)
dare-dare *adv* helter-skelter, straight
away, hurriedly
darne *nf cul* slice, steak (fish)
dartre *nf med* scurfy affection
date *nf* date; de longue ~ of long
standing, for a long time; en ~ de
under date of; faire ~ be a landmark
in history; prendre ~ pour fix a date
for
dater *vt+vi* date
datif *nm gramm* dative case
datte *nf* date
dattier *nm* date-palm
daube *nf cul* stew

**dauber** vt cul stew, braise

**dauphin** nm dolphin; Dauphin; fig successor-designate

**daurade** nf see dorade

**davantage** adv more; **pas ~** no more; no longer

**de** prep from; of; out of; by, with; **~ cette façon** in this way; **~ lui-même** off his own bat; **~ sa propre main** with his own hand; **d'un air drôle** with a strange air, strange-looking; **c'est bien ~ lui** that's just like him; **cette pièce est ~ Sartre** that play is by Sartre; **large ~ trois mètres** three metres wide; **pleurer ~ joie** cry for joy; **quelque chose ~ bon** something good

**dé** nm thimble; dice; tee (golf)

**déambuler** vi coll stroll about

**débâcle** nf downfall, collapse, rout; breaking up (ice on river)

**débâcler** vt clear of ice; vi break up (ice)

**déballage** nm unpacking; coll confession

**déballer** vt unpack; get sth off one's chest, confess

**déballeur** nm hawker

**débandade** nf rout; stampede; **à la ~** in confusion

**débander** vt relax; unbend (bow); unbandage; rout; disband

**débarbouiller** vt wash (usu face); **se ~** wash one's face

**débarcadère** nm landing-stage

**débarder** vt unload

**débardeur** nm docker, stevedore; tight-fitting sleeveless pullover

**débarquement** nm disembarking, landing; unloading

**débarquer** vt unload, discharge (cargo); disembark, set off (passengers); coll sack, get rid of; vi disembark, land; alight; coll turn up; **il débarque de sa province** he's fresh from the country, he's still got straw in his hair

**débarras** nm riddance; lumber-room

**débarrasser** vt clear, disencumber; **se ~ de** get rid of

**débarrer** vt unbar

**débat** nm debate, discussion; dispute

**débattable** adj debatable

**débattre** vt debate, discuss; **se ~** struggle

**débauche** nf debauchery

**débauché** adj debauched

**débaucher** vt lead astray, corrupt, debauch; distract, entice from work; discharge

**débile** adj feeble, sickly; coll silly

**débilitant** adj debilitating

**débilité** nf debility, weakness

**débine** nf sl poverty

**débiner** vt coll run down, disparage; sl **se**

**~ hop it**, piss off

**débit** nm sale; shop; output, delivery; flow; delivery (speech); capacity

**débitant -e** n retailer

**débiter** vt sell, retail; cut up; produce, turn out; debit; recite, deliver

**débiteur -trice** n debtor

**déblai** nm cutting, excavation; **~s** earth cleared by excavation

**déblatérer** vt (6) **~ des injures** fling abuse; vi vituperate, rail

**déblayer** vt (7) clear away; clear (ground)

**débloquer** vt raise the blockade; unclamp; release, defreeze (assets); **se ~** become resolved; (traffic) flow more freely

**débobiner** vt elect unwind

**déboire(s)** nm (pl) disappointment; rebuff

**déboisement** nm deforestation

**déboiser** vt deforest, clear (woodland)

**déboîter** vt disconnect; dislocate; **se ~** come out of joint; mot filter

**débonnaire** adj affable, good-natured

**débordé** adj overwhelmed, snowed under

**débordement** nm overflowing; outburst; **~s** excesses

**déborder** vt project, protrude, overlap; outflank; untuck; remove the edging from; vi overflow; extend beyond; **~ de vie** be full of life

**débotter** vt unboot

**débouché** nm outlet; issue; opening, opportunity

**déboucher** vt clear, remove obstruction from; uncork; vi emerge; open out; result

**déboucler** vt unbuckle; uncurl

**débouler** vi coll fall head over heels, tumble down

**déboulonner** vt unrivet

**débourber** vt remove mud from; cleanse, clean out; pull out of the mud

**débourrer** vt strip; remove stuffing from

**débours** nmpl disbursement

**déboursement** nm disbursement

**débourser** vt pay out, disburse

**déboussolé** adj coll confused, disconcerted

**debout** adv standing, upright; out of bed; **tenir ~** make sense, hold water (argument); **vent ~** head wind

**débouter** vt leg reject (suit)

**déboutonner** vt unbutton

**débraillé** adj untidy, slovenly (dress); loose (morals)

**débrancher** vt elect disconnect; unhook (coaches)

**débrayage** nm disconnecting; declutching; downing tools

**débrayer** vt (7) disconnect; vi declutch;

down tools

**débrider** vt unbridle

**débris** nm fragment; nmpl débris, remains

**débrouillard** adj coll resourceful

**débrouiller** vt disentangle, unravel; clear up (matter); se ~ manage; get out of difficulty

**débusquer** vt drive out of cover or refuge

**début** nm beginning, start; first appearance; first turn (game); dès le ~ from the very beginning

**débutant -e** n beginner, novice; nf débutante

**débuter** vi begin, start; make one's first appearance

**deçà** adv on this side; ~ (et) delà on all sides; en ~ de this side of

**décacheter** vt (5) unseal

**décade** nf period of ten days; decade

**décadence** nf decadence, decline

**décagénaire** n coll teenager

**décalage** nm removal of wedge(s); alteration (time); discrepancy, variation

**décalaminer** vt decarbonize

**décaler** vt remove wedge(s) from; displace (in space or time); shift

**décalque** nm transferring; transfer (picture)

**décalquer** vt transfer (picture)

**décamper** vi decamp, run away

**décantation** nf decanting

**décanter** vt decant

**décapant** nm cleansing or scouring solution; paint remover

**décaper** vt scour, clean

**décapitation** nf decapitation, beheading

**décapiter** vt behead, decapitate

**décapsuler** vt remove the top from (bottle)

**décapsuleur** nm bottle-opener

**décarburer** vt decarbonize

**décarcasser (se)** v refl coll go to great trouble, tear one's guts out

**décasyllabe** nm decasyllable; adj decasyllabic

**décati** adj coll the worse for wear

**décatir** vt take the gloss off

**décaver** vt coll clean out (gambling)

**décédé** adj deceased

**décéder** vi (6) die

**déceler** vt (6) discover, unearth; disclose, divulge

**décembre** nm December

**décemment** adv decently

**décence** nf decency; propriety

**décennal** adj decennial

**décennie** nf decade, period of ten years

**décent** adj decent, modest; proper, becoming

**décentralisation** nf decentralization

**décentraliser** vt decentralize

**décentrer** vt put out of centre (lens)

**déception** nf disappointment; deceit

**décerner** vt award, bestow; decree

**décès** nm decease, death; acte de ~ death certificate

**décevant** adj disappointing; deceptive

**décevoir** vt disappoint

**déchaîné** adj furious, wild, mad

**déchaînement** nm letting loose; breaking loose; outburst

**déchaîner** vt unchain, let loose; se ~ break out; lose one's temper

**déchanter** vi coll climb down, lower one's tone

**décharge** nf unloading, discharge; overflow; relief; dumping-ground (refuse); témoin à ~ witness for the defence

**déchargement** nm unloading; discharging

**décharger** vt unload; discharge; tip; relieve of load; se ~ go off (gun); run down (battery); flow, empty (river); se ~ d'une affaire sur qn shift the responsibility for a matter onto s/o else

**déchargeur** nm docker, unloader

**décharné** adj emaciated, skinny, fleshless

**déchausser** vt take off s/o's shoes; lay bare the roots of (tree); se ~ take off one's shoes; become loose (teeth)

**dèche** nf sl poverty

**déchéance** nf decadence; downfall; expiration; forfeiture

**déchet** nm decrease, diminution, falling off; waste; scrap

**déchiffrable** adj decipherable; legible

**déchiffrer** vt decipher; decode; sight-read (music)

**déchiqueté** adj jagged; mangled

**déchiqueter** vt (5) cut, tear to pieces or shreds; mangle

**déchirant** adj harrowing, heart-rending

**déchirement** nm tearing, rending

**déchirer** vt tear, tear up, rend; se ~ tear, get torn

**déchirure** nf tear, rent, rip; laceration

**déchoir** vi (34) fall (from high position); decline

**déchu** adj fallen

**décidé** adj resolute, determined; decided

**de-ci de-là** adv phr here and there

**décidément** adv resolutely; positively, decidedly; obviously; ~, ça ne va pas aujourd'hui it's just not my day

**décider** vt decide, settle; determine; persuade; se ~ decide, resolve, make up one's mind

**décimale** nf decimal

**décimer** vt decimate

**décisif -ive** adj decisive, final; conclusive; peremptory (tone)

**décision** *nf* decision; resolve; determination

**déclamateur -trice** *n* declaimer, tub-thumper

**déclamation** *nf* declamation; ranting

**déclamatoire** *adj* declamatory; ranting

**déclamer** *vt* declaim; *vi* rant

**déclaration** *nf* declaration, proclamation; notification

**déclaré** *adj* declared, professed

**déclarer** *vt* declare, proclaim, announce; notify; **se ~** declare; break out (illness); declare one's feelings

**déclassement** *nm* change of class (in railway, etc)

**déclasser** *vt* unclass; transfer from one class to another; bring down; **se ~** lower one's social position

**déclenchement** *nm* releasing, disengaging; launching, setting in motion

**déclencher** *vt* release, disconnect; start, set in motion; launch

**déclic** *nm* catch, trigger; noise of catch, click

**déclin** *nm* decline, wane, falling off, decadence

**déclinaison** *nf gramm* declension; declination (star)

**décliner** *vt* decline; refuse; *vi* wane, decline

**déclivité** *nf* slope, declivity, incline

**décloisonner** *vt fig* remove the barriers in

**déclouer** *vt* unnail

**décocher** *vt* shoot, let fly

**décodage** *nm* decoding

**décoder** *vt* decode

**décoiffer** *vt* remove (s/o's) hat; disarrange (s/o's) hair

**décolérer** *vi* (6) calm down, become less angry

**décollage** *nm* unsticking; take-off (aircraft)

**décoller** *vt* unstick, unglue; loosen; *vi* take off (aircraft); get off to a start; **se ~** become unstuck, work loose

**décolleté** *adj* with a low neck (dress); with a low-necked dress (woman)

**décolleter** *vt* (5) cut out the neck of (a dress); cut (screw)

**décolorant** *nm* bleaching agent

**décoloration** *nf* discolouring, bleaching; discolouration, fading

**décolorer** *vt* discolour, bleach; take the colour out of

**décombres** *nmpl* débris, rubbish, ruins

**décommander** *vt* cancel (order, meeting), countermand

**décomplexé** *adj* free of complexes, relaxed

**décomposer** *vt* decompose; decay; distort (features); **se ~** rot, decay; become distorted (features)

**décomposition** *nf* decomposition, decay; distortion (features)

**décompte** *nm* discount, deduction; disappointment

**décompter** *vt* deduct as discount

**déconcerter** *vt* upset, confuse; disconcert

**déconfit** *adj* crestfallen, nonplussed

**déconfiture** *nf* discomfiture; failure

**décongeler** *vt* (5) thaw

**décongestionner** *vt* relieve congestion in; clear

**déconseiller** *vt* advise against, dissuade

**déconsidérer** *vt* (6) discredit, bring into disrepute

**décontaminer** *vt* decontaminate

**décontenancer** *vt* put out of countenance

**décontracté** *adj* relaxed; at ease, confident

**décontracter (se)** *v refl* relax

**déconvenue** *nf* disappointment; setback

**décor** *nm* decoration; *theat* set; scene

**décorateur -trice** *n* decorator; stage-designer

**décoratif -ive** *adj* decorative, ornamental

**décoration** *nf* decoration; ornamentation; medal

**décorer** *vt* decorate, ornament; bestow a medal on

**décortiquer** *vt* decorticate, peel bark, husk or shell from

**décorum** *nm invar* decorum, propriety

**décote** *nf* tax relief

**découcher** *vi* sleep away from home, sleep out

**découdre** *vt* (28) unstitch; **se ~** become unstitched or unsewn

**découler** *vi* drip; proceed, result, follow

**découpage** *nm* cutting up, carving up

**découper** *vt* cut up, carve; cut out; stamp, punch; **scie à ~** fret-saw; **se ~** stand out, show up

**découplé** *adj* strapping; **bien ~** well set up

**découpler** *vt* uncouple

**découpure** *nf* piece cut out, cutting; cutting out; punching, stamping; indentation

**découragement** *nm* discouragement

**décourager** *vt* discourage, dishearten; deter; **se ~** lose heart

**découronner** *vt* uncrown; pollard (tree)

**décousu** *p part* **découdre** +*adj* unsewn; disconnected, incoherent, scrappy, unmethodical

**découvert** *nm* overdraft; **à ~** in the red; uncovered; *adj* uncovered; unsheltered, open, exposed

**découverte** *nf* discovery; exposure, detection

**découvrir** *vt* (30) uncover; discover, find out; expose, disclose; discern; **se ~** take one's hat off; clear (sky, weather); expose oneself

**décrasser** *vt* clear, scour

**décrépi** *adj* unplastered; peeling

**décrépit** *adj* senile, decrepit

**décret** *nm* decree, order

**décréter** *vt* (6) decree, enact

**décret-loi** *nm* (*pl* **décrets-lois**) government decree with force of law ( = Order in Council)

**décrier** *vt* disparage, discredit, run down

**décrire** *vt* (42) describe

**décrocher** *vt* unhook; bring down, take down from the peg; take off, disconnect; lift (receiver); *coll* obtain, get; **se ~ la mâchoire** disconnect one's jaw; *vi* abandon contact, leave off; *fig* pack up

**décrochez-moi-ça** *nm invar coll* **acheter au ~** buy cheap ready-made clothes

**décroiser** *vt* uncross (legs)

**décroissance** *nf*, **décroissement** *nm* decrease, diminution; decline, wane

**décroît** *nm* last quarter (moon)

**décroître** *vi* (32) decrease, decline

**décrotter** *vt* clean (boots), remove the mud from; *coll* **~ qn** eradicate s/o's unpolished manners or ignorance

**décrottoir** *nm* shoe-scraper

**décrypter** *vt* decipher

**déçu** *p part* décevoir

**déculotter** *vt* take off (s/o's) breeches; **se ~** let down (take off) one's trousers

**décupler** *vt + vi* multiply tenfold

**dédaigner** *vt* disdain, scorn

**dédaigneux -euse** *adj* disdainful, scornful

**dédain** *nm* scorn, disdain

**dédale** *nm* maze, labyrinth

**dedans** *nm* inside, interior; **au ~** inside; *adv* inside, within; **en ~** inside

**dédicace** *nf* dedication; *eccles* consecration

**dédicacer** *vt* dedicate (book)

**dédicatoire** *adj* dedicatory

**dédier** *vt* consecrate, dedicate

**dédire (se)** *v refl* (74) retract; go back on one's word

**dédit** *nm* retraction; going back on one's word; forfeit (for non-fulfilment of contract)

**dédommagement** *nm* compensation, damages; indemnification

**dédommager** *vt* compensate, indemnify

**dédoré** *adj* tarnished

**dédouaner** *vt* clear (at customs); rehabilitate

**dédoubler** *vt* undouble; divide into two; run (train) in two portions

**déductif -ive** *adj* deductive

**déduction** *nf* inference; abatement, deduction

**déduire** *vt* (80) deduce, conclude; deduct

**déesse** *nf* goddess

**défaillance** *nf* weakening, lapse; absence, extinction

**défaillant** *adj* failing, waning; dying out

**défaillir** *vi* (36) become weak, lose strength, faint

**défaire** *vt* (46) undo; destroy, cancel, break off; defeat; rid; **~ ses cheveux** let one's hair down; **visage défait** distorted features; **se ~** come undone; **se ~ de** get rid of; part with

**défaite** *nf* defeat

**défaitisme** *nm* defeatism

**défaitiste** *n* defeatist

**défalquer** *vt* deduct (sum of money), write off (debt)

**défaut** *nm* fault, defect, flaw; lack, absence; **à ~ de** failing, for lack of; **faire ~** be absent, lacking

**défaveur** *nf* discredit, disfavour

**défavorable** *adj* unfavourable

**défavoriser** *vt* put at a disadvantage

**défectif -ive** *adj* defective (verb)

**défection** *nf* desertion

**défectueux -ueuse** *adj* faulty, defective

**défectuosité** *nf* defect, imperfection, flaw

**défendable** *adj* defensible

**défendeur -eresse** *n leg* defendant

**défendre** *vt* defend, uphold (opinion); protect; forbid, prohibit; **à son corps défendant** reluctantly; *coll* **se ~** acquit oneself quite well; stay young; **se ~ de faire qch** refrain from doing sth

**défenestrer** *vt* throw out of the window

**défense** *nf* defence; **~ contre avions** anti-aircraft defence; **~ de fumer** no smoking; **~ passive** air-raid precautions; **~ s** defences; tusks; prohibition; **sans ~** defenceless

**défenseur** *nm* defender, protector; *leg* counsel for the defence

**défensif -ive** *adj* defensive

**déférence** *nf* respect, regard

**déférer** *vt* (6) *leg* refer; *leg* hand over; **~ à** confer (honour) on; *vi* defer

**déferler** *vt* unfurl; *vi* break (waves); swarm (crowd)

**déferrer** *vt* unshoe (horse); remove fetters from

**défeuiller** *vt* defoliate

**défi** *nm* challenge; defiance; **mettre qn au ~** dare s/o; **relever un ~** take up a challenge

**défiance** *nf* mistrust, suspicion

**défiant** *adj* mistrustful, suspicious, wary

**déficeler** *vt* (5) untie (string)

**déficit** *nm* shortage; **être en** ~ be in the red

**déficitaire** *adj* adverse (balance, account)

**défier** *vt* challenge; defy, brave; **se** ~ **de** mistrust

**défiger** *vt* liquefy

**défiguration** *nf* disfigurement; defacing

**défigurer** *vt* disfigure; deface; distort

**défilé** *nm* defile; *mil* march-past, procession; ~ **de mannequins** manequin parade

**défiler** *vt* unthread; *sl* **se** ~ clear off; *vi* march past; defile; walk in file

**défini** *adj* clearly defined; definite; **passé** ~ past historic, preterite

**définir** *vt* define

**définissable** *adj* definable

**définitif -ive** *adj* final, permanent, definitive

**définition** *nf* description, definition

**définitivement** *adv* for good, definitively

**déflationniste** *adj* deflationary

**défleurir** *vi* lose blossoms (tree, bush)

**déflorer** *vt* take away the freshness of; deflower

**défolier** *vt* defoliate

**défoncer** *vt* smash in; break up (road)

**défoulement** *nm* liberation from complexes, letting oneself go

**défouler (se)** *v refl coll* get rid of one's complexes, let oneself go

**défourner** *vt* remove from the kiln, oven (pottery), bread)

**défraîchi** *adj* soiled (goods); faded (flower)

**défraîchir** *vt* soil, spoil the freshness of

**défrayer** *vt* (7) pay the expenses of; ~ **la chronique** be in the news; ~ **la conversation** take the major part in a conversation, be the subject of conversation

**défricher** *vt* clear, make ready for cultivation (ground); ~ **un sujet** break new ground in a subject

**défriser** *vt* uncurl

**défroisser** *vt* uncrease

**défroncer** *vt* undo the pleats of

**défroquer** *vt* unfrock

**défunt** *adj* defunct, deceased

**dégagé** *adj* free and easy; untrammelled; **vue** ~ **e** open view

**dégagement** *nm* disengagement; relieving, slackening; clearing; empty space; redemption (pledge); escape (gas, etc); clearance; ~ **de sa parole** going back on one's promise; **voie de** ~ relief road

**dégager** *vt* (3) disengage; free; clear; bring out (sense); redeem; emit (gas, etc); give out (heat, etc); ~ **sa parole** get out of one's promise; *vi* clear the way, move along; **se** ~ emerge, stand out

**dégainer** *vt* unsheathe; *vt* + *vi* draw (sword)

**déganter (se)** *v refl* take off one's gloves

**dégarni** *adj* empty; stripped; **il a le front** ~ his hair is receding

**dégarnir** *vt* dismantle, empty; strip; **se** ~ lose its leaves (tree); lose one's hair; empty

**dégâts** *nmpl* damage

**dégel** *nm* thaw; **barrière de** ~ restricted or barred road (after thaw)

**dégelée** *nf sl* shower of blows

**dégeler** *vt* + *vi* (5) thaw (out)

**dégénéré -e** *n* + *adj* degenerate

**dégénérer** *vi* (6) degenerate; lower oneself

**dégénérescence** *nf* degeneration

**dégingandé** *adj coll* awkward, ungainly

**dégivrer** *vt* defrost

**déglacer** *vt* (4) thaw, de-ice; *cul* de-glaze

**dégommer** *vt* unstick; *sl* sack, kick out

**dégonfler** *vt* deflate; **se** ~ *sl* be scared; back out, climb down

**dégorger** *vt* (3) disgorge; unstop; scour (wool); *vi* overflow; empty

**dégot(t)er** *vt sl* find

**dégouliner** *vi coll* drip, run

**dégourdi** *adj* sharp, wide-awake, quick

**dégourdir** *vt* remove numbness from, revive; smarten, waken up; take the chill off; **se** ~ stretch, lose one's stiffness; grow more alert

**dégoût** *nm* disgust, distaste; aversion

**dégoûtant** *adj* disgusting, loathsome

**dégoûter** *vt* disgust; put off

**dégoutter** *vi* drip, be dripping

**dégradant** *adj* degrading

**dégradation** *nf* degradation; dilapidation

**dégrader** *vt* degrade; dilapidate, damage; taper (hair); **se** ~ degrade oneself; fall into disrepair

**dégrafer** *vt* unfasten, undo (dress); **se** ~ come undone; unfasten one's dress

**dégraissage** *nm* dry-cleaning

**dégraisser** *vt* take the fat off; clean; *comm* cut costs in

**degré** *nm* degree, stage; stair, step; degree (heat, circle)

**dégrever** *vt* (6) diminish (tax), reduce; disencumber (estate)

**dégringolade** *nf coll* tumble; downfall, collapse

**dégringoler** *vt* rush down; *vi coll* tumble down

**dégriser** *vt* sober; remove (s/o's) illusions

**dégrossir** *vt* make roughly ready; rough

down; rough-hew; *coll* lick into shape

**déguenillé** *adj* tattered, ragged

**déguerpir** *vi* clear out

**dégueulasse** *adj sl* bloody awful; disgusting, filthy

**déguisé** *adj* disguised; *coll* got up

**déguisement** *nm* disguise; dissimulation

**déguiser** *vt* disguise; conceal (truth); **se ~ en** get oneself up as

**dégustation** *nf* tasting; **verre à ~** balloon glass

**déguster** *vt* taste, sample; savour, relish

**déhancher (se)** *v refl* sway one's hips (walking); dislocate hip

**dehors** *nm* exterior; outside; *pl* outward appearances; **au ~ (de)** outside, beyond; **en ~ (de)** outside; **en ~ de moi** without my knowledge, participation; *adv* outside, out of doors; *coll* **mettre qn ~** give s/o the sack

**déifier** *vt* deify

**déité** *nf* deity

**déjà** *adv* already; previously; as it is; **d'ores et ~** here and now, from now on

**déjeter** *vt* (5) make lop-sided, warp

**déjeuner** *nm* lunch; breakfast cup and saucer; **petit ~** breakfast; *vi* have breakfast; have lunch

**déjouer** *vt* thwart; frustrate

**delà** *prep* beyond; **au ~ de, par ~ de** beyond

**délabré** *adj* dilapidated, broken-down

**délabrement** *nm* disrepair

**délabrer** *vt* dilapidate, ruin; impair (health); **se ~** fall into decay

**délacer** *vt* undo (shoes), unlace

**délai** *nm* time allotted or allowed; **demander un ~** ask for extra time; **sans ~** immediately

**délaissement** *nm* abandonment; neglect; renunciation

**délaisser** *vt* abandon, desert; relinquish

**délassement** *nm* relaxation

**délasser** *vt* refresh, rest; **se ~** relax

**délateur -trice** *n* informer

**délavé** *adj* washed out

**délayer** *vt* (7) add liquid to; thin; mix; *coll* spin out (speech)

**delco** *nm* mot distributor

**délectable** *adj* delightful, pleasant

**délecter** *vt* delight; **se ~** enjoy oneself

**délégation** *nf* delegation; delegating, assignment

**délégué -e** *n* delegate

**déléguer** *vt* (6) delegate; depute

**délester** *vt* unballast; *coll* relieve of a burden, of money

**délétère** *adj* offensive; noxious; pernicious (doctrine)

**délibération** *nf* discussion, debate; decision, vote (assembly)

**délibéré** *adj* deliberate, intentional; determined; **de propos ~** purposely

**délibérer** *vt* (6) discuss, debate; reflect on; *vi* deliberate; reflect

**délicat** *adj* delicate; tasty; refined, discerning; sensitive, fragile; difficult, ticklish (situation); scrupulous

**délicatesse** *nf* delicacy; fineness; refinement; fragility; awkwardness, difficulty; scrupulousness, tact

**délice** *nm* delight; **~s** *fpl* delights; **faire les ~s de** be the delight of

**délicieux -ieuse** *adj* delicious, delightful

**délictueux -ueuse** *adj* punishable; felonious

**délié** *adj* slender; subtle (mind); *coll* **avoir la langue ~e** talk easily

**délier** *vt* untie, loose; release (s/o from a promise)

**délimiter** *vt* delimit; define (powers)

**délinquance** *nf* delinquency

**délinquant -e** *n* delinquent

**délirant** *adj* delirious, raving

**délire** *nm* delirium; transport; **foule en ~** frenzied crowd

**délirer** *vi* be delirious; wander; rave

**délit** *nm* offence

**délivrance** *nf* rescue, deliverance; handing over; relief

**délivrer** *vt* rescue, deliver, hand over; release; relieve

**déloger** *vt* drive out, dislodge; *vi* move out; go away

**déloyal** *adj* disloyal; false; dishonest

**déloyauté** *nf* treachery, disloyalty; treacherous act

**déluge** *nm* deluge; torrent, mass (insults, etc); *coll* downpour; **après moi le ~!** I couldn't care less what happens when I'm gone!

**déluré** *adj* sharp, smart; forward (girl)

**demain** *adv* tomorrow; in the future; **~ en huit (quinze)** tomorrow week (fortnight)

**démancher** *vt* remove the handle from; put out of joint

**demande** *nf* request, application; *comm* demand; **~s d'emploi** situations required; **~ en mariage** proposal of marriage

**demander** *vt* ask (for); inquire; demand; require; **on vous demande** someone is asking for you; **très demandé** in great demand; **se ~** wonder

**demandeur -eresse** *n leg* plaintiff

**démangeaison** *nf* itch; *coll* urge

**démanger** *vi* itch; *coll* **ça me démange de** I badly want to

**démantèlement** *nm* dismantling

**démanteler** *vt* (5) dismantle

**démantibuler** *vt coll* take to bits; dislocate (jaw)

**démarche** nf walk, gait; step; intervention

**démarrage** nm starting (vehicle); unmooring; fig beginning, start

**démarrer** vi start (up) (vehicle); start; **faire ~** start (car); cast off; drive off

**démarreur** nm mot starter

**démasquer** vt expose; unmask; **~ ses batteries** reveal one's plans

**démêlé** nm usu pl unpleasant dealings

**démêler** vt disentangle; clear up; fathom; **se ~** extricate oneself

**démembrement** nm dismembering, breaking up

**démembrer** vt dismember, divide up

**déménagement** nm removal

**déménager** vt (3) move; vi move house; sl be (going) crazy

**démence** nf madness, lunacy

**démener (se)** v refl (6) struggle, agitate oneself; coll make great efforts

**dément** adj mad, crazy

**démenti** nm denial; disappointment

**démentir** vt (59) give the lie to; deny; belie

**démerder (se)** v refl vulg get a move on; extricate oneself from a mess

**démériter** vi act in an unworthy manner

**démesuré** adj huge, inordinate, immoderate

**démettre** vt (60) dislocate; dismiss; **se ~** resign

**demeurant (au)** adv phr after all, all the same

**demeure** nf dwelling, place of residence; stay; **à ~** permanently; **dernière ~** grave; **mise en ~** summons

**demeuré** adj backward

**demeurer** vi stay, remain; dwell, live; **demeurons-en là** let's leave it at that

**demi** nm half; sp half-back; glass of beer; **à ~** half, by halves; adj half; **trois heures et ~** e half past three; three and a half hours; **~-** semi-, half-

**demi-botte** nf half-boot

**demi-bouteille** nf half-bottle

**demi-cercle** nm semi-circle

**demi-dieu** nm demigod

**demie** nf half-hour

**demi-finale** nf semi-final

**demi-fond** nm **course de ~** middle-distance race

**demi-frère** nm half-brother

**demi-gros** nm comm retail supply trade (carried out by middleman)

**demi-heure** nf half an hour

**demi-jour** nm half-light

**démilitariser** vt demilitarize

**demi-litre** nm half-litre

**demi-lune** nf half-moon

**demi-mondaine** nf demi-mondaine, woman of easy virtue

**demi-mot (à)** adv phr **comprendre ~** take a hint

**demi-pension** nf half-board

**demi-pensionnaire** n day-boarder

**demi-place** nf half-fare; half-price

**demi-saison** nf spring; autumn; **manteau de ~** spring (or autumn) coat

**demi-sœur** nf half-sister; step-sister

**demi-solde** nf mil half-pay; nm mil officer on half-pay

**démission** nf resignation; abandonment

**démissionnaire** n person resigning; adj resigning; outgoing

**démissionner** vi resign; coll give up

**demi-ton** nm semitone

**demi-tour** nm half-turn; about turn; **faire ~** turn back, turn about

**demi-voix (à)** adv phr softly, under one's breath

**démobiliser** vt demobilize; discharge

**démocrate** n democrat

**démocratie** nf democracy

**démocratique** adj democratic

**démocratiser** vt democratize

**démodé** adj old-fashioned

**démoder (se)** v refl go out of fashion

**demoiselle** nf single woman, spinster; young woman; dragonfly; paving beetle; **nom de ~** maiden name

**démolir** vt demolish, pull down; coll beat up, knock flat; coll ruin the reputation of

**démolisseur -euse** n demolition worker; demolisher

**démon** nm demon, devil; genius, spirit; **~ de midi** love in middle age

**démoniaque** adj demoniac

**démonstrateur -trice** n demonstrator

**démonstratif -ive** adj demonstrative, expansive; conclusive

**démonstration** nf demonstration; proof (by deduction)

**démontable** adj that can be taken to pieces; collapsible

**démonté** adj stormy (sea); flustered

**démonter** vt take to pieces; dismantle, unhinge; unhorse; upset, disconcert

**démontrable** adj demonstrable

**démontrer** vt demonstrate

**démoraliser** vt demoralize; **se ~** become demoralized

**démordre** vi let go one's hold; **ne pas ~ de son opinion** stick to one's opinion

**démouler** vt withdraw from the mould; turn out (cake, etc)

**démoustiquer** vt clear of mosquitoes

**démultiplication** nf gearing down; reduction ratio (gears)

**démultiplier** vt reduce the gear ratio of

**démuni** adj unprovided; short (of money)

**démunir** vt deprive; **se ~** deprive oneself, allow oneself to run short

**démystifier** vt undeceive; coll debunk

**dénantir** vt deprive of securities

**dénatalité** nf fall in the birth rate

**dénationaliser** vt denationalize

**dénaturé** adj unnatural; hard-hearted (parent); ungrateful (child)

**dénaturer** vt alter the nature of; misrepresent, distort

**dénégation** nf denial

**déneigement** nm clearing of snow

**déniaiser** vt teach (s/o) the ways of the world, initiate

**dénicher** vt remove from the nest; dislodge; coll discover

**denier** nm denarius; denier; ~s publics public funds; **de ses propres** ~s with one's own money; **jusqu'au dernier** ~ to the last farthing

**dénier** vt deny, disclaim; refuse

**dénigrer** vt disparage

**déniveler** vt (5) make uneven (surface); contour

**dénivellation** nf, **dénivellement** nm difference in level; gradient

**dénombrement** nm census; counting

**dénombrer** vt take a census of; count

**dénominateur** nm denominator

**dénomination** nf name, denomination

**dénommer** vt name, denominate

**dénoncer** vt denounce; inform against; proclaim, betray; **se** ~ give oneself up

**dénonciateur -trice** n informer; adj tell-tale

**dénonciation** nf denunciation; cancellation, annulment

**dénoter** vt denote, show

**dénouement** nm untying; outcome, result, ending

**dénouer** vt untie, unknot; undo (hair); ~ **une intrigue** unravel a plot; **se** ~ end (story)

**denrée** nf commodity; ~s **alimentaires** foodstuffs

**dense** adj dense, compact, crowded

**densité** nf density; denseness

**dent** nf tooth; cog, prong; **à belles** ~s with appetite, heartily; **avoir une** ~ **contre qn** bear s/o a grudge; **être sur les** ~s be harassed; **n'avoir rien à se mettre sous la** ~ have nothing to eat; **ne pas desserrer les** ~s not utter a word

**dentaire** adj dental

**dent-de-lion** nf (pl **dents-de-lion**) dandelion

**denté** adj cogged

**denteler** vt (5) jag, notch

**dentelle** nf lace

**dentellerie** nf lace manufacture

**dentellière** nf lace-maker; lace-making machine

**dentelure** nf indentation; serration

**dentier** nm set of false teeth, denture

**dentifrice** nm tooth-paste; adj **pâte** ~ tooth-paste

**dentiste** n dentist; **chirurgien** ~ dental surgeon

**dentition** nf dentition; teething; set of teeth

**denture** nf set of teeth; cogs

**dénudation** nf denudation, stripping

**dénuder** vt lay bare, denude

**dénué** adj devoid, deprived

**dénuement, dénûment** nm need, destitution; bareness

**dénuer** vt strip, divest

**déodoriser** vt deodorize

**dépannage** nm emergency repairs (to engine)

**dépanner** vt repair and get going again (engine); coll help out

**dépanneuse** nf breakdown lorry

**dépareiller** vt spoil (set); **service dépareillé** incomplete, unmatched service

**déparer** vt strip; spoil (beauty)

**déparier** vt break up, separate (a pair)

**départ** nm departure, start; separation, sorting out; **au** ~ at the outset

**départager** vt decide between (opinion, etc)

**département** nm department, section; French administrative region

**départemental** adj departmental; **route** ~ **e** secondary road

**départir** vt divide; distribute, dispense; **se** ~ **de** renounce, give up

**dépasser** vt go beyond, overtake, outstrip; project; exceed; coll **cela me dépasse** it beats me

**dépaysé** adj out of one's element; ill-at-ease

**dépayser** vt remove (s/o) from (his) natural surroundings; disorientate

**dépecer** vt (6,4) dismember, carve up

**dépêche** nf telegram; dispatch

**dépêcher** vt despatch; **se** ~ hasten, be quick

**dépeigner** vt ruffle hair of

**dépeindre** vt (55) depict, describe

**dépenaillé** adj ragged, tattered

**dépendance** nf dependence; dependency; ~ **s** outbuildings

**dépendre** vt take down (hanging object); vi depend; belong, be under the dependence; **il dépend de vous de** it's up to you to

**dépens** nmpl costs; **à ses** ~ to his cost; **aux** ~ **de** at the expense of

**dépense** nf expense, outlay; expenditure; consumption; pantry

**dépenser** vt spend; consume; **se** ~ make strenuous efforts; devote oneself

**dépensier -ière** *adj* extravagant, spendthrift

**déperdition** *nf* waste; loss

**dépérir** *vi* waste away; wither

**dépersonnaliser** *vt* depersonalize

**dépêtrer** *vt* extricate; **se ~** extricate oneself

**dépeupler** *vt* depopulate

**déphasé** *adj* *elect* out of phase; lagging behind; *coll* disoriented

**dépilatoire** *n* + *adj* depilatory

**dépiler** *vt* remove the hairs from

**dépiquer** *vt* unstitch; plant out

**dépistage** *nm* detection

**dépister** *vt* track down; detect; throw off the scent

**dépit** *nm* spite, resentment; **en ~ de** in spite of; **en ~ du bon sens** badly, stupidly

**dépiter** *vt* vex

**déplacé** *adj* displaced; ill-timed, uncalled-for

**déplacement** *nm* displacement, removing; altering; travelling, journey; **en ~** travelling (on business); **frais de ~** travelling expenses

**déplacer** *vt* (4) displace; transfer, move; alter; have a displacement of (ship)

**déplaire** *vi* (69) displease, offend; **ne vous en déplaise** whatever you may think

**déplaisant** *adj* unpleasant, disagreeable

**déplaisir** *nm* displeasure

**déplanter** *vt* take up, transplant

**déplantoir** *nm* garden trowel

**dépliant** *nm* prospectus, pamphlet; folder; folder insert (in book)

**déplier** *vt* unfold, open out

**déplisser** *vt* take out the folds or creases of

**déploiement** *nm* unfolding; deployment; display, show

**déplomber** *vt* remove the lead seals from

**déplorer** *vt* deplore; grieve over

**déployer** *vt* (7) unfold; spread (sails, wings); deploy

**déplumer** *vt* pluck (chicken); **se ~** moult; *coll* lose one's hair, go bald

**dépolariser** *vt* depolarize

**dépolir** *vt* dull (surface); frost (glass)

**dépolitiser** *vt* take out of politics, remove from the political arena

**déporter** *vt* deport; sweep off course; **se ~** swerve

**déposer** *vt* deposit, set down, lay down; lodge; register; depose; **marque déposée** registered trademark; *vi* give evidence

**dépositaire** *n* trustee; *comm* agent

**déposition** *nf* statement (of evidence); deposing

**déposséder** *vt* (6) dispossess, deprive

**dépôt** *nm* depositing; deposit; deposi-

tory, store, depot; sediment; **~ de marchandises** warehouse; **en ~** on deposit; in trust; **mandat de ~** order for arrest

**dépoter** *vt* decant; unpot, plant out

**dépotoir** *nm* sewage farm; rubbish dump

**dépouille** *nf* (cast off) skin; **~s** spoils, effects; **~ mortelle** mortal remains

**dépouiller** *vt* skin; cast off; strip, deprive; analyse; **~ le courrier** go through the mail; **se ~ de** divest oneself of

**dépourvu** *adj* devoid, destitute; **être pris au ~** be caught unawares

**dépravation** *nf* depravation; depravity

**dépraver** *vt* deprave

**dépréciateur -trice** *adj* disparaging

**dépréciation** *nf* fall in value; wear; disparagement

**déprécier** *vt* depreciate; belittle

**déprédateur -trice** *n* depredator; *adj* depredatory

**dépression** *nf* hollow; fall; depression

**déprimant** *adj* depressing

**déprime** *nf* *coll* depression

**déprimer** *vt* depress

**depuis** *adv* since then; later; *prep* since, for; from; **~ que** *conj* since

**dépuratif** *nm* depurative

**dépurer** *vt* cleanse, clear

**députation** *nf* delegating; deputation; office of deputy

**député** *nm* delegate, deputy; member of French parliament; **~-maire** member of French parliament and mayor

**députer** *vt* depute; appoint as deputy

**déraciner** *vt* uproot; eradicate

**déraillement** *nm* going off the rails; *fig* diverging from the normal

**dérailler** *vi* become derailed; *coll* be crazy, go off the rails; **faire ~** derail

**dérailleur** *nm* type of gear-change (bicycle)

**déraison** *nf* unreasonableness

**déraisonnable** *adj* unreasonable; senseless, foolish

**déraisonner** *vi* talk nonsense; rave

**dérangement** *nm* derangement; disordering; disturbance; upset

**déranger** *vt* disturb; derange; disarrange; upset; **se ~** move; put oneself out; get out of order (machine)

**dérapage** *nm* skid; dragging, tripping (anchor); *fig* turn for the worse

**déraper** *vi* skid; drag, trip (anchor); *fig* fall, take a bad turn, go off the rails

**dératiser** *vt* clear of rats

**derechef** *adv* once more

**dérèglement** *nm* disorder; irregularity; dissoluteness

**dérégler** *vt* (6) upset, disorder; unsettle; put (clock) out of order

**dérider** vt smooth wrinkles of; *coll* cheer up; se ~ cheer up

**dérision** nf mockery, derision; **tourner en ~** hold up to ridicule

**dérisoire** adj laughable; insignificant

**dérivation** nf diversion (of waters); derivation; drift

**dérive** nf drift; **à la ~** adrift

**dérivé** nm derivative; by-product

**dériver** vt divert (stream); vi drift, be carried away by the current

**dermatologie** nf dermatology

**derme** nm dermis

**dernier -ière** adj last; final; latest; abject; utmost; latter

**dernièrement** adv lately, recently

**dernier-né** ( *f* **dernière-née**) n last-born child

**derny** nm light motor-cycle used for pace-making in cycle races

**dérobade** nf escape, avoidance

**dérobé** adj secret, hidden; **à la ~e** furtively, secretly

**dérober** vt steal; hide; se ~ escape, slip away; refuse; give way

**dérogation** nf impairment; exception

**dérogatoire** adj derogatory

**déroger** vi (3) depart (from custom, etc); derogate

**dérouiller** vt take the rust off; *coll* freshen up, polish up

**déroulement** nm unrolling, unwinding; development

**dérouler** vt unroll, unwind; se ~ come unrolled; develop; unfold; occur

**déroute** nf rout; **en ~** in flight

**dérouter** vt change the route of; baffle, confuse

**derrière** nm back, rear; backside, bottom; adv behind, in the rear; **par ~** from the rear; **porte de ~** back door; *prep* behind

**derviche, dervis** nm dervish

**des = de + les**

**dès** prep since, from; as early as; ~ **aujourd'hui** this very day; ~ **lors** ever since, from then onwards; ~ **maintenant** already; from now on; ~ **que** conj as soon as

**désabusé** adj disillusioned

**désabuser** vt disillusion, undeceive

**désaccord** nm disagreement; clash (of interests); *mus* discord

**désaccorder** vt set at variance; *mus* put out of tune

**désaccoutumer** vt disaccustom

**désaffectation** nf putting to different use

**désaffecter** vt put to different use

**désaffection** nf discontent, disaffection

**désaffectionner** vt alienate the affections of

**désagréable** adj unpleasant; surly; offensive

**désagrégation** nf disintegration; breaking up

**désagréger** vt (6) disintegrate, disaggregate

**désagrément** nm source of annoyance

**désaltérant** adj thirst-quenching

**désaltérer** vt (6) quench, slake; se ~ quench one's thirst

**désamorcer** vt unprime, prevent the functioning of; *fig* defuse

**désappointer** vt disappoint

**désapprendre** vt (75) forget, unlearn

**désapprobateur -trice** adj disapproving, censorious

**désapprobation** nf disapproval

**désapprouver** vt + vi disapprove (of), object (to)

**désarçonnant** adj coll staggering

**désarçonner** vt unseat; *coll* dumbfound, stagger

**désargenter** vt de-silver; *coll* drain of cash

**désarmement** nm disarming; disarmament; laying up (ship)

**désarmer** vt disarm; unload (gun); lay up (ship); vi disarm; weaken, abandon objections

**désarrimer** vt unstow (cargo); put out of trim (ship)

**désarroi** nm confusion, disorder

**désarticuler** vt disjoint; dislocate

**désassocier** vt disassociate, dissociate

**désassortir** vt break up (collection); être **désassorti** have a reduced stock or selection

**désastre** nm disaster, catastrophe

**désastreux -euse** adj disastrous, catastrophic

**désavantage** nm disadvantage; detriment

**désavantager** vt put at a disadvantage, affect adversely

**désavantageux -euse** adj unfavourable, disadvantageous

**désaveu** nm denial, disavowal

**désavouer** vt repudiate, disavow, deny; disclaim; retract; condemn

**désaxer** vt put out of true (wheel); unbalance (mind)

**desceller** vt unseal, break the seal of; loosen

**descendance** nf lineage, descendants

**descendant -e** n descendant; adj descending, downward

**descendre** vt go down (stairs, etc); bring, take down; lower; shoot down; set down; vi come down, descend, fall; be sloping; raid (police); stay (at hotel); be descended (from); alight

**descente** nf descent, going down; lowering; raid (police); stay (at hotel); ~ **de**

lit bedside rug, mat
**descriptible** adj describable
**descriptif -ive** adj descriptive
**désembouteiller** vt mot clear, free of traffic-jams
**désemparé** adj crippled (ship); at a loss, baffled
**désemparer** vt disable (ship); vi sans ~ without interruption, ceaselessly
**désemplir** vt empty partially; vi usu ne pas ~ always be full
**désenchantement** nm disenchantment; disillusion
**désenchanter** vt disenchant; disillusion
**désenclaver** vt disenclose; improve communications in
**désencombrer** vt disencumber; clear
**désenfler** vi become less swollen; go down; se ~ become less swollen
**désenfumer** vt clear of smoke
**désengager** vt (3) free from an obligation
**désengorger** vt (3) unchoke, clear (pipe)
**désenivrer** vt sober
**désenneiger** vt (3) clear the snow from
**désennuyer** vt (7) relieve from boredom, amuse
**désensibiliser** vt reduce the sensitivity of, desensitize
**désenterrer** vt disinter, exhume
**déséquilibrer** vt unbalance
**désert** nm desert, wilderness; adj deserted; uninhabited, lonely
**déserter** vt desert
**déserteur** nm deserter
**désertique** adj barren, desert-like
**désescalade** nf de-escalation
**désespérant** adj heart-breaking; dreadful, hopeless
**désespéré** adj desperate; hopeless
**désespérer** vt (6) drive to despair; vi despair, lose hope, be without hope; se ~ be in despair
**désespoir** nm despair; en ~ de cause as a last resort
**déshabillé** nm négligée
**déshabiller** vt undress; se ~ take off one's clothes
**déshabilloir** nm changing room (in clothes shop)
**déshabituer** vt break of a habit
**désherbant** nm weed-killer
**déshérité** adj poor (in natural or material gifts), underprivileged
**déshériter** vt disinherit
**déshonneur** nm dishonour
**déshonorant** adj discreditable, dishonourable
**déshonorer** vt dishonour
**déshumaniser** vt dehumanize
**déshydrater** vt dehydrate
**desiderata** nmpl needs, requirements

**désignation** nf designation; indicating; nomination
**désigner** vt designate, show, point out; fix, appoint, detail
**désillusion** nf disillusion
**désillusionner** vt disillusion
**désinfectant** nm disinfectant
**désinfecter** vt disinfect
**désinfection** nf disinfection
**désintégration** nf disintegration
**désintégrer** vt (6) disintegrate, destroy; se ~ disintegrate
**désintéressé** adj disinterested, unselfish
**désintéressement** nm disinterestedness; impartiality; paying off (creditor)
**désintéresser** vt buy out, pay off; se ~ de lose interest in; take no part in
**désintoxication** nf med cure for intoxication or for addiction (alcohol, drugs); fig relief from the strains and pollution of modern life
**désintoxiquer** vt med cure of intoxication or of addiction (alcohol, drugs); fig se ~ gain relief from the strains and pollution of modern life
**désinvolte** adj free, easy; detached; cavalier
**désinvolture** nf ease, lack of constraint; cheek, off-hand manner
**désir** nm desire, wish
**désirer** vt desire, want, wish; covet
**désireux -euse** adj desirous
**désistement** nm desistance, withdrawal
**désister (se)** v refl desist, withdraw
**désobéir** vi disobey
**désobéissance** nf disobedience
**désobéissant** adj disobedient
**désobligeance** nf disobligingness; unpleasantness
**désobligeant** adj disobliging; unpleasant, ungracious
**désobliger** vt (3) offend; disoblige
**désodorisant** nm deodorant
**désodoriser** vt deodorize
**désœuvré** adj unoccupied, idle
**désœuvrement** nm idleness
**désolant** adj distressing, disheartening
**désolation** nf desolation; laying waste; grief
**désolé** adj desolate; devastated; very sorry
**désoler** vt desolate; devastate; distress; se ~ be very sad
**désopilant** adj hilarious, very funny
**désordonné** adj untidy, disorderly; disordered; dissolute
**désordonner** vt throw into disorder
**désordre** nm disorder, confusion; disorderliness; tumult; ~s disturbances
**désorganisation** nf disorganization
**désorganiser** vt disorganize
**désorienté** adj bewildered, at a loss

**désorienter** vt make (s/o) lose his way; disconcert

**désormais** adv henceforth, from now on

**désosser** vt bone

**désoxyder** vt deoxidize

**despote** nm despot

**despotique** adj despotic

**despotisme** nm despotism

**desquels** = de + lesquels

**dessaisir** vt leg dispossess; se ~ de drop, relinquish; part with; leg not proceed with

**dessalé** adj with the salt removed; sl wide-awake

**dessaler** vt remove the salt from; coll qn teach s/o a thing or two

**dessécher** vt (6) dry up; desiccate; wither, waste; se ~ dry up, wither, waste

**dessein** nm plan, project, design; à ~ on purpose

**desserrer** vt loosen, slacken; unclench; release; ne pas ~ les dents refuse to say anything; se ~ work loose

**dessert** nm dessert; sweet; pudding

**desservir** vt (89) eccles minister; ~ une ville serve a town (train, etc)

**dessin** nm drawing, sketch; pattern, design; profile; ~ animé cartoon film

**dessinateur -trice** n designer; draughtsman (-woman)

**dessiner** vt draw, sketch; design; outline; se ~ stand out, be outlined

**dessouder** vt unsolder

**dessoûler, dessaouler** vt sober; se ~ become sober

**dessous** adv underneath, lower part; ~-de-plat table-mat; ~ de robe underslip; avoir le ~ get the worst of it; les ~ the shady side, secret side; underwear; adv underneath, below; de ~ under(neath); en ~ furtively, in an underhand fashion

**dessus** nm upper surface, upper part; ~-de-lit bedspread; avoir le ~ get, have the upper hand; le ~ du panier the pick, the best; reprendre le ~ rally, get better; adv over, above; on top; bras ~ bras dessous arm in arm; de ~ upper, outer; en ~ on top

**destin** nm destiny, fate

**destinataire** n addressee; payee

**destinée** nf destiny

**destiner** vt destine; intend, assign; se ~ à une profession intend to take up a profession

**destituer** vt dismiss, remove

**destitution** nf dismissal

**destructeur -trice** adj destructive

**destructif -ive** adj destructive

**désuet -ète** adj obsolete, antiquated

**désuétude** nf disuse

**désuni** adj disunited; disjoined

**désunion** nf disunion; disconnection

**désunir** vt disunite, divide; disconnect

**détachant** nm stain-remover

**détaché** adj loose; detached, unconcerned; seconded

**détachement** nm detaching; indifference; detachment; secondment

¹**détacher** vt detach; unfasten, untie, unbind; separate; cut off; tear off; second

²**détacher** vt remove stains from

**détail** nm detail; dividing up; vendre au ~ sell retail

**détaillant -e** n retailer

**détailler** vt divide up, cut up; retail; enumerate; relate in detail

**détaler** vi run off, scamper away

**détaxe** nf remission of tax; tax refund

**détaxer** vt suppress (reduce) tax on

**détecter** vt detect

**détecteur** nm detector

**déteindre** vt (55) take the colour out of; vi lose colour, fade

**dételer** vt (5) unharness, unyoke

**détendre** vt loosen, relax; calm; se ~ become slack; relax; ease

**détendu** adj slack; relaxed

**détenir** vt (96) hold; be in possession of; detain; withhold

**détente** nf loosening, slackening, relaxing; easing; rest; trigger; coll dur à la ~ close-fisted; hard to get anything out of

**détenteur -trice** n holder; owner

**détention** nf holding; imprisonment

**détenu -e** n prisoner

**détérioration** nf deterioration; damage

**détériorer** vt worsen; damage; se ~ deteriorate

**déterminé** adj definite, specific, well-defined; resolute

**déterminer** vt determine; fix; cause, give rise to; se ~ make up one's mind

**déterrer** vt dig up, unearth; bring to light

**détersif** nm detergent

**détestable** adj detestable, hateful

**détester** vt hate, detest

**détonateur** nm detonator

**détoner** vi detonate, explode

**détonner** vi sing (play) out of tune; clash, jar

**détordre** vt untwist

**détortiller** vt untwist, disentangle

**détour** nm deviation; roundabout way; turn; curve; devious method; sans ~(s) frankly

**détourné** adj indirect, roundabout; unfrequented

**détournement** nm diversion; misappropriation; abduction; hi-jacking

**détourner** vt divert, turn; avert, turn

away; misappropriate; dissuade; hijack

**détracteur -trice** *n* detractor, disparager

**détraqué** *adj* deranged

**détraquement** *nm* putting out of order; breakdown

**détraquer** *vt* put out of order; upset

**détrempe** *nf* distemper

**détremper** *vt* soak, moisten

**détresse** *nf* distress; grief

**détriment** *nm* detriment, loss

**détritus** *nm* residue, refuse; rubbish

**détroit** *nm* straits

**détromper** *vt* undeceive

**détrôner** *vt* dethrone

**détrousser** *vt* untuck; rob; rifle

**détrousseur** *nm* footpad, highwayman

**détruire** *vt* (80) destroy, demolish; **se ~** kill oneself

**dette** *nf* debt; **faire des ~ s** run up debts

**deuil** *nm* mourning, sorrow; bereavement; mourning-clothes; period of mourning; funeral procession; **faire son ~ de qch** give sth up as lost, get along without sth; **quitter le ~** go out of mourning

**deux** *nm* two; second (dates); *adj* two; **à ~ pas d'ici** just near here; **à nous ~** it's a matter between you and me; **en moins de ~** in a jiffy; **tous (les) ~** both; **tous les ~ jours** every other day

**deuxième** *nm* second floor; *adj* second

**deux-mâts** *nm* two-master

**deux-pièces** *nm* two-piece suit

**deux-points** *nm* colon

**deux-roues** *nm* two-wheeled vehicle

**deux-temps** *nm mus* two–four time; **moteur ~** two-stroke engine

**dévaler** *vt* hurry down, race down; *vi* go down

**dévaliser** *vt* rob; rifle

**dévalorisation** *nf* drop in value

**dévaloriser** *vt* devalue

**dévaluer** *vt* devalue

**devancer** *vt* (4) precede, go before; overtake, outstrip, arrive before; forestall; anticipate

**devancier -ière** *n* predecessor; **~ s** forefathers

**devant** *nm* front (part); **prendre les ~ s** go on ahead; forestall, make the first move; *adv* ahead, in front; **comme ~** as before; **par ~** in front, the front way; **sens ~ derrière** back to front; *prep* in front of, before; in the presence of, in the face of; in view of

**devanture** *nf* front (shop); display (shop)

**dévastateur -trice** *n* ravager

**dévaster** *vt* devastate, lay waste, ravage

**déveine** *nf coll* bad luck

**développement** *nm* development,

growth; spreading out, expansion; spread; developing

**développer** *vt* develop; spread out, open out; unwrap; expound; **se ~** open out; develop

**devenir** *vi* (96) become, grow; grow into; **c'est à ~ fou!** it's enough to drive one mad!; **qu'est-il devenu?** what has become of him?

**dévergondage** *nm* profligate, extravagant behaviour

**dévergondé** *adj* profligate, shameless

**dévergonder (se)** *v refl* fall into dissolute ways

**dévers** *nm* inclination, slope; banking

**déversement** *nm* discharge; tipping

**déverser** *vt* pour, discharge; tip; divert; slope

**déversoir** *nm* overflow

**dévêtir** *vt* (97) undress, strip

**déviation** *nf* deviation; diversion; variation; curvature (spine)

**dévider** *vt* unwind; reel off

**dévié** *adj* diverted; **route ~ e** diversion

**dévier** *vt* deflect, turn aside; **se ~** grow crooked; warp; *vi* deviate, diverge

**devin** *nm* soothsayer

**deviner** *vt* guess; predict; **cela se devine** that's obvious

**devinette** *nf* riddle

**devis** *nm* estimate; specification

**dévisager** *vt* stare at

**devise** *nf* device; motto; slogan; *usu pl* currency

**deviser** *vi* chat, gossip

**dévisser** *vt* unscrew

**dévoiler** *vt* unveil; reveal, disclose, unmask

**devoir** *nm* duty; exercise; **~ s** homework; respects; **rentrer dans le ~** return to the path of duty; **se faire un ~ de faire qch** make a point of doing sth; **se mettre en ~ de** prepare to; *vt* (37) owe; *vi* should, ought, have to; be supposed to; must (probability); **il doit être là** he must be there

**dévolter** *vt* lower voltage

**dévolu** *nm coll* **jeter son ~ sur** have designs on; *adj* devolving

**dévolution** *nf* transmission (property); *eccles* lapsing

**dévorant** *adj* consuming, devouring

**dévorateur -trice** *adj* devouring, consuming

**dévorer** *vt* devour, consume

**dévot -e** *n* devout person; **faux ~** religious hypocrite; *adj* devout, religious

**dévotion** *nf* piety, devoutness

**dévoué** *adj* devoted, loyal; **votre ~** yours truly

**dévouer** *vt* dedicate; devote, sacrifice; **se**

~ devote oneself; throw oneself heart and soul

**dévoyé** *adj* led astray, perverted

**dévoyer** *vt* (7) lead astray, pervert; **se** ~ go astray

**dextérité** *nf* dexterity

**diabète** *nm med* diabetes

**diabétique** *n + adj* diabetic

**diable** *nm* devil; two-wheeled trolley; **bruit de tous les** ~ **s** hell of a din; **ce** ~ **de ...** that wretched ...; **du** ~ terrific; *coll* **faire le** ~ be noisy, troublesome; **faire qch à la** ~ do sth anyhow; **il habite au** ~ he lives miles away; **tirer le** ~ **par la queue** be hard up; *adj* mischievous

**diablement** *adv* awfully, tremendously

**diablerie** *nf* mischievousness; sorcery

**diablotin** *nm* little devil; imp

**diabolique** *adj* fiendish, diabolical

**diacre** *nm eccles* deacon

**diadème** *nm* diadem

**diagnostic** *nm* diagnosis

**diagonale** *nf* diagonal (line)

**diagramme** *nm* diagram

**dialecte** *nm* dialect

**dialoguer** *vi* converse; put into dialogue form; engage in talks

**diamant** *nm* diamond

**diamanté** *adj* set with diamonds

**diamétral** *adj* diametrical

**diamètre** *nm* diameter

**diane** *nf mil* reveille; **sonner la** ~ sound the reveille

**diantre** *interj obs* deuce!

**diapason** *nm* pitch; tuning-fork; range (voice); **se mettre au** ~ adapt

**diaphane** *adj* translucent

**diaphragme** *nm* diaphragm

**diapositive** *nf phot* slide, transparency

**diaprer** *vt* mottle, variegate, speckle

**diarrhée** *nf* diarrhoea

**diatonique** *adj mus* diatonic

**dichotomie** *nf* dichotomy

**dictame** *nm bot* dittany

**dictateur** *nm* dictator

**dictature** *nf* dictatorship

**dictée** *nf* dictation

**dicter** *vt* dictate

**diction** *nf* diction, delivery; elocution

**dictionnaire** *nm* dictionary

**dicton** *nm* maxim, common saying

**didactique** *adj* didactic

**diérèse** *nf* diaeresis

**dièse** *nm mus* sharp

**diète** *nf* diet

**diététicien -ienne** *n* dietician

**Dieu** *nm* God; *coll* **le bon** ~ God; **la maison du bon** ~ a hospitable house

**dieu** *nm* god, deity; **jurer ses grands** ~ **x** swear by all that's sacred

**diffamant** *adj* slanderous, libellous

**diffamateur -trice** *n* slanderer, libeller

**diffamation** *nf* slander, libel

**diffamatoire** *adj* slanderous, libellous

**diffamer** *vt* slander, libel

**différé** *adj* postponed; **en** ~ recorded (broadcast)

**différence** *nf* difference; **à la** ~ **de** unlike; **faire la** ~ distinguish, discriminate

**différencier** *vt* differentiate

**différend** *nm* difference, disagreement; **partager le** ~ split the difference, compromise

**¹différentiel** *nm mot* differential

**²différentiel -ielle** *adj* differential

**¹différer** *vt* (6) postpone, defer, hold over

**²différer** *vi* (6) differ

**difficile** *adj* difficult; trying; *coll* difficult to please, particular; **faire le** ~ be fussy

**difficilement** *adv* with difficulty

**difficulté** *nf* difficulty; objection

**difforme** *adj* deformed, misshapen

**difformité** *nf* deformity

**diffus** *adj* diffused; wordy (style)

**diffuser** *vt* diffuse; broadcast

**diffusion** *nf* diffusion; broadcasting; wordiness

**digérer** *vt* (6) digest; assimilate; *sl* put up with, bear, accept; stomach

**digeste** *adj* digestible

**digestif** *nm* digestive; liqueur (after meal)

**digital** *adj* digital; **empreinte** ~**e** fingerprint

**digitale** *nf bot* digitalis, foxglove

**digne** *adj* worthy, deserving; dignified; *coll* **c'est bien** ~ **de lui** that's just like him

**dignitaire** *nm* dignitary

**dignité** *nf* dignity; high position

**digue** *nf* dike, embankment; breakwater; jetty; *fig* obstacle

**dilapidation** *nf* wasting, squandering; peculation

**dilapider** *vt* waste, squander; misappropriate

**dilatation** *nf* dilation, expansion; distension

**dilater** *vt* dilate, expand; distend; **se** ~ swell; become distended

**dilemme** *nm* dilemma

**dilettante** *n* amateur, dilettante

**diligence** *nf* application, diligence; haste; stage-coach

**diligent** *adj* industrious, diligent; assiduous

**diluer** *vt* dilute, water down; weaken

**dilution** *nf* dilution, watering down

**diluvien -ienne** *adj* diluvian, diluvial; torrential (rain)

**dimanche** *nm* Sunday; **habits du** ~ Sunday best; **le** ~ on Sundays

**dîme** *nf* tithe

**diminuer** *vt* lessen, diminish, reduce; reduce the pay of; *vi* lessen, diminish, abate, fall off; **les jours diminuent** the days are getting shorter

**diminutif -ive** *adj* diminutive

**diminution** *nf* lessening, diminution, reduction, decrease; shortening (dress)

**dinde** *nf* turkey(-hen); *coll* silly woman

**dindon** *nm* turkey(-cock); **le ~ de la farce** the dupe

**dindonneau** *nm* young turkey

**dîner** *nm* dinner, evening meal; dinner-party; *vi* dine, have dinner; **qui dort dîne** sleep is as good as a meal

**dînette** *nf* children's dinner-party; playing at dinner (with dolls); light meal

**dîneur -euse** *n* diner

**dingue** *adj sl* crazy, cracked

**diocésain** *adj eccles* diocesan

**diphasé** *adj elect* two-phase

**diphtérie** *nf* diphtheria

**diphtongue** *nf* diphthong

**diplomate** *n* diplomat

**diplomatie** *nf* diplomacy

**diplôme** *nm* diploma; **~s** qualifications

**diplômer** *vt* grant a diploma to; **diplômé** certificated, qualified

**dipsomane** *n* dipsomaniac

**dire** *nm* assertion, statement; *vt* (38) say, tell; recite; express; think; **dis donc, ...** I say, ...; *coll* **à qui le dites-vous?** don't I know it?; **ce disant** with these words; **cela ne me dit rien** that doesn't convey anything to me; I'm not keen on that; **cela ne se dit pas** one doesn't say that; **il n'y a pas à** ~ one can't deny it; **il n'y a rien à** ~ **à cela** there's no objection to that; **on dirait un fou** he looks like a madman; **pour tout** ~ in a word; **si le cœur vous en dit** if you feel like it; **tenez-vous cela pour dit** don't let me have to tell you that again; **trouver à** ~ to object; **vouloir** ~ mean

**direct** *nm* fast train; live transmission; **en** ~ live; *adj* direct, straight; fast (train)

**directement** *adv* directly, straight

**directeur -trice** *n* director, directress, manager, manageress; head, chief; headmaster, headmistress, principal; leader; *adj* managing, controlling, directing

**direction** *nf* direction; management; control; conduct; leadership; *mot* steering

**directive** *nf usu pl* directive, guide-lines, rule(s); order(s)

**dirigeable** *nm* airship, dirigible

**dirigeant** *adj* guiding, directing, ruling

**diriger** *vt* (3) direct, control, manage; lead; conduct; edit; drive; level, aim; **se**

**~ vers** make one's way towards, head for

**discal** *adj* hernie **~e** slipped disc

**discernement** *nm* perception; distinguishing; discernment; understanding

**disciplinaire** *adj* disciplinary

**discipline** *nf* discipline; scourge; branch of study

**discipliner** *vt* discipline, bring under control

**discontinu** *adj* discontinuous

**discontinuation** *nf* discontinuance

**discontinuer** *vt* discontinue, cease; *vi* stop for a moment

**discontinuité** *nf* discontinuity

**disconvenance** *nf* disproportion, inequality; unsuitableness

**disconvenir** *vi* (96) not to agree

**discordance** *nf* discordance, dissonance; clashing (colours); disagreement

**discordant** *adj* discordant; grating, jarring; clashing (colours); conflicting

**discorde** *nf* discord, strife, dissension

**discoureur -euse** *n* talker, speechifier

**discourir** *vi* (29) make discourse, air opinions

**discours** *nm* talk; speech, address; discourse; diction; **parties du** ~ parts of speech; **prononcer un** ~ make a speech

**discourtois** *adj* discourteous, impolite

**discréditer** *vt* discredit, disparage

**discret -ète** *adj* discreet, cautious; quiet, unassuming, unobtrusive; modest (request)

**discrétion** *nf* discretion; prudence; **manger à** ~ eat as much as one likes

**discriminer** *vt* discriminate

**disculpation** *nf* exoneration

**disculper** *vt* exculpate, exonerate; **se ~** clear oneself

**discursif -ive** *adj* discursive

**discussion** *nf* discussion, debate; argument

**discutable** *adj* debatable

**discutailler** *vi coll* argue over trivialities, quibble

**discuté** *adj* contested; criticized

**discuter** *vt* discuss, debate, talk over, argue, question; **ça se discute** it's a debatable point; *vi* talk, chat

**disert** *adj* eloquent

**disette** *nf* dearth, scarcity

**diseur -euse** *n* reciter; **diseuse de bonne aventure** fortune-teller

**disgrâce** *nf* disgrace, fall from favour; misfortune; ugliness; plainness

**disgracier** *vt* dismiss from favour

**disgracieux -ieuse** *adj* uncouth, ungraceful; unpleasant; ugly

**disjoindre** *vt* (55) disjoin, sever

**disjoncteur** *nm* cut-out switch

**dislocation** *nf* dislocation; dismemberment

**disloquer** *vt* dislocate, put out of joint; dismember

**disparaître** *vi* (68) disappear, vanish; be hidden; pass away

**disparate** *adj* dissimilar; ill-assorted

**disparition** *nf* disappearance; death

**disparu** *adj + p part* disparaître *mil* missing; dead, departed; extinct; être porté ~ be listed as missing

**dispendieux -ieuse** *adj* costly, expensive

**dispensaire** *nm* dispensary; out-patients' department

**dispensation** *nf* dispensation, distribution

**dispense** *nf* exemption

**dispenser** *vt* exempt, dispense; distribute, give out; make up (medicine)

**dispersement** *nm* dispersing

**disperser** *vt* scatter, disperse, spread

**dispersion** *nf* dispersal; rout; scattering

**disponibilité** *nf* availability; readiness; state of not being committed; ~s available assets

**disponible** *adj* available; uncommitted

**dispos** *adj* fit, in good form; esprit ~ alert mind

**disposé** *adj* disposed, inclined; subject

**disposer** *vt* dispose, arrange, lay out; incline, influence; *vi* dispose, have at one's disposal; disposez de moi I am at your service; se ~ à make ready to; vous pouvez ~ you may go

**dispositif** *nm* device, appliance, gear

**disposition** *nf* disposition, arrangement, lay-out; frame of mind; propensity; tendency; aptitude; talent; disposal; ~s arrangements; *leg* provisions; prendre des ~s make arrangements

**disproportionné** *adj* disproportionate

**dispute** *nf* dispute; quarrel

**disputer** *vt* dispute, argue; scold, tell off; ~ un prix compete for a prize; *vi* quarrel; se ~ quarrel

**disqualifier** *vt* disqualify

**disque** *nm* disk, disc; (gramophone) record; discus; ~ de stationnement parking disc

**dissemblable** *adj* different, dissimilar

**dissemblance** *nf* dissimilarity

**dissémination** *nf* scattering, spreading

**disséminer** *vt* scatter, spread, disseminate

**dissentiment** *nm* disagreement, dissent

**disséquer** *vt* (6) dissect

**dissertation** *nf* dissertation; essay

**disserter** *vi* dissert; hold forth

**dissidence** *nf* dissidence, dissent

**dissident** *nm* dissentient; dissenter; *adj* dissident; disaffected

**dissimilaire** *adj* dissimilar, unlike

**dissimulateur -trice** *n* dissembler, dissimulator

**dissimulation** *nf* deceit, dissimulation; concealment

**dissimulé** *adj* secretive

**dissimuler** *vt* dissemble, dissimulate; conceal; se ~ hide

**dissipateur -trice** *n* squanderer, spendthrift

**dissipation** *nf* dissipation; dispersion; inattention

**dissiper** *vt* dissipate, scatter, disperse; dispel, clear up; squander; se ~ disappear, clear; amuse oneself; become dissipated; be inattentive

**dissocier** *vt* dissociate

**dissolu** *adj* dissolute, profligate

**dissolution** *nf* dissolution, disintegration, dissolving; breaking up; profligacy

**dissolvant** *nm* solvent; nail-varnish remover

**dissoudre** *vt* (8) dissolve, melt; disperse; decompose; se ~ dissolve, melt

**dissuader** *vt* dissuade

**dissyllabique** *adj* dissyllabic

**distance** *nf* distance; interval; à ~ at a distance

**distancer** *vt* (4) outrun, outstrip; se ~ keep one's distance; keep one's freedom of action

**distant** *adj* distant; stand-offish

**distendre** *vt* distend; strain

**distension** *nf* distension; straining

**distillateur** *nm* distiller

**distiller** *vt* distil; secrete

**distillerie** *nf* distillery; distilling

**distinct** *adj* distinct, separate; clear

**distinctif -ive** *adj* distinctive, characteristic

**distinction** *nf* distinction; honour; eminence; distinguished manner

**distinguable** *adj* distinguishable

**distingué** *adj* distinguished; eminent

**distinguer** *vt* distinguish; characterize; single out; perceive, discern; se ~ distinguish oneself, stand out

**distique** *nm* distich

**distorsion** *nf* distortion

**distraction** *nf* division; appropriation; inadvertence, absent-mindedness; entertainment, amusement; par ~ inadvertently

**distraire** *vt* (9) separate; misappropriate; entertain, divert; se ~ amuse oneself

**distrait** *adj* absent-minded

**distrayant** *adj* entertaining

**distribuer** *vt* distribute, issue; deliver (letters); deal (cards)

**distributeur -trice** *n* distributor; ~ automatique vending-machine

**distribution** *nf* distribution, allotment; delivery (letters); cast, casting; ~ **des prix** prize-giving

**dit** *adj+p part* **dire** agreed, appointed; (so-)called

**diurne** *adj* diurnal

**diva** *nf* prima-donna

**divagation** *nf* wandering; digression

**divaguer** *vi* wander; digress; talk nonsense, ramble

**divergence** *nf* divergence; disagreement

**diverger** *vi* (3) diverge

**divers** *adj pl* diverse, different; various, miscellaneous; *adj sing* **fait** ~ minor news item

**diversifier** *vt* diversify, vary

**diversion** *nf* diversion, change; **faire** ~ create a diversion

**diversité** *nf* diversity

**divertir** *vt* divert; entertain

**divertissant** *adj* amusing, entertaining

**divertissement** *nm* entertainment, recreation

**dividende** *nm* dividend

**divin** *adj* divine, holy; exquisite

**divinateur -trice** *n* soothsayer, diviner

**divination** *nf* soothsaying

**divinatoire** *adj* divinatory

**divinité** *nf* divinity; Godhead; deity

**diviser** *vt* divide, separate; **se** ~ break up

**diviseur** *nm* divisor; divider

**division** *nf* division, dividing; partition; section, part; department, branch; discord

**divisionnaire** *adj* belonging to a division

**divorce** *nm* divorce; disagreement

**divorcer** *vi* (4) divorce

**divulguer** *vt* divulge, reveal

**dix** *nm+adj* ten

**dix-huit** *nm+adj* eighteen

**dix-huitième** *n+adj* eighteenth

**dixième** *n+adj* tenth

**dix-neuf** *nm+adj* nineteen

**dix-neuvième** *n+adj* nineteenth

**dix-sept** *nm+adj* seventeen

**dix-septième** *n+adj* seventeenth

**dizaine** *nf* about ten

**do** *nm invar mus* C, do(h)

**docile** *adj* docile, submissive, tractable

**docilité** *nf* docility

**dock** *nm naut* dock; warehouse; shop (*usu* food)

**docte** *adj* learned

**docteur** *nm* doctor

**doctoral** *adj* doctoral; pompous

**doctorat** *nm* doctorate

**doctoresse** *nf* woman doctor

**documentaire** *nm* documentary film; *adj* documentary

**documentation** *nf* documentation; documents

**documenter** *vt* document; **se** ~ **sur** gather information about

**dodeliner** *vi* shake head (of elderly person)

**dodo** *nm coll* bye-byes; **aller au** ~ go to bye-byes; **faire** ~ sleep

**dodu** *adj* plump

**dogmatique** *adj* dogmatic

**dogme** *nm* dogma

**dogue** *nm* big watch-dog; mastiff

**doigt** *nm* finger; finger's breadth; ~ **de pied** toe; ~ **de vin** drop of wine; **à deux** ~**s de la mort** within an inch of death; **mettre le** ~ **dessus** discover the solution; **montrer du** ~ point at; **s'en mordre les** ~**s** regret it

**doigté** *nm* tact; *mus* fingering

**doit** *nm* debit, liability

**doléances** *nfpl* complaints, grouses

**dolent** *adj* whining, plaintive

**domaine** *nm* domain; estate; field, realm; ~ **de l'État**, ~ **public** public property; **dans le** ~ **public** out of copyright

**dôme** *nm* dome

**domesticité** *nf* domesticated state, domesticity; domestic staff

**domestique** *n* servant; *adj* domestic

**domestiquer** *vt* domesticate

**domicile** *nm* residence, domicile; **à** ~ at one's place of residence

**domicilié** *adj* resident

**dominance** *nf* dominance; predominance, preponderance

**dominant** *adj* dominant, ruling; prevailing

**dominateur -trice** *adj* domineering

**dominer** *vt* rule; dominate, control; overtake, tower above; master

**dominicain -e** *n+adj eccles* Dominican

**dominical** *adj* dominical, relating to Sunday

**dommage** *nm* damage, injury; *leg* ~**s et intérêts** damages; **quel** ~! what a pity!; **réparer les** ~**s** make good the damage

**domptable** *adj* tameable

**domptage** *nm* taming

**dompter** *vt* tame, break in; subdue, master

**dompteur -euse** *n* tamer

**don** *nm* giving, gift, present; talent

**donateur -trice** *n* giver; *leg* donor (donatrix)

**donc** *conj* therefore, hence, so; *adv* (used for emphasis) **allez** ~! go on!; do go!; **pensez** ~! just imagine!

**dondon** *nf coll* fat woman

**donjon** *nm* keep

**donnant** *adj* generous; ~, ~ fifty-fifty

**donne** *nf* deal (cards)

**donnée** *nf* premise; datum; ~**s** data

**donner** *vt* give; provide, furnish; yield;

attribute, ascribe; ~ **la main à qn** shake hands with s/o; ~ **le bonjour à qn** wish s/o good day; ~ **tort (raison) à qn** disagree (agree) with s/o; ~ **une pièce de théâtre** put on a play; **cela donne à penser** that gives one food for thought; **c'est donné** it's dirt cheap; **étant donné que** given that; **je vous le donne en mille** you'll never guess; **se ~ au plaisir** give oneself up to pleasure; **se ~ pour** claim to be; **s'en ~ à cœur joie** enjoy oneself no end; vi ~ **dans le luxe** like expensive things; ~ **dans un piège** fall into a trap; ~ **de la tête contre** bump one's head against; ~ **sur** look out on, lead into, shine on

**donneur -euse** n giver, donor; dealer (cards); sl informer, nark, sneak

**dont** rel pron from, by, with whom or which; of, concerning whom or which; whose

**donzelle** nf coll wench

**dopant** nm dope, stimulant

**doper** vt dope; reinforce, improve the quality of

**dorade** nf sea-bream; dolphin

**dorénavant** adv henceforth

**dorer** vt gild; glaze (cake); brown; ~ **la pilule** sugar the pill; **doré sur tranches** gilt-edged (book)

**dorique** adj Doric

**dorloter** vt fondle; pamper

**dormant** adj sleeping; dormant; stagnant

**dormeur -euse** n sleeper; sleepy-head

**dormir** vi (39) sleep, be asleep; be dormant; ~ **debout** be dead tired; ~ **sur les deux oreilles** be quite easy in one's mind; **eau qui dort** stagnant water; **histoire à ~ debout** tall story, boring tale

**dortoir** nm dormitory

**dorure** nf gilding

**doryphore** nm Colorado beetle

**dos** nm back; **avoir bon ~** be blamed unfairly; coll **en avoir plein le ~** be fed up; **se mettre tout le monde à ~** put everyone against oneself

**doser** vt proportion

**dossard** nm number (on back of competitor's clothing)

**dossier** nm back (of seat); documents, record

**dot** nf dowry

**dotation** nf endowment

**doter** vt give dowry to; endow

**douairière** nf dowager; pej old woman

**douane** nf customs; customs house

**douanier -ière** n customs official; adj customs

**doublage** nm cin dubbing; theat under-

studying; doubling; lining (clothes)

**double** nm double; duplicate; adj double, twofold; ar two-faced; **faire coup ~** kill two birds with one stone

**doubler** vt double; fold; line (garment); mot overtake; dub; vi double

**doublure** nf lining; theat understudy; cin stand-in

**douce** adj see **doux**

**douceâtre** adj sweetish, cloying

**doucement** adv softly, gently; smoothly

**doucereux -euse** adj sickly; smooth-tongued

**douceur** nf sweetness; smoothness; pleasantness; ~s sweets; gentleness; **en ~** gently

**douche** nf shower; shower-bath; ~ **écossaise** alternate hot and cold shower; nasty shock

**doucher** vt give (s/o) a shower

**doué** adj gifted

**douer** vt endow

**douille** nf socket; elect holder; case (cartridge)

**douillet -ette** adj soft; snug; liking comfort

**douillette** nf quilted coat

**douleur** nf pain, suffering; grief

**douloureuse** nf coll bill

**douloureux -euse** adj painful; distressing

**doute** nm uncertainty, doubt; **avoir des ~s** have misgivings; **mettre en ~** cast doubt on; **sans ~** probably; certainly

**douter** vi doubt; **à n'en point ~** undoubtedly; coll **il ne doute de rien** he's cocksure; **se ~ de** suspect

**douteux -euse** adj uncertain, doubtful; suspect; grubby

**douve** nf moat

**doux** (f **douce**) adj sweet; soft, pleasant; gentle, meek; **eau douce** fresh water; adv **filer ~** be submissive; **tout ~!** gently!, easy!

**douzaine** nf dozen, about twelve

**douze** nm + adj twelve

**douzième** nm + adj twelfth

**doyen -enne** n oldest, senior; nm dean

**draconien -ienne** adj draconian, harsh

**dragage** nm dredging; mine-sweeping

**dragée** nf sugared almond; **tenir la ~ haute à qn** make s/o pay dearly for something

**dragon** nm dragon; mil dragoon

**drague** nf dredge; drag-net

**draguer** vt dredge; drag, sweep; coll pick up; vi coll be out for a pick-up

**dragueur** nm dredger; ~ **de mines** mine-sweeper

**drain** nm drainage-tube

**drainer** vt drain

**dramatique** adj dramatic

**dramatiser** *vt* dramatize

**dramaturge** *n* dramatist

**drame** *nm* drama; tragic occurrence, disaster

**drap** *nm* cloth; sheet; *coll* être dans de beaux ~ s be in a fine mess

**drapeau** *nm* flag; être sous les ~ x be in the army

**draper** *vt* drape, cover

**draperie** *nf* drapery

**drapier** *nm* draper

**drastique** *adj* drastic

**drelin** *nm* ting-a-ling

**dressage** *nm* training; dressage; straightening

**dresser** *vt* set up, erect; lay (table); pitch (tent); draw up; arrange; train, break in (animal); se ~ rise, straighten up, stand

**dresseur -euse** *n* trainer; erector

**dressoir** *nm* dresser, sideboard

**drogue** *nf* drug; *coll* worthless medicine

**drogué -e** *n* drug addict; drugged person

**droguer** *vt* drug; *vi coll* be kept waiting

**droguerie** *nf* shop selling household goods, paint, dyes, etc

**droguiste** *n* manager, owner of droguerie

**droit** *nm* right; law; fee, charge; ~ s d'auteur royalties; à bon ~ with good reason; à qui de ~ to whom it may concern; être en ~ de be entitled to; faire son ~ study law; *adj* straight, direct; right; upright, frank; angle ~ right angle; *adv* straight

**droite** *nf* right hand; *pol* right

**droitier -ière** *adj* right-handed

**droiture** *nf* straightforwardness, upright character

**drolatique** *adj* comic

**drôle** *nm* rascal; *adj* funny; ~ de odd, strange, curious

**drôlerie** *nf* oddness; joke

**drôlesse** *nf* jade, hussy

**dromadaire** *nm* dromedary

**dru** *adj* thick, strong, dense; *adv* thickly, hard

**druide -esse** *n* druid, druidess

**du** = de le

**dû** *nm* due; *adj* (*f* due) owing, due, owed; *p part* devoir

**dubitatif -ive** *adj* dubitative

**duc** *nm* duke; horned owl

**duché** *nm* dukedom

**duchesse** *nf* duchess

**duègne** *nf* duenna

**dulcifier** *vt* sweeten

**dulcinée** *nf* lady-love

**dûment** *adv* duly, in due form

**duo** *nm* duet

**duper** *vt* trick, fool, dupe

**duperie** *nf* deception

**duplex** *nm* two-way communication system, duplex; two-storey flat

**duplicata** *nm invar* copy, duplicate

**duplicité** *nf* double-dealing

**duquel** = du + lequel

**dur** *nm coll* tough guy; *pol* hawk; *bui* concrete, stone, etc; *adj* hard, tough; harsh, severe; à la ~ e in a tough way; avoir la vie ~ e be very resistant, be hard to kill; have a hard life; être ~ d'oreille be hard of hearing; œuf ~ hard-boiled egg; *adv* hard

**durabilité** *nf* durability

**durant** *prep* during

**durcir** *vt* + *vi* harden

**durcissement** *nm* hardening

**durée** *nf* duration; life, lasting quality; de courte ~ short-lived

**durement** *adv* hard, harshly

**durer** *vi* last, endure, hold out

**dureté** *nf* hardness; difficulty; harshness

**durillon** *nm* callosity, corn

**duvet** *nm* down; eiderdown; down sleeping-bag, clothing

**duveteux -euse** *adj* downy

**dynamique** *adj* dynamic

**dynamiter** *vt* blow up, dynamite

**dynastie** *nf* dynasty

**dysenterie** *nf* dysentery

**dyslexie** *nf* dyslexia

**dyslexique** *adj* dyslexic

**dyspepsie** *nf* dyspepsia

**dyspepsique, dyspeptique** *adj* dyspeptic

# E

eau *nf* water; ~ **courante** running water; ~ **oxygénée** hydrogen peroxide; **château d'**~ water tower; **cours d'**~ stream; **faire** ~ spring a leak (ship); **il tombe de l'**~ it is raining; **jet d'**~ fountain; **laver à grande** ~ swill down; **mettre de l'**~ **dans son vin** draw in one's horns; **pièce d'**~ ornamental pond or lake; **tomber à l'**~ fall through; **ville d'**~ spa

eau-de-vie *nf* (*pl* eaux-de-vie) spirits, brandy

eau-forte *nf* (*pl* eaux-fortes) etching; nitric acid

ébahir *vt* astound, flabbergast

ébahissement *nm* astonishment, amazement

ébarber *vt* trim, clip

ébats *nmpl* frolic, gambols

ébattre (s') *v refl* frolic, gambol, frisk about

ébaubi *adj* staggered

ébauche *nf* outline; rough sketch; rough pressing, rough cast

ébaucher *vt* sketch out, outline; rough-hew

ébène *nf* ebony

ébéniste *nm* cabinet-maker

ébénisterie *nf* cabinet work

éberlué *adj* amazed, staggered

éblouir *vt* dazzle

éblouissement *nm* dazzling; dizziness

éborgner *vt* blind in one eye

éboueur *nm* dustman

ébouillanter *vt* scald; dip in boiling water

éboulement *nm* landslide; caving in; rock-fall

ébouler (s') *v refl* crumble, cave in, slip

éboulis *nm* mass of fallen earth and stones, scree

ébouriffer *vt* ruffle, dishevel; amaze, take aback

ébrancher *vt* lop off the branches of

ébranlement *nm* shock, shaking; agitation

ébranler *vt* shake, unsettle; loosen; s' ~ get under way

ébrécher *vt* (6) chip; *coll* damage, reduce

ébriété *nf* state of drunkenness

ébrouer (s') *v refl* snort (horse); clean oneself (bird)

ébruiter *vt* noise abroad, make known; s' ~ become known

ébullition *nf* boiling, ebullition

écaille *nf* scale (fish); shell; tortoise-shell; flake, splinter

¹écailler *vt* remove scales from; open (oyster); s' ~ scale off

²écailler -ère *n* person who sells or opens oysters

écailleux -euse *adj* scaly; splintery, flaky

écale *nf* husk, shell

écarlate *nf*+*adj* scarlet

écarquiller *vt* open wide (eyes); spread out (legs)

écart *nm* distance apart; divergence, variation; deviation, swerve; discarding, discard (cards); ~ **de jeunesse** youthful aberration; **à l'**~ aside, on one side; **faire le grand** ~ do the splits; **faire un** ~ shy, step aside suddenly; make a digression; **tenir qn à l'**~ keep s/o in the background

écarté *adj* isolated, remote

écarteler *vt* (5) *hist* quarter (criminal, shield); **être écartelé entre** be torn between

écartement *nm* spacing, setting aside; gap, separation

écarter *vt* separate, open, draw aside, ward off; exclude; ~ **un obstacle** get rid of an obstacle; s' ~ move aside; diverge, stray

ecchymose *nf* bruise

ecclésiastique *nm* member of clergy, cleric; *adj* ecclesiastical

écervelé *adj* scatter-brained, thoughtless

échafaud *nm* scaffold

échafaudage *nm* scaffolding; erection of scaffolding; constructing

échafauder *vt* erect scaffolding on; build up; ~ **des projets** make plans

échalas *nm* prop (for vine or other plant); long, skinny person

échalote *nf* shallot

échancrer *vt* cut out; notch

échancrure *nf* cut-out section, opening; notch, indentation

échange *nm* exchange

échangeable *adj* exchangeable

échanger *vt* (3) exchange, swap

échangeur *nm* motorway intersection

échanson *nm* cup-bearer

échantillon *nm* sample, specimen

échantillonner *vt* prepare patterns of; check or compare samples of

échappatoire *nf* way out, subterfuge; loop-hole

échappée *nf* escape; escapade; glimpse; brief moment

**échappement** *nm* escape (gas, water); escapement (clock); **tuyau d'** ~ exhaust-pipe

**échapper** *vi* escape; pass unnoticed; **cela m'a échappé** I said that quite unintentionally; **l'** ~ **belle** have a narrow escape; **s'** ~ escape; flee, run away; leak

**écharde** *nf* splinter

**écharpe** *nf* sash; scarf; **avoir le bras en** ~ have one's arm in a sling; **mot prendre en** ~ crash into the side of

**écharper** *vt* slash; hack to pieces

**échasse** *nf* stilt

**échassier** *nm orni* wader

**échauder** *vt* scald; plunge in boiling water; ~ **un client** fleece a customer; **se faire** ~ burn one's fingers

**échauffant** *adj* binding (food)

**échauffement** *nm* heating, overheating; overexcitement

**échauffer** *vt* overheat; *coll* ~ **la bile de qn** anger s/o; **s'** ~ get overheated; get excited

**échauffourée** *nf* scuffle; clash

**échauguette** *nf* watch-tower; bartizan

**échéance** *nf* date (for payment, etc); expiration; **à courte (longue)** ~ short-(long-)dated

**échéant** *adj* **le cas** ~ should the occasion arise

**échec** *nm* failure; check; ~ **s** chess; ~ **et mat** checkmate; **tenir en** ~ hold in check

**échelle** *nf* ladder; scale; ~ **mobile** sliding scale; **faire la courte** ~ **à qn** give s/o a leg-up, a helping hand; **il n'y a plus qu'à tirer l'** ~ you can't do better than that; you might as well give up

**échelon** *nm* rung; *mil* echelon

**échelonner** *vt* space out; spread out; stagger; dispose in echelon (troops)

**écheveau** *nm* hank, skein

**échevelé** *adj* dishevelled; disordered, wild

**échine** *nf* spike, backbone; *coll* **avoir l'** ~ **souple** be obsequious

**échiner** *vt* break the back of; *coll* **s'** ~ wear oneself out

**échiquier** *nm* chess-board; **Chancelier de l'Échiquier** Chancellor of the Exchequer

**écho** *nm* echo; **les** ~ **s** news items; **se faire l'** ~ **de** repeat

**échoir** *vi* (40) happen; fall due

**échoppe** *nf* street stall

**échouer** *vi* run aground; fail, fall through; *coll* stop, land (in a place)

**échu** *p part* échoir

**éclaboussement** *nm* splashing, spattering

**éclabousser** *vt* splash, spatter

**éclaboussure** *nf* splash, spatter

**éclair** *nm* flash of lightning; flash; *cul* éclair

**éclairage** *nm* lighting; illumination; light

**éclairant** *adj* lighting, illuminating

**éclaircie** *nf* opening, break (in clouds); clearing

**éclaircir** *vt* lighten; clear; solve, explain; thin, thin out; clarify; **s'** ~ clear up; become clearer; thin

**éclaircissement** *nm* explanation, enlightenment, clearing up

**éclairé** *adj* well-informed, enlightened

**éclairer** *vt* light, illuminate; enlighten; reconnoitre

**éclaireur** *nm* scout

**éclaireuse** *nf* girl-guide

**éclat** *nm* chip, splinter; burst; flash, brightness, brilliance, glare, show; scandal; **sans** ~ quietly

**éclatant** *adj* brilliant, shining, dazzling, bright; loud

**éclatement** *nm* bursting; dispersion

**éclater** *vi* splinter; burst, explode; break out; burst out; spill out

**éclectique** *adj* eclectic

**éclipser** *vt* eclipse; **s'** ~ disappear, vanish

**éclopé** *adj* lame, crippled

**éclore** *vi* (41) open, blossom; hatch out; appear

**éclosion** *nf* opening, blossoming; hatching

**écluse** *nf* lock (canal)

**éclusier -ière** *n* lock-keeper

**écœurant** *adj* sickening, disgusting

**écœurement** *nm* disgust

**écœurer** *vt* sicken, disgust; discourage

**école** *nf* school; instruction, training; **être à bonne** ~ be in good hands; **faire** ~ found a school (art, thought); **haute** ~ advanced horsemanship

**écolier -ière** *n* schoolboy(girl); **chemin des** ~ **s** long way round

**écologie** *nf* ecology

**écologique** *adj* ecological

**écologiste** *n* ecologist

**éconduire** *vt* (80) show (s/o) the door, get rid of; refuse, reject

**économat** *nm* stewardship, bursarship; bursar's office, steward's office; staff shop

**économe** *n* bursar, treasurer, steward; *adj* economical, thrifty, sparing

**économie** *nf* economy, management; saving, thrift; **faire des** ~ **s** save money

**économique** *adj* economic; economical, thrifty; inexpensive

**économiser** *vt* save, economize

**économiste** *n* economist

**écoper** *vt* bail out; *vi sl* be wounded; cop it

**écorce** *nf* bark; rind, peel, husk

**écorcer** *vt* remove bark (peel, husk) of

**écorcher** *vt* flay, skin; fleece (customer);

graze, bark; scrape; ~ **l'oreille** grate on the ear; ~ **une langue** murder a language

**écorchure** *nf* abrasion, scratch, graze

**écorner** *vt* break, remove horns of (animal); break, chip off the corner of; dog-ear; ~ **sa fortune** break into one's fortune

**écornifler** *vt coll* scrounge, sponge

**Écossais -e** *n* Scot

**écossais** *adj* Scottish, Scots

**Écosse** *nf* Scotland

**écosser** *vt* shell (peas, etc)

**écot** *nm* quota, share

**écoulement** *nm* outflow, discharge; waste-pipe; sale

**écouler** *vt* get rid of, dispose of, sell; **s' ~** flow out; elapse, pass

**écourter** *vt* shorten, curtail, cut short; dock, crop

¹**écoute** *nf* listening; **être aux ~s** eavesdrop; **mettre sur ~** bug; **se mettre à l' ~** listen in to the radio

²**écoute** *nf naut* sheet

**écouter** *vt + vi* listen (to); pay attention (to); **s' ~ beaucoup** pay excessive attention to one's health; **s' ~ parler** enjoy hearing oneself speak

**écouteur** *nm* receiver, ear-phone

**écoutille** *nf naut* hatchway

**écrabouiller** *vt coll* squash, crush

**écran** *nm* screen; filter (light); shade; **le petit ~** television, the box

**écrasant** *adj* crushing

**écrasement** *nm* crushing, squashing; defeat; crashing, collapsing

**écraser** *vt* squash, crush; run over; defeat; overburden; **s' ~** collapse, crash; *vi sl* **écrase!** forget it!

**écrémer** *vt* (6) cream; skim (milk); *fig* cream off

**écrémeuse** *nf* creamer, (cream) separator

**écrevisse** *nf* crayfish; **rouge comme une ~** red as a lobster (beetroot)

**écrier (s')** *v refl* cry out, exclaim

**écrin** *nm* casket, jewel-case

**écrire** *vt + vi* (42) write, write down; **il est écrit que** fate has decided that; **machine à ~** typewriter

**écrit** *nm* writing; written exam, written document; **par ~** in writing

**écriteau** *nm* notice, placard

**écritoire** *nf* writing desk

**écriture** *nf* handwriting; **~s** documents, papers; accounts; **Écriture Sainte** Holy Scripture

**écrivailler** *vi coll* scribble, write badly

**écrivailleur -euse** *n* scribbler, hackwriter

**écrivain** *nm* writer, author

¹**écrou** *nm* nut

²**écrou** *nm* committal to gaol; **lever l' ~** discharge

**écrouelles** *nfpl* scrofula

**écrouer** *vt* put in prison

**écroulement** *nm* collapse, falling in; downfall

**écrouler (s')** *v refl* collapse, fall down, give way

**écru** *adj* unbleached (material)

**écu** *nm* shield, escutcheon; crown; *hist* five-franc piece

**écueil** *nm* reef; obstacle, peril

**écuelle** *nf* basin, bowl

**éculé** *adj* down at heel

**écume** *nf* froth, foam, scum; dregs (of society); ~ **de mer** meerschaum

**écumeux -euse** *adj* frothy, foamy

**écumoire** *nf* skimmer

**écurer** *vt* clean, scour

**écureuil** *nm* squirrel

**écurie** *nf* stable; horses; writers working with a publisher; cars or cyclists racing for a firm

**écusson** *nm* shield, escutcheon, badge

**écuyer** *nm* squire; equerry; (*f* **-ère**) horse-rider; **monter à l'écuyère** ride astride

**édenté** *adj* toothless

**édicter** *vt* decree

**édifiant** *adj* edifying

**édification** *nf* building, setting up; edification; enlightenment

**édifice** *nm* building, edifice

**édifier** *vt* set up, erect; edify; inform, enlighten

**Édimbourg** *nm* Edinburgh

**édit** *nm* edict

**éditer** *vt* publish; edit

**éditeur -trice** *n* publisher; editor

**édition** *nf* edition, issue, impression; publishing; ~ **originale** first edition

**Édouard** *nm* Edward

**édredon** *nm* eiderdown

**éducateur -trice** *n* educator

**éducatif -ive** *adj* educative

**éducation** *nf* education, upbringing; training; rearing; **homme sans ~** ill-bred man

**édulcorant** *nm* sweetener

**édulcorer** *vt* sweeten; attenuate

**éduquer** *vt* educate, bring up; train

**effacé** *adj* unobtrusive, retiring; retired

**effacement** *nm* obliteration; wearing away; self-effacement, unobtrusiveness

**effacer** *vt* obliterate, rub out, delete; eclipse, surpass; **s' ~** wear away; come off; stand aside, give way

**effarant** *adj* incredible, fantastic

**effarer** *vt* scare, frighten

**effaroucher** *vt* startle, scare

**effectif** *nm mil* establishment; manpower; *usu pl mil* strength; *adj* (*f* **-ive**) effective, efficacious; real

**effectivement** *adv* indeed, yes; effectively; actually

**effectuer** *vt* carry out, effect, realize, accomplish

**efféminé** *adj* effeminate

**effervescence** *nf* effervescence; excitement, agitation

**effet** *nm* result; property, virtue; action; impression, effect; bill; ~ s belongings; **à cet** ~ to this end; **en** ~ indeed; **faire bon** ~ look well, give a good impression; **faire de l'** ~ impress, attract attention; **faire l'** ~ **de** give the impression of; **manquer son** ~ fall flat; **mettre à** ~ carry out, put into operation; **prendre** ~ become operative; **sans** ~ ineffective

**effeuiller** *vt* take off, thin out leaves, petals of; **s'** ~ shed leaves or petals

**effeuilleuse** *nf* stripper

**efficace** *adj* effective, efficacious

**efficacité** *nf* effectiveness, efficacy; efficiency

**effigie** *nf* effigy

**effilé** *adj* slim, slender; tapering

**effiler** *vt* taper; fray; **s'** ~ taper; fray

**effilocher** *vt* fray; ravel out

**efflanqué** *adj* skinny, lean

**effleurement** *nm* light touch, graze; skimming

**effleurer** *vt* touch lightly, graze; skim

**effluve** *nm* emanation

**effondré** *adj* prostrate, shattered

**effondrement** *nm* collapse; subsidence; slump

**effondrer** *vt* break down, bash in; **s'** ~ cave in, fall in, collapse

**efforcer** (s') *v refl* (4) try, strive

**effort** *nm* effort, exertion; strain

**effraction** *nf* breaking in, house-breaking

**effraie** *nf* barn owl, screech owl

**effranger** *vt* (3) fray out (material)

**effrayant** *adj* frightening, terrifying; dreadful; *coll* amazing, tremendous

**effrayer** *vt* (7) frighten, scare; put off, discourage; **s'** ~ be frightened

**effréné** *adj* unbridled; frantic; excessive

**effriter** *vt* reduce to powder, make crumble; **s'** ~ crumble away

**effroi** *nm* terror, fright

**effronté** *adj* bold, shameless, brazen

**effronterie** *nf* effrontery, insolence

**effroyable** *adj* dreadful, frightful; tremendous, awful

**effusion** *nf* effusion; outpouring, overflowing; shedding (blood)

**égailler** (s') *v refl* scatter, disperse

**égal** *adj* equal; same; level, smooth, even, constant; **à armes** ~ **es** on equal terms; **à l'** ~ **de** equally with; **cela m'est** ~ I don't mind, it's all the same to me; *coll* **c'est** ~ well, never mind, all the same; **traiter qn d'** ~ **à** ~ treat s/o as an equal

**également** *adv* equally; also

**égaler** *vt* equal, be equal to; rival

**égaliser** *vt* equalize; level, make even

**égalitaire** *adj* egalitarian

**égalité** *nf* equality; evenness, regularity; **à** ~ equal, even (in games); **à** ~ **de** given equality in; **sur un pied d'** ~ on an equal footing

**égard** *nm* regard; consideration, respect; **à l'** ~ **de** with regard to; **avoir** ~ à allow for

**égaré** *adj* stray, lost; distraught

**égarement** *nm* mislaying; straying; bewilderment; deviation, misconduct; frenzy

**égarer** *vt* lead astray; lose, mislay; bewilder; **s'** ~ lose one's way; become deranged

**égayer** *vt* (7) amuse, cheer up; enliven; brighten up

**égide** *nf* aegis, shield; *coll* protection

**églantier** *nm* wild rose bush

**églantine** *nf* wild rose

**église** *nf* church

**églogue** *nf* eclogue

**égoïsme** *nm* selfishness

**égoïste** *n* + *adj* selfish (person)

**égorger** *vt* (3) cut the throat of; butcher, slaughter

**égosiller** (s') *v refl* bawl, shout one's head off; sing loudly (birds)

**égout** *nm* drainage, draining; sewer, drain; *fig* sink; **tout-à-l'** ~ mains drainage

**égoutter** *vt* + *vi* drain; drip dry; **s'** ~ drain, drip

**égouttoir** *nm* drainer, plate-rack

**égratigner** *vt* scratch; graze; *fig* offend slightly

**égratignure** *nf* scratch; slight

**égrener** *vt* (6) shell; ~ **un chapelet** tell beads; **s'** ~ drop, fall; be dotted along

**égrillard** *adj* ribald, lewd; spicy

**Égypte** *nf* Egypt

**égyptien -ienne** *adj* Egyptian

**eh** *interj* hey!; ~ **bien!** well!

**éhonté** *adj* shameless

**éjecter** *vt* eject

**élaborer** *vt* elaborate; digest

**élaguer** *vt* prune, lop off; cut down

**élan** *nm* bound, spring; impetus; burst; **prendre son** ~ take off, take a run

**élancement** *nm* sudden twinge of pain; transport (feeling)

**élancer** (s') *v refl* (4) spring, bound forward, rush forward

**élargir** *vt* widen, let out, stretch, broaden, enlarge; set free

**élargissement** nm widening

**élasticité** nf elasticity

**élastique** nm elastic; adj elastic; springy, buoyant

**électeur -trice** n elector, voter

**électif -ive** adj elective

**élection** nf election, polling; choice, preference

**électoral** adj electoral

**électorat** nm electorate

**électricien -ienne** n electrician

**électricité** nf electricity

**électrifier** vt electrify

**électrique** adj electric

**électro-aimant** nm electro-magnet

**électrocardiogramme** nm electrocardiogram

**électrocuter** vt electrocute

**électrogène** adj generating; **groupe ~** generating plant

**électrolyse** nf electrolysis

**électroménager** nm electrical household appliance department, industry; adj (f -ère) **appareil ~** electrical household appliance

**électronique** adj electronic

**électrophone** nm record-player

**élégance** nf elegance, stylishness

**élégant** adj elegant, well-dressed, stylish

**élégiaque** adj elegiac

**élégie** nf elegy

**élément** nm element; ingredient, component; elect cell; **~ s** rudiments

**élémentaire** adj elementary; rudimentary

**élevage** nm raising, rearing

**élévateur** nm lift, hoist; elevator muscle

**élévation** nf elevation, lifting; setting up; rise; height, altitude; promotion

**élévatoire** adj elevatory, lifting

**élève** n pupil, student; apprentice; disciple; trainee

**élevé** adj high; lofty; **bien ~** well-bred; **peu ~** low

**élever** vt (6) raise, elevate; set up, build; rear, bring up; s' ~ rise; raise oneself; s' ~ à amount to; s' ~ contre object to, protest against

**éleveur -euse** n breeder; wine-producer

**éleveuse** nf battery (poultry)

**elfe** nm elf

**élider** vt elide

**éligibilité** nf eligibility

**élimer** vt wear (cloth); s' ~ wear out

**éliminateur -trice** adj eliminating

**éliminatoire** adj eliminatory

**éliminer** vt eliminate, get rid of

**élire** vt (56) elect, choose; ~ **domicile** take up residence

**élite** nf élite, pick, flower; **troupes d' ~** crack troops

**élitisme** nm élitism

**elle** (pl **elles**) pron she, they; it, they; her, it, them

**ellipse** nf ellipsis; ellipse

**éloge** nm praise; panegyric; **faire l' ~ de** praise

**élogieux -ieuse** adj eulogistic, laudatory

**éloigné** adj distant, faraway, remote; ~ **de trois kilomètres** three kilometres away; **peu ~** near

**éloignement** nm removal; distance, remoteness

**éloigner** vt remove, send away, put away; put out of the way, banish, set aside, dismiss; put back, postpone; s' ~ move away, off; deviate; differ (opinion); become detached

**éloquence** nf eloquence, oratory

**¹élu -e** n elected member; elect; chosen

**²élu** p part **élire**

**élucider** vt elucidate, clear up

**élucubration** nf lucubration; **~ s** wild utterances

**éluder** vt elude, evade

**Élysée** nm Elysium; (le palais de) l' ~ French President's palace

**émacié** adj emaciated

**émail** nm (pl **-aux**) enamel

**émailler** vt enamel; glaze; stud, spangle; dot (of flowers); enrich, embellish

**émailleur -euse** n enameller

**émancipateur -trice** n emancipator

**émancipé** adj free (in manner)

**émanciper** vt emancipate; s' ~ free oneself; coll get out of hand, behave too freely

**émaner** vi emanate, issue

**émarger** vt trim the margins of; sign or initial in margin (as acknowledgement); vi be on the payroll

**émasculer** vt emasculate, weaken

**emballage** nm wrapping, packing

**emballement** nm racing (of engine); coll sudden enthusiasm

**emballer** vt wrap, pack; coll delight; sl tell off; race (engine); s' ~ bolt, run; race (of engine); coll be keen, enthusiastic; fly into a rage

**emballeur -euse** n packer

**embarcadère** nm landing-stage; quay, wharf

**embarcation** nf (small) craft

**embardée** nf lurch; skid, swerve

**embarquement** nm embarkation, embarking; shipment; entraining (troops)

**embarquer** vt embark; ship; coll arrest, run in; involve, drag (into something); ~ **de l'eau** ship water; vi embark; s' ~ embark, go on board; launch (into)

**embarras** nm obstacle, obstruction; hold-up (traffic); impediment; shortage of money; trouble, difficulty; indecision, perplexity, hesitation, embarrassment; ~ **du choix** too much to choose from; ~ **gastrique** gastric upset; **faire des ~** make a fuss; **tirer qn d' ~** get s/o out of a tricky situation

**embarrassant** *adj* cumbersome; puzzling; awkward

**embarrasser** *vt* hamper; obstruct, encumber; inconvenience; perplex, embarrass, confuse; **s' ~ (de)** worry, trouble (about); be perplexed (about)

**embase** *nf* base, shoulder, base-plate

**embastiller** *vt* put into prison

**emboucher** *vt* take on, engage, hire; *coll* entice, hire

**embauchoir** *nm* boot-tree, shoe-tree

**embaumer** *vt* embalm; perfume, scent; *vi* exhale fragrance

**embellie** *nf* bright spell, lull

**embellir** *vt* embellish; *vi* improve in looks

**embellissement** *nm* embellishment; improvement in looks; ornament

**emberlificoter** *vt coll* trick, get round

**embêtant** *adj coll* annoying

**embêtement** *nm* annoyance; **avoir des ~s** be in a jam, have trouble

**embêter** *vt* annoy, be a nuisance to

**emblée (d')** *adv phr* straight away, directly

**emblème** *nm* emblem, device, badge; symbol

**embobiner** *vt coll* get round, coax; take in; put on a reel or bobbin

**emboîtage** *nm* packing into boxes

**emboîter** *vt* encase; fit together, dovetail; ~ **le pas** fall into step

**embolie** *nf* embolism, blood-clot

**embonpoint** *nm* plumpness; **prendre de l' ~** put on flesh

**embouché** *adj sl* **mal ~** coarse

**embouchure** *nf* mouth (river); mouthpiece (instrument)

**embourber** *vt* put into the mud, mire; **s' ~** get bogged down, caught up

**embourgeoiser (s')** *v refl* acquire bourgeois attitudes, get into bourgeois ways

**embout** *nm* ferrule, tip

**embouteillage** *nm* congestion, trafficjam; bottling; bottling up

**embouteiller** *vt* congest; bottle; bottle up

**emboutir** *vt* stamp (metal); emboss; bash in; **s' ~** crash

**embranchement** *nm* branching; branch; road junction; railway junction; pipe junction

**embrancher** *vt* join up (roads, etc); **s' ~** come together; branch off

**embrasement** *nm* burning, conflagration; illumination

**embraser** *vt* set on fire, set ablaze; illuminate; **s' ~** catch fire

**embrassade** *nf* embrace

**embrasse** *nf* curtain-loop

**embrassement** *nm* embrace

**embrasser** *vt* embrace, hug; kiss; adopt, take up, undertake; contain, include; take on

**embrasure** *nf* (window) recess; embrasure

**embrayage** *nm* engaging, connection; *mot* clutch

**embrayer** *vt* (7) connect, engage; *vi mot* let in the clutch; *fig* start

**embrigader** *vt* rope in; *ar* brigade, enrol

**embrocher** *vt* spit (meat); *coll* run through

**embrouillement** *nm* entanglement; confusion; intricacy

**embrouiller** *vt* entangle; confuse, muddle, mix up; **s' ~** get confused, muddled; become complicated; cloud over

**embroussaillé** *adj* covered with bushes; disordered (hair)

**embrumer** *vt* cover with mist; **s' ~** become misty; cloud over

**embrun** *nm usu pl* spray

**embryon** *nm* embryo

**embûche** *nf* ambush; pitfall

**embuer** *vt* steam over, cloud

**embuscade** *nf* ambush; **dresser une ~** lay an ambush

**embusqué** *nm coll* shirker (in army)

**embusquer** *vt* place in ambush; **s' ~** lie in ambush; *coll* shirk (active service)

**éméché** *adj coll* tipsy, slightly drunk

**émeraude** *nf* emerald; *adj invar* emerald green

**émerger** *vi* (3) emerge; come into view

**émeri** *nm* emery; **bouchon à l' ~** ground (glass) stopper

**émérite** *adj* retired; experienced, practised

**émerveillement** *nm* wonder, amazement

**émerveiller** *vt* amaze, fill with wonder

**émétique** *nm* emetic

**émetteur** *nm* issuer; transmitter; *adj* (*f* **-trice**) issuing; transmitting, broadcasting

**émettre** *vt* (60) emit, send out; utter; issue; express; transmit, broadcast

**émeute** *nf* riot

**émeutier -ière** *n* rioter

**émietter** *vt* crumble; fritter away; **s' ~** crumble

**émigrant -e** *n* emigrant

**émigration** *nf* migration; emigration

**émigré -e** *n* exile, emigrant; émigré

**émigrer** *vi* migrate; emigrate

**émincé** *nm* thin slice; thinly sliced meat in sauce

**émincer** *vt* (4) slice, shred

**éminence** *nf* eminence; high ground; protuberance; prominence

**éminent** *adj* eminent, distinguished

**émissaire** *nm* emissary; *adj* **bouc ~** scapegoat

**émission** *nf* emission; utterance; transmission, broadcasting; issue, issuing; broadcast

**emmagasiner** *vt* store; accumulate; take in (knowledge)

**emmailloter** *vt* swaddle; bind up

**emmancher** *vt* fix a handle to; *coll* start (an affair); **s' ~** fit

**emmanchure** *nf* arm-hole

**emmêler** *vt* mix up, tangle, muddle

**emménagement** *nm* moving in

**emménager** *vt* move in (furniture); settle in; *vi* move into a new place

**emmener** *vt* (6) lead away, take away, take off

**emmitoufler** *vt* muffle up, wrap up

**émoi** *nm* agitation; **en ~** agitated, all of a flutter

**émoluments** *nmpl* emoluments, salary

**émonder** *vt* prune, trim

**émotionnant** *adj* exciting, thrilling

**émotionner** *vt* move, thrill; **s' ~** get excited

**émoudre** *vt* (61) grind, sharpen

**émouleur** *nm* grinder, knife-grinder

**émoulu** *adj* **frais ~ de** just out of (school, etc)

**émousser** *vt* blunt; dull, deaden; attenuate

**émoustillant** *adj* exhilarating

**émoustiller** *vt* rouse, excite

**émouvant** *adj* moving, touching; thrilling

**émouvoir** *vt* (63) move, touch; rouse; **s' ~** be moved; be roused

**empailler** *vt* pack or stuff with straw; make (chair-seat) with straw

**empailleur -euse** *n* person who makes chair-seats with straw; taxidermist

**empaler** *vt* impale

**empanacher** *vt* adorn with a plume or plumes

**empaqueter** *vt* (5) pack up, make into a parcel

**emparer (s')** *v refl* take possession, lay hold

**empâté** *adj* bloated; **voix ~ e** thick voice

**empâtement** *nm* thickness; bloatedness; fattening

**empâter** *vt* fill with paste; clog, fatten, cram, bloat; **s' ~** become bloated, put on flesh

**empattement** *nm* footing (wall); wheelbase; *typ* serif

**empaumer** *vt* catch or strike with palm of the hand; *coll* take (s/o) in

**empêché** *adj* unable to be present

**empêchement** *nm* hindrance, obstacle, impediment

**empêcher** *vt* hinder, prevent, stop; **(il) n'empêche qu'elle vous a vu** nevertheless she saw you; **il ne peut s' ~ de rire** he can't help laughing; **s' ~ de** prevent oneself from

**empeigne** *nf* upper (shoe)

**empennage** *nm* feathers (arrow); vanes; fins

**empereur** *nm* emperor

**empesé** *adj* starchy, stiff, formal

**empeser** *vt* (6) starch

**empester** *vt* stink out; reek of

**empêtrement** *nm* entanglement

**empêtrer** *vt* hobble; entangle; **s' ~** become entangled, get caught up; become confused

**emphase** *nf* bombast, grandiloquence

**emphatique** *adj* bombastic, grandiloquent, turgid

**empierrer** *vt* metal, macadamize; ballast; pave

**empiètement** *nm* encroachment; infringement

**empiéter** *vi* (6) encroach; infringe

**empiffrer** *vt coll* stuff with food; **s' ~** stuff oneself, gorge

**empiler** *vt* pile up, put in a pile, stack; *coll* cheat, swindle

**empire** *nm* supreme authority, sway; control; empire

**empirer** *vt* make worse; *vi* grow worse

**empirique** *adj* empirical, empiric

**emplacement** *nm* site, location; place; emplacement

**emplâtre** *nm* plaster; *sl* incompetent idler

**emplette** *nf* purchase; **faire ses ~s** go shopping

**emplir** *vt* fill; **s' ~** fill up

**emploi** *nm* employment, use; occupation, post, job; **~ du temps** timetable; **être sans ~** be out of work; **faire double ~** be superfluous, useless; **offres d' ~** situations vacant

**employé -e** *n* employee

**employer** *vt* (7) use, employ; **s' ~** be used, be current; occupy oneself; exert oneself

**employeur -euse** *n* employer

**emplumé** *adj* feathered, adorned with feathers

**empocher** *vt* pocket, cash in

**empoigne** *nf* seizing; **foire d' ~** free-for-all

**empoigner** *vt* seize, grasp, grab; grip, thrill; *coll* arrest; **ils se sont empoignés** they quarrelled, they came to blows

**empois** *nm* starch

**empoisonnant** *adj coll* boring; annoying

**empoisonnement** *nm* poisoning

**empoisonner** vt poison; infect; pollute; *coll* annoy

**empoisonneur -euse** n poisoner

**emporté** adj quick-tempered, passionate, fiery

**emportement** nm transport (anger)

**emporte-pièce** nm invar punch (tool); **style à l' ~** trenchant style

**emporter** vt carry away, take away; sweep away, blow away; carry along, carry off; take; **l' ~** prevail, win; **se laisser ~** let oneself be carried away; **s' ~** get angry, lose one's temper

**empoté** adj coll awkward, clumsy

**empourprer** vt colour crimson, purple; **s' ~** flush scarlet, turn crimson

**empreindre** vt (55) impress, stamp

**empreint** adj marked, stamped

**empreinte** nf mark; imprint, stamp; print; **~s digitales** finger-prints; **prendre l' ~ de** take an impression of

**empressé** adj eager, zealous, assiduous

**empressement** nm eagerness, alacrity, zeal, assiduity; attention

**empresser (s')** v refl hurry, hasten; show eagerness; be assiduous, attentive

**emprise** nf influence, ascendancy; expropriation

**emprisonnement** nm imprisonment

**emprisonner** vt put in prison, imprison

**emprunt** nm loan; borrowing; loan-word; **nom d' ~** assumed name

**emprunté** adj awkward, stiff; assumed, false

**emprunter** vt borrow; take (road)

**emprunteur -euse** n borrower

**empuantir** vt stink out

**ému** adj moved, affected

**émulation** nf emulation, rivalry

**émule** n emulator, rival

**émulsionner** vt emulsify

**en** pron invar of, about it, them; by it, her, him, them; some, any; **j' ~ ai** I have some; **je n' ~ ai pas** I haven't any; **prenez-~** take some; adv from there; because of that, for that reason, on that account; prep in, to; by; within; into; while; of; as a; **~ Angleterre** in, to England; **~ attendant** in the meantime; while waiting; **~ essayant** by trying; **~ souriant** (while) smiling; **~ vacances** on holiday; **de jour ~ jour** from day to day, from one day to the next; **il l'a fait ~ huit jours** he did it in a week; **il m'a traité ~ ami** he treated me as a friend; **une bague tout ~ or** a solid gold ring

**énamourer (s')** v refl fall in love

**énarque** nm technocrat, top bureaucrat

**en-avant** nm invar forward pass (rugby)

**encablure** nf naut cable-length (approx two hundred metres)

**encadrement** nm framing; framework, frame; mil officering; straddling (target); **~ du crédit** credit squeeze

**encadrer** vt frame; surround; mil officer; straddle, bracket (target)

**encadreur** nm picture-framer

**encaisse** nf cash in hand

**encaissement** nm encashment, collection; encasing; embankment

**encaisser** vt encash, take in; pack into cases; coll receive, take (punishment); embank (river)

**encan** nm auction; **mettre à l' ~** put up for auction

**encanailler (s')** v refl go around with rogues; get into low habits

**encapuchonner** vt put a hood, cowl on

**en-cas** nm invar ar article kept for emergency; light meal kept ready in case of need

**encastrer** vt set in, embed

**encaustique** nf wax-polish

¹**enceinte** nf enclosure; surrounding, perimeter wall; **~ acoustique** speaker system

²**enceinte** adj f pregnant

**encens** nm incense

**encenser** vt burn incense to; flatter

**encensoir** nm censer

**encerclement** nm encirclement

**encercler** vt encircle

**enchaînement** nm chaining up; series, chain; sequence

**enchaîner** vt chain, put in chains; link up; tie; put in sequence; carry on; **s' ~** be linked together, hang together

**enchantement** nm magic, spell; charm; enchantment; delight; **comme par ~** as though by magic

**enchanté** adj enchanted, bewitched; delighted

**enchanter** vt enchant, bewitch; delight, charm

**enchanteur -eresse** n enchanter, enchantress; adj charming, delightful; entrancing

**enchère** nf bid, bidding; **folle ~** crazy, irresponsible bid; **vente aux ~s (à l' ~)** auction sale

**enchérir** vi grow dearer; make a higher bid; **~ sur qn** outbid s/o, go one further than s/o

**enchevêtrement** nm tangle; tangling up; confusion

**enchevêtrer** vt tangle up, mix up; confuse

**enclaver** vt enclave; wedge in

**enclenchement** nm interlocking; putting into gear

**enclencher** vt engage; put into gear; **s' ~** engage

**enclin** adj disposed, inclined

**enclore** vt (23) enclose, fence in

**enclos** nm enclosure; paddock; fence

**enclume** nf anvil; **entre l' ~ et le marteau** between the devil and the deep blue sea

**encoche** nf notch, nick

**encocher** vt notch, nick

**encoignure** nf corner; corner cupboard

**encoller** vt coat with glue, gum

**encolure** nf neck and withers (horse); neck (dress); neck; size of collar; **de forte ~** thick-set

**encombrant** adj cumbersome, bulky; in the way

**encombre** nm **sans ~** without incident, with no difficulty

**encombrement** nm jam, congestion, block; litter; bulkiness; space occupied

**encombrer** vt congest; encumber, obstruct; overload; **s' ~** saddle oneself

**encontre (à l')** adv phr to the contrary; **~ de** against, in opposition to

**encorbellement** nm overhang; corbelling

**encorder (s')** v refl rope one another together (climbers)

**encore** adv still, yet; (yet) another, one ... more; again, (once) more; moreover; **~ que** although; **~ qu'il soit malade** even if he is ill; **~ si (si ~) il faisait beau** at least if it were fine; **~ une fois** once again; **~ un peu** a little more; **cent francs! ~ faudrait-il les avoir** a hundred francs! I would need to have them first; **hier ~** only yesterday, as recently as yesterday; **il le vendra cinquante francs, et ~!** he'll sell it for fifty francs, if that!; **mais ~?** what else?, tell me more, out with it; **pas ~** not yet; **quoi ~?** what else?; interj what again?, Heavens!

**encourageant** adj encouraging, cheering

**encourager** vt (3) encourage, incite; foster, aid

**encourir** vt (29) incur, expose oneself to

**encrasser** vt dirty, foul; clog; **s' ~** get dirty; get clogged

**encre** nf ink; **~ de Chine** Indian ink; **~ sympathique** invisible ink; **écrire à l' ~** write in ink

**encrier** nm inkpot; inkstand

**encroûté** adj stuck in a rut; fig fossilized

**encroûter** vt encrust; **s' ~** become encrusted; get into a rut

**enculer** vt vulg sodomize, bugger

**encyclique** nf eccles encyclical

**encyclopédie** nf encyclopaedia

**encyclopédique** adj encyclopaedic

**endémique** adj endemic

**endetter** vt get (s/o) into debt; **s' ~** get into debt

**endeuiller** vt plunge into mourning

**endiablé** adj wild, frenzied

**endiguer** vt dam up; contain with dikes; slow up, obstruct

**endimancher (s')** v refl dress up in one's Sunday best

**endive** nf chicory; endive

**endoctriner** vt indoctrinate

**endolori** adj sore, tender

**endolorir** vt make painful, make ache

**endommager** vt (3) damage

**endormeur -euse** n flatterer, cajoler

**endormi** adj asleep; drowsy; indolent; calm, silent; dormant

**endormir** vt (39) put to sleep; anaesthetize; deaden; cajole; lull; bore; allay; **s' ~** fall asleep, drop off; become inactive; fail to be watchful

**endos** nm endorsement (on back of cheque)

**endosser** vt put on (clothes); endorse (cheque); assume responsibility for

**endroit** nm place, spot; passage (book, speech); aspect; right side (material); **à l' ~** right side up, out; **à l' ~ de** regarding; **par ~s** here and there

**enduire** vt (80) smear, coat

**enduit** nm coat, coating (paint, plaster, etc)

**endurance** nf endurance; resistance to wear; mot **épreuve d' ~** reliability trial

**endurant** adj resistant; patient

**endurci** adj hardened, inured; hard, hardened; callous, pitiless

**endurcir** vt harden; inure; **s' ~** grow accustomed; become tough, hard

**endurcissement** nm hardening; inuring; insensitivity

**endurer** vt endure, bear

**énergétique** adj relative to energy

**énergie** nf energy; vigour, determination, force; efficacy

**énergique** adj energetic

**énergumène** n energumen, fanatic

**énervant** adj aggravating; tiresome; enervating

**énervé** adj excited; annoyed

**énervement** nm nervous excitement, overexcitement

**énerver** vt annoy, aggravate; enervate, weaken; **s' ~** get excited; get irritable

**enfance** nf childhood; children; beginning, infancy; **c'est l' ~ de l'art** it's child's play; **tomber en ~** sink into dotage

**enfant** n child; **~s** descendants, posterity; **~ de chœur** choirboy; coll naïve person; **~ de Paris** native of Paris, true Parisian; **~ trouvé** foundling; **agir en ~** behave like a child; **bon ~** good-natured; **faire l' ~** act childishly

**enfantement** nm childbirth; creation (work of art)

**enfantillage** *nm* childish act, childish saying, nonsense

**enfantin** *adj* infantile, childish, puerile; absurdly easy

**enfariné** *adj* covered with flour

**enfer** *nm* hell, the underworld; place in library where licentious books are kept; **d' ~** terrific, infernal, mad, frenzied

**enfermer** *vt* shut up, confine, lock up; enclose, surround; **s' ~** lock oneself in; stay in one's room, house

**enferrer** *vt* run through; catch (a fish) on a hook; **s' ~** get oneself run through; get caught in one's own tangle of lies

**enfiévrer** *vt* (6) make feverish; excite, fire

**enfilade** *nf* succession, series; suit, row, enfilade

**enfiler** *vt* thread; string (beads); run through; take (street); *coll* slip on, put on (clothes); *vulg* fuck

**enfin** *adv* lastly, finally; in a word; at last; well

**enflammé** *adj* blazing; fiery; passionate

**enflammer** *vt* inflame; set on fire, ignite; fire, stir up, rouse

**enfler** *vt + vi* swell, puff up; exaggerate

**enflure** *nf* swelling; bombast, turgidity

**enfoncé** *adj* staved in; deep, sunken; low-lying

**enfoncement** *nm* breaking open, staving in; hollow; recess

**enfoncer** *vt* drive in, bang in; break in, stave in, break open; *coll* overcome, get the better of; *vi* sink, go down; **s' ~** collapse, give way; penetrate; go down, be ruined; become immersed, absorbed

**enfouir** *vt* bury; hide, conceal

**enfourcher** *vt* stick a pitchfork into; bestride, mount; *coll* **~ son dada** ride one's hobby-horse

**enfourner** *vt* put into the oven; *coll* stuff (food into one's mouth)

**enfreindre** *vt* (55) infringe

**enfuir (s')** *v refl* (52) flee, fly, run away; fly by

**enfumer** *vt* fill with smoke; blacken with smoke; smoke out

**engageant** *adj* engaging, charming, winning

**engagement** *nm* pawning, pledging; commitment; promise; obligation; appointment; engaging; engagement, fight, action; *mil* enlistment, throwing (troops) into battle

**engager** *vt* (3) put in pawn, pledge; commit; engage; begin; throw in (troops); incite, exhort; put in, thrust in, insert; **~ des pourparlers** start talks; **cela ne vous engage à rien** that does not bind you in any way; **s' ~** bind oneself, undertake, promise; take up employment; penetrate; enlist; begin; take up a precise position

**engainer** *vt* sheathe

**engeance** *nf coll* crew, breed

**engelure** *nf* chilblain

**engendrement** *nm* begetting; generation

**engendrer** *vt* beget; engender, cause, bring about; breed

**engin** *nm* machine; contrivance, device

**englober** *vt* embody, include, comprise

**engloutir** *vt* swallow, gulp down; engulf; **~ une fortune** get through a fortune

**engluer** *vt* smear, lime (birds); *fig* ensnare

**engoncé** *adj* tightly wrapped (in one's clothes)

**engorgement** *nm* choking, blocking, clogging; obstruction

**engorger** *vt* (3) obstruct, clog, block

**engouement** *nm* infatuation, craze

**engouer (s')** *v refl* become infatuated, go mad

**engouffrer** *vt* swallow up, engulf; absorb, get through; **s' ~** be engulfed; rush, dash

**engoulevent** *nm orni* nightjar

**engourdir** *vt* numb, benumb; dull; **s' ~** go numb, become dull

**engourdissement** *nm* numbness; dullness

**engrais** *nm* fertilizer, manure; fattening food

**engraisser** *vt* fatten, make fat; fertilize; make rich; *vi* grow fat, put on weight

**engranger** *vt* garner

**engraver (s')** *v refl* run aground

**engrenage** *nm* gears, gearing, gearwheels; mesh (of circumstances)

**engrener** *vt* (6) engage, connect

**engrosser** *vt sl* make pregnant

**engueulade** *nf sl* slanging, quarrel

**engueuler** *vt sl* slang, blow up; **ils s'engueulent toute la journée** they go on at each other all day long

**enhardir** *vt* embolden; **s' ~** pluck up courage

**énigmatique** *adj* enigmatic

**énigme** *nf* enigma, riddle, puzzle; difficult subject

**enivrant** *adj* intoxicating, heady

**enivrement** *nm* intoxication, drunken state; transport, ecstasy

**enivrer** *vt* intoxicate, make drunk; elate; **s' ~** get drunk, become intoxicated

**enjambée** *nf* stride

**enjambement** *nm* enjambment; flyover, overpass

**enjamber** *vt* step over; bestride; *vi* stride; encroach, project

**enjeu** *nm* stake

**enjoindre** *vt* (55) enjoin, charge

**enjôlement** *nm* cajoling; cajolery

**enjôler** *vt* cajole, wheedle, coax; trick

**enjôleur -euse** *n* cajoler, wheedler; *adj* coaxing, wheedling, cajoling

**enjoliver** *vt* embellish, beautify

**enjoliveur -euse** *n* beautifier, embellisher; *nm mot* hub-cap

**enjolivure** *nf* embellishment

**enjoué** *adj* sprightly, playful

**enjouement** *nm* cheerful good-humour

**enlacer** *vt* (4) interlace, entwine; hug

**enlaidir** *vt* disfigure, make ugly; *vi* grow ugly

**enlèvement** *nm* carrying away, removal; abduction, kidnapping; *mil* storming

**enlever** *vt* (6) take away, carry away, remove; take up; carry off, kidnap, abduct; raise, bear up; perform brilliantly; delight, enrapture; *mil* storm

**enlisement** *nm* getting bogged down

**enliser (s')** *v refl* sink, get bogged, stuck

**enluminer** *vt* illuminate (manuscript); colour vividly

**enluminure** *nf* illuminating (manuscript); colouring

**enneigé** *adj* covered with snow

**enneigement** *nm* being covered with snow; depth of snow

**ennemi -e** *n* enemy, foe; *adj* hostile

**ennoblir** *vt* ennoble

**ennui** *nm* boredom, tediousness, tedium; worry, anxiety; **quel ~ !** what a nuisance!

**ennuyer** *vt* (7) bore, weary, annoy, worry; *coll* bother, put out; **s' ~ be bored**; **s' ~ à mourir** be bored to tears; **s' ~ à ne rien faire** get fed up with doing nothing

**ennuyeux -euse** *adj* boring, tedious, annoying, unpleasant

**énoncé** *nm* statement (facts)

**énoncer** *vt* state; articulate

**énonciation** *nf* stating, expressing; enunciation

**enorgueillir** *vt* make proud; **s' ~ become proud**, draw pride

**énorme** *adj* huge, enormous; outrageous

**énormément** *adv* hugely; tremendously, terribly; **~ de** a great deal of

**énormité** *nf* enormity; vastness; gravity; blunder

**enquérir (s')** *v refl* (27) inquire, ask

**enquête** *nf* inquiry, investigation; **procéder à une ~** hold an inquiry

**enquêter** *vi* make inquiries, conduct investigations

**enquiquiner** *vt coll* annoy, plague

**enraciné** *adj* deep-rooted

**enraciner** *vt* dig in; implant, establish

**enragé** *adj* furious; *coll* enthusiastic, very keen; rabid, mad (dog); **manger**

de la vache **~ e** have a hard time of it

**enrageant** *adj* maddening, infuriating

**enrager** *vi* (3) rage, fume; **faire ~ qn** tease s/o, annoy s/o

**enrayer** *vt* (7) check, slow up; stop, jam

**enrégimenter** *vt* regiment; enlist, enrol

**enregistrement** *nm* registration, recording, booking, entering up; recording (sound, etc)

**enregistrer** *vt* register, record, enter up, take note of; record (sound, etc)

**enregistreur -euse** *adj* recording; registering

**enrhumer (s')** *v refl* catch a cold

**enrichi** *adj* newly rich; enriched

**enrichir** *vt* enrich

**enrichissement** *nm* enrichment

**enrober** *vt* coat, cover; disguise, wrap up

**enrôlement** *nm* enrolment; enlistment

**enrôler** *vt* enrol, recruit; enlist

**enroué** *adj* hoarse, husky

**enrouement** *nm* hoarseness, huskiness

**enrouer** *vt* make husky, hoarse

**enrouler** *vt* roll up, wind; wrap up

**enrouleur** *nm* **ceinture à ~** inertia-reel seat belt

**enrubanner** *vt* decorate, cover with ribbons

**ensabler** *vt* run aground; cover with sand, silt up

**ensanglanter** *vt* stain, cover with blood; make run with blood

**enseignant -e** *n* teacher; *adj* teaching; **corps ~** teaching profession

**enseigne** *nm* standard-bearer; *nf* sign, mark, token; sign-board; standard; **à bonne ~** on good authority; **à telle(s) ~ (s) que** so much so that, the proof being that; **être logé à la même ~** be in the same predicament

**enseignement** *nm* teaching; education; **être dans l' ~** be a teacher

**enseigner** *vt* teach; show, indicate

**ensemble** *nm* whole, entirety; group, ensemble; cohesion, unity; **avec ~ harmoniously**; **dans l' ~** on the whole; **dans son ~** viewed as a whole, globally; **d' ~** general; **grand ~** large housing development; **mouvement d' ~** combined movement; **vue d' ~** general, comprehensive view; *adv* together; at the same time; **être bien ~** get on well together; **être mal ~** get on badly together

**ensemencer** *vt* (4) sow (ground); stock (with fish)

**enserrer** *vt* enclose; hem in; squeeze; fit tight

**ensevelir** *vt* bury; shroud

**ensevelissement** *nm* burial; shrouding

**ensoleillé** *adj* sunny

**ensommeillé** *adj* sleepy

**ensorceler** *vt* (5) bewitch, cast a spell on; captivate, charm

**ensorceleur -euse** *n* sorcerer, sorceress; charmer

**ensorcellement** *nm* witchcraft, sorcery; charm, spell

**ensuite** *adv* then, next, afterwards

**ensuivre** (s') *v refl* (43) ensue, result, follow; *coll* **et tout ce qui s'ensuit** and all the rest; **il s'ensuit que** it follows that

**entablement** *nm* entablature

**entacher** *vt* cast a slur on

**entaille** *nf* notch, nick; groove, slot; gash

**entailler** *vt* notch, nick; groove, slot; gash, cut

**entame** *nf* first slice, first piece

**entamer** *vt* cut into, open, start, break into; begin; broach (subject) **~ une réputation** taint a reputation

**entartrer** *vt* encrust, fur

**entassement** *nm* piling-up, heaping-up; pile, accumulation; crowding-in, congestion

**entasser** *vt* pile up, heap up, stack up; amass, accumulate; pack, crowd in; **s' ~** accumulate; crowd together

**entendement** *nm* understanding; capacity for comprehension

**entendeur** *nm* **à bon ~ salut** a word to the wise is enough; if the cap fits, wear it

**entendre** *vt* hear; understand; intend, mean; **~ dire que** hear that; **~ faire qch** intend to do sth; **~ parler de** hear about; **à l' ~** if one is to believe him; **donner à ~ à qn** lead s/o to believe; **faire ~** utter; **il n'entend pas la plaisanterie** he can't take a joke; **ils ne sont pas faits pour s' ~** they don't get on together; **je n'entends rien à cela** I don't understand a thing about that; **laisser ~** insinuate; **on ne s'entend pas** we can't hear ourselves speak; **qu'entendez-vous par là?** what do you mean by that?; **s' ~** agree, understand one another, get on; be good, be skilled

**entendu** *adj* agreed, decided; intelligent, sensible, business-like; **(c'est) ~ !** (it's) agreed!; **bien ~** naturally; **d'un air ~** with a knowing air; **faire l' ~** pretend to know all about sth

**entente** *nf* understanding; agreement; good relations; interpretation; **mot à double ~** word with a double meaning, double entendre

**enter** *vt* graft

**entériner** *vt* confirm, ratify

**entérite** *nf med* enteritis

**enterrement** *nm* burial; funeral, funeral procession; abandonment

**enterrer** *vt* bury; abandon (project); **il**

**nous enterrera tous** he will survive us all

**entêtant** *adj* heady

**en-tête** *nm* heading; headline

**entêté** *adj* obstinate, pig-headed, stubborn

**entêtement** *nm* obstinacy, stubbornness

**entêter** (s') *v refl* be obstinate, persist, dig one's toes in

**enthousiasme** *nm* enthusiasm

**enthousiasmer** *vt* fill with enthusiasm; **s' ~** become enthusiastic

**enthousiaste** *n* enthusiast; *adj* enthusiastic

**entiché** *adj* infatuated, crazy, keen

**enticher** (s') *v refl* become infatuated, crazy

**entier** *nm* entirety; **en ~** in full; *adj* (*f* **-ière**) whole, entire; complete; intact, unaltered; frank, outspoken; **nombre ~** integer; **payer place entière** pay full fare

**entièrement** *adv* wholly, entirely, utterly

**entité** *nf* entity

**entoiler** *vt* mount on canvas or linen; cover with canvas

**entomologie** *nf* entomology

**entonner** *vt* begin to sing; intone

**entonnoir** *nm* funnel; shell-hole, crater; depression, hollow

**entorse** *nf* sprain, twist; **faire une ~ à** stretch, fail to observe (law, etc)

**entortiller** *vt* wind, twist, twine, express in complicated fashion; *coll* get round

**entour** *nm* **à l' ~** round about, around; **à l' ~ de** round

**entourage** *nm* surroundings, environment; setting; circle (friends, etc)

**entourer** *vt* surround, encircle; fence in; devote attention to

**entourloupette** *nf coll* nasty trick

**entournure** *nf* arm-hole; *coll* **être gêné dans les ~s** feel awkward, ill at ease, be in difficulties

**entracte** *nm theat* interval; interlude; pause, respite

**entraide** *nf* mutual aid

**entraider** (s') *v refl* help one another

**entrailles** *nfpl* bowels, entrails; compassion, feeling, soul; **sans ~** pitiless

**entr'aimer** (s') *v refl* love one another

**entrain** *nm* briskness, go, liveliness, spirit; **avec ~** with gusto; **sans ~** listlessly, half-heartedly

**entraînant** *adj* stirring, gripping

**entraînement** *nm* dragging, carrying away; leading astray; enthusiasm; training

**entraîner** *vt* drag along, carry away, off; drive (mechanism); train, coach; seduce, lure; lead to, produce; **s' ~** train

**entraîneur** *nm* trainer, coach

**entraîneuse** *nf* night-club hostess

**entrant** *adj* incoming; newly appointed

**entr'apercevoir** *vt* glimpse, catch a glimpse of

**entrave** *nf* fetter, shackle; hobble; hindrance, impediment

**entraver** *vt* fetter, shackle; hobble; hamper, impede

**entre** *prep* between; among, amongst; ~ **amis** between friends, among friends; ~ **les deux** neither one thing nor the other; **belle ~ toutes** beautiful above all others; **d' ~** of (before *pers pron*); **deux d' ~ eux** two of them; **femme ~ deux âges** middle-aged woman; **lui, ~ autres** he, for one; **tomber ~ les mains de qn** fall into the hands of s/o

**entrebâillement** *nm* small gap, chink, slit

**entrebâiller** *vt* half-open (door)

**entrechat** *nm* caper, little jump; entrechat

**entrechoquer** *vt* knock together; **s' ~** collide, knock against one another

**entrecôte** *nf* sirloin steak

**entrecouper** *vt* interrupt

**entrecroiser** *vt* intersect, cross; interlace

**entre-déchirer (s')** *v refl* tear one another apart

**entre-deux** *nm invar* space between; intermediate state or position; insertion (dressmaking); piece of furniture (placed between two windows)

**entre-deux-guerres** *nm invar* period between the two world wars

**entredévorer (s')** *v refl* devour one another, destroy one another

**entrée** *nf* entry, entering; entrance, way in; admission, admittance; entrance hall, vestibule; *cul* entrée; beginning; ~ **interdite** no admittance; ~ **libre** admission free (= no obligation to buy); **avoir ses ~ s** have free access; **d' ~ de jeu** from the word go

**entrefaite** *nf* **sur ces ~ s** at that moment, then

**entrefilet** *nm* short article, filler

**entregent** *nm* tact, savoir-faire

**entrelacement** *nm* interlacing, interweaving; network

**entrelacer** *vt* (4) interlace, intertwine, interweave

**entrelacs** *nm* interlacing or intertwining motif

**entrelardé** *adj* streaky (meat)

**entrelarder** *vt* lard (meat); interlard

**entremêler** *vt* intermingle, intermix, intersperse

**entremets** *nm* dessert, sweet

**entremetteur -euse** *n pej* intermediary, coupler, match-maker

**entremettre (s')** *v refl* intervene, interpose

**entremise** *nf* intervention; mediation, good offices; **par l' ~ de qn** through s/o

**entrepont** *nm naut* between decks

**entreposer** *vt* store, deposit

**entrepôt** *nm* warehouse, store; storehouse

**entreprenant** *adj* enterprising, bold; forward

**entreprendre** *vt* (75) undertake, embark on; contract for; try to persuade

**entrepreneur -euse** *n* contractor; ~ (de bâtiments) (en construction) building contractor; ~ **de pompes funèbres** undertaker

**entreprise** *nf* undertaking; concern; venture

**entrer** *vt* bring in, carry in; *vi* enter, go in, come in; be admitted; be an ingredient of; ~ **à l'université** start at university; ~ **dans le détail** examine closely; ~ **en colère** get angry; ~ **en matière** begin; ~ **en religion** take holy orders; **faire ~ qn** admit s/o

**entre-temps** *adv* meanwhile, in the meantime

**entretenir** *vt* (96) keep up, maintain, support; converse with; ~ **des soupçons** entertain suspicions; **femme entretenue** kept woman; **s' ~** talk, converse

**entretien** *nm* upkeep, maintenance, support; conversation

**entre-tuer (s')** *v refl* kill one another

**entrevoir** *vt* (99) catch sight of, a glimpse of; have an inkling of

**entrevue** *nf* interview

**entrouvert** *adj* ajar, half-open

**entrouvrir** *vt* (30) open slightly

**énumérateur -trice** *n* enumerator

**énumérer** *vt* (6) enumerate

**envahir** *vt* invade, overrun, assail

**envahissant** *adj* importunate, indiscreet

**envahissement** *nm* invading; encroaching

**envahisseur** *nm* invader

**envaser** *vt* choke with mud; run into the mud

**enveloppant** *adj* enveloping; charming, seductive

**enveloppe** *nf* envelope, cover, wrapper; exterior; budget

**envelopper** *vt* envelop, wrap up, encase; close in on, surround; disguise

**envenimer** *vt* envenom, poison; aggravate, irritate; **s' ~** fester; become nasty, unpleasant

**envergure** *nf* spread, breadth, span (wing, sail); scale, amplitude; **d' ~** impressive, large, far-reaching

¹**envers** *nm* wrong side, reverse, back; contrary; **l' ~ de la médaille** the other side of the coin; **à l' ~** inside out; the wrong way up, upside down

²**envers** *prep* as regards, towards; **~ et contre tous** in spite of everybody

**envi (à l')** *adv phr* emulously

**envie** *nf* desire, longing; envy; birthmark; **avoir ~ de** desire, want; wish to; **faire ~ à** make envious; **porter ~ à qn** envy s/o, be jealous of s/o

**envier** *vt* envy; covet; begrudge

**envieux -ieuse** *adj* envious, jealous

**environ** *adv* about, approximately

**environnement** *nm* surroundings, environment

**environner** *vt* surround; beset

**environs** *nmpl* surroundings, neighbourhood, vicinity; **aux ~ de Pâques** round about Easter

**envisager** *vt* (3) contemplate, consider; envisage; plan

**envoi** *nm* sending, dispatch; consignment; *poet* envoy; **coup d' ~** kick-off, start

**envol** *nm* taking flight, taking off, take-off

**envolée** *nf* flight (eloquence)

**envoler (s')** *v refl* fly off, away; take off; fly (time); rise steeply (prices)

**envoûtement** *nm* spell; charm

**envoûter** *vt* cast a spell on; charm

**envoyé** *nm* envoy; messenger

**envoyer** *vt* (44) send; dispatch; throw (ball); **~ chercher qn** send for s/o; **~ dire que** send word that; *coll* **~ promener (paître) qn** tell s/o to go to hell; **réplique envoyée** telling reply; *sl* **s' ~** take, consume, appropriate, have

**envoyeur -euse** *n* sender

**éolien -ienne** *adj* Aeolian

**épagneul** *nm* spaniel

**épais -aisse** *adj* thick; dense; dull, coarse; **avoir la langue épaisse** be thick of speech; *adv* **semer ~** sow thick

**épaisseur** *nf* thickness; depth; dullness, slowness

**épaissir** *vt* thicken, make dense; *vi* become thick; **s' ~** grow stout; grow dull; grow thicker

**épaississement** *nm* thickening; growing denser; growing plumper

**épanchement** *nm* discharge, pouring out; effusion; outpouring; **~ de synovie** water on the knee

**épancher** *vt* pour out; shed (blood); **s' ~** pour out; unburden oneself, come out with everything

**épandage** *nm* spreading fertilizer, spreading manure

**épandre** *vt* spread by scattering

**épanoui** *adj* in full bloom; **visage ~** beaming face

**épanouir** *vt* cause to bloom; **s' ~** bloom, open out; beam, light up (face)

**épanouissement** *nm* bloom, blooming; brightening up (face)

**épargnant -e** *n* saver

**épargne** *nf* saving, thrift; savings; **caisse d' ~** savings bank

**épargner** *vt* save, economize; be sparing with; spare; have mercy on; treat gently; dispense with

**éparpillement** *nm* scattering, dispersing

**éparpiller** *vt* scatter, disperse; dissipate (efforts)

**épars** *adj* scattered

**épatant** *adj coll* marvellous, fine, splendid

**épate** *nf coll* swank, showing off

**épaté** *adj* broad at the base; splay-footed; *coll* amazed

**épatement** *nm coll* stupefaction

**épater** *vt coll* astound, amaze

**épaulard** *nm* grampus, killer-whale

**épaule** *nf* shoulder; **donner un coup d' ~** give a helping hand; **fusil sur l' ~** rifle at the slope; **hausser les ~ s** shrug one's shoulders; **par-dessus l' ~** negligently

**épauler** *vt* bring (gun) to the shoulder; take aim; help, back up

**épaulette** *nf* shoulder-strap; epaulette

**épave** *nf* wreck; abandoned or unclaimed object

**épée** *nf* sword; swordsman; **passer au fil de l' ~** put to the sword

**épeler** *vt* (5) spell, spell out

**éperdu** *adj* distracted, bewildered; desperate, wild

**éperdument** *adv* distractedly; madly

**éperlan** *nm* smelt

**éperon** *nm* spur, buttress; ram (ship)

**éperonner** *vt* put spurs on; spur on, urge on

**épervier** *nm* sparrow-hawk; *fig* hawk; sweep-net

**éphémère** *nm* may-fly, ephemera; *adj* ephemeral, short-lived, transitory

**éphéméride** *nf* tear-off calendar; almanac

**épi** *nm* ear (grain); tuft (hair), cow-lick; **stationnement en ~** fishtail parking

**épice** *nf* spice; **pain d' ~** spiced cake

**épicé** *adj* spiced, highly seasoned; spicy

**épicer** *vt* (4) spice

**épicerie** *nf* grocer's shop; groceries; grocery business; spices

**épicier -ière** *n* grocer

**épicurien -ienne** *n* epicure; Epicurean

**épidémie** *nf* epidemic

**épidémique** *adj* epidemic

**épiderme** *nm* epidermis, skin

**épier** *vt* spy on, watch closely; be on the look-out for

**épieu** *nm* pike; boar-spear
**épigastre** *nm* pit of the stomach
**épigone** *nm* imitator, follower
**épigramme** *nf* epigram
**épigraphe** *nf* inscription; epigraph
**épilation** *nf* plucking, removal of surplus hairs
**épilepsie** *nf* epilepsy
**épileptique** *n + adj* epileptic
**épiler** *vt* remove superfluous hairs from, pluck
**épilogue** *nm* epilogue
**épiloguer** *vi* find fault, make carping criticism; ~ **sur** comment at length on
**épinard** *nm* (*usu pl*) spinach; *coll* **mettre du beurre dans les** ~ **s** make life easier
**épine** *nf* thorn; thorn-bush; difficulty, snag; ~ **dorsale** spinal column, backbone; **être sur des** ~ **s** be on tenterhooks; **tirer une** ~ **du pied** rid of a worry
**épinette** *nf* spinet; small cage, coop; *bot* spruce
**épineux -euse** *adj* thorny, prickly; ticklish, awkward
**épingle** *nf* pin; ~ **à cheveux** hair-pin; ~ **à linge** clothes-peg; ~ **de nourrice (de sûreté)** safety-pin; **coup d'** ~ petty annoyance; *coll* **monter en** ~ give excessive importance to; **tiré à quatre** ~ **s** meticulously dressed, dressed up to the nines; **tirer son** ~ **du jeu** get out of a difficult situation
**épingler** *vt* pin, fasten with a pin
**épinière** *adj f* **moelle** ~ spinal cord
**épinoche** *nf* stickleback
**Épiphanie** *nf* Epiphany
**épique** *adj* epic
**épiscopat** *nm* episcopate; episcopacy
**épistolaire** *adj* epistolary
**épitaphe** *nf* epitaph
**épithète** *nf* epithet; attributive adjective
**épitomé** *nm* epitome, abridgement
**épître** *nf* epistle
**éploré** *adj* tearful, grief-stricken
**éplucher** *vt* peel, pare; clean; examine closely
**éplucheur -euse** *n* peeler; cleaner
**épluchure** *nf* (*usu pl*) peelings
**épointer** *vt* break the point of
**éponge** *nf* sponge; *coll* **passer l'** ~ **sur** forgive, say no more about
**éponger** *vt* (3) sponge up, mop up, absorb; sponge down; *econ* wipe out
**épontille** *nf* stanchion; prop, pillar
**éponyme** *n + adj* eponymous (hero)
**épopée** *nf* epic poem; epic
**époque** *nf* period, age, epoch; time, date; **faire** ~ be remembered, be a landmark; **meubles d'** ~ period furniture
**époumoner (s')** *v refl* shout oneself hoarse

**épouse** *nf* wife
**épouser** *vt* marry; take up, espouse; fit
**épouseur** *nm coll* suitor
**épousseter** *vt* (5) dust
**époustouflant** *adj coll* staggering, amazing
**épouvantable** *adj* dreadful, appalling
**épouvantail** *nm* scarecrow; bogey
**épouvante** *nf* terror, fright
**épouvanter** *vt* terrify; **s'** ~ become terrified
**époux** *nm* husband
**éprendre (s')** *v refl* fall in love; take a fancy
**épreuve** *nf* test, trial; affliction, ordeal; proof; paper (examination); event (sport); **à l'** ~ **de** proof against; **à toute** ~ capable of withstanding anything
**épris** *adj* in love, enamoured
**éprouvant** *adj* hard, taxing
**éprouver** *vt* test, try; feel, experience; sustain; make suffer
**éprouvette** *nf* test-tube; test-piece
**épuisant** *adj* exhausting
**épuisé** *adj* exhausted; out of print; sold out
**épuisement** *nm* exhaustion; exhausting; using up; emptying, draining
**épuiser** *vt* exhaust; use up, empty, consume; tire out; **s'** ~ become exhausted; run dry, run out
**épuisette** *nf* landing-net; bailer
**épurateur** *nm* purifying apparatus, purifier
**épuration** *nf* purification; purging; expurgation
**épure** *nf* working drawing; finished design
**épurer** *vt* purify; filter; purge
**équanimité** *nf* equanimity
**équarrir** *vt* square (timber); broach (cask); quarter (carcass)
**équarrisseur** *nm* knacker
**Équateur** *nm* Ecuador
**équateur** *nm* equator
**équerre** *nf* square; ~ **à dessin** set-square; **d'** ~, **en** ~ at right angles
**équestre** *adj* equestrian
**équilibrage** *nm* balancing
**équilibre** *nm* balance; stability; **se tenir en** ~ keep one's balance
**équilibrer** *vt* balance
**équilibriste** *n* tightrope-walker, acrobat
**équin** *adj* equine
**équinoxe** *nm* equinox
**équipage** *nm* crew; equipment; retinue; attire; *coll* rig-out
**équipe** *nf* team; gang
**équipée** *nf* escapade
**équipement** *nm* equipment; fitting up; outfit

**équiper** *vt* equip; fit out

**équipier -ière** *n* member of a team or gang

**équitable** *adj* equitable, fair

**équitation** *nf* horse-riding, horsemanship

**équité** *nf* equity, fairness

**équivaloir** *vi* (95) be equivalent; be tantamount

**équivoque** *nf* ambiguity; uncertainty; double entendre; *adj* ambiguous; doubtful, questionable

**érable** *nm* maple-tree

**érafler** *vt* graze, scratch

**éraflure** *nf* graze

**éraillé** *adj* hoarse, raucous; bloodshot

**érailler** *vt* unravel; chafe, graze; make hoarse

**ère** *nf* era, epoch; **de notre ~** A.D.

**érection** *nf* erection; setting up

**éreintant** *adj* killing, tiring

**éreintement** *nm* violent criticism; exhaustion

**éreinter** *vt* exhaust, wear out; criticize violently

**ergot** *nm* spur (cock); stub (tree); ergot (grain)

**ergoter** *vi coll* quibble, split hairs

**ergoteur -euse** *adj* cavilling, quibbling

**ériger** *vt* (3) erect, set up, construct; establish; exalt; **s' ~ en** set (oneself) up as

**ermitage** *nm* hermitage

**ermite** *nm* hermit

**éroder** *vt* erode, eat away

**érosif -ive** *adj* erosive

**érotique** *adj* erotic

**érotisme** *nm* eroticism

**errant** *adj* wandering, roaming, rambling

**erratique** *adj* erratic

**erre** *nf naut* headway; **~s** track, spoor

**errements** *nmpl* erring ways

**errer** *vi* roam, wander; be mistaken, err

**erreur** *nf* mistake, slip; delusion, error; **induire en ~** mislead; **sauf ~** if I am not mistaken; **tirer qn de l' ~** undeceive someone

**erroné** *adj* erroneous, wrong

**ersatz** *nm invar* substitute

**éructer** *vi* eruct, belch

**érudit -e** *n* scholar, learned person; *adj* learned, erudite

**éruption** *nf* eruption; rash

**érysipèle** *nm med* erysipelas

**ès** (= en les) *prep* **docteur ~ sciences** doctor of science

**esbroufe** *nf sl* showing-off; **faire de l' ~** show off; **vol à l' ~** pickpocketing

**esbroufer** *vt sl* impress by one's airs

**escabeau** *nm* stool; step-ladder

**escadre** *nf naut* + *aer* squadron

**escadrille** *nf naut* flotilla; *aer* flight

**escadron** *nm mil* + *aer* squadron

**escalade** *nf* scaling, climbing; breaking in; escalation

**escalader** *vt* scale, climb

**escale** *nf* port of call, place at which one stops; **faire ~** put in, call; **sans ~** non-stop

**escalier** *nm* staircase, stairs; **~ de service** tradesmen's staircase; **~ mécanique (roulant)** escalator; **esprit de l' ~** slow wit

**escalope** *nf* slice (meat, etc)

**escamotable** *adj* disappearing, retractable

**escamoter** *vt* conjure away, make disappear; retract; remove subtly, filch; slur, pronounce badly; burke (question)

**escampette** *nf* **prendre la poudre d' ~** flee

**escarbille** *nf* clinker, cinder

**escarboucle** *nf* carbuncle

**escarcelle** *nf* pouch (for money)

**escargot** *nm* snail

**escarmouche** *nf* skirmish

**escarpe** *nf* escarp

**escarpé** *adj* steep, abrupt, sheer

**escarpement** *nm* escarpment

**escarpin** *nm* dancing-shoe, pump

**escarpolette** *nf* swing

**escarre** *nf* bed-sore; scab

**escient** *nm* **à bon ~** deliberately

**esclaffer (s')** *v refl* burst out laughing

**esclandre** *nm* scandal; quarrel; racket; **faire un ~** make a scene

**esclavage** *nm* slavery

**esclave** *n* slave

**escogriffe** *nm* lanky man

**escompte** *nm* discount, rebate; **taux d' ~** bank rate

**escompter** *vt* discount; count on, bank on

**escorte** *nf* escort; convoy

**escorter** *vt* escort; convoy

**escorteur** *nm naut* escort vessel

**escouade** *nf* squad, gang

**escrime** *nf* fencing

**escrimer (s')** *v refl* try hard, make every effort

**escrimeur -euse** *n* fencer

**escroc** *nm* crook, swindler

**escroquer** *vt* cheat, rob, swindle

**escroquerie** *nf* swindling; swindle

**ésotérique** *adj* esoteric

**espace** *nm* space; interval; *nf typ* space

**espacer** *vt* (4) space, space out; **s' ~** become rarer, fewer

**espadon** *nm* sword-fish

**espadrille** *nf* rope-soled shoe

**Espagnol -e** *n* Spaniard

**espagnol** *nm* Spanish (language); *adj* Spanish

**espagnolette** *nf* window fastener

**espèce** *nf* sort, type; species; *coll* ~ de (+*noun*) silly, stupid, blessed ...; **cas d'** ~ special case; **en l'** ~ in that case, in that matter; **payer en** ~s pay in cash

**espérance** *nf* hope, expectation

**espérer** *vt* + *vi* (6) hope, hope for; ~ **en** trust in

**espiègle** *adj* mischievous, roguish

**espièglerie** *nf* mischievousness; prank

**espion -ionne** *n* spy; *nm* bugging device

**espionnage** *nm* spying, espionage

**espionner** *vt* spy on

**esplanade** *nf* promenade; esplanade

**espoir** *nm* hope

**esprit** *nm* spirit; ghost, sprite; mind; intellect; wit; ~ **fort** free thinker; **bel** ~ cultured, well-read person; **faire de l'** ~ express oneself wittily; **mot d'** ~ witticism; **reprendre ses** ~s regain consciousness; recover one's composure; **Saint-Esprit** Holy Ghost

**esprit-de-vin** *nm invar* alcohol

**esquif** *nm* skiff, small boat

**esquille** *nf* splinter (bone)

**Esquimau -aude** *n* Eskimo

**esquimau** *nm* choc-ice; two-piece wool garment for children

**esquintant** *adj coll* exhausting, killing

**esquinter** *vt coll* exhaust; bust up, break, spoil; criticize severely

**esquisse** *nf* sketch, outline; ~ **d'un sourire** faint smile

**esquisser** *vt* sketch, outline; ~ **un sourire** give a slight smile

**esquive** *nf* dodging, ducking

**esquiver** *vt* avoid, dodge, duck; **s'** ~ slip away, make oneself scarce

**essai** *nm* trial, test; attempt; essay; try (rugby); **à l'** ~ on approval, on trial

**essaim** *nm* swarm (bees)

**essaimer** *vi* swarm (bees)

**essarter** *vt* clear undergrowth from (after deforestation)

**essayer** *vt* + *vi* (7) try, attempt; test; try on; **s'** ~ make an attempt, try one's hand

**esse** *nf* S-shaped hook; S-shaped hole in violin; linchpin

**essence** *nf* essence, essential being; concentrate, extract; petrol, *US* gas; gist, main aspect; species (tree)

**essentiel -ielle** *adj* essential

**esseulé** *adj* lonely, solitary

**essieu** *nm* axle

**essor** *nm* flight, soaring; progress, expansion; **prendre son** ~ take wing

**essorer** *vt* spin-dry, wring

**essoreuse** *nm* spin-dryer

**essoriller** *vt* crop the ears of

**essoufflement** *nm* breathlessness, panting

**essouffler** *vt* wind, blow; **s'** ~ get out of breath; *fig* lose momentum, go less well

**essuie-glace** *nm invar* windscreen-wiper

**essuie-mains** *nm invar* hand-towel

**essuyer** *vt* (7) wipe; mop up; endure, suffer; ~ **les plâtres** have problems; ~ **une défaite** suffer a defeat

**est** *nm* East; *adj invar* east, eastern

**estacade** *nf* line of stakes; stockade; mole, breakwater

**estafette** *nf* courier; *mil* dispatch-rider

**estafilade** *nf* gash, slash (*usu* in face)

**estagnon** *nm* drum (for olive oil, etc)

**estaminet** *nm* small café

**estampe** *nf* print, engraving

**estamper** *vt* stamp; impress; *coll* swindle

**estampeur -euse** *n* stamper; *coll* swindler

**estampille** *nf* official stamp; trade-mark

**estampiller** *vt* stamp, mark

**esthète** *n* aesthete

**esthétique** *adj* aesthetic

**estimateur -trice** *n* estimator; valuer

**estimatif -ive** *adj* estimated; estimative

**estimation** *nf* estimation; valuation

**estime** *nf* esteem, regard; *naut* reckoning; **à l'** ~ by guesswork, at a rough estimation; *naut* by dead reckoning

**estimer** *vt* estimate, value; calculate; esteem; consider, think

**estival** *adj* summer, estival

**estivant -e** *n* summer visitor

**estocade** *nf* stab-wound; fatal thrust (bull-fighting)

**estomac** *nm* stomach; *coll* **avoir de l'** ~ be plucky; be cheeky; **avoir l'** ~ **dans les talons** be starving hungry

**estomaquer** *vt coll* stagger, amaze, astound

**estomper** *vt arts* stump, shade off, soften off; **s'** ~ become blurred

**estonien -ienne** *adj* Estonian

**estouffade** *nf* braised meat

**estourbir** *vt sl* kill, do in

**estrade** *nf* platform, stage, dais

**estragon** *nm* tarragon

**estropier** *vt* cripple, lame; ~ **le français** murder French

**estuaire** *nm* estuary

**estudiantin** *adj* student

**esturgeon** *nm* sturgeon

**et** *conj* and; ~ ... ~ both ... and

**étable** *nf* cowshed, cattle-shed

**établi** *nm* work-bench

**établir** *vt* establish, institute; install, set up; construct, put up; fix; set; prove; draw up, work out; lay down, prescribe; found; **s'** ~ settle; become established

**établissement** *nm* establishment; installing, setting up; working out; proving; drawing up; creating, instituting, founding; institution

**étage** *nm* floor, storey; tier, stage; *geol* layer, formation; rank, station

**étager** *vt* (3) range in tiers

**étagère** *nf* what-not; set of shelves; shelf

**étai** *nm* strut, prop; *naut* stay

**étain** *nm* tin; pewter

**étal** *nm* (*pl* **étals**) meat stall; market display

**étalage** *nm* show, display; ostentation; **faire ~ de** show off, display

**étalager** *vt* (3) put on display

**étalagiste** *n* window-dresser; stall-holder

**étale** *adj naut* slack (water); without headway (ship)

**étalement** *nm* display; staggering (hours, holidays)

**étaler** *vt* display, expose for sale; spread out; space out, stagger; flaunt; *naut* weather out; *coll* flatten (s/o); **s' ~** *coll* stretch out; *coll* fall over, fall down

**¹étalon** *nm* standard; **~ or** gold standard

**²étalon** *nm* stallion

**étalonner** *vt* standardize, calibrate; gauge, test

**étambot** *nm naut* stern-post

**étamer** *vt* tin-plate; galvanize; silver

**¹étamine** *nf* coarse muslin

**²étamine** *nf bot* stamen

**étampe** *nf* stamp, die

**étamper** *vt* stamp, punch; drop-forge

**étamure** *nf* metal for tinning; tin coating

**étanche** *adj* watertight

**étanchéité** *nf* watertightness

**étancher** *vt* staunch, stop the flow of; quench; make watertight

**étang** *nm* pond, pool

**étape** *nf* stage; halting-place; lap

**état** *nm* state, condition; nation, state; report, list; trade, profession; estate, social rank; **~ civil** civil status; **~ d'âme** mood, mental state; **~ des lieux** inventory of fixtures; *Fr hist* **États Généraux** States General; **ce n'est pas une affaire d'État!** it's not very important: **de son ~** by trade, by profession; **en tout ~ de cause** whatever the circumstances; *coll* **être dans tous ses ~ s** be in a terrible state; **faire ~ de qch** take sth into account; **hors d' ~ de** incapable of; **remettre qch en ~** put sth right, overhaul; **tenir en ~** maintain, keep in good repair; *Fr hist* **tiers ~** third estate

**étatiser** *vt* put under state control

**étatisme** *nm* state control; statism

**état-major** *nm* (*pl* **états-majors**) general staff; staff headquarters

**état-providence** *nm* welfare state

**États-Unis** *nmpl* United States

**étau** *nm* vice

**étayer** *vt* (7) prop up, shore up; support, back up

**¹été** *nm* summer; **~ de la Saint-Martin** Indian summer

**²été** *p part* **être**

**éteignoir** *nm* candle snuffer; *coll* kill-joy, wet blanket

**éteindre** *vt* (55) put out, extinguish; switch off; turn off; exterminate; quench (thirst); soften, fade; deaden; appease; settle (debt); **s' ~** go out; pass away

**éteint** *adj* extinct; dull, dim; toneless (voice)

**étendard** *nm* standard; flag

**étendoir** *nm* clothes-line

**étendre** *vt* spread, stretch; spread out, lay out; stretch out; extend, increase; dilute with water; **s' ~** lie down; spread, stretch

**étendu** *adj* extensive; outspread

**étendue** *nf* area, size, extent; duration, length, importance; stretch

**Éternel (l')** *nm* God, the Lord

**éternel -elle** *adj* eternal, endless, everlasting

**éterniser** *vt* perpetuate; drag out; **s' ~** *coll* stay a very long time

**éternité** *nf* eternity; very long time; **de toute ~** from time immemorial

**éternuement** *nm* sneeze; sneezing

**éternuer** *vi* sneeze

**étêter** *vt* remove the head from; pollard (tree)

**éteule** *nf* stubble

**éthéré** *adj* ethereal

**Éthiopie** *nf* Ethiopia

**éthiopien -ienne** *adj* Ethiopian

**éthique** *nf* ethics; *adj* ethical

**ethnique** *adj* ethnic

**ethnologie** *nf* ethnology

**ethnologue** *n* ethnologist

**éthylisme** *nm* alcoholism

**Étienne** *nm* Stephen

**étinceler** *vi* (5) sparkle, glitter, throw out sparks

**étincelle** *nf* spark

**étincellement** *nm* sparkling, glittering; twinkling

**étiolement** *nm* drooping; fading; atrophy

**étioler** *vt* blanch; make pale; **s' ~** blanch; droop

**étique** *adj* emaciated; consumptive

**étiqueter** *vt* (5) label

**étiquette** *nf* label, docket; étiquette, ceremony, protocol

**étirer** *vt* draw out, stretch; **s' ~** stretch oneself

**étoffe** *nf* fabric, material, stuff; **il a de l' ~** he's got what it takes

**étoffé** *adj* abundant, ample, rich; plump

**étoffer** *vt* stiffen; enrich, fill out

**étoile** *nf* star; star-shaped decoration; film-star; decoration; crossing (of several roads or paths); **~ de mer** star-fish;

~ **filante** shooting star; **à la belle ~** in the open air; **né sous une bonne (mauvaise) ~** born under a lucky (unlucky) star

**étoilé** *adj* starlit, star-spangled; star-shaped

**étoiler** *vt* spangle with stars; star (glass, ice)

**étole** *nf* stole

**étonnant** *adj* surprising, astonishing; amazing

**étonnement** *nm* astonishment; amazement

**étonner** *vt* surprise, astonish; **s' ~** be surprised

**étouffant** *adj* stifling, stuffy; sweltering

**étouffée** *nf cul* **cuire à l' ~** braise

**étouffement** *nm* suffocation, smothering; breathlessness

**étouffer** *vt* suffocate, smother; stifle; stamp out; suppress; damp, deaden; hush up; *vi* choke, suffocate

**étoupe** *nf* tow

**étouper** *vt* caulk

**étourderie** *nf* thoughtlessness; blunder, oversight; **par ~** inadvertently

**étourdi** *adj* thoughtless; scatter-brained, stupid

**étourdir** *vt* stun, daze; deaden, allay; tire (with noise); **s' ~** dull oneself, stupefy oneself; intoxicate oneself

**étourdissement** *nm* giddiness, fit of dizziness; numbing, deadening

**étourneau** *nm* starling; scatter-brained person

**étrange** *adj* strange, peculiar

**étranger -ère** *n* foreigner, stranger; *adj* foreign; strange; irrelevant; **à l' ~** abroad

**étrangeté** *nf* strangeness, oddness

**étranglement** *nm* strangling; narrowing, constriction; bottle-neck

**étrangler** *vt* strangle, throttle; constrict; suppress; **~ au berceau** nip in the bud

**étrangleur -euse** *n* strangler

**étrave** *nf naut* stern-post

**être** *nm* being, existence; nature; individual; creature; *vi* (2) be, exist; go (in past); *aux* used to form past of certain verbs and passive; **~ à** belong to; **~ bien avec** be well in with; **~ de** hail from, originate from; **~ en noir** dressed in black; **c'en est trop** it's too much; **en ~** belong to, be one of; **en ~ pour sa peine** waste one's efforts; **il en est qui** there are some people who; **il était une fois …** once upon a time there was …; **il n'est que de** one needs only to; **j'en suis là** that's what I've come to; **j'en suis pour payer son dîner** I'll have to foot the bill for his dinner; **j'y suis** I get it, I understand; **n'était sa maladie** were it not for his illness; **n' ~ plus** be dead; **nous sommes le quatorze** it's the fourteenth; **soit** so be it, that is to say

**étreindre** *vt* (56) hug, embrace; oppress (emotion)

**étreinte** *nf* hug, embrace; grasp

**étrenne** *nf* (*usu pl*) New Year gift; Christmas box; first use

**étrenner** *vt* use for the first time; wear for the first time; be the first to buy from

**étrésillon** *nm* prop, strut

**étrier** *nm* stirrup; *anat* stirrup-bone (ear); **à franc ~** at full gallop; **avoir le pied à l' ~** be ready to go; **coup de l' ~** one for the road; stirrup cup

**étrille** *nf* curry-comb

**étriller** *vt* curry-comb; beat, thrash; *coll* overcharge

**étriper** *vt* disembowel, gut

**étriqué** *adj* tight (clothing); small-minded, petty

**étroit** *adj* narrow, confined; tight; limited; close; **à l' ~** in confined quarters

**étroitesse** *nf* narrowness; tightness; closeness

**étron** *nm* turd

**étrusque** *adj* Etruscan

**étude** *nf* study; office, practice (solicitor); prep; **à l' ~** under consideration; **faire ses ~s** study

**étudiant -e** *n + adj* student

**étudié** *adj* studied; elaborate

**étudier** *vt* study; prepare, swot up; read (a subject); investigate; observe closely; *vi* study; **s' ~** strive, apply oneself; observe oneself closely

**étui** *nm* case, cover, box

**étuve** *nf* sweating-room; drying-oven; hot place

**étuvée** *nf cul* **à l' ~** steamed, braised

**étuver** *vt* braise, dry

**étymologie** *nf* etymology

**eu** *p part* **avoir**

**eucharistie** *nf* Eucharist, Lord's Supper

**eunuque** *nm* eunuch

**euphémisme** *nm* euphemism

**euphonie** *nf* euphony

**eurasien -ienne** *adj* Eurasian

**Européen -éenne** *n* European

**européen -éenne** *adj* European

**euthanasie** *nf* euthanasia

**eux** *pron pl* them, they

**évacuer** *vt* evacuate; drain; withdraw from; vacate

**évadé** *adj* escaped

**évader (s')** *v refl* escape, run away

**évaluation** *nf* valuation, assessment, estimate

**évaluer** *vt* value, estimate, assess; reckon

**évangélique** *adj* evangelic; evangelical

**évangéliser** vt evangelize

**évangéliste** nm evangelist

**évangile** nm gospel

**évanouir (s')** v refl faint; disappear, die away

**évanouissement** nm fainting fit; disappearance, dying away

**évaporé** adj irresponsible, scatterbrained

**évaporer (s')** v refl evaporate, dry off

**évasé** adj wide-mouthed; flared

**évasement** nm widening out

**évaser** vt widen out, open out

**évasif -ive** adj evasive

**évasion** nf escape; **besoin d'** ~ need for a change

**évêché** nm bishopric, see; bishop's palace

**éveil** nm awakening; alertness; **donner l' ~** raise the alarm; **être en ~** be on the alert

**éveillé** adj awake; alert, sharp

**éveiller** vt awaken, wake up; arouse

**événement** nm event

**éventail** nm fan; range; **en ~** fanshaped

**éventaire** nm hawker's tray; display outside shop

**éventé** adj stale; flat

**éventer** vt air, expose to the air; fan; coll ~ **la mèche** twig, cotton on; **s' ~** go flat, stale

**éventrer** vt disembowel; gut; rip open, break open

**éventualité** nf possibility, eventuality

**éventuel -uelle** adj possible

**éventuellement** adv possibly; should the occasion arise

**évêque** nm bishop

**évertuer (s')** v refl try very hard, do one's utmost

**éviction** nf eviction, expulsion; leg dispossession, deprival

**évidé** adj hollow; cut away

**évidemment** adv evidently; certainly, of course, naturally

**évidence** nf obviousness, clearness; conspicuousness; **de toute ~** quite obviously; **mettre en ~** show off, display; **se rendre à l' ~** bow to reality

**évident** adj obvious, plain

**évider** vt scoop out, hollow out; cut away

**évier** nm sink

**évincer** vt (4) eject, thrust aside, turn out; leg dispossess

**éviscérer** vt (6) eviscerate, disembowel

**évitable** adj avoidable

**évitement** nm avoidance, shunning; **voie d' ~** siding

**éviter** vt avoid, keep clear of

**évocateur -trice** adj evocative

**évocatoire** adj evocatory

**évolué** adj developed, advanced

**évoluer** vi manoeuvre, go round; evolve, develop; change one's opinion(s)

**évolution** nf mil movement, manoeuvre; evolution, development

**évoquer** vt evoke, call forth, conjure up; recall

**exacerber** vt exacerbate

**exact** adj exact, accurate; correct; punctual; conscientious

**exactitude** nf exactness; correctness; punctuality

**ex aequo** adv phr equals, of equal merit

**exagération** nf exaggeration

**exagérer** vt (6) exaggerate; overstate; overrate

**exaltation** nf exaltation; glorifying; excitement; rapture; stimulation

**exalté** adj overexcited, passionate; quixotic

**exalter** vt exalt; extol; excite; **s' ~** enthuse, get very excited

**examen** nm examination, test; investigation, scrutiny

**examinateur -trice** n examiner

**examiner** vt examine, investigate; scrutinize

**exaspération** nf exasperation; aggravation

**exaspérer** vt (6) exasperate, provoke; aggravate; **s' ~** become exasperated

**exaucer** vt (4) grant the prayer of; fulfil

**excavation** nf digging out, excavation; pit, hole

**excaver** vt dig out, excavate

**excédant** adj surplus; exasperating, tiresome

**excédent** nm surplus, excess

**excédentaire** adj surplus

**excéder** vt (6) exceed; exhaust; exasperate

**excellence** nf excellence; excellency; **par ~** above all

**exceller** vi excel

**excentrique** adj eccentric; outlying, remote; odd, strange

**excepté** prep except, but for, save

**excepter** vt except, exclude

**exception** nf exception; leg incidental plea; ~ **faite de, à l' ~ de** with the exception of; **faire ~** be an exception; **sauf ~** with certain exceptions

**exceptionnel -elle** adj exceptional

**excès** nm excess; nmpl cruel conduct; excesses

**excessif -ive** adj excessive, extreme, inordinate; exorbitant

**exciser** vt excise, cut out

**excitant** nm stimulant; adj stimulating

**excitation** nf excitement; incitement, encouragement

**exciter** *vt* excite, arouse, stimulate; incite, inflame; **s' ~** get worked up

**exclamatif -ive** *adj* exclamatory

**exclamation** *nf* exclamation; **point d' ~** exclamation mark

**exclamer (s')** *v refl* exclaim; protest

**exclure** *vt* (25) exclude, leave out; be incompatible with

**exclusif -ive** *adj* exclusive, sole; dogmatic

**exclusivité** *nf* exclusiveness; sole rights; **en ~ (à, chez)** only (at)

**excommunier** *vt* excommunicate

**excorier** *vt* excoriate; peel off (skin)

**excréter** *vt* (6) excrete

**excroissance** *nf* excrescence

**excursionniste** *n* tripper, excursionist

**excuse** *nf* excuse; **~ s** apology; **faire des ~ s, présenter ses (des) ~ s** apologize

**excuser** *vt* apologize for; excuse, let off; absolve; act as an excuse for; **s' ~** apologize; excuse oneself; **se faire ~** decline; **qui s'excuse s'accuse** excuses are a sign of a guilty conscience

**exécration** *nf* execration; object of detestation; **avoir en ~** loathe

**exécrer** *vt* (6) detest, loathe

**exécutable** *adj* practicable, feasible

**exécutant -e** *n* agent; *mus* performer

**exécuter** *vt* execute, carry out, perform, fulfil; put to death; *leg* distrain upon; **s' ~** comply, submit, oblige; pay up

**exécuteur -trice** *n* **~ des hautes œuvres** executioner; *leg* **~ testamentaire** executor

**exécutif -ive** *adj* executive

**exécution** *nf* execution; performance, carrying out, fulfilment; **mettre à ~** carry out, put into effect

**exécutoire** *adj leg* enforceable

**exégèse** *nf* exegesis

**exemplaire** *nm* pattern; specimen; copy; *adj* exemplary

**exemple** *nm* example; lesson, warning; precedent, instance; **à l' ~ de** following the example of; **par ~** for example; **par ~!** goodness!, the idea!; **sans ~** unparalleled

**exempter** *vt* exempt

**exercé** *adj* practised, experienced

**exercer** *vt* (4) exercise; exert; practise, pursue, carry on; **s' ~** train, practise

**exercice** *nm* exercise; practice, carrying out; financial year; **~ s spirituels** devotions; **en ~** practising; **entrer en ~** enter upon one's duties; **faire l' ~** drill

**exergue** *nm* **mettre en ~** give prominence to; use (quotation) as epigraph

**exfolier** *vt* exfoliate

**exhalaison** *nf* exhalation

**exhaler** *vt* exhale, give out; vent (anger); **s' ~** be given off

**exhausser** *vt* raise, increase the height of

**exhiber** *vt* show, present; display, exhibit, show off; **s' ~** make an exhibition of oneself, expose oneself

**exhibition** *nf* showing, producing; exhibition; display, flaunting

**exhorter** *vt* exhort, urge

**exhumer** *vt* exhume, disinter; bring to light, unearth

**exigeant** *adj* hard to please; exacting

**exigence** *nf* demand, requirement; need, exigency; exactingness

**exiger** *vt* (3) demand, require; necessitate, call for

**exigu -uë** *adj* tiny, exiguous; scant, slender

**exiguïté** *nf* exiguity, smallness; scantiness, slenderness

**exil** *nm* exile, banishment; place of exile

**exilé -e** *n* exile

**exiler** *vt* exile, banish

**existant** *adj* existing, existent

**existence** *nf* being; life, existence

**exister** *vi* exist, live; count, be important

**exocet** *nm* flying-fish; *mil* exocet (missile)

**exode** *nm* exodus, mass-emigration; **~ rural** drift from the country

**exonération** *nf* exoneration; exemption, dispensation

**exonérer** *vt* (6) dispense, exempt; exonerate

**exorbité** *adj* **yeux ~ s** eyes popping out of the head

**exorciser** *vt* exorcize, cast out (devil)

**exorcisme** *nm* exorcizing; exorcism

**exorde** *nm* opening (of speech)

**exotique** *adj* exotic

**exotisme** *nm* exoticism

**expansif -ive** *adj* expansive

**expansion** *nf* expansion; expansiveness; development

**expatrier** *vt* expatriate; **s' ~** leave one's own country

**expectative** *nf* expectancy, expectation

**expectorer** *vt* expectorate

**expédient** *nm* expedient, device

**expédier** *vt* dispatch; expedite, hasten, rush; get rid of; *leg* draw up

**expéditeur -trice** *n* sender, consigner

**expéditif -ive** *adj* expeditious

**expédition** *nf* expedition; dispatch, sending; execution; *leg* copy; **bulletin d' ~** way-bill

**expéditionnaire** *n* sender (goods); *leg* copying clerk; *adj* expeditionary

**expérience** *nf* experience; experiment; **faire l' ~ de** experience

**expérimental** *adj* experimental

**expérimentateur -trice** *n* experimenter

**expérimenté** *adj* experienced

**expérimenter** *vt + vi* test, try

**expert -e** *n* expert; connoisseur;

appraiser; *adj* expert, skilled, skilful

**expert-comptable** *nm* (*pl* **experts-comptables**) chartered accountant

**expertise** *nf* valuation, expert appraisal; expert's report

**expertiser** *vt* carry out a valuation or survey of

**expiatoire** *adj* expiatory

**expier** *vt* expiate, atone for

**expiration** *nf* breathing out, expiration; expiry

**expirer** *vt* breathe out; *vi* expire; die

**explétif** *nm* expletive

**explicatif -ive** *adj* explanatory

**explication** *nf* explanation; **avoir une ~ avec qn** have it out with s/o

**explicite** *adj* explicit, clear, plain

**expliquer** *vt* explain, elucidate; **s'~** explain oneself; have it out; understand

**exploit** *nm* achievement, exploit; *leg* writ

**exploitable** *adj* workable; exploitable

**exploitant -e** *n* operator; cultivator

**exploitation** *nf* exploitation, exploiting; working; cultivation; farm

**exploiter** *vt* exploit; operate; work; cultivate; take undue advantage of

**exploiteur -euse** *n* exploiter

**explorateur -trice** *n* explorer

**explorer** *vt* explore; examine, study, probe

**exploser** *vi* explode, blow up; *fig* overflow, develop greatly

**explosif** *nm* explosive; *adj* (*f* **-ive**) explosive

**explosion** *nf* explosion; **faire ~** explode; **moteur à ~** internal combustion engine

**exportateur -trice** *n* exporter

**exporter** *vt* export

**exposant -e** *n* exhibitor

**exposé** *nm* statement, account

**exposer** *vt* show, exhibit; expose; expound, put forward; **s'~** expose oneself (to danger)

**exposition** *nf* exhibition, display; exposing, exposure; exposition, account; aspect (house)

**exprès -esse** *adj* express, distinct; *invar* express; *adv* intentionally, on purpose; **un fait ~** a tiresome coincidence

**express** *nm* fast train; express letter

**expressif -ive** *adj* expressive

**expression** *nf* expression; phrase; utterance

**exprimable** *adj* expressible

**exprimer** *vt* express, voice; show; **s'~** express oneself

**exproprier** *vt* expropriate

**expulser** *vt* expel, evict, turn out

**expurger** *vt* expurgate

**exquis** *adj* exquisite; beautiful; charming, delightful

**exsangue** *adj* very pale; bloodless

**exsuder** *vt + vi* exude

**extase** *nf* ecstasy; rapture; trance; **être en ~ devant qn** be full of admiration for s/o

**extasier (s')** *v refl* go into ecstasies, be overcome with admiration

**extatique** *adj* ecstatic

**extenseur** *nm* chest-expander; *anat* extensor

**extensif -ive** *adj* extensive; tensile

**extension** *nf* extension; stretching, extending; enlargement, spreading; *med* traction; **prendre de l'~** grow, expand

**exténuant** *adj* exhausting

**exténuer** *vt* exhaust

**extérieur** *nm* exterior, outside; **à l'~ de** outside; *adj* exterior, outer, external

**extérieurement** *adv* outwardly, externally; on the surface

**extérioriser** *vt* exteriorize; **s'~** show one's feelings

**exterminateur -trice** *n* exterminator; *adj* exterminating

**exterminer** *vt* exterminate

**externat** *nm* day-school; day attendance; non-residence; non-resident medical work

**externe** *n* day pupil; non-resident doctor; *adj* external

¹**extincteur** *nm* fire extinguisher

²**extincteur -trice** *adj* extinguishing

**extinction** *nf* extinction; extinguishing, putting out; suppression; **~ de voix** loss of voice

**extirper** *vt* extirpate; remove

**extorquer** *vt* extort, wring

**extra** *nm invar* extra; supplement; temporary domestic servant; *adj invar coll* extraordinarily good, very special, super

**extracteur** *nm* extractor

**extraction** *nf* extraction, drawing out; quarrying; origin, descent

**extrader** *vt* extradite

**extra-fin** *adj* superfine

**extra-fort** *nm* strong ribbon or tape

**extraire** *vt* (9) extract, pull out; quarry

**extrait** *nm* extract; excerpt; abstract; copy of legal document

**extra-muros** *adv* outside the town

**extraordinaire** *adj* extraordinary; special; unusual

**extrapoler** *vt + vi* extrapolate

**extravagance** *nf* extravagance; folly; immoderateness

**extravagant** *adj* extravagant; foolish; immoderate

**extravaguer** *vi* talk nonsense

**extraverti -e** *n* extrovert

**extrême** *nm* extreme, limit; *adj* extreme; utmost; excessive; drastic; farthest
**extrême-onction** *nf* extreme unction
**Extrême-Orient** *nm* Far East
**extrémisme** *nm* extremism
**extrémité** *nf* extremity, end; last degree; **en venir à des ~ s** give way to violence; **être à la dernière ~** be at death's door;

**pousser qch à l' ~** carry sth to extremes
**extrinsèque** *adj* extrinsic
**exubérance** *nf* exuberance; superabundance
**exubérant** *adj* exuberant; superabundant
**exulter** *vi* exult, rejoice
**exutoire** *nm* outlet

# F

**fa** *nm invar mus* F, fa; **clef de ~** bass clef
**fable** *nf* fable; tale; lie; **la ~ du village** the talk of the village
**fabricant -e** *n* manufacturer; maker
**fabricateur -trice** *n* forger; fabricator
**fabrication** *nf* manufacture; forging; fabrication
**fabrique** *nf* manufacture; factory, mill; **marque de ~** trade-mark
**fabriquer** *vt* manufacture; make; forge; fabricate; *coll* **qu'est-ce que tu fabriques?** what are you up to?
**fabuleux -euse** *adj* fabulous
**Fac** *nf coll* faculty; university
**façade** *nf* façade, front; *sl* **se refaire la ~** make up (face)
**face** *nf* face, surface, aspect; head (coin); side (dice); **~ à** facing; **à double ~** reversible (material); two-faced (person); **coll** **en ~** full-face; **en ~** opposite, to one's face, in the face; **en ~ de** opposite, in front of, in the presence of; **faire ~ à** face up to, cope with; **pile ou ~?** heads or tails?
**face-à-main** *nm* (*pl* **faces-à-main**) lorgnette
**facétie** *nf* joke
**facétieux -ieuse** *adj* facetious
**facette** *nf* facet
**fâché** *adj* sorry; angry; on bad terms
**fâcher** *vt* anger, irritate, displease, offend; **se ~** get angry; **se ~ avec** fall out with; **se ~ tout rouge** fly into a rage
**fâcheux -euse** *adj* regrettable, sad, unfortunate; tiresome, dreary
**facile** *adj* easy; easy-going; facile, fluent; **~ à vivre** easy to get on with
**facilité** *nf* easiness; facility; fluency; **~ s de paiement** easy terms, instalment plan; **solution de ~** line of least resistance, easy way out
**faciliter** *vt* facilitate
**façon** *nf* make, making; way, manner, fashion; shape, cut; **à la ~ de** after the manner of; **à sa ~** in one's own way; **de cette ~** in this (that) way, at this (that) rate; **de ~ à** so as to; **de ~ que** so that; **de toute ~** anyway, at any rate; **en aucune ~** by no means; **faire des ~s** stand on ceremony; **sans ~** without ceremony; **sans plus de ~s** without more ado; **tailleur à ~** bespoke tailor, *US* custom tailor
**faconde** *nf* fluency; *coll* gift of the gab
**façonner** *vt* work, fashion, shape, mould; *agr* dress
**facteur** *nm* postman, *US* mailman; porter; carrier; agent; factor
**factice** *adj* factitious, artificial
**factieux -ieuse** *adj* factious
**faction** *nf* sentry duty, guard; faction; **de (en) ~** on sentry duty
**factionnaire** *nm* sentry, sentinel
**factuel -uelle** *adj* factual
**facture** *nf* bill, invoice; structure, composition; workmanship; **suivant ~** as per invoice
**facturer** *vt* invoice
**facultatif -ive** *adj* optional; **arrêt ~** request stop
**faculté** *nf* faculty, power; option, right; faculty, department; *coll* **la Faculté** the Faculty of Medicine, doctors, medical opinion
**fada** *adj invar coll* crazy, cracked
**fadaise** *nf usu pl* nonsense, twaddle
**fade** *adj* insipid, flat, tasteless, wishy-washy
**fadeur** *nf* insipidity
**fading** *nm rad* fade
**fafiot** *nm sl* banknote

**fagot** *nm* faggot; **sentir le ~** be suspect, smack of heresy

**fagoté** *adj coll* got up, badly dressed

**faible** *nm* weakness, partiality; **les économiquement ~s** the lower-income groups, the underprivileged; *adj* feeble, weak, faint; low, slight

**faiblesse** *nf* feebleness, weakness; slightness; shortcoming, failing

**faiblir** *vi* weaken, grow weaker, abate

**faïence** *nf* earthenware; crockery; **se regarder en chiens de ~** glower at each other

**faille** *nf* fault, crack

**failli** *nm* + *adj* bankrupt

**faillibilité** *nf* fallibility

**faillible** *adj* fallible

**faillir** *vi* (45) fail; err; nearly do; **j'ai failli mourir** I nearly died

**faillite** *nf* failure, bankruptcy; **faire ~** go bankrupt

**faim** *nf* hunger; **avoir ~** be hungry; **manger à sa ~** eat one's fill

**faîne** *nf* beech-nut

**fainéant -e** *n* idler, lazybones; *adj* lazy, idle

**fainéantise** *nf* idleness

**faire** *vt* (46) make, create, form, beget; do, perform, cause; play, affect; imitate; travel, cover, go; do, clean, wash; be (profession, trade); **~ attention** pay attention; **~ cas de** think a great deal of; **~ comprendre** give to understand, insinuate; **~ dire** send word; **~ eau** leak; **~ entendre** hint, give to understand; **~ ~ qch** have sth done, have sth made; **~ l'affaire** be just the thing; **~ part de** notify of; **~ penser à** remind of; **~ savoir à** inform; **~ valoir** make the most of, display; **~ venir** send for; **~ voir** show; **cela ne fait rien** it doesn't matter; **il faut le ~** it takes some doing, not everyone can do it; **laisser ~** let things take their course; **pourquoi ~?** what for?; **prière de ~ suivre** please forward; **se laisser ~** put up no resistance; *vi* do, act; need; **bien, say; ~ bien de** do well to; **~ de son mieux** do one's best; **~ pour le mieux** act for the best; **avoir fort à ~** have one's hands full; **n'avoir que ~ de** have no need of, have no use for; **que ~?** what's to be done?; **qu'y ~?** how can it be helped?; *v impers* **il fait beau (chaud, froid, jour, nuit)** it is fine (hot, cold, light, dark); **il fait bon se reposer** it is pleasant to rest; **se ~** be made, be done; happen; become, get, grow; **cela ne se fait pas** that's not done; **comment se fait-il que ...?** how is it that ...?; **il pourrait se ~ que ...** it could be that ...; **s'en ~** worry, care;

**un bruit se fit entendre** a noise was heard

**faire-part** *nm invar* notice, announcement (birth, death, etc)

**faisable** *adj* feasible, practicable

**faisan -e** *n* pheasant

**faisandé** *adj* high (game); spicy (story, etc)

**faisander** *vt* hang (game); *sl* cheat

**faisceau** *nm* bundle; pencil (light); *mil* pile; **former les ~x** pile arms

**faiseur -euse** *n* maker, doer; *coll* swindler, crook; **bon ~** good tailor

**fait** *nm* fact, act, deed; event; matter; **~ divers** minor news item; **au ~** in fact; **au ~ de** informed about; **de (en) ~** in fact, truly; **dire son ~ à qn** give s/o a piece of one's mind; **en ~ de** with regard to; **en venir au ~** come to the point; **pris sur le ~** caught in the act; **voies de ~** assault and battery; *adj* made, done, formed, developed, accustomed; ripe (cheese); *sl* arrested, nabbed; **bien ~** shapely, well-built; **c'en est ~ de lui** it's all up with him; **c'est bien ~ pour vous** it serves you right; **tout ~** ready-made

**faîte** *nm* top, summit, ridge

**fait-tout** *nm invar* cooking-pot

**faix** *nm* burden

**falaise** *nf* cliff

**falbalas** *nmpl* flounces; showy trimmings

**fallacieux -ieuse** *adj* fallacious

**falloir** *v impers* (47) be necessary, be required; must, have to; **agir comme il faut** act correctly, suitably; **il faut partir** I (we, you, etc) must go; **il le faut** it is essential; **il lui faut ...** he must ...; he requires ...; **il m'a fallu deux heures pour venir** it took me two hours to get here; **un homme comme il faut** a well-bred man, gentleman; **s'en ~** be short, lacking; **il s'en est fallu de peu qu'il ne tombe** he came within an ace of falling; **il s'en faut de beaucoup** far from it; **il s'en faut de cinq minutes** there are five minutes to go; **peu s'en faut** very nearly

¹**falot** *nm* big lantern

²**falot** *adj* wan; tame

**falsifier** *vt* falsify, forge, adulterate

**falzar(d)** *nm sl* trousers

**famé** *adj* **mal ~** ill-famed

**famélique** *adj* hungry-looking, half-starved

**fameux -euse** *adj* famous; *coll* first-rate, terrific; **pas ~** nothing to write home about

**familial** *adj* family

**familiale** *nf* estate car

**familiariser** *vt* familiarize; **se ~ avec** master

**familiarité** *nf* familiarity, intimacy

**familier** *nm* close friend, intimate; *adj* (*f* **-ière**) familiar, intimate; well-known; colloquial

**familistère** *nm* co-operative store

**famille** *nf* family, household; **en ~** with one's family; **nom de ~** surname

**famine** *nf* famine, hunger

**fanal** *nm* lantern, light, beacon

**fanatique** *n* fanatic; *adj* fanatical

**fanatisme** *nm* fanaticism

**faner** *vt* toss, ted (hay); wither, make fade; *vi* make hay; **se ~** fade

**fanfare** *nf* fanfare, flourish; brass band

**fanfaron -onne** *n + adj* braggart

**fanfaronnade** *nf* brag, bragging

**fanfaronner** *vi* brag, boast

**fanfreluche** *nf* bauble, trifle; frill

**fange** *nf* mud, mire, filth

**fangeux -euse** *adj* muddy, miry, filthy

**fanion** *nm* pennant

**fanon** *nm* dewlap; wattle; fetlock

**fantaisie** *nf* fancy, imagination, whim; *mus* fantasia; *comm* fancy goods; **de ~** fancy

**fantaisiste** *n* capricious person; (music-hall) comedian; *adj* fanciful, whimsical

**fantasme** *nm* hallucination, phantasm

**fantasque** *adj* odd, whimsical

**fantassin** *nm* infantryman, foot-soldier

**fantastique** *adj* fantastic

**fantoche** *nm* puppet, marionette

**fantôme** *nm* ghost, phantom; *adj* imaginary; mysterious

**faon** *nm* fawn

**faquin** *nm* knave

**faramineux -euse** *adj coll* terrific, colossal

**faraud** *adj coll* snobbish, affected

¹**farce** *nf* farce; prank, practical joke

²**farce** *nf* stuffing

**farceur -euse** *n* practical joker, wag

**farcir** *vt* stuff; *sl* **se ~** treat oneself to; have it off with (a woman); put up with

**fard** *nm* make-up, paint; disguise; **parler sans ~** speak frankly

**fardeau** *nm* burden, load

**farder** *vt* paint; disguise; **se ~** make up

**farfelu** *adj* odd, crazy, hare-brained; surprising, funny

**farfouiller** *vi coll* rummage

**faribole** *nf* nonsense, idle talk

**farinacé** *adj* farinaceous

**farine** *nf* flour, meal; **~ de riz** ground rice; **gens de la même ~** birds of a feather

**farineux -euse** *adj* starchy, farinaceous

**farouche** *adj* shy, timid, unsociable; wild

**fart** *nm* wax (for skis)

**farter** *vt* wax (skis)

**fascicule** *nm print* number, part

**fascinateur -trice** *adj* fascinating, spell-binding

**fasciner** *vt* fascinate, charm

**fascisant** *adj* having fascist leanings, favouring fascism

**fascisme** *nm* fascism

**fasciste** *n + adj* fascist

¹**faste** *nm* pomp, show

²**faste** *adj* lucky, auspicious

**fastidieux -ieuse** *adj* tedious, irksome

**fastueux -ueuse** *adj* sumptuous; gaudy, showy

**fat** *nm* fop, self-satisfied individual; *adj* conceited, foppish, vain

**fatal** *adj* (*pl* **~s**) fatal; inevitable; fateful

**fatalisme** *nm* fatalism

**fataliste** *n* fatalist; *adj* fatalistic

**fatalité** *nf* fatality, fate

**fatidique** *adj* fateful

**fatigant** *adj* tiring; trying, tiresome

**fatigue** *nf* fatigue, weariness; strain; wear and tear

**fatiguer** *vt* tire, fatigue; strain, overtax; bore; mix (salad); *vi* labour; **se ~** tire, get tired

**fatras** *nm* rubbish; mess, hotch-potch

**fatuité** *nf* fatuity, self-conceit, foppishness

**faubourg** *nm* suburb

**faubourien -ienne** *adj* suburban; **accent ~** common accent

**fauché** *adj coll* broke, hard-up

**faucher** *vt* mow, scythe; mow down; *sl* pinch, knock off

**faucheur -euse** *n* mower, haymaker

**faucheuse** *nf* reaper, mowing-machine

**faucheux** *nm* daddy-long-legs

**faucille** *nf* sickle

**faucon** *nm* falcon, hawk

**faudra** *fut* **falloir**

**faufiler** *vt* tack, baste; **se ~** creep, edge, steal

¹**faune** *nm* faun

²**faune** *nf* fauna

**faussaire** *n* forger

**faussement** *adv* falsely

**fausser** *vt* falsify; bend, force, warp, distort; **~ compagnie à qn** give s/o the slip

¹**fausset** *nm* falsetto

²**fausset** *nm* spigot, *US* faucet

**fausseté** *nf* falsity; falseness; falsehood

**faut** *près* **falloir**

**faute** *nf* fault, mistake; misdeed, transgression; lack, want, need; **~ de mieux** for want of anything better; **~ de quoi** failing which; **~ d'impression** misprint; **à qui la ~?** whose fault is it?;

faire ~ à be lacking; **sans** ~ without fail; **se faire** ~ **de** fail to
**fauter** *vi coll* allow oneself to be seduced
**fauteuil** *nm* arm-chair, easy-chair; *theat* ~ **d'orchestre** stall; ~ **roulant** bath-chair, wheel-chair; *coll* **arriver dans un** ~ win in a canter, win easily
**fauteur -trice** *n* abettor; ~ **de guerre** warmonger; ~ **de troubles** agitator
**fautif -ive** *adj* faulty, defective; guilty
**fauve** *nm* fawn (colour); large wild animal; *adj* tawny, fawn-coloured; wild
**fauvette** *nf* warbler
¹**faux** *nm* falsehood; forgery, imitation; *adj* (*f* **fausse**) false, untrue, wrong, insincere; sham, faked; paste (jewels); counterfeit (coins); ~ **col** separate collar; *coll* froth on a glass of beer; ~ **départ** false start; ~ **frais** incidental expenses; ~ **numéro** wrong number; **faire fausse route** be on the wrong track; **fausse clef** skeleton key; **fausse couche** miscarriage; *adv* wrongly; *mus* out of tune; **à** ~ wrongly, out of true, beside the mark
²**faux** *nf* scythe
**faux-filet** *nm* sirloin
**faux-fuyant** *nm* shift, subterfuge, evasion, dodge
**faux-monnayeur** *nm* coiner, counterfeiter
**faux-semblant** *nm* false pretence; pretext
**faveur** *nf* favour, kindness; ribbon, favour; **à la** ~ **de** under cover of; **billet de** ~ complimentary ticket; **en** ~ in vogue; **en** ~ **de** in aid of; **prix de** ~ preferential price
**favorable** *adj* favourable, propitious
**favori -ite** *n* favourite, darling; *coll* blue-eyed boy, *US* fair-haired boy; *adj* favourite, pet
**favoris** *nmpl* side-whiskers; *coll* sideburns
**favoriser** *vt* favour
**fayot** *nm coll* haricot bean
**fébrile** *adj* feverish, febrile
**fécond** *adj* fertile, fruitful, prolific
**fécondation** *nf* fecundation; *med* impregnation; ~ **artificielle** artificial insemination
**féconder** *vt* fecundate; fertilize
**fécondité** *nf* fecundity; fertility
**fécule** *nf* fecula, starch
**féculent** *nm* starchy substance; starchy food
**fédérer** *vt* (6) federate; federalize
**fée** *nf* fairy; **conte de** ~ fairy-tale
**féerie** *nf* fairyland; fairy play
**féerique** *adj* fairy-like, enchanting
**feignant** *adj coll* idle, lazy
**feindre** *vt* (55) feign, sham, simulate,

pretend; *vi* limp (horse)
**feint** *adj* feigned, sham, mock
**feinte** *nf* feint; sham, pretence
**feinter** *vt* feint
**fêlant** *adj sl* very funny, killing
**fêlé** *adj sl* mad, cracked, crazy
**fêler** *vt* crack; **se** ~ crack
**félicitations** *nfpl* congratulations
**félicité** *nf* felicity, bliss
**féliciter** *vt* congratulate
**félin** *adj* feline
**félon -onne** *adj* felonious, treacherous
**félonie** *nf* felony, treason
**felouque** *nf* felucca
**fêlure** *nf* crack; *med* fracture
**femelle** *nf + adj* female
**féminin** *nm + adj* feminine
**féminisme** *nm* feminism
**féministe** *n + adj* feminist
**femme** *nf* woman; wife; ~ **de chambre** chambermaid, housemaid; ~ **de ménage** charwoman, daily help; ~ **d'intérieur** home-loving woman; ~ **du monde** woman who moves in fashionable society; **prendre** ~ marry
**femmelette** *nf* feeble, timid woman; *coll* effeminate man, cissy
**fenaison** *nf* hay-harvest, haymaking
**fendiller** *vt* crack; **se** ~ crack, craze
**fendoir** *nm* cleaver, chopper
**fendre** *vt* split, crack; cleave; chop; break (heart); force one's way through; **se** ~ lunge (fencing); *coll* **se** ~ **de** cough up, fork out, be generous; *sl* **se** ~ **la pipe** laugh like hell
**fenêtre** *nf* window
**fenil** *nm* hay-loft
**fenouil** *nm* fennel; ~ **bâtard** dill
**fente** *nf* crack, split, slot
**féodal** *adj* feudal
**féodalité** *nf* feudalism
**fer** *nm* iron; head, tip; sword; ferrule; ~**s** forceps; irons; ~ **à cheval** horseshoe; ~ **à repasser** iron (laundering); ~ **à souder** soldering iron; ~ **de lance** spearhead; ~ **forgé** wrought iron; **fil de** ~ wire; **tomber les quatre** ~**s en l'air** fall down backwards
**fer-blanc** *nm* tin; **boîte en** ~ tin, can; *coll* **en** ~ shoddy, cheap
**ferblanterie** *nf* ironmongery; ironmonger's shop
**ferblantier** *nm* tinsmith; ironmonger
**férié** *adj* **jour** ~ holiday
**férir** *vt* **sans coup** ~ without striking a blow
**ferler** *vt naut* furl
**fermage** *nm agr* rent; tenant farming
¹**ferme** *nf* farm, farmhouse; **prendre à** ~ rent (farm)
²**ferme** *adj* firm, fast, steady, strong; **de pied** ~ resolutely; **terre** ~ terra firma;

*adv* firmly, fast; hard; **tenez** ~! hold fast!

**fermenter** *vi* ferment

**fermer** *vt* shut, close; fasten; clench; draw (curtains); switch off; ~ **à clef** lock, lock up; ~ **boutique** shut up shop, sell up; *sl* **ferme-la!** shut up!, belt up!; ~ **la marche** bring up the rear; ~ **les yeux sur** turn a blind eye to, wink at; **ne pas** ~ **les yeux de la nuit** not sleep a wink all night; *vi* shut, close; **on ferme!** we're closing!, time!; **se** ~ shut, close

**fermeté** *nf* firmness, steadfastness

**fermette** *nf* small farm; country cottage

**fermeture** *nf* closing, shutting; fastener; closing-time; ~ **éclair** zip, *US* zipper

**fermier -ière** *n* farmer (farmer's wife)

**fermoir** *nm* clasp, fastener

**féroce** *adj* ferocious, savage

**férocité** *nf* ferocity

**ferraille** *nf* scrap-iron, old iron; *coll* small change; **bruit de** ~ rattling noise

**ferrailler** *vi* fight with swords

**ferrailleur** *nm* scrap-iron dealer

**ferré** *adj* iron-shod; hobnailed; *coll* ~ **sur** well up in; **voie** ~ **e** railway track

**ferrer** *vt* shoe (horse)

**ferret** *nm* tag (lace)

**ferreux -euse** *adj* ferrous

**ferronnerie** *nf* decorative ironwork; place where ironwork is made or sold

**ferronnier** *nm* art ironworker

**ferroviaire** *adj* railway

**ferrugineux -euse** *adj* ferruginous

**ferrure** *nf* (piece of) ironwork; shoeing (horses)

**fertile** *adj* fertile; fruitful

**fertilisant** *adj* fertilizing

**fertiliser** *vt* fertilize

**féru** *adj* ~ **de** infatuated with; set on

**férule** *nf* ferule, cane; *bot* ferule; **sous la** ~ **de qn** under s/o's thumb

**fervent -e** *n* devotee; *adj* fervent, zealous

**ferveur** *nf* fervour

**fesse** *nf* buttock; ~ **s** *coll* backside, arse; **avoir chaud aux** ~ **s** (**serrer les** ~ **s**) be dead scared; **histoire de** ~ **s** bawdy story, sexy anecdote

**fessée** *nf* spanking, thrashing

**fesser** *vt* spank

**fessier** *nm coll* buttocks, arse

**festin** *nm* feast, banquet

**feston** *nm* festoon, garland

**festonner** *vt* festoon

**festoyer** *vi* (7) feast, booze

**fêtard** *nm* reveller, boozer

**fête** *nf* feast, festival, holiday, fête; name-day; anniversary, birthday; **Fête-Dieu** Corpus Christi; ~ **légale** bank holiday, public holiday; **faire la** ~ à give a warm welcome to; **faire la** ~ go on the spree; **jour de** ~ feast-day, holiday; **se faire une** ~ **de** look forward to; **souhaiter bonne** ~ à wish many happy returns to

**fêter** *vt* celebrate; observe; fête

**fétiche** *nm* mascot; fetish

**fétide** *adj* fetid, putrid

**fétu** *nm* wisp of straw

**¹feu** *nm* fire, heat; hearth; light; ardour, passion; ~ **arrière** rear light; ~ **de joie** bonfire; *coll* ~ **de paille** flash in the pan; ~ **x d'artifice** fireworks; ~ **x (de circulation) (traffic) lights; **mot** ~ **x de position** parking lights; *naut + aer* navigation lights; ~ **x rouges** traffic lights; red light; **au coin du** ~ by the fireside; **au** ~ **!** fire!; **avoir le** ~ **vert** get the go-ahead; **cuire à petit** ~ cook on a low flame; **donner du** ~ **à qn** give s/o a light; **en** ~ on fire, flushed; **faire du** ~ light a fire; **faire la part du** ~ cut one's losses; **faire long** ~ misfire; **je n'y vois que du** ~ I can't make head or tail of it; **mettre le** ~ **à** set fire to; **ne pas faire long** ~ not last long; **prendre** ~ catch fire; **tuer à petit** ~ kill by inches; *adj invar* **rouge** ~ flame-coloured

**²feu** *adj* late, deceased; ~ **ma mère** my late mother; **la** ~ **e reine** the late queen

**feuillage** *nm* foliage

**feuille** *nf* leaf; petal; sheet; newspaper; *sl arg* ~ **de chou** cabbage leaf; *fig* rag, small newspaper; ~ **de garde** fly-leaf; ~ **de présence** time-sheet; ~ **de route** way-bill; *mil* marching orders; *arts* ~ **de vigne** fig-leaf; ~ **volante** loose-leaf

**feuilleté** *adj cul* **pâte** ~ **e** puff-pastry

**feuilleter** *vt* (5) turn over the pages of, flick through

**feuilleton** *nm* serial; (regular) newspaper column

**feutre** *nm* felt; felt hat; felt pen, felt pencil

**feutré** *adj* felt, felty; padded; soft (footsteps)

**fève** *nf* bean

**février** *nm* February

**fi** *interj obs* for shame!; **faire** ~ **de** turn up one's nose at

**fiacre** *nm* cab

**fiançailles** *nfpl* betrothal, engagement

**fiancer** *vt* (4) betrothe; **se** ~ become engaged

**fibre** *nf* fibre, texture

**fibreux -euse** *adj* fibrous

**fibrome** *nm* fibrous tumour

**ficelé** *adj* tied; *coll* dressed, got up

**ficeler** *vt* (5) tie up

**ficelle** *nf* string, twine; small thin loaf; *mil* (officer's) stripe; *coll* trick; trickster; **vieille** ~ old hand; *adj coll* knowing, slick

**fiche** *nf* index-card, slip; peg, pin; *elect*

plug; *coll* ~ **de consolation** booby-prize

**ficher, fiche** *vt* (*p part* **fiché**+**fichu**) stick, drive; card-index (s/o); *coll* ~ **dehors** chuck out, sack; *coll* **fichez le camp!** beat it!, get out!; *coll* **fichez-moi la paix!** shut up!, leave me alone!; *coll* **ne rien** ~ not do a stroke; *coll* **se** ~ **de** not give a damn about; make fun of; *sl* **se** ~ **dedans** make a blunder, slip up

**fichier** *nm* card-index, card-index box

**fichtre** *interj obs* well, I'm blowed!, heck!

¹**fichu** *nm* scarf, square

²**fichu** *adj coll* done for, finished; awful, godforsaken; dolled up; ~ **de** capable of, up to; **bien** ~ good-looking; **mal** ~ under the weather; badly made; badly built (person)

**fictif -ive** *adj* fictitious

**fidèle** *adj* faithful, loyal; accurate

**fidélité** *nf* fidelity, faithfulness; accuracy

**fiduciaire** *adj* fiduciary; held in trust

**fieffé** *adj* arrant, absolute

**fiel** *nm* gall, bitterness

**fielleux -euse** *adj* bitter, rancorous

**fiente** *nf* droppings (*usu* birds)

¹**fier** (*f* **fière**) *adj* proud, noble, fine

²**fier (se)** *v refl* rely, trust

**fièrement** *adv* proudly; *coll* famously

**fierté** *nf* pride, dignity

**fiesta** *nf coll* spree, feast

**fièvre** *nf* fever; **avoir de la** ~ have a temperature

**fiévreux -euse** *adj* feverish

**fifre** *nm* fife; fife-player

**figé** *adj* congealed; stiff; starchy; set

**figer (se)** *v refl* (3) congeal; curdle (milk); freeze (smile)

**fignoler** *vt* take great care over

**figue** *nf* fig; ~ **de Barbarie** prickly pear; **faire la** ~ **à qn** make a vulgar gesture at s/o; **mi-**~, **mi-raisin** neither one thing nor the other

**figuier** *nm* fig-tree

**figurant -e** *n theat* walk-on; *cin* extra; inactive participant

**figuratif -ive** *adj* figurative

**figure** *nf* figure; face; air, look; court card; **faire triste** ~ cut a poor figure

**figuré** *nm* figurative sense; **au** ~ figuratively; *adj* figurative; represented; decorated

**figurer** *vt* figure, represent; *vi* figure, appear; **se** ~ imagine, fancy; picture to oneself

**fil** *nm* thread, wire; grain (wood); edge (blade); *fig* thread; ~ **à plomb** plumb-line; ~ **de fer** wire; ~**s de la Vierge** gossamer; **au bout du** ~ on the phone; **au** ~ **de l'eau** with the current; *coll* **avoir un** ~ **à la patte** be tied down; be

married, hitched; **coup de** ~ phone call; **cousu de** ~ **blanc** obvious; **de** ~ **en aiguille** step by step; **donner du** ~ **à retordre à** give a lot of trouble to

**filage** *nm* spinning

**filandreux -euse** *adj* stringy; long-drawn-out

**filant** *adj* thick, ropy; shooting (star)

**filasse** *nf* tow; **cheveux de** ~ tow-coloured hair; *adj invar* tow-coloured (hair)

**filateur** *nm* owner of spinning-mill

**filature** *nf* spinning; spinning-mill; shadowing, *US* tailing; **prendre en** ~ shadow

**file** *nf* file, queue, *US* line; **à la** ~ in file; uninterruptedly, on end

**filer** *vt* spin; pay out (cable); sustain (note); *theat* run through; shadow, *US* tail; *coll* ~ **un mauvais coton** be in poor health; *vi* smoke (lamp); shoot (star); run out (cable); ladder, run; *coll* buzz off, make off; ~ **à l'anglaise** take French leave; ~ **doux** sing small; watch one's step

¹**filet** *nm* net, network; rack (luggage); string bag; streak, trickle

²**filet** *nm cul* fillet

**filiale** *nf* subsidiary (company)

**filiation** *nf* filiation; **en** ~ **directe** in a direct line

**filière** *nf* usual channels; sequence, chain, path

**filigrane** *nm* watermark; filigree

**fille** *nf* daughter; girl; prostitute; ~**-mère** unmarried mother; **jeune** ~ girl; **rester** ~ remain single; **vieille** ~ old maid

**fillette** *nf* little girl; *coll* half-bottle

**filleul -e** *n* godson, goddaughter

**film** *nm* film; ~ **annonce** trailer, *US* preview; ~ **d'actualités** newsreel

**filmer** *vt* film

**filmothèque** *nf* film library, film collection

**filon** *nm* vein, lode; *coll* cushy job, *US* bonanza

**filou** *nm* swindler, crook

**filouter** *vt* swindle, cheat, con

**fils** *nm* son; ~ **à papa** rich man's son; ~ **de famille** young man of good family; ~ **de ses œuvres** self-made man

**filtre** *nm* filter, strainer; cup of black coffee; **bout** ~ filter-tip

**filtrer** *vt* filter, strain; *vi* percolate; leak out (news)

¹**fin** *nf* end, close, conclusion; goal, aim; death; expiration (lease); ~ **courant** at the end of the present month; ~ **de mois** monthly statement; end of the month; *leg* ~ **de non-recevoir** legal demurrer; *fig* refusal; ~ **prochain** at

the end of next month; **à cette ~** with this end in view; **à la ~** in the end, at last; **à toutes ~s utiles** for whatever purpose it may serve; to whom it may concern; **en ~ de compte** when all is said and done; **mener à bonne ~** bring to a successful conclusion; **toucher à sa ~** be drawing to a close; be at the point of death

²**fin** *nm* ultimate, best; clever fellow; **jouer au plus ~** try to outsmart; **le ~ du ~** the ultimate in perfection; *adj* fine, slender, thin, delicate; sharp, shrewd, acute; keen, expert; **~e bouche** gourmet; **~e champagne** liqueur brandy; **~es herbes** herbs for seasoning; **~e mouche** shrewd customer; **au ~ fond de** in the depths of; **le ~ mot** the truth; *adv* fine, finely; **écrire ~** write small

**final** *adj* final, last

**finale** *nf sp* final

**finalité** *nf* finality

**finance** *nf* finance; money; financial circles; **ministère des Finances** = Treasury

**financement** *nm* financing

**financer** *vt* (4) finance, back

**financier** *nm* financier; *adj* (*f* -ière) financial

**finasser** *vi* use trickery

**finasserie** *nf* trickery; ruse

**finaud** *adj* sly

**fine** *nf* liqueur brandy

**finesse** *nf* fineness, delicacy, slenderness; finesse; shrewdness, cunning, sharpness, subtlety; nicety

**fini** *nm* finish; finite; *adj* finished, completed; done for; finite; absolute; arrant

**finir** *vt* finish, end; *vi* finish, come to an end; die; **~ mal** turn out badly, come to a bad end; **en ~ avec** have done with

**finition** *nf* finishing, finish

**Finlandais -e** *n* Finn

**finlandais** *nm* Finnish (language); *adj* Finnish

**Finlande** *nf* Finland

**finnois** *nm* Finnish (language); *adj* Finnish

**fiole** *nf* phial; *sl* head, mug

**fioriture** *nf* flourish

**firme** *nf* firm

**fisc** *nm* Inland Revenue, *US* Internal Revenue

**fiston** *nm coll* son; youngster

**fistule** *nf* fistula

**five o'clock** *nm* afternoon tea

**fixage** *nm* fixing

**fixateur** *nm* fixer; fixing bath

**fixation** *nf* fixing, settling; fixation

**fixe** *nm* fixed salary; *adj* fixed, perma-

nent; regular; set (eyes); **beau ~** set fair; **idée ~** obsession; **regard ~** stare; *interj* eyes front!

**fixé** *adj* fixed, appointed; **être ~** know where one stands; know what to think

**fixement** *adv* fixedly; **regarder ~** stare (at)

**fixer** *vt* fix; fasten, make fast; stare at; determine, appoint; **~ qn sur qch** give s/o precise information about sth; **se ~** settle; **se ~ sur qch** decide on sth

**fixité** *nf* fixity; steadiness

**flacon** *nm* bottle, flask

**fla-fla** *nm coll* show; **faire du ~** show off

**flageller** *vt* scourge, flog, whip

**flageoler** *vi* shake, tremble (legs)

**flageolet** *nm* small kidney bean

**flagorner** *vt* toady to, fawn on

**flagorneur -euse** *n* toady

**flagrant** *adj* flagrant; **en ~ délit** red-handed, in the act

**flair** *nm* scent; flair

**flairer** *vt* scent, nose out; suspect

**Flamand -e** *n* Fleming

**flamand** *nm* Flemish (language); *adj* Flemish

**flamant** *nm* flamingo

**flambant** *adj* blazing, flaming; **~ neuf** brand new

**flambé** *adj coll* done for, sunk; *cul* flambé

**flambeau** *nm* torch; candlestick

**flambée** *nf* blaze; sudden upsurge, violent upsurge

**flamber** *vt* singe; set alight; *vi* burn, blaze, blaze up

**flamboyant** *adj* flaming, blazing; flamboyant, dazzling

**flamboyer** *vi* (7) flame, blaze

**flamme** *nf* flame; pennant; *lit + obs* passion; **retour de ~** backfire, flashback

**flan** *nm* baked tart; custard tart

**flanc** *nm* flank, side; **prêter le ~ à** lay oneself open to; **sur le ~** laid up; *coll* **tirer au ~** take things easy, swing the lead

**flancher** *vi* flinch, give way

**Flandre** *nf* Flanders

**flanelle** *nf* flannel; **~ de coton** flannelette

**flâner** *vi* saunter, loiter, hang about

**flânerie** *nf* loitering; stroll

**flâneur -euse** *n* loiterer, idler

**flanquer** *vt* flank; *coll* chuck, fling; **~ à la porte** sack, kick out

**flaque** *nf* puddle

**flash** *nm* (*pl* **flashes**) *phot* flash-lamp; short interview; short news item

**flasque** *adj* flabby, flaccid

**flatter** *vt* flatter; stroke, caress

**flatterie** *nf* flattery; caress

**flatteur -euse** *n* flatterer; *adj* flattering

**fléau** *nm* flail; plague, scourge, pest

**fléchage** *nm* signposting

**flèche** *nf* arrow; spire; **en** ~ ·dead straight; very rapidly; at the forefront, trendy; **faire** ~ **de tout bois** use every possible means

**flécher** *vt* signpost, arrow

**fléchette** *nf* dart

**fléchir** *vt* bend; move to pity; *vi* bend, give way

**fléchissement** *nm* bending, giving way

**flegmatique** *adj* phlegmatic, stolid

**flegme** *nm* phlegm, coolness

**flemmard -e** *n coll* slacker, lazybones; *adj coll* slack, lazy

**flemmarder** *vi coll* slack, laze

**flemme** *nf coll* laziness; **avoir la** ~ feel lazy; **tirer sa** ~ slack, laze

**flétan** *nm* halibut

**flétri** *adj* withered, faded; tarnished (reputation)

**flétrir** *vt* wither, blight; corrupt; stigmatize, criticize; **se** ~ wither, fade

**flétrissure** *nf* withering, fading; stigma, condemnation

**fleur** *nf* flower, blossom, bloom; ~ **de l'âge** prime of life; *coll* **la** ~ **des pois** the cream, pick of the bunch; **à** ~ **de** on a level with; **à** ~ **de peau** on the surface; **à** ~ **de tête** prominent (eyes); **arriver comme une** ~ drop in unexpectedly; *coll* **faire une** ~ **à qn** do s/o an unexpected favour, show s/o a kindness

**fleurer** *vt* smell of

**fleuret** *nm* foil

**fleuri** *adj* in blossom, bloom; adorned with flowers; flowery

**fleurir** *vt* (49) decorate with flowers; *vi* blossom, bloom; flourish

**fleuriste** *n* florist

**fleuve** *nm* river

**flibuster** *vi* filibuster

**flibustier** *nm* filibuster, swindler

**flic** *nm coll* policeman, cop

**flingot** *nm sl* rifle, gun

**flinguer** *vt sl* shoot at; kill; tear a strip off, tell off

**flipper** *nm* pin-table machine

**flirt** *nm* flirting; flirtation; boy-friend, girl-friend; friendly overtures

**flirter** *vi* flirt; make overtures

**flocon** *nm* flake; flock (wool)

**floconneux -euse** *adj* fleecy, fluffy

**flopée** *nf coll* large quantity, masses

**floraison** *nf* flowering, blooming

**floralies** *nfpl* flower show

**flore** *nf* flora

**floréal** *nm hist* eighth month of the French Republican calendar (April to May)

**florissant** *adj* flourishing, prosperous

**flot** *nm* wave; flood, stream; **à** ~ afloat; **à** ~ **s** in torrents

**flottaison** *nf* floating; **ligne de** ~ water-line

**flottant** *adj* floating; full (garment); unsteady, wavering, undecided

**flotte** *nf* fleet, navy; float (fishing); *sl* water, rain

**flottement** *nm* flapping; wavering

**flotter** *vi* float, stream; waver; *sl* rain

**flotteur** *nm* float (fishing); ball (cistern)

**flottille** *nf* flotilla

**flou** *adj* blurred, hazy, indistinct; soft, fluffy (hair)

**flouer** *vt coll* swindle, dupe

**flouze** *nm sl* money

**fluctuer** *vi* fluctuate

**fluet -ette** *adj* slender, thin and delicate; tiny (voice)

**fluide** *nm+adj* fluid

**fluidité** *nf* fluidity, fluid nature

**fluor** *nm* fluorine

**fluorine** *nf* calcium fluoride

**fluorure** *nm* fluoride

¹**flûte** *nf* flute; long loaf; flute glass; *coll* ~ **s** long thin legs, matchsticks; **petite** ~ piccolo

²**flûte** *interj* damn!, bother!

**flûté** *adj* flute-like, piping (voice)

**flûteau** *nm* whistle, pipe

**flûter** *vi* play the flute

**flûtiste** *n* flautist, flute-player

**Fluviale** *nf* **la** ~ the river police

**flux** *nm* flow, flood, flux

**fluxion** *nf* inflammation; *math* fluxion; ~ **de poitrine** inflammation, congestion of the lungs

**foc** *nm naut* jib

**focaliser** *vt* concentrate

**fofolle** *adj see* **fou-fou**

**foi** *nf* faith; belief; confidence, trust; **ajouter** ~ **à** believe in; **de bonne (mauvaise)** ~ in good (bad) faith; **digne de** ~ trustworthy; **faire** ~ be authoritative; **ma** ~! well!, indeed!; **profession de** ~ profession of faith; electoral manifesto

**foie** *nm* liver; **crise de** ~ bilious attack

**foin** *nm* hay; *coll* grass (marijuana); *coll* **faire du** ~ kick up a row; **rhume des** ~ **s** hay fever

**foire** *nf* fair; *coll* rumpus

**foirer** *vi sl* misfire, fail; *sl* have the shits

**fois** *nf* time; **à la** ~ at the same time; **deux** ~ twice; **encore une** ~ once more; **une** ~ once

**foison** *nf* plenty, abundance; **à** ~ in abundance

**foisonnement** *nm* abundance

**foisonner** *vi* abound; teem

**fol** *adj see* **fou** *adj*

**folâtre** *adj* playful, frisky

**folâtrer** *vi* gambol, frolic

**folichon -onne** *adj* playful, frisky; **pas ~** unexciting, dull

**folie** *nf* madness; folly; act of folly; craze

**folklore** *nm* folklore; *fig* nonsense, pretence

**folklorique** *adj* pertaining to folklore; *fig* amusing, crazy, absurd

**folle** *n + adj* see **fou**

**follet -ette** *adj* gay, frolicsome; **feu ~** will o' the wisp

**fomenter** *vt* foment, stir up

**foncé** *adj* dark, deep (colour)

**foncer** *vt* (4) sink; drive in; darken; *vi* grow darker; rush, dash

**fonceur -euse** *n fig* determined person

**foncier -ière** *adj* fundamental, basic; landed, of the land

**fonction** *nf* function; occupation; **en ~ de** in terms of; hand in hand with; **être ~ de** be dependent on

**fonctionnaire** *n* civil servant, official

**fonctionnariser** *vt* give the status of civil servant to

**fonctionnel -elle** *adj* functional

**fonctionnement** *nm* functioning, working

**fonctionner** *vi* function, work, run

**fond** *nm* bottom; bed (sea); back, far end (room); background; foundation; basis; essence; **~ de teint** make-up foundation; **à ~** thoroughly; **à ~ de train** at top speed; **article de ~** leading article; **au ~ (dans le ~)** basically; **course de ~** long-distance race; **de ~ en comble** from top to bottom

**fondamental** *adj* fundamental, basic; radical

**fondant** *nm cul* fondant; *metal* flux; *adj* melting; juicy

**fondateur -trice** *n* founder

**fondé** *nm* **~ de pouvoir** proxy; *adj* founded; well-founded; entitled

**fondement** *nm* base, foundation; *coll* bottom; **sans ~** groundless

**fonder** *vt* found; set up; establish; base; **se ~** rest, be based

**fonderie** *nf* foundry; smelting-works; smelting

**fondeur** *nm* founder; smelter

**fondre** *vt* smelt; cast; melt; dissolve; blend; *vi* melt; dissolve; **~ en larmes** burst into tears; **~ sur** pounce on; bear down upon; **se ~** melt; dissolve; blend

**fondrière** *nf* bog, quagmire

**fonds** *nm* land, estate; fund; stock-in-trade; *pl* funds, stocks; **~ de commerce** business, goodwill; **~ publics** government stocks

**fondu** *nm + adj rad* fade

**fondue** *nf* fondue (Swiss cheese dish); **~ bourguignonne** meat fondue

**fongus** *nm med* fungus

**fontaine** *nf* fountain; spring

**¹fonte** *nf* melting; *metal* smelting; cast-iron

**²fonte** *nf* holster

**fonts** *nmpl* font

**footballeur, footballer -euse** *n* football player

**footing** *nm* walking

**for** *nm* **~ intérieur** heart of hearts

**forage** *nm* boring, drilling

**forain** *nm* stall-keeper; hawker; *adj* itinerant; **fête ~ e** fun-fair

**forçat** *nm* convict; **mener une vie de ~** lead a life of drudgery

**force** *nf* strength; power; violence; vigour; **~ s** troops, forces; **~ de frappe** nuclear strike force; **~ lui fut de** he had no option but to; **à bout de ~ s** exhausted; **à ~ de** by dint of, by means of; **à toute ~** at all costs; **de ~** forcibly, willy-nilly; **la ~ de l'âge** the prime of life; *adv* many, a lot of

**forcé** *adj* strained, forced

**forcément** *adv* necessarily, inevitably; of course

**forcené** *adj* frenzied, frantic; mad

**forcer** *vt* (4) force, compel; break open; storm; **se ~** force oneself; strain oneself

**forcing** *nm* sustained pressure

**forcir** *vi* put on weight; grow strong

**forer** *vt* drill; bore

**forestier -ière** *n* forester, ranger; *adj* forest, forestry

**foret** *nm* drill, brace-bit; gimlet

**forêt** *nf* forest

**foreuse** *nf* drill

**¹forfait** *nm* serious crime

**²forfait** *nm* forfeit; **déclarer ~** give up; *sp* scratch

**³forfait** *nm* contract; agreed price; **à ~** charter, contract, by contract; **voyage à ~** package-tour

**forfaitaire** *adj* contractual; **paiement ~** lump sum

**forfaiture** *nf* forfeiture; breach

**forfanterie** *nf* bragging

**forge** *nf* forge; smithy; ironworks

**forger** *vt* (3) forge; coin, invent

**forgeron** *nm* smith, blacksmith

**forgeur** *nm* forger, smith

**formaliser (se)** *v refl* take offence, take exception

**formaliste** *n* formalist; stickler for formality; *adj* formal, stiff

**formalité** *nf* form; formality

**formateur -trice** *n* creator; *adj* formative

**formation** *nf* formation; education; **~ professionnelle** vocational training

**forme** *nf* form, shape; pattern; formality; way of proceeding; mould; **dans les ~ s** according to protocol; **par ~ de** by way of; **pour la ~** for appearance's sake; **sous (la) ~ de** in the form of

**formel -elle** *adj* formal; strict; categorical

**former** *vt* form; shape, fashion; train, teach; **se ~** take shape; be formed

**formidable** *adj* formidable, fearful; *coll* terrific, great

**formulaire** *nm* form; collection of formulae

**formule** *nf* formula; recipe; form

**formuler** *vt* formulate; put into words; write (prescription)

**forniquer** *vi* fornicate

**fors** *prep lit + obs* save, except

**fort** *nm* strong man; stronghold; forte; height (season); **~ des Halles** market porter; **~ en thème** swot; hardworking person; *adj* strong; powerful; clever; stout; high (price, wind); hard (currency); large (sum); heavy (beard, rain); **~ e tête** obstinate individual; *coll* **c'est un peu ~** it's a bit thick; **esprit ~** freethinker; contester; **se faire ~ de** undertake to; *adv* very, extremely; hard, strongly; loud(ly); **y aller ~** go hard at it; exaggerate, overdo

**forteresse** *nf* fortress, stronghold

**fortifiant** *nm + adj* tonic

**fortifier** *vt* fortify; strengthen, invigorate; **se ~** fortify oneself; grow stronger

**fortin** *nm* small fort

**fortuit** *adj* chance, accidental; casual

**fortune** *nf* fortune, (piece of) luck; chance; wealth; **dîner à la ~ du pot** take pot-luck

**fortuné** *adj* fortunate; well-to-do, rich

**forum** *nm hist* forum; *fig* place for public discussion; symposium

**fosse** *nf* hole, pit; grave; den (lions); *mot* inspection pit; **~ d'aisance** latrine; **~ septique** septic tank

**fossé** *nm* ditch, trench; moat

**fossette** *nf* dimple

**fossile** *nm* fossil

**fossoyer** *vt* (7) trench, ditch

**fossoyeur** *nm* grave-digger

**fou** (*f* **folle**) *nm* lunatic, madman (madwoman); jester, fool; bishop (chess); *adj* (*m* **fou, fol,** *f* **folle**) mad, crazy, insane; foolish, silly; terrific (success); large (crowd); out of control (vehicle); **~ de** crazy about

¹**foudre** *nm* large barrel

²**foudre** *nf* thunderbolt, lightning; **coup de ~** thunderbolt; love at first sight

**foudroyant** *adj* overwhelming; lightning; crushing, withering

**foudroyer** *vt* (7) strike (lightning); strike down; dumbfound, overwhelm

**fouet** *nm* whip, lash; whisk; **coup de ~** lash; stimulus; **heurter de plein ~** collide head-on with

**fouetter** *vt* whip, flog; whisk; *vi* lash, beat (rain); **avoir d'autres chats à ~** have other fish to fry

**fou-fou** (*f* **fofolle**) *adj* foolish, silly

**fougère** *nf* fern

**fougue** *nf* spirit, dash, fire

**fougueux -euse** *adj* spirited, fiery

**fouille** *nf* excavation; search

**fouiller** *vt + vi* excavate, dig; search, ransack; *sl* **va te faire ~ !** go to hell!

**fouillis** *nm* jumble, muddle

**fouine** *nf* marten

**fouiner** *vi coll* ferret, nose about

**fouir** *vt* dig

**foulard** *nm* foulard; scarf

**foule** *nf* crowd, throng; mob; **prendre un bain de ~** (of public figures) mix with the crowd, *US* press the flesh

**foulée** *nf* tread; stride; **~ s** spoor; **dans la ~ de** in the wake of; **en une seule ~** in one go

**fouler** *vt* tread, trample on; crush; sprain (joint); full (cloth); **~ aux pieds** trample underfoot; *coll* **se ~** take trouble

**foulure** *nf* sprain, wrench

**four** *nm* oven, cooker; furnace; kiln; failure, flop; **faire (un) ~** be a flop

**fourbe** *n* cheat, swindler; *adj* deceitful, crafty

**fourberie** *nf* cheating; imposture; deceit

**fourbi** *nm coll* stuff, things, thing

**fourbir** *vt* polish, rub up

**fourbu** *adj* tired out; foundered (horse)

**fourche** *nf* fork; pitchfork; **en ~** forked

**fourcher** *vt* fork (soil, etc); *vi* fork; **la langue m'a fourché** I made a slip of the tongue

**fourchette** *nf* (table) fork; wishbone; range, bracket; **c'est une belle ~** he is a big eater

**fourchu** *adj* forked; cloven (hoof)

¹**fourgon** *nm* van, wagon; luggage van, *US* baggage car

²**fourgon** *nm* poker, rake

**fourgonner** *vt* poke, rake; *vi* poke the fire; *fig* poke about

**fourgonnette** *nf* light van

**fourmi** *nf* ant; **avoir des ~ s** have pins and needles

**fourmilier** *nm* ant-eater

**fourmilière** *nf* ant-hill; *fig* swarm

**fourmillement** *nm* swarming; tingling, pins and needles

**fourmiller** *vi* swarm; tingle

**fournaise** *nf* furnace

**fourneau** *nm* stove; cooker, kitchen

range; bowl (pipe); **haut** ~ blast-furnace

**fournée** *nf* batch

**fourni** *adj* well-stocked; thick; bushy

**fournil** *nm* bakehouse

**fourniment** *nm* kit, equipment

**fournir** *vt* furnish, supply, equip

**fournisseur -euse** *n* supplier, purveyor; tradesman

**fourniture** *nf* supplying; supplies, equipment

**fourrage** *nm* fodder; forage

**fourrager** *vt* ravage; *vi* forage; rummage

**fourragère** *nf* hay-wagon

**fourré** *nm* thicket; *adj* furry; wooded; stuffed, filled; **porter un coup ~ à qn** deal s/o a back-handed blow

**fourreau** *nm* sheath; scabbard; sheath-dress

**fourrer** *vt* line with fur; *cul* stuff; cram, shove, thrust; **se ~** thrust, stick oneself; *coll* ~ **son nez dans** poke one's nose into

**fourre-tout** *nm* hold-all

**fourreur** *nm* furrier

**fourrier** *nm* quarter-master

**fourrière** *nf* pound

**fourrure** *nf* fur; *eng* lining

**fourvoiement** *nm* going astray

**fourvoyer** *vt* (7) lead astray, mislead; **se ~** go astray, blunder

**foutaise** *nf coll* nonsense, rot

¹**foutre** *nm vulg* sperm, spunk

²**foutre** *vt coll in all meanings* do; throw, chuck; give; ~ **la paix à qn** leave s/o alone; ~ **le camp** get out, go away; **se ~ de** make fun of, take the piss out of; **s'en ~** not give a damn

³**foutre** *interj vulg* bugger it!, fuck me!

**foutu** *adj coll in all meanings* bloody; done for; **mal** ~ out of sorts, tired; badly dressed

¹**fox** *nm* fox-terrier

²**fox** *nm* fox-trot

**foyer** *nm* hearth, fire, fireplace; *fig* home, family; firebox (engine); furnace; focus; hotbed; seat (illness); lounge (hotel); ~ **des artistes** greenroom; ~ **des étudiants** students' hostel; students' union; **verres à double** ~ bifocal lenses

**frac** *nm* dress-coat

**fracas** *nm* crash; roar; din

**fracassant** *adj fig* resounding, sensational

**fracasser** *vt* shatter, smash

**fractionnaire** *adj* fractional; **nombre ~** improper fraction

**fractionnel -elle** *adj* divisive

**fracture** *nf* breaking; fracture

**fracturer** *vt* break open; force (lock); fracture

**fragile** *adj* fragile; frail; brittle

**fragilité** *nf* fragility; frailty; brittleness

**fragment** *nm* fragment, chip; snatch (song)

**fragmentaire** *adj* fragmentary

**fragmenter** *vt* fragment, divide

**frai** *nm* spawning; spawn; fry (fish)

**fraîchement** *adv* freshly; coolly; newly, recently

**fraîcheur** *nf* freshness; coolness; bloom

**fraîchir** *vi* freshen, turn cool

¹**frais** *nm* cool, coolness; **au ~** in a cool place; *adj* (*f* **fraîche**) fresh, cool; new, recent; new-laid; wet (paint); *adv* newly, just

²**frais** *nmpl* expense, expenses; charge, charges; cost, outlay; ~ **de port** (transport) carriage (freight) charges; **en être pour ses ~** get nothing for one's pains; **faire les ~ de** bear the cost of; contribute most to (conversation); **menus ~** petty expenses; **rentrer dans ses ~** cover one's costs, get one's money back; **se mettre en ~** go to great expense

¹**fraise** *nf* strawberry; strawberry mark

²**fraise** *nf* ruff; *cul* crow (lamb, calf); wattle (fowl)

³**fraise** *nf* countersink; milling cutter; (dentist's) drill

**fraiser** *vt* frill; countersink; mill; drill (tooth)

**framboise** *nf* raspberry

**framboisé** *adj* raspberry-flavoured

**framboisier** *nm* raspberry cane

**Franc** (*f* **Franque**) *n* Frank

¹**franc** *nm* Frankish (language); *adj* (*f* **franque**) Frankish

²**franc** (*f* **franche**) *adj* candid, frank; open, free; sincere, real; downright, arrant; clear; ~ **de port** postage-free; **aller ~ jeu** go about things openly; **avoir son ~-parler** be outspoken; *sp* **coup ~** free kick; **jouer ~ jeu** play a straightforward game; play fair; act fairly; **parler ~** speak frankly

**Français -e** *n* Frenchman (Frenchwoman)

**français** *nm* French (language); *adj* French

**franchement** *adv* frankly; boldly; downright

**franchir** *vt* jump over; cross; pass through; overcome (obstacle)

**franchise** *nf* frankness; freedom (city); exemption (from charges, duty, etc)

**Franciscain -e** *n* Franciscan

**franciscain** *adj* Franciscan

**franciser** *vt* gallicize

**franc-maçon** *nm* (*pl* **francs-maçons**) Freemason

**franc-maçonnerie** *nf* freemasonry

**franco** *adv* carriage free, duty paid

**francophone** *adj* native French-speaking

**franc-parler** *nm* plain-speaking

**franc-tireur** *nm* (*pl* **francs-tireurs**) franc-tireur, sniper; loner

**frange** *nf* fringe

**franger** *vt* (3) fringe

**franglais** *nm* French language with excessive content of English vocabulary

**franquette** *nf* **à la bonne** ~ simply, without ceremony

**frappant** *adj* striking, impressive

¹**frappe** *nf* minting; striking; stamp; touch; **faute de** ~ typing error; misprint

²**frappe** *nf sl* scoundrel, bad lot

**frapper** *vt* strike, hit; mint (money); chill (drink); impose (tax); *vi* knock; ~ **du pied** stamp one's foot; ~ **juste** strike home; **se** ~ strike oneself; *coll* worry

**frappeur -euse** *n* striker; tapper, stamper; *adj* **esprit** ~ rapping spirit

**frasque** *nf* escapade, prank

**fraternel -elle** *adj* fraternal, brotherly

**fraterniser** *vi* fraternize

**fraternité** *nf* fraternity, brotherhood

**fratricide** *adj* fratricidal

**fraude** *nf* fraud, deceit, deception; **passer en** ~ smuggle in, out

**frauder** *vt* + *vi* cheat, swindle

**fraudeur -euse** *n* defrauder; smuggler; *adj* fraudulent; bogus

**frauduleux -euse** *adj* fraudulent

**frayer** *vt* (7) open up, clear; *vi* spawn (fish); associate; **se** ~ **un chemin** clear a way for oneself

**frayeur** *nf* fright, dread, terror

**fredaine** *nf* prank, escapade

**fredonner** *vt* + *vi* hum

**freezer** *nm* ice-compartment

**frégate** *nf* frigate

**frein** *nm* brake; bit, bridle; curb, restraint; moderating influence; **donner un coup de** ~ apply the brake, put on the brakes; **mettre un** ~ **à** curb, bridle; **ronger son** ~ champ the bit

**freinage** *nm* braking

**freiner** *vt* brake; moderate; curb; slow down; *vi* brake

**frelater** *vt* adulterate

**frêle** *adj* frail, weak

**frelon** *nm* hornet

**freluquet** *nm coll* whipper-snapper; young puppy

**frémir** *vi* quiver, tremble, shudder; rustle

**frémissement** *nm* quivering, trembling, shuddering; rustling

**frêne** *nm* ash-tree

**frénésie** *nf* frenzy, madness

**frénétique** *adj* frantic, frenzied

**fréquemment** *adv* frequently

**fréquence** *nf* frequency, rate

**fréquent** *adj* frequent, rapid

**fréquentation** *nf* frequenting

**fréquenter** *vt* frequent; visit; associate with; court; *vi* visit; be courting

**frère** *nm* brother; friar

**fresque** *nf* fresco

**fret** *nm* freight, cargo

**fréter** *vt* (6) freight; charter; fit out (ship); hire (means of transport)

**frétillant** *adj* wriggling; frisky

**frétiller** *vi* wag; wriggle; fidget

**fretin** *nm* fry (fish); *fig* rubbish

**friable** *adj* crumbly

**friand** *adj* dainty; ~ **de** partial to

**friandise** *nf* titbit, delicacy

**fric** *nm sl* money, lolly

**fricassée** *nf* fricassee, hash

**fricasser** *vt* fricassee

**fric-frac** *nm sl* burglary

**friche** *nf* waste land, fallow land

**frichti** *nm coll* dish; meal; grub

**fricot** *nm coll* stew, dish

**fricoter** *vt coll* cook, stew; *fig* plot; *vi coll* cook, stew; *fig* be engaged in shady business, traffic

**fricoteur -euse** *n coll* trafficker, shady businessman (-woman)

**friction** *nf* friction; massage; *sp* rubdown

**frictionner** *vt* rub; give a rub-down to; massage

**frigidaire** *nm* refrigerator

**frigide** *adj* frigid

**frigidité** *nf* frigidity

**frigo** *nm coll* fridge, *US* ice-box; *coll* frozen meat

**frigorifier** *vt* chill, freeze

**frigorifique** *adj* refrigerating, chilling

**frileux -euse** *adj* sensitive to the cold, delicate

**frimaire** *nm hist* third month of the French Republican calendar (November to December)

**frimas** *nm* hoar-frost

**frime** *nf coll* sham, pretence, show

**frimer** *vi* bluff

**frimousse** *nf coll* face (*usu* child or girl)

**fringale** *nf coll* tremendous appetite

**fringant** *adj* frisky; smart, dashing

**fringuer** *vt sl* rig out, kit

**fringues** *nfpl sl* gear, rig-out

**friper** *vt* crumple, rumple; wrinkle; **se** ~ get crumpled; wrinkle

**fripier -ière** *n* old-clothes dealer

**fripon -onne** *n* rogue, rascal; minx; *adj* roguish

**friponnerie** *nf* (piece of) roguery

**fripouille** *nf coll* rogue, rotter

**frire** *vt* + *vi* (51) fry

**frise** *nf* frieze

**frisé** *adj* curly, frizzy

**friser** *vt* curl, frizz; graze; border on, verge on; *vi* curl, be curly

¹**frison** *nm* curl, wave

²**frison -onne** *adj* Friesian

**frisquet -ette** *adj* nippy, cold

**frisson** *nm* shiver, shudder; thrill

**frissonnement** *nm* shivering; quivering

**frissonner** *vi* shiver, shudder; quiver

**frit** *adj* fried; *coll* done for; (**pommes**) **frites** chips, French fried, *US* French fries

**friteuse** *nf* deep-fryer

**friture** *nf* frying; fried fish; frying fat; crackling (radio)

**frivole** *adj* frivolous; trifling

**frivolité** *nf* frivolity; trifle

**froc** *nm* cowl, habit, monk's gown; *sl* trousers

**froid** *nm* cold, coldness; **avoir ~** be cold; **battre ~ à** cold-shoulder; **coup de ~** chill; **être en ~** be on bad terms; **industrie du ~** refrigeration business; **ne pas avoir ~ aux yeux** be fearless; **prendre ~** catch cold; *adj* cold, chilly, cool, frigid; reserved, distant

**froideur** *nf* coldness, chilliness, frigidity; reserve

**froissement** *nm* rumpling; rustling; bruising; slight, annoyance

**froisser** *vt* rumple; bruise; offend, hurt; **se ~** get bruised; take offence

**frôlement** *nm* grazing, brushing

**frôler** *vt* graze, touch lightly, brush against; narrowly escape

**fromage** *nm* cheese; *fig* cushy job; **~ de tête** brawn, *US* headcheese

**fromager -ère** *n* cheese-maker; *adj* cheese

**fromagerie** *nf* cheese-factory, cheese-maker's

**froment** *nm* wheat

**fronce** *nf* crease; gather

**froncement** *nm* contraction, puckering; **~ des sourcils** frown

**froncer** *vt* (4) pucker, wrinkle; gather; **~ les sourcils** frown, scowl

**frondaison** *nf* foliation, foliage

**fronde** *nf* catapult, sling

**fronder** *vt* sling, catapult; criticize, sneer at

**frondeur -euse** *n* slinger; critic; fault-finder, grouser; *adj* fault-finding, irreverent

**front** *nm* forehead, brow; face; cheek, effrontery; **de ~** abreast; **faire ~ à** face up to

**frontal** *nm* headband; frontal bone

**frontalier -ière** *n* borderer; one who daily crosses a frontier to get to work; *adj* frontier

**frontière** *nf* frontier, border, boundary

**frontispice** *nm* frontispiece; title page

**fronton** *nm* fronton, pediment

**frottée** *nf coll* pasting, thrashing; bread rubbed with garlic

**frottement** *nm* rubbing; chafing; friction

**frotter** *vt* rub, polish; chafe; strike (match); **se ~** rub oneself; associate; **~ les oreilles à qn** box s/o's ears

**frottis** *nm* rubbing; *med* smear

**frottoir** *nm* polisher

**frou-frou** *nm* rustle, swish

**froussard** *adj sl* cowardly

**frousse** *nf sl* funk

**fructidor** *nm hist* twelfth month of the French Republican calendar (August to September)

**fructifier** *vi* bear fruit, fructify

**fructueux -ueuse** *adj* fruitful, profitable

**frugalité** *nf* frugality

**fruit** *nm* fruit; advantage, benefit; **~ sec** dried fruit; *fig* failure; **~s de mer** sea-food

**fruité** *adj* fruity

**fruiterie** *nf* fruit trade; fruiterer's, greengrocer's shop

**fruitier -ière** *n* fruiterer, greengrocer; *adj* fruit-bearing, fruit

**frusques** *nfpl sl* togs, clothes, gear

**fruste** *adj* worn, rough, coarse

**frustrer** *vt* frustrate; **~ qn de qch** deprive s/o of sth

**fugace** *adj* fleeting, transient

**fugitif -ive** *n + adj* fugitive

**fugue** *nf* fugue; *coll* flight; *coll* escapade

**fuir** *vt* (52) run away from, avoid, shun; *vi* run away, flee; leak

**fuite** *nf* flight, escape; leak, leakage; **~ des cerveaux** brain-drain; *pol* **~ en avant** precipitate action

**fulgurant** *adj* flashing, sharp; lightning

**fuligineux -euse** *adj* sooty; murky

**fulmicoton** *nm* gun-cotton

**fulminer** *vt* fulminate; *vi* fulminate, inveigh

¹**fumage** *nm* smoking; curing

²**fumage** *nm* dunging, manure-spreading

**fumant** *adj* smoking; *sl* smashing

**fume-cigarette** *nm invar* cigarette-holder

**fumée** *nf* smoke, steam; fumes

¹**fumer** *vt* smoke; cure; *vi* smoke, steam; fume

²**fumer** *vt* manure

**fumet** *nm* aroma; bouquet (wine)

**fumeur -euse** *n* smoker; curer; *nm coll* smoker, smoking-compartment

**fumeux -euse** *adj* smoky; vague

**fumier** *nm* dung, manure; dunghill; *sl* bastard, swine

**fumiger** *vt* (3) fumigate

**fumiste** *nm coll* fraud, hoaxer; heating engineer

**fumisterie** *nf coll* fraud, hoax; heating contractor's business

**fumoir** *nm* smoking-room; smoke-house

**funambule** *n* tight-rope walker

**funambulesque** *adj* fantastic, grotesque

**funèbre** *adj* funeral; funereal, gloomy

**funérailles** *nfpl* funeral; obsequies

**funéraire** *adj* funeral

**funeste** *adj* fatal, deadly; baleful

**funiculaire** *nm* funicular railway

**fur** *nm* **au ~ et à mesure** gradually, progressively

**furet** *nm* ferret; *fig* busybody; pass the slipper (game)

**fureter** *vi* (5) ferret; nose about

**fureteur -euse** *n* ferreter; *fig* Nosy Parker, busybody; *adj* prying

**fureur** *nf* fury, rage; frenzy, passion; **faire ~** be all the rage

**furibond** *adj* furious, wild

**furie** *nf* fury, .age; passion

**furieux -ieuse** *adj* furious, mad, wild

**furoncle** *nm* boil

**furtif -ive** *adj* furtive, stealthy

**fusain** *nm* spindletree; charcoal sketch; charcoal pencil

**fuseau** *nm* spindle; distaff; **~ horaire** time zone; *coll* **jambes en ~** spindly legs; **pantalon ~** tapered trousers, ski-trousers

**¹fusée** *nf* fuse; rocket; **~ de rires** ripple of laughter; **~ éclairante** flare; **~ gigogne** multi-stage rocket; **avion à ~** rocket-propelled aircraft

**²fusée** *nf* spindle

**fusée-porteuse** *nf* (*pl* **fusées-porteuses**) first-stage rocket

**fuselé** *adj* tapering, streamlined

**fuseler** *vt* (5) taper

**fuser** *vi* fuse, melt, run; burst out (laughter)

**fusible** *nm* fuse; fuse-wire

**fusil** *nm* rifle, gun; steel (tinder-box); whetstone; **coup de ~** shot; *coll* very high charge (hotel, restaurant)

**fusilier** *nm* fusilier; **~ marin** marine

**fusillade** *nf* fusillade; execution by shooting

**fusiller** *vt* shoot, execute

**fusil-mitrailleur** *nm* (*pl* **fusils-mitrailleurs**) light machine-gun

**fusion** *nf* fusion, melting; merger

**fusionner** *vt + vi* merge, amalgamate

**fustiger** *vt* (3) flog, thrash

**fût** *nm* stock (gun); stem (tree); shaft (column); cask

**futaie** *nf* forest, wood

**futaille** *nf* cask, barrel

**futé** *adj coll* sharp, crafty

**futile** *adj* futile; trifling, trivial

**futilité** *nf* futility; triviality

**futur -e** *n* future husband, future wife; *nm gramm* future; *adj* future

**futurisme** *nm* futurism

**futuriste** *adj* futuristic

**futurologie** *nf* futurology

**futurologue** *n* futurologist

**fuyant** *adj* fleeing, fleeting; receding; shifty (eyes)

**fuyard -e** *n* fugitive, deserter

# G

**gabardine** *nf* raincoat, gaberdine

**gabare** *nf* lighter; barge; drag-net

**gabarier** *nm* lighterman

**gabarit** *nm* model; mould; gauge

**gabelle** *nf ar* salt-tax

**gabelou** *nm coll* customs-officer

**gabier** *nm* topman

**¹gâche** *nf* staple; wall-hook

**²gâche** *nf* trowel; *cul* spatula

**gâcher** *vt* mix (mortar); botch, bungle, spoil

**gâchette** *nf* trigger

**gâchis** *nm* wet mortar; mud; *fig* mess

**gaélique** *nm* Gaelic (language); *adj* Gaelic

**gaffe** *nf* boat-hook, gaff; *coll* blunder, bloomer; *coll* sentry-duty; *sl* **faire ~** be on the look out

**gaffer** *vt* hook, gaff; *vi* blunder, drop a brick, *US* pull a boner

**gaffeur -euse** *n coll* blunderer

**gaga** *nm* dodderer; *adj* doddering, senile

**gage** *nm* pawn, pledge; deposit, security; forfeit; stake (gambling); ~ s wages, pay; **mettre en** ~ pawn

**gager** *vt* (3) wager, bet; stake; hire, engage; pay wages to

**gageur -euse** *n* better, wagerer

**gageure** *nf* wager, bet; challenge

**gagnant -e** *n* winner; *adj* winning

**gagne-pain** *nm invar* livelihood, daily bread; breadwinner

**gagner** *vt* gain, earn; win; reach, arrive at; win over; overtake; *vi* gain; improve; spread; **se** ~ be catching

**gai** *adj* gay, merry, jolly, cheerful

**gaieté** *nf* gaiety, cheerfulness, mirth

¹**gaillard** *nm naut* castle; ~ **d'arrière** quarter-deck; ~ **d'avant** forecastle

²**gaillard** *nm* fellow, chap; *adj* strong; jolly, merry; spicy, risky

**gaillarde** *nf* wench, lively girl

**gaillardise** *nf* jollity, liveliness; risky story

**gain** *nm* gain, profit; earnings; winnings

**gaine** *nf* sheath; case; corset, girdle

**gainer** *vt* sheathe

**gala** *nm* gala, fête; **en grand** ~ in state; **habit de** ~ full dress

**galamment** *adv* gallantly, courteously; gracefully

**galant** *nm* ladies' man; sweetheart; *adj* attentive to women; gallant, courteous; elegant, gay; ~ **homme** man of honour; **femme** ~ **e** courtesan

**galanterie** *nf* politeness; gallantry; love affair

**galbe** *nm* curve, contour

**gale** *nf* scabies; itch; mange; scab; *sl* shrew

**galère** *nf* galley; **qu'allait-il faire dans cette** ~? what was he doing there?; **vogue la** ~! let's risk it!

**galerie** *nf* gallery; arcade; *mot* roof-rack

**galérien** *nm* galley-slave, convict

**galet** *nm* pebble, shingle; roller

**galetas** *nm* garret, hovel

**galette** *nf* cake; ship's biscuit; *coll* lolly, dough

**galeux -euse** *adj* itchy; scabby; mangy; **brebis galeuse** black sheep

¹**Galilée** *nm* Galileo

²**Galilée** *nf* Galilaea, Galilee

**galimatias** *nm* nonsense, gibberish; rigmarole

**Galles** *nfpl* **pays de** ~ Wales

**gallicisme** *nm* gallicism

**Gallois -e** *n* Welshman, Welshwoman

**gallois** *nm* Welsh (language); *adj* Welsh

**galoche** *nf* clog, galosh, *US* rubber

**galon** *nm* braid; stripe

**galonner** *vt* trim with braid, lace; braid

**galop** *nm* gallop; **au grand** ~ at full gallop; **au petit** ~ at a canter

**galoper** *vi* gallop

**galopin** *nm* errand-boy; urchin

**galvaniser** *vt* galvanize; stimulate

**galvanoplastie** *nf* electroplating

**galvauder** *vt coll* botch; sully, dishonour; **se** ~ sully one's name

**gambade** *nf* gambol, caper

**gambader** *vi* gambol, caper, romp

**gamelle** *nf* mess-tin, dixie

**gamin** *nm* boy, urchin, youngster

**gamine** *nf* girl, hoyden, gamine

**gamme** *nf* gamut, scale, range

**gammée** *adj f* **croix** ~ swastika

**ganache** *nf* lower jaw (horse); *coll* booby, blockhead

**gandin** *nm* dandy, *US* dude

**gangrène** *nf* gangrene; *fig* corruption

**gangrener** *vt* (6) gangrene; mortify; corrupt

**ganse** *nf* braid; piping; loop

**gant** *nm* glove; gauntlet

**ganterie** *nf* glove-trade; glove-factory; glove-shop

**gantier -ière** *n* glover

**garage** *nm* garage; parking, shunting; **voie de** ~ siding

**garagiste** *nm* garage proprietor; garage mechanic

**garant -e** *n* guarantor, surety; guarantee, bail; **se porter** ~ **de** vouch for

**garantie** *nf* guarantee; security; pledge

**garantir** *vt* guarantee; vouch for; insure; *fig* protect

**garce** *nf sl* bitch

**garçon** *nm* boy, lad; young man, fellow; bachelor; waiter, steward; ~ **de bureau** office messenger; ~ **d'honneur** best man

**garçonne** *nf* bachelor girl

**garçonnet** *nm* little boy

**garçonnière** *nf* bachelor apartment

**garde** *nm* guard; guardsman; keeper; watchman; ~ **champêtre** country policeman; *nf* guard, defence; keeping, charge; watch; nurse; flyleaf, endpaper; hilt (sword); ~ **à vous!** look out!; **prendre** ~ beware, be careful; **prendre** ~ **à** take good care to; **prendre** ~ **de** be careful not to

**garde-à-vous** *nm* **au** ~ at attention

**garde-barrière** *nm* (*pl* **gardes-barrières**) gatekeeper at level-crossing

**garde-boue** *nm invar* mudguard, *US* fender

**garde-chasse** *nm* (*pl* **gardes-chasses**) gamekeeper

**garde-corps** *nm invar* handrail; *naut* life-line

**garde-côte(s)** *nm* (*pl* **garde(s)-côtes**) coastguard vessel

**garde-feu** *nm* (*pl* ~ or **garde-feux**) fireguard; fender

**garde-fou** *nm invar* parapet; handrail

**garde-frein** *nm* (*pl* **gardes-freins**) brakesman

**garde-malade** *n* (*pl* ~ or **gardes-malades**) nurse

**garde-manger** *nm invar* larder, pantry; meat-safe

**garde-meuble** *nm invar* furniture store-house

**garde-nappe** *nm* (*pl* **gardes-nappes**) table-mat

**garde-pêche** *nm invar* water bailiff, river-keeper

**garde-port** *nm* (*pl* **gardes-ports**) harbour-master

**garder** *vt* guard, defend; look after; keep, preserve; nurse; observe, respect; stay in; **se** ~ protect oneself; **se** ~ **de** beware of; refrain from; take care not to

**garde-robe** *nf* wardrobe

**gardeur -euse** *n* keeper, minder

**gardien -ienne** *n* guardian; keeper; warder; caretaker; attendant; goal-keeper; ~ **de la paix** policeman; *adj* **ange** ~ guardian angel

**gardiennage** *nm* caretaking; looking after children

¹**gare** *interj* look out!, take care!; **sans crier** ~ without warning

²**gare** *nf* station; ~ **de triage** marshalling yard; ~ **maritime** harbour-station; ~ **routière** bus station

**garenne** *nf* warren

**garer** *vt* shunt; garage; park; **se** ~ shunt; pull to one side; park; take cover

**gargariser (se)** *v refl* gargle

**gargote** *nf* cheap eating-house, cook shop

**gargouille** *nf* gargoyle

**gargouiller** *vi* rumble, gurgle

**gargouillis** *nm* gurgling

**garnement** *nm coll* **mauvais** ~ scamp, rogue

**garni** *nm* furnished room(s); *adj* furnished; garnished (with vegetables); well-filled

**garnir** *vt* furnish, stock; fill; garnish, trim

**garnison** *nf* garrison

**garniture** *nf* fittings, furnishings; trimmings; lagging; *cul* garnishing; packing; *mot* lining

**garrot** *nm* tongue (saw); *med* tourniquet; garrotte

**garrotter** *vt* pinion; garrotte

**gars** *nm coll* lad, young fellow

**Gascogne** *nf* Gascony; **Golfe de** ~ Bay of Biscay

**Gascon -onne** *n* Gascon; *fig* boaster, braggart; **histoire de** ~ tall story

**gascon -onne** *adj* Gascon

**gasconnade** *nf* boasting, bragging; boast, tall story

**gas-oil** *nm* diesel oil

**gaspiller** *vt* waste, squander

**gaspilleur -euse** *n + adj* spendthrift

**gastrique** *adj* gastric; **embarras** ~ stomach upset

**gastrite** *nf* gastritis

**gastro-entérite** *nf* gastro-enteritis

**gastronomie** *nf* gastronomy

**gastronomique** *adj* gastronomic

**gâteau** *nm* cake, tart; ~ **de miel** honeycomb; ~ **de riz** rice-pudding; ~ **des Rois** Twelfth-Night cake; ~ **sec** biscuit; **papa** ~ doting parent

**gâter** *vt* spoil, damage, injure; taint; **se** ~ deteriorate, spoil, be spoiled

**gâterie** *nf* over-indulgence, spoiling; ~ **s** goodies, dainties

**gâteux -euse** *n* dotard, dodderer; *adj* senile, doddering

**gâtisme** *nm* senile decay, dotage

**gauche** *nf* left; *adj* left; awkward, clumsy

**gaucher -ère** *n* left-handed person; *adj* left-handed

**gaucherie** *nf* awkwardness, clumsiness

**gauchir** *vi* warp, buckle

**gauchisant** *adj* of leftist tendencies

**gauchisme** *nm* leftism

**gauchiste** *n + adj* leftist

**gaudriole** *nf coll* broad joke

**gaufre** *nf cul* waffle

**gaufrer** *vt* crimp, goffer; emboss; corrugate

**gaufrette** *nf* wafer

**gaufrier** *nm* waffle-iron

**Gaule** *nf* Gaul

**gaule** *nf* long pole; switch; fishing-rod

**gauler** *vt* knock down (fruit) from tree

**gaullisme** *nm* Gaullism

**gaulliste** *n* Gaullist

**Gaulois -e** *n* Gaul

**gaulois** *nm* Gallic (language); *adj* Gallic; *fig* racy, spicy

**gauloise** *nf* popular brand of French cigarette

**gausser (se)** *v refl coll* laugh, make fun

**gave** *nm* mountain stream, torrent (in Pyrenees)

**gaver** *vt* cram, stuff; **se** ~ gorge

**gavroche** *nm* urchin, street-arab

**gaz** *nm* gas; wind; ~ **hilarant** laughing-gas

**gaze** *nf* gauze

¹**gazer** *vt* cover with gauze; veil; tone down

²**gazer** *vt* gas; *vi coll* go very fast, go like a bomb

**gazette** *nf* gazette, newspaper; *fig* gossip

**gazeux -euse** *adj* gaseous; aerated, fizzy

**gazier** *nm* gas-fitter

**gazoduc** *nm* gas pipeline

**gazogène** *nm* gas-generator; gazogene; *adj* gas-producing; aerating

**gazomètre** *nm* gasometer

**gazon** *nm* grass; turf; lawn

**gazouillement** *nm* twittering, chirping; babbling (brook); prattling (child)

**gazouiller** *vi* twitter, chirp; babble; prattle

**geai** *nm* jay

**géant -e** *n* giant(ess); *adj* giant, gigantic

**geignard -e** *n* whiner, sniveller; *adj* whining, querulous

**geindre** *vi* (55) whine, complain; snivel

**gel** *nm* frost; freezing; blocking, stopping

**gélatineux -euse** *adj* gelatinous

**gelé** *adj* frozen; frostbitten

**gelée** *nf* frost; jelly

**geler** *vt* (5) freeze; block; *vi* freeze, become frozen

**gelure** *nf* frostbite

**Gémeaux** *nmpl* Gemini

**gémir** *vi* groan, moan, wail

**gémissement** *nm* groan(ing), moan(ing), wail(ing)

**gemme** *nf* gem; resin; bud; **sel ~** rock-salt

**gemmer** *vi* bud

**gênant** *adj* inconvenient, in the way; embarrassing, awkward

**gencive** *nf* gum

**gendarme** *nm* policeman

**gendarmerie** *nf* constabulary; police barracks

**gendre** *nm* son-in-law

**gêne** *nf* embarrassment; difficulty, trouble; discomfort; financial straits; **sans ~** brazen

**généalogie** *nf* genealogy, pedigree

**généalogique** *adj* genealogical, family

**gêner** *vt* cramp, constrict; embarrass; inconvenience, trouble; **être gêné** be short of money; **se ~** inconvenience oneself, put oneself out; be shy, stand on ceremony

**général -aux** *nm* general; **~ de brigade** brigadier(-general); **~ de division** major-general; *adj* general

¹**générale** *nf* general's wife

²**générale** *nf theat* dress-rehearsal

**généraliser** *vt* generalize; **se ~** become general, spread

**généralissime** *nm* generalissimo, commander-in-chief

**généraliste** *n* general practitioner

**généralité** *nf* generality

**générateur -trice** *n* generator, dynamo; *adj* generating, generative

**généreux -euse** *adj* generous

**générique** *nm* credits; *adj* generic

**générosité** *nf* generosity

**genèse** *nf* genesis, origin

**genêt** *nm bot* broom

**génétique** *nf* genetics; *adj* genetic

**gêneur -euse** *n* intruder, spoilsport

**Genève** *nf* Geneva

**genévrier** *nm* juniper

**génial** *adj* inspired, brilliant

**génie** *nm* genius; spirit; *mil* engineers; **~ civil** civil engineering

**genièvre** *nm* juniper; gin

**génisse** *nf* heifer

**genou** *nm* knee

**genre** *nm* kind, sort; genus, type; gender; style; form; **le ~ humain** the human race, mankind; **se donner du ~** put on airs

**gens** *npl* people, folk; servants; **~ de bien** honest folk; **droit des ~** law of nations; **jeunes ~** young people; young men

**gent** *nf ar* race, tribe

**gentiane** *nf* gentian

¹**gentil** *nm* gentile

²**gentil -ille** *adj* nice; kind; amiable, pleasing; *ar* noble, gentle

**gentilhomme** *nm* (*pl* **gentilshommes**) nobleman

**gentillesse** *nf* graciousness; kindness; politeness; **~s** nice things

**gentiment** *adv* nicely; politely

**géographe** *n* geographer

**géographie** *nf* geography

**géographique** *adj* geographical

**geôle** *nf ar* gaol, prison

**geôlier -ière** *n ar* gaoler, warder

**géologie** *nf* geology

**géologue** *n* geologist

**géométrie** *nf* geometry

**géométrique** *adj* geometrical

**gérance** *nf* management; managership; board of directors

**gérant -e** *n* director, manager(ess); managing-director

**gerbe** *nf* sheaf (wheat); spray (flowers, water); shower (sparks)

**gercer** *vt + vi* (4) crack; chap (hands)

**gerçure** *nf* crack; chap (hands)

**gérer** *vt* (6) manage, administer

**gériatrie** *nf* geriatrics

**gériatrique** *adj* geriatric

**germain** *adj* first (cousin)

**germanique** *adj* Germanic

**germe** *nm* germ; eye (potato); *fig* seed; **dans le ~** in the bud

**germer** *vi* germinate; sprout, shoot

**germinal** *nm hist* seventh month of the French Republican calendar (March to April)

**gérondif** *nm* gerundive

**gérontologie** *nf* gerontology

**gésier** *nm* gizzard

**gésir** *vi* (53) lie; **ci-gît** here lies

¹**geste** *nm* gesture, motion, movement, wave

²**geste** *nf* **chanson de ~** medieval verse chronicle; **faits et ~ s** exploits

**gesticuler** *vi* gesticulate

**gestion** *nf* management, administration

**gibecière** *nf* game-bag; satchel

**gibelotte** *nf* *cul* fricassee of rabbit or hare

**giberne** *nf* wallet; pouch

**gibet** *nm* gibbet, gallows

**gibier** *nm* game; **~ de potence** gallows bird

**giboulée** *nf* sudden shower

**giboyeux -euse** *adj* abounding in game

**gicler** *vi* splash, spurt

**gicleur** *nm* nozzle, jet

**gifle** *nf* slap in the face; box on the ear

**gifler** *vt* slap, cuff

**gigantesque** *adj* gigantic

**gigantisme** *nm* over-development, over-expansion

**gigogne** *nf* **fusée ~** multi-stage rocket; **lit ~** truckle-bed; **table ~** nest of tables

**gigot** *nm* leg of mutton or lamb

**gigoter** *vi coll* kick; jig

**gigue** *nf* hind leg, haunch; *mus* jig

**gilet** *nm* waistcoat, *US* vest; **~ de corps** singlet; **~ de sauvetage** life-jacket

**gingembre** *nm* ginger

**gingivite** *nf* gingivitis

**girafe** *nf* giraffe

**giration** *nf* gyration

**giratoire** *adj* gyratory; **sens ~** traffic flow at roundabout

**girofle** *nm* clove

**giroflée** *nf* wallflower

**giron** *nm* lap; *fig* bosom

**girouette** *nf* weathercock

**gisant** *nm* recumbent effigy; *adj* lying, recumbent

**gisement** *nm* layer, stratum, vein

**gitan -e** *n + adj* gipsy

**gîte** *nm* resting-place, lodging; lair (deer); form (hare); stratum, deposit

**gîter** *vt* lodge, shelter; *vi* lodge, lie

**givre** *nm* hoarfrost

**glabre** *adj* smooth, hairless, clean-shaven

**glaçage** *nm* glazing; *cul* icing, frosting

**glace** *nf* ice; ice-cream; icing; glass, plate-glass; mirror; window (vehicle); flaw

**glacé** *adj* frozen; icy; iced (drinks); chilled (wine); glossy; glazed

**glacer** *vt* (4) freeze; ice; chill; glaze

**glaciaire** *adj* glacial

**glacial** *adj* icy, frozen, glacial

**glacier** *nm* glacier; ice-cream man

**glacière** *nf* ice-box, freezer; *ar* ice-house;

cette chambre est une **~** it's ice-cold in this room

**glacis** *nm* slope; glaze

**glaçon** *nm* block of ice; ice-floe; icicle; ice-cube; *fig* cold fish

**gladiateur** *nm* gladiator

**glaïeul** *nm* gladiolus

**glaire** *nf* white of egg; mucus, phlegm

**glaise** *nf* clay, loam

**glaisière** *nf* clay-pit

**glaive** *nm ar + lit* sword

**glanage** *nm* gleaning

**gland** *nm* acorn; tassel; *anat* glans

**glande** *nf* gland

**glaner** *vt* glean

**glaneur -euse** *n* gleaner

**glapir** *vi* yelp, yap; bark (fox)

**glas** *nm* knell

**glauque** *adj* glaucous, sea-green; bluish-green

**glèbe** *nf lit* land, soil

**glissade** *nf* slip, slide; sliding; glide (dancing)

**glissant** *adj* sliding; slippery

**glissement** *nm* sliding, slipping; gliding

**glisser** *vt* slip; insinuate; *vi* slip, slide; glide; *mot* skid; **~ sur** glance off; not dwell upon; **se ~** creep, steal

**glisseur -euse** *n* downhill skier

**glissière** *nf* groove, guide; **à ~s** sliding

**glissoir** *nm* slide

**glissoire** *nf* slide (ice)

**global** *adj* total, inclusive, aggregate

**globe** *nm* globe, sphere, orb, ball

**globulaire** *adj* globular

**globule** *nm* corpuscle

**gloire** *nf* glory, fame; pride; halo; **se faire ~ de** glory in

**glorieux -ieuse** *n* braggart, boaster; *adj* glorious, proud; vain, conceited

**glorifier** *vt* glorify; **se ~** boast

**gloriole** *nf* vainglory, vanity

**glose** *nf* gloss, commentary; criticism

**gloser** *vt* gloss; *vi* criticize, carp

**glossaire** *nm* glossary

**glotte** *nf* glottis

**glouglou** *nm* gurgle, gurgling; gobbling (turkey)

**glouglouter** *vi* gurgle; gobble (turkey)

**glousser** *vi* cluck; chuckle

**glouton -onne** *n* glutton; *adj* greedy, gluttonous

**gloutonnerie** *nf* gluttony

**glu** *nf* bird-lime

**gluant** *adj* sticky, gluey

**glutineux -euse** *adj* glutinous

**glycine** *nf* wistaria

**gnangnan, gnian-gnian** *n invar coll* wet (person); *adj invar* wet, feeble, namby-pamby

**gniole, gnôle** *nf sl* brandy

**go** *adv* **tout de** ~ straight off; all of a sudden

**goal** *nm* goal; goalkeeper

**goblet** *nm* goblet, cup; **verre** ~ tumbler

**gobe-mouches** *nm invar orni* fly-catcher; *bot* fly-trap; *fig* ninny

**gober** *vt* swallow, gulp down; like enormously; ~ **des mouches** stand gaping

**gobeur -euse** *n coll* simpleton, sucker

**godasses** *nfpl sl* boots

**godet** *nm* mug; cup; flare (cloth), pucker

**godiche** *adj coll* clumsy; stupid, silly

**godille** *nf* stern-oar; scull

**godiller** *vi* scull

**godillot** *nm sl* heavy shoe; *pol* fanatical Gaullist

**goéland** *nm* seagull

**goélette** *nf* schooner

**goémon** *nm* seaweed

**¹gogo** *nm sl* mug, sucker

**²gogo (à)** *adv phr* galore

**goguenard -e** *n* mocker, jeerer; *adj* bantering, mocking

**goinfre** *nm* glutton; *adj* gluttonous

**goinfrer (se)** *v refl coll* gorge

**goinfrerie** *nf* gluttony, guzzling

**golf** *nm* golf; **culottes de** ~ plus-fours

**golfe** *nm* gulf, bay

**gomme** *nf* gum; rubber, eraser

**gommer** *vt* rub out; attenuate; eradicate

**gommeux** *nm coll* swell, *US* dude; *adj* (*f* **-euse**) gummy, sticky

**gond** *nm* hinge; *coll* **sortir de ses** ~ s fly off the handle

**gondolant** *adj sl* screamingly funny

**gondole** *nf* gondola

**gondoler** *vi* warp, buckle; **se** ~ warp, buckle; *sl* split one's sides laughing

**gonflage** *nm* inflation

**gonflement** *nm* inflation, swelling

**gonfler** *vt* inflate, swell, blow up; *coll* **mot** hot up; *vi* **se** ~ swell, become inflated, become distended

**gonfleur** *nm* air-pump, inflator

**gordien** *adj* Gordian

**goret** *nm* piglet; *coll* dirty brat

**gorge** *nf* throat, gullet; bosom; breast; gorge, pass; **à pleine** ~ at the top of one's voice; **avoir la** ~ **serrée** have a lump in one's throat; **faire des** ~ s **chaudes de** gloat over; **mal à la** ~ sore throat; **rendre** ~ disgorge, stump up; **rire à** ~ **déployée** laugh heartily

**gorgée** *nf* mouthful, gulp

**gorger** *vt* (3) gorge, cram; **se** ~ stuff oneself

**gorille** *nm* gorilla; *coll* bodyguard; *coll* secret agent

**gosier** *nm* throat, gullet; **à plein** ~ loudly

**gosse** *n coll* kid, youngster

**gothique** *nm* + *adj* Gothic

**gouailler** *vt* + *vi* chaff, banter

**gouaillerie** *nf* love of bantering

**gouailleur -euse** *adj* bantering, mocking

**gouape** *nf sl* nasty piece of work, swine

**goudron** *nm* tar

**goudronnage** *nm* tarring

**goudronner** *vt* tar

**gouffre** *nm* gulf, abyss, pit; spendthrift

**goujat** *nm* boor, cad

**¹goujon** *nm* gudgeon (fish)

**²goujon** *nm* gudgeon, stud, pin

**goulet** *nm* narrow entrance, gut; neck (bottle); gully (mountain)

**goulot** *nm* neck (bottle); *fig* bottleneck

**goulu -e** *n* glutton; *adj* greedy, gluttonous

**goupille** *nf* (linch)pin

**goupiller** *vt* pin, key; *sl* contrive, fix

**goupillon** *nm* aspergillum, holy-water sprinkler

**gourbi** *nm* hut, hovel; *mil* dugout

**gourd** *adj* numb, stiff

**gourde** *nf* gourd; water-bottle, flask; *coll* idiot, dope

**gourdin** *nm* cudgel, club

**gourer (se)** *v refl sl* be wrong

**gourmand -e** *n* gourmand, glutton; *adj* greedy, gluttonous; *fig* ~ **de** very fond of

**gourmander** *vt* scold, reprimand

**gourmandise** *nf* greediness, gluttony; ~ s sweet things

**gourme** *nf* impetigo; **jeter sa** ~ sow one's wild oats

**gourmé** *adj* stiff, stuck-up

**gourmette** *nf* curb (horse); chain (watch, etc)

**gousse** *nf* shell, pod; ~ **d'ail** clove of garlic

**gousset** *nm* waistcoat pocket; gusset

**goût** *nm* taste; flavour; savour; liking; style, manner; ~ **du jour** prevailing fashion

**goûter** *nm* (afternoon) snack; *vt* taste, try; enjoy, relish; *vi* taste, try; have a snack

**¹goutte** *nf* drop; sip, dram; speck; ~ **à** ~ drop by drop; **il tombe quelques** ~ s it's drizzling; **n'entendre** ~ not understand at all; **n'y voir** ~ not make anything out; **se ressembler comme deux** ~ s **d'eau** be as like as two peas; **suer à grosses** ~ s sweat profusely

**²goutte** *nf* gout

**goutte-à-goutte** *nm invar med* drip

**gouttelette** *nf* small drop, droplet

**goutter** *vi* drip

**goutteux -euse** *adj* gouty

**gouttière** *nf* gutter, rainspout

**gouvernail** *nm* rudder, helm

**gouvernant** adj governing, ruling; les ~ s the ruling class

**gouvernante** nf governess; housekeeper

**gouverne** nf guidance, direction; aer ~ s rudders and ailerons

**gouvernement** nm government; management

**gouverner** vt govern, control; manage; steer

**gouverneur** nm governor; manager; tutor

**grabat** nm pallet, bed, litter

**grabuge** nm coll squabble, row; **faire du ~** kick up a row

**grâce** nf grace, gracefulness; favour; mercy, pardon; ~ s thanks; ~ **à** thanks to; **action de** ~ s thanksgiving; **avoir bonne ~ à faire qch** do sth with a good grace; **de mauvaise ~** ungraciously; **faire des ~ s à qn** make a fuss of s/o; **faire** ~ **à** spare

**gracier** vt pardon, reprieve

**gracieux -ieuse** adj graceful, gracious; **à titre ~** free, complimentary

**gracile** adj slender, slim

**grade** nm grade, rank; **monter en ~** be promoted

**gradé** nm non-commissioned officer

**gradin** nm step, tier

**graduation** nf graduation; scale

**gradué** adj graduated, progressive

**graduel -uelle** adj gradual

**graduer** vt graduate, grade

**grailler** vi speak huskily

¹**graillon** nm cul bits of fat; smell of fat

²**graillon** nm sl gob

¹**grain** nm grain; seed; bean, berry; particle, speck; coll bee in the bonnet; ~ **de beauté** beauty-spot; ~ **de poivre** peppercorn; ~ **de raisin** grape; **poulet de** ~ free-range chicken

²**grain** nm naut squall

**graine** nf seed; pej ~ **de** likely, potential; coll **c'est une mauvaise** ~ he's a bad lot; **en prendre de la** ~ benefit by the example; **monter en** ~ go to seed; (spinster) be getting on

**grainetier -ière** n corn-chandler, seedsman (-woman)

**graissage** nm greasing, lubrication, oiling

**graisse** nf grease, fat; ~ **de porc** lard; ~ **de rognon** suet; ~ **de rôti** dripping

**graisser** vt grease, lubricate, oil; coll ~ **la patte à qn** grease s/o's palm

**graisseux -euse** adj greasy, oily

**grammaire** nf grammar

**grammairien -ienne** n grammarian

**grand** nm grandee; great man; adult, grown-up; big boy; adj great, big, large, tall; high; grand; grown-up; **en ~ e partie** largely, mainly; adv **en ~** on a large scale; **faire (voir)** ~ do (see) things in a big way

**grand-angulaire** nm wide-angle lens; adj wide-angle

**grand-chose** n invar much

**Grande-Bretagne** nf Great Britain

**grandement** adv greatly, extremely; grandly, nobly

**grandeur** nf size; height; extent; magnitude; grandeur; **Votre Grandeur** Your Highness

**grandir** vt increase, magnify; enlarge; vi grow, increase; grow tall; grow up

**grand-maman** nf (pl **grands-mamans**) coll grandma, granny

**grand-mère** nf (pl **grands-mères**) grandmother

**grand-messe** nf High Mass

**grand-papa** nm (pl **grands-papas**) coll grandpa

**grand-peine (à)** adv phr with great difficulty

**grand-père** nm (pl **grands-pères**) grandfather

**grand-route** nf highway, high road

**grand-rue** nf high street, main street

**grands-parents** nmpl grandparents

**grange** nf barn; **mettre en** ~ garner

**granit** nm granite

**granulaire** adj granular

**granulé** adj granulated

**granuleux -euse** adj granular, granulous

**graphie** nf writing, way of writing

**graphique** nm diagram, graph; adj graphic

**grappe** nf bunch, cluster; string (onions)

**grappin** nm grapnel, hook; coll **mettre le** ~ **sur** get hold of

**gras** nm fat; adj (f **grasse**) fat, fatty; stout; greasy, oily; rich (food); thick; fig broad, racy

**gras-double** nm cul tripe

**grassement** adv generously, liberally

**grasseyer** vi(7) phon speak with fricative r

**grassouillet -ette** adj plump, chubby

**gratification** nf tip; bonus; gratification

**gratifier** vt bestow, confer

**gratin** nm cul burnt part; fig + coll upper crust; **au** ~ with bread-crumbs and grated cheese

**gratiné** adj with bread-crumbs and grated cheese; coll fantastic

**gratinée** nf onion soup with cheese

**gratte** nf coll pickings, perks

**gratte-ciel** nm invar skyscraper

**gratte-papier** nm invar pen-pusher

**gratte-pieds** nm invar shoe-scraper

**gratter** vt scratch, scrape; cross out (word); coll overtake; **ça me gratte** I'm itching; vi coll scrape

**gratuit** adj free; gratuitous; **à titre** ~ free of charge

**gratuité** *nf* gratuitousness; exemption from charge

**grave** *adj* grave, solemn; serious, severe; important; deep, low, low-pitched; *gramm* grave

**graveleux -euse** *adj* gravelly, gritty; *fig* smutty, racy

**graver** *vt* engrave, carve; ~ **à l'eau forte** etch

**graveur** *nm* engraver, carver

**gravier** *nm* gravel, grit

**gravillon** *nm* fine gravel; ~s loose chippings

**gravir** *vt* climb, ascend

**gravité** *nf* gravity; seriousness; severity; weight; deepness

**graviter** *vi* gravitate; revolve

**gravure** *nf* engraving; print; picture; ~ **à l'eau forte** etching; ~ **sur bois** wood cut

**gré** *nm* will, wish; liking; **à mon** ~ as I please; **au** ~ **de** at the mercy of; at the will of; **bon** ~, **mal** ~ willy-nilly; **de bon** ~ willingly; **de** ~ **à** ~ by mutual agreement; **de** ~ **ou de force** willy-nilly; **de mon propre** ~ of my own accord; **savoir** ~ **à qn de qch** be grateful to s/o for sth

**Grec** (*f* **Grecque**) *n* Greek

**grec** *nm* Greek (language); *adj* (*f* **grecque**) Greek; Grecian

**Grèce** *nf* Greece

**gredin** *nm* rascal, rogue

**gréement** *nm* *naut* rigging, gear

**gréer** *vt* *naut* rig

¹**greffe** *nm* office of the clerk of the court; registry

²**greffe** *nf* graft, grafting; *med* transplant

**greffer** *vt* graft; *med* transplant

**greffier** *nm* clerk of the court

**grégaire** *adj* gregarious

**grégorien -ienne** *adj* Gregorian

¹**grêle** *nf* hail; *fig* shower

²**grêle** *adj* slender, thin; shrill

**grêlé** *adj* pock-marked

**grêler** *v impers* hail

**grêlon** *nm* hailstone

**grelot** *nm* small bell; sleigh-bell; *coll* **attacher le** ~ bell the cat

**grelotter** *vi* shiver, tremble; tinkle

**grenade** *nf* pomegranate; *mil* grenade; ~ **sous-marine** depth-charge

**grenadier** *nm* pomegranate-tree; *mil* grenadier

**grenat** *nm* garnet; *adj* garnet(-red)

**grener** *vt* (6) granulate; grain; stipple; *vi* seed, corn

**grènetis** *nm* milled edge, milling

**grenier** *nm* granary; loft; attic

**grenouille** *nf* frog

**grès** *nm* sandstone; **poterie de** ~ earthenware

**grésil** *nm* sleet

**grésillement** *nm* pattering; shrivelling; crackling; sizzling

**grésiller** *vt* shrivel up; *vi* patter, crackle; sizzle; *v impers* sleet

**grève** *nf* shore, beach, strand; strike; ~ **d'avertissement** token strike; ~ **de solidarité** sympathy strike; ~ **de zèle** work to rule; ~ **perlée** go-slow; ~ **sauvage** wild-cat strike; ~ **sur le tas** sit-down strike; ~ **tournante** staggered strike; **faire** ~ be on strike; **se mettre en** ~ go on strike

**grever** *vt* (6) burden; encumber; *leg* entail

**gréviste** *n* striker

**gribouillage** *nm* scrawl, scribble

**gribouiller** *vt* + *vi* scrawl, scribble

**gribouillis** *nm* scrawl, scribble

**grief** *nm* grievance

**grièvement** *adv* severely, seriously

**griffe** *nf* claw; talon; paper-clip, clamp; signature, handwriting; label (fashion-house); *fig* ~s clutches

**griffer** *vt* scratch, claw

**griffonnage** *nm* scrawl, scribble

**griffonner** *vt* scrawl, scribble

**grignotage** *nm* eroding, rubbing away

**grignoter** *vt* nibble

**grigou** *nm* *coll* miser, skinflint

**gril** *nm* grill, gridiron; *fig* tenterhooks; ~ **-express** buffet-car

**grillade** *nf* grilling; grill, grilled meat

¹**grillage** *nm* grilling; toasting

²**grillage** *nm* grating; railings

**grillager** *vt* (3) surround with wire-netting; fit lattice-work to

**grille** *nf* grating; railings; grill; iron gate; *elect* grid; *mot* grille; cipher-key

¹**griller** *vt* grill; toast; roast (coffee); scorch; *vi* grill; toast; burn out (lamp)

²**griller** *vt* rail in, rail off, bar

**grillon** *nm* cricket

**grimace** *nf* grimace, wry face

**grimacer** *vi* (4) grimace, grin; make faces; simper

**grimacier -ière** *n* affected person; *adj* grimacing, grinning; simpering

**grimage** *nm* *theat* making-up

**grimer** *vt* *theat* make up; **se** ~ make up

**grimoire** *nm* magician's book; obscure book; scrawl

**grimpant** *adj* climbing, creeping; **plante** ~ **e** creeper

**grimpée** *nf* stiff climb

**grimper** *vt* + *vi* climb

**grimpeur -euse** *n* climber; *adj* climbing

**grincer** *vi* (4) grind; gnash (teeth); creak; scratch (pen)

**grincheux -euse** *n* grumbler, grouser; *adj* grumpy, surly, testy

137

**gringalet** *nm coll* puny individual, shrimp

**griotte** *nf* morello cherry

**grippe** *nf* influenza, flu; **prendre qn en ~** take a dislike to s/o

**grippé** *adj* suffering from influenza

**gripper** *vi* run hot; seize up; jam

**grippe-sou** *nm coll* miser, skinflint

**gris** *nm* grey; tobacco; *adj* grey; grey-haired; dull, cloudy; tipsy

**grisaille** *nf arts* grisaille; dreariness, monotony

**grisâtre** *adj* greyish

**grisbi** *nm sl* cash, dough

**griser** *vt* tint grey; intoxicate; make tipsy; **se ~** get tipsy

**griserie** *nf* tipsiness; intoxication; rapture, ecstasy

**grisonner** *vi* turn grey

**grisou** *nm* fire-damp

**grive** *nf* thrush; **faute de ~s on mange des merles** beggars can't be choosers

**grivois** *adj* broad, spicy, smutty

**grivoiserie** *nf* broad joke, smutty story

**Groënland** *nm* Greenland

**Groënlandais -e** *n* Greenlander

**groënlandais** *adj* of Greenland

**grognard** *nm* grumbler, grouser; *hist* soldier of Napoleon's Old Guard; *adj* grumbling, grousing

**grogne** *nf coll* grousing, complaining

**grognement** *nm* grunt, grunting; growl, growling; grumble, grumbling

**grogner** *vi* grunt; growl; grumble

**grognon -onne** *n* grumbler, grouser; *adj* (*f* ~ or -onne) grumbling, querulous

**groin** *nm* snout

**grommeler** *vi* (5) grumble, mutter

**grondement** *nm* growl, growling; rumble; roar

**gronder** *vt* scold, chide; *vi* growl; rumble; roar

**gronderie** *nf* scolding

**grondeur -euse** *n* grumbler; scold; *adj* grumbling; scolding

**groom** *nm* page-boy, *US* bell-hop; stable-lad

**gros** *nm* main part; bulk, mass; hardest part; **en ~** broadly speaking; in bulk, wholesale; *adj* (*f* **grosse**) big, large; stout, portly; thick, coarse; rough; heavy; gruff, loud; **~ mots** bad language; **femme grosse** pregnant woman

**groseille** *nf* currant (red, white); **~ à maquereau** gooseberry

**groseillier** *nm* currant-bush

**Gros-Jean** *nm* **être ~ comme devant** be back to square one

**grossesse** *nf* pregnancy

**grosseur** *nf* size, bulk, volume; thickness; *med* swelling

**grossier -ière** *adj* coarse, rough; rude, vulgar

**grossièreté** *nf* coarseness, roughness; rudeness, vulgarity; rude remark, offensive comment

**grossir** *vt* enlarge, increase, magnify; make look fat; *vi* increase, grow bigger

**grossissant** *adj* magnifying

**grossissement** *nm* increase; swelling; magnifying, enlargement

**grossiste** *n* wholesaler

**grotte** *nf* cave; grotto

**grouiller** *vi* swarm; *coll* **se ~** look lively, hurry up

**groupe** *nm* group, party; clump (trees); cluster (stars)

**groupement** *nm* grouping, group

**grouper** *vt* group; **se ~** form a group, gather

**groupuscule** *nm pol pej* small group

**gruau** *nm* wheat flour; gruel; **~ d'avoine** oatmeal, groats

**grue** *nf orni* crane; *eng* crane; *sl* prostitute, tart

**gruger** *vt* (3) eat; crunch; *coll* sponge on, fleece

**grumeau** *nm* clot; small lump

**grumeler (se)** *v refl* (5) clot

**gué** *nm* ford

**guenille** *nf* rag, tatter

**guenon** *nf* she-monkey; *fig* ugly woman

**guépard** *nm* cheetah

**guêpe** *nf* wasp

**guêpier** *nm* wasps' nest; *fig* **tomber dans un ~** stir up a hornet's nest

**guère** *adv* **ne ... ~** hardly, scarcely; hardly ever, not much; not many

**guéret** *nm* ploughed field

**guéridon** *nm* pedestal table

**guérilla** *nf* guerrilla; guerrilla band; guerrilla warfare

**guérir** *vt* cure; heal; *vi* recover, be cured; heal, heal up

**guérison** *nf* recovery, cure; healing

**guérissable** *adj* curable

**guérisseur -euse** *n* quack; healer

**guérite** *nf* sentry-box; signal-box; watchman's hut

**guerre** *nf* war; warfare; hostilities; strife; **~ de position** trench warfare; **~ éclair** blitzkrieg; **à la ~ comme à la ~** you must take the rough with the smooth; one can't fight a war with kid-gloves; *coll* **de bonne ~** perfectly fair; **de ~ lasse** for the sake of peace and quiet; **être en ~** be at war; **se mettre en ~** go to war

**guerrier -ière** *n* warrior; *adj* warlike, war

**guerroyer** *vi* (7) wage war

**guet** *nm* watch; look-out; **au ~** on the look-out

**guet-apens** *nm* (*pl* **guets-apens**) ambush, trap

guêtre *nf* gaiter
guetter *vt* lie in wait for, look out for, watch for
guetteur *nm* look-out (man)
¹gueulard *nm* mouth (blast-furnace)
²gueulard -e *n* bawler; *adj* bawling
gueule *nf* mouth (animals); *sl* mouth, mug; muzzle (gun); *coll* avoir de la ~ be impressive, look quite something; *sl* avoir la ~ de bois have a hang-over; *sl* casser la ~ à qn bash s/o's face in; *sl* se casser la ~ smash oneself up; get killed; *sl* ta ~! shut up!
gueule-de-lion *nf* (*pl* gueules-de-lion) antirrhinum
gueule-de-loup *nf* (*pl* gueules-de-loup) snapdragon; (chimney) cowl
gueuler *vt* + *vi* *coll* bawl, shout
gueuleton *nm* *coll* blow-out, tuck-in
gueux -euse *n* beggar; *adj* poor, poverty-stricken
gui *nm* mistletoe
guibol(l)e *nf* *sl* leg
guiches *nfpl* kiss-curls
guichet *nm* wicket-gate; entrance gate; turnstile; pay-desk; counter position; booking-office window
guide *nm* guide, conductor; guide-book; *nf* girl-guide; ~ s reins
guider *vt* guide, lead; drive, steer
guidon *nm* handle-bar; *mil* foresight; *naut* pennant
guigne *nf* *coll* bad luck
guigner *vt* ogle, peer at; look enviously at
guignol *nm* puppet; Punch; Punch and Judy show, puppet-show; *sl* policeman

guignolet *nm* cherry-brandy
guignon *nm* *coll* bad luck
Guillaume *nm* William
guillemet *nm* inverted comma, quotation mark
guilleret -ette *adj* brisk, perky, lively
guillotine *nf* guillotine; fenêtre à ~ sash-window
guillotiner *vt* guillotine
guimauve *nf* marshmallow
guimbarde *nf* *coll* ramshackle vehicle, old crock
guimpe *nf* wimple
guindé *adj* stiff, starchy
guindeau *nm* windlass
guinder *vt* hoist; se ~ assume a superior manner; become stilted
Guinée *nf* Guinea
guinéen -éenne *adj* Guinean
guingan *nm* gingham
guingois (de) *adv phr* askew, awry
guinguette *nf* open-air café where there is dancing
guipure *nf* point-lace, pillow-lace
guirlande *nf* garland, festoon
guirlander *vt* garland, festoon
guise *nf* way, manner; à sa ~ as one pleases; en ~ de by way of; instead of
guitare *nf* guitar
gus *nm* *mil* *sl* soldier; bloke
gymnase *nm* gymnasium
gymnaste *n* gymnast
gymnastique *nf* gymnastics; *adj* gymnastic; au pas (de) ~ at the double
gynécologie *nf* gynaecology
gynécologue *n* gynaecologist
gypse *nm* gypsum, plaster of Paris

# H

The letter *h* in French is never pronounced. An asterisk before a word indicates that the *h* is aspirate, i.e. that there is neither elision nor liaison

habile *adj* clever; skilful, expert, able; smart
habileté *nf* cleverness; skill; ability; smartness
habilité *nf* competency; *adj* entitled
habillage *nm* casing

habillement *nm* clothing; clothes
habiller *vt* clothe, dress; s' ~ dress, get dressed; have one's clothes made
habilleur -euse *n* dresser
habit *nm* coat, dress-coat; *eccles* habit, frock; ~ s clothes
habitacle *nm* *aer* cockpit; *naut* binnacle; *mot* passenger compartment
habitant -e *n* inhabitant; dweller; occupier
habitation *nf* dwelling, residence

**habiter** vt inhabit, dwell in, occupy; vi live, dwell, reside

**habitude** nf habit, custom, use, practice; **avoir l' ~ de** be in the habit of; **comme d' ~** as usual; **d' ~** usually

**habitué -e** n frequenter, regular customer

**habituel -uelle** adj usual, habitual

**habituer** vt accustom, get into the habit; **s' ~** get used, become accustomed

*\*hâblerie* nf boasting

*\*hâbleur -euse* n boaster, braggart

*\*hache* nf axe, hatchet

*\*haché* adj chopped up, minced; staccato, jerky

*\*hacher* vt chop up, mince, hash

*\*hachis* nm minced meat, mince, hash

*\*hachoir* nm chopper, mincer; chopping-board

*\*hagard* adj haggard, wild-looking

*\*haie* nf hedge, hedgerow; hurdle; row

*\*haillon* nm rag, tatter

*\*haine* nf hate, hatred; aversion

*\*haineux -euse* adj spiteful, full of hatred

*\*haïr* vt (54) hate, detest, loathe

*\*haïssable* adj hateful, odious

*\*halage* nm towing, hauling; **chemin de ~** towpath

*\*hâle* nm sunburn, tan

*\*hâlé* adj sunburnt, tanned; weather-beaten

**haleine** nf breath; wind; **tenir en ~** keep in suspense

*\*haler* vt tow, haul, heave

*\*hâler* vt tan, sunburn

*\*haleter* vi (5) pant, gasp for breath

*\*hall* nm entrance hall, lounge (hotel)

*\*halle* nf (covered) market

*\*hallebarde* nf halberd; **il pleut des ~ s** it's raining cats and dogs

*\*hallier* nm thicket, copse

*\*halte* nf halt, stop; resting-place

**haltère** nm dumb-bell

*\*hamac* nm hammock

*\*hameau* nm hamlet

**hameçon** nm hook; bait

*\*¹hampe* nf staff, pole; stem

*\*²hampe* nf flank of beef

*\*hanche* nf hip; haunch

*\*handicapé -e* n handicapped person

*\*handicaper* vt handicap

*\*hangar* nm outhouse, shed; hangar

*\*hanneton* nm cockchafer, may-bug

*\*hanter* vt haunt, frequent

*\*hantise* nf obsession

*\*happer* vt snap up, snatch

*\*haquet* nm dray

*\*haranguer* vt harangue, lecture

*\*haras* nm stud farm; stud

*\*harasser* vt exhaust, wear out

*\*harceler* vt (5) harass, pester, harry

*\*¹harde* nf herd; flock (birds)

*\*²harde* nf leash

*\*hardes* nfpl old clothes

*\*hardi* adj bold, daring, rash; impudent

*\*hardiesse* nf boldness, daring, rashness; impudence

*\*hareng* nm herring; **~ salé et fumé** kipper; **~ saur** red herring

*\*hargneux -euse* adj peevish, bad-tempered, surly

*\*haricot* nm kidney bean; **~s d'Espagne** scarlet runners; **~s verts** French beans, US string beans

*\*haridelle* nf coll old horse, nag; fig tall, gawky woman

**harmonie** nf harmony; accord; **en ~ avec** in keeping with

**harmonieux -ieuse** adj harmonious; melodious; in keeping

**harmonique** nf harmonics; adj harmonic

**harmoniser** vt harmonize; match; **s' ~** be in keeping, blend

*\*harnachement* nm harness, trappings

*\*harnais* nm harness, saddlery; **cheval de ~** draught-horse

*\*haro* nm hue and cry

*\*harpe* nf harp

*\*harpie* nf harpy, shrew

*\*harpiste* n harpist

*\*harpon* nm harpoon

*\*harponner* vt harpoon

*\*hasard* nm chance, luck; risk, danger; hazard (golf); **à tout ~** on the off chance; **au ~** at random; **coup de ~** stroke of luck; fluke; **de ~** chance; **par ~** accidentally, by chance

*\*hasarder* vt hazard, risk, venture; **se ~** venture

*\*hasardeux -euse* adj hazardous, risky; daring, venturesome

*\*hâte* nf haste, hurry; **à la ~** in a hurry, hastily; **avoir ~ de** be in a hurry to; be eager to

*\*hâter* vt hasten, hurry on; expedite; force (fruit); **se ~** hurry, make haste

*\*hâtif -ive* adj hasty, hurried; premature; early (fruit)

*\*hauban* nm naut shroud

*\*hausse* nf rise, US raise; block, prop; (back-)sight (rifle); range (gun); **jouer à la ~** speculate on a rising market

*\*haussement* nm raising, lifting; **~ d'épaules** shrug(ging) of the shoulders

*\*hausser* vt raise, lift; shrug; vi rise; **se ~** raise oneself; lift, clear (weather)

*\*haussier* nm comm bull

*\*haussière* nf hawser

*\*haut* nm height; top; upper part; head (table); **de ~ en bas** downwards; from top to bottom; **en ~** above; upstairs; **les ~s et les bas** ups and downs; **tomber de son ~** fall flat on the ground; fig be dumbfounded; **traiter**

qn de (son) ~ talk down to s/o, patronize s/o; *adj* high, tall, lofty; raised, elevated; upper, higher; eminent, important; loud (voice); ~e mer open sea; les ~s temps remote antiquity; lire à ~e voix read aloud; mer ~ e high tide; *adv* high, up, above; aloud, loud, loudly; back (in time); ~ les mains! hands up!

*hautain *adj* haughty, proud

*hautbois *nm* oboe

*haut-de-forme *nm* (*pl* hauts-de-forme) top hat

*hauteur *nf* height, elevation, altitude; eminence; hill(-top); haughtiness, arrogance; pitch (sound); *naut* bearing; à la ~ de a match for (person); equal to (task); *coll* être à la ~ be up to it; *aer* prendre de la ~ climb

*haut-fond *nm* (*pl* hauts-fonds) shoal, shallow

*haut-le-cœur *nm invar* heave (stomach); avoir un ~ retch

*haut-le-corps *nm invar* start, jump

*haut-lieu *nm* (*pl* hauts-lieux) centre, important place

*haut-parleur *nm* loudspeaker, amplifier

*hauturier -ière *adj* of the high seas; pilote ~ deep-sea pilot

*Havane *nf* Havana

*havane *nm* Havana (cigar); *adj invar* brown

*hâve *adj* haggard, gaunt, emaciated

*havre *nm* haven, harbour, port

*havresac *nm* knapsack, pack

*Haye (la) *nf* The Hague

*hé *interj* hey there!; hi!; I say!; well!

*heaume *nm hist* helmet

hebdomadaire *nm* + *adj* weekly

héberger *vt* (3) lodge, put up

hébété *adj* dazed, bewildered

hébéter *vt* (6) daze, dull, stupefy

hébraïque *adj* Hebrew, Hebraic

hébraïsant -e *n* Hebraist, Hebrew scholar

hébreu *nm* Hebrew (language)

hécatombe *nf* hecatomb, slaughter

hégémonie *nf* hegemony

*hein *interj* eh?, what?; isn't it?, etc

hélas *interj* alas!

Hélène *nf* Helen

*héler *vt* (6) hail, call

hélice *nf* propeller, screw; *aer* propeller; escalier en ~ spiral staircase

hélicoptère *nm* helicopter

hellénique *adj* Hellenic

helvétique *adj* Helvetic, Helvetian, Swiss

hémistiche *nm* hemistich

hémoglobine *nf* haemoglobin

hémophylie *nf* haemophilia

hémorragie *nf* haemorrhage

hémorroïdes *nfpl* haemorrhoids, piles

*henné *nm* henna

*hennir *vi* neigh, whinny

Henri *nm* Henry

hépatique *n med* hepatic; *nf bot* liverwort; *adj* hepatic

hépatite *nf* hepatitis

heptagone *nm* heptagon; *adj* heptagonal

héraldique *nf* heraldry; *adj* heraldic

*héraut *nm* herald

herbacé *adj* herbaceous

herbage *nm* grassland; pasture; *cul* greens

herbe *nf* herb; grass; blé en ~ corn in the blade; en ~ budding, in embryo; fines ~s herbs for seasoning; manger son blé en ~ spend one's money before getting it; mauvaise ~ weed; *fig* rascal

herbeux -euse *adj* grassy

herbicide *nm* weed-killer; *adj* weed-killing

herbier *nm* herbarium

herbivore *adj* herbivorous

herboriser *vi* gather plants, botanize

herboriste *n* herbalist

herbu *adj* grassy

Hercule *nm* Hercules

hercule *nm* strong-man, strong-arm man

herculéen -enne *adj* herculean

*hère *nm* pauvre ~ poor devil

héréditaire *adj* hereditary

hérédité *nf* heredity; hereditary right; inheritance, succession

hérésie *nf* heresy

hérétique *n* heretic; *adj* heretical

*hérissé *adj* bristling; bristly, prickly; shaggy

*hérisser *vt* bristle, ruffle; se ~ bristle, bristle up, stand on end

*hérisson *nm* hedgehog; *fig* prickly person; ~ de mer sea-urchin

héritage *nm* inheritance, heritage

hériter *vt* inherit; *vi* inherit; succeed to

héritier -ière *n* heir, heiress

hermétique *adj* hermetically sealed, airtight, water-tight

hermine *nf* ermine

*herniaire *adj* hernial; bandage ~ truss

*hernie *nf* hernia, rupture

¹héroïne *nf* heroine

²héroïne *nf chem* heroin

héroïque *adj* heroic

héroïsme *nm* heroism

*héros *nm* hero

*herse *nf* harrow; portcullis; ~s *theat* battens

*herser *vt* harrow

hésiter *vi* hesitate, falter; pause

hétéroclite *adj* peculiar, irregular

hétérodoxe *adj* heterodox

**hétérogène** *adj* heterogeneous, mixed
*__**hêtre** *nm* beech
**heure** *nf* hour; time; moment; o'clock; ~ H zero hour; à la bonne ~! right!, fine!; well done!; à l' ~ on time; à tout à l' ~ see you later, so long; de bonne ~ early; dernière ~ latest news, stop-press news; sur l' ~ at once; tout à l' ~ just now; in a few minutes
**heureux -euse** *adj* happy, delighted; lucky, fortunate; blessed; successful
*__**heurt** *nm* knock, bump, collision, shock; sans ~ smoothly
*__**heurter** *vt* knock against, bump into; shock, offend; clash with; *vi* strike, collide; se ~ collide; clash
*__**heurtoir** *nm* knocker; buffer
**hexagone** *nm* hexagon; l'Hexagone metropolitan France; *adj* hexagonal
**hiberner** *vi* hibernate
*__**hibou** *nm* owl
*__**hic** *nm* rub, snag
*__**hideur** *nf* hideousness
*__**hideux -euse** *adj* hideous
**hjer** *adv* yesterday
*__**hiérarchie** *nf* hierarchy
*__**hiérarchique** *adj* hierarchical; voie ~ official channels
*__**hiéroglyphe** *nm* hieroglyph
**Hilaire** *nm + nf* Hilary
**hilarant** *adj* screamingly funny; gaz ~ laughing-gas
**hilare** *adj* hilarious
**hilarité** *nf* hilarity, mirth
**Hindou -e** *n* Hindu
**hindou** *adj* Hindu
**hindouisme** *nm* Hinduism
**hindoustani** *nm lang* Hindustani, Hindi
**hippique** *adj* equine; concours ~ horse-show; race-meeting
**hippodrome** *nm* race-course; hippo-drome
**hippopotame** *nm* hippopotamus
**hirondelle** *nf* swallow
**hirsute** *adj* hairy, hirsute; shaggy
*__**hisser** *vt* hoist, lift, raise, run up; se ~ pull, hoist oneself (up)
**histoire** *nf* history; story, tale; *coll* fib, yarn; *coll* ~ de just to; faire des ~s make a fuss
**historien -ienne** *n* historian
**historier** *vt* illustrate, embellish
**historiette** *nf* anecdote, short tale
**historiographe** *n* historiographer
**historique** *nm* record, account; *adj* historic, historical
**histrionique** *adj* histrionic
**hiver** *nm* winter
**hivernage** *nm* laying up for the winter; winter season; wintering-place
**hivernal** *adj* winter, wintry
**hivernant -e** *n* winter visitor; *adj* winter-ing

**hiverner** *vi* winter, hibernate
**H.L.M.** *nm* = council flat, council dwelling
*__**hobereau** *nm* country squire
*__**hocher** *vt* shake, nod, toss
**hoirie** *nf* inheritance, succession
*__**Hollandais -e** *n* Dutchman, Dutch-woman
*__**hollandais** *nm* Dutch (language); *adj* Dutch
*__**Hollande** *nf* Holland
*__[1]**hollande** *nm* Dutch cheese
*__[2]**hollande** *nf* holland (cloth)
**holocauste** *nm* holocaust; sacrifice
*__**homard** *nm* lobster
**homélie** *nf* homily
**homéopathe** *n* homoeopath; *adj* ho-moeopathic
**homéopathie** *nf* homoeopathy
**Homère** *nm* Homer
**homérique** *adj* Homeric
**homicide** *nm* homicide (crime); ~ involontaire manslaughter; *n* homicide (person); *adj* murderous, homicidal
**hommage** *nm* homage, tribute; token of esteem; ~ s compliments, respects
**hommasse** *adj* mannish, masculine
**homme** *nm* man; mankind; *coll* hus-band, old man; ~ d'affaires business-man
**homme-grenouille** *nm* (*pl* hommes-grenouilles) frogman
**homme-sandwich** *nm* (*pl* hommes-sandwiches) sandwich-man
**homogène** *adj* homogeneous
**homogénéité** *nf* homogeneity
**homologue** *adj* homologous
**homologuer** *vt* sanction
**homonyme** *nm* homonym; namesake; *adj* homonymous
*__**hongre** *nm* gelding; *adj* gelded
*__**hongrer** *vt* geld
*__**Hongrie** *nf* Hungary
*__**Hongrois -e** *n* Hungarian
*__**hongrois** *nm* Hungarian (language); *adj* Hungarian
**honnête** *adj* honest, upright; decent, respectable; proper, seemly; reason-able (price)
**honnêteté** *nf* honesty; decency; respect-ability; fairness (price)
**honneur** *nm* honour, integrity; credit; distinction; faire ~ à honour, meet; *mil* rendre les ~ s present arms
*__**honnir** *vt* disgrace, dishonour; spurn
**honorable** *adj* honourable, respectable, reputable
**honoraire** *nm* ~ s fee, honorarium; *adj* honorary
**honorer** *vt* honour, respect; do credit to
**honorifique** *adj* honorary

*honte nf shame; disgrace; scandal; avoir ~ be ashamed; faire ~ à put to shame; fausse ~ self-consciousness

*honteux -euse adj ashamed, shame-faced; shy, bashful; disgraceful

hôpital nm (pl -aux) hospital; poorhouse

*hoquet nm hiccup

*hoqueter vi hiccup; have the hiccups

horaire nm timetable; adj hourly

*horde nf horde, pack

horloge nf clock

horloger -ère n clockmaker, watchmaker

horlogerie nf clockmaking, watchmaking; watchmaker's shop; clockwork

*hormis prep except, but, save

horreur nf horror; detestation; ~s atrocities; beastly things

horrible adj horrible, horrid

horrifier vt horrify

horrifique adj horrific, hair-raising

horripilant adj hair-raising; exasperating

horripiler vt make (s/o's) hair stand on end; exasperate

*hors prep out of, outside; except, but, save; ~ circuit cut off; ~ d'affaire out of danger; ~ de combat out of action, disabled; ~ de doute beyond doubt; ~ d'ici! get out!; ~ de prix exorbitant; ~ de soi beside oneself; ~ jeu offside; ~ ligne outstanding

*hors-bord nm invar speedboat

*hors-la-loi nm invar outlaw

*hors-texte nm invar plate (in book)

hortensia nm hydrangea

horticulteur nm horticulturist

hospice nm almshouse; children's home

hospitalier -ière n hospitaller; adj hospitable

hospitaliser vt send (admit) to hospital (home)

hospitalité nf hospitality

hostellerie nf inn

hostie nf bibl sacrificial victim; (eucharistic) host

hostile adj hostile, adverse

hostilité nf hostility, enmity

hôte -esse n host, hostess; landlord, landlady; guest, visitor

hôtel nm mansion, town house; hotel; ~ des ventes auction rooms; ~ de ville town hall, city hall; ~ garni, ~ meublé residential hotel, furnished lodgings; maître d'~ head waiter; butler

hôtel-Dieu nm (pl hôtels-Dieu) hospital

hôtelier -ière n hotel-keeper; innkeeper; landlord, landlady; adj hotel

hôtellerie nf inn, hostelry; guest rooms

(monastery); hotel trade

*hotte nf basket (carried on back); (bricklayer's) hod; ~ aspirante (chimney) hood

*houblon nm bot hop(s)

*houblonnière nf hopfield

*houe nf hoe

*houer vt hoe

*houille nf coal; ~ blanche hydro-electric power

*houiller -ère adj coal, coal-bearing

*houillère nf coal-mine, colliery

*houilleux -euse adj coal-bearing

*houle nf swell, surge

*houlette nf (shepherd's) crook; crozier; trowel

*houleux -euse adj surging; rough (sea); fig stormy

*houppe nf tuft, crest; powder-puff

*houppé adj tufted, crested

*houppelande nf great-coat, box-coat; cloak

*houppette nf small tuft; powder-puff

*hourra interj hurrah!; nm cheer

*houspiller vt hustle, manhandle; fig abuse, insult

*housse nf cover(ing); loose-cover, US slip-cover; dust-sheet; clothes bag; horse-cloth

*houssine nf switch, riding-switch

*houx nm holly

*hoyau nm mattock, grubbing-hoe

*hublot nm port-hole, scuttle

*huche nf kneading-trough

*hue interj gee-up!

*huée nf boo, hoot; ~s boos, jeers

*huer vt boo; vi boo; hoot (owl)

huilage nm oiling, lubrication

huile nf oil; sl les ~s the big shots

huiler vt oil, lubricate

huileux -euse adj oily, greasy

huilier nm oil-merchant; oil-can; cul oil and vinegar cruet

huis nm à ~ clos in camera, behind closed doors

huissier nm usher; sheriff's officer, bailiff

*huit nm eight, eighth; adj eight; ~ jours a week; d'aujourd'hui en ~ today week; donner ses ~ jours à qn give s/o a week's notice

*huitaine nf (about) eight; week

*huitante adj invar (Swiss, Belgian) eighty

*huitantième adj (Swiss, Belgian) eightieth

*huitième n eighth, eighth part; adj eighth

huître nf oyster; coll fool, idiot

huîtrière nf oyster-bed

humain nm les ~ mankind, humanity; adj human; humane

humaniser vt humanize, civilize; s'~

become more humane
**humanisme** *nm* humanism
**humaniste** *n* humanist, classical scholar; *adj* humanist
**humanitaire** *adj* humanitarian
**humanité** *nf* humanity
**humble** *adj* humble, lowly; meek
**humecter** *vt* damp, moisten
\***humer** *vt* suck in, suck up; breathe in, sniff
**humeur** *nf* humour, mood; temper; ill-humour
**humide** *adj* damp, moist, wet, humid
**humidité** *nf* damp, dampness, moisture, humidity; **craint l' ~** to be kept dry; **taches d' ~** mildew
**humiliation** *nf* humiliation; affront
**humilier** *vt* humiliate, humble
**humilité** *nf* humility, humbleness
**humoriste** *n* humorist; *adj* humorous
**humoristique** *adj* humorous
\***hune** *nf naut* top; **~ de vigie** crow's nest
\***hunier** *nm* topsail
\***huppe** *nf* tuft, crest
\***huppé** *adj* tufted, crested; *coll* smart, well-dressed
\***hure** *nf* head; *cul* brawn, US head-cheese; *sl* head, mug
\***hurlement** *nm* howl(ing), roar(ing), yell(ing)
\***hurler** *vt* bawl out; *vi* howl, roar, yell
**hurluberlu** *nm* scatterbrain, harum-scarum
\***hussard** *nm* hussar
\***hutte** *nf* hut, shed
**hybride** *nm + adj* hybrid

**hydraulique** *nf* hydraulics; *adj* hydraulic
**hydravion** *nm* sea-plane
**hydre** *nf* hydra
**hydrogène** *nm* hydrogen
**hydroglisseur** *nm* speedboat
**hydrophile** *adj* absorbent
**hydrophobie** *nf* hydrophobia, rabies
**hydropisie** *nf* dropsy
**hyène** *nf* hyena
**hygiène** *nf* hygiene; **~ publique** public health
**hygiénique** *adj* hygienic; sanitary; **papier ~** toilet paper
**hymnaire** *nm* hymnal, hymn-book
**hymne** *nm* patriotic song; national anthem; *nf* hymn
**hyperbole** *nf* hyperbole, exaggeration
**hyperbolique** *adj* hyperbolic
**hypersensible** *adj* over-sensitive
**hypertension** *nf* high blood-pressure
**hypnose** *nf* hypnosis
**hypnotiser** *vt* hypnotize
**hypnotisme** *nm* hypnotism
**hypocondriaque** *n + adj* hypochondriac
**hypocondrie** *nf* hypochondria
**hypocrisie** *nf* hypocrisy
**hypocrite** *n* hypocrite; *adj* hypocritical
**hypodermique** *adj* hypodermic
**hypotension** *nf* low blood-pressure
**hypothécaire** *adj* mortgage
**hypothèque** *nf* mortgage
**hypothéquer** *vt* (6) mortgage
**hypothèse** *nf* hypothesis, supposition
**hypothétique** *adj* hypothetical
**hystérie** *nf* hysteria
**hystérique** *adj* hysteric, hysterical

# I

**i** *nm* the letter i; now; **~ grec** (the letter) y; **mettre les points sur les ~** speak plainly
**iambe** *nm* iambus, iambic
**iambique** *adj* iambic
**ibérique** *adj* Iberian
**ici** *adv* here; now; **~-bas** here on earth; **d' ~** henceforth; **d' ~ là** between now and then; **d' ~ peu** before long; **jusqu'~** as far as here; until now; **par ~** this way
**icône** *nf* icon

**iconoclaste** *n* iconoclast; *adj* iconoclastic
**idéal** *nm + adj* (*pl* **~ s, idéaux**) ideal
**idéaliser** *vt* idealize
**idéalisme** *nm* idealism
**idéaliste** *n* idealist; *adj* idealistic
**idée** *nf* idea, notion, view, opinion, mind; *coll* touch, small amount; **~ fixe** obsession; **~ lumineuse** brain-wave; **~ s noires** gloomy thoughts; **faire à son ~** please oneself; **il me vient à l' ~** it occurs to me; **se faire des ~ s to**

imagine things
**idem** *adv* idem, ditto
**identifier** *vt* identify; regard as identical
**identique** *adj* identical
**identité** *nf* identity
**idéogramme** *nm* ideogram, ideograph
**idéologie** *nf* ideology
**idéologique** *adj* ideological
**idéologue** *n* ideologist
**idiomatique** *adj* idiomatic
**idiome** *nm* idiom; mode of speech
**idiot -e** *n* fool, clot; *med* idiot, imbecile; *adj* idiotic, stupid, absurd; *med* idiot (child)
**idiotie** *nf* idiocy; *med* imbecility
**idiotisme** *nm* idiomatic expression
**idolâtre** *n* idolater; *adj* idolatrous
**idolâtrer** *vt* idolize, adore
**idolâtrie** *nf* idolatry
**idole** *nf* idol
**idylle** *nf* idyll
**idyllique** *adj* idyllic
**if** *nm* yew, yew-tree
**igame** *nm* high official with special powers
**ignare** *n* ignoramus; *adj* ignorant
**igné** *adj* igneous
**ignifuge** *nm* fire-proofing material; *adj* fire-proof, non-inflammable
**ignifuger** *vt* fire-proof
**ignoble** *adj* ignoble, shameful, disgraceful
**ignominie** *nf* ignominy, shame
**ignominieux -ieuse** *adj* ignominious, disgraceful
**ignorant -e** *n* ignorant person, ignoramus; *adj* ignorant, ignoramus
**ignoré** *adj* unknown
**ignorer** *vt* not know, be ignorant of; ignore
**¹il** *pron m* he, it; (ship) she
**²il** *impers pron invar* it, there; ~ était une fois once upon a time there was; ~ vient un homme there comes a man; ~ y a there is, are
**île** *nf* island, isle
**ilex** *nm invar* ilex, evergreen oak
**illégal** *adj* illegal, unlawful
**illégalité** *nf* illegality
**illégitime** *adj* illegitimate, unlawful; unwarranted
**illégitimité** *nf* illegitimacy
**illettré** *adj* uneducated, untutored
**illicite** *adj* illicit
**illico** *adv coll* at once, like a flash
**illimitable** *adj* limitless, boundless
**illimité** *adj* unlimited; **congé** ~ indefinite leave
**illisibilité** *nf* illegibility
**illisible** *adj* illegible; unreadable
**illogique** *adj* illogical
**illuminant** *adj* illuminating

**illuminateur -trice** *n* illuminator; enlightener
**illumination** *nf* lighting; ~s lights, illuminations; enlightenment, illumination
**illuminé -e** *n* visionary
**illuminer** *vt* light up, illuminate; enlighten
**illusion** *nf* illusion, delusion; ~ d'optique optical illusion; **se faire** ~, **se faire des** ~s deceive oneself
**illusionner** *vt* delude; **s'** ~ labour under a delusion
**illusionniste** *n* illusionist, conjurer
**illusoire** *adj* illusory, deceptive
**illustrateur -trice** *n* illustrator
**illustratif -ive** *adj* illustrative
**illustration** *nf* illustriousness; making illustrious; illustration, picture; illustrious person
**illustre** *adj* illustrious, famous
**illustré** *nm* illustrated magazine
**illustrer** *vt* make illustrious, famous; illustrate
**îlot** *nm* small island; block of houses
**ils** *pron mpl* they
**image** *nf* image, picture; mental picture; likeness, resemblance; simile, metaphor; reflection; *comm* ~ de marque public image; **sage comme une** ~ as good as gold; **se faire une** ~ de imagine
**imagé** *adj* vivid, full of imagery
**imagerie** *nf* coloured print; print factory
**imaginable** *adj* imaginable
**imaginaire** *adj* imaginary, make-believe; **malade** ~ hypochondriac
**imaginatif -ive** *adj* imaginative
**imagination** *nf* imagination; fancy
**imaginer** *vt* imagine, suppose, fancy; conceive, devise; **s'** ~ suppose
**imbattable** *adj* unbeatable, invincible
**imbattu** *adj* unbeaten
**imbécile** *n* imbecile, half-wit; *adj* half-witted; idiotic
**imbécillité** *nf* imbecility, feeble-mindedness; silliness; ~s nonsense
**imberbe** *adj* beardless; callow
**imbiber** *vt* soak, saturate; soak up, imbibe; imbue, impregnate; **s'** ~ become saturated; become steeped
**imbriqué** *adj* overlapping
**imbrisable** *adj* unbreakable
**imbrûlable** *adj* fireproof
**imbu** *adj* imbued; soaked
**imbuvable** *adj* undrinkable; *sl* insufferable
**imitateur -trice** *n* imitator
**imitatif -ive** *adj* imitative
**imitation** *nf* imitation, copying; forgery, counterfeit; forging, counterfeiting; mimicry; **à l'** ~ **de** in imitation of

**imiter** vt imitate, copy; mimic, model oneself on; forge (signature), counterfeit

**immaculé** adj immaculate, spotless, unstained

**immangeable** adj uneatable

**immanquable** adj unavoidable, certain

**immatériel -ielle** adj immaterial, intangible

**immatriculation** nf registration, inscription, enrolment; mot plaque d' ~ number-plate

**immatriculer** vt register, enter (s/o, sth) on a register

**immédiat** nm present time; adj immediate, instant; direct; close; chem analyse ~ e proximate analysis

**immense** adj immense, vast; boundless

**immensité** nf immensity, vastness; boundlessness

**immerger** vt (3) immerse, dip

**immérité** adj undeserved, unmerited

**immersion** nf immersion, dipping; astron occultation

**immesurable** adj immeasurable

**immeuble** nm building; real estate; adj leg real, immovable

**immeuble-tour** nm (pl immeubles-tours) high-rise building

**immigré -e** n immigrant

**immigrer** vi immigrate

**immiscer** vt (4) mix up, involve; s' ~ interfere

**immiscible** adj unmixable

**immobile** adj motionless, still, immobile; firm

**¹immobilier** nm property, US real estate

**²immobilier -ière** adj leg real; agence immobilière estate agency, US real estate agency; agent ~ estate agent; biens ~ s real estate

**immobilisation** nf immobilization; ~ s fixed assets; leg conversion into real estate

**immobiliser** vt immobilize, bring to a stop; tie up (capital); leg convert into real estate

**immobilisme** nm policy of inaction

**immobiliste** n die-hard

**immobilité** nf immobility, fixity

**immodéré** adj immoderate, inordinate

**immodeste** adj immodest, shameless

**immodestie** nf immodesty, shamelessness

**immoler** vt immolate

**immonde** adj filthy, disgusting, foul

**immondices** nfpl refuse, dirt

**immoralité** nf immorality

**immortaliser** vt immortalize

**immortalité** nf immortality

**immortel -elle** n immortal; les Immortels members of the French Academy;

~ elle everlasting flower, immortelle; adj immortal

**immuable** adj immutable, unchanging, fixed

**immuniser** vt immunize, make immune from

**immunité** nf immunity

**immutabilité** nf immutability

**impact** nm impact; effect

**¹impair** nm coll blunder, US goof

**²impair** adj odd, uneven

**impardonnable** adj unpardonable, unforgivable

**imparfait** nm imperfect tense; adj imperfect, defective; unfinished

**imparité** nf inequality, disparity; unevenness

**impartageable** adj indivisible; which cannot be shared

**impartial** adj impartial, unbiased, equitable

**impartialité** nf impartiality

**impartir** vt leg bestow, grant

**impasse** nf dead-end, cul-de-sac; deadlock; dans une ~ in a dilemma; (cards) faire une ~ finesse

**impassibilité** nf impassivity

**impassible** adj impassive, unconcerned; unimpressionable

**impatience** nf impatience; eagerness

**impatient** adj impatient; eager

**impatienter** vt make (s/o) lose patience, provoke, irritate; s' ~ lose patience

**impatroniser** vt impose, set in authority; s' ~ impose oneself, take charge

**impayable** adj invaluable, priceless; coll very funny, priceless

**impayé** adj unpaid, outstanding (debt)

**impeccabilité** nf impeccability, faultlessness

**impeccable** adj impeccable, faultless

**impécunieux -ieuse** adj impecunious

**impénétrabilité** nf impenetrability; inscrutability

**impénétrable** adj impenetrable, impervious; inscrutable

**imper** nm coll raincoat

**¹impératif** nm imperative

**²impératif -ive** adj imperative; peremptory

**impératrice** nf empress

**imperfection** nf imperfection, flaw; incompleteness

**impériale** nf top deck of bus; imperial beard

**impérialisme** nm imperialism

**impérialiste** n + adj imperialist

**impérieux -ieuse** adj imperious, haughty, overbearing; urgent, imperative

**impérissable** adj imperishable, undying

**impéritie** nf incapacity, inefficiency

**imperméabiliser** *vt* proof, render water-proof

**imperméable** *nm* raincoat; *adj* impermeable; impervious

**impersonnalité** *nf* impersonality

**impersonnel -elle** *adj* impersonal

**impertinence** *nf* impertinence, rudeness; irrelevance

**impertinent** *adj* impertinent, rude; irrelevant

**impétrant -e** *n leg* grantee; candidate

**impétueux -ueuse** *adj* impetuous, impulsive; violent

**impétuosité** *nf* impetuosity, impetuousness, impulsiveness

**impie** *adj* impious, irreligious; blasphemous

**impiété** *nf* impiety, impiousness; impious action; undutifulness

**impitoyable** *adj* pitiless, merciless

**implacable** *adj* implacable, relentless

**implanter** *vt* plant, implant; graft; s' ~ take root; *coll* s' ~ **chez qn** foist oneself on s/o

**implicite** *adj* implicit, absolute

**impliquer** *vt* implicate, involve; ~ **contradiction** imply a contradiction

**imploration** *nf* entreaty, imploring

**implorer** *vt* implore, entreat

**imployable** *adj* inflexible

**impoli** *adj* impolite, rude, uncivil

**impolitesse** *nf* impoliteness, incivility; rude, discourteous action

**impolitique** *adj* impolitic, ill-advised

**impondéré** *adj* ill-considered

**impopulaire** *adj* unpopular

**impopularité** *nf* unpopularity

**importable** *adj* unwearable; importable

**importance** *nf* importance, significance; extent, gravity, consequence; social position; d' ~ momentous; *adv phr* d' ~ soundly

**important** *nm* what matters, main point; *adj* important; considerable; consequential, self-important; **peu** ~ unimportant, trifling

**importateur -trice** *n* importer; *adj* importing

**importation** *nf* importation; import

**¹importer** *vt* import

**²importer** *vi* matter, be of importance; **n'importe** no matter, never mind; **n'importe comment** no matter how; **n'importe qui** no matter who, anyone; **qu'importe?** what does it matter?

**importun** *adj* importunate; tiresome; inopportune, unreasonable

**importuner** *vt* importune; bother, be a nuisance to, pester; dun

**importunité** *nf* importunity; harassing

**imposable** *adj* taxable; rateable

**imposant** *adj* imposing, impressive; dig-nified

**imposé -e** *n* tax-payer; rate-payer

**imposer** *vt* impose, prescribe, lay down; tax, assess; ~ **un prix** fix a price; *vi* impress, command respect; **en** ~ **à qn** overawe s/o; deceive s/o, take s/o in; s' ~ assert oneself; be essential; s' ~ **à, chez qn** foist oneself on s/o

**imposition** *nf* imposing, prescribing; taxation, imposition of tax, assessment; tax, duty, rates

**impossibilité** *nf* impossibility; impossible thing; **être dans l'** ~ **de** be quite unable to

**impossible** *nm* what is impossible; **faire l'** ~ **pour** do one's utmost to; **par** ~ against all probability; *adj* impossible; **cela m'est** ~ I cannot; **c'est** ~ out of the question, it can't be done; **il m'est** ~ **de croire que ...** I can't believe that ...; **une idée** ~ an absurd idea

**imposteur** *nm* impostor, humbug

**imposture** *nf* imposture, deception, trickery

**impôt** *nm* tax; ~ **sur le revenu** income-tax; **frapper d'un** ~ levy a tax on

**impotence** *nf* impotence, helplessness, infirmity

**impotent -e** *n* cripple, invalid; *adj* helpless, infirm

**impraticable** *adj* impracticable, unworkable; impassable (road)

**imprécation** *nf* imprecation, curse

**imprécatoire** *adj* imprecatory

**imprécis** *adj* imprecise, inaccurate, vague

**imprécision** *nf* imprecision, vagueness

**imprégner** *vt* (6) impregnate, permeate; s' ~ become saturated, imbued

**imprémédité** *adj* unpremeditated

**imprenable** *adj* impregnable

**imprescriptible** *adj leg* imprescriptible, inalienable

**impression** *nf* impression, feeling; impressing, imprint; printing; print; ~ **en couleurs** colour-print; **à l'** ~ in the press

**impressionnable** *adj* impressionable, excitable; sensitized

**impressionnant** *adj* impressive, moving

**impressionner** *vt* impress, move, make an impression on; s' ~ be impressed

**impressionniste** *n* impressionist; *adj* impressionist, impressionistic

**imprévisible** *adj* unforeseeable

**imprévision** *nf* lack of foresight

**imprévoyable** *adj* unforeseeable

**imprévoyance** *nf* lack of foresight; improvidence

**imprévoyant** *adj* unforeseeing; improvident

**imprévu** *nm* unforeseen event; ~ s

unforeseen expenses, contingencies; **à moins d' ~ , sauf ~** unless something unforeseen occurs, barring accidents; **en cas d' ~** in case of emergency; *adj* unforeseen, unexpected

**imprimable** *adj* printable

**imprimante** *nf* printer (computer)

**imprimé** *nm* printed paper; printed form; cotton print, *US* calico; **~ s** printed matter

**imprimer** *vt* imprint, stamp; print; communicate (movement)

**imprimerie** *nf* printing-works, printing-press; (art of) printing

**imprimeur** *nm* printer, master-printer; **~ -éditeur** printer and publisher

**imprimeuse** *nf* printing-machine

**improbabilité** *nf* improbability, unlikelihood

**improbable** *adj* improbable, unlikely

**improbité** *nf* improbity, dishonesty

**improductif -ive** *adj* unproductive

**impromptu** *nm* impromptu; *adj invar* impromptu, extempore; *adv* impromptu, on the spur of the moment

**imprononçable** *adj* unpronounceable

**impropre** *adj* improper, unsuitable; unfit

**impropriété** *nf* impropriety

**improvisateur -trice** *n* improvisor

**improvisation** *nf* improvisation; improvised playing, speaking

**improvisé** *adj* improvised, makeshift

**improviser** *vt* improvise; **~ un discours** make an extempore speech; *vi* improvise

**improviste (à l')** *adv phr* unexpectedly, unawares

**imprudence** *nf* imprudence, rashness; rash, incautious act

**imprudent** *adj* imprudent, rash, ill-advised, careless

**impubère** *adj* under the age of puberty

**impubliable** *adj* unpublishable

**impudence** *nf* impudence, effrontery; piece of impudence

**impudent** *adj* impudent, pert

**impudeur** *nf* shamelessness, immodesty

**impudicité** *nf* impudicity, lewdness; indecent act

**impudique** *adj* lewd, immodest

**impuissance** *nf* impotence, powerlessness; impotence (sexual)

**impuissant** *adj* impotent, powerless; unavailing; impotent (sexually)

**impulser** *vt* stimulate, animate

**impulsif -ive** *adj* impulsive

**impulsion** *nf* elect + mech impulse; *fig* impulse, stimulus

**impunément** *adv* with impunity

**impuni** *adj* unpunished

**impunité** *nf* impunity

**impur** *adj* impure, tainted; unchaste

**impureté** *nf* impurity; lewdness

**imputable** *adj* imputable; chargeable

**imputation** *nf* imputation, accusation; charging up

**imputer** *vt* impute, ascribe; charge

**in** *adj invar* in, fashionable

**inabordable** *adj* unapproachable, inaccessible; prohibitive

**inaccentué** *adj* unstressed, unaccented

**inaccessibilité** *nf* inaccessibility

**inaccessible** *adj* inaccessible; proof against

**inaccompli** *adj* unaccomplished

**inaccordable** *adj* ungrantable, inadmissible; irreconcilable

**inaccoutumé** *adj* unaccustomed; unusual

**inachevé** *adj* unfinished

**inactif -ive** *adj* inactive, indolent; *chem* inert; *comm* sluggish

**inactivité** *nf* inactivity, indolence; *chem* inertness; sluggishness

**inadaptation** *nf* maladjustment

**inadapté -e** *n* misfit; *adj* maladjusted

**inadmissibilité** *nf* inadmissibility; failure in qualifying written examination

**inadmissible** *adj* inadmissible; having failed in qualifying written examination; **c'est ~** it's out of the question

**inaliéné** *adj* inalienated

**inalliable** *adj* non-alloyable; incompatible

**inaltérable** *adj* non-deteriorating; unfailing

**inaltéré** *adj* unimpaired

**inamical** *adj* unfriendly

**inamovibilité** *nf* leg fixity of tenure; irremovability

**inamovible** *adj* leg irremovable; built-in

**inanimé** *adj* inanimate, lifeless

**inanité** *nf* inanity, futility; inane remark

**inapaisable** *adj* unappeasable; unquenchable

**inapaisé** *adj* unappeased; unquenched, unassuaged

**inapercevable** *adj* unperceivable

**inaperçu** *adj* unperceived; **passer ~** escape notice

**inapparent** *adj* unapparent, inconspicuous

**inappliqué** *adj* lacking in application; unapplied, in abeyance

**inappréciable** *adj* imperceptible; inestimable

**inapprécié** *adj* unappreciated

**inapprêté** *adj* uncooked; unprepared; unrehearsed

**inapprivoisable** *adj* untamable

**inapprivoisé** *adj* untamed, wild

**inapte** *adj* inapt, unapt, unfit

**inaptitude** *nf* inaptitude, unfitness

**inarticulé** *adj* inarticulate; inarticulated

**inassouvi** *adj* unappeased, unsatisfied; unquenched

**inassouvissable** *adj* insatiable

**inattaquable** *adj* unassailable, unquestionable; ~ **par** resistant to

**inattendu** *adj* unexpected, unforeseen

**inattentif -ive** *adj* inattentive; careless, heedless

**inattention** *nf* inattention, absent-mindedness; carelessness

**inaugurateur -trice** *n* inaugurator

**inaugurer** *vt* inaugurate; open, initiate

**inauthentique** *adj* unauthentic

**inautorisé** *adj* unauthorized

**inaverti** *adj* unwarned; inexperienced

**inavouable** *adj* unavowable; shameful

**inavoué** *adj* unavowed, unacknowledged

**incapable** *n* incapable, incompetent person; *adj* incapable, incompetent; unfit; sexually impotent

**incapacité** *nf* incapacity, incompetence; unfitness; disability

**incarcérer** *vt* (6) incarcerate, imprison

**incarnadin** *adj* incarnadine, pink

**incarnat** *nm* flesh-colour, rosiness; *adj* flesh-coloured, rosy

**incarnation** *nf* incarnation; embodiment

**incarné** *adj* incarnate; ingrowing (nail)

**incarner** *vt* incarnate, embody; *theat* play the role of; **s' ~** become incarnate; become ingrowing

**incartade** *nf* outburst, tirade; prank; swerve

**incassable** *adj* unbreakable

**incendiaire** *n* incendiary; fire-brand; *adj* incendiary, inflammatory

**incendie** *nm* fire, conflagration; ~ **volontaire** arson; **bouche d' ~** hydrant; **pompe à ~** fire-engine; **poste d' ~** fire-station

**incendier** *vt* set fire to, burn down

**incertain** *adj* uncertain, doubtful; unreliable; indistinct; unsettled (weather)

**incertitude** *nf* uncertainty, doubt, indecision

**incessamment** *adv* at once, without delay; incessantly, unceasingly

**incessant** *adj* unceasing, ceaseless

**incessible** *adj* inalienable

**inceste** *nm* incest

**incestueux -ueuse** *adj* incestuous

**inchangé** *adj* unchanged

**inchoatif -ive** *adj* inceptive, inchoative

**incidence** *nf* consequence, influence

**incident** *nm* incident, happening; difficulty; ~ **de parcours** hitch; *adj* incidental; *gramm* parenthetical

**incidente** *nf* subordinate clause

**incinérateur** *nm* incinerator

**incinération** *nf* incineration; cremation

**incinérer** *vt* (6) incinerate; cremate

**inciser** *vt* incise; lance

**incisif -ive** *adj* incisive; cutting

**incision** *nf* incision, cut; lancing

**incisive** *nf* incisor

**incitateur -trice** *n* inciter, agitator; *adj* inciting

**incitation** *nf* incitement

**inciter** *vt* incite, urge on

**incivil** *adj* uncivil

**incivilisé** *adj* uncivilized

**incivilité** *nf* incivility, discourtesy; act of incivility

**inclassable** *adj* unclassifiable

**inclémence** *nf* inclemency

**inclinaison** *nf* tilting, incline, slope, gradient; *naut* list; *archi* pitch; *elect* dip

**inclination** *nf* inclination, bow, nod; propensity, attachment

**incliné** *adj* inclined, tilted; bowed; disposed

**incliner** *vt* incline, slant, tilt, bend; predispose; *vi* lean, slope, list; be inclined; **s' ~** lean, slope, bend over; bow; yield

**inclure** *vt* (25) enclose; include

**inclus** *adj* enclosed; inclusive

**incolore** *adj* colourless

**incollable** *adj* impossible to catch out

**incomber** *v impers* be incumbent upon, devolve on

**incombustible** *adj* fire-proof, incombustible

**incomestible** *adj* inedible

**incommensurable** *adj* math incommensurable; *coll* large, outsize; **racine ~** irrational root

**incommodant** *adj* annoying, unpleasant

**incommode** *adj* inconvenient, incommodious, uncomfortable; awkward

**incommoder** *vt* incommode, inconvenience, bother; make unwell

**incommutable** *adj* non-transferable; **propriétaire ~** owner who cannot be dispossessed

**incompatibilité** *nf* incompatibility

**incompatible** *adj* incompatible, inconsistent

**incomplet -ète** *adj* incomplete

**incompréhensibilité** *nf* incomprehensibility

**incompréhensif -ive** *adj* lacking in understanding

**incompris** *adj* misunderstood

**inconcevable** *adj* inconceivable

**inconciliable** *adj* irreconcilable

**inconditionnel -elle** *n* die-hard; *adj* unconditional

**inconduite** *nf* immoral behaviour; *leg* misconduct

**inconfort** nm lack of comfort, discomfort

**incongru** adj incongruous; unbecoming, out of place

**incongruité** nf incongruity, incongruousness; impropriety; improper remark

**inconnaissable** adj unknowable

**inconnu -e** n unknown person; stranger; ~ e math unknown quantity; adj unknown

**inconquis** adj unconquered

**inconscience** nf unconsciousness; unawareness

**inconscient** adj unconscious; unaware

**inconséquence** nf inconsequence, inconsistency; non sequitur

**inconséquent** adj inconsequent, inconsistent; rambling, unconnected

**inconsidéré** adj ill-considered; inconsiderate; thoughtless

**inconsistance** nf lack of cohesion, looseness; inconsistency

**inconsistant** adj lacking in cohesion, loose; inconsistent

**inconsolable** adj inconsolable; disconsolate

**inconstance** nf inconstancy, fickleness

**inconstitutionnel -elle** adj unconstitutional

**incontestable** adj incontestable, undeniable, incontrovertible

**incontesté** adj uncontested, undisputed

**incontinent** adv forthwith, at once

**incontrôlable** adj unverifiable

**incontrôlé** adj unverified

**inconvenance** nf unseemliness; indecorousness; indecency; unseemly act

**inconvenant** adj unseemly, indecorous; indecent

**inconvénient** nm disadvantage, drawback; **si vous n'y voyez pas d' ~** if you have no objection

**inconvertissable** adj incorrigible; past praying for

**incorporer** vt incorporate; mil embody; s' ~ incorporate, blend

**incorrect** adj incorrect, wrong; indecorous

**incorrection** nf incorrectness, error; impropriety

**incrédule** n unbeliever, infidel; adj incredulous; unbelieving

**incrédulité** nf incredulousness; unbelief

**increvable** adj mot unpuncturable; coll tireless; coll indestructible

**incriminable** adj indictable, liable to be charged

**incrimination** nf incrimination; leg indictment; charge

**incriminer** vt condemn, blame; leg incriminate, charge

**incrochetable** adj unpickable, burglarproof

**incroyable** adj incredible, unbelievable

**incroyance** nf unbelief

**incroyant -e** n unbeliever; adj unbelieving

**incrustation** nf incrustation; inlaid work; furring up (boiler)

**incruster** vt encrust; inlay; s' ~ become encrusted, furred up, engrained; coll dig oneself in

**incubateur** nm incubator

**incube** nm incubus

**inculpable** adj indictable, chargeable

**inculpation** nf indictment, charge

**inculpé -e** n defendant, accused

**inculper** vt indict, charge

**inculquer** vt inculcate, instil

**inculte** adj uncultivated; uncultured

**incurie** nf negligence; lack of interest

**incurieux -ieuse** adj incurious

**incuriosité** nf incuriosity

**incursion** nf incursion, raid; fig excursion

**Inde** nf India; **les ~ s** the Indies

**indébrouillable** adj impossible to untangle; inextricable

**indécence** nf indecency, immodesty; indecent act

**indécent** adj indecent, immodest

**indéchiffrable** adj indecipherable, illegible; unintelligible

**indéchirable** adj untearable

**indécis** adj undecided, hesitating; indistinct, uncertain; indecisive

**indécisif -ive** adj indecisive

**indéclinable** adj impossible to refuse; gramm indeclinable

**indécrottable** n coll oaf, hopeless clot; adj uncleanable; coll incorrigible, hopeless

**indéfendable** adj indefensible

**indéfini** adj indefinite; undefined; gramm indefinite

**indéfinissable** adj indefinable; nondescript

**indéformable** adj that will not lose its shape

**indéfrisable** nf permanent wave; adj that cannot come out of curl

**indélibéré** adj unpremeditated; undeliberated

**indélicat** adj indelicate, tactless, coarse; dishonest; unscrupulous

**indélicatesse** nf indelicacy, tactlessness, coarseness; dishonesty; unscrupulousness

**indémaillable** adj ladder-proof

**indemne** adj unhurt; undamaged; **sortir ~** be unhurt

**indemnisation** nf indemnification, compensation

**indemniser** *vt* indemnify, compensate

**indemnité** *nf* indemnity, compensation; allowance, grant; ~ **de chômage** unemployment benefit; ~ **de déplacement** travelling expenses; ~ **de logement** living-out allowance; ~ **parlementaire** parliamentary stipend

**indémontrable** *adj* undemonstrable

**indémontré** *adj* undemonstrated

**indépendant** *adj* independent, free; self-contained (flat)

**indéracinable** *adj* ineradicable

**indéréglable** *adj* fool-proof, that cannot go wrong

**indescriptible** *adj* indescribable

**indéterminé** *adj* undetermined; irresolute; *math* indeterminate

**indétraquable** *adj* fool-proof, that cannot go wrong

¹**index** *nm* forefinger, index-finger; pointer

²**index** *nm* index; *eccles* Index; **mettre à l'** ~ ban, black-list

¹**indicateur** *nm* time-table, guide, directory; indicator, gauge; *mot* ~ **de vitesse** speedometer; *adj* (*f* **-trice**) indicatory, indicating; **plaque indicatrice** street-sign; **poteau** ~ sign-post

²**indicateur -trice** *n* informer, police-spy

¹**indicatif** *nm* *gramm* indicative; *rad* call-sign, signature

²**indicatif -ive** *adj* indicative

**indication** *nf* indication, pointing out; information, instruction; **à titre d'** ~ for guidance; **sauf** ~ **contraire** unless otherwise stated

**indice** *nm* indication, sign, clue; index; *math* index; *opt* ~ **de réfraction** refractive index

**indicible** *adj* inexpressible; unspeakable

**Indien -ienne** *n + adj* Indian

**indien -ienne** *adj* Indian

**indienne** *nf* printed calico; chintz

**indifféremment** *adv* indifferently, unconcernedly; indiscriminately

**indifférence** *nf* indifference, unconcern

**indifférent** *adj* indifferent, unconcerned; of no consequence, trifling; **cela m'est** ~ it doesn't matter to me

**indigence** *nf* indigence, poverty, want

**indigène** *n* native; *adj* indigenous, native

**indigent -e** *n* pauper; *adj* indigent, poverty-stricken

**indigeste** *adj* indigestible, stodgy; heavy, undigested

**indigne** *adj* unworthy, undeserving; shameful

**indigner** *vt* make indignant; **s'** ~ be indignant

**indignité** *nf* indignity; unworthiness; baseness

**indiquer** *vt* indicate, point out, show;

fix, specify; recommend; betoken; **c'est très indiqué** it's very advisable; **c'était indiqué** it was the obvious thing to do

**indirect** *adj* indirect; oblique; *leg* circumstantial

**indiscipliné** *adj* undisciplined

**indiscret -ète** *n + adj* indiscreet, tactless (person); over-talkative (person)

**indiscrétion** *nf* indiscretion; indiscreetness, tactlessness; tactless remark; **sa** ~ without being indiscreet

**indiscutable** *adj* indisputable, unquestionable

**indisponible** *adj* unavailable; *leg* inalienable; *leg* entailed

**indisposé** *adj* indisposed, unwell; ill-disposed

**indisposer** *vt* make unwell, upset; antagonize

**indistinct** *adj* indistinct, faint, blurred, dim

**indistinctement** *adv* indistinctly, faintly; indiscriminately

**indistinguible** *adj* indistinguishable

**individu** *nm* individual, human being; *coll* (*usu pej*) chap, fellow, character

**individualiser** *vt* individualize, particularize; personalize; **s'** ~ assume individual characteristics

**individualité** *nf* individuality

**individuel -uelle** *adj* individual, personal; separate

**indivis** *adj* joint

**indivisibilité** *nf* indivisibility

**Indochine** *nf* Indo-China

**indocilité** *nf* indocility, untractableness

**indolence** *nf* indolence, idleness; *med* painlessness

**indolent** *adj* indolent, idle; *med* painless

**indolore** *adj* painless

**indomptable** *adj* unconquerable, untameable; indomitable

**indompté** *adj* unconquered, untamed

**Indonésie** *nf* Indonesia

**indu** *adj* undue, unwarranted; **à des heures** ~**es** at all hours

**inductif -ive** *adj* inductive

**induire** *vt* (80) induce, beguile; *elect* induce

**indulgence** *nf* indulgence, leniency, forbearance

**indulgent** *adj* indulgent, lenient, forbearing

**indûment** *adv* unduly

**industrialiser** *vt* industrialize

**industrialisme** *nm* industrialism

**industrie** *nf* industry; ingenuity, dexterity; trade, manufacture; trickery; **vivre d'** ~ live by one's wits

¹**industriel** *nm* manufacturer, industrialist

²**industriel -ielle** *adj* industrial; *coll* **en quantité ~ -ielle** galore

**industrieux -ieuse** *adj* industrious

**inébranlable** *adj* unshakeable, resolute

**inéclairé** *adj* unlit; unenlightened

**inédit** *nm* unpublished work; *adj* unpublished; novel, original; unprecedented

**ineffaçable** *adj* ineffaceable, indelible

**inefficace** *adj* ineffectual, inefficacious

**inefficacité** *nf* ineffectualness, inefficacy

**inégal** *adj* unequalled

**inégalité** *nf* inequality; unevenness, roughness; capriciousness

**inemployé** *adj* unemployed, unused

**inénarrable** *adj* indescribable, untellable; *coll* hilarious

**inepte** *adj* inept, foolish, stupid

**ineptie** *nf* ineptitude, incapacity; inept remark; ~ **s** nonsense

**inépuisable** *adj* inexhaustible, unfailing

**inépuisé** *adj* unexhausted

**inéquitable** *adj* inequitable, unfair

**inerte** *adj* inert, sluggish, dull

**inertie** *nf* inertia, sluggishness, apathy; **(force d')** ~ passive resistance

**inespéré** *adj* unhoped for, unexpected

**inévitabilité** *nf* inevitability

**inévitable** *adj* inevitable, unavoidable

**inexact** *adj* inexact, incorrect; unreliable; unpunctual

**inexactitude** *nf* inexactitude, inaccuracy, mistake; unpunctuality

**inexécutable** *adj* unfeasible, unworkable

**inexécuté** *adj* unexecuted, unperformed, unfulfilled

**inexercé** *adj* unexercised, unskilled

**inexistant** *adj* non-existent

**inexpérimenté** *adj* inexperienced, unskilled; untested

**inexpié** *adj* unexpiated

**inexpliqué** *adj* unexplained, unaccounted for

**inexploité** *adj* unexploited, unworked, uncultivated

**inexploré** *adj* unexplored

**inexplosible** *adj* non-explosive

**inexpressif -ive** *adj* inexpressive, expressionless

**inexprimable** *adj* inexpressible

**inexprimé** *adj* unexpressed

**inexpugnable** *adj* inexpugnable, impregnable

**inextinguible** *adj* inextinguishable; unquenchable; irrepressible

**inextirpable** *adj* ineradicable

**infaillibilité** *nf* infallibility

**infaillible** *adj* infallible, impracticable

**infamant** *adj* defamatory; degrading, dishonourable; *leg* involving loss of civil rights

**infâme** *adj* infamous, vile, unspeakable

**infamie** *nf* infamy, disgrace; infamous deed

**infanterie** *nf* infantry

**infanticide** *nm* infanticide, child-murder; *n* child-murderer; *adj* infanticidal

**infantilisme** *nm* infantilism

**infarctus** *nm med* infarctus; ~ **du myocarde** coronary (thrombosis)

**infatigable** *adj* indefatigable, tireless

**infatuation** *nf* self-importance, smugness

**infatuer (s')** *v refl* become infatuated

**infécond** *adj* barren, sterile

**infécondité** *nf* barrenness, sterility

**infect** *adj* stinking, noisome; filthy, vile; *coll* **il est** ~ he's a shit

**infecter** *vt* infect, pollute; corrupt

**infectieux -ieuse** *adj* infectious

**infection** *nf* infection; corruption; stink, stench

**inférer** *vt* (6) infer

**inférieur -e** *n* inferior; *adj* inferior; lower; poor

**infériorité** *nf* inferiority

**infernal** *adj* infernal; diabolical, devilish; *coll* bloody

**infertilité** *nf* infertility, barrenness

**infester** *vt* infest, overrun

**infidèle** *n* infidel; *adj* unfaithful, faithless; untrue, inaccurate; dishonest

**infiltrer (s')** *v refl* infiltrate, percolate, seep

**infime** *adj* infinitesimal, minute; low, mean

**infini** *nm* infinite; **à l'** ~ ad infinitum, without limit; *adj* infinite, boundless, unlimited, endless

**infiniment** *adv* infinitely; *coll* terribly, awfully; **je regrette** ~ I'm terribly sorry

**infinité** *nf* infinity

**infinitif** *nm* infinitive

**infirme** *n+adj* invalid, cripple(d), disabled (person); weak (person)

**infirmer** *vt* weaken, demonstrate the weakness of; *leg* annul, quash, invalidate

**infirmerie** *nf* infirmary, hospital, sick-room

**infirmier** *nm* male nurse, hospital attendant; *mil* medical orderly

**infirmière** *nf* nurse; ~ **en chef** matron

**infirmité** *nf* infirmity; disability

**inflammabilité** *nf* inflammability

**inflammable** *adj* inflammable, *US* flammable; excitable

**inflammation** *nf* inflammation; ignition; **point d'** ~ flashpoint

**inflammatoi:.e** *adj* inflammatory

**inflation** *nf* inflation; excessive growth

**inflationniste** *adj* inflationary

**infléchir** vt inflect, bend; gramm inflect; s' ~ bend, curve

**infléchissable** adj unbendable, rigid; inflexible

**infléchissement** nm modification, slight change

**inflexibilité** nf inflexibility

**infliger** vt (3) inflict, impose

**influençable** adj influenceable

**influence** nf authority, influence

**influencer** vt (4) influence, have an influence on, sway

**influent** adj influential

**influer** vi have an influence; ~ sur influence, have an effect on

**in-folio** nm + adj invar folio

**informateur -trice** n informant; informer

**informaticien -ienne** n computer scientist

**informatif -ive** adj informative

**information** nf leg investigation; ~ s information, news; rad news bulletin; agence d' ~ s news agency; leg ouvrir une ~ begin legal proceedings; mil service d' ~ s intelligence

**informatique** nf + adj data-processing

**informe** adj formless, shapeless; crude, unpolished

**informé** nm jusqu'à plus ample ~ pending further information

**informel -elle** adj informal

**informer** vt inform, tell; vi leg investigate; ~ contre lay information against; s' ~ make inquiries

**infortune** nf misfortune, trouble; tomber dans l' ~ fall on evil days

**infortuné** adj unfortunate, unlucky

**infraction** nf offence, infraction, infringement

**infranchissable** adj impassable; insuperable

**infrarouge** adj infra-red

**infréquenté** adj unfrequented

**infroissable** adj crease-resisting; wrinkle-proof

**infructueux -ueuse** adj unfruitful, barren; fruitless

**infus** adj infused; inborn; coll il croit avoir la science ~ e he thinks he knows it all

**infuser** vt infuse, steep in, instil; vi infuse; s' ~ infuse, draw (tea)

**ingambe** adj nimble, alert

**ingénier (s')** v refl strive, strain one's ingenuity

**ingénierie** nf engineering

**ingénieur** nm engineer; ~ conseil consulting engineer; ~ des ponts et chaussées government civil engineer; ~ du son recording engineer

**ingénieux -ieuse** adj ingenious, clever

**ingéniosité** nf ingenuity, ingeniousness

**ingénu** adj ingenious, artless, unsophisticated

**ingénue** nf theat ingenue

**ingénuité** nf ingenuousness, simplicity

**ingérence** nf interference, meddling

**ingérer** vt (6) med ingest, take (food) into the stomach; s' ~ interfere, meddle; s' ~ dans poke one's nose into

**ingouvernable** adj ungovernable, unruly, unmanageable

**ingrat -e** n ungrateful person; adj ungrateful; disagreeable; sterile; thankless; l'âge ~ the awkward age

**ingratitude** nf ingratitude; sterility; thanklessness

**inguérissable** adj incurable

**ingurgiter** vt swallow, gulp down, wolf

**inhabile** adj unpractised, unskilled; clumsy; leg incompetent

**inhabileté** nf lack of skill, clumsiness

**inhabilité** nf leg incompetence

**inhabitable** adj uninhabitable

**inhabité** adj uninhabited

**inhalateur** nm inhaler

**inhaler** vt inhale

**inharmonie** nf discordance

**inharmonieux -ieuse** adj discordant, inharmonious

**inhiber** vt inhibit

**inhospitalier -ière** adj inhospitable

**inhumain** adj inhuman

**inhumer** vt bury, inhume

**inimaginable** adj unimaginable

**inimitié** nf hostility, enmity

**inintelligence** nf lack of intelligence

**inintelligent** adj unintelligent

**inintelligible** adj unintelligible

**ininterrompu** adj uninterrupted, continuous

**inique** adj iniquitous

**iniquité** nf iniquity

**initiale** nf initial

**initiateur -trice** n initiator; adj initiating

**initiative** nf initiative; ~ privée private enterprise; syndicat d' ~ local tourist office

**initié -e** n initiate, someone in the know

**initier** vt initiate

**injecté** adj injected; bloodshot; congested

**injecter** vt inject; s' ~ become injected, bloodshot

**injonction** nf injunction, order

**injouable** adj unplayable; unactable

**injudicieux -ieuse** adj injudicious

**injure** nf insult; wrong; leg tort; ~ s abuse

**injurier** vt insult

**injurieux -ieuse** adj injurious, insulting, abusive

**injuste** adj unjust, unfair; unrighteous

**injustice** *nf* injustice, unfairness; unjust action

**injustifiable** *adj* unjustifiable

**injustifié** *adj* unjustified

**inlassable** *adj* tireless, indefatigable, untiring

**innavigable** *adj* unnavigable; unseaworthy

**inné** *adj* innate, inborn

**innocence** *nf* innocence, guiltlessness; artlessness; innocuousness

**innocent -e** *n* simple-minded person; innocent person; *adj* innocent, guiltless; simple, artless

**innocenter** *vt* prove innocent, clear; excuse

**innombrable** *adj* innumerable, countless

**innommable** *adj* unspeakable

**innom(m)é** *adj* unnamed, nameless

**innovateur -trice** *n* innovator; *adj* innovating

**innover** *vt* innovate

**inobservation** *nf* inobservance; non-compliance

**inobservé** *adj* unobserved, unnoticed; not complied with

**inoccupé** *adj* unoccupied, vacant; unemployed, idle

**inoculer** *vt* inoculate; instil into

**inodore** *adj* inodorous, odourless

**inoffensif -ive** *adj* inoffensive, harmless; innocuous

**inondable** *adj* liable to flooding

**inondation** *nf* inundation, flood

**inondé** *adj* inundated, flooded; overrun; ~ **de larmes** bathed in tears

**inonder** *vt* inundate, flood; overrun

**inopérant** *adj* inoperative

**inopiné** *adj* unexpected, unlooked-for

**inopportun** *adj* inopportune, ill-timed

**inorganique** *adj* inorganic

**inoubliable** *adj* unforgettable

**inouï** *adj* unheard of, unparalleled; outrageous

**inox** *nm* stainless steel

**inoxydable** *adj* inoxidizable, rustless; stainless (steel)

**inqualifiable** *adj* unqualifiable; unspeakable, infamous

**in-quarto** *nm* + *adj invar* quarto

**inquiet -iète** *adj* restless, uneasy; anxious, worried

**inquiétant** *adj* alarming, disquieting, disturbing

**inquiéter** *vt* worry, make anxious, disturb; s' ~ worry, become anxious

**inquiétude** *nf* restlessness; anxiety, disquiet, concern; **éprouver des ~ s** have qualms

¹**inquisiteur** *nm* inquisitor

²**inquisiteur -trice** *adj* inquisitorial

**insaisissable** *adj* impossible to seize; elusive; imperceptible; *leg* not distrainable

**insalissable** *adj* unsoilable

**insalubre** *adj* insalubrious, unhealthy

**insalubrité** *nf* insalubrity, unhealthiness

**insanité** *nf* insanity, lunacy; insane action

**insatiable** *adj* insatiable, unquenchable

**insatisfait** *adj* unsatisfied

**inscription** *nf* inscription; entry, registration, enrolment; **droits d'** ~ registration fee; **feuille d'** ~ entry form

**inscrire** *vt* (42) inscribe, write down; register, enter; s' ~ , se faire ~ enter, put one's name down

**inscrit** *adj* enrolled, registered

**insecte** *nm* insect

**insécurité** *nf* insecurity

**insensé -e** *n* madman (-woman); *adj* mad, insane; foolish, crazy

**insensibiliser** *vt* anaesthetize

**insensibilité** *nf* insensibility, unconsciousness; insensitiveness; indifference

**insensible** *adj* insensible; insentient, numb; imperceptible; indifferent

**inséparable** *nm* orni love-bird; *adj* inseparable

**insérer** *vt* (6) insert

**insertion** *nf* insertion; assimilation, integration

**inserviable** *adj* disobliging

**insidieux -ieuse** *adj* insidious

**insigne** *nm* sign, badge; ~ **s** insignia; *adj* distinguished, noteworthy; notorious, arrant

**insignifiance** *nf* insignificance

**insignifiant** *adj* insignificant, trivial; vacuous

**insinuant** *adj* insinuating, smooth, ingratiating

**insinuer** *vt* insinuate, imply, hint at; insert; s' ~ insinuate oneself, creep

**insipide** *adj* insipid, tasteless; dull, tame

**insipidité** *nf* insipidity, tastelessness

**insistance** *nf* emphasis, insistence

**insister** *vi* insist, stress; persist, press the point; ~ **auprès de qn** make strong representations to s/o

**insobriété** *nf* insobriety; interference

**insociable** *adj* unsociable

**insolation** *nf* sunstroke

**insolence** *nf* insolence, impudence, impertinence; insolent remark

**insolent** *adj* insolent, impudent; arrogant, haughty

**insolite** *adj* unwonted; unexpected

**insoluble** *adj* insoluble, unsolvable

**insolvabilité** *nf* insolvency

**insolvable** *adj* insolvent

**insomnie** *nf* insomnia, sleeplessness

**insondable** *adj* unsoundable, unfathomable

**insonore** *adj* sound-proof; sound-deadening

**insonorisation** *nf* sound-proofing

**insonoriser** *vt* sound-proof, insulate

**insouciance** *nf* unconcern, heedlessness

**insouciant** *adj* unconcerned, heedless

**insoucieux -ieuse** *adj* unmindful, careless

**insoumis** *nm mil* absentee, defaulter, *US* draft dodger; *adj* unsubdued; unsubmissive, unruly, insubordinate; *mil* absent, defaulting

**insoumission** *nf* unsubmissiveness, insubordination; *mil* defaulting

**insoupçonnable** *adj* above suspicion

**insoupçonné** *adj* unsuspected

**insoutenable** *adj* untenable, indefensible; unbearable, unendurable

**inspecter** *vt* inspect, survey, examine

**inspecteur -trice** *n* inspector, inspectress, detective-inspector; ~ **d'Académie** inspector of schools ( = H.M.I.); ~ **des contributions directes** inspector of taxes; ~ **sanitaire** public health officer; ~ **du travail** factory inspector

**inspection** *nf* examination, inspection, survey; inspectorate

**inspirateur -trice** *n* inspirer, source of inspiration; *adj* inspiring; *med* inspiratory

**inspiration** *nf* inspiration, impulse; *med* inspiration, inhaling; **sous l'** ~ **du moment** on the spur of the moment

**inspirer** *vt* inspire, encourage, prompt; *vi med* inspire, inhale; **s'** ~ **de** draw one's inspiration from, imitate

**instabilité** *nf* instability, shakiness; inconstancy

**instable** *adj* unstable, shaky, inconstant

**installation** *nf* installation, fitting up; plant, equipment; fittings, appointments; *eccles* induction

**installer** *vt* install, fit up; equip; *eccles* install, induct; **s'** ~ settle down

**instamment** *adv* insistently, urgently

**instance** *nf* instancy, solicitation; *leg* suit; ~ **s** entreaties; **en** ~ **de départ** on the point of departure; **en** ~ **de divorce** in the process of getting a divorce; *leg* **introduire une** ~ start proceedings; **tribunal de première** ~ court of first instance, lower court

**instant** *nm* instant, moment; **à l'** ~ just now, a moment ago; at once, immediately; **un** ~ ! wait a moment!; *coll* hang on!; *adj* instant, urgent

**instantané** *nm* snap(shot); *adj* instantaneous, sudden

**instar (à l'** ~ **de)** *prep phr* after the manner of, like, in imitation of

**instaurateur -trice** *n* founder

**instauration** *nf* founding, establishing

**instaurer** *vt* found, establish

**instigateur -trice** *n* instigator

**instiller** *vt* instil

**instinctif -ive** *adj* instinctive

**instituer** *vt* institute, found, establish

**institut** *nm* institute, institution; ~ **de beauté** beauty parlour

**instituteur** *nm* teacher (in primary school); founder

**institution** *nf* institution, founding; private school, academy

**institutrice** *nf* teacher (in primary school); governess; foundress

**instructeur -trice** *n* instructor; *nm mil* (drill-)instructor

**instructif -ive** *adj* instructive

**instruction** *nf* instruction; education, schooling; *mil* training; *leg* preliminary investigation of a case; **avoir de l'** ~ be educated; *leg* **juge d'** ~ examining magistrate; **sans** ~ uneducated

**instruire** *vt* (80) instruct, teach; inform; *mil* train, drill; *leg* examine; **s'** ~ educate oneself

**instruit** *adj* educated, well-read; *mil* trained

**instrument** *nm* instrument; implement

**instrumenter** *vt mus* score; *vi leg* draw up a deed, take legal proceedings

**instrumentiste** *n* instrumentalist

**insu** *nm* ignorance; **à l'** ~ **de** without the knowledge of; **à son** ~ without his knowledge

**insubordonné** *adj* insubordinate

**insubstantiel -ielle** *adj* insubstantial

**insuccès** *nm* lack of success; failure

**insuffisance** *nf* insufficiency, inadequacy; shortage; incompetence

**insuffisant** *adj* insufficient, inadequate; incapable, incompetent

**insufflateur** *nm* throat-spray, nose-spray

**insuffler** *vt* insufflate, blow air into, inflate; *med* spray.

**insulaire** *n* islander; *adj* insular

**insularité** *nf* insularity

**insuline** *nf* insulin

**insultant** *adj* insulting, offensive

**insulte** *nf* insult; **faire** ~ **à** insult

**insulter** *vt* insult, offend; *vi* ~ **à** jeer at, give insult to

**insupportable** *adj* unbearable, intolerable, insufferable

**insurgé -e** *n* insurgent, rebel

**insurger (s')** *v refl* (3) rise, revolt

**insurmontable** *adj* insurmontable, insuperable

**intact** *adj* intact, undamaged, whole; unblemished

**intaille** *nf* intaglio

**intangibilité** *nf* intangibility

**intarissable** *adj* inexhaustible, unfailing, perennial

**intégral** *adj* integral, full, complete; *math* **calcul** ~ integral calculus; **édition** ~ **e** unexpurgated edition; complete edition

**intégrale** *nf math* integral; complete works

**intégralité** *nf* integrality, completeness

**intégrant** *adj* integrant, integral; **partie** ~ **e** integral part

**intègre** *adj* honest, upright

**intégrer** *vt* (6) integrate; **s'** ~ join, combine

**intégrité** *nf* integrity, uprightness; completeness, entirety

**intellectuel -uelle** *n* intellectual, highbrow, *US coll* egg-head; *adj* intellectual, mental

**intelligence** *nf* intelligence, intellect; comprehension, understanding; intercourse; conspiring; ~ **s** communications, dealings; **avoir une bonne** ~ **des affaires** have a good grasp of business; **d'** ~ **avec** in collusion with; **en bonne** ~ **avec** on good terms with

**intelligent** *adj* intelligent, clever, brainy

**intelligibilité** *nf* intelligibility

**intelligible** *adj* intelligible, clear, understandable

**intempérant** *adj* intemperate

**intempéré** *adj* immoderate

**intempérie** *nf* inclemency; ~ **s** bad weather

**intempestif -ive** *adj* untimely, inopportune

**intendance** *nf* intendance, administration, management; *mil* commissariat, supply services

**intendant -e** *n* manager; (school) bursar; *nm hist* intendant

**intense** *adj* intense, severe; deep (colour); intensive; strong

**intensif -ive** *adj* intensive

**intensifier** *vt* intensify

**intensité** *nf* intensity; depth (colour); strength

**intenter** *vt leg* bring; ~ **un procès contre** bring an action against, sue

**intention** *nf* intention, purpose; will, wish; *leg* intent; ~ **arrêtée de** determination to; **à l'** ~ **de** destined for, for the sake of; **à son** ~ for him; **avec** ~ on purpose; **dans l'** ~ **de** with a view to; **sans** ~ unintentionally

**intentionné** *adj* **bien** ~ well-intentioned; **mal** ~ ill-intentioned

**intentionnel -elle** *adj* intentional, deliberate

**inter** *nm tel* trunk call, long-distance call; *sp* inside-forward

**interagir** *vi* interact

**interallié** *adj* allied

**intercalaire** *nm* guide-card (card-index); *adj* intercalated, interpolated; intercalary

**intercaler** *vt* intercalate, insert

**intercéder** *vi* (6) intercede, plead

**intercepter** *vt* intercept; cut off

**intercesseur** *nm* intercessor; mediator

**interdiction** *nf* interdiction, prohibition; *leg* injunction; ~ **de séjour** ban on residence (in a specified area)

**interdire** *vt* (74) forbid, prohibit, ban; amaze, disconcert; *leg* interdict, veto; ~ **qn de ses fonctions** suspend s/o from his functions

**interdisciplinaire** *adj* interdisciplinary

**interdit** *nm* interdict; *adj* forbidden, prohibited, banned; amazed, speechless, disconcerted; *leg* under restraint; ~ **de séjour** banned from residing (in a specified area)

**intéressant** *adj* interesting; attractive, satisfactory; **être dans un état** ~ be in the family way

**intéressé** *adj* interested; concerned, involved; self-interested, calculating; **amour** ~ cupboard love

**intéresser** *vt* interest, affect, concern; ~ **qn dans une affaire** give s/o an interest in a business; **s'** ~ **à** be interested in, have an interest in, concern oneself with

**intérêt** *nm* interest; advantage, benefit; attraction, charm; concern; *comm* interest, share; ~ **composé** compound interest; **à** ~ **s** interest-bearing; **avoir** ~ **à** be well advised to; **avoir un** ~ **au jeu** have a stake in the game; **il y a** ~ **à** it is desirable to; **ligne d'** ~ **local** branch line; **porter** ~ **à qn** take an interest in s/o; **sans** ~ dull, boring

**interfolier** *vt* interleave

**intérieur** *nm* interior, inside; home; household affairs; *pol* interior; **à l'** ~ inside; **d'** ~ indoor; **femme d'** ~ home-loving woman; **ministère de l'Intérieur** = Home Office; *adj* interior, inner, inside; inward, spiritual; domestic

**intérim** *nm* interim; **assurer l'** ~ carry on (during vacancy or absence); **par** ~ acting, deputizing

**intérimaire** *n* deputy, locum tenens; *adj* temporary, interim, provisional

**interjection** *nf gramm* interjection; *leg* lodging (appeal)

**interjeter** *vt* (5) interject, insert (remark); *leg* lodge (appeal)

**interligne** *nm* space between the lines; **double** ~ double spacing

**interligner** *vt* interline, write between the lines of

**interlocuteur -trice** *n* interlocutor

**interlocutoire** *nm leg* interlocutory judgement; *adj* interlocutory, provisional

**interlope** *nm naut* blockade-runner, interloper; *adj naut* illegal, unauthorized; shady, suspect

**interloquer** *vt* disconcert, take aback; *leg* grant an interlocutory decree; s' ~ be disconcerted, be overcome by shyness

**intermède** *nm* medium, intermediary; *theat* interlude

**intermédiaire** *nm* intermediary, medium, go-between; *comm* middleman, agent; **par l' ~ de** through the medium of; *adj* intermediate, intermediary

**intermittence** *nf* intermittence; **par ~** intermittently

**intermittent** *adj* intermittent, occasional; *med* irregular (pulse)

**internat** *nm* boarding-school; boarding, living-in; *med* post of house-man, *US* internship

**interne** *n* boarder; *med* house-man, *US* intern

**internement** *nm* internment, confinement

**interner** *vt* intern, confine

**internissable** *adj* untarnishable

**interpellateur -trice** *n* interpellant, questioner

**interpellation** *nf* interpellation; (peremptory) questioning; question (in Parliament); *mil* challenge

**interpeller** *vt* question (peremptorily); put a question to (a Minister in Parliament); *mil* challenge

**interphone** *nm* intercom, *US* interphone

**interplanétaire** *adj* interplanetary, space (travel)

**interpoler** *vt* interpolate

**interposer** *vt* interpose; **par personne interposée** through an intermediary; s' ~ interpose oneself, intervene

**interposition** *nf* interposition; intervention

**interprétation** *nf* interpretation, explanation; *theat* + *mus* rendering, performance

**interprète** *n* interpreter; one who explains, expounds; *theat* + *mus* performer

**interpréter** *vt* (6) interpret; explain, expound; *theat* + *mus* perform

**interrègne** *nm* interregnum

**interrogateur -trice** *n* interrogator; *adj* interrogatory, questioning

**interrogatif -ive** *adj* interrogative

**interrogation** *nf* interrogation; **point d' ~** question-mark

**interrogatoire** *nm leg* examination, questioning; **contre- ~** cross-examination

**interroger** *vt* (3) interrogate, examine, question; consult

**interrompre** *vt* (85) interrupt, intercept; break off, suspend; break (journey); *elect* break off, cut off, switch off (current); s' ~ break off, stop (speaking)

**interrupteur -trice** *n* interrupter; *nm elect* switch, contact-breaker; *adj* interrupting

**interruption** *nf* interruption, interception; stoppage, suspension; *elect* breaking, cutting, switching off (current)

**interurbain** *adj* interurban; *tel* trunk

**intervalle** *nm* interval, gap, space; period (time); **dans l' ~** in the meantime; **par ~ s** now and then

**intervenir** *vi* (96) intervene, interfere, step in; happen, take place, arise; **faire ~** call in; *v impers* **il intervint un compromis** a compromise was made

**intervention** *nf* intervention, interference; *med* operation

**interversion** *nf* inversion, transposition

**intervertir** *vt* invert, transpose

**interviewer** *vt* interview

**intervieweur** *n* interviewer

**intestat** *adj invar* intestate

**intestin** *nm* intestine, bowel; ~ **grêle** small intestine; **gros ~** large intestine; *adj* intestine

**intimation** *nf* intimation, notification

**intime** *n* intimate, close friend; *adj* intimate, close; interior, innermost; cosy; homely

**intimé -e** *n* respondent

**intimer** *vt* intimate, notify; *leg* summons

**intimidant** *adj* intimidating

**intimidateur -trice** *n* intimidator; *adj* intimidating, intimidatory

**intimider** *vt* intimidate, threaten; s' ~ become nervous, shy

**intimité** *nf* intimacy, familiarity; innermost part; **dans l' ~** in private

**intitulé** *nm* heading (chapter), title (book)

**intituler** *vt* entitle, give a title to; s' ~ call oneself

**intonation** *nf* intonation; *mus* pitch, modulation

**intox(e)** *nf pol* indoctrination

**intoxicant** *adj* poisonous, toxic

**intoxication** *nf* intoxication; *pol* indoctrination

**intoxiquer** *vt* poison; *pol* indoctrinate

**intraduisible** *adj* untranslatable

**intraitable** *adj* intractable, obstinate, uncompromising; *med* untreatable

**intransigeance** *nf* intransigence; strictness

**intransigeant -e** *n* die-hard; *adj* intransigent, uncompromising; strict

**intransitif -ive** *adj* intransitive

**intraveineux -euse** *adj* intravenous

**intrépide** *adj* intrepid, bold, dauntless; **menteur ~** brazen, bare-faced liar

**intrépidité** *nf* intrepidity, boldness, dauntlessness

**intrigant -e** *n* intriguer; *adj* intriguing, scheming

**intrigue** *nf* intrigue, plot, scheme; love-affair; *theat* plot

**intriguer** *vt* puzzle, intrigue, make curious; *vi* intrigue, scheme, plot

**intrinsèque** *adj* intrinsic

**introducteur -trice** *n* introducer

**introductif -ive** *adj* introductory

**introduction** *nf* introduction, introducing, bringing in; insertion; preface, foreword

**introduire** *vt* (80) introduce, bring in, usher in; insert; **s' ~** get in, penetrate

**intronisation** *nf* enthronement; establishment

**introniser** *vt* enthrone; establish, set up; **s' ~** become established; establish oneself

**introspectif -ive** *adj* introspective

**introuvable** *adj* undiscoverable

**introverti -e** *n* introvert; *adj* introverted

**intrus -e** *n* intruder; *coll* gatecrasher; *leg* trespasser; *adj* intruding

**intuitif -ive** *adj* intuitive

**inusable** *adj* hard-wearing, long-lasting

**inusité** *adj* unusual, uncommon; not in use (word, phrase)

**inutile** *adj* useless, unavailing, vain; **~ de dire** needless to say; **c'est ~** it's no use, don't bother

**inutilisable** *adj* unusable

**inutilisé** *adj* unused

**inutilité** *nf* inutility, uselessness; useless thing

**invaincu** *adj* unconquered

**invalide** *n* invalid; disabled person; *mil* pensioner

**invalider** *vt* invalidate, quash (election, will)

**invalidité** *nf* infirmity, disablement; *leg* invalidity

**invariabilité** *nf* invariability

**invariable** *adj* invariable; *math* constant

**invectiver** *vt* abuse, rail at; *vi* **~ contre** rail against, inveigh against

**invendable** *adj* unsaleable

**invendu** *adj* unsold

**inventaire** *nm* inventory, list of stock; **faire son ~** take stock

**inventer** *vt* invent, contrive, make up; *coll* **il n'a pas inventé la poudre** he'll never set the Thames on fire

**inventeur -trice** *n* inventor; *adj* inventive

**inventif -ive** *adj* inventive

**invention** *nf* invention, device, discovery; fabrication, lie

**inventorier** *vt* inventory, take stock

**invérifiable** *adj* unverifiable

**invérifié** *adj* unverified, unchecked

**inversable** *adj* uncapsizable

**inverse** *nm* inverse, opposite, reverse; **à l' ~ de** contrary to; *adj* inverse, inverted, opposite

**inverser** *vt* reverse, invert; *elect* reverse

**inverseur** *nm* reversing-device; *elect* change-over switch

**inversion** *nf* *gramm* + *math* inversion; sexual inversion; *elect* reversal (current)

**invertébré** *adj* invertebrate

**inverti -e** *n* (sexual) invert

**invertir** *vt* invert, reverse; *elect* reverse (current)

**investigateur -trice** *n* investigator; *adj* investigating, searching

**investir** *vt* invest, bestow; *comm* invest; *mil* invest, beleaguer; **investi de l'autorité** vested with power

**investisseur** *nm* investor

**invétéré** *adj* inveterate, deep-rooted; confirmed

**invétérer (s')** *v refl* (6) become inveterate, become deep-rooted

**invincibilité** *nf* invincibility

**inviolabilité** *nf* inviolability

**inviolé** *adj* inviolate

**invisibilité** *nf* invisibility

**invitation** *nf* invitation; **sans ~** uninvited

**invite** *nf* lead (cards), call (bridge); incitement; **répondre à l' ~ de qn** return s/o's lead

**invité -e** *n* guest

**inviter** *vt* invite, ask; call (cards)

**invivable** *adj* *coll* unbearable, impossible to live with

**invocatoire** *adj* invocatory

**involontaire** *adj* involuntary, unintentional

**invoquer** *vt* invoke, call upon; refer to, put forward, cite

**invraisemblable** *adj* unlikely, improbable, hard to credit

**invraisemblance** *nf* unlikelihood, improbability

**invulnérabilité** *nf* invulnerability

**iode** *nm* iodine; **teinture d' ~** tincture of iodine

**ionique** *adj* *archi* ionic

**iota** *nm* iota; *coll* jot, whit, tittle

**iouler** *vi* yodel

**irascibilité** *nf* irascibility, temper, testiness

**irascible** *adj* irascible, irritable, testy
**iris** *nm* iris (eye); prismatic halo; *bot* iris, flag
**irisation** *nf* irisation, iridescence
**irisé** *adj* iridescent
**iriser** *vt* make iridescent; **s'~** become iridescent
**Irlandais -e** *n* Irishman (-woman)
**irlandais** *nm* Irish, Erse (language); *adj* Irish
**Irlande** *nf* Ireland
**ironie** *nf* irony
**ironique** *adj* ironic, ironical
**ironiser** *vi* speak ironically, use irony
**ironiste** *n* ironist
**irradier** *vi* irradiate, radiate, spread
**irraisonnable** *adj* irrational
**irraisonné** *adj* unreasoned
**irrationnel -elle** *adj* irrational
**irréalisable** *adj* unrealizable
**irrecevable** *adj* inadmissible; unacceptable
**irrécouvrable** *adj* irrecoverable, unrecoverable; **créance ~** bad debt
**irrécupérable** *adj* irretrievable; beyond salvation
**irrécusable** *adj* irrecusable, unimpeachable
**irréductible** *adj* indomitable, unshakeable; *math + med* irreducible
**irréel -elle** *adj* unreal
**irréfléchi** *adj* rash, unconsidered, hasty
**irréflexion** *nf* thoughtlessness
**irréformable** *adj* unalterable
**irréfuté** *adj* unrefuted
**irrégularité** *nf* irregularity; unevenness; unpunctuality
**irrégulier -ière** *adj* irregular; uneven; unpunctual
**irréligieux -ieuse** *adj* irreligious
**irrémédiable** *adj* irremediable, irreparable
**irremplaçable** *adj* irreplaceable
**irréparable** *adj* irreparable; irretrievable
**irréprochable** *adj* irreproachable, faultless
**irrésolu** *adj* irresolute, wavering; unsolved
**irrespect** *nm* disrespect
**irrespectueux -euse** *adj* disrespectful
**irrespirable** *adj* irrespirable, unbreathable
**irresponsabilité** *nf* irresponsibility
**irresponsable** *adj* irresponsible
**irrétrécissable** *adj* unshrinkable
**irrévérencieux -ieuse** *adj* irreverent, disrespectful
**irrigateur** *nm* hose; *med* enema
**irriguer** *vt* irrigate
**irritable** *adj* irritable, sensitive

**irritant** *nm* irritant; *adj* irritating
**irriter** *vt* irritate; **s'~** grow angry; become inflamed
**irruption** *nf* irruption, invasion; overflowing (river); **faire ~ dans** burst into
**islamique** *adj* Islamic
**Islandais -e** *n* Icelander
**islandais** *nm* Icelandic (language); *adj* Icelandic
**Islande** *nf* Iceland
**isobare** *nf* isobar; *adj* isobaric
**isocèle** *adj* isosceles
**isolant** *nm* *elect* insulator; *adj* isolating; insulating; **bouteille ~e** thermos flask; *archi* **couche ~e** damp-course; *elect* **ruban ~** insulating tape
**¹isolateur** *nm* *elect* insulator
**²isolateur -trice** *adj* insulating
**isolé** *adj* isolated, detached, lonely; *elect* insulated
**isolement** *nm* isolation, loneliness; *elect* insulation
**isolément** *adv* separately, individually, singly
**isoler** *vt* isolate, detach; *elect* insulate; **s'~** cut oneself off
**isoloir** *nm* polling-booth; *elect* insulator
**Israélien -ienne** *n* Israeli
**israélien -ienne** *adj* Israeli
**Israélite** *n* Israelite, Jew
**israélite** *adj* Israelite, Jewish
**issu** *adj* descended, born
**issue** *nf* result, upshot, issue; exit, way out; **à l'~ de** at the end of; **chemin sans ~** dead-end, cul-de-sac; **situation sans ~** dead-lock
**isthme** *nm* isthmus
**Italie** *nf* Italy
**Italien -ienne** *n* Italian
**italien** *nm* Italian (language); *adj* (*f* -ienne) Italian
**italique** *nm* *typ* italic, italics; *adj* Italic (race)
**item** *adv* ditto, item
**itératif -ive** *adj* *leg* reiterated; *gramm* iterative
**itinéraire** *nm* itinerary, route; guide-book; *adj* itinerary
**itou** *adv* *sl* also, too
**ivoire** *nm* ivory; object made of ivory
**ivoirerie** *nf* ivory trade; ivory work
**ivoirin** *adj* ivory
**ivraie** *nf* *bot* darnel, tare; *bibl* tare
**ivre** *adj* drunk, intoxicated
**ivresse** *nf* drunkenness, intoxication; rapture, ecstasy; *leg* **en état d'~ publique** drunk and disorderly
**ivrogne -esse** *n* drunkard; *coll* boozer, pub-crawler; *adj* drunken
**ivrognerie** *nf* drunkenness

# J

**jabot** *nm* frill, ruffle, jabot; crop (bird); *coll* belly; **se remplir le ~** have a good tuck-in

**jaboter** *vi coll* jabber, chatter

**jacasse** *nf* magpie; *coll* chatterbox (woman)

**jacasser** *vi coll* jabber, chatter

**jacasserie** *nf coll* gossip, idle chatter

**jachère** *nf* fallow, unploughed land

**jacinthe** *nf* hyacinth; **~ des bois, sauvage** bluebell

**jacquerie** *nf hist* peasant rising, peasants' revolt

**Jacques** *nm* James; **Maître ~** Jack-of-all-trades, factotum

**jacquet** *nm* backgammon; backgammon board

**Jacquot** *nm* Jim, Jimmy; Poll (parrot)

**jactance** *nf* boastfulness, bragging

**jadis** *adv* formerly, of old, once upon a time

**jaillir** *vi* gush out, spout, spurt (liquids); shoot out (flames); fly (sparks); *fig* burst forth

**jaillissant** *adj* gushing, spouting; flying; **puits ~** (oil) gusher

**jaillissement** *nm* gushing out; gush, spurt; shooting out; *elect* flash, sparking

**jais** *nm* jet; **noir comme du ~** jet-black

**jalon** *nm* surveyor's staff, levelling-rod, pole; plan, preparation; **poser des ~s** prepare the way, blaze the trail

**jalonnement** *nm* marking out, staking out

**jalonner** *vt* mark out, stake out

**jalouser** *vt* envy, be jealous of

¹**jalousie** *nf* jealousy

²**jalousie** *nf* Venetian blind

³**jalousie** *nf* sweet-william

**jaloux -ouse** *adj* jealous, envious, watchful, careful; **~ de** anxious to

**Jamaïque** *nf* Jamaica

**jamais** *adv* ever (positive); never (negative); **~ de la vie!** never!, out of the question!; **ne ... ~** never

**jambage** *nm* down-stroke (writing); *archi* jamb; foundation-wall

**jambe** *nf* leg; *archi* strut, stay; *coll* **ça vous fera une belle ~!** a lot of good that'll do you!; *coll* **par dessous la ~** carelessly, perfunctorily; *coll* **prendre ses ~s à son cou** take to one's heels; **s'enfuir à toutes ~s** run away as fast as possible; *coll* **tirer dans les ~s de qn**

play a mean trick on s/o

**jambé** *adj* **bien ~** with good, well-shaped legs

**jambière** *nf mil* gaiter; *med* (elastic) stocking; *sp* shin-pad

**jambon** *nm* ham; **~ de Bayonne =** Parma ham

**jambonneau** *nm* knuckle of ham

**jante** *nf* rim

**janvier** *nm* January

**Japon** *nm* Japan

**japon** *nm* Japanese vellum; Japanese porcelain

**Japonais -e** *n* Japanese

**japonais** *nm lang* Japanese; *adj* Japanese

**japonerie** *nf* Japanese curio

**jappement** *nm* yelping, yapping

**japper** *vi* yelp, yap

**jaquette** *nf* jacket (woman); morning coat (man); dust-cover

**jardin** *nm* garden; **~ d'acclimatation** zoo; **~ d'enfants** kindergarten, nursery school; **~ potager** kitchen garden; *theat* **côté ~** prompt-side, stage right

¹**jardinage** *nm* gardening; garden produce

²**jardinage** *nm* flaw (diamond)

**jardiner** *vi* garden

**jardinet** *nm* small garden

**jardinier -ière** *n* gardener; *adj* horticultural

¹**jardinière** *nf* **~ d'enfants** kindergarten teacher

²**jardinière** *nf* flower-stand; hand-cart; *cul* mixed vegetables; vegetable soup

**jargon** *nm* jargon; cant, slang; **~ administratif** officialese; *coll* lingo

**jargonner** *vi* talk jargon

**Jarnac** *nm* **coup de ~** treacherous blow

**jarre** *nf* earthenware jar

**jarret** *nm* back of the knee; hock (horse); *cul* **~ de bœuf** shin of beef; **~ de veau** knuckle of veal; *coll* **avoir du ~** be strong in the legs; **couper le ~ à** hamstring

**jarretelle** *nf* suspender, *US* garter

**jarretière** *nf* garter

**jars** *nm* gander

**jaser** *vi* chatter, natter; gossip; twitter, cackle; *coll* blab, blow the gaff

**jaseur -euse** *n* chatterbox, gossip; *adj* chattering, talkative, gossiping

**jasmin** *nm* jasmine

**jaspe** *nm* jasper; marbling (bookbinding)

**jasper** *vt* marble, mottle

**jaspure** *nf* marbling

**jatte** *nf* bowl, basin

**jauge** *nf* gauge; *mot* petrol-gauge, *US* gasoline-gauge; dipstick; *naut* tonnage

**jauger** *vt* (3) gauge, measure; *fig* size up; *vi naut* draw; *naut* ~ **5.000 tonnes** be of 5,000 tons burden

**jaugeur** *nm* gauger

**jaunâtre** *adj* yellowish

**jaune** *nm* man (woman) of yellow race; *nm* yellow (colour); *coll* black-leg, scab, strike-breaker; ~ **d'œuf** yolk of egg; *adj* yellow; sallow; brown (shoes); **feu** ~ amber light; *pol* **livre** ~ = blue book; *adv* **rire** ~ give a sickly smile

**jaunir** *vi* turn yellow; fade; *vt* make yellow

**jaunisse** *nf* jaundice

**javel** *nf* **eau de** ~ bleach, bleaching-water

**javelot** *nm* javelin

**je** *pron* I

**Jean** *nm* John

**jean** *nm* jeans

**Jeanne** *nf* Jane, Joan, Jean

**Jeannette** *nf* Janet, Jenny

**¹jeannette** *nf* sleeve-board

**²jeannette** *nf* Brownie

**je-m'en-foutisme** *nm coll* indifference, couldn't-care-less attitude

**je-ne-sais-quoi** *nm invar* an indefinable something

**jérémiade** *nf coll* Jeremiad, lamentation

**jersey** *nm* jersey; stockinet

**jésuite** *nm* Jesuit; hypocrite; *adj coll* Jesuitical, hypocritical

**jésuitique** *adj* Jesuitical, plausible, specious

**Jésus** *nm* Jesus; **avant** ~ **Christ** B.C.

**jésus** *adj* imperial (paper format)

**jet** *nm* throwing, casting; throw; jet, gush, stream; burst, flush; *bot* shoot (plant); *naut* jettisoning; spout, nozzle; ~ **d'eau** fountain; **à un** ~ **de pierre** at a stone's throw from; **d'un seul** ~ at one go; **premier** ~ first attempt, rough sketch

**jeté** *nm* over (knitting)

**jetée** *nf* jetty, pier; breakwater

**jeter** *vt* (5) throw, cast, fling, throw away, jettison; drop (anchor); lay (foundations); utter, let out; *med* discharge; ~ **un sort** cast a spell; **le dé en est jeté** the die is cast; **se** ~ throw oneself, rush; flow (river); **se** ~ **au cou de qn** fall on s/o's neck; **elle s'est jetée à sa tête** she threw herself at him

**jeton** *nm* counter, token; *coll* **c'est un faux** ~ he's a bit of a crook

**jeu** *nm* game, play, sport; gambling, gaming; stake; *theat* acting; *mus* playing; (organ-)stop; set (chess); pack (cards); slack, looseness, play; ~ **d'adresse** sleight of hand; ~ **de fiches** card-index; ~ **de lumière** lighting effect; ~ **de mots** play on words; *theat* ~ **de scène** business; ~ **de société** parlourgame; ~ **d'esprit** witticism; *coll* crack; ~ **d'orgues** organ stop; *theat* switchboard; **avoir du** ~ be loose, slack; **double** ~ double-cross; **faire le** ~ **de qn** play into s/o's hands; **faites vos** ~ **x!** place your bets!; *sp* **hors** ~ out of play; off-side; **jouer franc** ~ play fair; **jouer gros** ~ play for high stakes; **mettre qch en** ~ call sth into play; **vieux** ~ old-fashioned; **y aller franc** ~ go right ahead

**jeudi** *nm* Thursday; ~ **saint** Maundy Thursday; *coll* **la semaine des quatre** ~ **s** a month of Sundays

**jeun (à)** *adv phr* fasting; on an empty stomach; sober

**jeune** *n* young person, young man, young girl; *adj* young, youthful; immature, callow; *theat* ~ **premier** juvenile lead; ~ **première** leading lady

**jeûne** *nm* fast, fasting

**jeûner** *vi* fast

**jeunesse** *nf* youth, boyhood, girlhood; young people; *coll* girl; **il faut que** ~ **se passe** youth will have its fling

**jeunet -ette** *adj* youngish

**joaillerie** *nf* jewellery; jeweller's trade

**joaillier -ière** *n* jeweller

**jobard** *nm coll* simpleton, mug, dupe

**jobarder** *vt coll* dupe, fool, take (s/o) in

**jobardise** *nf coll* gullibility

**jocrisse** *nm* clown; *coll* mug, simpleton

**joie** *nf* joy, gladness, enjoyment, delight; mirth, merriment; **à cœur** ~ to one's heart's content; **faire la** ~ **de qn** make s/o happy; **feu de** ~ bonfire; *coll* **fille de** ~ whore, tart

**joignant** *adj* next, adjoining; *prep* next to, adjoining

**joindre** *vt* (55) join, unite, combine; add; adjoin, be adjacent to; meet, come into contact with; enclose; clasp (hands); *eng* weld; **se** ~ join, unite; be adjacent, contiguous

**joint** *nm* join, joint; *coll* solution, way out; *mot* ~ **de culasse** gasket; *coll* **trouver le** ~ find the way; *adj* joined, united, combined; added; **ci**— ~ attached, enclosed; **pièces ci**— ~ **es** enclosures

**jointé** *adj* jointed

**jointement** *nm* jointing

**jointoyer** *vt* (7) point (brickwork)

**jointure** *nf* joint; ~ **des doigts** knuckles

**joli** *nm coll* **c'est du** ~ ! that's a fine mess!; **le** ~ **de l'affaire** the best of it; *adj* pretty, good-looking, nice; *coll* considerable, fair, tidy; **une** ~ **e somme** a tidy sum

# joliment

**joliment** *adv* prettily, nicely; *coll* awfully, terribly; **vous avez ~ raison** how right you are

**jonc** *nm bot* rush; **~ marin** furze; **canne de ~** Malacca cane

**jonchée** *nf* scattering, strewing

**joncher** *vt* strew, litter

**jonction** *nf* junction, joining

**jongler** *vi* juggle

**jonglerie** *nf* juggling; trickery

**jongleur** *nm* juggler; charlatan; *lit* jongleur, minstrel

**jonque** *nf naut* junk

**jonquille** *nf* daffodil; *adj invar* pale yellow

**Jordanie** *nf* Jordan

**jouable** *adj* playable

**joue** *nf* cheek, side; **mettre en ~** aim at (with rifle, gun)

**jouer** *vt* play; stake, gamble, back; *theat* act, play part; look like, imitate, pretend to be; risk; *coll* fool, trick; *mus* play, perform; **~ pique** play, lead, spades; **~ un cheval gagnant et placé** back a horse each way; **il joue le malheureux** he is pretending to be unhappy; *vi* play (games etc); *mus+theat* play; gamble, speculate; come into play, work; be loose, have (too much) play; be operative (law, etc); **~ à la baisse** bear; **~ à la hausse** bull; *coll* **~ de la fourchette** tuck in; **~ de malheur** have a run of bad luck; **~ la comédie** play a part, put on an act; **faire ~** set going, start; **faire qch en se jouant** make child's play of sth; **se ~ de** deceive; make light of, deride

**jouet** *nm* toy, plaything

**joueur -euse** *n* player; performer; gambler; speculator; **beau (mauvais) ~** good (bad) loser; *adj* fond of gambling; playful

**joufflu** *adj* chubby

**joug** *nm* yoke (oxen); yoke, influence

**jouir** *vi* enjoy; have an orgasm, *coll* come; **~ de** enjoy possession of, own

**jouissance** *nf* enjoyment, delight, pleasure; orgasm, sexual pleasure; *leg* possession, enjoyment; **à vendre avec ~ immédiate** for sale with vacant possession

**jouisseur -euse** *n* sensualist, pleasure-seeker; *adj* sensual

**joujou** *nm coll* toy, plaything

**jour** *nm* day; daylight, light; aspect, light; opening, crack; **~s** days, life; **~ de l'An** New Year's Day; **~ des Rois** Twelfth Night; *mil* **~ J** D-Day; **à ~** up-to-date; **attenter aux ~s de qn** attempt to kill s/o; **au ~ le ~** from day to day; **au grand ~** in broad daylight; **au premier ~** as soon as

possible; **à un de ces ~s!** so long!, see you soon!; **de ~** in the daytime; on day duty; **de nos ~s** these days, in our time; **de tous les ~s** everyday, humdrum; **donner le ~ à** give birth to; **du ~ au lendemain** soon, at any moment; **en plein ~** in broad daylight; *comm* **intérêts à ce ~** interest to date; **le ~ se lève** the sun is rising, the dawn is breaking; **mettre qch au ~** bring sth to light; **ourlet à ~s** hemstitch; *cul* **plat du ~** today's special dish; **se faire ~** emerge, come out; **sous un ~ intéressant** in an interesting light; **sur mes vieux ~s** in my old age

**journal** *nm* newspaper, paper, journal; diary, journal; *naut* logbook; *rad +* **parlé, télévisé** news, *US* newscast

**journalier** *nm* day-labourer, journeyman; *adj* (*f* **-ière**) daily, everyday; changing, uncertain

**journalisme** *nm* journalism; **style de ~** journalese

**journaliste** *n* journalist, reporter

**journalistique** *adj* journalistic

**journée** *nf* day, daytime; day's work; day's march; day's wages; **à la ~** by the day; **femme de ~** charwoman, daily help

**journellement** *adv* daily, every day

**joute** *nf obs* joust; contest, tournament

**jouter** *vi obs* joust; fight, dispute

**jouvence** *nf ar* youth

**jouvenceau** *nm ar* young boy; adolescent

**jouvencelle** *nf ar* young girl

**jovial** *adj* jovial, jolly, good-humoured

**jovialité** *nf* joviality, jollity, good-humour

**joyau** *nm* jewel, precious stone

**joyeuseté** *nf* pleasantry, prank, joke; mirth

**joyeux -euse** *adj* joyful, merry, joyous

**jubé** *nm archi* rood-screen, rood-loft

**jubilé** *nm* jubilee; golden wedding

**jubiler** *vi* jubilate, glory; *coll* gloat

**juché** *adj* roosting, perched

**jucher** *vt* place high up; *vi* roost, perch; **se ~** go to roost; *coll* perch oneself

**juchoir** *nm* perch, roosting-place

**judaïque** *adj* Judaic, Jewish

**judaïsme** *nm* Judaism

**judas** *nm* traitor; betrayer; spy-hole, peep-hole (in door)

**judéo-allemand** *adj* Yiddish

**judiciaire** *adj* judicial, judiciary; legal; **police ~** = C.I.D

**judicieux -ieuse** *adj* judicious, sensible; discreet

**juge** *nm* judge, magistrate; *sp* umpire, judge; **~ d'instruction** examining magistrate; **~ de paix** police-court

162

magistrate; ~ **de touche** touch-judge, linesman

**jugé** *nm* **au** ~ by guesswork

**jugement** *nm* judgement, opinion, discrimination; *leg* trial, award, judgement, sentence; *leg* **mettre qn en** ~ bring s/o to trial; **passer en** ~ to stand trial

**jugeote** *nf coll* gumption, nous, common-sense

**juger** *vt* (3) judge, consider, deem, estimate, think; *leg* judge, try, decide (case), pass sentence on; **mal** ~ misjudge; *vi* ~ **de** judge of; ~ **d'après** judge from; ~ **par** judge by

**jugulaire** *nf med* jugular vein; chinstrap; *adj* jugular

**juguler** *vt* strangle, throttle, jugulate

**Juif** (*f* **Juive**) *n* Jew(ess)

**juif** *nm coll* **petit** ~ funny-bone, *US* crazy-bone; *adj* (*f* **juive**) Jewish

**juillet** *nm* July

**juin** *nm* June

**juiverie** *nf pej* Jewry, the Jews; ghetto; usury

**Jules** *nm* Julius

**jules** *nm sl* chamber-pot, jerry; *sl* pimp; *sl* **mon** ~ my man

**julienne** *nf cul* vegetable soup

**jumeau -elle** *n* twin, twin-brother (sister); *adj* twin; **maison jumelle** semi-detached house

**jumelage** *nm* pairing, compiling; twinning

**jumeler** *vt* (5) pair, arrange in pairs; **ville jumelée** twinned town

**jumelles** *nfpl* binoculars, opera-glasses

**jument** *nf* mare

**junior** *adj* youthful, teenage

**jupe** *nf* skirt; *coll* **il est pendu aux** ~ **s de sa mère** he is tied to his mother's apron-strings; *sl* **il est toujours fourré dans ses** ~ **s** he's always hanging about her

**jupe-culotte** *nf* (*pl* **jupes-culottes**) culottes

**jupon** *nm* underskirt, slip; *coll* girl, woman

**juré -e** *n* juryman (-woman), juror; ~ **s** jury; *adj* sworn

**jurement** *nm* oath, swearing, bad language

**jurer** *vt* swear, take an oath; vow, promise; *vi* swear; clash, jar (colours); **il ne faut** ~ **de rien** you never can tell

**juridiction** *nf* jurisdiction; *coll* province

**juridique** *adj* juridical, judicial, legal; **texte** ~ instrument

**jurisconsulte** *nm* jurisconsult, legal expert

**juriste** *nm* jurist, legal writer

**juron** *nm* oath, swear-word

**jury** *nm* panel, board (examiners), selection committee, judges, jury

**jus** *nm* juice; *cul* gravy; *coll* electricity; *coll* petrol, *US* gas; *sl* water (*esp* dirty); *sl mil* coffee; ~ **de la treille** wine; *coll* **donner du** ~ step on the gas; *sl* **tomber dans le** ~ fall in (water)

**jusqu'auboutiste** *n* die-hard

**jusque** *prep* as far as, to, down to, up to; until; as much as; even including; **aller jusqu'à faire qch** go so far as to do sth; **jusqu'à quand?** until when?, how long for?; *conj phr* **jusqu'à ce que** until

**jusques** *prep poet* + *ar* = **jusque**

**justaucorps** *nm* jerkin

**juste** *n* just, righteous; **au** ~ exactly; *adj* just, righteous, upright; fair; right, exact; barely sufficient; tight (clothes); ~ **milieu** happy medium, middle of the road; *comm* **au plus** ~ **prix** at rock-bottom price; **c'est** ~ **!** quite so!, that's right!; **c'est tout** ~ **si je ne me suis pas blessé** I very nearly hurt myself; **le mot** ~ the right word; *adv* justly, rightly, correctly; exactly; ~ **ce qu'il fallait** just what was wanted; *coll* **ça a été** ~ **!** it was a near thing!; **comme de** ~ of course, naturally; **frapper** ~ hit the nail on the head

**justement** *adv* justly, rightly; exactly, precisely

**justesse** *nf* justness, soundness; exactness; **de** ~ barely

**justice** *nf* justice, right; *leg* justice, law, legal proceedings; *leg* **aller en** ~ go to law; **se faire** ~ commit suicide; avenge oneself; **faire** ~ **à qn** treat s/o as he deserves

**justiciable** *n* person under jurisdiction; *adj* amenable; subject

**justicier -ière** *n* pronouncer of judgements; *adj* justiciary

**justificateur -trice** *n* justifier; *adj* justifying, indicating

**¹justificatif** *nm comm* voucher

**²justificatif -ive** *adj* justificative; **pièce justificative** voucher, document of proof; *leg* relevant document

**justification** *nf* justification; *typ* indication; proof

**justifier** *vt* justify, vindicate; prove; *vi leg* ~ **de** account for; prove (identity); **se** ~ vindicate, clear oneself

**juter** *vi* be juicy; *vulg* come

**¹juteux** *nm sl mil* sergeant-major

**²juteux -euse** *adj* juicy; *sl* lucrative

**juvénilité** *nf* youthfulness, juvenility

**juxtaposer** *vt* juxtapose, place side by side

# K

**kakatoès** *nm* cockatoo
**¹kaki** *nm* + *adj invar* khaki
**²kaki** *nm* persimmon
**kaléidoscopique** *adj* kaleidoscopic
**kangourou** *nm* kangaroo
**keepsake** *nm* keepsake, souvenir; autograph album
**képi** *nm* peaked cap (French army), kepi
**kermesse** *nf* village fair
**kif** *nm* marijuana, *coll* pot
**kif-kif** *adj sl* all the same, much of a muchness
**kiki** *nm sl* throat, neck
**kilométrer** *vt* (6) measure in kilometres; mark off with kilometre stones
**kilométrique** *adj* kilometric

**kiosque** *nm* kiosk, stall, stand; *naut* conning-tower; ~ **à musique** bandstand; ~ **de jardin** summer-house
**klaxon** *nm* klaxon; *mot* horn, hooter; ~ **de route** horn (for open road); ~ **de ville** horn (for town)
**klaxonner** *vi mot* hoot, sound horn
**kleptomane** *n* + *adj* kleptomaniac
**kleptomanie** *nf* kleptomania
**Koweït** *nm* Kuwait
**krach** *nm comm* financial crash, failure, collapse
**kymrique** *adj* Cymric
**kyrielle** *nf* rigmarole, string of words
**kyste** *nm* cyst
**kysteux -euse** *adj* cystic

# L

**l'** *def art* + *pron* = **le** or **la** before vowel
**¹la** *def art f* the; *pron f* her; it
**²la** *nm invar mus* A, la; **donner le** ~ give the pitch
**¹là** *adv* there; then; that; **de** ~ whence; **d'ici** ~ until then; **il est un peu** ~ he's very much on the ball, he's all there; **il n'en est pas encore** ~ he's not yet come to that; **par-ci, par-** ~ here and there; **par** ~ this way; whereby
**²là** *interj* ~, ~! there now; gently; **oh** ~, ~! oh dear me!
**là-bas** *adv* over there; yonder
**labeur** *nm* work, toil
**laborantin -e** *n* laboratory assistant
**laboratoire** *nm* laboratory
**laborieux -ieuse** *adj* laborious, hardworking; laboured, heavy; hard, wearisome; **les classes laborieuses** the working classes
**labour** *nm* tilling, ploughing, tillage; ~ s ploughed fields
**labourable** *adj* arable
**labourage** *nm* tilling, ploughing
**labourer** *vt* plough; furrow; *naut* graze, drag (anchor)
**laboureur** *nm* ploughman
**labyrinthe** *nm* labyrinth, maze
**lac** *nm* lake; *coll* **tomber dans le** ~ fail

**lacer** *vt* (4) lace; *naut* belay; **se** ~ lace up
**lacération** *nf* laceration, tearing, mauling; defacing
**lacérer** *vt* (6) lacerate, tear; deface, slash
**lacet** *nm* shoe-lace, boot-lace; hairpin-bend; noose, snare; **route en** ~ s winding road; **tendre un** ~ set a snare
**lâchage** *nm* releasing, letting go; *coll* jilting, dropping
**lâche** *n* coward; *adj* cowardly, faint-hearted; loose, slack; lax, perfunctory
**lâcher** *vt* release; loosen, slacken; let off; leave, drop; let down; ~ **prise** let go; *coll* ~ **un juron** let out an oath; *vi* give up; run away
**lâcheté** *nf* cowardice; cowardly act; dastardliness; despicable action
**lâcheur -euse** *n coll* quitter, traitor (to friends)
**lacis** *nm* network
**laconique** *adj* laconic
**lacrymogène** *adj* tear-producing; **gaz** ~ tear gas
**lacs** *nm* noose, snare
**lacté** *adj* lacteous, milky; **voie** ~ **e** Milky Way
**lacune** *nf* lacuna, gap
**lacustre** *adj* lake-dwelling, lacustrine

**lad** *nm* stable-boy
**là-dedans** *adv* within, in there
**là-dessous** *adv* underneath, under there
**là-dessus** *adv* on that; thereupon
**ladite** *adj f see* **ledit**
**ladre** *n med* leper; miser; *adj med* leprous; miserly, stingy
**ladrerie** *nf* miserliness, avarice
**lagune** *nf* lagoon
**là-haut** *adv* up there
¹**lai** *nm lit* lay
²**lai** *adj eccles* lay
**laïcisation** *nf* secularization
**laïciser** *vt* secularize
**laïcisme** *nm* secularism
**laïcité** *nf* secularity
**laid** *adj* ugly, repulsive, plain; vile, mean, shabby
**laideron** *nm* plain girl, plain woman; *adj* (*f* -onne) ugly
**laideur** *nf* ugliness, plainness; meanness, shabbiness
**laie** *nf* wild sow
**lainage** *nm* woollen article; ~ s woollen goods, woollens
**laine** *nf* wool; woolly hair; ~ **peignée** worsted
**laineux -euse** *adj* woolly, fleecy
**laïque** *n* layman, laywoman; ~ s laity; *adj* lay, secular; **école** ~ state school, undenominational school
¹**laisse** *nf* leash, lead
²**laisse** *nf naut* foreshore, tide-mark
**laisser** *vt* leave, quit; leave out, omit; let, allow; let have; ~ **aller** let things slide; ~ **faire** not interfere; ~ **un bénéfice** yield a profit; ~ **voir** reveal; **je vous le laisserai pour 6.000 francs** you can have it for 6,000 francs, I will let it go for 6,000 francs; **ne pas** ~ **de** not fail to; **se** ~ let oneself; be easy to; **se** ~ **aller** let oneself go
**laisser-aller** *nm invar* abandon; neglect; slovenliness
**laisser-faire** *nm invar* laissez-faire, non-interference
**laissez-passer** *nm invar* permit, pass
**lait** *nm* milk; ~ **concentré** condensed milk; **cochon de** ~ sucking pig; **frère (sœur) de** ~ foster-brother (-sister)
**laitage** *nm* dairy produce
**laitance** *nf* soft roe
**laité** *adj* soft-roed (fish)
**laiterie** *nf* dairy; dairy farming
**laiteux -euse** *adj* milky
**laitier -ière** *n* milkman (-woman); *adj* dairy (industry); **vache laitière** milk cow
**laitière** *nf* milk-maid; milk-cart
**laiton** *nm* brass
**laitue** *nf* lettuce
**laïus** *nm coll* lengthy speech, lecture

**laïusser** *vi coll* speechify, jaw
**lambeau** *nm* rag, shred, scrap
**lambin -e** *n coll* idler, dawdler; *adj coll* idle, dawdling
**lambiner** *vi coll* dawdle, loaf
**lambrequin** *nm* valance, pelmet
**lambris** *nm* panelling, wainscoting; lining in marble; (panelled) ceiling
**lambrissage** *nm* panelling, wainscoting; lining
**lambrisser** *vt* panel, wainscot
**lame** *nf* blade (knife, sword); strip (metal); leaf (spring); wave; ~ **de fond** ground swell; **bonne** ~ good swordsman; **visage en** ~ **de couteau** hatchet-face
**lamé** *nm* ~ **d'or** gold lamé, gold spangles; *adj* spangled
**lamentable** *adj* lamentable, deplorable; dismal; pitiful, woeful
**lamentation** *nf* lamentation, lament, wailing
**lamenter (se)** *v refl* lament, wail; **se** ~ **sur** bewail, deplore
**laminer** *vt* laminate; erode
**laminoir** *nm* rolling-mill; rolling-press
**lampadaire** *nm* standard-lamp; street-lamp; candelabrum
**lampant** *adj* refined (oil)
**lampe** *nf* lamp; *rad* valve; ~ **à alcool** spirit lamp; ~ **à incandescence** fluorescent, strip lighting; ~ **à souder** blow-lamp; ~ **témoin** pilot lamp
**lampée** *nf* draught, gulp
**lamper** *vt* gulp down, swig
**lampion** *nm* fairy light; Chinese lantern
**lampiste** *nm* lamp-maker; lamp-lighter
**lamproie** *nf zool* lamprey
**lance** *nf* lance, spear, harpoon; nozzle (hose); **fer de** ~ spear-head
**lancé** *adj* started, going; launched
**lance-bombes** *nm aer* bomb-rack
**lancée** *nf* impetus; ~ s shooting pains
**lance-flammes** *nm mil* flame-thrower
**lance-fusées** *nm mil* rocket-launcher
**lancement** *nm* throwing, flinging; *naut* launching; *comm* launching, floating
**lance-pierres** *nm* catapult
**lancer** *vt* (4) throw, fling; drop (bombs); start, set moving; launch; *mot* + *aer* swing (engine, propeller); set (fashion); puff out (smoke); *leg* issue (warrant); **se** ~ rush; throw oneself; **se** ~ **dans** embark on
**lance-torpilles** *nm* torpedo-tube
**lancette** *nf med* lancet
**lanceur -euse** *n* thrower; *comm* promoter, floater; initiator
**lancier** *nm* lancer
**lancinant** *adj* shooting (pain)
**landau** *nm* (*pl* ~ s) pram; landau
**lande** *nf* moor, heath

**langage** *nm* language, speech; lingo

**lange** *nm* baby's napkin; ~ s swaddling-clothes

**langoureux -euse** *adj* languorous, languid

**langouste** *nf* spiny lobster, crayfish

**langoustine** *nf* (large) prawn, Pacific prawn

**langue** *nf* tongue; language; style; ~ **verte** slang; **avoir la** ~ **bien pendue** have a glib tongue; **donner sa** ~ **au chat** give up (riddle, etc); **écrire une belle** ~ have an elegant style; **mauvaise** ~ scandal-monger, back-biter

**langueur** *nf* languor, listlessness

**languir** *vi* languish, pine; flag, drag

**languissant** *adj* languid; languishing; flagging

**lanière** *nf* thin strap, thong; lash (whip); **en** ~ **s** in ribbons

**lanterne** *nf* lantern; **à la** ~ ! hang him!, string him up!

**lanterneau** *nm* sky-light

**lanterner** *vi* linger, dawdle, shilly-shally

**lapalissade** *nf* truism, cliché

**laper** *vt* lap, lap up

**lapereau** *nm* young rabbit

**lapidaire** *nm* + *adj* lapidary

**lapider** *vt* stone; *fig* vilify

**lapin** *nm* rabbit; ~ **de garenne** wild rabbit; *coll* **poser un** ~ **à qn** let s/o down, fail to turn up; **un chaud** ~ a lecherous character

**lapine** *nf* doe, female rabbit

**lapon -onne** *adj* Lapp

**Laponie** *nf* Lapland

**laps** *nm* ~ **de temps** lapse of time

**lapsus** *nm* slip (tongue, pen)

**laquais** *nm* lackey, footman

**laque** *nf* lac; lacquer (hair); **gomme** ~ shellac; *nm or f* lacquer; ~ **de Chine** japan

**laquelle** *pron f see* **lequel**

**laquer** *vt* lacquer, japan

**larbin** *nm* flunkey

**larcin** *nm* petty theft

**lard** *nm* (pork) fat; bacon; *coll* **faire du** ~ put on weight

**larder** *vt cul* lard; *fig* stab at; interlard, sprinkle

**lardon** *nm* piece of bacon; gibe, crack, taint; *sl* brat, kid

**large** *nm* breadth, width; space; *naut* open sea, offing; *naut* **au** ~ in the offing; ~ **de Marseille** off Marseilles; **de long en** ~ to and fro; **dix mètres de** ~ ten metres wide; **être au** ~ have plenty of space; have plenty of money; **mettre le cap au** ~ put out to sea; *coll* decamp, run off; **prendre le** ~ clear off; *adj* wide, broad; generous, liberal; loose, ample; bold; free; considerable, extensive; **avoir la main** ~ be generous, open-handed; **avoir l'esprit** ~ be broad-minded; **geste** ~ sweeping gesture; **peinture** ~ bold painting; *adv* loosely; **peindre** ~ paint boldly; **s'habiller** ~ wear loose clothes

**largement** *adv* broadly, widely; freely; fully, amply; **avoir** ~ **le temps** have plenty of time

**largesse** *nf* liberality; largesse; ~ s gifts

**largeur** *nf* breadth, width; *naut* beam

**larguer** *vt naut* loose, let go (rope); shake out (reef); let out (sail); *aer* drop (bomb, parachutist); *fig* ditch

**larme** *nf* tear; *coll* drop; **avoir une crise de** ~ s, **fondre en** ~ s burst into tears; **pleurer à chaudes** ~ s weep bitterly

**larmoyant** *adj* tearful, whimpering, lachrymose; watering (eyes); maudlin, sentimental; *coll* sloppy

**larmoyer** *vi* (7) water (eyes); snivel, whimper

**larron** *nm ar* robber, thief; **s'entendre comme** ~ s **en foire** be as thick as thieves

**larvaire** *adj zool* larval; immature

**larve** *nf* larva, grub

**laryngite** *nf* laryngitis

¹**las** *interj obs* alas!

²**las** (*f* **lasse**) *adj* tired, weary

**lascar** *nm coll* cunning rogue

**lascif -ive** *adj* lascivious, lewd

**lasciveté** *nf* lasciviousness, lewdness

**lassant** *adj* tiring, wearisome; tedious

**lasser** *vt* tire, weary; **se** ~ grow tired

**latent** *adj* latent, hidden, dormant

**latéral** *adj* lateral, sideways

**latin** *nm* Latin; ~ **de cuisine** dog-latin; *coll* **y perdre son** ~ be all at sea, be unable to make head or tail of it; *adj* Latin; *naut* lateen

**latitude** *nf geog* latitude; breadth, scope, freedom

**latte** *nf* lath, batten, slat

**latter** *vt* lath, batten; lag (pipe)

**lattis** *nm* lath-work; lagging

**laudatif -ive** *adj* laudatory

**lauréat -e** *n* + *adj* laureate

**laurier** *nm bot* laurel; bay-tree; ~ s laurels; **cueillir des** ~ s win glory

**laurier-rose** *nm* (*pl* **lauriers-roses**) *bot* oleander

**lavable** *adj* washable

**lavabo** *nm* wash-stand, wash-hand basin; wash-room

**lavage** *nm* washing

**lavallière** *nf* loosely tied bow, cravat

**lavande** *nf* lavender

**lavandière** *nf obs* washerwoman

**lavasse** *nf* watery soup; *coll* dish-water, slops

**lave** *nf* lava

**lavé** *adj* washed, cleaned; washy (colour); **dessin** ~ wash-drawing

**lave-glace** *nm* windscreen washer

**lavement** *nm* med enema

**laver** *vt* wash, clean, wash up; bathe (wound); disculpate, clear; *sl* sell off; ~ **à grande eau** swill; ~ **la tête à** rebuke, haul over the coals; **se** ~ wash, wash oneself

**laverie** *nf* washing plant; ~ **(automatique)** launderette

**lavette** *nf* dish-mop; ~ **métallique** scrubber

**laveur -euse** *n* washer(woman)

**lave-vaisselle** *nm* dish-washer

**lavis** *nm* washing, tinting; wash-drawing

**lavoir** *nm* wash-house

**lavure** *nf* dish-water, kitchen swill; *coll* thin soup

**laxatif** *nm* laxative, aperient; *adj (f* -ive) laxative, aperient

**laxité** *nf* slackness, laxity

**layette** *nf* baby-linen, layette; packing-case

**lazzi** *nm invar* (*usu pl*) gibes, jokes; *theat* piece of comic business

**le** *def art* m the; *pron* m him; it

**léchage** *nm* licking

**lèche** *nf coll* thin slice (bread, meat); *sl* licking; *sl* **faire de la** ~ **à qn** suck up to s/o

**lèche-cul** *nm invar sl* arse-creeper, bum-sucker

**lèchefrite** *nf cul* dripping-pan

**lécher** *vt* (6) lick

**lécheur -euse** *n coll* lickspittle, toady, creep

**lèche-vitrines** *nm* window-shopping

**leçon** *nf* lesson; warning; reading, interpretation (manuscript); **faire la** ~ **à qn** give s/o a lecture

**lecteur -trice** *n* reader; proof-reader; (foreign) assistant at university; *nm* **(de bande)** repro head

**lecture** *nf* reading; ~ **sonore** sound pick-up; **abonnement de** ~ **s** circulating library; *obs* **cabinet de** ~ lending library; **être d'une** ~ **agréable** make pleasant reading

**ledit** *adj m (f* **ladite**, *mpl* **lesdits**, *fpl* **lesdites**) aforesaid

**légal** *adj* legal, lawful, statutory

**légalisation** *nf* legalization, authentication

**légaliser** *vt* legalize, authenticate

**légalité** *nf* legality, lawfulness

**légat** *nm* legate

**légataire** *n leg* legatee; ~ **universel (-elle)** sole heir (heiress)

**légendaire** *adj* legendary

**légende** *nf* legend, fable; inscription, caption; key (map)

**léger -ère** *adj* light; slight; frivolous, flighty; mild (tobacco, beer, etc); **à la légère** lightly, thoughtlessly, flippantly; **avoir la main légère** be quick with one's hands; **propos** ~ **s** frivolous, idle talk

**légèreté** *nf* lightness; slightness; levity, frivolousness; mildness

**légion** *nf* legion; *coll* host, crowd

**légionnaire** *nm* legionary; *mil* soldier of the Foreign Legion

**législateur -trice** *n* legislator; *adj* legislative

**législature** *nf* legislature, sitting (of law-making assembly)

**légiste** *nm* jurist; **médecin** ~ pathologist

**légitimation** *nf* legitimation, official recognition

**légitime** *adj* legitimate, lawful; justifiable

**légitimer** *vt* legitimize; justify; recognize

**légitimité** *nf* lawfulness

**legs** *nm* legacy, bequest

**léguer** *vt* (6) bequeath, leave

**légume** *nm* vegetable; *nf sl* **grosse** ~ bigwig

**légumier** *nm* vegetable dish

**Léman** *nm* **le lac** ~ the Lake of Geneva

**lendemain** *nm* next day, morrow; **du jour au** ~ overnight; **succès sans** ~ short-lived success

**lénifier** *vt* soften; *med* assuage, soothe

**lénitif -ive** *adj* lenitive, soothing

**lent** *adj* slow; dull

**lente** *nf zool* nit

**lenteur** *nf* slowness; dullness; ~ **s** delays

**lentille** *nf* lentil; *opt* lens; *naut* side-light; ~ **d'eau** duck-weed

**léonin** *adj* leonine

**lépidoptère** *nm* lepidopteran; *adj* lepidopterous

**lèpre** *nf* leprosy

**lépreux -euse** *n* leper; *adj* leprous; dilapidated

**léproserie** *nf* leper-hospital

**lequel** *rel pron (f* **laquelle**, *mpl* **lesquels**, *fpl* **lesquelles**) (contracted with à = **auquel**, **auxquels**, **auxquelles**, with de = **duquel**, **desquels**, **desquelles**) who, whom (persons); which (things); *inter pron* which?; *adj* which

**lès**, **les**, **lez** *prep* (with place names) near, by, eg **Villeneuve-les-Avignon**

**lesbien -ienne** *adj* lesbian

**lesbienne** *nf* lesbian

**lesdits**, **lesdites** *see* **ledit**

**lèse-** *adj f* ~ **humanité** outrage against humanity; ~ **majesté** high treason

**léser** *vt* (6) injure, wrong; *leg* commit a tort against; **la partie lésée** the injured party

**lésine** *nf* stinginess, miserliness
**lésiner** *vi* be stingy, close-fisted; haggle
**lésinerie** *nf* stinginess; stingy act
**lésineur -euse** *n+adj* stingy, miserly (person)
**lésion** *nf med* lesion, injury; *leg* injury, wrong
**lesquels, lesquelles** *see* **lequel**
**lessivage** *nm* washing, cleaning; getting rid of; *coll* selling off, raising the wind; ~ **de crâne** brain-washing
**lessive** *nf* household washing; articles washed; washing powder, washing liquid
**lessivé** *adj sl* cleaned out, broke; *sl* exhausted
**lessiver** *vt* wash (clothes, etc); scrub (floor); *coll* eliminate; *coll* sell off, raise the wind; *coll* squander, blue (money); *coll* ~ **la tête à qn** rebuke s/o, tear a strip off s/o
**lessiveuse** *nf* washing-machine
**lest** *nm* (*no pl*) ballast; **jeter du** ~ make sacrifices, cut one's losses; *naut* **navire sur** ~ ship in ballast
**leste** *adj* light, nimble, smart; unscrupulous, sharp; **propos** ~ dubious, broad remark
**lester** *vt naut* ballast; fill
**léthargie** *nf* lethargy
**léthargique** *adj* lethargic
**lettre** *nf* letter, character; letter, epistle; ~**s** letters, literature; **à la** ~, **au pied de la** ~ literally; **avant la** ~ premature; **avoir des** ~**s** be well read; **passer comme une** ~ **à la poste** go through easily
**lettré -e** *n* scholar, well-read person; *adj* literate, well-read
**lettrine** *nf typ* head-letter, ornamental letter
**leu** *nm* **à la queue** ~ ~ in single file, one after the other
**leucémie** *nf med* leukaemia
**leucémique** *n med* leukaemia sufferer; *adj* leukaemic
**leur** *pron* to them; *poss pron* theirs, their own; *poss adj* their
**leurre** *nm* lure, decoy; allurement, catch
**leurrer** *vt* lure, decoy; allure, deceive, delude; **se** ~ delude oneself
**levage** *nm* lifting, hoisting, raising
**levain** *nm* yeast; leaven
**levant** *nm* east; *adj* rising
**levantin** *adj* Levantine
**¹levé** *nm* survey
**²levé** *adj* up, out of bed; raised; **au pied** ~ impromptu, at a moment's notice; **dessin à main** ~**e** freehand drawing
**levée** *nf* raising, lifting; clearing (letter-box); trick (cards); dyke, embankment; levying (taxes); breaking (seals);

*mil* levy; ~ **d'écrou** discharge from prison; *comm* ~ **d'une prime** taking up of an option; **la** ~ **du corps aura lieu à** the funeral will leave at
**lever** *nm* rising (from bed); levee; *theat* rise (curtain); *vt* (6) raise; remove, lift; clear (letter-box); levy (taxes); break (seals); start (hare), flush (bird); *comm* take up, exercise; ~ **l'ancre** weigh anchor; *coll* ~ **le pied** make oneself scarce, hop it; *coll* ~ **une fille** pick up a girl; ~ **un plan** draw a plan; *vi cul* rise; shoot, sprout (plant); **faire** ~ rouse, wake; **se** ~ get up; start up; rise (sun, wind); break (day)
**levier** *nm* lever; crow-bar; ~ **de commande** control-bar; ~**s de commande** reins of power
**levraut** *nm* leveret, young hare
**lèvre** *nf* lip; **rire du bout des** ~**s** give a forced laugh
**levrette** *nf* greyhound bitch
**lévrier** *nm* greyhound
**levure** *nf* yeast; ~ **artificielle** baking powder
**lexicographe** *n* lexicographer
**lexicographie** *nf* lexicography
**lexicologie** *nf* lexicology
**lexique** *nm* lexicon, glossary; vocabulary
**lez** *prep see* **lès**
**lézard** *nm* lizard; *coll* **faire le** ~ bask in the sun
**lézarde** *nf* crack, split, chink
**lézarder** *vt* crack, split; *vi coll* bask in the sun; **se** ~ crack, split
**liage** *nm* tying, binding
**liaison** *nf* linking, joining, binding; *archi* mortar, cement; connection, communication; liaison, (love-)affair; *gramm* liaison, joining of two words; *mus* tie, slur; *cul* thickening (sauce); **effectuer la** ~ **avec** liaise with
**liane** *nf bot* liana, creeper
**liant** *nm* winning manner, niceness; **avoir du** ~ be a good mixer; *adj* sociable; winning, engaging; good-natured; **peu** ~ unsociable, stand-offish
**liard** *nm* farthing
**liasse** *nf* bundle, packet; file; wad (bank-notes)
**Liban** *nm* Lebanon
**libelle** *nm* lampoon, coarse satire
**libellé** *nm* wording, lettering; *comm* trade description
**libeller** *vt* draw up, word (text, document)
**libelliste** *n* satirist, lampoonist
**libellule** *nf* dragon-fly
**libéral** *adj* liberal, generous; broad-minded, tolerant

**libéralité** *nf* liberality, generosity; generous act

**libérateur -trice** *n* liberator, rescuer; *adj* liberating, rescuing

**libération** *nf* liberation, freeing; release; discharge (prisoner, soldier); *comm* payment in full

**libéré** *nm* discharged prisoner, soldier

**libérer** *vt* (6) liberate, release, set free; discharge; *comm* pay up; **se ~** free oneself; *comm* pay off, redeem

**liberté** *nf* liberty, freedom; **leg ~ sous caution** release on bail; **jour de ~** day off, free day

**libertin -e** *n* libertine, rake; *obs* freethinker; *adj* licentious, dissolute

**libertinage** *nm* libertinage, dissoluteness; *obs* free-thinking

**libidineux -euse** *adj* libidinous, salacious, lustful

**libraire** *n* bookseller

**librairie** *nf* bookshop; booktrade, bookselling; **en ~** published

**libre** *adj* free; disengaged, unoccupied; clear, open; equivocal, loose; **~ à vous de penser** you may think what you like; **école ~** private (non-state) school (in France *usu* Catholic); **remarque un peu ~** somewhat improper remark

**libre-échange** *nm pol* free-trade

**libre-service** *nm invar* self-service (shop, restaurant)

**lice** *nf obs* lists

**licence** *nf* licence, permission; leave; licentiousness, licence; first (university) degree; **~ ès lettres** = Bachelor of Arts degree

**licencié -e** *n* graduate; licensee; **~ ès lettres, sciences** = Bachelor of Arts, Science

**licencier** *vt* disband, dismiss; lay off (workers)

**licencieux -ieuse** *adj* licentious, loose

**licher** *vt sl* lick; *coll* drink, booze

**licite** *adj* lawful, permissible, legal

**licol** *nm* halter

**licorne** *nf myth* unicorn

**lie** *nf* lees, dregs; **~ du peuple** scum, rabble

**lié** *adj* tied, bound; intimately acquainted; linked

**liège** *nm* cork

**lien** *nm* bond, tie; link

**lier** *vt* tie, fasten, bind; *cul* thicken; *gramm* link; *mus* tie; **~ connaissance avec qn** strike up an acquaintance with s/o; **se ~** make friends; *cul* thicken

**lierre** *nm* ivy

**liesse** *nf* gaiety, jollity

**lieu** *nm* place, locality; occasion, grounds, reason; **~ commun** commonplace; **~x (d'aisances)** W.C.,

privy; **au ~ de** instead of; **au ~ que** whereas; instead of; **avoir ~** take place, happen; **en aucun ~** nowhere; **en haut ~** in high places; **en quelque ~ que** wherever; **en temps et ~** in due course; **mauvais ~** shady place (often = brothel); **vider les ~x** clear out

**lieue** *nf* league

**lieur -euse** *n agr* binder (person); *adj* binding

**lieuse** *nf agr* mechanical binder

**lieutenant** *nm mil+naut* lieutenant; (air force) flying officer; *naut* **~ de vaisseau** lieutenant-commander

**lieutenant-colonel** *nm mil* (*pl* **lieutenants-colonels**) lieutenant-colonel; (air force) wing-commander

**lièvre** *nm zool* hare; **courir deux ~s à la fois** try to do two things at once; **prendre le ~ au gîte** catch s/o napping

**lifter** *vt* give (s/o) a face-lift

**liftier** *nm* liftman, lift boy; lift attendant

**liftière** *nf* lift girl

**lifting** *nm* face-lift

**ligature** *nf* ligature, binding, splice; *mus* tie

**ligaturer** *vt* ligature, bind, splice

**lignage** *nm* lineage, descent

**lignard** *nm coll mil* infantryman, footslogger

**ligne** *nf* line; row; cord; *sp* **~ de touche** touch-line; **aller à la ~** start a new paragraph, indent; *naut* **bâtiment de ~** capital ship; **descendre en ~ droite de** be a direct descendant of; **garder la ~** keep one's figure; (railway) **grande ~** main line; **hors ~** outstanding; **pilote de ~** airline pilot

**lignée** *nf* line, issue

**ligneux -euse** *adj* ligneous, woody

**ligot** *nm* bundle of firewood

**ligotage** *nm* binding, tying up

**ligoter** *vt* bind, tie up; bind hand and foot

**ligue** *nf* league

**liguer** *vt* league, bind together; **se ~** league, form a league

**lilas** *nm+adj invar* lilac

**limace** *nf* slug

**limaçon** *nm* snail; **escalier en ~** spiral staircase

**limage** *nm* (action of) filing

**limaille** *nf* filings

**limande** *nf* dab (fish)

**limbes** *nmpl* limbo

**lime** *nf* file; **~ à ongles** nail-file; **~ émeri** emery-board

**limer** *vt* file; work at, polish

**limier** *nm zool* bloodhound; *coll* sleuth, detective

**liminaire** *adj* preliminary, prefatory; **épître ~** foreword

**limitatif -ive** *adj* limiting; restrictive

**limitation** *nf* limit, limitation; marking off

**limite** *nf* limit, boundary, margin; **cas ~** borderline case; **charge ~** maximum load; **date ~** deadline; **vitesse ~** maximum speed

**limiter** *vt* limit, bound, restrict

**limitrophe** *adj* adjacent, adjoining, bordering

**limogeage** *nm* mil coll bowler-hatting

**limoger** *vt* (3) *mil coll* bowler-hat; sack

¹**limon** *nm* mud, clay, silt

²**limon** *nm bot* lime

**limonade** *nf* lemonade

**limonadier -ière** *n* dealer in soft drinks; café owner

**limoneux -euse** *adj* muddy; *geol* alluvial

**limpide** *adj* limpid, clear

**limpidité** *nf* limpidity, clarity

**lin** *nm* flax; linen; **huile de ~** linseed oil

**linceul** *nm* shroud, winding-sheet

**linéaire** *adj* linear; **dessin ~** geometrical drawing

**linge** *nm* linen; **~ de corps** underwear; **~ de table** table linen

**lingère** *nf* person in charge of linen-room

**lingerie** *nf* linen drapery; underclothing, lingerie; linen-room

**lingot** *nm* ingot

**linguiste** *n* linguist

**linguistique** *nf* linguistics; *adj* linguistic

**linon** *nm* lawn (cloth)

**linotte** *nf orni* linnet; *coll* **avoir une tête de ~** be feather-brained

**linteau** *nm* lintel

**lion** *nm* lion; *coll* celebrity

**lionceau** *nm* lion-cub

**lionne** *nf* lioness

**lippe** *nf* thick lower lip; **faire la ~** pout

**lippu** *adj* thick-lipped

**liquéfier** *vt* liquefy; **se ~** turn liquid

**liquette** *nf coll* shirt

**liqueur** *nf* liquor, alcoholic drink; liqueur; *chem* liquid solution; **~ s fortes** hard liquor; **~ titrée** standard solution

**liquidateur** *nm comm* liquidator

**liquidation** *nf* liquidation, winding-up; *comm* clearance sale; settlement

**liquide** *nm* liquid; drink; *nf gramm* liquid consonant; *adj* liquid; **argent ~** ready money

**liquider** *vt* liquidate, wind up; settle up; realize (assets), sell off; *coll* liquidate, get rid of; *coll* **~ son passé** wipe out one's past; **se ~** clear oneself (debt); be settled

**liquidité** *nf* liquidity

**liquoreux -euse** *adj* like a liqueur (wine, sweet)

**lire** *vt + vi* (56) read; *mus* **~ à première vue** sight-read; **cela se lit sur son visage** it shows on his face; **ce livre se lit facilement** this book makes easy reading

**lis, lys** *nm bot* lily; **~ d'eau** water-lily

**liseré, liséré** *nm* border, edge; piping (garment)

**liserer, lisérer** *vt* (6) border, edge; trim with piping

**liseron** *nm bot* bind-weed, convolvulus

**liseur -euse** *n* s/o fond of reading, great reader; **~ d'âmes** thought-reader; *adj* fond of reading

**liseuse** *nf* reading-lamp; book-rest; book-wrapper; bed-jacket

**lisibilité** *nf* legibility

**lisible** *adj* legible; readable

**lisière** *nf* edge, border (forest, field); list, selvedge (cloth); leading strings

**lissage** *nm* smoothing, polishing

**lisse** *adj* smooth, polished, glossy

**lisser** *vt* smooth, polish, gloss; glaze, burnish; **se ~** become smooth; **se ~ les plumes** preen feathers (bird)

**liste** *nf* list, register, roll; *pol* **scrutin de ~** voting for several candidates from a list

**lit** *nm* bed; layer; bed of river; **enfant de second ~** child of second marriage; **voiture (wagon)- ~** sleeping car

**litanie** *nf* litany; *coll* rigmarole, long list

**litée** *nf* litter (animals)

**literie** *nf* bedding

**lithographe** *n* lithographer

**lithographie** *nf* lithography

**lithographier** *vt* lithograph

**litière** *nf* stretcher, litter; (stable) litter

**litige** *nm leg* litigation; legal dispute; **en ~** at issue

**litigieux -ieuse** *adj* litigious

**litote** *nf* litotes, understatement

**littéraire** *adj* literary

**littéral** *adj* literal; *leg* **preuve ~ e** documentary evidence

**littérateur** *nm* man of letters, litterateur

**littérature** *nf* literature

**littoral** *nm* coastline; *adj* coastal

**liturgie** *nf* liturgy

**liturgique** *adj* liturgical

**livide** *adj* livid, ghastly

**lividité** *nf* lividity, lividness, ghastliness

**livrable** *adj comm* ready for delivery, deliverable

**livraison** *nf comm* delivery; instalment (serial)

¹**livre** *nf* pound (weight); pound (sterling)

²**livre** *nm* book; **~ à succès** bestseller; *naut* **~ de bord** log-book; **~ de poche** paper-back; *comm* **grand ~** ledger

**livrée** *nf* livery

**livrer** *vt* deliver; give up, surrender; join

(battle); hand over; betray, reveal; **se ~ à** surrender oneself to, indulge in; **se ~ à la boisson** take to drink; **se ~ au travail** devote oneself to work

**livresque** *adj* bookish, obtained from books

**livret** *nm* booklet; *mus* libretto; **~ de caisse d'épargne** savings-bank book; *mil* **~ militaire** service record

**livreur** *nm comm* delivery-man

**lobélie** *nf bot* lobelia

**lober** *vt sp* lob

**local** *nm* premises, building; *adj* local

**localiser** *vt* locate; localize; **se ~** fix one's abode; become localized

**localité** *nf* locality, inhabited place

**locataire** *n* tenant; lodger

**¹locatif** *nm gramm* locative

**²locatif -ive** *adj* pertaining to letting or renting; **réparations locatives** tenant's repairs; **valeur locative** rental value

**location** *nf* letting, hiring; rented dwelling; booking, reserving (seats in train, theatre, etc); **agent de ~** house-agent; *theat* **bureau de ~** box-office; **en ~** on hire; **être en ~** live in rented accommodation; **voiture en ~** coach on train with reserved seats

**location-vente** *nf* hire-purchase system

**loch** *nm naut* log

**lock-outer** *vt* lock out

**locomobile** *nf* transportable steam-engine; *adj* transportable; **grue ~** travelling crane

**locomoteur -trice** *adj med* locomotor

**locomotif -ive** *adj* locomotive

**locomotive** *nf* locomotive, engine; *fig* energetic person, dynamic person; driving force

**locuste** *nf* locust

**locution** *nf* phrase, expression, idiom

**lof** *nm naut* windward side; **aller au ~** sail into the wind; **virer ~ pour ~** wear ship

**lofer** *vi naut* luff

**logarithme** *nm* logarithm

**loge** *nf* hut, cabin; lodge (porter, free-masons); *theat* box; *theat* dressing-room; *fig* **être aux premières ~ s** have a front seat, be well placed

**logeable** *adj* inhabitable, fit for occupation

**logement** *nm* lodging, housing; accommodation; dwelling; *mil* quarters; *naut* berth; *eng* housing, socket; **crise du ~** housing shortage

**loger** *vt* (3) lodge, house, accommodate; put up; *mil* quarter; put; *vi* lodge, live; *mil* be quartered; **~ en garni** live in furnished lodgings; **se ~** lodge; take lodgings

**logeur** *nm* landlord, lodging-house

keeper

**logeuse** *nf* landlady

**logicien** *nm* logician

**logique** *nf* logic; *adj* logical, reasoned, consistent; **c'est ~** fair enough

**logis** *nm* dwelling, house, abode; hostelry; **corps de ~** main part of the building

**logistique** *nf* logistics

**loi** *nf* law; enactment, statute; **faire la ~ à** lay down the law to; **projet de ~** bill (parliament); **se faire une ~ de** make a point of

**loin** *adv* far (place, time); **~ des yeux, ~ du cœur** out of sight out of mind; **de ~ en ~** now and then; **du plus ~ que je me souvienne** as far as I can recall; *conj phr* **~ que** far from

**lointain** *nm* distance; *adj* distant, remote; far off

**loir** *nm* dormouse

**loisible** *adj* permissible, allowable, optional; **il vous est ~ de** you are free to

**loisir** *nm* leisure, spare time

**lombago** *nm* lumbago

**lombaire** *adj* lumbar; **ponction ~** lumbar puncture

**lombes** *nmpl med* loins

**lombric** *nm* earthworm

**Londonien -ienne** *n* Londoner

**londonien -ienne** *adj* of London

**Londres** *nm* London

**londrès** *nm* kind of Havana (cigar)

**long** *nm* length; **de ~ en large** to and fro, up and down; **deux mètres de ~** two metres long; **en ~** lengthwise; **étendu de tout son ~** stretched at full length; **le ~ de** along; *naut* alongside; **tout au ~** all the way along; at full length; **tout le ~ du jour** the whole day long; *adj* (*f* **longue**) long; *cul* thin (sauce); **~ de deux mètres** two metres long; *comm* **à longue échéance** long-dated; **avoir les dents longues** be ambitious, greedy; **de longue date** of long-standing; *adv* **en dire ~** speak volumes; **en savoir ~ sur** know a good deal about

**longanime** *adj* long-suffering, forbearing, patient

**longanimité** *nf* forbearance, patience

**long-courrier** *nm* ocean-going ship, liner; intercontinental plane; *adj invar* ocean-going; long-distance

**longe** *nf* tether; thong; *cul* loin

**longer** *vt* (3) skirt, keep close to

**longévité** *nf* longevity

**longtemps** *adv* long; a long time; **cela n'arrivera pas de ~** that won't happen for a long time

**longue** *nf gramm* long syllable; **à la ~** eventually, in the long run

**longuement** *adv* for a long time; lengthily; slowly, deliberately

**longuet -ette** *adj coll* longish, on the long side

**longueur** *nf* length; slowness, delay; boring passage; ~ **d'onde** wavelength; **deux mètres de** ~ two metres long; **en** ~ lengthwise; *sp* **gagner d'une** ~ win by a length; **traîner en** ~ drag on

**lopin** *nm* bit, piece, plot (land)

**loquace** *adj* loquacious, talkative

**loquacité** *nf* loquacity, talkativeness

**loque** *nf* rag; (human) wreck; **en** ~ **s** in tatters, falling apart; **être comme une** ~ be worn out

**loquet** *nm* latch

**loqueteux** *nm* ragamuffin; s/o dressed in rags; *adj* (*f* **-euse**) ragged, in rags, in tatters

**lorgnade** *nf* sidelong glance

**lorgner** *vt* cast sidelong glances at, ogle; look through opera-glasses at; have one's eye on

**lorgnette** *nf* opera-glasses

**lorgnon** *nm* pince-nez; eye-glasses; lorgnette

**lors** *adv obs* then; ~ **de** at the time of; ~ **même que** even though, even when; **depuis** ~ from then on, ever since then; **dès** ~ from that time; **dès** ~ **que** since, given that

**lorsque** *conj* when

**losange** *nm* lozenge; **en** ~ diamond-shaped

**lot** *nm* share, portion, lot; batch; fate, fortune; prize (lottery); **gros** ~ first prize in lottery

**loterie** *nf* lottery; raffle; gamble, matter of chance

**loti** *adj coll* **bien** ~ well provided for, well off; **mal** ~ badly off, poor

**lotissement** *nm* dividing into lots, parcelling out; allotment, building plot; selling of building plots

**louable** *adj* laudable, praiseworthy

**louage** *nm* hiring out, hiring, engaging; **voiture de** ~ hackney carriage, cab

**louange** *nf* praise, commendation; **chanter ses propres** ~ **s** blow one's own trumpet

**louanger** *vt* (3) praise, eulogize; over-praise

**louangeur -euse** *n* praiser; flatterer; *adj* laudatory; flattering

**loubar(d)** *nm* yobbo, hoodlum

**¹louche** *nf* soup-ladle

**²louche** *adj* cross-eyed, squint-eyed; *coll* shady, suspicious, shifty; cloudy (liquid)

**loucher** *vi* squint, be cross-eyed; *coll* make eyes

**loucherie** *nf* squinting

**¹louer** *vt* hire, let out; hire, rent; book, reserve (seats)

**²louer** *vt* praise; **se** ~ be pleased, be satisfied; congratulate oneself

**¹loueur -euse** *n* hirer-out

**²loueur -euse** *n* praiser; flatterer; *adj* flattering

**loufoque** *adj coll* crazy, daft

**loufoquerie** *nf coll* daftness; eccentricity

**louis** *nm obs* gold coin (of varying value)

**loukoum** *nm* Turkish delight

**loup** *nm* wolf; sea-dace; black-velvet mask, domino; flaw, fault; *theat* fluff; *naut* ~ **de mer** old salt; **à pas de** ~ stealthily; **avoir une faim de** ~ be ravenous; **connu comme le** ~ **blanc** known to everybody; **enfermer le** ~ **dans la bergerie** set the fox to keep the geese; **il fait un froid de** ~ it's bitterly cold; **les** ~ **s ne se mangent pas entre eux** dog doesn't eat dog; *coll* **mon petit** ~ my sweet, my darling; **tenir le** ~ **par les oreilles** be in a dilemma

**loup-cervier** *nm* (*pl* **loups-cerviers**) *zool* lynx

**loupe** *nf* lens, magnifying glass; *med* wen; gnarl, lump

**louper** *vt coll* bungle, botch; miss (train, chance); *theat* fluff

**loup-garou** *nm* (*pl* **loups-garous**) werewolf

**lourd** *adj* heavy, ponderous; clumsy, ungainly; dull-witted; severe, grievous; sultry (weather); ~ **de** fraught with; **poids** ~ heavy lorry; heavy-weight boxer; *adv* heavy; *coll* **il n'en reste pas** ~ there's not much left; **ne pas peser** ~ not count for a great deal

**lourdaud -e** *n* dolt, lout; blockhead; *adj* loutish, awkward; dull-witted

**lourderie** *nf* loutishness; gross blunder

**lourdeur** *nf* heaviness, ponderousness; weight; clumsiness, dullness; sultriness

**loustic** *nm coll* wag, joker

**loutre** *nf* otter

**louve** *nf* she-wolf

**louveteau** *nm* wolf-cub; (wolf) cub (scouting)

**louvoiement** *nm* evasiveness; *naut* tacking

**louvoyage** *nm* evasiveness; *naut* tacking

**louvoyer** *vi* (7) be evasive; *naut* tack

**lover** *vt naut* coil; **se** ~ coil up (snake)

**loyal** *adj* honest, fair, dependable; sincere, straightforward

**loyalisme** *nm* loyalty, loyalism

**loyaliste** *n* loyalist

**loyauté** *nf* honesty, fairness; straightforwardness; loyalty

**loyer** *nm* rent, rental

**lu** *p part* **lire**

**lubie** *nf* whim, fad

**lubricité** *nf* lubricity, lust
**lubrifiant** *nm* lubricant; *adj* lubricating
**lubrifier** *vt* lubricate, grease
**lubrique** *adj* lustful, lewd
**lucarne** *nf* dormer-window; sky-light
**lucide** *adj* lucid, clear
**lucidité** *nf* lucidity, clarity
**luciole** *nf zool* firefly
**lucratif -ive** *adj* lucrative, paying
**luette** *nf med* uvula
**lueur** *nf* gleam; glimmer; flash, ray
**lugubre** *adj* lugubrious, dismal; sad, sorrowful
**luge** *nf* sleigh, toboggan
**lui** *pron* to him, to her, to it; he, he himself
**luire** *vi* (57) shine, gleam, glint
**luisant** *nm* gloss, shine, sheen; *adj* shining, shiny, glossy; **ver ~** glow-worm
**lumière** *nf* light; enlightenment; luminary; **donner de la ~** turn the light on; **la ville ~** Paris; **le siècle des ~s** the age of enlightenment; **mettre en ~** bring out, bring to light
**lumignon** *nm* candle-end; snuff; dim light
**luminaire** *nm* luminary
**lumineux -euse** *adj* luminous; brilliant; **idée lumineuse** brilliant idea; **onde lumineuse** light wave
**luminosité** *nf* luminosity, sheen
**lunaire** *adj* lunar
**lunatique** *adj* whimsical, unbalanced, capricious
**lundi** *nm* Monday
**lune** *nf* moon; *sl* behind, bum; **~ de miel** honeymoon; close understanding; **~ rousse** April moon; **clair de ~** moonlight; **dans une bonne ~** in a good humour; **être dans la ~** be day-dreaming
**luné** *adj coll* **bien, mal ~** in a good, bad, mood
**lunetier** *nm* spectacle-maker, optician
**lunette** *nf* telescope, field-glass; spy-glass; hole of W.C.; *mot* rear-window; **~s** glasses, spectacles
**lunetterie** *nf* spectacle-making; optical trade

**lupanar** *nm* brothel
**lurette** *nf* **il y a belle ~** a long time ago
**luron** *nm* big, strapping fellow; **c'est un gai ~** he's quite a lad
**luronne** *nf* strapping girl; tomboy; girl who gets around
**lustrage** *nm* glazing, glossing; shininess
**¹lustre** *nm* chandelier
**²lustre** *nm* lustre, sheen, polish; gloss
**lustré** *adj* lustrous, glossy
**luth** *nm mus* lute
**luthier** *nm mus* stringed instrument maker
**lutin** *nm* elf, goblin; imp (child)
**lutiner** *vt* tease, plague; *coll* **~ les filles** fondle the girls; *sl* snog
**lutrin** *nm eccles* lectern
**lutte** *nf* struggle, contest, strife; *sp* wrestling; *sp* **~ à la corde de traction** tug-of-war; **de bonne ~** by fair means; **de haute ~** by force; *leg* **les parties en ~** the contending parties
**lutter** *vi* fight, struggle; *sp* wrestle; try to resist; *sp* **~ de vitesse** race
**lutteur -euse** *n* wrestler; fighter
**luxe** *nm* luxury; wealth, profusion; **~ de précautions** excessive precautions; **se payer (se donner) le ~ de** treat oneself to
**luxer** *vt med* luxate, dislocate, put out of joint
**luxueux -ueuse** *adj* luxurious, sumptuous
**luxure** *nf* lechery, lust, lewdness
**luxurieux -ieuse** *adj* lecherous, lustful, lewd
**luzerne** *nf bot* lucerne
**lycanthropie** *nf* lycanthropy
**lycée** *nm* = state secondary grammar school
**lycéen -enne** *n* pupil at a **lycée**
**lymphatique** *adj med* lymphatic
**lymphe** *nf med* lymph
**lynchage** *nm* lynching
**lyncher** *vt* lynch
**lyrique** *adj* lyric; poet; *adj* lyrical; **théâtre ~** opera-house
**lyrisme** *nm* lyricism; *coll* enthusiasm; gush
**lys** *nm see* **lis**

# M

**ma** *poss adj f* my; *see* **mon**
**maboul** *n + adj sl* loony, idiot
**macabre** *adj* macabre, gruesome, grim; **la danse ~** the Dance of Death

**macache** *interj sl* nothing doing!, not on your life!
**macadam** *nm* macadam; macadamized road

**macadamiser** *vt* macadamize

**macaron** *nm cul* macaroon; coil (hair); *coll* decoration, medal

**macaroni** *nm cul* macaroni; *sl* Wop, Italian

**macchabée** *nm sl* corpse, stiff

**Macédoine** *nf* Macedonia

**macédoine** *nf* diced or chopped vegetables; fruit-salad; *fig* hotch-potch

**macération** *nf* maceration, steeping, soaking; mortifying (flesh)

**macérer** *vt* (6) macerate; mortify (flesh); **faire ~** steep, soak

**mâchefer** *nm* clinker, slag

**mâcher** *vt* masticate, chew; champ; tear, chew up; **ne pas ~ ses mots** not mince one's words; **~ la besogne à qn** do half s/o's work for him

**machiavélique** *adj* Machiavellian

**mâchicoulis** *nm* machicolation

**machin** *nm coll* what's-it, thingummy-jig; **Monsieur ~** Mr What's his name; *vulg* prick

**machinal** *adj* mechanical, automatic; unconscious

**machinateur -trice** *n* machinator, plotter, schemer

**machine** *nf* machine; engine; *fig* machinery; *coll* contraption; **~s** (ship's) engines; **~ à calculer** adding-machine, calculating machine; **~ à composer** type-setting machine; **~ à coudre** sewing-machine; **~ à écrire** typewriter; **~ à laver** washing-machine; **~ à sous** one-armed bandit, fruit-machine; **~ routière** traction-engine; *theat* **pièce à ~s** play dependent on stage-effects

**machine-outil** *nf* (*pl* **machines-outils**) machine-tool

**machiner** *vt* machinate, plot, scheme, contrive; **affaire machinée d'avance** put-up job

**machinerie** *nf* machine construction; machine-shops, plant; *naut* engine-room

**machinisme** *nm* automation

**machiniste** *nm theat* stage-hand; *obs* bus-driver; **chef ~** stage-manager

**mâchoire** *nf* jaw; jaw-bone; *mot* brake-shoe; *eng* jaws (vice), flange (pulley)

**mâchonnement** *nm* chewing; mumbling

**mâchonner** *vt* chew, munch; *fig* mumble, mutter

**mâchurer** *vt* smudge, blacken; crush, bruise

**maçon** *nm* mason, bricklayer; (free-) mason

**maçonner** *vt* build; face (wall); wall up

**maçonnerie** *nf* masonry, brick-work, stone-work; freemasonry

**maçonnique** *adj* masonic

**macrobiotique** *adj* macrobiotic

**macrocéphale** *adj med* macrocephalic, large-headed

**macrocosme** *nm* macrocosm

**maculage** *nm* maculation, staining; *typ* blurring

**macule** *nf* macula, spot, stain; sun-spot; *typ* spoiled sheet

**maculer** *vt* maculate, mark with spots, stain; *typ* blur

**madame** *nf* (*pl* **mesdames**) Mrs; madam; **jouer à la ~** put on airs

**Madeleine** *nf* **pleurer comme une ~** weep bitterly, cry one's eyes out

**madeleine** *nf* sponge-cake, madeleine

**mademoiselle** *nf* (*pl* **mesdemoiselles**) Miss

**Madère** *nm* Madeira; Madeira wine

**madone** *nf* madonna

**madré** *adj* sly, wily

**madrier** *nm* beam, thick board, plank

**madrilène** *adj* of Madrid

**maestria** *nf* masterly skill, brio

**magasin** *nm* shop; warehouse; *mil* armoury; magazine (rifle, etc); **~ à succursales** chain-store; **~s généraux** bonded warehouse; **en ~** in stock; **grand ~** department store

**magasinage** *nm* storing, warehousing

**magasinier** *nm* warehouseman; *mil* storesman

**mage** *nm* Magus; seer; **les Rois ~s** the Magi, the Three Wise Men

**magicien -ienne** *n* wizard; sorcerer (sorceress); magician

**magie** *nf* magic, wizardry

**magique** *adj* magic, magical

**magistral** *adj* magisterial, skilful, masterly; *coll* first-rate, exemplary

**magistrat** *nm leg* judge; someone in judicial capacity

**magistrature** *nf leg* magistrature; **~ assise** the Judges; **~ debout** the body of public prosecutors, the law-officers of the State; **entrer dans la ~** be appointed judge or public prosecutor

**magnanime** *adj* magnanimous

**magnanimité** *nf* magnanimity

**magnat** *nm* magnate, tycoon

**magnésie** *nf* magnesia; **sulfate de ~** Epsom salts

**magnésium** *nm chem* magnesium; *obs* **lampe au ~** flash-lamp

**magnétique** *adj* magnetic

**magnétiser** *vt* magnetize; mesmerize, hypnotize

**magnétiseur** *nm* magnetizer; mesmerizer

**magnétisme** *nm* magnetism; mesmerism; *fig* magnetism

**magnéto** *nf* magneto; *nm coll* tape-recorder

**magnétophone** *nm* tape-recorder

**magnétoscope** *nm* video-tape-recorder

**magnifier** *vt* magnify; glorify

**magnifique** *adj* magnificent, splendid; sumptuous; grandiloquent, pompous; *ar* generous, liberal

¹**magot** *nm* *zool* Barbary ape; Chinese (grotesque) figure in porcelain

²**magot** *nm coll* hoard, pile (money)

**magouille** *nf* chicanery

**mahométan** *adj* Mohammedan, Muslim, Moslem

**mahométanisme** *nm* Mohammedanism

**mai** *nm* May

**maigre** *nm cul* lean (meat); **faire ~** abstain from meat; *adj* lean, skinny, thin; meagre, scanty, sparse; *eccles* meatless; **~ repas** scanty meal; **jour ~** fast-day; **repas ~** meatless meal

**maigrelet -ette** *adj* on the thin side, skinny

**maigreur** *nf* thinness, lankness; emaciation; scantiness, sparseness

**maigrichon -onne** *adj* on the thin side, skinny

**maigrir** *vt* make (s/o) thinner (illness); make (s/o) look thinner (garment); *vi* grow thin, lose flesh; **se faire ~** diet, slim

**mail** *nm* promenade, avenue; *ar* hammer

¹**maille** *nf* stitch; link (chain); mesh (net); **~ à l'endroit et à l'envers** plain and purl; **arrêter les ~s** cast off; **cotte de ~s** coat of mail

²**maille** *nf ar* small coin; *coll* **n'avoir ni sou ni ~** be broke; **avoir ~ à partir avec qn** have a bone to pick with s/o

**mailler** *vt* net; *naut* shackle

**maillet** *nm* mallet, maul; *sp* mallet

**maillon** *nm* link; *naut* shackle

**maillot** *nm sp* singlet, vest, jersey; *theat* tights; baby's napkin; **~ de bain** bathing-costume; *sp* **~ jaune** yellow jersey worn by winner of a stage in Tour de France cycle race; the winner of such a stage

**main** *nf* hand; hand(-writing); hand (cards); **~ courante** hand-rail; **~ de papier** quire; **à bas les ~s!** hands off!; **à ~ levée** free-hand; **avoir la haute ~ sur** have complete control of; **avoir la ~ large** be generous, open-handed; **coup de ~** raid, surprise attack; **de longue ~** for a long time past; **donner un coup de ~** give a helping hand; **en un tour de ~** in a jiffy; **en venir aux ~s** come to blows; **faire ~ basse sur** lay hands on, make a clean sweep of; **faire qch sous ~** do sth in an underhand way; **gagner haut la ~** win hands down; **haut les ~s!** hands up!; **homme de ~** thug; **je n'en mettrais pas la ~ au feu** I would not swear to it; **mariage de la ~ gauche** morganatic marriage; **mettre la ~ sur qn** get hold of s/o; **ne pas y aller de ~ morte** make no bones about it, go hard at it; **passer la ~** pass the deal (cards); **passer la ~ dans le dos de qn** soft-soap s/o, butter s/o up; **porter la ~ sur qn** lay a hand on s/o; **prêter ~ forte à** help; **se donner la ~** shake hands; **se faire la ~** get one's hand in; **se passer la ~ dans le dos** pat oneself on the back; **sous la ~** at hand

**main-d'œuvre** *nf* labour; manpower, labour-force

**mainmise** *nf leg* seizure, distraint; nefarious influence

**mainmorte** *nf leg* mortmain

**maint** *adj* many a; **à ~es reprises** time and time again

**maintenant** *adv* now; **dès ~** from now on, henceforth; *conj* **~ que** now that

**maintenir** *vt* (96) maintain, hold; hold up; keep up; affirm; **~ qn en fonction** keep s/o in office; **se ~** keep on; last, hold on; continue

**maintien** *nm* maintenance, upholding, keeping; bearing, deportment; **se donner un ~** keep countenance

**maire** *nm* mayor

**mairesse** *nf* mayoress

**mairie** *nf* town-hall; office of mayor, mayoralty

**mais** *conj* but; *adv* indeed, well, why; **~ oui!** why, certainly!, but of course!; **~ non!** not at all!; **~ vous voilà!** well you're here!; **n'en pouvoir ~** be at the end of one's tether, exhausted

**maïs** *nm* maize, Indian corn, *US* corn

**maison** *nf* house, home; household, staff; family; firm, business; dynasty; *cul* home-made; *sl* classic, prize; **~ close** brothel; **~ d'arrêt** prison; **~ de correction** approved school; **~ de fous** lunatic asylum; **~ d'habitation** dwelling-house; **~ de rapport** tenement; **~ de repos** convalescent home, mental home; **~ religieuse** convent; **à la ~** at home; **de bonne ~** of good family; **entrer en ~** go into (domestic) service; **être de la ~** be one of the family

**maisonnée** *nf* household, members of family

**maisonnette** *nf* small house, cottage

**maître** *nm* master; **Maître** (instead of **Monsieur**) applied to lawyers; *coll* **~ chanteur** blackmailer; **~ de conférences** = (university) lecturer; **~ d'école** schoolmaster; **~ de forges** iron-master, steel-manufacturer; **~ d'hôtel** head-waiter, butler; *coll* **Maître Jacques** Jack-of-all-trades, factotum;

~ queux master cook; être passé ~ en be a past master at; les ~s de la peinture the great masters; parler à qn en ~ speak authoritatively to s/o

maître-autel nm (pl maîtres-autels) eccles high altar

maîtresse nf mistress; lover; ~ d'école school-mistress; ~ de maison housewife, hostess; ~ femme very capable woman; idée ~ governing principle

maîtrise nf mastership; mastery; eccles choir-school; choir; ~ de conférences lectureship; ~ de soi self-control; agent de ~ foreman

maîtriser vt master, subdue, control; se ~ control oneself

majesté nf majesty, stateliness, grandeur; Sa Majesté His Majesty, Her Majesty

majestueux -ueuse adj majestic, stately

majeur nm second finger, longest finger; adj major, principal, important; of age; mus major; c'est un cas de force ~ e it's a case of absolute necessity, there is no choice; devenir ~ come of age, reach one's majority; Lac Majeur Lake Maggiore

majeure nf major premise

majolique nf majolica

major nm mil adjudant; mil medical officer, M.O.; mil ~ général chief of staff; (navy) ~ général Admiral Maritime Superintendent

majoration nf over-estimation, over-valuation; increase (price, salary); additional charge

majordome nm major-domo, manager of (large) household

majorer vt over-estimate, over-value; increase (charge, price)

majoritaire adj majority, pertaining to the majority

majorité nf majority, greater part; coming of age; mil adjutancy

majuscule nf capital letter; adj capital

mal nm (pl maux) evil; harm; hurt; pain; disease, illness; ~ au cœur sickness, nausea; ~ blanc gathering, sore; ~ de l'air air-sickness; ~ de mer sea-sickness; ~ du pays home-sickness; attraper du ~ catch an infection; avoir du ~ à faire qch find sth difficult to do; avoir ~ à have a pain in; il n'y a pas grand ~ there's not much harm done; ne pas penser à ~ have good intentions; prendre du ~ fall ill; prendre qch en ~ take sth amiss, take offence at sth; se donner du ~ take trouble, take pains; tourner qch en ~ put the worst construction onto sth, show up

the black side of sth; vouloir du ~ à qn wish s/o ill; adj bad, wrong; bon an, ~ an year in year out; bon gré, ~ gré willy-nilly, regardless; adv badly, ill; in bad health; on bad terms; ugly; uncomfortable; ~ léché raw, callow; aller ~ be ill, be in bad health; c'est ~ à lui de it's wrong for him to, it's too bad of him to; être au plus ~ avec qn be at daggers drawn with s/o; on n'est pas ~ ici it's not too bad here; coll pas ~ not bad looking; coll pas ~ de many, quite a lot of; prendre ~ qch take sth amiss; se mettre ~ avec qn fall out with s/o; se sentir (se trouver) ~ feel unwell; vous ne feriez pas ~ de it wouldn't be a bad idea for you to; vous ne trouverez pas ~ que you won't mind if

malade n invalid, sick person; patient; faire le ~ malinger; adj ill, unwell, sick; injured, in poor condition; ~ de ill with; en être ~ be upset about sth; être ~ du cœur, du foie have heart-trouble, liver-trouble

maladie nf illness, sickness, disease, malady

maladif -ive adj sickly, weakly; unhealthy, morbid

maladresse nf clumsiness, awkwardness; blunder

maladroit n clumsy person; blunderer; adj clumsy, awkward, maladroit; blundering

malais nm Malaysian (language); adj Malaysian

malaise nm indisposition, faintness, discomfort; uneasiness, unrest

malaisé adj difficult

Malaisie nf Malaysia

malappris -e n lout, boor, unmannerly person; adj boorish, rude, unmannerly

malard nm zool mallard

malavisé adj ill-advised, blundering, tactless

malaxage nm mixing (cement); kneading (dough); working (butter); med massage

malaxer vt mix (cement); knead (dough); work (butter); med massage

malaxeur nm cement-mixer; kneading machine; butter-worker

malbâti adj misshapen, ill-favoured

malchance nf bad luck; mishap; par ~ as ill luck would have it

malchanceux -euse n + adj unlucky, unfortunate (person)

malcommode adj coll inconvenient

maldonne nf misdeal (cards); coll error

mâle nm male; adj male; virile, manly, vigorous

**malédiction** *nf* curse, malediction; *interj* curse it!, damnation!

**maléfice** *nm* evil spell, malefice

**maléfique** *adj* maleficent, baleful

**malencontreux -euse** *adj* unlucky, unfortunate, untoward; ill-met

**mal-en-point** *adj invar* in a bad way, out of sorts

**malentendu** *nm* misunderstanding, misapprehension, dispute

**malfaçon** *nf* defect, bad workmanship

**malfaisant** *adj* maleficent, harmful; noxious

**malfaiteur -trice** *n* malefactor, wrong-doer; scoundrel

**malfamé** *adj* of bad repute, ill-famed, disreputable

**malgache** *nm* Madagascan (language); *adj* Madagascan, Malagasy

**malgré** *prep* in spite of, despite; ~ **moi** against my will; ~ **que** *conj phr coll* though, although; ~ **que vous en ayez** for all you can do

**malhabile** *adj* unskilful, awkward

**malheur** *nm* misfortune, bad luck; accident, calamity; **à qch** ~ **est bon** it's an ill wind that blows no one any good; **faire le** ~ **de qn** be the ruin of s/o; *coll* **faire un** ~ do something desperate; **jouer de** ~ be out of luck; **par** ~ as ill luck would have it, unfortunately; **porter** ~ bring bad luck

**malheureux -euse** *n* unfortunate person; unlucky person; *adj* unfortunate, unhappy; unlucky, ill-fated; wretched, paltry; **avoir la main malheureuse** be clumsy; be unlucky (cards); **c'est** ~ **que** it's a pity that; *coll* **te voici, ce n'est pas** ~ ! so you are here, and about time too!

**malhonnête** *adj* dishonest, shady; impolite, rude; improper, coarse

**malhonnêteté** *nf* dishonesty; shady transaction; impoliteness; improper remark, coarse expression

**malice** *nf* mischievousness, mischief; sly remark; malevolence; **faire des** ~**s à** play sly tricks on; **ne pas voir** ~ **à qch** see nothing wrong in sth

**malicieux -ieuse** *adj* malicious; mischievous, arch, sly

**malignité** *nf* malignity; spitefulness; mischievousness; *med* malignancy

**malin -igne** *n* cunning person; *coll* sharp one; *coll* **c'est un** ~ ! he's pretty sharp!; *coll* **faire le** ~ try to be smart; **le Malin** the Devil; *adj* malignant; malicious, wicked; mischievous; cunning, sly, shrewd; *coll* difficult; *coll* **ce n'est pas** ~ that's not very clever; it's not difficult

**malingre** *adj* puny, sickly

**malintentionné** *adj* ill-intentioned

**malle** *nf* trunk, box; *mot* boot, *US* trunk; *ar* mail-boat; **faire (défaire) sa** ~ **pack (unpack) one's trunk**

**malléable** *adj* malleable, soft; pliable, pliant

**malle-poste** *nf* (*pl* **malles-poste(s)**) mail-coach

**mallette** *nf* small suitcase, attaché-case

**malmener** *vt* (6) ill-treat, handle roughly, mishandle; harry, brow-beat

**malodorant** *adj* malodorous, evil-smelling

**malotru** *nm* boor, cad; *adj* coarse, uncouth, caddish

**malpeigné** *adj* tousled, unkempt

**malplaisant** *adj* unpleasant, displeasing

**malpropre** *adj* dirty, untidy, slovenly; smutty, dirty (remark)

**malpropreté** *nf* dirtiness, untidiness, slovenliness; smuttiness; **dire des** ~ **s** talk smut

**malsain** *adj* unhealthy, unwholesome; pernicious, unsound

**malséant** *adj* unseemly, indecorous

**malsonnant** *adj* offensive, objectionable

**malterie** *nf* malt-house

**maltraiter** *vt* maltreat, ill-treat

**malveillance** *nf* malevolence, ill-will

**malveillant** *adj* malevolent, ill-willed; spiteful

**malvenu** *adj* ill-advised, badly placed

**maman** *nf* mother, *coll* mama, mummy; **bonne** ~ grandmother, *coll* grandma, granny

**mamelle** *nf* breast; udder

**mamelon** *nm* nipple; dug, teat; *geog* hillock

**mamillaire** *adj* mamillary

**mammaire** *adj med* mammary

**mammifère** *nm zool* mammal; *adj* mammalian

**mammouth** *nm* mammoth

**mamours** *nmpl* billing and cooing; **faire des** ~ **à** caress, coax

**manade** *nf* herd of bulls; herd of horses

**manant** *nm ar* peasant, villager; *coll* yokel, churl, boor

¹**manche** *nf* sleeve; *sp* game, set, hand (cards); ~ **à air** *aer* windsock; *naut* ventilator; **avoir qn dans sa** ~ have s/o in one's pocket; **la Manche** the Channel; **une autre paire de** ~**s** a different kettle of fish

²**manche** *nm* handle, haft, stock; ~ **à balai** broomstick; *aer* control-column, *coll* joy-stick; **jeter le** ~ **après la cognée** give up

**manchette** *nf* cuff; headline (newspaper); **boutons de** ~ cuff-links; **mettre en** ~ splash (newspaper)

**manchon** *nm* muff; *eng* casing, sleeve; flange; gas-mantle

¹**manchot** **-ote** *n* one-armed person; *adj* one-armed; *fig* clumsy; **il n'est pas ~** he's clever with his hands; he's not clumsy

²**manchot** *nm* penguin

**mandant** **-e** *n* *leg* principal; *pol* constituent

**mandarine** *nf* tangerine, mandarin

**mandarinier** *nm* tangerine orange tree

**mandat** *nm* mandate; warrant; money-order; *leg* power of attorney; **~ d'arrêt** warrant for arrest; *leg* **~ de perquisition** search-warrant; **~ du Trésor** Treasury warrant; **~ international** international money-order; **lancer un ~** issue a warrant

**mandataire** *n* proxy; *leg* representative; authorized agent

**mandat-carte** *nm* (*pl* **mandats-cartes**) (French) postcard money-order

**mandat-lettre** *nm* (*pl* **mandats-lettres**) money-order

**Mandchou** **-e** *n* Manchurian

**mandchou** *adj* Manchurian

**Mandchourie** *nf* Manchuria

**mandement** *nm* mandate, instructions

**mander** *vt* summon; *ar* say by letter, report

**mandibule** *nf* *anat* mandible, lower jaw

**mandragore** *nf* mandragora, mandrake

**mandrin** *nm* *eng* mandrel; punch; drift-bolt

**manécanterie** *nf* choir-school

**manège** *nm* riding-school; training (horses); roundabout, merry-go-round; *fig* trick, device

**mânes** *nmpl* manes, shades

**manette** *nf* lever; *elect* key, morse-key; *naut* spoke (wheel)

**manganèse** *nm* manganese

**mangeable** *adj* edible, eatable

**mangeoire** *nf* manger, feeding trough

**manger** *nm* food; *vt* (3) eat; eat into, away; devour, consume; spend; **~ de l'argent** squander money; *sl* **~ le morceau** squeal, blow the gaff; **~ ses mots** mumble, swallow one's words; *vi* eat; **~ à sa faim** have enough to eat; **~ comme quatre** eat a huge meal

**mange-tout** *nm invar* sugar pea; French bean; *ar* spendthrift

**mangeur** **-euse** *n* eater

**mangouste** *nf* mongoose

**mangue** *nf* mango

**manguier** *nm* mango-tree

**maniabilité** *nf* handiness; ease of handling, manoeuvrability (car, plane)

**maniable** *adj* handy; manageable, easy to handle; tractable, pliable; **peu ~** awkward, unhandy

**maniaque** *n* crank, eccentric, faddist; *med* maniac; *adj* eccentric, faddy, fussy

**manichéen** **-éenne** *adj* manichean

**manie** *nf* mania, craze, fad; idiosyncrasy, trick; *med* mental derangement; **avoir la ~ de** be mad about, have a craze for; have a trick of

**maniement** *nm* handling, management

**manier** *vt* handle, ply, wield; manage, use

**manière** *nf* manner, way, guise; kind; *arts* style; **~ d'être** condition, state; *arts* **à la ~** in the style, manner of; *coll* **de la belle ~** thoroughly; **d'une ou d'une autre** in one way or another; **en ~ de** by way of; **en quelque ~** in a way; **faire des ~s** put on airs; *coll* affect reluctance; *conj phr* **de ~ à** so as to; **de ~ que** so that

**maniéré** *adj* affected, finicky, pretentious; *arts* mannered, finical

**maniérisme** *nm* mannerism

**manieur** *nm* handler, user; **~ d'argent** financier; *coll* tycoon

**manif** *nf coll* demo

**manifestant** **-e** *n* demonstrator

**manifestation** *nf* manifestation; public occasion; political demonstration; *sl* demo

**manifeste** *nm* manifesto; *naut* manifest; *adj* manifest, obvious, overt; palpable

**manifester** *vt* show, manifest, express; *vi* demonstrate, take part in demonstration; **se ~** appear, emerge

**manigance** *nf coll* wangling; **~s** intrigue, wiles

**manigancer** *vt* (4) *coll* wangle; intrigue, plot; *pol* gerrymander

¹**manille** *nf* Manilla cigar

²**manille** *nf* kind of card game

**manipulateur** **-trice** *n* manipulator, handler; *nm* sending-key (telegraphy)

**manipuler** *vt* manipulate, handle; operate; *coll* wangle

**manitou** *nm coll* bigwig, big shot

**manivelle** *nf* handle, crank; *mot* starting handle

¹**manne** *nf bibl* manna

²**manne** *nf* basket, hamper

**mannequin** *nm* tailor's dummy; mannequin

**manœuvrabilité** *nf* manoeuvrability

**manœuvrable** *adj* manoeuvrable, manageable

¹**manœuvre** *nm* labourer; **travail de ~** unskilled labour

²**manœuvre** *nf* working, handling; driving; *mil* exercise, drill; move, movement; shunting; intrigue, manoeuvre, scheme; **~ électorale** vote-catching device; **fausse ~** wrong move

**manœuvrer** *vt* work, handle, drive; shunt; manoeuvre; *vi mil + naut* manoeuvre

**manoir** *nm* manor; country-house

**manomètre** *nm* manometer, pressure-gauge

**manquant** *adj* absent, missing; **porté ~** reported missing

**manque** *nm* lack, want, insufficiency; breach; **~ de cœur** heartlessness; **~ de parole** breach of faith; **par ~ de** for want of

**manqué** *adj* missed; unsuccessful; **c'est un acteur ~** he ought to have been an actor; **coup ~** failure, abortive attempt; **garçon ~** tomboy; **vie ~e** wasted life

**manquement** *nm* failure, lapse, breach; **~ à l'appel** absence from roll-call

**manquer** *vt* miss; *vi* lack, be missing, run short, fail; miss, be missing; give way; just miss, come near to; **~ à qn** be missed by s/o; be disrespectful to s/o; **~ de faire qch** nearly do something; *coll* **cela n'a pas manqué!** of course, it happened!; **ne ~ de rien** want for nothing; **ne pas ~ de** not fail to; *v impers* **il me manque une chaussette** I am one sock short; **il ne manque plus que cela!** that's the last straw!

**mansarde** *nf* attic, garret; dormer-window

**mansardé** *adj* mansard-roofed; **chambre ~e** attic-room

¹**mante** *nf* mantle, sleeveless cloak

²**mante** *nf ent* mantis

**manteau** *nm* overcoat; cloak; *mil* greatcoat; *fig* cloak, covering; **~ de cheminée** mantelpiece; **sous le ~** secretly, confidentially

**mantille** *nf* mantilla

**manucure** *nf* manicure

**manucurer** *vt* manicure

**manuel** *nm* manual, text-book, handbook; *adj (f* -**uelle**) *adj* manual

**manufacture** *nf* factory, mill, plant, works

**manufacturer** *vt* manufacture

**manufacturier** *nm* manufacturer, mill-owner; *adj (f* -**ière**) manufacturing

**manuscrit** *nm* manuscript

**manutention** *nf* handling; administration

**manutentionner** *vt* handle

**maoïsme** *nm* maoism

**maoïste** *n* maoist

**mappemonde** *nf* map of the world

¹**maquereau** *nm* mackerel

²**maquereau** *nm coll* pimp, ponce, procurer

**maquerelle** *nf coll* procuress, madam (brothel)

**maquette** *nf* model, mock-up; *print* dummy

**maquignon** *nm* horse-dealer; *coll* spiv, go-between

**maquignonner** *vt* sell (horses) dishonestly; *coll* fix, fiddle

**maquillage** *nm* make-up; making-up; faking

**maquiller** *vt* make up; fake, disguise, distort; **se ~** make up; *coll* paint oneself

**maquilleur** -**euse** *n theat + cin* person who does make-up

**maquis** *nm* bush, undergrowth (in Corsica); resistance movement; *fig* tangle, maze; **prendre le ~** take to the maquis, go underground

**maquisard** *nm* resistance fighter, partisan

**maraîcher** -**ère** *n* market-gardener; *adj* market-gardening (industry, produce)

**marais** *nm* marsh, bog; **~ salant** salt-marsh; **le Marais** the Marais district in Paris

**marasme** *nm* stagnation; depression, despondency

**marasquin** *nm* maraschino

**marâtre** *nf ar* step-mother; cruel, harsh step-mother

**maraudage** *nm* pilfering; looting

**maraude** *nf* thieving; marauding; *coll* **taxi en ~** cruising taxi

**marauder** *vi* pilfer; maraud; *coll* cruise for fares (taxi)

**marbre** *nm* marble, marble statue; marbling (book); *typ* bed of press; **livre sur le ~** book in the press

**marbré** *adj* marbled, mottled

**marbrer** *vt* marble (book); mottle

**marbrerie** *nf* marble work; marble-working; monumental mason's workshop

**marbrier** *nm* marble-cutter, monumental mason; *adj (f* -**ière**) marble

**marbrière** *nf* marble quarry

**marbrure** *nf* marbling (book); mottling

**marc** *nm* residue from fruit-pressing; kind of brandy; **~ de café** coffee-grounds

**marcassin** *nm zool* young wild boar

**marchand** -**e** *n* tradesman (-woman), dealer, shopkeeper; merchant; **~ au détail** retailer; **~ des quatre saisons** costermonger, barrow-boy; **~ en gros** wholesaler; *adj* saleable, marketable; commercial, merchant; **navire ~** merchant-ship, cargo-boat; **prix ~** market price; **valeur ~e** market value

**marchandage** *nm* bargaining

**marchander** *vt* haggle over, bargain for; grudge

**marchandise** *nf* merchandise, goods;

commodity; **faire valoir sa** ~ present things in a favourable light

¹**marche** *nf* border, march, borderland

²**marche** *nf* step, stair; walking, gait; functioning, running; *mus* march; *mot* ~ **arrière** reverse; ~ **à suivre** course to be followed; **en** ~ moving; **en état de** ~ in working order; **fermer la** ~ bring up the rear; **mettre en** ~ start (engine), set moving

**marché** *nm* market; marketing; transaction, dealing, buying; ~ **aux puces** flea-market, junk-market; ~ **conclu!** it's a deal!; ~ **des valeurs** stockmarket; **(à) bon** ~ cheap; **faire bon** ~ **de qch** attribute little value to sth; **faire son** ~ do the shopping

**marchepied** *nm mot* running-board; step (railway-coach); pair of steps, step-ladder; *fig* stepping-stone

**marcher** *nm* gait, walking; *vi* walk, go, march; tread; function, go, work, run; *coll* agree; ~ **à quatre pattes** walk on all fours; *coll* **cela n'a pas marché** it didn't work, it didn't come off; **façon de** ~ gait; **faire** ~ **une affaire** run a business; **faire** ~ **une maison** run a house; **les affaires marchent** business is good; *coll* **on vous a fait** ~ you've been had

**marcheur -euse** *n* walker; *coll* **vieux** ~ old rake

**marcotte** *nf hort* layer; runner, sucker

**marcotter** *vt hort* layer

**mardi** *nm* Tuesday; ~ **gras** Shrove Tuesday

**mare** *nf* pond, pool

**marécage** *nm* marsh, swamp, quagmire

**marécageux -euse** *adj* marshy, swampy

**maréchal** *nm* blacksmith; *mil* marshal; *mil* ~ **des logis** sergeant

**maréchaussée** *nf hist* mounted constabulary

**marée** *nf* tide; fresh fish; **à** ~ tidal; **la** ~ **monte (descend)** the tide is coming in (going out); **train de** ~ fish train

**marelle** *nf* hopscotch

**marémoteur -trice** *adj* tidal (energy); **usine marémotrice** tide-power plant

**marennes** *nf* Marennes oyster

**mareyage** *nm* fish trade

**mareyeur -euse** *n* fishmonger

**marge** *nf* border, edge; margin; *comm* ~ **bénéficiaire** profit margin; **note en** ~ marginal note

**margelle** *nf* curb-stone of well

**margotin** *nm* bundle of firewood

**margoulette** *nf sl* mug, face; jaw

**margoulin** *nm* small tradesman; *coll* black-marketeer

**Marguerite** *nf* Margaret

**marguerite** *nf* daisy; **effeuiller la** ~ play

'she loves me, she loves me not'

**marguillier** *nm* churchwarden

**mari** *nm* husband

**mariable** *adj* marriageable

**mariage** *nm* marriage, matrimony; wedding; wedlock; **acte de** ~ marriage certificate; **demande en** ~ proposal of marriage; **donner en** ~ give away; **né en dehors du** ~ born out of wedlock; **promesse de** ~ engagement, betrothal

**Marie** *nf* Mary

**marié -e** *n* married person; **jeune** ~ bridegroom; **jeune** ~ **e** bride; **la** ~ **e est trop belle** it's too good to be true

**marier** *vt* marry; join in marriage (priest); marry off; *fig* join, unite; match (colours); **fille à** ~ eligible daughter; **se** ~ marry, get married; **se** ~ **avec** get married to; *fig* blend, harmonize, go with

**marie-salope** *nf* (*pl* **maries-salopes**) *sl* slattern; mud-barge (dredger)

**marieur -ieuse** *n* match-maker

**marin** *nm* sailor; *coll* ~ **d'eau douce** land-lubber; *adj* marine; **avoir le pied** ~ be a good sailor (i.e. not seasick); **carte** ~ **e** chart

**marinade** *nf cul* marinade, pickle

**marine** *nf* seamanship; sea-service; *arts* sea-scape; ~ **(de guerre)** navy; ~ **marchande** merchant navy; **terme de** ~ nautical term; *adj usu invar* navy-blue

**mariner** *vt cul* marinade, pickle; *vi coll* be in a pickle for a long time

**marinier** *nm* waterman; *adj* (*f* **-ière**) marine, naval; **officier** ~ petty officer

**marinière** *nf* jersey, blouse, tee-shirt; *sp* side-stroke (swimming); *cul* **sauce** ~ onion sauce

**mariol(le)** *nm sl* **faire le** ~ show off, talk big

**marionnette** *nf* puppet; **théâtre de** ~ **s** puppet-show

**maritime** *adj* maritime, seaborne; **agent** ~ shipping agent; **courtier** ~ shipbroker

**maritorne** *nf* ugly slattern

**marivaudage** *nm* witty and sophisticated conversation; mild flirting

**marivauder** *vi* make witty and sophisticated conversation; flirt

**marjolaine** *nf bot* marjoram

**marlou** *nm sl* pimp

**marmaille** *nf coll* children, kids, brats

**marmelade** *nf* compote (fruit); *coll* hell of a mess; ~ **d'oranges** marmalade; **en** ~ in shreds, pounded to a jelly

**marmitage** *nm coll mil* (heavy) bombardment

**marmite** *nf* pot, pan; dixie; *coll mil* heavy shell; *geol* pot-hole

**marmiter** *vt coll mil* bombard with heavy shells, shell

**marmiton** *nm* kitchen hand, cook's boy

**marmonner** *vt* mumble, mutter (discontentedly)

**marmoréen -éenne** *adj* marmoreal, marble; cold, glacial

**marmot** *nm* brat, urchin; **croquer le ~** be kept waiting

**marmotte** *nf* marmot; **dormir comme une ~** sleep like a log

**marmotter** *vt* mumble, mutter

**marmouset** *nm coll* urchin, kid

**marne** *nf* marl

**marner** *vt* fertilize with marl, marl; *sl* work like a horse

**marnière** *nf* marl-pit

**Maroc** *nm* Morocco

**Marocain -e** *n* Moroccan

**marocain** *adj* Moroccan

**maronner** *vi coll* grumble, growl

**maroquin** *nm* Morocco (leather); *coll* minister's portfolio

**maroquinerie** *nf* Morocco leather goods; fancy leather trade; shop selling fancy leather; process of dressing leather

**maroquinier** *nm* seller of fancy leather goods; dresser of Morocco leather

**marotte** *nf ar* court-jester's bauble; *coll* fad, fancy; **flatter la ~ de qn** humour s/o

**maroufle** *nf arts* mounting paste .

**maroufler** *vt arts* mount (picture)

**marquant** *adj* prominent, outstanding, striking

**marque** *nf* mark, stamp; brand, make; *fig* token; *sp* **à vos ~ s!** on your marks!; **~ de fabrique** trade-mark; **~ déposée** registered trade-mark; **~ d'origine** maker's signature; **personnages de ~** persons of note

**marqué** *adj* marked; unmistakeable, pronounced; **au jour ~** on the appointed day; **prix ~** list-price, price on label

**marquer** *vt* mark; label, stencil, brand; make a note of, record, put down; *sp* score; *mus* **~ la mesure** beat time; **~ le coup** celebrate (occasion); *mil* **~ le pas** mark time; *sp* **~ les points** keep the score; **~ un arbre** blaze a tree; *vi* stand out, make a mark, leave a mark; look; **~ mal** look unprepossessing; **~ son âge** look one's age

**marqueter** *vt* (5) inlay; speckle

**marqueterie** *nf* marquetry, inlaid work; *fig* patchwork

**marquise** *nf* marchioness; awning; glass roof; marquee

**marraine** *nf* godmother; sponsor

**marrant** *adj sl* side-splitting, creasing

**marre** *adv coll* **en avoir ~** be fed up, be fed to the teeth

**marrer (se)** *v refl sl* split one's sides laughing

**marri** *adj ar* sorry, sad

[1]**marron** *nm* chestnut; maroon, signal-rocket; chestnut colour; *coll* blow; **~ d'Inde** horse-chestnut; *adj invar* chestnut (colour)

[2]**marron -onne** *adj* unlicensed, unqualified; shady; **nègre ~** runaway slave

**marronnier** *nm* chestnut-tree; **~ d'Inde** horse-chestnut-tree

**mars** *nm* March

**marsouin** *nm* porpoise

**marteau** *nm* hammer; **~ à deux mains** sledgehammer; **~ à panne fendue** claw-hammer; **~ de porte** door-knocker; *coll* **avoir un coup de ~ , être un peu ~** be cracked, barmy; **passer sous le ~** be sold under the (auctioneer's) hammer, be knocked down

**marteau-pilon** *nm* (*pl* **marteaux-pilons**) *eng* power hammer

**martelage** *nm* hammering; blazing (tree)

**martelé** *adj* hammered, wrought; **vers ~** laboured verse, chiselled verse

**marteler** *vt* (5) hammer; beat out (metal)

**martial** *adj* martial, soldierly; warlike; *mil* **cour ~ e** court martial

**martinet** *nm* strap, whip; *orni* swift, martin

**martin-pêcheur** *nm* (*pl* **martins-pêcheurs**) *orni* kingfisher

**martre** *nf zool* marten

**martyr -e** *n* martyr; *adj* martyred

**martyre** *nm* martyrdom

**martyriser** *vt* martyr; *coll* torture, make suffer

**marxisme** *nm* marxism

**marxiste** *n + adj* marxist

**maryland** *nm* Maryland tobacco

**mas** *nm* farmhouse (in S. France)

**mascarade** *nf* masquerade ·

**mascaret** *nm* bore, tidal wave in river

**mascotte** *nf* mascot, lucky charm

**masculin** *nm gramm* masculine (gender); *adj* masculine, male

**masochisme** *nm* masochism

**masochiste** *n* masochist

[1]**masque** *nm* mask; expression of the face, features; *mil* screen (smoke); masked person (ball); **~ mortuaire** death-mask

[2]**masque** *nf coll* hussy, hag

**masquer** *vt* mask, disguise, hide; *naut* back (sail)

**massacrant** *adj* **d'une humeur ~ e** in a vile temper

**massacre** *nm* massacre, slaughter; **jeu de ~** Aunt Sally

**massacrer** *vt* massacre, slaughter, butcher; *fig* ruin, murder (music), botch

**massacreur -euse** *n* slayer, butcher; *fig* murderer, butcher

¹**masse** *nf* mass, heap, mound; multitude; *comm* fund, stock; *elect* mass, earth; *comm* ~ **active** assets; *comm* ~ **passive** liabilities; **en** ~ in a body (people), in bulk (goods); *elect* **mettre à la** ~ earth

²**masse** *nf* sledge-hammer; maul; mace

**massepain** *nm* marzipan

¹**masser** *vt* mass; **se** ~ mass, form a mound

²**masser** *vt* massage

**massif** *nm* clump (shrubs); flower-bed; *geog* group of mountains; *archi* solid mass; *adj* (*f* -**ive**) massive, bulky; mass, large-scale; solid (gold, silver)

**massue** *nf* club, bludgeon

**mastic** *nm* mastic; cement; putty; *med* dental filling; *mot* puncture solution; *fig* coll mess, muddle, mix-up; *adj invar* putty-coloured

**masticage** *nm* filling, puttying

¹**mastiquer** *vt* fill (crack), putty (window)

²**mastiquer** *vt* masticate

**mastoc** *adj invar* coll heavy, lumpish

**mastodonte** *nm* mastodon

**mastoïde** *adj med* mastoid

**mastroquet** *nm* coll bar-keeper, pub-keeper

**masturber** *vt* masturbate; **se** ~ masturbate

**m'as-tu-vu** *nm invar* coll swank (person)

**masure** *nf* hovel, tumbledown cottage

¹**mat** *nm* (check)mate (chess); *adj invar* checkmated

²**mat** *adj* dull, lustreless; matt; dead, dull (sound)

**mât** *nm naut* mast; pole; *naut* ~ **d'artimon** mizzen-mast; ~ **de charge** derrick; ~ **de cocagne** greasy pole; ~ **de hune** top-mast; ~ **de misaine** fore-mast; **grand**~ main-mast

**matamore** *nm* braggart, swash-buckler

**matelas** *nm* mattress; cushion, padding; ~ **pneumatique** air-mattress; **toile à** ~ tick, ticking

**matelasser** *vt* pad, cushion; **porte matelassée** baize door

**matelot** *nm* sailor, seaman; ship; sailor suit; ~ **d'avant (d'arrière)** next ship ahead (astern); ~ **de première (deuxième, troisième) classe** = leading (able-bodied, ordinary) seaman

**matelote** *nf cul* fish-stew

¹**mater** *vt* mat, dull

²**mater** *vt* checkmate (chess); *fig* tame, humble, break in

**mâter** *vt naut* mast

**matérialiser** *vt* symbolize; materialize; **se** ~ materialize

**matérialisme** *nm* materialism

**matérialiste** *n* materialist; *adj* materialistic

**matériau** *nm invar* (constructional, building) material

**matériaux** *nmpl* materials

**matériel** *nm* plant, equipment; working-stock (factory); ~ **d'école** school furniture; ~ **de guerre** war material; ~ **roulant** rolling-stock; *adj* (*f* -**ielle**) material, physical; materialistic, sensual; real; *leg* **dommages** ~**s** damage to property

**maternel** -**elle** *adj* maternal, motherly

**maternelle** *nf* infant-school

**maternité** *nf* maternity, motherhood; maternity hospital

**mathématicien** -**ienne** *n* mathematician

**mathématique** *adj* mathematical

**mathématiques** *nfpl* mathematics, *coll* maths

**matière** *nf* matter, material, basis, substance; subject, topic; *med* ~**s** faeces; ~**s premières** raw materials; **en** ~ **de** as regards; **il n'y a pas** ~ **à rire** it's no laughing matter; **table des** ~**s** table of contents

**matin** *nm* morning; **au petit** ~ in the small hours; **de bon (grand)** ~ early in the morning; **le** ~ in the morning; **un beau** ~ one of these days; *adv* early; **se lever** ~ get up early

**mâtin** *nm* mastiff, watchdog

**matinal** *adj* morning; early; **être** ~ be an early riser

**mâtiné** *adj* cross-bred, mongrel

**matinée** *nf* morning; *theat* matinée; *coll* **faire la grasse** ~ have a lie-in, sleep late

**mâtiner** *vt* cross (dogs)

**matines** *nfpl eccles* matins

**matois** *nm* crafty, artful person; **fin** ~ wily customer; *adj* crafty, artful, sly

**matou** *nm* tom-cat

**matraquage** *nm* bludgeoning: *comm* saturation publicity; *mil* heavy bombardment

**matraque** *nf* club, cosh; rubber truncheon

**matraquer** *vt* cosh, hit with truncheon; *comm* repeat (slogans, etc); *mil* bombard heavily

**matriarcal** *adj* matriarchal

**matrice** *nf anat* uterus, womb; matrix, die; master (gramophone record); standard (weights)

**matricide** *nm* matricide; *n* person committing matricide; *adj* matricidal

**matriculaire** *adj* pertaining to registration, enrolment; *mil* **feuille** ~ service record

**matricule** *nf* roll, register, list; registration certificate; *nm* official number, reference number; *mot* registration number; *mil* army number

**matriculer** *vt* register; give an official number to

**matrone** *nf* middle-aged mother; fat middle-aged woman

**mâture** *nf naut* masts, masts and spars; sheers (crane); **dans la ~** aloft

**maturité** *nf* maturity, ripeness

**maudire** *vt* (58) curse

**maudit** *nm eccles* **Le Maudit** The Evil One; **les ~ s** the damned; *adj* cursed, accursed; damnable, damned

**maugréer** *vi* curse, grumble; *coll* grouse

**Maure -esque** *n* Moor, Moorish woman

**maure -esque** *adj* Moorish

**Maurice** *nm* Maurice; **l'Île ~** Mauritius

**mausolée** *nm* mausoleum

**maussade** *adj* sullen, glum, peevish, surly; dull, depressing (weather)

**mauvais -e** *nm* evil, what is bad; *adj* bad; evil, ill, wicked; poor, nasty, displeasing; faulty; wrong; rough (sea); **~ e langue** malicious gossiper; **~ e plaisanterie** stupid practical joke; **avoir l'air ~** look fierce; **faire ~ e mine à** cold-shoulder; **prendre qch du ~ côté** put the wrong construction on sth; **prendre qch en ~ e part** take exception to sth; **prendre qn par le ~ bout** rub s/o up the wrong way; **voir d'un ~ œil** bear a grudge against; *adv* **faire ~** be bad (weather); **sentir ~** smell bad

**mauve** *nm+adj* mauve, purple; *nf bot* mallow

**maxillaire** *nm* jaw-bone; *adj* maxillary

**maximal** *adj* maximum

**maxime** *nf* maxim

**maximiser** *vt* maximize

**maximum** *nm* (*pl* **maxima, ~s**) maximum; **~ de rendement** highest efficiency; **faire son ~** do one's very best; *adj* maximum, greatest

**mazout** *nm* fuel oil

**me** *pers pron* me; to me; *refl pron* myself

**mea-culpa** *nm invar* **faire son ~** acknowledge one's faults, beat one's breast

**méandre** *nm* meander, winding (stream, path)

**mec** *nm sl* chap, bloke

**mécanicien** *nm* mechanic; engine-driver; **ingénieur ~** mechanical engineer

**mécanicienne** *nf* machinist, sewing-machine operator (factory)

**mécanique** *nf* mechanism; science of mechanics; *adj* mechanical; machine-made

**mécanisation** *nf* mechanization

**mécaniser** *vt* mechanize

**mécanisme** *nm* mechanism, works; *mus* technique

**mécano** *nm coll* mechanic

**mécanographe** *n* punch-card machine operator; business machine operator

**mécanographie** *nf* data processing; operation of business machines

**mécénat** *nm* patronage of the arts

**mécène** *nm* Maecenas, rich patron

**méchamment** *adv* wickedly, spitefully, naughtily

**méchanceté** *nf* wickedness, malice, spitefulness; spiteful act; malicious remark; naughtiness, mischievousness (child)

**méchant -e** *n* disagreeable person, spiteful person; naughty child; *adj* wicked, malicious, spiteful, ill-natured; naughty, mischievous; paltry, miserable, mean; **~ article** third-rate article; **article ~** spiteful article; **chien ~ !** beware of the dog!; **un ~ billet de dix francs** a paltry ten-franc note; **un ~ pantalon** a scruffy pair of trousers

**mèche** *nf* wick; fuse; lash (whip); lock (hair); bit (drill); *coll* **être de ~ avec** be in league with, be hand in glove with; **vendre la ~** give the show away, blow the gaff

**mécompte** *nm* miscalculation, error; disappointment, foiled expectation

**méconnaissable** *adj* unrecognizable

**méconnaissance** *nf* failure to recognize, appreciate; disavowal, repudiation

**méconnaître** *vt* (68) fail to recognize, ignore; disavow, repudiate; misunderstand; underrate; **se ~** underrate oneself

**méconnu** *adj* unrecognized, unappreciated, misunderstood

**mécontent -e** *n* grumbler; malcontent; *adj* discontented, displeased

**mécontentement** *nm* discontent, displeasure

**mécontenter** *vt* displease, annoy

**mécréant -e** *n* misbeliever, unbeliever; *adj* misbelieving, unbelieving

**médaille** *nf* medal, badge; *archi* medallion; **envers de la ~** reverse side of the coin

**médaillé -e** *n mil* medal-holder; medallist, prize-winner; *adj* decorated

**médailler** *vt* decorate, give medal to

**médaillon** *nm* medallion; locket; inset (newspaper); *cul* medallion (meat)

**médecin** *nm* doctor, physician; *naut* **~ du bord** ship's doctor

**médecine** *nf* medicine; **~ de groupe** group medical practice; **faire sa ~** study medicine

**médian** *adj* median; *sp* **ligne ~ e** half-way line

**médiateur -trice** *n* mediator; *adj* mediating, mediatory

**médiator** *nm mus* plectrum

**médicament** *nm* medicine, drug, medicament

**médicamenter** *vt* doctor, dose; **se ~** dose oneself

**médiéviste** *n* medievalist

**médiocre** *nm* what is mediocre, ordinary; nonentity; *adj* mediocre, indifferent, second-rate; moderate, average; unimpressive

**médiocrité** *nf* mediocrity; exiguousness (means); second-rate person, nonentity

**médire** *vi* (74) **~ de** vilify, speak ill of, run down

**médisance** *nf* slander, scandal; piece of scandal

**médisant -e** *n* slanderer, scandalmonger; *adj* slanderous, scandalmongering

**méditatif -ive** *adj* meditative

**méditation** *nf* meditation; cogitation, rumination

**méditer** *vi* meditate, muse; *vt* ponder, meditate on; contemplate, envisage, plan

**Méditerranée** *nf geog* Mediterranean

**méditerranéen -éenne** *adj* Mediterranean

**médius** *nm anat* middle finger

**méduse** *nf* jelly-fish

**méduser** *vt* petrify, paralyse with fear

**méfait** *nm* misdeed, wrong-doing; **~s** damage

**méfiance** *nf* mistrust, distrust

**méfiant** *adj* mistrustful, distrustful

**méfier (se)** *v refl* be on one's guard; **se ~ de** distrust, beware of

**mégalomane** *n* megalomaniac

**mégalomanie** *nf* megalomania

**mégarde** *nf* **par ~** inadvertently, through carelessness, by an oversight

**mégatonne** *nf* megaton

**mégère** *nf* shrew, termagant

**mégot** *nm coll* cigarette-end, butt

**meilleur** *nm* better; best; *adj* better; **le ~** the best; **de ~ cœur** more willingly; *adv* better; **il fera ~ demain** the weather will be better tomorrow

**méjuger** *vt* (3) misjudge; underestimate

**mélancolie** *nf* melancholy, dejection, gloom

**mélancolique** *adj* melancholy, dejected, gloomy

**mélange** *nm* mixing, blending; mixture, blend; *arts* miscellany

**mélanger** *vt* (3) mix, blend; **se ~** mix, get mixed; mingle

**mélangeur** *nm* mixing-machine; *cin+ rad* mixer

**mélasse** *nf* molasses, treacle; *sl* mess; **~ raffinée** golden syrup

**mêlé** *adj* mixed, tangled

**mêlée** *nf* conflict, scuffle; *sp* scrum

**mêler** *vt* mix, mix together; tangle, throw into confusion; involve, implicate; **~ les cartes** shuffle cards; **être mêlé à tout** have a finger in every pie; **se ~** mix, mingle; interfere, take a hand; **mêlez-vous de vos affaires** mind your own business; **ne vous en mêlez pas!** keep out of it!, *coll* keep your nose clean!

**mélèze** *nm bot* larch

**méli-mélo** *nm coll* jumble, hotch-potch

**mélodie** *nf* melody, tune; melodiousness

**mélodieux -ieuse** *adj* melodious, tuneful

**mélodique** *adj mus* melodic

**mélodramatique** *adj* melodramatic

**mélodrame** *nm* melodrama

**mélomane** *n* music enthusiast, *coll* music fan; *adj* very keen on music, music mad

**melon** *nm bot* melon; bowler-hat, bowler

**mélopée** *nf mus* recitative; melancholy chant

**membrane** *nf* membrane, film; diaphragm; web (bird's foot)

**membrané** membranous; webbed

**membre** *nm* member, limb; *math* side (equation); *naut* timber; **~ viril** penis

**membré** *adj* limbed

**membrure** *nf* limbs; framework

**même** *adj* same; very, self; (*after pers pron*) self (as **moi-~** myself); **c'est cela ~** that's just it; **en ~ temps** at the same time; **être la bonté ~** be kindness itself; **le jour ~** the very day; **revenir au ~** come to the same thing; *adv* even; **à ~ de** able to, capable of; **à ~ la peau** next to the skin; **boire à ~ la bouteille** drink straight out of the bottle; **de ~ que** just as; **faire de ~** do likewise; **tout de ~** all the same

**mémento** *nm* memorandum; note-book; memento, reminder

**mémoire** *nm* memorial; report; memoir, dissertation; *leg* written statement; *comm* detailed bill; **~s** memoirs; *nf* memory; recollection, remembrance; **de ~ d'homme** within living memory; **en ~ de** in memory of; **rappeler qch à la ~ de qn** give s/o a reminder about sth; **si j'ai bonne ~** if I remember rightly

**mémorable** *adj* memorable, note-worthy; eventful

**mémorandum** *nm* memorandum; note-book

**menaçant** *adj* menacing, threatening; forbidding

**menace** *nf* menace, threat; **~s en l'air** idle threats

**menacer** *vt* (4) menace, threaten

**ménage** *nm* housekeeping; household; housework; married couple; household furniture; ~ **à trois** domestic triangle; **entrer en** ~ set up home; **faire bon (mauvais)** ~ **ensemble** get on well (badly) together; **faire le** ~ do the housework; **femme de** ~ charwoman; **un** ~ **uni** a devoted couple

**ménagement** *nm* circumspection, prudence, care; **sans** ~ bluntly, roughly

¹**ménager** *-ère adj* household; thrifty; **(Salon des) Arts** ~**s** = Ideal Home Exhibition

²**ménager** *vt* (3) save, husband, use economically; deal tactfully with, treat considerately, humour; arrange, control

**ménagère** *nf* housewife, housekeeper; canteen of cutlery

**mendiant** *-e n* beggar; *nm cul* kind of sweet, dessert cake

**mendicité** *nf* mendicity, begging; beggary

**mendier** *vt* beg for; *vi* beg

**meneau** *nm archi* = **vertical** mullion; ~ **horizontal** transom

**menée** *nf* sly manoeuvre, intrigue; **déjouer les** ~**s de** outwit, outmanoeuvre

**mener** *vt* (6) lead; conduct, take; control, manage, carry out; drive (horse, vehicle), steer (boat); *math* draw (line); ~ **plusieurs choses de front** have several irons in the fire; ~ **qch à bien** carry sth through successfully; **bien** ~ **sa barque** manage one's affairs well; **cela me mène à croire** that leads me to think; **cela peut** ~ **loin** that may have considerable consequences; *coll* **ne pas en** ~ **large** be in a jam; *vi* lead

**ménestrel** *nm* minstrel

**meneur** *-euse n* leader; ring-leader; agitator; ~ **de jeu** compère; quiz-master

**méningite** *nf* meningitis

**menotte** *nf* (child's) hand; ~**s** handcuffs

**mensonge** *nm* lie, untruth, fib; fallacy, illusion

**mensonger** *-ère adj* lying, false, untrue; fallacious, illusory

**menstruel** *-uelle adj* menstrual

**mensualisation** *nf* changeover to monthly payment of salary

**mensualité** *nf* monthly payment; **payer par** ~**s** pay by monthly instalments

**mensuel** *-uelle adj* monthly

**mental** *adj* mental; **calcul** ~ mental arithmetic

**mentalité** *nf* mentality

**menteur** *-euse n* liar; *adj* lying; prone to lying; deceptive, illusory

**menthe** *nf* mint; **pastilles de** ~ peppermints

**mention** *nf* mention; endorsement; distinction (examination); **reçu avec** ~ **très bien (bien)** passed with distinction (with credit)

**mentionner** *vt* mention

**mentir** *vi* (59) lie, tell lies; *coll* fib

**menton** *nm* chin

**mentonnet** *nm eng* catch, stop; tappet, lug

**mentonnière** *nf* chin-strap; chin-rest (violin)

¹**menu** *nm* menu, bill of fare; **prendre le** ~ have the set meal

²**menu** *adj* small, slender, slight; trifling, minor; ~ **e monnaie** small change; ~**s frais** petty expenses; ~**s propos** small talk; **le** ~ **peuple** the humbler classes; **par le** ~ in detail; *adv* small, fine; **écrire** ~ write small; **hacher** ~ chop up fine

**menuet** *nm* minuet

**menuiser** *vt* plane down, whittle (wood); *vi* do woodwork

**menuiserie** *nf* joinery, woodwork; joiner's (work)shop

**menuisier** *nm* joiner; *adj* (*f* -**ière**) **ouvrier** ~ joiner

**méplat** *nm* flat part (*esp* of face)

**méprendre (se)** *v refl* (75) be mistaken; **il n'y a pas à s'y** ~ there can be no mistake about it; **imiter qn à s'y** ~ imitate s/o to the life

**mépris** *nm* contempt, scorn; **au** ~ **de** in contempt of; **tenir qn en** ~ despise s/o

**méprisable** *adj* contemptible, despicable

**méprisant** *adj* contemptuous, scornful

**méprise** *nf* mistake, misapprehension

**mépriser** *vt* despise, scorn

**mer** *nf* sea; *coll* **ce n'est pas la** ~ **à boire** it's not all that difficult; **en pleine** ~ on the open sea; **gens de** ~ seamen; **mal de** ~ seasickness; **pleine (basse)** ~ high (low) tide; **porter de l'eau à la** ~ carry coals to Newcastle; **prendre la** ~ put to sea

**mercanti** *nm coll* shark, profiteer

**mercantile** *adj* mercantile, commercial; mercenary, grabbing

**mercantilisme** *nm* mercantilism; mercenary spirit, money-grabbing

**mercenaire** *nm* + *adj mil* mercenary

**mercerie** *nf* haberdashery; haberdasher's shop

¹**merci** *nf* mercy; grace; **Dieu** ~ ! thank God!; **sans** ~ merciless, mercilessly

²**merci** *nm* thanks; *interj* thanks, thank you; no thank you

**mercier** *-ière n* haberdasher

**mercredi** *nm* Wednesday

**mercure** *nm* mercury

**mercuriale** *nf* reprimand, *coll* tearing off of a strip; *comm* market-price list

**mercuriel -ielle** *adj chem* mercurial

**merde** *nf vulg* shit; *interj vulg* shit!, hell!

**merdeux -euse** *n vulg* shit; conceited ass; *adj vulg* shitty; conceited

**merdier** *nm sl* mess, shambles

**mère** *nf* mother; source, origin; ~ **célibataire** unmarried mother; ~ **de tous les vices** root of all evil; *comm* **maison** ~ head-office, parent company

**méridien** *nm* meridian; *adj* (*f* **-ienne**) meridian

**méridienne** *nf* meridian line; *coll* siesta, midday nap; sofa

**Méridional -e** *n* (*mpl* **-aux**, *fpl* **-ales**) southerner

**méridional** *adj* southern, meridional

**mérinos** *nm* merino (sheep, wool, cloth)

**merise** *nf* wild cherry, merry

**merisier** *nm* wild cherry tree

**méritant** *adj* deserving, worthy (person)

**mérite** *nm* merit, desert, worth; type of award; **s'attribuer le** ~ **de** take the credit for

**mériter** *vt* merit, deserve; entitle; require, need; ~ **examen** be worth looking into

**méritoire** *adj* meritorious, deserving

**merlan** *nm* whiting; *coll* **yeux de** ~ **frit** blankly staring eyes

**merle** *nm* blackbird

**merlin** *nm* cleaving axe; *naut* marline

**merluche** *nf* hake; *cul* dried cod

**merveille** *nf* marvel, wonder; **à** ~ wonderfully, admirably; **dire des** ~**s de** speak in glowing terms of; **faire** ~ work wonders; **se porter à** ~ be wonderfully well

**merveilleux** *nm* the supernatural; *adj* (*f* **-euse**) marvellous, wonderful

**mes** *poss adj pl* my; *see* **mon**

**mésalliance** *nf* misalliance

**mésallier (se)** *v refl* marry beneath oneself

**mésange** *nf orni* tit

**mésaventure** *nf* misadventure, mishap

**mesdames** *nfpl see* **madame**

**mesdemoiselles** *nfpl see* **mademoiselle**

**mésentente** *nf* misunderstanding, disagreement

**mésestimation** *nf* underestimation, underrating

**mésestime** *nf* disesteem, low esteem

**mésestimer** *vt* underestimate, underrate; have a low opinion of

**mésintelligence** *nf* disagreement, misunderstanding; **être en** ~ **avec** be at variance with

**mesmérisme** *nm* mesmerism

**mesquin** *adj* mean, stingy; petty, narrow; **à l'esprit** ~ small-minded

**mesquinerie** *nf* meanness, stinginess; pettiness, narrow-mindedness; mean action

**messager** *nm* carrier; *n* (*f* **-ère**) messenger

**messagerie** *nf* carrying trade, transport service; ~**s aériennes** air-transport service; ~**s maritimes** sea-transport, shipping company; **bureau des** ~**s** parcels office (railway, etc)

**messe** *nf eccles* mass

**messeigneurs** *nmpl see* **monseigneur**

**messidor** *nm hist* tenth month of the French Republican calendar (June to July)

**Messie** *nm* Messiah

**messieurs** *nmpl see* **monsieur**

**mesurable** *adj* measurable

**mesure** *nf* measure, measurement, extent; arrangement; precaution, step, move; moderation; *mus* bar, time; **à** ~ **in proportion; à** ~ **que** as, in proportion as; *mus* **battre la** ~ beat time; **dans une certaine** ~ to some extent; **dépasser la** ~ overstep the bounds; **donner sa** ~ show what one is made of, capable of; **être en** ~ **de** be in a position to; **fait sur** ~ made-to-measure

**mesuré** *adj* measured; temperate, moderate

**mesurer** *vt* measure, gauge, calculate, measure out, measure off; stint, ration; ~ **qn des yeux** look s/o up and down; **se** ~ **(avec, contre)** pit oneself against, measure oneself against, try conclusions with

**mésuser** *vi* ~ **de** misuse, abuse

**métabolisme** *nm* metabolism

**métairie** *nf* small farm (where rent is paid in kind)

**métallique** *adj* metallic; **cable** ~ wire-rope; *econ* **encaisse** ~ gold and silver reserve

**métalliser** *vt* metallize

**métallo** *nm coll* metal-worker

**métallurgie** *nf* metallurgy

**métallurgique** *adj* metallurgic

**métallurgiste** *n* metallurgist

**métamorphose** *nf* metamorphosis

**métamorphoser** *vt* metamorphose, transform; **se** ~ change, be metamorphosed

**métaphore** *nf* metaphor

**métaphorique** *adj* metaphorical

**métaphysicien -ienne** *n* metaphysician

**métaphysique** *nf* metaphysics; *adj* metaphysical

**métayage** *nm* system of farm-rents paid in kind

**métayer** *nm* farmer paying rent in kind .
**métempsychose** *nf* metempsychosis
**météo** *nf coll* weather forecast; meteorological office; *nm coll* meteorologist
**météore** *nm* meteor
**météorique** *adj* meteoric
**météorologie** *nf* meteorology
**météorologique** *adj* meteorological
**météorologiste** *n* meteorologist
**métèque** *nm pej* foreigner, alien; *coll* dago, wog
**méthode** *nf* method, way, system; textbook, manual
**méthodique** *adj* methodical
**méthodisme** *nm eccles* Methodism
**méthodiste** *n eccles* Methodist
**méticuleux -euse** *adj* meticulous, painstaking, punctilious
**méticulosité** *nf* meticulousness
**métier** *nm* trade, profession, craft; skill, competence; professionalism; loom; ~ **mécanique** power-loom; **armée de** ~ regular army; **arts et** ~ **s** arts and crafts; **avoir du** ~ have experience, technique; *coll* **ce n'est pas mon** ~ that's not in my line; **corps de** ~ craft corporation; *ar* guild; **être du** ~ be in the trade; **faire** ~ **de** pride oneself on; **homme de** ~ professional; **manquer de** ~ lack experience; **ouvrage sur le** ~ work on the stocks, in progress; **parler** ~ talk shop
**métis -isse** *n* half-breed (person); crossbred (animal); *adj* half-bred, crossbred
**métisser** *vt* cross
**métonymie** *nf* metonymy
**métrage** *nm* measurement, measuring; length; *archi* quantity-surveying; *cin* footage; *cin* **court (long)** ~ short (fulllength) feature film
**¹mètre** *nm* metre; metre rule; ~ **pliant** folding rule; ~ **à ruban** measuring-tape
**²mètre** *nm* metre (verse)
**métrer** *vt* (6) measure; survey
**métreur -euse** *n* quantity-surveyor
**métrique** *nf* prosody, metrics; *adj* metric (system); metrical (verse)
**métro** *nm coll* (Paris) underground (railway) = tube
**métropole** *nf* metropolis, capital; mother-country
**métropolitain** *nm* (Paris) underground railway; *adj* metropolitan
**mets** *nm* prepared food, dish
**mettable** *adj* wearable
**metteur -euse** *n* s/o who puts; *nm rad* ~ **en ondes** radio-producer; *typ* ~ **en pages** type-setter; *theat* + *cin* ~ **en scène** director
**mettre** *vt* (60) put, place, set, lay; put on, wear; use; take; grant, admit, suppose;

*comm* invest; spend; ~ **à contribution** press into service, oblige to co-operate; *comm* ~ **à exécution** bring into force, implement; ~ **à la voile** set sail; ~ **à mort** put to death; ~ **à nu** lay bare; ~ **aux enchères** put up for auction; ~ **bas** (of animal) give birth to; ~ **des vers en musique** set verse to music; ~ **du français en anglais** translate French into English; ~ **du temps à** take some time to; **mettez que je n'ai rien dit** I take that back; **mettons que tous les deux nous avions tort** let's admit we were both wrong; **mettons vingt francs?** shall we say twenty francs?; *coll* **on les met?** shall we go?, let's get out of here!; **y** ~ **le temps nécessaire** take all the time in the world; **se** ~ put oneself, place oneself; begin, start; become; dress; **se** ~ **à l'œuvre** get down to work; **se** ~ **à pleurer** begin to cry; **se** ~ **à table** sit down to eat; **se** ~ **au lit** go to bed; **se** ~ **au pas** fall into step; **se** ~ **de la pommade** put some ointment on; **se** ~ **en rage** lose one's temper; **se** ~ **en route** start off; **se** ~ **en short** put shorts on; **s'y** ~ get down to it; **le temps se met au beau** the weather is turning out fine
**meublant** *adj* decorative, usable for furnishing
**¹meuble** *nm* piece of furniture; ~ **s** furniture; **être dans ses** ~ **s** have one's own furniture
**²meuble** *adj* movable; *leg* **biens** ~ **s** chattels, movables; **terre** ~ light soil
**meublé** *nm* furnished apartment; *adj* furnished; *fig* stocked; **hôtel** ~ hotel not providing board
**meubler** *vt* furnish; fill, stock; *vi* be decorative; **se** ~ furnish one's home
**meuglement** *nm* lowing, mooing
**meugler** *vi* low, moo
**¹meule** *nf* millstone; grindstone; ~ **de fromage** large round cheese
**²meule** *nf* hayrick, haystack
**meuler** *vt* bore, grind
**meunerie** *nf* milling, milling trade
**meunier -ière** *n* miller
**meurt-de-faim** *nm invar* down-and-out
**meurtre** *nm leg* murder, homicide, manslaughter; *fig* crime, scandal
**meurtrier -ière** *n* murderer (murderess); *adj* murderous, deadly
**meurtrière** *nf archi* loop-hole
**meurtrir** *vt* bruise; ~ **de coups** beat
**meurtrissure** *nf* bruise
**meute** *nf* pack of hounds; crowd, mob
**mévente** *nf comm* sale at a loss; slump
**¹mi** *nm invar mus* E, mi
**²mi-** *adj invar* half, mid-, semi-; **à** ~ **-chemin** half-way; **à** ~ **-corps** to the waist; **à** ~ **-côte** half-way up the hill; **à**

~ **-hauteur** half-way up; à ~ **-jambes** half-way up the legs; à ~ **-voix** in an undertone

**miaou** *nm* miaow, mew

**miasme** *nm* miasma

**miaulement** *nm* miaowing, mewing

**miauler** *vt* wail (song, etc); *vi* miaow, mew

**mi-carême** *nf* mid-Lent

**miche** *nf* round loaf

**micheline** *nf* rail-car, autorail

**micmac** *nm coll* trick, scheming, manoeuvre, fiddle

**micocoulier** *nm* kind of elm (found in Provence)

**micro** *nm coll* microphone, mike; **parler au** ~ speak on the air

**microbe** *nm med* microbe; *coll* brat, kid

**microbien -ienne** *adj med* microbial; **guerre microbienne** bacteriological warfare

**microbiologie** *nf* microbiology

**microcosme** *nm* microcosm

**micromètre** *nm* micrometer

**microphone** *nm* microphone; ~ **à perche** boom-microphone; ~ **électro-dynamique** moving-coil microphone

**microscopie** *nf* microscopy

**microscopique** *adj* microscopic

**microsillon** *nm* microgroove; long-playing record, *coll* L.P.

**miction** *nf med* micturition, urination

**midi** *nm* midday, twelve o'clock; noontide, culminating point; south; southern part of France; *coll* **chercher** ~ **à quatorze heures** be over-subtle, invent complications; **en plein** ~ in broad daylight; **sur le** ~ about midday

**midinette** *nf* dressmaker's apprentice, assistant; working girl

**¹mie** *nf ar* sweetheart

**²mie** *nf* crumb; inside of loaf

**miel** *nm* honey; **lune de** ~ honeymoon

**miellé** *adj* honeyed, sweetened with honey

**mielleux -euse** *adj* tasting of honey, honeyed; *fig* sugary, honeyed; bland, unctuous, oily

**mien** *nm* mine, what is mine, my property; *poss adj* (*f* **mienne**) *ar* **un** ~ **oncle** an uncle of mine; *poss pron* (*f* **mienne**) mine

**miette** *nf* crumb (bread); scrap, morsel, bit; *coll* **réduit en** ~ **s** smashed to bits

**mieux** *nm* best (plan); improvement; **le** ~ **est l'ennemi du bien** leave well alone; *adv* better; **à qui** ~ ~ vying with one another; **c'est on ne peut** ~ it couldn't be better; **de** ~ **en** ~ better and better; **être** ~ be more comfortable; **il ressemble à son frère, mais en** ~ he's like his brother, but better-

looking; **ne pas demander** ~ be delighted; **pour ne pas dire** ~ to say the least; **tant** ~ so much the better; *adv phr* **le** ~ que vous avez de ~ **à faire est** the best thing you can do is; **en mettant les choses au** ~ at best; **être le** ~ **du monde avec** be on the best of terms with; **faire de son** ~ do one's best; **faire pour le** ~ do one's best

**mièvre** *adj* delicate, frail; affected, effete

**mièvrerie** *nf* fragility, daintiness; affectedness

**mignard** *adj* affected; *coll* dainty

**mignardise** *nf* affectation, winsomeness; affected act; prettiness (style); *bot* pink

**mignon -onne** *n* darling, pet; *nm ar* favourite, minion; *adj* dainty, delicate, tiny, sweet; **péché** ~ besetting sin

**mignonnet -ette** *adj* dainty, delicate, tiny

**mignonnette** *nf* kind of lace; *bot* mignonnette

**migrateur -trice** *adj* migrant; *zool* migratory

**migratoire** *adj* migratory

**mijaurée** *nf* affected, pretentious woman or girl

**mijoter** *vt cul* stew slowly, let simmer; *coll* concoct, plan; *vi cul* simmer; *coll* **se** ~ be brewing, be in preparation

**mil** *adj* thousand

**milan** *nm orni* kite

**mildiou** *nm* mildew

**milice** *nf* militia

**milicien -ienne** *n* member of the militia

**milieu** *nm* middle, midst; mean, middle course; milieu, environment; ~ **x officiels** official circles; **au beau** ~ **de** right in the middle of; **il n'y a pas de** ~ there's no middle course, it's either one thing or the other; **juste** ~ happy medium; *coll* **le** ~ the underworld

**militaire** *nm* soldier, serviceman; *adj* military, soldierly; warlike; *coll* exact; **à huit heures, heure** ~ at eight o'clock sharp; **marine** ~ navy

**militarisation** *nf* militarization

**militariser** *vt* militarize

**militarisme** *nm* militarism

**militariste** *n* + *adj* militarist

**militer** *vi* militate; be active in; fight

**¹mille** *nm invar* thousand; *adj invar* thousand; ~ **fois** a thousand times; *coll* time and again; very much indeed

**²mille** *nm* mile; *naut* nautical mile

**mille-feuille** *nm cul* kind of pastry

**millénaire** *nm* thousand years, millennium; *adj* millenary

**mille-pattes** *nm* centipede

**millésime** *nm* date on coin; date of production

**millésimé** *adj* bearing date of production (*esp* wine)

**millet** *nm bot* millet; **grains de ~** bird-seed

**milliard** *nm* milliard, thousand million

**milliardaire** *n + adj* multi-millionaire

**millième** *n + adj* thousandth

**millier** *nm* thousand, about a thousand; **par ~ s** in thousands

**millionième** *n + adj* millionth

**milord** *nm* English nobleman; my lord (form of address); *coll* very wealthy man

**mime** *nm theat* mime, pantomime; mimic

**mimer** *vt theat* mime, act in a dumb-show; mimic

**mimétisme** *nm* mimesis, mimicry

**mimique** *nf* mimicry, art of mime; *adj* mimic, mimetic

**minable** *adj* shabby, pitiable, seedy, down at heel; *eng* minable

**minauder** *vi* simper, smirk

**minauderie** *nf* simpering; **~ s** mincing manner

**minaudier -ière** *n* simperer, affected person; *adj* simpering, smirking

¹**mince** *adj* thin, slender; slight, insignificant

²**mince** *interj sl* **~ alors!** well I'm damned!; *sl* **~ de** what a, what a lot of

**minceur** *nf* thinness, slenderness; slightness

¹**mine** *nf* mine; *mil + naut* mine; graphite, black lead; *fig* fund, stock; **~ de houille** coal-mine; **champ de ~ s** mine-field

²**mine** *nf* mien, appearance, look; **avoir bonne (mauvaise) ~** look well (unwell), be good-looking (ill-looking); **de bonne ~** good-looking; **faire bonne ~ à** be courteous to; **faire des ~ s** simper; **faire grise ~** look disgruntled; **faire ~ de** pretend to be, make a show of being

**miner** *vt* mine; undermine; **se ~** waste away, pine

**minérai** *nm* ore; mineral; *adj* mineral; *chem* inorganic

**minéralier** *nm* ore-carrying ship

**minéralogie** *nf* mineralogy

**minéralogique** *adj* mineralogical; *mot* **numéro ~** registration number

**minéralogiste** *n* mineralogist

**minet** *nm coll* pussy, puss; darling, sweet; camp young man

**minette** *nf coll* nymphet

¹**mineur** *nm* miner

²**mineur -e** *n* minor; *leg* infant; *adj* minor, lesser; *mus* minor

**miniaturiste** *n* miniaturist

**minier -ière** *adj* mining

**minière** *nf* open-cast mine

**mini-jupe** *nf* mini-skirt

**minime** *adj* tiny; trivial

**minimum** *nm* (*pl* **minima, ~ s**) minimum; **~ vital** subsistence wage; **au ~** at least; *adj* minimum

**ministère** *nm* help, agency; ministry; government; **~ de l'Intérieur** = Home Office; **former un ~** form a government; *leg* **le ~ public** the Public Prosecutor('s office); **par le ~ de** through the help of

**ministériel -ielle** *adj* ministerial; **crise ministérielle** cabinet crisis

**ministre** *nm* minister, secretary of state, agent; *eccles* (Protestant) minister, clergyman; **Ministre de l'Intérieur** = Home Secretary; **Ministre des Finances** = Chancellor of the Exchequer

**minium** *nm* red lead

**minois** *nm* face, pretty face

**minorité** *nf* minority; *leg* infancy

**minotaure** *nm* minotaur

**minoterie** *nf* flour-milling; flour-mill

**minotier** *nm* miller

**minuit** *nm* midnight

**minus** *n coll* half-wit, clot

**minuscule** *nf* small letter, lower-case letter; *adj* minute, small

**minus habens** *n invar coll* half-wit, clot

¹**minute** *nf* minute; **cocotte ~** pressure-cooker; **être à la ~** be punctual, be on the dot; *interj* just a minute!, hang on!

²**minute** *nf leg* draft, minute, record

¹**minuter** *vt* time

²**minuter** *vt* minute, record

**minuterie** *nf* movement (watch); *elect* time-switch (*esp* for lights on staircase, corridors)

**minutie** *nf* minute detail; attention to detail, scrupulousness; **~ s** minutiae

**minutieux -ieuse** *adj* scrupulous, thorough, punctilious

**mioche** *n coll* kid, youngster, mite

**mirabelle** *nf* mirabelle plum; liqueur made from mirabelle plums

**miracle** *nm* miracle; wonder; *theat* miracle-play; **par ~** miraculously

**miraculeux -euse** *adj* miraculous

**mirador** *nm* platform; *mil* observation post

**mirage** *nm* mirage; *fig* illusion

**mire** *nf mil* foresight (rifle, etc); surveyor's pole, staff; test pattern (television); *mil* **angle de ~** angle of elevation; **point de ~** target; *fig* cynosure, centre of attention; **prendre sa ~** take aim

**mirer** *vt coll* cast one's eye on; **se ~** look at oneself (in mirror); be reflected

**mirifique** *adj coll* wonderful, terrific

**mirliton** *nm* toy musical instrument

**mirobolant**

(blown into); cream puff; **vers de ~** doggerel verse
**mirobolant** *adj coll* wonderful, staggering, terrific
**miroir** *nm* mirror; **œufs au ~** fried eggs
**miroitant** *adj* gleaming, glistening, sparkling, shimmering
**miroiter** *vi* gleam, glisten, sparkle, shimmer; **faire ~** show to advantage
**miroiterie** *nf* mirror trade; manufacture of mirrors
**miroton** *nm* beef-stew with onions
**mis** *p part* mettre; **bien ~** well-dressed
**misaine** *nf naut* foresail; **mât de ~** foremast
**misanthrope** *n* misanthrope; *adj* misanthropic
**misanthropie** *nf* misanthropy
**mise** *nf* placing, putting, setting in place; dress, attire; stake, outlay; **~ à exécution** implementation; *naut* **~ à l'eau** launching; *coll* **~ à pied** sacking; **~ à prix** reserve (price); **~ au net** making a fair copy, revision of draft; **~ au point** tuning (engine); focusing; clarification; warning; **~ bas** dropping of young; **~ de fonds** putting up of money; **~ en demeure** formal notice, summons; **~ en marche** starting (engine, motor); **~ en ondes** radio production; *typ* **~ en pages** lay-out; **~ en plis** set (hair); *theat* **~ en scène** production, staging; **être de ~** be suitable, appropriate
**miser** *vt* stake, bet (a sum); bid (a sum); *vi* stake, bet; bid (auction); **~ sur** bank on
**misérable** *n* poor wretch; scoundrel, wretch; *adj* miserable, unhappy; unfortunate; despicable, mean, paltry
**misère** *nf* misery, misfortune, woe; need, extreme poverty; mere trifle; **~s** worries, troubles; **~ noire** abject poverty; **crier ~** complain of poverty; **être dans la ~** be poverty-stricken; *coll* **faire des ~s à qn** give s/o a rough time, tease s/o unmercifully; **reprendre le collier de la ~** get back to the grindstone; **vêtements qui crient ~** shabby clothes
**miséreux -euse** *n + adj* needy, destitute (person)
**miséricorde** *nf* mercy, mercifulness; *interj* mercy!, gracious me!
**miséricordieux -ieuse** *n + adj* merciful (person)
**misogyne** *n* misogynist; *adj* misogynous
**misogynie** *nf* misogyny
**missel** *nm eccles* missal
**mission** *nf* mission; (diplomatic) mission; *eccles* mission station; **en ~** on

detached service
**missionnaire** *n + adj* missionary
**mistigri** *nm coll* puss
**mistral** *nm* violent north wind in S. France
**mitaine** *nf* mitten
**mitard** *nm sl* disciplinary cell
**mite** *nf* moth; **~ du fromage** cheesemite
**mité** *adj* moth-eaten
**miter (se)** *v refl* get moth-eaten
**miteux -euse** *adj coll* shabby, seedy
**mitiger** *vt* (3) mitigate, soften; relax
**mitonner** *vt cul* let simmer; prepare carefully; *coll* devise, concoct; *vi* simmer
**mitoyen -enne** *adj* party; **mur ~** party wall; **cloison ~enne** interior, dividing wall; **puits ~** well used in common
**mitoyenneté** *nf* joint ownership, joint usage
**mitraille** *nf mil* machine-gun fire; *ar* grape-shot; *coll* small change
**mitrailler** *vt mil* machine-gun, tommy-gun
**mitrailleur** *nm* machine-gunner; *adj (f -euse) mil* **fusil ~** machine-gun
**mitrailleuse** *nf mil* machine-gun
**mitre** *nm eccles* mitre; *archi* cowl (chimney pot)
**mitron** *nm* baker's apprentice
**mixage** *nm* mixing
**mixeur** *nm cul* mixer
**mixité** *nf* co-education
**mixte** *adj* mixed, joint; **assurance ~** life and endowment assurance; **double ~** mixed doubles (tennis); **école ~** co-educational school; **train ~** passenger and goods train
**mixtion** *nf* mixing; mixture
**mnémonique** *nf + adj* mnemonic
**mobile** *nm* motive; motive power; prime mover; mobile; *adj* movable; mobile; **échelle ~** sliding-scale; *med* **rein ~** floating kidney
**mobilier** *nm* furniture, suite of furniture; *adj (f -ière)* movable, personal; *leg* **biens ~s** personal estate, chattels; **valeurs mobilières** stocks and shares; **vente mobilière** furniture sale
**mobilisable** *adj* mobilizable; *comm* disposable, available
**mobilisation** *nf* mobilization; *comm* liquidation (capital), conversion
**mobiliser** *vt* mobilize; *mil* call up; *comm* free (capital), convert
**mobilité** *nf* mobility; instability, changeableness
**mobylette** *nf* moped, power-assisted bicycle

**moche** *adj coll* ugly, dowdy; poor, rotten, lousy

**modalité** *nf* modality; *pl* methods, details; **~s de paiement** terms of payment

**mode** *nm* method, mode; *gramm* mood; *mus* mode; **~ d'emploi** directions for use; *nf* fashion, manner; **~s** millinery; **à la ~** fashionable; **gravure de ~** fashion-plate; **passer de ~** go out of fashion

**modelage** *nm* modelling, moulding

**modèle** *nm* model, pattern, style; artist's model; **~ déposé** registered pattern; **~ réduit** small-scale model; **grand ~** large size (garment); *adj* model

**modelé** *nm arts* relief

**modeler** *vt* (5) model, mould, shape; **se ~** model oneself, take as pattern

**modeleur -euse** *n arts* modeller; model-maker

**modéliste** *n* dress-designer

**modérateur -trice** *nm* regulator, governor; *n* (*f*-trice) moderator, restrainer; mediator; *adj* moderating, restraining

**modération** *nf* moderation, restraint; temperance

**modéré -e** *n* moderate person; *pol* moderate; *adj* moderate, temperate; gentle, subdued

**modérer** *vt* (6) moderate, lessen, restrain, soften; regulate; **se ~** control oneself; subside (storm)

**moderne** *nm* modern, modern style; *adj* modern, up-to-date

**moderniser** *vt* modernize

**modernité** *nf* modernity

**modeste** *n* modest person; *adj* modest, unassuming; quiet, unpretentious; **prix ~** moderate, reasonable, price

**modestie** *nf* modesty, unpretentiousness

**modicité** *nf* moderateness; paucity; lowness

**modifiant** *adj* modifying

**modificateur -trice** *n* modifier; *adj* modificatory, modifying

**modificatif -ive** *adj* modifying

**modifier** *vt* modify, qualify, alter; **se ~** change

**modique** *adj* moderate, small, reasonable (sum, cost); slender (means)

**modulation** *nf mus* modulation; inflexion; *elect* modulation (frequency); **~ de fréquence** V.H.F., frequency modulation

**module** *nm math* modulus; *archi* module

**moduler** *vt* modulate; *vi mus* modulate

**moelle** *nf* marrow; pith, core; *anat* medulla; *anat* **~ épinière** spinal cord; **jusqu'à la ~** to the bone, thoroughly

**moelleux** *nm* softness, mellowness; juiciness; *adj* (*f*-euse) soft, mellow; juicy

**moellon** *nm archi* quarry-stone

**mœurs** *nfpl* morals, manners; customs; **avoir de bonnes ~** be of good character; **être sans ~** be unprincipled

**moi** *nm* ego, self; **culte du ~** egotism; *pers pron* I; me; **à ~** mine; **à ~!** help!; **de vous à ~** between you and me

**moignon** *nm* stump (of amputated limb)

**moi-même** *refl pron* myself

**moindre** *adj* less, lesser; least, smallest

**moine** *nm* monk, friar

**moineau** *nm* sparrow; *coll* **vilain ~** dirty dog, rat

**moins** *nm* minus, minus-sign; *adv* less, fewer; least; **à ~ de** unless, barring; **à ~ que** unless; **à tout le ~** at least; **au ~** not less than, at least; **de ~ en** less and less; **du ~** at least; **en ~** less, missing; **en ~ de rien** in less than no time; **non ~ que** quite as much as; **rien ~ que** nothing less than; far from; *prep* less, minus, but for; **deux heures ~ vingt** twenty to two

**moins-value** *nf* depreciation, drop in value

**moire** *nf* watered silk, moiré; watering

**moiré** *nm* watered, clouded effect (on fabric or metal); *adj* watered

**moirer** *vt* water (fabric); cloud (metal)

**moirure** *nf* watered, clouded effect

**mois** *nm* month; month's pay

**moïse** *nm* cradle, basket cot

**moisi** *nm* mould, mildew, staleness; **sentir le ~** smell musty; *adj* mouldy, mildewed, musty, stale

**moisir** *vt* make mouldy; *vi* mildew, become mouldy; **se ~** become mouldy

**moisissure** *nf* mould, mildew; mouldiness

**moisson** *nf* harvest; harvest-time; crop

**moissonner** *vt* harvest, reap, gather; **être moissonné** be cut off, die

**moissonneur -euse** *n* harvester, reaper

**moissonneuse** *nf* reaping-machine, harvester

**moissonneuse-batteuse** *nf* (*pl* moissonneuses-batteuses) combine-harvester

**moite** *adj* moist, damp, clammy

**moiteur** *nf* moistness, dampness, clamminess

**moitié** *nf* half; *coll* **ma chère ~** my better half; **se mettre de ~ avec qn** go halves with s/o; *adv* half; **~ moins cher** half as dear; **~ plus cher** half as dear again

**moka** *nm cul* Mocha coffee; coffee-flavoured cake

**mol** *adj see* mou

**molaire** *nf + adj* molar

**môle** *nm* mole, breakwater

**moléculaire** *adj* molecular
**moleskine** *nf* imitation leather
**molester** *vt* molest
**moleter** *vt* (5) mill, knurl
**molette** *nf* pestle; knurling-tool, cutting wheel; rowel; **clef à ~** adjustable spanner
**mollasse** *adj coll* flabby, soft; spineless; slow, lazy
**molle** *adj see* **mou**
**mollesse** *nf* softness, flabbiness; spinelessness; slackness; indolence
¹**mollet** *nm anat* calf
²**mollet** **-ette** *adj* soft, softest; **œuf ~** soft-boiled egg
**molletière** *adj f* **bandes ~s** puttees
**molleton** *nm* flannelette, soft wool or cotton cloth; felting (ironing-board)
**molletonné** *adj* lined with flannelette; fleece-lined (gloves)
**mollir** *vt naut* ease (helm), slacken (rope); *vi* soften, become soft; slacken, die down, flag, deteriorate
**mollusque** *nm zool* mollusc
**molosse** *nm* mastiff, watch-dog
**môme** *n sl* brat, kid; *nf sl* bird, bint
**moment** *nm* moment, instant, while; **arriver au bon ~** arrive in the nick of time; **à tout ~** constantly; at any moment; **au ~ où** just when; **au ~ voulu** at the right moment; **à un ~ donné** at a certain time; **du ~ où, du ~ que** seeing that; **d'un ~ à l'autre** at any moment; **le ~ venu** in due course; **par ~s** now and again; **sur le ~** on the spur of the moment
**momentané** *adj* momentary, temporary
**momerie** *nf* mummery
**momie** *nf* mummy; *coll* old fossil
**momification** *nf* mummification
**momifier** *vt* mummify
**mon** *poss adj m* (*f* **ma**, *pl* **mes**) my
**monacal** *adj* monastic, monkish
**monade** *nf* monad
**monarchie** *nf* monarchy
**monarchique** *adj* monarchical
**monarchisme** *nm* monarchism
**monarchiste** *n + adj* monarchist
**monarque** *nm* monarch
**monastère** *nm* monastery
**monastique** *adj* monastic
**monceau** *nm* heap, stock, pile
**mondain** **-e** *n* worldly person; *nm* man about town; *nf* (**~ e**) society lady; *adj* worldly, mundane; fashionable
**mondanité** *nf* worldliness; taste for social life; **~s** social events
**monde** *nm* world, earth; people; (high) society; servants, domestic staff; **ainsi va le ~** such is the way of the world, that is how things are; **aller dans le ~** move in society; **connaître son ~**

know with whom one is dealing; **être de ce ~** be alive; **être le mieux du ~ avec** be on the best of terms with; **homme (femme) du ~** man (lady) of quality; **il y a du ~** there are (lots of) people there; **le beau (grand, haut) ~** high society; **mettre au ~** give birth to; **tout le ~** everyone
**mondial** *adj* world-wide, universal; **guerre ~e** world war
**mond(i)ovision** *nf* TV satellite broadcasting
**monégasque** *adj* of Monaco
**monétaire** *adj* monetary
**monétariste** *n + adj* monetarist
**monétiser** *vt* mint
**mongolien -ienne** *n + adj med* mongol
**moniteur -trice** *n* monitor; *sp* coach, instructor
**monnaie** *nf* money, currency; change, small change; mint; **bot ~ du pape** honesty; **~ forte** hard currency; **la Monnaie** the Mint; *coll* **payer qn en ~ de singe** let s/o whistle for his money
**monnayage** *nm* minting, coining
**monnayer** *vt* (7) mint, coin; *fig* exploit, cash in on
**monnayeur** *nm* maker of coins; **faux-~** counterfeiter, coiner
**monocorde** *adj* monotonous
**monogame** *adj* monogamous
**monogamie** *nf* monogamy
**monogramme** *nm* monogram
**monographie** *nf* monograph
**monokini** *nm* topless (costume)
**monolithe** *nm* monolith; *adj* monolithic
**monologuer** *vi* soliloquize, talk to oneself
**monomane** *n + adj* monomaniac
**monôme** *nm math* monomial; student's procession (single file)
**monophasé** *adj elect* single-phase, monophase
**monoplace** *n + adj aer + mot* singleseater
**monoplan** *nm* monoplane
**monopole** *nm* monopoly
**monopolisation** *nf* monopolization
**monopoliser** *vt* monopolize
**monosyllabe** *nm* monosyllable
**monosyllabique** *adj* monosyllabic
**monothéisme** *nm* monotheism
**monothéiste** *n* monotheist; *adj* monotheistic
**monotone** *adj* monotonous; humdrum
**monotonie** *nf* monotony
**monseigneur** *nm* (*pl* **messeigneurs**) (*depending on rank of person addressed or referred to*) Your Royal Highness, His Royal Highness; Your Eminence, His Eminence (cardinal); Your Grace, His Grace (archbishop,

duke); my Lord, your Lordship, his Lordship (bishop); **donner du ~ à** give the title of Monseigneur to

**Monsieur** *nm* (*pl* **Messieurs**) Mr; **monsieur** gentleman; sir

**monstre** *nm* monster; monstrosity; **~ sacré** star, celebrity; *coll* **petit ~** little rascal; *adj coll* huge, colossal, terrific

**monstrueux -ueuse** *adj* monstrous, prodigious; huge; shocking, outrageous

**monstruosité** *nf* monstrosity; monstrousness, outrageousness

**mont** *nm* mount, mountain; **être toujours par ~s et par vaux** be always on the move; **promettre ~s et merveilles** promise the earth

**montage** *nm* taking up, carrying up; assembling, mounting, setting; *cin* montage, cutting; **chaîne de ~** assembly-line

**montagnard -e** *n* mountain-dweller, highlander; *adj* mountain, highland

**montagne** *nf* mountain; mountain region; **~s russes** switchback, big dipper; **se faire une ~ de qch** exaggerate the difficulty of sth

**montagneux -euse** *adj* mountainous, hilly

**montant** *nm* upright, pole, post; riser (stair); *comm* amount, sum total; *cul* strong distinctive taste; strong smell; *sp* **~s de but** goal-posts; *adj* rising, ascending, up-hill; high (collar), high-necked (dress)

**mont-de-piété** *nm* (*pl* **monts-de-piété**) pawn-shop

**monte** *nf* covering, mounting (female animal); riding, horsemanship; *sp* **partants et ~s probables** probable starters and jockeys

**monté** *adj* mounted (soldier, photograph, gun, etc); organized, set up; provided, stocked; *theat* staged; *coll* **collet ~** prim and proper, stuffy; *coll* **coup ~** put-up job; **être ~ contre qn** be worked up against s/o

**monte-charge** *nm invar* hoist; goods-lift

**montée** *nf* rise, slope, gradient; going up, climb; *eng* up-stroke; **en ~** going upwards; *eng* **tuyau de ~** up-take pipe

**monte-en-l'air** *nm invar sl* cat-burglar

**monte-plats** *nm* service-lift, kitchen-lift

**monter** *vt* mount, climb, go up; raise, carry up; set, mount, fit on, assemble; found, set up (business, society); cover, serve (female animal); *theat* stage; *elect* wire up; **~ la tête à qn contre qn** set s/o against s/o; **~ les mailles** cast on stitches (knitting); **~ un coup** hatch a plot; *theat* **~ un décor** fit up; **~ un magasin** open a shop; *vi*

climb up, go up, mount, ascend; rise, slope up; get in, get on; *comm* amount; **~ à bicyclette** ride a bicycle; **~ en bateau** get into a boat; **~ sur un bateau** go on board ship; **~ sur la scène** go onto the stage; **faire ~ qch (qn)** have sth (s/o) brought up(stairs); **se ~** equip oneself, fit oneself out with; amount to; *coll* get worked up, get excited

**monteur -euse** *n* fitter, assembler; setter (jewellery); *comm* promoter

**montgolfière** *nf ar* hot-air balloon

**monticule** *nm* hillock, knoll

**montre** *nf* show, display; watch; *comm* shop-window, show-case; *sp* **course contre la ~** timed race; **faire ~ de** display; **mettre en ~** put in the shop-window

**montre-bracelet** *nf* (*pl* **montres-bracelet**) wrist-watch

**montrer** *vt* show, display; point out, indicate; show how, teach; **se ~** appear, show oneself; prove to be, show oneself to be

**montueux -ueuse** *adj* hilly

**monture** *nf* mount (horse, etc); setting; mounting, assembling; frame (spectacles, umbrella); stock (gun, pistol)

**monument** *nm* monument, memorial; historic building

**monumental** *adj* monumental; *coll* colossal

**moquer (se)** *v refl* mock, make fun, laugh; *coll* not care, not give a damn

**moquerie** *nf* mockery, scoffing; piece of mockery

**moquette** *nf* moquette, carpeting

**moqueur -ueuse** *n* mocker, scoffer; *adj* mocking, scoffing; sarcastic, waggish

**moral** *nm* state of mind, morale; moral faculties; **remonter le ~ de, à qn** raise s/o's morale; *adj* moral, ethical; mental, intellectual

**morale** *nf* morals, ethics; moral (of story); lecture, advice; **faire la ~ à qn** lecture s/o

**moralement** *adv* morally; virtually

**moralisateur -trice** *n* moralizer; *adj* moralizing; edifying

**moraliser** *vt* lecture, sermonize; *vi* moralize; **se ~** become moral

**moraliste** *n* moralist

**moralité** *nf* morality; morals, honesty; moral lesson; *arts* morality-play

**moratoire** *nm* moratorium; *adj leg* moratory, postponed

**morbide** *adj* morbid, unhealthy

**morbidité** *nf* morbidity, morbidness

**morbleu** *interj ar* 'sdeath!

**morceau** *nm* piece, bit, morsel; extract; piece of music; **~x choisis** selections;

emporter le ~ win; *coll* gober le ~ swallow the bait; *coll* manger le ~ blow the gaff; sucre en ~x lump-sugar

**morceler** *vt* (5) cut up into pieces, break up, carve up

**morcellement** *nm* cutting up, parcelling out

**mordant** *nm* pungency, sharpness, pointedness; vigour, dash; *chem* corrosiveness; *adj* pungent, sharp, mordant; corrosive

**mordicus** *adv coll* stubbornly, stoutly

**mordiller** *vt* bite playfully (puppy); nibble

**mordoré** *adj* bronze, golden-brown

**mordorer** *vt* bronze (leather)

**mordorure** *nf* bronze finish

**mordre** *vt* bite; sting; *chem* eat into (acid); *coll* s'en ~ les doigts regret sth bitterly; *vi* bite; *arts* etch; *coll* catch on, begin to understand

**mordu** *adj* bitter; *coll* ~ de set on, mad about

**morfondre (se)** *v refl* get bored waiting about; feel dejected

**morganatique** *adj* morganatic

**morgue** *nf* pride, arrogance, haughtiness

**moribond -e** *n* dying person; *adj* moribund, dying

**moricaud -e** *n coll* blackamoor; *adj coll* dark-skinned, dusky

**morigéner** *vt* (6) lecture, take to task; *coll* tear a strip off

**morille** *nf* morel (mushroom)

**morne** *adj* dismal, gloomy, dreary, doleful

**mornifle** *nf coll* slap

**morose** *adj* morose, gloomy, moody, sullen

**morosité** *nf* moroseness, sullenness

**morphine** *nf* morphia, morphine

**morphinomane** *n* morphine addict

**morphologie** *nf* morphology

**morphologique** *adj* morphological

**morpion** *nm coll* crab-louse, crab; *coll* brat

**mors** *nm* bit (horse); jaw (vice); prendre le ~ aux dents take the bit in its teeth (horse); *fig* take the bit between one's teeth (person)

**morse** *nm* walrus

**morsure** *nf* bite, biting; gnawing (hunger); nip (cold)

**¹mort** *nm* dummy (cards); faire le ~ be dummy

**²mort -e** *n* dead person; faire le ~ lie low; jour des ~s All Soul's Day; *nf* death; à ~ X! down with X!, death to X!; attraper la ~ catch one's death; avoir la ~ dans l'âme be sick at heart; être à l'article de la ~ be at the point of

death; faire une bonne ~ make a good (Christian) end; mourir de sa belle ~ die in one's bed, die a natural death; *adj* dead, lifeless; arriver au point ~ come to a stand-still; *sp* ballon ~ dead ball; *arts* nature ~e still-life; poids-~ dead weight; *mot* point ~ neutral

**mortaise** *nf* mortise

**mortaiser** *vt* mortise

**mortalité** *nf* mortality; number of deaths; taux de ~ death-rate

**mort-aux-rats** *nf invar* rat-poison

**morte-eau** *nf* (*pl* mortes-eaux) neap-tide

**mortel -elle** *n* mortal; *adj* mortal; fatal; deadly; boring, wearisome

**mortellement** *adv* mortally, fatally; *coll* s'ennuyer ~ be bored to death

**mortier** *nm* mortar; *mil* mortar; *eccles* + *leg* cap; *archi* ~ liquide grout

**mortifiant** *adj* mortifying

**mortification** *nf* mortification, humiliation, chagrin; *cul* hanging (game)

**mortifier** *vt* mortify, humiliate; *cul* hang (game)

**mort-né -e** *n* + *adj* stillborn (child); *fig* abortive (project)

**mortuaire** *adj* mortuary; concerning death, burial; acte ~ death certificate; avis ~ announcement of death; drap ~ pall; extrait ~ death-certificate

**morue** *nf zool* cod; *vulg* tart; huile de foie de ~ cod-liver oil

**morutier** *nm naut* cod-fishing boat; cod-fisherman

**morve** *nf* nasal mucus, *sl* snot; *vet* glanders

**morveux -euse** *n coll* brat; impudent puppy; *adj coll* snotty; *vet* glandered

**¹mosaïque** *nf* mosaic; test-card (television)

**²mosaïque** *adj* Mosaic

**Moscou** *n* Moscow

**moscoutaire** *adj pej* communist, *coll* red

**moscovite** *adj* Muscovite

**mosquée** *nf* mosque

**mot** *nm* word; key, clue; *mil* password; ~ à ~ word for word, literal; *mil* ~ d'ordre password; ~s croisés crossword; au bas ~ at the lowest estimate; avoir le ~ pour rire have a good sense of humour, have funny things to say; bon ~ witticism, *coll* crack; comprendre à demi-~ know how to take a hint, be quick on the uptake; dire deux ~s à qn have a word with s/o; dire son ~ have one's say; écrire un ~ à qn drop s/o a line; faire des ~s be witty; gros ~s swear words, coarse language; le fin ~ the real clue, the key; *coll* ne pas connaître un traître ~ d'anglais not know a single word of English; parler à ~s couverts hint, drop hints; **prendre qn au ~** take s/o at his word; **se donner le ~** pass the word round; **tranchons le ~** let's get this clear, let's have it out

**motard** *nm coll* motorcycle cop; motor-cyclist

**mot-clé** *nm* (*pl* **mots-clé(s)**) key-word, catch-word

**moteur** *nm* mover, instigator; motor, engine; **~ à deux temps** two-stroke engine; **~ à explosion** internal combustion engine; **premier ~** prime mover; *adj* (*f* -**trice**) motive, driving

**motif** *nm* motive, incentive; pattern, motif; *leg* grounds; *mus* theme; **sans ~** groundless; *adj* (*f* -**ive**) motive

**motion** *nf* proposal, motion; **adopter une ~** carry a motion

**motiver** *vt* justify, warrant; motivate; state reasons for; *comm* account for

**moto** *nf coll* motor-bike

**moto-cross** *nm* motocross

**motocyclette** *nf* motorcycle

**motocycliste** *n* motorcyclist

**motogodille** *nf* outboard motor

**motorisation** *nf* motorization

**motoriser** *vt* motorize

**mots-croisés** *nmpl* crossword

**motte** *nf* clod, lump of earth; pat, block (butter)

**motus** *interj* not a word!, keep it dark!

**¹mou** *nm naut* slack; *cul* lights

**²mou, mol** (*f* **molle**) *adj* soft, flabby, slack; feeble, languid; lax

**mouchard -e** *n coll* sneak, tell-tale; police informer; *sl* nark

**moucharder** *vt coll* spy on; squeal on

**mouche** *nf* fly; *ar* patch (embellishment of face); tuft of hair; *sp* button (foil), bull's-eye (shooting); **~ à miel** bee; **~ bleue** blue-bottle; **~ commune** horse-fly; *sp* **faire ~** score a bull; **fine ~** sly character, slick customer; **on aurait entendu voler une ~** you could have heard a pin drop; *sp* **poids ~** fly-weight; **prendre la ~** lose one's temper; *coll* **quelle ~ vous pique?** what's biting you?

**moucher** *vt* blow (nose), wipe (child's nose); snuff, trim (candle); **se ~** blow one's nose; **il ne se mouche pas du coude** he has a great opinion of himself

**moucheron** *nm* gnat, midge; *coll* kid, brat

**moucheté** *adj* speckled, dappled, spotty

**moucheter** *vt* (5) speckle, fleck; *sp* button (foil)

**moucheture** *nf* speckle, spot

**mouchoir** *nm* handkerchief; **~ de tête** head-scarf, kerchief

**mouchure** *nf* nasal mucus; snuff (candle)

**moudre** *vt* (61) grind, mill

**moue** *nf* pout; **faire la ~** pout

**mouette** *nf* seagull

**mouffette** *nf zool* skunk

**moufle** *nf* mitten, mitt; *eng* pulley-block

**mouillage** *nm* watering, adulterating; damping; *naut* anchoring, anchorage; *naut* laying of mine; *naut* **droits de ~** harbour dues; *naut* **être au ~** ride at anchor

**mouiller** *vt* wet, moisten, damp; water down, adulterate; *naut* drop (anchor), moor; *naut* stream (buoy); *naut* lay (mine); *phon* palatalize; **se ~** get wet; water (eyes); *coll* compromise oneself; **mouillé jusqu'aux os** soaked to the skin; *coll* **poule mouillée** milksop

**mouillette** *nf cul* finger of bread

**mouilleur** *nm naut* anchor tripper; **~ de mines** mine-layer

**mouillure** *nf* wetting, damping; damp mark; wetness

**mouise** *nf sl* poverty; **dans la ~** broke, up against it

**moulage** *nm* casting, moulding; cast

**¹moule** *nm* mould, matrix; **mettre au ~** cast in a mould, run into a mould

**²moule** *nf* mussel; *coll* fat-head, clot

**moulé** *adj* moulded, cast; having a good figure; **écriture ~e** copper-plate

**mouler** *vt* mould, cast; **robe qui moule** dress that shows off the figure, skin-tight dress

**moulin** *nm* mill; grinder; *coll* **~ à paroles** chatterbox; **apporter de l'eau au ~** bring grist to the mill

**moulinet** *nm* reel (fishing-rod); twirl, flourish

**moult** *adv ar* + *joc* much, very

**moulu** *adj* ground, powdered; *coll* dead-beat, *sl* creased

**moulure** *nf archi* moulding

**mourant -e** *n* dying person; *adj* dying; *fig* faint; *coll* killing, creasingly funny

**mourir** *vi* (62) die; *fig* die away, fade, wither; **~ d'ennui** be bored to death; **~ de rire** be tickled to death; **~ d'impatience de** be dying to; **se ~** be dying

**mouroir** *nm pej* old people's home

**mouron** *nm bot* chickweed

**mousquet** *nm mil* musket

**mousquetaire** *nm mil* musketeer; **gants à la ~** gauntlet gloves

**mousqueton** *nm mil ar* blunderbuss; snap-hook; carabiner (mountaineering)

**moussant** *adj* foamy, frothy

**¹mousse** *nm naut* ship's boy

**²mousse** *nf* moss; froth, foam, head (beer), lather (soap); *cul* whipped cream and eggs, mousse; **caoutchouc ~** foam rubber

³**mousse** *adj* blunt (knife, point)

**mousseline** *nf* muslin; ~ **de soie** chiffon; *cul* **pommes** ~ mashed potatoes

**mousser** *vi* froth, foam; sparkle, fizz (wine); lather (soap); *cul* **faire** ~ **de la crème** whip cream; *sl* **faire** ~ **qn** anger s/o; *coll* sing praise of s/o; **se faire** ~ sing one's own praises

**mousseron** *nm* kind of edible mushroom

**mousseux -euse** *adj* mossy; foaming; sparkling (wine), frothy (beer)

**mousson** *nf* monsoon

**moussu** *adj* mossy, moss-grown

**moustache** *nf* moustache; whiskers (cat)

**moustachu** *adj* moustached

**moustiquaire** *nf* mosquito-net

**moustique** *nm* mosquito

**moût** *nm* must (grapes)

**moutard** *nm sl* brat, kid

**moutarde** *nf* mustard

**moutardier** *nm* mustard-maker; mustard-pot

**mouton** *nm* sheep; mutton; *eng* ram, monkey (pile-driver); *naut* ~ **s** white horses; **revenons à nos** ~ **s** let's get back to the point; *adj* (*f* **-onne**) sheep-like

**moutonné** *adj* fleecy; covered with white horses (sea); **ciel** ~ mackerel sky; *geol* **roche** ~ **e** glaciated rock

**moutonner** *vt* curl (hair); *vi* foam, become covered with white horses (sea); **se** ~ become covered with white horses (sea); become covered with fleecy clouds (sky)

**moutonneux -euse** *adj* fleecy; foam-flecked, covered with white horses (sea)

**moutonnier -ière** *adj* ovine; sheep-like

**mouture** *nf* grinding, milling

**mouvant** *adj* moving, unstable; **sables** ~ **s** quick-sands, shifting sands

**mouvement** *nm* movement, motion, activity; *comm* trend; *mus* time; mechanism, works (clock); turnover, transfer (staff); traffic; change, evolution; emotion, impulse, outburst; ~ **acquis** impetus; *geog* ~ **s de terrain** hills and valleys; **chef de** ~ traffic manager (railway); **être dans le** ~ be up-to-date; **faire un faux** ~ strain a muscle; **mettre en** ~ set in motion, start (engine); **quantité de** ~ momentum

**mouvementé** *adj* animated, lively; full of incident, eventful; *geog* undulatory

**mouvementer** *vt* animate, enliven

**mouvoir** *vt* (63) move, set in motion, actuate; urge, prompt; **se** ~ move, stir

**moyen** *nm* means, way; *math* mean; **au** ~ **de** by means of; **grands** ~ **s** extreme measures; **il n'y a pas** ~ nothing doing, it can't be done; **le** ~ **de savoir?**

how can one know?; *leg* **voies et** ~ **s** ways and means; *adj* (*f* **-enne**) middle, average, mean; ordinary, moderate; *rad* medium; **Moyen-Âge** Middle Ages; **Moyen Orient** Middle East; **cours** ~ intermediate course (lessons); *comm* middle price; **l'homme** ~ the average man, the common man; **très** ~ middling

**moyenâgeux -euse** *adj* (quaintly) medieval; out-of-date, behind the times

**moyennant** *prep* thanks to, subject to, at the cost of; ~ **finance** for a consideration; ~ **que** provided that, on condition that; ~ **quoi** in consideration of which

**moyenne** *nf* average; pass-mark (examination); *math* mean; **mot faire 50 à l'heure de** ~ average fifty

**moyennement** *adv* moderately, fairly; on the average

**moyeu** *nm* hub (wheel); boss (propeller)

**muable** *adj* mutable, changeable

**mucilagineux -euse** *adj* mucilaginous, viscous

**mucosité** *nf* mucosity

**mue** *nf* moulting (bird); shedding of coat, hair, antlers, etc; breaking of voice; hen-coop

**muer** *vi* moult; shed coat, hair, antlers, etc; break (voice); **se** ~ change into

**muet -uette** *n* dumb person, mute; *adj* dumb, mute; intent, speechless; *geog* **carte muette** blank map; *theat* **jeu** ~ piece of business; mime; *theat* **rôle** ~ non-speaking part, walk-on

**muette** *nf gramm* mute letter, unsounded letter

**mufle** *nm* muzzle, nose (animal); *coll* boor; rotter

**muflerie** *nf coll* boorishness; dirty trick

**muge** *nm zool* mullet

**mugir** *vi* low, moo (cow); roar, boom (sea); howl (wind)

**mugissement** *nm* lowing, mooing (cow); roaring, booming (sea); howling (wind)

**muguet** *nm bot* lily of the valley; *fig ar* dandy

**muid** *nm* large barrel, hogshead

**mulâtre** *nm* + *adj* mulatto

**mulâtresse** *nf* mulatto woman

¹**mule** *nf* (she-)mule

²**mule** *nf* slipper; *med* chilblain

**mulet** *nm* mule

**muletier** *nm* mule-driver, muleteer; *adj* (*f* **-ière**) mule; **chemin** ~ mule-track

**mulot** *nm* field-mouse

**multicolore** *adj* multicoloured, variegated

**multiforme** *adj* multiform

**multiple** *nm math* multiple; **le plus petit**

**commun** ~ = lowest common multiple; *adj* multiple, manifold, multifarious

**multiplicateur** *nm math* multiplier; *adj* (*f* -**trice**) *math* multiplying

**multiplication** *nf math* multiplication; *eng* gear-ratio; *fig* increase; **grande (petite)** ~ high (low) gear

**multiplicité** *nf* multiplicity

**multiplier** *vt math* multiply; *eng* gear up; *fig* multiply, propagate; *vi* multiply; **se** ~ multiply, increase; be in half a dozen places at once

**multitude** *nf* multitude, crowd; multiplicity, heaps

**municipalité** *nf* municipality; town council

**munir** *vt* furnish, supply, provide; **se** ~ provide oneself

**munition** *nf ar* provisioning; ~**s** *mil* ammunition; ~**s de bouche** supplies, provisions

**muqueux -euse** *adj* mucous

**muqueuse** *nf med* mucous membrane

**mur** *nm* wall, barrier; ~ **d'appui** low wall; ~ **de clôture** surrounding wall; *coll* **faire le** ~ climb out, go out without permission; **franchir le** ~ **du son** break the sound barrier; **mettre qn au pied du** ~ drive s/o into a corner; oblige s/o to come to a decision

**mûr** *adj* ripe, mellow; seasoned; mature; ready, considered; *sl* nicely drunk, mellow; *coll* worn (cloth); **femme assez** ~ **e** woman well on in years

**murage** *nm* walling in, walling up

**muraille** *nf* high wall, solid wall; *naut* side (of ship)

**mural** *adj* mural; **carte** ~ **e** wall-map

**mûre** *nf* mulberry; blackberry

**murer** *vt* wall in, wall up; shut up

**mûrier** *nm* mulberry-tree

**mûrir** *vt* ripen, mature; give careful thought to; work out; *med* bring to a head (abscess); *vi* ripen, become ripe; mature; *med* come to a head (abscess)

**murmurant** *adj* murmuring, muttering, sighing (wind); babbling (stream)

**murmure** *nm* murmur, murmuring, muttering; sighing (wind); babbling (stream)

**murmurer** *vt* whisper (secret); *vi* murmur, whisper; grumble, complain; mutter; sigh (wind); babble (stream)

**musaraigne** *nf zool* shrew (mouse)

**musard -e** *n coll* dawdler; *adj coll* dawdling, idling

**musarder** *vi coll* idle, dawdle

**musardise** *nf* dawdling

**musc** *nm* musk

**muscade** *nf* nutmeg

**muscadet** *nm* dry white wine from the Nantes area

**muscadier** *nm* nutmeg-tree

**muscadin** *nm ar* dandy, beau

**muscat** *nm* muscat grape; muscatel (wine); *adj* muscat (grape, wine)

**musclé** *adj* muscular, brawny, athletic; *fig* tough, brutal

**musculaire** *adj med* muscular

**musculeux -euse** *adj* brawny

**museau** *nm* muzzle, snout (animal); *coll* nose

**musée** *nm* museum

**museler** *vt* (5) muzzle (dog); *fig* muzzle, silence

**muselière** *nf* muzzle

**muser** *vi* idle, dawdle, fritter away one's time

**musette** *nf* kind of bagpipes; nose-bag (horse); *mil* haversack; **bal** ~ popular dance (one with accordeon band)

**muséum** *nm* natural history museum

**musicalité** *nf* musicality

**musicien -ienne** *n* musician; player in band; *adj* musical

**musicographe** *n* musicographer

**musicologue** *n* musicologist

**musique** *nf* music; band; *theat* incidental music; **chef de** ~ band-master; *coll* **connaître la** ~ know the ropes; **faire de la** ~ make music; study music, go in for music; *coll* **faire une** ~ **du diable** make a hell of a row

**musiquette** *nf coll* cheap music, badly played music

**musqué** *adj* musky, scented with musk; affected, lush; **bœuf** ~ musk-ox; **rat** ~ musk-rat; **rose** ~ **e** musk-rose

**Musulman -e** *n* Moslem, Muslim

**musulman** *adj* Moslem, Muslim

**mutabilité** *nf* mutability

**mutation** *nf* change, alteration; transfer (job, footballers); *leg* transfer, change of ownership; *mus* + *biol* mutation

**muter** *vt* transfer (employee)

**mutilateur -trice** *n* mutilator; defacer

**mutilation** *nf* mutilation, maiming; defacement

**mutilé -e** *n* disabled soldier, disabled person; **grand** ~ badly disabled soldier (person); *adj* mutilated, disfigured; disabled

**mutiler** *vt* mutilate, maim, disfigure; deface; *fig* mangle

**mutin** *nm* mutineer; *adj* rebellious, unruly, insubordinate; *mil* + *naut* mutinous; *coll* pert, saucy

**mutiné** *nm* mutineer; *adj* rebellious, mutinous

**mutiner (se)** *v refl* revolt; be disobedient (child); *mil* + *naut* mutiny

**mutinerie** *nf* insubordination; *mil* +

**naut** mutiny; disobedience, unruliness (child)

**mutisme** *nm* muteness, dumbness; **s'enfermer dans le ~** maintain a stubborn silence

**mutualité** *nf* mutuality, reciprocity; *leg* mutual insurance

**mutuel -uelle** *adj* mutual; *sp* **pari ~** tote; *leg* **société de secours ~s** friendly society

**mutuelle** *nf* mutual insurance company

**mycologie** *nf bot* mycology

**myélite** *nf med* myelitis

**myocarde** *nm anat* myocardium

**myope** *n + adj* short-sighted (person)

**myopie** *nf* short-sightedness, myopia

**myosotis** *nm bot* forget-me-not

**myriade** *nf* myriad

**myrmidon** *nm coll* little man, midget

**myrrhe** *nf* myrrh

**myrte** *nm* myrtle

**myrtille** *nf* bilberry, whortleberry, *US* huckleberry

**mystère** *nm* mystery, secret; mysteriousness; *theat* mystery(-play)

**mystérieux -ieuse** *adj* mysterious

**mysticisme** *nm* mysticism

**mystificateur -trice** *n* mystifier; *coll* hoaxer, humbug; *adj* mystifying

**mystification** *nf* mystification; hoaxing, humbug

**mystifier** *vt* mystify; hoax, humbug, fool

**mystique** *n* mystic; *nf* mystical doctrine; mystique; *adj* mystical, mystic

**mythe** *nm* myth, legend

**mythique** *adj* mythical

**mythologie** *nf* mythology

**mythologique** *adj* mythological

**mythologue** *n* mythologist

**myxomatose** *nf* myxomatosis

# N

**na** *interj* there!, so there! (child language)

**nabab** *nm* nabob

**nabot -e** *n* dwarf, midget; *adj* dwarfish, tiny

**nacelle** *nf* basket (balloon); *lit* skiff

**nacre** *nf* mother of pearl

**nacré** *adj* pearly

**nage** *nf* swimming; sculling, rowing; **donner la ~** set the stroke; **être en ~** be bathed in perspiration; **traverser une rivière à la ~** swim across a river

**nageoire** *nf* fin; *sl* arm

**nager** *vi* (3) swim; float, be submerged; scull, row; *coll* be uncertain, be at a loss; **~ dans l'abondance** wallow in luxury; **~ entre deux eaux** swim under water; *coll* **savoir ~** be a smooth operator, know how to cope

**nageur -euse** *n* swimmer; oarsman; *adj* swimming

**naguère** *adv* not long ago, lately, a short while back

**naïade** *nf* naiad, water-nymph

**naïf** (*f* **naïve**) *n* simpleton; *adj* artless, naïve, ingenuous; simple, simple-minded

**nain -e** *n* dwarf, midget; *adj* dwarfish, undersized

**naissance** *nf* birth; descent; origin, beginning; *med* root (muscle, tongue, etc); **de ~ obscure** of humble birth; **prendre ~** originate

**naissant** *adj* new-born; incipient, nascent, budding

**naître** *vi* (64) be born; arise; begin, come up; **faire ~** give birth to; give rise to, cause

**naïveté** *nf* naïvety; artlessness, ingenuousness; simple-mindedness; *coll* greenness; artless remark

**naja** *nm zool* cobra

**nana** *nf coll* girl

**nanan** *nm coll obs* something good to eat, something sweet; *coll* **c'est du ~!** yum-yum!

**nankin** *nm* nankeen

**nantir** *vt* provide, furnish; *leg* give security to, secure; **se ~** provide oneself

**nantissement** *nm leg* security, pledge, cover

**naphtaline** *nf* moth-balls; *chem* naphthaline

**naphte** *nm* naphtha

**napoléon** *nm ar* twenty-franc (gold) coin

**napolitain** *adj* Neapolitan

**nappe** *nf* tablecloth, cloth; *fig* sheet (water, ice, etc); ~ **d'autel** altar-cloth

**napperon** *nm* table-mat; tray-cloth; **petit** ~ doily

**narcisse** *nm* narcissus

**narcissisme** *nm* narcissism

**narcose** *nf med* narcosis

**narcotique** *nm* narcotic, drug; *adj* narcotic

**narcotiser** *vt* narcotize, drug

**narguer** *vt* taunt; snap one's fingers at; flout

**narguilé** *nm* hookah

**narine** *nf* nostril

**narquois** *adj* mocking, sneering, bantering

**narrateur -trice** *n* narrator, teller of story

**narratif -ive** *adj* narrative

**narration** *nf* narration, narrative; composition (school); *gramm* **infinitif de** ~ historic infinitive; *gramm* **présent de** ~ historic present

**narrer** *vt* narrate

**nasale** *nf phon* nasal

**nasaliser** *vt* nasalize

**nasalité** *nf* nasality

**nasarde** *nf* fillip, flick on the nose; *fig* rebuff

**naseau** *nm* nostril (animal)

**nasillard** *adj* nasal

**nasillement** *nm* nasal twang

**nasiller** *vt* say through one's nose; *vi* speak through one's nose, snuffle

**nasilleur -euse** *n* one who talks with a nasal twang

**nasse** *nf* trap, wicker-trap (fish); net for catching birds

**natal** (*pl* ~ **s**) *adj* native; natal; **ville** ~ **e** birth-place

**natalité** *nf* birth-rate

**natation** *nf* swimming

**natif -ive** *n* native; *adj* native, born; *fig* innate, natural; **bon sens** ~ native wit

**national** *adj* national; **route** ~ **e** trunk-road, = A road

**nationaliser** *vt* nationalize

**nationalisme** *nm* nationalism

**nationaliste** *n* nationalist; *adj* nationalistic

**nationalité** *nf* nationality

**nationaux** *nmpl* nationals, citizens of a country

**nativité** *nf eccles* nativity

**natte** *nf* mat, rush-matting; plait, pigtail

**natter** *vt* furnish (room) with mats; weave (rushes); plait (hair)

**naturalisation** *nf* naturalization; acclimatization; taxidermy, stuffing

**naturaliser** *vt* naturalize; acclimatize; stuff; **se faire** ~ become naturalized

**naturalisme** *nm* naturalism

**naturaliste** *n* naturalist; taxidermist; *adj* naturalist, naturalistic

**nature** *nf* nature, temperament, sort, kind, character; *arts* ~ **morte** still-life; **contre** ~ unnatural; **de** ~ **à** of such kind as to; **payer en** ~ pay in kind; *arts* **peindre d'après** ~ paint from life; *adj invar* neat, pure; unaffected; **café** ~ black coffee; **grandeur** ~ life-size; **omelette** ~ plain omelette; **pommes** ~ boiled potatoes

**naturel** *nm* nature; nature, character, disposition; naturalness; *cul* **au** ~ boiled; **avoir un heureux** ~ have a happy disposition; **chassez le** ~, **il revient au galop** nature will tell; **voir les choses au** ~ see things as they are; *adj* (*f* **-elle**) natural; innate; simple, unaffected, plain; unfortified (wine)

**naturellement** *adv* naturally, by nature; of course

**naturisme** *nm* naturism, nudism

**naturiste** *n* + *adj* naturist, nudist

**naufrage** *nm* shipwreck; *fig* ruin; **faire** ~ be wrecked

**naufragé -e** *n* + *adj* shipwrecked (person), castaway, marooned (person)

**naufrageur** *nm* wrecker

**nauséabond** *adj* nauseous, nauseating; *fig* loathsome, repugnant

**nausée** *nf* nausea; **avoir des** ~ **s** feel sick

**nautique** *adj* nautical

**nautisme** *nm* sailing, yachting

**naval** (*pl* ~ **s**) *adj* naval, nautical

**navarin** *nm cul* mutton stew (with carrots, onions, etc)

**navet** *nm* turnip; *arts* daub; *theat* + *cin* flop

¹**navette** *nf* shuttle; train on shuttle service; ~ **spatiale** space shuttle; **faire la** ~ ply to and fro (vehicle, ship, etc), go to and fro

²**navette** *nf bot* rape; **huile de** ~ colza oil

**navigabilité** *nf* navigability (river, etc); seaworthiness

**navigable** *adj* navigable (river, etc); seaworthy

**navigateur -trice** *n* navigator (sea, air); sailor; *adj* seafaring

**navigation** *nf* navigation (sea, air), sailing; ~ **de plaisance** pleasure-cruising, yachting; **compagnie de** ~ shipping company

**naviguer** *vt* + *vi* navigate, sail

**navire** *nm* ship, vessel; ~ **de ligne** capital ship

**navire-citerne** *nm* (*pl* **navires-citernes**) *naut* tanker

**navrant** *adj* heartbreaking, harrowing

**navré** *adj* heartbroken, very distressed; terribly sorry

**navrer** *vt* grieve, hurt deeply

**nazisme** *nm pol* Nazism

**ne** *adv* not, nothing (found normally as part of expressions, *eg* **ne ... pas** not; **ne ... que** only; **ne ... rien** nothing)

**né** *adj* born; **premier** ~ first-born; **bien** ~ of good family

**néanmoins** *adv* none the less, nevertheless, however, yet, still

**néant** *nm* nothingness; naught; nil, nothing

**nébuleuse** *nf astron* nebula

**nébuleux -euse** *adj* nebulous; cloudy, overcast, hazy; muddy, cloudy (liquid); *fig* confused, vague

**nébulosité** *nf* nebulosity, cloud-covering; *fig* lack of clarity

**nécessaire** *nm* what is necessary, requisite; necessaries of life; outfit, kit; ~ **à ouvrage** work-box ~ **de toilette** dressing-case; **manquer du** ~ lack the necessities of life; *adj* necessary, needful; **peu** ~ needless, unnecessary

**nécessité** *nf* necessity, need; compulsion, inevitability; *obs* poverty; **denrées de première** ~ essential foodstuffs; **il est de toute** ~ **de** it is essential to

**nécessiter** *vt* necessitate, entail

**nécessiteux -euse** *n + adj* needy (person)

**nécrologie** *nf* obituary

**nécrologique** *adj* **notice** ~ obituary notice

**nécromancie** *nf* necromancy

**nécromancien -ienne** *n* necromancer

**nécrophilie** *nf* necrophilia

**nécropole** *nf* necropolis

**nécrose** *nf med* necrosis, gangrene; *bot* canker

**Néerlandais -e** *n* Dutchman (Dutchwoman)

**néerlandais** *nm* Dutch (language); *adj* Dutch

**nef** *nf* nave; *ar* vessel, ship

**néfaste** *adj* disastrous, fatal; harmful; unlucky, ill-fated

**nèfle** *nf bot* medlar; *sl* **des** ~ **s!** nothing doing!, not on your life!

**néflier** *nm bot* medlar-tree

**négateur -trice** *n* one who denies; *adj* denying

**négatif** *nm phot* negative; *adj* (*f* **-ive**) negative

**négation** *nf* negation, denial; *gramm* negative

**négligé** *nm* négligé(e); woman's light dressing-gown; *adj* neglected, unheeded, missed; careless, slovenly, untidy

**négligeable** *adj* negligible, insignificant

**négligence** *nf* negligence, carelessness, neglect; heedlessness; slovenliness, untidiness

**négligent** *adj* negligent, careless, neglectful; heedless; untidy

**négliger** *vt* (3) neglect, omit, fail, be careless about; disregard; ~ **de faire qch** fail to do sth; **se** ~ neglect oneself, become slovenly

**négoce** *nm* trade, business

**négociabilité** *nf comm* negotiability

**négociable** *adj comm* negotiable, transferable

**négociant -e** *n* merchant

**négociateur -trice** *n* negotiator, transactor

**négociation** *nf* negotiation, negotiating; transaction

**négocier** *vt* negotiate (treaty, bill, loan); *vi* negotiate

**nègre** *nm* negro, black; ghost (writer); **faire le** ~ ghost; **petit** ~ broken French, = pidgin English; *adj* negro, black

**négresse** *nf* negress

**négrier** *nm* slave-trader; slave-ship

**négrillon -onne** *n coll* nigger-boy (-girl)

**négroïde** *adj* negroid

**neige** *nf* snow; ~ **carbonique** dry ice; ~ **fondue** slush, sleet; *cul* **blanc d'œufs battus en** ~ whipped whites of eggs; **train de** ~ skiing excursion train

**neiger** *vi* (3) snow

**neigeux -euse** *adj* snowy, snow-covered; snow-white

**nénés** *nmpl sl* tits

**nenni** *adv ar* nay!

**nénuphar** *nm* water-lily

**néolithique** *adj* neolithic

**néologisme** *nm* neologism

**Néo-Zélandais -e** *n* New Zealander

**néo-zélandais** *adj* New Zealand

**néphrétique** *adj med* nephritic, renal

**néphrite** *nf med* nephritis; *min* jade, nephrite

**népotisme** *nm* nepotism

**nerf** *nm med* nerve; sinew, tendon; *fig* nerve, sinew; *archi* rib; ~ **de bœuf** whip; *ar* pizzle; **avoir les** ~ **s à vif** be on edge, jumpy; **manquer de** ~ be flabby, lack energy; **taper (porter) sur les** ~ **s de qn** get on s/o's nerves

**nerveux -euse** *n* excitable, highly strung person; *adj med* nerve; nervous; sinewy, wiry; forceful; nervy, highly strung; *mot* lively, responsive; *bot* nervate

**nervi** *nm sl* gangster; thug, killer

**nervosité** *nf* state of nerves, excitability, irritability

**nervure** *nf archi* rib, fillet; *bot* vein, rib (leaf)

**net** *nm* **mettre qch au ~** make a fair copy of sth; *adj* (*f* **nette**) clean, spotless, neat, tidy; clear, clear-cut, distinct; unequivocal, candid, unmistakable; *comm* net; **en avoir le cœur ~** get something clear; *phot* **image nette** sharp image; **revenu ~ d'impôts** tax-free income; *adv* clearly, plainly, flatly; **mille francs ~** a clear thousand francs; **refuser ~** refuse point-blank; **s'arrêter ~** stop dead

**nettement** *adv* clearly, distinctly; definitely, decidedly; cleanly

**netteté** *nf* cleanness, cleanliness; clearness, distinctness; decidedness

**nettoiement** *nm* cleaning, cleansing (streets, town); clearing (waste land); **service du ~** refuse collection

**nettoyage** *nm* cleaning, clearing; *mil* mopping-up; **~ à sec** dry-cleaning

**nettoyer** *vt* (7) clean, scour, wash out, wash up; cleanse (wound); *mil* mop up; *coll* clean out (money); **~ à grande eau** mop; **~ à sec** dry clean; **se ~** clean oneself, wash oneself; clean; **tissu qui se nettoie bien** fabric that washes well

**nettoyeur -euse** *n* cleaner; *adj* cleaning

¹**neuf** *nm* nine; *adj* nine; ninth

²**neuf** *nm* new; **habillé de ~** dressed in new clothes; **il y a du ~** there's some news, something new has occurred; **remettre qch à ~** make sth as good as new; *adj* (*f* **neuve**) new, newly bought, fresh, inexperienced

**neurasthénie** *nf* neurasthenia

**neurasthénique** *adj* neurasthenic

**neurologie** *nf* neurology

**neurologue** *n* neurologist

**neutralisant** *nm chem* neutralizing agent; *adj chem* neutralizing

**neutraliser** *vt* neutralize

**neutralité** *nf* neutrality; *chem* neutral state

**neutre** *nm* neutral; *gramm* neuter; *adj* neutral; *gramm* + *zool* neuter

**neuvaine** *nf eccles* novena

**neuvième** *n* ninth; *nm* ninth part; *nf mus* ninth; *adj* ninth

**névé** *nm geog* névé, consolidated snow

**neveu** *nm* nephew

**névralgie** *nf* neuralgia

**névralgique** *adj* neuralgic; *fig* sensitive; **point ~** nerve centre

**névrite** *nf* neuritis

**névritique** *adj* neuritic

**névrose** *nf* neurosis

**névrosé -e** *n* + *adj* neurotic

**névrotique** *adj* neurotic

**nez** *nm* nose; bows (ship); **avoir du ~** have a sense of smell; have flair; **avoir le ~ creux** have a sharp instinct for a bargain; *sl* **avoir qn dans le ~** be unable to stand s/o; *coll* **à vue de ~** roughly speaking, at a rough estimate; **chercher du ~** nose about; **faire qch au ~ de qn** do sth under s/o's very nose; **faire un pied de ~** cock a snook; *coll* **mener qn par le bout du ~** twist s/o round one's little finger; **montrer son ~** show one's face; **piquer du ~** nosedive (aircraft), sink by the bows (ship); **rire au ~ de qn** laugh in s/o's face; **se casser le ~ à la porte de qn** find no one in; be rebuffed; *coll* **se manger le ~** quarrel (two persons); *coll* **tirer les vers du ~ de qn** worm secrets out of s/o; *naut* **vaisseau sur le ~** ship down by the bows

**ni** *conj* **ni ... ni** neither ... nor

**niais -e** *n* simpleton, fool; *adj* simple, silly, foolish

**niaiserie** *nf* simplicity, silliness, foolishness; inane remark, twaddle

¹**niche** *nf* (dog-)kennel; *archi* niche

²**niche** *nf* trick, practical joke

**nichée** *nf* brood (mice), nest (birds); *coll* brood, swarm (children)

**nicher** *vt* put in a nest; *vi* nest, build a nest; *coll* live, hang out; **se ~** nest; *coll* perch himself, put oneself

**nichon** *nm sl* tit

**nickelage** *nm* nickel-plating

**nickeler** *vt* (5) nickel-plate; *coll* **avoir les pieds nickelés** refuse to budge, be lazy

**nid** *nm* nest; *naut* **~ de pie** crow's nest; **~ de poule** pot-hole in the road

¹**nielle** *nm* niello, inlaid enamel-work

²**nielle** *nf agr* blight

**nieller** *vt* inlay with niello

²**nieller** *vt agr* blight; **se ~** become blighted

¹**niellure** *nf* niello-work

²**niellure** *nf agr* blighting

**nier** *vt* deny; *leg* repudiate (debt)

**nigaud -e** *n* fool, ass, idiot, booby; *adj* silly, foolish

**nigauderie** *nf* silliness, foolishness; act of stupidity, tomfoolery

**nihilisme** *nm* nihilism

**nihiliste** *n* nihilist; *adj* nihilistic

**nimbe** *nm* nimbus, halo

**nipper** *vt coll* clothe, rig out; **se ~** *coll* rig oneself out

**nippes** *nfpl coll* togs

**Nippon -onne** *n* Japanese

**nippon -onne** *adj* Japanese

**nique** *nf* **faire la ~ à qch** despise sth, snap one's fingers at sth; **faire la ~ à qn** cock a snook at s/o

**nitouche** *nf* demure, coy girl; **sainte ~** little hypocrite; **faire la sainte ~** look as though butter wouldn't melt in one's mouth

**nitre** *nm* nitre, saltpetre

**nitreux -euse** *adj* nitrous

**nitrique** *adj* nitric

**nitrogène** *nm* nitrogen; *adj* nitrogen

**niveau** *nm* level, standard; floor; level (instrument); **~ à bulle d'air** spirit level; *mot* **~ d'essence (d'huile)** petrol (oil) gauge; **~ de vie** standard of living; **au ~ de** on a level with; with regard to, in the field of; **de ~ avec** on a level with; **mettre à ~** level, level up; **passage à ~** level-crossing

**niveler** *vt* (5) survey; level, level up, even up; **se ~** become level, settle down

**niveleur -euse** *n* leveller; *adj* levelling

**nivellement** *nm* surveying; levelling

**nivôse** *nm hist* fourth month of the French Republican calendar (December to January)

**nobiliaire** *nm* peerage list; *adj* nobiliary

**noble** *n* nobleman, noblewoman *adj* noble, aristocratic; august; generous; *mech* of high technology; *theat* **père ~** heavy father

**noblesse** *nf* nobility; nobleness

**noce** *nf* wedding, wedding festivities; *coll* spree; **~s** marriage; **épouser en secondes ~s** marry for the second time; *coll* **faire la ~** go on the spree; *coll* **ne pas être à la ~** be having a bad time; **voyage de ~s** honeymoon

**noceur -euse** *n* reveller, fast liver

**nocher** *nm poet* boatman, pilot

**nocif -ive** *adj* noxious, injurious, harmful

**nocivité** *nf* noxiousness

**noctambule** *n* night-bird, one with nocturnal habits; *obs* sleepwalker; *adj* noctambulist

**nocturne** *nm mus* nocturne; *eccles* nocturn; *adj* nocturnal

**nodosité** *nf* nodosity, knottiness; nodule

**nodulaire** *adj geol* nodular

**Noé** *nm bibl* Noah; **l'arche de ~** Noah's Ark

**Noël** *nm* Christmas; Noel

**noël** *nm* Christmas carol

**nœud** *nm* knot; bow, favour; *fig* crux; bond; nautical mile; *math + phys* node; **~s** coils (serpent); **~ coulant** slipknot; **~ ferroviaire** railway junction; **~ papillon** bow-tie

**noir -e** *n* black man (woman); *nm* black (colour); darkness; *sp* bull's eye; **broyer du ~** be depressed, be in the dumps; **prendre le ~** go into mourning; **tourner au ~** turn dark; **voir tout en ~** look on the black side of things; *adj* black; dark; gloomy; base, foul, dirty; *sl* drunk, plastered; *cul* **au beurre ~** with browned butter sauce; **bête ~e** pet aversion; **faire ~** be dark; *theat* **four ~** dismal flop; **humour ~** macabre humour; **idées ~es** depressing thoughts, *coll* blues; **misère ~e** extreme poverty; *med* **peste ~e** bubonic plague; **travail ~** work on the side

**noirâtre** *adj* blackish

**noiraud -e** *n* dark-skinned person; *adj* swarthy, dark-skinned

**noirceur** *nf* blackness; base action; *obs* melancholy

**noircir** *vt* blacken, darken; slander; *coll* **~ du papier** write; *vi* grow dark, turn black; **se ~** grow black, grow dark; *sl* get drunk

**noircissement** *nm* blackening, darkening

**noire** *nf* black (roulette); *mus* crotchet

**noise** *nf ar* quarrel; **chercher ~ à qn** pick a quarrel with s/o

**noisetier** *nm bot* hazel-tree

**noisette** *nf bot* hazel-nut; *adj invar* nut-brown, hazel

**noix** *nm* walnut; nut; **~ de coco** coconut; **~ de terre** peanut; *sl* **à la ~** useless, lousy

**nom** *nm* name; fame, reputation; *gramm* noun, substantive; **~ de baptême** Christian name; **~ de Dieu!** for God's sake!; **~ de famille** surname; **~ de guerre** pseudonym, assumed name; **~ de jeune fille** maiden name; *comm* **~ déposé** registered trade name; **~ et prénoms** full name; **appeler les choses par leur ~** call a spade a spade; **ça n'a pas de ~!** it's unspeakable; **petit ~** Christian name; **se faire un ~** achieve fame, make a name for oneself

**nomade** *n* nomad; **~s** nomadic tribes; *adj* nomadic, wandering, migratory

**nombre** *nm* number; numbers; total; *pros* harmony; **~ de** a good many; *leg* **~ requis** quorum; **en grand ~** in large numbers; **être au ~ de** be one of, be among; **sans ~** innumerable; **tout fait ~** every little helps

**nombreux -euse** *adj* numerous, many;

large; *pros* harmonious; **peu** ~ few in number, infrequent

**nombril** *nm* navel; eye (fruit)

**nomenclature** *nf* nomenclature; nominal rate; list of words

**nominal** *adj* nominal; **appel** ~ roll-call; *comm* **valeur** ~ **e** face-value

**nominatif** *nm gramm* nominative; *adj* (*f* -**ive**) nominal; *gramm* nominative; **état** ~ nominal roll; **titres** ~**s** registered securities

**nomination** *nf* nomination, appointment; (honourable) mention; **recevoir sa** ~ be appointed

**nominativement** *adv* by name

**nommé** -**e** *n leg* person named; *adj* named; appointed; **à point** ~ in the nick of time, at the right moment

**nommément** *adv* by name

**nommer** *vt* name, mention by name, call; appoint, promote; **se** ~ be called, be named; state one's name

**non** *nm invar* no; **les** ~ **l'emportent** the noes have it; *adv* no; not; (in compound words) non-, un-; **mais** ~ **!** oh no!; ~ **pas!** not at all!, not a bit of it!; **que** ~ **!** certainly not!

**nonagénaire** *n* + *adj* nonagenarian

**non-alcoolisé** *adj* non-alcoholic

**non-aligné** *adj* non-aligned

**nonante** *adj dial* ninety

**nonce** *nm eccles* nuncio

**nonchalance** *nf* nonchalance; languidness, languor

**nonchalant** *adj* nonchalant; languid

**nonchaloir** *nm lit* nonchalance; listlessness

**non-combattant** -**e** *n* + *adj* non-combatant

**non-conducteur** *nm phys* non-conductor; *adj* (*f* -**trice**) *phys* non-conducting

**non-conformisme** *nm eccles* nonconformity

**non-conformiste** *n* + *adj eccles* nonconformist

**non-disponibilité** *nf* unavailability

**non-disponible** *adj* unavailable

**non-ingérence** *nf* non-intervention

**non-lieu** *nm leg* no true bill, no case to be answered; **ordonnance de** ~ dismissal of case

**nonne** *nf* nun

**nonobstant** *adv* nevertheless; *prep* notwithstanding, despite; ~ **que** although

**nonpareil** -**eille** *adj* nonpareil, matchless, peerless

**non-pesanteur** *nf* weightlessness

**non-recevoir** *nm* **fin de** ~ objection

**non-sens** *nm* meaningless sentence;

absurdity in translation; ludicrous notion

**non-valeur** *nf* useless object, useless person; bad debt; non-productive land

**nord** *nm* north; **au** ~ in the north; **en plein** ~ due north; **étoile du** ~ Pole star; *coll* **perdre le** ~ lose one's bearings, be all at sea; *adj invar* north, northern

**Nord-Africain** -**e** *n* North African

**nord-africain** *adj* North African

**nord-est** *nm* + *adj invar* north-east

**nordique** *adj* nordic

**nord-ouest** *nm* + *adj invar* north-west

**noria** *nf eng* chain-pump; bucket conveyor

**normal** *adj* normal, ordinary, habitual, standard; **école** ~ **e** teachers' training college

**normalien** *nm usu* (male) student (or ex-student) of the École Normale Supérieure in Paris; (male) student at teachers' training college

**normalienne** *nf usu* (female) student (or ex-student) of the École Normale Supérieure at Sèvres; (female) student at teachers' training college

**normalisation** *nf* normalization, standardization

**normaliser** *vt* normalize, standardize

**normalité** *nf* normality

**Normand** -**e** *n* Norman; **réponse de** ~ ambiguous answer

**normand** *adj* Norman; **trou** ~ glass of spirits taken in the middle of a meal

**Normandie** *nf* Normandy

**normatif** -**ive** *adj* normative

**norme** *nf* norm, standard; **hors de la** ~ abnormal

¹**norois, noroît** *nm naut* north-west wind

²**norois, norrois** *adj* Norse

**Norvège** *nf* Norway

**Norvégien** -**ienne** *n* Norwegian

**norvégien** *nm* Norwegian (language); *adj* (*f* -**ienne**) Norwegian

**nos** *poss adj pl see* **notre**

**nostalgie** *nf* homesickness; nostalgia

**nostalgique** *adj* nostalgic, yearning; homesick

**nota (nota bene)** *nm* N.B.

**notabilité** *nf* notability; important person, V.I.P.

**notable** *nm* person of note; *coll* local bigwig; *adj* notable, signal; eminent, prominent

**notaire** *nm* solicitor, notary

**notamment** *adv* notably, especially

**notarié** *adj* drawn up by a notary

**note** *nf* note, memorandum; notice, annotation; mark; tone; *comm* bill, invoice; *mus* note; *coll* **changer de ~** change one's tune; **donner la ~** set the tone; *mus* give the key; give the lead; **forcer la ~** exaggerate; **prendre bonne ~** take due note

**noter** *vt* note, take notice of; take a note of, jot down, record; **~ qn d'infamie** brand s/o with infamy; *mus* **~ un air** write down a tune; **notez bien!** mind you!; **bien (mal) noté** of good (bad) repute

**notifier** *vt* notify, intimate

**notion** *nf* notion, idea; smattering; **premières ~s** rudiments

**notoire** *adj* notorious, acknowledged; manifest

**notoriété** *nf* notoriety, notoriousness; repute, reputation; *leg* **acte de ~** certificate of identity; **de ~ publique** of common knowledge

**notre** *poss adj* (*pl* **nos**) our

**nôtre** *nm* **le ~** our own; **les ~s** our friends, our people; **mettons-y du ~** let's help; **est-il des ~s?** is he one of us?; *poss pron* ours

**noué** *adj* knotted; stunted (mind)

**nouer** *vt* tie, knot, fasten; stiffen (joints); strike up (friendship); enter into (conversation); weave (plot of story, play); *vi bot* set (fruit); **se ~** become knotted; become stiffened (joints); *bot* set (fruit)

**noueux -euse** *adj* knotty, gnarled; arthritic

**nouille** *nf cul* noodle; *coll* idiot, ass

**nounou** *nf coll* nanny, nurse

**nourri** *adj* fed, nourished, nurtured; rich, copious, sustained; *coll* meaty; **être logé et ~** have board and lodging

**nourrice** *nf* nurse, wet-nurse; *eng + mot* auxiliary tank; **mettre un enfant en ~** put a child out to nurse

**nourricier -ière** *adj* nutritious, nourishing; foster; **mère nourricière** foster-mother; **père ~** foster-father

**nourrir** *vt* feed, nourish, suckle, nurse; nurture, bring up; foster, cherish; harbour, entertain (thoughts); strengthen, enrich; *arts* deepen (colour, tone); *vi* be nourishing; **se ~** feed, subsist; keep oneself

**nourrissant** *adj* nourishing

**nourrisson** *nm* infant, babe in arms

**nourriture** *nf* nourishment, feeding; suckling, nurture; food, sustenance; keep; *fig* (intellectual) nourishment

**nous** *pers pron* we; us; ourselves

**nouveau** *nm* news, something new; new boy (school); **y a-t-il du ~ ?** is there any news?; *adj* (*f* **-elle**) new, recent, newly; fresh, renewed; another; **à ~** again,

afresh; **de ~** again, once more; *comm* **solde à ~** balance carried forward

**nouveau-né -e** *n* new-born child; *adj* new-born

**nouveauté** *nf* novelty, newness; change, new invention; new publication; **~s** *comm* fancy goods, linen drapery; **magasin de ~s** draper's shop

**nouvel** *adj m* form of **nouveau** before vowel or mute h

**nouvelle** *nf* news, piece of news; short novel, short story; **~s** news, tidings; **aller prendre des ~s** go and inquire about; **envoyez-moi de vos ~s** let me hear from you, do write and tell me how you are; *coll* **vous aurez de mes ~s** you've not heard the last of this!; *coll* **vous m'en direz des ~s** you'll be delighted with it

**Nouvelle-Orléans** *nf* New Orleans

**Nouvelle-Zélande** *nf* New Zealand

**nouvelliste** *n* short-story writer

**novateur -trice** *n* innovator; *adj* innovating

**novembre** *nm* November

**novice** *n eccles* novice; beginner, apprentice; *adj* inexperienced, raw

**noviciat** *nm eccles* noviciate; apprenticeship

**noyade** *nf* drowning

**noyau** *nm* stone (fruit), kernel; *fig* nucleus, core, small group; *archi* newel; *metal* core; **~ communiste** communist cell

**noyautage** *nm fig* infiltration, creation of a nucleus; *metal* coring

**noyauter** *vt fig* infiltrate, create a nucleus

**noyé -e** *n* drowned person

¹**noyer** *nm* walnut (wood); walnut-tree

²**noyer** *vt* (7) drown; *fig* drown, submerge; dilute (wine); *mot* flood; *eng* countersink (screw); **se ~** drown, be drowned; *coll* flounder, become confused

**nu** *nm arts* nude; *adj* naked, nude, bare; plain, unvarnished; *mot* stripped; **~-tête, tête ~e** bare-headed; **~ comme un ver** stark naked; **~ comme la main** bare as the back of your hand; **~ intégral** full frontal nudity; **mettre qch à ~** strip sth bare

**nuage** *nm* cloud; **~ de lait** drop of milk (in tea, etc); **sans ~s** cloudless; unclouded, unalloyed

**nuageux -euse** *adj* cloudy, overcast; hazy, dim, nebulous

**nuance** *nf* nuance, shade of meaning; shade of colour; *mus* slight change of tone; tinge, touch

**nuancement** *nm* blending, shading

**nuancer** *vt* (4) blend, shade; vary, make

fine differentiation in
**nubile** *adj* nubile, marriageable
**nubilité** *nf* nubility
**nucléaire** *adj* nuclear
**nudisme** *nm* nudism
**nudiste** *n + adj* nudist
**nudité** *nf* nudity, nakedness; bareness
**nue** *nf lit* cloud; ~ s sky, heavens; **porter aux** ~ s praise to the skies; **tomber des** ~ s be taken aback, be thunderstruck
**nuée** *nf lit* thick cloud, storm cloud; mass, multitude
**nue-propriété** *nf leg* reversion
**nuire** *vi* (65) be hurtful, be harmful, be injurious; ~ **à qn** harm s/o; ~ **aux intérêts de qn** damage s/o's interests
**nuisance** *nf* harmful environmental factor
**nuisibilité** *nf* harmfulness
**nuisible** *adj* hurtful, harmful, injurious; **bêtes** ~ s vermin
**nuit** *nf* night; night-time; darkness; **boîte de** ~ night-club; **cette** ~ last night; tonight; **de** ~ by night; **il ne passera pas la** ~ he will not live till morning; **il se fait** ~ it is getting dark; **je n'ai pas dormi de la** ~ I didn't sleep a wink all night
**nuitamment** *adv* by night; nightly
**nuitée** *nf* night's stay (at hotel)
**nul** (*f* **nulle**) *adj* no; ~ **homme ne le sait** no man knows it; *adj* useless, worthless; of no account, non-existent; *leg* invalid, worthless; *leg* ~ **et de** ~ **effet,** ~ **et non avenu** null and void; *sp* **match** ~ drawn game; *pron* no one, nobody; ~ **ne le sait** nobody knows
**nullement** *adv* not at all, in no way
**nullifier** *vt* nullify
**nullité** *nf* nullity, incapacity; incompetent person, nonentity; *leg* nullity, invalidity
**numéraire** *nm* specie; **en** ~ in cash
**numérateur** *nm math* numerator
**numérique** *adj* numerical
**numéro** *nm* number; copy, number (magazine); *theat* turn, item; *coll* odd person
**numérotage** *nm* numbering (tickets, etc); pagination
**numéroter** *vt* number (tickets, etc); paginate
**numismate** *n* numismatist
**numismatique** *nf* numismatics; *adj* numismatic
**nuptial** *adj* wedding, nuptial, bridal
**nuque** *nf* nape of the neck
**nurse** *nf* children's nurse, nanny
**nutritif -ive** *adj* nutritious, nourishing; **valeur nutritive** food value
**nymphe** *nf* nymph
**nymphéa** *nm bot* water-lily
**nymphomane** *nf + adj* nymphomaniac

# O

**ô** *interj* O!, oh!
**obédience** *nf eccles* obedience; *coll* submission
**obéir** *vi* obey; yield, submit; **se faire** ~ enforce obedience
**obéissance** *nf* obedience, submission
**obéissant** *adj* obedient, submissive
**obélisque** *nm* obelisk
**obérer** *vt* (6) burden (s/o) with debt; encumber (sth) with debt
**obèse** *adj* obese, stout, corpulent
**obésité** *nf* obesity, stoutness, corpulence
**obituaire** *nm eccles* obituary, register of deaths; *adj m* obituary
**objecter** *vt* object; hold against; give as a pretext
**objectif** *nm* aim, objective, target; lens, object-glass; *adj* (*f* **-ive**) objective, unbiased
**objection** *nf* objection; **faire des** ~ s argue
**objectiver** *vt* objectivize, make objective, exteriorize
**objet** *nm* object, thing; objective, purpose; *gramm* object, complement; *leg* ~ s **immobiliers** real property; ~ s **trouvés** lost property
**obligataire** *n comm* bondholder, debenture-holder
**obligation** *nf* obligation, duty; favour,

gratefulness; *leg* recognizance; *comm* bond, debenture; *comm* ~ **au porteur** bearer-bond; **avoir des ~ s envers qn** be under obligation to s/o; **être dans l' ~ de** be bound to; **être d' ~** be obligatory; **se trouver dans l' ~ de** feel compelled to

**obligatoire** *adj* compulsory, obligatory, binding

**obligé -e** *n* person under obligation; *leg* obligee; *adj* obliged, bound; obligatory; grateful; inevitable

**obligeance** *nf* obligingness; **veuillez avoir l' ~ de** please be so kind as to

**obligeant** *adj* obliging, kind

**obliger** *vt* (3) oblige, constrain, compel; do a favour to; **s' ~** bind oneself, undertake

**oblique** *adj* oblique, slanting, sidelong; crooked, underhand

**obliquer** *vi* move obliquely, edge; slant

**obliquité** *nf* obliquity; crookedness

**oblitérateur** *nm* cancel (stamps, etc); *adj* (*f* -**trice**) obliterating

**oblitération** *nf* obliteration; cancelling (stamp)

**oblitérer** *vt* (6) obliterate; cancel (stamp)

**obnubiler** *vt* dim, obscure

**obole** *nf* obol; mite

**obscène** *adj* obscene, lewd, filthy

**obscénité** *nf* obscenity, lewdness; filth; ~ s filthy words, filthy expressions

**obscur** *adj* dark, gloomy, overcast; obscure, abstruse; little known, unassuming

**obscurantisme** *nm* obscurantism

**obscurcir** *vt* obscure, darken, dim; *fig* obscure, cloud, dim; **s' ~** grow dark; *fig* grow dim, wane, become obscure

**obscurcissement** *nm* darkening, dimming; black-out; *fig* obfuscation, bewildering

**obscurité** *nf* obscurity; darkness; humble situation; confusion, abstruseness

**obsédant** *adj* obsessing, haunting; pressing, urgent

**obséder** *vt* (6) obsess; worry, beset

**obsèques** *nfpl* funeral, obsequies

**obséquieux -ieuse** *adj* obsequious

**obséquiosité** *nf* obsequiousness

**observateur -trice** *n* observer, onlooker, spectator; keeper (rules); *adj* observant, observing

**observation** *nf* observation, remark; observance, fulfilment; reproof; **faire des ~ s à** reproach, find fault with

**observatoire** *nm* observatory; *mil* observation post

**observer** *vt* observe, point out, remark; watch, note; fulfil, keep; **faire ~** enforce (law); point out; **s' ~** be

circumspect; observe one another

**obsessif -ive** *adj* obsessive

**obstétrique** *nf med* obstetrics; *adj* obstetrical

**obstination** *nf* obstinacy, stubbornness

**obstiné** *adj* obstinate, stubborn; persistent, persevering

**obstiner (s')** *v refl* show obstinacy, become obstinate; **s' ~ à** persist in

**obstructif -ive** *adj* obstructive

**obstruction** *nf* obstruction, blocking, stopping up; *med* obstruction, stoppage

**obstruer** *vt* obstruct, block, choke; **s' ~** become blocked, choked up

**obtempérer** *vi* (6) comply, accede, obey

**obtenir** *vt* (96) obtain, get, procure; gain, achieve; ~ **de faire qch** get authorization to do sth; **s' ~** be obtained, be procurable

**obtention** *nf* obtainment, obtaining

**obturateur** *nm* closing device, stopper; *eng* stop-valve; *adj* (*f* -**trice**) obturating, closing

**obturation** *nf* obturation; filling (tooth)

**obturer** *vt* obturate, block up; fill (tooth)

**obtus** *adj* obtuse, dull; *math* obtuse

**obus** *nm mil* shell; ~ **à balles** shrapnel shell

**obusier** *nm mil* howitzer

**obvier** *vi* ~ **à** obviate

**occasion** *nf* occasion, opportunity; chance; circumstance, juncture; reason, motive, cause; bargain; **à l' ~** if the opportunity arises; at times; **avoir l' ~ de** happen to, have occasion to; **d' ~** second-hand; **en cette ~** at this juncture, in this instance; **en pareille ~** in similar circumstances; **par ~** now and again; by chance; **suivant l' ~** as occasion arises

**occasionnel -elle** *adj* fortuitous; casual

**occasionner** *vt* occasion, cause

**Occidental -e** *n* Westerner, Occidental

**occidental** *adj* western

**occire** *vt obs* (irregular and very rare) slay, kill

**occis** *obs p part* **occire** killed, slain

**occitan** *adj* of Languedoc

**occlusion** *nf med* obstruction; closure; *eng* cut off

**occulte** *adj* occult

**occulter** *vt astron* occult, eclipse

**occultisme** *nm* occultism

**occupant -e** *n* occupier, occupant

**occupation** *nf* occupation, tenure; business, job

**occuper** *vt* occupy, inhabit; fill, take up; employ; **occupé** engaged (lavatory, telephone number); ~ **qn** keep s/o busy; **être occupé à faire qch** be busy doing sth; **s' ~** keep oneself busy, employ oneself; **s'** ~ **à** be busy with; **s'** ~ **de** attend to, look after; **occupez-vous de vos affaires!** mind your own business!

**occurrence** *nf* occurrence, emergency; **en l'** ~ under the circumstances

**Océanie** *nf* Oceania, the South Sea Islands

**océanique** *adj* oceanic

**océanographe** *n* oceanographer

**océanographie** *nf* oceanography

**ocre** *nf* ochre

**octaèdre** *nm math* octahedron; *adj math* octahedral

**octante** *adj dial* eighty

**octobre** *nm* October

**octogénaire** *n + adj* octogenarian

**octogone** *nm* octagon

**octosyllabe** *nm* octosyllable; *adj* octosyllabic

**octroi** *nm* granting, concession; toll-office; local city toll, town dues

**octroyer** *vt* (7) grant, concede; **s'** ~ indulge in, grant oneself

**oculaire** *nm* eye-piece, ocular; *adj* ocular; **témoin** ~ eye-witness

**oculiste** *n* oculist

**odeur** *nf* smell, odour; scent, perfume

**odieux -ieuse** *adj* odious, hateful; shocking, heinous

**odorant** *adj* odorous, sweet-smelling, smelly

**odorat** *nm* sense of smell

**odoriférant** *adj* fragrant, sweet-smelling, odiferous

**odyssée** *nf* odyssey

**œcuménique** *adj* ecumenical

**œdème** *nm med* oedema

**œil** *nm* (*pl* **yeux**) eye; sight, look; view, opinion, observation; hole; speck of fat (on soup); *typ* face; ~ **au beurre noir** black eye; **à l'** ~ by eye; *sl* free, buckshee; **à mes yeux** in my view; **avoir du travail par-dessus les yeux** be up to one's eyes in work; **avoir les yeux hors de la tête** have one's eyes starting from one's head; *coll* **avoir les yeux plus gros que le ventre** bite off more than one can chew; **avoir l'** ~ **à tout** keep an eye on everything; **avoir l'** ~ **sur** have an eye on, keep tabs on; **à vue d'** ~ visibly; *coll* **ça crève les yeux** it's obvious; **chercher qn des yeux** look for s/o; **coup d'** ~ glance; view; *coll* **coûter les yeux de la tête** cost the earth; *comm* **donner de l'** ~ **à** give a bit of style to; **d'un bon (mauvais)** ~ with a favourable (unfavourable) eye; *coll* **entre quatre(-z-) yeux** between you and me; **faire de l'** ~ **à qn** make eyes at s/o; **faire les gros yeux** look sternly; **faire les yeux doux à** look lovingly at; *coll* **faire qch pour les**

**beaux yeux de qn** do sth for love of s/o; **fermer les yeux sur qch** wink at sth, connive at sth; *naut* **l'** ~ **du vent** the wind eye; *sl* **mon** ~! my foot!; **n'avoir pas froid aux yeux** be brave; *coll* **ne pas avoir les yeux dans sa poche** be all there, keep one's eyes skinned; **ne pas fermer l'** ~ **de la nuit** not sleep a wink at night; **sauter aux yeux** be obvious, be clear as daylight; *sl* **s'en battre l'** ~ not give a damn; **se rincer l'** ~ get an eyeful; **signer les yeux fermés** sign without question; *coll* **taper dans l'** ~ impress; **tourner de l'** ~ faint

**œil-de-bœuf** *nm* (*pl* **œils-de-bœuf**) bull's eye window

**œil-de-perdrix** *nm* (*pl* **œils-de-perdrix**) *med* soft corn

**œillade** *nf* glance; **lancer des** ~**s à** ogle

**œillère** *nf* blinker (horse); *med* eye-bath; *coll* **avoir des** ~**s** be blinkered, be narrow-minded

**œillet** *nm bot* carnation, pink; eyelet, eye-hole

**œsophage** *nm anat* oesophagus

**œstrogène** *nm* oestrogen

**œuf** *nm* egg; ovum; spawn, hard roe; ~ **à la coque** boiled egg; ~ **(à repriser)** darning egg; ~ **à thé** tea-infuser; ~ **s au lait** custard; ~ **au plat** fried egg; ~ **mollet** soft-boiled egg; **dans l'** ~ in the bud; *coll* **marcher sur des** ~**s** be on very thin ice; **plein comme un** ~ chock-full; **tondre un** ~ be very miserly

**œuvre** *nm sing* complete works (of artist); *mus* opus; *archi* main work; **gros** ~ main walls and foundations; **le grand** ~ the philosopher's stone; *nf* work, production, finished work; action, activity, occupation; works; charitable society; ~ **de chair** sexual congress; ~ **maîtresse** masterpiece, magnum opus; *naut* ~**s mortes** topsides; *naut* ~**s vives** vitals; **exécuteur des hautes** ~**s** executioner; **faire** ~ perform an action; **mettre à l'** ~ set to work; **mettre en** ~ bring into play; **mise en** ~ carrying out, implementation; **se mettre à l'** ~ set to work

**œuvrer** *vi* work

**offensant** *adj* offensive, insulting

**offense** *nf* offence, insult; sin, transgression; *leg* contempt

**offensé -e** *n* injured party

**offenser** *vt* offend, be offensive to, offend against; shock; **s'** ~ take offence

**offenseur** *nm* offender

**offensif -ive** *adj* offensive

**offertoire** *nm eccles* offertory

**office** *nm* office, duty, function; service; bureau, centre office; *eccles* service; ~ **des morts** burial service; ~ **de tourisme**

Tourist Information Bureau; **d' ~** automatically, as a matter of course; according to regulations; **faire ~ de** act as; **rendre des bons ~ s à** be helpful to; *nf* servants' hall, butler's pantry

**officiant** *nm eccles* celebrant; *adj* celebrating

**officiel** *nm* official personality, authority; *adj (f* **-ielle)** official; **rendre ~** make publicly known; **à titre ~** officially

**Officiel (l')** *nm* (official) gazette; **être à l' ~** be gazetted

¹**officier** *nm* officer; *leg* **~ de l'état civil** municipal magistrate, registrar; **~ de la paix** police officer; **~ de santé** health officer; *ar* one authorized to practise medicine without a degree; *leg* **~ du ministère public** public prosecutor; *naut* **~ marinier** petty-officer; *leg* **~ ministériel** member of the legal profession

²**officier** *vi* officiate

**officieux -ieuse** *adj* semi-official, informal; officious

**officinal** *adj* medicinal

**officine** *nf* chemist's dispensary; *coll* den (thieves)

**offrande** *nf* offering, gift; *eccles* offertory

**offrant** *nm* **le plus ~** the highest bidder

**offre** *nf* offer, proposal; *comm* tender; **~ publique d'achat (OPA)** take-over bid; **l' ~ et la demande** supply and demand

**offrir** *vt* (30) offer, give, present; furnish; offer up; bid; **~ la main à qn** hold out one's hand to s/o; **~ un verre à qn** stand s/o a drink; **s' ~** offer oneself, volunteer; offer itself, present itself

**offusquer** *vt* offend, shock; **s' ~** take offence, be touchy

**ogive** *nf archi* ogive, gothic arch, pointed arch; **~ nucléaire** nuclear warhead

**ogresse** *nf* ogress

**ohé** *interj* hi!, hullo!

**oie** *nf* goose; **jeu de l' ~** = game like snakes and ladders

**oignon** *nm* onion; *hort* bulb; bunion; *coll* **ce n'est pas mes ~ s** its nothing to do with me, it's not my cup of tea; **en rang d' ~ s** in a straight line; *coll* **occupez-vous de vos ~ s** mind your own business

**oindre** *vt* (55) anoint

**oint** *adj* anointed

¹**oiseau** *nm* bird; **~ de basse-cour** poultry; **à vol d' ~** as the crow flies; *coll* **drôle d' ~** queer fish; **être comme l' ~ sur la branche** be in an uncertain situation

²**oiseau** *nm* (bricklayer's) hod

**oiseau-mouche** *nm* (*pl* **oiseaux-mouches**) humming-bird

**oiseleur** *nm* fowler, bird-catcher

**oiselier** *nm* bird-seller, bird-fancier

**oisellerie** *nf* bird-catching; bird-fancier's shop; breeding of birds

**oiseux -euse** *adj* idle, useless, lazy, otiose; trivial, irrelevant

**oisif -ive** *n* idler, unemployed person; *adj* idle, lazy, unoccupied

**oisillon** *nm* fledgling

**oisiveté** *nf* idleness, laziness

**oison** *nm* gosling

**oléagineux -euse** *adj* oleaginous, oil-yielding

**oléoduc** *nm* oil pipeline

**olfactif -ive** *adj* olfactory

**olibrius** *nm coll* braggart

**oligarchie** *nf* oligarchy

**oligarchique** *adj* oligarchical

**olivaie** *nf see* **oliveraie**

**olivâtre** *adj* olive-coloured; sallow

**olive** *nf* olive; *archi* olive moulding; *adj invar* olive-coloured

**oliveraie, olivaie** *nf* olive-grove

**olivier** *nm* olive-tree

**olympiade** *nf* Olympiad, Olympic games

**olympien -ienne** *adj* Olympian

**olympique** *adj* Olympic

**ombilic** *nm* umbilicus, navel

**ombilical** *adj* umbilical

**omble** *nm zool* char

**ombrage** *nm* shade; *fig* umbrage; **prendre ~** shy (horses); *fig* take umbrage

**ombrager** *vt* give shade to, shade

**ombrageux -euse** *adj* touchy, quick to take offence; skittish (horse)

¹**ombre** *nf* shade, shadow; darkness; trace, bit; illusion, ghost; **~ d'espoir** ray of hope; *sl* **à l' ~** in jug, in prison; **à l' ~ de** in the shade of; protected by; **jeter une ~ sur** cast gloom over; **rester dans l' ~** stay in the background; *ar* **sous l' ~ de** under pretext of

²**ombre** *nm zool* grayling

**ombrelle** *nf* sunshade; *aer* umbrella, air-cover

**ombrer** *vt arts* shade, hatch; darken (eyelids)

**ombreux -euse** *adj* shady

**omelette** *nf* omelette; **faire une ~ sans œufs** make bricks without straw

**omettre** *vt* (60) omit, leave out; fail, neglect

**omnibus** *nm* omnibus; **(train) ~** stopping train

**omnium** *nm comm* general trading company; *sp* open race

**omnivore** *adj* omnivorous

**omoplate** *nf* shoulder-blade

**on** *indef pron* one, somebody, people;

I; you; he; she; we; they; ~ **demande une bonne dactylo** wanted, good typist; ~ **dit que** they say, it is alleged that; ~ **parle anglais** English spoken

**onanisme** *nm* onanism

¹**once** *nf* ounce; bit, scrap

²**once** *nf zool* snow-leopard, ounce

**oncial** *adj* uncial

**oncle** *nm* uncle

**oncques** *adv obs* never, ever

**onction** *nf* unction, anointing; unction, unctuousness

**onctueux -ueuse** *adj* greasy, oily; unctuous

**onctuosité** *nf* greasiness, oiliness; unctuousness, oiliness; watering (silk)

**onde** *nf lit* wave, billow; wavy line, corrugation; watering (silk); *rad* wave; ~ **de choc** sonic boom; **en** ~ wavy; *rad* **metteur en** ~**s** radio producer

**ondé** *adj* waved, wavy, undulating; watered (silk)

**ondée** *nf* heavy shower

**ondin -e** *n* water-spirit

**on-dit** *nm invar* hearsay, rumour

**ondoiement** *nm* undulation, wavy motion

**ondoyant** *adj* undulating, waving, flowing; changing, changeable

**ondoyer** *vi* (7) undulate, wave

**ondulant** *adj* undulating, waving, wavy

**ondulation** *nf* undulation, waving, flowing; wave (hair); **se faire faire une** ~ have one's hair waved

**ondulatoire** *adj* undulatory

**ondulé** *adj* undulating, wavy, corrugated

**onduler** *vt* wave (hair); **se faire** ~ have one's hair waved; *vi* undulate, wave, ripple

**onduleux -euse** *adj* wavy, sinuous

**onéreux -euse** *adj* onerous, costly; **à titre** ~ subject to payment

**ongle** *nm* nail; claw; talon; **coup d'** ~ scratch; **jusqu'au bout des** ~**s** to the fingertips; **se ronger les** ~**s** bite one's nails; *coll* be impatient

**onglée** *nf med* numbness, tingling of finger-tip

**onglet** *nm* nail hole on penknife; tab, thumb index (book); *carp* mitre

**onglier** *nm* manicure set

**onguent** *nm* ointment, unguent

**onomastique** *adj* onomastic

**onomatopée** *nf* onomatopoeia

**ontologique** *adj* ontological

**onze** *nm sp* eleven, team; *adj invar* eleven; eleventh

**onzième** *nm* eleventh part; *adj* eleventh

**opacité** *nf* opacity, denseness

**opale** *nf* opal

**opalin** *adj* opaline

**opéra** *nm* opera; ~ **bouffe** comic opera; ~ **comique** light opera

**opérable** *adj* operable

**opérateur -trice** *n* operator, technician; cameraman; *cin* + *rad* ~ **du son** sound engineer

**opératif -ive** *adj* operative

**opération** *nf* operation, process, working; transaction; surgical operation; **salle d'** ~ operating theatre

**opérationnel -elle** *adj* operational

**opéré -e** *n* patient operated on; *nm comm* deal

**opérer** *vt* (6) effect, bring out, achieve, carry out; *surg* operate on; ~ **à chaud** perform an emergency operation on; **se faire** ~ have an operation; *vi* operate, work; *surg* perform an operation; **s'** ~ take place, come about

**opérette** *nf* operetta, musical comedy

**ophtalmie** *nf* ophthalmia

**ophtalmique** *adj* ophthalmic

**ophtalmologie** *nf* ophthalmology

**ophtalmologue** *n* ophthalmologist

**opiacé** *adj* opiated

**opiner** *vi* opine, be of the opinion that; incline to the view that; ~ **de la tête** nod agreement

**opiniâtre** *adj* opinionated, stubborn, obstinate; persistent, unflagging, tenacious

**opiniâtreté** *nf* stubbornness, obstinacy; tenacity

**opinion** *nf* opinion, point of view; judgement, notion; opinion, esteem

**opiomane** *n* opium-eater, opium-addict; *adj* addicted to opium

**opportun** *adj* opportune, seasonable, timely; expedient; **en temps** ~ at the appropriate time

**opportunisme** *nm* opportunism, time-serving

**opportuniste** *n* opportunist, time-server; *adj* opportunist, time-serving

**opportunité** *nf* opportuneness, expediency, timeliness

**opposant -e** *n* opponent, antagonist; *adj* opposing

**opposé** *nm* opposite, reverse, contrary; **à l'** ~ **de** contrary to; *adj* opposite; opposed to, contrary, hostile

**opposer** *vt* oppose; set opposite to, contrast with; set against; ~ **une défense à** set up a defence against; ~ **une résistance à** put up a fight against; ~ **un véto** veto; **s'** ~ oppose, be opposed; be in conflict, be against

**opposite** *nm* **à l'** ~ **de** contrary to; opposite, facing

**opposition** *nf* opposition, resistance; contrast, clash; *leg* **faire ~ à** appeal against; *comm* **frapper d'~** stop payment; *leg* **mettre à ~** seek an injunction against; **par ~ à** in contrast with

**oppressé** *adj* breathless, having difficulty in breathing

**oppresser** *vt* impede (breathing); be heavy on; *fig* weigh down

**oppresseur** *nm* oppressor

**oppressif -ive** *adj* oppressive

**oppression** *nf* difficulty in breathing, sense of suffocation; oppression, tyranny

**opprimé -e** *n* oppressed person, victim; *adj* oppressed, down-trodden

**opprimer** *vt* oppress, crush, trample upon

**opprobre** *nm* opprobrium, disgrace, shame, infamy

**opter** *vi* choose, decide, opt

**opticien -ienne** *n* optician

**optimal** *adj* optimum

**optimisme** *nm* optimism

**optimiste** *n* optimist; *adj* optimistic, sanguine

**option** *nf* option, choice; *comm* option

**optionnel -elle** *adj* optional

**optique** *nf* optics; *fig* perspective; *adj* optical

**opulence** *nf* opulence, wealth; *fig* richness

**opulent** *adj* opulent, wealthy; *fig* buxom

**opuscule** *nm* opuscule, monograph, pamphlet

¹**or** *nm* gold; **her** or; **~ en barre** gold ingots, bullion; *comm* **affaire en ~** excellent bargain; **à prix d'~** extremely expensive, at a very high price; *coll* **c'est de l'~ en barre** it's dead safe, it's as good as cash; **d'~** golden; **livre d'~** V.I.P. visitors' book; **rouler sur l'~** be rolling in money; **vaisselle en ~** gold plate; *adj invar* gold (colour)

²**or** *conj* now, well, well now

**orage** *nm* thunderstorm, storm, tempest; *fig* disturbance, turmoil

**orageux -euse** *adj* stormy, tempestuous, thundery, sultry; *fig* stormy; violent

**oraison** *nf* prayer, orison; oration; **faire ses ~s** say one's prayers

**oral** *nm* oral examination, viva(-voce); *adj* oral

**orange** *nf* orange; *nm* orange (colour); *adj invar* orange-coloured

**orangé** *nm* orange (colour); *adj* orange-coloured

**oranger** *nm* orange-tree; **fleur d'~** orange blossom

**orangerie** *nf* orangery, orange hothouse

**orateur -trice** *n* orator, speaker; spokesman (-woman); *nm eccles* preacher

**oratoire** *nm* oratory, chapel; *adj* oratorical; **art ~** oratory, public speaking

¹**orbe** *nm* orb, globe

²**orbe** *adj* **mur ~** blind wall

**orbite** *nf* orbit; eye-socket

**orbiter** *vi* orbit

**Orcades** *nfpl* Orkneys

**orchestre** *nm mus* orchestra; (dance-) band; *theat* stalls; **chef d'~** conductor

**orchestrer** *vt mus* orchestrate, score for orchestra; *fig* harmonize; mount (campaign)

**orchidée** *nf* orchid

**ordinaire** *nm* normal practice, wont, custom; ordinary fare; normal meals; *mil* mess; *eccles* ordinary; **à l'~**, **d'~** usually; *adj* ordinary, usual, normal; common; humble; **expression ~** trite phrase

**ordinateur** *nm* computer

**ordonnance** *nf* order; ordering, management; ordinance, enactment; *leg* writ; *mil* orderly, batman; *med* prescription; **~ de police** police regulation; *mil* **officier d'~** A.D.C.; *naut* flag-lieutenant

**ordonnancement** *nm* order to pay

**ordonnateur -trice** *n* organizer, arranger; director; *comm* person authorized to make payment

**ordonnée** *nf math* ordinate

**ordonner** *vt* order, command; put in order, arrange, regulate; *med* prescribe; *eccles* ordain; *vi* dispose, arrange

**ordre** *nm* order, succession; orderliness, discipline, tidiness; command, warrant, instruction; category, class, association, sort; course; decoration; **~s** holy orders; *mil* **~ d'appel** call-up papers; **~ de chevalerie** order of knighthood; **~ du jour** agenda; *mil* orders of the day; **~ monastique** monastic order; **~ public** law and order; *comm* **billet à ~** promissory note, bill payable to order; **de l'~ de** about, of the order of; **de premier ~** first-class; *eccles* **entrer dans les ~s** take orders; **jusqu'à nouvel ~** until further notice; **l'~ des avocats** = the Bar; **mettre bon ~ à qch** see to sth; **numéro d'~** serial number; *mil* **porter à l'~ du jour** mention in despatches; **rappeler qn à l'~** call s/o to order; **rentrer dans l'~** be in order again; **rétablir l'~** restore order; **sans ~** untidy, untidily; **selon l'~ des choses** in the nature of things, in the course of events; **service d'~** police force on duty; riot-police

**ordure** *nf* excrement, dung; filth, muck, refuse, *US* trash; dirt, obscenity; **~s ménagères** refuse; *sl* **c'est une ~** he's a shit

**ordurier -ière** *adj* lewd, filthy, obscene; scurrilous, ribald

**orée** *nf* edge, border

**oreille** *nf* ear; hearing; handle, lug; **à l' ~** confidentially; *mus* **avoir de l' ~** have an ear for music; **avoir l' ~ de** have influence over, have a pull with; **avoir l' ~ fine** have good hearing; **dresser l' ~** prick up one's ears; **être dur d' ~** be hard of hearing; **faire la sourde ~** turn a deaf ear; **frotter (tirer) les ~s de qn** pull s/o up; **l' ~ basse** crest-fallen; **n'écouter que d'une ~** listen absent-mindedly; **ne pas l'entendre de cette ~** not see things in that light; **rebattre les ~s à qn de qch** drum sth into s/o; **se faire tirer l' ~** need persuading, need talking to

**oreiller** *nm* pillow

**oreillette** *nf* ear-flap; *med* auricle

**oreillons** *nmpl med* mumps

**ores** *adv obs* now; **d' ~ et déjà** here and now; from now on

**orfèvre** *nm* goldsmith

**orfèvrerie** *nf* goldsmith's trade; gold plate

**orfraie** *nf* osprey

**organe** *nm med* organ; part, component (machine); voice; agent, means, instrument; organ, mouthpiece

**organigramme** *nm* organization chart

**organique** *adj* organic

**organisateur -trice** *n* organizer; *adj* organizing

**organisation** *nf* organizing; organization, body

**organiser** *vt* organize, arrange, set up; **s' ~** become organized, get into working order, settle down

**organisme** *nm* organism; *med* physical structure, constitution; *comm* corporation

**organiste** *n* organist

**orgasme** *nm* orgasm

**orge** *nf* barley; *nm* **~ mondé** hulled barley; **~ perlé** pearl barley

**orgelet** *nm med* stye

**orgiaque** *adj* orgiastic

**orgie** *nf* orgy; profusion

**orgue** *nm mus* organ; **~ de Barbarie** barrel organ; **tenir l' ~** play the organ

**orgueil** *nm* pride, arrogance, conceit; pride, dignity; **mettre son ~ à faire qch** take a pride in doing sth

**orgueilleux -euse** *n + adj* proud, arrogant, conceited (person)

**orgues** *nfpl mus* organ; **grandes ~** church organ; *theat* **jeu d' ~** switchboard

**Orient** *nm geog* Orient, East; **Extrême- (Moyen-) ~** Far (Middle) East

**orient** *nm* orient (pearl); lodge (free-masonry)

**orientable** *adj* swivelling

**Oriental -e** *n* Oriental

**oriental** *adj* oriental, eastern

**orientalisme** *nm* orientalism

**orientaliste** *n* orientalist

**orientation** *nf* orientation; guidance, counselling; tendency, trend; *naut* trim (sails); **~ politique** political tendency; **table d' ~** panoramic landmark indicator

**orienter** *vt* orientate, orient; set, direct, guide; *naut* trim (sails); **s' ~** take one's bearings, find one's bearings; **~ vers** tend towards

**orifice** *nm* orifice, aperture, mouth; *mech* **~ d'admission** intake; **~ d'échappement** exhaust

**originaire** *adj* originating, native; innate; original, primary

**original** *nm* original, pattern, model; *n* (*f -e* ) eccentric, unconventional person; *adj* original, inventive, fresh; odd, eccentric

**originalité** *nf* originality; eccentricity

**origine** *nf* origin; beginning; source; extraction, birth; **à l' ~** originally; **bureau postal d' ~** despatching post-office; **dès l' ~** from the start; *comm* **d' ~** certified genuine; **il est d' ~ française** he is French by birth

**originel -elle** *adj* original (sin); primordial

**oripeau** *nm* foil, imitation gold foil; **~ x** tawdry finery

**orme** *nm* elm

**ornement** *nm* ornament, embellishment; *mus* grace-note

**ornemental** *adj* decorative, ornamental

**orner** *vt* decorate, embellish, adorn

**ornière** *nf* rut, groove; routine

**ornithologie** *nf* ornithology

**ornithologique** *adj* ornithological

**ornithologiste** *n* ornithologist

**orographie** *nf* orography

**oronge** *nf* agaric (fungus)

**orphelin -e** *n* orphan

**orphelinat** *nm* orphanage

**orphéon** *nm* male-voice choir; brass-band

**Orsay** *nm* **Quai d' ~** French Foreign Office

**orteil** *nm* toe

**orthodoxe** *adj* orthodox; correct, normal, conventional; **peu ~** unorthodox

**orthodoxie** *nf* orthodoxy; soundness, normality

**orthographe** *nf* orthography, spelling; **faute d' ~** spelling mistake

**orthographier** *vt* spell correctly

**orthographique** *adj* orthographic

**orthopédie** *nf med* orthopaedics

**orthopédique** *adj* orthopaedic

**ortie** *nf bot* nettle

**orvet** *nm* slow-worm

**os** *nm* bone; **en chair et en** ~ in the flesh

**oscillant** *adj* oscillating, fluctuating

**oscillateur** *nm* oscillator

**oscillation** *nf* oscillation, fluctuation; wavering

**oscillatoire** *adj* oscillatory

**osciller** *vi* oscillate, rock, sway; waver

**osé** *adj* bold, daring; broad, improper

**oseille** *nf bot* sorrel

**oser** *vt* dare, venture, dare to; *vi* dare

**osier** *nm* osier, wicker; **branche d'** ~ withy

**osmose** *nf* osmosis

**ossature** *nf* skeleton, frame; framework

**osselet** *nm* knuckle-bone

**ossements** *nmpl* bones, remains

**osseux -euse** *adj* bony

**ossifier** *vt* ossify; **s'** ~ become ossified

**ossuaire** *nm* charnel-house; heap of bones

**ostensible** *adj* conspicuous, obvious, patent

**ostensoir** *nm eccles* monstrance

**ostentation** *nf* ostentation, show, display; **faire** ~ **de parade**

**ostéologie** *nf med* osteology

**ostéologiste** *n med* osteologist

**ostéopathe** *n med* osteopath

**ostracisme** *nm* ostracism

**ostréiculture** *nf* oyster-breeding, ostreiculture

**Ostrogoth -e** *n* Ostrogoth; *coll* barbarian

**otage** *nm* hostage

**otarie** *nf zool* otary

**ôter** *vt* take away, take off, remove; *math* subtract; ~ **qch à qn** take sth away from s/o; deprive s/o of sth; **s'** ~ remove oneself, get away, get out

**otite** *nf med* otitis

**oto-rhino-laryngologiste** *n* ear, nose and throat specialist

**ottomane** *nf* ottoman, divan

**ou** *conj* or; ~ **bien** or else

**où** *adv* where; to what, what; ~ **en êtes-vous?** how far have you got?; ~ **que** wherever; ~ **voulez-vous en venir?** what are you getting at?, what do you mean?; **d'** ~ from where, whence; **d'** ~ **que** from wherever; **jusqu'** ~ how far, up to which point; **là** ~ where; **n'importe** ~ anywhere; **partout** ~ wherever; *rel pron* where; **le jour** ~ **il est venu** the day when he came; **par** ~ through which

**ouailles** *nfpl eccles* flock

**ouais** *interj obs* well!, my word!, I say!; *iron* yes

**ouate** *nf* cotton-wool; wadding, padding

**ouater** *vt* wad, pad; *fig* soften, deaden

**ouateux -euse** *adj* soft, fleecy

**oubli** *nm* oblivion, forgetting; forgetfulness, omission, oversight; **par** ~ inadvertently

**oublier** *vt* forget, omit; overlook, pardon; let pass; **s'** ~ forget oneself, lower oneself; be unmindful

**oublieux -ieuse** *adj* forgetful, unmindful

**oued** *nm geog* wadi

**ouest** *nm* west; *adj invar* west, western, westerly

**ouf** *interj* phew!, what a relief!

**oui** *adv* yes; **je crois que** ~ I think so

**ouï-dire** *nm invar* hearsay

**ouïe** *nf* hearing; ~ **s** sound holes (violin); *zool* gills

**ouïr** *vt* (66) hear

**ouistiti** *nm* marmoset

**ouragan** *nm* hurricane; **arriver comme un** ~ burst in

**Oural** *nm geog* Ural; **les monts** ~ the Ural mountains

**ourdir** *vt* warp (linen, cloth); weave, hatch (plot, etc)

**ourdou** *nm* Urdu

**ourler** *vt* hem

**ourlet** *nm* hem; edge, rim; **point d'** ~ hem stitch

**ours** *nm* bear; boor, uncouth person; ~ **en peluche** teddy-bear; ~ **mal léché** boor; **vendre la peau de l'** ~ count one's chickens before they are hatched

**ourse** *nf* she-bear; *astron* **la grande Ourse** the Great Bear, Ursa Major; *astron* **la petite Ourse** the little Bear, Ursa Minor

**oursin** *nm zool* sea-urchin

**ourson** *nm* bear-cub

**oust(e)** *interj coll* get out!; **allez** ~ ! hop it!, get out!

**outarde** *nf orni* bustard

**outil** *nm* tool, implement

**outillage** *nm* set of tools; plant, equipment; equipping, providing with tools

**outillé** *adj* provided with tools; equipped, set up

**outiller** *vt* provide with tools; equip; **s'** ~ provide oneself with tools, be equipped

**outrage** *nm* outrage, insult; offence; *leg* ~ **à la pudeur** indecent exposure; *leg* ~ **à magistrat (à la justice)** contempt of court; **faire subir un** ~ **à qn** commit an outrage against s/o

**outrageant** *adj* insulting; scurrilous

**outrager** *vt* (3) outrage, insult

**outrageux -euse** *adj* insulting; scurrilous

**outrance** *nf* excess, exaggeration; **à** ~ unremittingly, to the utmost extreme

**outrancier -ière** *adj* excessive; extreme, extremist

**¹outre** *nf* goatskin bottle

**²outre** *adv* beyond, further; **en ~** besides, moreover; **passer ~** proceed further, go on regardless, disregard; *prep* in addition to, beyond, besides; **~ mesure** inordinately; **~ que** apart from the fact that

**outrecuidance** *nf* presumption, bumptiousness; insolence

**outrecuidant** *adj* presumptuous, bumptious; insolent

**outre-Manche** *adv* on the other side of the Channel

**outremer** *nm* lapis lazuli; ultramarine; *adj* ultramarine

**outre-mer** *adv* overseas

**outrepasser** *vt* exceed, go beyond (rights, authority)

**outrer** *vt* exaggerate, carry to excess; scandalize, provoke greatly

**outre-tombe** *adv* beyond the grave; **d' ~** posthumous

**ouvert** *adj* open; frank, straightforward; **grand ~** wide open

**ouverture** *nf* opening, aperture, gap; width, span; commencement; overture, proposal; *mus* overture; **~ de la chasse** first day of the shooting season; **~ d'esprit** broadmindedness; **~ d'un testament** reading of a will; *comm* **heures d' ~** business hours

**ouvrable** *adj* **jour ~** working day

**ouvrage** *nm* work, piece of work; product, production; *eng* **~ d'art** constructional work; **gros ~s** main walls (building); **sans ~** unemployed; **se mettre à l' ~** set to work, get down to work

**ouvrager** *vt* (3) work (metal, wood, etc); adorn, embroider

**ouvré** *adj* wrought, worked

**ouvre-boîte(s)** *nm* tin-opener

**ouvre-bouteille(s)** *nm* bottle-opener

**ouvrer** *vt* work (metal, wood, etc); adorn, embroider

**ouvreuse** *nf* *theat+cin* usherette

**ouvrier** *nm* workman, worker, craftsman, mechanic; *fig* creator, architect; **~ à façons** jobber; *adj (f* **-ière)** **cheville ouvrière** lynchpin; *fig* mainspring; **classe ouvrière** working class; **conflits ~s** labour disputes

**ouvrière** *nf* working woman, factory girl; worker (bee, etc); **~ lingère** seamstress

**ouvrir** *vt* (30) open, open up; start, set in train; switch on, turn on; *surg* lance; *elect* break (circuit); **~ la marche** lead the way; **~ les rideaux** draw back the curtains; *vi* open; let in; **s' ~** open, become open; begin; **s' ~ à** confide in, talk freely to

**ouvroir** *nm* sewing-room

**ovaire** *nm* ovary

**ovale** *nm+adj* oval

**ovin** *adj* ovine; **les ~s** sheep

**ovipare** *adj* *zool* oviparous

**ovni** *nm* UFO

**oxalique** *adj* oxalic

**oxydable** *adj* oxidizable, liable to rust

**oxydant** *nm* oxidizer; *adj* oxidizing

**oxydation** *nf* oxidization

**oxyde** *nm* oxide

**oxyder** *vt* oxidize; **s' ~** oxidize

**oxygène** *nm* oxygen

**oxygéner** *vt* (6) oxygenate; bleach; **eau oxygénée** hydrogen peroxide

**oxyton** *nm* *gramm* oxytone

# P

**pacage** *nm* pasture, pasturage; grazing

**pacager** *vt* (3) pasture; *vi* graze

**pacha** *nm* pasha; **vie de ~** life of luxury

**pachyderme** *nm* pachyderm

**pacificateur -trice** *n* pacifier, peacemaker; *adj* pacifying, peace-making

**pacifier** *vt* pacify, calm, appease

**Pacifique** *nm* *geog* Pacific

**pacifique** *adj* pacific, peaceful, quiet, calm

**pacifisme** *nm* pacifism

**pacotille** *nf* shoddy goods; **de ~** shoddy

**pacte** *nm* pact, agreement, covenant

**pactiser** *vi* enter into an agreement, compromise

**paf** *adj invar sl* **être ~** be tight; *interj*

bang!, slap!

**pagaie** *nf* paddle (canoe)

**pagaïe (pagaille)** *nf coll* muddle, shambles, mess; **en ~** in disorder; in quantity

**paganiser** *vt* paganize

**paganisme** *nm* paganism

**pagayer** *vt* (7) paddle (canoe)

**pagayeur -euse** *n* paddler (canoe)

¹**page** *nm* page(-boy)

²**page** *nf* page; **à la ~** up-to-date; in the know; *typ* **mettre en ~** make up

**paginer** *vt* paginate, page

**pagne** *nm* loin-cloth

**pagode** *nf* pagoda

**paie** *nf see* **paye**

**paiement, payement** *nm* payment

**païen -ienne** *n + adj* pagan

**paillard -e** *n* rake, debauchee; *f coll* tart; *adj* lewd, lecherous, ribald

**paillardise** *nf* lewdness, lecherousness

¹**paillasse** *nm* clown, mountebank

²**paillasse** *nf* palliasse, straw mattress; draining board; *sl* belly, guts

**paillasson** *nm* mat, door-mat; **~ à grille** wire mat; *coll* **mettre la clef sous le ~** abscond, bilk

**paille** *nf* straw; **~ de fer** wire wool; **coucher (être) sur la ~** be extremely poor; **tirer à la courte ~** draw lots; *adj invar* straw-coloured

**pailler** *vt* cane (chair); mulch (tree)

**pailleté** *adj* spangled

**paillette** *nf* spangle

**paillote** *nf* straw hut

**pain** *nm* bread; cake (soap); loaf (sugar); *sl* blow; **~ d'épice** kind of spiced cake; **~ grillé** toast; *coll* **acheter pour une bouchée de ~** buy for a mere song; **avoir du ~ sur la planche** have a lot of work on hand; **ne pas manger de ce ~ -là** have no stomach for that; **petit ~** roll; **se vendre comme des petits ~s** sell like hot cakes

**pair** *nm* peer; equal; *comm* par; **de ~ avec** on a par with; *adj* even (number)

**paire** *nf* pair; **une autre ~ de manches** quite another matter

**pairesse** *nf* peeress

**pairie** *nf* peerage

**paisible** *adj* peaceful, peaceable, quiet; uneventful

**paître** *vt* (67) graze on, feed on; *vi* graze, feed; **faire ~** graze; *coll* **envoyer ~** send packing

**paix** *nf* peace; quiet, stillness, tranquillity; **faire la ~ avec** make peace with, be reconciled with; *coll* **ficher (foutre) la ~ à qn** leave s/o alone, let s/o alone, shut up

**pal** *nm* stake, pale; *her* pale

**palabre** *nm + f* palaver

**palabrer** *vi* palaver

**palace** *nm* luxury hotel

¹**palais** *nm* palace; *leg* law-court; lawyers; **terme de ~** legal jargon

²**palais** *nm* palate; **voile du ~** soft palate; **voûte du ~** hard palate

**palan** *nm naut* hoist, pulley and tackle

**palanche** *nf* yoke

**palanque** *nf* stockade

**palatale** *nf phon* palatal, front consonant, front vowel

**palatin** *adj anat* palatine

**Palatinat** *nm* Palatinate

¹**pale** *nf* blade (of oar, propeller); *mech* sluice-gate

²**pale** *nf eccles* pall

**pâle** *adj* pale, light, wan; colourless, sickly

**palefrenier** *nm* groom, ostler, stableman

**palefroi** *nm ar* palfrey

**paléographe** *n* palaeographer

**paléographie** *nf* palaeography

**paléographique** *adj* palaeographical

**paléolithique** *adj* palaeolithic

**paléontologie** *nf* palaeontology

**palet** *nm* quoit

**paletot** *nm* greatcoat, overcoat; coat

**palette** *nf* blade, paddle; ping-pong bat; *cul* shoulder of mutton; (painter's) palette

**palétuvier** *nm bot* mangrove

**pâleur** *nf* paleness, pallor, wanness

**pâlichon -onne** *adj coll* on the pale side

**palier** *nm* landing, stair-head; level, level stretch; degree, stage; *mech* bearing; **être voisins de ~** live on the same floor; **par ~s** graduated

**palière** *adj f* leading on to the landing

**palimpseste** *nm* palimpsest

**palinodie** *nf* palinode, recantation, retraction

**pâlir** *vt* bleach (colour), make pale; *vi* grow pale, pall, turn pale; fade, grow dim; be on the wane

**palis** *nm* pale, stake; enclosure

**palissade** *nf* palissade, structure; box-hedge

**palissandre** *nm* rosewood

**pâlissant** *adj* growing pale, waning

**palliatif** *nm* palliative; *adj* (*f* **-ive**) palliative

**pallier** *vt* palliate

**palmarès** *nm* prize list, honours list

**palme** *nf bot* palm-leaf; (swimming) flipper; **~s (académiques)** academic honour; **remporter la ~** bear the palm

**palmé** *adj* web-footed; *bot* palmate

**palmer** *nm* callipers

**palmeraie** *nf* palm grove

**palmette** *nf agr* fan espalier; *archi* palm-leaf, palmette

**palmier** *nm* palm-tree

**palmipède** *nm + adj zool* palmiped
**palmure** *nf* web (of web foot)
**palombe** *nf orni* ring-dove; wood-pigeon
**pâlot -otte** *adj coll* palish, peaky
**palourde** *nf zool* clam
**palpabilité** *nf* palpability
**palpe** *nm zool* palp, palpus, feeler
**palper** *vt* feel, finger; *med* palpate; *coll* receive (money)
**palpitant** *adj* palpitating, throbbing; exciting, thrilling
**palpiter** *vi* palpitate, quiver, throb; flutter (eyelid); thrill
**paltoquet** *nm* nonentity
**paludéen, -éenne** *adj* marsh; malarial, paludal
**paludisme** *nm* malaria, paludism
**palustre** *adj* marsh (plant); marshy, swampy (ground)
**pâmer (se)** *v refl* faint away, swoon; **se ~ de rire** die with laughter
**pâmoison** *nf* swoon, fainting fit
**pampa** *nf* pampas
**pamphlet** *nm* satirical pamphlet, lampoon
**pamphlétaire** *n* pamphleteer, lampoonist
**pamplemousse** *nm* grapefruit
**pampre** *nm* vine-branch; *archi* vine-branch motif
¹**pan** *nm* flap (garment), tail (coat, shirt); face, piece, section, side; patch (sky); wall
²**pan** *interj* bang!, clonk!
**panacée** *nf* panacea
**panache** *nm* panache, plume; wreath (smoke); dash, show, swagger
¹**panaché** *nm* lemonade shandy
²**panaché** *adj* parti-coloured, variegated; **bière ~e** shandy; **glace ~e** mixed ice-cream
**panacher** *vt* variegate; plume; *pol* spread one's votes
**panade** *nf* thin gruel made of bread, butter and water; *sl* **dans la ~** in need, in want
**panais** *nm* parsnip
**Paname** *n coll* Paris
**panard** *nm sl* foot
**panaris** *nm med* whitlow
**pancarte** *nf* bill, notice, placard, poster; show-card (shop)
**panchromatique** *adj* panchromatic
**pandit** *nm* pundit
**panégyrique** *nm + adj* panegyric
**panégyriste** *nm* panegyrist
**paner** *vt* cover with bread-crumbs
**panerée** *nf* basketful; *coll* load
**paneterie** *nf* bread-store
**panier** *nm* basket; basketful; *ar* pannier; **~ à salade** salad-washer; *coll*

Black Maria; **~ percé** spendthrift; **dessus du ~** elite
**panifier** *vt* turn into bread
**panique** *nf* panic, scare, stampede; *adj* panic
**paniquer** *vi* panic, flap
¹**panne** *nf* breakdown, mishap; *theat* minor part, poor part; **mot ~ d'allumage** ignition trouble; **~ d'électricité** power failure; **~ d'essence** running out of petrol; *coll* **être dans la ~** be reduced to poverty; **être en ~ mot** have a breakdown; *naut* be hove to; *coll* be unable to carry on; *coll* **être en ~ de qch** be lacking sth; **laisser qn en ~** leave s/o in the lurch
²**panne** *nf* plush, panne
³**panne** *nf* peen (hammer), blade; **~ fendue** claw (hammer)
⁴**panne** *nf bui* purlin
**panné** *adj sl* broke
**panneau** *nm* panel, board, cover, boarding; net, snare, trap; *naut* **~ d'écoutille** hatch cover; **~ de signalisation** road sign; **~ réclame** hoarding; **donner (tomber) dans le ~** fall into the trap
**panneton** *nm* web (key); catch (window)
**panonceau** *nm* name-plate; sign; road-sign
**panoplie** *nf* panoply; toy outfit
**panoramique** *adj* panoramic
**panse** *nf coll* paunch, pot, pot-belly; belly (vase, bottle)
**pansement** *nm* bandaging, dressing; bandage, dressing
**panser** *vt* bandage, dress; tend (patient); groom (horse)
**pansu** *adj* pot-bellied
**pantalon** *nm* trousers, pair of trousers, slacks; **~s ar** woman's drawers
**pantalonnade** *nf theat* farce involving character Pantaloon; piece of humbug
**pantelant** *adj* panting, out of breath; quivering
**panthéisme** *nm* pantheism
**panthéiste** *n + adj* pantheist
**panthère** *nf zool* panther
**pantin** *nm* jumping-jack (toy); marionette, puppet; nonentity, figure of fun
**pantographe** *nm* pantograph
**pantois** *adj invar* amazed, flabbergasted, speechless
**pantomime** *nf* dumb-show, mime, pantomime; *fig* affected behaviour
**pantouflard** *adj coll* stay-at-home, home-loving
**pantoufle** *nf* slipper
**panure** *nf cul* bread-crumbs
**paon** *nm* peacock; peacock-moth
**paonne** *nf* peahen

**papa** *nm* papa, daddy; ~ **gâteau** over-indulgent father; *coll* **à la** ~ easily, without hurry; *coll* **de** ~ out of date; **fils à** ~ rich man's son, playboy
**papauté** *nf* papacy
**pape** *nm* pope
**papelard** *nm coll* bit of paper, paper; *adj* sanctimonious; hypocritical
**paperasse** *nf* useless paper; ~**s** old papers
**paperasserie** *nf* accumulation of old papers; red tape
**paperassier -ière** *adj* fond of scribbling, fond of conserving papers; given to red tape
**papeterie** *nf* paper-making; paper-mill; stationery shop
**papetier -ière** *n* paper-maker; stationer
**papier** *nm* paper; piece of paper; article; feature story; write-up; *comm* bill; ~**s** documents; ~ **à en-tête** headed paper; ~ **à lettres** writing paper; ~ **à musique** music paper; ~ **buvard** blotting-paper; ~ **calque** tracing paper; *vulg* ~ **cul** bumf, shitting-paper; ~ **de soie** tissue paper; ~ **de verre** sandpaper; ~ **hygiénique** toilet paper; ~ **journal** newsprint; ~ **peint** wall-paper; ~ **timbré** (official) stamped paper; *coll* **être dans les petits** ~**s de qn** be in s/o's good books; **rayez cela de vos** ~**s** don't bank on that
**papillaire** *adj anat* + *bot* papillary
**papille** *nf anat* + *bot* papilla
**papillon** *nm* butterfly; bow-tie; butterfly stroke (swimming); *coll* parking-ticket; summons; *mech* butterfly-nut; *mot* butterfly-valve, throttle; inset (page), inset-map; corollary; butterfly, gaudily dressed person; changeable, unreliable person; ~ **de nuit** moth; *coll* **minute** ~! hold on!
**papillonner** *vi* flit about, flutter about; pass from one subject to another
**papillote** *nf* curl-paper; toffee-paper; *cul* greased paper
**papillotement** *nm* dazzle; flickering
**papilloter** *vi* dazzle; flicker; blink (eyes)
**papiste** *n* + *adj* papist
**papotage** *nm* chatter, gossip
**papoter** *vi* chatter, gossip
**papule** *nf bot* + *med* papula
**pâque** *nf* Jewish passover
**paquebot** *nm* liner, steamer; ~ **mixte** ship carrying both cargo and passengers
**pâquerette** *nf* daisy
**Pâques** *nfpl* 'Easter; ~ **fleuries** Palm Sunday; **faire ses** ~ take the sacrament at Easter; **joyeuses** ~ happy Easter; *nm sing* Easter, day of Easter; **semaine de** ~ week after Easter

**paquet** *nm* bundle, package, packet, parcel; bundle, mass; pack (rugby football); *typ* parcel; tough criticism; ~ **de mer** green sea; **donner (lâcher) son** ~ **à qn** give s/o a piece of one's mind; **faire son** ~ pack up; **mettre le** ~ throw everything in, use strong measures
**paquetage** *nm* parcelling; *mil* equipment (laid out for inspection)
**par** *prep* at, by, by means of; out of; per; through; in; on; ~**-ci**, ~**-là** here and there, now and then; ~ **ici** this way; ~ **là** that way; ~ **trop** far too; **de** ~ by reason of; **de** ~ **le monde** somewhere in the world; **de** ~ **le Roi** in the name of the King
**para** *nm mil* parachutist
**parabole** *nf* parable; *math* parabola
**parabolique** *adj* parabolic(al)
**parachever** *vt* (6) complete, finish off, perfect
**parachutage** *nm* parachuting
**parachuter** *vt* parachute
**parachutiste** *n* parachutist
**parade** *nf* display, parade; *mil* review; parry (fencing); sudden stop (horse); **de** ~ ostentatious, showy
**parader** *vi* parade, show off
**paradigme** *nm gramm* paradigm
**paradis** *nm* paradise; *theat* gods; ~ **fiscal** tax haven; *coll* **vous ne l'emporterez pas au (en)** ~ I'll get even with you yet
**paradoxal** *adj* paradoxical
**paradoxe** *nm* paradox
**parafe, paraphe** *nm* paraph, flourish; initials (signature)
**parafer, parapher** *vt* sign; initial
**paraffine** *nf* paraffin wax; *med* **huile de** ~ liquid paraffin
**parage** *nm ar* lineage; **de haut** ~ of high birth
**parages** *nmpl naut* area of sea; region, vicinity; district, area
**paragraphe** *nm* paragraph
**paraître** *vi* (68) appear, come into sight; look, seem; be published; come on stage; **chercher à** ~ show off; **vient de** ~ just published; *v impers* **il paraît** it seems; **à ce qu'il paraît** apparently, it would seem; **il y paraît** it's obvious; *coll* **paraît que** it looks as though
**parallaxe** *nf astron* parallax
**parallèle** *nf math* parallel; *elect* **montage en** ~ parallel connection; *nm* parallel, comparison; *geog* parallel; *adj* parallel
**parallélisme** *nm* parallelism
**paralysant** *adj* paralysing
**paralyser** *vt* paralyse, cripple
**paralysie** *nf* paralysis
**paralytique** *n* + *adj* paralytic

**paramilitaire** *adj* paramilitary
**parangon** *nm* paragon
**parangonner** *vi typ* justify different types
**paranoïaque** *adj* paranoid
**paraphe** *nm see* **parafe**
**parapher** *vt see* **parafer**
**paraphraser** *vt* paraphrase
**paraphrastique** *adj* paraphrastic
**paraplégie** *nf med* paraplegia
**paraplégique** *n + adj* paraplegic
**parapluie** *nm* umbrella
**parasitaire** *adj* parasitic
**parasite** *nm* parasite, hanger-on; *coll* sponger; *biol* parasite; *rad* interference; *adj* parasitic
**parasiter** *vt* sponge on
**parasitique** *adj* parasitic, parasitical
**parasitisme** *nm* parasitism
**paratonnerre** *nm* lightning-conductor
**paratyphoïde** *nf + adj med* paratyphoid
**paravent** *nm* screen
**parbleu** *interj* rather!, sure!
**parc** *nm* park, grounds; enclosure; bed (oysters); fold (sheep), paddock (horses), pen (cattle, sheep); *mil* depot; whole stock of vehicles possessed (by army, country); rolling-stock (railway); car-park
**parcage** *nm* parking
**parcelle** *nf* fragment, particle; plot (of land)
**parce que** *conj phr* because
**parchemin** *nm* parchment, vellum; document, title-deed; *coll* degree certificate; **papier ~** parchment paper
**parcheminé** *adj* parchment-like, shrivelled
**parcheminer (se)** *v refl* become shrivelled up
**parcimonie** *nf* parsimony
**parcimonieux -ieuse** *adj* parsimonious
**parc(o)mètre** *nm* parking meter
**parcourir** *vt* (29) go through, pass through; cover (distance), travel; look through (book), skim; **~ des yeux** glance over
**parcours** *nm* journey, trip; route; distance to be covered, distance to be covered (race); circuit; course (golf); *mil* **~ du combattant** assault-course; **~ d'essai** trial run
**par-derrière** *adv + prep* behind
**par-dessous** *adv + prep* underneath, beneath
**pardessus** *nm* overcoat
**par-dessus** *adv + prep* over; **~ le marché** into the bargain
**par-devant** *prep* in front of, before
**pardi** *interj* indeed!
**pardieu** *interj obs* indeed!
**pardon** *nm* forgiveness, pardon; *eccles* Breton religious festival; *interj* excuse me!, sorry!
**pardonnable** *adj* pardonable, forgivable
**pardonner** *vt* excuse, forgive, pardon; **une maladie qui ne pardonne pas** incurable illness
**pare-boue** *nm invar* mud-flap
**pare-brise** *nm invar* wind-screen
**pare-chocs** *nm* mot bumper, *US* fender
**pare-étincelles** *nm invar* fire-guard, fire-screen
**pare-feu** *nm invar* fire-screen; fire-belt (forest)
**pare-fumée** *nm invar* smoke-shield
**parégorique** *nm + adj* paregoric
**pareil -eille** *n* equal, like, match; *coll* **c'est du ~ au même** it's all the same; **rendre la pareille** give tit for tat; **sans pareil(le)** unequalled; *adj* alike, equal, like; such; **à nul autre ~** unequalled; *adv sl* in the same way
**pareillement** *adv* also, equally, likewise, in the same way
**parement** *nm* adornment, ornament; decoration, ornamentation; adorning; dressing (stone); cuff, lapel
**parent -e** *n* kinsman, kinswoman, relative; **~ s** parents; relatives; ancestors; *adj* related, similar
**parenté** *nf* kinship, relationship; affinity, analogy
**parenthèse** *nf* parenthesis, digression; bracket; **entre ~ s** by the way
**¹parer** *vt* adorn, deck, embellish, ornament; attribute (qualities); prepare, dress (meat); *naut* clear, prepare; **se ~** adorn oneself, dress oneself up
**²parer** *vt* avoid, fend off, parry, ward off; *naut* round (cape); **~ à nul autre** a guard against
**pare-soleil** *nm invar mot* sun-shield
**paresse** *nf* idleness, laziness; *med* sluggishness
**paresser** *vi* idle, laze
**paresseux -euse** *n* idle person, lazy person, sluggard; *adj* idle, lazy; *med* sluggish; *nm zool* sloth
**parfaire** *vt* (46) perfect
**parfait** *nm* perfection; *gramm* perfect; *cul* parfait; *adj* perfect, excellent, faultless; complete, thorough
**parfaitement** *adv* perfectly; quite so, exactly
**parfois** *adv* sometimes, occasionally
**parfum** *nm* perfume, scent; *cul* flavour; *sl* **être au ~** be in the know
**parfumer** *vt* perfume, scent; *cul* flavour
**parfumerie** *nf* perfumery
**parfumeur -euse** *n* perfumer
**pari** *nm* bet, wager; **~ mutuel** tote
**paria** *nm* pariah; outcast
**parier** *vt* bet, wager; affirm
**pariétaire** *nf bot* pellitory

**pariétal**

**pariétal** *adj anat* parietal; wall (paintings)

**parieur** *nm* better, punter

**parisien -ienne** *adj* Parisian

**paritaire** *adj* composed of equal numbers

**parité** *nf* parity; *math* evenness

**parjure** *nm* perjury; *n* perjurer; *adj* perjured, forsworn

**parjurer (se)** *v refl* perjure oneself

**parking** *nm* car-park; parking (action)

**parlant** *adj* speaking, talking; expressive

**parlé** *adj* spoken; *rad* **journal ~** (radio) news

**parlement** *nm Fr hist* high court of law; parliament

**parlementaire** *n* member of parliament; *adj* parliamentary

**parlementer** *vi* parley

**parler** *nm* speaking, speech, manner of speaking; language, dialect; *vi* speak, talk; chat, confer, converse; admonish, lecture, tell; **~ pour ne rien dire** talk for the sake of talking; **il ne veut pas en entendre ~** he won't hear of it; **n'en parlons plus** let's say no more about it, that's settled; **sans ~ de** not to speak of; **trouver à qui ~** meet one's match; *sl* **tu parles!** not half!, you've said it!; some hope!

**parleur -euse** *n* speaker; confident speaker

**parloir** *nm* parlour; visiting-room (convent, prison, school)

**parlot(t)e** *nf coll* empty chatter

**parmi** *prep* amid, amidst, among, amongst

**parodie** *nf* parody; travesty

**parodier** *vt* parody; burlesque, take-off

**paroi** *nf* partition-wall; surface of wall; rock-face; *anat + biol* wall

**paroisse** *nf* parish

**paroissial** *adj* parochial

**paroissien -ienne** *n* parishioner; *nm* missal

**parole** *nf* word, spoken word; promise, undertaking; (faculty of) speech; eloquence; *mil* parole; **adresser la ~ à** address, speak to; **avoir la ~ facile** have the gift of the gab; **de belles ~s** promises, mere words; **demander la ~** risk leave to speak (at meeting); **histoire sans ~s** drawing or cartoon that needs no caption; **n'avoir qu'une ~** keep one's promises; **passer ~** pass (cards); **prendre la ~** begin to speak, take the floor; **rendre sa ~ à qn** release s/o from a promise

**parotide** *nf + adj* parotid

**paroxysme** *nm* paroxysm, climax

**parpaillot -e** *n joc* Protestant

**parpaing** *nm bui* parpen, through stone; breeze block (cement)

**parquer** *vt* pen (animals); garrison (soldiers); coop up (people); park (car); **se ~** park (one's car); *vi* park

¹**parquet** *nm Fr leg* public prosecutor's office; *collect* corps of public prosecutors

²**parquet** *nm* floor, flooring, parquet

**parqueter** *vt* (5) lay (a floor) in

**parqueteur** *nm* floor-maker, floor-layer

**parrain** *nm* godfather; sponsor (club, society)

**parrainage** *nm* function of god-parent; sponsorship, patronage

**parrainer** *vt* sponsor, support

**parsemer** *vt* (6) sprinkle, strew, stud

¹**part** *nf* part, portion, share; concern, participation; allowance, consideration; *comm* share; *cul* helping, slice; *leg* portion; **à ~** aside, elsewhere; except; **autre ~** elsewhere; **d'autre ~** on the other hand, moreover; **de la ~ de** on behalf of; from; **de ~ en ~** through and through; **de toute(s) ~(s)** on all sides; **faire bande à ~** form a separate clique; **faire chambre à ~** sleep in separate rooms (of husband and wife); **faire la ~ de** make allowance for; **faire ~ de** acquaint with, inform about; **nulle ~** nowhere; **prendre qch en bonne (mauvaise) ~** take sth in good (bad) part; **quelque ~** somewhere

²**part** *nm ar* parturition; *leg* new-born child

**partage** *nm* division, partition, sharing, sharing out; portion, share; fate, lot; equality of votes; *geog* **ligne de ~ des eaux** divide, watershed

**partager** *vt* (3) divide, share, share out; **se ~** be shared, be divided up; divide; share; **amour partagé** requited love; **être mal partagé** be ill provided for

**partance** *nf* **en ~ pour** leaving for

¹**partant** *nm* person departing; starter (racing)

²**partant** *adv* consequently, therefore

**partenaire** *n* partner

**parterre** *nm* flower-bed; *theat* pit, pit-audience

**parthe** *adj* Parthian; **flèche du ~** Parthian shot

¹**parti** *nm* party, association, group; gang; match (marriage); choice, decision; **~ pris** bias, prejudice, obstinate view; **beau ~** desirable match, *coll* catch; **de ~ pris** deliberately, intentionally; **prendre ~** decide; **prendre son ~ de** resign oneself to; **tirer ~ de** exploit

²**parti** *adj* absent, gone; *coll* a bit drunk, lively; **bien ~** off to a good start; **mal**

218

~ off to a bad start, ill-conceived
**partial** *adj* partial; biased, unfair
**partialité** *nf* partiality; bias, unfairness
**participant -e** *n* participant; competitor; *adj* participating; competing
**participe** *nm gramm* participle
**participer** *vi* participate, collaborate; share, take part
**particularisation** *nf* particularization, differentiation
**particulariser** *vt* particularize, differentiate; specify; **se** ~ make oneself conspicuous
**particularité** *nf* particularity; characteristic, peculiarity
**particule** *nf* particle; **avoir la** ~ be of noble family (have the particle 'de' before one's name)
**particulier -ière** *n* private individual; *coll* chap, fellow; *nm* particular, specific; *adj* particular, special, strange; private; **à titre** ~ in a private capacity; **en** ~ in private
**partie** *nf* part, element, piece; party; game, match; *leg* party; *mus* part; ~ **s** parts, genitals; ~ **carrée** two couples who exchange partners; ~ **de campagne** picnic; ~ **de plaisir** outing, picnic; *comm* ~ **double** double entry; ~ **remise** pleasure to come; **faire** ~ **de** be part of; be a member of; *vulg* **il me casse les** ~**s** he sends me up the wall; **prendre qn à** ~ hold s/o responsible; **se mettre de la** ~ join in
**partiel -ielle** *adj* partial, incomplete
**partir** *vi* depart, go away, leave, set out, start; come off (button, etc); go off (gun); disappear, come out (stain); **à** ~ **de** from, since; **faire** ~ let off (gun, etc); start (engine); send (s/o) away
**partitif -ive** *adj gramm* partitive
**partition** *nf ar* partition; *mus* score
**partouse (partouze)** *nf sl* orgy
**partout** *adv* everywhere; ~ **où** wherever; **trente** ~ thirty all (tennis)
**parturiente** *nf* woman in labour
**parure** *nf* adornment, dress, toilette; set (jewellery, underclothes); string (pearls)
**parution** *nf* appearance, publication (book)
**parvenir** *vi* (96) attain, reach; succeed; arrive, come; manage; succeed in life
**parvenu -e** *n* parvenu, upstart; newly rich
**¹pas** *nm* pace, step, stride; footprint; step (stair); passage, strait; stage, step forward; manner of walking; *mech* pitch (propeller), thread (screw); **Pas-de-Calais** Straits of Dover; department of Pas-de-Calais; ~ **de gymnastique** double; ~ **de porte** key-money; **à**

~ **de loup** stealthily; **au** ~ dead slow, at a walking pace; in step; **céder le** ~ give way; **de ce** ~ at once; **faire les cent** ~ walk up and down; **faire les premiers** ~ take the initiative; **faux** ~ false step; blunder; *coll* black; **mauvais** ~ tight corner; dangerous, exposed passage (mountaineering); **prendre le** ~ **sur** get in front of, precede; **salle des** ~ **perdus** circulating area; **se mettre au** ~ get into step
**²pas** *adv* not; not any, no
**pascal** *adj* paschal
**passable** *adj* passable, fair, tolerable; **mention** ~ pass (examination)
**passade** *nf* brief love affair
**passage** *nm* passage, path, way; crossing, passing over, passing through; journey by sea; fare for journey by sea; passage, extract (book); ~ **à niveau** level-crossing; ~ **clouté** pedestrian crossing; ~ **protégé** sign on major road indicating that a minor road joining it is furnished with a halt sign; ~ **souterrain** subway; **au** ~ on the way through; **de** ~ in transit, passing through
**passager -ère** *n* passenger; *adj* fleeting, momentary, transitory; migratory
**¹passant -e** *n* passer-by; *adj* busy (road, etc), well-trodden; *her* passant
**²passant** *nm* frog (on belt)
**passation** *nf leg* drawing up (act, contract); transmission (powers)
**¹passe** *nm* master-key
**²passe** *nf* passing; channel, passage, pass; thrust (fencing); pass (football); excess; ~ **d'armes** passage of arms; *comm* ~ **de caisse** contingency float; **être dans une bonne (mauvaise)** ~ be in a strong (weak) position; **être en** ~ **de** be on the point of; **maison de** ~ brothel; **mot de** ~ password
**passé** *nm* past; *gramm* past; past life; *adj* past; faded; over-ripe; *prep* after, beyond
**passe-droit** *nm* illegitimate favour, improper promotion; *ar* injustice
**passement** *nm* thread of gold (silver, silk); braid
**passementer** *vt* trim with braid
**passe-montagne** *nm* balaclava helmet
**passe-partout** *nm invar* master-key; passe-partout, adhesive tape for framing; *adj* universally acceptable
**passe-passe** *nm invar* jugglery, juggling; **tour de** ~ sleight of hand, conjuring-trick; *fig* cunning trick, deception
**passe-plat** *nm* serving-hatch
**passeport** *nm* passport
**passer** *vt* pass, cross, go over, go past; carry across, ferry; hand, pass; put on

(coat, ring); go beyond, exceed, surpass; spend (time); ignore, omit, overlook; grant, pass over; take (examination); survive; show (film); *mot* change (gear); connect with (on telephone); percolate, strain; *leg* conclude (agreement), enter into (contract); ~ **à tabac** beat up (*esp* of police); ~ **l'éponge sur** pass the sponge over, erase, forget, wipe out; ~ **un coup de fil à qn** ring s/o up; ~ **un mauvais quart d'heure** have a rough time, have a nasty moment; *coll* ~ **un savon à qn** tear a strip off s/o; *vi* pass, go past; call, go, pass through; undergo; pass away; die, pass away; become, be promoted; be accepted, be passed; come up (trial); fade (colour); omit, skip over; go down (food); filter through (liquid); **passe encore** very well, all right so far; *mot* ~ **en** change into (gear); ~ **outre** pass on; disregard, ignore, take no notice of; ~ **par** go through; ~ **pour** seem, be looked on as; ~ **sur** overlook; **passons!** never mind!, let's forget it!; **en passant** by the way; **en** ~ **par** put up with; *coll* **y** ~ die

**passereau** *nm* sparrow

**passerelle** *nf* foot-bridge; gangway (ship, aircraft); *naut* bridge

**passe-rose** *nf bot* hollyhock

**passe-temps** *nm invar* pastime

**passe-thé** *nm invar* (tea-)strainer

**passeur -euse** *n* ferryman, ferrywoman; smuggler (of persons across frontier)

**passible** *adj* liable; *theol* capable of suffering

**passif** *nm comm* liabilities; *gramm* passive; *adj* (*f* -**ive**) passive; *gramm* passive

**passion** *nf theol* Passion; passion; love

**passionnant** *adj* entrancing, fascinating, thrilling

**passionné** *adj* passionate, impassioned; avid, fervent

**passionnel -elle** *adj* concerning the passions; **crime** ~ crime of jealousy

**passionner** *vt* excite, interest powerfully; impassion, make passionate; **se** ~ become enthusiastic, show great interest

**passivité** *nf* passivity

**passoire** *nf cul* strainer

**pastel** *nm bot* woad; pastel shade; pastel; drawing in pastel

**pastèque** *nf* water-melon

**pasteur** *nm* shepherd; protestant clergyman, minister, pastor

**pasteurisation** *nf* pasteurization

**pasteuriser** *vt* pasteurize

**pastiche** *nm* pastiche; imitation, parody

**pasticher** *vt* pastiche; imitate, parody

**pastille** *nf* pastille, lozenge; lozenge (design)

**pastorale** *nf* pastoral play; pastoral letter

**pastorat** *nm* pastorate

**pat** *nm* + *adj invar* (chess) stalemate

**patachon** *nm* **mener une vie de** ~ lead a gay life

**patapouf** *nm coll* fat person, fat child; *interj* flop!, bump!

**pataquès** *nm* faulty liaison in pronunciation

**patate** *nf* sweet potato; *coll* potato; *coll* idiot

**patati, patata** *interj* **et patati! et patata!** and so on and so forth

**patatras** *interj* crash!

**pataud -e** *n* clumsy child; *nm* puppy with large paws; *adj* clumsy, loutish

**patauger** *vi* (3) flounder about, splash about (in mud); *fig* flounder; *coll* get bogged down

**pâte** *nf* paste; pulp (paper); *cul* pastry; ~ **s** spaghetti, macaroni, etc; *arts* colours mixed on palette; ~ **de carton** papier-mâché; ~ **dentifrice** toothpaste; **être comme un coq en** ~ lie warm in bed; **mettre la main à la** ~ work; **vivre comme un coq en** ~ lead a very comfortable life

**pâté** *nm* pâté; pie; blot (ink); block of houses; sand-pie

**pâtée** *nf* mash (pigs, poultry), food for dogs, cats

¹**patelin** *nm coll* village, small town

²**patelin** *adj* fawning, smooth

**patenôtre** *nf ar* Lord's prayer; *iron* prayer, mumbling

**patent** *adj* evident, manifest, patent; *ar* open

**patentable** *adj* requiring a licence (trade, tradesman)

**patente** *nf* licence (to trade); *naut* ~ **de santé** bill of health

**patenté** *adj* licensed; *coll* qualified, recognized

**patenter** *vt* license

**pater** *nm invar* Lord's prayer

**patère** *nf* coat-peg, hat-peg

**paterne** *adj* benevolent, soft-spoken

**paternel -elle** *adj* paternal, fatherly

**paternité** *nf* paternity

**pâteux -euse** *adj* pasty; coated (tongue); dull, heavy

**pathétique** *nm* pathos; *adj* pathetic, touching

**pathogène** *adj med* pathogenic

**pathologie** *nf* pathology

**pathologique** *adj* pathological; abnormal, morbid

**pathologiste** *n* pathologist

**pathos** *nm* false pathos

**patibulaire** *adj* sinister (appearance); *ar* **fourches** ~ **s** gallows

**patience** *nf* patience; long-suffering, resignation, constancy, courage; patience (cards); *mil* button-stick; **jeu de** ~ jigsaw puzzle

**patient -e** *n* surgical case; patient; *adj* patient, long-suffering, persevering

**patienter** *vi* be patient

**patin** *nm* skate; flange (rail); runner (sledge); *mot* brake-shoe; ~ **à roulettes** roller-skate

**patinage** *nm* skating; *mot* skidding

¹**patiner** *vi* skate; slide; skid

¹˒²**patiner** *vt* give a patina to

**patinette** *nf* scooter (child's toy)

**patineur -euse** *n* skater

**patinoire** *nf* skating-rink

**pâtir** *vi* suffer, be suffering

**pâtisserie** *nf* pastry; pastry-shop; pastry-making; ~ **s** cakes

**pâtissier -ière** *n* pastry-cook

**patois** *nm* patois, provincial dialect; *coll* jargon

**patouiller** *vt coll* grope, paw; *vi coll* flounder, splash about (in mud)

**patraque** *adj* off-colour, not well

**pâtre** *nm* herdsman, shepherd

**patriarche** *nm* patriarch

**patricien -ienne** *n* + *adj* patrician

**patrie** *nf* native land, fatherland, home country; nation

**patrimoine** *nm* patrimony

**patriote** *n* patriot; *adj* patriotic

**patriotique** *adj* patriotic

**patriotisme** *nm* patriotism

**patristique** *adj* patristic

¹**patron -onne** *n* patron, patroness, protector, protectress; patron saint; employer, *coll* boss; proprietor, landlord, landlady (bar, hotel); *med* clinical professor, consultant in teaching-hospital; ~ **de thèse** supervisor (of thesis)

²**patron** *nm* pattern, model; stencil-plate

**patronage** *nm* patronage, support; benevolent society; youth organization; **comité de** ~ list of patrons; committee running benevolent society

**patronal** *adj* pertaining to a patron-saint; pertaining to employers

**patronat** *nm* employers, body of employers

**patronner** *vt* be a patron of, patronize, protect, support

**patronnesse** *nf* + *adj* patroness; **dame** ~ patroness

**patronyme** *nm* patronymic, surname

**patronymique** *adj* patronymic

**patrouille** *nf* patrol; *aer* ~ **de chasse** fighter patrol

**patrouiller** *vi* patrol

**patrouilleur** *nm* member of a patrol; *aer* reconnaissance aircraft; *naut* patrol-ship, corvette

**patte** *nf* paw, leg, foot (animals, birds); *coll* leg (human), hand (human); flap (pocket); tab, strap; clamp; fluke (anchor); ~ **s de mouche** scrawl; **à quatre** ~ **s** on all fours; **avoir de la** ~ be skilful with one's hands; *coll* **graisser la** ~ tip, bribe; *coll* **retomber sur ses** ~ **s** fall on one's feet; **tenir qn sous sa** ~ have a hold on s/o; **tirer dans les** ~ **s de qn** cause s/o difficulties

**patte-d'oie** *nf* (*pl* **pattes-d'oie**) crow's-foot; crossroads; *bot* goose-foot

**pâturage** *nm* pasture, grazing; right of pasture

**pâture** *nf* fodder, food (animals); *fig* pabulum; pasture

**paume** *nf* palm; royal tennis, real tennis

**paumé** *adj coll* bewildered, lost; *sl* destitute, poor

**paumelle** *nf* sail-maker's palm; door-hinge

**paumer** *vt sl* lose; **se faire** ~ get caught, get pinched

**paupérisme** *nm* pauperism

**paupière** *nf* eyelid

**paupiette** *nf cul* (meat-)olive

**pause** *nf* pause, stop; half-time (football, etc); rest

**pauvre** *n* poor person, pauper; beggar; *adj* poor, needy; unfortunate, wretched

**pauvresse** *nf* poor woman

**pauvret -ette** *adj* poor little

**pauvreté** *nf* poverty; humbleness; shabbiness; banality

**pavage** *nm* paving; pavement

**pavaner (se)** *v refl* strut about

**pavé** *nm* paving-stone; pavement; paved road; (stone) floor; block, chunk; long article; big book; **battre le** ~ loaf about; **tenir le haut du** ~ keep the best company

**paver** *vt* pave

**pavillon** *nm* detached house, lodge, villa; wing of building; horn (gramophone); bell (trumpet, etc); *naut* flag; *ar mil* pavilion, tent; **baisser** ~ **devant qn** yield to s/o; *naut* **battre** ~ **français** fly the French flag

**pavois** *nm hist mil* shield; *naut* bulwark; *naut* flags; *naut* **hisser le grand** ~ dress ship overall; **hisser sur le** ~ give power to, extol; *naut* **petit** ~ recognition flags

**pavoisement** *nm naut* dressing ship; decking with flags

**pavoiser** *vt naut* dress ship; deck with flags, put out (flags); decorate

**pavot** *nm* poppy

**payant -e** *n* payer; *adj* paying; charged for; lucrative

**paye, paie** *nf* pay, wages; payment

**payement** *nm see* **paiement**

**payer** *vt* (7) pay, remunerate; reward; ~ **d'audace** take a risk; ~ **de sa personne** make an effort oneself, take a share in the risk; ~ **les pots cassés** repair the damage; ~ **qn de la même monnaie** pay s/o back in his own coin; ~ **qn de paroles** pay s/o with fine words; ~ **qn de retour** give tit for tat; ~ **rubis sur l'ongle** pay cash on the nail; **ça ne paie pas de mine** it's nothing to look at; **être payé pour savoir** learn to one's cost; **je suis payé pour savoir** I have good reason to know; **qui casse les verres les paie** you must pay for what you damage; **se** ~ pay oneself; buy for oneself; **se** ~ **de mots** be satisfied with mere words; *coll* **se** ~ **la tête de qn** pull s/o's leg

**payeur -euse** *n* payer

**¹pays** *nm* country, land; native land; village, small town; **être en** ~ **de connaissance** be among friends; **mal du** ~ homesickness; **voir du** ~ travel around, get about

**²pays, payse** *n coll* fellow-countryman, fellow-countrywoman

**paysage** *nm* landscape, scenery; *arts* landscape (painting)

**paysagiste** *n* landscape painter; landscape gardener

**paysan -anne** *n* peasant; farmer; *adj* peasant, rustic

**paysannat** *nm* peasantry, peasant clan

**paysannerie** *nf* peasantry; *ar* status of being a peasant; *lit* rustic novel

**Pays-Bas** *nmpl* Netherlands

**péage** *nm* toll; toll-gate; **autoroute à** ~ motorway with toll

**péager** *nm* toll collector

**peau** *nf* skin; fur; hide; peel, skin; coating, film; *sl* bag, tart; *coll* ~ **d'âne** diploma, parchment; *vulg* ~ **de vache** swine, bastard; **à fleur de** ~ superficial; *coll* **attraper qn par la** ~ **du cou (des fesses)** stop s/o at the last moment; *coll* **avoir qn dans la** ~ be infatuated with s/o; *theat* **entrer dans la** ~ **d'un personnage** get right into a part; *coll* **faire la** ~ **à qn** get s/o; **faire** ~ **neuve** cast its skin (snake); *fig* turn over a new leaf; *coll* **j'aurai sa** ~ I'll get him; *coll* **se faire crever la** ~ get oneself killed

**Peau-Rouge** *n* (*pl* **Peaux-Rouges**) Red Indian

**peausserie** *nf* skin-dressing; dressed skin

**pécari** *nm zool* peccary

**peccadille** *nf* peccadillo

**¹pêche** *nf* peach; *sl* slap

**²pêche** *nf* fishing; fishery; *leg* fishing rights; catch (of fish); **grande** ~ deep-sea fishing; **la** ~ **miraculeuse** the miraculous draught of fishes

**péché** *nm* sin, transgression; ~ **mignon** besetting sin

**pécher** *vi* (6) sin; offend

**¹pêcher** *nm* peach-tree

**²pêcher** *vt* fish for; catch (a fish); *coll* find, dig out

**pécheresse** *nf* sinner

**pêcherie** *nf* fishery

**pêcheur** *nm* sinner

**pêcheur -euse** *n* fisherman, fisherwoman; *adj* fishing

**pécore** *nf coll* silly girl, stupid bitch; *ar* animal

**pectoral** *adj* pectoral; **sirop** ~ cough mixture

**pectoraux** *nmpl* pectoral muscles; cough lozenges

**pécule** *nm* nest-egg, savings; earnings (convict); gratuity (soldier)

**pécuniaire** *adj* pecuniary

**pédagogie** *nf* pedagogy, pedagogics

**pédagogique** *adj* pedagogic(al)

**pédale** *nf* pedal; *sl* pederast, queer; queer milieu; *sl* **perdre les** ~ **s** get all mixed up

**pédaler** *vi* pedal; *sl* walk fast, run; ~ **en danseuse** ride bicycle standing on the pedals

**pédaleur -euse** *n* cyclist

**pédalier** *nm* pedal-board, pedals (organ); crank gear (bicycle)

**pédalo** *nm* pedal-craft, pedalo

**pédant -e** *n* pedant; *adj* pedantic

**pédanterie** *nf* pedantry; pedantic action, pedantic phrase

**pédantisme** *nm* pedantry

**pédéraste** *nm* pederast, homosexual; *coll* queer

**pédérastie** *nf* pederasty, homosexuality

**pédestre** *adj* pedestrian, on foot

**pédiatre** *n* paediatrician, paediatrist

**pédiatrie** *nf* paediatrics

**pédicure** *n* chiropodist

**pedzouille** *n coll* ignorant provincial, rustic

**pégase** *nm* flying-fish

**pègre** *nf* crooks, underworld

**peignage** *nm* carding, combing (wool)

**peigne** *nm* comb; card (wool); *zool* pecten, scallop

**peigné** *nm* worsted; *adj* combed; carded (wool); affected (style), finicky; excessively groomed

**peignée** *nf* cardful (wool); *coll* thrashing

**peigner** *vt* comb; card (wool); **se** ~ comb one's hair; *coll* fight, have a set-to

**peignoir** *nm* lady's dressing-gown; bathing-wrap

**peinard** *adj sl* peaceful, quiet, sly

**peindre** *vt* (55) paint, coat with paint; paint, portray; **se ~** make oneself up; describe oneself; *fig* appear

**peine** *nf* penalty, punishment; affliction, distress, pain, sorrow; effort, work, trouble, difficulty; **à ~** barely, hardly, scarcely; **comme une âme en ~** alone and sadly; **donnez-vous la ~ d'entrer** be so good as to come in; **en être pour sa ~** have wasted one's time and trouble; **être en ~ de qn** be worried about s/o; **faire de la ~ à qn** grieve s/o, hurt s/o; **homme de ~** labourer; **pour votre ~** this is for you (in giving a tip); **purger sa ~** serve one's sentence; **sous ~ d'amende** under pain of a fine; **valoir la ~** be worth the trouble

**peiner** *vt* distress, grieve, pain, vex; *vi* drudge, labour, toil

**peintre** *n* painter; **~ décorateur** decorator; *theat* designer; **~ en bâtiment(s)** house-painter; **artiste ~** artist

**peinture** *nf* painting; picture; paint, colour; *lit* **~ de mœurs** portrayal of manners; **je ne peux pas le voir en ~** I can't stand him; *coll* **un vrai pot de ~** a girl with too much make-up on

**peinturer** *vt* apply a coat of paint to; paint clumsily

**peinturlurer** *vt coll* daub, paint badly in screaming colours

**péjoratif -ive** *adj* pejorative

¹**pékin** *nm* pekin (fabric)

²**pékin** *nm coll mil* civilian, civvy; **s'habiller en ~** be in civilian clothes

**pelade** *nf med* alopecia, pelade

**pelage** *nm* coat, fur, wool (animal)

**pélagique** *adj zool* pelagian, pelagic

**pelé -e** *n* bald-head; *coll* **il n'y avait que quatre ~ s et un tondu** there were very few people; *adj* bald, bare, hairless

**pêle-mêle** *nm invar + adv* pell-mell

**peler** *vt* (5) peel; *vi* peel, peel off

**pèlerin -e** *n* pilgrim

**pèlerinage** *nm* pilgrimage

**pèlerine** *nf* (woman's) mantle, cape; cape with hood

**pellagre** *nf med* pellagra

**pelle** *nf* scoop, shovel; blade (oar); spade (children's); **~ mécanique** mechanical shovel; *coll* **ramasser une ~** fall; fail; **remuer l'argent à la ~** be very rich, be rolling in it

**pelletée** *nf* shovelful

**pelleter** *vt* (5) shovel, turn with a shovel

**pelleterie** *nf* pelt; preparation of furs; fur-trade

**pelleteuse** *nf* mechanical shovel

**pelletier -ière** *n* fur-trader; furrier

**pelliculaire** *adj* pellicular

**pellicule** *nf* pellicle; skin (milk); film; **~ s** dandruff

**pelliculeux -euse** *adj* scurfy

**pellucide** *adj* pellucid, crystal clear, limpid

**pelotage** *nm coll* groping, pawing

**pelote** *nf* ball (string, wool); pincushion; ball used in pelota; **~ basque** game of pelota; **avoir les nerfs en ~** be on edge; *coll mil* **faire la ~** be in defaulter's squad; *coll* **faire sa ~** make one's pile

**peloter** *vt coll* grope, paw

**peloton** *nm* ball (string, wool); *mil* squad, platoon; main body of runners in a race (*esp* cycling); **~ d' exécution** firing-squad

**pelotonner** *vt* wind into a ball (string, wool); **se ~** curl oneself up, snuggle close; cluster together

**pelouse** *nf* lawn, plot of grass; public enclosure (racecourse)

**peluche** *nf* plush; speck of dust, piece of fluff

**pelucher, plucher** *vi* become fluffy, shed fluff

**pelucheux -euse, plucheux -euse** *adj* shaggy, fluffy

**pelure** *nf* peel, skin (fruit); paring (vegetable); *coll* piece of clothing, *esp* overcoat; **~ d'oignon** onion skin; name of reddish-brown wine; **papier ~** typing paper, flimsy

**pelvien -ienne** *adj anat* pelvic

**pénal** *adj* penal; *leg* **clause ~e** penalty clause

**pénalisation** *nf* penalization; free kick, penalty (football)

**pénaliser** *vt* penalize (games); *leg* inflict a penalty on

**pénalité** *nf* penalty

**pénates** *nmpl fig* home

**penaud** *adj* crestfallen, shamefaced

**penchant** *nm* inclination, propensity, tendency; affection; *ar* slope

**penché** *adj* leaning; stooping

**pencher** *vt* bend, incline, tilt; *vi* lean; slope downwards; incline towards; *naut* list; **se ~** bend, incline, stoop; **se ~ sur** interest oneself in, examine closely

**pendable** *adj* **cas ~** blameworthy action; **tour ~** dirty trick

**pendaison** *nf* hanging

**pendant** *nm* pendant, ear-drop; counterpart, match; *adj* hanging, pendant; *leg* pending; *prep* during; **~ que** while

**pendard -e** *n ar* rascal, rogue; hussy

**pendeloque** *nf* pendant; ear-drop

**pendentif** *nm archi* pendentive; pendant

**penderie** *nf* hanging-cupboard

**pendiller** *vi* dangle

**pendre** *vt* hang; hang up; *vi* hang, hang down; **se ~ à** hang on to, cling to

**pendu -e** *n* one who has been hanged; *adj* hanging, hung; **~ à** hanging from; **être ~ à** be stuck to

**¹pendule** *nm* pendulum; **~ de sourcier** water-diviner's rod

**²pendule** *nf* clock

**pendulette** *nf* small clock, travelling-clock

**pêne** *nm* bolt, latch

**pénétrabilité** *nf* penetrability

**pénétrable** *adj* penetrable; comprehensible

**pénétrant** *adj* penetrating, piercing, sharp; clear, perspicacious, profound, searching

**pénétration** *nf* penetration; acumen, insight, perspicacity

**pénétrer** *vt* (6) penetrate, pass through, traverse; impregnate, touch; comprehend; *vi* enter, get in; **~ dans** enter into; **faire ~** inculcate; **se ~ de** become imbued with, become impregnated with

**pénible** *adj* arduous, hard, laborious; distressing, painful, sad

**péniblement** *adv* with difficulty; with pain; barely, just

**péniche** *nf* barge, canal-boat, lighter; *ar* shallop

**pénicilline** *nf* penicillin

**péninsulaire** *adj* peninsular

**péninsule** *nf* peninsula

**pénitence** *nf* penitence, repentance; penance; punishment; forfeit; **mettre un enfant en ~** punish a child, put a child in the corner

**pénitencier** *nm* penitentiary

**pénitent -e** *n + adj* penitent

**pénitentiaire** *adj* penitentiary; **colonie ~** borstal

**pénitentiel -ielle** *adj* penitential

**penne** *nf* quill-feather; feather of arrow; *naut* peak

**pénombre** *nf* penumbra; half-light

**pensant** *adj* thinking; **bien ~** conventional, right-minded; **mal ~** unorthodox, subversive

**¹pensée** *nf* thought; point of view, standpoint; idea; aphorism, maxim

**²pensée** *nf bot* pansy

**penser** *vt* consider, think; admit, believe, imagine; presume, suppose; suspect; intend to, mean to; conceive; *vi* think, reflect; speculate, reason; **~ à** apply one's mind to, think about; be interested in, be concerned for; remember to

**penseur** *nm* thinker

**pensif -ive** *adj* thoughtful; meditative, preoccupied

**pension** *nf* pension, allowance; payment for board (and lodging); boarding-house; boarding-school; **~ de retraite** retirement pension; **~ d'un élève** boarding-school fees; **~ reversible** widow's pension; **~ viagère** annuity; **prendre ~** board; **prendre qn en ~** take in a lodger

**pensionnaire** *n* boarder, resident, inmate, lodger; *theat* actor (actress) at the Comédie Française; **prendre des ~s** take in lodgers

**pensionnat** *nm* boarding-school; boarders

**pensionner** *vt* pension

**pensum** *nm* imposition (school); boring task

**pentagone** *nm* pentagon; *adj* pentagonal

**pentamètre** *nm* pentameter

**Pentateuque** *nm* Pentateuch

**pente** *nf* gradient, incline, slope; inclination, propensity; **en ~** sloping; **être sur une mauvaise ~** be on a slippery slope

**Pentecôte** *nf* Whitsun, Whitsuntide

**pénultième** *adj* penultimate

**pénurie** *nf* penury, poverty; lack, shortage

**pépé** *nm coll* grandpa

**pépée** *nf sl* girl, young woman

**pépère** *nm coll* grandpa; *coll* quiet old fellow; *adj sl* big; pleasant; restful

**pépètes** *nfpl sl* money

**pépie** *nf vet* pip; **avoir la ~** be very thirsty

**pépier** *vi* chirp, tweet

**¹pépin** *nm* pip, stone; hitch, snag

**²pépin** *nm coll* umbrella

**pépinière** *nf* seed-bed, nursery; *fig* nursery, hotbed

**pépiniériste** *n* nurseryman, nurserywoman

**pépite** *nf* nugget of gold

**pepsine** *nf physiol* pepsin

**peptique** *adj physiol* peptic

**péquenaud -e** *n*, **péquenot** *nm sl* bumpkin, yokel

**perçage** *nm* boring, drilling, piercing

**perçant** *adj* keen, penetrating, piercing, sharp; high-pitched, shrill

**perce** *nf* borer, drill; *mus* hole (in wind instrument); **mettre en ~** broach (cask)

**percée** *nf* clearing, cutting, glade; *mil* breakthrough; opening (football)

**percement** *nm* boring; tunnelling

**perce-neige** *nm or f invar* snowdrop

**perce-oreille** *nm* earwig

**perce-pierre** *nf* saxifrage

**¹percepteur** *nm* tax-collector

**²percepteur -trice** *adj* discerning, perceiving

**perceptible** *adj* perceptible; collectable (tax)

**perceptif -ive** *adj* perceptive

**perception** *nf* perception; collection of taxes; tax-office; post of tax-collector

**percer** *vt* (4) bore, pierce; broach (cask); cut; perforate; soak through; penetrate, understand; *ar* stab; ~ **à jour** discover (secret, something hidden); *vi* break through; succeed, become famous; burst (abscess)

**perceur -euse** *n* borer, driller; *nf* drilling-machine

**percevable** *adj* perceivable; collectable, leviable (tax)

**percevoir** *vt* discern, distinguish, perceive; collect, levy

¹**perche** *nf zool* perch

²**perche** *nf* pole; *rad* microphone boom; *coll* tall thin person, maypole; *ar* perch (measure); **tendre la ~ à qn** help s/o get out of a fix

**percher** *vt coll* place high up; *vi* perch; *coll* live on upper floor; **se ~** perch

**percheron** *nm* cart-horse, percheron; *adj* (*f* -**onne**) from the Perche region

**perchoir** *nm* perch, roost

**perclus** *adj med* anchylotic; stiff; crippled; *fig* paralysed

**perçoir** *nm mech* borer, drill; awl, gimlet; punch

**percolateur** *nm* percolator

**percutant** *adj* percussive; shattering; exploding on impact; *fig* striking; energetic

**percuter** *vt* strike, tap; *med* sound; *vi* ~ **contre** strike, crash into

**percuteur** *nm* hammer (gun)

**perdable** *adj* losable

**perdant -e** *n* loser; *nm* ebb-tide; *adj* losing

**perdition** *nf* perdition; *naut* **navire en ~** ship in distress

**perdre** *vt* lose; destroy, dishonour; harm; spoil; waste; ~ **au change** lose by the exchange; ~ **de vue** lose sight of, lose touch with; *coll* ~ **le nord** lose one's bearings; *coll* ~ **les pédales** get mixed up; ~ **pied** lose one's footing; *naut* ~ **terre** lose sight of land; **se ~** lose oneself; harm oneself; be wasted; disappear; be mixed; *vi* leak; lose, deteriorate, lose value

**perdreau** *nm* young partridge

**perdrix** *nf* partridge; ~ **des neiges** ptarmigan

**perdu** *adj* lost; depraved; ruined; wasted; terminally ill; absorbed; stray (bullet); **à corps ~** recklessly; **moments ~s** leisure time

**père** *nm* father; ~ **de famille** head of a family; *theat* ~ **noble** heavy (father);

**le ~ X** old X

**péremptoire** *adj* peremptory, unanswerable

**pérenne** *adj* perennial

**pérennité** *nf* eternity, permanence

**perfectibilité** *nf* perfectibility

**perfectionnement** *nm* perfecting, improving

**perfectionner** *vt* perfect, improve; **se ~** improve; improve one's knowledge

**perfectionniste** *n* perfectionist

**perfide** *adj* perfidious, treacherous

**perfidie** *nf* perfidy, perfidiousness, treachery; treacherous act

**perforage** *nm* perforating, boring, drilling

**perforant** *adj* perforating

**perforateur** *nm mech* drill; punch; workman operating drill; *adj* (*f* -**trice**) boring, drilling; punching

**perforatrice** *nf* drilling-machine

**perforer** *vt* bore, drill; punch

**perforeuse** *nf* perforating-machine

**périanthe** *nm bot* perianth

**péricarde** *nm anat* pericardium

**péricarpe** *nm bot* pericarp

**péricliter** *vi* be in danger; be shaky, totter

**péril** *nm* peril, danger; hazard, risk; **faire qch à ses risques et ~s** do sth at one's own risk

**périlleux -euse** *adj* perilous; hazardous; **saut ~** somersault

**périmé** *adj* out-of-date; expired, lapsed

**périmer (se)** *v refl* lapse; lose validity

**périmètre** *nm* perimeter; area

**périnée** *nm anat* perineum

¹**période** *nf* period; epoch, era

²**période** *nm lit* **au plus haut ~ (au dernier ~)** at the highest point, at the height

**périodique** *nm* periodical; *adj* periodical, intermittent, recurring; *math* **fraction ~** recurring decimal

**péripatéticien -ienne** *n* + *adj* peripatetic; *nf coll* prostitute, tart

**péripatétique** *adj* peripatetic

**péripétie** *nf lit* peripeteia; vicissitude; ~ **s** ups and downs

**périphérie** *nf* periphery, circumference; outskirts

**périphérique** *adj* peripheral; **boulevard ~** ring-road

**périphrase** *nf* periphrasis

**périphrastique** *adj* periphrastic

**périple** *nm* circumnavigation; long journey

**périr** *vi* perish, die; *fig* disappear; **faire ~** kill

**périscopique** *adj* periscopic

**périssable** *adj* perishable

**périssoire** *nf* canoe

225

**péritoine** *nm anat* peritoneum

**péritonite** *nf med* peritonitis

**perle** *nf* pearl; *fig* pearl, treasure; *coll* blunder, howler; bead (amber, glass, etc)

**perlé** *adj* pearly; beaded; carefully executed, perfectly done; **grève ~ e** go-slow

**perler** *vt* execute with care, perform perfectly; *vi* form beads (sweat, tears)

**permanence** *nf* permanence, stability; twenty-four-hour service; office always open; committee-room

**permanent** *adj* permanent, constant, stable; continuous

**permanente** *nf* permanent wave

**perméabilité** *nf* permeability

**permettre** *vt* (60) permit, allow; put up with, tolerate; **~ à** allow; enable; **permettez! allow me!; excuse me!; vous permettez?** may I?; *coll* **est-il permis d'être si stupide?** can anyone really be such a clot?

**permis** *nm* authorization, permission; pass; licence; **~ de séjour** certificate of registration (foreigner); **passer son ~** pass one's driving test

**permission** *nf* permission, authorization; leave

**permissionnaire** *nm* serviceman on leave

**permutation** *nf* posting, transferring; permutation

**permuter** *vt* change over, permutate; *vi* exchange posts

**pernicieux -ieuse** *adj* pernicious, harmful; corrupting

**péroné** *nm anat* fibula

**péronnelle** *nf coll* silly talkative girl

**péroraison** *nf* peroration

**pérorer** *vi* perorate; speechify

**peroxyde** *nm* peroxide

**perpendiculaire** *nf + adj* perpendicular, upright

**perpendicularité** *nf* perpendicularity

**perpète, perpette (à)** *adv phr sl* for ever, for life

**perpétrer** *vt* (6) perpetrate

**perpétuel -uelle** *adj* perpetual, everlasting; endless, incessant

**perpétuer** *vt* perpetuate; **se ~** continue, endure, become established

**perpétuité** *nf* perpetuity; **à ~** for ever, for life

**perplexe** *adj* perplexed, puzzled

**perplexité** *nf* perplexity, indecision

**perquisition** *nf leg* search, perquisition; investigation

**perquisitionner** *vi leg* conduct a search

**perroquet** *nm* parrot; *naut* topgallant

**perruche** *nf* budgerigar; female parrot; *naut* mizzen topgallant; *coll* talkative woman

**perruque** *nf* wig; old fogey, reactionary

**perruquier** *nm* wig-maker

**pers** *adj m* bluish-green, sea-green

**Persan -e** *n* Persian

**persan** *nm* Persian language; *adj* Persian

**Perse** *nf* Persia

**¹perse** *adj* Persian

**²perse** *nf* chintz

**persécuter** *vt* persecute; importune, pester

**persécuteur -trice** *n* persecutor; *adj* persecuting

**persévérant** *adj* persevering, persisting

**persévérer** *vi* (6) persevere, persist

**persienne** *nf* slatted shutter, persienne

**persifler** *vt* banter, mock, rally

**persifleur -euse** *n* banterer, mocker; *adj* mocking

**persil** *nm* parsley

**persillade** *nf* parsley sauce (incl garlic, vinegar); cold sliced beef with parsley sauce

**persillé** *adj* with chopped parsley; blue-veined (cheese); marbled (meat)

**persistance** *nf* persistence, determination; continuance

**persistant** *adj* persistent; continuing

**persister** *vi* persist; continue

**personnage** *nm* personage, dignitary; character, role (novel, play); figure (picture); *pej* fellow

**personnaliser** *vt* personalize

**personnalité** *nf* personality, individuality; personage, dignitary

**¹personne** *nf* person, individual; personality; personal appearance; *gramm* person

**²personne** *pron invar* anyone, anybody; **~ ne le sait** no one knows; **connaissez-vous ~ qui puisse venir?** do you know anyone who can come?; **mieux que ~** better than anyone; **ne ... ~** no one, nobody; **il n'y a ~** there is no one; **qui est là? Personne** who is there? No one

**personnel** *nm* personnel, staff; *mil* complement; *adj* (*f* **-elle**) personal, individual, private

**personnifier** *vt* personify, incarnate

**perspectif -ive** *adj* perspective

**perspective** *nf* perspective, point of view; outlook, view

**perspicace** *adj* perspicacious

**perspicacité** *nf* perspicacity

**persuader** *vt* persuade, convince; **~ (à) qn de** induce s/o to; **se ~** become convinced, decide

**persuasif -ive** *adj* persuasive, convincing

**persuasion** *nf* persuasion; belief, conviction

**perte** *nf* loss; wastage, waste; destruction, ruin; **~ s** *med* excessive menstrual flow; **~ sèche** dead loss; **à ~ de vue** further than the eye can see; **en pure ~** to no purpose

**pertinemment** *adv* pertinently; **savoir ~** be precisely informed

**pertuis** *nm* sluice; *geog* narrows, strait; *ar* hole

**pertuisane** *nf hist* partisan, halberd

**perturbateur -trice** *n* disturber; *adj* disturbing

**perturbation** *nf* perturbation, agitation; disturbance (weather)

**pervenche** *nf bot* periwinkle

**pervers -e** *n*+*adj* perverse, depraved, vicious (person)

**perversité** *nf* perversity

**pervertir** *vt* pervert, corrupt; **se ~** become depraved, degenerate

**pesage** *nm* weighing; weighing-in (jockey); paddock (race-course)

**pesamment** *adv* heavily; slowly; with difficulty

**pesant** *adj* heavy, weighty; ponderous, sluggish

**pesanteur** *nf* weight, heaviness; *phys* gravity; dullness, sluggishness

**pèse-bébé** *nm* scales for weighing baby

**pesée** *nf* weighing; amount weighed at one time; leverage

**pèse-lettre** *nm* letter-balance

**peser** *vt* (6) weigh; *vi* be heavy; weigh; **~ à** be hard to bear; importune, tire; **~ sur** weigh on; press (lever, handle); **se ~** weigh oneself

**peseur -euse** *n* weigher; **~ juré** inspector of weights and measures

**pessaire** *nm* pessary

**pessimisme** *nm* pessimism

**pessimiste** *n* pessimist; *adj* pessimistic

**peste** *nf* plague, pestilence; infernal nuisance; *coll* **c'est une petite ~** she's a little bitch

**pester** *vi* curse, storm, vociferate

**pesteux -euse** *adj* plague-infected

**pestiféré -e** *n* victim of plague; *adj* plague-infected, plague-ridden

**pestilence** *nf* pestilence; putrid smell, stink

**pestilentiel -ielle** *adj* pestilential; stinking

**pet** *nm* fart; *sl* scandal, row; *coll* **ça ne vaut pas un ~ (de lapin)** it's of no importance at all; **lâcher un ~** fart

**pétale** *nm* petal

**pétanque** *nf* variant of French bowls (played in South)

**pétarade** *nf* series of bangs; series of farts (donkey, horse); crackling (rifle fire)

**pétarader** *vi* make series of bangs; back-fire; let off farts (donkey, horse); crackle (rifles)

**pétard** *nm* cracker, banger; blast, shot (mine, quarry); detonator (railway); *coll* din, row; *sl* revolver; *sl* arse

**pétaudière** *nf* meeting out of control, bear-garden

**pet-de-nonne** *nm* (*pl* **pets-de-nonne**) *cul* kind of small cream puff

**pet-en-l'air** *nm invar coll* short jacket, bum-freezer

**péter** *vi* (6) fart; break; explode, burst; *coll* **~ dans la soie** have very good clothes; **~ du feu** be full of energy; *coll* **~ plus haut que le cul** be very pretentious

**pètesec, pète-sec** *n*+*adj invar* disagreeably bossy (person)

**pétillant** *adj* sparkling; crackling

**pétillement** *nm* sparkling; crackling

**pétiller** *vi* bubble; sparkle; flash

**petit -e** *n* child; young animal, young bird; *nf* girl; *adj* little, small; insignificant, petty, slight, unimportant; mean, minor, paltry; small-minded; *rad* short (wave); *coll* nice little, precious; **~ coin (endroit)** lavatory; *mil* **~e tenue** undress uniform; **en ~ comité** in a small group; **mon ~ Michel** dear Michael (affection); **mon ~ monsieur** my dear good sir; *adv* **à ~ little by little; **en ~** in a small way

**petite-fille** *nf* (*pl* **petites-filles**) grand-daughter

**petitement** *adv* meanly; humbly

**petite-nièce** *nf* (*pl* **petites-nièces**) great-niece

**petitesse** *nf* littleness; pettiness; narrow-mindedness

**petit-fils** *nm* (*pl* **petits-fils**) grandson

**petit-gris** *nm* (*pl* **petits-gris**) *zool* kind of Siberian grey squirrel; fur of this grey squirrel; kind of snail

**pétition** *nf* request, petition

**petit-lait** *nm* whey

**petit-maître** *nm* (*pl* **petits-maîtres**) *hist* coxcomb, fop

**petit-nègre** *nm* incorrect (colonial) French ( = pidgin English)

**petit-neveu** *nm* (*pl* **petits-neveux**) great-nephew

**petits-enfants** *nmpl* grandchildren

**petit-suisse** *nm* (*pl* **petits-suisses**) small cream cheese

**pétoche** *nf sl* fear

**pétoire** *nf coll* (useless old) gun, pop-gun

**peton** *nm coll* little foot; tootsy-wootsy (child)

**pétrifier** *vt* petrify, turn into stone; *fig* freeze, paralyse; **se ~** turn into stone; become quite motionless

**pétrin** *nm* kneading-trough; *coll* mess, fix

**pétrir** *vt* knead; mould, shape; **pétri**

**d'ignorance** deeply ignorant; **pétri d'orgueil** consumed with pride

**pétrissage** *nm* kneading; moulding

**pétrisseur -euse** *n* kneader

**pétrochimie** *nf* petrochemistry

**pétrole** *nm* petroleum; paraffin; **bleu ~** blue-green

**pétrolette** *nf* light motorcycle

**pétrolier** *nm naut* tanker; oil-magnate; *adj* (*f* **-ière**) petrol (industry), oil (installations)

**pétrolifère** *adj* oil-bearing; **gisement ~** oil-field

**pétulance** *nf* ardour, liveliness

**pétulant** *adj* ardent, lively, sprightly

**peu** *nm* little, small quantity; **un ~** a little, a few, a bit; *adv* little, few, not enough; briefly; not very; **à ~** little by little; **~ de** a few, some; **~ s'en faut** very nearly; **avant ~** shortly; **de ~** narrowly; **depuis ~** lately, of late; **d'ici ~** a short time hence; **pour un ~** for two pins, for a little; **quelque ~** somewhat; **si ~ que** however little; **sous ~** shortly; **tant soit ~** just a little, the least bit

**peuh** *interj* pooh!

**peu ou prou** *adv phr see* **prou**

**peuplade** *nf* small tribe, small community

**peuple** *nm* people; nation; **bas ~** lower classes; **le ~** the people, the masses; **petit ~** humble people; *adj invar* plebeian, vulgar

**peuplement** *nm* peopling; stocking (with fish, game); afforestation

**peupler** *vt* people, populate; stock (fish, game); inhabit, throng; **se ~** become populous, fill with people

**peuplier** *nm* poplar

**peur** *nf* anguish, apprehension, fear, fright; **~ bleue** blue funk; **à faire ~** hideously; **avoir ~** be afraid; **de ~ de** for fear of; **de ~ que** lest; **en être quitte pour la ~** get off with a fright; **n'avoir pas ~ des mots** call things by their name, call a spade a spade

**peureux -euse** *adj* easily frightened, nervous, timid, timorous

**peut-être** *adv* maybe, perhaps, possibly

**pèze** *nm sl* money, dough

**phalange** *nf* phalanx; army, host; falange (Spain); finger-joint

**phalène** *nf or m ent* moth, phalena

**phallique** *adj* phallic

**phantasme** *nm see* **fantasme**

**pharamineux** *adj see* **faramineux**

**pharaon** *nm* Pharaoh; faro (card-game)

**phare** *nm* lighthouse; airport beacon; headlight; *rad* beacon; *aer* **~ d'atterrissage** landing light; **mot ~s** code dipped headlights

**pharisien -ienne** *n* Pharisee

**pharmaceutique** *nf* pharmaceutics; *adj* pharmaceutic(al)

**pharmacie** *nf* pharmacy; chemist's shop, dispensary; medicine cupboard; contents of medicine cupboard; **~ de poche** first-aid kit

**pharmacien -ienne** *n* chemist

**pharmacologie** *nf* pharmacology

**pharmacopée** *nf* pharmacopoeia

**pharyngite** *nf* pharyngitis

**phase** *nf* phase; aspect, stage

**phénix** *nm* phoenix

**phénoménal** *adj* phenomenal; *coll* marvellous, terrific

**phénomène** *nm* phenomenon; marvel, prodigy; freak (monster); *coll* odd character, queer fish

**philanthrope** *n* philanthropist

**philanthropie** *nf* philanthropy

**philanthropique** *adj* philanthropic

**philatélie** *nf* philately

**philatélique** *adj* philatelic

**philatéliste** *n* philatelist

**philharmonie** *nf* local orchestra

**philharmonique** *adj* philharmonic

**philippique** *nf* philippic

**philistin** *nm* + *adj m* Philistine

**philistinisme** *nm* Philistinism

**philo** *nf coll* philosophy

**philologie** *nf* philology

**philologique** *adj* philological

**philologue** *n* philologist

**philosophale** *adj f* **pierre ~** philosopher's stone

**philosophe** *n* philosopher; thinker; *adj* philosophical; resigned, sensible, wise

**philosopher** *vi* philosophize

**philosophie** *nf* philosophy; one of the top forms in lycée

**philosophique** *adj* philosophic(al)

**phlébite** *nf med* phlebitis

**phlogistique** *nm* phlogiston

**phobie** *nf med* phobia; aversion, fear

**phonème** *nm* phoneme, phone

**phonémique** *adj* phonemic

**phonéticien -ienne** *n* phonetician

**phonétique** *nf* phonetics; *adj* phonetic

**phonique** *adj* phonic

**phonographe** *nm* gramophone; *obs* phonograph

**phonographique** *adj* phonographic

**phonologie** *nf* phonology

**phonothèque** *nf* sound archives

**phoque** *nm zool* seal

**phosphater** *vt* fertilize (soil) with phosphates

**phosphore** *nm* phosphorus

**phosphorer** *vi coll* study, swot

**phosphoreux -euse** *adj* phosphorous

**phosphure** *nm* phosphide

**photochimie** *nf* photochemistry

**photochimique** *adj* photochemical
**photocopie** *nf* photocopying; photostat
**photocopier** *vt* photocopy
**photo-électrique** *adj* photo-electric
**photogénique** *adj* photogenic
**photographe** *n* photographer
**photographie** *nf* photography; photograph
**photographier** *vt* photograph; reproduce with minute accuracy
**photographique** *adj* photographic
**photograveur** *nm* photo-engraver; block-maker
**photogravure** *nf* photo-engraving; photogravure (process, print)
**photomécanique** *adj* photomechanical
**photomètre** *nm* photometer
**photométrie** *nf* photometry
**photométrique** *adj* photometric
**photostoppeur** *nm* street photographer
**photosynthèse** *nf* photosynthesis
**photothèque** *nf* photographic archives
**phrase** *nf* sentence; *mus* phrase; **faire des ~s** indulge in flowery language; **sans ~s** without comment
**phraséologie** *nf* phraseology
**phraser** *vt mus* phrase
**phraseur -euse** *n* declaimer, flowery speaker
**phrénologie** *nf* phrenology
**phrénologiste** *n* phrenologist
**phrygien -ienne** *adj* Phrygian; **bonnet ~** Phrygian cap worn by revolutionaries in 1789; symbol of liberty
**phtisie** *nf med* phthisis; *ar* consumption, pulmonary consumption
**phtisique** *n + adj ar* consumptive
**phylactère** *nm* phylactery
**physicien -ienne** *n* physicist; *ar* natural philosopher
**physico-chimie** *nf* physical chemistry
**physico-chimique** *adj* physico-chemical
**physiognomonie** *nf ar* study of physiognomy
**physiologie** *nf* physiology
**physiologique** *adj* physiological
**physiologiste** *n* physiologist
**physionomie** *nf* physiognomy; face, physical features; expression; appearance, aspect
**physionomiste** *n* one who has a memory for faces; good judge of faces
**physique** *nm* physique, physical qualities; *nf* physics; *adj* physical
**piaf** *nm sl* sparrow
**piaffement** *nm* pawing the ground (horse); prancing, stamping
**piaffer** *vi* paw the ground (horse); prance, stamp
**piaillement** *nm* chirp, squawk (bird); squall, squeal
**piailler** *vi* chirp, squawk (bird); *coll*

squall, squeal
**piailleur -euse** *n coll* child (person) given to squealing; *adj* chirping, squawking (bird)
**pianiste** *n* pianist
**piano** *adv mus* piano; *coll* gently
**pianoter** *vi* strum, play badly; rattle, tap
**piaule** *nf sl* room
**piauler** *vi* chirp; whimper
¹**pic** *nm* pick, pick-axe; peak; summit of mountain; naut peak; **à ~** sheer, vertical; *coll* at the right moment; **couler à ~** founder
²**pic** *nm* woodpecker
**pichenette** *nf* fillip
**pichet** *nm* jug, pitcher
**picoler** *vi sl* drink a lot, soak
**picorer** *vt* pick up (food) (bird); *vi* scratch about for food (of bird)
**picot** *nm* splinter (wood); pick-hammer; picot (needlework)
**picoté** *adj* pimpled, pock-marked
**picotement** *nm* prickling, tingling
**picoter** *vt* prick holes in, pit; peck; sting, cause (eyes) to smart
**picrique** *adj chem* picric
**pictural** *adj* to do with painting, pictorial
**picvert** *nm see* **pivert**
¹**pie** *nf* magpie
²**pie** *adj invar* piebald; **voiture ~** black and white police-car
³**pie** *adj f* pious
**pièce** *nf* fragment, piece; single piece, unit; head (cattle, game); coin; gun; certificate, document, papers; *theat* play; room; piece, part, patch; cask (wine); liquid measure of about forty-eight gallons; *her* ordinary; **~ à conviction** exhibit (criminal trial); **~ d'eau** ornamental lake, pond; **~ de musée** show-piece; **~ de rechange** spare part; **~ de terre** field, plot; **~s justificatives** supporting documents; **cul ~ montée** ornamental piece of confectionery; **deux ~s** two-piece costume; two-roomed flat; **être tout d'une ~** be uncomplicated; be all in one piece; **faire ~ à qn** play a nasty trick on s/o; **inventé de toutes ~s** completely untrue, totally fabricated; **six francs ~** six francs each; **travail aux ~s (à la ~)** piece-work
**piècette** *nf* small coin
**pied** *nm* foot; hoof; base, leg, stand; foothold; track (hunting); *hist* French unit of measurement = $12\frac{3}{4}$ inches; English foot; **~ de fer** cobbler's last; **à ~, à cheval et en voiture** in every possible way; **au petit ~** diminutive, pint-size; **au ~ levé** off the cuff, unprepared; **avoir le ~ marin** be a

good sailor (i.e. not seasick); *coll* **avoir les ~ s nickelés** refuse to budge, be lazy; *coll* **casser les ~ s** bother, be a bloody nuisance; *coll* **comme un ~** very badly; **coup de ~** kick; **coup de ~ de pénalité** penalty (football); **de ~ en cap** from tip to toe; **de ~ ferme** with determination; **en ~** full-length (portrait); **faire des ~ s et des mains** use every possible means; **faire du ~ à qn** give warning kick to s/o; play footsie with s/o; **faire les ~ s à** teach, give experience to; **fouler aux ~ s** trample (underfoot); **lâcher ~** give ground; **lever le ~** run off with the cash-box; **marcher sur les ~ s de qn** treat s/o without consideration; try to supplant s/o; **mettre les ~ s dehors** go outside; **mettre qn à ~** give s/o the sack; **mettre qn au ~ du mur** call for a straightforward answer from s/o; **ne pas savoir sur quel ~ danser** be undecided, be uncertain what line to take; **se lever du ~ gauche** get out of bed on the wrong side; **y mettre les ~ s** set foot there

**pied-bot** *nm see* **bot**

**pied-d'alouette** *nm* ( *pl* **pieds-d'alouette**) *bot* delphinium, larkspur

**pied-de-biche** *nm* ( *pl* **pieds-de-biche**) cabriole leg; kind of bell-pull or door knocker; *mech* nail-claw; guide on sewing-machine

**pied-de-poule** *nm* ( *pl* **pieds-de-poule**) + *adj invar* broken check (cloth)

**piédestal** *nm* pedestal

**pied-noir** *nm* ( *pl* **pieds-noirs**) *coll* French colonist in Algeria

**piège** *nm* snare, trap; ambush, hidden danger

**piéger** *vt* (6, 3) trap; arm (mine)

**pie-grièche** *nf* ( *pl* **pies-grièches**) *orni* shrike; *coll* harpy, shrew

**pierraille** *nf* rubble, small stones

**pierre** *nf* stone; rock; *med* stone; precious stone; **~ à aiguiser** whetstone; **~ à briquet** lighter-flint; **~ à fusil** gun-flint; **~ bleue** washing blue; **~ de taille** ashlar; **~ levée** raised stone (druidical, etc); **apporter sa ~ à l'édifice** contribute one's mite; **faire d'une ~ deux coups** kill two birds with one stone

**pierreries** *nfpl* jewels, precious stones

**pierreux -euse** *adj* stony; in stone; gritty (pear)

**pierrot** *nm* sparrow; pierrot, clown

**piété** *nf* piety, devotion; affection, respect, tenderness

**piétinement** *nm* stamping, trampling; sound of stamping crowd; marking time, stagnation

**piétiner** *vt* stamp on, trample on; **~ un cadavre** insult the memory of dead person; *vi* stamp one's feet, mark time; stamp along; *fig* make little or no progress

**piétisme** *nm hist* pietism

**piéton** *nm* + *adj* ( *f* -**onne**) pedestrian

**piètre** *adj lit* mediocre, miserable, wretched

¹**pieu** *nm* post, stake; *eng* pile

²**pieu** *nm sl* bed, kip

**pieuter** *vi sl* turn in, kip down

**pieuvre** *nf* octopus, devil-fish; *fig* limpet

**pieux -euse** *adj* devout, pious; *lit* devoted

**pif** *nm sl* big nose, nose, conk

**pifer, piffer** *vt sl* put up with, stand

**pige** *nf* measuring-rod; *sl* year (of age); *coll* payment by the line ( journalist); *sl* **faire la ~ à** go one better than

**pigeon** *nm* pigeon; *coll* dupe; **~ ramier** wood-pigeon; **~ voyageur** carrier pigeon, homing pigeon

**pigeonneau** *nm* young pigeon

**pigeonner** *vt coll* dupe

**pigeonnier** *nm* pigeon-loft, dovecot

**piger** *vt* (3) *sl* cotton on to, understand; pay; *ar* catch, get hold of

**pigmentaire** *adj* pigmentary

**pigmenté** *adj* pigmented

**pigne** *nf* pine-cone

**pignocher** *vi coll* peck at one's food; paint with small finicky brush-strokes

¹**pignon** *nm* gable, gable-end; **avoir ~ sur rue** have a flourishing business situated in a good position; *ar* have a house of one's own

²**pignon** *nm mech* pinion

³**pignon** *nm bot* pine-seed

**pignouf** *nm sl* uncouth bastard, lout

**pilastre** *nm* pilaster

¹**pile** *nf* heap, pile; pier (bridge); battery; pile (atomic)

²**pile** *nf coll* thrashing; crushing defeat

³**pile** *nf* **~ ou face** heads or tails; **jouer à ~ ou face** toss up

⁴**pile** *adv coll* exactly; **ça tombe ~** just what's wanted; **s'arrêter ~** stop dead

**piler** *vt* crush, grind, pound; *coll* thrash; defeat

**pileux -euse** *adj* pilose, hairy

**pilier** *nm* column, pillar; *fig* support; prop-forward (rugby football); **~ de cabaret** s/o always to be found propping up the bar

**pillage** *nm* looting, pillage

**pillard -e** *n* looter, pillager; plagiarist; *adj* looting, pillaging

**piller** *vt* loot, pillage; plagiarize

**pilleur -euse** *n* looter, pillager; plagiarist

**pilon** *nm* pestle; earth-rammer; steam-hammer; *cul* drumstick; wooden leg; **mettre un livre au ~** pulp a book

**pilonnage** *nm* crushing; heavy bombardment

**pilonner** *vt* crush; bombard heavily

**pilori** *nm* pillory; **mettre au ~** pillory, put in the pillory

**pilosité** *nf* pilosity, hairiness

**pilot** *nm eng* pile

**pilotage** *nm* piloting

**pilote** *nm* pilot; driver; pilot-fish; *adj* pilot, experimental, model

**piloter** *vt* pilot; drive; guide

**pilotis** *nm eng* piling

**pilou** *nm* flannelette

**pilule** *nf* pill

**pimbêche** *nf* uppish and disagreeable woman; *coll* affected bitch

**piment** *nm* capsicum, pimento; red pepper; *fig* seasoning, spice

**pimenter** *vt* season with red pepper; *fig* give spice to

**pimpant** *adj* smart, spruce

**pimprenelle** *nf bot* pimpernel

**pin** *nm* pine-tree

**pinacle** *nm archi* pinnacle; *fig* exalted position; **porter qn au ~** praise s/o to the skies

**pinard** *nm sl* wine

**pince** *nf* pincers, pliers, tongs; clip; *sl* hand; pleat, tuck; claw (crab, lobster); **~ à linge** clothes-peg; *sl* **aller à ~s** go on foot

**pincé** *adj* affected, constrained, prim; thin

**pinceau** *nm* (artist's) paint-brush; painting; technique of painter; beam (light); *sl* foot

**pincée** *nf* pinch

**pince-fesse(s)** *nm invar sl* cheap dance-hall

**pincement** *nm* pinching; *mus* plucking; pruning, topping; **~ au cœur** spasm of anguish

**pince-monseigneur** *nf* (*pl* **pinces-mon-seigneur**) (burglar's) jemmy

**pincer** *vt* (4) nip, pinch; *mus* pluck; pinch off; prune, top; *coll* catch, cop, nab; *coll* **ça pince** it's very cold; **en ~ pour qn** be in love with s/o

**pince-sans-rire** *n invar + adj* unsmilingly ironical (person)

**pincette** *nf* small pincers, tweezers; **~s** fire-tongs; **il n'est pas à prendre avec des ~s** he is filthy dirty; he is extremely bad-tempered

**pinçon** *nm* mark left by pinch

**pine** *nf vulg* penis, prick

**pinède** *nf* pine-wood

**pingouin** *nm* auk; penguin

**pingre** *n* miser; *adj* miserly

**pingrerie** *nf* miserliness

**pinot** *nm* kind of vine

**pinson** *nm* finch; **gai comme un ~** happy as a lark

**pintade** *nf* guinea-fowl

**pintadeau** *nm* young guinea-fowl

**pinte** *nf ar* (French) pint ( = 1¾ English pints); glass containing a pint; (English) pint

**pinter** *vi sl* drink hard, soak

**piochage** *nm* digging; *fig* hard study, swotting

**pioche** *nf* pick, pickaxe; mattock; *coll* **une tête de ~** a very obstinate person

**piocher** *vt* dig up; *coll* swot at; *vi coll* swot

**piocheur** *nm* navvy; *n* (*f* **-euse**) *coll* swot; hard worker

**piocheuse** *nf* scarifier

**piolet** *nm* ice-axe

**pion** *nm* pawn (chess); piece (draughts); *coll* junior master

**pioncer** *vi* (4) *sl* sleep, snooze

**pionne** *nf* junior mistress

**pionnier** *nm* pioneer

**pioupiou** *nm ar* young infantryman, tommy

**pipe** *nf* pipe; large cask; *ar* reed pipe, tube; pipeful; **~ d'aération** ventilation pipe; **~ d'alimentation** conveyor-pipe; *sl* **casser sa ~** die; *sl* **par tête de ~** per person; **se fendre la ~** burst with laughter

**pipeau** *nm* reed-pipe, shepherd's pipe

**pipelet -ette** *n sl* concierge

**piper** *vt* snare (birds); load (dice); *vi* **ne pas ~** say not a word

**piperade** *nf cul* Basque dish (eggs, tomatoes, peppers)

**pipi** *nm coll* (or child's term) pee, piss; **faire ~** pee, piss; **~ de chat** nasty wine

**pipistrelle** *nf zool* small bat

**piquage** *nm* stitching (with sewing machine); piercing, making small holes

**piquant** *nm* prickle, thorn; quill, spine; *fig* piquancy; *adj* pricking, stinging; pungent; stimulating; wounding

¹**pique** *nf* pike (weapon); wounding word, phrase

²**pique** *nm* spade (cards)

**piqué** *nm* piqué, quilting; nose-dive; **bombardement en ~** dive-bombing; *adj* quilted; stitched; fly-blown, mildewed; sour (wine); *mus* staccato; *coll* cracked, round the bend

**pique-assiette** *n invar* sponger, parasite

**pique-feu** *nm invar* poker

**pique-nique** *nm* picnic

**pique-niquer** *vi* picnic

**pique-niqueur -euse** *n* picnicker

**pique-notes** *nm invar* spike-file

**piquer** *vt* goad; prick, puncture; bite, sting; sew, stitch; inoculate; pin up, stitch; impress; nettle, pique; quilt; *coll* pinch, steal, acquire, take; *coll* arrest;

have an attack of; *mus* play staccato; ~ **au vif** cut to the quick; ~ **des deux** go at full gallop; ~ **une tête** rush head first, take a dive; ~ **un fard (un soleil)** blush; **ça me pique** that itches, I'm itching; **quelle mouche te pique?** what's biting you?; *vi* gallop; dive, fall; **se** ~ prick oneself; give oneself an injection; become mildewed; become sour (wine); become angry; **se** ~ **de** claim to be; *coll* **se** ~ **le nez** get drunk

**piquet** *nm* picket, post, stake; *mil* picket; punishment of standing in the corner; ~ **de grève** strike picket

**piqueter** *vt* (5) mark out with stakes; dot with

**piquette** *nf* beverage made from fermented marc with water; sharp, poor wine; **ce n'est pas de la** ~ it's not a trifling matter

**piqueur -euse** *n* stitcher; *nm* whipper-in (hunting); stable-lad; platelayer (railway); road engineer; workman using pneumatic drill

**piqûre** *nf* bite, sting; stitching, quilting; puncture, small hole; worm-hole; injection; patch of mildew

**pirate** *nm* pirate; *fig* unscrupulous businessman; shark, swindler; ~ **de l'air** hijacker; *rad* **poste radio** ~ pirate station

**pirater** *vi* be a pirate

**piraterie** *nf* piracy; swindle

**pire** *nm* **le** ~ the worst; **au** ~ at the worst; *adj* worse; worst

**pirogue** *nf* dug-out canoe

**pirouetter** *vi* pirouette

¹**pis** *nm* teat, udder

²**pis** *nm* **le** ~ the worst; *adj invar lit* worse; **dire** ~ **que pendre de qn** say the most appalling things about s/o; *adv* worse; worst; **au** ~ **aller** if the worst comes to the worst

**pis-aller** *nm invar* last resource, makeshift

**pisciculteur** *nm* one who breeds fish

**piscine** *nf* swimming-bath, swimming-pool

**pissaladière** *nf cul* Provençal dish like Italian pizza

**pisse** *nf vulg* piss

**pisse-froid** *nm invar coll* boring, morose individual

**pissenlit** *nm bot* dandelion; *coll* **manger les** ~ **s par la racine** push up the daisies

**pisser** *vt* piss (out); cause to flow; leak; *vi vulg* piss; *coll* **il pleut comme vache qui pisse** it's pissing with rain; **c'est comme si on pissait dans un violon** it's a complete waste of time, it's a quite pointless thing to do

**pisseur -euse** *n vulg* pisser; *nf coll* little girl; ~ **de copie** hack journalist

**pisseux -euse** *adj coll* impregnated with, smelling of urine; of the colour of urine

**pissoir** *nm coll* urinal

**pissotière** *nf coll* urinal

**pistache** *nf* + *adj invar* pistachio (nut)

**piste** *nf* track; cycle-track, race-track, running-track; *aer* runway; ring (circus); rink (skating); dance-floor; ~ **sonore** sound-track

**pister** *vt* track; shadow

**pistolet** *nm* pistol; spray-gun; bread roll (in Belgium); *naut* davit; *coll* queer fish; **pistolet-mitrailleur** *nm* (*pl* **pistolets-mitrailleurs**) sub-machine gun

**piston** *nm* piston; *mus* valve; *fig* influence, wire-pulling

**pistonner** *vt* back, pull strings for

**pistou** *nm cul* **soupe de (au)** ~ Provençal soup with chopped basil

**pitchpin** *nm* pitch-pine

**piteux -euse** *adj* piteous, pitiable, woeful; derisory; **en** ~ **état** in a bad way

**pitié** *nf* compassion, pity; **faire** ~ arouse pity; **par** ~ for pity's sake

**piton** *nm* ring, bolt; sharp peak; piton

**pitoyable** *adj* pitiable; paltry

**pitre** *nm* clown; buffoon

**pitrerie** *nf* clowning; buffoonery

**pittoresque** *nm* picturesqueness; brilliance, vividness; *adj* picturesque; brilliant, vivid

**pituitaire** *adj anat* pituitary

**pivert, picvert** *nm orni* green woodpecker

**pivoine** *nf bot* peony

**pivot** *nm* pivot, pin, swivel; *fig* centre; tap-root

**pivoter** *vi* pivot, swing round, wheel

**placage** *nm* facing (marble, stone), plating, veneering; tackle (rugby, football)

**placard** *nm* built-in cupboard; placard, poster; large advertisement in paper; *print* galley proof

**placarder** *vt* post up, stick up; placard; print (a galley proof)

**place** *nf* place, position; square (in town); garrison town; *comm* market; seat; room, space; job, situation; ~ **entière** full fare; ~ **forte** fortress; *comm* **avoir du crédit sur la** ~ be thought a sound man financially; **demi-** ~ half fare; **être à sa** ~ be in the right place; **être en** ~ have a job; **faire la** ~ do the rounds (as commercial traveller); **mise en** ~ arrangement, installing; **remettre qn à sa** ~ put s/o in his place; **rester en** ~ keep still; **sur** ~ on the spot; **voiture de** ~ taxi, hire-car

**placement** *nm* investing, investment; placing; seating (at table); **bureau de** ~ employment agency

**placer** *vt* (4) lay, place, put, set down; find (s/o) a job; locate, situate (story); insert (remark); sell; invest; seat (guests); post (sentries); land (blow); marry (daughter); **se ~** seat oneself; place oneself; take a job

**placeur -euse** *n* steward (meeting); usher (theatre); head of employment agency

**placide** *adj* placid

**placidité** *nf* placidity

**placier -ière** *n* agent, canvasser, seller

**plafond** *nm* ceiling; maximum; *aer* ceiling; *mot* maximum speed

**plafonnage** *nm* installation of ceiling; *archi* ceiling work

**plafonner** *vt* instal a ceiling in; *vi* reach ceiling (aircraft, price)

**plafonnier** *nm* ceiling light, ceiling fitting

**plage** *nf* beach, shore; seaside resort; *naut* freeboard deck; band (on gramophone record)

**plagiaire** *n* plagiarist

**plagiat** *nm* plagiarism, plagiary

**plagier** *vt* plagiarize; imitate

**plaid** *nm* travelling-rug

**plaidant** *adj leg* pleading

**plaider** *vt* plead (case); allege, put forward; *vi leg* go to law; plead

**plaideur -euse** *n leg* litigant

**plaidoirie** *nf leg* counsel's speech; plea

**plaidoyer** *nm leg* speech in defence; *fig* defence

**plaie** *nf* wound; cut, sore; *fig* wound, running sore; *fig* curse

**plaignant -e** *n leg* plaintiff; complainer; *adj leg* **partie ~ e** plaintiff

**plain** *adj ar* level

**plain-chant** *nm* (*pl* **plains-chants**) plainsong

**plaindre** *vt* (55) pity; **se ~** complain, protest

**plaine** *nf* plain, flat country

**plain-pied** *adv* **de ~** on the same level; *fig* with no trouble; **être de ~ avec qn** get on well with s/o

**plainte** *nf* groan, moan, sigh; complaint; *leg* complaint, indictment; **déposer une ~ (dresser ~ , porter ~)** bring an action

**plaintif -ive** *adj* plaintive; complaining, querulous

**plaire** *vi* (69) charm, content, fascinate, please, satisfy; be pleasant; be loved; **se ~** be pleased with oneself; take pleasure; enjoy oneself; like one another; flourish (plant); **s'il vous plaît** please; I'd have you know; **plaît-il?** pardon?, what did you say?

**plaisamment** *adv* agreeably, pleasantly; absurdly, ridiculously

**plaisance** *nf ar lit* pleasure; **bateau de ~** pleasure craft; **maison de ~** country retreat

**plaisant** *nm* amusing side, what is amusing; jester, joker; **mauvais ~** practical joker; one who makes jokes in bad taste; *adj* pleasant, agreeable; amusing, funny; absurd, ridiculous

**plaisanter** *vt* banter, chaff; *vi* jest, joke, not be serious

**plaisanterie** *nf* joke; joking; absurdity; something very easy; push-over; **mauvaise ~** silly joke, nasty trick

**plaisir** *nm* contentment, delight, enjoyment, pleasure; satisfaction, well-being; amusement; sexual pleasure; **à ~** as much as one wants; wantonly; **au ~ de vous revoir** (*coll* **au ~**) until we meet again (see you soon); *joc* **menus ~ s** minor amusements; **vous me ferez ~ de** you would be doing me a kindness by

¹**plan** *nm* plane, surface; *cin* take; *cin* **gros ~** close-up; **premier ~** foreground; *theat* downstage; *theat* **second ~** up-stage; **sur le ~ de** as regards; *adj* flat, smooth; plane

²**plan** *nm* plan; blue-print, drawing; street map; design, plan, project; **~ horizontal** ground-plan; **laisser qn en ~** leave s/o in the lurch; **laisser son travail en ~** stop working; **lever un ~** draw up a plan

**planche** *nf* board, plank; block, engraving, plate; strip of land; *coll* ski; **~ s** *theat* boards, stage; *naut* gang-plank; **~ à roulettes** skate-board; **~ à voile** wind-surf board; *aer* **~ de bord** instrument panel; **~ de salut** last resort, sheet anchor; **être cloué entre quatre ~ s** be in one's coffin; **faire la ~** float on one's back

**planchéier** *vt* board over, floor

**plancher** *nm* floor; **~ des vaches** terra firma; *coll* **débarrasser le ~** run for it, clear out; *coll mot* **mettre le pied au ~** put one's foot down; **prix ~** minimum authorized price

**planchette** *nf* small plank, shelf; plane-table

**plancton** *nm zool* plankton

**plané** *adj* **vol ~** glide; *coll* **faire un vol ~** fall, tumble

¹**planer** *vt* plane

²**planer** *vi* glide; float in the air, soar; *fig* be in the air, threaten

**planétaire** *adj* planetary

**planète** *nf* planet

¹**planeur -euse** *n* planisher; *nf* **planeuse** planing machine

²**planeur** *nm* glider

**planifier** *vt* plan

**planning** *nm* work schedule

**planque** *nf coll* cushy job; *sl* hideout, hiding-place

**planquer** *vt sl* hide; *sl se* ~ hide, lie low

**plant** *nm hort* (nursery) plantation (trees); bed (plants); slip (seedling)

**plantaire** *adj anat* plantar

**plantation** *nf* planting; plantation; *theat* fit-up

¹**plante** *nf* plant; ~s **potagères** vegetables; **jardin des** ~s botanical gardens

²**plante** *nf* sole (of the foot)

**planté** *adj* stuck; **bien** ~ well set up; **rester** ~ remain standing

**planter** *vt* plant; stick in; set up; knock in (nail); *theat* fit up; establish (character); ~ **là qn** leave s/o standing; **se** ~ be planted; stand stock still

**planteur** *nm* planter (*esp* tropics)

**planteuse** *nf* potato planting machine

**plantoir** *nm* dibble

**planton** *nm mil* orderly; orderly duty; *coll* **faire le** ~ stand waiting

**plantureux -euse** *adj* abundant, copious; buxom

**plaquage** *nm* tackle (rugby, football); *sl* ~ **de** walking out on (girl)

**plaque** *nf* plate, sheet; badge, plaque, sign; patch, blotch; ~ **d'identité** identity plate, identity disc; *mot* ~ **d'immatriculation (minéralogique)** number plate; ~ **tournante** turntable; important centre

**plaqué** *nm* (metal) plating; plated metal; **montre** ~ **or** gold-plated watch

**plaquer** *vt* plate, plaster, veneer; tackle (rugby, football); *mus* hold (chord); *coll* abandon, walk out on; push; thrust; **se** ~ lie flat; plaster (hair)

**plaquette** *nf* small plate, tablet; booklet, opuscule

**plaqueur -euse** *n* plater

**plasmatique** *adj* plasmatic

**plastic** *nm* plastic explosive

**plasticage, plastiquage** *nm* bomb outrage

**plasticité** *nf* plasticity

**plastique** *nm* plastic; *nf* plastic art; *adj* plastic; malleable

**plastiquer** *vt* blow up with plastic explosive

**plastron** *nm* breastplate; fencing jacket; shirt front, bodice front

**plastronner** *vt* protect (with breastplate); *vi* pose, strut, throw out one's chest

¹**plat** *nm* flat, flat part; board (bookbinding); *coll* **faire du** ~ **à qn** flatter s/o; *adj* even, flat, level; lank, straight (hair); low (heel); thin; dull; flat, mediocre; **angle** ~ angle of 180°; **à** ~ horizontally; **à** ~ **ventre** flat on one's face; obsequiously; **être à** ~ be exhausted; be broke; have a flat tyre; *lit*

**rimes** ~**es** couplets with alternating masculine and feminine rhymes

²**plat** *nm* dish, plate; *cul* course, dish; ~ **garni** meat (or fish) with vegetables; **mettre les petits** ~**s dans les grands** take a lot of trouble over entertaining s/o, bring out the red carpet; *coll* **mettre les pieds dans le** ~ drop a brick; **œufs au** ~, **œufs sur le** ~ fried eggs; **servir à qn un** ~ **de sa façon** tear s/o apart, tell s/o off

**platane** *nm bot* plane-tree

**plat-bord** *nm* (*pl* **plats-bords**) *naut* gunwale

**plateau** *nm* salver; tray; board (cheese); turntable (record player); *geog* plateau; platform; *theat* stage; *cin* set; ~ **continental** continental shelf

**plate-bande** *nf* (*pl* **plates-bandes**) flower-bed; *archi* flat moulding; flat lintel; **marcher sur les** ~**s de qn** encroach on s/o's preserves, tread on s/o's toes

**platée** *nf* dishful

**plate-forme** *nf* (*pl* **plates-formes**) platform, terrace; *mil* gun-platform; open wagon (railway); *pol* programme

¹**platine** *nm* platinum; *adj invar* platinum (coloured)

²**platine** *nf* plate (lock, watch); *typ* platen; stage (microscope)

**platiné** *adj* platinum-plated; dyed platinum

**platiner** *vt* plate with platinum

**platitude** *nf* flatness, mediocrity; banality, platitude; servility; servile act

**platonicien -ienne** *adj* Platonist

**platonique** *adj* Platonic; platonic, pure; theoretical

**platonisme** *nm* Platonism

**plâtrage** *nm* plastering; plaster-work

**plâtras** *nm* debris of plaster-work; rubble; weight (on stomach)

**plâtre** *nm* plaster; plaster-cast; ~**s** plaster-work; ~ **à mouler** plaster of Paris; **battre qn comme** ~ flatten s/o, reduce s/o to pulp; **essuyer les** ~**s** be the first occupant; suffer the initial consequences; **pierre à** ~ gypsum

**plâtrer** *vt* plaster, plaster up; put into plaster; lime (field); plaster (wine); *coll* make (one's face) up badly

**plâtrerie** *nf* plastering; plaster works

**plâtrier** *nm* plasterer

**plâtrière** *nf* gypsum quarry; gypsum kiln

**plausibilité** *nf* plausibility

**plèbe** *nf* plebs

**plébéien -ienne** *n* + *adj* plebeian

**plébiscite** *nm* plebiscite, referendum

**plébisciter** *vt* approve (sth), elect (s/o) by referendum; approve (sth) or elect (s/o) by overwhelming majority

**plein** *nm* fill; bull's eye; downstroke (handwriting); **battre son** ～ be at its height (tide); *fig* be in full swing; **donner son** ～ give of one's best; *mot* **faire le** ～ fill up with petrol; *adj* full; crowded; massive, solid; plump (cheeks); complete, total; fresh (air); ～**e** pregnant (animal); ～ **aux** as very rich, rolling in it; **à** ～ fully, totally; **à** ～**e gorge** at the top of one's voice; **avoir le nez** ～ have one's nose blocked up; **en avoir** ～ **la bouche de** be always talking about; *coll* **en avoir** ～ **le dos** be fed up with; *coll* **en avoir** ～ **les bottes** be tired out from walking; **en** ～ fully, totally; in the midst; **en** ～ **dans (sur)** exactly in (on), right in (on); **en** ～ **jour** in broad daylight; *sl* **être** ～ be drunk, be pissed; *coll* **un gros** ～ **de soupe** a very fat man; *adv* **sonner** ～ give out clear, full sound; *coll* **tout** ～ very

**plein-emploi** *nm invar* full employment

**plénier -ière** *adj* plenary

**plénipotentiaire** *nm* plenipotentiary

**plénitude** *nf* plenitude, fullness; ampleness

**plénum** *nm* plenary session

**pléonasme** *nm* pleonasm

**pléonastique** *adj* pleonastic

**plésiosaure** *nm* plesiosaurus

**pléthore** *nf* plethora, superabundance

**pléthorique** *adj* abundant, overcrowded; *med* plethoric

**pleur** *nm* tear; ～**s** tears, weeping

**pleurard -e** *n coll* weeper, whimperer; *adj* tearful, whimpering

**pleurer** *vt* mourn, regret; weep (tears); *coll* ～ **misère** complain; *vi* cry, shed tears, whine; water (eyes); ～ **à chaudes larmes** weep bitterly; ～ **comme une vache** (*coll* **comme un veau**) weep buckets; **à** ～ (**à faire** ～) extremely

**pleurésie** *nf* pleurisy

**pleurétique** *n + adj* pleuritic (patient)

**pleureur -euse** *n* weeper, person given to whining; *adj* tearful, weeping, whining; *bot* with drooping branches; **saule** ～ weeping willow

**pleurnichement** *nm,* **pleurnicherie** *nf coll* snivelling, whining

**pleurnicher** *vi coll* snivel, whine

**pleurnicheur -euse** *n* sniveller; *adj* snivelling, whining

**pleutre** *nm* coward; *adj* cowardly

**pleuvasser, pleuvoter** *vi* rain intermittently

**pleuviner, pluviner** *vi* drizzle

**pleuvoir** *vi* (70) *impers* rain; *vi* rain down, fall down; **il pleut à verse (à flots, à seaux, à torrents)** it's raining cats and dogs, it's raining buckets; *sl* **il**

**pleut des cordes** it's pouring with rain

**pleuvoter** *vi see* **pleuvasser**

**plèvre** *nf anat* pleura

**pli** *nm* fold, pleat; wrinkle; crease; fall, hang (of garment); cover, envelope; habit; trick (cards); *geol* fold; **faux** ～ crease; **mise en** ～**s** setting (hair); **prendre un** ～ acquire a habit

**pliable** *adj* easily folded, pliable

**pliage** *nm* folding

**pliant** *nm* camp-stool, folding stool; *adj* collapsible, folding

**plie** *nf zool* plaice

**plier** *vt* fold, fold up; roll up; strike (tent); bend; *fig* cause to bend, make obey; *vi* bend; give way; **se** ～ **à** give in to, give way to, obey, yield to

**plinthe** *nf* plinth

**plioir** *nm* folding machine; paper-knife; winder (fishing-line)

**plissage** *nm* folding, putting in creases

**plissé** *nm* pleating; *adj* folded, creased; pleated

**plissement** *nm* corrugation, creasing, wrinkling; *geog* folding

**plisser** *vt* fold, crease; pleat; *vi* crease, crumple; **se** ～ crease, be creased, wrinkle

**pliure** *nf* crease, mark made by crease; *typ* folding

**ploiement** *nm* bending, folding

**plomb** *nm* lead; *naut* lead; lead shot; leaden seal; *elect* fuse; *typ* type; **à** ～ upright, vertical; **n'avoir pas de** ～ **dans la tête** be feather-brained; **soldats de** ～ tin soldiers; **sommeil de** ～ deep sleep·

**plombage** *nm* sheathing with lead; applying of leaden seals, sealing; filling (tooth)

**plombagine** *nf* plumbago, black lead; graphite

**plombé** *adj* sheathed with lead; sealed; leaden (colour); filled (tooth)

**plomber** *vt* sheath with lead; seal; plumb (wall); fill (tooth); leaden (colour); **se** ～ take on leaden colour

**plomberie** *nf* lead industry; lead works; plumbing (installation)

**plombier** *nm* plumber

**plombières** *nf cul* ice-cream with candied fruit in it

**plonge** *nf coll* dish-washing

**plongeant** *adj* plunging

**plongée** *nf* dive, diving; submersion (submarine); downward view

**plongement** *nm* immersion

**plongeoir** *nm* diving-board

¹**plongeon** *nm orni* diver, loon

²**plongeon** *nm* dive, plunge; *coll* **faire le** ～ be in financial trouble

**plonger** *vt* (3) dip, immerse, plunge; *vi*

dive, plunge; *naut* dive, submerge; plunge into, look down into; slope downwards; **se ~ dans** be plunged in, be immersed in, immerse oneself in

**plongeur -euse** *n* dish-washer, washer-up; plunger; diver; *nm orni* diver

**plot** *nm elect* contact

**plouf** *interj* plop!

**ploutocrate** *nm* plutocrat

**ploutocratie** *nf* plutocracy

**ploutocratique** *adj* plutocratic

**ployer** *vt* (7) bend; tame; *vi* bend, bow; give way, yield

**plucher** *vi*, **plucheux** *adj see* **pelucher, pelucheux**

**pluie** *nf* rain; **en ~** in drops; **ennuyeux comme la ~** deeply boring; **faire la ~ et le beau temps** have a lot of influence; **parler de la ~ et du beau temps** make polite conversation

**plumage** *nm* plumage, feathers; plucking

**plumard** *nm sl* bed

**plumasserie** *nf* feather trade

**plume** *nf* feather, plume; pen; quill pen; *coll* **y laisser des ~s** sustain a loss

**plumeau** *nm* feather duster; tuft of feathers

**plumer** *vt* pluck; *coll* fleece; *vi* feather (rowing)

**plumet** *nm* plume

**plumeur -euse** *n* plucker

**plumeux -euse** *adj* feathery

**plumier** *nm* pen-case, pencil-box

**plumitif** *nm coll* pen-pusher; bureaucrat, petty official; hack writer

**plupart** *nf* greater part, greatest part, majority, most, most part; **la ~ du temps** normally

**pluralisme** *nm* pluralism

**pluraliste** *adj* pluralist

**pluralité** *nf* plurality

**pluriel** *nm gramm* plural; **~ de majesté** royal we; *adj* plural

¹**plus** *nm* more; most; **le ~ de** the greatest amount of; **au ~, tout au ~** at the most

²**plus** *adv* (1. *comparative*) more, the more; **~ il criait, ~ je ris** the more he shouted, the more I laughed; **beaucoup ~, bien ~** much more; **de ~** moreover; **de ~ en ~** more and more; **en ~** and in addition; **en ~ beau** more beautifully; **on ne peut ~ stupide** impossibly stupid, more stupid than one can imagine; **qui ~ est** and what is more; **sans ~** and nothing more, without ado; (2. *superlative*) **le, la, les ~** most, the most; **ce que j'ai de ~ précieux** the most precious thing I have; **des ~** among the most; (3. *negative*) **je ne veux ~ le voir** I don't want to see

him any more; **non ~, ne ... ~** no more; **pas ~ grand que moi** no bigger than I; **Vous ne partez pas? Moi non ~** You're not going? Nor am I

³**plus** *conj* plus; **deux ~ trois font cinq** two plus three make five

**plusieurs** *adj* several; **~ personnes** several people; *pron pl* several

**plus-que-parfait** *nm gramm* pluperfect

**plus-value** *nf* appreciation, increment, capital gain; budget surplus; increased payment

**plutonique** *adj geol* plutonic

**plutôt** *adv* rather, sooner, somewhat; **ou ~** or to be more exact

**pluvial** *adj* pluvial; rainy (season)

**pluvier** *nm orni* plover

**pluvieux -ieuse** *adj* rainy, wet

**pluviner** *vi see* **pleuviner**

**pluviomètre** *nm* rain-gauge

**pluviométrique** *adj* pluviometric

**pluviôse** *nm hist* fifth month of the French Republican calendar (January to February)

**pluviosité** *nf* raininess; rainfall

**pneu** *nm* tyre; express letter (Paris, sent by pneumatic tube)

**pneumatique** *nm* tyre; express letter (Paris, sent by pneumatic tube); *adj* pneumatic

**pneumologue** *n* lung specialist

**pneumonie** *nf* pneumonia

**pochade** *nf* quick sketch (painting or writing)

**pochard -e** *n coll* drunkard; *adj coll* drunken

**poche** *nf* pocket; bag, sack; pouch; sac; bagginess (trousers); *sl* **c'est dans la ~** it's in the bag; **en être de sa ~** sustain a loss; **mettre qn dans sa ~** overcome s/o; **mettre sa fierté dans sa ~** pocket one's pride; **n'avoir pas les yeux dans sa ~** be observant; **n'avoir pas sa langue dans sa ~** have plenty to say

**poché** *adj* black (eye); poached (egg)

**pocher** *vt* black (s/o's eye); poach (egg); sketch rapidly

**pochette** *nf* envelope, folder; book (matches); compendium (paper and envelopes); pocket handkerchief; (gramophone) record sleeve

**pochoir** *nm* stencil

**podagre** *nf* gout; *n + adj* gouty (person)

¹**poêle** *nm eccles* funeral pall

²**poêle** *nm* stove

³**poêle** *nf* frying-pan; *coll* **tenir la queue de la ~** be in control of sth

**poêler** *vt* fry; pot-roast

**poêlon** *nm* pan; casserole

**poème** *nm* poem

**poésie** *nf* poetry; poem

**poète** nm + adj poet
**poétesse** nf poetess
**poétique** nf poetics; adj poetic(al)
**poétiser** vt poeticize
**pognon** nm sl money
**poids** nm weight; heaviness; load; burden; importance, influence, moment; weight (boxing); ~ **coq** bantam-weight; ~ **léger** light-weight; ~ **lourd** heavy-weight; long, heavy vehicle; ~ **mi-lourd** light heavy-weight; ~ **mi-moyen** welter-weight; ~ **mouche** fly-weight; ~ **moyen** middle-weight; ~ **plume** feather-weight; ~ **spécifique** specific gravity; ~ **utile** pay-load; **ne pas faire le** ~ not make the weight (boxing); lack the necessary qualities
**poignant** adj poignant, heart-searching, gripping
**poignard** nm dagger
**poignarder** vt stab
**poigne** nf grasp, grip; command, energy, firmness; **à** ~ firm, strong
**poignée** nf handful; grip, handle; ~ **de main** hand-shake
**poignet** nm wrist; cuff; **à la force du** ~ by one's own efforts
**poil** nm coat, fur, hair (animals); bristle; nap (cloth), pile (velvet); ~ **s** hairs (human being); coll **à** ~ naked; **à un** ~ **près** very nearly; coll **au** ~ fine, super!; coll **avoir un** ~ **dans la main** be lazy; **de tout** ~ (**de tous** ~**s**) of all kinds; coll **être de bon** (**mauvais**) ~ be in a good (bad) temper; coll **ne pas avoir un** ~ **de sec** sweat profusely; **reprendre du** ~ **de la bête** recover oneself
**poiler (se)** v refl roar with laughter
**poilu** nm soldier (in First World War); adj hairy
**poinçon** nm awl, bradawl, pricker, stabber; punch (tickets); die; hall-mark; bui king-post
**poinçonnage, poinçonnement** nm perforating; punching; hall-marking
**poinçonner** vt perforate; punch; hall-mark, stamp
**poinçonneur -euse** n puncher; ticket-puncher
**poinçonneuse** nf punching machine, stamping machine
**poindre** vt (71) hurt, wound; vi appear (dawn); come up, sprout (plants)
**poing** nm fist; **coup de** ~ punch; **coup de** ~ **américain** knuckle-duster; **dormir à** ~**s fermés** sleep deeply; **serrer les** ~**s** summon up one's courage
**¹point** nm point, spot; naut position; moment, point; situation, state; argument; aspect; degree; question; reason;

lace, needlework, stitch; full-stop; dot (dice); score (game); mark (school); leg point of law; ~ **d'attache** link; naut base; ~ **de côté** stitch (in side); ~ **d'exclamation** exclamation mark; ~ **d'interrogation** question mark; ~ **d'orgue** rest; ~ **du jour** dawn; ~ **mot mort** neutral; ~ **noir** blackhead; fig problem; **à** ~ at the right moment; in the right state; cul to a turn; **à** ~ **nommé** at the right moment; **à ce** ~ to such an extent; **à ce** ~ **que** so much so that; **au** ~ ready, right; **de** ~ **en** ~ literally; **faire le** ~ sum up the position; aer + naut take a fix; **mal en** ~ in a bad way; **mettre au** ~ adjust, regulate; mot tune; **mettre les** ~**s sur les i** dot the i's and cross the t's; **mise au** ~ adjustment; summing-up of situation
**²point** adv not at all
**pointage** nm checking, checking in; mil aiming, laying; naut marking up (chart); pointing (telescope)
**pointe** nf extremity; head, point, spike; cape, headland; pointed object; point (compass); triangular scarf; mil advance, sally; wedge; pointed remark, sally; touch, trace; spurt; peak (period); ~ **des pieds** tip-toe; lit ~ **du jour** dawn; arts ~ **sèche** dry-point etching, etching; **en** ~ pointed; **faire des** ~**s** execute points (ballet); **heure de** ~ peak-hour, rush-hour
**pointeau** nm mech centre-punch; mot needle (carburettor)
**pointer** vt prod, sharpen; prick up (ears); stitch; vi point, soar; advance, sally forth; dawn; (**se**) ~ clock on
**pointeur -euse** n checker, tally-clerk; timekeeper (athletics); mil gun-layer
**pointillé** nm dotting, stippling; dotted line; perforation (paper)
**pointiller** vt dot; vi make dots, stipple
**pointilleux -euse** adj captious, finicky, fussy, fastidious, particular
**pointu** adj pointed; sharp, shrill; unpleasant; touchy
**pointure** nf size (shoes, etc)
**point-virgule** nm (pl **points-virgules**) semi-colon
**poire** nf pear; pear-shaped object; elect pear-switch; coll head, nut; coll dupe, idiot; coll **couper la** ~ **en deux** split the difference; **garder une** ~ **pour la soif** keep something in reserve
**poiré** nm perry
**poireau, porreau** nm bot leek; med wart; coll **faire le** ~ wait, hang around
**poireauter** vi coll wait, hang around
**poirée** nf white beet
**poirier** nm pear-tree
**pois** nm pea; polka dot, spot, ~ **cassés**

split peas; ~ **chiche** chick pea; ~ **de senteur** sweet pea

**poison** *nm* poison; *coll* damn nuisance; *n coll* pest

**poissard** *adj* low-life, vulgar

**poissarde** *nf* fish-wife

**poisse** *nf coll* bad luck

**poisser** *vt* coat with pitch, dirty, soil; *coll* arrest, catch, nab; **vin poissé** resinated wine, retsina

**poisseux -euse** *adj* sticky

**poisson** *nm* fish; ~ **d'avril** April fool; ~ **rouge** goldfish; *coll* **engueuler qn comme du ~ pourri** tear a strip off s/o; **être (heureux) comme un ~ dans l'eau** be in one's element; *mot* **faire une queue de ~ à qn** cut in on s/o; **finir en queue de ~** fizzle out

**poissonnerie** *nf* fish trade; fish market; fish shop

**poissonneux -euse** *adj* full of fish

**poissonnier -ière** *n* fish merchant

**poissonnière** *nf* fish kettle

**poitevin** *adj* of Poitou; of Poitiers

**poitrail** *nm* breast; *bui* breast-summer

**poitrinaire** *n* + *adj* consumptive(patient)

**poitrine** *nf* chest; breasts (woman); *cul* breast (meat)

**poivrade** *nf cul* sauce with pepper and vinegar; **à la ~** with salt and pepper

**poivre** *nm* pepper; ~ **et sel** dark hair streaked with white

**poivré** *adj* peppered, peppery; *fig* improper, spicy

**poivrer** *vt* pepper, season with pepper; *coll* **se ~** get drunk

**poivrier** *nm bot* pepper plant; pepper-pot

**poivrière** *nf* pepper plantation; pepper-pot; *archi* (conical) turret

**poivron** *nm bot* capsicum, pepper

**poivrot -e** *n sl* drunkard

**poix** *nf* pitch, resin

**poker** *nm* poker (game); four of a kind (at poker); ~ **d'as** poker-dice

**polaire** *adj geog* + *math* polar

**Polaque** *nm hist* Polack; *coll pej* Pole

**polariser** *vt* polarize

**polariseur** *nm* polarizer

**polarité** *nf* polarity

**pôle** *nm* pole; polar regions

**polémique** *nf* polemic, controversy; *adj* polemical

**polémiste** *n* polemist

¹**poli** *nm* gloss, polish; *adj* polished, smooth; burnished

²**poli** *adj* polite, civil, courteous, well-behaved

¹**police** *nf* police, police-force; policing; discipline; ~ **des mœurs** vice squad; ~ **judiciaire** = C.I.D.; ~ **parallèle** secret police; **appeler ~ secours** = dial

999, call the police; **commissariat (poste) de ~** police-station; *mil* **salle de ~** guardroom

²**police** *nf* insurance policy; ~ **tous risques** comprehensive policy

**policer** *vt* (4) *lit* civilize

**polichinelle** *nm* Punch, Punchinello; buffoon, puppet; **secret de ~** no secret; public knowledge

**policier** *nm* policeman; detective, private detective; *adj* (*f* -**ière**) police; **régime ~** police state; **roman ~** detective story

**policlinique** *nf* out-patient clinic; clinical training

**poliment** *adv* politely, courteously

**polio** *n med* polio patient; *nf* polio

**poliomyélite** *nf med* poliomyelitis

**polir** *vt* burnish, polish, shine; file

**polissable** *adj* polishable

**polissage** *nm* burnishing, polishing, shining

**polisseur -euse** *n* polisher (person); gem-polisher

**polisson -onne** *n* naughty child, scamp; *adj* improper, smutty, lascivious; sexy (glance)

**polissonner** *vi* be naughty (child); *ar* behave indecently

**polissonnerie** *nf* mischievousness, prank (child); dirty remark; lewd act

**politesse** *nf* politeness, courtesy, good manners; polite action; polite remark; **brûler la ~** leave abruptly, go without saying goodbye; **échange de ~s** exchange of compliments; **faire des ~s** be civil, be polite

**politicard** *nm pej* (unscrupulous) politician

**politicien -ienne** *n often pej* politician; *adj pej* typical of a politician

**politique** *nm* political figure, statesman; s/o with statesmanlike qualities; *nf* politics, policy; *adj* political; politic, prudent

**politiser** *vt* make politically aware, make political

**pollinisation** *nf* pollination

**polluer** *vt* defile, pollute

**polo** *nm* polo; open-necked sports shirt

**Polonais -e** *n* Pole

**polonais** *nm* Polish (language); *adj* Polish

**polonaise** *nf mus* polonaise; *cul* kind of meringue (containing candied fruit)

**poltron -onne** *n* coward; *ar* poltroon; *adj* cowardly, faint-hearted, fearful

**poltronnerie** *nf* cowardice

**polyandre** *adj* having several husbands; *bot* polyandrous

**polyandrie** *nf* polyandry; *bot* polyandria

**polychrome** *adj* polychrome, polychromatic

**polyclinique** *nf* general clinic, general hospital

**polycopie** *nf* cyclostyling, duplicating, mimeographing, stencilling

**polycopié** *nm* cyclostyled document; **cours ~** cyclostyled course of lectures

**polycopier** *vt* cyclostyle, duplicate

**polyculture** *nf* mixed farming

**polyèdre** *nm* polyhedron

**polyédrique** *adj* polyhedral

**polygame** *n* polygamist; *adj* polygamous

**polygamie** *nf* polygamy

**polyglotte** *n + adj* polyglot

**polygone** *nm* polygon; *mil* fortified place; artillery range

**polymorphe** *adj* polymorphous

**polype** *nm zool* polyp; *med* polypus, soft tumour

**polyphasé** *adj elect* multiphase, polyphase

**polyphonie** *nf mus* polyphony

**polyphonique** *adj mus* polyphonic

**polysyllabe, polysyllabique** *adj* polysyllabic

**polytechnicien -ienne** *n* student, former student, of the Paris École Polytechnique

**Polytechnique** *nf* École Polytechnique in Paris

**polytechnique** *adj* polytechnic

**polythéisme** *nm* polytheism

**polythéiste** *n + adj* polytheist

**polyvalence** *nf* polyvalency

**pomiculteur** *nm* fruit-grower (apples, pears)

**pommade** *nf* ointment; *ar* pomade, pomatum; **~ rosat** lip salve; *coll* **passer de la ~ à qn** flatter s/o grossly

**pommader** *vt joc + pej* plaster (hair)

**pomme** *nf* apple; knob (bedstead, walking-stick); head (cabbage, lettuce); potato; rose (hose-pipe, shower); **~ de pin** fir-cone, pine-cone; **~ de terre** potato; **~s frites** chips; *coll* **aux ~s** fine, splendid; **compote de ~s** stewed apples; apple sauce; apple jam; *sl* **ma ~, sa ~** myself, himself; *coll* **tomber dans les ~s** faint

**pommeau** *nm* knob (walking-stick); pommel

**pommelé** *adj* dappled (horse); dappled, mottled

**pommeler (se)** *v refl* (5) become dappled; become rounded

**pommer** *vi bot* form a head

**pommette** *nf* cheek-bone

**pommier** *nm* apple-tree

**pomoculture** *nf* fruit-growing (apples, pears)

**pompage** *nm* pumping

**¹pompe** *nf* ceremony, pomp; **~s funèbres** funeral arrangements; **conducteur (entrepreneur, ordonnateur) des ~s funèbres** undertaker

**²pompe** *nf* pump; *sl* shoe; **~ à incendie** fire engine; **~ à vide** vacuum pump; *coll* **à toute ~** at full speed; *sl* **avoir un coup de ~** feel whacked; **Château-la-Pompe** tap-water

**pomper** *vt* pump, suck in; *sl* drink; *sl* exhaust; *fig* attract, draw

**pompette** *adj coll* slightly drunk, merry

**pompeux -euse** *adj pej* declamatory, high-flown, pompous; *ar* dignified, solemn; imposing, stately

**¹pompier** *nm* fireman

**²pompier** *nm coll* bombastic writer or painter; *adj* (*f* **-ière**) *coll* bombastic, pretentious

**pompiste** *n* petrol-pump attendant

**pompon** *nm* pompom, tassel, tuft; **avoir le ~** succeed, win

**pomponner** *vt* doll up, dress up, trick out; **se ~** doll oneself up, dress up

**ponant** *nm lit* west

**ponce** *nf* pumice; *arts* pounce bag

**¹ponceau** *nm bot* poppy, poppy colour; *adj invar* poppy-coloured, flaming-red

**²ponceau** *nm* culvert

**poncer** *vt* (4) pumice; pounce (drawing)

**poncif** *nm* pounce (pattern); *arts + lit* banal work, conventional work

**ponction** *nf surg* puncture

**ponctionner** *vt surg* puncture

**ponctualité** *nf* punctuality; assiduity, exactitude

**ponctuel -uelle** *adj* punctual; assiduous, exact

**ponctuer** *vt* punctuate

**pondérable** *adj* ponderable, weighable

**pondérateur -trice** *adj* balancing

**pondération** *nf* balance; level-headedness

**pondéré** *adj* calm, level-headed

**pondérer** *vt* (6) balance, weigh up

**pondeur** *nm coll* prolific writer

**pondeuse** *nf* layer (eggs); *coll* prolific woman; *adj* egg-laying

**pondre** *vt* lay (eggs); *sl pej* give birth to; *coll* give birth to (article, book)

**poney** *nm* pony

**pont** *nm* bridge; *naut* deck; *mot* transmission; flap (hat, trousers); *fig* link; **~ aérien** air-lift; *mot* **~ de graissage** inspection-hoist; *naut* **~ d'envol** flight-deck; **~ en dos d'âne** hump-backed bridge; **~ roulant** travelling crane; **Ponts et Chaussées** = Highways Department; **être solide comme le Pont-Neuf** be very strong and active; **faire le ~** take an extra day off between two public holidays; **faire un ~ d'or à qn** offer s/o inducement of higher salary; *naut* **faux ~** orlop deck; *comm* **sur ~** f.o.b., free on board

¹**ponte** *nf* (egg-)laying; number of eggs laid at one sitting; *physiol* **~ ovarienne** ovulation

²**ponte** *nm* gambler not holding the bank (baccara, roulette, etc); *coll* big-shot

**ponté** *adj naut* decked

**ponter** *vt* wager; *vi* gamble against the bank

**pontife** *nm* pontiff; *coll often iron* pundit

**pontifiant** *adj* pontificating

**pontificat** *nm* pontificate; papacy

**pontifier** *vi* pontificate

**pont-levis** *nm* (*pl* **ponts-levis**) draw-bridge

**ponton** *nm* floating platform, pontoon; flat-bottomed barge; hulk

**pontonnier** *nm mil* bridge-builder, pioneer

**popeline** *nf* poplin

**popote** *nf mil coll* officers' mess; *coll* cooking; *adj coll* too home-loving, stay-at-home

**popotin** *nm sl* arse, backside

**populace** *nf pej* rabble, riff-raff

**populacier -ière** *adj* coarse, low, vulgar

**populaire** *nm ar* people; *adj* of the people; folk (culture, tradition); familiar, popular (expression, style); popular, well-liked

**populariser** *vt* popularize, vulgarize

**popularité** *nf* popularity

**populeux -euse** *adj* populous

**populo** *nm coll* people, populace; crowd

**poquet** *nm hort* seed-hole

**porc** *nm* pig; pork; pig-skin; *fig* hog, pig; *fig* dirty old man

**porcelaine** *nf* porcelain, china; object made of porcelain

**porcelet** *nm* piglet

**porc-épic** *nm* (*pl* **porcs-épics**) porcupine

**porche** *nm* porch; vestibule

**porcher -ère** *n* swineherd

**porcherie** *nf* piggery

**porcin** *nm* pig; *adj* porcine

**poreux -euse** *adj* porous

**porion** *nm* foreman (in mine)

**pornographe** *nm* pornographer

**pornographie** *nf* pornography

**pornographique** *adj* pornographic

**priorité** *nf* priority

**porphyre** *nm* porphyry

**porreau** *nm see* **poireau**

¹**port** *nm* harbour, port; haven, shelter; sea-port town; *naut* **~ d'attache** port of registry; **arriver à bon ~** come safe into port, arrive safely

²**port** *nm* carrying; wearing; bearing

(name); transporting; price of transport; postage; bearing, deportment; *mil* **~ d'armes** presenting arms; *mus* **~ de voix** glide, portamento; **franc de ~ (franco de ~)** post-paid, carriage-paid

**portable** *adj* portable; wearable

**portail** *nm* portal

**portant** *nm* trunk handle; *elect* armature (magnet); *theat* flat; batten, spot-bar; *naut* rowlock; *bui* mullion; *adj* supporting; bearing, carrying; **à bout ~** point-blank; **bien (mal) ~** in good (bad) health

**portatif -ive** *adj* portable; **glace portative** ice-cream to be consumed elsewhere

¹**porte** *nf* gate, gateway (town); door, doorway, gate; *geog* defile; **~ à ~** door-to-door selling, door-to-door canvassing; **de ~ en ~** door to door, house to house; **entrer (passer) par la grande ~** be appointed straight to a high post; **frapper à la bonne (mauvaise) ~** go to the right (wrong) place; get on to the right (wrong) person; **interdire sa ~ à qn** refuse to admit s/o, be not at home to s/o; **mettre qn à la ~** dismiss s/o; throw s/o out

²**porte** *adj anat* portal

**porte-à-faux** *nm bui* overhang; **en ~** overhanging, overhung; *fig* uncertain, unstable

**porte-aiguilles** *nm* needle-case

**porte-allumettes** *nm* match-holder, match-box

**porte-amarre** *nm naut* life-saving rocket, apparatus

**porte-avions** *nm* aircraft-carrier

**porte-bagages** *nm* luggage-rack; luggage-grid

**porte-balais** *nm elect* brush-holder (dynamo)

**porte-billets** *nm* note-case, small wallet

**porte-bonheur** *nm invar* amulet, lucky charm

**porte-bouteilles** *nm* bottle-rack, wine-bin

**porte-carte, porte-cartes** *nm* small wallet (for identity papers etc); map-case

**porte-chapeaux** *nm* hat-stand

**porte-cigares** *nm invar* cigar-case

**porte-cigarettes** *nm* cigarette-case

**porte-clefs, porte-clés** *nm invar* key-ring; *ar* turnkey, warder

**porte-couteau** *nm* knife-rest

**porte-crayon** *nm* pencil-holder

**porte-documents** *nm invar* flat briefcase

**porte-drapeau** *nm mil+fig* standard-bearer

**portée** *nf* litter; *naut* load; *archi* bearing; span (arch, bridge); *mus* stave; reach; range; comprehension, import; *naut* ~ **lourde** dead-weight; **à (la)** ~ **de** within range of; accessible to; understandable by; **hors de (la)** ~ **de** inaccessible to; beyond the understanding of

**porte-épée** *nm invar* frog

**porte-étendard** *nm invar mil* standard-bearer

**porte-faix, portefaix** *nm invar ar* porter

**porte-fenêtre** *nf* (*pl* **portes-fenêtres**) French window

**portefeuille** *nm* portfolio (ministerial); *comm* portfolio; wallet, *US* billfold; **lit en** ~ apple-pie bed

**porte-greffe** *nm hort* plant, tree on which a graft is placed

**porte-jarretelles** *nm* suspender-belt

**portemanteau** *nm* coat (and hat) stand; *naut* davit

**porte-menu** *nm invar* menu-holder

**porte-mine, portemine** *nm* propelling pencil

**porte-monnaie** *nm invar* purse

**porte-musique** *nm invar* music-case

**porte-objet** *nm* (microscope) object slide

**porte-parapluies** *nm* umbrella-stand

**porte-parole** *nm invar* spokesman; spokeswoman; mouthpiece

**porte-plume** *nm invar* pen-holder, pen

**porter** *vt* carry, support; bear, have; hold up, raise; wear; convey; give (blow); enter, inscribe, put down; refer, concern; deliver; register (complaint); show (age); incline, induce; feel; nominate, propose; *her* carry; **à** bring to; incite; **être porté à** be inclined to; **être porté sur** have a taste for; **être porté sur la chose** be of amorous temperament, like making love; **il n'est pas bien porté de** it is not done to, the best people do not; *vi* carry (sound); be effective, have effect; ~ **sur** lie on, weigh on; strike against; be about, concern; *coll* **cela me porte sur les nerfs** that gets on my nerves; **se** ~ go, proceed; be worn (clothes); be (ill, well); present oneself (as candidate)

**porte-savon** *nm invar* soap-dish

**porte-serviettes** *nm* towel-rail

**porteur -euse** *n* porter; messenger; holder; *comm* bearer; *med* carrier; *adj* bearing, carrying

**porte-voix** *nm* speaking-tube; megaphone, speaking trumpet

**portier -ière** *n* doorkeeper, janitor; hotel porter; *ar* concierge

**portière** *nf* door (vehicle); door curtain

**portillon** *nm* gate; ~ **automatique** automatic barrier

**portion** *nf* portion; share (inheritance); helping (food)

**portionner** *vt* portion out, apportion

**portique** *nm* porch, portico; crossbar; gantry (crane); (airport) magnetic check-point

**porto** *nm* port (wine)

**portraitiste** *n* portrait-painter

**portrait-robot** *nm* (*pl* **portraits-robots**) identikit picture

**port-salut** *nm* kind of mild, soft cheese

**portuaire** *adj* port, harbour

**Portugais -e** *n* Portuguese

**portugais** *nm* Portuguese (language); *adj* Portuguese

**pose** *nf* fitting up, installing, laying down, setting up; pose; position (body); affectation, pretention; *phot* exposure

**posé** *adj* calm, sober, steady; even (voice)

**posément** *adv* calmly, deliberately, gently

**poser** *vt* place, put, set down; fit, install, set up; establish; formulate; put forward, state (candidature); abandon, set down; *sl* ~ **culotte** have a shit; *vi* lie on, rest on; pose (artist's model); pose, attitudinize; **se** ~ alight, land; arise (question); **se** ~ **en** set oneself up as

**poseur -euse** *n* layer (carpets, floors, rails, etc); poseur, prig; *adj* posing, affected

**positif** *nm mus* choir-organ; positive, rational; *adj* (*f* **-ive**) positive; actual, real; certain, sure; affirmative, favourable; constructive

**position** *nf* position, disposition; job, situation; attitude, point of view, standpoint; statement (bank); *naut* **feu de** ~ navigation light; *mot* **feux de** ~ parking lights; **rester sur ses** ~ **s** remain unconvinced; maintain the same attitude

**positivement** *adv* positively; really, exactly

**positivisme** *nm philos* positivism

**positiviste** *n* + *adj philos* positivist

**posologie** *nf med* posology, dosage

**possédant -e** *n* + *adj* moneyed, propertied (person)

**possédé -e** *n* + *adj* possessed (person)

**posséder** *vt* (6) have, hold, possess; know well (subject); have, possess (sexually); *sl* fool, trick; **se** ~ control oneself, possess oneself; *coll* **se faire** ~ be had

**possesseur** *nm* possessor, owner, proprietor

**possessif** *nm gramm* possessive; *adj* (*f* **-ive**) *gramm* possessive

**possession** *nf* possession; self-possession; *leg* ~ **vaut titre** possession is nine points of the law

**possibilité** *nf* possibility

**possible** *nm* possible, what is possible; **au** ~ extremely, as can be; *adj* possible, allowable; conceivable; eventual; acceptable; *adv coll* maybe, perhaps

**postdater** *vt* post-date

¹**poste** *nf* post, postal services; post-office; *ar* relay (horses); **grande** ~ main post-office

²**poste** *nm mil* post; police-station; job; post; shift; *rad* set; transmitting station; *mil* guardroom; *comm* ledger entry; *naut* ~ **de combat** action stations

**poster** *vt* post; place, position; **se** ~ place oneself

**postérieur** *nm coll* backside, buttocks; *adj* posterior, subsequent, behind

**postérité** *nf* posterity; descendants; future generations

**posthume** *adj* posthumous

**postiche** *nm* postiche, hair-piece; *adj* false, imitation, sham; bogus, false

**postier -ière** *n* post-office employee

**postillon** *nm* postillion; *coll* speck of saliva

**postillonner** *vi coll* spit, splutter when speaking

**postopératoire** *adj med* post-operative

**postscolaire** *adj* after-school, continuation

**post-scriptum** *nm* postscript

**postulant -e** *n* applicant, candidate; *eccles* postulant

**postulat** *nm* assumption, postulate

**postuler** *vt* apply for; postulate; *vi leg* plead

**posture** *nf* posture; position, situation; **en bonne (mauvaise)** ~ well (badly) placed

**pot** *nm* can, jar, jug, pot; cooking pot, casserole; potful; *coll* good luck, luck; *sl* arse, backside; pot, potty (child); *coll* drink, glass; *coll* canteen, refectory; ~ **de chambre** chamber-pot; *mot* ~ **d'échappement** exhaust-pipe; silencer; **découvrir le** ~ **aux roses** find out the truth about sth; **payer les** ~ **s cassés** pay for the damage, take the blame; **sourd comme un** ~ deaf as a post; **tourner autour du** ~ beat about the bush; cunningly seek an advantage

**potable** *adj* drinkable, fit to drink; *coll* all right, passable

**potache** *nm coll* schoolboy

**potage** *nm* soup; *lit* **pour tout** ~ all in all

**potager** *nm* kitchen-garden; *adj* (*f* -**ère**) vegetable

**potasse** *nf* potash

**potasser** *vt coll* study hard, swot

**potasseur** *nm coll* swot

**potassique** *adj* potassic

**pot-au-feu** *nm invar cul* stew of boiled beef and vegetables, hot-pot; *adj invar coll* home-loving, stay-at-home

**pot-de-vin** *nm* (*pl* **pots-de-vin**) bribe, graft

**pote** *nm sl* friend, mate

**poteau** *nm* pole, post, stake; stake (execution); *sl* friend, mate; ~ **d'arrivée (de départ)** winning (starting) post (race); ~ **indicateur** signpost; **au** ~ ! death!

**potée** *nf* kind of meat and vegetable stew; founder's clay

**potelé** *adj* chubby, plump

**potence** *nf* gallows, gibbet; death by hanging; bracket, support

**potentat** *nm* potentate

**potentialité** *nf* potentiality

**potentiel** *nm* potential; *adj* (*f* -**ielle**) potential

**poterie** *nf* pottery, earthenware (objects)

**poterne** *nf* postern

**potiche** *nf* large (porcelain) vase (*esp* oriental); figure-head, man of straw

**potier** *nm* potter

**potin** *nm* din, row; ~ **s** gossip

**potiner** *vi* gossip

**potiron** *nm* pumpkin

**potron-jaquet, potron-minet** *nm invar coll* dawn, first light

**pou** *nm* louse; ~ **de mouton** tick; **chercher des** ~ **x dans la tête de qn (à qn)** nag s/o; *coll* **être laid comme un** ~ be as ugly as sin

**pouah** *interj coll* ugh!

**poubelle** *nf* dustbin; *coll* **jeter à la** ~ reject scornfully

**pouce** *nm* thumb; big toe; inch; **donner le coup de** ~ add finishing touch; **donner un coup de** ~ **à qn** help s/o on (career); *sl* **et le** ~ ! and a bit more on top!; **manger un morceau sur le** ~ eat a hasty snack; **mettre les** ~ s give in, throw in the sponge; **tourner ses** ~ s, se **tourner les** ~ s be idle, twiddle one's thumbs

**poucier** *nm* thumb-stall; thumb-piece (door latch)

**pouding, pudding** *nm* pudding

**poudingue** *nm geol* conglomerate, pudding stone

**poudrage** *nm agr* spraying of powder

**poudre** *nf* dust; powder; (cosmetic) powder; explosive, gunpowder; **cela sent la** ~ there is a threat of trouble; **il n'a pas inventé la** ~ he's not very bright; **jeter de la** ~ **aux yeux de qn** throw dust in s/o's eyes; **mettre le feu**

aux ~s cause a disaster, provoke violent reactions

**poudrer** vt powder

**poudrerie** nf gunpowder factory

**poudreux -euse** adj dusty, powdery; ar dust-covered

**poudrier** nm powder-case, compact

**poudrière** nf powder-magazine

**poudrin** nm naut spindrift

**poudroiement** nm dust-haze

**poudroyer** vi (7) form clouds of dust

**¹pouf** nm pouffe; bustle

**²pouf** interj plop!; faire ~ fall (children's phrase)

**pouffer** vi ~ de rire burst out laughing

**pouffiasse, poufiasse** nf sl tart; old bag

**pouilleux -euse** n+adj verminous (person); miserable (place); adj geog sterile

**poulailler** nm hen-house; coll theat gallery

**poulain** nm colt, foal; novice, promising newcomer, trainee; skid (for unloading barrels)

**poularde** nf cul chicken fattened for the table

**poulbot** nm urchin

**poule** nf hen; hen bird; coll tart; coll bird, girl; darling, dear; (gambling) pool; knock-out competition; orni ~ d'eau wader; ~ mouillée coward; chair de ~ goose-flesh; mère ~ over-fussy mother; quand les ~s auront des dents when pigs can fly; tuer la ~ aux œufs d'or kill the goose that lays the golden eggs

**poulet** nm chicken; coll love-letter; coll letter; coll parking ticket; darling; coll policeman

**poulette** nf coll girl, young woman; darling; ar young hen; cul sauce (à la) ~ sauce made of butter, yolk of egg and vinegar

**pouliche** nf filly

**poulie** nf pulley; block

**pouliner** vi vet foal (mare)

**poulinière** nf+adj f (jument) ~ brood-mare

**poulpe** nm zool octopus

**pouls** nm pulse; tâter le ~ de qn (de qch) sound out s/o (sth)

**poumon** nm lung; ~ d'acier iron lung; à pleins ~s at the top of one's voice; avoir des ~s have a powerful voice; have plenty of stamina

**poupard** nm plump baby; adj chubby

**poupe** nf naut poop; avoir le vent en ~ forge ahead, be doing fine

**poupée** nf doll; coll bird, girl; bandaged finger

**poupin** adj doll-like

**poupon** nm baby, small child

**pouponner** vi give cuddles

**pouponnière** nf crèche; nursery

**pour** nm le ~ et le contre the pros and cons; prep for; in exchange for, in place of; as; on behalf of; on account of; in favour of; as for, regarding; per (cent); about; for, at the price of; meant for; because; during; to, for, in order to; for, by; though; ~ ce qui est de as far as (that) is concerned; coll ~ de bon for good (and all); sl ~ de vrai honest, really, truly; ~ lors then; ~ peu que however little; ~ que for, in order that; ~ ... que however; sl c'est fait ~ it's meant, it's done, for that; en tout et ~ tout once and for all; et ~ cause! for obvious reasons!; être ~ be in favour of; être ~ + infin be on the point of; n'être pas ~ not be calculated to

**pourboire** nm tip, gratuity

**pourceau** nm ar+lit pig; hog, swine

**pourcentage** nm percentage, proportion

**pourchasser** vt pursue, track down; se ~ pursue one another

**pourfendeur** nm ar+joc slayer

**pourfendre** vt lit destroy; ar cleave in twain

**pourlécher** vt (6) complete, polish up; se ~ lick one's lips

**pourparler** nm (usu pl) diplomatic negotiation, parley

**pourpoint** nm doublet

**pourpre** nm crimson; nf purple; cloth of purple; hist consular dignity; royal dignity; cardinalate; adj crimson, purple; hêtre ~ copper beech

**pourpré** adj crimson, purple, purplish

**pourquoi** nm invar cause, reason; question; adv+conj why

**pourri** adj rotted, rotten, corrupt, corrupted; dank (weather); coll full

**pourrir** vt rot; corrupt; infect; spoil (child); vi decompose, go bad, rot, decay; addle (egg); se ~ rot away; become worse

**pourrissant** adj rotting

**pourrissement** nm deterioration, rotting

**pourriture** nf decay, putrefaction, rotting; corruption, rottenness; corrupt person

**poursuite** nf pursuit, seeking after; continuation; leg often pl action, law-suit

**poursuivant -e** n pursuer; leg plaintiff; ar her poursuivant

**poursuivre** vt (92) pursue, chase, follow; harass; obsess; continue, go on with, proceed with; leg proceed against, prosecute, sue

**pourtant** adv however, nevertheless, none the less, still, yet

**pourtour** *nm* circumference, periphery, surround

**pourvoi** *nm* leg appeal; ~ **en grâce** petition for clemency

**pourvoir** *vt* (72) furnish, give, provide; endow, equip, provide for; *leg se* ~ appeal to higher court; *se* ~ *de* provide oneself with

**pourvoyeur -euse** *n* provider, purveyor

**pourvu que** *conj phr* provided that, so long as; it is to be hoped that

**pousse** *nf* growth; short sprout

**poussé** *adj* deep, profound (study); exaggerated; *mot* **moteur** ~ hotted-up engine

**pousse-café** *nm invar* brandy, liqueur; chaser

**poussée** *nf* impulse, pressure, pushing; *archi* thrust; push, shove; eruption (skin); attack (fever); growth (plant)

**pousse-pousse (pousse)** *nm invar* rickshaw

**pousser** *vt* push, shove; open; close; drive, impel; prolong, pursue; utter; heave (sigh); sing; put out (foliage); cut (teeth); ~ **à bout** exasperate, infuriate; ~ **l'aiguille** sew; **à la va comme je te pousse** anyhow, in any manner; *vi* push, push on, push out; go further on; grow (plant); *se* ~ push oneself forward; get on, make one's way, make progress; get out of the way, make way; push one another

**poussette** *nf* push-chair (child)

**poussier** *nm* coal-dust

**poussière** *nf* dust; powder; human remains; **réduire en** ~ pulverize; annihilate; **tomber en** ~ disintegrate, fall apart

**poussiéreux -euse** *adj* dusty

**poussif .-ive** *adj vet* broken-winded (horse); short of breath, wheezy; uninspired

**poussin** *nm* child; *cul* spring chicken

**poussinière** *nf* coop; incubator

**poussoir** *nm* push-button; *mech* rod

**poutrage** *nm* framework of beams

**poutre** *nf* beam; girder

**poutrelle** *nf* small steel girder

**pouvoir** *nm* power; force, clout; means; authority, competence, competency; sovereignty; *leg* authority, power of attorney; ~ **d'achat** purchasing power; **fondé de** ~ agent, proxy; manager, managing director; *vt* (73) be able to, be in a position to; *vi* be able to, be capable of; be allowed to, have permission to; be possible; **il peut (il pourra)** there may be; **n'en** ~ **plus** be exhausted; **on ne peut mieux** best possible; **on ne peut plus** as much as possible; **puissiez-vous être ...** may you

be ...; *se* ~ be possible; *coll* **ça se peut** maybe

**pragmatique** *adj* pragmatic

**pragmatisme** *nm* pragmatism

**pragmatiste** *n + adj* pragmatist

**prairial** *nm hist* ninth month of the French Republican calendar (May to June)

**prairie** *nf* meadow, grassland; prairie

**praline** *nf* burnt almond

**praliné** *adj* browned in sugar; containing burnt almonds; **chocolat** ~ nut chocolate

**praliner** *vt* brown in sugar

**praticabilité** *nf* practicability

**praticable** *nm theat* ros; platform; *adj* practicable, feasible; possible; negotiable; suitable for vehicles

**praticien -ienne** *n med* practitioner; practical exponent

**pratiquant -e** *n + adj* practising (Christian, Mohammedan, etc)

**pratique** *nf* experience, practice; practising; habit; observance; business custom; customer; *leg* procedure; religious observances; *adj* practical; realistic; utilitarian; ingenious, useful

**pratiquer** *vt* observe, practise, put into practice, exercise; perform; construct; contrive; cut (opening); frequent (author); *se* ~ be the custom

**pré** *nm* field, meadow; **aller sur le** ~ fight a duel

**préalable** *nm* necessary condition, precondition; preliminary; **au** ~ to begin with, as a first step; *adj* preliminary, previous

**préalpin** *adj* pre-alpine

**préambule** *nm* preamble

**préau** *nm* playground, covered part of playground; inner courtyard (prison, hospital, monastery, etc)

**préavis** *nm* previous warning; notice (of dismissal); **appel avec** ~ personal call (telephone)

**prébende** *nf eccles* prebend; sinecure

**prébendier** *nm eccles* prebendary; holder of sinecure

**précaire** *adj* precarious, uncertain; delicate, fragile

**précarité** *nf* precariousness

**précaution** *nf* precaution; care, caution, circumspection, wariness; *coll* **prendre ses** ~ **s** go to the lavatory as a precautionary measure

**précautionner** *vt ar* caution against, warn against; *se* ~ **contre** take one's precautions against; *se* ~ **de** furnish oneself with

**précautionneux -euse** *adj* prudent, wary

**précédemment** *adv* already, before, previously

**précédent** *nm* precedent; **sans** ~ unheard of; *adj* preceding, previous

**précéder** *vt* (6) go before, precede; have precedence over

**précellence** *nf lit* supreme excellence

**précepte** *nm* precept

**précepteur -trice** *n* (private) tutor, (*f*) governess

**prêche** *nm eccles* sermon; boring moral discourse

**prêcher** *vt eccles* preach (gospel, sermon); advocate, preach; *eccles* evangelize (s/o); *coll* try to persuade; *vi eccles* preach; moralize boringly; ~ **d'exemple (par l'exemple)** practise what one preaches

**prêcheur -euse** *n* moralizer, sermonizer; *adj eccles* preaching (friar); moralizing, preaching, sermonizing

**prêchi, prêcha, prêchi-prêcha** *nm invar coll* tedious moralizing

**précieuse** *nf Fr lit hist* précieuse, exponent of preciosity

**précieux -ieuse** *adj* precious, valuable, invaluable; affected, over-refined, precious

**préciosité** *nf* preciosity, affectation, over-refinement

**précipitamment** *adv* hastily, headlong, precipitately

**précipitation** *nf* haste, hurry, precipitation

**précipité** *nm chem* precipitate; *adj* fast, rapid; hasty, hurried

**précipiter** *vt* hurl down, precipitate, throw down; force, push; hasten, hurry, precipitate; **se** ~ hurl oneself down; fall down; rush; hasten, hurry

**précis** *nm* précis, abstract, epitome; short manual; *adj* clear, precise; detailed, explicit

**précisément** *adv* clearly, precisely; in fact

**préciser** *vt* express precisely; specify; determine, establish; emphasize; make clear; **se** ~ become clearer

**précision** *nf* accuracy, exactness, precision, clarity; ~**s** details, precise facts

**précité** *adj* above, previously mentioned

**préclassique** *adj* pre-classical

**précoce** *adj* precocious; *hort* early

**précocité** *nf* precociousness, precocity

**précompter** *vt comm* deduct beforehand

**préconception** *nf* preconception, preconceived idea; prejudice

**préconçu** *adj* preconceived, pre-established; prejudiced

**préconiser** *vt* advocate, recommend

**précontraint** *nm + adj eng* pre-stressed (concrete)

**précontrainte** *nf eng* pre-stressing

**précurseur** *nm* forerunner, precursor;

*adj m* precursory, premonitory

**prédateur** *nm + adj* predatory (animal, insect)

**prédestiné -e** *n theol* elect; *adj theol* predestined, preordained

**prédestiner** *vt theol* predestine; destine

**prédéterminer** *vt* predetermine

**prédicant** *nm* protestant preacher; *adj* moralizing

**prédicat** *nm gramm* predicate

**prédicateur** *nm* preacher

**prédication** *nf* preaching; sermon

**prédiction** *nf* forecast, prediction; prophecy

**prédigéré** *adj* predigested

**prédilection** *nf* predilection, preference; **de** ~ favourite

**prédire** *vt* (74) forecast, foretell, predict

**prédisposer** *vt* incline, predispose; influence

**prédisposition** *nf* predisposition, tendency; aptitude, gift

**prédominant** *adj* predominant

**prédominer** *vi* predominate

**prééminence** *nf* pre-eminence

**prééminent** *adj* pre-eminent

**préemption** *nf leg* pre-emption, first refusal

**préexistant** *adj* pre-existent

**préexistence** *nf* pre-existence

**préexister** *vi* pre-exist

**préfabriqué** *adj* prefabricated; arranged in advance

**préfacer** *vt* (4) preface

**préfectoral** *adj* prefectorial

**préfecture** *nf* prefecture; area administered by a prefect; ~ **de police** (Paris) police headquarters; ~ **maritime** naval port

**préférable** *adj* preferable; wiser

**préféré -e** *n + adj* favourite

**préférence** *nf* preference; predilection, weakness; privilege; **de** ~ preferably; **de** ~ **à** rather than

**préférentiel -ielle** *adj* preferential

**préférer** *vt* (6) like better, prefer; adopt, choose

**préfet** *nm Rom hist* prefect; (French administration) prefect; priest in charge of discipline in French Catholic school; ~ **de police** chief of Paris police; ~ **maritime** admiral commanding naval district

**préfète** *nf* wife of prefect

**préfigurer** *vt* prefigure

**préfixe** *nm gramm* prefix; dialling code (telephone)

**préfixer** *vt* prefix

**prégnant** *adj* having implicit meaning, significant; *gramm* pregnant

**préhellénique** *adj* prehellenic

**préhistoire** *nf* prehistory

**préhistorique** *adj* prehistoric

**préjudice** *nm* detriment, wrong; *leg* tort; **porter ~ à** injure, wrong; **sans ~ de** without prejudice to, without referring to

**préjudiciable** *adj* detrimental, injurious, prejudicial

**préjugé** *nm* presumption; bias, preconception, prejudice

**préjuger** *vt* (3) *lit* prejudge; **~ de** prejudge

**prélart** *nm* tarpaulin

**prélasser (se)** *v refl* loll about; *ar* give oneself airs

**prélat** *nm* prelate

**prélèvement** *nm* taking of a part of sth, taking of a sample; appropriation; quantity appropriated

**prélever** *vt* (6) take a part of, take a sample of; appropriate, extract, remove; remove in advance

**préliminaire** *adj* preliminary

**préliminaires** *nmpl* preliminaries

**préluder** *vi mus* prelude; **~ à** lead up to; try out

**prématuré** *adj* premature, untimely

**préméditation** *nf* premeditation; *leg* **avec ~** with malice aforethought

**préméditer** *vt* premeditate; calculate; **~ de** plan to

**prémices** *nfpl hist* first-fruit (offering); *lit* beginning

**premier -ière** *n* first, the first; first (of month); British prime minister; first syllable in charade; **en ~** first of all, of first rank; *theat* **jeune ~** juvenile lead; **le ~ venu** anyone at all, no matter who; *adj* first, initial; prime (quality); former, original, pristine; best, highest; essential; primordial; *math* **+ philos** prime; **~ ministre** prime minister; **première nouvelle!** first I've heard of it!, I'd no idea!; **au (du) ~ coup** at the first attempt; **au ~ plan** in the foreround; **enfant d'un ~** *lit* child of first marriage; **enseignement du ~ degré** primary education; *math* **facteurs ~ s** prime factors; *theat* **grand ~ rôle** lead; **matières premières** raw materials; *math* **nombre ~** prime number

**première** *nf* first night; sixth form (school); first-class ticket; first-class cabin; first-class seat (train); *mot* first gear

**premier-né** (*f* **première-née**) *n + adj* (*pl* **premiers-nés**, **premières-nées**) firstborn (child)

**prémisse** *nf philos* premise, premises; affirmation

**prémonitoire** *adj* premonitory

**prémunir** *vt* protect from, warn against; **se ~** arm oneself, protect oneself

**prenable** *adj* seizable, takeable

**prenant** *adj* prehensile; captivating, engaging, interesting; *leg* **partie ~e** payee

**prendre** *vt* (75) take, take hold of; pick up, seize; go and get; carry, take along; consider, think about; enjoy, feel; accept (responsibility); assume, take on; drink, eat, take; ask, charge (a price); buy (seat, ticket); arrest, capture, catch; deceive, take; have, obtain; have, possess (woman); catch out; *coll* put up with; receive (blow); *coll* come over one; **~ au passage** intercept; **~ de l'âge** be getting old; **~ du poids** put on weight; **~ du ventre** develop a paunch; **~ en grippe** take a strong dislike to; **~ froid** catch a cold; **~ goût à** begin to like; develop a taste for; *naut* **~ le large (la mer)** put out to sea; **~ la parole** speak at a meeting; **prenez la peine de** be so good as to; **~ l'eau** leak (boat); **~ le deuil** go into mourning; **~ le lit** take to one's bed; **~ les armes** take up arms; **~ le voile** go into a convent; **~ mal** take badly; fall ill; **~ qch à qn** take sth from s/o; **~ qch sur soi** take sth upon oneself; **~ sur soi de** take it upon oneself to; **~ sur son compte** take full responsibility; **~ un baiser** steal a kiss; **à tout ~** in short, when all is said and done; *coll* **ça vous prend souvent?** do you often behave like this?; **c'est à ~ ou à laisser** it's take it or leave it; *coll* **c'est autant de pris** that's something anyway; **on ne sait pas où le ~** he's very touchy; *coll* **qu'est-ce qui vous prend?** what's biting you?, what's the matter?; *vi* congeal, curdle; freeze, set, take; stick (to pan); begin to burn (fire); succeed, catch on (fashion, habit); go in a given direction; **~ à gauche** turn left; **se ~** be taken; be caught; catch oneself out; freeze (water); hold one another; make love together; take from one another; **se ~ à** begin to; **se ~ de** begin to feel (affection, etc); **se ~ pour** think oneself to be; **s'en ~ à** hold responsible for; **s'y ~** go about sth; **se ~ aux cheveux** quarrel

**preneur -euse** *n* taker; purchaser; *comm* payee; *leg* lessee, lease-holder; **je suis ~ à 2.000 francs** my offer is 2,000 francs

**prénom** *nm* Christian name, first name

**prénommé -e** *n + adj* above named

**prénommer** *vt* give a first name to; **se ~** be called

**préoccupation** *nf* preoccupation, obsession, absorption; anxiety, care

**préoccupé** *adj* preoccupied, absorbed; anxious, concerned

**préoccuper** *vt* preoccupy, absorb, engross; disturb, make worried; **se ~ de** attend to, see to, take trouble over; worry about

**préparateur -trice** *n* research assistant (sciences); dispenser (chemist's shop)

**préparatifs** *nmpl* arrangements, preparations

**préparation** *nf* preparation, preparing; dressing (skins); **mil ~ d'artillerie** barrage; **annoncer sans ~** blurt out

**préparatoire** *adj* preparatory

**préparer** *vt* get ready, organize; fit, train; study for (examination); dress (skins); **se ~** get ready; be about to happen, be imminent

**prépondérant** *adj* preponderant; decisive, dominant; **voix ~e** casting vote

**préposé -e** *n* minor official (customs officer, postman, etc); attendant

**préposer** *vt* appoint, entrust with

**prépositif -ive** *adj gramm* prepositional

**préraphaélisme** *nm* preraphaelitism

**préromantique** *adj* preromantic

**préromantisme** *nm* preromanticism

**près** *adv* close, close by, near, nearby; **~ de** close to, near to; by the side of; beside; nearby; **naut ~ du vent** close-hauled; **à beaucoup ~** far from it, nothing near; **à cela ~** excepting; **à peu ~** about; **à peu de chose(s) ~** very nearly; **à ... ~** approximately, nearly, save; *naut* **au plus ~** close-hauled; **de ~** closely, carefully

**présage** *nm* omen, portent, presage

**présager** *vt* (3) presage; foresee

**pré-salé** *nm* (*pl* **prés-salés**) salt-meadow sheep; salt-meadow mutton

**presbyte** *n + adj* long-sighted (person)

**presbytéral** *adj* priestly; **conseil ~** presbytery (Protestant)

**presbytère** *nm* presbytery (Catholic); (also used for) vicarage (Anglican), manse (non-conformist)

**presbytérianisme** *nm* presbyterianism

**presbytérien -ienne** *n + adj* presbyterian

**presbytie** *nf med* long-sightedness

**prescience** *nf theol* divine prescience; foreknowledge

**prescription** *nf* prescription; regulation; instruction

**prescrire** *vt* (42) indicate, prescribe, recommend; *med* prescribe; *leg* bar, prescribe; acquire by prescription

**préséance** *nf* precedence

**présélection** *nf* pre-selection

**présence** *nf* presence; existence; actuality; personality; **en ~** face to face; **en ~ de** before, in front of; **faire acte de ~** be formally present

**¹présent** *nm* present; *gramm* present (tense); *adj* present; at hand, on hand; current; *gramm* present; **à ~** at this moment, now; **à ~ que** now that; **d'à ~** concurrent, of this time, present

**²présent** *nm lit* gift, present

**présentateur -trice** *n* presenter; promoter; *rad* compère

**présentation** *nf* presentation; introduction; *coll* appearance; presentin launching (exhibition, novel); manner of presentation

**présenter** *vt* present; introduce; propose (for employment); put in (candidate for examination); put up (candidate for election); display, exhibit; convey (congratulations, sympathy); describe, show; appear to have; *vi coll* **~ bien (mal)** have a good (bad) appearance; **se ~** appear, arrive, call on; introduce oneself; make oneself known; apply, be a candidate, present oneself; come to mind

**préservateur -trice** *adj* preserving

**préservatif** *nm* sheath; *coll* French letter

**préserver** *vt* preserve, protect, save, shelter; **se ~** protect oneself

**présidence** *nf* presidency; duration of presidency; presidential residence; chairmanship

**président** *nm pol* president; president (society); chairman (company, examiners, magistrates); **~-directeur général (P.D.G.)** chairman and managing director; **~ du conseil** (French) prime minister, head of government

**présidentiel -ielle** *adj* presidential

**présider** *vt* preside over; take the chair at; direct, watch over; *vi* preside

**présomptif -ive** *adj* presumptive; **héritier ~** heir apparent

**présomption** *nf* presumption, conjecture; supposition; pretentiousness

**présomptueux -ueuse** *adj* presumptuous, pretentious

**presque** *adv* almost, nearly; near; hardly, scarcely

**presqu'île** *nf* peninsula

**pressage** *nm* pressing

**pressant** *adj* pressing, urgent

**presse** *nf* crowd, press; press; (printing) press; press (newspapers); peak period, rush; **~ du cœur** women's magazines; **~ monétaire** minting press; **mettre sous ~** begin to print, go to press

**pressé** *nm* **aller au plus ~** deal with the most urgent thing first; *adj* pressed; in a hurry, pressed; pressing, urgent

**presse-bouton** *adj invar* push-button

**presse-citron** *nm invar* lemon squeezer

**pressée** *nf* pressing (fruit, etc)

**pressentiment** *nm* foreboding, intuition, presentiment

**pressentir** *vt* have a presentiment of; be aware of; sound out

**presse-papiers** *nm* paper-weight

**presser** *vt* press, squeeze; assail, beset, harass; expedite, hurry (s/o) on, quicken (step); clasp, embrace; encourage, urge; *vi* be urgent; **se** ~ press oneself; hasten, hurry

**presse-raquette** *nm invar* racket-press (tennis)

**presseur -euse** *n* presser; *adj* pressing, which presses

**pressing** *nm* cleaner's (shop)

**pression** *nf* pressure; **bière à la** ~ draught-beer; **sous** ~ pressurized; under pressure; under steam

**pressoir** *nm* cider-press, oil-press, wine-press; building housing cider-press, etc

**pressurer** *vt* press (fruit, etc); pressurize; exact money from; *coll* **se** ~ **le cerveau** torment oneself

**pressuriser** *vt* pressurize

**prestance** *nf* bearing, demeanour, imposing presence

**prestation** *nf hist* + *leg* taking of an oath; *mil* allowance; benefit (health service, insurance); war indemnity; *theat* turn, number; ~ **en espèces (en nature)** benefits in cash (in kind)

**preste** *adj* agile, alert, nimble, quick; **avoir la main** ~ be adroit

**prestidigitateur -trice** *n* conjuror

**prestidigitation** *nf* conjuring, sleight of hand

**prestige** *nm* glamour, prestige

**prestigieux -ieuse** *adj lit* glamorous, remarkable, wonderful

**présumé** *adj* presumed, supposed

**présumer** *vt* presume, suppose; guess, infer, think; ~ **trop de** over-estimate

**présupposer** *vt* presuppose

**présure** *nf* rennet

**présurer** *vt* curdle (milk)

¹**prêt** *nm* lending, loan; *mil* pay; advance (of salary)

²**prêt** *adj* prepared, ready; ~ **à** ready to, willing to; about to

**prétantaine** *nf see* **prétentaine**

**prêt-à-porter** *nm collect* ready-made clothes

**prêté** *nm* **c'est un** ~ **pour un rendu** it's tit for tat; *adj* lent

**prétendant -e** *n* claimant, pretender (throne); *nm* suitor

**prétendre** *vt* affirm, declare, maintain; intend to, mean to; claim; ~ **à** aspire to, lay claim to; **à ce qu'il prétend** according to him; **en prétendant que** on the pretext that; **se** ~ maintain that one is

**prétendu -e** *n* intended (fiancé, fiancée); *adj* alleged, so-called, would-be

**prête-nom** *nm* agent, proxy; *pej* man of straw

**prétentaine, prétantaine** *nf* **courir la** ~ get into scrapes; gad about, have a lot of love affairs, lead a wild life

**prétentieux -ieuse** *adj* affected, mannered; pretentious, vain

**prétention** *nf* pretentiousness, vanity; claim, demand; ambition, pretension; condition, request

**prêter** *vt* lend; give, grant; ascribe, attribute; *vi* give, stretch (material); ~ **à** give rise to; ~ **attention** pay attention; ~ **la main** help; ~ **sa voix à** speak for; ~ **serment** take an oath; **se** ~ **à** agree to; indulge in; be adapted to

**prétérit** *nm gramm* preterite

**préteur** *nm Rom hist* praetor

**prêteur -euse** *n* lender, money-lender; ~ **sur gages** pawnbroker; *adj* disposed to lend, willing to lend

**prétexte** *nm* pretext; excuse, reason; **sous aucun** ~ under no circumstances

**prétexter** *vt* allege, plead

**prétoire** *nm* court, court-room; *Rom hist* praetorium

**prétorien** *nm* + *adj* (*f* -ienne) praetorian

**prêtre** *nm* priest

**prêtresse** *nf* priestess

**prêtrise** *nf* priesthood

**preuve** *nf* proof; evidence, justification, sign, token; ~ **d'une opération** cross-check; *hist* ~ **par jugement de Dieu** trial by ordeal; ~ **par l'absurde** reductio ad absurdum; *hist* ~ **par le combat** trial by combat; *coll* **à** ~ example, witness; **à** ~ **que** the proof is that; **faire** ~ **de** show; **faire ses** ~s show one's mettle, prove oneself

**preux** *nm* champion, valiant knight; *adj m* brave, valiant

**prévaloir** *vi* (76) prevail, succeed, win; **se** ~ **de** take advantage of; pride oneself on

**prévaricateur -trice** *n* culpably negligent administrator or judge; *adj* culpably negligent

**prévarication** *nf* culpable negligence; breach of trust

**prévariquer** *vi leg* be guilty of culpable negligence; be guilty of breach of trust

**prévenance** *nf* consideration, kindness, kindly act

**prévenant** *adj* considerate, kindly, thoughtful

**prévenir** *vt* (96) anticipate, avert, forestall, ward off; bias, influence; apprise, inform, tell, warn

**préventif -ive** *adj* precautionary, preventive

**prévention** *nf* bias, preconceived idea, prejudice; prepossession; prevention; *leg* imprisonment awaiting trial; ~ **routière** road safety organization

**prévenu -e** *n* accused, prisoner; *adj* biased, prejudiced

**prévisible** *adj* foreseeable

**prévision** *nf* estimate, expectation, forecast; **en** ~ **de** in expectation of

**prévoir** *vt* (77) forecast, foresee; estimate, make provision for; plan ahead for; **être prévu pour** be designed for, meant for

**prévôt** *nm hist* provost; *mil* officer of the military police; privileged prisoner

**prévôté** *nf hist* provostship; *hist + mil* (service of) military police

**prévoyance** *nf* foresight, forethought; **société de** ~ provident society

**prévoyant** *adj* foreseeing, prudent, far-sighted

**prévu** *adj* anticipated, expected, foreseen; allowed for, provided for

**prie-Dieu** *nm invar* prayer-stool

**prier** *vt* pray to; beg, request; invite; **je vous prie** please; **je vous en prie** it doesn't matter in the least, not at all; **sans se faire** ~ willingly; without trouble; **se faire** ~ agree after persuasion; *vi* pray

**prière** *nf* prayer; entreaty, request; ~ **de** you are asked to

**prieur -e** *n* prior(ess)

**prieuré** *nm* priory; priory church

**primaire** *adj* primary education; *elect* primary current; narrow-minded individual; dimwit; person ruled by primitive instincts; *adj* primary; narrow-minded, pedantic; dim; primitive

**primat** *nm eccles* primate; primacy

**primauté** *nf* pre-eminence, primacy, supremacy

**prime** *nf comm* premium; bonus, subsidy; free gift; expenses; *eccles* prime; prime (fencing); **marché à** ~ option market; *adj math* prime; *ar* first; ~ **jeunesse** earliest youth; **de** ~ **abord** right from the start

**primer** *vt* award a prize to, give a bonus to; *vi* excel, take the lead

**primerose** *nf* hollyhock

**primesautier -ière** *n + adj* impulsive, spontaneous (person)

**primeur** *nf* novelty; *ar* newness; ~ **s** early vegetables, fruit before season

**primevère** *nf bot* primrose

**primitif -ive** *n anthrop + arts* primitive; *adj* primitive; initial, original; primary (colour, tense); crude, primitive

**primo** *adv* firstly, in the first place

**primordial** *adj* primordial; essential, of prime importance

**primulacées** *nfpl bot* primulaceae

**prince** *nm* prince; **être bon** ~ be generous and kindly

**prince de Galles** *nm invar* kind of woollen cloth

**princeps** *adj* **édition** ~ first edition (of old, rare work)

**princesse** *nf* princess; **aux frais de la** ~ expenses paid

**princier -ière** *adj* princely

**principal** *nm* essential, main thing; principal (college, etc); *comm* principal, capital sum; *adj* chief, leading, main, principal

**principauté** *nf* principality

**principe** *nm* principle; first principle; hypothesis, premise, proposition; cause, mainspring; principle, rule, rule of conduct; ~ **s** rudiments; moral principles; **de** ~ a priori; **en** ~ in theory; **par** ~ on principle, a priori; **pour le** ~ on principle

**printanier -ière** *adj* spring, spring-like; youthful

**printemps** *nm* spring, springtime; *ar* **avoir quinze** ~ be fifteen years old

**prioritaire** *n + adj* priority (holder)

**priorité** *nf* priority; *mot* right of way; *mot* ~ **à droite** (road sign) give way to traffic coming from the right; *comm* **action de** ~ preference share; *mot* **route à** ~ major road

**pris** *adj* caught, taken; engaged, occupied; affected; coagulated, set; **bien** ~ svelte, slender

**prise** *nf* grasp, grip; hold; capture, catching, taking; catch (fish); pinch (snuff); take; coagulation, setting; means of catching, means of taking; *elect* plug; socket; *naut* prize; ~ **d'armes** military parade; ~ **d'eau** tap; hydrant; ~ **de bec** altercation, dispute; *leg* ~ **de corps** arrest; *elect* ~ **de courant** plug; socket; *med* ~ **de sang** blood-test; taking of blood from donor; ~ **de son** recording; *cin* ~ **de vue(s)** take; *mot* ~ **directe** direct transmission; **avoir** ~ **sur** have a hold over; **donner** ~ **à** give a handle to, give an opening to; **être aux** ~ **s avec** be struggling with; *mot* **être en** ~ be in top gear; **lâcher** ~ let go; abandon; **mettre aux** ~ **s** set by the ears

¹**priser** *vt* admire, prize, rate highly, value; **se** ~ think well of oneself

²**priser** *vt + vi* take (snuff)

¹**priseur -euse** *n* snuff-taker

²**priseur** *nm see* **commissaire-priseur**

**prismatique** *adj* prismatic

**prisme** *nm* prism

**prison** *nf* gaol, jail, prison; imprisonment; prison-like building; *coll* **aim-**

**able comme une porte de ~** very disagreeable

**prisonnier -ière** *n* prisoner; *adj* captive, imprisoned

**privatif** *nm* + *adj* (*f* -ive) *gramm* privative (prefix)

**privation** *nf* deprivation, lack; privation

**privatiser** *vt* privatize

**privautés** *nfpl* familiarity, liberties

**privé** *nm* private life; *coll* private industry; *adj* private; intimate, personal; individual, particular

**priver** *vt* deprive; debar; **se ~** deny oneself; impose privations on oneself

**privilège** *nm* privilege; exclusive right; *leg* lien, preference; *Fr hist* authorization from the king to publish a book; grant, licence, preferential right

**privilégié** *adj* privileged; *comm* preference (shares); exceptionally gifted, favoured

**prix** *nm* cost, price, value; rate, tariff; importance, value, weight; prize, reward; **~ de détail** retail price; **~ de gros** wholesale price; **~ de revient** cost price; **~ fixe** fixed price; fixed price meal; **à aucun ~** on no account; **à tout ~** at all costs; **attacher du ~ à** regard as important; **au ~ de** at the cost of; **au ~ fort** at a very high price; **à vil ~** at a very low price; **de ~** valuable; **dernier ~** final price; last word; **donner du ~ à** cause to be valued; **être sans ~** be priceless, be very valuable; **hors de ~** extremely expensive; **mise à ~** reserve price (auction)

**probabilisme** *nm philos* probabilism

**probabilité** *nf* probability, likelihood; conjecture

**probant** *adj* conclusive; *leg* probative

**probe** *adj* honest, upright

**probité** *nf* probity; uprightness

**problématique** *adj* problematical, questionable

**problème** *nm* problem, puzzle; sum

**procédé** *nm* method, process; *pej* stereotyped method; behaviour, conduct, dealing, method of handling; cue-tip (billiards); **échange de bons ~s** mutual help; exchange of courtesies

**procéder** *vi* (6) proceed; originate; act, behave, proceed; **~ à** *leg* execute; proceed with

**procédure** *nf leg* procedure, proceedings; legal practice

**procédurier -ière** *n* compulsive litigant; *adj* fond of chicanery, pettifogging

**procès** *nm* case, cause; trial; *anat* process; **être en ~ avec qn** be fighting a case against s/o; **faire le ~ de** criticize; **intenter un ~ à** bring an action against; **sans autre forme de ~**

without further ado; **soutenir un ~** bring an action

**processif -ive** *adj* litigious

**procession** *nf* religious procession; stream of persons

**processionnel -elle** *adj* processional

**processus** *nm* development method; *anat* process

**procès-verbal** *nm* (*pl* procès-verbaux) formal (police) report; minutes, proceedings; **~ de contravention (P.V.)** (police) ticket; **dresser (un) ~** draw up a report; take particulars

**prochain -e** *n* fellow-creature, neighbour; *adj* near, nearest, neighbouring; approaching (in time), following, next; proximate; **à la ~ e!** be seeing you!

**proche** *adj* near, neighbouring; closely related; *adv* near, nearby; **de ~ en ~** by degrees, step by step

**proclamer** *vt* proclaim; announce, publish; affirm

**proclitique** *adj gramm* proclitic

**proconsulaire** *adj* proconsular

**proconsulat** *nm* proconsulate

**procréateur -trice** *n ar* + *joc* parent; *adj* procreating

**procréer** *vt* engender, procreate

**procurateur** *nm hist* procurator

**procuration** *nf leg* procuration, proxy; power of attorney; **par ~** by proxy

**procurer** *vt* procure; provide; cause; **se ~** acquire

¹**procureur -atrice** *n leg* proxy

²**procureur** *nm* law officer; **~ de la république** public prosecutor

**prodigalité** *nf* prodigality; extravagance

**prodige** *nm* marvel, prodigy, wonder; **enfant ~** infant prodigy

**prodigieux -ieuse** *adj* extraordinary, prodigious, wonderful

**prodigue** *n* prodigal, spendthrift; *adj* prodigal, wasteful; generous, lavish

**prodiguer** *vt* give too readily, give generously, be lavish with; **se ~** exert oneself generously

**prodrome** *nm* preamble, preliminary; *med* premonitory symptom

**producteur -trice** *n* producer; *cin* producer; *adj* producing, productive

**productible** *adj* producible

**productif -ive** *adj* productive

**production** *nf* production, producing, formation; yield; output, manufacturing; product(s)

**productivité** *nf* productivity

**produire** *vt* (80) bring forth, engender, produce; adduce, bring out, show; yield; generate, manufacture; cause; **se ~** happen, occur; *ar* appear

**produit** *nm* takings; yield; **~s** goods, produce

**proéminence** *nf* protuberance; prominence

**proéminent** *adj* protuberant; prominent

**prof** *n coll* teacher

**profanateur -trice** *n* profaner; *adj* profaning

**profane** *n* uninitiated person; ignoramus; *adj* profane; ignorant; uninitiated

**profaner** *vt* desecrate, profane; degrade, violate

**proférer** *vt* (6) emit, pour forth, utter

**professer** *vt* teach, declare; profess

**professeur** *nm* master, mistress, teacher; lecturer; professor

**profession** *nf* business, calling, occupation; profession; ~ **de foi** *pol* (electoral) manifesto

**professionalisme** *nm* professionalism

**professionnel -elle** *n + adj* professional; *nf coll* whore

**professoral** *adj* concerning teaching; professorial

**professorat** *nm* teaching, teaching profession; status of teacher or professor

**profil** *nm* profile; contour, outline, silhouette; *archi* section; **de** ~ from the side, side-face

**profiler** *vt* profile, draw in profile; shape, streamline; outline sharply; **se** ~ be outlined, be silhouetted

**profit** *nm* advantage, benefit, enrichment, profit; **au** ~ **de** in aid of; **être à** ~ be showing a profit; **faire son** ~ **de** take advantage of; **mettre à** ~ use profitably; **tirer** ~ **de** derive benefit from

**profiter** *vi* profit; *coll* become stronger, develop; ~ **à** benefit from, derive profit from; bring profit to, be useful to; ~ **de** benefit by, profit by; avail oneself of, take advantage of; ~ **de qch pour** use sth as a pretext for

**profiteur -euse** *n pej* profiteer

**profond** *nm* depth; *adj* deep, deep-seated, profound; penetrating; impenetrable; downright; *adv* deep

**profondément** *adv* deeply, profoundly; intensely; intimately; extremely

**profondeur** *nf* depth; profoundness, profundity

**profus** *adj* profuse

**profusion** *nf* profusion, abundance; prodigality; **à** ~ in abundance

**progéniture** *nf* offspring, progeny

**prognathe** *adj anthrop* prognathous, protruding

**programmateur -trice** *n rad* programme-planner; *adj* programming (computer, etc)

**programmation** *nf cin + rad* programme-planning, programming

**programme** *nm* programme; syllabus;

intention, project; (computer) program

**programmer** *vt + vi* programme

**programmeur -euse** *n* (computer) programmer

**progrès** *nm* improvement, progress; development, progress; worsening (disease)

**progresser** *vi* advance, improve, progress; develop, make progress; worsen (disease)

**progressif -ive** *adj* progressive; developing; gradual, graduated

**progression** *nf* advancement, forward movement, progress, progression; aggravation; *math + mus* progression

**progressiste** *n + adj* progressive

**progressivité** *nf* progressiveness

**prohiber** *vt* forbid, prohibit

**prohibitif -ive** *adj* prohibitory; prohibitive

**prohibitionnisme** *nm* protection (by customs duties); *US hist* prohibitionism

**proie** *nf* prey, quarry; victim; **de** ~ predatory; **en** ~ **à** tormented by, tortured by, obsessed by

**projecteur** *nm* projector; floodlight; spotlight

**projectionniste** *n cin* operator, projectionist

**projet** *nm* design, intention, plan, project; blue-print, preliminary plan; ~ **de loi** bill; **à l'état de** ~ at the planning stage; provisional

**projeter** *vt* (5) project; cast, throw, hurl; design, intend, plan

**prolapsus** *nm path* prolapse

**prolétaire** *nm* proletarian

**prolétarien -ienne** *adj* proletarian

**prolifère** *adj bot* proliferous

**proliférer** *vi* (6) proliferate; increase, multiply

**prolifique** *adj* prolific

**prolixe** *adj* prolix, verbose, wordy

**prolixité** *nf* prolixity

**prolongation** *nf* extension, prolongation, protraction; *mus* holding; *sp* **jouer les** ~ **s** play extra time

**prolongé** *adj* continued, prolonged, protracted; *coll* ~ **e** not yet married (girl)

**prolongement** *nm* extension, lengthening, prolongation; consequence, development

**prolonger** *vt* (3) extend, lengthen, prolong, protract; **se** ~ go on, last longer than expected

**promenade** *nf* avenue, promenade, public walk; excursion, outing; stroll, walk; ~ **à bicyclette**, ~ **à cheval** ride; ~ **à pied** walk; ~ **en bateau** row, sail; ~ **en voiture** drive

**promener** vt (6) show round, take about; take for a drive, ride, run, sail, walk; move, run up and down (fingers, hand); carry about; **se** ~ walk; go for a drive, ride, run, sail, walk; **allez vous** ~! go to hell!; *coll* **envoyer** ~ **qn** send s/o packing, turn s/o out; **envoyer tout** ~ abandon everything, give up

**promeneur -euse** n stroller, walker; nf children's nurse

**promenoir** nm ambulatory, courtyard (convent, prison, etc); *theat* foyer

**promesse** nf assurance, pledge, promise, undertaking; hope, promise

**prometteur -euse** adj promising

**promettre** vt (60) assure, pledge, promise, undertake; announce, predict, promise; ~ **la lune**, ~ **monts et merveilles** promise the earth; **se** ~ count on, hope for; promise one another; **se** ~ **de** plan to

**promis -e** n betrothed, fiancé(e); adj promised; ~ **à** destined for

**promiscuité** nf promiscuity

**promontoire** nm promontory

**promoteur -trice** n author, creator, instigator, promoter; property developer

**promotion** nf advancement, preferment, promotion; *collect* successful candidates in competitive examination or at end of course

**promouvoir** vt (78) promote; encourage, foster

**prompt** adj immediate, prompt; diligent; adroit, quick; **avoir la main** ~ **e** be always ready to strike

**promptitude** nf promptitude, readiness; rapidity

**promu -e** n + adj promoted (person)

**promulguer** vt promulgate; issue, publish

**prône** nm eccles homily, sermon

**prôner** vt extol, praise highly; advocate, recommend

**pronom** nm gramm pronoun

**prononcé** nm leg (text of) judgement; adj declared, pronounced; definite, marked, pronounced

**prononcer** vt (4) announce; deliver (judgement); pronounce (sentence); articulate, say, utter; deliver, give (speech); vi take a decision; come down in favour; give judgement; **se** ~ be pronounced, become pronounced

**prononciation** nf pronunciation; delivery of judgement

**pronostic** nm med prognosis; forecast, prediction, prognostication

**pronostiquer** vt med forecast, predict, prognosticate

**pronostiqueur -ueuse** n forecaster

**propagande** nf propaganda; publicity

**propagandiste** n + adj propagandist

**propagateur -trice** n propagator

**propager** vt (3) propagate; **se** ~ spread (ideas, illness)

**propédeutique** nf introductory study at university

**propension** nf inclination, propensity, tendency

**prophète** nm prophet, augur

**prophétesse** nf prophetess

**prophétie** nf prophecy; prophesying; prediction, forecast

**prophétique** adj prophetic, prophetical

**prophétiser** vt prophesy; foretell, predict

**prophylactique** adj prophylactic

**prophylaxie** nf prophylaxis

**propice** adj auspicious, favourable, propitious

**propitiatoire** adj propitiatory

**proportion** nf percentage, proportion, ratio; harmony, scale; ~ s dimensions, size; **à** ~ **(en** ~**)** in proportion, proportionately; **à** ~ **de** according to; **à** ~ **que** as, in proportion as

**proportionné** adj proportioned; well-proportioned; proportionate

**proportionnel -elle** adj proportional; **impôt** ~ ad valorem tax; *math* **moyenne** ~**elle** geometrical mean

**proportionner** vt adapt, adjust, proportion

**propos** nm purpose, resolution; matter, subject; pl remarks, words; **à** ~ by the way; at the right moment; appropriately enough; **à** ~ **de** concerning; **à ce** ~ with regard to this; **à quel** ~ **?** about what?; **à tout** ~ all the time, incessantly; **hors de** ~ inappropriate; **mal à** ~ inopportune, unfortunate

**proposer** vt offer, propose, show; present, propound, submit; announce; set (question, subject); propose (candidate); vi form a plan, propose; **se** ~ propose oneself, submit one's candidature; have as one's aim, intend, mean

**proposition** nf proposal, proposition; offer; motion; *math + philos* proposition; **sur** ~ **de** at the suggestion of, on a motion of

**propre** nm characteristic, property; **au** ~ in the literal sense, literally; *coll* **c'est du** ~ it's disgraceful, it's disgusting; **en** ~ in one's own right; adj own, particular, personal; proper (name); appropriate, apt, very; clean, neat; correct, immaculate; honest, honourable; house-trained (pet); ~ **à** conducive to, suitable for; apt; ~ **à rien** good for nothing; **être** ~ be in a fix, be in a fine mess; **mettre au** ~ make a clean copy; **sens** ~ exact meaning; correct usage

**proprement** *adv* correctly, properly; exactly, precisely, truly; carefully; cleanly; *coll* decently; **à ~ parler** to be quite precise; ~ **dit** properly speaking

**propret~ette** *adj* nice and clean, neat

**propreté** *nf* cleanliness, neatness, tidiness; *arts* cleanness of execution

**propriétaire** *n* proprietor, proprietress; owner, landlord (landlady) (house); ~ **foncier** landed proprietor

**propriété** *nf* ownership, possession; property; estate, holding; house; spacious house in own grounds; characteristic, specific quality; correctness, propriety

**propulser** *vt* propel

**propulseur** *nm* propeller, propelling mechanism; *adj invar* propelling, propulsive

**propulsif -ive** *adj* propelling, propulsive

**prorata** *nm invar* **au ~ de** in proportion to

**prorogatif -ive** *adj pol* proroguing

**prorogation** *nf* extension, postponement; *pol* prorogation

**proroger** *vt* (3) extend, postpone; *pol* prorogue

**prosaïque** *adj* inelegant, ordinary, prosaic, vulgar

**prosaïsme** *nm* flatness, ordinariness, vulgarity

**prosateur** *nm* prose-writer

**proscription** *nf* banishment, outlawry, proscription; condemnation; rejection

**proscrire** *vt* (42) banish, outlaw, proscribe; condemn; reject

**proscrit -e** *n* exile, outlaw; *adj* banished, outlawed

**prosélytisme** *nm* proselytizing

**prosodie** *nf* prosody

**prosodique** *adj* prosodic, prosodical

**prospecter** *vt* prospect; do market research on

**prospecteur -trice** *n* prospector; *fig* explorer

**prospectif -ive** *adj* prospective

**prospective** *nf* study of future trends

**prospection** *nf* prospection (minerals); *comm* canvassing, sounding

**prospectus** *nm* publicity hand-out; brochure, handbill; *lit* prospectus

**prospère** *adj* flourishing; prosperous

**prospérer** *vi* (6) flourish, prosper, thrive

**prospérité** *nf* prosperity, well-being

**prostatique** *n + adj med* prostatic (patient)

**prosternement** *nm* prostrate position; *fig* humiliation

**prosterner** *vt* prostrate; **se ~** prostrate oneself; *fig* behave humbly, be servile

**prostitué -e** *n* prostitute

**prostituer** *vt* prostitute; make into a prostitute; *fig* degrade; **se ~** be a prostitute; prostitute oneself; *fig* degrade oneself

**prostitution** *nf* prostitution; degradation

**prostration** *nf* lying prone, prostration; exhaustion

**prostré** *adj* exhausted; prostrate

**protagoniste** *nm* protagonist

**prote** *nm* foreman, owner (in factory works)

**protecteur -trice** *n* protector, protectress; patron, patroness; lover (maintaining a mistress); *adj* protecting; *econ* protectionist; condescending, protective

**protection** *nf* aid, protection; encouragement, patronage; *mil* armour plating; condescension

**protectionnisme** *nm econ* protectionism

**protectorat** *nm* protectorate

**protégé -e** *n* protégé(e); dependant

**protège-dents** *nm* boxer's gum shield

**protège-oreilles** *nm* scrum-cap (rugby football)

**protège-parapluie** *nm invar* umbrella cover

**protéger** *vt* (6, 3) help, protect; defend; shelter, shield; encourage, favour, patronize; give support to

**protéine** *nf* protein

**protestantisme** *nm* Protestantism

**protestataire** *n* objector, protester; *adj* protesting

**protestation** *nf* protest, protestation; assertion, profession; *leg* declaration of protest

**protester** *vt + vi* protest; ~ **de** assert, maintain

**protêt** *nm leg* protest

**prothèse** *nf med* prosthesis; ~ **dentaire** false teeth; **appareils de ~** artificial limbs

**protocolaire** *adj* in accordance with protocol; regarding formal etiquette

**protocole** *nm* protocol; ceremonial; etiquette; *fig* social convention; *typ* list of conventional signs in proof correcting

**protoplasma, protoplasme** *nm* protoplasm

**protoxyde** *nm* nitrous oxide; laughing gas

**protubérance** *nf* protuberance; *med* bump

**prou** *adv lit* **peu ou ~** more or less

**proue** *nf naut* bows, prow

**prouesse** *nf* bravery, prowess, valour; exploit

**prouver** *vt* demonstrate, establish,

prove, show; indicate, reveal; se ~ demonstrate to oneself

**provenance** *nf* origin, provenance, source; ~s imported goods; **en ~ de** (coming) from

**Provençal -e** *n* inhabitant of Provence

**provençal** *nm* Provençal language; *adj* Provençal; *cul* **à la ~e** cooked with garlic and parsley

**provende** *nf* fodder; *ar* provender

**provenir** *vi* (96) come; originate

**proverbe** *nm* proverb; *theat* comedy illustrating a proverb; **passer en ~** become proverbial

**providence** *nf* providence; one who brings succour, protection, saviour; **être la ~ de qn** be the cause of s/o's happiness

**providentiel -ielle** *adj* providential

**province** *nf* province; **la ~** the provinces

**provincialisme** *nm* *lang* provincialism; *pej* provincialism

**proviseur** *nm* **~ de lycée** headmaster of French lycée

**provision** *nf* provision, store, supply; ~s food, provisions, supplies; *leg* interim payment (to creditor); advance, retainer; *comm* cover, deposit; **chèque sans ~** cheque referred to drawer; **faire ~ de** stock up with; **faire ses ~s** do one's shopping

**provisionnel -elle** *adj leg* provisional; **acompte ~** advance instalment of tax (based on previous year's assessment)

**provisoire** *nm* what is provisional, provisional state of affairs; *leg* interim judgement; *adj* provisional; temporary, transitory; acting; **à titre ~** for the time being

**provocant** *adj* aggressive, provocative; alluring, tempting

**provocateur -trice** *n* (rare) instigator; person used to incite to crime or violence; *adj* instigating, inciting, provocative

**provocation** *nf* provocation, incitement; challenge, defiance

**provoquer** *vt* incite, provoke; excite (sexually); bring about, cause, give rise to, provoke

**proxénète** *n* go-between (in love affair); *nm* procurer; pimp

**proxénétisme** *nm* living off immoral earnings

**proximité** *nf* nearness, proximity; approach, imminence; **à ~ de** near, nearby

**prude** *adj* prudish; *ar* virtuous

**prudence** *nf* caution, discretion, prudence

**prudent** *adj* careful, cautious, prudent; judicious, sensible

**pruderie** *nf* prudery, prudishness

**prud'homme** *nm* arbitrator in labour dispute; **conseil des ~s** conciliation tribunal

**prudhommesque** *adj* pompously banal

**pruine** *nf* bloom (on fruit)

**prune** *nf* plum; *coll* **des ~s!** not on your life!; *coll* **pour des ~s** for no reason, for nothing; *adj invar* plum-coloured

**pruneau** *nm* dried plum, prune; *sl* bullet

**¹prunelle** *nf bot* sloe; sloe gin

**²prunelle** *nf* pupil (eye); **~ de ses yeux** apple of one's eye; **jouer de la ~** make eyes at

**prunier** *nm* plum-tree

**prurigineux -euse** *adj path* itching

**prurit** *nm path* pruritus; *lit* longing, urge

**Prussien -ienne** *n* Prussian

**prussien -ienne** *adj* Prussian

**prussique** *adj m chem* prussic

**prytanée** *nm* school for the sons of servicemen

**psalmodie** *nf eccles* psalmody; *lit* monotonous declamation or singing

**psalmodier** *vt* + *vi eccles* intone; *fig* speak monotonously

**psaume** *nm eccles* psalm; musical setting of psalm

**psautier** *nm* psalter

**pseudonyme** *nm* pseudonym; *adj* pseudonymous

**psittacose** *nf path* psittacosis

**psychanalyse** *nf* psychoanalysis; psychoanalytic treatment

**psychanalyser** *vt* psychoanalyse

**psychanalyste** *n* psychoanalyst

**psychanalytique** *adj* psychoanalytic

**psyché** *nf* cheval-glass; *psych* psyche

**psychédélique** *adj* psychedelic

**psychiatre** *n* psychiatrist

**psychiatrie** *nf* psychiatry

**psychiatrique** *adj* psychiatric

**psychique** *adj* psychic, psychical

**psychisme** *nm* psychic phenomena

**psycholinguistique** *nf* psycholinguistics; *adj* psycholinguistic

**psychologie** *nf* psychology; *coll* mentality

**psychologique** *adj* psychological

**psychologue** *n* psychologist

**psychopathe** *n* psychopath

**psychopathie** *nf* psychopathic state

**psychopathologie** *nf* psychopathology

**psychophysique** *nf* psychophysics

**psychose** *nf* psychosis; obsession

**psychosomatique** *adj* psychosomatic

**psychothérapie** *nf* psychotherapy

**psychotique** *n* + *adj* psychotic

**ptérodactyle** *nm* pterodactyl

**puant** *adj* evil-smelling, stinking; *fig* conceited, pretentious

**puanteur** *nf* bad smell, stink

**pubère** *adj* pubescent

**puberté** *nf* puberty

**pubien -ienne** *adj* pubic

**publiable** *adj* publishable

**public** *nm* public; audience; *adj (f -ique)* public; generally known; notorious

**publicitaire** *n* publicist; *coll* adman; *adj* advertising

**publicité** *nf* advertising, publicity; advertising matter

**publier** *vt* publish; write; issue (order)

**puce** *nf* flea; *coll* midget (person); **jeu de ~** tiddly-winks; **(marché aux) ~s** flea-market; **mettre la ~ à l'oreille de qn** intrigue s/o; make s/o suspicious; *coll* **sac à ~s** bed; **secouer les ~s à qn** reprimand s/o; *coll* **tear a strip off s/o**; **secouer ses ~s** stretch oneself on waking; *adj invar* puce (colour)

**puceau** *nm* (male) virgin

**pucelage** *nm coll* maidenhead, virginity

**pucelle** *nf* virgin

**puceron** *nm ent* greenfly; *coll* tiny child

**pucier** *nm sl* bed

**puddler** *vt eng* puddle

**pudeur** *nf* modesty; delicacy, reserve; **attentat à la ~** indecent assault

**pudibond** *adj* prudish; easily shocked

**pudibonderie** *nf* prudishness; false modesty

**pudicité** *nf* modesty; modest nature

**pudique** *adj* chaste, modest; discreet, reserved

**puer** *vt* give off a disgusting smell of, stink of; *vi* smell, stink

**puéricultrice** *nf* children's nurse

**puériculture** *nf* rearing of children; medical care of small children

**puéril** *adj* childish, puerile

**puérilisme** *nm med* infantilism

**puérilité** *nf* puerility

**puerpéral** *adj med* puerperal

**pugilat** *nm* fight, set-to; *ar* pugilism

**pugiliste** *nm lit* boxer; *ar* pugilist

**pugilistique** *adj lit* pugilistic

**pugnace** *adj lit* combative, pugnacious

**pugnacité** *nf lit* pugnaciousness, pugnacity

**puîné -e** *n + adj* younger (son, daughter)

**puis** *adv* after that, next, then; besides; further on; **et ~** moreover; **et ~ ?**, *coll* **et ~ après?, et ~ quoi?** well?; *coll* so what?

**puisard** *nm* sunk draining trap; *mech* sump; *naut* bilges

**puisatier** *nm* well-sinker

**puiser** *vt* draw, ladle out (liquid); *vi* **~ dans** dig into (sack, wallet); derive inspiration from, draw on

**puisque** *conj* as, considering that, seeing that, since

**puissamment** *adv* powerfully; *coll* extremely

**puissance** *nf* power, strength, ability, capacity; *philos* possibility; authority, force, sovereignty; nation, state; volume (sound); *phys* energy; **mot ~ administrative**, **~ fiscale** horse-power (for purpose of licensing); **en ~** potential; **volonté de ~** urge to dominate

**puissant** *nm* powerful individual; *adj* mighty, powerful, strong; effective

**puits** *nm* well; (mine-)shaft, pit; *fig* fount; **~ de pétrole** oil-well; **~ naturel** pothole

**pull** *nm* pullover

**pullulation** *nf*, **pullulement** *nm* multiplication, pullulation; swarming

**pulluler** *vi* pullulate; swarm; abound

**pulmonaire** *nf bot* lungwort; *adj* pulmonary

**pulpe** *nf* pulp; fleshy part of finger-tip

**pulpeux -euse** *adj* pulpy

**pulsative** *adj f med* **douleur ~** throbbing pain

**pulvérisable** *adj* reducible to powder or fine clay

**pulvérisateur** *nm* atomizer, spray, vaporizer

**pulvérisation** *nf* pulverization; spraying, vaporizing

**pulvériser** *vt* pulverize, grind into powder; spray, vaporize; *coll* crush, destroy; *coll* beat easily, flatten

**pulvériseur** *nm agr* pulverizer

**punaise** *nf ent* bed-bug, bug; drawing-pin

**punch** *nm* (of boxer) ability to punch; *coll* dynamism, energy, go; (drink) punch

**punique** *adj* Punic

**punir** *vt* punish

**punissable** *adj* punishable

**punitif -ive** *adj* punitive

**punition** *nf* punishing, punishment

**pupe** *nf ent* pupa

**¹pupille** *n leg* pupil, ward; orphan

**²pupille** *nf anat* pupil

**pupitre** *nm* desk (school); music-stand; lectern

**pur** *adj* pure; unalloyed, undiluted; spotless, unsullied; impeccable, perfect; chaste, innocent; mere, sheer

**purée** *nf cul* purée, mash; mashed potatoes; *coll* poverty; *sl* **~!** what a shambles!; **~ de pois** pea-souper, thick fog; *sl* **être dans la ~** be in the soup, be hard up

**purement** *adv* purely; entirely

**pureté** *nf* pureness, purity; innocence;

correctness (language, style); clearness
**purgatif** *nm* laxative, purge; *adj* (*f* -**ive**) purgative
**purgatoire** *nm* purgatory
**purge** *nf* purge, purging; draining, draining-off; *leg* redemption; cleaning (raw fabrics)
**purger** *vt* (3) purge; give laxative to; drain off; purify; get rid of, sweep away; *leg* redeem (mortgage); serve (sentence); **se ~** take a laxative
**purifiant** *adj* purifying
**purificateur** -**trice** *adj* purifying
**purifier** *vt* purify; clean, cleanse, refine
**purin** *nm* liquid manure; **fosse à ~** manure-pit (in farmyard)
**purisme** *nm* purism
**puriste** *n* + *adj* purist
**puritain** -**e** *n* Puritan; *adj* puritan, puritanical
**puritanisme** *nm* Puritanism
**purotin** *nm sl* s/o who is broke, hard-up
**purpurin** *adj* crimson, purplish
**pur-sang** *nm invar* thoroughbred (horse)
**purulent** *adj* festering, purulent; reprehensible
**pusillanime** *adj* faint-hearted, pusillanimous
**pusillanimité** *nf* faint-heartedness, pusillanimity
**pustuleux** -**euse** *adj* pustular
**putain** *nf sl* whore; *vulg as interj* shit!; *sl* ~ **de** bloody
**putatif** -**ive** *adj* putative

**pute** *nf sl* tart, whore
**putois** *nm zool* polecat
**putréfiable** *adj* liable to putrefy
**putréfier** *vt* decompose, putrefy, rot; **se ~** decompose, rot
**putrescible** *adj* liable to putrefy; corruptible
**putridité** *nf* putridness
**puy** *nm geog* peak (Auvergne)
**pygmée** *nm* pygmy
**pyjama** *nm* pyjamas
**pylône** *nm* pylon; *archi* pillar, pylon
**pylore** *nm anat* pylorus
**pyorrhée** *nf med* pyorrhoea
**pyramide** *nf* pyramid
**pyrénéen** -**éenne** *adj geog* Pyrenean
**pyrèthre** *nm bot* feverfew, pyrethrum; **poudre de ~** pyrethrum powder, insect powder
**pyrexie** *nf path* feverish condition, pyrexia
**pyrite** *nf chem* pyrites
**pyromane** *n* incendiary, fire-raiser, arsonist
**pyromanie** *nf* pyromania
**pyrotechnie** *nf* pyrotechnics
**pyrotechnique** *adj* pyrotechnic
**pyrrhonien** -**ienne** *n* + *adj philos* sceptic
**pyrrhonisme** *nm philos* doctrine of Pyrrho, scepticism
**pythagoricien** -**ienne** *n* + *adj* Pythagorean
**pythagorique** *adj* Pythagorean
**pythonisse** *nf* prophetess, clairvoyante

# Q

**quadragénaire** *n* + *adj* quadragenarian
**quadrangulaire** *adj* quadrangular
**quadratique** *adj* quadratic
**quadrilatère** *nm* quadrilateral
**quadrillage** *nm* cross-ruling; chequerwork; partitioning (area, for policing operations)
**quadriller** *vt* rule in squares; partition (area, for policing operations)
**quadrimoteur** *nm* four-engined aircraft; *adj m* four-engined
**quadrupède** *nm* quadruped
**quadrupler** *vt* + *vi* quadruple
**quai** *nm* quay, wharf; embankment;

platform; **Quai d'Orsay** French Foreign Office
**qualifiable** *adj* describable
**qualificatif** -**ive** *adj* qualifying
**qualification** *nf* naming, calling; qualifying; name; qualification
**qualifier** *vt* qualify; call, term; describe; **crime qualifié** aggravated crime; **ouvrier qualifié** skilled worker; **se ~** call oneself
**qualitatif** -**ive** *adj* qualitative
**qualité** *nf* quality; excellence; property; capacity, qualification; rank; **en ~ de** as, in the capacity of
**quand** *adv* when; ~ **même** nevertheless;

**à ~ votre départ?** when is your departure?; **de ~ est sa lettre?** when does his letter date from?; **n'importe ~** at any time; *conj* when; whenever; even if; *coll* **je vous le disais!** didn't I tell you so!

**quant à** *prep* as to, as regards

**quant-à-soi** *nm* reserve, dignity; **rester sur son ~** stand on one's dignity

**quantifier** *vt* quantify

**quantitatif -ive** *adj* quantitative

**quantité** *nf* quantity; large number

**quantum** *nm* (*pl* **quanta**) amount, proportion; *phys* quantum

**quarantaine** *nf* about forty; age of forty; quarantine; **mettre qn en ~** send s/o to Coventry; put s/o in quarantine

**quarante** *adj* forty; **les Quarante** the members of the French Academy; *sl* **s'en ficher comme de l'an ~** not care a damn about s/o (sth)

**quarantième** *adj* fortieth

**quart** *nm* quarter; *naut* watch; carafe, mug (holding quarter of a litre); *sl* police station; **aux trois ~s** largely, mainly; **moins le (un) ~** a quarter to; *coll* **passer un mauvais ~ d'heure** have a few nasty moments; *adj ar* fourth

**quarteron** *nm* small number

**quartier** *nm* quarter; district; **~s** quarters; **~ général** headquarters; **bureau de ~** branch office

**quartier-maître** *nm* (*pl* **quartiers-maîtres**) *mil* quartermaster

¹**quasi** *nm* chump-end (of loin)

²**quasi** *adv* almost

**quasiment** *adv coll* almost

**Quasimodo** *nf eccles* Low Sunday

**quatorze** *nm* fourteen; fourteenth; *adj* fourteen

**quatre** *nm* four; fourth; *adj* four; **~ à ~** four at a time; **à ~ pas** very near; **à ~ pattes** on all fours; **manger comme ~** eat greedily; **ne pas y aller par ~ chemins** get straight to the point; **se mettre en ~** do one's utmost; **un de ces ~ matins** one of these days

**quatre-saisons** *nf invar* variety of strawberry; **marchand des ~** costermonger

**quatre-vingts** *nm + adj* eighty

**quatrième** *nm* fourth floor; *nf* third-year class (at secondary school); *adj* fourth

**quatuor** *nm mus* quartet; quatuor

**que** *rel pron* whom, that; that which; as; *inter pron* whom?, what?; *adv* why?; how?; what a lot; only; **ne ... ~** only; *conj* that; lest; may ...; let ...; so that; before, until; since; when; as; than; whether; *coll* **~ si!** yes, surely

**quel** (*f* **quelle**) *pron* who, what; **~ que**

whoever, whatever; *adj* which, what; **what a ...!**

**quelconque** *adj* any; *coll* ordinary, commonplace

**quelque** *adj* any, some; whatsoever; whatever; **~s** a few, some; **~ chose** something, anything; **~ part** somewhere; *adv* about, some; **~ ... que** however

**quelquefois** *adv* sometimes, occasionally

**quelques-uns** (*f* **quelques-unes**) *pron pl* a few, some

**quelqu'un** (*f* **quelqu'une**) *pron* one (or other); somebody, someone, anyone; *coll* **se prendre pour ~** think oneself important

**quémander** *vt* beg for; *vi* beg

**qu'en-dira-t-on** *nm invar* gossip

**quenelle** *nf* fish ball, meat ball

**quenotte** *nf coll* child's tooth

**quenouille** *nf* distaff

**querelle** *nf* quarrel; controversy; **~ d'Allemand** trumped-up quarrel; **chercher ~ à qn** try to pick a quarrel with s/o

**quereller** *vt* quarrel with (s/o); **se ~** quarrel

**querelleur -euse** *adj* quarrelsome

**quérir** *vt* (79) fetch

**qu'est-ce que** *inter pron* what?; **~ c'est que ça?** what's that?; *coll* **qu'est-ce qu'il fait froid!** how cold it is!

**qu'est-ce qui** *inter pron* what?

**question** *nf* question, query; point; matter; torture (judicial); **être ~ de** be a matter of; **mettre en ~** question, challenge; **ne pas faire ~** be beyond doubt; **poser une ~** ask a question

**questionnaire** *nm* list of questions, questionnaire

**questionner** *vt* question

**quête** *nf* collection, fund-raising; *ar* search

**quêter** *vt* angle for, fish for; *vi* collect (alms), take collection

**quêteur -euse** *n* collector of alms

**queue** *nf* tail; queue; handle (pan); stalk; train (dress); pigtail; pin (brooch); cue (billiards); *vulg* prick; **à la ~ leu leu** one behind the other; **en ~** at the rear; **faire la ~** queue up; *mot* **faire une ~ de poisson à qn** cut in on s/o; **finir en ~ de poisson** fizzle out; **piano à ~** grand piano

**queue-d'aronde** *nf* (*pl* **queues-d'aronde**) *carp* dovetail

**queue-de-pie** *nf* (*pl* **queues-de-pie**) *coll* tails

**queue-de-rat** *nf* (*pl* **queues-de-rat**) rat-tailed file

**queux** *nm ar* **maître ~** cook, chef

**qui** *rel pron* who, which, that; whom, which; he who; him who; that which, what; **~ ... ~** one ... another; **~ que vous soyez** whoever you may be; *inter pron* who?; whom?

**quia (à)** *adv phr* at a loss, in a quandary

**quiche** *nf* kind of savoury flan

**quiconque** *pron* whoever, whosoever, anyone who; anyone else

**quidam** *nm* someone, individual

**qui est-ce que** *inter pron* whom?

**qui est-ce qui** *inter pron* who?

**quiétude** *nf* quietude, peace of mind

**quignon** *nm* chunk of bread

¹**quille** *nf* skittle, ninepin; *sl* demob

²**quille** *nf* keel

**quincaillerie** *nf* ironmongery; hardware shop

**quincaillier** *nm* ironmonger

**quinconce** *nm* quincunx; **en ~** quincuncial

**quinquagénaire** *adj* fifty years old

**quinquennal** *adj* five-year, quinquennial

**quinquet** *nm* kind of lamp; *sl* **~ s** eyes

**quinquina** *nm* Peruvian bark; chinchona

**quinte** *nf mus* fifth, quint; quint (cards, fencing); **~ de toux** fit of coughing

**quintessencié** *adj* oversubtle

**quinteux -euse** *adj* capricious

**quintupler** *vt + vi* increase fivefold

**quintuplés -ées** *npl* quintuplets

**quinzaine** *nf* about fifteen; fortnight

**quinze** *nm* fifteen, fifteenth; rugby fifteen; *adj* fifteen; **~ jours** a fortnight

**quinzième** *n + adj* fifteenth

**quiproquo** *nm* mistake, misunderstanding

**quittance** *nf* receipt

**quittancer** *vt* (4) receipt

**quitte** *adj* free, quit, rid; quits; **~ à** at the risk of; **en être ~ pour** get off with; **tenir ~** dispense

**quitter** *vt* leave, quit; give up; take off (clothing); **ne quittez pas** hold the line; **se ~** part, separate

**qui-vive** *nm invar mil* sentry's challenge; **être sur le ~** be on the alert

**quoi** *rel pron* what, which; *pron* **~ que** whatever; **~ que ce soit** anything; whatever it may be; **~ qu'il en soit** be that as it may; *coll* **comme ~** which goes to show that; **de ~** the wherewithal, enough to, something with which to; **il n'y a pas de ~** don't mention it; *inter pron* what?; **à ~ bon?** what's the use?; **en ~ est-il?** what is it made of?; **un je ne sais ~** an indefinable something; *interj* what!

**quoique** *conj* although

**quolibet** *nm* gibe, coarse joke

**quote-part** *nf* (*pl* **quotes-parts**) portion, quota

**quotidien** *nm* daily newspaper; *adj* (*f* **-ienne**) daily

**quotité** *nf* quota, amount of share

# R

**ra** *nm invar* drum-roll

**rabâchage** *nm* tiresome repetition

**rabâcher** *vt + vi* repeat again and again

**rabais** *nm* price reduction; **au ~** on the cheap, cheap

**rabaisser** *vt* lower; reduce; depreciate, disparage; humble

**rabat** *nm* bands (clergy, magistrates); flap

**rabat-joie** *nm invar* killjoy, spoilsport

**rabattage** *nm* beating up (game)

**rabatteur -euse** *n* tout (for customers); beater (shoot)

**rabattre** *vt* fold down, fold back; flatten; put down; shut down; turn down; reduce, diminish; beat up (game); **en ~** be less demanding, climb down; **se ~** fall back; fold back

**rabbin** *nm* rabbi

**rabelaisien -ienne** *adj* Rabelaisian

**rabiot** *nm coll* extra work, overtime; *sl mil* surplus rations, surplus; *mil* extra service

**rabique** *adj* rabid

**râble** *nm cul* back, saddle

**râblé** *adj* strapping; broad-backed

**rabot** *nm* plane

**raboter** *vt* plane, plane down

**raboteux -euse** *adj* uneven, rough

**rabougri** *adj* stunted

**rabouter** *vt* join end to end

**rabrouer** *vt* scold

**racaille** *nf* riff-raff

**raccommodage** *nm* mending, repairing; mend

**raccommodement** *nm* reconciliation

**raccommoder** *vt* mend, repair; reconcile; **se ~ avec qn** make it up with s/o

**raccompagner** *vt* escort back; run back

**raccord** *nm* join; joint, connection

**raccordement** *nm* joining, linking-up; junction

**raccorder** *vt* join, link up, connect; **se ~** connect, fit together

**raccourci** *nm* foreshortening; epitome; short cut

**raccourcir** *vt* shorten; abridge; *vi* become shorter, shrink; **à bras raccourcis** violently, vigorously

**raccourcissement** *nm* shortening, shrinking

**raccoutumer (se)** *v refl* reaccustom oneself

**raccroc** *nm* fluke; **par ~** by chance

**raccrocher** *vt* hang up again, hook up again; *vi* hang up, ring off; recover

**race** *nf* race; species; strain; breed; **chasser de ~** be true to type; **cheval de ~** thoroughbred horse; **chien de ~** pedigree dog

**racé** *adj* thoroughbred; distinguished, well-bred

**rachat** *nm* buying back; redemption; atonement

**racheter** *vt* (5) buy back; buy again; redeem; atone for; ransom; **se ~** atone

**rachitique** *adj* rachitic

**rachitisme** *nm* rickets

**racine** *nf* root; cause, origins; base

**racisme** *nm* racialism, racism

**raciste** *n* racialist, racist

**raclée** *nf coll* thrashing, hiding

**racler** *vt* scrape; rake over; **~ du violon** play the violin badly; **se ~ la gorge** clear one's throat

**raclette** *nf* scraper; *cul* melted cheese dish

**racolage** *nm* recruiting; touting; soliciting

**racoler** *vt* recruit, impress; catch, bring in; solicit

**racontar** *nm* piece of gossip

**raconter** *vt* relate, tell, tell about; **en ~** tell wild tales

**raconteur -euse** *n* narrator, story-teller; raconteur, raconteuse

**racornir** *vt* make hard as horn; **se ~** become hard; *coll* shrivel up

**radariste** *n* radar technician

**rade** *nf naut* roads; natural harbour

**radeau** *nm* raft

**radiateur** *nm* radiator

**radiation** *nf* erasing, striking off; erasure

**¹radier** *nm bui* frame, bed, floor

**²radier** *vt* erase, strike out; strike off, cross off

**radieux -ieuse** *adj* radiant; beaming

**radin** *adj coll* stingy

**radio** *nf* radio; X-ray; **passer à la ~** broadcast; X-ray

**radio-actif -ive** radio-active

**radio-activité** *nf* radio-activity

**radiodiffuser** *vt* broadcast

**radiodiffusion** *nf* radio broadcasting

**radiogramme** *nm* radio message

**radiographie** *nf* X-ray photograph

**radiographier** *vt* make an X-ray of

**radiologie** *nf* X-ray treatment, radiology

**radiophonique** *adj* radiophonic

**radio-reportage** *nm* radio-reporting, commentary on the radio

**radioscopie** *nf* radioscopy

**radiothérapie** *nf* radiotherapy

**radis** *nm* radish; *coll* **n'avoir pas un ~** not have a halfpenny, be broke

**radotage** *nm* nonsense, drivel; rambling

**radoter** *vi* drivel, talk nonsense

**radoteur -euse** *n* dotard

**radoub** *nm naut* refit, repair; **bassin de ~** dry dock

**radouber** *vt naut* repair the hull of; repair (net)

**radoucir** *vt* calm; make milder; mollify; assuage, appease; **se ~** become milder; calm down

**rafale** *nf* squall; burst of fire

**raffermir** *vt* make firmer, harden; strengthen, fortify

**raffinage** *nm* refining process

**raffiné** *adj* refined; subtle

**raffinement** *nm* refining; refinement

**raffiner** *vt + vi* refine; **~ sur** split hairs over

**raffinerie** *nf* refinery

**raffineur -euse** *n* refiner

**raffoler** *vi* be very fond, dote

**raffut** *nm coll* shindy, row

**rafiot** *nm coll* poor boat, old tub

**rafistolage** *nm coll* repairing, patching up

**rafistoler** *vt coll* repair, patch up

**rafle** *nf* looting, cleaning out; round-up, police raid

**rafler** *vt* carry off, take away; round up

**rafraîchir** *vt* refresh, cool; revive; do up, renovate; trim (hair); touch up; **se ~** become cooler, fresher; refresh oneself, have a drink

**rafraîchissant** *adj* refreshing, cooling

**rafraîchissement** *nm* cooling; cooling down; reviving, freshening up; refreshing; cool drink; **~ s** refreshments

**ragaillardir** *vt* cheer up; give strength to

**rage** *nf* rage, fury; violent pain; passion,

mania; rabies; **faire ~** rage, be raging

**rageant** *adj* infuriating

**rager** *vi* (3) fume, be furious, be wild with anger

**rageur -euse** *adj* choleric; angry

**ragot** *nm coll* piece of gossip

**ragoût** *nm* stew

**ragoûtant** *adj* appetizing; attractive

**raid** *nm* raid; long-distance run, flight

**raide, roide** *adj* stiff; steep; obstinate; starchy; **c'est un peu ~** it's a bit thick; *adv* violently, hard; **~ mort** stone dead

**raideur, roideur** *nf* stiffness; steepness; starchiness; inflexibility

**raidillon** *nm* short steep path

**raidir, roidir** *vt* stiffen; tauten

**raidissement** *nm* stiffening

¹**raie** *nf* line, stroke; stripe; parting (hair); ridge (between furrows)

²**raie** *nm* skate (fish), ray

**raifort** *nm* horseradish

**rail** *nm* rail; railway

**railler** *vt* laugh at, jeer at; *vi* speak lightly, in jest

**railleur -euse** *adj* mocking, bantering

**rainer** *vt* groove, slot

**rainette** *nf* tree-frog

**rainure** *nf* furrow, groove

**raisin** *nm* grape; **~ de Corinthe** currant; **~ sec** raisin

**raisiné** *nm* jam made with grape juice and other fruit

**raison** *nf* reason; motive, ground; good sense; argument; proof; **~ de plus** all the more reason; **~ sociale** name under which a firm trades; **âge de ~** age of discretion; **à plus forte ~** all the more reason; **à ~ de** at the rate of; **avoir ~ de** get the better of; **comme de ~** as one could expect; **demander ~ de** ask for satisfaction for; **en ~ de** in consideration of; **entendre ~** listen to reason; **perdre la ~** take leave of one's senses; **ramener qn à la ~** bring s/o back to his senses; **rendre ~ de qch** give an explanation of sth; **se faire une ~** resign oneself to the inevitable

**raisonnable** *adj* reasonable, sensible; adequate

**raisonnement** *nm* reasoning; argument; objection

**raisonner** *vt* reason out, consider; reason with; *vi* reason, argue; be argumentative

**raisonneur -euse** *n* argumentative person; *adj* reasoning; argumentative

**rajeunir** *vt* rejuvenate; make look younger; *vi* grow young again

**rajeunissement** *nm* rejuvenation

**rajouter** *vt* add (something further)

**rajuster** *vt* readjust; set right; modify; **se**

**~** adjust one's clothing

¹**râle** *nm* rattle; **~ de la mort** death-rattle

²**râle** *nm orni* rail

**ralenti** *nm* slow motion; **au ~** slowly; *mot* **tourner au ~** idle

**ralentissement** *nm* slowing down, slowing up

**râler** *vi* rattle; gasp; *coll* grumble

**ralliement** *nm* rally, rallying

**rallier** *vt* rally, assemble; rejoin; win over; get to; **se ~** rally; adhere

**rallonge** *nf* extension; extra leaf (table); *coll* supplement; *coll* rise; **nom à ~** double-barrelled name

**rallonger** *vt* (3) lengthen, make longer

**rallumer** *vt* light again; revive; **se ~** light up again, be relit; flare up again

**rallye** *nm* rally

**ramage** *nm* warbling; floral design, branch design

**ramassage** *nm* picking up; collecting; **~ scolaire** school transport

**ramassé** *adj* thick-set, stocky; concise, compact

**ramasse-miettes** *nm* crumb-scoop

**ramasse-poussière** *nm invar* dust-pan

**ramasser** *vt* pick up; gather, collect, gather up; condense (style); *coll* make (money); *coll* take in, arrest; **se ~** crouch; gather oneself; *sl* pick oneself up

**ramassis** *nm pej* pile, heap, collection

¹**rame** *nf* oar, scull

²**rame** *nf* ream (paper); string, group (carriages, barges); **~ de métro** tube train

**rameau** *nm* small branch; twig; branch, subdivision; **dimanche des Rameaux** Palm Sunday

**ramée** *nf ar* branches, twigs

**ramener** *vt* (6) bring back, bring again; win over, bring round

**ramequin** *nm* cheese tart; baking vessel

**ramer** *vi* row

**rameur -euse** *n* rower, oarsman (oarswoman)

**rami** *nm* rummy (cards)

**ramier** *adj* pigeon **~** wood pigeon

**ramifier (se)** *v refl* branch out, divide

**ramolli** *adj* soft; *coll* dull-witted

**ramollir** *vt* soften; weaken

**ramollissement** *nm* softening

**ramonage** *nm* chimney-sweeping

**ramoner** *vt* sweep (chimney); climb (rock chimney)

**ramoneur** *nm* chimney-sweep

**rampant** *adj* creeping, crawling; subservient, grovelling; *her* rampant

**rampe** *nf* ramp; slope; *theat* footlights; handrail; **~ de lancement** launching pad; *coll* **lâcher la ~** die; *theat* **passer**

la ~ get across

**ramper** *vi* creep, crawl; grovel

**ramure** *nf* branches; antlers

**rancart** *nm* **mettre au** ~ put aside, get rid of

**rance** *adj* rancid

**rancir** *vi* go rancid

**rancœur** *nf* bitterness, rancour

**rançon** *nf* ransom; price

**rançonner** *vt* ransom, hold to ransom

**rancune** *nf* rancour, malice, spite, resentment; **garder** ~ harbour resentment; **sans** ~ no ill feelings

**rancunier -ière** *adj* vindictive, spiteful

**randonnée** *nf* trip, outing, excursion

**rang** *nm* line, row; rank; station; **en** ~ **d'oignons** in a line; **rompre les** ~ **s** disperse; **se mettre en** ~ **s** fall in; **se mettre sur les** ~ **s** put in for; **serrer les** ~ **s** close up; **sortir du** ~ rise from the ranks; make one's name

**rangé** *adj* tidy; steady; **bataille** ~ **e** pitched battle

**rangée** *nf* row, line

**ranger** *vt* (3) arrange; draw up; put away, tidy; set in order; range, rank; put aside, set aside; subjugate; go alongside; **se** ~ line up; side, take sides; stand aside, get out of the way; calm down, settle down

**ranimer** *vt* revive, restore to life; **se** ~ revive, come to life again

**rapace** *adj* rapacious, grasping; predacious

**rapaces** *nmpl* birds of prey

**rapacité** *nf* rapacity

**rapatriement** *nm* repatriation

**rapatrier** *vt* repatriate, send home

**râpe** *nf* grater; rasp

**râpé** *adj* grated; worn out, threadbare; *coll* failed

**râper** *vt* grate; rasp

**rapetasser** *vt coll* patch up

**rapetisser** *vt* make smaller; make appear smaller; diminish the merit of; *vi* become smaller, shorter

**râpeux -euse** *adj* rough

**raphia** *nm* raffia

**rapiat** *adj coll* stingy, miserly

**rapide** *nm* express, fast train; rapids; *adj* fast, rapid; steep

**rapidité** *nf* speed, swiftness; steepness

**rapiécer** *vt* (6, 4) patch

**rapière** *nf* rapier

**rapin** *nm ar* art student; dauber

**rapiner** *vt* + *vi* pillage

**raplapla** *adj coll invar* washed out, exhausted

**raplatir** *vt* flatten again

**rappel** *nm* recall; reminder; *eng* return; back payment; **battre le** ~ call to arms

**rappeler** *vt* (5) recall, call back; bring

back; remind of, bring to mind; **se** ~ remember

**rappliquer** *vi sl* come back; come

**rapport** *nm* report; return, yield; relations; relationship, connection; proportion; *sl* ~ **à** regarding; **avoir** ~ **à** relate to; **avoir des** ~ **s avec** be in touch with; have sexual relations with; **en** ~ **avec** in keeping with; **mettre en** ~ **avec** put in touch with; **par** ~ **à** in relation to; **sous ce** ~ in this respect

**rapportage** *nm coll* tale-bearing, sneaking

**rapporter** *vt* bring back, carry back; bring in, yield; report; repeat; annul, call off; ascribe; *vi* sneak; **se** ~ agree, tally; refer, relate; **s'en** ~ **à** rely on, leave things to

**rapporteur -euse** *n* tale-bearer; *nm* reporter, recorder; *math* protractor

**rapproché** *adj* near, nearly

**rapprochement** *nm* bringing together; reconciling, reconciliation; comparing; bringing nearer, coming nearer

**rapprocher** *vt* bring nearer, bring closer, bring near again; compare; bring together; reconcile; **se** ~ draw nearer

**rapt** *nm* abduction

**raquette** *nf* racket; snow-shoe; prickly pear

**rare** *adj* rare; exceptional, uncommon; sparse, thin

**raréfaction** *nf* rarefaction; depletion

**raréfier** *vt* rarefy; deplete

**rareté** *nf* rarity, scarcity, dearth; singularity; rare occurrence; rare object

**rarissime** *adj* very rare

¹**ras** *nm see* **raz**

²**ras** *adj* cut short, close-shaven; **à poil** ~ short-haired; **à** ~ **bord** to the brim; **à (au)** ~ **de** level with; *sl* **en avoir** ~ **le bol** be fed up to the teeth; **en** ~ **e campagne** in the open country; **faire table** ~ **e** make a clean sweep; *adv* close; **couper** ~ cut very short

**rasade** *nf* full glass

**rasage** *nm* shaving

**rasant** *adj* low-lying; low (shooting); *coll* boring, tiresome

**rascasse** *nf* hog-fish

**rase-mottes** *nm invar* **vol en** ~ very low flight, hedge-hopping

**raser** *vt* shave, shave off; raze; skim over, graze; keep close to, hug; *coll* bore, annoy; **se** ~ shave; *coll* be bored

**raseur -euse** *n coll* bore

**rasibus** *adv sl* very close

¹**rasoir** *nm* razor; ~ **de sûreté** safety razor

²**rasoir** *adj coll* boring, tiresome

**rassasier** *vt* satisfy (hunger); sate, surfeit; **se** ~ eat one's fill

**rassemblement** *nm* assembling, gathering; *mil* fall-in; crowd; political grouping

**rassembler** *vt* assemble, gather together; muster; collect; **se ~** assemble; *mil* fall in

**rasseoir** *vt* (15) replace; **se ~** sit down again

**rasséréner** *vt* (6) make calm again; **se ~** become calm again; clear up

**rassis** *adj* calm, staid, sedate; **pain ~** stale bread

**rassortir** *vt* see **réassortir**

**rassurant** *adj* reassuring

**rassurer** *vt* reassure, cheer

**rasta(quouère)** *nm coll* flashy foreigner

**rat** *nm* rat; *coll* miserly person; *coll* **~ de bibliothèque** book-worm; **~ de cave** wax taper; **~ d'église** regular churchgoer; **~ d'hôtel** hotel thief; **~ de l'Opéra** ballet pupil at the Opéra; **être fait comme un ~** be caught out

**rata** *nm sl mil* grub

**ratafia** *nm* ratafia (liqueur)

**rataplan** *nm* rat-tat (of drum)

**ratatiner** *vt* shrivel up, diminish; **se ~** shrivel up

**ratatouille** *nf coll* stew; poor cooking; **~ niçoise** Provençal vegetables cooked in olive oil

**rate** *nf anat* spleen; *coll* **dilater la ~** make laugh; *coll* **se fouler la ~** make an effort

**raté -e** *n* failure, flop, unsuccessful person

**râteau** *nm* rake

**râteler** *vt* (5) rake up

**râtelier** *nm* rack (stable); rack; row of teeth; *coll* false teeth, dentures; *coll* **manger à plusieurs (tous les) ~s** have two strings to one's bow; have a foot in both camps

**rater** *vt* miss; fail in; *vi* misfire, fail to go off; miscarry, fail

**ratiboiser** *vt coll* pinch, snaffle; clean out (at gambling)

**ratier** *nm* ratter (dog)

**ratière** *nf* rat-trap

**ratification** *nf* ratification; confirmation

**ratifier** *vt* ratify; confirm

**ratine** *nf* ratteen, petersham

**ratiociner** *vi* cavil, ratiocinate

**rationaliser** *vt* rationalize

**rationalisme** *nm* rationalism

**rationnel -elle** *adj* rational

**rationnement** *nm* rationing

**rationner** *vt* ration

**ratisser** *vt* rake, rake over; rake in (stakes); *mil* search and destroy; hook (rugby football)

**raton** *nm* young rat; *coll + pej* wog; **~ laveur** raccoon

**rattacher** *vt* tie up, fasten; tie again; bind; link up

**rattraper** *vt* catch again, recapture; catch up; correct, make good; **se ~** catch hold; compensate oneself; catch up, make up lost time

**rature** *nf* crossing out

**raturer** *vt* cross out, strike out

**rauque** *adj* hoarse, raucous, harsh

**ravage** *nm* damage; destruction; deterioration

**ravager** *vt* (3) ravage, lay waste; play havoc with; undermine, take a toll of

**ravalement** *nm* resurfacing, cleaning up

**ravaler** *vt* swallow again; clean up; resurface (wall); reduce the height of; humble; **se ~** degrade oneself

**ravaudage** *nm* mending, darning

**ravauder** *vt* mend, patch, darn

**rave** *nf bot* rape

**ravenelle** *nf* wallflower; wild radish

**ravi** *adj* delighted

**ravier** *nm* hors-d'œuvres dish

**ravigoter** *vt coll* revive, refresh

**ravin** *nm* ravine

**raviner** *vt* gulley, hollow out, channel

**ravir** *vt* carry off, ravish; delight, ravish; **à ~** delightful; delightfully, admirably

**raviser (se)** *v refl* change one's mind

**ravissant** *adj* delightful; entrancing

**ravissement** *nm* rapture, delight; *ar* carrying off

**ravisseur -euse** *n* kidnapper; ravisher

**ravitaillement** *nm* provisioning; provisions, food

**ravitailler** *vt* provision, revictual; supply with food, fuel

**raviver** *vt* revive; brighten up

**ravoir** *vt* (1) get again, recover

**rayé** *adj* striped; scratched

**rayer** *vt* (7) scratch, score; strike out; exclude; rifle

**¹rayon** *nm* ray, beam; spoke; radius; *hort* drill, small furrow; **~ d'action** range, scope

**²rayon** *nm* shelf; department (shop); **~ de miel** honeycomb

**rayonnant** *adj* radiant; beaming

**rayonne** *nf* rayon

**rayonnement** *nm* radiance

**rayonner** *vi* radiate; beam, shine

**rayure** *nf* stripe, streak; striking off; erasure

**raz, ras** *nm.* strong sea current; **~ de marée** bore; tidal wave; upheaval

**razzia** *nf* raid, foray

**ré** *nm invar mus* D, re

**réabonner** *vt* renew (s/o's) subscription; **se ~** renew one's subscription

**réacteur** *nm* reactor; jet-engine

**réaction** *nf* reaction; **avion à ~** jet plane

**réactionnaire** *n + adj* reactionary

**réactiver** *vt* reactivate

**réaffirmer** *vt* reaffirm

**réagir** *vi* react; *fig* resist

**réalisateur -trice** *n cin* director; *rad* producer

**réaliser** *vt* realize; effect, execute, carry out; make (film, etc)

**réalisme** *nm* realism

**réaliste** *n* realist; *adj* realist, realistic

**réalité** *nf* reality; **en ~** in actual fact; **prendre ses désirs pour des ~s** entertain illusions

**réanimation** *nf* reanimation; **centre de ~** intensive care unit

**réanimer** *vt* revive, reanimate

**réapparaître** *vi* (68) reappear

**réapparition** *nf* reappearance

**réassortir** *vt* replenish, restock; **se ~** replenish one's stocks

**rébarbatif -ive** *adj* forbidding, grim; surly

**rebattre** *vt* (16) beat again; *coll* **~ les oreilles à qn de qch** tell s/o the same thing over and over again

**rebattu** *adj* hackneyed; **avoir les oreilles ~es de qch** have heard sth over and over again

**rebelle** *n* rebel; *adj* rebellious, unruly; stubborn; difficult to control

**rebeller (se)** *v refl* rebel

**rébellion** *nf* rebellion, revolt

**rebiffer (se)** *v refl* jib, kick

**reboiser** *vt* replant (with trees)

**rebond** *nm* bounce

**rebondi** *adj* plump; chubby

**rebondir** *vi* rebound; bounce; start up again

**rebondissement** *nm* new development; recurrence

**rebord** *nm* edge, rim; ledge; hem

**rebours** *nm* **à ~** against the grain; **à ~ de** contrary to; **compte à ~** countdown

**rebouteur, rebouteux -euse** *n coll* bonesetter

**reboutonner** *vt* button up again; **se ~** button one's clothes up again; adjust one's dress

**rebrousse-poil (à)** *adv phr* the wrong way; against the grain

**rebrousser** *vt* turn or brush up the wrong way; **~ chemin** retrace one's steps

**rebuffade** *nf* rebuff, snub

**rébus** *nm* picture puzzle; punning riddle

**rebut** *nm* throw-out, reject; dregs; **de ~** low-grade

**rebutant** *adj* disheartening, off-putting; tiresome

**rebuter** *vt* rebuff, repulse; discourage; put off, repel

**récalcitrant** *adj* recalcitrant

**recaler** *vt coll* fail; plough (candidate)

**récapituler** *vt* recapitulate, sum up

**recel** *nm* receiving; concealment

**receler, recéler** *vt* (5) receive; conceal; harbour; contain

**receleur -euse** *n* receiver

**récemment** *adv* recently, lately

**recensement** *nm* census; counting

**recenser** *vt* make a census of; count; check off

**récépissé** *nm* receipt; acknowledgement

**récepteur** *nm* receiver (phone); collector, recipient; *adj* (*f* **-trice**) receiving

**réceptif -ive** *adj* receiving

**réception** *nf* receipt, receiving; welcome; reception; reception-desk

**réceptionner** *vt* check and sign for goods on their arrival

**réceptionniste** *n* receptionist

**recette** *nf* receipts, takings; collection (of money due); office of tax-collector; tax-collector's function; receipt; **faire ~** be a draw

**recevable** *adj* allowable, receivable; *leg* admissible

**receveur -euse** *n* receiver; tax-collector; conductor (bus)

**recevoir** *vt* receive, get; welcome; admit; absorb; **être reçu à un examen** pass an examination; **être reçu médecin** qualify as a doctor; *vi* entertain, have visitors; **se ~** land (after a jump)

**rechange** *nm* replacement; **de ~** spare, replacement

**rechaper** *vt* retread (tyre)

**réchapper** *vi* escape

**recharge** *nf* recharging; refill

**rechargement** *nm* recharging; reloading; refilling

**recharger** *vt* (3) recharge; reload; make up (fire); charge again; re-metal (road)

**réchaud** *nm* small portable stove; plate warmer

**réchauffé** *nm* warmed-up food; *coll* rehash

**réchauffer** *vt* warm up, heat up; re-kindle, warm; **se ~** warm oneself up; become warmer

**rechausser** *vt* put shoes on again; *archi* bank up

**rêche** *adj* rough; cross-grained; difficult to get on with

**recherche** *nf* search, pursuit; refinement; affectation, studied elegance; research; **à la ~ de** in search of

**recherché** *adj* select, rare; in great demand; affected, mannered

**rechercher** *vt* search for; inquire into; look for again; seek after

**rechigné** *adj* sour-tempered, sour-faced

**rechigner** *vi* jib, show bad grace

**rechute** *nf* relapse

**récidive** *nf* backsliding; relapse into

crime; recurrence (of illness)

**récidiver** vi repeat the same crime; recur (of illness)

**récidiviste** n habitual criminal, old offender

**récif** nm reef

**récipiendaire** n new member (of learned body)

**récipient** nm container, receptacle

**réciprocité** nf reciprocity

**réciproque** nf **rendre la ~ à qn** get even with s/o; adj reciprocal

**récit** nm narration, narrative, relation

**récitant -e** n narrator

**récitation** nf recitation, reciting

**réciter** vt recite

**réclamation** nf complaint, objection

**réclame** nf advertising; advertisement; **en ~** at a reduced price; **faire de la ~** advertise

**réclamer** vt demand, claim; ask for, clamour for; beg for; vi protest, complain; intercede; **se ~ de qn** appeal to s/o, call s/o to witness

**reclassement** nm fresh classification; rearrangement

**reclasser** vt reclassify; rearrange

**reclus -e** n recluse

**réclusion** nf imprisonment, detention

**recoin** nm nook; recess

**récoler** vt leg verify, check; read out witness's testimony

**recoller** vt stick, glue again

**récolte** nf harvesting; harvest; collection

**récolter** vt harvest; get, receive

**recommandable** adj commendable, estimable; advisable

**recommandation** nf recommendation; advice; injunction; (postal) registration

**recommander** vt recommend; urge, enjoin; register (letter, etc); **se ~ à qn** ask for s/o's assistance, protection; **se ~ de qn** invoke s/o's assistance; give s/o as a reference

**recommencer** vt + vi begin again, start again

**récompense** nf reward, recompense

**réconciliateur -trice** n reconciler

**réconcilier** vt reconcile

**reconduction** nf renewal, continuation

**reconduire** vt (80) escort back; show out

**réconfort** nm comfort, consolation

**réconfortant** adj strengthening; comforting

**réconforter** vt strengthen; comfort

**reconnaissance** nf recognition; gratitude; acknowledgement; reconnoitring

**reconnaissant** adj grateful

**reconnaître** vt (68) recognize; acknowledge, admit; reconnoitre; be grateful for; **je ne m'y reconnais plus** I'm at sea, I'm lost; **je vous reconnais là** that's just like you; **se faire ~** make oneself known

**reconquérir** vt (27) reconquer; regain

**reconquête** nf reconquest

**reconstituant** nm + adj tonic

**reconstituer** vt reconstitute; reconstruct; restore

**reconstruire** vt (80) reconstruct, rebuild

**reconversion** nf changing over

**reconvertir** vt change over, convert; **se ~** train for another job

**recopier** vt copy again; make a clean copy of

**recorder** vt re-string; rope up again

**recordman, recordwoman** nm (pl **recordmen, recordwomen**) recordholder

**recouper** vt cut again; blend (wines); corroborate

**recourber** vt bend back; bend again

**recourir** vi (29) run again; have recourse, address oneself, resort

**recours** nm recourse, resort; leg **~ en grâce** appeal for mercy; **en dernier ~** as a last resort; **il n'y a aucun ~ contre cela** that is irremediable; **sans ~** unavoidable

¹**recouvrement** nm recovery; collection

²**recouvrement** nm covering

**recouvrer** vt recover, regain, retrieve; collect

**recouvrir** vt (30) cover again; cover, cover entirely; conceal

**récréation** nf recreation; amusement; break (in school); **cour de ~** playground

**récréer** vt entertain, amuse; refresh

**récrier (se)** v refl exclaim

**récriminer** vi recriminate

**recroquevillé** adj curled up, shrivelled

**recroqueviller (se)** v refl shrivel up, curl up, crumple up

**recru** adj exhausted, worn out

**recrue** nf recruit; new member

**recrutement** nm recruiting, recruitment

**recruter** vt recruit, enlist

**recta** adv coll punctually

**rectangle** nm rectangle; adj right-angled

**rectangulaire** adj rectangular

**recteur** nm head of university; eccles rector; parish priest (Brittany)

**rectification** nf rectification; straightening; correction; adjustment

**rectifier** vt rectify, correct, amend; straighten; adjust; re-distil (alcohol)

**rectiligne** adj rectilinear

**rectitude** nf straightness; rectitude; rightness; integrity, uprightness

**rectoral** adj rectorial

**rectorat** nm rectorate, rectorship

**reçu** nm receipt

**recueil** *nm* collection

**recueillement** *nm* meditation, contemplation; veneration

**recueilli** *adj* contemplative

**recueillir** *vt* (33) draw, gather, get; collect, gather up; take in, give refuge to; **se ~** reflect, meditate; turn one's thoughts to God

**recul** *nm* retreat; backing; recoil, kick; step back; position of detachment

**reculé** *adj* remote, distant

**reculer** *vt* move back, push back, draw back; defer, postpone; *vi* move back, fall back, back; recoil, kick; **ne ~ devant rien** shrink from nothing

**reculons (à)** *adv phr* backwards

**récupération** *nf* recovery; recoupment; recuperation

**récupérer** *vt* (6) recover; recoup; *vi* get one's strength back

**récurer** *vt* scour

**récusable** *adj leg* untrustworthy (witness); exceptionable

**récuser** *vt leg* object to, take exception to; impugn (evidence); **se ~** disclaim competence

**recyclage** *nm* recycling

**recycler** *vt* recycle

**rédacteur -trice** *n* writer, drafter; sub-editor; **~ en chef** editor

**rédaction** *nf* drawing up, drafting, writing; editing; composition, essay

**reddition** *nf* surrender; presenting of accounts

**redemander** *vt* ask for again

**rédempteur -trice** *n* redeemer

**redevable** *adj* indebted

**rédiger** *vt* (3) draw up, draft, write; edit

**redingote** *nf* frock-coat; woman's coat

**redire** *vt* (38) say again, repeat; **trouver à ~ à** find fault with

**redite** *nf* frequent and useless repetition

**redondance** *nf* wordiness; superfluity, redundance

**redondant** *adj* wordy; pleonastic

**redonner** *vt* give again; restore

**redorer** *vt* gild again; **~ son blason** (of poor nobleman) marry a rich woman

**redoublement** *nm* redoubling; starting the year in the same class as last

**redoubler** *vt* redouble, increase; **~ une classe** do a second year in the same class; *vi* redouble; **~ d'efforts** try harder than ever

**redoutable** *adj* formidable, redoubtable

**redoute** *nf* redoubt

**redouter** *vt* fear, dread

**redressement** *nm* setting up again, re-erecting; straightening; rectification; righting; recovery

**redresser** *vt* set up again, re-erect; straighten; rectify, right, redress; **se ~** sit up again; right oneself; draw oneself up

**réducteur -trice** *adj* reducing

**réductible** *adj* reducible

**réduction** *nf* cutting down, reduction; conquest, capture

**réduire** *vt* (80) reduce; **se ~ à** confine oneself to; amount to

¹**réduit** *nm* corner, retreat; fortress, redoubt

²**réduit** *adj* reduced; cheap

**rééditer** *vt* republish

**réel** *nm* reality; *adj* (*f* **réelle**) actual, real

**réélection** *nf* re-election

**réellement** *adv* really, actually

**réexpédier** *vt* send on, forward; send back

**réexporter** *vt* re-export

**refaire** *vt* (46) remake, make again; do again; do differently; repair; do up, restore; *sl* trick, dupe; **se ~** get one's health back, pick up

**réfection** *nf* remaking, rebuilding; doing up, restoration

**référé** *nm leg* summary procedure; injunction

**référence** *nf* reference, referring; recommendation; **~s** references

**référendaire** *nm leg* verifying magistrate

**référer** *vt* + *vi* (6) refer; **se ~** refer; **je m'en réfère à votre avis** I refer the matter to you

**refiler** *vt sl* pass on, slip, give

**réfléchi** *adj* thoughtful; considered; reflexive

**réfléchir** *vt* reflect; *vi* reflect, consider, ponder; **donner à ~** give food for thought, make one think

**réflecteur** *nm* reflector

**reflet** *nm* reflection; echo

**refléter** *vt* (6) reflect

**réflexe** *nm* reflex, reflex action

**réflexion** *nf* reflection; thought; **(toute) ~ faite** on thinking it over

**refluer** *vi* flow back, surge back

**reflux** *nm* flowing back, ebb

**refondre** *vt* melt again; recast

**refonte** *nf* melting again; recasting

**réformateur -trice** *n* reformer

**réforme** *nf* reformation, reform; *mil* invaliding out; exemption from military service (on physical grounds)

**réformé -e** *n* + *adj* Protestant

**réformer** *vt* reform; amend; discharge from military service, exempt from military service

**réformiste** *n* + *adj* reformist

**refoulé -e** *adj* repressed

**refoulement** *nm* forcing back, thrusting back; repression

**refouler** *vt* force back, drive back; compress; repress, suppress

# réfractaire

**réfractaire** *adj* refractory, rebellious; resistant; heat-resistant

**réfracter** *vt* refract

**réfracteur -trice** *adj* refracting

**refrain** *nm* refrain; **toujours le même ~** always the same old story

**refréner** *vt* (6) bridle, curb

**réfrigérant** *adj* refrigerating, cooling; icy

**réfrigérateur** *nm* refrigerator; **mettre qch au ~** put sth on ice

**réfrigération** *nf* refrigeration, chilling

**réfrigérer** *vt* (6) refrigerate, cool

**refroidir** *vt* cool; dampen; *vi* grow cool, cool off; **se ~** grow cool; catch cold

**refroidissement** *nm* cooling; chill

**refuge** *nm* shelter, refuge; street island

**réfugié -e** *n* refugee

**réfugier (se)** *v refl* take refuge

**refus** *nm* refusal; **ce n'est pas de ~** I won't say no

**refuser** *vt* refuse; reject, turn down; deny; turn away; **se ~** object, decline

**réfuter** *vt* refute, disprove

**regagner** *vt* regain, win back, recover; get back to

**régal** *nm* feast; treat

**régalade** *nf* **boire à la ~** pour drink down one's throat

**régaler** *vt* regale, feast; **se ~** eat well, feast

**regard** *nm* glance, look; man-hole, inspection-hole; **au ~ de** in comparison with; **chercher qn du ~** look round for s/o; **leg droit de ~** right of inspection; **en ~ de** opposite; in comparison with

**regardant** *adj* careful, stingy

**regarder** *vt* look at; look towards, face; regard; *vi* consider; **~ à un franc** think twice before spending a franc; **y ~ à deux fois** consider carefully; **y ~ de près** be very particular

**regarnir** *vt* regarnish; re-stock; retrim

**régate** *nf* regatta; (neck-)tie

**régence** *nf* regency

**régénérateur -trice** *n* regenerator

**régénérer** *vt* (6) regenerate

**régent -e** *n* regent

**régenter** *vt* lord it over, give orders to

**régie** *nf* public administration, state management; state corporation; theatre administration; excise; excise personnel; **en ~** under state control; **salle de ~** control room

**regimber** *vi* kick; jib

**régime** *nm* diet, regimen; form of government; organization, system; running, operation; flow; **être au ~** be on a diet

**régiment** *nm* regiment; *coll* mass of people; **au ~** in the army

**régimentaire** *adj* regimental

**région** *nf* region, area

**régionalisme** *nm* regionalism

**régir** *vt* govern, rule; direct; *gramm* govern

**régisseur** *nm* manager; steward; *theat* stage-manager

**registre** *nm* register; account-book

**réglable** *adj* adjustable

**réglage** *nm* ruling; adjusting, regulating, setting

**règle** *nf* ruler; rule; **~s** menstrual periods; **agir dans les ~s** act according to the rules; **en ~** in order

**réglé** *adj* ruled; regular

**règlement** *nm* adjustment, settlement; payment; regulation

**réglementaire** *adj* regular, prescribed

**réglementation** *nf* making of rules; regulating

**réglementer** *vt* regulate

**régler** *vt* rule (paper); regulate; settle, put in order; pay

**réglisse** *nf* liquorice

**régnant** *adj* ruling, dominating

**règne** *nm* reign, rule

**régner** *vi* (6) reign, rule; be prevalent, prevail

**regorger** *vi* (3) overflow, brim over; abound; be crowded

**régresser** *vi* regress; diminish

**régressif -ive** *adj* regressive

**régression** *nf* regression

**regret** *nm* regret; **à ~** regretfully; **avoir le ~ de** regret; **être au ~ (de)** regret, be sorry (for, that)

**regretter** *vt* regret, be sorry about; miss

**regrouper** *vt* assemble, group together; group again

**régularisation** *nf* regularizing; putting in order

**régulariser** *vt* regularize; put in order

**régularité** *nf* regularity; evenness; punctuality

**régulateur** *nm* regulator; *adj* (*f* **-trice**) regulating

**régulation** *nf* regulation, adjustment, setting

**régulier -ière** *adj* regular; punctual; even, equable

**régulièrement** *adv* regularly; evenly; normally

**régurgiter** *vt* regurgitate

**réhabilitation** *nf* rehabilitation; discharge (of bankrupt)

**réhabiliter** *vt* rehabilitate; discharge

**rehausser** *vt* raise; enhance; heighten

**réimpression** *nf* reprinting; reprint

**réimprimer** *vt* reprint

**rein** *nm anat* kidney; **avoir les ~s solides** be sturdy; *coll* be rich

**reine** *nf* queen

**reine-claude** *nf* (*pl* **reines-claudes**) greengage

**reine-marguerite** *nf* (*pl* **reines-marguerites**) china aster

**reinette** *nf* rennet (apple)

**réinstaller** *vt* reinstall

**réintégrer** *vt* (6) restore, reinstate; return to

**réitérer** *vt* (6) repeat; reiterate

**reître** *nm* brutal soldier

**rejaillir** *vi* spurt back, gush out; be reflected

**rejet** *nm* throwing out; casting up; rejection; displacement

**rejeter** *vt* (5) throw back; cast out; reject; shift, transfer; **se ~** fall back

**rejeton** *nm* shoot, sucker; offspring, descendant

**rejoindre** *vt* (55) rejoin; join, overtake; **se ~** meet

**réjoui** *adj* joyous, jolly

**réjouir** *vt* gladden, delight, amuse; **se ~** rejoice; look forward, be glad

**réjouissance** *nf* rejoicing

**réjouissant** *adj* cheering

¹**relâche** *nm* + *nf* slackening; *theat* no performance

²**relâche** *nf naut* call, putting in; **faire ~ à un port** put into a port

**relâché** *adj* slack, relaxed; loose, lax

**relâchement** *nm* relaxing, slackening; falling off; looseness

**relâcher** *vt* slacken, relax; loosen; release, set free; **se ~** slacken; abate; flag, fall off, diminish

**relais** *nm* relay; shift; stage, stopping-point; **~ gastronomique** good restaurant worth stopping at; **~ routier** service station with restaurant; **prendre le ~** take over

**relance** *nf* giving new life, boosting; recrudescence

**relancer** *vt* (4) throw back, throw again; start again (quarry); *coll* pester, pursue assiduously

**relaps -e** *n* relapsed heretic

**relater** *vt* relate, state

**relatif -ive** *adj* relative

**relation** *nf* relation; connection; report, account

**relax(e)** *nm* relaxation; *adj* relaxed

**relaxation** *nf* leg release, discharge; reduction (of sentence)

**relaxer** *vt* leg discharge, release

**relayer** *vt* (7) relay; relieve; **se ~** take over from each other, turn and turn about

**relégation** *nf* relegation; transportation (to a penal settlement)

**reléguer** *vt* (6) relegate; transport (to a penal settlement)

**relent** *nm* musty smell; trail

**relève** *nf* relief (troops), changing (guard); relief troops

¹**relevé** *nm* account, statement

²**relevé** *adj* raised; exalted, noble

**relèvement** *nm* raising up, raising again; picking up; restoring; recovery; relieving (sentry); rise

**relever** *vt* (6) raise up again, lift up again; pick up; rebuild; enhance, set off; point out; relieve; release; read (meter); *vi* depend; **~ de maladie** have just recovered from an illness; **se ~** get up again; revive, recover

**relier** *vt* tie again; connect; bind (book)

**relieur** *nm* book-binder

**religieuse** *nf* nun; kind of chocolate éclair

**religieux** *nm* monk, friar; *adj* (*f* **-euse**) religious, sacred

**religiosité** *nf* religiosity

**reliquaire** *nm* reliquary, shrine

**reliquat** *nm* remainder, residue; after-effects (of illness)

**relique** *nf* relic (of saint)

**relire** *vt* (56) re-read

**reliure** *nf* bookbinding; binding (book)

**reluire** *vi* (57) shine, glisten, gleam

**reluisant** *adj* shining; **peu ~** poor, mediocre

**reluquer** *vt coll* eye, ogle; have one's eye on

**remâcher** *vt* dwell on

**remailler** *vt* re-mesh; mend a ladder (in stocking)

**remaniement** *nm* change, modification

**remanier** *vt* change, alter, recast; re-handle

**remarquable** *adj* remarkable; distinguished

**remarque** *nf* remark; note; **digne de ~** noteworthy; **faire la ~ que** remark that

**remarquer** *vt* remark, notice; mark again; **faire ~ à qn** point out to s/o; **se faire ~** attract attention

**remballer** *vt* re-pack

**rembarquer** *vt* + *vi* re-embark

**rembarrer** *vt coll* tell off; contradict sharply

**remblai** *nm* filling material; mound, bank; filling up; banking up

**remblayer** *vt* (7) fill up; bank up

**remboîter** *vt* set (bone); re-bind (book)

**rembourrer** *vt* stuff; upholster

**remboursement** *nm* reimbursement, repayment

**rembourser** *vt* reimburse, refund, repay

**rembrunir** *vt* darken; make sad; **se ~** grow dark; grow sad

**remède** *nm* cure, remedy; **sans ~** beyond remedy; **il n'y a pas de ~**

there's no help for it

**remédier** vi ~ à remedy, put right

**remembrement** nm ~ des terres regrouping of land

**remembrer** vt regroup (land into larger plots)

**remémorer** vt bring back to mind; se ~ recall

**remerciement** nm thanking; thanks; se confondre en ~ s thank effusively

**remercier** vt thank; dismiss; refuse

**remettre** vt (60) put back (again); put on again; deliver, hand over; remit; postpone; set, put back into place; recall; ~ ça have another go; ~ en état repair; ~ qn recall s/o; ~ son âme à Dieu commit one's soul to God; coll en ~ do too much; say too much; partie remise pleasure deferred; se ~ put oneself back again; start again; recover; s'en ~ à qn rely on s/o

**remise** nf putting back into place; handing over, delivery; reduction (in price); remission; award; remittance; postponement; shed, coach-house

**remiser** vt put in a shed; put away

**rémission** nf remission; sans ~ relentlessly; uninterruptedly

**remontant** nm tonic

**remonte** nf going upstream; remounting

**remontée** nf climb

**remonte-pente** nm ski-lift

**remonter** vt take up again; go up again; raise, elevate; wind up; remount; reassemble; refurbish; ~ qn cheer s/o up; vi go up again; go back

**remontoir** nm winder

**remontrance** nf remonstrance, reprimand

**remontrer** vt show again; point out; en ~ à qn give advice to s/o; be superior to s/o

**rémora** nm remora, sucking-fish; pilot-fish

**remords** nm remorse, compunction

**remorque** nf towing; trailer; tow-line

**remorquer** vt tow, pull, draw

**remorqueur** nm tug (boat)

**rémoulade** nf cul sauce made with mustard, oil, garlic, etc

**rémouleur** nm knife-grinder

**remous** nm eddy, swirl, backwash

**rempailler** vt re-seat, re-bottom (chair)

**rempailleur -euse** n chair-mender

**rempart** nm rampart; bulwark

**rempiler** vt pile up again; vi sl re-engage for military service

**remplaçant -e** n substitute

**remplacement** nm replacement; de ~ substitute, spare

**remplacer** vt (4) replace; take the place of

**rempli** nm tuck (in a dress); adj full, filled

**remplier** vt make a tuck in

**remplir** vt fill up; fill in; occupy; fulfil, perform

**remplissage** nm filling; padding

**remplumer (se)** v refl get new feathers; coll pick up again; regain weight

**remporter** vt carry back, take away, carry off; ~ la victoire be victorious

**rempoter** vt repot (plant)

**remuant** adj restless

**remue-ménage** nm invar bustle, stir

**remuer** vt stir; move; vi move, change places; fidget; se ~ bestir oneself

**remugle** nm musty smell

**rémunérateur -trice** adj remunerative, profitable

**rémunération** nf payment, remuneration

**rémunérer** vt (6) remunerate; reward

**renâcler** vi snort; draw back, be reluctant

**renaître** vi (64) be born again; spring up again, revive

**renard** nm fox; cunning fellow

**renarde** nf viven

**renchérir** vi get dearer; outbid; outdo

**renchérissement** nm rise in price

**rencogner** vt coll drive into a corner; se ~ retreat into a corner

**rencontre** nf meeting; encounter; skirmish; occasion; aller à la ~ de go to meet

**rencontrer** vt meet; run across; se ~ meet; occur; tally

**rendement** nm yield, return, profit; productivity; à plein ~ at maximum output

**rendez-vous** nm appointment; meeting-place; prendre ~ make an appointment

**rendormir (se)** v refl fall asleep again

**rendre** vt give back, return; repay; deliver; vomit; surrender; express, reproduce; make; produce, give out; ~ grâce à give thanks to; ~ la justice dispense justice; ~ l'âme die, pass away; ~ les armes admit defeat; se ~ go, proceed; surrender

**¹rendu** nm rendering

**²rendu** adj exhausted; arrived

**rêne** nf rein

**renégat -e** n renegade

**renfermé** nm close smell, musty odour; adj uncommunicative

**renfermer** vt shut up again; lock up; contain, include; se ~ dans le silence withdraw into silence

**renflement** nm swelling, bulging

**renfler** vt + vi swell out, enlarge

**renflouer** vt refloat; set up again

**renfoncement** nm hollow, cavity, recess

**renfoncer** *vt* (4) knock in, drive in further

**renforcer** *vt* (4) strengthen, reinforce; intensify

**renfort** *nm* reinforcement; backing, stiffening piece; **à grand ~ de** with the help of plenty of

**renfrogné** *adj* frowning, sullen

**renfrogner (se)** *v refl* scowl, knit one's brows

**rengaine** *nf coll* old story; refrain

**rengainer** *vt* sheathe; suppress, bottle up

**rengorger (se)** *v refl* strut, swagger

**reniement** *nm* denial, repudiation; disavowal

**renier** *vt* disown; disavow

**reniflard** *nm mech* snifting valve; breather

**reniflement** *nm* sniffing; sniff

**renifler** *vt* + *vi* sniff

**renne** *nm* reindeer

**renom** *nm* renown, fame

**renommé** *adj* renowned, famous

**renommée** *nf* renown, fame; rumour

**renommer** *vt* re-appoint, re-elect

**renoncement** *nm* renouncing, renouncement; self-denial, renunciation

**renoncer** *vi* (4) **~ à** renounce, give up; **y ~** give it up as a bad job

**renonciateur -trice** *n* renouncer

**renonciation** *nf* renunciation

**renoncule** *nf* buttercup, ranunculus

**renouer** *vt* tie up again; renew, resume

**renouveau** *nm* springtide; renewal

**renouveler** *vt* (5) renew, renovate; revive; **se ~** be renewed; happen again

**renouvellement** *nm* renewal, replacement; renovation

**rénovateur -trice** *n* renovator

**rénovation** *nf* renovation, renewing

**renseignement** *nm* piece of information, indication; **prendre des ~s** make inquiries

**renseigner** *vt* inform; **se ~** find out, make inquiries

**rentabilité** *nf* profitability

**rentable** *adj* profitable, paying

**rente** *nf* revenue; pension, allowance; **vivre de ses ~s** live on one's (private) income

**rentier -ière** *n* person of independent means

**rentoiler** *vt* back (painting)

**rentrant** *adj* re-entrant (angle)

**rentré** *adj* sunken, hollow

**rentrée** *nf* return, home-coming; beginning of term, end of holidays; taking in, encashment; gathering in

**rentrer** *vt* bring in, take in; bottle up, suppress; *vi* re-enter, go in again, come back; come home; go home, return; resume, re-open; **~ dans ses droits** recover one's rights; **~ dedans** bang into sth, crash into sth; **~ en grâce** be forgiven; **faire ~** call in (debt)

**renversant** *adj coll* staggering, astounding

**renverse** *nf* **à la ~** backwards

**renversé** *adj* reversed; upset; **crème ~e** sweet made of eggs and cream

**renversement** *nm* inversion, reversal; overthrow, upsetting

**renverser** *vt* reverse, invert; upset, overturn; overthrow; **se ~** fall down; tip over, capsize

**renvoi** *nm* return, sending back, throwing back; dismissal, discharge; postponement; referring; reference mark; belch; *mus* repeat mark

**renvoyer** *vt* (7) send back, return, throw back; turn away; dismiss, discharge; postpone; refer

**réorganiser** *vt* reorganize

**réouverture** *nf* re-opening; resumption

**repaire** *nm* den, nest, haunt

**repaître** *vt* (81) feed (animal); **se ~** feed; eat one's fill

**répandre** *vt* pour out; shed; spread, scatter, broadcast; give off; **se ~** spread, gain ground; spill; **se ~ en excuses** apologize profusely

**répandu** *adj* widespread, prevalent; widely known

**reparaître** *vi* (68) reappear; turn up again

**réparateur -trice** *n* repairer; *adj* restorative

**réparation** *nf* reparation; repairing, repair; redress; **en ~** under repair

**réparer** *vt* repair, mend; restore; make amends for; rectify

**reparler** *vi* speak again

**repartie** *nf* retort

**repartir** *vt* (89) retort; *vi* set out again

**répartir** *vt* share out, distribute; allocate

**répartiteur** *nm* distributor; assessor of taxes

**répartition** *nf* sharing out, distribution; allocation; assessment (of taxes)

**repas** *nm* meal

**repassage** *nm* ironing; sharpening

**repasser** *vt* pass by again, cross again; go over again, look over again; sharpen; iron; *vi* pass by again; call again

**repasseuse** *nf* ironer; ironing machine

**repêcher** *vt* fish out again, pick up; give a bare pass to (exam candidate)

**repeindre** *vt* (55) repaint, paint over

**repenser** *vt* re-examine

**repenti** *adj* repentant

**¹repentir** *nm* repentance

**²repentir (se)** *v refl* (59) repent, be sorry

**repérage** *nm* locating, marking

**répercussion** *nf* repercussion; consequence

**répercuter** vt reflect back, reflect, reverberate; **se ~** have repercussions

**repère** nm mark, reference; **point de ~** landmark; guide mark

**repérer** vt (6) locate, spot; mark with guide marks; **se ~** take one's bearings

**répertoire** nm list, table; repertory

**répertorier** vt index, make a reference table for; enter in an index

**répéter** vt (6) repeat; do again; rehearse; **ne pas se faire ~ qch** not need to be told sth twice

**répétiteur -trice** n tutor, private coach; part-time teacher

**répétition** nf repetition; reproduction; rehearsal; lesson; **montre à ~** repeater watch

**repeupler** vt repopulate; restock; replant

**repiquer** vt prick again, sting again; plant out, transplant; restitch; nab again

**répit** nm respite, breathing-space

**replacer** vt (4) put back in place; reinvest; give another job to

**replâtrer** vt replaster; coll patch up

**replet -ète** adj stout

**réplétion** nf repletion; corpulence

**repli** nm retreat; crease; recess; meander, winding

**replier** vt fold again; fold up, coil up; tuck in; **se ~** turn back; fold up; bend; retreat

**réplique** nf rejoinder, answer; theat cue; **argument sans ~** unanswerable argument

**répliquer** vt + vi retort, answer back

**répondant** nm eccles server; n (f -e) leg surety, referee

**répondre** vt answer; eccles **~ la messe** make the responses at mass; vi answer; respond, comply; correspond; be answerable; **je vous en réponds** take my word for it

**répons** nm eccles response

**réponse** nf answer, reply; response

**report** nm carrying forward; sum carried forward; contango; postponement; transfer

**reportage** nm reporting; report

**reporter** vt carry back, take back; postpone; carry forward; **se ~** refer

**repos** nm rest; pause; peace; **~!** stand at ease!; **au ~** laid off; **de tout ~** absolutely safe

**reposant** adj restful

**reposé** adj rested; calm; **à tête ~e** deliberately, at leisure

**reposer** vt put back, place back, replace; rest; vi rest; lie buried; **~ sur** be founded on; **se ~** rest, have a rest; settle again; rely

**reposoir** nm temporary altar

**repoussant** adj repulsive, loathsome

**repousse** nf fresh growth (hair)

**repoussé** adj embossed; repoussé

**repousser** vt push back, drive off, repulse, repel; put aside; reject; emboss; work in repoussé; throw out (shoots); delay, postpone; vi grow again, sprout again

**repoussoir** nm carp, etc starting-punch; cuticle remover; fig foil; ugly person

**reprendre** vt (75) take again, take back, recapture; resume; revive (play); criticize; vi start again, revive; improve, pick up; **se ~** correct oneself; recover oneself; **se ~ à faire qch** begin again to do sth

**représailles** nfpl reprisals; **user de ~** carry out reprisals

**représentant -e** n representative; (commercial) traveller

**représentatif -ive** adj representative

**représentation** nf representation; theat performance; comm agency; protest; (official) state display; **frais de ~** entertainment expenses

**représenter** vt present again, reintroduce; represent; portray; theat perform; point out; vi have a good presence; **se ~** present oneself again; reappear; occur again; imagine

**répressif -ive** adj repressive

**réprimande** nf reprimand

**réprimander** vt reprimand, reprove

**réprimer** vt repress, check, quell

**repris** nm **~ de justice** old offender, habitual criminal

**reprise** nf retaking, recapture; renewal, revival, resumption; acceleration; round (boxing); darn; deduction (in part-exchange transaction); taking over of fittings (with flat); **à plusieurs ~s** repeatedly; on several occasions

**repriser** vt darn

**réprobateur -trice** adj reproachful

**reproche** nm reproach; **sans ~** blameless

**reprocher** vt reproach; grudge

**reproducteur -trice** n animal kept for breeding purposes; adj reproductive

**reproductif -ive** adj reproductive

**reproduire** vt (80) reproduce; **se ~** happen again; breed

**reprographie** nf reprography, duplicating of documents

**réprouvé -e** n outcast; damned

**réprouver** vt disapprove of; reject; damn

**reps** nm rep(p)

**repu** adj sated, full

**républicain -e** n + adj republican

**républicanisme** nm republicanism

**république** nf republic; **la ~ des lettres**

writers, literary men

**répudier** *vt* repudiate; renounce

**répugnance** *nf* repugnance, dislike, aversion

**répugnant** *adj* loathsome

**répugner** *vi* feel repugnance; be reluctant; inspire loathing

**répulsif -ive** *adj* repulsive

**réputation** *nf* reputation, repute; **perdre qn de ~** ruin s/o's reputation

**réputé** *adj* well-known

**réputer** *vt* repute, consider, think

**requérant -e** *n leg* plaintiff, petitioner

**requérir** *vt* (27) ask for, demand; call upon

**requête** *nf* request, petition, suit; **à la ~ de** at the suit of

**requin** *nm* shark; greedy person (business)

**requinquer** *vt* pep up; **se ~** smarten oneself up; recover

**requis** *adj* required, necessary

**réquisition** *nf* requisitioning; requisition

**réquisitionner** *vt* requisition, commandeer

**réquisitoire** *nm* indictment; violent reproach

**R.E.R.** *see* réseau

**rescapé -e** *n* survivor; *adj* saved

**rescinder** *vt leg* annul, rescind

**rescousse** *nf* **à la ~** to the rescue

**réseau** *nm* network, system; **~ express régional (R.E.R.)** fast train service between Paris and outer suburbs

**réséda** *nm* mignonette

**réséquer** *vt* (6) *med* resect (bone)

**réservation** *nf* reservation, reserving; reserve; **~ légale** part of inheritance that must go to heirs; **à la ~ de** except for; **de ~** reserve; **sans ~** without prejudice

**réserve** *nf* reserve; **sous ~ de** subject to

**réservé** *adj* discreet, reserved

**réserver** *vt* reserve, set aside, keep in store; **se ~** hold back, wait

**réserviste** *nm* reservist

**réservoir** *nm* reservoir; tank, container

**résidence** *nf* residence; residing; luxury housing development, luxury block of flats

**résident, -e** *n* foreign resident

**résider** *vi* reside, dwell

**résidu** *nm* residue

**résiduel -uelle** *adj* residual

**résignation** *nf* resignation; submissiveness

**résigner** *vt* resign; give up; **se ~** submit, resign oneself

**résiliation** *nf* cancellation, annulment

**résilience** *nf* resilience

**résilier** *vt* annul, cancel

**résille** *nf* hair-net

**résine** *nf* resin

**résiner** *vt* dip in resin; extract the resin from

**résineux -euse** *adj* resinous

**résistance** *nf* resistance, opposition; endurance; resistance movement; **pièce de ~** principal dish; main feature

**résistant -e** *n* resistance fighter, member of resistance movement; *adj* resistant, strong

**résister** *vi* **~ à** resist, withstand

**résolu** *adj* resolute, determined

**résoluble** *adj* solvable; terminable

**résolument** *adv* courageously

**résolution** *nf* resolution; solution; annulment; **adopter une ~** pass a resolution

**résonnement** *nm* resonance, reverberation

**résonner** *vi* resound, reverberate

**résorber** *vt* reabsorb, absorb

**résoudre** *vt* (82) resolve; dissolve; annul; clear up, solve, settle; persuade, induce; **se ~** determine, resolve; dissolve

**respect** *nm* respect, regard; **~ humain** fear of public opinion; **sauf votre ~** with all due respect; **tenir en ~** keep at a respectful distance; keep in awe

**respectabilité** *nf* respectability

**respecter** *vt* respect, treat with regard; **se ~** have self-respect

**respectif -ive** *adj* respective

**respectueuse** *nf* prostitute

**respectueux -ueuse** *adj* respectful

**respiratoire** *adj* respiratory

**respirer** *vt* + *vi* breathe, inhale

**resplendir** *vi* shine, be resplendent

**resplendissant** *adj* shining, resplendent

**responsabilité** *nf* responsibility; liability; **engager sa ~ personnelle** assume personal responsibility

**responsable** *adj* responsible, answerable

**resquiller** *vi coll* get in without paying; gate-crash

**resquilleur -euse** *n* person who avoids paying (train, cinema, etc); uninvited guest

**ressac** *nm* undertow; surf

**ressaisir** *vt* seize again; **se ~** regain one's self-control

**ressasser** *vt coll* repeat ceaselessly

**ressaut** *nm* projection

**ressemblance** *nf* resemblance, likeness

**ressemblant** *adj* like; faithful (portrait)

**ressembler** *vi* **~ à** resemble, look like; **ça ne ressemble à rien** it's like nothing on earth; *coll* **ça ne vous ressemble pas** that's not a bit like you

**ressemelage** *nm* re-soling

**ressemeler** *vt* (5) re-sole

**ressentiment** *nm* resentment

**ressentir** *vt* (59) feel; experience; resent; **se ~ de** feel the effects of

**resserre** *nf* store-room

**resserrer** *vt* tighten; tie again; contract; restrain, confine; put away again; draw closer; **se ~** shrink, contract; retrench

**resservir** *vt* serve again; *vi* be used again, be of use again

¹**ressort** *nm* spring; elasticity, springiness; motive, cause; **avoir du ~** be resilient

²**ressort** *nm* scope, competence; **cela n'est pas de mon ~** that's not within my competence; **en dernier ~** in the last resort

¹**ressortir** *vi* (83) go out again, come out again; stand out, be evident

²**ressortir** *vi* (83) come under the jurisdiction

**ressortissant -e** *n* national

**ressource -e** *nf* resource; resourcefulness; expedient; **~s** means

**ressuer** *vi* sweat (walls)

**ressusciter** *vt + vi* resuscitate; revive

**restant** *nm* remainder; *adj* remaining

**restaurateur -trice** *n* restorer; restaurant-keeper

**restauration** *nf* restoration, restoring; restaurant business

**restaurer** *vt* restore; refresh; **se ~** take refreshment

**reste** *nm* remainder, rest; **~s** remains; **au ~** moreover; **de ~** over, remaining; **du ~** moreover; **être en ~** be under an obligation; **jouir de son ~** make the most of what is left to one; **ne pas demander son ~** clear out; have enough

**rester** *vi* remain, stay; be left; **en ~ là** stop at that point; **il n'en reste pas moins que** nevertheless; **reste à savoir si** it remains to be seen whether

**restituer** *vt* restore; hand back, return

**restitution** *nf* restoration; restitution

**restoroute** *nm* motorway restaurant

**restreindre** *vt* (55) restrict, curtail; **se ~** cut down on one's expenses

**restreint** *adj* restricted, limited

**restrictif -ive** *adj* restrictive, limitative

**résultante** *nf math + mech* resultant

**résultat** *nm* result, outcome

**résulter** *vi* result, arise; **il en résulte que** consequently

**résumé** *nm* summary, abstract; **en ~** to sum up

**résumer** *vt* summarize, sum up; **se ~** sum up

**résurrection** *nf* resurrection; revival

**retable** *nm* reredos, altar-piece

**rétablir** *vt* re-establish, restore; reinstate; bring back into force; **se ~** get well again

**rétablissement** *nm* re-establishment; restoration; recovery

**rétamer** *vt* re-tin; re-silver

**rétameur** *nm* tinker

**retape** *nf sl* **faire la ~** solicit (prostitute)

**retaper** *vt coll* do up, touch up, mend; **coll se ~** get well again

**retard** *nm* delay, slowness; **avoir du ~** be late; **en ~** late, behind

**retardataire** *n* late-comer, late arrival, straggler; *adj* late, behindhand

**retardateur -trice** *adj* retarding

**retarder** *vt* delay, retard, hold up; put off, put back; *vi* be late, be slow; lag, be behind

**retenir** *vt* (96) hold back, keep back, detain; retain; engage, reserve; curb, check; carry (numbers); **~ l'attention** hold the attention; **se ~** hold on; restrain oneself

**rétention** *nf med* retention; carrying (number)

**retentir** *vi* resound, echo, reverberate

**retentissant** *adj* resounding

**retentissement** *nm* reverberation; resounding noise; repercussion

**retenue** *nf* deduction; detention (at school); confinement; discretion, reserve, restraint, holding back; damming; **mettre un élève en ~** keep a pupil in

**réticence** *nf* reserve, reticence

**réticule** *nm* hand-bag; *opt* reticle

**rétif -ive** *adj* stubborn, recalcitrant

**rétine** *nf anat* retina

**retiré** *adj* remote; retired

**retirer** *vt* pull out; withdraw; take away; get, obtain; **se ~** retire; withdraw; subside, recede, ebb

**retombée** *nf* falling down; **~s radioactives** radio-active fall-out

**retomber** *vi* fall down again; fall; hang down; *coll* **~ sur ses pieds** land on one's feet

**retordre** *vt* wring out again, twist again; **donner du fil à ~** give trouble

**rétorquer** *vt* retort

**retors** *adj* twisted; crafty; cunning

**rétorsion** *nf* retorting

**retouche** *nf* slight alteration; retouch; *phot* retouching

**retoucher** *vt* touch up, retouch

**retour** *nm* return; turn, twist; vicissitude, reversal; **~ d'âge** menopause; **~ de conscience** qualms of conscience; **~ de flamme** blow-back; **être de ~** be back; **être sur le ~** be on the way home; be past one's prime; **faire un ~ sur soi-même** think seriously about one's conduct; **par ~ du courrier** by return of post; **payer de ~** requite

**retourne** *nf* turned-up card

**retourner** *vt* turn inside out; return, send back; turn up, turn over; examine thoroughly; *coll* upset; *vi* return, go back; revert; **de quoi retourne-t-il?** what's it all about?; **se ~** turn over, overturn; look round, turn round; devise means; **se ~ contre** round on; **s'en ~** return

**retracer** *vt* (4) retrace, trace again

**retracter** *vt* retract; draw in; **se ~** recant, retract

**retrait** *nm* withdrawal; shrinkage; **en ~** set back; recessed

**retraite** *nf* retreat; tattoo; retirement; (retirement) pension; place of retirement; haunt; **battre en ~** beat a retreat; **caisse de ~** pension fund

**retraité -e** *n* retired person; *adj* retired

**retranchement** *nm* docking, cutting off; excision; entrenchment

**retrancher** *vt* cut off, retrench; strike out; fortify; **se ~** entrench oneself

**retransmettre** *vt* (60) retransmit, pass on; *rad* relay

**rétrécir** *vt* + *vi* narrow, contract, shrink; **se ~** shrink

**rétrécissement** *nm* narrowing, shrinking

**retremper** *vt* soak again; retemper; **se ~** acquire new strength

**rétribuer** *vt* remunerate, pay

**rétribution** *nf* remuneration, salary; reward

**rétro** *nm abbr* **rétroviseur**

**rétroactif -ive** *adj* retroactive

**rétrocéder** *vt* (6) reassign

**rétrocession** *nf leg* retrocession

**rétrofusée** *nf* retro-rocket

**rétrograder** *vi* move backwards; change down (gear)

**rétrospectif -ive** *adj* retrospective

**rétrospective** *nf* chronological exhibition of artist's work

**retrousser** *vt* turn up, roll up; curl up; tuck up

**retrouver** *vt* find again; find; meet, join; **se ~** meet again; meet; find one's bearings; be where one was before

**rétroviseur** *nm* driving-mirror

**rets** *nm ar* net; trap, ruse

**réunion** *nf* reunion; joining up again, junction; meeting, coming together

**réunir** *vt* reunite; unite, join together; **se ~** get together, meet; join forces

**réussi** *adj* successful

**réussir** *vt* make a success of; *vi* succeed, do well; **tout lui réussit** everything turns out well for him

**réussite** *nf* success, successful result; patience (cards)

**revaloir** *vt* (95) pay back, return in kind

**revaloriser** *vt* revalue

**revanche** *nf* revenge; return match; **en ~** on the other hand

**rêvasser** *vi* day-dream, muse

**rêvasserie** *nf* day-dreaming, musing

**rêve** *nm* dream; day-dream; **c'est le ~!** it's all one could wish

**revêche** *adj* cross-grained, difficult

**réveil** *nm* waking; re-awakening; alarm-clock; **sonner le ~** sound reveille

**réveille-matin** *nm invar* alarm-clock

**réveiller** *vt* wake, awake; stir up, rouse; **se ~** wake up; revive

**réveillon** *nm* midnight supper (on Christmas Eve and New Year's Eve)

**réveillonner** *vi* have a **réveillon**

**révélateur -trice** *n* revealer, indicator; *adj* revealing

**révélation** *nf* revelation, disclosure

**révéler** *vt* (6) reveal; show; betray; **se ~** reveal oneself; come to light

**revenant** *nm* ghost; s/o who has been away

**revendeur -euse** *n* second-hand dealer; retailer

**revendication** *nf* claim, demand; claiming

**revendiquer** *vt* claim, demand

**revenez-y** *nm* return; renewal; *coll* **goût de ~** appetizing taste

**revenir** *vi* (96) return, come back; start again; **~ à** cost, come to; **~ à soi** regain consciousness; **~ au même** come to the same thing; **~ de loin** have been at death's door; have escaped a great danger; **~ de ses craintes** get over one's fears; **~ sur ses pas** retrace one's footsteps; **ça me revient maintenant** I remember it now; **cela revient à dire** that is tantamount to saying; **cul faire ~** brown; **je n'en reviens pas** I can't get over it; **son visage ne me revient pas** I don't like his face; **y ~** return to a subject

**revente** *nf* resale

**revenu** *nm* income, yield; drawing the temper (out of steel)

**rêver** *vt* dream of; *vi* dream

**réverbère** *nm* street lamp; reflector

**réverbérer** *vt* (6) reverberate, reflect

**reverdir** *vi* grow green again; grow young again

**révérence** *nf* reverence; bow, curtsey; **tirer sa ~** bow, drop a curtsey; *coll* go off

**révérenciel -ielle** *adj* reverential

**révérencieux -ieuse** *adj* ceremonious, over-polite

**révérer** *vt* (6) revere

**rêverie** *nf* dreaming, musing

**revers** *nm* reverse side, other side; lapel; turn-over; reverse; back-hand stroke; **~ de la médaille** other side of the coin;

à ~ in the rear
**reverser** *vt* pour again; transfer
**réversible** *adj* reversible; revertible
**reversoir** *nm* weir
**revêtement** *nm* coating, covering, surface (road); revetment
**revêtir** *vt* (97) reclothe; dress; put on, don; face, coat; invest (with office, honour); ~ **l'aspect de** assume the appearance of
**rêveur -euse** *n* dreamer; *adj* dreamy, dreaming
**revient** *nm* prix de ~ cost price
**revirement** *nm* sudden change, change of direction
**réviser** *vt* revise; re-examine; overhaul
**réviseur** *nm* reviser; *typ* proof-reader
**révision** *nf* revising; re-examination; *typ* proof-reading; inspection; *mot* servicing, overhauling; **conseil de** ~ medical examination (for army recruits)
**révisionniste** *adj* revisionist
**revivre** *vi* (98) live again; revive; relive
**révocable** *adj* revocable; removable
**révocation** *nf* revocation; repeal; dismissal
**revoici** *prep + adv coll* me ~ ! here I am again!
**revoilà** *prep + adv coll* le ~ ! there he is again!
**revoir** *nm invar* seeing again; **au** ~ good-bye; *vt* (99) see again; revise, re-examine
**révoltant** *adj* revolting, sickening
**révolte** *nf* revolt, rebellion
**révolté -e** *n* insurgent
**révolter** *vt* arouse indignation, revolt; **se** ~ revolt
**révolu** *adj* completed
**révolution** *nf* revolution; upheaval
**révolutionnaire** *n + adj* revolutionary
**révolutionner** *vt* revolutionize
**révoquer** *vt* revoke, repeal; dismiss; recall
**revue** *nf* review, survey; magazine; *theat* revue; *coll* **être de la** ~ have one's hopes dashed; **passer en** ~ revue
**révulser** *vt* overturn, upset; **les yeux révulsés** eyes turned upwards
**révulsif -ive** *adj* revulsive, counter-irritating
**rez-de-chaussée** *nm invar* ground floor, *US* first floor
**rhabiller** *vt* repair, mend; dress again; **se** ~ get dressed again
**rhabilleur** *nm* repairer
**rhapsodie** *nf* rhapsody
**rhénan** *adj* Rhenish
**rhétoricien -ienne** *n* rhetorician
**rhétorique** *nf* rhetoric; *ar* class in lycée = lower sixth
**Rhin** *nm* Rhine

**rhodanien -ienne** *adj* of the Rhône
**rhombe** *nm* rhombus
**rhomboïde** *adj* rhomboid
**rhubarbe** *nf* rhubarb
**rhum** *nm* rum
**rhumatisant** *adj* rheumatic; afflicted with rheumatism
**rhumatismal** *adj* rheumatic
**rhumatisme** *nm* rheumatism
**rhume** *nm* cold; ~ **de cerveau** head cold
**riant** *adj* smiling; cheerful; pleasant
**ribambelle** *nf coll* string, swarm, collection
**ribote** *nf sl* drinking orgy
**ribouldingue** *nf sl* feasting
**ricanement** *nm* sneering
**ricaner** *vi* sneer, mock
**ricaneur -euse** *n* sneerer; *adj* sneering
**richard -e** *n coll* rich person
**riche** *adj* rich, wealthy; fertile; ~ **à millions** enormously wealthy
**richesse** *nf* wealth, riches; fertility; sumptuousness
**richissime** *adj* very wealthy
**ricin** *nm* castor-oil plant; **huile de** ~ castor oil
**ricocher** *vi* rebound, glance off; ricochet
**ricochet** *nm* rebound; ricochet
**rictus** *nm* grin; *anat* rictus
**ride** *nf* wrinkle; ripple
**ridé** *adj* wrinkled
**rideau** *nm* curtain; screen; ~ **de fer** iron curtain; *theat* safety curtain; **tirer le** ~ **sur** draw a veil over
**rider** *vt* wrinkle, line; shrivel; ripple; **se** ~ grow wrinkled; ripple
**ridicule** *nm* absurdity; ridiculous touch; **tomber dans le** ~ make oneself ridiculous; **tourner en** ~ hold up to ridicule; *adj* laughable, ridiculous
**ridiculiser** *vt* ridicule
**rien** *nm* trifle, mere nothing; tiny quantity; *indef pron* anything; very little; nothing, not anything; ~ **moins que** far from; ~ **que** nothing but, only; **ce n'est pas** ~ it's quite something; **de** ~ don't mention it; **en** ~ in no way; **il n'en est** ~ nothing of the kind; **un homme de** ~ a man of no account
**rieur -euse** *n* person who laughs; *adj* fond of laughter
**rififi** *nm sl* fight
[1]**riflard** *nm* plastering-trowel, paring-chisel; coarse file
[2]**riflard** *nm coll* umbrella
**rigaudon** *nm* see rigodon
**rigide** *adj* rigid, inflexible; tense
**rigidité** *nf* rigidity; tenseness
**rigodon, rigaudon** *nm* rigadoon
**rigolade** *nf coll* lark, fun
**rigole** *nf* drain, gutter, channel; trickle
**rigoler** *vi coll* laugh

**rigolo -ote** *n coll* amusing person; *nm coll* revolver; *adj coll* comical, funny
**rigoriste** *adj* strict (as regards morals)
**rigoureux -euse** *adj* rigorous
**rigueur** *nf* severity, harshness; strictness, exactness; **à la ~** if necessary; **de ~** compulsory, indispensable; **user de ~** be severe
**rikiki** *nm see* **riquiqui**
**rillettes** *nfpl* potted minced pork (cooked)
**rimailler** *vi* write poor poetry
**rime** *nf* rhyme
**rimer** *vt* put into rhyme; *vi* rhyme; write verse; *coll* **cela ne rime à rien** there's no sense in that
**rimeur -euse** *n* rhymester
**rince-doigts** *nm* finger-bowl
**rincer** *vt* (4) rinse, rinse out
**rincette** *nf coll* nip (in bottom of glass or coffee cup)
**ringard** *nm* poker, fire-iron
**ripaille** *nf coll* feasting; **faire ~** feast
**riper** *vt* scrape, polish; slip (chain); shift; *vi* scrape; skid
**ripoliner** *vt* paint with gloss paint
**riposte** *nf* riposte; counter; retort
**riposter** *vi* counter; retort
**riquiqui** *nm coll* tiny thing, tiny person
**rire** *nm* laughter, laughing; laugh; *vi* (84) laugh; joke; have a laugh; **~ de** make fun of; scorn; **à mourir de ~** killingly funny; **avoir le mot pour ~** tell good jokes; **histoire de ~** for fun, as a joke; **il n'y a pas de quoi ~** it's no laughing matter; **pour ~** for fun; **prêter à ~** give cause for laughter; **rira bien qui rira le dernier** he who laughs last laughs best; **vous voulez ~!** you're joking; **se ~ de** mock
¹**ris** *nm naut* reef
²**ris** *nm* **~ de veau** sweetbread
¹**risée** *nf* mockery; laughing-stock
²**risée** *nf* light squall
**risette** *nf* laugh (*usu* child); **fais ~!** smile!
**risible** *adj* laughable, ludicrous
**risque** *nm* risk; **assurance tous ~s** comprehensive insurance policy; **à vos ~s et périls** at your own risk
**risquer** *vt* risk, chance; *coll* **~ de** be likely to; **~ le coup** chance it
**risque-tout** *nm invar* dare-devil
**rissoler** *vt cul* brown
**ristourne** *nf* refund; rebate; rake-off, commission
**ristourner** *vt* refund; return; give as commission
**ritournelle** *nf mus* ritornelle; *coll* same old story
**ritualiste** *adj* ritualistic
**rituel -uelle** *adj* ritual

**rivage** *nm* bank, shore
**rivaliser** *vi* rival, compete
**rivalité** *nf* rivalry
**rive** *nf* bank, shore; edge, border
**rivelaine** *nf* miner's pick
**river** *vt* rivet; attach, fix; **~ son clou à qn** shut s/o up
**riverain -e** *n* riverain; resident; *adj* waterside, riverside; bordering
**riveter** *vt* (5) rivet
**rivière** *nf* river, stream; **~ de diamants** diamond necklace
**rivoir** *nm* riveting-machine; riveting-hammer
**rixe** *nf* brawl, scuffle
**riz** *nm* rice
**rizière** *nf* rice-plantation, rice-paddy
**rob, robre** *nm* rubber (cards)
**robe** *nf* dress, frock, gown; legal profession; skin, husk; coat (animal); **~ de chambre** dressing-gown; **pommes de terre en ~ de chambre (des champs)** potatoes in their jackets
**robinet** *nm* tap, *US* faucet
**robinetterie** *nf* taps and fittings
**robot** *nm* robot; automatic kitchen gadget
**robre** *nm see* **rob**
**robuste** *adj* robust, sturdy, hardy
**robustesse** *nf* sturdiness, hardiness
**roc** *nm* rock
**rocade** *nf* by-pass
**rocaille** *nf* rockery; rubble
**rocailleux -euse** *adj* rocky, stony; harsh, rugged
**rocambolesque** *adj* fantastic
**roche** *nf* rock; **clair comme de l'eau de ~** crystal clear; **il y a anguille sous ~** there's something brewing
**rocher** *nm* rock
**rochet** *nm* rachet
**rocheux -euse** *adj* rocky, stony
**rodage** *nm* grinding; running in; wearing; **en ~** running in
**roder** *vt* grind; polish; run in
**rôder** *vi* prowl, wander about
**rôdeur -euse** *n* prowler
**rodomontade** *nf* blustering, swaggering
**Rogations** *nfpl eccles* Rogation-days
**rogatons** *nmpl coll* scraps (food)
**rogne** *nf coll* anger; **être en ~** be angry
**rogner** *vt* clip, trim, cut back
**rognon** *nm cul* kidney
**rognures** *nfpl* cuttings, clippings
**rogomme** *nm coll* spirits, liquor; **voix de ~** husky voice
**rogue** *adj* arrogant, haughty
**roi** *nm* king; **morceau de ~** dish fit for a king; **Nuit des Rois** Twelfth Night
**roide** *adj + adv see* **raide**
**roideur** *nf see* **raideur**
**roidir** *vt see* **raidir**

**roitelet** *nm* king of tiny country; wren

**rôle** *nm* roll, list, register; *theat* part, rôle; **à tour de ~** in turn

**Romain -e** *n* Roman

**romain** *adj* Roman

¹**romaine** *nf* steelyard

²**romaine** *nf* cos lettuce

**roman** *nm* novel, (medieval) romance; romance language, Romanic; *adj archi* romanesque; Norman (in England)

**romance** *nf* sentimental song

**romancer** *vt* give a romantic turn to

**romanche** *nm* Romansh

**romancier -ière** *n* novelist

**romand** *adj* **Suisse ~ e** French Switzerland

**romanesque** *adj* romantic; of the novel

**roman-feuilleton** *nm* (*pl* **romans-feuilletons**) serial

**romanichel -elle** *n* gipsy

**romaniste** *n* student of Romance languages

**roman-photo** *nm* (*pl* **romans-photos**) story told in photographs

**romantique** *adj* of the Romantic school; romantic

**romantisme** *nm* Romanticism

**romarin** *nm bot* rosemary

**rombière** *nf* pretentious old bag

**rompre** *vt* (85) break, snap, break off; **~ la tête (les oreilles) à qn** deafen s/o; weary s/o; **à tout ~** noisily, frantically; *vi* break off, cease relations; **se ~** break, break off; **se ~ à** accustom oneself to

**rompu** *adj* broken; experienced

**romsteck, rumsteak** *nm* rump steak

**ronce** *nf* bramble

**ronceraie** *nf* ground overgrown with brambles

**ronchonner** *vi coll* grouse, grumble

**rond** *nm* circle, ring, round; disk, washer; *sl* penny, dime; **en ~** in a ring; in circles; **faire des ~s de jambe** be obsequious; *adj* round; plump; straightforward; *adv* **tourner ~** run true, run smoothly (engine); *coll* **ne pas tourner ~** not function properly; be unwell

**rond-de-cuir** *nm* (*pl* **ronds-de-cuir**) *pej* bureaucrat; clerk

**ronde** *nf* round; beat; round-hand; round dance; **à la ~** around; **chemin de ~** sentry's watch (on battlements); **faire la ~** go the rounds

**rondeau** *nm* rondo

**rondelet -ette** *adj* plumpish; **somme rondelette** tidy sum

**rondelle** *nf* washer; small round slice

**rondement** *adv* promptly, smartly, briskly; **y aller ~** go about things briskly

**rondeur** *nf* roundness; frankness

**rondin** *nm* billet, log; cudgel

**rondouillard** *adj coll* plump

**rond-point** *nm* (*pl* **ronds-points**) circus (roads); roundabout

**ronflant** *adj* snoring; booming, rumbling

**ronflement** *nm* snore; snoring; booming; humming

**ronfler** *vi* snore; roar, boom; hum

**ronfleur -euse** *n* snorer

**ronger** *vt* (3) gnaw, nibble; eat away, corrode; **~ son frein** chafe

**rongeur** *nm* rodent; *adj* (*f* **-euse**) rodent, gnawing

**ronron** *nm* purr, purring; hum, whirr

**ronronner** *vi* purr; hum, whirr

**roquefort** *nm* Roquefort cheese

**roquer** *vi* castle (in chess)

**roquet** *nm* yapping little dog; grumpy little fellow

**roquette** *nf* rocket

**rosace** *nf* rose-window

**rosacé** *adj* rosaceous

**rosaire** *nm* rosary

**rosâtre** *adj* pinkish

**rosbif** *nm* roast beef

**rose** *nf* rose; rose-window; **~ des vents** compass card; *adj* pink; rosy; **voir tout en ~** see everything through rose-tinted spectacles

**rosé** *adj* roseate; rosé

**roseau** *nm* reed

**rosée** *nf* dew

**roseraie** *nf* rose-garden

**rosette** *nf* bow (of ribbon); rosette; **~ de Lyon** particular type of **saucisson**

**rosier** *nm* rose-tree, rose-bush

**rosière** *nf* virtuous maiden

**rosir** *vi* turn pink

**rosse** *nf coll* nag, sorry steed; *coll* unpleasant person; *adj coll* nasty, ill-natured, spiteful

**rossée** *nf* thrashing

**rosser** *vt coll* thrash

**rosserie** *nf coll* nasty trick; nastiness

**rossignol** *nm* nightingale; skeleton key; *coll* piece of junk; white elephant

**rot** *nm coll* belch

**rôt** *nm ar* roast meat

**rotatif -ive** *adj* rotary

**rotation** *nf* rotary motion; rotation

**rotative** *nf* rotary printing-press

**roter** *vi coll* belch

**rôti** *nm* roast

**rôtie** *nf* toast

**rôtir** *vt + vi* roast, toast; dry up

**rôtisserie** *nf* eating-house; grill-room

**rôtisseur -euse** *n* meat-roaster

**rôtissoire** *nf* small portable oven

**rotonde** *nf* rotunda

**rotondité** *nf* rotundity; roundness; plumpness

**rotule** *nf* knee-cap; *mech* knee-joint

**roturier -ière** *n* commoner

**rouable** *nm* fire-rake

**rouage** *nm* wheel; cog

**rouan -anne** *adj* roan

**roublard** *adj coll* artful, cunning

**roublardise** *nf coll* cunning; piece of trickery

**roucouler** *vi* coo

**roue** *nf* wheel; ~ **de secours** spare wheel; **cinquième** ~ **d'un carrosse** useless person, useless thing; **faire la** ~ spread its tail (peacock); swagger, show off; do cartwheels; **pousser à la** ~ lend a helping hand

**roué -e** *n* rake, profligate; *adj* cunning

**rouelle** *nf* round slice

**rouer** *vt ar* break on the wheel; ~ **de coups** beat, thrash

**rouerie** *nf* piece of trickery

**rouet** *nm* spinning-wheel; pulley wheel

**rouflaquette** *nf coll* lovelock

**rouge** *nm* red; rouge; *coll* red wine; **porter un métal au** ~ make a metal red hot; *adj* red; *adv* **se fâcher tout** ~ become furious

**rougeâtre** *adj* reddish

**rougeaud** *adj* red-faced

**rouge-gorge** *nm* (*pl* **rouges-gorges**) robin (redbreast)

**rougeole** *nf* measles

**rougeoyer** *vi* (7) turn reddish

**rouge-queue** *nm* (*pl* **rouges-queues**) red-start

**rouget** *nm* red-mullet; swine disease

**rougeur** *nf* redness; blush; redspot

**rougir** *vt* redden; *vi* turn red; blush; ~ **de qch** be ashamed of sth

**rouille** *nf* rust; *agr* mildew, blight

**rouiller** *vt* rust; *agr* mildew; **se** ~ become rusty; *agr* become mildewed

**rouillure** *nf* rust; *agr* blight

**roulade** *nf mus* roulade; rolled slice of meat or fish

**roulage** *nm* rolling; cartage, haulage

**roulant** *adj* rolling; moving; travelling; smooth; *coll* funny; **matériel** ~ rolling stock

**rouleau** *nm* roller; roll; coil; spool; ~ **compresseur** steam-roller; **être au bout de son (du)** ~ have no more to say; have tried everything; be absolutely exhausted; be near the end; be broke

**roulement** *nm* rolling; rumbling; rattle; taking turns, alternation; ~ **à billes** ball-bearing; ~ **de fonds** circulation of capital; **fonds de** ~ working capital

**rouler** *vt* roll; *coll* trick, swindle; turn over (project); *vi* roll, roll along; drive, cruise along; rumble; roam, rove; ~ **sur l'or** be rolling in money

**roulette** *nf* caster, small wheel, tracing-

wheel; roulette; **patins à** ~s roller-skates

**rouleur** *nm* good long-distance cyclist

**rouleuse** *nf sl* prostitute

**roulis** *nm naut* rolling

**roulotte** *nf* caravan

**roulure** *nf* cupshake; *sl* prostitute

**Roumain -e** *n* Romanian

**roumain** *nm* Romanian (language); *adj* Romanian

**Roumanie** *nf* Romania

¹**roupie** *nf* rupee

²**roupie** *nf* drop (on person's nose)

**roupiller** *vi coll* sleep

**roupillon** *nm coll* sleep

**rouquin -e** *n* redhead; *adj* red-haired

**rouspéter** *vi* (6) *coll* grumble

**rouspéteur -euse** *adj* grumbling

**rousseur** *nf* redness; **taches de** ~ freckles

**roussi** *nm* smell of burning; **ça sent le** ~ there's a smell of burning; *coll* there's trouble brewing

**roussin** *nm* cob (horse)

**roussir** *vt* redden, turn brown; *cul* brown; singe; *vi* turn brown

**routage** *nm* routing (mail, papers)

**route** *nf* road, track; way, route; ~ **nationale** main road; **code de la** ~ highway code; **en** ~ **!** off we go!; off you go!; **faire fausse** ~ lose one's way; take the wrong course; **mettre en** ~ start, start up; **se mettre en** ~ set out

**router** *vt* route (mail, papers)

**routier** *nm* long-distance lorry-driver; road racer (cyclist); **vieux** ~ old stager; *adj* (*f* **-ière**) road, roadside; **carte routière** road map; **relai** ~ roadside restaurant, pull-up

**routinier -ière** *adj* routine

**rouvrir** *vt* + *vi* (30) reopen

¹**roux** *nm* russet; *cul* brown sauce

²**roux** (*f* **rousse**) *adj* red, russet, brown; red-haired

**royal** *adj* royal, regal, kingly

**royaliste** *n* + *adj* royalist

**royaume** *nm* kingdom; ~ **des cieux** kingdom of heaven

**royauté** *nf* royalty

**ru** *nm* little stream

**ruade** *nf* kicking out (horse)

**ruban** *nm* ribbon; metal strip; tape; ~ **bleu** Blue Riband

**rubéole** *nf* German measles, rubella

**rubicond** *adj* rubicund

**rubis** *nm* ruby

**rubrique** *nf* heading; imprint; column (newspaper)

**ruche** *nf* bee-hive

**rude** *adj* rough, coarse; harsh, rugged; uncouth; arduous; tough; redoubtable

**rudement** *adv* harshly; roughly, coarsely

**rudesse** *nf* roughness, coarseness; harshness, severity
**rudimentaire** *adj* rudimentary
**rudoyer** *vt* (7) treat roughly
**rue** *nf* street; **grand' ~ , grande ~** high street
**ruée** *nf* onrush; rush
**ruelle** *nf* alley, back street; space between the bed and the wall
**ruer** *vi* kick, lash out; **se ~** rush, fling oneself
**rugir** *vi* roar
**rugissement** *nm* roar
**rugosité** *nf* ruggedness, rugosity; wrinkle
**rugueux -ueuse** *adj* rough, rugged; gnarled
**ruine** *nf* ruin; downfall
**ruiner** *vt* ruin, destroy
**ruineux -euse** *adj* ruinous
**ruisseau** *nm* stream, brook; gutter
**ruisseler** *vi* (5) stream, run, run down, trickle
**rumeur** *nf* confused murmur; rumour; **~ publique** opinion of the crowd
**ruminer** *vt* ruminate; *coll* ponder over; *vi* chew the cud

**rumsteak** *nm see* romsteck
**rupin** *adj sl* rich, luxurious
**rupteur** *nm elect* contact breaker, make-and-break
**rupture** *nf* breaking, rupture; bursting; breaking off; breach
**ruse** *nf* trick, dodge, ruse
**rusé** *adj* crafty, cunning, wily
**ruser** *vi* use cunning
**Russe** *n* Russian
**russe** *nm* Russian (language); *adj* Russian
**Russie** *nf* Russia
**rustaud** *adj* boorish
**rusticité** *nf* rusticity; primitiveness; hardiness (plant)
**rustique** *adj* rustic; hardy (plant)
**rustre** *adj* boorish, coarse
**rustrerie** *nf* boorishness
**rut** *nm* rutting
**rutabaga** *nm* swede
**rutilant** *adj* glowing red; gleaming
**rutiler** *vi* glow red; gleam
**rythme** *nm* rhythm
**rythmer** *vt* give rhythm to
**rythmique** *adj* rhythmic

# S

**s** *nm* **sentier en ~** winding path
**sa** *poss adj see* son
**sabayon** *nm cul* zabaglione
**sabbat** *nm* Sabbath; witches' sabbath; *coll* row, shindy
**sabbatique** *adj* sabbatical
**sabir** *nm* lingo; Mediterranean lingua franca
**sable** *nm* sand; **~s mouvants** quicksands; **le marchand de ~ a passé** he (she) is nodding off
**sablé** *nm* kind of shortbread
**sabler** *vt* sand; **~ le champagne** drink champagne (to celebrate an occasion)
**sableux -euse** *adj* mixed with sand
**sablier** *nm* hour-glass; egg-timer
**sablière** *nf* gravel-pit, sand-pit; sand-box
**sablonner** *vt* sprinkle with sand; sand
**sablonneux -euse** *adj* sandy, gritty
**sablonnière** *nf* sand-pit
**sabord** *nm naut* (gun-)port

**saborder** *vt* scuttle
**sabot** *nm* clog, wooden shoe; hoof; whipping-top; shoe (brake); useless tool or machine
**sabotage** *nm* clog-making; botching; sabotage
**saboter** *vt* botch; damage, sabotage
**saboteur -euse** *n* saboteur; botcher
**sabotier -ière** *n* clog-maker
**sabrer** *vt* sabre, hack down; cut drastically; *coll* criticize
**¹sac** *nm* sack, bag; sackful; sackcloth; **~ à dos** rucksack; **~ à main** handbag; **~ à vin** drunkard; *coll* **~ percé** spendthrift; *coll* **l'affaire est dans le ~** it's in the bag, the affair is as good as settled; *coll* **prendre qn la main dans le ~** catch s/o red-handed; **vider son ~** hold nothing back, unbosom oneself
**²sac** *nm* sacking, pillaging
**saccade** *nf* jolt, jerk; **par ~s** in jerks
**saccadé** *adj* jerky, abrupt

**saccager** *vt* (3) pillage; ransack; *coll* put in disorder
**sacerdoce** *nm* priesthood; calling
**sacerdotal** *adj* priestly
**sachée** *nf* sackful
**sachet** *nm* small bag
**sacoche** *nf* satchel; wallet
**sacquer** *vt coll* sack, dismiss
**sacramentel -elle** *adj* sacramental
**sacre** *nm* consecration; coronation
**¹sacré** *adj* sacred, consecrated; *coll* blessed, confounded; inviolable; **feu ~** zeal
**²sacré** *adj anat* sacral
**sacrement** *nm* sacrament; marriage
**sacrer** *vt* consecrate; anoint, crown; *vi coll* swear
**sacrificateur -trice** *n* sacrificer
**sacrificatoire** *adj* sacrificial
**sacrifier** *vt* sacrifice; give
**sacrilège** *nm* sacrilege; *adj* sacrilegious
**sacripant** *nm* scoundrel, rascal
**sacristain** *nm* sacristan, sexton
**sacristi, sapristi** *interj coll* Lord!
**sacristie** *nf eccles* vestry
**sacro-saint** *adj* sacrosanct
**sadique** *n* sadist; *adj* sadistic
**sadisme** *nm* sadism
**safran** *nm* saffron
**sagace** *adj* sagacious
**sagacité** *nf* sagacity, shrewdness
**sagaie** *nf* assegai
**sage** *adj* wise; discreet, judicious; well-behaved, good; chaste; **~ comme une image** as good as gold
**sage-femme** *nf* (*pl* **sages-femmes**) midwife
**sagesse** *nf* wisdom; discretion, prudence; good behaviour; chasteness
**sagou** *nm* sago
**sagouin** *nm* squirrel-monkey; *coll* dirty, slovenly person
**saignant** *adj* bleeding; underdone (meat)
**saignée** *nf* bleeding, bloodletting; bend (of the arm); trench; drain (resources)
**saigner** *vt* bleed; draw blood from; *vi* bleed; **se ~** make great sacrifices
**saillant** *nm* salient; *adj* projecting; striking, outstanding
**saillie** *nf* projection, ledge; flash of wit; **en ~** projecting
**saillir** *vt* (86) cover, mount; *vi* jut out, project
**sain** *adj* healthy; sound; wholesome; **~ et sauf** safe and sound
**saindoux** *nm* lard
**saint -e** *n* saint; **~e nitouche** little hypocrite; **ne plus savoir à quel ~ se vouer** not know where to turn; **prêcher pour son ~** have an eye to one's own interest; *adj* holy; godly, saintly; *coll* **toute la ~e journée** the whole

wretched day; **vendredi saint** Good Friday
**Saint-Esprit** *nm* Holy Ghost
**sainteté** *nf* holiness, saintliness; sanctity
**saint-frusquin** *nm invar sl* **tout le ~** the whole damn lot
**saint-glinglin (à la)** *adv phr coll* never
**saint-honoré** *nm* kind of cream cake
**Saint-Office** *nm* Holy Office; *hist* Inquisition
**Saint-Siège** *nm* Holy See
**Saint-Sylvestre** *nf* New Year's Eve
**saisie** *nf* seizure; *leg* distraint, attachment
**saisir** *vt* seize; take hold of, grasp, grip; *leg* distrain, attach; *leg* place before (court); understand; *cul* seal; **être saisi d'étonnement** be startled; **se ~ de** lay hands on, take possession of
**saisissement** *nm* sudden chill; seizure
**saison** *nf* season; **de ~** in season; timely; **hors de ~** out of place, inopportune
**saisonnier -ière** *n* seasonal worker; *adj* seasonal
**salace** *adj* salacious
**salade** *nf* salad; *coll* jumble
**saladier** *nm* salad-bowl
**salage** *nm* salting (roads)
**salaire** *nm* wage, pay; reward
**salaison** *nf* salting; curing; **~s** provisions
**salamalec** *nm coll* salaam, deep bow
**salamandre** *nf* salamander; slow-combustion stove
**salant** *adj* salt-producing; **marais ~s** salt marshes
**salarial** *adj* concerning wages
**salariat** *nm* wage-earning; wage-earners
**salarié -e** *n* wage-earner
**salarier** *vt* pay, give a wage to
**salaud** *nm sl* swine, shit
**sale** *adj* dirty, filthy; rotten, nasty, beastly; dishonest; **~ comme un peigne** filthy
**salé** *nm* salt pork; **petit ~** cooked salt pork; *adj* salt; salted; salty; spicy; *coll* exaggerated, exorbitant; **prés ~s** saltings
**salement** *adv* dirtily; *sl* very, extremely
**saler** *vt* salt; cure (pork); *coll* punish excessively; sell at an excessive price
**saleté** *nf* dirt, filth; dirtiness; rubbish; obscenity; nasty trick
**salière** *nf* salt-cellar; hollow above collar-bone (in skinny person)
**saligaud** *nm sl* swine, shit
**salin** *nm* salt-marsh; *adj* saline, salt-bearing
**saline** *nf* salt-pan
**salinité** *nf* saltness
**salique** *adj* Salic
**salir** *vt* dirty; defile; tarnish

**salissant** *adj* dirty, messy; easily dirtied
**salissure** *nf* stain
**salivaire** *adj* salivary
**salive** *nf* saliva, spittle; *coll* perdre sa ~ waste one's breath
**saliver** *vi* salivate
**salle** *nf* hall; large room; audience, house; ~ à manger dining-room; ~ d'armes fencing school; ~ d'attente waiting-room; ~ de bains bathroom; ~ des fêtes local hall; ~ des pas perdus waiting-hall; ~ des ventes auction rooms
**salmigondis** *nm* mixed stew; *coll* miscellany
**salmis** *nm cul* salmi, game stew
**saloir** *nm* salting-tub
**salon** *nm* drawing-room; art exhibition; show, exhibition; ~ de thé tea-room; fréquenter les ~s move in society
**salopard** *nm sl* bastard, shit
**salope** *nf sl* slut
**saloper** *vt sl* botch
**saloperie** *nf sl* filthiness; dirt; trash, rubbish; dirty trick
**salopette** *nf* overalls, dungarees.
**salpêtre** *nm* saltpetre
**salsifis** *nm* salsify
**saltimbanque** *n* tumbler, circus acrobat
**salubre** *adj* salubrious, healthy, wholesome
**salubrité** *nf* salubriousness, healthiness, wholesomeness
**saluer** *vt* salute; greet, hail; acclaim
**salure** *nf* saltness; tang
**salut** *nm* salvation; safety; saving; salute; greeting; *eccles* evening service; ~! hullo!; Armée du Salut Salvation Army; faire son ~ seek salvation
**salutaire** *adj* salutary, beneficial
**salutation** *nf* greeting
**salutiste** *n* member of the Salvation Army
**salve** *nf* salvo; ~ d'applaudissements burst of applause
**samaritain** *adj* Samaritan
**samedi** *nm* Saturday
**sanctificateur -trice** *n* sanctifier; *adj* sanctifying
**sanctifier** *vt* sanctify, make holy, hallow
**sanction** *nf* sanction; approval, consent; punishment; consequence; prendre des ~s take repressive measures
**sanctionner** *vt* sanction; approve; *coll* punish
**sanctuaire** *nm* sanctuary
**sandale** *nf* sandal
**sang** *nm* blood; race; *coll* avoir du ~ dans les veines be energetic; avoir le ~ chaud be quick-tempered; bon ~! Heavens!, Good God!; coup de ~ stroke; pur ~ thoroughbred; se faire du mauvais ~ worry; suer ~ et eau slave away
**sang-froid** *nm invar* composure, calm
**sanglant** *adj* bloody; blood-stained; cruel, scathing
**sangle** *nf* strap; lit de ~s camp bed
**sangler** *vt* girth (horse); strap
**sanglier** *nm* wild boar
**sanglot** *nm* sob
**sangloter** *vi* sob
**sangsue** *nf* blood-sucker, leech
**sanguin** *adj* of the blood; full-blooded
**sanguinaire** *adj* sanguinary, bloody; bloodthirsty
**sanguine** *nf* red chalk; drawing in red chalk; bloodstone; blood orange
**sanguinolent** *adj* tinged with blood
**sanie** *nf med* pus
**sanieux -ieuse** *adj med* purulent
**sanitaire** *nm* plumbing installation; *adj* sanitary
**sans** *prep* without; but for; ~ cela otherwise; ~ mentir to tell the truth; ~ plus nothing more; ~ quoi otherwise; être ~ le sou be penniless; je ne suis pas ~ le savoir I do know; *conj* ~ que without
**sans-abri** *n invar* homeless person
**sans-cœur** *n invar coll* heartless person
**sans-façon** *nm invar* straightforwardness; *adj invar* homely
**sans-filiste** *n* wireless enthusiast, radio ham
**sans-gêne** *nm invar* excessive familiarity; cheek; *adj invar* unceremonious, rude
**sans-le-sou** *n invar coll* penniless person
**sans-logis** *n* homeless person
**sansonnet** *nm* starling
**sans-souci** *n invar* carefree person
**sans-travail** *n invar* unemployed person
**santal** *nm* sandalwood-tree
**santé** *nf* health; maison de ~ mental home
**santon** *nm* small painted clay figure of saint
**saoul** *adj* see soûl
**saouler** *vt* see soûler
**sape** *nf* undermining, sapping
**saper** *vt* undermine, sap
**saperlipopette** *interj obs* Good Lord!
**sapeur** *nm mil* sapper
**sapeur-pompier** *nm* (*pl* sapeurs-pompiers) fireman
**saphir** *nm* sapphire
**sapin** *nm* fir-tree; bois de ~ deal; *coll* sentir le ~ not have long to live
**sapinière** *nf* fir plantation
**sapristi** *interj* see sacristi
**saquer** *vt* see sacquer
**sarabande** *nf* saraband

**sarbacane** *nf* blow-pipe

**sarcasme** *nm* taunt, piece of sarcasm

**sarcastique** *adj* sarcastic

**sarcelle** *nf* teal

**sarcler** *vt + vi* hoe, weed

**sarcloir** *nm* hoe

**sarcome** *nm* sarcoma

**sarcophage** *nm* sarcophagus

**Sardaigne** *nf* Sardinia

**sardane** *nf* Catalan dance

**sarde** *adj* Sardinian

**sardine** *nf* sardine; pilchard; *mil coll* stripe

**sardinier** *nm* sardine-boat; sardine-net

**sardonique** *adj* sardonic

**sargasse** *nf* gulf-weed, sargasso

**sarment** *nm* climbing stem; vine-shoot

¹**sarrasin** *nm* buckwheat

²**sarrasin** *adj* Saracen

**sarrasine** *nf* portcullis

**sarrau** *nm* (*pl* **sarraus** *or* **sarraux**) smock

**sas** *nm* sieve, riddle; air lock; flooding chamber

**sasser** *vt* sift; screen (flour); lock (boat)

**satané** *adj coll* damned, confounded

**satanique** *adj* satanic, diabolical

**satelliser** *vt* put into orbit

**satiété** *nf* satiety; surfeit

**satiner** *vt* give a glossy surface to

**satinette** *nf* sateen

**satirique** *adj* satirical

**satiriser** *vt* satirize

**satisfaction** *nf* satisfaction; reparation

**satisfaire** *vt* (46) satisfy; gratify; *vi* satisfy; make amends; meet; fulfil

**satisfaisant** *adj* satisfying; acceptable

**satisfait** *adj* satisfied

**saturer** *vt* saturate; sate

**saturnin** *adj* saturnine

**satyre** *nm* satyr; *coll* sex-maniac

**sauce** *nf* sauce; soft black crayon; accompaniment; manner; **mettre qn à toutes les ~s** use s/o in all kinds of ways

**saucée** *nf coll* shower

**saucer** *vt* (4) dip in the sauce; drench

**saucier** *nm* sauce-cook

**saucière** *nf* sauce-boat, gravy-boat

**saucisse** *nf* sausage; observation balloon; *coll* **ne pas attacher son chien avec des ~s** be careful with one's money

**saucisson** *nm* French sàlami

¹**sauf, sauve** *adj* safe, unhurt

²**sauf** *prep* except, save, but for; saving; **~ avis contraire** unless I (you, we, etc) hear to the contrary; **~ imprévu** barring any unforeseen occurrence

**sauf-conduit** *nm* safe-conduct, pass

**sauge** *nf bot* sage

**saugrenu** *adj* preposterous, absurd

**saule** *nm* willow; **~ pleureur** weeping willow

**saumâtre** *adj* brackish, briny

**saumon** *nm* salmon

**saumoné** *adj* **truite ~e** salmon-trout

**saumure** *nf* brine (for pickling)

**saunier** *nm* salt-maker

**saupiquet** *nm cul* spiced sauce

**saupoudrer** *vt* sprinkle, dust; *fig* disperse (resources)

**saur** *adj m* **hareng ~** bloater

**saurer** *vt* cure, bloat

**saurien** *adj* saurian

**saut** *nm* jump, leap; waterfall; **~ en hauteur** high jump; **~ en longueur** long jump; **~ périlleux** somersault in mid-air; **au ~ du lit** on getting out of bed; **faire le ~** take the plunge; **faire un ~ chez** pop over to

**saut-de-lit** *nm* (*pl* **sauts-de-lit**) dressing gown

**saut-de-loup** *nm* (*pl* **sauts-de-loup**) deep ditch

**saute** *nf* sudden change, jump

**sauté** *adj* fried, sauté

**saute-mouton** *nm invar* leap-frog

**sauter** *vt* jump over, clear; leave out; skip; *vi* jump, leap; explode, blow up; change (wind); **~ au plafond** be very surprised; be furious; **faire ~** make (s/o) jump; blow up; burst; **faire ~ qn** deprive s/o of his turn; **se ~ la cervelle** blow one's brains out

**sauterelle** *nf* grasshopper; *carp* bevel square

**sauterie** *nf coll* hop, dance

**saute-ruisseau** *nm invar* errand boy, messenger boy

**sauteuse** *nf* shallow saucepan (for frying); *coll* trollop, tart

**sautiller** *vi* hop about, jump about

**sautoir** *nm* long chain necklace; **en ~** crosswise; over the shoulder

**sauvage** *n* savage; *adj* savage, wild; uncivilized; barbarous; shy; unsociable; wild-cat (strike)

**sauvageon -onne** *n* shy, unsociable child; *nm* wild stock

**sauvagerie** *nf* unsociable nature; savagery

**sauvagine** *nf* waterfowl

**sauvegarde** *nf* safeguard, safekeeping; *naut* life-line

**sauvegarder** *vt* safeguard

**sauve-qui-peut** *nm invar* panic flight; stampede

**sauver** *vt* save, rescue; preserve; **se ~** escape, flee; clear off; boil over

**sauvetage** *nm* rescue, life-saving; **bateau de ~** lifeboat; **ceinture de ~** life-belt

**sauveteur** *nm* rescuer, life-saver

**sauvette (à la)** *adv phr* hastily; **marchand ~** illicit street vendor

**savamment** *adv* knowingly; learnedly

**savane** *nf* savanna

**savant** *nm* scientist; scholar; *adj* learned, scholarly; clever, skilful

**savate** *nf* old shoe, old slipper; *coll* **traîner la ~** be poor; be idle

**savetier** *nm ar* cobbler

**saveur** *nf* taste, savour, flavour

**savoir** *nm* knowledge, learning; *vt* (87) know, be aware of; learn, get to know; know how to, be able to; **à ~** namely, that is to say; **en ~ long sur** know a lot about; **faire ~** inform; **il ne veut rien ~** he won't hear of it; **je ne sache pas** I am not aware; **je ne saurais** I can't; **que je sache** that I know of; **que sais-je!** goodness knows!; **reste à ~ il** it remains to be seen; **un je ne sais quoi** something

**savoir-faire** *nm invar* ability

**savoir-vivre** *nm invar* knowledge of the world, good manners

**savon** *nm* soap; *coll* reprimand

**savonner** *vt* soap, wash

**savonnerie** *nf* soap-works; soap-trade

**savonnette** *nf* cake of toilet-soap

**savonneux -euse** *adj* soapy

**savourer** *vt* enjoy, relish

**savoureux -euse** *adj* tasty, savoury; rich (story, joke)

**savoyard** *adj* of Savoy

**saynète** *nf* playlet

**sbire** *nm pej* hired thug; tough policeman

**scabieux -ieuse** *adj* scabby

**scabreux -euse** *adj* ticklish, difficult; indelicate; improper

**scalper** *vt* scalp

**scandale** *nm* scandal, disgrace; **faire ~** shock

**scandaleux -euse** *adj* disgraceful, scandalous

**scandaliser** *vt* scandalize; **se ~** be indignant

**scander** *vt* scan (verse); stress, emphasize

**scandinave** *adj* Scandinavian

**scaphandre** *nm* diving-suit; space-suit; **~ autonome** aqualung

**scaphandrier** *nm* (deep-sea) diver

**scapulaire** *nm eccles* scapular; *adj anat* scapular

**scarabée** *nm* beetle; scarab

**scare** *nm* parrot-fish

**scarificateur** *nm agr* scarifier; *surg* scarificator

**scarifier** *vt agr + surg* scarify

**scarlatine** *nf* scarlet fever

**scarole** *nf bot* endive

**scatologique** *adj* scatological

**sceau** *nm* seal; mark, stamp; **Garde des Sceaux** = Lord Chancellor

**scélérat -e** *n* villain, scoundrel; *adj* villainous; crafty

**sceller** *vt* seal, seal up; confirm

**scellés** *nmpl* **apposer (mettre) les ~** affix the seals

**scénario** *nm* scenario, script

**scénariste** *n* script-writer

**scène** *nf* stage; scene; row; *theat* **mettre en ~** produce; *theat* **mise en ~** production

**scénique** *adj* scenic; theatrical

**scepticisme** *nm* scepticism

**sceptique** *n* sceptic; *adj* sceptical

**schéma** *nm* diagram, sketch-plan

**schématique** *adj* schematic, diagrammatic

**schisme** *nm* schism

**schiste** *nm* schist, shale

**schizophrénie** *nf* schizophrenia

**schlass** *adj invar sl* drunk

**schnaps** *nm coll* spirits

**schuss** *nm* direct descent (skiing)

**sciatique** *nf* sciatica; *adj* sciatic

**scie** *nf* saw; *coll* bore; **~ à découper** fret-saw; **~ à métaux** hack-saw

**sciemment** *adv* knowingly, wittingly

**science** *nf* knowledge, learning; science

**scientifique** *adj* scientific

**scier** *vt* saw, saw off

**scierie** *nf* saw-mill

**scieur** *nm* sawyer

**scinder** *vt* split up, divide

**scintiller** *vi* sparkle, scintillate, twinkle

**scission** *nf* split, scission; secession

**sciure** *nf* sawdust

**scléreux -euse** *adj* sclerosed, hard

**sclérose** *nf* sclerosis; hardening

**scléroser** *vt* harden; **se ~** harden

**sclérotique** *nf* sclera

**scolaire** *adj* school; **groupe ~** (large) school

**scolariser** *vt* provide with schools; give schooling to

**scolastique** *adj* scholastic

**scoliose** *nf* scoliosis

**scolopendre** *nf* scolopendra, centipede; *bot* hart's tongue

**sconse** *nm* skunk

**scorbut** *nm* scurvy

**scorbutique** *adj* scurvied

**scorie** *nf usu pl* slag, cinders

**scorsonère** *nf* black salsify

**scotch** *nm* (Scotch) whisky; adhesive tape

**scoutisme** *nm* Boy Scout movement

**script** *nm* script handwriting, copperplate

**scripte** *nf* continuity girl

**scrofule** *nf* scrofula

**scrofuleux -euse** *adj* scrofulous

**scrupule** *nm* scruple; **se faire ~** scruple

**scrupuleux -euse** *adj* scrupulous

**scrutateur -trice** *n* teller, scrutineer; *adj* searching, scrutinizing

**scruter** *vt* scrutinize, examine closely

**scrutin** *nm* poll, voting; **procéder au ~** take the votes; divide

**scull** *nm* double-sculler

**sculpter** *vt* sculpture, carve

**sculpteur** *nm* sculptor

**scythe** *adj* Scythian

**se** *refl pron* oneself; himself; herself; themselves; each other; one another

**séance** *nf* session; meeting; sitting; performance; seance; **lever la ~** close the meeting

¹**séant** *nm* bottom, behind, posterior

²**séant** *adj* becoming, fitting

**seau** *nm* pail; pailful; **~ hygiénique** sanitary pail; **pleuvoir à ~x** rain very hard

**sébacé** *adj* sebaceous

**sébile** *nf* wooden bowl

**sec** (*f* **sèche**) *adj* dry; lean, gaunt; dull; brusque; **à ~** dry; broke; **boire ~** drink hard; have one's drink neat; **coup ~** sharp blow; **mettre à ~** dry, dry up; **parler ~** speak frankly; **perte sèche** dead loss

**sécateur** *nm* pruning scissors, secateurs

**sèche-cheveux** *nm* hair-drier

**sèchement** *adv* drily, curtly

**sécher** *vt+vi* (6) dry, dry up; *coll* cut (lecture); fail to answer

**sécheresse** *nf* drought; dryness; leanness; curtness; lack of feeling

**sécherie** *nf* drying establishment, drying-place

**séchoir** *nm* drier; clothes-horse; drying-place

**second -e** *n* second; *nm* second floor; assistant, second-in-command; **sans ~** peerless, unparalleled; *adj* second

**secondaire** *nm* secondary education; *adj* secondary; minor, accessory

**seconde** *nf* second; jiffy

**seconder** *vt* help, support

**secouer** *vt* shake; shake up; shake down; **se ~** shake oneself; *coll* buck up, bestir oneself

**secourable** *adj* helpful

**secourir** *vt* (29) help

**secourisme** *nm* first-aid

**secouriste** *n* first-aid worker

**secours** *nm* help, assistance, relief; **au ~!** help!; **sortie de ~** emergency exit

**secousse** *nf* shake, shaking; jolt, jerk; shock; tremor

**secret** *nm* secret; secrecy; hidden spring; *adj* (*f* **-ète**) secret; hidden

**secrétaire** *n* secretary; *nm* writing-desk; secretary-bird

**secrétariat** *nm* secretariat; office of secretary

**sécréter** *vt* (6) secrete

**sectaire** *adj* sectarian

**sectarisme** *nm* sectarianism

**secte** *nf* sect

**secteur** *nm* district; sector

**section** *nf* cutting; section; branch; department; platoon; subdivision

**sectionner** *vt* cut, sever; divide into sections

**séculaire** *adj* century-old; occurring once a century; secular

**séculariser** *vt* secularize; deconsecrate

**séculier -ière** *adj* secular

**secundo** *adv* secondly

**sécurité** *nf* security; safety

**sédatif** *nm* sedative; *adj* (*f* **-ive**) sedative

**sédentaire** *adj* sedentary; stationary, fixed

**sédimentaire** *adj* sedimentary

**séditieux -ieuse** *adj* seditious; rebellious

**sédition** *nf* mutiny; sedition

**séducteur -trice** *n* seducer; *adj* seductive

**séduction** *nf* seduction; charm; leading astray

**séduire** *vt* (80) charm, captivate; seduce; lead astray

**segmenter** *vt* segment, divide into segments

**ségrégation** *nf* segregation; isolation

**seiche** *nf* cuttle-fish

**seigle** *nm* rye

**seigneur** *nm* lord; master; **le Seigneur** God, the Lord; **faire le grand ~** give oneself airs

**seigneurie** *nf* domain, manor; lordship

**seille** *nf* *dial* bucket

**sein** *nm* breast, bosom; *fig* heart; **donner le ~ à** suckle

**seing** *nm* leg **acte sous ~ privé** simple contract, private agreement

**séisme** *nm* earthquake, seism

**seize** *nm + adj* sixteen; sixteenth

**seizième** *n + adj* sixteenth

**séjour** *nm* stay; place, residence

**séjournant -e** *n* holiday-maker

**séjourner** *vi* stay, stop, sojourn

**sel** *nm* salt; *fig* wit; **~ gemme** rock-salt; **~s** smelling-salts

**sélectif -ive** *adj rad* selective

**sélection** *nf* choice, selection

**self** *nm* *coll* self-service restaurant; *nf elect* inductance coil

**selle** *nf* saddle; *med* stool; **être bien en ~** be firmly established

**seller** *vt* saddle

**sellette** *nf* small seat, stool; stool for accused; **être sur la ~** be accused; be in the hot seat

**sellier** *nm* saddler

**selon** *prep* according to; **~ que** according as; **c'est ~** it all depends

**semailles** *nfpl* sowing; sowing-time

**semaine** *nf* week; week's wages; ~ **anglaise** five-day week; **prêter à la petite** ~ lend money on a weekly interest basis

**semainier -ière** *n* person on duty for a week; *nm* bracelet with seven links; piece of furniture with seven drawers

**sémantique** *nf* semantics; *adj* semantic

**sémaphore** *nm* semaphore

**semblable** *n* equal, like; fellow-man; *adj* similar, like; such

**semblant** *nm* appearance, semblance; **faire** ~ **de** pretend; **faux** ~ pretence; **sans faire** ~ **de rien** surreptitiously; pretending not to be aware of anything

**sembler** *vi* seem, appear; **à ce qu'il me semble** as it strikes me; **que vous en semble?** what do you think of it?

**semelle** *nf* sole; *bui* ground-sill; *coll* **battre la** ~ stamp (to warm one's feet); *coll* **ne pas reculer d'une** ~ not yield an inch

**semence** *nf* seed

**semer** *vt* (6) sow; disseminate, scatter, spread; *sl* shake off; ~ **son argent** spend one's money freely

**semestre** *nm* semester; half-year; six months' pay

**semestriel -ielle** *adj* half-yearly

**semeur -euse** *n* sower; disseminator

**semi-circulaire** *adj* semi-circular

**sémillant** *adj* bright, sprightly

**séminaire** *nm* seminary; seminar; **petit** ~ Catholic school

**séminariste** *nm* seminarist

**sémiotique** *nf* semiotics

**semis** *nm* sowing; sowing-plot; seedlings

**sémitique** *adj* Semitic

**semoir** *nm* seed-bag; sowing-machine

**semonce** *nf* reprimand; **verte** ~ good dressing-down

**semoule** *nf* semolina

**sempiternel -elle** *adj* never-ending

**sénat** *nm* senate; senate-house

**sénateur** *nm* senator; **train de** ~ slow, solemn walk

**séné** *nm* senna

**séneçon** *nm* groundsel

**sénégalais** *adj* Senegalese

**sénevé** *nm bot* mustard

**sénilité** *nf* senility

**sens** *nm* sense; intelligence, judgement; meaning; direction; ~ **dessus dessous** upside down; ~ **devant derrière** back to front; ~ **interdit** no entry; ~ **unique** one-way (street); **abonder dans le** ~ **de qn** be in agreement with s/o, be of the same opinion as s/o; **à mon** ~ to my way of thinking; **en dépit du bon** ~ against all reason

**sensass** *adj invar coll* terrific, super

**sensation** *nf* feeling, sensation; excite-

ment; **faire** ~ create a sensation

**sensationnel -elle** *adj* sensational; *coll* terrific

**sensé** *adj* sensible

**sensibilisateur** *nm phot* sensitizer

**sensibiliser** *vt* make aware, arouse (opinion); *phot* sensitize

**sensibilité** *nf* sensibility; sensitiveness; compassion

**sensible** *adj* sensitive, susceptible; perceptible; tender, sore; **d'une manière** ~ appreciably

**sensiblement** *adv* appreciably

**sensiblerie** *nf* sentimentalism

**sensitif -ive** *adj* sensitive; sensory

**sensoriel -ielle** *adj* relating to the senses

**sensualisme** *nm* sensualism

**sensualité** *nf* sensuality

**sensuel -uelle** *adj* sensual

**sente** *nf* footpath, little path

**sentence** *nf* maxim; judgement, sentence

**sentencieux -ieuse** *adj* sententious

**senteur** *nf* perfume, aroma

**senti** *adj* strongly felt

**sentier** *nm* path

**sentiment** *nm* feeling; sensation; opinion; **faire du** ~ sentimentalize

**sentimentalité** *nf* sentimentality

**sentine** *nf naut* bilge; *fig* cess-pit

**sentinelle** *nf* sentry, sentinel

**sentir** *vt* (59) feel; be aware of; smell; **faire** ~ make felt; *vi* smell of; smack of; ~ **bon (mauvais)** smell nice (bad); **se** ~ feel; **il ne se sent pas de joie** he is beside himself with joy; **il se sent du courage** he feels brave; **se** ~ **de qch** be affected by sth

**seoir** *vi* (88) suit, become

**séparateur** *nm* separator; *elect* separating-plate

**séparatif -ive** *adj* separating, separative

**séparation** *nf* separation, parting; dispersal; ~ **de biens** separate ownership (in marriage); ~ **de corps** legal separation

**séparatisme** *nm* separatism

**séparé** *adj* separate, distinct; separated

**séparément** *adv* separately

**séparer** *vt* separate, part; keep apart; **se** ~ separate, part; divide; disperse, break up

**sépia** *nf* cuttle-fish; sepia (colour)

**sept** *nm* + *adj* seven; seventh

**septante** *adj* seventy (in Belgium and Switzerland)

**septembre** *nm* September

**septennal** *adj* septennial

**septentrional** *adj* northern

**septicémie** *nf* septicaemia

**septième** *n* + *adj* seventh

**septique** *adj* septic

**septuagénaire** *n* + *adj* septuagenarian

**Septuagésime** nf Septuagesima
**septuor** nm septet
**septupler** vt multiply by seven
**sépulcral** adj sepulchral
**sépulcre** nm sepulchre
**sépulture** nf burial, interment; burial-place
**séquelle** nf usu pl results, consequences (of illness)
**séquence** nf sequence
**séquentiel -ielle** adj sequential
**séquestration** nf isolation; sequestration; seclusion
**séquestre** nm leg sequestration
**séquestrer** vt sequestrate; seclude, isolate
**sérail** nm seraglio
**séraphin** nm seraph
**séraphique** adj seraphic
**serein** adj calm, serene; cheerful
**sérénité** nf serenity, calmness
**séreux -euse** adj serous
**serf** (f serve) n serf; adj in bondage
**serfouette** nf combined hoe and fork tool
**sergent** nm sergeant; ar ~ **de ville** policeman
**sériciculture** nf silkworm breeding
**série** nf series, succession; line (samples); **fabrication en** ~ mass production; **fin de** ~ remnant, oddment; **hors** ~ specially manufactured; exceptional
**sérier** vt arrange in series
**sérieux** adj seriousness, gravity; **manque de** ~ irresponsibility; adj (f -ieuse) serious, grave; serious-minded; earnest, sincere; important; reliable
**serin** nm canary
**seriner** vt coll repeat ad nauseam
**seringue** nf syringe
**seringuer** vt syringe; squirt
**serment** nm oath; **prêter** ~ swear an oath, be sworn
**sermonner** vt sermonize, lecture; reprimand
**sérosité** nf serosity
**serpe** nf bill-hook
**serpent** nm snake, serpent; spiteful, cunning person
**serpenter** vi wind, meander
**serpentin** nm coil of tubing; paper streamer; adj serpentine
**serpette** nf pruning-knife
**serpillière** nf floor cloth; sacking
**serpolet** nm wild thyme
**¹serre** nf greenhouse
**²serre** nf grip, squeezing; claw, talon
**serré** adj tight, close, dense; **avoir le cœur** ~ be sad; adv **jouer** ~ play carefully; act cautiously
**serre-livres** nm book-end

**serrement** nm squeezing; ~ **de cœur** pang
**serrer** vt squeeze, grasp; tighten, screw up; close; put away, shut away; clench; keep close to, hug; ~ **la main à qn** shake hands with s/o; ~ **les freins** apply the brakes; **se** ~ crowd together; tighten
**serre-tête** nm invar headband
**serrure** nf lock
**serrurerie** nf locksmith's trade; metal-work
**serrurier** nm locksmith
**sertir** vt set (jewel, etc); metal crimp
**sertissure** nf setting
**servage** nm serfdom
**servant** adj m **chevalier (cavalier)** ~ faithful admirer
**servante** nf servant-girl, servant-woman
**serveur** nm waiter
**serveuse** nf waitress
**serviabilité** nf obliging nature
**serviable** adj obliging
**service** nm service; **chef de** ~ head of department; **entrée de** ~ staff entrance; **être de** ~ be on duty; **hors de** ~ out of action; **offrir ses** ~s offer one's good offices; **premier** ~ first sitting (meal); **rendre (un)** ~ **à qn** do s/o a good turn
**serviette** nf table napkin; towel; brief-case
**serviette-éponge** nf (pl **serviettes-éponges**) Turkish towel
**servilité** nf servility; slavishness
**servir** vt (89) serve; wait on; serve up; help, be of service to; satisfy; ~ **la messe** serve at mass; ~ **une rente** pay out a yearly income; vi serve, be of use; ~ **à qch** be useful for some purpose; **cela ne sert à rien de ...** it's no use ...; **rien ne sert de ...** it's no use ...; **se** ~ help oneself; supply oneself; **se** ~ **de** use, make use of
**serviteur** nm servant; **votre** ~ your obedient servant
**servitude** nf servitude, slavery; charge, financial obligation
**servofrein** nm servo-assisted brake
**ses** poss adj see **son**
**session** nf sitting, session
**sétacé** adj bristly, setaceous
**seuil** nm threshold; door-step; geog shelf
**seul** adj single, only; alone; mere, very; ~ **et unique** one and only; **parler** ~ **à** ~ **à qn** speak to s/o alone, with no one else present
**seulement** adv only; even
**sève** nf sap; vigour
**sévère** adj strict; severe; stern
**sévérité** nf severity; strictness

**sévices** *nmpl* brutality, ill-treatment

**sévir** *vi* inflict severe punishment; rage, be rife

**sevrer** *vt* (6) wean; deprive

**sexagénaire** *n + adj* sexagenarian

**sexe** *nm* sex; sexual organ

**sexisme** *nm* sexism

**sexiste** *n + adj* sexist

**sexologie** *nf* sexology

**sextupler** *vt* increase sixfold

**sexualité** *nf* sexuality '

**sexué** *adj* sexed

**sexuel -uelle** *adj* sexual

**seyant** *adj* becoming, attractive

**shampooing** *nm* shampoo

**shooter** *vi* kick (football)

**¹si** *nm invar mus* B, ti, te

**²si** *adv* so; so much; such; yes (after *neg*); **~ bien que** with the result that; **~ fait** yes; **~ grand qu'il soit** however big he may be; **que ~** yes, of course (after *neg*)

**³si** *conj* if; whether; how much; what if; **~ ce n'est** but for; **~ je le connais!** of course I know him!; **~ tant est que** + *subj* if indeed ...

**siamois** *adj* Siamese

**sibylle** *nf* sibyl

**sibyllin** *adj* sybilline

**siccatif -ive** *adj* quick-drying

**sicilien -ienne** *adj* Sicilian

**SIDA** *nm med* Aids

**sidéral** *adj* sidereal

**sidérant** *adj* staggering

**sidéré** *adj* amazed, staggered

**sidérer** *vt* (6) dumbfound, amaze

**sidérurgie** *nf* metallurgy of iron and steel

**sidérurgique** *adj* **industrie ~** iron and steel industry

**sidi** *nm pej* North African

**siècle** *nm* century; period; *theol* world; **le Grand Siècle** the age of Louis XIV

**siège** *nm* seat; centre; siege; chair; **~ social** registered office; **bain de ~** hip bath; **état de ~** martial law; **lever le ~** raise the siege; **mettre le ~** lay siege; **Saint-Siège** Holy See

**siéger** *vi* (6,3) sit, be in session; be seated; have a seat

**sien** (*f* **sienne**) *n* one's own; **faire des siennes** be up to one's tricks; **les ~ s** one's friends; one's kin; **y mettre du ~** make one's contribution; *pron* his; hers; its; one's

**sieste** *nf* siesta

**sieur** *nm leg* Mr

**sifflant** *adj* hissing, whistling

**sifflement** *nm* whistling, whistle

**siffler** *vt* whistle; whistle for; boo; *sl* swig down; *vi* whistle; hiss; wheeze; boo

**sifflet** *nm* whistle; **coup de ~** whistle blast; *sl* **couper le ~ à qn** cut s/o's throat; shut somebody up

**siffleur -euse** *n* whistler; *adj* whistling; hissing; wheezing

**siffloter** *vi* whistle gently, whistle to oneself

**sigle** *nm* set of initials

**signal** *nm* signal; **donner le ~ de** cause, start

**signalement** *nm* description (person), particulars

**signaler** *vt* point out; draw attention to; report; signal; give a description of; **se ~** distinguish oneself, attract notice

**signalétique** *adj* descriptive; **fiche ~** police record card

**signaleur** *nm* signaller

**signalisation** *nf* signalling; signalling system

**signataire** *n* signatory

**signature** *nf* signing; signature

**signe** *nm* sign; indication, mark; symbol; gesture; **en ~ de** as a sign of; **faire ~ à qn** beckon to s/o, motion to s/o; **placé sous le ~ de** the theme (keynote) of which is

**signer** *vt* sign; **se ~** cross oneself

**signet** *nm* book-mark

**significatif -ive** *adj* significant

**signification** *nf* meaning, significance, sense; *leg* notification

**signifier** *vt* mean, signify; notify quite clearly; give notice of

**silence** *nm* silence; **faire ~** be quiet, stop talking; **passer qch sous ~** fail to mention sth

**silencieux** *nm mot* silencer; *adj* (*f* -ieuse) silent; taciturn; peaceful

**silex** *nm* flint

**silhouetter** *vt* silhouette, outline

**silice** *nf* silica

**sillage** *nm* wake, wash; slipstream

**sillon** *nm* furrow; drill; track, trace; groove (record); **~ s** wrinkles; **faire (creuser) son ~** carry out one's self-allotted task

**sillonner** *vt* furrow; streak; wrinkle

**silurien -ienne** *adj* Silurian

**simagrée** *nf coll* pretence; **faire des ~ s** mince; make a fuss

**simien -ienne** *adj* Simian

**simiesque** *adj* monkey-like

**similaire** *adj* similar, like

**similarité** *nf* similarity

**simili** *nm* half-tone block; *coll* imitation; *pref* imitation

**similigravure** *nf* process engraving, half-tone

**similitude** *nf* resemblance, likeness; similitude

**simonie** *nf* simony

**simoun** *nm* simoon

**simple** *nm* singles (tennis); **~ s** medicinal herbs; *adj* simple; single; unaffected;

straightforward, easy; plain; ordinary; naïve, ingenuous; ~ **comme bonjour** simple as can be; ~ **d'esprit** stupid; ~ **soldat** private soldier; **corps** ~ element; **passé** ~ past definite, past historic

**simplet -ette** *adj coll* naïve, a bit simple

**simplicité** *nf* simplicity

**simplificateur -trice** *n* simplifier; *adj* simplifying

**simplifier** *vt* simplify

**simplisme** *nm* over-simplification; superficial argumentation

**simpliste** *adj* over-simple

**simulacre** *nm* semblance, appearance, show

**simulateur -trice** *n* shammer; *nm* simulator

**simuler** *vt* sham, feign

**simultané** *adj* simultaneous

**sinapiser** *vt* add mustard to

**sinapisme** *nm* mustard poultice; mustard plaster

**sincère** *adj* sincere; frank; genuine

**sincérité** *nf* sincerity; frankness; genuineness

**singe** *nm* monkey, ape

**singer** *vt* (3) ape, mimic

**singerie** *nf* monkey trick, antic; clumsy mimicry; monkey-house

**singulariser** *vt* make conspicuous

**singularité** *nf* singularity; peculiarity; oddness

**singulier -ière** *adj* singular; remarkable; peculiar, strange; **combat** ~ single combat

**sinistre** *nm* disaster, calamity; *adj* sinister, ominous

**sinistré -e** *n* victim of a disaster; *adj* distressed, destroyed by a disaster

**sinologie** *nf* sinology

**sinologue** *n* China specialist

**sinon** *conj* otherwise, or else; except

**sinueux -euse** *adj* winding, sinuous, meandering

**sinuosité** *nf* winding, sinuosity; bend (river)

**sinusite** *nf* sinusitis

**sioniste** *n + adj* Zionist

**siphon** *nm* siphon; trap (sink-pipe)

**siphonner** *vt* siphon

**sire** *nm ar* sir, Lord; sire; **un triste** ~ a miserable rogue

**sirène** *nf* siren, hooter; mermaid

**sirop** *nm* syrup

**siroter** *vt* sip

**sis** *adj* situated

**sismique** *adj* seismic

**sismographie** *nf* seismography

**site** *nm* site; beauty spot

**sitôt** *adv* straightaway, so soon; **de** ~ soon; ~ **que** as soon as

**situation** *nf* situation; position, site; condition, state; job

**situer** *vt* situate

**sixième** *n + adj* sixth

**Sixtine** *adj* Sistine

**sizain** *nm* six-line stanza

**ski** *nm* ski; skiing; **faire du** ~ go skiing

**skieur, skieuse** *n* skier

**slave** *adj* Slav, Slavonic

**slip** *nm* briefs; *naut* slipway; ~ **de bain** bathing trunks

**slovaque** *adj* Slovakian

**smala** *nf coll* large family; Arab chief's household

**smicard -e** *n* minimum wage-earner

**smoking** *nm* dinner-jacket

**snack** *nm coll* snack-bar

**snober** *vt* treat with disdain

**sobre** *adj* moderate; abstemious; sparing; simple, sober

**sobriété** *nf* moderation; temperateness; sobriety, simplicity

**sobriquet** *nm* nickname

**soc** *nm* ploughshare

**sociabilité** *nf* sociableness

**social** *adj* social; **capital** ~ registered capital; **raison** ~ **e** name of company; **siège** ~ head office

**socialisant** *adj* with socialist tendencies

**socialiser** *vt* socialize

**socialisme** *nm* socialism

**socialiste** *n + adj* socialist

**sociétaire** *n* member

**société** *nf* society; community; company; association; ~ **à responsabilité limitée** limited (liability) company; ~ **par actions** joint-stock company

**sociologie** *nf* sociology

**socle** *nm* base, pedestal; stand

**socque** *nm* clog, patten

**socquette** *nf* ankle-sock

**sodomie** *nf* sodomy

**sœur** *nf* sister; ~ **de lait** foster-sister; **bonne** ~ nun

**soi** *pron* oneself; himself, herself, itself; **aller de** ~ create no problem, present no obstacle

**soi-disant** *adj invar* so-called; self-styled; *adv* allegedly

**soie** *nf* silk; pig's bristle; **papier de** ~ tissue paper

**soierie** *nf* silk article; silk factory

**soif** *nf* thirst; **avoir** ~ be thirsty; **avoir** ~ **de** be eager for; **boire à sa** ~ slake one's thirst

**soigné** *adj* carefully done, polished

**soigner** *vt* take care of, look after; nurse; take care with; **se** ~ take care of oneself; *coll* do oneself well

**soigneur** *nm* second (boxing)

**soigneux -euse** *adj* painstaking, meticulous, careful

**soin** *nm* care; charge; attention, trouble; ~ s medical attention; **avoir ~ de faire qch** take good care to do sth; **avoir ~ de qch** take care of sth; **être aux petits ~ s pour qn** be full of attentions for s/o; **premiers ~ s** first aid; **prendre ~ de** take care of; **sans ~** careless, untidy; untidily

**soir** *nm* evening; **à ce ~!** see you tonight!

**soirée** *nf* evening; social evening; ~ **dansante** dancing-party

**soit** *adv* so be it, agreed; suppose; *conj* ~ ... ~ either ... or; ~ **que ... ~ que** whether ... or; **tant ~ peu** very little

**soixantaine** *nf* about sixty; the sixties (age)

**soixante** *nm + adj* sixty

**soixante-dix** *nm + adj* seventy

**soixantième** *n + adj* sixtieth

¹**sol** *nm* ground, earth

²**sol** *nm invar mus* G, so(h)

**sol-air** *adj invar* ground-to-air

**solaire** *adj* solar; **cadran ~** sundial

**soldat** *nm* soldier; ~ **de plomb** tin soldier

**soldatesque** *nf pej* soldiery; *adj* barrack-room

¹**solde** *nf* soldier's pay; **être à la ~ de qn** be in s/o's pay

²**solde** *nm comm* balance; sale; ~ s goods sold in sale

**solder** *vt* settle the balance of, pay off (account); sell off cheap; remainder; **se ~ par** have as a result

**solécisme** *nm* solecism

**soleil** *nm* sun; sunshine; sunflower; catherine-wheel; ~ **couchant** setting sun; ~ **levant** rising sun; **avoir du bien au ~** have landed property; **faire (du) ~** be sunny; **grand ~** bright sunshine; *coll* **piquer un ~** go red, blush

**solennel -elle** *adj* solemn; grave

**solenniser** *vt* solemnize

**solennité** *nf* solemnity; solemn ceremony

**solénoïde** *nm elect* solenoid

**solfège** *nm* rudiments of music

**solidaire** *adj* interdependent; *leg* jointly responsible

**solidariser (se)** *v refl* make common cause

**solidarité** *nf* solidarity; interdependence; *leg* joint responsibility

**solide** *nm* solid body; *adj* solid; resistant, strong

**solidifier** *vt* solidify; **se ~** become solid

**solidité** *nf* solidity; soundness; stability

**soliloque** *nm* soliloquy

**soliste** *n* soloist

**solitaire** *n* hermit; solitaire; old male boar; *adj* solitary, lonely

**solive** *nf* beam, joist

**soliveau** *nm* small beam

**sollicitation** *nf* entreaty, solicitation

**solliciter** *vt* solicit, beg for; apply for; attract, provoke

**solliciteur -euse** *n* solicitant, petitioner

**sollicitude** *nf* anxiety, concern; solicitude

**solubiliser** *vt* make soluble

**solubilité** *nf* solubility

**solutionner** *vt* solve

**solvabilité** *nf* solvency

**solvable** *adj* solvent

**somatique** *adj* somatic

**sombre** *adj* dark; gloomy; dull; dismal

**sombrer** *vi* sink, go down; fall

**sommaire** *nm* summary; *adj* concise, summary; hasty

**sommation** *nf leg* summons; demand, urgent request

¹**somme** *nf* amount, sum; sum total; ~ **toute** when all's said and done; **en ~** in short

²**somme** *nf* **bête de ~** beast of burden

³**somme** *nm* nap, short sleep; **faire un ~** take a nap

**sommeil** *nm* sleep; sleepiness; inactivity; **avoir le ~ léger** be a light sleeper; **avoir le ~ lourd** be a sound sleeper; **avoir ~** be sleepy

**sommeiller** *vi* doze, sleep lightly; be dormant

**sommelier** *nm* wine-waiter; cellarman

**sommer** *vt* call on; summon

**sommes** *first pers pl pres ind* **être**

**sommet** *nm* summit, top; crest; pinnacle; **conférence au ~** summit conference

**sommier** *nm* box-mattress; lintel

**sommité** *nf* top, extremity; top personality

**somnambule** *n* sleep-walker; *adj* somnambulistic

**somnambulisme** *nm* sleep-walking

**somnifère** *nm* soporific, sleeping tablet; *adj* sleep-inducing

**somnolent** *adj* drowsy, sleepy

**somnoler** *vi* doze

**somptueux -ueuse** *adj* sumptuous

**somptuosité** *nf* sumptuousness

¹**son** (*f* **sa**, *pl* **ses**) *adj* his, her, its, one's

²**son** *nm* sound; **mur du ~** sound barrier

³**son** *nm* bran; **taches de ~** freckles

**sonate** *nf* sonata

**sonatine** *nf* sonatina

**sondage** *nm* sounding; boring; investigation; ~ **d'opinion** opinion poll

**sonde** *nf* sounding-line; probe; sounding-rod

**sonder** *vt* sound; probe, examine; ~ **le terrain** try to find out what is going on

**sondeur** *nm* pollster

**songe** *nm* dream

**songe-creux** *nm* dreamer, visionary

**songer** *vi* (3) dream; day-dream; think; remember; intend

**songerie** *nf* day-dreaming; reverie

**songeur -euse** *adj* dreamy; thoughtful

**sonnant** *adj* **espèces ~ es** hard cash; **horloge ~ e** striking clock; **huit heures ~ es** eight o'clock precisely

**sonné** *adj* announced by a bell; *sl* crazy, barmy; **il est midi ~** it has struck twelve

**sonner** *vt* ring, ring for; play (trumpet, etc); *coll* bash, knock out; *vi* sound; strike, ring

**sonnerie** *nf* ringing; set of bells; chiming mechanism

**sonnette** *nf* little bell, hand bell; house bell; **coup de ~** ring; **serpent à ~s** rattlesnake

**sonneur** *nm* bell-ringer

**sonore** *adj* sonorous, loud; resonant, resounding; **bande ~** sound track; **consonne ~** voiced consonant; **fond ~** sound background

**sonoriser** *vt* sound; add sound to; equip for sound reproduction

**sonorité** *nf* sonorousness, sound quality

**sont** *third pers pl pres ind* être

**sophisme** *nm* sophism

**sophistication** *nf* sophistication; adulteration

**soporifique** *adj* soporific; *coll* tedious

**sorbet** *nm* water-ice, sorbet

**sorbetière** *nf* freezer (for making sorbets)

**sorbier** *nm bot* sorb, service-tree

**sorcellerie** *nf* witchcraft

**sorcier** *nm* wizard, sorcerer; *adj coll* (*f* -ière) clever

**sorcière** *nf* witch, sorceress

**sordide** *adj* filthy, sordid

**sordidité** *nf* sordidness

**Sorlingues** *nfpl* Isles of Scilly

**sornettes** *nfpl obs* nonsense

**sort** *nm* destiny, fate; lot; chance; spell; **faire un ~ à** show to advantage; *coll* finish with; **jeter un ~** cast a spell; **tirer au ~** draw lots

**sortable** *adj* presentable, decent

**sortant** *adj* going out; outgoing; retiring; **numéro ~** winning number

**sorte** *nf* kind, sort; manner, way; **de la ~** like that, in that way; **de ~ que** so that; **en quelque ~** as it were; **en ~ que** so that

**sortie** *nf* exit, way out; going out, departure; excursion, outing; sally; outburst; *theat* exit

**sortie-de-bain** *nf* (*pl* **sorties-de-bain**) bathgown

**sortilège** *nm* spell, charm

**sortir** *nm* **au ~ de** on coming out of, on leaving; at the end of; *vt* (59) take out, bring out; *vi* go out; come out; get out;

protrude, stick out; spring from, be descended from; turn up (lottery number); **~ de faire qch** have just done sth; **~ d'embarras** escape from an awkward situation; **d'où sors-tu?** wherever have you been?; **faire ~** take out; send out; **laisser ~** let out; **ne pas ~ de là** persist in one's opinion; **s'en ~** get out of a jam

**sosie** *nm* double (person)

**sot, sotte** *n* fool; *adj* stupid, silly; embarrassed; absurd

**sottise** *nf* stupidity; foolish act, stupid word; insult

**sou** *nm* five centimes piece, sou; **cent ~s** five francs; **être près de ses ~s** be very careful with money; **être sans le ~** be penniless; **machine à ~s** fruit-machine; **n'avoir pas le ~** be penniless; **pas ... pour deux ~s** not in the least ...; **question de gros ~s** matter of hard cash

**soubassement** *nm* base, sub-foundation (building)

**soubresaut** *nm* leap, bound; sudden movement, jerk

**soubrette** *nf coll* maid; *theat* maid, waiting-maid

**souche** *nf* stump, stock; founder (family); counterfoil, stub; stack (chimney); **faire ~** found a family; *coll* **rester comme une ~** remain inactive

**¹souci** *nm* care; worry, anxiety

**²souci** *nm* marigold

**soucier** *vt* worry; **se ~** worry

**soucieux -ieuse** *adj* anxious, concerned

**soucoupe** *nf* saucer

**soudage** *nm* soldering, welding

**soudain** *adj* sudden; *adv* suddenly, all of a sudden

**soudaineté** *nf* suddenness

**soudard** *nm ar* mercenary soldier, professional soldier; old trooper, coarse fighting man

**soude** *nf* soda

**souder** *vt* solder, weld; **se ~** fuse together, join together, knit

**soudoyer** *vt* (7) hire, bribe

**soudure** *nf* soldering, welding; soldering joint; join; solder

**soue** *nf* pigsty

**soufflage** *nm* blowing; glass-blowing

**souffle** *nm* breath; blast; puff; breathing; *coll* **avoir du ~** have a cheek; **couper le ~ à qn** wind s/o; take s/o's breath away; **effet de ~** blast (explosion); **être à bout de ~** be exhausted; **manquer de ~** be short of breath; be short of (poetic) inspiration

**souffler** *vt* blow, blow up; blow out; utter, breathe (word); *theat* prompt; huff (draughts); suggest; *coll* **~ qch à qn** do s/o out of sth; *vi* blow; breathe; puff, pant; **~ comme un bœuf** breathe heavily

**soufflerie** *nf* blower; bellows

¹**soufflet** *nm* bellows; vestibule (railway coach)

²**soufflet** *nm* blow, box on the ear; affront

**souffleter** *vt* (5) slap, deal a blow to

¹**souffleur -euse** *n theat* prompter; *theat* **trou du ~** prompt-box

²**souffleur** *nm* glass-blower

**soufflure** *nf* blister, bubble

**souffrance** *nf* suffering; **en ~** in abeyance; held up in transit

**souffrant** *adj* suffering; unwell, indisposed

**souffre-douleur** *nm invar* butt

**souffreteux -euse** *adj* sickly, weak

**souffrir** *vt* (30) suffer; endure, put up with; allow, brook; *vi* suffer, be in pain; feel ill effects

**soufre** *nm* sulphur

**soufrer** *vt* treat with sulphur, sulphur

**soufrière** *nf* sulphur-mine

**souhait** *nm* wish, desire; **à ~** according to one's desire; **à vos ~s!** bless you!

**souhaitable** *adj* desirable

**souhaiter** *vt* wish, desire

**souiller** *vt* dirty, make filthy; defile; tarnish (reputation)

**souillon** *n* filthy person; slattern

**souillure** *nf* stain; blemish

**soûl** *adj* drunk; glutted, surfeited; **tout son ~** as much as one can, as much as one wants

**soulagement** *nm* relief; comfort

**soulager** *vt* (3) relieve; lighten the burden of; alleviate; **se ~** obtain relief; *coll* relieve oneself

**soûlard -e** *n sl* drunkard

**soûler** *vt coll* make drunk, intoxicate; *coll* **se ~** get drunk; surfeit oneself

**soûlerie** *nf sl* drinking-bout; drunkenness

**soulèvement** *nm* rising, heaving, uprising, revolt; surge of indignation; **~ de cœur** nausea

**soulever** *vt* (6) raise; lift, lift up; arouse, excite; stir up, rouse; **~ le cœur** disgust; **se ~** rise; lift oneself; revolt

**soulier** *nm* shoe; *coll* **être dans ses petits ~s** be in an awkward situation

**souligner** *vt* underline; emphasize, stress

**soumettre** *vt* (60) subdue; submit; subject; **se ~** submit, give in

**soumis** *adj* submissive; dutiful; subject

**soumission** *nf* submission; obedience; submissiveness; tender

**soumissionnaire** *n* party or person making a tender

**soumissionner** *vt* tender

**soupape** *nf* valve; **~ d'admission** inlet valve; **~ d'échappement** outlet valve; **~ de sûreté** safety valve; **~ en tête** overhead valve; **~ latérale** side valve

**soupçon** *nm* suspicion; conjecture; slight appearance, trace; *coll* small quantity, dash

**soupçonner** *vt* suspect; surmise

**soupçonneux -euse** *adj* distrustful, of a suspicious nature

**soupe** *nf* soup; bread soaked in broth; *coll* grub, meal; **~ au lait** bread and milk; **~ populaire** soup kitchen; **à la ~!** grub's up!

**soupente** *nf* garret; recess (under stairs)

**souper** *nm* supper; *vi* have supper, sup; *sl* **avoir soupé de qch** be fed up with sth

**soupeser** *vt* (6) weigh, feel the weight of

**soupière** *nf* soup-tureen

**soupir** *nm* sigh; crotchet rest; **pousser un ~** heave a sigh

**soupirail -aux** *nm* air-hole, ventilator

**soupirant** *nm obs iron* wooer, gallant, suitor

**soupirer** *vi* sigh; **~ après qch** long for sth

**souple** *adj* supple; flexible; lithe; pliant, tractable

**souplesse** *nf* suppleness; flexibility; litheness; pliancy, tractability

**souquer** *vt naut* haul taut; *vi* row hard

**source** *nf* source; spring, well; cause, origin; **couler de ~** be the natural result

**sourcier** *nm* water-diviner

**sourcil** *nm* eyebrow

**sourciller** *vi* frown, knit one's brows; flinch; **sans ~** without turning a hair

**sourcilleux -euse** *adj* haughty; fussy

**sourd -e** *n* deaf person; **crier comme un ~** shout one's head off; *adj* deaf; dull, muffled; secret; veiled; **~ comme un pot** deaf as a post; **consonne ~ e** voiceless consonant; **faire la ~ e oreille** pretend not to hear

**sourdement** *adv* with a dull sound; secretly

**sourdine** *nf mus* mute; **en ~** secretly, unobtrusively; **mettre une ~ à** tone down, be less noisy with

**sourd-muet** *n* (*f* **sourde-muette,** *mpl* **sourds-muets,** *fpl* **sourdes-muettes**) deaf mute; *adj* deaf and dumb

**sourdre** *vi* (90) well up; spring, arise

**souriant** *adj* smiling, cheerful

**souricier** *nm* mouse-catcher

**souricière** *nf* mouse-trap; trap, police-trap

**sourire** *nm* smile; *vi* (84) smile; be favourable, be attractive

¹**souris** *nf* mouse; knuckle-end of leg of mutton; *coll* girl

²**souris** *nm obs* smile

**sournois** *adj* sly, crafty, cunning

**sournoiserie** *nf* craftiness, cunning

**sous** *prep* under, beneath, below; within the time of; **~ ce rapport** in this respect;

~ **clef** under lock and key; ~ **le nom de** by the name of; ~ **mes yeux** before my eyes; ~ **peine de** on pain of; ~ **peu** in a short time; ~ **un mauvais jour** in a bad light; **être** ~ **les drapeaux** serve with the colour

**sous-alimentation** *nf* malnutrition
**sous-alimenté** *adj* undernourished
**sous-bois** *nm* undergrowth
> **sous-chef** *nm* deputy chief, assistant head
**sous-comité** *nm* sub-committee
**sous-commission** *nf* sub-commission
**souscripteur -trice** *n* subscriber
**souscription** *nf* signing; subscription, signature; contribution
**souscrire** *vt* (42) sign, execute; take out a subscription; contribute; ~ **à** subscribe to; agree, consent to
**sous-cutané** *adj* subcutaneous
**sous-développé** *adj* underdeveloped, developing (nation)
**sous-diacre** *nm* sub-deacon
**sous-directeur -trice** *n* assistant manager, assistant manageress; vice-principal
**sous-emploi** *nm* underemployment
**sous-entendre** *vt* imply
**sous-entendu** *nm* implication
**sous-équipé** *adj* under-equipped
**sous-estimer** *vt* underestimate
**sous-exposer** *vt phot* under-expose
**sous-garde** *nf* trigger-guard
**sous-genre** *nm* sub-group
**sous-jacent** *adj* underlying
**sous-jupe** *nf* underslip, underskirt
**sous-lieutenant** *nm* sub-lieutenant, second lieutenant
**sous-locataire** *n* subtenant
**sous-location** *nf* sub-letting; sub-let
**sous-louer** *vt* sub-let
**sous-main** *nm invar* blotting-pad; **en** ~ secretly
**sous-marin** *nm* submarine; *adj* submarine, underwater, deep-sea
**sous-maxillaire** *adj* submaxillary
**sous-nappe** *nf* under-tablecloth
**sous-œuvre** *nm bui* underpinning
**sous-off** *nm coll* non-commissioned officer
**sous-officier** *nm* non-commissioned officer; petty officer
**sous-ordre** *nm* subordinate
**sous-peuplé** *adj* under-populated
**sous-pied** *nm* under-strap (gaiters); trouser-strap
**sous-préfecture** *nf* sub-prefecture; town where the sub-prefect resides
**sous-préfet** *nm* sub-prefect
**sous-préfète** *nf* sub-prefect's wife
**sous-production** *nf* under-production
**sous-produit** *nm* by-product
**sous-secrétaire** *nm* under-secretary

**sous-seing** *nm invar* private contract
**soussigné** *adj* undersigned
**soussigner** *vt* sign, undersign
**sous-sol** *nm* basement; subsoil
**sous-station** *nf* sub-station
**sous-titre** *nm* subtitle
**soustractif -ive** *adj* subtractive
**soustraction** *nf* taking away, removal; subtraction
**soustraire** *vt* (9) take away, withdraw; shield, preserve; subtract; **se** ~ **à** escape, avoid
**sous-traitant** *nm* sub-contractor
**sous-traiter** *vt* sub-contract
**sous-verre** *nm invar* passe-partout picture
**sous-vêtement** *nm* undergarment
**soutache** *nf* braid
**soutacher** *vt* braid
**soutane** *nf* cassock; **prendre la** ~ go into the priesthood
**soute** *nf naut* store-room, bunker
**soutenable** *adj* bearable; tenable, arguable
**soutènement** *nm* supporting, propping, holding up; **mur de** ~ retaining wall
**souteneur** *nm* pimp; *obs* upholder
**soutenir** *vt* (96) support, sustain; hold up; back, help; maintain, uphold; affirm, assert; bear; withstand; **se** ~ stand on one's feet; hold oneself up; support one another; continue, last
**soutenu** *adj* sustained; constant, unflagging
**souterrain** *nm* underground passage; vault; *adj* underground
**soutien** *nm* support; supporter; ~ **de famille** bread-winner
**soutien-gorge** *nm* (*pl* **soutiens-gorge**) brassière, bra
**soutier** *nm naut* coal-trimmer
**soutirer** *vt* draw off, tap; squeeze, wheedle (money out of s/o)
**souvenance** *nf* avoir ~ **de** remember
**souvenir** *nm* memory, recollection; memento, souvenir; **veuillez me rappeler au bon** ~ **de Jean** please remember me to John; *v impers* **il me souvient que** I remember; **se** ~ *v refl* (96) remember
**souvent** *adv* often, frequently
**souverain -e** *n* sovereign, ruler; *adj* sovereign
**souverainement** *adv* highly, extremely
**souveraineté** *nf* sovereignty; supreme authority
**soviétique** *adj* Soviet
**soyeux -euse** *adj* silky
**spacieux -ieuse** *adj* roomy, spacious
**spadassin** *nm* bravo, ruffian
**sparadrap** *nm med* adhesive plaster
**sparte** *nm* esparto grass

**Sparte** *nf* Sparta
**Spartiate** *n* Spartan
**spartiate** *nf* sandal; *adj* Spartan
**spasme** *nm* spasm
**spasmodique** *adj* spasmodic
**spath** *nm* min spar
**spatule** *nf* spatula
**speaker** (*f* **speakerine**) *n* speaker, announcer
**spécialisé** *adj* specialized; **ouvrier ~** semi-skilled worker
**spécialiser** *vt* specialize; **se ~** specialize
**spécialiste** *n* specialist
**spécialité** *nf* speciality; special feature
**spécieux -ieuse** *adj* specious
**spécifier** *vt* specify; determine
**spécifique** *nm + adj* specific
**spéciosité** *nf* speciousness
**spectacle** *nm* sight, spectacle; *theat* play, show; display; **pièce à grand ~** spectacular; **salle de ~** theatre; **se donner en ~** make an exhibition of oneself
**spectaculaire** *adj* spectacular
**spectateur -trice** *n* spectator; onlooker, beholder
**spectral** *adj* spectral, ghost-like; **couleurs ~es** colours of the spectrum
**spectre** *nm* ghost, spectre; spectrum
**spéculaire** *adj* specular; **écriture ~** mirror writing
**spéculateur -trice** *n* speculator
**spéculatif -ive** *adj* speculative
**spéculation** *nf* speculation; theory
**spéculer** *vi* speculate; cogitate
**spéléologie** *nf* speleology
**spéléologue** *n* speleologist
**spencer** *nm* short jacket
**spermatozoïde** *nm* spermatozoon
**sperme** *nm* sperm
**sphère** *nf* sphere; globe; orbit, field
**sphérique** *adj* spherical
**sphinx** *nm* sphinx; hawk-moth
**spirale** *nf* spiral
**spirante** *nf* ling spirant consonant, fricative
**spire** *nf* whorl; twirl
**spirite** *n + adj* spiritualist
**spiritisme** *nm* spiritualism
**spiritualiser** *vt* spiritualize
**spiritualisme** *nm philos* spiritualism
**spiritualiste** *n + adj* spiritualist
**spirituel -uelle** *adj* spiritual; religious; witty
**spiritueux** *nm* alcoholic spirit; *adj* (*f* **-ueuse**) spirituous
**spirochète** *nm biol* spirochaeta
**splendeur** *nf* splendour; brilliance; grandeur
**splendide** *adj* splendid; brilliant, magnificent
**splénique** *adj* splenic

**spoliateur -trice** *n* despoiler
**spolier** *vt* despoil, rob, plunder
**spongieux -ieuse** *adj* spongy
**spongiosité** *nf* sponginess
**spontané** *adj* spontaneous
**spontanéité** *nf* spontaneity
**sporadique** *adj* sporadic
**sport** *nm* sport; *adj invar* sportsmanlike; *coll* sporty
**sportif -ive** *n* lover of sport; *adj* sporting
**sportsman** *nm* (*pl* **sportsmen**) racegoer
**spot** *nm* spotlight, spot; television commercial
**spumeux -euse** *adj* foamy, frothy
**squale** *nm* dog-fish
**squame** *nf* scale (skin)
**squelette** *nm* skeleton; framework; bare outline
**squelettique** *adj* skeletal
**squirr(h)e** *nm med* scirrhus
**stabilisateur** *nm* stabilizer; *adj* (*f* **-trice**) stabilizing
**stabiliser** *vt* stabilize; **se ~** become stable
**stabilité** *nf* stability, steadiness; firmness
**stable** *adj* stable, steady; firm; lasting, durable
**stabulation** *nf* stabling (horses), stalling (cattle)
**stade** *nm* stadium, sports-ground; stage
**stage** *nm* period of training
**stagiaire** *n + adj* trainee
**stalle** *nf* stall (church); box (stable)
**staminé** *adj bot* staminate
**stance** *nf* stanza
**stand** *nm* shooting-stand; booth, stall, stand (exhibition)
**standard** *nm* standard; switchboard
**standardiser** *vt* standardize
**standing** *nm* social status; (**de**) **grand ~** luxurious, luxury
**staphylocoque** *nm biol* staphylococcus
**star** *nf* film-star
**starlette** *nf* starlet
**starter** *nm mot* choke; *sp* starter
**station** *nf* station; standing; stop, halt; stage; position; **~ thermale** spa; **en ~** stationed
**stationnaire** *adj* stationary
**stationnement** *nm* stopping; parking
**stationner** *vi* park; stop
**statique** *adj* static
**statisticien -ienne** *n* statistician
**statuaire** *n + adj* statuary
**statuer** *vi* ordain, decree; **~ sur** pronounce on, settle
**statufier** *vt coll* erect a statue to
**statu quo** *nm invar* status quo
**statut** *nm* statute; rule; status
**statutaire** *adj* statutory
**stéarique** *adj* stearic (acid)
**stèle** *nf* stele, column

**stellaire** *adj* stellar
**sténo** *nf coll* shorthand; *coll* shorthand-writer
**sténodactylo(graphe)** *nf* shorthand-typist
**sténodactylo(graphie)** *nf* shorthand and typing
**sténographe** *n* shorthand-writer
**sténographie** *nf* shorthand
**sténographier** *vt* take down in shorthand
**sténotypie** *nf* shorthand-typing
**stercoraire** *adj* stercoraceous
**stère** *nm* cubic metre of wood
**stéréophonie** *nf* stereophony
**stéréophonique** *adj* stereophonic
**stéréotypé** *adj* stereotyped, ordinary, hackneyed
**stéréotyper** *vt* stereotype
**stérile** *adj* barren, sterile; fruitless, unprofitable
**stérilet** *nm* loop, coil (contraception)
**stérilisateur** *nm* sterilizer
**stériliser** *vt* sterilize
**stérilité** *nf* sterility
**sternutation** *nf* sneezing
**sternutatoire** *adj* causing sneezing
**stéroïde** *nm* + *adj* steroid
**stick** *nm* swagger-stick
**stigmate** *nm* stigma; trace, stain, mark; stigmata
**stigmatiser** *vt* stigmatize; brand; stain
**stimulant** *nm* stimulant; stimulus, incentive; *adj* stimulating
**stimulateur -trice** *adj* stimulative
**stimuler** *vt* stimulate, incite
**stipendié -e** *n* + *adj* mercenary
**stipendier** *vt* have in one's pay
**stipuler** *vt* stipulate
**stockage** *nm* stocking, laying in stocks
**stocker** *vt* stock; stock-pile
**stockiste** *nm* stocker; wholesale warehouseman
**stoïcisme** *nm* stoicism
**stoïque** *n* + *adj* stoic
**stolon** *nm bot* runner, sucker
**stomacal** *adj* gastric, stomachal
**stop** *nm* stop; stop-sign; *coll* hitch-hiking
**stoppage** *nm* invisible mending
¹**stopper** *vt* repair by invisible mending
²**stopper** *vt* stop; check; *vi* stop
¹**stoppeur -euse** *n* invisible mender
²**stoppeur -euse** *n coll* hitch-hiker
**store** *nm* blind
**strabique** *adj* squint-eyed
**strabisme** *nm* squinting
**strapontin** *nm* folding seat
**stratagème** *nm* stratagem
**stratège** *nm* strategist
**stratégie** *nf* strategy
**stratégique** *adj* strategic

**stratifier** *vt* stratify
**streptocoque** *nm biol* streptococcus
**strette** *nf mus* stretto
**strict** *adj* severe, strict; **le ~ nécessaire** the barest essential
**stridence** *nf* harshness, stridency
**striduler** *vi* chirr, stridulate
**strie** *nf* scratch, ridge
**strié** *adj* striped, scored
**strier** *vt* score, scratch; groove
**strige** *nf* vampire
**striure** *nf* scratch; groove
**strophe** *nf* verse, stanza
**structuralisme** *nm* structuralism
**structurer** *vt* give a structure to
**stuc** *nm* stucco
**studieux -ieuse** *adj* studious
**studio** *nm* studio; one-room flat
**stupéfaction** *nf* stupefaction, amazement
**stupéfait** *adj* stupefied, amazed
**stupéfiant** *nm* narcotic, drug
**stupéfier** *vt* stupefy; amaze, astound
**stupeur** *nf* stupor; amazement
**stupide** *adj* stupid, silly; stunned, bemused
**stupidité** *nf* stupidity; piece of stupidity
**stupre** *nm* debauchery
**stuquer** *vt* stucco
**stygien -ienne** *adj* Stygian
**style** *nm* style; stylus
**styler** *vt* train
**stylet** *nm* stiletto; *surg* probe
**styliser** *vt* stylize
**styliste** *n* stylist
**stylistique** *nf* stylistics
**stylo** *nm* fountain-pen; ~ **à bille** ballpoint pen
**styptique** *nm* + *adj* styptic
**su** *nm* **au vu et au ~ de** known to
**suaire** *nm* shroud, winding-sheet
**suave** *adj* pleasant, sweet
**suavité** *nf* sweetness; suavity
**subalterne** *adj* subordinate, minor, inferior
**subconscient** *nm* + *adj* subconscious
**subdiviser** *vt* subdivide
**subéreux -euse** *adj bot* corky
**subir** *vt* undergo; suffer, sustain; **faire ~** inflict, put through
**subit** *adj* sudden, unexpected
**subito** *adv coll* suddenly
**subjectif -ive** *adj* subjective
**subjonctif** *nm* subjunctive; *adj* (*f* -ive) subjunctive
**subjuguer** *vt* subjugate, subdue; dominate; charm
**sublimé** *nm chem* sublimate
**sublimer** *vt* sublimate
**sublimité** *nf* sublimity
**submerger** *vt* (3) submerge; flood; swamp; *coll* overwhelm

293

**submersible** *nm obs* submarine; *adj* submersible; sinkable

**subordonné** *adj* subordinate (clause)

**subordonner** *vt* subordinate

**suborner** *vt* suborn, instigate

**subreptice** *adj* surreptitious, clandestine

**subrogation** *nf leg* substitution, delegation

**subroger** *vt* (3) *leg* subrogate, appoint as deputy

**subside** *nm* subsidy

**subsidiaire** *adj* subsidiary, auxiliary

**subsistance** *nf* subsistence, maintenance; keep; ~ s provisions

**subsistant** *adj* subsisting, remaining in existence

**subsister** *vi* subsist, remain in existence; ~ de live on

**substance** *nf* substance; material; en ~ substantially

**substantiel -ielle** *adj* substantial, important; nourishing

**substantif** *nm* noun, substantive; *adj* (*f* -ive) substantive; substantial

**substituer** *vt* substitute; *leg* ~ un héritier appoint an heir in another's place; se ~ à qn take s/o else's place

**substitut** *nm leg* deputy magistrate; substitute

**substrat** *nm* substratum

**subtil** *adj* subtle; tenuous; shrewd, discerning; acute

**subtiliser** *vt coll* pinch, sneak

**subtilité** *nf* subtlety; shrewdness; subtle argument

**suburbain** *adj* suburban

**subvenir** *vi* (96) come to the help; supply, provide

**subvention** *nf* subsidy, grant

**subventionner** *vt* subsidize

**subversif -ive** *adj* subversive

**suc** *nm* sap; juice; essence

**succédané** *nm* substitute

**succéder** *vi* (6) succeed, come after

**succès** *nm* happy issue; success

**successeur** *nm* successor

**successif -ive** *adj* successive

**succession** *nf* succession; sequence; inheritance; **droits de** ~ estate duty; **prendre la** ~ **de** succeed; take over from

**succin** *nm* yellow amber

**succion** *nf* suction

**succomber** *vi* succumb; yield; die

**succube** *nm* succubus

**succursale** *nf* branch; sub-office; **magasin à** ~ s **multiples** chain store

**sucer** *vt* (4) suck; *coll* suck dry

**sucette** *nf* baby's dummy; lollipop

**suçoir** *nm ent + bot* sucker

**suçon** *nm* kiss-mark (on skin); love-bite

**suçoter** *vt* suck away at

**sucre** *nm* sugar; ~ **cristallisé** granulated sugar; ~ **en poudre** caster sugar

**sucré** *adj* sweet; sugared, sweetened; sugary

**sucrer** *vt* sweeten, sugar; *coll* se ~ take a good cut, do well out of s/o

**sucrerie** *nf* sugar-refinery

**sucrier** *nm* sugar-basin; sugar-manufacturer

**sud** *nm* south; *adj invar* southern, southerly

**sudation** *nf med* sweating

**sud-est** *nm* south-east; *adj invar* south-east

**Sudiste** *n US* southerner

**sud-ouest** *nm* south-west; *adj invar* south-west

**Suède** *nf* Sweden

**Suédois -e** *n* Swede

**suédois** *nm* Swedish (language); *adj* Swedish

**suée** *nf coll* sweating

**suer** *vi* sweat; perspire; exude, ooze; *coll* reek; be steeped; *sl* **faire** ~ **qn** annoy s/o; *vt coll* ~ **sang et eau** make tremendous efforts

**sueur** *nf* sweat, perspiration; **être en** ~ be sweating

**suffire** *vi* (91) suffice, be enough; **suffit!** that'll do!; **à chaque jour suffit sa peine** sufficient unto the day is the evil thereof; **il suffit de ...** all that is needed is to ...; **il suffit d'une fois** once is enough; se ~ be self-sufficient, support oneself

**suffisance** *nf* sufficiency; conceit; **à** ~ in plenty

**suffisant** *adj* sufficient, enough; conceited, self-important, presumptuous

**suffixe** *nm* suffix

**suffocant** *adj* stifling, suffocating

**suffoquer** *vt* suffocate, stifle; *coll* astonish; *vi* suffocate, choke

**suffragant** *nm + adj eccles* suffragan

**suffrage** *nm* vote, suffrage

**suggérer** *vt* (6) suggest

**suggestibilité** *nf* suggestibility

**suggestif -ive** *adj* suggestive

**suicidé -e** *n* suicide

**suicider (se)** *v refl* commit suicide

**suie** *nf* soot

**suif** *nm* tallow

**suint** *nm* wool grease

**suinter** *vi* ooze, seep; leak, run

**suis** *first pers sing pres ind* être

**Suisse** *nf* Switzerland; *n* (*f* Suissesse) Swiss (person)

¹**suisse** *adj* Swiss

²**suisse** *nm* hall porter; church official; **boire en** ~ drink alone; **petit** ~ small cream cheese

**suite** *nf* continuation; train, retinue; sequence, series; result; *mus* suite; **à la**

~ de following, after; **avoir de la ~ dans les idées** be capable of perseverance; **de** ~ in succession, on end; **donner** ~ à carry out; give effect to; **esprit de** ~ methodical perseverance; **et ainsi de** ~ and so on; **par la** ~ later on, subsequently; **par** ~ consequently; **sans** ~ incoherent; **tout de** ~ immediately

**suivant -e** *n* follower; *adj* next, following; **au** ~ ! and the next!; *prep* according to; ~ **que** according as

**suivi** *adj* connected; sustained; continuous

**suivre** *vt* (92) follow; escort; pursue; succeed, come after; keep up with; result; **à** ~ to be continued; **faire** ~ **une lettre** forward a letter

**sujet** *nm* topic, subject; cause, reason; individual; **au** ~ **de** concerning; **bon** ~ good chap; **mauvais** ~ bad lot; *n* (*f* -ette) subject; *adj* (*f* -ette) subject; prone, liable

**sujétion** *nf* subjection, servitude; obligation

**sulfate** *nm* sulphate

**sulfater** *vt* sulphate; treat with copper sulphate

**sulfure** *nm* sulphide

**sulfuré** *adj* sulphuretted

**sulfureux -euse** *adj* sulphureous; sulphurous

**sulfurique** *adj* sulphuric

**sultane** *nf* sultana

**summum** *nm* height, highest degree

¹**super** *nm abbr* **supercarburant**

²**super** *adj coll* terrific, first-rate

³**super** *vt* suck in (pump)

**superbe** *nf lit + obs* pride; *adj* superb, splendid, magnificent; *lit + obs* arrogant, proud

**supercarburant** *nm* high-octane petrol

**supercherie** *nf* deceit, fraud

**supérette** *nf* small supermarket

**superfétation** *nf* superfluity; redundancy

**superficie** *nf* surface; area; superficial aspect

**superficiel -ielle** *adj* superficial; shallow

**superfin** *adj* superfine; of very fine quality

**superflu** *nm* superfluity; *adj* superfluous, unnecessary

**superfluité** *nf* superfluity

**supérieur** *nm* superior, head; *adj* upper; superior; higher

**supériorité** *nf* superiority

**superlatif** *nm* superlative; *adj* (*f* ~ive) superlative

**supermarché** *nm* supermarket

**superposer** *vt* superimpose, place on top of

**superposition** *nf* superimposition

**supersonique** *adj* supersonic

**superstitieux -ieuse** *adj* superstitious

**superviser** *vt* supervise, check

**supin** *nm gramm* supine

**supplanter** *vt* supplant, supersede

**suppléance** *nf* temporary post, interim post

**suppléant -e** *n* substitute; deputy; *adj* acting, temporary

**suppléer** *vt* make up, supply; take the place of; *vi* make up, compensate

**supplément** *nm* supplement; extra payment, additional charge, excess fare; extra; **en** ~ additional, extra

**supplémentaire** *adj* supplementary, additional, extra; **heures** ~ **s** overtime

**suppliant -e** *n* supplicant; *adj* suppliant, imploring, pleading

**supplice** *nm* torture, punishment; violent pain; **être au** ~ suffer agony, be on the rack; **mettre au** ~ torture

**supplicié -e** *n* executed criminal; criminal under torture

**supplicier** *vt* put to the torture, torture; execute by torture

**supplier** *vt* implore, beseech; **je vous en supplie** I beg of you

**supplique** *nf* petition

**support** *nm* prop, support; stand, mount, holder; backing, back-up material

**supportable** *adj* bearable, endurable

**supporter** *vt* support; hold up; bear, endure; stand, put up with, tolerate

**supposer** *vt* suppose, assume; imply, presuppose; **supposé que** supposing that

**suppositoire** *nm* suppository

**suppôt** *nm* tool, agent; ~ **de Satan** fiend, wicked person

**suppression** *nf* suppression; discontinuance, cancellation

**supprimer** *vt* suppress, abolish; leave out; cut out; kill; withhold, conceal; ~ **qch à qn** deprive s/o of sth

**suppurer** *vi* run, ooze pus, suppurate

**supputation** *nf* calculation

**supputer** *vt* compute, calculate

**supraliminaire** *adj psych* supraliminal

**suprématie** *nf* supremacy

**suprême** *adj* supreme; highest; last; **moment (heure)** ~ moment (hour) of death

¹**sur** *adj* sour, tart

²**sur** *prep* on, upon; towards; over, above; about; out of; by; after, upon; ~ **ce**, ~ **quoi** whereupon

**sûr** *adj* sure; safe, secure; reliable, trustworthy; certain; ~ **et certain** absolutely certain; **à coup** ~ certainly, without fail; **avoir le pied** ~ be sure-footed; **bien** ~! of course!; **jouer au plus** ~ play safe; **peu** ~ unsafe;

uncertain; *coll* pour ~ ! to be sure!

**surabondance** *nf* superabundance, excess

**surabondant** *adj* superabundant

**surabonder** *vi* be very abundant

**suraigu -uë** *adj* very shrill, very high-pitched

**surajouter** *vt* add extra

**suralimentation** *nf* feeding up; over-feeding; supercharging

**suralimenter** *vt* feed up; overfeed; supercharge

**suranné** *adj* out-of-date, old-fashioned

**surbaissé** *adj* mot low-slung; *archi* depressed

**surboum** *nf coll* party

**surcharge** *nf* overloading; extra load; excess luggage weight; overcharge; weight-handicap; additional charge, surcharge

**surcharger** *vt* (3) overload; overcharge; overtax; surcharge

**surchauffe** *nf* overheating; overheating of economy; superheat

**surchauffer** *vt* overheat; superheat

**surchauffeur** *nm mech* superheater

**surchoix** *nm* best quality

**surclasser** *vt* outclass

**surcomposé** *adj gramm* double-composed

**surcompression** *nf mech* supercharging

**surcomprimé** *adj mech* supercharged

**surcontre** *nm* redouble (bridge)

**surcontrer** *vt* redouble (bridge)

**surcouper** *vt* overtrump

**surcroît** *nm* increase; **par** ~ into the bargain, in addition

**surdité** *nf* deafness

**sureau** *nm* elder; **baie de** ~ elderberry

**surélévation** *nf* heightening, raising; additional floor

**surélever** *vt* (6) heighten, raise

**sûrement** *adv* certainly, surely; confidently; steadily; safely

**surenchère** *nf* overbid; outbidding

**surenchérir** *vi* bid higher, overbid; go one higher; promise too much

**surérogation** *nf* supererogation

**surestimer** *vt* overestimate, overvalue; overrate

**suret -ette** *adj* slightly sour, tart

**sûreté** *nf* safety, security; sureness; guarantee, surety; **La Sûreté** = Criminal Investigation Department; **être en** ~ be in a safe place; **pour plus de** ~ to make absolutely sure; **rasoir de** ~ safety razor

**surexcitation** *nf* agitation, excitement

**surexciter** *vt* excite; over-stimulate

**surexposer** *vt phot* over-expose

**surexposition** *nf phot* over-exposure

**surface** *nf* surface; **grande** ~ supermarket

**surfaire** *vt* (46) overprice, overcharge; overrate, overestimate

**surfiler** *vt* oversew

**surfin** *adj* of very fine quality

**surgeler** *vt* (6) deep-freeze, *US* quick-freeze

**surgeon** *nm hort* sucker

**surgir** *vi* rise, loom, come into view

**surhausser** *vt* heighten, raise; cant; bank; force up (price)

**surhomme** *nm* superman

**surhumain** *adj* superhuman

**surimposer** *vt* increase the tax on; over-tax; *ar* superimpose

**surimposition** *nf* superimposition; increase of taxation; over-taxation

**surintendance** *nf hist* stewardship

**surintendant** *nm hist* overseer, steward

**surir** *vi* turn sour

**surjet** *nm* overcasting; overcast seam

**surjeter** *vt* (5) overcast, whip (seam)

**sur-le-champ** *adv* immediately

**surlendemain** *nm* next day but one

**surmenage** *nm* overworking

**surmener** *vt* (6) overwork; **se** ~ overwork, work too hard

**surmonter** *vt* surmount, overcome, get over; **se** ~ control one's feelings

**surmultiplié** *adj* vitesse ~e overdrive

**surnager** *vi* (3) float on the surface; subsist, survive

**surnaturel -elle** *adj* supernatural; extraordinary

**surnom** *nm* nickname

**surnombre** *nm* excess number, number over the regulation number; **en** ~ in excess

**surnommer** *vt* name; nickname

**surnuméraire** *adj* supernumerary

**suroffre** *nf* better offer

**suroît** *nm naut* south-west wind, sou'wester

**surpasser** *vt* surpass; exceed, outdo; **se** ~ excel oneself

**surpaye** *nf* extra pay

**surpayer** *vt* (7) overpay

**surpeuplé** *adj* overpopulated

**surpeuplement** *nm* overpopulation; overcrowding

**surplis** *nm* surplice

**surplomb** *nm* overhang; **être en** ~ overhang

**surplomber** *vt* overhang; *vi* jut out, overhang

**surplus** *nm* excess, surplus; **au** ~ besides, after all

**surpopulation** *nf* overpopulation

**surprenant** *adj* surprising, astonishing

**surprendre** *vt* (75) surprise, catch unawares; catch in the act; come upon unexpectedly, take by surprise; astonish; overhear; take advantage of; disconcert; **se ~ à faire qch** catch oneself doing sth

**surpression** *nf* high pressure, excessive pressure

**surpris** *adj* surprised, amazed

**surprise** *nf* surprise, astonishment; unexpected present

**surprise-partie** *nf* bottle-party

**surproduction** *nf* overproduction

**surréalisme** *nm* surrealism

**surréaliste** *n + adj* surrealist

**surrénal** *adj* suprarenal; **les glandes ~ es** adrenal glands

**sursalaire** *nm* supplementary wage, extra pay

**sursaturer** *vt* supersaturate

**sursaut** *nm* start, jump; **en ~** with a start

**sursauter** *vi* start; **faire ~ qn** startle s/o

**surseoir** *vi* (93) **~ à** defer, delay, put off

**sursis** *nm leg* delay, stay of proceedings; reprieve, deferment; **deux ans de prison avec ~** two years' suspended sentence

**surtaux** *nm* excessive rate

**surtaxe** *nf* surcharge; extra tax

**surtension** *nf elect* surge of voltage

¹**surtout** *nm* overcoat; centre-piece (table)

²**surtout** *adv* particularly, especially

**surveillance** *nf* supervision; watch, watching

**surveillant -e** *n* supervisor, overseer; teacher on duty

**surveiller** *vt* supervise; tend; watch over, look after

**survenir** *vi* (96) happen, occur; arise; arrive unexpectedly

**survêtement** *nm* warm overgarment

**survie** *nf* survival; life after death

**survireur -euse** *adj mot* with a tendency to over-steer

**survivance** *nf* survival; relic; reversion

**survivant -e** *n* survivor

**survivre** *vi* (98) survive

**survol** *nm* flying over; flight over

**survoler** *vt* fly over

**survolter** *vt elect* boost

**survolteur** *nm elect* booster

**sus (en)** *adv phr* in addition, extra

**susceptibilité** *nf* susceptibility; irritability

**susceptible** *adj* susceptible; sensitive; touchy; **~ de** liable to; capable of

**susciter** *vt* give rise to; rouse

**suscription** *nf* address (on letter)

**susdit** *adj* aforesaid

**susmentionné** *adj* above-mentioned

**susnommé** *adj* above-named

**suspect** *nm* suspect; *adj* suspicious, doubtful, suspect

**suspecter** *vt* suspect, doubt

**suspendre** *vt* suspend; hang up; postpone, adjourn; interrupt

**suspendu** *adj* suspended, hanging; **bien ~** well sprung; **pont ~** suspension bridge

**suspens** *nm* **en ~** in suspense, in uncertainty; in abeyance

**suspension** *nf* suspension, hanging; interruption, discontinuance; hanging lamp; *mot* springs

**sustentation** *nf* sustenance; support

**sustenter** *vt* sustain, support, nourish

**susurrement** *nm* murmuring; rustling

**susurrer** *vi* murmur, whisper

**suture** *nf anat* suture, join; **point de ~** stitch

**suturer** *vt* stitch, stitch up (wound)

**suzeraineté** *nf* suzerainty

**svastika** *nm* swastika

**svelte** *adj* slim, slender

**sveltesse** *nf* slimness, slenderness

**sycomore** *nm* sycamore

**sycophante** *nm* sycophant

**syllabe** *nf* syllable

**syllabique** *adj* syllabic

**syllepse** *nf* syllepsis

**syllogisme** *nm* syllogism

**sylphe** *nm* sylph

**sylphide** *nf* sylph; lovely woman

**sylvestre** *adj* woodland

**sylviculture** *nf* forestry

**symbiose** *nf* symbiosis

**symbole** *nm* symbol; conventional sign; creed

**symbolique** *adj* symbolic

**symboliser** *vt* symbolize

**symbolisme** *nm* symbolism

**symétrie** *nf* symmetry

**symétrique** *adj* symmetrical

**sympathie** *nf* sympathy; attraction; **avoir de la ~ pour qn** like s/o

**sympathique** *nm anat* **le grand ~** the sympathetic nerve; *adj* likeable, attractive, congenial; **encre ~** invisible ink

**sympathiser** *vi* have friendly feelings; sympathize

**symphonie** *nf* symphony

**symphonique** *adj* symphonic

**symptomatique** *adj* symptomatic

**symptôme** *nm* symptom; sign, indication

**synchroniser** *vt* synchronize

**syncope** *nf med* syncope, faint, swoon; *mus* syncopation; **tomber en ~** swoon

**syncoper** *vt mus* syncopate

**syndic** *nm* syndic, representative

**syndical** *adj* trade-union; syndical

**syndicalisme** *nm* trade-unionism; trade unions; trade-union action

**syndicat** *nm* (trade) union; syndicate; **~**

**d'initiative** local tourist office; ~ **ouvrier** trade union, *US* labor union
**syndiquer** *vt* enrol in a union; syndicate; **syndiqué** belonging to a union; **se ~** combine; form a trade union
**synecdoque** *nf* synecdoche
**synode** *nm eccles* synod
**synonyme** *nm* synonym; *adj* synonymous
**synoptique** *adj* synoptic
**synovie** *nf anat* synovia
**syntaxe** *nf* syntax
**syntaxique** *adj* syntactical

**synthèse** *nf* synthesis
**synthétique** *adj* synthetic
**synthétiser** *vt* synthesize
**Syrie** *nf* Syria
**syrien -ienne** *adj* Syrian
**systématique** *adj* systematic; dogmatic, hide-bound
**systématiser** *vt* systematize
**système** *nm* system; scheme, method; *coll* ~ **D** resourcefulness; *sl* **il me tape sur le** ~ he gets on my nerves; **par** ~ in a set way, deliberately

# T

**ta** *poss adj f see* **ton**
**tabac** *nm* tobacco; tobacconist's shop; ~ **à priser** snuff; **bureau (débit) de** ~ tobacconist's shop; *coll* **passer qn à** ~ grill s/o, treat s/o roughly
**tabagie** *nf* place that reeks of tobacco smoke
**tabasser** *vt coll* beat up
**tabatière** *nf* snuff-box
**tabellion** *nm leg + ar* scrivener
**tablature** *nf mus* notation
**table** *nf* table; eating, board; slab; tablet; list; ~ **d'écoute** bugging device; ~ **de nuit** bedside table; ~ **de toilette** dressing table; ~ **roulante** tea (dinner) trolley; **la sainte** ~ the communion table; **mettre la** ~ lay the table; **se mettre à** ~ sit down to dinner (or lunch); **service de (par) petites** ~s separate tables
**tableau** *nm* board; notice-board; painting; list, table; ~ **d'avancement** promotion list; ~ **de bord** fascia; instrument panel; ~ **de chasse** bag (hunting); ~ **de contrôle** control panel; ~ **noir** blackboard
**tableautin** *nm* small picture
**tablée** *nf* group of people seated round a table
**tabler** *vi* ~ **sur qch** count on sth
**tablette** *nf* shelf; sill; slab; bar (chocolate); ~s tablets; **mettre qch sur ses** ~s make a note of sth
**tabletterie** *nf* fancy-goods industry; inlaid ware
**tablier** *nm* apron; smock; blower (fire-

place); steel shutter; superstructure; roadway (on bridge); *coll* **rendre son** ~ stop doing one's job
**tabou** *nm* taboo
**tabouret** *nm* stool; footstool
**tabulateur** *nm* tabulator
**tabulatrice** *nf* punch-card machine
**tac** *nm* click; **répondre du** ~ **au** ~ answer quickly in the same vein
**tache** *nf* stain, spot; blemish, flaw; blot; **faire** ~ jar, stand out as a blemish
**tâche** *nf* task; à la ~ on piece-work; **prendre à** ~ **de** make every effort to
**tacher** *vt* stain; blemish, sully
**tâcher** *vi* try, endeavour
**tâcheron** *nm* hard-worker; *bui* jobber, sub-contractor
**tacheter** *vt* (5) stain with spots; fleck, speckle
**tachycardie** *nf med* tachycardia, rapid heart-beat
**tachygraphe** *nm* tachograph
**tachymètre** *nm* tachometer, speedometer
**tacite** *adj* tacit, implied, understood
**taciturne** *adj* taciturn, uncommunicative
**taciturnité** *nf* taciturnity
**tacot** *nm coll* old crock (car)
**tact** *nm* touch; tact; **manquer de** ~ be tactless, act tactlessly
**tacticien -ienne** *n* tactician
**tactique** *nf* tactics; *adj* tactical
**tadorne** *nm orni* sheldrake
**taffetas** *nm* taffeta
**taïaut** *interj* tally-ho!

**taie** *nf* ~ **d'oreiller** pillow-case; speck (in eye), leucoma

**taillable** *adj hist* liable to pay the **taille**; ~ **et corvéable à merci** exploited on all sides

**taillade** *nf* cut, gash

**taillader** *vt* slash, gash

**taillanderie** *nf* edge-tool industry

**taillandier** *nm* edge-tool maker

**taillant** *nm* cutting edge

**taille** *nf* cutting; pruning, trimming; cut; edge (sword); trees growing again (after being cut); stature, height; waist; tally; *hist* direct tax; **être de** ~ **à** be strong enough to; **pierre de** ~ rough-hewn stone; **tour de** ~ waist measurement

**taillé** *adj* ready, prepared; ~ **pour** suitable for, made for; **bien** ~ well built

**taille-crayon** *nm* (*pl invar or* **taille-crayons**) pencil-sharpener

**taille-douce** *nf* copper-plate engraving

**tailler** *vt* cut; hew; prune, trim, clip; ~ **une armée en pièces** hack an army to pieces; *sl* **se** ~ clear off

**tailleur** *nm* tailor; cutter; hewer; **(costume)** ~ woman's suit; **s'asseoir en** ~ sit cross-legged

**tailleuse** *nf* dressmaker

**taillis** *nm* coppice, copse

**tailloir** *nm* trencher

**tain** *nm* silvering (mirror)

**taire** *vt* (69) keep silent about, suppress, hush up; **faire** ~ **qn** silence s/o; **se** ~ be silent, say nothing

**talc** *nm* French chalk; talc; **poudre de** ~ talcum powder

**talé** *adj* bruised (fruit)

**talent** *nm* talent, gift; **avoir du** ~ be gifted, be talented

**talentueux -ueuse** *adj coll* talented

**talkie-walkie** *nm* (*pl* **talkies-walkies**) walkie-talkie

**talle** *nf agr + hort* sucker

**taller** *vi agr + hort* throw out suckers

**taloche** *nf coll* cuff, clout

**talon** *nm* heel; crust; counterfoil; **être sur les** ~ **s de qn** dog s/o's footsteps; **montrer (tourner) les** ~ **s** clear off, run away

**talonner** *vt* follow closely, dog; spur on; *sp* heel

**talonnette** *nf* heel-piece; reinforcement (for bottom of trouser-leg)

**talonneur** *nm sp* hooker

**talonnière** *nf* heel-wing

**talquer** *vt* cover or sprinkle with talcum powder

**talus** *nm* slope; bank, embankment

**tamarinier** *nm* tamarind(-tree)

**tamaris** *nm bot* tamarisk

**tambour** *nm* drum; drummer; winding-drum, barrel; revolving door; ~ **de basque** tambourine; ~ **de frein** brake-drum; ~ **de ville** town-crier; *coll* **mener qn** ~ **battant** jolly s/o along; **sans** ~ **ni trompette** without fuss; secretly

**tambourin** *nm* long narrow drum; tambourine

**tambouriner** *vt* make known by beating on a drum; make known; *vi* beat a drum; drum, beat a tattoo

**tambour-major** *nm* (*pl* **tambours-majors**) drum-major

**tamia** *nm* chipmunk

**tamis** *nm* sieve; riddle; **passer au** ~ sift

**Tamise** *nf* Thames

**tamiser** *vt* sift, bolt (flour); strain, filter

**tampon** *nm* stopper, plug, bung; wad, plug; rubber-stamp; pad; wall-plug; buffer; ~ **hygiénique** tampon, sanitary towel

**tamponnement** *nm* collision; plugging; dabbing

**tamponner** *vt* bang into, run into; plug; dab

**tam-tam** *nm* tom-tom; *coll* **faire du** ~ make a great noise

**tan** *nm* tanner's bark

**tancer** *vt* (4) reprimand, scold

**tanche** *nf* tench

**tandis que** *conj phr* whereas; whilst

**tangage** *nm* pitching (ship)

**tangent** *adj* tangential

**tangente** *nf* tangent; *coll* **s'échapper par la** ~ dodge the question; slip away

**tangentiel -ielle** *adj* tangential

**tango** *nm* tango; *adj invar* orange-coloured

**tanguer** *vi naut* pitch

**tanière** *nf* den, lair

**tanin** *nm* tannin

**tanne** *nf* blackhead

**tanné** *nm* tan; *adj* tanned (leather, face)

**tannée** *nf* spent tan; *coll* thrashing

**tanner** *vt* tan; *coll* bore, pester; *sl* thrash

**tannerie** *nf* tannery

**tanneur** *nm* tanner

**tannique** *adj* tannic

**tant** *adv* so much; as much; as long; ~ **et plus** ever so many; ever so much; ~ **mieux!** so much the better!, good!; ~ **pis** so much the worse; it can't be helped; *coll* ~ **qu'à faire** while one's about it; ~ **que** as long as; ~ **s'en faut que** far from; ~ **soit peu** ever so little; **en** ~ **que** in the capacity of, qua; in so far as; **faire** ~ **et si bien que** work to such good effect that; **si** ~ **est que** if indeed; *coll* **vous m'en direz** ~! you don't say so!

**tante** *nf* aunt; *sl* homosexual; *coll* **ma** ~ pawnshop

**tantième** *nm* share, percentage

**tantinet** *nm coll* small quantity, tiny bit, dash, touch

**tantôt** *nm coll* afternoon; *adv* soon, presently; a short time ago, just now; ~ ... ~ at one time ... at another time; à ~ see you presently, so long

**taon** *nm* horse-fly

**tapage** *nm* noise, din; *leg* ~ **nocturne** disturbing of the peace at night

**tapageur -euse** *adj* rowdy, noisy; showy, flashy

**tapant** *adj* striking; à **midi** ~ on the stroke of noon

**¹tape** *nf* tap, pat, rap

**²tape** *nf* stopper, plug

**tapé** *adj* dried (fruit); *coll* **bien** ~ successful

**tape-à-l'œil** *adj invar coll* flashy

**tapecul** *nm* see-saw; boneshaking carriage

**tapée** *nf sl* large quantity, mass

**taper** *vt* strike, pat; type; *coll* borrow money from; *sl* **se** ~ **qch** get oneself sth; *vi* ~ **sur** hit; *coll* ~ **dans** help oneself from; ~ **sur qn** slang s/o

**tapette** *nf* mallet; swatter; carpet-beater; *coll* tongue; *sl* queer, fairy

**tapin** *nm sl* **faire le** ~ walk the street (prostitute)

**tapinois (en)** *adv phr* stealthily

**tapir (se)** *v refl* cower, squat, crouch

**tapis** *nm* carpet; cover; ~ **roulant** conveyor belt; ~ **vert** gaming table; **aller au** ~ get knocked down (boxing); **amuser le** ~ keep the company amused; **être sur le** ~ be under discussion; **mettre qch sur le** ~ bring sth up for discussion

**tapis-brosse** *nm* door-mat

**tapisser** *vt* hang with tapestry; paper (wall); plaster (with adverts)

**tapisserie** *nf* tapestry, hangings; tapestry-making; wallpaper; **faire** ~ be a wall-flower (at a dance)

**tapissier -ière** *n* tapestry-worker; paper-hanger; upholsterer

**tapoter** *vt coll* pat, thrum

**taquet** *nm* bracket; angle-block

**taquin** *adj* fond of teasing

**taquiner** *vt* tease

**taquinerie** *nf* teasing; teasing nature

**tarabiscoté** *adj* heavily ornamented; affected

**tarabuster** *vt* plague, pester

**tarare** *nm* winnowing-machine

**taratata** *interj* fiddlesticks!

**taraud** *nm mech* tap

**tarauder** *vt mech* tap, thread

**tard** *nm* **sur le** ~ late in life; at a late hour; *adv* late

**tarder** *vi* delay; be a long time; ~ **à faire qch** be a long time doing sth; defer doing sth; **il me tarde de** I am longing to; **sans** ~ without delay

**tardif -ive** *adj* belated, late; slow, tardy

**tardiveté** *nf* lateness, backwardness

**tare** *nf* defect, blemish; allowance for weight, tare; **faire la** ~ allow for the tare

**taré** *adj* tainted, blemished, spoilt

**tarentelle** *nf* tarantella

**tarentule** *nf* tarantula

**tarer** *vt comm* tare, ascertain (weight of packing)

**targette** *nf* small (flat) bolt

**targuer (se)** *v refl* boast, pride oneself

**tarière** *nf* auger; drill; *ent* terebra

**tarif** *nm* price-list, tariff; charge, price; *coll* **c'est le** ~ that's what it costs; that's what you must expect

**tarifer** *vt* fix the price of

**tarir** *vt* dry up; exhaust; *vi* run dry; stop, cease; **ne pas** ~ **sur** not cease talking about

**tarse** *nm anat + zool* tarsus

**tartine** *nf* slice of bread and butter; *coll* long speech

**tartiner** *vt* spread (with butter); **fromage à** ~ cheese spread

**tartre** *nm* tartar; scale, fur

**tartreux -euse** *adj* tartarous

**tartrique** *adj* tartaric (acid)

**tartuf(f)e** *nm* hypocrite

**tartuf(f)erie** *nf* hypocrisy

**tas** *nm* pile, heap; *coll* great deal, lot; **dans le** ~ from the mass; *fig* **sur le** ~ at work; **tirer dans le** ~ fire at random

**tasse** *nf* cup; cupful

**tassé** *adj* abundant, slap-up; strong

**tasseau** *nm* cleat, batten; bracket; lug

**tasser** *vt* compress, squeeze together, pack; **se** ~ settle, subside; *coll* settle down, calm down

**taste-vin, tâte-vin** *nm invar* pipette or cup for tasting wine

**tâter** *vt* feel, touch, handle; ~ **de (à)** sample, try; ~ **le terrain** sound out the ground; **se** ~ examine oneself; *coll* hesitate

**tatillon -onne** *adj* fussy, finicky, meddlesome

**tâtonner** *vi* grope, feel one's way

**tâtons (à)** *adv phr* gropingly

**tatouage** *nm* tattooing

**tatouer** *vt* tattoo

**taudis** *nm* hovel, miserable lodging

**taule, tôle** *nf sl* room; *sl* prison

**taulier -ière, tôlier -ière** *n sl* hotel-keeper

**taupe** *nf* mole

**taupé** *adj feutre* ~ velours felt

**taupier** *nm* mole-catcher

**taupière** *nf* mole-trap

**taupinière** *nf* mole-hill

**taureau** *nm* bull

**taurillon** *nm* bull-calf
**tauromachie** *nf* bull-fighting
**tautologie** *nf* tautology
**taux** *nm* rate, fixed price
**taveler** *vt* (5) speckle, spot
**taverne** *nf* café; café with old-world décor
**taxateur** *nm* taxer, assessor
**taxation** *nf* fixing (prices, wages); taxing; assessment
**taxe** *nf* fixed price; fixed rate; charge; tax, duty; taxing; ~ **à (sur) la valeur ajoutée (T.V.A.)** value added tax (V.A.T.)
**taxer** *vt* regulate (price, rate); charge; tax, accuse
**taxidermie** *nf* taxidermy
**taximètre** *nm* taximeter, *coll* clock
**taxiphone** *nm* public telephone
**tchécoslovaque** *adj* Czechoslovak
**Tchécoslovaquie** *nf* Czechoslovakia
**Tchèque** *n* Czech
**tchèque** *nm* Czech (language); *adj* Czech
**te** (t' before vowel) *pers pron* you; to you; thee, thyself
**¹té** *interj* (S. France) Well!, Fancy!
**²té** *nm* T-shaped object; T-square; T-bracket
**technicien -ienne** *n* qualified person, technician
**technique** *nf* technics; technique; *adj* technical
**technocrate** *n* technocrat; partisan of technocracy
**technologie** *nf* technology
**technologique** *adj* technological
**teck, tek** *nm* teak
**teckel** *nm* dachshund
**tectonique** *nf* tectonics; *adj* tectonic
**teigne** *nf* moth; scalp disease; *coll* nasty person, pest
**teigneux -euse** *n + adj* (person) suffering from scalp disease
**teiller** *vt* strip (flax)
**teindre** *vt* (55) dye; **se** ~ dye one's hair
**teint** *nm* dye; complexion
**teinte** *nf* shade, hue; slight touch, tinge
**teinter** *vt* tint
**teinture** *nf* dyeing; tinting; dye, colour, hue; tincture
**teinturerie** *nf* dyeing; dry-cleaners
**teinturier -ière** *n* dry-cleaner; dyer
**tek** *nm see* **teck**
**tel** (*f* **telle**) *adj* such; so great; like, as; ~ **quel** just as it is; **de** ~ **le sorte que** so that, in such a way that; *pron* such a one, such; ~ **et** ~ this man and that; ~ **qui** he who; **un** ~ so-and-so
**télé** *nf abbr coll* television
**télébenne** *nf see* **télécabine**
**télécabine** *nf* cable-car; cable railway

**télécommande** *nf* remote control
**télécommander** *vt* control by remote control
**téléférique, téléphérique** *nm* cable-car railway
**télégénique** *adj* that looks good on the TV screen
**télégramme** *nm* telegram
**télégraphe** *nm* telegraph
**télégraphie** *nf* telegraphy; ~ **sans fil** wireless telegraphy
**télégraphier** *vt + vi* telegraph, wire
**télégraphique** *adj* telegraphic
**télégraphiste** *n* telegraphist
**téléguidage** *nm* remote control, radio control
**téléguider** *vt* guide by remote control, radio control; **engin téléguidé** guided missile
**téléimprimeur** *nm* teleprinter, *US* teletypewriter
**télémécanique** *nf* telemechanics
**télémètre** *nm* range-finder
**téléobjectif** *nm* telescopic lens
**téléologie** *nf* teleology
**télépathie** *nf* telepathy
**télépathique** *adj* telepathic
**téléphérique** *nm see* **téléférique**
**téléphone** *nm* telephone; ~ **arabe** bush telegraph, grape-vine; ~ **rouge** hot line (White House–Kremlin); **coup de** ~ phone call
**téléphoner** *vt + vi* telephone, *US* call
**téléphonie** *nf* telephony
**téléphonique** *adj* telephonic
**téléphoniste** *n* telephonist
**télescopage** *nm* telescoping
**télescoper** *vt + vi* telescope
**télescopique** *adj* telescopic
**téléscripteur** *nm* teleprinter, *US* teletypewriter
**télésiège** *nm* chairlift
**téléski** *nm* ski-lift
**téléspectateur -trice** *n* viewer
**télétype** *nm* teleprinter, *US* teletypewriter
**téléviser** *vt* televize
**téléviseur** *nm* television set
**tellement** *adv* so, in such a way, to such an extent; *coll* a lot, a great deal
**tellurien -ienne** *adj* tellurian, earth
**téméraire** *adj* rash, reckless, foolhardy
**témérité** *nf* temerity, foolhardiness
**témoignage** *nm* testimony, evidence; mark, token; **en** ~ **de** as a token of; **rendre** ~ **à** bear grateful witness to; give evidence in favour of
**témoigner** *vt* testify, bear witness to; *vi* testify, bear witness; ~ **de** bear witness to; show, display
**témoin** *nm* witness; sign, proof; boundary-mark; *sp* baton; **appartement** ~

show (model) flat; **barre des** ~ **s** witness box; **leg en** ~ **de quoi** in witness whereof; **lampe** ~ pilot light; **prendre qn à** ~ call s/o to witness

**tempe** *nf anat* temple

**tempérament** *nm* temperament; constitution; **avoir du** ~ be lusty; **vente à** ~ hire-purchase

**tempérance** *nf* moderation, temperance; abstinence (from drink)

**tempérant** *adj* moderate, temperate

**température** *nf* temperature

**tempéré** *adj* mild, temperate; restrained

**tempérer** *vt* (6) moderate, temper

**tempête** *nf* storm, tempest

**tempêter** *vi* rage, fulminate

**tempêtueux -ueuse** *adj* tempestuous, stormy

**temple** *nm* temple; Protestant church; **Ordre du Temple** Order of the Knights Templars

**templier** *nm hist* Templar

**temporaire** *adj* temporary, provisional

**temporel -elle** *adj* temporal, secular

**temporisateur -trice** *n* temporizer

**temporiser** *vi* temporize

**temps** *nm* time; weather; *gramm* tense; *mus* beat; **à** ~ in good time; **avant le** ~ prematurely; **avec le** ~ in the course of time; **avoir fait son** ~ be worn out; **de** ~ **à autre (de** ~ **en** ~**)** from time to time; **en même** ~ at the same time; **en** ~ **et lieu** at the appropriate time and place; **gros** ~ stormy weather at sea; **il est grand** ~ **de** it is high time to; **le** ~ **de m'habiller, je descends** just give me time to dress, and I'll come down; **marquer un** ~ pause; **moteur à deux** ~ two-stroke engine; **par tous les** ~ in all kinds of weather; *coll* **se donner du bon** ~ enjoy oneself, have a good time

**tenable** *adj* bearable

**tenace** *adj* tough; tenacious, persistent, stubborn

**ténacité** *nf* tenacity; toughness; adhesiveness

**tenaille** *nf usu pl* pincers

**tenancier -ière** *n* lessee manager(ess)

**tenant** *nm* champion, supporter (opinion); *sp* holder (title); **d'un seul** ~ in one block; **les** ~ **s et les aboutissants** adjacent parts; full details, all relevant details; **adj séance** ~ **e** immediately

**tendance** *nf* tendency, propensity

**tendancieux -ieuse** *adj* tendentious

[1]**tendeur -euse** *n* layer; hanger

[2]**tendeur** *nm* stretcher, tightener; elastic strap (for luggage); chain-adjuster (bicycle)

**tendoir** *nm* drying-line

[1]**tendre** *vt* stretch; set, fix up; hold out; pitch (tent); paper (room); ~ **l'oreille** prick up one's ears; *vi* tend, conduce

[2]**tendre** *adj* tender, soft, delicate; early (age); affectionate, loving

**tendresse** *nf* tenderness, fondness

**tendron** *nm cul* gristle (veal)

**tendu** *adj* tense; taut, tight

**ténèbres** *nfpl* darkness, gloom; *fig* ignorance

**ténébreux -euse** *adj* gloomy, dark; mysterious

**teneur** *nf* purport, tenor; content, amount

**ténia** *nm* tapeworm

**tenir** *vt* (96) hold; take up, occupy; keep, maintain; contain; run, manage; restrain, hold back; ~ **la chambre** be confined to one's room; ~ **la (sa) droite (gauche)** keep to the right (left); ~ **qch de qn** have sth from s/o; **tenez-vous le pour dit** I shan't tell you again; **tiens!** fancy!, well!; *vi* hold, stick fast; be contained, fit into; ~ **à** be fond of, be keen on; value; result from; ~ **à ce qu'on fasse qch** be insistent that sth should be done; ~ **bon** hold fast, stand fast; ~ **pour** be in favour of; **il ne tient qu'à vous** it all depends on you; **ne pas** ~ **en place** be restless; **qu'à cela ne tienne!** never mind that!; **un tiens vaut mieux que deux tu l'auras** a bird in the hand is worth two in the bush; **se** ~ remain; contain oneself; **se** ~ **tranquille** keep quiet; **ne pas savoir à quoi s'en** ~ not know what to believe; **s'en** ~ **à qch** abide by sth, want nothing more; **tenez-vous bien** mind out, watch it; **tiens-toi** behave yourself

**tension** *nf* tension; stretching; tightness; tenseness

**tentaculaire** *adj* tentacular

**tentacule** *nm* tentacle

**tentant** *adj* tempting, alluring

**tentateur -trice** *n* tempter (temptress); *adj* tempting

**tentatif -ive** *adj* tentative

**tentation** *nf* temptation

**tentative** *nf* attempt

**tente** *nf* tent

**tenter** *vt* tempt; try, attempt

**tenture** *nf* hangings, tapestry

**tenu** *adj* **bien** ~ well-kept, neat, tidy; **être** ~ **de (à)** be obliged to; **mal** ~ neglected, untidy

**ténu** *adj* tenuous, slender

**tenue** *nf* keeping, maintaining; behaviour, bearing; dress; *mus* sustained note; ~ **de livres** book-keeping; ~ **de route** road-holding; **avoir de la** ~ have good manners; **d'une seule** ~ without interruption; **en grande ~** in full dress; *coll* **en petite ~** scantily dressed; **en ~** in uniform; **tout d'une ~** without interruption

**ténuité** *nf* tenuity; slenderness; fineness

**ter** *adv* three times

**tératologie** *nf* teratology

**térébenthine** *nf* turpentine

**tergiverser** *vi* beat about the bush, tergiversate

**terme** *nm* term; end, limit; appointed time; date for paying (rent, etc); rent, payment; expression, word; **~s** terms, footing; conditions; wording; **à court ~** short-term; short-dated; **à long ~** long-term; long-dated; **marché à ~** forward transaction; **mettre un ~ à** put an end to; **né avant ~** premature

**terminaison** *nf* termination, ending

**terminale** *nf* last year at secondary school ( = Upper Sixth)

**terminer** *vt* terminate, finish, conclude; complete; **se ~** come to an end

**terminologie** *nf* terminology

**ternaire** *adj* ternary

¹**terne** *nm* tern, set of three

²**terne** *adj* dull, flat, colourless

**ternir** *vt* tarnish; dull; **se ~** grow dull; become tarnished

**terrain** *nm* ground; plot, piece of ground; *sp* field; **connaître le ~** know the people one has to deal with; **être sur son ~** be on familiar ground; **véhicule tout ~** cross-country vehicle

**terrasse** *nf* terrace; **en ~** terraced

**terrassement** *nm* banking; terracing; earthwork

**terrasser** *vt* crush, knock down, beat; dismay

**terrassier** *nm* navvy

**terre** *nf* earth; world; land, ground; soil; **~s** property, estate; **à ~** matter-of-fact, down-to-earth; ordinary; **~ cuite** terra cotta; **être sur ~** be alive, exist; *elect* **mettre à la ~** earth; **par ~** on the ground; to the ground; **porter qn en ~** bury s/o

**terreau** *nm* vegetable mould

**Terre-Neuve** *nf* Newfoundland

**terre-neuve** *nm invar* Newfoundland dog

**terre-plein** *nm* terrace, earth platform

**terrer** *vi* earth up; cover with earth; **se ~** go to ground, hide below ground; hide, stay concealed

**terrestre** *adj* terrestrial; earthly, worldly

**terreur** *nf* terror, dread

**terreux -euse** *adj* earthy; dirty; sickly, ashy

**terrible** *adj* terrible; *coll* marvellous, terrific

**terrien -ienne** *n* earth-dweller; land-dweller; *adj* land-owning; of the land

**terrier** *nm* burrow, earth, hole; terrier

**terrifiant** *adj* terrifying

**terrifier** *vt* terrify

**terrine** *nf* earthenware pot; earthenware vessel; terrine

**territoire** *nm* territory

**terroir** *nm* soil; **sentir le ~** betray one's native origins

**terroriser** *vt* terrorize

**terrorisme** *nm* terrorism

**terroriste** *nm* terrorist

**tertiaire** *adj* tertiary

**tertre** *nm* hillock, mound

**tes** *poss adj pl see* **ton**

**tesson** *nm* piece (broken glass, etc), shard

**test** *nm see* **têt**

**testament** *nm* will, testament; **mettre (coucher) qn sur son ~** mention s/o in one's will

**testamentaire** *adj* testamentary

**testateur -trice** *n* testator (testatrix)

¹**tester** *vi* make one's will

²**tester** *vt* test, examine

**testicule** *nm* testicle

**têt, test** *nm chem* small fire-clay cup, crucible

**tétanique** *adj med* tetanic

**tétanos** *nm med* tetanus, lock-jaw

**têtard** *nm* tadpole; pollard

**tête** *nf* head; top; beginning; front; brains, imagination; leader; *coll* face; **~ baissée** rashly, headlong; **~ brûlée** desperate character; **~ de bielle** big end; **~ de lecture** repro head; **~ de ligne** rail-head; starting point; **~ de mort** skull; **avoir mal à la ~** have a headache; **courber la ~** submit; *coll* **en avoir par-dessus la ~** be fed up; **en faire à sa ~** have one's way, do as one likes; **faire une ~** pull a long face; **femme de ~** capable woman; **forte ~** unruly character; **ne pas savoir où donner de la ~** not know where to turn; **se casser la ~** rack one's brains; **signe de ~** nod; **tenir ~ à qn** stand up to s/o; **tourner la ~ à qn** drive s/o mad

**tête-à-queue** *nm invar* mot **faire un ~** spin right round

**tête-à-tête** *nm invar* private conversation; **en ~** alone together

**tête-bêche** *adv* head to foot (alongside)

**tête-de-loup** *nf* (*pl* **têtes-de-loup**) long-handled brush, wall-broom

**tête-de-nègre** *nm + adj invar* dark brown

**tétée** *nf* suck, feeding; milk drunk at one feed

**téter** *vt + vi* (6) suck, feed

**têtière** *nf* head-stall; head-rest; anti-macassar

**tétin** *nm* nipple
**tétine** *nf* dug, udder; teat
**téton** *nm coll* tit, nipple
**tétrarchie** *nf* tetrarchy
**tétras** *nm* grouse
**tette** *nf* dug, teat
**têtu** *adj* stubborn, obstinate
**teuf-teuf** *nm invar coll* vintage car
**teutonique** *adj* Teutonic
**texte** *nm* text
**textuel -uelle** *adj* textual
**thaumaturge** *nm* miracle-worker
**thé** *nm* tea; tea-party
**théâtral** *adj* theatrical
**théâtre** *nm* theatre; scene, stage; dramatic art; dramatic works; **coup de ~** dramatic turn of events, startling event; **faire du ~** act; **pièce de ~** play
**thébaïde** *nf* wilderness; solitary retreat
**théière** *nf* tea-pot
**théisme** *nm* theism
**théiste** *n* theist; *adj* theistic
**thématique** *adj* thematic
**thème** *nm* topic, theme; prose composition; **fort en ~** swot, bookworm
**théocratie** *nf* theocracy
**théologal** *adj* relating to theology
**théologie** *nf* theology
**théologien** *nm* theologian
**théologique** *adj* theological
**théorème** *nm* theorem
**théoricien -ienne** *n* theorist
**théorie** *nf* theory; group in procession
**théorique** *adj* theoretical
**théoriser** *vi* theorize
**théosophie** *nf* theosophy
**thérapeutique** *nf* therapeutics; *adj* therapeutic
**thermes** *nmpl* hot springs, thermal baths; Roman baths
**thermidor** *nm hist* eleventh month of the French Republican calendar (July to August)
**thermie** *nf* therm
**thermique** *adj* thermic
**thermo-dynamique** *nf* thermodynamics
**thermogène** *adj* heat-producing
**thermomètre** *nm* thermometer
**thésauriser** *vt* pile up, hoard (money)
**thèse** *nf* thesis; argument, proposition
**thibaude** *nf* coarse hair-cloth, underlay
**thon** *nm* tunny, tuna
**thoracique** *adj* thoracic
**thrombose** *nf* thrombosis
**thuriféraire** *nm* incense-bearer; flatterer
**thym** *nm* thyme
**thyroïde** *nf* thyroid gland
**tiare** *nf* tiara
**Tibétain -e** *n* Tibetan
**tibétain** *nm* Tibetan (language); *adj* Tibetan
**tic** *nm* twitching, tic; mannerism, trick

**ticket** *nm* ticket, voucher, coupon, slip; **~ modérateur** part-payment of French health service charges; *coll* **avoir un (le) ~ avec** be a hit with
**tic-tac** *nm invar* tick-tock, ticking
**tiède** *adj* tepid, lukewarm
**tiédeur** *nf* tepidity, lukewarmness; lack of enthusiasm
**tiédir** *vt* make lukewarm; *vi* become lukewarm
**tien** (*f* **tienne**) *n* yours; thine; your property; **les ~s** your family and relatives; *pron* yours; thine
**tiens** *interj* fancy!; well!; hullo!
**tierce** *nf mus* third; tierce (fencing); run of three cards; *print* final proof
**tiercé** *nm* bet (to forecast first three horses in race)
**tiercelet** *nm* male falcon
**tiers** *nm* third; third party, third person; **~ provisionnel** third of income tax (to be paid in advance); **le ~ et le quart** anybody; *adj* (*f* **tierce**) *hist* **~ état** third estate, bourgeoisie; **~ monde** third world
**tige** *nf* stalk, stem; spindle, shaft
**tignasse** *nf* mop of hair
**tigré** *adj* striped; speckled
**tigresse** *nf* tigress
**tillac** *nm naut ar* upper deck
**tilleul** *nm* lime-tree; lime-blossom tea; **vert ~** lime-coloured
**tilt** *nm coll* **faire ~** have a shock effect
**timbale** *nf* kettledrum; metal mug; circular pie-dish; kind of vol-au-vent
**timbrage** *nm* franking
**timbre** *nm* bell; timbre (voice); (postage-)stamp; stamp duty; shell (helmet); **~ de la poste** postmark
**timbré** *adj* stamped; *coll* cracked, crackbrained; sonorous
**timbrer** *vt* stamp
**timide** *adj* timid; timorous; shy
**timidité** *nf* timidity
**timon** *nm* pole (cart, etc); *naut + ar* rudder
**timonier** *nm naut* helmsman; wheel-horse
**timoré** *adj* fearful, timorous
**tin** *nm naut* chock, stocks
**tinette** *nf* soil-tub; *coll* lavatory
**tintamarre** *nm coll* racket, din
**tintement** *nm* ringing
**tinter** *vt* ring, toll; *vi* tinkle; chink; ring
**tintin** *nm sl* nothing at all
**tintinnabuler** *vi* tinkle
**tintouin** *nm coll* worry, trouble; din
**tique** *nf ent* tick
**tiquer** *vi coll* show surprise, show annoyance
**tiqueté** *adj* speckled, mottled

**tiqueur -euse** *n* person with a mannerism

**tir** *nm* shooting; gunnery; firing; shooting-gallery, rifle-range; **à ~ rapide** quick-firing

**tirade** *nf* declamation, long speech; tirade

**tirage** *nm* pulling; draught; drawing; draw; number of copies printed; *print* + *phot* printing off; circulation

**tiraillement** *nm* tugging; *coll* quarreling, wrangling

**tirailler** *vt* pull, tug; *fig* pester; (pain) stab at; *vi* shoot wildly

**tirailleur** *nm* sharp-shooter

**tirant** *nm* purse-string; boot-tag; sinew (meat); tie-beam, tie-rod; *naut* ~ **d'eau** displacement

**tire** *nf* **voleur à la** ~ pickpocket

**tiré** *adj* drawn, haggard

**tire-au-cul** *nm invar sl* shirker

**tire-au-flanc** *nm invar coll* shirker

**tire-botte** *nm* boot-jack

**tire-bouchon** *nm* corkscrew

**tire-bouton** *nm* button-hook

**tire-d'aile (à)** *adv phr* swiftly, flying fast

**tire-fesses** *nm coll* ski-lift

**tire-fond** *nm invar* long bolt; ring (screwed into ceiling)

**tire-laine** *nm invar obs* robber, footpad

**tire-larigot (à)** *adv phr coll* abundantly, copiously

**tire-ligne** *nm* drawing-pen; scribing awl

**tirelire** *nf* money-box; *sl* stomach

**tirer** *vt* pull, tug, haul; stretch, pull out; extract; pull off; draw; print off; fire, let off; gain; ~ **d'embarras** get out of an awkward situation; ~ **parti de qch** take advantage of sth; *vulg* ~ **un coup** have it off; ~ **une conséquence** conclude; *vi* pull; tend, verge; draw (chimney); shoot; ~ **à sa fin** draw to an end; *sl* **se** ~ scram, clear off; **se** ~ **de** extricate oneself from

**tiret** *nm* dash

**tirette** *nf* flue damper; tablet, sliding shelf

**tireur -euse** *n* drawer; marksman; **tireuse de cartes** fortune-teller

**tiroir** *nm* drawer; slide-valve

**tiroir-caisse** *nm* (*pl* **tiroirs-caisses**) till, cash register

**tisane** *nf* herb tea

**tison** *nm* fire-brand; fusee

**tisonner** *vt* poke, stir (fire)

**tisonnier** *nm* poker

**tisser** *vt* weave

**tisserand -e** *n* weaver

**tisseur -euse** *n* weaver

**tissu** *nm* tissue; cloth, fabric; *adj ar* woven; mixed

**tissu-éponge** *nm* (*pl* **tissus-éponge**) towelling

**tissure** *nf* texture

**titane** *nm* titanium

**titi** *nm sl* urchin, cheeky little fellow

**titiller** *vt* titillate; tickle

**titrage** *nm chem* titration; assaying; sizing

**titre** *nm* title; diploma, certificate; claim; heading; right; grade (ore); titre, strength (chemical solution); ~ **s** stocks and shares; **à juste** ~ rightly; **à quel** ~? by what right?; **à** ~ **de** by right of; **en** ~ titular

**titré** *adj* titled; titrated, standard (solution)

**titrer** *vt* give a title to; titrate; assay; size; give sub-titles to

**tituber** *vi* stagger, reel about

**titulaire** *n* holder; incumbent; bearer; *adj* titular

**titulariser** *vt* establish, confirm the appointment of

**toboggan** *nm* toboggan; slide, chute; temporary overpass

¹**toc** *nm coll* cheap imitation (jewellery, etc)

²**toc** *interj* tap!

**tocante** *nf see* **toquante**

**tocard** *nm* poor race-horse; *sl* useless individual; *adj coll* ugly, poor

**toge** *nf* toga; gown, robe (judge)

**tohu-bohu** *nm* confusion; hubbub

**toi** *pers pron* you; thou

**toile** *nf* linen, cloth; canvas; oil painting; sail; ~ **d'araignée** spider's web; ~ **de coton** calico; ~ **de fond** backcloth

**toilette** *nf* wash-stand; toilet-table, dressing-table; washing, dressing; toilet; dress, costume; tailor's wrapper; ~ **s** lavatory; **en grande** ~ in full dress

**toi-même** *pers pron* yourself; thyself

**toise** *nf* measuring instrument; *ar* fathom

**toiser** *vt* measure; size up, eye from head to foot

**toison** *nf* fleece; mop of hair

**toit** *nm* roof; house, home; **crier qch sur les** ~ **s** shout sth all over the place, broadcast sth

**toiture** *nf* roofing, roof

¹**tôle** *nf* sheet-metal, sheet-iron; ~ **ondulée** corrugated iron

²**tôle** *nf see* **taule**

**tolérable** *adj* bearable, tolerable

**tolérance** *nf* tolerance; toleration; **maison de** ~ brothel

**tolérer** *vt* (6) tolerate; wink at, close one's eyes to

**tôlerie** *nf* sheet-iron; sheet-iron works

**tolet** *nm naut* thole-pin

**¹tôlier** *nm* sheet-iron dealer; sheet-iron worker; *mot* panel-beater

**²tôlier -ière** *n see* taulier -ière

**tollé** *nm* furious cries, hue and cry

**tomate** *nf* tomato

**tombal** *adj* relating to tombs; **pierre ~ e** tombstone

**tombant** *adj* falling; drooping; **à la nuit ~ e** at nightfall

**tombée** *nf* fall

**tomber** *nm* **au ~ du jour** at nightfall; *vt sl* throw to the ground, make fall; *sl* seduce; *coll* **~ la veste** take off one's jacket; *vi* fall, fall down, drop down; abate, drop, decline; fail; hang down, hang; lapse; **~ bien** come at the right time; **~ de sommeil** be dead-tired; **~ sous le sens** be evident; **~ sur** attack, fall upon; light on, meet; **faire ~ qn** knock s/o down, knock s/o over; **laisser ~** drop; *coll* **laisser ~ qn** drop s/o; **se laisser ~** drop, sink

**tombereau** *nm* tip-cart, tumbril

**tombeur** *nm* wrestler who overthrows his opponent; *coll* seducer

**tombola** *nf* lottery

**tomme** *nf* fat cheese from S.E. France

**tom-pouce** *nm invar coll* tiny man; small collapsible umbrella

**¹ton** *nm* tone; intonation; breeding, manners; *mus* pitch; *mus* key; colour, tint; **bon ~** good form; **donner le ~** set the fashion; **faire baisser le ~ à qn** make s/o sing small, take s/o down a peg

**²ton** *poss adj* (*f* ta, *pl* tes) your; thy

**tonalité** *nf* tonality; shade; dialling tone

**tondeur -euse** *n* shearer, clipper

**tondeuse** *nf* lawn-mower; hair-clippers; shears, shearing machine

**tondre** *vt* shear, clip; mow; *coll* fleece, rook

**tonifiant** *adj* tonic, bracing

**tonifier** *vt* brace, tone up, invigorate

**tonique** *nm* tonic; tonic accent; *nf mus* key-note; *adj mus* tonic

**tonitruant** *adj* stentorian, thunderous

**tonne** *nf* (metric) ton; tun

**tonneau** *nm* barrel, cask; *naut* ton; somersault; *aer* roll

**tonnelet** *nm* small barrel

**tonnelier** *nm* cooper

**tonnelle** *nf* arbour, bower

**tonner** *vi* thunder; boom; fulminate

**tonnerre** *nm* thunder; thunderbolt, lightning; rumble; *coll* **c'est du ~** it's terrific; **coup de ~** thunderclap

**tonsurer** *vt* tonsure

**tonte** *nf* sheep-shearing; shearing-time; clip

**tonton** *nm coll* uncle

**tonus** *nm* tone (muscle); *coll* energy

**top** *nm rad* pip

**topaze** *nf* topaz

**toper** *vi* agree, shake hands on it; **tope!** done!, agreed!

**topinambour** *nm* Jerusalem artichoke

**topique** *nm* topical remedy; commonplace; *adj med* topical

**topo** *nm* speech, exposé; plan, sketch-plan

**topographe** *nm* topographer

**topographie** *nf* topography

**topographique** *adj* topographical

**toponymie** *nf* toponymy

**toquade** *nf coll* passing fancy, infatuation

**toquante** *nf sl* watch

**toque** *nf* cap, toque

**toqué** *adj coll* crazy, mad; **être ~ de qn** be infatuated with s/o

**toquer (se)** *v refl coll* **~ de qn** become infatuated with s/o

**torche** *nf* torch; twist of straw

**torcher** *vt* wipe, wipe clean; *coll* botch, skimp

**torchère** *nf* candelabrum; standard-lamp

**torchis** *nm bui* daub

**torchon** *nm* dish-cloth, floor-cloth, duster, rag; **le ~ brûle** they are quarrelling

**torchonner** *vt coll* botch, skimp

**tordant** *adj coll* screamingly funny

**tord-boyaux** *nm coll* strong spirits, rot-gut

**tordre** *vt* twist; wring; **se ~** writhe, twist; **se ~ de rire** split one's sides with laughter; **se ~ les mains** wring one's hands

**tordu** *adj* twisted; *coll* strange; *coll* crazy

**toréer** *vi* engage in bull-fighting

**torgnole** *nf coll* slap, blow, cuff

**tornade** *nf* tornado

**torpédo** *nf mot* open tourer

**torpeur** *nf* torpor

**torpille** *nf* torpedo

**torpiller** *vt* torpedo

**torpilleur** *nm* torpedo-boat; torpedo man

**torréfaction** *nf* roasting (coffee, etc)

**torréfier** *vt* roast (coffee, etc); scorch

**torrentiel -ielle** *adj* torrential

**torrentueux -ueuse** *adj* torrent-like

**torride** *adj* torrid; scorching

**tors** *adj* twisted

**torsade** *nf* twisted fringe; cable moulding; **~ de cheveux** coil of hair

**torsader** *vt* twist

**torse** *nm* bust

**torsion** *nf* twisting, torsion

**tort** *nm* wrong; fault; harm, injury; **à ~** wrongly; **à ~ et à travers** without rhyme or reason, indiscriminately;

**avoir** ~ be wrong; **donner** ~ **à qn** decide against s/o; **faire** ~ **à** harm, injure; **se mettre dans son** ~ put oneself in the wrong

**torticolis** *nm* crick in the neck, stiff neck

**tortillage** *nm* quibbling

**tortillard** *nm* slow local train (on light railway)

**tortiller** *vt* twist; *vi* quibble, prevaricate; **se** ~ writhe, wriggle

**tortillon** *nm* pad (for carrying loads on the head); twist (rag, paper)

**tortionnaire** *nm* torturer, tormentor; *adj* torturing

**tortu** *adj* crooked

**tortue** *nf* tortoise; ~ **marine** turtle

**tortueux -euse** *adj* winding, tortuous; crooked, underhand

**torturer** *vt* torture; twist (meaning)

**torve** *adj* **regard** ~ menacing look

**toscan** *adj* Tuscan

**tôt** *adv* early; ~ **ou tard** sooner or later; **le plus** ~ **sera le mieux** the sooner the better

**totalement** *adv* totally, wholly

**totalisateur** *nm* adding-machine; *adj* (*f -trice*) adding, calculating

**totaliser** *vt* totalize

**totalitaire** *adj* totalitarian

**totalité** *nf* totality, whole

**totémisme** *nm* totemism

**toton** *nm* teetotum, small top

**toubib** *nm coll* doctor

**touchant** *adj* touching, affecting; *prep* concerning, about

**touche** *nf* touch, touching; key (piano, typewriter); dab; goad; manner (painter); hit (fencing); appearance; *coll* **faire (avoir) une** ~ **avec** make a hit with

**touche-à-tout** *nm invar* busybody, meddler

**toucher** *nm* touch; *vt* touch; move, affect; concern; draw, receive (money); touch on, allude to; *vi* touch; ~ **à** be in touch with; be close to, border on; start, make a start on; change, alter; meddle, interfere; **je lui en toucherai un mot** I'll mention it to him; **n'avoir pas l'air d'y** ~ put on an innocent air

**touchette** *nf* fret (guitar)

**toue** *nf* flat-bottomed barge; towing

**touer** *vt* tow

**touffe** *nf* tuft; clump

**touffeur** *nf* suffocating heat

**touffu** *adj* bushy, thick; involved, obscure

**touiller** *vt coll* stir

**toujours** *adv* always, ever; still; just the same, nevertheless, all the same; ~ **est-il que ...** the fact remains that...; **allez** ~ go on, go ahead; **pour** ~ for ever

**toundra** *nf* tundra

**toupet** *nm* tuft of hair, quiff; toupet; *coll* cheek, nerve

**toupie** *nf* top, spinning-top; milled cutter; **vieille** ~ old trout, trump

**toupiller** *vt* shape (wood); *vi coll* spin round

**¹tour** *nf* tower; castle (chess); tall block (flats)

**²tour** *nm* turn; revolution; trip; stroll; circuit, circumference; lathe; adornment; trick, feat; turn of phrase; shape; course, turn (of events); ~ **à** ~ by turns, alternately; ~ **de main** knack; ~ **de poitrine** chest measurement; **à qui le** ~ ? whose turn is it?; **à** ~ **de bras** hard, with all one's might; **à** ~ **de rôle** in turn; **donner un** ~ **de clef à** lock; **en un** ~ **de main** in an instant; **faire le** ~ **de** go round; **faire un** ~ go for a walk

**tourangeau -elle** *adj* of Tours; of Touraine

**tourbe** *nf* peat

**tourbeux -euse** *adj* peaty

**tourbière** *nf* peat-bog

**tourbillon** *nm* whirlwind; whirlpool; eddy; bustle, whirl

**tourbillonner** *vi* whirl, swirl

**tourelle** *nf* small tower; gun-turret

**tourie** *nf* carboy

**tourisme** *nm* tourism; touring

**touriste** *n* tourist; **classe** ~ economy class

**touristique** *adj* touristic

**tourment** *nm* torture; torment, anguish

**tourmente** *nf* storm, tempest; turmoil

**tourmenté** *adj* irregular; tormented; laboured (style)

**tourmenter** *vt* torture; torment; worry, trouble; pester, plague; **se** ~ worry

**tournage** *nm* turning (on lathe); *cin* shooting

**tournailler** *vi* prowl about, wander round and round

**tournant** *nm* turning; bend, corner; turning point; *adj* turning; revolving

**tourné** *adj* turned; **bien** ~ well set up; well disposed; **mal** ~ cross-grained; soured

**tournebroche** *nm* roasting-jack; turn-spit

**tourne-disque** *nm* record-player

**tournedos** *nm* fillet steak

**tournée** *nf* tour, round; **payer une** ~ stand a round of drinks

**tournemain** *nm* **en un** ~ in a trice

**tourner** *vt* turn; shape, fashion; revolve, rotate; shoot (film); act in (film); convert; evade, get round; ~ **la tête à qn** arouse s/o's admiration; arouse s/o's affections; *vi* revolve, go round; turn,

turn off; result, turn out; ~ **autour de
qn** hang around s/o; ~ **autour du pot**
beat about the bush; ~ **court** stop
suddenly, stop short, finish inconclu-
sively; *coll* ~ **de l'œil** die; ~ **en
ridicule** hold up to ridicule; **mal** ~ go
to the bad; turn out badly; **se** ~ turn,
turn round

**tournesol** *nm* sunflower

**tourneur -euse** *n* lathe-operator; *adj*
**derviche** ~ dancing dervish

**tourne-vent** *nm invar* chimney-cowl

**tournevis** *nm* screwdriver

**tourniole** *nf* whitlow

**tourniquer** *vi* wander about

**tourniquet** *nm* turnstile; turn-buckle;
whirligig; *surg* tourniquet

**tournis** *nm vet* staggers

**tournoi** *nm* tournament

**tournoiement** *nm* whirling

**tournoyer** *vi* (7) whirl, swirl, turn round
and round

**tournure** *nf* turn, course; figure, appearance; *metal* turnings; bustle (dress);
turn (mind, phrase)

**tourte** *nf* tart; *sl* fool, idiot

**tourteau** *nm* round loaf; oil-cake; edible
crab; *her* roundel

**tourtereau** *nm* young turtle-dove; *fig* ~ x
love-birds

**tourterelle** *nf* turtle-dove

**tourtière** *nf* pie-dish; baking-tin

**tous** *pron* + *adj see* **tout**

**Toussaint** *nf* All Saints' day

**tousser** *vi* cough

**toussoter** *vi* cough slightly and frequently

**tout** *nm* whole; total; **risquer le** ~ **pour
le** ~ stake everything; *pron* (*pl* **tous,
toutes**) all, everything; **c'est** ~ **dire** I
needn't say more; *adj* (*pl* **tous, toutes**)
all, every; any; all the, the whole; ~ **
autre que vous** anyone other than
yourself; ~ **le monde** everyone; **à** ~ **e
vitesse** at full speed; **à** ~ **prendre** all
things considered; **c'est** ~ **e une histoire** it's a long story; **de** ~ **e beauté**
extremely beautiful; **le Tout-Paris**
fashionable Paris society; **somme** ~ **e**
all in all, all things considered; **tous
(les) deux** both; **tous les jours** every
day; **tous les deux jours** every other day; *adv* quite,
wholly, entirely; very; ~ **à fait** quite,
utterly; ~ **agréable qu'elle est** however pleasant she is; ~ **au moins** at
least; ~ **au plus** at most; ~ **droit**
straight on; quite straight; **c'est** ~ **le
portrait de son père** he (she) is the living
image of his (her) father

**tout-à-l'égout** *nm invar* mains drainage

**toutefois** *adv* nevertheless, yet, however

**toute-puissance** *nf* omnipotence

**toutou** *nm* doggie

**Tout-Paris** *nm* fashionable Paris society

**Tout-Puissant** *nm* **le** ~ the Almighty

**tout-puissant** *adj* (*f* **toute-puissante**)
all-powerful, almighty

**toux** *nf* cough

**toxémie** *nf* blood-poisoning, toxaemia

**toxicité** *nf* toxic nature, toxicity

**toxicologie** *nf* toxicology

**toxicomane** *n* drug-addict

**toxicomanie** *nf* drug addiction

**toxine** *nf* toxin

**toxique** *nm* poison; *adj* toxic

**trac** *nm* stage-fright; **tout à** ~ thoughtlessly

**traçage** *nm* tracing

**traçant** *adj* running, creeping; **balle** ~ **e**
tracer bullet

**tracas** *nm* trouble, worry, bother

**tracasser** *vt* worry, bother; **se** ~ worry

**tracasserie** *nf* worry; pestering

**tracassier -ière** *adj* pestering; vexatious;
bothersome; fussy

**trace** *nf* trace; trail, track; mark, scar;
impression; **marcher sur les** ~ **s de qn**
follow in s/o's footsteps

**tracé** *nm* tracing, plotting; outline;
lay-out; diagram, sketch

**tracer** *vt* (4) trace; lay out, mark out,
plot; write out, describe; set out

**traceur -euse** *adj* tracer

**trachée** *nf* trachea, windpipe

**trachée-artère** *nf* (*pl* **trachées-artères**)
trachea, windpipe

**trachéen -éenne** *adj anat* trachean

**trachéotomie** *nf* tracheotomy

**trachome** *nm* trachoma

**tractation** *nf* dealing, bargaining

**tracteur** *nm* tractor

**tractif -ive** *adj* tractive

**traction** *nf* traction; pulling; draught;
~ **(avant)** front-wheel drive car

**tradition** *nf* tradition; *leg* handing over

**traditionnel -elle** *adj* traditional, customary

**traducteur -trice** *n* translator

**traduction** *nf* translating; translation

**traduire** *vt* (80) translate; interpret,
explain, express; ~ **en justice** prosecute

**traduisible** *adj* translatable

**trafic** *nm* trafficking, illegal trading;
trading; traffic

**trafiquant -e** *n* trafficker

**trafiquer** *vi* traffic, deal

**tragédie** *nf* tragedy

**tragédien -ienne** *n* tragic actor, tragedian

**tragi-comédie** *nf* tragi-comedy

**tragi-comique** *adj* tragi-comic

**tragique** *nm* tragic side; tragic art; tragic
author; **prendre qch au** ~ make a

tragedy of sth; *adj* tragic

**trahir** *vt* betray; reveal, disclose; distort; let down

**trahison** *nf* treason, betrayal

**train** *nm* train; string, line; pace, rate; ~ **d'atterrissage** landing gear; ~ **de derrière** hindquarters; ~ **de maison** household expenses; ~ **de vie** style of living; **à fond de** ~ at full speed; **aller bon** ~ go at a good speed; **être en** ~ be in good form; **être en** ~ **de faire qch** be doing sth, be occupied in doing sth; **être mal en** ~ be out of sorts, be in poor shape; **mener bon** ~ hustle along; **mener grand** ~ live on a grand scale; **mettre en** ~ get ready, start, get going

**traînage** *nm* hauling; dragging

**traînant** *adj* trailing; languid; drawling

**traînard -e** *n coll* straggler, dawdler

**traînasser** *vi* loiter, dawdle

**traîne** *nf* dawdling; being dragged; dragnet; train (dress); **à la** ~ in tow; *coll* in disorder, in disarray; **pêcher à la** ~ troll

**traîneau** *nm* sledge, sleigh

**traînée** *nf* trail; ground-line (fishing); *coll* slut

**traîner** *vt* pull, drag, haul, draw; drag out; drawl; *vi* trail; lag, trail behind; lie around; loiter, dawdle; drag; ~ **en longueur** drag on and on; ~ **la jambe** limp

**traîneur -euse** *n* straggler

**train-train** *nm coll* routine

**traire** *vt* (9) milk

**trait** *nm* pulling; trace (harness); line, stroke; draught, gulp; deed; *mus* brilliant passage; ~**s** features; ~ **d'esprit** flash of wit; ~ **de génie** stroke of genius; ~ **d'union** hyphen; **avaler d'un** ~ swallow at one go; **avoir** ~ **à** be relevant to, have reference to; **partir comme un** ~ be off like a flash

**traitable** *adj* manageable, tractable

**traitant** *adj* **médecin** ~ doctor treating a case; family doctor

**traite** *nf* stretch, stage; trading; *comm* draft, bill of exchange; milking; ~ **des blanches** white slave traffic; ~ **des noirs** slave trade; **d'une** ~ at a stretch, at one stretch

**traité** *nm* treaty; treatise

**traitement** *nm* treatment; salary, remuneration

**traiter** *vt* treat; negotiate; deal with; ~ **d'un sujet** deal with a subject, write about a subject; ~ **qn de voleur** call s/o a thief

**traiteur** *nm* caterer

**traître -esse** *n* traitor (traitress); **en** ~ treacherously; *adj* treacherous; **ne pas dire un** ~ **mot** not say a single word

**traîtreusement** *adv* treacherously

**traîtrise** *nf* treachery

**trajectoire** *nf* trajectory

**trajet** *nm* journey, trip; *anat* course (nerve, vessel)

**tralala** *nm coll* fuss, exaggerated ceremony

**trame** *nf* woof, weft; plot, intrigue; *fig* web, thread

**tramer** *vt* weave; plot; **se** ~ be afoot, be brewing

**tramontane** *nf* north wind from the mountains

**tranchant** *nm* cutting edge; *adj* cutting, sharp; trenchant

**tranche** *nf* slice; block, group; instalment; slab; edge (book); round (beef); **livre doré sur** ~ gilt-edged book; *coll* **s'en payer une** ~ have a fling

**tranchée** *nf* trench; cutting

**trancher** *vt* cut, slice; decide, settle; ~ **le mot** speak out, speak plainly; *vi* decide; contrast strongly, stand out clearly

**tranchet** *nm* paring knife

**tranchoir** *nm* cutting-board

**tranquille** *adj* calm, quiet, still; peaceful, undisturbed; unworried, untroubled

**tranquillisant** *nm* tranquillizer

**tranquilliser** *vt* reassure, set at rest

**tranquillité** *nf* tranquillity, quiet, calm

**transactionnel -elle** *adj* transactional

**transalpin** *adj* transalpine

**transat** *nm abbr* deck-chair

**transatlantique** *nm* transatlantic liner; deck-chair; *adj* transatlantic

**transbordement** *nm* trans-shipment; transfer of goods

**transborder** *vt* trans-ship; transfer (goods)

**transbordeur** *nm* **(pont)** ~ transporter bridge

**transcendance** *nf* transcendency

**transcendant** *adj* transcendent, surpassing

**transcendantal** *adj* transcendental; speculative

**transcender** *vt* transcend, be superior to

**transcripteur** *nm* transcriber

**transcription** *nf* transcribing, transcription; copy, transcript

**transcrire** *vt* (42) transcribe, write out

**transe** *nf* trance; anxiety; **entrer en** ~ get all worked up

**transférer** *vt* (6) transfer; move, shift

**transfert** *nm* transfer; transference; making over, assignment, conveyance

**transfigurer** *vt* transfigure

**transformateur** *nm* transformer; *adj* (*f* **-trice**) transforming

**transformer** vt transform, change, convert; **se ~** change, turn

**transfuge** nm deserter; n turncoat

**transfuser** vt transfuse

**transgresser** vt transgress, contravene

**transhumance** nf movement of cattle to mountain pastures

**transhumer** vt move to mountain pastures

**transi** adj numb with cold

**transiger** vi (3) compromise

**transir** vt chill; paralyse (with fear, cold)

**transit** nm transit, passage of goods; through traffic

**transitaire** nm forwarding agent; adj through which goods are conveyed

**transiter** vt send through (goods); vi pass through (goods)

**transitif -ive** adj transitive

**transitoire** adj transient

**translation** nf leg transferring, conveyance

**translucide** adj translucent

**translucidité** nf translucence

**transmetteur** nm transmitter

**transmettre** vt (60) transmit; pass on; leg transfer

**transmigrer** vi transmigrate

**transmission** nf transmission; passing on; handing down; mot transmission (gear); leg making over, assignment; communication; **arbre de ~** driving-shaft

**transmuer, transmuter** vt transmute

**transparaître** vi (68) show through, appear

**transparence** nf transparency

**transpercer** vt (4) pierce, transfix

**transpiration** nf perspiring; perspiration; bot transpiration

**transpirer** vi perspire; transpire

**transplanter** vt transplant

**transport** nm transport, conveyance; troop transport, troop-ship; leg transfer, making over; rapture, outburst; **~ s en commun** public transport, US public transportation

**transporter** vt transport, convey; leg transfer; enrapture; **se ~** betake oneself

**transporteur** nm carrier, forwarding agent; transporter; conveyor

**transposer** vt transpose

**transsexuel -uelle** adj transsexual

**transsuder** vi ooze through

**transvaser** vt decant

**transvider** vt pour into another container

**trapèze** nm trapeze; trapezium

**trappe** nf trap; trap-door

**trappeur** nm trapper

**trappiste** nm Trappist monk

**trapu** adj thickset, stocky

**traquenard** nm trap, pitfall, ambush

**traquer** vt hunt down, track down; beat up (game)

**traqueur** nm beater; tracker

**traumatique** adj traumatic

**traumatiser** vt traumatize

**traumatisme** nm traumatism

**travail** nm (pl **-aux**) work; labour; working; piece of work; workmanship, craftsmanship; employment; fermenting; **travaux forcés** hard labour; **attention travaux!** road works ahead!; **avoir le ~ facile** work easily; **sans ~** out of work; **se mettre au ~** get down to work

**travaillé** adj wrought; elaborate

**travailler** vt work, shape, fashion; torment, obsess; stir up, work up; vi work, toil; make efforts; ferment; warp (animals)

**travailleur -euse** n worker; adj hard-working

**travailleuse** nf work-table

**travaillisme** nm pol Labour doctrine

**travailliste** n pol member of Labour party, Labour supporter; adj Labour

**travée** nf span; archi bay; row of seats

**travers** nm fault, quirk, bad habit; **à ~** through; across; **au ~ de** through, right through; **de ~** the wrong way; amiss; **en ~** athwart; **prendre qch de ~** take sth wrongly, put a bad construction on sth; **regarder qn de ~** look askance at s/o

**traverse** nf cross-piece, cross-bar; sleeper (railway); **~ s** obstacles; **chemin de ~** short cut; **se mettre à la ~** oppose, provide obstacles

**traversée** nf crossing, passage

**traverser** vt cross, pass through, traverse, go through; span

**traversier -ière** adj cross, crossing

**traversin** nm bolster

**traversine** nf cross-bar; cross-beam

**travesti** nm disguise; theat man playing woman's part or vice versa; transvestite

**travestir** vt disguise; travesty, parody; **bal travesti** fancy-dress ball; **se ~** dress up (esp as member of opposite sex)

**travestisme** nm transvestism

**travestissement** nm disguise; transvestism

**trayeur -euse** n milker

**trayeuse** nf milking machine

**trébuchant** adj stumbling; **espèces sonnantes et ~ es** hard cash

**trébucher** vt test for weight (coin); vi stumble, totter

**tréfilerie** nf wire-works

**trèfle** nm clover, trefoil; clubs (cards); **(carrefour en) ~** motorway intersection

**tréfonds** nm deepest part, heart; subsoil

**treillage** nm trellis-work, lattice-work

**treillager** vt (3) trellis

**treille** *nf* vine-arbour; climbing-vine; *coll* **jus de la ~** wine

**treillis** *nm* trellis; grating; sacking

**treillisser** *vt* trellis

**treize** *nm* + *adj* thirteen; thirteenth

**treizième** *n* + *adj* thirteenth

**tréma** *nm* diaeresis

**tremblant** *adj* trembling, quivering; unsteady; flickering

**tremble** *nm* aspen

**tremblé** *adj* shaky (handwriting); trembling (voice)

**tremblement** *nm* trembling, shaking; tremor; **~ de terre** earthquake; *coll* **tout le ~** the whole caboodle

**trembler** *vi* tremble, shake; quake; quiver

**trembleur** *nm elect* trembler, vibrator

**tremblote** *nf* **avoir la ~** have the shivers; quake with fear

**trembloter** *vi* tremble slightly, quiver

**trémie** *nf* mill-hopper; loading funnel; hopper

**trémière** *adj f* **rose ~** holly-hock

**trémousser (se)** *v refl* jump up and down; fidget

**trempe** *nf* soaking, dipping; tempering; temper (steel); quality; *coll* scolding

**tremper** *vt* soak, steep, drench; dilute with water; harden, temper; **~ sa soupe** put bread in one's soup; *vi* soak; **~ dans** dabble in; **trempé jusqu'aux os** soaked to the skin

**trempette** *nf* **faire ~** take a quick dip; dip (bread, biscuit, etc) in milk, wine, etc

**tremplin** *nm* spring-board; diving-board

**trentaine** *nf* about thirty; thirties (age)

**trente** *nm* + *adj* thirty; thirtieth; *coll* **se mettre sur son ~ et un** put on one's best clothes

**trentième** *n* + *adj* thirtieth

**trépan** *nm* rock-drill; trepan

**trépanation** *nf* trepanning

**trépaner** *vt* bore, drill; trepan

**trépas** *nm obs* + *lit* death

**trépasser** *vi obs* + *lit* die; **les trépassés** the dead

**trépidant** *adj* agitated, bustling

**trépidation** *nf* agitation, flurry

**trépider** *vi* shake, vibrate

**trépied** *nm* tripod; three-legged stool

**trépigner** *vi* stamp (with rage)

**trépointe** *nf* welt (shoe)

**très** *adv* very, very much; most

**Très-Haut** *nm* Almighty

**trésor** *nm* treasure; treasure-house; **le Trésor** national financial resources

**trésorerie** *nf* treasury; office of treasurer

**trésorier -ière** *n* treasurer

**tressaillement** *nm* start, quiver

**tressaillir** *vi* (14) start, jump; shudder, quiver

**tressauter** *vi* start, jump

**tresse** *nf* plait, braid

**tresser** *vt* plait, braid, weave

**tréteau** *nm* trestle, support; **~x** stage, boards

**treuil** *nm* winch

**trêve** *nf* truce; *coll* **~ de** enough of; **sans ~** unremittingly

**tri** *nm* sorting, sorting out

**triade** *nf* triad

**triage** *nm* sorting; sorting place; **gare de ~** marshalling yard

**triangulaire** *adj* triangular

**tribalisme** *nm* tribalism

**tribord** *nm naut* starboard

**tribu** *nf* tribe

**tribun** *nm Rom hist* tribune; popular orator

**tribunal** *nm* law-court; tribunal; bar (public opinion); **en plein ~** in open court

**tribune** *nf* tribune, platform; forum; gallery (church); **~s** stands

**tribut** *nm* tribute

**tributaire** *adj* tributary

**tricentenaire** *nm* + *adj* tercentenary

**tricher** *vi* cheat

**tricherie** *nf* cheating, trickery

**tricheur -euse** *n* cheat; *adj* cheating

**tricolore** *nm* tricolour; *adj* tricolour, three-coloured

**tricorne** *nm* three-cornered hat

**tricot** *nm* knitting; jumper; **~ (de corps)** (under)vest

**tricoter** *vt* + *vi* knit; *vi sl* walk very fast; pedal

**tricoteuse** *nf* knitting-machine; knitter

**trictrac** *nm* backgammon

**triennal** *adj* triennial; lasting three years

**trier** *vt* sort, sort out

**trifouiller** *vi coll* rummage

**trigonométrie** *nf* trigonometry

**trilingue** *adj* trilingual

**trille** *nm mus* trill

**triller** *vi mus* trill

**trilogie** *nf* trilogy

**trimarder** *vi sl* tramp, be a vagabond

**trimardeur** *nm sl* vagabond

**trimbaler** *vt coll* cart around, carry

**trimer** *vi coll* work hard, slave away

**trimestre** *nm* three-month period, trimester; (school) term; termly pay; termly fees

**trimestriel -ielle** *adj* three-monthly

**tringle** *nf* rod, metal rod; *coll* **se mettre la ~** go without

**trinité** *nf* trinity

**trinquer** *vi* clink glasses; *coll* drink; *sl* get the worst of things

**trinqueur** *nm coll* drinker

**triolet** *nm* triolet; *mus* triplet

**triomphal** *adj* triumphal

**triomphant** adj triumphant

**triomphe** nm triumph; **arc de ~** triumphal arch; **porter qn en ~** carry s/o shoulder high

**triompher** vi triumph; exult; **~ de qch** overcome sth; **~ de qn** get the better of s/o

**tripaille** nf coll offal

**tripatouiller** vt coll tamper with; paw, mishandle

**tripe** nf tripe; coll bowel; inside of cigar; coll **~s** innards; **avoir la ~ royaliste** be a royalist at heart

**triperie** nf tripe-shop

**tripette** nf sl **ne pas valoir ~** be worthless

**triphasé** adj elect three-phase

**tripier -ière** n tripe-dealer

**triple** adj treble, triple; coll very great, extreme

**tripler** vt + vi treble, triple

**triplicata** nm third copy

**triporteur** nm carrier-tricycle

**tripot** nm gambling den

**tripotage** nm shady dealing; coll fiddling about

**tripotée** nf coll thrashing; great quantity

**tripoter** vt coll handle, paw; fiddle with; vulg touch up; vi coll fiddle around; engage in shady dealing

**tripoteur -euse** n coll shady dealer

**triptyque** nm triptych; mot triptyque

**trique** nf cudgel, truncheon

**trisaïeul -e** n (mpl **trisaïeuls** or **trisaïeux**) great-great-grandfather (great-great-grandmother)

**trisannuel -uelle** adj triennial, three yearly

**trisser** vi sl go away; sl **se ~** clear off, escape

**triste** adj sad, sorrowful; poor, wretched; vile; unhappy; gloomy; **c'est une ~ affaire** it's a bad business; **faire ~ mine** look sad; **faire ~ mine à qn** give s/o a poor reception

**tristesse** nf sadness; gloom; dullness, dreariness

**triturer** vt triturate, reduce to powder; handle roughly

**triumvirat** nm triumvirate

**trivial** adj low, coarse

**trivialité** nf coarseness, vulgarity

**troc** nm barter, exchange

**troène** nm bot privet

**trogne** nf coll ruddy, bloated face

**trognon** nm stump (cabbage, etc); core (apple); sl **jusqu'au ~** completely

**Troie** nf Troy

**trois** nm + adj three; third

**trois-étoiles** nm three-star (hotel, restaurant); **Monsieur ~** Mr X

**troisième** n third; nm third floor; nf fourth form; third class; adj third

**trois-mâts** nm three-masted vessel

**trois-quarts** nm child's violin; three-quarter-length coat; sp three-quarter

**trolley** nm coll trolleybus

**trombe** nf whirlwind; **~ d'eau** torrential downpour; **arriver (passer) en ~** arrive (go past) at lightning speed

**trombine** nf sl face

**tromblon** nm blunderbuss

**trombone** nm trombone; trombone-player; paper-clip

**trompe** nf horn; trunk, proboscis; anat tube; eng aspirator

**trompe-la-mort** n invar person who escapes death, dare-devil

**trompe-l'œil** nm invar art trompe l'œil; dummy window; illusion, eyewash

**tromper** vt deceive; cheat; be unfaithful to, betray; outwit; while away; **se ~** be wrong, be mistaken; **se ~ de chemin** take the wrong way

**tromperie** nf deception, deceit; fraud

**trompeter** vt (5) trumpet abroad, shout from the rooftops

**trompette** nf trumpet; nm trumpeter

**trompettiste** n trumpet-player

**trompeur -euse** adj deceptive, misleading

**tronc** nm trunk; stem, body; drum (column); offertory-box; **~ commun** common curriculum (in early years at French secondary school)

**tronçon** nm stub, broken end, stump; section, stage

**tronçonner** vt cut into sections, cut into lengths

**tronçonneuse** nf chain saw

**trône** nm throne

**trôner** vi be enthroned; sit in state; coll lord it

**tronquer** vt truncate; mutilate; curtail

**trop** nm excess; too much, too many; adv too much; **de ~** too much; coll **en ~** in excess; **être de ~** be unwelcome; be superfluous; coll **par ~** too much

**trophée** nm trophy

**tropique** nm tropic

**trop-plein** nm excess liquid; excess; overflow

**troquer** vt exchange, barter

**trotte** nf coll stretch, distance to walk

**trotter** vi trot; coll walk fast; sl **se ~** clear off

**trotteur -euse** n trotter; trotting horse

**trottiner** vi trot about; toddle; walk fast with short steps

**trottinette** nf scooter; coll little car

**trottoir** nm pavement, footpath, US sidewalk; **faire le ~** walk the streets (prostitute)

**trou** *nm* hole; cavity; *coll* dump, backwater; ~ **d'air** air pocket; ~ **du souffleur** prompter's box; **avoir un** ~ **de mémoire** have a lapse of memory; **boucher un** ~ pay back a debt

**troublant** *adj* disturbing, disquieting

**trouble** *nm* confusion; agitation, anxiety; *med* trouble; ~ **s** uprising, revolt; **jeter le** ~ **dans** upset, disturb; *adj* cloudy, turbid; dim; murky; confused; *adv* **voir** ~ not see clearly

**trouble-fête** *n invar* spoil-sport, kill-joy

**troubler** *vt* make cloudy; blur; perturb, worry; disturb, upset; interrupt, interfere with; **se** ~ become cloudy; cloud over; go dim, become blurred; falter; get confused

**trouée** *nf* opening; breach; *geog* gap

**trouer** *vt* make a hole in, perforate

**troufignon** *nm vulg* arse

**troufion** *nm sl* soldier

**trouille** *nf sl* funk, fear

**trou-madame** *nm* (*pl* **trous-madame**) kind of bagatelle

**troupe** *nf* company, band; troupe of actors; soldiery; troup (scouts)

**troupeau** *nm* herd, flock

**troupier** *nm ar* soldier; *coll* trooper

**trousse** *nf* case, kit; **être aux** ~ **s de qn** be on s/o's heels

**trousseau** *nm* outfit, trousseau; ~ **de clefs** bunch of keys

**trousser** *vt* tuck up, turn up; truss (fowl); *coll* dispatch, get through fast; *coll* seduce; *coll* **bien troussé** well done, well executed; **se** ~ tuck up one's clothes

**trouvaille** *nf* lucky find, windfall

**trouver** *vt* find, discover; invent; feel; consider, think; ~ **à qui parler** meet one's match; ~ **à redire** find fault; ~ **bon (mauvais)** approve (disapprove); ~ **la mort** be killed; ~ **le temps long** get bored; **aller** ~ **qn** go and look s/o up, go and see s/o; **bien trouvé** felicitous, clever; **il se trouve que** it so happens that; *coll* **la** ~ **mauvaise** dislike sth, disapprove of sth; **objets trouvés** lost property; **se** ~ be, be situated; turn out, happen; **se** ~ **mieux** feel better

**trouvère** *nm* minstrel (N. France)

**troyen -enne** *adj* Trojan

**truand** *nm* rogue, crook; vagabond (in Middle Ages)

**trublion** *nm* trouble-maker

**truc** *nm coll* knack, skill; trick; thing; what's-it, thingummy

**trucage** *nm see* **truquage**

**truchement** *nm* intermediary, go-between

**truelle** *nf* trowel

**truffe** *nf* truffle; end of dog's nose

**truffer** *vt* stuff with truffles; fill, pack

**truie** *nf* sow

**truisme** *nm* truism

**truite** *nf* trout

**truité** *adj* speckled; crackled; spotted

**trumeau** *nm* pier-glass; chimney-breast, panel; leg of beef

**truquage, trucage** *nm* faking; *cin* trick picture

**truquer** *vt* fake

**tsar** *nm* czar

**tsé-tsé** *nf* (**mouche**) ~ tsetse fly

**tu** *pers pron* you; thee; **être à** ~ **et à toi avec qn** be on familiar terms with s/o

**tuant** *adj* exhausting; trying

**tuba** *nm* diver's respiration tube

**tube** *nm* tube; *sl* top-hat; duct; hit (song, record)

**tubercule** *nm bot* tuber; *med* tubercle

**tuberculeux -euse** *n* tuberculosis sufferer; *adj* tubercular

**tuberculose** *nf* tuberculosis

**tubéreuse** *nf* tuberose

**tubéreux -euse** *adj* tuberous

**tubulaire** *adj* tubular

**tubulure** *nf* tubulature; pipe; nozzle

**tudesque** *adj* Germanic

**tue-mouche(s)** *adj* (**papier**) ~ fly-paper

**tuer** *vt* kill, slay, slaughter; tire out

**tuerie** *nf* slaughter, carnage

**tue-tête (à)** *adv phr* **crier** ~ bawl out, shout at the top of one's voice

**tueur -euse** *n* killer; *nm* slaughterman

**tuf** *nm* tufa; bed-rock, foundation

**tuffeau, tufeau** *nm* calcareous tufa

**tuile** *nf* tile; *coll* misfortune, piece of bad luck

**tuilerie** *nf* tile-works

**tulipe** *nf* tulip; tulip-shaped ornament

**tuméfaction** *nf* swelling, tumefaction

**tuméfier** *vt* tumefy, make swell

**tumeur** *nf* tumour, growth

**tumulaire** *adj* tumular; sepulchral

**tumulte** *nm* uproar, tumult; hubbub

**tumultueux -ueuse** *adj* tumultuous, noisy

**tungstène** *nm* tungsten

**tunique** *nf* tunic

**Tunisie** *nf* Tunisia

**Tunisien -ienne** *n* Tunisian

**tunisien -ienne** *adj* Tunisian

**turbidité** *nf* turbidity, cloudiness

**turbin** *nm sl* work

**turbiner** *vi sl* work

**turbo-alternateur** *nm elect* turbo-alternator

**turbocompresseur** *nm* turbocompressor

**turbomoteur** *nm* turbine; steam turbine

**turbotrain** *nm* train driven by gas turbine

**turbulence** *nf* unruliness; boisterousness; turbulence

**turbulent** *adj* unruly, restless; boisterous; turbulent

**Turc** (*f* **Turque**) *n* Turk; **fort comme un ~** strong as a horse; **tête de ~** whipping-boy

**turc** *nm* Turkish (language); *adj* (*f* **turque**) Turkish

**turf** *nm* race-course

**turfiste** *n* race-goer

**turlupiner** *vt coll* worry, torment

**turlutaine** *nf* constant theme

**turlututu** *interj* fiddlesticks!

**turne** *nf sl* squalid digs; *coll* room, study

**turnep(s)** *nm* kohl-rabi

**Turquie** *nf* Turkey

**turquin** *adj* kind of blue marble

**tussilage** *nm bot* coltsfoot

**tussor** *nm* tussore (silk)

**tutélaire** *adj* tutelary

**tutelle** *nf* guardianship, tutelage; protection

**tuteur -trice** *n* guardian, tutor; *nm hort* support, stake

**tutoyer** *vt* (7) address (s/o) as **tu**, be on familiar terms with

**tutu** *nm* ballet skirt

**tuyau** *nm* pipe; barrel (quill); stalk (corn); tubing, tube; *coll* tip; **~ d'arrosage** hose-pipe; **~ d'incendie** fire-hose

**tuyauter** *vt* goffer; *coll* inform, give a tip to

**tuyauterie** *nf* pipes, pipes and fittings

**tuyère** *nf metal* twyer, blast-pipe, nozzle

**tympan** *nm* ear-drum; *archi* tympanum

**type** *nm* type; pattern; personality; *sl* fellow, bloke

**typhoïde** *nf* + *adj* typhoid

**typhon** *nm* typhoon

**typique** *adj* typical

**typographe** *n* typographer

**typographie** *nf* typography

**typographique** *adj* typographical

**tyran** *nm* tyrant

**tyranneau** *nm* petty tyrant

**tyrannie** *nf* tyranny

**tyrannique** *adj* tyrannical

**tyranniser** *vt* tyrannize

**tyrolien -ienne** *adj* Tyrolean

# U

**ubiquité** *nf* ubiquity

**ukase** *nm* edict, ukase

**ukrainien -ienne** *adj* Ukrainian

**ulcère** *nm* ulcer

**ulcéré** *adj* embittered; ulcerated

**ulcérer** *vt* (6) ulcerate; embitter

**ulcéreux -euse** *adj* ulcerous

**ultérieur** *adj* ulterior; subsequent, later; farther

**ultérieurement** *adv* subsequently, later on

**ultime** *adj* final, ultimate

**ultra** *n pol* extremist; *adv* (*usu* with hyphen) extremely, very, ultra-

**ululement** *nm* hooting, hoot (owl)

**ululer** *vi* hoot (owl)

**Ulysse** *nm* Ulysses

**un** (*f* **-une**) *indef art* (*pl* **des**), *num adj*, *pron* a, an; one; some, someone; **~ à ~** one by one; **~ d'entre nous** one of us; **~ par ~** one by one; *coll* **c'est d' ~ fini!** it really is most polished!; **c'est tout ~** it all comes to the same; **chambre à ~** lit single (bed)room; *coll* **en savoir plus d' ~ e** know a thing or two; *coll* **et d' ~ (e)!** so much for that one!, that's one done (gone)!; **il n'a fait ni ~ e ni deux** he didn't hesitate a moment; **ils sont d' ~ égoïsme!** they are incredibly selfish!; **la ~ e** front page of the newspaper(s); **les ~ s ... les autres** some ... others; **le ~** number one; **l' ~ et l'autre** both; **l' ~ l'autre** each other; *coll* **ne faire qu' ~** be one and the same, be indistinguishable; be hand in glove

**unanime** *adj* unanimous

**unanimité** *nf* unanimity; **à l' ~** unanimously

**uni** *adj* united; even, level, smooth; plain, uniform; equable, calm

**unicorne** *nm* unicorn

**unième** *adj* **vingt** (**trente**, etc) **-et-~** twenty-(thirty-, etc)first

**unificateur -trice** *n* unifier; *adj* unifying

**unification** *nf* unification; standardization; amalgamation

**unifier** *vt* unify; consolidate; standardize; s' ~ become united, unite

**uniforme** *nm* uniform; **grand** ~ full-dress uniform; *coll* **quitter l'** ~ leave the service; *adj* uniform, even, unvarying; consistent

**uniformément** *adv* uniformly; consistently

**uniformisation** *nf* standardization

**uniformiser** *vt* make uniform, standardize

**uniformité** *nf* uniformity

**unijambiste** *n + adj* one-legged (person)

**unilatéral** *adj* one-sided, unilateral

**uniment** *adv* smoothly, evenly, plainly

**union** *nf* union, association; combination; unity; agreement; marriage; **l' ~ fait la force** unity is strength

**unionisme** *nm pol* unionism

**unioniste** *adj* unionist

**unipersonnel** *adj gramm* impersonal

**unique** *adj* only, single, sole; unique, matchless, unrivalled; *coll* priceless; **rue à sens** ~ one-way street; **seul et** ~ one and only

**unir** *vt* unite, combine, join; level, smoothe; ~ **le geste à la parole** suit the action to the word; s' ~ unite, join forces; become level; s' ~ **à qn** marry s/o

**unisexe** *adj invar* unisex

**unisexué** *adj biol* unisexual

**unisson** *nm* unison; **à l'** ~ in unison; in keeping

**unitaire** *adj* unitary; *eccles* Unitarian

**unitarisme** *nm* unitarianism

**unité** *nf* unity, one; unit; consistency, uniformity; (examination) ~ **de valeur** credit; **prix de l'** ~ price per article

**univers** *nm* universe, world

**universaliser** *vt* universalize, make universal

**universalité** *nf* universality

**universel -elle** *adj* universal, worldwide; **homme** ~ man who knows everything; **légataire** ~ residuary legatee

**universitaire** *n* academic; *adj* university, academic; **cité** ~ students' halls of residence

**université** *nf* university

**upériser** *vt* uperize

**urbain** *adj* urban, town; urbane; **central** ~ local telephone exchange

**urbanisation** *nf* town planning, urbanization

**urbaniser** *vt* urbanize; **zone à** ~ area destined for residential occupation; s' ~ become polite, become more polished

**urbanisme** *nm* town planning

**urbaniste** *n* town planner; *adj* urban

**urbanité** *nf* urbanity

**urée** *nf* urea

**urémie** *nf med* uraemia

**uretère** *nm anat* ureter

**urétral** *adj anat* urethral

**urètre** *nm anat* urethra

**urgence** *nf* urgency, urgent nature; emergency (hospital) case; **état d'** ~ state of emergency; **être appelé d'** ~ receive an urgent call; **salle des** ~ s emergency ward; **transporter d'** ~ **un malade à l'hôpital** rush a patient to hospital

**urger** *vi* (3) *coll* be urgent

**urinaire** *adj* urinary

**uriner** *vi* urinate

**urinoir** *nm* urinal

**urique** *adj* uric

**urne** *nf* urn; ~ **de scrutin** ballot box; **aller aux** ~ s go to the polls

**urologie** *nf* urology

**urologue** *n* urologist

**urticaire** *nf* nettle-rash

**us** *nmpl obs* customs; **les** ~ **et coutumes** the ways and customs

**usage** *nm* custom, practice; use, employment; ~ **du monde** good breeding; **à l'** ~ with use; **à l'** ~ **de** for the use of; **à** ~ **s multiples** multi-purpose; **d'** ~ customary, usual; **faire** ~ **de** make use of; **garanti à l'** ~ guaranteed to wear well; **hors d'** ~ worn out; **manquer d'** ~ be lacking in breeding; **à** ~ **externe** for external use only

**usagé** *adj* used, worn; secondhand; **non** ~ new

**usager -ère** *n* user; *adj* everyday, for common use

**usé** *adj* worn, worn-out, shabby; hackneyed, stale

**user** *nm* wear; **être d'un bon** ~ wear well; *vt* use up; wear out; *vi* ~ **de** use, make use of, have recourse to; ~ **de force** resort to force; ~ **de son droit** exercise one's rights; **en** ~ **bien (mal) avec qn** treat s/o well (badly); s' ~ wear, wear away, wear out

**usinage** *nm* machining

**usine** *nf* factory, works, plant, mill

**usiner** *vt* machine, machine-finish; manufacture

**usinier -ière** *n* manufacturer, mill owner

**usité** *adj* used, in current use; **peu** ~ rarely used

**ustensile** *nm* utensil, tool, implement

**usuel -uelle** *adj* usual, customary, everyday

**usufruit** *nm leg* usufruct, life interest

**usuraire** *adj* usurious, exorbitant

**¹usure** *nf* usury

**²usure** *nf* wear and tear; ~ **en magasin** shelf depreciation; *coll* **avoir qn à l'** ~ wear s/o down; **guerre d'** ~ war of attrition; **résister à l'** ~ be resistant to wear

**usurier -ière** *n* usurer; *adj* usurious

**usurpateur -trice** *n* usurper; *adj* usurping

**usurpatoire** *adj* usurpatory

**usurper** *vt* usurp, encroach upon; *vi* ~ **sur** encroach upon

**ut** *nm invar mus* C, do(h)

**utérin** *adj* uterine; **frère** ~ half-brother

**utile** *nm* utility; **joindre l'** ~ **à l'agréable** combine business with pleasure; *adj* useful, of use, serviceable; advisable **charge** ~ carrying capacity; **en temps** ~ in good time; duly; **être** ~ **à qn** be of service to s/o; **prendre toutes les dispositions** ~s take all the necessary steps

**utilement** *adv* usefully, profitably, advantageously

**utilisable** *adj* usable, fit for use, utilizable

**utilisateur -trice** *n* user

**utiliser** *vt* use, utilize, make use of; turn to account, make the best of

**utilitaire** *adj* utilitarian

**utilitarisme** *nm* utilitarianism

**utilité** *nf* utility, usefulness; service; advisability; *theat* bit part; **d'** ~ **publique** of public interest; **n'être d'aucune** ~ be of no earthly use

**utopie** *nf* utopia

**utopique** *adj* utopian

**utopiste** *n* dreamer

**uvulaire** *adj phon* uvular

**uvule** *nf anat* uvula

# V

**va** *third pers pres indic* **aller**

**vacance** *nf* vacancy, vacant post; (mind) vacuity; ~s holidays, vacation; ~s **de neige** winter holidays in the mountains; **entrer en** ~s break up; **en** ~s on holiday; **les grandes** ~s the summer holidays

**vacancier -ière** *n* holiday-maker

**vacarme** *nm* din, noise, row, uproar

**vacation** *nf* sitting (of public officials); *leg* recess; (rights) abeyance; *leg* ~s fees

**vaccin** *nm* vaccine

**vaccine** *nf* cowpox; cowpox vaccination

**vacciner** *vt* vaccinate

**vache** *nf* cow; cowhide; *sl* fat woman; *sl fig* swine; *sl* pig (policeman); ~ **à lait** milch-cow; sucker; *sl* **être** ~ be a swine; *coll* **le plancher des** ~ s dry land, terra firma; **manger de la** ~ **enragée** have a rough time; *naut* **nœud de** ~ granny knot; **parler français comme une** ~ **espagnole** speak dreadful French; **pleurer comme une** ~ cry one's eyes out; *adj sl* mean, disgusting, swinish

**vachement** *adv sl* bloody, damned, tremendously

**vacher** *nm* cowherd, cowman

**vachère** *nf* cowgirl

**vacherie** *nf ar* cowshed; *sl* dirty trick

**vacherin** *nm* type of sweet made with ice-cream and meringue; type of cheese

**vachette** *nf* young cow; calfskin (leather)

**vacillant** *adj* vacillating, wavering; unsteady, uncertain; flickering

**vacillation** *nf* vacillation, wavering; unsteadiness; flickering

**vacillement** *nm see* **vacillation**

**vaciller** *vi* vacillate, waver; be unsteady; be undecided; flicker; stagger, wobble

**va-comme-je-te-pousse (à la)** *adv phr* haphazardly

**vacuité** *nf* vacuity, emptiness

**vadrouille** *nf naut* deck-swab; *coll* **aller en** ~ go on the spree

**vadrouiller** *vi coll* gallivant, knock around, gad about

**vadrouilleur -euse** *n* roamer

**va-et-vient** *nm invar* coming and going; to-and-fro movement, swinging movement; *elect* two-way wiring; *elect* **commutateur** ~ two-way switch; **faire le** ~ **entre** ply between; **porte** ~ swing door

**vagabond -e** *n* tramp, vagrant, vagabond; *adj* vagrant, roving

**vagabondage** *nm* vagrancy

**vagabonder** *vi* tramp, rove, roam, wander

**vagin** *nm anat* vagina

**vagir** *vi* wail, cry

**vagissement** *nm* wailing

¹**vague** *nf* wave; *coll* **faire des ~ s** shock, scandalize

²**vague** *nm* vagueness, imprecision; *adj* vague, indefinite; hazy, dim; sketchy; **quelque ~ ...** some ... or other

³**vague** *nm* emptiness; *adj* empty, vacant; **terrain ~** waste land

**vaguelette** *nf* little wave

**vaguer** *vi* wander, roam

**vaillamment** *adv* valiantly, bravely, courageously

**vaillance** *nf* valour, bravery, courage

**vaillant** *adj* valiant, brave, courageous

**vain** *adj* vain, fruitless, useless; unreal, empty, sham; conceited; **~e gloire** vainglory; **en ~** in vain

**vaincre** *vt* (94) conquer, vanquish, defeat, beat; master, get the better of; **s'avouer vaincu** admit defeat; **se laisser ~ par** give way to; *vi* conquer

**vaincu -e** *n* vanquished person; *adj* vanquished

**vainement** *adv* vainly, fruitlessly, to no purpose

**vainqueur** *nm* victor, conqueror; *sp* winner; *adj m* conquering, victorious

**vair** *nm her* vair; (Cinderella) **pantoufle de ~** glass slipper

**vairon** *nm* minnow; *adj* **aux yeux ~ s** with eyes of different colours

**vaisseau** *nm* ship, vessel; receptacle; (blood) vessel; nave; **~ amiral** flagship; **le ~ fantôme** the Flying Dutchman

**vaisseau-école** *nm* (*pl* **vaisseaux-écoles**) training ship

**vaisselier** *nm* dresser

**vaisselle** *nf* crockery, plates and dishes; **~ d'or (d'argent)** gold (silver) plate; **eau de ~** dishwater; **faire la ~** wash up; **machine à laver la ~** dishwasher

**val** *nm* (*pl* **~s** *or* **vaux**) valley, vale, dale; **par monts et par vaux** up hill and down dale

**valable** *adj* valid, good, cogent

**valence** *nf chem* valency

**valériane** *nf* valerian

**valet** *nm* valet, manservant; support, stand; jack (cards); weight (door); clamp; **~ de chambre** manservant; **~ d'écurie** groom; **~ de ferme** farmhand; **âme de ~** servile nature; **tel maître tel ~** like master like man

**valetaille** *nf pej* menials, varletry

**valétudinaire** *n + adj* valetudinarian

**valeur** *nf* value, worth, price; meaning, import; courage, valour; *comm* **~ s** securities; **avoir de la ~** be of value; *fig* carry weight; **homme de ~** man of ability, man of merit; **mettre en ~** show to advantage; develop, exploit;

**objets de ~** valuables; **sans ~** worthless

**valeureux -euse** *adj* gallant, brave

**valide** *adj* able-bodied, fit; valid

**valider** *vt* validate, authenticate

**validité** *nf* validity

**valise** *nf* suitcase, grip; **~ diplomatique** diplomatic bag

**vallée** *nf* valley

**vallon** *nm* small valley

**vallonné** *adj* undulating

**vallonnement** *nm* foothills; laying out in dells

**valoir** *vt + vi* (95) be worth; deserve, merit; be equal to, be as good as; be valid, hold good; procure, gain; **~ mieux** be better; **à ~ on** account; **autant vaut** one may as well; *coll* **ça se vaut** it's the same either way; *coll* **ça vaut le coup** it's worth it; it's worth trying; **cela ne vaut rien** that's no use, that's not worth anything, that's no good; **cela vaut pour** that goes for; **(en) ~ la peine** be worth it; **faire ~ que** point out that; **faire ~ qch** make the most of sth, set sth to advantage; show off sth, set off sth; emphasize sth; **mieux vaut tard que jamais** better late than never; **ne pas ~ cher** not be worth much; *coll* not be much good; **rien qui vaille** nothing worth mentioning; **se faire ~** make the most of oneself; put oneself forward; **vaille que vaille** for better or for worse

**valoriser** *vt* valorize; stabilize

**valse** *nf* waltz

**valser** *vi* waltz; *coll* **faire ~ qch** send sth flying; **faire ~ qn** do the waltz with s/o; *coll fig* lead s/o a dance

**valseur -euse** *n* waltzer; *nfpl sl* testicles

**valve** *nf* valve

**valvulaire** *adj* valvular

**vamper** *vt coll* vamp

**van** *nm* winnowing-basket; winnowing-machine

**vandale** *n* vandal

**vandalisme** *nm* vandalism

**vanille** *nf* vanilla

**vanillé** *adj* vanilla-flavoured

**vanité** *nf* vanity; conceit; futility, emptiness; **sans ~** without wanting to boast; **tirer ~ de qch** take an empty pride in sth

**vaniteux -euse** *adj* vain, conceited

**vannage** *nm* winnowing

**vanne** *nf* sluice, flood-gate; **~ de décharge** overflow weir; **~ d'entrée** inlet valve; **~ de réglage** regulating valve; **lever les ~s** open the floodgates

**vanneau** *nm* lapwing, peewit

¹**vanner** *vt* winnow; sift; *coll* exhaust, tire out

²**vanner** vt fit sluices to, sluice

**vannerie** nf basket-making; basket-work

**vanneur -euse** n winnower

**vannier** nm basket-maker

**vannure** nf chaff, winnowings

**vantail** nm leaf (of door)

**vantard -e** n boaster, braggart; adj boasting

**vantardise** nf bragging, boasting; boast

**vanter** vt praise, extol, vaunt; **se ~** brag, boast; **il ne s'en vante pas** he keeps quiet about it

**vanterie** nf bragging, boasting

**va-nu-pieds** n beggar, barefooted vagabond

**vapeur** nm steamship; nf vapour; steam; haze; **~s** fumes; obs vapours; **à la ~** by steam; **à toute ~** at full speed; **bateau à ~** steamship; cul **cuire à la ~** steam; **machine à ~** steam engine

**vaporeux -euse** adj vaporous; misty; hazy; nebulous

**vaporisateur** nm atomizer, spray

**vaporiser** vt vaporize; atomize; spray; **se ~** vaporize, turn to vapour; spray oneself

**vaquer** vi be vacant; be in recess; **~ à** attend to, concern oneself with, go about

**varappe** nf rock-climbing

**varapper** vi climb rock-faces

**varappeur** nm rock-climber

**varech** nm seaweed, wrack

**vareuse** nf sailor's jersey, jumper; mil tunic

**variabilité** nf variability, changeableness

**variable** adj variable, changeable

**variant** adj variable, fickle

**variante** nf variant

**varice** nf varicose vein

**varicelle** nf chicken-pox

**varié** adj varied, varying; variegated; miscellaneous

**varier** vt vary, change; diversify; variegate; vi vary, change; differ in opinion

**variété** nf variety, diversity; choice, range; **spectacle de ~s** variety show

**variole** nf smallpox

**variolé** adj pock-marked

**variqueux -euse** adj varicose

**Varsovie** nf Warsaw

**vasculaire** adj vascular

¹**vase** nm vase; vessel; receptacle; **~ de nuit** chamber pot; **en ~ clos** in isolation

²**vase** nf mud, slime, sludge

**vasectomie** nf vasectomy

**vaseux -euse** adj muddy, slimy; sl washed-out, off-colour; woolly

**vasistas** nm fanlight

**vasomoteur -trice** adj vasomotor

**vasouiller** vi sl be at sea, be all confused

**vasque** nf basin (fountain); bowl

**vaste** adj vast, immense; spacious

**vaticiner** vi lit + pej prophesy

**va-tout** nm invar one's whole stake; **jouer son ~** stake one's all

**vaudou** nm voodoo

**vau-l'eau (à)** adv phr with the stream; **aller ~** go to rack and ruin, degenerate

**vaurien -ienne** n good-for-nothing, lay-about

**vautour** nm vulture

**vautrer (se)** v refl wallow, sprawl

**va-vite (à la)** adv phr fait **~** rushed, botched

**veau** nm calf; veal; calf-leather; sl fool; **~ marin** seal; **le ~ gras** the fatted calf; **pleurer comme un ~** blubber, cry like a baby; **reliure en ~** calf binding; **ris de ~** sweetbread; **s'étendre comme un ~** sprawl, loll about

**vecteur** nm carrier (disease); vehicle

**vécu** p part **vivre**; adj experienced; true-to-life

**vedette** nf sentry, scout; cin star; motor-boat, patrol boat, launch; **en ~** in the limelight; **imprimer en ~** print in bold type, make stand out; **mettre en ~** highlight

**végétal** nm plant; adj vegetable, plant

**végétarien -ienne** n + adj vegetarian

**végétarisme** nm vegetarianism

**végétatif -ive** adj vegetative; cabbage-like (existence)

**végétation** nf vegetation; coll **~s** adenoids

**végéter** vi (6) vegetate

**véhémence** nf vehemence

**véhément** adj vehement, violent

**véhiculaire** adj vehicular

**véhicule** nm vehicle

**véhiculer** vt transport, carry

**veille** nf watching, sitting up, staying up; late night, vigil; eve, day before; coll **ce n'est pas demain la ~** not likely, it won't be for ages; **être à la ~ de** be on the brink of; **la ~ au soir** the evening before

**veillée** nf evening; watching, night nursing, vigil

**veiller** vt watch over, sit up with, attend to; **~ un mort** keep vigil over a dead body; vi sit up, stay awake, keep watch; **~ à** see to, watch over; **~ à ses intérêts** attend to one's interests

**veilleur** nm watcher, guard; **~ de nuit** night watchman

**veilleuse** nf night-light; pilot-light (heater, etc); **mettre en ~** turn low (gas); dim (lights); shelve, put off (plans, etc)

**veinard -e** *n coll* lucky person; *adj* lucky

**veine** *nf* vein; seam; inspiration; *fig* luck; **avoir de la ~** be lucky; **avoir une ~ de cocu** have the devil's own luck; **c'est bien ma ~!** just my luck!; **coup de ~** stroke of luck; **être en ~ de faire qch** be in the mood for sth; **porter ~ à** bring good luck to

**veiner** *vt* vein, grain

**veineux -euse** *adj* veinous, veined

**veinure, vêlement** *nf* veining

**vêlage** *nm* calving

**vélaire** *adj ling* velar

**vêlement** *nm see* **vêlage**

**vêler** *vi* calve

**vélin** *nm* vellum

**velléitaire** *adj* erratic, hesitant

**velléité** *nf* whim, fancy, impulse; slight desire; half-hearted attempt

**vélo** *nm coll* bike; **aller à (en) ~** cycle; **faire du ~** cycle

**véloce** *adj lit* swift

**vélocité** *nf* speed, velocity

**vélodrome** *nm* cycle-racing track

**vélomoteur** *nm* light motor-cycle

**vélomotoriste** *nm* rider of light motor-cycle

**vélo-pousse** *nm* bicycle rickshaw

**velours** *nm* velvet; **~ côtelé (à côtes)** corduroy velvet; **~ de coton** velveteen; **c'est du ~** it's delicious; *sl* it's a pushover; **faire patte de ~** draw in claws (cat); *fig* show the velvet glove; **jouer sur le ~** take no risks, act without risks

**velouté** *nm* velvet quality, softness; bloom (fruit); *cul* thick soup; *adj* velvety, downy

**velouter** *vt* make like velvet, give a velvety appearance to

**velouteux -euse** *adj* velvety

**veloutier** *nm* velvet-maker

**Velpeau** *nf* **bande ~** crape bandage

**velu** *adj* hairy, shaggy

**velum, vélum** *nm* awning

**venaison** *nf* venison

**vénal** *adj* venal; mercenary

**vénalité** *nf* venality

**venant** *nf* **à tous ~s (à tout ~)** to all and sundry

**vendable** *adj* saleable, marketable

**vendange** *nf* grape-harvest; vintage; **faire les ~s (la ~)** gather in the grapes

**vendanger** *vt + vi* (3) gather, harvest (grapes)

**vendangeur -euse** *n* wine-harvester; *nf* aster

**vendémiaire** *nm hist* first month of the French Republican calendar (September to October)

**vendeur -euse** *n* seller, vendor; salesman (saleswoman), shop assistant, *US* sales clerk

**vendre** *vt* sell; *fig* betray, give away; **à ~** for sale; **se ~** sell, be sold; **se ~ comme des petits pains** sell like hot cakes

**vendredi** *nm* Friday; **~ saint** Good Friday

**vendu** *nm* traitor; *sl* double-crosser

**venelle** *nf* alley

**vénéneux -euse** *adj* poisonous

**vénérer** *vt* (6) venerate, reverence

**vénerie** *nf* venery, hunting

**vénérien -ienne** *adj* venereal

**vengeance** *nf* revenge; retribution; **crier ~** cry aloud for vengeance; **tirer ~ de** be revenged for

**venger** *vt* (3) avenge; **se ~** take revenge, be revenged

**vengeur -euse** *n* avenger; *adj* avenging

**venimeux -euse** *adj* poisonous; spiteful

**venin** *nm* venom, poison; spite

**venir** *vi* (96) come; originate; occur, happen; grow, thrive; *fig* **~ à** happen to; **~ au monde** be born; *fig* **~ de** have just; **d'où vient que ...?** how is it that ...?; **en ~ à faire qch** come to the point of doing sth; be reduced to doing sth; **en ~ aux mains** come to blows; **faire ~** summon, call, send for; (crops) grow; **je vous vois ~** I see what your game is; **la semaine qui vient** next week; **ne faire qu'aller et ~** be right back, be just a moment; **où veut-il en ~?** what is he driving at?; *fig* **voir ~** wait and see

**Venise** *nf* Venice

**vénitien -ienne** *adj* Venetian

**vent** *nm* wind; scent; *med* flatulence; **~ debout** head wind; **~ du nord (du sud, etc)** north (south, etc) wind; **aller (faire) ~ arrière** sail before the wind; **au ~** in the wind; **au ~ de** to the leeward of; *fig* **avoir le ~ en poupe** be on a successful course; *coll* have everything going for one; **avoir ~ de** get wind of; suspect; **ce n'est que du ~** it's all hot air; **côté du ~** weather side; **coup de ~** gust of wind; **donner ~ à** give vent to; **en coup de ~** hurriedly; **en plein ~** in the open air; **être dans le ~** be with it, be up-to-date; **faire du ~** be windy; **mettre au ~** hang out to dry; **prendre le ~** catch the wind; *coll* see how the land lies; **quel bon ~ vous amène?** how nice to see you!; **tomber sous le ~** drop to leeward; **virer à tout ~** be a weathercock

**vente** *nf* sale, selling; tree-felling; timber; **~ aux enchères** auction; **~ par correspondance** mail-order business; **en ~** for sale; **en ~ chez** for sale at; **en ~ libre** unrationed; **mettre en ~**

put up for sale, put on sale; **point de ~** sales outlet; **salle des ~s** auction rooms

**venter** *v impers* blow, be windy

**venteux -euse** *adj* windy

**ventilateur** *nm* ventilator; **~ électrique** electric fan

**ventiler** *vt* ventilate, air

**ventôse** *nm hist* sixth month of the French Republican calendar (February to March)

**ventouse** *nf med* cupping-glass; suction pad; air-hole, air-vent; **faire ~** adhere by suction; *coll* **voiture ~** car that stays parked in one spot

**ventre** *nm* abdomen, belly; paunch; womb; bulge; **~ à terre** at full speed, at full tilt; **à plat ~** flat on one's face, flat on the ground; **avoir le ~ creux** have an empty stomach; **avoir mal au ~** have a bellyache; *coll* **avoir qch dans le ~** have guts; **faire ~** bulge out; **prendre du ~** grow stout; **se mettre à plat ~ devant qn** grovel before s/o; **serrer le ~** tighten one's belt

**ventricule** *nm* ventricle

**ventriloque** *n* ventriloquist

**ventru** *adj* portly, corpulent

**venu -e** *n* comer; **le dernier ~** the last to arrive; **le premier ~** the first arrival; anybody; **un nouveau ~** a newcomer; *adj* **bien ~** sturdy; pleasing; **mal ~** stunted, displeasing

**venue** *nf* coming, arrival; growth

**vêpres** *nfpl eccles* vespers, evensong

**ver** *nm* worm; maggot, grub, mite; **~ à soie** silkworm; **~ de terre** earthworm; **~ luisant** glow-worm; **~ solitaire** tapeworm; **nu comme un ~** stark naked; **rongé (piqué) des ~s** worm-eaten; **tirer les ~s du nez à qn** worm secrets out of s/o

**véracité** *nf* veracity, truthfulness

**verbalement** *adv* verbally, by word of mouth

**verbalisation** *nf leg* entry of charge; *coll* taking down of particulars

**verbaliser** *vi* draw up an official report; *coll* take down particulars; verbalize

**verbe** *nm* tone of voice, speech; verb; **avoir le ~ haut** talk in a loud voice; talk in a peremptory manner

**verbeux -euse** *adj* verbose, wordy, prolix

**verbomanie** *nf* verbal diarrhoea

**verbosité** *nf* verbosity

**verdâtre** *adj* greenish

**verdelet -ette** *adj* tart (wine); hale and hearty

**verdeur** *nf* greenness; tartness; vigour

**verdier** *nm* greenfinch

**verdir** *vt* make green, colour green; *vi* grow green, turn green

**verdissement** *nm* turning green, going green

**verdoiement** *nm* turning green

**verdoyant** *adj* green, verdant

**verdoyer** *vi* (7) become green

**verdure** *nf* greenness, greenery; vegetables for salad

**véreux -euse** *adj* worm-eaten, maggoty; *coll* fishy, dubious

**verge** *nf* switch, wand, rod, cane; shank (anchor); *anat* penis; *coll bot* **~ d'or** golden rod

**vergé** *adj* laid (paper); worm-eaten

**verger** *nm* orchard

**vergette** *nf* small cane, switch

**verglacé** *adj* icy

**verglas** *nm* coating of ice, black ice

**vergogne** *nf obs* shame; **sans ~** shameless(ly)

**vergue** *nf naut* yard

**véridique** *adj* truthful, veracious

**vérificateur -trice** *n* checker, examiner, verifier

**vérification** *nf* inspection, check, checking, examination

**vérifier** *vt* check, verify, examine, inspect; *comm* audit; confirm, prove

**vérin** *nm mech* jack

**véritable** *adj* true; genuine, real

**vérité** *nf* truth; fact; authenticity; likeness; **à la ~** as a matter of fact; **c'est la ~** it's the truth; it's a fact; **dire ses (quatre) ~s à qn** tell s/o a few home truths; **en ~** actually, verily; **être en dessous de la ~** fall short of the truth

**verjus** *nm* verjuice

**vermeil** *nm* silver-gilt; *adj* (*f* **-eille**) vermilion, rosy, bright red

**vermicelle** *nm* vermicelli

**vermicide** *nm* vermicide; *adj* vermicidal

**vermiculé** *adj* vermiculated

**vermillon** *nm* vermilion, bright red

**vermine** *nf* vermin

**vermineux -euse** *adj* infested with vermin, verminous

**vermoulu** *adj* worm-eaten; decrepit

**vermoulure** *nf* worm-hole

**vermout(h)** *nm* vermouth

**verni** *adj* varnished; (leather) patent; *coll* lucky

**vernir** *vt* varnish, lacquer, japan

**vernis** *nm* varnish, polish, gloss; veneer; **~ à ongles** nail varnish; **~ au tampon** French polish; **~ gras** oil varnish

**vernissage** *nm* varnishing; japanning; private viewing at opening of exhibition

**vernisser** *vt* glaze

**vernisseur -euse** *n* varnisher

**vernissure** *nf* varnishing; glazing

**vérole** *nf coll* syphilis, pox; **petite ~** smallpox

**véronique** *nf* veronica

**verre** *nm* glass; glassful; lens; ~ **à boire** drinking glass, tumbler; ~ **à dents** tooth glass; ~ **à glace** plate glass; ~ **à pied** stemmed glass; ~ **ballon** brandy balloon; ~ **dépoli** frosted glass; ~ **grossissant** magnifying glass; **boire un** ~ have a drink; **papier de** ~ sandpaper; **porter des** ~ **s** wear glasses

**verrerie** *nf* glassware; glass-works

**verrier** *nm* glassmaker, glassblower; artist in stained glass

**verrière** *nf* glass casing; glass roof; glass wall

**verroterie** *nf* glass trinkets, glass beads

**verrou** *nm* bolt, bar; **être sous les** ~ **s** be in custody; **fermer au** ~ bolt

**verrouillage** *nm* bolting, locking; stop

**verrouiller** *vt* bolt, lock; stop; lock up

**verrue** *nf* wart, verruca

**verruqueux -euse** *adj* warty

¹**vers** *nm* verse, line of verse; *pl* poetry

²**vers** *prep* towards; approximately, about (time); in the area of

**versant** *nm* slope, hill-side, bank

**versatile** *adj* fickle, changing, changeable

**versatilité** *nf* inconstancy, fickleness

**verse** *nf* beating down (corn); **pleuvoir à** ~ **pour** with rain

**versé** *adj* versed, experienced

**Verseau** *nm astrol* Aquarius

**versement** *nm* pouring; payment, deposit

**verser** *vt* pour, pour out; spill; shed (blood, tears); overturn, upset; pay in, deposit; flatten, beat down (corn); *mil* incorporate; *vi* overturn; be laid flat (corn); ~ **dans** drift into, fall into

**verset** *nm* verse (Bible)

**verseur** *adj m* pouring

**verseuse** *nf* coffee-pot

**versificateur -trice** *n* versifier

**versifier** *vt* + *vi* versify

**version** *nf* version, account; translation, unseen; ~ **anglaise** (film) dubbed into English

**verso** *nm* reverse, back, verso; **voir au** ~ see overleaf

**vert** *nm* green; **prendre qn sans** ~ catch s/o napping; *adj* green; unripe; vigorous; sharp; acid, tart (wine); unroasted (coffee); **en raconter des** ~ **es** tell some crude stories; **en voir des** ~ **es et des pas mûres** have a rough time; **langue** ~ **e** slang

**vert-de-gris** *nm* verdigris

**vertébral** *adj* vertebral; **colonne** ~ **e** spine

**vertèbre** *nf anat* vertebra

**vertébré** *adj* vertebrate

**vertical** *adj* vertical, perpendicular, upright

**verticale** *nf* vertical; vertical position

**vertige** *nm* vertigo; dizziness, giddiness; **avoir le** ~ feel dizzy; have no head for heights; **cela me donne le** ~ it makes me feel giddy

**vertigineux -euse** *adj* vertiginous, dizzy; breakneck

**vertigo** *nm vet* staggers

**vertu** *nf* virtue; chastity; property; *obs* valour; *coll* **ce n'est pas une** ~ she's no angel; **en** ~ **de** by virtue of; **faire de nécessité** ~ make a virtue of necessity

**vertueux -ueuse** *adj* virtuous; chaste

**verve** *nf* animation, zest, verve; **être en** ~ be in excellent form

**verveine** *nf* verbena

**verveux -euse** *adj* lively, animated

**vésicule** *nf* vesicle, bladder; ~ **biliaire** gall-bladder

**vespasienne** *nf* public urinal

**vessie** *nf* bladder; **prendre des** ~ **s pour des lanternes** believe the moon is made of green cheese

**vestale** *nf* vestal virgin

**veste** *nf* jacket; **retourner sa** ~ be a turncoat; *coll* **tomber la** ~ take off one's jacket

**vestiaire** *nm* cloak-room; changing-room; clothes-locker

**vestibule** *nm* hall, lobby, vestibule

**vestige** *nm* trace, vestige; remains

**vestimentaire** *adj* vestimentary

**veston** *nm* jacket; ~ **croisé (droit)** double-breasted (single-breasted) jacket; **complet** ~ lounge suit

**Vésuve** *nm* Vesuvius

**vêtement** *nm* garment, article of clothing; ~ **s** clothes

**vétérinaire** *n* veterinary surgeon, *coll* vet; *adj* veterinary

**vétille** *nf* trifle, bagatelle

**vêtir** *vt* (97) clothe, dress; **se** ~ get dressed

**vétuste** *adj* decrepit, ancient

**vétusté** *nf* decrepitude, decay

**veuf** *nm* widower; *adj* (*f* **veuve**) widowed

**veule** *adj* soft, flabby, weak, sluggish

**veulerie** *nf* slackness, sluggishness

**veuvage** *nm* widowhood; widowerhood

**veuve** *nf* widow

**vexant** *adj* annoying, provoking

**vexation** *nf* humiliation, mortification

**vexatoire** *adj* vexatious, oppressive

**vexer** *vt* annoy, vex, provoke, irritate; **se** ~ **de qch** be annoyed, offended about sth

**viabilisé** *adj* **terrain** ~ site with roads, mains, drainage, etc

**viabiliser** *vt* put in roads, drains, etc (on site)

¹**viabilité** *nf* viability

# viabilité

²**viabilité** *nf* practicability (road); development (site)

¹**viable** *adj* capable of living, viable

²**viable** *adj* fit for traffic

**viaduc** *nm* viaduct

**viager** *nm* life interest, life annuity; **mettre en ~** invest so as to bring in annuity for life; *adj* (*f* -**ère**) for life

**viande** *nf* meat, flesh

**viatique** *nm eccles* last sacrament

**vibrant** *adj* vibrating, vibrant; stirring, rousing

**vibrateur** *nm* vibrator

**vibratoire** *adj* vibratory

**vibrer** *vi* vibrate

**vibromasseur** *nm* vibrator (massage)

**vicaire** *nm* curate; **~ de Dieu** vicar of Christ, Pope

**vicariat** *nm* vicariate; = curacy

**vice** *nm* vice, depravity; defect; fault

**vice-amiral** *nm* vice-admiral

**vice-chancelier** *nm* vice-chancellor

**vice-gérant -e** *n* assistant manager

**vice-présidence** *nf* vice-presidency

**vice-roi** *nm* viceroy

**vicié** *adj* vitiated, corrupt, tainted; polluted

**vicier** *vt* corrupt, spoil, pollute

**vicieux -ieuse** *adj* depraved; faulty, imperfect; restive (horse)

**vicinal** *adj* local (road, path)

**vicomte** *nm* viscount

**vicomtesse** *nf* viscountess

**victime** *nf* victim

**victoire** *nf* victory; **crier (chanter) ~** triumph, crow victory; **remporter la ~** gain the victory

**victorien -ienne** *adj* Victorian

**victorieux -ieuse** *adj* victorious

**victuailles** *nfpl* victuals

**vidage** *nm* emptying; gutting

**vidange** *nf* emptying, draining; *mot* oil-change; **~ s** night-soil; sludge

**vidanger** *vt* (3) empty, drain

**vidangeur** *nm* cesspool-emptier

**vide** *nm* empty space, vacuum, blank; void; **à ~** empty; **emballage sous ~** vacuum packing; *coll* **faire le ~ autour de qn** isolate s/o; **regarder dans le ~** stare into space; **son départ laisse un ~** his departure creates a gap; **taper dans le ~** miss the mark; *adj* empty; vacant, unoccupied; void; **~ de sens** devoid of meaning; **revenir les mains ~ s** return empty-handed

**vide-ordures** *nm invar* rubbish-chute

**vide-poches** *nm invar* receptacle (for odds and ends)

**vider** *vt* empty; clear out; vacate; drain; end, settle; draw (poultry); clean (fish); *coll* exhaust; *coll* dismiss, chuck out; ruin; *cóll* **~ les lieux** clear out; *coll*

**~ son sac** get sth off one's chest; **se ~** become empty, empty

**vie** *nf* life, existence; lifetime; living; **à ~** for life; **avoir la ~ dure** be hard to kill, die hard; **changer de ~** change one's way of life; **de toute sa ~** all his life; **donner la ~ à** give birth to; **en ~** alive; **faire la ~** lead a fast life; **femme de mauvaise ~** prostitute; **il y va de la ~** it's a matter of life and death; **jamais de la ~** ! never!, not on your life!; **mener la grande ~** live it up; **niveau de ~** standard of living; **rendre la ~ dure à qn** make things tough for s/o; **sans ~** lifeless

**vieil** *adj see* **vieux**

**vieillard** *nm* old man

**vieille** *adj see* **vieux**

**vieillerie** *nf* old thing, out-of-date thing, old junk

**vieillesse** *nf* old age; *coll* old people; **bâton de ~** support in old age

**vieilli** *adj* grown old; old-looking; old-fashioned

**vieillir** *vt* make old; age, make look old; *vi* grow old; age; become out-of-date

**vieillissement** *nm* growing old, ageing; making old

**vieillot -otte** *adj* quaint, old-fashioned

**vielle** *nf ar* ancient stringed instrument

**Vienne** *nf* Vienna (Austria); Vienne (France)

**viennois** *adj* Viennese

**vierge** *nf* virgin, maid; **la Sainte Vierge** the Blessed Virgin; *adj* virgin; unsoiled, pure; empty, blank

**vietnamien -ienne** *adj* Vietnamese

**vieux** (*f* **vieille**) *n* old man (old woman); *coll* father (mother); **mon ~** old chap; **un ~ de la vieille** one of the old brigade; *adj* (**vieil**) (*f* **vieille**) old, elderly, aged; ancient; **~ jeu** old-fashioned; *coll* **prendre un coup de ~** get old all of a sudden; **se faire ~** be getting on in years; **une vieille fille** an old maid; **un ~ garçon** a bachelor; **vivre ~** live to a ripe old age

**vif** *nm* leg living person; quick; **avoir les nerfs à ~** be all on edge; **blessé au ~** stung to the quick; **le ~ de la question** the heart of the matter; **pêcher au ~** fish with live bait; **sur le ~** from (real) life; *adj* (*f* **vive**) alive, living; animated; quick, lively, bright; vivid; keen, intense; brisk, sharp, hasty; **chaux vive** quicklime; **de vive voix** by word of mouth; **eau vive** running water, spring water; **haie vive** quickset hedge

**vif-argent** *nm invar* quicksilver, mercury

**vigie** *nf* look-out; watch-tower; observation box

**vigilant** *adj* vigilant, alert, watchful

**vigile** *nm* watchman; *nf eccles* vigil

**vigne** *nf* vine; vineyard; ~ **vierge** Virginia creeper; *coll* **être dans les** ~ **s du Seigneur** be drunk

**vigneron -onne** *n* vine-grower

**vignette** *nf* vignette; text illustration; small label; *mot* tax label

**vignoble** *nm* vineyard; vine-growing area

**vigogne** *nf* vicuna; vicuna wool

**vigoureux -euse** *adj* vigorous, strong, sturdy

**vigueur** *nf* vigour, strength; **entrer en** ~ come into effect; **en** ~ in force

**vil** *adj* low, mean, base; cheap; **à** ~ **prix** dirt cheap

**vilain -e** *n* rogue, villain; naughty boy (girl); *hist* villein; *coll* **il y aura du** ~ there's trouble brewing; *adj* ugly; nasty, unpleasant; low, mean; shabby, sordid; **il fait (un)** ~ **(temps)** the weather's filthy; *sl* **un** ~ **coco** a nasty piece of work

**vilebrequin** *nm* brace, brace and bit; *mech* crankshaft

**vilenie** *nf* mean trick, vile action

**vilipender** *vt* vilify, abuse; run down

**villageois -e** *n* villager; *adj* village, country

**ville** *nf* town, city; ~ **d'eaux** spa; **à la** ~ in town (as opposed to country); **costume de** ~ lounge suit; **dîner en** ~ dine out; **en** ~ in town; **hôtel de** ~ town hall

**ville-dortoir** *nf* (*pl* **villes-dortoirs**) dormitory town

**villégiature** *nf* stay in the country, holiday in the country; **en** ~ on holiday

**ville-satellite** *nf* (*pl* **villes-satellites**) satellite town

**vin** *nm* wine; ~ **cacheté** better-quality wine; ~ **chaud** mulled wine; ~ **cuit** aperitif wine; ~ **de marque** fine wine, vintage wine; ~ **de messe** communion wine; ~ **mousseux** sparkling wine; ~ **ouvert** carafe wine; **avoir le** ~ **triste (gai)** be sad (merry) when drunk; **cuver son** ~ sleep it off; **entre deux** ~ **s** half seas over, tight; **être pris de** ~ be drunk; **quand le** ~ **est tiré, il faut le boire** it's too late to draw back now; **mettre de l'eau dans son** ~ water one's wine; *coll fig* reduce one's expectations; **offrir un** ~ **d'honneur à qn** hold a reception in s/o's honour; **tache de** ~ strawberry mark

**vinaigre** *nm* vinegar

**vinaigrer** *vt* add vinegar to

**vinaigrerie** *nf* vinegar factory; vinegar trade

**vinaigrette** *nf* French dressing, oil and vinegar

**vinaigrier** *nm* vinegar manufacturer; vinegar-cruet

**vinasse** *nf coll* poor wine

**vindas** *nm naut* windlass

**vindicatif -ive** *adj* vindictive

**viner** *vt* fortify, add alcohol to

**vineux -euse** *adj* the colour of red wine; wine-flavoured

**vingt** *nm* + *adj invar* twenty, a score; **le** ~ **mars** 20 March; **les années** ~ the twenties; **trois heures moins** ~ twenty to three; *coll* ~ **-deux (les flics)!** look out!

**vingtaine** *nf* a score, about twenty

**vingtième** *n* + *adj* twentieth

**vinicole** *adj* wine-growing, wine-producing

**vinyle** *nm* vinyl

**vinylique** *adj* of vinyl

**vioc, vioque** *adj sl* old

**viol** *nm* rape; violation

**violacé** *adj* purplish-blue

**violateur -trice** *n* infringer, transgressor; violator

**violation** *nf* violation; infringement

**violâtre** *adj* purplish

**viole** *nf mus* viol

**violemment** *adv* violently

**violence** *nf* violence, force; **faire** ~ **à qch** violate sth; **faire** ~ **à qn** do violence to s/o; **faire subir des** ~ **s à une femme** assault a woman; **se faire une douce** ~ agree willingly to sth after a show of resistance; **se faire** ~ go against one's feelings

**violenter** *vt* do violence to; rape

**violer** *vt* violate; transgress; break (oath); rape

**violet** *nm* violet colour; *adj* (*f* **-ette**) violet, purple

**violette** *nf bot* violet

**violeur** *nm* rapist

**violiste** *n* viol-player

**violon** *nm* violin; violin-player; *sl* lock-up cells; ~ **d'Ingres** sideline; *fig* **accordez vos** ~ s make sure you all agree on your story; *sl* **c'est comme si on pissait dans un** ~ it's a waste of breath; **payer les** ~ s pay the piper

**violoncelle** *nm* cello; cello-player

**violoncelliste** *n* cellist

**violoneux** *nm* fiddler

**violoniste** *n* violinist

**viorne** *nf bot* viburnum

**vipère** *nf* viper, adder; *coll fig* snake

**vipérin** *adj* viperish

**virage** *nm* curve, turning, bend; cornering, swinging round; changing of colour; *naut* tacking; change of opinion

**virée** *nf coll* trip, outing

**virement** *nm* turning; *naut* tacking; transfer (banking)

**virer** *vt* turn over; transfer (banking); *phot* tone; *coll* chuck out; *vi* turn; *naut* tack, veer; change colour; bank (plane)

**virevolte** *nm* spinning round, half turn; *fig* volte-face

**virevolter** *vi* spin round, wheel round suddenly

**virginité** *nf* virginity, maidenhood

**virgule** *nf* comma; decimal point

**viril** *adj* virile; male; **l'âge ~** manhood; **parties ~ es** male sex organs

**viriliser** *vt* make virile

**virilité** *nf* virility; manhood; manliness

**virole** *nf* ferrule; *mech* collar, sleeve

**virtuel -uelle** *adj* virtual

**virtuose** *n* virtuoso

**virtuosité** *nf* virtuosity

**vis** *nf* screw; **~ à droite (à gauche)** right-handed (left-handed) screw; **~ à papillon** wing screw; **~ de réglage** adjusting screw; **mot ~ platinées** contact points; **~ sans tête** grub screw; **escalier à ~** spiral staircase; **pas de ~** thread; *fig* **serrer la ~ à qn** be very strict with s/o

**visa** *nm* visa; certificate

**visage** *nm* face, countenance; aspect; **à deux ~s** two-faced; **à ~ découvert** with one's face uncovered; barefacedly; **faire bon ~** smile in adversity; **faire bon ~ à qn** be amiable with s/o; **se faire le ~** make one's face up; **voir les choses sous leur vrai ~** see things in their true light

**visagiste** *n* beautician

**vis-à-vis** *nm* person opposite; partner (cards); *adv* opposite; *prep* **~ de** facing, opposite; with regard to, with respect to

**viscéral** *adj* visceral; deep-seated

**viscères** *nmpl* viscera, entrails

**viscosité** *nf* viscosity, stickiness

**visée** *nf* aiming; aim, end; **homme à grandes ~s** ambitious man

¹**viser** *vt* aim at, take aim at; refer to; take a sight on; *fig* aspire to; *sl* look at; *vi* aim

²**viser** *vt* put a visa in; countersign; stamp

**viseur** *nm* sight; viewfinder

**visibilité** *nf* visibility

**visible** *adj* visible; obvious, perceptible; *coll* able to receive visitors

**visière** *nf* vizor, eye-shade; peak (cap); gun-sight; **mettre sa main en ~** shade one's eyes with one's hand; **rompre en ~ à (avec) qn** quarrel violently with s/o; contradict s/o violently

**vision** *nf* vision, eyesight; dream, fancy; sight, view; *cin* **en première ~** first showing

**visionnaire** *n* visionary, dreamer

**visionner** *vt cin* view, preview

**visionneuse** *nf cin + phot* viewer

**visite** *nf* visit; call; inspection, examination; **~ dirigée (accompagnée)** conducted tour; **carte de ~** visiting card; *leg* **droit de ~** right of access; *naut* right of search; **être en ~ chez qn** be visiting s/o; **faire la ~** go on a tour of inspection, inspect; **heures de ~** visiting hours; **passer la ~** have one's medical; **recevoir des ~s** have visitors; **rendre (faire) ~ à qn** pay s/o a visit; **trou de ~** manhole

**visiter** *vt* visit; call on; examine, inspect; search

**visiteur -euse** *n* visitor; examiner, inspector; **infirmière visiteuse** district nurse

**vison** *nm* mink; mink coat

**visqueux -euse** *adj* viscous, sticky

**visser** *vt* screw, screw on, screw down; *coll fig* treat severely; **être vissé sur sa chaise** be sitting glued to one's chair

**visualiser** *vt cin* translate into visual terms

**visuel -uelle** *adj* visual; appealing to the eye; **champ ~** field of vision

**vitalité** *nf* vitality

**vitamine** *nf* vitamin

**vite** *adj* fast (sport); *adv* quickly, fast, rapidly; soon; **au plus ~** as quickly as possible; **avoir ~ fait de faire qch** be quick about doing sth; **faites ~ !** look sharp!; **on a ~ fait de** it's easy to

**vitesse** *nf* speed, quickness, rapidity; **à toute ~** at full speed; *mot* **boîte de ~s** gear-box; *mot* **changer de ~** change gear; **en ~** speedily, in haste; **être en perte de ~** be slowing down, be flagging; **excès de ~** exceeding the speed limit; **faire de la ~** speed; **gagner (prendre) qn de ~** outstrip s/o; **grande (petite) ~** by passenger (goods) train (rail freight); *mot* **passer les ~s** go through the gears; **prendre de la ~** gather speed

**viticole** *adj* wine-growing

**viticulteur** *nm* wine-grower

**viticulture** *nf* wine-growing

**vitrage** *nm* glazing; glass windows

**vitrail** *nm* stained glass window

**vitre** *nf* pane, window-pane; *mot* **~ arrière** rear window; *mot* **~ avant** windscreen; *fig* **casser les ~s** kick up a row

**vitrer** *vt* glaze; **porte vitrée** glass door

**vitreux -euse** *adj* glassy, glazed, vitreous

**vitrier** *nm* glazier

**vitrifier** *vt* vitrify; coat with transparent plastic

**vitrine** *nf* shop-window; glass case, show case

**vitrioler** *vt* throw vitriol at; add sulphuric acid to

**vitupérateur -trice** *n* vituperator; *adj* vituperative

**vitupérer** *vi* (6) vituperate, protest

**vivable** *adj coll* that can be lived (in); bearable; *coll* **elle n'est pas ~** she's impossible

**vivace** *adj* long-lived; hardy; persistent, tenacious

**vivacité** *nf* vivacity, liveliness; spirit; promptness; hastiness; acuteness of feeling

**vivandière** *nf mil + hist* canteen-keeper

**vivant** *nm* lifetime; living person; **bon ~** person who enjoys life; **de son ~** during his lifetime; **du ~ de** during the lifetime of; *adj* living, alive; animated, lively; life-like

**vivat** *nm* cheer, hurrah; *interj obs* hurrah!

**¹vive** *nf* weaver-fish

**²vive** see **²vivre**

**vivement** *adv* briskly, sharply; suddenly; keenly, acutely; *interj* **~ les vacances!** roll on the holidays!; **~ qu'il arrive!** I wish he'd arrive!

**viveur** *nm* pleasure-seeker

**vivier** *nm* fish-pond; fish-tank

**vivifiant** *adj* bracing, invigorating

**vivifier** *vt* quicken, vitalize; invigorate

**vivipare** *adj* viviparous

**vivoter** *vi* live sparely, subsist; just manage, struggle along

**¹vivre** *nm usu pl* supplies, provisions; *fig* **couper les ~ s à qn** stop s/o's allowance

**²vivre** *vt* (98) live, live through, experience; **~ sa vie** live one's own life; **~ une expérience unique** live through a unique experience; *vi* live, be alive; survive; **~ bien** eat well; **~ de** live on, live by means of; **vive le joie** take life easy; **apprendre à ~ à qn** teach s/o manners; **avoir de quoi ~** have enough to live on; **elle a beaucoup vécu** she has seen life; **facile à ~** easy to get on with; **faire ~ les siens** support one's family; **ne rencontrer âme qui vive** not meet a soul; *mil* **qui vive?** who goes there?; **qui vivra verra** time will show; **savoir ~** know how to behave; **se laisser ~** take life easy; **vive la joie!** let's all be merry!; **vive le roi!** long live the King!

**vizir** *nm* vizier

**vlan, v'lan** *interj* wham!, bang!, smack!

**vocabulaire** *nm* vocabulary; word list, short dictionary

**vocalement** *adv* vocally, orally

**vocalique** *adj* vocalic

**vocalise** *nf mus* vocalization exercise

**vocaliser** *vt + vi* vocalize

**vocatif** *nm* vocative

**vocation** *nf* calling, vocation; inclination

**vociférer** *vi* (6) vociferate, cry out, yell

**vœu** *nm* vow; wish; **accomplir un ~** fulfil a vow; **émettre un ~** express a wish; **faire des ~ x pour** wish ardently for; **faire (le) ~ de faire qch** vow to do sth

**vogue** *nf* fashion, vogue; **en ~** in fashion; **mettre en ~** bring into fashion

**voguer** *vi* sail; **vogue la galère!** let's risk it; come what may!

**voici** *prep* here is, here are; this is, these are; **~ l'heure!** it's time!; **~ pourquoi** this is the reason; **quatre ans qu'il est parti** he's been gone four years; **qui est facile** here's something easy; **~ qu'il se met à chanter** and now he's started to sing; **en ~ bien d'une autre** here's something new; **la dame que ~** this lady here; **la ~ qui vient** here she comes!; **le ~!** here he is!; **les ~!** here they are!

**voie** *nf* way, road, route; track, line; means, course; passage, duct; *chem* process; **~ de garage** railway siding; *fig* dead end; **~ ferrée** railway; **~ publique** public thoroughfare; **~ s de fait** acts of violence; **en ~ de** in the process of; nearing; **être en bonne ~** de be in a fair way to; **faire ~ d'eau** spring a leak; **mettre qn sur la ~** put s/o on the right track; **par la ~ des airs** by air; **pays en ~ de développement** developing country

**voilà** *prep* there is, there are; **~!** there!; **~ ce que c'est que d'aller trop vite** that's what you get for going too fast; **~, monsieur!** coming, sir!; **~ qui est fait!** that's done!; **~ qu'il se met à hurler** there he goes and starts shouting; **~ tout** that's all; **~ trois jours qu'il est parti** he's been gone for three days; **comme vous ~ beau!** how nice you look!; **en ~ assez!** that'll do!, no more of that!; **en ~ des manières!** what bad manners!; **le ~ bien!** that's him all over!; **le ~ qui vient!** here he comes!; **me ~!** here I am!

**¹voile** *nm* veil; *phot* fog; *anat* **~ du palais** velum; **avoir un ~ devant les yeux** have a mist before one's eyes; **prendre le ~** take holy orders; **sous le ~ de** under the guise of

**²voile** *nf* sail; **bateau à ~ s** sailing boat; **faire de la ~** sail, go sailing; **faire ~** set sail

**voilé** *adj* veiled; clouded; dim, obscure; husky

¹**voiler** vt veil; cloud, obscure; disguise, conceal; muffle; *phot* fog; **se ~** wear a veil; grow dim

²**voiler** vt *naut* equip with sails; vi obs warp; **se ~** warp

**voilette** nf veil (hat)

**voilier** nm sailing boat; sailmaker

**voilure** nf sails, canvas

**voir** vt (99) see; inspect; visit; understand; attend to; look after; look into; regard; **~ du pays** travel; **~ venir qn** see what s/o is after; **à le ~** judging by his appearance; **aller ~** go and see; **c'est à ~** that's worth seeing; that remains to be seen; *coll* **écoutez ~** just listen; *coll* **en faire ~ à qn** lead s/o a dance; **faire ~** show; **je ne peux pas le ~** I can't stand him; **je n'y vois rien** I can't see a thing; **je vois ça d'ici** I can visualize what it's like; **ni vu ni connu** without anyone being any the wiser; **se faire mal ~** get a bad reputation; vi see; **~ c'est croire** seeing is believing; **cela n'a rien à ~ avec** that has nothing to do with; **on verra bien** we'll see; **voyez un peu** just look; **voyons!** look here!, now, now!; **se ~** see oneself; see one another (each other); **cela se voit** that's obvious

**voire** adv indeed, even, nay; **~ même** and even

**voirie** nf public highway; administration of public thoroughfare; refuse-dump

**voisin -e** n neighbour; adj neighbouring, next-door; adjoining; next; akin

**voisinage** nm neighbourhood, vicinity; proximity, nearness

**voisiner** vi obs visit one's neighbours; **~ avec** be sitting next to

**voiture** nf carriage, conveyance, vehicle; (motor-)car; cart, wagon; railway coach; **~ cellulaire** prison van; **~ de livraison** delivery van; **~ de malade** invalid chair; **~ d'enfant** pram; **~ de place** cab; **en ~!** all aboard!; take your seats!; *comm* **lettre de ~** waybill

**voiture-pie** nf (pl **voitures-pies**) police car, = panda car

**voiturer** vt transport by car

**voiture-restaurant** nf (pl **voitures-restaurants**) restaurant-car, dining-car

**voiturette** nf small car; small cart, trap

**voiturier** nm carter, carrier

**voix** nf voice; tone; vote; *gramm* voice; speech; **à haute ~** aloud; **à portée de ~** within earshot; **à ~ basse** softly, in an undertone; **de vive ~** by word of mouth; **donner de la ~** give tongue; **d'une commune ~** by common consent; **mettre aux ~** put to the vote; **n'avoir pas ~ au chapitre** have no say in the matter

¹**vol** nm flight; flying; flock (of birds); **à ~ d'oiseau** as the crow flies; **de haut ~** high-class; lofty; **en plein ~** in full flight; **prendre son ~** take flight; **saisir l'occasion au ~** jump at the opportunity

²**vol** nm theft, stealing, larceny; robbery; **~ à la tire** bag-snatching, purse-snatching; **~ à l'étalage** shop-lifting; **~ à main armée** armed robbery; **~ avec agression** robbery with violence; **~ avec effraction** housebreaking; **~ qualifié** aggravated theft; *coll* **c'est un ~ manifeste** it's daylight robbery

**volage** adj fickle, flighty, inconstant

**volaille** nf poultry

¹**volant** nm shuttlecock; flounce, frill; *mech* flywheel; *mot* steering-wheel; tear-off leaf; **être tué au ~** be killed in a car accident; **jouer au ~** play at battledore and shuttlecock; **tenir le ~** drive

²**volant** adj flying; movable; loose; fluttering; **table ~e** occasional table; **vivre en camp ~** live in makeshift accommodation, camp out

**volatil** adj volatile

**volatile** nm winged creature, bird; farmyard bird

**volatiliser** vt volatilize; **se ~** fade away, vanish

**volatilité** nf volatility

**volcan** nm volcano

**volcanique** adj volcanic

**volcanologue** n vulcanologist

**vole** nf **faire la ~** win all the tricks (cards)

**volée** nf flight; flock, bevy, brood; volley, salvo; peal of bells; hail of blows; rank; **à la ~** in flight, on the wing; **de haute ~** of high rank; **lancer à toute ~** hurl; **semer à la ~** broadcast seed; **sonner à toute ~** ring out loudly

¹**voler** vt steal; rob; swindle, cheat; **il ne l'a pas volé** it serves him right; **je suis volé** I've been swindled

²**voler** vi fly; *fig* rush, go very fast; *fig* **entendre ~ une mouche** hear a pin drop; **faire ~ qch** send sth flying

**volet** nm shutter; sorting-board; *aer* flap; *coll* **trié sur le ~** hand-picked

**voleter** vi (5) flutter, flutter about

**voleur -euse** n thief; robber; burglar; **~ à la tire** bag-snatcher; **~ à l'étalage** shop-lifter; **~ de grand chemin** highway robber; **au ~!** stop thief!; adj thieving

**volière** nf aviary

**volige** nf bui batten

**voliger** vt (3) bui batten; lath

**volontaire** n volunteer; adj voluntary; headstrong, self-willed

326

**volonté** *nf* will; will-power; pleasure, wish; **à ~** at will; ad lib; **dernières ~s** last will and testament; **faire ses quatre ~s** do as one pleases; **mauvaise ~** unwillingness; **n'en faire qu'à sa ~** refuse to listen to reason

**volontiers** *adv* willingly, gladly; readily

**volte-face** *nf invar* turning about, volte-face; **faire ~** face about, turn right about

**voltige** *nf* acrobatics (rope, trapeze); *aer* aerobatics

**voltiger** *vi* (3) flit, hover, fly about; perform acrobatics (rope, trapeze)

**voltigeur -euse** *n* acrobat (rope, trapeze); *nm ar* light infantryman

**volubile** *adj* voluble

**volubilis** *nm bot* convolvulus

**volubilité** *nf* volubility

**volume** *nm* bulk, volume, mass; tome; volume, sound level; capacity

**volumétrique** *adj* volumetric

**volumineux -euse** *adj* voluminous

**volupté** *nf* voluptuousness; pleasure, delight

**voluptueux -ueuse** *adj* voluptuous

**volute** *nf* volute, scroll; wreath (smoke); whorl; curl (wave)

**vomir** *vt* vomit, belch out, spew up; *vi* vomit, be sick; **c'est à ~** it's enough to make one sick

**vomissement** *nm* vomiting

**vomissure** *nf* vomit

**vomitif** *nm* emetic

**vorace** *adj* voracious, ravenous

**voracité** *nf* voracity

**vos** *poss adj pl see* **votre**

**votant -e** *n* voter

**votation** *nf* voting

**vote** *nm* vote, voting, suffrage; **droit de ~** franchise

**voter** *vt* pass, carry; *vi* vote

**votif -ive** *adj* votive

**votre** *poss adj* (*pl* **vos**) your; **vos père et mère** your father and mother

**vôtre** *pron* yours; **à la ~!** your very good health!; **il faut y mettre du ~** you must do your bit; *comm* **j'ai reçu la ~ du 15 avril** I am in receipt of yours of 15 April

**vouer** *vt* vow, dedicate, devote; **ne pas (plus) savoir à quel saint se ~** not know which way to turn; **voué à l'échec** destined to fail

**vouloir** *nm* will; **de son bon ~** of one's own accord; *vt* (100) want, wish; desire, wish for; require; **combien en veut-il?** how much is he asking for it?; **en veux-tu en voilà** as much as you like; **en ~ à qn** bear s/o a grudge; **il l'a voulu** he wanted it; he asked for it; **que lui voulez-vous?** what do you want of

him?; **que voulez-vous?** what do you want?; what do you expect?; **que voulez-vous que j'y fasse?** how can I help it?; **qu'il le veuille ou non** willy-nilly; **sans le ~** unintentionally; **s'en ~** be annoyed with oneself; **se ~** claim; *vi* will; want; wish; be willing; **~ c'est pouvoir** where there's a will there's a way; **~ de qch** want sth; **~ dire** mean; **c'est comme vous voudrez** as you please; **Dieu veuille** God grant, please to God; **il en veut à mon argent** he has designs on my money; **je ne veux pas de ça** I want none of that; **je veux bien** willingly; **je veux bien que tu l'aies vu** you may well have seen him; **je veux qu'il vienne** I want him to come; **voulez-vous bien me passer le sel** please (kindly) pass me the salt

**voulu** *adj* required, requisite; intentional, deliberate

**vous** *pron* you; yourself; to you; one; **c'est à ~** it's yours; it's your turn; **de ~ à moi** between ourselves

**vous-même** *pron* yourself

**voussure** *nf* curve of arch

**voûte** *nf* vault, arch

**voûté** *adj* vaulted, arched; bent, stooping

**voûter (se)** *v refl* become round-shouldered, grow bent

**vouvoiement** *nm* use of 'vous' in addressing people

**vouvoyer** *vt* (7) use 'vous' in addressing people

**voyage** *nm* journey, voyage; travel; *coll* trip; **~ accompagné** conducted tour; **~ d'agrément** pleasure trip; **~ de noces** honeymoon; **bon ~!** have a good journey!; **être en ~** be travelling; be away; **partir en ~** set off on a journey

**voyager** *vi* (3) travel; *coll* have a trip

**voyageur -euse** *n* traveller; passenger; fare (taxi); **~ (de commerce)** (commercial) traveller; **pigeon ~** carrier pigeon

**¹voyant** *nm* signal, mark; signal light, indicator light; *adj* gaudy, garish, showy, loud

**²voyant -e** *n* seeing person; clairvoyant

**voyelle** *nf* vowel

**voyou** *nm* hooligan, layabout

**voyouterie** *nf* hooliganism; gutter wit

**vrac** *nm* **en ~** loose (goods)

**vrai** *nm* truth; reality; **être dans le ~** be in the right; **il y a du ~ là-dedans** there's some truth in that; *adj* true, real; genuine; correct; realistic; **pour de ~** really, seriously; *adv* truly, indeed, really; *coll* **~ de ~** really and truly; **à ~ dire** to tell the truth

**vraiment** *adv* really, truly
**vraisemblable** *adj* probable, likely; plausible; **au delà du** ~ beyond the bounds of probability
**vraisemblance** *nf* probability, likelihood; plausibility
**vrille** *nf* tendril; *eng* gimlet, borer; *aer* spin; **tomber en** ~ come down in a spin
**vrillé** *adj* curled; twisted; *bot* with tendrils
**vrillée** *nf coll bot* bindweed
**vriller** *vt* bore; *vi* whirl; *aer* climb in a spiral; snarl, shrink
**vrillette** *nf* deathwatch beetle
**vrombir** *vi* buzz, zoom, hum, purr
**vrombissement** *nm* buzzing, zooming, humming, purring
**vu** *nm* **au** ~ **et au su de tous** openly; *p part* **voir**; *prep* considering, seeing, in view of
**vue** *nf* sight, eyesight; view, aspect, prospect; intention; opinion; view; slide; ~ **d'oiseau** bird's eye view; **à la** ~ **de** at the sight of; **à première** ~ at first sight; **avoir des** ~s **sur** have designs on; **avoir la** ~ **basse (longue)** be short-sighted (long-sighted); **à** ~ **de nez** at a rough guess; **à** ~ **d'œil** visibly; **du point de** ~ **de** with regard to; **en mettre plein la** ~ **à qn** try to impress s/o; **entrer dans les** ~s **de qn** agree with s/o; **en** ~ **de** with an eye to; **être très en** ~ be very much in the public eye; **garder à** ~ keep in sight; **payable à** ~ payable on sight; **perdre de** ~ lose sight of
**vulcaniser** *vt* vulcanize
**vulcanologie** *nf* vulcanology
**vulgaire** *nm obs* the common people; *adj* vulgar, common; ordinary; **la langue** ~ the vernacular
**vulgarisateur -trice** *n* popularizer
**vulgarisation** *nf* popularization, vulgarization
**vulgariser** *vt* popularize; make vulgar
**vulgarité** *nf* vulgarity
**vulnérabilité** *nf* vulnerability
**vulve** *nf anat* vulva

# W

**wagnérien -ienne** *adj* Wagnerian
**wagon** *nm* carriage, coach, car; wagon, truck; wagon-load; ~ **à bagages** luggage-van, *US* baggage car; ~ **à caisse** goods-truck, *US* freight-car; ~ **à chevaux** horse-box, *US* horse-car; ~ **de marchandises** goods-wagon, *US* freight-car; ~ **en plate-forme** flat goods-truck, *US* flat-car; ~ **frein** brake-van; ~ **frigorifique** refrigerator-car; ~ **rail-route** road railer
**wagon-citerne** *nm* (*pl* **wagons-citernes**) tank-car, tank-wagon
**wagon-foudre** *nm* (*pl* **wagons-foudres**) tank-car, tank-wagon
**wagon-lit** *nm* (*pl* **wagons-lits**) sleeping-car, *coll* sleeper
**wagonnet** *nm* tip-truck, tip-wagon
**wagon-poste** *nm* (*pl* **wagons-poste**) mail-van
**wagon-restaurant** *nm* (*pl* **wagons-restaurants**) restaurant-car, dining-car
**wallon -onne** *adj* Walloon
**waters** *nmpl coll* water-closet, W.C., *coll* loo
**wattman** *nm obs* tram-driver
**western** *nm* cowboy film, western

# X

X *nm invar* **avoir les jambes en** ~ be knock-kneed; **l'** ~ the École Polytechnique; **rayons** ~ X-rays
**xénophobie** *nf* xenophobia

**Xérès** *nm* sherry
**xérographie** *nf* xeroxing
**xylographie** *nf* wood-engraving; woodcut

# Y

y *adv* there; here; thither; **il** ~ **a** there is, there are; *coll* **je n'** ~ **suis pas du tout** I'm all at sea; *coll fig* **j'** ~ **suis!** I've got it!; *coll* **j'** ~ **suis, j'** ~ **reste!** here I am and here I stay!; *pron invar* at it, to it, about it, of it, etc; **ça** ~ **est!** it's done!, that's it!, all right!; **il** ~ **est pour quelque chose** he has a hand in it; **je n'** ~ **manquerai pas** I shall not fail to do so; **je n'** ~ **suis pour personne** I'm not at home to anyone; **je n'** ~ **suis pour rien** it is none of my doing; **pendant que j'** ~ **suis** while I'm about it; **pensez-** ~ think of it; **rien n'** ~ **fait** it's no good; **vas-**~**!** go there!, get on with it!

**yaourt** *nm* yogurt; *coll* **mot pot de** ~ bubble-car
**yeuse** *nf* ilex, holm-oak, holly-oak
**yeux** *nmpl* eyes (*pl* of **œil**)
**yé-yé** *n* with-it teenager, hipster, raver
**yole** *nf naut* yawl
**yougoslave** *adj* Yugoslav
**Yougoslavie** *nf* Yugoslavia
**youpin -e** *n sl pej* Yid
**youyou** *nm* dinghy
**ypérite** *nf chem* yperite, mustard-gas
**ypréau** *nm* broad-leaved elm; white poplar

# Z

**zazou** *nm* teddy-boy
**zèbre** *nm* zebra; *coll* chap
**zébré** *adj* striped
**zébrer** *vt* (6) mark with stripes; streak

**zébrure** *nf* stripe; series of stripes; zebra-markings
**zélateur -trice** *n* zealot; *adj* zealous
**zèle** *nm* zeal, ardour; **brûler de** ~ be fired

with enthusiasm; *coll* **faire du** ~ be over-zealous

**zélé** *adj* zealous

**zélote** *nm* zealot

**zéro** *nm* cipher, nought; *coll sp* nil, love; **c'est un** ~ he's a nobody; **partir de** ~ start from scratch

**zeste** *nm cul* zest, outer skin (of orange, lemon); *coll* very small quantity

**zézaiement** *nm* lisping, lisp

**zézayer** *vi* (7) lisp

**zibeline** *nf zool* **(martre)** ~ sable

**zig, zigue** *nm sl* fellow, chap; **un bon** ~ a decent fellow

**zigoteau, zigoto** *nm sl* fellow, chap

**zigouiller** *vt sl* kill, murder, knife

**zigzag** *nm* zigzag; **éclair en** ~ forked lightning

**zigzaguer** *vi* zigzag; drive erratically

**zinc** *nm* zinc; *coll* counter (of a bar); *coll* café, bar; **pommade à l'oxyde de** ~ zinc ointment

**zinguer** *vt* cover with zinc; *metal* galvanize

**zingueur** *nm* zinc-worker; zinc-roofer

**zinzin** *nm coll* thing; *adj coll* barmy

**zizanie** *nf* discord

**zizi** *nm coll* thing; *sl* penis; *sl* vagina

**zob** *nm vulg* penis

**zodiaque** *nm* zodiac

**zona** *nm med* shingles, zona

**zone** *nf* zone; sphere, area; *coll* outskirts of Paris; *mot* ~ **bleue** area of restricted parking; *meteor* ~ **de dépression** trough of low pressure; *geog* ~ **des alizés** trade wind belt; *mil* ~ **des armées** war zone; ~ **verte** green belt

**zoologie** *nf* zoology

**zoologique** *adj* zoological; **jardin** ~ zoological garden, zoo

**zoologiste** *n* zoologist

**zouave** *nm mil* zouave; *coll* **faire le** ~ play the fool

**zozoter** *vi coll* lisp

**zut** *interj* blast!; oh, hell!; ~ **pour vous!** go to blazes!

**zyeuter, zieuter** *vt sl* stare at, have a look at

ENGLISH-FRENCH

# A

**a** *n* (la lettre) a; *mus* la *m*; **A 1** en parfait état

**a, an** *indef art* un (*f* une)

**aback** *adv naut* masqué, pris vent debout; **taken ~** dérouté, déconcenancé

**abacus** *n* abaque *m*, boulier compteur *m*; *archi* abaque *m*

**abaft** *adv naut* vers l'arrière; *prep naut* derrière

**abandon** *n* nonchalance *f*, abandon *m*, laisser-aller *m invar*; *vt* abandonner, lâcher, délaisser; **~ oneself** s'abandonner, se livrer

**abandonment** *n* abandon *m*; (casualness) laisser-aller *m invar*; renonciation *f*

**abase** *vt* humilier, mortifier, abaisser

**abasement** *n* humiliation *f*, abaissement *m*

**abash** *vt* déconcerter, confondre

**abate** *vt* diminuer; (price) rabattre; (lessen) affaiblir; *leg* annuler; *vi* diminuer, s'affaiblir

**abatement** *n* diminution *f*; rabais *m*; *leg* annulation *f*

**abattoir** *n* abattoir *m*

**abbatial** *adj* abbatial

**abbess** *n* abbesse *f*

**abbey** *n* abbaye *f*; (church) (église) abbatiale *f*

**abbot** *n* abbé *m*, supérieur *m* d'un monastère

**abbreviate** *vt* abréger, écourter

**abbreviation** *n* abréviation *f*

**A B C** *n* alphabet *m*; **A B C** *m*, rudiments *mpl* de connaissances

**abdicate** *vt* abdiquer, renoncer à; *vi* abdiquer

**abdication** *n* abdication *f*

**abdomen** *n* abdomen *m*

**abdominal** *adj* abdominal

**abduct** *vt* enlever, kidnapper

**abduction** *n* enlèvement *m*, rapt *m*; (minor) détournement *m*; *med* abduction *f*

**abductor** *n* ravisseur -euse; *med* (muscle) abducteur *m*

**abeam** *adj naut* par le travers

**abed** *adv* au lit

**aberrance** *n* aberrance *f*

**aberrant** *adj* aberrant

**aberration** *n* aberration *f*, déviation *f*, égarement *m*

**abet** *vt* inciter, aiguillonner, encourager;

**aid and ~** être complice de, prendre part à

**abetter, abettor** *n* complice

**abeyance** *n* suspension *f*; **fall into ~** tomber en désuétude

**abhor** *vt* détester, exécrer, abhorrer

**abhorrence** *n* exécration *f*, horreur *f*

**abhorrent** *adj* détestable, exécrable

**abidance** *n* persistance *f*; conformité *f*

**abide** *vt* (wait for) attendre; souffrir; supporter; *vi* durer, continuer; **~ by** rester fidèle à, respecter

**abiding** *adj* permanent, constant

**ability** *n* compétence *f*, capacité *f*; (cleverness) habileté *f*

**abiogenesis** *n* génération spontanée

**abject** *adj* abject, ignoble, répugnant

**abjection** *n* abjection *f*, avilissement *m*, indignité *f*

**abjuration** *n* abjuration *f*

**abjure** *vt* abjurer

**ablation** *n geol+surg* ablation *f*

**ablative** *n gramm* ablatif *m*; *adj gramm* ablatif -ive

**ablaze** *adj* embrasé, en feu, en flammes; *fig* excité, enflammé

**able** *adj* intelligent, habile; capable, compétent; *med* sain; *leg* compétent

**able-bodied** *adj* robuste, fort; **~ seaman** matelot *m* de deuxième classe

**ablution** *n* ablution *f*

**abnegate** *vt* (responsibility) renier; (rights) renoncer à

**abnegation** *n* abnégation *f*; renoncement *m*

**abnormal** *adj* anormal, singulier -ière; exceptionnel -elle; insolite

**abnormality** *n* anomalie *f*, singularité *f*; (oddness) bizarrerie *f*

**abnormity** *n* anomalie *f*; monstruosité *f*

**aboard** *adv* à bord; **take ~** embarquer; *prep* à bord de

**abode** *n* habitation *f*, domicile *m*, demeure *f*

**abolish** *vt* abolir, supprimer

**abolition** *n* abolition *f*, suppression *f*

**abolitionist** *n* abolitionniste

**A-bomb** *n* bombe *f* atomique

**abominable** *adj* abominable, monstrueux -ueuse

**abominate** *vt* abominer, exécrer, détester

**abomination** *n* abomination *f*, exécration *f*

**aboriginal** n aborigène, indigène; adj aborigène, indigène

**aborigines** npl aborigènes pl, indigènes pl

**abort** vt faire avorter; mil (operation) interrompre; vi avorter; échouer

**abortion** n avortement m; (creature) avorton m

**abortionist** n avorteur -euse; coll faiseuse f d'anges

**abortive** adj prématuré, avorté; rudimentaire

**aboulia, abulia** n aboulie f

**abound** vi abonder, foisonner, regorger; coll grouiller

**about** adv de tous côtés, ça et là; (around) environ; à peu près, vers; (near) près; (all round) autour; (opposite direction) à rebours; mil ~ turn! demi-tour, marche!; be ~ to être sur le point de; naut go ~ virer de bord; out and ~ sur pied; put sth ~ lancer un canard, faire courir un bruit; prep (near to) autour de, aux alentours de; (concerning) au sujet de, à propos de; (concerned with) occupé à; how ~ a walk? si l'on allait se promener?; what's it ~ ? de quoi s'agit-il?; while I'm ~ it pendant que j'y suis

**above** adv (higher up) au-dessus, en haut, plus haut; (heaven) au ciel; (in text) plus haut; (more than) à partir de; over and ~ en sus de; prep (higher than) au-dessus de, plus haut que; (more than) plus de; (upstream) en amont de; (better) supérieur à

**above-board** adj franc (f franche), ouvert; adv ouvertement

**abrade** vt gratter, racler, user en frottant; éroder

**abrasion** n abrasion f; érosion f; (scratch) écorchure f

**abreast** adv de front, côte à côte; ~ of à la hauteur de; keep ~ of se tenir au courant de

**abridge** vt abréger, résumer; (lessen) diminuer; leg priver

**abridgement** n abrégé m, résumé m; diminution f; leg privation f

**abroach** adv + adj (cask) en perce

**abroad** adv (in another country) à l'étranger; (outside) dehors, à l'extérieur; (far and wide) au loin

**abrogate** vt abroger

**abrupt** adj brusque; (style) décousu; abrupt, escarpé

**abruptness** n brusquerie f; (haste) précipitation f; (slope) raideur f

**abscess** n abcès m

**abscond** vi filer, se sauver, s'enfuir; coll déguerpir, décamper

**absence** n absence f; (lack) manque m; leg défaut m; ~ of mind distraction f; in the ~ of faute de; mil leave of ~ permission f

**absent** vt ~ oneself s'absenter; adj absent; manquant; distrait

**absentee** n absent -e, absentéiste

**absenteeism** n absentéisme m

**absent-minded** adj distrait, absent, rêveur -euse, étourdi

**absent-mindedness** n distraction f, absence f, étourderie f

**absinth** n absinthe f

**absolute** n absolu m; adj absolu, complet -ète, parfait; entier -ière, intransigeant; indépendant

**absolutely** adv absolument, parfaitement; entièrement; coll (agreed) d'accord, oui

**absolution** n absolution f

**absolutism** n absolutisme m

**absolve** vt absoudre; leg acquitter

**absonant** adj discordant; mus dissonant

**absorb** vt absorber, assimiler; (noise, shock) amortir

**absorbent** n absorbant m; adj absorbant

**absorber** n shock ~ amortisseur m

**absorbing** adj absorbant; fig passionnant

**absorption** n absorption f; (sounds) amortissement m

**abstain** vi s'abstenir; ~ from se priver de, renoncer à

**abstainer** n pol abstentionniste; total ~ personne f qui ne boit jamais d'alcool

**abstemious** adj sobre, frugal, modéré

**abstention** n abstention f

**abstinence** n privation f; eccles abstinence f

**abstinent** adj sobre, frugal, modéré

**abstract** n résumé m, abrégé m; philos abstrait m; abstraction f; vt abstraire; euph soustraire, voler; adj abstrait

**abstracted** adj distrait, rêveur -euse; dégagé

**abstraction** n abstraction f; (absent-mindedness) distraction f; euph vol m; leg soustraction f

**abstruse** adj abstrus

**absurd** n absurde m; ridicule m; adj absurde, déraisonnable; ridicule

**absurdity** n absurdité f

**abundance** n abondance f, profusion f; foisonnement m; richesse f

**abundant** adj abondant, foisonnant; (lavish) plantureux -euse, riche

**abuse** n abus m, excès m; (verbal) injure f, insulte f; vt maltraiter, faire mauvais usage de; (verbally) injurier, insulter; (privilege) abuser de

**abusive** adj injurieux -ieuse, insultant; abusif -ive

**abut** vi être contigu -üe, être limitrophe

**abysmal** *adj* insondable; *coll* exécrable; (ignorance) profond

**abyss** *n* abîme *m*; *geog* abysse *m*

**abyssal** *adj* abyssal

**acacia** *n* acacia *m*

**academic** *n* personne *f* exerçant une fonction dans l'enseignement supérieur (universitaire); *adj* académique; (learned) savant, érudit; *pej* pédant, théorique; universitaire

**academician** *n* membre *m* d'une académie savante

**academy** *n* académie *f*

**acanthus** *n* acanthe *f*

**accede** *vi* accéder, atteindre; (agree to) accepter, agréer

**accelerate** *vt + vi* accélérer, hâter, presser; activer

**acceleration** *n* accélération *f*

**accelerator** *n* accélérateur *m*; *coll* mot champignon *m*

**accent** *n* accent *m*; inflexion *f*, intonation *f*; *ling* accent *m* tonique; *vt* accentuer; intensifier

**accentual** *adj* accentuel -uelle

**accentuate** *vt* accentuer; augmenter, intensifier

**accentuation** *n* accentuation *f*

**accept** *vt* accepter; (agree to) accueillir, agréer; adhérer à; se résigner à, souffrir; (adopt) adopter, approuver

**acceptable** *adj* acceptable, recevable, satisfaisant; (welcome) opportun, bienvenu

**acceptance** *n* acceptation *f*; consentement *m*, agrément *m*

**acceptation** *n* acceptation *f*

**acceptor** *n comm* accepteur *m*

**access** *n* accès *m*, abord *m*; entrée *f*, ouverture *f*; *med* accès *m*, crise *f*

**accessary** *n* complice; adjoint -e; *adj* accessoire

**accessible** *adj* accessible; abordable; compréhensible; ouvert

**accession** *n* accession *f*; (joining) adhésion *f*; *leg* accession *f*; (addition) accroissement *m*

**accessory** *n* (person) complice; *theat + comm* accessoire *m*; *adj* accessoire, secondaire, auxiliaire

**accidence** *n gramm* morphologie *f*; rudiments *mpl*

**accident** *n* accident *m*; chance *f*, hasard *m*

**accidental** *n mus* accident *m*, signe accidentel; *adj* accidentel -elle, contingent, fortuit; accessoire; extrinsèque; *mus* accidentel -elle

**acclaim** *n* acclamation *f*; *vt* acclamer, applaudir; (announce) proclamer

**acclamation** *n* acclamation *f*

**acclimatization** *n* acclimatation *f*

**acclimatize** *vt* acclimater, habituer; *vi* s'acclimater, s'habituer

**acclivity** *n* montée *f*

**accolade** *n* accolade *f*; *mus* accolade *f*

**accommodate** *vt* accommoder, adapter, ajuster; harmoniser, mettre d'accord, réconcilier; (arrange) agencer, disposer; (assist) aider, rendre service à; (put up) loger, abriter

**accommodating** *adj* obligeant, serviable; (helpful) accommodant, débonnaire, complaisant

**accommodation** *n* accommodation *f*, ajustement *m*; adaptation *f*; accommodement *m*, arrangement *m*, compromis *m*; (lodging) logement *m*; (train, ship, etc) place *f*; (hotel) chambre *f*; (loan) prêt *m* d'argent; *naut* ~ **ladder** échelle *f* de coupée

**accompaniment** *n* accompagnement *m*

**accompanist** *n* accompagnateur -trice

**accompany** *vt* accompagner

**accomplice** *n* complice

**accomplish** *vt* accomplir, achever, terminer; exécuter, réaliser

**accomplished** *adj* accompli, consommé, incomparable

**accomplishment** *n* accomplissement *m*, réalisation *f*; (success) réussite *f*; ~ **s** talents *mpl*; (social) talents *mpl* de société

**accord** *n* accord *m*, consentement *m*; harmonie *f*; (agreement) traité *m*; *vt* accorder; ajuster; octroyer; (bring to agreement) mettre d'accord; *vi* s'accorder, être d'accord

**accordance** *n* accord *m*, compatibilité *f*, conformité *f*; **in** ~ **with** suivant, selon, conformément à

**accordant** *adj* conforme

**according** *adv conj phr* ~ **as** selon que, suivant que; *prep phr* ~ **to** suivant, selon, conformément à

**accordingly** *adv* donc; en conséquence

**accordion** *n* accordéon *m*

**accordionist** *n* accordéoniste

**accost** *vt* accoster, aborder; *coll* draguer; racoler

**account** *n* compte *m*; (part payment) acompte *m*; (narrative) récit *m*, description *f*, relation *f*; (significance) estime *f*, égard *m*, importance *f*; ~ **s** comptabilité *f*, écritures *fpl*; **bank** ~ compte *m* en banque; **by all** ~ **s** de l'avis général; **call s/o to** ~ demander des comptes à qn; **current** ~ compte courant; **give a good** ~ **of oneself** se défendre bien; **keep the** ~ **s** tenir la comptabilité; **on** ~ à valoir; **on** ~ **of** à cause de; *vt* estimer, considérer; *vi* ~ **for** rendre compte de, expliquer, justifier; **there's no** ~ **ing for tastes** des

goûts et des couleurs on ne dispute pas
**accountable** *adj* responsable, comptable; explicable
**accountant** *n* comptable, agent comptable; **chartered** ~ = expert *m+f* comptable
**accoutre** *vt lit* accoutrer
**accoutrement** *n* accoutrement *m*
**accredit** *vt* accréditer, attribuer
**accrete** *vt* accroître; *vi* adhérer, s'accroître, s'attacher
**accretion** *n* accroissement *m*
**accrue** *vi* revenir, échoir; s'accroître
**accumulate** *vt* accumuler, amasser, amonceler, entasser; *vi* s'accumuler, s'entasser
**accumulation** *n* accumulation *f*, entassement *m*, amoncellement *m*; (capital) accroissement *m*; *leg* cumul *m*
**accumulative** *adj* (person) qui accumule; (miserly) avare; qui s'accumule; *comm* cumulatif -ive
**accumulator** *n* accumulateur *m*; *coll* accu *m*
**accuracy** *n* exactitude *f*, précision *f*
**accurate** *adj* exact, précis
**accursed** *adj* maudit; détestable
**accusal** *n* accusation *f*
**accusation** *n* accusation *f*; *leg* (indictment) acte *m* d'accusation
**accusative** *n gramm* accusatif *m*; *adj* à l'accusatif
**accusatory** *adj* accusateur -trice; *leg* accusatoire
**accuse** *vt* accuser, inculper, incriminer
**accuser** *n* accusateur -trice
**accustom** *vt* accoutumer, habituer; *vi* s'accoutumer, s'habituer
**accustomed** *adj* accoutumé, habitué; habituel -uelle
**ace** *n* as *m*; **within an ~ of** à deux doigts de
**acephalous** *adj* acéphale
**acerbity** *n* acerbité *f*, aigreur *f*
**acetate** *n* acétate *m*
**acetic** *adj* acétique
**acetify** *vt* acétifier; *vi* aigrir
**acetone** *n* acétone *f*
**acetylene** *n* acétylène *m*
**ache** *n* mal *m*, douleur *f*; peine *f*; *vi* avoir mal, souffrir; ~ **for** désirer, avoir envie de; **my head** ~ **s** j'ai mal à la tête
**achieve** *vt* accomplir, achever; effectuer, exécuter; atteindre, mener à bien
**achievement** *n* accomplissement *m*, exécution *f*; réalisation *f*; (success) réussite *f*
**aching** *adj* endolori, douloureux -euse; **have an ~ heart** avoir le cœur gros
**achromatic** *adj opt + biol* achromatique
**acid** *n* acide *m*; *adj* acide; (bitter) aigre; (criticism) acerbe

**acidify** *vt* acidifier; *vi* s'acidifier
**acidosis** *n med* acidose *f*
**acidulated** *adj* acidulé
**acidulous** *adj* acidulé, aigrelet -ette
**acknowledge** *vt* reconnaître, admettre, avouer; accuser réception de; (gift) remercier de *or* pour
**acknowledg(e)ment** *n* reconnaissance *f*; accusé *m* de réception; *comm* récépissé *m*; aveu *m*; remerciement *m*
**acme** *n* acmé *f*, comble *m*, summum *m*
**acne** *n* acné *f*
**acolyte** *n* acolyte *m*
**aconite** *n* aconit *m*
**acorn** *n* gland *m*
**acoustic** *adj* acoustique
**acoustics** *npl* acoustique *f*
**acquaint** *vt* renseigner, informer, aviser; **be ~ed with** connaître
**acquaintance** *n* (person) connaissance *f*, relation *f*; (knowledge) familiarité *f*; **have some ~ with** avoir une certaine connaissance de; **make the ~ of** faire la connaissance de; **upon further ~** en connaissant mieux
**acquiesce** *vi* acquiescer, accepter, consentir, déférer
**acquiescence** *n* acquiescement *m*, assentiment *m*, consentement *m*
**acquire** *vt* acquérir, gagner; (learn) apprendre
**acquired** *adj* acquis
**acquisition** *n* acquisition *f*
**acquisitive** *adj* avide, cupide, âpre au gain
**acquit** *vt* acquitter, payer; absoudre, acquitter; ~ **oneself well** se comporter bien
**acquittal** *n* acquittement *m*; (duty) exécution *f*
**acquittance** *n* acquittement *m*; *leg* quittance *f*; *comm* acquit *m*
**acre** *n* acre *f*, arpent *m*, demi-hectare *m*; ~ **s of** des hectares de; **God's ~** cimetière *m*
**acrid** *adj* acre; acerbe, sarcastique, caustique
**acrimonious** *adj* acrimonieux -ieuse
**acrimony** *n* acrimonie *f*
**acrobat** *n* acrobate
**acrobatic** *adj* acrobatique
**across** *adv* en travers, de l'autre côté, *prep* à travers, au travers de; de l'autre côté de; **come ~** (person) rencontrer; (thing) tomber sur; **get sth ~** faire comprendre qch; **put sth ~ s/o** faire marcher qn
**acrostic** *n* acrostiche *m*
**act** *n* acte *m*; action *f*; (law) loi *f*, décret *m*; (acting turn) numéro *m*; ~ **of God** force majeure; **caught in the ~** pris en flagrant délit; **in the ~ of** en train de;

**put on an** ~ jouer la comédie, feindre; *vt theat* jouer; (pretend) feindre, simuler; *vi* agir; (behave) se comporter, se tenir; ~ **for** représenter

**acting** *n* action *f*; *theat* jeu *m*, art *m* de jouer, métier *m* d'acteur; *adj* suppléant, intérimaire, provisoire

**actinic** *adj* actinique

**action** *n* action *f*; acte *m*, fait *m*; influence *f*; activité *f*, effort *m*; *leg* action *f*, procès *m*; *mil* **go into** ~ aller au feu; *mil* **killed in** ~ mort au champ d'honneur; **out of** ~ hors d'usage, en panne; **put into** ~ mettre à exécution; **take** ~ prendre des mesures; *leg* **take** ~ **against** citer, poursuivre; *vt leg* actionner

**actionable** *adj leg* donnant matière à procès

**activate** *vt* activer, accélérer, hâter; rendre radio-actif -ive

**active** *adj* actif -ive; travailleur -euse, efficace, diligent

**activism** *n* activisme *m*

**activist** *n* activiste

**activity** *n* activité *f*; occupation *f*; dynamisme *m*

**actor** *n* acteur *m*, comédien *m*

**actress** *n* actrice *f*, comédienne *f*

**actual** *adj* réel -elle, concret -ète; actuel -uelle

**actuality** *n* réalité *f*, fait *m*, actualité *f*; circonstances actuelles

**actualize** *vt* réaliser; décrire avec réalisme

**actually** *adv* de fait, vraiment; (right now) pour l'instant, actuellement; même; (really) véritablement

**actuary** *n* actuaire

**actuate** *vt* actionner; faire agir, pousser

**acuity** *n* acuité *f*

**acumen** *n* pénétration *f*, sagacité *f*, perspicacité *f*

**acuminate** *vt* aiguiser; *adj bot* acuminé

**acupuncture** *n* acuponcture *f*, acupuncture *f*

**acute** *adj* aigu -üe, pointu; (clever) perspicace, avisé, pénétrant

**acuteness** *n* acuité *f*, intensité *f*; pénétration *f*, sagacité *f*, perspicacité *f*

**ad** *n coll abbr* réclame *f*

**adage** *n* adage *m*, maxime *f*

**Adam** *n* Adam *m*; ~ **'s apple** pomme *f* d'Adam; **not to know from** ~ ne pas connaître ni d'Ève ni d'Adam

**adamant** *adj* inflexible

**adamantine** *adj* adamantin

**adapt** *vt* adapter, accommoder; mettre en harmonie

**adaptability** *n* souplesse *f*, maniabilité *f*

**adaptable** *adj* adaptable, souple

**adaptation** *n* adaptation *f*; *mus* arrangement *m*

**adapter, adaptor** *n* adapteur -trice; *elect* prise *f* multiple

**add** *vt* ajouter; ~ **to** augmenter, accroître; ~ **up** additionner; ~ **up to** se résumer à, signifier; ~ **ed to which** au surplus; *vi* **that** ~ **s up** cela concorde

**addendum** *n* (*pl* **addenda**) addenda *mpl*

**adder** *n* vipère *f*

**addict** *n* drogué -e, toxicomane; *fig* fanatique; *vt* vouer, consacrer; ~ **oneself** se vouer à

**addiction** *n* toxicomanie *f*; (taste) goût *m*, penchant *m*

**addictive** *adj* qui mène à la toxicomanie; qui crée une dépendance

**addition** *n* addition *f*; (increase) augmentation *f*; (of collaborators) adjonction *f*

**additional** *adj* additionnel -elle, supplémentaire

**additive** *n* additif *m*; *adj* additif -ive

**addle** *vt* brouiller, troubler; (egg) pourrir; *vi* se pourrir

**addled** *adj* (egg) pourri; *fig* brouillé, confus, troublé

**address** *n* adresse *f*, domicile *m*; (speech) discours *m*, allocution *f*; (skill) habileté *f*, dextérité *f*; (flair) doigté *m*; **form of** ~ titre *m*; **of no fixed** ~ sans domicile; **pay** ~ **es** to faire la cour à; *vt* adresser; apostropher; mettre l'adresse sur; (encounter) aborder; (talk to) s'adresser à

**addressee** *n* destinataire

**adduce** *vt* citer, alléguer; mettre en avant

**adducent** *adj med* adducteur *m*

**adduction** *n* allégation *f*; *med* adduction *f*

**adductor** *n med* adducteur *m*

**adenoidal** *adj* adénoïde

**adenoids** *npl* végétations *fpl* adénoïdes

**adept** *n* expert *m*; *ar* initié -e; *adj* expert

**adequacy** *n* à-propos *m*, justesse *f*

**adequate** *adj* adéquat, juste, congru; (all right) suffisant

**adhere** *vi* adhérer, tenir; persister, maintenir

**adherent** *n* adhérent -e, membre *m*; *adj* adhérent

**adhesion** *n* (support) adhésion *f*; (sticking) adhérence *f*; *med* adhérence *f*

**adhesive** *adj* adhésif -ive, collant

**adieu** *n* + *interj* adieu *m*

**adipose** *adj* adipeux -euse

**adiposity** *n* adiposité *f*

**adit** *n* entrée *f*; accès *m*

**adjacent** *adj* adjacent, attenant, contigu -üe

**adjectival** *adj* adjectif -ive

**adjective** *n* adjectif *m*, épithète *f*

**adjoin** *vt* adjoindre, joindre; toucher à; être adhérent à
**adjoining** *adj* limitrophe
**adjourn** *vt* ajourner, différer, renvoyer; *vi* s'ajourner; se déplacer
**adjournment** *n* ajournement *m*, renvoi *m*; suspension *f*
**adjudge** *vt leg* juger; condamner; (reward) décerner, adjuger
**adjudicate** *vt* juger; *leg* décider, arrêter
**adjudication** *n leg* décision *f*; jugement *m*
**adjudicator** *n* juge *m*
**adjunct** *n* (person) adjoint -e; (thing) accessoire *m*; *gramm* complément *m*; *adj* accessoire, ajouté
**adjuration** *n* adjuration *f*
**adjure** *vt* adjurer
**adjust** *vt* ajuster, régler, arranger
**adjustable** *adj* ajustable, réglable; ~ **spanner** clef *f* à molette
**adjutant** *n mil* = adjudant-major *m* (*pl* adjudants-major)
**ad lib** *vt + vi coll theat* improviser; *adj* improvisé, impromptu; *adv* à volonté
**adman** *n coll* publicitaire *m*, publiciste *m*
**admass** *n comm* clientèle *f* influençable (par la publicité)
**administer** *vt* administrer; gérer; (oath) faire prêter
**administration** *n* administration *f*, gestion *f*
**administrative** *adj* administratif -ive
**admirable** *adj* admirable, merveilleux -euse
**admiral** *n* amiral *m*; *ent* vulcain *m*
**Admiralty** *n* amirauté *f*; = ministère *m* de la Marine
**admiration** *n* admiration *f*
**admire** *vt* admirer; estimer
**admirer** *n* admirateur -trice; soupirant *m*
**admissibility** *n* admissibilité *f*, acceptabilité *f*
**admissible** *adj* admissible, acceptable
**admission** *n* admission *f*; (way in) accès *m*, entrée *f*; (confession) aveu *m*, acceptation *f*; **by his own** ~ de son propre aveu; **free** ~ entrée gratuite
**admit** *vt* admettre, avouer; laisser entrer; accepter; reconnaître, concéder; ~ **bearer** laissez passer; ~ **of** permettre; **one must** ~ on doit avouer; *vi* admettre
**admittance** *n* admission *f*; *elect* admittance *f*
**admittedly** *adv* de l'aveu général
**admix** *vt* mélanger; *vi* se mélanger
**admixture** *n* mélange *m*, dosage *m*
**admonish** *vt* admonester, réprimander; avertir

**admonition** *n* admonition *f*, admonestation *f*, réprimande *f*
**admonitory** *adj* qui admoneste
**ado** *n* agitation *f*; difficulté *f*, embarras *m*; **much** ~ **about nothing** beaucoup de bruit pour rien; **without further** ~ sans plus d'histoires
**adobe** *n* adobe *m*
**adolescence** *n* adolescence *f*
**adolescent** *n + adj* adolescent -e
**adopt** *vt* adopter; choisir
**adoption** *n* adoption *f*
**adoptive** *adj* adopté; adoptif -ive
**adorable** *adj* adorable
**adoration** *n* adoration *f*
**adore** *vt* adorer
**adorer** *n* adorateur -trice
**adorn** *vt* orner, parer
**adornment** *n* ornement *m*, parure *f*
**adrenal** *adj med* surrénal
**adrenalin** *n* adrénaline *f*
**adrift** *adj* à la dérive, en dérive; *fig* **be** ~ divaguer
**adroit** *adj* adroit
**adroitness** *n* adresse *f*
**adulate** *vt* aduler, flatter, flagorner
**adulation** *n* adulation *f*, flagornerie *f*
**adulator** *n* adulateur -trice
**adulatory** *adj* adulateur -trice, flatteur -euse
**adult** *n + adj* adulte
**adulterate** *vt* adultérer, frelater; *adj* adultéré, frelaté; (child) adultérin
**adulteration** *n* altération *f*, frelatage *m*
**adulterer** *n* adultère *m*
**adulteress** *n* adultère *f*
**adulterine** *adj* adultérin
**adulterous** *adj* adultère
**adultery** *n* adultère *m*
**adumbrate** *vt* esquisser; prédire
**adumbration** *n* esquisse *f*
**advance** *n* avance *f*, progression *f*; (rise) hausse *f*; (salary) acompte *m*; paiement anticipé; *vt* avancer, faire progresser; (money) prêter; faire avancer; (price) augmenter; *vi* avancer, progresser; s'avancer; augmenter
**advance-guard** *n* avant-garde *f*
**advancement** *n* avance *f*, avancement *m*
**advantage** *n* avantage *m*, supériorité *f*; gain *m*, profit *m*; *sp* avantage *m*; **show to** ~ avantager; **take** ~ **of** profiter de; *pej* abuser de; **turn to** ~ tirer parti de; *vt* avantager, favoriser
**advantageous** *adj* avantageux -euse, favorable; profitable, intéressant
**advent** *n* arrivée *f*, venue *f*; **Advent** *eccles* Avent *m*, Avènement *m*
**adventitious** *adj* adventice
**adventure** *n* aventure *f*, risque *m*; *vt* aventurer, risquer; *vi* s'aventurer
**adventurer** *n* aventurier *m*

**adventuresome** *adj* aventureux -euse
**adventuress** *n* aventurière *f*
**adventurous** *adj* aventureux -euse
**adverb** *n* adverbe *m*
**adverbial** *adj* adverbial
**adversary** *n* adversaire
**adverse** *adj* adverse, hostile, contraire
**adversity** *n* adversité *f*, malheur *m*
**¹advert** *n coll abbr* annonce *f*, réclame *f*
**²advert** *vi* faire allusion
**advertise** *vt* faire de la publicité pour, faire de la réclame pour; afficher, annoncer; *vi* faire de la publicité; (in paper) mettre une annonce
**advertisement** *n* annonce *f*; (poster) affiche *f*; (classified) petite annonce; publicité *f*
**advertiser** *n* annonceur *m*
**advice** *n* avis *m*, conseils *mpl*; *comm* avis *m*; **act on s/o's ~** suivre les conseils de qn; **piece of ~** conseil *m*; **seek ~ from** demander conseil à
**advisable** *adj* recommandable; prudent; opportun
**advise** *vt* conseiller; (inform) aviser; *vi* conseiller
**advised** *adj* avisé; délibéré
**advisedly** *adv* délibérément, en pleine connaissance de cause
**adviser** *n* conseiller -ère
**advisory** *adj* consultatif -ive
**advocacy** *n* profession *f* d'avocat; (plea) plaidoyer *m*, justification *f*
**advocate** *n* avocat -e, défenseur *m*; **devil's ~** avocat *m* du diable; *vt* recommander, préconiser
**adze** *n* (h)erminette *f*
**aegis** *n* égide *f*
**aeolian** *adj* éolien -ienne
**aerate** *vt* aérer; (liquids) gazéifier; **~ d water** eau gazeuse
**aeration** *n* aération *f*
**aerial** *n rad* antenne *f*; *adj* aérien -ienne
**aerie** *n see* eyrie
**aerify** *vt* aérifier
**aerobatics** *npl* acrobatie aérienne
**aerobic** *adj* aérobique
**aerodrome** *n* aérodrome *m*
**aerodynamic** *adj* aérodynamique
**aerodynamics** *npl* aérodynamique *f*
**aerolite, aerolith** *n* aérolit(h)e *m*
**aerology** *n* aérologie *f*
**aeronaut** *n* aéronaute
**aeronautics** *npl* aéronautique *f*
**aeroplane** *n* avion *m*, aéroplane *m*
**aerosol** *n* aérosol *m*, bombe *f*
**aerostat** *n* aérostat *m*
**aerostatics** *npl* aérostatique *f*
**aertex** *n* cellular *m*
**aesthete** *n* esthète
**aesthetic** *adj* esthétique
**aestheticism** *n* esthétisme *m*
**aesthetics** *npl* esthétique *f*

**aestivation** *n zool* estivation *f*
**aestival, estival** *adj* estival
**aether** *n see* ether
**aetiology** *n* étiologie *f*
**afar** *adv* loin
**affability** *n* affabilité *f*
**affable** *adj* affable
**affair** *n* (business) affaire *f*, occupation *f*; (matter) affaire *f*, question *f*; (love) affaire *f* de cœur, liaison *f*
**¹affect** *vt* (assume) affecter, adopter; (like) affectionner; (pretend) feindre
**²affect** *vt* affecter, influencer; (change) affecter, modifier; (move) affecter, toucher, émouvoir; *med* affecter, intéresser
**affectation** *n* affectation *f*
**affected** *adj* affecté, maniéré; (put on) feint; (moved) ému, touché
**affecting** *adj* émouvant, touchant
**affection** *n* affection *f*, tendresse *f*; état *m* d'âme, émotion *f*; *med* maladie *f*
**affectionate** *adj* affectueux -euse
**affectionately** *adv* affectueusement
**affective** *adj* affectif -ive
**afferent** *adj physiol* afférent
**affiance** *vt* fiancer
**affidavit** *n leg* déclaration *f* sous serment
**affiliate** *vt* affilier; *leg* attribuer la paternité; **~ oneself** s'affilier
**affiliation** *n* affiliation *f*; *leg* attribution *f* de paternité; **~ order** jugement *m* en constatation de paternité
**affinity** *n* affinité *f*; ressemblance *f*; attrait *m*
**affirm** *vt* affirmer, maintenir, soutenir; *vi* affirmer
**affirmation** *n* affirmation *f*, assertion *f*; *leg* confirmation *f*
**affirmative** *n* affirmatif *m*; *adj* affirmatif -ive
**affix** *n* prolongement *m*; *gramm* affixe *m*; *vt* (signature) apposer; ajouter; attacher
**afflatus** *n poet* inspiration divine
**afflict** *vt* affliger
**affliction** *n* affliction *f*, détresse *f*; (disaster) désastre *m*
**affluence** *n* richesse *f*; abondance *f*
**¹affluent** *n geog* affluent *m*
**²affluent** *adj* riche, prospère; abondant
**afflux** *n* afflux *m*
**afford** *vt* (give, bestow) fournir, procurer; (be able to pay for) avoir les moyens d'acheter, pouvoir s'offrir; (time) avoir le temps
**afforest** *vt* boiser, reboiser
**afforestation** *n* boisement *m*, reboisement *m*
**affranchise** *vt* affranchir
**affray** *n* bagarre *f*, rixe *f*
**affright** *n poet* effroi *m*; *vt poet* effrayer
**affront** *n* affront *m*, insulte *f*; *vt* insulter; (confront) braver, affronter
**afield** *adv* au loin; **far ~** très loin

**afire** *adj + adv lit* enflammé, en feu

**aflame** *adj + adv lit* embrasé, en flammes

**afloat** *adv* sur l'eau, à flot; en mer; *fig* (rumour) en circulation; *fig comm* à flot, hors de dettes; **keep ~** maintenir à flot

**afoot** *adv* en voie de préparation, imminent; (on foot) à pied; **there is sth ~** il se prépare qch

**aforementioned, aforesaid** *adj* susdit, susmentionné

**aforethought** *adj* prémédité; *leg* **with malice ~** avec préméditation criminelle

**afraid** *adj* effrayé, pris de peur, apeuré; **be ~ to** avoir peur de; **be ~ that** (regret) regretter, être désolé

**afresh** *adv* de nouveau, encore, de plus belle

**Africa** *n* Afrique *f*

**African** *n* Africain -e; *adj* africain

**Afrikaaner** *n* Afrikander

**Afrikaans** *n* afrikans *m*

**afro** *adj coll* afro *invar*

**Afro-Asian** *adj* afro-asiatique

**aft** *adv naut* à l'arrière; vers l'arrière

**after** *adj* (time) subséquent; *naut* arrière; *adv* après, ensuite; d'après; *prep* après; **be ~ s/o** chercher qn; *US* **half ~ six** six heures et demie; **take ~** ressembler à; **what are you ~?** que voulez-vous?; *conj* après, après que

**afterbirth** *n* arrière-faix *m*, placenta *m*

**after-care** *n* postcure *f*

**after-effect** *n med* séquelle *f*; répercussion *f*

**afterglow** *n* (sunset) dernières lueurs

**afterlife** *n* vie future

**aftermath** *n* suites *fpl*, conséquences *fpl*

**afternoon** *n* après-midi *m + f invar*

**afters** *npl coll* dessert *m*

**after-sales** *adj* après-vente *invar*

**aftershave** *n* after-shave *m*, lotion *f* après-rasage

**aftertaste** *n* arrière-goût *m*

**afterthought** *n* pensée *f* après coup

**afterwards** *adv* plus tard, après, ensuite

**again** *adv* encore, de nouveau, encore une fois; (in addition) une fois de plus; (moreover) d'ailleurs; **~ and ~** maintes et maintes fois, à plusieurs reprises; **and there ~** et puis alors; **as much ~** deux fois plus; **never ~** jamais plus; **not ~!** encore!; **now and ~** de temps en temps

**against** *prep* contre, à l'encontre de; (bump) sur; (in preparation for) en vue de, en prévision de; **over ~** en face de

¹**agape** *n hist eccles* agape *f*

²**agape** *adv* bouche bée

**agaric** *n bot* agaric *m*

**agate** *n* agate *f*

**age** *n* âge *m*; (period) époque *f*, ère *f*; *coll* (long time) éternité *f*, siècle *m*; **come of ~** atteindre sa majorité; **middle ~** un certain âge; **old ~** vieillesse *f*; **over ~** trop vieux (*f* vieille); **under ~** trop jeune; *vt* vieillir; *vi* vieillir, prendre de l'âge; (metal) fatiguer

**age-bracket** *n* tranche *f* d'âge

**aged** *npl* gens âgés; *adj* (old) âgé, vieux (*f* vieille); (of the age of) âgé de; (grown old) vieilli

**age-group** *n* groupe *m* de personnes du même âge

**ageless** *adj* sans âge

**age-long** *adj* pérenne

**agency** *n* (means) entremise *f*, intermédiaire *m*; *comm* agence *f*, bureau *m*

**agenda** *n* ordre *m* du jour

**agent** *n* agent *m*; (for product) concessionnaire

**age-old** *adj* antique

**agglomerate** *n* agglomérat *m*; *vt* agglomérer; *vi* s'agglomérer

**agglomeration** *n* agglomération *f*

**agglutinant** *n* agglutinant *m*; *adj* agglutinant

**agglutinate** *vt* agglutiner; *vi* s'agglutiner; *adj* agglutiné

**agglutination** *n* agglutination *f*

**aggrandize** *vt* agrandir

**aggrandizement** *n* agrandissement *m*

**aggravate** *vt* aggraver; (quarrel) envenimer; (irritate) agacer, exaspérer

**aggravating** *adj* aggravant; (irritating) agaçant, exaspérant

**aggravation** *n* aggravation *f*; (irritation) agacement *m*, exaspération *f*

**aggregate** *n* total *m*, ensemble *m*; *geol + phys* agrégat *m*; **in the ~** au total; *vt* agréger, rassembler; *vi* s'agréger; *adj* total, global; *geol* agrégé

**aggress** *vi* être l'agresseur

**aggression** *n* agression *f*

**aggressive** *adj* agressif -ive; *mil* offensif -ive

**aggressor** *n* agresseur *m*

**aggrieved** *adj* blessé, affligé

**aggro** *n sl* agressivité *f*, violence *f*; grabuge *m*

**aghast** *adj* ahuri, abasourdi, atterré

**agile** *adj* agile, leste

**agility** *n* agilité *f*, souplesse *f*

**agio** *n* agio *m*

**agiotage** *n* agiotage *m*

**agitate** *vt* (stir) agiter, remuer; (emotion) troubler, émouvoir; *vi* faire de l'agitation, exciter l'opinion publique, attirer l'attention publique

**agitated** *adj* troublé; inquiet -iète

**agitation** *n* agitation *f*; (emotion) trouble *m*, agitation *f*

**agitator** *n* agitateur -trice; *mech* agitateur *m*

**aglow** *adj* embrasé; (person) rayonnant

**agnostic** *n* + *adj* agnostique

**agnosticism** *n* agnosticisme *m*

**ago** *adv* il y a; **ten years** ~ il y a dix ans

**agog** *adj* + *adv* en émoi

**agonize** *vi* (try) s'efforcer; être au supplice, souffrir le martyre

**agonizing** *adj* déchirant, agonisant

**agony** *n* angoisse *f*; (physical pain) paroxysme *m*; (death) agonie *f*; (newspaper) ~ **column** rubrique *f* des messages personnels; *coll* **pile on the** ~ en rajouter, exagérer

**agrarian** *n* + *adj hist* agrarien -ienne

**agree** *vt* accepter, consentir à; (opinion) convenir de; (admit) avouer; *vi* être d'accord, être du même avis; (come to terms) se mettre d'accord; (coincide) concorder, correspondre; *gramm* s'accorder; ~ **to differ** rester sur ses positions; (health) ~ **with** être bon (*f* bonne) pour

**agreeable** *adj* agréable, aimable; (willing) consentant; **be** ~ **to** vouloir bien

**agreed** *adj* d'accord, entendu; *coll* d'accord

**agreement** *n* accord *m*, harmonie *f*; *comm* contrat *m*; *leg* accommodement *m*; *gramm* accord *m*; **be in** ~ être d'accord; **by mutual** ~ d'un commun accord; **enter into an** ~ signer un accord

**agricultural** *adj* agricole

**agriculturalist** *n* agronome *m*; (farmer) agriculteur *m*

**agriculture** *n* agriculture *f*

**agronomics** *npl* agronomie *f*

**agronomist** *n* agronome

**aground** *adj naut* échoué

**ague** *n* fièvre intermittente

**ah** *interj* ah!

**aha** *interj* eh voilà!, tiens!

**ahead** *adv* en avant, devant; (time) en avance, d'avance; ~ **of** (time) avant; (place) devant; **draw** ~ gagner de l'avant; **get** ~ avancer; **go** ~ prendre de l'avance; **look** ~ considérer l'avenir

**ahoy** *interj naut* ohé!

**aid** *n* aide *f*, assistance *f*, secours *m*; (person) aide, assistant -e; **deaf** ~ appareil *m* acoustique; **first** ~ secours *mpl* d'urgence; **in** ~ **of** à l'appui de; (charity) au profit de; **legal** ~ assistance *f* judiciaire; *coll* **what's this in** ~ **of?** qu'est-ce que ça signifie?; *vt* aider, assister, secourir; *leg* ~ **and abet** être complice de, avoir part à

**aide-de-camp** *n* aide *m* de camp

**Aids** *n med* SIDA *m*

**aigrette** *n* aigrette *f*

**ail** *vt ar* + *poet* affliger; *vi* souffrir

**aileron** *n* aileron *m*

**ailing** *adj* souffrant, en mauvaise santé

**ailment** *n* indisposition *f*

**aim** *n* action *f* de viser; (purpose) but *m*, objet *m*, visées *fpl*; **take** ~ viser; *vt* (gun) braquer; (blow) allonger; (remark) diriger; *vi* (intend) viser, aspirer; ~ **high** être ambitieux -ieuse; ~ **to** aspirer à

**aimless** *adj* sans but; futile

**ain't** *dial* + *sl abbr* = **am not, are not, is not, has not, have not**

**air** *n* air *m*, atmosphère *f*; (breeze) brise *f*; *fig* air *m*, aspect *m*, mine *f*; *mus* air *m*; ~**s** minauderies *fpl*; ~ **traffic control** contrôle *m* de la circulation aérienne; **be in the** ~ être à l'état de projet; **by** ~ par avion; **give oneself (put on)** ~**s** se donner de grands airs; **have an** ~ **about one** avoir de l'allure; *coll* **hot** ~ blablabla *m*; **on the** ~ à la radio, sur les ondes; **open** ~ plein air; **there's sth in the** ~ le bruit court; **tread on** ~ être aux anges; *vt* aérer, sécher; (opinions) exprimer, faire connaître

**air-base** *n* base aérienne, base *f* d'aviation

**air-bed** *n* matelas *m* pneumatique

**airborne** *adj* aéroporté; (plane) **be** ~ avoir décollé

**air-brake** *n* frein *m* à air comprimé; *aer* aérofrein *m*

**airbus** *n* airbus *m*, aérobus *m*

**air-chamber** *n* chambre *f* à air

**Air-Chief-Marshal** *n* = général *m* d'armée aérienne

**Air-Commodore** *n* = général *m* de brigade aérienne

**air-conditioned** *adj* climatisé

**air-conditioning** *n* climatisation *f*

**air-cooled** *adj* à refroidissement par air

**air-cooling** *n* refroidissement *m* par air

**aircraft** *n* avion *m*

**aircraft-carrier** *n* porte-avions *m*

**aircraft(s)man** *n* = soldat *m* de deuxième classe (de l'armée de l'air)

**air-crew** *n* équipage *m* (d'un avion)

**air-cushion** *n* coussin *m* pneumatique

**airdrome** *n US see* **aerodrome**

**airdrop** *n* parachutage *m*

**air-ferry** *n* avion transbordeur

**airfield** *n* terrain *m* d'aviation, aérodrome *m*

**air-filter** *n* filtre *m* à air

**air-force** *n* = armée *f* de l'air

**air-gun** *n* fusil *m* à air comprimé

**air-hole** *n* soupirail *m*

**air-hostess** *n* hôtesse *f* de l'air

**airily** *adv* légèrement, d'un ton dégagé, avec désinvolture

**airiness** *n* aération *f*; (behaviour)

désinvolture *f*, insouciance *f*

**airing** *n* aération *f*; (problem) discussion *f*

**air-lane** *n* couloir *m* de navigation aérienne

**airless** *adj* mal ventilé, privé d'air

**airline** *n* compagnie *f* d'aviation

**airliner** *n* avion *m* de ligne

**airlock** *n* bulle *f* d'air; (caisson) sas *m*

**airmail** *n* poste aérienne; *adj* + *adv* par avion

**airman** *n* aviateur *m*; soldat *m* de l'armée de l'air

**Air-Marshal** *n* = général *m* de corps aérien

**air-mattress** *n* matelas *m* pneumatique

**airplane** *n US see* **aeroplane**

**air-pocket** *n* trou *m* d'air

**airport** *n* aéroport *m*

**air-pressure** *n* pression *f* atmosphérique

**air-pump** *n* compresseur *m*

**air-raid** *n* attaque aérienne; ~ **precautions** défense aérienne passive

**air-screw** *n* hélice *f*

**airshaft** *n* min puits *m* d'aérage

**airship** *n* dirigeable *m*

**air-sickness** *n* mal *m* de l'air

**air-space** *n* espace aérien; (room) cubage *m* d'air

**airstrip** *n* piste *f* d'atterrissage

**airtight** *adj* étanche, hermétique

**air-to-air** *adj* avion-avion *invar*

**air-to-ground** *adj* air-sol *invar*

**Air-Vice-Marshal** *n* = général *m* de division aérienne

**airway** *n* (shaft) conduit *m* d'air; (route) voie aérienne

**airwoman** *n* aviatrice *f*; = auxiliaire *f* de l'armée de l'air

**airworthiness** *n* navigabilité *f*; **certificate of** ~ certificat *m* de navigabilité

**airworthy** *adj* navigable; muni d'un certificat de navigabilité

**airy** *adj* (ventilated) aéré; (light) léger -ère; (casual) désinvolte

**aisle** *n* nef latérale, bas-côté *m*; allée centrale, passage *m*, couloir *m*

**ajar** *adj* entrebâillé, entr'ouvert

**akimbo** *adv* **arms** ~ les mains *fpl* sur les hanches

**akin** *adj* apparenté; ~ **to** qui ressemble à

**alabaster** *n* albâtre *m*; *adj* d'albâtre

**alack** *interj poet* hélas!

**alacrity** *n* entrain *m*, empressement *m*, alacrité *f*

**alarm** *n* alarme *f*, alerte *f*; (fear) alarme *f*, agitation *f*; inquiétude *f*; *joc* ~ **s and excursions** branle-bas *m* de combat; *vt* alarmer, alerter; faire peur à

**alarm-bell** *n* sonnerie *f* d'alarme

**alarm-clock** *n* réveil *m*, réveille-matin *m* *invar*

**alarming** *adj* déconcertant, alarmant

**alarmist** *n* + *adj* alarmiste

**alas** *interj* hélas!

**alb** *n eccles* aube *f*

**albatross** *n* albatros *m*

**albeit** *conj lit* encore que, bien que

**albino** *n* albinos

**album** *n* album *m*

**albumen, albumin** *n* (egg) albumen *m*, blanc *m* de l'œuf; *physiol* albumine *f*

**albuminous** *adj* albumineux -euse

**alchemic** *adj* alchimique

**alchemist** *n* alchimiste *m*

**alchemy, alchymy** *n* alchimie *f*

**alcohol** *n* alcool *m*

**alcoholic** *n* alcoolique; *adj* alcoolique; (drink) alcoolisé

**alcoholism** *n* alcoolisme *m*

**alcove** *n* alcôve *f*; (summerhouse) tonnelle *f*

**aldehyde** *n chem* aldehyde *m*

**alder** *n* aulne *m*, aune *m*

**alderman** *n* = conseiller -ère municipal -e (ou) général -e d'une certaine ancienneté; *hist* échevin *m*

**Alderney** *n geog* Aurigny *f*

**ale** *n* bière *f*, ale *f*

**aleatory** *adj* aléatoire

**alembic** *n* alambic *m*

**alert** *n* alerte *f*; *adj* alerte, vigilant; (sharp) éveillé; *vt* alerter, éveiller l'attention de

**alexandrine** *n lit* alexandrin *m*

**alexia** *n* cécité verbale, alexie *f*

**alfa** *n* alfa *m*

**alfalfa** *n* luzerne *f*

**alfresco** *adv* en plein air

**alga** *n* (*pl* **algae**) algue(s) *f* (*pl*)

**algebra** *n* algèbre *f*

**algebraic** *adj* algébrique

**algebrist** *n* algébriste

**Algeria** *n geog* Algérie *f*

**alias** *n* nom *m* d'emprunt; *adv* alias

**alibi** *n* alibi *m*

**alien** *n* + *adj* étranger -ère

**alienable** *adj leg* aliénable

**alienate** *vt* aliéner

**alienation** *n* *leg* + *med* aliénation *f*; éloignement *m*; désaffection *f*

**alienist** *n* aliéniste

¹**alight** *vi* descendre, mettre pied à terre

²**alight** *adj* en feu, allumé

**align** *vt* aligner, mettre en ligne; *vi* s'aligner

**alignment** *n* alignement *m*

**alike** *adj* semblable, pareil -eille; *adv* pareillement, de même; de la même façon

**aliment** *n* aliment *m*; *vt* alimenter, nourrir

**alimentary** *adj* alimentaire; ~ **canal** tube digestif

**alimentation** n alimentation f

**alimony** n leg pension f alimentaire

**alive** adj vivant, en vie; (lively) vif (f vive); (sensitive) sensible; (alert) alerte, actif -ive; ~ **with** grouillant de; **keep** ~ maintenir, préserver

**alkali** n alcali m

**alkaline** adj alcalin

**alkaloid** n alcaloïde m

**all** n tout m; (everyone) tous les hommes, tout le monde, tous (f toutes); ~ **clear** signal m de fin d'alerte; ~ **in** ~ à tout prendre; **after** ~ après tout; **at** ~ du tout; **for good and** ~ pour toujours; **in** ~ en tout; **once for** ~ une fois pour toutes; sp **three** ~ (tennis) trois partout; (other games) trois à trois; pron tout (mpl tous, fpl toutes); adj tout (mpl tous, fpl toutes); (utmost) le plus possible; ~ **the** tout le (f toute la, mpl tous les, fpl toutes les); **for** ~ **that** malgré tout; **on** ~ **fours** à quatre pattes; adv tout, tout à fait, entièrement; ~ **at once** tout d'un coup; ~ **but** presque; ~ **over** (finished) fini; (everywhere) partout; ~ **right** bien, très bien; (health) en bonne santé; (agreement) d'accord; ~ **the better** tant mieux; coll ~ **there** intelligent, malin (f maligne); coll ~ **up with** ruiné, fichu

**allay** vt apaiser, calmer, modérer; (suspicion) dissiper

**allegation** n allégation f

**allege** vt alléguer, prétendre

**alleged** adj prétendu; (criminal) présumé

**allegiance** n hist allégeance f; fidélité f, obéissance f

**allegoric, allegorical** adj allégorique

**allegory** n allégorie f

**allegretto** n allegretto m; adv allegretto

**allegro** n allegro m; adv allegro

**alleluia, hallelujah** interj alléluia!

**allemande** n mus allemande f

**allergic** adj allergique

**allergy** n med allergie f

**alleviate** vt alléger, calmer, soulager

**alley** n (in garden) allée f; (between buildings) ruelle f; **blind** ~ cul-de-sac m (pl culs-de-sac), impasse f; fig impasse f; **bowling** ~ bowling m

**alleyway** n ruelle f

**alliance** n alliance f, pacte m

**allied** adj allié; (related) apparenté

**alligator** n alligator m

**all-in** adj coll épuisé; ~ **(insurance) policy** police f (d'assurances) tous risques; ~ **wrestling** lutte f libre, catch m; adv tout compris

**alliteration** n allitération f

**alliterative** adj allitératif -ive

**all-night** adj de nuit, durant toute la nuit

**allocate** vt allouer, attribuer, affecter

**allocation** n allocation f; (sum) affectation f; (amount) part f; (distribution) répartition f

**allocution** n allocution f

**allopathy** n allopathie f

**allot** vt (share out) répartir; (assign) attribuer, assigner

**allotment** n répartition f, assignation f; (share) part f; mil délégation f de solde; (plot of land) lopin de terre loué pour la culture

**allotropic** adj chem allotropique

**allotropy** n chem allotropie f

**all-out** adj total; coll tous azimuths; coll ~ **effort** effort m maximum; adv coll **go** ~ faire son possible, mettre toutes ses forces

**allow** vt permettre; (admit) admettre, concéder; (grant) allouer, accorder; ~ **for** tenir compte de

**allowable** adj admissible, permis

**allowance** n allocation f, rente f, pension f; (rent, lodging, etc) indemnité f; (discount) rabais m, réduction f; mech tolérance f; **make** ~ **for s/o** se montrer indulgent à l'égard de qn; **make** ~ **for sth** prendre qch en considération

**allowed** adj permis; (true) reconnu, accepté; **not** ~ interdit

**alloy** n alliage m; vt allier; fig altérer, corrompre

**all-round** adj complet -ète, sur toute la ligne

**all-rounder** n coll esp sp qn ayant des talents (sportifs) très variés

**all-star** adj (cast) de vedettes

**all-time** adj coll sans précédent, inouï

**allude** vi faire allusion

**allure** n charme m, attirance f; vt séduire, charmer, attirer

**allurement** n attrait m, fascination f

**alluring** adj séduisant, attrayant

**allusion** n allusion f

**allusive** adj allusif -ive

**alluvial** adj alluvial

**alluvium** n alluvion f

**ally** n allié -e; hist **the Allies** les Alliés; vt allier; ~ **oneself with** s'allier avec

**almanac** n almanach m

**almighty** n **the Almighty** le Tout-Puissant; adj tout-puissant, omnipotent; coll extrême, énorme, fameux -euse

**almond** n amande f; (tree) amandier m; adj en amande

**almoner** n (in a hospital) assistant -e social -e

**almost** adv presque, à peu près

**almshouse** n hospice m; maison f de retraite

**aloe** n aloès m; ~ **s** aloès médicinal

**aloft** *adv* en haut, en l'air; *naut* dans la mâture

**alone** *adj* seul; **let s/o ~** laisser qn tranquille; **let well ~** le mieux est l'ennemi du bien; *adv* seulement; *conj* **let ~** sans parler de

**along** *adv* en avant; **~ with** avec; **all ~** (time) du début à la fin; (space) d'un bout à l'autre; **come ~** allons; **get ~** se débrouiller, s'arranger; **get ~ with you!** sans blague!; **move ~!** circulez!; *prep* le long de

**alongside** *adv naut* bord à bord; *prep* le long de, à côté de, près de; **come ~** *naut* accoster

**aloof** *adj* distant, réservé; *adv* à distance; **stand ~ from** se tenir à l'écart de

**aloofness** *n* réserve *f*

**aloud** *adv* à haute voix, à voix haute, tout haut

**alp** *n* (mountain pasture) alpe *f*, pâturage *m* de montagne; **the Alps** les Alpes *fpl*

**alpaca** *n* alpaga *m*

**alpha** *n* alpha *m*; (mark at school, university) = très bonne note; **~ particle** particule *f* alpha

**alphabet** *n* alphabet *m*

**alphabetical** *adj* alphabétique

**alpine** *adj* alpin

**already** *adv* déjà

**alright** *see* **all right**

**Alsatian** *n* Alsacien -ienne; **~ (dog)** chien *m* loup, berger allemand; *adj* alsacien -ienne, d'Alsace

**also** *adv* aussi, d'ailleurs, également

**also-ran** *n sp* cheval non classé; *fig* raté -e

**altar** *n* autel *m*; **high ~** maître-autel *m* (*pl* maîtres-autels); **lead to the ~** épouser

**altar-bread** *n* hostie *f*

**altar-cloth** *n* nappe *f* d'autel

**altar-piece** *n* retable *m*

**altar-rail(s)** *n* balustre *m* du chœur

**alter** *vt* changer, modifier; (touch up) retoucher, remanier; *vi* changer

**alterable** *adj* modifiable, transformable

**alterant** *n* altérogène *m*; *adj* altérant

**alteration** *n* changement *m*, modification *f*

**altercation** *n* altercation *f*

**alter ego** *n* alter ego *m*

**alternate** *adj* alterné, alternatif -ive; (every other) tous les deux; *vt* faire alterner; *vi* alterner

**alternating** *adj* alternant; *elect* **~ current** courant alternatif

**alternation** *n* alternance *f*

**alternative** *n* alternative *f*, choix *m*; *adj* alternatif -ive, autre

**alternator** *n elect* alternateur *m*

**although** *conj* quoique, bien que, encore que

**altimeter** *n* altimètre *m*

**altitude** *n* altitude *f*, hauteur *f*

**alto** *n mus* (male voice) haute-contre *f* (*pl* hautes-contre); (female voice) contralto *m*

**altogether** *adv* tout à fait, entièrement, absolument; (on the whole) tout compte fait, au total; (in total) en tout

**altruism** *n* altruisme *m*

**altruist** *n* altruiste

**altruistic** *adj* altruiste

**alum** *n* alun *m*

**aluminium** *n* aluminium *m*

**aluminum** *n US see* **aluminium**

**alumna** *n* (*pl* **alumnae**) *US* ancienne élève (d'une école, d'une université)

**alumnus** *n* (*pl* **alumni**) *US* ancien élève (d'une école, d'une université)

**alveolar** *adj* alvéolaire

**alveole, alveolus** *n* alvéole *m* or *f*

**always** *adv* toujours

**am** *see* **be**

**amain** *adv ar poet* violemment, de toutes ses forces, à toute vitesse

**amalgam** *n* amalgame *m*

**amalgamate** *vt* amalgamer, unifier; *vi* s'amalgamer, s'unifier

**amalgamation** *n* amalgamation *f*, unification *f*, fusion *f*

**amanuensis** *n* (*pl* **amanuenses**) secrétaire, copiste

**amaranth** *n bot* amarante *f*

**amaranthine** *adj* amarante *invar*

**amaryllis** *n* amaryllis *f*

**amass** *vt* amasser, accumuler, amonceler

**amateur** *n* amateur *m*; *adj* d'amateur

**amateurish** *adj pej* d'amateur, de dilettante

**amatory** *adj* amoureux -euse; lascif -ive

**amaze** *vt* ébahir, étonner, frapper de stupeur

**amazement** *n* ébahissement *m*, étonnement *m*, stupeur *f*

**amazing** *adj* ahurissant, étonnant; merveilleux -euse

**Amazon** *n myth* Amazone *f*; *sp* athlète *f*

**ambassador** *n* ambassadeur *m*

**ambassadress** *n* ambassadrice *f*

**amber** *n* ambre *m*; *adj* d'ambre; (colour) ambré; *mot* **~ light** feu *m* jaune

**ambergris** *n* ambre gris

**ambidextrous** *adj* ambidextre

**ambience** *n* ambiance *f*

**ambient** *adj* ambiant

**ambiguity** *n* ambiguïté *f*, équivoque *f*

**ambiguous** *adj* ambigu -uë, équivoque; obscur

**ambiguousness** *n* ambiguïté *f*, équivoque *f*

**ambit** *n* pourtour *m*, limites *fpl*; étendue *f*, sphère *f* d'influence

**ambition** *n* ambition *f*

**ambitious** *adj* ambitieux -ieuse

**ambivalence** *n* ambivalence *f*

**ambivalent** *adj* ambivalent

**amble** *vi* (horse) ambler, aller l'amble; (person) flâner

**ambrosia** *n* ambroisie *f*

**ambrosial** *adj* au parfum d'ambroisie

**ambulance** *n* ambulance *f*

**ambulant** *adj* ambulant

**ambulatory** *n* cloître *m*; (apse) abside *f*; *adj* ambulatoire

**ambuscade** *n* embuscade *f*; *vt* embusquer; *vi* s'embusquer

**ambush** *n* embuscade *f*, guet-apens *m* (*pl* guets-apens); *vt* attirer dans une embuscade

**ameliorate** *vt* améliorer; *vi* s'améliorer

**amen** *n* amen *m invar*; *interj* amen!

**amenable** *adj* (responsive) sensible, raisonnable, maniable; (responsible) responsable

**amend** *vt* amender, corriger, modifier; *vi* s'amender

**amendment** *n* amendement *m*, rectification *f*

**amends** *npl* réparation *f*, compensation *f*; **make ~** faire réparation; (admit wrong) faire amende honorable; **make ~ to** dédommager

**amenity** *n* agrément *m*, charme *m*; (place, district) **amenities** commodités *fpl*, agréments *mpl*

**America** *n* Amérique *f*

**American** *n* Américain -e; *adj* américain

**americanism** *n* américanisme *m*

**americanize** *vt* américaniser

**amethyst** *n* améthyste *f*

**Amharic** *n ling* amharique *m*

**amiability** *n* amabilité *f*, gentillesse *f*

**amiable** *adj* aimable, gentil -ille

**amicable** *adj* amical

**amice** *n eccles* amict *m*

**amid** *prep* parmi, au milieu de

**amidships** *adv naut* au milieu du navire

**amidst** *prep* parmi, au milieu de

**amino-acid** *n* amino-acide *m*, acide aminé

**amiss** *adj* incorrect, mal à propos; *adv* mal, mal à propos, incorrectement; **it wouldn't come ~** ça ne ferait pas de mal; **take sth ~** prendre qch en mauvaise part; **there is sth ~** il y a qch qui cloche

**amity** *n* amitié *f*, concorde *f*

**ammeter** *n elect* ampèremètre *m*

**ammonia** *n* ammoniac *m*; **~ solution** ammoniaque *f*

**ammoniac** *adj* ammoniac -aque

**ammunition** *n* munitions *fpl*; *fig* armes *fpl*

**amnesia** *n* amnésie *f*

**amnesic** *adj* amnésique

**amnesty** *n* amnistie *f*; *vt* amnistier

**amoeba** *n* amibe *f*

**amoebic** *adj* amibien -ienne

**amok** *adv see* **amuck**

**among(st)** *prep* parmi; (between) au milieu de

**amoral** *adj* amoral

**amorous** *adj* amoureux -euse, lascif -ive

**amorousness** *n* lasciveté *f*

**amorphous** *adj* amorphe; *fig* sans forme, mal organisé

**amortization** *n* amortissement *m*

**amortize** *vt* amortir

**amount** *n* quantité *f*; (sum) montant *m*, somme *f*, total *m*; (meaning) signification *f*; **any ~ of** des quantités de; *vi* **~ to** s'élever à, se chiffrer à; (be equivalent to) se réduire à, se ramener à; **it ~ s to the same thing** ça revient au même

**amour** *n* liaison *f*, intrigue amoureuse

**amperage** *n elect* intensité *f* d'un courant exprimé en ampères

**ampere** *n* ampère *m*

**ampersand** *n* esperluète *f*

**amphetamine** *n* amphétamine *f*

**amphibia** *npl zool* amphibiens *mpl*, batraciens *mpl*

**amphibian** *n zool* amphibie *m*; *mil* char *m* amphibie, avion *m* amphibie; *adj* amphibie

**amphibious** *adj* amphibie

**amphitheatre** *n* amphithéâtre *m*; *coll* amphi *m*

**amphora** *n* (*pl* **amphorae**) amphore *f*

**ample** *adj* abondant, sans bornes; (garment) ample; bien assez de; **have ~ means** avoir une grosse fortune; **have ~ time** avoir largement le temps

**amplification** *n* amplification *f*

**amplifier** *n* amplificateur *m*, *coll* ampli *m*

**amplify** *vt* amplifier, augmenter; (view) développer

**amplitude** *n* amplitude *f*

**amply** *adv* amplement, largement

**ampoule** *n* ampoule *f*

**amputate** *vt* amputer

**amputation** *n* amputation *f*

**amuck, amok** *adv* **run ~** s'abandonner à l'amok, être pris d'un accès de folie meurtrière; *fig* perdre tout contrôle de soi-même

**amulet** *n* amulette *f*

**amuse** *vt* amuser, divertir, faire rire

**amusement** *n* amusement *m*, divertissement *m*; (pastime) distraction *f*, amusement *m*; **~ arcade** luna-park *m*

**amusing** *adj* amusant, drôle, divertissant

**amusingly** *adv* drôlement, d'une manière amusante

**amyl** *n* amyle *m*; ~ **alcohol** alcool *m* amylique

¹**an** *indef art see* **a**

²**an** *conj ar* si

**Anabaptist** *n* anabaptiste

**anabolism** *n physiol* anabolisme *m*

**anachronism** *n* anachronisme *m*

**anachronistic** *adj* anachronique

**anacoluthon** *n* (*pl* **anacolutha**) anacoluthe *f*

**anaconda** *n* anaconda *m*

**anacreontic** *adj* anacréontique

**anaemia** *n* anémie *f*

**anaemic** *adj* anémique

**anaesthesia** *n* anesthésie *f*

**anaesthetic** *n* anesthésique *m*; *adj* anesthésique

**anaesthetist** *n* anesthésiste

**anaesthetize** *vt* anesthésier

**anagram** *n* anagramme *f*

**anal** *adj* anal

**analgesia** *n* analgésie *f*

**analgesic** *n* analgésique *m*; *adj* analgésique

**analog** *n US see* **analogue**

**analogical** *adj* analogique

**analogous** *adj* analogue

**analogue** *n* analogue *m*; ~ **computer** calculateur *m* analogique

**analogy** *n* analogie *f*

**analyse, analyze** *vt* analyser, faire l'analyse de; *gramm* faire l'analyse logique de; *psych* psychanalyser

**analysis** *n* (*pl* **analyses**) analyse *f*; *psych* psychanalyse *f*

**analyst** *n chem* analyste; *psych* psychanalyste

**analytic, analytical** *adj* analytique

**analytics** *n* analytique *f*

**anapaest** *n pros* anapeste *m*

**anaphrodisiac** *n* anaphrodisiaque *m*; *adj* anaphrodisiaque

**anarchic, anarchical** *adj* anarchique

**anarchism** *n* anarchisme *m*

**anarchist** *n* + *adj* anarchiste

**anarchy** *n* anarchie *f*

**anathema** *n eccles* + *fig* anathème *m*

**anathematize** *vt* frapper d'anathème, maudire

**anatomical** *adj* anatomique

**anatomist** *n* anatomiste

**anatomize** *vt* disséquer; examiner minutieusement

**anatomy** *n* anatomie *f*; *fig* analyse détaillée

**ancestor** *n* ancêtre *m*, aïeul *m* (*pl* aïeux)

**ancestral** *adj* ancestral

**ancestress** *n* aïeule *f*

**ancestry** *n* ascendance *f*, ancêtres *mpl*

**anchor** *n* ancre *f*; *fig* soutien *m*; **cast** ~,

**come to** ~ jeter l'ancre, mouiller; **weigh** ~ lever l'ancre; *vt* mettre à l'ancre; *fig* ancrer; *vi* mouiller, se mettre à l'ancre

**anchorage** *n* mouillage *m*, ancrage *m*; (dues) droits *mpl* de mouillage

**anchored** *adj* ancré

**anchorite** *n* anachorète *m*

**anchovy** *n* anchois *m*

**anchylosis** *n* ankylose *f*

**anchylotic** *adj* ankylosé

**ancient** *n* **the** ~**s** les anciens; *adj* (antiquity) antique; (dated) ancien -ienne

**ancillary** *adj* auxiliaire

**and** *conj* et; ~ **so forth**, ~ **so on** et ainsi de suite; **faster** ~ **faster** de plus en plus vite; **go** ~ **ask** allez demander; **more** ~ **more** de plus en plus; **one hundred** ~ **ten** cent dix; **wait** ~ **see** attendez voir

**andante** *n mus* andante *m*

**andiron** *n* chenet *m*

**androgynous** *adj* androgène

**anecdotal** *adj* anecdotique

**anecdote** *n* anecdote *f*

**anemometer** *n* anémomètre *m*

**anemone** *n* anémone *f*; **sea** ~ actinie *f*, anémone *f* de mer

**aneroid** *n* baromètre *m* anéroïde; *adj* anéroïde

**aneurism** *n path* anévrisme *m*

**anew** *adv* encore, de nouveau

**angel** *n* ange *m*; *coll* amour *m*

**angel-fish** *n* ange *m* de mer

**angelic** *adj* angélique

**angelica** *n* angélique *f*

**angelical** *adj* angélique

**angelus** *n* angélus *m*

**anger** *n* colère *f*, fureur *f*; *lit* courroux *m*; *vt* irriter, mettre en colère; *lit* courroucer

**angina** *n* angine *f*; ~ **pectoris** angine *f* de poitrine

¹**angle** *n* angle *m*; *fig* point *m* de vue, aspect *m*, angle *m*; **at an** ~ de biais; *vt* *coll* (news, information) présenter avec parti-pris, donner des renseignements tendancieux

²**angle** *vi* pêcher à la ligne; *fig* manœuvrer

**angler** *n* pêcheur -euse à la ligne

**Angles** *npl hist* Angles *mpl*

**Anglican** *n* + *adj* anglican -e

**Anglicanism** *n* anglicanisme *m*

**anglicism** *n* anglicisme *m*

**anglicize** *vt* angliciser

**angling** *n* pêche *f* à la ligne

**anglomania** *n* anglomanie *f*

**anglophile** *n* + *adj* anglophile

**anglophobe** *n* + *adj* anglophobe

**anglophobia** *n* anglophobie *f*

**Anglo-Saxon** *n* (person) Anglo-Saxononne; *ling* anglo-saxon *m*; *adj* anglo-saxon -onne

**angora** *n* (wool) laine *f* angora, angora *m*; (animal) chat *m* angora, lapin *m* angora, chèvre *f* angora

**angostura, angustura** *n* angusture *f*; ~ **bitters** bitter *m* à base d'angusture

**angry** *adj* en colère, furieux -ieuse, irrité, fâché; *med* enflammé, irrité

**anguish** *n* angoisse *f*, anxiété *f*; *vt* angoisser, inquiéter

**angular** *adj* anguleux -euse, pointu

**aniline** *n* aniline *f*; *adj* à base d'aniline

**animadversion** *n* animadversion *f*, observation *f* hostile

**animadvert** *vi* blâmer, critiquer

**animal** *n* animal *m*, bête *f*; *adj* animal; ~ **magnetism** hypnotisme *m*; ~ **spirits** vivacité *f*, entrain *m*

**animality** *n* animalité *f*

**animalize** *vt* brutaliser, animaliser

**animate** *adj* vivant; (lively) vivace; *vt* animer, stimuler, encourager

**animated** *adj* animé; ~ **cartoon** dessin animé

**animation** *n* animation *f*, vivacité *f*, entrain *m*

**animator** *n* animateur -trice

**animism** *n* animisme *m*

**animist** *n* + *adj* animiste

**animosity** *n* animosité *f*, hostilité *f*

**animus** *n* *see* **animosity**

**anise** *n* anis *m*

**aniseed** *n* graine *f* d'anis

**ankle** *n* cheville *f*

**anklet** *n* bracelet *m* de cheville

**annalist** *n* annaliste *m*

**annals** *npl* annales *fpl*

**anneal** *vt* *metal* recuire

**annex, annexe** *n* annexe *f*; *vt* annexer, incorporer

**annexation** *n* incorporation *f*

**annexe** *n* *see* **annex**

**annihilate** *vt* annihiler, anéantir

**annihilation** *n* annihilation *f*, anéantissement *m*

**anniversary** *n* anniversaire *m*

**annotate** *vt* annoter

**annotation** *n* annotation *f*

**announce** *vt* annoncer, proclamer; faire savoir; (birth, death, etc) faire part de

**announcement** *n* annonce *f*, avis *m*; (birth, death, etc) faire-part *m invar*

**announcer** *n* *rad* + *T V* speaker -ine

**annoy** *vt* ennuyer, vexer, agacer, contrarier, irriter

**annoyance** *n* contrariété *f*, irritation *f*, ennui *m*

**annoying** *adj* ennuyeux -euse, agaçant, fâcheux -euse, contrariant

**annual** *n* publication annuelle; *bot* plante annuelle; *adj* annuel -elle

**annuity** *n* annuité *f*, rente viagère, viager *m*

**annul** *vt* annuler; *leg* abroger

**annular** *adj* annulaire

**annulary** *n* annulaire *m*

**annulment** *n* annulation *f*; *leg* abrogation *f*

**Annunciation** *n* Annonciation *f*

**anode** *n* *elect* anode *f*

**anodize** *vt* anodiser

**anodyne** *n* analgésique *m*; *adj* analgésique, calmant; *fig* inoffensif -ive

**anoint** *vt* oindre, consacrer; (king) sacrer

**anomalous** *adj* irrégulier -ière, anormal

**anomaly** *n* anomalie *f*

**¹anon** *adv* *ar* *joc* bientôt, tout à l'heure

**²anon** *adj* *abbr* anonyme

**anonymity** *n* anonymat *m*

**anonymous** *adj* anonyme

**anopheles** *n* *ent* anophèle *m*

**anorak** *n* anorak *m*

**anorexia** *n* anorexie *f*

**another** *adj* (one more) encore un(e), un(e) de plus; (different) un(e) autre; *pron* un(e) autre, encore un(e)

**answer** *n* (reply) réponse *f*; (solution) solution *f*; *vt* répondre à, répliquer à; (prayer) exaucer; ~**ing machine** répondeur *m* téléphonique ~ **the door** aller ouvrir la porte; *vi* répondre; *coll* ~ **back** donner une réponse impertinente

**answerable** *adj* responsable; (question) susceptible de réponse

**ant** *n* fourmi *f*

**antacid** *n* antiacide *m*, alcalin *m*; *adj* anti-acide, alcalin

**antagonism** *n* antagonisme *m*

**antagonist** *n* antagoniste, adversaire

**antagonize** *vt* contrarier, éveiller l'hostilité de

**Antarctic** *n* Antarctique *m*; *adj* antarctique, austral

**Antarctica** *n* Antarctique *m*, Terres Australes

**ante-** *pref* anté-, anti-

**ant-eater** *n* fourmilier *m*

**antecede** *vt* précéder

**antecedent** *n* antécédent *m*; ~**s** (person) passé *m*; *adj* antérieur

**antechamber** *n* antichambre *f*

**antedate** *vt* antidater; (precede) précéder

**antediluvian** *adj* antédiluvien -ienne

**antelope** *n* antilope *f*

**antenatal** *adj* prénatal

**antenna** *n* (*pl* antennae) antenne *f*

**antepenultimate** *adj* antépénultième

**anterior** *adj* antérieur

**anteroom** *n* antichambre *f*

**ant-heap** *n* fourmilière *f*

**anthem** *n* motet *m*, hymne *m* + *f*; **national** ~ hymne national

**ant-hill** *n* fourmilière *f*
**anthologist** *n* éditeur -trice d'anthologie
**anthology** *n* anthologie *f*
**anthracite** *n* anthracite *m*
**anthrax** *n biol* anthrax *m*; *vet* charbon *m*
**anthropocentric** *adj* anthropocentrique
**anthropoid** *n* anthropoïde *m*; *adj* anthropoïde
**anthropological** *adj* anthropologique
**anthropologist** *n* anthropologiste, anthropologue
**anthropology** *n* anthropologie *f*
**anthropometry** *n* anthropométrie *f*
**anthropomorphic** *adj* anthropomorphique
**anthropomorphism** *n* anthropomorphisme *m*
**anthropophagi** *npl* anthropophages *mpl*, cannibales *mpl*
**anthropophagous** *adj* anthropophage, cannibale
**anthropophagy** *n* anthropophagie *f*, cannibalisme *m*
**anti-** *pref* anti-; *adv coll* contre
**anti-aircraft** *adj* antiaérien -ienne; ~ **defence** défense *f* contre avions
**antibiotic** *n* antibiotique *m*; *adj* antibiotique
**antibody** *n* anticorps *m*
**antic** *adj* grotesque; ~**s** *npl* cabrioles *fpl*, gambades *fpl*; *fig* bouffonneries *fpl*
**anti-carbon** *n* ~ **additive** décalaminant *m*
**Antichrist** *n* Antéchrist *m*
**antichristian** *adj* antichrétien -ienne
**anticipate** *vt* prévoir, s'attendre à; prévenir, devancer
**anticipation** *n* attente *f*, pressentiment *m*; **in** ~ d'avance
**anticlerical** *adj* anticlérical
**anticlericalism** *n* anticléricalisme *m*
**anticlimax** *n* chute *f*, déception *f*
**anticlinal** *adj* anticlinal
**anticline** *n* anticlinal *m*
**anti-clockwise** *adj* dans le sens inverse des aiguilles d'une montre
**anticoagulant** *n* anticoagulant *m*; *adj* anticoagulant
**anticyclone** *n* anticyclone *m*
**anti-dazzle** *adj* mot anti-éblouissant
**antidemocratic** *adj* antidémocratique
**antidote** *n* antidote *m*, contrepoison *m*
**antifreeze** *n* mot antigel *m*
**antigen** *n* antigène *m*
**antihistamine** *n* antihistaminique *m*
**anti-icer** *n aer* antigivrant *m*
**anti-knock** *n* mot produit antidétonant
**antilogarithm** *n* antilogarithme *m*
**antimacassar** *n* têtière *f*
**antimony** *n* antimoine *m*
**antinomy** *n* antinomie *f*
**anti-particle** *n* antiparticule *f*

**antipathetic, antipathetical** *adj* antipathique
**antipathy** *n* antipathie *f*, aversion *f*
**anti-personnel** *adj mil* antipersonnel *invar*
**antiphlogistic** *adj med* antiphlogistique
**antiphon** *n* antienne *f*
**antiphonal** *n* antiphonaire *m*; *adj* antiphoné
**antiphony** *n* chant *m* d'antiennes
**antipodal, antipodean** *adj* antipodal
**antipodes** *npl* antipode *m*
**antipope** *n eccles* antipape *m*
**anti-proton** *n* antiproton *m*
**antiquarian** *n* amateur *m* d'antiquités; (dealer) antiquaire; *adj* d'antiquaire; ~ **bookseller** libraire spécialisé en vieilles éditions
**antiquary** *n* archéologue; collectionneur -euse d'antiquités
**antiquated** *adj* vieilli, vieillot -otte
**antique** *n* objet *m* d'époque; (furniture) meuble *m* d'époque, meuble ancien; *adj* (old) ancien -ienne; (antiquity) antique
**antiquity** *n* antiquité *f*; **antiquities** antiquités *fpl*, objets *mpl* d'art antiques
**antirrhinum** *n* muflier *m*, gueule-de-loup *f* (*pl* gueules-de-loup)
**antiscorbutic** *adj* antiscorbutique
**anti-semite** *n* antisémite
**anti-semitic** *adj* antisémite, antisémitique
**anti-semitism** *n* antisémitisme *m*
**antisepsis** *n* antisepsie *f*
**antiseptic** *n* antiseptique *m*; *adj* antiseptique
**antisocial** *adj* antisocial
**anti-tank** *adj* antichar
**antithesis** *n* antithèse *f*; contraire *m*
**antithetic, antithetical** *adj* antithétique
**antitoxic** *adj* antitoxique
**antitoxin** *n* antitoxine *f*
**anti-vivisectionist** *n* adversaire de la vivisection; *adj* contre la vivisection
**antler** *n* andouiller *m*; ~**s** ramure *f*, bois *mpl*
**antonym** *n* antonyme *m*
**antrum** *n* (*pl* **antra**) *anat* antre *m*
**anus** *n* anus *m*
**anvil** *n* enclume *f*
**anxiety** *n* (worry) anxiété *f*, inquiétude *f*, souci *m*; (eagerness) grand désir
**anxious** *adj* (worried) anxieux -ieuse, soucieux -ieuse, troublé, inquiet -iète; (eager) anxieux -ieuse, désireux -euse, impatient
**any** *adj* (no matter what) n'importe quel (*f* quelle), tout, quelconque; (some) un peu de, quelque; (with neg) aucun; ~ **person who** toute personne qui; **at** ~ **moment** à tout moment; **have you** ~

348

**comments to make?** avez-vous des remarques à faire?; **I haven't ~ reason to think** je n'ai aucune raison de croire; *pron* (no matter who) n'importe qui; (no matter which) n'importe lequel (*f* laquelle); (some) en; (someone) quelconque; (with neg) aucun; **have you ~?** en avez-vous?; **if ~ of you know** si quelconque d'entre vous sait; *adv* (a little) un peu; (not at all) nullement, aucunement; **at ~ rate, in ~ case** en tout cas; **can you walk ~ faster?** pouvez-vous marcher un peu plus vite?; **he is not ~ cleverer than you** il n'est nullement plus intelligent que vous

**anybody** *pron* (somebody) quelqu'un, n'importe qui; (with *neg*) personne

**anyhow** *adv* (in any case) en tout cas, de toute façon; (carelessly) n'importe comment, tant bien que mal

**anyone** *pron see* **anybody**

**anything** *pron* (no matter what) n'importe quoi; *inter* quelque chose; (with *neg*) rien

**anywhere** *adv* n'importe où, partout; *inter* quelque part; (with *neg*) nulle part

**aorist** *n* aoriste *m*

**aorta** *n* aorte *f*

**apace** *adv lit* vite, rapidement

**Apache** *n* Apache; **apache** *obs* apache *m*, voyou *m*

**apanage, appanage** *n* apanage *m*

**apart** *adv* à distance, à l'écart, de côté, à part; (separately) séparément; (in pieces) en morceaux; **~ from** en dehors de; **come ~** se détacher; **live ~** être séparé; **take ~** démonter; **tell ~** distinguer

**apartheid** *n* apartheid *m*

**apartment** *n* (room) pièce *f*; *US* appartement *m*; **~s** logement (meublé); **~ house** immeuble (divisé en appartements), maison *f* de rapport

**apathetic** *adj* apathique, indifférent

**apathy** *n* apathie *f*, indifférence *f*

**ape** *n* (grand) singe; *vt* singer

**aperient** *n* laxatif *m*; *adj* laxatif -ive

**aperitif** *n* apéritif *m*

**aperture** *n* trou *m*, orifice *m*; *phot* ouverture *f*

**apex** *n* (*pl* **apices**) sommet *m*

**aphasia** *n* aphasie *f*

**aphis** *n* (*pl* **aphides**) aphis *m*

**aphonia, aphony** *n* aphonie *f*

**aphonic** *adj* aphone

**aphorism** *n* aphorisme *m*

**aphrodisiac** *n* aphrodisiaque *m*; *adj* aphrodisiaque

**aphtha** *n* aphte *m*

**apiarist** *n* apiculteur *m*

**apiary** *n* rucher *m*

**apiculture** *n* apiculture *f*

**apiece** *adv* (person) par personne, par tête, chacun; (thing) chacun, la pièce

**apish** *adj* comme un singe, singeant

**aplomb** *n* sang-froid *m invar*, aplomb *m*, assurance *f*

**Apocalypse** *n* Apocalypse *f*

**apocalyptic** *adj* apocalyptique

**apocope** *n* apocope *f*

**Apocrypha** *n* apocryphes *mpl*

**apocryphal** *adj* apocryphe

**apogee** *n* apogée *m*

**apologetic** *adj* d'excuse, plein de déférence; *eccles* apologétique

**apologetics** *npl* apologétique *f*

**apologia** *n* apologie *f*

**apologist** *n* apologiste

**apologize** *vi* s'excuser

**apologue** *n* apologue *m*, fable *f*

**apology** *n* excuses *fpl*; expédient *m*; apologie *f*

**apoplectic** *n* + *adj* apoplectique; **~ fit** attaque *f* d'apoplexie

**apoplexy** *n* apoplexie *f*

**apophthegm, apothegm** *n* maxime *f*, apophtegme *m*

**apostasy** *n* apostasie *f*

**apostate** *n* apostat *m*; *adj* apostat

**apostatic** *adj* apostatique

**apostatize** *vi* apostasier

**a posteriori** *adv* a posteriori

**apostle** *n* apôtre *m*; **~'s creed** symbole *m* des apôtres

**apostrophe** *n* apostrophe *f*

**apostrophize** *vt* apostropher

**apothecary** *n ar* apothicaire *m*

**apothegm** *n see* **apophthegm**

**apotheosis** *n* apothéose *f*

**appal** *vt* consterner, choquer

**appalling** *adj* consternant, choquant; horrible, épouvantable

**appanage** *n see* **apanage**

**apparatus** *n* appareil *m*, mécanisme *m*

**apparel** *n* habillement *m*; *vt* habiller

**apparent** *adj* apparent; (obvious) apparent, évident; **heir ~** héritier -ière présomptif -ive

**apparition** *n* apparition *f*

**appeal** *n* appel *m*; (request) supplication *f*; (attraction) attrait *m*; **Court of Appeal** cour *f* d'appel; *vi* (for money) lancer un appel; (request) faire appel; *leg* se pourvoir en appel; (attract) plaire, attirer

**appealing** *adj* émouvant, attendrissant; (attractive) attirant; (asking) implorant

**appear** *vi* (become visible) apparaître, se montrer, arriver; *leg* comparaître; (book) paraître, sortir; (actor) jouer; (seem) sembler, paraître

**appearance** *n* (action of appearing) apparition *f*, arrivée *f*; (look) apparence *f*, aspect *m*, mine *f*; **leg** comparution *f*; (book) parution *f*; **at first ~** au premier abord; **keep up ~ s** sauver les apparences; **judge by ~ s** se fier aux apparences; **make one's first ~** débuter

**appease** *vt* apaiser, calmer, assouvir

**appeasement** *n* apaisement *m*, assouvissement *m*, conciliation *f*

**appellant** *n* leg appelant -e; *adj* appelant

**appellate** *adj* leg d'appel

**appellation** *n* appellation *f*

**append** *vt* ajouter, joindre

**appendage** *n* appendice *m*, prolongement *m*

**appendicitis** *n* appendicite *f*

**appendix** *n* (*pl* **appendices**) appendice *m*

**appertain** *vi* appartenir, faire partie, relever

**appetence** *n* appétence *f*

**appetite** *n* appétit *m*

**appetizer** *n* (liquid) apéritif *m*; (food) amuse-gueule *m invar*

**appetizing** *adj* appétissant, alléchant

**applaud** *vt* applaudir, approuver

**applause** *n* applaudissements *mpl*, acclamation *f*

**apple** *n* pomme *f*; **be the ~ of s/o's eye** être le chouchou de qn

**apple-brandy** *n* eau-de-vie *f* (*pl* eaux-de-vie) de pommes; (Normandy) calvados *m*

**apple-cart** *n coll* **upset the ~** tout ficher en l'air

**apple-dumpling** *n* pomme *f* au four

**applejack** *n US* eau-de-vie *f* (*pl* eaux-de-vie) de pommes

**apple-pie** *n* tarte *f* aux pommes; **~ bed** lit *m* en portefeuille; **~ order** ordre parfait

**apple-tree** *n* pommier *m*

**appliance** *n* appareil *m*, dispositif *m*

**applicable** *adj* applicable

**applicant** *n* candidat -e, demandeur -euse

**application** *n* (request) demande *f*; (post, etc) candidature *f*; (use) application *f*; (ointment) enduit *m*; (hard work) assiduité *f*

**applied** *adj* appliqué

**appliqué** *n* application *f*, travail *m* d'application

**apply** *vt* (put on) appliquer, mettre; **~ the brakes** freiner; **~ pressure** faire pression; *vi* s'adresser; (refer) s'appliquer; **~ for** faire une demande de, poser sa candidature pour; **~ oneself** s'appliquer

**appoggiatura** *n mus* appoggiature *f*

**appoint** *vt* (elect) nommer, désigner; (fix) fixer, désigner; **well ~ed** bien aménagé

**appointment** *n* (meeting) rendez-vous

*m*; (election) nomination *f*, désignation *f*; (post) emploi *m*, poste *m*; **by ~ to** fournisseur *m* de; (fitments) **~ s** ameublement *m*, mobilier *m*

**apportion** *vt* répartir, partager, assigner

**apposite** *adj* juste, à propos

**apposition** *n* apposition *f*

**appraisal** *n* évaluation *f*, appréciation *f*

**appraise** *vt* évaluer

**appreciable** *adj* appréciable, considérable

**appreciate** *vt* (esteem) apprécier, goûter; (value) évaluer, estimer; être sensible à, être reconnaissant de; *vi* monter, s'apprécier, augmenter de valeur

**appreciation** *n* (judgement) appréciation *f*, évaluation *f*; (gratitude) reconnaissance *f*; *fin* hausse *f*

**appreciative** *adj* sensible; reconnaissant

**apprehend** *vt* (understand) comprendre, percevoir; (arrest) arrêter, appréhender

**apprehension** *n* appréhension *f*, crainte *f*; (arrest) arrestation *f*; (understanding) compréhension *f*

**apprehensive** *adj* appréhensif -ive, craintif -ive

**apprentice** *n* apprenti -e, élève; *vt* mettre en apprentissage

**apprenticeship** *n* apprentissage *m*

**apprise** *vt* informer, prévenir

**approach** *n* approche *f*, arrivée *f*; (access) abord *m*, voie *f* d'accès; **make ~ es to s/o** faire des avances à qn; *vt* approcher de; s'adresser à; *vi* approcher, s'approcher; **be easy to ~** être d'un abord facile

**approachable** *adj* avenant, approchable, accessible

**approbation** *n* approbation *f*

**appropriate** *adj* juste, opportun, convenable, approprié; *vt* s'approprier, s'emparer de

**appropriateness** *n* justesse *f*, à-propos *m*

**appropriation** *n* appropriation *f*

**approval** *n* approbation *f*, assentiment *m*; **on ~** à l'essai

**approve** *vt* approuver, confirmer, ratifier, homologuer; *vi* approuver

**approved** *adj* approuvé, estimé; **~ school** centre *m* d'éducation surveillée

**approving** *adj* approbateur -trice

**approximate** *adj* approximatif -ive; *vi* se rapprocher, s'approcher

**approximation** *n* approximation *f*

**appurtenance** *n usu pl* dépendances *fpl*, accessoires *mpl*, installations *fpl*

**apricot** *n* abricot *m*; (tree) abricotier *m*; **~ tart** tarte *f* aux abricots

**April** *n* avril *m*; **~ fool** poisson *m* d'avril; **~ shower** giboulée *f* de mars

**a priori** *adv* a priori
**apron** *n* tablier *m*; *theat* avant-scène *f*; *aer* aire *f* de stationnement
**apron-strings** *npl* **tied to his mother's ~** pendu aux jupes de sa mère
**apropos** *adj* opportun; *adv* à propos, opportunément
**apse** *n* abside *f*
**apsidal** *adj* absidal
**apt** *adj* (suitable) approprié, juste; (intelligent) doué, intelligent; **~ to** enclin à, porté à
**aptitude** *n* aptitude *f*
**aptly** *adv* avec justesse, à propos
**aptness** *n* justesse *f*
**aqualung** *n* scaphandre *m* autonome
**aquamarine** *n* (stone) aigue-marine *f* (*pl* aigues-marines); (colour) bleu-vert *m* *invar*
**aquaplane** *n* aquaplane *m*; *vi* faire de l'aquaplane
**aquarelle** *n* aquarelle *f*
**aquarium** *n* aquarium *m*
**Aquarius** *n* *astrol* le Verseau
**aquatic** *adj* aquatique; *sp* nautique
**aquatint** *n* aquatinte *f*
**aqueduct** *n* aqueduc *m*
**aqueous** *adj* aqueux -euse
**aquiline** *adj* aquilin
**Arab** *n* Arabe; cheval *m* arabe; *adj* arabe; **street arab** gamin -e des rues
**arabesque** *n* arabesque *f*
**Arabia** *n* Arabie *f*
**Arabian** *adj* arabe; **~ Gulf** golfe *m* Arabique; **the ~ Nights** les Mille et Une Nuits
**Arabic** *n* *ling* arabe *m*; *adj* arabe; **~ numerals** chiffres *mpl* arabes
**Arabist** *n* arabisant -e
**arable** *adj* arable, cultivable
**arachnid** *n* ~ **s** arachnides *mpl*
**Aramaic** *n* *ling* araméen *m*; *adj* araméen -enne
**arbiter** *n* arbitre *m*, juge *m*
**arbitrariness** *n* arbitraire *m*
**arbitrary** *adj* arbitraire
**arbitrate** *vt* arbitrer, juger; *vi* arbitrer
**arbitration** *n* arbitrage *m*
**arbitrator** *n* arbitre *m*, juge *m*
**arboreal** *adj* arboricole
**arborescent** *adj* arborescent
**arboretum** *n* (*pl* **arboreta**) arboretum *m*
**arboriculture** *n* arboriculture *f*
**arborist** *n* arboriculteur -trice
**arbour** *n* tonnelle *f*, charmille *f*
**arc** *n* arc *m*; **~ lamp** lampe *f* à arc; **~ welding** soudure *f* à arc (voltaïque)
**arcade** *n* arcade *f*; (shops) galerie marchande, passage *m*
**Arcadian** *adj* arcadien -ienne
**arcanum** *n* (*pl* **arcana**) arcane *m*
**¹arch** *n* *archi* voûte *f*, arc *m*, cintre *m*;

(bridge) arche *f*; *anat* arcade *f*, cambrure *f*; *vt* arquer, cambrer; *vi* s'arquer
**²arch** *adj* espiègle; malicieux -ieuse
**³arch-** *pref* archi-
**Archaean** *adj* *geol* archéen -éenne
**archaeological** *adj* archéologique
**archaeologist** *n* archéologue
**archaeology** *n* archéologie *f*
**archaic** *adj* archaïque
**archaism** *n* archaïsme *m*
**archangel** *n* archange *m*
**archbishop** *n* archevêque *m*
**archbishopric** *n* archevêché *m*
**archdeacon** *n* archidiacre *m*
**archdiocese** *n* archidiocèse *m*
**archduchess** *n* archiduchesse *f*
**archduchy** *n* archiduché *m*
**archduke** *n* archiduc *m*
**archer** *n* archer *m*
**archery** *n* tir *m* à l'arc
**archetypal** *adj* archétype
**archetype** *n* archétype *m*
**archiepiscopal** *adj* archiépiscopal
**archimandrite** *n* archimandrite *m*
**archipelago** *n* archipel *m*
**architect** *n* architecte *m*
**architectonic** *adj* architectonique
**architectural** *adj* architectural
**architecture** *n* architecture *f*
**architrave** *n* *archi* architrave *f*; (frame) encadrement *m*
**archival** *adj* archivistique
**archives** *npl* archives *fpl*
**archivist** *n* archiviste
**archness** *n* espièglerie *f*, malice *f*
**archway** *n* passage voûté; voûte *f*, porche *m*
**Arctic** *adj* arctique
**ardent** *adj* ardent; passionné, fervent
**ardour** *n* ardeur *f*, ferveur *f*
**arduous** *adj* ardu, laborieux -ieuse, pénible
**arduously** *adv* laborieusement, péniblement
**arduousness** *n* difficulté *f*, peine *f*
**are** *see* **be**
**area** *n* superficie *f*; région *f*, zone *f*; (scope) domaine *m*, champ *m*; **dining ~** coin *m* salle-à-manger; *adj* **~ manager** directeur régional, chef *m* de secteur; **~ office** agence régionale
**arena** *n* arène *f*
**arete** *n* *geog* arête *f*
**Argentina** *n* Argentine *f*
**Argentine** *adj* argentin
**Argentinian** *n* Argentin -e; *adj* argentin
**argillaceous** *adj* argileux -euse
**argon** *n* argon *m*
**Argonaut** *n* Argonaute *m*
**argosy** *n* *ar* galion *m*
**arguable** *adj* discutable; **it is ~ that** on peut soutenir que

**argue** vt (debate) discuter, débattre; (denote) dénoter, indiquer; (maintain) soutenir; (persuade) persuader; (dissuade) dissuader; (case) présenter; vi raisonner, argumenter; (dispute) se disputer; **don't ~!** pas de discussion!; **that ~s well for you** cela parle en votre faveur

**argument** n (reason) argument m; (discussion) discussion f, débat m; (synopsis) sommaire m, résumé m, argument m

**argumentation** n argumentation f

**argumentative** adj raisonneur -euse; logique

**aria** n mus aria f

**Arian** n Arien -ienne; adj arien -ienne

**Arianism** n arianisme m

**arid** adj aride

**aridity** n aridité f

**Aries** n astrol le Bélier

**aright** adv correctement, bien

**arise** vi (get up) se lever; (come about, appear) survenir, se présenter; (problem, question) se poser; (result) résulter, provenir; **~ out of** résulter de; **arising from that** à partir de cela; **if the question ~s** le cas échéant; **should the need ~** en cas de besoin

**aristocracy** n aristocratie f

**aristocrat** n aristocrate

**aristocratic** adj aristocratique

**arithmetic** n arithmétique f

**arithmetical** adj arithmétique

**arithmetician** n arithméticien -ienne

**ark** n arche f; **Ark of the Covenant** arche d'alliance, arche sainte; **Noah's ~** arche f de Noé

¹**arm** n (limb) bras m; **~ in ~** bras dessus bras dessous; **child in ~** s enfant au berceau; **keep at ~'s length** tenir à distance; **with open ~s** à bras ouverts

²**arm** n (weapon) arme f; (military career) **~s** armes fpl; **her ~s** armes fpl, armoiries fpl; **~s race** course f aux armements; **be up in ~s against** s'insurger contre; **lay down one's ~s** se rendre, déposer les armes; **take up ~s** prendre les armes; vt (person) armer; (missile) munir d'une ogive; vi s'armer

**armada** n armada f

**armament** n armement m; matériel m de guerre; (preparation for war) armement m

**armature** n mil armure f; (armour-plating) blindage m; elect armature f; zool carapace f

**arm-band** n brassard m

**armchair** n fauteuil m

**armed** adj armé

**armful** n brassée f

**arm-hole** n emmanchure f

**armistice** n armistice m

**armless** adj sans bras

**armlet** n brassard m

**armorial** n armorial m; adj armorial

**armory** n US fabrique f d'armes

**armour** n hist armure f; (plating) blindage m; (armoured forces) forces blindées

**armour-bearer** n hist écuyer m

**armoured** adj blindé; **~ car** voiture blindée

**armourer** n armurier m

**armour-piercing** adj (gun) antichar (f invar; mpl+fpl antichars); (shell, bullet) perforant

**armour-plate** n blindage m

**armour-plated** adj blindé

**armoury** n dépôt m d'armes

**armpit** n aisselle f

**arm-rest** n accoudoir m

**army** n armée f; fig foule f, multitude f; **join the ~** s'engager

**army-corps** n corps m d'armée

**army-list** n annuaire m militaire

**arnica** n arnica f

**aroma** n arôme m

**aromatic** n aromate m; adj aromatique

**aromatize** vt aromatiser

**around** adv autour; (near) alentour, dans les parages; **be ~** être dans les parages; prep autour de; (about) environ, à peu près

**arouse** vt éveiller, réveiller; (cause) susciter, provoquer

**arpeggio** n mus arpège m

**arraign** vt leg poursuivre en justice; accuser, blâmer

**arraignment** n leg assignation f; critique f, attaque f

**arrange** vt arranger, aménager; organiser; régler; vi s'arranger, prendre des mesures

**arrangement** n arrangement m; aménagement m, disposition f; (agreement) accommodement m, entente f; **~s** mesures fpl, préparations fpl; **by ~ with** avec l'accord de, avec l'autorisation de

**arrant** adj notoire, fieffé

**arras** n tapisserie f

**array** n ordre m, rang m; vt mil ranger, déployer

**arrears** npl arriéré m; **be in ~** s'arriérer, être en retard

**arrest** n arrestation f; leg (judgement) suspension f; **close ~** arrêts mpl de rigueur; **house ~** assignation f à domicile; **open ~** arrêts mpl simples; **under ~** en état d'arrestation; mil aux arrêts; vt arrêter, appréhender

**arresting** adj frappant, impressionnant

**arrival** *n* arrivée *f*; (person) arrivant -e;
**on ~** à l'arrivée; (letter) **to await ~**
prière de ne pas faire suivre

**arrive** *vi* arriver; *fig* réussir

**arrogance** *n* arrogance *f*, morgue *f*

**arrogant** *adj* arrogant

**arrogate** *vt* (claim wrongly) s'arroger,
revendiquer à tort; (attribute unfairly)
attribuer injustement

**arrogation** *n* usurpation *f*

**arrow** *n* flèche *f*

**arrow-head** *n* pointe *f* de flèche

**arrowroot** *n* arrow-root *m*

**arse** *n sl* cul *m*; *vi sl* **~ about, around**
faire l'imbécile

**arse-hole** *n sl* trou *m* du cul

**arsenal** *n* arsenal *m*

**arsenic** *n* arsenic *m*

**arsenical** *adj* arsenical

**arson** *n* incendie criminel

**arsonist** *n* incendiaire

**art** *n* art *m*; (cunning) ruse *f*, artifice *m*;
(skill) adresse *f*, habileté *f*; **black ~s**
magie noire; **fine ~s** beaux arts

**artefact** *n* objet fabriqué

**arterial** *adj* artériel -ielle; **~ road** voie *f*
à grande circulation

**arteriosclerosis** *n* artériosclérose *f*

**artery** *n* artère *f*

**artesian** *adj* artésien -ienne

**art-form** *n* moyen *m* d'expression artistique

**artful** *adj* malin -igne, astucieux -ieuse,
rusé; ingénieux -ieuse

**arthritic** *adj* arthritique

**arthritis** *n* arthrite *f*

**arthropoda** *npl* arthropodes *mpl*

**artichoke** *n* artichaut *m*; **Jerusalem ~**
topinambour *m*

**article** *n* article *m*; objet *m*; *vt* mettre en
apprentissage; *leg* stipuler

**articulate** *vt + vi* articuler; *adj* articulé;
(speech) bien articulé

**articulation** *n* articulation *f*

**artifice** *n* artifice *m*, stratagème *m*

**artificer** *n* artisan *m*

**artificial** *adj* artificiel -ielle, synthétique;
(affected) affecté, factice

**artificiality** *n* insincérité *f*, manque *m* de
naturel

**artillery** *n* artillerie *f*

**artillery-man** *n* artilleur *m*

**artisan** *n* artisan *m*

**artist** *n* artiste

**artistic** *adj* artistique

**artistry** *n* talent *m* artistique, art *m*

**artless** *adj* (simple) ingénu; (crude) grossier -ière

**artlessness** *n* (simplicity) ingénuité *f*;
grossièreté *f*

**art-silk** *n* rayonne *f*

**arty** *adj coll* qui affecte le genre artistique

**arty-crafty,** *US* **artsy-craftsy** *adj coll pej*
artisanal

**Aryan** *n* Aryen -enne; *adj* aryen -enne

**as** *adv* si, aussi; *conj* comme; (time)
alors que, tandis que; (since) puisque,
étant donné que; (in the capacity of ) en
tant que; **~ for, ~ to** quant à; **~
good ~** aussi bon que; **~ long ~**
pourvu que; (time) aussi longtemps
que; **~ many ~** autant que; (all who)
tous ceux qui; **~ well ~** aussi bien
que; **be dressed ~** être habillé en;
**much ~** en dépit du fait que

**asbestos** *n* amiante *f*, asbeste *m*

**ascend** *vt* gravir, monter; *vi* monter,
s'élever

**ascendancy** *n* ascendant *m*, emprise *f*

**ascendant** *n astrol* ascendant *m*; **be in
the ~** monter; *adj astrol* ascendant;
dominant

**ascension** *n* ascension *f*

**ascent** *n* montée *f*, ascension *f*

**ascertain** *vt* établir, vérifier; s'informer de

**ascetic** *n* ascète; *adj* ascétique

**asceticism** *n* ascétisme *m*

**ascorbic** *adj* ascorbique, antiscorbutique; **~ acid** acide *m* ascorbique,
vitamine *f* C

**ascribable** *adj* attribuable, imputable

**ascribe** *vt* attribuer, imputer

**ascription** *n* attribution *f*, imputation *f*

**asdic** *n mil* asdic *m*

**asepsis** *n* asepsie *f*

**aseptic** *adj* aseptique

**asexual** *adj* asexué

**asexuality** *n* asexualité *f*

¹**ash** *n* frêne *m*; **mountain ~** sorbier *m*

²**ash** *n* cendre *f*; **~es** (cremated body)
cendres *fpl*; **~ blond** blond cendré;
**sackcloth and ~es** le sac et la cendre;
**turn to dust and ~es** être anéanti

**ashamed** *adj* honteux -euse, confus

**ash-bin, ash-can** *n* poubelle *f*, boîte *f* à
ordures

¹**ashen** *adj* cendreux -euse, terreux -euse

²**ashen** (wood) en frêne

**ashlar** *n* pierre *f* de taille

**ashore** *adv* à terre; **go ~** débarquer; **run
~** échouer

**ash-pan** *n* cendrier *m*

**ash-tray** *n* cendrier *m*

**Ash-Wednesday** *n* mercredi *m* des Cendres

**ashy** *adj* cendré; (pale) cendreux -euse;
couvert de cendres

**Asia** *n* Asie *f*

**Asian** *n* Asiatique; *adj* asiatique

**Asiatic** *n* Asiatique; *adj* asiatique

**aside** *n* aparté *m*; *adv* de côté, à part; *leg*
**set ~** casser

**asinine** *adj* idiot, sot ( *f* sotte)

**ask** *vt* (inquire, request) demander;

(invite) inviter; (prices) vouloir; *vi* demander; **~ after (about)** demander des nouvelles de; **~ for s/o** demander à voir qn; *sl* **~ for it** chercher des ennuis; **~ for sth** demander qch; **~ for sth back** demander qu'on rende qch; **~ s/o in** prier qn d'entrer; **~ out** inviter à sortir

**askance** *adv* de côté, de biais; **look ~** regarder de travers, regarder d'un œil désapprobateur

**askew** *adv* de travers, obliquement

**asking** *n* it's there for the **~** on l'a comme on veut; *coll* that's **~**! je ne vous dirai pas!

**aslant** *adv* de biais, de travers

**asleep** *adj* endormi; (limb) engourdi; **fall ~** s'endormir

**asp** *n* aspic *m*

**asparagus** *n* asperge *f*

**aspect** *n* aspect *m*, air *m*; (question) aspect *m*, angle *m*; (building) orientation *f*, exposition *f*; *gramm+astrol* aspect *m*

**aspen** *n* tremble *m*

**asperge** *vt* asperger

**aspergillum** *n* goupillon *m*

**asperity** *n* aspérité *f*, dureté *f*; (person) rudesse *f*

**aspersion** *n* calomnie *f*

**asphalt** *n* asphalte *m*; *vt* asphalter

**asphodel** *n* asphodèle *m*

**asphyxia** *n* asphyxie *f*

**asphyxiate** *vt* asphyxier; *vi* s'asphyxier

**asphyxiation** *n* asphyxie *f*

**aspic** *n* cul gelée *f*

**aspidistra** *n* aspidistra *m*

**aspirant** *n* aspirant -e

**aspirate** *n* consonne aspirée; *adj* aspiré; *vt* aspirer

**aspiration** *n* aspiration *f*

**aspirator** *n* aspirateur *m*

**aspire** *vi* aspirer, viser, ambitionner

**aspirin** *n* aspirine *f*; (tablet) comprimé d'aspirine

**aspiring** *adj* ambitieux -ieuse

¹**ass** *n* âne *m* (*f* ânesse); *coll* idiot -e, imbécile

²**ass** *n* US *vulg* cul *m*

**assail** *vt* assaillir, attaquer

**assailant** *n* aggresseur *m*

**assassin** *n* assassin *m*

**assassinate** *vt* assassiner

**assassination** *n* assassinat *m*

**assault** *n mil* assaut *m*; *leg* agression *f*; **~ and battery** voies *fpl* de fait; **~ course** parcours *m* du combattant; **~ craft** chaland *m* de débarquement; **indecent ~** attentat *m* à la pudeur; *vt mil* attaquer; *leg* agresser

**assay** *n* essai *m*; *vt* essayer

**assemblage** *n* assemblage *m*, montage

*m*; (people) réunion *f*, foule *f*

**assemble** *vt* assembler; (people) réunir; *vi* s'assembler, se réunir

**assembly** *n* assemblée *f*, réunion *f*

**assent** *n* assentiment *m*, consentement *m*; *vi* consentir

**assert** *vt* affirmer, soutenir; (maintain) défendre; (claim) revendiquer; **~ oneself** faire valoir ses droits, se pousser

**assertion** *n* assertion *f*, affirmation *f*

**assertive** *adj* péremptoire, tranchant

**assess** *vt* estimer, évaluer; (payment) fixer

**assessment** *n* estimation *f*, évaluation *f*, détermination *f*

**assessor** *n leg* assesseur *m*

**asset** *n* avantage *m*, atout *m*; (possession) avoir *m*; **~s** biens *mpl*; *comm* actif *m*

**asseverate** *vt* affirmer solennellement, déclarer

**asseveration** *n* affirmation solennelle, déclaration *f*

**assiduity** *n* assiduité *f*, zèle *m*

**assiduous** *adj* assidu

**assiduousness** *n* assiduité *f*

**assign** *n leg* ayant-droit *m* (*pl* ayants-droit); *vt* assigner, fixer; attribuer; (appoint) nommer, affecter; *leg* céder

**assignation** *n* (meeting) rendez-vous *m*; attribution *f*; *leg* cession *f*

**assignee** *n leg* cessionnaire, mandataire

**assignment** *n* (task) mission *f*; attribution *f*, allocation *f*; *leg* cession *f*

**assimilable** *adj* assimilable

**assimilate** *vt* assimiler; *vi* s'assimiler

**assimilation** *n* assimilation *f*, rapprochement *m*

**assist** *vt* assister, aider, secourir; *vi* aider

**assistance** *n* assistance *f*, aide *f*, secours *m*

**assistant** *n* assistant -e, aide, auxiliaire; *adj* auxiliaire; (deputy) adjoint; sous-

**assize** *n obs* **~ s** assises *fpl*

**associate** *n* associé -e, collègue; (crime) complice; (club, society) membre *m*; *adj* associé; US **~ professor** = maître *m* de conférences; *vt* associer; *vi* **~ with** s'associer avec, fréquenter

**association** *n* association *f*; fréquentation *f*

**assonance** *n* assonance *f*

**assonant** *adj* assonant

**assort** *vt* ranger, classer, assortir; *vi* s'assortir, s'accorder; **~ with** fréquenter

**assorted** *adj* assorti

**assortment** *n* assortiment *m*, collection *f*

**assuage** *vt* assouvir, calmer, soulager, apaiser

**assume** *vt* assumer, endosser, prendre sur soi; (accept) présumer, supposer; (air) prendre

**assumed** *adj* faux (*f* fausse); ~ **name** nom *m* d'emprunt

**assuming** *conj* en supposant que

**assumption** *n* supposition *f*; hypothèse *f*; *eccles* **Assumption** Assomption *f*

**assurance** *n* assurance *f*; (promise) promesse *f*; affirmation *f*; (cheek) toupet *m*

**assure** *vt* assurer, affirmer; convaincre; (life) assurer

**assured** *adj* assuré

**assuredly** *adv* assurément, certainement

**aster** *n* aster *m*

**asterisk** *n* astérisque *m*; *vt* marquer d'un astérisque

**astern** *adv naut* en poupe, à l'arrière; **go** ~ faire marche arrière

**asteroid** *n* astéroïde *m*

**asthenia** *n med* asthénie *f*

**asthenic** *adj med* asthénique

**asthma** *n* asthme *m*

**asthmatic** *n* + *adj* asthmatique

**astigmatic** *adj* astigmate

**astigmatism** *n* astigmatisme *m*

**astir** *adv* en mouvement; **be** ~ être levé; **set** ~ mettre en branle

**astonish** *vt* étonner, ébahir, ahurir

**astonishing** *adj* étonnant, ahurissant

**astonishingly** *adv* incroyablement, remarquablement

**astonishment** *n* étonnement *m*, ahurissement *m*

**astound** *vt* ébahir, abasourdir

**astounding** *adj* ahurissant

**astragal** *n anat* + *archi* astragale *m*

**astrakhan** *n* astrakan *m*

**astral** *adj* astral

**astray** *adv* égaré; **go** ~ s'égarer; **lead** ~ dévoyer

**astride** *adv* à califourchon; *prep* à califourchon sur

**astringency** *n* astringence *f*

**astringent** *adj* astringent

**astrolabe** *n* astrolabe *m*

**astrologer** *n* astrologue *m*

**astrology** *n* astrologie *f*

**astronaut** *n* astronaute *m*

**astronautics** *npl* astronautique *f*

**astronomer** *n* astronome *m*

**astronomic, astronomical** *adj* astronomique

**astronomy** *n* astronomie *f*

**astrophysics** *npl* astrophysique *f*

**astute** *adj* astucieux -ieuse, malin (*f* maligne), rusé; (mind) pénétrant

**astuteness** *n* astuce *f*, ruse *f*

**asunder** *adv* en morceaux; éloigné, à distance

**asylum** *n* asile *m*, refuge *m*; (mental) asile *m* d'aliénés

**asymmetrical** *adj* asymétrique

**at** *prep* (place, time, price) à; (at the house of) chez; (towards) vers;

(because of) à propos de, à cause de; ~ **all events** tout de même; ~ **first** d'abord; ~ **his request** sur sa demande; ~ **home** chez soi, à la maison; ~ **night** la nuit; ~ **once** tout de suite, immédiatement; ~ **one** en accord; ~ **sea** en mer; *fig* perdu; *coll* ~ **that** encore; ~ **the same time** en même temps; **be** ~ être occupé à; **be hard** ~ **it** travailler ferme; **he's always** ~ **me** il me casse les pieds tout le temps; **while you're** ~ **it** pendant que vous y êtes

**ataraxy** *n* ataraxie *f*

**atavism** *n* atavisme *m*

**atavistic** *adj* atavistique

**ataxia, ataxy** *n* ataxie *f*

**ate** *see* **eat**

**atheism** *n* athéisme *m*

**atheist** *n* athée

**atheistic, atheistical** *adj* athée

**athlete** *n* athlète

**athletic** *adj* athlétique

**athletics** *n pl* athlétisme *m*

**athwart** *adv* en travers; *naut* par le travers; *prep* en travers de

**Atlantic** *n* Atlantique *m*; *adj* atlantique

**atlas** *n* atlas *m*

**atmosphere** *n* atmosphère *f*; *fig* atmosphère *f*, ambiance *f*

**atmospheric** *adj* atmosphérique

**atmospherics** *npl rad* parasites *mpl*

**atoll** *n* atoll *m*

**atom** *n* atome *m*; *fig* grain *m*, brin *m*; **smash to** ~**s** réduire en miettes

**atom-bomb** *n* bombe *f* atomique

**atomic** *adj* atomique

**atomicity** *n* atomicité *f*

**atomize** *vt* atomiser, vaporiser

**atomizer** *n* atomiseur *m*

**atonal** *adj* atonal

**atonality** *n* atonalité *f*

**atone** *vi* expier, racheter

**atonement** *n* expiation *f*

**atonic** *adj pros* atone; *anat* atonique

**atrocious** *adj* atroce; *coll* horrible, affreux -euse

**atrociousness** *n* conduite *f* atroce

**atrocity** *n* atrocité *f*

**atrophy** *n* atrophie *f*; *vt* atrophier; *vi* s'atrophier

**atropine** *n* atropine *f*

**attach** *vt* (fasten) attacher, joindre, lier; (appoint) affecter, attacher; *fig* attribuer; *leg* (person) arrêter; saisir; **be** ~**ed to** être attaché à; *vi* être imputé à

**attaché** *n* attaché -e

**attaché-case** *n* mallette *f*, attaché-case *m invar*

**attachment** *n* (fastening) fixation *f*; (accessory) accessoire *m*; (feelings) attachement *m*, affection *f*; *leg* (person) arrestation *f*; (goods) saisie *f*; (appointment) affectation *f*; (temporary work) stage *m*; action *f* d'attacher

**attack** *n* attaque *f*; *med* crise *f*, attaque *f*; *vt* attaquer, assaillir; (tackle) s'attaquer à

**attacker** *n* agresseur *m*, attaquant *m*, assaillant *m*

**attain** *vt* atteindre, parvenir à, arriver à

**attainable** *adj* susceptible d'être atteint

**attainment** *n* (accomplishment) travail *m*, réalisation *f*, accomplissement *m*; (knowledge) acquisition *f*

**attempt** *n* tentative *f*, effort *m*, essai *m*; (attack) attentat *m*; *vt* essayer, tenter; *mil* attaquer; (difficult task) entreprendre, s'attaquer à

**attend** *vt* (look after) servir; accompagner; (doctor) soigner; (be present at) assister à; (church, school) aller à, fréquenter; *vi* faire attention; **~ to** s'occuper de

**attendance** *n* présence *f*; (audience) assistance *f*; **dance ~ on** être aux petits soins pour

**attendant** *n* domestique, suivant -e; (guide) gardien -ienne; *adj* qui accompagne, qui suit; concomitant

**attention** *n* attention *f*; (care) attentions *fpl*; *mil* garde-à-vous *m*; **stand at ~** être au garde-à-vous

**attentive** *adj* attentif -ive; (careful) empressé

**attenuate** *vt* atténuer, modérer; (make thin) amincir; (dilute) raréfier; *vi* s'atténuer, diminuer; *adj* atténué, raréfié; mince

**attenuation** *n* atténuation *f*, diminution *f*

**attest** *vt* attester, témoigner de; *leg* (signature) légaliser; (put on oath) faire prêter serment à; *vi* prêter serment; (vouch for) témoigner de

**attestation** *n* attestation *f*, témoignage *m*; *leg* (signature) légalisation *f*

¹**attic** *n* grenier *m*; **~ room** mansarde *f*

²**attic** *adj* attique

**attire** *n* vêtements *mpl*; *vt* vêtir, parer

**attitude** *n* attitude *f*, disposition *f*; **strike an ~** poser

**attitudinize** *vi* poser, prendre un air affecté

**attorney** *n leg* mandataire *m*, *US* avoué *m*; **Attorney General** = Procureur Général; *US* = Garde *m* des Sceaux; **power of ~** procuration *f*

**attract** *vt* attirer; *fig* plaire à, séduire; charmer

**attraction** *n* attraction *f*; **~s** attractions *fpl*, attraits *mpl*

**attractive** *adj* attirant, attrayant;

charmant; (price) intéressant; *phys* attractif -ive

**attractiveness** *n* attraction *f*, attrait *m*, charme *m*

**attribute** *n* attribut *m*; *gramm* épithète *f*; *vt* attribuer, imputer, prêter

**attribution** *n* attribution *f*, imputation *f*

**attributive** *n* attribut *m*; *gramm* épithète *f*; *adj* attributif -ive; *gramm* qualicatif -ive

**attrition** *n* usure *f*, attrition *f*

**attune** *vt* mettre à l'unisson, accorder

**atypical** *adj* atypique

**aubade** *n* aubade *f*

**aubergine** *n* aubergine *f*

**auburn** *adj* auburn *invar*

**auction** *n* vente *f* aux enchères; **Dutch ~** enchères *fpl* au rabais; *vt* vendre aux enchères

**auctioneer** *n* adjudicateur -trice, commissaire-priseur *m* (*pl* commissaires-priseurs)

**audacious** *adj* audacieux -ieuse, hardi; impudent, effronté

**audacity** *n* audace *f*, hardiesse *f*; impudence *f*, effronterie *f*

**audibility** *n* audibilité *f*

**audible** *adj* audible

**audience** *n* (entertainment) spectateurs *mpl*, public *m*; *theat* salle *f*; (lecture) assistance *f*; *rad* auditeurs *mpl*; (television) téléspectateurs *mpl*; (hearing) audience *f*; *rad* + *T V* **~ rating** indice *m* d'audience

**audio-visual** *adj* audio-visuel -elle; **~ aids** moyens audio-visuels

**audit** *n* vérification *f*; *vt* vérifier, apurer

**audition** *n* audition *f*; *vt* + *vi theat* auditionner

**auditive** *adj* auditif -ive

**auditor** *n* (listener) auditeur -trice; *comm* expert-comptable *m* (*pl* experts-comptables), vérificateur *m* (de comptes)

**auditorium** *n* auditorium *m*; *theat* salle *f*

**auditory** *adj* auditif -ive

**auger** *n* vrille *f*

**aught** *n lit* quoi que ce soit *m*, quelque chose *m*; *adv* **for ~ I know** pour autant que je sache

**augment** *vt* augmenter, accroître; *vi* augmenter, s'accroître

**augmentation** *n* augmentation *f*, accroissement *m*

**augur** *n* augure *m*; *vt* prédire, présager; *vi* **~ well (ill)** être de bon (de mauvais) augure

**augury** *n* augure *m*, présage *m*

**August** *n* août *m*

**august** *adj* auguste

**Augustan** *adj* *hist* d'Auguste; (neo-classical) néo-classique

**Augustinian** *n* augustin -e
**auk** *n orni* guillemot *m*; **little** ~ mergule *m*
**aunt** *n* tante *f*; ~ **Sally** (game) jeu *m* de massacre; (person) tête *f* de turc
**auntie** *n coll* tatie *f*
**au pair** *adj+adv* au pair
**aura** *n* aura *f*, ambiance *f*
**aural** *adj* auriculaire
**aureola, aureole** *n* auréole *f*
**auricle** *n anat* (heart) oreillette *f*; (ear) pavillon *m* auriculaire
**auricular** *adj* auriculaire
**aurochs** *n* aurochs *m*
**aurora borealis** *n* aurore boréale
**auroral** *adj* auroral
**auscultation** *n* auscultation *f*
**auspice** *n* augure *m* favorable; ~ s auspices *mpl*, patronage *m*
**auspicious** *adj* propice, de bon augure
**Aussie** *n+adj coll see* **Australian**
**austere** *adj* austère, sévère
**austerity** *n* austérité *f*, sévérité *f*; (wartime) restrictions *fpl*; *adj* d'austérité, de restrictions
**austral** *adj* austral (*pl* -als)
**Australasia** *n* Australasie *f*
**Australia** *n* Australie *f*
**Australian** *n* Australien -ienne; *adj* australien -ienne
**authentic** *adj* authentique
**authenticate** *vt* vérifier, valider
**authentication** *n* authentification *f*
**author** *n* auteur *m*; (writer) écrivain *m*
**authoress** *n* femme *f* auteur, femme *f* écrivain
**authoritarian** *n* partisan -e de l'autorité; *adj* autoritaire
**authoritarianism** *n* tyrannie *f*, despotisme *m*
**authoritative** *adj* autoritaire; (definitive) qui fait autorité
**authority** *n* autorité *f*, pouvoir *m*, compétence *f*; (right) autorisation *f*; (person, book, etc) autorité *f*; **authorities** autorités *fpl*, administration *f*
**authorization** *n* autorisation *f*; *leg* mandat *m*
**authorize** *vt* autoriser, sanctionner
**authorship** *n* paternité *f*; (profession) métier *m* d'écrivain
**autism** *n* autisme *m*
**autistic** *adj* autistique
**autobahn** *n* autoroute *f*
**autobiographical** *adj* autobiographique
**autobiography** *n* autobiographie *f*
**autocade** *n US* cortège *m* d'automobiles
**autochthon** *n+adj* autochtone
**autoclave** *n* autoclave *m*
**autocracy** *n* autocratie *f*
**autocrat** *n* autocrate *m*

**autocratic** *adj* autocratique
**auto-cycle** *n* cyclomoteur *m*; ~ **rider** cyclomotoriste
**auto-da-fé** *n* (*pl* **autos-da-fé**) autodafé *m*
**auto-erotism** *n* auto-érotisme *m*
**autograph** *n* autographe *m*; ~ **album** album *m* d'autographes; *vt* autographier, dédicacer
**autography** *n* autographie *f*
**auto-intoxication** *n* auto-intoxication *f*
**autolysis** *n bioch* autolyse *f*
**automate** *vt* automatiser
**automated** *adj* automatisé
**automatic** *n* automatique *m*; ~ s automatique *f*; *adj* automatique
**automation** *n* automatisation *f*
**automatism** *n* automatisme *m*
**automaton** *n* (*pl* **automata**) automate *m*, robot *m*
**automobile** *n* automobile *f*, auto *f*; *US* voiture *f*
**autonomist** *n* autonomiste
**autonomous** *adj* autonome
**autonomy** *n* autonomie *f*
**autopsy** *n* autopsie *f*
**auto-suggestion** *n* autosuggestion *f*
**autumn** *n* automne *m*; *adj* d'automne
**autumnal** *adj* d'automne
**auxiliary** *n* auxiliaire *m*; *gramm* auxiliaire *m*; *adj* auxiliaire, subsidiaire
**avail** *n* secours *m*, utilité *f*, avantage *m*; **be of little** ~ ne pas servir à grand-chose; **be to no** ~ ne servir à rien; **of no** ~ sans résultats; *vt* aider, secourir; ~ **oneself of** utiliser; *vi* être utile, être efficace
**availability** *n* disponibilité *f*
**available** *adj* disponible
**avalanche** *n* avalanche *f*; *vi* tomber en avalanche
**avant-garde** *n* avant-garde *f*
**avarice** *n* avarice *f*
**avaricious** *adj* avare
**avariciousness** *n* avarice *f*
**avatar** *n* avatar *m*
**avaunt** *interj lit* hors d'ici!
**ave** *n* avé *m*, avé Maria *m*
**avenge** *vt* venger; ~ **oneself on** prendre sa revanche sur
**avenue** *n* avenue *f*, boulevard *m*; *fig* possibilité *f*
**aver** *vt* affirmer; *leg* démontrer
**average** *n* moyenne *f*; *adj* moyen -enne; *vt* faire la moyenne de; ~ **out at** revenir à la moyenne de
**averse** *adj* peu disposé, ennemi, opposé
**aversion** *n* aversion *f*, dégoût *m*, répugnance *f*; objet *m* d'aversion
**avert** *vt* éviter, prévenir; (eyes) détourner
**aviary** *n* volière *f*

**aviation** n aviation f
**aviator** n aviateur -trice
**aviculture** n aviculture f
**avid** adj avide
**avidity** n avidité f
**avionics** npl avionique f
**avocado** n avocat m
**avocation** n métier m, profession f; passe-temps m, violon m d'Ingres
**avoid** vt éviter, échapper à, esquiver; leg résilier, annuler
**avoidance** n réserve f, attitude distante, évitement m; évasion f
**avoirdupois** n poids commercial; (overweight) excès m de poids, embonpoint m
**avouch** vt se porter garant de, garantir; affirmer; vi confesser
**avow** vt avouer, confesser
**avowal** n aveu m
**avowed** adj déclaré
**avowedly** adv nettement
**avuncular** adj avunculaire
**await** vt attendre; être réservé à
**awake** adj éveillé, réveillé; en éveil; vt éveiller, réveiller; vi s'éveiller, se réveiller
**awaken** vt réveiller; vi s'éveiller
**awakening** n réveil m
**award** n prix m, récompense f; leg décision f; (scholarship) bourse f; vt décerner, attribuer
**aware** adj conscient, averti; (knowledgeable) avisé
**awareness** n conscience f
**awash** adj naut à fleur d'eau
**away** adj sp ~ **match** match m à l'extérieur; adv au loin, très loin; (continuously) sans arrêt; interj hors d'ici!; ouste!; be ~ être absent; coll be well ~ être parti; **far and** ~ de beaucoup; **twenty kilometres** ~ à

vingt kilomètres de distance; **we must** ~ nous devons partir
**awe** n crainte f, effroi m; vt inspirer de la crainte à
**awe-inspiring** adj imposant, terrible
**awesome** adj mystérieux -ieuse, étrange, épouvantable
**awestruck** adj frappé de terreur; épouvanté
**awful** adj affreux -euse, terrible, horrible; ~ **cheek!** quel culot!
**awfully** adv terriblement; coll très, vraiment, comme tout, rudement
**awhile** adv un instant; quelque temps
**awkward** adj peu commode, difficile, peu maniable; gênant, embarrassant; (clumsy) gauche, maladroit; ~ **age** âge ingrat; ~ **customer** type m pas commode
**awkwardness** n gaucherie f, maladresse f; (circumstance) embarras m
**awl** n poinçon m
**awning** n taud m; store m
**awry** adj de travers, de guingois
**axe**, US **ax** n hache f; coll (money) coupe f sombre; coll **have an** ~ **to grind** prêcher pour son saint, agir dans un but intéressé
**axiom** n axiome m
**axiomatic, axiomatical** adj axiomatique
**axis** n axe m
**axle** n axe m; mot essieu m, pont m
**axle-box** n boîte f d'essieu
**axle-pin** n clavette f d'essieu
**aye** n pol vote m pour; **the** ~ **s have it** les oui l'emportent; interj oui; dial toujours
**azalea** n azalée f
**azimuth** n azimut m
**azote** n azote m
**Aztec** n Astèque; adj astèque
**azure** n azur m; adj azuré, d'azur

# B

**baa** n bêlement m; vi bêler
**babble** n babil m, babillage m, bavardage m; (stream) gazouillement m; vt débiter; (secrets) divulguer; vi babiller; (stream) gazouiller, murmurer
**babbler** n babillard -e, bavard -e

**babe** n bébé m; naïf -ive; débutant -e
**baboon** n babouin m
**babouche** n babouche f
**baby** n bébé m; enfant, gosse; US coll chérie f; sl **hold the** ~ payer les pots cassés; adj de bébé; petit, de taille

réduite; ~ **grand (piano)** crapaud *m*, (piano *m*) demi-queue *m invar*
**babyhood** *n* première enfance
**babyish** *adj* enfantin, puéril
**baby-sit** *vi* faire du baby-sitting
**baby-sitter** *n* baby-sitter
**baby-sitting** *n* baby-sitting *m*
**baby-talk** *n* langage enfantin
**baccalaureate** *n* baccalauréat *m*
**bacchic** *adj* bachique
**bachelor** *n* célibataire *m*; *hist* bachelier *m*; **Bachelor of Arts** licencié -e
**bachelor-girl** *n* célibataire *f*
**bachelorhood** *n* célibat *m*
**bacillary** *adj* bacillaire
**bacillus** *n* bacille *m*
**back** *n* (human being, animal, knife, book, etc) dos *m*; (head, building) derrière *m*; (chair) dossier *m*; (cloth, mountain range) envers *m*; (coin, medal) revers *m*; (page) verso *m*; (hall, theatre) fond *m*; *sp* arrière *m*; *naut* quille *f*; ~ **to** ~ dos à dos; **at the** ~ **of beyond** au fin fond du bled; **be on one's** ~ être sur le flanc; *fig* **break one's** ~ s'éreinter; **break the** ~ **of sth** en faire le plus dur; **put one's** ~ **into** donner un coup de collier à, en mettre un coup; **put s/o's** ~ **up** vexer qn, froisser qn; **turn one's** ~ **on s/o** tourner le dos à qn; **with one's** ~ **to the wall** au pied du mur, acculé au mur; *vt* faire reculer; (bet) parier pour; financer; (plan) avaliser; épauler, encourager; ~ **up** soutenir; *vi* reculer, faire marche arrière; *naut* (tide, wind) renverser; ~ **down**, ~ **out** se retirer, lâcher la partie; *adj* de derrière, arrière *invar*; (out-of-date) arriéré; ~ **seat** siège *m* arrière; ~**-seat driver** personne *f* prodigue de conseils superflus; **take a** ~ **seat** être au second plan; *adv* en arrière; plus tôt, au passé; (from journey) de retour; ~ **and forth** en allant et venant; **answer** ~ rétorquer, objecter; **go** ~ **on** (principle) répudier; (promise) violer; (friend) trahir; **pay s/o** ~ payer qn de retour; **take** ~ rétracter
**back-bench(es)** *n*(*pl*) (British Parliament) banc(s) *m*(*pl*) où s'assoient les deputés qui n'ont pas de position ministérielle
**back-bencher** *n* (British Parliament) deputé *m* sans portefeuille
**backbite** *vt* médire de, décrier; *vi* médire
**backbiter** *n* médisant -e
**backbone** *n* épine dorsale, colonne vertébrale; *fig* pivot *m*; *fig* caractère *m*, courage *m*
**back-breaking** *adj* épuisant, éreintant
**back-chat** *n coll* réplique impertinente
**back-cloth** *n theat* + •*g* toile *f* de fond

**backdoor** *adj* secret; louche
**back-drop** *n theat* toile *f* de fond
**backer** *n comm* commanditaire *m*; soutien *m*; *sp* parieur -ieuse, turfiste
**backfire** *n mot* pétarade *f*, retour *m* de flamme; *vi mot* pétarader, avoir des retours de flamme; *coll fig* échouer
**backgammon** *n* trictrac *m*
**background** *n* arrière-plan *m*, fond *m*; (person) origines *fpl*; (experience) acquis *m*; (epoch) climat culturel; *adj* de fond
**backhand** *n* (tennis, etc) revers *m*; (writing) écriture renversée; *adj* de revers; renversé
**backhanded** *adj* (writing) renversé; *fig* (compliment) douteux -euse, équivoque
**backhander** *n* (blow) revers *m*; reproche *m*; *coll* (bribe) dessous *m* de table
**backing** *n* soutien *m*; (going backwards) recul *m*
**backlash** *n mech* secousse *f*; *pol* réaction brutale
**backlog** *n* arriéré *m*
**back-number** *n* (newspaper, etc) ancien numéro; *fig* personne *f* qui ne compte plus
**back-pedal** *vi* rétropédaler; *fig* faire machine arrière
**back-room** *adj* ~ **boy** expert *m* (qui travaille à l'arrière-plan)
**back-scratcher** *n* gratte-dos *m invar*
**backside** *n* derrière *m*, *sl* cul *m*
**backsight** *n* cran *m* de mire
**backslapping** *n* grandes démonstrations d'amitié
**backslide** *vi* rechuter, récidiver
**backslider** *n* récidiviste
**backstage** *adj* + *adv theat* en coulisse
**backstairs** *n* escalier *m* de service; *adj fig* louche, clandestin
**backstays** *npl* haubans *mpl*
**backstitch** *n* point *m* arrière
**backstroke** *n* nage *f* sur le dos
**backward** *adj* en arrière; (outmoded) arriéré; (child) retardé
**backward(s)** *adv* (motion) en arrière; à rebours, à l'envers; **know sth** ~ connaître qch à fond
**backwardness** *n* retard *m*; *med* arriération *f*, faiblesse *f* d'esprit
**backwash** *n* remous *m*
**backwater** *n* (river) bras mort; *fig* trou *m* de province, bled *m*
**backwoods** *npl* forêt *f* vierge
**backwoodsman** *n* bûcheron *m*; *pej* rustre *m*
**bacon** *n* lard *m*, bacon *m*
**bacterial** *adj* bactérien -ienne
**bactericide** *n* produit *m* bactéricide
**bacteriological** *adj* bactériologique

**bacteriologist** *n* bactériologiste
**bacteriology** *n* bactériologie *f*
**bacterium** *n* (*pl* **-ia**) bactérie *f*
**bad** *n* mauvais *m*; (evil) mal *m*; **be £500 to the** ~ être en déficit de £500; **go to the** ~ mal tourner; *adj* mauvais; défectueux -euse, imparfait; inférieur; (behaviour) méchant, vicieux -ieuse, cruel -elle; (food) avarié, pourri; (harmful) désagréable, nuisible; (ill) malade; (word, language) grossier -ière; (mistake, cold) gros (*f* grosse); ~ **blood** hostilité *f*; ~ **debt** dette *f* irrécouvrable; ~ **form** manque *m* d'éducation; **be** ~ **at** ne pas réussir à; **be** ~ **for** ne rien valoir à; **go** ~ se gâter, tourner; **in a** ~ **way** en mauvaise posture; **look** ~ faire mauvaise impression; **too** ~! dommage!, tant pis!
**baddish** *adj* assez mauvais
**badge** *n* insigne *m*, badge *m*
¹**badger** *n* blaireau *m*
²**badger** *vt* taquiner, harceler; importuner
**badinage** *n* badinage *m*
**badly** *adv* mal; cruellement; (hopelessly) désespérément; (very much) beaucoup; ~ **beaten** battu à plate(s) couture(s); **do** ~ mal réussir
**badminton** *n* badminton *m*
**badness** *n* mauvaise qualité, mauvais état; (evil) méchanceté *f*
¹**baffle** *n* déflecteur *m*; *rad* baffle *m*
²**baffle** *vt* confondre, dérouter; frustrer
**baffling** *adj* déroutant, déconcertant
**bag** *n* sac *m*; sacoche *f*; (purse) bourse *f*; (eye) poche *f*; *sp* tableau *m* de chasse; *sl* putain *f*, vioquarde *f*; ~**s** *coll obs* pantalon *m*; ~ **and baggage** tout le bazar; ~ **of bones** paquet *m* d'os; **be in the** ~ être dans le sac; **diplomatic** ~ valise *f* diplomatique; **let the cat out of the** ~ vendre la mèche; **sleeping** ~ sac *m* de couchage; *vt* mettre en sac, ensacher; *sp* tuer à la chasse; *coll* mettre le grappin sur; *vi* (garment) bouffer, faire des poches
**bagatelle** *n* bagatelle *f*, fadaise *f*; *mus* divertissement *m*; (game) espèce *f* de jeu de billard
**baggage** *n* bagages *mpl*; *coll* traînée *f*
**baggy** *adj* bouffant, gonflé; (trousers) faisant poche
**bagpipe(s)** *n* cornemuse *f*
**bah** *interj* bah!
¹**bail** *n* *leg* caution *f*, cautionnement *m*; (person) répondant *m*, caution *f*, garant -e *f*; **go** ~ **for** s/o se porter caution pour qn; *vt leg* cautionner, se rendre caution pour; *leg* ~ **s/o out** obtenir moyennant caution la liberté

provisoire de qn; *fig* tirer qn d'une situation difficile
²**bail** *n naut* écope *f*; *vt naut* écoper
**bailiff** *n* bailli *m*; *leg* huissier *m*; *agr* intendant *m*
**bairn** *n dial* enfant
**bait** *n* amorce *f*, appât *m*; *fig* tentation *f*; **rise to the** ~ mordre à l'hameçon; *vt* (hook) appâter; (horse) donner à manger à; *fig* harceler
**baize** *n* (green) tapis vert
**bake** *vt* cuire au four; (skin) bronzer; *vi* cuire
**bakehouse** *n* boulangerie *f*
**Bakelite** *n* Bakélite *f*
**baker** *n* boulanger -ère; ~'**s dozen** treize
**bakery** *n* boulangerie *f*
**baking** *n* cuisson *f*; (bread) fournée *f*; *adj* très chaud; ~ **powder** levure *f*
**baksheesh, bakshish** *n* bakchich *m*
**balaclava** *n* passe-montagne *m*
**balalaika** *n* balalaïka *f*
**balance** *n* balance *f*; contrepoids *m*; (clock, watch) balancier *m*; *comm* balance *f*; *fig* équilibre *m*, accord *m*; ~ **of payments** balance *f* des paiements; ~ **sheet** bilan *m*; **hang in the** ~ être en balance; **on** ~ tout considéré; *vt* mettre en équilibre, balancer; équilibrer; *comm* balancer, équilibrer; *vi* balancer, hésiter; se balancer
**balcony** *n* balcon *m*
**bald** *adj* chauve; (statement, style) simple, sec (*f* sèche)
**balderdash** *n* balivernes *fpl*
**baldness** *n* calvitie *f*; *fig* simplicité *f*, sécheresse *f*
¹**bale** *n* balle *f*, ballot *m*; *vt* emballotter
²**bale** *vi aer* ~ **out** faire un saut en parachute
**baleful** *adj* nuisible; sinistre, funeste
**balk, baulk** *n bui* solive *f*; *agr* billon *m*; *fig* obstacle *m*, pierre *f* d'achoppement; *vt* éviter, esquiver; (thwart) entraver, contrecarrer; *vi* (horse) se dérober; ~ **at sth** reculer devant qch
**Balkan** *adj* balkanique
**Balkans** *npl* Balkans *mpl*
¹**ball** *n* (golf, tennis) balle *f*; (football) ballon *m*; (billiards) bille *f*; (hockey, snow) boule *f*; *cul* boulette *f*; (eye) prunelle *f*; (wool) pelote *f*; *sl* ~**s** couilles *fpl*; *sl* ~ **s!** conneries! *fpl*; *fig* **be on the** ~ être dégourdi; **keep the** ~ **rolling** soutenir la conversation; faire le boute-en-train; **play** ~ coopérer, être de mèche; *vt* (wool) peloter; *sl* ~ **up** embrouiller, bousiller
²**ball** *n* bal *m*; **fancy-dress** ~ bal costumé; *US coll* **have a** ~ s'amuser énormément, rire aux éclats
**ballad** *n* ballade *f*; poème narratif *m*; *mus*

**ballast** *n* *naut+aer* lest *m*; (railway) ballast *m*; *fig* pondération *f*; *vt* lester; empierrer
**ball-bearing** *n* *eng* bille *f*
**ball-cock** *n* flotteur *m* (de chasse d'eau)
**ballerina** *n* ballerine *f*
**ballet** *n* ballet *m*
**ballistic** *adj* balistique
**ballistics** *npl* balistique *f*
**ballocks** *npl* *sl* couilles *fpl*; *sl* conneries! *fpl*
**balloon** *n* ballon *m*; ~ **barrage** ballons *mpl* de protection, ballons *mpl* de barrage; ~ **glass** verre *m* ballon; *vt* ballonner; *vi* monter en ballon
**ballot** *n* (paper) bulletin *m* de vote; (method of voting) scrutin *m*; *pol* scrutin *m*; (lots) tirage *m* au sort; *vi* voter au scrutin; ~ **for** élire par scrutin
**ballot-box** *n* urne électorale
**ball-point** *n* stylo *m* à bille
**ballroom** *n* salle *f* de bal; *adj* ~ **dancing** danse *f* de salon
**balls-up** *n* *sl* make a ~ of bousiller
**ballyhoo** *n* (publicity) battage *m*; (nonsense) bobard *m*
**balm** *n* baume *m*
**balmy** *adj* embaumé, parfumé; *fig* calmant; (weather) doux (*f* douce); *coll* cinglé
**balsa** *n* balsa *m*
**balsam** *n* *med+fig* baume *m*; *bot* balsamine *f*
**balsamic** *adj* balsamique
**baluster** *n* balustre *m*; ~s rampe *f*, main courante
**balustrade** *n* balustrade *f*
**bamboo** *n* bambou *m*
**bamboozle** *vt* *coll* embobiner, rouler
**ban** *n* interdiction *f*, exclusive *f*; *eccles* interdit *m*, excommunication *f*; *vt* interdire, défendre, proscrire
**banal** *adj* insignifiant, banal (*pl* banals)
**banality** *n* banalité *f*
**banana** *n* banane *f*
**¹band** *n* (cloth, paper, metal, *rad*, etc) bande *f*
**²band** *n* (group) bande *f*; *mil* troupe *f*; *mus* orchestre *m*; brass ~ fanfare *f*; **military** ~ musique *f* militaire
**³band** *vt* bander; grouper; *vi* se grouper
**bandage** *n* pansement *m*, bandage *m*; *vt* bander, mettre un pansement à
**bandeau** *n* bandeau *m*
**banderole, banderol** *n* banderole *f*
**bandit** *n* bandit *m*; **one-armed** ~ machine *f* à sous
**bandmaster** *n* chef *m* de musique
**bandolier** *n* bandoulière *f*, cartouchière *f*
**band-saw** *n* scie *f* sans fin

**bandstand** *n* kiosque *m* à musique
**bandwagon** *n* *US* char *m* (de carnaval) portant des musiciens; *coll* climb on the ~ se mettre du côté du manche
**¹bandy** *vt* renvoyer, relancer; ~ **words** ergoter, se disputer; *usu pej* have one's name bandied about défrayer la chronique
**²bandy** *adj* tors, tordu; ~ **legged** bancal (*pl* bancals)
**bane** *n* ruine *f*, fléau *m*; *ar* poison *m*; be the ~ of s/o's life empoisonner la vie de qn
**baneful** *adj* injurieux -ieuse; (poisonous) vénéneux -euse
**¹bang** *n* détonation *f*, explosion *f*; coup *m*; bruit sec; (supersonic) bang *m*; *vulg* have a ~ baiser; with a ~ avec grand succès, précisément, exactement; *vt* cogner, marteler; (door) claquer; *vi* faire un bruit sec; *adv phr coll* ~ on juste, exact; *interj* ~ ! paf!
**²bang** *n* (hair) frange *f*
**bangle** *n* bracelet *m*
**banian, banyan** *n* *bot* banian *m*
**banish** *vt* exiler, bannir; expulser, chasser
**banishment** *n* exil *m*, bannissement *m*
**banister, bannister** *n* rampe *f* (d'escalier)
**banjo** *n* banjo *m*
**¹bank** *n* (mound) talus *m*, remblai *m*; (river, lake) bord *m*, berge *f*, rive *f*; (sand, cloud) banc *m*; (camber) bombement *m*; *vt* remployer, (heap up) amonceler; *vi* s'amonceler, s'entasser; *aer* virer sur l'aile
**²bank** *n* (galley) banc *m* des rameurs; (oars) rangée *f*; *mus* clavier *m*
**³bank** *n* banque *f*; ~ **card** carte *f* d'identité bancaire; Bank Holiday fête légale; ~ **rate** taux *m* d'escompte; break the ~ faire sauter la banque; *vt* déposer en banque; *vi* ~ **on**, ~ **upon** compter sur; ~ **with** avoir un compte en banque à
**bank-book** *n* carnet *m* de banque
**banker** *n* banquier *m*
**¹banking** *n* finance *f*, banque *f*
**²banking** *n* remblai *m*; (camber) bombement *m*; *aer* virage *m* sur l'aile
**bank-note** *n* billet *m* de banque
**bankrupt** *n* failli -e; **fraudulent** ~ banqueroutier -ière; *vt* faire faire faillite à; *adj* failli, en faillite; *fig* ~ **of** privé de; go ~ faire faillite
**bankruptcy** *n* faillite *f*; **fraudulent** ~ banqueroute *f*
**banner** *n* bannière *f*; étendard *m*; ~ **headline** titre *m* sur cinq colonnes à la une
**bannister** *n* see **banister**
**bannock** *n* (espèce *f* de) galette *f*

**banns** npl bans mpl

**banquet** n banquet m; vt régaler; vi banqueter

**bantam** n coq m; sp ~ **weight** poids m coq

**banter** n plaisanterie f, badinerie f; vt railler, plaisanter; vi plaisanter, badiner

**ban-the-bomb** adj ~ **campaign** campagne f contre la bombe atomique

**banyan** n see banian

**baobab** n baobab m

**baptism** n baptême m; ~ **of fire** baptême m du feu

**baptismal** adj baptismal

**Baptist** n baptiste

**baptistery** n baptistère m

**baptize** vt baptiser

¹**bar** n (wood, metal, etc) barre f; (gate, window) barreau m; (for drinking) bar m; leg barreau m; naut barre f; mus barre f; fig obstacle m; entrave f; her bande f; her ~ **sinister** barre f de bâtardise; leg **be called to the** ~ être inscrit au barreau; vt barrer; fermer; (stripe) rayer; (exclude) exclure; leg interdire; prep sauf; ~ **none** sans exception

²**bar** n zool bar m

**barb** n zool+bot barbe f; (hook, arrow) pointe f; fig pointe f, flèche f; vt aiguiser, effiler

**barbarian** n+adj barbare

**barbaric** adj barbare, rude; de mauvais goût, inculte

**barbarism** n barbarie f; brutalité f; ling barbarisme m

**barbarity** n barbarie f, brutalité f

**barbarize** vt rendre barbare; ling corrompre

**barbarous** adj barbare, sauvage; cruel -elle; ling barbare, inculte; grossier -ière, bruyant

**barbecue** n barbecue m; vt griller sur barbecue

**barbed** adj barbelé; fig mordant, acéré

**barbel** n zool (fish) barbeau m; zool (bristle) barbillon m

**barber** n coiffeur m; ar barbier m

**barbican** n barbacane f

**barbitone** n véronal m

**barbiturates** npl chem dérivés mpl de l'acide barbiturique, somnifères mpl

**barbituric** adj barbiturique

**barcarole, barcarolle** n barcarolle f

¹**bard** n poet barde m

²**bard** n cul barde f; vt cul barder

**bare** adj nu, dénudé; dégarni; (empty) vide; simple, peu orné; à peine suffisant; **earn a** ~ **living** gagner à peine de quoi vivre; vt dénuder, mettre à nu; (sword) dégainer; fig révéler, montrer

**bareback** adj ~ **rider** cavalier -ière à cru; adv à cru, à poil

**barefaced** adj à visage découvert; fig effronté, éhonté

**barefoot** adj+adv nu-pieds; adj phr+adv phr pieds nus

**bare-headed** adj nu-tête invar

**barely** adv à peine, juste; pauvrement

**bargain** n comm marché m, accord m; (cheap purchase) occasion f; **into the** ~ par-dessus le marché; aussi; vi marchander; ~ **for** s'attendre à

**bargain-basement** n rayon m des soldes

**barge** n péniche f, chaland m; (navy) canot m major; vi coll ~ **in** arriver comme un chien dans un jeu de quilles; s'immiscer dans; coll ~ **into** se cogner contre, se heurter contre

**bargee** n marinier m; **swear like a** ~ jurer comme un charretier

**baritone** n baryton m; adj de baryton

**barium** n chem baryum m

¹**bark** n (tree) écorce f; vt (tree) écorcer; (skins) tanner; coll s'écorcher

²**bark** n aboiement m; coll toux f; **his** ~ **is worse than his bite** tous les chiens qui aboient ne mordent pas; vi aboyer; coll tousser; ~ **up the wrong tree** se tromper, se tromper de but

³**bark** n see barque

**barley** n orge f; **pearl** ~ orge perlé

**barley-sugar** n sucre m d'orge

**barley-water** n infusion f d'orge perlé, orgeat m

**barmaid** n barmaid f, serveuse f de bar

**barman** n barman m

**barmy** adj coll toqué

**barn** n grange f; coll **a** ~ **of a place** une grande baraque

**barnacle** n (shellfish) anatife m, bernache f; (goose) bernacle f; coll fig crampon m, importun -e

**barn-door** n porte f d'une grange; coll cible si grande qu'on ne peut pas la manquer

**barn-owl** n effraie f

**barn-stormer** n theat cabotin -e

**barograph** n baromètre m à cadran

**barometer** n baromètre m

**baron** n baron m; ~ **of beef** double aloyau m

**baronage** n collect noblesse f; hist Gotha m

**baroness** n baronne f

**baronet** n baronnet m

**baronial** adj de baron

**barony** n baronnie f

**baroque** n baroque m; adj baroque

**barque, bark** n naut trois-mâts carré

**barrack** vt+vi sp applaudir ironiquement

**barracking** n sp applaudissements mpl ironiques

**barrack(s)** n mil caserne f; fig grande baraque; mil **barrack room** chambrée f; vt **barrack** caserner

**barrage** n eng barrage m; mil tir m de barrage

**barratry** n leg baraterie f

**barrel** n (small) baril m; (larger) barrique f, tonneau m; (herring) caque f; (firearm) canon m; (watch, clock, lock) barillet m; ~ **vault** archi arc m en berceau

**barrel-organ** n orgue m de Barbarie

**barren** adj med stérile; stérile, inculte, aride; fig sans intérêt, sans idées

**barrenness** n med stérilité f; aridité f; fig manque m d'idées

**barricade** n barricade f; vt barricader

**barrier** n barrière f; fig obstacle m, empêchement m

**barring** prep sauf, excepté

**barrister** n leg = avocat -e

**¹barrow** n arch tumulus m

**²barrow** n charrette f à bras; **wheel ~** brouette f

**barrow-boy** n marchand m des quatre-saisons

**barter** n troc m; vt troquer; fig échanger; ~ **away** vendre, faire trafic de

**basalt** n geol basalte m

**bascule** n eng bascule f

**¹base** n base f; archi assise f, fondation f; phil racine f; fig point m de départ, principe m; vt baser, fonder, appuyer; ~ **oneself on** se baser sur

**²base** adj (birth) de basse extraction; vil, abject, bas (f basse)

**baseball** n US base-ball m

**baseless** adj sans fondement

**basement** n sous-sol m

**baseness** n bassesse f, abjection f

**bash** n coll coup m; coll **have a ~** essayer; vt coll cogner; ~ **in** enfoncer; coll ~ **up** tabasser; vi ~ **on** continuer, se résigner

**bashful** adj timide, transi

**bashfulness** n timidité f

**basic** adj de base; chem basique

**basil** n bot basilic m

**basilica** n basilique f

**basilisk** n basilic m

**basin** n bassin m, cuvette f; (for food) bol m; geog+naut bassin m; geol cuvette f; **wash ~** lavabo m

**basinful** n pleine cuvette; coll **have a ~** en avoir ras le bol

**basis** n base f, fondement m

**bask** vi ~ **in the sun** paresser au soleil, coll lézarder; fig se plaire

**basket** n panier m, corbeille f

**basketball** n sp basket-ball m, basket m

**basketful** n panier m

**basket-work, basketry** n vannerie f

**Basque** n Basque; (language) basque m; adj basque

**bas-relief, bass-relief** n bas-relief m

**¹bass** n mus basse f; adj mus de basse, grave

**²bass** n (freshwater) perche f; (sea) bar m

**basset** n basset m

**basset-horn** n mus cor m de basset

**bassoon** n basson m

**bassoonist** n basson m, bassoniste

**bastard** n bâtard -e, enfant naturel -elle; sl fig salaud m; sl (nuisance) emmerdement m; sl fig **stupid ~** ! crétin!; adj bâtard, illégitime; fig faux (f fausse), anormal

**bastardize** vt déclarer illégitime

**bastardy** n bâtardise f

**baste** vt cul arroser

**bastion** n bastion m

**¹bat** n chauve-souris f (pl chauves-souris); fig **have ~ s in the belfry** avoir une araignée au plafond

**²bat** n sp batte f; (table-tennis) raquette f; **off one's own ~** sans aide; vt (eyelid) cligner; vi sp manier la batte

**batch** n (baking) fournée f; tas m; (persons) groupe m

**bate** vt baisser; vt diminuer; **with ~ d breath** anxieusement

**bath** n baignoire f; (action of taking a bath) bain m; ~ **s** établissement m de bains; **have a ~** prendre un bain; vt baigner, donner un bain à; vi prendre un bain

**bath-chair** n fauteuil roulant (pour malade)

**bathe** n bain m, baignade f; vt baigner; (flood) inonder; vi se baigner

**bather** n baigneur -euse

**bathetic** adj rhet qui tombe dans le ridicule

**bathing** n baignade f, bain m de mer (de rivière)

**bathing-costume** n maillot m de bain; slip m

**bath-mat** n tapis m de bain

**bathos** n rhet chute f dans lè ridicule

**bathroom** n salle f de bains

**bath-towel** n serviette f de bain

**bathtub** n baignoire f

**bathyscaphe** n bathyscaphe m

**bathysphere** n bathysphère f

**batiste** n batiste f

**batman** n mil ordonnance f or m

**baton** n mus bâton m; (police) matraque f

**bats** adj coll cinglé, toqué

**battalion** n bataillon m

**¹batten** n planche f, latte f; theat herse f;

*vt* latter; *naut* ~ **down hatches** fermer les écoutilles

²**batten** *vi* s'engraisser; *fig* ~ **on** prospérer aux dépens de

¹**batter** *n cul* pâte *f* à frire; *print* caractère écrasé

²**batter** *vt* rouer de coups; *sl* tabasser; (deform) cabosser, bosseler; *mil* battre en brèche; ~ **down** démolir; ~ **in** défoncer

**battering-ram** *n mil ar* bélier *m*

**battery** *n leg* voie *f* de fait; *mil* + *elect* + *agr* batterie *f*; ~ **hen** poulet *m* de batterie; **dry** ~ pile (sèche)

**battle** *n* bataille *f*, combat *m*; **give** ~ livrer bataille; **killed in** ~ mort au champ d'honneur; *vi* ~ **against** lutter contre; ~ **for** batailler pour, combattre pour

**battle-axe** *n hist* hache *f* d'armes; *fig* mégère *f*

**battle-cruiser** *n naut* croiseur lourd

**battle-cry** *n* cri *m* de guerre; *fig* slogan *m*

**battle-dress** *n mil* tenue *f* de combat, tenue *f* de campagne

**battlefield** *n* champ *m* de bataille

**battlement** *n* créneau *m*

**battleship** *n naut* cuirassé *m*

**batty** *adj coll* cinglé, toqué

**bauble** *n hist* marotte *f*; *fig* babiole *f*, colifichet *m*

**baulk** *n* + *vt* + *vi see* **balk**

**bauxite** *n min* bauxite *f*

**bawd** *n obs* proxénète *m*

**bawdry** *n* grivoiseries *fpl*

**bawdy** *n* gauloiserie *f*; *adj* gaulois, grivois, leste

**bawdy-house** *n obs* bordel *m*

**bawl** *n* braillement *m*; *vt* brailler, beugler; *vi* brailler, beugler; *coll* ~ **out** engueuler

¹**bay** *n* golfe *m*; baie *f*, anse *f*

²**bay** *bot* laurier *m*

³**bay** *n archi* travée *f*; ~ **window** bay-window *f*, oriel *m*; *naut* **sick** ~ hôpital *m* de bord

⁴**bay** *n* aboiement *m*; abois *mpl*; **at** ~ aux abois; **keep at** ~ tenir en échec; *vi* aboyer

⁵**bay** *adj* (horse) bai

**bayonet** *n* baïonnette *f*; *vt* donner un coup de baïonnette à

**bazaar, bazar** *n* (department store) bazar *m*; vente *f* de charité; (oriental) souk *m*, bazar *m*

**bazooka** *n mil* bazooka *m*

**be** *vi* (exist) être, exister, se trouver; (come, go) être, venir, aller; (well, ill) aller, se porter; (age) avoir; (feel) avoir; (remain) rester; *math* faire; (have to) devoir; (cost) coûter, valoir; **here is** voici; **how are you?** comment

allez-vous?, comment vous portez-vous?; **how long are you here for?** vous restez combien de temps ici?; **how much is this hat?** combien coûte-t-il, ce chapeau?, combien vaut-il, ce chapeau?; **I am afraid** j'ai peur; **I am here** je suis ici; **I am hot** j'ai chaud; **I am to say** je dois dire; **I am twenty years old** j'ai vingt ans; **I have been to London** je suis allé à Londres; **no one has been here today** personne n'est venu ici aujourd'hui; **there is** il y a; *lit* il est; (pointing out) voilà; **two and two are four** deux et deux font quatre; *v aux* être; *v impers* (weather) **it is fine** il fait beau; **it is time to go** il est temps de partir

**beach** *n* plage *f*, grève *f*; *vt naut* échouer

**beachcomber** *n obs* (Pacific Islands) colon blanc appauvri; (wave) lame déferlante

**beachhead** *n mil* tête *f* de pont

**beacon** *n* signal lumineux; fanal *m*; phare *m*; *naut* balise *f*; *vt naut* baliser

**bead** *n* perle *f*; (rosary) grain *m*; (sweat) goutte *f*; *mil* cran *m* de mire; *archi* baguette *f*; ~**s** collier *m*; *eccles* chapelet *m*; **draw a** ~ **on** viser; **tell one's** ~**s** égrener son chapelet; *vt* enfiler; orner de perles

**beading** *n carp* baguette *f*; garniture *f* de perles

**beady** *adj* (eye) perçant

**beagle** *n* beagle *m*; *vi* chasser avec des beagles

**beagling** *n* chasse *f* avec des beagles

**beak** *n* bec *m*; *sl* nez crochu; *sl* magistrat *m*, juge *m*

**beaked** *adj* pointu

**beaker** *n lit* coupe *f*; *chem* vase *m*

**be-all** *n* ~ **and end-all le** fin fond

**beam** *n* (light) rayon *m*, faisceau *m*; *bui* poutre *f*; (plough) timon *m*; *naut* largeur *f*; *naut* (side) travers *m*; (scales) fléau *m*; *phys* + *rad* + *aer* + *naut* faisceau *m*; *fig* grand sourire, sourire rayonnant; ~ **navigation** navigation *f* radiogonométrique; **on the port (starboard)** ~ par le travers bâbord (tribord); *vt* émettre, diriger; *vi* sourire; rayonner

**beaming** *adj* rayonnant; *phys* + *rad* directionnel -elle

**bean** *n* haricot *m*; fève *f*; *coll* sou *m*; **broad** ~ fève *f*; **runner** ~ haricot vert; *coll* **spill the** ~**s** vendre la mèche

¹**bear** *n zool* + *fig* ours *m*; (Stock Exchange) baissier *m*; *astron* **Great Bear** Grande Ourse; **Little Bear** Petite Ourse; *vi* jouer à la baisse

²**bear** *vt* porter, transporter; (endure) supporter, tolérer, endurer;

(child) porter, enfanter, accoucher; (responsibility) porter; (remembering) mériter; (grudge) éprouver, ressentir; (relation) avoir rapport à; ~ **away** enlever, emmener; ~ **out** confirmer; ~ **with** supporter avec patience; ~ **witness** témoigner; *vi* ~ **down on** foncer sur; *naut* s'approcher rapidement de; ~ **hard on** peser sur; *naut* ~ **off** prendre le large, s'éloigner de; ~ **right** prendre à droite; ~ **up** montrer du courage, faire preuve de courage

**bearable** *adj* supportable, tolérable

**beard** *n* barbe *f*; *vt* tirer par la barbe; confronter, défier

**bearded** *adj* barbu

**beardless** *adj* imberbe

**bearer** *n* porteur *m*; *comm* porteur *m*, titulaire *m*; *adj* ~ **bond** titre *m* au porteur

**bear-garden** *n* pétaudière *f*

**bearing** *n* port *m*, allure *f*; (behaviour) maintien *m*; (relevance) rapport *m*, portée *f*; (endurance) endurance *f*, patience *f*; (child) enfantement *m*; (direction) relèvement *m*; *archi* appui *m*, portée *f*; *eng* cône *m*, galet *m*; *her* pièce *f* honorable; **lose one's** ~ **s** s'égarer, perdre le nord

**bearish** *adj* bourru, grincheux -euse; (Stock Exchange) tendant à la baisse

**beast** *n* bête *f*; *fig* brute *f*; *coll* abruti -e, vache *f*; ~ **s** bétail *m*, bestiaux *mpl*

**beastliness** *n* méchanceté *f*; obscénité *f*; *coll* saloperie *f*

**beastly** *adj* dégoûtant, infect; brutal; abominable

¹**beat** *n* battement *m*; coup *m*; *mus* temps *m*, battement *m*; (hunting) battue *f*; (policeman) secteur *m*, ronde *f*; *vt* battre, frapper; (defeat) battre, vaincre; *mus* + *cul* battre; *mil* ~ **a retreat** se retirer; (price) ~ **down** faire rabattre; ~ **in** enfoncer; *coll* ~ **it** foutre le camp; ~ **off** repousser; ~ **out** marteler; ~ **time** battre la mesure; ~ **up** rosser; *coll* **that ~ s me!** ça me dépasse; *vi naut* louvoyer; ~ **about the bush** tergiverser

²**beat** *adj coll* beatnik

**beaten** *adj* battu; (metal) martelé; (exhausted) éreinté

**beater** *n* batteur -euse; (carpet) battoir *m*; *sp* rabatteur -euse

**beatific** *adj* béatifique

**beatification** *n eccles* béatification *f*

**beatify** *vt eccles* béatifier

**beating** *n* battement *m*; *naut* louvoiement *m*; volée *f* de coups; défaite *f*; **take a** ~ se faire battre à plate(s) couture(s); **take some** ~ être difficile à battre

**beatitude** *n* béatitude *f*

**beatnik** *n* + *adj* beatnik (*f sing invar*, *m* + *fpl* beatniks)

**beau** *n* dandy *m*, élégant *m*

**beauteous** *adj* beau (*f* belle)

**beautician** *n US* esthéticien -ienne

**beautiful** *n* the ~ le beau; *adj* beau (*f* belle), admirable

**beautify** *vt* rendre beau (*f* belle)

**beauty** *n* beauté *f*; **the ~ of it is...** le plus beau, c'est que...; **the Sleeping Beauty** la Belle au bois dormant

**beauty-parlour** *n* institut *m* de beauté

**beauty-sleep** *n* sommeil *m* d'avant minuit

**beauty-spot** *n* grain *m* de beauté; (patch) mouche *f*; endroit *m* de beauté naturelle

**beaver** *n* castor *m*; *coll* **eager** ~ personne *f* qui fait du zèle; *vi coll* ~ **away** travailler avec persévérance

**be-bop** *n* be-bop *m*

**becalm** *vt* calmer; *naut* **be** ~ **ed** être encalminé

**because** *conj* parce que; ~ **of** en raison de, à cause de

**béchamel** *n cul* béchamel *f*

**beck** *n* signe *m*, appel *m*; **at the** ~ **and call of** prêt à obéir à; *vt* + *vi see* **beckon**

**beckon** *vt* faire signe à; *vi* faire signe

**become** *vt* (suit) convenir à; *vi* devenir, se faire

**becoming** *adj* convenable; (clothes, etc) seyant

**bed** *n* lit *m*; *lit* couche *f*; (plants) plate-bande *f* (*pl* plates-bandes), parterre *m*; *geol* couche *f*, gisement *m*; (base) assiette *f*; *fig* rapport sexuel; ~ **and board** le logement et la nourriture, pension complète; **be brought to** ~ accoucher; **double** ~ grand lit; **get out of** ~ **on the wrong side** se lever du pied gauche; **go to** ~ se coucher, aller se coucher; **put to** ~ coucher; **take to one's** ~ s'aliter; *vt* planter, repiquer; *bui* asseoir; *sl* baiser; *vi bui* s'asseoir

**bedaub** *vt* barbouiller

**bed-bug** *n* punaise *f*

**bed-clothes** *npl* draps *mpl* et couvertures *fpl*

**bedding** *n* literie *f*; *agr* litière *f*; (plants) repiquage *m*; *geol* stratification *f*

**bedeck** *vt* orner, parer

**bedevil** *vt* abîmer, gâter; harceler; tourmenter; (bewitch) envoûter

**bedevilment** *n* (confusion) désordre *m*; (bewitching) envoûtement *m*

**bedfellow** *n* compagnon *m* de lit; *fig* associé *m*

**bedim** *vt* obscurcir

**bedlam** *n obs* maison *f* de fous; *fig* tumulte *m*

**bed-linen** *n* draps *mpl* de lit et taies *fpl* d'oreiller

**Bedouin** *n* Bédouin -e

**bed-pan** *n* bassin *m* (hygiénique)

**bedpost** *n* (of four-poster) colonne *f*; *coll* **between you and me and the ~** strictement entre nous deux

**bedraggle** *vt* crotter, tacher de boue

**bedridden** *adj* alité

**bed-rock** *n geol* soubassement *m* (rocheux); *fig* fondement *m*

**bedside** *n* chevet *m*; **~ lamp** lampe *f* de chevet; (doctor) **have a good ~ manner** savoir inspirer confiance à un malade

**bedsitter, bedsit** *n coll*, **bedsitting room** *n* studio *m*, chambre meublée

**bed-socks** *npl* chaussettes *fpl* de nuit

**bedsore** *n* escarre *f*

**bedspread** *n* couvre-lit *m*

**bedstead** *n* châlit *m*, bois *m* de lit

**bedtime** *n* heure *f* de se coucher

**bedwetting** *n* incontinence *f* nocturne

**bee** *n* abeille *f*; *fig* personne affairée; **have a ~ in one's bonnet** avoir une marotte, avoir une araignée au plafond

**beech** *n* hêtre *m*

**beef** *cul* bœuf *m*; *fig* force *f* musculaire, vigueur *f*

**beef-steak** *n* bifteck *m*

**beefy** *adj* musculaire

**beehive** *n* ruche *f*

**bee-keeper** *n* apiculteur *m*

**bee-keeping** *n* apiculture *f*

**bee-line** *n* **make a ~ for** se diriger tout droit vers

**beer** *n* bière *f*; **small ~** petite bière; (person) personne *f* sans importance

**beer-mat** *n* dessous *m* de verre (de bière)

**beery** *adj* qui sent la bière; un peu parti

**beeswax** *n* cire *f* d'abeille

**beet** *n* betterave *f*; *US* **red ~** betterave (potagère)

**¹beetle** *n* maillet *m*, masse *f*

**²beetle** *n* coléoptère *m*, cafard *m*; (scarab) scarabée *m*

**³beetle** *vi* (cliff) surplomber; *coll* **~ off** s'en aller; *adj* surplombant

**beetling** *adj* surplombant; proéminent

**beetroot** *n* betterave (potagère)

**befall** *vt* arriver à; *vi* arriver

**befit** *vt* convenir à, être digne de

**befog** *vt* brouiller, embrouiller

**before** *adv* devant, en avant; (time) avant, auparavant; (in the past) déjà; **day ~** veille *f*; *prep* (place) devant; (time) avant de; de préférence à; *leg* par-devant; *conj* avant que; (rather than) plutôt que de

**beforehand** *adv* d'avance, préalablement

**befoul** *vt* souiller; *fig* salir

**befriend** *vt* nouer une amitié avec; aider

**beg** *vt* mendier; (request) solliciter, demander; (urge) prier, supplier; **~ off** s/o solliciter la grâce de qn; **~ the question** présumer vrai ce qui est en question; *vi* mendier, demander l'aumône; (dog) faire le beau; **~ to** avoir l'honneur de

**beget** *vt* engendrer, procréer; *fig* produire

**beggar** *n* mendiant -e; *coll* type *m*; *vt* ruiner, réduire à la mendicité; *fig* dépasser

**beggarly** *adj* pauvre, misérable, sordide

**beggary** *n* mendicité *f*

**begin** *vt* commencer, entamer; inaugurer; *vi* commencer, s'y mettre; **~ at the beginning** commencer par le commencement; **~ by doing** commencer par faire; **to ~ with** d'abord

**beginner** *n* débutant -e

**beginning** *n* commencement *m*, début *m*; (origin) principe *m*, origine *f*

**begonia** *n* bégonia *m*

**begrudge** *vt* envier; donner à contre-cœur

**beguile** *vt* tromper; (trick out of) soutirer; charmer, ensorceler; (time) passer agréablement

**behalf** *n* **on ~ of** au nom de; pour le compte de; (representing) de la part de

**behave** *vi* se conduire, se comporter; **~ oneself** se conduire bien, se comporter bien

**behaviour** *n* comportement *m*, conduite *f*, façon *f* d'agir; *mech* fonctionnement *m*

**behead** *vt* décapiter

**behest** *n obs* ordre *m*, commandement *m*

**behind** *n* derrière *m*; *coll* cul *m*; *adv* en arrière, derrière; (time) dans le passé; (late) en retard; **fall ~** rester en arrière, se laisser distancer; **put ~ one** refuser de considérer; **stay ~** rester; *prep* derrière, en arrière de; (time) en retard sur; **~ the scenes** en coulisse; **~ the times** arriéré, suranné; **~ time** en retard

**behindhand** *adj* **be ~** être en retard; (old-fashioned) être suranné; *adv* en retard; (payment) en retard

**behold** *vt + vi* regarder, contempler; voir; **~!** regardez!, voyez!

**beholden** *adj* obligé, redevable

**beholder** *n* spectateur -trice

**behove** *v impers* incomber

**beige** *n* tissu écru; (colour) beige *m*; *adj* beige

**being** *n* être *m*, créature *f*; vie *f*, existence *f*

**bel** *n phys* bel *m*

**belabour** *vt* rouer de coups; (words) invectiver

**belated** *adj* tardif -ive; (not on schedule) en retard, retardé

**belay** *n* (mountaineering) point *m*

d'appui; *vt naut* amarrer; ~! ferme!, stop!

**belaying-pin** *n naut* cabillot *m*

**belch** *n* éructation *f*, *sl* rot *m*; *vt fig* cracher, vomir; *vi* éructer, *sl* rôter

**beleaguer** *vt* assiéger, investir, bloquer

**belfry** *n* beffroi *m*, clocher *m*

**Belgian** *n* Belge; *adj* belge

**Belgium** *n* Belgique *f*

**belie** *vt* (misrepresent) mentir au sujet de; (mislead) donner une impression fausse de; (hopes) décevoir, démentir

**belief** *n* croyance *f*, conviction *f*; (confidence) confiance *f*; foi (religieuse)

**believable** *adj* croyable

**believe** *vt* croire, penser; ajouter foi à; *vi* croire; ~ **in** croire à

**believer** *n eccles* croyant -e; partisan -e

**belittle** *vt* rapetisser; déconsidérer, dénigrer

**bell** *n* cloche *f*; (hand-bell, electric bell) sonnette *f*; (bicycle, typewriter) timbre *m*; (on harness) grelot *m*; *mus* (trumpet, trombone, etc) pavillon *m*; *naut* ~ s coups *mpl* de cloche; **ring a** ~ faire penser à qch, faire souvenir de qch; **ring the** ~ gagner un prix; **sound as a** ~ en parfaite santé; *vt* mettre une cloche à; ~ **the cat** attacher le grelot

**belladonna** *n bot* belladone *f*

**bell-bottomed** *adj* (trousers) à patte d'éléphant

**bell-boy** *n* chasseur *m*, groom *m*

**belle** *n* belle *f*, beauté *f*

**bell-founder** *n* fondeur *m* de cloches

**bell-hop** *n US* chasseur *m*, groom *m*

**bellicose** *adj* belliqueux -euse

**belligerence** *n* belligérance *f*

**belligerent** *n* belligérant -e; *adj* belligérant

**bellow** *n* (animal) beuglement *m*, mugissement *m*; hurlement *m*; *vt* beugler; *vi* beugler, mugir; hurler

**bellows** *npl* soufflet *m*; *mus* (organ) soufflerie *f*

**belly** *n* ventre *m*; estomac *m*, abdomen *m*; *lit* (womb) sein *m*; *mus* table *f* d'harmonie; *vi* se gonfler, s'enfler

**belly-ache** *n* colique *f*, mal *m* de ventre; *vi sl* rouspéter, ronchonner

**belly-button** *n sl* nombril *m*

**bellyflop** *n* plat-ventre *m*

**bellyful** *n* quantité plus que suffisante; *coll* **have a** ~ en avoir plein le dos, *sl* en avoir ras le bol

**bellyland** *vi aer* atterrir sur le ventre

**bellylanding** *n aer* atterrissage *m* sur le ventre

**belong** *vi* appartenir; faire partie; (born in) être originaire; (fit in with) aller ensemble, s'accorder ensemble; ~ **with** dépendre de, relever de

**belongings** *npl* possessions *fpl*, biens *mpl*

**beloved** *n* bien-aimé -e; *adj* bien-aimé, chéri

**below** *adv* au-dessous, en bas; (lower) plus bas; en dessous; (downstream) en aval; (in book) ci-dessous, infra; (on earth) sur terre; (in hell) en enfer; *naut* en bas; *prep* au-dessous de; inférieur à

**belt** *n* ceinture *f*; *mech* courroie *f*; *mil* ceinturon *m*; (machine-gun) bande *f* de mitrailleuse; *geog* zone *f*; **conveyor** ~ chaîne *f* de fabrication, chaîne *f* de montage; **green** ~ ceinture verte; **blow below the** ~ coup *m* de Jarnac; **aer+mot seat** ~ ceinture *f* de sécurité; **tighten one's** ~ faire des économies, réduire ses dépenses; *vt* ceinturer; donner une raclée à; *vi sl* ~ **on** courir vite; *sl* ~ **up** se taire

**belting** *n coll* raclée *f*; *collect* ceintures *fpl*; courroies *fpl*

**belvedere** *n* belvédère *m*

**bemoan** *vt+vi* pleurer, lamenter

**bemuse** *vt* hébéter; déconcerter

**bench** *n* banc *m*; (work) établi *m*, table *f*; *leg* banc *m* des magistrats, banc *m* d'un juge; *leg collect* juges *mpl*, magistrats *mpl*; *pol* **front** ~ banc *m* des ministres

**bench-mark** *n* repère *m* de niveau

**bend** *n* courbe *f*; (road) virage *m*; *her* bande *f*; *naut* nœud *m*; ~ s maladie *f* des caissons; *her* ~ **sinister** barre *f*; *coll* **round the** ~ cinglé -e; *vt* courber, ployer, plier; (gaze) diriger; (stretch) tendre; *fig* faire plier, faire dévier; tendre; *naut* (rope, etc) amarrer; *naut* (sail) enverguer; **be bent upon** s'acharner à; *vi* se courber, s'incliner, (se) plier; (road) faire un coude

**benediction** *n* bénédiction *f*; (grace at meal) bénédicité *m*

**benefaction** *n* (gift) don *m*; (good deed) bienfait *m*

**benefactor** *n* donateur *m*, bienfaiteur *m*

**benefactress** *n* donatrice *f*, bienfaitrice *f*

**benefice** *n eccles* bénéfice *m*

**beneficence** *n* bienfaisance *f*

**beneficent** *adj* bienfaisant

**beneficial** *adj* salutaire; avantageux -euse, favorable; utile

**beneficiary** *n* bénéficiaire *f*; *eccles* possesseur *m* d'un bénéfice

**benefit** *n* profit *m*, avantage *m*, bénéfice *m*; *leg* bénéfice *m*; *eccles hist* privilège *m*; (social) allocation *f*; *theat* représentation *f* au profit d'une œuvre; *vt* faire du bien à; profiter à; *vi* profiter, bénéficier

**Benelux** *n* Bénélux *m*

**benevolence** *n* bienveillance *f*, bonté *f*, générosité *f*

**benighted** *adj* surpris par la nuit; *fig* ignorant, arriéré

**benign** *adj* bon (*f* bonne), gentil -ille, affable; (favorable) propice; *med* bénin (*f* bénigne)

**benignant** *adj* bon (*f* bonne), affable; bienveillant

¹**bent** *n* disposition *f*, aptitude *f*; **follow one's ~** poursuivre ses propres intérêts; **to the top of one's ~** au maximum possible

²**bent** *adj* tordu, courbé; *sl* (crooked) malhonnête; *sl* (stolen) volé; *sl* homosexuel -elle

**benumb** *vt* engourdir, paralyser

**benzine** *n* benzine *f*

**bequeath** *vt* léguer

**bequest** *n* legs *m*

**berate** *vt* morigéner

**bereave** *vt* priver, déposséder; priver (par la mort)

**bereaved** *n* **the ~** la famille du disparu

**bereavement** *n* perte *f*; dépossession *f*; isolement *m*

**beret** *n* béret *m*

**bergamot** *n bot* (tree) bergamotier *m*; (fruit) bergamote *f*; (oil) essence *f* de bergamote

**bergschrund** *n* rimaye *f*

**beriberi** *n path* béribéri *m*

**berlin** *n* berline *f*

**berry** *n* baie *f*; (coffee) grain *m*; (roe) œuf *m*; **brown as a ~** tout bronzé; *vi* produire des baies; cueillir des baies

**berserk** *adj* frénétique; **go ~** devenir fou furieux

**berth** *n naut* mouillage *m*; (travel) lit *m*; (folding) couchette *f*; (job) poste *m*; **give a wide ~ to** éviter soigneusement; *vt naut* amarrer; *vi naut* mouiller

**beryl** *n* béryl *m*

**beryllium** *n chem* béryllium *m*

**beseech** *vt* implorer, supplier, conjurer

**beset** *vt* assiéger, serrer de près; *fig* assaillir; (adornments) parsemer

**besetting** *adj* habituel -elle; **~ sin** péché mignon

**beside** *prep* à côté de, près de; (like) comparé à; (irrelevant to) sans rapport avec; (wide of) loin de; **~ oneself** hors de soi, furieux -ieuse

**besides** *adv* en outre, de plus; (moreover) d'ailleurs, d'autre part; (else) d'autre; *prep* outre, en dehors de; (except) hormis

**besiege** *vt* assiéger

**besieger** *n* assiégeant -e

**besmear** *vt* souiller; *fig* calomnier

**besmirch** *vt* salir; ternir; *fig* salir, flétrir

**besom** *n* balai *m* (de brindilles)

**besotted** *adj* saoul, hébété; *fig* entiché, épris; idiot

**bespatter** *vt* éclabousser; crotter; *fig* salir

**bespeak** *vt* commander, réserver; indiquer, suggérer

**bespoke** *adj* fait sur commande

**best** *n* mieux *m*; meilleur -e; **~ man** garçon *m* d'honneur; **at ~** au mieux; **be at one's ~** être en excellente forme; **do one's ~** faire de son mieux; **for the ~** pour le mieux; **have the ~ of it** l'emporter; **look one's ~** être en beauté; **make the ~ of** s'arranger de; **make the ~ of a bad job** faire contre mauvaise fortune bon cœur; **to the ~ of my knowledge** autant que je sache; *adj superl* meilleur, plus grand; sans égal; plus beau (*f* belle); **it would be ~ to** le mieux serait de; *adv superl* mieux, le mieux; **as ~ I can** de mon mieux; **you know ~** vous êtes le mieux placé pour savoir; *vt* vaincre, battre

**bestial** *adj* bestial

**bestiality** *n* bestialité *f*

**bestiary** *n* bestiaire *m*

**bestir** *vt* **~ oneself** se remuer, se démener

**bestow** *vt* conférer, accorder; ranger, placer; loger

**bestowal** *n* don *m*

**bestrew** *vt* joncher, éparpiller

**bestride** *vt* être à cheval sur; (horse) enfourcher; (stride across) enjamber

**best-seller** *n* best-seller *m*

**bet** *n* pari *m*; *vt + vi* parier; *coll* **you ~!** pour sûr

**beta** *n* bêta *m*

**betake** *vt* (place, person) **~ oneself** se rendre

**betatron** *n phys* bêtatron *m*

**bethink** *vt* **~ oneself** réfléchir

**betimes** *adv* de bonne heure; (quickly) vite

**betoken** *vt* présager; indiquer, révéler

**betray** *vt* trahir, livrer; révéler; (trust, hope) décevoir; (emotion) manifester, montrer

**betrayal** *n* trahison *f*; traîtrise *f*

**betroth** *vt* fiancer

**betrothal** *n* fiançailles *fpl*

**betrothed** *n* fiancé -e

¹**better** *n* **~(s)** supérieur(s) *m*(*pl*); **get the ~ of** avoir le dessus sur, avoir l'avantage sur; *vt* améliorer; **~ oneself** s'améliorer; *adj comp* meilleur, supérieur; plus grand; plus convenable; (health) mieux; guéri; *coll* (wife) **~ half** moitié *f*; **be ~ than** valoir mieux que; **hope for ~ things** espérer mieux; *adv comp* mieux; plus; **~ and ~** de mieux en mieux; **~ still** encore mieux; (illness) **be ~** aller mieux; **be ~ off** être plus riche; **know ~** en savoir plus long; **make sth ~**

améliorer qch; **think ~ of sth** se raviser, changer d'avis; **you had ~ leave** vous feriez mieux de partir

²**better** *n* parieur -ieuse

**betterment** *n* amélioration *f*

**betting** *n* activité *f* de parieur; *adj* ~ **shop** bureau *m* de paris

**between** *adv* entre; au milieu; ~ **whiles** entretemps; **betwixt and** ~ entre les deux; *prep* entre, au milieu de

**betwixt** *adv* + *prep see* **between**

**bevel** *n* biseau *m*; *vt* biseauter, couper en biais; *adj* biseauté

**beverage** *n* boisson *f*, *esp* boisson non-alcoolisée

**bevy** *n* essaim *m* (de jeunes filles); (birds) vol *m*

**bewail** *vt* lamenter, déplorer; *vi* se lamenter

**beware** *vt* prendre garde à, se méfier de; *vi* prendre garde, se méfier; ~ ! attention!

**bewilder** *vt* déconcerter, dérouter

**bewildering** *adj* déconcertant, déroutant

**bewilderment** *n* ahurissement *m*, confusion *f*

**bewitch** *vt* ensorceler; *fig* fasciner, ensorceler

**beyond** *n* au-delà *m*; **at the back of ~** au fin fond; *adv* là-bas; (on the other side) de l'autre côté, (further off) plus loin; *prep* au delà de, de l'autre côté de; outre; hors de; (more than) au dessus de; (time) plus de; ~ **belief** incroyable; **it's ~ me** cela me dépasse; **that's a ~ joke** cela dépasse les bornes

**bezel** *n* (chisel) biseau *m*; (setting of jewel) chaton *m*; (face of jewel) facette *f*; *vt* biseauter

**bezique** *n* bésigue *m*

**biannual** *adj* (twice a year) semestriel -ielle; (every two years) biennal

**bias** *n* inclination *f*, préjugé *m*, penchant *m*; (cloth) biais *m*; *sp* (bowls) déviation *f*; *vt* influencer; ~ **against** prévenir contre

**biased, biassed** *adj* influencé

¹**bib** *n* bavette *f*; **best ~ and tucker** habits *mpl* du dimanche

²**bib** *vt* + *vi* boire, *coll* biberonner

**bible** *n* bible *f*; livre *m* qui fait autorité

**biblical** *adj* biblique

**bibliographer** *n* bibliographe

**bibliography** *n* bibliographie *f*

**bibliophile** *n* bibliophile

**bibulous** *adj* adonné à la boisson

**bicarbonate** *n* bicarbonate *m*

**bicentenary** *n* bicentenaire *m*

**bicephalous** *adj* bicéphale

**biceps** *n* biceps *m*

**bicker** *vi* se disputer, se chamailler

**bickering** *n* prise *f* de bec, querelle *f*

**bicycle** *n* bicyclette *f*, vélo *m*; *vi* aller à bicyclette, faire du vélo

**bicyclist** *n* cycliste

**bid** *n* offre *f*, enchère *f*; (bridge) annonce *f*; *fig* effort *m*, tentative *f*; *vt* inviter, prier; (order) ordonner, commander; (auction) offrir; (bridge) annoncer; *vi* faire une offre; enchérir; ~ **fair to** paraître devoir

**biddable** *adj* soumis, docile

**bidder** *n* enchérisseur *m*

**bidding** *n* enchères *fpl*; (bridge) annonces *fpl*; (order) ordre *m*

**bide** *vt* tolérer; ~ **one's time** attendre, patienter; *vi* tolérer

**bidet** *n* bidet *m*

**biennial** *n bot* plante bisannuelle; *adj* biennal, bisannuel -uelle

**bier** *n* civière *f*

**biff** *n coll* tape *f*; *sl* gnon *m*; *vt coll* cogner, taper

**bifocal** *adj* bifocal

**bifocals** *npl* lunettes bifocales, verres *mpl* à double foyer

**bifurcate** *vt* faire bifurquer; *vi* bifurquer; *adj* bifurqué

**bifurcation** *n* bifurcation *f*

**big** *adj* grand; (bulk) gros (*f* grosse); (powerful) fort; *fig* important; noble; *coll* généreux -euse; *sl* ~ **bug**, ~ **noise**, ~ **shot** grosse légume; ~ **business** grosses affaires; ~ **game** gros gibier; ~ **with child** enceinte; **earn ~ money** gagner gros; **talk ~** se vanter, faire l'important; **too ~ for one's boots** vaniteux -euse, prétentieux -ieuse

**bigamist** *n* bigame

**bigamous** *adj* bigame

**bigamy** *n* bigamie *f*

**big-end** *n mot* tête *f* de bielle

**big-head** *n coll* vaniteux -euse

**big-headed** *adj coll* vaniteux -euse

**bight** *n geog* baie *f*; (river) boucle *f*; *naut* (knot) boucle *f*

**bigot** *n* bigot -e; fanatique

**bigoted** *adj* bigot; fanatique

**bigwig** *n coll* grosse légume, huile *f*

**bijou** *n* bijou *m*; *adj* (often *iron*) petit; élégant

**bike** *n coll* vélo *m*; *vi coll* aller en vélo

**bikini** *n* bikini *m*

**bilateral** *adj* bilatéral

**bilberry** *n* myrtille *f*

**bile** *n* bile *f*; *fig* bile *f*, colère *f*

**bilge** *n naut* sentine *f*; eaux *fpl* de sentine; (cask) fond *m*; *coll fig* absurdité *f*, *sl* connerie *f*

**biliary** *adj med* biliaire

**bilingual** *adj* bilingue

**bilious** *adj* bilieux -ieuse; *fig* colérique; ~ **attack** crise *f* de foie

**bilk** *vt* escroquer; (taxi, hotel, etc) filer

sans payer; frauder, tromper

¹**bill** *n* facture *f*; (restaurant, etc) addition *f*, note *f*; *pol* projet *m* de loi; *leg* plainte *f*; (poster) affiche *f*; *comm* billet *m*, effet *m*; ~ **of exchange** effet *m* de commerce, lettre *f* de change; ~ **of fare** menu *m*; *naut* ~ **of health** patente *f* de santé; *naut* ~ **of lading** connaissement *m*; *bui* ~ **of quantities** devis descriptif; **fill the** ~ être au niveau requis, convenir; **foot the** ~ solder; *coll* payer les pots cassés

²**bill** *n zool* + *naut* bec *m*; *geog* cap *m*; *vi* ~ **and coo** se bécoter

³**bill** *n hist* hallebarde *f*; *agr* serpe *f*; *vt* élaguer

⁴**bill** *vt* afficher; *theat* annoncer en vedette

**billboard** *n* panneau *m* d'affichage

**billet** *n mil* logement *m* chez l'habitant; *mil* billet *m* de logement; *fig* emploi *m*, poste *m*; *vt mil* loger

**bill-hook** *n* serpe *f*

**billiards** *npl* jeu *m* de billard

**billiard-table** *n* billard *m*

¹**billing** *n fig* ~ **and cooing** roucoulements *mpl*

²**billing** *n theat* **star** ~ mise *f* en vedette

**billion** *n* billion *m*; *US* milliard *m*

**billow** *n poet* lame *f*; *vi* onduler

**bill-poster, bill-sticker** *n* colleur *m* d'affiches

**billy-can** *n* gamelle *f*

**billy-goat** *n* bouc *m*

**bimetallism** *n* bimétallisme *m*

**bimonthly** *adj* bi-mensuel -elle

**bin** *n* huche *f*; coffre *m*; (wine) casier *m*; ~ **end** fin *f* de série; *vt* mettre dans un coffre; (wine) mettre dans un casier

**binary** *adj* binaire

**bind** *n mus* ligature *f*; *sl* embêtement *m*; corvée *f*; *sl* (person) crampon *m*; *vt* lier, lier ensemble; (tie) attacher, ficeler; (prisoner) ligoter; (book) relier; constiper; (agreement) ratifier; engager; *leg* obliger; *vi* durcir; *mech* se coincer; **bound up in** absorbé dans

**binder** *n agr* (person) lieur (*f* lieuse); (machine) lieuse *f*; relieur -ieuse ·

**binding** *n* reliure *f*; action *f* de lier; *adj* qui lie; obligatoire; *med* constipant

**bind-weed** *n* liseron *m*

**binge** *n sl* bombe *f*

**bingo** *n* loto *m*

**binnacle** *n* habitacle *m*

**binocular** *adj* binoculaire

**binoculars** *npl* jumelle *f*

**binomial** *n math* binôme *m*; *adj* binôme

**biochemistry** *n* biochimie *f*

**biographer** *n* biographe

**biographic, biographical** *adj* biographique

**biography** *n* biographie *f*

**biological** *adj* biologique

**biologist** *n* biologiste

**biology** *n* biologie *f*

**biometrics** *npl*, **biometry** *n* biométrie *f*

**biophysics** *npl* biophysique *f*

**biopsy** *n med* biopsie *f*

**bipartite** *adj* biparti

**biped** *n* bipède *m*; *adj* bipède

**bipolar** *adj* bipolaire

**birch** *n bot* bouleau *m*; (for punishment) faisceau *m* de verges; *vt* fouetter (avec des verges)

**bird** *n* oiseau *m*; *sl* fille *f*, poule *f*; ~ **of passage** oiseau migrateur; *fig* voyageur -euse, vagabond -e; *pej* ~ **s of a feather** gens *mpl* du même acabit; **a little** ~ **told me** mon petit doigt me l'a dit; **give s/o the** ~ *theat* huer qn, siffler qn; envoyer paître qn; *cul* **veal** ~ paupiette *f* de veau

**bird-cage** *n* cage *f*; (large) volière *f*

**bird-fancier** *n* oiselier -ière

**bird-lime** *n* glu *f*

**bird-nesting, bird's nesting** *n* **go** ~ aller dénicher des oiseaux

**bird's-eye** *adj* ~ **view** vue *f* à vol d'oiseau; *fig* résumé *m*

**bird's-nest** *n* nid *m* d'oiseau

**bird's-nester** *n* dénicheur -euse d'oiseaux

**bird-watcher** *n* ornithologiste, ornithologue

**biretta** *n eccles* barrette *f*

**Biro** *n* stylo *m* à bille; pointe *f* Bic

**birth** *n* naissance *f*; origine *f*, extraction *f*; *med* accouchement *m*; *fig* commencement *m*, genèse *f*

**birth-control** *n* contrôle *m* des naissances

**birthday** *n* anniversaire *m*; **in one's** ~ **suit** tout nu, dans la tenue d'Adam

**birthmark** *n* tache *f* de vin, envie *f*

**birthplace** *n* lieu *m* de naissance; pays natal; maison natale

**birth-rate** *n* natalité *f*

**birthright** *n* droit *m* d'aînesse; patrimoine *m*

**Biscay** *n geog* **Bay of** ~ golfe *m* de Gascogne

**biscuit** *n* biscuit *m*, gâteau sec

**bisect** *vt* couper en deux; *vi* bifurquer

**bisection** *n* division *f* en deux parties; *geom* bissection *f*

**bisector** *n geom* bissecteur -trice

**bisexual** *adj* bisexuel -elle

**bisexuality** *n* bisexualité *f*

**bishop** *n* évêque *m*; (chess) fou *m*

**bishopric** *n* (diocese) évêché *m*; (office) épiscopat *m*

**bisk** *n cul* bisque *f*

**bissextile** *n* année *f* bissextile; *adj* bissextile

**bistoury** *n surg* bistouri *m*

**bit** *n* morceau *m*, bout *m*, bribe *f*; (food) bouchée *f*; (time) petit moment; *coll* fille *f*; *mech* mèche *f*; (bridle) mors *m*; *vt* mettre le mors à; *fig* brider; *adj theat* ~ **part** petit rôle, panne *f*

**bitch** *n* chienne *f*, *coll* chipie *f*, femme *f* acariâtre; *vi US* rouspéter

**bite** *n* morsure *f*, (insect) piqûre *f*; (mouthful) bouchée *f*; (action) coup *m* de dents; (fishing) touche *f*; *vt* mordre; (insect) piquer; *fig* prendre, attraper; *mot* adhérer; (cold) piquer, mordre; ~ **the dust** tomber par terre, être vaincu; *vi* mordre; (insect) piquer

**biting** *adj* (cold) âpre, mordant; (irony) caustique, cinglant

**bitter** *n* bière blonde; *adj* amer -ère; *fig* cruel -elle; violent; (style) mordant, acéré; (criticism) acerbe; (wind) cinglant

**bittern** *n zool* butor *m*

**bitters** *npl* bitter *m*

**bitter-sweet** *adj* aigre-doux (*f* aigre-douce)

**bitumen** *n* bitume *m*

**bituminous** *adj* bitumineux -euse

**bivalent** *adj chem* bivalent

**bivalve** *n* bivalve *m*; *adj* bivalve

**bivouac** *n* bivouac *m*; *vi* bivouaquer

**bizarre** *adj* bizarre, grotesque; excentrique

**blab** *vt* divulguer; *vi* cancaner; *sl* manger le morceau

**black** *n* noir *m*; (mourning) deuil *m*; (person) noir -e, nègre (*f* négresse); *adj* noir, sombre, obscur; (dirty) sale; *fig* mortel -elle; infâme; (angry) menaçant; ~ **and blue** fortement ecchymosé, plein de bleus; ~ **art** nécromancie *f*; ~ **eye** œil *m* au beurre noir; *coll* **Black Maria** panier *m* à salade; ~ **market** marché noir; **in** ~ **and white** par écrit; *vt* noircir; (shoes) cirer; *fig* calomnier

**blackball** *vt* blackbouler; évincer

**black-beetle** *n* blatte *f*, cafard *m*

**blackberry** *n* mûre *f*; *vi* cueillir des mûres

**blackbird** *n* merle *m*

**blackboard** *n* tableau noir

**blackcurrant** *n* cassis *m*

**blacken** *vt* + *vi* noircir

**blackguard** *n* vaurien *m*, malfaiteur *m*; *vt* vilipender, injurier

**blackhead** *n* point noir

**blacking** *n* cirage noir

**blacklead** *n* graphite *m*

**blackleg** *n* jaune *m*

**blacklist** *n* liste noire; *vt* porter sur la liste noire

**blackmail** *n* chantage *m*; *vt* faire chanter

**blackmailer** *n* maître chanteur

**blackout** *n med* étourdissement *m*; *theat* noir *m*; (wartime) black-out *m*; (lighting

failure) panne *f* d'électricité; (news) censure *f*; *vt* (wartime) faire le blackout de

**black-pudding** *n* boudin *m*

**blackshirt** *n* fasciste

**blacksmith** *n* forgeron *m*

**blackthorn** *n* prunellier *m*

**bladder** *n* (urinary) vessie *f*; (vesicle) vésicule *f*; (football) vessie *f* (de ballon); **gall** ~ vésicule *f* biliaire

**blade** *n* (grass) brin *m*; (sword) épée *f*, lame *f*, (of knife) lame *f*; (oar, propeller) pale *f*; *coll obs* gandin *m*, dandy *m*

**blamable** *adj* blâmable

**blame** *n* blâme *m*; responsabilité *f*; *vt* blâmer, reprocher à; **be to** ~ être responsable, mériter le blâme

**blameless** *adj* irréprochable, sans tache

**blameworthy** *adj* blâmable, méritant le blâme

**blanch** *vt* blanchir; (hair) faire blanchir; *vi* blémir, pâlir

**bland** *adj* suave, poli; (ingratiating) doucereux -euse; (weather, drink) doux (*f* douce)

**blandish** *vt* cajoler, flatter

**blandishment** *n* cajolerie *f*, flatterie *f*

**blank** *n* blanc *m*, vide *m*; *mil* cartouche *f* à blanc; **draw a** ~ ne pas réussir; *adj* blanc (*f* blanche), vide; (page) vierge; (cartridge) à blanc; (verse) blanc; (cheque) en blanc; *fig* catégorique, total, absolu; (look) vide, morne

**blanket** *n* couverture *f*, (layer) couche *f*; **wet** ~ éteignoir *m*, rabat-joie *m invar*; *adj* intégral, complet -ète; *vt* couvrir d'une couverture; couvrir

**blankly** *adv* sans expression; (boldly) carrément

**blare** *n* tintamarre *m*; (trumpet) sonnerie *f*; *vi* corner; sonner de la trompette; ~ **out** (music) faire retentir; (news) claironner

**blarney** *n coll* boniment *m*; *vt coll* flagorner; *vi* bonimenter

**blaspheme** *vt* + *vi* blasphémer

**blasphemer** *n* blasphémateur -trice

**blasphemous** *adj* blasphématoire

**blasphemy** *n* blasphème *m*

**blast** *n* (wind) rafale *f*, souffle *m*; (trumpet, horn) sonnerie *f*; explosion *f*; *vt* (explosive) faire sauter; (shatter) fracasser; flétrir; ruiner

**blasted** *adj* désolé; *coll* sacré; (hopes) anéanti

**blast-furnace** *n* haut fourneau

**blasting** *n* (quarry) action *f* de faire sauter, tir *m* de mines

**blast-off** *n* (rocket, spacecraft) lancement *m*

**blatancy** *n* vulgarité criarde

**blatant** *adj* criard, vulgaire; flagrant

**¹blaze** n flambée f, flamboiement m; feu m; (fire) incendie m; (light) éclat m; coll **go to ~ s!** diable!; coll **like ~ s** vigoureusement; vi flamber, flamboyer; briller, étinceler; **~ away** tirer sans arrêt; fig travailler avec acharnement; **~ up** s'embraser; fig s'emporter

**²blaze** n (horse) étoile f; (tree) encoche f; vt marquer; **~ the trail** frayer la piste

**blazer** n blazer m

**blazing** adj flamboyant; éblouissant; fig furieux -euse

**blazon** n blason m; vt blasonner; **~ abroad** proclamer

**bleach** n eau f de Javel; vt + vi blanchir

**¹bleak** n zool ablette f

**²bleak** adj (bare) nu; (cold) froid; (dreary) morne, désolé

**bleary** adj **~ -eyed** aux yeux chassieux

**bleat** n bêlement m; vi bêler; fig geindre

**bleb** n (blister) ampoule f; (bubble) bulle f

**bleed** vt saigner; vi saigner; (colour) déteindre; bot suinter; **my heart ~ s** je suis désolé

**bleeder** n hémophile; coll salaud m

**bleeding** n saignement m; perte f de sang; (blood-letting) saignée f; adj saignant; coll sacré

**bleep** n top m; vt biper

**blemish** n tache f; vt entacher, gâter, endommager

**blench** vi broncher, reculer

**blend** n mélange m; vt mélanger; vi se mêler, se mélanger

**bless** vt bénir; être reconnaissant à; favoriser, douer

**blessed, blest** adj béni; doué; coll sacré

**blessing** n bénédiction f; (luck) chance f; avantage m; **~ in disguise** avantage inattendu

**blight** n nielle f; fig fléau m; vt nieller; fig flétrir, miner

**blighter** n sl salaud m

**blind** n (window) store m; coll soûlerie f; **the ~** les aveugles; **Venetian ~** store vénitien; adj aveugle; (dark) sombre, obscur; (door, window) aveugle, faux (f fausse); aer sans visibilité; coll saoul; **~ alley** rue f sans issue, impasse f; (job) poste m sans avenir; **~ spot** angle mort; **turn a ~ eye** faire semblant de ne pas voir; vt aveugler; **~ oneself** s'aveugler; vi sl mot foncer à l'aveuglette

**blindfold** adj aux yeux bandés; adv les yeux bandés; vt bander les yeux à, aveugler

**blinding** adj éblouissant

**blindness** n cécité f; fig aveuglement m

**blind-side** n côté m de l'angle mort; fig point m faible

**blink** n lueur f, clignotement m; vi cligner des yeux; (light) clignoter; vaciller

**blinker(s)** n(pl) œillère(s) f(pl)

**blinking** adj coll euph sacré

**bliss** n félicité f, joie f, contentement m

**blissful** adj bienheureux -euse; coll merveilleux -euse

**blister** n ampoule f; cloque f; coll emmerdeur -euse; vt provoquer des ampoules sur; fig flétrir; vi développer des ampoules

**blistering** n (skin) formation f d'ampoules; (paint) boursouflure f; adj (heat) étouffant; (attack) cinglant

**blithe** adj heureux -euse, gai, folâtre

**blithering** adj coll **~ idiot** crétin -e

**blitz** n bombardement aérien; vt bombarder

**blizzard** n tourmente f de neige; (polar) blizzard m

**¹bloat** vt (herring) fumer

**²bloat** vt gonfler, enfler, bouffir; vi enfler

**bloated** adj gonflé, boursouflé; (face) bouffi

**bloater** n hareng saur

**blob** n tache f; (ink) pâté m

**bloc** n pol bloc m

**block** n bloc m; (tree) souche f; (scaffold, cobbler, ship-yard) billot m; (butcher) hachoir m; (pulley) chape f; (hatter) forme f; (buildings) îlot m, pâté m; print planche f; fig obstacle m, blocage m, obstruction f; **~ s** jeu m de cubes; vt bloquer, barrer, boucher; entraver; **~ out** (obstruct) boucher; (sketch out) ébaucher; adj **~ grant** subvention f fixe; **~ letters** lettres fpl majuscules

**blockade** n blocus m; **raise the ~** lever le blocus; **run the ~** forcer le blocus; vt faire le blocus de

**blockbuster** n coll bombe f de gros calibre; (film, etc) superproduction f

**blockhead** n crétin -e

**blockhouse** n blockhaus m

**bloke** n coll type m

**blond** n blond m; adj blond

**blonde** n blonde f

**blood** n sang m; (bloodshed) meurtre m, mort f; (relationship) parenté f, race f, descendance f; tempérament m, colère f; coll obs dandy m; **bad ~** haine f, malveillance f; **blue ~** sang bleu; **first ~** avantage initial; **flesh and ~** parents mpl; **in cold ~** délibérément; **make s/o's ~ boil** faire bouillir le sang à qn; **one's ~ is up** on est en colère; vt faire une saignée à; fig initier; adj; **~ bank** banque f du sang; **~ count** numération f globulaire; **~ feud** vendetta f; **~ orange** sanguine f; **~ pressure** tension artérielle; **~ sports** chasse f

**blood-bath** n massacre m, bain m de sang

**blood-curdling** *adj* horrible, à faire frémir

**blood-donor** *n* donneur -euse de sang

**blood-group** *n* groupe sanguin

**bloodhound** *n* limier *m*; *fig* limier *m*, détective *m*

**bloodless** *adj med* exsangue; pâle; sans vitalité; sans effusion de sang

**blood-letting** *n* saignée *f*

**bloodlust** *n* désir *m* de sang, soif *f* de sang

**blood-money** *n* prix *m* du sang

**blood-poisoning** *n med* empoisonnement *m* du sang

**blood-pudding** *n* boudin *m*

**blood-red** *adj* rouge sang *invar*

**blood-relation** *n* parent -e par le sang

**bloodshed** *n* meurtre *m*, carnage *m*, effusion *f* de sang

**bloodshot** *adj* injecté de sang

**blood-stained** *adj* taché de sang

**bloodstock** *n* pur-sang *m invar*

**bloodstone** *n* sanguine *f*, héliotrope *m*

**blood-sucker** *n* sangsue *f*

**blood-test** *n* examen *m* du sang

**blood-thirsty** *adj* sanguinaire

**blood-transfusion** *n* transfusion sanguine

**blood-vessel** *n* vaisseau sanguin

**bloody** *adj* ensanglanté; (battle) sanguinaire; *coll* sacré, foutu

**bloody-mary** *n* vodka *f* au jus de tomate

**bloody-minded** *adj coll* hargneux -euse

**bloody-mindedness** *n coll* hargne *f*

**bloom** *n* fleur *f*; (flowering) floraison *f*; (certain fruit) velouté *m*; *vi* fleurir; *fig* être resplendissant

**bloomer** *n coll* gaffe *f*

**bloomers** *npl obs* culotte bouffante

**blooming** *n* floraison *f*; *adj* fleuri, épanoui, rayonnant; *coll* sacré

**blossom** *n* fleur *f*; *vi* fleurir; s'épanouir; *fig* ~ **out** s'épanouir; avoir du succès

**blot** *n* pâté *m*, tache *f*; *vt* (stain) tacher; (dry) sécher (au buvard); *fig* tacher; ~ **out** effacer

**blotch** *n* tache *f*; *vt* couvrir de taches

**blotchy** *adj* taché, tacheté

**blotter** *n* buvard *m*

**blotting-paper** *n* papier *m* buvard, buvard *m*

**blotto** *adj coll* parti, ivre

**blouse** *n* blouse *f*

¹**blow** *n* coup *m*; choc *m*

²**blow** *n* coup *m* de vent; souffle *m*; *vt* souffler; faire souffler; (trumpet, etc) sonner de; *elect* faire sauter; ~ **one's own trumpet** se vanter; ~ **the gaff** révéler des secrets, vendre la mèche; ~ **the lid off** exposer; *vi* souffler, venter; *mus* sonner; ~ **hot and cold** vaciller, souffler le chaud et le froid; *coll* ~ **off steam** exprimer ses sentiments; ~ **up**

faire sauter; *fig* exagérer; *coll phot* élargir; *vi* ~ **over** se calmer, s'apaiser; ~ **up** exploser; *coll* devenir furieux

**blower** *n* (fireplace) tablier *m*; *coll* bigophone *m*

**blow-hole** *n* évent *m*

**blow-lamp** *n* chalumeau *m*

**blow-out** *n* (tyre) éclatement *m*; *coll* gueuleton *m*; *elect* **there's a** ~ les plombs ont sauté

**blow-pipe** *n* chalumeau *m*; (weapon) sarbacane *f*

**blow-up** *n phot coll* agrandissement *m*

**blowzy** *adj* échevelé, malpropre; (face) rougeâtre

**blub** *vi coll* chialer

¹**blubber** *n* graisse *f* de baleine

²**blubber** *vi* pleurnicher, pleurer

³**blubber** *adj* (lips) lippu

**bludgeon** *n* matraque *f*; trique *f*; *vt* matraquer

**blue** *n* bleu *m*, azur *m*; *adj* bleu; *fig* misérable, malheureux -euse; *sl* grivois, obscène, porno; ~ **chip shares** valeurs *fpl* de tout repos; *coll* ~ **funk** frousse *f*; **once in a** ~ **moon** tous les trente-six du mois; **true** ~ fidèle, loyal; *vt* (laundry) passer au bleu; *coll* (money) gaspiller

**bluebell** *n* jacinthe *f* des bois

**blue-book** *n pol* livre bleu

**bluebottle** *n* mouche bleue; *coll* flic *m*

**blue-eyed** *adj coll* préféré, favori -ite

**bluejacket** *n* matelot *m*

**blue-pencil** *vt* censurer, couper; (delete) barrer

**blueprint** *n* plan *m*, épure *f*; *fig* schéma *m*

**blues** *npl mus* blues *m*; *fig* cafard *m*, idées noires

**blue-stocking** *n* bas-bleu *m*

¹**bluff** *n* escarpement *m*; *adj* à pic, escarpé; *fig* brusque, franc (*f* franche)

²**bluff** *n* bluff *m*; *coll* **call s/o's** ~ relever le défi de qn, mettre qn au pied du mur; *vt* + *vi* bluffer

**bluffer** *n* bluffeur -euse

**bluish** *adj* bleuâtre

**blunder** *n* erreur *f*, bévue *f*, balourdise *f*, gaffe *f*; (social) impair *m*; *vt* gâcher; *vi* faire une gaffe; ~ **on** avancer à l'aveuglette; ~ **upon** découvrir par hasard

**blunderbuss** *n hist* tromblon *m*

**blunderer** *n* balourd -e; *coll* gaffeur -euse

**blunt** *vt* émousser; épointer; *fig* émousser, engourdir; *adj* émoussé; épointé; (mind) lourd; (speech) brusque, cassant

**bluntness** *n* épointement *m*; brusquerie *f*

**blur** *n* tache *f*; barbouillage *m*; aspect indistinct; *vt* brouiller, barbouiller, ternir; *vi* se brouiller

**blurb** *n coll* bande *f* publicitaire, texte *m* de lancement

**blurt** vt dire spontanément, dire sans réfléchir; (secret) ~ **out** révéler

**blush** n rougeur f; couleur f rose; lueur f; **at the first** ~ au premier regard; vi rougir, devenir rouge

**blushing** adj rougissant; fig timide

**bluster** n fracas m; fanfaronnade f; vi (wind) souffler fort, mugir; fig déblatérer, tonitruer

**blusterer** n fanfaron -onne

**blustering, blustery** adj (wind, sea) furieux -ieuse; (manner) fanfaron-onne

**boa** n boa m

**boar** n (hog) verrat m; (wild) sanglier m

¹**board** n planche f; (notices) panneau m; (blackboard) tableau noir; (cardboard) carton m; theat obs ~ s scène f, plateau m; vt planchéier

²**board** n nourriture f, pension f; table f avec couverts; (directors, etc) conseil m (d'administration); **above** ~ honnête, juste; **sweep the** ~ tout gagner; vt nourrir; vi être en pension

³**board** n naut bord m; **go by the** ~ tomber à l'eau; **on** ~ à bord; vt (ship) monter à bord de; (train, bus) monter dans; fig monter

**boarder** n (lodging-house) pensionnaire; (school) interne

**boarding** n planchéiage m; aer ~**ing card** carte f d'accès à bord

**boarding-house** n pension f de famille

**boarding-school** n pensionnat m, internat m

**boast** n vantardise f; hâblerie f; objet m d'orgueil; vt se vanter de; se faire gloire de posséder; vi se vanter

**boastful** adj vantard

**boastfulness** n vantardise f

**boat** n bateau m; (small) canot m, embarcation f; (steamer) paquebot m; cul saucière f; **be in the same** ~ être dans le pétrin ensemble, être logé à la même enseigne; **burn one's** ~ **s** s'engager à fond; coll **miss the** ~ manquer le coche

**boater** n canotier m

**boatful** n cargaison f, plein bateau

**boathook** n gaffe f

**boat-house** n hangar m à canots

**boating** n canotage m

**boatman** n batelier m; (hirer) loueur m de canots

**boatswain** n naut maître m d'équipage

¹**bob** n (horse) queue écourtée; (hairstyle) coiffure f à la Jeanne d'Arc; (curl) boucle f; (pendulum) poids m; vt (hair) écourter

²**bob** n tape f; vt taper, faire taper

³**bob** n (curtsy) révérence f; vi faire une révérence

⁴**bob** n coll obs shilling m

⁵**bob, bob-sled, bobsleigh** n sp traîneau m, bobsleigh m, bob m

**bobbed** adj (hair) à la Jeanne d'Arc

**bobbin** n bobine f; fuseau m

**bobby** n coll flic m

**bobbysoxer** n US coll minette f

**bob-sled, bobsleigh** n see bob⁵

**bobstay** n naut sous-barbe f

**bob-tail** n (horse) queue écourtée; pej **rag-tag and** ~ quatre pelés et un tondu

**Boche** n pej Boche m; adj boche

**bode** vt présager; vi ~ **well (ill)** être de bon (mauvais) augure

**bodice** n corsage m

**bodily** adj corporel -elle, physique; adv en personne, en chair et en os; en masse, tout ensemble

**bodkin** n poinçon m

**body** n corps m; (dead) cadavre m; mot carrosserie f; (bodice) corsage m; (main part) corps m; (people) groupe m, masse f; (organization) corps m, corporation f, groupement m; (solidity) consistance f; (wine) corps m; coll type m; ~ **politic** l'Etat m; ~ **(repair) shop** atelier m de carrosserie; **heavenly** ~ corps m céleste

**body-builder** n mot carrossier m; (food) aliment nourrissant; appareil m pour développer les muscles

**bodyguard** n garde m du corps; coll barbouze f

**body-snatcher** n ar déterreur m de cadavres

**bodywork** n mot carrosserie f

**boffin** n coll chercheur m (à la solde des forces armées)

**bog** n marais m; sl latrines fpl; vulg chiottes fpl; vt embourber; **get bogged down** s'embourber

**bogey, bogie, bogy** n épouvantail m

**boggle** vi hésiter; avoir peur; ~ **at** avoir des scrupules concernant; **the mind** ~ s on croit rêver

**boggler** n peureux -euse; (stickler) tatillon -onne

**boggy** adj marécageux -euse

**bogie, bogey, bogy** n (railway) bogie m

**bogus** adj factice, faux (f fausse)

¹**boil** n furoncle m; coll clou m

²**boil** n ébullition f; vt faire bouillir; (egg) faire bouillir à la coque; vi bouillir; fig bouillonner

**boiled** adj bouilli; (egg) à la coque; coll ~ **shirt** plastron m

**boiler** n chaudière f; (kettle) bouilloire f; (chicken) poule f à bouillir

**boiler-suit** n bleu m de travail

**boiling** n ébullition f; coll **the whole** ~ tout le bazar; adj bouillonnant

**boiling-point** n température f de bouillonnement

**boisterous** *adj* turbulent, tapageur -euse; exubérant; (sea) houleux -euse

**bold** *adj* courageux -euse, hardi, brave, audacieux -ieuse; impudent, effronté; (cliff) à pic, escarpé; **make so ~ as to** présumer

**bold-face** *n print* gras *m*

**boldness** *n* courage *m*, audace *f*; impudence *f*, effronterie *f*

**bollard** *n naut* bitte *f* d'amarrage, bollard *m*; *mot* borne (lumineuse)

**Bolshevik** *n* Bolchevik, Bolcheviste; *adj* bolchevique

**Bolshevism** *n* bolchevisme *m*

**Bolshy** *adj coll* bolchevique

**bolshy** *adj coll* pas commode, difficile

**bolster** *n* traversin *m*; *bui* traverse *f*; *mech* coussin *m*; *vt* soutenir, étayer; **~ up** soutenir; couvrir, protéger

**bolt** *n* (lock) verrou *m*, pêne *m*; (screw) boulon *m*; (thunderbolt) coup *m* de foudre; (cloth) coupe *f*, pièce *f*; *mil* culasse *f* mobile; départ *m* brusque; **~ from the blue** coup *m* de tonnerre; **shoot one's ~** faire un dernier effort; *vt* verrouiller; (food) engloutir; *vi* partir brusquement; (horse) s'emballer; *adv* **~ upright** droit comme un i

**bolt-hole** *n* terrier *m*

**bomb** *n* bombe *f*; *coll* **cost a ~** coûter les yeux de la tête; *vt* bombarder; **~ed out** sinistré (par bombardement)

**bombard** *vt* bombarder

**bombardier** *n mil* caporal *m* d'artillerie

**bombast** *n* emphase *f*, grandiloquence *f*

**bombastic** *adj* emphatique, ampoulé, grandiloquent

**Bombay duck** *n cul* poisson salé (dans un curry)

**bomb-disposal** *n* désamorçage *m* (de bombes)

**bombe** *n cul* bombe *f*

**bomber** *n aer* + *mil* bombardier *m*

**bomb-proof** *adj* blindé, protégé contre les bombes

**bombshell** *n mil* obus *m*; *fig* surprise ahurissante

**bomb-sight** *n* viseur *m* de bombardement

**bomb-site** *n* lieu bombardé

**bona fide** *adj* de bonne foi; authentique

**bonanza** *n min* filon *m* riche; *fig* aubaine *f*

**bond** *n* lien *m*; *leg* engagement *m*; contrat *m*; *comm* titre *m*, valeur *f*; (customs) entrepôt *m*; *bui* appareil *m*; *vt* lier; (customs) entreposer; *bui* appareiller; *adj* en esclavage

**bondage** *n* esclavage *m*, asservissement *m*

**bonded** *adj* entreposé; **~ warehouse** entrepôt *m*

**bondsman, bondswoman** *n* esclave

**bone** *n* os *m*; (fish) arête *f*; (whale) fanon *m*; **~ s** corps *m*, cadavre *m*; (dice) dés *mpl*; (castanets) castagnettes *fpl*; **~ of contention** pomme *f* de discorde; **have a ~ to pick with** avoir maille à partir avec; **make no ~ s** ne pas hésiter; **to the ~** jusqu'à l'os; (roots) jusqu'au minimum; *vt* désosser; *sl* voler; *coll* **~ up on** potasser, bûcher

**bone-dry** *adj* complètement sec (*f* sèche)

**bone-head** *n sl* crétin -e

**bone-idle** *adj* extrêmement paresseux -euse

**boneless** *adj* sans os, désossé; *fig* faible

**bonemeal** engrais *m* d'os (broyés)

**bone-setter** *n* rebouteux *m*

**bonfire** *n* feu *m* de joie; feu *m* de jardin

**bonhomie** *n* bonhomie *f*

**bonkers** *adj coll* cinglé

**bonnet** *n* bonnet *m*; (chimney) capuchon *m*; *mot* capot *m*

**bonny** *adj* joli, beau (*f* belle)

**bonus** *n* prime *f*, gratification *f*; *fig* aubaine *f*; **cost of living ~** indemnité *f* de vie chère; **no-claim ~** bonification *f* pour non-sinistre

**bony** *adj* osseux -euse

**bonze** *n* bonze *m*

**boo** *interj* hou!; *vt* huer, chahuter; *vi* pousser des huées

**boob** *n sl* idiot -e, crétin -e; *sl* (breast) néné *m*; *vi sl* gaffer

**booby** *n* idiot -e, crétin -e, benêt *m*

**booby-prize** *n* prix *m* de consolation

**booby-trap** *n* attrape-nigaud *m*; *mil* objet piégé

**boodle** *n sl* fric *m*

**boogie-woogie** *n* boogie-woogie *m*

**book** *n* livre *m*, bouquin *m*; *mus* livret *m*; (exercise book) cahier *m*; *sp* livre *m* de paris; *comm* registre *m*; **bring s/o to ~** demander des comptes à qn; **in s/o's good (bad) ~s** bien (mal) vu de qn; **keep the ~s** tenir la comptabilité; **suit one's ~** convenir à qn, plaire à qn; **take a leaf out of s/o's ~** imiter qn; *vt* inscrire; (seat, place) louer, retenir, réserver; (performer, speaker) engager; *sp* (referee) prendre le nom de; *US* (police) donner une contravention à

**bookbinder** *n* relieur *m*

**bookbinding** *n* reliure *f*

**bookcase** *n* bibliothèque *f*

**book-ends** *npl* serre-livres *mpl*

**booking** *n* inscription *f*, location *f*, réservation *f*; *sp* **he got a ~ from the referee** l'arbitre a pris son nom

**booking-office** *n* guichet *m*

**bookish** *adj* studieux -euse; livresque

**book-keeper** *n* comptable

**book-keeping** n comptabilité f
**book-learning** n connaissances fpl livresques
**booklet** n livret m
**bookmaker** n bookmaker m
**bookmark** n signet m
**bookmobile** n US bibliobus m
**book-plate** n ex-libris m
**bookseller** n libraire
**bookshop** n librairie f
**bookstall** n kiosque m; (station) bibliothèque f de gare
**bookstore** n librairie f
**book-token** n chèque-livre m (pl chèques-livres)
**bookworm** n coll fig rat m de bibliothèque
¹**boom** n (harbour) estacade f; naut gui m; rad perche f; (crane) flèche f
²**boom** n grondement m, mugissement m; vi gronder, mugir
³**boom** n comm boom m; vi prospérer, augmenter brusquement de valeur
**boomerang** n boomerang m; vi fig faire boomerang
**boon** n aubaine f; ar faveur f; adj ~ **companion** joyeux compère, grand copain
**boor** n paysan -anne; fig butor m
**boorish** adj balourd, rustre
**boost** n coll aide f; coll éloge m publicitaire; vt élever, prôner, faire de la réclame pour; augmenter; elect survolter
**booster** n elect survolteur m; fusée f gigogne; med piqûre f supplémentaire, rappel m
¹**boot** n botte f; (ankle boot) botillon m; (buttoned) bottine f; mot coffre m; **bet one's** ~ **s** être sûr de; **get the** ~ être licencié; **the** ~ **is on the other foot** les rôles sont renversés; vt donner un coup de pied à; coll ~ **out** licencier; flanquer à la porte
²**boot** n to ~ d'ailleurs, par surcroît
**booth** n baraque f; (election) isoloir m; (telephone) cabine f
**bootlace** n lacet m
**bootleg** vt US vendre ou importer en contrebande; vi faire de la contrebande (d'alcools)
**bootlegger** n US hist bootlegger m
**bootless** adj sans profit, inutile; (without boots) sans bottes
**boots** n garçon m d'hôtel
**booty** n butin m
**booze** n coll boisson f alcoolique; vi boire beaucoup
**boozed** adj coll saoul, parti
**boozer** n coll (person) ivrogne; coll bar m, bistro m
**bop** n bop m, be-bop m
**boracic** adj chem borique

**borage** n bot bourrache f
**borax** n chem borax m
**border** n bord m, côté m; marge f; frontière f; (garden) bordure f; (dress) galon m; vt border, entourer; ~ **on** être contigu à; ressembler à, avoisiner, friser
**borderer** n frontalier -ière
**borderland** n zone f frontière
**borderline** n frontière f; ligne f de démarcation; adj douteux -euse, incertain; ~ **case** cas m limite
¹**bore** n (gun) calibre m; mot alésage m; vt vriller, percer, perforer, creuser; forer; mot aléser
²**bore** n fâcheux -euse; coll raseur -euse, casse-pieds; (thing) barbe f, scie f; vt ennuyer; coll ~ **s/o stiff** casser les pieds à qn
³**bore** n (river) mascaret m
**boreal** adj boréal
**boredom** n ennui m
**borehole** n trou m de sondage
**borer** n vrille f; foret m; insecte térébrant
**boric** adj chem borique
**boring** adj ennuyeux -euse; coll barbant, assommant
**born** adj né; (innate) inné; naturel -elle
**boron** n chem bore m
**borough** n ville f; (England) ville administrée par un maire et un conseil municipal; (England) **parliamentary** ~ ville f formant une circonscription électorale
**borrow** vt emprunter
**borrower** n emprunteur -euse
**borrowing** n emprunt m
**borsch, bortsch** n cul bortsch m
**bosh** n coll idiotie f, absurdité f; interj avec ça!
**bosk, bosket, bosquet** n bosquet m, fourré m
**bosky** adj touffu
**bosom** n sein m; ~ **of the family** intimité familiale; adj familier -ière, intime
¹**boss** n bosse f, bossage m; vt bosseler
²**boss** n coll patron m; (foreman) contremaître m; US coll manitou m politique; vt contrôler, gérer; coll dominer; ~ **about** régenter
³**boss** vt sl bousiller
**boss-eyed** adj coll louche, bigle; fig tortueux -euse
**boss-shot** n coll bousillage m
**bossy** adj autoritaire
**botanic, botanical** adj botanique
**botanist** n botaniste
**botanize** vi faire de la botanique, herboriser
**botany** n botanique f

**botch** *n* défaut *m*, tache *f*; travail bâclé; *vt coll* bousiller, bâcler

**both** *pron* tous (*f* toutes) les deux, l'un (*f* l'une) et l'autre; *adj* les deux; *adv* à la fois, aussi bien; ~ ... **and** non seulement ... mais aussi

**bother** *n* ennui *m*; tracas *m*, souci *m*; *coll* embêtement *m*; *vt* ennuyer, importuner; (worry) tracasser; *coll* embêter; *vi* se tourmenter, se tracasser; ~ ! zut!

**botheration** *n* tracas *m*; *coll* embêtement *m*; ~ ! zut!

**bothersome** *adj* gênant, agaçant

**bottle** *n* bouteille *f*; (child) biberon *m*; (hot-water) bouillotte *f*; *fig* boisson *f*, habitude *f* de boire; ~ **party** réunion *f* intime où chacun apporte à boire; *vt* embouteiller, mettre en bouteille; ~ **up** retenir, contenir

**bottled** *adj* en bouteille; ~ **by** mis en bouteille par

**bottle-green** *adj* vert bouteille *invar*

**bottleneck** *n mot* bouchon *m*; goulot *m*

**bottle-washer** *n* plongeur *m*; **head cook and** ~ factotum *m*

**bottom** *n* fond *m*; (hill, tree) pied *m*; (page) bas *m*; *fig* fondement *m*, base *f*; *coll* derrière *m*, cul *m*; *naut* quille *f*; *naut* navire *m*; **be at the** ~ **of** être la cause de; **get to the** ~ **of** examiner en détail; *adj* le plus bas; (last) dernier -ière; ~ **gear** première vitesse; ~ **half** deuxième moitié *f*; *vt* mettre un fond à; *vi* toucher le fond

**bottomless** *adj* sans fond; insondable

**boudoir** *n* boudoir *m*

**bough** *n* rameau *m*

**bouillon** *n* bouillon *m*

**boulder** *n* roche *f*, bloc *m*; *geol* roche *f* erratique; *geol* ~ **clay** dépôt argileux; *geol* ~ **period** période *f* glaciaire

**boulevard** *n* boulevard *m*

**bounce** *n* bond *m*, rebondissement *m*; (ball) rebond *m*; *coll* jactance *f*; élasticité *f*; *vt* faire rebondir; *vi* rebondir, sauter, bondir; *coll* (cheque) être retourné sans provision

**bouncer** *n* (lie) mensonge éhonté; (liar) hâbleur -euse; *coll* videur *m*

**bouncing** *adj* qui rebondit; *fig* plantureux -euse, robuste

**¹bound** *n* limite *f*, borne *f*; **out of** ~ **s** accès interdit; *vt* borner, limiter; *vi* être limitrophe de, avoir ses limites

**²bound** *n* bond *m*, saut *m*; *vi* bondir, rebondir

**³bound** *adj* prêt à partir; *naut* en partance

**⁴bound** *adj* ~ **to** obligé à

**boundary** *n* limite *f*, frontière *f*

**bounden** *adj ar* ~ **duty** devoir absolu

**bounder** *coll obs* salaud *m*

**boundless** *adj* sans limite, infini

**bounteous** *adj* généreux -euse; abondant

**bounteousness** *n* générosité *f*; abondance *f*

**bountiful** *adj* généreux -euse, libéral; **lady** ~ dame patronnesse

**bounty** *n* générosité *f*, libéralité *f*; prime *f*

**bouquet** *n* (flower, wine) bouquet *m*

**Bourbon** *n* (espèce *f* de) whisky américain

**bourdon** *n* bourdon *m*

**bourgeois** *n + adj* bourgèois -e

**bourgeoisie** *n* bourgeoisie *f*

**bout** *n* coup *m*; (boxing, wrestling, etc) match *m*; *med* accès *m*; période *f*; *coll* (drink) cuite *f*

**boutique** *n* boutique *f*

**bovine** *adj* bovin

**¹bow** *n* arc *m*; *mus* archet *m*; (knot) boucle *f*; *coll* **draw the long** ~ exagérer; **have many strings to one's** ~ avoir plusieurs cordes à son arc; *vi mus* tirer l'archet

**²bow** *n* salut *m*, inclination *f* de la tête; **make one's** ~ apparaître; (withdraw) se retirer; *vt* incliner, courber; (knee) fléchir; faire ployer; *vi* saluer, s'incliner; fléchir, se courber; ~ **and scrape** faire des courbettes; ~ **down** se baisser; ~ **out** tirer sa révérence

**³bow(s)** *n naut* avant *m*, proue *f*

**bowdlerize** *vt* expurger

**bowel(s)** *n*(*pl*) intestin(s) *m*(*pl*); ~ **s** *fig* entrailles *fpl*; *lit* émotions *fpl*; ~ **s of mercy** sentiments *mpl* de piété

**¹bower** *n* tonnelle *f*; *poet* boudoir *m*; maison *f* rustique

**²bower** *n naut* ancre *f*

**¹bowl** *n* bol *m*; (wine) coupe *f*; (washing) cuvette *f*; assiette *f* à soupe, assiette creuse; (pipe) fourneau *m*

**²bowl** *n* boule *f*; *vt* rouler, faire rouler, lancer; *fig* ~ **out** battre; ~ **over** renverser; *fig* déconcerter, décontenancer; *vi* ~ **along** rouler

**bow-legged** *adj* bancal

**bowler** *n sp* joueur -euse de boules

**bowler(-hat)** *n* (chapeau *m*) melon *m*

**bowline** *n* nœud de chaise

**bowling** *n* jeu *m* de boules

**bowling-alley** *n* bowling *m*

**bowling-green** *n* boulingrin *m*

**bowls** *n* jeu *m* de boules

**bowsprit** *n naut* beaupré *m*

**bow-wow** *n* aboiement *m*; (child language) toutou *m*

**¹box** *n* boîte *f*; (cardboard) carton *m*; (sizable) caisse *f*; *theat* loge *f*, baignoire *f*; (horse) box *m*; *leg* (jury, press) banc *m*; (witness) barre *f* (des témoins); *mot* (gears, differential) carter *m*; *sl* télé (*f*); (railway) ~ **car** fourgon *m*; ~ **number**

boîte postale; **Christmas** ~ étrennes *fpl*; *vt* mettre en boîte, mettre en caisse; *leg* déposer; ~ **in** cerner; *fig* circonscrire; ~ **off** circonscrire; ~ **up** mettre en boîte

²**box** *n* claque *f*, gifle *f*, soufflet *m*; *vt* boxer; souffleter; *vi* boxer

³**box** *n bot* buis *m*

**box-calf** *n* box-calf *m*

¹**boxer** *n* boxeur *m*

²**boxer** *n* (dog) boxer *m*

**boxing** *n* boxe *f*

**Boxing-Day** *n* le lendemain de Noël

**box-office** *n theat* bureau *m* de location

**box-spanner** *n* clef *f* en tube

**box-tree** *n* buis *m*

**boy** *n* garçon *m*; jeune homme *m*; (servant) boy *m*; ~ **friend** petit ami, amoureux *m*; **old** ~ ancien élève; *coll* mon vieux

**boycott** *n* boycottage *m*; *vt* boycotter

**boyhood** *n* enfance *f*; adolescence *f*

**boyish** *n* d'un garçon; *fig* puéril

**bra** *n coll* soutien-gorge *m* (*pl* soutiens-gorge)

**brace** *n* étai *m*, attache *f*; *bui* étrésillon *m*; (tool) vilebrequin *m*; (pair) couple *m*, paire *f*; ~ **s** bretelles *fpl*; *vt* attacher; appuyer; étayer; *naut* brasser; revigorer, tonifier; ~ **oneself up** rassembler ses forces; *coll* prendre un petit verre

**bracelet** *n* bracelet *m*; *coll* ~s menottes *fpl*

**bracken** *n* fougère *f*

**bracket** *n bui* support *m*, poterne *f*, tasseau *m*; *print* (square) crochet *m*; (round) parenthèse *f*; *vt* mettre entre crochets; mettre entre parenthèses; *mil* encadrer; *fig* grouper ensemble

**brackish** *adj* saumâtre

**bradawl** *n* poinçon *m*

**brag** *n* vanterie *f*, hâblerie *f*; *vi* se vanter

**braggart** *n + adj* hâbleur -euse

**Brahmin, Brahman** *n* brahmane *m*

**braid** *n* (plait) tresse *f*; (trimming) soutache *f*; *mil* galon *m*; *vt* tresser; soutacher; galonner

**Braille** *n* braille *m*

**brain** *n* cerveau *m*; *fig* as *m*; ~ **s** intelligence *f*; *cul* cervelle *f*; **blow out one's** ~ **s** se brûler la cervelle; **have something on the** ~ être obsédé par quelque chose; **pick s/o's** ~ **s** utiliser les idées d'un autre; **rack one's** ~ **s** se creuser la cervelle; *vt* défoncer le crâne à

**brain-child** *n* invention personnelle

**brain-drain** *n* brain-drain *m*, émigration *f* des cerveaux (des chercheurs)

**brain-fever** *n med* fièvre cérébrale,

méningite *f*

**brainless** *adj* stupide, crétin

**brain-storm** *n* congestion cérébrale, transport *m* au cerveau; *fig* idée géniale

**brains-trust** *n coll* brain-trust *m*

**brainwash** *vt* faire un lavage de cerveau à

**brainwashing** *n* lavage *m* de cerveau

**brainwave** *n coll* trouvaille *f*, idée géniale

**brainy** *adj* intelligent

**braise** *vt cul* braiser

¹**brake** *n* frein *m*; *vt* freiner

²**brake** *n ar* break *m*

³**brake** *n bot* fougère *f*

**brake-drum** *n mot* tambour *m* de frein

**bramble** *n* ronce *f*; mûre *f*

**bran** *n* son *m*

**branch** *n* branche *f*; (railway) embranchement *m*; *comm* succursale *f*; (river) affluent *m*; *mil* arme *f*; **root and** ~ entièrement, complètement; *vi bot* pousser des branches; ~ **out** se ramifier, se séparer

**brand** *n* brandon *m*, tison *m*; fer *m* à marquer; *fig* flétrissure *f*; *comm* marque *f*; *vt* marquer au fer rouge; *fig* dénoncer; *fig* ~ **on the memory** graver dans la mémoire

**brandish** *vt* brandir

**brand-new** *adj* tout à fait neuf (*f* tout à fait neuve), flambant neuf (*f* flambant neuve)

**brandy** *n* eau-de-vie *f* (*pl* eaux-de-vie); *usu* cognac *m*

**brash** *adj* outrecuidant, impudent, vulgaire

**brass** *n* laiton *m*; bronze *m*; *mus* cuivres *mpl*; *fig* impudence *f*, effronterie *f*; *coll* (money) fric *m*; *mil sl* **top** ~ huiles *fpl*; ~ **tacks** réalités *fpl*

**brassard** *n* brassard *m*

**brass-band** *n* fanfare *f*

**brass-hat** *n coll* officier supérieur

**brassière** *n* soutien-gorge *m* (*pl* soutiens-gorge)

**brassy** *adj* de bronze; *fig* effronté

**brat** *n* moutard *m*; *cont* morveux -euse

**bravado** *n* bravade *f*; *ar* spadassin *m*

**brave** *adj* courageux -euse, brave; élégant, beau (*f* belle); *vt* braver, défier

**bravery** *n* courage *m*, bravoure *f*

**bravo** *interj* bravo!

**brawl** *n* bagarre *f*, rixe *f*; *vi* beugler; se bagarrer; (stream) bruire

**brawler** *n* braillard -e; bagarreur *m*

**brawling** *adj* braillard, gueulard

**brawn** *n cul* fromage *m* de tête; muscle *m*; *fig* force *f*

**brawny** *adj* musclé, costaud, fort

¹**bray** *n* braiment *m*; *vi* braire

²**bray** *vt* (crush) broyer

**brazen** *adj* d'airain, de bronze; (sound) cuivré; *fig* impudent, effronté

**brazen-faced** *adj* impudent, effronté

**brazier** *n* brasero *m*

**Brazil** *n* Brésil *m*

**Brazilian** *n* Brésilien -ienne; *adj* brésilien -ienne

**breach** *n* rupture *f*, cassure *f*; *mil* brèche *f*; *leg* infraction *f*, violation *f*; *fig* rupture *f*, brouille *f*; ~ **of promise** rupture *f* d'un mariage; ~ **of the peace** désordre *m*; ~ **of trust** abus *m* de confiance; *vt* ouvrir une brèche dans, percer

**bread** *n* pain *m*; *fig* subsistance *f*, gagne-pain *m invar*; *eccles* hostie *f*; *sl* fric *m*; ~ **and butter** tartine (beurrée); *fig* gagne-pain *m invar*; **earn one's** ~ **and butter** gagner son pain

**bread-basket** *n* corbeille *f* à pain; *sl* estomac *m*, bide *m*

**breadcrumb** *n* miette *f*; *cul* ~s chapelure *f*

**breadth** *n* largeur *f*; *fig* largeur *f*, ampleur *f*; tolérance *f*

**break** *n* cassure *f*, rupture *f*; (gap) trou *m*; interruption *f*; (rest) repos *m*, répit *m*, pause *f*; (school) récréation *f*; (hiatus) solution *f* de continuité; (billiards) série *f*; (prison) évasion *f*; *sl* (luck) veine *f*; *sl* (bad luck) malchance *f*; *vt* briser, casser, rompre; (burst) crever, faire éclater; séparer; (law) violer, enfreindre; (news) annoncer; (journey) interrompre; *mil* (resistance) rompre; (enemy) anéantir; (reduce to ranks) casser; (promise) manquer à; (bank in gambling) faire sauter; *fig* briser, anéantir; ~ **down** démolir, abattre; (analyse) analyser, compartimenter; ~ **in** défoncer; (animal) mater; ~ **into** cambrioler; *fig* percer; ~ **in upon** interrompre; ~ **off** casser; *fig* rompre, faire cesser; ~ **open** ouvrir avec violence; ~ **through** percer; ~ **up** démolir; (soil) ameublir; faire disperser, dissoudre; *vi* se briser, se casser, se rompre; (day) poindre; (health) se détériorer, s'altérer; (voice) muer; ~ **down** (actor, speaker) s'interrompre, *coll* sécher; *mot* avoir une panne; ~ **even** couvrir ses frais; ~ **in** interrompre; (building) entrer par effraction; ~ **off** s'interrompre, cesser; rompre avec; ~ **out** s'évader; (war, fire, storm, epidemic, scandal, etc) éclater; (disease) se répandre, faire éruption; (skin) ~ **out into** se couvrir de; ~ **up** se disperser; (school) fermer pour les vacances; ~ **with** rompre avec

**breakable** *adj* fragile, cassable

**breakage** *n* casse *f*; objets cassés; dégâts *mpl*

**breakdown** *n* *mot* + *med* panne *f*; (negotiation) rupture *f*; (health) effondrement *m*, dépression nerveuse; analyse *f*; (dividing up) compartimentage *m*; ~ **service** service *m* de dépannage

**breaker** *n* *naut* brisant *m*; (person) casseur *m*; *elect* interrupteur *m*; *naut* baril *m*

**breakfast** *n* petit déjeuner; **English** ~ breakfast *m*; *vi* prendre le petit déjeuner

**breakneck** *adj* (speed) à se casser le cou, dangereux -euse

**break-out** *n* (prison) évasion *f*, cavale *f*

**breakthrough** *n* *mil* percée *f*; *fig* découverte majeure

**break-up** *n* désintégration *f*; effondrement *m*; (ice) dégel *m*; (school) fin *f* des cours

**breakwater** *n* brise-lames *m invar*, môle *m*

**bream** *n* *zool* brème *f*

**breast** *n* *anat* poitrine *f*; (woman) sein *m*; *fig* cœur *m*; **make a clean** ~ **of it** tout avouer; *vt* affronter, faire face à; opposer; (crest) surmonter

**breast-feed** *vt* nourrir au sein

**breast-feeding** *n* allaitement *m* au sein

**breast-plate** *n* *hist* plastron *m*

**breast-stroke** *n* brasse *f*

**breast-work** *n* *mil* parapet *m*

**breath** *n* souffle *m*, haleine *f*; respiration *f*; *fig* vie *f*; souffle *m*, brise *f*; **catch one's** ~ retenir son souffle; **draw** ~ respirer; **draw one's last** ~ rendre le dernier soupir; **hold one's** ~ retenir son souffle; **out of** ~ essoufflé; **take s/o's** ~ **away** alarmer qn, surprendre qn; **under one's** ~ à voix basse

**breathalyser** *n* *mot* alcoo(l)test *m*

**breathe** *vt* respirer; (out) exhaler; murmurer; (courage, desire) insuffler; *vi* respirer; être vivant; soupirer; *fig* ~ **freely** n'avoir plus peur, être soulagé

**breather** *n* bol *m* d'air; moment *m* de répit

**breathing** *n* respiration *f*

**breathing-space** *n* moment *m* de répit

**breathless** *adj* essoufflé, haletant; sans vie, inanimé

**breathlessness** *n* essoufflement *m*

**bred** *adj* engendré; élevé; **well** ~ de bonne souche

**breech** *n* culasse *f*; cul *m*; ~**es** culotte *f*, *coll* pantalon *m*

**breech-block** *n* bloc *m* de culasse

**breed** *n* espèce *f*, race *f*; (kind) type *m*; *vt* produire, porter; engendrer, procréer; (animals) faire l'élevage de; *vi* se reproduire; avoir des enfants; (animal) avoir des petits

**breeder** n éleveur m

**breeding** n élevage m; éducation f; bonnes manières

**breeze** n brise f; coll dispute f; vi coll ~ **in** entrer en coup de vent

**breeze-block** n bui parpaing m

**breezy** adj aéré; fig désinvolte

**Bren** n mil (espèce f de) mitrailleuse légère

**brethren** npl frères mpl

**Breton** n Breton -onne; adj breton -onne

**breve** n mus carrée f

**brevet** n brevet m

**breviary** n bréviaire m

**brevity** n brièveté f, concision f

**brew** n breuvage m; (beer) brassin m; vt (beer) brasser; (tea) faire (infuser); fig tramer, mijoter; vi infuser; (beer) fermenter; fig se préparer, se mijoter

**brewer** n brasseur -euse

**brewery** n brasserie f

**brewing** n brassage m

¹**briar** n bot églantier m; ~ **s** ronces fpl

²**briar** n (pipe) pipe f en racine de bruyère

**bribable** adj corruptible

**bribe** n pot-de-vin m (pl pots-de-vin); vt corrompre, acheter; vi donner des pots-de-vin

**bribery** n corruption f

**brick** n brique f; coll brave type m; ~ **s** (toy) jeu m de construction; coll **drop a** ~ faire une gaffe; vt murer de briques

**brickbat** n fig critique f

**bricklayer** n ouvrier m maçon

**brickwork** n briquetage m

**brickyard** n briqueterie f

**bridal** n poet noce f; adj (bed) conjugal; nuptial, de mariée

**bride** n (jeune) mariée f, promise f

**bridegroom** n (jeune) marié m, promis m

**bridesmaid** n demoiselle f d'honneur

¹**bridge** n pont m; (gangway) passerelle f; mus chevalet m; (nose) dos m; (dentistry) bridge m; vt faire un pont sur; fig faire la soudure entre

²**bridge** n (cards) bridge m

**bridgehead** n mil tête f de pont

**bridle** n bride f; vt brider, freiner; vi se rebiffer

**bridle-path** n sentier m

¹**brief** n leg dossier m, résumé m, cause f; eccles bref m; leg + fig **hold a** ~ **for** plaider pour; **hold no** ~ **for** ne pas être du côté de; leg **take a** ~ accepter une cause; vt leg confier une cause à; mil donner des instructions à; fig documenter

²**brief** adj bref (f brève), prompt, court, concis; **in** ~ bref

**briefcase** n serviette f

**briefing** n briefing m

**briefness** n brièveté f

**briefs** npl coll slip m

**brig** n naut brick m

**brigade** n brigade f

**brigadier** n mil général m de brigade

**brigand** n brigand m

**brigandage** n brigandage m

**brigantine** n naut brigantin m

**bright** adj brillant, vif (f vive); (shiny) luisant; (light) clair; intelligent, doué

**brighten** vt faire briller; fig ranimer, raviver; vi s'animer; (weather) s'éclaircir

**brightness** n éclat m, brillant m; intelligence f; vivacité f

**brill** n zool barbue f

**brilliance** n éclat m, brillant m; intelligence f; excellence f

**brilliant** adj brillant, éclatant, scintillant

**brilliantine** n brillantine f

**brim** n bord m; vi être plein à déborder; ~ **over** déborder

**brimful** adj plein à déborder; tout à fait plein

**brimstone** n soufre m; bibl **fire and** ~ les feux mpl de l'enfer

**brine** n saumure f

**bring** vt (person, animal) amener, faire venir, conduire; (object) apporter; (cause) causer, entraîner, engendrer; persuader; ~ **about** causer; ~ **back** (memories) rappeler; (person) ramener; ~ **down** abattre; faire tomber; ~ **forward** avancer; (figures) reporter; ~ **in** (money) rapporter; ~ **off** réussir; ~ **on** causer; ~ **out** (qualities) faire valoir; (book) publier; (emphasize) souligner; ~ **round** ranimer; rallier; ~ **to** naut mettre en panne; med ranimer; ~ **up** soulever; (children) élever; (data) avancer; (food) vomir; naut mettre en panne

**brink** n bord m

**briny** n coll obs mer f; adj saumâtre

**brio** n brio m

**briquette** n briquette f

**brisk** adj vif (f vive); alerte, animé; (business, trade) actif -ive; mil (fire) nourri; vt animer, activer

**brisket** n cul poitrine f

**bristle** n poil m; vi (animal) se hérisser; fig se fâcher; (problems) être rempli

**Bristol-board** n bristol m

**Britain** n Grande-Bretagne f

**Britannia** n metall métal anglais; poet Albion f

**Britannic** adj britannique

**British** npl Anglais mpl, Britanniques mpl; adj britannique

**Britisher** n US Anglais -e

**Briton** n Anglais -e; hist Celte, Breton -onne

**Brittany** *n* Bretagne *f*

**brittle** *adj* fragile

**broach** *n mech* foret *m*, perçoir *m*; (leather) alène *f*; *cul* broche *f*; *vt* entamer, ouvrir; percer; *fig* aborder, entamer

**broad** *n sl* poule *f*; *adj* large, vaste, étendu; (accent) fort, prononcé; *fig* clair, manifeste; tolérant; (improper) sale, grivois; ~ **bean** fève *f*; **have a** ~ **back** avoir bon dos; *coll* **it's as** ~ **as it's long** c'est kif-kif, cela revient au même

**broadcast** *n rad* transmission *f*, émission *f*; *vt* diffuser, émettre; *fig* diffuser, répandre; (seed) semer à la volée; *adj rad* diffusé; *fig* diffusé, répandu; (seed) semé à la volée

**broadcaster** *n* quelqu'un qui parle à la radio; (announcer) speaker *m* (*f* speakerine), annonceur *m*

**broadcasting** *n* radiodiffusion *f*; télévision *f*

**broaden** *vt* élargir; *vi* s'élargir

**broad-minded** *adj* large d'esprit, tolérant

**broadsheet** *n* placard *m*, affiche *f*

**broadside** *n naut* (salvo) bordée *f*; *fig* sortie *f*, invective *f*; ~ **on** *naut* par le travers

**brocade** *n* brocart *m*; *vt* brocher

**broccoli** *n* brocoli *m*

**brochure** *n* brochure *f*, dépliant *m*

**broil** *vt cul* griller; *fig* cuire, rôtir

**broiler** *n cul* gril *m*; *cul* poulet *m* à rôtir

**broke** *adj coll* fauché

**broken** *adj* brisé, cassé; (ground) accidenté; (speech) incorrect, défectueux -euse; *fig* brisé, rompu; (humble) ruiné; (voice) mué

**broken-down** *adj* délabré; *med* en panne; *fig* infirme

**broken-hearted** *adj* au cœur brisé, inconsolable

**broker** *n* courtier *m*; brocanteur *m*

**brokerage** *n* courtage *m*

**broking** *n* courtage *m*

**bromide** *n chem* bromure *f*; sédatif *m*; *fig* (person) raseur -euse; (remark) platitude *f*

**bromine** *n chem* brome *m*

**bronchial** *adj* bronchique

**bronchitis** *n* bronchite *f*

**broncho-pneumonia** *n* bronco-pneumonie *f*

**brontosaurus** *n* brontosaure *m*

**bronze** *n* bronze *m*; ~ **age** âge *m* de bronze; *vt* bronzer; *vi* se bronzer

**brooch** *n* broche *f*

**brood** *n* (birds) couvée *f*, nichée *f*; (children) nichée *f*, *coll* couvée *f*; *vi* (hen) couver; *fig* couver, ruminer, broyer du noir; ~ **on** (**over**) ruminer

**broody** *adj* (hen) prête à couver; *fig* cafardeux -euse

**¹brook** *n* ruisseau *m*

**²brook** *vt* supporter, tolérer

**broom** *n* balai *m*; *bot* genêt *m*; **a new** ~ **sweeps clean** tout nouveau tout beau

**broomstick** *n* manche *m* à balai

**broth** *n* bouillon *m*

**brothel** *n* bordel *m*

**brother** *n* frère *m*; camarade *m*, compagnon *m*

**brotherhood** *n* fraternité *f*, confraternité *f*; *eccles* confrérie *f*

**brother-in-law** *n* beau-frère *m* (*pl* beaux-frères)

**brotherly** *adj* fraternel -elle

**brow** *n* sourcil *m*; front *m*; (hill) sommet *m*

**browbeat** *vt* malmener, rudoyer, rabrouer

**brown** *n* brun *m*; *adj* brun; (person) bronzé, hâlé; ~ **bread** pain bis; ~ **study** rêverie *f*; *vt* brunir; (person) bronzer; *cul* dorer; *coll* ~ **ed off** cafardeux -euse

**brownish** *adj* brunâtre

**browse** *vi* brouter; (book) lire au hasard; (bookshop) bouquiner

**bruise** *n* contusion *f*, ecchymose *f*; *coll* bleu *m*; *vt* meurtrir, contusionner; *vi* être meurtri, se meurtrir

**bruit** *vt* ébruiter

**brunette** *n* brune *f*

**brunt** *n* choc *m*; attaque principale

**brush** *n* brosse *f*; coup *m* de brosse; (painter) pinceau *m*; *elect* balai *m*; (undergrowth) broussailles *fpl*; (verbal) prise *f* de bec; *mil* + *fig* escarmouche *f*; ~ **work** (painter) peinture *f*; **shaving** ~ blaireau *m*; *vt* brosser; effleurer; ~ **aside** écarter; ~ **away** balayer; *coll* ~ **off** liquider; ~ **up** donner un coup de brosse à; réviser; *fig* rafraîchir; *vi* ~ **past** frôler en passant

**brush-off** *n coll* refus *m*

**brushwood** *n* broussailles *fpl*

**brusque** *adj* brusque

**brusqueness** *n* brusquerie *f*

**Brussels** *n* Bruxelles *m*; ~ **sprouts** choux *mpl* de Bruxelles

**brutal** *adj* brutal

**brutality** *n* brutalité *f*, férocité *f*

**brutalize** *vt* abrutir; brutaliser

**brute** *n* brute *f*; *coll* salaud *m*; *adj* brutal; ~ **force** vive force

**bubble** *n* bulle *f*; *fig* chimère *f*; *vi* faire des bulles; ~ **over** bouillonner

**bubbly** *n coll obs* champagne *m*; *adj* plein de bulles, pétillant

**bubo** *n med* bubon *m*

**bubonic** *adj* bubonique

**buccaneer** *n* flibustier *m*

**buck** *n* daim *m*, chevreuil *m*; mâle *m* (du lapin, du lièvre, de l'antilope, du chamois, etc); *fig* dandy *m*; *coll US* dollar *m*;

*sl* **pass the** ~ esquiver une obligation; *vt coll* ~ **s/o up** remonter qn, encourager qn; *vi* (horse) ruer; *coll* ~ **up** se hâter

**bucket** *n* seau *m*; (dredger) godet *m*; *sl* **kick the** ~ mourir, crever; *vt* (horse) surmener; *vi* ~ **about** être ballotté

**bucketful** *n* plein seau

**bucket-shop** *n* bureau *m* de courtier marron

**buckle** *n* boucle *f*; *vt* boucler; *vi* (bend) se voiler; *coll* ~ **down to** s'y mettre

**buckled** *adj* bouclé *e*; (bent) voilé, faussé

**buckler** *n* bouclier *m*

**buckram** *n* bougran *m*

**buckshee** *n sl* ce qu'on n'a pas payé; *adj* aux frais de la princesse, à l'œil, gratuit

**buckskin** *n* peau *f* de daim

**buckwheat** *n* sarrasin *m*, blé noir

**bucolic** *adj* bucolique

**bud** *n* bourgeon *m*, bouton *m*; *fig* **nip in the** ~ tuer dans l'œuf; *vt* écussonner; *vi* bourgeonner

**Buddha** *n* Bouddha *m*

**Buddhism** *n* bouddhisme *m*

**Buddhist** *n* Bouddhiste; *adj* bouddhiste

**budding** *n* bourgeonnement *m*; *adj* bourgeonnant; *fig* en herbe

**buddy** *n coll US* copain *m*; *sl* pote *m*

**budge** *vt* faire bouger; *vi* bouger

**budgerigar** *n* perruche *f*

**budget** *n* budget *m*; *vi* estimer; ~ **for** inscrire à son budget

**buff** *n* peau *f* de buffle; (colour) chamois *m*; *coll fig* **to the** ~ tout nu (*f* toute nue); *vt* polir

**buffalo** *n* buffle *m*; bison *m*

¹**buffer** *n* (railway) tampon *m*; pare-chocs *m*; ~ **state** état *m* tampon

²**buffer** *n coll* croulant *m*

¹**buffet** *n* (punch) coup *m* de poing, bourrade *f*; *fig* malheur *m*, coup *m* du sort; *vt* souffleter, bourrer de coups; (waves) ~ **ed by** ballotté par

²**buffet** *n* (refreshment bar, sideboard) buffet *m*; ~ **car** gril-express *m*; ~ **lunch** lunch *m*

**buffeting** *n* série *f* de coups

**buffoon** *n* pitre *m*

**bug** *n zool* punaise *f*; *coll* virus *m*; *coll* **big** ~ grosse légume; *vt* mettre sur écoute, brancher sur table d'écoute

**bugbear** *n* épouvantail *m*

**bugger** *n leg* sodomite *m*; *coll* idiot *m*; (silly) crétin *m*; *vt leg* sodomiser; *sl* enculer; *vi sl* ~ **off** foutre le camp

**buggery** *n leg* sodomie *f*

**bugle** *n mil* clairon *m*

**bugler** *n mil* clairon *m*

**build** *n* (person) carrure *f*, charpente *f*; structure *f*; *vt* bâtir, construire, élever; *fig* bâtir, établir, développer; *fig* ~ **on** se baser sur; ~ **up** développer, amé-

liorer, fortifier; construire, bâtir

**builder** *n* entrepreneur *m* (en bâtiments)

**building** *n* bâtiment *m*, édifice *m*, immeuble *m*; ~ **society** société *f* qui accorde des prêts pour l'achat d'une maison (d'un appartement)

**build-up** *n coll mil* préparatifs *mpl* pour une offensive; *coll fig* campagne *f* publicitaire

**built-in** *adj* (cupboards, etc) encastré; *fig* garanti

**built-up** *adj* ~ **area** agglomération *f*

**bulb** *n bot* bulbe *m*, oignon *m*; *elect* ampoule *f*

**bulbous** *adj* bulbeux -euse

**bulge** *n* bosse *f*; *mil* saillant *m*; *vi* bomber

**bulging** *adj* gonflé, archi-plein

**bulk** *n* masse *f*; (person) corpulence *f*; volume *m*; majeure partie; **in** ~ en gros; *naut* en vrac; *vt* entasser (en vrac); *vi* tenir de la place; *fig* sembler important, apparaître signifiant

**bulkhead** *n naut* cloison *f*

**bulky** *adj* encombrant, volumineux -euse; (person) corpulent

¹**bull** *n* taureau *m*; mâle *m* (de l'éléphant, de la baleine, etc); *comm* haussier *m*; (target) noir *m*, mille *m*; *mil sl* astiquage *m*; *sl* balivernes *fpl*; ~ **in a china shop** éléphant *m* dans un magasin de porcelaine; **take the** ~ **by the horns** prendre le taureau par les cornes; *vt* essayer de faire hausser le cours de; *vi* jouer à la hausse

²**bull** *n eccles* bulle *f*

**bull-calf** *n* jeune taureau *m*

**bulldog** *n* bouledogue *m*

**bulldoze** *vt* passer au bulldozer; *fig US* intimider, persuader de force

**bulldozer** *n* bulldozer *m*

**bullet** *n* balle *f*

**bulletin** *n* bulletin *m*, communiqué *m*

**bullet-proof** *adj* blindé

**bullfight** *n* course *f* de taureaux, corrida *f*

**bullfighter** *n* matador *m*, torero *m*

**bullfinch** *n orni* bouvreuil *m*

**bullfrog** *n* grosse grenouille (d'Amérique)

**bullion** *n* (gold) or *m* en barre, or *m* en lingot(s); (silver) argent *m* en barre, argent *m* en lingot(s)

**bullish** *adj comm* tendant à la hausse

**bullock** *n* bœuf *m*

**bull-ring** *n* arène *f* (de corrida), arènes *fpl*

**bull's-eye** *n* (target) mille *m*; (sweet) bonbon *m* à la menthe; *bui* œil-de-bœuf *m* (*pl* œils-de-bœuf); **get a** ~ faire mouche

**bullshit** *n sl mil* astiquage *m*; *sl* balivernes *fpl*

¹**bully** n tyranneau m; vt brimer, persécuter, intimider
²**bully** adj coll ar épatant, sensas invar
³**bully (beef )** n coll singe m; (viande f de) bœuf m en conserve
**bulrush** n jonc m
**bulwark** n rempart m; naut pavois m; brise-lames m invar; fig défense f; protecteur m
¹**bum** n sl fesses fpl, cul m
²**bum** n sl US (idler) flemmard m; (vagrant) clochard m; vt sl US écornifler; vi sl US vivre aux crochets des autres; ~ **around** fainéanter
**bumble-bee** n bourdon m
**bumf** n sl torche-cul m; coll paperasses fpl
**bump** n choc m, coup m; bosse f; vt (strike) cogner; (bump into) tamponner; vi (car) être cahoté; sl ~ **off** descendre, démolir
**bumper** n mot pare-chocs m invar; plein verre; adj abondant
**bumpkin** n pej péquenot m
**bumptious** adj satisfait, suffisant, arrogant
**bumpy** adj (surface) bosselé; (ride) cahoteux -euse
**bun** n (espèce f de) brioche f; (hair) chignon m; coll **have a** ~ **in the oven** avoir un polichinelle dans le tiroir
**bunch** n groupe m; (flowers) bouquet m; (keys) trousseau m; (grapes) grappe f; sl bande f; vt grouper; nouer; vi se grouper, se serrer
**bundle** n ballot m; paquet m; (papers) liasse f; (asparagus, carrots) botte f; vt empaqueter, emballer; ~ **away (off, out)** expédier, renvoyer; vi coll ~ **away** décamper; ~ **in** s'entasser
**bung** n bonde f; vt mettre une bonde à; sl jeter; ~ **up** (pipe) obstruer; ~**ed up** (eyes) gonflé; (nose) bouché
**bungalow** n bungalow m
**bungle** vt bâcler, brouiller; vi travailler d'une façon incompétente
**bunion** n oignon m
¹**bunk** n (ship, train) couchette f; sl **do a** ~ foutre le camp; vi sl foutre le camp; ~ **down** se coucher
²**bunk** n sl balivernes fpl
**bunker** n naut soute f à charbon; mil bunker m, casemate f; vt naut (coal, oil) mettre en soute; (coal) charbonner; (oil) mazouter
**bunkum** n coll sornettes fpl, balivernes fpl
**bunny** n (child's language) lapin m
**Bunsen-burner** n bec m Bunsen
¹**bunting** n (cloth) étamine f; (flag) drapeau m; collect drapeaux mpl
²**bunting** n orni bruant m

**buoy** n naut bouée f; vt baliser; fig ~ **up** soutenir, épauler
**buoyancy** n flottabilité f; fig gaieté f, animation f; comm (prices) fermeté f
**buoyant** n flottable; fig gai, animé; comm (prices) ferme
¹**bur(r)** n bot bardane f; coll (person) crampon m
²**bur(r)** n grasseyement m
**burble** n gloussement m; vi glousser, bafouiller
**burden** n fardeau m, faix m; naut tonnage m; fig fardeau m, charge f; ~ **of proof** obligation f de faire la preuve; **beast of** ~ bête f de somme; vt charger; opprimer
**burdensome** adj lourd, pesant
**burdock** n bot bardane f
**bureau** n (desk) bureau m; US commode f; (office) bureau m
**bureaucracy** n bureaucratie f
**bureaucrat** n bureaucrate
**bureaucratic** adj bureaucratique
**burglar** n cambrioleur -euse
**burglary** n cambriolage m; leg cambriolage m nocturne
**burgle** vt cambrioler
**Burgundy** n geog Bourgogne f; (wine) bourgogne m
**burial** n enterrement m
**burial-ground** n cimetière m
**burin** n burin m
**burlap** n toile f d'emballage
**burlesque** n burlesque m, parodie f; adj burlesque; vt satiriser, parodier
**burly** adj costaud, solide
¹**burn** n ruisseau m
²**burn** n brûlure f; vt brûler; consumer; (set fire to) incendier, mettre la flamme à; (acid) corroder; (put to death) brûler vif (f vive), faire mourir sur le bûcher; ~ **one's fingers** se brûler les doigts; vi brûler, être en flammes, flamber; (feel hot) avoir très chaud; sl ~ **up** se fâcher tout rouge
**burner** n brûleur m, bec m
**burning** n incendie m; adj brûlant, enflammé, en feu; fig ardent, brûlant; ~ **bush** buisson ardent
**burnish** n lustre m; cati m; vt brunir, polir
**burnt** adj brûlé; (colour) jaune foncé
**burp** n sl rot m; vi sl roter
**burr** n see bur(r)
**burrow** n terrier m; vt creuser
**bursar** n (school, university) économe, intendant -e
**bursary** n (grant) bourse f; bureau m de l'économe
**burst** n éclatement m, explosion f; (pipe) fuite f; mil (fire) rafale f; (flames) jaillissement m; fig élan m; (enthusiasm)

accès *m*; (applause) tonnerre *m*; *sp* (speed) sprint *m*, emballage *m*; *vt* crever; (explode) faire sauter; (banks) déborder; (break) rompre; ~ **in** (door, etc) enfoncer; *vi* sauter, éclater, exploser; crever; déborder; ~ **into flower** s'épanouir

**burton** *n sl* gone for a ~ mort, crevé

**bury** *vt* ensevelir, enterrer, inhumer; dissimuler, celer; (quarrel) oublier; ~ **oneself in** se plonger dans; ~ **the hatchet** se réconcilier

**bus** *n* autobus *m*; (coach) car *m*; *coll* mot bagnole *f*; ~ **station** gare routière; *vt US* transporter en car; *vi coll* aller en autobus

¹**bush** *n* buisson *m*; (undergrowth) broussailles *fpl*; (Africa, Australia) brousse *f*; (Corsica) maquis *m*; ~ **telegraph** téléphone *m* arabe; **beat about the** ~ tergiverser; *vi* pousser en broussailles

²**bush** *n eng* bague *f*

**bushel** *n* boisseau *m*; **hide one's light under a** ~ être trop modeste

**bushy** *adj* broussailleux -euse, touffu

**business** *n* (task) affaire *f*; (trade) affaires *fpl*; métier *m*, travail *m*, profession *f*; (commercial undertaking) commerce *m*, maison *f*, entreprise *f*; *fig* affaire *f*, question sérieuse; *theat* jeux *mpl* de scène

**businesslike** *adj* méthodique, efficace

**businessman** *n* homme *m* d'affaires, businessman *m*

**busman** *n* (driver) conducteur *m* d'autobus; (conductor) receveur *m* d'autobus

¹**bust** *n* buste *m*; *anat* poitrine *f*; (woman) gorge *f*

²**bust** *vt sl* briser, rompre; *sl* (catch) prendre sur le fait; (arrest) arrêter; *adj sl* fauché

**bustard** *n zool* outarde *f*

¹**bustle** *n* tournure *f*

²**bustle** *n* remue-ménage *m invar*; *vt* bousculer; activer; *vi* s'affairer, s'empresser, se démener

**bust-up** *n sl* bagarre *f*

**busy** *n sl* flic *m*; *adj* occupé, affairé; (day) chargé; (street, town, etc) animé; *pej* officieux -ieuse, important; *vt* ~ **oneself with** s'activer à, se mêler de

**busybody** *n* officieux -ieuse; *sl* emmerdeur -euse

**but** *n* mais *m*; **ifs and** ~ **s** les si et les mais; *adv* seulement, ne … que; **could you** ~ **understand!** si seulement vous pouviez comprendre!; **it is** ~ **a short distance away** ce n'est qu'à deux pas d'ici; *prep* sauf, excepté; sans, sinon; **no one** ~ **you** could do that personne sauf (excepté) vous ne pourrait faire

cela; **no one came** ~ **him of course** bien sûr personne n'est venu sinon lui; **you could have gone** ~ **for me** sans moi vous seriez parti; *conj* mais

**butane** *n* butane *m*

**butch** *n sl* gouine *f*; homosexuel -uelle actif (*f* active)

**butcher** *n* boucher -ère; *fig* boucher -ère, assassin -e; *vt* massacrer

**butchery** *n* (slaughter-house) abattoir *m*; métier *m* de boucher; (massacre) boucherie *f*

**butler** *n* maître d'hôtel *m*

¹**butt** *n* bout *m*; (rifle) crosse *f*; (cigarette) mégot *m*; *coll US* derrière *m*

²**butt** *n* barrique *f*

³**butt** *n mil* ouvrage *m* de terre devant les cibles d'un champ de tir; *fig* bouc *m* émissaire, victime *f*; *mil* ~ **s** champ de tir

⁴**butt** *n* coup *m* de corne, coup *m* de tête; *vt* encorner, donner un coup de corne (de tête) à; *vi* donner des cornes, donner de la tête; ~ **in** intervenir, dire son mot

**butt-end** *n* extrémité inférieure, gros bout

**butter** *n* beurre *m*; *fig* flatterie *f*; *vt* beurrer; *fig* ~ **s/o up** flatter qn

**buttercup** *n* bouton d'or *m*

**butter-dish** *n* beurrier *m*

**butterfly** *n* papillon *m*; *fig* dandy *m*; *adj* frivole

**buttermilk** *n* babeurre *m*, lait *m* de beurre

**butter-muslin** *n* étamine *f*

**butterscotch** *n* (espèce *f* de) caramel *m* au beurre

**buttock** *n* fesse *f*.

**button** *n* bouton *m*; ~ **mushroom** champignon *m* de Paris; *vt* boutonner; *vi* se boutonner; *coll* ~ **up** ne plus rien dire

**button-hole** *n* boutonnière *f*; fleur *f*; *vt* faire une boutonnière à; *fig* retenir, importuner; *coll* cramponner

**buttress** *n* contrefort *m*; *fig* pilier *m*, soutien *m*; (mountain) contrefort *m*; **flying** ~ arc-boutant *m* (*pl* arcs-boutants)

**buxom** *adj* plantureux -euse, dodu, bien en chair

**buy** *n coll* achat *m*; (bargain) occasion *f*; *vt* acheter; acquérir; *sl* accepter, adapter; ~ **dear** payer cher; ~ **in** racheter; ~ **s/o off** acheter qn, soudoyer qn; ~ **s/o out** acheter les droits de qn; ~ **up** acheter en bloc

**buyer** *n* acheteur -euse; acquéreur *m*

**buzz** *n* bourdonnement *m*; *coll* (rumour) canard *m*, bruit *m*; *coll* (telephone) coup *m* de fil; *vt coll* (rumour) répandre;

*coll* lancer; *coll* téléphoner; *aer* frôler; *vi* bourdonner; *coll* ~ **off** se barrer, filer

**buzzard** *n* buse *f*, busard *m*

**buzzer** *n* (factory) sirène *f*; *elect* vibrateur *m*

**by** *adv* près, auprès; ~ **the** ~ à propos; **put** ~ mettre de côté; *prep* par, de; près de; (time) à, pendant, vers; (measure) à, de, sur; ~ **and** ~ bientôt; ~ **chance** par hasard; ~ **day** pendant le jour; ~ **far** de beaucoup; ~ **means of** au moyen de; ~ **oneself** tout seul (*f* toute seule); ~ **the minute** à la minute; ~ **then** avant ce moment; ~ **the ton** à la tonne; **near** ~ tout près; **ten** ~ **six** dix sur six

**by-election** *n* élection partielle

**bygone** *n* événement passé; **let** ~ **s be** ~ **s!** oubliez et pardonnez!; *adj* du passé, d'autrefois, du temps jadis

**by-law** *n* *leg* arrêté administratif local

**by-pass** *n* *mot* bretelle *f* de contournement; voie *f* de dérivation, by-pass *m*; *mech* conduit *m* de dérivation; *elect* dérivation *f*; *vt* contourner, éviter

**bypath** *n* chemin écarté

**by-play** *n* *theat* jeux *mpl* de scène en aparté

**by-product** *n* sous-produit *m*, dérivé *m*

**byre** *n* étable *f*

**bystander** *n* spectateur -trice

**by-way** *n* route *f* secondaire; *fig* à-côté *m*

**by-word** *n* dicton *m*; objet *m* de dérision; **become a** ~ passer en proverbe

# C

**cab** *n* *ar* fiacre *m*; taxi *m*; (railway, lorry) cabine *f*; ~ **rank** station *f* de taxis

**cabal** *n* cabale *f*, intrigue *f*; *vi* comploter, intriguer

**cabala, cabbala** *n* cabale *f*

**cabaret** *n* *obs* estaminet *m*, bistrot *m*; cabaret *m*, café-concert *m* (*pl* cafésconcerts), boîte *f* de nuit

**cabbage** *n* chou *m*; *coll* lourdaud -e; ~ **butterfly** papillon blanc

**cabby** *n* *obs* *coll* chauffeur *m* de taxi

**cab-driver** *n* chauffeur *m* de taxi

**cabin** *n* cabine *f*; (hut) cabane *f*; *naut* ~ **class** deuxième classe *f*

**cabin-boy** *n* mousse *m*

**cabinet** *n* cabinet *m*, bureau *m*; (furniture) cabinet *m*; *pol* conseil *m* des ministres; **filing** ~ classeur *m*

**cabinet-maker** *n* ébéniste *m*

**cable** *n* câble *m*; *naut* (distance) encablure *f*; *vt* + *vi* télégraphier, câbler

**cablegram** *n* télégramme *m*

**cable-railway** *n* funiculaire *m*; (carried on pylons) téléférique *m*

**caboodle** *n* *coll* **the whole** ~ tout le bazar

**cabotage** *n* *naut* cabotage *m*

**cab-rank** *n* station *f* de taxis

**cacao** *n* cacao *m*

**cache** *n* cache *f*; cachette *f*; objet caché;

*vt* cacher, mettre en réserve

**cachet** *n* cachet *m*

**cachou** *n* cachou *m*

**cackle** *n* caquet *m*; gloussement *m*; **cut the** ~! en voilà assez!; *vi* caqueter; glousser

**cacophonous** *adj* discordant

**cacophony** *n* discordance *f*

**cactus** *n* cactus *m*

**cad** *n* goujat *m*, malotru *m*

**cadaver** *n* corps *m*, mort -e

**cadaveric, cadaverous** *adj* cadavérique; (pale) blême

**caddie, caddy** *n* (golf) cadet *m*, caddie *m*

**caddish** *n* *coll* grossier -ière, de goujat

**caddy** *n* boîte *f* à thé

**cadence** ~ cadence *f*

**cadet** *n* cadet *m*; *mil* aspirant *m*

**cadge** *vt* écornifler, quémander; *vi* quémander

**cadger** *n* écornifleur -euse

**cadmium** *n* *chem* cadmium *m*

**cadre** *n* cadre *m*

**caecum** *n* *anat* caecum *m*

**Caesarean, Caesarian** *n* *surg* césarienne *f*; *adj* *surg* (operation) césarienne; *hist* césarien -ienne

**caesura** *n* césure *f*

**café** *n* café *m*, café-restaurant *m* (*pl*

cafés-restaurants)

**cafeteria** *n* cafétéria *f*, cafeteria *f*, (restaurant *m*) libre-service *m* (*pl* libres-services); *coll* self *m*

**caffeine** *n chem* caféine; ~-**free** décaféiné

**caftan, kaftan** *n* caftan *m*, cafetan *m*

**cage** *n* cage *f*; *vt* mettre en cage; encager

**cagey** *adj coll* prudent, finaud

**caginess** *n coll* prudence *f*, finauderie *f*

**cahoot** *n coll* in ~ s de mèche

**cairn** *n* cairn *m*

**Cairo** *n* Le Caire

**caisson** *n* caisson *m*

**cajole** *vt* cajoler

**cajolery** *n* cajolerie *f*

**cake** *n* gâteau *m*, galette *f*; *agr* tourteau *m*; (soap) pain *m*; *coll* **a piece of** ~ du gâteau; *coll* **take the** ~ être la fin des haricots; *vt* durcir, coaguler, couvrir d'une croûte; *vi* se coaguler, faire croûte

**calamine** *n chem* calamine *f*

**calamitous** *adj* calamiteux -euse

**calamity** *n* calamité *f*, catastrophe *f*; malheur *m*

**calcareous** *adj* calcaire

**calcedony** *n see* **chalcedony**

**calcification** *n* calcification *f*

**calcify** *vt* calcifier; *vi* se calcifier

**calcine** *vt* calciner; *vi* se calciner

**calcium** *n chem* calcium *m*

**calculable** *adj* calculable

**calculate** *vt* calculer; régler, organiser; *vi* calculer, faire des calculs; ~ **on** compter sur

**calculated** *adj* calculé; réfléchi, délibéré

**calculating** *adj* prudent; calculateur -trice; ~ **machine** calculatrice *f*

**calculation** *n* calcul *m*

**calculator** *n* (person) calculateur -trice; (machine) calculatrice *f*

**calculous** *adj med* calculeux -euse

**calculus** *n med* + *math* calcul *m*

**calendar** *n* calendrier *m*; *leg* rôle *m*; *vt* classer, indexer

**calends, kalends** *npl Rom hist* calendes *fpl*; **at the Greek** ~ aux calendes grecques

**¹calf** *n* (*pl* calves) veau *m*; (seal, whale, buffalo, etc) petit *m*; *fig* blanc-bec *m* (*pl* blancs-becs); (leather) veau *m*, box(-calf) *m*

**²calf** *n* (*pl* calves) (muscle) mollet *m*

**calfskin** *n* cuir *m* de veau

**calibrate** *vt* calibrer

**calibration** *n* calibrage *m*

**calibre** *n* calibre *m*

**calico** *n* calicot *m*

**calif, caliph** *n* calife *m*

**calipers** *n see* **callipers**

**calisthenics, callisthenics** *npl* gymnastique *f* rythmique

**calix** *n* (*pl* calices) *biol* calice *m*

**¹calk** *n* crampon *m* (à glace); *vt* ferrer

**²calk** *vt* calquer, décalquer

**³calk** *vt see* **caulk**

**call** *n* (shout) cri *m*; appel *m*; appel *m* téléphonique, communication *f*; vocation *f*; *leg* sommation *f*; courte visite; (need) besoin *m*; (cards) demande *f*; *theat* (curtain) rappel *m*; *comm* appel *m* de fonds; *mil* sonnerie *f*; *naut* escale *f*; *comm* ~ **option** option *f*; **on** ~ disponible, prêt; *comm* payable à vue; **within** ~ tout près; *vt* appeler, faire venir; (wake) réveiller; (cards) annoncer; appeler par téléphone; (meeting) convoquer; ~ **a halt to** mettre fin à; ~ **aside** prendre à part; ~ **attention to** attirer l'attention sur; ~ **for** demander, réclamer; ~ **forth** faire naître, soulever; ~ **in** faire entrer; *comm* faire rentrer, rappeler; ~ **in question** mettre en question; ~ **into play** faire agir; ~ **it a day** cesser le travail pour la journée; ~ **names** dénigrer, bafouer; ~ **off** annuler; ~ **out** (duel) provoquer; (workers) faire mettre en grève; *mil* faire intervenir; ~ **over** faire appel; ~ **over the coals** réprimander; *eccles* ~ **the banns** proclamer les bans; ~ **to mind** rappeler; ~ **to the bar** inscrire au barreau; *mil* ~ **up** appeler, mobiliser; *vi* appeler, crier; (visit) passer; *naut* faire escale; ~ **out** appeler

**call-box** *n* cabine *f* téléphonique

**caller** *n* visiteur -euse; (telephone) personne *f* qui appelle

**call-girl** *n* prostituée *f* qu'on retient par téléphone, call-girl *f*

**calligraphist** *n* calligraphe

**calligraphy** *n* calligraphie *f*

**calling** *n* profession *f*, vocation *f*; (meeting) convocation *f*

**callipers, calipers** *n* compas *m*

**callosity** *n* callosité *f*

**callous** *adj* (skin) calleux -euse; *fig* dur, brutal, insensible

**callousness** *n* dureté *f*, brutalité *f*, insensibilité *f*

**callow** *adj zool* sans plumes; *fig* naïf -ïve, inexpérimenté

**call-up** *n mil* appel *m*

**callus** *n med* cal *m* (*pl* cals), durillon *m*

**calm** *n* calme *m*, tranquillité *f*; *adj* calme, tranquille; *vt* calmer; *vi* se calmer; ~ **down** s'apaiser, se calmer

**calmness** *n* calme *m*, sang-froid *m invar*

**calomel** *n med* calomel *m*

**calorie** *n* calorie *f*

**calorific** *adj* calorifique

**calorimeter** *n phys* calorimètre *m*

**calumniate** *vt* calomnier

calumniator *n* calomniateur -trice
calumnious *adj* calomnieux -ieuse
calumny *n* calomnie *f*
calvary *n* calvaire *m*
calve *vt zool* mettre bas; *vi* vêler
Calvinism *n* calvinisme *m*
Calvinist *n* + *adj* calviniste
calypso *n* calypso *m*
calyx *n* (*pl* calyces) *bot* calice *m*
cam *n mech* came *f*
camber *n* (road) bombement *m*; *archi* cambrure *f*; *vt* bomber; cambrer; *vi* se bomber; se cambrer
Cambrian *adj* gallois; *geol* cambrien -ienne
cambric *n* batiste *f*
camel *n* chameau *m* (*f* chamelle); *naut* chameau *m*; (colour) couleur *f* fauve; *mil* Camel Corps = méharistes *mpl*
camel-driver *n* chamelier *m*
camel-hair *n* poil *m* de chameau
camellia *n* camélia *m*
cameo *n* camée *m*
camera *n* appareil *m* de photo; (film, television) caméra *f*; *leg* in ~ à huis clos
camisole *n obs* camisole *f*
camomile *n bot* camomille *f*; ~ tea camomille *f*
camouflage *n* camouflage *m*; *vt* camoufler
¹camp *n* camp *m*, campement *m*; *fig* vie *f* militaire; faction *f*, parti *m*; strike ~ lever le camp; *vi* camper; go ~ing faire du camping
²camp *adj sl* affecté, efféminé; *theat* cabotin; *vi sl theat* ~ it up faire le cabotin, cabotiner
campaign *n mil* campagne *f*; *vi* faire campagne, militer
campaigner *n* militant -e; *mil* old ~ vétéran *m*
campanile *n* campanile *m*
campanology *n art m* de sonner les cloches; art *m* de la fonte des cloches
campanula *n bot* campanule *f*
camp-bed *n* lit *m* de camp
camp-chair *n* chaise pliante
camper *n* campeur -euse
camp-follower *n mil hist* cantinière *f*; personne *f* qui vit aux crochets d'une armée; prostituée *f*
camphor *n* camphre *m*
camphorated *adj* camphré
camping *n* camping *m*; ~ site (terrain *m* de) camping *m*
camp-stool *n* pliant *m*
campus *n* campus *m*
camshaft *n mech* arbre *m* à cames
¹can *n* boîte *f* en fer blanc, boîte *f* de conserve; (milk, petrol) bidon *m*; (oil) burette *f*; (beer) canette *f*; *sl* carry the

~ payer les pots cassés; *vt* mettre en conserve; *coll rad* enregistrer; *sl* ~ it! ta gueule!
²can *v aux* pouvoir; (allow oneself to) se permettre de; avoir la permission de; (know how to) savoir
Canada *n* Canada *m*
canal *n* canal *m*
canalization *n* canalisation *f*
canalize *vt* canaliser
canary *n* canari *m*, serin *m*; *adj* ~ yellow jaune serin *invar*
canasta *n* canasta *f*
can-can *n* cancan *m*
cancel *vt* annuler; oblitérer; (delete) barrer, rayer; (arrangement) décommander; (will) révoquer; *vi* ~ out s'annuler
cancellation *n* annulation *f*; contre-ordre *m*
cancer *n* cancer *m*; Cancer Cancer *m*
cancerous *adj med* cancéreux -euse
candelabrum, candelabra *n* candélabre *m*
candid *adj* franc (*f* franche)
candidate *n* candidat -e, postulant -e
candidature *n* candidature *f*
candied *adj cul* candi *adj m*, confit
candle *n* (wax) bougie *f*; (tallow) chandelle *f*; *eccles* cierge *m*; burn the ~ at both ends brûler la chandelle par les deux bouts; not fit to hold a ~ to très inférieur à; *coll* the game is not worth the ~ ça ne vaut pas le coup
candlelight *n* lumière *f* d'une chandelle (des chandelles)
candlepower *n obs phys* bougie *f*
candlestick *n* chandelier *m*
candour *n* candeur *f*, franchise *f*, sincérité *f*
candy *n* sucre *m* candi; *US* bonbon(s) *m*(*pl*); *vt* confire, candir; *vi* se candir
candy-floss *n* barbe *f* à papa
cane *n* canne *f*, bâton *m*; férule *f*; (plant) tige; get the ~ être fouetté; *vt* fouetter; (chair) canner
canine *n* canine *f*; *adj* canin
caning *n* volée *f* de coups de bâton
canister *n* (tea, coffee, etc) boîte *f* métallique
canker *n med* ulcère *m*, chancre *m*; gangrène *f*; *bot* + *fig* chancre *m*; *vt* ulcérer, ronger, gangrener; *vi* se gangrener
cankered *adj fig* ulcéré, aigri
cannabis *n* marihuana *f*, marijuana *f*; cannabis *m*
canned *adj* en conserve; *coll mus* enregistré; *coll* ivre, parti
cannery *n* conserverie *f*
cannibal *n* cannibale
cannibalism *n* cannibalisme *m*
cannibalize *vt mech* démonter pour

obtenir des pièces de rechange

¹**cannon** n canon m; ~ **fodder** chair f à canon

²**cannon** n (billiards) carambolage m; vi caramboler; fig ~ **into** se heurter contre, heurter

**cannonade** n canonade f; vi tirer un canon contre

**cannon-ball** n hist boulet m (de canon)

**cannot** = can not see **can**

**canny** adj rusé, finaud

**canoe** n canoë m; (Africa, S.E. Asia) pirogue f; vi faire du canoë

**canoeist** n canoéiste

¹**canon** n (church law) canon m; critère m, règle f; mus canon m; œuvre m authentique

²**canon** n (cathedral) chanoine m

**canonical** adj canonique

**canonicals** npl vêtements mpl sacerdotaux

**canonization** n eccles canonisation f

**canonize** vt eccles canoniser

**canonry** n canonicat m

**canoodle** vt sl peloter; vi sl se peloter

**can-opener** n ouvre-boîte(s) m

**canopy** n baldaquin m, dais m, ciel m de lit; fig voûte f; vt surmonter d'un baldaquin, d'un dais, etc

¹**cant** n surface inclinée; inclinaison f; (bevel) biseau m; (movement) poussée déviatrice; vt pencher, incliner; biseauter; vi pencher, s'incliner

²**cant** n jargon m; hypocrisie f; vi employer un jargon; parler hypocritement

**cantaloup(e)** n cantaloup m

**cantankerous** adj revêche, hargneux -euse

**cantankerousness** n hargne f, mauvaise humeur

**cantata** n mus cantate f

**canteen** n cantine f; mil (mess-tin) gamelle f; mil (water-bottle) bidon m; (cutlery) ménagère f

**canter** n canter m; **win in a ~** gagner facilement; coll arriver dans un fauteuil; vt mener au canter; vi aller au canter

**canticle** n cantique m

**cantilever** n eng cantilever m; adj cantilever invar

**canto** n chant m

**canton** n canton m

**cantonment** n mil cantonnement m

**canvas** n grosse toile f; (tapestry) canevas m; arts tableau m, toile f; fig canevas m; **under ~** sous la tente; naut sous voiles

**canvass** n pol campagne électorale; campagne f publicitaire; vt pol (elector) solliciter la voix de; (customer) visiter; vi pol solliciter des voix; comm visiter

la clientèle

**canvassing** n pol démarchage électoral

**canyon** n cañon m

**cap** n (baby, lace, bathing) bonnet m; (judge, fur) toque f; (officer, jockey, schoolboy) casquette f; (bottle, tube) capsule f; eccles calotte f; (fountain pen) capuchon m; (mot bouchon m; ~ **in hand** humblement; **percussion ~** amorce f; **set one's ~ at** jeter son dévolu sur; vt (person) coiffer; (bottle) capsuler; sp choisir pour l'équipe nationale; couvrir; fig surpasser; renchérir sur

**capability** n compétence f, capacité f; **capabilities** moyens mpl, possibilités fpl

**capable** adj capable, compétent; ~ **of** capable de; (likely) susceptible de

**capacious** adj spacieux -ieuse, vaste

**capaciousness** n grande capacité

**capacity** n capacité f, faculté f; aptitude f, talent m; (size) capacité f, contenance f; (position) qualité f

¹**cape** n cape f, pèlerine f

²**cape** n geog cap m, promontoire m

¹**caper** n (shrub) câprier m; cul câpre f

²**caper** n cabriole f, entrechat m; vi cabrioler, gambader

**capillary** n capillaire m; adj capillaire

¹**capital** n archi chapiteau m

²**capital** n geog capitale f; (letter) majuscule f; comm capital m, capitaux mpl; **working ~** fonds mpl de roulements; adj (crime) capital; important, signifiant, essentiel -ielle; (mistake) désastreux -euse, fatal (pl fatals); coll au poil; naut ~ **ship** cuirassé m

**capitalism** n capitalisme m

**capitalist** n capitaliste

**capitalization** n capitalisation f

**capitalize** vt capitaliser; fig tourner à son avantage

**capitation** n capitation f

**capitulate** vi capituler

**capitulation** n capitulation f

**capon** n chapon m

**caprice** n caprice m

**capricious** adj capricieux -ieuse

**capriciousness** n caprice m, inconstance f

**Capricorn** n Capricorne m

**capsize** n chavirement m; vt faire chavirer; vi chavirer

**capstan** n naut cabestan m

**capsular** adj capsulaire

**capsule** n med + anat capsule f; (bottle) capsule f

**captain** n mil + sp + naut capitaine m; (navy) capitaine m de vaisseau; comm chef m; vt mil commander; fig diriger

**captaincy** n mil grade m de capitaine

**caption** n (title-heading) en-tête m; (illustration) légende f; (film) sous-titre m

**captious** adj (person) vétilleux -euse, pointilleux -euse; (argument) critique

**captivate** vt fasciner, captiver, séduire

**captivating** adj fascinant, enchanteur (f enchanteresse)

**captive** n captif -ive, prisonnier -ière; adj captif -ive, prisonnier -ière

**captivity** n captivité f

**captor** n personne f qui capture

**capture** n capture f, prise f; vt capturer

**car** n voiture f, automobile f; (railway) wagon m, voiture f; ~ car = carte grise; ~ **park** parking m; ~ **sleeper** train m autocouchettes

**carafe** n carafe f

**caramel** n caramel m

**carat** n carat m

**caravan** n (desert) caravane f; (gipsy) roulotte f; mot caravane f

**caraway** n cumin m, carvi m

**carbide** n chem carbure m

**carbine** n carabine f

**carbohydrate** n chem hydrate m de carbone, glucide m

**carbolic** adj chem phénique; ~ **acid** phénol m

**carbon** n chem + elect carbone m; graphite m; (typing) (papier m) carbone m

**carbon-copy** n double m au carbone, carbone m

**carbonic** adj chem carbonique

**carboniferous** adj carbonifère

**carbonize** vt carboniser

**carborundum** n carborundum m

**carboy** n bonbonne f

**carbuncle** n (jewel) escarboucle f; (boil) anthrax m invar

**carburettor, carburetter** n mot carburateur m

**carcass, carcase** n carcasse f

**carcinoma** n med carcinome m

¹**card** n carte f; carte postale; carte f de visite; (compass) rose f des vents; coll (person) numéro m, original -e; **get one's ~ s** être licencié; **on the ~ s** probable; **play one's ~ s well** manœuvrer habilement; **put one's ~ s on the table** jouer cartes sur table, jouer franc jeu

²**card** n carde f; vt carder

**cardboard** n carton m; adj fig factice; raide

**cardiac** adj cardiaque

**cardigan** n cardigan m

¹**cardinal** n eccles cardinal m

²**cardinal** adj cardinal; (colour) rouge vif invar

**card-index** n fichier m, catalogue m sur fiches

**cardiogram** n cardiogramme m

**cardiograph** n cardiographe m

**cardiography** n cardiographie f

**cardiology** n cardiologie f

**cardsharper** n bonneteur m, tricheur -euse

**card-table** n table f de jeu

**care** n attention f, soin m, sollicitude f; précaution f; (anxiety) souci m; ~ **of** aux bons soins de; **take** ~ faire attention, prendre garde; **take** ~ **of** prendre soin de; vi se soucier; ~ **for** avoir de l'affection pour, avoir de la sympathie pour; prendre soin de; **I couldn't** ~ **less** je m'en fiche; **not** ~ être indifférent

**careen** vt naut caréner; vi naut donner de la bande

**careenage** n naut carénage m

**career** n carrière f, profession f; course f; vi aller à toute vitesse, se ruer

**careerist** n arriviste

**carefree** adj insouciant, sans souci

**careful** adj attentif -ive; prudent, circonspect; (work) soigné; (worker) soigneux -euse

**careless** adj insouciant, sans souci; négligent, inattentif -ive; naturel -elle, spontané

**caress** n caresse f; vt caresser; (soothe) câliner, cajoler

**caressing** adj caressant

**caretaker** n gardien -ienne, concierge

**car-ferry** n car-ferry m

**cargo** n cargaison f

**cargo-boat** n cargo m

**caribou** n caribou m

**caricature** n caricature f; vt caricaturer

**caries** n med carie f

**carillon** n carillon m

**carious** adj med carié

**carmine** n carmin m; adj carmin invar

**carnage** n carnage m

**carnal** adj charnel -elle, sensuel -elle; sexuel -elle; ~ **knowledge** rapports sexuels

**carnality** n sensualité f

**carnation** n bot œillet m; (colour) incarnat m; adj incarnat

**carnival** n carnaval m (pl carnavals), fête f

**carnivore** n carnivore m

**carnivorous** adj carnivore, carnassier -ière

**carol** n mus chant m allègre; (Christmas) noël m; vt chanter; vi chanter allègrement

**carotid** n anat carotide f; adj carotide

**carousal** n beuverie f

**carouse** n beuverie f; vi faire la noce

¹**carp** n zool carpe f

²**carp** vi critiquer, trouver à redire

**carpenter** n charpentier m; (joiner)

menuisier *m*; *vi* faire de la menuiserie

**carpentry** *n* charpenterie *f*; menuiserie *f*

**carpet** *n* tapis *m*; **on the ~** (under discussion) sur le tapis; *coll* (rebuke) sur la sellette; *vt* recouvrir d'un tapis; *coll* mettre sur la sellette

**carpet-slipper** *n* pantoufle *f*

**carpet-sweeper** *n* balai *m* mécanique

**carping** *n* chicanerie *f*; *adj* chicanier -ière

**carriage** *n* transport *m*; port *m*; (charges) frais *mpl* de port; (bearing) maintien *m*, posture *f*; wagon *m*, voiture *f*; (typewriter) chariot *m*; (gun) affût *m*; **~ forward** port dû; **~ paid** port payé

**carriageway** *n* chaussée *f*

**Carribean** *n* mer *f* des Antilles (des Caraïbes)

**carrier** *n* roulier *m*, voiturier *m*; *med* porteur *m* de microbes, vecteur *m*; (bicycle) porte-bagages *m*

**carrier-bag** *n* sac *m* en papier (en plastique)

**carrier-pigeon** *n* pigeon voyageur

**carrion** *n* chair *f* en putréfaction

**carrot** *n* carotte *f*

**carroty** *adj* roux (*f* rousse)

**carry** *n* (ball, bullet) portée *f*; *vt* porter, transporter, charrier; (capture) enlever, emporter; (bear child) porter; (include) comporter; *archi* supporter, soutenir; (pipe) amener; *math* reporter; **~ all before one** marcher en vainqueur; **~ down** descendre; *comm* **~ forward**, **~ over** reporter; **~ in** rentrer; **~ off** (s/o) enlever; (sth) emporter; (prize) remporter; **~ off well** se tirer d'affaire avec aisance; **~ on** poursuivre, continuer; (trade, business) exercer; **~ out** emporter; exécuter, accomplir; **~ the day** gagner la bataille; **~ through** mener à terme; **~ up** monter; **~ weight** avoir de l'influence; *vi* effectuer des transports; (voice) porter; **~ on** continuer, persister; *coll* se comporter d'une façon idiote; flirter; **~ oneself** se tenir

**carry-cot** *n* lit d'enfant portatif

**cart** *n* charrette *f*; **hand ~** charrette *f* à bras; **put the ~ before the horse** mettre la charrue devant les bœufs

**carte (à la)** *adv phr* à la carte

**carte-blanche** *n* carte blanche *f*

**cartel** *n* cartel *m*

**carthorse** *n* cheval *m* de trait

**Carthusian** *n* chartreux -euse

**cartilage** *n* *anat* cartilage *m*

**cartographer** *n* cartographe

**cartography** *n* cartographie *f*

**cartomancy** *n* cartomancie *f*

**carton** *n* carton *m*; (target) blanc *m*, mouche *f*

**cartoon** *n* *arts* carton *m*; caricature *f*; dessin *m* satirique; *cin* dessin animé

**cartoonist** *n* caricaturiste

**cartridge** *n* (small-arms) cartouche *f*; (gun) gargousse *f*; (record player) cellule *f*; **blank ~** cartouche *f* à blanc

**cartridge-paper** *n* papier *m* à cartouche

**cart-track** *n* chemin muletier

**cart-wheel** *n* roue *f* de charrette; (somersault) roue *f*

**carve** *vt* sculpter, ciseler, tailler; *cul* découper; **~ out** tailler; **~ up** dépecer

**carving** *n* sculpture *f*; *cul* découpage *m*

**carving-knife** *n* couteau *m* à découper

**caryatid** *n* cariatide *f*

**cascade** *n* cascade *f*; *vi* cascader

**¹case** *n* cas *m*, fait *m*, circonstance *f*; (plight) état *m*, position *f*; argument *m*; *leg* affaire *f*, procès *m*; *med* **~ history** dossier médical; **~ in point** bon exemple; **as the ~ may be** selon le cas; **in any ~** en tout cas; **in ~** au besoin; dans le cas où; **in ~ of** en cas de; **in that ~** dans ce cas, si cela arrive; **put the ~ that** supposez que

**²case** *n* caisse *f*, boîte *f*; (casing) enveloppe *f*; (cigarettes, glasses) étui *m*; (jewels) écrin *m*; (display) vitrine *f*; *print* casse *f*; *print* **lower ~** bas *m* de casse; *print* **upper ~** haut *m* de casse; *vt* mettre en caisse

**casein** *n* caséine *f*

**case-law** *n* *leg* précédents *mpl*

**casemate** *n* *mil* casemate *f*

**casement** *n* *bui* fenêtre *f* à battants

**cash** *n* argent *m* liquide (comptant), espèces *fpl*; *coll* fric *m*; **~ on delivery**, **c.o.d.** livraison *f* contre remboursement; **pay ~ down** payer comptant; *coll* payer cash; *vt* (cheque) encaisser, toucher; **~ in on** profiter de

**cash-book** *n* livre *m* de caisse

**cash-flow** *n* cash-flow *m*

**¹cashier** *n* caissier -ière

**²cashier** *vt* *mil* casser; renvoyer

**cashmere** *n* cachemire *m*

**cash-register** *n* caisse enregistreuse

**casing** *n* enveloppe *f*; *mech* revêtement *m*

**casino** *n* casino *m*

**cask** *n* barrique *f*, tonneau *m*

**casket** *n* écrin *m*, coffret *m*

**cassava** *n* manioc *m*

**casserole** *n* *cul* (pot) cocotte *f*; (food) ragoût *m* en cocotte

**cassock** *n* soutane *f*

**cast** *n* lancement *m*, jet *m*; (dice) coup *m*; (angling) lancer *m*; *theat* distribution *f*; (metal) fonte *f*; (mould) moule *m*; *med* plâtre *m*; *med* strabisme *m*; (snake) dépouille *f*; *fig* trempe *f*; disposition *f*; *vt* lancer, jeter; (glance, anchor) jeter; (shed) perdre; *arts + eng* mouler; *theat* distribuer les rôles de; ~ **aside** mettre de côté, rejeter; ~ **away** rejeter, repousser; ~ **off** rejeter; (knitting) arrêter (les mailles); *naut* larguer; ~ **out** chasser, expulser; ~ **up** (sea) rejeter; vomir; (eyes) lever au ciel; ~ **a vote** voter; *vi* (angling) jeter la ligne; (eyes) loucher; ~ **about for how to** chercher le moyen de; ~ **off** *naut* larguer les amarres; (knitting) arrêter les mailles

**castanets** *npl* castagnettes *fpl*

**castaway** *n* naufragé -e

**caste** *n* caste *f*; *fig* élite *f*

**castellated** *adj* crénelé

**caster, castor** *n* (salt, sugar, etc) saupoudroir *m*; (furniture) roulette *f*; ~ **sugar** sucre *m* en poudre

**castigate** *vt* châtier, punir

**castigation** *n* châtiment *m*, punition *f*

**casting** *n* *mech* fonte *f*; *mech* pièce fondue; *arts* moulage *m*; *theat* distribution *f* des rôles

**casting-vote** *n* voix prépondérante

**cast-iron** *n* fonte *f*; *adj fig* de fer, certain

**castle** *n* château fort; (chess) tour *f*; ~ **in the air**, ~ **s in Spain** châteaux *mpl* en Espagne; *vi* (chess) roquer

**cast-off** *n* ~ **s** (clothes) frusques *fpl*; *adj* rejeté

¹**castor** *n see* **caster**

²**castor** *n zool* castor *m*

**castor-oil** *n* huile *f* de ricin

**castrate** *vt* châtrer, émasculer, castrer

**castration** *n* castration *f*

**casual** *adj* (chance) fortuit, de hasard; (uncaring) insouciant, désinvolte; (clothes) de sport; ~ **labourer** travailleur *m* temporaire; ~ **ward** asile *m* de nuit

**casualty** *n* *med* accidenté -e; victime *f*; *mil* **casualties** pertes *fpl*; *mil* ~ **list** état *m* des pertes; ~ **(ward)** service *m* des urgences

**casuist** *n* casuiste

**casuistic** *adj* de casuiste

**casuistry** *n* casuistique *f*

**cat** *n* chat *m* (*f* chatte); *zool* félin -e; *coll pej* (woman) chipie *f*; *naut* bossoir *m*; *sl* joueur *m* de swing; *abbr* (cat o' nine tails) chat *m* à neuf queues; **a** ~ **may look at a king** même les plus humbles ont des droits; **enough to make a** ~ **laugh** extrêmement drôle; *coll* **it's raining** ~ **s and dogs** il pleut à verse; **see which way the** ~ **jumps** attendre le déroulement des événements; **when the** ~ **'s away the mice will play** quand le chat n'est pas là les souris dansent; *vt naut* lever (l'ancre) au bossoir; *vi sl* dégueuler

**cataclysm** *n* cataclysme *m*

**catacomb** *n* catacombe *f*

**catafalque** *n* catafalque *m*

**catalepsy** *n* catalepsie *f*

**cataleptic** *adj* cataleptique

**catalogue** *n* catalogue *m*; *vt* cataloguer

**Catalonia** *n* Catalogne *f*

**catalysis** *n* *chem* catalyse *f*

**catalyst** *n* *chem* catalyseur *m*

**catamaran** *n* *naut* catamaran *m*

**cataplasm** *n* cataplasme *m*

**catapult** *n* catapulte *f*; *vt* catapulter

**cataract** *n* *geog + med* cataracte *f*; cascade *f*; torrent *m*; trombe *f*, déluge *m*

**catarrh** *n* catarrhe *m*

**catarrhal** *adj* catarrheux -euse

**catastrophe** *n* catastrophe *f*

**catastrophic** *adj* catastrophique, désastreux -euse

**cat-burglar** *n* cambrioleur -euse; *sl* monte-en-l'air *m invar*

**catcall** *n* sifflet *m*, huée *f*

**catch** *n* prise *f*, capture *f*; (buckle) ardillon *m*; (lock) loquet *m*; (window) loqueteau *m*; (cog-wheel) cliquet *m*; (fish) pêche *f*; *mus* chanson *f* à reprises; (trick) attrape *f*; (snag) hic *m*, difficulté *f*; *coll* (marriage) beau parti; *vt* attraper; (seize) prendre, capturer, saisir; (deceive) attraper, prendre; (surprise) surprendre; (attention) saisir, attirer; (glance) apercevoir; *coll* ~ **it** écoper; *coll* ~ **me doing that again!** on ne m'y reprendra plus; ~ **out** surprendre, prendre; ~ **up** rattraper; *vi* s'accrocher; s'enchevêtrer; (key) accrocher; (fire) prendre; *cul* attacher; *coll* ~ **on** piger; prendre, devenir à la mode

**catching** *adj* contagieux -ieuse; (appealing) prenant

**catchment** *n* captage *m*; ~ **area** *geog* bassin *m*; *fig* aire *f*

**catchword** *n* *print* réclame *f*; slogan *m*

**catchy** *adj* (tune) facile à retenir; (question) insidieux -ieuse

**catechism** *n* catéchisme *m*

**catechist** *n* catéchiste

**catechize** *vt* catéchiser; endoctriner

**categorical** *adj* catégorique

**categorize** *vt* ranger par catégories

**category** *n* catégorie *f*

**cater** *vi* approvisionner; ~ **for** pourvoir à

**caterer** *n* traiteur *m*

**catering** *n* activité *f* de traiteur

**caterpillar** *n* chenille *f*

**caterwaul** *vi* (cat) miauler; (person) brailler

**catgut** *n* *surg* catgut *m*; corde *f* à violon; *sp* corde *f* de raquette

**catharsis** *n* *med + lit* purgation *f*

**cathartic** *adj* purgatif -ive

**cathead** n naut bossoir m
**cathedral** n cathédrale f; adj cathédral
**catherine-wheel** n soleil m; (somersault) roue f; bui rosace f
**catheter** n cathéter m, sonde creuse
**cathode** n elect cathode f; adj cathodique; ~ **ray tube** tube m cathodique
**catholic** n catholique; adj universel -elle; libéral, large d'esprit; (Roman) catholique; **Catholic church** Église catholique (romaine)
**catholicism** n catholicisme m
**catholicity** n universalité f, compréhension f; catholicité f
**catkin** n bot chaton m
**catlick** n toilette f de chat
**cat-like** adj félin
**catnap** n petit somme
**cat-o' nine-tails** n chat m à neuf queues
**cat's-eyes** npl clous mpl à catadioptre
**cats-paw** n coll dupe f; naut vent léger, bouffée f
**cattle** n bétail m; bestiaux mpl; ~ **crossing** passage m de troupeaux
**catty** adj méchant, rosse
**caucus** n groupe m de pression
**caudal** adj caudal
**cauldron** n cul chaudron m
**cauliflower** n chou-fleur m (pl choux-fleurs)
**caulk, calk** vt calfeutrer; naut calfater
**causal** adj causal
**causality** n causalité f
**causation** n causalité f
**cause** n cause f, raison f; motif m; **give ~ for** donner lieu à; **have ~ for** avoir lieu de; **make common ~** agir de concert; vt causer, produire, provoquer; ~ **s/o to do sth** faire faire qch à qn
**causeway** n digue f, chaussée f
**caustic** n caustique m; adj caustique; acerbe, moquant
**cauterization** n cautérisation f
**cauterize** vt cautériser
**cautery** n cautère m
**caution** n prudence f, circonspection f; avertissement m; ~ **money** cautionnement m; vt avertir, donner des conseils de prudence à, mettre en garde
**cautionary** adj avertisseur -euse; moral
**cautious** adj prudent, circonspect
**cautiousness** n prudence f, circonspection f
**cavalcade** n cavalcade f
**cavalier** n cavalier m; hist partisan m du roi Charles 1er d'Angleterre; adj sans souci, libre; dédaigneux -euse
**cavalry** n cavalerie f
**cave** n caverne f; vi ~ **in** s'effondrer; coll fig se soumettre, céder
**cave** interj coll pet!
**caveat** n avertissement m; leg notification f d'opposition
**cave-man** n homme m des cavernes
**cavern** n caverne f
**cavernous** adj caverneux -euse
**caviar, caviare** n caviar m
**cavil** n ergoterie f, chicane f; vi chicaner, ergoter
**cavity** n cavité f, creux m, trou m (pl trous)
**cavort** vi coll cabrioler
**caw** n croassement m; vi croasser
**cayenne** n cul poivre m de Cayenne
**cease** n without ~ sans cesse; vt cesser, arrêter; vi cesser, s'arrêter
**cease-fire** n mil cessez-le-feu m invar
**cedar** n cèdre m
**cede** vt céder
**cedilla** n gramm cédille f
**ceiling** n plafond m
**celebrant** n eccles célébrant m
**celebrate** vt célébrer, solenniser, fêter; vi célébrer; coll s'amuser
**celebrated** adj célèbre, éminent
**celebration** n célébration f, commémoration f; coll bringue f
**celebrity** n célébrité f; coll grosse légume
**celeriac** n céleri-rave m
**celerity** n célérité f
**celery** n céleri m
**celesta** n mus célesta m
**celestial** adj céleste
**celibacy** n célibat m
**celibate** n + adj célibataire
**cell** n cellule f
**cellar** n cave f
**cellist** n mus violoncelliste
**cello** n mus violoncelle m
**cellophane** n cellophane f
**cellular** adj cellulaire
**celluloid** n celluloïd m
**cellulose** n cellulose f; adj en (de) cellulose
**Celt** n Celte
**Celtic** n celtique m; adj celtique, celte
**cement** n ciment m; vt cimenter
**cement-mixer** n bétonnière f
**cemetery** n cimetière m
**cenotaph** n cénotaphe m
**censer** n eccles encensoir m
**censor** n censeur m; vt censurer
**censorial** adj censorial
**censorious** adj pointilleux -euse, désapprobateur -trice, dénigreur -euse
**censorship** n censure f
**censure** n blâme m, réprobation f; critique f, censure f; vt censurer, blâmer
**census** n recensement m
**centaur** n centaure m
**centenarian** n + adj centenaire
**centenary** n centenaire m
**centigrade** adj centigrade
**centigramme** n centigramme m

**centilitre** *n* centilitre *m*

**centimetre** *n* centimètre *m*

**centipede** *n* mille-pattes *m invar*

**central** *adj* central

**centralization** *n* centralisation *f*

**centralize** *vt* centraliser; *vi* se centraliser

**centre** *n* centre *m*; foyer *m*; *sp* ~ **for-ward** avant-centre *m* (*pl* avants-centres); *sp* ~ **half** demi-centre *m*; ~ **of attraction** point *m* de mire; ~ **of gravity** centre *m* de gravité; *adj* central; *vt* centrer; (hopes, etc) concentrer; *vi* se concentrer; (converge) se rassembler

**centre-board** *n naut* quille *f* mobile, dérive *f*

**centric** *adj* central

**centrifugal** *adj* centrifuge

**centrifuge** *n* centrifugeur *m*, centrifugeuse *f*

**centripetal** *adj* centripète

**centuple** *adj* centuple; *vt* centupler

**centurion** *n* centurion *m*

**century** *n* siècle *m*

**ceramic** *adj* céramique

**ceramics** *npl arts* céramique *f*

**cereal** *n* céréale *f*; ~ **s** (breakfast food) flocons *mpl* de céréales

**cerebellum** *n anat* cervelet *m*

**cerebral** *adj* cérébral

**cerebration** *n* activité *f* du cerveau; *coll* **do a little** ~ se creuser la cervelle

**cerebro-spinal** *adj* cérébro-spinal

**cerebrum** *n* cerveau *m*

**ceremonial** *n* cérémonial *m* (*pl* cérémonials); *eccles* rituel *m*; *adj* de cérémonie

**ceremonious** *adj* cérémonieux -ieuse

**ceremony** *n* cérémonie *f*; **stand on** ~ faire des façons

**cert** *n sl* bon tuyau; **it's a (dead)** ~ c'est du tout cuit

**certain** *adj* certain, sûr; assuré; précis; indiscutable, indéniable; (quantity) certain, appréciable; **for** ~ assurément; **make** ~ **of** s'assurer de

**certainly** *adv* certainement, sans doute; ~ **!** mais bien sûr!

**certainty** *n* certitude *f*; conviction *f*; ce qui est sûr d'arriver, fait certain

**certifiable** *adj* certifiable; *coll* dingue

**certificate** *n* certificat *m*; (examination) diplôme *m*; **bankrupt's** ~ concordat *m*; *vt* donner un certificat à; diplômer

**certify** *vt* certifier; garantir; *med* interner

**certitude** *n* certitude *f*

**cessation** *n* cessation *f*; interruption *f*

**cession** *n leg* cession *f*

**cesspit, cesspool** *n* fosse *f* d'aisance

**cetacean** *n zool* cétacé *m*

**chaconne** *n mus* chaconne *f*

**chafe** *n* éraflure *f*, écorchure *f*; *fig* irritation *f*; *vt* frotter; érafler, irriter; *vi* s'érafler, s'écorcher; *fig* s'irriter; ~ **against** s'érafler contre

**chaff** *n* balle *f*; paille hâchée; *coll* taquinerie *f*; *fig* vétille *f*; *vt* taquiner

**chaffer** *n* marchandage *m*; *vi* marchander

**chaffinch** *n* pinson *m*

**chafing-dish** *n cul* chaufferette *f*

**chagrin** *n* chagrin *m*, contrariété *f*; irritation *f*; déception *f*; *vt* chagriner, contrarier

**chain** *n* chaîne *f*; (fetters) ~ **s** fers *mpl*; *vt* enchaîner; barrer à l'aide d'une chaîne

**chain-bridge** *n* pont suspendu

**chain-drive** *n eng* transmission *f* par chaîne

**chain-gang** *n* forçats *mpl* à la chaîne

**chain-mail** *n* armure *f* de mailles

**chain-reaction** *n* réaction *f* en chaîne

**chain-saw** *n* scie *f* à chaînette

**chain-smoker** *n* fumeur -euse invétéré -e

**chain-store** *n* magasin *m* à succursales multiples

**chair** *n* chaise *f*, siège *m*; (university) chaire *f*; (meeting) fauteuil *m* du président; *US coll* chaise *f* électrique; *vt* porter en triomphe; (meeting) présider

**chairman** *n* (meeting, company) président -e; **Madam** ~ Madame la présidente

**chairmanship** *n* présidence *f*

**chairperson** *n* président -e

**chalcedony, calcedony** *n* calcédoine *f*

**chalet** *n* chalet *m*

**chalice** *n eccles* + *bot* calice *m*; coupe *f*

**chalk** *n* craie *f*; (piece) bâton *m* de craie; **by a long** ~ de beaucoup, de loin; **French** ~ talc *m*; **not know** ~ **from cheese** ne pas savoir distinguer entre le jour et la nuit; *vt* marquer à la craie; ~ **out** tracer; ~ **up** (tally) porter sur l'ardoise

**chalk-pit** *n* carrière *f* de craie

**chalky** *adj* crayeux -euse

**challenge** *n* défi *m*; *sp* challenge *m*; *mil* sommation *f*; *leg* récusation *f*; *fig* provocation *f*, épreuve *f*; *vt* défier; provoquer en duel; mettre en question, contester; *mil* faire une sommation à; *leg* récuser

**challenger** *n* provocateur -trice; *sp* challenger *m*

**challenging** *adj* qui provoque

**chamber** *n* chambre *f*; salle *f*; (firearm) chambre *f*; *med* chambre *f*, cavité *f*; *leg* ~ **s** cabinet *m* de juge (ou d'avocat); *vt* évider

**chamberlain** *n hist* chambellan *m*

**chambermaid** *n* femme *f* de chambre

**chamber-music** *n* musique *f* de chambre

**chamber-pot** *n* pot *m* de chambre, vase *m* de nuit

**chameleon** *n* caméléon *m*

**chamfer** *n* chanfrein *m*; *vt* chanfreiner

**chammy-leather** *n* chamois *m*

**chamois** *n zool* chamois *m*; (leather) chamois *m*; ~ **leather** peau *f* de chamois

**champ** *vt* + *vi* mâchonner, mâcher; ~ **at the bit** ronger son frein

**champagne** *n* champagne *m*

**champion** *n* champion -ionne; défenseur *m*; *adj coll* de première classe, suprême; *coll* fantastique, fameux -euse, au poil; *vt* défendre comme champion; *fig* défendre, soutenir

**championship** *n* championnat *m*; *fig* défense *f*

**chance** *n* chance *f*, hasard *m*; bonne chance; possibilité *f*, occasion *f*; risque *m*; **take one's** ~ courir sa chance; the main ~ possibilité *f* de gain personnel; *adj* fortuit, accidentel -elle; *vt* risquer, courir la chance de; *vi* (happen) arriver; avoir l'occasion de; ~ **upon** trouver par hasard, rencontrer par hasard

**chancel** *n eccles* chœur *m*

**chancellery** *n* chancellerie *f*

**chancellor** *n* chancelier *m*; *pol* Chancellor of the Exchequer = ministre *m* des Finances

**chancery** *n leg* section *f* de la Haute Cour en Angleterre

**chancre** *n med* chancre *m*

**chancy** *adj coll* incertain, douteux -euse, chanceux -euse

**chandelier** *n* lustre *m*

**chandler** *n* marchand *m* de chandelles; *naut* ships' ~ marchand *m* de fournitures pour bateaux

**change** *n* changement *m*; variété *f*, distraction *f*; (replacement) rechange *m*; échange *m*; (money) monnaie *f*; vicissitudes *fpl*, hauts *mpl* et bas *mpl*; ~ of life retour *m* d'âge, ménopause *f*; get no ~ out of ne pouvoir rien tirer de; it makes a ~ ça vous change les idées; just for a ~ pour changer un peu; *fig* ring the ~s répéter en variant; *vt* transformer; modifier; échanger; changer; (clothes) changer de; *mot* ~ gear changer de vitesse; *vi* changer; se transformer, se modifier; *mot* ~ down rétrograder; ~ over passer de; *mot* ~ up passer à une vitesse supérieure

**changeability** *n* inconstance *f*

**changeable** *adj* changeant, variable, inconstant

**changeless** *adj* constant, immuable

**channel** *n* (river-bed) lit *m*; *naut* chenal *m*; *geog* détroit *m*; (groove) cannelure *f*; canal *m*, conduit *m*; *rad* (television) chaîne *f*; voie *f* de communication; the English Channel la Manche; usual ~ s

voie *f* hiérarchique; *vt* creuser des canaux dans; canaliser; canneler

**chant** *n eccles* psalmodie *f*, plain-chant *m* (*pl* plains-chants); chant *m* monotone; *vt eccles* psalmodier; (verse) réciter; (celebrate) chanter

**chaos** *n* chaos *m*

**chaotic** *adj* chaotique

¹**chap** *n coll* type *m*

²**chap** *n* gerçure *f*; *vt* gercer; *vi* se gercer

**chapel** *n* chapelle *f*; (non-conformist) temple *m*; *typ* association syndicale

**chaperon** *n* chaperon *m*; *hist* duègne *f*; *vt* chaperonner

**chaplain** *n eccles* chapelain *m*; *mil* aumônier *m*

**chapped** *adj* gercé

**chaps** *npl* mâchoire *f*

**chapter** *n* chapitre *m*; *eccles* chapitre *m*; ~ of accidents suite *f* de malheurs; give ~ and verse citer ses autorités

¹**char** *n zool* ombre *m*, omble *m*

²**char** *n coll* thé *m*

³**char** *n coll* femme *f* de ménage; *vi coll* faire des ménages

⁴**char** *vt* charbonner; roussir; *vi* roussir

**charabanc** *n obs* car *m*, autocar *m*

**character** *n* caractère *m*, naturel *m*, nature *f*, tempérament *m*; (writing) caractère *m*, écriture *f*; *print* lettre *f*; (type) genre *m*, caractéristique *f*; fermeté *f*, volonté *f*, énergie *f*; réputation *f*; personnalité *f*; (literature) personnage *m*; *coll* type *m*, numéro *m*; (testimonial) certificat *m* (de bonnes mœurs), attestation *f*; *theat* ~ part rôle *m* de composition; in ~ typique

**characteristic** *n* caractéristique *f*; *adj* caractéristique, typique

**characterization** *n* caractérisation *f*

**characterize** *vt* caractériser; décrire; dépeindre

**characterless** *adj* sans caractère; sans certificat

**charade** *n* charade *f*

**charcoal** *n* charbon *m* de bois; (colour) gris foncé

**charge** *n* charge *f*; (burden) faix *m*, fardeau *m*; responsabilité *f*; soin *m*; recommandation *f*; fonction *f*, emploi *m*; (cost) coût *m*, prix *m*; **give in** ~ livrer à la police; **in** ~ **of** responsable de; **in the** ~ **of** confié aux soins de; *vt* charger; faire responsable; *leg* accuser, inculper; (price) compter, faire payer; *fig* imputer; *vi mil* charger; donner l'ordre

**chargeable** *adj* imputable, à la charge; *leg* accusable

¹**charger** *n* grand plat

²**charger** *n* cheval *m* de bataille

**chariness** *n* prudence *f*

**chariot** n chariot m; char m

**charisma** n charisme m

**charitable** adj charitable; indulgent

**charity** n charité f; indulgence f, bienveillance f; générosité f; (alms) aumône f; œuvre f de bienfaisance; **cold as ~** insensible, négligent; adj charitable; de charité

**charlady** n femme f de ménage

**charlatan** n charlatan m

**charlatanism** n charlatanisme m

**charlotte** n cul charlotte f

**charm** n charme m; (spell) enchantement m; séduction f; amulette f, talisman m; (on bracelet) breloque f; **like a ~** parfaitement; vt charmer, enchanter; calmer; plaire à

**charmer** n charmeur -euse; enchanteur m (f enchanteresse)

**charming** adj charmant, enchanteur (f enchanteresse)

**charnel-house** n charnier m

**chart** n naut carte f; plan m; graphique m; med courbe f; **organization ~** organigramme m; vt naut (position) établir

**charter** n charte f; leg statuts mpl; vt (plane, ship, etc) affréter; accorder une charte à; **~ed accountant** expert-comptable m (pl experts-comptables)

**charter-flight** n (vol m) charter m

**charter-party** n naut charte-partie f (pl chartes-parties)

**chartreuse** n chartreuse f

**charwoman** n femme f de ménage

**chary** adj prudent; (frugal) chiche

¹**chase** n chasse f, poursuite f; vt chasser, poursuivre; fig dissiper; **~ after** courir après

²**chase** vt enchâsser, ciseler

**chasm** n gouffre m; abîme m

**chassis** n châssis m

**chaste** adj chaste, pudique; fig pur, raffiné

**chasten** vt châtier, éprouver; modérer

**chastening** n châtiment m; adj qui corrige; purifiant

**chastise** vt battre, fouetter; punir

**chastisement** n correction f

**chastity** n chasteté f; hist **~ belt** ceinture f de chasteté

**chasuble** n eccles chasuble f

**chat** n bavardage m, causette f; **~ show** entretien radiodiffusé (télévisé); vi bavarder, causer; coll **~ up** flatter, amadouer

**chattels** npl possessions fpl; leg biens mpl meubles; **goods and ~** biens mpl et effets mpl

**chatter** n bavardage m; babil m; (teeth) claquement m; vi bavarder; babiller; (teeth) claquer

**chatterbox** n bavard -e; coll moulin m à paroles

**chatty** adj bavard, causeur -euse, familier -ière

**chauffeur** n chauffeur m

**chauvinism** n chauvinisme m

**cheap** adj bon marché, pas cher (f chère), avantageux -euse; pej sans valeur, de pauvre qualité; (person) vulgaire; **dirt ~** vraiment pas cher; **on the ~** au rabais; adv à bon marché

**cheapen** vt baisser le prix de; **~ oneself** se déconsidérer; vi baisser

**cheapness** n bon marché; fig médiocrité f, vulgarité f

**cheat** n trompeur -euse, filou m, escroc m; tricheur -euse; vt tromper, duper, rouler, escroquer; vi tromper, tricher

**check** n arrêt m, obstacle m; contrôle m, vérification f; (cloakroom, baggage) ticket m; (pattern) carreau m, damier m; US chèque m; US (bill) note f; (restaurant) addition f; adj à carreaux, à damiers; vt arrêter, enrayer; vérifier; contrôler; examiner; (chess) faire échec à; US **~ out** vérifier; **~ up** vérifier; vi s'arrêter; hésiter; **~ in** (hotel) s'inscrire; (airport) présenter son billet; (hotel) **~ out** payer sa note; **~ up on** se renseigner sur

**checkbook** n US see **cheque-book**

**check-list** n liste f de contrôle

**checkmate** n (chess) échec m et mat m; fig échec m, défaite f; vt (chess) mater; frustrer, circonvenir

**check-out** n (supermarket) caisse f

**checkpoint** n contrôle m

**check-room** n US vestiaire m

**check-up** n contrôle m, vérification f; med check-up m invar, bilan m de santé

**cheek** n joue f; coll toupet m, effronterie f; coll (buttock) fesse f; **~ by jowl with** s/o côte à côte avec qn

**cheekbone** n pommette f

**cheeky** adj effronté, impudent

**cheep** n gazouillis m; vi gazouiller

**cheer** n gaieté f, allégresse f; état m d'esprit; (food) chère f, nourriture f; (solace) soulagement m; acclamations fpl; **of good ~** heureux -euse, content; vt encourager, réconforter; acclamer, applaudir; égayer; **~ up** réconforter; vi encourager; applaudir; **~ up** s'égayer

**cheerful** adj gai, allègre, heureux -euse

**cheeriness** n gaieté f, allégresse f, bonne humeur

**cheering** n acclamations fpl, applaudissements mpl; adj réconfortant, réjouissant

**cheerio** interj coll au revoir!, ciao!

cheerless

**cheerless** *adj* morne, triste, misérable
**cheers** *interj coll* à la vôtre!
**cheery** *adj* animé, gai, allègre; *pej* trop empressé
**¹cheese** *n* fromage *m*
**²cheese** *vt sl* ~ **it** ta gueule!; halte-là!
**cheesecake** *n* tarte *f* au fromage blanc; *coll* photo *f* de pin-up
**cheesed** *adj coll* ennuyé, emmerdé
**cheesemonger** *n* marchand -e de fromages
**cheeseparing** *n* avarice *f*, pingrerie *f*; *adj* avare, pingre
**cheesy** *adj* caséeux -éeuse
**cheetah** *n zool* guépard *m*
**chef** *n* chef *m*, cuisinier *m*, chef *m* de cuisine
**chef-d'œuvre** *n* (*pl* chefs-d'œuvre) chef-d'œuvre *m* (*pl* chefs-d'œuvre)
**chemical** *n* produit *m* chimique; *adj* chimique
**chemise** *n* (for women) chemise *f*
**chemist** *n* (researcher) chimiste *f*; (dispenser) pharmacien -ienne
**chemistry** *n* chimie *f*
**chemotherapy** *n* chimiothérapie *f*
**cheque** *n* chèque *m*
**cheque-book** *n* carnet *m* de chèques, chéquier *m*
**chequer** *n* carreau *m*, damier *m*; *vt* orner de carreaux (de damiers), quadriller; diversifier; ~ **ed career** vie mouvementée, vie *f* avec des hauts et des bas
**cherish** *vt* chérir; *fig* entretenir; nourrir
**cherry** *n* cerise *f*; (tree) cerisier *m*; *adj* (colour) cerise *invar*
**cherry-brandy** *n* cherry-brandy *m*, liqueur *f* de cerises
**cherub** *n* chérubin *m*
**cherubic** *adj* de chérubin; (child) dodu; sage
**chervil** *n bot* cerfeuil *m*
**chess** *n* échecs *mpl*
**chessboard** *n* échiquier *m*
**chessmen** *npl* pièces *fpl* de jeu d'échecs
**chest** *n* caisse *f*, boîte *f*, coffre *m*; *anat* poitrine *f*; ~ **of drawers** commode *f*
**chesterfield** *n* sofa capitonné
**chestnut** *n* châtaigne *f*, marron *m*; (horse-chestnut) marron *m* d'Inde; (colour) châtain *m*; (horse) alezan *m*; *coll* (joke) anecdote archi-connue; *adj* châtain *invar*
**chevalier** *n* chevalier *m*
**chevron** *n* chevron *m*
**chew** *n* mâchonnement *m*; *vt* mâcher, mâchonner; (tobacco) chiquer; *vi* chiquer; *fig* ~ **over** ruminer, ressasser
**chewing-gum** *n* chewing-gum *m*, gomme *f* à mâcher
**chiaroscuro** *n* clair-obscur *m* (*pl* clairs-obscurs)

**chic** *n* chic *m*; *adj* chic *invar*
**chicane** *n* chicane *f*; *vt* + *vi* chicaner
**chicanery** *n* chicane *f*, chicanerie *f*, ergoterie *f*
**chichi** *adj coll pej* délicat, affecté
**chick** *n* (chicken) poussin *m*; (young bird) oisillon *m*; *coll US* nana *f*
**chicken** *n* poulet *m*, poularde *f*, poule *f*; *fig* naïf -ïve, tendron *m*; *sl* lâche; **no** ~ d'un certain âge
**chicken-feed** *n* pâtée *f*; *coll fig* qch sans aucune valeur
**chicken-hearted** *adj* peureux -euse
**chickenpox** *n* varicelle *f*
**chicken-run** *n* cage *f* à poules
**chickweed** *n bot* mouron *m*
**chicory** *n* chicorée *f*; (vegetable) endive *f*
**chide** *vt* + *vi* gronder
**chiding** *n* grondement *m*
**chief** *n* chef *m*; *coll* patron -onne; *adj* principal, en chef, plus grand
**chiefly** *adv* surtout, principalement
**chieftain** *n* chef *m*
**chiffon** *n* mousseline *f* de soie
**chignon** *n* chignon *m*
**chilblain** *n* engelure *f*
**child** *n* enfant; *fig* disciple *m*
**childbearing** *n* gestation *f*; (state) grossesse *f*
**childbirth** *n* accouchement *m*
**childhood** *n* enfance *f*; **second** ~ gâtisme *m*, affaiblissement *m*, sénilité *f*
**childish** *adj* enfantin, puéril
**childishness** *n* enfantillage *m*
**childless** *adj* sans enfants
**childlike** *adj* innocent, candide
**chill** *n* refroidissement *m*; froid *m*; *adj* froid, transi, glacé; *vt* refroidir, transir; congeler; *vi* se refroidir
**chilled** *adj* refroidi; congelé
**chilli, chili** *n* piment *m*
**chilliness** *n* froid *m*; froideur *f*
**chilly** *adj* frais (*f* fraîche), frisquet -ette; froid, glacial
**chime** *n* carillon *m*; mélodie *f*; *vt* carillonner; (hour) sonner; *vi* carillonner; *fig* s'accorder
**chimera** *n* chimère *f*
**chimerical** *adj* chimérique
**chimney** *n* cheminée *f*; (lamp) verre *m*
**chimney-breast** *n* trumeau *m*
**chimney-corner** *n* coin *m* du feu
**chimney-piece** *n* manteau *m* de cheminée
**chimney-pot** *n* pot *m* de cheminée, cheminée *f*
**chimney-stack** *n* cheminée *f*; cheminée *f* d'usine
**chimpanzee** *n* chimpanzé *m*
**chin** *n* menton *m*
**China** *n* Chine *f*

**china** *n* porcelaine *f*; vaisselle *f*; *adj* de porcelaine
**china-clay** *n* kaolin *m*
**Chinaman** *n* Chinois *m*
**chinchilla** *n* chinchilla *m*
**chin-chin** *interj* *coll* à la vôtre!
¹**chine** *n* ravin *m*
²**chine** *n* échine *f*
**Chinese** *n* (language) chinois *m*; *adj* chinois; ~ **lantern** lanterne vénitienne
¹**chink** *n* (crack) fente *f*, lézarde *f*
²**chink** *n* (sound) tintement *m*; *vt* faire tinter; *vi* tinter
**chinstrap** *n* mentonnière *f*
**chintz** *n* perse *f*, cretonne imprimée
**chip** *n* fragment *m*, copeau *m*, éclat *m*; (crack) brèche *f*; (gambling) jeton *m*; (potatoes) ~s pommes frites; *US* chips *mpl*; ~ **off the old block** digne rejeton; **have a** ~ **on one's shoulder** en vouloir à tout le monde; **pass in one's** ~s mourir; **silicon** ~ plaquette *f* de silicium; *vt* (wood) faire des copeaux; (glass, plate) ébrécher, écorner; tailler, sculpter; *vi* s'ébrécher, s'écorner; *coll* ~ **in** (conversation) intervenir; (cost) contribuer aux frais; (participate) coopérer dans une entreprise
**chippings** *npl* gravillons *mpl*
**chiromancy** *n* chiromancie *f*
**chiropodist** *n* pédicure *f*
**chiropractic** *n* chiropraxie *f*, chiropractie *f*
**chiropractor** *n* chiropracteur *m*
**chirp** *n* gazouillis *m*, pépiement *m*; *vi* gazouiller, pépier
**chirpy** *adj* *coll* allègre
**chisel** *n* ciseau *m*; (engraving) burin *m*; *vt* ciseler; (engrave) buriner; *fig* *sl* escroquer
**chiselled** *adj* ciselé, buriné; (clear-cut) précis, clair
**chiseller** *n* *sl* escroc *m*
¹**chit** *n* *coll* gamine *f*
²**chit** *n* note *f*, certificat *m*
**chitchat** *n* bavardage *m*
**chitterlings** *npl* tripes *fpl* de porc
**chivalric** *adj* chevaleresque
**chivalrous** *adj* chevaleresque
**chivalry** *n* chevalerie *f*; qualités *fpl* chevaleresques
**chive** *n* *cul* ciboulette *f*, cive *f*, civette *f*
**chivvy**, **chivy** *vt* harceler
**chloral** *n* *chem* chloral *m*
**chlorate** *n* *chem* chlorate *m*
**chloric** *adj* *chem* chlorique
**chloride** *n* *chem* chlorure *m*
**chlorinate** *vt* javelliser
**chlorination** *n* javellisation *f*
**chlorine** *n* *chem* chlore *m*
**chloroform** *n* *med* chloroforme *m*; *vt* chloroformer

**chlorophyll** *n* *bot* chlorophylle *f*
**chlorosis** *n* chlorose *f*
**chlorotic** *adj* chlorotique
**choc-ice** *n* esquimau *m*
**chock** *n* cale *f*; *vt* caler, coincer
**chock-a-block** *adj* plein à craquer
**chock-full** *adj* bondé, plein à craquer
**chocolate** *n* chocolat *m*; *adj* au chocolat; (colour) brun foncé
**choice** *n* choix *m*; assortiment *m*; **Hobson's** ~ aucun choix; *adj* choisi, raffiné; *comm* de première qualité, sélectionné
**choir** *n* *mus* chœur *m*, chorale *f*; *mus* + *eccles* maîtrise *f*; *archi* chœur *m*
**choirboy** *n* enfant *m* de chœur
**choke** *n* étranglement *m*, étouffement *m*; obstruction *f*; *mot* starter *m*; *sl* taule *f*; *vt* étouffer, étrangler; boucher, obstruer; *coll* ~ **off** envoyer promener, décourager; ~ **up** obstruer; *vi* étouffer, s'étrangler
**choker** *n* (necklace) collier *m*; (scarf) foulard *m*
**choky** *adj* étouffant, suffocant
**choler** *n* *ar* bile *f*; colère *f*
**cholera** *n* *med* choléra *m*
**choleric** *adj* colérique, coléreux -euse
**cholesterol** *n* *med* cholestérol *m*
**choose** *vt* choisir; élire; *vi* choisir, décider; **I cannot** ~ **but** je ne peux faire autrement que; **pick and** ~ sélectionner, choisir avec attention
**choosy** *adj* difficile à plaire, chichiteux -euse
¹**chop** *n* (tree) coup *m* de hache; (butcher) coup *m* de hachoir; *cul* côtelette *f*; *coll* **get the** ~ être licencié; *vt* trancher; (tree) donner un coup de hache à; (butcher) donner un coup de hachoir à, hacher; ~ **down** abattre; *vi* donner un coup de hache (de hachoir)
²**chop** *vt* changer; ~ **and change** changer souvent; ~ **logic** ergoter, discutailler; *vi* (wind) varier
**chopper** *n* hache *f*, hachoir *m*; *coll* hélicoptère *m*
**choppy** *adj* (sea) agité
**chops** *npl* mâchoires *fpl*
**chopstick** *n* baguette *f*
**chopsuey** *n* ragoût *m* à la chinoise
**choral** *adj* choral
**chorale** *n* *mus* choral *m* (*pl* chorals)
**chord** *n* corde *f*; *mus* accord *m*; *fig* **strike a** ~ toucher la corde, faire vibrer la corde
**chore** *n* corvée *f*; ~s travaux *mpl* domestiques
**choreographer** *n* chorégraphe *n*
**choreographic** *adj* chorégraphique
**choreography** *n* chorégraphie *f*
**chorister** *n* enfant *m* de chœur

**chortle** n gloussement m; vi glousser

**chorus** n theat + mus chœur m; (in song) refrain m; fig chœur m, concert m

**chorus-girl** n girl f

**chosen** adj choisi; élu; **the ~ people** les Juifs, le peuple élu

**chough** n zool crave m

**chow** n zool chow-chow m

**chowder** n US cul (sorte f de) soupe f de poissons

**Christ** n Christ m

**christen** vt baptiser; donner le nom de

**Christendom** n chrétienté f

**christening** n baptême m

**Christian** n chrétien -ienne; adj chrétien -ienne; fig charitable, bienfaisant, indulgent; **~ name** nom m de baptême, prénom m; **~ Science** scientisme chrétien

**Christianity** n christianisme m

**christianize** vt christianiser

**Christlike** adj semblable au Christ

**Christmas** n Noël m, jour m de Noël; **~ card** carte f de Noël; **Father ~** père m Noël

**Christmas-box** n cadeau m de Noël (en espèces), = étrennes fpl

**Christmastide, Christmas-time** n temps m de Noël, saison f de Noël

**Christmas-tree** n arbre m de Noël

**Christology** n christologie f

**chromatic** adj chromatique

**chromatics** n chromatique f

**chrome** n chrome m, chromate m de plomb; **~ steel** acier chromé

**chromic** adj chem chromique

**chromium** n chem chrome m; **~ plating** chromage m

**chromosome** n biol chromosome m

**chronic** adj med chronique, invétéré; fig chronique; sl terrible

**chronicle** n chronique f; vt écrire (des chroniques), enregistrer (des faits)

**chronicler** n chroniqueur m, historien m

**chronological** adj chronologique

**chronology** n chronologie f

**chronometer** n chronomètre m

**chrysalis** n ent chrysalide f

**chrysanthemum** n bot chrysanthème m

**chrysolite** n chrysolithe f

**chrysoprase** n chrysoprase f

**chub** n zool chevesne f, chevaine f

**chubby** adj joufflu

¹**chuck** n (under the chin) petite tape; action f de lancer; sl **give s/o the ~** balancer qn; vt tapoter; coll lancer, jeter; coll **~ it!** en voilà assez!, ça suffit!; coll **~ out** vider; coll **~ up** renoncer à

²**chuck** n coll (endearment) poulet m, poule f

**chucker-out** n sl videur m

**chuckle** n gloussement m; vi glousser

**chuckling** n gloussements mpl

**chuffed** adj sl vain, content

**chug** n halètement m; teuf-teuf m (pl teufs-teufs); vi haleter, faire teuf-teuf

**chum** n coll copain m; vi coll **~ up with** se lier d'amitié avec

**chummy** adj liant, sociable

**chump** n souche f, bloc m de bois; gros bout; coll idiot -e, balourd -e; **~ chop** côte première de mouton; sl **off one's ~** dingue

**chunk** n gros morceau; (bread) quignon m

**church** n église f; (protestant) temple m; clergé m, ordres mpl; **enter the ~** devenir prêtre, devenir pasteur

**church-goer** n pratiquant -e

**church-service** n office m, service m, culte m

**churchwarden** n marguillier m

**churchyard** n cimetière m

**churl** n malotru -e; avare

**churlish** adj (bad-mannered) grossier -ière; (surly) revêche, grincheux -euse; (mean) avaricieux -ieuse

**churn** n bidon m; (butter-making) baratte f; vt (milk) baratter; battre; fig brasser, agiter; **~ out** produire abondamment; vi bouillonner

**chute** n (river) rapide m; (water overflow) chenal m; (snow) glissoire f

**chutney** n condiment m (à base de fruits, etc), chutney m

**cicada** n zool cigale f

**cicatrice** n cicatrice f

**cicatrize** vt cicatriser; vi se cicatriser

**cider** n cidre m

**cigar** n cigare m

**cigarette** n cigarette f

**cigarette-case** n porte-cigarettes m invar

**cigarette-end** n mégot m

**cigarette-holder** n fume-cigarette m invar

**cinch** n US coll **it's a ~!** c'est du tout cuit!

**cinder** n cendre f; (furnace) scories fpl

**Cinderella** n Cendrillon f

**cinder-path, cinder-track** n piste cendrée

**cine-camera** n caméra f

**cinema** n cinéma m

**Cinemascope** n cinémascope m

**cinematic** adj du cinéma, relatif -ive au cinéma

**cinematograph** n cinématographe m

**cinematography** n cinématographie f

**cine-projector** n projecteur m (de cinéma)

**Cinerama** n cinérama m

**cinerary** adj cinéraire

**Cingalese** adj see Sing(h)alese

**cinnabar** n chem cinabre m

**cinnamon** *n* (tree) cinnamome *m*, cannelier *m*; (spice) cannelle *f*

**cipher** *n math* chiffre *m* arabe; zéro *m*; (code) chiffre *m*; monogramme *m*; *vt* chiffrer; *vi* calculer

**circa** *adv* autour de; *prep* autour de

**circle** *n* cercle *m*; *theat* (premier) balcon; *fig* cercle *m*, sphère *f*; *theat* **upper ~** deuxième balcon *m*; **vicious ~** cercle vicieux; *vt* encercler, entourer; *vi* tourner autour (de)

**circs** *npl coll* circonstances *fpl*

**circuit** *n* circuit *m*, tour *m*; (line or distance round) pourtour *m*; *leg* tournée *f*; *elect* circuit *m*; **closed ~** circuit fermé; **short ~** court circuit; *vt* **short ~** court-circuiter

**circuitous** *adj* indirect, qui fait un détour; *fig* détourné

**circular** *n* circulaire *f*; *adj* circulaire

**circularize** *vt* envoyer des circulaires à

**circulate** *vt* faire circuler; *vi* circuler

**circulation** *n* circulation *f*; (newspaper) tirage *m*

**circumambient** *adj* ambiant

**circumcise** *vt* circoncire

**circumcision** *n* circoncision *f*

**circumference** *n* circonférence *f*

**circumflex** *n gramm* accent *m* circonflexe

**circumlocution** *n* périphrase *f*, circonlocution *f*

**circumnavigate** *vt* faire le tour de

**circumnavigation** *n* circumnavigation *f*

**circumscribe** *vt* circonscrire; encercler

**circumscription** *n* circonscription *f*; délimitation *f*; (coin) légende *f*

**circumspect** *adj* prudent, avisé, circonspect

**circumspection** *n* prudence *f*, circonspection *f*

**circumstance** *n* circonstance *f*, événement *m*; détail *m*, fait *m*; pompe *f*; **~ s** situation *f* de fortune

**circumstantial** *adj* circonstancié, détaillé

**circumstantiate** *vt* fournir des détails comme preuve de

**circumvent** *vt* circonvenir

**circumvention** *n* finesse *f*, duperie *f*; mise *f* en échec

**circumvolution** *n* enroulement *m*, circonvolution *f*

**circus** *n* cirque *m*; (roads) rond-point *m* (*pl* ronds-points)

**cirque** *n* cirque *m*

**cirrhosis** *n med* cirrhose *f*

**cirro-cumulus** *n* cirro-cumulus *m*

**cirro-stratus** *n* cirro-stratus *m*

**cirrus** *n* cirrus *m*

**cisalpine** *adj* cisalpin

**cissy, sissy** *n coll* efféminé *m*

**cistern** *n* réservoir *m*; (W.C.) chase *f* d'eau

**citadel** *n* citadelle *f*

**citation** *n* citation *f*

**cite** *vt* citer

**citizen** *n* citoyen -enne; *leg* ressortissant -e, sujet -ette

**citizenship** *n* nationalité *f*

**citrate** *n chem* citrate *m*

**citric** *adj chem* citrique

**citron** *n bot* cédrat *m*; (tree) cédratier *m*

**citronella** *n bot* citronnelle *f*

**citrous** *adj* relatif -ive aux agrumes

**citrus** *n* citrus *mpl*

**city** *n* ville *f*, cité *f*; **the City** la Cité de Londres

**civet** *n* civette *f*

**civic** *adj* civique; **~ centre** bâtiments municipaux

**civics** *npl* instruction *f* civique

**civil** *adj* civil; **~ defence** défense passive; **~ law** droit civil; (in England) **~ list** sommes votées par le Parlement anglais pour le maintien de la famille royale; **~ servant** fonctionnaire; **the Civil Service** la fonction publique

**civilian** *n* civil -e; *adj* civil

**civility** *n* civilité *f*

**civilization** *n* civilisation *f*

**civilize** *vt* civiliser

**civvies** *npl coll* vêtements *mpl* de pékin

**civvy** *adj coll* civil, de pékin; **~ street** vie civile

**clack** *n* claquement *m*; *mech* clapet *m*; *vi* jacasser

**clad** *adj* vêtu

**claim** *n* revendication *f*; demande *f*, réclamation *f*; *leg* droit *m*, titre *m*; **disputed ~s office** contentieux *m*; *vt* revendiquer, exiger; prétendre à; affirmer

**claimant** *n leg* requérant -e

**clairvoyance** *n* voyance *f*

**clairvoyant** *n* voyant -e

**clam** *n zool* palourde *f*; *coll fig* taciturne

**clamber** *vi* grimper

**clammy** *adj* humide, suintant

**clamorous** *adj* criard, braillard

**clamour** *n* clameur *f*; revendication *f*; *vi* clamer, vociférer

**¹clamp** *n* crampon *m*, serre-joint(s) *m*, sergent *m*, pince *f*; *vt* serrer, cramponner; *fig* **~ down on** supprimer; (expenditure) freiner

**²clamp** *n* piétinement *m*; trépignement *m*; *vt* piétiner; *vi* trépigner

**clan** *n* clan *m*

**clandestine** *adj* clandestin

**clang** *n* bruit *m* métallique; son *m* de cloche; *vt* faire retentir, faire résonner; *vi* retentir, résonner

**clanger** *n coll* bévue *f*, gaffe *f*; *coll* **drop a ~ gaffer**

**clank** *n* cliquetis *m*; *vt* faire cliqueter; *vi* cliqueter

**clannish** *adj* ayant l'esprit de clan

¹**clap** *n* claquement *m*; battement *m*; battements *mpl* de mains; tape *f*; (thunder) coup *m*; *vt* battre, claquer; applaudir; **~ eyes on** voir; **~ on** surajouter, coller sur; *vi* applaudir, battre des mains

²**clap** *n sl* chaude-pisse *f*

**clapper** *n* qui applaudit; (bell) battant *m*

**claptrap** *n* boniment *m*, baratin *m*

**claque** *n* claque *f*

**claret** *n* (vin *m* de) bordeaux *m* rouge

**clarification** *n* clarification *f*

**clarify** *vt* clarifier, éclaircir; *vi* se clarifier, s'éclaircir

**clarinet** *n* clarinette *f*

**clarion** *n mus* clairon *m*; **~ call** appel vibrant

**clarity** *n* clarté *f*

**clash** *n* choc *m*, heurt *m*; fracas *m*; bruit *m* métallique, cliquetis *m*; *fig* conflit *m*, clash *m*; (colours) disparate *f*, discordance *f*; *vt* heurter, choquer; faire cliqueter; *vi* se heurter; cliqueter; (colours) jurer, détonner; *fig* se heurter

**clasp** *n* agrafe *f*, fermoir *m*; (person) étreinte *f*; (hands) serrement *m*; *vt* agrafer, fermer; étreindre, serrer

**clasp-knife** *n* couteau *m* de poche

**class** *n* classe *f*, catégorie *f*; (school) classe *f*; (order of merit) classement *m*; *fig* qualité *f*; *adj* de haute qualité; *vt* classer, classifier

**class-conscious** *adj* ayant l'esprit de classe

**class-consciousness** *n* esprit *m* de classe

**class-distinction** *n* sens *m* des différences de classe

**classic** *n* classique *m*; (studies) **~s** études *fpl* de l'antiquité grecque et latine; *adj* classique

**classical** *adj* classique

**classicism** *n* classicisme *m*

**classicist** *n* humaniste *m*

**classification** *n* classification *f*

**classified** *adj* classé, classifié; *mil* secret -ète

**classify** *vt* classifier, classer

**classless** *adj* sans classe; dénué d'esprit de classe

**class-war** *n* lutte *f* des classes

**classy** *adj coll* chic *invar*

**clatter** *n* fracas *m*; (talk) brouhaha *m*; *vt* choquer; *vi* cliqueter; (talk) jacasser

**clause** *n gramm* membre *m* de phrase; *leg* disposition *f*; *pol* clause *f*

**claustrophobia** *n* claustrophobie *f*

**clavichord** *n* clavecin *m*

**clavicle** *n anat* clavicule *f*

**clavier** *n mus* clavier *m*

**claw** *n* (bird) serre *f*; (lobster, etc) pince *f*; (cat, etc) griffe *f*; *carp* arrache-clou *m*; *vt* griffer; *vi* s'agripper; *naut* louvoyer au vent

**claw-hammer** *n* pied-de-biche *m* (*pl* pieds-de-biche), arrache-clou *m*

**clay** *n* argile *f*, glaise *f*; *fig* terre *f*; cadavre *m*; **~ pigeon shoot** ball-trap *m*

**clean** *adj* propre, lavé, net (*f* nette); *fig* honnête, pur; (skilful) adroit, achevé; **come ~** avouer; *adv* absolument; *vt* nettoyer, laver; (brush) brosser; (polish) polir; **~ out** nettoyer; *coll* plumer, dépouiller; **~ up** nettoyer

**clean-cut** *adj* précis, bien défini

**cleaner** *n* dégraisseur -euse; femme *f* de ménage; détergent *m*, détersif *m*

**cleaning** *n* nettoyage *m*; *adj* détersif -ive

**clean-limbed** *adj* bien bâti

**clean-living** *adj* chaste; honnête

**cleanly** *adj* propre, net (*f* nette); *adv* proprement

**cleanness** *n* propreté *f*, netteté *f*

**clean-out** *n* nettoyage *m*, déblaiement *m*

**cleanse** *vt* nettoyer, décrotter; *fig* purifier

**cleansing** *n* nettoiement *m*; *fig* purification *f*

**clean-up** *n* nettoyage *m*; *fig* épuration *f*, assainissement *m*; (person) débarbouillage *m*

**clear** *n* **be in the ~** être au-dessus de tout soupçon; *adj* clair, brillant; (sky) dégagé; (complexion) frais (*f* fraîche); transparent; distinct; (free) libre; évident, manifeste; (entire) entier -ière, absolu; (lucid) lucide; innocent; *vt* clarifier, éclaircir; (obstruction) débarrasser; **leg** innocenter, disculper; (obstacle) sauter, franchir; (cheque) solder; **~ away** dégager; **~ off** liquider; **~ out** désencombrer; **~ up** ranger; (resolve) élucider; *vi* (sky) se dégager, s'éclaircir; **~ off** se libérer; s'en aller, *sl* foutre le camp; **~ out** s'en aller; **~ up** (weather) s'éclaircir

**clearage** *n naut* dédouanement *m*

**clearance** *n* débarras *m*; *naut* dédouanement *m*; *mech* dégagement *m*, jeu *m*

**clear-cut** *adj* précis, bien défini

**clearing** *n* clairière *f*; (weather) éclaircie *f*; dédouanement *m*

**clearing-house** *n comm* chambre *f* de compensation (de clearing)

**clearing-station** *n mil* poste *m* de secours

**clearness** *n* clarté *f*

**clear-out** *n see* **clean-out**

**clear-sighted** *adj* qui voit clair; qui prévoit

**clearway** *n mot* voie *f* à stationnement interdit

**cleat** *n naut* taquet *m*

**cleavage** *n* clivage *m*; scission *f*; (woman) décolleté *m*

¹**cleave** *vt* cliver, fendre; *vi* se fendre

²**cleave** *vi* coller, adhérer; *fig* s'attacher

**cleaver** *n* (butcher's) hachoir *m*, couperet *m*

**clef** *n mus* clef *f*, clé *f*

**cleft** *n* fissure *f*, fente *f*; *adj* fendu, fourbu

**cleft-palate** *n anat* palais fendu

**clematis** *n bot* clématite *f*

**clemency** *n* clémence *f*; (gentleness) douceur *f*

**clement** *adj* clément; (gentle) doux (*f* douce)

**clench** *vt* crisper, serrer; *mech* rabattre, river; (bargain, deal) conclure; *vi* se crisper; se rabattre

**clerestory** *n archi* claire-voie *f* (*pl* claires-voies)

**clergy** *n* clergé *m*

**clergyman** *n* pasteur *m*, clergyman *m*

**cleric** *n* clerc *m*, ecclésiastique *m*

**clerical** *adj* clérical

**clericalism** *n* cléricalisme *m*

**clerihew** *n lit* = petit poème (quatre vers) satirique ou fantaisiste

**clerk** *n* commis *m*, employé -e; *eccles* ecclésiastique *m*; *ar* érudit *m*; (solicitor's) clerc *m*

**clever** *adj* intelligent, astucieux -ieuse; adroit, habile; savant

**cleverness** *n* intelligence *f*, habileté *f*

**clew** *n* (thread) pelote *f*; *naut* point *m* d'écoute; *vt* pelotonner; *naut* carguer

**cliché** *n* cliché *m*, poncif *m*; *typ* cliché *m*

**click** *n* déclic *m*, claquement *m*; (tongue) clappement *m*; *vt* claquer; (tongue) clapper de; *vi* cliqueter, claquer; *sl* faire une touche

**client** *n* client -e

**clientele** *n* coll clientèle *f*

**cliff** *n* falaise *f*; paroi *f*

**cliff-hanging** *adj coll* (story) à suspense

**climacteric** *n* climatérique *f*; ménopause *f*

**climactic** *adj* à son apogée

**climate** *n* climat *m*

**climatic** *adj* climatique

**climatology** *n* climatologie *f*

**climax** *n* apogée *m*, sommet *m*; orgasme *m*

**climb** *n* montée *f*, ascension *f*; *vt* grimper, escalader, gravir; monter; *vi* grimper; monter

**climber** *n* grimpeur -euse; alpiniste; *bot* plante grimpante; *fig* arriviste

**climbing** *n* alpinisme *m*; (rock-climbing) varappe *f*; *adj* grimpeur -euse; *bot* grimpant

**clinch** *n* (boxing) corps à corps *m*; (grip) étreinte *f*; (riveting) rivetage *m*; (rivet) rivet *m*; *vt* (nail) river; *fig* boucler; (bargain) conclure; *vi* s'accrocher, se prendre corps à corps

**cling** *vi* s'accrocher, se cramponner; adhérer, se coller; *fig* rester attaché, se maintenir

**clinging** *adj* collant; tenace; possessif -ive

**clinic** *n* clinique *f*

**clinical** *adj* clinique; ~ **thermometer** thermomètre médical

¹**clink** *n* tintement *m*; *vt* faire tinter; *vi* tinter

²**clink** *n sl* taule *f*

**clinker** *n* mâchefer *m*

**clinometer** *n* clinomètre *m*

¹**clip** *n* attache *f*, pince *f*, agrafe *f*; (paper) trombone *m*; *cin* séquence *f*; (jewel) clip *m*; *vt* agrafer, serrer; *vi* être agrafé

²**clip** *n* (wool) tonte *f*; (blow) coup *m*; *sl* pas *m* rapide; *vt* tondre, couper; (wings) rogner; (words) manger; (ticket) poinçonner

**clip-joint** *n coll* restaurant *m*, etc où l'on vous assassine, restaurant *m*, etc coup de fusil

**clipper** *n naut* clipper *m*; (sheep) tondeur *m*; (tool) tondeuse *f*

**clippie** *n coll* receveuse *f* (d'autobus)

**clipping** *n* coupe *f*, tonte *f*; coupure *f* de presse

**clique** *n* clique *f*, coterie *f*

**cliquish** *adj* exclusif -ive

**clitoris** *n* clitoris *m*

**cloaca** *n* cloaque *m*

**cloak** *n* capote *f*, manteau *m*; *fig* apparence *f*; ~ **and dagger story** roman *m* de cape et d'épée; *vt* couvrir d'un manteau; déguiser

**cloakroom** *n theat* vestiaire *m*; (railway) consigne *f*

**clobber** *vt sl* arrêter; attaquer; rouer de coups

**cloche** *n* cloche *f*

¹**clock** *n* horloge *f*; (small) pendule *f*; *vt sp* chronométrer; *vi* ~ **in** (**on**) (se) pointer

²**clock** *n* (stocking) baguette *f*

**clockwise** *adj* dans le sens des aiguilles d'une montre

**clockwork** *n* mouvement *m* d'horlogerie; mécanisme *m*; **like** ~ précis, régulier -ière; *adj* mécanique

**clod** *n* motte *f*; *coll* balourd *m*

**clod-hopper** *n* rustre *m*, cul-terreux *m* (*pl* culs-terreux)

**clog** *n* sabot *m*; *fig* entrave *f*; *vt* entraver; obstruer

**cloisonné** adj cloisonné

**cloister** n cloître m; vt cloîtrer; ~ one-self se cloîtrer

**¹close** n (enclosure) enclos m; (cathedral) enceinte f; (quadrangle) cour f; adj proche; intime; clos; (reticent) renfermé; (compact) serré; étroit; concis, précis; (thorough) minutieux -ieuse; (stingy) avaricieux -ieuse; (weather) lourd, étouffant; ~ **season** période f où l'on n'a pas le droit de chasser; ~ **vowel** voyelle fermée; **have a** ~ **call** (shave) l'échapper belle; adv près; ~ **by** tout près; ~ **on** tout près de

**²close** n fin f, conclusion f; vt fermer, clore; **elect** fermer; (finish) achever, terminer; ~ **down** finir, fermer; ~ **in** cerner, envelopper; ~ **up** boucher, bloquer; vi terminer, finir, clore; se fermer; (agree) s'accorder, se mettre d'accord; ~ **down** rad cesser de transmettre; fermer; ~ **in** s'approcher; (night) tomber

**closed** adj fermé; limité; (blocked) barré; ~ **circuit** circuit fermé; ~ **shop** atelier m (usine f) qui n'engage que des employés syndiqués, monopole m d'embauche (d'un syndicat); **road** ~ route barrée

**close-down** n fermeture f; rad fin f des émissions

**close-fisted** adj grippe-sou invar

**close-hauled** adj naut au plus près

**closely** adv de près, étroitement

**closeness** n (weather) lourdeur f; intimité f; (miserliness) pingrerie f

**close-quarters** npl mil contact m avec l'ennemi; espace restreint; **come to** ~ **with** en venir aux mains avec

**close-stool** n chaise percée

**closet** n (room) cabinet m; (cupboard) penderie f

**closeted** adj en petit comité

**close-up** n cin gros plan

**closing** n fermeture f, clôture f

**closing-time** n heure f de fermeture

**closure** n (business, etc) fermeture f; (debate, parliament) clôture f; vt clôturer

**clot** n caillot m; coll idiot -e, lourdaud -e; vi cailler, coaguler

**cloth** n tissu m, étoffe f, drap m; theat toile f; (cleaning) chiffon m, torchon m; **the** ~ le clergé

**clothe** vt habiller, vêtir; fig revêtir, couvrir

**clothes** npl vêtements mpl, habits mpl; **in plain** ~ en civil

**clothes-basket** n panier m à linge

**clothes-brush** n brosse f à habits

**clothes-horse** n séchoir m

**clothes-line** n étendoir m

**clothes-peg** n pince f à linge

**clothier** n (marchand m) drapier m

**clothing** n vêtements mpl

**clotted** adj coagulé

**cloud** n nuage m; lit nuée f, nue f; (mirror) buée f; fig ombre f; **have one's head in the** ~s être dans les nuages; **under a** ~ soupçonné, en butte aux soupçons; vt couvrir de nuages, obscurcir; (reputation) ternir; vi se couvrir de nuages; s'obscurcir; (reputation) se ternir

**cloudburst** n pluie battante, déluge m; trombe f d'eau

**clouded** adj couvert de nuages; obscurci; fig terne, mélancolique

**cloudiness** n aspect nuageux; (liquid) aspect m trouble

**cloudless** adj sans nuages, serein

**cloudy** adj nuageux -euse, couvert, sombre; (liquid) trouble; fig sombre; vague, nébuleux -euse

**clout** n torchon m; morceau d'étoffe; coll gifle f, soufflet m, torgnole f; coll (power) pouvoir m; influence f; vt gifler; rapiécer

**¹clove** n gousse f

**²clove** n bot clou m de girofle

**cloven** adj fendu, fourchu; ~ **foot** pied fourchu

**clover** n trèfle m; **be in** ~ être comme un coq en pâte

**cloverleaf** n mot échangeur m

**clown** n pitre m; (circus) clown m; ar bouffon m; rustre m; vi bouffonner, faire le clown

**clowning** n bouffonnerie f, pitrerie f

**clownish** adj gauche, balourd

**cloy** vt rassasier, blaser; fig lasser; vi se blaser

**club** n (weapon) matraque f, trique f, gourdin m; club m, société f, cercle m, association f; (cards) trèfle m; (golf) crosse f; vt matraquer; vi se réunir; ~ **together** cotiser

**clubbable** adj sociable

**club-foot** n pied-bot m (pl pieds-bot)

**club-room** n salle f de réunion

**cluck** n gloussement m; vi glousser

**clue** n indice m; **not have a** ~ n'en avoir pas la moindre idée

**clueless** adj coll crétin; incapable; **he's** ~ il ne sait jamais rien

**clump** n touffe f, massif m, bosquet m; (footsteps) bruit m de pas; coll coup m, gifle f; vt grouper en massif; coll gifler; vi marcher d'un pas lourd

**clumsiness** n gaucherie f, maladresse f; lourdeur f; manque m de tact

**clumsy** adj gauche, maladroit, lourd, incommode; inélégant

**cluster** n (fruit) grappe f; (flowers)

bouquet *m*; (trees) massif *m*; groupe *m*; (houses) pâté *m*; *vi* se grouper

¹**clutch** *n* mot embrayage *m*; (grasp) étreinte *f*, prise *f*; (snatch) griffe *f*; *vt* saisir, étreindre; *vi* se cramponner, s'accrocher

²**clutch** *n* (eggs) couvée *f*

**clutter** *n* désordre *m*, *coll* pagaïe *f*; *vt* mettre en désordre, *coll* mettre en pagaïe

**clyster** *n* clystère *m*

**coach** *n* carrosse *m*; coche *m*; (railway) wagon *m*, voiture *f*; *mot* car *m*; *sp* entraîneur *m*; (tutor) répétiteur -trice; *vt sp* entraîner; (teach) préparer (à un examen)

**coachbuilder** *n* mot carrossier *m*

**coach-built** *adj* mot à carrosserie hors série

**coaching** *n sp* entraînement *m*; enseignement *m*, préparation *f*

**coachman** *n* cocher *m*

**coachwork** *n* mot carrosserie *f*

**coagulant** *n* coagulant *m*; *adj* coagulant

**coagulate** *vt* coaguler; *vi* se coaguler

**coal** *n* charbon *m*, houille *f*; **carry ~ s to Newcastle** apporter de l'eau à la mer; **haul s/o over the ~s** réprimander qn; **heap ~s of fire on s/o's head** rendre le bien pour le mal; *vt naut* fournir en charbon; *vi naut* s'approvisionner en charbon

**coalblack** *adj* noir comme du charbon

**coal-bunker** *n naut* soute *f* à charbon

**coal-cellar** *n* cave *f* à charbon

**coalesce** *vi* (substances) se souder, fusionner; *fig* s'unir

**coal-face** *n* banc *m* de houille

**coalfield** *n* bassin houiller

**coal-gas** *n* gaz *m* de houille

**coaling** *n naut* approvisionnement *m* en charbon

**coalition** *n* coalition *f*

**coal-mine** *n* houillère *f*, mine *f* de charbon

**coal-miner** *n* mineur *m*

**coal-pit** *n* houillère *f*, mine *f* de charbon

**coal-scuttle** *n* seau *m* à charbon

**coal-tar** *n* coaltar *m*, goudron *m*

**coarse** *adj* vulgaire, commun; (substance) grossier -ière, rude; (joke) indécent

**coarsen** *vt* rendre vulgaire; (substance) rendre grossier -ière; *vi* devenir vulgaire; (substance) devenir grossier -ière

**coarseness** *n* vulgarité *f*; grossièreté *f*

**coast** *n* côte *f*; littoral *m*; **the ~ is clear** il n'y a pas de danger; *vi* (vehicle) descendre en roue libre

**coastal** *adj* côtier -ière

**coaster** *n naut* caboteur *m*

**coastguard** *n* garde-côte *m*

**coastline** *n* littoral *m*

**coat** *n* habit *m*; veste *f*, veston *m*; (overcoat) manteau *m*, pardessus *m*; (tails) habit *m*; (layer) couche *f*; (animal) pelage *m*; *anat* membrane *f*; **~ of arms** blason *m*, armoiries *fpl*; *vt* enduire, couvrir; *cul* + *med* enrober

**coax** *vt* cajoler, amadouer, entortiller

**coaxer** *n* cajoleur -euse, flatteur -euse

**co-axial** *adj math* coaxial

**coaxing** *adj* cajoleur -euse

**cob** *n* (coal) tête *f* de moineau; (maize) épi *m*; (nut) noisette *f*; (horse) bidet *m*; *zool* cygne *m* mâle; *vt coll* frapper, battre

**cobalt** *n* cobalt *m*

¹**cobble** *n* pavé rond; *vt* paver

²**cobble** *vt* réparer (des chaussures); rafistoler

**cobbler** *n* cordonnier *m*, savetier *m*

**cobble-stone** *n* pavé rond

**co-belligerent** *n* cobelligérant *m*; *adj* cobelligérant

**cob-loaf** *n* pain arrondi, boule *f*

**cob-nut** *n* noisette *f*

**cobra** *n* cobra *m*, naja *m*

**cobweb** *n* toile *f* d'araignée

**Coca-Cola** *n* Coca-Cola *m*

**cocaine** *n* cocaïne *f*

**coccyx** *n anat* coccyx *m*

**cochineal** *n* cochenille *f*

**cock** *n* coq *m*; oiseau *m* mâle, mâle *m*; (tap) robinet *m*; (rifle) chien *m*; (balance) aiguille *f*; (sundial) style *m*; (weather-vane) girouette *f*; *agr* meulon *m*; *coll* type *m*, bonhomme *m*; *sl* (penis) queue *f*, bite *f*; **~ of the walk** coq *m* du village; **go off at half ~** commencer prématurément; *coll* **old ~** mon vieux; *sl* **talk ~** déconner; *vt* dresser, redresser; (rifle) armer; *sl* **~ up** bousiller

**cockade** *n* cocarde *f*

**cock-a-hoop** *adj* triomphant, allègre; *adv* allègrement, triomphalement

**cockatoo** *n zool* cacatoès *m*

**cockatrice** *n* basilic *m*

**cock-crow** *n* aube *f*

**cocked** *adj* (rifle) armé; (ears) dressé; **~ hat** chapeau *m* à cornes

**cocker** *n* (dog) cocker *m*

**cockerel** *n* coquelet *m*

**cock-eyed** *adj coll* louche, bigle; *sl* (crooked) de travers; (drunk) ivre

**cock-fight** *n* combat *m* de coqs

**cockiness** *n* suffisance *f*

**cockle** *n zool* coque *f*; (boat) coquille *f* de noix; **warm the ~s of one's heart** réconforter

**Cockney** *n* Cockney; *adj* cockney

**cockpit** *n naut* + *aer* cockpit *m*; *fig* arène *f*

**cockroach** n zool blatte f, cafard m
**cockscomb** n crête f de coq; bot crête-de-coq f (pl crêtes-de-coq)
**cock-sparrow** n moineau m (mâle); fig pej freluquet m
**cocksure** adj suffisant
**cocktail** n (drink) cocktail m; (horse) courtaud -e; ~ **party** cocktail m
**cock-up** n sl pagaïe f, pagaille f
**cocky** adj arrogant, suffisant
**coco** n bot cocotier m
**cocoa** n cacao m
**coconut, cocoanut** n noix f de coco; ~ **butter** beurre m de coco; ~ **matting** tapis m de fibre (de noix de coco)
**cocoon** n cocon m
**cod** n morue f
**coda** n mus coda f
**coddle** vt dorloter, choyer; cul faire mijoter
**code** n code m; (cypher) chiffre m; (telephone) indicatif m; vt coder
**codeine** n med codéine f
**codfish** n zool morue f
**codger** n coll croulant m
**codicil** n leg codicille m
**codification** n codification f
**codify** vt codifier
**co-director** n (managing) codirecteur -trice; coadministrateur -trice
**cod-liver-oil** n huile f de foie de morue
**co-ed** n US coll étudiante f dans un collège mixte
**co-education** n éducation f mixte
**co-educational** adj mixte
**coefficient** n coefficient m
**coerce** vt contraindre
**coercion** n contrainte f
**coercive** adj coercitif -ive
**coeval** n contemporain -e; adj contemporain, du même âge
**coexist** vi coexister
**coexistence** n coexistence f
**coffee** n café m; **black** ~ café m nature; **white** ~ café au lait, café crème
**coffee-bean** n grain m de café
**coffee-grounds** n marc m de café
**coffee-mill** n moulin m à café
**coffee-pot** n cafetière f
**coffee-table** n table basse; ~ **book** grand livre illustré
**coffer** n coffre m, caisse f; eng caisson m; ~s ressources financières
**coffin** n cercueil m, bière f
¹**cog** n dent f; carp tenon m
²**cog** vt (dice) manipuler en trichant; vi tricher
**cogency** n puissance f, bien-fondé m
**cogent** adj puissant, convaincant, péremptoire
**cogitate** vt + vi méditer
**cogitation** n méditation f, réflexion f

**cognac** n cognac m
**cognate** n leg cognat m; gramm analogue m; adj leg parent; gramm analogue
**cognition** n perception f; philo cognition f
**cognizance** n connaissance f; leg compétence f, ressort m
**cognizant** adj instruit, ayant connaissance
**cognomen** n nom m de famille; (nickname) surnom m
**cog-wheel** n roue f à dents
**cohabit** vi cohabiter
**cohere** vi se tenir; adhérer
**coherence** n cohérence f
**coherent** adj cohérent, logique
**cohesion** n cohésion f
**cohesive** adj cohésif -ive
**cohort** n cohorte f
**coiffure** n coiffure f
**coil** n rouleau m, tour m; (hair) chignon m; elect bobine f; (contraceptive) stérilet m; vt enrouler; elect bobiner; vi s'enrouler
**coin** n pièce f (de monnaie); numéraire m; **pay s/o in his own** ~ rendre à qn la monnaie de sa pièce; vt frapper; (words) inventer; coll ~ **money** s'enrichir
**coinage** n monnaie f; frappe f; (words) invention f
**coincide** vi coïncider
**coincidence** n coïncidence f
**coincident** adj coïncident
**coincidental** adj de coïncidence
**coiner** n faux-monnayeur m
**coitus, coition** n coït m
¹**coke** n coke m; vt cokéfier
²**coke** n sl cocaïne f; coll coca m
**col** n col m
**colander** n passoire f
**cold** n froid m; med rhume m; **catch** ~ s'enrhumer; **out in the** ~ négligé, à l'écart; adj froid; fig froid, indifférent, détaché; ~ **comfort** maigre consolation f; ~ **sweat** sueur froide; ~ **war** guerre froide; **have** ~ **feet** avoir peur; **in** ~ **blood** de sang-froid; coll **it leaves me** ~ ça ne me fait aucun effet, ça ne m'intéresse point; **throw** ~ **water on** refroidir, décourager
**cold-blooded** adj zool à sang froid; fig cruel -elle, insensible, dur
**cold-chisel** n burin m, ciseau m à froid
**cold-cream** n cold-cream m
**cold-frame** n agr châssis m
**cold-front** n meteor masse f d'air froid
**coldish** adj frisquet -ette, frais (f fraîche)
**coldness** n froideur f
**cold-shoulder** n indifférence voulue,

rebuffade f; vt faire grise mine à
**cold-storage** n conservation f en congélateur; fig **put into** ~ différer sine die
**coleslaw** n salade f de chou cru
**colibri** n colibri m
**colic** n med colique f; adj med du côlon;
de colique
**colitis** n med colite f
**collaborate** vi collaborer
**collaboration** n collaboration f
**collaborator** n collaborateur -trice
**collage** n collage m
**collapse** n chute f, effondrement m,
écroulement m; med collapsus m; vi
s'effondrer, s'écrouler, tomber
**collapsible** adj pliant
**collar** n col m, collet m; (detachable)
faux col; (blouse) collerette f; (dog)
collier m; mech collet m; vt coll saisir,
prendre au collet; coll rafler
**collar-bone** n anat clavicule f
**collate** vt collationner; eccles nommer
**collateral** n nantissement m; adj parallèle; leg collatéral; secondaire; comm
subsidiaire
**collation** n collation f
**colleague** n collègue
¹**collect** n eccles collecte f; US ~ **call**
appel m en P.C.V.
²**collect** vt grouper, rassembler, réunir;
collectionner; (pick up) ramasser;
(gather) recueillir; vi se rassembler; ~
**oneself** se recueillir
**collected** adj groupé, ramassé; (calm)
calme, recueilli; ~ **works** œuvres com-
plètes
**collection** n collection f; eccles quête f,
collecte f; (group) groupement m, rassemblement m; (mail) levée f
**collective** adj collectif -ive
**collectivism** n collectivisme m
**collectivization** n collectivisation f
**collector** n collectionneur -euse; (tax)
percepteur m, receveur m; (railway
ticket) contrôleur -euse
**college** n collège m; (school) école
privée; **electoral** ~ collège électoral;
**military** ~ école f militaire; **naval** ~
école navale; **technical** ~ collège m
technique
**collegial** adj de collège
**collegiate** adj de collège; eccles collégial;
~ **church** collégiale f
**collide** vi se heurter, se tamponner; ~
**with** heurter, tamponner; fig se heurter
contre, être en conflit avec
**collie** n colley m
**collier** n mineur m; naut charbonnier m
**colliery** n mine f de charbon, houillère f
**collision** n collision f, choc m, heurt m,
tamponnement m; fig conflit m
**collocate** vt arranger, juxtaposer

**collocation** n arrangement m, juxtaposition f
**collodion** n chem collodion m
**colloquial** adj familier -ière, parlé
**colloquialism** n tournure familière
**colloquy** n colloque m; dialogue m
**collude** vi agir de connivence
**collusion** n collusion f, complicité f
**collusive** adj collusoire, complice
**collywobbles** n coll mal m d'estomac,
coliques fpl
¹**colon** n anat côlon m
²**colon** n gramm deux-points mpl
**colonel** n colonel m
**colonial** n colonial -e; adj colonial
**colonialism** n colonialisme m
**colonic** adj du côlon; ~ **irrigation** lavement m
**colonist** n colon m
**colonization** n colonisation f
**colonize** vt coloniser
**colony** n colonie f
**Colorado** n Colorado m; zool ~ **beetle**
doryphore m
**coloration** n coloration f, coloris m
**colossal** adj colossal
**colossus** n colosse m
**colour** n couleur f, teinte f, coloris m;
teinture f; (complexion) teint m; mus
ton m, timbre m; fig aspect m; vivacité
f; ~**s** sp couleurs fpl; mil drapeau m;
~ **problem** problème racial; **change**
~ changer de visage; **off** ~ malade,
souffrant; **with flying** ~**s** triomphalement; vt colorer; (dye) teindre; (paint)
colorier, peindre; fig colorer; (distort)
dénaturer; vi se colorer, changer de
couleur; (flush) rougir
**colourable** adj spécieux -ieuse, plausible
**colour-bar** n discrimination raciale
**colour-blind** adj daltonien -ienne
**colour-blindness** n daltonisme m
**coloured** adj coloré; (person) de couleur; fig dénaturé; influencé
**colourful** adj éclatant, vif (f vive); fig
pittoresque, original, gai
**colouring** n pigment m; (hue) coloration
f; complexion f; fig aspect m, apparence f
**colourist** n coloriste
**colourless** adj incolore; fig fade, terne
¹**colt** n poulain m
²**colt** n colt m, pistolet m
**coltish** adj fringant; inexpérimenté
**columbine** n bot colombine f
**column** n colonne f
**columnist** n (newspaper) collaborateur
-trice régulier -ière d'un journal
**coma** n coma m
**comatose** adj comateux -euse
**comb** n peigne m; (wool) carde f; (cock)
crête f; (honey) rayon m; vt peigner;

carder; *fig* fouiller; ~ **out** démêler; sélectionner

**combat** *n* combat *m*; *vt* combattre; *vi* se battre

**combatant** *n + adj* combattant -e

**combative** *adj* combatif -ive

**comber** *n* (person) peigneur -euse; (machine) peigneuse *f*; (wave) vague déferlante

**combination** *n* combinaison *f*; association *f*; (garment) combinaison *f*; **motor-cycle** ~ side-car *m*

**combine** *n comm* trust *m*, consortium *m*; *agr* moissonneuse-batteuse *f* (*pl* moissonneuses-batteuses); *vt* combiner, unir; *vi* s'unir, se grouper ensemble

**combine-harvester** *n* moissonneuse-batteuse *f* (*pl* moissonneuses-batteuses)

**combustible** *n* combustible *m*; *adj* combustible

**combustion** *n* combustion *f*

**come** *vi* venir, approcher; arriver, paraître; (happen) se produire, advenir, arriver, survenir; (cause) être causé par; *coll* jouer le rôle de; *sl* (orgasm) jouir, juter; ~! voyons!, tout de même!; ~ **about** arriver, advenir; *naut* virer; ~ **across** rencontrer, trouver par hasard; *sl* ~ **across with** (lend) prêter; (cough up) casquer; ~ **along** avancer rapidement, se presser; ~ **at** attaquer, atteindre; ~ **away** s'en aller, partir; se détacher; ~ **back** retourner; *sl* riposter; ~ **between** séparer, brouiller; ~ **by** obtenir; *coll* ~ **clean** avouer; ~ **down** descendre; *fig* tomber bas; (be transmitted) se transmettre; ~ **down on** blâmer, gronder; ~ **forward** offrir de l'aide; se proposer, s'offrir; ~ **from** venir de, provenir de; ~ **in** entrer, arriver; devenir à la mode; *coll* ~ **in for** obtenir; encourir; ~ **into** hériter; ~ **off** réussir, advenir, avoir lieu; se détacher; ~ **off it!** dis la vérité!; ~ **on** avancer, faire des progrès; (pain) commencer; *theat* entrer en scène, faire une entrée; ~ **out** être révélé, se divulguer; sortir, paraître; (book) paraître, être publié; (in society) débuter; (strike) se mettre en grève; ~ **out with** (words) lâcher; ~ **over** passer à l'autre camp; (feel) se sentir; ~ **round** *med* revenir à soi, se ranimer; (accept) se résigner, donner son accord; *coll* visiter, faire un saut; ~ **through** survivre; ~ **to** *med* revenir à soi; (bill, amount) revenir à; ~ **under** (list) se trouver sous la mention de; être sous l'autorité de; ~ **up** (plant) pousser, pointer; (conversation) être mentionné, venir sur le tapis; monter; ~

**upon (on)** trouver par hasard, tomber sur; ~ **up to** égaler; ~ **up with** (catch up) rejoindre; (idea) proposer

**come-back** *n coll* rentrée *f*; *coll* riposte *f*

**comedian** *n* (music-hall) comique; *theat* acteur -trice comique; comédien -ienne

**come-down** *n* déchéance *f*, humiliation *f*

**comedy** *n* comédie *f*; **musical** ~ opérette *f*

**comeliness** *n* beauté *f*, charme *m*, grâce *f*

**comely** *adj* avenant, beau (*f* belle)

**comestible** *n* comestible *m*; *adj* comestible

**comet** *n* comète *f*

**comfort** *n* confort *m*; aises *fpl*; (consolation) réconfort *m*, encouragement *m*; (ease) bien-être *m*, aisance *f*; ~ **station** *US* toilettes *fpl* publiques; *vt* consoler, soulager; encourager, réconforter

**comfortable** *adj* confortable, commode; (thought) rassurant; (money) aisé

**comforter** *n* consolateur -trice; (scarf) cache-nez *m*; (child) sucette *f*

**comfortless** *adj* sans confort, incommode; (cheerless) triste

**comfy** *adj coll* confortable, douillet -ette

**comic** *n coll* (performer) comique; *coll* (magazine, strip) bande(s) dessinée(s); *adj* comique; amusant

**comical** *adj* comique, drôle; (absurd) cocasse

**comic-strip** *n* bande dessinée

**Cominform** *n pol* Cominform *m*

**coming** *n* venue *f*, arrivée *f*; *eccles* événement *m*; *adj* à venir, futur; (week, month, year) prochain; (promising) qui promet, d'avenir

**comity** *n* courtoisie *f*; *pol* ~ **of nations** nations *fpl* ayant de bons rapports entre elles

**comma** *n* virgule *f*; **inverted** ~**(s)** guillemet(s) *m(pl)*

**command** *n* ordre *m*; autorité *f*; commandement *m*; *mil* troupes *fpl*; *mil* **high** ~ haut commandement; *vt* ordonner; (respect) exiger; (control) commander, dominer, contrôler; (overlook) donner sur; (price) atteindre; (respect) inspirer

**commandant** *n mil* commandant *m*

**commandeer** *vt* réquisitionner

**commander** *n* chef *m*, commandant *m*; *naut* = capitaine *m* de frégate; *aer* chef *m* de bord; ~ **in chief** commandant *m* en chef

**commanding** *adj* (tone, etc) de commandement; (presence) imposant; (height, position) dominant, élevé; *mil* ~ **officer** commandant *m*

**commandment** *n* ordre *m*; *eccles* commandement *m*

**commando** n mil commando m
**commemorate** vt commémorer
**commemoration** n commémoration f
**commence** vt + vi commencer
**commencement** n commencement m
**commend** vt louer; (recommend) recommander; (entrust) confier; ~ **oneself** se recommander; ~ **itself** (idea, plan) faire bonne impression
**commendable** adj louable
**commendation** n louange f, approbation f
**commendatory** adj laudatif -ive, approbatif -ive
**commensurability** n commensurabilité f
**commensurable** adj commensurable
**commensurate** adj de même mesure, proportionné; en accord
**comment** n commentaire m, observation f, remarque f; (note) annotation f; vi faire des remarques
**commentary** n commentaire m; rad **running** ~ reportage m en direct
**commentate** vt commenter; vi faire un reportage
**commentator** n commentateur -trice; rad radio-reporter m
**commerce** n commerce m
**commercial** n spot m publicitaire; adj commercial, de commerce; ~ **traveller** voyageur m de commerce
**commercialism** n pej esprit m mercantile; pratique f du commerce
**commercialize** vt commercialiser
**commination** n commination f
**comminatory** adj comminatoire
**commingle** vt mélanger; vi se mélanger
**commiserate** vi avoir de la commisération, compatir aux malheurs
**commiseration** n commisération f
**commissariat** n mil intendance f; ravitaillement m
**commissary** n commissaire m
**commission** n commission f, comité f; mil brevet m; (artist) commande f; comm commission f; naut armement m; eccles commission f; vt donner pouvoir à, déléguer; (artist) passer une commande à; naut armer
**commissionaire** n commissionaire m d'hôtel (de restaurant, etc)
**commissioner** n membre m d'une commission
**commit** vt commettre, perpétrer; (entrust) confier, livrer; leg écrouer; ~ **oneself** s'engager
**commitment** n engagement m; (handing over) action f de confier; perpétration f; leg incarcération f; leg mandat m de dépôt; engagement financier
**committal** n action f de perpétrer; ~ **to the earth** enterrement m

**committee** n comité m, commission f
**committee-room** n salle f de réunion; (electoral) permanence f
**commode** n commode f; chaise percée
**commodious** adj spacieux -ieuse
**commodity** n denrée f, produit m
**commodore** n commodore m; président m d'un yacht-club
**common** n (city) espace vert; (village) terrain communal; adj commun (widespread) général, public (f publique); (well-known) familier -ière, habituel -uelle, ordinaire; fréquent, normal; (low) vulgaire, bas (f basse); gramm + math commun; mus parfait; ~ **decency** simple politesse f; ~ **ground** faits incontestés; leg ~ **law** droit coutumier; ~ **people** commun m; ~ **sense** sens commun, bon sens; ~ **soldier** simple soldat m
**commonalty** n commun m; gens mpl du peuple
**commoner** n roturier -ière
**commonly** adv généralement, ordinairement
**commonness** n vulgarité f
**commonplace** n cliché m, lieu commun, banalité f; adj banal, ordinaire, quelconque
**commons** npl gens mpl du peuple, commun m; (rations) quantité f fixe de vivres; **House of Commons** Chambre f des Communes; **short** ~ portion congrue
**commonweal** n bien public
**commonwealth** n nation f démocratique; confédération f de nations; **the Commonwealth** le Commonwealth (britannique)
**commotion** n commotion f, agitation f; tumulte m
**communal** adj communal; commun
¹**commune** n commune f
²**commune** vi communier, converser; US eccles communier; ~ **with oneself** se recueillir
**communicable** adj communicable
**communicant** n eccles communicant -e; informateur -trice
**communicate** vt communiquer, transmettre; vi communiquer, se mettre en rapport; eccles communier
**communication** n communication f; transmission f; message m, information f, renseignement m; ~ **s** système m de transmission de messages; moyens mpl de communication; (railway) ~ **cord** signal m d'alarme; ~ **satellite** satellite-relais m (pl satellites-relais)
**communicative** adj communicatif -ive, expansif -ive
**communicator** n communicateur -trice, transmetteur -trice

**communion** *n* communion *f*, communion *f* d'idées; relations *fpl* intimes; *eccles* communion *f*
**communiqué** *n* communiqué *m*
**communism** *n* communisme *m*
**communist** *n* + *adj* communiste
**communistic** *adj* communiste; (tendency) communisant
**community** *n* communauté *f*, collectivité *f*; société *f*; *eccles* communauté *f*, ordre *m*; *leg* communauté *f* (de biens)
**commutability** *n* permutabilité *f*
**commutable** *adj* permutable
**commutation** *n* permutation *f*, commutation *f*
**commute** *vt* échanger; *leg* commuer; *elect* modifier; *vi* faire la navette
**commuter** *n* personne *f* qui fait la navette; ~ **belt** grande banlieue
¹**compact** *n* accord *m*, contrat *m*, convention *f*
²**compact** *n* poudrier *m*
³**compact** *n* *US* petite voiture; *adj* compact, dense; *fig* concis, bref (*f* brève); *vt* rendre compact, tasser, comprimer
**compacted** *adj* comprimé, tassé
**compactness** *n* densité *f*, concision *f*
¹**companion** *n* compagnon *m*, compagne *f*; dame *f* de compagnie; (book) guide *m*, manuel *m*; (pair) pendant *m*; *adj* qui se fait pendant; *vt* accompagner
²**companion** *n* *naut* capot *m*; ~ **hatch** écoutille *f*; ~ **ladder** échelle *f* des cabines
**companionable** *adj* sociable
**companionship** *n* camaraderie *f*
**company** *n* compagnie *f*; (guests) invités -ées *pl*; camaraderie *f*; **bad** ~ mauvaises fréquentations; **be good** ~ être très agréable; **keep** ~ **with** frayer avec; **keep s/o** ~ tenir compagnie à qn; **part** ~ **with** se séparer de; ne plus être d'accord avec
**comparable** *adj* comparable
**comparative** *adj* comparatif -ive; relatif -ive; *gramm* comparatif -ive; (literature, linguistics, etc) comparé
**compare** *n* comparaison *f*; **beyond** ~ incomparable; *vt* comparer, mettre en comparaison; *vi* se comparer
**comparison** *n* comparaison *f*
**compartment** *n* compartiment *m*
**compass** *n* *naut*, *etc* boussole *f*; *fig* étendue *f*; (scope) champ *m*, rayon *m*; *mus* portée *f*; *math* ~es compas *m*; *vt* faire le tour de; entourer; (scheme) projeter, comploter; (achieve) réaliser, accomplir
**compass-card** *n* rose *f* des vents
**compassing** *adj* entourant; (achieving) accomplissant

**compassion** *n* compassion *f*
**compassionate** *adj* compatissant
**compatibility** *n* compatibilité *f*
**compatible** *adj* compatible
**compatriot** *n* compatriote
**compel** *vt* obliger, contraindre, forcer
**compelling** *adj* irrésistible
**compendious** *adj* compendieux -ieuse, succinct
**compendium** *n* abrégé *m*
**compensate** *vt* compenser, indemniser; *mech* compenser; *vi* ~ **for** être une compensation de
**compensation** *n* compensation *f*, dédommagement *m*, indemnité *f*; *mech* compensation *f*
**compensatory** *adj* compensateur -trice, compensatoire
**compete** *vi* concourir; (rival) faire concurrence; participer
**competence** *n* compétence *f*, capacité *f*; aisance *f*; *leg* compétence *f*
**competent** *adj* compétent, capable; qualifié; *leg* compétent, habile
**competition** *n* compétition *f*, concurrence *f*; (contest) concours *m*
**competitive** *adj comm* compétitif -ive; de concours
**competitor** *n* concurrent -e
**compilation** *n* compilation *f*
**compile** *vt* compiler, recueillir
**complacence, complacency** *n* satisfaction *f*, contentement *m* de soi, suffisance *f*
**complacent** *adj* satisfait, suffisant
**complain** *vi* se plaindre, se lamenter; formuler une plainte
**complainant** *n* *leg* plaignant -e
**complaint** *n* plainte *f*, lamentation *f*; (grievance) grief *m*, réclamation *f*; maladie *f*; *leg* plainte *f*
**complaisance** *n* complaisance *f*, obligeance *f*; (courtesy) courtoisie *f*
**complaisant** *adj* complaisant, obligeant; (polite) courtois
**complement** *n* complément *m*; *mil* + *naut* effectif *m*; *gramm* complément *m*, attribut *m*; *vt* compléter, complémenter
**complementary** *adj* complémentaire
**complete** *adj* complet -ète, entier -ière; (finished) achevé, fini; *coll* parfait, consommé; *vt* achever, finir; compléter
**completeness** *n* plénitude *f*
**completion** *n* achèvement *m*; réalisation *f*; plénitude *f*
**complex** *n* complexe *m*; *adj* complexe
**complexion** *n* complexion *f*; *fig* aspect *m*, nature *f*
**complexity** *n* complexité *f*, complication *f*
**compliance** *n* acquiescement *m*;

(conformity) conformité *f*; (submission) complaisance *f*; **in ~ with** conformément à

**compliant** *adj* accommodant, complaisant; servile

**complicate** *vt* compliquer

**complication** *n* complication *f*

**complicity** *n* complicité *f*

**compliment** *n* compliment *m*, louange *f*; **~ s** compliments *mpl*, hommages *mpl*; vœux *mpl*; *vt* complimenter, féliciter

**complimentary** *adj* flatteur -euse, élogieux -ieuse; (free) gratuit; **~ copy** (book) exemplaire offert en hommage; **~ ticket** billet *m* de faveur

**compline** *n eccles* complies *fpl*

**comply** *vi* céder, se plier; **~ with** se conformer à, observer

**component** *n* élément *m*; *chem* composant *m*; *adj* composant

**comport** *vt* **~ oneself** se comporter, se conduire; *vi* s'accorder

**compose** *vt* composer, constituer, former; (calm) arranger, apaiser; (order) disposer, organiser

**composed** *adj* composé; calme, tranquille

**composer** *n* compositeur -trice

**composite** *n* composé *m*; *bot* composée *f*; *archi* composite *m*; *adj* composite, divers, hétéroclite; mixte

**composition** *n* composition *f*, œuvre *f*; rédaction *f*, dissertation *f*; *leg* accommodement *m*, compromis *m*; *fig* composé *m*, nature *f*

**compositor** *n print* compositeur -trice

**compos mentis** *adj phr* sain d'esprit

**compost** *n* compost *m*

**composure** *n* calme *m*, flegme *m*

**compote** *n cul* compote *f*

**¹compound** *n* enclos *m*

**²compound** *n* composé *m*; *chem* composé *m*; *adj* composé, complexe; *med* **~ fracture** fracture compliquée; **~ interest** intérêts composés; *gramm* **~ sentence** phrase *f* complexe; **~ word** mot composé

**³compound** *vt* mêler, mélanger; *chem* composer; *leg* régler à l'amiable; *leg* (felony) pactiser avec; *vi* composer; transiger; s'arranger à l'amiable

**comprehend** *vt* comprendre; inclure, contenir

**comprehensibility** *n* compréhensibilité *f*, intelligibilité *f*

**comprehensible** *adj* compréhensible, intelligible

**comprehension** *n* compréhension *f*, intelligence *f*; inclusion *f*

**comprehensive** *n* = C.E.S. (Collège *m* d'Enseignement Secondaire); *adj* compréhensif -ive, large, ample

**compress** *n med* compresse *f*; *vt* comprimer

**compressed** *adj* comprimé; (made smaller) réduit; (terse) concis

**compressible** *adj* compressible

**compression** *n* compression *f*; concision *f*, concentration *f*

**compressive** *adj* compressif -ive

**compressor** *n* compresseur *m*

**comprise** *vt* contenir, comprendre, comporter

**compromise** *n* compromis *m*, arrangement *m*; *vt* transiger, régler par un compromis; (endanger) compromettre, mettre en danger; **~ oneself** se compromettre; *vi* transiger

**compulsion** *n* contrainte *f*; *psych* compulsion *f*

**compulsive** *adj* irrésistible; *psych* compulsif -ive

**compulsory** *adj* obligatoire, forcé; (required) exigé

**compunction** *n* remords *m*; hésitation *f*, scrupule *m*; *eccles* componction *f*

**computable** *adj* calculable

**computation** *n* calcul *m*, évaluation *f*

**compute** *vt* calculer, évaluer

**computer** *n* ordinateur *m*

**computerize** *vt* calculer au moyen d'un ordinateur; équiper d'un ordinateur

**comrade** *n* camarade

**comradeship** *n* camaraderie *f*

**¹con** *vt* étudier; apprendre par cœur

**²con** *vt naut* gouverner

**³con** *n sl* escroquerie *f*; **~ man** escroc *m*; *vt sl* escroquer

**concatenate** *vt* enchaîner

**concatenation** *n* enchaînement *m*

**concave** *adj* concave

**concavity** *n* concavité *f*; (hollow) creux *m*

**conceal** *vt* celer, cacher; garder secret -ète

**concealment** *n* action *f* de cacher; (place) cachette *f*; *fig* dissimulation *f*

**concede** *vt* concéder, admettre, reconnaître; *vi* céder

**conceit** *n* suffisance *f*, vanité *f*, prétention *f*; *lit* trait *m* d'esprit; **~ s** concetti *mpl*

**conceited** *adj* suffisant, vaniteux -euse

**conceivable** *adj* concevable, imaginable

**conceive** *vt* concevoir, imaginer; exprimer, formuler; (child) concevoir; *vi* penser; concevoir

**concentrate** *n* concentré *m*; *vt* concentrer; *vi* se concentrer

**concentration** *n* concentration *f*; **~ camp** camp *m* de concentration

**concentric** *adj* concentrique

**concept** *n* concept *m*, idée *f*

**conception** *n* conception *f*

conceptive

conceptive *adj philos* capable de concevoir
conceptual *adj* conceptuel -elle
conceptualize *vt* former un concept au sujet de
concern *n* souci *m*, inquiétude *f*; (business) affaire *f*; responsabilité *f*; soin *m*; *comm* entreprise *f*, firme *f*, établissement *m*; *vt* concerner, regarder; intéresser; (upset) affliger, inquiéter; ~ oneself s'inquiéter; (take trouble) se donner du mal
concerned *adj* intéressé; impliqué; inquiet -iète, soucieux -ieuse
concerning *prep* concernant, regardant, à propos de, au sujet de
concert *n* concert *m*; concorde *f*, harmonie *f*, accord *m*; *vt* concerter, arranger, organiser
concerted *adj* concerté; *mus* orchestré
concert-grand *n mus* piano *m* de concert
concertina *n mus* concertina *m*
concerto *n mus* concerto *m*
concert-pitch *n mus* diapason *m* de concert; at ~ *mus* au diapason; *fig* en pleine forme
concession *n* concession *f*
concessionaire *n* concessionnaire
concessionary *adj* concessionnaire
conch *n zool* + *anat* conque *f*
conchology *n* conchyliologie *f*
conciliate *vt* concilier; gagner, amener
conciliation *n* conciliation *f*
conciliatory *adj* conciliatoire
concise *adj* concis
conciseness, concision *n* concision *f*
conclave *n eccles* conclave *m*; discussion secrète
conclude *vt* conclure, finir, achever, terminer; (deduce) conclure, déduire; *vi* conclure; se terminer, s'achever; décider
conclusion *n* conclusion *f*, fin *f*; déduction *f*; décision *f*; foregone ~ affaire réglée d'avance; in ~ finalement; try ~ s with se mesurer contre
conclusive *adj* conclusif -ive, concluant
concoct *vt cul* confectionner; *fig* inventer, fabriquer
concoction *n* mélange *m*, confection *f*; *pej* médicament *m* désagréable
concomitant *n* fait concomitant; *adj* concomitant
concord *n* concorde *f*, entente *f*; harmonie *f*; *gramm* + *mus* accord *m*
concordance *n* concordance *f*; index *m*
concordant *adj* concordant, harmonieux -ieuse
concordat *n eccles* concordat *m*
concourse *n* concours *m*; affluence *f*, foule *f*; *US* (street) boulevard *m*; (station) salle *f* des pas perdus, hall *m*

concrete *n* béton *m*; reinforced ~ béton armé; *adj* concret -ète; *bui* en béton; ~ mixer bétonnière *f*; ~ music musique concrète; *vt* bétonner; solidifier; *vi* se solidifier
concreteness *n* concrétion *f*; solidité *f*
concretion *n med* calcul *m*
concubinage *n* concubinage *m*
concubine *n* concubine *f*
concupiscence *n* concupiscence *f*
concupiscent *adj* concupiscent
concur *vi* être d'accord; concourir, coïncider
concurrence *n* accord *m*, assentiment *m*; concurrence *f*, concours *m*, coïncidence *f*
concurrent *n* circonstance concourante; *adj* simultané, concourant; (agreeing) concordant, d'accord; convergent
concuss *vt* secouer, frapper; *med* commotionner
concussion *n med* commotion cérébrale; choc *m*, secousse *f*
condemn *vt* condamner; blâmer, censurer; (building) déclarer inhabitable; (food) interdire la consommation de
condemnation *n* condamnation *f*
condemnatory *adj* condamnatoire
condensation *n* condensation *f*
condense *vt* condenser, concentrer; résumer; ~ d milk lait concentré
condenser *n* condensateur *m*; *phys* condenseur *m*
condescend *vi* daigner, condescendre; s'abaisser, descendre
condescending *adj* condescendant
condescension *n* condescendance *f*
condign *adj* mérité, juste
condiment *n cul* condiment *m*
condition *n* condition *f*, stipulation *f*; (state) état *m*, circonstance *f*; (rank) rang *m*, position *f*; ~s circonstances *fpl*, ambiance *f*; on ~ pourvu que; *vt* stipuler; (influence) conditionner, déterminer
conditional *n gramm* conditionnel *m*; *adj* conditionnel -elle, dépendant; *gramm* conditionnel -elle; be ~ on dépendre de
conditioned *adj* conditionné, déterminé; *psych* ~ reflex réflexe conditionné; well ~ en bonne condition, en bonne forme
conditioning *n psych* modification *f* des réflexes
condole *vi* prendre part à la douleur, offrir ses condoléances
condolence *n* condoléance *f*
condom *n* préservatif *m*; *coll* capote anglaise
condominium *n pol* condominium *m*

**condone** *vt* pardonner; (adultery) passer sous silence

**condor** *n zool elect* condor *m*

**conduce** *vi* ~ **to** tendre à, produire

**conducive** *adj* tendant, contribuant

**conduct** *n* (management, behaviour) conduite *f*, comportement *m*, attitude *f*; **safe** ~ sauf-conduit *m*; *vt* conduire, mener; (guide) diriger; *mus* diriger; *elect* conduire; ~ **oneself** se conduire, se comporter; ~ **ed tour** visite guidée

**conductance** *n elect* conductance *f*

**conductibility** *n phys* conductibilité *f*

**conductible** *adj phys* conductible

**conduction** *n phys* + *physiol* conduction *f*

**conductive** *adj elect* + *phys* conducteur -trice

**conductor** *n* conducteur -trice; (bus) receveur *m*; *mus* chef *m* d'orchestre; *phys* + *elect* conducteur *m*

**conductress** *n* (bus) receveuse *f*

**conduit** *n* conduit *m*, tuyau *m*, tube *m*

**cone** *n math* + *geol* cône *m*; *bot* pomme *f* de pin; (ice-cream) cornet *m*

**cone-bearing** *adj* conifère

**confabulation** *n* discussion amicale

**confection** *n* fabrication *f*; *cul* friandise *f*, petit gâteau; article *m* de Paris

**confectioner** *n* confiseur -euse

**confectionery** *n* confiserie *f*

**confederacy** *n* confédération *f*; fédération *f*; conspiration *f*

**confederate** *n* confédéré *m*; complice; *adj* confédéré, allié; *vt* confédérer; *vi* se confédérer

**confederation** *n* confédération *f*

**confer** *vt* conférer, accorder; *vi* conférer, s'entretenir

**conferment** *n* action *f* de conférer, octroi *m*

**confess** *vt* avouer, confesser, admettre; *eccles* confesser (qn); *vi* passer aux aveux; *eccles* confesser, se confesser

**confession** *n* aveu *m*; confession *f*; *eccles* confession *f*; secte *f*

**confessional** *n eccles* confessionnal *m*; *adj* confessionnel -elle

**confessor** *n eccles* confesseur *m*

**confetti** *n* confetti *mpl*

**confidant** *n* confident *m*; ~ **e** confidente *f*

**confide** *vt* confier; *vi* ~ **in** se fier à, s'ouvrir à

**confidence** *n* confiance *f*, espoir *m*, assurance *f*; secret *m*, confidence *f*; ~ **trick** escroquerie *f*; **in** ~ confidentiel -ielle

**confidential** *adj* confidentiel -ielle, intime, particulier -ière; (trustworthy) de confiance; ~ **secretary** secrétaire particulier -ière

**confiding** *adj* confiant

**configuration** *n* configuration *f*

**confine** *vt* confiner, enfermer; emprisonner; limiter, retenir; *med* **be** ~ **d** être en couches

**confinement** *n* emprisonnement *m*, réclusion *f*; *med* couches *fpl*

**confines** *npl* confins *mpl*, bornes *fpl*; *fig* limites *fpl*

**confirm** *vt* confirmer, corroborer; affirmer, renforcer; ratifier; *eccles* confirmer

**confirmation** *n* confirmation *f*; ratification *f*

**confirmative, confirmatory** *adj* qui confirme

**confirmed** *adj* confirmé; (inveterate) invétéré, durci; (habitual) habituel -elle

**confiscate** *vt* confisquer; *adj leg* confisqué

**confiscation** *n* confiscation *f*

**conflagration** *n* conflagration *f*; incendie *m*

**conflict** *n* conflit *m*, combat *m*; désaccord *m*; *vi* s'opposer, se heurter

**confluence** *n geog* + *fig* confluence *f*

**confluent** *n geog* affluent *m*; *adj* qui se rejoignent

**conform** *vt* conformer; adapter; *vi* se conformer, s'adapter

**conformation** *n* conformation *f*, configuration *f*, structure *f*

**conformist** *n* conformiste

**conformity** *n* conformité *f*; accord *m*; (submission) soumission *f*

**confound** *vt* confondre, brouiller, rendre confus; (overthrow) détruire; *coll* ~ **it!** diable!

**confounded** *adj* confus; (abashed) déconcerté; *coll* sacré

**confoundedly** *adv coll* extrêmement, très, diablement

**confraternity** *n* confraternité *f*, confrérie *f*

**confront** *vt* affronter, braver; (compare texts) collationner; confronter, mettre en présence

**confrontation** *n* confrontation *f*

**Confucian** *n* confucianiste; *adj* confucianiste

**confuse** *vt* (bewilder) effarer, obscurcir; (mix) brouiller, mêler; (fail to distinguish) confondre, ne pas distinguer; embarrasser

**confused** *adj* ahuri, embarrassé; confus

**confusion** *n* confusion *f*, désordre *m*; embarras *m*, désarroi *m*

**confutation** *n* réfutation *f*

**confute** *vt* réfuter

**congeal** *vt* (freeze) congeler; (blood)

coaguler; (milk) cailler; (oil) figer; *vi* (freeze) se congeler; (blood) se coaguler; (milk) se cailler; (oil) se figer

**congelation** *n* congélation *f*

**congenial** *adj* sympathique, aimable, agréable; approprié, de même tempérament

**congenital** *adj* congénital

**conger** *n zool* ~ (**eel**) congre *m*

**congest** *vt* (pack) entasser; (crowd) encombrer, congestionner; *med* congestionner

**congestion** *n* encombrement *m*; (traffic) embouteillage *m*; *med* congestion *f*

¹**conglomerate** *n geol* + *fig* conglomérat *m*

²**conglomerate** *vt* conglomérer; *vi* se conglomérer

**conglomeration** *n* conglomération *f*

**congratulate** *vt* féliciter, congratuler

**congratulation** *n* félicitation *f*, congratulation *f*; ~ **s!** félicitations!

**congregate** *vt* rassembler, réunir; *vi* se rassembler, se réunir

**congregation** *n* assemblée *f*; *eccles* congrégation *f*

**congregationalism** *n eccles* (protestant) congrégationalisme *m*

**congress** *n* congrès *m*; *US* **Congress** Congrès *m*

**congressman** *n US* membre *m* du Congrès

**congruence** *n* accord *m*, conformité *f*; *math* congruence *f*

**congruent** *adj* d'accord, en conformité; convenable; *math* congru

**congruous** *adj* convenable, approprié, consistant

**conic** *adj* conique; *math* ~ **section** section *f* conique

**conical** *adj* conique

**conifer** *n* conifère *m*

**coniferous** *adj* conifère

**conjectural** *adj* conjectural

**conjecture** *n* conjecture *f*, supposition *f*; *vt* conjecturer, supposer; *vi* conjecturer, faire des conjectures

**conjoin** *vt* adjoindre, conjoindre; *vi* s'unir

**conjoint** *adj* uni, combiné, joint

**conjugal** *adj* conjugal

**conjugate** *adj* conjugué; *vt gramm* conjuguer; *vi* se conjuguer

**conjugation** *n* conjugaison *f*

**conjunction** *n* conjonction *f*; jonction *f*, union *f*

**conjunctive** *adj* unissant; *gramm* + *med* conjonctif -ive

**conjunctivitis** *n med* conjonctivite *f*

**conjuncture** *n* conjoncture *f*, circonstance *f*; crise *f*

¹**conjure** *vt* conjurer

²**conjure** *vt* escamoter; ~ **up** faire apparaître

**conjurer, conjuror** *n* prestidigitateur -trice

**conjuring** *n* prestidigitation *f*; *adj* de passe-passe

¹**conk** *n coll* nez *m*; *coll* gnon *m* (sur le nez)

²**conk** *vi mot* ~ **out** caler, rester en panne

**connect** *vt* joindre, unir; relier; *elect* connecter; *vi* se relier, se raccorder; (train) correspondre

**connecting-rod** *n eng* bielle *f*

**connection, connexion** *n* union *f*, connexion *f*; (relationship) rapport *m*, lien *m*, association *f*; rapports sexuels; *elect* prise *f*, connexion *f*; (railway) correspondance *f*

**conning** *n naut* commandement *m*; *adj* ~ **tower** tourelle *f* de commandement

**connivance** *n* connivence *f*, complicité *f*

**connive** *vi* ~ **at** être de connivence dans; (pretend not to notice) fermer les yeux sur

**connoisseur** *n* connaisseur -euse

**connotation** *n* implication *f*, associations *fpl*; *philos* connotation *f*

**connote** *vt* impliquer, suggérer; *coll* signifier

**connubial** *adj* conjugal

**conquer** *vt* vaincre, battre; subjuguer; (overcome) surmonter, conquérir

**conqueror** *n* vainqueur *m*, conquérant -e

**conquest** *n* conquête *f*

**consanguineous** *adj* consanguin

**consanguinity** *n* consanguinité *f*

**conscience** *n* conscience *f*

**conscientious** *adj* consciencieux -ieuse; ~ **objector** objecteur *m* de conscience

**conscious** *adj* conscient; intentionnel -elle; embarrassé, gêné

**conscript** *n* conscrit *m*; *adj* conscrit; *vt mil* enrôler par conscription

**conscription** *n mil* conscription *f*

**consecrate** *adj eccles* consacré; *vt* consacrer; (king, bishop) sacrer

**consecration** *n* consécration *f*; (king, bishop) sacre *m*

**consecutive** *adj* consécutif -ive, successif -ive

**consensus** *n* accord général, consensus *m*

**consent** *n* consentement *m*, assentiment *m*, accord *m*; permission *f*; **age of** ~ nubilité *f*, âge *m* nubile; *vi* consentir, acquiescer

**consequence** *n* conséquence *f*; effet *m*; importance *f*, valeur *f*

**consequent** *n philos* conséquent *m*; *adj* conséquent, résultant; logique

**consequential** *adj* résultant, dérivé; (pompous) suffisant, prétentieux -ieuse

**conservancy** *n* = administration *f* des eaux et forêts; protection *f* écologique

**conservation** *n* conservation *f*, préservation *f*

**conservatism** n conservatisme m; pol (Britain) idées fpl du parti conservateur

**conservative** n pol (Britain) membre m du parti conservateur; adj conservateur -trice; prudent, modéré

**conservatoire** n conservatoire m

**conservatory** n serre f; conservatoire m

**conserve** n (jam) confiture f; fruits confits; vt conserver, préserver

**conshy, conshie, conchy** n coll obs mil objecteur m de conscience

**consider** vt considérer, examiner; estimer, respecter; peser; vi réfléchir, méditer

**considerable** adj considérable, notable; important, remarquable

**considerate** adj attentionné, prévenant

**considerateness** n égards mpl, gentillesse f, humanité f

**consideration** n considération f; réflexion f, étude f; estime f; (money) compensation f, dédommagement m; sollicitude f

**considered** adj pondéré, réfléchi; estimé

**considering** prep vu, étant donné; en raison de; adv coll quand on y pense

**consign** vt consigner, confier, remettre; expédier

**consignation** n expédition f; consignation f

**consignee** n destinataire

**consigner, consignor** n expéditeur -trice, consignateur -trice

**consignment** n envoi m; (despatch) expédition f; quantité f de marchandises

**consist** vi ~ **in** consister en; ~ **of** consister de, se composer de; ~ **with** être consistant avec

**consistence, consistency** n consistance f; (unchanging character) stabilité f, fermeté f, uniformité f

**consistent** adj consistant, stable, logique, régulier -ière; ~ **with** compatible avec, en accord avec

**consistory** n eccles consistoire m

**consolable** adj consolable

**consolation** n consolation f

**consolatory** adj consolateur -trice

¹**console** n archi + mus + rad console f

²**console** vt consoler

**consolidate** vt consolider; fusionner, joindre; vi se consolider

**consolidation** n consolidation f

**consols** n consolidés mpl

**consommé** n cul consommé m

**consonance** n accord m; harmonie f; mus consonance f

¹**consonant** n gramm consonne f

²**consonant** adj d'accord, en harmonie; mus consonant

¹**consort** n conjoint -e; naut navire m voyageant de conserve

²**consort** vi s'associer, frayer; (agree) s'accorder

**consortium** n consortium m

**conspectus** n sommaire m, tableau m synoptique

**conspicuous** adj évident, très visible; frappant, remarquable; insigne, exceptionnel -elle; pej voyant; **make oneself** ~ se faire remarquer

**conspiracy** n conspiration f, conjuration f

**conspirator** n conspirateur -trice, conjuré -e

**conspire** vi conspirer, comploter

**constable** n (Britain) constable m; agent m de police, gendarme m; **chief** ~ = préfet m de police

**constabulary** n police f; agents mpl de police (d'une ville, d'une région)

**constancy** n constance f, fermeté f, fidélité f; stabilité f

**constant** n math constante f; adj constant, fidèle, ferme; stable

**constantly** adv fréquemment, constamment; fidèlement

**constellation** n constellation f

**consternation** n atterrement m, désarroi m

**constipate** vt constiper

**constipation** n constipation f

**constituency** n circonscription f

**constituent** n (component) élément m, composant m; pol électeur -trice; adj constituant, composant

**constitute** vt établir, constituer, former; (make up) composer; (appoint) désigner, instituer

**constitution** n constitution f; pol + med constitution f; tempérament m; leg statuts mpl

**constitutional** n promenade f; adj constitutionnel -elle

**constitutionally** adv constitutionnellement; naturellement

**constrain** vt contraindre, réprimer; forcer; (restrict) restreindre

**constrained** adj embarrassé, gêné; gauche, contraint

**constraint** n contrainte f, force f; embarras m

**constrict** vt comprimer, serrer; (contract) rétrécir; (inhibit) retenir, restreindre

**constriction** n constriction f

**constrictor** n anat constricteur m; zool boa constricteur

**construct** n construction f; vt construire, édifier, bâtir

**construction** n construction f; édifice m, bâtiment m; interprétation f

**constructional** adj de construction

**constructive** adj constructif -ive, créateur -trice; inféré, déduit; implicite
**constructor** n constructeur -trice
**construe** vt gramm faire l'analyse grammaticale de; traduire mot à mot; fig interpréter; vi faire une analyse grammaticale
**consubstantial** adj consubstantiel -ielle
**consubstantiation** n theol consubstantiation f
**consul** n consul m
**consular** adj consulaire
**consulate** n consulat m
**consult** vt consulter, demander l'avis de; (book) se référer à; (take into account) considérer, prendre en considération; vi conférer; se consulter
**consultant** n med médecin consultant; leg avocat m conseil; eng ingénieur m conseil
**consultation** n consultation f
**consultative** adj consultatif -ive
**consulting** adj med consultant; conseil invar
**consumable** adj consommable
**consume** vt consumer, brûler; user, gaspiller; (food, drink) consommer; fig obséder, consumer; vi se consumer
**consumer** n consommateur -trice; ~ durables appareils ménagers; ~ goods denrées fpl de consommation; ~ research études fpl de marchés
**consummate** vt (marriage) consommer; (complete) achever, parfaire; adj achevé, parfait, consommé
**consummation** n consommation f; achèvement m, fin f; perfection f; résultat m
**consumption** n consommation f; med tuberculose f
**consumptive** n + adj med tuberculeux -euse, phtisique
**contact** n contact m; (person) relation f; (relationship) rapport m; ~ lenses verres mpl de contact; vt coll contacter
**contact-breaker** n interrupteur m, conjoncteur m
**contagion** n contagion f
**contagious** adj contagieux -ieuse
**contagiousness** n contagiosité f
**contain** vt contenir, renfermer; math être divisible par; fig contenir, réprimer; se contenir
**container** n (goods) containeur m; boîte f; récipient m
**containment** n endiguement m, limitation f
**contaminate** vt contaminer
**contamination** n contamination f
**contango** n report m
**contemplate** vt contempler; envisager, considérer; (plan) projeter; vi méditer,

réfléchir
**contemplation** n contemplation f; (deep thought) méditation f
**contemplative** adj pensif -ive, méditatif -ive, songeur -euse; eccles contemplatif -ive
**contemporaneous** adj contemporain
**contemporary** n + adj contemporain -e
**contempt** n mépris m; dédain m; ~ of court outrage m à magistrat
**contemptibility** n ignominie f, bassesse f
**contemptible** adj méprisable, indigne
**contemptuous** adj méprisant, dédaigneux -euse
**contemptuousness** n mépris m, dédain m
**contend** vi lutter; (argue) discuter, disputer; (maintain) maintenir, assurer
¹**content** n contenu m; capacité f, volume m; sens m, signification f; ~ s contenu m; table of ~ s table f des matières
²**content** n contentement m, satisfaction f; adj content, satisfait, heureux -euse; vt contenter, satisfaire; ~ oneself se contenter, être satisfait
**contention** n contention f, controverse f, démêlé m; affirmation f, prétention f
**contentious** adj querelleur -euse, ergoteur -euse; (issue) controversé; leg contentieux -ieuse
**contentment** n contentement m
**conterminous, co-terminous** adj contigu -üe, limitrophe; (time) de même durée; (space) de même étendue
**contest** n lutte f, compétition f; conflit m; sp épreuve f; vt contester, discuter; disputer
**contestant** n contestant -e
**contestation** n contestation f
**context** n contexte m
**contiguity** n contiguïté f
**contiguous** adj contigu -üe, adjacent, limitrophe
**continence** n continence f, retenue f
¹**continent** n continent m; coll (continent m d') Europe f
²**continent** adj continent; sobre
**continental** n Européen -éenne; adj continental; ~ breakfast café complet
**contingency** n éventualité f; philos contingence f
**contingent** adj éventuel -uelle, imprévu; philos contingent; be ~ (up)on dépendre de
**continual** adj continuel -uelle
**continuance** n continuation f; durée f
**continuation** n continuation f, prolongement m, extension f
**continuator** n continuateur -trice
**continue** vt continuer, poursuivre;

persister; prolonger; (start again) reprendre; *vi* continuer; (remain) rester, demeurer, persister

**continued** *adj* continu; prolongé; (restarted) repris

**continuing** *adj* durable

**continuity** *n* continuité *f*

**continuity-girl** *n cin* scripte *f*

**continuous** *adj* continu; *cin* permanent

**contort** *vt* tordre; déformer; dénaturer

**contortion** *n* torsion *f*, contorsion *f*

**contortionist** *n* contorsionniste

**contour** *n* contour *m*; profil *m*; *geog* ~ **(line)** courbe *f* de niveau; courbe *f* hypsométrique; ~ **map** carte *f* hypsométrique; *vt* dessiner le contour de

**contra** *n* contrepartie *f*; *prep* contre

**contraband** *n* contrebande *f*; *adj* de contrebande

**contrabandist** *n* contrebandier -ière

**contrabass** *n mus* contrebasse *f*

**contraception** *n* contraception *f*

**contraceptive** *n* contraceptif *m*, préservatif *m*; *adj* contraceptif -ive, anticonceptionnel -elle

¹**contract** *n* contrat *m*; (agreement) accord *m*, pacte *m*; contrat *m* de mariage; ~ **bridge** bridge *m* contrat; ~ **work** travail *m* à forfait; *vt* contracter; *vi* s'engager; ~ **in (out)** accepter (refuser) de participer; ~ **to do sth** s'engager à faire qch

²**contract** *vt* contracter, crisper; (shorten) écourter; *vi* se contracter, se crisper

**contractible** *adj* qui peut être contracté

**contractile** *adj* contractile

**contracting** *adj* contractant; *pol* **high ~ powers** hautes parties contractantes

**contraction** *n* contraction *f*

**contractor** *n* entrepreneur *m*; contractant *m*; *anat* muscle *m* contractile

**contractual** *adj* contractuel -uelle

**contracture** *n med* contracture *f*

**contradict** *vt* contredire; (rumour) démentir

**contradiction** *n* contradiction *f*

**contradictory** *adj* contradictoire, inconsistant

**contradistinction** *n* contraste *m*

**contra-indicate** *vt med* contre-indiquer

**contra-indication** *n med* contre-indication *f*

**contralto** *n mus* contralto *m*

**contraption** *n coll* truc *m*, machin *m*, gadget *m*

**contrapuntal** *adj* en contrepoint

**contrariety** *n* opposition *f*; (setback) entrave *f*

**contrarily** *adv* contrairement; (perversely) avec perversité

**contrariness** *n coll* esprit *m* de contradiction

**contrariwise** *adv* en sens contraire

¹**contrary** *n* contraire *m*, opposé *m*; **on the** ~ pas du tout, au contraire; **unless you hear to the** ~ sauf avis contraire; *adj* contraire, opposé; hostile, défavorable

²**contrary** *adj* contrariant, obstiné

**contrast** *n* contraste *m*, opposition *f*; *vt* faire contraster; contraster, opposer; *vi* faire contraste, contraster

**contravene** *vt* violer, désobéir à; contredire

**contretemps** *n* contretemps *m*

**contribute** *vt* contribuer, donner; (articles) écrire; *vi* souscrire, contribuer

**contribution** *n* contribution *f*, souscription *f*, cotisation *f*; (paper) article *m*

**contributor** *n* collaborateur -trice, auteur *m*; (subscriber) souscripteur -trice

**contributory** *adj* qui contribue; accessoire

**contrite** *adj* contrit

**contrition** *n* contrition *f*

**contrivance** *n* invention *f*; dispositif *m*, machin *m*; plan *m*, procédé *m*; idée ingénieuse

**contrive** *vt* réussir, concevoir; arranger, organiser; *fig* machiner, combiner

**control** *n* autorité *f*; restriction *f*, limitation *f*; contrôle *m*; réglementation *f*; (spiritualism) esprit *m* contrôleur; *mech* commande *f*; ~ **s** instruments *mpl* de commande; *vt* commander, diriger; contrôler; vérifier; régler; (restrain) maîtriser, contenir

**controller, comptroller** *n* contrôleur *m*

**controversial** *adj* controversable

**controversy** *n* controverse *f*; dispute *f*

**controvert** *vt* contredire, opposer, argumenter, disputer

**controvertible** *adj* controversable, contestable

**contumacious** *adj* rebelle, réfractaire; *leg* contumace

**contumacy** *n* insubordination *f*; *leg* contumace *f*

**contumely** *n* injure *f*, insolence *f*; (scorn) mépris *m*, dédain *m*

**contuse** *vt med* contusionner, meurtrir

**contusion** *n med* contusion *f*, meurtrissure *f*

**conundrum** *n* devinette *f*

**conurbation** *n* conurbation *f*

**convalesce** *vi* être en convalescence, se remettre

**convalescence** *n* convalescence *f*

**convalescent** *adj* convalescent

**convection** *n* convection *f*

**convector** *n* appareil *m* de chauffage à convection

**convene** *vt* convoquer; *vi* se réunir

**convenience**

**convenience** *n* convenance *f*, opportunité *f*; (usefulness) utilité *f*; (comfort) commodité *f*, confort *m*; (lavatory) toilettes *fpl*; **at one's ~** à loisir; **at your earliest ~** dans les meilleurs délais
**convenient** *adj* commode; acceptable; loisible; *coll* tout près
**convent** *n* couvent *m*
**convention** *n* convention *f*, usage *m*; (meeting) assemblée *f*
**conventional** *adj* de convention, conventionnel -elle; **~ weapons** armes *fpl* classiques
**conventionality** *n* bienséance *f*; usage conventionnel
**conventionalize** *vt* rendre conventionnel
**conventual** *n + adj eccles* conventuel -elle
**converge** *vt* faire converger; *vi* converger
**convergence** *n* convergence *f*
**convergent** *adj* convergent
**conversable** *adj* sociable, causeur -euse
**conversant** *adj* familier -ière; (experienced) versé, expérimenté, compétent
**conversation** *n* conversation *f*, entretien *m*
**conversational** *adj* de conversation; (style) coulant, facile
**conversationalist** *n* causeur -euse; raconteur -euse
**¹converse** *n* conversation *f*, entretien *m*; *vi* converser, s'entretenir
**²converse** *n* contraire *m*, inverse *m*; *adj* contraire, inverse
**conversion** *n* conversion *f*, transformation *f*, mutation *f*; (building) aménagement *m*
**convert** *n* converti -e; *vt* transformer, convertir, changer
**converter** *n mech + elect* convertisseur *m*
**convertible** *n mot* voiture *f* décapotable; *adj* convertissable; *comm* convertible
**convex** *adj* convexe
**convexity** *n* convexité *f*
**convey** *vt* transporter, porter; amener; transmettre, communiquer; exprimer, rendre; *leg* aliéner, transférer
**conveyance** *n* transport *m*; moyen *m* de transport, véhicule *m*; *leg* cession *f*, transfert *m*
**conveyancer** *n leg* personne *f* qui opère un transfert
**conveyancing** *n leg* cession *f* de biens, transfert *m*, aliénation *f*
**conveyer, conveyor** *n* (person) porteur *m*; (thing) transporteur *m*, convoyeur *m*; **~ belt** convoyeur *m*, tapis roulant
**convict** *n* condamné -e, forçat *m*; *vt* condamner, déclarer coupable
**conviction** *n* conviction *f*, croyance *f*; *leg* condamnation *f*
**convince** *vt* convaincre, persuader

**convincing** *adj* convaincant, plausible
**convivial** *adj* sociable, jovial; *coll* un peu parti
**convocation** *n* convocation *f*; *eccles* synode *m*
**convoke** *vt* convoquer
**convolute, convoluted** *adj* convoluté
**convolution** *n* convolution *f*
**convolvulus** *n bot* volubilis *m*
**convoy** *n naut* convoi *m*; *vt naut* convoyer
**convulse** *vt* convulsionner; *med* convulser; **~ with laughter** faire tordre de rire
**convulsion** *n* convulsion *f*; agitation *f*
**convulsive** *adj* convulsif -ive
**cony** *n* lapin *m*; (fur) fourrure *f* de lapin
**coo** *n* roucoulement *m*; *vi* roucouler; **bill and ~** se bécoter; *interj coll* tiens!
**cook** *n* cuisinier -ière; chef *m*; *vt* cuire, faire cuire; *coll* (fake) cuisiner, falsifier; **~ s/o's goose** ruiner qn; **~ up** inventer, falsifier; *vi* cuisiner, faire la cuisine; cuire
**cooker** *n* cuisinière *f*; **pressure ~** cocotte *f* minute, autocuiseur *m*
**cookery** *n* cuisine *f*; **~ book** livre *m* de cuisine
**cook-house** *n mil* cuisine *f*
**cookie** *n* petit gâteau
**cooking** *n* cuisine *f*; (process) cuisson *f*
**cool** *n* fraîcheur *f*; *sl* calme *m*; **keep one's ~** garder son sang-froid, rester calme; *adj* frais (*f* fraîche); calme, froid, indifférent, tiède; *coll* sans gêne; (with it) chic *invar*; (no less than) au moins; *vt* rafraîchir, refroidir; *sl* **~ it** se calmer; **~ one's heels** être obligé d'attendre; *vi* se refroidir
**cooler** *n* glacière *f*; (apparatus) refroidisseur *m*; *sl* taule *f*
**coolie** *n* coolie *m*
**coolness** *n* fraîcheur *f*; calme *m*; (estrangement) froideur *f*
**coombe** *n* combe *f*
**coon** *n zool* laveur raton *m*; *obs pej* nègre (*f* négresse)
**coop** *n* poulailler *m*, mue *f*; *vt* enfermer; mettre en cage; **~ up** enfermer
**cooper** *n* tonnelier *m*
**co-operate** *vi* coopérer, contribuer
**co-operation** *n* coopération *f*
**co-operative** *n* coopérative *f*; *adj* coopératif -ive
**co-opt** *vt* coopter
**co-option** *n* cooptation *f*
**co-ordinate** *n math* coordonnées *fpl*; *adj* coordonné; *vt* coordonner
**co-ordination** *n* coordination *f*
**coot** *n zool* foulque *f*; *coll* idiot -e; **bald as a ~** chauve comme un œuf
**cop** *n sl* (policeman) flic *m*; *sl* prise *f*; **it's not much ~** ça ne vaut pas grand-

416

chose; *vt sl* coincer; ~ **it** être puni

¹**cope** *n eccles* chape *f*; *vt* couvrir d'une chape; *archi* chaperonner

²**cope** *vi* se débrouiller; ~ **with** se charger de; (successfully) venir à bout de

**coper** *n* maquignon *m*

**copier** *n* copiste; machine *f* à photocopier

**co-pilot** *n* copilote *m*

**coping** *n bui* chaperon *m*

**coping-stone** *n archi* couronnement *m*

**copious** *adj* copieux -ieuse, abondant

**copiousness** *n* abondance *f*, profusion *f*

¹**copper** *n* cuivre *m*; (small coin) sou *m*; couleur *f* cuivre; (cauldron) chaudron *m*; *adj* de cuivre, cuivré; *vt* cuivrer

²**copper** *n sl* flic *m*

**copper-beech** *n* hêtre *m* pourpre

**copper-bottomed** *adj fig* absolument sûr

**copperplate** *n* plaque *f* de cuivre; (engraving) taille-douce *f* (*pl* tailles-douces); (writing) écriture moulée

**coppersmith** *n* fabricant *m* de dinanderie

**coppery** *adj* cuivré

**coppice, copse** *n* taillis *m*, bosquet *m*

**copra** *n* copra *m*

**copse** *n see* **coppice**

**copula** *n gramm* copule *f*

**copulate** *vi* copuler

**copulation** *n* copulation *f*, coït *m*

**copulative** *adj* copulatif -ive

**copy** *n* copie *f*, imitation *f*; reproduction *f*, transcription *f*; (book) exemplaire *m*; (journalism) copie *f*; *leg* certified ~ copie *f* conforme; *vt* copier, imiter; reproduire, transcrire; *vi* copier, faire une copie

**copy-book** *n* cahier *m* (d'écriture); **blot one's** ~ endommager sa réputation

**copyist** *n* copiste

**copyright** *n* copyright *m*, propriété *f* littéraire; *adj* aux droits réservés; *vt* réserver les droits de reproduction de

**copywriter** *n* personne *f* qui compose des textes publicitaires, publiciste

**coquet, coquette** *vi* flirter

**coquetry** *n* coquetterie *f*

**coquette** *n* coquette *f*

**cor** *interj sl* mince alors!

**coral** *n* corail *m*; couleur *f* corail; *adj* de corail, en corail; couleur de corail

**coralline** *adj* corallien -ienne; *obs* corallin

**coral-reef** *n* récif *m* de corail

**cor anglais** *n mus* cor anglais, hautbois *m* alto

**corbel** *n archi* corbeau *m*, console *f*; *vt* soutenir par une console

**cord** *n* corde *f*; ~ **s** (corduroy) pantalon *m* de velours côtelé; **spinal** ~ moelle épinière; *vt* encorder, lier

**cordage** *n naut* cordages *mpl*

**corded** *adj* ligoté; (cloth) côtelé

**cordial** *n* cordial *m*; *adj* cordial

**cordiality** *n* cordialité *f*

**cordite** *n* cordite *f*

**cordon** *n* cordon *m*; *archi* + *mil* cordon *m*; *joc* ~ **bleu** cordon-bleu *m* (*pl* cordons-bleus); *vt* établir un cordon autour de; ~ **off** isoler

**corduroy** *n* velours côtelé; *adj* en velours côtelé

**core** *n* cœur *m*; (fruit) trognon *m*; *elect* noyau *m*; *med* (boil) bourbillon *m*, *fig* cœur *m*, tréfonds *m*; **hard** ~ ceux que l'on ne peut pas convaincre; **rotten to the** ~ pourri jusqu'à la moelle; *vt* enlever le cœur de, évider

**co-religionist** *n* coreligionnaire

**co-respondent** *n* partenaire d'un homme (d'une femme) adultère

**coriander** *n bot* coriandre *f*

**cork** *n* (substance) liège *m*; (bottle) bouchon *m*; *adj* de liège; *vt* (bottle) boucher; *fig* enrayer; noircir au bouchon

**corked** *adj* (wine) qui sent le bouchon

**corker** *n coll* (lie) craque *f*; argument *m* massue; (person) type *m* formidable; (girl) beau morceau (de fille)

**corking** *adj coll* énorme, formidable

**corkscrew** *n* tire-bouchon *m*; *adj* en tire-bouchon, spiral; *vi* se tire-bouchonner, se tortiller

**cork-tree** *n bot* chêne-liège *m* (*pl* chênes-lièges)

**cormorant** *n zool* cormoran *m*

¹**corn** *n* grain *m*; (wheat) blé *m*; (oats) avoine *f*; *US* maïs *m*; *coll* banalité *f*, cliché *m*

²**corn** *n med* cor *m*

**corn-chandler** *n* grainetier *m*

**corn-cob** *n* épi *m* de maïs

**corn-crake** *n orni* râle *m*

**cornea** *n anat* cornée *f*

**corned-beef** *n* bœuf *m* en conserve; *coll* singe *m*

**cornelian** *n* cornaline *f*

**corner** *n* coin *m*, angle *m*; *comm* accaparement *m*; *sp* (football, hockey) corner *m*; **drive into a** ~ coincer, mettre au pied du mur; **round the** ~ tout près; **turn the** ~ commencer à se remettre; *vt* mettre dans un coin; mettre au pied du mur, coincer; *mot* prendre un virage; *comm* accaparer

**cornered** *adj* à coins; acculé

**corner-stone** *n* pierre *f* angulaire

**cornet** *n mus* cornet *m* à pistons; (ice-cream) cornet *m*; *eccles* (nun's head-dress) cornette *f*; *mil ar* cornette *f*

**cornflakes** *npl* cornflakes *fpl*

**cornflour** *n* maïzena *f*

417

**cornice** *n archi* corniche *f*

**cornucopia** *n* corne *f* d'abondance

**corny** *adj coll* banal (*pl* banals)

**corolla** *n bot* corolle *f*

**corollary** *n* corollaire *m*; *adj* corollaire

**corona** *n astron* couronne *f*, halo *m*; (tooth) couronne *f*

**coronary** *adj med* coronaire; **~ thrombosis** thrombose *f* coronaire

**coronation** *n* couronnement *m*

**coroner** *n* coroner *m*

**coronet** *n* diadème *m*, couronne *f*

**¹corporal** *n mil* caporal *m*

**²corporal** *adj* corporel -elle; **~ punishment** châtiment corporel

**corporate** *adj* constitué

**corporation** *n* corporation *f*; = conseil municipal; *coll* (paunch) bide *m*

**corporeal** *adj* corporel -elle; matériel -ielle; tangible

**corps** *n mil* corps *m*; **~ de ballet** corps *m* de ballet

**corpse** *n* cadavre *m*

**corpulence** *n* corpulence *f*

**corpulent** *adj* corpulent

**corpus** *n* corpus *m*, recueil *m*; *comm* capital *m*; **Corpus Christi** Fête-Dieu *f*

**corpuscle** *n med* corpuscule *m*; *phys* molécule *f*

**corpuscular** *adj med* corpusculaire; *phys* moléculaire

**corral** *n* corral *m*

**correct** *adj* correct, exact, juste; *vt* corriger, redresser; améliorer; rectifier

**correction** *n* correction *f*, rectification *f*; (punishment) peine *f*, châtiment *m*; **house of ~** maison *f* de correction

**corrective** *adj* correctif -ive

**correctness** *n* exactitude *f*; (propriety) correction *f*, convenance *f*, justesse *f*

**corrector** *n* correcteur -trice; *print* corrigeur -euse

**correlate** *n* corrélatif *m*; *vt* mettre en corrélation avec; *vi* être en corrélation avec

**correlation** *n* corrélation *f*

**correlative** *n* corrélatif *m*; *adj* corrélatif -ive

**correspond** *vi* correspondre, communiquer; correspondre, être conforme

**correspondence** *n* correspondance *f*; corrélation *f*; **~ column** (newspaper) rubrique *f* des lettres; **~ course** cours *m* par correspondance

**correspondent** *n + adj* correspondant -e

**corresponding** *adj* correspondant

**corridor** *n* corridor *m*, couloir *m*

**corrigendum** *n* erratum *m*

**corroborate** *vt* corroborer

**corrode** *vt* corroder; *vi* se corroder

**corrosion** *n* corrosion *f*

**corrosive** *n* corrosif *m*; *adj* corrosif -ive

**corrugate** *vt* onduler; (wrinkle) rider; *vi* onduler; se rider

**corrugated** *adj* ondulé; **~ iron** tôle ondulée

**corrupt** *adj* corrompu, pourri; (bribed) acheté; *vt* corrompre; soudoyer, acheter; *vi* se corrompre; pourrir

**corrupter** *n* corrupteur -trice

**corruptible** *adj* corruptible

**corrupting** *adj* corrupteur -trice

**corruption** *n* corruption *f*; putréfaction *f*; (depravation) avilissement *m*

**corruptly** *adv* d'une façon corrompue

**corruptness** *n* corruption *f*

**corsage** *n* corsage *m*

**corsair** *n* corsaire *m*

**corset** *n* corset *m*, gaine *f*

**cortège** *n* cortège *m*

**cortex** *n bot* écorce *f*; *anat* cortex *m*

**cortical** *adj bot + anat* cortical

**cortisone** *n med* cortisone *f*

**corundum** *n* corindon *m*

**coruscate** *vi* scintiller

**coruscation** *n* scintillement *m*

**corvette** *n naut* corvette *f*

**coryza** *n med* coryza *m*

**¹cos** *n bot* romaine *f*

**²cos** *n abbr math* cosinus *m*

**cosecant** *n geom* cosécante *f*

**cosh** *n coll* matraque *f*, trique *f*; *vt coll* matraquer

**co-signatory** *n + adj* cosignataire

**cosily** *adv* douillettement

**cosine** *n math* cosinus *m*

**cosiness** *n* confort *m*

**cosmetic** *n* cosmétique *m*; **~s** produits *mpl* de beauté; *adj* cosmétique

**cosmetician** *n* esthéticien -ienne

**cosmic** *adj* cosmique

**cosmogony** *n* cosmogonie *f*

**cosmographer** *n* cosmographe

**cosmography** *n* cosmographie *f*

**cosmology** *n* cosmologie *f*

**cosmonaut** *n* cosmonaute

**cosmopolitan** *n + adj* cosmopolite

**cosmos** *n* cosmos *m*

**Cossack** *n* cosaque *m*

**cosset** *vt* choyer, dorloter

**cost** *n* prix *m*, coût *m*, frais *mpl*; **~s** *fig leg* dépens *mpl*; *leg* frais *mpl* judiciaires; **~ of living** coût *m* de la vie; **~ price** prix coûtant; **at the ~ of** aux dépens de; **to one's ~** à ses dépens; *vt* coûter, valoir

**coster, costermonger** *n* marchand -e des quatre-saisons

**costing** *n* établissement *m* d'un devis

**costive** *adj* constipé; *fig* lent, indolent

**costly** *adj* cher -ère, coûteux -euse; (valuable) de prix

**costume** *n* costume *m*; deux-pièces *m*; **~ jewellery** bijoux *mpl* en toc; *vt* costumer

**costumier** *n* costumier -ière

**cosy** *n* petit lainage qu'on met sur une théière, ou sur un œuf à la coque (pour conserver la chaleur); *adj* douillet -ette, confortable, chaud

¹**cot** *n* lit *m* d'enfant, petit lit; *naut* cadre *m*

²**cot** *n poet* cabane *f*

**cotangent** *n math* cotangente *f*

**coterie** *n* coterie *f*

**co-terminous** *adj see* **conterminous**

**cotillion** *n* cotillon *m*

**cottage** *n* petite maison rustique; ~ **industry** artisanat *m*; *cul* ~ **pie** mélange *m* de viande hachée et pommes purée cuit au four; **country** ~ cottage *m*; **thatched** ~ chaumière *f*

**cottager** *n* campagnard -e

**cotter** *n* clavette *f*; ~ **pin** goupille fendue

**cotton** *n* coton *m*; (fabric) cotonnade *f*; (plant) cotonnier *m*; *adj* de coton; *vi* aimer, avoir bonne impression; ~ **on** comprendre; *coll* piger

**cotton-cake** *n agr* tourteau *m*

**cotton-print** *n* percale *f*, indienne *f*

**cotton-wool** *n* ouate *f*; coton *m* hydrophile; **wrap in** ~ dorloter

¹**couch** *n* (bed) couche *f*; divan *m*; *vt* coucher; *fig* (words) exprimer, rédiger

²**couch, couch-grass** *n* chiendent *m*

**couchant** *adj her* couchant

**cough** *n* toux *f*; *vi* tousser; ~ **up** cracher, expectorer (en toussant); *coll* (money) casquer; *coll* (information) révéler

**cough-drop** *n* pâte pectorale

**could** *see* can *v aux*

**coulomb** *n elect* coulomb *m*

**council** *n* conseil *m*, assemblée *f*; *eccles RC* concile *m*; *fig* conseil *m*, débat *m*

**council-chamber** *n* salle *f* de réunion (d'un conseil municipal)

**council-flat** *n* = appartement *m* H.L.M. (habitation *f* à loyer modéré)

**council-house** *n* maison louée à la municipalité

**councillor** *n* conseiller -ère (municipal -e)

**council-school** *n* école *f* primaire, école communale

**counsel** *n* conseil *m*, avis *m*; consultation *f*; = avocat -e; ~ **of perfection** conseil idéal mais peu pratique; *vt* conseiller

**counsellor** *n* conseiller -ère; (social services, etc) orienteur *m*

¹**count** *n* compte *m*, calcul *m*; *leg* chef *m* d'accusation; *sp* (boxing) compte *m*; **on all** ~ **s** de tous les points de vue; **take no** ~ **of** négliger; *vt* compter, calculer, dénombrer; *fig* tenir pour, considérer; ~ **in** inclure; ~ **out** ajourner; *sp* déclarer K.O.; *coll* exclure; *vi* compter; avoir de l'importance; ~ **down** faire le compte à rebours; ~ **for** être considéré comme; ~ **on** se fier à

²**count** *n* (title) comte *m*

**count-down** *n* compte *m* à rebours

**countenance** *n* visage *m*, air *m*, expression *f*; (bearing) contenance *f*; appui *m*, encouragement *m*; **keep one's** ~ cacher ses sentiments; **lose** ~ se décontenancer; **out of** ~ déconcerté; *vt* approuver, encourager; tolérer

¹**counter** *n* (machine) compteur *m*; jeton *m*; **revolution** ~ compte-tours *m*

²**counter** *n* (shop, etc) comptoir *m*; **under the** ~ subrepticement, furtivement; illégalement

³**counter** *n* (horse) poitrail *m*; *naut* poupe *f*

⁴**counter** *adj* contraire, opposé; *adv* à l'encontre, à contresens, contrairement; *vt* contrarier, contrer; déjouer; *vi* contrer

**counteract** *vt* neutraliser, contrecarrer; limiter

**counteraction** *n* contre-mesure *f*, neutralisation *f*

**counter-attack** *n mil* contre-attaque *f*; *vt* contre-attaquer

**counter-attraction** *n* attraction rivale

**counterbalance** *n* contrepoids *m*; *vt* contrebalancer

**counterblast** *n* riposte *f*

**countercharge** *n leg* contre-accusation *f*

**counter-espionage** *n* contre-espionnage *m*

**counterfeit** *n* contrefaçon *f*; *adj* faux (*f* fausse); *vt* contrefaire; simuler

**counterfeiter** *n* faux-monnayeur *m*

**counterfoil** *n* (cheque, receipt, etc) talon *m*

**countermand** *vt* révoquer, annuler

**countermarch** *n* contremarche *f*; *vi* faire une contremarche

**countermine** *n mil* contre-mine *f*; *vt* contreminer

**counter-offensive** *n mil* contre-offensive *f*

**counterpane** *n* couvre-lit *m*

**counterpoint** *n mus* contrepoint *m*

**counterpoise** *n* contrepoids *m*; *vt* contrebalancer; *vi* faire contrepoids à

**counter-productive** *adj* qui produit un résultat opposé (à celui désiré)

**counter-revolution** *n* contre-revolution *f*

¹**countersign** *n mil* mot *m* d'ordre, consigne *f*

²**countersign** *vt* contresigner; ratifier, confirmer

**countersink** *n mech* fraise *f*; *vt* fraiser

**counter-tenor** *n* (voice) haute-contre *f*; (singer) haute-contre *m*

**countess** *n* comtesse *f*

**countless** *adj* innombrable, sans nombre

**countrified** *adj* campagnard, provincial

**country** *n* pays *m*, nation *f*, patrie *f*; (landscape) contrée *f*; (countryside) campagne *f*; ~ **cousin** provincial -e; **go to**

**country-dance**

the ~ consulter la nation; *US* God's own ~ les États-Unis; *adj* campagnard, rustique, provincial

**country-dance** *n* contredanse *f*, quadrille *m*

**countryman** *n* compatriote *m*; paysan *m*, campagnard *m*

**country-seat** *n* manoir *m*

**countryside** *n* campagne *f*, paysage *m*

**countrywoman** *n* compatriote *f*; paysanne *f*, campagnarde *f*

**county** *n* (England) comté *m*; (people) aristocratie terrienne; ~ **town** chef-lieu *m* (*pl* chefs-lieux) de comté; *adj coll* snob

**coup** *n* coup *m*

**coupé** *n* coupé *m*

**couple** *n* couple *m*, paire *f*; mari *m* et femme *f*; (hounds) laisse *f*; *vt* coupler; accoupler; *fig* associer; *vi* s'accoupler

**coupler** *n mech* coupleur *m*; personne *f* qui couple

**couplet** *n* distique *m*

**coupling** *n* accouplement *m*, union *f*; *elect* couplage *m*; (railway) chaîne *f* d'attelage

**coupon** *n* coupon *m*, ticket *m*

**courage** *n* courage *m*

**courageous** *adj* courageux -euse

**courier** *n* courrier *m*

**course** *n* (time) cours *m*, progrès *m*; (direction) route *f*, voie *f*, direction *f*; développement *m*; (studies) programme, cours *m*; *cul* service *m*, plat *m*; *sp* terrain *m*; (bricks) assise *f*; *naut* route *f*; **in due ~** en temps voulu; **of ~** certainement, bien sûr; *vt* faire courir, courir; *vi* courir; couler

**coursing** *n* chasse *f* au lièvre

**court** *n* cour *f*; *leg* cour *f*; *sp* terrain *m*; (tennis) court *m*; (courtyard) cour *f*; **out of ~** en défaveur; *vt* courtiser, faire la cour à; (risk) courir; chercher; *vi* faire la cour; **be ~ing** sortir ensemble, se fréquenter

**court-card** *n* figure *f*

**courteous** *adj* courtois

**courtesan** *n* courtisane *f*, cocotte *f*, prostituée *f*

**courtesy** *n* courtoisie *f*, politesse *f*; **by ~ of** avec la permission de

**courtier** *n* courtisan *m*

**courting** *adj* ~ **couple** couple *m* d'amoureux

**courtly** *adj* courtois, distingué, poli

**court-martial** *n* conseil *m* de guerre, tribunal *m* militaire; *vt* traduire en conseil de guerre

**courtship** *n* cour *f*

**courtyard** *n* cour *f*

**cousin** *n* cousin -e; **first ~** cousin -e germain -e; **second ~** cousin -e issu -e de

germains

¹**cove** *n geog* anse *f*, crique *f*; *archi* cintre *m*

²**cove** *n coll* type *m*

**covenant** *n* pacte *m*, convention *f*

**cover** *n* couverture *f*; (lid) couvercle *m*; (chair) housse *f*; enveloppe *f*; (at table) couvert *m*; (shelter) abri *m*; *leg* nantissement *m*; *comm* couverture *f*; (journalism) reportage *m*; **break ~** déboucher; **take ~** se mettre à l'abri; **under ~ of** protégé par, caché par; (pretence) sous prétexte de; **under separate ~** sous pli séparé; *vt* couvrir; protéger, abriter; (distance) couvrir, parcourir; (hide) cacher, dissimuler; (subject) comprendre, traiter; (journalism) faire un reportage sur; (firearm) mettre en joue; ~ **in** remplir; ~ **over** couvrir, envelopper; ~ **up** couvrir, envelopper; cacher, déguiser

**coverage** *n* reportages *mpl*; (insurance) risques couverts

**cover-charge** *n* couvert *m*

**cover-girl** *n* cover-girl *f*

**covering** *n* couverture *f*; protection *f*; *adj* qui couvre; ~ **letter** lettre explicative

**coverlet** *n* couvre-lit *m*

¹**covert** *n* fourré *m*; gîte *m*, terrier *m*

²**covert** *adj* secret -ète, déguisé

**covet** *vt* convoiter

**covetous** *adj* avide; avaricieux -ieuse

**covetousness** *n* convoitise *f*; avidité *f*, avarice *f*

¹**cow** *n* vache *f*; femelle *f*; *coll* (woman) vache *f*, salope *f*

²**cow** *vt* intimider, mater

**coward** *n* lâche, couard -e, poltron -onne

**cowardice** *n* lâcheté *f*, couardise *f*, poltronnerie *f*

**cowardly** *adj* lâche, poltron -onne

**cowboy** *n* cowboy *m*

**cower** *vi* s'accroupir; s'aplatir

**cowherd** *n* vacher *m*

**cowhide** *n* cuir *m* de vache; (whip) fouet *m*

**cowl** *n* capuchon *m*, cagoule *f*; *archi* mitre *f*

**cow-pox** *n* vaccine *f*

**cowslip** *n bot* coucou *m*

**cox** *n* barreur -euse

**coxcomb** *n ar* casquette *f* de bouffon; *obs* dandy *m*, fat *m*

**coxswain** *n* patron *m* de barque; barreur *m*

**coy** *adj* timide, effarouché

**coyness** *n* timidité *f*

**cozen** *vt* filouter, escroquer; *vi* tricher

¹**crab** *n* crabe *m*; *astron* cancer *m*; (louse) morpion *m*; *vi* pêcher le crabe; *aer* dériver

²**crab** n pomme f sauvage; (person) grincheux -euse; vt déblatérer contre; vi rouspéter

**crabbed** adj grincheux -euse, acariâtre; (writing) griffonné, gribouillé

**crab-louse** n morpion m

**crab-pot** n casier m, nasse f

**crack** n (noise) craquement m, bruit sec; fissure f, fêlure f, fente f; coll effort m, essai m; coll riposte f, bon mot; coll (expert) crack m; ~ **of dawn** moment m de l'aube; ~ **of doom** Jugement dernier; adj coll expert, formidable; vt fendre, fêler; (bone) fracturer; (skin) crevasser; (wall) lézarder; faire craquer; faire claquer; casser; (joke) débiter; (problem) résoudre; (bottle) boire; sl ~ **a crib** cambrioler une maison; ~ **down on** mettre un frein à; ~ **up** louer beaucoup; vi (noise) craquer; (whip) claquer; (split) se fendre, se fêler; (bone) se fracturer; (skin) se crevasser; (wall) se lézarder; (voice) muer; naut ~ **on** mettre (toutes les voiles); coll ~ **up** s'effondrer, flancher; coll **be ~ed** être fêlé, être toqué

**crack-brained** adj coll fêlé, toqué

**cracked** adj fêlé, plein de fissures; (voice) cassé; coll fêlé, toqué

**cracker** n (firework) pétard m; (paper) diablotin m; (biscuit) craquelin m; US biscuit m; ~ **s** casse-noisette m

**crackers** adj coll fêlé, toqué

¹**cracking** n chem cracking m, craquage m

²**cracking** adj très rapide; adv remarquablement

**crackle** n crépitement m; vi crépiter

**crackling** n crépitement m; cul couenne f

**cradle** n berceau m; med arceau m; naut ber m, bers m; fig enfance f; vt bercer; coucher dans un berceau; vi bercer

**craft** n adresse f, habileté f, dextérité f; (cunning) ruse f, astuce f; art manuel, métier m; naut bâtiment m, embarcation f; aer appareil m

**craftily** adv habilement, astucieusement

**craftiness** n habileté f, astuce f

**craftsman** n artisan m

**craftsmanship** n artisanat m

**crafty** adj habile, astucieux -ieuse

**crag** n rocher m

**craggy** adj escarpé, à pic

**cragsman** n varappeur -euse

**cram** n (examination) bachotage m; coll mensonge m; vt bourrer, bonder; (poultry) gaver, gorger; (subject) potasser; vi se bourrer, se gaver; (examination) bachoter

**crammer** n coll bachoteur -euse; répétiteur -trice; ~ **'s** boîte f à bachot

¹**cramp** n med crampe f; (spasm) crispation f; vt donner des crampes à

²**cramp** n crampon m, étau m; vt cramponner; (fig) comprimer, restreindre

**cramped** adj resserré, comprimé; restreint; (writing) illisible

**crampon** n crampon m

**cranberry** n airelle f

**crane** n orni + mech grue f; vt + vi tendre (le cou)

**cranial** adj anat cranien -ienne

**cranium** n anat crâne m

**crank** n mech manivelle f; bizarrerie f de langage; (person) eccentrique; vt couder; faire partir à la manivelle

**crankiness** n eccentricité f

**cranky** adj eccentrique, fêlé, toqué

**cranny** n fissure f, petit trou

**crap** n vulg merde f; sl fig balivernes fpl; vi vulg chier

**crapulence** n crapule f

**crash** n fracas m; heurt m, collision f, impact m; comm krach m; fig ruine f, effondrement m; vt fracasser; vi s'écraser; retentir avec fracas; s'effondrer; ~ **into** percuter, tamponner

**crash-helmet** n casque m (de motocycliste)

**crashing** n fracas m; adj écrasant; coll total

**crash-landing** n aer atterrissage forcé

**crass** adj épais (f épaisse); crasse, grossier -ière; stupide

**crate** n cageot m, caisse f; vt mettre dans un cageot, emballer

**crater** n cratère m; (bomb) entonnoir m

**cravat** n foulard m

**crave** vt souhaiter, désirer beaucoup; solliciter

**craven** n + adj lâche, poltron -onne

**craving** n désir m intense, aspiration f; adj intense, dévorant

**crawfish** n see crayfish

**crawl** n rampement m; (snake) reptation f; allure lente; sp crawl m; vi ramper, se traîner (à quatre pattes); avancer lentement; (insects, etc) grouiller, fourmiller; coll fig s'aplatir

**crawler** n (baby-clothes) barboteuse f; coll fig (idler) paresseux -euse; flatteur -euse

**crawling** adj rampant; (swarming) grouillant, foisonnant

**crayfish, crawfish** n (freshwater) écrevisse f; (sea) langouste f

**crayon** n fusain m, pastel m; vt dessiner au fusain, crayonner

**craze** n manie f, mode f; vt rendre cinglé; vi devenir cinglé

**crazed** adj cinglé, toqué

**crazy** adj fou (f folle), toqué; coll enthousiaste; ~ **paving** dalles irrégulières

**creak** n grincement; vi grincer

**creaky** *adj* grinçant
**cream** *n* crème *f*; *fig* crème *f*, élite *f*; **cold ~** cold-cream *m*; *vt* écrémer; (butter, etc) battre
**cream-cake** *n* pâtisserie *f* à la crème
**cream-cheese** *n* fromage blanc
**creamer** *n* écrémeuse *f*; (pot) pot *m* à la crème
**creamery** *n* (shop) crémerie *f*; (dairy) laiterie *f*
**creamy** *adj* crémeux -euse
**crease** *n* pli *m*; (unintentional) faux pli; *vt* plisser, froisser; *vi* se plisser
**create** *vt* créer; *vi coll* rouspéter
**creation** *n* création *f*
**creative** *adj* créateur -trice
**creativeness, creativity** *n* pouvoir créateur
**creator** *n* créateur -trice; **the Creator** Dieu *m*
**creature** *n* créature *f*, animal *m*; personne *f*; **~ comforts** confort matériel
**crèche** *n* crèche *f*
**credence** *n* créance *f*
**credentials** *npl* lettre *f* de créance
**credibility** *n* crédibilité *f*
**credible** *adj* croyable, plausible
**credit** *n* crédit *m*; réputation *f*; honneur *m*; (balance) crédit *m*; *cin+TV* **~s** générique *m*; **do ~ to** faire honneur à; **letter of ~** accréditif *m*; *vt* créditer; croire; attribuer à, imputer
**creditable** *adj* louable; estimable
**creditor** *n* créancier -ière; (bookkeeping) compte créditeur
**credo** *n* foi *f*, credo *m*
**credulity** *n* crédulité *f*
**credulous** *adj* crédule
**creed** *n* foi *f*, credo *m*; **apostle's ~** symbole *m* des apôtres
**creek** *n* crique *f*, anse *f*; *sl* **be up the ~** être en difficulté
**creep** *n sl* salaud *m*; **~s** chair *f* de poule; *vi* ramper, se faufiler, se glisser; *bot* grimper; (flesh) avoir la chair de poule; *fig* s'abaisser, ramper
**creeper** *n* personne *f* qui rampe; *bot* plante grimpante; *coll* flatteur -euse; **~s** chaussures *fpl* à semelle de caoutchouc
**creepiness** *n* effroi *m*
**creeping** *n* (serpent) reptation *f*; action *f* de ramper; *adj* rampant
**cremate** *vt* incinérer
**cremation** *n* incinération *f*, crémation *f*
**crematorium** *n* four *m* crématoire, crématoire *m*
**crematory** *adj* crématoire
**crenellated** *adj* crénelé
**crenellation** *n* créneau *m*
**creole** *n + adj* créole
**creosote** *n* créosote *f*

**crêpe** *n* crêpe *m*; **~ de Chine** crêpe *m* de Chine; **~ paper** papier gaufré; **~ rubber** crêpe *m*; **~ sole** semelle *f* de crêpe
**crepitate** *vi* crépiter
**crepuscular** *adj* crépusculaire
**crescendo** *n* crescendo *m*; *adv* crescendo
**crescent** *n* croissant *m*; rue *f* en demi-lune; *adj* croissant, en croissant
**cresol** *n* crésol *m*
**cress** *n* cresson *m*
**crest** *n* crête *f*; (helmet) panache *m*, cimier *m*; *her* écusson *m*; *vt* orner d'un panache; atteindre la crête de; *vi* (wave) moutonner
**crestfallen** *adj* penaud, mortifié
**cretin** *n* crétin -e
**cretinism** *n* crétinisme *m*
**cretinous** *adj* crétin
**cretonne** *n* cretonne *f*
**crevasse** *n* crevasse *f*
**crevice** *n* fissure *f*
**crew** *n* équipage *m*; *sp* équipe *f*; *coll* bande *f*; *vt naut* faire partie de l'équipage de
**crew-cut** *n* coupe *f* en brosse
**crib** *n* (manger) mangeoire *f*; (cradle) berceau *m*; *eccles* crèche *f*; *coll* (school) traduction *f* juxtalinéaire; *vt coll* copier, plagier; *vi* (examination) tricher
**crick** *n* (neck) torticolis *m*; (back) lumbago *m*; *vt* **~ one's neck (back)** causer un torticolis (un lumbago)
¹**cricket** *n zool* grillon *m*
²**cricket** *n sp* cricket *m*; **not ~** pas de jeu
**crier** *n* crieur *m*; *leg* huissier *m*; **town ~** crieur public
**crime** *n* crime *m*
**criminal** *n* criminel -elle; malfaiteur *m*; *adj* criminel -elle; *leg* **~ conversation** adultère *m*
**criminality** *n* criminalité *f*
**criminologist** *n* criminologiste
**criminology** *n* criminologie *f*
**crimp** *n* pli *m*; *vt* gaufrer, crêper; (hair) friser; *cul* (fish) taillader
**crimson** *n* cramoisi *m*, pourpre *m*; *adj* cramoisi, pourpre; *vt* teindre en pourpre; *vi* s'empourprer
**cringe** *vi* s'abaisser, s'aplatir, faire des courbettes
**crinkle** *n* ride *f*, ondulation *f*; *vt* onduler, plisser; *vi* onduler, se plisser, se chiffonner
**crinoline** *n* crinoline *f*
**cripple** *n* estropié -e, infirme; *vt* estropier; *fig* paralyser, endommager
**crisis** *n* crise *f*
**crisp** *n cul* **potato ~s** pommes *fpl* chips; *adj* sec (*f* sèche); (air) vif (*f* vive); *cul* croustillant, croquant; (hair) crépu; *fig* net (*f* nette), précis, alerte; *vt* crêper;

*cul* rendre croustillant; *vi* se crêper; *cul* devenir croustillant

**criterion** *n* (*pl* **criteria**) critérium *m*, critère *m*

**critic** *n* critique *m*; (hostile) censeur *m*

**critical** *adj* critique; (demanding) exigeant, difficile; (situation) dangereux -euse, crucial, délicat

**criticism** *n* critique *f*; (reproach) blâme *m*; **textual ~** examen *m* critique de manuscrits

**criticize** *vt* critiquer; analyser, juger

**critique** *n* critique *f*

**croak** *n* (frog) coassement *m*; (raven) croassement *m*; *vt* dire d'une voix enrouée; *vi* (frog) coasser; (raven) croasser; *fig* grommeler, grogner; *sl* crever

**croaker** *n* grognon -onne; pessimiste, rabat-joie *m invar*

**croaky** *adj* rauque, enroué

**crochet** *n* crochet *m*; *vt* faire au crochet; *vi* faire du crochet

**crock** *n* cruche *f*; (horse) rosse *f*; *coll* (person) débris *m*; (car) guimbarde *f*; *vt* claquer; *vi* se claquer

**crockery** *n* vaisselle *f*

**crocodile** *n* crocodile *m*; *coll* groupe *m* d'élèves marchant deux par deux; *adj* de crocodile

**crocus** *n* crocus *m*; (colour) safran *m*

**croft** *n* clos *m*; petite ferme

**crofter** *n* fermier *m*

**cromlech** *n* cromlech *m*

**crone** *n* vieille ratatinée

**crony** *n* compagnon *m*, ami *m*; *coll* copain *m*

**crook** *n* houlette *f*; *eccles* crosse *f*; (hook) croc *m*; (bend) virage *m*; *coll* escroc *m*; *adj* fourbe, malhonnête; *vt* recourber; *vi* se recourber

**crooked** *adj* courbé, recourbé; tordu, tors; sinueux -euse; tortueux -euse, malhonnête

**croon** *vt* + *vi* (sing softly) fredonner

**crooner** *n* chanteur -euse de charme

**crop** *n* récolte *f*; *zool* jabot *m*; (whip) manche *m*; (hair) coupe *f*; *geol* affleurement *m*; *fig* quantité *f*; **neck and ~** totalement; *vt* (graze) brouter; (cut) couper, tondre; (plant) semer de; *vi* produire; *geol* **~ out**, **~ up** affleurer; *coll* **~ up** paraître à l'imprévu

**crop-eared** *adj* essorillé

**cropper** *n* plante productrice; (person) agriculteur *m*; *coll* **come a ~** tomber lourdement, ramasser une pelle; (fail) manquer

**croquet** *n* croquet *m*

**croquette** *n* *cul* croquette *f*

**crosier, crozier** *n* *eccles* crosse *f*

**cross** *n* croix *f*; (race) croisement *m*, métis -isse; *hist* **take the ~** devenir croisé;

**take up one's ~** supporter patiemment ses malheurs; *adj* transversal, en biais; (breed) croisé, métis -isse; (angry) fâché, en colère; (opposite) contraire; *vt* croiser; (intersect) couper; rencontrer; (go across) traverser; (thwart) contrecarrer; *eccles* signer; (letter t) barrer; (cheque) barrer; **~ one's fingers** conjurer le sort; **~ one's heart** jurer ses grands dieux; **~ one's mind** *impers* venir en tête; **~ the palm of** graisser la patte de; **~ the path of** rencontrer; *vi* se croiser; *eccles* se signer; **~ off** barrer, biffer

**crossbar** *n* traverse *f*

**crossbeam** *n* traverse *f*

**cross-bow** *n* arbalète *f*

**crossbred** *adj* métissé

**crossbreed** *n* métis -isse; *vt* métisser

**cross-channel** *adj* (service) à travers la Manche

**cross-check** *vt* recouper; *vi* se recouper

**cross-country** *adj* **~ race** cross-country *m*

**crosscut** *n* coupe *f* en travers; **~ saw** scie *f* à deux mains; *vt* couper en travers

**cross-examination** *n* *leg* interrogatoire *m*

**cross-examine** *vt* *leg* interroger

**cross-eyed** *adj* louche, bigle

**cross-fire** *n* *mil* feu croisé

**cross-grained** *adj* (wood) à fibres torses; (person) grincheux -euse

**cross-hatch** *vt* hacher, hachurer

**cross-hatching** *n* hachure *f*

**crossing** *n* croisement *m*; (sea, desert, etc) traversée *f*; **level ~** passage *m* à niveau; **pedestrian ~, zebra ~** passage clouté

**crossness** *n* irritation *f*, mauvaise humeur

**cross-over** *n* (road) passage supérieur

**crosspatch** *n* grincheux -euse, chipie *f*

**crosspiece** *n* entretoise *f*, entrait *m*

**cross-purpose** *n* but opposé; **be at ~s** être en désaccord

**cross-question** *vt* *leg* interroger

**cross-reference** *n* renvoi *m*

**crossroad** *n* carrefour *m*, intersection *f*

**cross-section** *n* coupe transversale; tranche *f*

**cross-stitch** *n* point *m* de croix

**cross-talk** *n* *coll* répliques *fpl*

**crossways, crosswise** *adv* en croix; en travers

**crossword** *n* mots croisés *pl*

**crotch** *n* fourche *f*

**crotchet** *n* *mus* noire *f*

**crotchety** *adj* grincheux -euse

**crouch** *n* accroupissement *m*; *vi* s'accroupir

**¹croup** *n* *med* croup *m*

**²croup** *n* (horse) croupe *f*

**croupier** *n* croupier *m*

**¹crow** *n* corbeau *m*, corneille *f*; **as the ~**

**flies** à vol d'oiseau, en ligne droite

²**crow** *n* cocorico *m*; (baby) gazouillis *m*, gazouillement *m*; *vi* faire cocorico; (baby) gazouiller; *fig* exulter, triompher

**crowbar** *n* barre *f* de fer, levier *m*

**crowd** *n* foule *f*, cohue *f*, presse *f*; masse *f*; *coll* bande *f*; *vt* assembler, attrouper; (pile) entasser, empiler; (fill) bonder, encombrer; ~ **out** repousser faute de place; *vi* s'assembler, s'attrouper

**crown** *n* couronne *f*; monarchie *f*; (hill) sommet *m*; (garland) guirlande *f*, diadème *m*; (road) axe *m*; (head) tête *f*; (tooth) couronne *f*; *fig* couronnement *m*; *adj* de la Couronne; *vt* couronner; (reward) récompenser, combler; (dentist) couronner; (complete) achever; *sl* cogner

**crown-court** *n* (England) = cour *f* d'assises

**crowned** *adj* couronné

**crowning** *n* couronnement *m*; *adj* le plus haut, parfait

**crown-wheel** *n* couronne *f*

**crow's-feet** *npl* patte-d'oie *f* (*pl* pattes-d'oie)

**crow's-nest** *n naut* nid *m* de pie

**crozier** *n see* **crosier**

**crucial** *adj* décisif -ive, critique, capital, crucial

**crucible** *n* creuset *m*

**crucifix** *n* crucifix *m*

**crucifixion** *n* crucifixion *f*

**cruciform** *adj* cruciforme

**crucify** *vt* crucifier, mettre en croix; *fig* torturer; mortifier

**crude** *adj* cru; brut; (vulgar) grossier -ière; brutal; (botched) sommaire

**crudity**, **crudeness** *n* crudité *f*; grossièreté *f*

**cruel** *adj* cruel -elle; (painful) douloureux -euse; *adv coll* mal

**cruelty** *n* cruauté *f*

**cruet** *n cul* poivrier *m*, salière *f* et pot *m* de moutarde; *eccles* burette *f*

**cruise** *n* croisière *f*; *vi naut* croiser; (taxi) marauder; ~ **along** rouler tranquillement; **cruising speed** vitesse *f* de croisière

**cruiser** *n naut* croiseur *m*

**crumb** *n* miette *f*; (inside of loaf ) mie *f*; (scrap) brin *m*

**crumble** *vt* émietter, effriter; *vi* s'émietter, s'effriter; *fig* se désagréger

**crumbly** *adj* friable

**crump** *n* bruit *m* d'explosion; *vi* faire un bruit d'explosion

**crumpet** *n* crêpe beurrée; *sl* poule *f*

**crumple** *vt* froisser, chiffonner; *fig* flancher, céder; *vi* se froisser, se chiffonner

**crunch** *n* craquement *m*; *coll fig* moment décisif; *vt* broyer, écraser; (chew) croquer; *vi* mâchonner

**crupper** *n* croupe *f*; (harness) croupière *f*

**crusade** *n* croisade *f*; *vi* partir en croisade; ~ **for** militer pour

**crusader** *n* croisé *m*

**crush** *n* presse *f*, foule *f*; (act of crushing) écrasement *m*; *coll* béguin *m*; *vt* écraser, broyer; *fig* écraser, dominer, mater, réprimer; *vi* s'écraser, se tasser

**crushing** *adj* total, absolu; (overwhelming) écrasant, accablant

**crust** *n* croûte *f*, croûton *m*; (wine) dépôt *m*; couche *f*; *geol* écorce *f* terrestre; *vt* former croûte sur; *vi* former croûte

**crustacea** *npl* crustacés *mpl*

**crustacean** *n* crustacé *m*; *adj* crustacé

**crusted** *adj* couvert d'une croûte; (wine) ayant un dépôt; *fig* vieux ( *f* vieille)

**crusty** *adj* croquant; *fig* grincheux -euse

**crutch** *n* béquille *f*; support *m*; *anat* fourche *f*

**crux** *n* point crucial, nœud *m*

**cry** *n* cri *m*; (call) appel *m*; (tears) larmes *fpl*, crise *f* de larmes; (request) prière *f*, demande *f*; slogan *m*; (hounds) clabaudage *m*; **a far** ~ une grande distance, loin; **in full** ~ acharné; *vt* crier; pleurer; implorer; proclamer, publier; ~ **down** dénigrer; *vi* crier; s'écrier; (tears) pleurer; (hounds) clabauder; ~ **for** solliciter, demander; ~ **off** se décommander, se retirer; ~ **out** crier, pousser des cris

**cry-baby** *n* (enfant) pleurnicheur -euse

**crying** *adj* criant; *fig* notoire, patent

**crypt** *n* crypte *f*

**cryptic** *adj* cryptique, abscons, abstrus

**cryptogam** *n bot* cryptogame *m* or *f*

**cryptogram** *n* cryptogramme *m*

**cryptographer** *n* cryptographe

**crystal** *n* cristal *m*; *adj* de cristal, cristallin

**crystal-gazing** *n* art *m* de la voyante

**crystalline** *adj* cristallin

**crystallization** *n* cristallisation *f*

**crystallize** *vt* cristalliser

**crystallography** *n* cristallographie *f*

**crystalloid** *n* cristalloïde *m*; *adj* cristalloïde

**cub** *n* petit *m*; (fox) renardeau *m*; (wolf) louveteau *m*; (lion) lionceau *m*; (bear) ourson *m*; (scout movement) louveteau *m*; *coll* gosse *m*; *vi* chasser des renardeaux; (give birth) mettre bas

**cubby-hole** *n* taule *f*

**cube** *n* cube *m*; *cul* bouillon *m* cube; *adj* ~ **root** racine *f* cubique; *vt* cuber

**cubic** *adj* cubique; cube

**cubicle** *n* box *m*, alcôve *f*; (baths) cabine *f*

**cubism** n cubisme m

**cuckold** n cocu m; vt faire cocu; sl cocufier

**cuckoldry** n cocuage m

**cuckoo** n coucou m; adj coll toqué; ~ **clock** pendule f à coucou

**cuckoo-flower** n bot cardamine m des prés

**cucumber** n concombre m; **cool as a ~** très maître de soi

**cud** n chew the ~ ruminer

**cuddle** n enlacement m, étreinte f; vt caresser, peloter; vi s'entrelacer; ~ **up** se pelotonner, coucher dans les bras l'un de l'autre

**cuddly** adj coll qu'on a envie de caresser

**cudgel** n matraque f; take up the ~ s for défendre vigoureusement; vt matraquer; ~ **one's brains** se creuser la cervelle

¹**cue** n theat réplique f; mus signal m d'entrée; fig indication f, mot m d'ordre; vt theat donner la réplique à

²**cue** n (billiards) queue f

¹**cuff** n poignet m, manchette f; US revers m de pantalon; sl ~ s menottes fpl; coll **off the ~** à l'improviste

²**cuff** n gifle f, calotte f; vt gifler, calotter

**cuff-link** n bouton m de manchette

**cuirass** n mil cuirasse f

**cuirassier** n mil cuirassier m

**cuisine** n cuisine f

**cul-de-sac** n impasse f, cul-de-sac m (pl culs-de-sac)

**culinary** adj culinaire

**cull** vt cueillir, sélectionner; (animals) tuer pour diminuer le nombre

**cullander** n see colander

**culminate** vi culminer

**culmination** n culmination f

**culpability** n culpabilité f

**culprit** n coupable; leg prévenu -e

**cult** n culte m; mode f

**cultivate** vt cultiver

**cultivated** adj cultivé; raffiné

**cultivation** n culture f

**cultivator** n cultivateur -trice; (machine) cultivateur m

**cultural** adj agr cultural; arts culturel -elle

**culture** n culture f

**culvert** n conduit m

**cumbersome** adj encombrant, lourd

**cumbrous** adj encombrant, lourd

**cumin** n bot cumin m

**cummerbund** n large ceinture f (en étoffe)-

**cumulate** vt accumuler; leg cumuler; vi s'accumuler

**cumulation** n accumulation f; leg cumul m

**cumulative** adj qui s'ajoute; leg cumulatif -ive; (vote) plural; (interest) composé

**cumulo-nimbus** n cumulo-nimbus m

**cumulus** n cumulus m

**cuneiform** adj cunéiforme

**cunning** n ruse f, astuce f, fourberie f; ar adresse f; adj rusé, astucieux -ieuse, fourbe; habile, adroit, malin (f maligne)

**cunt** n vulg + sl fig con m

**cup** n tasse f; (prize) coupe f; eccles + bot calice m; mélange de vin et de fruits; fig (pleasant) coupe f; (unpleasant) calice m; surg ventouse f; **in one's ~ s** ivre; coll **one's ~ of tea** ce qu'on aime; vt ~ **one's hands** mettre ses mains en coupe

**cupboard** n placard m, armoire f; ~ **love** amour intéressé

**cupful** n tasse f

**cupidity** n cupidité f

**cupola** n coupole f, dôme m

**cupper, cuppa** n coll tasse f de thé

**cupric** adj cuprique

**cupro-nickel** n cupro-nickel m

**cup-tie** n match m (de football) éliminatoire

**cur** n chien bâtard; coll clebs m; fig salaud m

**curaçoa, curaçao** n curaçao m

**curacy** n eccles vicariat m

**curare** n curare m

**curate** n vicaire m

**curative** adj curatif -ive

**curator** n conservateur -trice

**curb** n (harness) gourmette f; frein m; (pavement) bord m du trottoir; vt restreindre, freiner, contraindre

**curd** n lait caillé, caillebotte f; vt cailler; vi se cailler

**curdle** vt cailler; coaguler; vi se cailler; se coaguler; **make s/o's blood ~** terrifier qn, effrayer qn

**cure** n (remedy) remède m; (treatment) cure f; guérison f; eccles charge f; vt guérir; cul saler; cul fumer; fig remédier à; (rubber) vulcaniser

**curfew** n couvre-feu m

**curia** n eccles curie f

**curio** n bibelot m, objet curieux

**curiosity** n curiosité f; bizarrerie f; objet curieux, rareté f

**curious** adj curieux -ieuse; étrange, singulier -ière; avide de savoir, indiscret -ète; extraordinaire

**curl** n boucle f; spirale f, volute f; vt boucler, faire boucler, friser; vi boucler, friser; ~ **up** (person) se pelotonner; s'enrouler; coll s'effondrer

**curler** n bigoudi m

**curlew** n zool courlis m

¹**curling** adj à friser; qui frise; ~ **irons**, ~ **tongs** fer m à friser; ~ **pin** bigoudi m

curling

**²curling** *n sp* curling *m*
**curl-paper** *n* papillote *f*
**curly** *adj* frisé, bouclé
**curmudgeon** *n* grincheux *m*
**currant** *n* raisin *m* de Corinthe; groseille *f*; **black ~** cassis *m*; **red ~** groseille rouge
**currency** *n* circulation *f*; monnaie *f* ayant cours; devise *f*; (general acceptance) cours *m*; **foreign ~** devises étrangères
**current** *n* (stream, air) courant *m*; (water) cours *m*; *adj* courant, commun; (accepted) admis; reçu; en cours; *comm* **~ account** compte courant; **~ events** actualités *fpl*
**curriculum** *n* programme *m* scolaire; **~ vitae** curriculum vitae *m*, *abbr* C.V.
**¹curry** *n* curry *m*, cari *m*; *vt* assaisonner au cari
**²curry** *vt* (horse) étriller; (leather) corroyer; **~ favour with s/o** amadouer qn par flatterie
**curse** *n* malédiction *f*; (oath) juron *m*, imprécation *f*; *eccles* excommunication *f*; *fig* désastre *m*, calamité *f*; *coll* (period) règles *fpl*; *vt* maudire; *eccles* excommunier; *vi* jurer, blasphémer
**cursed, curst** *adj* maudit, abominable, odieux -ieuse, *coll* sacré, irritant; obstiné
**cursive** *n* cursive *f*; *adj* cursif -ive
**cursoriness** *n* hâte *f*, rapidité *f*
**cursory** *adj* sommaire, superficiel -ielle, hâtif -ive, rapide
**curt** *adj* brusque, sec (*f* sèche), cassant
**curtail** *vt* écourter, raccourcir; réduire, diminuer
**curtailment** *n* raccourcissement *m*; diminution *f*
**curtain** *n* rideau *m*; *fig* voile *m*; *mil* courtine *f*; *mil* **~ of fire** tir *m* de barrage; *fig* **draw a ~ over** cacher, ne plus rien dire sur; **iron ~** rideau de fer; **it's ~ s** c'est la fin; *vt* garnir de rideaux; **~ off** cacher par un rideau
**curtain-call** *n theat* rappel *m*
**curtain-raiser** *n theat* lever *m* de rideau
**curtness** *n* brusquerie *f*
**curtsey, curtsy** *n* révérence *f*; *vi* faire la (une) révérence
**curvature** *n* courbure *f*
**curve** *n* courbe *f*; *mot* virage *m*; **~ s** rondeurs *fpl*; *vt* courber; *vi* se courber; décrire une courbe
**cushion** *n* coussin *m*; (billiards) bande *f*; **air ~** matelas *m* d'air; *vt* orner de coussins; (stuff) matelasser; *fig* amortir
**cushy** *adj coll* pépère
**cusp** *n geom* sommet *m*; *archi* lobe *m*; *astron* corne *f*
**cuspidor** *n* crachoir *m*

**cuss** *n coll* juron *m*; *coll* type *m*; *vt + vi* jurer
**cussed** *adj coll* obstiné; (annoying) emmerdant
**cussedness** *n* esprit *m* de contradiction
**custard** *n cul* crème anglaise
**custodian** *n* gardien -ienne; concierge
**custody** *n* garde *f*; état *m* d'arrestation; **take into ~** écrouer
**custom** *n* coutume *f*, usage *m*, habitude *f*; **~ s** douane *f*; (officials) douaniers -ières; **~ s duty** droits *mpl* de douane
**customary** *adj* normal, habituel -elle, coutumier -ière
**custom-built, custom-made** *adj US* fait sur commande; (clothes) fait sur mesure
**customer** *n* client -e; *coll* type *m*
**custom-house** *n* douane *f*
**cut** *n* coupe *f*; coupure *f*, entaille *f*; (wound) plaie *f*; incision *f*; (slash) estafilade *f*; (slice) tranche *f*; (abridgement) coupure *f*, réduction *f*, passage coupé; *sl* pot-de-vin *m* (*pl* pots-de-vin), pourcentage *m*; **a ~ above** supérieur à; **short ~** raccourci *m*; *adj* divisé, coupé; gravé; réduit; coupé en tranches; (castrated) châtré; **~ and dried** préparé d'avance; *vt* couper, trancher, tailler; (notch) entailler, encocher; croiser, traverser; (chisel) ciseler; (reduce) réduire; censurer; (castrate) couper; *sp* couper; *coll* (class, lesson) sécher; **~ a dash** faire de l'épate; (argument) **~ both ways** être à double tranchant; **~ down** tuer; (reduce) réduire, raccourcir; (trees) abattre; (text) tronquer; *coll* **~ fine** laisser peu de temps, laisser peu de marge; *coll* **~ it out!** en voilà assez!, ta gueule!; **~ no ice** rester sans effet, ne rien changer; **~ off** couper, découper, prélever; *surg* amputer; *elect* couper le courant à; **~ off with a shilling** déshériter; **~ out** couper, tailler, émonder; sculpter; *coll* évincer, supplanter; **~ short** abréger; **~ s/o dead** faire semblant de ne pas voir qn; **~ up** découper; (criticize) éreinter; **be ~ off** être coupé; **be ~ out for** avoir l'étoffe de; **have one's work ~ out** avoir du mal vers; *vi* **~ back** to revenir sur ses pas à; **~ in** interrompre; **~ in on** (cards, dance) prendre la place de; *mot* faire une queue de poisson à; **~ loose** rompre avec, jeter sa gourme; **~ out** *eng* découpler; *mot* caler; **~ up rough** se fâcher
**cutaneous** *adj* cutané
**cute** *adj coll* malin (*f* maligne), déluré; *US* mignon -onne, charmant
**cuteness** *n coll* finesse *f*; *US* gentillesse *f*
**cuticle** *n bot* cuticule *f*; *anat* épiderme *m*

426

**cutlass** *n* coutelas *m*
**cutler** *n* coutelier *m*
**cutlery** *n* coutellerie *f*
**cutlet** *n* côtelette *f*
**cut-off** *n eng* obturateur *m*, valve *f*; (rifle) cran *m* de sûreté
**cut-out** *n elect* coupe-circuit *m invar*; mot échappement *m* libre; (wood, etc) découpage *m*
**cut-price** *adj* au rabais
**cutter** *n* (tailor) coupeur -euse; (stone) tailleur *m*; *naut* cotre *m*, canot *m*
**cut-throat** *n* assassin *m*; *coll* rasoir *m* à main; *adj* meurtrier -ière
**cutting** *n* action *f* de couper; coupe *f*; percement *m*; *hort* bouture *f*; (wood) percée *f*; (newspaper) coupure *f*; *cin* découpage *m*; (railway, road) tranchée *f*; *adj* coupant, tranchant; (rain) cinglant; (cold) piquant; (words) blessant, mordant
**cuttle-fish** *n zool* seiche *f*
**cutwater** *n naut* étrave *f*
**cyanide** *n chem* cyanure *m*
**cyanosis** *n med* cyanose *f*
**cybernetics** *n* cybernétique *f*
**cyclamen** *n bot* cyclamen *m*
**cycle** *n* cycle *m*; *lit* cycle *m*; bicyclette *f*, vélo *m*; *elect* cycle *m*; *vi* revenir par cycles; faire de la bicyclette
**cyclic, cyclical** *adj* cyclique
**cycling** *n* cyclisme *m*

**cyclist** *n* cycliste
**cyclometer** *n* compteur *m* kilométrique
**cyclone** *n* cyclone *m*
**cyclonic** *adj* cyclonal
**cyclopean** *adj* cyclopéen -éenne
**Cyclops** *n* Cyclope *m*
**cyclostyle** *n* duplicateur *m* à stencils; *vt* reproduire, polycopier
**cyclotron** *n phys* cyclotron *m*
**cygnet** *n zool* jeune cygne *m*
**cylinder** *n* cylindre *m*
**cylindrical** *adj* cylindrique
**cymbal** *n mus* cymbale *f*
**cynic** *n philos* cynique; sceptique
**cynical** *adj* cynique
**cynicism** *n* scepticisme *m*; causticité *f*
**cynosure** *n* point *m* de mire; centre *m* d'attraction
**cypress** *n bot* cyprès *m*
**Cypriot** *n* Cypriote
**Cyprus** *n* Chypre *f*
**cyst** *n* kyste *m*
**cystitis** *n med* cystite *f*
**cystotomy** *n surg* cystotomie *f*
**cytology** *n* cytologie *f*
**czar, tzar** *n* tsar *m*, czar *m*
**czarina** *n* tsarine *f*
**Czech** *n* Tchèque; *adj* tchèque
**Czechoslovak** *n* Tchécoslovaque; *adj* tchécoslovaque
**Czechoslovakia** *n* Tchécoslovaquie *f*

# D

**d** *n mus* ré *m*; **D-day** le jour J
¹**dab** *n* tape *f*; tache *f*; *coll* ~ s empreintes digitales; *vt* tapoter; tamponner
²**dab** *n zool* limande *f*
³**dab** *adj coll* calé, expert; **be a ~ hand at** être doué pour
**dabble** *vi* ~ **in (at)** donner dans, s'occuper un peu de
**dabbler** *n* amateur *m*; (writer) écrivailleur *m*
**dachshund** *n* dachshund *m*
**dactyl** *n* dactyle *m*
**dad, daddy** *n coll* papa *m*
**daddy-long-legs** *n zool* tipule *f*
**dado** *n* lambris *m*; (pedestal) dé *m*; plinthe *f*

**daffodil** *n* jonquille *f*; *adj* (colour) jonquille *invar*
**daft** *adj* toqué, cinglé; faible d'esprit
**dagger** *n* dague *f*; poignard *m*; *print* croix *f*; **at ~ s drawn** à couteaux tirés; **look (speak) ~ s** regarder (parler) avec haine
**dahlia** *n bot* dahlia *m*
**daily** *n* (newspaper) quotidien *m*; (maid) femme *f* de journée; *adj* quotidien -ienne, journalier -ière; *adv* tous les jours, quotidiennement, journellement
**daintiness** *n* délicatesse *f*, raffinement *m*; élégance *f*; finesse *f*
**dainty** *n cul* friandise *f*, mets fin; *adj*

délicat, raffiné; élégant, fin, choisi

**dairy** n (installation) laiterie f; (shop) crémerie f, laiterie f; adj laitier -ière

**dairy-cattle** npl vaches laitières

**dairy-farm** n laiterie f

**dairymaid** n laitière f

**dairyman** n laitier m

**daïs** n estrade f

**daisy** n paquerette f, marguerite f

**dale** n vallée f

**dalliance** n (amorous) badinage m; (sophisticated) marivaudage m, pej libertinage m

**dally** vi (amorously) badiner; jouer; (idly) flâner, traînasser; ~ with considérer, envisager

**dalmatic** n eccles dalmatique f

**daltonism** n daltonisme m

¹**dam** n barrage m (de retenue); reversoir m; vt construire un barrage sur

²**dam** n zool femelle f

**damage** n dommage m; (material) dégâts mpl; coll what's the ~? ça fait combien?; leg ~s dommages-intérêts mpl; vt endommager; fig léser; vi causer des dégâts

**damageable** adj dommageable

**damascene** vt damasquiner

**Damascus** n Damas f

**damask** n damas m; (colour) incarnat m; adj (fabric) damassé; (steel) damasquiné; vt damasquiner

**dame** n US coll femme f

**damn** n juron m; not care a ~ s'en ficher totalement; adj damné, sacré; vt condamner; maudire; eccles damner; fig désapprouver; interj zut!

**damnable** adj exécrable

**damnation** n damnation f; interj malheur!

**damned** n eccles damnés mpl; adj eccles damné; maudit; coll sacré

**damning** adj accablant, écrasant

**damp** n humidité f; (mining) grisou m; fig découragement m, abattement m; adj humide, mouillé; vt humecter, mouiller; (fire) étouffer; (sound) étouffer, amortir; fig décourager, déprimer

**damp-course** n bui couche isolante

**dampen** vt see damp vt

**damper** n (stamps) mouilleur m; (piano) étouffoir m; (stove) registre m; fig (person) rabat-joie m invar; put a ~ on jeter un froid sur

**dampness** n humidité f

**damp-proof** adj imperméable

**damsel** n jeune fille f, demoiselle f

**damson** n prune f de Damas

**dance** n danse f; bal m; ~ of death danse f macabre; lead s/o a ~ en faire voir à qn, faire des difficultés à qn; St Vitus's ~ danse f de Saint-Guy; vt + vi danser;

~ **attendance on** faire l'empressé auprès de, être au petits soins avec

**dance-band** n orchestre m de danse

**dance-hall** n dancing m

**dancer** n danseur -euse

**dancing** n danse f

**dandelion** n bot pissenlit m

**dandle** vt faire sauter

**dandruff** n pellicules fpl

**dandy** n dandy m; fat m; adj bien habillé; coll au poil

**dandyism** n dandysme m

**Dane** n Danois -e

**danger** n danger m, péril m; be in ~ of risquer de

**danger-money** n prime f de risque

**dangerous** adj dangereux -euse, périlleux -euse

**dangle** vt laisser pendiller; vi pendiller, brimbaler

**Danish** n (language) danois m; adj danois

**dank** adj humide

**dankness** n humidité f

**dapper** adj pimpant; actif -ive

**dapple** vt tacheter

**dapple-grey** adj gris pommelé invar

**dare** n coll défi m; vt oser; (challenge) défier; vi oser; I ~ say cela se peut bien, il me semble que, très probablement

**daredevil** n casse-cou m invar; adj audacieux -ieuse

**daring** n courage m, audace f; adj courageux -euse, audacieux -ieuse

**dark** n obscurité f; noir m, nuit f; fig ignorance f; adj obscur, sombre, noir; (colour) foncé; (hair) noir, brun; fig lugubre, sinistre; mystérieux -ieuse; hist **Dark Ages** première partie du Moyen Âge; fig ~ **horse** outsider m; keep ~ tenir secret -ète; keep s/o in the ~ laisser qn dans l'ignorance

**darken** vt obscurcir; (colour) foncer; fig obscurcir, assombrir; noircir; vi s'obscurcir; (colour) foncer; fig s'obscurcir, s'assombrir, se rembrunir

**darkling** adj qui devient sombre; lugubre

**darkly** adv d'un air sombre, d'un air lugubre; mystérieusement

**darkness** n obscurité f; ténèbres fpl; fig ignorance f

**darling** n chéri -e; adj bien aimé

**darn** n reprise f; vt repriser

**darning** n ravaudage m

**darning-ball** n œuf m à repriser

**darning-needle** n aiguille f à repriser

**dart** n javelot m; sp fléchette f; (insect) dard m; (movement) brusque élan m; vt lancer; vi foncer, avancer vite

**dartboard** n cible f du jeu de fléchettes

**darts** npl jeu m de fléchettes

**dash** n ruée f; (punctuation, Morse) trait m; (liquid) goutte f; (colour) touche f;

*fig* élan *m*; entrain *m*, énergie *f*;
**cut a** ~ faire de l'effet, sembler important; **make a** ~ prendre ses jambes à
son cou; *vt* lancer, jeter avec violence; *fig* (hopes) abattre; (person)
démoraliser; ~ **off** bâcler, enlever; *vi*
s'élancer, se précipiter, se ruer; ~
**away**, ~ **off** partir vite
**dashboard** *n* *mot* tableau *m* de bord
**dashing** *adj* fringant, élégant, dynamique
**dastard** *n* *obs* lâche, poltron -onne
**dastardly** *adj* lâche, couard, infâme
**data** *npl* données *fpl*
**data-bank** banque *f* de données
**datable** *adj* datable
¹**date** *n* datte *f*; époque *f*; *coll* rendez-vous
*m*; **out of** ~ démodé; **up to** ~
moderne, à la page; *vt* dater; *coll US*
fixer un rendez-vous avec; *vi* dater; être
démodé
²**date** *n* datte *f*
**date-line** *n* méridien *m* 180°; (newspaper, etc) date *f* de publication
**date-palm** *n* dattier *m*
**dative** *n* *gramm* datif *m*
**datum** *n* (*pl* **data**) donnée *f*; (mark, line)
repère *m*
**daub** *n* badigeonnage *m*, enduit *m*; *arts*
croûte *f*; *vt* badigeonner, enduire; *arts*
barbouiller
**dauber** *n* peintre *m* médiocre, barbouilleur *m*
**daughter** *n* fille *f*
**daughter-in-law** *n* belle-fille *f* (*pl* belles-filles), bru *f*
**daunt** *n* décourager, abattre
**dauntless** *adj* courageux -euse, intrépide
**dauphin** *n* dauphin *m*
**davit** *n* *naut* bossoir *m* d'embarcations,
portemanteau *m*
**daw** *n* *orni* choucas *m*
**dawdle** *vi* flâner, traîner
**dawdler** *n* flâneur -euse
**dawn** *n* aube *f*, aurore *f*; *fig* aube *f*, commencement *m*; *vi* poindre, se lever; *fig*
naître, commencer; ~ **upon** devenir
clair à
**dawning** *n* aube *f*, aurore *f*; *fig* commencement *m*, naissance *f*; *adj* naissant
**day** *n* (*usu* unit of time) jour *m*; (*usu*
daylight hours, working) journée *f*;
~**s** jours *mpl*, époque *f*; ~ **by** ~ tous
les jours; ~**s of grace** délai *m* de grâce;
**any** ~ **now** d'un jour à l'autre; **call it**
**a** ~ cesser le travail; **every other** ~
tous les deux jours; **name the** ~ fixer la
date d'un mariage, prendre la décision
de se marier; **one of these** ~**s** bientôt;
**pass the time of** ~ se saluer, faire un
bout de conversation; **the good old** ~ **s**

le bon vieux temps; *adj* de jour; (ticket,
etc) valable un jour seulement
**day-bed** *n* divan *m*
**day-boy** *n* (school) externe *m*
**daybreak** *n* aube *f*, point *m* du jour
**daydream** *n* rêverie *f*; *vi* rêver, rêvasser
**day-girl** *n* (school) externe *f*
**day-labour** *n* travail *m* à la journée
**day-labourer** *n* journalier -ière
**daylight** *n* jour *m*, lumière *f* du jour; **in**
**broad** ~ en plein jour; **see** ~ commencer à comprendre
**day-nursery** *n* crèche *f*, garderie *f* (d'enfants)
**day-school** *n* externat *m*
**day-shift** *n* équipe *f* de jour
**day-time** *n* jour *m*, journée *f*
**daze** *n* étourdissement *m*, abrutissement
*m*; *vt* étourdir, abrutir
**dazzle** *n* éblouissement *m*; *vt* éblouir,
aveugler
**dazzling** *adj* éblouissant
**deacon** *n* *eccles* diacre *m*
**deaconess** *n* *eccles* diaconesse *f*
**dead** *n* *collect* morts *mpl*; *fig* ~ **of night**
milieu *m* de la nuit; *adj* mort, sans vie;
crevé; (numbed) engourdi; (colour)
terne, neutre; (sound) sourd, assourdi;
*coll* total; *elect* à plat; (calm) plat; *bui*
(door, window) faux (*f* fausse), condamné; ~ **end** impasse *f*, cul-de-sac *m*
(*pl* culs-de-sac); *mil* ~ **ground** angle
mort; *sp* ~ **heat** égalité *f*; ~ **letter**
(mail) rebut *m*; ~ **loss** perte sèche; *coll*
(useless person) bon (*f* bonne) à rien;
~ **march** marche *f* funèbre; *coll* ~
**men** bouteilles *fpl* vides; *naut* ~ **reckoning** estime *f*; ~ **set** attaque poussée;
*coll* effort *m* de séduction; ~ **shot**
tireur *m* hors ligne; *adv* absolument,
très; ~ **slow** au pas
**dead-and-alive** *adj* (place) triste, mort;
(person) sans entrain
**dead-beat** *n* *US* *coll* écornifleur -euse;
*adj* *coll* épuisé, éreinté
**dead-centre** *n* *eng* point mort
**deaden** *vt* amortir; (sound) assourdir;
(blunt) émousser; ternir
**dead-end** *n* impasse *f*; *adj* ~ **job** métier
*m* sans avenir
**deadline** *n* date *f* limite
**deadlock** *n* impasse *f*
**deadly** *adj* mortel -elle, fatal; (weapon)
meurtrier -ière; *coll* rasant; *adv coll* extrêmement
**deadly-nightshade** *n* *bot* belladone *f*
**deadness** *n* mort *f*; stagnation *f*, engourdissement *m*; apathie *f*
**deadpan** *n* visage *m* sans expression; *adj*
sans expression
**dead-weight** *n* poids mort, masse lourde
**deaf** *n* *collect* sourds *mpl*; *adj* sourd; *fig*

indifférent, insensible; ~ **and dumb** sourd-muet (*pl* sourds-muets) (*f* sourde-muette, *pl* sourdes-muettes); ~ **as a post** sourd comme un pot

**deaf-aid** *n* prothèse auditive, appareil *m* acoustique

**deafen** *vt* assourdir; étouffer

**deaf-mute** *n* sourd-muet *m* (*pl* sourds-muets), sourde-muette *f* (*pl* sourdes-muettes)

**deafness** *n* surdité *f*

¹**deal** *n* quantité *f*; affaire *f*, transaction *f*; (cards) donne *f*; *vt* distribuer, répartir; (blow) asséner, allonger; (cards) donner; *vi* (cards) donner; ~ **in** faire le commerce de; ~ **with** concerner, s'agir de; discuter avec; (resolve) résoudre, maîtriser; *comm* (order) régler; être client de

²**deal** *n* bois blanc, sapin *m*

**dealer** *n* marchand -e, négociant -e; (cards) joueur -euse qui donne les cartes

**dealing** *n* comportement *m*, manière *f* d'agir; commerce *m*

**dean** *n* doyen -enne

**deanery** *n eccles* doyenné *m*

**dear** *n* cher (*f* chère), chéri -e; *coll* amour *m*; *adj* cher (*f* chère), aimé, chéri; précieux -ieuse; (cost) cher (*f* chère), coûteux -euse; *adv* trop cher; *interj* mon Dieu!

**dearly** *adv* affectueusement; cher, chèrement

**dearness** *n* affection *f*, attachement *m*; (price) cherté *f*, coût élevé

**dearth** *n* manque *m*; pénurie *f*

**death** *n* mort *f*; *lit* trépas *m*; décès *m*; *fig* fin *f*; **at ~ 's door** à l'article de la mort; **be in at the ~** (hunting) être présent à la mise à mort; *fig* assister à la phase finale, voir le dénouement; *coll* **catch one's ~** attraper la crève

**deathbed** *n* lit *m* de mort; *adj* in extremis

**death-blow** *n* coup mortel

**death-duties** *n leg* droits *mpl* de succession

**death-knell** *n* glas *m*

**deathless** *adj* immortel -elle

**deathlike** *adj* de mort, cadavéreux -euse

**deathly** *adj* mortel -elle, de mort; *adv* mortellement; ~ **pale** pâle comme la mort

**death-mask** *n* masque *m* mortuaire

**death-rate** *n* mortalité *f*

**death-rattle** *n* râle *m*

**death-roll** *n* liste *f* des morts; nombre *m* de morts

**death's-head** *n* tête *f* de mort; ~ **moth** sphinx *m*, tête *f* de mort

**death-trap** *n* casse-cou *m invar*

**death-watch** (**beetle**) *n* vrillette *f*

**debacle** *n* débâcle *f*

**debar** *vt* exclure; (prevent) interdire, empêcher

**debark** *vt* + *vi* débarquer

**debase** *vt* avilir; (coinage) déprécier

**debatable** *adj* discutable

**debate** *n* débat *m*; discussion *f*, controverse *f*; *vt* débattre, discuter; examiner; *vi* discuter; réfléchir

**debater** *n* argumentateur -trice

**debauch** *n* débauche *f*, partie *f* de débauche; *vt* débaucher, corrompre

**debauchee** *n* débauché -e

**debauchery** *n* débauche *f*, luxure *f*

**debenture** *n* obligation *f*

**debilitate** *vt* débiliter

**debilitating** *adj* débilitant

**debility** *n* débilité *f*

**debit** *n* débit *m*; *vt* débiter

**debonair** *adj* gai, riant; affable

**debouch** *vi* déboucher

**debris** *n* débris *mpl*, décombres *mpl*

**debt** *n* dette *f*; **in ~** endetté

**debtor** *n* débiteur -trice

**debunk** *vt coll* dégonfler, déboulonner

**début, debut** *n* début *m*

**débutante** *n* débutante *f*

**decade** *n* décennie *f*

**decadence** *n* décadence *f*

**decadent** *adj* décadent

**décalogue** *n bibl* décalogue *m*

**decamp** *vi* décamper

**decant** *vt* décanter

**decanter** *n* carafe *f*, carafon *m*

**decapitate** *vt* décapiter

**decapitation** *n* décapitation *f*

**decarbonize** *vt mot* décalaminer

**decasyllable** *n* décasyllabe *m*

**decay** *n* décomposition *f*, pourriture *f*; (teeth) carie *f*; désintégration *f*, déclin *m*, déchéance *f*; *vi* se détériorer, pourrir; décliner; (teeth) se carier

**decease** *n* décès *m*; *vi* décéder

**deceased** *n* défunt -e; *adj* décédé, défunt

**deceit, deceitfulness** *n* duperie *f*, supercherie *f*, duplicité *f*

**deceitful** *adj* trompeur -euse, fourbe; illusoire

**deceive** *vt* tromper, duper; *vi* se tromper

**deceiver** *n* trompeur -euse, fourbe

**decelerate** *vt* + *vi* ralentir

**deceleration** *n* décélération *f*, ralentissement *m*

**December** *n* décembre *m*

**decency** *n* décence *f*, modestie *f*; (seemliness) convenance *f*, bienséance *f*

**decent** *adj* décent, modeste, respectable; (seemly) convenable, bienséant; *coll* passable; (nice) gentil -ille

**decentralization** *n* décentralisation *f*

**decentralize** *vt* décentraliser

**deception** *n* duperie *f*, supercherie *f*,

duplicité *f*; (trick) leurre *m*

**deceptive** *adj* trompeur -euse; décevant

**deceptiveness** *n* apparence trompeuse

**decibel** *n* décibel *m*

**decide** *vt* décider, déterminer; (arrange) résoudre, régler; *vi* se décider, se résoudre, décider

**decided** *adj* défini, déterminé; décidé, résolu; précis, net (*f* nette)

**decidedly** *adv* nettement, incontestablement

**decider** *n sp* belle *f*

**deciduous** *adj bot* (tree) à feuilles caduques

**decimal** *n* décimale *f*; *adj* décimal; ~ **point** virgule *f*; **recurring** ~ fraction *f* périodique; **two** ~ **five** deux virgule cinq

**decimate** *vt* décimer

**decimation** *n* décimation *f*

**decipher** *vt* déchiffrer

**decision** *n* décision *f*; détermination *f*, résolution *f*

**decisive** *adj* décisif -ive, concluant, probant; (determined) résolu, ferme

**decisiveness** *n* décision *f*, fermeté *f*

**¹deck** *n naut* pont *m*; (cards) jeu *m* de cartes; **aer** *coll* sol *m*; **clear the** ~ **s** *naut* faire le branle-bas; *fig* se préparer à agir; **top** ~ (bus) impériale *f*

**²deck** *vt* orner, parer; *naut* ponter

**deck-chair** *n* transat *m*, transatlantique *m*

**declaim** *vt* + *vi* déclamer

**declamation** *n* déclamation *f*

**declamatory** *adj* déclamatoire

**declarable** *adj* à déclarer

**declaration** *n* déclaration *f*

**declarative** *adj* explicatif -ive

**declaratory** *adj* déclaratoire; explicatif -ive

**declare** *vt* déclarer, assurer; faire connaître, proclamer; ~ **for** prendre parti pour; *vi* se déclarer

**declared** *adj* déclaré, ouvert

**déclassé** *adj* déclassé

**declension** *n* déclin *m*, détérioration *f*; *gramm* déclinaison *f*

**declinable** *adj gramm* déclinable

**declination** *n* inclination *f*, pente *f*; *astron* déclinaison *f*

**decline** *n* déclin *m*, baisse *f*; *fig* déclin *m*, décadence *f*; *vt* décliner; *vi* pencher, s'incliner; baisser, décliner

**declivity** *n* déclivité *f*

**declutch** *vi* mot débrayer

**decoction** *n* décoction *f*

**decode** *vt* déchiffrer, décoder

**decoder** *n* déchiffreur -euse; appareil *m* qui décode

**decoke** *vt* mot coll décalaminer

**decolleté** *n* décolleté *m*; *adj* décolleté

**decolorant** *n* décolorant *m*

**decolour, decolourize** *vt* décolorer

**decompose** *vt* décomposer; analyser; *vi* se décomposer

**decomposition** *n* décomposition *f*

**decompress** *vt* décomprimer

**decompression** *n* décompression *f*

**deconsecrate** *vt eccles* séculariser, désaffecter

**decontaminate** *vt* décontaminer

**decontamination** *n* décontamination *f*

**decontrol** *vt* libérer de contrôle

**décor** *n theat* décor *m*

**decorate** *vt* décorer, orner; (medal) décorer

**decoration** *n* décoration *f*

**decorative** *adj* décoratif -ive; joli

**decorator** *n* décorateur -trice, ensemblier *m*; (painter) peintre *m*

**decorous** *adj* bienséant, comme il faut

**decorum** *n* décorum *m*, tenue *f*; bienséance *f*

**decoy** *n* appeau *m*, leurre *m*; (person) compère *m*; *vt* leurrer, piper; attirer dans un piège

**decrease** *n* décroissance *f*, diminution *f*; *vt* + *vi* diminuer, décroître

**decree** *n* arrêt *m*, décret *m*, ordonnance *f*; *eccles* décret *m*; *leg* ~ **nisi** jugement *m* provisoire (de divorce); *vt* décréter; *vi* faire un décret

**decrepit** *adj* décrépit, délabré

**decrepitude** *n* décrépitude *f*

**decretal** *n eccles* décrétale *f*

**decry** *vt* décrier, dénigrer

**decuple** *n* décuple *m*; *vt* décupler

**dedicate** *vt eccles* dédier, consacrer; (devote) dédier, vouer; (book) dédier

**dedication** *n* dédicace *f*; (devotion) dévouement *m*

**dedicatory** *adj* dédicatoire

**deduce** *vt philos* déduire

**deduct** *vt math* déduire, soustraire, défalquer

**deduction** *n math* + *philos* déduction *f*; (money) défalcation *f*

**deductive** *adj* déductif -ive

**¹deed** *n* action *f*, exploit *m*

**²deed** *n leg* contrat *m*, acte notarié

**deem** *vt* croire, juger, estimer; *vi* avoir une opinion

**deep** *n* ce qui est profond; *poet* océan *m*; (abyss) gouffre *m*, abîme *m*; ~ **s** profondeurs *fpl*; *adj* profond; (colour) foncé, riche; (sound) grave; *fig* sérieux -ieuse, intense, profond; obscur; extrême, total; *coll* malin (*f* maligne), fourbe; ~ **in** absorbé par, enfoncé dans; **go off the** ~ **end** s'emballer, se mettre en colère; **in** ~ **water** en difficulté; *adv* profondément

**deep-dyed** *adj fig* profondément coupable

**deepen** *vt* approfondir; intensifier; *mus* rendre plus grave; *vi* s'approfondir; (colour) se foncer; s'intensifier

**deep-freeze** *n* congélateur *m*, freezer *m*; *vt* surgeler, congeler

**deep-fry** *vt* faire cuire en friteuse

**deep-laid** *adj* bien préparé

**deep-rooted** *adj* profondément enraciné

**deep-sea** *adj* au grand large; de haute mer

**deep-seated** *adj* profondément enraciné, ancré

**deer** *n* (species) cervidé *m*; (red) cerf *m*; (fallow) daim *m*; (roe) chevreuil *m*

**deerskin** *n* daim *m*

**deface** *vt* défigurer, lacérer; (make illegible) effacer, rendre illisible

**defacement** *n* lacération *f*; effacement *m*

**de facto** *adj* de facto

**defalcate** *vt* détourner

**defamation** *n* diffamation *f*

**defamatory** *adj* diffamatoire

**defame** *n* diffamer

**default** *n* défaut *m*; *leg* défaut *m*, non-comparution *f*, contumace *f*; **in ~ of** dans l'absence de, faute de; **judgement by ~** jugement *m* par contumace; *vt leg* condamner par défaut; *vi leg* faire défaut; (debt) manquer à ses engagements

**defaulter** *n leg* contumace, défaillant -e; *mil* réfractaire *m*, puni *m*

**defeat** *n* défaite *f*; (setback) échec *m*; *vt* vaincre, défaire; faire échec à; *pol* mettre en minorité

**defeatism** *n* défaitisme *m*

**defecate** *vi* déféquer

**defecation** *n* défécation *f*

**defect** *n* défaut *m*, défectuosité *f*, imperfection *f*; *vt* abandonner, déserter

**defection** *n* défection *f*, abandon *m*

**defective** *adj* défectueux -euse; *gramm* défectif -ive; *med* déficient

**defence** *n* défense *f*; *mil* **~ s** défenses *fpl*, ouvrages défensifs, fortifications *fpl*; *psych* **~ mechanism** réflexe *m* de défense

**defenceless** *adj* sans défense

**defencelessness** *n* impuissance *f*

**defend** *vt* défendre, protéger; *leg* défendre

**defendant** *n leg* défendeur *m*, défenderesse *f*

**defensible** *adj* défendable

**defensive** *n* défensive *f*; *adj* défensif -ive

**¹defer** *vt* différer, remettre; *vi* différer, atermoyer

**²defer** *vi* déférer, accéder

**deference** *n* déférence *f*, respect *m*

**deferential** *adj* déférent, humble; *pej* servile

**deferment** *n* sursis *m*

**deferred** *adj* différé; *mil* ajourné

**defiance** *n* défi *m*, bravade *f*; **in ~ of** au mépris de

**defiant** *adj* intraitable; (reply) provocant

**deficiency** *n* déficience *f*; *comm* défaut *m*; **~ disease** avitaminose *f*

**deficient** *adj* déficient, insuffisant; **be ~ in** manquer de; **mentally ~** déficient

**deficit** *n* déficit *m*, découvert *m*

**¹defile** *n geog* défilé *m*

**²defile** *vt* polluer, souiller; *fig* violer

**³defile** *vi mil* défiler

**definable** *adj* définissable

**define** *vt* définir; (limit) délimiter

**definite** *adj* défini, explicite; (clear) clair, précis; délimité; sûr; *gramm* **~ article** article défini; *gramm* **past ~** passé défini

**definitely** *adv* définitivement, avec précision; (surely) assurément, certainement

**deflagration** *n* déflagration *f*

**deflate** *vt* dégonfler

**deflation** *n* dégonflement *m*; déflation *f*

**deflationary** *adj* déflationniste

**deflect** *vt* détourner, dévier; *vi* dévier, se détourner

**deflection** *n* déviation *f*, détournement *m*

**deflector** *n* déflecteur *m*

**defloration** *n bot* défloraison *f*; (woman) défloration *f*

**deflower** *vt bot* défleurir; (woman) déflorer

**defoliation** *n* défoliation *f*

**deforest** *vt* déboiser

**deforestation** *n* déboisement *m*

**deform** *vt* déformer, contrefaire; enlaidir

**deformation** *n* déformation *f*

**deformity** *n* difformité *f*, laideur *f*

**defraud** *vt* frauder, escroquer

**defray** *vt* payer, couvrir (les frais)

**defreeze** *vt* (food) décongeler

**defrock** *vt eccles* défroquer

**defrost** *vt* dégivrer; (food) décongeler

**deft** *adj* adroit, habile

**deftness** *n* adresse *f*, habileté *f*, dextérité *f*

**defunct** *n* défunt -e; *adj* défunt

**defuse** *vt* désamorcer

**defy** *vt* défier, mettre au défi; braver; désobéir à

**degeneracy** *n* dégénérescence *f*

**degenerate** *n* dégénéré -e; *adj* dégénéré; *vi* dégénérer, détériorer

**degeneration** *n* dégénération *f*

**degradation** *n* dégradation *f*, avilissement *m*

**degrade** *vt* dégrader, avilir

**degrading** *adj* dégradant, avilissant

**degree** *n* degré *m*, rang *m*; (university) grade *m*; diplôme *m*; *math*+*gramm*+*phys*+*geog* degré *m*; **by ~ s** peu à peu; **third ~** passage *m* à tabac; **to a ~** considérablement

**degression** *n* dégrèvement *m*

**degressive** *adj* dégressif -ive

**dehumanize** *vt* déshumaniser

**dehydrate** *vt* déshydrater

**dehydration** *n* déshydratation *f*

**de-ice** *vt* dégivrer

**deify** *vt* déifier

**deign** *vt* daigner

**deism** *n* déisme *m*

**deist** *n* déiste

**deity** *n* déité *f*, divinité *f*

**déjà-vu** *n* illusion *f* d'avoir déjà vu

**deject** *vt* déprimer

**dejection** *n* déjection *f*; abattement *m*

**de jure** *adj*+*adv* de jure

**delate** *vt leg* dénoncer

**delation** *n* délation *f*

**delay** *n* délai *m*, retard *m*; (waiting) attente *f*; *vt* retarder, différer

**delectable** *adj* délicieux -ieuse, agréable; *cul* délectable

**delectation** *n* délectation *f*

**delegacy** *n* commission *f*, délégation *f*

**delegate** *n* délégué -e; *vt* déléguer

**delegation** *n* commission *f*, délégation *f*; (act of delegating) délégation *f*

**delete** *vt* biffer, rayer, supprimer

**deleterious** *adj* délétère, nocif -ive

**deletion** *n* rature *f*; suppression *f*

**deliberate** *adj* délibéré, pondéré; voulu, intentionnel -elle; prudent; (slow) lent; *vt* délibérer de, décider; *vi* délibérer, réfléchir

**deliberation** *n* délibération *f*; (consideration) réflexion *f*, pondération *f*; (slowness) lenteur *f*

**deliberative** *adj* délibérant; (with power to decide) délibératif -ive

**delicacy** *n* (food) friandise *f*; (tact) délicatesse *f*, finesse *f*, tact *m*; modestie *f*, sensibilité *f*

**delicate** *adj* délicat; fin; (colour) pâle, tendre; fragile, frêle; (refined) raffiné, sensible

**delicatessen** *n* (shop) épicerie fine; (food) produits *mpl* d'épicerie fine

**delicious** *adj* délicieux -ieuse

**delight** *n* délice *m*, plaisir *m*; **Turkish ~** loukoum *m*; *vt* charmer, ravir; *vi* se délecter

**delightful** *adj* délicieux -ieuse, charmant, agréable; (sight) ravissant

**delimit** *vt* délimiter

**delimitation** *n* délimitation *f*

**delineate** *vt* esquisser, ébaucher; décrire

**delineation** *n* esquisse *f*; description *f*

**delinquency** *n* délinquance *f*

**delinquent** *n* délinquant -e

**deliquesce** *vi chem* se liquéfier

**deliquescence** *n* déliquescence *f*

**deliquescent** *adj* déliquescent

**delirious** *adj* délirant

**delirium** *n med* délire *m*; *fig* délire *m*, transport *m*, excitation *f*; **~ tremens** délirium *m* tremens

**deliver** *vt* délivrer, libérer; (mail) distribuer; transmettre; (speech) prononcer; (goods) livrer; *med* délivrer; *leg* signifier; **be ~ed of** accoucher de; **stand and ~ !** la bourse ou la vie!

**deliverance** *n* délivrance *f*, libération *f*; *leg* déclaration *f*

**deliverer** *n* libérateur -trice

**delivery** *n* (mail) distribution *f*; (goods) livraison *f*; (speech) débit *m*; *leg* prononcé *m*; (manner of speech) élocution *f*; *med* accouchement *m*, délivrance *f*

**dell** *n* vallon *m*

**delouse** *vt* épouiller

**delousing** *n* épouillage *m*

**delphinium** *n* dauphinelle *f*, pied *m* d'alouette

**delta** *n geog* delta *m*; *aer* **~ wing** aile *f* (en) delta

**deltoid** *n anat* deltoïde *m*; *adj* deltoïde

**delude** *vt* tromper

**deluge** *n* déluge *m*; *vt* inonder, submerger

**delusion** *n* illusion *f*; *psych* hallucination *f*

**delusive** *adj* décevant, irréel -elle, trompeur -euse

**delusory** *adj* illusoire

**delve** *vt* bêcher; **~ into** creuser, fouiller (dans)

**demagogic** *adj* démagogique

**demagogue** *n* démagogue *m*

**demand** *n* demande *f*; exigence *f*; (claim) prétention *f*; **in great ~** très recherché; **payable on ~** payable sur demande; *vt* exiger, réclamer; avoir besoin de

**demarcate** *vt* délimiter, démarquer

**demarcation** *n* démarcation *f*, délimitation *f*

**demarche, démarche** *n* démarche *f*

**demean** *v refl* (degrade) s'abaisser, s'avilir

**demeanour** *n* comportement *m*, conduite *f*

**demented** *adj* fou (*f* folle)

**dementia** *n med* démence *f*; **~ praecox** schizophrénie *f*

**demerara** *n* cassonade *f*

**demesne** *n* domaine *m*

**demi-john** *n* dame-jeanne *f* (*pl* damesjeannes)

**demilitarize** *vt* démilitariser

**demise** *n* décès *m*; *leg* cession *f* par legs;

**433**

*vt leg* (estate) léguer; (honour, sovereignty) transmettre

**demission** *n* démission *f*

**demister** *n mot* dispositif *m* antibuée

**demiurge** *n* démiurge *m*

**demo** *n coll* manif *f*

**demobilization** *n mil* démobilisation *f*

**demobilize** *vt mil* démobiliser

**democracy** *n* démocratie *f*

**democrat** *n* démocrate

**democratic** *adj* démocratique

**demodé, démodé** *adj* démodé

**demographic** *adj* démographique

**demography** *n* démographie *f*

**demolish** *vt* démolir; *coll* bouffer

**demolition** *n* démolition *f*

**demon** *n* démon *m*

**demonetization** *n* démonétisation *f*

**demonetize** *vt* démonétiser

**demoniac** *n* + *adj* démoniaque

**demoniacal** *adj* démoniaque

**demonic** *adj* possédé

**demonism** *n* démonisme *m*

**demonology** *n* démonologie *f*

**demonstrable** *adj* démontrable

**demonstrably** *adv* indiscutablement

**demonstrate** *vt* démontrer; *vi* (in public) manifester

**demonstration** *n* démonstration *f*; (public) manifestation *f*

**demonstrative** *adj* probant; (feelings) démonstratif -ive; *gramm* démonstratif -ive

**demonstrator** *n* démonstrateur -trice; *sci* préparateur -trice; (in public) manifestant -e

**demoralization** *n* démoralisation *f*, découragement *m*

**demoralize** *vt* démoraliser, décourager; (pervert) corrompre

**demote** *vt* rétrograder

**demotic** *adj* démotique

**demotion** *n* rétrogradation *f*

**demur** *n* hésitation *f*; objection *f*; *vi* hésiter; soulever des objections; *leg* opposer une exception

**demure** *adj* pudique, réservé; *pej* d'une modestie affectée

**demureness** *n* air *m* pudique, réserve *f*; *pej* modestie affectée

**den** *n* antre *m*, tanière *f*; (thieves) repaire *m*; *coll* piaule *f*

**denationalize** *vt* dénationaliser

**denaturalize** *vt* dénaturaliser

**denature** *vt* dénaturer

**dene** *n* ravin *m*, ravine *f*

**denial** *n* démenti *m*, dénégation *f*; (disavowal) reniement '*m*; refus *m*

**denigrate** *vt* dénigrer

**denigration** *n* dénigrement *m*

**denim** *n* toile *f* de jean, treillis *m*; ~ **s** (trousers) jean(s) *m*(*pl*); (overalls) bleu

*m* (de travail); *mil* treillis *m*

**denizen** *n* habitant -e; étranger -ère ayant un permis de séjour; *bot* plante acclimatée; *zool* animal naturalisé; *gramm* mot *m* d'emprunt

**denominate** *vt* dénommer

**denomination** *n* dénomination *f*, appellation *f*; (money) valeur *f*; *eccles* confession *f*

**denominational** *adj eccles* confessionnel -elle

**denominative** *adj* dénominatif -ive

**denominator** *n math* dénominateur *m*; **common** ~ *math* facteur commun; *fig* ce que les membres d'un groupe ont en commun

**denotation** *n* dénotation *f*, notation *f*, signe *m*; symbole *m*; sens *m*

**denouement, dénouement** *n* dénouement *m*

**denounce** *vt* dénoncer; critiquer, condamner

**dense** *adj* dense, tassé; épais (*f* épaisse); *phot* opaque; *coll* lourd, stupide

**density** *n* densité *f*, épaisseur *f*

**dent** *n* bosse *f*, creux *m*; *vt* bosseler, cabosser

**dental** *n phon* dentale *f*; *adj med* dentaire; *phon* dental

**dentate** *adj* denté, dentelé

**dentifrice** *n* dentifrice *m*

**dentine** *n anat* dentine *f*

**dentist** *n* dentiste

**dentistry** *n* chirurgie *f* dentaire

**dentition** *n* dentition *f*

**denture** *n* dentier *m*, *coll* râtelier *m*

**denudation** *n* mise *f* à nu

**denude** *vt* dénuder; (deprive) dépouiller

**denunciation** *n* dénonciation *f*; critique violente; condamnation *f*

**denunciator** *n* dénonciateur -trice

**deny** *vt* nier; (declare untrue) démentir; (faith) renier; (refuse) refuser; (deprive) priver; **there's no** ~ **ing it** c'est indéniable

**deodorant** *n* désodorisant *m*, déodorant *m*; *adj* désodorisant, déodorant

**deodorize** *vt* désodoriser

**deodorizer** *n* désodorisant *m*, déodorant *m*

**depart** *vi* partir, s'en aller; (deviate) s'écarter; (die) mourir

**departed** *n* mort -e; **the** ~ les morts *mpl*; *adj* (finished) disparu, achevé; (dead) mort

**department** *n* section *f*; (administration) service *m*; *pol* ministère *m*; *pol* + *comm* département *m*; (shop) rayon *m*; ~ **store** grand magasin

**departmental** *adj* départemental; d'un service

**departmentalism** *n* méthodes *fpl* bureaucratiques

**departure** *n* départ *m*; déviation *f*; innovation *f*

**depend** *vi* ~ **on** dépendre de; (rely on) se fier à; *leg* être pendant; ~ **on it** vous pouvez compter là-dessus; **that** ~ **s** peut-être

**dependable** *adj* de confiance, sûr

**dependant, dependent** *n* protégé -e; subordonné -e, domestique

**dependence** *n* dépendance *f*; subordination *f*; confiance *f*

**dependency** *n* dépendance *f*

**dependent** *adj* dépendant, subordonné; (for support) à charge; (hanging) pendant

**depending** *adj* (hanging on) pendant; dépendant; *leg* pendant

**depersonalize** *vt* dépersonnaliser; *vi* se dépersonnaliser

**depict** *vt* dépeindre, peindre; décrire

**depiction** *n* peinture *f*; description *f*

**depilatory** *n* dépilatoire *m*; *adj* dépilatoire

**deplete** *vt* (exhaust) épuiser; (empty) vider, dégarnir; *med* décongestionner

**deplorable** *adj* déplorable, lamentable

**deplore** *vt* déplorer, désapprouver

**deploy** *vt* *mil* déployer; *vi* se déployer

**deployment** *n* *mil* déploiement *m*

**depone** *vi* *leg* déposer

¹**deponent** *n* *leg* déposant -e

²**deponent** *n* *gramm* déponent *m*; *adj* déponent

**depopulate** *vt* dépeupler; *vi* se dépeupler

**depopulation** *n* dépeuplement *m*

**deport** *vt* expulser, déporter; ~ **oneself** se comporter

**deportation** *n* expulsion *f*, déportation *f*

**deportee** *n* déporté -e

**deportment** *n* (behaviour) comportement *m*; (bearing) port *m*, maintien *m*

**depose** *vt* déposer, détrôner; *vi leg* déposer

**deposit** *n* (money) dépôt *m*; (security) cautionnement *m*; (on account) arrhes *fpl*; (sediment) dépôt *m*; *geol* gisement *m*; *vt* déposer, verser

**depositary** *n* (person) dépositaire

**deposition** *n* déposition *f*; *eccles* descente *f* de croix; (sediment) dépôt *m*

**depositor** *n* déposant -e

**depository** *n* entrepôt *m*; lieu *m* de dépôt

**depot** *n* dépôt *m*, entrepôt *m*; *mil* caserne *f*; (bus, locomotive) dépôt *m*; *US* gare *f*

**depravation, depravity** *n* dépravation *f*, corruption *f*

**deprave** *vt* dépraver, pervertir, corrompre

**deprecate** *vt* désapprouver, déplorer

**deprecatory** *adj* désapprobateur -trice

**depreciate** *vt* déprécier, dévaloriser; dénigrer; *vi* se déprécier

**depreciation** *n* dépréciation *f*; *fig* dénigrement *m*

**depredate** *vt* piller, dévaster

**depredation** *n* déprédation *f*, dévastation *f*, pillage *m*

**depress** *vt* (lower) baisser; (pedal, handle) appuyer sur, abaisser; (person) déprimer, abattre; (price) faire baisser

**depressant** *n* *med* sédatif *m*

**depressed** *adj* (person) déprimé, découragé; (business) en crise; ~ **area** région *f* pauvre ayant beaucoup de chômeurs

**depressing** *adj* morne, déprimant

**depression** *n* dépression *f*; *econ* crise *f*

**depressive** *adj* dépressif -ive

**depressor** *n* *anat* abaisseur *m*

**deprivation** *n* privation *f*; (loss) perte *f*; (office, rank) destitution *f*

**deprive** *vt* priver, déposséder, destituer

**depth** *n* profondeur *f*; *mus* gravité *f*; *fig* profondeur *f*, intensité *f*; (night, winter) milieu *m*; **in** ~ en profondeur; (thoroughly) de façon approfondie; **in the** ~ **s of** au fin fond de; *fig* au comble de; **out of one's** ~ ayant perdu pied; *fig* dépassé

**depth-charge** *n* *naut* grenade sous-marine

**depth-gauge** *n* sondeur *m*

**deputation** *n* députation *f*

**depute** *vt* députer; déléguer

**deputize** *vt* députer; *vi* assurer l'intérim

**deputy** *n* suppléant -e; *pol* député *m*

**deracinate** *vt* déraciner

**derail** *vt* faire dérailler; *vi* dérailler

**derange** *vt* déranger, bouleverser; distraire

**derangement** *n* maladie mentale

**derelict** *n* *naut* + *leg* + *fig* épave *f*; *adj* abandonné, délaissé

**dereliction** *n* abandon *m*; (duty) négligence *f*, manquement *m* au devoir

**derequisition** *vt* déréquisitionner

**deride** *vt* tourner en dérision, ridiculiser; traiter avec mépris; faire peu de cas de

**derision** *n* dérision *f*

**derisive** *adj* railleur -euse, moqueur -euse

**derisory** *adj* dérisoire

**derivation** *n* dérivation *f*

**derivative** *n* dérivé *m*; *adj* dérivé

**derive** *vt* tirer, trouver, puiser; *vi* tracer son origine; ~ **from** émaner de

**dermatitis** *n* dermatite *f*, dermite *f*

**dermatologist** *n* dermatologiste, dermatologue

**dermatology** *n* dermatologie *f*

**derogate** *vi* amoindrir, nuire à, déroger à

**derogation** n dénigrement m, diminution f; amoindrissement m
**derogatory** adj dénigrant, irrespectueux -euse, qui abaisse
**derrick** n (oil) derrick m; naut mât m de charge, palan m
**derv** n gas-oil m
**dervish** n derviche m
**descale** vt détartrer
**descant** n mus déchant m; vi mus exécuter un déchant
**descend** vt descendre; vi descendre; (originate) être issu; dégénérer; ~ upon se jeter sur; visiter à l'improviste; ~ to s'abaisser à
**descendant** n descendant -e
**descent** n descente f; pente f; (lineage) descendance f; attaque f
**describe** vt décrire, relater; tracer
**description** n description f, récit m; sorte f, espèce f; (personal) signalement m
**descry** vt apercevoir, discerner de loin
**desecrate** vt profaner
**desecration** n profanation f
¹**desert** n désert m, région f désertique; adj désertique, inculte, inhabité
²**desert** n mérite m; ~ s dû m
³**desert** vt abandonner, quitter; mil déserter; vi déserter
**desertion** n abandon m; mil désertion f
**deserve** vt + vi mériter
**deservedly** adv à bon droit, à juste titre
**deserving** adj digne, méritoire; méritant
**desiccate** vt dessécher
**desiccation** n dessèchement m, dessiccation f
**desiderata** npl desiderata mpl
**design** n dessein m, projet m, plan m; intention f; theat décors mpl; pej dessein m sinistre; (painting) dessin m, motif m; (sketch) esquisse f; comm modèle m; by ~ délibérément; vt (sketch) esquisser, ébaucher; faire le plan de; avoir l'intention de, projeter de; vi créer des modèles; (sketch) faire des esquisses
**designate** adj désigné; vt désigner, nommer; spécifier
**designation** n désignation f
**designer** n dessinateur -trice; theat décorateur -trice
**designing** n dessin m, création f de modèles; theat création f de maquettes, création f de décors; adj intrigant
**desirable** adj désirable, souhaitable
**desire** n désir m; envie f; concupiscence f; vœu m; demande f; vt désirer, souhaiter; (covet) convoiter; (ask) demander
**desirous** adj désireux -euse; ambitieux -ieuse
**desist** vi désister

**desk** n bureau m, secrétaire m; (school) pupitre m; mus pupitre m; (cash) caisse f; US ~ clerk réceptionniste
**desolate** adj désolé, ravagé; inhabité, désert; seul, affligé; vt dépeupler; rendre désert; (sadden) désoler, rendre malheureux -euse
**desolation** n désolation f, dévastation f; (abandonment) abandon m, solitude f
**despair** n désespoir m; vi désespérer
**despatch, dispatch** n (message) dépêche f; (sending) expédition f, envoi m; (speed) rapidité f, promptitude f; (newspaper) reportage m; (killing) exécution f; ~ box valise f qui contient des documents, valise officielle; ~ rider estafette f (à motocyclette); vt (messenger) dépêcher; (letter) envoyer; (goods) acheminer; (hasten) expédier; (kill) achever
**desperado** n bandit m, desperado m
**desperate** adj capable de tout, acharné; (without hope) désespéré; (illness) mortel -elle; coll terrible, énorme
**desperation** n désespoir m
**despicable** adj méprisable
**despise** vt mépriser, dédaigner
¹**despite** n dépit m; dédain m; in ~ of malgré
²**despite** prep malgré, en dépit de
**despoil** vt dépouiller, spolier
**despoliation** n dépouillement m, spoliation f
**despond** n ar désespoir m; vi perdre courage, être déprimé
**despondency** n découragement m, dépression f
**despondent** adj découragé, déprimé
**despot** n despote m, tyran m
**despotic** adj despotique, tyrannique
**despotism** n despotisme m, tyrannie f
**dessert** n dessert m
**dessert-spoon** n cuillère f à dessert
**destination** n destination f
**destine** vt destiner, prédestiner; déterminer, fixer; ~ d for voué à
**destiny** n destinée f; (fate) destin m
**destitute** adj dénué, dépourvu, indigent
**destroy** vt détruire, démolir; ruiner
**destroyer** n naut destroyer m, contre-torpilleur m; (person) destructeur -trice
**destructible** adj destructible
**destruction** n destruction f, perte f; démolition f
**destructive** adj destructif -ive; destructeur -trice
**destructor** n incinérateur m
**desuetude** n désuétude f
**desultory** adj décousu, sans suite, sans méthode

**detach** *vt* détacher, séparer
**detached** *adj* détaché, séparé; impartial
**detachment** *n* détachement *m*
**detail** *n* détail *m*; *mil* détachement *m*; **in ~** en détail, dans le détail; *vt* détailler; *mil* détacher
**detailed** *adj* détaillé; *mil* détaché
**detain** *vt* détenir; (delay) retarder, retenir
**detainee** *n* leg détenu
**detainer** *n* leg détention *f*; *leg* mandat *m* de dépôt
**detect** *vt* déceler, découvrir, détecter; se rendre compte de
**detection** *n* découverte *f*, détention *f*
**detective** *n* inspecteur *m* de police, détective *m*; *adj* policier -ière; **~ story** roman policier
**detector** *n* détecteur *m*
**detente, détente** *n* détente *f*
**detention** *n* détention *f*; (school) retenue *f*; *mil* **~ barracks** prison *f* militaire
**deter** *vt* détourner, décourager
**detergent** *n* détergent *m*, détersif *m*; *adj* détersif -ive, détergent
**deteriorate** *vt* détériorer, déprécier; *vi* se détériorer, baisser, dégénérer; empirer
**deterioration** *n* détérioration *f*, altération *f*; (worsening) aggravation *f*
**determent** *n* détournement *m*; dissuasion *f*
**determinable** *adj* déterminable
**determinant** *n* *math* + *gramm* déterminant *m*; *adj* déterminant
**determinate** *adj* déterminé, fixé; (conclusive) établi, définitif -ive
**determination** *n* détermination *f*, résolution *f*; décision *f*, résolution *f*; délimitation *f*; *leg* résiliation *f*
**determinative** *n* *gramm* + *math* déterminant *m*; *adj* déterminant
**determine** *vt* déterminer, décider, résoudre; (set limits to) délimiter; (fix) régler; *leg* résilier; *vi* se déterminer, se résoudre; *leg* expirer
**determined** *adj* déterminé, résolu; fixe
**determinism** *n* déterminisme *m*
**determinist** *n* déterministe
**deterrence** *n* dissuasion *f*, découragement *m*
**deterrent** *n* *mil* forces *fpl* de dissuasion; **act as a ~** avoir un effet dissuasif; *adj* de dissuasion, dissuasif -ive
**detest** *vt* détester
**detestable** *adj* détestable
**detestation** *n* détestation *f*; objet *m* d'horreur
**dethrone** *vt* détrôner
**detonate** *vt* faire éclater, faire détoner; *vi* éclater, détoner
**detonation** *n* détonation *f*, explosion *f*
**detonator** *n* détonateur *m*, amorce *f*;

(railway) pétard *m*
**detour** *n* détour *m*
**detract** *vt* ôter; *vi* **~ from** diminuer
**detraction** *n* détraction *f*, dénigrement *m*, calomnie *f*
**detractor** *n* détracteur -trice, accusateur -trice
**detrain** *vt* + *vi esp mil* débarquer (d'un train)
**detriment** *n* détriment *m*, dommage *m*, préjudice *m*
**detrimental** *adj* préjudiciable, nuisible
**detrition** *n* détrition *f*
**detritus** *n geol* détritus *mpl*, roches *fpl* détritiques; *fig* détritus *mpl*
**deuce** *n* (tennis) égalité *f*, quarante à; *interj* diable!
**deuced** *adj coll* du diable; *adv coll* diablement
**deuterium** *n chem* deutérium *m*
**devaluate** *vt* dévaluer
**devaluation** *n* dévaluation *f*
**devalue** *vt* + *vi* dévaluer
**devastate** *vt* dévaster
**devastating** *adj* dévastateur -trice; *coll* foudroyant, efficace
**devastation** *n* dévastation *f*
**develop** *vt* développer; (set forth) exposer, élaborer; (strengthen) développer, fortifier; (exploit) mettre en valeur, exploiter; (habit, disease) contracter; (skill) faire preuve de, manifester; *vi* se développer, s'amplifier, évoluer, progresser; **~ing country** pays *m* en voie de développement
**developer** *n phot* révélateur *m*
**development** *n* développement *m*; évolution *f*, extension *f*, progrès *m*; exposé *m*; *mus* développement *m*; **~ area** zone *f* à urbaniser en priorité (Z.U.P. *f*)
**deviate** *vi* dévier
**deviation** *n* déviation *f*, divergence *f*, écart *m*; (compass, traffic, *math*) déviation *f*
**deviationist** *n* + *adj pol* déviationniste
**device** *n* expédient *m*, moyen *m*; (trick) truc *m*, astuce *f*; *mech* dispositif *m*, appareil *m*, invention *f*; *her* devise *f*; **leave s/o to his own ~s** laisser qn se débrouiller tout seul, laisser qn suivre sa pente
**devil** *n* diable *m*, démon *m*; (lawyer's) apprenti *m*; (printer, writer) nègre *m*; **~'s advocate** avocat *m* du diable; **be a ~!** laissez-vous tenter!; **between the ~ and the deep blue sea** entre l'enclume et le marteau; **go to the ~** être ruiné; *interj* foutez-moi le camp!; **play the ~ with** ruiner, léser; **poor ~** pauvre diable *m*; **raise the ~** faire un bruit de tous les diables; **talk of the ~**

quand on parle du loup on en voit la queue; **there'll be the ~ to pay** ça nous (vous, etc) coûtera cher; *vt cul* griller en ajoutant beaucoup d'épices; *vi* faire le nègre

**devilish** *adj* diabolique; *adv coll* extrêmement, diablement

**devil-may-care** *adj* téméraire; insouciant

**devilment** *n* diablerie *f*

**devilry** *n* (black magic) magie noire; satanisme *m*; (wickedness) méchanceté *f*, cruauté *f*; (daring) témérité *f*

**devious** *adj* tortueux -euse

**devise** *vt* concevoir, inventer; (plot) manigancer

**devitalization** *n* dévitalisation *f*

**devitalize** *vt* dévitaliser

**devoid** *adj* dépourvu, dénué

**devolution** *n* transmission *f*, délégation *f*; *biol* dégénérescence *f*; *pol* décentralisation *f*

**devolve** *vt* transmettre, déléguer; *vi* ~ **on** incomber à; *leg* être dévolu à

**devote** *vt* vouer, consacrer; ~ **oneself** s'adonner, se livrer, se consacrer

**devoted** *adj* dévoué, fidèle; (dedicated) voué, consacré

**devotee** *n* fervent -e, partisan -e

**devotion** *n eccles* dévotion *f*, piété *f*; dévouement *m*, attachement *m*; ~ **s** dévotions *fpl*

**devour** *vt* dévorer

**devout** *adj* (person) pieux (*f* pieuse), dévot; (prayer, etc) fervent

**dew** *n* rosée *f*

**dewdrop** *n* goutte *f* de rosée

**dewlap** *n* fanon *m*; (human) double menton *m*

**dewy** *adj* humide de rosée

**dewy-eyed** *adj* aux grands yeux ingénus

**dexter** *adj* dextre

**dexterity** *n* dextérité *f*

**dexterous, dextrous** *adj* habile, adroit, plein de dextérité

**dextrose** *n chem* dextrose *m*

**diabetes** *n* diabète *m*

**diabetic** *n + adj* diabétique

**diabolic, diabolical** *adj* diabolique; (evil) méchant; *coll* difficile, désagréable

**diabolism** *n* satanisme *m*; (sorcery) sorcellerie *f*; action *f* diabolique

**diachronic** *adj ling* diachronique

**diaconal** *adj eccles* diaconal

**diaconate** *n eccles* diaconat *m*

**diacritic, diacritical** *adj* diacritique

**diadem** *n* diadème *m*

**diaeresis** *n phon* diérèse *f*

**diagnose** *vt* diagnostiquer

**diagnosis** *n* diagnostic *m*; *biol* diagnose *f*

**diagnostic** *adj* diagnostique

**diagnostician** *n* diagnostiqueur *m*

**diagonal** *n* diagonale *f*; *adj* diagonal, oblique

**diagram** *n geom* figure *f*; diagramme *m*, plan *m*, schéma *m*

**diagrammatic** *adj* schématique

**dial** *n* (sun) cadran *m* solaire; (clock, gauge, telephone, etc) cadran *m*; *coll* (face) gueule *f*; *vt* (telephone number) composer

**dialect** *n* dialecte *m*; (regional) patois *m*

**dialectal** *adj* dialectal

**dialectic** *n* dialectique *f*; *adj* dialectique

**dialectical** *adj* dialectique; ~ **materialism** matérialisme *m* marxiste

**dialectician** *n* dialecticien -ienne

**dialling** *n* action *f* de composer un numéro de téléphone; ~ **tone** tonalité *f*; **subscriber trunk ~ (S.T.D.)** automatique *m*

**dialogue** *n* dialogue *m*

**diameter** *n* diamètre *m*

**diametric, diametrical** *adj* diamétral; (opposite) opposé

**diametrically** *adv* diamétralement; *fig* tout à fait, absolument

**diamond** *n* diamant *m*; *math* losange *m*; (cards) carreau *m*; (baseball) terrain *m*; ~ **drill** diamant *m* (de vitrier, de miroitier); ~ **jubilee** soixantième anniversaire *m* de l'accession au trône; ~ **wedding** noces *fpl* de diamant; **be a rough ~** avoir bon cœur et mauvais caractère; **black ~** charbon *m*; *adj* de diamant, en diamant; *vt* diamanter

**diamonded** *adj* diamanté

**diapason** *n mus* registre *m*, diapason *m*; (tuning fork) diapason *m*; *fig* harmonie majestueuse

**diaper** *n* (baby) couche *f*; *archi* décoration *f* en losanges; *her* losange *m*; *vt* décorer de losanges

**diaphanous** *adj* diaphane, transparent

**diaphragm** *n* diaphragme *m*

**diarist** *n* personne *f* qui tient un journal intime

**diarrhoea** *n* diarrhée *f*; **verbal ~** verbomanie *f*

**diary** *n* journal *m*; carnet *m*; agenda *m*

**diatonic** *adj mus* diatonique

**diatribe** *n* diatribe *f*

**dibber** *n agr* plantoir *m*

**dibble** *n agr* plantoir *m*; *vt* trouer au plantoir; *vi* se servir d'un plantoir

**dice** *npl* dés *mpl*; *vt cul* couper en dés; *vi* jouer aux dés

**dice-box** *n* cornet *m* à dés

**dicey** *adj coll* pas sûr, dangereux -euse

**dichotomous** *adj* divisé en deux

**dichotomy** *n* dichotomie *f*

**dicing** *n* activité *f* de jouer aux dés; *cul* action *f* de couper en dés

**dick** *n coll obs* type *m*; *sl obs* détective *m*; *vulg obs* bite *f*

**dickens** *interj coll* diable!

¹**dicky, dickey** *n mot obs* spider *m*; (shirt front) plastron *m*

²**dicky** *adj coll* peu sûr; (unwell) un peu malade; (financially) peu solide

**dicky-bird** *n* (child language) oiseau *m*

**dictaphone** *n* dictaphone *m*

**dictate** *n pol* diktat *m*; *vt* dicter; ordonner; *vi* donner des ordres, s'imposer

**dictation** *n* dictée *f*

**dictator** *n* dictateur *m*

**dictatorial** *adj* dictatorial

**dictatorship** *n* dictature *f*

**diction** *n* diction *f*, élocution *f*; choix *m* de mots; **poetic ~** langage *m* de la poésie

**dictionary** *n* dictionnaire *m*

**dictum** *n* dicton *m*; maxime *f*; (statement) affirmation *f*

**didactic** *adj* didactique; pédantesque

**didacticism** *n*, **didactics** *npl* didactique *f*

**diddle** *vt coll* carotter, escroquer; *vi* tricher

¹**die** *n* (*pl* **dice**) dé *m*; (*pl* **~ s**) (minting) coin *m*; **the ~ is cast** les jeux sont faits

²**die** *vi* mourir, expirer; disparaître, s'éteindre; **~ away** se dissiper, s'éteindre; *bot* **~ back** se flétrir; **~ down** diminuer; **~ hard** avoir la vie dure; **~ in harness** mourir en plein travail; **~ off** mourir un à un; **~ out** s'éteindre; **~ the death** souffrir la peine de mort; **be dying to** mourir d'envie de

**diehard** *n + adj* réactionnaire; intransigeant -e

**diesel** *n* diesel *m*; **~ oil** gas-oil *m*

¹**diet** *n* régime *m*; (normal food) alimentation *f*; *vt* mettre au régime; *vi* suivre un régime

²**diet** *n pol* diète *f*

**dietary** *n* régime *m*; *adj* de régime

**dietetic** *adj* diététique

**dietetics** *npl* diététique *f*

**dietician** *n* diététicien -ienne

**differ** *vi* différer, se différencier, être différent; (quarrel) se brouiller; **agree to ~** rester sur ses positions

**difference** *n* différence *f*, divergence *f*, disparité *f*; (gap) écart *m*; querelle *f*, dispute *f*; **split the ~** couper la poire en deux

**different** *adj* différent, dissemblable; varié, divers

**differential** *n elect + eng* différentiel *m*; *math* différentielle *f*; *adj* différentiel -ielle

**differentiate** *vt* différencier; *vi* se différencier

**differing** *adj* contradictoire

**difficult** *adj* difficile

**difficulty** *n* difficulté *f*; obstacle *m*; objection *f*; (trouble) ennui *m*; **be in difficulties** avoir des problèmes; **make difficulties** soulever des objections

**diffidence** *n* manque *m* d'assurance, timidité *f*

**diffident** *adj* dépourvu d'assurance, timide, embarrassé

**diffraction** *n* diffraction *f*

**diffuse** *adj* diffus; *vt* diffuser; *vi* se diffuser

**diffusible** *adj* diffusible

**diffusion** *n* diffusion *f*

**diffusive** *adj* qui diffuse; (verbose) verbeux -euse, bavard, prolixe

**dig** *n* bêchage *m*; *arch* fouilles *fpl*; *coll* sarcasme *m*, brocard *m*; **~ s** logement *m*; *vt* bêcher, piocher; creuser; excaver; extraire; (vegetables) arracher; (nails) enfoncer; *fig* découvrir; *coll* brocarder; *sl* comprendre; approuver; aimer; *sl* travailler; *vi* creuser; faire des fouilles; *sl* loger; *sl* comprendre; **~ in** enterrer; *mil* se creuser un abri; s'incruster; *coll* **~ into** travailler dur à; **~ out, ~ up** découvrir, trouver

¹**digest** *n* digest *m*; résumé *m*; *hist leg* digeste *m*

²**digest** *vt* digérer; assimiler; (summarize) abréger, résumer; *vi* être digéré

**digestible** *adj* digestible

**digestion** *n* digestion *f*

**digestive** *n* digestif *m*; *adj* digestif -ive

**digger** *n* (person) bêcheur -euse; chercheur *m* d'or; *mech* plantoir *m*; *agr* arrachoir *m*; *sl* Australien -ienne

**digit** *n* chiffre *m*; *anat + astron* doigt *m*

**digital** *adj* digital

**digitalin** *n med* digitaline *f*

**digitalis** *n bot* digitale *f*; *med* digitaline *f*

**dignified** *adj* solennel -elle, digne, imposant

**dignitary** *n* dignitaire *m*

**dignity** *n* dignité *f*, gravité *f*; rang *m*, dignité *f*

**digress** *vi* faire une digression; (deviate) dévier

**digression** *n* digression *f*

**digressive** *adj* décousu, avec des digressions

**digs** *n coll* logement *m*

**dihedral** *n* dièdre *m*; *adj* dièdre

**dike** *n + vt see* **dyke**

**dilapidate** *vt* abîmer, dégrader, délabrer; (fortune) dilapider; *vi* se délabrer

**dilapidation** *n* délabrement *m*, dégradation *f*; (fortune) dilapidation *f*

**dilatable** *adj* dilatable, expansible

**dilatation** *n* dilatation *f*

**dilate** *vt* dilater

**dilation** *n* dilatation *f*

**dilator** *n med* dilatant *m*; dilatateur *m*

**dilatory** *adj* dilatoire

**dilemma** *n* dilemme *m*; **on the horns of a** ~ enfermé dans un dilemme

**dilettante** *n* (*pl* **dilettanti**) + *adj* dilettante

**dilettantism** *n* dilettantisme *m*

¹**diligence** *n* diligence *f*, application *f*; persévérance *f*

²**diligence** *n* (coach) diligence *f*

**diligent** *adj* diligent

**dill** *n bot* fenouil *m*

**dilly-dally** *vi* vaciller, lambiner

**diluent** *n* dissolvant *m*

**dilute** *vt* diluer, noyer; (wine) couper, baptiser; *fig* affaiblir; *adj* dilué, affaibli

**dilution** *n* dilution *f*; affaiblissement *m*

**diluvial** *adj* diluvial; diluvien -ienne

**diluvium** *n geol* diluvium *m*

**dim** *adj* terne, faible, pâle; (sight) trouble; (sound) sourd; indistinct, confus; *coll* bête, stupide; *coll* (boring) ennuyeux -euse, *sl* emmerdant; *vt* ternir, obscurcir; *vt* tremper, plonger; (sound) assourdir; *mot* baisser, *mot* mettre en code; *vi* (glory) se ternir, s'obscurcir

**dime** *n US* (pièce *f* de) dix cents *mpl*

**dimension** *n* dimension *f*

**diminish** *vt* diminuer, réduire; raccourcir; *vi* diminuer, décliner

**diminuendo** *n mus* diminuendo *m*

**diminution** *n* diminution *f*

**diminutive** *n gramm* diminutif *m*; *adj* minuscule, tout petit

**dimness** *n* aspect *m* terne; (weakness) faiblesse *f*; *coll* stupidité *f*, bêtise *f*

**dimple** *n* fossette *f*

**dimwit** *n coll* crétin -e, idiot -e

**din** *n* potin *m*, boucan *m*; bruit *m*; *vt* rabâcher; *vi* faire du potin

**dine** *vi* inviter à dîner; *vi* dîner

**diner** *n* dîneur -euse; *US* wagon-restaurant *m* (*pl* wagons-restaurants); *coll* restaurant *m*

**diner-out** *n* mondain -e

**ding** *n* son *m* de cloche; *vi* résonner

**ding-dong** *n* son *m* de cloche; *adj* à qui mieux mieux

**dinghy** *n naut* canot *m*, youyou *m*

**dinginess** *n* aspect *m* minable

**dingle** *n* vallon *m*

**dingy** *adj* terne, minable

**dining-car** *n* wagon-restaurant *m* (*pl* wagons-restaurants)

**dining-hall** *n* réfectoire *m*

**dining-room** *n* salle *f* à manger

**dining-table** *n* table *f* de salle à manger

**dinky** *adj coll* chou *invar*, chouette

**dinner** *n* dîner *m*; ~ **dress** robe longue; ~ **jacket** smoking *m*; ~ **time** heure *f* du dîner

**dinosaur** *n* dinosaure *m*

**dint** *n* bosse *f*, creux *m*; **by** ~ **of** à force

de; *vt* bosseler, cabosser

**diocesan** *n* diocésain *m*; *adj* diocésain

**diocese** *n* diocèse *m*

**diode** *n elect* diode *f*

**dioxide** *n chem* bioxyde *m*

**dip** *n* (bathe) baignade *f*; (immersion) plongée *f*; (incline) déclivité *f*, inclinaison *f*; *vt* tremper, plonger; *mot* baisser; *vi* plonger, se plonger; *mot* se mettre en code

**diphase** *adj elect* diphasé

**diphtheria** *n med* diphtérie *f*

**diphthong** *n phon* diphtongue *f*

**diploma** *n* diplôme *m*

**diplomacy** *n* diplomatie *f*

**diplomat** *n* diplomate *m*

**diplomatic** *adj* diplomatique; ~ **corps** corps *m* diplomatique

**diplomatics** *npl* diplomatique *f*

**dipper** *n* plongeur -euse; *cul* louche *f*; *orni* merle *m*; *mot* basculeur *m*; (fair) montagnes *fpl* russes

**dipsomania** *n* dipsomanie *f*

**dipsomaniac** *n* dipsomane *m*

**dipstick** *n mot* jauge *f* (d'huile)

**diptera** *npl zool* diptères *mpl*

**diptych** *n* diptyque *m*

**dire** *adj* terrible, désastreux -euse

**direct** *adj* direct; (straight) droit; (frank) net (*f* nette), franc (*f* franche), immédiat; absolu, complet -ète; *elect* continu; *gramm* direct; ~ **action** recours *m* à la grève; ~ **input** entrée directe; *adv* directement, tout droit; *vt* diriger; (lead) mener, conduire; (point) braquer; administrer; *theat* mettre en scène; *cin* réaliser; (letters) adresser

**direction** *n* direction *f*, conduite *f*, administration *f*; sens *m*, orientation *f*; (letter) adresse *f*; *theat* mise *f* en scène; *cin* réalisation *f*; ~ **s instructions** *fpl*; **in the** ~ **of** vers; *rad* ~ **finder** radiogoniomètre *m*; *mot* ~ **indicator** (winker) clignotant *m*; (pointer) flèche *f*

**directional** *adj rad* directionnel -elle; directeur -trice

**directive** *n* directive *f*, instruction *f*; *adj* directeur -trice

**directly** *adv* directement, immédiatement; *conj* dès que

**directness** *n* netteté *f*, franchise *f*

**director** *n* directeur -trice

**directorate** *n* conseil *m* d'administration

**directorial** *adj* directorial

**directorship** *n* direction *f*, présidence *f*

**directory** *n* annuaire *m*; *US* conseil *m* d'administration; *adj* directeur -trice

**directress** *n* directrice *f*

**direful** *adj* terrible, désastreux -euse

**dirge** *n* lamentation *f*; hymne *m* funèbre; mélodie *f* triste

**dirigible** *n* dirigeable *m*; *adj* dirigeable

**dirk** *n obs* poignard *m*

**dirt** *n* saleté *f*, crasse *f*; (mud) boue *f*, fange *f*; (dust) poussière *f*; obscénité *f*, pornographie *f*, ordures *fpl*; ~ **cheap** pour rien, à vil prix; *sl* **do** ~ **to** escroquer, jouer un sale tour à; **throw** ~ **at** traîner dans la boue

**dirtiness** *n* saleté *f*

**dirt-track** *n* piste *f*; *sp* cendrée *f*

**dirty** *adj* sale, crasseux -euse; boueux -euse, crotté; obscène, grossier -ière, ordurier -ière; (weather) vilain, sale; *coll* **do the** ~ **on** jouer un sale tour à; *vt* salir; *vi* se salir

**disability** *n* incapacité *f*; invalidité *f*

**disable** *vt* estropier; rendre inapte; (put out of action) mettre hors d'état; *naut* désemparer; *leg* frapper d'incapacité

**disablement** *n* incapacité *f* physique

**disabuse** *vt* désabuser

**disaccord** *n* désaccord *m*; *vi* différer

**disadvantage** *n* désavantage *m*; *vt* désavantager

**disadvantageous** *adj* désavantageux -euse

**disaffect** *vt* aliéner, mécontenter

**disaffected** *adj* mécontent, mal disposé, dissident

**disaffectedness, disaffection** *n* désaffection *f*

**disagree** *vi* différer, ne pas être d'accord; (argue) se disputer, se quereller; ~ **with** ne pas convenir à, rendre malade

**disagreeable** *adj* désagréable

**disagreeableness** *n* hargne *f*

**disagreement** *n* désaccord *m*; dispute *f*, querelle *f*; (discrepancy) discordance *f*

**disallow** *vt* rejeter, repousser; défendre

**disappear** *vi* disparaître

**disappearance** *n* disparition *f*

**disappoint** *vt* décevoir, désappointer; (thwart) faire échouer, contrecarrer

**disappointment** *n* déception *f*, désappointement *m*; (hitch, snag) contretemps *m*

**disapprobation** *n* désapprobation *f*

**disapproval** *n* désapprobation *f*

**disapprove** *vt* désapprouver, condamner; *vi* trouver à redire

**disarm** *vt* désarmer

**disarmament** *n* désarmement *m*

**disarming** *adj* désarmant, touchant

**disarrange** *vt* déranger, bouleverser

**disarrangement** *n* dérangement *m*, bouleversement *m*

**disarray** *n* désordre *m*, confusion *f*, désarroi *m*; négligé *m*; *vt* mettre en désordre, bouleverser; dévêtir

**disassociate** *vt* dissocier

**disassociation** *n* dissociation *f*

**disaster** *n* désastre *m*, catastrophe *f*

**disastrous** *adj* désastreux -euse, catastrophique

**disavow** *vt* désavouer

**disband** *vt* disperser; *mil* licencier; *vi* se disperser; *mil* se débander

**disbandment** *n mil* licenciement *m*

**disbar** *vt leg* exclure du barreau

**disbelief** *n* incrédulité *f*

**disburden** *vt* décharger

**disburse** *vt* + *vi* débourser

**disbursement** *n* déboursement *m*

**disc, disk** *n* disque *m*; **slipped** ~ hernie discale; *rad* ~ **jockey** présentateur -trice de disques

**discal** *adj* discal

**discard** *n* action *f* de jeter; (cards) écart *m*; *vt* jeter, mettre de côté, écarter; (clothes) enlever, ôter, rejeter; (cards) écarter, se défausser de; *vi* se défausser

**discern** *vt* discerner, percevoir, distinguer

**discernible** *adj* discernable, perceptible

**discerning** *adj* judicieux -ieuse, pénétrant, fin

**discernment** *n* discernement *m*, discrimination *f*

**discharge** *n* (dismissal) renvoi *m*, congédiement *m*; (unloading) déchargement *m*; libération *f*, licenciement *m*; (firearm) décharge *f*; *elect* décharge *f*; *med* suppuration *f*; *leg* acquittement *m*; *comm* (debt) règlement *m*; *eng* débit *m*; (duty) exercice *m*; (prisoner) élargissement *m*; *vt* (dismiss) renvoyer, congédier; (unload) décharger, libérer; *mil* (weapon) décharger; (soldier) démobiliser, licencier; (unfit soldier) réformer; *elect* décharger; *leg* acquitter; *comm* régler; (prisoner) élargir; *eng* débiter; (duty) accomplir; *vi med* suppurer; se déverser

**disciple** *n* disciple *m*

**disciplinable** *adj* disciplinable

**disciplinarian** *n* personne *f* très sévère en matière de discipline

**disciplinary** *adj* disciplinaire, de discipline

**discipline** *n* discipline *f*; *vt* discipliner, punir

**disclaim** *vt* rejeter, désavouer; *leg* renoncer à

**disclaimer** *n* désaveu *m*, déni *m*; *leg* désistement *m*, renonciation *f*

**disclose** *vt* découvrir, révéler, divulguer

**disclosure** *n* révélation *f*

**discoid** *adj* discoïde

**discoloration, discolouration** *n* décoloration *f*

**discolour** *vt* décolorer

**discomfit** *vt* déconcerter, décontenancer; *mil* battre

**discomfiture** *n* déconvenue *f*, déconfiture *f*, échec *m*; *mil* défaite *f*

**discomfort** *n* inconfort *m*; *med* malaise *m*; *vt* incommoder

**discommode** *vt* incommoder, gêner

**discompose** *vt* troubler, bouleverser

**discomposure** *n* trouble *m*; embarras *m*, gêne *f*

**disconcert** *vt* déconcerter, décontenancer; (embarrass) gêner; frustrer

**disconnect** *vt* disjoindre, séparer; (telephone) couper; *elect* débrancher

**disconnected** *adj* séparé; incohérent

**disconnection, disconnexion** *n* séparation *f*; *elect* débranchement *m*

**disconsolate** *adj* triste, inconsolable, misérable

**discontent** *n* mécontentement *m*; *adj* mécontent; *vt* mécontenter

**discontented** *adj* mécontent

**discontinuance** *n* interruption *f*, discontinuation *f*

**discontinuation** *n* interruption *f*, discontinuation *f*

**discontinue** *vt* discontinuer, interrompre, cesser; *vi* prendre fin

**discontinuity** *n* discontinuité *f*

**discontinuous** *adj* discontinu

**discophile** *n* + *adj* discophile

**discord** *n* discorde *f*, division *f*; discordance *f*; *mus* dissonance *f*

**discordance, discordancy** *n* discorde *f*; désaccord *m*

**disco(theque)** *n* disco(thèque) *f*

**discount** *n* escompte *m*; rabais *m*, réduction *f*; at a ~ au rabais; (unimportant) de peu de valeur; *vt* rabattre, décompter; escompter; faire peu de cas de, ne pas tenir compte de

**discourage** *vt* décourager, rebuter; dissuader

**discouragement** *n* découragement *m*

**discourse** *n* discours *m*; conversation *f*; dissertation *f*; *vi* discourir, disserter; s'entretenir

**discourteous** *adj* discourtois, impoli

**discourtesy** *n* discourtoisie *f*, impolitesse *f*

**discover** *vt* découvrir, trouver; *ar* révéler

**discovery** *n* découverte *f*

**discredit** *n* discrédit *m*; doute *m*; *vt* discréditer; mettre en doute, douter de

**discreditable** *adj* honteux -euse

**discreet** *adj* discret -ète, circonspect, réservé

**discrepance, discrepancy** *n* contradiction *f*, discordance *f*

**discrete** *adj* séparé, discontinu; *med* + *bot* discret -ète

**discretion** *n* discrétion *f*, prudence *f*; jugement *m*, discernement *m*; latitude *f*; at the ~ of selon l'avis de; years of ~ âge *m* de raison

**discretionary** *adj* discrétionnaire

**discriminate** *adj* distinct, discriminatoire; *vt* discriminer, distinguer; *vi* établir une discrimination

**discriminating** *adj* judicieux -ieuse, avisé, perceptif -ive; (tariff) différentiel -ielle

**discrimination** *n* discrimination *f*; discernement *m*

**discriminatory** *adj* discriminatoire

**disculpate** *vt* disculper

**discursive, discursory** *adj* décousu, incohérent

**discus** *n* *sp* disque *m*

**discuss** *vt* discuter, s'entretenir de

**discussion** *n* discussion *f*

**disdain** *n* dédain *m*, mépris *m*; *vt* dédaigner, mépriser

**disease** *n* maladie *f*, mal *m*; *fig* mal *m*

**disembark** *vt* + *vi* débarquer

**disembarkation** *n* débarquement *m*

**disembodiment** *n* séparation *f* du corps

**disembody** *vt* *mil* licencier; séparer du corps

**disembowel** *vt* étriper, éviscérer

**disenchant** *vt* désenchanter; désillusionner

**disenchantment** *n* désenchantement *m*, désillusion *f*

**disencumber** *vt* désencombrer

**disenfranchise** *vt* *see* **disfranchise**

**disengage** *vt* dégager, détacher; *vi* se dégager

**disengagement** *n* dégagement *m*

**disentangle** *vt* démêler, débrouiller; dénouer; *coll* dépêtrer; *vi* se dénouer; *coll* se dépêtrer

**disentanglement** *n* démêlage *m*; dénouement *m*

**disequilibrium** *n* déséquilibre *m*, instabilité *f*

**disestablish** *vt* (church) séparer de l'état

**disestablishment** *n* (church) séparation *f* de l'état

**disesteem** *n* défaveur *f*; *vt* mésestimer

**disfavour** *n* défaveur *f*; disgrâce *f*, déconsidération *f*; *vt* désapprouver, ne pas aimer

**disfiguration** *n* *see* **disfigurement**

**disfigure** *vt* défigurer, enlaidir

**disfigurement** *n* défiguration *f*, enlaidissement *m*

**disfranchise, disenfranchise** *vt* priver des droits civiques, priver du droit de vote

**disfranchisement** *n* privation *f* des droits civiques, privation *f* du droit de vote

**disgorge** *vt* dégorger; (give back) rendre; (river) déverser

**disgrace** *n* disgrâce *f*; déshonneur *m*, honte *f*; *vt* disgracier, déshonorer

**disgraceful** *adj* honteux -euse, déshonorant

**disgruntled** *adj* mécontent, de mauvaise humeur

**disguise** *n* déguisement *m*, travesti *m*; *fig* travestissement *m*, faux-semblant *m*; *vt* déguiser, travestir; dissimuler

**disgust** *n* dégoût *m*, écœurement *m*; *vt* dégoûter, écœurer

**disgusting** *adj* dégoûtant, écœurant; révoltant, indigne

**dish** *n* (plate, food, plateful) plat *m*; *cul* mets *m*; (hollow) cuvette *f*; *sl* homme *m*, femme *f* ayant du chien; *vt cul* apprêter, servir (un plat); *coll* (spoil) couler, enfoncer; ~ **out** servir à manger; *coll* distribuer; ~ **up** servir à table dans un plat; *coll* présenter avec goût

**dish-cloth** *n* torchon *m*

**dish-cover** *n* couvercle *m*

**dishearten** *vt* décourager, démoraliser, déprimer

**disheartening** *adj* décourageant, déprimant

**dished** *adj* concave; *mot* désaxé; *coll* cuit, fichu

**dishevelled** *adj* (hair) échevelé, ébouriffé; (person) mal tenu, débraillé

**dishful** *n* plat *m*, platée *f*

**dish-mat** *n* dessous-de-plat *m invar*

**dishonest** *adj* malhonnête

**dishonesty** *n* malhonnêteté *f*

**dishonour** *n* déshonneur *m*, disgrâce *f*, honte *f*, ignominie *f*; *vt* déshonorer; (woman) séduire; insulter; *comm* (cheque) refuser d'honorer; (bill) protester; (promise) ne pas tenir; ~ **ed** cheque chèque *m* sans provision

**dishonourable** *adj* honteux -euse, déshonorant

**dishwasher** *n* plongeur -euse

**dish-water** *n* eau *f* de vaisselle; *coll pej* (soup, coffee, etc) lavasse *f*

**dishy** *adj sl* excitant, sexy

**disillusion** *n* désillusion *f*; *vt* désillusionner

**disillusionment** *n* désillusionnement *m*

**disincentive** *n* qch qui décourage l'action ou l'initiative

**disinclination** *n* répugnance *f*, aversion *f*

**disincline** *vt* rendre peu enthousiaste; *vi* devenir peu enthousiaste

**disinfect** *vt* désinfecter

**disinfectant** *n* désinfectant *m*

**disinfection** *n* désinfection *f*

**disinfest** *vt* dératiser; (lice) épouiller

**disinfestation** *n* dératisation *f*; (lice) épouillage *m*

**disingenuous** *adj* insincère, faux (*f* fausse)

**disingenuousness** *n* insincérité *f*, finasserie *f*

**disinherit** *vt* déshériter

**disinheritance** *n leg* exhérédation *f*

**disintegrate** *vt* désintégrer, désagréger; *vi* se désagréger

**disintegration** *n* désintégration *f*, désagrégation *f*

**disinter** *vt* déterrer, exhumer; *fig* révéler

**disinterested** *adj* désintéressé; impartial; *sl* ennuyé

**disinterestedness** *n* désintéressement *m*; impartialité *f*

**disinterment** *n* déterrement *m*, exhumation *f*

**disjoin** *vt* disjoindre, désunir

**disjoint** *vt* disloquer; désunir, détraquer

**disjointed** *adj* disloqué; *fig* incohérent, décousu

**disjunction** *n* disjonction *f*, séparation *f*

**disjuncture** *n gramm* disjonctive *f*; *adj* disjonctif -ive

**disk** *n see* disc

**dislike** *n* antipathie *f*, aversion *f*; dégoût *m*; *vt* ne pas aimer; avoir de l'aversion pour

**dislocate** *vt* disloquer; *med* désarticuler; désorganiser, bouleverser

**dislocation** *n* dislocation *f*; *med* luxation *f*; dérangement *m*; désorganisation *f*

**dislodge** *vt* déloger; (object) déplacer, faire bouger

**disloyal** *adj* déloyal; infidèle

**disloyalty** *n* déloyauté *f*

**dismal** *adj* morne, terne, sombre

**dismantle** *vt mil* démanteler; *naut* dégréer; *mech* démonter

**dismast** *vt naut* démâter

**dismay** *n* consternation *f*, atterrement *m*; effroi *m*; *vt* consterner, atterrer; effrayer

**dismember** *vt* démembrer

**dismemberment** *n* démembrement *m*

**dismiss** *vt* congédier, renvoyer; (official) révoquer; *leg* (case) classer; (appeal) rejeter; *fig* cesser de considérer; *mil* ~ ! rompez!

**dismissal** *n* renvoi *m*; (official) révocation *f*

**dismissive** *adj* qui signifie un renvoi; méprisant

**dismount** *vt* faire descendre, démonter, désarçonner; *vi* descendre de, mettre pied à terre

**disobedience** *n* désobéissance *f*

**disobedient** *adj* désobéissant

**disobey** *vt* + *vi* désobéir

**disoblige** *vt* désobliger; (offend) offenser, peiner

**disobliging** *adj* désobligeant, désagréable

**disorder** *n* désordre *m*, tumulte *m*; désordres *mpl*; *med* maladie *f*, trouble *m*;

*vt* mettre en désordre; mettre en confusion; rendre malade

**disorderliness** *n* désordre *m*; esprit *m* de désordre

**disorderly** *adj* en désordre, désordonné; (mob) turbulent; ~ **house** maison *f* de prostitution, bordel *m*; (gambling) maison *f* de jeu

**disorganization** *n* désorganisation *f*

**disorganize** *vt* désorganiser

**disorientate** *vt* désorienter

**disorientation** *n* égarement *m*, désorientation *f*

**disown** *vt* désavouer; nier

**disparage** *vt* dénigrer; discréditer, déprécier

**disparagement** *n* dénigrement *m*, dépréciation *f*

**disparate** *adj* disparate

**disparity** *n* disparité *f*

**dispassionate** *adj* sans émotion, calme, froid; (unbiased) sans préjugés

**dispatch** *n* + *vt see* **despatch**

**dispel** *vt* dissiper, chasser

**dispensable** *adj* superflu, dont on peut se passer; dispensable; *eccles* pardonnable

**dispensary** *n* dispensaire *m*; (chemist's shop) officine *f*

**dispensation** *n* distribution *f*; *leg* + *eccles* dispense *f*; (decree) décret *m*; disposition providentielle

**dispense** *vt* distribuer, administrer; *med* préparer; dispenser, exempter; *vi* se dispenser, se passer

**dispenser** *n* (person) pharmacien -ienne; (device) distributeur *m*

**dispersal** *n* dispersion *f*

**disperse** *vt* disperser, éparpiller; dissiper; (spread) répandre; *opt* décomposer; *vi* se disperser

**dispersion** *n* dispersion *f*; *opt* décomposition *f*

**dispirit** *vt* déprimer, décourager

**displace** *vt* déplacer; (from office) remplacer, évincer

**displaced** *adj* déplacé; ~ **person** réfugié -e

**displacement** *n* déplacement *m*; (from office) remplacement *m*; destitution *f*; *naut* + *phys* déplacement *m*; *geol* faille *f*

**display** *n* (spreading) étalement *m*, déploiement *m*; manifestation *f*; (show) étalage *m*, exposition *f*; parade *f*; *print* mise *f* en vedette; *vt* étaler, déployer; manifester; mettre à l'étalage, étaler; *print* mettre en vedette

**displease** *vt* mécontenter; déplaire à; *vi* déplaire

**displeasure** *n* déplaisir *m*, mécontentement *m*

**disport** *vt* ~ **oneself** s'ébattre, s'amu-

ser; *vi* jouer

**disposable** *adj* à jeter

**disposal** *n* action *f* de disposer; (selling) vente *f*; *leg* cession *f*; (rubbish) enlèvement *m*; (ordering) arrangement *m*; (bomb) désamorçage *m*; **at one's** ~ à sa disposition

**dispose** *vt* disposer, arranger; (regulate) régler; (make willing) disposer, incliner; préparer; *vi* disposer; ~ **of** disposer de; (settle) régler; *comm* céder, vendre; *coll* (food) manger; ~ **of s/o** se débarrasser de qn

**disposition** *n* disposition *f*, arrangement *m*; *leg* disposition *f* testamentaire; disposition *f* entre vifs; droit *m* de disposition; (nature) tempérament *m*, disposition *f*, caractère *m*; tendance *f*, inclination *f*

**dispossess** *vt* déposséder; (oust) faire sortir; *leg* exproprier

**dispossession** *n* dépossession *f*; *leg* expropriation *f*

**dispraise** *n* blâme *m*, dénigrement *m*; *vt* blâmer, dénigrer

**disproof** *n* réfutation *f*

**disproportion** *n* disproportion *f*; *vt* rendre disproportionné

**disproportional, disproportionate** *adj* disproportionné

**disprove** *vt* réfuter; démontrer la fausseté de

**disputable** *adj* discutable, douteux -euse

**disputant** *n* interlocuteur -trice; contradicteur -trice; *eccles* controversiste

**disputation** *n* débat *m*, discussion *f*; *hist* + *theol* dispute *f*

**disputatious** *adj* ergoteur -euse; raisonneur -euse

**dispute** *n* querelle *f*, dispute *f*; discussion *f*, débat *m*; **beyond** ~ incontestable, réglé; **in** ~ en discussion, incertain; **industrial** ~ conflit industriel; *vt* discuter, disputer, débattre; (oppose) contester; *vi* discuter, disputer; se disputer

**disqualification** *n* inaptitude *f*, incapacité *f*; *sp* disqualification *f*

**disqualify** *vt* *sp* disqualifier; rendre inapte; *mot* retirer le permis à

**disquiet** *n* inquiétude *f*; agitation *f*, trouble *m*; *vt* inquiéter, troubler

**disquieting** *adj* inquiétant, troublant

**disquietude** *n* inquiétude *f*

**disquisition** *n* traité *m*, étude *f*, dissertation *f*

**disregard** *n* négligence *f*; déconsidération *f*; *leg* violation *f*; (danger) insouciance *f*; *vt* déconsidérer; négliger; manquer d'égards envers; (danger) mépriser

**disrepair** *n* délabrement *m*, état *m* de

délabrement; **fall into** ~ se délabrer

**disreputable** *adj* louche; peu estimable; mal famé; (action) honteux -euse

**disrepute** *n* discrédit *m*; mauvaise réputation

**disrespect** *n* manque *m* de respect, irrespect *m*; impolitesse *f*

**disrespectful** *adj* irrespectueux -euse; impoli

**disrobe** *vt* dévêtir; *vi* se dévêtir

**disrupt** *vt* faire éclater; disloquer; interrompre, disperser

**disruption** *n* éclatement *m*; dislocation *f*; interruption *f*

**disruptive** *adj* qui cherche à disloquer, perturbateur -trice

**dissatisfaction** *n* insatisfaction *f*; mécontentement *m*

**dissatisfied** *adj* insatisfait, mécontent

**dissatisfy** *vt* mécontenter

**dissect** *vt* découper; *anat* disséquer; *fig* analyser, dépouiller

**dissection** *n* découpement *m*; *anat* dissection *f*; *fig* analyse *f*, dépouillement *m*

**dissector** *n anat* (person) disséqueur *m*; (instrument) scalpel *m*

**dissemble** *vt* dissimuler, déguiser; *vi* dissimuler

**dissembler** *n* dissimulateur -trice

**disseminate** *vt* disséminer

**dissemination** *n* dissémination *f*

**dissension** *n* dissension *f*, désaccord *m*

**dissent** *n* désaccord *m*, dissentiment *m*; dissidence *f*; *eccles hist* non-conformisme *m*; *vi* être d'un avis contraire, ne pas être d'accord; *eccles* être dissident

**dissenter** *n eccles* (England, Scotland) non-conformiste

**dissentient** *n* dissident -e; *adj* dissident; minoritaire

**dissertation** *n* dissertation *f*, mémoire *m*, étude *f*

**disserve** *vt* desservir

**disservice** *n* mauvais service

**dissident** *n* dissident -e; *adj* dissident

**dissimilar** *adj* dissemblable

**dissimilarity** *n* dissemblance *f*

**dissimilate** *vt* différencier

**dissimulate** *vt* + *vi* dissimuler

**dissimulation** *n* dissimulation *f*

**dissimulator** *n* dissimulateur -trice

**dissipate** *vt* dissiper; chasser, disperser; (waste) gaspiller; *vi* se dissiper; se livrer à la débauche

**dissipation** *n* dissipation *f*; dispersion *f*; vie dissipée, débauche *f*

**dissociate** *vt* dissocier, séparer, désagréger; ~ **oneself from** se séparer de, se désolidariser de; se désintéresser de

**dissociation** *n* séparation *f*; disassociation *f*

**dissolute** *adj* dissolu, débauché

**dissolution** *n* dissolution *f*, désagrégation *f*; (in liquid) fonte *f*; *leg* résiliation *f*

**dissolve** *n cin* + *TV* fondu (enchaîné); *vt* dissoudre, faire fondre; dissiper, disperser; *leg* résilier; *vi* se dissoudre, fondre; *cin* enchaîner

**dissolvent** *n* dissolvant *m*; *adj* dissolvant

**dissonance** *n mus* dissonance *f*; désaccord *m*

**dissonant** *adj mus* dissonant; *adj* en désaccord

**dissuade** *vt* dissuader; déconseiller

**dissuasion** *n* dissuasion *f*

**distaff** *n* quenouille *f*; ~ **side** côté maternel

**distance** *n* distance *f*, éloignement *m*; lointain *m*; *mus* intervalle *m*; *fig* distance *f*, froideur *f*; **at a** ~, **in the** ~ loin, distant; **keep at a** ~ traiter avec froideur; **keep one's** ~ tenir ses distances; *vt* distancer; éloigner; (painting) reculer, donner un effet de profondeur

**distant** *adj* distant, séparé, éloigné; *fig* froid

**distantly** *adv* de loin; avec froideur

**distaste** *n* dégoût *m*, aversion *f*

**distasteful** *adj* dégoûtant, répugnant

**distastefulness** *n* dégoût *m*, sens *m* d'aversion

¹**distemper** *n* maladie *f* de Carré; *obs* malaise *m*; *fig* mécontentement *m*; désordre *m*

²**distemper** *n* (paint) détrempe *f*, badigeon *m*; *vt* peindre en détrempe

**distend** *vt* distendre; *vi* se distendre

**distension** *n* distension *f*

**distil** *vt* distiller; faire couler goutte à goutte; *fig* distiller, répandre, épancher; *vi* se distiller, couler goutte à goutte

**distillation** *n* distillation *f*; *fig* essence *f*

**distiller** *n* distillateur *m*; (home) bouilleur *m* de cru

**distillery** *n* distillerie *f*

**distinct** *adj* distinct, séparé; précis, net (*f* nette)

**distinction** *n* distinction *f*; discrimination *f*; (honour) décoration *f*; (refinement) raffinement *m*; (quality) valeur *f*

**distinctive** *adj* distinctif -ive

**distinctly** *adv* distinctement; (undoubtedly) nettement, indubitablement

**distinctness** *n* netteté *f*, clarté *f*

**distingué** *adj* distingué

**distinguish** *vt* distinguer; différencier; caractériser; apercevoir

**distinguishable** *adj* perceptible; que l'on peut distinguer

**distinguished** *adj* distingué

**distort** vt déformer, dénaturer; (twist) tordre

**distortion** n déformation f, contorsion f; dénaturation f; (sound) distorsion f; (TV picture) déformation f

**distract** vt distraire; (divert) détourner; (drive mad) rendre fou (f folle)

**distracted** adj affolé, perplexe; (mad) fou (f folle); (absent-minded) distrait

**distraction** n distraction f; inattention f; diversion f, amusement m; folie f

**distrain** vi leg ~ **upon s/o's goods** saisir les biens de qn

**distraint** n leg saisie f

**distraught** adj affolé, égaré; fou (f folle)

**distress** n détresse f, angoisse f, désarroi m; (poverty) misère f; péril m, danger m; leg droit m de saisie; ~ **gun** canon m porte-amarre invar; ~ **signal** signal m de détresse; naut **in** ~ en perdition; vt affliger, désoler; leg saisir

**distressed** adj troublé, affolé, (exhausted) épuisé; misérable

**distressful** adj (painful) douloureux -euse; (unpleasant) angoissant

**distressing** adj pénible, pitoyable, lamentable

**distribute** vt distribuer, dispenser; (divide out) répartir

**distribution** n distribution f; (dividing out) répartition f; (newspaper) diffusion f

**distributive** adj qui distribue; gramm distributif -ive

**distributor** n distributeur -trice; comm concessionnaire; mot distributeur m

**district** n district m; région f; unité administrative; ~ **nurse** infirmière visiteuse

**distrust** n défiance f; (suspicion) méfiance f; vt se méfier de; soupçonner

**distrustful** adj méfiant; soupçonneux -euse

**disturb** vt troubler, déranger; (disquiet) inquiéter, rendre perplexe

**disturbance** n trouble m, dérangement m; (anxiety) inquiétude f; (riot) soulèvement m, désordre m

**disturbing** adj inquiétant

**disunite** vt désunir; vi se désunir

**disunity** n désunion f

**disuse** n abandon m, désuétude f; vt ne plus utiliser

**disyllabic, dissyllabic** adj dissyllabique

**ditch** n fossé m; **die in the last** ~ défendre une position jusqu'à la fin; vt creuser des fossés dans; entourer d'un fossé; coll jeter, abandonner; coll aer (plane) faire descendre en mer; coll mot faire verser dans un fossé; vi creuser des fossés; coll mot verser dans le fossé

**ditch-water** n eau stagnante, eau bourbeuse; **as dull as** ~ assommant au possible; **clear as** ~ obscur

**dither** n coll tremblotement m, agitation f; vi coll s'agiter; trembler; hésiter, tergiverser

**dithyrambic** adj dithyrambique

**ditto** adv idem; **say** ~ **to** être d'accord avec

**ditty** n petite chanson

**diuresis** n med diurèse f

**diuretic** n med diurétique m; adj med diurétique

**diurnal** n eccles diurnal m; adj diurne

**diva** n (opera) diva f

**divagate** vi divaguer; (wander) errer; (digress) s'écarter du sujet

**divagation** n divagation f

**divan** n divan m

**dive** n sp plongeon m; plongée f; aer piqué m; coll bistrot m, gargote f; (gambling den) maison f de jeu; vi plonger; aer piquer; se plonger; se précipiter

**dive-bomb** vt + vi bombarder en piqué

**dive-bomber** n avion m qui bombarde en piqué

**dive-bombing** n bombardement m en piqué

**diver** n sp plongeur -euse; (deep sea) scaphandrier m; orni plongeon m

**diverge** vt bifurquer; dévier

**divergence** n divergence f

**divergent** adj divergent

**divers** adj pl plusieurs, divers

**diverse** adj divers, différent; varié

**diversification** n diversification f

**diversify** vt diversifier

**diversion** n déviation f; mil diversion f; diversion f, divertissement m

**diversity** n diversité f

**divert** vt détourner, dévier; distraire, divertir; mot dévier

**diverting** adj divertissant, amusant

**divest** vt dépouiller; priver, déposséder

**divide** n geog ligne f de partage des eaux; vt diviser; séparer; (share) partager; (distribute) répartir, distribuer; (parliament) faire voter; vi se diviser; se séparer, se partager; math être divisible; voter, procéder au scrutin

**divided** adj divisé

**dividend** n dividende m

**dividers** npl compas m

**divination** n divination f

**divinatory** adj divinatoire

**divine** n eccles théologien m; coll prêtre m, pasteur m; adj divin; vt + vi deviner

**diviner** n (water) sourcier -ière; devin m, devineresse f

**diving-bell** n caisson m, cloche f à plongeur

**diving-board** n plongeoir m
**diving-suit** n scaphandre m
**divining-rod** n baguette f de sourcier
**divinity** n divinité f; théologie f
**divisible** adj divisible
**division** n division f; séparation f; (partition) cloison f; (sharing out) partage m, distribution f; section f, subdivision f; désaccord m, dissension f; (parliament, meeting) scrutin m, vote m; mil division f; math ~ **sign** signe conventionnel de division
**divisive** adj qui entraîne la division, qui cause le désaccord
**divisor** n math diviseur m
**divorce** n divorce m; fig séparation f; vt divorcer d'avec; vi divorcer
**divorcee** n divorcé -e
**divulge** vt révéler, divulguer
**dixie** n gamelle f
**dizziness** n vertige m; étourdissement m
**dizzy** adj pris de vertige, ayant un vertige; (height) vertigineux -euse; coll stupide; vt donner le vertige à, faire tourner la tête à
**djinn, jinn** n djinn m
¹**do** n coll réception f; réunion f, soirée f; (trick) escroquerie f; **fair ~s parts** égales; vt faire; (perform) accomplir, effectuer; (work at) travailler à, étudier; (distance) faire, parcourir; (speed) faire, atteindre; (destroy) ruiner, éreinter; (finish) terminer, finir; (harm) faire, causer; (hair) arranger; (shoes) polir, nettoyer; (nails) couper; (tour) faire, visiter; (justice) faire, rendre; (suit) convenir; theat (play) monter; (time in prison) faire; coll (cheat) escroquer; coll (hit) frapper, battre; ~ **down** coll rouler; ~ **in** coll éreinter, épuiser; sl descendre, zigouiller; ~ **out** nettoyer; ~ **s/o out of sth** escroquer qch à qn; ~ **over** coll décorer, enduire; sl passer à tabac; ~ **to death** tuer; ~ **up** ficeler, emballer; (refurbish) refaire, remettre à neuf; cul accommoder, réchauffer; vi+v aux (behave) agir, se comporter; (suffice) suffire; (health) aller, se porter; ~ **away with** abolir, supprimer, tuer; ~ **badly** aller mal; ~ **by** agir aux égards de; coll ~ **for** détruire, tuer; (char) tenir le ménage de; ~ **go away!** partez, je vous prie!; ~ **well** prospérer, progresser; ~ **with sth** (need) avoir besoin de qch; tolérer qch; ~ **without** se passer de; **did he come?** est-il venu?; **have to ~ with** avoir affaire à; **he did come** il est venu en effet; **he did not come** il n'est pas venu; **he drank that wine faster than I could have done** il a bu ce vin plus vite

que je n'aurais pu le faire; **He drinks a lot of wine.** - **Does he?** Il boit beaucoup de vin. - Vraiment?; **I could ~ with** j'ai besoin de; **make ~** se débrouiller; **nothing ~ing!** rien à faire!; **nothing to ~ with** rien à voir avec; **you ~ love me, don't you?** vous m'aimez, n'est-ce pas?; **you don't love me, ~ you?** vous ne m'aimez pas, n'est-ce pas?
²**do** n mus do m, ut m
³**do** adv abbr idem
**docile** adj docile
**docility** n docilité f
¹**dock** n naut bassin m, dock(s) m(pl); (quayside) quai m; (landing-stage) embarcadère m; **dry ~**, **graving ~** cale sèche; **floating ~** dock flottant; **tidal ~** bassin ouvert; vt (bring to quayside) mettre à quai; (put in dock) faire entrer au(x) dock(s); vi naut (come alongside quay) se mettre à quai; (go in dock) entrer au(x) dock(s); coll mot **be in ~** être en réparation
²**dock** n bot patience f
³**dock** n (tail) tronçon m; (harness) trousse-queue m invar; vt (tail) écourter, couper; (wages) retrancher, rogner
⁴**dock** n leg banc m des accusés
**docker** n docker m
**docket** n fiche f; (abstract) bordereau m; leg registre m des jugements; récépissé m de douane; vt résumer; faire une fiche pour; attacher une fiche à
**dockyard** n chantier naval (pl navals); **naval ~** arsenal m
**doctor** n med médecin m, docteur m, femme f médecin; (law, letters, music, philosophy, etc) docteur m; vt med soigner, traiter; donner des remèdes à; fig falsifier, truquer; coll (domestic animal) châtrer
**doctoral** adj doctoral
**doctorate** n doctorat m
**doctrinaire** n+adj doctrinaire
**doctrinal** adj doctrinal
**doctrine** n doctrine f
**document** n document m; vt documenter
**documentary** n cin documentaire m; adj documentaire
**documentation** n documentation f
**dodder** vi chanceler, flageoler, tituber
**dodderer** n gâteux -euse
**dodecagon** n geom dodécagone m
**dodecahedron** n geom dodécaèdre m
**dodge** n coll tour m, truc m; mouvement m de côté; vt esquiver, éluder; (task, etc) éviter; vi se jeter de côté; (disappear) s'esquiver; (trick) biaiser
**dodgem** n coll auto tamponneuse f
**dodger** n coll roublard -e; (military

service) embusqué *m*

**dodgy** *adj* malin (*f* maligne); *sl* difficile
**doe** *n* (deer) daine *f*; (hare) hase *f*;
(rabbit) lapine *f*
**doer** *n* personne active; (action) auteur
*m*
**doeskin** *n* daim *m*
**doff** *vt* ôter, enlever
**dog** *n* chien *m*; *pej* salaud *m*, lâche *m*;
*coll* type *m*; (live wire) boute-en-train
*m invar*; *mech* crampon *m*; **(fire)** ~ s
chenet *m*; ~ **eat** ~ rivalité acharnée;
~ **in the manger** chien *m* du jardinier;
**a hair of the** ~ **that bit you** un petit
verre pour guérir la gueule de bois; **be
top** ~ avoir le dessus; **die like a** ~
mourir comme un chien; **every** ~ **has
his day** à chacun vient sa chance; *coll*
**go and see a man about a** ~ aller faire
pipi; **go to the** ~ s mal tourner,
dégénérer; **hot** ~ hot-dog *m*; **lead a**
~ **'s life** avoir une vie de chien; **let
sleeping** ~ s **lie** il ne faut pas réveiller le
chat qui dort; **lucky** ~ veinard -e; **the**
~ s courses *fpl* de levrettes; *vt* suivre de
très près, filer; ~ **s/o's footsteps**
talonner qn
**dog-collar** *n* collier *m* de chien; *coll* col
*m* d'ecclésiastique
**dog-days** *npl* canicule *f*
**doge** *n* doge *m*
**dog-eared** *adj* corné
**dogfight** *n aer* duel aérien
**dogfish** *n zool* chien *m* de mer
**dogged** *adj* obstiné; déterminé
**doggedness** *n* persévérance *f*, obstination *f*
**doggerel** *n* vers *mpl* de mirliton; *adj* de
mirliton
**doggie, doggy** *n coll* toutou *m*
**dogginess** *n* ressemblance *f* aux chiens;
amour *m* des chiens
**doggo** *adv* sans mouvement
**doggone** *adj US coll* sacré
**dog-house** *n* chenil *m*; *sl* **in the** ~ en
disgrâce
**dog-latin** *n* latin *m* de cuisine
**dogma** *n* dogme *m*
**dogmatic, dogmatical** *adj* dogmatique
**dogmatism** *n* dogmatisme *m*
**dogmatist** *n* dogmatiseur *m*
**dogmatize** *vi* dogmatiser
**dog-rose** *n* (flower) églantine *f*; (bush)
églantier *m*
**dogsbody** *n sl* souillon *f*, factotum *m*
**dog-show** *n* exposition canine
**dog-star** *n astron* Sirius *m*
**dog-tired** *adj* fourbu, vanné
**dog-watch** *n naut* petit quart
**doily** *n* napperon *m*
**doings** *npl* activités *fpl*; (behaviour)
façons *fpl*, conduite *f*; *coll* truc *m*,

machin *m*
**doldrums** *npl naut* zone *f* des calmes; *fig*
cafard *m*, dépression *f*
**dole** *n* charité *f*; (unemployment) allocation *f* de chômage; **be on the** ~ être
au chômage, toucher l'allocation de
chômage; *vt* ~ **out** distribuer parcimonieusement
**doleful** *adj* morne, lugubre, triste, mélancolique
**dolefulness** *n* mélancolie *f*, tristesse *f*
**doll** *n* (toy) poupée *f*; *coll* (pretty girl)
poupée *f*; *sl* (girl) nana *f*, pépée *f*; *vt*
orner; ~ **up** se bichonner
**dollar** *n* dollar *m*
**dollop** *n coll* tas *m*, gros morceau
**dolly** *n* poupée *f*; (laundry) agitateur *m*;
(sailing) plate-forme *f*; (filming)
chariot *m*; *vi* (filming) se servir d'un
chariot; ~ **in** se rapprocher; ~ **out** se
distancer
**dolmen** *n* dolmen *m*
**dolomite** *n min* dolomite *f*; **Dolomites**
*npl* Dolomites *fpl*
**dolorous** *adj* lugubre; (painful) douloureux -euse
**dolour** *n* affliction *f*, chagrin *m*
**dolphin** *n* dauphin *m*
**dolt** *n* crétin -e; *sl* andouille *f*
**domain** *n* domaine *m*
**dome** *n* dôme *m*, coupole *f*; *coll* tête *f*
**domestic** *n* domestique; *adj* domestique,
ménager -ère; (home-loving) casanier
-ière
**domesticate** *vt* domestiquer
**domestication** *n* domestication *f*
**domesticity** *n* vie *f* de famille, amour *m*
du foyer
**domicile** *n* domicile *m*
**dominance, dominancy** *n* prédominance
*f*, autorité *f*
**dominant** *n mus* dominante *f*; *adj* dominant
**dominate** *vt* dominer
**domination** *n* domination *f*
**domineer** *vi* dominer tyranniquement;
se conduire avec arrogance
**Dominican** *n* + *adj eccles* dominicain -e
**dominion** *n* dominion *m*
**domino** *n* domino *m*; ~ es jeu *m* de
dominos
¹**don** *n* (academic) professeur *m*
²**don** *vt* revêtir, mettre, enfiler
**donate** *vt* donner, faire don de; (blood)
donner
**donation** *n* donation *f*
**donator** *n* donateur -trice
**done** *adj* fini, achevé; (cooked) cuit;
(worn out) usé; *coll* (exhausted) fourbu;
*sl* (tricked) escroqué; ~ **for** ruiné;
mourant; ~ **in**, ~ **up** épuisé, fourbu;
~ **up** fini, ruiné; **have** ~ **with**

renoncer à, en finir avec; **not** ~ contre les bonnes manières; **the** ~ **thing** ce qui se fait

**donkey** n âne m, baudet m; coll crétin -e, idiot -e; coll ~ **work** travail m de routine; coll **for** ~ **'s years** très longtemps

**donnish** adj professoral; pédant

**donor** n donateur -trice; donneur -euse; **blood** ~ donneur -euse de sang

**doodle** vi gribouiller

**doodle-bug** n hist bombe volante

**doom** n leg + eccles jugement m; destin m; mort f; ruine f; **crack of** ~ fin f du monde; vt condamner; vouer à une fin terrible

**doomsday** n jour m du jugement dernier

**door** n porte f; (large) portail m; (car, train) portière f; ~ **to** ~ porte à porte; **answer the** ~ ouvrir la porte à un visiteur; **lay sth at s/o's** ~ imputer qch à qn; **lie at the** ~ **of** être imputable à; **next** ~ la maison voisine; **next** ~ **to** à côté de; (almost) presque; fig **open the** ~ **to** ouvrir la voie à; **out of** ~s au dehors, en plein air; **show s/o the** ~ congédier qn, chasser qn

**doorbell** n sonnette f

**door-frame** n chambranle m

**door-handle** n poignée f de porte

**door-keeper** n portier -ière; (flats) concierge

**door-knob** n bouton m de porte

**doorman** n portier m

**doormat** n paillasson m

**door-plate** n plaque f de propreté

**doorstep** n seuil m; coll tranche épaisse de pain

**door-stop** n butoir m

**doorstrip** n bourrelet m

**doorway** n ouverture f de porte; moyen m d'accès

**dope** n coll drogue f, stupéfiant m; sp doping m; coll (information) tuyau m, détails mpl; aer enduit m, laque f; phot révélateur m; sl crétin -e, idiot -e; US sl (drug-addict) drogué -e; vt aer enduire, laquer; coll doper; calmer; ~ **oneself** se droguer

**dopey, dopy** adj coll drogué; (stupid) lent, abruti

**dorado** n zool daurade f

**Doric** adj archi dorique

**Dorien** adj geog + mus dorien -ienne

**dormant** adj dormant, assoupi

**dormer** n archi lucarne f

**dormitory** n dortoir m; ~ **suburb** banlieue-dortoir f (pl banlieues-dortoirs); ~ **town** ville-dortoir f (pl villes-dortoirs)

**dormouse** n loir m

**dorsal** adj dorsal

**dosage** n dosage m; posologie f

**dose** n dose f; sl maladie vénérienne; vt donner un médicament à; vi mesurer une dose; prendre un médicament

**doss** n sl lit m dans un asile de nuit; vi sl dormir dans un asile de nuit; coll ~ **down** dormir dans un lit de fortune

**doss-house** n asile m de nuit

**dossier** n dossier m

**dot** n point m; **in the year** ~ il y a très longtemps; coll **on the** ~ pile, recta; vt mettre un point sur; (line) pointiller; (scatter) éparpiller, parsemer; mus pointer; coll frapper; coll ~ **and carry one** clopiner; coll ~ **one's i's** fig être très méticuleux -euse; mettre les points sur les i; **sign on the** ~ **ted line** donner son accord; accepter aveuglément

**dotage** n radotage m

**dotard** n gâteux -euse, radoteur -euse

**dote** vi être gâteux -euse; ~ **on** raffoler de

**doting** adj qui adore, entiché; gâteux -euse, sénile

**dotty** adj coll cinglé, toqué; pointillé

**double** n double m, sosie m; (bridge) contre m; (running) pas m de gymnastique; theat doublure f; (tennis) ~ **s** double m; adj double; doublé, redoublé; (room) à deux, pour deux personnes; fig ambigu; fourbe, à deux faces; ~ **bed** grand lit; ~ **time** tarif m heures supplémentaires; **play a** ~ **game** jouer double jeu; adv double; à deux; vt (fold) doubler, plier en deux, replier; (speed) redoubler; theat doubler; (bridge) contrer; vi doubler, se doubler; (run) prendre le pas de course; ~ **back** (return) revenir sur ses pas; ~ **up** se plier en deux; coll partager une chambre, partager un lit

**double-barrelled** adj à deux coups; (name) à tiroirs

**double-bass** n contrebasse f

**double-breasted** adj croisé

**double-chin** n double menton m

**double-cross** n escroquerie f; vt rouler, trahir

**double-dealer** n fourbe

**double-dealing** n duplicité f, fourberie f

**double-decker** n autobus m à impériale

**double-declutch** vi mot faire un double débrayage

**double-Dutch** n coll baragouin m, charabia m

**double-edged** adj à double tranchant

**double-entry** n comptabilité f en partie double

**double-faced** adj à double face, hypocrite

**double-glazing** n **put in** ~ poser des doubles fenêtres

**double-jointed** adj désarticulé

**double-lock** *vt* fermer à double tour

**double-park** *vi* se garer en double file

**double-quick** *adj* très vite; au pas de gymnastique

**double-stop** *vi mus* jouer à double corde

**doublet** *n hist* pourpoint *m*; *ling* doublet *m*

**double-talk** *n* balivernes *fpl*; *pol* slogans *mpl* vides

**doublethink** *n* acceptation simultanée de deux notions contradictoires

**doubling** *n* multiplication *f* par deux; (fold) pli *m*; (lining) doublure *f*

**doubly** *adv* doublement, deux fois plus

**doubt** *n* doute *m*, incertitude *f*; (worry) inquiétude *f*; **beyond ~** sans aucun doute; **give s/o the benefit of the ~** accorder à qn le bénéfice du doute; **in ~** incertain; **without ~** sans aucun doute; *vt* douter de, mettre en doute; *vi* douter, être incertain, se demander

**doubtful** *adj* douteux -euse, incertain, problématique; hésitant; (unclear) peu clair, ambigu -uë; (suspect) équivoque, louche

**doubtless** *adv* sans doute; probablement

**douceur** *n* (tip) pourboire *m*; (bribe) pot-de-vin *m* (*pl* pots-de-vin)

**douche** *n med* injection *f*; douche *f*; **cold ~** surprise *f* désagréable; découragement *m*; *vt* doucher; donner une injection à; *vi* prendre une douche, se doucher

**dough** *n cul* pâte *f*; *sl* fric *m*

**dough-boy** *n US coll* soldat américain

**doughnut** *n cul* sorte *f* de beignet

**doughty** *adj* vaillant

**doughy** *adj cul* pâteux -euse

**dour** *adj* obstiné; (gloomy) austère, sombre

**dourness** *n* obstination *f*; austérité *f*, humeur *f* sombre

**douse, dowse** *vt* arroser, tremper; *coll* (light) éteindre

**dove** *n zool + fig* colombe *f*

**dove-colour** *adj* gorge-de-pigeon *invar*

**dovecot** *n* colombier *m*

**dovetail** *n carp* queue-d'aronde *f* (*pl* queues-d'aronde); *vt* assembler à queue-d'aronde; *fig* joindre facilement; *vi* se raccorder, s'engrener; *fig* s'accorder

**dowager** *n* douairière *f*

**dowdiness** *n* manque *m* d'élégance

**dowdy** *adj* (woman) mal habillée, mal fichue; (clothes) (shabby) fripé; (out of fashion) démodé

**dower** *n* (wife) dot *f*; (widow) douaire *m*; *vt* doter; assigner un douaire à

**¹down** *n* duvet *m*

**²down** *n* colline dénudée

**³down** *n* infortune *f*; *coll* antipathie *f*;

**have a ~ on** avoir une dent contre; *adj* qui descend; *mus* (beat) fort; (sad) triste, déprimé; (train) d'aller; (tyre) à plat; **~ payment** acompte *m*; *adv* en bas; vers le bas; (time) le long de; **~ and out** sans le sou; **~ at heel** minable; pauvre; misérable; **~ in the mouth** la mine longue, avec triste mine; **~ on** en colère contre, hostile à; **~ on one's luck** en difficulté; à court d'argent; **~ to the ground** entièrement; *coll* **~ under** en Australie, en Nouvelle Zélande; **~ with** souffrant de; **~ with!** à bas!; *prep* au bas de; en descendant; le long de; **~ stream** en aval; **~ wind** au vent

**downbeat** *n mus* temps frappé

**downcast** *adj* abattu, triste; (look) baissé

**down-draught** *n* courant *m* d'air descendant

**downfall** *n* chute *f*; *fig* effondrement *m*

**downgrade** *n* descente *f*; déchéance *f*; **on the ~** sur le déclin; *vt* rétrograder, mettre (réduire) à un niveau inférieur

**downhearted** *adj* découragé

**downhill** *n* pente *f*, descente *f*; *adj* en pente, descendant; *adv* en pente; sur le déclin

**downpipe** *n* tuyau *m* de descente

**downpour** *n* pluie battante

**downright** *adj* franc (*f* franche); complet -ète, total; absolu; *adv* carrément, nettement; tout à fait

**downstairs** *n* rez-de-chaussée *m invar*; *adj* du bas; *adv* en bas de l'escalier; au rez-de-chaussée

**downstream** *adv* en aval

**downtrodden** *adj* piétiné; *fig* opprimé, subjugué

**downward** *adj* (slope) descendant; (time) postérieur

**downward(s)** *adv* en bas, vers le bas

**downy** *adj* duveté; *sl* avisé, pas con

**dowry** *n* dot *f*

**¹dowse** *vt see* douse

**²dowse** *vi* faire le sourcier

**dowsing-rod** *n* baguette *f* de sourcier

**doxology** *n* doxologie *f*

**doxy** *n sl* putain *f*, traînée *f*

**doyen** *n* doyen *m*, doyenne *f*

**doyenne** *n* doyenne *f*

**doze** *n* petit somme; *vi* somnoler

**dozen** *n* douzaine *f*; **baker's ~** treize; **daily ~** gymnastique quotidienne; **talk nineteen to the ~** parler vite et sans arrêt

**doziness** *n* somnolence *f*

**dozy** *adj* somnolent

**¹drab** *n ar* prostituée *f*, souillon *f*

**²drab** *n* (fabric) bure *f*; *adj* terne, monotone; (colour) fauve

**drabble** *vt* crotter, salir; *vi* se crotter

**drabness** *n* monotonie *f*; (colour) grisaille *f*

**drachm** *n* drachme *f*

**drachma** *n* drachme *f*

**draconian** *adj* draconien -ienne

**draft** *n* brouillon *m*; (sketch) esquisse *f*; *comm* trait *m*; *mil* contingent *m*; *vt* faire un brouillon de; esquisser; *mil* affecter; *US* appeler

**draftee** *n US mil* conscrit *m*

**draftsman** *n see* **draughtsman**

**drag** *n aer* ralentissement *m*; (brake) frein *m*; *naut* gaffe *f*; *agr* herse *f*; *ar* calèche *f*, drag *m*; (hindrance) entrave *f*; *coll* (bore) emmerdement *m*; *coll* bouffée *f* de cigarette; *sl* **in** ~ en travesti; *vt* traîner, tirer, entraîner; (river) draguer; *agr* herser; *naut* ~ **anchor** chasser sur l'ancre; *coll* (conversation) ~ **in** introduire (un sujet) mal à propos; ~ **one's feet** hésiter, ne pas montrer d'entrain; (children) ~ **up** élever plutôt mal; *vi* traîner à terre; se traîner; *naut* (anchor) chasser; ~ **on** traîner

**draggle** *vt* traîner dans la boue, crotter; *vi* se crotter; traîner

**drag-net** *n* seine *f*

**dragon** *n* dragon *m*; *coll* (woman) dragon *m* de vertu

**dragon-fly** *n* libellule *f*

**dragon's teeth** *npl mil* fortifications *fpl* antichar

**dragoon** *n mil* dragon *m*; *vt* gendarmer; (compel) contraindre

**drain** *n* tuyau *m* d'écoulement; *agr* fosse *f* d'écoulement; *med* drain *m*; *comm* (money) drainage *m*; *fig* perte *f*, écoulement *m*, fuite *f*; (drink) goutte *f*; ~ **s** (dregs) lie *f*; *vt* faire écouler; (glass) vider; (marsh) assécher, assainir; *mot* (sump) vidanger; *med* drainer; *fig* épuiser; *coll* ~ **s/o dry** saigner qn à blanc; *vi* s'écouler

**drainage** *n agr* drainage *m*, assainissement *m*; *med* drainage *m*; réseau *m* d'égouts; eaux *fpl* d'égout; *geol* drainage *m*

**drainer** *n cul* égouttoir *m*

**draining-board** *n* paillasse *f*, égouttoir *m*

**draining-rack** *n* égouttoir *m*

**drainpipe** *n* tuyau *m* de vidange; (rainwater) descente *f*; *sl* ~ **s** pantalon collant, pantalon *m* cigarette

**drake** *n* canard *m*

**dram** *n* drachme *f*; *coll* petit verre, goutte *f*

**drama** *n* drame *m*; théâtre *m*, art *m* dramatique

**dramatic** *adj* dramatique; théâtral; excitant

**dramatics** *npl* activité théâtrale; *coll* (histrionics) comédie *f*

**dramatist** *n* auteur *m* dramatique

**dramatization** *n* adaptation théâtrale; *fig* dramatisation *f*

**dramatize** *vt* dramatiser; adapter pour le théâtre (le cinéma, la télévision)

**dramaturge, dramaturgist** *n* dramaturge *m*

**drape** *n* (cloth) façon *f* de pendre; *theat* toile *f*, ~ **s** tentures *fpl*; *US* rideaux *mpl*; *vt* draper; *vi* se draper

**draper** *n* drapier *m*, marchand -e de draps

**drapery** *n* draperie *f*; commerce *m* de draperie; métier *m* de drapier

**drastic** *adj* énergique, violent; efficace; *med* (purge) drastique; (measure) draconien -ienne

**drat** *interj coll* zut!

**dratted** *adj coll* misérable, sacré

**draught** *n* traction *f*; (drinking) trait *m*, gorgée *f*; (chimney) tirage *m*; (current of air) courant *m* d'air, vent *m* coulis; *naut* tirant *m* d'eau; (fish) coup *m* de filet, pêche *f*; *med* potion *f*; (game) ~ **s** dames *fpl*; ~ **beer** bière *f* à la pression; *coll fig* **feel the** ~ rencontrer des difficultés

**draught-board** *n* damier *m*

**draught-excluder** *n* bourrelet *m*

**draughtiness** *n* présence *f* de courants d'air

**draughtsman, draftsman** *n* dessinateur industriel; (documents) rédacteur *m*; (game) pion *m*

**draughty** *adj* plein de courants d'air

**draw** *n* traction *f*; loterie *f*, tirage *m* au sort; *sp* match nul; *theat* pièce *f* à succès; *coll* attraction *f*; *vt* tirer, traîner; (water, strength, information) puiser; (pull out) extraire, arracher; (lots) tirer au sort, tirer à la courte paille; (cheque, money) tirer; (sword) dégainer; (sketch) dessiner; (map) dresser; (write) tracer; *cul* (bird) vider; (tea) faire infuser; (abscess) faire mûrir; (attract) attirer; (conclusion) tirer; (comparison) établir; (face) contracter; ~ **a blank** faire un coup nul, faire chou blanc; être déçu; ~ **breath** respirer; ~ **down** encourir; ~ **in** entraîner; (liquid) ~ **off** tirer; ~ **oneself up** se tenir droit; ~ **out** faire parler; ~ **the line** avoir des scrupules; *fig* ~ **the longbow** exagérer, mentir; ~ **the teeth of** rendre inoffensif -ive; ~ **up** (document) rédiger; (account) établir; (troops) aligner; *vi* tirer; (sketch) dessiner; (chimney) tirer; *naut* (sails) porter; (tea) infuser; (abscess) mûrir; ~ **aside** s'écarter; ~ **back** se retirer; ~ **in** (days) raccourcir; s'approcher; ~ **level** arriver à la même hauteur; ~ **near** se rapprocher; ~ **on** (time) avancer; ~ **out** devenir plus long, se prolonger; ~ **up** s'arrêter

**drawback** *n* inconvénient *m*; *comm* drawback *m*

**drawbridge** *n hist* pont-levis *m* ( *pl* ponts-levis), pont basculant

**drawer** n (cheque) tireur m; (sketch) dessinateur -trice; (furniture) tiroir m; ~s (man) caleçon m; (woman) culotte f; **chest of** ~s commode f

**drawing** n dessin m; metal étirage m

**drawing-board** n planche f à dessin

**drawing-pin** n punaise f

**drawing-room** n salon m, living m

**drawl** n manière de parler traînante; vt dire d'un ton traînant; vi parler d'un ton traînant

**drawn** adj (weapon) dégainé, tiré; sp nul (f nulle); (appearance) fatigué, tendu; (disembowelled) éviscéré

**dray** n haquet m

**dray-horse** n cheval m de trait

**dread** n épouvante f, effroi m; appréhension f; adj redoutable, terrifiant; vt redouter, craindre

**dreadful** adj terrible, redoutable; coll terrible, épouvantable

**dreadfully** adv d'une manière terrible; coll très

**dream** n rêve m, songe m; (daydream) rêverie f; idéal m, ambition f; **wet** ~ émission f nocturne; adj coll idéal; vt rêver, songer; imaginer; coll ~ **up** inventer, concevoir; vi rêver, faire un rêve; songer; imaginer, se figurer

**dreamer** n rêveur -euse; idéaliste; songecreux m invar

**dreamland** n pays m des songes

**dreamless** adj (sleep) sans rêves

**dreamlike** adj comme un rêve; irréel -elle, vague

**dreamy** adj rêveur -euse, songeur -euse; vague, distrait

**drear** adj see dreary

**dreariness** n tristesse f, mélancolie f; aspect m lugubre

**dreary, drear** adj terne, morne, mélancolique, lugubre

¹**dredge** n naut drague f; vt + vi draguer

²**dredge** n cul saupoudreuse f; vt saupoudrer

**dregs** npl lie f

**drench** n vet breuvage médicinal; vt tremper, inonder; vet faire boire

**drencher** n vet entonnoir m; coll saucée f

**drenching** adj ~ **rain** pluie battante

**Dresden** n (china) porcelaine f de Saxe; geog Dresde

**dress** n habits mpl, vêtements mpl, habillement m; (woman) robe f; (formal) tenue f, mise f; theat ~ **circle** corbeille f, premier balcon; ~ **coat** habit m, frac m; theat ~ **rehearsal** générale f; ~ **suit** tenue f de soirée, smoking m; **evening** ~ tenue f de soirée; **morning** ~ jaquette f et pantalon rayé; vt habiller, vêtir; (decorate) orner, parer, décorer; mil aligner; carp dégrossir; (stone) équarrir; préparer, apprêter; cul apprêter; (poultry, fish, etc) habiller, accommoder; (salad) assaisonner; med panser; ~ **a window** faire l'étalage; ~ **down** (horse) panser; coll arranger, engueuler; ~ **up** parer, attifer; déguiser; vi s'habiller; mil s'aligner; ~ **up** s'habiller avec soin; pej se déguiser; (Sunday best) s'endimancher; (fancy dress) se costumer

**dressage** n dressage m

¹**dresser** n habilleur -euse; theat habilleuse f; surg assistant -e; mech équarrissoir m

²**dresser** n buffet m de cuisine, dressoir m

**dressing** n toilette f; action f de s'habiller; cul assaisonnement m; sauce f; (salad) mayonnaise f; med pansement m; mil alignement m; préparation f, apprêt m

**dressing-case** n nécessaire m de toilette

**dressing-down** n coll savon m, engueulade f

**dressing-gown** n robe f de chambre

**dressing-room** n vestiaire m; theat loge f

**dressing-table** n coiffeuse f

**dressmaker** n couturier -ière

**dressy** adj chic invar, à la mode

**dribble** n (saliva) bave f; (liquid) égouttement m; sp dribble m; vt faire couler goutte à goutte, faire dégoutter; sp dribbler; vi couler goutte à goutte, dégoutter; (saliva) baver; sp dribbler

**driblet** n petite quantité

**dribs and drabs** n in ~ au comptegouttes

**drier** n séchoir m; (substance) siccatif m

**drift** n poussée f, traînée f; naut + aer dérive f; tendance f; (meaning) sens m, portée f, intention f; (pile) tas m, amoncellement m; (snow) congère f; (mining) galerie f; vt charrier, entraîner; faire entasser, faire amonceler; vi naut + aer aller à la dérive, dériver; s'amonceler, s'entasser; se laisser aller; coll flâner

**drift-anchor** n naut ancre flottante

**driftwood** n bois flotté

¹**drill** n mech foret m; (bit) mèche f; (machine) foreuse f, perforatrice f; (dentist) roulette f, fraise f; vt forer, percer; (dentist) fraiser; vi se servir d'un foret, d'une foreuse, etc

²**drill** n mil exercice m, drill m; entraînement m physique; (lesson repeated) drill m; vt mil faire faire l'exercice à; vi mil faire l'exercice

³**drill** n agr sillon m; (machine) semoir m; vt semer, creuser des sillons dans

⁴**drill** n (fabric) coutil m, treillis m

**drill-sergeant** n mil sergent instructeur m

**drily** adv see dryly

**drink** n boisson f; (glass of sth alcoholic) verre m, petit verre, drink m; (soft) boisson non-alcoolisée; sl (sea) mer f; **drive to** ~ pousser à la boisson; **take to** ~ s'adonner à la boisson; vt boire; (soup) manger; fig boire, absorber; ~ **in** (words) boire; ~ **like a fish** boire comme un trou; ~ **off** vider; ~ **to** porter un toast à, boire à la santé de; vi boire; boire beaucoup; (customer) consommer

**drinkable** adj (good) buvable; (safe) potable

**drinker** n buveur -euse

**drinking** n boire m; (habit) boisson f, ivrognerie f; adj qui boit

**drinking-bout** n beuverie f

**drinking-fountain** n fontaine publique

**drinking-song** n chanson f à boire

**drinking-water** n eau f potable

**drip** n goutte f, égouttement m; med goutte-à-goutte m invar; sl nouille f; archi larmier m; vt faire couler goutte à goutte, faire égoutter; vi couler goutte à goutte, égoutter, dégoutter

**drip-dry** adj ne nécessitant aucun repassage

**drip-feed** vt med nourrir au goutte-à-goutte, alimenter par perfusion

**dripping** n égouttement m, gouttes fpl; cul graisse f (de viande); adj ~ **wet** mouillé jusqu'à l'os

**drive** n coup violent; dynamisme m, énergie f, allant m, entrain m; mech transmission f; mot promenade f en voiture; comm campagne f; (road) voie privée; sp drive m; mot **front-wheel** ~ traction f avant; **rear-wheel** ~ propulsion f arrière; **right-hand** ~ conduite f à droite; vt pousser, chasser; propulser; mech faire marcher, actionner; mot conduire, transporter; comm (bargain) passer, conclure; fig obliger, forcer; (push) pousser, amener; (overwork) surmener; sp (ball) renvoyer, driver; ~ **back** refouler; (nail) ~ **in** enfoncer; ~ **mad** rendre fou (f folle); ~ **off**, ~ **out** chasser; vi avancer vigoureusement; mot conduire, rouler; fig s'acharner, s'atteler; ~ **at** avoir comme but; (mean) vouloir dire; ~ **home** insister sur; ~ **off** partir en voiture

**drive-in** n drive-in m invar

**drivel** n radotage m, balivernes fpl; vi baver, radoter

**driver** n (car, taxi) chauffeur m; (car, bus, train, etc) conducteur -trice; (train) mécanicien m; (carriage) cocher m

**driving** n conduite f; adj qui transmet le mouvement; (rain) battant

**driving-licence** n permis m de conduire

**driving-school** n auto-école f

**driving-wheel** n mech roue motrice

**drizzle** n bruine f, crachin m; vi bruiner

**droll** n bouffon m; adj drôle, bizarre

**drollery** n drôlerie f, bouffonnerie f

**dromedary** n dromadaire m

**drone** n zool abeille f mâle, faux bourdon; fig oisif m, parasite m; (sound) bourdonnement m; (speech) ronronnement m; vt dire sur un ton monotone; vi (bees) bourdonner; fig bourdonner, ronronner

**drool** n radotage m, balivernes fpl; vi dire des bêtises; baver; (drivel) radoter; (lick lips) s'en lécher les babines

**droop** n (eyelids) abaissement m; (spirits) abattement m; vt pencher, baisser; vi se pencher, se baisser; fig languir, s'affaiblir

**drop** n goutte f; pendant m; (chandelier) pendeloque f; (sweet) bonbon m; (descent) dénivellation f; précipice m; hauteur f de chute; (price, number, temperature) baisse f; coll (drink) goutte f, doigt m; **a** ~ **in the ocean** une quantité insignifiante, une goutte d'eau dans la mer; **at the** ~ **of a hat** tout de suite, sans hésiter; vt laisser tomber, faire tomber, lâcher; (let fall in drops) laisser tomber goutte à goutte; (eyes, voice) baisser; (omit) omettre; (set down) déposer; math abaisser; coll abandonner, délaisser; (animal) mettre bas; fig laisser, cesser, interrompre; coll laisser tomber; coll ~ **a brick** faire une gaffe; ~ **down on** gronder, morigéner; ~ **it!** en voilà assez!, laisse tomber!; ~ **s/o a line** envoyer un mot à qn; **let** ~ dire en passant, faire savoir; vi couler goutte à goutte, s'égoutter; tomber; (wind, voice, price) baisser; fig cesser, prendre fin; ~ **away** diminuer; ~ **behind** se laisser devancer; ~ **in** entrer en passant; ~ **off** piquer un somme, s'endormir; (diminish) diminuer; sl ~ **out** renoncer, abandonner; sp drop(p)er; ~ **out of** sortir de, disparaître de

**drop-kick** n sp drop m

**drop-leaf** n volet m de table

**droplet** n gouttelette f

**drop-out** n sl drop-out, dropé -e

**dropping** n chute f; aer parachutage m; ~ **s** fiente f, crottes fpl

**dropsical** adj med hydropique

**dropsy** n med hydropisie f

**dross** n scories fpl; immondices fpl, ordures fpl; fig camelote f, toc m

**drought** n sécheresse f

**drove** n troupeau m en marche

**drover** n toucheur m

**drown** vt noyer; fig inonder, submerger;

**drowning**

(sound) étouffer, assourdir; *vi* se noyer

**drowning** *n* noyade *f*; *adj* qui se noie

**drowse** *n* somme *m*, somnolence *f*; *vt* assoupir; *vi* somnoler, s'assoupir

**drowsiness** *n* somnolence *f*

**drowsy** *adj* somnolent

**drub** *vt* battre; rosser; (abuse) engueuler

**drubbing** *n* volée *f* de coups, raclée *f*; *coll* tripotée *f*

**drudge** *n* domestique surmené -e; *vi* trimer

**drudgery** *n* travail dur et monotone

**drug** *n* produit *m* pharmaceutique, médicament *m*, drogue *f*; (addictive) drogue *f*, stupéfiant *m*; ~ **addict** toxicomane; ~ **addiction** toxicomanie *f*; *fig* ~ **on the market** article *m* invendable; *vt* droguer; administrer un narcotique à; *vi* se droguer

**druggist** *n* pharmacien -ienne

**drugstore** *n* *US* drugstore *m*

**druid** *n* druide *m*

**druidic** *adj* druidique

**drum** *n* *mus* tambour *m*; *anat* tympan *m*; *mech* tambour *m*, cylindre *m*; (container) baril *m*, b̆don *m*; *archi* tambour *m*; *elect* bobine *f*; *mus* **big ~** grosse caisse; *vt* *mus* tambouriner, pianoter; ~ **into** enseigner à force de répétitions; *mil* ~ **up** battre le rappel de; (support) faire du battage pour; *vi* battre du tambour

**drum-major** *n* tambour-major *m* (*pl* tambours-majors)

**drummer** *n* *mus* tambour *m*; *US* commis-voyageur *m*

**drumstick** *n* baguette *f* de tambour; *cul* pilon *m*

**drunk** *n* ivrogne *m*; *sl* soulard -e; *adj* saoul, ivre; *fig* ivre, enivré

**drunkard** *n* ivrogne *m*, ivrognesse *f*

**drunkenness** *n* ivrognerie , saoulerie *f*

**dry** *adj* sec (*f* sèche); desséché; (answer, style, humour) froid; *US* à régime sec; ~ **battery** pile sèche; ~ **goods** textiles *mpl*, nouveautés *fpl*; ~ **land** terre *f* ferme; ~ **rot** pourriture sèche; ~(-**stone**) **wall** mur *m* en pierres sèches; *vt* faire sécher; essuyer; *vi* sécher, se sécher; tarir; *theat* sécher; ~ **up** se sécher; *coll* cesser de parler

**dryad** *n* dryade *f*

**dry-clean** *vt* nettoyer à sec

**dry-cleaning** *n* nettoyage *m* à sec

**dry-dock** *n* cale sèche

**dryer** *n* see **drier**

**dry-eyed** *adj* sans larmes

**dry-ice** *n* *chem* neige *f* carbonique

**dryly, drily** *adv* sèchement; ironiquement

**dryness** *n* sécheresse *f*

**dry-shod** *adj* à pied sec

**dual** *adj* double, à deux, jumelé

**dual-carriageway** *n* mot route *f* à deux voies

**dualism** *n* dualisme *m*

**dualistic** *adj* dualiste

**duality** *n* dualité *f*

**dual-purpose** *adj* utilisable de deux façons, à double usage

**dub** *vt* conférer le titre de chevalier à; donner un surnom à; *cin* doubler; (recording) copier; (leather) graisser

**dubbing** *n* *cin* doublage *m*; (recording) copie *f*

**dubious** *adj* douteux -euse; hésitant; discutable, vague; suspect, louche; (unclear) ambigu -uë

**ducal** *adj* ducal

**ducat** *n* ducat *m*

**duchess** *n* duchesse *f*

**duchy** *n* duché *m*

**¹duck** *n* canard *m*; (female) cane *f*; *coll* chou *m*, chéri -e; *coll mil* camion *m* amphibie; **lame ~** canard boiteux; **like a ~ takes to water** naturellement, facilement; **like a dying ~ in a thunderstorm** faible, impuissant, inerte; **like water off a ~'s back** sans faire la moindre impression; **play ~s and drakes** faire des ricochets sur l'eau; **play ~s and drakes with one's money** gaspiller son argent; **wild ~** canard *m* sauvage; *vt* (head) baisser vivement; ~ **s/o** plonger qn dans l'eau; *vi* se courber, s'esquiver en se courbant; se plonger

**²duck** *n* toile *f*; ~ **s** pantalon *m* de toile

**duck-bill** *n* ornithorynque *m*

**duck-board** *n* caillebotis *m*

**ducking** *n* bain forcé

**duckling** *n* caneton *m*

**duckweed** *n* bot lentille *f* d'eau

**duct** *n* conduite *f*; *anat* canal *m*, conduit *m*; canalisation *f*

**ductile** *adj* (metal) ductile; *fig* souple, influençable

**ductless** *adj* anat à sécrétion interne; ~ **gland** glande endocrine

**dud** *n* *coll mil* obus non éclaté; objet *m* inutile, rossignol *m*; (coin) pièce fausse; (person) raté -e; *adj* inutile, qui ne marche pas; ~ **cheque** chèque *m* sans provision

**dude** *n* *US sl* poseur *m*, gommeux *m*

**dude-ranch** *n* hôtel *m* ranch

**dudgeon** *n* colère *f*, ressentiment *m*

**due** *n* dû *m*; ~ **s** droits *mpl*; *adj* dû (*f* due); (fallen due) échu; juste, mérité; (arrival) attendu, prévu; ~ **to** à cause de; *adv* ~ **north, east, etc** plein nord, est, etc

**duel** *n* duel *m*; *vi* se battre en duel

**dueller, duellist** *n* duelliste *m*

454

**duenna** *n* duègne *f*

**duet** *n mus* duo *m*

**duffel, duffle** *n* molleton *m*; ~ **coat** duffel-coat *m*

**duffer** *n coll* (schoolboy) cancre *m*; crétin -e, gourde *f*

**dug** *n* tétine *f*; (cow) pis *m*

**dugout** *n naut* pirogue *f*; *mil* abri souterrain

**duke** *n* duc *m*

**dukedom** *n* duché *m*; titre *m* de duc

**dulcet** *adj* mélodieux -ieuse, doux (*f* douce)

**dulcimer** *n mus* tympanon *m*

**dull** *adj* lourd, lent, bête, borné; (colour) terne, morne; (appearance) sans éclat; (sound) sourd, mat; (weather) couvert; (boring) ennuyeux -euse, insipide; (inactive) sans entrain; (bored) ennuyé; (pain) sourd; (blunt) émoussé; *vt* alourdir, hébéter; (blunt) émousser; (colour) ternir; (sound) assourdir; (pain) amortir; *vi* s'alourdir; se ternir; s'assourdir; s'émousser; s'amortir

**dullard** *n* balourd -e, crétin -e

**dullness** *n* lourdeur *f*, lenteur *f*; aspect *m* terne; (appearance) manque *m* d'éclat; caractère *m* insipide; insipidité *f*

**duly** *adv* dûment, correctement

**dumb** *adj* muet -ette; silencieux -ieuse; *coll* borné, gourde, crétin; ~ **blonde** blonde évaporée; ~ **show** pantomime *f*

**dumb-bell** *n* haltère *m*

**dumbfound** *vt* ébahir, désarçonner, étonner

**dumbness** *n* mutisme *m*

**dumb-waiter** *n* table roulante; (stand) plateau tournant; *US* monte-plats *m invar*

**dum-dum** *n mil* dum-dum *f invar*

**dummy** *n* simulacre *m*; (draper's model) mannequin *m*; (cards) mort *m*; (baby) sucette *f*; *mech* ~ **run** essai *m*; **tailor's** ~ mannequin *m*; *sl* m'as-tu vu *m invar*, m'as-tu vue *f invar*

**dump** *n* (rubbish) dépotoir *m*; (pile) tas *m*, amas *m*; *mil* dépôt *m*; *coll* trou *m*; *vt* décharger, déverser; *comm* faire du dumping pour; *coll* se débarrasser de; *vi* se décharger

**dumpling** *n cul* boulette *f* de pâte; **apple** ~ pomme entourée de pâte

**dumps** *npl* cafard *m*

**dumpy** *adj* courtaud, rondouillard

¹**dun** *n* couleur *f* gris-foncé; *adj* gris foncé *invar*

²**dun** *n* huissier *m*; *vt* (debtor) relancer

**dunce** *n* cancre *m*, âne *m*

**dune** *n* dune *f*

**dung** *n* fiente *f*, crotte *f*; **cow** ~ bouse *f*; **horse** ~ crottin *m*; *vt* fumer

**dungaree** *n* treillis *m*; ~ **s** bleu *m* de travail, *coll* salopette *f*

**dungeon** *n* cachot *m*, oubliette *f*; *hist* donjon *m*

**dunghill** *n* tas *m* de fumier

**dunk** *vt* tremper

**duo** *n mus* duo *m*

**duodecimal** *adj math* duodécimal

**duodecimo** *n* (book) in-douze *m invar*

**duodenal** *adj med* duodénal

**duodenum** *n anat* duodénum *m*

**duologue** *n* dialogue *m*

**dupe** *n* dupe *f*; *vt* duper

**duplex** *n US* ~ **apartment** appartement *m* à deux étages, duplex *m*; *adj* double; *elect* + *rad* duplex

**duplicate** *n* double *m*, copie exacte; *adj* double, en double; *vt* faire en double exemplaire; reproduire

**duplication** *n* reproduction *f* par duplicateur

**duplicator** *n* duplicateur *m*

**duplicity** *n* duplicité *f*

**durability** *n* durabilité *f*

**durable** *adj* durable

**duralumin** *n* duralumin *m*

**duration** *n* durée *f*

**duress** *n* emprisonnement *m*, captivité *f*; *leg* constrainte *f*

**during** *prep* pendant, durant

**dusk** *n* crépuscule *m*; obscurité *f*, ombre *f*; *adj poet* sombre; *vt poet* assombrir; *vi poet* s'assombrir

**dusky** *adj* sombre; (complexion) hâlé, brun

**dust** *n* poussière *f*; poudre *f*; (corpse) cendres *fpl*; **gold** ~ poudre *f* d'or; **lick the** ~ ramper; **shake the** ~ **off one's feet** quitter dédaigneusement un endroit; **throw** ~ **in the eyes** jeter de la poudre aux yeux; *vt* épousseter; (sprinkle) saupoudrer; *vi* enlever la poussière

**dustbin** *n* poubelle *f*, boîte *f* à ordures

**dust-bowl** *n* région *f* à sol dénudé, désert *m* de poussière

**dust-cart** *n* camion *m* des boueux

**dust-cover** *n* (book) couvre-livre *m*; (furniture) housse *f*

**duster** *n* chiffon *m*

**dusting** *n* époussetage *m*; *coll* raclée *f*; *med* poudre *f* antiseptique

**dust-jacket** *n* couvre-livre *m*

**dustman** *n* boueux *m*, éboueur *m*

**dustpan** *n* pelle *f* à ordures, pelle *f* à poussière

**dust-proof** *adj* protégé contre la poussière

**dust-sheet** *n* housse *f*

**dust-up** *n coll* bagarre *f*, querelle *f*

**dust-wrapper** *n* couvre-livre *m*

**dusty** *adj* poussiéreux -euse, poudreux -euse; *sl* **not so ~** pas si moche
**Dutch** *n* hollandais *m*; *adj* hollandais, néerlandais; **~ cap** pessaire *m*; **~ courage** courage *m* d'ivrogne; *coll* **~ treat** repas *m* où l'on partage les frais; *coll* **double ~** charabia *m*, baragouin *m*; *coll* **go ~** partager les frais; **talk to s/o like a ~ uncle** réprimander qn, tancer qn
**Dutchman** *n* Hollandais *m*
**Dutchwoman** *n* Hollandaise *f*
**duteous** *adj* obéissant; respectueux -euse
**dutiable** *adj* sujet -ette aux droits de douane
**dutiful** *adj* respectueux -euse, déférent; obéissant; consciencieux -ieuse
**duty** *n* devoir *m*, obligation *f*; déférence *f*; (tax) droits *mpl*; **duties** fonctions *fpl*; **do ~ for** remplacer; *mil* **on ~** de service
**duty-free** *adj* en franchise, exempt de droits de douane
**dwarf** *n* nain -e; *adj* nain; (stunted) rabougri; *vt* rapetisser; éclipser; *bot* rabougrir, étioler
**dwarfish** *adj* rabougri; minuscule
**dwell** *vi* habiter, demeurer; rester; **~ on** réfléchir sur; insister sur
**dweller** *n* habitant -e
**dwelling** *n* habitation *f*, demeure *f*; **~ place** demeure *f*
**dwindle** *vi* diminuer; s'étioler; perdre de l'importance
**dye** *n* teinture *f*; teinte *f*; *vt* teindre; *vi* se teindre
**dyeing** *n* teinture *f*; teinturerie *f*
**dyer** *n* teinturier -ière
**dyestuffs** *npl* teintures *fpl*
**dying** *adj* mourant
**¹dyke, dike** *n* digue *f*; (ditch) fossé *m*; *geol* filon *m*, dyke *m*; *vt* endiguer
**²dyke** *n sl* (lesbian) gouine *f*
**dynamic** *adj phys* dynamique; *med* fonctionnel -elle; *fig* dynamique, énergique
**dynamics** *npl phys* dynamique *f*
**dynamism** *n philos* dynamisme *m*
**dynamite** *n* dynamite *f*; *vt* faire sauter à la dynamite, dynamiter
**dynamiter** *n* dynamiteur -euse
**dynamo** *n* dynamo *f*; **human ~** personne *f* énergique
**dynamometer** *n* dynamomètre *m*
**dynast** *n ar* dynaste *m*, souverain *m* héréditaire
**dynastic** *adj* dynastique
**dynasty** *n* dynastie *f*
**dyne** *n phys* dyne *f*
**dysentery** *n med* dysenterie *f*
**dyslexia** *n med* dyslexie *f*
**dyslexic** *n + adj med* dyslexique
**dyspepsia** *n* dyspepsie *f*
**dyspeptic** *adj med* dyspepsique, dyspeptique; *fig* lugubre

# E

**each** *adj* chaque; *pron* chacun -e; **~ other** l'un l'autre; **ten francs ~** dix francs pièce, dix francs chaque
**eager** *adj* ardent, impatient; enthousiaste; avide; *coll* **~ beaver** personne *f* qui fait du zèle
**eagerness** *n* impatience *f*; zèle *m*, enthousiasme *m*
**eagle** *n* aigle *m*; **golden ~** aigle royal
**eagle-eyed** *adj* perspicace, qui voit tout
**eaglet** *n* aiglon *m*
**¹ear** *n* oreille *f*; (hearing) ouïe *f*; **be all ~s** être tout oreilles; **keep one's ~s to the ground** être aux écoutes; **play by ~** (music) jouer à l'oreille; *fig* improviser le moment venu; **set by the ~s** semer le désaccord; **turn a deaf ~** faire la sourde oreille; *coll* **up to the ~s** extrêmement, jusqu'au cou
**²ear** *n bot* épi *m*; *vi* épier
**earache** *n* mal *m* d'oreilles, mal *m* aux oreilles
**eardrum** *n* tympan *m*
**earl** *n* = comte *m*
**earldom** *n* = comté *m*
**early** *adj* de bonne heure, matinal; *bot* précoce, de primeur; *hist* primitif -ive; *coll* **~ bird** personne *f* qui se lève de bonne heure; personne *f* qui arrive tôt; **~ closing day** jour *m* où les magasins

sont fermés l'après-midi; ~ **times** passé lointain; **in the ~ nineteenth century** au début du dix-neuvième siècle; *adv* tôt, de bonne heure; au début; (right from) **as ~ as** dès; **as ~ as possible** le plus tôt possible

**earmark** *n* (sheep) marque *f* à l'oreille; *fig* signe distinctif, caractéristique *f*; *vt* (sheep) marquer à l'oreille; réserver, affecter

**earn** *vt* (money) gagner; (interest) rapporter; *fig* mériter

**¹earnest** *n* arrhes *fpl*; gage *m*

**²earnest** *n* sérieux *m*; **in ~** sérieusement; *adj* sérieux -ieuse; sincère; (assiduous) empressé, zélé

**earnings** *npl* (salary) appointements *mpl*, salaire *m*; (wages) gages *mpl*; (profits) bénéfices *mpl*

**earphone** *n* écouteur *m*

**earring** *n* boucle *f* d'oreille

**earshot** *n* portée *f* de la voix

**ear-splitting** *adj* assourdissant

**earth** *n* terre *f*, monde *m*; (soil) terre *f*, sol *m*; (burrow) terrier *m*; **down to ~** réaliste; **run to ~** se terrer; **where on ~?** où diable?; *vt* couvrir de terre; *elect* mettre à la terre

**earth-born** *adj* mortel -elle

**earth-bound** *adj* terrestre; prosaïque; *eccles* mondain

**earthen** *adj* en terre, de terre

**earthenware** *n* faïence *f*

**earthly** *adj* terrestre; *eccles* mondain; profane, matérialiste; *coll* possible; **no ~ use** sans aucune utilité; *sl* **not an ~** rien à faire

**earthly-minded** *adj* profane, matérialiste

**earthquake** *n* tremblement *m* de terre

**earthwork** *n* *eng* terrassement *m*; *mil* ouvrage *m* de terre

**earthworm** *adj* ver *m* de terre

**earthy** *n* terreux -euse; (crude) grossier -ière

**ear-trumpet** *n* cornet *m* acoustique

**earwax** *n* cérumen *m*

**earwig** *n* perce-oreille *m*

**ease** *n* (well-being) bien-être *m*; confort *m*, aises *fpl*; (facility) aisance *f*; **at ~** à l'aise; *mil* repos!; *vt* apaiser, alléger; réconforter; *naut* mollir; *vi* se détendre

**easel** *n* chevalet *m*

**easily** *adv* facilement; (possibly) bien

**easiness** *n* facilité *f*, aisance *f*; confort *m*; nonchalance *f*

**east** *n* est *m*, levant *m*; Orient *m*; **Far East** Extrême-Orient *m*; **Middle East** Moyen-Orient *m*; *adj* à l'est, de l'est; *adv* à l'est

**Easter** *n* Pâques *fpl* or *m sing*; **~ egg** œuf *m* de Pâques

**easterly** *adj* d'est; *adv* de l'est

**eastern** *adj* face à l'est; oriental; de l'Orient

**eastward, eastwards** *adv* vers l'est

**easy** *adj* facile, aisé, simple; (chair, clothes) confortable; (relaxed) à l'aise; (understanding) souple; tolérant; tranquille, calme; *comm* peu demandé; **on the eye** bien balancé; **by ~ stages** par petites étapes; **in ~ circumstances** prospère; *adv* à l'aise, sans effort; *coll* **~ does it!** doucement!, on a le temps!; *coll* **take it ~** faire se la couler douce

**easy-chair** *n* fauteuil *m*

**easy-going** *adj* tolérant, accommodant, facile à vivre

**eat** *vt* manger; dévorer; *fig* manger; ronger; *sl* tracasser, irriter; **~ away** dévorer peu à peu; corroder; **~ one's heart out** se consumer de chagrin; **~ one's words** se rétracter; **~ out of s/o's hand** faire les quatre volontés de qn; **~ up** dévorer; tout manger; *vi* manger; **~ into** ronger, corroder, pénétrer dans; **be ~en** se manger

**eatable** *adj* mangeable, comestible

**eatables** *npl* victuailles *fpl*

**eater** *n* mangeur -euse

**eating** *n* manger *m*; *adj* comestible; **~ apple** pomme *f* à couteau

**eating-house** *n* restaurant pas cher

**eau-de-Cologne** *n* eau *f* de Cologne

**eau-de-vie** *n* eau-de-vie *f* (*pl* eaux-de-vie)

**eaves** *npl* avant-toit *m*

**eavesdrop** *vi* écouter aux portes

**eavesdropper** *n* écouteur -euse aux portes

**ebb** *n* reflux *m*; *fig* déclin *m*, diminution *f*; *vi* refluer; *fig* décliner

**ebb-tide** *n* jusant *m*, reflux *m*

**ebonist** *n* ébéniste

**ebonite** *n* ébonite *f*

**ebony** *n* ébène *f*; *adj* d'ébène; tout à fait noir

**ebullience, ebulliency** *n* ébullition *f*; exubérance *f*

**ebullient** *adj* bouillonnant; exubérant

**ebullition** *n* ébullition *f*; *fig* éclatement *m*, débordement *m*

**eccentric** *n* original -e; *adj* excentrique

**eccentricity** *n* eccentricité *f*

**ecchymosis** *n* ecchymose *f*

**ecclesiastic** *n* ecclésiastique *m*; *adj* ecclésiastique

**echelon** *n* *mil* échelon *m*

**echo** *n* écho *m*; *vt* répéter; *vi* faire écho

**éclair** *n* cul éclair *m*

**eclectic** *n* + *adj* éclectique

**eclecticism** *n* éclectisme *m*

**eclipse** *n* éclipse *f*; *vt* éclipser; *vi* s'éclipser

**eclogue** *n* églogue *f*

457

**ecological** *adj* écologique
**ecologist** *n* écologiste
**ecology** *n* écologie *f*
**economic** *adj* économique
**economical** *adj* économique; (person) économe
**economics** *npl* économique *f*; économie *f* politique
**economist** *n* économiste; personne *f* économe
**economize** *vt* économiser; *vi* faire des économies, économiser
**economy** *n* économie *f*; système *m* économique
**ecstasy** *n* extase *f*, joie *f* intense, ravissement *m*, transport *m*
**ecstatic** *adj* extatique
**ectoplasm** *n* ectoplasme *m*
**Ecuador** *n* Équateur *m*
**ecumenical, oecumenical** *adj* œcuménique
**ecumenism, oecumenism** *n* œcuménisme *m*
**eczema** *n med* eczéma *m*
**eddy** *n* remous *m*, tourbillon *m*; *vi* tourbillonner
**edema** *n see* oedema
**Eden** *n* Éden *m*, paradis *m* terrestre
**edge** *n* (blade) tranchant *m*, fil *m*; (border) bord *m*, extrémité *f*, marge *f*; *geog* arête *f*; *fig* enthousiasme *m*, mordant *m*; **have the ~ on** devancer mais de peu; **on ~** crispé, irrité, exaspéré; **set the teeth on ~** irriter, agacer; **take the ~ off** émousser; *vt* (sharpen) aiguiser, affiler; border, ourler; **~ out** évincer; *vi* **~ away** s'éloigner peu à peu; **~ into** s'insinuer dans
**edgeways, edgewise** *adv* de biais, de côté; **be unable to get a word in ~** ne pouvoir placer un mot
**edging** *n* bordure *f*
**edgy** *adj* tranchant; *fig* crispé, nerveux -euse; *arts* sans contours accusés
**edible** *adj* comestible, mangeable
**edict** *n* édit *m*, décret *m*
**edification** *n* édification *f*
**edifice** *n* édifice *m*
**edify** *adj* édifier
**edifying** *adj* édifiant
**Edinburgh** *n* Édimbourg
**edit** *vt* (text, book) éditer, préparer pour la publication; (newspaper) diriger, être le rédacteur -trice en chef de
**edition** *n* édition *f*; (number of copies) tirage *m*
**editor** *n* (text) éditeur -trice; (newspaper) rédacteur -trice en chef; (department of newspaper) rédacteur -trice
**editorial** *n* éditorial *m*, article *m* de fond
**editorship** *n* (publishing) profession *f* d'éditeur -trice; (newspaper) profession *f* de rédacteur -trice en chef
**educable** *adj* éducable
**education** *n* éducation *f*; (teaching) enseignement *m*, instruction *f*
**educational** *adj* éducateur -trice, éducatif -ive
**educationalist, educationist** *n* pédagogue
**educator** *n* éducateur -trice
**edulcorate** *vt* édulcorer
**eel** *n* anguille *f*
**eerie, eery** *adj* sinistre, effrayant; mystérieux -ieuse
**efface** *vt* effacer; **~ oneself** s'effacer
**effacement** *n* effacement *m*
**effect** *n* effet *m*, résultat *m*; influence *f*; impression *f*, sens *m*; **~ s** effets *mpl*; *theat + cin* (sound) bruitage *m*; (visual) truquage *m*; **put into ~** mettre en application; **to no ~** en vain; **to the same ~** dans le même sens; *vt* causer, effectuer; accomplir
**effective** *n mil* effectif *m*; *adj* efficace, efficient; *mil* effectif -ive
**effectiveness** *n* efficacité *f*
**effectual** *adj* efficace; (valid) valable
**effectuate** *vt* effectuer
**effeminacy** *n* caractère efféminé; manque *m* de virilité
**effeminate** *n* efféminé *m*; *adj* efféminé
**effervesce** *vi* être en effervescence, bouillonner
**effervescence** *n* effervescence *f*
**effervescent** *adj* effervescent
**effete** *adj* épuisé; sans force; stérile
**effeteness** *n* épuisement *m*; faiblesse *f*
**efficacious** *adj* efficace
**efficaciousness, efficacy** *n* efficacité *f*
**efficiency** *n* efficacité *f*; (productivity) capacité *f* de rendement; compétence *f*; *phys + mech + econ* rendement *m*
**efficient** *adj* efficace, efficient; capable, compétent
**effigy** *n* effigie *f*
**effloresce** *vi bot* être en fleurs; *chem* effleurir
**efflorescence** *n bot* floraison *f*; *chem* efflorescence *f*
**efflorescent** *adj bot* en fleurs; *chem* efflorescent
**effluent** *n* effluent *m*
**effluvium** *n* effluve *m*
**efflux** *n* écoulement *m*
**effort** *n* effort *m*; *coll* accomplissement *m*
**effortless** *adj* sans effort; facile, naturel -elle, aisé
**effrontery** *n* effronterie *f*, audace *f*
**effulgence** *n* éclat *m* (de lumière)
**effulgent** *adj* éclatant, rayonnant
**effusion** *n* effusion *f*, déversement *m*, épanchement *m*; *lit* flot *m* de paroles;

écrit plein d'épanchements; *med* effusion *f*

**effusive** *adj* exubérant, démonstratif -ive

**effusiveness** *n* effusion *f*, épanchement *m*

**egalitarian** *adj* égalitaire

**egalitarianism** *n* égalitarisme *m*

**egality** *n* égalité *f*

**¹egg** *n* œuf *m*; *biol* ovule *m*; *coll* **good ~** brave type *m*; **hard-boiled ~** œuf dur; **soft-boiled ~** œuf *m* à la coque

**²egg** *vt* inciter, pousser; **~ on** pousser

**egg-cup** *n* coquetier *m*

**egg-flip** *n* lait *m* de poule

**egg-head** *n* + *adj sl cont US* intellectuel -elle

**egg-nog** *n* flip *m*

**egg-plant** *n* aubergine *f*

**eggshell** *n* coquille *f* d'œuf

**egg-timer** *n* sablier *m*

**egg-whisk** *n cul* fouet *m*

**eglantine** *n bot* églantine *f*

**ego** *n* ego *m*, moi *m*

**egocentric** *adj* égocentrique

**egoism** *n* égoïsme *m*; suffisance *f*

**egoist** *n* égoïste; égotiste

**egoistic** *adj* égoïste

**egotism** *n* égotisme *m*

**egregious** *adj* terrible, très mauvais, notoire

**egress , egression** *n* sortie *f*

**Egypt** *n* Égypte *f*

**Egyptian** *n* Égyptien -ienne; *adj* égyptien -ienne

**egyptologist** *n* égyptologue

**egyptology** *n* égyptologie *f*

**eh** *interj* hé!, hein?

**eider** *n zool* eider *m*

**eiderdown** *n* édredon *m*, duvet *m*

**eight** *n* huit *m invar*; *sp* (rowing) équipe *f* de huit personnes; (skating) **figure of ~** huit *m*; *sl* **have one over the ~** boire un coup de trop; *adj* huit *invar*

**eighteen** *n* dix-huit *m invar*; *adj* dix-huit *invar*

**eighteenth** *n* dix-huitième; (date) dix-huit *m*; *adj* dix-huitième

**eighth** *n* huitième; (date) huit *m*; *adj* huitième

**eightieth** *n* + *adj* quatre-vingtième

**eighty** *n* quatre-vingts *m*; *adj* quatre-vingts

**either** *adj* + *pron* l'un ou l'autre; **not ~ of them** ni l'un ni l'autre; *adv* non plus; *conj* **~ ... or** ou ... ou, soit ... soit

**ejaculate** *vt* (cry) pousser (un cri); *vi* s'exclamer, s'écrier; *physiol* éjaculer

**ejaculation** *n* exclamation *f*; *physiol* éjaculation *f*

**eject** *vt* éjecter; émettre, lancer; (person) chasser, expulser

**ejection** *n* éjection *f*; expulsion *f*

**ejector** *n* éjecteur *m*; *aer* **~ seat** siège *m*

**ejectable**

**eke** *vt* **~ out** augmenter, supplémenter; faire durer

**elaborate** *adj* compliqué; soigné; *vt* élaborer

**elaboration** *n* élaboration *f*

**elan** *n* élan *m*

**elapse** *vi* (time) passer, s'écouler

**elastic** *n* élastique *m*; *adj* élastique, souple

**elasticity** *n* élasticité *f*

**elate** *vt* exciter, ravir, enthousiasmer

**elation** *n* ravissement *m*, transport *m*, enivrement *m*

**elbow** *n* coude *m*; **at one's ~** à portée de la main; **out at the ~s** déguenillé; *vt* coudoyer; pousser du coude; frayer à coups de coude; **~ one's way through** se frayer un passage à travers; *vi* jouer des coudes

**elbow-grease** *n* huile *f* de coude, travail *m* physique

**elbow-room** *n* espace *m*; **have ~** avoir les coudées franches

**¹elder** *n* aîné -e; supérieur *m*; *adj* plus âgé, aîné; plus ancien -ienne; **~ statesman** ancien ministre qu'on consulte toujours

**²elder** *n bot* sureau *m*

**elderly** *adj* mûr; vieux (*f* vieille)

**eldest** *adj* aîné, le plus âgé

**elect** *n* élu -e; *adj* élu; *vt* élire; (choose) choisir

**election** *n* élection *f*

**electioneer** *vi* faire une campagne électorale, faire de la propagande électorale

**electioneering** *n* campagne électorale, propagande électorale

**elective** *adj* électif -ive

**elector** *n* électeur -trice

**electoral** *adj* électoral

**electorate** *n* corps électoral; (constituency) circonscription électorale

**electric** *adj* électrique; *fig* chargé d'émotion; **~ blue** bleu *m* métallique; *zool* **~ eel** gymnote *m*; **~ field** champ *m* électrique; **~ shock** décharge *f* électrique

**electrical** *adj* électrique

**electrician** *n* électricien *m*

**electricity** *n* électricité *f*

**electrification** *n* électrification *f*; (charge) électrisation *f*

**electrify** *vt* électrifier, électriser; *fig* étonner, exciter, électriser

**electrocardiogram** *n med* électrocardiogramme *m*

**electrocute** *vt* électrocuter

**electrocution** *n* électrocution *f*

**electrode** *n* électrode *f*

**electrolysis** *n* électrolyse *f*

**electromagnet** *n* électro-aimant *m*
**electromagnetic** *adj* électromagnétique
**electromagnetism** *n* électromagnétisme *m*
**electron** *n* électron *m*; ~ **microscope** microscope *m* électronique
**electronic** *adj* électronique
**electronics** *npl* électronique *f*
**electroplate** *n* plaqué *m*; *vt* plaquer par électrolyse
**electroscope** *n* électroscope *m*
**electrostatic** *adj* électrostatique
**electrotherapy** *n* électrothérapie *f*
**elegance** *n* élégance *f*
**elegant** *adj* élégant
**elegiac, elegiacal** *adj* élégiaque
**elegy** *n* élégie *f*
**element** *n* élément *m*; *elect* résistance *f*; ~ **s** éléments *mpl*, rudiments *mpl*; *eccles* espèces *fpl*
**elemental** *adj* des éléments; primordial, fondamental, simple
**elementary** *adj* élémentaire, rudimentaire; *ar* ~ **school** école primaire
**elephant** *n* éléphant *m*; *fig* white ~ rossignol *m*
**elephantiasis** *n med* éléphantiasis *f*
**elephantine** *adj* éléphantin, très lourd
**elevate** *vt* élever, hausser; (rank, morals) élever; exalter
**elevation** *n* élévation *f*, érection *f*; promotion *f*; dignité *f*, noblesse *f*; éloquence *f*; exaltation *f*; *geog* altitude *f*
**elevator** *n* monte-charge *m invar*, élévateur *m*; *US* ascenseur *m*
**eleven** *n* onze *m invar*; *sp* équipe *f* de onze personnes; *adj* onze *invar*
**elevenses** *npl coll* snack *m* vers onze heures du matin
**eleventh** *n* onzième *m*; (date) onze *m*; *adj* onzième; ~ **hour** dernière minute
**elf** *n* elfe *m*, génie *m*; *fig* jeune enfant grêle
**elfin** *adj* féerique
**elfish** *adj* féerique; espiègle
**elicit** *vt* dévoiler; (draw out) arracher, tirer; (facts) tirer au clair
**elide** *vt gramm* élider
**eligibility** *n* éligibilité *f*
**eligible** *adj* éligible; ~ **man** bon parti
**eliminate** *vt* éliminer
**elimination** *n* élimination *f*
**elision** *n gramm* élision *f*
**élite** *n* élite *f*
**elixir** *n* élixir *m*
**Elizabethan** *n* Élisabéthain -e; *adj* élisabéthain
**elk** *n zool* élan *m*
**ell** *n ar* aune *f*
**ellipse** *n geom* ellipse *f*
**ellipsis** *n gramm* ellipse *f*
**elliptic, elliptical** *adj* elliptique

**elm** *n* orme *m*
**elocution** *n* diction *f*; élocution *f*
**elocutionist** *n* diseur -euse; professeur *m* de diction
**elongate** *vt* allonger; *vi* s'allonger
**elongation** *n* élongation *f*, allongement *m*
**elope** *vi* partir avec un amant (une amante)
**elopement** *n* fugue amoureuse
**eloquence** *n* éloquence *f*
**eloquent** *adj* éloquent
**else** *adv* autre, d'autre; **anywhere** ~ ailleurs; **everything** ~ tout autre chose; **or** ~ autrement, sinon; **what** ~ ? quoi d'autre?; **who** ~ ? qui d'autre?
**elsewhere** *adv* ailleurs, autre part
**elucidate** *vt* élucider
**elucidation** *n* élucidation *f*
**elude** *vt* éluder; éviter, esquiver
**elusive, elusory** *adj* évasif -ive; difficile à saisir; difficile à comprendre
**Elysian** *adj* élyséen -éenne; ~ **fields** Champs-Élysées *mpl*
**Elysium** *n* Élysée *m*
**emaciate** *vt* amaigrir, émacier; creuser; *vi* s'émacier
**emaciation** *n* émaciation *f*
**emanate** *vi* émaner
**emanation** *n* émanation *f*
**emancipate** *vt* émanciper, affranchir, libérer
**emancipated** *adj* libéré, émancipé; *coll* émancipé, affranchi
**emancipation** *n* émancipation *f*, libération *f*
**emancipator** *n* libérateur -trice
**emasculate** *vt* émasculer
**emasculation** *n* émasculation *f*
**embalm** *vt* embaumer; *fig* conserver pieusement le souvenir de; parfumer
**embankment** *n* (river) digue *f*; (road, railway) remblai *m*
**embargo** *n* embargo *m*; **under an** ~ sous séquestre; *vt* mettre l'embargo sur
**embark** *vt* embarquer; *vi* s'embarquer
**embarkation** *n* embarquement *m*
**embarrass** *vt* embarrasser, gêner; (disconcert) décontenancer; *fig* (financial) mettre en difficulté
**embarrassment** *n* embarras *m*; difficulté *f*, anicroche *f*
**embassy** *n* ambassade *f*
**embattle** *vt* ranger en bataille
**embed** *vt* fixer; *mech* emboîter, encastrer
**embellish** *vt* embellir
**embellishment** *n* embellissement *m*
**ember** *n* tison *m*, braise *f*
**embezzle** *vt* détourner
**embezzlement** *n* détournement *m* de fonds

**embitter** vt (quarrel) envenimer, aggraver; (person) aigrir
**emblazon** vt blasonner
**emblem** n emblème m; her devise f
**emblematic** adj emblématique
**embodiment** n incorporation f, incarnation f
**embody** vt incorporer, incarner
**embolden** vt enhardir
**embolism** n med embolisme m
**emboss** vt (leather) gaufrer; (metal) bosseler, estamper
**embossment** n (leather) gaufrage m; (metal) bosselage m
**embrace** n embrassement m, étreinte f; vt embrasser, étreindre; (comprise) embrasser, englober, contenir; (perceive) saisir; (adopt) adopter
**embrasure** n embrasure f
**embrocation** n embrocation f
**embroider** vt broder; fig enjoliver
**embroidery** n broderie ·f; fig enjolivement m
**embroil** vt (affairs) embrouiller; (person) brouiller
**embroilment** n (confusion) embrouillement m; (discord) brouille f
**embryo** n embryon m; adj embryonnaire
**embryology** n embryologie f
**embryonic** adj embryonnaire
**embus** vt mil faire monter en car; vi monter en car
**emend** vt corriger
**emendation** n correction f
**emerald** n émeraude f; adj émeraude invar
**emerge** vi émerger, surgir, sortir; (appear) apparaître, se faire jour
**emergence** n émergence f
**emergency** n état m d'urgence, crise f, situation f critique; in case of ~ en cas d'urgence; rise to the ~ être à la hauteur des circonstances; adj d'urgence; de secours; (temporary) de fortune, provisoire; ~ exit sortie f de secours
**emeritus** adj émérite, honoraire
**emersion** n émersion f
**emery** n émeri m; ~ board lime f en carton; ~ cloth toile f émeri; ~ paper papier m d'émeri
**emetic** n émétique m; adj émétique
**emigrant** n émigrant -e
**emigrate** vi émigrer
**emigration** n émigration f; (persons) émigrants mpl, émigrantes fpl
**émigré** n Fr hist émigré -e
**eminence, eminency** n éminence f; (ground) élévation f; (position) grandeur f; anat saillie f
**eminent** adj éminent
**emir** n émir m

**emissary** n émissaire m
**emission** n émission f
**emit** vt émettre; (fumes) dégager; (smell) exhaler; (water) décharger
**emollient** n émollient m; adj émollient
**emolument** n traitement m, émoluments mpl, appointements mpl
**emote** vi coll s'épancher excessivement
**emotion** n émotion f, émoi m
**emotional** adj émotif -ive; émotionnable, impressionnable; psych émotionnel -elle
**emotionalism** n émotivité f, impressionnabilité f; pej sensiblerie f
**emotionalize** vt traiter avec (un excès d')émotion
**emotive** adj émotif -ive, émouvant
**empanel, impanel** vt leg ~ a jury dresser la liste des jurés; inscrire sur la liste des jurés
**empathy** n psych intuition f psychologique; coll état m d'être sur la même longueur d'ondes,. communion f d'idées
**emperor** n empereur m; ent paon m de nuit; ~ penguin manchot m empereur
**emphasis** n force f, intensité f; gramm accent m, accentuation f; fig importance f, poids m
**emphasize** vt mettre en valeur, souligner; gramm accentuer
**emphatic** adj catégorique, formel -elle; gramm accentué
**empire** n empire m; adj empire invar
**empiric** n med empirique m; adj empirique
**empirical** adj empirique
**empiricism** n empirisme m
**empiricist** n + adj empiriste
**emplacement** n position f; mil emplacement m
**employ** n emploi m, service m; vt employer, utiliser, faire usage de
**employable** adj utilisable, employable
**employee** n employé -e
**employer** n employeur -euse, patron -onne; ~'s union syndicat patronal
**employment** n emploi· m, travail m, occupation f
**emporium** n grand magasin; centre commercial
**empower** vt autoriser; rendre capable; leg nantir d'un pouvoir, habiliter
**empress** n impératrice f
**emptiness** n vide m, néant m
**empty** n coll (bottle) bouteille f vide; (case) caisse f vide; adj vide; vt vider; vi se vider
**empty-handed** adj les mains vides, bredouille
**empty-headed** adj à la tête creuse, sans cervelle

**empyrean** *n* empyrée *m*
**emu** *n orni* émeu *m*, ému *m*
**emulate** *vt* être l'émule de, rivaliser avec, tenter d'égaler
**emulation** *n* émulation *f*
**emulator** *n* émule
**emulous** *adj* plein d'émulation, rivalisant; ambitieux -ieuse
**emulsifier** *n* (apparatus) émulseur *m*; (substance) émulsifiant *m*
**emulsify** *vt* émulsionner
**emulsion** *n* émulsion *f*
**enable** *vt* rendre capable, mettre à même, permettre; *leg* habiliter
**enabling** *adj leg* habilitant
**enact** *vt* décréter; *leg* promulguer; (perform) accomplir; *theat* représenter
**enactment** *n* décret *m*; *leg* promulgation *f*
**enamel** *n* émail *m*; vernis *m*; (paint) peinture laquée, ripolin *m*; *adj* émaillé, vernissé; *vt* émailler, vernisser
**enamelling** *n* émaillage *m*, vernissage *m*
**enamour** *vt* enamourer, captiver; be ~ed of être épris de
**encamp** *vt mil* mettre dans un camp; *vi* camper, dresser des tentes
**encampment** *n* campement *m*
**encase** *vt* encaisser, enfermer; (box) mettre dans un étui; (machinery) blinder
**encash** *vt* encaisser
**encashment** *n* encaissement *m*
**encaustic** *n* encaustique *f*; *adj* encaustique
**encephalic** *adj* encéphalique
**encephalitis** *n* encéphalite *f*
**enchain** *vt* enchaîner; *fig* captiver
**enchant** *vt* enchanter; *fig* captiver, enchanter
**enchanter** *n* enchanteur *m*, enchanteresse *f*; magicien -ienne
**enchanting** *adj* enchanteur (*f* enchanteresse); charmant
**enchantment** *n* enchantement *m*
**enchantress** *n* enchanteresse *f*; sorcière *f*
**enchase** *vt* enchâsser
**encircle** *vt* encercler
**encirclement** *n* encerclement *m*
**enclave** *n* enclave *f*
**enclitic** *n gramm* enclitique *m*
**enclose, inclose** *vt* enclore, enfermer; (surround) entourer; (put inside) inclure, joindre; ~d sous ce pli, ci-joint
**enclosure, inclosure** *n* (act) clôture *f*; (space) enclos *m*, enceinte *f*; (fence) clôture *f*; (in letter) pièce jointe
**encomium** *n* panégyrique *m*
**encompass** *vt* encercler, entourer, contenir
**encore** *n theat* bis *m*; *vt* bisser; *interj* bis!
**encounter** *n* rencontre *f*; *mil* combat *m*; *vt* rencontrer, rencontrer par hasard, tomber sur

**encourage** *vt* encourager, aider, soutenir; (urge) pousser, stimuler
**encouragement** *n* encouragement *m*
**encouraging** *adj* encourageant
**encroach** *vi* empiéter; ~ on empiéter sur
**encrust, incrust** *vt* encroûter, incruster
**encrustation, incrustation** *n* incrustation *f*, encroûtement *m*
**encumber** *vt* encombrer, gêner, obstruer; *leg* grever
**encumbrance** *n* encombrement *m*, gêne *f*; *leg* charge *f*
**encyclical, encyclic** *n eccles* encyclique *f*; *adj* encyclique
**encyclop(a)edia** *n* encyclopédie *f*
**encyclop(a)edic** *adj* encyclopédique
**encyclop(a)edist** *n* encyclopédiste *m*
**end** *n* fin *f*, bout *m*; limite *f*; conclusion *f*, terme *m*; (death) mort *f*; (purpose) but *m*, intention *f*; at a loose ~ désœuvré; be at an ~ être terminé; bring to an ~ achever, terminer; come to an ~ s'achever, se terminer; get hold of the wrong ~ of the stick comprendre de travers; go off the deep ~ s'emporter, se mettre en colère; keep one's ~ up tenir bon; latter ~ (old age) vieillesse *f*; (death) mort *f*; make an ~ of mettre fin à; make ~s meet joindre les deux bouts; coll no ~ extrêmement, à n'en plus finir, à gogo; no ~ of un tas de; on ~ debout; (without stopping) de suite; there's no ~ to it cela n'en finit plus; with that ~ in view dans ce but; *vt* finir, terminer, achever; *vi* finir, se terminer, prendre fin; mourir
**end-all** *n* fin *f* de tout; but final
**endanger** *vt* mettre en péril, exposer au danger
**endear** *vt* rendre cher (*f* chère); ~ one-self to se faire aimer de
**endearing** *adj* attachant
**endearment** *n* affection *f*, caresse *f*; ~s (words) paroles *fpl* tendres
**endeavour** *n* effort *m*, tentative *f*; *vi* essayer, tâcher, s'efforcer
**endemic** *adj* endémique
**end-game** *n* fin *f* de partie
**ending** *n* fin *f*, conclusion *f*; *gramm* désinence *f*, terminaison *f*; happy ~ dénouement heureux
**endive** *n* (straight) endive *f*; (curly) chicorée *f*
**endless** *adj* sans fin, infini; continuel -elle, incessant; (too long) interminable
**endocardium** *n anat* endocarde *m*
**endocrine** *n anat* glande *f* endocrine; *adj* endocrine
**endorse, indorse** *vt* (cheque) endosser; *fig* soutenir, approuver; (passport) viser; *mot* ~ a driving licence (in Eng-

land) inscrire les détails d'un délit au verso d'un permis de conduire

**endorsee, indorsee** n endossataire

**endorsement, indorsement** n endos m, aval m; fig soutien m, appui m; mot (in England) contravention portée sur un permis de conduire

**endow** vt faire une dotation à; fig douer, pourvoir

**endowment** n dotation f; fig don m, qualité f

**endpapers** npl feuilles fpl de garde

**end-product** n résultat final

**endue** vt douer, investir

**endurable** adj endurable, supportable

**endurance** n endurance f, résistance f

**endure** vt endurer, souffrir, subir; supporter; vi (last) durer; (hold out) endurer

**enduring** adj durable; éternel -elle

**endways, endwise** adv debout

**enema** n lavement m, clystère m

**enemy** n ennemi -e; adj ennemi

**energetic** adj énergique, vigoureux -euse

**energize** vt stimuler, donner de l'énergie à

**energy** n énergie f, force f, vigueur f, fermeté f; adj énergétique

**enervate** vt abattre, amollir, affaiblir

**enervation** n amollissement m, affaiblissement m

**enfeeble** vt affaiblir

**enfilade** n mil tir m d'enfilade; vt prendre en enfilade

**enfold** vt enrouler, envelopper; embrasser

**enforce** vt imposer par la force; (law) faire respecter, appliquer

**enforcement** n contrainte f; (law) application f

**enfranchise** vt donner le droit de vote à; (slave) affranchir; (landed property) affranchir

**enfranchisement** n octroi m du droit de vote; affranchissement m

**engage** vt engager; (reserve) louer, retenir; (betroth) fiancer; (employ) embaucher, employer; (attract) attirer, séduire; mil attaquer, engager le combat contre; mech engager; vi s'engager; (pledge) promettre; mech s'engager, s'embrayer

**engaged** adj (betrothed) fiancé; (telephone, lavatory, etc) occupé; (employee) embauché

**engagement** n engagement m; (betrothal) fiançailles fpl; (appointment) engagement m, rendez-vous m; mil engagement m, bataille f; mech embrayage m, engrenage m

**engaging** adj attirant, engageant, charmant

**engender** vt engendrer, produire

**engine** n machine f; mot moteur m; (railway) locomotive f; mil hist engin m

**engine-driver** n mécanicien m

**engineer** n ingénieur m; mil officier m du génie, soldat m du génie; rad sound ~ ingénieur m du son; vt construire; exécuter; pej manigancer

**engineering** n ingénierie f, génie m; fig pej machinations fpl; **civil** ~ génie civil; **military** ~ génie m militaire; **production** ~ technique f de la production

**engine-room** n salle f des machines

**English** n (language) anglais m; (people) Anglais mpl; adj anglais; vt traduire en anglais; angliciser

**Englishism** n anglicisme m

**Englishman** n Anglais m

**Englishwoman** n Anglaise f

**engorge** vt engloutir, dévorer

**engraft** vt greffer; fig implanter

**engrain** vt teindre

**engrained** adj see ingrained

**engrave** vt graver

**engraver** n graveur m

**engraving** n gravure f

**engross** vt absorber, accaparer; leg grossoyer

**engrossing** adj absorbant, passionnant

**engrossment** n accaparement m; leg grosse f

**engulf** vt engouffrer

**enhance** vt rehausser, intensifier, relever

**enhancement** n rehaussement m

**enigma** n énigme f

**enigmatic, enigmatical** adj énigmatique

**enjambment** n pros enjambement m

**enjoin** vt ordonner à, enjoindre à

**enjoy** vt prendre plaisir à, jouir de, aimer; (have use of) jouir de, posséder; ~ **oneself** s'amuser, prendre du plaisir

**enjoyable** adj agréable

**enjoyment** n plaisir m, agrément m; leg possession f, jouissance f

**enkindle** vt allumer; fig enflammer

**enlace** vt enlacer

**enlarge** vt agrandir, développer; phot agrandir; vi s'agrandir; ~ **upon** développer, s'étendre sur

**enlargement** n agrandissement m; accroissement m

**enlarger** n phot agrandisseur m

**enlighten** vt éclairer, édifier

**enlightenment** n lumières fpl, édification f; lit hist **the Enlightenment** le Siècle des lumières

**enlist** vt mil enrôler; fig gagner, obtenir; vi s'enrôler

**enlistment** n enrôlement m

**enliven** vt animer, stimuler

**enmesh** vt prendre au filet; fig enchevêtrer, embrouiller

**enmity** n inimitié f, hostilité f

ennoble vt anoblir; *fig* ennoblir, élever

ennoblement n anoblissement m; *fig* ennoblissement m

ennui n ennui m

enormity n monstruosité f; atrocité f; (size) énormité f

enormous adj énorme, immense

enough n suffisance f; adj assez de, suffisant; adv assez, suffisamment; *interj* assez!, en voilà assez!, ça suffit!

enounce vt prononcer; proclamer

enquire vt + vi see inquire

enquiry n see inquiry

enrage vt enrager, rendre furieux -ieuse

enrapture vt ravir, enchanter

enrich vt enrichir; (soil) fertiliser

enrichment n enrichissement m

enrol vt porter sur une liste, enrôler

enrolment n inscription f sur une liste, enrôlement m

ensconce vt placer, mettre en sûreté; ~ oneself bien s'installer

ensemble n ensemble m

enshrine vt *eccles* enchâsser; *fig* révérer

enshrinement n *eccles* enchâssement m

enshroud vt ensevelir (dans un linceul); (conceal) cacher; (veil) voiler

ensign n (badge) insigne m; *naut* pavillon m; *ar mil* enseigne m; *US naut* enseigne m de vaisseau

enslave vt réduire en esclavage, asservir

enslavement n asservissement m

ensnare vt prendre au piège, piéger

ensue vi résulter, s'ensuivre

ensure vt assurer, rendre certain

entablature n *archi* entablement m

entail n leg substitution f d'héritiers; leg bien substitué; vt entraîner, occasionner; leg substituer

entangle vt enchevêtrer, embrouiller; *fig* compliquer

entanglement n enchevêtrement m, embrouillement m; *mil* réseau m de barbelés; *fig* complication f

entente n entente f

enter vt entrer dans, pénétrer (dans); (join) s'inscrire à, s'enrôler à; (name, etc) inscrire; leg intenter; (cargo) déclarer; (protest) formuler; vi entrer, pénétrer; *theat* entrer en scène; ~ for s'inscrire pour; ~ into prendre part à, participer à; (start) entamer; ~ upon commencer, entreprendre; prendre possession de

enteric adj intestinal

enteritis n entérite f

enterprise n entreprise f; esprit m d'entreprise

enterprising adj entreprenant, aventureux -euse

entertain vt divertir, amuser; (guest) recevoir; (idea) considérer; (doubt, hope) nourrir; vi recevoir, donner une réception

entertainer n amuseur m, diseur -euse, comique m

entertaining adj divertissant, amusant

entertainment n réception f; hospitalité f; (amusement) divertissement m, distraction f; *theat* spectacle m

enthral, enthrall vt captiver, fasciner; *ar* asservir

enthralling adj captivant, fascinant

enthrone vt *eccles* introniser; (king) placer sur le trône

enthuse vi *coll* s'enthousiasmer

enthusiasm n enthousiasme m

enthusiast n enthousiaste, fervent -e

enthusiastic adj enthousiaste, fervent

entice vt tenter, seduire; (attract) attirer

enticement n attrait m; tentation f

enticing adj attirant, alléchant, séduisant

entire adj entier -ière, complet -ète

entirety n entièreté f, totalité f

entitle vt intituler; donner droit à

entity n entité f

entomb vt enterrer; *fig* ensevelir

entomological adj entomologique

entomologist n entomologiste

entomology n entomologie f

entourage n entourage m

entr'acte n *theat* entracte m

entrails npl intestins mpl; *lit fig* entrailles fpl

entrain vt mettre dans un train; *mil* faire monter dans un train; emporter; vi monter dans un train

¹entrance n entrée f; ~ fee prix m d'entrée; tradesman's ~ entrée f de service

²entrance vt ravir, transporter

entrancement n ravissement m

entrancing adj ravissant

entrant n sp participant -e; (examination) candidat -e

entrap vt prendre au piège

entreat vt supplier, conjurer

entreaty n supplication f

entrechat n entrechat m

entrée n entrée f

entremets n *cul* entremets m

entrench vt *mil ar* retrancher; *fig* ~ oneself s'établir; se défendre

entrenchment n retranchement m

entrepot n entrepôt m

entrepreneur n entrepreneur m

entrepreneurial adj d'entrepreneur

entrust vt (person) charger; (thing) confier

entry n entrée f; (list) inscription f; leg entrée f en possession, jouissance f; double ~ partie f double; no ~ entrée interdite; single ~ partie f simple

**entwine** *vt* enlacer, entrelacer; *vi* s'entre-lacer
**enumerate** *vt* énumérer
**enumeration** *n* énumération *f*
**enunciate** *vt* énoncer, articuler; proclamer, formuler
**enunciation** *n* énonciation *f*, articulation *f*; proclamation *f*
**enuresis** *n* énurésie *f*
**envelop** *vt* envelopper
**envelope** *n* enveloppe *f*
**envelopment** *n* enveloppement *m*; (wrapper) enveloppe *f*
**envenom** *vt* envenimer, empoisonner; (embitter) aigrir
**enviable** *adj* enviable
**envious** *adj* envieux -ieuse, jaloux -ouse
**environ** *vt* environner, entourer
**environment** *n* environnement *m*; milieu *m*
**environmental** *adj* écologique; environnemental
**environs** *npl* alentours *mpl*, environs *mpl*
**envisage** *vt* envisager, considérer
**envoy** *n poet* envoi *m*; émissaire *m*, plénipotentiaire *m*
**envy** *n* envie *f*; *vt* envier
**enwrap** *vt* envelopper
**enzyme** *n* enzyme *f*
**eon** *n* éon *m*
**epaulet, epaulette** *n mil* épaulette *f*
**epergne** *n* milieu *m* de table, surtout *m*
**ephemera** *n ent* éphémère *m*
**ephemeral** *adj* éphémère
**epic** *n* épopée *f*, poème *m* épique; *adj* épique
**epicene** *n* hermaphrodite *m*; *adj* hermaphrodite; *gramm* épicène
**epicentre** *n* épicentre *m*
**epicure** *n* gourmet *m*; épicurien -ienne
**epicurean** *n + adj* épicurien -ienne
**epicureanism** *n* épicurisme *m*
**epicycle** *n* épicycle *m*
**epidemic** *n* épidémie *f*; *adj* épidémique
**epidermal** *adj* épidermique
**epidermis** *n* épiderme *m*
**epidiascope** *n* épidiascope *m*
**epiglottis** *n anat* épiglotte *f*
**epigram** *n* épigramme *f*
**epigrammatic(al)** *adj* épigrammatique
**epigrammatist** *n* auteur *m* d'épigrammes
**epigraph** *n* épigraphe *f*
**epigraphy** *n* épigraphie *f*
**epilepsy** *n* épilepsie *f*
**epileptic** *n + adj* épileptique; ~ **fit** crise *f* d'épilepsie
**epilogue** *n* épilogue *m*
**Epiphany** *n eccles* Épiphanie *f*, jour *m* des Rois; **epiphany** *fig* moment transcendant

**episcopacy** *n* épiscopat *m*
**episcopal** *adj* épiscopal
**episcopalian** *adj* épiscopalien -ienne
**episcopate** *n* épiscopat *m*
**episode** *n* épisode *m*
**episodic** *adj* épisodique
**epistemology** *n* épistémologie *f*
**epistle** *n* épître *f*
**epistolary** *adj* épistolaire
**epitaph** *n* épitaphe *f*
**epithalamium** *n* épithalame *m*
**epithelium** *n biol + bot* épithélium *m*
**epithet** *n* épithète *f*
**epitome** *n* abrégé *m*, résumé *m*
**epitomize** *vt* abréger, faire un résumé de
**epoch** *n* époque *f*
**epoch-making** *adj* qui fait époque; très important
**eponymous** *adj* éponyme
**Epsom salts** *npl* sulfate *m* de magnésie
**equability** *n* uniformité *f*; sérénité *f*
**equable** *adj* uniforme; serein
**equal** *n* égal -e; *adj* égal; (capable) à la hauteur, de force; **other things being** ~ toutes choses égales; *vt* égaler, être l'égal de
**equality** *n* égalité *f*
**equalization** *n* égalisation *f*
**equalize** *vt* égaliser; *vi sp* égaliser
**equally** *adv* également, au même degré
**equanimity** *n* équanimité *f*, égalité *f* d'âme
**equate** *vt* égaler, donner comme équivalent; *math* mettre en équation
**equation** *n* égalisation *f*; *math + chem + astron* équation *f*
**equator** *n* équateur *m*
**equatorial** *adj* équatorial
**equerry** *n* officier *m* de la maison du roi; *ar* écuyer *m*
**equestrian** *n* cavalier -ière; *adj* équestre
**equidistant** *adj* équidistant
**equilateral** *n geom* figure équilatérale; *adj geom* équilatéral
**equilibrate** *vt* équilibrer; *vi* s'équilibrer
**equilibration** *n* équilibrage *m*
**equilibrist** *n* équilibriste
**equilibrium** *n* équilibre *m*, aplomb *m*
**equine** *adj* équin
**equinoctial** *adj* équinoxial, d'équinoxe
**equinox** *n* équinoxe *m*
**equip** *vt* équiper
**equipment** *n* équipement *m*, matériel *m*; (action) équipement *m*, aménagement *m*; (tools) outillage *m*; *naut* armement *m*
**equipoise** *n* équilibre *m*; (object) contrepoids *m*
**equitable** *adj* équitable
**equitation** *n* équitation *f*
**equity** *n* équité *f*; *comm* **equities** actions *fpl* ordinaires

**equivalence** n équivalence f

**equivalent** adj équivalent

**equivocal** adj équivoque, ambigu -uë, douteux -euse; (conduct) louche

**equivocate** vi équivoquer, biaiser

**equivocation** n ambiguïté f, faux-fuyant m

**equivocator** n ergoteur -euse

**era** n ère f

**eradicate** vt déraciner, extirper; (destroy) supprimer, détruire

**eradication** n éradication f; extirpation f

**erase** vt effacer, raturer, gommer

**eraser** n gomme f

**erasure** n rature f

**ere** prep + adv poet avant; conj avant que

**erect** adj droit, debout, dressé; vt dresser, mettre debout; archi ériger, construire; math élever

**erectile** adj érectile

**erection** n érection f; (building) bâtiment m

**erector** n mech ajusteur-monteur m (pl ajusteurs-monteurs); anat muscle érecteur

**erg** n erg m

**ergonomics** npl ergonomie f

**ergot** n bot ergot m

**ermine** n hermine f

**erode** vt éroder; corroder

**erosion** n érosion f

**erotic** adj érotique

**erotica** npl littérature f érotique

**eroticism** n érotisme m

**err** vi errer, se tromper; (sin) pécher

**errand** n course f, commission f

**errand-boy** n garçon m de courses

**errant** adj errant

**erratic** adj (odd) fantasque, excentrique, original; (results, performance) irrégulier -ière; geol + med erratique

**erratum** n (pl **errata**) erratum m (pl errata)

**erroneous** adj erroné, incorrect

**error** n erreur f, méprise f; opinion fausse; (sin) errement m, faute f; **in ~** par méprise; **printer's ~** coquille f; **see the ~ of one's ways** revenir de ses erreurs

**ersatz** n ersatz m

**Erse** n erse m, gaélique m

**erstwhile** adj ar d'autrefois; adv ar autrefois, jadis

**erubescence** n érubescence f

**erubescent** adj érubescent

**eruct, eructate** vi éructer

**eructation** n éructation f

**erudite** adj érudit

**erudition** n érudition f

**erupt** vi (volcano) faire éruption; fig se déchaîner; (teeth) percer

**eruption** n (volcano) éruption f; fig explosion f; (teeth) percée f; med éruption f

**eruptive** adj éruptif -ive

**erysipelas** n med érysipèle m

**escalade** vt escalader

**escalate** vt augmenter; intensifier; vi faire escalade; augmenter

**escalation** n escalade f

**escalator** n escalier roulant, escalier m mécanique

**escapade** n escapade f

**escape** n évasion f, action f d'échapper, fuite f; (leak) fuite f, échappement m; (pipe) tuyau m d'échappement; **leg ~ clause** échappatoire f; vt échapper à, fuir; vi s'échapper, s'enfuir, s'évader; (leak) s'échapper, fuir

**escapee** n évadé -e

**escapement** n mech échappement m

**escapism** n fig évasion f

**escapist** n personne f qui fuit la réalité; adj d'évasion

**escarpment** n escarpement m

**eschatology** n theol eschatologie f

**eschew** vt éviter, se détourner de

**escort** n escorte f; (male companion) cavalier m; vt escorter, accompagner

**escritoire** n secrétaire m

**escutcheon** n her + naut écusson m; **blot on one's ~** tache f sur son nom

**Eskimo** n Esquimau -aude; adj esquimau -aude

**esoteric** adj ésotérique

**espalier** n espalier m

**esparto** n spart(e) m, alfa m

**especial** adj spécial, particulier -ière

**especially** adv en particulier; (very) très, fort, spécialement

**Esperantist** n + adj espérantiste

**Esperanto** n espéranto m

**espionage** n espionnage m

**esplanade** n esplanade f, promenade f

**espousal** n épousailles fpl; fig ralliement m

**espouse** vt épouser; fig adopter, se rallier à

**espresso** n (café m) express m

**espy** vt discerner, apercevoir

**Esquire** n (abbr **Esq.**) (après le nom de famille sur une adresse) = Monsieur

**essay** n dissertation f, rédaction f, composition f; (attempt) essai m, tentative f; vt essayer; éprouver, mettre à l'essai

**essayist** n essayiste

**essence** n essence f

**essential** n essentiel m; adj essentiel -ielle

**essentially** adv essentiellement, au fond

**establish** vt établir, fonder, installer; fig établir, prouver, démontrer, faire reconnaître

**establishment** n établissement m, fondation f; institution f; fig établissement *m*, démonstration *f*; *coll pej* **the Establishment** l'establishment *m*, les gens *mpl* en place

**estate** *n* (land) propriété *f*, domaine *m*; (rank) état *m*; *leg* (possessions) biens *mpl*; *coll* **the fourth ~** la presse; **man's ~** l'âge *m* d'homme; **real ~** propriété foncière; *hist* **the Third Estate** le Tiers État

**estate-agency** *n* agence immobilière
**estate-agent** *n* agent immobilier
**estate-car** *n* break *m*
**esteem** *n* estime *f*; *vt* estimer, priser, considérer
**ester** *n chem* ester *m*
**esthete** *n see* **aesthete**
**esthetic** *adj see* **aesthetic**
**estimable** *adj* estimable, respectable
**estimate** *n* estimation *f*, évaluation *f*; *comm* devis *m*; *pol* **~s** crédits *mpl* budgétaires, budget *m*; *vt* estimer, évaluer; calculer; *fig* estimer, jauger
**estimation** *n* estimation *f*; (opinion) avis *m*, jugement *m*; (esteem) estime *f*
**estrange** *vt* s'aliéner l'estime (l'affection) de; détourner; **they have become ~d** ils sont brouillés
**estrangement** *n* désaffection *f*, éloignement *m*, brouille *f*
**estuary** *n* estuaire *m*
**etcetera** *n* (*abbr* **etc**) et caetera (cetera) *m invar*; **~s** extras *mpl*
**etch** *vt* graver
**etching** *n* gravure *f*
**eternal** *adj* éternel -elle, sans fin; (without change) éternel -elle, immuable; (endless) éternel -elle, incessant; **Eternal City** = Rome *f*; **~ triangle** ménage *m* à trois
**eternalize** *vt* éterniser; rendre immortel -elle
**eternity** *n* éternité *f*
**ethane** *n chem* éthane *m*
**ether** *n chem* + *phys* éther *m*; *fig ar* ciel *m* (*pl* cieux)
**ethereal** *adj* éthéré, céleste, léger -ère; *chem* éthéré
**etherealize** *vt* rendre éthéré, spiritualiser
**etherize** *vt* éthériser
**ethic** *n* éthique *f*, morale *f*; *adj* éthique
**ethical** *adj* éthique, moral
**ethics** *npl* éthique *f*
**Ethiopian** *n* Ethiopien -ienne; *adj* éthiopien -ienne
**ethnic(al)** *adj* ethnique
**ethnographer** *n* ethnographe
**ethnographic** *adj* ethnographique
**ethnography** *n* ethnographie *f*
**ethnological** *adj* ethnologique
**ethnologist** *n* ethnologue
**ethnology** *n* ethnologie *f*
**ethology** *n* éthologie *f*

**ethos** *n* caractéristiques morales (d'un groupe, d'une société)
**ethyl** *n chem* éthyle *m*
**ethylene** *n chem* éthylène *m*
**etiolate** *vt* étioler
**etiology** *n* étiologie *f*
**etiquette** *n* étiquette *f*, protocole *m*; bonnes manières; **medical ~** déontologie médicale
**Eton crop** *n phr* coiffure *f* à la garçonne
**etymological** *adj* étymologique
**etymologize** *vi* étudier l'étymologie; proposer une étymologie
**etymology** *n* étymologie *f*
**etymon** *n* étymon *m*
**eucalyptus** *n* eucalyptus *m*
**Eucharist** *n* Eucharistie *f*
**Euclidean** *adj* euclidien -ienne
**eugenic** *adj* eugénique
**eugenics** *npl* eugénique *f*
**eugenist** *n* eugéniste
**eulogist** *n* panégyriste
**eulogistic** *adj* laudatif -ive
**eulogize** *vt* louer hautement, exalter
**eulogy** *n* panégyrique *m*
**eunuch** *n* eunuque *m*
**euphemism** *n* euphémisme *m*
**euphemistic** *adj* euphémique
**euphemize** *vt* exprimer par un euphémisme; *vi* se servir d'euphémismes
**euphonious** *adj* euphonique
**euphonium** *n* saxhorn *m*
**euphony** *n* euphonie *f*
**euphorbia** *n bot* euphorbe *f*
**euphoria** *n* euphorie *f*
**euphoric** *adj* euphorique
**euphuism** *n* euphuisme *m*
**Eurasia** *n* Eurasie *f*
**Eurasian** *n* Eurasien -ienne; *adj* eurasien -ienne
**eurhythmics** *npl* gymnastique *f* rythmique
**Europe** *n* Europe *f*
**European** *n* Européen -éenne; *adj* européen -éenne
**Eurovision** *n* Eurovision *f*; **on ~** en Eurovision
**Eustachian** *adj anat* **~ tube** trompe *f* d'Eustache
**euthanasia** *n* euthanasie *f*
**evacuate** *vt* évacuer
**evacuation** *n* évacuation *f*
**evacuee** *n* évacué -e
**evade** *vt* éviter, éluder, échapper à
**evaluate** *vt* évaluer
**evaluation** *n* évaluation *f*
**evanesce** *vi* disparaître
**evanescence** *n* évanescence *f*
**evanescent** *adj* évanescent
**evangelic, evangelical** *adj* évangélique
**evangelical** *n* protestant -e évangélique
**evangelism** *n* évangélisme *m*

**evangelist** n évangéliste m
**evangelize** vt évangéliser
**evaporate** vt évaporer, faire évaporer; vi s'évaporer; fig disparaître
**evaporation** n évaporation f
**evaporator** n évaporateur m
**evasion** n évasion f, dérobade f; (excuse) faux-fuyant m
**evasive** adj évasif -ive
**evasiveness** n (reply) caractère évasif
**eve** n veille f
**¹even** n ar soir m
**²even** adj (smooth) uni, plat; (equal) uniforme, égal; (calm) tranquille, calme, serein, équilibré; (like) semblable, identique; (right) juste, équitable; math pair; adv même; ~ so précisément; vt aplanir, unifier, égaliser
**even-handed** adj impartial, équitable
**evening** n soir m; soirée f; ~ **dress** tenue f de soirée; ~ **gown** robe f de soirée; **the** ~ **before** la veille au soir
**evenness** n égalité f, uniformité f
**evensong** n eccles = vêpres fpl
**event** n événement m; conséquence f, résultat m; sp épreuve f; **after the** ~ après coup; **at all** ~ **s** en tout cas; **in the** ~ **of** au cas où
**even-tempered** adj calme, placide, d'humeur égale
**eventful** adj mémorable, important; (full of incidents) mouvementé
**eventide** n poet soir m
**eventual** adj final; éventuel -elle
**eventuality** n éventualité f
**ever** adv jamais; toujours; coll ~ **so** très; coll ~ **so much** beaucoup; **for** ~ pour toujours, sans cesse; **if** ~ **there was one** s'il en fut jamais; **what** ~ **can I say?** qu'est-ce que je peux bien dire?; **when** ~? quand donc?; **yours** ~ bien cordialement vôtre
**evergreen** n arbre toujours vert; adj toujours vert
**everlasting** adj éternel -elle, sans fin; (repeated) perpétuel -uelle, incessant
**evermore** adv toujours
**every** adj chaque, chacun de, tout; tous (f toutes) les; ~ **now and then** de temps en temps; ~ **other** tous (f toutes) les deux
**everybody** n chacun, tout le monde, tous
**everyday** adj de tous les jours; habituel -elle
**everyone** n chacun, tout le monde, tous
**everything** n tout m, toutes choses
**everyway** adv de toutes manières
**everywhere** adv partout
**evict** vt leg expulser
**eviction** n leg éviction f
**evidence** n leg déposition f, témoignage m, preuve f; (clearness) évidence f;

(sign) marque f; **circumstantial** ~ preuves indirectes; **turn queen's (king's)** ~ témoigner contre un complice
**evident** adj évident, clair
**evidently** adv évidemment, manifestement
**evil** n mal m; malheur m, désastre m; adj mauvais, méchant; (causing harm) néfaste, nuisible; **the Evil One** le Malin
**evil-doer** n malfaiteur m, méchant -e
**evilly** adv mal
**evil-minded** adj malintentionné, malveillant
**evince** vt montrer, démontrer
**eviscerate** vt éviscérer, éventrer; fig affaiblir, vider de sa substance
**evocation** n évocation f
**evocative** adj évocateur -trice
**evoke** vt évoquer, rappeler
**evolution** n évolution f, développement m
**evolutionary** adj d'évolution
**evolutionism** n évolutionnisme m
**evolve** vt faire évoluer, développer; vi évoluer, se développer
**ewe** n brebis f
**ewer** n broc m
**exacerbate** vt exacerber, exaspérer, irriter
**exacerbation** n exacerbation f
**¹exact** adj exact, précis, juste, rigoureux -euse
**²exact** vt exiger, demander; extorquer
**exacting** adj (person) exigeant; (task) ardu, dur, pénible
**exaction** n exaction f, extorsion f
**exactitude** n exactitude f, précision f
**exactly** adv exactement, précisément; interj parfaitement!
**exactness** n exactitude f
**exaggerate** vt + vi exagérer; (fashion, etc) outrer
**exaggeration** n exagération f
**exalt** vt exalter, glorifier, porter aux nues
**exaltation** n exaltation f, glorification f; (excitement) transport m, excitation f
**exalted** adj noble, élevé; (elated) exalté
**exam** n coll abbr examen m
**examination** n examen m; inspection f, contrôle m; leg instruction f; (customs) visite f; leg cross- ~ interrogatoire m; **medical** ~ visite médicale
**examine** vt examiner, inspecter, contrôler; leg (case) instruire, (witness) interroger; (baggage) visiter
**examinee** n candidat -e
**examiner** n examinateur -trice, membre m du jury (d'examen)
**example** n exemple m; **for** ~ par exemple; **make an** ~ **of** punir de façon exemplaire; **set an** ~ donner

l'exemple; **without** ~ sans précédent
**exasperate** *vt* exaspérer; aggraver
**exasperating** *adj* exaspérant, énervant
**exasperation** *n* exaspération *f*; fureur *f*
**excavate** *vt* creuser; *vi arch* faire des fouilles
**excavation** *n* creusement *m*; *arch* fouilles *fpl*
**excavator** *n* personne *f* qui creuse; (machine) excavateur *m*, excavatrice *f*
**exceed** *vt* excéder, dépasser, surpasser; *vi* dépasser les bornes
**exceeding** *adj* très grand
**exceedingly** *adv* extrêmement
**excel** *vt* surpasser, dépasser; *vi* exceller
**excellence** *n* excellence *f*, supériorité *f*, mérite *m*
**excellency** *n* excellence *f*
**excellent** *adj* excellent
**except** *vt* excepter; *prep* excepté, hormis, sauf; ~ **for** sauf; *conj ar* à moins que, sauf que
**excepting** *prep* hormis, sauf, à l'exception de
**exception** *n* exception *f*; **take** ~ élever des objections, trouver à redire; **with certain** ~ s sauf exceptions
**exceptionable** *adj* critiquable, blâmable
**exceptional** *adj* exceptionnel -elle, rare, remarquable
**excerpt** *n* extrait *m*, fragment *m*, morceau choisi; *vt* extraire, choisir
**excess** *n* excès *m*; (quantity) excédent *m*; (charge) supplément *m*; *adj* excédentaire
**excessive** *adj* excessif -ive
**exchange** *n* échange *m*, troc *m*; (telephone) central *m*; (currency) change *m*; **Stock Exchange** Bourse *f*; *vt* échanger, troquer; (currency) changer; *vi* s'échanger
**exchequer** *n hist* échiquier *m*; trésor public; **Chancellor of the Exchequer** = ministre *m* des Finances
**excisable** *adj* imposable
¹**excise** *n* impôt indirect; *vt* imposer
²**excise** *vt* exciser, retrancher
**exciseman** *n* employé *m* des contributions indirectes
**excision** *n* excision *f*; *fig* rejet *m*
**excitable** *adj* excitable
**excitant** *n* excitant *m*
**excitation** *n* excitation *f*
**excite** *vt* exciter, agiter; inciter, stimuler, émouvoir; **get** ~ **d** s'exciter
**excitement** *n* excitation *f*, agitation *f*, fièvre *f*
**exciting** *adj* excitant, émouvant, passionnant, impressionnant
**exclaim** *vi* s'écrier, s'exclamer; ~ **against** protester contre
**exclamation** *n* exclamation *f*; ~ **mark**

point *m* d'exclamation
**exclamatory** *adj* exclamatif -ive
**exclude** *vt* exclure, rejeter; (prevent) empêcher
**excluding** *prep* à l'exclusion de
**exclusion** *n* exclusion *f*
**exclusive** *adj* exclusif -ive; snob *invar*; (keeping others out) fermé, select (no *f*); ~ **of** sans compter; **mutually** ~ incompatible
**exclusiveness** *n* exclusivité *f*
**excogitate** *vt* imaginer, combiner
**excommunicate** *vt* excommunier
**excommunication** *n* excommunication *f*
**excoriate** *vt* excorier, écorcher
**excoriation** *n* excoriation *f*, écorchure *f*
**excrement** *n* excrément *m*
**excremential** *adj* excrémentiel -ielle
**excrescence** *n* excroissance *f*
**excrescent** *adj* qui forme une excroissance, superflu
**excreta** *npl* excrétions *fpl*
**excrete** *vt* excréter; (plant) sécréter
**excretion** *n* excrétion *f*; (plant) sécrétion *f*
**excretory** *adj* excréteur -trice
**excruciate** *vt* torturer, mettre au supplice
**excruciating** *adj* très douloureux -euse; atroce
**excruciation** *n* supplice *m*, torture *f*
**exculpate** *vt* disculper
**exculpation** *n* disculpation *f*
**excursion** *n* excursion *f*; *obs mil* sortie *f*; *fig* digression *f*; *fig* **alarms and** ~ s confusion *f*, commotion *f*
**excursionist** *n* excursionniste
**excursive** *adj* décousu, digressif -ive
**excursus** *n* digression *f*, appendice *m*
**excusable** *adj* excusable
**excuse** *n* excuse *f*, prétexte *m*; *vt* excuser; pardonner; dispenser, exempter; ~ **me** pardon, permettez
**execrable** *adj* exécrable, abominable
**execrate** *vt* exécrer, détester
**execration** *n* exécration *f*, détestation *f*
**executant** *n* exécutant -e
**execute** *vt* exécuter, accomplir; (criminal, will, etc) exécuter
**execution** *n* exécution *f*, accomplissement *m*; *leg* (criminal, will, etc) exécution *f*
**executioner** *n* bourreau *m*; *hist* exécuteur *m* des hautes œuvres
**executive** *n* (pouvoir *m*) exécutif *m*; (person) administrateur -trice; *adj* exécutif -ive
**executor** *n leg* exécuteur *m* testamentaire
**executrix** *n leg* exécutrice *f* testamentaire
**exegesis** *n* exégèse *f*
**exegetic** *adj* exégétique
**exegetics** *npl* exégétique *f*

**exemplar** *n* modèle *m*

**exemplary** *adj* exemplaire, parfait; (warning) exemplaire

**exemplification** *n* exemple *m*, illustration *f* au moyen d'exemples; *leg* ampliation *f*

**exempt** *adj* exempt; *vt* exempter

**exemption** *n* exemption *f*

**exercise** *n* exercice *m*; (task) devoir *m*; *vt* exercer; (puzzle) rendre perplexe; *vi* s'exercer, faire de l'exercice

**exert** *vt* employer, déployer, exercer; ~ oneself se dépenser, se donner du mal, se remuer

**exertion** *n* effort *m*; emploi *m*, usage *m*

**exfoliate** *vt* exfolier

**exfoliation** *n* exfoliation *f*

**exhalation** *n* exhalaison *f*; émanation *f*, effluve *m*

**exhale** *vt* exhaler, émettre, évaporer; *vi* expirer

**exhaust** *n* échappement *m*; tuyau *m* d'échappement; *vt* épuiser, exténuer; (use up) épuiser; vider; *fig* (subject) épuiser

**exhaustible** *adj* épuisable

**exhausting** *adj* exténuant, épuisant

**exhaustion** *n* épuisement *m*, grande fatigue

**exhaustive** *adj* exhaustif -ive

**exhaust-pipe** *n* tuyau *m* d'échappement

**exhibit** *n* objet exposé; *leg* document *m*; *vt* exhiber, exposer, montrer; *leg* exhiber; *vi* faire une exposition

**exhibition** *n* exposition *f*; *leg* exhibition *f*; (education) bourse *f*

**exhibitionism** *n* exhibitionnisme *m*

**exhibitor** *n* exposant -e

**exhilarate** *vt* animer, vivifier, émoustiller

**exhilarating** *adj* vivifiant, émoustillant

**exhilaration** *n* gaieté *f* de cœur, animation *f*, joie *f* de vivre

**exhort** *vt* exhorter, inciter; recommander; avertir

**exhortation** *n* exhortation *f*

**exhumation** *n* exhumation *f*

**exhume** *vt* exhumer

**exigence, exigency** *n* exigence *f*, urgence *f*; nécessité *f*

**exigent** *adj* urgent, exigeant

**exiguity** *n* exiguïté *f*

**exiguous** *adj* exigu -uë

**exiguousness** *n* exiguïté *f*

**exile** *n* exil *m*, bannissement *m*; (person) exilé -e; *vt* exiler, bannir

**existence** *n* existence *f*

**existent** *adj* existant

**existential** *adj* existentiel -ielle

**existentialism** *n* *philos* existentialisme *m*

**existentialist** *n* + *adj* *philos* existentialiste

**exit** *n* sortie *f*; *vi* sortir; *fig* mourir

**exodus** *n* exode *m*

**ex-officio** *adj* nommé d'office; *adv* ex officio, d'office

**exonerate** *vt* exonérer, dispenser; (blame) disculper

**exoneration** *n* exonération *f*, dispense *f*; (blame) disculpation *f*

**exorbitance** *n* extravagance *f*

**exorbitant** *adj* exorbitant, extravagant

**exorcism** *n* exorcisme *m*

**exorcist** *n* exorciste

**exordium** *n* exorde *m*

**exoteric** *adj* exotérique, populaire

**exotic** *adj* exotique

**expand** *vt* étendre, élargir; développer; *physiol* dilater; *vi* s'étendre, s'élargir; se développer, s'épanouir; *physiol* se dilater

**expander** *n* extenseur *m*

**expanse** *n* étendue *f*

**expansible** *adj* expansible, extensible

**expansion** *n* expansion *f*, extension *f*; élargissement *m*; *fig* développement *m*

**expansionism** *n* expansionnisme *m*

**expansive** *adj* expansible; *phys* expansif -ive; *fig* expansif -ive, démonstratif -ive

**expatiate** *vi* disserter, discourir, s'étendre

**expatiation** *n* long discours, dissertation *f*

**expatriate** *n* + *adj* expatrié -e; *vt* expatrier, exiler

**expatriation** *n* expatriation *f*

**expect** *vt* attendre, compter sur; *coll* supposer, présumer; *coll* be ~ing être enceinte; **know what to** ~ savoir à quoi s'en tenir

**expectancy** *n* attente *f*, expectative *f*; (possession) espérance *f*

**expectant** *adj* d'attente, d'expectative, expectant; ~ **mother** femme enceinte

**expectation** *n* expectative *f*; perspective *f*, probabilité *f*; espérance *f*; ~ **of life** espérance *f* de vie

**expectorant** *n* expectorant *m*; *adj* expectorant

**expectorate** *vt* expectorer, cracher; *vi* cracher

**expectoration** *n* expectoration *f*

**expedience, expediency** *n* convenance *f*, à-propos *m*; opportunité *f*; opportunisme *m*

**expedient** *n* expédient *m*; *adj* expédient, politique; avantageux -euse

**expedite** *vt* accélérer, activer; expédier

**expedition** *n* expédition *f*

**expeditionary** *adj* *mil* expéditionnaire

**expeditious** *adj* prompt, expéditif -ive

**expel** *vt* expulser, refouler; (school) renvoyer

**expend** *vt* dépenser

**expendable** *adj* remplaçable, de

consommation; *mil* à sacrifier
**expenditure** *n* dépense *f*
**expense** *n* dépense *f*; prix *m*; *fig* dépens *mpl*; ~ s frais *mpl*; ~ **account** frais *mpl* de représentation; **at the** ~ **of** aux dépens de
**expensive** *adj* coûteux -euse, cher (*f* chère)
**experience** *n* expérience *f*; *vt* éprouver, faire l'expérience de
**experiment** *n* expérience *f*; *vi* expérimenter, faire une expérience
**experimental** *adj* expérimental
**experimentalist** *n* expérimentateur -trice
**experimenter** *n* expérimentateur -trice
**expert** *n* expert *m*, spécialiste; *adj* expert, habile, adroit
**expertise** *n* expertise *f*
**expertly** *adv* de façon experte
**expertness** *n* adresse *f*, habileté *f*
**expiable** *adj* expiable
**expiate** *vt* expier
**expiation** *n* expiation *f*
**expiatory** *adj* expiatoire
**expiration** *n* expiration *f*
**expiratory** *adj* expirateur -trice
**expire** *vt* + *vi* expirer
**expiry** *n* expiration *f*
**explain** *vt* expliquer, élucider; expliquer, donner l'explication de; ~ **away** justifier, rendre raison de; ~ **oneself** s'expliquer
**explanation** *n* explication *f*, éclaircissement *m*
**explanatory** *adj* explicatif -ive
**expletive** *n* juron *m*; *gramm* explétif *m*; *adj* superflu; *gramm* explétif -ive
**explicable** *adj* explicable
**explicate** *vt* expliquer, élucider
**explication** *n* explication *f*, élucidation *f*
**explicative**, **explicatory** *adj* explicatif -ive
**explicit** *adj* explicite, défini, clair; (outspoken) catégorique
**explicitness** *n* précision *f*, caractère *m* explicite
**explode** *vt* faire exploser, faire sauter, faire détoner; *fig* réfuter, discréditer; *vi* exploser, sauter
¹**exploit** *n* exploit *m*, haut fait
²**exploit** *vt* exploiter
**exploitable** *adj* exploitable
**exploitation** *n* exploitation *f*
**exploiter** *n* (developer, cultivator) exploitant -e; *pej* exploiteur -euse
**exploration** *n* exploration *f*
**exploratory** *adj* de recherche, de découverte; exploratoire
**explore** *vt* explorer; *vi* faire des explorations
**explorer** *n* explorateur -trice
**explosion** *n* explosion *f*

**explosive** *n* explosif *m*; *phon* explosive *f*; *adj* explosif -ive
**exponent** *n* interprète, explicateur -trice; *math* exposant *m*
**export** *n* exportation *f*; (goods) article *m* d'exportation; *adj* d'exportation; *vt* exporter
**exportable** *adj* exportable
**exportation** *n* exportation *f*
**exporter** *n* exportateur -trice
**expose** *vt* exposer, mettre au jour; (crime, scandal) dévoiler
**exposé** *n* exposé *m*, relation *f*; révélation *f*, mise *f* à jour
**exposed** *adj* exposé, ouvert, sans protection; révélé, dévoilé
**exposition** *n* exposition *f*; explication *f*, exposé *m*
**expositor** *n* commentateur -trice, interprète
**expository** *adj* descriptif -ive
**expostulate** *vi* protester
**expostulation** *n* remontrance *f*
**exposure** *n* exposition *f*; *phot* pose *f*; *fig* révélation *f*; *phot* ~ **meter** posemètre *m*; **indecent** ~ attentat *m* à la pudeur
**expound** *vt* expliquer, interpréter, exposer
¹**express** *n* (railway) rapide *m*; (letter) exprès *m*; *adj* exprès (*f* expresse); (railway) rapide; *adv* par exprès; très rapidement
²**express** *vt* exprimer, émettre, formuler, communiquer; ~ **oneself** s'exprimer
**expressible** *adj* exprimable
**expression** *n* expression *f*
**expressionism** *n* expressionnisme *m*
**expressionist** *n* + *adj* expressionniste
**expressionistic** *adj* expressionniste
**expressive** *adj* expressif -ive, significatif -ive
**expressly** *adv* expressément, explicitement, exprès
**expropriate** *vt* déposséder; *leg* exproprier
**expropriation** *n* expropriation *f*
**expulsion** *n* expulsion *f*; (school, etc) renvoi *m*
**expunge** *vt* effacer, supprimer
**expurgate** *vt* expurger
**expurgation** *n* expurgation *f*
**expurgator** *n* celui (celle) qui expurge
**exquisite** *n* dandy *m*; *ar* petit-maître (*pl* petits-maîtres); *adj* exquis, délicat, parfait, raffiné
**exquisiteness** *n* perfection *f*, délicatesse *f*
**ex-serviceman** *n* ancien combattant
**extant** *adj* existant, qui existe encore, subsistant
**extemporaneous**, **extemporary**, **extempore** *adj* improvisé, impromptu
**extemporaneously**, **extemporarily**,

**extempore** adv impromptu, à l'improviste

**extemporization** n improvisation f

**extemporize** vt + vi improviser

**extend** vt étendre, allonger, prolonger; fig (help, comfort) apporter, offrir; (sympathy) manifester; vi s'étendre; se prolonger

**extendible, extensible, extensile** adj extensible

**extension** n extension f, étendue f, prolongement m; (building) annexe f; (time) prolongation f; (telephone) poste m; carp rallonge f; ~ **ladder** échelle f à coulisse

**extensive** adj étendu, vaste; compréhensif -ive

**extensor** n anat extenseur m

**extent** n étendue f; (dimension) grandeur f, longueur f; (degree) mesure f, portée f; **to some** ~ dans une certaine mesure; **to such an** ~ **that** à tel point que; **to the full** ~ entièrement, le maximum possible

**extenuate** vt diminuer, atténuer, minimiser

**extenuating** adj ~ **circumstances** circonstances atténuantes

**extenuation** n diminution f, atténuation f

**exterior** n extérieur m; adj extérieur, du dehors

**exteriorize** vt psych extérioriser

**exterminate** vt exterminer

**extermination** n extermination f

**exterminator** n exterminateur -trice

**exterminatory** adj exterminateur -trice

**external** n extérieur m; ~s apparences fpl; adj extérieur, du dehors; visible; superficiel -ielle; med externe

**externalization** n extériorisation f

**externalize** vt extérioriser

**extinct** adj éteint, disparu

**extinction** n extinction f

**extinguish** vt éteindre

**extinguisher** n (fire) extincteur m; (candle) éteignoir m

**extirpate** vt extirper, déraciner

**extirpation** n extirpation f, déracinement m

**extirpator** n agr extirpateur m, scarificateur m

**extol** vt exalter, porter aux nues

**extort** vt extorquer, soutirer; arracher

**extortion** n extorsion f, exaction f

**extortionate** adj exorbitant, excessif -ive

**extra** n extra m, supplément m; (newspaper) édition spéciale; theat + cin figurant -e; adj supplémentaire; adv en plus, en sus, en supplément; extra, d'extra

**extract** n extrait m; cul extrait m, concentré m; vt extraire; (money) extorquer, soutirer; (promise) arracher

**extractable** adj qu'on peut extraire

**extraction** n extraction f

**extractor** n extracteur m

**extraditable** adj susceptible d'extradition

**extradite** vt extrader

**extradition** n extradition f

**extramural** adj extra-muros invar; (course) hors faculté

**extraneous** adj étranger -ère

**extraordinariness** n extraordinaire m

**extraordinary** adj extraordinaire, rare, remarquable, exceptionnel -elle

**extrapolate** vt + vi extrapoler

**extrapolation** n extrapolation f

**extrasensory** adj extra-sensoriel -ielle

**extra-special** adj coll très spécial, extra

**extraterritorial** adj d'extra-territorialité

**extraterritoriality** n extra-territorialité f

**extravagance** n extravagance f; prodigalité f; dévergondage m

**extravagant** adj extravagant; prodigal; dévergondé

**extravaganza** n theat + mus fantaisie f; débauche f d'imagination; histoire abracadabrante

**extravasation** n med extravasation f

**extraversion** n see extroversion

**extravert** n + adj see extrovert

**extreme** n extrême m; (extremity) extrémité f; plus haut point; **go to** ~**s** pousser les choses à l'extrême; **in the** ~ à l'extrême; adj extrême; dernier -ière, le plus éloigné; intense; excessif -ive, abusif -ive; rigoureux -euse, sévère; ~ **penalty** peine f de mort; ~ **unction** extrême-onction f

**extremely** adv extrêmement, très

**extremism** n extrémisme m

**extremist** n + adj extrémiste

**extremity** n extrémité f

**extricate** vt dégager, libérer

**extrication** n dégagement m, libération f

**extrinsic** adj extrinsèque

**extroversion, extraversion** n extroversion f, extraversion f

**extrovert, extravert** n + adj extraverti -e, extroverti -e

**extrude** vt mech refouler; expulser

**extrusion** n mech extrusion f

**exuberance, exuberancy** n exubérance f

**exuberant** adj exubérant; luxuriant, abondant

**exude** vt + vi exsuder

**exult** vi exulter, se réjouir

**exultancy** n exultation f

**exultant** adj exultant, triomphant

**exultation** n exultation f

**eye** n œil m (pl yeux); vision f; estimation f, faculté f d'observation; fig point m de vue, jugement *m*; (needle) chas *m*; *elect* + *bot* + *zool* œil *m*; (loop) œillet *m*; *mil* — s front! fixe!; *mil* — s right! tête à droite!; *coll* all my — baliver- nes!; **be in the public** — être très en vue; *sl* **do in the** — gâcher; *coll* **easy on the** — agréable à reluquer; **glad** — regard lascif; **have an** — **for** remar- quer; être bon juge de; *naut* **in the** — **of the wind** contre le vent; **keep an** — **on** surveiller; protéger; **keep one's** — s **open (skinned, peeled)** ouvrir l'œil; **make** — s **at** faire de l'œil à; *sl* **my** — ! mince alors!; (contradiction) mon œil!; **open the** — s **of s/o** faire com- prendre à qn; **see** — **to** — **with** être complètement d'accord avec; **see with half an** — voir facilement; **sheep's** — s yeux *mpl* de merlan frit, regards amou- reux; **the mind's** — l'imagination *f*; **turn a blind** — **to** ignorer; **up to the** — s **in** très occupé avec, débordé de; **with an** — **to** en prévision de; *vt* dévisager; regarder souvent

**eyeball** *n* globe *m* de l'œil, globe *m* oculaire; — **to** — face à face

**eye-bath** *n* bain *m* oculaire, œillère *f*

**eyebrow** *n* sourcil *m*; **not raise an** — ne pas sourciller

**eyeful** *n* ce qu'on peut voir d'un regard; *coll* **get an** — se rincer l'œil, s'en mettre plein la vue

**eye-glass** *n* monocle *m*; — es pince-nez *m*

**eyelash** *n* cil *m*

**eyelet** *n* œillet *m*

**eyelid** *n* paupière *f*

**eye-opener** *n coll* révélation surprenante

**eyepiece** *n* oculaire *m*

**eyeshade** *n* visière *f*

**eyeshadow** *n* rimmel *m*

**eyeshot** *n* portée *f* du regard

**eyesight** *n* vue *f*

**eyesore** *n* objet déplaisant, ce qui blesse la vue; *coll* horreur *f*

**eye-tooth** *n* (dent) canine *f*; **cut one's eye-teeth** sortir de l'enfance

**eyewash** *n med* collyre *m*; *coll* boniment *m*, bourrage *m* de crâne

**eye-witness** *n* témoin *m* oculaire

**eyot** *n* îlot *m*

**eyrie** *n* aire *f*, nid *m* d'aigle

# F

**fa** *n mus* fa *m*

**fab** *adj sl* sensas

**fable** *n* fable *f*; légende *f*, mythe *m*; in- vention *f*

**fabled** *adj* légendaire, fabuleux -euse; inventé

**fabric** *n* structure *f*, charpente *f*; (cloth) tissu *m*, étoffe *f*; *archi* édifice *m*; *fig* base *f*

**fabricate** *vt* construire, fabriquer; in- venter; *pej* fabriquer, forger

**fabrication** *n* invention *f*; *pej* fabrica- tion *f*

**fabricator** *n* constructeur *m*; *pej* fabrica- teur -trice, faussaire

**fabulist** *n* fabuliste *m*

**fabulous** *adj* fabuleux -euse; *coll* mer- veilleux -euse, sensationnel -elle

**façade** *n* façade *f*

**face** *n* visage *m*, figure *f*, face *f*; expres- sion *f*, mine *f*, contenance *f*; grimace *f*; (impudence) effronterie *f*, toupet *m*;

apparence *f*; (surface) surface *f*, plat *m*, face *f*; (clock) cadran *m*; *typ* œil *m*; (coal) front *m* de taille; — **to** — face à face; — **value** valeur nominale; **fly in the** — **of** défier; **have the** — **to** avoir le toupet (culot) de; **in the** — **of** opposé à, au nez de; **keep a straight** — garder son sérieux; **look s/o in the** — faire face à qn; **lose** — perdre contenance, perdre la face; **make (pull) a** — grimacer; **on the** — **of it** apparemment; **pull (wear) a long** — faire triste mine; **put a bold** — **on** faire bonne contenance devant; **save one's** — sauver les apparences (la face); **set one's** — **against** opposer résolument; **show one's** — faire une apparition; **to one's** — ouvertement; *vt* faire face à, regarder; affronter, faire front à, se trouver devant; (surface) revêtir; (stone) aplanir; (window) donner sur; — **both ways** ménager la chèvre et le chou; — **out** payer

face-ache

d'audace; ~ **the music** répondre de ses actions; *vi* être tourné vers; être orienté à; *US mil* ~ **about** faire demi-tour; ~ **up to** faire face à

**face-ache** *n* névralgie faciale
**face-cloth** *n* gant *m* de toilette
**face-cream** *n* crème *f* de toilette
**faceless** *adj pej* anonyme
**face-lifting** *n* chirurgie *f* esthétique du visage, lifting *m*
**face-pack** *n* masque *m* anti-rides
**face-powder** *n* poudre *f* de riz
**facer** *n coll* (blow) gifle *f*; problème *m*, difficultés *fpl*
**facet** *n* facette *f*; *fig* aspect *m*
**facetious** *adj* facétieux -ieuse
**facetiousness** *n* bouffonnerie *f*, humeur facétieuse
**facial** *n* traitement *m* anti-rides (du visage); *adj* facial, du visage
**facile** *adj* facile, aisé; influençable, accommodant; (talk) patelin, coulant; superficiel -ielle
**facilitate** *vt* faciliter
**facility** *n* facilité *f*, aisance *f*; talent *m*, aptitude *f*; dextérité *f*; **facilities** facilités *fpl*, possibilités *fpl*
**facing** *n bui* revêtement *m*; ~ **s** parements *mpl*
**facsimile** *n* fac-similé *m*
**fact** *n* fait *m*; réalité *f*, vérité *f*; *leg* fait *m*; ~ **and fiction** le vrai et le faux; **as a matter of** ~, **in point of** ~ de fait, à vrai dire, en réalité; **know for a** ~ savoir de source sûre; **stick to the** ~ **s** s'en tenir aux faits; **the** ~ **of the matter is that** le fait est que; **the** ~ **remains that** le fait est que
**fact-finding** *adj* qui enquête
**faction** *n* faction *f*
**factious** *adj* factieux -ieuse, séditieux -ieuse
**factiousness** *n* esprit *m* de faction
**factitious** *adj* factice
¹**factor** *n* facteur *m*; *math* **common** ~ facteur commun
²**factor** *n comm* agent *m* de vente; (Scotland) intendant *m*
**factorial** *adj math* factoriel -ielle
**factory** *n* usine *f*, fabrique *f*; (trading-post) comptoir *m*
**factotum** *n* factotum *m*
**factual** *adj* effectif -ive, réel -elle, positif -ive
**facultative** *adj* facultatif -ive
**faculty** *n* faculté *f*; (ability) don *m*; *eccles* dispense *f*
**fad** *n* marotte *f*, manie *f*
**faddy** *adj* capricieux -ieuse
**fade** *n rad* fading *m*; *cin* fondu *m*; *vt* faner, flétrir, décolorer; *vi* se faner, se flétrir; (colours) déteindre, pâlir; *fig*

s'évanouir, disparaître; ~ **away** mourir, s'éteindre
**fadeless** *adj* (cloth) bon teint *invar*
**faecal, fecal** *adj med* fécal
**faeces, feces** *npl med* fèces *fpl*
**faerie, faery** *n lit* pays *m* des fées; *adj* féerique
**fag** *n coll* corvée *f*; fatigue *f*; *sl* cigarette *f*, clope *m*, sèche *f*; (school) petit *m* (qui fait des corvées pour les grands); *vt* éreinter, fatiguer; *vi* s'éreinter, se fatiguer
**fag-end** *n* mégot *m*; *fig* bout *m*
**fagged** *adj* crevé
**faggot** *n* fagot *m*; *bui*+*mil* fascine *f*; *cul* boulette *f* de foie; *sl* pédé *m*; *vt* fagoter
**Fahrenheit** *n* Fahrenheit *m*; *adj* Fahrenheit *invar*
**faience** *n* faïence *f*
**fail** *n* échec *m*; faute *f*; **without** ~ sans faute; *vt* (test, examination) échouer à, *coll* rater; (candidate) refuser, *coll* coller; (let down) manquer à; (omit) omettre, négliger; *vi* manquer, faillir; négliger, omettre; échouer; baisser, diminuer; *comm* faire faillite; *mech* tomber en panne; ~ **to do sth** ne pas réussir à faire qch
**failing** *n* faiblesse *f*, défaut *m*, faute *f*; *prep* sans, à défaut de, faute de
**failsafe** *adj* à sûreté intégrale
**failure** *n* échec *m*; (person) raté -e; négligence *f*; manque *m*; *mech* panne *f*
**fain** *adj ar* prêt, disposé; ~ **to** obligé à; *adv* heureusement
**faint** *n* évanouissement *m*, pâmoison *f*; *adj* faible, sans vigueur, timide; vague, indistinct, peu clair; défaillant, prêt à s'évanouir; *vi* s'évanouir; (weaken) s'affaiblir
**faint-hearted** *adj* peureux -euse, pusillanime, timide
**fainting** *n* évanouissement *m*
**faintly** *adv* faiblement; vaguement; *coll* un peu
**faintness** *n* faiblesse *f*; malaise *m*
¹**fair** *n* foire *f*, foire commerciale; (amusement) fête foraine
²**fair** *adj* beau (*f* belle); (weather) clair, ensoleillé; (colour) clair, blond; (honest) juste, impartial, franc (*f* franche), honnête, équitable; *fig* pur, prometteur -euse; plausible, passable, moyen -enne; (wind) propice; ~ **and square** direct, honorable; ~ **copy** copie *f* au net; ~ **enough** ça va!, d'accord!; ~ **game** proie *f* légitime; ~ **play** franc-jeu *m*, fair-play *m*; **in a way to** de nature à; (barometer) **set** ~ au grand beau (temps); *adv* honorablement, bien, convenablement,

carrément, franchement; **bid** ~ **to** avoir des chances de

**fairground** n champ m de foire

**fair-haired** adj aux cheveux blonds

**fairly** adv assez, justement; complètement

**fair-minded** adj équitable, juste

**fairness** n équité f, droiture f, franchise f, loyauté f; blancheur f, beauté f, clarté f

**fair-spoken** adj poli, avenant; plausible

**fairway** n naut chenal m navigable, passe f; (golf) parcours normal

**fair-weather** adj des beaux jours

**fairy** n fée f; sl pédé m, tapette f; adj féerique, enchanteur (f enchanteresse)

**fairy-lamp** n lampion m

**fairyland** n royaume m des fées

**fairy-like** adj féerique

**fairy-story** n conte m de fées

**faith** n foi f, croyance f; loyauté f, honneur m, fidélité f, parole f; confiance f; promesse f; **bad** ~ mauvaise foi; **in good** ~ sincèrement

**faithful** n collect fidèles mpl; adj fidèle, loyal, dévoué; juste, exact

**faithfully** adv fidèlement; loyalement; exactement; **yours** ~ veuillez agréer l'expression de mes sentiments les plus distingués

**faithfulness** n fidélité f; loyauté f; exactitude f

**faith-healing** n guérison f par la foi

**faithless** adj infidèle, inconstant, déloyal; eccles infidèle, incroyant

**fake** n imitation f, faux m, falsification f; adj faux (f fausse), truqué, falsifié; vt truquer, falsifier

**fakir** n fakir m

**falcon** n faucon m

**falconer** n fauconnier m

**falconry** n fauconnerie f

**fall** n chute f, tombée f; (decline) baisse f; mil chute f, reddition f; comm baisse f, dépréciation f; theat (curtain) baisser m; fig chute f, défaite f; (sin) péché m; (waterfall) cascade f; US automne m; **head for a** ~ courir à l'échec; **try a** ~ **with** se mesurer contre; vi tomber; lit (collapse) s'écrouler; (ground) s'incliner, descendre; (river) déboucher, se jeter; (event) arriver, survenir; (categories) se diviser, se classer; (value, health, sight) baisser, diminuer, être en baisse; (night) tomber, approcher; (face) s'allonger; (star) filer; (sea, wind) se calmer; fig tomber, déchoir; décroître; (morally) pécher, succomber, s'avilir; (blame) retomber; sl ~ **about** rire aux éclats; ~ **away** (ground) s'affaisser; (follower, soldier) déserter; theol apostasier; (thin) s'amaigrir; ~

back se replier; ~ **back on** se rabattre sur; ~ **behind** rester en arrière; (payment) s'arriérer; coll ~ **down (on)** (fail) échouer; (go wrong) faire une grande erreur; ~ **flat** faillir, ne produire aucun effet; ~ **for** donner dans, se laisser prendre à; (love) s'amouracher de; ~ **foul of** naut entrer en collision avec; fig se heurter à; ~ **in** mil former les rangs; (collapse) s'effondrer; (lease) expirer; (debt) échoir; ~ **in with** consentir à; (meet) rencontrer par hasard; ~ **off** baisser, diminuer; naut ne pas obéir à la barre; ~ **on** attaquer; (incumbent) incomber à; ~ **out** advenir, arriver; mil rompre les rangs; (quarrel) se brouiller; ~ **over backwards** se mettre en quatre; ~ **short** rester en deçà, être insuffisant; ~ **short of** ne pas être à la hauteur de; ~ **through** tomber à l'eau; ~ **to** commencer, entamer; attaquer; commencer à manger; ~ **under** être classé comme

**fallacious** adj fallacieux -ieuse

**fallacy** n opinion fausse, raisonnement erroné; argument fallacieux; philos sophisme m

**fallen** adj coupable, déchu, ~ **woman** prostituée f; **the** ~ les morts mpl au champ d'honneur

**fall-guy** n US bouc m émissaire

**fallibility** n faillibilité f

**fallible** adj faillible

**Fallopian** adj anat de Fallope; ~ **tube** trompe f de Fallope

**fall-out** n retombée(s) radioactive(s)

¹**fallow** n agr jachère f, friche f; adj agr en jachère, en friche; fig inculte; vt agr laisser en jachère

²**fallow** adj fauve

**fallow-deer** n daim m

**false** adj faux (f fausse), erroné; (lying) menteur -euse, trompeur -euse; traître -esse; (sham) factice, contrefait; artificiel -ielle, postiche; ~ **bottom** double fond m; ~ **position** situation fausse; ~ **pretences** prétextes frauduleux; ~ **step** faux pas; adv **play s/o** ~ tromper qn

**false-hearted** adj déloyal, traître -esse

**falsehood** n (lie) mensonge m; (falseness) fausseté f

**falseness** n fausseté f

**falsetto** n mus fausset m; adj mus de fausset

**falsies** npl sl seins mpl postiches

**falsification** n falsification f

**falsify** vt falsifier; déformer, dénaturer

**falsity** n fausseté f; mensonge m; malhonnêteté f, traîtrise f

**falter** vi (trip) trébucher; (wobble) vaciller, chanceler; hésiter, balancer; (speech) bredouiller, balbutier

**fame** n réputation f, gloire f; renom m,

renommée f; ar bruit m qui court; **house of ill** ~ bordel m
**famed** adj renommé, célèbre
**familiar** n (friend) familier -ière, intime; (demon) esprit familier; eccles familier m; adj familier -ière, amical, intime; impudent, libre; ordinaire, commun; (well-known) connu; **be** ~ **with** être au courant de
**familiarity** n familiarité f
**familiarize** vt familiariser
**family** n famille f; ~ **allowance** allocation familiale; ~ **man** homme m d'intérieur; **her** ~ **tree** arbre m généalogique; **in the** ~ **way** enceinte; adj familial
**famine** n famine f, disette f
**famish** vt affamer; vi être réduit à la famine; **be** ~ **ed** avoir très faim
**famous** adj célèbre, fameux -euse; coll excellent, fameux -euse
**famously** adv coll très bien
¹**fan** n éventail m; (mechanical) ventilateur m; agr van m; ~ **vaulting** voûte f en éventail; vt éventer; (flames) souffler sur; (fire) attiser; agr vanner; fig exciter, attiser, envenimer; vi se déployer en éventail
²**fan** n fan, admirateur -trice; ~ **mail** courrier m des fans
**fanatic** n fanatique, fervent -e, enthousiaste, coll fana; adj fanatique, fervent
**fanatical** adj fanatique, fervent, coll fana
**fanaticism** n fanatisme m
**fanaticize** vt fanatiser
**fancier** n amateur -trice, connaisseur -euse; (animals, birds, etc) éleveur -euse, marchand -e
**fanciful** adj imaginatif -ive, rêveur -euse; capricieux -ieuse, fantaisiste; fantastique, étrange
**fancy** n chimère f, illusion f; caprice m, lubie f; goût m, inclination f; lit fantaisie f, imagination f; **take the** ~ **of** attirer, plaire à; **the** ~ **took him** il a eu envie; adj de fantaisie; fantaisiste, extravagant; de luxe, cher (f chère); imaginatif -ive; ~ **dress** travesti m, déguisement m; ~ **goods** articles mpl de Paris; sl ~ **man** proxénète m, maquereau m; ~ **woman** maîtresse f; prostituée f; ~ **work** broderie f; vt imaginer, s'imaginer; avoir du goût pour, coll avoir le béguin pour; supposer, croire; ~ **oneself** avoir bonne opinion de soi
**fancy-free** adj libre, avec le cœur libre
**fandango** n fandango m
**fanfare** n fanfare f
**fang** n (animal) croc m; (snake) crochet m (à venin); (of tooth) racine f

**fanlight** n imposte f (en éventail)
**fanny** n sl cul m; vulg con m
**fantasia** n mus fantaisie f
**fantastic, fantastical** adj fantastique, grotesque; imaginaire, chimérique; fantasque; coll sensationnel -elle
**fantasy, phantasy** n fantaisie f, caprice m, lubie f; illusion f; mus + lit fantaisie f
**far** adj éloigné, lointain, distant; (other) autre, plus éloigné; ~ **cry** grande distance; **Far East** Extrême Orient m; ~ **side** autre côté m; adv loin; (much) beaucoup; ~ **and away** de beaucoup; ~ **and wide** partout; ~ **back** loin dans le passé; ~ **be it from me** to loin de moi l'idée de; ~ **from it!** tant s'en faut!; ~ **gone** bien parti, avancé; ~ **into** très avant dans; ~ **off** au loin; **by** ~ de loin; fig go ~ réussir; go ~ **towards** beaucoup contribuer à; go too ~ aller trop loin, dépasser les bornes; **how** ~ **is it to London?** Londres est à quelle distance?; **in so** ~ **as** dans la mesure où; **thus** ~ jusqu'ici; (time) jusqu'à présent
**faraway** adj lointain, éloigné; fig rêveur -euse, vague
**farce** n farce f; vt cul farcir
**farcical** adj de farce; bouffon -onne; grotesque
**fare** n (bus, train, aircraft) prix m de la place, prix m du voyage; (taxi) prix m de la course; (taxi passenger) client -e; cul nourriture f, chère f; **excess** ~ supplément m; **full** ~ plein tarif; vi aller, se trouver; advenir, résulter; cul se nourrir, manger; ar voyager
**farewell** n adieu m; interj adieu!
**far-fetched** adj recherché, tiré par les cheveux
**far-flung** adj vaste, très étendu
**farinaceous** adj farinacé
**farm** n ferme f, exploitation f agricole; vt cultiver, exploiter; ~ **out** (work) confier, affermer; (children) donner à garder; ~ **out work** céder un travail en sous-traitance; vi être fermier -ière
**farmer** n fermier -ière, exploitant -e agricole, cultivateur -trice
**farm-hand** n ouvrier m agricole
**farm-house** n maison f de ferme
**farming** n agriculture f, culture f; (rearing) élevage m; ~ **out** affermage m; (sub-contracting) sous-traitance f
**farm-labourer** n ouvrier m agricole
**farmstead** n ferme f
**farmyard** n cour f de ferme, basse-cour f (pl basses-cours)
**farrago** n fouillis m, méli-mélo m (pl mélis-mélos)
**far-reaching** adj de grande envergure

**farrier** *n* maréchal-ferrant *m* (*pl* maréchaux-ferrants)

**farrow** *n* portée *f* de cochons; *vt* mettre bas (des cochons); *vi* cochonner

**far-sighted** *adj* presbyte; *fig* prévoyant

**fart** *n vulg* pet *m*; *vi* péter

**farther** *adj* plus éloigné; plus avancé; *adv* plus loin; (moreover) de plus

**farthermost** *adj* le plus éloigné

**farthest** *adj* le plus éloigné; *adv* le plus loin

**farthing** *n obs* le quart d'un ancien penny; *fig* sou *m*

**fascicule** *n* fascicule *m*

**fascinate** *vt* fasciner, charmer, éblouir

**fascination** *n* fascination *f*, enchantement *m*

**Fascism** *n* fascisme *m*

**Fascist** *n* + *adj* fasciste

**fashion** *n* habitude *f*, coutume *f*; mode *f*, vogue *f*; (way) façon *f*, manière *f*; (garment) forme *f*; ~ **magazine** journal *m* de mode; **after a** ~ tant bien que mal; **in** ~ à la mode; **out of** ~ démodé; *vt* façonner, former; **fully** ~**ed** diminué, proportionné

**fashionable** *adj* à la mode, élégant, chic *invar*

**fashion-plate** *n* gravure *f* de mode; *coll* élégant -e

¹**fast** *n* jeûne *m*, période *f* de jeûne; *vi* jeûner; (partially) faire maigre

²**fast** *adj* solide, ferme; rapide, prompt; (colour) bon teint *invar*; (clock) en avance; *fig* loyal, fidèle; (dissipated) dévergondé, émancipé; ~ **train** rapide *m*; *coll* **pull a** ~ **one on s/o** avoir qn; *adv* solidement, fermement; rapidement, vite, promptement; (thoroughly) complètement; **be** ~ **asleep** dormir à poings fermés; *naut* **make** ~ amarrer; **play** ~ **and loose with s/o** se jouer de qn; **stand** ~ tenir bon

**fasten** *vt* fixer, attacher; (bind) lier; (clasp) agrafer; ~ **on** saisir; imputer à, rejeter sur; *vi* se fixer, s'attacher, s'agrafer

**fastener** *n* attache *f*, fermeture *f*; (clasp) agrafe *f*; **paper** ~ trombone *m*

**fastening** *n* attache *f*

**fastidious** *adj* délicat, difficile

**fastidiousness** *n* délicatesse exagérée; (food) goût *m* difficile

**fasting** *n* jeûne *m*

**fast-living** *adj* dissolu

**fastness** *n* forteresse *f*; fermeté *f*, solidité *f*; rapidité *f*

**fat** *n* graisse *f*; (meat) gras *m*; *chem* glycéride *f*; **live off the** ~ **of the land** vivre comme un coq en pâte; **the** ~ **is in the fire** on a mis le feu aux poudres; *adj* gros (*f* grosse), corpulent; (greasy) gras (*f* grasse); (soil) fertile, riche; (salary)

élevé; *coll* lourd, idiot; *coll* **a** ~ **lot** beaucoup; (ironical) rien du tout

**fatal** *adj* fatal, inévitable; funeste, désastreux -euse; mortel -elle

**fatalism** *n* fatalisme *m*

**fatalist** *n* fataliste

**fatality** *n* mort accidentelle; calamité *f*; fatalité *f*

**fate** *n* destin *m*, sort *m*, destinée *f*; (death) mort *f*; *myth* **Fates** Parques *fpl*

**fated** *adj* destiné, voué; décrété par le destin

**fateful** *adj* décisif -ive, important; fatal, mortel -elle

**fat-head** *n* idiot -e, imbécile

**father** *n* père *m*; *fig* créateur *m*, fondateur *m*; *eccles* (title) père *m*; **from** ~ **to son** de père en fils; **the Father** Dieu *m* le père; **Holy-Father** Saint-Père; *vt* engendrer, être le père de; *fig* créer, inventer, enfanter; prendre la responsabilité de; ~ **sth on s/o** attribuer la responsabilité de qch à qn

**fatherhood** *n* paternité *f*

**father-in-law** *n* beau-père *m* (*pl* beaux-pères)

**fatherland** *n* patrie *f*

**fatherless** *adj* orphelin -e de père, sans père

**fatherly** *adj* paternel -elle

**fathom** *n naut* = brasse *f*; *ar* toise *f*; *vt* sonder; *fig* comprendre

**fathomless** *adj* insondable; incompréhensible

**fatigue** *n* fatigue *f*, épuisement *m*; *mil* corvée *f*; *mech* fatigue *f*; *vt* fatiguer

**fatness** *n* grosseur *f*, embonpoint *m*; fertilité *f*; abondance *f*

**fatted** *adj* ~ **calf** veau gras

**fatten** *vt* + *vi* engraisser

**fatty** *adj* graisseux -euse

**fatuous** *adj* sot (*f* sotte), idiot

**faucet** *n* (barrel) cannelle *f*; *US* robinet *m*

**fault** *n* défaut *m*, imperfection *f*; (sin) faute *f*, péché *m*; erreur *f*; *geol* faille *f*; **be at** ~ être fautif -ive, être en défaut; **find** ~ **with** critiquer, trouver à redire à; *vt* blâmer, critiquer; *geol* provoquer une faille; **I can't** ~ **him** je ne peux pas le prendre en défaut; *vi* relever une faute, noter une erreur; *geol* présenter une faille

**fault-finder** *n* critiqueur -euse, mécontent -e

**fault-finding** *n* critique *f*

**faultiness** *n* imperfection *f*

**faultless** *adj* sans défaut, sans faille

**faulty** *adj* défectueux -euse, imparfait

**faun** *n* faune *m*, faunesse *f*

**fauna** *n* faune *f*

**favour** *n* faveur *f*; (kindness) service *m*, considération *f*; approbation *f*, aide *f*;

## favourable

(partiality) bienfait *m*, décision indulgente; préférence *f*; (token) faveur *f*, ruban *m* souvenir; *comm* lettre *f*; ~ s (sexual) faveurs *fpl*, complaisances *fpl*; **as a** ~ pour rendre service; *coll* **do me a** ~ ! je t'en prie!; **in** ~ **of** pour; *vt* considérer favorablement, être pour; favoriser; aider, appuyer, préférer; faciliter

**favourable** *adj* favorable, bien disposé; approbateur -trice

**favoured** *adj* avantagé, privilégié; favorisé; (lucky) fortuné

**favouring** *adj* favorable, propice

**favourite** *n* favori -ite, préféré -e; *adj* favori -ite, préféré

**favouritism** *n* favoritisme *m*

¹**fawn** *n zool* faon *m*; *adj* fauve

²**fawn** *vi* ramper, s'aplatir; *fig* ~ (up)on s/o flatter qn, lécher les bottes de qn

**fear** *n* peur *f*, crainte *f*; **for** ~ **of** de peur de; *coll* no ~ ! jamais de la vie!; **put the** ~ **of God into s/o** passer à qn une semonce qu'il n'oubliera pas de sitôt; (alarm) faire une peur bleue à qn; *vt* craindre, avoir peur de, redouter; *vi* avoir peur, craindre; **never** ~ ne vous en faites pas

**fearful** *adj* craintif -ive, peureux -euse, effrayé; (terrible) effrayant, terrible

**fearfulness** *n* crainte *f*, timidité *f*; caractère *m* terrible

**fearless** *adj* sans peur, intrépide, courageux -euse

**fearlessness** *n* intrépidité *f*, courage *m*

**fearsome** *adj* effrayant, terrible

**feasibility** *n* praticabilité *f*, possibilité *f*; plausibilité *f*

**feasible** *adj* faisable, praticable; probable

**feast** *n eccles* fête *f*; banquet *m*, festin *m*; *fig* fête *f*, régal *m*; *vt* fêter, régaler; *vi* banqueter, se régaler; *fig* se délecter

**feast-day** *n* jour *m* de fête

**feat** *n* haut fait, exploit *m*

**feather** *n* plume *f*; (arrow) penne *f*; **a** ~ **in one's cap** de quoi être fier; **birds of a** ~ gens *mpl* du même acabit; **in high** ~ vigoureux -euse, en pleine forme; de bonne humeur; **show the white** ~ avoir la frousse, être lâche; *vt* emplumer, empenner; (rowing) ramener à plat; ~ **one's nest** s'enrichir, se remplir les poches; *vi* mettre les plumes

**feather-bed** *n* lit *m* de plume(s); *fig* délice *m*; ~ **industry** compagnie (industrie) protégée et subventionnée par le gouvernement; *vt* favoriser, dorloter

**feather-brained** *adj* sans cervelle, écervelé, étourdi

**feathered** *adj* emplumé, garni de plumes; **our** ~ **friends** les oiseaux *mpl*

**feathering** *n* plumage *m*; (rowing) nage plate

**feather-weight** *n sp* poids *m* plume

**feathery** *adj* couvert de plumes; plumeux -euse; très léger -ère

**feature** *n* trait *m*, trait *m* caractéristique; (facial trait) trait *m* du visage, particularité *f*; *cin* grand film, long métrage; (newspaper) article *m* (à sensation); *vt* caractériser, marquer; dépeindre; *cin* + *rad* + *theat* présenter, mettre en vedette

**feature-length** *adj cin* de long métrage

**featureless** *adj* monotone, terne, uniforme

**febrile** *adj* fébrile; *fig* agité

**February** *n* février *m*

**fecal** *adj*, **feces** *npl see* **faecal**, **faeces**

**feckless** *adj* insouciant, irréfléchi, étourdi; incapable, mou (*f* molle)

**feculence** *n* féculence *f*; crasse *f*

**feculent** *adj* crasseux -euse, fétide, féculent

**fecund** *adj* fécond

**fecundate** *vt* féconder

**fecundity** *n* fécondité *f*

**federal** *adj* fédéral

**federalism** *n* fédéralisme *m*

**federalize** *vt* fédérer; *vi* se fédérer

**federate** *vt* fédérer; *vi* se fédérer

**federation** *n* fédération *f*

**fee** *n* émoluments *mpl*; (doctor, lawyer) honoraires *mpl*; (actor) cachet *m*; (school) frais *mpl* (de scolarité); (entrance) droits *mpl* (d'entrée); *hist* fief *m*; *vt* payer des droits à, louer

**feeble** *adj* faible, débile; timide; influençable; fragile; *fig* irrésolu; (joke, story) piètre

**feeble-minded** *adj* d'esprit faible, pauvre d'esprit

**feed** *n* action *f* de nourrir; alimentation *f*; *agr* fourrage *m*, pacage *m*; (poultry) pâtée *f*; *coll* gueuleton *m*; *vt* nourrir, donner à manger à; alimenter; *agr* faire paître, engraisser; *theat* donner la réplique à; *fig* alimenter, nourrir; satisfaire; ~ **on** manger habituellement; ~ **up** engraisser; *vi* se nourrir, manger; *agr* paître; *coll* **be fed up with** en avoir marre de, en avoir ras-le-bol de

**feedback** *n elect* feed-back *m invar*, rétroaction *f*; *fig* feed-back *m invar*

**feeder** *n* mangeur -euse; (for baby) biberon *m*; (tributary river) affluent *m*; (road) route *f* secondaire; *elect* feeder *m*

**feed-pipe** *n* tuyau *m* d'alimentation

**feel** *n* toucher *m*; sensation *f*; attouchement *m*; *vt* sentir, avoir la sensation de; (touch) palper, tâter, manier; éprouver; ressentir, être affecté par; *coll* tripoter; ~ **one's way** tâtonner; *vi* (think)

478

penser, considérer, trouver, avoir le sentiment; se sentir ému; (state) se sentir, se trouver; ~ **for** éprouver de la pitié pour; ~ **like** avoir envie de; ~ **up to** se sentir le courage de

**feeler** n antenne f, palpe m; fig ballon m d'essai

**feeling** n toucher m, tact m; (act) palpage m; sensation f; sentiment m, sensibilité f, gentillesse f; susceptibilité f; (hostile) irritation f, ressentiment m; intuition f, conviction f; adj sensible, émotionné

**fee-simple** n leg pleine propriété; bien m en toute propriété

**feet** npl see **foot**

**feign** vt feindre, simuler; vi feindre

**feint** n feinte f; vi faire semblant

**feldspar, felspar** n min feldspath m

**felicitate** vt féliciter

**felicitation** n félicitation f

**felicitous** adj heureux -euse

**felicity** n félicité f

**feline** n félin m; adj félin

¹**fell** n colline rocheuse

²**fell** adj poet féroce, cruel -elle, meurtrier -ière

³**fell** vt abattre, faire tomber

**fellah** n fellah m

**fellatio** n fellation f

**fellow** n camarade m, compagnon m, coll copain m; complice m; homme m, individu m, quidam m, coll type m; professeur m (à Oxford ou à Cambridge); membre m (d'une académie savante); adj pareil -eille, égal

**fellow-feeling** n sentiment m réciproque, sympathie f

**fellowship** n camaraderie f, fraternité f, solidarité f; compagnie f, association f; poste m de professeur (à Oxford ou à Cambridge); titre m de membre (d'une académie savante)

**fellow-traveller** n compagnon m (f compagne) de voyage; pol communiste -e

¹**felon** n criminel -elle; adj poet vil

²**felon** n panaris m

**felonious** adj criminel -elle; vil

**felony** n crime m

**felspar** n see **feldspar**

**felt** n feutre m; adj de feutre; vt feutrer; vi se feutrer

**felting** n feutrage m; étoffe feutrée

**felucca** n felouque f

**female** n femelle f; femme f; joc femelle f

**feminine** n gramm féminin m; adj féminin

**femininity** n fémininité f

**feminism** n féminisme m

**feminist** n féministe

**feminize** vt féminiser; vi se féminiser

**femoral** adj anat fémoral

**femur** n anat fémur m

**fen** n marais m, marécage m

**fence** n clôture f, claie f, palissade f, barrière f; sl (receiver) receleur -euse; mech garde f; **be on the other side of the** ~ ne pas être du même bord; **sit on the** ~ ménager la chèvre et le chou; vt clôturer, enclore; protéger; ~ **off** parer; vi faire de l'escrime; sl (stolen goods) receler; fig ~ **with** esquiver, se dérober

**fencer** n escrimeur -euse

**fencing** n palissade f, clôture f, barrière f; sp escrime f; sl (stolen goods) recel m

**fend** vt repousser, parer; vi ~ **for oneself** se débrouiller, s'arranger tout seul

**fender** n garde-feu m invar; naut défense f; US mot pare-chocs m

**fennel** n fenouil m

**feoff** n see **fief**

¹**feral** adj fatal; funèbre

²**feral** adj sauvage; féroce

**ferment** n ferment m, levure f; fermentation f; fig agitation f, excitation f; vt faire fermenter; fig exciter, agiter; vi fermenter

**fermentation** n fermentation f

**fern** n fougère f

**ferocious** adj féroce, cruel -elle

**ferociousness** n férocité f, cruauté f

**ferocity** n férocité f

**ferrate** n chem ferrate m

**ferreous** adj ferreux (no f)

**ferret** n furet m; vt prendre au furet; ~ **out** détecter, dénicher; vi chasser au furet; ~ **about** fureter, fouiner

**ferrety** adj de furet, fureteur -euse

**ferric** adj ferrique

**ferro-concrete** n béton armé

**ferrous** adj ferreux -euse

**ferruginous** adj ferrugineux -euse

**ferrule** n bout ferré; virole f

**ferry** n (river) bac m; (sea) ferry m; (place) lieu m de passage en bac; vt (passengers, cars, etc) faire traverser en bac, faire traverser en bateau

**ferryman** n passeur m

**fertile** adj fertile

**fertility** n fertilité f

**fertilization** n fertilisation f

**fertilize** vt agr fertiliser; biol + bot féconder

**fertilizer** n engrais m

**ferule** n férule f

**fervency** n ferveur f

**fervent** adj passionné, fervent; brûlant, incandescent

**fervid** adj passionné, intense

**fervour** n ferveur f, ardeur f; chaleur f intense

**festal** adj de fête

**fester** n pustule f; vt med rendre

purulent; gâter, envenimer; *vi med + fig* s'envenimer

**festival** *n* festival *m; eccles* fête *f; adj* gai

**festive** *adj* gai, de fête

**festivity** *n* fête *f;* festival *m;* **festivities** festivités *fpl*

**festoon** *n* feston *m,* guirlande *f; vt* festonner

**fetch** *n coll* ruse *f; vt* (s/o) amener; (sth) apporter, ramener, chercher; (induce) tirer; (blows) asséner, flanquer; *comm* atteindre, rapporter; *coll* séduire, attirer; *fig* ~ **and carry for s/o** faire des courses pour qn, être aux ordres de qn; *naut* ~ **away** larguer; ~ **back** ramener; ~ **out** faire sortir; *coll* ~ **up** vomir; *coll naut* ~ **up at** arriver à

**fetching** *adj coll* séduisant

**fête** *n* festival *m,* fête *f; vt* fêter

**fetich** *n see* fetish

**fetid, foetid** *adj* fétide, puant

**fetish, fetich** *n* fétiche *m*

**fetishism** *n* fétichisme *m*

**fetlock** *n* (joint) boulet *m;* (hair) fanon *m*

**fetter** *vt* mettre aux fers; *fig* entraver

**fetters** *npl* fers *mpl*

**fettle** *n* condition *f,* état *m;* santé *f*

**feud** *n* inimitié *f,* vendetta *f*

**feudal** *adj* féodal

**feudalism** *n* féodalité *f*

**feudalistic** *adj* féodal

**feudality** *n* féodalité *f*

**feudalize** *vt* inféoder

**feudatory** *n* feudataire; *adj* féodal

**fever** *n* fièvre *f*

**feverish** *adj* fiévreux -euse; fébrile

**few** *n* minorité *f,* peu *m* de gens; **a good** ~ un assez grand nombre de, *coll* pas mal de; *adj* peu de, quelques; ~ **and far between** rares; **every** ~ **days** à quelques jours d'intervalle; **some** ~ quelques; **with** ~ **exceptions** à quelques exceptions près

**fey** *adj* voué à la mort; *coll* farfelu

**fez** *n* fez *m*

**fiancé** *n* fiancé *m*

**fiancée** *n* fiancée *f*

**fiasco** *n* fiasco *m*

**fiat** *n* autorisation *f;* ordre *m,* décret *m*

**fib** *n* petit mensonge, craque *f; vi* en conter

**fibre** *n* fibre *f; fig* trempe *f*

**fibre-glass** *n* plexiglas(s) *m,* altuglas *m*

**fibrous** *adj* fibreux -euse

**fibula** *n anat* péroné *m*

**fichu** *n* fichu *m*

**fickle** *adj* inconstant, volage, capricieux -ieuse

**fickleness** *n* inconstance *f*

**fiction** *n* fiction *f;* invention *f;* **legal** ~ fiction légale

**fictitious** *adj* fictif -ive, imaginaire; faux (*f* fausse)

**fictive** *adj* fictif -ive

**fid** *n naut* épissoir *m*

**fiddle** *n mus + naut* violon *m; sl* combine *f;* **as fit as a** ~ en pleine santé; **play second** ~ **to** jouer en sous-fifre auprès de, jouer un rôle secondaire auprès de; *vt coll* truquer, maquiller; *vi* jouer du violon, violonner

**fiddler** *n* violoniste; *coll* escroc *m,* filou *m*

**fiddlestick** *n mus* archet *m;* ~**s!** balivernes!

**fiddling** *adj* insignifiant, sans valeur; (annoying) tâtillon -onne

**fidelity** *n* fidélité *f;* **high** ~ haute fidélité

**fidget** *n* agité -e; **be a** ~ avoir la bougeotte; *vt* agacer, irriter; *vi* s'agiter, se démener, se trémousser

**fidgety** *adj* agité, remuant; impatient, nerveux -euse

**fiduciary** *n* fiduciaire *m; adj* fiduciaire

**fie** *interj* fi!

**fief, feoff** *n hist* fief *m*

**field** *n* champ *m;* terrain *m;* (extent) étendue *f;* (oil, mineral, etc) gisement *m; sp* **a strong** ~ beaucoup de concurrents valables; **hold the** ~ se maintenir en position; être maître du champ; **mil in the** ~ en campagne; **take the** ~ se mettre en campagne; *vt mil* mettre en campagne; *sp* faire jouer (une équipe); (ball) attraper

**field-artillery** *n mil* artillerie *f* de campagne

**field-battery** *n mil* batterie *f* de campagne

**field-day** *n mil* jour *m* de manœuvres; *fig* jour *m* de grands succès

**field-gun** *n mil* canon *m* de campagne

**field-hospital** *n mil* antenne chirurgicale

**field-marshal** *n mil* maréchal *m*

**field-mouse** *n* mulot *m*

**field-officer** *n mil* (in British army) officier *m* au-dessus du rang de capitaine

**field-sports** *npl* sports *mpl* de plein air; la chasse et la pêche

**field-work** *n mil* ouvrage *m* de campagne; travaux *mpl* pratiques; *geol* recherches *fpl* sur le terrain

**fiend** *n* démon *m,* diable *m; coll* (drugs, etc) intoxiqué -e

**fiendish** *adj* diabolique

**fierce** *adj* féroce; (desire) ardent, brûlant; acharné; violent, furieux -ieuse; *mot* (clutch) brutal

**fierceness** *n* férocité *f;* violence *f*

**fiery** *adj* flamboyant, embrasé; (person) ardent, fougueux -euse, enflammé; (temper) bouillant

**fife** *n* fifre *m*

filter-tip

**fifteen** *n* quinze *m invar*; *sp* (rugby) quinze *m*; *adj* quinze *invar*

**fifteenth** *n* quinzième; (date) quinze *m*; *adj* quinzième

**fifth** *n* cinquième; (date) cinq *m*; *mus* quinte *f*; *adj* cinquième

**fiftieth** *n + adj* cinquantième

**fifty** *n* cinquante *m invar*; **the fifties** (epoch) les années cinquante; (age) la cinquantaine; *adj* cinquante *invar*

**fifty-fifty** *adj + adv* kif-kif *invar*, fifty-fifty *invar*; **go ~** partager également ment

**fig** *n* figue *f*; (tree) figuier *m*; **I don't give a ~** ça m'est égal, je m'en fous

**fight** *n* combat *m*, lutte *f*, bataille *f*; (fighting spirit) combativité *f*; **free ~** bagarre *f*; **put up a good ~** se défendre bien; **show ~** accepter le conflit; *vt* combattre, se battre contre, lutter pour; (battle) livrer; **~ down** réprimer, écraser; **~ off** lutter contre; chasser; **~ one's way** avancer; *vi* se battre, combattre, lutter; **~ back** se défendre bien; **~ it out** lutter jusqu'au bout

**fighter** *n* combattant -e; batailleur -euse *m*; *aer* chasseur *m*

**fighting** *n* lutte *f*, bataille *f*; rixe *f*; *adj* combatif -ive, agressif -ive; qui se bat; *fig* (speech) enflammé

**fig-leaf** *n bot* feuille *f* de figuier; (statue) feuille *f* de vigne

**figment** *n* invention *f*

**fig-tree** *n* figuier *m*

**figuration** *n* figuration *f*; configuration *f*, forme *f*

**figurative** *adj* figuratif -ive; symbolique; (style) imagé

**figure** *n* forme *f*; figure *f*, apparence *f*; (important) personnage *m*; représentation *f*, imitation *f*; *arts* motif *m*, dessin *m*, illustration *f*; symbole *m*, emblème *m*; (money) somme *f* d'argent; *math* chiffre *m*; (shape of body) ligne *f*; *astrol* horoscope *m*; **at a low (high) ~** bon marché (cher, *f* chère); **have no head for ~s** ne rien comprendre aux chiffres; *vt* figurer, représenter, dépeindre; décorer; *US* calculer, penser; **~ out** calculer, penser; *vi* figurer; *coll* **that doesn't ~** ça ne tient pas debout

**figured** *adj* figuré, à dessins; *mus* chiffré

**figurehead** *n naut* figure *f* de proue; *fig* personnalité majeure, figure *f* de proue

**figure-of-eight** *n* huit *m invar*

**figurine** *n* figurine *f*

**filament** *n* filament *m*; *bot* filet *m*

**filature** *n* filature *f*; (machine) dévidoir *m*

**filbert** *n* (tree) avelinier *m*; (nut) aveline *f*, noisette *f*

**filch** *vt* chiper, chaparder

**filcher** *n* chapardeur -euse

<sup>1</sup>**file** *n* (documents, etc) classeur *m*, casier *m*; (card-index) fichier *m*; archives *fpl*, dossier *m*; *leg* **~ one's petition** déposer son bilan

<sup>2</sup>**file** *n* (tool) lime *f*; *vt* limer

<sup>3</sup>**file** *n* file *f*, colonne *f*; **Indian ~** file indienne; **in ~** en file, à la file; **the rank and ~** *mil* les hommes *mpl* de troupe; le commun, les gens *mpl* ordinaires; *vt* *mil* faire défiler; *vi* défiler

**filial** *adj* filial

**filiation** *n* filiation *f*

**filibuster** *n* (pirate) flibustier *m*; *pol* tactique *f* obstructionniste; *vi* flibuster; *pol* faire de l'obstructionnisme

**filiform** *adj* filiforme

**filigree** *n* filigrane *m*

<sup>1</sup>**filing** *n* classement *m*; *adj* **~ cabinet** classeur *m*

<sup>2</sup>**filing** *n* limage *m*; (particle) limaille *f*

**fill** *n* quantité *f* pour remplir; ce qu'il faut (pour remplir); (enough) saoul *m*, soûl *m*; **I've had my ~ of that** j'en ai assez de cela; *vt* remplir, emplir; (gap) combler; (post, office) occuper; (vacancy) pourvoir à; (balloon) gonfler; (tooth) plomber, obturer; *naut* (sails) mettre le vent dans; **~ in** (form) remplir; (hole) combler; *coll* **~ the bill** être à la hauteur; **~ up** remplir tout à fait; (form) remplir; *vi* se remplir, s'emplir; **~ out** grossir; se gonfler; **~ up** s'emplir

**filler** *n* (person) remplisseur -euse; (funnel) entonnoir *m*; (painting) mastic *m*

**fillet** *n* (meat, fish, etc) filet *m*; (hair) bandeau *m*, serre-tête *m invar*; *vt* lever les filets de; (bone) désosser; (head) orner d'un bandeau

**filling** *n* remplissage *m*; (teeth) plombage *m*, obturation *f*; *cul* farce *f*

**filling-station** *n* station-service *f* (*pl* stations-service), poste *m* d'essence

**fillip** *n* chiquenaude *f*; *fig* stimulant *m*, encouragement *m*; *vt* donner une chiquenaude à; *fig* stimuler, encourager; *vi* donner une chiquenaude

**filly** *n* pouliche *f*; *coll* (girl) jeune fille alléchante

**film** *n* film *m*; (coating) pellicule *f*, couche *f*; *phot* pellicule *f*; *vt* filmer; couvrir d'une pellicule; *vi* se couvrir d'une pellicule

**filmic** *adj* du cinéma, filmique

**film-star** *n* vedette *f*, star *f*

**filmy** *adj* couvert d'une pellicule

**filter** *n* filtre *m*; *vt + vi* filtrer

**filter-paper** *n* papier-filtre *m* (*pl* papiers-filtres)

**filter-tip** *n* bout *m* filtre

**filth** *n* ordure *f*, immondices *mpl*; *fig* obscénité *f*

**filthy** *adj* sale; ordurier -ière, obscène

**filtrate** *n* filtrat *m*; *vt* filtrer

**filtration** *n* filtration *f*

**fin** *n* (fish) nageoire *f*; (shark) aileron *m*; *aer* aileron *m*; *mech* ailette *f*

**final** *n sp* finale *f*; ~ **s** = examens *mpl* de dernière année; *adj* final, ultime; déterminant, conclusif -ive; définitif -ive

**finale** *n* conclusion *f*; *mus* finale *m*

**finalist** *n* finaliste

**finality** *n* caractère définitif; *philos* finalité *f*

**finalization** *n* règlement *m*, arrangement définitif

**finalize** *vt* régler définitivement, conclure

**finance** *n* finance *f*; *vt* financer, commanditer

**financial** *adj* financier -ière

**financier** *n* financier -ière, commanditaire *m*

**finch** *n* pinson *m*

**find** *n* découverte *f*, trouvaille *f*; *vt* trouver, découvrir; constater, établir; considérer, estimer; (supply) fournir, pourvoir; ~ **out** découvrir, apprendre, venir à savoir; ~ **s/o out** démasquer qn; *vi leg* rendre un verdict; *leg* ~ **for s/o** retourner un verdict en faveur de qn

**finder** *n* trouveur -euse *phot* viseur *m*; *astron* chercheur *m*

**finding** *n* découverte *f*; *leg* verdict *m*; décision *f*, conclusion *f*

¹**fine** *n* amende *f*; (key-money) pas *m* de porte; *vt* infliger une amende à, mettre à l'amende

²**fine** *adj* beau (*f* belle), superbe, excellent, splendide; (sharp) aigu -uë, fin; (pure) fin, pur; délicat, élégant, raffiné; (distinction) subtil; (weather) beau (*f* belle); *coll* + *iron* joli; ~ **arts** beaux arts; *coll* **one** ~ **day** un de ces jours, un de ces quatre matins; *adv coll* bien; **cut it** ~ y arriver de justesse; *vt* (gold) affiner; (liquid) clarifier; *fig* affiner; *vi* s'affiner

**fine-draw** *vt* stopper; (wire) étirer

**fine-drawn** *adj* stoppé; (wire) étiré; *fig* subtil, délié; (athlete) amaigri

**fine-looking** *adj* beau (*f* belle)

**finely** *adv* admirablement; (small pieces) menu

**fineness** *n* beauté *f*, finesse *f*, subtilité *f*, délicatesse *f*

¹**finery** *n* atours *mpl*

²**finery** *n mech* fourneau *m* d'affinage

**fine-spun** *adj* ténu, fragile; *fig* trop subtil

**finesse** *n* finesse *f*, habileté *f*; (bridge) impasse *f*; *vi* (bridge) ~ **against** faire l'impasse à

**finger** *n* doigt *m*; (bread) mouillette *f*; **first** ~ **index** *m*; **have a** ~ **in sth** y être pour qch; **lay a** ~ **on** toucher, faire du mal à; **middle** ~ médius *m*; **not lift a** ~ **to** ne pas remuer le petit doigt pour; **put one's** ~ **on** mettre le doigt sur; **ring** ~ annulaire *m*; *coll* **take one's** ~ **out** faire un effort; **twist s/o round one's little** ~ dominer qn, influencer qn, mener qn par le bout du nez; *vt* manier du doigt, toucher du doigt, palper; *mus* (instrument) toucher de; *mus* (give fingering) doigter

**finger-alphabet** *n* alphabet *m* des sourds-muets

**fingerboard** *n mus* (violin, etc) touche *f*; (piano) clavier *m*

**fingerbowl** *n* rince-doigts *m*

**fingering** *n mus* doigté *m*; (handling) maniement *m*

**fingernail** *n* ongle *m*

**fingerplate** *n* plaque *f* de propreté

**fingerpost** *n* poteau indicateur

**fingerprint** *n* empreinte digitale

**fingerstall** *n med* doigtier *m*

**fingertip** *n* bout *m* du doigt; **have at one's** ~ **s** savoir sur le bout des doigts

**finical, finicking, finicky** *adj* précieux -ieuse, pointilleux -euse, difficile

**fining** *n* clarification *f*; (metal) affinage *m*

**finis** *n* fin *f*

**finish** *n* fin *f*; (polish, paint) fini *m*; **fight to the** ~ combat *m* à l'outrance; *vt* finir, terminer, achever, compléter, accomplir; (perfect) perfectionner, parachever; ~ **off** donner le dernier coup de main à; ~ **up** finir; *vi* finir, achever, cesser, s'achever, prendre fin

**finished** *adj* fini, terminé; parfait, soigné, achevé; (done for) fichu

**finisher** *n mech* finisseur -euse; *coll* coup *m* de grâce

**finishing** *n* parachèvement *m*, finissage *m*; *adj* qui finit, dernier -ière; ~ **touch** coup *m* de fion

**finite** *adj* fini

**fink** *n US sl* salaud *m*, mouchard -e, salope *f*; *vt* moucharder contre; *vi* moucharder

**Finland** *n* Finlande *f*

**Finn** *n* Finlandais -e

**finnan** *n* haddock fumé

**Finnish** *n* (language) finnois *m*; *adj* finnois

**finny** *adj* à nageoires; poissonneux -euse

**fiord, fjord** *n* fjord *m*

**fir** *n* sapin *m*

**fire** *n* feu *m*; (conflagration) incendie *m*; *mil* feu *m*; *fig* flamme *f*, énergie *f*, passion *f*; (glow) lueur *f*; **be under** ~ essuyer le feu; **catch** ~ prendre feu; **go through** ~ **and water** faire face à de grands périls; **hang** ~ (guns) faire long feu; (project, etc) traîner en longueur;

lay a ~ préparer le feu; **on** ~ en feu, en flammes; **open** ~ ouvrir le feu; **play with** ~ jouer avec le feu; *mil* **running** ~ tir *m* rapide; **set** ~ **to, set on** ~ allumer, mettre le feu à; **set the Thames on** ~ inventer la poudre; *vt* mettre le feu à, incendier; (firearm) tirer; (rocket) lancer; (explosive, mine) faire exploser; (pottery) cuire; *fig* enflammer, exciter; (employee) balancer; (questions) lancer; *vi* prendre feu; *mot*+*mech* marcher, tourner; *fig* s'enflammer; ~ **up** s'emporter

**fire-alarm** *n* avertisseur *m* d'incendie; signal *m* d'incendie

**firearm** *n* arme *f* à feu

**firebox** *n* foyer *m*

**firebrand** *n* tison *m*, brandon *m*; *fig* boutefeu *m*

**firebreak** *n* (forest) pare-feu *m invar*

**firebrick** *n* brique *f* réfractaire

**fire-brigade** *n* corps *m* des sapeurs-pompiers, pompiers *mpl*

**fire-bug** *n* luciole *f*; *sl* (arsonist) incendiaire

**fireclay** *n* argile *f* réfractaire, terre *f* réfractaire

**firedamp** *n* grisou *m*

**firedog** *n* chenet *m*

**fire-eater** *n* avaleur *m* de feu; *fig* grognon -onne, batailleur -euse

**fire-engine** *n* pompe *f* à incendie

**fire-escape** *n* échelle *f* d'incendie

**fire-extinguisher** *n* extincteur *m*

**fire-fighter** *n* pompier *m*

**firefly** *n* luciole *f*

**fireguard** *n* garde-feu *m invar*

**fire-insurance** *n* assurance *f* contre l'incendie

**fire-irons** *npl* garniture *f* de foyer

**fireless** *adj* sans feu

**firelight** *n* lumière *f* du feu

**firelighter** *n* allume-feu *m invar*

**fireman** *n* pompier *m*; (stoker) chauffeur *m*

**fireplace** *n* âtre *m*, cheminée *f*

**fire-plug** *n* bouche *f* d'incendie

**fireproof** *adj* ininflammable, ignifuge

**fire-raiser** *n* pyromane *m*

**fire-raising** *n* pyromanie *f*

**fire-screen** *n* écran *m*

**fireside** *n* coin *m* du feu, foyer *m*

**fire-station** *n* caserne *f* de pompiers, poste *m* d'incendie

**firewater** *n coll* gnôle *f*

**firewood** *n* bois *m* de chauffage

**firework** *n* pièce *f* d'artifice; ~s feu *m* d'artifice

**firing** *n mil* fusillade *f*; *mech* chauffage *m*, chauffe *f*; (pottery) cuite *f*, cuisson *m*; (fuel) combustible *m*; mise *f* à feu, allumage *m*; ~ **line** ligne *f* de feu; ~

**party,** ~ **squad** peloton *m* d'exécution

**firkin** *n* barillet *m*

¹**firm** *n comm* compagnie *f*, maison *f*, firme *f*

²**firm** *adj* ferme, solide, résolu; stable, fort; déterminé

**firmament** *n* firmament *m*

**firmness** *n* fermeté *f*

**first** *n* premier -ière; commencement *m*, début *m*; *adj* premier -ière; principal; le plus haut; unième; original, primordial; ~ **thing** en premier lieu, tout de suite; ~ **thing in the morning** dès le matin; *adv* premièrement, au début, d'abord; plutôt

**first-aid** *n* premiers secours

**firstborn** *n*+*adj* premier-né (*f* première-née)

**first-class** *adj* de première classe, excellent, de premier ordre; *adv* très bien

**first-floor** *n* premier étage; *US* rez-de-chaussée *m invar*

**first-fruits** *npl* prémices *fpl*

**first-hand** *adj* de première main

**first-night** *n theat* première *f*

**first-rate** *adj* de première classe, excellent, de premier ordre; *adv* très bien

**firth** *n* estuaire *m*, bras *m* de mer

**fiscal** *n Scots* = procureur *m* de la République; *adj* fiscal

¹**fish** *n* poisson *m*; *coll* type *m*; **cry stinking** ~ se déprécier; *coll* **feed the** ~**es** (drown) se noyer; (be seasick) avoir le mal de mer; *coll fig* **have other** ~ **to fry** avoir d'autres chats à fouetter; *coll fig* **pretty kettle of** ~ jolie affaire, beau gâchis; *vt* pêcher; *coll* ~ **for** pêcher, quêter; ~ **out** repêcher, tirer de l'eau; *vi* pêcher; *fig* ~ **in troubled waters** pêcher en eau trouble

²**fish** *n naut* jumelle *f*; *vt* jumeler

**fishball, fishcake** *n* boulette *f* de poisson

**fisher** *n* pêcheur *m*; (boat) bateau *m* de pêche

**fisherman** *n* pêcheur *m*; (boat) bateau *m* de pêche

**fisherwoman** *n* pêcheuse *f*

**fishery** *n* pêche *f*; (fishing ground) pêcherie *f*; leg droit *m* de pêche

**fish-glue** *n* colle *f* de poisson

**fish-hook** *n* hameçon *m*

**fishiness** *n* goût *m* de poisson; odeur *f* de poisson; *coll fig* caractère *m* louche

**fishing** *n* pêche *f*; droit *m* de pêche; ~ **boat** bateau *m* de pêche

**fish-kettle** *n cul* poissonnière *f*

**fish-knife** *n* couteau *m* à poisson

**fishmonger** *n* marchand -e de poisson

**fishpaste** *n* pâté *m* d'anchois, pâté *m* de saumon, pâté *m* de homard, pâté *m* de crabe

**fishplate** *n* éclisse *f*

**fish-slice** *n* truelle *f* à poisson
**fishwife** *n* marchande *f* de poisson; *fig* harengère *f*
**fishy** *adj* de poisson; *fig* louche, véreux -euse
**fissile** *adj* fissile
**fission** *n* fission *f*
**fissionable** *adj* fissile
**fissure** *n* fissure *f*; *vt* fissurer; *vi* se fissurer
**fist** *n* poing *m*; *coll* écriture *f*; *vt* cogner; *naut* empoigner
**fistful** *n* poignée *f*
**fisticuffs** *npl* rixe *f* à coups de poing
**fistula** *n path* fistule *f*
¹**fit** *n* accès *m*, attaque *f*, crise *f*; (coughing) quinte *f*; *fig* accès *m*, caprice *m*; ~ s convulsions *fpl*; **by ~ s and starts** par à-coups, par saccade; *coll* **throw a ~** piquer une crise
²**fit** *n* ajustement *m*; **this coat is a good ~ for me** ce veston est à ma taille; *adj* convenable, approprié; apte, propre; en bonne santé, dispos; ~ **as a fiddle** en pleine forme; *vt* (clothes) aller à; (suit) être propre à; adapter, ajuster; (match) répondre à; (clothes) ~ **on** essayer; ~ **out** équiper; *naut* armer; ~ **up** équiper, aménager; *vi* s'ajuster, s'adapter; (clothes) aller bien; ~ **in with** s'adapter à, accorder avec
**fitful** *adj* irrégulier -ière, changeant, capricieux -ieuse
**fitment** *n* meuble *m* à demeure; *mech* accessoire *m*, pièce *f*
**fitness** *n* aptitude *f*; (appropriateness) justesse *f*, à-propos *m*; (health) santé *f*, bonne forme
**fitter** *n* ajusteur *m*, monteur *m*; (clothes) essayeur -euse
**fitting** *n* ajustage *m*, ajustement *m*; montage *m*; (clothes) essayage *m*; *adj* convenable, approprié; (proper) bienséant
**fit-up** *n theat* pose *f* des décors
**five** *n* cinq *M invar*; *adj* cinq *invar*
**five-fold** *adj* quintuple; *adv* au quintuple
**fiver** *n coll* billet *m* de cinq livres
**fives** *npl sp* jeu anglais semblable à la pelote basque
**fivescore** *n* cent *m*
**fix** *n coll* embarras *m*, difficulté *f*; *naut* + *aer* détermination *f*; position déterminée; *sl* piqûre *f* de drogue; **be in a ~** être dans le pétrin; *vt* fixer; (arrange) arrêter, décider; *US* arranger, préparer; (repair) réparer; (bribe) soudoyer; (election) truquer
**fixate** *vt* fixer
**fixation** *n* fixation *f*
**fixative** *n* fixatif *m*; *adj* fixatif -ive
**fixed** *adj* fixe, arrêté; constant, invariable; ~ **idea** idée *f* fixe

**fixer** *n* personne *f* qui arrange les choses; *phot* fixateur *m*
**fixing** *n* fixation *f*; *phot* fixage *m*; *coll* ~ s accessoires *mpl*
**fixity** *n* fixité *f*
**fixture** *n* meuble *m* à demeure, meuble *m* fixe; *sp* engagement *m*, match prévu; *leg* ~ s biens *mpl* par destination
**fizz** *n* pétillement *m*; effervescence *f*; *coll* champagne *m*; boisson gazeuse; *vi* pétiller
**fizzle** *n* pétillement *m*; *coll* fiasco *m*; *vi* pétiller; ~ **out** finir en queue de poisson, avorter
**fizzy** *adj* pétillant, gazeux -euse
**fjord** *n see* **fiord**
**flabbergast** *vt coll* abasourdir, étonner; déconcerter, dérouter
**flabbiness** *n* mollesse *f*
**flabby** *adj* mou (*f* molle), flasque, avachi
**flaccid** *adj* flasque
**flaccidity** *n* flaccidité *f*
¹**flag** *n* drapeau *m*; *naut* pavillon *m*; (small) fanion *m*; (bookmarker) signet *m*; *coll* **show the ~** se manifester, être présent; **yellow ~** pavillon *m* de quarantaine; **white ~** parlementaire *m*; *vt* pavoiser; transmettre par signaux (au moyen de fanions); faire signe à; ~ **down** faire signe de s'arrêter à
²**flag** *n bot* iris *m*
³**flag** *n* (stone) dalle *f*; *vt* daller
⁴**flag** *vi* (hang down) pendre mollement; (weaken) s'affaiblir, diminuer; (zeal) défaillir, fléchir; (interest) faiblir; (plant) languir
**flag-day** *n* jour *m* de quête
**flagellant** *n* flagellant *m*
**flagellate** *vt* flageller, fouetter
**flagellation** *n* flagellation *f*
**flageolet** *n mus* flageolet *m*
¹**flagging** *n* dallage *m*, carrelage *m*
²**flagging** *adj* languissant
**flagitious** *adj* infâme, abominable, vil
**flag-lieutenant** *n naut* lieutenant *m* de pavillon
**flag-officer** *n naut* officier général
**flagon** *n* grande bouteille; pot *m* (pour le vin)
**flagrance, flagrancy** *n* énormité *f*, caractère scandaleux; *leg* flagrance *f*
**flagrant** *adj* flagrant, énorme, scandaleux -euse
**flagship** *n naut* vaisseau *m* amiral
**flagstaff** *n* mât *m* (de drapeau)
**flagstone** *n* dalle *f*
**flagwagging** *n coll mil* + *naut* signalisation *f* (au moyen de fanions); *coll fig* chauvinisme *m*, patriotisme exagéré
**flail** *n* fléau *m*; *vt* battre au fléau
**flair** *n* flair *m*, don *m*; perspicacité *f*
**flake** *n* (snow, etc) flocon *m*; (layer)

écaille *f*, lamelle *f*; *cul* feuillette *f*; (soap) paillette *f*; *vi* s'écailler

**flake-white** *n* blanc *m* de céruse

**flaky** *adj* floconneux -euse; lamellé; *cul* feuilleté

**flamboyance** *n* caractère flamboyant; panache *m*

**flamboyant** *adj* flamboyant

**flame** *n* flamme *f*; *fig* flamme *f*, ardeur *f*, passion *f*; *coll* béguin *m*, flirt *m*, amoureux -euse; *vi* flamber, flamboyer; s'enflammer

**flamenco** *n* flamenco *m*

**flame-thrower** *n mil* lance-flammes *m*

**flaming** *adj* flambant, flamboyant; *fig* ardent, passionné; *coll* sacré

**flamingo** *n* flamant *m*

**flammable** *adj* inflammable

**flan** *n* flan *m*

**flange** *n* (wheel) boudin *m*; (tube) collerette *f*; (pulley) joue *f*; *vt* brider

**flank** *n* flanc *m*; *vt* flanquer; *mil* prendre de flanc; *vi* être aux flancs, être à côté

**flannel** *n* flanelle *f*; (face-cloth) gant *m* de toilette; ~s pantalon *m* de flanelle; *vi coll* baratiner

**flannelette** *n* finette *f*

**flap** *n* (movement) battement *m*; (pocket, envelope) rabat *m*; (table) battant *m*; *coll fig* panique *f*; *coll* be in a ~ s'affoler; *vt* (wings) battre; *vi* battre, claquer; *coll fig* paniquer

**flapjack** *n* crêpe épaisse

**flapper** *n* (fly-whisk) émouchoir *m*; *ar* adolescente *f*

**flare** *n* flamboiement *m*; (signal) feu *m*, signal lumineux; *mil* fusée éclairante; (dress) évasement *m*; *vi* flamber, flamboyer; (dress) s'évaser

**flare-path** *n aer* rampe *f* de balisage

**flare-up** *n* flamboiement *m*, flambée soudaine; *fig* altercation *f*

**flash** *n* éclat *m*; (lightning, inspiration) éclair *m*; (camera, news) flash *m*; *mil* parement *m*; ~ **in the pan** feu *m* de paille; **in a** ~ tout de suite, en un clin d'œil; *adj coll* (showy) voyant, criard; (suspect) louche; *vt* (light) projeter; (news, etc) transmettre (par radio, etc); *mot* ~ **one's headlights** faire une appel de phares; *pej* (display) étaler; *sl* (look) reluquer; *vi* (bright object) étinceler; *mot* (lights) clignoter; ~ **past** passer comme un éclair

**flashback** *n* retour *m* en arrière

**flasher** *n mot* clignotant *m*; exhibitionniste *m*

**flashiness** *n* clinquant *m*

**flashlight** *n* (torch) lampe *f* électrique; *phot* flash *m*

**flashpoint** *n* point *m* d'ignition

**flashy** *adj* clinquant, voyant

**flask** *n* flacon *m*; *chem* fiole *f*

**flat** *n* appartement *m*; (mud) marécage *m*; *mus* bémol *m*; *theat* portant *m*; (racing) plat *m*; *adj* plat, monotone; *mus* faux (*f* fausse); (beer, lemonade) éventé; (categorical) net (*f* nette); (tyre) crevé; *coll* (absolute) net (*f* nette), catégorique; *coll* ~ **broke** fauché; ~ **race** course *f* de plat; *mus* **A** ~ **A bémol**; *coll* **be in a** ~ **spin** être dans tous ses états; **fall** ~ **on one's face** tomber sur le nez; *coll* **that's** ~ un point c'est tout; *adv* à plat; *coll* (definitely) carrément, sans ambages; *mus* faux; **be** ~ **out** être à plat; *coll* **go** ~ **out** (runner) courir à fond de train; (car) être à sa vitesse de pointe; *fig* donner son maximum; **work** ~ **out** travailler d'arrache-pied

**flatfish** *n* poisson plat

**flat-footed** *adj* aux pieds plats; *fig* balourd

**flat-iron** *n* fer *m* à repasser

**flatlet** *n* studio *m*

**flatly** *adv* carrément; (deny) catégoriquement

**flatness** *n* égalité *f*, aspect plat; (dullness) monotonie *f*

**flatten** *vt* (smooth) aplanir; (press, hammer) aplatir; (crops) coucher; (trees) abattre; *vi* ~ **out** s'aplanir; *aer* se redresser

**flatter** *vt* flatter; ~ **oneself** se flatter

**flatterer** *n* flatteur -euse

**flattery** *n* flatterie *f*

**flattish** *adj* assez plat

**flatulence, flatulency** *n* flatulence *f*

**flaunt** *vt* étaler, faire étalage de; *pej* faire parade de

**flautist** *n* flûtiste *m*

**flavour** *n* arôme *m*, goût *m*, saveur *f*; (ice-cream, etc) parfum *m*; (meat) fumet *m*; *fig* atmosphère *f*; *vt* donner du goût à; (season) assaisonner; (sweet, ice-cream, etc) parfumer

**flavouring** *n* (seasoning) assaisonnement *m*; (sweet, ice-cream, etc) parfum *m*

**flaw** *n* défaut *m*, imperfection *f*; *leg* vice *m* de forme; *fig* (blemish) faille *f*; (snag) inconvénient *m*; *vt* abîmer

**flawed** *adj* imparfait

**flawless** *adj* parfait, sans faille, impeccable

**flax** *n* lin *m*

**flaxen** *adj* de lin

**flay** *vt* écorcher; (beat) fouetter, battre; (criticize) éreinter

**flea** *n* puce *f*; *fig* ~ **in one's ear** rebuffade *f*

**flea-bag** *n coll* sac *m* de couchage

**flea-bite** *n* piqûre *f* de puce; *fig* vétille *f*, broutille *f*

**flea-bitten** *adj* mordu par les puces; *coll* moche, miteux -euse

**flea-pit** *n coll* (cinema) ciné miteux

**fleck** *n* particule *f*, petite tache; *vt* tacheter, moucheter, pommeler

**flection** *n see* **flexion**

**fledged** *adj* fully ~ (bird) qui a toutes ses plumes; *fig* qualifié, diplômé; adulte

**fledgeling** *n* oiselet *m*; (novice) blanc-bec *m* (*pl* blancs-becs)

**flee** *vt* fuir, s'enfuir de; *vi* fuir, s'enfuir

**fleece** *n* toison *f*; *vt* (sheep) tondre; *fig* escroquer, filouter

**fleecy** *adj* (wool) laineux -euse; (clouds) floconneux -euse

**¹fleet** *n* flotte *f*

**²fleet** *adj* rapide

**fleet-footed** *adj* au pied léger

**Fleming** *n* Flamand -e

**Flemish** *n* (language) flamand *m*; *adj* flamand

**flesh** *n* chair *f*; (fruit) pulpe *f*; *cul* viande *f*; *poet* être humain; **go the way of all ~** payer le tribut de la nature; **in the ~** en chair et en os; **make one's ~ creep** donner la chair de poule à qn; **one's own ~ and blood** sa famille; **pound of ~** dû *m*

**flesh-coloured** *adj* couleur chair *invar*

**fleshly** *adj* charnel -elle

**fleshpots** *npl* bonne chère

**fleshy** *adj* charnu

**¹flex** *n* fil *m* (souple)

**²flex** *vt* fléchir; (muscles) bander

**flexibility** *n* flexibilité *f*, souplesse *f*

**flexible** *adj* flexible, souple; *fig* (person) accommodant, souple

**flexion** *n* flexion *f*, courbure *f*

**flexor** *n anat* fléchisseur *m*

**flibbertigibbet** *n* hurluberlu *m*, écervelé -e, tête *f* de linotte

**flick** *n* (finger) chiquenaude *f*; (light blow) petit coup; *coll* ~s ciné *m*; *vt* donner un petit coup à; ~ **off** enlever d'une chiquenaude; (book, etc) ~ **through** feuilleter, lire en diagonale

**flicker** *n* vacillement *m*; (hope) lueur *f*; *vi* vaciller, trembloter, danser

**flick-knife** *n* couteau *m* à cran d'arrêt

**flier** *n see* **flyer**

**¹flight** *n* vol *m*; (bullet, etc) trajectoire *f*; (fancy) essor *m*, envol *m*; (birds) vol *m*, volée *f*; (planes) escadrille *f*; (stairs) volée *f*; **in the first (top) ~** de pointe; **two ~s up** (on second floor) au deuxième étage; deux étages plus haut

**²flight** *n* fuite *f*; **put to ~** mettre en fuite; **take to ~** s'enfuir

**flight-deck** *n naut* pont *m* d'envol; *aer* poste *m* de pilotage

**flight-lieutenant** *n* = capitaine *m* de l'armée de l'air

**flighty** *adj* volage, capricieux -ieuse

**flimsiness** *n* fragilité *f*, minceur *f*; (excuse) faiblesse *f*

**flimsy** *n coll* papier *m* pelure *invar*; *adj* mince; (excuse) faible, piètre

**flinch** *vi* broncher, reculer

**flinders** *npl* éclats *mpl*

**fling** *n* action *f* de lancer; mouvement *m* brusque; *fig* (taunt) raillerie *f*; *coll* **have a ~** faire la noce; **youth must have its ~** il faut que jeunesse se passe; *vt* jeter, lancer; ~ **away** jeter; ~ **in s/o's teeth** reprocher à qn; *fig* ~ **off** se débarrasser de; ~ **oneself at s/o** se jeter à la tête de qn; ~ **oneself into** se lancer à corps perdu dans; ~ **out** jeter, se débarrasser de; ~ **up** jeter en l'air; *vi* se précipiter

**flint** *n* silex *m*; (cigarette lighter) pierre *f* (à briquet); *adj* de pierre

**flinty** *adj* à silex; *fig* dur, de pierre

**flip** *n* chiquenaude *f*, pichenette *f*; *sl aer* petit tour en zinc; *adj coll* désinvolte; (record) ~ **side** autre face *f* (d'un disque); *vt* donner une chiquenaude à; ~ **over**, ~ **through** (book) feuilleter

**flippancy** *n* désinvolture *f*

**flippant** *adj* désinvolte

**flipper** *n* (animal) nageoire *f*; ~**s** (swimmer) palmes *fpl*

**flipping** *adj coll* maudit

**flirt** *n* flirteur -euse; *vi* flirter

**flirtation** *n* flirt *m*, amourette *f*

**flirtatious** *adj* flirteur -euse, flirt *invar*

**flit** *n* déménagement *m*; **do a moonlight ~** déménager à la cloche de bois; *vi* voleter, voltiger; (move house) déménager à la cloche de bois

**flitch** *n cul* flèche *f*

**flitting** *n* déménagement *m*

**flivver** *n coll* bagnole *f*, tacot *m*, guimbarde *f*

**float** *n* (fishing, seaplane, carburettor) flotteur *m*; (raft) radeau *m*; (cart) char *m*; *theat* ~**s** rampe *f*; *vt* (boat) faire flotter; (company) créer, fonder; (loan, idea) lancer; *vi* flotter, être à flot; (swimmer) faire la planche; ~ **around** circuler; ~ **away** partir à la dérive

**floatation** *n* flottaison *f*; *comm* lancement *m*

**floating** *adj* flottant; *fig* instable; ~ **assets** capitaux courants; ~ **voter** électeur -trice indécis -e

**flocculent** *adj* floconneux -euse

**¹flock** *n* (animals, geese) troupeau *m*; (birds) vol *m*; (people) foule *f*; *eccles* ouailles *fpl*; *vi* affluer, venir en masse; ~ **round** se grouper autour de; ~ **together** s'assembler

**²flock** *n* bourre *f* (de laine, de coton)

**floe** *n* banquise *f*

**flog** vt fouetter, fustiger; *coll* (sell) vendre; *fig* ~ **a dead horse** enfoncer une porte ouverte, perdre sa peine

**flogging** n flagellation f; *leg* fouet m

**flood** n inondation f; (spate) crue f; (tide) flux m; *fig* flot m, déluge m, torrent m; *fig* **at the** ~ au moment le plus propice; *eccles* **the Flood** le déluge; vt inonder, submerger; *mot* noyer; vi (river) déborder; (crowd) affluer

**floodgate** n vanne f; *fig* **open the** ~**s** ouvrir les vannes

**flooding** n inondation f

**floodlight** n projecteur m; vt illuminer, éclairer; *fig* mettre en lumière

**floodlighting** n illumination f, éclairage m

**floodtide** n flux m

**floor** n plancher m; parquet m; (tiled) carrelage m; (storey) étage m; (sea-bed) fond m; (dance) piste f; *fig comm* plancher m; **on the** ~ par terre, sur le sol; **take the** ~ prendre la parole; vt planchéier, parqueter; (knock to the ground) terrasser, envoyer au tapis; *coll* réduire au silence, déconcerter

**floorboard** n planche f, latte f

**floorcloth** n (cleaning) serpillière f; (covering) revêtement m de sol

**floor-polish** n encaustique f

**floor-polisher** n cireuse f

**floor-show** n attractions fpl

**floosie, floozy** n sl poule f

**flop** n floc m; *fig* (disaster) four m, fiasco m; **be a** ~ échouer; vi (collapse) s'effondrer, s'affaler; *theat* faire un four; (scheme) être un fiasco

**flop-house** n US asile m de nuit

**floppy** adj flottant, flou

**flora** n flore f

**floral** adj floral

**florescence** n floraison f

**florescent** adj en fleurs

**floriculture** n floriculture f

**florid** adj (complexion) rubicond, rougeaud; (style) fleuri

**florist** n fleuriste

**floss** n bourre f de soie

**flotation** n *see* **floatation**

**flotilla** n flotille f

**flotsam** n épave flottante

¹**flounce** n mouvement m brusque; vi avoir des mouvements vifs, faire un mouvement brusque; ~ **in** entrer brusquement; ~ **out** sortir brusquement

²**flounce** n volant m; vt garnir de volants

¹**flounder** n flet m, plie f, carrelet m

²**flounder** vi patauger, barboter; (struggle) se débattre; *fig* hésiter, bredouiller

**flour** n farine f; vt fariner; (face) enfariner

**flourish** n fioriture f, ornement m; *mus*

fanfare f; vt (stick) brandir; vi fleurir, prospérer; (develop) s'épanouir, bien venir

**flourishing** adj florissant, prospère; (health) en bonne santé

**floury** adj enfariné; (foodstuff) farineux -euse

**flout** n moquerie f; vt se moquer de, faire fi de

**flow** n (liquid) écoulement m; (words) flot m; (current) courant m; (tide) flux m; vi couler; (current) circuler; (tide) monter; *fig* résulter; (hair) flotter

**flower** n fleur f; floraison f; *fig* (best part) crème f, élite f; ~ **people** hippies mpl; vt faire fleurir; vi fleurir

**flowerbed** n plate-bande f (pl plates-bandes), parterre m

**flowered** adj fleuri

**flowering** n floraison f; adj en fleurs

**flowerpot** n pot m à fleurs

**flower-shop** n boutique f de fleuriste

**flower-show** n floralies fpl

**flowery** adj fleuri, couvert de fleurs; (style) orné

**flowing** adj coulant; (tide) montant; (beard) long (f longue); (movement) gracieux -ieuse

**flu** n *coll* grippe f

**fluctuate** vi fluctuer, varier

**fluctuating** adj variant, vacillant

**fluctuation** n fluctuation f, variation f

¹**flue** n conduit m de cheminée, tuyau m de cheminée

²**flue** vt évaser; vi s'évaser

**fluency** n aisance f, facilité f

**fluent** adj aisé, coulant; **speak** ~ **French** parler couramment le français

**fluently** adv couramment

**fluff** n peluche f; (bird, etc) duvet m; sl (girl) nénette f; vt ébouriffer; *theat* (line) louper; vi *theat* louper

**fluffy** adj duveteux -euse

**fluid** n fluide m, liquide m; adj fluide, liquide

**fluidity** n fluidité f

¹**fluke** n coup m de veine

²**fluke** n *naut* patte f (d'ancre)

³**fluke** n (fish) carrelet m

**flummery** n *coll* flagornerie f

**flummox** vt *coll* déconcerter

**flunk** vt US (examination) être collé à

**flunkey** n laquais m; *fig* larbin m

**fluoresce** vi devenir fluorescent

**fluorescence** n fluorescence f

**fluorescent** adj fluorescent

**fluoride** n *chem* fluorure m

**fluorine** n *chem* fluor m

**fluorite** n *chem* fluorine f

**flurry** n (wind) rafale f; *fig* agitation f; vt agiter, effarer

¹**flush** n (redness) rougeur f; (shy)

rougeoiement *m*; (blood) flux *m*; (lavatory) chasse *f* (d'eau); *fig* (excitement) élan *m*, ivresse *f*; (health) éclat *m*; *med* hot ~ bouffée *f* de chaleur; *vt* nettoyer à grande eau; ~ the lavatory tirer la chasse (d'eau); *vi* rougir, s'empourprer

²flush *n* (birds) envolée *f*; *vt* (birds) lever

³flush *n* (cards) flush *m*

⁴flush *adj* (full) plein à déborder; (level) au même niveau, à ras; *coll* ~ with money plein de fric; *adv* de niveau, à ras; *vt* mettre au niveau

fluster *n* trouble *m*, agitation *f*, énervement *m*; in a ~ énervé; *vt* troubler, agiter, énerver

flute *n* flûte *f*; (player) flûtiste; *archi* cannelure *f*; *vt archi* canneler; *vi* jouer de la flûte; chanter d'un ton flûté

fluted *adj archi* cannelé

fluting *n archi* cannelure *f*

flutist *n* see flautist

flutter *n* (movement) battement *m*; (heart) palpitation *f*; (worry) agitation *f*, émoi *m*; *coll* have a ~ (bet) parier de petites sommes; (speculation) boursicoter; *vt* (wings, eyelids) battre de; *vi* (fly) voleter, voltiger; (wings) battre; (heart) palpiter; (flag) flatter; (person) virevolter, être agité

fluvial *adj* fluvial

flux *n* (flow) flot *m*, flux *m*; (change) vicissitudes *fpl*, fluctuation *f*; *med* / *phys* flux *m*; be in a state of ~ changer sans arrêt

fluxion *n med* fluxion *f*

¹fly *n* (insect, fishing) mouche *f*; *fig* ~ in the ointment hic *m*, ennui *m*; *coll* there are no flies on him il n'est pas né d'hier; *adj coll* malin (*f* maligne), rusé

²fly *n* (flying) vol *m*; (trousers) braguette *f*; (tent) auvent *m*; (flag) battant *m*; (carriage) fiacre *m*; *theat* flies cintres *mpl*; *coll* (trousers) braguette *f*; *vt* (aircraft) piloter; (passenger, goods) transporter en avion; ~ a kite faire voler un cerf-volant; *fig* lancer un ballon d'essai; ~ the country s'enfuir du pays; *naut* ~ the French flag battre pavillon français; *vi* (bird, aircraft, etc) voler; (passenger) voyager en avion; (time) passer vite; (flee) fuir, s'enfuir; (move fast) se précipiter, courir; (spark) jaillir; ~ at attaquer violemment; *coll* ~ high être ambitieux -ieuse; ~ in the face of lancer un défi à; ~ into a rage s'emporter, se mettre en colère; ~ off the handle sortir de ses gonds, s'emporter; ~ out at insulter violemment; ~ over survoler; I must ~ il faut que je file; let ~ at s/o prendre qn violemment à partie

flyaway *adj* (hair) intraitable

flyblown *adj* couvert de chiures de mouche; *fig* gâté

fly-button *n* bouton *m* de braguette

fly-by-night *n* débiteur -trice qui décampe en douce

fly-catcher *n orni* gobe-mouches *m*; *bot* plante *f* carnivore; (trap) attrape-mouches *m*

flyer, flier *n aer* aviateur -trice; *fig* doué -e

fly-fishing *n* pêche *f* à la mouche

fly-half *n sp* demi *m* d'ouverture

flying-boat *n* hydravion *m*

flying-bomb *n* bombe volante

flying-buttress *n* arc-boutant *m* (*pl* arcs-boutants)

flying-fish *n* poisson volant

flying-saucer *n* soucoupe volante

flying-squad *n* brigade volante de la police judiciaire

flyleaf *n* page *f* de garde

fly-over *n* autopont *m*, toboggan *m*; *US* défilé aérien

fly-paper *n* papier *m* tue-mouches

fly-past *n* défilé aérien

fly-sheet *n* feuille volante

fly-swatter *n* tapette *f*

flyweight *n sp* poids *m* mouche

fly-wheel *n* volant *m*

foal *n* (horse) poulain *m*; (ass) ânon *m*; *vi* mettre bas

foam *n* (sea) écume *f*; (beer) mousse *f*; ~ rubber caoutchouc *m* mousse; ~ sprayer extincteur *m* à mousse; *vi* (sea) écumer, moutonner; (soapy water) mousser; (sparkling wine) mousser, pétiller; ~ at the mouth (animal) baver; *fig* (person) écumer de rage

foamy *adj* (sea) écumeux -euse; (beer) mousseux -euse

fob *n ar* gousset *m*; *vt* tricher; ~ s/o off with promises payer qn de promesses; ~ sth off on s/o refiler qch à qn

focal *adj* focal; ~ length distance focale; ~ point foyer *m*; *fig* point central

focus *n* foyer *m*; *fig* centre *m*; in ~ au point; *vt fig* concentrer; *vi* (light, rays) converger

fodder *n* fourrage *m*

foe *n* ennemi -e

foehn, föhn *n* foehn *m*, föhn *m*

foetal *adj* fœtal

foetid *adj see* fetid

foetus *n* fœtus *m*

fog *n* brouillard *m*; *naut* brume *f*; *phot* voile *m*; *vt* (windows, glasses, etc) embuer; *phot* voiler; *fig* obscurcir; *vi* (windows, glasses, etc) s'embuer; (landscape) s'embrunir; *phot* se voiler

fogbank *n* banc *m* de brume

fogbound *adj* pris dans le brouillard

**fogey, fogy** *n coll* **old** ~ vieux bonze, vieille baderne

**foggy** *adj* brumeux -euse; *fig* (idea) vague, confus; **I haven't the foggiest idea!** aucune idée!

**foghorn** *n* sirène *f* de brume

**foglamp** *n mot* phare *m* antibrouillard

**fog-signal** *n* (railway) pétard *m*

**fogy** *n see* **fogey**

**föhn** *n see* **foehn**

**foible** *n* marotte *f*, petite manie

¹**foil** *n* feuille *f* de métal, lame *f* de métal; (mirror) tain *m*; *cul* papier *m* d'aluminium; *archi* lobe *m*; *fig* (contrast) repoussoir *m*

²**foil** *n sp* fleuret *m*

³**foil** *vt* contrecarrer, déjouer

**foist** *vt* refiler, repasser; ~ **oneself on** s'imposer à

¹**fold** *n* (sheep) parc *m* à moutons; *eccles* bercail *m*; *vt* (sheep) parquer

²**fold** *n* pli *m*; *geol* plissement *m*; (hollow) repli *m*; *vt* plier; (wrap) envelopper, entourer; ~ **in two** plier en deux; ~ **one's arms** se croiser les bras; ~ **s/o in one's arms** étreindre qn; *vi* (chair, table, etc) se replier; *coll theat* faire un four, tomber; (business) fermer ses portes; ~ **up** (business) échouer

**folder** *n* (file) chemise *f*; (circular) brochure *f*, dépliant *m*

**folding** *adj* pliant; ~ **door** porte *f* en accordéon; ~ **seat** pliant *m*; *mot*+*theat* strapontin *m*

**foliage** *n* feuillage *m*

**foliate** *adj bot* folié; *vt* (book) folioter; *archi* décorer de lobes

**foliation** *n bot* foliation *f*, feuillaison *f*; (book) foliotage *m*

**folio** *n* folio *m*; (book) in-folio *m*

**folk** *n* (people) gens *mpl*; (people in general) les gens *mpl*; **old** ~ les vieux; **young** ~ les jeunes; *coll* ~ **s** (relatives) parents *mpl*, famille *f*; *adj* traditionnel -elle, populaire, folklorique

**folk-dance, folk-dancing** *n* danse *f* folklorique, danse *f* rustique

**folklore** *n* folklore *m*

**folk-music** *n* musique *f* folklorique; (contemporary) musique *f* folk

**folksinger** *n* chanteur -euse de musique folklorique (de musique folk)

**folksong** *n* chanson *f* folklorique

**folksy** *adj coll* populaire, rustique; (person) gentil -ille

**folktale** *n* conte *m* populaire, conte *m* folklorique

**follicle** *n* follicule *m*

**follow** *vt* suivre, marcher derrière; (pursue) poursuivre; (suspect) filer; (profession) suivre, exercer; (understand) suivre, comprendre; (fashion) se

conformer à, suivre; ~ **out** poursuivre jusqu'au bout; ~ **suit** fournir une carte; *fig* faire de même; (inquiries) ~ **up** poursuivre, continuer; *vi* suivre; (understand) suivre, comprendre; (result) s'ensuivre; ~ **on** suivre; résulter; (meal) **what's to** ~ ? qu'est-ce qu'il y a après?

**follower** *n* disciple *m*, partisan -e; (retainer) suivant -e; *coll ar* admirateur *m*, amoureux *m*

**following** *n* suite *f*; partisans *mpl* (*fpl* partisanes), adeptes *pl*; *adj* suivant, ce qui suit

**follow-up** *n* suite *f*; (circular) rappel *m*; *med* ~ **care** soins post-hospitaliers; ~ **study** étude *f* complémentaire

**folly** *n* folie *f*, absurdité *f*, sottise *f*; *archi* folie *f*

**foment** *vt* fomenter

**fomentation** *n* fomentation *f*

**fond** *adj* tendre, affectueux -euse; (doting) trop indulgent; (hope) fervent; (belief) naïf (*f* naïve); **be** ~ **of** aimer, aimer beaucoup

**fondle** *vt* caresser

**fondly** *adv* affectueusement; (credulously) naïvement

**fondness** *n* (people) affection *f*, tendresse *f*; (things) penchant *m*, prédilection *f*

**font** *n* fonts baptismaux

**food** *n* nourriture *f*, aliment *m*, de quoi manger; (cattle) pâture *f*; (poultry, domestic animals, etc) pâtée *f*; *fig* nourriture *f*, pâture *f*; ~ **s** aliments *mpl*; ~ **chain** chaîne *f* alimentaire; ~ **for thought** matière *f* à réflexion; ~ **shop** magasin *m* d'alimentation; ~ **supplies** ravitaillement *m*; ~ **convenience** ~ **s** aliments *mpl* à préparation rapide

**foodstuff** *n* denrée *f* alimentaire; ~ **s** denrées *fpl* alimentaires, vivres *mpl*, comestibles *mpl*

¹**fool** *n* imbécile, idiot -e, sot (*f* sotte); (jester) bouffon *m*; ~ **'s paradise** bonheur *m* illusoire; **make a** ~ **of** duper; **make a** ~ **of oneself** se rendre ridicule; **play the** ~ faire l'idiot -e; *vt* duper, berner, *coll* avoir; *vi* faire l'imbécile; ~ **about** perdre son temps, faire l'idiot

²**fool** *n cul* mousse *f* de fruits

**foolery** *n* ânerie *f*, bêtises *fpl*, bouffonnerie *f*

**foolhardiness** *n* témérité *f*, imprudence *f*

**foolhardy** *adj* téméraire, imprudent

**foolish** *adj* bête, idiot, stupide; (rash) imprudent, insensé; (simple) simple d'esprit; (behaviour) **be** ~ faire l'idiot -e

**foolishly** *adv* bêtement, sottement

**foolishness** *n* bêtise *f*, sottise *f*

**foolscap** *n* papier écolier, papier *m* ministre

**foot** n (pl **feet**) pied m; (animal) patte f; mil infanterie f; (page) bas m; (table, bed) bout m; fig **at one's feet** fasciné; **fall on one's feet** avoir de la chance; **find one's feet** trouver le joint; **get off on the wrong ~** commencer mal; **get one's ~ in the door** établir un premier contact; coll **my ~!** balivernes!; **one ~ in the grave** un pied dans la tombe; **put one's best ~ forward** allonger le pas, faire de son mieux; **put one's ~ down** faire acte d'autorité; **mot** appuyer sur le champignon; coll **put one's ~ in it** mettre ses pieds dans le plat; **set on ~** mettre en train; vt (stocking) rempiéter; ~ **it** aller à pied; coll ~ **the bill** casquer

**footage** n cin = métrage m

**foot-and-mouth (disease)** n fièvre aphteuse

**football** n ballon m; (game) football m

**footballer** n joueur m de football

**footboard** n marchepied m

**foot-bridge** n passerelle f

**footfall** n pas m; (sound) bruit m de pas

**footgear** n chaussures fpl

**foothill** n contrefort m

**foothold** n prise f de pied, point m d'appui; fig pied m

**footing** n prise f de pied, point m d'appui; fig (status) position f, situation f; (contact) relation f

**footle** vi coll faire l'âne

**footlights** npl theat rampe f

**footling** adj coll futile

**foot-loose** adj libre comme l'air

**footman** n valet m de pied

**footmark** n empreinte f (de pied)

**footnote** n note f en bas de la page; vt annoter

**footpad** n ar voleur m de grands chemins

**footpath** n sentier m

**footplate** n plate-forme f (pl plates-formes) (d'une locomotive)

**footprint** n empreinte f (de pied)

**foot-slog** vi coll marcher d'un pas lourd

**footsore** adj aux pieds endoloris

**footstep** n pas m; **follow in the ~s of** imiter

**footstool** n tabouret m

**footway** n sentier m

**footwear** n chaussures fpl

**footwork** n jeu m de jambes

**fop** n dandy m, petit-maître m (pl petits-maîtres), fat m

**foppery** n fatuité f

**foppish** adj dandy invar

**for** prep pour; au profit de; (because of) pour, en raison de; (instead of) à la place de; (time) pour, pendant, depuis; (distance) pendant, sur; (considering) pour; (in spite of) malgré; (towards) dans la direction de, vers; ~ **all that** malgré tout; ~ **my part** quant à moi; **be all ~** être tout à fait pour; **what ~?** pourquoi?; **what is that ~?** à quoi ça sert?; **you're ~ it!** qu'est-ce que tu vas prendre!; conj car

**forage** n fourrage m; vi fourrager, fouiller

**forage-cap** n mil calot m

**forasmuch** conj ~ **as** vu que, étant donné que

**foray** n raid m, razzia f, incursion f; vi faire un raid

¹**forbear, forebear** n ancêtre m

²**forbear** vi s'abstenir; ~ **to** se garder de

**forbearance** n tolérance f, longanimité f, patience f

**forbearing** adj tolérant, patient

**forbid** vt défendre, interdire; (refuse access) interdire l'accès de; **God ~!** j'espère bien que non!

**forbidden** adj défendu, interdit; ~ **fruit** fruit défendu

**forbidding** adj menaçant, sombre; (person) rebutant, sévère

**force** n force f, violence f, énergie f, vigueur f; (influence) influence f; mil force f; mil ~ **s** forces armées; **brute ~** violence f physique; **by brute ~** de vive force; **by sheer ~** of à force de; **in ~** en vigueur; **police ~** forces fpl de police; vt contraindre, forcer, obliger; (lock, entry) forcer; (rape) violer; (extort) arracher, extorquer; hort forcer, hâter; (push) pousser; ~ **back** faire reculer, repousser; (aircraft) ~ **down** forcer à atterrir; ~ **in** faire entrer de force; ~ **out** faire sortir de force

**forced** adj forcé, contraint, artificiel -ielle

**force-feed** vt nourrir de force

**forceful** adj puissant; vigoureux -euse, énergique

**forcemeat** n cul farce f, hâchis m

**forceps** n forceps m

**forcible** adj de force, par force; (forceful) puissant; (language) vigoureux -euse

**ford** n gué m; vt passer à gué

**fordable** adj guéable

**fore** n naut avant m; **to the ~** en évidence; adj à l'avant, antérieur; naut ~ **and aft** (rig, sail) aurique; adv à l'avant

**forearm** n avant-bras m

**forebear** n see ¹**forbear**

**forebode** vt annoncer, prédire; présager

**foreboding** n prémonition f

**forecast** n prévision f; sp pronostic m; **weather ~** bulletin m météorologique, prévisions fpl météorologiques, coll météo f; vt prévoir

**forecastle** n *naut* gaillard m d'avant, poste m d'équipage

**foreclose** vt *leg* saisir; ~ **on a mortgage** saisir un bien hypothéqué

**foreclosure** n *leg* saisie f

**forecourt** n avant-cour f; (petrol station) devant m

**forefather** n ancêtre m

**forefinger** n index m

**forefoot** n (large animal) pied antérieur; (dog, etc) patte antérieure, patte f de devant

**forefront** n premier rang; (progress) avant-garde f

**foregather, forgather** vi s'assembler, se réunir

**forego, forgo** vt se priver de, renoncer à, se passer de

**foregoing** adj précédent; déjà cité

**foregone** adj déjà réglé; ~ **conclusion** qch de réglé à l'avance

**foreground** n premier plan

**forehand** n sp coup droit

**forehead** n front m

**foreign** adj étranger -ère; (trade) extérieur

**foreigner** n étranger -ère

**foreknowledge** n préconnaissance f

**foreland** n promontoire m, cap m

**foreleg** n (large animal) jambe antérieure; (dog, etc) patte antérieure, patte f de devant

**forelock** n mèche f; **take time by the** ~ sauter sur l'occasion; **touch one's** ~ saluer obséquieusement

**foreman** n contremaître m; (jury) président m

**foremast** n naut mât m de misaine

**forementioned** adj déjà cité, précité

**foremost** adj principal, le plus en vue; adv **first and** ~ avant tout

**forenoon** n matinée f

**forensic** adj leg du barreau; ~ **evidence** expertise médico-légale; ~ **medicine** médecine légale

**forerunner** n précurseur m

**foresail** n naut voile f de misaine

**foresee** vt prévoir

**foreseeable** adj prévisible

**foreshadow** vt présager, annoncer, augurer

**foreshore** n laisse f de mer; leg lais m

**foreshorten** vt phot faire un raccourci de

**foreshortening** n phot raccourci m

**foresight** n prévoyance f

**foreskin** n prépuce m

**forest** n forêt f

**forestall** vt anticiper, devancer

**forester** n garde forestier

**forestry** n sylviculture f

**foretaste** n avant-goût m

**foretell** vt prédire

**forethought** n prévoyance f

**forever** adv toujours, sans cesse

**forewarn** vt prévenir, avertir

**foreword** n avant-propos m, préface f

**forfeit** n peine f; (game) ~s gages mpl; vt perdre, payer de

**forfeiture** n perte f par confiscation

**forgather** vi see **foregather**

**forge** n forge f; vt (metal, alliance, friendship) forger; (counterfeit) contrefaire, faire un faux de; vi ~ **ahead** pousser de l'avant

**forger** n faussaire

**forgery** n contrefaçon f, falsification f; (thing forged) faux m

**forget** vt oublier; (leave behind) oublier, laisser; ~ **it!** n'y pensez plus!; ~ **oneself** se comporter mal; vi oublier; **not forgetting** sans oublier

**forgetful** adj distrait, étourdi

**forgetfulness** n étourderie f, distraction f

**forging** n falsification f

**forgivable** adj pardonnable

**forgive** vt pardonner

**forgiveness** n pardon m; miséricorde f

**forgiving** adj indulgent, clément

**forgo** vt see **forego**

**forgotten** adj oublié

**fork** n agr fourche f; (cutlery) fourchette f; (junction) fourche f, embranchement m, bifurcation f; anat fourche f; vt fourcher; vi bifurquer; coll ~ **out** casquer

**forked** adj fourchu; ~ **lightning** éclair m en zigzag

**fork-lift** n ~ **truck** chariot m de levage, chariot élévateur

**forlorn** adj délaissé, abandonné, triste; ~ **hope** mince espoir m; (last effort) tentative désespérée

**form** forme f, genre m; (document to be filled in) formule f, formulaire m; (fitness) forme f, condition f; (school) classe f; (bench) banc m; **be good (bad)** ~ se faire (ne pas se faire); (racing) **study** ~ établir un pronostic; coll **what's the** ~? qu'est-ce qu'on doit faire?; vt former, modeler, construire, façonner; (train) former, éduquer, contracter; (organize) constituer, composer; mil se mettre, s'aligner; vi prendre forme, se former; ~ **up** se mettre en ligne

**formal** adj formel -elle, officiel -ielle, explicite; (stiff) austère, guindé; (ceremonial) cérémonieux -ieuse; (superficial) de forme, pour la forme

**formaldehyde** n chem formaldéhyde m

**formalin** n chem formol m

**formalism** n formalisme m

**formality** n formalité f; (stiffness)

raideur *f*, cérémonie *f*

**formalize** *vt* formaliser

**formally** *adv* officiellement; cérémonieusement

**format** *n* format *m*

**formation** *n* formation *f*; création *f*, organisation *f*

**formative** *adj* formateur -trice

**forme** *n* print forme *f*

**former** *adj* précédent, ancien -ienne; (first mentioned) premier -ière; *pron* celui-là (*f* celle-là, *mpl* ceux-là, *fpl* celles-là)

**formerly** *adv* autrefois, jadis

**formic** *adj chem* formique

**Formica** *n* Formica *m*

**formidable** *adj* redoutable, terrible, énorme

**formless** *adj* informe

**formula** *n* formule *f*

**formularize** *vt* formuler

**formulate** *vt* formuler

**formulation** *n* formulation *f*

**formulize** *vt* formuler

**fornicate** *vi* forniquer

**fornication** *n* fornication *f*

**fornicator** *n* fornicateur *m*

**fornicatress** *n* fornicatrice *f*

**forrard** *adv naut* vers le devant

**forsake** *vt* délaisser, quitter; (give up) renoncer à

**forsaken** *adj* délaissé

**forsooth** *adv ar +* *joc* en vérité; *interj* par exemple!

**forswear** *vt* abjurer, renoncer à, désavouer; ~ **oneself** se parjurer

**forsworn** *adj* parjure

**forsythia** *n bot* forsythia *m*

**fort** *n* fort *m*

¹**forte** *n* fort *m*

²**forte** *adv mus* forte

**forth** *adv* en avant; **and so** ~ et ainsi de suite; **from this day (time, moment)** ~ dorénavant, désormais; **go back and** ~ aller et venir; **hold** ~ parler longuement; **set** ~ se mettre en route

**forthcoming** *adj* à paraître, à venir; (available) disponible; (frank) ouvert, accueillant, avenant

**forthright** *adj* direct, franc (*f* franche), carré

**forthwith** *adv* aussitôt, sur-le-champ

**fortieth** *n +* *adj* quarantième

**fortification** *n* fortification *f*

**fortify** *vt* fortifier, armer; (food) renforcer en vitamines; (drink) augmenter la teneur en alcool de

**fortitude** *n* courage *m*, force *f* d'âme

**fortnight** *n* quinzaine *f*, quinze jours *mpl*

**fortnightly** *adj* bimensuel -elle; *adv* tous les quinze jours

**fortress** *n* fort *m*, forteresse *f*

**fortuitous** *adj* fortuit, imprévu

**fortuitousness** *n* chance *f*, hasard *m*

**fortunate** *adj* heureux -euse, favorable, propice

**fortune** *n* fortune *f*, chance *f*; (wealth) fortune *f*, richesse *f*

**fortune-hunter** *n* coureur *m* de dot

**fortune-teller** *n* diseur -euse de bonne aventure

**forty** *n* quarante *m invar*; **the forties** les années quarante; *geog* **the roaring forties** les quarantièmes rugissants; *adj* quarante *invar*; *coll* ~ **winks** petit somme

**forum** *n* forum *m*, tribune *f*

**forward** *n sp* avant *m*; *vt* favoriser; (goods, etc) expédier, faire suivre; *adj* en avant; (well advanced) en avance, précoce; (presumptuous) effronté, insolent; (long-term) à long terme; *naut* vers le devant; *mot* ~ **gears** vitesses *fpl* avant; *adv* en avant

**forwarding** *adj* ~ **address** adresse *f* pour faire suivre le courrier; ~ **agent** transitaire *m*

**forward-looking** *adj* progressif -ive, tourné vers l'avenir

**forwardness** *n* précocité *f*; *pej* audace *f*, effronterie *f*

**forwards** *adv see* forward *adv*

**fossil** *n* fossile *m*; *coll* croulant *m*; *adj* fossile; ~ **fuel** combustible *m* fossile

**fossilize** *vt* fossiliser; *vi* se fossiliser

¹**foster** *vt* nourrir, élever; *fig* encourager, chérir; (harbour) entretenir

²**foster** *adj* adoptif -ive, nourricier -ière, de lait

**foster-brother** *n* frère adoptif, frère *m* de lait

**foster-father** *n* père adoptif

**foster-mother** *n* mère adoptive

**foster-parent** *n* parent adoptif

**foster-sister** *n* sœur adoptive, sœur *f* de lait

**foul** *n sp* coup irrégulier; *adj* infect, immonde, crasseux -euse; (smell) fétide; (air) vicié; *fig* vil, infâme, abominable; (language) grossier -ière, ordurier -ière; ~ **play** meurtre *m*, assassinat *m*; **fall** ~ **of** *naut* aborder, entrer en collision avec; *fig* attirer l'hostilité de; *vt* polluer, infecter; (block) obstruer; *naut* aborder, entrer en collision avec; (entangle) embrouiller, entortiller; *vi* (rope, etc) s'emmêler, s'embrouiller

**foul-mouthed** *adj* (language) ordurier -ière; (person) au langage ordurier

**foulness** *n* saleté *f*

¹**found** *vt* fonder, créer, établir

²**found** *vt metal* fondre

**foundation** *n* fondation *f*, création *f*,

établissement *m*; (basis) base *f*, fondement *m*; (make-up) fond *m* de teint; *bui* ~ **s** fondations *fpl*; ~ **garment** gaine *f*, combiné *m*; ~ **stone** pierre commémorative

¹**founder** *n* fondateur -trice

²**founder** *n metal* fondeur *m*

³**founder** *vi* (horse) se mettre à boiter; (ship) sombrer, chavirer; *fig* s'effondrer, échouer

**foundling** *n* enfant trouvé -e

**foundry** *n* fonderie *f*

**fount** *n* source *f*; *typ* fonte *f*

**fountain** *n* fontaine *f*, jet *m* d'eau; (drinking) source *f* d'eau potable, fontaine publique

**fountain-head** *n* source *f*, origine *f*

**fountain-pen** *n* stylo *m*

**four** *n* quatre *m invar*; **in** ~ **figures** dans les milliers; **on all** ~ **s** à quatre pattes; *adj* quatre *invar*

**four-door** *adj* à quatre portes

**four-engined** *adj* ~ **plane** quadrimoteur *m*

**four-figure** *adj* ~ **salary** traitement *m* de plus de mille livres

**four-fold** *adj* quadruple; *adv* au quadruple

**four-letter** *adj* ~ **word** obscénité *f*, parole grossière

**four-poster (bed)** *n* lit *m* à baldaquin

**fourscore** *n* quatre-vingts *m*

**four-seater** *n* voiture *f* à quatre places

**foursome** *n sp* partie *f* à quatre; deux couples *mpl*; partie carrée

**foursquare** *adj* carré; *fig* ferme, inébranlable

**fourteen** *n* quatorze *m invar*; *adj* quatorze *invar*

**fourth** *n* quatrième; (fraction) quart *m*; *adj* quatrième

**four-wheel** *adj* ~ **drive** propulsion *f* à quatre roues motrices

**fowl** *n* volatile *m*, volaille *f*; *collect* volaille *f*, oiseaux *mpl* de basse-cour; *cul* **roast** ~ poulet rôti; *vt* (birds) chasser

**fowling-piece** *n* fusil de chasse léger

**fox** *n* renard; *fig* rusé *m*, malin *m*; *vt coll* mystifier; (fool) berner

**fox-cub** *n* renardeau *m*

**fox-earth** *n* terrier *m* de renard

**foxed** *n* (paper) marqué de rousseurs; *coll* mystifié

**foxglove** *n bot* digitale *f*

**foxhole** *n* terrier *m* de renard; *mil* petite tranchée, gourbi *m*

**foxhound** *n* foxhound *m*

**foxhunt** *n* chasse *f* au renard

**foxhunter** *n* chasseur *m* (de renard)

**foxhunting** *n* chasse *f* au renard; *adj* adonné à la chasse au renard

**fox-terrier** *n* fox *m*

**fox-trot** *n* slow *m*, slow-fox *m*

**foxy** *adj* rusé, finaud

**foyer** *n* foyer *m*, hall *m*

**fracas** *n* fracas *m*

**fraction** *n* fraction *f*, partie *f*

**fractional** *adj* infime; *math* fractionnaire; *chem* fractionné

**fractionally** *adv* un tout petit peu

**fractious** *adj* grincheux -euse, hargneux -euse

**fracture** *n* fracture *f*; *vt* fracturer; *vi* se casser, se fracturer

**fragile** *adj* fragile, frêle, précaire

**fragility** *n* fragilité *f*

**fragment** *n* fragment *m*, morceau *m*; **reduce to** ~ **s** réduire en miettes; *vt* fragmenter; *vi* se fragmenter

**fragmental** *adj* fragmentaire; *geol* clastique

**fragmentary** *adj* fragmentaire

**fragmentation** *n* fragmentation *f*

**fragrance** *n* parfum *m*, senteur *f*

**fragrant** *adj* parfumé; *fig* doux (*f* douce)

**frail** *adj* fragile, frêle, délicat

**frailty** *n* fragilité *f*, faiblesse *f*

**frame** *n* (picture) cadre *m*; (window, car) châssis *m*; (door) encadrement *m*; (spectacles) monture *f*; *hort* châssis *m*, cloche *f*; *cin* image *f*; (bone structure) ossature *f*, charpente *f*; *fig* ~ **of mind** disposition *f*; *vt* (surround) encadrer; (construct) bâtir; (plan, etc) formuler, concevoir; *coll* monter un coup contre

**frame-house** *n* maison *f* à charpente de bois

**frame-rucksack** *n* sac *m* à dos à armature

**frame-up** *n coll* coup monté

**framework** *n* cadre *m*, ossature *f*, structure *f*

**franc** *n* franc *m*

**France** *n* France *f*

**franchise** *n* droit *m* de suffrage

**Franciscan** *n* franciscain *m*; *adj* franciscain

**francophile** *n* + *adj* francophile

**francophobe** *n* + *adj* francophobe

**frangipane** *n* frangipane *f*

**Frank** *n hist* Franc *m* (*f* Franque)

¹**frank** *adj* franc (*f* franche), ouvert, sincère

²**frank** *vt* affranchir

**frankfurter** *n* saucisse *f* de Francfort

**frankincense** *n* encens *m*

**Frankish** *adj* franc (*f* franque)

**frankness** *n* franchise *f*, sincérité *f*

**frantic** *adj* frénétique, effréné; (person) hors de soi, fou (*f* folle)

**fraternal** *adj* fraternel -elle

**fraternity** *n* fraternité *f*; *US* (students) confrérie *f*

**fraternization** *n* fraternisation *f*

**fraternize** vi fraterniser
**fratricidal** adj fratricide
**fratricide** n fratricide m
**fraud** n (money) escroquerie f; (crime) imposture f, tromperie f, fraude f; (person) imposteur m, charlatan m; (cheat) escroc m; coll **he's a bit of a ~** c'est un fumiste
**fraudulence, fraudulency** n caractère frauduleux
**fraudulent** adj frauduleux -euse; leg **~ conversion** malversation f
**fraught** adj plein, chargé; fig lourd, tendu; coll tendu, risqué
¹**fray** n rixe f, conflit m; fig **enter the ~** entrer en lice
²**fray** vt effilocher; (cuff) effranger; naut (rope) raguer; fig exaspérer; vi s'effilocher, s'effiler; naut se raguer
**frazzle** n **to a ~** complètement, tout à fait; vt US coll éreinter, crever
**freak** n monstre m, phénomène m; (whim) lubie f; (behaviour) caprice m; sl dingue; adj anormal, insolite, bizarre; vi (also **~ out**) sl (drugs) se défoncer; (drop out) se défouler, devenir hippie
**freakish** adj insolite, anormal, bizarre, saugrenu
**freckle** n tache f de rousseur, tache f de son; vt marquer de taches de rousseur; vi se couvrir de taches de rousseur
**freckled** adj taché de son, couvert de taches de rousseur
**free** adj libre; indépendant, autonome; (without payment) gratuit, libre; (lavish) généreux -euse, prodigue; **~ and easy** décontracté; **~ church** église f nonconformiste; **~ fight** mêlée f, rixe f; **~ hand** carte blanche; sp **~ kick** coup franc; comm **~ on board (f.o.b.)** franco à bord; coll **feel ~!** sers-toi!, fais ce que tu veux!; coll **for ~** à l'œil; **get ~ of** se débarrasser de; **give ~ rein to** donner libre cours à; go **~** être relâché; **make ~ with** se permettre des libertés avec; vt libérer, affranchir; (exempt) exempter, exonérer; (burden) soulager
**freeboard** n naut franc-bord m (pl francs-bords)
**freebooter** n pirate m, flibustier m
**freeborn** adj né libre
**freedom** n liberté f; (exemption) franchise f
**free-for-all** n foire f d'empoigne
**free-hand** adj à main levée
**free-handed** adj généreux -euse, large
**free-hearted** adj ouvert, généreux -euse
**freehold** n propriété foncière libre; adj tenu en propriété perpétuelle et libre
**freeholder** n propriétaire foncier -ière

sans obligation
**freelance** n + adj indépendant -e
**freeman** n hist homme m libre; **~ of a city** citoyen -enne d'honneur d'une ville
**Freemason** n franc-maçon m (pl francs-maçons)
**freemasonry** n franc-maçonnerie f
**free-range** adj **~ eggs** œufs mpl de ferme; **~ poultry** poulets mpl de ferme
**freesia** n bot freesia m
**free-spoken** adj franc (f franche); (forthright) carré
**free-standing** adj non encastré
**freestone** n pierre f de taille
**freestyle** adj sp **~ swimming** nage f libre
**freethinker** n libre-penseur -euse (mpl libres-penseurs, fpl libres-penseuses)
**freethinking** n libre pensée f; adj libre-penseur (pl libres-penseurs)
**free-thought** n libre pensée f
**freeway** n US autoroute f (sans péage)
**free-wheel** n (bicycle) roue f libre; vi (bicycle) être en roue libre; mot rouler au point mort
**free-will** n philos libre arbitre m; adj volontaire
**freeze** n gel m, temps m de gel; vt geler; (food) congeler; (prices) bloquer, stabiliser; (credit) geler; **~ out** exclure; vi geler; fig se figer; US coll **~!** bouge pas!; coll **~ on to** s/o se cramponner à qn; **~ to death** mourir de froid; **~ up** se prendre en glace; mot (windscreen) se givrer
**freezer** n congélateur m; (compartment in refrigerator) freezer m
**freeze-up** n grand gel
**freezing** adj glacial; **~ cold** froid m de canard; **~ mixture** antigel m; **~ point** point m de congélation
**freight** n fret m, cargaison f; transport m; (chartering of ship) affrètement m; **air ~** fret m par avion; **by ~** par petite vitesse; adj US **~ car** wagon m de marchandises; **~ train** train m de marchandises; vt (ship) affréter, charger
**freightage** n fret m
**freighter** n naut cargo m; aer avion m de fret
**French** n (language) français m; **the ~** les Français; adj français; **~ bean** haricot vert; **~ Canadian** Canadien -ienne français -e; **~ chalk** craie f de tailleur; cul **~ dressing** vinaigrette f; **~ fried, US ~ fries** pommes frites; **~ horn** cor m d'harmonie; coll **~ letter** capote anglaise; **~ polish** vernis m à l'alcool; **~ window** porte-fenêtre f (pl portes-fenêtres); **take ~ leave** filer à l'anglaise

**frenchify** vt franciser

**Frenchman** n Français m

**French-speaking** adj francophone

**Frenchwoman** n Française f

**frenetic** adj frénétique, effréné

**frenzied** adj frénétique, effréné; (enthusiastic) délirant

**frenzy** n frénésie f; (delight) transport m de joie

**frequency** n fréquence f; ~ **modulation** modulation f de fréquence

**frequent** adj fréquent, courant; vt fréquenter

**frequentation** n fréquentation f

**fresco** n fresque f

**fresh** adj frais (f fraîche); (new) nouveau (f nouvelle); (colour) gai; (lively) fringant, plein d'entrain; coll familier -ière, culotté; inexpérimenté, naïf (f naïve); ~ **as a daisy** frais (f fraîche) comme une rose; adv ~ **from** frais émoulu de, fraîchement arrivé de

**freshen** vt rafraîchir, débarbouiller; rendre plus clair; vi (wind) fraîchir; ~ **up** faire un brin de toilette; (woman) se refaire une beauté

**fresher, freshman** n coll (student) conscrit m, bleu m, bizuth m

**freshness** n fraîcheur f; fig franchise f, spontanéité f; nouveauté f

**freshwater** adj d'eau douce

¹**fret** n anxiété f, tension nerveuse; vt corroder; (wind) rider; vi se tourmenter, se tracasser; (baby) geindre

²**fret** n (guitar) touchette f; (design) motif m; vt découper, chantourner

**fretful** adj pleurnicheur -euse, mécontent, geignard

**fretfulness** n pleurnicherie f

**fret-saw** n scie f à découper

**fretwork** n découpage m

**Freudian** adj freudien -ienne

**friability** n friabilité f

**friable** adj friable

**friar** n religieux m, frère m

**fricassee** n fricassée f

**fricative** n fricative f; adj fricatif -ive

**friction** n friction f, frottement m; désaccord m

**Friday** n vendredi m; **Good** ~ vendredi saint; m

**fridge** n abbr frigo m, frigidaire m

**friend** n ami -e; (school, work, etc) camarade, copain m, copine f; **a** ~ **in need is a** ~ **indeed** c'est dans le besoin qu'on connaît ses vrais amis; **boy** ~ petit ami; **girl** ~ petite amie; **have** ~ **s at court** avoir des amis influents; (parliament) **my honourable** ~, leg **my learned** ~ mon honorable confrère; **Society of Friends** Quakers mpl

**friendless** adj seul, sans amis

**friendliness** n bienveillance f, amabilité f

**friendly** adj amical, gentil -ille, affectueux -euse; bienveillant

**friendship** n amitié f

¹**frieze** n archi frise f, bordure f

²**frieze** n ratine f

**frigate** n naut frégate f

**fright** n effroi m, peur f; coll (person) horreur f, épouvantail m; **give s/o a** ~ effrayer qn; **have a** ~ avoir peur; **take** ~ s'épouvanter, s'effrayer

**frighten** vt effrayer, faire peur à, épouvanter; ~ **away**, ~ **off** effaroucher

**frightened** adj effrayé; **don't be** ~ n'ayez pas peur

**frightful** adj épouvantable, effroyable

**frightfully** adv effroyablement, affreusement; coll terriblement; **be** ~ **sorry** être absolument désolé

**frightfulness** n atrocité f, horreur f

**frigid** adj glacial, froid, glacé; (woman) frigide

**frigidity** n froideur f; (sexual) frigidité f

**frigorific** adj frigorifique

**frill** n ruche f; (shirt) jabot m; fig fanfreluche f; coll ~ **s** façons fpl, manières fpl

**frilly** adj à fanfreluches

**fringe** n (edging, hair) frange f; (border) bord m, lisière f; **on the** ~ **of** en marge de; adj sur le bord de la légalité; peu orthodoxe; ~ **benefits** avantages mpl accessoires, petits bénéfices; ~ **group** groupe marginal

**frippery** n colifichets mpl; fig préciosité f

**frisk** vt fouiller; vi gambader, folâtrer

**friskiness** n animation f, vivacité f

**frisky** adj animé, vif (f vive)

¹**fritter** n cul beignet m

²**fritter** vt ~ **away** gaspiller, perdre

**frivolity** n frivolité f

**frivolous** adj frivole

**frivolousness** n frivolité f

**frizz** n boucles désordonnées; vt faire friser

¹**frizzle** vt (hair) faire friser

²**frizzle** vt faire griller; vi grésiller; ~ **d up** calciné

**frizzy** adj crépu, crêpelé

**fro** adv **to and** ~ de long en large; **go to and** ~ **between** faire la navette entre

**frock** n robe f; (monk) froc m

**frock-coat** n ar redingote f

**frog** n grenouille f; coll pej Français -e; (loop) brandebourg m; (in throat) chat m

**frogman** n homme-grenouille m (pl hommes-grenouilles)

**frog-march** vt amener (qn) de force; (carry) amener (qn) en le prenant par les quatre membres

**frolic** n ébats mpl, réjouissances fpl;

(prank) espièglerie *f*; *vi* folâtrer, gambader

**frolicsome** *adj* folâtre, gai

**from** *prep* de; (beginning at) à partir de; (person) de la part de, d'après; (price) à partir de; (time) depuis; (keep, take) à; ~ **a novel by Balzac** d'après un roman de Balzac; ~ **150 francs a day** à partir de 150 francs par jour; ~ **now on** à partir de maintenant; ~ **the mayor** de la part du maire; **take that glass** ~ **the child** enlevez ce verre à l'enfant

**frond** *n* fronde *f*

**front** *n* devant *m*, avant *m*; (first row) premier rang; (beginning) début *m*; *mil* front *m*; (seaside) bord *m* de mer; (promenade) front *m* de mer; (figure-head) homme *m* de paille; (cover) couverture *f*; *theat* salle *f*; (shirt) plastron *m*; *coll* effronterie *f*; **be in** ~ mener, être en tête; *fig* **come to the** ~ percer; **put on a bold** ~ faire bonne contenance; *adj* de devant, premier -ière; de face; ~ **door** porte *f* d'entrée; *archi* ~ **elevation** élévation frontale; **have a** ~ **seat** avoir une place au premier rang; *fig* être aux premières loges; *mil* **eyes** ~ ! fixe!; *vt bui* donner une façade à; *vi* ~ **on to** faire face à, donner sur

**frontage** *n* (shop) devanture *f*; (house) façade *f*

**frontal** *adj med* frontal; *mil* de front; **full** ~ **nude** nu(e) de face

**frontier** *n* frontière *f*; *adj* de frontière

**frontiersman** *n* frontalier *m*

**frontispiece** *n* frontispice *m*

**front-page** *adj* ~ **news** nouvelles importantes; **be** ~ **news** être à la une

**frontwards** *adv* vers l'avant, en avant

**front-wheel** *adj mot* ~ **drive** traction *f* avant

**frost** *n* gel *m*, gelée *f*, givre *m*; *coll* four *m*; *vt* geler; (glass) givrer; *US* (cake) glacer

**frostbite** *n* gelure *f*

**frostbitten** *adj* gelé

**frosted** *adj* givré; ~ **glass** verre dépoli

**frosting** *n US cul* glaçage *m*

**frosty** *adj* glacial

**froth** *n* écume *f*, mousse *f*; *fig* vent *m*, futilités *fpl*; *vi* écumer, mousser

**frothy** *adj* écumeux -euse, mousseux -euse; (clothing) vaporeux -euse; *fig* creux *f* creuse)

**frown** *n* froncement *m* de sourcils; *vi* froncer les sourcils, se renfrogner; ~ **upon** désapprouver

**frowsty, frowzy** *adj* qui sent le renfermé

**frozen** *adj* gelé, glacé; (food) congelé

**fructification** *n* fructification *f*

**fructify** *vt* faire fructifier; *vi* fructifier

**frugal** *adj* économe; (meal) frugal

**frugality** *n* frugalité *f*; (thrift) parcimonie *f*, économie *f*

**frugally** *adv* parcimonieusement, simplement, sobrement

**fruit** *n* fruit *m*; *fig* **bear** ~ porter fruit; ~ **machine** machine *f* à sous; ~ **salad** salade *f* de fruits; ~ **salts** sels purgatifs; *vi* (tree) donner, porter des fruits

**fruit-cake** *n* cake *m*

**fruiterer** *n* marchand -e de fruits, fruitier -ière

**fruitful** *adj* fécond, fertile; (useful) fructueux -euse, profitable, utile

**fruitfulness** *n* fécondité *f*, fertilité *f*; *fig* utilité *f*, profit *m*

**fruitiness** *n* caractère fruité

**fruitless** *adj* infécond, stérile; *fig* stérile, vain

**fruitlessness** *n* infécondité *f*, stérilité *f*; *fig* stérilité *f*

**fruity** *adj* fruité; (voice) moelleux -euse; *coll* corsé

**frump** *n* bonne femme mal fagotée

**frustrate** *vt* frustrer, tromper; (foil) contrecarrer, déjouer

**frustration** *n* frustration *f*, déception *f*

¹**fry** *n* (fish) fretin *m*; **small** ~ (unimportant people) le menu fretin; (children) marmaille *f*

²**fry** *n* friture *f*; *vt* frire, faire frire; **fried egg** œuf *m* sur le plat; *vi* frire

**fryer** *n* poêle *f* à frire; **deep** ~ friteuse *f*

**frying-pan** *n* poêle *f* à frire; **out of the** ~ **into the fire** de Charybde en Scylla

**fuchsia** *n bot* fuchsia *m*

**fuck** *n vulg* baisage *m*; **she's a good** ~ elle baise bien; *vt vulg* baiser; ~!, ~ **it!** putain *f* de merde!; ~ **me!** merde alors!; ~ **you!** va te faire foutre!; **feel** ~ **ed** être mal foutu; *vi vulg* baiser; ~ **about** déconner; ~ **off** foutre le camp; ~ **up** foutre la merde dans

**fuck-all** *n vulg* rien *m* de rien

**fucking** *adj vulg* putain *f* de; ~ **hell** putain *f* de bordel; **this** ~ **car** cette putain de voiture

**fuddled** *adj* brouillé, confus; (tipsy) éméché, gris

**fuddy-duddy** *n* vieux machin; *sl* croulant -e

**fudge** *n cul* fondant *m*; (newspaper) dernières nouvelles; *interj* balivernes!; *vt* monter, truquer; (work) bâcler

**fuel** *n* combustible *m*; *mot* carburant *m*; *fig* **add** ~ **to the flames** jeter de l'huile sur le feu; *vt* alimenter, ravitailler en combustible

**fuelling** *n* combustible *m*; ravitaillement *m* en combustible

**fuel-oil** *n* mazout *m*

**fug** *n* odeur *f* de renfermé

**fugitive** *n* fugitif -ive, fuyard -e; *adj* fugitif -ive; *fig* éphémère
**fugue** *n mus+psych* fugue *f*
**fulcrum** *n* pivot *m*, point *m* d'appui
**fulfil** *vt* accomplir, réaliser, satisfaire; (prayer) exaucer
**fulfilment** *n* accomplissement *m*, réalisation *f*, satisfaction *f*; (prayer) exaucement *m*
**full** *n* in ~ en toutes lettres; intégralement; **to the** ~ tout à fait, pleinement; *adj* plein, rempli; (crowded) comble; (clothes) large, ample; (plump) rondelet -ette; (hotel) complet -ète; (face) rond, joufflu; *coll* (having eaten) rempli, rassasié; ~ **dress** *mil* grande tenue; tenue *f* de soirée; ~ **face portrait** portrait *m* de face; ~ **fare** place entière; ~ **house** *theat* salle *f* comble; (cards) full *m*; ~ **of** préoccupé de; ~ **of oneself** satisfait; (punctuation) ~ **stop** point *m*; arrêt complet; ~ **up** plein à craquer; (noise) **at** ~ **blast** à pleins tubes; **at** ~ **speed** à toute vitesse; **be in** ~ **swing** battre son plein; **fall** ~ **length** tomber de tout son long; **in** ~ **blast** très actif -ive; **in** ~ **cry** suivant de très près; *adv* complètement, directement; ~ **in the face** en plein visage; **go** ~ **out** aller à toute vitesse
**fullback** *n sp* arrière *m*
**full-blooded** *adj* vigoureux -euse, robuste
**full-bodied** *adj* corpulent; (wine) corsé
**full-dress** *adj* (clothes) de cérémonie; (discussion, etc) dans les règles
**fuller** *n* fouleur -euse
**fuller's earth** *n* terre *f* à foulon
**full-fledged** *adj US see* **fully-fledged**
**full-grown** *adj* grand, adulte
**full-length** *adj* étendu; *cin* de long métrage; (portrait) en pied
**fullness** *n* abondance *f*, ampleur *f*; **in the** ~ **of time** (eventually) avec le temps; (at the appointed time) en temps et lieu
**full-scale** *adj* grandeur nature *invar*; de grande envergure
**full-time** *n sp* fin *f* de match; *adj* à plein temps
**fully** *adv* entièrement, pleinement; (at least) au moins, largement
**fully-fashioned** *adj* entièrement diminué
**fully-fledged** *adj* (bird) ayant toutes ses plumes; *fig* qualifié; (entire) à part entière
**fulmar** *n orni* fulmar *m*
**fulminant** *adj* fulminant
**fulminate** *n chem* fulminate *m*; *vi* exploser; *fig* fulminer, pester
**fulmination** *n* explosion *f*; *fig* fulmination *f*

**fulsome** *adj* exagéré, plein d'effusions
**fumarole** *n* fumerolle *f*
**fumble** *vt* manier maladroitement; *vi* fouiller; (grope) chercher à tâtons; ~ **for words** chercher ses mots
**fume** *n* ~s fumées *fpl*, exhalaisons *fpl*; *vi* exhaler des vapeurs; *fig* être furieux -ieuse, rager
**fumigate** *vt* fumiger
**fumigation** *n* fumigation *f*
**fumigator** *n* fumigateur *m*
**fun** *n* amusement *m*, divertissement *m*; (joke) plaisanterie *f*; *euph* rapport sexuel; **be** ~ être amusant; **for** ~ pour rire; **have good** ~ s'amuser bien; **in** ~ par plaisanterie; *sl* **like** ~ *iron* pas du tout; très vite; **make** ~ **of** se moquer de; *adj coll* marrant
**funambulist** *n* funambule
**function** *n* fonction *f*, charge *f*; (meeting) réunion *f*, réception *f*; *vi* fonctionner, marcher; ~ **as** jouer le rôle de
**functional** *adj* fonctionnel -elle
**functionary** *n* (public) fonctionnaire; employé -e
**fund** *n* fonds *m*, caisse *f*; (charity, etc) souscription *f*; *fig* (stock) fond *m*, quantité *f*; capitaux *mpl*; ~**s** (public) fonds publics; *vt* consolider; financer
**fundament** *n* fesses *fpl*; anus *m*
**fundamental** *n mus* fondamental *m*; principe essentiel; *adj* fondamental, de principe, de base
**fundamentalist** *n* fondamentaliste
**funeral** *n* enterrement *m*, obsèques *fpl*; (large-scale) funérailles *fpl*; **state** ~ funérailles nationales; *coll* **that's your** ~! tant pis pour toi!; *adj* funèbre
**funerary** *adj* funéraire
**funereal** *adj* funèbre, lugubre, sépulcral
**fun-fair** *n* fête foraine
**fungoid** *adj med* fongueux -euse; *bot* cryptogamique
**fungus** *n* champignon *m*; (mould) moisissure *f*; *med* fungus *m*; *joc* moustaches *fpl* et barbe *f*
**funicular** *n* funiculaire *m*; *adj* funiculaire
**funk** *n coll* froussard -e, poltron -onne; **be in a blue** ~ avoir la frousse; *vt* avoir peur de; *vi* se dégonfler, caner
**funky** *adj coll* froussard
**funnel** *n* entonnoir *m*; (ship) cheminée *f*; *vt* faire passer dans un entonnoir; *fig* canaliser
**funnily** *adv* drôlement; (curiously, oddly) curieusement, bizarrement; ~ **enough** c'est drôle
**funny** *adj* drôle, amusant, comique; (odd) curieux -ieuse, bizarre, drôle de; (slightly unwell) indisposé, drôle; ~ **business** qch de louche; **don't try to be**

~ ce n'est pas le moment de faire de l'esprit

**funnybone** n coll petit juif

**fur** n poil m, fourrure f; (clothing) fourrure(s) f(pl); (kettle) incrustation f; **have ~ on one's tongue** avoir la langue empâtée; **make the ~ fly** faire du grabuge; vt revêtir de fourrures; vi ~ **up** s'incruster; (tongue) être chargée

**furbelow** n falbala m; fanfreluches fpl

**furbish** vt (rust) dérouiller; astiquer, remettre à neuf

**furious** adj furieux -ieuse; (raging) déchaîné; (struggle) acharné; (speed) fou (f folle)

**furiousness** n fureur f

**furl** vt naut ferler; (umbrella, flag) rouler

**furlong** n = 200 mètres (à peu près)

**furlough** n congé m, permission f

**furnace** n fourneau m; fig fournaise f

**furnish** vt (house, etc) meubler; (supply) fournir, munir

**furnisher** n marchand -e de meubles

**furnishing** n installation f de meubles; ~s mobilier m, meubles mpl, ameublement m

**furniture** n mobilier m, meubles mpl, ameublement m; **piece of ~** meuble m; ~ **remover** déménageur m; ~ **shop** magasin m de meubles; ~ **store** garde-meuble m; ~ **van** camion m de déménagement

**furore**, US **furor** n débordement m d'enthousiasme, admiration f sans bornes

**furrier** n fourreur m

**furrow** n sillon m, rayon m; (wrinkle) ride f; vt sillonner; (face) rider

**furry** adj à poil; (toy) en peluche

**further** adj plus éloigné; additionnel -elle, supplémentaire; (education) post-scolaire; **until ~ notice** jusqu'à nouvel ordre; **without ~ delay** sans plus attendre; adv plus loin; (more) davantage, plus; (moreover) de plus, d'ailleurs; comm ~ **to your letter** par suite à votre lettre; vt avancer, favoriser

**furtherance** n avancement m

**furthermore** adv en outre, par ailleurs, de plus

**furthermost** adj le plus éloigné

**furthest** adj le plus éloigné; adv le plus loin

**furtive** adj furtif -ive, sournois

**fury** n fureur f, furie f; myth furie f; fig mégère f; **like ~** d'arrache-pied

**furze** n ajoncs mpl

**fuse** n elect fusible m, plomb m; min cordeau m, mèche f; (bomb) amorce f, détonateur m; vt (metal) fondre, mettre en fusion; fig fusionner, unifier; elect faire sauter; (bomb) amorcer; vi (metal) fondre; fig s'unifier, fusionner; elect sauter

**fuse-box** n elect coupe-circuit m invar

**fuselage** n fuselage m

**fusel-oil** n huile f de fusel

**fuse-wire** n elect fusible m

**fusibility** n fusibilité f

**fusible** adj fusible

**fusilier** n fusilier m

**fusillade** n fusillade f

**fusion** n (metal) fonte f, fusion f; phys fusion f; fig fusionnement m

**fuss** n agitation f, tapage m; embarras m; coll **kick up a ~** faire un tas d'histoires; **make a ~ about** faire des histoires pour; **make a ~ of** être aux petits soins pour; vi ennuyer, embêter; vi s'agiter; (worry) se tracasser, s'en faire; ~ **about** s'affairer

**fuss-pot** n coll enquiquineur -euse, coupeur -euse de cheveux en quatre

**fussy** adj pointilleux -euse, tâtillon -onne; enquiquinant; (over elegant) tarabiscoté; **I'm not ~** ça m'est égal, je ne suis pas difficile

**fustian** n futaine f

**fustigate** vt joc fouetter, fustiger

**fusty** adj de moisi, renfermé; fig suranné

**futile** adj futile

**futility** n futilité f

**future** n avenir m; gramm futur m; comm ~**s** marchandises achetées à terme; adj futur, à venir

**futureless** adj sans avenir

**futurism** n futurisme m

**futuristic** adj futuriste

**futurity** n avenir m

**fuzz** n cheveux crépus; (on body) duvet m; sl **the ~** la flicaille

**fuzzy** adj (hair) crépu; (blurred) flou; (muddled) déconcerté; (drunk) un peu parti; **feel ~** avoir la tête qui tourne

# G

G *n mus* sol *m*

**gab** *n coll* tapette *f*, loquacité *f*; *coll* bec *m*, gueule *f*; **have the gift of the ~** avoir la langue bien pendue; *vi* bavarder, bonimenter

**gabble** *n* bredouillement *m*, jacasserie *f*; *vt* bredouiller; *vi* bredouiller, jacasser

**gabbler** *n* bredouilleur -euse

**gable** *n* pignon *m*; **~ end** pignon *m*; *vt* mettre des pignons à; *vi* être à pignons

**gabled** *adj* à pignons

¹**gad** *n* aiguillon *m*; (spear) pointe *f*

²**gad** *n* flâne *f*, balade *f*; *vi* vadrouiller; courailler

**gadabout** *n* vadrouilleur -euse; coureur -euse

**gadfly** *n* taon *m*

**gadget** *n* truc *m*, machin *m*; (device) dispositif *m*, gadget *m*

**Gaelic** *n* (language) gaélique *m*; *adj* gaélique

¹**gaff** *n* gaffe *f*; harpon *m*; *naut* corne *f*; *vt* gaffer

²**gaff** *n coll* **blow the ~** manger le morceau, vendre la mèche

**gaffer** *n* vieux *m*; *coll* croulant *m*; (foreman) contremaître *m*; (boss) patron *m*

**gag** *n* bâillon *m*; *theat* gag *m*, lazzi *m*; *vt* bâillonner, museler; *vi coll theat* improviser; *theat* faire des gags

**gaga** *adj coll* gaga, gâteux -euse; cinglé

**gage** *n* gage *m*; *leg* nantissement *m*; *ar* défi *m*; *vt* donner en gage

**gaggle** *n* troupeau *m* (d'oies); *vi* cacarder

**gaiety** *n* gaieté *f*, allégresse *f*, enjouement *m*

**gaily** *adv* gaiement, allègrement, avec entrain

**gain** *n* profit *m*, gain *m*, bénéfice *m*; accroissement *m*; avantage *m*, amélioration *f*; (clock) avance *f*; *vt* gagner; atteindre; acquérir; (information) obtenir; **~ ground** gagner du terrain, faire des progrès; **~ time** gagner du temps, se procurer un sursis; *vi* gagner; augmenter; (clock) avancer; **~ by** trouver avantage à; **~ on** prendre de l'avance sur, rattraper, gagner du terrain sur

**gain-control** *n rad* bouton *m* de puissance

**gainer** *n* celui *m* (*f* celle) qui gagne

**gainful** *adj* rémunérateur -trice, rentable

**gainfully** *adv* **~ employed** ayant un emploi rémunérateur

**gainsay** *vt* contredire

**gait** *n* démarche *f*, manière *f* de marcher, allure *f*

**gaiter** *n* guêtre *f*

**gaitered** *adj* guêtré

**galactic** *adj* galactique; *med* lactaire

**galaxy** *n astron* galaxie *f*; *fig* constellation *f*; pléiade *f*

**gale** *n* vent violent, tempête *f*

**galena** *n* galène *f*

**Galilean** *n* Galiléen -éenne; *adj* galiléen -éenne

**galiot** *n see* **galliot**

¹**gall** *n med* bile *f*; (of animals) fiel *m*; *fig* amertume *f*, fiel *m*

²**gall** *n* écorchure *f*; enflure *f*; *vet* (*esp* of horse) gale *f*, rouvieux *m*; *bot* galle *f*; *vt* écorcher, excorier; *fig* irriter

**gallant** *n* galant *m*; soupirant *m*, élégant *m*; *adj* courageux -euse, vaillant; élégant, noble; galant; *vi* faire le galant, faire la cour

**gallantly** *adv* courageusement, vaillamment; galamment

**gallantry** *n* courage *m*, vaillance *f*; galanterie *f*; propos flatteur, compliment *m*, douceur *f*

**gall-bladder** *n* vésicule *f* biliaire

**galleon** *n* galion *m*

**gallery** *n* galerie *f*, tribune *f*; *eng* galerie *f*; musée *m*, galerie *f*; *theat* paradis *m*, galerie *f*, *coll* poulailler *m*; **play to the ~** poser pour la galerie

**galley** *n naut* (ship) galère *f*; (rowing-boat) yole *f*; (ship's kitchen) coquerie *f*; *print* placard *m*

**galley-proof** *n print* placard *m*

**galley-slave** *n* galérien *m*

**galliard** *n* gaillarde *f*

**Gallic** *adj* gaulois

**gallic** *adj chem* gallique

**gallicism** *n* gallicisme *m*

**gallicize** *vt* franciser

**gallimaufry** *n* salmigondis *m*, galimatias *m*

**gallinaceous** *adj* gallinacé

**galling** *adj* irritant, mortifiant

**galliot, galiot** *n naut* galiote *f*

**gallivant** *vi* vadrouiller; couraller; flirter

**gallon** *n* gallon *m* (= 4.54 litres)

**gallop** *n* galop *m*; *vt* faire galoper; *vi* galoper; courir vite, aller vite; faire vite

**gallows** n gibet m, potence f; peine f de mort; ~ **bird** gibier m de potence; ~ **tree** gibet m, potence f

**gall-stone** n med calcul m biliaire

**galop** n galop m; vi danser un galop

**galore** adv à foison, à profusion, en quantité; coll à gogo

**galoshes** npl botillons mpl de caoutchouc, caoutchoucs mpl

**galumph** vi coll gambader, caracoler

**galvanic** adj elect galvanique; fig convulsif -ive; frénétique

**galvanism** n elect galvanisme m; med galvanisation f

**galvanization** n galvanisation f, zingage m

**galvanize** vt galvaniser, zinguer; fig électriser, galvaniser

**galvanometer** n galvanomètre m

**gambit** n (chess) gambit m; ruse f, astuce f

**gamble** n action f de miser; fig entreprise risquée; **it's a** ~ c'est un risque; vt jouer, miser; risquer; vi jouer; prendre des risques

**gambler** n joueur -euse

**gambling** n jeu m

**gamboge** n gomme-gutte f (pl gommes-guttes)

**gambol** n gambade f, cabriole f; vi gambader, cabrioler, sautiller

**¹game** n jeu m, amusement m; match m, partie f; (hunting) gibier m; cul gibier m; fig jeu m, manège m, manigance f, artifice m; **big** ~ grands fauves; **fair** ~ proie f légitime; **make** ~ **of** se moquer de; **one** ~ **all** un partout; **paying** ~ entreprise lucrative; **play a good** ~ jouer bien; **play the** ~ jouer franc jeu; **the** ~ **is up** tout est raté; vi (gamble) jouer

**²game** adj estropié; coll brave, crâne, culotté; prêt, disposé; **be** ~ **for anything** n'avoir peur de rien, avoir du cran

**game-bag** n gibecière f

**game-cock** n coq m de combat

**gamekeeper** n garde-chasse m (pl gardes-chasse(s))

**game-laws** n code m de la chasse

**gamely** adv courageusement

**gameness** n crânerie f

**gamesmanship** n utilisation f d'astuces pour gagner

**gamester** n joueur -euse

**gaming** n (gambling) jeu m

**¹gammon** n quartier de porc fumé; jambon fumé; vt (pork, ham) fumer

**²gammon** n coll baliverne f, bourde f; vt mettre en boîte, tromper; vi coll dire des balivernes, dire des bourdes

**gammy** adj coll estropié

**gamut** n mus gamme f; fig gamme f,

étendue f

**gamy** adj faisandé; coll crâne, culotté

**gander** n jars m; niais m; coll coup m d'œil

**gang** n bande f, équipe f, clan m, clique f; (criminals) gang m; (tools) jeu m; vi coll former une bande; ~ **up on** se liguer contre

**ganger** n contremaître m

**gangling** adj dégingandé

**ganglionique** adj ganglionnaire

**gang-plank** n naut planche f

**gangrene** n gangrène f; vt gangrener; vi se gangrener

**gangrenous** adj gangreneux -euse

**gangster** n gangster m, bandit m, malfaiteur m

**gangway** n passage m; (in seats) couloir m; naut passerelle f; interj dégagez!

**gannet** n orni fou m

**gantry** n eng portique m; (railway) portique m à signaux; (barrels) chantier m

**gaol, jail** n prison f

**gaol-bird** n récidiviste, cheval m de retour

**gaoler, jailer** n geôlier -ière, gardien -ienne

**gaol-fever** n typhus m

**gap** n trou m, vide m; (between mountains, in hedge, etc) brèche f; (time) intervalle m; fig trou m, lacune f, interruption f, hiatus m, solution f de continuité; **bridge the** ~ faire la soudure, combler le vide; **credibility** ~ crise f de confiance

**gape** n bâillement m; ouverture f; vi bâiller; béer, bayer aux corneilles; fig s'ouvrir, rester ouvert; ~ **at** regarder bouche bée

**garage** n garage m; vt mettre au garage, garer

**garb** n accoutrement m, costume m; vt accoutrer, vêtir

**garbage** n ordures fpl, détritus mpl; saleté f

**garble** vt dénaturer, fausser

**garden** n jardin m; ~**s** jardin public; **flower** ~ jardin m d'agrément; **kitchen** ~ potager m; **market** ~ maraîcher m; **lead s/o up the** ~(**-path**) duper qn, berner qn; adj (plants) de jardin; (tools) de jardinage; vi jardiner

**garden-city** n cité-jardin f (pl cités-jardins)

**gardener** n jardinier -ière

**gardenia** n gardénia m

**gardening** n jardinage m

**gargantuan** adj gargantuesque

**gargle** n gargarisme m; vi se gargariser

**gargoyle** n gargouille f

**garish** adj (colour, appearance) criard, voyant; (light) cru

**garishness** *n* aspect criard, couleur criarde; (light) crudité *f*

**garland** *n* guirlande *f*, feston *m*; *fig* palme *f*; *vt* enguirlander; *fig* couronner

**garlic** *n* ail *m*

**garment** *n* vêtement *m*; ~ s habillement *m*

**garner** *n* grenier *m*, fenil *m*, grange *f*; anthologie *f*; *vi* engranger, accumuler

**garnet** *n* grenat *m*

**garnish** *n* ornementation *f*; *cul* garniture *f*; *vt* orner, garnir, parer; *cul* garnir

**garnishing** *n* ornementation *f*; *cul* garniture *f*

**garniture** *n* ornementation *f*

**garret** *n* mansarde *f*, grenier *m*

**garrison** *n* garnison *f*; *vt* (town) installer une garnison dans; (troops) mettre en garnison

**garrotte** *n* garrot *m*; *vt* étrangler

**garrulity** *n* loquacité *f*

**garrulous** *adj* loquace, bavard

**garrulousness** *n* loquacité *f*

**garter** *n* jarretière *f*

**garth** *n* cour *f*, enclos *m*

**gas** *n* gaz *m*; *US* essence *f*; *coll* bavardage *m*, baratin *m*; **coal** ~ gaz *m* de houille; **laughing** ~ gaz hilarant; **marsh** ~ gaz *m* du marais, méthane *m*; **natural** ~ gaz naturel, gaz *m* du pétrole; **poison** ~ gaz asphyxiant; *coll* **step on the** ~ accélérer, *coll* appuyer sur le champignon; **tear** ~ gaz *m* lacrymogène; *vt mil* gazer; asphyxier; *vi coll* bavarder, baratiner

**gas-bag** *n* enveloppe *f* d'un aérostat; *coll* baratineur -euse

**gas-bracket** *n* applique *f* à gaz

**gas-burner** *n* bec *m* de gaz

**gas-chamber** *n* chambre *f* à gaz

**gas-cooker** *n* cuisinière *f* à gaz

**gaseous** *adj* gazeux -euse

**gas-fire** *n* radiateur *m* à gaz

**gas-fitter** *n* gazier *m*

**gas-fittings** *npl* installations *fpl* de gaz

**gash** *n* balafre *f*, entaille *f*, estafilade *f*, taillade *f*; *vt* balafrer, entailler, taillader

**gasification** *n* gazéification *f*

**gasify** *vt* gazéifier; *vi* passer à l'état de gaz

**gas-jet** *n* bec *m* de gaz

**gasket** *n* mot joint *m* de culasse; *naut* raban *m* de ferlage

**gaslight** *n* lumière *f* de gaz

**gas-main** *n* conduite *f* de gaz

**gas-mantle** *n* manchon *m* à incandescence

**gas-mask** *n* masque *m* à gaz

**gas-meter** *n* compteur *m* à gaz

**gasoline** *n* gazoline *f*; *US* essence *f*

**gasometer** *n* gazomètre *m*

**gasp** *n* halètement *m*, souffle *m*; **at the last** ~ au bout des forces, sur le point de mourir, à l'agonie; *vt* parler en soufflant; *vi* haleter, souffler

**gasper** *n sl* sèche *f*

**gasping** *n* halètement *m*; *adj* essoufflé; spasmodique

**gas-ring** *n* réchaud *m* à gaz

**gas-station** *n US* poste *m* d'essence, station-service *f* (*pl* stations-service)

**gas-stove** *n* (cooker) cuisinière *f* à gaz; (heater) fourneau *m* à gaz

**gassy** *adj* gazeux -euse; *coll* loquace

**gasteropod** *n zool* gastéropode *m*

**gastric** *adj med* gastrique

**gastritis** *n med* gastrite *f*

**gastro-enteritis** *n med* gastro-entérite *f*

**gastronome, gastronomer, gastronomist** *n* gastronome *m*

**gastronomic** *adj* gastronomique

**gastronomy** *n* gastronomie *f*

**gas-works** *npl* usine *f* a gaz

**gat** *n US coll* revolver *m*, *coll* pétard *m*

**gate** *n* porte *f*, (in field) barrière *f*, (*usu* metal) grille *f*; (lock, dock) vanne *f*; *geog* porte *f*, défilé *m*; (crowd at match) entrées *fpl*, public *m*; (money paid by crowd at match) entrées *fpl*, recette *f*; (slalom) porte *f*; *vt* (student) consigner

**gate-crash** *vt* assister à (une réception ou réunion privée) sans être invité; (without paying) resquiller

**gate-crasher** *n* intrus -e qui assiste (à une réception ou réunion privée) sans être invité -e; (without paying) resquilleur -euse

**gate-house** *n* loge *f*; *mil* corps *m* de garde

**gate-keeper** *n* portier -ière, concierge

**gate-legged** *adj* (table) à battants

**gate-post** *n* montant *m*

**gateway** *n* porte *f*, portail *m*; *fig* porte *f*

¹**gather** *n* (pleat) fronce *f*

²**gather** *vt* assembler, grouper, rassembler, recueillir; acquérir, prendre, reprendre; (flowers, fruit) cueillir, (corn) récolter; (skirt) froncer; *typ* (pages) assembler; ~ **breath** reprendre haleine; ~ **speed** prendre de la vitesse; *vt* conclure, déduire, induire, inférer; *vi* s'assembler, se grouper, se rassembler, se réunir; (increase) augmenter, s'entasser, grandir; *med* (boil, abscess) mûrir

**gathering** *n* assemblage *m*, rassemblement *m*, réunion *f*, assemblée *f*; *med* abcès *m*

**gatling** *n obs* mitrailleuse *f*

**gaud** *n* colifichet *m*, babiole *f*

**gaudiness** *n* éclat *m* vulgaire, clinquant *m*

¹**gaudy** *n* banquet *m* d'anciens élèves

²**gaudy** *adj* voyant, criard; éclatant, rutilant

**gauge** *n* étalon *m*; (bore) calibre *m*; (fluid level) jauge *f*; (railway) écartement *m*; indicateur *m*, mesureur *m*; *fig* étendue *f*; portée *f*, capacité *f*; *naut* point *m*; (railway) **loading** ~ gabarit *m*; (railway) **narrow** ~ voie étroite; **petrol** ~ jauge *f* à essence; **pressure** ~ manomètre *m*; **rain** ~ pluviomètre *m*; **wind** ~ anémomètre *m*; *vt* mesurer, calibrer, jauger; *fig* mesurer, estimer, jauger

**gauger** *n* jaugeur *m*

**Gaul** *n geog* Gaule *f*; (inhabitant) Gaulois -e

**gaunt** *adj* décharné, anguleux -euse; sévère, lugubre

¹**gauntlet** *n* gantelet *m*; *sp+mot* gant *m* à crispin; **take up the** ~ relever un défi, relever le gant; **throw down the** ~ lancer un défi, jeter le gant

²**gauntlet** *n* **run the** ~ *hist* passer par les baguettes; *fig* essuyer des critiques

**gauntness** *n* maigreur *f* extrême

**gauze** *n* (film) gaze *f*; (metal) toile *f* métallique

**gauzy** *adj* diaphane

**gavel** *n* marteau *m*

**gawk** *n coll* lourdaud -e, balourd -e, maladroit -e

**gawkiness** *n* lourdeur *f*, balourdise *f*

**gawky** *adj* lourdaud, balourd, maladroit

**gay** *n* homosexuel -elle; *adj* gai, joyeux -euse; (colour) vif (*f* vive), éclatant, gai; frivole; homosexuel -elle, *coll* de la pédale

**gaze** *n* regard *m* fixe; *vi* regarder fixement, fixer du regard

**gazebo** *n* belvédère *m*

**gazette** *n* journal officiel; journal *m*, revue *f*; **the London Gazette** = l'Officiel; *vt* publier à l'Officiel

**gazetteer** *n* dictionnaire *m* géographique

**gear** *n* équipement *m*, outils *mpl*, utensiles *mpl*; (harness) harnachement *m*; (clothing) habillement *m*; *mech* engrenage *m*; *mot* vitesse *f*; **change** ~ changer de vitesse; **first** ~ première vitesse; **in** ~ engrené, enclenché; **out of** ~ *mot* au point mort, déclenché; *fig* détraqué; **reverse** ~ marche *f* arrière; *vt* engrener, équiper; *fig* ~ **to** adapter à, lier à; *vi* s'engrener

**gear-box** *n* boîte *f* de vitesse

**gearing** *n* engrenage *m*

**gear-lever** *n* levier *m* de vitesse

**gear-wheel** *n* roue *f* d'engrenage; (bicycle) pignon *m*

**gee** *interj* hue!; *US* tiens!

**gee-gee** *n* (child's language) dada *m*

**gee-up** *interj* hue!

**geezer** *n sl* type *m*, zèbre *m*, zig *m*, zigue *m*

**gehenna** *n* géhenne *f*, enfer *m*

**Geiger counter** *n* compteur *m* Geiger

**gel** *n chem* colloïde *m*; *vi* se coaguler

**gelatine** *n* gélatine *f*

**gelatinous** *adj* gélatineux -euse

**geld** *vt* châtrer

**gelding** *n* castration *f*; animal châtré; (horse) hongre *m*

**gelid** *adj* gelé, transi

**gelidity, gelidness** *n* froid *m* intense

**gelignite** *n* gélignite *f*

**gem** *n min* gemme *f*; pierre précieuse, joyau *m*, bijou *m*; *fig* joyau *m*, bijou *m*, perle *f*; *vt* orner de pierres précieuses

**geminate** *vt* géminer; *adj* géminé

**Gemini** *n astron* Gémeaux *mpl*

**gemma** *n bot* bourgeon *m*, gemme *f*

**gemmate** *vi bot* bourgeonner, gemmer

**gemmation** *n* gemmation *f*

**gen** *n coll* vérité vraie, tuyau *m*, coordonnées *fpl*; *vt* ~**s/o up on** mettre qn au parfum de; *vi* ~ **up on sth** se renseigner sur qch

**gender** *n gramm* genre *m*; *coll* sexe *m*

**gene** *n biol* gène *m*

**genealogical** *adj* généalogique; ~ **tree** arbre *m* généalogique

**genealogist** *n* généalogiste

**genealogy** *n* généalogie *f*

¹**general** *n mil+eccles* général *m*; *coll* bonne *f* à tout faire

²**general** *adj* général; non spécialisé; ~ **election** élections législatives; **in** ~ en général

**generalissimo** *n* généralissime *m*

**generality** *n* généralité *f*, majorité *f*, commun *m*

**generalization** *n* généralisation *f*

**generalize** *vt* généraliser, rendre général; *vi* généraliser

**generally** *adv* généralement, en général, pour la plupart

**generalship** *n mil* (rank) généralat *m*; habileté *f* stratégique, compétence *f* tactique

**generate** *vt* engendrer, causer, produire

**generating** *adj* générateur -trice; ~ **station** centrale *f* électrique

**generation** *n* engendrement *m*; génération *f*

**generative** *adj* générateur -trice, producteur -trice

**generator** *n* générateur -trice; *elect* génératrice *f*

**generic, generical** *adj* générique

**generosity** *n* générosité *f*; acte généreux

**generous** *adj* généreux -euse, charitable, libéral; brave, élevé, humain; (wine)

généreux -euse, corsé
**genesis** n genèse f
**genet** n zool genette f
**genetic, genetical** adj génétique
**genetics** npl génétique f
**Geneva** n Genève f; **lake of ~** Lac m Léman, Lac m de Genève
**geneva** n genièvre m
**genial** adj bienveillant, amical, cordial, ouvert; (climate) doux (f douce), favorable, mitigé
**geniality** n bienveillance f, cordialité f, bonhomie f
**genic** adj génétique
**genie** n génie m, djinn m
**genista** n bot genêt m
**genital** adj génital
**genitalia, genitals** npl parties génitales
**genitive** n gramm génitif m
**genius** n (pl **geniuses**) (characteristic) génie m, aptitude f remarquable, caractère distinctif; (person) génie m; (pl **genii**) génie m, lutin m, démon m; **evil ~** mauvais génie
**genocide** n génocide m
**genre** n genre m
**gent** n coll chic type m
**genteel** adj ar bien élevé, distingué; pej distingué, délicat
**gentian** n bot gentiane f
**gentile** n gentil m; adj des gentils
**gentility** n bonne naissance, distinction f; pej distinction f, délicatesse f
¹**gentle** adj doux (f douce), aimable, modéré, tendre, docile; obs bien né, noble; her ayant droit aux armoiries
²**gentle** n asticot m
**gentlefolk** npl gens mpl comme il faut, gens bien nés
**gentleman** n gentleman m, homme m du monde, galant homme, monsieur m; ar noble m, gentilhomme m; **~'s agreement** convention f tacite
**gentleman-at-arms** n gentilhomme m de la garde royale
**gentleman-farmer** n gentleman-farmer m (pl gentlemen-farmers)
**gentlemanlike, gentlemanly** adj (behaviour) courtois, poli, de bon ton; (person) bien élevé, bien né
**gentleness** n douceur f; amabilité f, tendresse f, docilité f
**gentlewoman** n dame f, demoiselle f, dame f du monde; obs grande dame
**gently** adv doucement, aimablement, tendrement, docilement
**genuflect** vi faire une génuflexion
**genuflection, genuflexion** n génuflexion f
**genuine** adj vrai, authentique, véridique; sincère, franc (f franche); zool de pure race

**genuineness** n authenticité f; sincérité f, franchise f
**genus** n biol genre m
**geocentric, geocentrical** adj géocentrique
**geodesic** adj géodésique
**geodesy** n géodésie f
**geographer** n géographe
**geographic, geographical** adj géographique
**geography** n géographie f; topographie f, configuration f; livre m de géographie
**geological** adj géologique
**geologist** n géologue
**geologize** vt étudier la géologie de; vi faire de la géologie
**geology** n géologie f
**geometer** n géomètre m
**geometric, geometrical** adj géométrique; fig régulier -ière, symétrique, angulaire
**geometrician** n géomètre
**geometry** n géométrie f
**geophysical** adj géophysique
**geophysics** npl géophysique f
**geopolitical** adj géopolitique
**geopolitics** npl géopolitique f
**George** n Georges m; **by ~!** mon Dieu!
**georgette** n crêpe m georgette
**georgic** n géorgique f
**geranium** n bot géranium m
**gerfalcon** n orni gerfaut m
**geriatric** adj gériatrique
**geriatrics** npl gériatrie f
**germ** n med bacille m, microbe m, germe m; fig source f, origine f, germe m; **~ warfare** guerre f bactériologique
**German** n Allemand -e; hist Germain -e; (language) allemand m; adj allemand, germanique; hist germain; **~ measles** rubéole f
**german** adj (cousin) germain
**germane** adj apparenté; **~ to** se rapportant à
**Germanic** n germanique m; adj germanique
**Germanism** n germanisme m
**Germanist** n germaniste
**Germanize** vt germaniser
**German silver** n argentan m, maillechort m
**Germany** n Allemagne f
**germen** n bot germe m
**germicidal** adj germicide, bactéricide, microbicide
**germicide** n microbicide m; adj germicide, bactéricide, microbicide
**germinal** adj biol germinal; en germe
**germinant** adj qui germe
**germinate** vt faire germer; vi germer
**germination** n germination f

**germon** n germon m, thon blanc
**gerontology** n gérontologie f
**gerrymander** n modification f de circonscriptions pour des raisons électorales, *coll* cuisine électorale; *vt* truquer (une élection), *coll* cuisiner (une élection)
**gerrymandering** n action f de truquer une élection
**gerund** n *gramm* (English) substantif verbal; (Latin, French) gérondif m
**gerundive** n *gramm* (English) adjectif formé d'après un substantif verbal
**gestalt** n gestaltisme m
**gestation** n gestation f
**gestatory** adj gestatoire
**gesticulate** vi gesticuler, faire des gestes
**gesticulation** n gesticulation f, geste m
**gesticulatory** adj gesticulant
**gesture** n geste m, signe m; acte m; *vt* exprimer par gestes; *vi* gesticuler, faire des gestes
**get** vt obtenir, acquérir; recevoir; (bring) amener, apporter; (succeed in doing) réussir, atteindre; (illness) attraper; (cause to do) faire faire; (cause) faire; (persuade) persuader, arranger; *ar* engendrer; *coll* (understand) piger; (notice) remarquer; (annoy) irriter; (impress) impressionner; *sl* exciter; *coll* (kill) tuer; (stop) arrêter; ~ **across** faire comprendre; communiquer; ~ **away** entraîner, faire partir; ~ **back** recouvrer, faire revenir; ~ **back into** faire rentrer dans; ~ **down** descendre, faire descendre; (food) avaler; (on paper) noter; (depress) décourager; ~ **in** faire entrer, introduire, rentrer; (word) placer; (harvest) rentrer, engranger; ~ **into** faire entrer, introduire; *coll* ~ **it** piger, comprendre; ~ **off** ôter, enlever; *leg* faire acquitter; (send) expédier; *naut* (refloat) renflouer; ~ **on** mettre, enfiler; faire progresser; ~ **oneself up** s'attifer, se déguiser; ~ **one's hand in** se faire la main; ~ **one's own back** prendre sa revanche; ~ **out** enlever; (cork) tirer; (tooth) enlever; (book) sortir; (account) dresser; (list) établir; (problem) résoudre; ~ **over** en finir avec; ~ **round** persuader; ~ **s/o into trouble** causer des ennuis à qn; (girl) faire un enfant à; ~ **s/o out of trouble** tirer qn du pétrin; *coll* ~ **s/o's back up** agacer qn, emmerder qn; ~ **sth on the brain** n'avoir que ça dans la tête; ~ **through** (law) faire adopter; (pupil) faire réussir; ~ **up** (person) faire monter, obliger à se lever; (thing) monter; (role, part) apprendre, préparer; (play) monter; ~ **with child** engrosser; he

~ **s me down** il me tape sur les nerfs; **have got** posséder; **have got to** être obligé à; *vi* (become) devenir; (be) être; ~ **about** (person) se déplacer, circuler; (news) s'ébruiter; ~ **ahead** prospérer, faire des progrès, prendre de l'avance; ~ **along** s'en aller, avancer; (manage) se débrouiller; ~ **along with s'**accorder avec; ~ **along with you!** allez!, c'est ridicule!; *coll* ~ **around** s'amuser; être connu; (news) se disséminer; ~ **at** parvenir à, atteindre, toucher; *coll* (bribe) acheter, corrompre; ~ **away** partir, se sauver; sortir indemne, s'en tirer; *coll* ~ **away with you!** pas vrai!; ~ **back** revenir, retourner; ~ **back at** rendre la pareille à; ~ **by** se débrouiller, se tirer d'affaire; ~ **cracking** démarrer; ~ **down** descendre; ~ **down to** se mettre à; ~ **hold of** obtenir; (understand) comprendre; ~ **home** rentrer à la maison; ~ **in** entrer, rentrer; *pol* être élu; (examination) être reçu; ~ **into** (clothes) mettre; (enter) pénétrer dans; ~ **into the habit of** prendre l'habitude de; ~ **into trouble** s'attirer des ennemis; (girl) fauter; ~ **in with s/o** entrer dans les bonnes grâces de qn; *coll* ~ **it** piger; ~ **nowhere** ne faire aucun progrès; ~ **off** (dismount) descendre; (accusation) se tirer d'affaire; *coll* ~ **off with** faire une touche avec; ~ **on** continuer, poursuivre, avancer; (vehicle) monter dans; (agree) s'entendre; (make progress) progresser, réussir; ~ **on one's feet** se lever, se mettre debout; *coll* ~ **on s/o's nerves** taper sur les nerfs de qn; ~ **on top** vaincre, être à la hauteur; ~ **on to s/o** (telephone) avoir qn; ~ **on with** s'entendre avec; ~ **out** sortir, descendre; (rumour, news) s'ébruiter, se propager; *coll* ~ **out!** fous le camp!; ~ **out of sth** se tirer d'affaire, se soustraire à qch; ~ **over** se remettre de, se rétablir de, se faire à; (obstacle) franchir; ~ **past** passer; ~ **round** faire le tour de, contourner; ~ **there** réussir; ~ **through** passer à travers; (examination) être reçu; (money, task) arriver au bout de; ~ **through to** établir la communication avec; ~ **together** s'assembler, se réunir; ~ **under** passer par-dessous; *naut* ~ **under way** appareiller; ~ **up** monter; (from bed, chair, etc) se lever; (sea) grossir; (wind) se lever; ~ **up to** faire; ~ **wind of** avoir vent de; *coll* **tell s/o where he** ~ **s off** remettre qn à sa place; **what are you** ~ **ting at?** où voulez-vous en venir?
**get-at-able** adj *coll* accessible

**getaway** n coll fuite f, départ m; mot démarrage m

**get-out** n coll échappatoire m

**get-together** n réunion f

**get-up** n coll accoutrement m, habillement m

**gewgaw** n colifichet m, babiole f

**geyser** n geol geyser m; (water heater) chauffe-bain m

**ghastliness** n aspect m sinistre; extrême pâleur f

**ghastly** adj effroyable, atroce; (pale) blême

**gherkin** n cornichon m

**ghetto** n ghetto m

**ghost** n spectre m, fantôme m, revenant m; (soul) âme f; phys image f secondaire; fig ombre f, soupçon m, trace f; (writer) nègre m; **give up the** ~ rendre l'âme; **Holy Ghost** Saint Esprit

**ghostliness** n aspect spectral

**ghostly** adj spectral

**ghoul** n goule f; déterreur m de cadavres

**ghoulish** adj morbide, macabre

**giant** n géant m; adj géant, énorme

**giantess** n géante f

**gib** n + vi see jib

**gibber** vi baragouiner; émettre des sons inarticulés

**gibberish** n baragouinage m, charabia m

**gibbet** n gibet m, potence f

**gibbon** n gibbon m

**gibbose, gibbous** adj gibbeux -euse, bossu

**gibe, jibe** n moquerie f, raillerie f; vi se moquer, railler

**giblets** npl abattis mpl

**giddiness** n vertige m, étourdissement m; fig frivolité f, légèreté f

**giddy** adj pris de vertige, étourdi; (height) vertigineux -euse; (whirling) giratoire; fig frivole, léger -ère

**gift** n don m, cadeau m; fig don m, talent m; comm prime f; coll aubaine f

**gifted** adj doué

**gift-horse** n look a ~ **in the mouth** faire le difficile

**gig** n cabriolet m; naut yole f

**gigantic** adj gigantesque, géant, colossal

**gigantism** n med gigantisme m

**giggle** n gloussement m; vi glousser

**gigolo** n gigolo m

**gigue** n gigue f

¹**gild** n see guild

²**gild** vt dorer; fig embellir, illuminer; ~ **the lily** ajouter des ornements superflus; ~ **the pill** dorer la pilule

**gilded** adj doré; ~ **youth** jeunesse dorée

**gilding** n dorure f

**gill** n (fish) branchie f; ~s ouïes fpl

**gillyflower** n giroflée f

**gilt** n feuille f d'or, peinture f d'or; éclat m, brillant m; adj doré

**gilt-edged** adj (book) doré sur tranche; ~ **security** rente f à intérêts fixes; fig placement m de tout repos

**gimcrack** n babiole f; adj de camelote

**gimlet** n vrille f

**gimmick** n truc m, dispositif m; (advertising) astuce f publicitaire

¹**gin** n gin m

²**gin** n obs piège m, collet m; eng chèvre f

**ginger** n gingembre m; (colour) roux m; fig entrain m; ~ **group** groupe m de pression; adj (colour) roux (f rousse), coll rouquin; vt parfumer au gingembre; fig ~ **up** animer, secouer

**ginger-ale, ginger-beer** n boisson gazeuse au gingembre

**gingerbread** n gâteau m au gingembre; **take the gilt off the** ~ enlever l'attraction

**gingerly** adj prudent, circonspect; adv prudemment, avec circonspection

**ginger-nut** n biscuit m au gingembre

**ginger-wine** n boisson alcoolisée au gingembre

**gingery** adj ayant un goût de gingembre; (colour) roux (f rousse); fig irascible, coléreux -euse

**gingham** n (cloth) vichy m

**gingival** adj gingival

**gingivitis** n gingivite f

**gipsy, gypsy** n bohémien -ienne, gitan -e; fig vagabond -e, coquin -e; adj de bohémien, gitan

**giraffe** n girafe f

**girandole** n girandole f

**gird** vt ceindre, entourer, cercler

**girder** n poutre f métallique, poutrelle f, longeron m

¹**girdle** n ceinture f; (corset) gaine f; vt ceinturer, entourer

²**girdle** n see griddle

**girl** n fille f, jeune fille f; (little) fillette f; (servant) bonne f; ~ **friend** petite amie; (school) **old** ~ ancienne élève; **old** ~! ma vieille!

**girlhood** n enfance f, jeunesse f

**girlish** adj de jeune fille, de petite fille

**girlishness** n enfance f, jeunesse f

**girth** n tour m de taille; circonférence f; (horse) sangle f

**gist** n fond m, essentiel m

**give** n élasticité f, flexibilité f; ~ **and take** échange m de bons procédés; vt donner, offrir; occasionner, causer, provoquer; exécuter, formuler, faire; conférer, infliger; concéder; payer; (shout) pousser; (judgement) rendre; ~ **away** donner; (prizes) distribuer; coll (betray) moucharder, dénoncer; (secret) trahir; (oneself) se trahir; ~ **back** rendre, restituer; ~ **chase** poursuivre; ~ **forth** annoncer, proclamer; ~ **ground** céder, reculer, battre en retraite; ~ **in** remettre; *coll* ~ **it to** punir; (scold) engueuler; ~ **off** émettre, dégager; ~ **oneself out for** s'intituler, se dire; ~ **oneself up** se rendre, se constituer prisonnier -ière; ~ **oneself up to** s'adonner à; ~ **out** distribuer; (announce) faire connaître, proclamer; ~ **rise to** remplacé par; *med* ~ **s/o best** reconnaître la supériorité de qn; ~ **s/o out for** faire passer qn pour; *med* ~ **s/o up** condamner; ~ **tongue** parler fort; (dog) aboyer; ~ **up** abandonner, délaisser; renoncer à, cesser de; (post) se démettre de; (seat) céder; *vi* donner; céder; ~ **and take** transiger, faire des concessions mutuelles; ~ **in** renoncer, abandonner; ~ **into** donner accès à, donner sur; ~ **in to s/o** céder à qn; ~ **onto** donner sur; ~ **out** faire défaut, venir à manquer; finir; ~ **over** renoncer; *coll* arrêter; ~ **up** renoncer, abandonner

**given** *adj* donné, déterminé; *Scots + US* ~ **name** prénom *m*; ~ **to** adonné à, enclin à, porté à

**giving** *n* action *f* de donner; *adj* généreux -euse; flexible

**gizzard** *n* gésier *m*

**glabrous** *adj* glabre

**glacé** *adj* glacé

**glacial** *adj* glacial; *geol* glaciaire

**glaciation** *n* glaciation *f*

**glacier** *n* glacier *m*

**glacis** *n* glacis *m*

**glad** *adj* content, heureux -euse, joyeux -euse, enchanté; *coll* **give the** ~ **eye to** reluquer, faire de l'œil à; *coll* ~ **rags** beaux atours

**gladden** *vt* réjouir, rendre heureux -euse

**glade** *n* clairière *f*

**gladiator** *n* gladiateur *m*

**gladiatorial** *adj* de gladiateur

**gladiolus** *n* (*pl* **gladioli**) glaïeul *m*

**gladly** *adv* avec plaisir, volontiers, de bon cœur; avec joie

**gladness** *n* contentement *m*, joie *f*

**gladsome** *adj ar* joyeux -euse

**glair** *n cul* blanc m d'œuf; matière blanche et visqueuse; *med* glaire *f*; *vt* glairer

**glamorize** *vt* exalter; porter aux nues

**glamorous** *adj* romantique, séduisant; enchanteur -eresse, ensorcelant

**glamour** *n* éclat *m*, enchantement *m*; sex-appeal *m*; ensorcellement *m*

**glance** *n* coup *m* d'œil; (blow) coup *m* de biais; **have a** ~ **at** jeter un coup d'œil à; *vi* regarder rapidement, jeter un coup d'œil; (glint) étinceler, briller; ~ **off** effleurer; être dévié; (book) ~ **at,** ~

**through** feuilleter

**glancing** *adj* (blow) oblique

**gland** *n* glande *f*

**glanders** *npl vet* morve *f*

**glandular** *adj* glandulaire; ~ **fever** mononucléose infectieuse

**glandule** *n* glandule *f*; tumeur *f*

**glare** *n* lumière crue, éclat éblouissant; (look) regard furieux; *vi* briller; (look) jeter un regard furieux

**glaring** *adj* (light) éblouissant, aveuglant; (colour) éclatant, criard; (mistake) manifeste, flagrant

**glass** *n* verre *m*; (drinking) verre *m*; baromètre *m*; (mirror) glace *f*, miroir *m*; télescope *m*; ~**es** lunettes *fpl*; **cut** ~ cristal taillé; **hour** ~ sablier *m*; **looking** ~ glace *f*, miroir *m*; **magnifying** ~ loupe *f*; **opera** ~**es** jumelles *fpl*; **pane of** ~ carreau *m*, vitre *f*; *adj* de verre, en verre; (door) vitré

**glassblower** *n* souffleur *m*

**glass-cloth** *n* essuie-verres *m*

**glasscutter** *n* vitrier *m*; (tool) diamant *m*

**glass-frame** *n hort* châssis *m*

**glassful** *n* verre *m*, plein verre

**glasshouse** *n* serre *f*; *coll* prison *f* militaire

**glass-paper** *n* papier *m* de verre

**glassware** *n* verrerie *f*, articles *mpl* de verre

**glass-wool** *n* laine *f* de verre

**glass-works** *n* verrerie *f*

**glassy** *adj* vitreux -euse; (smooth) uni, lisse

**glauber's salt** *n med* sulfate *m* de soude

**glaucoma** *n med* glaucome *m*

**glaucous** *adj* glauque

**glaze** *n* vernis *m*, glaçure *f*, enduit *m*; *cul* glace *f*; *vt* (insert glass) vitrer; *obs* vernisser; (tiles) vitrifier; *cul* glacer; *vi* (expression) devenir impassible; (eye) devenir vitreux

**glazed** *adj* vitré; vernissé; *cul* glacé

**glazier** *n* vitrier *m*

**glazing** *n* (trade) vitrerie *f*; (inserting glass) pose *f* des vitres; vernissage *m*; vernis *m*, enduit *m*; *cul* glace *f*; **double** ~ double vitrage *m*

**gleam** *n* lueur *f*; *vi* luire

**gleaming** *adj* luisant

**glean** *vt* glaner

**gleaner** *n* glaneur -euse

**gleanings** *npl* glanure *f*

**glebe** *n lit* glèbe *f*

**glee** *n* allégresse *f*, joie *f*; *mus* chant à plusieurs voix non accompagné

**gleeful** *adj* allègre, joyeux -euse

**glen** *n* ravin *m*, petite vallée

**glib** *adj* plausible, spécieux -ieuse; facile

**glibness** *n* plausibilité *f*; facilité *f*

**glide** *n* glissement *m*, glissade *f*;

(dancing) glissade f, glissé m
**glider** n aer planeur m
**gliding** n glissement m; aer vol m à voile, vol plané
**glimmer** n lueur f; vi jeter une lueur; vaciller
**glimmering** n lueur f; adj vacillant
**glimpse** n coup m d'œil; vt entr'evoir
**glint** n lueur f, reflet m; vi luire
**glissade** n glissade f
**glisten** vi étinceler, scintiller; briller, miroiter
**glistening** adj étincelant, scintillant; brillant, miroitant
**glister** n + vi obs see **glitter**
**glitter** n scintillement m; fig éclat m, brillant m; vi briller, chatoyer, étinceler; (sea) brasiller
**glittering** adj brillant, chatoyant, étincelant
**gloaming** n crépuscule m
**gloat** vi triompher; coll faire des gorges chaudes
**global** adj global, universel -elle, achevé
**globe** n globe m; sphère f; geog mappemonde f; (glass) bocal m sphérique
**globe-trotter** n globe-trotter m
**globular** adj globulaire, globuleux -euse
**globule** n med globule m; gouttelette f
**globulin** n globuline f
**glockenspiel** n mus glockenspiel m
**glomerate** adj congloméré
**gloom, gloominess** n obscurité f, noir m; fig mélancolie f, dépression f
**gloominess** n see **gloom**
**gloomy** adj obscur, sombre, ténébreux -euse; fig mélancolie, sombre
**gloria** n eccles gloria m invar
**glorification** n glorification f
**glorify** vt glorifier, célébrer; (adorn) enrichir, parer
**gloriole** n auréole f
**glorious** adj glorieux -ieuse, illustre; célèbre, magnifique; (weather) radieux -ieuse; coll fameux -euse, épatant
**gloriously** adv glorieusement; magnifiquement; coll fameusement
**glory** n gloire f, magnificence f, splendeur f; (halo) auréole f; **be in one's ~** se savoir bon gré, triompher; **Old Glory** drapeau m des États-Unis
**glory-hole** n débarras m; naut cambuse f
**¹gloss** n glose f, commentaire m; vt gloser, commenter; **~ over** atténuer, justifier tant bien que mal
**²gloss** n brillant m, éclat m, lustre m; fig vernis m; apparence trompeuse; vt lustrer, polir
**glossary** n glossaire m
**glossiness** n brillant m, lustre m
**glossy** adj brillant, lustré, vernissé; phot glacé; coll **~ magazine** magazine chic

(imprimé sur papier glacé)
**glottal** adj glottique, glottal; **~ stop** coup m de glotte
**glottis** n anat glotte f
**glove** n gant m; **be hand in ~** s'entendre comme larrons en foire; **fit like a ~** aller comme un gant; **throw down the ~** lancer un défi; **with ~s off** à outrance
**glove-maker** n gantier -ière
**glover** n gantier -ière
**glow** n rougeur f, embrasement m; fig ardeur f; (well-being) bien-être m; vi rougeoyer; (fire) couver; fig sentir une chaleur; être radieux -ieuse, rayonner
**glower** vi se renfrogner, faire grise mine
**glowing** adj rougeoyant, embrasé; (complexion) rouge; fig chaleureux -euse, enthousiaste
**glow-lamp** n lampe f à incandescence
**glow-worm** n ver luisant
**glucose** n glucose m
**glue** n colle f; vt coller
**gluey** adj collant, gluant
**glum** adj morose, renfrogné, sombre
**glumness** n humeur chagrine, morosité f
**glut** n excès m; comm surabondance f; vt comm saturer; rassasier
**glutinosity** n viscosité f
**glutinous** adj glutineux -euse, visqueux -euse
**glutton** n glouton -onne, goinfre m; fig enthousiaste
**gluttonous** adj glouton -onne, goinfre, goulu
**gluttony** n gloutonnerie f, goinfrerie f
**glycerine** n glycérine f, glycérol m
**glycerol** n chem glycérol m, glycérine f
**glycogen** n chem glycogène m
**glycol** n chem glycol m
**gnarl** n bot nœud m
**gnarled** adj noueux -euse; rugueux -euse
**gnash** vt **~ one's teeth** grincer des dents
**gnashing** n grincement m
**gnat** n moucheron m
**gnaw** vt ronger, grignoter
**gnawing** n grignotement m, rongement m; adj rongeur -euse
**gneiss** n geol gneiss m
**gnome** n gnome m, homme petit et contrefait
**gnomic** adj gnomique
**gnosis** n gnose f
**Gnostic** n gnostique
**gnostic** adj gnostique
**gnosticism** n gnosticisme m
**gnu** n zool gnou m
**go** n mouvement m, action f; (attempt) essai m, coup m, tentative f; dynamisme m, énergie f, allant m, entrain m; **at one ~** d'un seul coup; **be always on the ~** être toujours sur la brèche;

# goad

have a ~! allez-y toujours!; *coll* it's all the ~ c'est le dernier cri; it's your ~ c'est votre tour; make a ~ of it réussir qch; no ~ rien à faire; that was a near ~ on l'a échappé belle; *vi* aller, marcher; (depart) partir, s'en aller; (road) conduire; (yield) céder, se casser; (work) marcher, fonctionner; (eyesight) baisser; (evolve) se présenter, se développer, tourner; (become) devenir; (time) s'écouler, passer; (disappear) disparaître; (wear out) s'user; ~ about voyager; (rumour) courir; (undertake) vaquer à; *naut* virer de bord; ~ after courir après, poursuivre; ~ against s'opposer à; (current) remonter; ~ ahead avancer, progresser; (start) commencer; ~ (all) out for s'efforcer d'obtenir; ~ along continuer, avancer; along with accompagner; *coll* accepter; ~ and get aller chercher; ~ at attaquer; ~ away s'en aller, partir; ~ back retourner en arrière; (memory) remonter; ~ back on one's word manquer à sa parole; *leg* ~ bail for se porter caution pour; ~ beyond dépasser; ~ by passer; (time) s'écouler; (name) être connu sous (le nom de); ~ down descendre; (wind) tomber; (ship) sombrer, couler; (in history) être perpétué; (university) quitter l'université, finir ses études; ~ for aller chercher; (sale) être vendu pour; *coll* attaquer; (fall for) être entiché de; ~ for one another se prendre aux cheveux; ~ forward avancer; (plan) être en voie de réalisation; going! going! gone! une fois, deux fois, trois fois, adjugé! (vendu!); ~ hard with aller mal pour; ~ in entrer; (sun) se cacher; ~ in for se présenter à, affronter; (habit) s'adonner à; *pej* se livrer à; ~ into entrer en, entrer dans, se lancer dans; (examine) approfondir; ~ into hiding se cacher; ~ into mourning prendre le deuil; ~ off s'en aller, partir; (food) s'abîmer, se gâter; (milk) tourner; *theat* faire une sortie; ~ on continuer, poursuivre, avancer; (take place) se dérouler; *theat* faire une entrée; ~ on at harceler, gronder; ~ on for (be nearly) approcher; ~ out sortir, quitter; (light) s'éteindre; (fashion) passer de mode; ~ out of office quitter le pouvoir; (heart) ~ out to sympathiser avec; ~ over verser, basculer; (check) vérifier, repasser, revoir; ~ round faire le tour; ~ through traverser; (book) dépouiller; (endure) subir, souffrir; ~ through with mener à bien, achever; ~ to aller à, aller

trouver, s'adresser à; ~ together aller ensemble; ~ to show servir à montrer; ~ to the country en appeler à la nation, provoquer des élections législatives; ~ to the trouble of se donner la peine de; ~ towards aller vers; (fund) être une contribution à; ~ under sombrer, couler; ~ up monter, augmenter; (university) entrer dans; (price) ~ up to aller jusqu'à; *coll* ~ west être foutu; (die) crever; ~ with (match) aller avec, s'assortir avec; (accompany) accompagner; ~ without se passer de; ~ without saying aller de soi, aller sans dire; be ~ing to être sur le point de; let ~ laisser aller, lâcher prise, relâcher; let oneself ~ se laisser aller, s'abandonner; the meat will ~ round il y aura assez de viande pour tout le monde

**goad** *n* aiguillon *m*; *fig* stimulant *m*; *vt* aiguillonner; *fig* stimuler, aiguillonner, provoquer

**go-ahead** *n* signal *m* du départ; autorisation *f* du départ; *adj* entreprenant

**goal** *n* but *m*

**goal-keeper** *n* gardien *m* de but

**goal-line** *n* ligne *f* de but

**goal-post** *n* montant *m* (de but)

**goat** *n* bouc *m*, chèvre *f*; *fig* satyre *m*; *coll* idiot -e; **act the (giddy) ~** *sl* faire des conneries; *coll* **get s/o's ~** irriter qn, emmerder qn

**goatee** *n* (beard) bouc *m*

**goatherd** *n* chevrier -ière

**goatish** *adj* de bouc; *fig* libidineux -euse, lubrique

**gob** *n* *sl* (mouth) gueule *f*; *sl* (spit) glaviot *m*; *US sl* matelot *m*

**gobbet** *n* morceau *m*

**gobble** *vt* engloutir, dévorer; *vi* se gaver, s'empiffrer; (turkey) glouglouter

**gobbledygook** *n* *sl* charabia *m*, baragouin *m*

**go-between** *n* intermédiaire; (pimp) entremetteur *m*

**goblet** *n* gobelet *m*

**goblin** *n* lutin *m*

**go-by** *n* give s/o the ~ éviter qn

**go-cart** *n* poussette *f*; chariot *m* d'enfant; charrette *f* à bras

**god** *n* dieu *m*; **God** Dieu *m*; **God's acre** cimetière *m*; *leg* **act of God** cas *m* de force majeure; **house of God** église *f*; *coll theat* **the ~s** le paradis, le poulailler; *coll* **tin ~** tyranneau *m*

**godchild** *n* filleul -e

**goddam** *adj* damné, maudit

**goddaughter** *n* filleule *f*

**goddess** *n* déesse *f*

**godfather** *n* parrain *m*

508

**godfearing** *adj* pieux (*f* pieuse), religieux -ieuse

**godforsaken** *adj* sinistre, désert, misérable; (wicked) mauvais; *coll* ~ **place** trou perdu

**godhead** *n* divinité *f*

**godless** *adj* impie, irréligieux -ieuse, athée

**godlessness** *n* impiété *f*, irréligion *f*, athéisme *m*

**godlike** *adj* divin, comme un dieu

**godly** *adj* pieux (*f* pieuse), dévot, religieux -ieuse

**godmother** *n* marraine *f*; **fairy** ~ bienfaitrice *f*, protectrice *f*

**godparent** *n* parrain *m*, marraine *f*

**godsend** *n* aubaine *f*

**godson** *n* filleul *m*

**god-speed** *n* bonne chance

**goer** *n* personne qui va; cheval *m* (voiture *f*, etc) qui va vite; *coll* as *m*

**gofer** *n* US factotum *m*

**goffer** *n* tuyauté *m*; *vt* (clothes) tuyauter; (paper, leather) gaufrer

**goffering** *n* tuyauté *m*

**go-getter** *n* *coll* arriviste, ambitieux -ieuse

**goggle** *vi* bayer aux corneilles, ouvrir de grands yeux; (eye) être saillant

**goggle-eyed** *adj* aux yeux saillants

**goggles** *npl* lunettes *fpl* de protection, lunettes *fpl* de motocycliste; *coll* lunettes *fpl*, besicles *fpl*

**going** *n* action *f* d'aller, action *f* de partir, départ *m*; (ground) état *m* du terrain; **while the** ~ **is good** pendant que les circonstances sont favorables; *adj* prospère, en bon ordre; en état de marche

**going-over** *n* *coll* interrogatoire *m*; passage *m* à tabac; correction *f*

**goings-on** *npl* *coll* *pej* manigance *f*, micmac *m*

**goitre** *n* goitre *m*

**goitrous** *adj* goitreux -euse

**gold** *n* or *m*; *fig* richesses *fpl*; ~ **standard** étalon-or *m*; *adj* en or

**goldbearing** *adj* aurifère

**goldbeater** *n* batteur *m* d'or

**gold-digger** *n* chercheur *m* d'or; *coll* femme *f* qui cherche un mari riche

**gold-dust** *n* poudre *f* d'or

**golden** *adj* en or; d'or, doré; ~ **age** âge *m* d'or; ~ **syrup** mélasse raffinée

**gold-field** *n* terrain *m* aurifère

**goldfinch** *n* chardonneret *m*

**goldfish** *n* poisson *m* rouge

**gold-foil** *n* feuille *f* d'or

**gold-lace** *n* galon *m* d'or

**gold-leaf** *n* feuille *f* d'or

**gold-mine** *n* mine *f* d'or

**gold-plate** *n* vaisselle *f* d'or

**gold-rush** *n* ruée *f* vers l'or

**goldsmith** *n* orfèvre *m*

**golf** *n* golf *m*; *vi* faire du golf

**golf-club** *n* (object) club *m*, canne *f*, crosse *f* (de golf); (place) golf *m*

**golf-course**, **golf-links** *n* terrain *m* de golf

**golfer** *n* golfeur -euse

**golliwog** *n* poupée *f* représentant un nègre

**golly** *interj* *coll* ciel!, mon Dieu!, ça alors!

**golosh** *n* (*usu pl*) botillons *mpl* de caoutchouc, caoutchoucs *mpl*

**gonad** *n* *biol* gonade *f*

**gondola** *n* gondole *f*; (airship) nacelle *f*

**gondolier** *n* gondolier *m*

**gone** *adj* parti; *coll* perdu; *sl* foutu; (dead) mort; *coll* ~ **on** entiché de

**goner** *n* *sl* homme foutu, type perdu

**gonfalon** *n* gonfalon *m*

**gong** *n* gong *m*; *sl* médaille *f*; *vt* appeler par un coup de gong; *vi* frapper sur un gong

**gonorrhoea** *n* blennorragie *f*

**goo** *n* *sl* *pej* douceur mielleuse, sentimentalité *f*

**good** *n* bon *m*, bien *m*; vertu *f*; avantage *m*, profit *m*; ~s marchandises *fpl*, biens *mpl*; **be up to no** ~ préparer un mauvais coup; *coll* **deliver the** ~s remplir une promesse; (perform satisfactorily) prouver ses capacités; **for** ~ pour de bon; **it's no** ~ **doing that** inutile de faire cela; **so much to the** ~ autant de gagné; (object) **that's no** ~ cela ne vaut rien; **the** ~ (persons) les bons; **what's the** ~ **of?** à quoi bon?; *adj* bon (*f* bonne), brave; bien *invar*; (fine) beau (*f* belle), joli; (kind) bienveillant, aimable; (child) sage; (beneficial) salutaire; compétent, expert; (worthy) honorable, digne; (saintly) pieux (*f* pieuse); **Good Friday** vendredi saint; ~ **turn** service *m*; **a** ~ **deal** beaucoup; **a** ~ **many** beaucoup; **a** ~ **while** longtemps; **as** ~ **as** pour ainsi dire, pratiquement; **be as** ~ **as** valoir; *coll* **be on to a** ~ **thing** trouver le filon; **have a** ~ **time** s'amuser bien; **in** ~ **time** bien à l'heure; **make** ~ prospérer; (mend) réparer; (loss) compenser; (promise) remplir, tenir

**goodbye** *n* + *interj* adieu *m*, au revoir *m*

**good-for-nothing** *n* + *adj* bon (*f* bonne) à rien

**good-humoured** *adj* de bonne humeur, allègre, gai

**goodish** *adj* assez bon (*f* bonne)

**good-looking** *adj* beau (*f* belle), *coll* bien *invar*

**goodly** *adj* beau (*f* belle); gracieux

-ieuse, avenant; (sizable) grand, considérable

**good-natured** adj aimable, sympathique

**goodness** n bonté f; gentillesse f; interj mon Dieu!, vraiment!: ~ **gracious**!, ~ **me**!, **my** ~! mon Dieu!

**good-tempered** adj de bon caractère, de caractère égal

**goodwill** n bienveillance f; bonne volonté; leg réputation f d'une maison de commerce

**goody** n (usu pl) friandise f

**goody-goody** n coll petit -e saint -e, dévot -e

**gooey** adj gluant; coll fig sentimental

**goof** n toqué -e; vt ~ **up** bousiller; vi faire une gaffe

**goofy** adj sl idiot

**goon** n coll bouffon m

**goose** n oie f; coll imbécile; (girl) oie f, pécore f; coll **cook s/o's** ~ régler son compte à qn

**gooseberry** n groseille f à maquereau; coll chaperon m; coll **play** ~ être le tiers incommode

**gooseflesh** n chair f de poule

**goose-neck** n eng col m de cygne

**goose-step** n mil pas m de l'oie

¹**gore** n sang m

²**gore** n godet m; vt mettre un godet dans

³**gore** vt corner, donner un coup de corne à

**gorge** n geog+physiol gorge f; **my** ~ **rises at it** cela m'écœure; vt gorger, rassasier; vi se gorger, s'empiffrer

**gorgeous** adj fastueux -euse, somptueux -euse; coll splendide, épatant; (woman) plantureux -euse

**gorgeousness** n magnificence f, faste m, splendeur f

**Gorgon** n myth Gorgone f; fig mégère f

**gorilla** n gorille m

**gormandize** vi s'empiffrer, se bourrer

**gormless** adj coll lourdaud

**gorse** n ajonc m

**gory** adj ensanglanté; fig sanglant

**gosh** interj ça alors!, pas possible!

**goshawk** n autour m

**gosling** n oison m

**go-slow** n travail m au ralenti; (work to rule) grève perlée

**gospel** n évangile m; bibl Évangile m; ~ **truth** parole f d'évangile

**gospeller** n évangéliste m, prédicateur m

**gossamer** n (cobweb) fils mpl de la vierge; gaze légère

**gossip** n commérage m, cancans mpl; (person) bavard -e; ar compère m, commère f; vi caqueter; pej cancaner

**gossipy** adj (person) cancanier -ière; (conversation) de commérages

**Goth** n Goth m; fig barbare m

**Gothic** n gothique m; adj gothique

**gouache** n gouache f

**gouge** n gouge f

**goulash** n cul goulasch (goulache) m or f

**gourd** n gourde f

**gourmand** n gourmand -e

**gourmet** n gourmet m

**gout** n goutte f

**gouty** adj goutteux -euse

**gov** n sl patron m; (address) m'sieu

**govern** vt gouverner; (affairs) administrer, diriger; fig régler, déterminer, guider; gramm régir; (temper) maîtriser, dominer; vi gouverner

**governable** adj gouvernable

**governess** n préceptrice f, institutrice f à domicile

**governing** adj gouvernant; ~ **body** conseil m d'administration, conseil m de gestion; ~ **idea** idée dominante

**government** n gouvernement m; régime m; conseil m des ministres, cabinet gouvernemental

**governmental** adj gouvernemental, du gouvernement

**governor** n (country, province, bank) gouverneur m; (in general) administrateur m; mech régulateur m; coll père m; coll patron m

**governor-general** n gouverneur général

**governorship** n fonction f de gouverneur

**gown** n robe f; (official, academic) toge f

**grab** n mouvement m pour saisir; empoigne f; mech poigne f mécanique; vt empoigner, agripper; (acquire) accaparer, saisir; usurper

**grace** n grâce f, distinction f; (favour) faveur f; (forgiveness) pardon m, clémence f; (before meal) bénédicité m; (after meal) grâces fpl; leg **act of** ~ amnistie f; **airs and** ~s manières affectées; **in the bad (good)** ~s **of** mal (bien) vu de; **with bad (good)** ~ de mauvaise (bonne) grâce; vt orner, honorer

**graceful** adj gracieux -ieuse, élégant

**gracefulness** n grâce f, élégance f, distinction f

**graceless** adj sans grâce, gauche, inélégant; eccles hors de l'état de grâce

**gracelessness** n manque m de grâce, gaucherie f, inélégance f

**grace-note** n mus agrément m

**gracile** adj gracile, mince

**gracious** adj gracieux -ieuse, aimable, bienveillant; condescendant; interj mon Dieu!, vraiment!

**graciousness** n grâce f, amabilité f, bienveillance f; condescendance f

**gradation** n gradation f

**grade** n degré m, rang m, grade m; qualité f; catégorie f; US (school)

classe *f*; (mark) note *f*; **make the ~**
réussir, se montrer à la hauteur; *vt*
classifier, classer, trier; graduer; *US*
(school) noter

**gradient** *n* pente *f*

**gradual** *adj* graduel -elle, progressif -ive

**gradually** *adv* peu à peu, petit à petit,
progressivement

**gradualness** *n* progression *f*, lent développement

**graduate** *n* (university) diplômé -e, licencié -e; *vt* classer en grades; graduer;
*vi* (university) obtenir sa licence; se
changer graduellement

**graduation** *n* graduation *f*; (university)
obtention *f* de licence

**graffiti** *npl* graffiti *mpl*

**graft** *n* greffe *f*, greffon *m*; *coll* pot-de-vin
*m* (*pl* pots-de-vin), tripotage *m*; *sl*
boulot *m*; *vt* greffer; *vi coll* tripoter; *sl*
travailler dur

**grafter** *n* (person) greffeur *m*; (instrument) greffoir *m*; *coll* tripoteur *m*

**grafting** *n* greffage *m*

**grail** *n* graal *m*

**grain** *n* (small particle) grain *m*; (corn)
blé *m*; (cloth, paper, etc) grain *m*;
(weight) grain *m*; (wood) fibres *fpl*;
**against the ~** à rebours; *vt* granuler,
grener, marbrer

**graining** *n* grain *m*, marbrure *f*

**gram** *n* gramme *m*

**graminaceous** *adj* graminé

**grammar** *n* grammaire *f*; **~ school** =
collège *m*, lycée *m*

**grammarian** *n* grammairien -ienne

**grammatic(al)** *adj* grammatical

**gramme** *n* gramme *m*

**gramophone** *n* phonographe *m*, électrophone *m*

**grampus** *n zool* épaulard *m*; *coll*
(person) poussif *m*

**granary** *n* grenier *m*

**grand** *n coll US* mille dollars *mpl* ; *coll*
piano *m* à queue; **baby ~** piano *m*
demi-queue; *adj* splendide, imposant,
important, magnifique, grandiose;
(duke, cross, master) grand; (main)
principal; prétentieux -ieuse; *coll*
épatant; **~ piano** piano *m* à queue

**grandchild** *n* petit-fils *m* (*f* petite-fille, *pl*
petits-enfants)

**grand-dad, grandad** *n coll* grand-père *m*
(*pl* grands-pères), bon papa

**granddaughter** *n* petite-fille *f* (*pl* petites-
filles)

**grandee** *n* grand *m* d'Espagne; noble *m*

**grandeur** *n* grandeur *f*; splendeur *f*, magnificence *f*

**grandfather** *n* grand-père *m* (*pl* grands-
pères); **~ clock** horloge *f* de parquet

**grandiloquence** *n* grandiloquence *f*,
emphase *f*

**grandiloquent** *adj* grandiloquent

**grandiose** *adj* grandiose, imposant,
prétentieux -ieuse

**grandiosity** *n* prétention *f*

**grandly** *adv* avec grandeur; grandiose-
ment

**grandma** *n coll* grand-maman *f* (*pl*
grands-mamans), mémé *f*

**grandmother** *n* grand-mère *f* (*pl* grands-
mères)

**grand-nephew** *n* petit-neveu *m* (*pl*
petits-neveux)

**grandness** *n* grandeur *f*

**grand-niece** *n* petite-nièce *f* (*pl* petites-
nièces)

**grandpapa, grandpa** *n coll* grand-papa
*m* (*pl* grands-papas), pépé *m*

**grandparent** *n* grand-père *m* (*f* grand-
mère, *pl* grands-parents)

**grandson** *n* petit-fils *m* (*pl* petits-fils)

**grandstand** *n* tribune *f*

**grand-uncle** *n* grand-oncle *m* (*pl* grands-
oncles)

**grange** *n* manoir *m*; *ar* grenier *m*

**granite** *n* granit(e) *m*; *adj* de granit(e)

**granitic** *adj* granitique

**granny** *n coll* grand-maman *f* (*pl*
grands-mamans), mémé *f*; **~ knot**
nœud plat fait incorrectement, nœud
*m* de vache

**grant** *n* don *m*; allocation *f*; subvention
*f*; concession *f*; *leg* cession *f*, acte *m* de
donation; bourse *f* (d'études); *vt*
donner; accorder, octroyer; *leg* céder;
(admit) admettre, concéder; **~ ed that**
étant donné que

**grantee** *n leg* donataire

**grantor** *n leg* donateur -trice

**granular** *adj* granuleux -euse, granulaire

**granulate** *vt* granuler; *vi* se granuler

**granulated** *adj* granuleux -euse, granulé;
(sugar) cristallisé

**granulation** *n* granulation *f*

**granule** *n* granule *m*

**granulous** *adj* granuleux -euse

**grape** *n* grain *m* de raisin; **~ s** raisin *m*,
raisins *mpl*

**grapefruit** *n* pamplemousse *m*

**grapeshot** *n* mitraille *f*

**grape-sugar** *n* glucose *m*, sucre *m* de
raisin

**grapevine** *n* vigne *f*, treille *f*; *coll* téléphone *m* arabe

**graph** *n* graphique *m*, courbe *f*

**graphic(al)** *adj* graphique; *fig* pittoresque, expressif -ive

**graphics** *npl* procédés *mpl* graphiques

**graphite** *n* graphite *m*, plombagine *f*

**graphology** *n* graphologie *f*

**grapnel** *n naut* grappin *m*

**grapple** *n naut* grappin *m*; (struggle)

corps à corps *m*; *vt naut* saisir au grappin; (clutch) empoigner à bras le corps, agripper; *vi* lutter corps à corps, lutter à bras le corps; *fig* se débattre; *naut* jeter le grappin

**grappling-iron** *n naut* grappin *m*

**grasp** *n* étreinte *f*, poigne *f*; *fig* compréhension *f*, entendement *m*; *vt* empoigner, saisir; *fig* comprendre, saisir; *vi* ~ **at** essayer de saisir

**grasping** *adj* avide (de gain, de pouvoir), âpre (au gain); avare, cupide

**grass** *n* herbe *f*; pelouse *f*; (pasture) pâturage *m*, herbage *m*; *sl* (marijuana) herbe *f*; *sl* (informer) mouchard *m*; **out to** ~ en pâture; *coll* au repos; *vt* mettre en herbe, gazonner; (cattle) faire paître; (prey) abattre; (fish) prendre, gaffer; *coll* descendre, abattre; *vi sl* ~ **on** moucharder sur

**grass-cutter** *n* tondeuse *f* à gazon

**grass-green** *adj* vert pré *invar*

**grasshopper** *n* sauterelle *f*

**grassland** *n* herbage *m*; prairie *f*

**grass-plot** *n* pelouse *f*

**grass-roots** *npl fig* électeurs moyens; (workers) base *f*

**grass-snake** *n* couleuvre *f*

**grass-widow** *n* femme *f* dont le mari est absent

**grass-widower** *n* mari *m* dont la femme est absente

**grassy** *adj* herbeux -euse

**¹grate** *n* grille *f* en fonte (de cheminée); foyer *m*

**²grate** *vt* râper; *vi* grincer; *fig* ~ **on** agacer

**grateful** *adj* reconnaissant

**gratefully** *adv* avec reconnaissance

**gratefulness** *n* reconnaissance *f*, gratitude *f*

**grater** *n* râpe *f*

**gratification** *n* gratification *f*, contentement *m*, cause *f* de contentement; *ar* + *joc* (tip) pourboire *m*

**gratify** *vt* (person) faire plaisir à, satisfaire; (wish) contenter

**gratifying** *adj* satisfaisant, acceptable; agréable

**gratin** *n cul* gratin *m*

**¹grating** *n* grille *f*, grillage *m*

**²grating** *n* (sound) grincement *m*; *adj* grinçant

**gratis** *adv* gratis, gratuitement

**gratitude** *n* gratitude *f*, reconnaissance *f*

**gratuitous** *adj* gratuit, bénévole, gracieux -ieuse; *fig* gratuit, arbitraire

**gratuity** *n* pourboire *m*; gratification *f*, prime *f*; *mil* pécule *m*

**¹grave** *n* fosse *f*, tombe *f*; tombeau *m*

**²grave** *adj* grave, sérieux -ieuse, solennel -elle; important; *phon* grave

**³grave** *vt naut* radouber

**grave-digger** *n* fossoyeur *m*

**gravel** *n* gravier *m*, gravillon *m*; *med* gravelle *f*; *vt* couvrir de gravier; *fig* déconcerter

**gravelly** *adj* de gravier

**gravely** *adv* gravement, sérieusement

**graven** *adj ar* gravé, sculpté

**graver** *n* (person) graveur *m*; (tool) outil *m* de graveur, burin *m*

**gravestone** *n* pierre tombale

**graveyard** *n* cimetière *m*

**gravid** *adj* enceinte; (female animal) pleine

**graving-dock** *n* bassin *m* de radoub

**gravitate** *vi* graviter; être attiré

**gravitation** *n* gravitation *f*

**gravity** *n* gravité *f*

**gravy** *n* jus *m*, sauce *f*

**gravy-boat** *n* saucière *f*

**gray** *n* + *adj* + *vi see* **grey**

**grayling** *n zool* ombre *m*

**¹graze** *vt* (grass) paître, brouter; (cattle) faire paître, paître; *vi* paître, brouter

**²graze** *n* effleurement *m*, frôlement *m*; (scratch) égratignure *f*, éraflure *f*; *vt* effleurer, frôler; (scratch) égratigner, érafler

**grazing** *n* pâturage *m*

**grease** *n* graisse *f*, lubrifiant *m*; (wool) suint *m*; *coll* (bribe) pot-de-vin *m* (*pl* pots-de-vin); *coll* flatterie *f*; *vt* graisser; *coll* (bribe) graisser la patte à; *coll* flatter, lécher les bottes à

**greasepaint** *n theat* fard *m*

**greaseproof** *adj* résistant à la graisse; (paper) sulfurisé

**greaser** *n* graisseur *m*; *US coll* Mexicain -e; Sud-américain -e

**grease-remover** *n* (substance) dégraissant *m*; (person) dégraisseur -euse

**greasiness** *n* graisse *f*; *fig* flagornerie *f*

**greasy** *adj* graisseux -euse; glissant; *fig* onctueux -euse

**great** *adj* grand, important, nombreux -euse, principal, excellent, grandiose, supérieur; éminent, haut placé, illustre, noble; *coll* agréable, épatant, fameux -euse; ~ **at** expert en; **Great Dane** (chien) danois *m*; **Greater London** l'agglomération londonienne; ~ **on** s'intéressant beaucoup à, connaissant fort bien

**great-aunt** *n* grand-tante *f* (*pl* grand(s)-tantes)

**great-coat** *n* pardessus *m*; *mil* capote *f*

**great-grandchild** *n* arrière-petit-fils *m* (*f* arrière-petite-fille, *pl* arrière-petits-enfants)

**great-granddaughter** *n* arrière-petite-fille *f* (*pl* arrière-petites-filles)

**great-grandfather** *n* arrière-grand-père

*m* (*pl* arrière-grands-pères), bisaïeul *m*

**great-grandmother** *n* arrière-grand-mère *f* (*pl* arrières-grands-mères), bisaïeule *f*

**great-grandparent** *n* arrière-grand-père *m* (*f* arrière-grand-mère, *pl* arrière-grands-parents), bisaïeul -e (*pl* bisaïeuls)

**great-grandson** *n* arrière-petit-fils *m* (*pl* arrière-petits-fils)

**great-hearted** *adj* magnanime, généreux -euse

**greatly** *adv* beaucoup, très, fort, grandement, énormément

**great-nephew** *n* petit-neveu *m* (*pl* petits-neveux)

**greatness** *n* grandeur *f*

**great-niece** *n* petite-nièce *f* (*pl* petites-nièces)

**grebe** *n orni* grèbe *m*

**Grecian** *adj* grec (*f* grecque)

**Greece** *n* Grèce *f*

**greed** *n* avidité *f*; (eating) gloutonnerie *f*

**greedily** *adv* avidement; (eating) gloutonnement

**greediness** *n* avidité *f*; (eating) gloutonnerie *f*

**greedy** *adj* avide; (eating) glouton -onne

**greedy-guts** *n sl* goinfre *m*

**Greek** *n* Grec (*f* Grecque); (language) grec *m*; **it's all ~ to me** c'est de l'hébreu pour moi; *adj* grec (*f* grecque)

**green** *n* vert *m*; verdure *f*; (lawn) gazon *m*; **~ s** légumes verts; *adj* vert, verdoyant; (unripe) vert, pas mûr; (complexion) vert, blême; *fig* jaloux -ouse, envieux -ieuse; *coll* inexpérimenté, naïf -ïve; *fig* florissant, vivace; **~ belt** ceinture verte; *mot* **~ light** feu vert

**greenback** *n US coll* billet *m* de banque

**greenery** *n* verdure *f*, feuillage *m*

**greenfinch** *n* verdier *m*

**greenfly** *n* puceron *m*

**greengage** *n* reine-claude *f* (*pl* reines-claudes)

**greengrocer** *n* marchand -e de fruits et légumes, fruitier -ière

**greengrocery** *n* fruiterie *f*; (wares) fruits *mpl* et légumes *mpl*

**greenhorn** *n* blanc-bec *m* (*pl* blancs-becs), débutant -e; dupe *f*

**greenhouse** *n* serre *f*

**greenish** *adj* verdâtre

**greenness** *n* verdeur *f*

**green-room** *n theat* foyer *m* des artistes

**green-sickness** *n med* chlorose *f*

**greenstick** *n med* **~ fracture** fracture incomplète

**greenstuff** *n* légumes verts, verdure *f*

**greensward** *n ar* tapis *m* de verdure, pelouse *f*

**greet** *vt* saluer, accueillir; envoyer des vœux à

**greeting** *n* salut *m*, accueil *m*; **~ s card** carte *f* de vœux

**gregarious** *adj* grégaire

**gregariousness** *n* grégarisme *m*

**Gregorian** *adj* grégorien -ienne; **~ chant** chant grégorien

**grenade** *n* grenade *f*

**grenadier** *n* grenadier *m*

**grenadine** *n* grenadine *f*

**grey, gray** *n* gris *m*; (horse) cheval gris; *adj* gris; *coll* (person) fade, incolore; **~ matter** matière grise; *vi* (hair) grisonner

**grey-beard** *n* grison *m*, barbon *m*

**greyhound** *n* lévrier *m*

**greyish** *adj* grisâtre

**greyness** *n* grisaille *f*, teinte grise

**grid** *n* grille *f*, grillage *m*; *cul* + *naut* + *theat* gril *m*; réseau *m* électrique

**griddle, girdle** *n* plaque *f* de four

**griddle-cake** *n* galette *f*

**gridiron** *n cul* gril *m*

**grief** *n* affliction *f*, chagrin *m*; **come to ~** avoir un accident

**grievance** *n* grief *m*

**grieve** *vt* affliger, chagriner, peiner; *vi* s'affliger, se désoler

**grievous** *adj* atroce, cruel -elle, douloureux -euse, pénible; **charged with causing ~ bodily harm** inculpé pour coups et blessures

**grievousness** *n* gravité *f*

**griffin, griffon, gryphon** *n her* + *myth* + *orni* griffon *m*

**grill** *n cul* gril *m*; (food) grillade *f*; **grill-room** *m*, rôtisserie *f*; (grating) grille *f*; *vt cul* griller, faire griller; *coll* (question) cuisiner, passer à tabac; *vi cul* griller

**grille** *n* grille *f*

**grill-room** *n* grill-room *m*, rôtisserie *f*

**grim** *adj* austère, sévère; lugubre, sinistre; *coll* désagréable

**grimace** *n* grimace *f*; *vi* grimacer

**grime** *n* crasse *f*, saleté *f*; *vt* encrasser, noircir, salir

**griminess** *n* crasse *f*, saleté *f*

**grimness** *n* caractère *m* sinistre, sévérité *f*

**grimy** *adj* crasseux -euse, sale

**grin** *n* (smile) large sourire *m*; (forced) grimace *f*; (hostile) ricanement *m*; *vi* (smile) sourire franchement; (forced) grimacer; (hostile) ricaner **~ and bear it** supporter un malheur en souriant

**grind** *n* broyage *m*, trituration *f*; *coll* (hard work) corvée *f*; *vt* broyer, moudre, triturer; polir, buriner; (teeth) grincer de; (barrel-organ) moudre; **~ down** opprimer; *vi* se broyer, se moudre; (teeth) grincer; *coll* (study) bûcher, potasser; *coll* (work) boulonner

**grindstone** *n* meule *f*; **keep one's nose to the ~** travailler ferme

**grip** n étreinte f; poigne f; fig compréhension f; (control) emprise f; (tool, handle) prise f, poignée f; (suitcase) petite valise, mallette f; **get to ~ s with** se mettre à; **in the ~ of** en proie à; fig **lose one's ~** vt saisir, empoigner; fig comprendre

**gripe** n colique aiguë; vt provoquer des coliques; vi avoir des coliques; sl ronchonner

**gripping** adj saisissant, excitant

**grisliness** n macabre m; horreur f

**grisly** adj macabre, sinistre; horrible

**grist** n blé m à moudre; **it is all ~ to my mill** je fais flèche de tout bois

**gristle** n cartilage m

**gristly** adj cartilagineux -euse

**grit** n gravier m; gros sable; (courage) cran m; vt sabler; **~ one's teeth** serrer les dents; fig tenir bon

**gritstone** n geol grès m

**gritty** adj graveleux -euse, sablonneux -euse

¹**grizzle** n (colour) gris m

²**grizzle** vi coll pleurnicher; se plaindre

**grizzled** adj grisonnant; (hair) poivre et sel invar

¹**grizzly** n zool ours gris

²**grizzly** adj (hair) grisonnant

**groan** n gémissement m, geignement m; (complaint) grognement m; vi gémir, geindre; (complain) grogner

**grocer** n épicier -ière

**grocery** n épicerie f, magasin m d'alimentation; **groceries** épicerie f

**grog** n grog m

**grogginess** n coll faiblesse f; défaillance f

**groggy** adj coll chancelant, titubant, défaillant

**groin** n aine f; archi arête f, nervure f

**grommet, grummet** n naut anneau m de cordage

**groom** n valet m d'écurie, palefrenier m; (bridegroom) marié m; vt (horse) panser, étriller; soigner, parer; **~ oneself** se soigner

**groove** n rainure f, cannelure f; (pulley) gorge f; (record) sillon m; coll **get into a ~** s'encroûter; sl **in the ~** en pleine forme; vt canneler, rainer

**groovy** adj sl dans le vent; sexy

**grope** vt chercher à tâtons; sl peloter; vi tâtonner

**groping** n tâtonnement m; adj tâtonnant

¹**gross** n grosse f

²**gross** n tout m; majorité f; adj gros (f grosse), lourd; vulgaire, grossier -ière; total, brut; flagrant, évident; vt totaliser

**grotesque** n grotesque m; adj grotesque, bizarre

**grotesqueness** n grotesque m

**grotto** n grotte f

**grotty** adj sl moche

**grouch** n coll grognement m; vi coll grogner

**ground** n terre f, sol m, terrain m; (basis) fond m, base f; (picture) champ m; **~ s** raison f, motif m; leg considérants mpl; parc m; (coffee) marc m; **~ floor** rez-de-chaussée m invar; **~ landlord** propriétaire foncier; (airport) **~ staff** personnel m au sol; **break new ~** faire les premiers pas; **common ~** point acquis; **down to the ~** complètement; **get in on the ~ floor** être d'une affaire dès le début; **give ~** lâcher du terrain; **on the ~ s that** sous prétexte que; **stand one's ~** se défendre; adj broyé, concassé; poli; (coffee, etc) moulu; vt (base) fonder, baser; mettre à terre; aer empêcher de voler; naut échouer; vi naut (s')échouer

**ground-bass** n mus basse continue

**grounding** n action f de mettre qch à terre; naut échouage m; aer interdiction f de voler; fig base f, connaissance f élémentaire

**groundless** adj dénué de fondement, mal fondé

**groundling** n hist spectateur -trice du parterre; fig personne f inculte

**groundnut** n arachide f

**ground-plan** n archi plan horizontal; fig plan m de base

**ground-rent** n redevance foncière; rente foncière

**groundsel** n bot séneçon m

**groundsheet** n tapis m de sol

**groundsman** n responsable m d'un terrain de sport, gardien m de stade

**groundswell** n lame f de fond

**groundwork** n fondement m, base f; travail m préliminaire; (painting) fond m

**group** n groupe m; (mountains) massif m; aer **~ captain** colonel m d'aviation; adj de groupe; vt grouper, classifier; vi se grouper

**grouping** n groupement m

¹**grouse** n orni coq m de bruyère, grouse f

²**grouse** n coll grief m, rogne f; vi rouspéter

**grouser** n rouspéteur -euse

**grout** n mortier m, gâchis m; vt remplir de mortier

**grove** n bosquet m

**grovel** vi se vautrer, s'aplatir; courber l'échine, s'humilier

**groveller** n personne f qui s'humilie

**grovelling** adj abject; rampant

**grow** vt faire pousser, faire croître, cultiver; vi croître, grandir, pousser; se développer, augmenter; (become) devenir; ~ **on** plaire de plus en plus à; ~ **out of** (clothes) devenir trop grand pour; (habits) perdre en grandissant; ~ **to** en venir à; ~ **up** devenir adulte; (spread) se répandre

**grower** *n* cultivateur -trice, producteur -trice

**growing** *n* croissance *f*; *agr* culture *f*

**growl** *n* grognement *m*; *vt* + *vi* grogner, gronder

**growler** *n* ronchonneur -euse

**grown** *adj* adulte

**grown-up** *n* adulte *m*, grande personne; *adj* adulte

**growth** *n* croissance *f*; (plant) pousse *f*; (wine) crû *m*; *med* tumeur *f*, (external) excroissance *f*; *fig* développement *m*, expansion *f*

**groyne** *n naut* brise-lames *m*

¹**grub** *n* larve *f*, asticot *m*; (drudge) gratte-papier *m invar*; *sl* (food) boustifaille *f*

²**grub** *vt* fouiller; ~ **up** déraciner, extirper; *vi* fouiller; (work) trimer

**grubber** *n* (person) défricheur *m*; (tool) scarificateur *m*

**grubbiness** *n* crasse *f*, saleté *f*

**grubby** *adj* crasseux -euse, sale; (fruit) véreux -euse

**grudge** *n* rancune *f*; grief *m*; **bear s/o a** ~ en vouloir à qn; *vt* donner à contrecœur à; envier à; reprocher à

**grudging** *adj* donné à regret, donné à contrecœur; pingre, avare

**gruel** *n* gruau *m*; *coll* punition *f*

**gruelling** *n sl* raclée *f*; *adj coll* éreintant; sévère

**gruesome** *adj* horrible, macabre, horrifiant

**gruff** *adj* bourru, brusque; (voice) éraillé, rauque

**gruffness** *n* brusquerie *f*

**grumble** *n* grief *m*, grognement *m*, bougonnement *m*; *vi* grogner, bougonner; *coll* ronchonner, rouspéter; ~ **about** se plaindre de

**grumbler** *n* grogneur -euse, *coll* rouspéteur -euse

**grumbling** *n* grognement *m*, bougonnement *m*; *adj* grognon -onne, mécontent, ronchon -onne; (pain) intermittent

**grummet** *n see* **grommet**

**grumpiness** *n* grogne *f*, maussaderie *f*

**grumpy** *adj* grincheux -euse, grognon -onne, maussade

**grunt** *n* grognement *m*; *vt* + *vi* grogner

**gryphon** *n see* **griffin**

**g-string** *n* cache-sexe *m invar*

**guana** *n zool* iguane *m*

**guano** *n* guano *m*

**guarantee, guaranty** *n* caution *f*, garantie *f*; (person) garant -e; *vt* cautionner, garantir; *fig* (answer for) répondre de

**guarantor** *n leg* garant -e

**guaranty** *n see* **guarantee** *n*

**guard** *n* garde *f*, protection *f*; (person) garde *m*; *mil* sentinelle *f*; (railway) chef *m* de train; (fire) garde-feu *m invar*; **be caught off one's** ~ être pris au dépourvu; **be on one's** ~ être sur ses gardes; *mil* **on** ~ en garde; *vt* garder, protéger; *vi* se garder, se prémunir

**guarded** *adj* gardé; *fig* circonspect

**guardedly** *adv* prudemment, avec circonspection

**guardhouse** *n mil* corps *m* de garde

**guardian** *n* gardien -ienne, protecteur -trice; *leg* tuteur -trice; *adj* gardien -ienne, protecteur -trice

**gudgeon** *n* goujon *m*; *mech* tourillon *m*; *mot* ~ **pin** goupille *f*

**guelder-rose** *n bot* boule-de-neige *f* (*pl* boules-de-neige)

**Guernsey** *n* Guernesey *m*

**guerrilla** *n* guérillero *m*, franc-tireur *m* (*pl* francs-tireurs); ~ **band** guérilla *f*; ~ **warfare** guérilla *f*

**guess** *n* conjecture *f*, supposition *f*; **at a** ~ au jugé; **at a rough** ~ à vue de nez; **have a** ~ deviner; **have a** ~ **!** devinez!; **my** ~ **is** d'après moi; *vt* deviner, conjecturer, supposer; (calculate) estimer, évaluer; *US* (believe) croire, penser, avoir l'impression; *vi* deviner; ~ **right** deviner juste; ~ **wrong** tomber à côté; **keep s/o** ~ **ing** laisser qn dans le doute

**guesswork** *n* conjecture *f*, hypothèse *f*; **by** ~ par flair

**guest** *n* hôte, invité -e; (meal) convive; (hotel) client -e; ~ **room** chambre *f* d'amis

**guest-house** *n* pension *f*

**guff** *n coll* bêtises *fpl*

**guffaw** *n* gros rire *m*; *vi* s'esclaffer

**guidance** *n* conduite *f*, direction *f*

**guide** *n* (person, book) guide *m*; indication *f*; *mech* glissière *f*; **girl** ~ guide *f*; *vt* guider, diriger

**guided** *adj* (missile) téléguidé

**guidelines** *npl* directives *fpl*

**guild, gild** *n hist* guilde *f*; corporation *f*

**guilder** *n* gulden *m*

**guildhall** *n* hôtel *m* de ville

**guile** *n* astuce *f*, ruse *f*; (deceit) fourberie *f*

**guileful** *adj* astucieux -ieuse, rusé; (deceitful) fourbe

**guileless** *adj* candide, naïf -ïve, franc (*f* franche)

**guilelessness** *n* candeur *f*, naïveté *f*; franchise *f*

515

**guillemot** n guillemot m
**guillotine** n guillotine f; vt guillotiner
**guilt** n culpabilité f
**guiltiness** n culpabilité f
**guiltless** adj innocent
**guiltlessness** n innocence f
**guilty** adj coupable; ~ **conscience** mauvaise conscience
**guinea** n ar guinée f
**guinea-fowl** n pintade f
**guinea-pig** n zool + fig cobaye m
**guise** n apparence f, aspect m; costume m
**guitar** n guitare f
**guitarist** n guitariste
**gulch** n US ravin m
**gules** n her gueules fpl
**gulf** n golfe m; fig abîme m, gouffre m
¹**gull** n orni goëland m, mouette f
²**gull** n dupe f, imbécile; sl poire f; vt duper, rouler
**gullet** n œsophage m, gosier m
**gulley** n see gully
**gullibility** n crédulité f
**gullible** adj crédule
**gully, gulley** n rigole f; (mountain) couloir m; vt creuser une rigole dans
**gulp** n action f d'avaler; (liquids) gorgée f; (food) bouchée f; serrement m de gorge; vt avaler, engloutir; ~ **sth out** dire qch la gorge serrée
¹**gum** n gencive f
²**gum** n gomme f, colle f, résine f; **chewing** ~ chewing-gum m; vt gommer, coller; coll ~ **up** bousiller, rendre inutilisable
**gumboil** n abcès m aux gencives
**gumboots** npl bottes fpl en caoutchouc
**gummy** adj gommeux -euse, collant, gluant
**gumption** n coll bon sens, jugeotte f, initiative f
**gum-tree** n bot gommier m; sl **up a** ~ foutu, perdu
**gun** n mil canon m; (rifle) fusil m; fusil m de chasse; revolver m; (spraying) pistolet m; ~ **dog** chien m d'arrêt, retriever m; coll **big** ~ grosse légume; **stick to one's** ~**s** ne pas fléchir, ne pas démordre; vt + vi chasser, tirer; vi sl ~ **for s/o** viser qn, chercher qn
**gunboat** n canonnière f
**gun-carriage** n affût m (de canon)
**gun-cotton** n coton-poudre m (pl cotons-poudre), fulmicoton m
**gun-fire** n tir m d'artillerie
**gunman** n bandit armé, gangster m
**gunner** n mil artilleur m, canonnier m
**gunnery** n balistique f; tir m d'artillerie
**gunpowder** n poudre f (à canon)
**gunrunner** n contrebandier m d'armes
**gunrunning** n contrebande f d'armes
**gunshot** n coup m de feu; **within** ~ à portée de canon; adj (wound) causé par un projectile
**gunsmith** n armurier m
**gun-stock** n fût m
**gunwale** n naut plat-bord m (pl platsbords)
**gurgle** n gargouillement m, glouglou m; vi gargouiller, glouglouter
**gush** n jaillissement m, ruissellement m, flot m; fig effusion sentimentale, épanchement m; vi jaillir, ruisseler; fig pej s'épancher
**gushing** adj jaillissant, ruisselant; fig pej trop expansif -ive
**gusset** n (clothes) soufflet m; (bracket) tasseau m
**gust** n coup m de vent; fig accès m
**gustatory** adj gustatif -ive
**gusto** n entrain m
**gusty** adj venteux -euse; fig émotif -ive
**gut** n boyaux mpl, intestin m; mus corde f; ~**s** ventre m; coll fig cran m; vt étriper, vider; (fire) ravager
**gutta-percha** n gutta-percha f
**gutter** n (roof) gouttière f; (street) caniveau m, ruisseau m; (groove) rainure f; fig boue f, pauvreté f sordide; ~ **press** presse f à sensation; vt mettre des gouttières à; rainer; vi (candle) couler
**guttering** n gouttières fpl
**guttersnipe** n gamin -e des rues, petit voyou
**guttural** n gutturale f; adj phon guttural; rauque
¹**guy** n naut hauban m, étai m; (tent) corde f d'attache; vt naut haubaner
²**guy** n (strangely dressed person) épouvantail m; coll type m
³**guy** vt ridiculiser, tourner en ridicule
**guy-rope** n corde f de tente
**guzzle** vt manger gloutonnement; coll bâfrer; vi se goinfrer, s'empiffrer
**guzzler** n glouton -onne, goinfre m
**gybe** vi naut empanner
**gym** n (place) gymnase m; (activity) gymnastique f
**gymnasium** n gymnase m
**gymnast** n gymnaste
**gymnastic** adj gymnastique
**gymnastics** npl gymnastique f
**gynaecological** adj gynécologique
**gynaecologist** n gynécologue
**gynaecology** n gynécologie f
**gypsum** n gypse m
**gypsy** n + adj see gipsy
**gyrate** vi tournoyer
**gyration** n giration f, rotation f
**gyratory** adj giratoire, rotatif -ive
**gyrocompass** n gyrocompas m
**gyroscope** n gyroscope m
**gyrostat** n gyrostat m

# H

ha *interj* ha!
haberdasher *n* mercier -ière
haberdashery *n* mercerie *f*
¹habit *n* habitude *f*; coutume *f*
²habit *n* ar + eccles habit *m*
habitability *n* habitabilité *f*
habitable *adj* habitable
habitat *n* habitat *m*
habitation *n* habitation *f*
habitual *adj* habituel -elle
habituate *vt* habituer
habitué *n* habitué -e
hachures *npl* hachure *f*
¹hack *n* coupure *f*, entaille *f*; (kick) coup *m* de pied (à la jambe); *med* toux sèche; (tool) pioche *f*; *vt* couper, entailler, taillader; (kick) donner un coup de pied (à la jambe); piocher
²hack *n* cheval *m* de louage; cheval *m* de selle; *coll* canasson *m*; *fig* forçat *m* du travail; (writer) écrivailleur -euse; *vi* aller au petit trot
hacking *adj* (cough) sec (*f* sèche)
hackle *n* orni plumes *fpl* du cou; with ~ s up sur ses ergots; *fig* en colère
hackney *n* cheval *m* de louage; cheval *m* de selle
hackney-carriage *n* voiture *f* de louage, voiture *f* de place
hackneyed *adj* banal (*pl* banals), insignifiant, plat
hacksaw *n* scie *f* à métaux
hackwork *n* travail *m* monotone
hack-writer *n* écrivailleur -euse
haddock *n* haddock *m*, aiglefin *m*
haemoglobin *n* hémoglobine *f*
haemophilia *n* med hémophilie *f*
haemorrhage, hemorrhage *n* hémorragie *f*
haemorrhoid, hemorrhoid *n* hémorroïde *f*
haft *n* manche *m*, poignée *f*
¹hag *n* sorcière *f*; *coll* vieille bique
²hag *n* (marsh) fondrière *f*; (peat) tourbière *f*
haggard *adj* hagard; défait, hâve
haggle *vi* marchander
haggler *n* marchandeur -euse
hagiarchy *n* gouvernement *m* par des prêtres; hiérarchie *f* des saints
hagiographer *n* hagiographe
hagiographic *adj* hagiographique
hagiography *n* hagiographie *f*
hagiology *n* littérature *f* hagiographique
hag-ridden *adj* obsédé; sujet -ette à des cauchemars
Hague (The) *n* La Haye
¹hail *n* grêle *f*; *vt* déverser, décharger; *vi* grêler; tomber rapidement
²hail *n* appel *m*; salut *m*; within ~ à portée de voix; *vt* appeler, héler; saluer; *vi naut* + *coll* ~ from venir de, être en provenance de
³hail *interj* salut!
hailstone *n* grêlon *m*
hailstorm *n* tempête *f* de grêle
hair *n* (human body, animal) poil *m*; (human head) cheveu *m*; *collect* (human head) cheveux *mpl*, chevelure *f*; (animal) pelage *m*; do one's ~ se coiffer; *coll* keep one's ~ on rester calme; let one's ~ down parler sans gêne; agir sans inhibitions; make s/o's ~ stand on end faire dresser les cheveux sur la tête de qn; not turn a ~ ne pas broncher; put one's ~ up se coiffer en toupet; split ~ s couper les cheveux en quatre; tear one's ~ s'arracher les cheveux; to a ~ exactement, tout à fait
hairbreadth *n* épaisseur *f* d'un cheveu; by a ~ de justesse; *adj* de l'épaisseur d'un cheveu, très étroit
hairbrush *n* brosse *f* à cheveux
haircloth *n* tissu *m* de crin
hair-cut *n* coupe *f* de cheveux; have a ~ se faire couper les cheveux
hair-do *n coll* coiffure *f*
hairdresser *n* coiffeur -euse
hairdressing *n* coiffure *f*
hairiness *n* (head) aspect chevelu; (body) aspect poilu
hairline *n* ligne *f* très mince; naissance *f* des cheveux; ~ fracture fêlure *f*
hairnet *n* résille *f*
hairpin *n* épingle *f* à cheveux; ~ bend virage *m* en épingle à cheveux
hair-raising *adj* horrifique, effrayant
hair-shirt *n* haire *f*, cilice *m*
hair-slide *n* barrette *f*
hair-splitting *n* ergotage *m*
hairspring *n* spiral *m* (de montre)
hairy *adj* (head) chevelu; (body, animal) poilu, velu
hake *n* merlu *m*, colin *m*
halberd *n* hallebarde *f*
halberdier *n* hallebardier *m*
halcyon *adj* serein, tranquille; ~ days temps *m* de paix et de bonheur
¹hale *adj* costaud, vigoureux -euse
²hale *vt* tirer, traîner

# half

**half** n moitié f, demi m, demie f; sp demi m; (match) mi-temps f; joc **better ~** moitié f; **by halves** partiellement; **go halves** être de moitié, partager; **too clever by ~** trop habile de moitié, beaucoup trop habile; adj demi (invar before noun); adv demi-, à demi; coll **not ~ !** certainement!, bien sûr!; coll **not ~ bad** pas mal du tout, très bien

**half-and-half** adv moitié-moitié

**half-back** n demi m

**half-baked** adj à demi-cuit; fig (person) étourdi; (idea) inconsidéré

**half-breed** n métis -isse, sang-mêlé invar; (horse) demi-sang m invar; adj métis -isse

**half-brother** n demi-frère m

**half-caste** n + adj métis -isse

**half-cock** n **go off at ~** exploser prématurément; fig mal partir

**half-crown** n obs demi-couronne f

**half-dollar** n US demi-dollar m; coll ar demi-couronne f

**half-fare** n demi-place f; adj à demi-tarif

**half-hearted** adj peu empressé, peu enthousiaste

**half-heartedness** n manque m d'enthousiasme

**half-hitch** n naut demi-clef f

**half-holiday** n congé m d'une demi-journée

**half-length** n portrait m en buste; adj en buste

**half-light** n demi-jour m

**half-mast** n **at ~** en berne

**half-moon** n demi-lune f

**half-nelson** n sp clef f du cou

**half-pay** n mil demi-solde f; adj mil en demi-solde

**halfpenny** n demi-penny m, sou m

**half-seas-over** adj sl parti, éméché

**half-sister** n demi-sœur f

**half-timbered** adj aux poutres apparentes

**half-time** n sp mi-temps f; (work) **be on ~** travailler (être) à mi-temps

**half-tone** n arts demi-teinte f; mus demi-ton m

**half-track** n half-track m

**half-truth** n demi-vérité f

**half-volley** n demi-volée f

**halfway** adj + adv à mi-chemin

**half-wit** n coll crétin -e, idiot -e

**halibut** n flétan m

**halitosis** n med mauvaise haleine

**hall** n salle f, grande salle; (dining) réfectoire m; (hotel) hall m; (house) vestibule m; (students' hostel) maison f d'étudiants, pavillon f; **town ~** hôtel m de ville

**hallelujah** interj alléluia!

**halliard** n see **halyard**

**hallmark** n (gold, silver) poinçon m de garantie; fig preuve f de grande qualité, garantie f

**hallo, hello, hullo** interj hola!; allo!

**hallow** vt sanctifier, bénir

**Hallowe'en** n veille f de la Toussaint

**hallucination** n hallucination f

**hallucinatory** adj hallucinatoire

**halo** n auréole f, nimbe m; astron halo m; vt auréoler; astron entourer d'un halo

**halogen** n chem halogène m

¹**halt** n halte f, arrêt m; interj halte!; vt arrêter, faire arrêter; vi faire halte, s'arrêter

²**halt** npl ar estropiés mpl; adj boiteux -euse; vi boiter, clopiner; (speech) balbutier

**halter** n licol m, licou m; vt mettre un licou à

**halting** adj boiteux -euse; hésitant

**halve** vt diviser en deux, partager entre deux

**halyard, halliard** n naut drisse f

**ham** n jambon m; theat cabotin -e; coll radio-amateur m; **~ s** fesses fpl; vt theat charger; vi theat cabotiner

**hamburger** n hamburger m; US **~ meat** viande hachée

**ham-fisted** adj maladroit

**ham-handed** adj maladroit

**hamlet** n hameau m

**hammer** n marteau m; (firearm) percuteur m; **~ and tongs** avec acharnement; **come under the ~** être vendu aux enchères; vt marteler, pilonner; frapper fort; coll attaquer, battre; (Stock Exchange) proclamer comme failli; **~ in** enfoncer à coups de marteau; fig faire apprendre à force de répéter; **~ out** résoudre; vi **~ away at** s'acharner à

**hammer-head** n tête f de marteau; zool (shark) requin m marteau

**hammock** n hamac m

**hammy** adj coll theat cabotin

¹**hamper** n banne f, manne f, panier m

²**hamper** vt entraver, gêner, obstruer

**hamster** n hamster m

**hamstring** n tendon m de jarret; vt couper le jarret à; fig couper les moyens à

**hand** n main f; (share) part f; (person) ouvrier m, travailleur m; naut marin m; agr valet m de ferme; (handwriting) écriture f; (dial) aiguille f; (measure) palme f; (help) aide f; (cards held) jeu m; (card game) partie f; (card player) joueur -euse; (applause) applaudissements mpl; **~ in glove** comme larrons en foire, coll de mèche; **~ in ~** la main dans la main; **~ s off!** pas d'intervention!; *coll* bas les pattes!; ~ over ~ avec une main après l'autre; ~ to ~ corps à corps; ~s up! haut les mains!; at first ~ de première main; at ~ à proximité; by ~ à la main; par livraison personnelle; cash in ~ encaisse *f*; change ~s changer de mains; come to ~ être arrivé, être retrouvé; eat out of s/o's ~ être totalement soumis à qn; from ~ to ~ de la main à la main; from ~ to mouth au jour le jour; get one's ~ in se faire la main; have a free ~ avoir carte blanche; have a ~ in avoir un doigt dans; in ~ sur le chantier, en train; keep one's ~ in s'entretenir la main; lay ~s on saisir; (find) mettre la main sur; *eccles* laying on ~s imposition *f* des mains; lend a ~ donner un coup de main; lost with all ~s péri corps et biens; not to do a ~'s turn ne rien faire de ses dix doigts; off one's ~s n'étant plus sa responsabilité; old ~ vétéran *m*; on all ~s de tous côtés; on one's ~s sur les bras; on the one ~ ... on the other ~ d'une part ... d'autre part; out of ~ de suite, sans hésitation; hors des gonds; play into the ~s of faire le jeu de; shake ~s with serrer la main à; show one's ~ dévoiler son jeu; take a ~ in participer à; take in ~ s'occuper de; upper ~ dessus *m*; wash one's ~s of se laver les mains de; win ~s down gagner facilement; with a heavy ~ avec poigne; with a high ~ autoritairement; *adj* fait (à la) main; à main, qu'on tient dans la main; *vt* passer, donner, transmettre; ~ down (inheritance, tradition) transmettre; ~ in remettre; *sl* ~ it to tirer son chapeau à; ~ on transmettre, envoyer; ~ out distribuer; ~ over livrer; ~ round distribuer

**handbag** *n* sac *m* à main

**handbarrow** *n* brouette *f*; charrette *f* à bras

**handbell** *n* clochette *f*, sonnette *f*

**handbill** *n* prospectus *m*, avis *m*

**handbook** *n* (instruction) manuel *m*; (guide) guide *m*

**handbrace** *n mech* vilebrequin *m*

**handbrake** *n mot* frein *m* à main

**handcart** *n* charrette *f* à bras

**handcuff** *vt* mettre les menottes à

**handcuffs** *npl* menottes *fpl*

**handful** *n* poignée *f*; *fig* petit nombre; that child is a real ~ cet enfant est une vraie peste

**hand-glass** *n* miroir *m* à main, glace *f* à main

**hand-grenade** *n* grenade *f* à main

**handgrip** *n* poignée *f* de main; prise *f*

**handhold** *n* prise *f*

**handicap** *n* handicap *m*, désavantage *m*; *vt* handicaper, désavantager

**handicraft** *n* travail *m* d'artisanat

**handicraftsman** *n* artisan *m*

**handily** *adv* adroitement; commodément

**handiness** *n* (skill) adresse *f*; (convenience) commodité *f*; proximité *f*

**handiwork** *n* travail fait à la main; objet fait à la main; *fig* œuvre *f*, ouvrage *m*

**handkerchief** *n* mouchoir *m*

**handle** *n* (basket) anse *f*; (door) poignée *f*; (axe, broom, knife, etc) manche *m*; (pan) queue *f*; *coll* fly off the ~ sortir de ses gonds; give a ~ to donner prise à; have a ~ to one's name avoir un nom à particule; *vt* manier, manipuler; contrôler; *comm* trafiquer de; (subject) traiter; I can ~ him je sais le prendre

**handlebar(s)** *n* guidon *m*; ~ moustache moustache *f* en croc

**handling** *n* maniement *m*; traitement *m*

**handmade** *adj* fait (à la) main

**handmaid** *n ar* servante *f*; *fig* subordonnée *f*, aide *f*

**hand-me-down** *adj US* (ready-made) de confection; (cheap) bon marché; (secondhand) d'occasion

**hand-mill** *n cul* moulin *m*

**handout** *n* (statement) communiqué *m*; *US* aumône *f*

**hand-picked** *adj* sélectionné (à la main)

**handrail** *n* main courante

**handsaw** *n* scie *f* à main

**handshake** *n* poignée *f* de main

**handsome** *adj* beau (*f* belle); généreux -euse; *coll* come down ~ être généreux

**handsomeness** *n* beauté *f*; générosité *f*

**handspring** *n* saut périlleux

**handwork** *n* travail fait à la main

**handwriting** *n* écriture *f*

**handy** *adj* (near) accessible, sous la main; (convenient) commode, pratique; (skilled) adroit, habile; *adv* tout près

**handyman** *n* bricoleur *m*

**hang** *n* (clothes, curtains, etc) drapé *m*; *coll* get the ~ of comprendre; *vt* pendre; accrocher, suspendre; (drape) tendre; (painting) exposer; (wallpaper) poser; (execute) pendre; ~ fire (firearm) faire long feu; *fig* être retardé; ~ oneself se pendre; ~ one's head baisser la tête; ~ out (flag) arborer; ~ up accrocher, suspendre; (telephone) raccrocher; ~ upon s'appuyer sur; (words) écouter avidement; *vi* pendre, être accroché; (curtains) tomber; (recline) pencher, s'incliner; (on gallows) être pendu; ~ about (around) traîner, musarder; ~ back hésiter; rester en arrière; ~ by a

**thread** ne tenir qu'à un fil; ~ **on** s'accrocher; *fig* tenir bon; *coll* attendre; ~ **out** pendre dehors; *coll* habiter, percher; ~ **together** se tenir les coudes; (story, etc) tenir debout; **be hung up** être retardé

**hangar** *n* hangar *m*

**hangdog** *adj* ~ **look** air *m* coupable

**hanger** *n* crochet *m*; (coat) cintre *m*, portemanteau *m*; (on hat stand) patère *f*; (handwriting) jambage *m*

**hanger-on** *n* parasite *m*

**hanging** *n* pendaison *f*; accrochage *m*; (wallpaper) pose *f*; ~**s** draperies *fpl*; *adj* pendant, suspendu, tombant; ~ **garden** jardin suspendu; ~ **matter** cas *m* pendable

**hangman** *n* bourreau *m*

**hangover** *n* gueule *f* de bois

**hang-up** *n* complexe *m*

**hank** *n* écheveau *m*

**hanker** *vi* ~ **after, for** avoir envie de, soupirer après

**hankering** *n* envie forte, grand désir

**hanky** *n coll* mouchoir *m*

**hanky-panky** *n coll* roublardise *f*

**Hansard** *n* le Hansard, transcription *f* des débats du parlement britannique

**Hanseatic** *adj hist* hanséatique

**hansom** *n obs* cab *m*

**ha'penny** *n see* **halfpenny**

**haphazard** *adj* fortuit, au hasard

**hapless** *adj* infortuné, malchanceux -euse

**haplessness** *n* infortune *f*, malchance *f*

**happen** *vi* arriver, advenir, avoir lieu, se produire, survenir; *coll* ~ **along** arriver par hasard; ~ **on (upon)** trouver par hasard; ~ **to be** se trouver par hasard

**happening** *n* événement *m*

**happiness** *n* bonheur *m*, contentement *m*, satisfaction *f*

**happy** *adj* heureux -euse, content, enchanté, satisfait

**happy-go-lucky** *adj* insouciant, nonchalant

**hara-kiri** *n* harakiri *m*; **commit** ~ faire harakiri

**harangue** *n* harangue *f*, *coll* laïus *m*; *vt* haranguer; *vi* prononcer une harangue; *coll* faire un laïus

**harass** *vt* harceler, tourmenter, tracasser

**harassment** *n* harcèlement *m*, tourment *m*, tracas *m*

**harbinger** *n* avant-coureur *m*, annonciateur -trice

**harbour** *n* port *m*; *vt* abriter, héberger; (criminal) receler; (feelings) nourrir; *vi* se mettre à l'abri, se réfugier

**harbour-bar** *n naut* barre *f*

**harbour-master** *n* capitaine *m* de port

**hard** *n naut* quai *m*, cale *f*; *coll* travaux forcés; *vulg* **have a** ~ **on** bander; *adj* dur, solide; difficile; ardu, fatigant, pénible, rude; brutal; exigeant, implacable, sévère; (words) amer -ère, violent; (fate) injuste; (weather) inclément, rigoureux -euse; (water) calcaire; ~ **and fast** inflexible, ferme; ~ **cash** liquide *m*; ~ **court** tennis asphalté; ~ **currency** devises fortes; ~ **drinking** beuverie *f*; ~ **labour** travaux forcés; ~ **lines!** dommage!, tant pis!; ~ **luck** malchance *f*; ~ **of hearing** dur d'oreille; ~ **up** fauché; **be** ~ **on** traiter durement; *adv* dur, durement, ferme, fort; énergiquement, sévèrement, violemment; ~ **by** tout près; ~ **hit** très affecté; **die** ~ mettre longtemps à disparaître; **it will go** ~ **with you** vous aurez bien des ennuis

**hardback** *n* livre relié

**hard-baked** *adj* cuit longuement au four; *coll fig* dur, endurci

**hard-bitten** *adj* implacable, inexorable

**hardboard** *n* carton-cuir *m*

**hard-boiled** *adj* (egg) dur; *coll* implacable, inexorable; (shrewd) astucieux -ieuse

**hardcore** *n bui* blocaille *f*

**hard-core** *adj* impénitent, inébranlable

**hard-earned** *adj* durement gagné

**harden** *vt* durcir, rendre dur, endurcir; *med* indurer, scléroser; (steel) tremper; *vi* durcir, se durcir, s'endurcir; *med* s'indurer, se scléroser; (prices) monter

**hardened** *adj fig* impénitent, invétéré

**hardening** *n* durcissement *m*; *med* induration *f*, sclérose *f*; (steel) trempe *f*

**hard-faced, hard-favoured, hard-featured** *adj* aux traits durs; *sl* pète-sec *invar*

**hard-fisted** *adj* pingre

**hard-headed** *adj* perspicace; pratique, terre à terre

**hard-hearted** *adj* cruel -elle, insensible

**hardihood** *n* courage *m*, hardiesse *f*

**hardily** *adv* audacieusement, fermement

**hardiness** *n* audace *f*, hardiesse *f*; résistance *f*

**hard-liner** *n* faucon *m*, dur *m*

**hardly** *adv* à peine, guère, tout juste; durement, rudement

**hardness** *n* dureté *f*, rigueur *f*, sévérité *f*; ~ **of heart** sécheresse *f* de cœur

**hard-pressed** *adj* aux prises *fpl* avec des problèmes; (short of money) gêné

**hard-set** *adj* (cement, etc) durci; *fig* obstiné, têtu

**hardship** *n* épreuve *f*, privation *f*, rigueur *f*

**hardtop** *n mot* hard-top *m*

**hardware** *n* quincaillerie *f*; (computers)

hardware *m*; (communication, teaching) audio-visuel *m*; *US* ~ **store** quincaillerie *f*

**hardwood** *n* bois dur

**hardy** *adj* résistant, robuste; hardi, intrépide

**hare** *n* lièvre *m*; *sl* projet *m* chimérique; **start a** ~ intervenir mal à propos dans un argument; *vi coll* courir vite; ~ **off** détaler

**harebell** *n bot* campanule *f*

**hare-brained** *adj* écervelé, étourdi

**hare-lip** *n* bec-de-lièvre *m* (*pl* becs-de-lièvre)

**harem** *n* harem *m*, sérail *m*

**haricot** *n bot* haricot blanc; *cul* navarin *m*

**hark** *vi* écouter; ~ **back to** revenir sur

**harken** *vi see* **hearken**

**Harlequin** *n* Arlequin *m*

**harlequin** *adj* bigarré, d'arlequin

**harlequinade** *n* arlequinade *f*

**harlot** *n* prostituée *f*, putain *f*

**harlotry** *n* prostitution *f*

**harm** *n* dommage *m*, mal *m*, préjudice *m*, tort *m*; *vt* endommager, faire du mal à, nuire à; *leg* léser

**harmful** *adj* malfaisant, néfaste, nocif -ive, nuisible

**harmless** *adj* anodin, inoffensif -ive

**harmlessness** *n* innocuité *f*

**harmonic** *n* harmonique *m or f*; ~ **s** harmonique *m or f*; *adj* harmonique; ~ **series** série *f* harmonique

**harmonica** *n* harmonica *m*

**harmonious** *adj* harmonieux -ieuse, mélodieux -ieuse; (pleasant) plaisant; bien arrangé, bien construit

**harmoniousness** *n* harmonie *f*

**harmonist** *n* harmoniste

**harmonium** *n* harmonium *m*

**harmonization** *n* harmonisation *f*

**harmonize** *vt* harmoniser; *vi* s'harmoniser

**harmony** *n* harmonie *f*; *fig* concordance *f*, entente *f*

**harness** *n* harnachement *m*, harnais *m*; (parachute) ceinture *f*; **die in** ~ travailler jusqu'à la mort; **get back in** ~ reprendre le collier; *vt* harnacher; (river) aménager; (energy, etc) exploiter

**harp** *n* harpe *f*; *vi mus* jouer de la harpe; ~ **on** rabâcher

**harpist** *n* harpiste

**harpoon** *n* harpon *m*; *vt* harponner

**harpsichord** *n* clavecin *m*

**harpy** *n myth* harpie *f*; *fig* mégère *f*

**harquebus, arquebus** *n hist* arquebuse *f*

**harridan** *n* vieille sorcière, vieille chipie

**harrier** *n* (bird) busard *m*; (dog) braque *m*; (runner) coureur *m* de fond, coureur *m* de cross

**harrow** *n agr* herse *f*; *vt agr* herser; *fig* affliger, tourmenter

**harrowing** *adj* affligeant, angoissant

**harry** *vt* dévaster, piller; (pester) harceler

**harsh** *adj* sévère, cruel -elle; (touch) rêche, rugueux -euse; (voice) rauque; (sound) discordant; (colour) criard; (taste) râpeux -euse

**harshness** *n* sévérité *f*, cruauté *f*; (touch) rudesse *f*, rugosité *f*; (sound) discordance *f*; (colour) aspect criard; (taste) âpreté *f*

**hart** *n* cerf *m*

**harum-scarum** *n + adj* écervelé -e

**harvest** *n* moisson *f*, récolte *f*; ~ **festival** service *m* d'action de grâces au moment de la récolte; ~ **moon** pleine lune de l'équinoxe d'automne; *vt* moissonner, récolter; *vi* faire la moisson

**harvester** *n* (person) moissonneur -euse; (machine) moissonneuse *f*; ~ **bug** aoûtat *m*

**harvest-home** *n* rentrée *f* de la moisson; festin *m* de la moisson

**harvest-mouse** *n* mulot *m*

**has-been** *n coll* croulant *m*

**hash** *n cul* hachis *m*; *coll* (mess) gâchis *m*, pagaïe *f*; *coll* (repetition) rabâchage *m*; *coll* haschisch *m*; *coll* **settle s/o's** ~ régler son compte à qn; *vt cul* hacher; *coll* (mess up) gâcher

**hashish** *n* hachisch *m*, haschisch *m*

**haslets** *npl* fressure *f*

**hasp** *n* (door, lock) loquet *m*, morailon *m*; (window) espagnolette *f*; (thread) écheveau *m*; *vt* fermer au loquet

**hassock** *n* coussin *m* (d'agenouilloir)

¹**haste** *n* hâte *f*; précipitation *f*

²**haste** *vt + vi see* **hasten**

**hasten** *vt* hâter, presser; *vi* se hâter, se dépêcher, se presser

**hastily** *adv* hâtivement, à la hâte; à la légère

**hastiness** *n* hâte *f*, précipitation *f*; brusquerie *f*

**hasty** *adj* hâtif -ive, précipité; inconsidéré, irréfléchi

**hat** *n* chapeau *m*; *coll* **keep it under your** ~ n'en dites pas un mot; **my** ~! vraiment!; *coll* **talk through one's** ~ dire n'importe quoi

**hatband** *n* ruban *m* de chapeau

¹**hatch** *n* trappe *f*; *naut* écoutille *f*; *coll* **down the** ~! à la vôtre!; **serving** ~ passe-plat *m*; *naut* **under** ~**es** dans la cale; *fig* emprisonné

²**hatch** *n* (arts) hachure *f*; *vt* hachurer

³**hatch** *n* éclosion *f*; couvée *f*; *vt* couver; *fig* ourdir, tramer; *vi* éclore

**hatcher** *n* couveuse *f*

**hatchery** *n* alevinier *m*

**hatchet** *n* hachette *f*; ~ **face** visage *m* en lame de couteau; ~ **man** tueur *m* à gages; **bury the** ~ faire la paix

**hatchway** *n naut* écoutille *f*

**hate** *n* haine *f*, exécration *f*; (person) objet *m* de haine; *vt* haïr, détester, exécrer

**hateful** *adj* détestable, haïssable, odieux -ieuse

**hatefulness** *n* aspect *m* détestable, aspect *m* haïssable

**hatpin** *n* épingle *f* à chapeau

**hatrack** *n* porte-chapeaux *m*

**hatred** *n* haine *f*, exécration *f*

**hatstand** *n* porte-chapeaux *m*

**hatted** *adj* coiffé d'un chapeau

**hatter** *n* chapelier *m*; **mad as a** ~ complètement cinglé

**haughtiness** *n* hauteur *f*, morgue *f*

**haughty** *adj* altier -ière, hautain

**haul** *n* traction *f*; *naut* bordée *f*; (fish) prise *f*; *vt* + *v* haler, tirer, traîner

**haulage** *n* halage *m*; (road) camionnage *m*; ~ **contractor** entrepreneur *m* de transport, transporteur *m*

**haulier** *n* (coal-mining) herscheur *m*; transporteur *m*

**haunch** *n* hanche *f*; *cul* (venison) cuissot *m*

**haunt** *n* lieu *m* de prédilection; (den) repaire *m*; *vt* fréquenter, visiter souvent; (ghost) hanter; *fig* hanter, obséder

**haunted** *adj* hanté

**haunting** *adj* fascinant, inoubliable, qui hante

**hautboy** *n ar* hautbois *m*

**have** *n coll* attrape *f*; ~ **s** riches *mpl*; **the** ~ **s and the** ~ **-nots** les riches et les pauvres; *vt* avoir, posséder; (hold) tenir, saisir; (feel) éprouver, sentir; (undergo) subir; (take) prendre; (drink) boire; (eat) manger; (get) obtenir; (cause) faire; (allow) permettre, supporter, tolérer; *coll* (trick) avoir, duper; *vulg* faire l'amour avec, baiser; *v aux* avoir; ~ **better** faire mieux; *coll* ~ **had it** être cuit; *sl* être foutu; (die) mourir, crever; ~ **in** inviter (à la maison); *coll* ~ **it in for** en vouloir à, garder une dent contre; ~ **it out** s'expliquer; ~ **just** venir de; ~ **s/o on** canuler qn; ~ **sth done** faire faire qch; ~ **sth on** avoir qch à faire; ~ **to** avoir à, devoir, être obligé de; ~ **to do with** avoir à faire à; *coll* ~ **up** faire passer en correctionnelle, poursuivre en justice

**haven** *n* port *m*; *fig* asile *m*, havre *m*

**have-not** *n* pauvre *m*, démuni -e

**haver** *vi* hésiter; *Scots* déraisonner

**haversack** *n* havresac *m*

**havoc** *n* dévastation *f*

¹**haw** *n bot* fleur *m* d'aubépine

²**haw** *vi* hum and ~ *see* hum

¹**hawk** *n* faucon *m*; *fig* escroc *m*; *pol* faucon *m*; *vi* chasser au faucon

²**hawk** *vi* expectorer

³**hawk** *vt* colporter

**hawker** *n* colporteur *m*; (fruit, vegetables) marchand -e des quatre saisons

**hawk-eyed** *adj* aux yeux de lynx

**hawkmoth** *n* sphinx *m*

**hawser** *n naut* haussière *f*, câble *m*

**hawthorn** *n* aubépine *f*

**hay** *n* foin *m*; *coll* **hit the** ~ aller se coucher; **make** ~ faner; **make** ~ **of** embrouiller; **make** ~ **while the sun shines** saisir l'occasion

**hay-fever** *n* rhume *m* des foins

**haymaker** *n* faneur -euse

**haymaking** *n* fanage *m*

**hayrick** *n* meule *f* de foin

**haystack** *n* meule *f* de foin

**haywire** *adj coll* fou (*f* folle); embrouillé, en pagaïe

**hazard** *n* hasard *m*, chance *f*; obstacle *m*; péril *m*, risque *m*; *vt* hasarder, risquer; exposer à un risque

**hazardous** *adj* hasardeux -euse; périlleux -euse, risqué

¹**haze** *n* brume *f*, brouillard *m*; *fig* incertitude *f*

²**haze** *vt* brimer, railler; *naut* accabler de corvées

**hazel** *n bot* coudrier *m*, noisetier *m*; couleur *f* noisette; *adj* (couleur) noisette *invar*

**hazel-nut** *n* noisette *f*

**hazy** *adj* brumeux -euse; *fig* nébuleux -euse, vague

**H-bomb** *n* bombe *f* H

¹**he** *n* mâle *m*; *adj* mâle

²**he** *pron 3rd pers sing masc nom* il; lui; ~ **is** il est, c'est; ~ **who** celui qui

**head** *n* tête *f*; chef *m*, directeur -trice; (front) devant *m*; (top) haut *m*; *geog* cap *m*, promontoire *m*; (section, heading) partie *f*, chef *m*; (boil, pimple) tête *f*; (froth) mousse *f*, faux-col *m*; (steam) pression *f*; *fig* idée *f*, intelligence *f*, raison *f*; *coll* mal *m* de tête; (coin) ~ **s** face *f*; ~ **and shoulders above** loin au-dessus; ~ **of water** hauteur *f* de chute; ~ **over heels** cul pardessus tête *m*; **above one's** ~ trop difficile à comprendre; **be off one's** ~ être cinglé; **bring matters to a** ~ amener une crise; **come to a** ~ aboutir à une crise; (boil, pimple) mûrir; **give s/o his** ~ donner carte blanche à qn; **keep one's** ~ rester calme; **keep one's** ~ **above water** surnager, se maintenir; **lose one's** ~ perdre la tête, s'affoler; **not make** ~ **or tail of it** n'y comprendre rien; **put** ~ **s**

**together** conférer; **talk s/o's ~ off** casser la tête à qn; **turn s/o's ~** tourner la tête à qn; **under that ~** sous cette rubrique; *adj* principal; *vt* (direct) diriger, mener; (article, chapter) intituler, mettre en tête de; (football) donner un coup de tête à; (lead) être à la tête de, venir en tête de; **~ off** détourner, faire dévier; *vi* **~ for** se -diriger vers, courir vers; *naut* mettre le cap sur; **~ for disaster** aller vers la ruine

**headache** *n* mal *m* de tête; *coll fig* casse-tête *m invar*

**headband** *n* bandeau *m*

**head-dress** *n* coiffure *f*

**headed** *adj* à tête; (paper) à en-tête

**header** *n* (dive) plongeon *m*; (football) coup *m* de tête; *bui* boutisse *f*

**head-first, head-foremost** *adv* la tête la première, tête baissée; impétueusement, témérairement

**headgear** *n* coiffure *f*

**head-hunter** *n* chasseur *m* de têtes

**headiness** *n* excitation *f*, ivresse *f*

**heading** *n* (writing-paper) en-tête *m*; (title) intitulé *m*; (article) rubrique *f*

**headlamp** *n* phare *m*

**headland** *n* cap *m*, promontoire *m*

**headlight** *n* phare *m*; **drive with dipped ~ s** rouler en code

**headline** *n* en-tête *m*, titre *m*; *coll* **hit the ~ s** défrayer la chronique

**headlong** *adj* impétueux -euse, précipité, téméraire; à la tête la première, tête baissée; impétueusement

**headman** *n* chef *m*; contremaître *m*

**headmaster** *n* directeur *m*; (French lycée) proviseur *m*

**headmistress** *n* directrice *f*

**head-office** *n* siège central

**head-on** *adj* + *adv* de front

**headphone** *n* écouteur *m*; **~ s** casque *m*

**headpiece** *n* coiffure *f*, couvre-chef *m*; *coll* tête *f*, cervelle *f*

**headquarters** *npl* quartier général; *comm* siège social

**headrest** *n* appui-tête *m invar*

**headroom** *n* hauteur *f* libre, dégagement *m*

**headship** *n* poste *m* de chef (school); poste *m* de directeur (proviseur, directrice)

**headsman** *n* bourreau *m*

**headstone** *n* pierre tombale; *archi* pierre *f* angulaire

**headstrong** *adj* entêté, têtu; impétueux -euse

**headway** *n* progrès *m*; *archi* hauteur *f* libre, dégagement *m*

**headwind** *n* *naut* vent *m* debout, vent *m* contraire

**headword** *n* mot *m* souche

**heady** *adj* capiteux -euse, enivrant, excitant; impétueux -euse

**heal** *vt* (person) guérir; (wound) cicatriser; *fig* réparer; apaiser; *vi* (person) se guérir; (wound) se cicatriser; *fig* s'apaiser

**healer** *n* guérisseur *m*

**healing** *n* guérison *f*; (wound) cicatrisation *f*; *fig* apaisement *m*; *adj* curatif -ive; apaisant

**health** *n* santé *f*; hygiène *f*; toast *m*; **~ insurance** assurance *f* maladie; **~ resort** station *f* climatique; **drink s/o's ~** boire à la santé de qn, porter un toast à qn

**healthiness** *n* salubrité *f*

**healthy** *adj* sain; (climate, etc) salubre; (beneficial) salutaire; (prosperous) florissant; (appetite) robuste

**heap** *n* tas *m*, amas *m*, amoncellement *m*; **~ s** beaucoup; *coll* **struck all of a ~** bouleversé, étonné; *vt* amonceler, entasser; (bestow) combler

**heaps** *adv coll* beaucoup

**hear** *vt* entendre; (listen to) écouter; (learn) apprendre, entendre dire; (concert, lecture, etc) assister à; **~ out** entendre jusqu'au bout; *vi* entendre; **~ about** avoir connaissance de, entendre parler de; **~ from** recevoir des nouvelles de, recevoir une lettre de; **~ of** entendre parler de; **he will not ~ of it** il ne veut rien savoir

**hear! hear!** *interj* bravo!, d'accord!

**hearer** *n* auditeur -trice

**hearing** *n* ouïe *f*; (action) audition *f*; *leg* audience *f*; **in my ~** en ma présence; **within ~** à portée de voix

**hearing-aid** *n* prothèse auditive, appareil *m* acoustique

**hearken, harken** *vi* écouter attentivement

**hearsay** *n* ouï-dire *m invar*; *adj* par ouï-dire

**hearse** *n* corbillard *m*

**heart** *n* cœur *m*; affection *f*, émotion *f*, sentiment *m*; humanité *f*; courage *m*, énergie *f*; (soul) âme *f*, for intérieur; centre *m*, noyau *m*; (artichoke) cœur *m*, fond *m*; **~ and soul** corps et âme; **~ to ~ intime; after my own ~** selon mon cœur; **at ~** au fond du cœur; **break s/o's ~** briser le cœur à qn; **by ~** par cœur; **eat one's ~ out** se ronger; **have at ~** attacher grande importance à; **have one's ~ in one's mouth** être plein d'appréhension; **have one's ~ in the right place** avoir le cœur bien placé; **have the ~ to** être assez dur pour; **in his ~ of ~ s** au plus profond de son cœur (de lui-même); **lose one's ~ to** tomber amoureux -euse de; **set one's ~ on** désirer fort, se résoudre à obtenir; **take ~** prendre courage; **to one's ~'s content** à cœur joie; **with all one's ~** de tout son cœur

**heartache** *n* chagrin persistant, peine *f* de cœur

**heartbeat** *n* battement *m* de cœur

**heartbreak** *n* déchirement *m* de cœur, déception amère

**heartbreaking** *adj* déchirant; *coll* épuisant

**heartbroken** *adj* le cœur brisé, navré

**heartburn** *n med* pyrosis *m*, brulûres *fpl* d'estomac

**heartburning** *n* envie dissimulée; amertume *f*

**hearten** *vt* encourager

**heartening** *adj* encourageant

**heartfelt** *adj* sincère

**hearth** *n* âtre *m*, foyer *m*; (home) foyer *m*

**hearthstone** *n* foyer *m*, dalle *f* de foyer

**heartiness** *n* cordialité *f*, empressement *m*; vigueur *f*

**heartless** *adj* sans cœur, cruel -elle, dur

**heartlessness** *n* manque *m* de cœur, cruauté *f*, dureté *f*

**heart-rending** *adj* touchant, qui fend le cœur

**heart-searching** *n* examen *m* de conscience

**heart-strings** *npl fig* sentiments profonds

**heart-throb** *n sl* béguin *m*

**hearty** *n sl* sportif -ive; *pej* béotien -icnne; *adj* cordial, empressé; vigoureux -euse; (appetite) gros (*f* grosse); (meal) copieux -ieuse; *pej* béotien -ienne

**heat** *n* chaleur *f*; (race) manche *f*; *fig* ardeur *f*, enthousiasme *m*; (temper) colère *f*, indignation *f*; (animal) rut *m*; ~ **stroke** coup *m* de chaleur; ~ **wave** vague *f* de chaleur; *sp* **dead** ~ deadheat *m*; **on** ~ en chaleur, en rut; *fig* **turn the** ~ **on s/o** exercer une pression sur qn; *vt* + *vi* chauffer

**heated** *adj* chaud, chauffé; *fig* animé, excité; (word) vif (*f* vive); **become** ~ *coll* s'échauffer

**heater** *n* appareil *m* de chauffage, radiateur *m*; **water** ~ chauffe-eau *m invar*

**heath** *n* lande *f*, bruyère *f*

**heathen** *n* païen -ïenne; *coll* agnostique; barbare; *adj* païen -ïenne; *coll* agnostique; barbare

**heathenish** *adj* païen -ïenne; *coll* barbare

**heathenism** *n* paganisme *m*

**heather** *n* bruyère *f*

**heating** *n* chauffage *m*; ~ **engineer** installateur *m* de chauffage; *adj* chauffant

**heave** *n* soulèvement *m*; *med* nausée *f*; *vt* soulever; (throw) jeter, lancer; (sigh) pousser; *naut* haler; *vi* se gonfler, se soulever; *med* avoir des nausées; *naut* ~ **to** se mettre en panne

**heaven** *n* ciel *m*, paradis *m*; *coll* félicité *f*;

**Heaven** Dieu *m*; ~ **s** ciel *m*; **for** ~ **'s sake!** pour l'amour de Dieu!; **move** ~ **and earth** remuer ciel et terre

**heavenly** *adj* céleste, du ciel; *coll* divin, épatant

**heavenward** *adj* + *adv* vers le ciel

**heaver** *n* déchargeur *m*

**heavily** *adv* lourdement; fortement; **rain** ~ pleuvoir dru

**heaviness** *n* lourdeur *f*, pesanteur *f*; *fig* appesantissement *m*, abattement *m*

**heavy** *adj* lourd, pesant; (eater, rain, cold, etc) gros (*f* grosse); (sea) houleux -euse; (sky) couvert; (weather) lourd, orageux -euse; (gunfire) violent; (drinker) grand; (soil) gras (*f* grasse); *fig* lourd, pénible, triste; (day) chargé; ~ **with young** grosse; *adv* lourd, lourdement

**heavy-handed** *adj* gauche, maladroit

**heavy-laden** *adj* chargé; opprimé

**heavyweight** *n* poids lourd

**Hebraic** *adj* hébraïque

**Hebraism** *n* judaïsme *m*; culture *f* hébraïque; (idiom) hébraïsme *m*

**Hebrew** *n* (person) Hébreu *m*, Juif -ive, Israélite; (language) hébreu *m*; *adj* hébreu (*m* only), juif -ive

**hecatomb** *n* hécatombe *f*

**heck** *interj* diable!

**heckle** *vt* interpeller; *vi* porter la contradiction

**heckler** *n* interpellateur -trice

**hectare** *n* hectare *m*

**hectic** *adj* fiévreux -euse, mouvementé

**hectogram** *n* hectogramme *m*

**hectolitre** *n* hectolitre *m*

**hectometre** *n* hectomètre *m*

**hector** *vt* rudoyer; *vi* faire l'autoritaire

**hedge** *n* haie *f*; *fig* protection *f*; *vt* entourer d'une haie; ~ **in** entourer, restreindre; *coll* ~ **one's bets** placer des paris secondaires comme assurance; prendre ses précautions; *vi* planter une haie; *coll* refuser de se déclarer, parler (agir) d'une manière équivoque

**hedgehog** *n* hérisson *m*

**hedge-hop** *vi coll aer* voler en rase-mottes

**hedgerow** *n* haie *f*

**hedonic** *adj* hédoniste

**hedonism** *n* hédonisme *m*, recherche *f* du plaisir

**hedonist** *n* hédoniste

**hedonistic** *adj* hédoniste

**heed** *n* attention *f*, soin *m*; prudence *f*; (obedience) obéissance *f*; **take** ~ faire attention; *vt* faire attention à, noter; *vi* faire attention, prendre garde

**heedful** *adj* circonspect, prudent; attentif -ive; obéissant

**heedfulness** *n* circonspection *f*,

prudence *f*; attention *f*; obéissance *f*

**heedless** *adj* étourdi, insouciant; inattentif -ive

**heedlessness** *n* étourderie *f*, insouciance *f*; inattention *f*

**hee-haw** *n* hi-han *m*; *vi* braire

¹**heel** *n* talon *m*; *coll US* canaille *f*, salaud *m*; **Achilles'** ~ talon *m* d'Achille; **at (upon) s/o's** ~**s** juste derrière qn; **come to** ~ (dog) venir à côté de son maître; *fig* se soumettre; **cool (kick) one's** ~**s** être obligé d'attendre, faire le pied de grue; **down at** ~ minable; **lay by the** ~**s** attraper, capturer; **out at** ~ minable; **show a clean pair of** ~**s** détaler; **take to one's** ~**s** prendre ses jambes à son cou; *vt* talonner

²**heel** *vi naut* gîter, donner de la bande; pencher

**heel-tap** *n* fond *m* de verre

**hefty** *adj coll* costaud; *fig* considérable

**heftiness** *n coll* force *f*

**hegemony** *n* hégémonie *f*

**heifer** *n* génisse *f*

**height** *n* hauteur *f*; altitude *f*; (person) taille *f*; *fig* apogée *m*, comble *m*

**heighten** *vt* rehausser, relever; (increase) augmenter; *vi* s'élever, se rehausser

**heinous** *adj* exécrable, odieux -ieuse

**heinousness** *n* énormité *f*

**heir** *n* héritier *m*; ~ **apparent** héritier assuré; ~ **presumptive** héritier présomptif

**heiress** *n* héritière *f*

**heirloom** *n* objet reçu en héritage; bijou *m* de famille

**helical** *adj* hélicoïdal

**helicopter** *n* hélicoptère *m*

**heliocentric** *adj* héliocentrique

**heliography** *n* héliographie *f*

**heliotrope** *n bot* héliotrope *m*

**heliport** *n* héliport *m*

**helium** *n chem* hélium *m*

**helix** *n* hélice *f*, spirale *f*; *anat+zool* hélix *m*

**hell** *n* enfer *m*; *coll* **a** ~ **of a** un sacré; *coll* **for the** ~ **of it** pour rire, pour s'amuser; *coll* **give** ~ **to** rudoyer, faire passer un mauvais quart d'heure à; **go** ~ **for leather** aller ventre à terre; *coll* **like** ~ beaucoup, énormément, *iron* pas du tout, mais non

**hellbent** *adj US* acharné

**hellcat** *n* harpie *f*

**hellebore** *n bot* ellébore *f*

**Hellene** *n* Hellène *m*; *adj* hellène

**Hellenic** *adj* (language) hellénique; (race) hellène

**Hellenism** *n* hellénisme *m*

**Hellenist** *n* helléniste *m*

**Hellenistic** *adj* hellénistique

**hellhound** *n* suppôt *m* d'enfer

**hellish** *adj* infernal; *coll* très désagréable; *adv coll* très désagréablement; extrêmement

**hellishly** *adv* infernalement

**hello** *interj + v* see **hallo**

¹**helm** *n naut* barre *f*, gouvernail *m*; *fig* contrôle *m*

²**helm** *n hist* heaume *m*

**helmet** *n* casque *m*

**helmeted** *adj* casqué

**helmsman** *n* timonier *m*, homme *m* de barre

**helot** *n* ilote *m*

**help** *n* aide *f*, assistance *f*, secours *m*; remède *m*; (person) aide; (household) femme *f* de ménage; *vt* aider, assister, secourir, venir en aide à; (ease) faciliter; (at table) servir; (avoid, prevent) éviter, empêcher; ~ **out** aider, *coll* dépanner; **I can't** ~ **it** je n'y peux rien; *vi* aider

**helper** *n* aide, assistant -e, auxiliaire

**helpful** *adj* secourable, serviable; salutaire, utile

**helpfulness** *n* serviabilité *f*

**helping** *n* portion *f*; *adj* secourable; **lend a** ~ **hand** donner un coup de main

**helpless** *adj* impuissant, incapable; incompétent; sans protection

**helplessness** *n* impuissance *f*, incapacité *f*; manque *m* de protection

**helpmate, helpmeet** *n* collaborateur -trice; (wife) moitié *f*

**helter-skelter** *adj* débridé, désordonné; *adv* pêle-mêle, à la débandade

¹**hem** *n* bord *m*, ourlet *m*; *vt* border, ourler; ~ **in** encercler, entourer

²**hem, hum, h'm** *interj* hem!, hum!; *vi* faire hem, faire hum

**he-man** *n coll* costaud *m*

**hemicycle** *n* hémicycle *m*

**hemiplegia** *n med* hémiplégie *f*

**hemisphere** *n* hémisphère *m*

**hemistich** *n* hémistiche *m*

**hem-line** *n* hauteur *f* (du sol) d'une jupe

**hemlock** *n bot* ciguë *f*

**hemorrhage** *n see* **haemorrhage**

**hemorrhoid** *n see* **haemorrhoid**

**hemp** *n* (plant, fibre) chanvre *m*; (drug) ha(s)chich *m*, *coll* kif *m*

**hempen** *adj* de chanvre

**hemstitch** *n* ourlet *m* à jour; *vt* ourler à jour

**hen** *n* poule *f*; (birds in general) femelle *f*; *coll* mijaurée *f*

**hence** *adv* (therefore) donc, ainsi, d'où; (place) d'ici; (time) dorénavant; *interj ar* allez!, partez!

**henceforth, henceforward** *adv* désormais, dorénavant

**henchman** *n* suivant *m*; partisan *m* fidèle

hen-coop, hen-house n poulailler m

henna n henné m

hen-party n réunion f de femmes

henpeck vt (wife) dominer

hep adj sl qui aime le swing; à la page

hepatic adj hépatique; jaune, olivâtre

hepatitis n med hépatite f

hep-cat n sl fanatique du swing; joueur -euse de swing

heptagon n heptagone m

heptagonal adj heptagonal

her poss adj son (f sa, mpl + fpl ses); pron elle; la; lui; celle; give ~ the book donnez-lui le livre; I see ~ je la vois; I thought of ~ j'ai pensé à elle; to ~ who came à celle qui est venue

herald n héraut m; messager m; vt proclamer; annoncer

heraldic adj héraldique

heraldry n blason m, science f héraldique

herb n herbe f; ~s cul fines herbes; med herbes médicinales

herbaceous adj herbacé; ~ border parterre m de plantes herbacées

herbage n herbage m; leg (droit m de) pâturage m

herbal n traité m de botanique; adj d'herbes

herbalist n botaniste; med herboriste

herbarium n herbier m

herbivorous adj herbivore

Herculean adj herculéen -éenne

Hercules n Hercule m; fig hercule m

herd n troupeau m; (people) foule f; vt mettre en troupeau, rassembler en troupeau; vi s'attrouper, se rassembler

herdsman n bouvier m, pâtre m

here adv ici, en ce lieu; ~ and there ça et là; neither ~ nor there hors de propos; ~ goes! allons-y donc!; ~ I am! me voici!; ~'s to vive; ~ you are voici ce qu'il vous faut

hereabout(s) adv près d'ici, aux alentours

hereafter n au-delà m; vie future; adv plus tard; dans l'autre monde

hereby adv en ceci, par ceci, par ces moyens; leg par les présentes

hereditament n leg bien m transmissible, patrimoine m

hereditary adj héréditaire; ~ factor gène m

heredity n hérédité f

herein adv en ceci, sur ce point; dans ce bien, ici; (enclosed) ci-inclus

hereof adv de ceci

heresy n hérésie f

heretic n hérétique

heretical adj hérétique

hereunder adv ci-après, ci-dessous

hereupon adv sur ce point; (then) sur ce;

(above) ci-dessus

herewith adv avec ceci, ci-joint

heritage n héritage m

hermaphrodite n hermaphrodite m; adj hermaphrodite

hermetic adj hermétique

hermit n ermite m, solitaire m; ~ crab bernard-l'(h)ermite m invar

hermitage n ermitage m

hernia n med hernie f

hernial adj med herniaire

hero n héros m; ~ worship culte m des héros

heroic adj héroïque; (style) grandiloquent; ~ age temps mpl héroïques; ~ couplet deux décasyllabes rimés; ~ verse vers mpl héroïques, vers mpl épiques; mock ~ héroï-comique, burlesque

heroical adj héroïque

heroics npl emphase f, grandiloquence f

heroin n héroïne f

heroine n héroïne f

heroism n héroïsme m

heron n héron m

herring n hareng m; red ~ argument m hors de propos servant à détourner l'attention

herring-bone n arête f de hareng; adj (stitch) au point de chausson; archi en épi

hers pron le sien (f la sienne), à elle

herself refl pron se; emph elle-même; by ~ toute seule

Hertzian adj hertzien -ienne

hesitance, hesitancy n hésitation f, incertitude f, indécision f

hesitant adj hésitant, indécis

hesitate vi hésiter; balancer, osciller

hesitation n hésitation f, indécision f

hessian n toile f d'emballage, toile f de jute

heterodox adj hétérodoxe

heterodoxy n hétérodoxie f

heterogeneity n hétérogénéité f

heterogeneous adj hétérogène

heterosexual adj hétérosexuel -elle

heterosexuality n hétérosexualité f

het-up adj coll excité, énervé; tourmenté

hew vt tailler, tailladier; (stone) équarrir

hewer n tailleur m

hewn adj taillé

hexagon n hexagone m

hexagonal adj hexagonal

hexameter n hexamètre m

hexametric(al) adj hexamètre

hey interj hé!, ohé!

heyday n apogée m, comble m; (youth) fleur f

hi interj hé!, ohé!

hiatus n hiatus m; lacune f, solution f de continuité

**hibernal** *adj* hivernal

**hibernate** *vi* hiverner, hiberner; *fig* somnoler

**hibernation** *n* hibernation *f*; *fig* somnolence *f*

**hibiscus** *n* hibiscus *m*

**hiccup, hiccough** *n* hoquet *m*; *vt* dire en hoquetant; *vi* avoir le hoquet, hoqueter

**hick** *n* US *sl* péquenot *m*

**hickory** *n* hickory *m*

**hidalgo** *n* hidalgo *m*

¹**hide** *n* cuir *m*, peau *f*; *coll* **have a thick ~** être insensible; **tan the ~ off s/o** rosser qn; *vt* écorcher; *coll* rosser

²**hide** *n* cachette *f*; *mil* observatoire caché; *vt* cacher, tenir secret -ète; *vi* se cacher

**hide-and-seek** *n* cache-cache *m invar*

**hidebound** *adj* conservateur -trice, réactionnaire; (limited) borné

**hideous** *adj* hideux -euse, horrible; (crime) abominable, atroce

**hideousness** *n* hideur *f*; (crime) atrocité *f*

**hideout** *n* cachette *f*, *sl* planque *f*

¹**hiding** *n* action *f* de cacher; **~ place** cachette *f*; **in ~** caché

²**hiding** *n* volée *f* de coups

**hierarchal, hierarchic, hierarchical** *adj* hiérarchique

**hierarchy** *n* hiérarchie *f*

**hieroglyphic** *adj* hiéroglyphique

**hieroglyphics** *npl* écriture *f* hiéroglyphique

**hi-fi** *n* hi-fi *f*, haute fidélité

**higgledy-piggledy** *adj* + *adv* en désordre

**high** *adj* haut, grand, de haute taille; élevé; (rank) élevé, puissant, supérieur; (main) principal; excellent; (voice, note) aigu -guë; (meat) faisandé; *coll* (drunk) saoul, parti; (drugged) exalté; (life) luxueux -euse, mondain; (words) violent; **~ altar** maître-autel *m* (*pl* maîtres-autels); **~ and dry** *naut* échoué; *fig* abandonné; (safe) en sûreté; **~ and low** partout; **~ colour** teint fleuri; **~ court** haute cour; **~ explosive** explosif puissant; **~ living** grand train de vie, luxe *m*; **~ noon** midi exactement; **~ priest** grand prêtre; **~ school** école *f* d'enseignement secondaire; **~ seas** haute mer; **~ street** rue principale, grand-rue *f*; **~ tea** repas substantiel servi vers six heures du soir; **~ tide** marée haute; **be ~ and mighty** se donner de grands airs; **get on one's ~ horse** monter sur ses grands chevaux, prendre qch de haut; **it is ~ time** c'est le moment, ce n'est pas trop tôt; **the Most High** le Très-Haut; *adv* haut, en haut; de haut

**highball** *n* US *coll* whisky *m* soda, fine *f*

à l'eau de Seltz

**highborn** *adj* de haute naissance

**highbrow** *n* *coll* *pej* intellectuel -uelle; *adj* *coll* intellectuel -uelle

**high-class** *adj* chic *invar*; de classe; de haute qualité

**highday** *n* jour *m* de fête

**high-fidelity** *adj* haute fidélité

**high-flier** *n* ambitieux -ieuse

**highflown** *adj* prétentieux -ieuse

**high-frequency** *adj* *elect* à haute fréquence

**high-grade** *adj* de qualité supérieure; **~ petrol** super *m*

**high-handed** *adj* arbitraire, autoritaire

**high-hat** *n* + *adj* US *coll* snob

**high-jump** *n* saut *m* en hauteur; *coll* **he's for the ~** ça va aller très mal pour lui

**highland(s)** *n*(*pl*) pays *m* de montagne; hautes terres

**high-life** *n* vie *f* du monde, vie mondaine

**highlight** *n* (painting, etc) rehaut *m*; *fig* trait marquant; *vt* rehausser, éclairer

**highly** *adv* fort, hautement, extrêmement

**highly-strung** *adj* nerveux -euse, surexcitable

**high-mettled** *adj* courageux -euse

**high-minded** *adj* noble, d'âme noble, d'esprit noble

**high-mindedness** *n* noblesse *f* d'âme

**highness** *n* élévation *f*, hauteur *f*; (title) altesse *f*

**high-pitched** *adj* (voice) aigu -uë; *archi* pointu; *fig* noble

**high-powered** *adj* puissant; efficace

**high-pressure** *adj* à haute pression; *fig* dynamique, énergique

**high-principled** *adj* honorable

**high-rise** *adj* **~ building** tour *f* d'habitation

**highroad** *n* route principale

**high-sounding** *adj* grandiloquent; *coll* ronflant; *pej* ampoulé

**high-spirited** *adj* intrépide; animé, gai; (horse) fougueux -euse

**high-up** *n* *coll* personnage important, grosse légume

**high-water** *n* marée haute; **~ mark** limite atteinte par la marée haute; *fig* apogée *m*

**highway** *n* voie publique; grande route

**highwayman** *n* voleur *m* de grand chemin

**hijack** *vt* (plane) détourner; US *coll* (person) détrousser; *orig* voler des spiritueux de contrebande

**hijacker** *n* pirate *m* de l'air; US *coll* détrousseur *m*

**hijacking** *n* piraterie *f* de l'air; *US coll* vol *m*

**hike** *n* randonnée *f* à pied; *vt* traîner; *vi* faire une randonnée à pied

**hiker** *n* excursionniste à pied

**hiking** *n* marche *f*

**hilarious** *adj* hilare, très gai

**hilarity** *n* hilarité *f*

**hill** *n* colline *f*, coteau *m*; (slope) côte *f*, descente *f*, montée *f*; *mil* côte *f*; **old as the** ~**s** vieux (*f* vieille) comme le monde

**hillbilly** *n* + *adj US coll* montagnard -e

**hillock** *n* mamelon *m*

**hillside** *n* flanc *m* de coteau

**hilly** *adj* accidenté, vallonné

**hilt** *n* garde *f*, poignée *f*; **up to the** ~ jusqu'à la garde; *fig* complètement

**him** *pron* le; lui; celui; **I see** ~ je le vois; **I thought of** ~ j'ai pensé à lui; **show** ~ **the book** montrez-lui le livre; **to** ~ **who came** à celui qui est venu

**himself** *refl pron* se; *emph* lui-même; **by** ~ tout seul

¹**hind** *n zool* biche *f*

²**hind** *adj* postérieur, de derrière

**hinder** *vt* entraver, gêner, retarder, retenir

**hindmost** *n* dernier -ière; *adj* dernier -ière, ultime

**hindquarters** *npl* arrière-train *m*; fesses *fpl*

**hindrance** *n* empêchement *m*, entrave *f*, obstacle *m*

**hindsight** *n* sagesse rétrospective; (rifle, gun) hausse *f*

**Hindu** *n* Hindou -e; *adj* hindou

**Hinduism** *n* hindouisme *m*

**Hindustani** *n* (language) hindi *m*; Hindou -e; *adj* hindou

**hinge** *n* charnière *f*, gond *m*; *fig* plaque tournante; *vt* (door) mettre dans ses gonds; *vi* pivoter; *fig* ~ **on** dépendre de, être axé sur

**hint** *n* allusion *f*, insinuation *f*; (advice) conseil *m*; *fig* nuance *f*, soupçon *m*; *vt* insinuer, laisser entendre, suggérer; *vi* ~ **at** faire allusion à

**hinterland** *n* arrière-pays *m*

¹**hip** *n* hanche *f*; *bui* arête *f*; ~ **and thigh** sans merci; *coll* **on the** ~ acculé, en mauvaise posture

²**hip** *n bot* gratte-cul *m invar*

**hip-bath** *n* bain *m* de siège

**hip-bone** *n anat* os coxal; (os *m* de) la hanche

**hipped** *adj coll* démoralisé, emmerdé

**hippo** *n coll* hippopotame *m*

**hippocampus** *n zool* hippocampe *m*

**hippopotamus** *n* hippopotame *m*

**hippy** *n* hippie

**hire** *n* location *f*; (payment) prix *m* de location; *US* embauchage *m*; *vt* louer; *US* embaucher

**hireling** *n* mercenaire

**hire-purchase** *n* achat *m* à crédit (à tempérament)

**hirsute** *adj* hirsute

**his** *poss adj* son (*f* sa, *mpl* + *fpl* ses); *poss pron* le sien (*f* la sienne); à lui

**Hispanic** *adj* hispanique

**hiss** *n* sifflement *m*; *theat* sifflet *m*; *vt* + *vi* siffler

**hissing** *n* sifflement *m*

**histamine** *n med* histamine *f*

**histological** *adj* histologique

**histology** *n* histologie *f*

**historian** *n* historien -ienne

**historic** *adj* célèbre, historique

**historical** *adj* historique

**historiographer** *n* historiographe *m*

**history** *n* histoire *f*; (story) récit *m*; (play) drame *m* historique; ~ **book** livre *m* d'histoire; **make** ~ entrer dans l'histoire, créer un précédent

**histrionic** *adj* théâtral

**histrionics** *npl* technique *f* du jeu théâtral; *pej* cabotinage *m*

**hit** *n* coup *m*; (fencing) touche *f*; (success) succès *m*, réussite *f*; **make a** ~ **with** impressionner, *coll* accrocher avec; *vt* battre, frapper; (knock against) heurter; (reach) atteindre, toucher; (hurt) blesser, toucher; ~ **and run driver** chauffard *m*; *coll* ~ **it** deviner correctement; *sl* foutre le camp; *coll* ~ **it off with** s'entendre bien avec; ~ **off** (likeness) attraper, saisir; (imitate) imiter; *vi* ~ **at** attaquer, condamner; ~ **back** riposter; ~ **out at** cogner sur, s'attaquer à; ~ **upon** (on) trouver par hasard, tomber sur

**hitch** *n* secousse *f*; (setback) accroc *m*, contretemps *m*, obstacle *m*; *naut* demi-clef *f*; *coll* trajet *m* en auto-stop; *vt* accrocher, attacher, fixer; *naut* amarrer; *vi* s'accrocher; *coll* faire de l'auto-stop; *coll* ~ **up with** épouser

**hitched** *adj coll* marié

**hitch-hike** *vi* faire de l'auto-stop, faire du stop

**hitch-hiker** *n* auto-stoppeur -euse

**hitch-hiking** *n* auto-stop *m*

**hither** *adv* ici; ~ **and thither** ça et là

**hitherto** *adv* jusqu'ici, jusqu'à présent

**hit-or-miss** *adj* fortuit, au hasard

**hitter** *n* personne *f* qui frappe

**hive** *n* ruche *f*; *vt* mettre dans une ruche, recevoir dans une ruche; ~ **off** séparer; *vi* entrer dans une ruche, être dans une ruche; ~ **off** se séparer

**hoar** *n* givre *m*, gelée blanche; *adj* givré

**hoard** *n* accumulation *f*, amas *m*; trésor *m*; *vt* accumuler, amasser, entasser; *vi*

528

économiser, thésauriser

**hoarder** *n* personne *f* qui amasse

¹**hoarding** *n* accumulation *f*, thésaurisation *f*

²**hoarding** *n* panneau *m* (d'affichage); clôture *f* en bois

**hoarfrost** *n* givre *m*, gelée blanche

**hoarse** *adj* enroué, rauque

**hoarseness** *n* enrouement *m*

**hoary** *adj* ayant les cheveux gris (blancs); grisonnant; *fig* vénérable

**hoax** *n* attrape *f*, canular *m*; *vt* duper, attraper, berner

**hoaxer** *n* personne *f* qui monte une attrape (un canular)

**hobble** *vt* (horse) entraver; *vi* boiter, clocher

**hobby** *n* hobby *m*, passe-temps *m*, violon *m* d'Ingres

**hobby-horse** *n* cheval *m* de bois; (toy) tête de cheval en bois montée sur un bâton; *fig* manie *f*, dada *m*

**hobgoblin** *n* lutin *m*

**hobnail** *n* caboche *f*

**hobnailed** *adj* ferré (de caboches)

**hobnob** *vi* frayer; boire ensemble; bavarder ensemble

**hobo** *n US coll* clochard *m*

¹**hock** *n* (animal) jarret *m*; *vt* couper le jarret à

²**hock** *n* vin blanc allemand, vin *m* du Rhin

³**hock** *n US sl* in ~ (pawn) au clou; (prison) en taule; *vt US sl* mettre au clou

**hockey** *n* hockey *m*

**hocus-pocus** *n* charabia *m*; mystification *f*, tour *m* de passe-passe

**hod** *n* hotte *f*; seau *m* à charbon

**hodge-podge** *n see* **hotchpotch**

**hoe** *n* binette *f*, houe *f*; *vt+vi* biner, houer

**hog** *n* cochon *m*, porc *m*, pourceau *m*; *coll fig* goinfre *m*; *coll* go the whole ~ y aller à fond; road ~ chauffard *m*; *vt* prendre pour soi-même, monopoliser; *vi* se goinfrer

**hogback, hogsback** *n* dos *m* d'âne

**hoggish** *adj* glouton -onne, goinfre; égoïste

**hogmanay** *n Scots* nuit *f* de la nouvelle année, Saint-Sylvestre *f*; réveillon *m*

**hogshead** *n* barrique *f*

**hogwash** *n* pâtée *f*; *coll* (gossip) cancan *m*, ragot *m*; *sl* vinasse *f*

**hoick** *vt* soulever abruptement; *vi* se soulever abruptement

**hoist** *n* action *f* de hisser; *naut* palan *m*; *mech* monte-charge *m invar*; *vt* hisser, remonter

**hoity-toity** *adj* arrogant, hautain

¹**hold** *n naut* cale *f*

²**hold** *n* prise *f*, étreinte *f*; contrôle *m*, autorité *f*; get ~ of obtenir; have a ~ on avoir prise sur; avoir un moyen de faire du chantage à; *vt* tenir; (contain) contenir; (hold back) retenir; (support) soutenir; (seize) saisir; (preserve) conserver; (mass) célébrer; (funds) détenir; (post) occuper, remplir; (court) présider; (record) détenir; (attention) retenir; (deem) estimer, juger, considérer; ~ back retenir; ~ down tenir baissé, subjuguer; ~ in retenir; ~ it! ne bougez pas!; ~ off tenir éloigné; (postpone) retarder; ~ on maintenir, saisir; ~ one's own se défendre bien; ~ one's tongue ne rien dire; ~ out tendre; tenir, offrir; ~ over ajourner, différer; *coll* the baby payer les pots cassés; ~ the line! ne quittez pas!; *ar* ~ them up! haut les mains!; ~ up relever, soutenir; retenir; (delay) différer; (rob) dévaliser; (as example) citer; *fig* ~ water tenir debout; *vi* tenir, rester ferme, se maintenir; (last) demeurer, durer; (continue) persister; (believe) croire, être de l'avis de; ~ back rester en arrière, se retenir; ~ forth faire un discours, pérorer; ~ good être valable, être vrai; ~ hard! attendez!, doucement!; ~ off se tenir éloigné; *naut* tenir le large; ~ on se cramponner, se maintenir; (resist) tenir bon, tenir le coup; ~ on! attendez!, minute!; ~ out tenir, résister; ~ out on cacher l'essentiel à; ~ to maintenir; ~ with approuver

**holdall** *n* sac *m* de voyage, fourre-tout *m invar*

**holder** *n* qui tient; qui contient; (office) titulaire; (record) détenteur -trice; (funds, stocks) détenteur -trice

**holding** *n* action *f* de tenir; possession *f*; (investments) portefeuille *m*, fonds *mpl*

**hold-up** *n* attaque *f* à main armée, hold-up *m invar*; (delay) entrave *f*, retard *m*

**hole** *n* trou *m*; (hollow) creux *m*; excavation *f*, fosse *f*; brèche *f*; orifice *m*; ouverture *f*; *bui* boulin *m*; (button) œillet *m*; (rabbit) terrier *m*; (argument) défaut *m*; (awkward situation) embarras *m*; *coll* trou perdu; *coll* make a ~ in entamer; pick ~ s in relever les points faibles; *vt* faire un trou dans, percer; (clothes) trouer; *vi* se trouer

**hole-and-corner** *adj* furtif -ive, fait en sous-main

**holiday** *n* jour *m* de congé, congé *m*; *eccles* fête *f*, jour *m* de fête; ~ s vacances *fpl*; Bank (public) ~ jour férié; ~ s with pay congés payés; *adj* de fête;

allègre; *vi* passer des vacances

**holiday-maker** *n* estivant -e; touriste

**holiness** *n* sainteté *f*; **His Holiness** Sa Sainteté

**Holland** *n* Hollande *f*

**holland** *n* (cloth) hollande *f*

**hollandaise** *n cul* sauce hollandaise

**holler** *vi* crier, hurler

**hollow** *n* creux *m*; vallon *m*; cavité *f*, cuvette *f*; *adj* creux (*f* creuse); (eye) cave; (voice) caverneux -euse; (sound) sourd; *fig* faux (*f* fausse), vain, vide; *adv coll* **to beat** ~ battre à plate(s) couture(s); *vt* creuser

**hollowness** *n* creux *m*; *fig* fausseté *f*, vide *m*

**holly** *n* houx *m*

**hollyhock** *n* rose trémière

**holocaust** *n* holocauste *m*

**holster** *n* étui *m* de revolver

**holy** *adj* (Alliance, City, Father, Land, person, Scriptures, Spirit, Trinity, Week) saint; (sacred) sacré; (water) bénit; **Holy Ghost** Saint Esprit; *coll* ~ **terror** enfant terrible; personne *f* redoutable; **Holy Writ** la Bible, les Saintes Écritures

**holy-day** *n eccles* fête *f*

**holystone** *n naut* brique *f*

**homage** *n* hommage *m*; **pay** ~ rendre hommage

**home** *n* demeure *f*, maison *f*; chez-soi *m invar*, foyer *m*, home *m*; intérieur *m*; famille *f*; pays natal; (institution) asile *m*, hospice *m*; (sailors, students, etc) foyer *m*; **at** ~ à la maison; *fig* à son aise; **be at** ~ recevoir (des visiteurs); **make oneself at** ~ faire comme chez soi; *coll* **nothing to write** ~ **about** peu intéressant; *adj* de famille, familial; domestique; fait à la maison; du pays, national; ~ **counties** environs *mpl* de Londres; **Home Office** = ministère *m* de l'Intérieur; *adv* à la maison, chez soi; au pays; (fully) à fond; **bring** ~ **to** faire comprendre pleinement à; **drive sth** ~ souligner qch; **go** ~ rentrer chez soi; *fig* (argument, idea) porter; **send** ~ renvoyer à la maison; rapatrier; *vi* revenir chez soi; (pigeon) revenir au colombier

**homecoming** *n* retour *m* au pays, retour *m* chez soi

**homeland** *n* pays natal

**homeless** *adj* sans abri, sans foyer

**homeliness** *n* manque *m* de façons, simplicité *f*; *US* manque *m* d'attraits

**homely** *adj* sans façons, simple; *US* sans attraits

**home-made** *adj* fait à la maison; (fait) maison *invar*

**Homeric** *adj* homérique

**homesick** *adj* nostalgique

**homesickness** *n* mal *m* du pays, nostalgie *f*

**homespun** *n* homespun *m*; *adj* filé à la main; *fig* sans façons, simple

**homestead** *n* manoir *m*

**homestretch** *n* dernière partie d'une course

**home-thrust** *n* botte enfoncée; *fig* (remark) flèche *f*

**homeward** *adj* de retour; *adv* vers la maison, vers la patrie; ~ **bound** sur le chemin du retour

**homework** *n* devoirs *mpl* (du soir)

**homey** *adj see* homy

**homicidal** *adj* homicide

**homicide** *n* homicide *m*

**homily** *n* homélie *f*

**homing** *adj* (pigeon) voyageur; (missile) à tête chercheuse

**hominy** *n US* bouillie *f* de farine de maïs

**homo** *n sl* homosexuel -elle, inverti -e, (male) pédé *m*, (female) lesbienne *f*; *adj sl* homosexuel -elle, inverti

**homoeopath** *n* homéopathe

**homoeopathic, homeopathic** *adj* homéopathique

**homoeopathy, homeopathy** *n* homéopathie *f*

**homogeneity** *n* homogénéité *f*

**homogeneous** *adj* homogène

**homogenize** *vt* homogénéiser

**homologous** *adj* homologue

**homologue** *n* homologue *m*

**homonym** *n* homonyme *m*

**homosexual** *n* homosexuel -elle; *adj* homosexuel -elle

**homosexuality** *n* homosexualité *f*

**homy, homey** *adj* familial, comme à la maison; intime

**hone** *n* pierre *f* à aiguiser, meule *f* à aiguiser; *vt* affiler, affûter, aiguiser

**honest** *adj* honnête, intègre, loyal, probe; franc (*f* franche), sincère; (woman) chaste; **make an** ~ **woman of** épouser

**honestly** *adv* honnêtement; *coll* franchement, vraiment

**honest-to-goodness** *adj coll* véritable

¹**honesty** *n* honnêteté *f*, intégrité *f*, probité *f*; franchise *f*, sincérité *f*, vertu *f*; (woman) chasteté *f*

²**honesty** *n bot* lunaire *f*, monnaie-du-pape *f* (*pl* monnaies-du-pape)

**honey** *n* miel *m*; *coll* chéri -e; *adj* de miel

**honey-bee** *n* abeille *f*

**honeycomb** *n* rayon *m* de miel; motif hexagonal; *vt* cribler, percer de trous

**honeydew** *n bot* miellée *f*; *poet* ambroisie *f*

**honeyed** *adj* couvert de miel; *fig*

mielleux -euse, doucereux -euse

**honeymoon** *n* lune *f* de miel; *vi* passer sa lune de miel

**honeysuckle** *n* chèvrefeuille *m*

**honk** *n* coup *m* de klaxon; *vi* klaxonner

**honky-tonk** *n US sl* bastringue *m*, boîte *f*

**honorarium** *n* (*pl* **honoraria**) honoraires *mpl*

**honorary** *adj* honoraire, honorifique, d'honneur

**honorific** *adj* honorifique

**honour** *n* honneur *m*, estime *f*; gloire *f*, réputation *f*; distinction *f*, titre *m* honorifique; dignité *f*; privilège *m*; honnêteté *f*, pudeur *f*; **do the ~ s** faire les honneurs, faire les présentations; **maid of ~** demoiselle *f* d'honneur; **on one's ~** sur son honneur, engagé d'honneur; *vt* honorer, rendre honneur à; estimer, respecter, révérer; *comm* honorer, acquitter

**honourable** *adj* honorable, digne, estimable, respectable

**hooch** *n US sl* whisky *m*

**hood** *n* capuchon *m*; (monk) capuchon *m*, cagoule *f*; (university, etc) épitoge *f*; *US mot* capot *m*; *mot* capote *f*; *bui* (fireplace) hotte *f*, (cowl) capot *m*; *vt* couvrir d'un capuchon

**hoodlum** *n US sl* voyou *m*

**hoodoo** *n* porte-malheur *m invar*; (bad luck) malchance *f*; *coll* guigne *f*, guignon *m*; *vt* porter malchance à; (curse) maudire

**hoodwink** *vt fig* berner, duper

**hoof** *n* (*pl* **hooves**) *zool* sabot *m*; *joc* pied *m*; (cattle) **on the ~** vivant; *vt sl* **~ it** marcher, danser; **~ out** chasser, vider

**hoo-ha** *n coll* bruit *m*; dispute *f*; (fuss) histoires *fpl*

**hook** *n* crochet *m*; croc *m*, grappin *m*; (meat) pendoir *m*; (fishing) hameçon *m*; (boxing) crochet *m*; (clothes) agrafe *f*; **~ , line and sinker** absolument tout; **by ~ or by crook** par n'importe quel moyen; *coll* **let s/o off the ~** épargner qn; *vt* accrocher, agrafer; (fish) prendre; (boxing) donner un crochet à; (rugby football) talonner; *fig* agripper, happer, saisir; *sl* **~ it** déguerpir; *coll* **get ~ ed** se marier; être drogué; *sl* **get ~ ed on** prendre goût à; *vi* s'accrocher; **~ on** to se cramponner à

**hookah** *n* houka *m*, narguilé *m*

**¹hooker** *n* (rugby) talonneur *m*; *US sl* putain *f*

**²hooker** *n coll naut* navire *m*

**hookey** *n US coll* **play ~** faire l'école buissonnière

**hookup** *n rad* relais *m*

**hookworm** *n* ankylostome *m*

**hooligan** *n* voyou *m*, crapule *f*

**hooliganism** *n* conduite *f* de voyou

**¹hoop** *n* cerceau *m*, cercle *m*; (croquet) arceau *m*; *coll* **go through the ~** passer un mauvais quart d'heure

**²hoop, whoop** *n* quinte *f*; (shout) cri *m* rauque; *vi* avoir une quinte (de toux); (shout) pousser un cri rauque

**hooping-cough, whooping-cough** *n* coqueluche *f*

**hooray** *vi* pousser des hourras; *interj* hourra!

**hoot** *n* huée *f*; (bird) (h)ululement *m*; (siren) mugissement *m*; *mot* coup *m* de klaxon; (train) coup *m* de sifflet; *sl* qch de très drôle; *coll* **not care a ~ about** se ficher de; *vt* huer; *vi* huer; (bird) (h)ululer; (siren) mugir; *mot* klaxonner; (train) siffler

**hooter** *n* sirène *f*; *mot* klaxon *m*, avertisseur *m*

**Hoover** *n* aspirateur *m*

**hoover** *vt* passer l'aspirateur sur

**¹hop** *n* sautillement *m*, saut *m*; *coll* sauterie *f*; *aer* étape *f*; **on the ~** au dépourvu, à l'improviste; *vt* sauter; *coll* **~ it!** fiche le camp!; *vi* sautiller, sauter, sauter à cloche-pied; **~ across to** faire un saut à

**²hop** *n bot* houblon *m*; fleur *f* de houblon

**hope** *n* espérance *f*, espoir *m*; *coll* **what a ~ !** aucune chance!; *vi* espérer, avoir de l'espoir; **~ against ~** espérer contre toute attente

**hopeful** *n joc* **young ~** jeune espoir *m*, poulain *m*; *adj* optimiste, plein d'espoir; encourageant, prometteur -euse

**hopefulness** *n* espoir *m*, espérance *f*

**hopeless** *adj* désespérant, désespéré, navrant; *coll* incorrigible

**hopelessly** *adv* sans espoir, désespérément, irrémédiablement

**hopelessness** *n* désespoir *m*; vanité *f*

**hopper** *n* sauteur *m*; *med* trémie *f*; (railway) wagon *m* à fond ouvrant

**hop-picker** *n* cueilleur -euse de houblon

**hopscotch** *n* marelle *f*

**horde** *n* horde *f*; *coll* des tas *mpl*, des masses *fpl*

**horizon** *n* horizon *m*; *geol* **soil ~** horizon *m* du sol; *astron* **true ~** horizon *m* astronomique

**horizontal** *adj* horizontal

**hormone** *n* hormone *f*

**horn** *n* corne *f*; (deer) bois *m*; (shoehorn) chausse-pied *m*; *mot* avertisseur *m*, klaxon *m*; *cul* cornet *m* de pâtisserie; *mus* cor *m*; **~ of plenty** corne *f* d'abondance; **draw in one's ~s** faire des économies; *coll* **English ~** cor anglais; **on the ~s of a dilemma** enfermé dans un dilemme; **take the bull by the ~s**

prendre le taureau par les cornes; *adj* de corne; *vt* encorner; *coll* ~ **in on** s'immiscer dans, mettre son grain de sel dans

**hornbeam** *n bot* charme *m*

**hornblende** *n* hornblende *f*

**horned** *adj* cornu

**hornet** *n* frelon *m*; *coll* **stir up a** ~ **'s nest** tomber dans un guêpier

**hornpipe** *n* matelote *f*

**hornrimmed** *adj* à monture de corne

**horny** *adj* corné, cornu, en corne; (hands) calleux -euse; *US vulg* excité

**horoscope** *n* horoscope *m*

**horrible** *adj* horrible, abominable, affreux -euse, atroce, hideux -euse, monstrueux -ueuse

**horrid** *adj* horrible, horrifiant, répugnant, révoltant; *coll* désagréable

**horrific** *adj* horrible, terrifiant

**horrify** *vt* horrifier

**horror** *n* horreur *f*, épouvante *f*, peur *f*; abomination *f*, répugnance *f*; infamie *f*; ~ **comic** comique *m* d'épouvante; ~ **s** peur irrationnelle

**horror-stricken** *adj* frappé d'horreur, effrayé

**hors d'œuvre** *n* hors-d'œuvre *m invar*

**horse** *n* cheval *m*; (stallion) étalon *m*; (gymnasium) cheval *m* d'arçons; *mil* cavalerie *f*; séchoir *m* à lessive; chevalet *m*; ~ **of another colour** une toute autre question; **back the wrong** ~ faire un mauvais choix; **dark** ~ outsider *m*; **eat like a** ~ manger comme quatre; **flog a dead** ~ vouloir ranimer une vieille controverse; **hold your** ~ **s!** du calme!, rien ne presse!; **on one's high** ~ sur ses grands chevaux; (waves) **white** ~ **s** moutons *mpl*; *adj* de cheval; *mil* (guards, artillery) monté

**horseback** *n* dos *m* de cheval; **on** ~ à cheval

**horsebox** *n* wagon (camion) affecté au transport des chevaux

**horse-chestnut** *n* marron *m* d'Inde; (tree) marronier *m* d'Inde

**horse-cloth** *n* housse *f*, couverture *f* de cheval

**horse-coper** *n* maquignon *m*

**horsedrawn** *adj* hippomobile

**horseflesh** *n* viande *f* de cheval; *collect* chevaux *mpl*

**horsefly** *n* taon *m*

**horsehair** *n* crin *m* de cheval

**horse-laugh** *n coll* gros rire

**horseman** *n* cavalier *m*, écuyer *m*

**horsemanship** *n* équitation *f*

**horseplay** *n* tapage *m*, jeu turbulent

**horse-power** *n* puissance *f* en chevaux; *mot* cheval-vapeur *m* (*pl* chevaux-vapeur)

**horse-race** *n* course *f* de chevaux

**horse-racing** *n* courses *fpl* de chevaux

**horseradish** *n* raifort *m*

**horse-sense** *n* bon sens, finesse *f*

**horseshoe** *n* fer *m* à cheval

**horseshow** *n* concours *m* hippique

**horsetail** *n* queue *f* de cheval

**horsewhip** *n* cravache *f*; *vt* cravacher

**horsewoman** *n* amazone *f*, cavalière *f*

**horsy** *adj* passionné de chevaux; *joc* + *pej* ayant des traits chevalins

**hortative**, **hortatory** *adj* persuasif -ive, encourageant

**horticultural** *adj* horticole

**horticulturalist** *n* horticulteur *m*

**horticulture** *n* horticulture *f*

**hosanna** *n* hosanna *m*

¹**hose** *n* tuyau *m* d'arrosage; *vt* arroser

²**hose** *n ar* chausses *fpl*; (stockings) bas *m*

**hosepipe** *n* tuyau *m* d'arrosage

**hosier** *n* bonnetier -ière

**hosiery** *n* bonneterie *f*

**hospice** *n* asile *m*, hospice *m*

**hospitable** *adj* hospitalier -ière, accueillant

**hospitableness** *n* disposition hospitalière, générosité *f*

**hospital** *n* hôpital *m*; hospice *m*

**hospitality** *n* hospitalité *f*

**hospitalization** *n* hospitalisation *f*

**hospitalize** *vt* hospitaliser

¹**host** *n bibl* armée *f*; foule *f*

²**host** *n* hôte *m*; aubergiste *m*

³**host** *n eccles* hostie *f*

**hostage** *n* otage *m*

**hostel** *n* maison *f* d'étudiants, maison *f* du marin, maison *f* du soldat; **youth** ~ auberge *f* de (la) jeunesse

**hosteller** *n* touriste fréquentant les auberges de (la) jeunesse, *coll* ajiste

**hostelry** *n* auberge *f*

**hostess** *n* hôtesse *f*; **air** ~ hôtesse *f* de l'air

**hostile** *adj* hostile

**hostility** *n* hostilité *f*

**hot** *adj* chaud; *fig* ardent, impétueux -euse, passionné, violent; (sauce) piquant; (jazz) hot; *sl* (clever) calé, expert; *sl* sexy; ~ **air** balivernes *fpl*; ~ **dog** hot-dog *m*; ~ **favourite** grand favori; ~ **line** téléphone *m* rouge; ~ **news** dernières nouvelles, information sensationnelle; ~ **on the track of** serrant de près; *coll* ~ **stuff** formidable; (get near) **get** ~ brûler; *coll* **have got into** ~ **water** être dans le pétrin; *coll* **not so** ~ pas fameux -euse; *adv* chaleureusement, chaudement; vigoureusement; coléreusement; **blow** ~ **and cold** être indécis; *vt coll* ~ **up** chauffer, animer; (engine) surcomprimer; *vi coll* ~ **up** chauffer, s'échauffer, s'animer

**hotbed** n *hort* couche f; *fig* (intrigue, etc) foyer m

**hot-blooded** adj au sang chaud, passionné

**hotchpotch, hodge-podge** n *cul*+*fig* salmigondis m; *coll fig* méli-mélo m (*pl* mélis-mélos)

**hotel** n hôtel m

**hotelier** n hôtelier -ière

**hotfoot** adv hâtivement, précipitamment

**hot-head** n exalté -e, tête brûlée

**hot-headed** adj exalté, à tête brûlée

**hot-house** n serre chaude; adj cultivé en serre chaude; *fig* fragile

**hotly** adv chaleureusement, chaudement; vigoureusement; coléreusement

**hot-plate** n (cooker) plaque chauffante; (dishes) chauffe-plats m

**hotpot** n pot-au-feu m invar

**hound** n chien courant; ~s meute f; *fig* vaurien m; vt poursuivre, s'acharner sur

**hour** n heure f; **at the eleventh** ~ au dernier moment, in extremis; **in the small** ~s au petit matin; **keep good (late)** ~s se coucher tôt (tard); **office** ~s heures fpl de bureau; **the** ~ **has come** le moment est venu

**hour-glass** n sablier m

**hour-hand** n aiguille f des heures

**hourly** adj à chaque heure, de toutes les heures; qui dure une heure; *fig* fréquent, incessant; adv toutes les heures; fréquemment

**house** n maison f, demeure f, habitation f; hôtel m, pension f; famille f; (household) maisonnée f, ménage m; (parliament) chambre f; ~ **of ill-fame** maison close, bordel m; ~ **to** ~ **canvassing** porte-à-porte m; **bring the** ~ **down** provoquer rires et applaudissements; *theat* **full (good)** ~ salle f comble; **keep** ~ tenir le ménage; **keep open** ~ être très hospitalier -ière; **like a** ~ **on fire** très vite; fameusement; *coll* **on the** ~ aux frais de la princesse; **safe as** ~s tout à fait sûr; **set one's** ~ **in order** mettre de l'ordre dans ses affaires (dans sa vie); vt héberger, loger; vi loger, habiter, loger

**house-agent** n agent immobilier

**houseboat** n péniche f

**housebound** adj obligé de rester à la maison

**housebreaker** n cambrioleur m; démolisseur m

**housebreaking** n cambriolage m

**housecoat** n robe f d'intérieur

**house-dog** n chien m de garde

**houseful** n maisonnée f

**household** n maison f, maisonnée f; famille f; gens mpl de maison; adj domestique, de ménage, du ménage; *mil* **Household Troops** régiments mpl de la garde royale anglaise; ~ **word** mot très répandu; nom très connu

**householder** n chef m de famille; occupant -e

**housekeeper** n gouvernante f; (large household) intendante f

**housekeeping** n ménage m; (money) sous mpl du ménage, économie f domestique

**housemaid** n bonne f, domestique f; ~ **'s knee** épanchement m de synovie

**house-party** n invités réunis dans une maison de campagne

**house-physician** n interne

**houseproud** adj coll popote invar

**houseroom** n logement m, place f

**house-surgeon** n chirurgien m interne

**house-trained** adj (animal) propre

**house-warming** n pendaison f de crémaillère

**housewife** n maîtresse f de maison; ménagère f; (sewing) trousse f à couture

**housewifery** n soins mpl du ménage

**housework** n travaux ménagers

**housing** n logement m; ~ **estate** cité f; (council) groupe m de H.L.M.; ~ **shortage** crise f du logement

**hovel** n baraque f, bouge m, taudis m

**hover** vi planer, voltiger; *fig* s'attarder, tourner autour; hésiter

**hovercraft** n aéroglisseur m, hovercraft m

**how** n comment m, manière f; adv (manner) comment, de quelle façon; (extent) combien; comme; que; *coll* ~ **come?** comment ça se fait?; ~ **far is it to X?** combien de kilomètres y a-t-il d'ici à X?; ~ **he talks!** comme il parle!; ~ **long has he been here?** depuis combien de temps est-il ici?; ~ **long is the journey?** le voyage dure combien de temps?; ~ **long is the ship?** de quelle longueur est le navire?; ~ **many?** combien?; ~ **much?** combien?; ~ **often?** combien de fois?; ~ **old is he?** quel âge a-t-il?; ~ **pleased I am!** que je suis content!

**how-do-you-do, how-d'ye-do** n coll here's a fine ~! en voilà une histoire!

**however** adv de quelque façon (manière) que; quelque ... que, pour ... que, si ... que; *inter* comment?; ~ **good he is** quelque bon qu'il soit, si bon qu'il soit; *conj* cependant, néanmoins, pourtant, toutefois

**howitzer** n obusier m

**howl** n hurlement m; huées fpl; (laughter) éclat m de rire; vi hurler; ~ **down** huer

**howler** *n* hurleur *m*; *coll* bourde *f*, perle *f*

**howling** *n* hurlement *m*; *adj* hurlant; *coll* énorme, fantastique

**howsoever** *adv* + *conj see* **however**

**hoy** *interj* ohé!

**hoyden** *n* garçon manqué

**hub** *n* moyeu *m*; *fig* centre *m*, pivot *m*

**hubbub** *n* brouhaha *m*, tumulte *m*, vacarme *m*

**hubby** *n coll* époux *m*, mari *m*

**hub-cap** *n mot* enjoliveur *m*

**hubris** *n* arrogance *f*, insolence *f*

**huckleberry** *n US bot* myrtille *f*

**huckster** *n* colporteur *m*; *vi* marchander

**huddle** *n* foule *f*, tas *m*; **go into a** ~ discuter en petit comité; *vt* empiler, entasser; *vi* s'empiler, s'entasser

**¹hue** *n* teinte *f*

**²hue** *n* ~ **and cry** haro *m*; poursuite acharnée; protestation *f*

**huff** *n* bouderie *f*, irritation *f*; accès *m* de mauvaise humeur; **be in a** ~ bouder; *vt* brimer, malmener; insulter, offenser; (draughts) souffler; *vi* (breathing) souffler; bouder, se formaliser, s'offusquer; s'emporter

**huffiness, huffishness** *n* mauvaise humeur, irritation *f*

**huffish, huffy** *adj* de mauvaise humeur, irrité

**hug** *n* embrassement *m*, étreinte *f*; (wrestling) prise *f*; *vt* embrasser, étreindre, serrer dans ses bras; *fig* chérir; (ship) ~ **the coast** serrer la côte

**huge** *adj* énorme, immense, vaste

**hugeness** *n* immensité *f*

**Huguenot** *n* Huguenot -e; *adj* huguenot

**hulk** *n naut* ponton *m*; ~ **s** galères *fpl*; *coll* lourdaud *m*

**hulking** *adj* lourdaud; encombrant, énorme

**¹hull** *n naut* coque *f*

**²hull** *n bot* cosse *f*, gousse *f*; *vt* écosser

**hullabaloo** *n coll* tapage *m*, vacarme *m*

**hullo** *interj* + *vi see* **hallo**

**¹hum** *n* bourdonnement *m*; (music) fredonnement *m*; (engine) ronflement *m*; (aircraft) vrombissement *m*; *vt* (tune) fredonner; *vi* bourdonner; (engine) ronfler; (aircraft) vrombir; ~ **and haw** bafouiller, bredouiller; **make things** ~ activer les choses; *coll* **things are humming** ça gaze

**²hum** *vi sl* puer, schlinguer

**³hum** *interj see* **²hem**

**human** *n* être humain; *adj* humain

**humane** *adj* humain, bon (*f* bonne), gentil -ille; humaniste

**humaneness** *n* humanité *f*, bonté *f*

**humanism** *n* humanisme *m*

**humanist** *n* humaniste

**humanistic** *adj* humaniste

**humanitarian** *n* + *adj* humanitaire

**humanity** *n* humanité *f*; genre humain; bonté *f*; **humanities** études *fpl* classiques; études *fpl* littéraires

**humanization** *n* humanisation *f*

**humanize** *vt* + *vi* humaniser, civiliser

**humanly** *adv* humainement; avec humanité

**humble** *adj* humble, effacé, modeste, obscur; *vt* abaisser, humilier, rabaisser

**humble-bee** *n* bourdon *m*

**humble-pie** *n* **eat** ~ s'humilier, s'excuser humblement

**humbly** *adv* humblement

**humbug** *n* hypocrisie *f*, insincérité *f*; charlatanisme *m*; (person) blagueur *m*, charlatan *m*; *cul* bonbon *m* à la menthe; *vt* duper hypocritement; entortiller

**humdinger** *n US sl* **it's a real** ~ c'est sensationnel

**humdrum** *adj* monotone, ordinaire; ennuyeux -euse

**humectation** *n med* humectage *m*

**humeral** *adj anat* huméral

**humerus** *n anat* humérus *m*

**humid** *adj* humide

**humidification** *n* humidification *f*

**humidifier** *n* humidificateur *m*

**humidify** *vt* humidifier

**humiliate** *vt* abaisser, humilier, rabaisser

**humiliation** *n* humiliation *f*, mortification *f*; disgrâce *f*

**humility** *n* humilité *f*

**humming** *n* (insects) bourdonnement *m*; (tune) fredonnement *m*; (engine) ronflement *m*; (aircraft) vrombissement *m*; *adj* bourdonnant; fredonnant; ronflant; vrombissant

**humming-bird** *n* colibri *m*, oiseau-mouche *m* (*pl* oiseaux-mouches)

**hummock** *n* mamelon *m*, monticule *m*, tertre *m*

**humorist, humourist** *n* humoriste

**humoristic** *adj* comique, humoristique

**humorous** *adj* amusant, comique, divertissant; (person) humoriste; (account) humoristique

**humorousness** *n* comique *m*, humour *m*

**humour** *n* humour *m*, amusement *m*; disposition *f*, humeur *f*; *med ar* humeur *f*; **out of** ~ fâché, irrité; *vt* ménager, passer les caprices à, ne plus contrarier

**humourless** *adj* dépourvu de sens de l'humour

**hump** *n* bosse *f*; *geog* monticule *m*; *coll* mauvaise humeur; *vt* arrondir, voûter; *sl* charger sur son dos

**humpback** *n* bossu -e; *zool* baleine *f* à bosse

**humpbacked** *adj* bossu

**humph** *interj* hum!

**humpy** *adj* bosselé, bossu

**humus** *n* humus *m*

**Hun** *n hist* Hun *m*; *sl obs* Boche *m*

**hunch** *n* bosse *f*; (chunk) morceau *m*; *coll* intuition *f*, pressentiment *m*; *vt* arrondir, voûter

**hunchback** *n* bossu -e

**hunchbacked** *adj* bossu

**hundred** *n* centaine *f*; *hist* (England) canton *m*; ~ s grand nombre; *adj* cent

**hundredfold** *adv* au centuple

**hundredth** *n + adj* centième

**hundredweight** *n* mesure de poids anglaise (environ cinquante kilogrammes)

**Hungarian** *n* Hongrois -e; (language) hongrois *m*; *adj* hongrois

**Hungary** *n* Hongrie *f*

**hunger** *n* faim *f*; famine *f*; *fig* désir *m*; soif *f*; ~ **strike** grève *f* de la faim; *vi* avoir faim; ~ **after** désirer, avoir soif de

**hungry** *adj* ayant faim; affamé; (soil) infertile; *fig* avide

**hunk** *n* morceau *m*; (bread) quignon *m*

**hunt** *n* chasse *f*; *vt* chasser; (area) battre, courir; *fig* pourchasser, poursuivre; ~ **down** traquer; ~ **out** dénicher, déterrer; *vi* chasser; *mech* vibrer excessivement

**hunter** *n* chasseur *m*; cheval *m* de chasse

**hunting** *n* chasse *f*

**hunting-box** *n* pavillon *m* de chasse

**hunting-crop** *n* cravache *f*

**hunting-ground** *n* terrain *m* de chasse; *fig* terrain *m* riche; *fig* **happy** ~ terrain *m* propice, lieu *m* propice

**hunting-lodge** *n* pavillon *m* de chasse

**huntress** *n* chasseuse *f*, *lit* chasseresse *f*

**huntsman** *n* chasseur *m*; veneur *m*

**hurdle** *n* claie *f*; (athletics) haie *f*; *fig* obstacle *m*; *vt* entourer de claies; *vi* (athletics) faire une course de haies

**hurdler** *n* (athletics) coureur -euse de course de haies

**hurdy-gurdy** *n* orgue *m* de barbarie

**hurl** *vt* jeter violemment, lancer

**hurling** *n* lancement *m*

**hurly-burly** *n* brouhaha *m*; confusion *f*, tohu-bohu *m*

**hurrah, hurray** *n* hourra *m*; *interj* hourra!

**hurricane** *n* ouragan *m*

**hurricane-lamp** *n* lampe-tempête *f* (*pl* lampes-tempête)

**hurried** *adj* précipité, rapide

**hurry** *n* hâte *f*, empressement *m*, précipitation *f*; **in a** ~ empressé, impatient; **there's no** ~ rien ne presse; *vt* hâter,

précipiter, presser; *vi* se dépêcher, se presser; ~ **up** se hâter

**hurt** *n* mal *m*, blessure *f*; *fig leg* dommage *m*, tort *m*; *adj* blessé; *fig* affligé, attristé, navré; *vt* blesser, faire du mal à; *fig* affliger, attrister; *leg* faire du tort à; léser; *vi* faire mal, faire souffrir

**hurtful** *adj* nocif -ive; blessant, offensant

**hurtfulness** *n* nocivité *f*; ce qui cause du chagrin

**hurtle** *vi* s'élancer, se lancer, voler

¹**husband** *n* époux *m*, mari *m*

²**husband** *vt* économiser, ménager

**husbandry** *n* agriculture *f*; économie *f*; bonne gestion

**hush** *n* silence *m*, tranquillité *f*; *vt* faire taire, tranquilliser; ~ **up** étouffer; *vi* se taire; *interj* chut!

**hush-hush** *adj coll* secret -ète

**hush-money** *n* argent obtenu par chantage; prix *m* du silence

**husk** *n* (cereals) balle *f*; *vt* décortiquer

**huskiness** *n* enrouement *m*

¹**husky** *n* chien esquimau

²**husky** *adj* enroué, rauque; *US* costaud

**hussar** *n mil* hussard *m*

**hussy** *n pej* chipie *f*; garce *f*; *sl* salope *f*, traînée *f*

**hustings** *npl* estrade *f* en plein air pour réunions électorales

**hustle** *n* bousculade *f*; *vt* bousculer, forcer, pousser; faire avancer; *vi* se dépêcher, se hâter, se précipiter

**hustler** *n* personnage *m* dynamique; *sl* (male) prostitué *m*

**hut** *n* cabane *f*, hutte *f*; *mil* baraquement *m*

**hutch** *n* (rabbit) clapier *m*; wagonnet *m*; coffre *m*, huche *f*

**hutment** *n mil* baraquement *m*

**hyacinth** *n* jacinthe *f*; (stone) hyacinthe *f*

**hyaena** *n see* hyena

**hybrid** *n + adj* (person) métis -isse; hybride

**hydra** *n myth + zool* hydre *f*; *fig* monstre *m*

**hydrangea** *n* hortensia *m*

**hydrant** *n* bouche *f* d'incendie

**hydrate** *n chem* hydrate *m*; *vt* hydrater; *vi* s'hydrater

**hydration** *n* hydratation *f*

**hydraulic** *adj* hydraulique

**hydric** *adj chem* hydrogéné

**hydro** *n* établissement thermal

**hydrocarbon** *n chem* hydrocarbure *m*

**hydrocephalic** *adj* hydrocéphale

**hydrocephalus, hydrocephaly** *n med* hydrocéphalie *f*

**hydrochloric** *adj* chlorhydrique

**hydrodynamic** *adj* hydrodynamique

**hydrodynamics** *npl* hydrodynamique *f*

**hydro-electric** *adj* hydro-électrique

**hydro-electricity** *n* énergie *f* hydro-électrique

**hydrofoil** *n* hydrofoil *m*

**hydrogen** *n* hydrogène *m*; ~ **peroxide** eau oxygénée; **sulphuretted** ~ sulfure *m* d'hydrogène

**hydrogenation** *n* hydrogénation *f*

**hydrogen-bomb** *n* bombe *f* à hydrogène

**hydrogenize** *vt* hydrogéner

**hydrogenous** *adj* hydrogéné

**hydrographer** *n* hydrographe

**hydrographic** *adj* hydrographique

**hydrography** *n* hydrographie *f*

**hydrology** *n* hydrologie *f*

**hydrolysis** *n* hydrolyse *f*

**hydrometer** *n* hydromètre *m*

**hydrometry** *n* hydrométrie *f*

**hydropathic** *adj* hydrothérapique

**hydropathy** *n* hydrothérapie *f*

**hydrophobe** *n* hydrophobe

**hydrophobia** *n* hydrophobie *f*

**hydrophobic** *adj* hydrophobe

**hydropic** *adj* hydropique

**hydroplane** *n naut* bateau glisseur; *aer* hydravion *m*; (submarine) barre *f* de plongée

**hydrosphere** *n* hydrosphère *f*

**hydrostat** *n* indicateur *m* de niveau d'eau

**hydrostatic** *adj* hydrostatique

**hydrostatics** *n* hydrostatique *f*

**hydrous** *adj* aqueux -euse

**hydroxide** *n chem* hydroxyde *m*

**hyena, hyaena** *n zool* + *fig* hyène *f*

**hygiene** *n* hygiène *f*

**hygienic** *adj* hygiénique

**hygrometer** *n* hygromètre *m*

**hygroscope** *n* hygroscope *m*

**hygroscopic** *adj* hygroscopique

**hymen** *n* hymen *m*

**hymn** *n eccles* hymne *m* or *f*, cantique *m*; *lit* hymne *m*; *vt* célébrer, chanter, glorifier; *vi* chanter des hymnes

**hymnal** *n* recueil *m* d'hymnes

**hymn-book** *n* recueil *m* d'hymnes

**hype** *n coll* battage *m* publicitaire, publicité *f* tapageuse

**hyperbola** *n geom* hyperbole *f*

**hyperbole** *n rhet* hyperbole *f*

**hyperbolic, hyperbolical** *adj* hyperbolique

**hyperborean** *adj lit* hyperboréen -éenne

**hypercritical** *adj* hypercritique

**hyperphysical** *adj* surnaturel -elle

**hypersensitive** *adj* hypersensible

**hypersonic** *adj* hypersonique

**hypertension** *n med* hypertension *f*

**hyperthyroidism** *n med* hyperthyroïdie *f*

**hypertrophied** *adj* hypertrophié

**hypertrophy** *n* hypertrophie *f*

¹**hyphen** *n* trait *m* d'union

²**hyphen, hyphenate** *vt* mettre un trait d'union à

**hypnosis** *n* hypnose *f*; hypnotisme *m*

**hypnotic** *n* hypnotique *m*; sujet *m* hypnotique; *adj* hypnotique; *coll* fascinant

**hypnotism** *n* hypnotisme *m*; *fig* fascination *f*

**hypnotist** *n* hypnotiseur *m*

**hypnotize** *vt* hypnotiser; *fig* éblouir, fasciner

**hypo** *n chem* hyposulfite *m* de soude; *phot* fixateur *m*

**hypochondria** *n* hypocondrie *f*

**hypochondriac** *n* + *adj* hypocondriaque

**hypocrisy** *n* hypocrisie *f*

**hypocrite** *n* hypocrite

**hypocritical** *adj* hypocrite

**hypodermic** *n* piqûre *f* hypodermique; seringue *f* hypodermique; *adj* hypodermique

**hypodermis** *n* hypoderme *m*

**hypostasis** *n med* + *philos* + *theat* hypostase *f*

**hypotenuse** *n geom* hypoténuse *f*

**hypothesis** *n* hypothèse *f*

**hypothesize** *vt* supposer; *vi* émettre une hypothèse

**hypothetic, hypothetical** *adj* hypothétique

**hypothyroidism** *n med* hypothyroïdie *f*

**hypsometer** *n* hypsomètre *m*

**hyssop** *n bibl* hysope *f*

**hysterectomy** *n surg* hystérectomie *f*

**hysteria** *n* hystérie *f*

**hysteric, hysterical** *adj* hystérique

**hysterics** *npl* crise *f* hystérique

**hysterotomy** *n surg* hystérotomie *f*, césarienne *f*

# I

**I** *pron* je, (before vowel) j'; (stressed) moi; ~ **myself** think moi je pense; **you and** ~ vous et moi
**iambic** *n* iambe *m*; *adj* iambique
**Iberia** *n* Ibérie *f*
**Iberian** *n* Ibérien -ienne; (language) ibérien *m*; *adj* ibérien -ienne
**ibex** *n* ibex *m*, bouquetin *m*
**ibid(em)** *adv* ibid(em)
**ibis** *n* orni ibis *m*
**ice** *n* glace *f*; (ice-cream) glace *f*; **be on thin** ~ être sur la corde raide; **black** ~ verglas *m*; **break the** ~ briser la glace; *fig* commencer une démarche délicate; **cut no** ~ **with** laisser froid, ne faire aucun effet sur; **keep sth on** ~ mettre qch à la glacière; *fig* mettre qch en attente; *vt* (chill) rafraîchir; (cake) glacer; ~ **up** (windscreen, etc) givrer; *vi* ~ **over** (lake, river) geler; ~ **up** (windscreen, etc) givrer
**ice-age** *n* période *f* glaciaire
**ice-axe** *n* piolet *m*
**iceberg** *n* iceberg *m*
**icebound** *adj* (ship) pris dans les glaces; (port) fermé par les glaces
**icebox** *n* glacière *f*; *US* frigidaire *m*; **this room is like an** ~ on gèle dans cette pièce
**ice-breaker** *n* brise-glaces *m*
**ice-cap** *n* calotte *f* glaciaire
**ice-cream** *n* glace *f*
**ice-field** *n* champ *m* de glace
**ice-floe** *n* banquise *f*
**ice-house** *n* glacière *f*
**Iceland** *n* Islande *f*
**Icelander** *n* Islandais -e
**Icelandic** *n* (language) islandais *m*; *adj* islandais
**iceman** *n* *US* livreur *m* de glace, marchand *m* de glace
**ice-pack** *n* banquise *f*
**ice-rink** *n* patinoire *f*
**ice-skate** *n* patin *m* à glace; *vi* patiner sur glace
**ice-skating** *n* patinage *m* sur glace
**ichthyology** *n* ichtyologie *f*
**icicle** *n* glaçon *m*
**icily** *adv* (speech) d'un ton glacial; (manner) d'un air glacial
**iciness** *n* air glacial; (road, etc) verglas *m*
**icing** *n* (windscreen, aircraft) givre *m*; *cul* glaçage *m*; ~ **sugar** sucre *m* glace
**icon, ikon** *n* icône *f*
**iconoclasm** *n* iconoclasme *m*

**iconoclast** *n* iconoclaste
**iconoclastic** *adj* iconoclaste
**iconographer** *n* iconographe
**iconography** *n* iconographie *f*
**icy** *adj* glacial, glacé
**id** *n* *psych* ça *m*
**idea** *n* idée *f*; (vague) notion *f*; (thought) pensée *f*; (opinion) opinion *f*, avis *m*; plan *m*; **I've got the general** ~ j'ai compris à peu près; **that's the** ~! c'est ça!; **the** ~ **is to** il s'agit de; **the very** ~! quelle idée!; *coll* **what's the big** ~? qu'est-ce que c'est que cette histoire?
**ideal** *n* idéal *m*; *adj* idéal, parfait
**idealism** *n* idéalisme *m*
**idealist** *n* + *adj* idéaliste
**idealize** *vt* idéaliser
**ideally** *adv* idéalement, d'une manière idéale
**idem** *adv* idem
**identical** *adj* identique; ~ **twins** vrais jumeaux, vraies jumelles
**identifiable** *adj* identifiable
**identification** *n* identification *f*
**identify** *vt* identifier, établir l'identité de; *vi* ~ **oneself with** s'identifier avec
**identikit** *adj* ~ **portrait** portrait-robot *m* (*pl* portraits-robots)
**identity** *n* identité *f*; ~ **card** carte *f* d'identité
**ideogram, ideograph** *n* idéogramme *m*
**ideological** *adj* idéologique
**ideologist** *n* idéologue
**ideology** *n* idéologie *f*
**ides** *n* Rom hist ides *fpl*
**idiocy** *n* idiotie *f*, stupidité *f*, imbécillité *f*
**idiom** *n* (phrase) idiotisme *m*; (mode of language) idiome *m*
**idiomatic** *adj* idiomatique; (colloquial) de la langue populaire; ~ **expression** idiotisme *m*
**idiosyncrasy** *n* caractéristique *f*, particularité *f*, excentricité *f*
**idiosyncratic** *adj* caractéristique, particulier -ière
**idiot** *n* imbécile, crétin -e
**idiotic** *adj* imbécile, crétin, bête, stupide
**idle** *adj* paresseux -euse, fainéant, oisif -ive; (unemployed) en chômage; (unoccupied) désœuvré, sans occupation; (trivial) oiseux -euse, frivole, futile; *mech* ~ **wheel** roue folle; *vi mech* tourner au ralenti; ~ **(about)** fainéanter, paresser; ~ **away one's time**

gaspiller son temps

**idleness** n paresse f, oisiveté f, désœuvrement m

**idler** n fainéant -e, oisif -ive, paresseux -euse; *mech* (wheel) roue folle

**idly** adv paresseusement; (without thinking) négligemment

**idol** n idole f

**idolater** n idolâtre

**idolatrous** adj idolâtre

**idolatry** n idolâtrie f

**idolize** vt idolâtrer, adorer

**idyll** n idylle f

**idyllic** adj idyllique

**if** n ~s and buts les si mpl et les mais mpl; conj si; **as** ~ comme si

**igloo** n igloo m, iglou m

**igneous** adj igné

**ignitable** adj inflammable

**ignite** vt mettre le feu à, enflammer; vi prendre feu, s'enflammer

**ignition** n ignition f; mot allumage m

**ignoble** adj ignoble, infâme, vil

**ignominious** adj ignominieux -ieuse, honteux -euse

**ignominy** n ignominie f

**ignoramus** n ignorant -e, ignare

**ignorance** n ignorance f

**ignorant** adj ignorant

**ignore** vt (make no mention of) passer sous silence, ne pas relever; (person) faire semblant de ne pas reconnaître; (rule) ne pas respecter

**iguana** n iguane m

**ikon** n see icon

**ilex** n yeuse f; (genus) houx m

**ilk** adj Scots of that ~ de cet acabit

**ill** n mal m; adj (unwell) malade, souffrant; (evil) méchant, mauvais; ~ **luck** malchance f; **it's an** ~ **wind that blows nobody any good** à quelque chose malheur est bon; adv mal; ~ **at ease** mal à l'aise; **speak** ~ **of** dire du mal de

**ill-advised** adj malavisé, peu judicieux -ieuse

**ill-affected** adj mal disposé

**ill-bred** adj mal élevé; (birth) mal né

**ill-breeding** n manque m d'éducation, manque m de savoir-vivre

**ill-conditioned** adj mal conditionné

**illegal** adj illégal

**illegality** n illégalité f

**illegally** adv illégalement

**illegible** adj illisible

**illegitimacy** n illégitimité f

**illegitimate** adj illégitime; (wrongful) erroné, illogique

**ill-fated** adj malheureux -euse, infortuné; (occasion) néfaste, fatal

**ill-favoured** adj laid, déplaisant, répugnant

**ill-gotten** adj mal acquis

**ill-humoured** adj maussade, de mauvaise humeur

**illiberal** adj (petty) mesquin; intolérant; (miserly) ladre

**illicit** adj illicite

**illimitable** adj illimité, sans bornes

**illiteracy** n analphabétisme m

**illiterate** n analphabète, illettré -e; adj analphabète, illettré

**ill-judged** adj peu judicieux -ieuse, malavisé

**ill-mannered** adj impoli, mal élevé, grossier -ière

**ill-natured** adj désagréable, fruste, revêche

**illness** n maladie f; (ill-health) mauvaise santé

**illogical** adj illogique

**illogicality** n illogisme m

**ill-omened** adj de mauvais augure

**ill-starred** adj désastreux -euse, néfaste; (person) infortuné

**ill-tempered** adj grincheux -euse, de mauvaise humeur

**ill-timed** adj malencontreux -euse, inopportun, mal à propos

**ill-treat** vt malmener, maltraiter, brutaliser

**ill-treatment** n mauvais traitement

**illuminate** vt illuminer, éclairer; fig éclairer, faire la lumière sur; (manuscript) enluminer

**illuminating** adj révélateur -trice, éclairant

**illumination** n (lighting) éclairage m; (flood-lighting) illumination f; (manuscript) enluminure f; fig lumière f, inspiration f; ~s illuminations fpl

**illumine** vt éclairer, faire la lumière sur

**ill-usage** n mauvais traitement

**illusion** n illusion f; **be under an** ~ se faire des illusions

**illusionist** n illusionniste

**illusive** adj qui cause une illusion; (caused by illusion) illusoire; (deceptive) trompeur -euse

**illustrate** vt illustrer; fig illustrer, éclairer

**illustration** n illustration f; fig illustration f, exemple m

**illustrative** adj qui illustre, explicatif -ive

**illustrator** n illustrateur -trice

**illustrious** adj illustre, célèbre, glorieux -ieuse

**illustriousness** n gloire f, renommée f

**ill-will** n malveillance f, hostilité f

**image** n image f; (mirror, etc) réflexion f; (public impression of sth) image f de marque; coll **he is the spit** ~ **of his father** c'est son père tout craché; vt imager; refléter; imaginer

**imagery** n images fpl

**imaginable** adj imaginable

**imaginary** *adj* imaginaire, fictif -ive

**imagination** *n* imagination *f*

**imaginative** *adj* imaginatif -ive, plein d'imagination

**imaginativeness** *n* imagination *f*, esprit créateur

**imagine** *vt* (suppose) supposer, imaginer, croire; (to oneself) s'imaginer, se figurer

**imbalance** *n* déséquilibre *m*

**imbecile** *n* imbécile, idiot -e; *adj* imbécile, idiot, stupide

**imbecility** *n* imbécillité *f*, stupidité *f*

**imbibe** *vt* boire, absorber; *fig* assimiler; *vi coll* lever le coude, picoler

**imbricate** *vt* imbriquer; *vi* s'imbriquer; *adj* imbriqué

**imbroglio** *n* imbroglio *m*

**imbue** *vt* imprégner; *fig* imprégner, inculquer

**imitable** *adj* imitable

**imitate** *vt* imiter

**imitation** *n* imitation *f*; (counterfeit) contrefaçon *f*

**imitative** *adj* imitatif -ive; peu original

**imitator** *n* imitateur -trice

**immaculate** *adj* (pure) immaculé; (clean) tout propre; (faultless) irréprochable, impeccable; *theol* immaculé; **the Immaculate Conception** l'Immaculée Conception

**immanence, immanency** *n* immanence *f*

**immanent** *adj* immanent

**immaterial** *adj* insignifiant, négligeable, sans importance; (spiritual) immatériel -ielle

**immateriality** *n* insignifiance *f*

**immature** *adj* (person) jeune, peu avancé; (fruit) vert, pas mûr; **be ~** manquer de maturité

**immaturity** *n* manque *m* de maturité, immaturité *f*

**immeasurability** *n* incommensurabilité *f*

**immeasurable** *adj* incommensurable; énorme, vaste

**immediacy** *n* caractère immédiat

**immediate** *adj* immédiat, direct, instantané

**immemorial** *adj* immémorial

**immense** *adj* immense, vaste, énorme; *sl* épatant

**immensely** *adv* immensément, extrêmement

**immensity** *n* immensité *f*

**immensurable** *adj* incommensurable

**immerse** *vt* immerger, plonger; (baptism) baptiser par immersion; *fig* **~ oneself in** se plonger dans, être absorbé dans

**immersion** *n* immersion *f*; (baptism) baptême *m* par immersion; **~ heater** chauffe-eau *m invar* à élément chauffant

**immigrant** *n* immigrant -e; *adj* immigré

**immigrate** *vi* immigrer

**immigration** *n* immigration *f*

**imminence** *n* imminence *f*

**imminent** *adj* imminent

**immobile** *adj* immobile

**immobility** *n* immobilité *f*

**immobilize** *vt* immobiliser

**immoderate** *adj* excessif -ive, immodéré

**immoderation** *n* immodération *f*, excès *m*

**immodest** *adj* immodeste, impudique; arrogant, présomptueux -euse

**immodesty** *n* immodestie *f*, impudeur *f*; arrogance *f*, présomption *f*

**immolate** *vt* immoler

**immolation** *n* immolation *f*

**immoral** *adj* immoral

**immorality** *n* immoralité *f*; acte immoral

**immortal** *n* immortel -elle; *adj* immortel -elle, impérissable

**immortality** *n* immortalité *f*

**immortalize** *vt* immortaliser

**immortelle** *n bot* immortelle *f*

**immovability** *n* (officials) inamovibilité *f*; (immutability) immuabilité *f*; fixité *f*

**immovable** *adj* fixe; (resolution) inébranlable, immuable, impossible à déplacer; *leg* immobilier -ière; **~ s** *npl* immeubles *mpl*

**immune** *adj* immunisé, à l'abri

**immunity** *n* immunité *f*

**immunization** *n* immunisation *f*

**immunize** *vt* immuniser

**immure** *vt* emmurer, enfermer; **~ oneself** s'isoler

**immutability** *n* immutabilité *f*, immuabilité *f*

**immutable** *adj* immuable, inaltérable

**imp** *n* lutin *m*, diablotin *m*; (child) petit espiègle

**impact** *n* impact *m*, choc *m*; *vt* enfoncer; **~ ed tooth** dent incluse

**impair** *vt* (senses) affaiblir, abîmer; (injure) détériorer, diminuer

**impale** *vt* empaler

**impalpable** *adj* impalpable

**impanel** *v see* empanel

**impart** *vt* communiquer, transmettre, faire connaître

**impartial** *adj* impartial, objectif -ive

**impartiality** *n* impartialité *f*

**impassable** *adj* infranchissable

**impasse** *n* impasse *f*

**impassibility** *n* impassibilité *f*

**impassible** *adj* impassible

**impassion** *vt* exalter

**impassioned** *adj* exalté, fervent, passionné

**impassive** *adj* impassible

**impassivity** *n* impassibilité *f*

**impatience** *n* impatience *f*; intolérance *f*

**impatient** *adj* impatient; intolérant

**impeach** *vt pol* + *leg* mettre en accusation, entamer la procédure de destitution contre; (discredit) mettre en doute; *leg* ~ **a witness** récuser un témoin

**impeachment** *n pol* + *leg* mise *f* en accusation; (character) dénigrement *m*

**impeccable** *adj* impeccable, irréprochable

**impecuniosity** impécuniosité *f*, indigence *f*

**impecunious** *adj* impécunieux -ieuse, nécessiteux -euse

**impede** *vt* empêcher, gêner, entraver

**impediment** *n* (speech) défaut *m* de prononciation, défaut *m* d'élocution; obstacle *m*, entrave *f*

**impedimenta** *npl* bagages *mpl*

**impel** *vt* pousser, faire avancer; *fig* obliger, forcer, pousser

**impend** *vi* être imminent; planer

**impending** *adj* imminent, prochain; menaçant

**impenetrability** *n* impénétrabilité *f*

**impenetrable** *adj* impénétrable

**impenitence** *n* impénitence *f*

**impenitent** *adj* impénitent

**imperative** *n* exigence *f*, impératif *m*; *gramm* impératif *m*; *adj* impératif -ive, urgent, pressant; autoritaire

**imperceptibility** *n* imperceptibilité *f*

**imperceptible** *adj* imperceptible, minuscule

**imperceptive** *adj* peu perspicace

**imperfect** *n gramm* imparfait *m*; *adj* imparfait, incomplet -ète, défectueux -euse; *gramm* imparfait

**imperfectibility** *n* imperfectibilité *f*

**imperfectible** *adj* imperfectible

**imperfection** *n* imperfection *f*, défectuosité *f*

**imperforate** *adj* non perforé

**imperial** *n* (beard) barbe *f* à l'impériale; *adj* impérial; grandiose

**imperialism** *n* impérialisme *m*

**imperialist** *n* impérialiste

**imperialistic** *adj* impérialiste

**imperil** *vt* mettre en péril

**imperious** *adj* impérieux -ieuse, autoritaire; (need) urgent, pressant

**imperishable** *adj* impérissable; immortel -elle

**impermanence** *n* caractère *m* éphémère

**impermanent** *adj* éphémère, transitoire

**impermeable** *adj* imperméable, étanche; *fig* impénétrable

**impersonal** *adj* impersonnel -elle

**impersonality** *n* impersonnalité *f*

**impersonate** *vt* imiter; se faire passer pour; *leg* usurper l'identité de

**impersonation** *n* imitation *f*; *leg* usurpation *f* d'identité

**impersonator** *n* imitateur -trice; *leg* usurpateur -trice d'identité; **female** ~ travesti *m*

**impertinence** *n* impertinence *f*, insolence *f*; (irrelevance) manque *m* de rapport

**impertinent** *adj* impertinent, insolent; (irrelevant) sans rapport, hors de propos

**imperturbability** *n* imperturbabilité *f*

**imperturbable** *adj* imperturbable

**impervious** *adj* imperméable, étanche; ~ **to** sourd à

**impetigo** *n* impétigo *m*

**impetuosity, impetuousness** *n* impétuosité *f*, imprudence *f*, fougue *f*

**impetuous** *adj* impétueux -ueuse, imprudent, fougueux -euse

**impetuousness** *n see* **impetuosity**

**impetus** *n* force *f* d'impulsion; (momentum) élan *m*, vitesse *f*; *fig* élan *m*, impulsion *f*

**impiety** *n* impiété *f*

**impinge** *vi* ~ **on** toucher, affecter; (encroach) empiéter sur; (strike) frapper

**impingement** *n* empiètement *m*

**impious** *adj* impie

**impish** *adj* espiègle

**impishness** *n* espièglerie *f*

**implacability** *n* implacabilité *f*

**implacable** *adj* implacable

**implant** *n med* implant *m*; *vt* implanter; *fig* inculquer, inspirer

**implantation** *n* implantation *f*

**implausibility** *n* invraisemblance *f*

**implausible** *adj* invraisemblable, peu plausible

**implement** *n* outil *m*, instrument *m*; ~ **s** matériel *m*; *vt* exécuter, accomplir; (complete) achever

**implementation** *n* exécution *f*, accomplissement *m*

**implicate** *vt* impliquer, compromettre

**implication** *n* implication *f*; insinuation *f*

**implicit** *adj* implicite, tacite; (absolute) absolu, aveugle

**implied** *adj* sous-entendu, tacite

**implode** *vt* causer l'implosion de; *vi* imploser

**implore** *vt* implorer, supplier

**imploring** *adj* implorant, suppliant

**implosion** *n* implosion *f*

**imply** *vt* impliquer, suggérer, laisser entendre, insinuer

**impolite** *adj* impoli

**impoliteness** *n* impolitesse *f*

**impolitic** *adj* impolitique, malavisé

**imponderability** *n* impondérabilité *f*

**imponderable** *n* impondérable *m*; *adj* impondérable

**import** n comm importation f; (meaning) sens m, signification f; importance f; ~ **duty** droit m d'entrée; comm ~ s articles mpl d'importation; vt comm importer; (meaning) signifier
**importable** adj importable
**importance** n importance f
**important** adj important
**importantly** adv d'un air important
**importation** n importation f
**importer** n importateur -trice
**importunate** adj importun; (insistent) harcelant
**importune** vt importuner; harceler; (prostitute) racoler; vi (prostitute) racoler
**importunity** n importunité f
**impose** vt imposer; (tax) imposer, taxer; (penalty) infliger; vi ~ **on (upon)** (mislead) tromper, duper; (take advantage of) abuser de
**imposing** adj imposant, impressionnant
**imposition** n imposition f, taxe f; (school) punition f
**impossibility** n impossibilité f
**impossible** n impossible m; adj impossible; (person) impossible, insupportable; coll invivable
**impost** n impôt m
**impostor** n imposteur m, charlatan m
**imposture** n imposture f
**impotence** n impuissance f, faiblesse f; (sexual) impuissance f; med impotence f
**impotent** adj impuissant, faible
**impound** vt saisir, confisquer; (confine) enfermer
**impoverish** vt appauvrir
**impoverishment** n appauvrissement m
**impracticability** n impraticabilité f
**impracticable** adj impraticable, impossible
**impractical** adj (person) peu pratique; (thing) pas pratique
**imprecation** n imprécation f, malédiction f
**imprecatory** adj imprécatoire
**impregnable** adj imprenable, inexpugnable; fig invincible
**impregnate** vt féconder; (saturate) imprégner
**impregnation** n fécondation f; imprégnation f
**impresario** n impresario m
**imprescriptible** adj leg imprescriptible
**impress** n empreinte f, marque f; vt (mark) imprimer, marquer; (make impression) impressionner, faire impression sur
**impression** n impression f; (mark) empreinte f, trace f; **be under the** ~ avoir une vague idée, avoir l'impression

**impressionability** n impressionnabilité f
**impressionable** adj impressionnable, sensible
**impressionism** n impressionnisme m
**impressionist** n + adj impressionniste
**impressionistic** adj impressionniste; subjectif -ive
**impressive** adj impressionnant, frappant, imposant
**impressiveness** n caractère impressionnant
**imprimatur** n imprimatur m
**imprint** n empreinte f, marque f; **under the** ~ **of** édité chez; vt imprimer, marquer
**imprison** vt emprisonner
**imprisonment** n emprisonnement m; **one month's** ~ un mois de prison
**improbability** n improbabilité f, invraisemblance f
**improbable** adj improbable, invraisemblable
**impromptu** n impromptu m; adj + adv impromptu
**improper** adj malséant, de mauvais goût; indécent, scabreux -euse; (dishonest) malhonnête
**impropriety** n inconvenance f
**improvable** adj susceptible d'amélioration
**improve** vt améliorer, perfectionner; (fortune, knowledge) augmenter, accroître; (land) bonifier; (landscape) embellir; (make good use of) tirer parti de, profiter de; vi s'améliorer; augmenter, s'accroître; ~ **on** faire mieux que
**improvement** n amélioration f, perfectionnement m; progrès m
**improvidence** n imprévoyance f
**improvident** adj imprévoyant; (spendthrift) prodigue
**improving** adj édifiant, moralisant
**improvisation** n improvisation f
**improvise** vt + vi improviser
**imprudence** n imprudence f
**imprudent** adj imprudent
**impudence** n impudence f, effronterie f
**impudent** adj impudent, effronté
**impudicity** n impudeur f
**impugn** vt attaquer, critiquer
**impulse** n impulsion f, élan m; (thrust) poussée f; **rash** ~ coup m de tête
**impulsion** n impulsion f
**impulsive** adj impulsif -ive, spontané, primesautier -ière; (force) irrésistible
**impulsively** adv sur impulsion
**impulsiveness** n impulsivité f
**impunity** n impunité f; **with** ~ impunément
**impure** adj impur; (immoral) impudique
**impurity** n impureté f; (immorality) impudicité f

**imputable** *adj* imputable
**imputation** *n* imputation *f*, accusation *f*
**impute** *vt* imputer, attribuer
**in** *n* **the** ~s **and outs** les tenants et les
aboutissants; *prep* (place) dans, en, à;
(during) en, dans, pendant; (after)
dans, au bout de; (made of) en; (dress)
en, de; (towns) à; (countries) en, au(x);
~ **a week's time** dans une semaine, au
bout d'une semaine; ~ **cotton** en
coton; ~ **England** en Angleterre; ~
**Portugal** au Portugal; ~ **Rome** à
Rome; ~ **shorts** en short; ~ **so far as**
dans la mesure où; ~ **spring** au printemps; ~ **the country** à la campagne;
~ **the evening** le soir, dans la soirée,
pendant la soirée; ~ **the house** dans la
maison; ~ **town** en ville; ~ **winter** en
hiver; ~ **writing** par écrit; **dressed** ~
**wool** vêtu de laine; *adv* dedans, à
l'intérieur; **be** ~ (at home) être chez
soi, être là; (government) être au pouvoir; (candidate) être élu; *coll* être à la
mode; **be** ~ **for** aller avoir; (candidature) être candidat pour; *coll* **be** ~ **for
it** aller écoper; **be** ~ **on sth** (informed)
être au courant de qch; être dans le
coup; **be well** ~ être en bons
termes avec; *coll* **have it** ~ **for** s/o
avoir une dent contre qn; *adj* intérieur
**inability** *n* incapacité *f*, impuissance *f*
**inaccessibility** *n* inaccessibilité *f*
**inaccessible** *adj* inaccessible; (person)
inabordable
**inaccuracy** *n* inexactitude *f*, imprécision
*f*
**inaccurate** *adj* inexact, imprécis; (wrong)
incorrect
**inaction** *n* inaction *f*, inactivité *f*;
paresse *f*
**inactive** *adj* inactif -ive; inerte
**inactivity** *n* inactivité *f*
**inadaptability** *n* incapacité *f* de
s'adapter
**inadaptable** *adj* incapable de s'adapter
**inadequacy** *n* insuffisance *f*, médiocrité
*f*, incompétence *f*
**inadequate** *adj* insuffisant, médiocre, incompétent; *psych* mal adapté
**inadmissibility** *n* inadmissibilité *f*
**inadmissible** *adj* inadmissible, inacceptable; *leg* (evidence) irrecevable
**inadvertence, inadvertency** *n* inattention *f*, inadvertence *f*, mégarde *f*
**inadvertent** *adj* inattentif -ive, par mégarde
**inadvisability** *n* inopportunité *f*
**inadvisable** *adj* inopportun, peu recommandable
**inalienable** *adj* inaliénable
**inane** *adj* stupide, inepte, vide; ~
**remark** ineptie *f*

**inanimate** *adj* inanimé
**inanition** *n* inanition *f*
**inanity** *n* ineptie *f*
**inappetence** *n* inappétence *f*, indifférence *f*
**inapplicability** *n* impossibilité *f* d'être
mis en vigueur (pratique); (relevance)
manque *m* de rapport
**inapplicable** *adj* inapplicable
**inapplication** *n* inapplication *f*, défaut
*m* d'application
**inapposite** *adj* sans rapport, hors de
propos
**inappreciable** *adj* inappréciable
**inapproachable** *adj* réservé, distant
**inappropriate** *adj* inopportun, mal à
propos
**inappropriateness** *n* inopportunité *f*
**inapt** *adj* inapte, incapable
**inaptitude, inaptness** *n* inaptitude *f*,
incapacité *f*
**inarticulate** *adj* (speech) mal prononcé,
inarticulé; (person) incohérent, qui
s'exprime avec difficulté; *anat* inarticulé
**inarticulateness** *n* incohérence *f*
**inartistic** *adj* peu artistique; (person)
peu artiste
**inasmuch** *adv* ~ **as** vu que, attendu que
**inattention** *n* inattention *f*, manque *m*
d'attention
**inattentive** *adj* inattentif -ive, distrait
**inaudibility** *n* imperceptibilité *f*
**inaudible** *adj* inaudible
**inaugural** *adj* inaugural
**inaugurate** *vt* inaugurer; (person) investir de ses fonctions
**inauguration** *n* inauguration *f*; (person)
investiture *f*
**inauspicious** *adj* de mauvais augure, peu
propice; (unfavourable) malencontreux -euse
**inboard** *adj naut* intérieur; *adv naut* à
bord, à l'intérieur
**inborn** *adj* inné
**inbred** *adj* inné; (engendering) né de
parents consanguins
**inbreed** *vt* croiser; *vi* être croisé
**inbreeding** *n* unions consanguines
**incalculable** *adj* incalculable, imprévisible
**incandescence** *n* incandescence *f*
**incandescent** *adj* incandescent
**incantation** *n* incantation *f*
**incapability** *n* incapacité *f*
**incapable** *adj* incapable, incompétent;
(physically helpless) impotent; *leg* incapable; ~ **of proof** impossible à
prouver
**incapacitate** *vt* rendre incapable; *leg*
frapper d'incapacité
**incapacitation** *n* incapacité *f*

**incapacity** *n* incapacité *f*, incompétence *f*; (helplessness) impotence *f*; *leg* incapacité *f*
**incarcerate** *vt* incarcérer
**incarceration** *n* incarcération *f*, emprisonnement *m*
**incarnadine** *adj* incarnat
**incarnate** *adj* incarné; *vt* incarner
**incarnation** *n* incarnation *f*
**incautious** *adj* imprudent, inconsidéré
**incautiousness** *n* imprudence *f*
**incendiarism** *n* incendie criminel
**incendiary** *n* (person) incendiaire; (bomb) bombe *f* incendiaire; *fig* agitateur -trice; *adj* incendiaire
**¹incense** *n* encens *m*; *vt* encenser
**²incense** *vt* exaspérer, rendre furieux -ieuse, mettre en colère
**incensory** *n* encensoir *m*
**incentive** *n* motivation *f*, bonne raison; *comm* **provide** ~**s** donner des primes; *adj* stimulant, encourageant; ~ **bonus** prime *f* d'encouragement; (pieceworker) prime *f* de rendement
**incertitude** *n* incertitude *f*, doute *m*
**incessant** *adj* incessant, ininterrompu, continu
**incest** *n* inceste *m*
**incestuous** *adj* incestueux -ueuse
**inch** *n* pouce *m*; ~ **es** hauteur *f*; ~ **by** ~, **by** ~ **es** petit à petit; **be every** ~ **an artist** être artiste jusqu'au bout des ongles; **within** ~ **es of** à deux doigts de; *vt* ~ **sth forward** faire avancer qch peu à peu; *vi* ~ **forward** avancer peu à peu
**inchoate** *adj* naissant, débutant; (undeveloped) rudimentaire; *vt* + *vi* commencer
**inch-tape** *n* = centimètre *m*
**incidence** *n* fréquence *f*; *phys* incidence *f*
**incident** *n* incident *m*, événement *m*; (fiction) épisode *m*; *adj* associé; *leg* attaché
**incidental** *n* chose fortuite; *adj* fortuit, accidentel -elle; (subordinate) accessoire; ~ **expenses** frais *mpl* accessoires; ~ **music** *theat* musique *f* de scène; *cin* musique *f* de film
**incidentally** *adv* incidemment; (by the way) à propos
**incinerate** *vt* incinérer
**incineration** *n* incinération *f*
**incinerator** *n* incinérateur *m*
**incipient** *adj* naissant, commençant
**incise** *vt* inciser; (engrave) graver
**incision** *n* incision *f*, coupure *f*; *surg* incision *f*; *fig* tranchant *m*
**incisive** *adj* incisif -ive, acéré, tranchant; lucide
**incisiveness** *n* tranchant *m*, pénétration *f*, lucidité *f*
**incisor** *n* incisive *f*

**incitation** *n* incitation *f*
**incite** *vt* inciter, pousser, encourager
**incitement** *n* incitation *f*
**incivility** *n* incivilité *f*, impolitesse *f*
**inclemency** *n* inclémence *f*, rigueur *f*
**inclement** *adj* inclément, rigoureux -euse
**inclination** *n* inclination *f*, pente *f*, inclinaison *f*; (liking) inclination *f*, penchant *m*
**incline** *n* inclinaison *f*, pente *f*; *vt* incliner, pencher; *vi* s'incliner, pencher, se courber; **be** ~ **d to** incliner à, être enclin à; **be well** ~ **d towards s/o** être bien disposé à l'égard de qn
**inclose** *v see* **enclose**
**inclosure** *n see* **enclosure**
**include** *vt* inclure, comprendre, englober; *sl* ~ **out** exclure
**including** *prep* inclus, y compris; ~ **service** service compris
**inclusion** *n* inclusion *f*
**inclusive** *adj* inclus, compris; ~ **charge** prix *m* tout compris
**incognito** *n* incognito *m*; *adj* dans l'incognito; *adv* incognito
**incoherence** *n* incohérence *f*
**incoherent** *adj* incohérent
**incoherently** *adv* d'une façon incohérente
**incohesive** *adj* sans cohésion
**incombustibility** *n* incombustibilité *f*
**incombustible** *adj* incombustible
**income** *n* revenu *m*; (unearned) rente(s) *f(pl)*; ~ **tax** impôt *m* sur le revenu; ~ **tax collector** percepteur *m* des contributions directes; ~ **s policy** politique *f* des revenus; **taxable** ~ revenu *m* imposable
**incomer** *n* arrivant -e; (immigrant) immigrant -e
**incoming** *adj* entrant, qui arrive, nouveau (*f* nouvelle); ~ **tide** marée montante
**incommensurable** *adj* incommensurable
**incommensurate** *adj* sans rapport, disproportionné; (inadequate) insuffisant; incommensurable
**incommode** *vt* incommoder, gêner
**incommodious** *adj* incommode; (small) trop petit
**incommodity** *n* incommodité *f*
**incommunicable** *adj* incommunicable
**incommunicado** *adj* tenu au secret; *adv* au secret
**incomparable** *adj* incomparable, sans pareil -eille
**incompatibility** *n* incompatibilité *f*
**incompatible** *adj* incompatible
**incompetence** *n* incompétence *f*, incapacité *f*
**incompetent** *adj* incompétent, incapable

**incomplete** *adj* incomplet -ète, inachevé
**incompleteness** *n* état incomplet
**incomprehensibility** *n* incompréhensibilité *f*
**incomprehensible** *adj* incompréhensible; (hand-writing) indéchiffrable
**incomprehension** *n* incompréhension *f*
**incomprehensive** *adj* incompréhensif -ive; incomplet -ète
**inconceivable** *adj* inconcevable
**inconceivably** *adv* à un degré inconcevable
**inconclusive** *adj* peu concluant; sans résultat
**incongruity** *n* incongruité *f*, inconvenance *f*, disproportion *f*
**incongruous** *adj* incongru, déplacé; (unsuitable) peu convenable; absurde; incompatible, disparate
**inconsequence** *n* inconséquence *f*
**inconsequent** *adj* inconséquent, illogique
**inconsequential** *adj* inconséquent, sans importance
**inconsiderable** *adj* insignifiant
**inconsiderate** *adj* (person) qui manque d'égards; (action, speech) inconsidéré, irréfléchi
**inconsistency** *n* inconsistance *f*, inconséquence *f*
**inconsistent** *adj* inconsistant, inconséquent
**inconsolable** *adj* inconsolable
**inconspicuous** *adj* peu voyant, qui passe inaperçu
**inconstancy** *n* inconstance *f*
**inconstant** *adj* inconstant, changeant; (fickle) volage
**incontestability** *n* incontestabilité *f*
**incontestable** *adj* incontestable, indiscutable
**incontinence** *n* incontinence *f*
**incontinent** *adj* incontinent; qui ne peut se retenir
**incontrollable** *adj* irrésistible, qui ne peut être contenu
**incontrovertible** *adj* indéniable, irréfutable
**inconvenience** *n* inconvénient *m*, désagrément *m*; (trouble) dérangement *m*; *vt* déranger, incommoder
**inconvenient** *adj* inopportun, gênant; (uncomfortable) incommode
**inconvertibility** *n econ* non-convertibilité *f*, inconvertibilité *f*
**inconvertible** *adj econ* inconvertible
**incorporate** *adj* incorporel -elle; uni; *vt* incorporer, contenir; *leg* ~ **with** former une société avec; *vi leg* se constituer en société
**incorporation** *n* incorporation *f*
**incorporeal** *adj* incorporel -elle

**incorrect** *adj* incorrect, inexact, erroné; (conduct) incorrect, déplacé
**incorrectness** *n* incorrection *f*, inexactitude *f*, erreur *f*
**incorrigible** *adj* incorrigible
**incorruptibility** *n* incorruptibilité *f*
**incorruptible** *adj* incorruptible
**increase** *n* augmentation *f*; (growth) croissance *f*, accroissement *m*, agrandissement *m*; **on the** ~ en augmentation; *vt* augmenter, accroître, agrandir; *vi* augmenter, croître, monter
**increasing** *adj* croissant
**increasingly** *adv* de plus en plus
**incredibility** *n* incrédibilité *f*
**incredible** *adj* incroyable, inimaginable; *coll fig* extraordinaire, fantastique
**incredulity** *n* incrédulité *f*
**incredulous** *adj* incrédule
**incredulousness** *n* incrédulité *f*
**increment** *n* (salary) augmentation *f*
**incremental** *adj* par augmentation; ~ **scale** échelle *f* des salaires
**incriminate** *vt* incriminer; accuser d'un crime
**incrimination** *n* incrimination *f*; accusation *f*
**incriminatory** *adj* compromettant
**incrust** *v see* **encrust**
**incrustation** *n see* **encrustation**
**incubate** *vt* couver, incuber; *vi* couver
**incubation** *n* incubation *f*
**incubator** *n* incubateur *m*, couveuse *f*
**incubus** *n* incube *m*; (anxiety) poids *m*; (nightmare) cauchemar *m*
**inculcate** *vt* inculquer
**inculcation** *n* inculcation *f*
**inculpate** *vt* (accuse) inculper; incriminer
**inculpation** *n* inculpation *f*
**incumbency** *n eccles* charge *f*
**incumbent** *n eccles* titulaire *m* (d'une charge); *adj* obligatoire; **be** ~ **on s/o** incomber à qn
**incunabula** *npl* incunables *mpl*
**incur** *vt* (be liable to) encourir, s'attirer; (debts) contracter
**incurability** *n* incurabilité *f*
**incurable** *n* incurable; *adj* incurable, inguérissable
**incurious** *adj* incurieux -ieuse, sans curiosité
**incursion** *n* incursion *f*
**indebted** *adj* redevable
**indebtedness** *n* dette(s) *f* (*pl*)
**indecency** *n* indécence *f*; *leg* outrage *m* à la pudeur
**indecent** *adj* indécent; (unseemly) malséant; *leg* ~ **assault** attentat *m* à la pudeur; *leg* ~ **exposure** outrage *m* à la pudeur

indecipherable *adj* indéchiffrable
indecision *n* indécision *f*
indecisive *adj* indécisif -ive, irrésolu, incertain
indeclinable *adj gramm* indéclinable
indecorous *adj* inconvenant, peu convenable
indecorousness *n* inconvenance *f*
indecorum *n* inconvenance *f*, manquement *m* aux usages
indeed *adv* (truly) vraiment; (corroboration) en effet; *interj* (corroboration) en effet!; mais certainement!; *iron* vraiment?
indefatigable *adj* infatigable, inlassable
indefeasible *adj leg* qui ne peut pas être annulé
indefensible *adj* indéfendable, injustifiable, insoutenable
indefinable *adj* indéfinissable
indefinite *adj* indéfini, incertain, vague; (unlimited) illimité
indelibility *n* indélébilité *f*
indelible *adj* indélébile; *fig* ineffaçable
indelicacy *n* indélicatesse *f*; (words) grossièreté *f*
indelicate *adj* indélicat; (coarse) grossier -ière; indécent
indemnification *n* indemnisation *f*; (sum) indemnité *f*, dédommagement *m*
indemnify *vt* indemniser, dédommager; (safeguard) garantir
indemnity *n* indemnité *f*, dédommagement *m*; (insurance) garantie *f*, assurance *f*
indent *n* (notch) encoche *f*; (dent) bosselure *f*; (edge) dentelure *f*; *comm* commande *f*; *leg see* indenture; *vt* encocher; bosseler; denteler; *vi comm* ~ for commander
indentation *n* (notch) encoche *f*; (dent) bosselure *f*; (edge) dentelure *f*; (imprint) empreinte *f*; *comm* acte *m* de passer une commande
indenture *n leg* contrat *m* synallagmatique; (apprentice) contrat *m* d'apprentissage; *vt leg* lier par contrat (d'apprentissage)
independence *n* indépendance *f*, autonomie *f*
independent *n pol* député non inscrit; *adj* indépendant, autonome; (uninfluenced) original; have ~ means vivre de ses rentes, avoir une fortune personnelle
indescribable *adj* indescriptible; inexprimable, indicible
indestructibility *n* indestructibilité *f*
indestructible *adj* indestructible
indeterminable *adj* indéterminable
indeterminate *adj* indéterminé; vague, incertain

indetermination *n* indétermination *f*, irrésolution *f*, hésitation *f*
index *n* (*pl* indices, indexes) (book) index *m*, table *f* des matières; (library) catalogue *m*; (pointer) aiguille *f*, index *m*; *math* exposant *m*; *fig* indice *m*, signe *m*; *ar eccles* the Index l'Index *m*; *vt* (book) mettre un index à; (word) mettre dans l'index
index-finger *n* index *m*
India *n* Inde *f*, les Indes *fpl*
Indian *n* Indien -ienne; (American) Indien -ienne d'Amérique; Red ~ Peau-Rouge (*pl* Peaux-Rouges); *adj* indien -ienne; (American) amérindien -ienne; ~ club massue *f* de gymnastique; ~ corn maïs *m*; ~ file file indienne; ~ ink encre *f* de Chine; ~ summer été *m* de la Saint-Martin
india-paper *n* papier *m* bible
indiarubber *n* (substance) caoutchouc *m*; (eraser) gomme *f*
indicate *vt* indiquer, montrer; (reveal) révéler, dénoter; (be a sign of) dénoter, être l'indice de; (make known) faire connaître, signaler; *med* indiquer
indication *n* indication *f*, indice *m*, signe *m*
indicative *n gramm* indicatif *m*; *adj* indicatif -ive
indicator *n* indicateur *m*; (pointer) aiguille *f*, index *m*; *mot* clignotant *m*
indict *vt leg* accuser, mettre en accusation; *fig* porter une accusation contre
indictable *adj leg* ~ offence délit pénal
indictment *n leg* acte *m* d'accusation; *fig* accusation *f*
indifference *n* indifférence *f*
indifferent *adj* indifférent; médiocre, quelconque
indigence *n* indigence *f*
indigenous *adj* indigène, autochtone
indigent *adj* indigent, très pauvre
indigestible *adj* indigeste
indigestion *n* indigestion *f*, dyspepsie *f*; attack of ~ indigestion *f*
indignant *adj* indigné, furieux -ieuse; grow ~ s'indigner
indignation *n* indignation *f*
indignity *n* indignité *f*, affront *m*
indigo *n* indigo *m*; *adj* indigo *invar*
indirect *adj* indirect; (route, etc) détourné; ~ taxes contributions indirectes
indirectness *n* caractère indirect
indiscernible *adj* indiscernable, imperceptible
indiscipline *n* indiscipline *f*
indiscreet *adj* indiscret -ète; imprudent
indiscretion *n* indiscrétion *f*; imprudence *f*; youthful ~ péché *m* de jeunesse
indiscriminate *adj* qui manque de

discernement; (without distinctions) fait au hasard; confus

**indispensable** *adj* indispensable, essentiel -ielle

**indispose** *vt* mécontenter, indisposer; rendre malade

**indisposed** *adj* souffrant, indisposé

**indisposition** *n* indisposition *f*, malaise *m*; (unwillingness) manque *m* de bonne volonté

**indisputable** *adj* indiscutable, incontestable

**indissoluble** *adj* indissoluble; *chem* insoluble

**indistinct** *adj* indistinct, peu clair; vague, confus, faible

**indistinguishable** *adj* qu'on ne distingue pas; imperceptible, insaisissable

**individual** *n* individu *m*; *adj* individuel -elle; original, particulier -ière

**individualism** *n* individualisme *m*

**individualist** *n* + *adj* individualiste

**individuality** *n* individualité *f*

**individualize** *vt* individualiser

**individually** *adv* individuellement, séparément

**indivisibility** *n* indivisibilité *f*

**indivisible** *adj* indivisible

**Indo-China** *n* Indo-Chine *f*

**indocile** *adj* indocile

**indoctrinate** *vt* endoctriner

**indoctrination** *n* endoctrinement *m*

**Indo-European** *n ling* indo-européen *m*; *adj* indo-européen -éenne

**indolence** *n* indolence *f*, nonchalance *f*

**indolent** *adj* indolent, nonchalant, paresseux -euse

**indomitable** *adj* indomptable, invincible

**Indonesian** *n* Indonésien -ienne; (language) indonésien *m*; *adj* indonésien -ienne

**indoor** *adj* d'intérieur; (swimming-pool) couvert; (game) pratiqué en intérieur

**indoors** *adv* à l'intérieur, à la maison

**indorse** *v see* endorse

**indorsee** *n see* endorsee

**indorsement** *n see* endorsement

**indubitable** *adj* indubitable, incontestable

**induce** *vt* persuader; causer, provoquer, amener; *philos* induire, conclure; *elect* produire par induction; *med* ~ **labour** déclencher l'accouchement

**inducement** *n* motif *m*, encouragement *m*; (incentive) motivation *f*; (bribe) pot-de-vin *m* (*pl* pots-de-vin)

**induct** *vt* installer; *US mil* incorporer

**induction** *n philos* + *elect* induction *f*; *eccles* installation *f*; *psych* provocation *f*; *elect* ~ **coil** bobine *f* d'induction

**inductive** *adj* inductif -ive; *elect* inducteur -trice

**inductor** *n* inducteur *m*

**indulge** *vt* (spoil) gâter; (yield to) céder à; (desire) satisfaire, donner libre cours à; *vi* ~ **in** s'adonner à, se permettre

**indulgence** *n* indulgence *f*, complaisance *f*, satisfaction *f*; *eccles* indulgence *f*

**indulgent** *adj* indulgent, complaisant, compréhensif -ive, accommodant

**indurate** *vt med* indurer; *vi med* s'indurer

**induration** *n med* induration *f*

**industrial** *adj* industriel -ielle; (disease) professionnel -elle; ~ **action** action revendicative, grève *f*; ~ **medicine** médecine *f* du travail

**industrialism** *n* industrialisme *m*

**industrialist** *n* industriel *m*

**industrialization** *n* industrialisation *f*

**industrialize** *vt* industrialiser

**industrious** *adj* travailleur -euse, industrieux -ieuse, courageux -euse

**industriousness** *n* assiduité *f*

**industry** *n* industrie *f*; (hard work) assiduité *f*, zèle *m*

**inebriate** *n* ivrogne, alcoolique; *adj* saoul, ivre; *vt* saouler, griser

**inebriation, inebriety** *n* ébriété *f*, ivresse *f*

**inedible** *adj* non comestible; (disgusting) immangeable

**ineffable** *adj* inexprimable, indicible

**ineffaceable** *adj* ineffaçable, indélébile

**ineffective, ineffectual, inefficacious** *adj* inefficace, sans effet; inutile, plat; incompétent

**inefficacy** *n* inefficacité *f*

**inefficiency** *n* inefficacité *f*, incompétence *f*

**inefficient** *adj* inefficace, incompétent, incapable

**inelastic** *adj* inélastique; rigide

**inelasticity** *n* inélasticité *f*

**inelegance** *n* inélégance *f*, manque *m* d'élégance

**inelegant** *adj* inélégant, sans élégance

**ineligibility** *n* inéligibilité *f*

**ineligible** *adj* inéligible; (without rights) n'ayant pas droit

**ineluctable** *adj* inéluctable, inévitable

**inept** *adj* inepte, stupide, absurde

**ineptitude** *n* ineptie *f*, sottise *f*

**inequality** *n* inégalité *f*

**inequitable** *adj* inéquitable, injuste

**inequity** *n* inéquité *f*, injustice *f*

**ineradicable** *adj* indéracinable, tenace

**inerrable** *adj* infaillible

**inert** *adj* inerte

**inertia** *n* inertie *f*, apathie *f*; ~ **reel belt** ceinture *f* de sécurité à enrouleurs; *comm* ~ **selling** vente *f* par envoi forcé

**inescapable** *adj* inévitable, inéluctable

5

**inessential** *adj* non-essentiel -ielle, superflu

**inestimable** *adj* inestimable, incalculable

**inevitability** *n* inévitabilité *f*

**inevitable** *adj* inévitable, inéluctable

**inexact** *adj* inexact, erroné

**inexactitude** *n* inexactitude *f*

**inexcusable** *adj* inexcusable, impardonnable

**inexhaustible** *adj* inépuisable

**inexhaustive** *adj* peu approfondi

**inexorability** *n* inexorabilité *f*

**inexorable** *adj* inexorable

**inexpedient** *adj* malavisé

**inexpensive** *adj* peu cher (*f* chère), bon
marché

**inexperience** *n* inexpérience *f*, manque
*m* d'expérience

**inexperienced** *adj* inexpérimenté

**inexpert** *adj* inexpert, maladroit

**inexpiable** *adj* inexpiable

**inexplicable** *adj* inexplicable

**inexpressible** *adj* inexprimable

**inexpugnable** *adj* inexpugnable; invincible

**inextinguishable** *adj* inextinguible

**inextricable** *adj* inextricable

**infallibility** *n* infaillibilité *f*

**infallible** *adj* infaillible

**infamous** *adj* infâme, abominable

**infamy** *n* infamie *f*

**infancy** *n* petite enfance, bas âge; *leg*
minorité *f*

**infant** *n* (baby) nouveau-né (*f* -née),
bébé *m*; *leg* mineur -e; *adj* infantile

**infanta** *n* infante *f*

**infante** *n* infant *m*

**infanticide** *n* infanticide *m*; (person) infanticide

**infantile** *adj* infantile, enfantin, puéril;
~ **paralysis** poliomyélite *f*

**infantilism** *n* infantilisme *m*

**infantry** *n* infanterie *f*

**infantryman** *n* fantassin *m*

**infatuate** *vt* tourner la tête à

**infatuated** *adj* entiché; **be** ~ **with**
(person) avoir le béguin pour; (idea)
s'engouer de

**infatuation** *n* béguin *m*; (idea) engouement *m*

**infect** *vt* infecter, contaminer; (disease)
transmettre; *fig* corrompre

**infection** *n* infection *f*, contamination *f*,
contagion *f*; **ear** ~ otite *f*; **throat** ~
angine *f*

**infectious** *adj* infectieux -ieuse, contagieux -ieuse

**infectiousness** *n med* nature infectieuse;
*fig* contagion *f*

**infective** *adj* infectueux -euse

**infelicitous** *adj* malheureux -euse; (inap-

propriate) mal à propos; fâcheux -euse

**infelicity** *n* malheur *m*; inopportunité
*f*, maladresse *f*

**infer** *vt* inférer, conclure, déduire

**inference** *n* inférence *f*, conclusion *f*,
déduction *f*

**inferential** *adj* déductif -ive

**inferior** *n* inférieur -e; (rank) subalterne;
*adj* inférieur

**inferiority** *n* infériorité *f*; ~ **complex**
complexe *m* d'infériorité

**infernal** *adj* infernal, diabolique; ~
**machine** bombe *f* à retardement; objet
piégé

**inferno** *n* enfer *m*

**infertile** *adj* infertile, infécond, stérile

**infest** *vt* infester

**infestation** *n* infestation *f*

**infidel** *n* infidèle, païen -ïenne

**infidelity** *n* infidélité *f*

**infighting** *n* corps à corps *m*; *fig* luttes *fpl*
internes

**infiltrate** *vt* (liquid) infiltrer; (troops)
faire s'infiltrer; (spy, etc) noyauter

**infiltration** *n* infiltration *f*; *pol* noyautage *m*

**infinite** *n* infini *m*; *adj* infini, sans bornes

**infinitesimal** *adj* infinitésimal, infime

**infinitive** *n gramm* infinitif *m*; *adj* infinitif -ive

**infinitude** *n* infinité *f*

**infinity** *n* infinité *f*

**infirm** *adj* infirme; (hesitant) irrésolu,
indécis

**infirmary** *n* hôpital *m*; (sick bay) infirmerie *f*

**infirmity** *n* infirmité *f*; (disease) maladie
*f*; (hesitation) irrésolution *f*, indécision *f*

**infix** *vt* insérer

**inflame** *vt* enflammer, mettre en feu;
*med* enflammer; *fig* envenimer, exacerber; *vi* s'enflammer, prendre feu; *med*
s'enflammer; *fig* s'échauffer

**inflammable** *adj* inflammable; *US* ignifuge

**inflammation** *n* inflammation *f*

**inflammatory** *adj* incendiaire; *med* in-
flammatoire

**inflate** *vt* (air, gas) gonfler; (prices) hausser; *econ* augmenter la quantité de
(monnaie en circulation); *fig* enfler

**inflated** *adj* (air, gas) gonflé; (prices)
gonflé, exagéré; (style) enflé, boursouflé

**inflation** *n* (air, gas) gonflement *m*;
(prices) hausse *f*; *econ* inflation *f*

**inflationary** *adj* inflationniste

**inflationism** *n* politique *f* inflationniste

**inflationist** *adj* inflationniste

**inflect** *vt* (bend) courber, fléchir; (voice)
moduler; *gramm* modifier la désinence
de; *vi gramm* prendre une désinence

**inflection** *n see* **inflexion**

**inflectional** *adj see* **inflexional**
**inflexibility** *n* rigidité *f*; *fig* inflexibilité *f*
**inflexible** *adj* rigide; *fig* inflexible
**inflexion, inflection** *n* (voice) modulation *f*; *gramm* (process) modification *f* de désinence; (ending) désinence *f*
**inflexional, inflectional** *adj ling* flexionnel -elle, désinentiel -ielle
**inflict** *vt* infliger, faire subir
**infliction** *n* infliction *f*
**inflow** *n* afflux *m*
**influence** *n* influence *f*; (drink, drugs, etc) **under the ~ of** sous l'effet de, sous l'empire de; *vt* influencer, influer sur, persuader
**influential** *adj* influent
**influenza** *n* grippe *f*
**influx** *n* afflux *m*, flot *m*; (confluence) confluent *m*
**info** *n sl abbr* tuyaux *mpl*
**inform** *vt* informer, avertir, aviser, tenir au courant; *vi* ~ **against** dénoncer, informer contre
**informal** *adj* simple, sans façons; informel -elle, dénué de formalité; (unofficial) officieux -ieuse; ~ **dress** tenue *f* de ville
**informality** *n* simplicité *f*, absence *f* de formalité
**informant** *n* informateur -trice
**information** *n* information(s) *f(pl)*, renseignements *mpl*; (knowledge) connaissances *fpl*; *leg* dénonciation *f*; **for your ~** à titre de renseignement
**informative, informatory** *adj* instructif -ive
**informed** *adj* informé; (enlightened) éclairé
**informer** *n* dénonciateur -trice, délateur -trice; (police) indicateur -trice
**infra** *adv* au-dessous; *coll* ~ **dig** au-dessous de sa dignité
**infraction** *n* infraction *f*
**infrangible** *adj* incassable
**infra-red** *adj* infrarouge
**infrequency** *n* rareté *f*
**infrequent** *adj* peu fréquent, rare; peu normal
**infringe** *vt* enfreindre, transgresser, contrevenir à
**infringement** *n* infraction *f*, contravention *f*; ~ **of patent** contrefaçon *f* d'une fabrication brevetée
**infuriate** *vt* rendre furieux -ieuse, exaspérer
**infuriating** *adj* exaspérant
**infuse** *vt* infuser; *fig* inspirer, insuffler
**infusion** *n* infusion *f*
**ingenious** *adj* ingénieux -ieuse, astucieux -ieuse
**ingenue** *n* ingénue *f*
**ingenuity** *n* ingéniosité *f*

**ingenuous** *adj* ingénu, naïf (*f* naïve); (candid) sincère, ouvert
**ingenuousness** *n* ingénuité *f*, naïveté *f*; sincérité *f*
**ingest** *vt* ingérer
**ingestion** *n* ingestion *f*
**ingle-nook** *n* coin *m* du feu
**inglorious** *adj* peu glorieux -ieuse, honteux -euse
**ingot** *n* lingot *m*
**ingrained** *adj* invétéré, enraciné, ancré
**ingratiate** *vt* ~ **oneself with s/o** s'insinuer dans les bonnes grâces de qn
**ingratiating** *adj* insinuant
**ingratitude** *n* ingratitude *f*
**ingredient** *n* ingrédient *m*
**ingress** *n* entrée *f*
**ingrowing** *adj* ~ **nail** ongle incarné
**ingurgitate** *vt* ingurgiter, avaler
**inhabit** *vt* habiter
**inhabitable** *adj* habitable
**inhabitant** *n* habitant -e
**inhabitation** *n* habitation *f*
**inhalation** *n* inhalation *f*, aspiration *f*
**inhale** *vt* aspirer, inhaler, avaler; *vi* (smoking) avaler la fumée
**inhaler** *n* inhalateur *m*
**inharmonious** *adj* inharmonieux -ieuse, discordant
**inhere** *vi* être inhérent
**inherence** *n* inhérence *f*
**inherent** *adj* inhérent
**inherently** *adv* en soi
**inherit** *vt* hériter, hériter de; *vi* hériter
**inheritable** *adj* qu'on peut recevoir en héritage
**inheritance** *n* héritage *m*, patrimoine *m*; (process of inheriting) succession *f*
**inheritor** *n* héritier -ière
**inhibit** *vt* entraver, empêcher; (desire) maîtriser; *psych* inhiber; (forbid) interdire
**inhibited** *adj* inhibé, ayant des inhibitions
**inhibition** *n* inhibition *f*; *leg* interdiction *f*
**inhibitory** *adj* inhibiteur -trice; *leg* prohibitif -ive
**inhospitable** *adj* (climate, etc) inhospitalier -ière; (person) peu accueillant, désagréable
**inhuman** *adj* inhumain
**inhumane** *adj* cruel (*f* cruelle), inhumain, brutal
**inhumanity** *n* inhumanité *f*, cruauté *f*, brutalité *f*
**inhumation** *n* inhumation *f*, enterrement *m*
**inhume** *vt* inhumer, enterrer
**inimical** *adj* inamical, hostile, ennemi
**inimitable** *adj* inimitable; *coll* impayable

**iniquitous** *adj* inique
**iniquity** *n* iniquité *f*
**initial** *n* (lettre) initiale *f*; ~s initiales *fpl*; *adj* initial, premier -ière; *vt* parafer, parapher
**initially** *adv* au début, au commencement, initialement
**initiate** *n* initié -e; *adj* initié; *vt* (admit) initier; (originate) inaugurer, lancer, amorcer; *leg* intenter
**initiation** *n* (admission) initiation *f*, admission *f*; (beginning) commencement *m*, début *m*
**initiative** *n* initiative *f*
**initiator** *n* initiateur -trice
**inject** *vt* injecter, faire une piqûre à (qn); *fig* insuffler
**injection** *n* injection *f*, piqûre *f*
**in-joke** *n coll* plaisanterie comprise seulement par les initiés
**injudicious** *adj* malavisé, peu judicieux -ieuse
**injunction** *n leg* injonction *f*; ordre *m*
**injure** *vt* (hurt) blesser; (wrong) faire un tort à; *leg* léser
**injured** *adj* blessé; *fig* offensé; *leg* lésé
**injurious** *adj* nuisible, préjudiciable
**injury** *n* blessure *f*; (wrong) tort *m*; *leg* lésion *f*
**injustice** *n* injustice *f*
**ink** *n* encre *f*; *vt* encrer; ~ **in** repasser à l'encre
**inkling** *n* soupçon *m*, idée *f* vague; **have no** ~ ne pas avoir la moindre idée
**inkstand** *n* encrier *m*
**inkwell** *n* encrier *m* (de pupitre)
**inky** *adj* taché d'encre; (darkness) noir comme de l'encre
**inland** *adj* intérieur; ~ **revenue** fisc *m*; (money received) contributions directes; *adv* à l'intérieur
**in-laws** *npl* belle famille
**inlay** *n* incrustation *f*; (wood) marqueterie *f*; (floor) parquet *m*; *vt* incruster; marqueter; parqueter
**inlet** *n* crique *f*, bras *m* de mer; *mech* arrivée *f*; ~ **pipe** tuyau *m* d'arrivée
**inly** *adv* secrètement, intimement
**inmate** *n* (hospital) hospitalisé -e; (asylum) interné -e; (prison) détenu -e
**inmost** *adj* le plus profond, le plus secret (*f* la plus secrète)
**inn** *n* auberge *f*; **Inns of Court** écoles *fpl* de droit à Londres
**innards** *npl coll* entrailles *fpl*
**innate** *adj* inné, naturel -elle
**innateness** *n* innéité *f*
**inner** *n* (target) zone *f* autour du mille; *adj* intérieur, interne; *fig* intime, secret -ète; *mot* ~ **tube** chambre *f* à air
**innermost** *adj* le plus profond, le plus secret (*f* la plus secrète)

**innings** *n sp* tour *m* de batte; *fig* tour *m*, période *f*
**innkeeper** *n* aubergiste
**innocence** *n* innocence *f*; (simplicity) naïveté *f*, candeur *f*
**innocent** *n* innocent -e; *adj* innocent; (simple) naïf (*f* naïve), candide; ~ **of** dépourvu de
**innocuous** *adj* inoffensif -ive
**innovate** *vi* innover
**innovation** *n* innovation *f*, changement *m*
**innovator** *n* innovateur -trice, novateur -trice
**innuendo** *n* insinuation (malveillante), allusion (malveillante)
**innumerable** *adj* innombrable, sans nombre
**inobservance** *n* manque *m* d'observance
**inoculate** *vt* inoculer, vacciner; *fig* inculquer
**inoculation** *n* inoculation *f*
**inodorous** *adj* inodore
**inoffensive** *adj* inoffensif -ive
**inoperable** *adj* inopérable
**inoperative** *adj* inopérant
**inopportune** *adj* inopportun, déplacé, intempestif -ive
**inordinate** *adj* excessif -ive, démesuré, immodéré
**inorganic** *adj* inorganique
**in-patient** *n* malade hospitalisé -e
**input** *n elect* puissance *f*; (computer) données *fpl*
**inquest** *n leg* enquête *f* judiciaire
**inquietude** *n* inquiétude *f*
**inquire, enquire** *vt* demander, s'enquérir, poser des questions; *vi* demander, s'enquérir, s'informer; (health) ~ **after** demander des nouvelles de; ~ **into** faire des recherches sur, enquêter sur
**inquiring, enquiring** *adj* curieux -ieuse; interrogateur -trice
**inquiry, enquiry** *n* demande *f* (de renseignements); (official) enquête *f*, investigation *f*
**inquisition** *n* enquête *f*, investigation *f*; *eccles* **the Inquisition** l'Inquisition *f*
**inquisitive** *adj* curieux -ieuse; *pej* trop curieux -ieuse
**inquisitiveness** *n* curiosité *f*; *pej* indiscrétion *f*
**inquisitor** *n* enquêteur *m*; *eccles* inquisiteur *m*
**inquisitorial** *adj* inquisitorial
**inroad** *n* incursion *f*; **make** ~**s upon** empiéter sur, entamer
**insalubrious** *adj* insalubre, malsain
**insalubrity** *n* insalubrité *f*
**insalutary** *adj* qui n'est pas salutaire
**insane** *n med* **the** ~ *npl* les aliénés *mpl*;

*adj* fou (*f* folle); *med* aliéné, dément; *fig* insensé

**insanitary** *adj* insalubre, malsain

**insanity** *n* folie *f*, insanité *f*; *med* aliénation *f*, démence *f*

**insatiable** *adj* insatiable

**inscribe** *vt* inscrire, graver; (dedicate) dédicacer

**inscription** *n* inscription *f*; (dedication) dédicace *f*

**inscrutability** *n* impénétrabilité *f*

**inscrutable** *adj* impénétrable

**insect** *n* insecte *m*; ~ **spray** aérosol *m* insecticide, bombe *f* insecticide

**insecticide** *n* insecticide *m*; *adj* insecticide

**insecure** *adj* (object) peu solide, qui tient mal; (future) incertain; (worried) anxieux -ieuse; (unsafe) peu sûr

**insecurity** *n* insécurité *f*

**inseminate** *vt* inséminer

**insemination** *n* insémination *f*

**insensate** *adj* insensé; (not alive) inanimé

**insensibility** *n* insensibilité *f*, indifférence *f*; *med* inconscience *f*

**insensible** *adj* insensible, indifférent; *med* inconscient

**insensitive** *adj* insensible

**insensitiveness** *n* insensibilité *f*

**inseparable** *adj* inséparable

**insert** *n typ* encart *m*; (newspaper) insertion *f*; *vt* insérer; *typ* encarter; (jewel) incruster

**insertion** *n* insertion *f*

**inset** *n typ* encart *m*; (map, diagram, etc, inserted on page) carte *f* (schéma *m*) en cartouche; *vt* insérer (en cartouche); (jewel) incruster

**inshore** *adj* côtier -ière; *adv* près de la côte, vers la côte

**inside** *n* dedans *m*, intérieur *m*; *coll* ventre *m*; ~ **out** à l'envers, sens dessus dessous; (completely) à fond; *adj* intérieur, d'intérieur; (secret) secret -ète; ~ **information** renseignements obtenus à la source; *coll* ~ **job** coup monté de l'intérieur; *mot* ~ **lane** (in England) voie *f* de gauche; (in France) voie *f* de droite; ~ **leg measurement** hauteur *f* d'entre-jambes; *adv* dedans, au-dedans, à l'intérieur; *coll* en prison, en taule; *prep* à l'intérieur de, dans; (time) en moins de

**inside-forward** *n sp* intérieur *m*

**insider** *n* initié -e

**insidious** *adj* insidieux -ieuse, spécieux -ieuse

**insight** *n* perspicacité *f*

**insignia** *npl* insignes *mpl*

**insignificance** *n* insignifiance *f*

**insignificant** *adj* insignifiant

**insincere** *adj* insincère, de mauvaise foi

**insincerity** *n* insincérité *f*, manque *m* de sincérité, mauvaise foi

**insinuate** *vt* insinuer, laisser entendre; *vi* s'insinuer

**insinuation** *n* insinuation *f*, allusion *f*

**insipid** *adj* insipide, fade

**insipidity** *n* insipidité *f*, fadeur *f*

**insist** *vt* insister, affirmer, maintenir; *vi* insister

**insistence** *n* insistance *f*

**insistent** *adj* insistant, pressant, persistant

**insobriety** *n* ivrognerie *f*

**insofar** *adv* à tel point

**insolation** *n* exposition *f* au soleil; (sunstroke) insolation *f*

**insole** *n* semelle *f*

**insolence** *n* insolence *f*

**insolent** *adj* insolent

**insolubility** *n* insolubilité *f*

**insoluble** *adj* insoluble

**insolvency** *n* insolvabilité *f*, faillite *f*

**insolvent** *adj* insolvable, en faillite; **become** ~ faire faillite; **declare oneself** ~ déposer son bilan

**insomnia** *n* insomnie *f*

**insomniac** *n* insomniaque

**insomuch** *adv* à tel point; ~ **as** d'autant que

**insouciance** *n* insouciance *f*

**inspect** *vt* inspecter, examiner, vérifier; *med* passer en revue

**inspection** *n* inspection *f*, examen *m*, vérification *f*; *mil* inspection *f*, revue *f*

**inspector** *n* inspecteur -trice; (bus, train) contrôleur -euse

**inspectorate** *n* corps *m* des inspecteurs

**inspiration** *n* inspiration *f*

**inspire** *vt* inspirer, stimuler

**inst** *adj abbr comm* courant

**instability** *n* instabilité *f*

**install** *vt* installer, établir

**installation** *n* installation *f*

**instalment** *n comm* acompte *m*, versement partiel; (serial) épisode *m*; **buy on the** ~ **plan** acheter à tempérament; **pay by** ~ **s** payer par traites échelonnées

**instance** *n* cas *m*, exemple *m*; circonstance *f*; *leg* demande *f*, instance *f*; **for** ~ par exemple; **in the first** ~ en premier lieu; *vt* donner en exemple, illustrer

**instant** *n* instant *m*, moment *m*; **this** ~ tout de suite; *adj* immédiat, instantané; ~ **coffee** café *m* soluble; ~ **soup** potage instantané en poudre

**instantaneous** *adj* instantané

**instanter** *adv* immédiatement

**instantly** *adv* immédiatement

**instate** *vt* installer

**instead** *adv* au lieu de cela, à la place de

cela, plutôt; ~ **of** à la place de, au lieu de

**instep** n cou-de-pied m (pl cous-de-pied); (shoe) cambrure f

**instigate** vt inciter, pousser

**instigation** n instigation f, incitation f

**instigator** n instigateur -trice

**instil** vt insuffler, inculquer, instiller

**instillation** n instillation f

**instilment** n instillation f

**instinct** n instinct m

**instinctive** adj instinctif -ive

**institute** n institut m; vt instituer, établir; (found) fonder, créer; **leg ~ proceedings** entamer un procès

**institution** n institution f, fondation f, établissement m; **leg** mise f en train; (hospital) hôpital m; (mental hospital) hôpital m psychiatrique; (workhouse) asile m

**institutional** adj institutionnel -elle

**institutionalize** vt institutionnaliser; (person) garder dans un établissement (dans un hôpital, dans un asile, etc)

**instruct** vt (teach) instruire, enseigner; (order) donner des ordres à; **leg ~ counsel** confier une cause à un(e) avocat(e)

**instruction** n instruction f, enseignement m; ~ s (directions) directives fpl, instructions fpl; indications fpl; **mil** (orders) consigne f; (method of use) mode m d'emploi

**instructive** adj instructif -ive, révélateur -trice

**instructor** n maître m; **mil** instructeur m; **sp** moniteur m

**instructress** n maîtresse f; **sp** monitrice f

**instrument** n instrument m, outil m, ustensile m; vt orchestrer

**instrumental** adj **mus** instrumental; **be ~ in** être pour quelque chose dans

**instrumentalist** n instrumentiste

**instrumentation** n orchestration f

**insubordinate** adj insubordonné, indiscipliné, rebelle

**insubordination** n insubordination f, rébellion f

**insubstantial** adj irréel -éelle; peu substantiel -ielle, sans substance

**insufferable** adj insupportable, intolérable

**insufficiency** n insuffisance f

**insufficient** adj insuffisant

**insufflate** vt insuffler

**insufflation** n insufflation f

**insular** adj insulaire; **fig** étroit

**insularity** n insularité f; étroitesse f

**insulate** vt isoler; (sound) insonoriser; (heat) calorifuger; **fig** isoler, séparer

**insulation** n isolation f; (sound) insonorisation f; (heat) calorifugeage m; (substance) isolant m

**insulator** n (substance) isolant m; (device) isolateur m

**insulin** n insuline f; ~ **shock** choc m insulinique

**insult** n insulte f, injure f, affront m; **add ~ to injury** porter l'insulte à son comble; vt insulter, injurier

**insulting** adj injurieux -ieuse, insultant

**insuperable** adj insurmontable

**insupportable** adj insupportable

**insurable** adj assurable

**insurance** n assurance f, garantie f; **comprehensive ~** assurance f tous risques; **fire ~** assurance-incendie f (pl assurances-incendie); **life ~** assurance-vie f (pl assurances-vie); **take out ~** s'assurer; **third-party ~** assurance f au tiers

**insure** vt assurer; (make sure) garantir, assurer

**insurer** n assureur m

**insurgency** n rébellion f

**insurgent** n insurgé -e, rebelle; adj insurgé, en révolte

**insurmountable** adj insurmontable

**insurrection** n insurrection f, rébellion f, émeute f

**insurrectionary** adj insurrectionnel -elle

**insusceptibility** n insensibilité f

**insusceptible** adj insensible, peu susceptible

**intact** adj intact

**intake** n (school, etc) admission(s) f (pl); **mil** contingent m; (inlet, tube, etc) prise f, adduction f; (food, liquid) consommation f; **mech ~ valve** soupape f d'admission

**intangible** adj intangible

**integer** n nombre entier

**integral** n **math** intégrale f; adj intégral, complet -ète; (essential) intégrant; ~ **part** partie intégrante

**integrate** vt intégrer, compléter, coordonner; **US** (school) imposer la déségrégation raciale

**integration** n intégration f; **US** déségrégation raciale

**integrity** n intégrité f, probité f; (wholeness) intégrité f, totalité f, intégralité f

**integument** n tégument m

**intellect** n intellect m; intelligence f, esprit m; (person) intelligence f, esprit m

**intellectual** n + adj intellectuel -uelle

**intellectualism** n intellectualisme m

**intellectuality** n intellectualité f

**intellectualize** vt intellectualiser

**intelligence** n intelligence f; (news) information(s) f (pl), renseignement(s) m (pl); **mil** renseignements mpl; ~ **service** service m de renseignements; ~ **test** test m d'aptitude intellectuelle

**intelligent** adj intelligent

**intelligentsia** n élite intellectuelle

**intelligibility** *n* intelligibilité *f*
**intelligible** *adj* intelligible
**intemperance** *n* excès *m*, manque *m* de modération, intempérance *f*; (drunkenness) ivrognerie *f*
**intemperate** *adj* immodéré, excessif -ive; (drunken) adonné à la boisson; (climate) rigoureux -euse
**intend** *vt* avoir l'intention de, penser, projeter; destiner
**intended** *n coll* (future husband, future wife) promis -e, futur -e; *adj* intentionnel -elle, voulu, délibéré
**intense** *adj* intense, extrême; ardent; violent, excessif -ive
**intensification** *n* intensification *f*
**intensify** *vt* intensifier; *vi* s'intensifier
**intensity** *n* intensité *f*; puissance *f*
**intensive** intensif -ive; *med* ~ **care unit** service *m* de réanimation
¹**intent** *n* intention *f*, dessein *m*, but *m*; **to all ~s and purposes** virtuellement, en fait
²**intent** *adj* résolu, absorbé, attentif -ive
**intention** *n* intention *f*, but *m*, dessein *m*
**intentional** *adj* intentionnel -elle, voulu, délibéré
**interact** *vi* réagir réciproquement
**interaction** *n* interaction *f*
**interbreed** *vt* croiser; *vi* se croiser
**intercalary** *adj* intercalaire
**intercalate** *vt* intercaler
**intercalation** *n* intercalation *f*
**intercede** *vi* intercéder
**intercept** *vt* intercepter; (halt) arrêter au passage
**interception** *n* interception *f*
**interceptor** *n* intercepteur *m*
**intercession** *n* intercession *f*
**intercessor** *n* intercesseur *m*
**interchange** *n* échange *m*; (alteration) alternance *f*; *mot* (motorway) échangeur *m*; *vt* échanger, faire alterner; (exchange places) changer de place
**interchangeable** *adj* interchangeable
**intercom** *n* interphone *m*
**intercommunicate** *vi* communiquer réciproquement
**intercommunication** *n* intercommunication *f*
**intercommunion** *n eccles* intercommunion *f*
**interconnect** *vt* connecter; *vi* communiquer
**intercontinental** *adj* intercontinental
**intercostal** *adj anat* intercostal
**intercourse** *n* commerce *m*, rapports *mpl*, relations *fpl*; **sexual ~** rapports sexuels, copulation *f*
**interdenominational** *adj eccles* interconfessionnel -elle

**interdepend** *vi* dépendre l'un de l'autre (les uns des autres)
**interdependence** *n* interdépendance *f*
**interdependent** *adj* interdépendant
**interdict** *n leg* interdiction *f*; *eccles* interdit *m*; *vt leg* interdire; *eccles* jeter l'interdit sur
**interdiction** *n* interdiction *f*
**interest** *n* intérêt *m*; (benefit) avantage *m*, profit *m*; *comm* (share in) intérêts *mpl*, participation *f*; (on capital) intérêt(s) *m(pl)*; (hobby) passe-temps *m*; *vt* intéresser, s'intéresser à; (concern) intéresser, concerner, toucher, préoccuper
**interested** *adj* intéressé; *leg* ~ **party** ayant-droit *m* (*pl* ayants-droit)
**interesting** *adj* intéressant; *coll obs* **in an ~ condition** enceinte
**interface** *n* interface *f*
**interfere** *vi* s'occuper, s'ingérer, s'immiscer, se mêler; *phys* interférer; ~ **with** empêcher, contrecarrer; (molest) importuner; *leg* (sexually) attenter à la pudeur de
**interference** *n* ingérance *f*, intrusion *f*; *phys* interférence *f*; *rad* parasites *mpl*
**interfering** *adj* importun
**interim** *n* intérim *m*; (dividend) dividende *m* intérimaire; *adj* provisoire, intérimaire; ~ **payment** acompte *m*
**interior** *n* intérieur *m*; *arts* (tableau *m* d')intérieur *m*; *adj* intérieur
**interject** *vt* placer, lancer
**interjection** *n* interjection *f*
**interlace** *vt* entrelacer, entrecroiser; *vi* s'entrelacer, s'entrecroiser
**interlard** *vt* entrelarder
**interleave** *vt* interfolier
**interline** *vt typ* interligner; (clothing) mettre une doublure intermédiaire à
**interlinear** *adj* interlinéaire
**interlining** *n* doublure *f* intermédiaire
**interlock** *vt* enclencher; *vi* s'enclencher
**interlocutor** *n* interlocuteur -trice
**interlocutory** *adj* interlocutoire
**interloper** *n* intrus -e; *comm* commerçant -e marron -onne
**interlude** *n mus* interlude *m*; (interval) intervalle *m*; *theat* intermède *m*
**intermarriage** *n* mariage *m* entre personnes de races (religions, nationalités) différentes; mariage *m* entre membres de la même famille, de la même tribu
**intermarry** *vi* se marier avec une personne de race (religion, nationalité) différente; se marier avec une personne de la même famille, de la même tribu
**intermediary** *n* + *adj* intermédiaire
**intermediate** *adj* intermédiaire
**interment** *n* enterrement *m*, inhumation *f*

**intermezzo** n mus intermezzo m; intermède m
**interminable** adj interminable
**intermingle** vt entremêler, mélanger; vi s'entremêler, se mélanger
**intermission** n interruption f, trêve f, pause f; theat entracte m; med intermission f
**intermittent** adj intermittent
¹**intern** n US interne
²**intern** vt interner
**internal** adj interne, intérieur; (intrinsic) intrinsèque; ~ **combustion engine** moteur m à combustion interne
**international** n sp (match, player) international m; adj international; ~ **date line** ligne f de changement de date
**Internationale** n the ~ l'Internationale f
**internationalism** n internationalisme m
**internationalize** vt internationaliser
**internecine** adj de destruction mutuelle
**internee** n interné -e
**internment** n internement m
**interpellate** vt interpeller
**interpellation** n interpellation f
**interpenetrate** vt interpénétrer
**interpenetration** n interpénétration f
**interphone** n interphone m
**interplanetary** adj interplanétaire
**interplay** n effet m réciproque
**interpolate** vt (text) corrompre; (insert) interpoler
**interpolation** n interpolation f
**interpose** vt intercaler, insérer; (veto) objecter; vi s'interposer, intervenir
**interposition** n interposition f, intervention f
**interpret** vt interpréter; vi interpréter, faire l'interprète
**interpretation** n interprétation f
**interpretative** adj interprétatif -ive
**interpreter** n interprète
**interracial** adj entre races différentes
**interregnum** n interrègne m
**interrelate** vt mettre en corrélation
**interrelation** n corrélation f
**interrogate** vt interroger
**interrogation** n interrogation f; (grilling) interrogatoire m
**interrogative** n gramm interrogatif m; adj interrogateur -trice; gramm interrogatif -ive
**interrogator** n interrogateur -trice
**interrogatory** n interrogatoire m; adj interrogateur -trice
**interrupt** vt interrompre, couper; (obstruct) gêner, cacher
**interruption** n interruption f
**intersect** vt couper, croiser; math intersecter; vi s'entrecouper, s'entrecroiser
**intersection** n croisement m, carrefour

m; math intersection f
**intersperse** vt parsemer, répandre
**interstellar** adj interstellaire
**interstice** n interstice m
**intertwine** vt entrelacer; vi s'entrelacer
**interurban** adj interurbain
**interval** n intervalle m, pause f; theat entracte m; (space) intervalle m, écartement m; at ~ s par intervalles
**intervene** vi intervenir; (occur) survenir, arriver; (time) passer, s'écouler
**intervention** n intervention f
**interview** n entrevue f; (media) interview f; vt avoir une entrevue avec; (media) interviewer
**interviewer** n (media) interviewer m; (opinion poll, etc) enquêteur -euse
**interweave** vt tisser ensemble, entrelacer; fig entremêler; vi s'entrelacer
**intestacy** n état produit quand quelqu'un meurt intestat
**intestate** adj intestat invar
**intestinal** adj intestinal
**intestine** n intestin m; large ~ gros intestin; small ~ intestin m grêle; adj fig interne, intestin
**intimacy** n intimité f; rapports sexuels, rapports mpl intimes
¹**intimate** n intime, familier -ière; adj intime, proche; (knowledge) approfondi; be ~ with avoir des rapports sexuels (intimes) avec
²**intimate** vt faire savoir, annoncer; (hint) suggérer, laisser entendre
**intimation** n annonce f, avis m; (hint) indice m, indication f
**intimidate** vt intimider
**intimidation** n intimidation f
**into** prep dans, en; coll be ~ donner dans; far ~ très avant dans; (dividing) two ~ ten dix divisé par deux
**intolerable** adj intolérable, insupportable
**intolerance** n intolérance f
**intolerant** adj intolérant
**intonation** n intonation f
**intone** vt + vi psalmodier
**intoxicant** n boisson f alcoolique; adj enivrant
**intoxicate** vt saouler; fig griser, enivrer
**intoxication** n ivresse f; med intoxication f; fig ivresse f, griserie f
**intractability** n opiniâtreté f
**intractable** adj intractable, opiniâtre, indocile
**intramural** adj intra-muros invar
**intransigence** n intransigeance f
**intransigent** n intransigeant -e; adj intransigeant
**intransitive** n gramm intransitif m; adj gramm intransitif -ive
**intravenous** adj intraveineux-euse

**intrepid** *adj* intrépide
**intrepidity** *n* intrépidité *f*
**intricacy** *n* complexité *f*
**intricate** *adj* complexe
**intrigue** *n* intrigue *f*; (love affair) liaison *f*; *vt* intriguer, intéresser; *vi* intriguer, comploter
**intrinsic** *adj* intrinsèque
**introduce** *vt* (bring in) introduire; (socially) présenter; (put into) introduire, insérer; (bring into use) établir, faire adopter; (bill in parliament) déposer; (make known) initier, faire connaître, lancer
**introduction** *n* introduction *f*; (social) présentation *f*; (book) introduction *f*, avant-propos *m*; (elementary textbook) introduction *f*, manuel *m* élémentaire, cours *m* de base
**introductory** *adj* préliminaire, préalable
**introit** *n eccles* introït *m*
**introspection** *n* introspection *f*
**introspective** *adj* introspectif -ive
**introversion** *n* introversion *f*
**introvert** *n* introverti -e; *adj* introverti; *vt* (turn inwards) tourner sur soi-même
**intrude** *vt* entrer de force; entrer sans permission; (views) imposer; *vi* (person) s'imposer; ~ **on** s'ingérer dans, s'immiscer dans; (encroach) empiéter sur
**intruder** *n* intrus -e; avion (navire) isolé
**intrusion** *n* intrusion *f*, imposition *f*
**intrusive** *adj* importun, gênant
**intuition** *n* intuition *f*
**intuitive** *adj* intuitif -ive
**intumescence** *n* intumescence *f*
**inundate** *vt* inonder
**inundation** *n* inondation *f*
**inure, enure** *vt* accoutumer, endurcir
**inutility** *n* inutilité *f*
**invade**,*vt* envahir
**invader** *n* envahisseur -euse
¹**invalid** *n* malade; *adj* malade, infirme; ~ **chair** fauteuil *m* de malade; *vt mil* ~ **out** démobiliser pour blessures (pour raisons de santé)
²**invalid** *adj* non valable; (ticket) périmé
**invalidate** *vt* invalider, annuler; *leg* casser
**invalidation** *n* invalidation *f*
**invalidity** *n* invalidité *f*, état périmé
**invaluable** *adj* inestimable, hors de prix
**invariable** *adj* invariable
**invariably** *adv* invariablement, toujours
**invasion** *n* invasion *f*, envahissement *m*; (rights) empiètement *m*
**invective** *n* invective *f*
**inveigh** *vi* ~ **against** invectiver contre, tonner contre
**inveigle** entraîner, cajoler, attirer
**invent** *vt* inventer

**invention** *n* invention *f*; (lie) invention *f*, mensonge *m*
**inventive** *adj* inventif -ive
**inventiveness** *n* esprit *m* d'invention
**inventor** *n* inventeur -trice
**inventory** *n* inventaire *m*; stock *m*; *vt* inventorier
**inverse** *n* inverse *m*; *adj* inverse; **in** ~ **ratio to** en raison inverse de
**inversion** *n* inversion *f*; *mus* renversement *m*
**invert** *n* inverti -e; *vt* intervertir, renverser; ~ **ed commas** guillemets *mpl*
**invertebrate** *n* invertébré *m*; *adj* invertébré
**invest** *vt* (money) investir, placer; *mil* investir; *fig* (clothes) revêtir; (endow) investir; *vi* (money) placer de l'argent, investir
**investigate** *vt* examiner, sonder, enquêter sur
**investigation** *n* examen *m*, enquête *f*, investigation *f*
**investigator** *n* investigateur -trice
**investiture** *n* investiture *f*
**investment** *n* investissement *m*, placement *m*; *mil* investissement *m*; investiture *f*
**investor** *n* investisseur *m*; (shareholder) actionnaire
**inveterate** *adj* invétéré, acharné; ~ **liar** fieffé menteur
**invidious** *adj* propre à susciter la jalousie; (task) ingrat
**invigilate** *vt* (examination) surveiller; *vi* être de surveillance à un examen
**invigilation** *n* surveillance *f* d'un examen
**invigilator** *n* surveillant -e à un examen
**invigorate** *vt* revigorer, fortifier, tonifier, vivifier
**invigorating** *adj* tonifiant
**invigoration** *n* revigoration *f*
**invincibility** *n* invincibilité *f*
**invincible** *adj* invincible
**inviolability** *n* inviolabilité *f*
**inviolable** *adj* inviolable
**inviolate** *adj* inviolé
**invisibility** *n* invisibilité *f*
**invisible** *adj* invisible; ~ **ink** encre *f* sympathique; ~ **mending** stoppage *m*
**invitation** *n* invitation *f*
**invite** *n coll* invitation *f*; *vt* inviter; (seek) demander, solliciter; (provoke) appeler, chercher; ~ **in** inviter à entrer; ~ **out** inviter à sortir; ~ **over** inviter à venir
**inviting** *adj* invitant, attrayant, engageant; (food) alléchant, appétissant
**invocation** *n* invocation *f*
**invocatory** *adj* invocatoire
**invoice** *n* facture *f*; *vt* facturer
**invoke** *vt* invoquer; demander l'aide de; (spirits) évoquer

**involuntary** adj involontaire

**involve** vt (entangle) impliquer, entraîner, mêler; (imply) entraîner, nécessiter

**involved** adj compliqué, complexe; **be ~ être en jeu; be ~ in** être mêlé à

**involvement** n participation f; (commitment) engagement m, rôle m

**invulnerability** n invulnérabilité f

**invulnerable** adj invulnérable

**inward** adj intérieur; (mind, soul) intime; (towards the interior) vers l'intérieur; adv **~ s** vers l'intérieur; **turn ~ s upon oneself** rentrer en soi-même

**inwardly** adv intérieurement, au-dedans, à l'intérieur; (privately) secrètement

**inwards** adv see **inward**

**iodine** n iode m; **tincture of ~** teinture f d'iode

**iodize** vt ioder

**iodoform** n iodoforme m

**ion** n phys ion m

**Ionian** adj ionien -ienne

**Ionic** adj archi ionique

**ionic** adj phys ionique

**ionization** n ionisation f

**ionize** vt ioniser

**ionosphere** n ionosphère f

**iota** n iota m, brin m

**I.O.U.** n reconnaissance f de dette(s)

**ipecacuanha** n ipéca m

**Iran** n Iran m

**Iranian** n Iranien -ienne; (language) iranien m; adj iranien -ienne

**Iraq** n Iraq m

**Iraqi** n Irakien -ienne; adj irakien -ienne

**irascibility** n irascibilité f

**irascible** adj irascible, colérique

**irate** adj courroucé, furieux -ieuse

**ire** n courroux m, colère f, ire f

**Ireland** n Irlande f; **Northern ~** Irlande f du Nord; **Republic of ~** République f d'Irlande

**iridescence** n chatoiement m

**iridescent** adj irisé

**iridium** n iridium m

**iris** n bot + anat iris m

**Irish** n (language) irlandais m; **the ~** les Irlandais; adj irlandais; **~ stew** ragoût m de mouton à l'irlandaise

**Irishman** n Irlandais m

**Irishwoman** n Irlandaise f

**irk** vt ennuyer, contrarier, embêter

**irksome** adj ennuyeux -euse, assommant

**iron** n fer m; (tool) fer m; (clothes) fer m à repasser; (golf) fer m; sl pétard m; **~ s** (fetters) fers mpl, chaînes fpl; (for legs) entraves fpl; **have many ~ s in the fire** avoir beaucoup d'affaires en train; **man of ~** homme m de fer; **scrap ~** ferraille f; **strike while the ~ is hot** battre le fer pendant qu'il est chaud; **the ~ has**

entered his soul (bitterness) il est plein d'amertume; (grief) il a la mort dans l'âme; adj de fer; chem ferreux -euse; **the Iron Age** l'âge m de fer; pol **~ curtain** rideau m de fer; **~ lung** poumon m d'acier; **~ rations** vivres mpl de réserve; vt repasser, donner un coup de fer à; **~ out** (creases) faire disparaître au fer; fig (difficulties) aplanir, faire disparaître

**ironclad** n naut cuirassé m

**iron-founder** n fondeur m

**iron-grey** n + adj gris fer invar

**ironic, ironical** adj ironique

**ironing** n repassage m; **~ board** planche f à repasser

**ironist** n ironiste

**ironmaster** n maître m de forges

**ironmonger** n quincaillier; **~ 's shop** quincaillerie f

**ironmongery** n quincaillerie f

**ironware** n quincaillerie f

**ironwork** n ferronerie f; **wrought ~** ferronerie f d'art; **~ s** usine f sidérurgique

**irony** n ironie f

**irradiate** vt (expose to radiation) irradier; fig illuminer; vi irradier, émettre de la lumière

**irradiation** n irradiation f, illumination f

**irrational** adj irrationnel -elle; (person) pas rationnel -elle; (belief) déraisonnable, absurde

**irrationality** n irrationalité f

**irrationalize** vt rendre irrationnel -elle

**irrealizable** adj irréalisable

**irreclaimable** adj incorrigible; (land) incultivable

**irrecognizable** adj impossible à reconnaître

**irreconcilable** adj irréconciliable; (hostile) implacable; incompatible

**irrecoverable** adj irrécupérable; irréparable

**irrecusable** adj irrécusable

**irredeemable** adj irrémédiable; comm non remboursable

**irredentism** n irrédentisme m

**irreducible** adj irréductible

**irrefutable** adj irréfutable, irrécusable

**irregular** adj irrégulier -ière, asymétrique; (conduct) déréglé

**irregularity** n irrégularité f, asymétrie f

**irrelevance** n manque m d'à-propos, manque m de rapport

**irrelevant** adj sans rapport, hors de propos

**irreligion** n irreligion f

**irreligious** adj irreligieux -ieuse

**irremediable** adj irrémédiable

**irremovable** adj immuable; (official, judge) inamovible

**irreparable** adj irréparable

555

**irreplaceable** adj irremplaçable
**irrepressible** adj irrépressible, irrésistible
**irreproachable** adj irréprochable
**irresistibility** n état m d'être irrésistible
**irresistible** adj irrésistible
**irresolute** adj irrésolu, indécis
**irresoluteness, irresolution** n irrésolution f, hésitation f
**irresolvable** adj qu'on ne peut pas résoudre
**irrespective** adj ~ of sans tenir compte de
**irresponsibility** n irresponsabilité f
**irresponsible** adj irréfléchi, inconsidéré; irresponsable
**irresponsive** adj qui réagit peu; peu aimable
**irresponsiveness** n réserve f; manque m d'amabilité
**irretrievable** adj irréparable, irrémédiable; (lost) introuvable
**irreverence** n irrévérence f
**irreverent** adj irrévérencieux -ieuse
**irreversibility** n irréversibilité f
**irreversible** adj irréversible
**irrevocability** n irrévocabilité f
**irrevocable** adj irrévocable
**irrigable** adj irrigable
**irrigate** vt irriguer
**irrigation** n irrigation f
**irrigator** n (machine) irrigateur m
**irritability** n irritabilité f, irascibilité f
**irritable** adj irritable, irascible, coléreux -euse
**irritant** n irritant m; adj irritant
**irritate** vt irriter, agacer
**irritating** adj irritant, agaçant
**irritation** n irritation f
**irruption** n irruption f
**isinglass** n cul gélatine f
**Islam** n Islam m
**Islamic** adj islamique
**island** n île f; small ~ îlot m; traffic ~ refuge m; adj insulaire
**islander** n insulaire, habitant -e d'une île
**isle** n île f
**islet** n îlot m
**ism** n pej théorie f, doctrine f
**isobar** n isobare f
**isolate** vt isoler
**isolation** n isolement m; solitude f
**isolationism** n isolationnisme m
**isolationist** n isolationniste
**isosceles** adj isocèle
**isotherm** n isotherme f
**isotope** n isotope m
**Israel** n Israël m
**Israeli** n Israélien -ienne; adj israélien -ienne
**Israelite** n Israélite

**issue** n (publication) sortie f, parution f; (distributing) livraison f, émission f; (copy) numéro m; (problem, question) problème m, question f, sujet m; (result) issue f, résultat m; med écoulement m; leg descendance f, progéniture f; at ~ sous discussion; cloud the ~ brouiller les cartes; evade the ~ prendre la tangente; join ~ with engager une controverse avec; make an ~ of sth monter qch en épingle; point at ~ point controversé; vt (book) publier, faire paraître; (give out) distribuer, mettre en circulation, émettre, fournir; vi (originate) émaner, descendre
**isthmus** n isthme m
**it** n coll perfection f, idéal m; sl sex-appeal m; (game) you're ~ c'est toi le chat; coll abbr vermouth italien; pron il, elle; (accusative case) le, la, (before vowel) l'; (dative case) lui; impers il, ce, cela, ça; above ~ au-dessus; below ~ au-dessous; coll be with ~ être dans le vent; coll have had ~ être fichu; coll have ~ in for s/o avoir une dent contre qn; coll have what ~ takes être à la hauteur; let's face ~ regardons les choses en face, pour dire vrai; of ~ en; to ~ y; coll you'll catch ~, you're for ~ tu vas écoper
**Italian** n Italien -ienne; (language) italien m; adj italien -ienne
**italic** adj print italique; npl ~s italique m
**italicize** vt mettre (imprimer) en italique
**itch** n démangeaison f; désir m, envie f; vi éprouver des démangeaisons; avoir très envie
**itchy** adj qui démange; coll have ~ feet avoir la bougeotte; coll have ~ fingers avoir les doigts collants
**¹item** n (article) article m; (in programme) numéro m; (agenda) question f, numéro m
**²item** adv de plus; comm item
**itemize** vt détailler, spécifier
**iterate** vt répéter
**iterative** adj itératif -ive
**itinerant** adj itinérant, errant
**itinerary** n itinéraire m
**its** poss adj son (f sa, pl ses)
**itself** pron lui-même m, elle-même f
**ivory** n ivoire m; (colour) ivoire m; coll ivories (piano) touches fpl; sl dents fpl; sl (dice) dés mpl; sl (billiard balls) boules fpl de billard; Ivory Coast Côte f d'Ivoire; coll black ~ esclaves pl de l'Afrique noire
**ivy** n lierre m; US Ivy League ensemble m de certaines grandes universités de l'est des États-Unis
**izard** n isard m

# J

**jab** *n* coup *m* de pointe; *coll* piqûre *f*; (boxing) coup droit; *vt* pousser, donner un coup de doigt à; (stab) poignarder; (boxing) lancer un coup droit à

**jabber** *vi* jacasser, bavarder

**jabbering** *n* jacasserie *f*, bavardage *m*

**jabot** *n* jabot *m*

**jacaranda** *n bot* jacaranda *m*

**jack** *n* mot cric *m*; (cards) valet *m*; (bowls) cochonnet *m*; *elect* fiche *f* d'alimentation; (flag) drapeau *m*; ~ **of all trades** homme *m* à tout faire; **Jack Tar** matelot *m*; **before you can say Jack Robinson** tout de suite, en un clin d'œil; **every man** ~ chacun, tous; **Union Jack** drapeau *m* britannique; *vt* ~ **up** soulever avec un cric; (prices) faire monter; *coll* renoncer, plaquer

**jackal** *n* chacal *m* (*pl* chacals)

**jackanapes** *n* polisson *m*

**jackass** *n* âne *m*; *coll* crétin *m*

**jackboot** *n* botte *f* à l'écuyère

**jackdaw** *n* choucas *m*

**jacket** *n* (man) veston *m*, veste *f*; (woman) jaquette *f*; (book) couverture *f*; (boiler, tank, etc) enveloppe *f*; (potato) peau *f*, pelure *f*; **potatoes baked in their** ~**s** pommes de terre *fpl* en robe de chambre

**jack-in-office** *n coll pej* petit fonctionnaire satisfait, rond-de-cuir *m* (*pl* ronds-de-cuir) qui joue à l'important

**jack-in-the-box** *n* diable *m* à ressort

**jack-knife** *n* couteau *m* de poche; (dive) saut *m* de carpe; *vi* (trailer) se mettre en travers

**jack-o'-lantern** *n* feu follet

**jackpot** *n* (cards) pot *m*; gros lot; *coll* **hit the** ~ gagner le gros lot, avoir de la veine

**Jacobean** *adj* de l'époque de Jacques I<sup>er</sup> (d'Angleterre)

**Jacobite** *n* Jacobite

**jactation** *n* vantardise *f*

**¹jade** *n* (horse) haridelle *f*; (whore) prostituée *f*

**²jade** *n* jade *m*; *adj* (colour) jade; ~ **green** vert jade *invar*

**jag** *n* pointe *f*, saillie *f*; *sl* cuite *f*; *vt* déchirer, déchiqueter

**jagged** *adj* déchiqueté, dentelé

**jaguar** *n* jaguar *m*

**jail** *n see* **gaol**

**jailer** *n see* **gaoler**

**jalopy** *n coll* vieux tacot

**jalousie** *n* jalousie *f*

**¹jam** *n* confiture *f*; ~ **jar** pot *m* à confiture; ~ **roll** roulé *m* à la confiture; ~ **session** séance *f* de jazz improvisé; ~ **tart** tarte *f* à la confiture; **money for** ~ de l'argent gagné sans peine

**²jam** *n* foule *f*; (traffic) embouteillage *m*, bouchon *m*; *coll* (tight spot) pétrin *m*; ~ **full** plein à craquer; *vt* (squeeze) serrer, écraser; (wedge) coincer; (block) bloquer; (gun) enrayer; (thrust into) enfoncer, fourrer; (obstruct) encombrer; (with traffic) embouteiller; *rad* brouiller; ~ **the brakes on** bloquer les freins; *vi* (crowd) s'entasser; (become stuck) se bloquer, se coincer; (gun) s'enrayer

**Jamaica** *n* Jamaïque *f*

**Jamaican** *n* Jamaïquain -e; *adj* jamaïquain

**jamb** *n bui* jambage *m*, montant *m*

**jamboree** *n* (scouts) jamboree *m*; grande fête

**jamming** *n rad* brouillage *m*

**jangle** *n* cliquetis *m*, bruit confus; dispute *f*; *vt* faire cliqueter, faire faire un bruit de ferraille à; *vi* retentir avec un bruit de ferraille

**janissary** *n* janissaire *m*

**janitor** *n* portier *m*, gardien *m*; concierge

**Jansenism** *n* Jansénisme *m*

**January** *n* janvier *m*

**Jap** *n coll abbr* Japonais -e

**Japan** *n* Japon *m*

**japan** *n* laque *m*; *vt* laquer

**Japanese** *n* Japonais -e; (language) japonais *m*; *adj* japonais

**jape** *n coll* farce *f*, blague *f*

**japonica** *n* cognassier *m* du Japon

**¹jar** *n* pot *m*; (earthenware) jarre *f*; (glass) bocal *m*

**²jar** *n* (sound) son discordant; (shock) choc *m*, secousse *f*; *vt* (shake) ébranler; ~ **on** agacer, irriter; *vi* (sound) faire un bruit discordant, grincer; (vibrate) vibrer; (colour) jurer; *mus* détonner; (ideas) se heurter

**jargon** *n* jargon *m*; charabia *m*

**jarring** *adj* discordant, rauque; irritant; (colour) qui jure

**jasmine** *n* jasmin *m*

**jasper** *n* jaspe *m*

**jaundice** *n* jaunisse *f*; *fig* amertume *f*, jalousie *f*

**jaundiced** adj amer -ère, aigri; jaloux -ouse; **have a ~ view of things** voir les choses en noir; **with a ~ eye** d'un mauvais œil

**jaunt** n balade f; vi aller se balader

**jauntiness** n désinvolture f, insouciance f; (swagger) crânerie f

**jaunty** adj désinvolte, insouciant; (swaggering) crâneur -euse

**javelin** n javelot m

**jaw** n mâchoire f; sl (sermon) laïus m; coll (chat) causette f; **~s** gueule f; mech mâchoires fpl; vt coll sermonner; vi coll faire un sermon; coll (chat) bavarder

**jaw-bone** n (os m) maxillaire m

**jay** n geai m

**jay-walker** n piéton indiscipliné

**jazz** n jazz m; adj de jazz; vt arranger en style de jazz; sl **~ up** animer, rajeunir; vi danser sur un rythme de jazz

**jazzy** adj de jazz; (colour) tapageur -euse

**jealous** adj jaloux -ouse; (watchful) vigilant

**jealousness** n jalousie f

**jealousy** n jalousie f

**jeans** n blue-jean m, jean m; (overalls) bleu m de travail

**jeep** n jeep f

**jeer** n sarcasme m, raillerie f; vt huer; vi railler, huer; **~ at** insulter, se moquer de

**jeering** adj railleur -euse, moqueur -euse

**Jehovah** n Jéhovah m; **~'s witness** témoin m de Jéhovah

**jejune** adj ennuyeux -euse; (meagre) maigre

**jell** vi cul épaissir; coll prendre tournure

**jellied** adj en gelée

**jelly** n cul gelée f; sl gélignite f

**jelly-fish** n méduse f

**jemmy** n pince-monseigneur f (pl pinces-monseigneur)

**jeopardize** vt mettre en danger, exposer à des risques, compromettre

**jeopardy** n danger m, péril m; **in ~** menacé, en péril

**jeremiad** n jérémiade f

**jerk** n secousse f, saccade f; med crispation nerveuse; sl pauvre type m; coll **physical ~s** gymnastique f; vt secouer, donner une secousse à; vi cahoter; **~ along** avancer par saccades

**jerkily** adv par saccades

**jerkin** n blouson m; hist justaucorps m

**jerky** adj saccadé

**Jerry** n coll Fritz m invar

**jerry** n coll Jules m, pot m de chambre

**jerry-builder** n constructeur m de maisons en carton-pâte

**jerry-built** adj construit en carton-pâte

**jerry-can** n jerrycan m

**Jersey** n Jersey f

**jersey** n tricot m; vache f de Jersey

**Jerusalem** n Jérusalem f; **~ artichoke** topinambour m

**jest** n plaisanterie f; **in ~** pour rire; vi plaisanter

**jester** n hist bouffon m; plaisantin m

**Jesuit** n Jésuite m

**jesuitical** adj jésuitique

¹**jet** n jais m; adj de jais

²**jet** n (spurt) jet m, giclée f; aer avion m à réaction, jet m; (burner) brûleur m; mot gicleur m; **~ engine** moteur m à réaction, réacteur m; **~ fighter** chasseur m à réaction; **~ lag** décalage m horaire; **~ set** clientèle f des jets; vt faire gicler, faire jaillir; vi gicler, jaillir; voyager en jet

**jet-black** adj noir comme (du) jais

**jet-propelled** adj à réaction

**jet-propulsion** n propulsion f à réaction

**jetsam** n naut objets jetés à la mer (pour alléger un navire); fig rebut m

**jettison** vt naut jeter par dessus bord, se délester de; aer larguer; fig abandonner, se délester de

**jetty** n embarcadère m, débarcadère m, jetée f

**Jew** n Juif (f Juive); coll pej avare m, grippe-sou m (pl grippe-sou(s))

**jewel** n bijou m, joyau m; (watch) rubis m; fig perle f, trésor m; vt sertir

**jeweller** n bijoutier m, joaillier m; **~'s shop** bijouterie f, joaillerie f

**jewellery** n bijouterie f, bijoux mpl

**Jewess** n Juive f

**jew's harp** n guimbarde f

¹**jib** n naut foc m; coll **the cut of one's ~** sa tournure

²**jib** vi renâcler, répugner; (horse) se refuser

**jib-boom** n naut gui m de beaupré, bout-dehors m (pl bouts-dehors) de foc

**jibe** n + vi see gibe

**jiffy** n coll instant m; coll **in a ~** en moins de deux

**jig** n (dance) gigue f; mech (template) gabarit m; (sieve) tamis m; vt mech tamiser; vi danser la gigue, sautiller

¹**jigger** n mech tamis m

²**jigger** n zool pou m des sables

**jiggered** adj coll étonné; **well! I'll be ~!** ça alors!

**jiggery-pokery** n manigances fpl

**jiggle** vt secouer légèrement

**jigsaw** n mech scie f à chantourner; (puzzle) puzzle m

**jilt** vt laisser tomber, rompre avec

**Jim Crow** n US politique f raciste envers les noirs; obs zool nègre m

**jimjams** npl coll délirium m tremens;

have the ~ avoir les chocottes, avoir le trac

**jingle** n (noise) tintement m, cliquetis m; (verse) petit couplet; (advertising) couplet m publicitaire; vt faire tinter; vi tinter

**jingo** n chauvin m; coll by ~! nom d'une pipe!

**jingoism** n chauvinisme m

**jingoistic** adj chauvin

**jink** vi se faufiler; sp faire une esquive

**jinks** npl coll high ~ ébats bruyants

**jinx** n coll porte-guigne m invar

**jitney** n US coll pièce f de cinq cents; adj US coll bon marché

**jitter** vi coll avoir la frousse

**jitterbug** n boogie-woogie m; fig frous-sard -e; vi danser le boogie-woogie

**jitters** npl coll frousse f, trac m

**jittery** adj coll froussard

**jiu-jitsu** n see ju-jutsu

**jive** n swing m; vi danser le swing

**job** n (piece of work) travail m, tâche f; (employment) poste m, travail m, coll boulot m; (difficulty) mal m, peine f; coll (criminal act) combine f, vol m; ~ lot objets divers; coll ~ s for the boys des planques fpl pour les petits copains; a good ~! à la bonne heure!; have a ~ doing sth avoir du mal à faire qch; just the ~! juste ce qu'il faut!; it's a bad ~ c'est une sale affaire; it's a good ~ that c'est une chance que; know one's ~ connaître son affaire; coll on the ~ occupé; out of a ~ en chômage; put up ~ coup monté; sl the blonde ~ over there isn't bad elle n'est pas mal la nana blonde en face; vt (work) sous-traiter; travailler à la pièce, faire de petits travaux; faire le courtier en bourse; (peculate) détour-ner des fonds publics

**jobber** n (Stock Exchange) inter-médiaire m; (piece-worker) ouvrier -ière à la pièce; pej tripoteur -euse

**jobbery** n tripotage m (de fonds publics)

**jobbing** n travail m à la pièce; tripotage m (de fonds publics); (Stock Exchange) activité f de courtier; ~ gardener jar-dinier -ière à la journée

**jockey** n jockey m; **Jockey Club** Jockey-Club m; vt manœuvrer; vi intriguer, manœuvrer

**jock-strap** n suspensoir m

**jocose** adj enjoué, facétieux -ieuse, jovial

**jocular** adj enjoué, facétieux -ieuse, jovial

**jocularity** n jovialité f

**jocund** adj jovial, joyeux -euse

**jocundity** n jovialité f

**jodhpurs** n jodhpurs mpl, culotte f de cheval

**jog** n secousse f, cahot m; (elbow) coup m de coude; vt secouer, pousser; ~ s/o's memory rafraîchir la mémoire de qn; vi sp faire du jogging; ~ along aller son chemin

**jogging** n sp jogging m

**joggle** vt secouer; vi branler

**jog-trot** n petit trot

**John** n Jean m; ~ **Bull**, US ~ **Doe** = Monsieur Dupont, Monsieur Durand

**john** n US cabinets mpl

**join** n ligne f de raccord; (sewing) couture f; vt joindre, unir, relier; (become member of) devenir membre de, s'inscrire à, adhérer à; (meet) re-joindre; (go into the company of) aller avec; vi se joindre, s'unir, se rejoindre

**joiner** n menuisier m

**joinery** n menuiserie f

**joint** n anat + carp articulation f; cul rôti m; coll (bar, restaurant, etc) bistrot m, boîte f; (night club) boîte f de nuit; sl (drugs) joint m; clip ~ endroit m (boîte f) où l'on se fait estamper; anat **out of** ~ démis, luxé; fig disloqué; **put s/o's nose out of** ~ défriser qn, évincer qn; adj commun, réuni; vt joindre, articuler

**jointed** adj articulé; (rod, etc) démon-table; **double** ~ désarticulé

**jointly** adv en commun, conjointement

**joint-stock** n ~ **company** société f par actions

**jointure** n douaire m

**joist** n solive f

**joke** n plaisanterie f, blague f; (trick) tour m; (laughing-stock) risée f; **no** ~ une affaire sérieuse; **practical** ~ farce f; **the** ~ **is that** le plus drôle c'est que; vi plaisanter, blaguer; coll **you must be joking!** tu veux rire!, tu plaisantes!

**joker** n blagueur -euse; (cards) joker m

**jollification** n réjouissances fpl

**jollity** n gaieté f

**jolly** adj gai, enjoué; agréable; adv coll drôlement; sl vachement; vt enjôler, flatter

**jolt** n secousse f, choc m, coup m; vt secouer, cahoter; vi cahoter

**Jonah** n Jonas m; porte-malheur m invar

**jonquil** n bot jonquille f, narcisse m

**josh** n US coll mise f en boîte; canular m; vt mettre en boîte; faire un canular à; vi blaguer

**joss-stick** n bâton m d'encens

**jostle** n bousculade f; vt bousculer; vi se bousculer, se cogner

**jot** n iota m, brin m; vt ~ **down** noter

**jotter** n cahier m, bloc-notes m invar

**jottings** npl notes fpl

**journal** n (diary) journal m; (newspaper) journal m; (periodical) revue f; naut livre m de bord
**journalese** n pej jargon m journalistique
**journalism** n journalisme m
**journalist** n journaliste
**journalistic** adj journalistique
**journey** n voyage m; (distance travelled) trajet m, parcours m; vi voyager
**journeyman** n compagnon m
**joust** n joute f; vi jouter
**Jove** n Jupiter m; coll by ~ ! mon Dieu!, sapristi!
**jovial** adj jovial, enjoué
**joviality** n jovialité f
**jowl** n (jaw) mâchoire f; (cheek) joue f; (flabby cheek) bajoue f; (cattle) fanon m; **cheek by ~** côte à côte
**joy** n joie f, bonheur m; ~ **s** plaisirs mpl; **get no ~** ne rien gagner; iron **I wish you ~** je vous souhaite bien du plaisir
**joyful** adj joyeux -euse
**joyless** adj morne, sans joie
**joyous** adj joyeux -euse
**joyousness** n joie f, bonheur m
**joy-ride** n coll virée f, balade f
**joystick** n aer manche m à balai
**jubilant** adj radieux -ieuse, débordant de joie, triomphant, allègre
**jubilate** vi se réjouir, triompher
**jubilation** n jubilation f, exultation f, allégresse f
**jubilee** n eccles jubilé m; **diamond ~** soixantième anniversaire m; **golden ~** cinquantième anniversaire m; **silver ~** vingt-cinquième anniversaire m
**Judaic** adj judaïque
**Judaism** n judaïsme m
**Judas** n Judas m; traître m, judas m
**judas** n (peephole) judas m
**judge** n juge m; connaisseur m; **be a good ~ of** s'y connaître en; **sober as a ~** pas ivre du tout; vt juger, estimer, considérer; vi juger, penser
**judicatory** n tribunal m, cour f; adj judiciaire
**judicature** n justice f; (judges) magistrature f; (system) organisation f judiciaire
**judicial** adj leg judiciaire; fig juste, impartial; **~ murder** assassinat légal
**judicious** adj judicieux -ieuse
**judo** n judo m
**jug** n pot m, cruche f, broc m; sl (prison) taule f; vt cul cuire à l'étuvée; coll (imprison) coffrer; **~ged hare** civet m de lièvre
**jugful** n contenu m d'un pot
**juggernaut** n (lorry) mastodonte m; fig force meurtrière
**juggins** n niais -e, cruche f
**juggle** vt jongler avec; vi jongler

**juggler** n jongleur -euse, prestidigitateur -trice
**jugglery** n jonglerie f, tours mpl de passe-passe
**Jugoslav, Yugoslav** n Yougoslave; adj yougoslave
**Jugoslavia, Yugoslavia** n Yougoslavie f
**jugular** n jugulaire f; adj jugulaire
**juice** n jus m; physiol suc m; coll elect courant m
**juiciness** n juteux m
**juicy** adj juteux -euse; (story) savoureux -euse; (spicy story) salé
**jujube** n jujube m
**ju-jutsu, jiu-jitsu** n jiu-jitsu m
**jukebox** n juke-box m
**julep** n sirop m; US **mint ~** bourbon glacé à la menthe
**July** n juillet m
**jumble** n mélange m, fouillis m; **~ sale** vente f d'objets usagés; vt mélanger, brouiller
**jumbo** n (child language) éléphant m; **~ jet** avion géant, Boeing m 747
**jump** n saut m; (nervous movement) sursaut m; vt sauter, franchir d'un bond; vi bondir; (nervousness) sursauter, tressauter; **~ at** sauter sur; **~ down** descendre d'un bond; **~ on** s/o prendre qn à partie; **~ the gun** partir avant le départ; **~ the lights** passer au rouge; **~ the rails** dérailler; **~ up and down** sautiller
**jumped-up** adj parvenu, prétentieux -ieuse
**jumper** n pullover m; naut vareuse f
**jumpy** adj nerveux -euse
**junction** n jonction f; (road) bifurcation f; (crossroads) carrefour m; (railway) embranchement m; (rivers) confluent m; (station) gare f de correspondance; elect **~ box** boîte f de dérivation
**juncture** n jointure f; fig conjoncture f; **at this ~** maintenant
**June** n juin m
**jungle** n jungle f
**junior** n cadet -ette; adj plus jeune, cadet -ette; (subordinate) subalterne; US **John Smith ~** John Smith fils
**juniper** n genévrier m
**¹junk** n ferraille f, vieilleries fpl, bric-à-brac m invar; fig âneries fpl; sl (drugs) camé f
**²junk** n (boat) jonque f
**junket** n cul lait caillé m
**junketing** n bringue f; US voyage m (banquet m) aux frais de la princesse
**junkie** n sl drogué -e, camé -e, toxicomane
**junta** n junte f
**Jurassic** adj jurassique
**juridical** adj juridique

**jurisdiction** n juridiction f
**jurisprudence** n jurisprudence f
**jurist** n juriste m, légiste m
**juror** n juré m, femme jurée
¹**jury** n jury m, jurés mpl
²**jury** adj naut improvisé, de fortune
¹**just** adj juste, équitable, mérité, légitime
²**just** adv exactement, juste, parfaitement, précisément; (nearly) de justesse; (quite) juste; (simply) tout simplement; (absolutely) tout simplement; ~ **about here** à peu près ici; ~ **as** tout aussi; ~ **look!** regardez un peu ça!; ~ **now** tout à l'heure; en ce moment; ~ **the same** tout de même; **have** ~ venir de; **it's** ~ **as well!** heureusement!; **it's** ~ **one of those things** c'est la vie; **that's** ~ **the point!**

justement!
**justice** n justice f; équité f; (magistrate) juge m; **do oneself** ~ se montrer à sa juste valeur
**justiciary** n justicier -ière
**justifiable** adj justifiable
**justification** n justification f
**justificative** adj justificatif -ive
**justify** vt justifier, légitimer, prouver
**justly** adv avec raison
**jut** vi faire saillie, dépasser; ~ **out** dépasser, saillir
**jute** n jute m
**juvenile** n adolescent -e, jeune; adj juvénile; pej puéril; ~ **delinquency** délinquence f juvénile
**juvenilia** n œuvres fpl de jeunesse
**juxtapose** vt juxtaposer
**juxtaposition** n juxtaposition f

# K

**Kaffir** n Cafre
**kale** n chou frisé (d'Écosse)
**kaleidoscope** n kaléidoscope m
**kaleidoscopic** adj kaléidoscopique
**kangaroo** n kangourou m
**kaolin** n geol kaolin m
**kapok** n kapok m, capoc m
**karate** n karaté m
**kedge** n ancre f de touée
**keel** n quille f; fig navire m; vi ~ **over** chavirer
**keen** adj aiguisé, affilé, tranchant; (cold, mind, feelings) vif (f vive); fig ardent, acharné, intense; enragé; ~ **appetite** appétit dévorant; coll **be** ~ **on s/o** avoir le béguin pour qn; **be** ~ **on sth** être enthousiaste de qch; **have a** ~ **ear** avoir l'ouïe fine
**keenly** adv avidement, vivement
**keenness** n acuité f; (cold) âpreté f; ardeur f, enthousiasme m; (mind) finesse f
**keep** n donjon m; nourriture f; coll **for** ~ **s** pour de bon; **300 francs a week and his** ~ 300 francs par semaine logé et nourri; vt garder; (promise) tenir; (rules, etc) suivre, observer; (preserve) préserver, protéger, défendre; (festival) célébrer; (maintain) maintenir, en-

tretenir; (retain) conserver; (reserve) retenir, réserver; (prevent) empêcher; (delay) retarder; ~ **an appointment** aller à un rendez-vous; (not to miss) ne pas manquer à un rendez-vous; ~ **away** tenir éloigné; ~ **back** retenir; (hide) cacher; ~ **company with** fréquenter; ~ **down** réprimer; (prices) maintenir bas; ~ **from** empêcher de; ~ **in** tenir enfermé; (school) mettre en retenue; ~ **off** éloigner; (repel) repousser; ~ **on** (retain) garder; ~ **one's hand in** s'entretenir la main; ~ **one's temper** ne pas s'emporter; ~ **out** empêcher d'entrer; ~ **s/o waiting** faire attendre qn; ~ **sth from s/o** cacher qch à qn; ~ **under** tenir dans la soumission; ~ **up** (hold up) soutenir; (price) maintenir; (appearances) sauver; (maintain) entretenir; (keep from going to bed) faire veiller; vi (last) se garder, se conserver; (stay) rester, se tenir; coll ~ **at it** travailler ferme; ~ **away** rester éloigné; ~ **back** rester en arrière; ~ **down** se tapir; ~ **from** s'abstenir de; ~ **off** se tenir à l'écart; ~ **off the grass** défense de marcher sur le gazon; ~ **on** (doing) continuer (à faire); (go forward) avancer; (stay fixed on) tenir; ~ **out** rester dehors; ~ **straight on** continuer tout droit; ~ **to** s'en tenir à, se conformer à; ~ **together** rester ensemble; ~ **to one-self** faire bande à part, se tenir à l'écart; ~ **to the right** tenir la droite; ~ **up with** marcher de front avec; suivre; ~ **up with the times** être de son temps

**keeper** n garde m, gardien m; surveillant m; (museum) conservateur m

**keeping** n garde f; **in** ~ **with** en rapport avec; **in safe** ~ sous bonne garde

**keepsake** n souvenir m

**keg** n caque f, baril m; (beer) (bière f) pression f

**kelp** n varech m

**ken** n connaissance f

**kennel** n niche f; (dogs' home) ~s chenil m

**kerb** n rebord m du trottoir; bord m, bordure f

**kerbstone** n rebord m du trottoir

**kerchief** n fichu m

**kernel** n amande f; fig noyau m

**kerosene** n kérosène m

**kestrel** n crécerelle f

**ketch** n ketch m

**ketchup** n ketchup m

**kettle** n bouilloire f; **a pretty** ~ **of fish!** voilà une belle affaire!

**kettledrum** n timbale f

¹**key** n clef f, clé f; (piano, typewriter) touche f; mus ton m; mech clavette f; ~ **money** pas m de porte; **under lock and** ~ sous clef; adj essentiel -ielle; ~ **person** personnage m clef; vt mus ~ **up** accorder; ~ **ed up** tendu

²**key** n îlot m à fleur d'eau

**keyboard** n clavier m

**keyhole** n trou m de serrure

**keynote** n ton m; fig idée principale

**key-ring** n porte-clefs m invar

**keystone** n clef f de voûte

**khaki** n kaki m; adj kaki invar

**kibbutz** n (pl **kibbutzim**) kibboutz m

**kibosh** n sl bêtises fpl; sl **put the** ~ **on** mettre fin à

**kick** n coup m de pied; (gun) recul m; (thrill) plaisir violent; **for** ~s histoire de rire; **free** ~ coup franc; **penalty** ~ coup m de pénalité; vt donner un coup de pied à; ~ **a goal** marquer un but; ~ **one's heels** poireauter; ~ **out** chasser à coups de pied; sl ~ **s/o up the arse** botter les fesses à qn; coll ~ **the bucket** mourir, coll crever; ~ **up a row** faire du tapage; vi donner des coups de pied; (gun) reculer; (horse, etc) ruer; ~ **against** regimber contre; ~ **off** donner le coup d'envoi

**kick-off** n coup m d'envoi

¹**kid** n chevreau m; coll (child) gosse,

mioche m; ~ **brother** petit frère: **handle s/o with** ~ **gloves** ménager qn

²**kid** vt coll faire marcher, tromper

**kid-glove** adj délicat

**kidnap** vt enlever, kidnapper

**kidnapper** n ravisseur -euse, kidnappeur -euse

**kidnapping** n enlèvement m, vol m d'enfant

**kidney** n anat rein m; cul rognon m; **of the same** ~ du même acabit

**kidney-bean** n haricot m

**kill** n mise f à mort; (hunting) tableau m (de chasse); vt tuer, abattre; (destroy) détruire; (sound) amortir; ~ **off** exterminer; ~ **or cure remedy** remède m héroïque; ~ **two birds with one stone** faire d'une pierre deux coups; coll **be dressed to** ~ être en grand tralala

**killer** n tueur -euse; meurtrier -ière

**killer-whale** n épaulard m

**killing** n tuerie f; (Stock Exchange) **make a** ~ faire un grand bénéfice; adj meurtrier -ière; (work) tuant; (joke) tordant; coll crevant

**killjoy** n rabat-joie m invar, trouble-fête m invar

**kiln** n four m

**kilo** n kilo m

**kilocycle** n rad + elect kilohertz m

**kilogram(me)** n kilogramme m, kilo m

**kilolitre** n kilolitre m

**kilometre** n kilomètre m

**kilowatt** n kilowatt m

**kilowatt-hour** n kilowatt-heure m (pl kilowatts-heures)

**kilt** n kilt m

**kimono** n kimono m

**kin** n parents mpl; parenté f, famille f; **inform the next of** ~ prévenir la famille

¹**kind** n genre m, sorte f, espèce f; (nature) nature f; coll ~ **of** en quelque sorte; **in a** ~ **of way** en quelque sorte; **nothing of the** ~ rien de la sorte; **of its** ~ dans son genre; **pay in** ~ payer en nature; **repay s/o in** ~ rendre à qn la monnaie de sa pièce

²**kind** adj bon (f bonne), aimable, gentil -ille, bienveillant; **give my** ~ **regards to** faites mes amitiés à; **it's very** ~ **of you** c'est très aimable à vous

**kindergarten** n école maternelle, jardin m d'enfants

**kind-hearted** adj bienveillant; **be** ~ avoir bon cœur

**kindle** vt allumer, enflammer; susciter; vi prendre feu, s'enflammer

**kindling** n allumage m; bois m d'allumage

**kindly** adj bon (f bonne), aimable, bienveillant; adv avec bonté; ~ **close the**

**door** veuillez fermer la porte
**kindness** *n* bonté *f*, amabilité *f*; service *m*
**kindred** *n* parenté *f*, parents *mpl*; *adj* du même genre, apparenté; ~ **spirit** âme *f* sœur
**kinetic** *adj* cinétique
**kinetics** *npl* cinétique *f*
**king** *n* roi *m*; (draughts) dame *f*
**kingdom** *n* royaume *m*; **animal** ~ règne animal; **United Kingdom** Royaume-Uni
**kingfisher** *n* martin-pêcheur *m* (*pl* martins-pêcheurs)
**kingly** *adj* royal, de roi
**king-pin** *n* cheville ouvrière
**kingship** *n* royauté *f*
**king-size(d)** *adj* géant
**kink** *n* nœud *m*; faux pli; lubie *f*
**kinky** *adj* (rope) noué; (hair) crépu; *coll* (person) bizarre, pas normal
**kinsfolk** *npl* parents *mpl*
**kinship** *n* parenté *f*
**kinsman** *n* parent *m*
**kinswoman** *n* parente *f*
**kiosk** *n* kiosque *m*
**kip** *n coll* plumard *m*; *vi* se pieuter
**kipper** *n* kipper *m*
**kirk** *n Scots* église *f*
**kiss** *n* baiser *m*; ~ **of life** bouche à bouche *m*; *vt* embrasser, donner un baiser à, baiser; ~ **the dust** mordre la poussière
**kiss-curl** *n* accroche-cœur *m*
**kisser** *n sl* gueule *f*
**kissing** *n* baisers *mpl*, embrassement *m*
**kit** *n* effets *mpl*; *mil* (equipment) *m*; bagage *m*; outils *mpl*; (assembly) kit *m*; **repair** ~ nécessaire *m* de réparation
**kit-bag** *n* sac *m* de voyage; *mil* ballot *m*
**kitchen** *n* cuisine *f*; ~ **utensils** batterie *f* de cuisine; **soup** ~ soupe *f* populaire; **thieves'** ~ repaire *m* de voleurs
**kitchenette** *n* petite cuisine
**kitchen-garden** *n* jardin potager
**kitchen-maid** *n* fille *f* de cuisine
**kite** *n orni* milan *m*; cerf-volant *m* (*pl* cerfs-volants); *fig* **fly a** ~ lancer un ballon d'essai, tâter le terrain
**kith** *n* ~ **and kin** amis *mpl* et parents *mpl*, famille *f*
**kitten** *n* chaton *m*; petit(e) chat(te)
**¹kitty** *n see* **kitten**
**²kitty** *n* cagnotte *f*
**klaxon** *n* klaxon *m*
**kleptomania** *n* kleptomanie *f*
**kleptomaniac** *n* kleptomane
**knack** *n* don *m*; chic *m*; tour *m* de main
**knacker** *n* abatteur *m* de chevaux, équarrisseur *m*
**knapsack** *n* havresac *m*
**knave** *n* fripon *m*, coquin *m*; (cards)

**valet** *m*
**knavery** *n* fourberie *f*
**knavish** *adj* fourbe, de coquin
**knead** *vt* pétrir; (clay) travailler
**kneading-trough** *n* pétrin *m*
**knee** *n* genou *m*; **on one's** ~ s à genoux; *vt* pousser du genou
**knee-breeches** *npl* culotte courte
**knee-cap** *n anat* rotule *f*
**knee-deep** *adj* + *adv* jusqu'aux genoux, à hauteur du genou
**kneel** *vi* s'agenouiller, se mettre à genoux
**kneeler** *n eccles* agenouilloir *m*
**kneeling** *n* agenouillement *m*; *adj* agenouillé
**knell** *n* glas *m*
**knickerbockers** *npl* culotte bouffante; knickerbockers *mpl*
**knickers** *npl* culotte *f*; pantalon *m* de femme
**knick-knack** *n* (cheap) colifichet *m*; bibelot *m*
**knife** *n* couteau *m*; *surg* bistouri *m*; **have one's** ~ **into** s/o s'acharner contre (après) qn; **war to the** ~ guerre *f* à outrance; *vt* donner un coup de couteau à; poignarder
**knife-edge** *n* arête *f* en lame de couteau
**knife-grinder** *n* rémouleur *m*
**knife-rest** *n* porte-couteau *m*
**knife-sharpener** *n* affiloir *m*, fusil *m*
**knight** *n* chevalier *m*; (chess) cavalier *m*; *vt* créer chevalier
**knight-errant** *n* chevalier errant
**knighthood** *n* chevalerie *f*; titre *m* de chevalier
**knightly** *adj* chevaleresque
**knit** *vt* tricoter; joindre, unir; ~ **one's brows** froncer les sourcils; *vi* tricoter; ~ **together** se souder
**knitting** *n* tricot *m*; tricotage *m*; soudure *f*
**knitting-machine** *n* machine *f* à tricoter
**knitting-needle** *n* aiguille *f* à tricoter
**knob** *n* bosse *f*; bouton *m*; (door) poignée *f*; (walking-stick) pomme *f*
**knobb(l)y** *adj* noueux -euse
**knock** *n* coup *m*, heurt *m*; **hear a** ~ entendre frapper; *vt* frapper, heurter; *coll* critiquer; ~ **about** maltraiter, malmener; *sl* ~ **back** s'envoyer; ~ **down** renverser, abattre; (at auction) adjuger; ~ **in** enfoncer; défoncer; ~ **off** faire tomber de; achever; *sl* faucher; ~ **out** faire sortir; supprimer; mettre knock-out; éliminer; ~ **over** renverser, faire tomber; *coll* ~ **up** construire rapidement; (awaken) réveiller; *vi* frapper, taper; cogner; ~ **about** bourlinguer; ~ **against** se heurter contre; *coll* ~ **off** débrayer

**knockabout** n bateleur m, clown m; adj bruyant, violent

**knock-down** adj (price) minimum; de réclame

**knocker** n marteau m (de porte)

**knock-kneed** adj cagneux -euse

**knock-out** n knock-out m

**knoll** n tertre m, monticule m

**knot** n nœud m; groupe m; vt nouer, faire un nœud à; vi se nouer

**knotty** adj noueux -euse; difficile

**know** vt (facts) savoir; connaître; reconnaître; distinguer; ~ **best** être le meilleur juge de; ~ **better than to** se garder de, être trop avisé pour; ~ **how to do sth** savoir faire qch; ~ **of** connaître; connaître de réputation; avoir entendu parler de; **don't I** ~ **it!** à qui le dites-vous!; **get to** ~ apprendre à connaître; faire la connaissance de; **let s/o** ~ faire savoir à qn; **not that I** ~ pas que je sache

**knowable** adj connaissable; reconnaissable

**know-all** n personne f qui prétend tout savoir

**know-how** n connaissance f technique

**knowing** adj malin (f maligne), rusé; **without my** ~ à mon insu

**knowingly** adv sciemment, à bon escient

**knowledge** n connaissance f; savoir m, connaissances fpl; **not to my** ~ pas que je sache; **without my** ~ à mon insu

**knowledgeable** adj bien informé

¹**knuckle** n jointure f du doigt; ~ **of veal** jarret m de veau

²**knuckle** vi ~ **down** s'y mettre; ~ **under** se soumettre

**knucklebone** n osselet m

**knuckleduster** n coup-de-poing (pl coups-de-poing) américain

**knurl** n mech molette f

**koala, koolah** n zool koala m

**kohlrabi** n bot chou-rave m (pl choux-raves)

**Koran** n Coran m

**Korean** adj coréen -éenne

**kosher** adj kascher invar, cascher invar

**kow-tow** vi se prosterner, s'aplatir

**Kremlin** n Kremlin m

**kudos** n gloire f, gloriole f

**kummel** n kummel m

# L

**la** n mus la m

**lab** n labo m

**label** n étiquette f; vt étiqueter

**labial** adj labial

**laboratory** n laboratoire m; ~ **assistant** laborantin -e

**laborious** adj laborieux -ieuse, travailleur -euse; pénible

**labour** n travail m, labeur m, peine f; main d'œuvre f; pol **Labour** les travaillistes; ~ **exchange** bureau public de placement; adj pol travailliste; vt ~ **a point** s'étendre sur qch; vi travailler, peiner; ~ **under a delusion** être victime d'une illusion

**laboured** adj pénible; travaillé

**labourer** n travailleur m, manœuvre m

**labouring** adj ouvrier -ière

**labour-saving** adj qui allège le travail

**labrador** n terre-neuve m invar

**laburnum** n bot cytise m

**labyrinth** n labyrinthe m, dédale m

**lace** n dentelle f; (shoe) lacet m; galon m; vt lacer; garnir de dentelles; (drink) arroser

**lacerate** vt lacérer, déchirer

**laceration** n lacération f, déchirure f

**lachrymose** adj larmoyant

**lack** n manque m, défaut m; **for** ~ **of** faute de; vt manquer de; vi manquer

**lackadaisical** adj apathique, languissant

**lackey** n laquais m

**lacking** adj dépourvu (de), dénué (de)

**laconic** adj laconique

**lacquer** n laque f, peinture laquée; vt laquer; vernir

**lacrosse** n crosse canadienne

**lacuna** n lacune f

**lad, laddie** n garçon m, jeune homme m

**ladder** n échelle f; (stocking) maille f qui file

**ladder-proof** adj indémaillable

**laddie** n see lad

**lade** vt naut charger

**laden** adj chargé

**la-di-da** adj coll affecté

**lading** n naut bill of ~ connaissance m

**ladle** n louche f; vt ~ out servir

**lady** n dame f; dame bien élevée; **Lady Day** Fête f de l'Annonciation; ~ **doctor** femme f médecin; **ladies and gentlemen!** mesdames, mesdemoiselles, messieurs!; **ladies' man** homme galant; **Our Lady** Notre-Dame f, la Sainte Vierge; **young ~** demoiselle f, jeune femme f

**ladybird**, US **lady-bug** n coccinelle f; coll bête f à bon Dieu

**lady-in-waiting** n dame f d'atour

**lady-killer** n tombeur m de femmes

**ladylike** adj distingué, comme il faut, de dame

**ladyship** n your (her) ~ madame la comtesse (marquise, etc)

**¹lag** n coll old ~ repris m de justice

**²lag** vi traîner, rester en arrière; retarder

**³lag** vt garnir, envelopper

**lager** n bière blonde allemande

**laggard** n traînard -e; adj lent, paresseux -euse

**lagging** n enveloppe f, garniture f; enveloppe isolante

**lagoon** n lagune f; (coral) lagon m

**laid** adj coll ~ **back** calme, imperturbable

**lair** n repaire m, tanière f

**laissez-faire**, **laisser-faire** n laisser-faire m invar

**laity** n les laïques mpl

**lake** n lac m

**lake-dwelling** adj lacustre

**lakeland** n la Région des Lacs (en Angleterre)

**lama** n lama m

**lamb** n agneau m; ~ **chop** côtelette f d'agneau; bot ~'s **lettuce** mâche f; vi mettre bas

**lame** adj boiteux -euse; (crippled) estropié; (excuse) faible, pauvre; **be ~** boiter; vt rendre boiteux -euse; estropier

**lameness** n boitement m; (excuse) faiblesse f

**lament** n lamentation f; vt pleurer; vi se lamenter

**lamentable** adj lamentable, déplorable

**lamentation** n lamentation f

**lamented** adj **late ~** regretté

**laminate** vt laminer; diviser en lamelles

**lamination** n laminage m

**lamp** n lampe f; mot phare m; (cycle) lanterne f; **ceiling ~** plafonnier m; **table ~** lampe f de table; **wall ~** applique f

**lamp-bracket** n applique f

**lamp-holder** n douille f

**lamplighter** n allumeur m de réverbères

**lampoon** n libelle m, satire f; vt lancer des satires contre

**lamp-post** n réverbère m

**lamprey** n lamproie f

**lampshade** n abat-jour m invar

**lance** n lance f; vt med (abscess) percer

**lancer** n mil lancier m

**lancet** n med lancette f, bistouri m

**land** n terre f; (country) pays m; (ground) terrain m, sol m; **dry ~** terre f ferme; **native ~** patrie f; vt mettre à terre, débarquer; ~ **a blow** porter un coup; **be ~ed with sth** rester avec qch sur les bras; vi atterrir; descendre à terre, débarquer; tomber, retomber; (on moon) alunir; ~ **on one's feet** retomber sur ses pieds

**land-agent** n intendant m d'un domaine

**landed** adj (proprietor) terrien -ienne; (property) foncier -ière

**landfall** n naut arrivée f en vue de terre

**land-girl** n femme f agriculteur

**landing** n naut débarquement m; mise f à terre; aer atterrissage m; (on sea) amerrissage m; (on moon) alunissage m

**landing-craft** n péniche f de débarquement

**landing-ground** n terrain m d'atterrissage

**landing-net** n épuisette f

**landing-stage** n débarcadère m; ponton m

**landlady** n propriétaire f; logeuse f; hôtelière f; patronne f

**land-line** n câble aérien, câble m téléphonique

**landlocked** adj enfermé dans les terres

**landlord** n propriétaire m; aubergiste m; hôtelier m

**landlubber** n terrien -ienne; marin m d'eau douce

**landmark** n point m de repère; borne f, limite f; fig événement marquant

**landowner** n propriétaire foncier

**land-rover** n voiture f tout-terrain invar; tout-terrain m invar

**landscape** n paysage m

**landscape-painter** n paysagiste m

**landslide** n éboulement m; pol victoire écrasante

**landslip** n glissement m de terrain

**lane** n chemin m; ruelle f; naut route f de navigation; (for traffic) voie f; **three-~ motorway** autoroute f à trois voies

**lang syne** n Scots le temps jadis; adv jadis, autrefois

**language** n langue f; (expression) langage m; **bad ~** langage grossier; **modern ~s** langues vivantes

**languid** adj languissant, langoureux -euse

**languish**

**languish** *vi* languir
**languishing** *adj* languissant
**languor** *n* langueur *f*
**lank** *adj* maigre; pendant; (animal) efflanqué
**lanky** *adj* maigre, grand et maigre
**lantern** *n* lanterne *f*; *naut* fanal *m*; **Chinese ~** lampion *m*; **magic ~** lanterne *f* magique
**lanyard** *n* aiguillette *f*; *naut* cordon *m*
**¹lap** *n* giron *m*; (clothing) pan *m*, basque *f*; **in the ~ of the gods** impossible à prévoir; **on s/o's ~** sur les genoux de qn
**²lap** *n* tour *m* de piste, circuit *m*
**³lap** *vt* laper; **~ up** avaler; *vi* clapoter
**⁴lap** *vt* **~ over** recouvrir; **~ round** enrouler autour; *vi* **~ over** chevaucher
**lapdog** *n* chien *m* d'appartement; bichon -onne
**lapel** *n* revers *m*
**lapidary** *n* lapidaire *m*; *adj* lapidaire
**Lapp** *n* Lapon -one; *adj* lapon -one
**lapse** *n* (time) cours *m*; laps *m* de temps; (mistake) erreur *f*, faute *f*; *leg* déchéance *f*; *vi* manquer à ses devoirs; faire un faux pas; *leg* tomber en désuétude
**lapsed** *adj* déchu; (ticket) périmé; *leg* périmé; caduc (*f* caduque)
**lapwing** *n* vanneau *m*
**larceny** *n* larcin *m*, vol *m*
**larch** *n* *bot* mélèze *m*
**lard** *n* saindoux *m*; *vt* larder
**larder** *n* garde-manger *m* invar
**large** *adj* grand; gros (*f* grosse); (extensive) étendu; considérable; (numerous) nombreux -euse; **~ sum** forte somme; **at ~** libre, en liberté; **grow ~** grandir; grossir; **in (a) ~ measure** en grande partie; **on a ~ scale** en grand; **set at ~** élargir
**large-hearted** *adj* magnanime; généreux -euse
**largely** *adv* en grande partie
**large-scale** *adj* grand
**largess(e)** *n* largesse *f*
**lariat** *n* lasso *m*
**¹lark** *n* *orni* alouette *f*; **sing like a ~** chanter comme un rossignol
**²lark** *n* *coll* rigolade *f*; **for a ~** pour s'amuser, histoire de rigoler; *vi coll* rigoler; faire des farces
**larkspur** *n* *bot* pied-d'alouette *m* (*pl* pieds-d'alouette)
**larva** *n* larve *f*
**laryngitis** *n* *med* laryngite *f*
**larynx** *n* *anat* larynx *m*
**lascivious** *adj* lascif -ive
**lasciviousness** *n* lasciveté *f*
**laser** *n* *phys* laser *m*
**¹lash** *n* coup *m* de fouet; (of whip) lanière *f*; (eye) cil *m*; *vt* fouetter, cingler; *vi* **~**

**~ out** (animal) ruer; **~ out against s/o** se déchaîner contre qn
**²lash** *vt* attacher, lier, ligoter; *naut* amarrer
**¹lashing** *n* coups *mpl* de fouet; **~s of** des masses de, des tas de; *adj* cinglant
**²lashing** *n* *naut* amarrage *m*
**lass** *n* *esp Scots* jeune fille *f*
**lassitude** *n* lassitude *f*
**lasso** *n* lasso *m*; *vt* prendre au lasso
**¹last** *n* (shoe) forme *f*
**²last** *adj* dernier -ière; **~ but one** avant-dernier -ière; **~ night** hier soir; (in the night) cette nuit; **~ year** l'année passée (dernière); **at ~** enfin; **in the ~ resort** en dernier ressort; **the ~ straw** le bouquet; *fig* **the ~ word** le dernier cri; **to the ~** jusqu'au bout; **we shall never hear the ~ of it** on ne nous le laissera pas oublier; *adv* la dernière fois
**³last** *vi* durer; **it will ~ me six months** ça me fera six mois
**lasting** *adj* durable; résistant
**lastly** *adv* en dernier lieu
**¹latch** *n* loquet *m*
**²latch** *vi coll* **~ on to sth** piger qch
**latch-key** *n* clef *f* de maison
**late** *adj* tard; (not on time) en retard; (delayed) retardé; tardif -ive; récent; (deceased) décédé, feu; (former) ancien -ienne; **it is getting ~** il se fait tard; **latest** dernier -ière; **of ~** dernièrement; *adv* tard; en retard; **get up ~** faire la grasse matinée; **see you later!** à tout à l'heure!; **sooner or later** tôt ou tard
**late-comer** *n* retardataire
**lately** *adv* dernièrement
**lateness** *n* retard *m*; heure tardive; arrivée tardive; (fruit) tardiveté *f*
**latent** *adj* latent; caché
**lateral** *adj* latéral
**latex** *n* *bot* latex *m*
**lath** *n* *bui* latte *f*
**lathe** *n* tour *m*
**lather** *n* mousse *f* de savon; (horse) écume *f*; *vt* savonner; *vi* mousser
**Latin** *n* (language) latin *m*; *adj* latin
**latitude** *n* latitude *f*
**latrine** *n* latrines *fpl*
**latter** *adj* dernier -ière; second; *pron* **the ~** celui-ci (*f* celle-ci, *mpl* ceux-ci)
**latterly** *adv* dernièrement
**lattice-window** *n* fenêtre treillagée
**lattice(-work)** *n* treillis *m*; *vt* treillisser, treillager
**Latvian** *adj* letton -on(n)e
**laud** *vt* louer
**laudable** *adj* louable, digne d'éloges
**laudanum** *n* laudanum *m*
**laudatory** *adj* élogieux -ieuse
**laugh** *n* rire *m*; **with a ~** en riant; *vi* rire; **~ at s/o** se moquer de qn; **~ at sth** rire

566

de qch; ~ **heartily** rire de bon cœur; ~ **in s/o's face** rire au nez de qn; ~ **sth off** tourner qch en plaisanterie; ~ **to oneself** rire tout bas; **burst out ~ing** éclater de rire; **don't make me ~!** laissez-moi rire!

**laughable** *adj* risible, ridicule

**laughing** *adj* rieur ( *f* rieuse); ~ **gas** gaz hilarant; **it's no ~ matter** il n'y a pas de quoi rire

**laughing-stock** *n* risée *f*

**laughter** *n* rire *m*, rires *mpl*; **roar with ~** rire aux éclats

¹**launch** *n* chaloupe *f*

²**launch** *vt* lancer; ~ **an attack** déclencher une attaque; *vi* ~ **out into** se lancer dans

**launching** *n* lancement *m*

**launching-pad** *n* aire *f* de lancement

**launder** *vt* blanchir

**launderette** *n* laverie *f* (automatique)

**laundering** *n* blanchissage *m*

**laundress** *n* blanchisseuse *f*

**laundry** *n* blanchisserie *f*; (linen, etc) linge *m*; (wash-place) buanderie *f*

**laureate** *n* + *adj* lauréat -e

**laurel** *n bot* laurier *m*; **rest on one's ~s** se reposer sur ses lauriers

**lava** *n* lave *f*

**lavatory** *n obs* cabinet *m* (de toilette), lavabo *m*; (W.C.) waters *mpl*, cabinets *mpl*, toilettes *fpl*

**lavender** *n* lavande *f*; ~ **water** eau *f* de lavande

**lavish** *adj* prodigue; abondant, somptueux -euse; *vt* prodiguer

**lavishness** *n* prodigalité *f*

**law** *n* loi *f*; (system of laws, profession) droit *m*; ~ **and order** ordre public; ~ **court** tribunal *m*; **be a ~ unto oneself** n'en faire qu'à sa tête; **be at ~** être en procès; **common ~** droit coutumier; **go to ~** avoir recours (recourir) à la justice; **lay down the ~** faire la loi; **she thinks she's above the ~** elle se croit tout permis; **study ~** étudier le droit, faire son droit

**law-abiding** *adj* respectueux -euse des lois

**law-breaker** *n* transgresseur *m*

**lawful** *adj* légal; licite, permis; légitime

**lawgiver** *n* législateur -trice

**lawless** *adj* sans loi; déréglé

**lawlessness** *n* dérèglement *m*, anarchie *f*

¹**lawn** *n* pelouse *f*, gazon *m*

²**lawn** *n* (textile) batiste *f*

**lawn-mower** *n* tondeuse *f*

**lawn-tennis** *n* tennis *m*, lawn-tennis *m*

**lawsuit** *n* procès *m*

**lawyer** *n* homme *m* de loi; juriste *m*; (solicitor) notaire *m*; (barrister) avocat -e

**lax** *adj* (person) négligent; (behaviour) relâché; (authority) mou ( *f* molle); (limp) flasque; **become ~** se relâcher

**laxative** *n* laxatif *m*; *adj* laxatif -ive

**laxity** *n* relâchement *m*

¹**lay** *n* lai *m*, chanson *f*

²**lay** *adj* laïque

³**lay** *vt* mettre, poser, placer; coucher; (eggs) pondre; (dust) abattre; (bet) parier; (fire) préparer; *sl* coucher avec; ~ **aside** mettre de côté; ~ **bare** mettre à nu; ~ **down** déposer, poser; (arms) rendre; (give up) renoncer à; (rules) établir; (ship) mettre en chantier; ~ **down the law** faire la loi; ~ **hold of** saisir; ~ **in** faire provision de; *fig* ~ **it on thick** y aller fort; ~ **off** licencier, congédier; ~ **out** arranger, disposer; (spend) dépenser; (corpse) faire la toilette de; *coll* étendre d'un coup; ~ **the table** mettre la table (le couvert); ~ **up** amasser; mettre en réserve; (car) remiser; (ship) désarmer; **be laid up** être alité; *vi coll* ~ **off** cesser

**layabout** *n* fainéant -e

**layby** *n* terre-plein *m* de stationnement; (railway) voie *f* de garage

¹**layer** *n* (stratum) couche *f*; (hen) pondeuse *f*; (plant) marcotte *f*; poseur -euse

²**layer** *vt hort* marcotter

**layman** *n* laïc *m*, laïque *m*

**lay-off** *n* mise *f* en chômage technique

**layout** *n* disposition *f*, arrangement *m*

**laze** *vi* paresser

**laziness** *n* paresse *f*

**lazy** *adj* paresseux -euse, indolent

**lazybones** *n* fainéant -e

¹**lead** *n* (metal) plomb *m*; sonde *f*; (pencil) mine *f*; *coll* **swing the ~** tirer au flanc

²**lead** *n* conduite *f*; *theat* premier rôle *m*; (dog) laisse *f*; *elect* câble *m*, branchement *m*; **give the ~** montrer la voie

³**lead** *vt* conduire, mener; guider; diriger, commander; (induce) porter; (cards) jouer; ~ **astray** égarer; ~ **away** emmener; ~ **back** ramener; ~ **on** entraîner; ~ **the way** montrer le chemin; ~ **to** amener à; *vi* mener; (cards) jouer le premier ( *f* la première); ~ **onto** donner sur

**leaden** *adj* de plomb

**leader** *n* conducteur -trice; guide *m*; chef *m*; (agitator) meneur -euse; (newspaper) article *m* de fond

**leadership** *n* direction *f*; conduite *f*

**leading** *adj* principal; premier -ière; ~ **article** article *m* de fond; ~ **idea** idée maîtresse; *theat* ~ **man** premier rôle

**leaf** *n* ( *pl* **leaves**) feuille *f*; (book) feuillet *m*; (door) battant *m*; (table) rallonge *f*;

take a ~ out of s/o's book prendre
exemple sur qn; **turn over a new ~**
changer de conduite; **turn over the
leaves of a book** feuilleter un livre
**leafless** *adj* sans feuilles
**leaflet** *n* feuillet *m*; (advertising) papillon *m*; *pol* tract *m*
**leafy** *adj* couvert de feuilles; feuillu
¹**league** *n* ligue *f*; *hist* League of Nations
Société *f* des Nations; **be in ~ with** être
ligué (de coalition) avec
²**league** *n* (distance) lieue *f*
³**league** *vi* ~ **together** se liguer
**leak** *n* fuite *f*; (water) écoulement *m*;
infiltration *f*; **have a ~** fuir; *coll* pisser;
**spring a ~** faire (une voie d')eau; *vt*
(news) laisser filtrer; *vi* fuir, avoir une
fuite; (ship) faire eau; prendre l'eau;
~ **out** s'ébruiter
**leakage** *n* fuite *f*; perte *f*
**leaky** *adj* qui fuit; (ship) qui fait eau; qui
laisse entrer l'eau
¹**lean** *vt* appuyer; *vi* s'appuyer; se pencher; s'adosser; ~ **back in one's chair**
se renverser dans son fauteuil; ~ **forward** se pencher en avant; *fig* ~ **over
backwards** faire le maximum de concessions
²**lean** *adj* maigre; (animal) efflanqué
**leaning** *n* penchant *m*; inclination *f*; *adj*
penché
**leanness** *n* maigreur *f*
**lean-to** *n* appentis *m*
**leap** *n* saut *m*, bond *m*; *vi* sauter, bondir;
~ **over** franchir d'un bond
**leap-frog** *n* saute-mouton *m*; *vi* jouer à
saute-mouton
**leap-year** *n* année *f* bissextile
**learn** *vt* apprendre; savoir
**learned** *adj* savant, érudit, instruit
**learner** *n* débutant -e
**learning** *n* science *f*, savoir *m*
**lease** *n* bail *m* (*pl* baux); concession *f*;
**take on a new ~ of life** renaître à la vie;
*vt* louer; (land) affermer
**leasehold** *n* tenure *f* à bail; *adj* tenu à bail
**lease-lend** *n* prêt-bail *m*
**leash** *n* laisse *f*; *vt* mettre à l'attache
**leasing** *n* location *f* à bail; (land)
affermage *m*
**least** *adj* moindre, plus petit; le moins
important; **at the very ~** tout au
moins; **not in the ~** pas le moins du
monde; **to say the ~** pour le moins;
*adv* le moins
**leather** *n* cuir *m*; **(fancy) ~ goods**
maroquinerie *f*; *vt* garnir de cuir;
(thrash) rosser
**leatherette** *n* similicuir *m*
**leather-neck** *n US sl* fusilier marin
**leathery** *adj* qui ressemble au cuir;
(meat) coriace

**leave** *n* permission *f*, autorisation *f*;
congé *m*; **by your ~** avec votre permission; **sick ~** congé *m* de maladie;
**take French ~** filer à l'anglaise;
~ **of s/o** prendre congé de qn; **take
one's ~** prendre congé; *vt* quitter;
laisser; partir de; (desert) abandonner;
(deposit) déposer; (bequeath) léguer;
~ **about** laisser traîner; ~ **behind**
laisser; oublier; ~ **go** lâcher; ~ **it to
me** laissez-moi faire; **be left** rester; **I ~
it to you** je m'en remets à vous; **three
from ten ~s seven** dix moins trois
égale (reste) sept; *vi* partir
**leaven** *n* levain *m*; *vt* faire lever
**leavings** *npl* restes *mpl*
**Lebanese** *n* Libanais -e; *adj* libanais
**Lebanon** *n* Liban *m*
**lecher** *n* débauché *m*
**lecherous** *adj* lascif -ive, débauché
**lechery** *n* lasciveté *f*
**lectern** *n* lutrin *m*
**lecture** *n* conférence *f*; *coll* semonce *f*;
**give a ~** faire une conférence; *vt* sermonner; faire la morale à; *vi* faire une
conférence (des conférences); faire un
cours
**lecturer** *n* conférencier -ière; (university)
maître *m* de conférences, chargé -e de
cours
**ledge** *n* rebord *m*; saillie *f*; (building)
corniche *f*
**ledger** *n* grand livre
**lee** *n* abri *m*; *naut* côté *m* sous le vent
**leech** *n* sangsue *f*
**leek** *n* poireau *m*
**leer** *n* mauvais regard; *vi* regarder d'un
air méchant; lancer des œillades
**lees** *npl* lie *f*; *fig* rebut *m*
**leeward** *adj* + *adv* sous le vent
**leeway** *n naut* dérive *f*; retard *m*; liberté
*f* d'action
**left** *n* gauche *f*; **keep to the ~** tenir la
gauche; **on the ~** à gauche; *adj* gauche
**left-hand** *adj* gauche; ~ **drive** conduite
*f* à gauche
**left-handed** *adj* gaucher -ère; ~ **compliment** compliment douteux
**leftist** *n* + *adj* gauchiste
**left-luggage office** *n* consigne *f*
**leftward** *adv* vers la gauche
**left-wing** *adj pol* de gauche
**leg** *n* jambe *f*; (animal) patte *f*; (chicken)
cuisse *f*; (mutton) gigot *m*; (furniture)
pied *m*; **be on one's ~s** être sur pied,
être debout; **pull s/o's ~** faire marcher
qn
**legacy** *n* legs *m*
**legal** *adj* légal; licite; ~ **department** service *m* du contentieux; ~ **document**
acte *m* authentique; **take ~ advice**
consulter un avocat

**legality** *n* légalité *f*
**legalize** *vt* légaliser, rendre légal
**legate** *n* légat *m*
**legatee** *n* légataire
**legation** *n* légation *f*
**legend** *n* légende *f*; inscription *f*; explication *f*
**legendary** *adj* légendaire
**legerdemain** *n* tour *m* de passe-passe; prestidigitation *f*
**leggings** *npl* jambières *fpl*, guêtres *fpl*
**legibility** *n* lisibilité *f*
**legible** *adj* lisible
**legion** *n* légion *f*; **they are ~** ils sont innombrables
**legislate** *vi* légiférer, faire des lois
**legislation** *n* législation *f*
**legislative** *adj* législatif -ive
**legislator** *n* législateur *m*
**legislature** *n* législature *f*
**legitimacy** *n* légitimité *f*
**legitimate** *adj* légitime
**legitimatize, legitimize** *vt* légitimer
**leg-pull** *n* mystification *f*
**leguminous** *adj* légumineux -euse
**leg-up** *n* **give s/o a ~** faire la courte échelle à qn; aider qn à monter en selle
**leisure** *n* loisir *m*; **~ hours** heures *fpl* de loisir, moments perdus
**leisurely** *adj* (person) qui n'est pas pressé; lent, mesuré
**leitmotiv** *n* leitmotiv *m*
**lemon** *n* citron *m*; **~ sole** limande *f*; **~ squash** citronnade *f*
**lemonade** *n* citronnade *f*; **fizzy ~** limonade *f*
**lemon-drop** *n* bonbon acidulé au citron
**lemon-squeezer** *n* presse-citron *m invar*
**lend** *vt* prêter; **~ a hand** prêter secours; **~ an ear** prêter l'oreille; **~ oneself to** se prêter à
**lender** *n* prêteur -euse
**lending-library** *n* bibliothèque *f* de prêt
**lend-lease** *n* prêt-bail *m*
**length** *n* longueur *f*; (time) durée *f*; (string) bout *m*; (material) métrage *m*; **at ~** enfin; **at full ~** d'un bout à l'autre; **at some ~** assez longuement; **fall full ~** tomber de tout son long; **go to great ~s** pousser les choses bien loin; **go to the ~ of doing sth** aller jusqu'à faire qch
**lengthen** *vt* allonger; rallonger; (time) prolonger; *vi* s'allonger; croître, grandir
**lengthways, lengthwise** *adv* en longueur; en long
**lengthy** *adj* long (*f* longue); qui traîne en longueur
**leniency** *n* indulgence *f*; clémence *f*
**lenient** *adj* indulgent; clément
**lens** *n* lentille *f*; *phot* objectif *m*

**Lent** *n* carême *m*
**Lenten** *adj* de carême
**lentil** *n* lentille *f*
**leopard** *n* léopard *m*; **American ~** jaguar *m*
**leopardess** *n* léoparde *f*
**leper** *n* lépreux -euse
**leprechaun** *n* lutin *m*
**leprosy** *n* lèpre *f*
**leprous** *adj* lépreux -euse
**lesbian** *n* lesbienne *f*; *adj* lesbien -ienne
**lesion** *n* lésion *f*
**less** *adj* moindre; plus petit; *adv* moins; **~ and ~** de moins en moins; **grow ~** diminuer, s'amoindrir; **he continued none the ~** il n'en continua pas moins; **nothing ~ than** rien moins que
**lessee** *n* locataire; tenancier -ière
**lessen** *vt* diminuer, amoindrir; *vi* diminuer, s'amoindrir, s'atténuer
**lesser** *adj* moindre; petit
**lesson** *n* leçon *f*; **let that be a ~ to you** que cela vous serve de leçon; **object ~** (school) leçon *f* de choses; exemple *m*; **private ~** leçon particulière
**lest** *conj* de peur (de crainte) que ... ne
**¹let** *n ar* empêchement *m*; (tennis, etc) balle *f* de filet
**²let** *n* location *f*; *vt* (allow) permettre, laisser; (hire out) louer; **~ alone** laisser tranquille; **~ down** laisser; laisser descendre; *fig* faire faux bond à; **~ go** lâcher, lâcher prise; **~ him come** qu'il vienne; **~ in** faire entrer; laisser passer; **~ off** (pardon) faire grâce à; (gun) tirer; (firework) faire partir; (cry) laisser échapper; *coll* **~ on about sth** aller dire qch; **~ oneself in for sth** s'engager à qch; **~ out** laisser sortir; (release) lâcher; (secret) trahir; (hire) louer; (fire) laisser éteindre; **~ s/o do sth** permettre à qn de faire qch; **~ s/o into the secret** mettre qn dans le secret; **~ s/o off from doing sth** dispenser qn de faire qch; **~'s see** voyons; **~ up** diminuer; **~ us go** allons; **~ us hear about it** racontez-nous cela; **~ us know** faites-nous savoir
**let-down** *n* déception *f*
**lethal** *adj* mortel -elle; **~ weapon** arme meurtrière
**lethargic** *adj* léthargique
**lethargy** *n* léthargie *f*
**letter** *n* lettre *f*; caractère *m*; **capital ~** majuscule *f*; **man of ~s** homme *m* de lettres; **small ~** minuscule *f*; *vt* mettre des lettres sur, graver avec des lettres
**letter-box** *n* boîte *f* aux lettres
**letter-card** *n* carte-lettre *f* (*pl* cartes-lettres)
**letterhead** *n* en-tête *m*
**lettering** *n* lettrage *m*

**letter-press** *n* impression *f* typographique; texte *m*
**lettuce** *n* laitue *f*, salade verte
**let-up** *n* diminution *f*
**leukaemia** *n med* leucémie *f*
**Levant** *n* Levant *m*
**level** *n* niveau *m*; **at eye ~** à la hauteur des yeux; **at ministerial ~** à l'échelon ministériel; **come down to s/o's ~** se mettre au niveau de qn; **on a ~ with** à la hauteur de; *archi* de plain-pied avec; **on the ~** à plat; *coll* de bonne foi; *mot* **speed on the ~** vitesse *f* en palier; *adj* de niveau, horizontal; (ground) uni; **~ with** à fleur de, au ras de; **be ~** être de niveau; **do one's ~ best** faire tout son possible; **keep a ~ head** garder son sang-froid; *vt* niveler, aplanir; (gun) pointer; (direct) diriger; (raze) raser; **~ an accusation** lancer une accusation; **~ out** égaliser
**level-crossing** *n* passage *m* à niveau
**level-headed** *adj* qui a la tête bien équilibrée
**levelling** *n* nivellement *m*
**lever** *n* levier *m*; **gear ~** levier *m* de vitesse; *vt* soulever (manœuvrer) au moyen d'un levier
**leverage** *n* force *f* de levier
**leveret** *n* levraut *m*
**leviathan** *n* Léviathan *m*
**levity** *n* légèreté *f*
**levy** *n* levée *f*; (tax) impôt *m*; *vt* lever; (tax) percevoir
**lewd** *adj* impudique; ignoble
**lewdness** *n* impudicité *f*
**lexicographer** *n* lexicographe *m*
**lexicography** *n* lexicographie *f*
**liability** *n* responsabilité *f*; (tendency) susceptibilité *f*, tendance *f*; **liabilities** dettes *fpl*, obligations *fpl*; **assets and liabilities** actif *m* et passif *m*; **be a ~** être un poids mort
**liable** *adj* responsable; sujet -ette, exposé; (likely) susceptible; **~ to tax** soumis à l'impôt
**liaise** *vi* effectuer la liaison, établir le contact
**liaison** *n* liaison *f*
**liar** *n* menteur -euse
**libel** *n* diffamation *f*; écrit *m* diffamatoire; *vt* diffamer
**libellous** *adj* diffamatoire
**liberal** *adj* libéral; d'esprit large; généreux -euse, prodigue; (plentiful) abondant; **Liberal** *n* + *adj pol* libéral -e
**liberalism** *n* libéralisme *m*
**liberality** *n* libéralité *f*; générosité *f*
**liberalize** *vt* libéraliser
**liberally** *adv* libéralement
**liberate** *vt* libérer; mettre en liberté, lâcher

**liberation** *n* libération *f*
**liberator** *n* libérateur -trice
**libertine** *n* libertin *m*, débauché *m*
**liberty** *n* liberté *f*; **at ~** en liberté; **be at ~ to do sth** être libre de faire qch; **take liberties** prendre des libertés; **take the ~ of doing sth** se permettre de faire qch
**libido** *n* libido *f*
**librarian** *n* bibliothécaire
**library** *n* bibliothèque *f*; **photographic ~** photothèque *f*; **public ~** bibliothèque municipale; **record ~** discothèque *f*
**libretto** *n* livret *m*
**licence** *n* permis *m*; (trade) patente *f*; (permission) permission *f*, autorisation *f*; (freedom) licence *f*; (immorality) débauche *f*; **car ~** carte grise; **driving ~** permis *m* de conduire; **game ~** permis *m* de chasse; **marriage ~** dispense *f* de bans
**license** *vt* accorder un permis (une patente) à; autoriser; **~d** patenté
**licensee** *n* détenteur -trice d'une patente; (pub, café) patron -onne
**licentious** *adj* licencieux -ieuse, dévergondé
**licentiousness** *n* licence *f*, dévergondage *m*
**lichen** *n* lichen *m*
**licit** *adj* licite
**lick** *n* coup *m* de langue; *coll* **at a great ~** à grande vitesse; *vt* lécher; *coll* battre; **~ up** laper; **that's got me ~ed** ça me dépasse
**licking** *n* léchage *m*; *coll* raclée *f*, défaite *f*
**lid** *n* couvercle *m*; (eye) paupière *f*; *coll* **that puts the ~ on it!** ça c'est le comble!
**lido** *n* lido *m*, piscine *f* en plein air
**¹lie** *n* mensonge *m*; **give s/o the ~** donner un démenti à qn; **tell ~s** mentir; **white ~** mensonge innocent; *vi* mentir
**²lie** *n* position *f*, disposition *f*; **~ of the land** configuration *f* du terrain; *vi* être couché (étendu); (be situated) se trouver; (consist) résider; **~ about** traîner; **~ asleep** être endormi; *naut* **~ at anchor** être à l'ancre; **~ down** se coucher, s'étendre; (rest) se reposer; **~ in** faire la grasse matinée; **~ in ambush** se tenir en embuscade; **~ in wait** guetter; **~ over** rester en suspens; *coll* **~ up** garder le lit; **ar ~ with** coucher avec; **a great future ~s before him** un grand avenir s'ouvre devant lui; **here ~s** ci-gît; **take sth lying down** se laisser faire; **the difference ...** la différence réside en ceci que ...; **time**

**lay heavy on his hands** le temps lui pesait
**lie-detector** *n* machine *f* à déceler le mensonge
**liege** *n hist* seigneur *m; adj* lige
**lie-in** *n coll* **have a ~** faire la grasse matinée
**lieutenant** *n* lieutenant *m*
**life** *n (pl* **lives)** vie *f;* (object) durée *f;* biographie *f;* **~ and soul of the party** boute-en-train *m invar* de la compagnie; **~ imprisonment** prison *f* à perpétuité; **a matter of ~ and death** une question de vie ou de mort; **at my time of ~** à mon âge; **early ~** enfance *f;* **flee for one's ~** se sauver à toutes jambes; **for ~** à vie; **from ~** d'après nature; **high ~** grande vie; *coll* **how's ~?** que devenez-vous?; **lay down one's ~** donner sa vie; **not on your ~!** jamais de la vie!; **put new ~ into** ranimer; **run for your lives!** sauve qui peut!; **save s/o's ~** sauver la vie à qn; **such is ~** c'est la vie, ainsi va la vie; **take one's ~** se suicider; **the prime of ~** la fleur de l'âge; **true to ~** tout à fait naturel -elle
**lifebelt** *n* ceinture *f* de sauvetage
**life-blood** *n fig* âme *f*
**lifeboat** *n* canot *m* de sauvetage
**lifebuoy** *n* bouée *f* de sauvetage
**life-cycle** *n* cycle *m* d'évolution
**life-giving** *adj* vivifiant
**life-guard** *n* garde *m* du corps
**life-jacket** *n* gilet *m* de sauvetage
**lifeless** *adj* sans vie, mort; sans vigueur, sans entrain
**lifelike** *adj* vivant, ressemblant
**lifelong** *adj* de toute la vie
**life-preserver** *n* casse-tête *m invar; US* ceinture *f* de sauvetage
**life-size** *adj* de grandeur naturelle
**lifetime** *n* vie *f;* **in my ~** de mon vivant
**lift** *n* haussement *m;* (in building) ascenseur *m;* **~ attendant** liftier -ière; **give s/o a ~** faire monter qn (dans sa voiture); **goods ~** monte-charge *m invar;* **hitch (thumb) a ~** faire de l'auto-stop; *vt* lever, soulever, élever; *agr* lever, arracher; *coll* voler; **~ one's hand against s/o** lever la main contre qn; **~ sth down** descendre qch; **~ up one's head** redresser la tête; *vi* (fog) se disperser, se lever
**liftboy, liftman** *n* liftier *m*
**lift-off** *n* lancement *m*
**ligament** *n anat* ligament *m*
¹**light** *n* lumière *f;* (day) jour *m;* lueur *f;* lampe *f,* bougie *f;* (match) feu *m;* (window) fenêtre *f;* (skylight) lucarne *f;* **according to one's ~s** selon ses lumières; **against the ~** à contre-jour;

by the **~ of** à la lumière de; **give ~** éclairer; **in this ~** sous cet angle; **it is ~** il fait jour; **navigation ~s** feux *mpl* de bord; **parking ~s** feux *mpl* de stationnement (position); **throw ~ on a matter** éclairer une question; **traffic ~s** feux *mpl* rouges, signaux lumineux; *adj* clair; bien éclairé; (hair) blond; *vt* allumer; illuminer, éclairer; *vi* s'allumer; prendre feu; s'éclairer; **~ up** (face) s'éclairer; *coll* allumer sa pipe; *coll* lit up éméché
²**light** *adj* léger -ère; (wind) faible; (easy) facile; **be a ~ sleeper** avoir le sommeil léger; **make ~ of** faire peu de cas de, traiter à la légère
³**light** *vi* se poser; **~ on** trouver, rencontrer, tomber sur
¹**lighten** *vt* éclairer; *vi* s'éclairer; (lightning) faire des éclairs
²**lighten** *vt* alléger; (relieve) soulager
¹**lighter** *n* briquet *m;* (person) allumeur -euse
²**lighter** *n naut* chaland *m,* péniche *f*
**light-fingered** *adj* aux doigts agiles
**light-headed** *adj* étourdi, écervelé
**light-hearted** *adj* enjoué, au cœur gai
**lighthouse** *n* phare *m*
**lighting** *n* éclairage *m,* allumage *m*
**lightness** *n* légèreté *f*
**lightning** *n* éclairs *mpl,* foudre *f;* **~ conductor** paratonnerre *m;* **~ strike** grève *f* surprise; **flash of ~** éclair *m; adj* rapide, foudroyant, éclair *invar*
**lights** *npl cul* mou *m*
**lightship** *n* bateau-phare *m (pl* bateaux-phares)
**lightweight** *n* (boxing) poids léger; *adj* léger -ère; *fig* insignifiant
**light-year** *n* année-lumière *f (pl* années-lumières)
¹**like** *n* pareil *m;* chose *f* semblable; *adj* semblable, pareil -eille; **tel** (*f* **telle**); (portrait) ressemblant; **~ father, ~ son** tel père, tel fils; *coll* **~ hell!** jamais de la vie!; **a man ~ him** un homme tel que lui; **do the ~** en faire autant; **he's ~ that** il est ainsi; **I never saw anything ~ that** je n'ai jamais rien vu de pareil; **look ~** ressembler à; **nothing ~ as** loin de; **sth ~ ten** à peu près dix; **that's just ~ a man** voilà bien les hommes; **that's just ~ him** c'est bien lui; **there's nothing ~ a good holiday** rien ne vaut de bonnes vacances; **very ~,** *prep* comme; probablement; **what's he ~?** comment est-il?; **what's it ~?** comment est-ce?; *adv* comme; probablement; *prep* comme
²**like** *n* **~s** goûts *mpl,* préférences *fpl; vt* aimer; (person) aimer bien; (food) trouver bon; **~ it or not** bon gré, mal

gré; ~ **to do sth** aimer (à) faire qch; **as much as you** ~ tant (autant) que vous voudrez; **do as one** ~**s** en faire à sa tête; **he would** ~ **nothing better** il ne demande pas mieux; **how do you** ~ **it?** comment le trouvez-vous?; **if you** ~ si vous voulez; **I** ~ **him** il me plaît, je le trouve sympathique

**likeable** *adj* sympathique, agréable

**likelihood** *n* probabilité *f*

**likely** *adj* probable, vraisemblable; ~ **to** susceptible de; *coll* **that's a** ~ **one!** en voilà une bonne!; *adv* **most** ~ très probablement

**like-minded** *adj* du même avis, partageant le même point de vue

**liken** *vt* comparer

**likeness** *n* ressemblance *f*; portrait *m*

**likewise** *adv* également, aussi, pareillement, de même

**liking** *n* goût *m*; penchant *m*; **acquire a** ~ **for sth** prendre goût à qch; **take a** ~ **to s/o** prendre qn en amitié

**lilac** *n* lilas *m*

**lilt** *n* rythme *m*, cadence *f*

**lily** *n* lis *m*; *US sl* tapette *f*; ~ **of the valley** muguet *m*; **water** ~ nénuphar *m*

**lily-livered** *adj* poltron -onne

**lily-white** *adj* blanc (*f* blanche) comme le lis

**limb** *n* membre *m*; (tree) branche *f*; ~ **of the law** homme *m* de loi; agent *m* de police; *coll* **out on a** ~ en plan

¹**limber** *n* avant-train *m*

²**limber** *vi* ~ **up** se dégourdir

**limbless** *adj* sans membres, sans bras ni jambes

**limbo** *n* limbes *mpl*; **descend into** ~ tomber dans l'oubli

¹**lime** *n* chaux *f*; **bird** ~ glu *f*; *vt* gluer

²**lime** *n* (tree) tilleul *m*; (fruit) lime *f*

**lime-kiln** *n* four *m* à chaux

**limelight** *n* in the ~ *fig* très en vue; sous les feux de la rampe

**limerick** *n* poème comique, souvent scabreux, en cinq vers

**limestone** *n* pierre *f* à chaux

**limey** *n US* (English sailor) marin anglais; *Aust sl* (Englishman) Anglais *m*

**limit** *n* limite *f*, borne *f*; *eng* tolérance *f*; *coll* **that's the** ~ ! ça c'est le comble!; *vt* limiter, borner

**limitation** *n* limitation *f*, restriction *f*

**limited** *adj* (mind, views) borné; ~ **edition** édition *f* à tirage restreint; ~ **liability company** compagnie *f* à responsabilité limitée

**limousine** *n* limousine *f*

¹**limp** *adj* flasque, mou (*f* molle)

²**limp** *n* boitement *m*; *vi* boiter, clopiner

**limpet** *n* patelle *f*; *coll fig* **cling like a** ~ être crampon *f invar*

**limpid** *adj* limpide

**limpidity** *n* limpidité *f*

**limpness** *n* mollesse *f*

**linchpin** *n eng* esse *f*, clavette *f* de bout d'essieu; *fig* clef *f* de voûte

**linctus** *n* sirop *m* pharmaceutique, sirop *m* pour la toux

**linden(-tree)** *n* tilleul *m*

¹**line** *n* ligne *f*; (wire) fil *m*; (row) rang *m*, rangée *f*; corde *f*; file *f*; (wrinkle) ride *f*; (drawing) trait *m*; (stroke) raie *f*; (transport) service *m*, ligne *f*; (railway) voie *f*; (poetry) vers *m*; (note) mot *m*; *geog* équateur *m*; (descent) lignée *f*; spécialité *f*, genre *m*; queue *f*, file *f*; ~ **drawing** dessin *m* au trait; ~ **of argument** raisonnement *m*; ~ **of business** partie *f*; **draw the** ~ **at sth** ne pas aller jusqu'à; **drop s/o a** ~ envoyer un petit mot à qn; **fall into** ~ **with** se conformer à; (paragraph) **first** ~ alinéa *m*; **leading** ~ article *m* de réclame; **main** ~ grande ligne; **marriage** ~**s** acte *m* de mariage; *vt* (paper) régler; (face) rider; ~ **up** aligner; *vi* ~ **up** s'aligner; **faire la queue**

²**line** *vt* doubler, fourrer; (edge) border; (pocket) remplir; garnir

**lineage** *n* lignée *f*

**lineament** *n* trait *m*

**linear** *adj* linéaire

**linen** *n* toile *f* (de lin); linge *m*; **table** ~ linge *m* de table; *adj* de toile

**liner** *n* transatlantique *m*, paquebot *m*

**linesman** *n* (sport) arbitre *m* de lignes; (railway) poseur *m* de lignes

**line-up** *n* alignement *m*, mise *f* en rangs

**linger** *vi* s'attarder, tarder; traîner; (sick person) languir, traîner; ~ **on** subsister

**lingerie** *n* lingerie *f*

**lingering** *adj* lent, languissant; ~ **death** mort lente; ~ **look** regard prolongé

**lingo** *n* langue *f* du pays; baragouin *m*

**lingua franca** *n* sabir *m*

**linguist** *n* linguiste

**linguistic** *adj* linguistique

**linguistics** *n* linguistique *f*

**liniment** *n* liniment *m*

**link** *n* chaînon *m*, maillon *m*; (chain) anneau *m*; lien *m*; *vt* relier, enchaîner; *vi* ~ **on to sth** s'unir à qch

**links** *npl* terrain *m* de golf

**linnet** *n orni* linotte *f*

**lino, linoleum** *n* linoléum *m*

**linseed** *n* graine *f* de lin; ~ **oil** huile *f* de lin

**lint** *n* tissu *m* de pansement, charpie *f*

**lintel** *n* linteau *m*

**lion** *n* lion *m*; *coll* célébrité *f*; ~ **cub** lionceau *m*

**lioness** *n* lionne *f*

**lion-hearted** *adj* au cœur de lion
**lionize** *vt coll* traiter comme une personne célèbre
**lip** *n* lèvre *f*; (animal) babine *f*; (cup) bord *m*; (jug) bec *m*; *coll* toupet *m*, insolence *f*; saillie *f*, rebord *m*; **hang on s/o's ~s** boire les paroles de qn; **he never opened his ~s** il n'a pas desserré les dents; **keep a stiff upper ~** rester impassible; **smack one's ~s** se lécher les babines
**lip-read** *vi* lire sur les lèvres
**lip-reading** *n* lecture *f* sur les lèvres
**lip-service** *n* **pay ~** payer de paroles
**lipstick** *n* bâton *m* de rouge; rouge *m* à lèvres
**liquefy** *vt* liquéfier; *vi* se liquéfier
**liqueur** *n* liqueur *f*
**liquid** *n* liquide *m*; *adj* liquide
**liquidate** *vt* liquider
**liquor** *n* boisson *f* alcoolique; *cul* eau *f* de cuisson; *US* alcool *m*; **in ~** ivre
**liquorice, licorice** *n* réglisse *f*
**Lisbon** *n* Lisbonne *f*
**lisp** *n* zézaiement *m*; *vt* + *vi* zézayer
**lissom** *adj* souple, agile
¹**list** *n* liste *f*, rôle *m*; **be on the danger ~** être dans un état grave; **mailing ~** liste *f* d'envoi; **waiting ~** liste *f* d'attente; *vt* cataloguer
²**list** *n naut* bande *f*; **have a ~** donner de la bande; *vi* donner de la bande
**listen** *vi* écouter; faire attention; **~ to** écouter
**listener** *n* auditeur -trice
**listless** *adj* apathique; nonchalant
**lists** *npl* lice *f*
**litany** *n* litanie *f*
**literacy** *n* aptitude *f* à lire et écrire
**literal** *adj* littéral; **in the ~ sense of the word** au sens propre du mot
**literally** *adv* littéralement; **take sth ~** prendre qch au pied de la lettre
**literary** *adj* littéraire
**literate** *adj* qui sait lire et écrire; (well-read) lettré
**literature** *n* littérature *f*; documentation *f*
**lithe** *adj* agile, souple
**litheness** *n* souplesse *f*
**lithograph** *n* lithographie *f*; *vt* lithographier
**Lithuania** *n* Lithuanie *f*
**Lithuanian** *n* Lithuanien -ienne; *adj* lithuanien -ienne
**litigate** *vi* plaider
**litigation** *n* litige *m*
**litre** *n* litre *m*
**litter** *n* (straw, vehicle) litière *f*; (refuse) papiers *mpl* sales; désordre *m*; (animals) portée *f*; *vt* mettre en désordre; **~ed with** encombré de

**litter-bin** *n* boîte *f* à ordures
**little** *n* peu, peu de; **a ~** un peu (de); **a ~ more** encore un peu; **think ~ of sth** faire peu de cas de qch; *adj* petit; **~ ways** manières *fpl*; **I know his ~ game** je sais ce qu'il manigance; **tiny ~** tout petit; *adv* peu; **~ by ~** peu à peu; **a ~** un peu; **for a ~ (while)** pendant un certain temps
**littleness** *n* petitesse *f*
**littoral** *n* littoral *m*
**liturgic(al)** *adj* liturgique
**liturgy** *n* liturgie *f*
**livable, liveable** *adj* vivable; (house, etc) habitable
**live** *vt* **~ a life of** mener une vie de; *coll* **~ it up** mener grand train; *vi* vivre; (dwell) demeurer, habiter; **~ on** continuer à vivre; **~ on sth** se nourrir de qch; **~ sth down** faire oublier qch; **~ well** faire bonne chère; **enough to ~ on** de quoi vivre; **one ~s and learns** qui vivra verra; *adj* vivant, en vie; *elect* en charge, sous tension; **~ broadcast** émission *f* en direct; **~ cartridge** cartouche chargée; *fig* **he's a ~ wire** il est dynamique
**livelihood** *n* vie *f*; gagne-pain *m invar*
**liveliness** *n* vivacité *f*, animation *f*
**livelong** *adj* **the ~ day** toute la journée
**lively** *adj* vif (*f* vive), animé, gai; **take a ~ interest in** s'intéresser vivement à
¹**liver** *n anat* foie *m*
²**liver** *n* personne *f* qui vit
**liveried** *adj* en livrée
**livery** *n* livrée *f*
**livid** *adj* livide, blême
**living** *n* vie *f*; *eccles* bénéfice *m*; **make a good ~** gagner bien sa vie; *adj* vivant, en vie; **~ or dead** mort ou vif; **~ wage** salaire minimum vital; **no one ~** personne au monde
**living-room** *n* salle *f* de séjour, living (-room) *m*
**living-space** *n* espace vital
**lizard** *n* lézard *m*
**llama** *n* lama *m*
**load** *n* charge *f*; (burden) fardeau *m*; **have a ~ on one's conscience** avoir un poids sur la conscience; **~s of** des quantités de; **that's a ~ off my mind** c'est un grand soulagement pour moi; **we have ~s of time** nous avons largement le temps; *vt* charger; (dice) piper; *vi* **~ up** prendre un chargement
**loaded** *adj* chargé; **~ question** question *f* piège; **~ up with** encombré de; **~ with cares** accablé de soucis
**loader** *n* chargeur *m*
**loadstone, lodestone** *n* aimant (naturel)
¹**loaf** *n* pain *m*, miche *f* (de pain); *coll*

tête f; coll use your ~ ! réfléchis un peu!

²**loaf** vi flâner; ~ **about** faire le (la) fainéant -e

**loafer** n fainéant -e, flâneur -euse; (shoe) mocassin m

**loam** n terre grasse, terre végétale

**loan** n prêt m; (borrowing) emprunt m; **on ~ from** prêté par; vt US + coll prêter

**loan-word** n mot m d'emprunt

**loath** adj be ~ **to do sth** répugner à faire qch; **nothing ~** très volontiers

**loathe** vt détester, avoir horreur de

**loathsome** adj odieux -ieuse, répugnant

**lob** n lob m; vt lober

**lobby** n vestibule m; (parliament) couloir m; pol groupe m de pression; US trust m; vt pol chercher à influencer; vi pol intriguer dans les couloirs de la Chambre

**lobe** n lobe m

**lobelia** n bot lobélie f

**lobster** n homard m

**lobster-pot** n casier m à homards

**local** n habitant -e de l'endroit (du pays); coll bistrot m du coin; adj local; ~ **government** administration locale; ~ **road** route départementale

**locality** n localité f, voisinage m; caractère local

**localize** vt localiser

**locate** vt découvrir; situer; localiser

**location** n (locating) repérage m; emplacement m, situation f; (S. Africa) réserve f indigène; cin be on ~ tourner hors des studios

**loch** n Scots lac m

¹**lock** n mèche f (de cheveux)

²**lock** n serrure f; (padlock) cadenas m; mot angle m de braquage; (wrestling) étreinte f; (waterway) écluse f; (gun) platine f; ~, **stock and barrel** tout sans exception; **under ~ and key** sous clef; (person) sous les verrous; vt fermer à clef; (wheels) bloquer; ~ **in** enfermer (à clef); ~ **out** empêcher d'entrer (en fermant la porte à clef); (industry) lockouter; ~ **up** mettre sous clef, enfermer; fermer à clef; (capital) immobiliser

**locker** n coffre m

**locket** n médaillon m

**lockjaw** n tétanos m, trismus m

**lock-keeper** n éclusier -ière

**locksmith** n serrurier m

**locomotion** n locomotion f

**locomotive** n locomotive f

**locum(-tenens)** n remplaçant -e; (doctor) suppléant -e

**locust** n criquet m

**locution** n locution f

**lode** n filon m

**lodestar** n étoile f polaire

**lodge** n loge f; **shooting** (**hunting**) ~ pavillon m de chasse; vt loger, héberger;

(deposit) placer; ~ **a complaint** porter plainte; vi se loger; ~ **with** s/o demeurer chez qn

**lodge-keeper** n concierge

**lodger** n locataire

**lodging** n logement m; ~s logement m, appartement meublé; **let** ~s louer des chambres; **live in furnished** ~s habiter en garni

**lodging-house** n hôtel garni

**loft** n grenier m, soupente f

**loftiness** n hauteur f; élévation f

**lofty** adj haut, élevé; (manner) hautain

¹**log** n (fire) bûche f; (timber) bille f; naut loch m

²**log** n logarithme m

³**log** vt noter, porter au journal

**loganberry** n ronce-framboise f (pl ronces-framboises)

**logarithm** n logarithme m

**log(-book)** n mot carnet m de route; (in France) carte grise; (ship) journal m de bord

**log-cabin** n cabane f en rondins

**loggerhead** n be at ~s **with** s/o être en désaccord avec qn

**loggia** n loggia f

**logic** n logique f

**logical** adj logique; (person) qui a de la logique

**logician** n logicien -ienne

**logistics** npl logistique f

**loin** n (lamb, veal) filet m; longe f (de veau); ~s reins mpl

**loin-cloth** n pagne m

**loiter** vi traîner, flâner; (linger) s'attarder

**loiterer** n flâneur -euse

**loitering** n flânerie f; vagabondage m

**loll** vt (head) laisser pendre; vi ~ **about** se vautrer; ~ **back** se renverser; ~ **out** pendre

¹**lolly, lollipop** n sucette f

²**lolly** n sl argent m; sl pognon m, sl fric m

**London** n Londres m; **Greater** ~ l'agglomération londonienne; adj londonien -ienne, de Londres

**Londoner** n Londonien -ienne

**lone** adj solitaire, seul; be a ~ **wolf** aimer agir seul

**loneliness** n solitude f

**lonely** adj solitaire, isolé

**lonesome** adj solitaire

¹**long** n before ~ avant peu; **for** ~ pendant longtemps; adj long (f longue); **a** ~ **time** longtemps; **be two metres** ~ avoir deux mètres de long; **get** ~ **er** rallonger; **how** ~ **is their garden?** quelle est la longueur de leur jardin?; **how** ~ **are the holidays?** quelle est la durée des vacances?; **in the** ~ **run** à la longue; **that's a** ~ **time ago** il y a longtemps de cela; adv longtemps; ~ **live the Queen!**

vive la Reine!; as ~ as tant que; **don't be** ~ dépêchez-vous, ne me faites pas attendre; **how** ~ **has he been here?** depuis combien de temps est-il ici?; **she won't be** ~ elle ne tardera pas; **so** ~ ! à bientôt!; **so** ~ **as** pourvu que; **they were not** ~ **in doing sth** ils eurent vite fait de faire qch

²**long** vi ~ **for sth** avoir grande envie de qch; ~ **to do sth** avoir bien envie de faire qch

**long-distance** adj ~ **runner** coureur -euse de fond; ~ **telephone** (téléphone) interurbain m

**longevity** n longévité f

**longhand** n écriture courante

**longing** n grande envie

**longish** adj assez long (f longue)

**longitude** n longitude f

**long-jump** n saut m en longueur

**long-playing** adj ~ **record** (disque m) microsillon m

**long-range** adj à longue portée

**long-sighted** adj presbyte; fig prévoyant

**long-standing** adj de longue date

**long-suffering** adj patient; indulgent

**long-term** adj à longue échéance

**longways** adv en long

**long-winded** adj interminable; (boring) ennuyeux -euse

**loo** n coll cabinets mpl

**look** n regard m; air m, mine f; aspect m; coup m d'œil; **good** ~ **s** belle mine; **have a** ~ **at sth** regarder qch; vi regarder; (appear) paraître, avoir l'air, sembler; ~ **about one** regarder autour de soi; ~ **after** s'occuper de; (nurse) soigner; ~ **at** regarder; ~ **away** détourner les yeux (le regard); ~ **back** regarder en arrière; (turn round) se retourner; ~ **down on s/o** mépriser qn; ~ **down on s/o** mépriser qn; ~ **for** chercher; ~ **forward to sth** attendre qch avec plaisir; ~ **here!** écoutez!; ~ **in** passer, s'arrêter (chez qn) en passant; ~ **into sth** examiner qch; ~ **like** ressembler à; ~ **on** regarder; ~ **out** regarder au dehors; (take care) faire attention; ~ **out!** attention!; ~ **out for** être à la recherche de; ~ **out on** donner sur; ~ **over** examiner; ~ **sharp!** dépêchez-vous!; ~ **s/o up and down** toiser qn; ~ **the part** avoir le physique de l'emploi; ~ **through** parcourir, examiner; ~ **to s/o** compter sur qn; ~ **to sth** s'occuper de qch; ~ **up** lever les yeux; chercher; (call on) passer chez; (improve) reprendre; ~ **up to s/o** respecter qn; ~ **well** avoir bonne mine; **it** ~ **s like rain** on dirait qu'il va pleuvoir; **not be much to** ~ **at** ne pas payer de mine; **to** ~ **at him** à le regarder

**looker-on** n spectateur -trice; curieux -ieuse

**look-in** n he won't get a ~ il n'a aucune chance

**looking-glass** n glace f, miroir m

**look-out** n guet m; poste m d'observation; (person) guetteur m; **be on the** ~ être sur ses gardes; **keep a good** ~ faire bonne garde; **that's a poor** ~ ! voilà une triste perspective!; **that's his** ~ c'est son affaire

**look-see** n sl coup m d'œil rapide

¹**loom** n métier m

²**loom** vi se dessiner; ~ **ahead** menacer; ~ **up** surgir

**loony** n + adj fou (f folle), timbré -e

**loop** n boucle f; (stream) méandre m; vt boucler; ~ **the** ~ boucler la boucle

**loophole** n (fortress) meurtrière f; fig ouverture f, trou m; fig **find a** ~ trouver une échappatoire

**loose** adj (slack) lâche, mal assujetti; détaché; (escaped) évadé; (page) détaché; (morals) relâché; (knot) défait; (screw) desserré; (vague) vague; (tooth, etc) branlant; (translation) approximatif- ive; **at a** ~ **end** désœuvré; **come** ~ se détacher; **let** ~ lâcher; vt délier, détacher; (knot) dénouer; (arrow) décocher

**loose-leaf** adj à feuilles mobiles

**loose-limbed** adj démanché, dégingandé

**loosen** vt détacher, relâcher; (screw) desserrer; (untighten) détendre; vi se délier, se défaire

**looseness** n relâchement m; (clothes) ampleur f; (play) jeu m; imprécision f

**loot** n butin m, pillage m

**lop** vt élaguer

**lope** vi ~ **along** courir à petits bonds

**lop-eared** adj aux oreilles pendantes

**lop-sided** adj déjeté, de guingois

**loquacious** adj loquace

**loquacity** n loquacité f

**lord** n seigneur m, maître m; ~ **of the manor** châtelain m; **live like a** ~ vivre en seigneur; **the Lord** le Seigneur; **the Lord's Prayer** le Pater invar, l'oraison dominicale; vt ~ **it over s/o** agir en maître avec qn

**lordly** adj majestueux -euse; hautain

**lordship** n suzeraineté f; **your** ~ votre Seigneurie; (to nobleman) monsieur le comte, etc

**lore** n savoir m

**lorgnette** n face-à-main m (pl faces-à-main)

**lorry** n camion m; **heavy** ~ poids lourd

**lorry-driver** n routier m

**lorryload** n a ~ **of** un plein camion de

**lose** vt perdre, égarer; (waste) gaspiller; ~ **face** perdre la face; ~ **oneself**

s'égarer; ~ **one's temper** se mettre en colère; ~ **sight of s/o** perdre qn de vue; **my watch** ~**s five minutes a day** ma montre retarde de cinq minutes par jour; *vi* perdre; ~ **out** ne pas réussir

**loser** *n* perdant -e; **good (bad)** ~ bon (mauvais) joueur, bonne (mauvaise) joueuse

**losing** *adj* perdant; ~ **game** partie perdue d'avance

**loss** *n* perte *f*; ~ **of voice** extinction *f* de voix; **be at a** ~ être embarrassé, ne savoir que faire; **dead** ~ perte sèche; **sell at a** ~ vendre à perte

**lost** *adj* perdu, égaré; ~ **property office** bureau *m* (service *m*) des objets trouvés; **be** ~ **in thought** être absorbé dans ses pensées

**lot** *n* sort *m*, destin *m*; (share) partage *m*; quantité *f*; beaucoup; (auction, ground) lot *m*; **a** ~ beaucoup, bien; **draw** ~**s** tirer au sort; **it fell to my** ~ **to ...** le sort voulut que je ...; **such a** ~ tellement, tant, un si grand nombre; **what a** ~ **of ...!** que de ...!

**lotion** *n* lotion *f*

**lottery** *n* loterie *f*

**lotto** *n* loto *m*

**lotus, lotos** *n* lotus *m*

**loud** *adj* bruyant; (voice) fort, haut; (colours) voyant, criard; **in a** ~ **voice** à haute voix; *adv* haut

**loudhailer** *n* porte-voix *m*

**loudly** *adv* à voix haute, haut

**loudmouthed** *adj sl* fort en gueule

**loudspeaker** *n* haut-parleur *m*

**lounge** *n* flânerie *f*; salon *m*; (hotel) hall *m*; **sun** ~ véranda *f*; *vi* flâner; (in chair) s'étaler

**lounger** *n* flâneur -euse

**lounge-suit** *n* complet *m*, costume *m*

**lour** *vi see* **lower** *vi*

**louse** *n* (*pl* lice) pou *m*; *sl* salaud *m*

**lousy** *adj* pouilleux -euse; *sl* miteux -euse, moche

**lout** *n* rustre *m*, lourdaud *m*

**lovable** *adj* aimable; sympathique

**love** *n* amour *m*; affection *f*, tendresse *f*; chéri -e; (tennis) zéro *m*; ~ **game** jeu blanc; **fall in** ~ **with** s'éprendre de; **give my** ~ **to** faites mes amitiés à; **make** ~ faire l'amour; **not for** ~ **nor money** à aucun prix; **play for** ~ jouer pour le plaisir; *vt* aimer; (be in love with) aimer d'amour; adorer; affectionner

**love-affair** *n* affaire *f* de cœur, aventure amoureuse

**love-bird** *n* perruche *f*; *fig* ~**s** tourtereaux *mpl*

**love-child** *n* enfant naturel -elle

**loveless** *adj* sans amour

**love-letter** *n* billet doux

**love-life** *n* vie sentimentale; vie sexuelle

**loveliness** *n* beauté *f*, charme *m*

**love-lorn** *adj* délaissé

**lovely** *adj* beau (*f* belle); ravissant

**love-making** *n* amour *m*; (courtship) cour amoureuse

**love-match** *n* mariage *m* d'amour

**lover** *n* amoureux -euse; fiancé -e; amant -e; *arts* amateur *m*

**lovesick** *adj* malade d'amour

**love-story** *n* histoire *f* d'amour; roman *m* d'amour

**loving** *adj* tendre, affectueux -euse

¹**low** *n* **all-time** ~ point le plus bas; *adj* bas (*f* basse); (deep) profond; (spirits) abattu; (voice) grave; (vulgar) vulgaire; (dress) décolleté; **lie** ~ rester caché; ~**est price** dernier prix; **the Low Countries** les Pays-Bas; **the** ~ **est of the** ~ le dernier des derniers; *adv* bas; à voix basse

²**low** *vi* meugler

**low-born** *adj* de basse naissance

**lowbrow** *adj* peu intellectuel -elle

**low-down** *n coll* **give s/o the** ~ **on** renseigner qn sur

¹**lower** *adj* inférieur, plus bas (*f* basse); *geog* bas (*f* basse); **the** ~ **regions** les régions infernales; *vt* baisser; abaisser; (lessen) diminuer, réduire; rabattre; (bring down) descendre; ~ **oneself** s'abaisser

²**lower** *vi* froncer les sourcils; (sky) s'assombrir, se couvrir, menacer

¹**lowering** *adj* menaçant, sombre

²**lowering** *adj* dégradant, humiliant

**lowing** *n* meuglement *m*

**lowland** *n* plaine basse; ~**s** pays plat

**lowliness** *n* humilité *f*

**lowly** *adj* humble, modeste

**low-lying** *adj* situé en bas, bas (*f* basse)

**lowness** *n* situation basse; (moral) bassesse *f*; (spirits) abattement *m*; (sound) gravité *f*; (volume) faiblesse *f*; (price) modicité *f*

**low-pitched** *adj* grave

**low-priced** *adj* bon marché *invar*

**low-spirited** *adj* triste, abattu

**loyal** *adj* fidèle, dévoué, loyal

**loyalist** *n* loyaliste

**loyalty** *n* fidélité *f*

**lozenge** *n* pastille *f*; (shape) losange *m*

**lubber** *n* lourdaud *m*

**lubricant** *n* lubrifiant *m*; *adj* lubrifiant

**lubricate** *vt* lubrifier; graisser

**lubrication** *n* graissage *m*

**lucid** *adj* lucide, clair

**lucidity** *n* (mind) lucidité *f*; transparence *f*

**luck** *n* chance *f*, hasard *m*; (favourable) bonheur *m*, bonne fortune; **as** ~

**would have it** par bonheur; **bad ~** mauvaise chance, déveine *f*; **be in ~** avoir de la chance; **be out of ~** jouer de malheur; **good ~!** bonne chance!; **hard ~!** pas de chance!, tant pis!; **stroke of ~** coup *m* de chance; **worse ~!** tant pis!

**luckily** *adv* par bonheur, heureusement

**luckless** *adj* malheureux -euse, infortuné

**lucky** *adj* heureux -euse; chanceux -euse; (bringing luck) porte-bonheur *invar*; *coll* **~ dog** veinard *m*

**lucrative** *adj* lucratif -ive

**lucre** *n* lucre *m*; **for filthy ~** par amour du gain

**ludicrous** *adj* risible, grotesque

**luff** *vi naut* lofer

¹**lug** *n coll* + *mech* oreille *f*

²**lug** *vt* tirer, traîner, trimbaler

**luggage** *n* bagages *mpl*

**luggage-rack** *n* porte-bagages *m invar*; . *mot* galerie *f*

**luggage-van** *n* fourgon *m*

**lugubrious** *adj* lugubre

**lukewarm** *adj* tiède

**lull** *n* moment *m* de calme; (weather) accalmie *f*; *vt* bercer, endormir; calmer

**lullaby** *n* berceuse *f*

**lumbago** *n* lumbago *m*

**lumbar** *adj* lombaire

**lumber** *n* fatras *m*; *US* bois *m* de charpente; *vt* encombrer, embarrasser; *vi* **~ along** avancer lourdement

**lumbering** *adj* lourd

**lumberjack**, *US* **lumberman** *n* bûcheron *m*

**lumber-room** *n* débarras *m*, grenier *m*

**luminous** *adj* lumineux -euse

¹**lump** *n* (piece) morceau *m*; (swelling) bosse *f*; (earth) motte *f*; masse *f*; (in soup, etc) grumeau *m*; *med* grosseur *f*; *sl* (person) pataud *m*; **~ sugar** sucre *m* en morceaux; **~ sum** somme globale; *vt* **~ together** mettre ensemble, réunir

²**lump** *vt coll* **he can ~ it!** tant pis pour lui!, qu'il s'arrange!

**lumpish** *adj* lourd

**lumpy** *adj* (soup, etc) grumeleux -euse; (soil) rempli de mottes; (person) difforme, gros (*f* grosse)

**lunacy** *n* folie *f*, démence *f*

**lunar** *adj* lunaire; **~ landing** alunissage *m*

**lunatic** *n* fou (*f* folle), aliéné -e; **~ asylum** asile *m* d'aliénés; *adj* de fou (*f* folle)

**lunch** *n* déjeuner *m*; **have ~** déjeuner; *vt* offrir à déjeuner à; *vi* déjeuner

**luncheon** *n* déjeuner *m*

**lunch-hour** *n* heure *f* du déjeuner

**lung** *n* poumon *m*; **iron ~** poumon *m* d'acier

**lunge** *n* mouvement *m* en avant; (fencing) botte *f*; *vi* (fencing) se fendre; **~ forward** se précipiter en avant; **~ out at** s/o allonger un coup de poing à qn

**lupin** *n* lupin *m*

¹**lurch** *n* **leave** s/o **in the ~** planter là qn

²**lurch** *n* embardée *f*; *mot* cahot *m*; *vi* (person) tituber; faire une embardée

**lure** *n* leurre *m*, piège *m*; attrait *m*; *vt* leurrer; attirer

**lurid** *adj* sinistre, effrayant; (sky) rougeoyant

**lurk** *vi* se cacher, rôder

**luscious** *adj* délicieux -ieuse, succulent

**lush** *adj* plein de sève; *coll* abondant; *coll* agréable, confortable

**lust** *n* luxure *f*; convoitise *f*; *vi* **~ after** convoiter; **~ for** avoir soif de, avoir envie de

**lustful** *adj* lascif -ive

**lustily** *adv* vigoureusement

**lustiness** *n* vigueur *f*

**lustre** *n* éclat *m*, splendeur *f*, brillant *m*

**lustrous** *adj* éclatant, brillant

**lusty** *adj* vigoureux -euse, robuste, fort

**lute** *n* luth *m*

**Lutheran** *adj* luthérien -ienne

**luxate** *vt* luxer

**luxuriance** *n* exubérance *f*, luxuriance *f*

**luxuriant** *adj* luxuriant

**luxurious** *adj* luxueux -euse

**luxury** *n* luxe *m*; objet *m* de luxe

¹**lying** *n* mensonge *m*; *adj* faux (*f* fausse)

²**lying** *adj* couché, étendu

**lying-in** *n* accouchement *m*

**lymph** *n anat* lymphe *f*; *med* vaccin *m*

**lymphatic** *adj* lymphatique

**lynch** *vt* lyncher

**lynx** *n* lynx *m*

**lyre** *n* lyre *f*

**lyric** *n* poème *m* lyrique; chanson *f*; **~ s** couplets *mpl* de chanson; *adj* lyrique

**lyrical** *adj* lyrique

**lyricism** *n* lyrisme *m*

# M

ma *n coll* maman *f*
ma'am *n see* madam
mac *n imper* mach *m*
macabre *adj* macabre
macadam *n* macadam *m*
macaroni *n cul* macaroni(s) *m(pl)*
macaroon *n* macaron *m*
¹mace *n* masse *f*; *hist* (weapon) massue *f*
²mace *n* (spice) macis *m*
Macedonia *n* Macédoine *f*
macerate *vt* + *vi* macérer
mach *n aer* mach *m*
machiavellian *adj* machiavélique
machinate *vi* comploter
machination *n* complot *m*, machination *f*
machine *n* machine *f*, appareil *m*; organisation *f*; *vt* façonner; (sewing) piquer à la machine
machine-gun *n* mitrailleuse *f*; *vt* mitrailler
machinery *n* mécanisme *m*, machines *fpl*; *fig* rouages *mpl*
machine-tool *n* machine-outil *f* (*pl* machines-outils)
machinist *n* machiniste
mackerel *n* maquereau *m*
mackintosh *n* imperméable *m*; *obs* manteau *m* en caoutchouc
macrocosm *n* macrocosme *m*
mad *adj* fou (*f* folle), dément; (animal) enragé; (angry) furieux -ieuse; (plan, etc) insensé; **be ~ about** raffoler de; **drive s/o ~** rendre qn fou (*f* folle); **go ~** devenir fou (*f* folle); **raving ~** fou furieux (*f* folle furieuse), fou (*f* folle) à lier
madam, ma'am *n* madame *f*
madcap *n* + *adj* écervelé -e
madden *vt* rendre fou (*f* folle), exaspérer
made *adj* fabriqué, fait; **~-up** (face) maquillé; (story) inventé; *US coll* **have it ~** avoir réussi; **ready-~** confectionné
madhouse *n* maison *f* de fous, asile *m* d'aliénés; **the place is like a ~** on se croirait chez les fous
madly *adv* follement; furieusement
madman *n* fou *m*
madness *n* folie *f*, démence *f*
madonna *n* madone *f*
madrigal *n* madrigal *m*
madwoman *n* folle *f*
maelstrom *n* maelström *m*; tourbillon *m*

maestro *n* maître *m*, maestro *m*
mafia *n* maf(f)ia *f*
magazine *n* revue *f*, magazine *m*; (rifle) magasin *m*; *mil* magasin *m* d'armes
magenta *n* + *adj* rouge violacé
maggot *n* ver *m*, asticot *m*
Magi *n* **the ~** les Rois *mpl* mages
magic *n* magie *f*, enchantement *m*; *adj* magique
magical *adj* magique
magician *n* magicien -ienne
magisterial *adj* magistral
magistracy *n* magistrature *f*
magistrate *n* magistrat *m*
magnanimity *n* magnanimité *f*
magnanimous *adj* magnanime
magnate *n* magnat *m*
magnesium *n* magnésium *m*
magnet *n* aimant *m*
magnetic *adj* magnétique; **~ tape** bande *f* magnétique
magnetism *n* magnétisme *m*
magnetize *vt* magnétiser
magneto *n* magnéto *f*
magnification *n* grossissement *m*
magnificence *n* magnificence *f*
magnificent *adj* magnifique; somptueux -euse
magnifier *n* loupe *f*
magnify *vt* grossir; *phot* agrandir; amplifier; **~ing glass** loupe *f*
magnitude *n* grandeur *f*
magnolia *n* magnolia *m*
magnum *n* magnum *m*
magpie *n* pie *f*
mahogany *n* acajou *m*
Mahometan *n* + *adj see* Mohammedan
maid *n* jeune fille *f*, vierge *f*; (servant) bonne *f*, servante *f*; **~ of all work** bonne *f* à tout faire; **~ of honour** demoiselle *f* d'honneur; **lady's ~** femme *f* de chambre; **old ~** vieille fille; **the Maid of Orleans** la Pucelle d'Orléans
maiden *n* jeune fille *f*, vierge *f*; **~ aunt** tante non mariée; **~ lady** demoiselle *f*; **~ name** nom *m* de jeune fille; **~ voyage** premier voyage
maidenhead *n* hymen *m*
maidenhood *n* virginité *f*
maidenly *adj* modeste; de jeune fille
maidservant *n* servante *f*, bonne *f*
¹mail *n* courrier *m*; **~ boat** courrier postal; **~ train** train-poste *m* (*pl* trains-poste); *vt* envoyer par la poste

²**mail** *n* maille *f*

**mailbag** *n* sac postal

**mail-box** *n US* boîte *f* aux lettres

**mail-coach** *n obs* malle-poste *f* (*pl* malles-poste)

**mailing-list** *n* liste *f* d'adresses

**mail-man** *n US* facteur *m*

**mail-order** *n* commande *f* par poste; ~ **firm** maison *f* de vente par correspondance

**maim** *vt* estropier, mutiler

**main** *n* conduite principale; *lit* (sea) océan *m*; *elect* ~s câble *m* de distribution; ~s water eau *f* de la ville; **in the** ~ en général; **with might and** ~ de toutes ses forces; *adj* principal, essentiel -ielle; ~ **dish** plat *m* de résistance; ~ **line** voie principale, grande ligne; ~ **road** grande route, route principale; **the** ~ **body** le gros; **the** ~ **point** le point capital, l'essentiel *m*

**mainland** *n* continent *m*; *adj* continental

**mainline** *adj coll* important, essentiel -ielle

**mainly** *adv* principalement, surtout

**mainmast** *n* grand mât

**mainspring** *n* grand ressort; *fig* mobile essentiel

**mainstay** *n* soutien principal

**mainstream** *adj* important, essentiel -ielle

**maintain** *vt* maintenir, soutenir; (affirm) prétendre; (keep) conserver, entretenir; (attitude) garder

**maintenance** *n* maintien *m*; (upkeep, family) entretien *m*; (machine) maintenance *f*; (money allowance) pension *f* alimentaire

**maisonnette** *n* appartement *m* dans une maison; duplex *m*; maisonnette *f*

**maize** *n* maïs *m*

**majestic** *adj* majestueux -euse

**majesty** *n* majesté *f*

¹**major** *n mil* commandant *m*

²**major** *adj* majeur *m*; (older) aîné; ~ **road** route *f* à priorité

³**major** *vi US* ~ **in** obtenir sa licence en

**Majorca** *n* Majorque *f*

**major-domo** *n* majordome *m*

**majority** *n* majorité *f*; plupart *f*, plus grande partie; **be in the** ~ être en majorité; *adj* majoritaire

**make** *n* construction *f*, fabrication *f*; (brand) marque *f*; *coll* **on the** ~ intéressé; *vt* faire, créer, construire; (manufacture) fabriquer; (clothes) confectionner; (render) rendre; (force) forcer, faire; (gain) gagner; (reach) atteindre; (estimate) estimer; (friends) se faire; ~ **fast** amarrer; ~ **good** réparer; ~ **it** réussir; ~ **it up to s/o** dédommager qn; ~ **it up with s/o** se

réconcilier avec qn; ~ **oneself up** se maquiller, *theat* se maquiller, se grimer; ~ **over** céder; ~ **s/o out** comprendre qn; ~ **sth into sth** transformer qch en qch; ~ **sth out** (recognize) distinguer qch; (prove) prouver qch; ~ **the best of** s'accommoder de; ~ **the most of** tirer le meilleur parti de; ~ **up** compléter; (deficit) combler; (invent) inventer; (face) maquiller; (actor) grimer; (prescription) préparer; ~ **up one's mind** se décider; **what do you** ~ **the time?** quelle heure avez-vous?; **what do you** ~ **of it?** qu'en pensez-vous?; *vi* ~ **away** s'éloigner; ~ **away with** (kill) détruire, supprimer; (escape with) disparaître avec; ~ **for** se diriger vers; (tend) contribuer à; ~ **good** réussir; ~ **off** filer, se sauver; ~ **up for lost time** rattraper le temps perdu; *coll* ~ **up to s/o** faire des avances à qn

**make-and-break** *n elect* conjoncteur-disjoncteur *m* (*pl* conjoncteurs-disjoncteurs)

**make-believe** *n* semblant *m*; trompe-l'œil *m invar*

**maker** *n* faiseur -euse; (manufacturer) fabricant *m*, constructeur *m*; **Maker** Créateur *m*

**makeshift** *n* pis-aller *m invar*, moyen *m* de fortune; *adj* de fortune, de rencontre

**make-up** *n* maquillage *m*, fard *m*; (composition) composition *f*

**makeweight** *n* complément *m* de poids; **he's there as a** ~ il est là pour faire le nombre

**making** *n* création *f*, fabrication *f*; construction *f*; (clothes) façon *f*; ~s petits profits; **have the** ~s **of** avoir (tout) ce qu'il faut pour faire

**maladjusted** *adj* inadapté

**maladministration** *n* mauvaise administration

**maladroit** *adj* maladroit

**malady** *n* maladie *f*, mal *m*

**malaise** *n* malaise *m*

**malaria** *n* paludisme *m*, malaria *f*

**malcontent** *n* + *adj* mécontent -e

**male** *n* mâle *m*; *adj* mâle

**malediction** *n* malédiction *f*

**malefactor** *n* malfaiteur -trice

**malevolence** *n* malveillance *f*

**malevolent** *adj* malveillant

**malformation** *n* malformation *f*

**malice** *n* malveillance *f*, méchanceté *f*; **bear** ~ **towards s/o** en vouloir à qn; **with** ~ **aforethought** avec préméditation

**malicious** *adj* méchant, malveillant; rancunier -ière

¹**malign** *adj* nuisible

²**malign** vt diffamer, calomnier

**malignancy, malignity** n malignité f

**malignant** adj méchant; malin (f maligne)

**malignity** n see **malignancy**

**malinger** vi faire le (f la) malade

**malingerer** n faux (f fausse) malade

**malleable** adj malléable

**mallet** n maillet m

**malnutrition** n sous-alimentation f

**malodorous** adj malodorant

**malpractice** n méfait m; (doctor) négligence f; leg malversation f

**malt** n malt m

**Maltese** n Maltais -e; adj maltais

**maltreat** vt maltraiter

**maltreatment** n mauvais traitement

**mammal** n mammifère m

**mammoth** n mammouth m; adj géant, énorme

**man** n homme m; (workman) ouvrier m; (servant) domestique m, valet m; (chess) pièce f; (draughts) pion m; ~ **proposes, God disposes** l'homme propose, Dieu dispose; ~ **to** ~ d'homme à homme; **come on, old** ~ viens, mon vieux; **he's a big** ~ c'est qn; **he's not the** ~ **for that** il n'est pas fait pour cela; **the** ~ **in the street** l'homme moyen; **they died to a** ~ ils moururent jusqu'au dernier; vt naut équiper; (gun) servir; pourvoir de main-d'œuvre

**manacle** n ~s menottes fpl; vt mettre les menottes à

**manage** vt gérer, diriger, administrer; (handle) manier; (person) mater; (animal) maîtriser; (business) arranger; (cope with) venir à bout de; **can you** ~ **another cup?** pouvez-vous en boire encore une tasse?; **I can** ~ **him** je sais le prendre; **I can't** ~ **any more money** je ne peux plus payer d'argent; vi s'en tirer, s'y prendre, se débrouiller; ~ **to do** réussir à faire; **how do you** ~ **to …?** comment faites-vous pour …?; **I'll** ~ je m'arrangerai

**manageable** adj maniable; (person) docile, traitable; (possible) faisable

**management** n conduite f, direction f, administration f; (property) gestion f; (things, men) maniement m

**manager** n directeur m; gérant m; (property) régisseur m; sp manager m; (household) ménagère f

**manageress** n directrice f; gérante f

**managing** adj directeur -trice; ~ **director** administrateur directeur, directeur général = P.D.G.

¹**mandarin** n (person) mandarin m

²**mandarin(e)** n (fruit) mandarine f

**mandate** n mandat m; vt mandater

**mandatory** adj mandataire

**mandolin(e)** n mandoline f

**mane** n crinière f

**man-eater** n (cannibal) anthropophage m; (animal) mangeur m d'hommes

**manful** adj viril, vaillant, courageux -euse

**manganese** n manganèse m

**mange** n gale f

**manger** n mangeoire f, crèche f; **the dog in the** ~ le chien du jardinier

¹**mangle** n essoreuse f; vt (clothes) essorer

²**mangle** vt mutiler; (tear) déchirer; (language) estropier

**mango** n mangue f

**mangrove** n bot manglier m

**mangy** adj galeux -euse; (poor) minable; coll moche

**manhandle** vt manutentionner; coll malmener

**manhater** n misanthrope

**manhole** n trou m de visite; ~ **cover** plaque f d'égout

**manhood** n humanité f; âge m d'homme, âge viril

**man-hour** n heure f de main-d'œuvre

**manhunt** n chasse f à l'homme

**mania** n manie f; folie f; **have a** ~ **for doing sth** avoir la passion de faire qch

**maniac** n+adj fou furieux (f folle furieuse); maniaque

**manic** adj atteint de manie

**manicure** n soin m des mains; vt soigner les mains à

**manicurist** n manucure

**manifest** n manifeste m; adj manifeste, évident; vt manifester, témoigner; naut déclarer

**manifestation** n manifestation f

**manifesto** n manifeste m

**manifold** n mot tubulure f d'échappement; adj divers, varié; vt obs polycopier

**manipulate** vt manipuler; manœuvrer

**manipulation** n manipulation f; manœuvre f

**mankind** n le genre humain, les hommes mpl

**manly** adj viril, d'homme

**man-made** adj artificiel -ielle

**manna** n manne f

**mannequin** n mannequin m

**manner** n manière f, façon f; (bearing) air m, maintien m; (sort) sorte f, espèce f; ~**s** (customs) mœurs fpl; **in a** ~ **of speaking** pour ainsi dire; **in such a** ~ **that** de telle sorte que; **in this** ~ de cette façon (manière)

**mannered** adj maniéré; (style) précieux -ieuse

**mannerism** n affectation f; maniérisme m

**mannerless** *adj* sans éducation
**mannerly** *adj* poli, bien élevé, courtois
**mannish** *adj* hommasse
**manoeuvre** *n* manœuvre *f*; *vt* manœuvrer
**man-of-war** *n* vaisseau *m* de guerre
**manor** *n* manoir *m*, château seigneurial
**manpower** *n* main-d'œuvre *f* (*pl* mains-d'œuvre), effectifs *mpl*
**manservant** *n* domestique *m*
**mansion** *n* (in country) château *m*; (in town) hôtel (particulier)
**manslaughter** *n* homicide *m* involontaire
**mantelpiece** *n* cheminée *f*; tablette *f* de cheminée
**mantelshelf** *n* tablette *f* de cheminée
**mantilla** *n* mantille *f*
**mantis** *n* mante *f*; **praying** ~ mante religieuse
**mantle** *n* cape *f*, pèlerine *f*; (covering) manteau *m*; (gas) manchon *m*; *vt* couvrir d'un manteau; *vi* se répandre
**manual** *n* manuel *m*; *adj* manuel -elle
**manufacture** *n* fabrication *f*; (clothes) confection *f*; (article) produit manufacturé; *vt* fabriquer
**manure** *n* engrais *m*; (farmyard) fumier *m*; **liquid** ~ purin *m*; *vt* fumer, engraisser
**manuscript** *n* manuscrit *m*
**many** *n* un grand nombre, une multitude; *adj*+*adv* beaucoup (de), bien des, un grand nombre (de); ~ **a** maint; ~ **of you** beaucoup d'entre vous; **as** ~ autant (de); **how** ~ combien (de); **one too** ~ un (*f* une) de trop; **so** ~ tant (de); **too** ~ trop (de)
**many-sided** *adj* complexe; (object) à plusieurs côtés; (person) aux talents variés
**map** *n* carte *f* (géographique); (town) plan *m*; **put sth on the** ~ mettre qch en vedette; *vt* dresser une carte (un plan) de; ~ **out** tracer
**maple** *n* érable *m*
**mar** *vt* gâter, gâcher; **make or** ~ **matters** tout arranger ou tout gâcher
**marathon** *n* marathon *m*
**maraud** *vt* piller; *vi* marauder
**marauder** *n* maraudeur -euse
**marble** *n* marbre *m*; (toy) bille *f*; **play** ~ **s** jouer aux billes
**marcasite** *n* marcassite *f*
**March** *n* mars *m*; **in** ~ au mois de mars
¹**march** *n* marche *f*; **quick** ~ pas cadencé; *vi* marcher; ~ **along** marcher; ~ **in** entrer; ~ **off** se mettre en marche; *coll* décamper; **quick** ~! en avant, marche!
²**march** *n ar* marche *f*; *vi ar* ~ **with** être

limitrophe de
**marchioness** *n* marquise *f*
**march-past** *n* défilé *m*
**mare** *n* jument *f*; ~ **'s nest** découverte *f* illusoire
**margarine** *n* margarine *f*
**margin** *n* marge *f*, bord *m*; (divergence) écart *m*; *vt* annoter en marge; **faire une marge à**
**marginal** *adj* en marge, marginal
**marguerite** *n* marguerite *f*
**marigold** *n* souci *m*
**marijuana, marihuana** *n* marihuana *f*, marijuana *f*
**marina** *n* marina *f*
**marinade** *n* marinade *f*; *vt*+*vi* mariner
**marine** *n* marine *f*; *mil* fusilier marin; **tell that to the** ~**s!** à d'autres!; *adj* marin
**mariner** *n* marin *m*
**marionette** *n* marionnette *f*
**marital** *adj* marital, matrimonial
**maritime** *adj* maritime
**marjoram** *n* marjolaine *f*, origan *m*
¹**mark** *n* marque *f*; (sign) signe *m*, témoignage *m*; (aim) but *m*, cible *f*; (school) note *f*, point *m*; (for signature) croix *f*; **as a** ~ **of my esteem** en témoignage de mon estime; **be up to the** ~ être à la hauteur; (health) être dans son assiette; **be wide of the** ~ être loin du compte; **make one's** ~ se distinguer, se faire une réputation; *vt* marquer; indiquer; (note) observer, noter; (underline) souligner; ~ **down** baisser le prix de; (note) inscrire; ~ **my words!** écoutez bien ce que je dis!; vous verrez!; (on list) ~ **off** cocher; ~ **out** délimiter; distinguer; ~ **time** marquer le pas; ~ **up** augmenter le prix de
²**mark** *n* (coin) mark *m*
**marked** *adj* marqué, évident, prononcé
**marker** *n* marqueur -euse; (book) signet *m*; repère *m*
**market** *n* marché *m*; (covered) halle *f*, halles *fpl*; (price) cours *m*; ~ **square** place *f* du marché; **be in the** ~ **for** être acheteur -euse de; **find a** ~ **for** trouver un débouché pour; *vt* lancer sur le marché, vendre
**market-garden** *n* jardin maraîcher
**market-gardener** *n* maraîcher -ère
**marketing** *n* marketing *m*
**market-price** *n* prix courant
**marking** *n* marquage *m*; marque *f*, tache *f*; (school) correction *f*
**marksman** *n* bon tireur
**marl** *n* marne *f*
**marmalade** *n* confiture *f* d'oranges
**marmot** *n* marmotte *f*
¹**maroon** *n* marron *m*; *adj* marron *invar*
²**maroon** *vt* abandonner sur une île dé-

serte; ~ ed by floods isolé par les inondations

marquee n grande tente

marquis, marquess n marquis m

marriage n mariage m; ~-lines acte m de mariage; ~ service bénédiction nuptiale; by ~ par alliance

marriageable adj (girl) nubile; mariable

married adj marié; ~ couple ménage m; ~ name nom m de femme mariée

marrow n moelle f; cul amourettes fpl; (vegetable) courge f

marry vt épouser, se marier avec; (priest) marier; ~ money faire un mariage d'argent; vi se marier

marsh n marais m, marécage m

marshal n maréchal m; US commissaire m de police; vt ranger, placer en rang; (rolling-stock) trier

marshalling-yard n gare f de triage

marshmallow n guimauve f

marshy adj marécageux -euse

marsupial n marsupial m; adj marsupial

marten n martre f

martial adj martial; declare ~ law proclamer l'état de siège

martin n house ~ hirondelle f (de toit, de fenêtre)

martinet n officier m sévère; sl pète-sec m invar

martyr n martyr -e; vt martyriser

martyrdom n martyre m

marvel n merveille f; vi s'émerveiller

marvellous adj merveilleux -euse

Marxism n marxisme m

Mary n Marie f

marzipan n massepain m

mascara n mascara m

mascot n mascotte f, porte-bonheur m invar

masculine adj masculin, mâle

masculinity n masculinité f

mash n purée f, pâte f; (farm animals) pâtée f; vt brasser, mélanger, écraser; (potatoes) mettre en purée

mask n masque m; (velvet) loup m; throw off the ~ lever le masque; vt masquer; cacher, voiler

masochism n masochisme m

mason n maçon m; (freemason) franc-maçon m (pl francs-maçons)

masonic adj maçonnique

masonry n maçonnerie f

masque n masque m

masquerade n mascarade f

¹mass n eccles messe f; high ~ grand-messe f; low ~ messe basse

²mass n masse f; (people) foule f, multitude f; (majority) majorité f, plus grande partie f; the ~es les masses; vt masser; vi se masser

massacre n massacre m; vt massacrer

massage n massage m; vt masser

masseur n masseur m

masseuse n masseuse f

massif n massif m

massive adj massif -ive

mass-produce vt fabriquer en série

mass-production n fabrication f en série

¹mast n naut mât m; pylône m

²mast n (beech) faîne f; (oak) gland m

master n maître m; (teacher) professeur m; (boss) patron m; (ship) capitaine m; ~-card carte maîtresse; ~ of fox-hounds grand veneur; be a past ~ être passé maître; be ~ of a subject posséder à fond un sujet; form ~ professeur principal; old ~ tableau m de maître; vt maîtriser, dompter; (learn well) apprendre à fond; ~ a difficulty surmonter une difficulté

masterful adj autoritaire, impérieux -ieuse

master-key n passe-partout m invar; coll passe m

masterly adj magistral, de maître

mastermind n esprit supérieur m; vt organiser

masterpiece n chef-d'œuvre m (pl chefs-d'œuvre)

masterstroke n coup m de maître

mastery n maîtrise f, domination f; (of a subject) connaissance approfondie; (skill) grande habileté; gain the ~ over l'emporter sur

masticate vt mâcher, mastiquer

mastication n mastication f

mastiff n mâtin m

mastodon n mastodonte m

mastoid adj mastoïde

mastoids n mastoïdite f

masturbate vi se masturber

¹mat n natte f, paillasson m; carpette f; (table) dessous m de plat; be on the ~ être sur la sellette; vt natter, tresser; (hair) emmêler

²mat adj mat

matador n matador m

¹match n allumette f; safety ~ allumette suédoise; strike a ~ frotter une allumette

²match n égal -e, pareil -eille; sp match m, partie f, lutte f; (marriage) alliance f, mariage m; be a good ~ aller bien ensemble; be a ~ for s/o être de force à lutter avec qn; make a good ~ faire un beau mariage; vt égaler, être l'égal de; (oppose) opposer; (pairs) apparier; (colours) assortir; vi s'assortir, s'harmoniser

matchbox n boîte f à allumettes

matchet n machette f

matchless adj incomparable; sans pareil -eille

**matchmaker** *n* marieur -ieuse

**matchwood** *n* bois *m* d'allumettes; **smashed to ~** brisé en petits morceaux

¹**mate** *n* camarade, compagnon *m* (*f* compagne); *coll* copain *m* (*f* copine); (couple) époux (*f* épouse); (animals) mâle *m*, femelle *f*; *naut* officier *m*; *vt* accoupler; unir; *vi* s'accoupler; **mating season** saison *f* des amours

²**mate** *n see* **checkmate**

**material** *n* matière *f*, matériau *m*; (textile) tissu *m*, étoffe *f*; **~s** fournitures *fpl*; **raw ~s** matières premières; *adj* matériel -ielle; grossier -ière, terre-à-terre *invar*; (important) essentiel -ielle, important; (germane) pertinent

**materialism** *n* matérialisme *m*

**materialist** *n* + *adj* matérialiste

**materialize** *vt* matérialiser; *vi* se réaliser; (appear) apparaître

**materially** *adv* matériellement, essentiellement

**maternal** *adj* maternel -elle

**maternity** *n* maternité *f*; **~ hospital** maternité *f*

**matey** *adj coll* amical

**mathematical** *adj* mathématique

**mathematician** *n* mathématicien -ienne

**mathematics** *npl* mathématiques *fpl*

**maths** *npl* math(s) *fpl*

**matins** *npl* matines *fpl*

**matriarch** *n* matrone *f*

**matricide** *n* matricide *m*; (person) matricide

**matriculate** *vi* (university) se faire inscrire

**matriculation** *n* (university) inscription *f*

**matrimonial** *adj* matrimonial, conjugal

**matrimony** *n* mariage *m*

**matrix** *n* matrice *f*

**matron** *n* matrone *f*, mère *f* de famille; (hospital) infirmière *f* en chef; (institution) intendante *f*

**matronly** *adj* opulent, de matrone, plantureux -euse

**matter** *n* matière *f*; (business) affaire *f*; (subject) sujet *m*; (case) cas *m*; (thing) chose *f*; *med* pus *m*; **as a ~ of course** cela va sans dire; **as a ~ of fact** en fait; **as if nothing was the ~** comme si de rien n'était; **for that ~** quant à cela; **hanging ~** cas *m* pendable; **it's no laughing ~** il n'y a pas de quoi rire; **no ~ how much you try** vous avez beau essayer; **printed ~** imprimé *m*; **reading ~** de quoi lire, lecture *f*; **sth must be the ~** il doit y avoir qch; **what's the ~?** qu'est-ce qu'il y a?; **what's the ~ with you?** qu'avez-vous?; *vi* importer; avoir de l'importance; *med* suppurer; **it doesn't ~** cela ne fait rien, n'im-porte; **what does it ~?** qu'importe?

**matter-of-fact** *adj* positif -ive

**matting** *n* nattes *fpl*

**mattock** *n* pioche *f*

**mattress** *n* matelas *m*; **air ~** matelas *m* pneumatique

**maturation** *n* maturation *f*

**mature** *adj* mûr, mûri; *vt* mûrir; *vi* mûrir; (bill) arriver à échéance

**maturity** *n* maturité *f*

**maudlin** *adj* larmoyant, pleurard; (drink) **be ~** avoir le vin triste

**maul** *vt* malmener, meurtrir

**maunder** *vi* divaguer

**mausoleum** *n* mausolée *m*

**mauve** *n* mauve *m*; *adj* mauve

**maverick** *n coll* non-conformiste

**maw** *n* (animal) estomac *m*; (bird) jabot *m*; (jaws) gueule *f*

**mawkish** *adj* insipide, fade; excessivement sentimental

**maxi** *adj* maxi

**maxim** *n* maxime *f*

**maximize** *vt* exploiter à fond

**maximum** *n* maximum *m* (*pl* maximums *or* maxima); *adj* maximum (*f* maximum *or* maxima, *pl* maximums *or* maxima)

¹**may** *n* (hawthorn) aubépine *f*; **May** mai *m*

²**may** *v aux* (*p* **might**) **~ he never know!** puisse-t-il ne jamais savoir!; **~ I come in?** puis-je entrer?; **be that as it ~** quoi qu'il en soit; **he ~ come tonight** il peut venir ce soir; **I might try** je pourrais essayer; **it ~ be that …** il se peut que …; **it ~ rain** il peut pleuvoir; **it might be that …** il se pourrait que …; **long ~ you wait!** puissiez-vous attendre longtemps!; **that's as ~ be** c'est selon; **they ~ have phoned** ils ont pu téléphoner; **they might have phoned** ils auraient pu téléphoner; **whoever it ~ be** qui que ce soit; **you might say good morning** vous pourriez bien dire bonjour

**maybe** *adv* peut-être

**may-bug** *n* hanneton *m*

**May-day** *n* le premier mai; **~!** = signal international de détresse

**may-fly** *n* éphémère *f*

**mayhem** *n US* **commit ~ on s/o** se livrer à des voies de fait contre qn

**mayonnaise** *n* mayonnaise *f*

**mayor** *n* maire *m*; **deputy ~** maire adjoint

**mayoress** *n* mairesse *f*, femme *f* du maire; (holder of office) Madame le Maire

**maze** *n* labyrinthe *m*, dédale *m*

**mazurka** *n* mazurka *f*

**me** *pron* me; moi; **dear ~!** mon Dieu!; **tell him from ~** dites-lui de ma part

**mead** n hydromel m

**meadow** n pré m, prairie f

**meagre** adj maigre, peu copieux -ieuse

**¹meal** n repas m; **make a ~ of it** en faire son repas; coll **make a ~ of s/o** ne faire qu'une bouchée de qn

**²meal** n farine f

**mealy** adj farineux -euse

**mealy-mouthed** adj doucereux -euse, patelin

**¹mean** n milieu m; (average) moyenne f; **~ s** moyen m; (resources) moyens mpl; **by all ~s!** mais certainement!; **by fair ~s** honnêtement; **by ~s of** au moyen de; **by no ~s** pas du tout; **find ~s to do sth** trouver le moyen de faire qch; **live beyond one's ~s** vivre au-dessus de ses moyens; **man of ~s** homme aisé; **private ~s** fortune personnelle; **there's no ~s of doing it** il n'y a pas moyen de le faire; adj moyen -enne

**²mean** adj misérable, mesquin; (avaricious) avare; (low) bas (f basse); **~ trick** vilain tour

**³mean** vt signifier, vouloir dire; (intend) avoir l'intention de, entendre; (destine) destiner; **~ s/o harm** vouloir du mal à qn; **~ well** avoir de bonnes intentions; **be meant to** être censé; **do you really ~ it?** êtes-vous vraiment sérieux -ieuse?; **he didn't ~ to do it** il ne l'a pas fait exprès; **he ~s no harm** il ne pense pas à mal; **that ~s nothing to me** cela ne me dit rien; **what do you ~ by that?** qu'entendez-vous par cela?; **you don't ~ it!** vous plaisantez!

**meander** n méandre m; vi serpenter, faire des méandres

**meaning** n signification f, sens m; adj significatif -ive

**meaningful** adj significatif -ive

**meaningless** adj dénué de sens

**meanness** n avarice f; (character) bassesse f, mesquinerie f; (poorness) pauvreté f, médiocrité f

**means-test** n enquête f sur la situation (de fortune)

**meantime, meanwhile** adv en attendant

**measles** npl rougeole f; **German ~** rubéole f

**measly** adj coll misérable

**measurable** adj mesurable

**measure** n mesure f; (step) démarche f; math diviseur m; (bound) limite f; **beyond ~** outre mesure; **in great ~** en grande partie; **in some ~** jusqu'à un certain point, en partie; **made to ~** fait sur mesure; vt mesurer; (tailor) prendre la mesure de; **~ one's words** peser ses mots; **~ out** distribuer

**measured** adj mesuré, déterminé; (language) modéré

**measureless** adj infini

**measurement** n mesurage m; (size) dimension f, mesure f

**meat** n viande f; (food) aliment m, nourriture f

**meatless** adj maigre

**meat-safe** n garde-manger m invar

**meaty** adj charnu; fig plein de substance

**Mecca** n la Mecque

**mechanic** n mécanicien -ienne, monteur -euse

**mechanical** adj mécanique; (action) machinal, automatique

**mechanism** n mécanisme m; appareil m

**mechanization** n mécanisation f

**mechanize** vt mécaniser

**medal** n médaille f

**medallion** n médaillon m

**medallist** n médailleur m; sp gagnant -e de médaille(s)

**meddle** vi **~ in** s'immiscer dans; **~ with** toucher à, se mêler de

**meddler** n officieux -ieuse, touche-à-tout m invar

**meddlesome** adj intrigant

**media** npl media mpl, média mpl; **mass ~** mass-media mpl

**mediate** vi s'interposer, servir de médiateur -trice

**mediation** n médiation f

**mediator** n médiateur -trice

**medical** adj médical; **~ inspection** visite médicale; **~ officer** médecin m du travail; **~ profession** corps médical; **~ student** étudiant -e en médecine

**medicate** vt médicamenter

**medicinal** adj médicinal

**medicine** n médecine f, médicament m; (remedy) remède m

**medicine-chest** n pharmacie f

**medicine-man** n sorcier guérisseur

**medieval, mediaeval** adj médiéval, du moyen âge

**mediocre** adj médiocre

**mediocrity** n médiocrité f

**meditate** vt + vi méditer

**meditation** n méditation f

**meditative** adj méditatif -ive

**Mediterranean** n Méditerranée f; adj méditerranéen -éenne

**medium** n milieu m; véhicule m; (intermediary) intermédiaire m, agent m; (spirit) médium m; **happy ~** juste milieu m; adj moyen -enne

**medlar** n bot nèfle f

**medley** n mélange m; mus pot-pourri m (pl pots-pourris)

**meek** adj humble, doux (f douce)

**meekness** n humilité f, soumission f

**¹meet** n rendez-vous m de chasseurs; vt rencontrer; (first time) faire la connaissance de; (join) rejoindre; (problem, demand) faire face à; (death) trouver; (danger) affronter; (requirement) satisfaire à; ~ s/o half-way faire des concessions à qn; **arrange to ~ s/o** donner rendez-vous à qn; **go and ~ s/o** aller au devant de qn; **my eyes met his** nos regards se croisèrent; **pleased to ~ you** enchanté de faire votre connaissance; **there's more here than ~s the eye** il y a quelque anguille sous roche; *vi* se rencontrer, se voir, se réunir; **~ with** rencontrer; **~ with a loss** essuyer une perte; **make both ends ~** joindre les deux bouts; **till we ~ again!** au revoir!

²**meet** *adj lit* convenable, à propos; **as is ~** comme il convient

**meeting** *n* rencontre *f*; réunion *f*, assemblée *f*; *sp+pol* meeting *m*; (roads) croisement *m*

**meeting-house** *n* (Quakers) temple *m*

**meeting-place** *n* lieu *m* de réunion; lieu *m* de rendez-vous

**megalomania** *n* mégalomanie *f*, folie *f* des grandeurs

**megaphone** *n* porte-voix *m invar*

**megaton** *n* mégatonne *f*

**melancholic** *adj* mélancolique

**melancholy** *n* mélancolie *f*; *adj* mélancolique

**mellifluous** *adj* mielleux -euse, douceureux -euse

**mellow** *adj* mûr; (wine) moelleux -euse; (voice) doux (*f* douce); (drunk) gris; *vt* mûrir, faire mûrir; (wine) rendre moelleux -euse; adoucir; *vi* mûrir; (character) s'adoucir

**melodic** *adj* mélodique

**melodious** *adj* mélodieux -ieuse, harmonieux -ieuse

**melodrama** *n* mélodrame *m*

**melodramatic** *adj* mélodramatique

**melody** *n* mélodie *f*, air *m*

**melon** *n* melon *m*

**melt** *vt* fondre, faire fondre; *fig* attendrir, émouvoir; **~ down** fondre; *vi* fondre; se fondre, se dissoudre; (crowd) se disperser; **~ into tears** fondre en larmes

**melting** *n* fonte *f*, fusion *f*; *fig* attendrissement *m*; *adj* fondant

**melting-point** *n* point *m* de fusion

**melting-pot** *n* creuset *m*

**member** *n* membre *m*, adhérent -e; *anat* membre *m*, organe *m*; **Member of Parliament** = député *m*

**membership** *n* qualité *f* de membre; (total) nombre *m* des membres; **~ card** carte *f* de membre (d'adhérent -e)

**membrane** *n* membrane *f*; **mucous ~** muqueuse *f*

**memento** *n* souvenir *m*

**memo** *n* mémorandum *m*

**memoir** *n* étude *f*; **~s** mémoires *fpl*, autobiographie *f*

**memorable** *adj* mémorable

**memorandum** *n* mémorandum *m*, note *f*

**memorial** *n* monument (commémoratif); **war ~** monument *m* aux morts; *adj* commémoratif -ive

**memorialist** *n* mémorialiste

**memorize** *vt* apprendre par cœur

**memory** *n* (faculty) mémoire *f*; souvenir *m*; **from ~** de mémoire; **have a good ~** avoir de la mémoire, avoir une bonne mémoire; **in ~ of** en souvenir de, en mémoire de; **to the best of my ~** autant que je m'en souvienne; **within living ~** de mémoire d'homme

**menace** *n* menace *f*; *coll* **he's a ~** il est terrible; *vt* menacer

**menagerie** *n* ménagerie *f*

**mend** *n* (clothes) reprise *f*; **be on the ~** (patient) être en voie de guérison; (business) reprendre; *vt* (clothes) repriser, raccommoder; réparer; (rectify) corriger, rectifier; (matters) arranger; **~ one's ways** changer de conduite; *vi* (health) se rétablir; (weather) se remettre; (reform) s'amender; (improve) s'améliorer

**mendacious** *adj* mensonger -ère

**mendacity** *n* penchant *m* au mensonge

**mender** *n* raccommodeur -euse; (machines, etc) réparateur -trice; **invisible ~** stoppeur -euse

**mendicant** *n+adj* mendiant -e

**mending** *n* raccommodage *m*; **invisible ~** stoppage *m*

**menfolk** *npl* les hommes *mpl* (de la famille)

**menhir** *n* menhir *m*

**menial** *n* domestique; *adj* servile; domestique

**meningitis** *n* méningite *f*

**menopause** *n* ménopause *f*

**menstrual** *adj* menstruel -elle

**menstruate** *vi* avoir ses règles

**mental** *adj* mental; *coll* fou (*f* folle); **~ case** aliéné -e; **~ defective** minus habens *m*; **~ home** hospice *m* d'aliénés; **~ hospital** hôpital *m* psychiatrique; **~ specialist** médecin *m* aliéniste

**mentality** *n* mentalité *f*

**mention** *n* mention *f*; *vt* mentionner, faire mention de; (quote) citer; **don't ~ it!** il n'y a pas de quoi!; **not to ~** sans parler de; **not worth ~ing** sans aucune importance

**menu** *n* menu *m*

**mercantile** *adj* mercantile, marchand

**mercenary** *n+adj* mercenaire

**merchandise** *n* marchandises *fpl*

**merchant** *n* négociant -e, commerçant

~-e, marchand -e; *coll* type *m*; *adj* marchand, de commerce; ~ **bank** banque *f* d'affaires

**merciful** *adj* miséricordieux -ieuse

**merciless** *adj* impitoyable

**mercurial** *adj* vif (*f* vive); inconstant

**mercury** *n* mercure *m*

**mercy** *n* miséricorde *f*, grâce *f*, pitié *f*; **ask for** ~ demander grâce; **at the** ~ **of** à la merci de; **for** ~'**s sake!** par pitié!; **Sister of Mercy** sœur *f* de la Charité; **what a** ~! quelle chance!

¹**mere** *n* lac *m*, étang *m*, mare *f*

²**mere** *adj* pur, simple, seul

**merely** *adv* simplement, seulement

**merge** *vt* fondre; amalgamer; ~ **into** englober dans; *vi* se fondre, se confondre; (firms) fusionner

**merger** *n* fusion *f*, amalgamation *f*

**meridian** *n* méridien *m*

**meringue** *n* meringue *f*

**merino** *n* mérinos *m*

**merit** *n* mérite *m*, valeur *f*; *vt* mériter

**meritorious** *adj* méritoire; (person) méritant

**mermaid** *n* sirène *f*

**merriment** *n* gaieté *f*, hilarité *f*

**merry** *adj* gai, joyeux -euse; ~ **Christmas!** joyeux Noël!; *coll* be ~ être éméché; **make** ~ s'amuser; **the more the merrier** plus on est de fous, plus on rit

**merry-go-round** *n* chevaux *mpl* de bois, carrousel *m*

**merry-making** *n* réjouissances *fpl*

**mesh** *n* maille *f*; *mech* engrenage *m*, prise *f*; (tangle) rets *mpl*; *vt* prendre au filet; *mech* engrener

**mesmerize** *vt* hypnotiser

**mess** *n* (muddle) gâchis *m*, fouillis *m*; (dirt) saleté *f*; *mil* (officers) mess *m*, (men) popote *f*; *ar* (dish) plat *m*; **be in a** ~ (person) être dans de beaux draps; (room) être en désordre; **make a** ~ **of** (dirty) salir; (create confusion) gâcher; *vt* gâcher; salir; *vi mil* faire popote; ~ **about** bricoler; faire l'idiot -e; ~ **about with** (girl) tripoter

**message** *n* message *m*; (phone) communication *f*; (writer) enseignement *m*; *coll* **get the** ~ piger; **give the** ~ faire la commission; **leave a** ~ laisser un mot

**messenger** *n* messager -ère; commissionnaire *m*; (hotel) chasseur *m*; garçon *m* de bureau

**Messiah** *n* Messie *m*

**messmate** *n* camarade *m* de table

**Messrs** *npl* Messieurs *mpl*

**mess-tin** *n* gamelle *f*

**mess-up** *n* gâchis *m*; (misunderstanding) malentendu *m*

**messy** *adj* malpropre, sale

**metal** *n* métal *m*; *vt* ~ **a road** empierrer une route

**metallic** *adj* métallique

**metallurgy** *n* métallurgie *f*

**metamorphosis** *n* métamorphose *f*

**metaphor** *n* métaphore *f*

**metaphoric** *adj* métaphorique

**metaphysical** *adj* métaphysique

**metaphysics** *n* métaphysique *f*

**mete** *vt* ~ **out** assigner, distribuer

**meteor** *n* météore *m*

**meteoric** *adj* météorique; atmosphérique

**meteorite** *n* météorite *m* or *f*

**meteorological** *adj* météorologique

**meteorology** *n* météorologie *f*

**meter** *n* compteur *m*; **parking** ~ parcomètre *m*, compteur *m*

**methane** *n* méthane *m*

**method** *n* méthode *f*; (manner) manière *f*; procédé *m*

**methodical** *adj* méthodique

**Methodism** *n* méthodisme *m*

**methodology** *n* méthodologie *f*

**methylated** *adj* ~ **spirit** alcool *m* à brûler

**meticulous** *adj* méticuleux -euse

**metonymy** *n* métonymie *f*

¹**metre** *n pros* mètre *m*, mesure *f*

²**metre** *n* mètre *m*

**metric, metrical** *adj* métrique

**metro** *n* métro *m*

**metronome** *n* métronome *m*

**metropolis** *n* métropole *f*

**metropolitan** *n eccles* métropolitain *m*; *adj* métropolitain

**mettle** *n* courage *m*, ardeur *f*; **be on one's** ~ se piquer d'honneur; **show one's** ~ faire preuve de courage

¹**mew** *n* (bird) mouette *f*

²**mew** *n* + *vi see* miaow

**mews** *n* écuries *fpl*; (street) ruelle *f*; écuries transformées en habitations

**Mexican** *n* Mexicain -e; *adj* mexicain

**Mexico** *n* le Mexique

**mezzanine** *n* entresol *m*

**mi** *n mus* mi *m*

**miaow, mew** *n* miaulement *m*, miaou *m*; *vi* miauler

**miasma** *n* miasme *m*

**mica** *n* mica *m*

**Michael** *n* Michel *m*

**Michaelmas** *n* la Saint-Michel; ~-**daisy** aster *m*, marguerite *f* d'automne

**mickey** *n coll* **take the** ~ **out of** s/o se payer la tête de qn

**microbe** *n* microbe *m*

**microbiology** *n* microbiologie *f*

**microcosm** *n* microcosme *m*

**microfilm** *n* microfilm *m*

**microgroove** *n* microsillon *m*

**microphone** *n* microphone *m*

**microscope** *n* microscope *m*

**microscopic** *adj* microscopique
**mid** *adj* du milieu, mi-; **in ~ -air** (high) en plein ciel; en l'air; **in ~ -July** à la mi-juillet; **in ~ -winter** au cœur de l'hiver
**midday** *n* midi *m*; *adj* de midi
**middle** *n* milieu *m*, centre *m*; **be in the ~ of doing sth** être en train de faire qch; **in the ~ of** au milieu de; *adj* du milieu, central; (intermediate) moyen -enne; **Middle Ages** moyen âge; **~ class** bourgeoisie *f*; **Middle East** Moyen-Orient *m*; **~ finger** médius *m*; **~ -sized** de grandeur moyenne; **take a ~ course** prendre le parti moyen
**middle-aged** *adj* d'un certain âge
**middleman** *n* intermédiaire *m*
**middle-weight** *n sp* poids moyen
**middling** *adj* médiocre, passable; (health) pas mal, comme ci comme ça; (quality) de qualité moyenne; *adv* passablement
**midge** *n* moucheron *m*
**midget** *n* nain -e; *adj* tout petit, minuscule
**midnight** *n* minuit *m*; *adj* de minuit
**midriff** *n* diaphragme *m*
**midshipman** *n* = aspirant *m* (de marine)
**midst** *n* milieu *m*; **in our ~** parmi nous; **in the ~ of** en plein milieu de; **in the ~ of doing sth** en train de faire qch; **in the ~ of winter** en plein hiver, au cœur de l'hiver
**midstream** *n* **in ~** au milieu du courant
**midsummer** *n* cœur *m* de l'été
**midway** *adv* à mi-chemin
**midwife** *n* (*pl* **midwives**) sage-femme *f* (*pl* sages-femmes)
**midwifery** *n* obstétrique *f*
**midwinter** *n* fort *m* de l'hiver, cœur *m* de l'hiver
**mien** *n* mine *f*, air *m*
**might** *n* force *f*, puissance *f*; **~ is right** la raison du plus fort est toujours la meilleure; **with all one's ~** de toutes ses forces; *vi see* **may**
**mighty** *adj* puissant, fort; (big) grand, vaste; *adv* fort, bien, extrêmement
**mignonette** *n* réséda *m*
**migraine** *n* migraine *f*
**migrant** *n + adj* migrateur -trice
**migrate** *vi* émigrer
**migration** *n* migration *f*
**migratory** *adj* migrateur -trice
**mild** *adj* doux (*f* douce); léger -ère; (illness) bénin (*f* bénigne); modéré; **~ beer** bière brune
**mildew** *n* (wheat) rouille *f*; (vine) mildiou *m*; moisissure *f*
**mildness** *n* douceur *f*; (illness) bénignité *f*; (weather) clémence *f*
**mile** *n* mille *m*

**mileage** *n* distance *f* en milles
**milestone** *n* borne *f* milliaire; = borne *f* kilométrique
**milieu** *n* milieu *m*
**militancy** *n* attitude militante, esprit militant
**militant** *n + adj* militant -e
**militarism** *n* militarisme *m*
**military** *n* **the ~** les militaires *mpl*; *adj* militaire; **~ age** âge *m* de servir
**militate** *vi* militer
**militia** *n* milice *f*
**milk** *n* lait *m*; **~ and water** lait coupé d'eau; **land flowing with ~ and honey** pays *m* de cocagne; **malted ~** farine lactée; *vt* traire; *fig* exploiter
**milk-bar** *n* milk-bar *m*
**milk-float** *n* voiture *f* de laitier
**milkiness** *n* couleur laiteuse
**milking** *n* traite *f*
**milk-jug** *n* pot *m* à lait
**milkmaid** *n* laitière *f*
**milkman** *n* laitier *m*
**milksop** *n coll* poule mouillée
**milk-tooth** *n* dent *f* de lait
**milky** *adj* laiteux -euse
**mill** *n* moulin *m*; (modern) minoterie *f*; (factory) usine *f*, manufacture *f*; (spinning) filature *f*; *vt* moudre; (cloth) fouler; *mech* fraiser; *vi* (crowd) fourmiller
**millennium** *n* millénaire *m*, mille ans *mpl*
**miller** *n* meunier *m*; minotier *m*; *mech* (person) fraiseur *m*; (machine) fraiseuse *f*
**millet** *n* millet *m*, mil *m*
**milligram(me)** *n* milligramme *m*
**millimetre** *n* millimètre *m*
**milliner** *n* modiste *f*
**millinery** *n* articles *mpl* de mode
**million** *n* million *m*
**millionaire** *n* millionnaire
**millionth** *n* millionième; (fraction) millionième *m*; *adj* millionième
**millipede, millepede** *n* mille-pattes *m*
**millstone** *n* meule *f*; (encumbrance) boulet *m*
**mime** *n* mime *m*; *vt* mimer
**mimic** *n* mime *m*, imitateur -trice; *adj* mimique; *vt* imiter, mimer; (ape) singer
**mimicry** *n* imitation *f*
**mimosa** *n* mimosa *m*
**minaret** *n* minaret *m*
**mince** *n* hachis *m*; *vt* hacher; **~ one's words** parler du bout des lèvres; **not to ~ one's words** ne pas mâcher ses mots; *vi* minauder; marcher à petits pas
**mincemeat** *n* (meat) hachis *m*; espèce *f* de compote anglaise; *fig* **make ~ of** détruire

**mince-pie** *n* tartelette *f* contenant du mincemeat

**mincer** *n* hachoir *m*

**mincing-machine** *n* hachoir *m*, hache-viande *m invar*

**mind** *n* esprit *m*, âme *f*; (memory) souvenir *m*, mémoire *f*; (thought) pensée *f*, idée *f*; (intention) intention *f*, envie *f*; **bear in** ~ ne pas oublier; **be in one's right** ~ avoir toute sa raison; **be in two** ~**s about sth** être indécis sur qch; **be out of one's** ~ avoir perdu la raison; **call to** ~ se rappeler; **change one's** ~ changer d'avis; **give s/o a piece of one's** ~ dire son fait à qn; **have a good** ~ **to** avoir envie de; **have sth in** ~ avoir qch en vue; **he has sth on his** ~ il a qch qui le préoccupe (tracasse); **it came to my** ~ **that** il m'est venu à l'esprit que; **it went out of my** ~ cela m'est sorti de l'esprit; **know one's own** ~ savoir ce qu'on veut; **make up one's** ~ prendre son parti, se décider; **sound of** ~ sain d'esprit; **put sth out of one's** ~ ne plus penser à qch; **speak one's** ~ dire ce qu'on pense; **to my** ~ à mon avis; **turn of** ~ tour *m* d'esprit; *vt + vi* faire attention à; (look after) veiller sur, garder; (be concerned with) s'occuper de, se mêler de; (take care of) avoir soin de; (worry over) se soucier de; ~ **(out)!** attention!; ~ **the step** attention à la marche; ~ **you** remarquez, ~ **you don't fall** prenez garde de tomber; ~ **your own business** mêlez-vous de ce qui vous regarde; **I don't** ~ cela m'est égal; **I wouldn't** ~ **a chocolate** je prendrais volontiers un chocolat; **never** ~ n'importe, tant pis; **never** ~ **the money** ne regardez pas à l'argent; **Will you have a cake?** – **I don't** ~ **if I do** Voulez-vous prendre un gâteau? – Je veux bien; **would you** ~ **moving on a bit?** voudriez-vous avancer un peu?

**minded** *adj* disposé

**mindful** *adj* attentif -ive

**mindless** *adj* insouciant, indifférent; (stupid) imbécile, stupide

**mind-reader** *n* liseur -euse de pensées

¹**mine** *n* mine *f*; **lay** ~**s** mouiller des mines; *vt* miner

²**mine** *poss pron* le mien (*f* la mienne, *mpl* les miens, *fpl* les miennes); **a brother of** ~ un de mes frères; **this chair is** ~ cette chaise est à moi

**minefield** *n* champ *m* de mines

**mine-layer** *n* mouilleur *m* de mines

**miner** *n* mineur *m*

**mineral** *n* minéral *m*; (ore) minerai *m*; *adj* minéral; ~ **water** eau minérale

**mineralogy** *n* minéralogie *f*

**minesweeper** *n* dragueur *m* de mines

**mingle** *vt* mêler, mélanger; *vi* se mêler, se mélanger

**mingy** *adj coll* misérable, pauvre

**mini** *n* + *adj* mini

**mini-** *prefix* mini-

**miniature** *n* miniature *f*; ~ **painter** miniaturiste; *adj* en miniature, (de) petit format

**minibus** *n* minibus *m*

**minim** *n* (measure) goutte *f*; *mus* blanche *f*

**minimal** *adj* minimal

**minimize** *vt* réduire au minimum, minimiser

**minimum** *n* minimum *m* (*pl* minimums or minima); *adj* minimum (*f* minimum or minima, *pl* minimums or minima)

**mining** *n* exploitation minière; *adj* minier -ière

**minion** *n* favori -ite; (subject) subordonné -e

**minister** *n* ministre *m*; *eccles* pasteur *m*; *vi* ~ **to s/o's needs** soigner qn, pourvoir aux besoins de qn

**ministerial** *adj* ministériel -ielle; exécutif -ive; *eccles* sacerdotal

**ministry** *n* ministère *m*; (good offices) entremise *f*

**mink** *n* vison *m*

**minnow** *n* vairon *m*

**minor** *n* mineur -e; *adj* moindre, mineur; (unimportant) peu important, petit

**Minorca** *n* Minorque *f*

**minority** *n* minorité *f*; *adj* minoritaire

**minster** *n* cathédrale *f*

**minstrel** *n hist* ménestrel *m*; poète *m*, musicien *m*

¹**mint** *n* **the Mint** la Monnaie; **be worth a** ~ **of money** (person) rouler sur l'or; (thing) valoir des millions; **fresh from the** ~ tout battant neuf (*f* neuve); **make a** ~ **of money** gagner un argent fou; *adj* **in** ~ **condition** tout neuf (*f* toute neuve); *vt* (money) battre; (gold) monnayer; (invent) inventer

²**mint** *n bot* menthe *f*; ~ **-sauce** vinaigrette *f* à la menthe

**minuet** *n* menuet *m*

**minus** *n* (sign) moins *m*; ~ **quantity** quantité négative; *prep* moins

¹**minute** *n* minute *f*; (moment) moment *m*; (note) note *f*; ~ **s of a meeting** procès-verbal d'une séance; **he is due any** ~ il doit arriver d'un instant à l'autre; **I shan't be a** ~ j'en ai pour une seconde; **ten** ~ **s past three** trois heures dix; **ten** ~ **s to three** trois heures moins dix; **this very** ~ à l'instant même; *vt* minuter

²**minute** *adj* tout petit, minuscule;

(precise) minutieux -ieuse

**minute-book** *n* registre *m* des procès-verbaux

**minute-hand** *n* grande aiguille

**minutely** *adv* minutieusement; en détail

**minuteness** *n* petitesse *f*; (exactitude) minutie *f*

**minutiae** *npl* petits détails

**minx** *n* coquine *f*

**miracle** *n* miracle *m*

**miraculous** *adj* miraculeux -euse; extraordinaire

**mirage** *n* mirage *m*

**mire** *n* bourbier *m*; (mud) boue *f*; *fig* fange *f*; **sink into the ~** s'embourber

**mirror** *n* miroir *m*, glace *f*; **driving-~** rétroviseur *m*; *vt* refléter

**mirth** *n* gaieté *f*, allégresse *f*

**mirthful** *adj* joyeux -euse, gai

**mirthless** *adj* triste, sans gaieté

**misadventure** *n* mésaventure *f*

**misalliance** *n* mésalliance *f*

**misanthrope** *n* misanthrope

**misanthropic** *adj* misanthropique

**misanthropist** *n see* **misanthrope**

**misanthropy** *n* misanthropie *f*

**misapply** *vt* mal appliquer, mal employer; (funds) détourner

**misapprehend** *vt* mal comprendre

**misapprehension** *n* malentendu *m*, méprise *f*

**misappropriate** *vt* détourner

**misappropriation** *n* détournement *m*

**misbegotten** *adj* (child) illégitime; *fig* misérable

**misbehave** *vi* se conduire mal

**misbehaviour** *n* mauvaise conduite.

**miscalculate** *vt* mal calculer

**miscalculation** *n* mauvais calcul

**miscall** *vt* mal nommer

**miscarriage** *n* (failure) insuccès *m*; *med* fausse couche; (loss) égarement *m*; **~ of justice** erreur *f* judiciaire

**miscarry** *vi* (go astray) s'égarer; *med* faire une fausse couche; (fail) échouer

**miscellaneous** *adj* divers, varié

**miscellany** *n* mélange *m*

**mischance** *n* mauvaise chance; mésaventure *f*, malheur *m*

**mischief** *n* (harm) mal *m*, tort *m*; (child) espièglerie *f*; malice *f*; **be up to some ~** méditer un mauvais coup; **keep s/o out of ~** empêcher qn de faire des sottises; **make ~** semer la discorde

**mischief-maker** *n* brandon *m* de discorde

**mischievous** *adj* méchant; (thing) nuisible; (child) espiègle; malicieux -ieuse

**misconceive** *vt* mal concevoir

**misconception** *n* malentendu *m*; conception fausse

**misconduct** *n* (business) mauvaise gestion; (person) mauvaise conduite; (adultery) adultère *m*; *vt* mal gérer; **~ oneself** se conduire mal

**misconstruction** *n* fausse interprétation

**misconstrue** *vt* mal interpréter

**miscount** *n* erreur *f* d'addition; *pol* erreur *f* dans le dépouillement du scrutin; *vt* mal compter

**miscreant** *n* scélérat -e

**misdeal** *n* maldonne *f*; *vt* maldonner

**misdeed** *n* méfait *m*

**misdemeanour** *n leg* délit *m*; écart *m* de conduite

**misdirect** *vt* (letter) mal adresser; (aim) mal viser; (direction) mal diriger; (misinform) mal renseigner

**miser** *n* avare

**miserable** *adj* misérable, malheureux -euse, triste

**miserly** *adj* avare

**misery** *n* misère *f*, détresse *f*; (suffering) supplice *m*

**misfire** *vi* rater, faire long feu; (engine) avoir des ratés; (joke) manquer son effet

**misfit** *n* vêtement manqué; (social) inadapté -e

**misfortune** *n* malheur *m*, infortune *f*

**misgiving** *n* pressentiment *m*, doute *m*; (fear) crainte *f*

**misgovern** *vt* mal gouverner

**misguided** *adj* peu judicieux -ieuse, mal avisé, malencontreux -euse

**mishandle** *vt* maltraiter; (business) mal conduire

**mishap** *n* contretemps *m*, accident *m*, mésaventure *f*

**misinform** *vt* mal renseigner

**misinterpret** *vt* mal interpréter

**misinterpretation** *n* fausse interprétation

**misjudge** *vt* mal juger; méconnaître

**mislay** *vt* égarer

**mislead** *vt* tromper; (lead astray) égarer

**misleading** *adj* trompeur -euse

**mismanage** *vt* mal conduire; mal gérer

**mismanagement** *n* mauvaise gestion

**misname** *vt* mal nommer

**misnomer** *n* erreur *f* de nom; fausse appellation

**misogynist** *n* misogyne

**misplace** *vt* mal placer; **~d remark** remarque déplacée

**misprint** *n* faute *f* d'impression, coquille *f*; *vt* faire une faute d'impression dans

**mispronounce** *vt* mal prononcer

**mispronunciation** *n* faute *f* de prononciation, mauvaise prononciation

**misquotation** *n* citation incorrecte

**misquote** *vt* citer à faux

**misread** *vt* mal lire; (misinterpret) mal interpréter

**misrepresent** vt mal représenter; (facts) dénaturer, travestir

**misrule** n mauvais gouvernement; désordre m; vt mal gouverner

**Miss** n Mademoiselle f; ~ **World** Miss Monde; **miss** demoiselle f

**miss** n coup manqué; **give sth a** ~ omettre qch; vt manquer, rater; (omit) omettre, passer; (not see) ne pas voir; remarquer l'absence de; coll fig ~ **the bus** rater l'occasion; ~ **the point** ne pas comprendre; **he** ~**ed his wallet** il ne trouva pas son portefeuille; **I** ~**ed my footing** le pied me manqua; **I** ~ **my mother** ma mère me manque; **my pen is** ~**ing** mon stylo a disparu; **narrowly** ~ **doing sth** faillir faire qch; coll **you haven't** ~**ed much** vous n'avez pas raté grand-chose; **we** ~ **the car** nous regrettons la voiture; vi ~ **out** échouer

**missal** n eccles missel m

**misshapen** adj difforme

**missile** n projectile m; mil missile m; **guided** ~ engin téléguidé

**missing** adj absent, manquant; ~ **link** forme intermédiaire disparue

**mission** n mission f

**missionary** n+adj missionnaire

**missive** n missive f, lettre f

**misspell** vt mal épeler

**misspent** adj mal employé

**misstate** vt rapporter incorrectement

**misstatement** n rapport inexact

**missus** n coll the ~ la vieille, la bourgeoise

**mist** n brume f; (on glass) buée f; **the** ~**s of time** la nuit des temps; vt couvrir de buée; vi disparaître sous la brume; se couvrir de buée

**mistakable** adj facile à confondre

**mistake** n erreur f, méprise f, faute f; **make a** ~ se tromper; **there's no** ~ **about it** c'est bien le cas de dire, il n'y a pas à dire; vt mal comprendre; (intentions) se méprendre sur; ~ **one's way** se tromper de chemin; ~ **s/o for s/o else** prendre qn pour qn d'autre

**mistaken** adj (idea) erroné; (misunderstood) mal compris; **be** ~ se tromper, faire erreur; **if I am not** ~ sauf erreur

**Mister** n see **Mr**

**mistime** vt faire à contretemps; mal calculer

**mistimed** adj inopportun

**mistiness** n état brumeux

**mistletoe** n gui m

**mistranslate** vt mal traduire

**mistreat** vt maltraiter

**mistress** n maîtresse f; (teacher) institutrice f; (boss) patronne f; **be one's own** ~ être indépendante

**mistrust** n méfiance f, manque m de confiance; vt se méfier de

**misty** adj brumeux -euse; (eye) voilé

**misunderstand** vt mal comprendre, mal interpréter; méconnaître

**misunderstanding** n malentendu m; (quarrel) mésentente f, brouille f

**misuse** n abus m, mauvais usage; vt abuser de, faire un mauvais usage de; (use wrongly) employer incorrectement; (ill-treat) maltraiter

**mite** n (small gift) obole f; (insect) mite f; (child) mioche m; (small quantity) miette f

**mitigate** vt adoucir, atténuer, amoindrir; (heat) tempérer; **mitigating circumstances** circonstances atténuantes

**mitigation** n adoucissement m; amoindrissement m; (penalty) atténuation f

**mitre** n mitre f

**mitten** n mitaine f

**mix** n mélange m, proportions fpl; vt mêler, mélanger; (drink) préparer; (salad) retourner; ~ **ed up in sth** être mêlé à une affaire; **he** ~**es everything up** il embrouille tout; vi se mêler, se mélanger; ~ **with people** fréquenter les gens

**mixed** adj mêlé, mélangé; (school, bathing, etc) mixte; (colours) assorti

**mixer** n mélangeur m, mixe(u)r m; rad opérateur m des sons; **be a good (bad)** ~ être (peu) sociable

**mixture** n mélange m; (pharmacy) mixture f

**mix-up** n confusion f, embrouillement m; coll pagaille f; (fight) coll bagarre f

**mnemonic** n mnémonique f; adj mnémonique

**moan** n gémissement m, plainte f; vi gémir

**moat** n douve f

**mob** n (crowd) foule f; (rabble) populace f; vt malmener; (fans) assiéger; vi s'attrouper

**mobile** n mobile m; adj mobile; (character) changeant

**mobility** n mobilité f

**mobilization** n mobilisation f

**mobilize** vt mobiliser; vi entrer en mobilisation

**moccasin, moccassin** n mocassin m

**mock** n **make a** ~ **of s/o** se moquer de qn; adj faux (f fausse), contrefait, d'imitation; vt se moquer de; narguer; tromper; (mimic) imiter, singer

**mockery** n moquerie f, raillerie f; (pretence) semblant m; objet m de dérision

**mock-up** n maquette f

**mod** n sl jeune homme (fille) habillé(e) avec recherche (à motocyclette); adj sl moderne

**mode** n (manner) façon f, mode m,

manière *f*; (fashion) mode *f*

**model** *n* modèle *m*; maquette *f*; (dressmaking) patron *m*; **scale ~** modèle réduit; *adj* modèle; *vt* modeler; *vi* (fashions) être mannequin

**modelling** *n* modelage *m*

¹**moderate** *adj* modéré; médiocre, ordinaire; (character) raisonnable; (price) modique

²**moderate** *vt* modérer, tempérer; présider, arbitrer; *vi* se modérer

**moderation** *n* modération *f*, mesure *f*; **in ~** modérément

**moderator** *n* président *m*

**modern** *adj* moderne; **~ languages** langues vivantes

**modernism** *n* modernisme *m*; nouveauté *f*

**modernistic** *adj* moderniste

**modernity** *n* modernité *f*

**modernize** *vt* moderniser

**modest** *adj* modeste; (prudish) pudique

**modesty** *n* modestie *f*; (prudery) pudeur *f*; (expense) modicité *f*; (demand) modération *f*; absence *f* de prétention

**modicum** *n* petite quantité

**modification** *n* modification *f*; (attenuation) atténuation *f*

**modify** *vt* modifier; (attenuate) atténuer

**modish** *adj* élégant, à la mode

**modulate** *vt* moduler

**modulation** *n* modulation *f*

**module** *n* module *m*; **command ~** module *m* de commande; **service ~** module *m* de service

**mohair** *n* mohair *m*

**Mohammedan, Mahometan** *n* Musulman -e; *adj* musulman, mahométan

**moil** *vi* **toil and ~** travailler dur

**moist** *adj* humide, mouillé; (skin) moite

**moisten** *vt* humecter, mouiller

**moisture** *n* humidité *f*; (skin) moiteur *f*

**molar** *n* molaire *f*; *adj* molaire

**molasses** *npl* mélasse *f*

¹**mole** *n zool* taupe *f*

²**mole** *n* (pier) môle *m*, jetée *f*

³**mole** *n* (spot) envie *f*, grain *m* de beauté

**molecular** *adj* moléculaire

**molecule** *n* molécule *f*

**molehill** *n* taupinière *f*

**molest** *vt* molester; rudoyer

**mollify** *vt* apaiser, adoucir

**mollusc** *n* mollusque *m*

**mollycoddle** *vt* dorloter, choyer

**molten** *adj* fondu

**molybdenum** *n* molybdène *m*

**moment** *n* moment *m*, instant *m*; **a ~ ago** il y a un moment; **at the present ~** en ce moment; **from the ~ when** ... dès l'instant où ...; **I have just this ~ arrived** j'arrive à l'instant, je viens tout

juste d'arriver; **it all happened in a ~** cela se passa en un clin d'œil; **just one ~, please** un petit instant, s'il vous plaît; **not for one ~!** jamais de la vie!; **of great ~** de (d'une) grande importance; **the ~ he arrives** dès qu'il viendra

**momentary** *adj* passager -ère, momentané

**momentous** *adj* important, capital

**momentum** *n* vitesse acquise, élan *m*; *phys* quantité *f* de mouvement

**monarch** *n* monarque *m*

**monarchist** *n* + *adj* monarchiste

**monarchy** *n* monarchie *f*

**monastery** *n* monastère *m*

**monastic(al)** *adj* monastique

**monasticism** *n* monachisme *m*, vie *f* monastique

**Monday** *n* lundi *m*

**monetary** *adj* monétaire

**money** *n* argent *m*, monnaie *f*; **be coining ~** ramasser l'argent à la pelle; **be rolling in ~** rouler sur l'or; **bring in big ~** rapporter gros; **buy sth with one's own ~** acheter qch de ses propres deniers; **come into ~** hériter d'une fortune; **get one's ~ back** être remboursé; **have one's ~'s worth** en avoir pour son argent; *coll* **have pots of ~** *sl* être plein aux as; **paper ~** papier-monnaie *m*; **part with one's ~** débourser; **pocket ~** argent *m* de poche; **ready ~** argent *m* liquide; **there's ~ in it** c'est une bonne affaire; **your ~ or your life!** la bourse ou la vie!

**money-box** *n* tirelire *f*

**money-changer** *n* changeur *m*, cambiste *m*

**moneyed** *adj* riche

**money-grubber** *n* grippe-sou *m* (*pl* grippe-sou(s))

**money-lender** *n* prêteur -euse d'argent

**money-market** *n* marché *m* monétaire

**money-order** *n* mandat *m*

**money-spinner** *n coll* chose *f* qui rapporte beaucoup d'argent; personne *f* qui gagne beaucoup d'argent

**mongol** *n* + *adj* mongolien -ienne

**Mongolian** *n* Mongol -e; *adj* mongol

**mongoose** *n* mangouste *f*

**mongrel** *n* + *adj* (human) métis -isse; (dog) bâtard *m*

**monitor** *n* moniteur -trice; *rad* opérateur -trice d'interception; **~ screen** écran *m* témoin; **~ speaker** haut-parleur *m* témoin; *vt* contrôler

**monk** *n* moine *m*, religieux *m*

**monkey** *n* singe *m*; **female ~** guenon *f*; *sl* **get one's ~ up** piquer une colère; *coll* **I'm not having any ~ business** on ne va pas me la faire; *vi* **~ about** faire

l'idiot -e; ~ **about with** tripoter; toucher à
**monkey-nut** n cacahouète f
**monkey-puzzle** n bot araucaria m
**monkey-wrench** n clef f (clé f) à molette,
US clef (clé) anglaise
**mono** adj coll mono
**monochrome** n monochrome m; adj
monochrome
**monocle** n monocle m
**monogamy** n monogamie f
**monogram** n monogramme m
**monograph** n monographie f
**monolith** n monolithe m
**monologue** n monologue m
**monomania** n monomanie f
**monoplane** n monoplan m
**monopolist** n monopolisateur -trice
**monopolize** vt monopoliser
**monopoly** n monopole m
**monorail** n monorail m
**monosyllable** n monosyllabe m
**monotone** n bruit m monotone, son m
monotone
**monotonous** adj monotone; ennuyeux
-euse, fastidieux -ieuse
**monotony** n monotonie f
**monsoon** n mousson f
**monster** n monstre m; adj énorme, colossal
**monstrosity** n monstruosité f; monstre
m; énormité f
**monstrous** adj monstrueux -euse
**montage** n montage m
**month** n mois m; by the ~ au mois;
**calendar** ~ mois m du calendrier; get
**one's** ~ 's pay toucher son mois; in the
~ of au mois de; once a ~ une fois par
mois
**monthly** n revue mensuelle; adj mensuel
-elle; (ticket, etc) valable (pour) un
mois; ~ **pay** mois m; ~ **payment** (instalment) mensualité f; physiol ~
**period** règles fpl; adv mensuellement,
par mois; **be paid** ~ être payé au mois
**monument** n monument m; pierre tombale
**monumental** adj monumental; ~ **mason**
marbrier m
**moo** n meuglement m, beuglement m; vi
meugler, beugler; interj meuh!
**mooch** vi ~ **about** flâner, rôder
**mood** n humeur f, disposition f; gram
mode m; **be in a good (bad)** ~ être de
bonne (mauvaise) humeur; **be in no** ~
**for** n'avoir aucune envie de; **be in the**
**for** être d'humeur à; **have** ~ s être lunatique
**moodiness** n humeur changeante
**moody** adj d'humeur incertaine
**moon** n lune f; **landing on the** ~ aluni-
sage m; **land on the** ~ alunir; **many** ~ s

ago il y a longtemps; **once in a blue** ~
tous les trente-six du mois; vi ~ **about**
muser
**moonbeam** n rayon m de lune
**moonlight** n clair m de lune; **in the** ~ au
clair de la lune
**moonlit** adj éclairé par la lune
**moonshine** n clair m de lune; (nonsense)
balivernes fpl, blague f; US alcool m de
contrebande
**moonshot** n envoi m d'une fusée vers la
lune
**moonstruck** adj coll toqué
**moony** adj rêveur -euse
**Moor** n Maure m, Mauresque f
¹**moor** n lande f, bruyère f
²**moor** vt amarrer; vi s'amarrer
**moorhen** n poule f d'eau
**mooring** n amarrage m; **ship at her** ~ s
navire m sur ses amarres
**moorland** n lande f
**moose** n élan m du Canada
¹**moot** adj discutable
²**moot** vt (question) soulever; **be** ~ ed être
mis sur le tapis
**mop** n balai m à franges, balai m à laver;
~ **of hair** tignasse f; vt essuyer; ~
**one's brow** s'éponger le front; ~ **up**
éponger; (absorb) absorber
**mope** vi être triste; s'ennuyer
**moped** n cyclomoteur m, vélomoteur m
**mopping-up** n épongeage m, essuyage m
**moral** n morale f, moralité f; ~ s moralité f, mœurs fpl; adj moral; (morally
good) conforme aux bonnes mœurs
**morale** n moral m
**moralist** n moraliste
**morality** n moralité f; (good conduct)
bonnes mœurs
**moralize** vi moraliser, faire de la morale
**morally** adv moralement
**morass** n marais m, fondrière f
**moratorium** n moratoire m
**morbid** adj morbide
**morbidity** n morbidité f
**more** n davantage, plus; encore; ~ **than**
**five** plus de cinq; **a little** ~ encore un
peu; **be no** ~ être mort; **one** ~ un de
plus, encore un; **say no** ~ n'en parlez
plus; **the** ~ **he tries, the** ~ **he loses** plus
il essaie, plus il perd; **what is** ~ qui plus
est; adj plus de; adv plus, davantage; ~
**and** ~ de plus en plus; **all the** ~ d'autant plus; **don't come any** ~ ne venez
plus; **once** ~ encore une fois
**moreover** adv d'ailleurs, du reste, de plus
**morgue** n morgue f
**moribund** adj moribond
**Mormon** n + adj mormon -e
**morning** n matin m; matinée f; **all the** ~
toute la matinée; **early in the** ~ de bon
matin; **good** ~! bonjour!; **in the** ~ le

matin; **the ~ before** la veille au matin; **the next ~** le lendemain matin; **two o'clock in the ~** deux heures du matin; *adj* matinal, du matin

**Morocco** *n* le Maroc; (leather) maroquin *m*

**moron** *n* idiot -e; minus habens *m invar*

**morose** *adj* morose

**morphia, morphine** *n* morphine *f*

**morphinomaniac** *n* + *adj* morphinomane

**morphology** *n* morphologie *f*

**morris-dance** *n* danse folklorique anglaise

**morse** *n* (code) morse *m*

**morsel** *n* morceau *m*, petit morceau

**mortal** *adj* mortel -elle

**mortality** *n* mortalité *f*

**mortar** *n* mortier *m*

**mortar-board** *n* planche *f* à mortier

**mortgage** *n* hypothèque *f*; *vt* hypothéquer

**mortification** *n* mortification *f*

**mortify** *vt* mortifier; humilier; *med* gangrener

**mortuary** *n* morgue *f*; (hospital) salle *f* mortuaire

**mosaic** *n* mosaïque *f*; *adj* en mosaïque

**Moscow** *n* Moscou *m*

**Moslem, Muslim** *n* Mahométan -e, Musulman -e; *adj* mahométan, musulman

**mosque** *n* mosquée *f*

**mosquito** *n* moustique *m*

**mosquito-net** *n* moustiquaire *f*

**moss** *n bot* mousse *f*; (bog) marais *m*

**mossy** *adj* moussu

**most** *n* le plus; la plupart, la majeure partie; **~ of them** la plupart d'entre eux; **at the ~** tout au plus; **make the ~ of sth** tirer le meilleur parti possible de qch, profiter au maximum de qch; (eke out) ménager le plus possible qch; *adj* le plus de; **~ people** la plupart des gens; **for the ~ part** pour la plupart; *adv* le plus; (very much) très, fort, bien, on ne peut plus, tout ce qu'il y a de plus

**motel** *n* motel *m*

**moth** *n* (clothes) mite *f*; papillon *m* de nuit

**moth-ball** *n* boule *f* de naphtaline

**moth-eaten** *adj* mité, mangé des mites; *fig* miteux -euse

**mother** *n* mère *f*; **~ country** mère patrie *f*; **~ naked** nu comme un ver; **~ of five** mère *f* de cinq enfants; **Mother's Day** la fête des Mères; **~ tongue** langue maternelle; **every ~'s son** tous sans exception; **unmarried ~** mère *f* célibataire, *pej* fille-mère *f* (*pl* filles-mères); *vt* servir de mère à; (fuss over) dorloter

**motherhood** *n* maternité *f*

**mother-in-law** *n* belle-mère *f* (*pl* belles-mères)

**motherland** *n* patrie *f*

**motherless** *adj* sans mère, orphelin de mère

**motherly** *adj* maternel -elle

**mother-of-pearl** *n* nacre *f*

**moth-killer** *n* antimite *m*

**mothproof** *adj* antimite(s)

**motion** *n* mouvement *m*; déplacement *m*; (sign) signe *m*, geste *m*; (proposal) proposition *f*, motion *f*; *med* évacuation *f*; **~-picture** film *m*; **carry a ~** adopter une motion; **go through the ~s of doing sth** faire semblant de faire qch; **propose a ~** faire une proposition; **set in ~** mettre en mouvement; *vt* faire signe à

**motionless** *adj* immobile

**motivate** *vt* motiver

**motivation** *n* motivation *f*

**motive** *n* motif *m*; (action) mobile *m*; ressort *m*; *adj* moteur -trice

**motley** *adj* (colours) bariolé; (varied) divers

**motor** *n* moteur *m*; (car) auto *f*, voiture *f*; **~-coach** autocar *m*; **~ show** salon *m* de l'auto; *vi* voyager en automobile

**motorbike** *n* motocyclette *f*

**motorboat** *n* canot *m* automobile

**motorcade** *n US* défilé *m* de voitures

**motorcar** *n* auto *f*, voiture *f*

**motorcycle** *n* motocyclette *f*

**motoring** *n* automobilisme *m*; **school of ~** auto-école *f*

**motorist** *n* automobiliste

**motorize** *vt* motoriser

**motor-scooter** *n* scooter *m*

**motorway** *n* autoroute *f*

**mottle** *n* tache *f*; (marbling) marbrure *f*; *vt* tacheter, marbrer; **~d** (sky, horse) pommelé; (skin) marbré

**motto** *n* devise *f*

**¹mould** *n* (soil) terre *f*, terreau *m*

**²mould** *n* (mildew) moisi *m*, moisissure *f*; *vi* moisir

**³mould** *n* (shape) moule *m*; *vt* mouler; former

**moulder** *vi* tomber en poussière; moisir

**mouldiness** *n* moisissure *f*

**moulding** *n* moulage *m*; (character) formation *f*; (decoration, etc) moulure *f*

**mouldy** *adj* moisi; **go ~** moisir; **smell ~** sentir le moisi

**moult** *vi* muer

**moulting** *n* mue *f*

**mound** *n* butte *f*, tertre *m*

**¹mount** *n* mont *m*, montagne *f*

**²mount** *n* (horse) monture *f*; montage *m*, support *m*; (photo) carton *m*; (machine) armement *m*; (stamp) charnière *f*; *vt* monter, monter sur; **~ guard**

monter la garde; *vi* monter; (horse) monter à cheval; (rise) s'élever, augmenter; **~ed** à cheval; **~ up** augmenter

**mountain** *n* montagne *f*; **~ range** chaîne *f* de montagnes; **make ~s out of molehills** se noyer dans un verre d'eau; *adj* (mountainous) montagneux -euse; (of mountain), montagnard

**mountaineer** *n* alpiniste; *vi* faire de l'alpinisme

**mountaineering** *n* alpinisme *m*

**mountainous** *adj* montagneux -euse

**mountebank** *n* saltimbanque *m*; (quack) charlatan *m*

**mourn** *vt* pleurer, prendre le deuil pour; *vi* pleurer

**mourner** *n* personne *f* qui suit le cortège funèbre

**mournful** *adj* lugubre, triste

**mourning** *n* deuil *m*; (clothes) habits *mpl* de deuil; **be in ~ for** porter le deuil de; **go into ~** prendre le deuil; **in deep ~** en grand deuil

**mouse** *n* souris *f*; *vi* chasser les souris

**mouse-colour** *n* gris *m* de souris

**mouse-hole** *n* trou *m* de souris

**mouse-like** *adj* insignifiant

**mouse-trap** *n* souricière *f*; *coll* fromage *m* de qualité inférieure

**mousse** *n* mousse *f*

**moustache** *n* moustache *f*

**mousy** *adj* gris souris *invar*; timide

**mouth** *n* bouche *f*; (animal) gueule *f*; (opening) ouverture *f*; (river) embouchure *f*; (bottle) goulot *m*; **by word of ~** de vive voix; **down in the ~** triste; **make s/o's ~ water** faire venir l'eau à la bouche de qn; **put words into s/o's ~** attribuer des paroles à qn; *vt* déclamer; grimacer

**mouthful** *n* bouchée *f*; (liquid) gorgée *f*; (swimming) **swallow a ~** boire la tasse

**mouth-organ** *n* harmonica *m*

**mouthpiece** *n* (instrument) embouchure *f*; (person) porte-parole *m invar*

**movable** *adj* mobile; **~s** *npl* biens mobiliers

**move** *n* (house) déménagement *m*; mouvement *m*; (chess) coup *m*; (intervention) démarche *f*; **be on the ~** être en mouvement; **get a ~ on** *coll* se dépêcher; *sl* se grouiller; **it's your ~** (c'est) à vous de jouer; **make a ~** (game) jouer; (depart) se mettre en route, partir; **make the first ~** faire le premier pas; *vt* déplacer, bouger, remuer; (goods) transporter; (furniture) déménager; (feelings) toucher, émouvoir; (opinion) faire changer d'avis à; (resolution) proposer; **~ back** faire reculer; **~ forward** faire

avancer; **~ heaven and earth** faire des pieds et des mains; **~ on** faire circuler; **~ out** déloger, faire sortir; **~ over** écarter; **~ s/o to anger** provoquer la colère de qn; **~ s/o to do sth** inciter qn à faire qch; *vi* se déplacer; bouger; **~ away** s'éloigner; **~ back** reculer; **~ forward** avancer; (house) **~ in** emménager; **~ off** s'en aller; **~ on** circuler; aller plus loin; **~ out** sortir; (house) déménager; **~ over** s'écarter

**movement** *n* mouvement *m*; (shift) déplacement *m*; **watch s/o's ~s** surveiller les allées et venues de qn

**mover** *n* moteur *m*; auteur *m*

**movie** *n* *coll US* film *m*; **go to the ~s** aller au cinéma

**moving** *adj* en mouvement; mobile; (feeling) touchant, émouvant; (force) moteur -trice

**mow** *vt* (lawn) tondre; (field) faucher

**mower** *n* (person) faucheur -euse; (lawn) tondeuse *f*

**Mr** *n* M., Monsieur *m*

**Mrs** *n* Mme, Madame *f*

**much** *n* une bonne (grande) partie; beaucoup, grand-chose; **~ has happened** il s'est passé beaucoup de choses; **he's not ~ of a teacher** ce n'est pas un très bon professeur; **I don't think ~ of him** je ne l'estime pas beaucoup; **I don't think ~ of it** j'en fais peu de cas; **make ~ of sth** faire grand cas de qch; vanter qch; **that's not up to ~** cela ne vaut pas grand-chose; **this is too ~!** c'est trop fort!; **twice as ~ as** deux fois plus que; *adj* beaucoup de, bien du (de la, des); **as ~ as** autant de; **how ~?** combien de?; **so ~** tant de; **too ~** trop de; *adv* beaucoup, bien; **~ to his surprise** à son grand étonnement; **~ the best de** beaucoup le meilleur; **~ the same** à peu près la même chose; **as ~** autant; **as ~ as to say** avec l'air de vouloir dire; **how ~?** combien?; **it doesn't matter ~** cela n'a pas grande importance; **so ~** tant; **too ~** trop; **very ~** beaucoup

**muchness** *n* **much of a ~** pareil -eille; *coll* kif-kif *invar*

**muck** *n* fumier *m*; (mire) fange *f*; (animal) crotte *f*; (filth) ordures *fpl*; *coll fig* cochonneries *fpl*; bêtises *fpl*; *vt* salir, crotter; **~ up sth** gâcher qch; (work) cochonner; *vi* **~ about** flâner; *sl* **~ in with s/o** partager la chambre de qn, partager les repas de qn

**muckiness** *n* saleté *f*

**muck-raking** *n* publication *f* de scandales; colportage *m* de potins

**mucky** *adj* sale, crotté

**mud** *n* boue *f*; bourbe *f*; (mire) fange *f*; (liquid) vase *f*; **drag s/o's name in the**

~ traîner qn dans la boue; **stuck** . ¡ the ~ embourbé

**muddle** *n* fouillis *m*, confusion *f*; **be in a ~** être en désordre; (person) avoir les idées brouillées; **get into a ~** s'embrouiller; *vt* embrouiller, brouiller; *vi* ~ **through** se débrouiller, s'en tirer tant bien que mal

**muddle-headed** *adj* à l'esprit confus; (idea) embrouillé

**muddler** *n* brouillon -onne

**muddy** *adj* boueux -euse, crotté, couvert de boue

**mudguard** *n* garde-boue *m invar*

**mud-slinging** *n* médisance *f*

¹**muff** *n* manchon *m*

²**muff** *n* (person) empoté -e; *vt* rater, louper

**muffin** *n* sorte *f* de galette

**muffle** *vt* emmitoufler, envelopper; (sound) étouffer; (bell) assourdir; *vi* ~ **up** s'emmitoufler

**muffler** *n* cache-nez *m invar*

¹**mug** *n* pot *m*, chope *f*; grosse tasse; gobelet *m*; *sl* (face) binette *f*, gueule *f*

²**mug** *n sl* nigaud -e, andouille *f*

³**mug** *vt* dévaliser, agresser et dévaliser; *coll* ~ **up** bûcher, piocher

**muggy** *adj* lourd, mou ( *f* molle)

**mulberry** *n* mûre *f*; ~ **-tree** mûrier *m*

**mulch** *n hort* paillis *m*; *vt* pailler

**mulct** *vt* frapper d'une amende; priver de

¹**mule** *n* mulet *m*, mule *f*

²**mule** *n* (slipper) mule *f*

**muleteer** *n* muletier *m*

**mulish** *adj* têtu, entêté

¹**mull** *vt* chauffer avec des épices

²**mull** *vt* ~ **over** réfléchir sur

**mullet** *n* muge *m*; **red** ~ rouget *m*

**mulligatawny** *n* potage *m* au curry

**mullion** *n* meneau *m*

**multicoloured** *adj* multicolore

**multifarious** *adj* divers, multiple

**multilateral** *adj* multilatéral

**multimillionaire** *n* multimillionnaire *m*; *adj* multimillionnaire

**multiple** *n* multiple *m*; *adj* multiple

**multiplication** *n* multiplication *f*

**multiplicity** *n* multiplicité *f*

**multiply** *vt* multiplier; *vi* se multiplier

**multitude** *n* multitude *f*, foule *f*; multiplicité *f*

**multitudinous** *adj* innombrable, nombreux -euse

¹**mum** *n coll* maman *f*

²**mum** *interj* chut!; ~**'s the word!** motus!; **keep** ~ ne pas souffler mot

**mumble** *vt* + *vi* marmonner, marmotter

**mumbo-jumbo** *n* baragouin *m*; culte superstitieux

**mummify** *vt* momifier

¹**mummy** *n* momie *f*

²**mummy** *n coll* maman *f*

**mumps** *n* oreillons *mpl*

**munch** *vt* mâcher, mâchonner

**mundane** *adj* mondain

**municipal** *adj* municipal

**municipality** *n* municipalité *f*

**munificence** *n* munificence *f*

**munificent** *adj* libéral, généreux -euse

**munitions** *npl* munitions *fpl*

**mural** *n* peinture murale; *adj* mural

**murder** *n* meurtre *m*, assassinat *m*; *vt* assassiner; (song) massacrer; (language) estropier

**murderer** *n* meurtrier *m*, assassin *m*

**murderess** *n* meurtrière *f*

**murderous** *adj* meurtrier -ière

**murk, mirk** *n* obscurité *f*

**murkiness** *n* obscurité *f*

**murky** *adj* obscur, sombre; *fig* ténébreux -euse

**murmur** *n* murmure *m*; *vt* + *vi* murmurer, susurrer

**muscatel** *n* muscat *m*

**muscle** *n* muscle *m*

**muscular** *adj* musculaire

¹**muse** *n* muse *f*

²**muse** *vi* rêver, méditer

**museum** *n* musée *m*; ~ **-piece** pièce *f* de musée

**mush** *n coll* bouillie *f*; *rad* friture *f*

**mushroom** *n* champignon *m*; ~ **spawn** blanc *m* de champignon; *vi* proliférer, se propager

**mushroom-bed** *n* champignonnière *f*

**mushroom-grower** *n* champignonniste

**mushrooming** *n* **go** ~ aller cueillir des champignons

**mushy** *adj* (ground) détrempé; (fruit) blet ( *f* blette); *fig* plein de sensiblerie

**music** *n* musique *f*; *fig* **face the** ~ accepter les conséquences de ses actes; tenir tête à l'orage; **programme** ~ musique *f* de genre; **set to** ~ mettre en musique

**musical** *n* opérette *f*; *adj* musical; (person) musicien -ienne; harmonieux -ieuse; ~ **box** boîte *f* à musique; ~ **comedy** opérette *f*

**musically** *adv* du point de vue musical

**music-hall** *n* music-hall *m*

**musician** *n* musicien -ienne

**music-stand** *n* pupitre *m* à musique

**music-stool** *n* tabouret *m* à piano

**musk** *n* musc *m*

**musket** *n* mousquet *m*

**musky** *adj* musqué

**Muslim** *n* + *adj see* **Moslem**

**muslin** *n* mousseline *f*

**musquash** *n* rat musqué

**mussel** *n* moule *f*

¹**must** *n* moisi *m*

²**must** *n* (wine) moût *m*

³**must** *n coll* **it's a** ~ c'est absolument

595

essentiel, c'est une nécessité; *vi* (necessity) falloir; devoir; **I ~ go now** il faut que je parte maintenant; **she ~ have seen him** elle a dû le voir, elle l'aura vu; **that ~ be my mother** ce doit être ma mère

**mustang** *n* mustang *m*

**mustard** *n* moutarde *f*

**mustard-gas** *n* ypérite *f*

**mustard-plaster** *n* sinapisme *m*

**mustard-pot** *n* moutardier *m*

**muster** *n* (assembly) rassemblement *m*; *mil* revue *f*; **pass ~** être passable; *vt* rassembler; (comprise) compter; *mil* passer en revue; **~ one's strength** rassembler ses forces; *vi* se rassembler, se réunir

**mustiness** *n* remugle *m*, odeur *f* de moisi

**musty** *adj* **~ smell** remugle *m*, odeur *f* de moisi; **smell ~** sentir le moisi; (room) sentir le renfermé

**mutable** *adj* muable, variable, changeant

**mutate** *vi* subir une mutation

**mutation** *n* mutation *f*; changement *m*

**mute** *n* + *adj* muet -ette; *n* (funeral attendant) croque-mort *m*; *mus* sourdine *f*; *vt* amortir, étouffer

**mutilate** *vt* mutiler, estropier

**mutilation** *n* mutilation *f*

**mutineer** *n* mutin *m*, rebelle *m*

**mutinous** *adj* mutin, rebelle

**mutiny** *n* révolte *f*, mutinerie *f*; *vi* se mutiner, se révolter

**mutt** *n coll* imbécile

**mutter** *vt* + *vi* marmonner, marmotter

**mutton** *n* mouton *m*; **dead as ~** tout à fait mort; **leg of ~** gigot *m*; **roast ~** rôti *m* de mouton

**mutual** *adj* réciproque, mutuel -elle; **~ benefit society** société *f* de secours mutuels; **~ friend** ami -e commun -e

**mutuality** *n* mutualité *f*

**Muzak** *n* musique enregistrée et continue

**muzzle** *n* museau *m*; (for dogs) muselière *f*; (gun) bouche *f*; *vt* museler, bâillonner

**muzzy** *adj* (idea) confus, vague; (person) brouillé dans ses idées; (outline) flou; (dazed) hébété; (weather) brumeux -euse; (tipsy) gris

**my** *adj* mon (*f* ma, *pl* mes); **~ arm hurts** le bras me fait mal; (emphatic) **~ car** ma voiture à moi; **I have broken ~ arm** je me suis cassé le bras

**myopic** *adj* myope

**myriad** *n* myriade *f*

**myrrh** *n* myrrhe *f*

**myrtle** *n* myrte *m*

**myself** *pron* moi-même; **all by ~** (moi) tout seul (*f* toute seule)

**mysterious** *adj* mystérieux -ieuse

**mystery** *n* mystère *m*; **make a ~ of sth** faire mystère de qch

**mystic** *n* + *adj* mystique

**mystical** *adj* mystique

**mysticism** *n* mysticisme *m*

**mystification** *n* mystification *f*; embrouillement *m*

**mystify** *vt* mystifier, dérouter

**mystique** *n* mystique *f*

**myth** *n* mythe *m*

**mythical** *adj* mythique

**mythological** *adj* mythologique

**mythology** *n* mythologie *f*

**myxomatosis** *n* myxomatose *f*

# N

**nab** *vt coll* pincer; (thing) chiper; **get ~ bed** se faire pincer

**nabob** *n* nabab *m*

**nadir** *n* nadir *m*

**¹nag** *n* bidet *m*, canasson *m*

**²nag** *vt* gronder, quereller

**nagging** *adj* hargneux -euse, querelleur -euse; (pain) agaçant

**naiad** *n* naïade *f*

**nail** *n* (metal) clou *m*; (finger) ongle *m*; **bite one's ~s** se ronger les ongles; **he's hard as ~s** c'est un dur; il est sans pitié; **hit the ~ on the head** tomber juste; **pay on the ~** payer comptant; *vt* clouer; (shoes, etc) clouter; **~ down** clouer; *coll* attraper

**nail-brush** *n* brosse *f* à ongles

**nail-file** *n* lime *f* à ongles

**nail-scissors** *n* ciseaux *mpl* à ongles, coupe-ongles *m*

**nail-varnish** n vernis m à ongles

**naïve** adj naïf (f naïve), ingénu

**naïvety** n naïveté f

**naked** adj nu; dégarni, dénudé; ~ **truth** vérité f sans fard; **stark** ~ nu comme un ver

**nakedness** n nudité f

**namby-pamby** n + adj maniéré -e, minaudier -ière

**name** n nom m; réputation f; (firm) raison sociale; ~-**day** fête f; **call s/o** ~ s dire des injures à qn; **Christian** ~, **first** ~, US **given** ~ prénom m; **in the** ~ **of** au nom de; **know s/o by** ~ connaître qn de nom; **maiden** ~ nom m de jeune fille; **mention no** ~ s ne nommer personne; **my** ~ **is** je m'appelle; **put down one's** ~ s'inscrire; (be a candidate) poser sa candidature; **what is your** ~? comment vous appelez-vous?; vt nommer; désigner; (quote) citer; (day) fixer

**nameless** adj sans nom, inconnu; (anonymous) anonyme; (horrible) inexprimable, indicible; **a person who shall be** ~ une personne dont je tairai le nom

**namely** adv à savoir, c'est-à-dire

**nameplate** n plaque f

**namesake** n homonyme m

**nancy, nancy-boy** n sl homosexuel m

**nankeen** n nankin m

**nanny** n nurse f, bonne f d'enfants, nounou f

**nanny-goat** n chèvre f, coll bique f

¹**nap** n petit somme; vi sommeiller; **catch s/o** ~ **ping** prendre qn au dépourvu

²**nap** n (cloth) poil m; **against the** ~ à rebrousse-poil; vt garnir, gratter

³**nap** n (cards) nap m

**napalm** n napalm m

**nape** n nuque f

**naphtha** n naphte m

**naphthalene** n naphtaline f

**napkin** n serviette f; (baby) couche f; ~-**ring** rond m de serviette

**Napoleonic** adj napoléonien -ienne

**nappy** n couche f

**narcissus** n (pl **narcissi**) narcisse m

**narcosis** n narcose f

**narcotic** n stupéfiant m, narcotique m; adj narcotique

**nark** n sl mouchard m; vt (annoy) irriter; ~ **it!** fiche-nous la paix!; vi sl moucharder

**narrate** vt raconter, narrer

**narration** n narration f

**narrative** n récit m

**narrator** n narrateur -trice; adj narratif -ive

**narrow** adj étroit, resserré; (ideas) borné; ~ **majority** faible majorité f;

**have a** ~ **escape** l'échapper belle; vt limiter, restreindre; rétrécir; vi devenir plus étroit, se rétrécir, se resserrer

**narrowly** adv étroitement; (only just) tout juste; (closely) de près

**narrow-minded** adj à l'esprit étroit, borné

**narrows** npl passe étroite; (river) étranglement m

**nasal** adj nasal; ~ **twang** accent nasillard

**nascent** adj naissant

**nasturtium** n capucine f

**nasty** adj désagréable, sale, vilain; ~ **piece of work** sale type m; ~ **trick** vilain tour; **have a** ~ **mind** avoir l'esprit mal tourné

**natality** n natalité f

**nation** n nation f; **the United Nations** les Nations Unies

**national** n ressortissant -e; adj national; ~ **service** service m militaire

**nationalism** n nationalisme m

**nationalist** n + adj nationaliste

**nationality** n nationalité f

**nationalization** n nationalisation f

**nationalize** vt nationaliser

**nationally** adv du point de vue national, nationalement

**nationwide** adj répandu dans tout le pays

**native** n natif -ive, indigène, originaire; adj (place) natal; natif -ive, naturel -elle, inné; (language) maternel -elle; (indigenous) originaire, indigène

**nativity** n nativité f

**Nato** n Otan f (abbr Organisation f du Traité de l'Atlantique du Nord)

**natter** n causette f; vi jacasser, bavarder

**natty** adj (dress) coquet -ette; (woman) pimpant

**natural** n mus note naturelle; adj naturel -elle; (inherent) inhérent, inné; **as is** ~ comme de raison

**naturalism** n naturalisme m

**naturalist** n naturaliste

**naturalization** n naturalisation f

**naturalize** vt naturaliser; (plant) acclimater

**naturally** adv naturellement; (by nature) de nature; **die** ~ mourir de sa belle mort

**nature** n nature f; (character) caractère m; (kind) sorte f, espèce f; **by** ~ par tempérament; **draw from** ~ dessiner d'après nature

**nature-study** n histoire naturelle

**naught** n néant m, rien m

**naughtiness** n méchanceté f, mauvaise conduite

**naughty** adj méchant, vilain; (story) grivois

**nausea** *n* nausée *f*; *fig* dégoût *m*

**nauseate** *vt* écœurer, dégoûter

**nauseating** *adj* dégoûtant, nauséabond

**nauseous** *adj see* **nauseating**

**nautical** *adj* nautique, marin; **~ term** terme *m* de navigation

**naval** *adj* naval (*pl* navals); *mil* **~ forces** marine *f*; **~ officer** officier *m* de marine

**nave** *n* (church) nef *f*

**navel** *n* nombril *m*

**navigable** *adj* navigable

**navigate** *vt* (ship) gouverner; naviguer sur; *vi* naviguer

**navigation** *n* navigation *f*; (ship) conduite *f*

**navigator** *n* navigateur *m*

**navvy** *n* terrassier *m*

**navy** *n* marine *f* (militaire); **merchant ~** marine marchande

**navy-blue** *adj* bleu marine *invar*

**nay** *adv* non

**Nazi** *n* Nazi -e

**neap** *adj* **~ tide** morte-eau *f* (*pl* morteseaux)

**near** *adj* proche, voisin; (friend) cher (*f* chère); (stingy) parcimonieux -ieuse, chiche; **~ offer** offre approchante; *mot* **on the ~ side** du côté du trottoir; **that was a ~ thing for us** nous l'avons échappé belle; **the ~ est way** le chemin le plus court; **to the ~ est centimetre** à un centimètre près; *adv* près, de près; (almost) presque; **~-by** tout près; **as ~ as I can remember** autant que je puisse m'en souvenir; **be ~ to doing sth** être sur le point de faire qch; **she came ~ to being killed** elle a failli être tuée; *vt* (s')approcher de; *prep* près de, auprès de; **~ death** près de mourir

**near-by** *adj* proche, voisin

**nearly** *adv* presque, à peu près, peu s'en faut; **I ~ fell** j'ai manqué (de) tomber, j'ai failli tomber; **it is ~ six** il est bientôt six heures; **pretty ~** peu s'en faut, à peu de chose près; **they are not ~ so rich as you** ils sont loin d'être aussi riches que vous

**nearness** *n* proximité *f*; (accuracy) exactitude *f*

**near-sighted** *adj* myope

**neat** *adj* (person) ordonné; (tidy) soigné, propre, bien rangé; (drink) sec (*f* sèche); (writing) net (*f* nette); (style) élégant

**neatly** *adv* (tidily) avec ordre; (skilfully) adroitement; (dressing) avec soin

**neatness** *n* simplicité *f*; (dress) bon goût; (tidiness) bon ordre; (skill) adresse *f*; (writing) netteté *f*

**nebulous** *adj* nébuleux -euse

**necessary** *n* nécessaire *m*; *adj* nécessaire;

**do everything ~** faire (tout) ce qu'il faut; **if ~** s'il le faut; **make all the ~ arrangements** prendre toutes les dispositions utiles

**necessitate** *vt* nécessiter, rendre nécessaire

**necessitous** *adj* nécessiteux -euse

**necessity** *n* nécessité *f*, besoin *m*; obligation *f*; (poverty) indigence *f*; **bare necessities** strict nécessaire; **case of absolute ~** cas *m* de force majeure; **of ~** de nécessité; **out of ~** par nécessité

**neck** *n* cou *m*; (bottle) goulot *m*; (vase) col *m*; (land) langue *f*; (violin) manche *m*; (horse) encolure *f*; **~ and ~** à égalité; **~ measurement** encolure *f*; **be up to one's ~ in work** avoir du travail par-dessus la tête; **fling one's arms round s/o's ~** sauter au cou de qn; **get it in the ~** écoper; *coll* **he's a pain in the ~** il est casse-pieds; **it's ~ or nothing** il faut jouer le tout pour le tout; **low ~** décolleté *m*; **save one's ~** sauver sa peau; **stiff ~** torticolis *m*; *vi coll* se peloter, se faire des mamours

**neckerchief** *n* fichu *m*

**necking** *n* pelotage *m*

**necklace** *n* collier *m*

**necktie** *n* cravate *f*

**necromancy** *n* nécromancie *f*

**necropolis** *n* nécropole *f*

**nectar** *n* nectar *m*

**nectarine** *n* brugnon *m*

**née** *adj f* née

**need** *n* besoin *m*; (poverty) embarras *m*, adversité *f*, indigence *f*; **be in ~ of** avoir besoin de; **have no ~ to do sth** n'avoir que faire de qch; **if ~ be** au besoin, en cas de besoin; **what ~ is there to see her?** à quoi bon la voir?; *vt* avoir besoin de; (thing) demander, exiger; **I ~ n't go** je ne suis pas tenu d'y aller; **it ~ s a screwdriver** il faut un tournevis; **no ~** to inutile de; **you ~ only knock** vous n'avez qu'à frapper

**needful** *n coll* argent *m*; *adj* nécessaire

**needle** *n* aiguille *f*; (carburettor) pointeau *m*; *vt* piquer d'une aiguille; *coll* chiner, irriter

**needless** *adj* inutile; **~ to say** ... il va sans dire que ...

**needlewoman** *n* couturière *f*

**needlework** *n* travaux *mpl* à l'aiguille; couture *f*

**needs** *adv* **if ~ must** s'il le faut; **I must ~ go** je suis obligé de partir

**needy** *adj* nécessiteux -euse, besogneux -euse

**ne'er** *adv poet* jamais

**ne'er-do-well** *n* propre à rien

**nefarious** *adj* infâme, scélérat

**negate** *vt* nier; (law) nullifier

**negation** n négation f
**negative** n négative f; gramm négation f; phot négatif m; **answer in the ~** répondre de façon négative; adj négatif -ive; vt réfuter; nier; (reject) rejeter; (cancel) annuler
**neglect** n négligence f; manque m de soins; manque m d'égards; (machine) mauvais entretien; vt négliger; manquer de soins pour; manquer d'égards envers; **~ an opportunity** laisser échapper une occasion; **~ to do sth** négliger de faire qch
**neglectful** adj négligent
**négligé** n négligé m
**negligence** n négligence f; manque m de soins
**negligent** adj négligent
**negligible** adj négligeable
**negotiable** adj négociable; (track, etc) praticable
**negotiate** vt négocier; (obstacle) franchir; (difficulty) surmonter; **~ a bend** prendre un virage
**negotiation** n négociation f; (obstacle) franchissement m; **enter into ~s with s/o** entamer des négociations avec qn; **price by ~** prix m à débattre; **under ~** en négociation
**negotiator** n négociateur -trice
**Negress** n négresse f
**Negro** n nègre m
**negroid** adj négroïde
**neigh** n hennissement m; vi hennir
**neighbour** n voisin -e; bibl prochain -e
**neighbourhood** n voisinage m, proximité f; (locality) quartier m; (district) environs mpl
**neighbouring** adj voisin, avoisinant
**neighbourly** adj (person) amical; **in a ~ fashion** en bon voisin (f en bonne voisine)
**neither** adj+pron aucun (f aucune), ni l'un ni l'autre; adv non plus; conj ni; **~ ... nor** ni ... ni
**neologism** n néologisme m
**neon** n néon m; **~ lighting** éclairage m au néon
**neophyte** n eccles néophyte; débutant -e
**nephew** n neveu m
**nephritis** n néphrite f
**nepotism** n népotisme m
**Neptune** n Neptune m
**nerve** n nerf m; (courage) audace f; (cheek) toupet m; **it gets on my ~s** ça me porte (tape) sur les nerfs; **strain every ~ to** déployer tous ses efforts pour; vt **~ oneself to** s'armer de courage pour
**nerveless** adj sans force, sans vigueur
**nerve-racking** adj énervant, horripilant
**nervous** adj (frightened) peureux -euse,

timide; (worried) inquiet -iète; (excitable) excitable; anat nerveux -euse; **it makes me ~** cela m'intimide
**nervy** adj irritable, énervé; (action) nerveux -euse; peureux -euse
**nest** n nid m; (den) repaire m; (eggs) nichée f; **~ of shelves** casier m; **~ of tables** table f gigogne; vi faire son nid, nicher
**nest-egg** n (savings) magot m, pécule m
**nestle** vi se nicher, se blottir; **~ close up to s/o** se serrer contre qn
**nestling** n oisillon m
**net** n filet m; (fabric) tulle m; vt prendre au filet; (ball) envoyer dans le filet
**net(t)** adj net (f nette); **~ cash** argent comptant; vt (person) toucher net; (deal) rapporter net
**netball** n basket m
**nether** adj inférieur
**Netherlands** npl Pays-Bas mpl
**netting** n filet m; (fabric) tulle m; pose f de filet
**nettle** n ortie f
**nettle-rash** n urticaire f
**network** n réseau m; **railway ~** réseau m ferroviaire; **road ~** réseau routier
**neural** adj neural
**neuralgia** n névralgie f
**neuralgic** adj névralgique
**neurasthenia** n neurasthénie f
**neuritis** n névrite f
**neurologist** n neurologue
**neurology** n neurologie f
**neurosis** n névrose f
**neurotic** adj névrosé
**neuter** adj neutre; vt châtrer
**neutral** n+adj neutre
**neutrality** n neutralité f
**neutralize** vt neutraliser
**never** adv jamais, ne ... jamais; **~!** jamais de la vie!; **~ again** (ne ...) plus jamais, jamais plus (... ne); **I ~ expected this** je ne m'attendais aucunement à cela; **~ mind** n'importe; **well I ~!** par exemple!
**never-ending** adj interminable
**nevermore** adv (ne ...) plus jamais, jamais plus (... ne)
**nevertheless** adv néanmoins, pourtant, quand même
**new** adj (unused) neuf (f neuve); (changed) nouveau (f nouvelle); **~ bread** pain frais; **New Year** Nouvel An; **as ~** à l'état de neuf; **brand ~** tout neuf (f toute neuve)
**newborn** adj nouveau-né
**newcomer** n nouveau venu (f nouvelle venue), nouvel arrivé (f nouvelle arrivée)
**newfangled** adj d'un moderne outré
**Newfoundland** n Terre-Neuve f

**new-laid** *adj* du jour; frais (*f* fraîche)
**newly** *adv* récemment, nouvellement; fraîchement
**newly-weds** *npl* nouveaux mariés
**newness** *n* nouveauté *f*; (inexperience) inexpérience *f*; (article) état neuf
**news** *npl* nouvelle *f*, nouvelles *fpl*; (broadcasting) informations *fpl*; ~ **film** film *m* d'actualités; **be in the** ~ défrayer la chronique; **make** ~ faire sensation
**news-agency** *n* agence *f* d'informations
**newsagent** *n* marchand -e de journaux
**newscaster** *n* speaker *m*, speakerine *f*
**newspaper** *n* journal *m*, quotidien *m*; ~**-stall** kiosque *m*; **weekly** ~ hebdomadaire *m*
**newsprint** *n* papier *m* de journal
**newsreel** *n* film *m* d'actualités
**news-room** *n* salle *f* de rédaction
**news-sheet** *n* feuille *f*
**news-stand** *n* kiosque *m*
**news-theatre** *n* ciné-actualités *m*
**newsy** *adj* plein de nouvelles
**newt** *n* triton *m*
**next** *adj* prochain; (following) suivant; (neighbouring) voisin; (nearest) le (*f* la) plus proche; (adjacent) attenant; ~ **door** (d')à côté; ~ **week** la semaine prochaine; **and the** ~ au suivant; **for** ~ **to nothing** pour presque rien; **the** ~ **day** le lendemain; **the** ~ **morning** le lendemain matin; **the** ~ **week** la semaine suivante; **what** ~! par exemple!; **who's** ~? à qui le tour?; *adv* ensuite, après; *prep* à côté de; ~ **to me** à côté de moi
**next of kin** *n* famille *f*, proche parenté *f*
**nib** *n* bec *m* de plume
**nibble** *n* grignotement *m*; *vt + vi* grignoter, mordiller
**nice** *adj* bon (*f* bonne); joli, agréable; (person) gentil -ille, sympathique, aimable; (particular) difficile; (question) délicat; (respectable) convenable; ~ **and ...** bien ...; **a** ~ **sum** une somme rondelette; **be** ~ **to s/o** se montrer aimable envers qn
**nice-looking** *adj* beau (*f* belle), avenant
**nicely** *adv* joliment, bien, gentiment; **get on** ~ (patient) faire des progrès; (business) marcher bien; **that will do** ~ cela fera bien mon affaire
**nicety** *n* précision *f*; subtilité *f*; **niceties** minuties *fpl*; **to a** ~ exactement, à la perfection
**niche** *n* niche *f*
**nick** *n* cran *m*, entaille *f*; *sl* taule *f*; **in the** ~ **of time** juste à temps; *vt* encocher, entailler; *coll* pincer, faucher; *vi* ~ **in** s'insinuer
**nickel** *n* nickel *m*; *US* pièce *f* de cinq

cents; *vt* nickeler
**nickname** *n* sobriquet *m*; *vt* surnommer
**nicotine** *n* nicotine *f*
**niece** *n* nièce *f*
**nifty** *adj coll* adroit, agile; (smelly) puant
**niggardly** *adj* (person) pingre, chiche; (sum) mesquin
**nigger** *n pej* nègre (*f* négresse); **there's a** ~ **in the woodpile** il y a quelque anguille sous roche
**niggle** *vi* couper les cheveux en quatre; ~ **over trifles** s'attarder à des détails insignifiants
**niggling** *adj* (detail) insignifiant; (person) tatillon -onne
**nigh** *adj lit + ar* proche; *adv* près, proche; *prep* près de
**night** *n* nuit *f*; (evening) soir *m*; **at** ~ la nuit; **by** ~ de nuit; **eleven o'clock** ~ onze heures du soir; *theat* **first** ~ première *f*; **have a good (bad)** ~ dormir bien (mal); **have a late** ~ aller se coucher tard; **in the** ~ la nuit; **it is** ~ il fait nuit; **last** ~ hier (au) soir; **make a** ~ **of it** continuer toute la nuit; **the** ~ **before last** avant-hier (au) soir; **the** ~ **train** le train de nuit; **tomorrow** ~ demain soir
**night-bird** *n* oiseau *m* de nuit
**night-blindness** *n* héméralopie *f*
**nightcap** *n* bonnet *m* de nuit; boisson prise avant de se coucher
**night-club** *n* boîte *f* de nuit
**night-dress** *n* chemise *f* de nuit
**nightfall** *n* tombée *f* de la nuit; **at** ~ à la nuit tombante
**nightgown** *n* chemise *f* de nuit
**nightingale** *n* rossignol *m*
**nightjar** *n* engoulevent *m*
**night-light** *n* veilleuse *f*
**nightly** *adj* nocturne, de nuit; (every night) de tous les soirs, (de) chaque nuit; *adv* tous les soirs, toutes les nuits
**nightmare** *n* cauchemar *m*
**night-school** *n* cours *mpl* du soir
**nightshade** *n* morelle noire; **deadly** ~ belladone *f*
**night-shift** *n* équipe *f* de nuit
**nightshirt** *n* chemise *f* de nuit
**night-soil** *n* vidanges *fpl*
**night-time** *n* nuit *f*
**nightwatchman** *n* veilleur *m*, gardien *m* de nuit
**nigritude** *n* négritude *f*
**nihilism** *n* nihilisme *m*
**nihilist** *n* nihiliste
**nil** *n* rien *m*, zéro *m*, néant *m*
**Nile** *n* Nil *m*
**nimble** *adj* agile, leste; (mind) subtil, prompt
**nimbus** *n* auréole *f*; *meteor* nimbus *m*

**nincompoop** *n* niais -e, nigaud -e, imbécile

**nine** *n* neuf *m invar*; *adj* neuf *invar*

**nineteen** *n* dix-neuf *m invar*; *adj* dix-neuf *invar*

**nineteenth** *n* dix-neuvième; (date) dix-neuf *m*; *adj* dix-neuvième

**ninetieth** *n* + *adj* quatre-vingt-dixième

**ninety** *n* quatre-vingt-dix *m invar*; *adj* quatre-vingt-dix *invar*

**ninny** *n coll* imbécile, niais -e

**ninth** *n* neuvième; (date) neuf *m*; *adj* neuvième

**¹nip** *n* pincement *m*; (bite) morsure *f*; *vt* pincer; mordre; *vi* ~ **in** passer en courant; ~ **off** filer; ~ **out** sortir un instant; ~ **round to s/o's (house)** courir chez qn

**²nip** *n* goutte *f*, petit coup

**nipper** *n* pince *f*; *coll* gosse, gamin -e

**nippers** *npl* pinces *fpl*, tenailles *fpl*

**nipple** *n* mamelon *m*; (feeding bottle) tétine *f*

**nippy** *adj coll* leste, vif (*f* vive); (air) âpre; **be ~ about it!** *sl* grouillez-vous!

**nirvana** *n* nirvāna *m*

**¹nit** *n ent* lente *f*

**²nit** *n coll* andouille *f*

**nitrate** *n* nitrate *m*

**nitrogen** *n* azote *m*

**nitroglycerin(e)** *n* nitroglycérine *f*

**nitwit** *n coll* andouille *f*, crétin -e

**nix** *n coll* rien *m* du tout

**no** *n* non; **not take ~ for an answer** ne pas admettre le refus; **the ~es have it** le vote est contre; *adj* (ne ...) nul (*f* nulle), pas de, (ne ...) aucun (*f* aucune); ~ **admittance** entrée interdite; ~ **doubt** sans doute; ~ **longer** (ne ...) plus; ~ **matter** n'importe; ~ **more** (ne ...) plus; ~ **nonsense!** pas de bêtises!; ~ **one** (ne ...) personne; ~ **smoking** défense de fumer; **he is ~ teacher** il n'est pas professeur; il n'a aucune des qualités voulues pour être professeur; **in less than ~ time** en moins de rien; **of ~ importance** sans importance; **this is ~ easy problem** ce problème n'est pas facile du tout; *adv* non; ~ **better than I** pas mieux que moi

**Noah** *n* Noé *m*; ~ **'s ark** l'arche *f* de Noé

**nobble** *vt coll* (horse) écloper; (person) soudoyer; (pinch) chiper; (approach) aborder; (catch) pincer

**nobility** *n* noblesse *f*

**noble** *n* noble *m*; *adj* noble

**nobleman** *n* noble *m*, gentilhomme *m*

**noblewoman** *n* aristocrate *f*

**nobly** *adv* noblement, magnifiquement

**nobody** *n* zéro *m*, nullité *f*; *pron* (ne ...) personne, nul (ne ...), (ne ...) aucun

**nocturnal** *adj* nocturne

**nocturne** *n* nocturne *m*

**nod** *n* signe de tête affirmatif; **give a ~** faire un signe de tête (affirmatif); **on the ~** à l'œil; *vt* + *vi* faire un signe de tête; (with sleep) somnoler; (make mistake) se tromper; ~ **to s/o** faire un signe de tête à qn

**nodule** *n* nodule *m*

**noggin** *n* petit pot; (drink) petit coup

**no-good** *n* vaurien -ienne; *adj* d'aucune valeur

**noise** *n* bruit *m*; tapage *m*, fracas *m*; *coll* **he's a big ~** c'est un grand manitou; *vt* ~ **abroad** ébruiter, répandre

**noiseless** *adj* silencieux -ieuse, sans bruit

**noisiness** *n* vacarme *m*; (children) turbulence *f*

**noisome** *adj* nuisible, nocif -ive; (smell) fétide, malsain; (work) désagréable

**noisy** *adj* bruyant; (child) turbulent

**nomad** *n* nomade *m*

**nomadic** *adj* nomade

**no-man's-land** *n mil* zone *f* neutre; terrain *m* vague

**nom de plume** *n* pseudonyme *m*

**nomenclature** *n* nomenclature *f*

**nominal** *adj* nominal

**nominate** *vt* nommer, désigner; (candidate) présenter

**nomination** *n* nomination *f*; (candidate) présentation *f*

**nominative** *n gramm* nominatif *m*; *adj* nominatif -ive

**nominee** *n* candidat -e désigné -e

**non-acceptance** *n* non-acceptation *f*

**nonagenarian** *n* + *adj* nonagénaire

**non-aggression** *n* non-agression *f*

**non-alcoholic** *adj* non-alcoolique

**non-appearance** *n* non-comparution *f*

**non-attendance** *n* absence *f*

**nonchalance** *n* nonchalance *f*

**nonchalant** *adj* indifférent, nonchalant

**non-combatant** *n* non-combattant *m*; *adj* non-combattant

**non-commissioned** *adj* ~ **officer** sous-officier *m*

**non-committal** *adj* qui n'engage à rien

**non-conformist** *adj eccles* dissident

**non-denominational** *adj* n'adhérant à aucune confession

**nondescript** *adj* indéfinissable; (ordinary) quelconque

**none** *pron* (ne ...) aucun (*f* aucune); ~ **but he ...** il n'y a que lui qui ..., lui seul ...; ~ **can say** personne ne le sait; ~ **of this is correct** rien de ceci n'est juste; ~ **of you** aucun (*f* aucune) (personne) d'entre vous; ~ **the less** néanmoins; **I have ~** je n'en ai point (pas); **it was ~ other than his father** ce n'était autre que son père; **these apples are ~ of the best** ces pommes ne sont pas des

meilleures; *adv* ~ **too** ... (far from)
rien moins que; (not very) pas très; ~
**too soon** juste à temps; **he is** ~ **the
richer for that** il n'en est pas plus riche
**nonentity** *n* personne insignifiante, nullité *f*
**non-essential** *adj* non essentiel -ielle
**non-existent** *adj* inexistant, non-existant
**non-fiction** *n* documentaire *m*
**non-fulfilment** *n* non-exécution *f*
**non-intervention** *n* non-intervention *f*
**non-payment** *n* non-paiement *m*
**nonplus** *vt* embarrasser
**non-resident** *n* + *adj* non-résident -e
**non-returnable** *adj* non repris
**nonsense** *n* non-sens *m*, absurdité *f*, sottise *f*; ~ ! pas possible!; **no** ~ ! pas de
bêtises!; **piece of** ~ bêtise *f*; **talk** ~
dire des bêtises
**nonsensical** *adj* absurde
**non sequitur** *n* illogicité *f*
**non-skid** *adj* antidérapant
**non-smoker** *n* non-fumeur *m*; (railway)
compartiment *m* non-fumeurs
**non-smoking** *adj* ~ **compartment** compartiment *m* non-fumeurs
**non-stop** *adj* direct; *adv* (air travel) sans
escale; (train) sans arrêt
**non-violence** *n* non-violence *f*
¹**noodle** *n coll* nigaud -e, andouille *f*
²**noodle** *n cul* nouille *f*
**nook** *n* coin *m*, recoin *m*
**noon** *n* midi *m*
**noose** *n* nœud coulant; (snare) lacet *m*
**nor** *conj* ni; ~ **do I wish** ... de plus, je ne
souhaite pas ...; ~ **you neither** ni vous
non plus; **neither** ... ~ ni ... ni; **they
don't know,** ~ **do they care** ils ne
savent pas et ils ne s'en soucient pas
**Nordic** *adj* nordique, scandinave
**norm** *n* norme *f*
**normal** *adj* normal, régulier -ière
**normalcy** *n US* normalité *f*
**normality** *n* normalité *f*
**normalize** *vt* normaliser
**normally** *adv* normalement; *coll* régulièrement
**Norman** *n* Normand -e; *adj* normand;
~ **architecture** (in England) architecture romane; (in Normandy) architecture normande
**Normandy** *n* Normandie *f*
**normative** *adj* normatif -ive
**north** *n* nord *m*; **to the** ~ **of** au nord de;
*adj* nord *invar*, septentrional; (north-
facing) exposé au nord; ~ **wind** vent *m*
du nord; *adv* du nord
**north-east** *n* nord-est *m*; *adj* nord-est
*invar*
**northerly** *adj* du nord; (direction) vers le
nord
**northern** *adj* du nord, septentrional; ~

lights aurore boréale
**northernmost** *adj* le plus au nord
**northward** *adj* au nord, du nord, vers le
nord
**northwards** *adv* vers le nord
**north-west** *n* nord-ouest *m*; *adj* nord-
ouest *invar*
**Norway** *n* Norvège *f*
**Norwegian** *n* Norvégien -ienne; (language) norvégien *m*; *adj* norvégien
-ienne
**nose** *n* nez *m*; (animals) museau *m*;
(sense of smell) odorat *m*; **blow one's**
~ se moucher; **lead s/o by the** ~
mener qn par le bout du nez; **look
down one's** ~ **at** regarder avec mépris;
(fowl) **parson's** ~ croupion *m*; **pay
through the** ~ payer le prix fort; **poke
one's** ~ **into** fourrer son nez dans;
**speak through the** ~ nasiller, parler du
nez; **turn up one's** ~ **at** faire fi de;
**under his very** ~ à son nez; *vt* flairer,
sentir; ~ **out** flairer, dépister; *vi* ~
**about** fureter, fouiner
**nosebag** *n* musette *f*
**nose-bleed** *n* saignement *m* de nez
**nose-cone** *n* (rocket) ogive *f*
**nose-dive** *n* piqué *m*; *vi* descendre en
piqué
**nosey, nosy** *adj* fouinard; ~ **parker** indiscret -ète
**nosh** *n sl* boustifaille *f*; *vt sl* bouffer, boulotter
**nostalgia** *n* nostalgie *f*
**nostalgic** *adj* nostalgique
**nostril** *n* narine *f*; (animal) naseau *m*
**nosy** *adj see* nosey
**not** *adv* (ne ...) pas, (ne ...) point; ~ **a
few** pas mal de; ~ **at all** pas du tout; *sl*
~ **half!** tu parles!, et comment!; ~
**that** ... non (pas) que ...; *coll* ~ **to
worry!** ne vous en faites pas!; **am I** ~ ?
(aren't I?, aren't you?, isn't he?, etc)
n'est-ce pas?; **I think** ~ je crois que
non; **Thank you very much. – Not at all**
Merci beaucoup. – De rien; **why** ~ ?
pourquoi pas?
**notability** *n* notabilité *f*
**notable** *adj* notable, considérable;
(person) éminent
**notation** *n* notation *f*
**notch** *n* entaille *f*, encoche *f*, cran *m*;
(blade) brèche *f*; *US* défilé *m*; *vt* entailler, encocher; (blade) ébrécher
**note** *n* note *f*; (mark) marque *f*, signe *m*;
(piano) touche *f*; *comm* bordereau *m*;
(short letter) mot *m*, billet *m*; (bank-
note) billet *m*; ~ **credit** ~ note *f* de
crédit; **make a** ~ **of sth** prendre note
de qch; **man of** ~ homme *m* de renom;
**nothing of** ~ rien d'important; **take**
~ **of** constater, remarquer; **take** ~ **s**

prendre des notes; *vt* noter, constater, remarquer; (mistake) relever; ~ **sth down** inscrire qch, noter qch

**notebook** *n* carnet *m*

**noted** *adj* éminent, célèbre, distingué

**notepad** *n* bloc-notes *m* (*pl* blocs-notes)

**notepaper** *n* papier *m* à lettres (à écrire)

**noteworthy** *adj* remarquable, digne d'attention

**nothing** *n* néant *m*, zéro *m*, rien *m*; ~ **at all** rien du tout; ~ **but** rien que; ~ **doing!** rien à faire!; ~ **else** rien d'autre; ~ **much** pas grand-chose; ~ **new** rien de nouveau; ~ **to do** rien à faire; **come to** ~ aboutir à rien; **do** ~ **but** ne faire que; **get** ~ **out of sth** en être pour ses frais; **I have** ~ **to do with it** je n'y suis pour rien; **it's** ~ **to do with me** cela ne me regarde pas; **that has** ~ **to do with my work** cela n'a rien à voir avec mon travail; **that's** ~ **to me** cela m'est égal; **there's** ~ **for it but to go** il n'y a qu'à partir; **there's** ~ **more to be said** il n'y a plus rien à dire; **think** ~ **of doing sth** ne pas se faire scrupule de faire qch; **think** ~ **of sth** ne faire aucun cas de qch; *adv* aucunement, nullement

**nothingness** *n* néant *m*

**notice** *n* avis *m*, notification *f*; (poster) affiche *f*; (newspaper) annonce *f*; (book) revue *f*; **at a day's** ~ du jour au lendemain; **at short** ~ à bref délai; **attract** ~ se faire remarquer; **at two days'** ~ dans un délai de deux jours; **bring to the** ~ **of** porter à l'attention de; **give** ~ **that** prévenir que; **give one's** ~ donner son congé; **give s/o** ~ donner son congé a qn; **he takes no** ~ il n'y prend pas garde; **public** ~ avis *m* au public; **take** ~ **of** tenir compte de; **until further** ~ jusqu'à nouvel avis; **without** ~ sans préavis; *vt* remarquer, observer, s'apercevoir de; (take notice) prendre garde à; **get oneself** ~ **d** attirer l'attention sur soi

**noticeable** *adj* perceptible; (not inconsiderable) digne d'attention

**notice-board** *n* écriteau *m*; (institution) tableau *m* d'annonces

**notification** *n* avis *m*, annonce *f*, notification *f*

**notify** *vt* notifier, déclarer, faire savoir

**notion** *n* idée *f*, notion *f*; opinion *f*; (whim) caprice *m*; *US* ~ **s** mercerie *f*; **have a** ~ **that** avoir dans l'idée que; **have a** ~ **to do sth** s'aviser de faire qch

**notional** *adj* imaginaire, spéculatif -ive; *econ* fictif -ive

**notoriety** *n* notoriété *f*

**notorious** *adj* insigne; (place) mal famé

**notwithstanding** *adv* quand même, tout de même, pourtant; *prep* malgré, en dépit de

**nougat** *n* nougat *m*

**nought** *n* zéro *m*

**noun** *n* nom *m*, substantif *m*

**nourish** *vt* nourrir, alimenter; (hope) entretenir

**nourishment** *n* nourriture *f*

**nous** *n coll* intelligence *f*

¹**novel** *n* roman *m*

²**novel** *adj* nouveau -elle; original

**novelist** *n* romancier -ière

**novelty** *n* nouveauté *f*, innovation *f*

**November** *n* novembre *m*

**novena** *n eccles* neuvaine *f*

**novice** *n* débutant -e; *eccles* novice

**noviciate, novitiate** *n* noviciat *m*

**now** *adv* maintenant, à présent, en ce moment, actuellement; (not referring to time) or; (meaning 'then', in narrative) alors, à ce moment-là; ~ **and then** de temps en temps, de temps à autre; ~ ... ~ tantôt ... tantôt; ~ **then!** allons!; **between** ~ **and then** d'ici là; **by** ~ à l'heure qu'il est; **even** ~ même à cette heure tardive; **in three days from** ~ d'ici trois jours; **right** ~ tout de suite; **until** ~ jusqu'ici; *conj* maintenant que, à présent que

**nowadays** *adv* de nos jours, aujourd'hui, au jour d'aujourd'hui

**noway(s)** *interj coll* pas du tout

**nowhere** *adv* nulle part; ~ **else** nulle part ailleurs; ~ **near** loin d'être

**noxious** *adj* nuisible, nocif -ive; malfaisant

**nozzle** *n* jet *m*; (pipe) lance *f*; (spout) bec *m*; (jet) ajutage *m*

**nuance** *n* nuance *f*

**nub** *n* (coal, etc) petit morceau; (question) essentiel *m*

**nubile** *adj* nubile

**nuclear** *adj* nucléaire

**nucleus** *n* noyau *m*

**nude** *n* (drawing) nu *m*; **in the** ~ nu; *adj* nu

**nudge** *n* coup *m* de coude; *vt* pousser du coude

**nudism** *n* nudisme *m*

**nudist** *n* nudiste

**nudity** *n* nudité *f*

**nugget** *n* pépite *f*

**nuisance** *n* désagrément *m*; *coll* peste *f*, fléau *m*; *leg* dommage *m*; **be a** ~ **to s/o** embêter qn; **what a** ~ ! que c'est embêtant!

**null** *adj* ~ **and void** nul et non avenu

**nullify** *vt* nullifier, annuler

**nullity** *n* nullité *f*

**numb** *adj* engourdi; *vt* engourdir

**number** *n* (quantity) nombre *m*; (symbol) numéro *m*; *math* nombre *m*, chiffre *m*; *theat* numéro *m*; **a large** ~ **of**

beaucoup de; **a** ~ **of times** plusieurs fois; **back** ~ vieux numéro; **few in** ~ peu nombreux -euse; **five in** ~ au nombre de cinq; *coll* **his** ~**'s up** il est fichu; **in small** ~**s** en petit nombre; *coll* **look after** ~ **one** prendre soin de sa petite personne; **one of our** ~ un (*f* une) d'entre nous; **swell the** ~ faire nombre; **without** ~ innombrable; *vt* numéroter; (count) compter; (amount to) se monter à, compter; **his days are** ~ **ed** il n'a plus longtemps à vivre

**numberless** *adj* innombrable

**number-plate** *n* plaque *f* minéralogique, plaque *f* d'immatriculation

**numbness** *n* engourdissement *m*; (mind) torpeur *f*

**num(b)skull** *n* nigaud -e, idiot -e, *coll* cornichon *m*

**numeral** *n* chiffre *m*, nombre *m*; *adj* numéral

**numerate** *adj* connaissant les éléments de l'arithmétique

**numerical** *adj* numérique

**numerous** *adj* nombreux -euse

**numismatics** *npl* numismatique *f*

**nun** *n* religieuse *f*, nonne *f*

**nuncio** *n* nonce *m*

**nunnery** *n* couvent *m*

**nuptial** *adj* nuptial

**nurse** *n* (wet-nurse) nourrice *f*; (children's nurse) bonne *f* d'enfants, nurse *f*; (hospital) infirmière *f*; (sick-nurse) garde-malade *f* (*pl* gardes-malades); **male** ~ infirmier *m*; *vt* soigner, garder; (grief, etc) nourrir, entretenir; (child) bercer; (fondle) dorloter

**nursemaid** *n* bonne *f* d'enfants

**nursery** *n* nursery *f*, chambre *f* des enfants; (public) crèche *f*; (plants) pépinière *f*; ~ **rhyme** chanson *f* de nourrice; ~ **school** maternelle *f*

**nurseryman** *n* pépiniériste *m*

**nursing** *n* (medical) soins *mpl*; (profession) profession *f* de garde-malade (d'infirmière); **take up** ~ se faire infirmière

**nursing-home** *n* clinique *f*, hôpital privé

**nursling** *n* nourrisson *m*

**nurture** *n* nourriture *f*; éducation *f*; *vt* nourrir; élever

**nut** *n* noix *f*; (hazel-nut) noisette *f*; *mech* écrou *m*; *sl* tête *f*, *coll* caboche *f*; **be** ~ **s** être timbré; **be off one's** ~ être timbré; **he's a tough** ~ c'est un dur; **you can't play for** ~**s** vous ne savez pas jouer du tout

**nut-brown** *adj* couleur noisette *invar*

**nutcracker** *n* casse-noisette(s) *m*

**nutmeg** *n* muscade *f*

**nutriment** *n* nourriture *f*

**nutrition** *n* nutrition *f*

**nutritious** *adj* nutritif -ive, nourrissant

**nutritive** *adj* nutritif -ive, nourrissant

**nutshell** *n* coquille *f* de noix; **in a** ~ en un mot

**nutty** *adj* ayant le goût de noix; *sl* timbré, toqué

**nuzzle** *vi* (animal) mettre son museau contre; (person) se blottir contre; (pig) fouiller avec le groin

**nylon** *n* nylon *m*

**nymph** *n* nymphe *f*

**nymphomaniac** *n* nymphomane *f*

# O

**o** *interj* ô!, oh!

**oaf** *n* lourdaud -e

**oak** *n* chêne *m*

**oaken** *adj* de chêne, en chêne

**oakum** *n* étoupe *f*

**oar** *n* aviron *m*, rame *f*; **put (stick) one's** ~ **in** intervenir

**oarsman** *n* rameur *m*

**oasis** *n* oasis *f*

**oath** *n* serment *m*; (curse) juron *m*; **on** ~ sous serment; **take the** ~ prêter serment

**oatmeal** *n* farine *f* d'avoine

**oats** *n* avoine *f*; **sow one's wild** ~ faire des fredaines

**obduracy** *n* entêtement *m*, opiniâtreté *f*

**obdurate** *adj* têtu, opiniâtre; inflexible

**obedience** *n* obéissance *f*

**obedient** *adj* obéissant, soumis

**obeisance** *n* révérence *f*; *hist* hommage *m*

**obelisk** *n* obélisque *m*

**obese** *adj* obèse

**obesity** *n* obésité *f*

**obey** *vt* obéir à; *vi* obéir

**obituary** *n* notice *f* nécrologique; *adj* nécrologique

¹**object** *n* objet *m*, chose *f*; (aim) but *m*; (reason) raison *f*; *gramm* complément *m* d'objet; ~ **lesson** leçon *f*, exemple *m*; **expense is no ~ for me** je ne regarde pas à la dépense; **there's no ~ in going there** cela ne sert à rien d'y aller; **with this ~ in view** dans ce but

²**object** *vt* objecter; *vi* s'opposer, trouver à redire, faire objection; ~ **to doing sth** se refuser à faire qch

**objection** *n* objection *f*; inconvénient *m*; **have no ~ to** ne pas s'opposer à; **if you have no ~** si cela ne vous fait rien; **raise an ~** soulever une objection; **see no ~ to sth** ne voir aucun inconvénient à qch

**objectionable** *adj* répréhensible; désagréable; choquant

**objective** *n* but *m*, objectif *m*; *adj* objectif -ive

**objectivity** *n* objectivité *f*

**objector** *n* protestataire, contestataire; **conscientious ~** objecteur *m* de conscience

**obligate** *vt* imposer une obligation à

**obligation** *n* obligation *f*; **be under an ~ to s/o** devoir de la reconnaissance à qn; **fail to meet one's ~s** manquer à ses engagements; **put s/o under an ~ to do sth** imposer à qn l'obligation de faire qch

**obligatory** *adj* obligatoire

**oblige** *vt* obliger; (do a favour) rendre service à; **can you ~ me with a match?** voudriez-vous me donner du feu?; **do sth to ~** faire qch par complaisance; **he is ~d to go away** il faut qu'il parte; **I am much ~d to you** je vous suis très reconnaissant

**obliging** *adj* complaisant, serviable

**oblique** *adj* oblique; indirect; *vi* obliquer

**obliterate** *vt* oblitérer, effacer; (ticket) composter

**oblivion** *n* oubli *m*

**oblivious** *adj* oublieux -ieuse; **be ~ of** ignorer

**oblong** *adj* oblong (*f* oblongue)

**obnoxious** *adj* odieux -ieuse, détestable, exécrable

**oboe** *n* hautbois *m*

**obscene** *adj* obscène

**obscenity** *n* obscénité *f*

**obscurantism** *n* obscurantisme *m*

**obscure** *adj* obscur, peu clair; *vt* obscurcir

**obscurity** *n* obscurité *f*

**obsequies** *npl* obsèques *fpl*, funérailles *fpl*

**obsequious** *adj* obséquieux -ieuse

**observable** *adj* visible, perceptible

**observance** *n* observance *f*

**observant** *adj* observateur -trice

**observation** *n* observation *f*; remarque *f*; ~ **car** voiture *f* panoramique; **under ~** en observation

**observatory** *n* observatoire *m*

**observe** *vt* observer, regarder, apercevoir; (note) noter; (say) dire, faire remarquer; (rule, etc) se conformer à

**observer** *n* observateur -trice

**obsess** *vt* obséder

**obsession** *n* obsession *f*, hantise *f*, idée *f* fixe

**obsessive** *adj* obsédant

**obsolescence** *n* vieillissement *m*

**obsolescent** *adj* qui tombe en désuétude

**obsolete** *adj* désuet -ète, suranné, tombé en désuétude

**obstacle** *n* obstacle *m*; **be an ~ to** faire obstacle à

**obstetric** *adj* obstétrique, obstétrical

**obstetrician** *n* médecin accoucheur; obstétricien -ienne

**obstetrics** *n* obstétrique *f*

**obstinacy** *n* entêtement *m*, obstination *f*

**obstinate** *adj* entêté, obstiné, opiniâtre

**obstreperous** *adj* bruyant, tapageur -euse; (unruly) indiscipliné, turbulent

**obstruct** *vt* obstruer, encombrer; (block) boucher; (hinder) gêner; (prevent) empêcher; ~ **the traffic** entraver la circulation

**obstruction** *n* obstacle *m*, empêchement *m*; *med* obstruction *f*, occlusion *f*; *mot* stationnement gênant; (navigation) entrave *f*; *pol* obstruction *f*

**obstructionism** *n* *pol* obstructionnisme *m*

**obstructive** *adj* obstructif -ive; *pol* obstructionniste

**obtain** *vt* obtenir, se procurer; *vi* (prevail) prévaloir; avoir cours, régner, être en vigueur

**obtainable** *adj* qu'on peut se procurer

**obtrude** *vt* mettre en avant, imposer; *vi* s'imposer; ~ **oneself on s/o** importuner qn

**obtrusion** *n* importunité *f*; intrusion *f*

**obtrusive** *adj* importun, indiscret -ète

**obtuse** *adj* obtus

**obtuseness** *n* stupidité *f*

**obverse** *n* avers *m*, obvers *m*, face *f*

**obviate** *vt* éviter, obvier à

**obvious** *adj* évident, clair; **it's the ~ thing to do** c'est la chose à faire, cela s'impose

**occasion** *n* cause *f*, occasion *f*, raison *f*; (need) besoin *m*; occurrence *f*; **as ~ requires** au besoin; **have no ~ to**

complain n'avoir aucun sujet de se plaindre; **have ~ to** avoir à; **on ~** à l'occasion; **on several ~s** plusieurs fois, à plusieurs reprises; **on such an ~** en pareille occasion; **on the ~ of** à l'occasion de; **should (the) ~ arise** le cas échéant; vt occasionner, provoquer

**occasional** adj qui se produit de temps en temps; (chance) fortuit

**occasionally** adv de temps en temps

**occidental** adj occidental

**occlude** vt boucher, fermer

**occlusion** n occlusion f

**occult** n the ~ le surnaturel; adj occulte

**occupancy** n occupation f, habitation f

**occupant** n habitant -e; (tenant) locataire; (post) titulaire

**occupation** n occupation f; (job) emploi m, métier m; (possession) possession f

**occupational** adj professionnel -elle; ~ **hazards** risques mpl du métier

**occupier** n locataire, occupant -e, habitant -e

**occupy** vt occuper; (house) habiter; (time) employer

**occur** vi avoir lieu, arriver, se produire; (be found) se trouver; **don't let it ~ again!** que cela n'arrive plus!; **if the opportunity ~s** si l'occasion se présente; **it ~s to me** il me vient à l'esprit

**occurrence** n (event) événement m; (circumstance) occurrence f; **be of frequent ~** arriver souvent

**ocean** n océan m

**ocean-going** adj ~ **ship** navire m au long cours

**Oceania** n Océanie f

**oceanic** adj océanique

**oceanography** n océanographie f

**ochre** n ocre f; (colour) ocre m

**o'clock** adv **one (two) ~** une (deux) heure(s)

**octagon** n octogone m

**octagonal** adj octogonal

**octane** n octane m

**octave** n octave f

**octavo** n in-octavo m invar

**octet** n mus octuor m

**October** n octobre m

**octogenarian** n + adj octogénaire

**octopus** n pieuvre f, poulpe m

**ocular** adj oculaire

**oculist** n oculiste

**odd** adj (number) impair; (unmatched) dépareillé; (single) seul; (queer) singulier -ière, drôle, curieux -ieuse, bizarre; ~ **job man** homme m à tout faire; ~ **moments** moments perdus; **a hundred ~** une centaine; **at ~ times** à diverses reprises; **be ~ man out** rester en surnombre; **the ~ game** (cards) la

belle; **twenty pounds ~** vingt et quelques livres

**oddity** n singularité f; (person) original -e

**oddly** adv singulièrement; ~ **enough** chose curieuse

**oddments** npl fins fpl de série; restes mpl

**odds** n avantages mpl, chances fpl; (difference) différence f, inégalité f; ~ **and ends** petits bouts, restes mpl; **be at ~ with** s/o (quarrel) être brouillé avec qn; (differ) ne pas être d'accord avec qn; **it doesn't make the slightest ~** cela ne fait rien du tout; **lay ~** parier; **the ~ are that** il y a à parier que

**ode** n ode f

**odious** adj odieux -ieuse, détestable

**odium** n détestation f, réprobation f

**odorous** adj odorant

**odour** n odeur f, parfum m

**odourless** adj inodore

**Odyssey** n odyssée f

**oecumenical** adj see ecumenical

**oedema, edema** n œdème m

**Oedipus** n ~ **complex** complexe m d'Œdipe

**oesophagus** n œsophage m

**of** prep de; ~ **a Saturday** le samedi; ~ **late** dernièrement; ~ **necessity** obligatoirement; ~ **old** d'autrefois; ~ **the hundred ten were useless** sur les cent dix étaient inutilisables; **all ~ a sudden** tout à coup; US **a quarter ~ six** six heures moins le (un) quart; **I'm a friend ~ his** je suis de ses amis; **it's very good ~ you** c'est très gentil de votre part; **she's one ~ us** elle est des nôtres; **the fifth ~ June** le cinq juin; **what ~ it?** et alors?, et après?

**off** adv (away) éloigné de; (aside) à l'écart; (cancelled) annulé, rompu; (removed from) détaché, séparé; (food) pas frais (f fraîche), avarié; naut au large; (tap, etc) fermé; (current) coupé; ~ **he goes!** le voilà parti; **be badly ~** être dans la gêne; **beef is ~** il n'y a plus de bœuf; **be ~** partir, se sauver; **be ~!** allez-vous-en!, va-t'en!; **be well ~** être riche (aisé); **be worse ~** être moins bien qu'avant; **come ~** se détacher; **far ~** très éloigné; **go ~ to sleep** s'endormir; **hats ~!** chapeaux bas!; **have a day ~** avoir un jour de congé; coll **have it ~ with** faire l'amour avec; **keep ~** se tenir éloigné; (abstain) s'abstenir; **leave ~** cesser; **on and ~** de temps à autre; **straight ~** tout de suite; prep de; naut au large de; **be ~ one's food** n'avoir pas d'appétit; **be ~ work** être malade, ne pas pouvoir travailler; **eat ~ a plate** manger dans une assiette

**offal** n (rubbish) ordures fpl; (waste)

déchets *mpl*; (animal) abats *mpl*

**offbeat** *adj coll* original; *mus* syncopé

**off-chance** *n* vague possibilité *f*; **on the ~** à tout hasard

**off-colour** *adj coll* peu bien; *sl* grivois, grossier -ière

**off-day** *n* mauvais jour

**offence** *n* offense *f*, faute *f*; (crime) délit *m*; **give ~ to s/o** offenser (blesser) qn; **mean no ~** ne vouloir offenser personne; **second ~** récidive *f*; **take ~** se froisser

**offend** *vt* offenser, déplaire à, froisser; **~ the eye** choquer la vue; **be easily ~ed** être très susceptible; **be ~ed at sth** se fâcher de qch

**offender** *n* délinquant -e; offenseur *m*; (guilty person) coupable; **old ~** repris *m* de justice

**offensive** *n* offensive *f*; *adj mil* offensif -ive; choquant, désagréable, repoussant

**offensively** *adv mil* offensivement; désagréablement

**offer** *n* offre *f*, proposition *f*; **~ of marriage** demande *f* en mariage; *vt* offrir, présenter; **~ an opinion** avancer une opinion; *vi* s'offrir; **~ to do sth** offrir de faire qch

**offering** *n* offre *f*

**offertory** *n* (part of service) offertoire *m*; (collection) quête *f*

**off-hand, off-handed** *adj* désinvolte, cavalier -ière; spontané, impromptu

**office** *n* bureau *m*; (public position) charge *f*, fonctions *fpl*; (lawyer) étude *f*; (duty) devoir *m*; *eccles* office *m*; **~ hours** heures *fpl* de bureau; **be in ~** (government) être au pouvoir; **head ~** siège social; **hold ~** remplir un emploi; **Home Office** = ministère *m* de l'Intérieur; **through the good ~s of** grâce aux bons offices de

**office-boy** *n* garçon *m* de bureau

**officer** *n* officier *m*; (public) fonctionnaire *m*; (police) agent *m* de police

**official** *n* fonctionnaire; employé -e; *adj* officiel -ielle

**officialdom** *n* bureaucratie *f*; administration *f*

**officialese** *n coll* jargon administratif

**officialism** *n* bureaucratie *f*

**officially** *adv* officiellement

**officiate** *vi* officier

**officious** *adj* (meddlesome) empressé; autoritaire; (unofficial, informal) officieux -ieuse

**offing** *n naut* large *m*; *fig* **in the ~** en perspective

**off-licence** *n* débit *m* de boissons

**off-peak** *adj* **~ hours** heures creuses

**off-putting** *adj coll* déconcertant, rébarbatif -ive

**off-season** *n* morte-saison *f* (*pl* mortes-saisons)

**offset** *n* compensation *f*; *hort* rejeton *m*; *typ* offset *m*; *vt* compenser; *vi hort* pousser des rejetons

**offshoot** *n* rejeton *m*

**offshore** *adj* éloigné de la côte, qui se trouve au large

**off-side** *n sp* hors-jeu *m invar*; *adv sp* hors jeu; *mot* du côté de la route

**offspring** *n* rejeton *m*, descendant *m*; *coll* progéniture *f*

**offstage** *adv* dans les coulisses

**off-white** *n* blanc cassé; *adj* blanc cassé *invar*, quasi-blanc (*f* quasi-blanche)

**oft** *adv poet* mainte fois, souvent

**often** *adv* souvent, fréquemment; **every so ~** de temps en temps; **how ~?** combien de fois?

**ogle** *vt* lorgner, lancer des œillades à

**ogre** *n* ogre *m*

**ogress** *n* ogresse *f*

**oh** *interj* oh!

**oil** *n* huile *f*; (mineral) pétrole *m*; (fuel) mazout *m*; **~ industry** industrie pétrolière; *mot* **change the ~** faire la vidange; *vt* huiler, graisser, lubrifier

**oil-bearing** *adj geol* pétrolifère

**oil-can** *n* (pouring) burette *f* à huile; (storing) bidon *m* à huile

**oil-cloth** *n* toile cirée

**oil-colour, oil-paint** *n* couleur *f* à l'huile

**oil-field** *n* gisement *m* pétrolifère

**oil-fired** *adj* **~ heating** chauffage *m* au mazout

**oil-gauge** *n* jauge *f* de niveau d'huile

**oiliness** *n fig* onctuosité *f*

**oil-lamp** *n* lampe *f* à huile (pétrole)

**oil-paint** *n see* **oil-colour**

**oil-painting** *n* peinture *f* à l'huile

**oilskin** *n* toile cirée; **~ cape** cape *f* en toile cirée

**oil-stove** *n* (heater) réchaud *m* à pétrole; (cooker) fourneau *m* à pétrole

**oil-tanker** *n* pétrolier *m*

**oil-well** *n* puits *m* à (de) pétrole

**oily** *adj* huileux -euse, graisseux -euse, gras (*f* grasse); *fig* onctueux -euse

**ointment** *n* pommade *f*, onguent *m*; **fly in the ~** ombre *f* au tableau

**O.K., okay, okey-doke** *n coll* approbation *f*, feu vert; *adj invar* + *interj coll* O.K., très bien; *vt coll* approuver

**old** *adj* vieux, vieil (*f* vieille), âgé; (former) ancien -ienne; **~ age** vieillesse *f*; **~ age pension** retraite *f* de vieillesse; **~ boy** ancien élève; **~ chap** mon vieux; **~ man** vieillard *m*, vieil homme; *coll* mari *m*; **~ salt** loup *m* de mer; **~ woman** vieille *f*; *coll* femme *f*; **any ~ thing** la première chose venue; **be an ~ hand** avoir une longue expérience; **be**

~ **enough to do sth** être d'âge à (en âge de) faire qch; **good ~ age** âge avancé; **grow ~** vieillir; **how ~ are you?** quel âge avez-vous?; **I am ~ er than you** je suis votre aîné, je suis plus âgé que vous; **she is five years ~** elle a cinq ans; **the good ~ days** le bon vieux temps; **the ~ man (dad)** papa; **(boss)** patron *m*; *naut* capitaine *m*

**olden** *adj* **in ~ times** au temps jadis

**old-fashioned** *adj* (out-of-date) démodé, suranné; à l'ancienne mode

**old-world** *adj* de l'ancien temps

**oleander** *n bot* laurier-rose *m* (*pl* lauriers-roses)

**oligarchy** *n* oligarchie *f*

**olive** *n* olive *f*; (tree) olivier *m*; *cul* **meat-~** paupiette *f*; *adj* olive *invar*, olivâtre

**olive-branch** *n* rameau *m* d'olivier

**olive-green** *adj* couleur d'olive

**olive-oil** *n* huile *f* d'olive

**Olympian** *adj* olympien -ienne

**Olympic** *n* **the ~ s** les Jeux *mpl* olympiques; *adj* olympique

**ombudsman** *n* = haut fonctionnaire chargé d'enquêter dans les cas d'injustice bureaucratique

**omelet(te)** *n* omelette *f*

**omen** *n* présage *m*, augure *m*

**ominous** *adj* de mauvais augure, sinistre, menaçant

**omission** *n* omission *f*; négligence *f*, oubli *m*

**omit** *vt* omettre; (not mention) passer sous silence

**omnibus** *n* autobus *m*

**omnipotence** *n* toute-puissance *f*, omnipotence *f*

**omnipotent** *adj* omnipotent, tout-puissant (*f* toute-puissante)

**omnipresence** *n* omniprésence *f*

**omnipresent** *adj* omniprésent

**omniscient** *adj* omniscient

**omnivorous** *adj* omnivore

**on** *adv* (forward) en avant; (light) allumé; (tap) ouvert; (engine) en marche; **and so ~** et ainsi de suite; (actor) **be ~** être sur scène; **from then ~** à partir de ce moment; **go ~** continuer; (happen) se passer; **go ~!** pas vrai!; **have nothing ~** être tout(e) nu(e); *fig* ne pas avoir de projet; *coll* être libre; **have sth ~** porter qch; (plan) projeter qch; *coll* **it's not ~** il n'y a pas moyen; **keep ~ doing sth** continuer à faire qch; **later ~** plus tard; **put ~** mettre; **what's ~ ?** *cin* qu'est-ce se donne?; *theat* qu'est-ce qu'on joue?; *prep* sur; à, de, en; ~ **arrival** en arrivant; ~ **foot** à pied; ~ **Friday** vendredi; ~ **horse-back** à cheval; ~ **page two** à la page

deux; ~ **pain of** sous peine de; ~ **purpose** exprès; ~ **sale** en vente; ~ **strike** en grève; ~ **the left (right)** à gauche (droite); ~ **the other side** de l'autre côté; ~ **the phone** au téléphone; ~ **the train** dans le train; **be ~ the staff** faire partie du personnel; **just ~ two years ago** il y a près de deux ans

**onanism** *n* onanisme *m*

**once** *adv* une fois; (formerly) autrefois; ~ **again** encore une fois; ~ **a week** une fois par semaine; **at ~** tout de suite; (simultaneously) en même temps; **just for ~** pour cette fois-ci; *conj* aussitôt que

**once-over** *n coll* examen *m* rapide

**one** *n* un *m* (*f* une); **it's all ~ to me** ça m'est égal; **the good ~** le bon (*f* la bonne); **you're a ~!** vous dites!; *adj* seul, unique; *num* un; **a hundred and ~** cent un; *coll* **be ~ up on** avoir l'avantage sur; **have ~ drink too many** boire un verre de trop; *sl* **number ~** soi-même; **twenty-~** vingt-et-un; *pron* on; ~ **another** les un(e)s les autres; ~ **Mr X** un certain Monsieur X; ~ **'s** son (*f* sa, *pl* ses); **that ~** celui-là (*f* celle-là); **the ~ who** celui (*f* celle) qui; **this ~** celui-ci (*f* celle-ci); **which ~ ?** lequel (*f* laquelle)?

**one-armed** *adj* manchot; *coll* ~ **bandit** machine *f* à sous

**one-eyed** *adj* borgne

**one-horse** *adj US coll* misérable, de rien

**oneness** *n* unité *f*, accord *m*

**onerous** *adj* onéreux -euse

**oneself** *pron* soi, soi-même; se; **be beside ~** être hors de soi

**one-sided** *adj* unilatéral; (partial) partial, injuste; (lop-sided) de biais, asymétrique

**one-track** *adj* ~ **mind** esprit obsédé par une seule idée

**one-upmanship** *n coll* art *m* de surpasser les autres

**one-way** *adj* à sens unique; *US* ~ **ticket** billet *m* simple

**onion** *n* oignon *m*; *coll* **know one's ~ s** connaître son affaire; **spring ~** ciboule *f*; **string of ~s** chapelet *m* d'oignons

**onlooker** *n* spectateur -trice, assistant -e

**only** *adj* seul, unique; ~ **child** enfant unique; **the ~ one** le seul (*f* la seule); *adv* seulement, ne ... que; ~ **this morning** pas plus tard que ce matin; ~ **to imagine it** il rien que de l'imaginer; ~ **you can say** seul vous êtes à même de le dire; **he has ~ to ask** il n'a qu'à demander; **he ~ tried** il n'a fait qu'essayer; *conj* mais

**onomatopoeia** *n* onomatopée *f*

**onrush** *n* ruée *f*, attaque *f*

**onset** *n* assaut *m*, attaque *f*; choc *m*; **at the first** ~ de prime abord

**onslaught** *n* assaut *m*, attaque *f*

**onto** *prep* sur

**onus** *n* responsabilité *f*, charge *f*

**onward** *adj* progressif -ive

**onwards** *adv* en avant; **from now** ~ à partir de maintenant

**onyx** *n* onyx *m*

**oodles** *npl coll* une grande quantité, des masses

**ooze** *n* (oozing) suintement *m*; (mud) limon *m*; *vi* suinter

**opal** *n* opale *f*

**opaque** *adj* opaque

**open** *adj* ouvert; (bottle) débouché; (frank) franc (*f* franche); (question) discutable; (disposed) disposé, prêt; (public) manifeste; (unobstructed) libre; ~ **to the winds** exposé au vent; **break** ~ éventrer; **half** ~ entrouvert; **in the** ~ **air** en plein air; **in the** ~ **country** en pleine campagne; **it is** ~ **to you** to il vous est loisible de; **keep** ~ **house** tenir table ouverte; **lay oneself** ~ **to** s'exposer à; **wide** ~ grand ouvert; *vt* ouvrir; (bottle) déboucher; (parcel) défaire; (uncover) découvrir, exposer; (begin) commencer; (legs) écarter; (hole) percer; ~ **out** ouvrir; (orifice, sleeve) évaser; ~ **up** ouvrir; *vi* s'ouvrir; (shop) ouvrir (ses portes); (begin) commencer, débuter; (flowers) s'épanouir; ~ **on to** donner sur; ~ **out** s'élargir; **half** ~ entrouvrir

**open-cast** *adj* à ciel ouvert

**open-eared** *adj* attentif -ive

**opener** *n* ouvreur -euse; (tin) ouvre-boîte(s) *m*

**open-eyed** *adj* qui voit clair; vigilant

**open-handed** *adj* généreux -euse

**open-hearted** *adj* franc (*f* franche); (sympathetic) compatissant

**opening** *n* ouverture *f*; (beginning) commencement *m*; (wood) clairière *f*; (clouds) éclaircie *f*; (opportunity) occasion *f* favorable; *comm* débouché *m*; (flower) épanouissement *m*; (uncorking) débouchage *m*; *adj* inaugural, d'ouverture, de début

**openly** *adv* ouvertement, franchement

**open-minded** *adj* impartial, sans parti pris

**open-mouthed** *adj* bouche bée

**openness** *n* franchise *f*; aspect découvert

**open-plan** *adj* sans cloisons

**opera** *n* opéra *m*

**operable** *adj* opérable

**opera-glasses** *npl* jumelles *fpl*, lorgnette *f*

**opera-house** *n* opéra *m*

**operate** *vt* effectuer; faire fonctionner, faire manœuvrer, actionner; *vi* opérer; agir; fonctionner; ~ **on** s/o opérer qn

**operatic** *adj* d'opéra

**operating** *adj med* d'opération

**operation** *n* opération *f*; *surg* intervention *f*; (functioning) fonctionnement *m*; **be in** ~ (rule) être en vigueur; (machine) fonctionner, être en marche; **undergo an** ~ se faire opérer, subir une intervention (chirurgicale)

**operational** *adj* opérationnel -elle

**operative** *n* ouvrier -ière; *adj* opératif -ive, actif -ive; **become** ~ entrer en vigueur

**operator** *n* opérateur -trice; **telephone** ~ standardiste

**operetta** *n* opérette *f*

**ophthalmic** *adj* ophtalmique

**ophthalmology** *n* ophtalmologie *f*

**opinion** *n* opinion *f*, avis *m*; **ask s/o's** ~ consulter qn; **form an** ~ se faire une opinion; **I am of the** ~ **that** je suis d'avis que; **in my** ~ à mon avis

**opinionated** *adj* imbu de ses opinions

**opium** *n* opium *m*; ~ **den** fumerie *f*

**opponent** *n* adversaire *m*

**opportune** *adj* opportun, à propos

**opportunely** *adv* à propos

**opportuneness** *n* opportunité *f*

**opportunism** *n* opportunisme *m*

**opportunity** *n* occasion *f* (favorable); **at the earliest** ~ à la première occasion; **take the** ~ profiter de l'occasion

**oppose** *vt* (resist) s'opposer à; (contrast) opposer

**opposed** *adj* opposé, hostile; **as** ~ **to** par opposition à

**opposite** *n* opposé *m*, contraire *m*; *adj* opposé; (facing) vis-à-vis, en face; (contrary) contraire; **in the** ~ **direction** en sens inverse; **on the** ~ **side** de l'autre côté; **their** ~ **neighbours** leurs voisins d'en face; *adv* vis-à-vis, en face; *prep* en face de; (level with) à la hauteur de

**opposition** *n* opposition *f*; résistance *f*; *comm* concurrence *f*

**oppress** *vt* opprimer; (mind) oppresser

**oppression** *n* oppression *f*; (mind) accablement *m*

**oppressive** *adj* oppressif -ive, tyrannique; (weather) lourd

**oppressor** *n* oppresseur *m*, opprimant *m*

**opprobrious** *adj* injurieux -ieuse

**opprobrium** *n* opprobre *m*

**opt** *vi* opter

**optic** *adj* optique

**optical** *adj* optique; ~ **illusion** illusion *f* d'optique; ~ **instrument** instrument *m* d'optique

**optician** *n* opticien -ienne

**optics** n optique f

**optimism** n optimisme m

**optimist** n optimiste

**optimistic** adj optimiste

**optimize** vt + vi tirer le meilleur parti (de)

**optimum** n optimum m (pl optimums or optima); adj optimum (f optimum or optima, pl optimums or optima)

**option** n option f, choix m

**optional** adj facultatif -ive

**opulence** n opulence f

**opulent** adj opulent

**opus** n mus opus m

**opuscule** n opuscule m

**or** conj ou; (with neg) ni; ~ **else** ou bien; **a kilometre** ~ **so** environ un kilomètre; **either...** ~ ou ... ou; **without...** ~ sans ... ni

**oracle** n oracle m

**oracular** adj équivoque; d'oracle

**oracy** n capacité f de s'exprimer

**oral** adj oral; ~ **examination** (examen m) oral m; ~ **vaccine** vaccin buccal

**orally** adv oralement, de vive voix; med par voie buccale

**orange** n orange f; **blood** ~ sanguine f; **Seville** ~ orange amère; adj orange

**orangeade** n orangeade f

**orange-blossom** n fleurs fpl d'oranger

**orange-house** n orangerie f

**orange-peel** n pelure f d'orange

**orang-outang, orang-utan** n orang-outang m (pl orangs-outangs)

**orate** vi pej pérorer

**oration** n discours m, allocution f

**orator** n orateur -trice

**oratorical** adj oratoire; (speech) verbeux -euse

**oratorio** n oratorio m

¹**oratory** n éloquence f

²**oratory** n eccles oratoire m

**orb** n orbe m, sphère f

**orbit** n orbite f; vt décrire une orbite autour de, orbiter autour de

**orchard** n verger m

**orchestra** n orchestre m; ~ **stalls** fauteuils mpl d'orchestre

**orchestral** adj orchestral

**orchestrate** vt orchestrer

**orchid** n orchidée f

**orchitis** n med orchite f

**ordain** vt ordonner, décréter; eccles ordonner

**ordeal** n épreuve f

**order** n ordre m; comm commande f; (rule) règlement m; (sequence) suite f, succession f; mil commandement m; eccles ~ **s** ordres mpl; **call s/o to** ~ rappeler qn à l'ordre; **in good** ~ en bon état; (affairs) en règle; **in** ~ dans les règles; **in** ~ **that** pour que, afin que; **in** ~ **to** pour, afin de; **made to** ~ fait

sur commande; **out of** ~ (machine) détraqué; (on public notice) en panne; (telephone) en dérangement; (irregular) irrégulier -ière; **postal** ~, **money** ~ mandat-poste m (pl mandats-poste); **the lower** ~ **s** les classes inférieures; **the old** ~ l'ancien régime; **until further** ~ **s** jusqu'à nouvel ordre; vt ordonner; comm commander; (tidy) ranger, arranger; ~ **about** envoyer à droite et à gauche; (posting) ~ **s/o** to envoyer qn à; ~ **s/o to do sth** ordonner (commander) à qn de faire qch; **just what the doctor** ~ **ed** tout à fait ce qu'il faut

**ordering** n mise f en ordre, disposition f

**orderliness** n bon ordre; habitude f d'ordre

**orderly** n mil ordonnance f; (hospital) infirmier m; adj ordonné, méthodique; (life) tranquille, rangé

**ordinal** adj ordinal

**ordinance** n ordonnance f

**ordinary** n ordinaire m; **out of the** ~ exceptionnel -elle; adj ordinaire; normal, habituel -elle; pej quelconque

**ordination** n arrangement m; eccles ordination f

**ordnance** n artillerie f; ~ **survey map** carte f d'état-major

**ordure** n ordure f, excrément m; saleté f

**ore** n minerai m

**organ** n anat organe m; mus orgue m, orgues fpl; (publication) journal m; **barrel (street)** ~ orgue m de Barbarie; **preside at the** ~ tenir l'orgue (les orgues)

**organdie** n organdi m

**organ-grinder** n joueur -euse d'orgue de Barbarie

**organic** adj organique

**organism** n organisme m

**organist** n organiste

**organization** n organisation f; pol organisme m

**organize** vt organiser

**organizer** n organisateur -trice

**orgasm** n orgasme m

**orgiastic** adj orgiaque

**orgy** n orgie f

**Orient** n Orient m

**Oriental** n Oriental -e; adj oriental, d'Orient

**orientate** vt orienter

**orientation** n orientation f

**orienteering** n sp traversée f de terrain en se servant de moyens d'orientation

**orifice** n ouverture f, orifice m

**origin** n origine f, provenance f

**original** n original m; adj (primitive) originel -elle, primitif -ive, originaire; original

**originality** n originalité f

**originally** adv à l'origine, originairement; (at first) originalement

**originate** vt être l'auteur de, donner naissance à; vi avoir son origine, provenir, tirer son origine

**originator** n créateur -trice, auteur m; initiateur -trice

**ormolu** n chrysocale m, similor m

**ornament** n ornement m; vt orner, décorer

**ornamental** adj ornemental

**ornamentation** n décoration f, embellissement m

**ornate** adj surchargé (d'ornements); (style) fleuri

**ornithologist** n ornithologiste, ornithologue

**ornithology** n ornithologie f

**orphan** n orphelin -e; vt rendre orphelin -e

**orphanage** n orphelinat m

**orthodox** adj orthodoxe

**orthodoxy** n orthodoxie f

**orthography** n orthographe f

**orthopaedic** adj orthopédique

**Oscar** n cin Oscar m

**oscillate** vt faire osciller; vi osciller

**oscillation** n oscillation f

**osmosis** n osmose f

**osprey** n orfraie f

**ossify** vt ossifier; vi s'ossifier

**ostensible** adj prétendu, feint

**ostensibly** adv en apparence

**ostentation** n ostentation f, apparat m; bravade f

**ostentatious** adj fastueux -euse

**osteopath** n chiropracteur m

**osteopathy** n chiropraxie f

**ostler** n garçon m d'écurie

**ostracism** n ostracisme m

**ostracize** vt frapper d'ostracisme

**ostrich** n autruche f

**other** adj autre; ~ people d'autres; ~ things being equal toutes choses égales; each ~ l'un (f l'une) l'autre; every ~ week toutes les deux semaines; the habits of ~ people les mœurs fpl d'autrui; the ~ ones les autres; the ~ three les trois autres; pron autre; has he any ~ s? en a-t-il d'autres?; one or ~ of us l'un (f l'une) de nous; some... ~ s les uns (f les unes)... les autres; adv autrement

**otherwise** adv autrement; dans le cas contraire; ~, he is quite normal sous d'autres égards, il est tout à fait normal; be ~ engaged être occupé à faire autre chose; except where ~ stated sauf indication contraire

**otherworldly** adj détaché de ce monde

**otiose** adj inutile, superflu

**otter** n loutre f

**Ottoman** n Ottoman -e; adj ottoman

**ottoman** n ottomane f

**ouch** interj aïe!

**ought** vi devoir, falloir; my father ~ to know mon père est bien placé pour le savoir; one ~ to keep calm il faut rester calme; you ~ not to have left vous n'auriez pas dû partir; you ~ really to try it vous devriez vraiment l'essayer

**ounce** n once f

**our** adj notre (pl nos)

**ours** pron le (la) nôtre; a friend of ~ un de nos amis (f une de nos amies); that's ~ c'est à nous

**ourselves** pron nous-mêmes; refl pron nous

**oust** vt déloger; (take the place of) évincer, supplanter

**out** adj ~ tray corbeille f pour le courrier à expédier, corbeille f dépant; vt coll sortir, mettre à la porte; adv dehors; (away from home) sorti; (fire, etc) éteint; (book) paru; (on strike) en grève; (discovered) découvert; sp hors jeu; (aloud) à haute voix; (plant, etc) en fleur; ~ at sea au large; ~ of parmi, de; ~ with it! dites-le!; ~ all ~ à toute vitesse; be ~ and about être sur pied; before the year is ~ avant la fin de l'année; be ~ in one's reckoning être loin du compte; far ~ loin; go all ~ to mettre tout en œuvre pour; go ~ sortir; have an evening ~ faire une sortie le soir; have a tooth ~ se faire arracher une dent; have it ~ with s/o avoir une explication (des explications) avec qn; hear s/o ~ écouter qn jusqu'au bout; mil lights ~ extinction f des feux; put s/o ~ dérouter qn; that's ~ (excluded) c'est exclu; (old-fashioned) c'est vieux jeu; the journey ~ l'aller m; the sun is ~ il fait du soleil; you are far ~ vous vous trompez de beaucoup; prep ~ of hors de, au dehors de; ~ of doors dehors; ~ of gear débrayé; ~ of patience à bout de patience; ~ of print épuisé; ~ of respect par respect; ~ of sight hors de vue; ~ of sight, ~ of mind loin des yeux, loin du cœur; ~ of tune (singing) faux (f fausse); (instrument) désaccordé; be ~ of it ne pas être de la partie; être laissé à l'écart; be ~ of one's mind avoir perdu la raison; drink ~ of a glass boire dans un verre; it's ~ of the question! jamais de la vie!; look ~ of the window regarder par la fenêtre; turn ~ of doors mettre à la porte

**out-and-out** adj consommé, achevé

**outbid** vt enchérir sur; (outdo) surpasser

**outboard** adj ~ **motor** moteur m hors-bord invar; ~ **motor boat** hors-bord m invar

**outbreak** n (riot) révolte f, émeute f; (illness) épidémie f; (from confinement) éruption f; (feelings) explosion f

**outbuilding** n dépendance f; (shed) hangar m

**outburst** n éruption f; (laughter) éclat m; (anger) déchaînement m

**outcast(e)** n + adj proscrit -e, exilé -e, expulsé -e

**outclass** vt surclasser

**outcome** n résultat m, conséquence f

**outcrop** n geol affleurement m

**outcry** n clameur f, cri m, cri m d'indignation

**outdated** adj démodé, suranné

**outdistance** vt distancer

**outdo** vt surpasser, l'emporter sur

**outdoor** adj extérieur, au grand air

**outdoors** adv dehors, en plein air

**outer** adj extérieur

**outermost** adj le plus à l'extérieur

**outface** vt dévisager

**outfit** n (gear) équipement m, attirail m; (clothes) trousseau m; (kit) trousse f; coll organisation f

**outfitter** n confectionneur -euse

**outflank** vt détourner, déborder

**outflow** n écoulement m; décharge f

**outgoing** n sortie f; ~ **s** dépenses fpl; adj sortant; (official) démissionnaire

**outgrow** vt dépasser en croissance, devenir plus grand que; (clothes) devenir trop grand pour; (habit) perdre

**outgrowth** n excroissance f

**outhouse** n dépendance f; (shed) hangar m

**outing** n sortie f, excursion f, promenade f

**outlandish** adj bizarre, étrange; (place) retiré

**outlast** vt durer plus longtemps que, survivre à

**outlaw** n proscrit m, hors-la-loi m invar; vt proscrire

**outlay** n frais mpl, dépenses fpl; (first expense) mise f de fonds

**outlet** n issue f, sortie f; comm débouché m

**outline** n contour m, silhouette f; (sketch) dessin m, esquisse f; (rough idea) aperçu m; vt esquisser, ébaucher

**outlive** vt survivre à

**outlook** n vue f, perspective f

**outlying** adj écarté

**outmanoeuvre** vt déjouer

**outmatch** vt surpasser

**outmoded** adj démodé

**outnumber** vt être plus nombreux -euses que, surpasser en nombre

**out-of-date** adj passé de mode, vieilli; (ticket, etc) périmé

**out-of-door** adj en plein air, de plein air

**out-of-school** adj extra-scolaire

**out-of-the-way** adj (situation) écarté; (unusual) peu ordinaire

**outpace** vt dépasser, devancer

**out-patient** n malade qui vient consulter à l'hôpital

**outplay** vt jouer mieux que

**outpost** n avant-poste m

**outpouring** n épanchement m; (feeling) effusion f

**output** n rendement m; production f; (author) débit m

**outrage** n outrage m; attentat m; vt outrager

**outrageous** adj outrageant; (price) excessif -ive; immodéré

**outrider** n piqueur m

**outrigger** n outrigger m

**outright** adj (manner) franc (f franche); absolu, total; adv complètement, tout à fait; **kill s/o** ~ tuer qn raide

**outrun** vt dépasser, distancer

**outset** n commencement m, début m; **at the** ~ dès le début

**outshine** vt éclipser, dépasser

**outside** n extérieur m, dehors m; **at the** ~ tout au plus; adj extérieur, du dehors; (price) maximum (f maximum or maxima, pl maximums or maxima); adv dehors, au dehors, en dehors; prep à l'extérieur de, en dehors de

**outsider** n étranger -ère; (racing) outsider m

**outsize** adj pointure f (taille f) hors série; (very big) géant

**outskirts** npl (town) faubourgs mpl, banlieue f; (forest) lisière f; (surroundings) abords mpl

**outsmart** vt déjouer les intentions de, duper

**outspoken** adj franc (f franche); **be** ~ ne pas mâcher ses mots

**outspokenness** n franchise f

**outspread** adj étendu; (wings) déployé

**outstanding** adj (jutting) saillant; (excellent) éclatant; (person) marquant, éminent; (debt) dû, à payer; (matter) en suspens

**outstay** vt rester plus longtemps que

**outstretched** adj étendu; (wings) déployé

**outstrip** vt dépasser, devancer; surpasser

**outvote** vt obtenir la majorité sur; **be** ~ **d** être mis en minorité

**outward** adj extérieur; en dehors, de dehors; ~ **journey** voyage m d'aller

**outwardly** adv à l'extérieur; en apparence

**outwards** *adv* au dehors; vers l'extérieur

**outweigh** *vt* peser plus que; *fig* avoir plus d'influence que, l'emporter sur

**outwit** *vt* duper, déjouer les intentions de

**outwork** *n mil* ouvrage avancé

**outworn** *adj* démodé

**oval** *n* ovale *m*; *adj* oval

**ovary** *n* ovaire *m*

**ovation** *n* ovation *f*

**oven** *n* four *m*

**ovenware** *n* vaisselle *f* allant au four

**over** *adv* par-dessus; (finished) fini, passé; (remaining) de reste; (too much) trop; (more) davantage; ~ **and above** en outre; ~ **and** ~ à maintes reprises; ~ **there** là-bas; **all** ~ partout; **it's all** ~ **with us** c'en est fait de nous; **that's you all** ~ c'est typique de vous; *prep* sur; par-dessus; au-dessus de; (more than) plus de; (on the other side of ) de l'autre côté de; (during) au cours de; ~ **the way** en face; **all** ~ **England** partout en Angleterre

**overact** *vt* + *vi theat* charger, outrer

**overall** *n* blouse *f*; ~ **s** salopette *f*, bleus *mpl*; *adj* global, total

**overawe** *vt* intimider

**overbalance** *vt* renverser; *vi* perdre l'équilibre

**overbearing** *adj* arrogant, impérieux -ieuse

**overblown** *adj* trop épanoui

**overboard** *adv* par-dessus bord

**overburden** *vt* surcharger, accabler

**overcast** *adj* couvert, obscurci; *vt* obscurcir

**overcharge** *n* prix excessif; *elect* surcharge *f*; *vt* (battery) surcharger; ~ **s/o** faire payer qn trop cher

**overcloud** *vt* couvrir de nuages; *fig* obscurcir

**overcoat** *n* pardessus *m*

**overcome** *adj* accablé; *vt* (enemy) vaincre; (difficulty) surmonter

**overconfidence** *n* confiance excessive

**overconfident** *adj* trop confiant de soi, trop assuré

**overcrowd** *vt* trop remplir; (with people) surpeupler

**overcrowded** *adj* (vehicle) bondé; (place) surpeuplé

**overdo** *vt* exagérer, outrer; *cul* faire trop cuire; ~ **it** se surmener; (exaggerate) exagérer

**overdose** *n* dose trop forte; dose mortelle

**overdraft** *n* découvert *m*

**overdraw** *vt* mettre à découvert

**overdress** *vt* habiller avec trop de recherche; *vi* s'habiller avec trop de recherche

**overdrive** *n mot* vitesse surmultipliée *f*

**overdue** *adj* en retard; (account) arriéré

**overeat** *vi* trop manger

**overestimate** *vt* surestimer

**overexcite** *vt* surexciter

**overexcitement** *n* surexcitation *f*

**over-expose** *vt* surexposer

**overfeed** *vt* suralimenter

**overflow** *n* débordement *m*; trop-plein *m*; (cistern) déversoir *m*; *vi* déborder

**overgrow** *vt* couvrir, envahir

**overgrown** *adj* couvert

**overhang** *n* surplomb *m*; *vt* surplomber

**overhanging** *adj* en surplomb, surplombant

**overhaul** *n* révision *f*, remise *f* en état; *vt* examiner à fond; *mech* réviser, remettre en état; (overtake) rattraper

**overhead** *adj* aérien -ienne; ~ **expenses,** ~ **s** frais généraux; ~ **valves** soupapes *fpl* en tête; *adv* en haut, au-dessus

**overhear** *vt* entendre par hasard; (conversation) surprendre

**overheat** *vt* surchauffer; ~ **oneself** s'échauffer; *vi* trop chauffer

**overjoyed** *adj* ravi, rempli de joie

**overladen** *adj* surchargé

**overland** *adj* ~ **route** voie *f* de terre; *adv* par voie de terre

**overlap** *n* chevauchement *m*; (duplication) double emploi *m*; *vt* + *vi* chevaucher, recouvrir

**overlay** *n* matelas *m*; *vt* recouvrir, couvrir

**overleaf** *adv* au verso

**overload** *vt* surcharger

**overlook** *vt* dominer, donner sur; (forgive) laisser passer, pardonner; (forget) oublier; (not see) ne pas voir; (neglect) négliger; (watch) surveiller

**overlord** *n* suzerain *m*

**overmuch** *adv* trop, par trop

**overnight** *adj* de nuit; *adv* (pendant) la nuit; la veille au soir; (until next day) jusqu'au lendemain; (suddenly) du jour au lendemain

**overpaid** *adj* trop payé

**overpass** *n* viaduc routier

**overpopulate** *vt* surpeupler

**overpower** *vt* maîtriser, vaincre; *fig* accabler

**overpowering** *adj* accablant, écrasant

**overproduction** *n* surproduction *f*

**overrate** *vt* surestimer, surfaire

**overreach** *vt* (deceive) duper; ~ **oneself** aller trop loin

**override** *vt* outrepasser; (horse) surmener

**overrider** *n mot* banane *f*

**overrule** *vt* annuler, rejeter

**overrun** *vt* envahir; (infest) infester; (go past) dépasser; *typ* reporter à la ligne (page) suivante

**overseas** *adj* d'outre-mer; *adv* outre-mer, par delà les mers

**oversee** *vt* surveiller

**overseer** *n* surveillant *m*

**overshadow** *vt* ombrager; *fig* éclipser

**overshoe** *n* galoche *f*; **rubber ~s** caoutchoucs *mpl*

**overshoot** *vt* dépasser; **~ the mark** dépasser le but

**oversight** *n* oubli *m*, inadvertance *f*; (supervision) surveillance *f*

**oversleep** *vi* dormir trop longtemps

**overspend** *vi* dépenser trop

**overspill** *n* déversement *m* de population

**overstate** *vt* exagérer

**overstatement** *n* exagération *f*

**overstay** *vt* dépasser

**oversteer** *vi mot* survirer

**overstep** *vt* dépasser, outrepasser

**overstock** *vt* encombrer, surcharger

**overstrain** *vt* surmener

**overstrung** *adj* énervé

**overt** *adj* évident, manifeste

**overtake** *vt* (catch up) rattraper; (pass) doubler, dépasser; (surprise) surprendre; (happen to) arriver à

**overtax** *vt* trop exiger de; **~ one's strength** se surmener

**overthrow** *n* renversement *m*; (defeat) défaite *f*; *vt* renverser; (enemy) vaincre

**overtime** *n* heures *fpl* supplémentaires; **work ~** faire des heures supplémentaires

**overtire** *vt* surmener

**overtly** *adv* ouvertement

**overtone** *n mus* harmonique *m* or *f*; *fig* nuance *f*

**overture** *n* ouverture *f*

**overturn** *vt* renverser; (boat) faire chavirer; *vi* se renverser; (boat) chavirer

**overvalue** *vt* surévaluer, surestimer

**overweening** *adj* outrecuidant, présomptueux -ueuse

**overweight** *n* surpoids *m*, excédent *m*; **be ~** être trop lourd; être trop gros (*f* grosse)

**overwhelm** *vt* accabler; (with kindness) combler; (surprise) étonner

**overwork** *n* surmenage *m*; *vt* surmener; *vi* se surmener

**overwrought** *adj* surmené, excédé

**ovine** *adj* ovin

**owe** *vt* devoir, être redevable de

**owl** *n* hibou *m*

**owlish** *adj* de hibou

**¹own** *n* **all one's ~** original; **be (all) on one's ~** être tout seul (*f* toute seule); **come into one's ~** entrer en possession de son bien; **do sth on one's ~** faire qch tout seul (*f* toute seule); (taking responsibility for) faire qch de son propre chef; **my ~** à moi, le mien (*f* la mienne); *adj* propre

**²own** *vt* posséder; (confess) avouer; (acknowledge) reconnaître

**owner** *n* propriétaire

**owner-driver** *n* conducteur *m* propriétaire

**owner-occupier** *n* propriétaire qui habite sur place

**ownership** *n* possession *f*, droit *m* de propriété

**ox** *n* bœuf *m*

**oxide** *n* oxyde *m*

**oxidize** *vt* oxyder

**oxtail** *n* queue *f* de bœuf

**oxyacetylene** *adj* oxyacétylénique

**oxygen** *n* oxygène *m*

**oxygen-mask** *n* masque *m* à oxygène

**oxygen-tent** *n* tente *f* à oxygène

**oyster** *n* huître *f*

**oyster-bed** *n* parc *m* à huîtres, banc *m* d'huîtres

**oyster-shell** *n* écaille *f* d'huître

**ozone** *n* ozone *m*

# P

**pace** *n* pas *m*; (speed) train *m*, allure *f*; **at a good ~** à vive allure; **at a walking ~** au pas; **keep ~ with** marcher de pair avec; **put s/o through his ~s** mettre qn à l'épreuve; **set the ~** mener le train; *vt* arpenter; *vi* **~ up and down** faire les cent pas

**pacemaker** *n* entraîneur *m*; *med* stimulateur *m* cardiaque

**pacific** *adj* pacifique

**pacification** *n* pacification *f*, apaisement *m*

**pacifism** n pacifisme m
**pacifist** n pacifiste
**pacify** vt pacifier, apaiser
**pack** n paquet m; (group) bande f; (collection) tas m; (cards) jeu m; (hounds) meute f; sp mêlée f; (wool) balle f; med emplâtre m; vt emballer; (luggage) faire; (cram) serrer, tasser, bourrer; ~ed hall salle f comble; ~ s/o off expédier qn; send s/o ~ing envoyer promener qn; the train was ~ed le train était bondé; vi se tasser, se presser; ~ up plier bagage; fig cesser
**package** n paquet m, colis m; ~ tour voyage organisé, voyage m à forfait; vt conditionner
**packaging** n conditionnement m
**packer** n emballeur -euse
**packet** n paquet m, colis m; obs (boat) paquebot m
**packhorse** n cheval m de somme
**pack-ice** n glace f de banquise
**packing** n emballage m; (snow) tassement m
**packing-case** n boîte f (caisse f) d'emballage
**packing-paper** n papier m d'emballage
**pact** n pacte m
**¹pad** n (cushion, stuffing) coussinet m, bourrelet; mech tampon m; mot (bearing) coussinet m; (paper) bloc m; (blotter) sous-main m invar; (certain animals) patte f; sl (bed) pieu m; sl (room) piaule f
**²pad** vt rembourrer; capitonner; ~ out délayer
**³pad** vi aller à pied
**padding** n rembourrage m; fig remplissage m; (speech) délayage m; (substance) bourre f, ouate f; (writing) cheville f
**paddle** n pagaie f; (steamship) aube f; vt + vi pagayer; vi (wade) barboter, patauger
**paddle-steamer** n vapeur m (navire m) à aubes
**paddle-wheel** n roue f à aubes
**paddock** n enclos m; (horse-racing) paddock m, pesage m
**paddyfield** n rizière f
**padlock** n cadenas m; vt cadenasser
**padre** n aumônier m
**paederast, pederast** n pédéraste m
**paederasty, pederasty** n pédérastie f
**paediatrician, pediatrician** n pédiatre m
**paediatrics, pediatrics** n pédiatrie f
**paeony** n see peony
**pagan** n + adj païen -ïenne
**paganism** n paganisme m
**¹page** n page m; (hotel) chasseur m; vt (call) appeler
**²page** n page f; vt paginer, numéroter

**pageant** n spectacle m
**pageantry** n pompe f, apparat m
**pagination** n pagination f
**pagoda** n pagode f
**pail** n seau m
**pailful** n seau m, plein seau
**pain** n douleur f, souffrance f; (mental) peine f; be a ~ in the neck être enquiquinant; be in ~ souffrir, avoir mal; have a ~ in avoir mal à; on ~ of sous peine de; take ~s to se donner du mal pour; vt (mental) faire de la peine à; (physical) faire souffrir
**pained** adj peiné
**painful** adj douloureux -euse
**pain-killer** n calmant m, analgésique m
**painless** adj sans douleur
**painstaking** adj soigneux -euse; (work) soigné
**paint** n peinture f; vt peindre; (describe) dépeindre; med badigeonner; ~ one's face se farder; ~ the town red faire une noce du tonnerre
**paint-box** n boîte f de couleurs
**paint-brush** n pinceau m
**¹painter** n peintre m
**²painter** n naut amarre f
**painting** n peinture f; (picture) tableau m, peinture f
**paint-remover** n décapant m
**paint-sprayer** n pistolet m (à peindre)
**Pakistan** n Pakistan m
**Pakistani** n Pakistanais -e; adj pakistanais
**pal** n coll copain m (f copine)
**palace** n palais m; (of bishop) évêché m
**palatable** adj agréable au goût
**palate** n palais m
**palatial** adj magnifique, grandiose
**palaver** n palabre m
**¹pale** n pieu m, pal m; beyond the ~ au ban de la société
**²pale** adj pâle, blême; ~ blue bleu pâle invar; turn ~ pâlir; vi pâlir
**paleness** n pâleur f
**Palestinian** n Palestinien -ienne; adj palestinien -ienne
**palette** n palette f
**paling** n palissade f, clôture f à claire-voie
**palisade** n palissade f
**¹pall** n drap m mortuaire, poêle m
**²pall** vi devenir fade, s'affadir
**pallbearer** n porteur m d'un cordon du poêle
**palliate** vt pallier, atténuer
**palliative** n palliatif m; adj palliatif -ive
**pallid** adj pâle, blafard, blême
**pallor** n pâleur f
**pally** adj coll be ~ with être copain (f copine) avec
**¹palm** n (tree) palmier m; (branch) palme

*f*; **Palm Sunday** le dimanche des Rameaux

²**palm** *n* (hand) paume *f*; **grease s/o's ~** graisser la patte à qn

³**palm** *vt* (card) escamoter; **~ off** refiler

**palmist** *n* chiromancien -ienne

**palmistry** *n* chiromancie *f*

**palpability** *n* palpabilité *f*; évidence *f*

**palpable** *adj* palpable; clair, évident

**palpate** *vt med* palper

**palpitate** *vi* palpiter

**palsy** *n* paralysie *f*

**paltry** *adj* misérable, mesquin

**pamper** *vt* dorloter, choyer

**pamphlet** *n* brochure *f*; (scurrilous) pamphlet *m*

¹**pan** *n* casserole *f*, poêlon *m*; (scales) plateau *m*; (lavatory) cuvette *f*

²**pan** *vt coll* éreinter

**panacea** *n* panacée *f*

**panache** *n* panache *m*, bravoure *f*

**Panama** *n* Panama *m*

**panama** *n* panama *m*

**pancake** *n* crêpe *f*; **~ day** mardi gras; *aer* **~ landing** atterrissage *m* sur le ventre

**panchromatic** *adj* panchromatique

**pancreas** *n* pancréas *m*

**panda** *n* panda *m*

**pandemonium** *n* vacarme *m*, pandémonium *m*

**pander** *n* entremetteur -euse; *vi* **~ to** encourager; (person) flatter bassement

**pane** *n* carreau *m*, vitre *f*

**panegyric** *n* panégyrique *m*

**panel** *n* panneau *m*; *leg* liste *f* du jury, jury *m*; *vt* diviser en panneaux; recouvrir de panneaux, lambrisser

**panel-beater** *n* tôlier *m*

**panel-game** *n* jeu *m* de groupe

**panelist** *n* membre *m* d'un groupe (dans un jeu, une discussion)

**panelling** *n* division *f* en panneaux; lambris *m*, boiserie *f*

**pang** *n* douleur *f*; angoisse subite; **~s of death** affres *fpl* de la mort

**panic** *n* panique *f*, terreur *f*, affolement *m*; *vt* remplir de panique; *vi* s'affoler, paniquer

**panicky** *adj* (person) sujet -ette à la panique

**panic-stricken** *adj* affolé, pris de panique

**pannier** *n* panier *m*

**panoply** *n* panoplie *f*

**panorama** *n* panorama *m*

**panoramic** *adj* panoramique

**pansy** *n* pensée *f*; *sl* (homosexual) tapette *f*

**pant** *vi* haleter; (heart) palpiter; **~ for sth** soupirer après qch

**pantechnicon** *n* camion *m* de déménagement; (store) garde-meuble *m* (*pl* garde-meuble(s))

**pantheism** *n* panthéisme *m*

**pantheon** *n* panthéon *m*

**panther** *n* panthère *f*

**panties** *npl* slip *m*

**pantomime** *n* pantomime *f*; revue-féerie *f* (*pl* revues-féeries) (en Grande-Bretagne à l'époque de Noël)

**pantry** *n* garde-manger *m invar*; **butler's ~** office *f*

**pants** *npl* caleçon *m*; (short) `slip *m* (d'homme); *US* (trousers) pantalon *m*; **be caught with one's ~ down** se trouver en mauvaise posture; **kick in the ~** coup *m* de pied au derrière; *US* **short ~s** culotte *f*, short *m*

**pap** *n* bouillie *f*

**papa** *n* papa *m*

**papacy** *n* papauté *f*

**papal** *adj* papal

**paper** *n* papier *m*; (newspaper) journal *m*; (essay) article *m*; (exam) composition *f*, épreuve *f*; (learned) mémoire *m*; **~ bag** sac *m* en papier; **~ money** billets *mpl* de banque; **it looks good on ~** cela paraît bien en théorie; **old ~s** papèrasse *f*; **read a ~** faire un exposé; *vt* (room) tapisser; **~ up** recouvrir de papier

**paperback** *n* livre *m* de poche

**paper-boy** *n* garçon *m* livreur de journaux

**paper-chase** *n* rallye-paper *m*

**paper-clip** *n* trombone *m*

**paper-fastener** *n* agrafe *f*

**paper-knife** *n* coupe-papier *m invar*

**papermill** *n* fabrique *f* de papier, papeterie *f*

**paperweight** *n* presse-papiers *m invar*

**papier-mâché** *n* papier mâché *m*

**papist** *n* papiste

**paprika** *n* paprika *m*

**papyrus** *n* papyrus *m*

**par** *n* pair *m*, égalité *f*; **above (below) ~** `au-dessus (au-dessous) du pair; **at ~** au pair; **be on a ~ with** aller de pair avec; **feel below ~** ne pas être dans son assiette

**parable** *n* parabole *f*

**parabola** *n* parabole *f*

**parachute** *n* parachute *m*; *vt + vi* parachuter

**parachutist** *n* parachutiste

**parade** *n* parade *f*; (procession) défilé *m*; *mil* rassemblement *m*; promenade *f*, esplanade *f*; **on ~** à l'exercice; *vt* faire parade de, afficher; *mil* faire défiler; *vi* parader; défiler

**parade-ground** *n* place *f* d'armes

**paradigm** *n* paradigme *m*

**paradise** *n* paradis *m*

**paradox** *n* paradoxe *m*

**paradoxical** *adj* paradoxal

**paraffin** *n* pétrole *m*; *med* paraffine *f*; ~ **lamp** lampe *f* à pétrole; **liquid** ~ huile *f* de paraffine

**paragon** *n* modèle *m*, parangon *m*

**paragraph** *n* paragraphe *m*; *vt* diviser en paragraphes

**parakeet, paroquet** *n* perruche *f*

**parallax** *n astron* parallaxe *f*

**parallel** *adj* parallèle; (similar) semblable, pareil -eille; *vt* égaler

**parallelism** *n* parallélisme *m*

**parallelogram** *n* parallélogramme *m*

**paralyse** *vt* paralyser

**paralysis** *n* paralysie *f*; **creeping** ~ paralysie progressive; **infantile** ~ poliomyélite *f*

**paralytic** *adj* paralytique

**para-military** *adj* paramilitaire

**paramount** *adj* souverain, éminent; **of** ~ **importance** de première importance

**paranoia** *n* paranoia *f*

**paranoiac** *n* + *adj* paranoïaque

**parapet** *n* parapet *m*; (safety wall) garde-fou *m*

**paraphernalia** *npl* attirail *m*, effets *mpl*; **all the** ~ tout le bataclan

**paraphrase** *n* paraphrase *f*; *vt* paraphraser

**paraplegic** *adj* paraplégique

**parasite** *n* parasite *m*; (sponger) pique-assiette *m invar*

**parasitic(al)** *adj* parasite; (illness) parasitaire

**parasol** *n* ombrelle *f*, parasol *m*

**paratrooper** *n* (soldat *m*) parachutiste *m*

**paratroops** *npl* (soldats *mpl*) parachutistes *mpl*

**paratyphoid** *n* paratyphoïde *f*

**parcel** *n* paquet *m*, colis *m*; (ground) parcelle *f*; ~ **post** service *m* des colis postaux; **send sth by** ~ **post** envoyer qch comme colis postal; *vt* ~ **out** partager, morceler; ~ **up** emballer, empaqueter

**parch** *vt* sécher, dessécher; **be** ~**ed with thirst** avoir une soif terrible; *vi* se dessécher

**parchment** *n* parchemin *m*

**pardon** *n* pardon *m*; **I beg your** ~ je vous demande pardon; *vt* (crime, etc) pardonner; ~ **s/o** pardonner à qn; *leg* gracier qn

**pardonable** *adj* pardonnable, excusable

**pare** *vt* (nails) rogner; (fruit, etc) éplucher, peler; ~ **down** rogner

**parent** *n* (father) père *m*; (mother) mère *f*; ~**s** père *m* et mère *f*; ~ **establishment** maison *f* mère

**parentage** *n* naissance *f*, origine *f*

**parental** *adj* des parents, paternel -elle, maternel -elle

**parenthesis** *n* parenthèse *f*

**parenthood** *n* paternité *f*, maternité *f*

**pariah** *n* paria *m*

**paring** *n* rognage *m*; ~**s** rognures *fpl*

**Paris** *n* Paris *m*

**parish** *n* paroisse *f*; (civil) commune *f*; ~ **priest** (catholic) curé *m*; (protestant) pasteur *m*

**parishioner** *n* paroissien -ienne

**parish-pump** *adj* d'intérêt local

**Parisian** *n* Parisien -ienne; *adj* parisien -ienne

**parity** *n* égalité *f*, parité *f*

**park** *n* parc *m*, jardin public; **car** ~ parc *m* de stationnement, parking *m*; *vt* enfermer dans un parc; *mot* garer, parquer; ~ **oneself** s'installer; *vi* stationner, se garer

**parking** *n* stationnement *m*; ~ **attendant** gardien *m* d'autos; ~ **lights** *mpl* de position; ~ **lot** (place) parc *m* de stationnement; ~ **ticket** papillon *m*

**parking-meter** *n* parc(o)mètre *m*

**Parkinson** *n* ~'**s disease** maladie *f* de Parkinson

**parlance** *n* langage *m*

**parley** *n* pourparlers *mpl*; *vi* parlementer

**parliament** *n* parlement *m*

**parliamentarian** *n* + *adj* parlementaire

**parliamentary** *adj* parlementaire

**parlour** *n* petit salon, parloir *m*; *US* salon *m*

**parlous** *adj* précaire, dangereux -euse; alarmant

**parochial** *adj eccles* paroissial; communal; *pej* provincial

**parochialism** *n* esprit *m* de clocher

**parody** *n* parodie *f*, pastiche *m*

**parole** *n* parole *f* (d'honneur); **be put on** ~ être libéré sur parole

**paroquet** *n see* **parakeet**

**paroxysm** *n* paroxysme *m*, crise *f*

**parquet** *n* parquet *m*

**parricide** *n* (person) parricide; (crime) parricide *m*

**parrot** *n* perroquet *m*

**parry** *vt* parer, détourner

**parsimonious** *adj* parcimonieux -ieuse

**parsimony** *n* parcimonie *f*

**parsley** *n* persil *m*

**parsnip** *n* panais *m*

**parson** *n* (protestant) pasteur *m*

**parsonage** *n* presbytère *m*

¹**part** *n* partie *f*; (share) part *f*; (side) parti *m*; (district) quartier *m*; (region) région *f*; *theat* rôle *m*; ~ **and parcel** partie intégrante; **a man of** ~**s** un homme très doué; **for my** ~ quant à moi; **have no** ~ **in sth** n'y être pour rien; **in** ~ partiellement, en partie; **in these** ~**s** dans cette région; **take** ~ **in** prendre part à; **take sth in good** ~ prendre qch

en bonne part; *adv* partiellement, en partie

²**part** *vt* séparer (en deux); (divide) diviser; ~ one's hair se faire une raie; *vi* se séparer, se diviser, se quitter; (break) céder; ~ with céder

**partake** *vi* ~ of (in) sth participer à qch

**partial** *adj* partiel -ielle; (unjust) partial; be ~ to aimer bien

**partiality** *n* (bias) partialité *f*; (fondness) prédilection *f*

**partially** *adv* en partie; (unjustly) partialement

**participant** *n+adj* participant -e

**participate** *vi* participer, prendre part

**participation** *n* participation *f*

**participle** *n* participe *m*

**particle** *n* particule *f*

**parti-coloured** *adj* bigarré

**particular** *n* détail *m*; ~s détails *mpl*, renseignements *mpl*; (personal) coordonnées *fpl*; *adj* particulier -ière, spécial; (fussy) difficile; (careful) minutieux -ieuse, méticuleux -euse; (exact) précis, exact; a ~ friend un ami (*f* une amie) intime; he's very ~ about it il y tient beaucoup; nothing ~ rien de spécial

**particularity** *n* particularité *f*

**particularize** *vt* particulariser

**parting** *n* séparation *f*; (leaving) départ *m*; (farewell) adieux *mpl*; (hair) raie *f*; *adj* d'adieu; (last) dernier -ière

**partisan, partizan** *n* partisan *m*; *adj* de parti pris

**partition** *n* partage *m*; (wall) cloison *f*; *vt* partager, morceler; ~ a room cloisonner une pièce

**partly** *adv* partiellement, en partie

**partner** *n* associé -e; (games) partenaire; (dance, outing) cavalier -ière, danseur -euse; **sleeping** ~ commanditaire *m*; *vt* être associé à; *sp* être le (*f* la) partenaire de

**partnership** *n* association *f*; take s/o into ~ prendre qn comme associé

**part-owner** *n* copropriétaire

**partridge** *n* perdrix *f*; (young) perdreau *m*

**part-song** *n* chanson *f* à plusieurs voix

**part-time** *n+adj* ~ work travail *m* à mi-temps; be on ~ être en chômage partiel

**party** *n* parti *m*; (pleasure) partie *f*; (group) bande *f*, groupe *m*; (accomplice) complice; (telephone) ~ line ligne partagée; ~ politics politique *f* de partis; ~ wall mur mitoyen; a third ~ un tiers; be a small ~ être peu nombreux -euse; be no ~ to sth ne pas s'associer à qch; private ~ réunion *f* intime; third ~ insurance assurance *f*

au tiers

¹**pass** *n* (mountain) col *m*, défilé *m*

²**pass** *n* passe *f*; (permit) permis *m*, laissez-passer *m invar*; come to a pretty ~ être dans un bel état; *coll* make a ~ at faire des avances à; obtain a ~ obtenir la moyenne; *fig* sell the ~ vendre la mèche

³**pass** *vt* passer; franchir; (overtake) dépasser; *mot* doubler; (from opposite direction) croiser; (exam) être reçu à; (candidate) recevoir; (approve) approuver; (law) adopter; (hand over) transmettre, donner; ~ a remark faire une observation; ~ off for faire passer pour; ~ sentence prononcer le jugement; ~ on répéter qch; (hand on) transmettre qch; ~ sth round faire circuler qch; *coll* ~ the buck se débrouiller sur le voisin; ~ through traverser; ~ water uriner; *vi* passer; (time) s'écouler; (storm) se dissiper; ~ along! circulez!, avancez!; ~ away (die) mourir, disparaître; ~ off se passer; ~ on passer son chemin; ~ out s'évanouir; come to ~ arriver; that will never ~ ça ne prendra jamais

**passable** *adj* passable; (road) praticable

**passage** *n* passage *m*; (sea) traversée *f*; (corridor) couloir *m*, corridor *m*; (small street) ruelle *f*; (fare) prix *m* du billet; (music) morceau *m*; have a rough (sea) ~ faire une mauvaise traversée; *fig* avoir beaucoup de mal

**pass-book** *n* carnet *m* de banque

**passé** *adj* passé de mode; (faded) défraîchi

**passenger** *n* (by sea or air, in car) passager -ère; (by train) voyageur -euse; *coll* be a ~ être la cinquième roue du carrosse

**passer-by** *n* passant -e

**passion** *n* passion *f*; (love) amour *m*; (fury) emportement *m*, colère *f*; fly into a ~ se mettre en colère

**passionate** *adj* passionné; (angry) emporté, irascible

**passion-flower** *n* fleur *f* de la passion

**passive** *n gramm* passif *m*; *adj* passif -ive

**passivity** *n* passivité *f*

**pass-key** *n* passe-partout *m invar*; *coll* passe *m*

**Passover** *n* Pâque *f* (des Juifs)

**passport** *n* passeport *m*

**password** *n* mot *m* de passe

¹**past** *n* passé *m*; be a thing of the ~ ne plus exister; in the ~ autrefois, au passé; *adj* passé, ancien -ienne; (recent) dernier -ière; for some time ~ depuis quelque temps

²**past** *prep* au-delà de; (more than) plus de; *coll* be ~ caring s'en ficher

complètement; *coll* **be ~ it** être trop
vieux (*f* vieille), ne plus y arriver; **five
~ four** quatre heures cinq; **go ~**
passer devant; **half ~ five** cinq heures
et demie; **it's ~ belief** c'est incroyable;
**I wouldn't put it ~ him** il en est bien
capable; **just ~ the house** un peu plus
loin que la maison

**paste** *n* (glue) colle *f*; pâte *f*; **tooth ~**
pâte *f* dentifrice; *vt* coller

**pastel** *n* pastel *m*; crayon *m* pastel,
couleur *f* pastel

**pasteurize** *vt* pasteuriser

**pastiche** *n* pastiche *m*

**pastille** *n* pastille *f*

**pastime** *n* passe-temps *m invar*

**past-master** *n* expert *m*

**pastor** *n* pasteur *m*

**pastoral** *n* pastorale *f*; poème pastoral;
*adj* pastoral

**pastry** *n* pâtisserie *f*; (for cooking) pâte
*f*; *US* **~ shop** pâtisserie *f*

**pastry-cook** *n* pâtissier -ière

**pasture** *n* pâturage *m*; *vt* faire paître; *vi*
paître

**¹pasty** *n* petit pâté

**²pasty** *adj* pâteux -euse; pâle

**¹pat** *n* tape *f*; caresse *f*; (butter) coquille
*f*; *fig* **give s/o a ~ on the back** encourager qn; *vt* taper, tapoter; caresser;
(animal) flatter

**²pat** *adv* à propos; **answer ~** répondre
sur-le-champ

**patch** *n* pièce *f*; (land) parcelle *f*; (tyre)
pastille *f*; (colour) tache *f*; (vegetable)
carré *m*; **strike a bad ~** être en déveine;
**that's not a ~ on mine** ce n'est rien à
côté du mien (*f* de la mienne); *vt* rapiécer, raccommoder; **~ up** rafistoler

**patchiness** *n* manque *m* d'harmonie

**patchwork** *n* rapiéçage *m*; ouvrage fait
de pièces et de morceaux d'étoffe

**patchy** *adj* inégal

**pâté** *n* pâté *m*

**patent** *n* brevet *m* d'invention; (thing
patented) invention brevetée; **take out
a ~ on sth** faire breveter qch; *adj* (obvious) manifeste; (patented) breveté;
**~ leather** cuir verni; **~ medicine**
spécialité *f* pharmaceutique; *vt* faire
breveter

**patently** *adv* manifestement

**paternal** *adj* paternel -elle

**paternalism** *n* paternalisme *m*

**paternally** *adv* paternellement

**paternity** *n* paternité *f*

**path** *n* chemin *m*, sentier *m*; (garden)
allée *f*; (route) route *f*; (course) course
*f*, trajectoire *f*; (orbit) orbite *f*

**pathetic** *adj* touchant, pathétique; *coll*
pitoyable

**pathfinder** *n* pionnier *m*

**pathological** *adj* pathologique

**pathologist** *n* pathologiste; *leg* médecin
*m* légiste

**pathology** *n* pathologie *f*

**pathos** *n* pathétique *m*

**pathway** *n* sentier *m*

**patience** *n* patience *f*; (cards) réussite *f*;
**his ~ is exhausted** il est à bout de patience; **play ~** faire des réussites

**patient** *n* malade, patient -e; *adj* patient

**patina** *n* patine *f*

**patio** *n* patio *m*

**patois** *n* patois *m*

**patriarch** *n* patriarche *m*

**patrician** *n* patricien -ienne

**patricide** *n* (person) parricide; (crime)
parricide *m*

**patrimony** *n* patrimoine *m*

**patriot** *n* patriote

**patriotic** *adj* patriote

**patriotism** *n* patriotisme *m*

**patrol** *n* patrouille *f*; **~ wagon** voiture *f* cellulaire; *vt* faire la patrouille
dans; *vi* patrouiller

**patrol-car** *n* voiture policière, voiture pie
*f* (*pl* voitures pie)

**patron** *n* protecteur *m*; (arts) mécène *m*;
(charity) patron *m*; (customer) client
-e; **~ saint** patron -onne

**patronage** *n* protection *f*, patronage *m*;
(of establishment) clientèle *f*

**patroness** *n* (arts) protectrice *f*; (charity)
patronnesse *f*

**patronize** *vt* patronner; (artist) protéger;
(shop) accorder sa clientèle à; (be condescending) traiter d'un air protecteur

**patronymic** *n* nom *m* patronymique,
patronyme *m*; *adj* patronymique

**¹patter** *n* petit bruit de pas; (rain) fouettement *m*; *vi* trottiner; (rain) fouetter

**²patter** (fast sales talk) boniment *m*, *sl*
baratin *m*; (chatter) bavardage *m*; *vi*
bavarder sans arrêt, caqueter

**pattern** *n* modèle *m*; (design) dessin *m*;
(sample) échantillon *m*; (paper) patron
*m*; *vt* façonner, modeler

**paucity** *n* manque *m*, rareté *f*

**paunch** *n* ventre *m*, panse *f*, *coll* bedaine
*f*

**pauper** *n* indigent -e

**pause** *n* pause *f*; hésitation *f*; **give ~ to**
faire hésiter; *vi* faire une pause,
s'arrêter (un instant); hésiter; **make s/o
~** donner à réfléchir à qn

**pave** *vt* paver; **~ the way** ouvrir la voie,
préparer le terrain

**pavement** *n* trottoir *m*; pavé *m*; *US*
chaussée *f*

**pavilion** *n* pavillon *m*

**paving** *n* dallage *m*; **~ stone** pavé *m*

**paw** *n* patte *f*; *sl* **~ s off!** bas les pattes!; *vt*
(horse) piaffer; *coll pej* tripoter, peloter

**pawl** n mech cliquet m

¹**pawn** n gage m; vt mettre en gage, engager

²**pawn** n (chess) pion m

**pawnbroker** n prêteur -euse sur gages

**pawnshop** n mont-de-piété m (pl monts-de-piété), établissement m de prêt sur gages

**pawn-ticket** n reconnaissance f (de dépôt sur gages)

**pay** n paie f, salaire m, traitement m; (wages) gages mpl; mil solde f; US ~ **phone** téléphone public; US ~ **station** cabine f (à la banque) verser; ~ **in** (to bank) verser; congés payés; **in the** ~ **of** à la solde de; vt payer; (visit) faire, rendre; (bill) régler, acquitter; ~ **attention** faire attention; ~ **back** rembourser, rendre; ~ **dearly** payer cher; ~ **for sth** payer qch; ~ **in** (to bank) verser; ~ **off** (debts) acquitter; (dismiss) congédier; ~ **one's way** se suffire, joindre les deux bouts; ~ **out** débourser; coll ~ **through the nose** payer le prix fort; **I'll** ~ **him for that** je le lui paierai; **it** ~**s him to …** il gagne à …; vi payer, être rentable

**payable** adj payable

**pay-as-you-earn** n (système m de) retenue f de l'impôt à la source

**pay-day** n jour m de paie

**payee** n bénéficiaire

**pay-envelope** n US enveloppe f contenant la paie de la semaine

**pay-load** n charge commerciale

**payment** n paiement m; (instalment) versement m; (settlement) règlement m

**pay-off** n paiement (versement) final; fig le fin mot de l'histoire

**pay-packet** n enveloppe f contenant la paie de la semaine

**pay-roll** n liste f des employé(e)s (d'une compagnie, etc); **he is on the** ~ il émarge au budget

**pay-slip** n feuille f de paie

**pea** n pois m; **be as like as two** ~**s** se ressembler comme deux gouttes d'eau; **green** ~**s** petits pois; **split** ~**s** pois cassés

**peace** n paix f; (of mind) tranquillité f; **at** ~ en paix; **break the** ~ troubler l'ordre public; **hold one's** ~ se taire, garder le silence; **sleep in** ~ dormir tranquille

**peaceable** adj pacifique

**peaceful** adj paisible, calme

**peacemaker** n pacificateur -trice

**peace-offering** n cadeau m de réconciliation

¹**peach** n pêche f; (tree) pêcher m

²**peach** vi sl moucharder

**peacock** n paon m

**pea-green** adj vert feuille invar

**peahen** n paonne f

**peak** n cime f, pic m; (cap) visière f; (high point) pointe f, apogée f; ~ **hours** heures fpl de pointe; ~ **load** charge f maximum

**peaked** adj à visière

**peal** n (bells) carillon m; (thunder) coup m, grondement m; ~ **of laughter** éclat m de rire; vt sonner à toute volée; vi (bells) carillonner; (thunder) gronder

**peanut** n arachide f, cacahouète f; coll ~**s** rien du tout

**pear** n poire f; (tree) poirier m

**pearl** n perle f; **mother of** ~ nacre f

**pearl-barley** n orge perlé

**pearl-diver** n pêcheur -euse de perles

**peasant** n paysan -anne, campagnard -e

**pea-shooter** n sarbacane f

**pea-souper** n brouillard m jaune

**peat** n tourbe f

**peat-bog** n tourbière f

**pebble** n caillou m; (on beach) galet m; fig **you're not the only** ~ **on the beach** vous n'êtes pas unique au monde

**pebble-dash** n crépi m

**pebbly** adj caillouteux -euse; ~ **beach** plage f de galets

**peccadillo** n peccadille f, vétille f

**peck** n coup m de bec; (kiss) bise f, bécot m; vt donner des coups (un coup) de bec à; (bird) picoter

**peckish** adj **be** ~ avoir faim; **feel** ~ avoir le ventre creux

**pectoral** adj pectoral

**peculation** n détournement m de fonds

**peculiar** adj particulier -ière, spécial; (unusual) étrange, singulier -ière; (odd) bizarre

**peculiarity** n particularité f, singularité f; (oddness) bizarrerie f

**pecuniary** adj pécuniaire

**pedagogic** adj pédagogique

**pedagogue** n pédagogue m; pej pédant -e

**pedagogy** n pédagogie f

**pedal** n pédale f; vi pédaler

**pedant** n pédant -e

**pedantic** adj (person) pédant; (thing) pédantesque

**pedantry** n pédantisme m

**peddle** vt colporter; vi faire le (du) colportage

**pederast** n see paederast

**pederasty** n see paederasty

**pedestal** n piédestal m, socle m

**pedestrian** n piéton m; adj pédestre; fig prosaïque; ~ **crossing** passage clouté

**pediatrician** n see paediatrician

**pediatrics** n see paediatrics

**pedigree** n généalogie f; (tree) arbre m généalogique; (certificate) pedigree m; adj de race

**pedlar** *n* colporteur *m*; **drug ~** trafiquant *m* en stupéfiants

**pee** *vi coll* faire pipi

**peek** *n + vi see* ¹**peep**

**peel** *n* pelure *f*, écorce *f*, peau *f*; *cul* zeste *m*; *vt* peler, éplucher; **~ off one's clothes** se déshabiller; *vi* peler; (paint) s'écailler

**peeler** *n* (person) éplucheur -euse; (thing) éplucheur *m*

**peelings** *npl* épluchures *fpl*

¹**peep** *n* coup *m* d'œil; **at ~ of day** au point du jour; *vi* donner un coup d'œil; **~ at sth** regarder quelque chose à la dérobée; **~ out** se montrer, se laisser entrevoir

²**peep** *n* pépiement *m*; *vi* (bird) pépier; (mouse) crier

**peep-hole** *n* judas *m*

¹**peer** *n* pair *m*; (equal) pareil -eille

²**peer** *vi* **~ at** scruter du regard

**peerage** *n* (rank) pairie *f*; *collect* noblesse *f*

**peeress** *n* pairesse *f*

**peerless** *adj* sans pareil -eille, incomparable

**peeve** *vt* irriter, vexer, fâcher

**peevish** *adj* grognon -onne, grincheux -euse

**peevishness** *n* mauvaise humeur

**peewit** *n see* pewit

**peg** *n* cheville *f*; (for clothes) patère *f*; épingle *f*; *coll* (drink) coup *m*; **be a square ~ in a round hole** n'être pas dans son emploi; **clothes off the ~** vêtements *mpl* de confection; **take s/o down a ~** remettre qn à sa place; *vt* cheviller; (prices) stabiliser; *vi* **~ away at sth** persévérer à qch, travailler ferme à qch; *coll* **~ out** casser sa pipe

**pejorative** *adj* péjoratif -ive

**pekinese, pekingese** (chien *m*) pékinois *m*

**pelican** *n* pélican *m*

**pellet** *n* boulette *f*; *med* pilule *f*; (lead shot) grain *m* de plomb

**pell-mell** *adj* en désordre; *adv* pêle-mêle

**pellucid** *adj* transparent, pellucide, clair, lucide

**pelmet** *n* lambrequin *m*

¹**pelt** *n* peau *f*, fourrure *f*

²**pelt** *n* **at full ~** à toute vitesse; *vt* lancer à, lancer contre; *vi* tomber à verse; **~ along** aller à toute vitesse; **~ing rain** pluie battante

**pelvis** *n* bassin *m*

**pemmican** *n* pemmican *m*

¹**pen** *n* enclos *m*, parc *m*; *US* (cattle) étable *f*, (pigs) porcherie *f*; *vt* (animals) parquer; (people) confiner

²**pen** *n* plume *f*; **make a living by one's ~** vivre de sa plume; *vt* écrire

**penal** *adj* (law) pénal; (crime) qui entraîne une pénalité; **~ servitude** travaux forcés

**penalize** *vt sp* pénaliser; infliger une peine à

**penalty** *n* peine *f*, pénalité *f*; (fine) amende *f*; (rugby) pénalité *f*; (soccer) penalty *m* (*pl* penalties); **death ~** peine *f* de mort

**penance** *n* pénitence *f*

**penchant** *n* penchant *m*

**pencil** *n* crayon *m*; **~ of light** faisceau lumineux; **in ~** au crayon; **propelling ~** porte-mines *m invar*; *vt* marquer au crayon; (draw) dessiner au crayon; **~ a note** crayonner un billet

**pencil-sharpener** *n* taille-crayon(s) *m invar*

**pendant, pendent** *n* (necklace) pendentif *m*; (lamp) pendeloque *f*; (counterpart) pendant *m*; *adj* suspendu

**pending** *adj leg* en instance; *prep* en attendant

**pendulous** *adj* pendant; (swinging) oscillant

**pendulum** *n* pendule *m*, balancier *m*

**penetrability** *n* pénétrabilité *f*

**penetrable** *adj* pénétrable

**penetrate** *vt + vi* pénétrer

**penetrating** *adj* pénétrant

**penetration** *n* pénétration *f*; perspicacité *f*

**pen-friend** *n* correspondant -e

**penguin** *n* pingouin *m*

**pen-holder** *n* porte-plume *m invar*

**penicillin** *n* pénicilline *f*

**peninsula** *n* péninsule *f*, presqu'île *f*

**penis** *n* pénis *m*

**penitence** *n* pénitence *f*

**penitent** *n + adj* pénitent -e

**penitential** *adj* pénitentiel -ielle

**penitentiary** *n* pénitencier *m*, prison *f*

**penitently** *adv* d'un air contrit

**penknife** *n* canif *m*

**penmanship** *n* calligraphie *f*

**pen-name** *n* pseudonyme *m*

**pennant** *n* flamme *f*

**penniless** *adj* sans le sou

**penny** *n* penny *m*; *fig* deux sous *mpl*; **~ dreadful** roman *m* à quatre sous; **cost a pretty ~** coûter cher; **he's a bad ~** c'est un mauvais sujet; **spend a ~** faire pipi; *coll* **the ~ has dropped** ça y est, il a compris (elle a compris, etc)

**penny-in-the-slot (machine)** *n* distributeur *m* automatique; (entertainment) machine *f* à sous

**penny-wise** *adj* qui fait des économies de bouts de chandelle

**pension** *n* pension *f*, retraite *f*; (boarding-house) pension *f* (de famille); **old-age ~** retraite *f* de vieillesse (des vieux); **retire on a** ~ prendre sa retraite; *vt* pensionner; ~ **off** mettre à la retraite

**pensionable** *adj* ayant droit à une pension

**pensioner** *n* retraité -e, titulaire d'une pension

**pensive** *adj* pensif -ive, songeur -euse

**pent** *adj* ~ **up** enfermé

**pentagon** *n* pentagone *m*

**pentathlon** *n* pentathlon *m*

**Pentecost** *n* la Pentecôte

**penthouse** *n* appentis *m*; ~ **flat** appartement *m* sur le toit, entouré d'une terrasse; ~ **roof** auvent *m*

**penultimate** *adj* avant-dernier -ière, pénultième

**penumbra** *n* pénombre *f*

**penurious** *adj* (poor) pauvre; (stingy) mesquin, parcimonieux -ieuse

**penury** *n* (poverty) indigence *f*; (shortage) pénurie *f*

**peony, paeony** *n* pivoine *f*

**people** *n* (of a country) nation *f*, peuple *m*; gens *mpl* or *fpl*; (citizens) citoyens *mpl*, habitants *mpl*; (persons) personnes *fpl*; (crowd) monde *m*; *coll* (relatives) parents *mpl*; ~ **say** on dit; *vt* peupler

**pep** *n coll* allant *m*, entrain *m*; *vt* ~ **s/o up** ragaillardir qn; ~ **sth up** donner de l'entrain à qch

**pepper** *n* poivre *m*; *vt* poivrer; *fig* cribler

**peppercorn** *n* grain *m* de poivre; ~ **rent** loyer nominal

**pepper-mill** *n* moulin *m* à poivre

**peppermint** *n* bonbon *m* à la menthe

**pepper-pot** *n* poivrier *m*

**peppery** *adj* poivré; *fig* irascible

**pep-talk** *n* petit discours d'encouragement

**peptic** *adj* peptique

**per** *prep* par; ~ **annum** par an; ~ **capita** par tête; ~ **cent** pour cent; **as** ~ conformément à

**perambulate** *vt* parcourir, inspecter; *vi* se promener

**perambulator** *n* voiture *f* d'enfant, landau *m*

**perceivable** *adj* perceptible

**perceive** *vt* percevoir; (notice) s'apercevoir de

**percentage** *n* pourcentage *m*, proportion *f*

**perceptibility** *n* perceptibilité *f*

**perceptible** *adj* perceptible

**perception** *n* perception *f*; (sensitiveness) sensibilité *f*

**perceptive** *adj* perceptif -ive

**perceptivity** *n* perceptivité *f*

¹**perch** *n* perchoir *m*; *vi* (se) percher, jucher

²**perch** *n* (fish) perche *f*

**percipient** *n* sujet *m* télépathique; *adj* percepteur -trice

**percolate** *vt* filtrer, passer; *vi* filtrer, percoler

**percolator** *n* filtre *m* à café

**percussion** *n* percussion *f*; ~ **cap** amorce *f*; *mus* ~ **instruments** batterie *f*

**perdition** *n* perdition *f*, ruine *f*, perte *f*

**peregrination** *n* pérégrination *f*

**peremptoriness** *n* intransigeance *f*

**peremptory** *adj* péremptoire; (total) absolu

**perennial** *n bot* plante *f* vivace; *adj* (constant) perpétuel -elle; *bot* vivace

**perfect** *n gramm* parfait *m*; **in the** ~ **(tense)** au parfait; *adj* parfait; *coll* (first-rate) impeccable; *vt* achever, parachever; (make perfect) perfectionner, rendre parfait; (device) mettre au point

**perfectibility** *n* perfectibilité *f*

**perfectible** *adj* perfectible

**perfection** *n* perfection *f*; (finishing) achèvement *m*, accomplissement *m*; **to** ~ à la perfection

**perfectionism** *n* perfectionnisme *m*

**perfectly** *adv* parfaitement; tout à fait

**perfidious** *adj* perfide, traître -esse

**perfidy** *n* perfidie *f*

**perforate** *vt* percer; *med* perforer

**perforation** *n* perforation *f*; (piercing) percement *m*; (little hole) petit trou

**perforce** *adv* forcément

**perform** *vt* accomplir, exécuter, effectuer; (ceremony) célébrer; *theat* jouer, représenter; (dance) exécuter; (role) remplir

**performance** *n mus* exécution *f*; *theat* représentation *f*; *cin* séance *f*; (task) accomplissement *m*; (action) action *f*, exploit *m*; *sp* performance *f*; (ceremony) célébration *f*; (machine) fonctionnement *m*, marche *f*; **afternoon** ~ matinée *f*; *cin* **continuous** ~ spectacle permanent; **evening** ~ soirée *f*; **no** ~ relâche *f*

**performer** *n* artiste; *theat* acteur -trice; *mus* exécutant -e

**perfume** *n* parfum *m*; *vt* parfumer

**perfunctory** *adj* (person) négligent, léger -ère; (examination) fait pour la forme

**perhaps** *adv* peut-être

**peril** *n* péril *m*, danger *m*; **at one's own** ~ à ses risques et périls

**perilous** *adj* périlleux -euse, dangereux -euse

**perimeter** *n* périmètre *m*

**period** *n* période *f*, durée *f*; (school) cours *m*, heure *f* de cours; époque *f*, âge *m*; *gramm* point *m*; *med* ~**(s)**

règles *fpl*; *US* **I'm not going,** ~ je n'y vais pas, un point c'est tout

**periodic** *adj* périodique

**periodical** *n* publication *f* périodique, périodique *m*; *adj* périodique

**periodicity** *n* périodicité *f*

**peripatetic** *adj* péripatéticien -ienne, péripatétique

**peripheral** *adj* périphérique

**periphery** *n* périphérie *f*

**periphrasis** *n* périphrase *f*

**periscope** *n* périscope *m*

**perish** *vi* mourir, périr; (substance) se détériorer

**perishable** *adj* périssable

**perished** *adj* détérioré

**perishing** *adj coll* it's ~ **cold** il fait un froid de canard

**peritonitis** *n* péritonite *f*

¹**periwinkle** *n bot* pervenche *f*

²**periwinkle** *n* bigorneau *m*

**perjure** *vt* ~ **oneself** se parjurer

**perjurer** *n* parjure

**perjury** *n* parjure *m*; **commit** ~ faire (rendre) un faux témoignage

¹**perk** *n sl* avantage *m*, casuel *m*

²**perk** *vt* ~ **s/o up** requinquer qn; *vi* ~ up se ranimer, redresser la tête

**perky** *adj* éveillé

**perm** *n coll* permanente *f*; *vt coll* **have one's hair** ~ed se faire faire une permanente

**permanence** *n* permanence *f*, stabilité *f*

**permanency** *n* emploi permanent

**permanent** *adj* permanent; ~ **address** résidence *f* fixe

**permeability** *n* perméabilité *f*

**permeable** *adj* perméable

**permeate** *vt* pénétrer, s'insinuer dans; *vi* pénétrer, s'insinuer

**permissible** *adj* permis, autorisé

**permission** *n* permission *f*, autorisation *f*

**permit** *n* permis *m*, autorisation *f*; (customs) passavant *m*; *vt* permettre, autoriser; ~ **s/o to do sth** permettre à qn de faire qch; *vi* this ~s of no reply cela n'admet pas de réplique

**permutation** *n* permutation *f*

**pernicious** *adj* pernicieux -ieuse

**pernickety** *adj* (person) pointilleux -euse, difficile; (task) délicat

**perorate** *vi* pérorer

**peroration** *n* péroraison *f*

**peroxide** *n* peroxyde *m*, eau oxygénée

**perpendicular** *n* fil *m* à plomb; (line) perpendiculaire *f*; *adj* perpendiculaire

**perpetrate** *vt* perpétrer, commettre

**perpetrator** *n* auteur *m*

**perpetual** *adj* perpétuel -elle, éternel -elle

**perpetuate** *vt* perpétuer

**perpetuation** *n* perpétuation *f*

**perpetuity** *n* perpétuité *f*

**perplex** *vt* embarrasser

**perplexed** *adj* perplexe

**perplexity** *n* embarras *m*, perplexité *f*

**perquisite** *n* avantage *m*, casuel *m*

**perry** *n* cidre *m* de poire

**persecute** *vt* persécuter; tourmenter

**persecution** *n* persécution *f*

**persecutor** *n* persécuteur -trice

**perseverance** *n* persévérance *f*

**persevere** *vi* persévérer

**persevering** *adj* assidu, persévérant

**Persian** *n* Persan -e; *adj* persan; ~ **Gulf** golfe *m* Persique

**persimmon** *n bot* kaki *m*

**persist** *vi* persister, s'obstiner; (continue) continuer

**persistence, persistency** *n* persistance *f*, obstination *f*

**persistent** *adj* persistant, tenace

**person** *n* personne *f*; (often *pej*) individu *m*; ~**s** gens *mpl*; **in** ~ en personne

**personable** *adj* qui présente bien, bien fait de sa personne

**personage** *n* personnage *m*, personnalité *f*

**personal** *adj* personnel -elle; ~ **property** biens mobiliers; **don't be** ~ ne faites pas de personnalités; **make a** ~ **application** se présenter en personne

**personality** *n* personnalité *f*, personnage *m*

**personalize** *vt* (personify) personnifier; personnaliser

**personally** *adv* personnellement; (for my part) pour moi, quant à moi

**personalty** *n leg* biens meubles *mpl*

**personification** *n* personnification *f*

**personify** *vt* personnifier; **she is stupidity personified** elle est la stupidité même

**personnel** *n* personnel *m*

**perspective** *n* perspective *f*; **see a matter in its true** ~ voir une affaire sous son vrai jour

**perspex** *n* perspex *m*

**perspicacious** *adj* perspicace

**perspicacity** *n* perspicacité *f*, discernement *m*

**perspicuity** *n* clarté *f*, lucidité *f*

**perspicuous** *adj* lucide, clair

**perspiration** *n* transpiration *f*; **bathed in** ~ trempé de sueur

**perspire** *vi* transpirer

**persuade** *vt* persuader, convaincre; ~ **s/o to do sth** persuader qn de faire qch

**persuasion** *n* persuasion *f*; (conviction) croyance *f*, conviction *f*; (religious) confession *f*

**persuasive** *adj* persuasif -ive

**pert** *adj* effronté, impertinent

**pertain** vi appartenir; ~ing to ayant rapport à
**pertinacious** adj obstiné, entêté, opiniâtre
**pertinacity** n obstination f, entêtement m, opiniâtreté f
**pertinence, pertinency** n pertinence f, à-propos m
**pertinent** adj pertinent, à propos
**pertly** adv avec impertinence, d'un air effronté
**pertness** n effronterie f, impertinence f
**perturb** vt inquiéter, troubler
**perturbation** n inquiétude f, trouble m
**Peru** n Pérou m
**perusal** n lecture f, examen m
**peruse** vt lire attentivement, examiner
**pervade** vt pénétrer, s'infiltrer dans, se répandre dans
**pervasion** n pénétration f, infiltration f
**pervasive** adj pénétrant
**perverse** adj pervers, méchant; (wayward) contrariant
**perverseness, perversity** n perversité f; (contrariness) caractère m revêche
**perversion** n perversion f; ~ of justice travestissement m de la vérité
**perversity** n see **perverseness**
**pervert** n perverti -e; vt pervertir; dépraver; détourner
**perverter** n pervertisseur -euse
**pessary** n pessaire m
**pessimism** n pessimisme m
**pessimist** n pessimiste
**pessimistic** adj pessimiste
**pest** n ent insecte m nuisible; (plague) fléau m, peste f; **he's an absolute ~!** quel casse-pieds, celui-là!
**pester** vt tourmenter, ennuyer, importuner
**pesticide** n pesticide m
**pestiferous** adj pestifère; nuisible
**pestilence** n peste f
**pestilential** adj pestilentiel -ielle; (disease) contagieux -ieuse; (idea) pernicieux -ieuse
**pestle** n pilon m
**¹pet** n animal familier; enfant gâté, enfant choyé; **my ~** mon petit chou; adj favori, choyé; **~ aversion** bête noire; **~ name** nom m d'amitié; vt choyer, chouchouter; coll peloter
**²pet** n accès m de mauvaise humeur
**petal** n pétale m
**Peter** n Pierre m
**peter** vi **~ out** s'épuiser, disparaître; (plan) s'en aller en fumée
**petite** adj petite f
**petition** n pétition f, supplique f, requête f; **~ for divorce** demande f en divorce; vt présenter (adresser) une pétition (requête) à

**petrel** n pétrel m; fig stormy **~** émissaire m de discorde
**petrify** vt pétrifier; vi se pétrifier
**petrochemical** adj pétrochimique
**petrol** n essence f; **premium grade ~** supercarburant m, coll super m; **~ station** station f d'essence; **run out of ~** avoir une panne d'essence
**petrol-can** n bidon m à essence
**petroleum** n pétrole m; **~ industry** industrie pétrolière; **~ jelly** vaseline f
**petticoat** n jupon m
**pettifogging** adj chicanier -ière, avocassier -ière
**pettiness** n mesquinerie f, petitesse f
**petty** adj (mean) mesquin; (trifling) insignifiant, sans importance; **~ cash** petite caisse; **~ expenses** menus frais; naut **~ officer** sous-officier m
**petulance** n irritabilité f
**petunia** n pétunia m
**pew** n banc m d'église
**pewit, peewit** n vanneau m
**pewter** n étain m
**phalanx** n phalange f
**phallic** adj phallique
**phallus** n phallus m
**phantasmagoria** n fantasmagorie f
**phantom** n fantôme m, spectre m
**Pharaoh** n Pharaon m
**Pharisee** n Pharisien -ienne
**pharmaceutical** adj pharmaceutique
**pharmaceutics** npl pharmaceutique f
**pharmacist** n pharmacien -ienne
**pharmacology** n pharmacologie f
**pharmacy** n pharmacie f
**pharynx** n pharynx m
**phase** n phase f
**pheasant** n faisan m
**phenol** n phénol m
**phenomenal** adj phénoménal
**phenomenon** n phénomène m
**phial** n fiole f, flacon m
**philander** vi flirter, conter fleurette à
**philanderer** n galant m; flirteur m
**philanthropic** adj philanthropique; (person) philanthrope
**philanthropist** n philanthrope
**philanthropy** n philanthropie f
**philatelist** n philatéliste
**philately** n philatélie f
**philharmonic** adj philharmonique
**Philistine** n Philistin m
**philological** adj philologique
**philology** n philologie f
**philosopher** n philosophe
**philosophic(al)** adj philosophique
**philosophize** vi philosopher
**philosophy** n philosophie f
**phlebitis** n phlébite f
**phlegm** n flegme m
**phlegmatic** adj flegmatique

phlox *n bot* phlox *m*

phobia *n* phobie *f*

phoenix *n* phénix *m*

phone *n coll* téléphone *m*; be on the ~ (have the ~) avoir le téléphone; (be speaking) être au téléphone; *vt* téléphoner à; *vi* téléphoner

phoneme *n* phonème *m*

phonetic *adj* phonétique

phonetician *n* phonéticien -ienne

phonetics *n* phonétique *f*

phoney, phony *n coll* imposteur *m*; *adj coll* faux (*f* fausse); ~ war drôle de guerre *f*

phonograph *n US* phonographe *m*

phonology *n* phonologie *f*

phosgene *n* phosgène *m*

phosphate *n* phosphate *m*

phosphorescence *n* phosphorescence *f*

phosphorous *adj* phosphoreux -euse

phosphorus *n* phosphore *m*

photo *n* photo *f*

photocopier *n* photocopieur *m*; photocopieuse *f*

photocopy *n* photocopie *f*

photoelectric *adj* photo-électrique

photo-finish *n* photo *f* à l'arrivée

photogenic *adj* photogénique

photograph *n* photographie *f*; *vt* photographier, prendre en photo

photographer *n* photographe *m*

photographic *adj* photographique

photography *n* photographie *f*

photostat *n* photocopie *f*, photostat *m*; *vt* photocopier

phrase *n* expression *f*, locution *f*; *vt* exprimer; *mus* phraser

phraseology *n* phraséologie *f*

phrenetic *adj* frénétique

phrenology *n* phrénologie *f*

phut *adv coll go* ~ claquer

physical *adj* physique; ~ impossibility impossibilité matérielle

physician *n* médecin *m*

physicist *n* physicien -ienne

physics *n* physique *f*

physiognomy *n* physionomie *f*

physiological *adj* physiologique

physiologist *n* physiologue *m*

physiology *n* physiologie *f*

physiotherapist *n* kinésithérapeute

physiotherapy *n* kinésithérapie *f*

physique *n* physique *m*

pianist *n* pianiste

piano *n* piano *m*

pianola *n* pianola *m*

piano-stool *n* tabouret *m* de piano

picaresque *adj* picaresque

piccalilli *n* pickles *mpl* à la moutarde

piccolo *n* piccolo *m*

¹pick *n* pioche *f*, pic *m*

²pick *n* choix *m*; élite *f*; *vt* (gather)

cueillir; (choose) choisir; (lock) crocheter; ~ a bone enlever la chair d'un os; ~ and choose se montrer difficile; ~ a quarrel with s/o chercher querelle à qn; ~ off descendre; ~ one's teeth se curer les dents; ~ on s/o accuser qn; ~ out choisir, sélectionner; (spot) repérer; ~ pockets pratiquer le vol à la tire; ~ up ramasser; (learn) apprendre; (buy cheaply) acheter à bon marché; (s/o) prendre, rejoindre; *sl* (s/o) draguer; have a bone to ~ with s/o avoir maille à partir avec qn; *vi* ~ up (recover) se rétablir, se ressaisir; (engine) reprendre

pickaback *adv* sur le dos, sur les épaules

pickax(e) *n* pioche *f*

picker *n* cueilleur -euse, récolteur -euse

picket *n* piquet *m*; *mil* poste *m*; ~ fence palissade *f*; strike ~ piquet *m* de grève; *vt* mettre au piquet; (factory, etc) installer (poster) des piquets de grève devant

picking *n* (fruit) cueillette *f*; (birds) picotage *m*; (selecting) triage *m*; ~s (remainder) restes *mpl*; fat ~s beaux bénéfices

pickle *n* marinade *f*; (brine) saumure *f*; ~s pickles *mpl*, conserves *fpl* au vinaigre; *coll* be in a (pretty) ~ être dans de beaux draps; *vt* conserver dans du vinaigre

pick-me-up *n coll* remontant *m*

pickpocket *n* voleur *m* à la tire, pickpocket *m*

pick-up *n* (recovery) reprise *f*; (record-player) pick-up *m invar*

picnic *n* pique-nique *m*; *vi* pique-niquer

picnicker *n* pique-niqueur -euse

pictorial *adj* illustré; (description) pittoresque

picture *n* image *f*; (painting) tableau *m*, peinture *f*; (engraving) gravure *f*; (likeness) portrait *m*; *cin* film *m*; be a ~ of health respirer la santé; *coll* be in the ~ être au courant, être au parfum; put s/o in the ~ mettre qn au courant; *vt* représenter, dépeindre; ~ to oneself se figurer

picture-book *n* livre *m* d'images

picture-frame *n* cadre *m*

picture-postcard *n* carte postale illustrée

picturesque *adj* pittoresque

piddling *adj coll* sans importance

pidgin, pigeon *n* ~ English pidgin *m*; talk ~ parler petit nègre

pie *n* (meat) pâté *m*; tarte *f*

piebald *adj* (horse) pie; (motley) bigarré

piece *n* morceau *m*, bout *m*; (part) partie *f*; (chip) éclat *m*; (land) parcelle *f*; fragment *m*; (from book) passage *m*; (coin) pièce *f*; *coll* fille *f*; ~ of advice conseil *m*; ~ of clothing vêtement *m*; ~ of

**luggage** valise f, colis m; ~ **of news** nouvelle f; ~ **of work** ouvrage m; **all of a** ~ tout d'une pièce; **fall into** ~ s s'en aller en morceaux; **fly into** ~ s voler en éclats; fig **give s/o a** ~ **of one's mind** dire son fait à qn; **take to** ~ s démonter; **tear to** ~ s déchirer; (argument) démolir; vt rapiécer; ~ **together** raccommoder, rassembler

**piecemeal** adv par morceaux, pièce à pièce

**piece-work** n travail m à la pièce; **be on** ~ être payé à la pièce, coll être aux pièces

**pie-crust** n croûte f de pâté

**pied** adj bigarré

**pied-à-terre** n pied-à-terre m invar

**pie-dish** n plat m allant au four, terrine f; tourtière f

**pier** n jetée f, digue f; (at resort) jetée f promenade; (for landing) débarcadère m; bui pilier m

**pierce** vt percer, transpercer, pénétrer

**piercing** adj perçant, pénétrant; (shout) aigu

**piety** n piété f

**piffle** n coll bêtises fpl

**pig** n cochon m, porc m, pourceau m; metal gueuse f; **bleed like a** ~ saigner comme un bœuf; **buy a** ~ **in a poke** acheter un chat en poche; **make a** ~ **of oneself** manger gloutonnement

¹**pigeon** n pigeon m; **carrier (homing)** ~ pigeon voyageur; coll **that's my** ~ c'est mon affaire; **wood** ~ pigeon ramier

²**pigeon** n see **pidgin**

**pigeon-hole** n case f; vt classer, caser

**pigeon-house, pigeon-loft** n colombier m, pigeonnier m

**pigeon-toed** adj qui marche les pieds tournés en dedans

**piggery** n porcherie f

**piggish** adj désagréable; (dirty) sale

**piggy** n (child's language) petit cochon

**pigheaded** adj entêté, têtu

**pig-iron** n fer m en fonte

**piglet** n porcelet m, cochon m de lait

**pigment** n colorant m, pigment m

**pigmy** n see **pygmy**

**pigskin** n peau f de porc

**pigsty** n porcherie f; coll bauge f; fig taudis m

**pigtail** n natte f; (tobacco) tabac m en corde

¹**pike** n pique f

²**pike** n (fish) brochet m

**pikestaff** n **plain as a** ~ parfaitement clair

**pilaf** n pilaf m

**pilchard** n (espèce f de) sardine f

¹**pile** n pieu m; **built on** ~ s bâti sur pilotis

²**pile** n (heap) tas m, pile f, monceau m; (arms) faisceau m; (funeral) bûcher m; (atomic) pile f; édifice m; **make one's** ~

faire sa pelote; vt entasser, amasser; empiler; coll ~ **it on** exagérer; vi ~ **up** s'amonceler, s'accumuler

³**pile** n (carpet) poil m

**pile-driver** n sonnette f

**piles** npl hémorroïdes fpl

**pile-up** n mot accident m multiple

**pilfer** vt chaparder, chiper

**pilfering** n chapardage m

**pilgrim** n pèlerin -e

**pilgrimage** n pèlerinage m

**pill** n pilule f; **sugar the** ~ dorer la pilule

**pillage** n pillage m; vt piller, saccager

**pillar** n pilier m, colonne f

**pillar-box** n boîte f aux lettres

**pill-box** n boîte f à pilules; mil réduit m en béton armé, blockhaus m

**pillion** n (motor-cycle) siège m arrière; **ride** ~ monter derrière

**pillory** n pilori m; vt mettre au pilori

**pillow** n oreiller m

**pillow-case, pillow-slip** n taie f d'oreiller

**pilot** n pilote m; vt piloter, conduire

**pilot-boat** n bateau m pilote

**pilotless** adj sans pilote; ~ **plane** avion m robot

**pilot-light** n veilleuse f

**pilot-officer** n sous-lieutenant m aviateur

**pimento** n piment m

**pimp** n proxénète m, coll maquereau m

**pimpernel** n mouron m

**pimple** n bouton m

**pimply** adj boutonneux -euse

**pin** n épingle f; carp cheville f; mech goupille f; coll ~ s jambes fpl; ~ s **and needles** fourmillements mpl; **hear a** ~ **drop** entendre voler une mouche; **not care two** ~ s **about it** s'en moquer comme de l'an quarante; **safety** ~ épingle f de sûreté (nourrice); vt épingler; carp cheviller; (fasten) attacher, fixer; (nail) clouer; ~ **one's faith in s/o** se fier à qn; **be** ~ **ned down** être (se trouver) pris

**pinafore** n tablier m

**pince-nez** n pince-nez m, lorgnon m

**pincers** npl tenailles fpl, pince f; zool pinces fpl

**pinch** n action f de pincer; (small amount) pincée f; (snuff) prise f; **at a** ~ au besoin; vt pincer; (shoe) blesser; coll (steal) chiper, faucher; coll (arrest) pincer; ~ **and scrape** se priver

**pincushion** n pelote f à épingles

¹**pine** n pin m; bois m de pin

²**pine** vi languir, dépérir

**pineapple** n ananas m

**pine-cone** n pomme f de pin

**pine-needle** n aiguille f de pin

**ping-pong** n tennis m de table, ping-pong m

**pinhead** n tête f d'épingle; coll crétin -e

**pinhole** n trou m d'épingle

¹**pinion** n aileron m; poet aile f; vt rogner les ailes à; (tie up) lier

²**pinion** n mech pignon m

¹**pink** n bot œillet m; (colour) rose m; **in the ~** en parfaite santé; adj rose

²**pink** vt toucher; (dressmaking) denteler les bords de

³**pink** vi mot cliqueter

**pinnace** n pinasse f

**pinnacle** n sommet m; archi pinacle m; fig faîte m, apogée m

**pinpoint** n pointe f d'épingle; vt mettre le doigt sur; définir de façon précise

**pinprick** n piqûre f d'épingle; fig tracasserie f; **it's a mere ~** ce n'est rien

**pin-stripe** n **~ trousers** pantalon rayé

**pint** n pinte f

**pin-table** n flipper m, billard m électrique

**pint-sized** adj coll tout petit

**pin-up** n pin-up f invar

**pioneer** n pionnier m; vt introduire, être à l'avant-garde dans

**pious** adj pieux (f pieuse)

¹**pip** n (poultry disease) pépie f; coll **give s/o the ~** donner le cafard à qn

²**pip** n (fruit) pépin m

³**pip** n (cards) point m; mil galon m

⁴**pip** n (time signal) top m

⁵**pip** vt vaincre; (exam) échouer à

**pipe** n tuyau m, conduit m; mus pipeau m, chalumeau m; (smoking) pipe f; (birdsong) chant m; vt jouer (un air); (water, etc) canaliser; vi jouer du chalumeau; coll **~ down** sl la boucler; coll **~ up** se faire entendre

**pipe-cleaner** n cure-pipe m

**pipe-dream** n rêve m impossible, chimère f

**pipeful** n **~ (of tobacco)** pipe f (de tabac)

**pipeline** n canalisation f, conduite f; (oil) oléoduc m, pipe-line m

**pipe-organ** n grand orgue m

**piper** n joueur -euse de chalumeau; **he who pays the ~ calls the tune** celui qui paie a le droit de choisir; **pay the ~** payer les violons

**pipette** n pipette f

**piping** n son m du chalumeau (de la cornemuse); (whistle) sifflement m; (pipes) canalisation f, tuyauterie f; **~ cord** ganse f, passepoil m; adj (voice) flûté; **~ hot** tout chaud (f toute chaude)

**pipit** n pipi m, pipit m

**pippin** n (pomme f) reinette f

**pip-squeak** n coll rien m du tout invar

**piquancy** n piquant m

**piquant** adj piquant

**pique** n pique f, ressentiment m

**piracy** n piraterie f; (plagiarism) plagiat m

**pirate** n pirate m; (book) plagiaire

**piratical** adj de pirate; (book) de plagiaire

**pirouette** n pirouette f; vi pirouetter

**piss** n sl urine f; (animal) pissat m; vt coll pisser; sl **~ ed** ivre; vi uriner, pisser, coll faire pipi; vulg **~ off** foutre le camp

**pistachio** n pistache f

**pistol** n pistolet m

**piston** n piston m

**pit** n fosse f, trou m; (stomach) creux m; theat parterre m; (quarry) carrière f; (mine-shaft) puits m; vt (acid) piquer, trouer; med marquer; **~ s/o against s/o** opposer qn à qn

**pit-a-pat** adv **go ~** (heart) palpiter; (rain) crépiter; (feet) trottiner

¹**pitch** n poix f, bitume m, goudron m; vt enduire de poix

²**pitch** n (throwing) lancement m; (street-vendor) place f; naut tangage m; sp terrain m; (degree) point m, degré m; mus diapason m; **reach the highest ~** atteindre son comble; **to such a ~ that** à tel point que; vt (throw) lancer, jeter; (tent) dresser; coll **~ a yarn** débiter une histoire; mus **~ one's voice higher (lower)** hausser (baisser) le ton de sa voix; **~ed battle** bataille rangée; vi (ship) tanguer; **~ into** s'attaquer à; (criticize) dire son fait à

**pitch-black** adj noir comme poix

**pitchblende** n pechblende f

**pitch-dark** adj très noir; **it is ~** il fait nuit noire

¹**pitcher** n lanceur -euse

²**pitcher** n (vessel) cruche f

**pitchfork** n fourche f; vt lancer avec la fourche; coll fig bombarder

**pitch-pine** n pitchpin m

**piteous** adj pitoyable, piteux -euse

**pitfall** n piège m

**pith** n moelle f; fig vigueur f, ardeur f; (book) essence f

**pit-head** n carreau m

**pithy** adj plein de moelle; fig vigoureux -euse, nerveux -euse, concis

**pitiable** adj pitoyable

**pitiful** adj pitoyable; (compassionate) compatissant; pej lamentable

**pitiless** adj sans pitié, impitoyable, cruel -elle

**pit-prop** n poteau m de mine

**pittance** n maigre salaire m

**pitter-patter** n (rain) fouettement m

**pituitary** n hypophyse f; adj hypophisaire

**pity** n pitié f, compassion f; **out of ~**

par pitié; **take ~ on** s/o prendre pitié de qn; **that's a ~** c'est dommage; **what a ~!** quel dommage!; *vt* avoir pitié de, plaindre

**pivot** *n* pivot *m*; *vi* pivoter, tourner

**pixie** *n* fée *f*, lutin *m*

**pizzicato** *n* pizzicato (*pl* pizzicati *or* pizzicatos); *adj+adv* pizzicato

**placard** *n* écriteau *m*, affiche *f*, panneau *m*; *vt* afficher

**placate** *vt* calmer, apaiser

**place** *n* endroit *m*, lieu *m*, localité *f*; (seat) place *f*; (rank) position *f*; (employment) place *f*, poste *m*, emploi *m*; (home) demeure *f*, domicile *m*; (at meal) couvert *m*; **all over the ~** partout; **at my ~** chez moi; **be out of ~** ne pas être à sa place; *fig* être mal à propos; **change ~s with** changer de place avec; **give ~ to** faire place à; **in high ~s** en haut lieu; **in my ~** à ma place; **in the first ~** d'abord; **it's not his ~ to** ce n'est pas à lui de; **put s/o in his (her) ~** remettre qn à sa place; **take ~** avoir lieu; *vt* placer, mettre, poser; donner un rang à; (recognize) remettre; **~ an order** passer une commande; *sp* **be ~d** être classé; (horse) être placé

**place-kick** *n* coup placé

**placement** *n* placement *m*, arrangement *m*

**placenta** *n* placenta *m*

**placid** *adj* placide, calme, tranquille

**placidity** *n* placidité *f*, calme *m*

**placidly** *adv* tranquillement, avec calme

**plagiarism** *n* plagiat *m*

**plagiarist** *n* plagiaire

**plagiarize** *vt* plagier

**plague** *n* peste *f*; *fig* fléau *m*; **the ten ~s** les dix plaies *fpl*; *vt* tourmenter; (bore) embêter, raser

**plaice** *n* carrelet *m*, plie *f*

**plaid** *n* plaid *m*

**plain** *n* plaine *f*; *adj* simple; (clear) évident, clair; (smooth) uni; (face) sans attraits; (ugly) laid; (frank) franc (*f* franche); **~ cooking** cuisine *f* simple; **~ dealing** procédés *mpl* honnêtes; **in ~ clothes** en civil; **that's as ~ as daylight** c'est clair comme le jour; *adv* clairement, distinctement

**plain-chant** *n* plain-chant *m*

**plainness** *n* (simplicity) simplicité *f*; (clearness) clarté *f*, netteté *f*; (frankness) franchise *f*; (features) manque *m* d'attraits

**plain-song** *n* plain-chant *m*

**plain-spoken** *adj* franc (*f* franche)

**plaintiff** *n* demandeur -eresse, plaignant -e

**plaintive** *adj* plaintif -ive

**plait** *n* natte *f*, tresse *f*; *vt* natter, tresser

**plan** *n* plan *m*, projet *m*; **go according to ~** marcher selon les prévisions; **your best ~ is to go away** le mieux serait que vous partiez; *vt* faire le plan de; (intend) projeter, arranger

¹**plane** *n* (tool) rabot *m*; *vt* raboter

²**plane** *n coll* avion *m*

³**plane, plane-tree** *n* platane *m*

⁴**plane** *n* (surface) plan *m*; *adj* plan, uni, plat

**planet** *n* planète *f*

**plane-table** *n* planchette *f*

**planetarium** *n* planétarium *m*

**planetary** *adj* planétaire

**plank** *n* planche *f*, madrier *m*; *vt* planchéier; *coll* **~ down** jeter, déposer

**planking** *n* (action) planchéiage *m*; (planks) planches *fpl*

**plankton** *n* plancton *m*

**planning** *n* organisation *f*, planification *f*; **family ~** contrôle *m* des naissances

**plant** *n* plante *f*; *mech* matériel *m*; **~ life** vie végétale; *vt* planter; **~ a bomb** déposer une bombe; **~ an idea** implanter une idée

**plantation** *n* plantation *f*

**planter** *n* planteur *m*; propriétaire *m* d'une plantation

**plaque** *n* plaque *f*

**plasma** *n biol* plasma *m*

**plaster** *n* plâtre *m*; *med* emplâtre *m*; *med* **adhesive ~** sparadrap *m*; **~ cast** moulage *m* au plâtre, plâtre *m*; **~ of Paris** plâtre *m*; *vt* plâtrer; *med* mettre un emplâtre sur; (hair) **~ down** plaquer; **~ up** plâtrer

**plastered** *adj* plâtré; *coll* ivre

**plasterer** *n* plâtrier *m*

**plastic** *n* matière *f* plastique, plastique *m*; (explosive) plastic *m*; *adj* plastique; malléable, souple; **~ surgery** chirurgie *f* plastique

**Plasticine** *n* pâte *f* à modeler

**plasticity** *n* plasticité *f*

**plastics** *n* matières *fpl* plastiques; industrie *f* plastique

**plate** *n* assiette *f*; (metal, etc) plaque *f*, feuille *f*; (book) planche *f*; (gold, silver) vaisselle *f* d'or (d'argent); (dental) dentier *m*; **dinner ~** assiette plate; **hot ~** plaque chauffante; *mot* **number ~** plaque *f* minéralogique; *phot* **sensitive ~** plaque *f* sensible; **soup ~** assiette creuse; *vt* plaquer; blinder

**plateau** *n* plateau *m*

**plateful** *n* assiettée *f*

**plate-glass** *n* glace *f*, verre *m* à vitre

**platform** *n* plate-forme *f* (*pl* plates-formes), terrasse *f*; (railway) quai *m*; (public) estrade *f*, tribune *f*; *pol* programme *m*, plate-forme *f* (*pl* plates-formes)

**plating** *n* revêtement *m* en métal; plaquage *m*

**platinum** *n* platine *m*

**platitude** *n* platitude *f*

**platitudinous** *adj* (style) banal, plat; (person) qui débite des banalités

**Platonic** *adj* (love) platonique; *philos* platonicien -ienne

**platoon** *n* *mil* section *f*

**platter** *n* assiette *f* (en bois); *US* plat *m*

**platypus** *n* ornithorynque *m*

**plaudit** *n* applaudissement *m*

**plausibility** *n* plausibilité *f*

**plausible** *adj* plausible, vraisemblable; (specious) spécieux -ieuse; (person) enjôleur -euse

**play** *n* jeu *m*; *theat* pièce *f* (de théâtre), spectacle *m*; (fun) amusement *m*; ~ **on words** calembour *m*; **come into** ~ entrer en jeu; **give full** ~ **to** donner libre cours à; *sp* (ball) **out of** ~ hors jeu; *vt* jouer; (game) jouer à; (instrument) jouer de; (direct) diriger; (match) disputer; (fish) manœuvrer; ~ **along with** coopérer avec; ~ **back** faire repasser; *coll* ~ **ball** marcher; ~ **down** minimiser; ~ **s/o off against s/o** opposer qn à qn; ~ **the fool** faire l'imbécile; ~ **up** (annoy) agacer; *vi* jouer; (animals) gambader; s'amuser; ~ **fair** jouer franc jeu; (cards) ~ **first** entamer; ~ **on** continuer de jouer; **on s/o's credulity** abuser de la crédulité de qn; ~ **out** jouer jusqu'au bout; ~ **up** (try) faire de son mieux

**playable** *adj* qu'on peut jouer; (ground) sur lequel on peut jouer

**play-act** *vi* jouer la comédie

**playback** *n* play-back *m*, lecture *f* sonore

**play-bill** *n* affiche *f*, annonce *f* de spectacle

**playboy** *n* play-boy *m*, bon vivant

**player** *n* joueur -euse; *theat* acteur -trice, comédien -ienne; *mus* exécutant -e

**playfellow** *n* camarade de jeu

**playful** *adj* enjoué, badin

**playgoer** *n* amateur *m* de théâtre

**playground** *n* cour *f* (terrain *m*) de récréation

**playing** *n* jeu *m*; *theat* interprétation *f*; *mus* exécution *f*

**playing-card** *n* carte *f* (à jouer)

**playing-field** *n* terrain *m* de jeux (sport)

**playmate** *n* camarade de jeu

**play-off** *n* belle *f*

**playpen** *n* parc *m* pour enfants

**plaything** *n* jouet *m*, *coll* joujou *m*

**playtime** *n* récréation *f*

**playwright** *n* auteur *m* dramatique, dramaturge *m*

**plea** *n* excuse *f*, prétexte *m*; *leg* défense *f*; **on the** ~ **of** sous prétexte de; **submit**

the ~ **that** plaider que

**plead** *vt* (cause) plaider; (allege) invoquer, alléguer; *vi* plaider; *leg* ~ **(not) guilty** plaider (non) coupable; ~ **with** plaider auprès de

**pleading** *n* art *m* de plaider; plaidoirie *f*, supplication *f*

**pleasant** *adj* agréable, aimable

**pleasantry** *n* plaisanterie *f*

**please** *vt* plaire à, faire plaisir à; (satisfy) contenter; ~ **d** satisfait, content; ~ **do!** je vous en prie!; ~ **God!** plaise à Dieu!; ~ **yourself** faites à votre guise; **as you** ~ comme vous voudrez; **be as** ~ **d as Punch** être heureux comme un roi; **be** ~ **d to** être heureux -euse de; **be** ~ **d with** être content de; **do as one** ~ **s** n'en faire qu'à sa tête; **hard to** ~ difficile; **if you** ~ s'il vous plaît; *adv + interj* s'il vous (te) plaît

**pleasing** *adj* agréable

**pleasurable** *adj* agréable

**pleasure** *n* plaisir *m*; (wish) volonté *f*, bon plaisir; **at your** ~ à votre gré; **take** ~ **in** éprouver du plaisir à

**pleasure-loving** *adj* qui aime le plaisir

**pleasure-trip** *n* voyage *m* d'agrément

**pleat** *n* pli *m*; *vt* plisser

**plebeian** *adj* plébéien -ienne

**plebiscite** *n* plébiscite *m*

**plectrum** *n* plectre *m*

**pledge** *n* gage *m*; (promise) promesse *f*, vœu *m*; **take the** ~ faire vœu de tempérance; *vt* mettre en gage, engager; (toast) boire à la santé de

**plenary** *adj* entier -ière, complet -ète; ~ **assembly** assemblée plénière; ~ **powers** pleins pouvoirs

**plenipotentiary** *n* plénipotentiaire; *adj* plénipotentiaire

**plenitude** *n* plénitude *f*

**plenteous** *adj* abondant

**plentiful** *adj* abondant, copieux -ieuse

**plenty** *n* abondance *f*; ~ **of** bien assez de, beaucoup de; **land of** ~ pays *m* de cocagne; **live in** ~ vivre très à l'aise; *adv coll* ~ **big enough** bien assez gros (*f* grosse)

**plethora** *n* pléthore *f*, surabondance *f*

**pleurisy** *n* pleurésie *f*

**pliability** *n* flexibilité *f*; (character) souplesse *f*

**pliable, pliant** *adj* flexible; (character) souple, complaisant

**pliers** *npl* pinces *fpl*

**plight** *n* condition *f*, état *m*; **be in a sorry** ~ être dans de beaux draps; *vt lit* ~ **one's troth** engager sa foi

**Plimsoll** *n* ~ **line** ligne *f* de Plimsoll

**plimsolls** *npl* chaussures *fpl* de gymnastique

**plinth** *n* plinthe *f*

**plod** *vi* marcher péniblement, marcher lourdement; ~ **away at sth** travailler laborieusement à qch; ~ **on** persévérer

**plodder** *n* piocheur -euse

¹**plonk** *n* bruit sourd; *vt* ~ **sth down** déposer qch bruyamment

²**plonk** *n coll* vin *m* ordinaire, *coll* pinard *m*

**plop** *vi* tomber en faisant plouf; *interj* plouf!

**plot** *n* (conspiracy) complot *m*; (story) intrigue *f*, action *f*; (ground) parcelle *f*, lopin *m*; *vt* comploter, conspirer; tracer, faire le plan de; (record) relever; *vi* comploter

**plotter** *n* conspirateur -trice; traceur *m*

**plough** *n* charrue *f*; *astron* **the Plough** le Chariot; *vt* labourer; (ship) sillonner; *coll* (candidate) recaler; ~ **back profits** reverser des bénéfices dans une affaire; ~ **into the ground** enterrer en labourant; *coll* **be ~ ed** échouer à un examen

**ploughman** *n* laboureur *m*

**ploughshare** *n* soc *m* de charrue

**ploy** *n coll* (dodge) tour *m*, truc *m*

**pluck** *n* courage *m*, cran *m*; *vt* (flower) cueillir; (feathers) arracher; (hairs) épiler; ~ **out** arracher; ~ **up courage** s'armer de courage

**plucky** *adj* courageux -euse; *coll* crâne

**plug** *n* tampon *m*, bouchon *m*; *elect* fiche *f*; sl coup *m* de poing; (lavatory) chasse *f* d'eau; *coll* (advertising) réclame *f*; *mot* bougie *f*; **wall** ~ prise *f* de courant; *vt* boucher, tamponner; *coll* (advertise) faire une campagne de publicité pour; *sl* (shoot) tirer sur; *sl* (punch) donner un coup de poing à; ~ **in** brancher; *vi* ~ **away** persévérer

**plum** *n* prune *f*; *coll* (job) meilleur poste

**plumage** *n* plumage *m*

**plumb** *n* plomb *m*; aplomb *m*; *adj* droit, d'aplomb; ~ **in the middle** en plein milieu; *adv US* complètement; *vt* sonder, plomber

**plumber** *n* plombier *m*

**plumbing** *n* plomberie *f*

**plumb-line** *n* fil *m* à plomb

**plume** *n* plume *f*; (ornamental) panache *m*; *vt* orner de plumes; (bird) ~ **itself** se lisser les plumes; (person) ~ **oneself on sth** se piquer de qch

**plummet** *n* plomb *m*; *vi* descendre à pic

¹**plump** *adj* rebondi, grassouillet -ette, dodu, potelé; *vt* + *vi* engraisser

²**plump** *n* bruit sourd

³**plump** *vt* flanquer; *vi* tomber lourdement; ~ **for** choisir; *pol* voter pour un seul candidat

**plum-pudding** *n* plum-pudding *m*

**plum-tree** *n* prunier *m*

**plunder** *n* pillage *m*; (booty) butin *m*; *vt* piller, dépouiller

**plunderer** *n* pillard *m*

**plunge** *n* plongeon *m*; **take the** ~ faire le plongeon; *vt* plonger, immerger; *vi* plonger; (penetrate) s'enfoncer; (rush) se précipiter; ~ **forward** s'élancer en avant

**plunger** *n* plongeur *m*; *coll* (gaming) joueur effréné; *coll* (speculator) risque-tout *m invar*

**plural** *n* pluriel *m*; **in the** ~ au pluriel; *adj* pluriel -ielle; ~ **vote** vote pluriel

**plurality** *n* pluralité *f*

**plus** *n* plus *m*; quantité positive; *adj* positif -ive; *prep* plus

**plus-fours** *npl* culotte *f* de golf

**plush** *n* peluche *f*; *adj sl* rupin

**plushy** *adj* peluché; *sl* rupin

**plutocracy** *n* ploutocratie *f*

**plutocrat** *n* ploutocrate *m*

**plutocratic** *adj* ploutocratique

**plutonium** *n* plutonium *m*

¹**ply** *n* (fold) pli *m*; (thickness) épaisseur *f*; (strand) fil *m*, brin *m*

²**ply** *vt* (use) manier énergiquement; (trade) exercer; (person) presser; *vi* faire le service, faire la navette

**plywood** *n* contre-plaqué *m*

**pneumatic** *adj* pneumatique; ~ **drill** foreuse *f* (perceuse *f*) à air comprimé

**pneumonia** *n* pneumonie *f*, fluxion *f* de poitrine

¹**poach** *vt cul* pocher

²**poach** *vt* (game) braconner

**poacher** *n* braconnier *m*

**pock** *n* pustule *f*

**pocket** *n* poche *f*; (bag) sac *m*, sacoche *f*; **air** ~ trou *m* d'air; **be out of** ~ en être de sa poche; **breast** ~ poche intérieure; *fig* **I've got him in my** ~ je le tiens; **line one's** ~ se faire sa pelote; *vt* empocher, mettre dans sa poche; *pej* chiper; (billiards) blouser; (insult) avaler; ~ **one's pride** mettre son orgueil dans sa poche

**pocket-book** *n* carnet *m* de poche

**pocket-handkerchief** *n* mouchoir *m* de poche

**pocket-knife** *n* couteau *m* de poche, canif *m*

**pocket-money** *n* argent *m* de poche

**pock-marked** *adj* variolé

**pod** *n* cosse *f*, gousse *f*

**podgy** *adj* boulot -otte; (finger) boudiné

**podium** *n* (dais) podium *m*

**poem** *n* poème *m*, poésie *f*

**poet** *n* poète *m*

**poetess** *n* poétesse *f*

**poetic(al)** *adj* poétique

**poetry** *n* poésie *f*

**po-faced** *adj sl* à l'air solennel

**pogrom** *n* pogrom *m*

**poignancy** *n* (grief) acuité *f*; (feeling) violence *f*; (satire) mordant *m*

**poignant** *adj* (feeling) vif (*f* vive); (thoughts) angoissant; piquant

**point** *n* point *m*; (sharp end) pointe *f*; (decimal) virgule *f*; (question) question *f*; (feature) trait *m*, détail *m*; *elect* prise *f* de courant; (railway) ~ s aiguilles *fpl*; ~ of the compass aire *f* de vent; ~ of view point *m* de vue; a case in ~ un cas topique; a sore ~ un endroit sensible; at the ~ of death à l'article de la mort; be on the ~ of doing sth être sur le point de faire qch; beside the ~ hors de propos, sans rapport; from every ~ of view sous tous les rapports; gain one's ~ atteindre son but; in ~ of fact en fait, par le fait; make a ~ of doing sth s'obliger à faire qch; off the ~ hors de propos; on this ~ à cet égard; score ~ s marquer des points; see the ~ comprendre (la signification); stretch a ~ faire une exception (concession); there's no ~ in inutile de; to the ~ à propos; up to a ~ jusqu'à un certain point; what's the ~ ? à quoi bon?; *vt* (sharpen) tailler (en pointe), aiguiser; (way) indiquer, montrer; (gun) braquer; (wall) jointoyer; (dot) marquer de points; ~ out a fact faire ressortir un fait; ~ sth out montrer qch du doigt; *vi* (gun) pointer; ~ at (to) sth indiquer qch du doigt; ~ towards être tourné vers; ~ up souligner; this ~ s to his guilt cela laisse supposer qu'il est coupable

**point-blank** *adj* direct; *adv* (shooting) à bout portant; ask ~ demander à brûle-pourpoint; refuse ~ refuser net

**point-duty** *n* be on ~ être de service à point fixe

**pointed** *adj* pointu; (answer) mordant; (reference) direct

**pointer** *n* (dog) chien *m* d'arrêt; (on dial) aiguille *f*; (stick) baguette *f*; (information) renseignement *m*, *coll* tuyau *m*

**pointing** *n* ponctuation *f*; (gun) braquage *m*; *bui* jointoiement *m*

**pointless** *adj* (remark) qui ne rime à rien; (joke) fade; (futile) futile, inutile

**poise** *n* équilibre *m*, aplomb *m*; *vt* équilibrer, balancer

**poison** *n* poison *m*; *vt* empoisonner, intoxiquer; *fig* corrompre

**poisonous** *adj* toxique; empoisonné; (animal) venimeux -euse; (plant) vénéneux -euse; *fig* (tongue) venimeux -euse

**poke** *n* poussée *f*; (elbow) coup *m* de coude; (finger) coup *m* du bout du doigt; (poker) coup *m* de tisonnier; buy a pig in a ~ acheter un chat en poche;

*vt* pousser du doigt (du coude); (fire) attiser, tisonner; (push) passer, fourrer; ~ fun at s/o se moquer de qn; ~ one's head out of the window passer la tête par la fenêtre; *vi* ~ about fureter, farfouiller; ~ at sth tâter qch

¹**poker** *n* tisonnier *m*

²**poker** *n* (card game) poker *m*

**poker-face** *n* visage *m* impassible

**poky** *adj* étroit, misérable; (job) mesquin

**Poland** *n* Pologne *f*

**polar** *adj* polaire

**polarity** *n* polarité *f*

**polarization** *n* polarisation *f*

**polarize** *vt* polariser; *vi* se polariser

**Pole** *n* Polonais -e

¹**pole** *n* perche *f*; (telegraph) poteau *m*; (mast) mât *m*; (cart) timon *m*; *coll* be up the ~ être timbré, être toqué

²**pole** *n* *geog* pôle *m*; Pole Star étoile *f* polaire

**pole-axe** *n* assommoir *m*

**polecat** *n* putois *m*

**pole-jump, pole-vault** *n* saut *m* à la perche; *vi* sauter à la perche

**polemic** *n* polémique *f*; *adj* polémique

**pole-vault** *n* + *vi see* **pole-jump**

**police** *n* police *f*; (rural) gendarmerie *f*; ~ constable agent *m* de police; ~ station poste *m* de police, commissariat *m* de police; (rural) gendarmerie *f*; *adj* policier -ière; *vt* policer, maintenir l'ordre dans

**policeman** *n* agent *m* de police; (rural) gendarme *m*

**policewoman** *n* femme-agent *f* (de police) (*pl* femmes-agents)

¹**policy** *n* politique *f*; think it ~ to juger prudent de

²**policy** *n* (insurance) police *f*; take out a ~ s'assurer, prendre une police

**polio** *n* polio *f*

**poliomyelitis** *n* poliomyélite *f*

**Polish** *n* (language) polonais *m*; *adj* polonais

**polish** *n* poli *m*, brillant *m*; (shoe) cirage *m*; (nail) vernis *m*; (floor) encaustique *f*; (manners) politesse *f*; *vt* polir; (shoes) cirer; (floor) encaustiquer; *coll* ~ off (work) expédier, bâcler; (person) régler le compte de; (food) ne rien laisser de; ~ up astiquer; ~ up one's French dérouiller son français

**polisher** *n* (person) polisseur -euse; (machine) cireuse *f*; (tool) polissoir *m*

**polite** *adj* poli, courtois

**politeness** *n* politesse *f*

**politic** *adj* avisé, politique; (skilful) adroit, habile

**political** *adj* politique

**politician** *n* homme *m* politique

**politics** n politique f
**polka** n polka f
**poll** n vote m, scrutin m; (opinion) sondage m; **declare the ~** proclamer le résultat du scrutin; **go to the ~s** aller aux urnes; vt (votes) réunir; (horns) écorner; (tree) étêter; vi voter
**pollen** n pollen m
**pollinate** vt polliniser
**pollination** n pollinisation f
**polling-booth** n isoloir m
**polling-station** n bureau m de vote
**pollster** n sondeur m
**pollute** vt polluer, souiller; (corrupt) corrompre
**pollution** n pollution f
**polo** n polo m
**polonaise** n polonaise f
**polo-neck** n col roulé
**poltergeist** n esprit frappeur
**polygamist** n polygame
**polygamous** adj polygame
**polygamy** n polygamie f
**polyglot** n + adj polyglotte
**polymath** n homme très savant
**polymer** n chem polymère m
**polyp** n polype m
**polystyrene** n polystyrène m
**polysyllabic** adj polysyllabique
**polytechnic** n (école f) polytechnique; adj polytechnique
**polythene** n polyéthylène m
**pomegranate** n grenade f
**pommel, pummel** n pommeau m; vt bourrer de coups
**pomp** n pompe f, faste m, éclat m
**pompon** n pompon m
**pomposity** n suffisance f
**pompous** adj (person) suffisant; (style) pompeux -euse
**poncho** n poncho m
**pond** n étang m, mare f; (artificial) pièce f d'eau
**ponder** vt réfléchir sur, peser; vi méditer
**ponderous** adj pesant, lourd
**pong** n sl mauvaise odeur; vi sl puer, schlinguer
**pontiff** n pontife m
**pontifical** adj pontifical
**pontificate** vi pontifier; faire l'important
**¹pontoon** n ponton m
**²pontoon** n (cards) vingt-et-un
**pontoon-bridge** n pont m de bateaux
**pony** n poney m; sl (glass) petit verre
**pony-tail** n queue f de cheval
**poodle** n caniche m
**poof** n sl tapette f
**pooh-pooh** vt faire peu de cas de; (advice) repousser
**¹pool** n mare f; (swimming) piscine f; (puddle) flaque f
**²pool** n (cards) poule f, cagnotte f;

(game) billard américain; pol + econ pool m; **typing ~** équipe f de dactylos; vt mettre en commun
**poop** n poupe f
**poor** adj pauvre; (bad) mauvais; (wretched) malheureux -euse; (quality) médiocre; (weak) faible; **~ quality** basse qualité
**poor-box** n eccles tronc m
**poorhouse** n hospice m, asile m des pauvres
**poorly** adj indisposé, souffrant
**poorness** n pauvreté f
**poor-spirited** adj pusillanime
**¹pop** n coll papa m
**²pop** adj coll populaire; **~ music** musique f pop
**³pop** n bruit sec; coll (drink) boisson gazeuse; vt (put) mettre, fourrer; (burst) crever; (cork) faire sauter; sl (put in pawn) mettre au clou; **~ one's head out of the window** passer la tête par la fenêtre; vi péter, éclater; **~ in** entrer en passant; **~ out** sortir; **~ over** passer; **~ round** faire un saut; **~ up** surgir, apparaître; interj crac!, pan!
**popcorn** n maïs éclaté, pop-corn m
**Pope** n Pape m
**popery** n pej papisme m
**pop-eyed** adj coll aux yeux protubérants
**popgun** n pistolet m d'enfant
**poplar** n peuplier m
**poplin** n popeline f
**poppy** n pavot m; **field ~** coquelicot m
**poppycock** n coll bêtises fpl
**pop-singer** n chanteur -euse pop
**popsy** n coll fille f
**populace** n peuple m; pej populace f
**popular** adj populaire, du peuple; en vogue; (error) courant
**popularity** n popularité f
**popularization** n popularisation f; (knowledge) vulgarisation f
**popularize** vt populariser; (knowledge) vulgariser
**popularly** adv de façon courante, couramment
**populate** vt peupler
**population** n population f
**populous** adj populeux -euse
**porcelain** n porcelaine f
**porch** n porche m, portique m; US véranda f
**porcupine** n porc-épic m (pl porcs-épics)
**¹pore** n pore m
**²pore** vi **~ over** regarder attentivement; **~ over a book** s'absorber dans la lecture d'un livre
**pork** n porc m, viande f de porc; **~ chop** côte f (côtelette f) de porc; **~ pie** pâté m de porc
**pork-butcher** n charcutier -ière; **~'s**

**shop** charcuterie *f*
**porker** *n* jeune porc gras
**porky** *adj coll* gras (*f* grasse), gros (*f* grosse)
**pornographer** *n* pornographe *m*
**pornographic** *adj* pornographique
**pornography** *n* pornographie *f*
**porosity** *n* porosité *f*
**porous** *adj* poreux -euse
**porpoise** *n* marsouin *m*
**porridge** *n* porridge *m*, bouillie *f* d'avoine
¹**port** *n* port *m*; (ship) bâbord *m*; ~ **charges** droits *mpl* de port; ~ **of call** port *m* d'escale, escale *f*; **come into** ~ entrer au port; **naval** ~ port *m* militaire; **put into** ~ faire escale; *vt* mettre à bâbord; *vi* venir sur bâbord
²**port** *n naut* (for guns) sabord *m*; (porthole) hublot *m*
³**port** *n* (wine) porto *m*
⁴**port** *vt mil* porter; ~ **arms** présenter les armes pour l'inspection
**portable** *adj* portatif -ive, transportable
**portage** *n* transport *m*, port *m*; (charges) frais *mpl* de port
**portal** *n* portail *m*, portique *m*
**portcullis** *n* herse *f*
**portend** *vt* présager, augurer
**portent** *n* mauvais présage
**portentous** *adj* de mauvais augure, sinistre; (marvellous) prodigieux -ieuse
¹**porter** *n* (house) portier *m*, concierge *m*; ~ **'s lodge** loge *f* du concierge
²**porter** *n* (station) porteur *m*; *obs* portefaix *m*; (market) fort *m* des Halles
³**porter** *n* (beer) bière brune, porter *m*
**porterhouse** *n* ~ **steak** filet *m* de bœuf
**portfolio** *n* (brief-case) serviette *f*; *pol+comm* portefeuille *m*
**porthole** *n* hublot *m*
**portion** *n* portion *f*; (part) partie *f*; (destiny) destinée *f*; (inheritance) part *f*; **marriage** ~ dot *f*; *vt* répartir, distribuer
**portliness** *n* corpulence *f*, embonpoint *m*
**portly** *adj* corpulent, ventru
**portmanteau** *n obs* valise *f*
**portrait** *n* portrait *m*; **full-length** ~ portrait *m* en pied
**portraiture** *n* art *m* du portrait; portrait *m*
**portray** *vt* (paint) peindre, faire le portrait de; (describe) dépeindre
**portrayal** *n* peinture *f*, description *f*
**Portugal** *n* le Portugal
**Portuguese** *n* Portugais -e; (language) portugais *m*; *adj* portugais
**pose** *n* pose *f*; attitude *f*; (affectation) affectation *f*; *vt* (question) poser; *vi* (model) poser; se donner des airs affectés; ~ **as** se faire passer pour
**poser** *n* question *f* difficile, *coll* colle *f*

**posh** *adj coll* chic (*f invar*); *vi* ~ **oneself up** se faire beau (*f* belle)
**position** *n* position *f*; attitude *f*; (place) place *f*, situation *f*; (employment) poste *m*, emploi *m*; (order) rang *m*, classement *m*; ~ **of trust** poste *m* de confiance; **be in a** ~ **to** être à même de; **he's in a better** ~ **to** il est mieux placé pour; **in a high** ~ haut placé; **in** ~ en place; **keep up one's** ~ tenir son rang; **put yourself in my** ~ mettez-vous à ma place; **take up a** ~ prendre position; *vt* placer, mettre en position; (find) déterminer la position de, situer
**positive** *adj* positif -ive, (sure) certain, assuré, convaincu; (absolute) absolu
**positively** *adv* positivement, (certainly) certainement, sûrement, absolument
**positiveness** *n* certitude *f*, assurance *f*; (manner) ton décisif
**positivism** *n* positivisme *m*
**posse** *n* (crowd) foule *f*, troupe *f*, bande *f*; (police) détachement *m*
**possess** *vt* posséder, être en possession de; ~ **oneself of sth** s'emparer de qch; **be** ~ **ed of a quality** être doué d'une qualité; **be** ~ **ed with** être obsédé de; **whatever** ~ **ed you to …?** qu'est-ce qui vous a pris de …?
**possession** *n* possession *f*; (property) jouissance *f*; ~ **s** biens *mpl*, avoir *m*; **be in** ~ **of** disposer de, posséder; **enter into** ~ **of** entrer en possession de; **take** ~ **of** s'emparer de
**possessive** *adj* qui aime posséder entièrement; *gramm* possessif -ive
**possessor** *n* possesseur *m*, propriétaire
**possibility** *n* possibilité *f*; (possible event) éventualité *f*; **within the range of** ~ dans la limite du possible
**possible** *adj* possible; **as early as** ~ le plus tôt possible; **as far as** ~ dans la mesure du possible, autant que possible; le plus loin possible; **do everything** ~ faire tout son possible; **if** ~ si possible, si c'est possible; **it's just** ~ il y a une chance
**possibly** *adv* peut-être; **do all one** ~ **can** faire tout son possible; **I can't** ~ **come** je ne peux absolument pas venir
¹**post** *n* (wooden) poteau *m*; (door) montant *m*, pilier *m*; **as deaf as a** ~ sourd comme un pot; *fig* **be left at the** ~ manquer le départ; *vt* placarder, coller, afficher; ~ **no bills** défense d'afficher
²**post** *n* (duty) poste *m*; (employment) situation *f*, emploi *m*; **take up one's** ~ entrer en fonctions; *vt* poster; (sentinel) mettre en faction; **be** ~ **ed to a command** être affecté à un commandement
³**post** *n* (letters) courrier *m*; (postal

organization) poste *f*; ~ **office** bureau *m* de poste; ~ **office clerk** employé(e) des postes; **Post Office Savings Bank** = Caisse Nationale d'Épargne; ~ **paid** port payé, franco; **by** ~ par la poste; **by return of** ~ par retour du courrier; **first-class** ~ = tarif normal; **miss the** ~ manquer le courrier; manquer la levée; **open one's** ~ dépouiller son courrier; **second-class** ~ = tarif réduit; **the (General) Post Office** = les Postes *fpl* et Télécommunications *fpl*; **the** ~ **has come** le facteur est passé; *vt* mettre à la poste, poster; ~ **sth to s/o** envoyer qch à qn par la poste; **keep s/o** ~ **ed** tenir qn au courant

**¹post** *n mil* **last** ~ sonnerie *f* aux morts

**postage** *n* port *m*, affranchissement *m*

**postage-stamp** *n* timbre-poste *m* (*pl* timbres-poste); timbre *m*

**postal** *adj* postal; ~ **order** mandat-poste *m* (*pl* mandats-poste)

**postbag** *n* (mail) courrier *m*; sac postal

**post-box** *n* boîte *f* aux lettres

**postcard** *n* carte postale

**post-date** *vt* postdater

**poster** *n* affiche *f*

**poste restante** *n* poste restante

**posterior** *n* postérieur *m*, derrière *m*; *adj* postérieur

**posterity** *n* postérité *f*

**postern** *n* poterne *f*

**post-free** *adj* franc de port *invar*

**post-graduate (student)** *n* licencié -e qui poursuit ses études

**post-haste** *adv* en toute hâte

**posthumous** *adj* posthume

**postman** *n* facteur *m*

**postmark** *n* cachet *m* de la poste

**postmaster** *n* receveur *m* (des Postes)

**postmistress** *n* receveuse *f* (des Postes)

**post-mortem** *n* ~ **(examination)** autopsie *f*; *adj* après décès

**postpone** *vt* remettre, ajourner, différer, reporter (à plus tard)

**postponement** *n* ajournement *m*, renvoi *m*

**postscript** *n* post-scriptum *m invar*

**postulant** *n eccles* postulant -e

**postulate** *vt* postuler

**posture** *n* attitude *f*, posture *f*; (state) état *m*; *vi* prendre une posture

**post-war** *adj* d'après-guerre; **the** ~ **period** l'après-guerre *m*

**posy** *n* petit bouquet

**pot** *n* pot *m*; (cooking) marmite *f*; *coll* marihuana *f*; ~ **s and pans** batterie *f* de cuisine; *coll* ~ **s of money** des tas *mpl* d'argent; *coll* **go to** ~ aller à la ruine; *vt* mettre en pot; *coll* (shoot) tirer, abattre; (billiards) blouser; (child) mettre sur le pot; *vi* ~ **at** tirer un coup de fusil sur

**potash** *n* potasse *f*

**potassium** *n* potassium *m*

**potato** *n* (*pl* ~ **es**) pomme *f* de terre; ~ **crisps**, *US* ~ **chips** pommes *fpl* chips; **boiled** ~ **es** pommes *fpl* (de terre) à l'anglaise; **baked** ~ **es** pommes *fpl* de terre au four; **chipped (French fried)** ~ **es** pommes (de terre) frites, *coll* frites *fpl*; **mashed** ~ **es** purée *f* de pommes de terre; **roast** ~ **es** pommes *fpl* de terre au four

**pot-belly** *n* panse *f*, bedon *m*

**pot-boiler** *n* œuvre *f* qui fait bouillir la marmite

**potency** *n* force *f*, puissance *f*; (medicine) efficacité *f*; *physiol* virilité *f*

**potent** *adj* (drug, etc) puissant, efficace; (argument, etc) convaincant; viril

**potentate** *n* potentat *m*

**potential** *n* potentiel *m*; *adj* potentiel -ielle; latent, en puissance

**potentiality** *n* potentialité *f*

**potently** *adv* puissamment

**pothole** *n* trou *m* dans une route, *coll* nid *m* de poule; *geol* gouffre *m*

**potholer** *n* spéléologue

**potholing** *n* spéléologie *f*

**pot-hook** *n* crémaillère *f*; (writing) bâton *m*

**potion** *n* potion *f*, dose *f*

**potluck** *n* **take** ~ manger à la fortune du pot

**pot-pourri** *n* pot-pourri *m* (*pl* pots-pourris)

**pot-shot** *n coll* **take a** ~ **at sth** tirer au petit bonheur un coup de fusil sur qch; *fig* faire qch au petit bonheur

**potted** *adj* en pot, conservé *f* de

**¹potter** *n* potier *m*; ~ **'s wheel** tour *m* de potier

**²potter** *vi* ~ **about** (do odd jobs) bricoler; (wander) flâner; ~ **along** aller son petit bonhomme de chemin

**pottery** *n* poterie *f*

**potting** *n hort* mise *f* en pots; (jam, etc) mise *f* en conserve

**¹potty** *n coll* pot *m* de chambre

**²potty** *adj coll* (mad) timbré, toqué; (small) petit

**pouch** *n* petit sac; (animal) poche (ventrale); (under eyes) poche *f*

**pouf, pouffe** *n* (furniture) pouf *m*; (dress) bouffant

**poulterer** *n* marchand -e de volaille

**poultice** *n* cataplasme *m*; *vt* mettre un cataplasme sur

**poultry** *n* volaille *f*

**pounce** *vi* ~ **on** s'abattre sur, se jeter sur

**¹pound** *n* (money, weight) livre *f*; ~ **sterling** livre *f* sterling; **by the** ~ à la livre

**²pound** *n* (animals) fourrière *f*

³**pound** vt broyer, piler; vi ~ **on** frapper sur

**pour** vt verser; vi (rain) tomber à verse; ~ **in** (people) affluer; ~ **into** (liquid) entrer à flots dans; (people) entrer en foule dans; **it is ~ ing** il pleut à verse; **it never rains but it ~ s** un malheur ne vient jamais seul

**pourer** n verseur -euse

**pout** n moue f; vi faire la moue

**poverty** n pauvreté f; (lack) pénurie f; ~ **of ideas** dénuement m d'idées

**poverty-stricken** adj indigent, dans la misère

**powder** n poudre f; vt (face) poudrer; (sprinkle with) saupoudrer; pulvériser; coll fig ~ **one's nose** aller aux toilettes

**powder-box** n poudrier m

**powder-compact** n poudrier m

**powderpuff** n houppe f (à poudre)

**powder-room** n toilette f pour dames

**power** n pouvoir m; (nation, machine) puissance f; (ability) faculté f, capacité f; (strength) force f, vigueur f; (authority) autorité f; **a ~ of good** grand bien; **all in my ~** tout ce qui est en mon pouvoir; **come to ~** arriver au pouvoir; **it's beyond my ~** cela ne m'est pas possible; **the ~ s that be** les autorités fpl; vt fournir d'énergie

**power-driven** adj automoteur -trice

**powered** adj mû (f mue); **high-(low-) ~** de haute (faible) puissance

**powerful** adj puissant, fort

**power-house** n see power-station

**powerless** adj impuissant

**powerlessness** n impuissance f

**power-mower** n tondeuse f à moteur

**power-point** n prise f de courant

**power-station, power-house** n centrale f électrique

**pox** n vérole f, syphilis f

**practicability** n praticabilité f

**practicable** adj praticable, faisable, pratique

**practical** adj pratique; ~ **consideration** considération f d'ordre pratique; ~ **joke** farce f; ~ **joker** farceur -euse

**practicality** n (plan, etc) caractère m pratique

**practically** adv pratiquement; (almost) presque, pour ainsi dire

**practicalness** n sens m pratique

**practice** n pratique f; (usage) habitude f, coutume f; (exercise) exercice m; (clients) clientèle f; ~ **makes perfect** c'est en forgeant qu'on devient forgeron; ~ **match** match m d'entraînement; **be in ~** être entraîné; **do sth for ~** faire qch pour s'exercer; **put into ~** mettre en pratique

**practise** vt pratiquer; (profession) exercer; (train at) s'exercer à; ~ **what one preaches** prêcher d'exemple; vi mus s'exercer; sp s'entraîner; (doctor, lawyer) exercer

**practised** adj expérimenté, exercé

**practising** adj qui exerce, exerçant; (religion) pratiquant

**practitioner** n praticien -ienne

**pragmatic(al)** adj pragmatique

**prairie** n prairie f

**praise** n louange f, éloge m; ~ **be to God!** Dieu soit loué!; **be loud in s/o's ~** prodiguer des éloges à qn; **beyond all ~** au-dessus de tout éloge; vt louer, faire l'éloge de; ~ **to the skies** porter aux nues

**praiseworthy** adj digne d'éloges; (work) méritoire

**pram** n voiture f d'enfants

**prance** vi (person) se pavaner; (horse) caracoler

**prank** n tour m, farce f; (mischief) frasque f, fredaine f; **play a ~ on s/o** jouer un tour à qn, faire une farce à qn

**prate** vi bavarder, jaser

**prattle** n babil m, babillage m; vi (esp child) babiller; (chatter) jaser, bavarder

**prattler** n babillard -e; bavard -e

**prawn** n bouquet m

**pray** vt + vi prier, supplier, implorer; ~ **come in** veuillez entrer; **be past ~ ing for** être perdu sans retour; coll être incorrigible

**prayer** n prière f; **say one's ~ s** faire ses dévotions; **the Lord's Prayer** l'oraison dominicale, le Pater

**preach** vt + vi prêcher

**preacher** n prédicateur m; pej prêcheur -euse

**preaching** n prédication f; pej prêcherie f

**preamble** n préambule m

**prebend** n prébende f

**precarious** adj précaire

**precaution** n précaution f

**precautionary** adj de précaution

**precede** vt précéder; (bring before) faire précéder; (have precedence) avoir la préséance sur

**precedence** n préséance f, priorité f

**precedent** n précédent m

**precentor** n eccles maître m de chapelle

**precept** n précepte m

**precinct** n enceinte f, enclos m; ~ **s** pourtour m, limite f; **shopping ~** centre commercial (interdit à la circulation)

**preciosity** n préciosité f

**precious** adj précieux -ieuse; (style) affecté; adv ~ **few** très peu

**precipice** n précipice m

**precipitance, precipitancy** n précipita-

tion *f*, empressement *m*
**precipitate** *adj* précipité, irréfléchi; *vt* (cast down) précipiter; (hurry) hâter, accélérer, précipiter
**precipitation** *n* précipitation *f*
**precipitous** *adj* escarpé
**précis** *n* précis *m*, résumé *m*, abrégé *m*
**precise** *adj* précis, exact; (person) pointilleux -euse, méticuleux -euse
**precision** *n* précision *f*
**preclude** *vt* exclure, empêcher
**precocious** *adj* précoce
**precociousness, precocity** *n* précocité *f*
**precognition** *n* préconnaissance *f*
**preconceive** *vt* préconcevoir
**preconception** *n* préconception *f*; (bias) préjugé *m*
**precondition** *n* condition *f* préalable
**precursor** *n* précurseur *m*, devancier *m*
**pre-date** *vt* antidater; (come before) venir avant
**predatory** *adj* rapace
**predecessor** *n* prédécesseur *m*
**predestination** *n* prédestination *f*
**predestine** *vt* prédestiner, destiner d'avance
**predetermine** *vt* déterminer d'avance
**predicament** *n* embarras *m*, situation *f* difficile
**predicate** *n gramm* attribut *m*
**predict** *vt* prédire
**predictable** *adj* prévisible, qui peut être prédit
**prediction** *n* prédiction *f*
**predilection** *n* prédilection *f*
**predispose** *vt* prédisposer
**predisposition** *n* prédisposition *f*
**predominance** *n* prédominance *f*
**predominant** *adj* prédominant
**predominate** *vi* prédominer
**pre-eminence** *n* prééminence *f*
**pre-eminent** *adj* prééminent
**pre-empt** *vt* préempter; acquérir d'avance
**pre-emption** *n* (droit *m* de) préemption *f*
**pre-emptive** *adj* préemptif -ive; préventif -ive
**preen** *vt* (bird) lisser, nettoyer; ~ one-self se bichonner; *fig* se montrer satisfait
**prefab** *n coll* maison préfabriquée
**prefabricate** *vt* préfabriquer
**preface** *n* préface *f*, avant-propos *m*; introduction *f*; *vt* préfacer; préluder
**prefatory** *adj* préliminaire
**prefect** *n* préfet *m*; (school) élève qui aide à maintenir la discipline, moniteur -trice
**prefer** *vt* préférer; (promote) nommer; ~ a complaint déposer une plainte
**preferable** *adj* préférable

**preference** *n* préférence *f*; *econ* ~ stock actions privilégiées; in ~ to de préférence à
**preferential** *adj* préférentiel -ielle, de préférence
**preferment** *n* avancement *m*
**prefigure** *vt* préfigurer
**pregnancy** *n* grossesse *f*
**pregnant** *adj* enceinte, grosse
**prehensile** *adj* préhensile
**prehistoric** *adj* préhistorique
**prehistory** *n* préhistoire *f*
**prejudge** *vt* préjuger; (condemn in advance) condamner d'avance
**prejudice** *n* prévention *f*, préjugé *m*; (injury) préjudice *m*; have a ~ against être prévenu contre; without ~ sous toutes réserves; *vt* prévenir, prédisposer; (injure) nuire à, porter préjudice à
**prejudiced** *adj* prévenu
**prejudicial** *adj* préjudiciable, nuisible
**prelate** *n* prélat *m*
**preliminary** *n* prélude *m*; **preliminaries** préliminaires *mpl*; *adj* préliminaire, préalable
**prelude** *n* prélude *m*; *vt* préluder à, précéder; *vi* préluder
**premarital** *adj* avant le mariage
**premature** *adj* prématuré
**prematurely** *adv* prématurément, de façon prématurée; (birth) avant terme
**prematureness, prematurity** *n* prématurité *f*
**premeditate** *vt* préméditer
**premeditation** *n* préméditation *f*
**premier** *n* premier ministre; *adj* premier -ière
**premiership** *n* fonction *f* de premier ministre
**premise** *n log* prémisse *f*; ~s local *m*, locaux *mpl*; on the ~s sur les lieux; *vt* poser en principe; citer en guise d'introduction
**premium** *n* (prize) prix *m*, récompense *f*; (insurance) prime *f*; (initial payment) droit *m*; be at a ~ (be scarce) être très recherché; (be expensive) se vendre très cher; (stock) faire prime; put a ~ on donner une prime à
**premolar** *n* prémolaire *f*
**premonition** *n* pressentiment *m*, prémonition *f*
**prenatal** *adj* prénatal
**preoccupation** *n* préoccupation *f*
**preoccupy** *vt* préoccuper, absorber
**pre-ordain** *vt* ordonner d'avance
**prep** *n coll* étude *f*; ~ school école *f* préparatoire
**pre-packed** *adj* préconditionné
**preparation** *n* préparation *f*; (school) devoirs *mpl*; ~s préparatifs *mpl*

**preparatory** *adj* préparatoire
**prepare** *vt* préparer; (dish) accommoder; ~ **a surprise for s/o** ménager une surprise à qn; *vi* se préparer, s'apprêter; ~ **for an examination** préparer un examen
**prepared** *adj* préparé, prêt; **be ~ for** être prêt à, s'attendre à
**prepay** *vt* payer d'avance (à l'avance); (letter) affranchir
**preponderance** *n* prépondérance *f*
**preponderant** *adj* prépondérant
**preponderate** *vi* l'emporter, emporter la balance
**preposition** *n* préposition *f*
**prepossessing** *adj* agréable, prévenant
**preposterous** *adj* absurde, déraisonnable
**prerequisite** *n* nécessité *f* préalable
**prerogative** *n* prérogative *f*, privilège *m*
**presage** *n* présage *m*, pressentiment *m*; *vt* présager; (person) prédire
**Presbyterian** *n* + *adj* presbytérien -ienne
**Presbyterianism** *n* presbytérianisme *m*
**presbytery** *n* presbytère *m*, cure *f*; (chancel) chœur *m*
**prescience** *n* prescience *f*
**prescribe** *vt* prescrire, ordonner
**prescription** *n* prescription *f*; *med* ordonnance *f*; **make out a ~** rédiger une ordonnance
**presence** *n* présence *f*; (person) air *m*; (impressive) prestance *f*, allure *f*; ~ **of mind** sang-froid *m*, présence *f* d'esprit; **in the ~ of** en la présence de; *ar* **saving your ~** sauf votre respect
¹**present** *n* présent *m*; **at ~** à présent; **for the ~** pour le moment; *adj* présent; **all those ~** toute l'assistance, tous les assistants; **at the ~ time** à l'époque actuelle; **be ~ at** être présent à, assister à; **the ~ tense** le (temps) présent
²**present** *n* don *m*, cadeau *m*, présent *m*; **is it for a ~?** c'est pour offrir?; **make s/o a ~ of sth** faire cadeau de qch à qn; *vt* présenter, offrir, donner
**presentable** *adj* présentable; (clothing) portable
**presentation** *n* présentation *f*
**present-day** *adj* actuel -elle, d'aujourd'hui
**presentiment** *n* pressentiment *m*
**presently** *adv* bientôt, tout à l'heure; *US* maintenant
**preservation** *n* conservation *f*; (from danger, etc) préservation *f*
**preservative** *n* agent *m* de conservation; *adj* préservatif -ive
**preserve** *vt* conserver; (from danger, etc) préserver; (peace) maintenir; ~ **appearances** sauver les apparences

**preside** *vi* présider; ~ **over** présider (à)
**presidency** *n* présidence *f*
**president** *n* président -e
**presidential** *adj* présidentiel -ielle
**press** *n* (papers) presse *f*; (crowd) foule *f*; (pressure) pression *f*; (printing) imprimerie *f*; (grapes) pressoir *m*; ~ **conference** conférence *f* de presse; ~ **release** communiqué *m* de presse; **have a good ~** avoir bonne presse; **in the ~** sous presse; *vt* presser; (press on) appuyer sur, peser sur; (squeeze out) exprimer; (squash) pressurer; (clothes) repasser; ~ **down** enfoncer; ~ **for a reply** insister sur une réponse; ~ **into service** enrôler; ~ **one's advantage** poursuivre son avantage; *vi* se serrer, se presser; ~ **back** refouler; ~ **on** avancer, continuer
**press-agency** *n* agence *f* de presse
**press-agent** *n* agent *m* de publicité
**press-box** *n* stand *m* pour la presse
**press-button** *adj* presse-bouton *invar*
**press-clipping, press-cutting** *n* coupure *f* de journal
**pressed** *adj* pressé, serré, comprimé; ~ **for time** très pressé; **be very ~** être débordé; **hard ~** serré de près
**press-gallery** *n* tribune *f* de la presse
**pressing** *adj* urgent, pressant
**press-stud** *n* bouton-pression *m* (*pl* boutons-pression)
**pressure** *n* pression *f*; ~ **of business** poids *m* des affaires; **act under ~** agir par contrainte; **blood ~** tension artérielle; **bring ~ to bear** exercer une pression
**pressure-cooker** *n* autocuiseur *m*, cocotte *f* minute
**pressure-gauge** *n* jauge *f* de pression
**pressurize** *vt* pressuriser
**prestige** *n* prestige *m*
**prestigious** *adj* prestigieux -ieuse
**presumable** *adj* présumable
**presume** *vt* présumer; *vi* ~ **to do sth** se permettre de faire qch, présumer de faire qch
**presuming** *adj* présomptueux -euse
**presumption** *n* présomption *f*; arrogance *f*
**presumptuous** *adj* présomptueux -euse
**presuppose** *vt* présupposer
**presupposition** *n* présupposition *f*
**pretence** *n* semblant *m*, prétexte *m*; (claim) prétention *f*; **make a ~ of doing sth** faire semblant de faire qch; **on the ~ of** sous prétexte de; **under false ~s** par des moyens frauduleux
**pretend** *vt* simuler, feindre; (claim) prétendre; *vi* faire semblant; (act) jouer la comédie; ~ **to be deaf** jouer le sourd

(*f* la sourde); ~ **to do sth** faire semblant de faire qch

**pretended** *adj* simulé, feint, faux (*f* fausse); (person) prétendu, supposé

**pretender** *n* (to the throne, etc) prétendant; simulateur -trice

**pretension** *n* prétention *f*

**pretentious** *adj* prétentieux -ieuse

**preterite** *n gramm* prétérit *m*

**preternatural** *adj* surnaturel -elle

**pretext** *n* prétexte *m*; **on the ~ of** sous prétexte de; *vt* prétexter, alléguer comme prétexte

**prettily** *adv* joliment, gentiment

**prettiness** *n* gentillesse *f*

**pretty** *adj* joli, gentil -ille; ~ **as a picture** joli à croquer; *coll* **be sitting ~** avoir la bonne place; **cost a ~ penny** coûter assez cher; **this is a ~ state of affairs!** c'est du joli!; *adv* assez, passablement; ~ **nearly** à peu près

**pretzel** *n cul* bretzel *m*

**prevail** *vi* (win) prévaloir; (dominate) prédominer; (be prevalent) régner; ~ **upon s/o to do sth** décider qn à faire qch; **be ~ed upon to do sth** se laisser persuader de faire qch

**prevailing** *adj* dominant; (fashion) en vogue

**prevalence** *n* prédominance *f*

**prevalent** *adj* général, répandu; dominant

**prevaricate** *vi* équivoquer, biaiser

**prevarication** *n* tergiversation *f*; (lies) mensonge *m*

**prevaricator** *n* tergiversateur -trice; (liar) menteur -euse

**prevent** *vt* empêcher; (forestall) prévenir, éviter; ~ **s/o from doing sth** empêcher qn de faire qch

**preventable** *adj* évitable

**preventative** *adj* préventif -ive

**prevention** *n* empêchement *m*

**preventive** *n* empêchement *m*; *med* médicament préventif; *adj* préventif -ive

**preview** *n cin* + *theat* avant-première *f*; (art gallery) vernissage *m*

**previous** *adj* préalable, antérieur; *coll* trop pressé; **the ~ day** la veille, le jour précédent; *adv* ~ **to** avant, antérieurement à

**previously** *adv* préalablement, auparavant

**prewar** *adj* d'avant-guerre

**prey** *n* proie *f*; **be a ~ to** être en proie à; **beasts of ~** carnassiers *mpl*; **birds of ~** oiseaux *mpl* de proie; **fall a ~ to** tomber en proie à; *vi* ~ **upon** faire sa proie de; (mind) tourmenter, travailler, ronger

**price** *n* prix *m*; **at any ~** à tout prix, coûte que coûte; **at a reduced ~** au rabais; **cost ~** prix coûtant; **fixed ~**

prix *m* fixe; **not at any ~** pour rien au monde; **what ~ …?** que dites-vous de …?; *vt* fixer le prix de; estimer, évaluer; (inquire) s'informer du prix de; (show price) marquer le prix de; **be ~d at ten francs** être marqué dix francs

**priceless** *adj* inestimable, hors de prix; *coll fig* inouï, (person) impayable

**price-list** *n* tarif *m*, prix courant

**pricey** *adj coll* coûteux -euse, cher (*f* chère)

**prick** *n* piqûre *f*; coup *m* d'épingle; *sl* queue *f*; **kick against the ~s** regimber; *vt* piquer; (conscience) causer des remords; *hort* ~ **out** repiquer; ~ **up one's ears** (person) tendre l'oreille; (animal) dresser les oreilles; *vi* picoter

**pricking** *n* piquage *m*; ~ **s of conscience** remords *mpl* de conscience

**prickle** *n* piquant *m*, épine *f*; *vt* piquer, picoter; *vi* fourmiller

**prickling** *n* picotement *m*, fourmillement *m*

**prickly** *adj* (plant) épineux -euse; (animal) armé de piquants; ~ **pear** figue *f* de Barbarie

**pride** *n* orgueil *m*, fierté *f*; (self-esteem) amour-propre *m*; (*pl* amours-propres); (zenith) comble *m*; **be the ~ of** faire l'orgueil de; **take ~ in doing sth** faire qch avec amour; *vt* ~ **oneself on sth** se piquer de qch, s'enorgueillir de qch

**priest** *n* prêtre *m*

**priestess** *n* prêtresse *f*

**priesthood** *n* sacerdoce *m*, prêtrise *f*

**prig** *n* poseur -euse; petit saint (*f* petite sainte)

**priggish** *adj* poseur -euse; bégueule

**prim** *adj* guindé; (person) collet monté *invar*

**primacy** *n* primauté *f*

**prima donna** *n* prima donna *f invar*

**primaeval** *adj see* primeval

**prima facie** *adj* + *adv* à première vue, de prime abord

**primarily** *adv* principalement; primitivement

**primary** *n US* élection *f* préliminaire qui permet de choisir les candidats à la présidence; *adj* premier -ière, originel -elle; primaire; (chief) principal; ~ **product** produit *m* de base

**primate** *n eccles* primat *m*; *zool* primate *m*

¹**prime** *n* perfection *f*; commencement *m*; (best) choix *m*; **be past one's ~** être sur le retour; **in the ~ of life** dans la force (fleur) de l'âge; *adj* premier -ière, principal; (quality) de première qualité; primitif -ive; (very important) primordial; ~ **minister** premier ministre

²**prime** *vt* (gun, pump) amorcer;

(instruct) mettre au courant; (surface) apprêter

**primeval, primaeval** *adj* primitif -ive, primordial; **~ forest** forêt *f* vierge

**primitive** *adj* primitif -ive

**primly** *adv* d'un air guindé

**primness** *n* air *m* collet monté

**primogeniture** *n* primogéniture *f*; **right of ~** droit *m* d'aînesse

**primordial** *adj* primordial

**primrose** *n* primevère *f*

**primula** *n* primevère *f*

**primus** *n* **~ (stove)** réchaud *m* à pétrole

**prince** *n* prince *m*

**princely** *adj* princier -ière, de prince; *fig* magnifique

**princess** *n* princesse *f*

**principal** *n* directeur -trice; (boss) chef *m*, patron -onne; (money) capital *m*; *leg* auteur *m*; *theat* rôle principal; *adj* principal

**principality** *n* principauté *f*

**principally** *adv* principalement

**principle** *n* principe *m*; **do sth as a matter of ~** faire qch par principe; **on ~** par principe

**prink** *vt* (bird) **~ its feathers** se lisser les plumes; *vi* prendre des airs

**print** *n* (finger, foot) empreinte *f*; (engraving) gravure *f*, estampe *f*; (printed matter) imprimé *m*, matière imprimée; *phot* épreuve *f*, copie *f*; (cloth) indienne *f*, cotonnade *f*; **be in ~** être imprimé; **large (small) ~** gros (petits) caractères; **out of ~** épuisé; *vt* imprimer; (make impression) marquer d'une empreinte; *phot* tirer; **~ed matter** imprimés *mpl*; **~ off a newspaper** tirer un journal; **~ out** imprimer

**printable** *adj* imprimable

**printer** *n* imprimeur *m*; (workman) (ouvrier *m*) typographe *m*; (computer) printer; **~'s error** faute *f* d'impression, coquille *f*; **~'s ink** encre *f* d'imprimerie; **~'s reader** correcteur -trice d'épreuves

**printing** *n* impression *f*; (art) imprimerie *f*; *phot* tirage *m*

**printing-press** *n* presse *f* (d'imprimerie)

**¹prior** *n eccles* prieur *m*

**²prior** *adj* préalable, antérieur, précédent; *adv* **~ to** avant, antérieurement à

**prioress** *n eccles* prieure *f*

**priority** *n* priorité *f*; **according to ~** selon l'ordre de priorité; *adj* prioritaire

**priory** *n* prieuré *m*

**prise, prize** *vt* **~ open** forcer; **~ up** soulever à l'aide d'un levier

**prism** *n* prisme *m*

**prismatic** *adj* prismatique

**prison** *n* prison *f*; **have been in ~** avoir

fait de la prison

**prison-camp** *n* camp *m* de prisonniers

**prisoner** *n* prisonnier -ière; détenu -e; **~ at the bar** prévenu -e, accusé -e; **take ~** faire prisonnier

**prison-van** *n* voiture *f* cellulaire, *coll* panier *m* à salade

**pristine** *adj* premier -ière, primitif -ive

**privacy** *n* vie privée; retraite *f*; intimité *f*; **have no ~** n'être jamais seul

**private** *n mil* simple soldat *m*; **~s** parties (génitales); **in ~** (meeting) en séance privée; dans l'intimité, en famille; *adj* privé; (personal) particulier -ière, personnel -elle; (secret) secret -ète; défense d'entrer, entrée interdite; **~ lesson** leçon particulière; **~ opinion** avis personnel; **~ person** particulier *m*; **~ residence** domicile particulier

**privation** *n* privation *f*

**privet** *n bot* troène *m*

**privilege** *n* privilège *m*, prérogative *f*

**privy** *n leg* partie intéressée; *ar* (toilet) cabinets *mpl*; *adj* privé; **Privy Council =** Conseil *m* du Roi; **be ~ to sth** avoir connaissance de qch

**¹prize** *n* prix *m*; (lottery) lot *m*; (navy) prise *f*; *vt* priser, estimer, évaluer; **~ highly** faire grand cas de

**²prize** *vt see* prise

**prize-fight** *n* match *m* de boxe (professionnelle)

**prize-winner** *n* lauréat -e

**pro** *n sp* pro, professionel -elle

**²pro** *n* **the ~s and cons** le pour et le contre; *prep* **~ forma** pour la forme

**probability** *n* probabilité *f*; (plausibility) vraisemblance *f*; **in all ~** selon toute probabilité

**probable** *adj* probable; (plausible) vraisemblable

**probate** *n* (will) homologation *f*

**probation** *n* temps *m* d'épreuve; liberté *f* sous surveillance; **be on ~** être mise à l'épreuve, être en liberté surveillée; **~ officer** délégué -e à la liberté surveillée

**probationary** *adj* d'épreuve; (person) stagiaire

**probationer** *n* stagiaire; *eccles* novice; *leg* personne *f* en liberté surveillée

**probe** *n* sonde *f*; coup *m* de sonde; (inquiry) enquête *f*; **space ~** sonde *f* cosmique; *vt* sonder, explorer; fouiller, examiner

**probity** *n* probité *f*

**problem** *n* problème *m*; **~ child** enfant difficile

**problematic(al)** *adj* problématique

**procedure** *n* procédé *m*, manière *f* d'agir; *leg* procédure *f*

**proceed** *vi* aller; (go on) avancer, passer, poursuivre son chemin; (continue) continuer; (act) procéder; ~ **against** s/o procéder contre qn; ~ **from** provenir de; **be ~ing** être en cours, suivre son train

**proceeding** n procédé m, façon f d'agir; ~**s** (meeting) séance f; (deliberation) débats mpl; **take ~s against** s/o intenter un procès contre qn

**proceeds** n produit m; (money) recette f

¹**process** n processus m; (method) procédé m, méthode f; (work) travail m; **in the ~ of** en cours de; **in the ~ of time** avec le temps; vt traiter, transformer

²**process** vi coll aller en cortège

**processing** n traitement m d'une matière première; **data ~** traitement m des informations; **food ~** industrie f alimentaire; **information ~** informatique f

**procession** n cortège m; (religious) procession f

**proclaim** vt proclamer, déclarer

**proclamation** n proclamation f, déclaration f

**proclivity** n penchant m, tendance f

**procrastinate** vi temporiser, remettre les choses à plus tard

**procrastinator** n temporisateur -trice

**procreate** vt procréer

**procreation** n procréation f

**procurable** adj procurable

**procuration** n acquisition f; leg procuration f

**procure** vt obtenir, procurer; ~ **sth (for oneself)** se procurer qch; vi (prostitution) faire le métier de proxénète

**procurement** n acquisition f

**procurer** n acquéreur -euse; (for s/o else) personne f qui procure; (prostitution) proxénète m

**prod** n coup m; vt donner un petit coup à; fig stimuler, aiguillonner

**prodigal** n+adj prodigue

**prodigality** n prodigalité f

**prodigious** adj prodigieux -ieuse

**prodigy** n prodige m, merveille f; **infant ~** enfant prodige

**produce** n produit m; (production) rendement m; vt produire; (show) présenter; (industry) fabriquer; cin+theat mettre en scène; (create) créer; (profit) rapporter

**producer** n producteur -trice; theat metteur m en scène; cin+TV réalisateur -trice; rad metteur m en ondes

**producible** adj productible

**product** n produit m

**production** n production f; (showing) présentation f; (manufacture) fabrication f; theat mise f en scène; rad mise f en ondes; (show, film, etc) réalisation f

**productive** adj productif -ive; (land)

fécond

**productivity** n productivité f

**profanation** n profanation f

**profane** adj profane; impie; vt profaner, polluer

**profess** vt professer; (profession) exercer; ~ **oneself** se déclarer; (falsely) se faire passer pour

**professed** adj déclaré; (falsely) prétendu, soi-disant

**profession** n profession f, métier m; déclaration f; **by ~** de profession

**professional** n professionnel -elle; adj professionnel -elle; expert; ~**s** gens mpl du métier; ~ **classes** membres mpl des professions libérales

**professionalism** n professionnalisme m

**professor** n professeur m (titulaire d'une chaire)

**professorial** adj professoral

**professorship** n chaire f; **obtain a ~** être nommé à une chaire

**proffer** vt offrir, présenter

**proficiency** n compétence f, capacité f

**proficient** adj compétent, capable

**profile** n profil m, silhouette f; (newspaper) portrait m; **maintain a low ~** se comporter avec réserve; vt profiler

**profit** n profit m, bénéfice m; avantage m; ~ **and loss** profits mpl et pertes fpl; **sell at a ~** vendre à profit; vt profiter à; vi bénéficier, profiter

**profitability** n rentabilité f

**profitable** adj profitable, avantageux -euse

**profiteer** n profiteur m

**profitless** adj sans profit

**profit-sharing** n participation f aux bénéfices

**profligacy** n libertinage m, débauche f

**profligate** n+adj débauché -e, libertin -e

**profound** adj profond, approfondi

**profundity, profoundness** n profondeur f

**profuse** adj prodigue; abondant

**profusion** n profusion f, abondance f

**progenitor** n ancêtre m

**progeniture** n progéniture f

**progeny** n progéniture f; (descendants) descendants mpl, lignée f

**prognosis** n med diagnostic m, pronostic m

**prognostic** n pronostic m, présage m; adj pronostique

**prognosticate** vt pronostiquer, prédire

**prognostication** n pronostication f, prédiction f

**programme**, US **program** n programme m; vt programmer

**programme-music** n musique f de genre

**programmer** n programmeur -euse

**progress** n progrès m; (movement) marche f en avant; **in ~** en cours; **make ~** faire des progrès; vi s'avancer; (improve) faire des progrès; (illness) progresser

**progression** n progression f

**progressive** adj progressif -ive

**prohibit** vt interdire, défendre; **smoking ~ed** défense f de fumer

**prohibition** n interdiction f, défense f, prohibition f; US hist prohibition f

**prohibitive** adj prohibitif -ive; **~ price** prix m inabordable

**project** n projet m; vt projeter; (throw) lancer, projeter; vi s'avancer, faire saillie

**projectile** n projectile m

**projecting** adj en saillie

**projection** n projection f; (jutting out) saillie f, avancement m; cin **~ room** cabine f de projection

**projectionist** n projectionniste

**projector** n projecteur m; cin appareil m de projection

**proletarian** n prolétaire; adj prolétarien -ienne

**proletariat(e)** n prolétariat m

**proliferate** vi proliférer

**proliferation** n prolifération f

**prolific** adj prolifique, fécond

**prolix** adj diffus, prolixe

**prolixity** n prolixité f

**prologue** n prologue m

**prolong** vt prolonger

**prolongation** n prolongation f

**prom** n coll (seaside) esplanade f; US bal m d'étudiants; = **promenade concert**

**promenade** n (walk) promenade f; lieu m de promenade, esplanade f; theat promenoir m; **~ concert** concert m où une partie des auditeurs restent debout; vt promener; vi se promener; parader

**promenade-deck** n pont m promenade

**prominence** n proéminence f; fig distinction f, éminence f

**prominent** adj saillant, proéminent; (noteworthy) remarquable; (famous) éminent; **~ personality** personnage m très en vue; **play a ~ part** jouer un rôle important

**promiscuity** n promiscuité f

**promiscuous** adj mêlé, confus; (indiscriminate) sans distinction; **be ~** coucher avec tout le monde

**promise** n promesse f; **break one's ~** manquer à sa promesse; **full of ~** qui promet; vt promettre; vi promettre; **~ well** s'annoncer bien

**promising** adj prometteur -euse, qui promet bien

**promissory** adj **~ note** billet m à ordre

**promontory** n promontoire m

**promote** vt (person) donner de l'avancement à, nommer; (arts) encourager; (company) lancer, fonder; (interests) avancer; (make easier) faciliter; (advertise) faire de la publicité (réclame) pour

**promoter** n instigateur -trice; comm promoteur m

**promotion** n avancement m; promotion f; (arts) encouragement m; comm lancement m

¹**prompt** adj prompt, exact; (quick) rapide; (immediate) immédiat; adv promptement, à l'heure

²**prompt** n suggestion f; vt theat souffler; (urge) exciter; (inspire) inspirer; **~ s/o to do sth** suggérer qch à qn, inciter qn à faire qch; **be ~ed by sth** être mû (f mue) par qch

**prompt-box** n theat trou m du souffleur

**prompt-corner** n theat côté m jardin

**prompter** n instigateur -trice; theat souffleur m; **~'s box** trou m du souffleur

**promptitude** n promptitude f, empressement m

**promptly** adv promptement; immédiatement

**promulgate** vt promulguer; (news, idea) répandre

**promulgation** n promulgation f; (news, idea) dissémination f

**prone** adj (person) couché sur le ventre, couché la face contre terre; (inclined) enclin, disposé

**proneness** n disposition f, inclination f

**prong** n fourchon m; (fork) dent f

**pronged** adj à dents

**pronoun** n pronom m

**pronounce** vt prononcer; (declare) déclarer

**pronounceable** adj prononçable

**pronounced** adj marqué, prononcé, très fort

**pronouncement** n déclaration f

**pronunciation** n prononciation f

**proof** n (evidence) preuve f; (test) épreuve f; phot + print épreuve f; **give (show) ~ of** faire preuve de; **in ~ of** en preuve de; **put to the ~** mettre à l'épreuve de; adj résistant; **~ against sth** à l'épreuve de qch

**proof-reader** n correcteur -trice

¹**prop** n (support) appui m, support m, étai m; (plant) tuteur m; vt **~ up** soutenir; étayer

²**prop** n theat accessoire m

³**prop** n coll (propeller) hélice f

**propaganda** n propagande f

**propagandize** vt soumettre à la propagande

641

**propagate** *vt* propager; (ideas) répandre, disséminer; *vi* se propager, se reproduire
**propagation** *n* propagation *f*, reproduction *f*
**propagator** *n* propagateur -trice
**propane** *n* propane *m*
**propel** *vt* propulser; donner une impulsion à
**propellant** *n* combustible *m*; *adj* propulseur (no *f*)
**propeller** *n* (screw) hélice *f*; propulseur *m*
**propensity** *n* penchant *m*, tendance *f*, inclination *f*
**proper** *adj* propre; (suitable) convenable, juste, approprié; (correct) correct, comme il faut; (real) vrai; ~ to sth particulier -ière à qch; at the ~ time en temps utile; do as you think ~ faites comme bon vous semble; *adv coll* vraiment
**properly** *adv* proprement; (correctly) correctement; (well) bien, comme il faut; (very much) absolument
**property** *n* propriété *f*; biens *mpl*; *theat* accessoire *m*; landed ~ biens fonciers; lost ~ objets trouvés
**prophecy** *n* prophétie *f*
**prophesy** *vt* prophétiser, prédire
**prophet** *n* prophète *m*
**prophetess** *n* prophétesse *f*
**prophetic(al)** *adj* prophétique
**prophylactic** *n* prophylactique *m*; *adj* prophylactique
**prophylaxis** *n* prophylaxie *f*
**propinquity** *n* proximité *f*
**propitiate** *vt* rendre propice; (appease) apaiser
**propitiation** *n* propitiation *f*; apaisement *m*
**propitiator** *n* propitiateur -trice
**propitiatory** *adj* propitiatoire
**propitious** *adj* propice, favorable
**proportion** *n* proportion *f*, partie *f*; in ~ as à mesure que; in ~ to en proportion à; out of ~ mal proportionné; out of ~ to disproportionné à; *vt* proportionner; (ingredients) doser
**proportional** *adj* proportionnel -elle, en proportion
**proportionate** *adj* proportionné
**proposal** *n* proposition *f*; offre *f*; (marriage) demande *f* en mariage
**propose** *vt* proposer, offrir; ~ s/o's health proposer un toast à qn; *vi* (intend) compter; (marriage) faire une demande en mariage; ~ to do sth se proposer (avoir l'intention) de faire qch
**proposition** *n* proposition *f*; (business) affaire *f*; a tough ~ un problème

difficile
**propound** *vt* proposer; (idea) émettre; (question) poser
**proprietary** *adj* de propriétaire, de propriété; ~ article article breveté; ~ medicine spécialité *f* pharmaceutique
**proprietor** *n* propriétaire *m*
**proprietress** *n* propriétaire *f*
**propriety** *n* (suitability) propriété *f*; bienséance *f*, décence *f*; (correctness) justesse *f*, correction *f*, rectitude *f*
**propulsion** *n* propulsion *f*
**prorogation** *n* prorogation *f*
**prorogue** *vt* proroger
**prosaic** *adj* prosaïque
**proscenium** *n theat* avant-scène *f*, proscenium *m*
**proscribe** *vt* proscrire; (forbid) interdire, défendre
**prose** *n* prose *f*; (translation into foreign language) thème *m*
**prosecute** *vt* poursuivre en justice
**prosecution** *n leg* poursuites *fpl*; (continuation) continuation *f*; (execution) exercice *m*; the Prosecution (state) le ministère public; (private) les plaignants *mpl*; witness for the ~ témoin *m* à charge
**prosecutor** *n* plaignant *m*, demandeur *m*; Public Prosecutor procureur *m* de la République
**proselyte** *n* prosélyte
**proselytize** *vt* convertir
**prosiness** *n* prosaïsme *m*; (person) verbosité *f*
**prosody** *n* prosodie *f*
**prospect** *n* vue *f*; *fig* perspective *f*; (prospects) espérances *fpl*, avenir *m*; (chance) chance *f*; *vt* + *vi* prospecter
**prospecting** *n* recherche *f*
**prospective** *adj* prospectif -ive, en perspective
**prospector** *n* prospecteur -trice, chercheur -euse
**prospectus** *n* prospectus *m*
**prosper** *vi* prospérer, réussir
**prosperity** *n* prospérité *f*
**prosperous** *adj* prospère; (favourable) favorable
**prostate** *n* prostate *f*
**prostitute** *n* prostituée *f*; *vt* prostituer
**prostitution** *n* prostitution *f*
**prostrate** *adj* prosterné; *fig* abattu, accablé; *vt* abattre; ~ oneself se prosterner
**prostration** *n* prostration *f*; *fig* abattement *m*
**prosy** *adj* prosaïque; (person) ennuyeux -euse; (wordy) verbeux -euse
**protagonist** *n* protagoniste *m*
**protect** *vt* protéger, défendre; (interests) sauvegarder
**protection** *n* protection *f*, défense *f*;

(interests) sauvegarde *f*; (patronage) patronage *m*; (shelter) abri *m*

**protective** *adj* protecteur -trice

**protector** *n* protecteur -trice

**protectorate** *n* protectorat *m*

**protégé** *n* protégé -e

**protein** *n* protéine *f*

**protest** *n* protestation *f*; **raise a** ~ élever une protestation; **under** ~ en protestant; *vt* + *vi* protester

**Protestant** *n* + *adj* protestant -e

**Protestantism** *n* protestantisme *m*

**protestation** *n* protestation *f*; (affirmation) déclaration *f*

**protocol** *n* protocole *m*

**protoplasm** *n* protoplasme *m*

**prototype** *n* prototype *m*

**protract** *vt* prolonger, traîner en longueur

**protraction** *n* prolongation *f*

**protractor** *n geom* rapporteur *m*

**protrude** *vi* s'avancer, faire saillie

**protruding** *adj* saillant

**protrusion** *n* saillie *f*

**protuberance** *n* protubérance *f*

**protuberant** *adj* protubérant

**proud** *adj* fier (*f* fière), orgueilleux -euse; (haughty) hautain; *coll* **do oneself** ~ ne se priver de rien; *coll* **do s/o** ~ se mettre en frais pour qn

**provable** *adj* prouvable, démontrable

**prove** *vt* prouver, démontrer; (test) éprouver; (check) vérifier; *leg* homologuer; ~ **oneself** faire ses preuves; **to** ~ **my case** comme preuve à l'appui; *vi* se montrer, être; (turn out to be) s'avérer

**provender** *n* fourrage *m*

**proverb** *n* proverbe *m*

**proverbial** *adj* proverbial

**provide** *vt* fournir, munir, nantir; ~ **s/o with sth** fournir qch à qn; *vi* ~ **against** se prémunir contre; ~ **for oneself** se suffire; (feeding) se nourrir; ~ **for s/o** pourvoir aux besoins de qn; ~ **for sth** prévoir qch

**provided** *adj* pourvu, muni; *conj* ~ **that** pourvu que

**providence** *n* providence *f*; (foresight) prévoyance *f*; (economy) économie *f*

**provident** *adj* prévoyant; (thrifty) économe

**providential** *adj* providentiel -ielle

**province** *n* province *f*; (sphere) ressort *m*, domaine *m*

**provincial** *adj* provincial, de province

**provincialism** *n* provincialisme *m*

**provision** *n* provision *f*; stipulation *f*; *comm* prestation *f*; (law) clause *f*; ~ **s** vivres *mpl*, provisions *fpl*; (in shop) produits *mpl* d'alimentation; **come within the** ~ **s of the law** tomber sous le coup de la loi; **make** ~ **against** prendre

des mesures contre; **make** ~ **for s/o** pourvoir aux besoins de qn; **make** ~ **for sth** pourvoir à qch; *vt* ravitailler, approvisionner

**provisional** *adj* provisoire, temporaire

**proviso** *n* condition *f*, stipulation *f*

**provisory** *adj* conditionnel -elle; provisoire

**provocation** *n* provocation *f*

**provocative** *adj* provocateur -trice; provocant; (annoying) agaçant

**provoke** *vt* provoquer, inciter; (annoy) irriter, contrarier, agacer; (curiosity) exciter

**provoking** *adj* irritant, exaspérant

**prow** *n* proue *f*

**prowess** *n* prouesse *f*

**prowl** *n* **be on the** ~ rôder; *vi* rôder

**prowl-car** *n US* voiture *f* de patrouille

**prowler** *n* rôdeur -euse

**proximity** *n* proximité *f*

**proxy** *n leg* procuration *f*; (person) fondé -e de pouvoir(s), délégué -e

**prude** *n* prude *f*; *adj* prude, *coll* bégueule

**prudence** *n* prudence *f*, sagesse *f*

**prudent** *adj* prudent, sage

**prudery** *n* pruderie *f*, *coll* bégueulerie *f*

**prudish** *adj* prude, pudibond, *coll* bégueule

¹**prune** *n* pruneau *m*

²**prune** *vt* tailler, élaguer

**pruning** *n* taille *f*

**pruning-knife** *n* serpette *f*

**prurience, pruriency** *n* lasciveté *f*, luxure *f*

**prurient** *adj* lascif -ive

**Prussian** *n* Prussien -ienne; *adj* prussien -ienne

**prussic** *adj* prussique

**pry** *vi* fureter, fouiller, *coll* fourrer le nez

**prying** *adj* trop curieux -ieuse

**psalm** *n* psaume *m*

**psalmist** *n* psalmiste *m*

**psalmody** *n* psalmodie *f*

**psalter** *n* psautier *m*

**pseudo** *adj coll* fumiste

**pseudonym** *n* pseudonyme *m*

**psyche** *n* psyché *f*

**psychedelic** *adj* psychédélique

**psychiatric** *adj* psychiatrique

**psychiatrist** *n* psychiatre *m*

**psychiatry** *n* psychiatrie *f*

**psychic(al)** *adj* psychique

**psychoanalyse** *vt* psychanalyser

**psychoanalysis** *n* psychanalyse *f*

**psychoanalyst** *n* psychanalyste *m*

**psychological** *adj* psychologique

**psychologist** *n* psychologue

**psychology** *n* psychologie *f*

**psychopath** *n* psychopathe

**psychosis** *n* psychose *f*

**psychosomatic** *adj* psychosomatique

**psychotherapy** *n* psychothérapie *f*
**psychotic** *n+adj* psychotique
**ptarmigan** *n* lagopède *m*
**ptomaine** *n chem* ptomaïne *f*
**pub** *n coll* pub *m*, bar *m*
**pub-crawl** *n* tournée *f* des bistrots
**puberty** *n* puberté *f*
**pubescent** *adj* pubère
**pubic** *adj* pubien -ienne; ~ **hair** poils *mpl* (du pubis)
**public** *n* public *m*; **in** ~ en public; **the general** ~ le grand public; *adj* public (*f* publique); ~ **holiday** fête légale; ~ **library** bibliothèque municipale; ~ **ownership** nationalisation *f*; ~ **school** = lycée indépendant et privé d'une certaine catégorie; *US* école *f* d'état; ~ **spirit** civisme *m*; ~ **transport** transports publics, transports *mpl* en commun
**publican** *n* patron -onne de café (de bistrot), aubergiste
**publication** *n* publication *f*; (of book) parution *f*; (decree) promulgation *f*
**public-house** *n* café *m*, bistrot *m*, pub *m*
**publicity** *n* publicité *f*; ~ **department** service *m* de presse
**publicize** *vt* faire connaître au public; *comm* faire de la publicité autour de
**publicly** *adv* publiquement, en public
**publish** *vt* publier; (book) faire paraître, sortir; **just** ~ed vient de paraître
**publishable** *adj* publiable
**publisher** *n* éditeur -trice
**publishing** *n* publication *f*; (trade) édition *f*
**puce** *n* puce *m*; *adj* puce *invar*
**puck** *n* (ice-hockey) palet *m*
**pucker** *n* plissement *m*; *vt* rider; (crease) plisser; (sewing) faire goder; *vi* ~ **up** faire des plis
**pudding** *n* pudding *m*, pouding *m*; **black** ~ boudin (noir); **rice** ~ riz *m* au lait
**puddle** *n* flaque *f* (d'eau); *vt* (clay) corroyer; (metal) puddler
**pudgy** *adj* boulot -otte, grassouillet -ette
**puerile** *adj* puéril
**puerility** *n* puérilité *f*
**puff** *n* souffle *m*; (air) bouffée *f*; (dress) bouffant *m*; *cul* gâteau feuilleté; (publicity) boniment *m*; *vt* (swell) gonfler, faire gonfler; (exaggerate) faire mousser; ~ **a cigarette** fumer une cigarette (par petites bouffées); *vi* souffler; lancer des bouffées; (shirt) bouffer; ~ **and blow** haleter
**puffin** *n* macareux *m*
**puffiness** *n* boursouflure *f*, enflure *f*
**puff-pastry** *n* pâte feuilletée
**puffy** *adj* (swollen) bouffi, boursouflé; (wind) qui souffle par bouffées

¹**pug** *n* (dog) carlin *m*, roquet *m*
²**pug** *n* (clay) argile malaxée; *vt* malaxer, corroyer
**pugilism** *n* pugilat *m*, boxe *f*
**pugilist** *n* pugiliste *m*, boxeur *m*
**pugnacious** *adj* batailleur -euse, querelleur -euse
**pugnacity** *n* humeur batailleuse
**pug-nose** *n* nez épaté
**puke** *vi* vomir; *sl* dégobiller
**pull** *n* traction *f*, tirage *m*; (advantage) avantage *m*; (coll) (influence) piston *m*; (rowing) coup *m* d'aviron; *coll* (drink) gorgée *f*; (magnet) force *f* d'attraction; *vt* tirer; ~ **about** tirailler; ~ **a face** faire une grimace; ~ **apart** détacher, séparer; ~ **away** arracher; ~ **down** faire descendre; (illness) affaiblir; (topple) renverser; (demolish) démolir; ~ **in** rentrer; *coll* (police) arrêter; *coll* (succeed) ~ **it off** réussir; ~ **off** enlever, arracher, retirer; *sp* gagner; ~ **oneself together** se reprendre; ~ **out** sortir, tirer, retirer; (tooth) arracher; ~ **round** ranimer; (after illness) remettre sur pied; ~ **s/o back** empêcher qn de progresser; (restrain) retenir; ~ **s/o's leg** taquiner qn, faire marcher qn; ~ **s/o through** aider qn à se remettre; ~ **up** remonter; (tell off) réprimander; *coll* ~ **up one's socks** s'activer; *coll* **he** ~ed **a fast one on me** il m'a eu; *vi* tirer; ~ **ahead** se détacher, prendre de l'avance; ~ **at** tirer sur; ~ **away** s'éloigner; ~ **in** (train) entrer en gare; *mot* se ranger près du trottoir; *mot* ~ **out** démarrer; prendre le milieu de la chaussée; sortir pour doubler; *coll* (give up) *sl* se dégonfler; abandonner; ~ **out of** se retirer de; *mot* ~ **over** se ranger; ~ **round** se ranimer; (after illness) se remettre, guérir; ~ **through** s'en tirer; ~ **together** agir de concert; (agree) s'entendre; ~ **up** *mot* s'arrêter; (recover) se rattraper
**puller** *n* tireur -euse
**pullet** *n* poularde *f*, poulette *f*
**pulley** *n* poulie *f*
**pull-in** *n* parking *m*; restaurant routier, café *m* pour routiers
**Pullman** *n* (voiture *f*) pullman *m*; *US* wagon-lit *m* (*pl* wagons-lits)
**pullover** *n* pullover *m*
**pulmonary** *adj* pulmonaire
**pulp** *n* pulpe *f*; (paper) pâte *f* (à papier); *vt* réduire en pulpe
**pulp-fiction** *n US* roman *m* à quatre sous
**pulpit** *n* chaire *f*
**pulpy** *adj* pulpeux -euse, charnu
**pulsate** *vi* battre; palpiter
**pulsation** *n* pulsation *f*
**pulse** *n* pouls *m*, battement *m* du cœur;

**feel s/o 's** ~ tâter le pouls à qn; *vi* battre, palpiter

**pulverize** *vt* pulvériser, réduire en poudre; *fig* réduire à néant

**puma** *n* puma *m*

**pumice-stone** *n* pierre *f* ponce

**pummel** *n* + *vt see* **pommel**

**pump** *n* pompe *f*; **petrol** ~ pompe *f* à essence; *vt* pomper; (person) sonder, faire causer; ~ **up** faire monter en pompant; (tyre) gonfler; *vi* pomper

**pumpkin** *n* potiron *m*, citrouille *f*

**pump-room** *n* (at a spa) pavillon *m* de la source

**pun** *n* calembour *m*, jeu *m* de mots; *vi* faire des jeux de mots

¹**punch** *n* (tool) poinçon *m*; *vt* poinçonner; (pierce) percer; ~ **in** enfoncer; ~ **out** découper à l'emporte-pièce

²**punch** *n* coup *m* de poing; *fig* énergie *f*; *vt* donner un coup de poing à

³**punch** *n* (drink) punch *m*

**Punch** *n* ~ **and Judy show** théâtre *m* de guignol

**punch-ball** *n* punching-ball *m*

**punch-bowl** *n* bol *m* à punch; *geog* cuvette *f*

**punch-card** *n* carte perforée

**punch-drunk** *adj* abruti de coups

**punch-line** *n* mot *m* de la fin

**punch-up** *n* bagarre *f*

**punctilious** *adj* pointilleux -euse

**punctual** *adj* ponctuel -elle, exact, à l'heure

**punctuality** *n* ponctualité *f*, exactitude *f*

**punctually** *adv* ponctuellement, exactement

**punctuate** *vt* ponctuer

**punctuation** *n* ponctuation *f*; ~ **mark** signe *m* de ponctuation

**puncture** *n* (tyre) crevaison *f*; perforation *f*; *surg* ponction *f*

**pundit** *n* pandit *m*; *coll* ponte *m*

**pungency** *n* goût piquant; (smell) odeur forte; (speech) âcreté *f*; (tale) saveur *f*

**pungent** *adj* (smell, taste) fort, piquant; (feeling) poignant

**punish** *vt* punir, châtier; (child) corriger; ~ **an engine** forcer un moteur

**punishable** *adj* punissable

**punishment** *n* punition *f*, châtiment *m*; **as a** ~ par punition; **capital** ~ peine capitale, peine *f* de mort; **corporal** ~ châtiment corporel

**punitive** *adj* punitif -ive

¹**punt** *n* bateau *m* à fond plat; *vt* transporter dans un bateau à fond plat; *vi* pousser un bateau à la perche

²**punt** *n* (rugby) coup *m* (de pied) de volée

³**punt** *vi* (racing) parier; (cards) ponter

**punter** *n* (racing) parieur -ieuse; (cards) ponte *m*

**puny** *adj* chétif -ive; (tiny) menu, petit; (wretched) mesquin

**pup** *n* petit chien, chiot *m*

¹**pupil** *n* élève, écolier -ière; *leg* (ward) pupille

²**pupil** *n anat* pupille *f*

**puppet** *n* marionnette *f*; (person) pantin *m*, fantoche *m*

**puppet-show** *n* spectacle *m* de marionnettes; théâtre *m* de marionnettes

**puppy** *n* petit chien, jeune chien *m*, chiot *m*

**purblind** *adj* myope; *fig* obtus

**purchase** *n* achat *m*, acquisition *f*; (leverage) prise *f*; **take** ~ **on** prendre appui sur; *vt* acheter, acquérir

**purchaser** *n* acheteur -euse, acquéreur -euse

**pure** *adj* pur

**purgation** *n* purgation *f*

**purgative** *adj* purgatif -ive

**purgatory** *n* purgatoire *m*

**purge** *n* purge *f*; épuration *f*, nettoyage *m*; *vt* purger; (clean) nettoyer; épurer

**purification** *n* purification *f*, épuration *f*

**purificatory** *adj* purificatoire

**purify** *vt* purifier, épurer

**purism** *n* purisme *m*

**purist** *n* puriste

**Puritan** *n* + *adj* puritain -e

**Puritanism** *n* puritanisme *m*

**purity** *n* pureté *f*

**purl** *n* (lace) picot *m*; ~ **stitch** maille *f* à l'envers; *vt* (knitting) tricoter à l'envers; **knit one,** ~ **one** une maille à l'endroit, une maille à l'envers

**purloin** *vt* soustraire, détourner; voler, dérober

**purple** *n* pourpre *f*, violet *m*; *adj* violet -ette; ~ **passage** morceau *m* de bravoure

**purport** *n* sens *m*, signification *f*; *vt* impliquer, vouloir dire; ~ **to be** avoir la prétention d'être

**purpose** *n* but *m*, dessein *m*, intention *f*, fin *f*; **answer the** ~ répondre au but; **for the** ~ **of** dans le but de; **for this** ~ à cet effet; **on** ~ à dessein, exprès; **serve no** ~ ne servir à rien; **speak to the** ~ parler à propos; **to no** ~ en vain, inutile; **to some** ~ utilement; **to what** ~ ? à quoi bon? ; *vt* avoir l'intention

**purposeful** *adj* (person) tenace; (act) prémédité, réfléchi

**purposeless** *adj* inutile

**purposely** *adv* exprès, à dessein

**purr** *n* ronron *m*; (engine) ronflement *m*; *vi* ronronner; (engine) ronfler

¹**purse** *n* porte-monnaie *m invar*, bourse *f*; *sp* prix *m*; **well-lined** ~ bourse bien garnie

²**purse** *vt* ~ **one's lips** pincer les lèvres

**purser** n naut commissaire m
**purse-strings** npl fig hold the ~ tenir les cordons de la bourse
**pursue** vt poursuivre; (continue) continuer; (course) suivre; (seek) rechercher; ~ **a profession** exercer une profession
**pursuer** n poursuivant -e
**pursuit** n poursuite f; (knowledge) recherche f; (occupation) occupation f; **in** ~ **of** en quête de, à la recherche de; **set out in** ~ **of** se mettre à la poursuite de
**purulence** n purulence f
**purulent** adj purulent
**purvey** vt fournir, pourvoir
**purveyor** n fournisseur -euse, pourvoyeur -euse
**purview** n limites fpl, portée f
**pus** n pus m
**push** n poussée f; impulsion f; effort m; (go) allant m, dynamisme m; mil attaque f; coll **at a** ~ au besoin; **when it comes to the** ~ à l'instant critique; vt pousser; (goods) pousser la vente de; (advantage) poursuivre; (urge) presser; (push about) bousculer; (use influence for) pistonner; ~ **away** repousser, éloigner; ~ **forward** pousser en avant, faire avancer; ~ **in** enfoncer; ~ **oneself forward** se mettre en avant; ~ **out** pousser au dehors, faire sortir; ~ **through** faire passer à travers; (complete) terminer, mener à bien; ~ **up** relever; **be** ~**ed for money** être à court d'argent; vi pousser; ~ **forward** avancer; ~ **off** coll s'en aller; naut pousser au large; ~ **on** se remettre en route; continuer
**push-bike** n vélo m, bécane f
**push-button** n bouton m de contact
**push-cart** n charrette f à bras, poussette f
**push-chair** n fauteuil roulant
**pusher** n personne f qui pousse; (drugs) trafiquant -e; coll arriviste
**pushing, pushy** adj entreprenant
**pushover** n coll **it's a** ~ c'est du gâteau
**pusillanimity** n pusillanimité f
**pusillanimous** adj pusillanime
**puss, pussy** n minet m; **Puss in Boots** le Chat Botté
**pussy** n US vulg con m
**pustule** n pustule f
**¹put** vt mettre; (lay down) poser, déposer; (place) placer; (question) poser; (apply) appliquer; (express) dire; (estimate) évaluer; (resolution) présenter; naut ~ **about** virer; ~ **a matter right** arranger une affaire; ~ **aside** mettre de côté; (save) économiser; ~ **away** (tidy) ranger; (save) économiser; ~ **by**

(money) mettre de côté; (store up) mettre en réserve; ~ **down** déposer; (write) noter, mettre par écrit; (ascribe) attribuer; (person) humilier; (animal) endormir, abattre; ~ **forward** proposer; avancer; ~ **in** insérer, introduire; ~ **in a word** placer un mot; ~ **it to s/o** présenter la chose à qn; ~ **money on sth** parier sur qch; ~ **off** ôter, retirer; (postpone) remettre, différer; (disconcert) déconcerter; (discourage) décourager; ~ **on** mettre; (add) ajouter; (clock) avancer; (flesh) prendre; (light) allumer; (assume) prendre; (play) monter; ~ **out** mettre dehors, faire sortir; (hand) tendre; (fire) éteindre; (disturb) déranger, gêner; (upset) contrarier, vexer; (leaves, shoots) pousser; ~ **out one's tongue** tirer la langue; coll ~ **s/o on to sth** donner un tuyau à qn; ~ **the weight** lancer le poids; ~ **through** (complete) mener à bonne fin; (telephone) mettre en communication, passer; ~ **together** mettre ensemble, rassembler; (machine) monter; (compare) comparer; ~ **up** relever, lever; (install) installer; (fix) fixer; (lodge) loger; (offer) offrir, faire; (price) augmenter; (umbrella) ouvrir; ~ **up for sale** mettre en vente; **be hard** ~ **to it to** avoir fort à faire à; **I** ~ **it to you** je vous le demande; **to** ~ **it bluntly** pour parler franc; vi naut ~ **back** revenir au port; naut ~ **in faire relâche**; ~ **in for** poser sa candidature pour, postuler; ~ **into port** entrer au port, faire escale dans un port; naut ~ **off** pousser au large; ~ **to sea** prendre le large; ~ **up** loger; (at a hotel) descendre; ~ **up with s/o** supporter qn; ~ **up with sth** se résigner à qch
**²put** vt see **put(t)**
**putative** adj putatif -ive
**putrefaction** n putréfaction f
**putrefy** vt putréfier; vi se putréfier, pourrir
**putrescence** n putrescence f
**putrid** adj putride
**putsch** n putsch m
**put(t)** vt (golf) frapper très doucement
**puttees** npl bandes molletières fpl
**putty** n mastic m; vt mastiquer
**put-up** adj coll ~ **job** coup monté
**puzzle** n (mystery) énigme f; (dilemma) embarras m, perplexité f; (jigsaw) puzzle m; (problem) problème m, devinette f; **crossword** ~ problème m de mots croisés; vt intriguer; (confuse) embarrasser; ~ **out** éclaircir, déchiffrer, trouver la solution de; vi ~ **over sth** se creuser la tête pour comprendre qch

**puzzler** *n* question embarrassante; casse-tête *m invar*; (school) colle *f*
**pygmy, pigmy** *n* pygmée *m*
**pyjamas** *npl* pyjama *m*
**pylon** *n* pylône *m*
**pyorrhea** *n* pyorrhée *f*

**pyramid** *n* pyramide *f*
**pyre** *n* bûcher *m*
**pyrex** *n* pyrex *m*
**pyrotechnic** *adj* pyrotechnique
**python** *n* python *m*
**pyx** *n eccles* ciboire *m*

# Q

**qua** *adv* comme
¹**quack** *n* coin-coin *m invar*; *vi* faire coin-coin
²**quack** *n* (doctor) charlatan *m*
**quad** *n abbr* **quadrangle**; *abbr* **quadruplet**
**quadragenarian** *n* quadragénaire *m*
**quadrangle** *n geom* quadrilatère *m*; (school) cour *f*
**quadrant** *n* quart *m* de cercle, quadrant *m*
**quadratic** *adj* quadratique
**quadrille** *n* quadrille *m*
**quadruped** *n* quadrupède *m*
**quadruple** *adj* quadruple
**quadruplet** *n* quadruplé -e
**quaff** *vt* boire à grands traits; *coll* lamper
**quagmire** *n* fondrière *f*, marécage *m*
¹**quail** *n* caille *f*
²**quail** *vi* fléchir, faiblir, trembler
**quaint** *adj* bizarre, étrange; (old) vieillot -otte
**quake** *n* tremblement *m*; *coll* tremblement *m* de terre; *vi* trembler, frémir
**Quaker** *n* quaker -eresse *f*
**qualification** *n* qualification *f*; (for a post) qualité *f*, compétence *f*, aptitude *f*; (modification) réserve *f*, restriction *f*
**qualified** *adj* qualifié; diplômé; (authorised) autorisé; **be ~ to do sth** avoir les capacités pour faire qch
**qualify** *vt* qualifier; (make reservations) apporter des réserves à; (modify) modifier; **~ oneself for sth** acquérir la compétence nécessaire pour faire qch; **~ s/o to do sth** rendre qn propre à faire qch; *vi* se qualifier; **~ for (as)** passer l'examen de
**qualitative** *adj* qualitatif -ive
**quality** *n* qualité *f*; **~ products** produits *mpl* de qualité
**qualm** *n* scrupule *m*, remords *m*; (worry)

inquiétude *f*; nausée *f*; **without any ~ s** sans le moindre scrupule
**quandary** *n* embarras *m*, dilemme *m*; **be in a ~** ne trop savoir que faire
**quantify** *vt* quantifier; déterminer la quantité de
**quantitative** *adj* quantitatif -ive
**quantity** *n* quantité *f*
**quantity-surveyor** *n* métreur (vérificateur)
**quantum** *n* quantum *m*; **~ theory** théorie *f* des quanta
**quarantine** *n* quarantaine *f*; *vt* mettre en quarantaine
**quarrel** *n* querelle *f*, dispute *f*, brouille *f*; **have no ~ with s/o** n'avoir rien à reprocher à qn; **I have no ~ with that** je ne trouve rien à redire à cela; **pick a ~ with s/o** chercher querelle à qn; *vi* se quereller, se disputer; (find fault) trouver à redire
**quarrelsome** *adj* querelleur -euse, batailleur -euse
¹**quarry** *n* (pit) carrière *f*; *vt* tirer de la carrière; *vi* creuser une carrière
²**quarry** *n* (prey) proie *f*
**quart** *n* quart *m* (de gallon)
**quarter** *n* quart *m*; (district) quartier *m*; (three months) trimestre *m*; (meat, moon) quartier *m*; **~ s** logement *m*, appartements *mpl*; **~ of an hour** quart *m* d'heure; **a ~ past five** cinq heures et quart; **a ~ to four** quatre heures moins le (un) quart; **ask for ~** demander quartier; **at close ~ s** de près; **divide into ~ s** diviser en quartiers; **from all ~ s** de tous (les) côtés, de partout, de toutes parts; **give ~** faire quartier; **take up one's ~ s** s'installer; *vt* diviser en quatre; *mil* cantonner, loger; *leg + her* écarteler
**quarter-day** *n* jour *m* du terme, terme *m*

**quarter-deck** *n* gaillard *m* d'arrière

**quarterly** *adj* trimestriel -ielle

**quartermaster** *n mil* maréchal *m* des logis; *naut* quartier-maître *m* (*pl* quartiers-maîtres) de timonerie; *US* ~ **corps** service *m* de l'intendance

**quartet(te)** *n* quatuor *m*

**quarto** *n* in-quarto *m invar*

**quartz** *n* quartz *m*

**quasar** *n astron* quasar *m*

**quash** *vt* casser, annuler; (suppress) écraser

**quatrain** *n* quatrain *m*

**quaver** *n mus* croche *f*; *mus* (tremor) trille *f*; (trembling) tremblement *m*; *vi* (voice) trembloter, chevroter; (singer) faire des trilles

**quay** *n* quai *m*, appontement *m*

**queasy** *adj* sujet -ette à des nausées

**queen** *n* (cards) dame *f*; *coll* homosexuel *m*; ~ **bee** reine *f* des abeilles; **beauty** ~ reine *f* de beauté; *vi coll* ~ **it** faire la reine

**queenly** *adj* de reine

**¹queer** *n coll* homosexuel *m*, *sl* tapette *f*; *adj* étrange, bizarre, drôle; (unwell) peu bien; (suspicious) suspect; *coll* homosexuel -elle

**²queer** *vt* ~ **the pitch for s/o** faire échouer les plans de qn, mettre les bâtons dans les roues à qn

**quell** *vt* réprimer; (feeling) calmer; (passion) étouffer

**quench** *vt* (thirst) étancher; (fire) éteindre; *fig* refroidir

**querulous** *adj* plaintif -ive, maussade

**query** *n* question *f*; *vt* mettre en question, mettre en doute

**quest** *n* recherche *f*; **in** ~ **of** à la recherche de

**question** *n* question *f*; (doubt) doute *m*; **ask a** ~ poser une question; **beyond** ~ hors de question; **it is a** ~ **of** il s'agit de; **out of the** ~ impossible, exclu; **that's not the** ~ il ne s'agit pas de cela; **without** ~ sans aucun doute; *vt* questionner, interroger; (doubt) mettre en doute, mettre en question

**questionable** *adj* discutable; douteux -euse

**question-mark** *n* point *m* d'interrogation

**question-master** *n rad* + *TV* meneur *m* de jeu

**questionnaire** *n* questionnaire *m*

**queue** *n* queue *f*; **form a** ~ faire la queue; *vi* ~ **up** faire la queue

**quibble** *n* chicane *f*; *vi* chicaner, ergoter

**quibbling** *n* chicane *f*

**quick** *n* vif *m*; **cut s/o to the** ~ blesser qn au vif; **the** ~ les vivants *mpl*; *adj* rapide; prompt; (sharp) vif (*f* vive), éveillé; **as**

~ **as lightning** comme un éclair; **be** ~ faire vite, se dépêcher; **have a** ~ **ear** avoir l'oreille fine; **have a** ~ **temper** s'emporter facilement; **the** ~ **est way** le chemin le plus court; *adv* vite, rapidement

**quicken** *vt* (hasten) hâter, presser; (bring (back) to life) (r)animer; (stimulate) stimuler, exciter; *vi* (hope, etc) s'animer; (pace) devenir plus rapide; (foetus) donner des signes de vie

**quick-firing** *adj* à tir rapide

**quicklime** *n* chaux vive

**quickly** *adv* vite, rapidement

**quickness** *n* rapidité *f*, vitesse *f*; (ear) finesse *f*; (eye) acuité *f*; (mind) vivacité *f*

**quicksand** *n* sable mouvant

**quickset** *adj* ~ **hedge** haie vive

**quicksilver** *n* vif-argent *m*, mercure *m*

**quickstep** *n* (dance) fox-trot *m*

**quick-tempered** *adj* coléreux -euse

**quick-witted** *adj* à l'esprit prompt

**¹quid** *n coll* livre *f*

**²quid** *n* (tobacco) chique *f*

**quiescence** *n* repos *m*, tranquillité *f*

**quiescent** *adj* tranquille, en repos

**quiet** *n* tranquillité *f*; repos *m*, calme *m*; *adj* tranquille, calme; (silent) silencieux -ieuse; (character) doux (*f* douce); (unassuming) simple, sobre; (without worry) tranquille, sans inquiétude; **be** ~ **!** taisez-vous!; **keep** ~ se tenir tranquille; **on the** ~ en cachette, à la dérobée

**quiet(en)** *vt* calmer, apaiser, faire taire; (fears) dissiper

**quietly** *adv* tranquillement, doucement, silencieusement; **be married** ~ se marier dans l'intimité

**quietness** *n see* **quiet** *n*

**quietude** *n* quiétude *f*

**quiff** *n* mèche *f*

**quill** *n* (pen) plume *f*; (porcupine) piquant *m*

**quilt** *n* couvre-pieds *m invar*, couverture piquée *f*; *vt* capitonner, ouater, piquer

**quince** *n* coing *m*; (tree) cognassier *m*

**quinine** *n* quinine *f*

**quinquennial** *adj* quinquennal

**quins** *npl* quintuplé(e)s

**quinsy** *n* angine *f*

**quintessence** *n* quintessence *f*

**quintet(te)** *n* quintette *m*

**quintuple** *adj* quintuple

**quintuplet** *n* quintuplé -e

**quip** *n* repartie *f*, raillerie *f*, sarcasme *m*

**quire** *n* (paper) main *f*

**quirk** *n* équivoque *f*; (character) bizarrerie *f* de caractère

**quirky** *adj* **have** ~ **habits** avoir des habitudes vraiment bizarres

**¹quit** *adj* quitte; **be** ~ **for** en être quitte

pour; **be ~ of s/o (sth)** être débarrassé de qn (qch)

²**quit** *vt* quitter; (acquit) **~ oneself** se comporter; *vi coll* abandonner; ´*US* **~ doing sth** cesser de faire qch; **notice to ~** congé *m*

**quite** *adv* tout à fait, tout, entièrement; (at least) bien, au moins; (fairly) assez; **~ as much** tout autant; **~ a surprise** une vraie surprise; **~ right** tout à fait, très bien, très juste; **~ so** parfaitement; **it's been ~ a day!** quelle journée!

**quits** *adj* **we are ~** nous sommes quittes

**quitter** *n coll* lâcheur -euse

¹**quiver** *n* (arrows) carquois *m*

²**quiver** *n* tremblement *m*, frémissement *m*; (eyelid) battement *m*; *vi* trembler, frémir

**quixotic** *adj* exalté

**quiz** *n* quiz *m*; *vt* poser des colles à

**quizmaster** *n rad + TV* meneur *m* de jeu

**quizzical** *adj* (laughable) risible; (mocking) railleur -euse

**quod** *n sl* taule *f*

**quoit** *n* palet *m*

**quorum** *n* quorum *m*

**quota** *n* quote-part *f* ( *pl* quotes-parts)

**quotable** *adj* citable

**quotation** *n* citation *f*; (price) prix *m*, cours *m*

**quote** *n coll* quotation *f*; *vt* citer; **~ an example** fournir un exemple; **~ a price** fixer (établir) un prix

**quotient** *n math* quotient *m*

# R

**rabbi** *n* rabbin *m*

**rabbit** *n* lapin *m*; (person) poltron *m*; **tame ~** lapin *m* domestique; **wild ~** lapin *m* de garenne

**rabbit-hole** *n* terrier *m* de lapin

**rabbit-hutch** *n* clapier *m*

**rabbit-warren** *n* garenne *f*

**rabble** *n* cohue *f*; (populace) canaille *f*, populace *f*

**rabble-rouser** *n* agitateur -trice

**rabid** *adj* furieux -ieuse, acharné; (dog) enragé

**rabies** *n vet* rage *f*

¹**race** *n* course *f*; (water) raz *m*; **arms ~** course *f* aux armements; **long-distance ~** course *f* de fond; **run a ~** disputer une course; *vt* (person) lutter de vitesse avec; (horse) faire courir; *mot + eng* emballer; *vi* (go fast) filer à toute vitesse; faire la course; *mot + eng* s'emballer; **~ along** aller grand train

²**race** *n* (breed) race *f*, espèce *f*; (lineage) descendance *f*, lignée *f*; **~ relations** rapports *mpl* entre les races

**racecourse** *n* champ *m* de courses

**racegoer** *n* turfiste *f*

**racehorse** *n* cheval *m* de course

**racer** *n* coureur -euse; (horse) cheval *m* de course; (car) voiture *f* de course

**race-track** *n* piste *f*

**racial** *adj* racial; de race

**racialism** *n* racisme *m*

**racily** *adv* d'une façon piquante

**raciness** *n* (style) piquant *m*; (wine) bouquet *m*

**racing** *n* course *f*, courses *fpl*; (engine) emballement *m*; **~ car** voiture *f* de course

**racist, racialist** *n + adj* raciste

**rack** *n* (stable) râtelier *m*; (for coats) portemanteau *m*; (railway carriage) filet *m*; (car) porte-bagages *m*, galerie *f*; chevalet *m* (de torture); **~ and pinion** crémaillère *f*; **be on the ~** être au supplice; **go to ~ and ruin** tomber en ruine; *vt* tourmenter, torturer; (extort) extorquer; **~ one's brains** se creuser le cerveau

¹**racket** *n sp* raquette *f*

²**racket** *n* (din) vacarme *m*, tapage *m*; (swindle) escroquerie *f*; (crime) racket *m*; **stand the ~** subir les conséquences; *coll* payer les pots cassés; *vi* **~ about** faire du tapage

**racketeer** *n* gangster *m*, racketter *m*

**raconteur** *n* raconteur *m*

**racy** *adj* (person) vif ( *f* vive); **~ anecdote** anecdote savoureuse; **~ style** style plein de verve

**radar** *n* radar *m*; ~ **screen** écran *m* de radar

**raddled** *adj* grossièrement fardé

**radial** *n* (radial-ply tyre) pneu *m* à armature (carcasse) radiale; *adj* radial

**radiance, radiancy** *n* rayonnement *m*, éclat *m*

**radiant** *adj* (emit) émettre, dégager; *vi* rayonner

**radiate** *vt* (emit) émettre, dégager; *vi* rayonner

**radiation** *n* rayonnement *m*; (subjecting to) irradiation *f*; (emitting of rays) radiation *f*

**radiator** *n* radiateur *m*; **mot** ~ **cap** bouchon *m* de radiateur

**radical** *n* radical *m*; *adj* radical

**radio** *n* radio *f*, T.S.F. *f*; ~ **set** poste *m* de radio, radio *f*; ~ **station** poste émetteur (de) radio; *vt* radiotélégraphier, envoyer par radio

**radioactive** *adj* radio-actif -ive

**radioactivity** *n* radio-activité *f*

**radio-astronomy** *n* radio-astronomie *f*

**radio-control** *n* téléguidage *m*

**radio-controlled** *adj* téléguidé

**radiogram** *n* poste *m* de radio avec tourne-disques (pick-up)

**radiography** *n* radiographie *f*

**radiology** *n* radiologie *f*

**radiotherapy** *n* radiothérapie *f*

**radish** *n* radis *m*

**radium** *n* radium *m*

**radius** *n* rayon *m* (de cercle); *anat* radius *m*; **within a** ~ **of** dans un rayon de

**raffia** *n* raphia *m*

**raffle** *n* loterie *f*, tombola *f*; *vt* mettre en loterie

**raft** *n* radeau *m*

**rafter** *n* chevron *m*

¹**rag** *n* chiffon *m*; *coll* (newspaper) feuille *f* de chou; ~ **s** haillons *mpl*, guenilles *fpl*, loques*fpl*; **be in** ~ **s** être en guenilles; **the** ~ **trade** l'industrie *f* de l'habillement

²**rag** *n* chahut *m*, farce *f*; (student) monôme *m*; *vt* (teacher) chahuter; (fellow-student) brimer; *vi* chahuter

**ragamuffin** *n* gueux -euse; (rascal) mauvais garnement

**rag-and-bone** *n* ~ **man** chiffonnier *m*

**rag-bag** *n* *fig* mélange *m*

**rage** *n* rage *f*, fureur *f*; (mania) manie *f*; **be all the** ~ faire fureur; **fly into a** ~ s'emporter, se mettre en colère; *vi* être furieux -ieuse, rager; (wind) faire rage; (epidemic) sévir

**ragged** *adj* (person) en haillons; (torn) déchiré, en lambeaux; (disorderly) en désordre

**raging** *n* rage *f*, fureur *f*; *adj* furieux -ieuse; ~ **thirst** soif ardente

**ragtime** *n* rag-time *m*

**raid** *n* raid *m*; incursion *f*; (police) rafle *f*, descente *f* de police; (bandits) razzia *f*; *vt* (police) faire une rafle dans; faire une incursion dans; ~ **the larder** aller se servir dans le garde-manger

**raider** *n* pillard *m*; (plane) avion *m* en raid

¹**rail** *n* (bar) barre *f*; (stairs) rampe *f*; (railing) grille *f*; (railway) rail *m*; (parapet) garde-fou *m*, parapet *m*; (balcony) balustrade *f*; **British Rail** Chemins *mpl* de Fer Britanniques; **go off the** ~ **s** dérailler; **live** ~ rail conducteur (de contact); **send sth by** ~ envoyer qch par chemin de fer (par le rail); **travel by** ~ voyager en chemin de fer; *vt* ~ **in** fermer avec une grille, griller; entourer d'une grille; ~ **off** protéger par une grille; séparer avec une grille

²**rail** *vi* proférer des injures; ~ **at s/o** crier contre qn, s'en prendre à qn

**railhead** *n* tête *f* de ligne

**railing** *n* (abuse) injures *fpl*

**railing(s)** *n* grille *f*, palissade *f*

**raillery** *n* raillerie *f*

**railroad** *n* voie ferrée; *vt* *US* forcer; (bill) faire voter en vitesse

**railway** *n* chemin *m* de fer

**railwayman** *n* employé *m* des chemins de fer, cheminot *m*

**raiment** *n* habillement *m*

**rain** *n* pluie *f*; **driving** ~ pluie battante; **it looks like** ~ le temps est à la pluie; *vt* + *vi* pleuvoir; ~ **hard** pleuvoir à verse; **it is** ~ **ing** il pleut

**rainbow** *n* arc-en-ciel *m* (*pl* arcs-en-ciel)

**raincoat** *n* imperméable *m*

**raindrop** *n* goutte *f* de pluie

**rainfall** *n* précipitation *f*

**rain-gauge** *n* pluviomètre *m*

**rainproof** *adj* imperméable; *vt* imperméabiliser

**rainy** *adj* pluvieux -ieuse; ~ **season** saison *f* des pluies; **put sth by for a** ~ **day** garder une poire pour la soif

**raise** *n* *US* augmentation *f* (de salaire); *vt* lever, élever; (lift up) soulever; (pole, ladder, etc) dresser; (erect) ériger; (build) bâtir; (breed, bring up) élever; (produce) produire; (plants) cultiver; (cry) pousser; (prices, salary) augmenter; (money) se procurer; (dead) ressusciter; (hopes) faire naître; (objection) soulever; (spirit) évoquer; ~ **an army** lever une armée; ~ **one's glass to one's lips** porter son verre à ses lèvres; ~ **one's voice** élever la voix

**raisin** *n* raisin sec

¹**rake** *n* viveur *m*, noceur *m*

²**rake** *n* (slope) inclinaison *f*

³**rake** *n* (tool) râteau *m*; (fire) fourgon

*m*; **thin as a ~** maigre comme un clou; *vt* (leaves) ratisser; (soil) râteler; (guns) prendre en enfilade; (money) **~ in** amasser; **~ out the ashes** retirer les cendres du feu; **~ up the past** revenir sur le passé

**rake-off** *n* gratte *f*

**¹rakish** *adj* dissolu, libertin; **~ appearance** air *m* bravache

**²rakish** *adj naut* élancé

**¹rally** *n* ralliement *m*; *mot* rallye *m*; (health) reprise *f* des forces, retour *m* d'énergie; (prices) reprise *f*; *vt* rallier; *vi* se rallier; (health) reprendre des forces; (team) se reprendre

**²rally** *vt ar* (mock) railler

**ram** *n* bélier *m*; *naut* éperon *m*; *vt* cogner, heurter; (ship) éperonner; (stake) enfoncer; **~ down** (soil) tasser; (stake) enfoncer

**ramble** *n* excursion *f* à pied, promenade *f*, balade *f*; *vi* (wander) errer à l'aventure; faire des excursions à pied; (speech) divaguer

**rambler** *n* promeneur -euse; (rose) rosier grimpant

**rambling** *adj* vagabond, errant; (speech) décousu; **~ house** grande maison pleine de recoins

**ramification** *n* ramification *f*

**ramify** *vi* se ramifier

**¹ramp** *n* (on road) rampe *f*; (slope) pente *f*

**²ramp** *n comm* coup monté, combine *f*

**rampage** *n* **be on the ~** agir comme un fou (*f* une folle); *vi* se conduire comme un fou (*f* une folle)

**rampant** *adj* (person) déchaîné, violent; *her* rampant; (disease) **be ~** sévir

**rampart** *n* rempart *m*

**ramrod** *n* baguette *f* (de fusil); (cannon) écouvillon *m*; **straight as a ~** droit comme un piquet

**ramshackle** *adj* délabré

**ranch** *n US* ranch *m*; ferme *f* d'élevage

**rancid** *adj* rance

**rancorous** *adj* rancunier -ière

**rancour** *n* rancune *f*

**random** *n* **at ~** au hasard; *adj* fait (tiré) au hasard

**randy** *adj coll* porté sur la bagatelle, lascif -ive; *Scots* bruyant

**range** *n* (extent) étendue *f*; (reach) portée *f*; (mountain) chaîne *f*; (spread) gamme *f*; (plane) rayon *m* d'action, autonomie *f*; (salary) éventail *m*; *US* grand pâturage; (shooting) champ *m* de tir; (kitchen) fourneau *m*, cuisinière *f*; **at long ~** à longue portée; **out of ~** hors d'atteinte, hors de portée; *vt* ranger, aligner; (order) disposer en ordre;

(scan) parcourir; **~ oneself with s/o** se ranger du côté de qn; *vi* (extend) s'étendre; (wander) errer; (vary) varier; **~ over** (roam) parcourir; (cover) s'étendre sur

**range-finder** *n* télémètre *m*

**ranger** *n* garde forestier; gardien *m*; *US* ranger *m*

**¹rank** *n* rang *m*; (social) classe *f*; *mil* grade *m*; (taxis) station *f*; **close ~s** serrer les rangs; *mil* **other ~s** simples soldats *mpl*; **the ~ and file** *mil* les simples soldats *mpl*; le commun des mortels; *vt* ranger, compter; *vi* se ranger, être classé; **he ~s among the finest writers** il compte parmi les meilleurs écrivains

**²rank** *adj* (growth) luxuriant; (fierce) violent, fort; (smell) répugnant; (downright) vrai; (rancid) rance

**rankle** *vi* rester sur le cœur, ronger le cœur

**ransack** *vt* saccager, piller; (search) fouiller (dans)

**ransom** *n* rançon *f*; **hold s/o to ~** rançonner qn; *vt* racheter, payer la rançon de; (hold to ransom) mettre à rançon, rançonner

**rant** *n* déclaration extravagante, rodomontade *f*; *vi* déclarer avec extravagance

**¹rap** *n* tape *f*, petit coup; *vt* frapper, donner un petit coup à; *vi* **~ at** donner un (petit) coup à

**²rap** *n coll* **not care a ~** s'en ficher

**rapacious** *adj* rapace

**rapacity** *n* rapacité *f*

**¹rape** *n* viol *m*; *vt* violer

**²rape** *n bot* colza *m*

**rapid** *n geog* rapide *m*; *adj* rapide

**rapidity** *n* rapidité *f*, vitesse *f*

**rapidly** *adv* rapidement

**rapier** *n* rapière *f*

**rapist** *n* auteur *m* d'un viol, violeur *m*

**rapprochement** *n* rapprochement *m*

**rapt** *adj* (delighted) ravi; (absorbed) absorbé

**rapture** *n* ravissement *m*; **go into ~s over** s'extasier sur

**rapturous** *adj* d'extase, frénétique

**¹rare** *adj* rare; *coll* (famous) fameux -euse

**²rare** *adj* (steak) saignant

**rarebit** *n* **Welsh ~ (rabbit)** fondue *f* au fromage sur canapé

**rarefy** *vt* raréfier

**rarely** *adv* rarement

**rareness** *n* rareté *f*

**rarity** *n* rareté *f*; (thing) chose *f* rare

**rascal** *n* coquin -e, fripon -onne

**rascally** *adj* vilain, de coquin

**¹rash** *n* éruption *f*

²**rash** *adj* téméraire, imprudent, ir-réfléchi

**rasher** *n* tranche *f* de lard

**rashness** *n* témérité *f*, imprudence *f*, étourderie *f*

**rasp** *n* râpe *f*; *vt* râper; *vi* grincer; *fig* irriter

**raspberry** *n* framboise *f*; *fig* rebuffade *f*; **give s/o a ~** engueuler qn

**rat** *n* rat *m*; **~ poison** mort *f* aux rats; **smell a ~** flairer un piège, soupçonner quelque anguille sous roche; *vi* faire la chasse aux rats; *coll fig* abandonner son parti (ses amis); **~ on s/o** vendre qn

**ratable** *adj see* **rateable**

**rat-catcher** *n* preneur *m* de rats

**ratchet** *n* cliquet *m*

¹**rate** *n* (speed) vitesse *f*, allure *f*; nombre proportionnel, taux *m*; (exchange) cours *m*; **~s** impôts locaux; **~ of interest** taux *m* d'intérêt; **at that ~** à ce taux-là, à ce compte-là; **at the ~ he's going** au train où il va; **at the ~ of** à raison de; **bank ~** taux *m* d'escompte; **birth ~** (taux *m* de la) natalité *f*; **growth ~** taux *m* de croissance; *vt* estimer, évaluer; (assess) taxer; (consider) considérer; *vi* être classé

²**rate** *vt* (scold) tancer, gronder

**rateable, ratable** *adj* imposable

**rate-collector** *n* receveur municipal

**ratepayer** *n* contribuable

**rather** *adv* plutôt; (somewhat) un peu, assez; (preferably) de préférence; **I would ~** j'aimerais mieux; **I would ~ not** veuillez m'excuser; *interj* et comment!, pour sûr!

**ratification** *n* ratification *f*

**ratify** *vt* ratifier

**rating** *n* évaluation *f*; classement *m*; *sp* classe *f*; (scolding) semonce *f*; (navy) classe *f*; (navy) **~s** les matelots *mpl* et gradés

**ratio** *n* proportion *f*, rapport *m*

**ration** *n* ration *f*; *vt* rationner

**rational** *adj* raisonnable; (able to think) doué de raison; (reasoned) raisonné

**rationale** *n* analyse raisonnée

**rationalism** *n* rationalisme *m*

**rationalist** *n* rationaliste

**rationality** *n* rationalité *f*

**rationalization** *n* rationalisation *f*

**rationalize** *vt* rationaliser

**rationally** *adv* raisonnablement

**ration-book** *n* carte *f* d'alimentation

**rat-race** *n coll* foire *f* d'empoigne, course *f* au biftck

**rattle** *n* crécelle *f*, (child's toy) hochet *m*; (noise) bruit *m*, fracas *m*; (metal) cliquetis *m*; (death) râle *m*; *vt* agiter avec bruit; (metal) faire cliqueter; (shake) secouer; *coll fig* consterner; *vi* (metal) cliqueter; (windows) trembler; (be noisy) faire du bruit; *med* râler

**rattler, rattlesnake** *n* serpent *m* à sonnettes

**rattling** *n* bruit *m*, fracas *m*; (metal) cliquetis *m*; *adj* bruyant; (fine) épatant; *coll* **at a ~ pace** à vive allure

**ratty** *adj* infesté de rats; *coll* fâché

**raucous** *adj* rauque

**ravage** *n* ravage *m*; *vt* ravager, dévaster

**rave** *n coll* louange *f* enthousiaste; *sl* béguin *m*; **~ notices** (review) critique très élogieuse; *vi* être en délire; *coll* battre la campagne; **~ about sth** s'extasier sur qch; **~ at s/o** pester (tempêter) contre qn

**ravel** *vt* embrouiller, emmêler; *vi* s'embrouiller

**raven** *n* corbeau *m*

**ravenous** *adj* vorace; **be ~** avoir une faim de loup

**ravine** *n* ravin *m*

**raving** *adj* **~ mad** fou furieux (*f* folle furieuse)

**ravioli** *n* ravioli *mpl*

**ravish** *vt* ravir; (kidnap) enlever; (rape) violer

**ravishing** *adj* ravissant, enchanteur -eresse

**raw** *adj* cru; (inexperienced) sans expérience; (wound) à vif; (uncouth) grossier -ière; (weather) froid et humide; (commodity) brut; **~ materials** matières premières; **it's a ~ deal** c'est dur à avaler; **touch s/o on the ~** piquer qn au vif

**raw-boned** *adj* décharné, maigre

**rawhide** *n* cuir vert; *adj* en cuir vert

¹**ray** *n* rayon *m*

²**ray** *n* (fish) raie *f*

**rayon** *n* rayonne *f*

**raze** *vt* raser, démolir

**razor** *n* rasoir *m*; **~ blade** lame *f* de rasoir; **safety ~** rasoir *m* de sûreté

**razor-edge** *n* fil *m* du rasoir

**reach** *n* (of hand) extension *f*; (extent) étendue *f*, portée *f*, atteinte *f*; **out of ~** (range) hors de portée; (safety) hors d'atteinte; **within easy ~ of** tout près de, à proximité de; **within one's ~** à sa portée; **within ~ of everyone** accessible à tous; *vt* (place) arriver à; (goal) atteindre; (give) passer, donner; *vi* (extend) s'étendre; **~ down to** descendre jusqu'à; **~ out (with one's hand) for sth** avancer la main pour prendre qch; **~ to** arriver à; **~ up to** monter jusqu'à

**reach-me-downs** *npl coll* costume *m* de confection; *coll* **wear ~** s'habiller au décrochez-moi-ça

**react** *vi* réagir

**reaction** *n* réaction *f*

**reactionary** *adj* réactionnaire

**reactor** *n* réacteur *m*

**read** *n* **have a quiet ~** lire tranquillement; *vt* lire; (study at university) étudier; **~ aloud** lire à haute voix; **~ into** trouver un sens caché dans; **~ law** faire son droit; **~ on** continuer de lire; **~ the gas meter** relever le compteur à gaz; **~ through** parcourir; **~ up** étudier; *vi* **~ to s/o** faire la lecture à qn; **this story ~s like a poem** cette histoire fait l'effet d'un poème

**readable** *adj* lisible

**readdress** *vt* (letter) faire suivre; changer l'adresse de

**reader** *n* liseur -euse, lecteur -trice; (proofs) correcteur -trice; (book) livre *m* de lecture; (university) = maître *m* de conférences

**readership** *n* nombre *m* de lecteurs, public *m*

**readily** *adv* volontiers, avec empressement

**readiness** *n* empressement *m*; promptitude *f*; (ease) facilité *f*

**reading** *n* lecture *f*; (interpretation) interprétation *f*; (meter) relevé *m*; (instruments) observation *f*

**reading-desk** *n* pupitre *m*

**reading-lamp** *n* lampe *f* de bureau

**reading-room** *n* salle *f* de lecture

**readjust** *vt* rajuster; (ways) réadapter; *vi* se réadapter

**readmission, readmittance** *n* réadmission *f*

**readmit** *vt* réadmettre

**readmittance** *n see* **readmission**

**ready** *n sl* fric *m*; *adj* prêt; (and willing) disposé; (eager) empressé; (finished) fini; (quick) prompt; (near) sous la main; (meal) servi; (prone) porté; **~ money** argent comptant; **~ reckoner** barème *m*; **make ~** se préparer, s'apprêter

**ready-made** *adj* tout fait; (clothes) de confection

**ready-to-wear** *adj* prêt-à-porter

**reaffirm** *vt* réaffirmer

**real** *adj* réel -elle; (true) vrai; (genuine) véritable, authentique; **~ estate** propriété immobilière; **~ silk** soie naturelle; *adv US coll* très

**realism** *n* réalisme *m*

**realist** *n* réaliste

**realistic** *adj* réaliste

**reality** *n* réalité *f*

**realizable** *adj* réalisable; imaginable

**realization** *n* réalisation *f*

**realize** *vt* (achieve) réaliser; (understand) se rendre compte de, bien comprendre, prendre conscience de

**really** *adv* vraiment, réellement

**realm** *n* royaume *m*; *fig* domaine *m*

**realty** *n US* propriété immobilière

¹**ream** *n* rame *f*

²**ream** *vt metal* aléser

**reap** *vt* moissonner, récolter; *fig* recueillir; (advantage) retirer; **we ~ as we sow** on recueille ce qu'on a semé

**reaper** *n* moissonneur -euse

**reappear** *vi* réapparaître, reparaître

**reappoint** *vt* réintégrer dans ses fonctions

¹**rear** *n* arrière *m*, derrière *m*; (end) dernier rang *m*, queue *f*; *mil* arrière-garde *f*; *mil* **bring up the ~** fermer la marche; *adj* de derrière, arrière; **at the ~ end of the train** en queue du train

²**rear** *vt* élever; (plants) cultiver; *vi* (horse) se cabrer

**rear-admiral** *n* contre-amiral *m*

**rearguard** *n* arrière-garde *f*

**rearm** *vt* réarmer

**rearmament** *n* réarmement *m*

**rearmost** *adj* dernier -ière

**rearrange** *vt* réarranger, arranger de nouveau

**rear-view** *adj mot* **~ mirror** rétroviseur *m*

**rearward** *adj* situé à l'arrière

**rearwards** *adv* à l'arrière; vers l'arrière

**rear-window** *n mot* lunette *f* arrière

**reason** *n* raison *f*, cause *f*; motif *m*; (good sense) bon sens; **all the more ~ for doing it** raison de plus pour le faire; **by ~ of** à cause de; **for no ~** sans motif; **for the same ~** au même titre; **for (very) good ~** et pour cause; **have ~ to be glad** avoir sujet d'être content; **it stands to ~** cela va de soi; **listen to ~** entendre raison; **with good ~** à bon droit, à juste titre; **within ~** jusqu'à un certain point, raisonnablement; *vi* raisonner, arguer; **try to ~ with him** essayez de le raisonner

**reasonable** *adj* raisonnable

**reasoning** *n* raisonnement *m*; *adj* doué de raison

**reassemble** *vt* rassembler, assembler de nouveau; (machine) remonter; *vi* se rassembler

**reassert** *vt* réaffirmer

**reassessment** *n* réévaluation *f*

**reassurance** *n* action *f* de rassurer

**reassure** *vt* rassurer, tranquilliser

**rebate** *n* rabais *m*; (refund) remboursement *m*, ristourne *f*

**rebel** *n* rebelle, insurgé -e; *adj* insurgé, rebelle; *vi* se rebeller, se révolter

**rebellion** *n* rébellion *f*, révolte *f*

**rebellious** *adj* rebelle

**rebirth** *n* renaissance *f*

**rebore** n mech réalésage m; vt mech réaléser
**reborn** adj né de nouveau
**rebound** n rebondissement m; vi rebondir
**rebuff** n rebuffade f; (setback) échec m; vt repousser
**rebuild** vt reconstruire, rebâtir
**rebuilding** n reconstruction f
**rebuke** n réprimande f; vt réprimander
**rebus** n rébus m
**rebut** vt réfuter
**rebuttal** n réfutation f
**recalcitrance** n récalcitrance f
**recalcitrant** adj récalcitrant
**recall** n rappel m; **beyond ~** irrévocablement; vt rappeler; (remember) se rappeler; (evoke) évoquer
**recant** vt rétracter, abjurer; vi se rétracter
**recantation** n rétractation f, abjuration f
**recap** n coll récapitulation f; vt + vi coll récapituler
**recapitulate** vt récapituler
**recapitulation** n récapitulation f
**recapture** n reprise f; vt reprendre
**recast** vt metal refondre; theat faire une nouvelle distribution des rôles de
**recce** n coll mil reconnaissance f
**recede** vi s'éloigner, se retirer
**receding** adj qui s'éloigne; **~ forehead** front fuyant
**receipt** n réception f; (for money) reçu m, quittance f, récépissé m; US cul recette f; **~s** recettes fpl; **acknowledge ~ of** accuser réception de; **on ~ of** au reçu de; **pay on ~** payer à la réception
**receive** vt recevoir; (stolen goods) receler; **~d with thanks** pour acquit
**receiver** n personne f qui reçoit; (letters) destinataire; (administration) receveur -euse; (stolen goods) receleur -euse; (telephone) récepteur m; rad poste m (récepteur de radio)
**recent** adj récent
**receptacle** n récipient m
**reception** n réception f; (welcome) accueil m; **~ centre** centre m d'accueil; (hotel) **~ desk** réception f; **~ room** salle f de réception; (flat, house) pièce f
**receptionist** n réceptionniste
**receptive** adj réceptif -ive
**receptivity** n réceptivité f
**recess** n (building, wall) recoin m, enfoncement m; (window) embrasure f; (holiday) vacances fpl; vt pratiquer un enfoncement dans
**recession** n (withdrawing) recul m, retraite f; econ récession f
**recharge** n recharge f; vt recharger
**recidivism** n rechute f, récidive f
**recipe** n recette f

**recipient** n personne f qui reçoit; (letter) destinataire; (gift) donataire
**reciprocal** adj réciproque
**reciprocate** vt (feeling) payer de retour; (service) se rendre mutuellement; vi retourner le compliment; rendre la pareille
**reciprocation** n action f de payer de retour, retour m
**reciprocity** n réciprocité f
**recital** n (story) narration f, récit m; (poetry) récitation f; mus récital m
**recitative** n mus récitatif m
**recite** vt réciter, raconter
**reciter** n déclamateur m
**reckless** adj (bold) téméraire; (careless) insouciant; (incautious) imprudent
**recklessness** n insouciance f; manque m de précaution
**reckon** vt + vi compter, calculer; (estimate) estimer, juger; **~ up** additionner, calculer; vi **~ with s/o** compter avec qn
**reckoner** n (person) calculateur -trice; barème m
**reckoning** n compte m, calcul m; (bill) note f; fig expiation f
**reclaim** vt (person) réformer; (land) défricher
**reclamation** n (persons) réforme f; (land) défrichement m; réclamation f
**recline** vt appuyer, reposer; vi être couché, être appuyé
**reclining** adj étendu, allongé; **~ seat** siège m réglable
**recluse** n + adj reclus -e, solitaire
**recognition** n reconnaissance f; **beyond ~** méconnaissable
**recognizable** adj reconnaissable
**recognize** vt reconnaître; (admit) admettre, avouer
**recoil** n recul m; mouvement m de recul; vi reculer; (spring) se détendre; fig retomber
**recollect** vt se rappeler, se souvenir de
**recollection** n souvenir m, mémoire f; **to the best of my ~** autant que je m'en souvienne
**recommence** vt recommencer
**recommend** vt recommander; **have little to ~ one** n'avoir pas grand-chose pour soi; **not to be ~ed** à déconseiller
**recommendable** adj recommandable
**recommendation** n recommandation f
**recompense** n récompense f; (damage) dédommagement m; vt récompenser; dédommager; (service) payer de retour
**recompose** vt recomposer
**reconcilable** adj conciliable
**reconcile** vt réconcilier; (facts) concilier; **~ oneself** se résigner; **~ s/o to sth** faire accepter qch à qn

**reconciliation** *n* réconciliation *f*; (opinions, facts) conciliation *f*

**recondite** *adj* abstrus; (obscure) mystérieux -ieuse; (style) obscur

**recondition** *vt* rénover, remettre à neuf

**reconnaissance** *n* reconnaissance *f*

**reconnoitre** *vt mil* reconnaître; *vi* faire une reconnaissance

**reconsider** *vt* reconsidérer, considérer de nouveau; (problem) repenser; (decision) revenir sur

**reconstitute** *vt* reconstituer

**reconstruct** *vt* reconstruire, rebâtir; (crime) reconstituer

**reconstruction** *n* reconstruction *f*

**reconversion** *n* reconversion *f*

**record** *n* enregistrement *m*; (written) registre *m*; (mention) mention *f*; *sp* record *m*; (gramophone) disque *m*; (of sth) souvenir *m*; (police) dossier *m*; (career) carrière *f*, passé *m*; **break the ~** battre le record; **have a clean ~** avoir un casier judiciaire vierge; **hold the ~** détenir le record; **make a ~ of sth** noter qch; **off the ~** à titre confidentiel; entre nous; **Public Record Office** = Archives Nationales; *adj* record *invar*; *vt* enregistrer; (note down) consigner par écrit; (report) rapporter

**record-breaking** *adj* qui bat tous les records

**recorder** *n* magnétophone *m*; *mus* flûte *f* à bec; archiviste; *leg* magistrat *m*

**record-holder** *n* recordman (*f* recordwoman)

**recording** *n* enregistrement *m*; **~ head** tête enregistreuse

**record-player** *n* tourne-disque *m*, électrophone *m*

**recount** *vt* (narrate) raconter

**re-count** *n* (votes) nouveau dépouillement du scrutin; *vt* recompter

**recoup** *vt* rembourser, dédommager; **~ one's losses** se rattraper de ses pertes

**recourse** *n* recours *m*; **have ~ to sth** recourir à qch

**recover** *vt* (get back) recouvrer, regagner; (appetite) retrouver; **~ lost ground** reprendre le terrain perdu; **lost time** rattraper le temps perdu; **~ one's balance** retrouver son équilibre; **~ one's breath** reprendre haleine; **~ one's health** se rétablir, guérir; *vi* (health) se rétablir, se remettre, guérir; (prices) se relever

**re-cover** *vt* recouvrir; (upholstery) regarnir

**recoverable** *adj* recouvrable

**recovery** *n* (getting back) recouvrement *m*; (health) rétablissement *m*, guérison *f*; *econ* redressement *m*; **be past ~** être dans un état désespéré

**recreant** *n* apostat *m*

**re-create** *vt* recréer

**recreation** *n* récréation *f*, divertissement *m*

**recreational, recreative** *adj* récréatif -ive

**recriminate** *vi* récriminer

**recrimination** *n* récrimination *f*

**recriminatory** *adj* récriminatoire

**recrudescence** *n* recrudescence *f*

**recruit** *n* recrue *f*; *vt* recruter

**recruiting-officer** *n* officier recruteur

**recruitment** *n* recrutement *m*

**rectal** *adj* rectal

**rectangle** *n* rectangle *m*

**rectangular** *adj* rectangulaire

**rectifiable** *adj* rectifiable

**rectification** *n* rectification *f*

**rectifier** *n* rectificateur *m*

**rectify** *vt* rectifier, corriger; (omission) réparer

**rectilineal** *adj* rectiligne

**rectitude** *n* rectitude *f*; (character) droiture *f*

**recto** *n* recto *m*

**rector** *n* (priest) curé *m*; *Scots* (headmaster) directeur *m*

**rectum** *n* rectum *m*

**recumbent** *adj* couché

**recuperable** *adj* recouvrable

**recuperate** *vt* remettre, rétablir; *vi* se remettre, se rétablir

**recuperation** *n* récupération *f*

**recuperative** *adj* (beneficial) restauratif -ive; **~ powers** pouvoirs *mpl* de rétablissement

**recur** *vi* revenir; (event) se reproduire; (opportunity) se représenter

**recurrence** *n* réapparition *f*, retour *m*

**recurrent, recurring** *adj* périodique, qui revient souvent

**red** *n* rouge *m*; *coll* **be in the ~** avoir une balance (un compte) déficitaire; *adj* rouge; (hair) roux (*f* rousse); (lips) vermeil -eille; *fig* **~ tape** paperasserie *f*; tracasseries administratives; **go (turn) ~** rougir; *coll* **see ~** voir rouge

**red-blooded** *adj* (person) vigoureux -euse

**redbreast** *n* rouge-gorge *m* (*pl* rouges-gorges)

**red-cap** *n coll mil* soldat *m* de la police militaire

**redden** *vt* + *vi* rougir

**reddish** *adj* rougeâtre

**redecorate** *vt* repeindre

**redeem** *vt* (buy back) racheter; (from pawn) retirer, dégager; (promise) tenir; (debt) amortir

**redeemable** *adj* rachetable, amortissable, remboursable

**Redeemer** *n* Rédempteur *m*

**redemption** *n* rédemption *f*; remboursement *m*, amortissement *m*; rachat *m*

**red-haired** *adj* roux (*f* rousse)

**red-handed** *adj* **be caught** ~ être pris en flagrant délit, être pris la main dans le sac

**red-head** *n* rouquin -e

**red-hot** *adj* (chauffé au) rouge; *fig* ardent; (person) acharné

**redirect** *vt* (letter) faire suivre

**rediscover** *vt* redécouvrir

**redistribute** *vt* redistribuer

**redistribution** *n* redistribution *f*

**red-lead** *n* minium *m*

**red-letter** *adj* ~ **day** jour *m* mémorable

**redness** *n* rougeur *f*; (hair) rousseur *f*

**redo** *vt* refaire

**redolence** *n* parfum *m*, odeur *f* suave

**redolent** *adj* odorant, parfumé; *fig* ~ **of** évocateur -trice de

**redouble** *vt* + *vi* redoubler

**redoubt** *n* redoute *f*

**redoubtable** *adj* redoutable, formidable

**redound** *vi* contribuer, résulter

**redress** *n* réparation *f*, redressement *m*; (abuse) réforme *f*; **seek** ~ demander justice; *vt* (balance) rétablir; (wrong) réparer; (abuse) réformer

**redskin** *n* peau-rouge (*pl* peaux-rouges)

**reduce** *vt* réduire, diminuer; (length) raccourcir; (attenuate) atténuer; (humiliate) ravaler; ~ **speed** ralentir; *mil* ~ **to the ranks** casser; **be** ~**d to doing sth** en être réduit à faire qch; *vi* maigrir

**reducible** *adj* réductible

**reduction** *n* réduction *f*, diminution *f*; (making smaller) rapetissement *m*; (temperature) baisse *f*; *comm* rabais *m*, remise *f*

**redundance, redundancy** *n* surabondance *f*, surplus *m*, excédent *m*; (style) redondance *f*; (unemployment) licenciement *m*

**redundant** *adj* surabondant; (style) redondant; (person) **be** ~ être en surnombre; (unemployed) être licencié, être au chômage

**reduplicate** *vt* redoubler, répéter

**reduplication** *n* redoublement *m*

**redwood** *n bot* séquoia *m*

**re-echo** *vt* (repeat) répéter; *vi* retentir, résonner

**reed** *n bot* roseau *m*; (pipe) chalumeau *m*; *mus* anche *f*

**re-edit** *vt* rééditer

**re-educate** *vt* rééduquer

**reedy** *adj* plein de roseaux, couvert de roseaux; ~ **voice** voix flûtée

¹**reef** *n* récif *m*; **submerged** ~ écueil *m*

²**reef** *n naut* ris *m*; *vt* prendre un ris dans

**reefer** *n sl* cigarette *f* de marijuana

**reef-knot** *n* nœud plat

**reek** *n* exhalaison *f*; odeur forte; *vi* fumer; exhaler une mauvaise odeur; ~ **of sth**

puer (empester) qch

¹**reel** *n* (cotton, etc) bobine *f*; (winder) dévidoir *m*; (fishing-line) moulinet *m*; (film) rouleau *m*; *vt* (wind) dévider, bobiner; *fig* ~ **off sth** réciter qch d'un trait

²**reel** *n* (dance) danse écossaise; *vi* tournoyer; (totter) chanceler, tituber; **my head** ~**s** la tête me tourne

**re-elect** *vt* réélire

**re-embark** *vt* + *vi* rembarquer

**re-enact** *vt* reproduire; (law) remettre en vigueur

**re-engage** *vt* rengager

**re-enter** *vt* rentrer dans; (on document) réinscrire; *vi* rentrer

**re-entry** *n* rentrée *f*

**re-establish** *vt* rétablir

**re-examination** *n* nouvel examen

**re-examine** *vt* examiner à nouveau

**re-export** *vt* réexporter

**ref** *n coll* arbitre *m*

**reface** *vt* (building) ravaler

**refashion** *vt* refaçonner

**refectory** *n* réfectoire *m*

**refer** *vt* rapporter; (send back) renvoyer; (submit) soumettre; ~ **a matter to s/o** s'en référer à qn d'une question; ~ **s/o to s/o** adresser qn à qn; *vi* se référer; (be relevant) se rapporter, avoir trait; (allude) faire allusion; **I won't** ~ **to it again** je n'en reparlerai plus

**referee** *n* arbitre *m*; (sponsor) répondant *m*; *vt* ~ **a match** arbitrer un match

**reference** *n* référence *f*; renvoi *m*; (allusion) allusion *f*; (relation) rapport *m*; **give s/o as a** ~ se recommander de qn; **terms of** ~ mandat *m*; **with** ~ **to** en ce qui concerne; **with** ~ **to my letter of** comme suite à ma lettre de; **work of** ~ ouvrage *m* à consulter, instrument *m* de travail

**referendum** *n* référendum *m*, referendum *m*

**refill** *n* objet *m* de rechange; (pen) recharge *f*; (battery) pile *f* de rechange; (pencil) mine *f* de rechange; (file) feuilles *fpl* de rechange; *vt* remplir (à nouveau)

**refine** *vt* raffiner, affiner; (purify) épurer

**refined** *adj* raffiné; (person) distingué

**refinement** *n* (action) raffinage *m*; (taste) raffinement *m*; (person) distinction *f*, raffinement *m*

**refinery** *n* raffinerie *f*

**refit** *n* rajustement *m*; *naut* radoub *m*; *vt* rajuster; *naut* radouber, réarmer; (factory) réaménager

**reflect** *vt* refléter, réfléchir; *vi* réfléchir, méditer

**reflection, reflexion** *n* réflexion *f*; reflet *m*, image *f*; **cast a** ~ **on s/o** critiquer qn;

on ~ réflexion faite; **that's a ~ on his honour** cela porte atteinte à son honneur

**reflective** *adj* réfléchissant; (person) réfléchi

**reflector** *n* réflecteur *m*; *mot US* (on road) cataphote *m*

**reflex** *n* réflexe *m*; *adj* réflexe

**reflexion** *n* see reflection

**reflexive** *adj* *gramm* réfléchi

**refloat** *vt* renflouer

**reform** *n* réforme *f*; *vt* réformer, corriger; *vi* se réformer, se corriger

**re-form** *vt* reformer; *vi* se reformer

**reformation** *n* réformation *f*; *eccles* réforme *f*

**reformative** *adj* ~ **measures** mesures *fpl* de réforme

**reformatory** *n* maison *f* de correction

**reformer** *n* réformateur -trice

**refract** *vt* réfracter

**refraction** *n* réfraction *f*

**refractory** *adj* réfractaire, indocile, insoumis

¹**refrain** *n* refrain *m*

²**refrain** *vi* se retenir, s'abstenir; **he can't ~ from talking** il ne peut s'empêcher de bavarder

**refresh** *vt* rafraîchir; (rest) délasser

**refresher** *n* chose *f* qui rafraîchit; (fees) supplément *m* d'honoraires; ~ **course** cours *m* de perfectionnement

**refreshing** *adj* rafraîchissant; *fig* agréable

**refreshment** *n* rafraîchissement *m*; (rest) délassement *m*; (railway) ~ **room** buffet *m*

**refrigerate** *vt* réfrigérer, frigorifier

**refrigeration** *n* réfrigération *f*, frigorification *f*

**refrigerator** *n* réfrigérateur *m*, frigidaire *m*, *coll* frigo *m*

**refuel** *vt* réapprovisionner en combustible (en essence, en fuel); *vi* se réapprovisionner en combustible (en fuel); *mot* prendre de l'essence, faire le plein d'essence

**refuge** *n* refuge *m*, abri *m*; lieu *m* de refuge; **seek ~** chercher refuge; **take ~** se réfugier

**refugee** *n* réfugié -e

**refulgence** *n* éclat *m*, splendeur *f*

**refulgent** *adj* éclatant, resplendissant

**refund** *n* remboursement *m*; (rebate) ristourne *f*; *vt* rembourser; (rebate) ristourner; restituer; ~ **s/o** rembourser qn

**refurbish** *vt* remettre à neuf

**refurnish** *vt* remeubler

**refusal** *n* refus *m*; **a flat ~** un refus net; **meet with a ~** essuyer un refus

¹**refuse** *n* rebut *m*, déchets *mpl*, ordures *fpl*; ~ **bin** poubelle *f*; ~ **dump** décharge (publique) *f*; **household ~** ordures ménagères

²**refuse** *vt* refuser; (reject) rejeter; ~ **s/o sth** refuser qch à qn; ~ **to do sth** refuser de faire qch; *vi* refuser

**refutation** *n* réfutation *f*

**refute** *vt* réfuter

**regain** *vt* regagner; (health) recouvrer; ~ **consciousness** reprendre connaissance

**regal** *adj* royal

**regale** *vt* régaler

**regalia** *n* insignes *mpl* de la royauté; *joc* atours *mpl*

**regally** *adv* royalement

**regard** *n* (consideration) égard *m*; (esteem) respect *m*, estime *f*; **give my kind ~s to** faites mes amitiés à; **have no ~ for** faire peu de cas de; **having ~ to** eu égard à; **in this ~** à cet égard; **out of ~ for** par égard pour; **with ~ to** pour ce qui concerne; *vt* considérer; (take into consideration) tenir compte de; (concern) concerner; **as ~s** en ce qui concerne

**regarding** *prep* quant à, à l'égard de, concernant

**regardless** *adj* inattentif -ive; peu soigneux -euse; ~ **of** sans se soucier de; ~ **of expense** sans regarder à la dépense

**regatta** *n* régates *fpl*

**regency** *n* régence *f*

**regenerate** *vt* régénérer

**regeneration** *n* régénération *f*

**regent** *n* régent -e

**regicide** *n* (person) régicide; (crime) régicide *m*

**régime** *n* régime *m*

**regimen** *n* régime *m*

**regiment** *n* régiment *m*; *vt* enrégimenter

**regimental** *adj* du régiment, régimentaire

**regimentation** *n* réglementation *f*

**region** *n* région *f*; **in the ~ of five hundred francs** dans les cinq cents francs

**regional** *adj* régional

**register** *n* registre *m*; matricule *f*; ~ **of voters** liste électorale; *vt* enregistrer; (name) inscrire; (letter) recommander; (births, etc) déclarer; (emotion) témoigner; (patent) déposer; (luggage) enregistrer; *vi* (fit) coïncider exactement; (in hotel) s'inscrire sur le registre; *coll* être compris, pénétrer

**registrar** *n* *leg* greffier *m*; (births, etc) officier *m* de l'état civil

**registration** *n* enregistrement *m*; inscription *f*; (patent) dépôt *m*; (vehicle) immatriculation *f*; (letter) recommandation *f*; ~ **number** numéro *m* matricule; ~ **plate** plaque *f* minéralogique

**registry** *n* enregistrement *m*; bureau *m* d'enregistrement; bureau *m* de l'état civil; (employment) bureau *m* de placement

**registry-office** *n* bureau *m* de l'état civil

**regress** *n* retour *m* en arrière; *vi* régresser

**regression** *n* régression *f*

**regressive** *adj* régressif -ive

**regret** *n* regret *m*; **much to my** ~ à mon grand regret; **with** ~ à regret; *vt* regretter

**regretful** *adj* (person) plein de regrets; (thing) à regretter

**regrettable** *adj* regrettable

**regroup** *vt* regrouper; reclasser

**regular** *n* (customer) habitué -e, bon client (*f* bonne cliente); (at pub, café) *coll* pilier *m* de café; *mil* ~ s troupes *fpl* de l'active; *adj* régulier -ière; (correct) en règle, dans les règles; (character) réglé, rangé; (usual) ordinaire; (downright) vrai, véritable

**regularity** *n* régularité *f*

**regularize** *vt* régulariser

**regularly** *adv* régulièrement

**regulate** *vt* régler, ajuster; (business) diriger; (make rules) fixer les règles pour

**regulation** *n* règlement *m*, réglementation *f*; (technical) réglage *m*; *adj* réglementaire

**regulator** *n* (person) régulateur -trice; (device) régulateur *m*

**regurgitate** *vt* régurgiter

**regurgitation** *n* régurgitation *f*

**rehabilitate** *vt* réhabiliter; réadapter

**rehabilitation** *n* réhabilitation *f*; (injured) rééducation *f*; (refugees) réadaptation *f*; ~ **centre** centre *m* de rééducation professionnelle

**rehash** *n* réchauffé *m*; *fig* + *pej* resucée *f*; *vt* réchauffer

**rehearsal** *n* répétition *f*; **dress** ~ répétition générale

**rehearse** *vt* répéter; (go over) énumérer

**rehouse** *vt* reloger

**reign** *n* règne *m*; **in the** ~ **of** sous le règne de; *vi* régner

**reimburse** *vt* rembourser

**reimbursement** *n* remboursement *m*

**reimport** *vt* réimporter

**rein** *n* rêne *f*, guide *f*; **give** ~ **to** lâcher la bride à; *fig* donner libre cours à; **keep a tight** ~ **on** s/o tenir la bride serrée à qn; *vt* ~ **in a horse** serrer la bride à un cheval; *vi* ~ **in** ramener son cheval au pas

**reincarnate** *vt* réincarner

**reincarnation** *n* réincarnation *f*

**reindeer** *n* renne *m*

**reinforce** *vt* renforcer; (request) appuyer; ~ **d concrete** béton armé

**reinforcement** *n* renforcement *m*; *mil* ~ s renforts *mpl*

**reinstate** *vt* réintégrer

**reinsure** *vt* réassurer

**reinvest** *vt* replacer, trouver un nouveau placement pour

**reissue** *n* nouvelle édition *f*; *vt econ* émettre de nouveau; (book) publier une nouvelle édition de

**reiterate** *vt* réitérer, répéter

**reiteration** *n* réitération *f*, répétition *f*

**reiterative** *adj* réitératif -ive

**reject** *n* pièce *f* de rebut; **export** ~ article *m* impropre à l'exportation; *vt* rejeter, repousser; (applicant) refuser

**rejection** *n* rejet *m*; refus *m*

**rejoice** *vt* réjouir; *vi* se réjouir

**rejoicing** *n* réjouissance *f*, allégresse *f*; *adj* réjouissant

**rejoin** *vi* répliquer, répondre

**re-join** *vt* rejoindre, réunir; *mil* rallier; *vi* se rejoindre, se réunir

**rejoinder** *n* réplique *f*, repartie *f*

**rejuvenate** *vt* rajeunir

**rejuvenation** *n* rajeunissement *m*

**rekindle** *vt* rallumer; (hope) ranimer; *vi* se rallumer; (hope) se ranimer

**relapse** *n* rechute *f*; *vi med* faire une rechute; retomber; ~ **into crime** retomber dans le crime

**relate** *vt* raconter; (connect) rapporter, rattacher; *vi* avoir rapport, se rapporter

**related** *adj* ayant rapport; (person) apparenté; (by marriage) allié

**relation** *n* (kin) parent -e; (story) récit *m*; (connection) rapport *m*, relation *f*; **bear a** ~ **to** avoir rapport à; **break off** ~ **s with** cesser tout rapport avec; **public** ~ **s** relations publiques; **this bears no** ~ **to** ceci n'a rien à voir avec

**relationship** *n* (connection) rapport *m*; (kin) parenté *f*

**relative** *n* parent -e; *adj* relatif -ive

**relatively** *adv* relativement

**relativism** *n* relativisme *m*

**relativity** *n* relativité *f*

**relax** *vt* relâcher, détendre; (mind) délasser; (hold) desserrer; *vi* (muscles) se relâcher; (person) se détendre, se décontracter

**relaxation** *n* (discipline, muscles) relâchement *m*; (from work) délassement *m*, détente *f*, repos *m*

**relaxing** *adj* délassant, décontractant; (climate) débilitant

**relay** *n* relais *m*; *vt* relayer

**release** *n* délivrance *f*; (from obligation) libération *f*; (from debt) décharge *f*; (film) mise *f* en circulation; (gas) dégagement *m*; (spring) déclenchement *m*; **press** ~ communiqué *m* de presse; *vt* libérer; (from obligation) acquitter, décharger; (let go) lâcher; (film) mettre en circulation; (mechanism) déclencher; ~ **one's hold** lâcher prise

**relegate** vt reléguer

**relegation** n leg + sp relégation f; (putting aside) mise f à l'écart

**relent** vi s'attendrir; revenir sur une décision

**relentless** adj implacable, impitoyable

**re-let** vt relouer; (sublet) sous-louer

**relevance, relevancy** n pertinence f, à-propos m

**relevant** adj applicable, pertinent; ~ **to** qui touche à, qui a rapport à

**reliability** n sûreté f, honnêteté f; (statement) crédibilité f; (machine) sécurité f de fonctionnement, régularité f de marche

**reliable** adj sûr; (person) digne de confiance; (friend) solide; (machine) d'un fonctionnement sûr

**reliance** n confiance f; **place** ~ **on s/o** se fier à qn, compter sur qn

**reliant** adj confiant

**relic** n eccles relique f; (remnant) reste m

¹**relief** n (pain) soulagement m; (from distress) allégement m; (help) secours m; mil (guard) relève f; (siege) dégagement m; leg réparation f; ~ **train** train m supplémentaire; **go to s/o's** ~ aller au secours de qn

²**relief** n relief m; **stand out in** ~ **against sth** se détacher sur qch

**relieve** vt (pain) soulager; (help) aider, secourir; (rid) débarrasser, délester; mil (soldiers) relever, (town) dégager; ~ **boredom** dissiper l'ennui; ~ **oneself** faire ses besoins; ~ **one's feelings** se décharger le cœur

**religion** n religion f; (denomination) confession f

**religious** adj religieux -ieuse, pieux (f pieuse)

**re-line** vt (clothes) remettre une doublure à; (brakes) regarnir

**relinquish** vt abandonner; (claim, plan, etc) renoncer à; (let go) lâcher

**relish** n saveur f, goût m; **do sth with** ~ se plaire (se délecter) à faire qch; **eat with** ~ manger de bon appétit; ~ savourer, goûter; (give taste to) relever le goût de; ~ **doing sth** trouver du plaisir à faire qch

**relive** vt revivre

**reluctance** n répugnance f; **with** ~ à contre-cœur

**reluctant** adj qui agit à contre-cœur; **be** ~ **to do sth** être peu disposé à faire qch

**rely** vi ~ **on** compter sur

**remain** vi rester, demeurer; ~ **behind** ne pas partir; **I** ~, **Sir, yours faithfully**

agréez, Monsieur, mes salutations distinguées; **it** ~ **s to be seen whether** reste à savoir si; **the fact** ~ **s that** il n'en est pas moins vrai que

**remainder** n restant m, reste m; (book) livre soldé; **the** ~ les autres; vt (books) solder

**remains** npl restes mpl; débris mpl; **mortal** ~ dépouille mortelle

**remake** n cin remake m; vt refaire

**remand** n leg renvoi m à une autre audience; ~ **home** maison f de correction; vt leg renvoyer à une autre audience

**remark** n remarque f, observation f, commentaire m; vt remarquer, observer; (point out) faire observer; vi faire une remarque

**remarkable** adj remarquable, frappant

**remarry** vi se remarier

**remediable** adj remédiable

**remedial** adj (treatment) curatif -ive; réparateur -trice

**remedy** n remède m; leg recours m; vt remédier à

**remember** vt se rappeler, se souvenir de; ~ **doing sth** se souvenir d'avoir fait qch; ~ **me to Mr X** rappelez-moi au bon souvenir de Monsieur X; ~ **what I told you** n'oubliez pas ce que je vous ai dit; **as far as I can** ~ autant qu'il m'en souvienne (souvient); **if I** ~ **rightly** si j'ai bonne mémoire

**remembrance** n souvenir m, mémoire f

**remind** vt faire penser à, rappeler; ~ **me to tell him** faites-moi penser à lui dire; ~ **s/o of sth** rappeler qch à qn; **that** ~ **s me!** à propos!

**reminisce** vi raconter des souvenirs

**reminiscence** n réminiscence f

**reminiscent** adj ~ **of** qui rappelle, qui fait penser à

**remiss** adj négligent

**remission** n rémission f; (punishment) remise f

**remit** vt remettre; (sins) pardonner; leg renvoyer; vi diminuer d'intensité

**remittance** n remise f, envoi m de fonds

**remitter** n comm remetteur m

**remnant** n reste m, restant m; (cloth) coupon m; (shop) ~ **s** soldes mpl

**remodel** vt remodeler; (work) remanier, refondre

**remonstrance** n remontrance f

**remonstrate** vi faire des remontrances, protester

**remorse** n remords m

**remorseful** adj plein de remords

**remorseless** adj sans remords; impitoyable

**remote** adj éloigné, lointain, écarté; (hazy) vague; ~ **control** télécommande *f*; **not the ~st chance** pas la moindre chance

**remoteness** *n* éloignement *m*

**remould** *n* mot pneu rechapé

**remount** *n* cheval *m* de remonte; *vt* remonter; *vi* remonter à cheval; (bicycle) enfourcher son vélo à nouveau

**removal** *n* enlèvement *m*; (house) déménagement *m*; (abuse) suppression *f*; (dismissal) révocation *f*, renvoi *m*; (pain) soulagement *m*

**remove** *n* distance *f*; **at one ~** tout près; *vt* (take away) enlever; (take off) ôter; (suppress) supprimer; (furniture) déménager; (dismiss) renvoyer, révoquer; (objection) résoudre; *vi* déménager

**remunerate** *vt* rémunérer

**remuneration** *n* rémunération *f*

**remunerative** *adj* rémunérateur -trice

**renaissance** *n* renaissance *f*

**renal** *adj* rénal

**rename** *vt* rebaptiser

**rend** *vt* déchirer; **a cry rent the air** un cri fendit l'air

**render** *vt* rendre; (translate) traduire; (interpret) interpréter

**rendering** *n* (work) interprétation *f*; (translation) traduction *f*; (surrender, giving) reddition *f*

**rendez-vous** *n* rendez-vous *m*

**rendition** *n* reddition *f*; US traduction *f*

**renegade** *n* renégat *m*

**renegotiate** *vt* renégocier

**renew** *vt* renouveler; (begin again) recommencer; **~ acquaintance with s/o** renouer connaissance avec qn; **~ a subscription** se réabonner

**renewable** *adj* renouvelable

**renewal** *n* renouvellement *m*; **~ of subscription** réabonnement *m*

**renounce** *vt* renoncer à, abandonner; (treaty) dénoncer; (child) renier; (belief) répudier

**renovate** *vt* rénover, remettre à neuf

**renovation** *n* rénovation *f*, remise *f* à neuf

**renovator** *n* rénovateur -trice

**renown** *n* renommée *f*, célébrité *f*

**renowned** *adj* renommé, célèbre

¹**rent** *n* (tear) déchirure *f*

²**rent** *n* (lodging) loyer *m*, location *f*; *vt* (let, hire) louer; (hire) prendre en location

**rental** *n* loyer *m*, prix *m* de location

**rent-free** *adj* **live ~** habiter sans payer (sans avoir à payer) de loyer

**renunciation** *n* renoncement *m*, renonciation *f*

**reopen** *vt* rouvrir; **~ hostilities** reprendre les hostilités; *vi* rouvrir; (wound) se rouvrir

**reorganization** *n* réorganisation *f*

**reorganize** *vt* réorganiser; *vi* se réorganiser

**reorientation** *n* réorientation *f*

¹**rep** *n* reps *m*

²**rep** *n theat abbr* **repertory**; *abbr* **representative**

**repaint** *vt* repeindre

¹**repair** *vi* (go) se rendre

²**repair** *n* réparation *f*; *naut* radoub *m*; **be under ~** être en réparation; **in bad ~** mal entretenu; **in good ~** en bon état; *vt* réparer; (machine) remettre en état; (clothing) raccommoder; *naut* radouber

**repairer** *n* réparateur -trice

**re-paper** *vt* retapisser

**reparable** *adj* réparable

**reparation** *n* réparation *f*

**repartee** *n* repartie *f*

**repartition** *n* répartition *f*

**repast** *n lit* repas *m*

**repatriate** *vt* rapatrier

**repatriation** *n* rapatriement *m*

**repay** *vt* (money) rembourser, rendre; (reward) récompenser; (person) rembourser; **~ an obligation** s'acquitter d'une obligation; **~ s/o's kindness** payer de retour la bonté de qn; **~ s/o with ingratitude** payer qn d'ingratitude; **how can I ever ~ you?** comment pourrai-je jamais m'acquitter envers vous?

**repayable** *adj* remboursable

**repayment** *n* remboursement *m*; (for service) récompense *f*

**repeal** *n* abrogation *f*, révocation *f*; *vt* abroger, annuler, révoquer

**repeat** *n* reprise *f*; *adj* repris, renouvelé; *vt* répéter, réitérer; (renew) renouveler; (class) redoubler

**repeater** *n* (watch) montre *f* à répétition

**repel** *vt* repousser

**repellent** *adj* répulsif -ive, repoussant

**repent** *vi* se repentir

**repentance** *n* repentir *m*

**repentant** *adj* repenti, repentant

**repercussion** *n* répercussion *f*, contrecoup *m*

**repertoire** *n* répertoire *m*

**repertory** *n theat* théâtre *m* de répertoire

**repetition** *n* répétition *f*; (music-playing) reprise *f*; (effort) renouvellement *m*

**repetitive** *adj* (person) qui se répète; (book) plein de répétitions

**replace** *vt* (put back) remettre en place, replacer; remplacer; **~ the receiver** raccrocher (le récepteur)

**replacement** *n* (action) remise *f* en place; remplacement *m*, substitution *f*; **~s** pièces *fpl* de rechange

**replant** *vt* replanter

**replay** *n sp* match rejoué; *vt* rejouer

**replenish** *vt* remplir (à nouveau); (stock) réapprovisionner

**replenishment** *n* remplissage *m*; réapprovisionnement *m*

**replete** *adj* rempli, plein

**repletion** *n* réplétion *f*

**replica** *n* reproduction *f*, copie *f*; (picture) réplique *f*

**reply** *n* réponse *f*; *vt* + *vi* répondre, répliquer

**reply-coupon** *n* coupon-réponse *m* (*pl* coupons-réponse)

**repoint** *vt bui* repointoyer

**repopulate** *vt* repeupler

**report** *n* rapport *m*, compte rendu; (rumour) bruit *m*; détonation *f*, coup *m* de fusil (de canon); (repute) réputation *f*; *comm* **annual ~** rapport *m* de gestion; **policeman's ~** procès-verbal *m*; **weather ~** bulletin *m* météorologique; *vt* rapporter, rendre compte de; (notify) signaler; (media) faire un reportage sur; (denounce) dénoncer; **nothing to ~** rien à signaler; *vi* ~ **sick** se porter malade; **~ to a place** se présenter à un endroit

**reportage** *n* reportage *m*

**reporter** *n* reporter *m*, journaliste

¹**repose** *n* repos *m*; calme *m*; *vi* se reposer; dormir

²**repose** *vt* ~ **one's trust in s/o** mettre sa confiance en qn

**repository** *n* dépôt *m*, entrepôt *m*; (information) répertoire *m*; (of secret) dépositaire; **furniture ~** garde-meuble *m*

**reprehend** *vt* réprimander, blâmer

**reprehensible** *adj* répréhensible, blâmable

**represent** *vt* représenter; (play) jouer; (indicate) faire remarquer, signaler

**representation** *n* représentation *f*; **make ~ s** faire une démarche; protester

**representative** *n* représentant -e; délégué -e; *US pol* = député *m*; *adj* représentatif -ive

**repress** *vt* réprimer; *psych* refouler

**repressed** *adj* réprimé, contenu; *psych* refoulé

**repression** *n* répression *f*; *psych* refoulement *m*

**repressive** *adj* répressif -ive

**reprieve** *n* sursis *m*; répit *m*; commutation *f* de la peine capitale; *vt* accorder un délai à; donner du répit à; accorder une commutation de la peine capitale à

**reprimand** *n* réprimande *f*; *vt* réprimander; *leg* blâmer publiquement

**reprint** *n* réimpression *f*, nouveau tirage; *vt* réimprimer

**reprisals** *npl* représailles *fpl*; **carry out**

~ user de représailles

**reproach** *n* reproche *m*; (shame) honte *f*, opprobre *m*; *vt* faire des reproches à, blâmer

**reproachful** *adj* réprobateur -trice

**reprobate** *n* vaurien -ienne

**reproduce** *vt* reproduire, copier; *vi* se reproduire

**reproduction** *n* reproduction *f*

**reproductive** *adj* reproducteur -trice, reproductif -ive

**reproof** *n* reproche *m*, réprimande *f*

**reprove** *vt* réprimander, reprendre, condamner, blâmer

**reptile** *n* reptile *m*

**reptilian** *adj* reptilien -ienne

**republic** *n* république *f*

**republican** *n* + *adj* républicain -e

**republicanism** *n* républicanisme *m*

**republish** *vt* rééditer

**repudiate** *vt* répudier, désavouer

**repudiation** *n* répudiation *f*, désaveu *m*; (debt) reniement *m*

**repugnance** *n* répugnance *f*, antipathie *f*

**repugnant** *adj* répugnant

**repulse** *n* échec *m*; (refusal) refus *m*; (rebuff) rebuffade *f*; *vt* repousser, refouler

**repulsion** *n* répulsion *f*, aversion *f*

**repulsive** *adj* répulsif -ive, repoussant

**repurchase** *n* rachat *m*; *vt* racheter

**reputable** *adj* honorable, estimé

**reputation** *n* réputation *f*, renom *m*

**repute** *n* réputation *f*, renom *m*

**reputed** *adj* réputé, supposé; **be ~ rich** passer pour riche, avoir la réputation d'être riche

**request** *n* demande *f*; **~ stop** arrêt facultatif; **at the ~ of** à la demande de; **on ~** sur demande; *vt* demander, prier; **~ s/o to do sth** demander à qn de faire qch; **~ sth of s/o** demander qch à qn

**requiem** *n* requiem *m invar*; **~ mass** messe *f* des morts

**require** *vt* demander, réclamer; (desire) vouloir; (necessitate) nécessiter; (need) avoir besoin de; **if ~ d** s'il le faut; **the ~ d sum** la somme nécessaire; **what does he ~ of me?** que veut-il de moi?

**requirement** *n* besoin *m*, exigence *f*; demande *f*; nécessité *f*

**requisite** *n* chose *f* nécessaire; **toilet ~ s** accessoires *mpl* de toilette; *adj* nécessaire, requis, indispensable

**requisition** *n* demande *f*; *mil* réquisition *f*

**requital** *n* récompense *f*; (revenge) revanche *f*

**requite** *vt* récompenser; (revenge) venger; **~ s/o's love** répondre à l'amour de qn

**reredos** *n* retable *m*

**resale** n revente f; ~ **price maintenance** système m de prix imposés

**rescind** vt annuler; (law) abroger

**rescue** n délivrance f; (at sea) sauvetage m; ~ **team** équipe f de secours; **come to s/o's** ~ venir au secours de qn

**rescuer** n naut sauveteur m; libérateur -trice

**research** n recherche f; ~ **work** travaux mpl de recherche; recherches fpl; ~ **worker** chercheur -euse; vi faire des recherches

**reseat** vt rasseoir, faire rasseoir; (chair) refaire un fond à

**resell** vt revendre

**resemblance** n ressemblance f

**resemble** vt ressembler à

**resent** vt s'offenser de; être froissé de

**resentful** adj rancunier -ière; irrité, froissé

**resentment** n ressentiment m, rancœur f

**reservation** n réserve f; (seat) place retenue (louée), location f (des places); **have you a** ~? avez-vous retenu?

**reserve** n réserve f; (land) terrain réservé; restriction f; (sale) mise f à prix; (aloofness) discrétion f; vt réserver; (seat) retenir; ~ **the right to do sth** se réserver le droit de faire qch

**reserved** adj réservé

**reservist** n mil réserviste m

**reservoir** n réservoir m

**reset** vt replacer, remettre en place; (jewels) remonter; (limb) remettre; (watch) remettre à l'heure

**resettle** vt réinstaller; vi se réinstaller

**resettlement** n transfert m de population; nouvelle colonisation

**reshuffle** n remaniement m; (cards) nouveau battement; vt (cards) rebattre; (posts, people) remanier

**reside** vi résider

**residence** n demeure f, résidence f; leg domicile m; (stay) séjour m

**resident** n résident -e, habitant -e; adj résidant; ~ **population** population f fixe

**residential** adj résidentiel -ielle

**residual** adj résiduel -elle

**residue** n fig + chem résidu m; reste m

**residuum** n résidu m

**resign** vt résigner, se démettre de; (give up) abandonner; ~ **oneself to doing sth** se résigner à faire qch; ~ **sth to s/o** céder qch à qn; vi démissionner; ~! démission!

**resignation** n (from office) démission f; (rights) abandon m; (submission) résignation f

**resigned** adj résigné; **become** ~ **to sth** prendre son parti de qch

**resilience, resiliency** n (thing) élasticité f; (person) ressort m

**resilient** adj élastique; (person) **be** ~ avoir du ressort

**resin** n résine f

**resinous** adj résineux -euse

**resist** vt résister à; **not be able to** ~ **doing sth** ne (pas) pouvoir s'empêcher de faire qch

**resistance** n résistance f; ~ **fighter** résistant -e

**resistant** adj résistant

**resistless** adj irrésistible

**re-sole** vt (shoes) ressemeler

**resolute** adj résolu, déterminé

**resolutely** adv résolument

**resoluteness** n résolution f

**resolution** n résolution f; décision f

**resolvable** adj résoluble

**resolve** vt résoudre; (doubt) dissiper; vi se résoudre; ~ **to do sth** se décider à faire qch

**resolved** adj décidé, résolu

**resonance** n résonance f

**resonant** adj résonnant; (voice) sonore

**resort** n recours m, ressource f; (meeting-place) (lieu m de) rendez-vous m; (holiday, etc) station f; **in the last** ~ en dernier ressort; vi avoir recours, recourir; ~ **to a place** (go) se rendre à un endroit; (frequent) fréquenter

**resound** vi résonner, retentir

**resounding** adj résonnant, retentissant

**resource** n ressource f

**resourceful** adj habile, plein de ressources; coll débrouillard

**respect** n respect m; (reference) rapport m, égard m; **command** ~ se faire respecter; **give my** ~ **s to** présentez mes hommages à; **in every** ~ à tous égards; **in some** ~ **s** en quelque sorte, sous certains rapports; **pay one's** ~ **s to** présenter ses respects à; **with** ~ **to** quant à

**respectability** n respectabilité f

**respectable** adj respectable, honorable, digne de respect; (decent) convenable

**respecter** n **be no** ~ **of persons** ne se laisser impressionner par personne

**respectful** adj respectueux -euse

**respecting** prep quant à, relativement à, à l'égard de

**respective** adj respectif -ive

**respectively** adv respectivement

**respiration** n respiration f

**respirator** n respirateur m; masque m à gaz

**respiratory** adj respiratoire

**respire** vt + vi respirer

**respite** n répit m, sursis m; vt accorder un sursis à; (sentence) différer

**resplendence, resplendency** n splendeur f

**resplendent** adj resplendissant, éblouissant

**respond** vi répondre; ~ **to affection** être sensible à l'affection; ~ **to music** apprécier la musique

**respondent** n leg défendeur -eresse; adj qui répond, répondant

**response** n réponse f, réplique f; eccles répons m; (reaction) réaction f; **meet with a warm** ~ être très bien accueilli

**responsibility** n responsabilité f

**responsible** adj (capable) capable, compétent; (answerable) responsable, chargé; (post) important, plein de responsabilités; (trustworthy) sérieux -ieuse; **be** ~ **for one's actions** être maître (f maîtresse) de ses actes; **be** ~ **for sth** avoir la charge de qch; être cause de qch; **be** ~ **for sth to s/o** avoir à rendre compte à qn de qch

**responsive** adj sensible, impressionnable

**rest** n (repose) repos m; (support) appui m, support m; (shelter) abri m, asile m; mus pause f, silence m; ~ **home** maison f de repos; US ~ **room** toilettes fpl; **at** ~ au repos; (stopped) à l'arrêt; **come to** ~ s'arrêter, s'immobiliser; **have a good night's** ~ passer une bonne nuit; **have a little** ~ se reposer un peu (un moment); **set s/o's mind** ~ dissiper les inquiétudes de qn; vt reposer; (lean) appuyer; (base) baser; vi se reposer, reposer; (lean) s'appuyer; ~ **in God** s'en remettre à Dieu; **it** ~ **s with you to** c'est à vous de; **the matter** ~ **s there** l'affaire en reste là; **we won't let it** ~ **there** nous ne permettrons pas que la chose se passe ainsi; **you may** ~ **assured that** soyez sûr (assuré) que

**restate** vt réaffirmer; exposer de nouveau

**restatement** n réaffirmation f

**restaurant** n restaurant m; (railway) ~ **car** wagon-restaurant m (pl wagons-restaurants)

**rest-cure** n cure f de repos

**restful** adj reposant, paisible; (quiet) tranquille

**resting-place** n lieu m de repos; **last** ~ dernière demeure

**restitution** n restitution f

**restive** adj (person) inquiet -iète; rétif -ive, indocile

**restless** adj agité, troublé; (night) sans repos; (child) remuant; (worried) inquiet -iète; **become** ~ s'impatienter, s'énerver

**restlessness** n agitation f; (worry) inquiétude f; nervosité f

**restock** vt repeupler; (goods) réapprovisionner; (river) rempoissonner

**restoration** n (building, monarch) restauration f; (giving back) restitution f; (health) rétablissement m

**restorative** n med fortifiant m; adj fortifiant

**restore** vt (building, monarch) restaurer; (give back) restituer, rendre; (freedom, order, health, etc) rétablir; (place) remettre

**restorer** n restaurateur -trice

**restrain** vt (check) réprimer, retenir, restreindre; (prevent) empêcher; (bottle up) contenir; (slow down) freiner

**restrained** adj contenu, mesuré

**restraining** adj restrictif -ive

**restraint** n contrainte f, entrave f; **lack of** ~ manque m de réserve; **speak without** ~ parler en toute liberté

**restrict** vt limiter, restreindre

**restriction** n restriction f; (reduction) réduction f

**restrictive** adj restrictif -ive

**result** n résultat m, suite f; **as a** ~ **of** par suite de; vi résulter; aboutir; ~ **in nothing** ne mener à rien

**resultant** adj résultant

**resume** vt (continue) reprendre, continuer; (sum up) résumer; ~ **work** se remettre au travail; vi reprendre

**résumé** n résumé m

**resumption** n reprise f, continuation f

**resurface** vt ~ **a road** refaire le revêtement d'une route; vi faire surface, revenir à la surface

**resurgence** n résurrection f

**resurrect** vt ressusciter, faire revivre

**resurrection** n résurrection f

**resuscitate** vt + vi ressusciter

**resuscitation** n ressuscitation f

**retail** n détail m, vente f au détail; ~ **dealer** détaillant -e; ~ **price** prix m de détail; **sell** ~ vendre au détail; vt détailler, vendre au détail; (repeat) colporter, répéter

**retailer** n détaillant -e; (of gossip) colporteur -euse

**retain** vt retenir, conserver, garder; (maintain) maintenir; (engage) engager; (remember) garder en mémoire

**retainer** n dispositif m de retenue; (fee) arrhes fpl; leg honoraires mpl; ~ **s** gens mpl, suite f

**retaining** adj ~ **dam** barrage m de retenue; ~ **fee** provision f; ~ **wall** mur m de soutènement

**retake** n reprise f; cin réplique f; vt reprendre

**retaliate** vi rendre la pareille

**retaliation** n représailles fpl

**retaliatory** adj de représailles

**retard** vt retarder

**retardation** n retardement m, retard m, ralentissement m

**retch** vi faire des efforts pour vomir

**retention** n conservation f, maintien m; med rétention f

**retentive** adj (memory) fidèle

**rethink** vt repenser

**reticence** n réticence f

**reticent** adj réticent, peu communicatif -ive

**reticular** adj réticulaire

**retina** n rétine f

**retinue** n suite f

**retire** vt mettre à la retraite; vi se retirer; (give up post) se démettre de ses fonctions; (on a pension) prendre sa retraite; (withdraw) abandonner; ~ to bed aller se coucher; ~ into oneself se replier sur soi-même

**retired** adj retiré; (person) retraité, en (à la) retraite

**retirement** n retraite f

**retiring** adj (person) réservé; (from office) sortant

¹**retort** n réplique f, riposte f; vt répliquer, riposter

²**retort** n chem cornue f

**retouch** n retouche f; vt retoucher

**retrace** vt (past) reconstituer; remonter à l'origine de; ~ one's steps revenir sur ses pas

**retract** vt rétracter; vi se rétracter

**retractable** adj rétractable; (undercarriage) escamotable

**retraction** n retrait m, rétraction f

**retranslate** vt retraduire

¹**retread** vt fouler de nouveau; ~ the same path repasser par le même chemin

²**retread** n (tyre) pneu rechapé; vt (tyre) rechaper

**retreat** n retraite f; (shelter) abri m; (home) asile m; vi se retirer, s'éloigner; mil battre en retraite

**retrench** vt retrancher; (expenses) réduire, restreindre

**retrenchment** n retranchement m; (expenses) réduction f

**retrial** n leg nouveau procès

**retribution** n châtiment m

**retributive** adj vengeur -eresse

**retrievable** adj recouvrable; (mistake) réparable

**retrieve** vt (get back) recouvrer; (fetch back) rapporter; (find) retrouver; (restore) rétablir; (mistake) réparer

**retriever** n (dog) retriever m

**retroactive** adj rétroactif -ive

**retrograde** adj rétrograde

**retrogress** vi rétrograder

**retrogression** n mouvement m rétrograde

**retrogressive** adj rétrogressif -ive, rétrograde

**retro-rocket** n rétrofusée f

**retrospect** n examen rétrospectif; in ~ en regardant dans le passé

**retrospection** n rétrospection f

**retrospective** adj rétrospectif -ive

**retry** vt leg juger à nouveau

**return** n retour m; (home, after holidays) rentrée f; (sending back) renvoi m; (giving back) restitution f; (profit) profit m, bénéfice m; (receipts) recettes fpl; (account) rapport m; (election) élection f; (putting back) remise f; (election) ~s résultat m du scrutin; **match** revanche f; ~ **ticket** billet m aller et retour; **by** ~ par retour du courrier; **in** ~ **for** (exchange) en échange de; (reward) en récompense de; **many happy** ~s **(of the day)** meilleurs vœux pour votre anniversaire; **on his** ~ à son retour; vt (give back) rendre; (send back) renvoyer; (money) rembourser; (put back) remettre; (candidate) élire; (stolen object) restituer; (report) déclarer, rapporter; (answer) répliquer, répondre; ~ s/o's feelings répondre aux sentiments de qn; vi (come back) revenir; (go back) retourner; (home, after holidays) rentrer

**returnable** adj restituable; ~ **bottle** bouteille consignée; ~ **goods** marchandises fpl de retour

**reunion** n réunion f, assemblée f; coll **a touching** ~ de touchantes retrouvailles

**reunite** vt unir de nouveau, réunir; vi se réunir

**rev** n abbr **revolution** coll mot tour m; vt coll mot faire tourner (plus) vite; vi ~ **up** tourner vite, s'emballer

**revaluation** n réévaluation f

**reveal** vt révéler, faire connaître, laisser voir

**revealing** adj révélateur -trice

**reveille** n mil diane f

**revel** n usu pl réjouissances fpl; orgie f; vi se réjouir; coll faire bombance; ~ **in** se délecter à, aimer beaucoup

**revelation** n révélation f; **(the Book of) Revelations** l'Apocalypse f (de Jean)

**reveller** n joyeux -euse convive, noceur -euse

**revelry** n festin m, bombance f

**revenge** n vengeance f; **have one's** ~ se venger; **take** ~ **for sth on** s/o se venger de qch sur qn; vt venger; ~ **oneself** se venger

**revengeful** adj vindicatif -ive

**revenue** n revenu m, rentes fpl; **excise** ~ contributions indirectes; **the Inland Revenue** = le fisc

**reverberant** adj retentissant, réverbérant

**reverberate** *vi* (light) réverbérer; (sound) résonner, retentir

**reverberation** *n* (light) réverbération *f*; (sound) répercussion *f*

**revere** *vt* révérer, vénérer

**reverence** *n* révérence *f*, vénération *f*; *vt* révérer

**reverend** *adj* révérend

**reverent** *adj* respectueux -euse

**reverential** *adj* révérenciel -ielle

**reverie** *n* rêverie *f*

**reversal** *n* *leg* annulation *f*; renversement *m*, inversion *f*

**reverse** *n* contraire *m*, opposé *m*; (other side) revers *m*, dos *m*; (page) verso *m*; (defeat) échec *m*; *mot* go (get) into ~ faire (mettre en) marche arrière; *mot* in ~ en marche arrière; *adj* contraire, inverse, opposé; ~ **charge call** communication *f* en P.C.V.; **in ~ order** en ordre inverse; *vt* renverser; (order) invertir; (clothing) retourner; *leg* révoquer, annuler; *vi* *mot* faire marche arrière; (go backwards) reculer

**reversed** *adj* renversé; contraire, opposé

**reversible** *adj* réversible

**reversion** *n* réversion *f*, retour *m*

**revert** *vi* revenir, retourner

**review** *n* revue *f*; (book) critique *f*, analyse *f*; *leg* révision *f*; *vt* réviser; (troops) passer en revue; (book) faire la critique de

**reviewer** *n* critique *m* littéraire

**revile** *vt* injurier, insulter

**revise** *n* *typ* épreuve *f* de révision; *vt* revoir, relire; (correct) corriger; (laws) réviser; ~ **a lesson** revoir une leçon

**revision** *n* révision *f*

**revisionist** *n* révisionniste

**revisit** *vt* revisiter, visiter de nouveau

**revitalize** *vt* revivifier

**revival** *n* retour *m* à la vie; (arts) renaissance *f*; (religion) réveil *m*; (play, business) reprise *f*; (renewal) renouvellement *m*

**revive** *vt* faire revivre, ressusciter; (renew) renouveler; (hope) ranimer, faire renaître; (desire) réveiller; (play) reprendre; *vi* reprendre connaissance, ressusciter; (feelings) renaître, se ranimer; (custom) reprendre

**revivify** *vt* revivifier

**revocable** *adj* révocable

**revocation** *n* révocation *f*

**revoke** *vt* révoquer; (promise) rétracter

**revolt** *n* révolte *f*; *vt* révolter, indigner; *vi* se révolter, se rebeller

**revolting** *adj* révoltant, dégoûtant

**revolution** *n* révolution *f*; (motor) tour *m*; ~ **counter** compte-tours *m*

**revolutionary** *n* + *adj* révolutionnaire

**revolutionize** *vt* révolutionner

**revolve** *vt* faire tourner; (thoughts) ruminer; *vi* tourner

**revolver** *n* revolver *m*

**revolving** *adj* en rotation; ~ **chair** fauteuil pivotant; ~ **door** porte *f* à tambour

**revue** *n* *theat* revue *f*

**revulsion** *n* revirement *m*; *med* révulsion *f*

**reward** *n* récompense *f*; *vt* récompenser

**rewarding** *adj* (money) rémunérateur -trice; qui en vaut la peine

**rewind** *vt* rebobiner; (film) réembobiner; (clock) remonter à nouveau

**rewire** *vt* refaire toute la canalisation électrique de

**reword** *vt* recomposer

**rewrite** *n* remaniement *m*; *cin* rewriting *m*; *vt* récrire, remanier

**rhapsodize** *vi* ~ **over sth** s'extasier sur qch

**rhapsody** *n* rhapsodie *f*

**rheostat** *n* *elect* rhéostat *m*

**rhesus** *n* rhésus *m*

**rhetoric** *n* rhétorique *f*, éloquence *f*

**rhetorical** *adj* de rhétorique; ~ **question** question *f* pour la forme

**rhetorician** *n* rhétoricien -ienne

**rheumatic** *n* rhumatisant -e; *adj* (pain) rhumatismal; (person) rhumatisant; ~ **fever** rhumatisme articulaire aigu

**rheumatism** *n* rhumatisme *m*

**Rhine** *n* Rhin *m*

**rhinoceros** *n* rhinocéros *m*

**Rhodesia** *n* Rhodésie *f*

**rhododendron** *n* rhododendron *m*

**rhombus** *n* *geom* losange *m*, rhombe *m*

**rhubarb** *n* rhubarbe *f*

**rhumba** *n* *see* **rumba**

**rhyme, rime** *n* rime *f*; **in ~** en vers; *vt* faire rimer; *vi* rimer

**rhythm** *n* rythme *m*, cadence *f*

**rhythmic(al)** *adj* rythmique, cadencé

**rib** *n* *anat* côte *f*; (support) support *m*; (umbrella) baleine *f*; (ship) membrure *f*; *vt* garnir de côtes; *coll* (tease) taquiner

**ribald** *adj* grossier -ière, licencieux -ieuse

**ribaldry** *n* grivoiseries *fpl*

**ribbon** *n* ruban *m*; **tear sth to ~s** mettre qch en lambeaux

**rice** *n* riz *m*; ~ **pudding** riz *m* au lait; **ground ~** farine *f* de riz

**rice-paper** *n* papier *m* de riz

**rice-plantation** *n* rizière *f*

**rich** *adj* riche; (soil) fertile; (food) difficile à digérer; (story) impayable

**riches** *npl* richesse *f*

**richly** *adv* richement, abondamment; (very) bien

**richness** n richesse f, abondance f; (soil) fertilité f

¹**rick** n (hay) meule f

²**rick** n entorse f; ~ **in the neck** torticolis m; vt ~ **one's ankle** se fouler la cheville; ~ **oneself** se donner une entorse

**rickets** npl rachitisme m

**rickety** adj (chair) bancal; (stair) branlant; med rachitique

**rickshaw** n pousse-pousse m invar

**ricochet** n ricochet m; vi ricocher

**rid** vt débarrasser, délivrer; ~ **oneself of sth** se débarrasser de qch; **get** ~ **of** se débarrasser de; (sack) renvoyer; (suppress) faire disparaître

**riddance** n good ~! bon débarras!

¹**riddle** n énigme f, devinette f

²**riddle** n (sieve) crible m; vt cribler; passer au crible

**ride** n promenade f à cheval (en auto, à bicyclette, etc); trajet m, course f; **take s/o for a ~** (kidnap) enlever qn; (dupe) duper qn; vt monter; (waves) voguer sur; ~ **down** écraser; ~ **out the storm** naut étaler la tempête; fig surmonter la crise; vi se promener (aller) à cheval (en auto, à bicyclette, etc); (astride) chevaucher; ~ **at anchor** être mouillé; ~ **away** partir; (horse) ~ **behind** monter en croupe; ~ **by** passer; ~ **up** arriver à cheval; ~ **well** monter bien à cheval, être bon cavalier (f bonne cavalière); fig **be riding for a fall** courir à un échec

**rider** n cavalier -ière f; (racing) jockey m; (document) annexe f

**riderless** adj sans cavalier

**ridge** n (mountains) crête f, arête f; (roof) faîte m; agr billon m

**ridicule** n moquerie f, dérision f; **hold s/o up to** ~ se moquer de qn; **lay oneself open to** ~ s'exposer au ridicule; vt se moquer de, tourner en ridicule

**ridiculous** adj (absurd) absurde; ridicule

**riding** n équitation f

**riding-school** n manège m

**riding-whip** n cravache f

**rife** adj be ~ sévir, régner

**riff-raff** n canaille f, racaille f

¹**rifle** n fusil m; (hunting) carabine f; ~ **s** (soldiers) fusiliers mpl; **magazine** ~ fusil m à répétition; vt rayer

²**rifle** vt (rob) piller; (empty) vider

**rifling** n rayure f

**rift** n fente f, fissure f; ~ **in the clouds** éclaircie f

¹**rig** n naut gréement m; coll toilette f; équipement m

²**rig** vt naut gréer; équiper; ~ **out** équiper; coll attifer

³**rig** vt truquer; ~ **the market** provoquer une hausse (ou une baisse) factice

**rigging** n naut gréement m

**right** n droit m; bien m; justice f; (of possession) titre m; (side) côté droit, droite f; (boxing) coup m du droit; ~ **s** droits mpl; **be in the** ~ avoir raison; **be within one's** ~ **s** être dans son droit; **by** ~ **s** en toute justice; **by what** ~? de quel droit?; **have a** ~ **to sth** avoir droit à qch; **on the** ~ à droite; **set things to** ~ **s** rétablir les choses; adj droit; (proper) bon (f bonne), juste; (correct) correct, juste, exact; (true) vrai; (required) qu'il faut, bon (f bonne), voulu; ~ **side up** à l'endroit; sl **a bit of all** ~ qch d'épatant; (girl) un beau brin de fille; **all** ~! très bien!, à la bonne heure!; (enough) c'est bon!; **as** ~ **as rain** en parfait état; **be in one's** ~ **mind** avoir toute sa raison; **be in the** ~ **place** (well placed) être bien placé; (correct place) être à sa place; **be** ~ avoir raison; coll **come** ~ s'arranger; **more than is** ~ plus que de raison; **put** ~ corriger, rectifier, réparer; **put s/o** (direct) mettre qn sur le bon chemin; (correct) détromper qn; **set things** ~ rétablir les choses; **that's** ~! c'est bien cela!; **the** ~ **time** l'heure exacte; **think it** ~ **to** le croire bon de; adv droit; (well) bien; (correctly) correctement; (to the right) à droite; ~ **away** tout de suite, sur-le-champ; ~ **in the middle** au beau milieu; ~ **now**, US ~ **off** tout de suite; ~ **round** tout autour; ~ **to the end** jusqu'au bout; **do** ~ bien agir; **go** ~ réussir; **it's** ~ **here!** le voilà!; **see** ~ voir juste; vt redresser, réparer; (mistake) corriger, rectifier

**right-about** n demi-tour m à droite; **turn** ~ faire demi-tour

**right-angled** adj à angle droit

**righteous** adj juste, droit; vertueux -euse

**righteousness** n droiture f

**rightful** adj légitime, juste

**right-hand** adj de droite; (thumb, etc) de la main droite; ~ **man** bras droit

**right-handed** adj (person) droitier -ière f

**right-ho** interj coll d'accord!

**rightly** adv légitimement; (correctly) correctement; ~ **or wrongly** à tort ou à raison; **act** ~ bien agir

**right-minded** adj sensé; pej bien pensant

**rightness** n rectitude f, justesse f

**right-of-way** n droit m de passage

**right-wing** adj de droite

**right-winger** n (football) ailier droit; pol homme m de droite

**rigid** adj rigide, raide; (behaviour) strict

**rigidity** n rigidité f, raideur f; sévérité f

**rigmarole** n discours m sans suite, galimatias m

**rigor** n med (fever) frissons mpl; ~

**mortis** rigidité *f* cadavérique
**rigorous** *adj* rigoureux -euse
**rigour** *n* rigueur *f*, sévérité *f*; exactitude *f*; (religion) austérité *f*
**rig-out** *n coll* toilette *f*
**rile** *vt* agacer, énerver
**rim** *n* bord *m*; (wheel) jante *f*; (spectacles) monture *f*
**rime** *n see* **rhyme** *n*
**rind** *n* écorce *f*; (fruit) peau *f*, pelure *f*; (cheese) croûte *f*; (bacon) couenne *f*
¹**ring** *n* anneau *m*; (finger) bague *f*; (serviette) rond *m*; (circle) cercle *m*; (clique) coterie *f*, groupe *m*; (round eyes) cerne *m*; (boxing) ring *m*; *comm* cartel *m*; (circus) piste *f*; **form a ~** se former en cercle; **in a ~** en rond; *coll* **make ~s round s/o** se montrer nettement supérieur à qn; *vt* (bird) baguer
²**ring** *n* sonnerie *f*; (sound) son *m*; (voice) timbre *m*, intonation *f*; (bell) coup *m* de sonnette; (telephone) coup *m* de téléphone; *vt* sonner, faire sonner; *coll* **that ~s a bell** cela me rappelle qch; *vi* sonner, tinter; **~ for the maid** sonner la bonne; **~ off** raccrocher (l'appareil); **~ out** retentir; **~ up s/o** téléphoner à qn, appeler qn au téléphone; **that does not ~ true** cela sonne faux
**ringer** *n* sonneur *m*
**ring-finger** *n* annulaire *m*
**ringing** *n* son *m*; tintement *m*; retentissement *m*; *adj* (bell) qui tinte; (cheers, etc) retentissant
**ringleader** *n* meneur *m*, chef *m*
**ringlet** *n* (hair) boucle *f*
**ringmaster** *n* maître *m* de manège
**ring-road** *n* route *f* de ceinture; (round Paris) boulevard *m* périphérique
**ringside** *n* **have a ~ seat** avoir une place au premier rang
**ringworm** *n* teigne *f*
**rink** *n* (skating) patinoire *f*
**rinse** *n* rinçage *m*; *vt* rincer
**riot** *n* émeute *f*, bagarre *f*; (abundance) orgie *f*; **it's a ~** (funny) c'est tordant; **run ~** se déchaîner; *vi* s'ameuter, faire une émeute; (be noisy) faire du vacarme
**rioter** *n* émeutier -ière
**riotous** *adj* tumultueux -euse, turbulent; (person) bruyant; **~ living** vie dissipée
**rip** *n* fente *f*, déchirure *f*; *vt* fendre, déchirer; **~ off** arracher; **~ open** éventrer, ouvrir en déchirant; **~ up** éventrer, arracher; *vi* se déchirer, se fendre; *coll* **~ along** aller bon train, aller à toute vitesse; *coll* **mot let her ~** laissez-la filer; *coll* **let ~** être déchaîné, laisser déchaîner sa colère
**rip-cord** *n* cordelette *f* de déclenchement
**ripe** *adj* mûr; (cheese) bien fait; **a ~ old age** un bel âge
**ripen** *vt* faire mûrir, mûrir; *vi* mûrir; (cheese) se faire
**ripeness** *n* maturité *f*
**rip-off** *n coll* coup *m* de fusil
**riposte** *n* riposte *f*
**ripper** *n* éventreur *m*
**ripping** *adj coll fig* épatant
**ripple** *n* (water) ride *f*; (sound) murmure *m*; *vt* rider; *vi* (water) se rider; onduler
**rise** *n* ascension *f*; (road, hill) montée *f*; (price) hausse *f*; (water) crue *f*; (increase) augmentation *f*; (promotion) avancement *m*; *coll* **get a ~ out of s/o** se payer la tête de qn; **give ~ to** faire naître, donner lieu à, provoquer; *vi* (get up) se lever; (price) monter, augmenter; (building, etc) se dresser, s'élever; (go upwards) monter; (revolt) se soulever; (river) prendre (sa) source; (spring) naître; (cake, etc) lever; (from the dead) ressusciter; **~ in price** augmenter de prix; **~ in the world** faire son chemin; **~ to it (the occasion)** se montrer à la hauteur de l'occasion
**riser** *n* (step) contremarche *f*; **be an early ~** être matinal
**risible** *adj* (laughable) risible; enclin au rire
**rising** *n* lever *m*; (revolt) soulèvement *m*; (water) crue *f*; *adj* (sun) levant; (anger) croissant; (going upwards) montant
**risk** *n* risque *m*, péril *m*; **at your own ~** à vos risques et périls; *coll* **not be worth the ~** ne pas valoir le coup; **run the ~** courir le risque; *vt* risquer, hasarder
**risky** *adj* risqué, hasardeux
**risotto** *n* risotto *m*
**risqué** *adj* risqué, scabreux -euse
**rissole** *n* croquette *f*
**rite** *n* rite *m*, cérémonie *f*; **last ~s** derniers sacrements
**ritual** *n* rites *mpl*; *adj* rituel -elle
**ritualism** *n* ritualisme *m*
**ritualistic** *adj* ritualiste
**ritually** *adv* selon les rites
**rival** *n* rival -e; *comm* concurrent -e; *adj* rival; *comm* concurrentiel -ielle
**rivalry** *n* rivalité *f*
**river** *n* fleuve *m*; (tributary) rivière *f*; **down ~** en aval; *coll* **sell s/o down the ~** trahir qn; **up ~** en amont
**river-bed** *n* lit *m* de rivière
**river-side** *n* rive *f*, bord *m* de l'eau; *adj* situé au bord de la rivière
**rivet** *n* rivet *m*; *vt* riveter, river; (attention) capter
**rivulet** *n* ruisseau *m*
**roach** *n* gardon *m*
**road** *n* (main) route *f*; (secondary) chemin *m*, voie *f*; *fig* voie *f*; (roadway) chaussée *f*; (street) rue *f*; *naut* **~s** rade

*f*; **be on the right** ~ être sur la bonne voie; **be on the** ~ être en route; (commercial traveller) être en tournée; *adj* routier -ière

**roadblock** *n* barrage (routier)

**road-hog** *n* chauffard *m*

**roadhouse** *n* relais *m*

**road-map** *n* carte routière

**road-sense** *n* sens *m* pratique des dangers de la route

**roadside** *n* bord *m* de la route; *adj* situé au bord de la route

**road-user** *n* usager *m* de la route

**roadway** *n* chaussée *f*

**roadworthy** *adj* mot en état de marche

**roam** *vt* parcourir; *vi* errer, rôder; ~ **about the world** rouler sa bosse

**roan** *n* (cheval) rouan *m*

**roar** *n* (animal) rugissement *m*; (thunder) grondement *m*; (person) hurlement *m*; (laughter) éclat *m*; *vt* vociférer; *vi* (animal) rugir; (thunder) gronder; (person) hurler; (engine) ronfler, vrombir; ~ **with laughter** éclater de rire

**roaring** *n see* **roar** *n*; *adj coll* **do a** ~ **trade** faire des affaires d'or

**roast** *n* rôti *m*; (beef) rosbif *m*; *vt* faire rôtir, rôtir; (coffee) griller; *vi* rôtir

**roaster** *n* (machine) rôtissoire *f*; (poultry) poulet *m* à rôtir, volaille *f* à rôtir

**rob** *vt* voler, dévaliser; ~ **s/o of sth** voler qch à qn

**robber** *n* voleur -euse

**robbery** *n* vol *m*, vol qualifié; **armed** ~ vol *m* à main armée; **highway** ~ vol *m* de grand chemin; *fig* escroquerie *f*

**robe** *n* robe *f*; (clothing) vêtement *m*; **bath** ~ peignoir *m* de bain

**robin** *n* rouge-gorge *m* (*pl* rouges-gorges)

**robot** *n* robot *m*, automate *m*

**robust** *adj* robuste, vigoureux -euse

**robustness** *n* robustesse *f*

**rock** *n* rocher *m*, roche *f*, roc *m*; *fig* **be on the** ~**s** être dans la dèche; (drink) **on the** ~**s** avec des glaçons; *vt* (cradle, child) bercer, balancer; (tip over) basculer; *fig* ~ **the boat** créer des ennuis; *vi* balancer; (person) se balancer; ~ **with laughter** se tordre de rire

**rock-and-roll, rock-n-roll** *n* rock and roll *m*

**rock-bottom** *n* fond rocheux; ~ **price** prix le plus bas; **reach** ~ toucher le fond, tomber au plus bas

**rock-cake** *n* petit gâteau aux raisins secs

¹**rocker** *n* bascule *f*; *eng* culbuteur *m*; *sl* **be off one's** ~ être un peu toqué

²**rocker** *n* (youth) blouson noir

**rockery** *n* rocaille *f*, jardin *m* de rocaille

**rocket** *n* fusée *f*; *mil* roquette *f*; *vi* se lancer; monter comme une fusée;

(prices) monter en flèche; ~ **to fame** devenir célèbre du jour au lendemain

**rocket-launcher** *n* lance-fusées *m*, lance-roquettes *m*

**rock-fall** *n* chute *f* de pierres, éboulement *m*

**rock-garden** *n* jardin *m* de rocaille

**rocking** *n* branlement *m*, balancement *m*; *adj* (unsteady) branlant; oscillant

**rocking-chair** *n* fauteuil *m* à bascule

**rocking-horse** *n* cheval *m* à bascule

¹**rocky** *adj* rocheux -euse, rocailleux -euse; (of rock) de roche

²**rocky** *adj coll* chancelant

**rococo** *n* rococo *m*; *adj* rococo *invar*

**rod** *n* baguette *f*, verge *f*; (fishing) canne *f* (à pêche); (curtain) tringle *f*; *eng* tige *f*; **fish with a** ~ **and line** pêcher à la ligne; **rule s/o with a** ~ **of iron** mener qn à la baguette; **spare the** ~ **and spoil the child** qui aime bien châtie bien

**rodent** *n* rongeur *m*; *adj* rongeur -euse

**rodeo** *n* rodéo *m*

¹**roe** *n* (deer) chevreuil *m*; (female) chevrette *f*

²**roe** *n* (hard) œufs *mpl* de poisson; (soft) laitance *f*

**rogue** *n* coquin -e, fripon -onne; *adj* (animal) solitaire

**roguery** *n* coquinerie *f*, friponnerie *f*

**roguish** *adj* coquin, fripon -onne; (mischievous) espiègle

**roisterer** *n* fêtard -e

**roistering** *adj* tapageur -euse

**role** *n* rôle *m*

**roll** *n* rouleau *m*; (list) liste *f*, état *m*; (bread) petit pain; (film) bobine *f*; (ship) roulis *m*; (thunder) grondement *m*; (drum) roulement *m*; ~ **of fat** bourrelet *m*; **call the** ~ faire l'appel; *vt* rouler; ~ **off** (print) imprimer; ~ **one's r's** rouler les r; ~ **over** retourner; ~ **up** enrouler, rouler; (sleeves) retrousser; *vi* rouler; (thunder) gronder; ~ **about** rouler çà et là; ~ **back** rouler en arrière; ~ **by** passer en roulant; ~ **down** (tears) couler; ~ **on** continuer de rouler; (time) s'écouler; *coll* ~ **on to-morrow** vivement demain; ~ **over** se retourner; *coll* ~ **up** arriver; ~ **up into a ball** se mettre en boule; **be** ~ **ing in money** rouler sur l'or

**roll-call** *n* appel *m*

**roller** *n* rouleau *m*; (road) rouleau compresseur; *eng* galet *m*

**roller-coaster** *n* montagnes *fpl* russes

**roller-skate** *n* patin *m* à roulettes; *vi* faire du patin à roulettes

**roller-towel** *n* essuie-mains *m* à rouleau

**rollicking** *n* jovial, rigoleur -euse, exubérant

**rolling** *n* roulement *m*; (ship) roulis *m*;

*adj* roulant; (sea) houleux -euse; (countryside) accidenté; **a ~ stone gathers no moss** pierre qui roule n'amasse pas mousse

**rolling-pin** *n* rouleau *m* à pâtisserie

**rolling-stock** *n* matériel roulant

**roll-top** *adj* **~ desk** bureau *m* à cylindre

**roly-poly** *adj coll* boulot -otte

**Roman** *n* Romain -e; *adj* romain; **~ Catholic** catholique

**romance** *n* (medieval) roman *m*; (story) histoire *f* romanesque; (affair) idylle *f*; *vi* exagérer

**romancer** *n pej* brodeur -euse

**Romania, Romanian** *n + adj see* **Roumania, Roumanian**

**romantic** *adj* romanesque, romantique

**romanticism** *n* romantisme *m*

**romp** *n* gambades *fpl*; *vi* s'ébattre; *coll* **~ home** gagner haut la main; *coll fig* **~ through** réussir facilement

**rompers** *npl* barboteuse *f*

**roneo** *n* ronéo *f*; *vt* ronéotyper, polycopier

**roof** *n* toit *m*, toiture *f*; (tunnel) voûte *f*; (mouth) dôme *m* du palais; *fig* **raise the ~** (be noisy) faire du vacarme; (applaud) applaudir à tout casser; *mot* **sunshine ~** toit ouvrant; *vt* couvrir (recouvrir) d'un toit

**roof-garden** *n* jardin *m* sur le toit

**roofing** *n* toiture *f*

**roofless** *adj* sans toit; (person) sans abri

**roof-light** *n mot* plafonnier *m*

¹**rook** *n* corneille *f*

²**rook** (chess) tour *f*

³**rook** *vt coll* rouler, refaire

**rookery** *n* colonie *f* de corneilles

**room** *n* (space) espace *m*, place *f*; (in house) pièce *f*; (bedroom) chambre *f*; (large) salle *f*; (grounds) lieu *m*; **~s** appartement *m*; **double ~** chambre *f* à deux personnes; **single ~** chambre *f* à une personne; **take up ~** prendre de la place; **there is ~ for improvement** cela laisse à désirer; *vi US* loger, vivre en garni

**roomful** *n* salle pleine, chambrée *f*

**roominess** *n* dimensions spacieuses

**rooming-house** *n US* maison *f* où on loue des chambres meublées

**room-mate** *n* compagnon (*f* compagne) de chambre

**roomy** *adj* spacieux -ieuse

**roost** *n* perchoir *m*, juchoir *m*; *fig* **come home to ~** se retourner contre son auteur; **go to ~** se jucher; *coll* aller coucher; **rule the ~** être le maître chez soi; *vi* se percher, se jucher

**rooster** *n* coq *m*

¹**root** *n* racine *f*; (origin) source *f*; **~ and branch** de fond en comble; **~ cause**

cause première; **lie at the ~ of** être à la source de; **pull up by the ~s** déraciner; **take ~** prendre racine; *vt* enraciner; **~ up** déraciner; *vi* s'enraciner

²**root, rout** *vt* **~ out** dénicher, déterrer; *vi* **~ among** fouiller parmi

**rooted** *adj* ancré, enraciné

**rope** *n* corde *f*; *naut* cordage *m*; (onions) chapelet *m*; *fig* **give s/o plenty of ~** lâcher la bride à qn; *fig* **know the ~s** connaître son affaire; *fig* **show s/o the ~s** mettre qn au courant; *vt* corder, attacher avec une corde; **~ in** entourer de cordes; (catch) prendre; (enrol) embrigader; *vi* (mountaineering) **~ up** s'encorder

**rope-ladder** *n* échelle *f* de corde

**ropey** *adj coll* pas fameux -euse, assez moche

**rosary** *n* chapelet *m*, rosaire *m*

**rose** *n* rose *f*; (colour) rose *m*; (wateringcan) pomme *f* (d'arrosoir); **ceiling ~** rosace *f* de plafond; **under the ~** en cachette, en confidence; **wild ~** églantine *f*

**rosebud** *n* bouton *m* de rose

**rose-bush** *n* rosier *m*

**rose-coloured** *adj* rose, rosé; **see things through ~ spectacles** voir tout en rose

**rose-garden** *n* roseraie *f*

**rosemary** *n* romarin *m*

**rose-tree** *n* rosier *m*

**rosette** *n* cocarde *f*, rosette *f*

**rosewood** *n* palissandre *m*

**rosiness** *n* teint rosé

**roster** *n* liste *f*; *mil* tableau *m* de service

**rostrum** *n* tribune *f*

**rosy** *adj* rose, rosé; **~ cheeks** joues vermeilles; **he has a ~ future** il a un bel avenir

**rot** *n* pourriture *f*; *fig* démoralisation *f*; (trees) carie *f*; (vine) mildiou *m*; *coll* (nonsense) bêtises *fpl*; **dry ~** carie sèche; **stop the ~** enrayer une progression dangereuse; **wet ~** carie *f* humide; *vt* faire pourrir, décomposer; *vi* pourrir, se décomposer

**rota** *n* liste *f*, tableau *m* de service

**rotary** *n US* rond-point *m* (*pl* rondspoints); *adj* rotatif -ive; **Rotary Club** Rotary Club *m*; **~ press** rotative *f*

**rotate** *vt* faire tourner; *agr* alterner; *vi* tourner, pivoter

**rotation** *n* rotation *f*; mouvement *m* rotatoire; **in ~** à tour de rôle

**rote** *n* **by ~** par cœur

**rotor** *n* rotor *m*

**rotten** *adj* pourri, carié; *coll* mauvais, moche, misérable

**rotter** *n coll* sale type *m*

**rotund** *adj* rond, arrondi

**rotunda** *n* rotonde *f*

**rotundity** n rondeur f, rotondité f

**rouble** n rouble m

**rouge** n rouge m, fard m

**rough** n (person) voyou m; (ground) terrain accidenté; **in the ~** à l'état brut; **take the ~ with the smooth** prendre le bénéfice avec les charges; adj rude; (coarse) grossier -ière; (surface) rugueux -euse, inégal; (conduct) brutal, brusque; (weather) gros (f grosse); (wind) violent; (sea) agité; (approximate) approximatif -ive; (voice) rauque; (unpolished) brut; (path) raboteux -euse; coll **~ customer** type violent; **~ draft (work)** brouillon m; **~ sketch** ébauche f; **be ~ with s/o** brutaliser qn; **give s/o a ~ handling** malmener qn; coll **have a ~ time** en baver; adv see **roughly**; vt coll **~ it** vivre à la dure; (have a bad time) en voir de dures; **~ up** (hair) ébouriffer; (glass) dépolir; coll (ill-treat) malmener

**roughage** n genre m d'aliments stimulant l'intestin

**rough-and-ready** adj (work) fait à la hâte; (person) sans façon

**rough-and-tumble** n bagarre f, mêlée f

**rough-cast** n crépi m

**roughen** vt rendre rude

**rough-handle** vt malmener

**rough-hew** vt dégrossir; **~ n stone** pierre f de taille

**rough-house** n bagarre f

**roughish** adj assez rude; (surface) rugueux -euse; (sea) assez houleux -euse

**roughly** adv rudement; (coarsely) grossièrement; brutalement; (about) approximativement, à peu près

**roughness** n rudesse f; (surface) rugosité f, aspérité f; (coarseness) grossièreté f; (manner) brusquerie f; (taste) âpreté f; (sea) agitation f; (roads) état raboteux; (violence) violence f

**roughshod** adj (horse) ferré à glace; fig **ride ~ over s/o** traiter qn sans ménagement

**rough-spoken** adj au langage grossier

**roulette** n roulette f

**Roumania, Romania** n Roumanie f

**Roumanian, Romanian** n Roumain -e; (language) roumain m; adj roumain

**round** n (cercle m, rond m; tour m, circuit m; (patrol) ronde f; (ladder) échelon m; (applause) salve f; (boxing) round m, reprise f; (golf, drinks, postman) tournée f; **~ of toast** rôtie f; **daily ~** train-train quotidien; **fire a ~** tirer un coup; **go on (make) one's ~s** faire sa tournée; adj rond, circulaire; **~ dance** ronde f; **~ robin** pétition revêtue de signatures en rond; **~ shoul-**

ders épaules voûtées; **~ sum** forte somme; US **~ trip** aller et retour m; **a ~ dozen** une bonne douzaine; **in ~ figures** en chiffres ronds; **make ~** arrondir; adv en rond; **~ about** tout autour, alentour; **all the year ~** pendant toute l'année; **a long way ~** un grand détour; **ask s/o ~** inviter qn (à venir chez soi); **bring ~** apporter; fig ranimer; **come ~** (visit) passer; (recover) reprendre connaissance; (return) revenir; **fifty metres ~** cinquante mètres de tour; **get ~ a problem** résoudre un problème; **get ~ s/o** enjôler qn; **get ~ to doing sth** finir par faire qch; **go ~** tourner; (call) passer, y aller; **hand ~** faire passer; **turn ~** and **~** tournoyer; **walk ~** faire le tour de; prep autour de; (near) aux abords de, près de; **go ~ sth** tourner autour de qch; (avoid) contourner qch; (visit) visiter qch; coll **go ~ the bend** devenir fou (f folle); **take s/o ~ a place** faire visiter un endroit à qn; vt arrondir; (cape) doubler; (obstacle) contourner; **~ off** arrondir; fig finir; **~ up** rassembler; (police) rafler; vi s'arrondir; coll **~ on s/o** s'en prendre brusquement à qn

**roundabout** n manège m, carrousel m, chevaux mpl de bois; (road) rond-point m (pl ronds-points); adj détourné, indirect; **~ way** détour m; **in a ~ way** de façon détournée

**rounders** npl balle f au camp

**roundly** adv rondement, vivement

**roundness** n rondeur f

**round-shouldered** adj au dos voûté

**roundsman** n livreur m

**round-table** adj **~ conference** table ronde f

**round-up** n (cattle) rassemblement m; (police) rafle f

**rouse** vt (awaken) réveiller; (provoke) provoquer; (indignation) soulever; (stimulate) exciter; (admiration) susciter; (from idleness) secouer; **~ oneself** se secouer; **~ s/o to action** inciter qn à l'action; **be ~ d** être monté, être furieux -ieuse

**rousing** adj (cheers) chaleureux -euse; (speech) vibrant, émouvant

**¹rout** n déroute f; **put to ~** mettre en déroute; vt mettre en déroute, disperser

**²rout** see **²root**

**route** n itinéraire m; route f, voie f; (bus) ligne f

**routine** n routine f; **~ questions** questions fpl d'usage; **daily ~** train-train quotidien

**roux** n cul roux m

**rove** vt parcourir; vi rôder, errer

**rover** *n* rôdeur -euse, vagabond -e; *naut* écumeur *m* de mer

**roving** *n* vagabondage *m*; *adj* vagabond, nomade

¹**row** *n* rang *m*, rangée *f*, ligne *f*; (figures) colonne *f*; (cars) file *f*; **in ~ s** par rangs; **in the front ~** au premier rang

²**row** *n* (on water) promenade *f* en barque (en canot); *vt* conduire à l'aviron; **~ s/o across** transporter qn en barque à l'autre rive; *vi* ramer, faire du canotage; *naut* nager

³**row** *n* (noise) tapage *m*, chahut *m*, vacarme *m*; (quarrel) scène *f*, dispute *f*; **get into a ~** se faire attraper; *coll* se faire passer un savon; **kick up a ~** faire du chahut; *vi* se quereller

**rowdy** *n* (troublemaker) voyou *m*; (noisy person) chahuteur *m*; *adj* tapageur -euse

**rowdyism** *n* chahutage *m*

**rowing** *n* (sport) canotage *m*

**rowing-boat** *n* bateau *m* à rames, barque *f* à rames

**rowlocks** *npl* tolets *mpl*

**royal** *adj* royal

**royalist** *n* + *adj* royaliste

**royally** *adv* royalement

**royalty** *n* royauté *f*; **(author's) royalties** droits *mpl* d'auteur

**rub** *n* frottement *m*; (dusting) coup *m* de torchon; (snag) hic *m*; *vt* frotter; (massage) frictionner; **~ away** user en frottant; **~ down** frotter; (person) frictionner; **~ out (off)** effacer; **~ shoulders with** frayer avec; *fig* **~ s/o up the wrong way** prendre qn à rebrousse-poil; **~ up** donner un coup de torchon à; *vi* frotter; (person) se frotter; **~ along** se débrouiller

¹**rubber** *n* (instrument) frottoir *m*; (person) frotteur -euse

²**rubber** *n* (substance) caoutchouc *m*; (eraser) gomme *f*; *US* **~ s** caoutchoucs *mpl*; **~ band** élastique *m*; **~ gloves** gants *mpl* en caoutchouc; **~ stamp** tampon *m*; **foam ~** caoutchouc *m* mousse

³**rubber** *n* (cards) robre *m*

**rubberize** *vt* caoutchouter

**rubberneck** *n US coll* badaud -e

**rubbery** *adj* caoutchouteux -euse

**rubbing** *n* frottement *m*; friction *f*

**rubbish** *n* détritus *mpl*; (household) ordures *fpl*; (old things) vieilleries *fpl*; (nonsense) bêtises *fpl*; (valueless) camelote *f*; **talk ~** dire des bêtises; *vt coll* dénigrer

**rubbish-dump** *n* décharge publique

**rubbishy** *adj* sans valeur

**rubble** *n* (in ruins) décombres *mpl*; *bui* moellons *mpl*; (for roads) blocaille *f*

**rub-down** *n* friction *f*

**rubicund** *adj* rubicond

**rubric** *n* rubrique *f*

**ruby** *n* rubis *m*; *adj* couleur de rubis

¹**ruck** *n* (racing) peloton *m*; **the ~** le commun du peuple

²**ruck** *n* faux pli; *vt* froisser, chiffonner; *vi* se chiffonner

**rucksack** *n* sac *m* à dos

**ructions** *npl coll* **there will be ~** il y aura du grabuge

**rudder** *n* gouvernail *m*; *aer* palonnier *m*

**rudderless** *adj* sans gouvernail

**ruddiness** *n* rougeur *f*

**ruddy** *adj* (cheeks) vermeil -eille; (complexion) coloré; *coll* sacré

**rude** *adj* (crude) primitif -ive, rude; (impolite) impoli, mal élevé; (vulgar) grossier -ière; (obscene) obscène; (sudden) brusque

**rudeness** *n* rudesse *f*; (person) impolitesse *f*; (coarseness) grossièreté *f*

**rudiment** *n* rudiment *m*; (basic knowledge) **~ s** premières notions

**rudimentary** *adj* rudimentaire, élémentaire

¹**rue** *n bot* rue *f*

²**rue** *vt* regretter amèrement, se repentir de

**rueful** *adj* triste, lugubre

**ruff** *n* fraise *f*, collerette *f*

**ruffian** *n* bandit *m*, brute *f*

**ruffianly** *adj* brutal

**ruffle** *n* (wrist) manchette *f* en dentelle; (neck) fraise *f*; (chest) jabot plissé; *vt* (hair) ébouriffer; (vex) irriter; (dress) plisser; (water) troubler, rider

**rug** *n* couverture *f*; (floor) carpette *f*; (bedside) descente *f* (de lit)

**rugby** *n* rugby *m*

**rugged** *adj* (ground) raboteux -euse, accidenté; (bark) rugueux -euse; (person) rude

**rugger** *n coll* rugby *m*

**ruin** *n* ruine *f*; *vt* ruiner; (spoil) abîmer; (seduce) séduire

**ruination** *n* ruine *f*, perte *f*

**ruinous** *adj* ruineux -euse; (in ruins) délabré

**rule** *n* règle *f*; gouvernement *m*, autorité *f*; *leg* décision *f*; **~ of the road** code *m* de la route; **~ of thumb** méthode *f* empirique; **~ s and regulations** règlements *mpl*; **as a ~** en général; **do things by ~** faire les choses selon les règles; **hard and fast ~** règle rigoureuse; *vt* gouverner; *leg* décider; (lines) régler, tracer; *vi* (prices) se pratiquer

**ruler** *n* souverain -e; gouverneur *m*; (for lines) règle *f*

**ruling** *adj* dominant; **~ classes** classes dirigeantes

**¹rum** *n* rhum *m*

**²rum** *adj coll* bizarre, drôle

**rumba, rhumba** *n* rumba *f*

**rumble** *n* (traffic) roulement *m*; (thunder) grondement *m*; (stomach) gargouillement *m*; *US* mot spider *m*; *vi* (traffic) rouler; (thunder) gronder; (stomach) gargouiller

**rumbling** *n see* **rumble**

**rumbustious** *adj* chahuteur -euse, bruyant

**ruminant** *n* ruminant *m*

**ruminate** *vt* + *vi* ruminer

**rumination** *n* rumination *f*

**ruminative** *adj* méditatif -ive

**rummage** *n* fouille *f*; (things) vieilleries *fpl* de rebut; *vt* + *vi* fouiller

**rummage-sale** *n* vente *f* d'objets usagés

**rumour** *n* rumeur *f*, bruit *m*; ~ **has it that** le bruit court que

**rumoured** *adj* allégué, présumé; **it is** ~ **that** le bruit court que

**rump** *n* (animal) croupe *f*; (person) derrière *m*; *cul* (beef) culotte *f*; *fig* reste *m*

**rumple** *vt* chiffonner, froisser

**rumpsteak** *n* romsteck *m*, rumsteck *m*

**rumpus** *n coll* vacarme *m*, chahut *m*

**run** *n* course *f*; (train) trajet *m*; *naut* parcours *m*; (outing) promenade *f*, tour *m*; (course) cours *m*; (rush to buy) descente *f*; (duration) durée *f*; (succession) suite *f*; (generality) commun *m*; *mus* roulade *f*; **an hour's** ~ **from** à une heure de; **at a** ~ au pas de course; **break into a** ~ se mettre à courir; **give s/o a** ~ **for his money** en donner à qn pour son argent; **have a long** ~ tenir longtemps; *theat* rester longtemps à l'affiche; **have a** ~ **of luck** être en veine; **have the** ~ **of the house** avoir libre accès dans la maison; **in the long** ~ à la longue; (criminal) **on the** ~ recherché par la police; **there's a** ~ **on sugar** tout le monde achète du sucre; **trial** ~ cours *m* d'essai; *vt* (risk) courir; (animal) faire courir; (wires, pipes) faire passer; (drive) conduire; (engine) faire marcher; (organization, service) diriger; (errand) faire; (house, car) entretenir; (shop, hotel) tenir; (liquid) verser, faire couler; (train, bus) mettre en service; ~ **down** (run over) écraser; (knock over) renverser; (find) dépister; *fig* dénigrer; ~ **in** conduire au poste (de police); (engine) roder; ~ **off** réciter; (liquid) faire couler; (letter) taper; ~ **one's car into a tree** heurter un arbre avec sa voiture; ~ **one's eye over sth** jeter un coup d'œil sur qch; (rope) ~ **out** laisser filer; ~ **over** (document) parcourir; (search) fouiller; (with vehicle) écraser; ~ **s/o**

through transpercer qn, passer son épée à travers le corps de qn; ~ **s/o to the station** conduire qn à la gare; ~ **up debts** laisser accumuler des dettes; *vi* courir; (escape) se sauver, filer; (machine) marcher, fonctionner; (liquid) couler; (leak) fuir; (bus, train) circuler; (eyes) pleurer; (rope) glisser; (nose) couler; (wound) suppurer; (play) jouer, tenir l'affiche; (colour) déteindre; ~ **about** courir de côté et d'autre; ~ **across** traverser en courant; ~ **across s/o** tomber sur qn; ~ **after** courir après; ~ **aground** échouer; ~ **along** (flank) longer; (go away) filer; ~ **at** se jeter sur; ~ **away** se sauver, s'enfuir; ~ **away with** (kidnap) enlever; ~ **away with the idea that** aller s'imaginer que; ~ **down** descendre en courant; (flow) ruisseler; (battery) se décharger; ~ **for sth** courir chercher qch; (sea) ~ **high** être grosse; ~ **into** (figures) s'élever à; (collide) heurter; ~ **into debt** s'endetter; ~ **into s/o** tomber sur qn; ~ **off** fuir; ~ **out** sortir en courant; (time) expirer; (supplies) s'épuiser; ~ **through** traverser en courant; (read quickly) parcourir; (money) dissiper; ~ **up** monter en courant

**runabout** *n mot* petite voiture; (person) vagabond -e

**runaway** *n* + *adj* fugitif -ive; ~ **marriage** mariage clandestin; ~ **victory** victoire *f* facile

**run-down** *n* résumé *m*; diminution *f* d'activité; *adj* épuisé, affaibli; (battery) à plat

**rune** *n* rune *f*

**rung** *n* échelon *m*; (chair) bâton *m*

**runic** *adj* runique

**runnel** *n* ruisseau *m*

**runner** *n* coureur -euse; (sledge) patin *m*; (messenger) messager *m*; **scarlet** ~ **bean** haricot *m* d'Espagne

**runner-up** *n* second -e

**running** *n* course *f*; (machine) fonctionnement *m*; (hotel, etc) direction *f*; (water) ruissellement *m*; (wound) suppuration *f*; **be out of the** ~ n'avoir plus aucune chance; **make the** ~ mener la course; *adj* courant; (wound) qui suppure; (continuous) continu; ~ **cold** rhume *m* de cerveau; ~ **commentary** reportage *m* en direct; ~ **expenses** dépenses courantes; ~ **jump** saut *m* avec élan; **in** ~ **order** en état de fonctionnement

**running-board** *n mot* marchepied *m*

**runny** *adj* liquide; (nose) qui coule

**runt** *n* bœuf *m* de petite race; *coll* nabot *m*

**run-through** *n* répétition *f*

**runway** *n aer* piste *f* d'envol; *eng* chemin *m* de roulement
**rupture** *n* rupture *f*; (hernia) hernie *f*; *vt* rompre; **be ~ d** avoir une hernie; *vi* se rompre
**rural** *adj* rural
**ruse** *n* ruse *f*, stratagème *m*
¹**rush** *n* jonc *m*
²**rush** *n* ruée *f*, course précipitée; (people) presse *f*, bousculade *f*; (haste) hâte *f*; *cin* **~ es** projection *f* d'essai; **~ hour** heure *f* d'affluence (de pointe); **~ job** travail urgent; *vt* (person) entraîner, faire dépêcher; (transport) transporter d'urgence; (invade) envahir; *coll* (charge high price) estamper; **~ up** (build) bâtir à la hâte; *vi* se précipiter, s'élancer; **~ at s/o** se jeter sur qn; **~ into** se précipiter dans; **~ out** sortir précipitamment; **~ through** traverser à toute vitesse; **~ to conclusions** conclure hâtivement
**rusk** *n* biscotte *f*
**russet** *n* (apple) reinette (grise); *adj* (colour) roussâtre
**Russia** *n* Russie *f*
**Russian** *n* Russe; (language) russe *m*; *adj* russe
**rust** *n* rouille *f*; *vt* rouiller; *vi* se rouiller, rouiller

**rustic** *n* paysan -anne; *pej* rustre; *adj* rustique
**rusticate** *vt* (student) renvoyer temporairement; *vi* habiter à la campagne; se retirer à la campagne
**rustication** *n* (student) renvoi *m* temporaire; résidence *f* à la campagne
**rusticity** *n* rusticité *f*
**rustle** *n* (leaves, etc) bruissement *m*; (paper) froissement *m*; (silk) frou-frou *m*; *vt* (leaves, etc) faire bruire; (paper) froisser; (silk) faire froufrouter; *US* (steal cattle) voler du bétail; *coll* **~ up** se débrouiller pour trouver (pour faire); *vi* (leaves, etc) bruire; (silk) faire frou-frou; (paper) produire un bruissement
**rustless** *adj* (rustproof) inoxydable; (not rusted) sans rouille
**rust-preventive** *n* anti-rouille *m*
**rustproof** *adj* inoxydable
**rusty** *adj* rouillé; (colour) couleur de rouille; (voice) rauque, éraillé; **get ~** se rouiller
¹**rut** *n* ornière *f*; *vt* sillonner d'ornières
²**rut** *n* (of animals) chaleur *f*; *vt* couvrir; *vi* être en chaleur
**ruthless** *adj* impitoyable, sans merci
**rye** *n* seigle *m*
**rye-grass** *n* ray-grass *m*

# S

**Sabbath** *n* sabbat *m*
**sabbatical** *adj eccles* sabbatique; **~ year** année *f* de congé
**sable** *n* (animal) zibeline *f*
**sabotage** *n* sabotage *m*; *vt* saboter
**saboteur** *n* saboteur -euse
**sabre** *n* sabre *m*
**sabre-rattling** *n* menaces *fpl* de guerre
**saccharin** *n* saccharine *f*
**sacerdotal** *adj* sacerdotal
**sachet** *n* sachet *m*
¹**sack** *n* sac *m*; *coll* **get the ~** recevoir son congé; *coll* **give s/o the ~** congédier qn; *vt* mettre en sac; *coll* (fire) congédier
²**sack** *n* (pillage) pillage *m*, sac *m*; *vt* saccager, mettre à sac
**sackcloth** *n* toile *f* à sac

**sackful** *n* plein sac *m*
¹**sacking** *n* mise *f* en sac; *coll* (firing) congédiement *m*
²**sacking** *n* (pillage) sac *m*
**sacrament** *n* sacrement *m*
**sacramental** *adj* sacramentel -elle
**sacred** *adj* sacré, saint; **~ to** consacré à
**sacredness** *n* sainteté *f*
**sacrifice** *n* sacrifice *m*; (giving up) renoncement *m*; (offering) victime *f*; **at a great ~** au prix de grands sacrifices; *vt* sacrifier; (giving up) renoncer à
**sacrificial** *adj* sacrificatoire
**sacrilege** *n* sacrilège *m*
**sacrilegious** *adj* sacrilège
**sacristan** *n* sacristain *m*
**sacristy** *n* sacristie *f*
**sacrosanct** *adj* sacro-saint

**sacrum** *n* sacrum *m*

**sad** *adj* triste; (regrettable) déplorable; (loss) cruel -elle; (place) morne; **make s/o ~** attrister qn

**sadden** *vt* attrister, affliger

**saddle** *n* selle *f*; (mountain) col *m*; (mutton) selle *f*; (hare) râble *m*; **in the ~ en selle**; *vt* seller; *coll* **~ s/o with sth** mettre qch sur le dos de qn

**saddle-bag** *n* sacoche *f* de selle

**saddler** *n* bourrelier *m*, sellier *m*

**saddlery** *n* bourrellerie *f*, sellerie *f*

**sadism** *n* sadisme *m*

**sadist** *n* sadiste

**sadistic** *adj* sadique

**sadly** *adv* tristement; (greatly) beaucoup, vraiment

**sadness** *n* tristesse *f*

**safari** *n* safari *m*

¹**safe** *n* coffre-fort *m* ( *pl* coffres-forts)

²**safe** *adj* (in safety) en sûreté; (place) sûr; (not dangerous) sans danger; (out of danger) hors de danger; **~ and sound** sain et sauf; **be on the ~ side** être du bon côté; **get home ~** rentrer sans accident; **in a ~ place** en lieu sûr; **it's quite ~ to** il n'y a aucun danger à

**safe-conduct** *n* sauf-conduit *m*

**safeguard** *n* sauvegarde *f*; *vt* sauvegarder, protéger

**safekeeping** *n* bonne garde

**safely** *adv* sans accident; sûrement; (without risk) sans danger; (securely) en sûreté

**safety** *n* sûreté *f*, sécurité *f*; **~ device** dispositif *m* de sûreté; **~ first!** soyez prudents!; **road ~** sécurité routière

**safety-belt** *n* mot ceinture *f* de sécurité

**safety-catch** *n* cran *m* de sécurité

**safety-lamp** *n* lampe *f* de sûreté

**safety-match** *n* allumette suédoise

**safety-pin** *n* épingle *f* de sûreté (de nourrice)

**safety-razor** *n* rasoir *m* de sûreté

**safety-valve** *n* soupape *f* de sûreté

**saffron** *n* safran *m*

**sag** *n* affaissement *m*, fléchissement *m*; *vi* s'affaisser, fléchir; (lean over) pencher d'un côté; (cord, cable) se détendre

**saga** *n* *lit* saga *f*; suite *f* d'événements extraordinaires

**sagacious** *adj* sagace, perspicace, avisé

**sagacity, sagaciousness** *n* sagacité *f*

¹**sage** *n* sage *m*, philosophe *m*; *adj* sage

²**sage** *n* *bot* sauge *f*

**sago** *n* sagou *m*

**Sahara** *n* the **~** le Sahara

**sail** *n* voile *f*; (windmill) aile *f*; (trip) promenade *f* à la voile, promenade *f* en mer; **hoist ~** hisser une voile; **lower ~** amener une voile; **set ~** appareiller,

prendre la mer; **under full ~** toutes voiles dehors; (sea) parcourir; *vi* faire de la voile, naviguer; (glide) planer; (leave) partir; **~ at five knots** filer cinq nœuds; **down** descendre

**sailing** *n* navigation *f*; (departure) départ *m*; **he likes ~** il aime la voile; **it's plain ~** cela va tout seul

**sailing-boat** *n* canot *m* à voiles

**sailing-ship** *n* voilier *m*, bateau *m* à voiles

**sailor** *n* marin *m*, matelot *m*; **be a bad ~** être sujet -ette au mal de mer; **be a good ~** avoir le pied marin

**saint** *n* saint -e; **All Saints' Day** la Toussaint; *adj* saint

**saintly** *adj* saint

¹**sake** *n* cause *f*; **art for art's ~** l'art pour l'art; **for God's ~** pour l'amour de Dieu; **for his ~** à cause de lui; **for pity's ~ !** pour l'amour de Dieu!; **for the ~ of** à cause de, pour l'amour de

²**sake** *n* (drink) saké *m*, saki *m*

**salacious** *adj* lubrique

**salad** *n* salade *f*; **~ days** années *fpl* de jeunesse; **fruit ~** macédoine *f* de fruits; **mixed ~** salade panachée

**salad-bowl** *n* saladier *m*

**salad-dressing** *n* vinaigrette *f*

**salamander** *n* salamandre *f*

**salami** *n* salami *m*

**salaried** *adj* rétribué, rémunéré, salarié

**salary** *n* traitement *m*, appointements *mpl*

**sale** *n* vente *f*; (clearance) solde *m*; (auction) vente *f* aux enchères; *US* **~ s clerk** vendeur -euse; **~ s promotion** campagne *f* de vente; **for ~** à vendre; **on ~** en vente; **put up for ~** mettre en vente

**saleable** *adj* vendable

**sale-price** *n* prix *m* de solde

**saleroom** *n* salle *f* des ventes

**salesgirl** *n* vendeuse *f*

**salesman** *n* vendeur *m*

**salesmanship** *n* art *m* de vendre

**sales-resistance** *n* hésitation *f* à acheter; **there is a lot of ~** la clientèle boude

**sales-talk** *n* boniment *m*

**saleswoman** *n* vendeuse *f*

**salient** *n* *mil* saillant *m*; *adj* saillant; *fig* frappant

**saline** *n* marais *m* salant; (saltworks) saline *f*; *med* sel purgatif; *adj* salin, salé

**salinity** *n* salinité *f*

**saliva** *n* salive *f*

**salivary** *adj* salivaire

**salivate** *vi* saliver

**salivation** *n* salivation *f*

**sallow** *adj* jaune, jaunâtre

**sally** *n* *mil* sortie *f*; (wit) saillie *f*; *vi* *mil* faire une sortie; ~ **forth** se mettre en route

**salmon** *n* saumon *m*; *adj* saumon *invar*

**salmon-trout** *n* truite saumonée

**salon** *n* salon *m*; **beauty** ~ institut *m* de beauté

**saloon** *n* salle *f*, salon *m*; *mot* conduite intérieure; *US* bar *m*; ~ **deck** pont *m* de première classe

**saloon-bar** *n* = bar plus cher dans un pub anglais

**salt** *n* sel *m*; **an old** ~ un loup de mer; **kitchen** ~ gros sel; **not worth one's** ~ inutile; **rock** ~ sel *m* gemme; **spirits of** ~ esprit *m* de sel; **with a pinch of** ~ avec un grain de sel; *adj* salé; *vt* saler

**salt-cellar** *n* salière *f*

**saltiness** *n* salinité *f*, salure *f*

**salt-marsh** *n* marais salant

**saltpetre** *n* salpêtre *m*

**salt-tax** *n hist* gabelle *f*

**salt-water** *adj* de mer

**salty** *adj* salé

**salubrious** *adj* salubre

**salutary** *adj* salutaire

**salutation** *n* salutation *f*

**salute** *n* salut *m*, salutation *f*; **fire a** ~ tirer une salve; **take the** ~ passer les troupes en revue; *vt* saluer

**salvage** *n* sauvetage *m*; (money) prime *f* de sauvetage; (things) objets sauvés; (materials) récupération *f*; *vt* sauver; effectuer le sauvetage de; (waste materials) récupérer

**salvation** *n* salut *m*; **Salvation Army** Armée *f* du Salut

**salve** *n* pommade *f*, baume *m*; *vt* adoucir, apaiser

**salver** *n* plateau *m*

**salvo** *n* salve *f*

**samba** *n* samba *f*

**same** *adj* + *pron* même; ~ **here!** moi aussi!; **and the** ~ **to you** à vous de même; **at the** ~ **time** en même temps; (simultaneously) à la fois; **do the** ~ en faire autant; **he looks just the** ~ il n'a pas changé du tout; **in the** ~ **way de** même; **it comes to the** ~ **thing** cela revient au même; **it's all the** ~ c'est tout un; **it's all the** ~ **to me** cela m'est égal; *adv* de même; **all the** ~ malgré tout, quand même

**sameness** *n* identité *f*; monotonie *f*

**sample** *n* échantillon *m*; **as a** ~ à titre d'échantillon; *vt* échantillonner; (taste) déguster, goûter; (try out) essayer

**sanatorium** *n* (*pl* **sanatoria**) sanatorium *m*; (school) infirmerie *f*

**sanctification** *n* sanctification *f*

**sanctify** *vt* sanctifier, consacrer

**sanctimonious** *adj* papelard, cagot

**sanctimoniousness, sanctimony** *n* cagoterie *f*, papelardise *f*

**sanction** *n* sanction *f*; *vt* sanctionner, approuver

**sanctity** *n* sainteté *f*

**sanctuary** *n* sanctuaire *m*; *fig* refuge *m*; **right of** ~ droit *m* d'asile; **take** ~ chercher asile

**sanctum** *n* sanctuaire *m*; (private room) cabinet privé

**sand** *n* sable *m*; ~ **s** plage *f*; *vt* sabler; *vi* ~ **up** s'ensabler

**sandal** *n* sandale *f*

**sandbag** *n* sac *m* de sable, sac *m* de terre; *vt* protéger avec des sacs de sable

**sandbank** *n* banc *m* de sable

**sand-blast** *n* jet *m* de sable; *vt* passer au jet de sable

**sandcastle** *n* château *m* de sable

**sand-dune** *n* dune *f*

**sandiness** *n* nature sablonneuse

**sandman** *n* **the** ~ **is coming** le marchand de sable passe

**sandpaper** *n* papier *m* de verre; *vt* frotter au papier de verre

**sandstone** *n* grès *m*

**sandstorm** *n* tempête *f* de sable

**sandwich** *n* sandwich *m* (*pl* sandwiches); *vt* intercaler; **be** ~ **ed between** être pris entre

**sandwichman** *n* homme-sandwich *m* (*pl* hommes-sandwiches)

**sandy** *adj* sableux -euse, sablonneux -euse; (hair) roux (*f* rousse)

**sane** *adj* sain d'esprit, sensé

**sanguinary** *adj* sanguinaire

**sanguine** *adj* (temperament) sanguin; (complexion) rubicond; (optimistic) optimiste, confiant

**sanitary** *adj* sanitaire, hygiénique; ~ **towel** serviette *f* hygiénique

**sanitation** *n* hygiène *f*; système *m* sanitaire; (in house) sanitaire *m*

**sanity** *n* santé *f* d'esprit; bon sens

**Sanskrit** *n* sanskrit *m*

**Santa Claus** *n* le Père Noël

¹**sap** *n bot* sève *f*

²**sap** *n coll* idiot -e, nigaud -e

³**sap** *vt* miner, saper

**sapless** *adj* sans sève, desséché

**sapling** *n* jeune arbre *m*

**sapper** *n mil* sapeur *m*

**sapphire** *n* saphir *m*

**sappy** *adj* plein de sève

**saraband** *n mus* sarabande *f*

**sarcasm** *n* sarcasme *m*, ironie *f*

**sarcastic** *adj* sarcastique, mordant

**sarcoma** *n med* sarcome *m*

**sardine** *n* sardine *f*; **packed like** ~ **s** serrés comme des harengs

**sardonic** *adj* sardonique

**sari, saree** *n* sari *m*

**sarong** n sarong m
**sartorial** adj de tailleur
¹**sash** n écharpe f, ceinture f
²**sash** n (window) châssis m
**sash-window** n fenêtre f à guillotine
**Satan** n Satan m
**satanic** adj diabolique, satanique
**satchel** n (bag) sacoche f; (school) cartable m
**sate** vt assouvir, rassasier
**satellite** n satellite m; ~ **town** ville f satellite
**satiate** vt rassasier
**satiety** n satiété f
**satin** n satin m; adj de satin; (like satin) satiné
**satire** n satire f
**satiric(al)** adj satirique
**satirist** n auteur m satirique
**satirize** vt satiriser
**satisfaction** n satisfaction f; (payment) paiement m, acquittement m; (reparation) réparation f; (passion) assouvissement m; (reason for satisfaction) motif m de satisfaction; **give s/o** ~ faire réparation à qn; **to his** ~ de manière à le satisfaire
**satisfactorily** adv de façon satisfaisante
**satisfactory** adj satisfaisant
**satisfied** adj content, satisfait; (convinced) convaincu
**satisfy** vt satisfaire, contenter; (convince) convaincre; (condition) remplir; (honour) satisfaire à; (make reparation to) faire réparation à; (desire) assouvir; **done to** ~ **one's conscience** fait par acquit de conscience
**saturate** vt saturer, tremper
**saturation** n saturation f
**Saturday** n samedi m
**Saturn** n Saturne m
**saturnine** adj taciturne, sombre
**satyr** n satyre m
**sauce** n sauce f; coll (impertinence) culot m, toupet m; **what is** ~ **for the goose is** ~ **for the gander** ce qui est bon pour l'un est bon pour l'autre
**sauce-boat** n saucière f
**saucepan** n casserole f
**saucer** n soucoupe f; **flying** ~ soucoupe volante
**saucy** adj impertinent; (roguish) fripon -onne
**Saudi Arabia** n Arabie Saoudite f
**sauerkraut** n choucroute f
**sauna** n sauna m
**saunter** vi flâner, se balader; ~ **up** s'approcher sans se presser
**sausage** n saucisse f; (dry) saucisson m
**sausage-meat** n chair f à saucisse
**sausage-roll** n saucisse enrobée de pâte
**sauté** adj cul sauté; vt faire sauter

**savage** n sauvage; adj sauvage, barbare; (animal) féroce; vt attaquer
**savagery**, **savageness** n sauvagerie f, barbarie f, brutalité f
**savant** n savant -e
¹**save** n sp arrêt m; vt sauver; (save up) économiser; (put aside) mettre de côté; (time) gagner; (protect) protéger; (avoid) éviter; (look after) ménager; (reserve) réserver; (from danger, etc) préserver; ~ **appearances** sauvegarder (sauver) les apparences; ~ **oneself for sth** se ménager pour qch; ~ **s/o the trouble of doing sth** épargner à qn la peine de faire qch
²**save** prep excepté, sauf
**saveloy** n cervelas m
**saver** n (saviour) sauveur m; (rescuer) sauveteur m; (economiser) personne f économe
¹**saving** n (rescue) sauvetage m; (freeing) délivrance f; (souls) salut m; (money) économie f; ~**s** économies fpl
²**saving** prep sauf
**savings-bank** n caisse f d'épargne
**saviour** n sauveur m
**savory** n bot sarriette f
**savour** n saveur f, goût m; (trace) trace f; vt savourer; ~ **of sth** tenir de qch
**savoury** n entremets non sucré; adj savoureux -euse, succulent
¹**saw** n scie f; **power** ~ scie f mécanique; (for trees) tronçonneuse f; vt scier; ~ **the air** battre l'air; ~ **up** débiter
²**saw** n ar (saying) dicton m, maxime f
**sawdust** n sciure f
**saw-mill** n scierie f
**sawyer** n scieur m
**saxifrage** n saxifrage f
**Saxon** n Saxon -onne; adj saxon -onne
**Saxony** n Saxe f
**saxophone** n saxophone m
**say** n parole f, mot m; **have one's** ~ dire ce qu'on a à dire; **have no** ~ **in the matter** ne pas avoir voix au chapitre; vt dire; (prayers) faire; ~ **no more!** n'en dites pas davantage!; **didn't I** ~ **so!** quand je vous le disais!; **have plenty to** ~ **for oneself** ne pas avoir la langue dans sa poche; **I must** ~ **that** j'avoue que; **it is said that** on dit que; **let's** ~ **five pounds** disons cinq livres; **so to** ~ pour ainsi dire; **that is to** ~ c'est à dire; **there's much to be said for doing this** il y a de bonnes raisons pour faire cela; **to** ~ **nothing of** sans parler de; **what did you** ~? comment?, que dites-vous?; **what do you** ~ **to a walk?** si on faisait une promenade?; **without** ~**ing a word** sans mot dire; vi as one might ~ comme qui dirait; **I** ~ **!** dites donc!; **so to** ~ pour ainsi dire; **that is to** ~ c'est

à dire; **you don't ~**! pas possible!, par exemple!

**saying** n dicton m; (action) énonciation f

**scab** n (disease) gale f; (over wound) croûte f; coll (workman refusing to strike) jaune m; vi former une croûte

**scabbard** n fourreau m, gaine f

**scabby** adj galeux -euse; (sore) croûteux -euse; coll (worthless) méprisable

**scabies** n gale f

**scabious** n bot scabieuse f

**scabrous** adj rugueux -euse; (story, etc) scabreux -euse

**scaffold** n échafaud m; (for speaker) estrade f

**scaffolding** n échafaudage m

**scald** n échaudure f; vt échauder, ébouillanter

**scalding** n échaudage m; adj bouillant

¹**scale** n (fish, skin) écaille f; (deposit) dépôt m; (on teeth) tartre m; vt écailler; (teeth) détartrer; vi s'écailler; (boiler) s'incruster

²**scale** n (of balance) plateau m; ~s balance f; **bathroom-~s** pèse-personne m (pl pèse-personne(s)); **letter ~** pèse-lettre m; **tip the ~s at** peser plus de; fig **turn the ~s** faire pencher la balance; vi peser

³**scale** n échelle f; (extent) étendue f; mus gamme f; **on a large (small) ~** en grand (petit); **on the ~ of** à l'échelle de; vt (climb) escalader; (map) tracer à l'échelle; **~ up (down)** augmenter (réduire) à l'échelle

**scalene** adj scalène

**scaliness** n squamosité f

**scallop** n zool pétoncle m, coquille f Saint-Jacques; (needlework) feston m; vt faire cuire en coquille; festonner

**scallywag** n coll propre à rien

**scalp** n cuir chevelu; vt scalper

**scalpel** n scalpel m

**scaly** adj écailleux -euse; (boiler) tartreux -euse

**scamp** n mauvais garnement, vaurien -ienne; **young ~** petit galopin; vt bâcler

**scamper** vi courir allègrement; **~ away (off)** détaler, se sauver à toutes jambes

**scampi** npl scampi mpl

**scan** vt scruter, examiner; (verse) mesurer; cin+TV balayer; (read quickly) parcourir rapidement

**scandal** n scandale m, honte f; (slander) médisance f; **create a ~** faire un scandale; **talk ~** cancaner

**scandalize** vt scandaliser

**scandalmonger** n médisant -e, mauvaise langue

**scandalous** adj scandaleux -euse, honteux -euse

**Scandinavian** n Scandinave; adj scandinave

**scanner** n scrutateur -trice; elect appareil explorateur; **radar ~** déchiffreur m de radar

**scansion** n scansion f

**scant** adj insuffisant, peu abondant

**scanty** adj insuffisant; (meal) maigre; (news, hair) rare

**scapegoat** n bouc m émissaire

**scar** n cicatrice f; (face) balafre f; vt laisser une cicatrice sur; balafrer; vi se cicatriser

**scarce** adj rare, peu abondant; **grow ~** se faire rare; coll **make oneself ~** filer

**scarcely** adv à peine; **~ ever** presque jamais; **he can ~ walk** c'est à peine s'il peut marcher; **he ~ goes out** il ne sort guère; **I can ~ believe it** j'ai de la peine à le croire

**scarcity, scarceness** n pénurie f, manque m, rareté f

**scare** n panique f, alarme f; **give s/o a ~** faire peur à qn; vt effrayer, alarmer, faire peur à; **~ away** effaroucher; vi s'effrayer, s'alarmer

**scarecrow** n épouvantail m

**scaremonger** n alarmiste

**scarf** n écharpe f; (woman's) fichu m; (silk) foulard m; (man's) cache-col m invar

**scarifier** n scarificateur m

**scarify** vt scarifier

**scarlet** n écarlate f; adj écarlate; **~ fever** scarlatine f

**scarred** adj portant des cicatrices; balafré

**scary** adj coll épouvantable, effrayant

**scat** interj file!, filez!

**scathing** adj mordant, cinglant

**scatological** adj scatologique

**scatology** n scatologie f

**scatter** n dispersion f; vt disperser; (put to flight) mettre en fuite; (clouds) dissiper; (seeds) semer à la volée; (throw about) éparpiller; vi (mob) se disperser; (clouds) se dissiper; s'éparpiller

**scatter-brain** n étourdi -e

**scattered** adj dispersé, épars

**scattering** n dispersion f; éparpillement m; (small number) petite quantité

**scatty** adj coll étourdi, timbré

**scavenge** vt+vi balayer, nettoyer

**scavenger** n boueur m, balayeur m des rues; (creature) animal m nécrophage

**scenario** n scénario m

**scene** n scène f; (event) théâtre m, lieu m; (theatre set) décor m; (landscape) paysage m; sl ambiance f; **behind the ~s** dans la coulisse (les coulisses); **make a ~** faire une scène; **on the ~ of the accident** sur les lieux de l'accident scenery n (landscape) paysage m; theat décors mpl

scenic adj scénique; théâtral

scent n odeur f, parfum m, senteur f; (track) piste f, trace f; (sense) odorat m; (dog) flair m; **be on the right ~** être sur la piste; vt (smell out) flairer; (perfume) parfumer, embaumer

scented adj parfumé; (air) embaumé

scentless adj sans odeur, inodore

sceptic n sceptique

sceptical adj sceptique

scepticism n scepticisme m

sceptre n sceptre m

schedule n liste f; (timetable) horaire m; (to law) annexe f; note explicative; (inventory) inventaire m; (taxes) cédule f; (plan) plan m d'exécution; **according to ~** selon les provisions; **be behind ~** être en retard sur l'horaire prévu; **on ~** à l'heure; **up to ~** comme prévu, à la date voulue; vt (law) ajouter comme annexe; (put on list) inscrire sur une liste; (plan) dresser le programme de; aer **~d service** vol régulier

schema n (pl schemata) schéma m

schematic adj schématique

scheme n plan m, projet m; arrangement m; pej intrigue f, machination f; vt combiner, machiner; vi intriguer, comploter

schemer n intrigant -e

scheming adj intrigant

scherzo n scherzo m

schism n schisme m

schismatic adj schismatique

schizoid adj schizoïde

schizophrenia n schizophrénie f

schizophrenic adj schizophrène

schmaltzy adj coll d'un sentimentalisme exagéré

schnap(p)s n schnaps m

schnorkel n see snorkel

scholar n écolier -ière, élève; (learned) savant -e, érudit -e; (holder of scholarship) boursier -ière

scholarly adj savant, érudit

scholarship n savoir m, érudition f; (for studies) bourse f

scholastic adj scolastique, érudit

scholasticism n scolastique f

¹school n école f, groupe m scolaire; (grammar) lycée m, collège m; (boarding) pension f, pensionnat m; (schooling) études fpl scolaires, les classes fpl; (higher education) académie f, institut m; **~ year** année f scolaire; **church ~** = école f libre; **comprehensive ~** = collège m d'enseignement secondaire (C.E.S.); **go to ~** aller en classe; **independent ~** collège privé; **night ~** cours mpl du soir; **public ~** collège privé; US école f d'état; **state ~** école f d'état; vt discipliner, former, instruire; **~ed in** habitué à

²school n (fish) banc m, bande f

schoolbook n livre m scolaire

schoolboy n écolier m, élève m

schoolday n jour m de classe; **in my ~s** pendant mes années d'école

schoolfellow n camarade d'école

schoolgirl n écolière f, élève f

schooling n éducation f, instruction f

schoolmarm n coll maîtresse f d'école

schoolmaster n (secondary) professeur m; (primary) instituteur m

schoolmate n copain (f copine) d'école

schoolmistress n (secondary) professeur m; (primary) institutrice f

schoolroom n salle f de classe

schoolteacher n (secondary) professeur m; (primary) instituteur -trice

schoolteaching n enseignement m scolaire

schooner n naut schooner m, goélette f; grand verre (à Xérès)

sciatic adj sciatique

sciatica n sciatique f

science n science f

science-fiction n science-fiction f

scientific adj scientifique

scientist n savant -e, homme m de science, scientifique

Scilly Isles npl Sorlingues fpl

scimitar n cimeterre m

scintillate vi scintiller, étinceler

scion n descendant -e; bot rejeton m

scissors npl ciseaux mpl

sclerosis n sclérose f; **multiple ~** sclérose f en plaques

sclerotic adj sclérosé

¹scoff vi se moquer; **~ at** se moquer de

²scoff vt bouffer

scold n mégère f; vt + vi gronder, réprimander

sconce n bougeoir m

scone n pain m au lait

scoop n (shovel) pelle f; (spoon) grande cuiller; (news) scoop m; vt (scoop out) évider; (liquid) écoper; (news) faire un scoop de

scoot vi coll décamper, filer

scooter n (child's) trottinette f; (motor-scooter) scooter m

scope n (extent) étendue f, portée f; (space) espace m; (freedom) liberté f; **fall within the ~ of a work** rentrer dans le plan d'un ouvrage; **give ~ for** donner carrière à; **have full ~ to** avoir toute latitude pour

scorbutic adj scorbutique

scorch vt roussir, brûler; (sun) rôtir, dessécher; vi coll **~ along** brûler le pavé, rouler comme un fou

**scorcher** *n coll* journée *f* torride; (remark) riposte cinglante

**scorching** *adj* brûlant; (weather) torride

**score** *n* (notch) entaille *f*, encoche *f*; (game) nombre *m* de points, score *m*; (twenty) vingtaine *f*; *mus* partition *f*; (subject) question *f*, point *m*; **~ of people** des masses de gens; **keep ~** marquer les points; *coll* **know the ~** s'y connaître; **on that ~** à cet égard; **pay off old ~s** régler de vieux comptes; **pay one's ~** régler son compte; *vt* (scratch) érafler, rayer; (notch) entailler, cocher; (goal, point) marquer; *mus* noter; (success) remporter; *vi* (game) marquer un but (un point); **~ off s/o** marquer des points aux dépens de qn; **~ over s/o** l'emporter sur qn

**scorer** *n* marqueur *m*

**scoria** *n* scorie *f*, scories *fpl*

**scorn** *n* dédain *m*, mépris *m*

**scornful** *adj* méprisant, dédaigneux -euse

**scorpion** *n* scorpion *m*

**Scot** *n* Écossais -e

**Scotch** *adj* écossais

**¹scotch** *n* (whisky) scotch *m*

**²scotch** *vt* (plan) faire avorter, déjouer

**scotfree** *adj* **get off ~** s'en tirer indemne

**Scotland** *n* Écosse *f*

**Scots** *n* dialecte écossais; *adj* écossais

**Scotsman** *n* Écossais *m*

**Scotswoman** *n* Écossaise *f*

**Scottish** *adj* écossais

**scoundrel** *n* scélérat *m*, gredin *m*, voyou *m*

**scour** *n* nettoyage *m*, récurage *m*; *vt* nettoyer, frotter; (greasy object) dégraisser; (saucepan) récurer; (country) battre, parcourir

**scourer** *n* nettoyeur -euse, récureur -euse; (for pans) éponge *f* métallique

**scourge** *n* fléau *m*; *vt* fouetter; *fig* châtier

**¹scout** *n* éclaireur *m*; *vi* aller en reconnaissance

**²scout** *vt* repousser avec mépris

**scoutmaster** *n* chef *m* de troupe

**scowl** *n* air renfrogné; *vi* froncer les sourcils, se renfrogner

**scrabble** *vi* **~ about** gratter; (search) chercher à quatre pattes

**scrag** *n* (person) personne *f* maigre; (animal) bête efflanquée; **~ of mutton** collet *m* de mouton; *vt* tordre le cou à

**scraggy** *adj* maigre, décharné

**scram** *vi coll* filer, ficher le camp, se débiner

**scramble** *n* (walking) marche *f* pénible; (struggle) mêlée *f*, bousculade *f*; *vt* brouiller; *vi* avancer péniblement; **~ for sth** se bousculer pour avoir qch; **~**

**up** grimper à quatre pattes

**scrambler** *n* (telephone) brouilleur *m*

**¹scrap** *n* petit morceau, bout *m*, fragment *m*; (land) parcelle *f*; (conversation) bribe *f*; (comfort) brin *m*; (newspaper) coupure *f*; **~s** (left-overs) restes *mpl*; (materials) déchets *mpl*; *vt* mettre au rebut; (plan, etc) mettre au rancart

**²scrap** *n coll* bagarre *f*; *vi* se battre

**scrapbook** *n* album *m*

**scrape** *n* coup *m* de grattoir; *coll* mauvais pas, embarras *m*; (violin) grincement *m*; *coll* mince couche *f* de beurre (de margarine); **get into a ~** se mettre dans le pétrin; **get out of a ~** se tirer d'affaire; *vt* gratter, racler; (flesh) écorcher; (shoes) décrotter; **~ away (off)** enlever en raclant; (violin) **~ the bow** faire grincer l'archet; **~ together** amasser; *vi* gratter, racler; **~ against** (passing by) raser; (rubbing) frotter contre; **~ on the violin** racler du violon; **~ through** passer tout juste; (exam) réussir de justesse

**scraper** *n* (tool) grattoir *m*, racloir *m*

**scrap-heap** *n* tas *m* de ferraille

**scraping** *n* éraflement *m*, raclage *m*; **bowing and ~** courbettes *fpl*

**scrap-iron** *n* ferraille *f*

**scrap-merchant** *n* marchand *m* de ferraille

**scrappy** *adj* hétérogène, disparate; (speech) décousu

**¹scratch** *n* égratignure *f*; (with nail) coup *m* d'ongle; (with claw) coup *m* de griffe; (on surface) rayure *f*; (sound) grattement *m*, grincement *m*; (sport) scratch *m*; **come up to ~** se montrer à la hauteur de l'occasion; **start from ~** partir de zéro; *vt* griffer, égratigner, donner un coup de griffe à; (skin) écorcher; (surface) rayer; (body) gratter; (sport) scratcher; **~ one's head** se gratter la tête; **~ out** rayer; **~ the surface of a problem** ne pas aller jusqu'au fond d'un problème; *vi* grincer, gratter

**²scratch** *adj* improvisé

**scratchy** *adj* qui gratte, qui grince; (rough) rugueux -euse

**scrawl** *n* gribouillage *m*, griffonnage *m*; *vt + vi* gribouiller, griffonner

**scrawny** *adj* maigre, décharné

**scream** *n* cri *m*, cri perçant; *coll fig* chose amusante; **~ of laughter** éclat *m* de rire; **give a ~** pousser un cri; *coll* **he's a ~** il est tordant; *vi* pousser des cris, crier; **~ with laughter** rire aux éclats

**screaming** *n* cris *mpl*, hurlements *mpl*; *adj* criard

**scree** *n* éboulis *m*; (rocky) clapier *m*

**screech** *n* cri perçant; *vi* pousser des cris perçants

**screech-owl** *n* chouette *f*

**screed** *n* longue liste

**screen** *n* écran *m*; (folding) paravent *m*; (trees) rideau *m*; (sieve) crible *m*; (profession) cinéma *m*; *vt* (give screen to) munir d'un écran; (hide) cacher, masquer; (protect) abriter, protéger; (sift) passer au crible; (film) mettre à l'écran

**screenplay** *n* scénario *m*

**screw** *n* vis *f*; (propeller) hélice *f*; (with screwdriver) coup *m* de tournevis; *coll* (miser) avare, grippe-sou *m* (*pl* grippe-sou(s)); *coll* (wages) salaire *m*, gages *mpl*; *sl* (warder) gardien *m*; *vt* visser; *sl* baiser; ~ **down** visser; ~ **off** dévisser; ~ **on** visser, fixer; *coll* ~ **sth out of** s/o tirer qch de qn; ~ **up one's courage** prendre son courage à deux mains; ~ **up one's face** faire la (une) grimace; ~ **up sth** resserrer qch, visser qch à fond; ~ **se visser**

**screwball** *n* *US* cinglé -e, loufoque

**screw-cap** *n* bouchon vissé

**screwdriver** *n* tournevis *m*

**screwed** *adj coll* ivre; *US coll* fichu

**screwy** *adj US coll* timbré, cinglé

**scribble** *n* griffonnage *m*; *vt* griffonner

**scribbler** *n* griffonneur -euse; *coll* (office clerk) gratte-papier *m* (*pl* gratte-papier(s))

**scribe** *n* scribe *m*

**scrimmage** *n* mêlée *f*, bousculade *f*

**scrimp** *vi* faire des économies de bouts de chandelle

**scrip** *n* *ar* besace *f*; (Stock Exchange) ~ **issue** émission *f* d'actions gratuites

**script** *n* manuscrit *m*; (exam) copie *f*; *cin*+*TV* scénario *m*; (handwriting) écriture *f*

**scriptural** *adj* scriptural

**Scripture** (Holy) ~ (s) Écriture Sainte

**script-writer** *n* *cin*+*TV* scénariste

**scroll** *n* rouleau *m* (de papier, de parchemin)

**scrotum** *n* *anat* scrotum *m*

**scrounge** *n* *coll* be on the ~ être à la recherche de choses à chiper; *coll* chiper, chaparder; *vi coll* ~ **on** s/o vivre aux crochets de qn

**scrounger** *n* *coll* chapardeur -euse, rabioteur -euse

¹**scrub** *n* brousse *f*, broussailles *fpl*

²**scrub** *n* friction *f*, nettoyage *m*; *vt* (floor) frotter; (pan) récurer; *coll* (cancel) annuler

**scrubbing-brush** *n* brosse dure

**scrubby** *adj* (stunted) rabougri; (ground) couvert de broussailles

**scruff** *n* nuque *f*; peau *f* de la nuque; by

the ~ **of the neck** par la peau du cou

**scruffy** *adj coll* mal soigné

**scrum, scrummage** *n coll* bousculade *f*; (rugby) mêlée *f*

**scrum-half** *n* demi *m* de mêlée

**scrummage** *n see* **scrum**

**scrumptious** *adj coll* délicieux -ieuse, excellent

**scruple** *n* scrupule *m*; *vi* ~ **to do sth** avoir des scrupules à faire qch

**scrupulous** *adj* scrupuleux -euse; (very careful) méticuleux -euse

**scrupulousness** *n* scrupules *mpl*

**scrutinize** *vt* scruter, examiner minutieusement

**scrutiny** *n* examen minutieux; (votes) vérification *f*

**scud** *n* (squall) rafale *f*; *vi* courir vite, filer; ~ **away** s'enfuir

**scuff** *vt* racler avec les pieds; *vi* traîner les pieds

**scuffle** *n* mêlée *f*, rixe *f*; *vi* se battre

**scull** *n* (oar) aviron *m*; (stern) godille *f*; *vi* ramer, godiller

**sculler** *n* rameur *m* de couple; (boat) scull *m*

**scullery** *n* arrière-cuisine *f*; ~ **maid** laveuse *f* de vaisselle

**sculpt** *vt*+*i* sculpter

**sculptor** *n* sculpteur *m*

**sculptress** *n* femme *f* sculpteur

**sculpture** *n* sculpture *f*; *vt* sculpter; (decorate) orner de sculptures

**scum** *n* écume *f*, mousse *f*; *coll* rebut *m*; *vt*+*vi* écumer

**scummy** *adj* écumeux -euse

**scupper** *n* *naut* dalot *m*; *vt* *naut* saborder; *coll* ruiner; saboter

**scurf** *n* (dandruff) pellicules *fpl*

**scurfy** *adj* (head) pelliculeux -euse; (hair) plein de pellicules

**scurrility** *n* grossièreté *f*

**scurrilous** *adj* (person) ignoble; (language) grossier -ière

**scurry** *n* débandade *f*; *vi* courir à toutes jambes; ~ **off** détaler

¹**scurvy** *n* scorbut *m*

²**scurvy** *adj* vilain, misérable, indigne

¹**scuttle** *n* (coal) seau *m* à charbon

²**scuttle** *n* *naut* écoutille *f*; (porthole) hublot *m*; *vt* *naut* saborder

³**scuttle** *vi* ~ **off** déguerpir, détaler

**scythe** *n* faux *f*; *vt* faucher

**sea** *n* mer *f*; *fig* infinité *f*, multitude *f*; *fig* be at ~ être perdu, ne pas y être du tout; beyond the ~ outre-mer; by ~ par voie de mer; by the ~ au bord de la mer; go to ~ se faire marin; on the high ~ s en pleine mer; the open ~ le large, la haute mer

**sea-anemone** *n* actinie *f*

**seabird** *n* oiseau *m* de mer

**seaboard** n littoral m

**sea-breeze** n brise f de mer

**sea-captain** n capitaine m au long cours

**sea-coast** n côte f, littoral m

**sea-dog** n loup m de mer, vieux marin

**seafarer** n marin m

**seafaring** adj ~ **man** marin m

**seafood** n fruits mpl de mer

**sea-front** n esplanade f

**sea-going** adj de haute mer

**sea-green** adj vert de mer invar, glauque

**seagull** n mouette f

**sea-horse** n hippocampe m

**¹seal** n zool phoque m

**²seal** n sceau m; (letter) cachet m; leg affix (remove) the ~s poser (lever) les scellés; vt (deeds, etc) sceller; (letter) cacheter; (decide) décider; ~ **a bargain** confirmer une affaire; ~ **up** fermer hermétiquement; **his fate is ~ed** c'en est fait de lui

**sea-legs** npl **have one's ~** avoir le pied marin

**sea-level** n niveau m de la mer

**sealing-wax** n cire f à cacheter

**sea-lion** n otarie f

**sealskin** n peau f de phoque

**seam** n couture f; min couche f, gisement m; (face) ride f; vt coudre

**seaman** n matelot m, marin m

**seamanship** n navigation f, manœuvre f

**sea-mile** n mille marin

**seamless** adj sans couture

**sea-monster** n monstre marin (des mers)

**seamstress, sempstress** n ouvrière couturière f

**seamy** adj the ~ **side of life** le mauvais côté de la vie

**séance** n séance f de spiritisme

**seaplane** n hydravion m

**seaport** n port m de mer

**sea-power** n puissance f maritime

**sear** adj desséché, sec (f sèche); vt dessécher, flétrir; (wound) cautériser

**search** n recherche f; leg perquisition f; (customs) visite f; **in ~ of** à la recherche de; vt chercher dans, fouiller; leg perquisitionner dans; (customs) visiter; vi leg faire une perquisition; ~ **for** chercher

**searcher** n chercheur -euse

**searching** adj (look) pénétrant; (examination) minutieux -ieuse

**searchlight** n projecteur m

**search-party** n expédition f de secours

**search-warrant** n mandat m de perquisition

**seascape** n marine f

**sea-serpent** n serpent m de mer

**sea-shell** n coquillage m

**sea-shore** n rivage m, plage f

**sea-sick** adj be ~ avoir le mal de mer

**sea-sickness** n mal m de mer

**seaside** n bord m de la mer; adj (resort) balnéaire; (place) situé au bord de la mer

**season** n saison f; (period) temps m, période f; (abbr season-ticket) abonnement m; **be in ~** être en saison; (animal) être en chaleur; **for a ~** pendant quelque temps; **holiday ~** saison f des vacances; **off ~** morte-saison f; **remark in ~** remarque faite à propos; **remark out of ~** remarque déplacée; vt assaisonner, relever; (timber) sécher; (allow to mature) mûrir; (person) acclimater, endurcir; (temper) tempérer

**seasonable** adj de saison; (opportune) à propos

**seasonal** adj saisonnier -ière, des saisons

**seasoned** adj assaisonné; (wood) sec (f sèche); **become ~** s'aguerrir

**seasoning** n assaisonnement m; (wood) séchage m; (person) acclimatement m

**season-ticket** n abonnement m

**seat** n siège m; (vehicle) banquette f; (chair) chaise f; (seat-space) place f; (sitting part of chair, trousers) fond m; (bench) banc m; (illness) foyer m; (residence) château m; ~ **belt** ceinture f de sécurité; ~ **in the House** siège m au Parlement (à la Chambre); **take a ~** s'asseoir; vt faire asseoir; asseoir, placer; (chair) mettre un fond à; (find room for) trouver une place pour; (have room for) tenir; **please be ~ed** veuillez vous asseoir

**seating** n allocation f des places; (accommodation) nombre m des places; (seats) bancs mpl, sièges mpl; (machine) lit m de pose

**sea-trout** n truite saumonnée

**sea-wall** n digue f

**seaward** adj (tide) qui porte au large; adv vers la mer

**seawards** adv vers la mer, vers le large

**seaweed** n algue f, varech m

**seaworthiness** n bon état de navigabilité

**seaworthy** adj en bon état de navigabilité

**secant** n math sécante f

**secateurs** npl sécateur m

**secede** vi se séparer, faire sécession

**secession** n sécession f

**seclude** vt tenir éloigné

**secluded** adj retiré, écarté

**seclusion** n retraite f, solitude f

**¹second** n (time) seconde f; moment m, instant m

**²second** n second -e, deuxième; (duel) témoin m; (boxing) second m; ~ **s** articles mpl de deuxième qualité; adj second, deuxième; (other) autre,

**secondary**

nouveau (*f* nouvelle); (dates, kings) deux; *US* (floor) premier; **every ~ day** tous les deux jours; **take ~ place** passer second; **the ~ nicest house** la plus belle maison sauf une; *vt* (support) seconder, appuyer; *mil* détacher; **~ a motion** appuyer une proposition

**secondary** *adj* secondaire

**second-best** *n* **be ~** être un pis-aller; **come off ~** être battu; *adj* numéro deux; (everyday) de tous les jours

**second-class** *adj* (quality) de deuxième qualité; (traveller) de seconde (classe); de second ordre, de deuxième rang; **~ mail rate** = tarif réduit; *adv* **travel ~** voyager en seconde

**seconder** *n* **be the ~ of** appuyer

¹**second-hand** *n* aiguille *f* des secondes

²**second-hand** *adj* d'occasion; (news) de seconde main; **~ dealer** brocanteur -euse

**secondly** *adv* deuxièmement, en second lieu

**second-rate** *adj* inférieur, médiocre

**secrecy** *n* secret *m*, discrétion *f*; **in ~** en secret

**secret** *n* secret *m*; **in ~** en secret; **make a ~ of sth** faire mystère de qch; **open ~** secret *m* de Polichinelle; *adj* secret -ète, caché; **the Secret Service** = le Deuxième Bureau; **top ~** très secret -ète

**secretarial** *adj* de secrétaire

**secretariat** *n* secrétariat *m*

**secretary** *n* secrétaire; *pol* ministre *m*; **Secretary of State** secrétaire *m* d'État; *US* Ministre *m* des Affaires étrangères; **principal private ~** (of minister) chef *m* de cabinet; **private ~** secrétaire particulier -ière

¹**secrete** *vt* (exude) sécréter

²**secrete** *vt* (hide) cacher

**secretion** *n* sécrétion *f*

**secretive** *adj* cachottier -ière, dissimulé

**secretly** *adv* secrètement, en secret

**sect** *n* secte *f*

**sectarian** *n* + *adj* sectaire

**section** *n* section *f*, division *f*, tranche *f*; (drawing) coupe *f*, profil *m*; *vt* diviser en sections, sectionner

**sectional** *adj* (drawing) en coupe; en sections

**sector** *n* secteur *m*

**secular** *adj* séculier -ière; (school) laïc (*f* laïque); (time) séculaire

**secularization** *n* laïcisation *f*

**secularize** *vt* séculariser; (school) laïciser

**secure** *adj* sûr, assuré; (safe) en sûreté, sauf (*f* sauve); (well fixed) solide, ferme, bien fixé; **~ against** à l'abri de; *vt* mettre en sûreté, mettre à l'abri; (fasten) fixer, assujettir; (window) fermer bien; (guard) garder; (obtain) se

procurer; (get possession of) s'emparer de; (debt) garantir

**security** *n* sécurité *f*, sûreté *f*; (protection) sauvegarde *f*; *comm* caution *f*, garantie *f*; **securities** valeurs *fpl*, titres *mpl*; **Security Council** Conseil *m* de sécurité; **~ device** dispositif *m* de sûreté; **~ police** police secrète; **~ risk** personne *f* présentant des risques pour la sécurité de l'État; **give sth as ~** donner qch comme gage; **government securities** fonds *mpl* d'État

**sedan** *n* *US* (voiture *f* à) conduite intérieure

**sedan-chair** *n* chaise *f* à porteurs

**sedate** *adj* (person) posé; (bearing) composé; (mind) rassis

**sedation** *n* sédation *f*

**sedative** *n* calmant *m*; *adj* sédatif -ive

**sedentary** *adj* sédentaire

**sedge** *n* laîche *f*

**sediment** *n* dépôt *m*, sédiment *m*; (wine) lie *f*

**sedimentary** *adj* sédimentaire

**sedimentation** *n* sédimentation *f*

**sedition** *n* sédition *f*

**seditious** *adj* séditieux -ieuse

**seduce** *vt* séduire; (corrupt) corrompre

**seducer** *n* séducteur -trice

**seduction** *n* séduction *f*; corruption *f*; attraction *f*, charme *m*

**seductive** *adj* séduisant

**sedulity, sedulousness** *n* assiduité *f*, diligence *f*

**sedulous** *adj* assidu, diligent, appliqué

¹**see** *n eccles* siège épiscopal, évêché *m*

²**see** *vt* voir; (visit) visiter; (notice) remarquer; (doctor) consulter; (understand) comprendre; (make sure) s'assurer; (judge) juger, apprécier; **~ fit to** juger convenable de; **~ s/o home** reconduire qn chez lui; **~ s/o off** accompagner qn (jusqu') à la porte; **~ s/o to the station** accompagner qn jusqu'à la gare; **~ sth out** mener qch à bonne fin; voir la fin de qch; **~ you soon!** à bientôt!; **he can't ~ a joke** il n'entend pas la plaisanterie; **nothing to be ~ n** rien à voir; **what can you ~ in her?** qu'est-ce que vous lui trouvez?; *vi* voir; **~ about sth** s'occuper de qch; **~ into** examiner; **~ through** s/o pénétrer les intentions de qn; **~ to it that** veiller à ce que; **to read** voir assez clair pour lire; **as far as the eye can ~** à perte de vue; **I'll ~ about it** j'y réfléchirai, je verrai; **let me ~ !** (show) faites voir!; *fig* attendez un peu!

**seed** *n agr* + *bot* graine *f*; *collect* + *fig* semence *f*; (descendants) lignée *f*; **go to ~** monter en graine; *vt* semer, ensemencer; *sp* sélectionner, trier; **~ed**

682

**players** têtes *fpl* de série; *vi* (plant) monter en graine; (cereal) s'égrener

**seedbed** *n* couche *f* de semis

**seedcake** *n* gâteau *m* au carvi (cumin)

**seediness** *n coll* apparence *f* minable; (state) malaise *m*

**seedless** *adj* (fruit) sans pépins

**seedling** *n* jeune plant *m*

**seedy** *adj* (full of seeds) plein de graines; *coll* (shabby) râpé; *coll* miteux -euse; *coll* (out of sorts) mal en train, peu bien

**seeing** *n* vue *f*, vision *f*; ~ **is believing** voir c'est croire; **that is worth** ~ cela vaut la peine d'être vu

**seeing that** *conj phr* vu que

**seek** *vt* chercher, rechercher; (request) demander; *vi* ~ **after** rechercher, poursuivre; ~ **to do sth** essayer de faire qch

**seeker** *n* chercheur -euse

**seem** *vi* sembler, paraître, avoir l'air; **how does it** ~ **to you?** que vous en semble?; **it** ~ **s that** il semble que; **so it** ~ **s** à ce qu'il paraît

**seeming** *adj* apparent, soi-disant

**seemingly** *adv* en apparence

**seemly** *adj* convenable, bienséant

**seep** *vi* suinter, filtrer

**seepage** *n* suintement *m*, infiltration *f*

**seer** *n* prophète *m*

**see-saw** *n* bascule *f*, balançoire *f*, tape-cul *m*; *adj* de bascule; *vi* basculer, osciller

**seethe** *vi* bouillonner; (mass) grouiller

**segment** *n* segment *m*; *vt* partager en segments

**segmentation** *n* segmentation *f*

**segregate** *vt* isoler, séparer; *vi* se mettre à part

**segregation** *n* ségrégation *f*; séparation *f*

**segregationist** *n* partisan -e de la ségrégation raciale

**seismic** *adj* séismique, sismique

**seismograph** *n* sismographe *m*

**seismology** *n* sismologie *f*

**seize** *vt* saisir, s'emparer de; (person) appréhender; (capture) capturer; **be** ~ **d with** être pris de; *vi mech* gripper; ~ **on** se saisir de; ~ **up** caler

**seizure** *n leg* (things) saisie *f*; *leg* (persons) appréhension *f*; confiscation *f*; *med* attaque *f*

**seldom** *adv* rarement

**select** *adj* choisi, de choix, d'élite; (circle) fermé; *vt* choisir; sélectionner

**selection** *n* choix *m*, sélection *f*; (extracts) morceaux choisis

**selective** *adj* sélectif -ive

**selectivity** *n* sélectivité *f*

**selector** *n* sélecteur *m*

**self** *n* moi *m*; **be one's old** ~ **again** être rétabli; **one's better** ~ notre meilleur côté; **pay** ~ payez à moi-même; *pron* (compounded with *adj*: **my** ~, **your** ~ etc) -même; **by my** ~, **your** ~, **him** ~, etc tout seul (*f* toute seule); **everyone for him** ~ chacun pour soi; **he is kindness it** ~ il est la bonté même; *refl pron* **my** ~, **your** ~, etc me, te, etc

**self-abuse** *n* masturbation *f*, onanisme *m*

**self-accusation** *n* auto-accusation *f*

**self-adjusting** *adj* à autoréglage

**self-assertion** *n* caractère impérieux, autoritarisme *m*

**self-assertive** *adj* autoritaire

**self-assurance** *n* assurance *f*, aplomb *m*

**self-centred** *adj* égocentrique

**self-closing** *adj* à fermeture automatique

**self-complacent** *adj* satisfait, content de soi

**self-conceit** *n* vanité *f*, suffisance *f*

**self-confidence** *n* assurance *f*, confiance *f* en soi

**self-conscious** *adj* gêné, embarrassé; (manners) contraint

**self-contained** *adj* (person) réservé; indépendant; (flat) ayant son entrée particulière

**self-control** *n* maîtrise *f* de soi

**self-deception** *n* illusion *f*

**self-defence** *n* défense personnelle; *leg* légitime défense *f*

**self-denial** *n* abnégation *f*; (economy) frugalité *f*

**self-determination** *n* auto-détermination *f*

**self-drive** *adj* ~ **car hire** location *f* de voitures sans chauffeur

**self-educated** *adj* autodidacte

**self-effacing** *adj* modeste

**self-employed** *adj* indépendant

**self-esteem** *n* amour-propre *m*

**self-evident** *adj* évident, qui saute aux yeux

**self-explanatory** *adj* qui s'explique de soi-même

**self-expression** *n* expression *f* de soi-même

**self-governing** *adj* autonome

**self-government** *n* autonomie *f*

**self-importance** *n* suffisance *f*, présomption *f*

**self-indulgence** *n* sybaritisme *m*

**self-interest** *n* égoïsme *m*, intérêt personnel

**selfish** *adj* égoïste, intéressé

**selfless** *adj* désintéressé

**self-made** *adj* qui est arrivé par lui-même (*f* elle-même)

**self-opinionated** *adj* opiniâtre

**self-pity** *n* pitié *f* pour soi-même

**self-portrait** *n* autoportrait *m*, portrait *m* de l'artiste par lui-même (*f* elle-même)

**self-possessed** *adj* maître (*f* maîtresse) de soi

**self-preservation** *n* conservation *f* de soi-même

**self-propelled** *adj* autopropulsé

**self-propulsion** *n* autopropulsion *f*

**self-raising** *adj* ~ **flour** farine préparée à la levure chimique

**self-reliant** *adj* confiant en soi, indépendant

**self-respect** *n* amour-propre *m*, respect *m* de soi

**self-respecting** *adj* qui se respecte

**self-restraint** *n* retenue *f*; **exercise ~** faire preuve de modération

**self-righteous** *adj* pharisaïque

**self-sacrifice** *n* abnégation *f* de soi

**self-same** *adj* identique, exactement le (la) même

**self-satisfied** *adj* content de soi, suffisant

**self-seeking** *adj* égoïste, intéressé

**self-service** *n* libre-service *m invar*; ~ **store** (**restaurant**) magasin *m* (restaurant *m*) libre-service, libre-service (*pl* libres-services), self-service *m* (*pl* self-services), *coll* self *m*

**self-starter** *n* mot démarreur *m*

**self-styled** *adj* soi-disant

**self-sufficiency** *n* indépendance *f*

**self-sufficient** *adj* indépendant

**self-supporting** *adj* qui vit de son travail; indépendant

**self-taught** *adj* autodidacte

**self-willed** *adj* obstiné, entêté, volontaire

**self-winding** *adj* à remontage automatique

**sell** *n* (swindle) escroquerie *f*; *coll* déception *f*; *vt* vendre; *coll* (trick) duper; ~ **off** solder, liquider; ~ **out** vendre tout son stock de; ~ **short** vendre à découvert; ~ **sth for ten francs** vendre qch dix francs; *coll* **be sold on sth** être entiché de qch; **sold out** épuisé; (person) avoir tout vendu; **to be sold** à vendre; *vi* se vendre; ~ **up** vendre tout

**seller** *n* (vendeur -euse, marchand -e; **be a good ~** se vendre bien

**selling** *n* vente *f*; *comm* écoulement *m*

**sell-out** *n* trahison *f*

**semantic** *adj* sémantique

**semantics** *n* sémantique *f*

**semaphore** *n* sémaphore *m*; *vt* + *vi* transmettre par sémaphore

**semblance** *n* semblant *m*, apparence *f*

**semeiology** *n* sém(é)iologie *f*

**semen** *n* semence *f*, sperme *m*

**semester** *n* semestre *m*

**semi** *n* (house) maison jumelle (jumelée)

**semi-** *pref* semi-

**semibreve** *n mus* ronde *f*

**semicircle** *n* demi-cercle *m*

**semicircular** *adj* demi-circulaire, semi-circulaire

**semicolon** *n* point-virgule *m* (*pl* points-virgules)

**semi-conscious** *adj* à demi conscient

**semi-detached** *adj* ~ **house** maison jumelle (jumelée)

**semi-final** *n* demi-finale *f*

**seminal** *adj* séminal

**seminar** *n* séminaire *m*

**seminary** *n* séminaire *m*

**semi-official** *adj* officieux -ieuse, semi-officiel -ielle

**semi-precious** *adj* (stones) fin

**semiquaver** *n mus* double croche *f*

**Semitic** *adj* sémitique

**semitone** *n* demi-ton *m*

**semi-tropical** *adj* subtropical

**semolina** *n* semoule *f*

**senate** *n* sénat *m*

**senator** *n* sénateur *m*

**send** *vt* envoyer; (dispatch) expédier; *sl* exciter; ~ **away** expédier; (person) congédier; ~ **back** renvoyer; ~ **down** (person) faire descendre; (student) expulser; ~ **for** envoyer chercher; ~ **forth** (give off) répandre; jeter; ~ **in** envoyer; présenter, soumettre; ~ **off** envoyer, expédier; ~ **on** faire suivre; ~ **out** (person) faire sortir; (things) expédier; (emit) émettre; ~ **round** faire circuler; (person) envoyer; ~ **s/o packing** envoyer promener qn; ~ **up** faire monter; *coll* se moquer de, parodier; ~ **word** faire dire, faire savoir

**sender** *n* expéditeur -trice

**send-off** *n* fête *f* d'adieu; **give s/o a good ~** être nombreux -euses au départ de qn

**senescence** *n* sénescence *f*

**senile** *adj* sénile

**senility** *n* sénilité *f*

**senior** *n* aîné -e; doyen -enne; (pupil) grand; *US* étudiant -e en dernière année; *adj* aîné; (rank) supérieur; **she is two years ~ to me** elle est mon aînée de deux ans; **the Senior Service** la marine

**seniority** *n* ancienneté *f*, priorité *f* d'âge

**senna** *n* séné *m*

**sensation** *n* sensation *f*; sentiment *m*, impression *f*; **create a ~** faire sensation

**sensational** *adj* sensationnel -elle

**sensationalism** *n* recherche *f* du sensationnel

**sense** *n* sens *m*; (feeling) sentiment *m*; (meaning) signification *f*; (intelligence) intelligence *f*; ~ **of humour** sens *m* de l'humour; **bring s/o to his ~s** ramener qn à la raison; **common ~** bon sens,

sens commun; **have the good ~ to** avoir l'intelligence de; **in a ~** d'un certain point de vue; **in the literal ~** au sens propre; **lose one's ~ s** perdre connaissance; **make ~** avoir un sens; **make ~ of** comprendre; **take leave of one's ~ s** perdre la tête (la raison); **talk ~** parler raison; *vt* percevoir, sentir intuitivement; (in advance) pressentir; (understand) comprendre

**senseless** *adj* (person) sans connaissance, inanimé; (silly) absurde, insensé

**sensibility** *n* sensibilité *f*

**sensible** *adj* (reasonable) sensé, raisonnable; (aware) sensible; (perceptible) perceptible; (appreciable) appréciable; (clothing) pratique

**sensibly** *adv* raisonnablement; perceptiblement; sensiblement

**sensitive** *adj* sensible; (touchy) susceptible; **~ plant** sensitive *f*

**sensitivity, sensitiveness** *n* sensibilité *f*; (touchiness) susceptibilité *f*

**sensitize** *vt* sensibiliser

**sensory** *adj* sensoriel -ielle

**sensual** *adj* sensuel -elle; voluptueux -euse

**sensualism** *n* sensualisme *m*

**sensuality** *n* sensualité *f*

**sensuous** *adj* voluptueux -euse; (charm) capiteux -euse

**sentence** *n gramm* phrase *f*; *leg* jugement *m*, sentence *f*; (punishment) peine *f*; **serve one's ~** purger sa peine; *vt leg* condamner

**sententious** *adj* sentencieux -ieuse

**sentient** *adj* sensible

**sentiment** *n* sentiment *m*; (opinion) avis *m*; (mawkish) sensiblerie *f*

**sentimental** *adj* sentimental

**sentimentalism** *n* sensiblerie *f*

**sentimentalist** *n* personne sentimentale

**sentimentality** *n* sensiblerie *f*

**sentimentalize** *vt* apporter du sentiment à; *vi* faire du sentiment

**sentinel** *n* sentinelle *f*, factionnaire *m*; **stand ~** monter la garde

**sentry** *n* sentinelle *f*, factionnaire *m*; **be on ~-go** être de faction, monter la garde

**sentry-box** *n* guérite *f*

**separability** *n* séparabilité *f*

**separable** *adj* séparable

**separate** *adj* séparé, détaché; (distinct) distinct; (room, etc) individuel -elle, particulier -ière; *vt* séparer, détacher; (disunite) désunir; *vi* se séparer, se détacher; (part) se quitter

**separation** *n* séparation *f*; (gap) écart *m*

**separatist** *n + adj* séparatiste

**separator** *n* séparateur *m*; (cream) écrémeuse *f*

**sepia** *n* sépia *f*

**sepsis** *n med* septicémie *f*; putréfaction *f*

**September** *n* septembre *m*

**septet** *n mus* septuor *m*

**septic** *adj* septique; *sl* infecte; **~ tank** fosse *f* septique

**septicaemia** *n* septicémie *f*

**septuagenarian** *n + adj* septuagénaire

**Septuagesima** *n eccles* Septuagésime *f*

**sepulchral** *adj* sépulcral

**sepulchre** *n* sépulcre *m*

**sequel** *n* suite *f*

**sequence** *n* suite *f*, succession *f*, chaîne *f*; **~ of tenses** concordance *f* des temps; **in ~** en série

**sequential** *adj* consécutif -ive

**sequester** *vt* séquestrer, mettre sous séquestre

**sequestered** *adj* retiré, isolé; *leg* sous séquestre

**sequestrate** *vt* séquestrer

**sequestration** *n* retraite *f*; *leg* mise *f* sous séquestre

**sequin** *n* sequin *m*

**seraglio** *n* sérail *m*

**seraph** *n* séraphin *m*

**seraphic** *adj* séraphique

**Serbia** *n* Serbie *f*

**Serbo-Croat(ian)** *n* (language) serbo-croate *m*

**serenade** *n* sérénade *f*; *vt* donner une sérénade à

**serendipity** *n* don *m* de faire des trouvailles; *coll* veine *f*

**serene** *adj* serein, calme; (title) sérénissime

**serenity** *n* sérénité *f*, calme *m*

**serf** *n* serf (*f* serve)

**serfdom** *n* servage *m*

**serge** *n* serge *f*

**sergeant** *n* sergent *m*

**sergeant-major** *n* adjudant *m*

**serial** *n* feuilleton *m*, roman-feuilleton *m* (*pl* romans-feuilletons); **~ rights** droits *mpl* de reproduction en feuilleton; **~ writer** feuilletoniste; *adj* **~ number** numéro *m* de série

**serialize** *vt* publier en feuilleton; (film) passer en feuilleton

**serially** *adv* en série

**series** *n* série *f*, suite *f*

**serious** *adj* sérieux -ieuse; (wound, illness) grave

**seriousness** *n* sérieux *m*; (illness) gravité *f*

**sermon** *n* sermon *m*; *fig* remontrance *f*

**sermonize** *vt* sermonner, chapitrer; *vi* sermonner

**serous** *adj* séreux -euse

**serpent** *n* serpent *m*

**serpentine** *adj* serpentin, sinueux -euse

**serrate** *vt* denteler

**serrated** *adj* en dents de scie, dentelé

**serried** *adj* serré

**serum** *n* sérum *m*

**servant** *n* domestique; serviteur *m* (*f* servante); (maid) bonne *f*; (employee) employé -e; **civil ~** fonctionnaire

**serve** *vt* servir; (suffice) suffire à; (treat) traiter; (bus, train, etc) desservir; (breeding) couvrir; **~ one's apprenticeship** faire un apprentissage; **~ out** distribuer; **~ s/o with sth** servir qch à qn; **~ the purpose** faire l'affaire; **~ time** faire de la prison; **~ up** servir; **are you being ~ d?** est-ce qu'on vous sert?; *mil* **he has ~ d twenty years** il a vingt ans de service; **I'll ~ you out for that** vous me le payerez; **it ~ s him right** c'est bien fait pour lui; *vi* **~ as** servir de; **~ to** servir à

**service** *n* service *m*; (employ) emploi *m*; *eccles RC* office *m*; *eccles* (Protestant) culte *m*; (usefulness) utilité *f*; **~ charge** service *m*; **be at s/o's ~** être à la disposition de qn; **be of ~ to** être utile à; **be in ~** être en condition; **be in the civil ~** être fonctionnaire (de l'État); **do good ~** faire bon usage; **postal ~s** Postes *fpl* et Télécommunications *fpl*; **the armed ~s** les forces armées; **the public service** l'administration *f*; *vt* *mot* entretenir et réparer

**serviceable** *adj* pratique, utile; (usable) utilisable; (durable) durable; (person) serviable

**service-flat** *n* appartement *m* avec service

**service-hatch** *n* passe-plat *m*

**service-station** *n* *mot* station-service (*pl* stations-service)

**servicing** *n* *mot* entretien *m*, maintenance *f*

**serviette** *n* serviette *f* de table

**servile** *adj* servile

**servility** *n* servilité *f*

**servitude** *n* servitude *f*, esclavage *m*; **~ penal** travaux forcés

**servobrake** *n* servofrein *m*

**servomechanism** *n* servomécanisme *m*

**sesame** *n* *bot* sésame *m*

**session** *n* séance *f*, session *f*; trimestre *m* (année *f*) scolaire (universitaire)

**sestet** *n* *see* **sextet**

**set** *n* série *f*, assortiment *m*, collection *f*; (china) service *m*; (buttons, ornaments) garniture *f*; (jewels) parure *f*; (false teeth) dentier *m*; (people) bande *f*, clique *f*, société *f*; *rad* + *TV* poste *m*; (hairdressing) mise *f* en plis; *cin* + *theat* décor *m*; (chess) jeu *m*; (tennis) set *m*; *coll* **make a dead ~ at s/o** attaquer qn furieusement; *theat* **on the ~** sur le plateau; **the smart ~** le monde élégant;

*adj* (firm) résolu, ferme; (prices) fixe; (time) fixe, fixé; (speech) préparé; (motionless) immobile; (expression) figé; (fruit) noué; (imposed) imposé, assigné; **~ book** livre *m* au programme; **~ fair** au beau fixe; **~ phrase** expression consacrée; **be dead ~ against sth** être totalement opposé à qch; **be ~ on sth** être résolu à qch, tenir à qch; *vt* (put) poser, mettre, placer; (task) imposer; (bone) remettre; (watch) régler; (example) donner; (trap) tendre, dresser; (tool) affiler, affûter; (signature) apposer; (jewels) sertir; (sail) déployer; **~ aside** mettre de côté; (reject) rejeter; (will) annuler; **~ down** déposer; **~ down (forth) in writing** coucher par écrit; **~ eyes on s/o** voir qn, apercevoir qn; **~ fire to sth** mettre le feu à qch; **~ limits to** assigner des limites à; **~ off** faire ressortir; (debt) compenser; (show to advantage) faire valoir; **~ oneself against sth** s'opposer à qch; **~ oneself up as** se poser en; **~ one's teeth** serrer les dents; **~ out** (display) étaler; (arrange) ranger; (reasons) présenter; **~ right** arranger; rectifier; **~ s/o doing sth** mettre qn à faire qch; **~ sth going** mettre qch en train; **~ the dog on s/o** lancer le chien contre qn; **~ to music** mettre en musique; **~ up** monter, dresser, établir; (type) composer; *coll US* (frame) faire accuser faussement; **have one's hair ~** se faire faire une mise en plis; *vi* (sun) se coucher; (jelly, etc) prendre; (flowers) se nouer; **~ about doing sth** se mettre à faire qch; **~ about s/o** attaquer qn; **~ forth** se mettre en route; **~ in** commencer; **~ off** se mettre en route, partir; **~ on (upon) s/o** attaquer qn; **~ out for** partir pour; **~ to** s'y mettre, se mettre au travail; *coll* (fight) en venir aux mains; **~ up as** s'établir

**setback** *n* échec *m*, revers *m* de fortune; (business) recul *m*; (illness) rechute *f*

**set-square** *n* équerre *f*

**settee** *n* canapé *m*, causeuse *f*

**setter** *n* (person) monteur *m*; (jewels) sertisseur *m*; (dog) setter *m*

**setting** *n* mise *f*, pose *f*; (arrangement) disposition *f*, arrangement *m*; (sun) coucher *m*; (jewels) monture *f*; (type) composition *f*; *mech* réglage *m*; (hair) mise *f* en plis; (sharpening) aiguisage *m*; (tools) affûtage *m*; (task) imposition *f*; (fracture) réduction *f*; (cement, jelly) prise *f*; (story) cadre *m*

**settle** *vt* établir, installer; (fix) fixer; (dispute) arranger; (accounts) régler, payer; (question) résoudre, décider;

(quieten) calmer; (country) coloniser; ~ **property on s/o** assigner des biens à qn; **it's all ~d** tout est réglé; **that ~s it!** c'est réglé; cela me décide; *vi* (residence) s'établir, s'installer; (perch) se poser; (sink) se précipiter; (weather) se remettre au beau; (quieten) se calmer; *fig* (ground) se tasser; ~ **down** se ranger; (marry) entrer en ménage; *coll* (get quieter) se tasser; ~ **down to work** se mettre au travail; ~ **in** s'installer; ~ **up** régler un compte; ~ **upon sth** se décider pour qch; ~ **with s/o** s'arranger avec qn

**settlement** *n* établissement *m*, installation *f*; (colony) colonie *f*; (accounts) règlement *m*; (question) résolution *f*; (subsidence) tassement *m*; **deed of ~** acte *m* de disposition; **marriage ~** contrat *m* de mariage; **reach a ~** arriver à un accord amical

**settler** *n* colon *m*

**set-to** *n coll* combat *m*, empoignade *f*; **have a ~** en venir aux mains

**set-up** *n coll* arrangement *m*, organisation *f*

**seven** *n* sept *m invar*; *adj* sept *invar*

**seventeen** *n* dix-sept *m invar*; *adj* dix-sept *invar*

**seventeenth** *n* dix-septième; (date) dix-sept *m*; *adj* dix-septième

**seventh** *n* septième; (date) sept *m*; *adj* septième

**seventieth** *n + adj* soixante-dixième

**seventy** *n* soixante-dix *m invar*; *adj* soixante-dix; (Belgium, Switzerland) septante

**sever** *vt* (divide) désunir; (break off) rompre; (cut) couper, trancher, sectionner

**several** *adj* différent, séparé; *pl* plusieurs, divers; *pron* plusieurs

**severally** *adv* séparément

**severance** *n* séparation *f*, rupture *f*; ~ **pay** indemnité *f* de départ

**severe** *adj* sévère; rigoureux -euse; (weather) dur; (pain) vif (*f* vive)

**severity** *n* sévérité *f*; (illness) gravité *f*; (weather) rigueur *f*; (pain) violence *f*

**sew** *vt* coudre; (bookbinding) brocher

**sewage** *n* eaux *fpl* d'égouts; ~ **farm** champ *m* d'épandage; ~ **system** système *m* du tout à l'égout; ~ **works** usine *f* d'épuration

¹**sewer** *n* (person) personne *f* qui coud, couseuse *f*; (bookbinding) brocheuse *f*

²**sewer** *n* (drain) égout *m*

**sewerage** *n* système *m* d'égouts

**sewing** *n* couture *f*; (bookbinding) brochage *m*; ~ **cotton** fil *m* à coudre; ~ **needle** aiguille *f* à coudre

**sewing-machine** *n* machine *f* à coudre

**sex** *n* sexe *m*; amour *m* physique, coïtion *f*; **have ~ with s/o** coucher avec qn; **the fair ~** le beau sexe; *vt* déterminer le sexe de

**sexagenarian** *n + adj* sexagénaire

**sex-appeal** *n* sex-appeal *m*, *coll* chien *m*

**sexed** *adj* sexué; **be highly ~** avoir du tempérament

**sexily** *adv* de manière très sexy

**sexless** *adj* asexué; *coll* froid

**sex-maniac** *n* obsédé sexuel (*f* obsédée sexuelle)

**sextant** *n* sextant *m*

**sextet** *n* sextuor *m*

**sexton** *n* sacristain *m*; (bell-ringer) sonneur *m* de cloches; (gravedigger) fossoyeur *m*

**sextuple** *adj* sextuple; *vt* sextupler

**sexual** *adj* sexuel -elle

**sexuality** *n* sexualité *f*

**sexually** *adv* d'une manière sexuelle

**sexy** *adj* sexy, excitant, aguichant; **be ~** (attractive) avoir du chien; (highly sexed) avoir du tempérament

**sh** *interj* chut!

**shabby** *adj* (clothes) râpé, usé; (mean) mesquin; (poor) pauvre; *coll* moche

**shack** *n* hutte *f*, cabane *f*; *vi* ~ **up with** *coll* cohabiter avec; *coll* partager un logement avec

**shackle** *vt* mettre les fers à

**shackles** *npl* fers *mpl*; *fig* entraves *fpl*

**shade** *n* ombre *f*; (tree) ombrage *m*; (colour, meaning) nuance *f*; (lamp) abat-jour *m invar*; *US* (blind) store *m*; **a ~ better** un tout petit peu mieux; **put s/o in(to) the ~** éclipser qn; **the Shades** les enfers; *vt* ombrager; (protect) abriter, mettre à l'abri de; (drawing) ombrer; *vi* ~ **into** se fondre en

**shadiness** *n* ombre *f*, ombrage *m*; (suspicious character) aspect *m* louche

**shading** *n* projection *f* d'une ombre; (drawing) ombres *fpl*

**shadow** *n* ombre *f*; ~ **government** gouvernement *m* fantôme; **be reduced to a ~** être un pâle reflet de soi-même; **cast a ~** projeter une ombre; **have ~s under one's eyes** avoir les yeux cernés; **in the ~ of** à l'ombre de; *vt* (follow) filer

**shadowy** *adj* (plan) indécis, vague; chimérique

**shady** *adj* (shaded) ombragé; (giving shade) ombreux -euse; (suspicious) louche

¹**shaft** *n* (spear, arrow) hampe *f*; (handle) manche *m*; (spear) bois *m*; (arrow) flèche *f*, trait *m*; (light) rayon *m*; *mech* arbre *m*; (cart) brancard *m*

²**shaft** *n* (mine) puits *m*; (lift) cage *f*

³**shag** *n coll* tabac fort

**shagged** adj sl crevé
**shaggy** adj poilu; (beard) touffu; (eyebrows) en broussailles
**shah** n chah m
**shake** n secousse f; (hand) poignée f (de main); (trembling) tremblement m; (head) hochement m de tête; mus trille m; coll ~ s délirium m tremens; coll **be no great ~ s** ne pas valoir grand-chose; vt secouer, agiter; (make weaker) ébranler; (frighten) effrayer; (rouse) réveiller; ~ **down** faire tomber; ~ **hands on sth** toper; ~ **hands with s/o** serrer la main à qn; ~ **off** secouer; (get rid of) se débarrasser de; ~ **one's fist at s/o** menacer qn du poing; ~ **out** secouer; (empty) vider (en secouant); ~ **up** remuer, secouer; coll stimuler; vi trembler; (totter) branler, chanceler; (voice) trembloter; ~ **all over** trembler de tout son corps; ~ **down** s'installer
**shake-down** n coll lit improvisé
**shaken** adj secoué, ébranlé; **be ~ by sth** se ressentir de qch
**shaker** n trembleur m; **cocktail ~ shaker** m; **salad ~** panier m à salade
**shake-up** n remaniement m
**shakily** adv (weakly) faiblement; (unsteadily) à pas chancelants; (writing) d'une main tremblante
**shakiness** n tremblement m; manque m de stabilité; (voice) chevrotement m
**shaky** adj (building, etc) peu solide; (health) faible; (legs) chancelant; (voice) mal assuré; **feel ~** se sentir patraque; **his maths are ~** il est faible en mathématiques
**shale** n schiste argileux
**shall** aux v fut **I ~ give** je donnerai; (immediate fut) **I ~ be with you in a minute** je vais être chez vous dans un instant; (obligation) devoir; ~ **I come?** dois-je venir?; **should I come?** devrais-je venir?; (strong obligation) **all boys ~ be dressed in blue** tous les garçons sont tenus d'être habillés en bleu; (must) **they ~ not do this** il ne faut pas qu'ils fassent cela; (polite request) ~ **I help you?** voulez-vous que je vous aide?; (in answers) **Will you go?** – **I ~ (I shan't)** Irez-vous? – Oui (Non)
**shallot** n échalote f
**shallow** n bas-fond m; adj peu profond; (dish) plat; (person) superficiel -ielle
**shallowness** n manque m de profondeur; (person) caractère superficiel
**sham** n feinte f; coll chiqué m; imposture f; adj simulé, feint, faux (f fausse); vt feindre, simuler
**shamble** vi ~ **along** marcher (aller) à pas traînants
**shambles** n abattoir m; coll désordre m,

pagaille f
**shame** n honte f; **for ~!** fi donc!; **it's a ~!** c'est honteux!; **put s/o to ~** faire honte à qn; **what a ~!** quel dommage!; vt faire honte à, humilier
**shamefaced** adj penaud, honteux -euse, timide
**shameful** adj honteux -euse, scandaleux -euse
**shameless** adj (person) éhonté, effronté; (action) honteux -euse
**shampoo** n shampooing m; **dry ~** friction f; vt faire un shampooing à
**shamrock** n trèfle m
**shandy** n bière panachée
**shanghai** vt naut enlever après avoir enivré (drogué); forcer
**shank** n tige f; coll ~ s jambes fpl, coll quilles fpl; **go on ~ 's pony** aller à pied
¹**shanty** n baraque f, cabane f
²**shanty** n sea ~ chanson f de bord
**shantytown** n bidonville m
**shape** n forme f; (clothes) coupe f; (style) façon f; (mould) moule m; **be in good (bad) ~** être en bonne (mauvaise) forme; **keep in ~** garder sa forme; **out of ~** déformé; **take ~** prendre forme, se dessiner; vt façonner, former; (plan) inventer; ~ **one's course** diriger ses pas; vi se développer; ~ **well** promettre, prendre bonne tournure
**shaped** adj façonné, taillé, en forme de
**shapeless** adj sans forme, difforme
**shapely** adj bien fait, bien tourné
**shard** n tesson m
**share** n portion f, part f; (contribution) contribution f, écot m; (Stock Exchange) action f, titre m; ~ **in the profits** participation f aux bénéfices; **go ~ s** partager; **have ~ s** être intéressé dans; vt partager; (profits) avoir part à; ~ **out** répartir; vi ~ **in** participer à
**shareholder** n actionnaire
**share-out** n partage m, répartition f
**shark** n requin m; (cheat) escroc m, filou m; vt escroquer
**sharkskin** n peau f de requin; peau f de chagrin
¹**sharp** n mus dièse m
²**sharp** adj tranchant; (point) pointu, aigu -uë; (taste) acide, aigre; (cold) vif (f vive); (features) anguleux -euse; (clever) intelligent, éveillé; (cunning) rusé, fin; (sound) perçant, acerbe; (pain) violent; (hearing) fin; (distinct) net (f nette); (glance) pénétrant; ~ **corner** tournant m brusque; mot virage serré; ~ **practice** procédé m peu honnête; ~ **tongue** langue acérée; **at seven ~** à sept heures précises; **keep a ~ look-out** avoir l'œil bien ouvert

**sharpen** vt aiguiser, affiler, affûter; (pencil) tailler; (wits) dégourdir; cul relever; vi s'aiguiser; (sound) devenir plus aigu -uë

**sharpener** n (instrument) dispositif m d'affûtage

**sharper** n coll escroc m, tricheur -euse

**sharp-eyed** adj aux yeux perçants

**sharpish** adj coll plus vite que ça

**sharply** adv (clearly) nettement; (suddenly) brusquement; (briskly) vivement

**sharpshooter** n tirailleur m

**sharp-sighted** adj à la vue perçante

**sharp-witted** adj éveillé, dégourdi

**shatter** vt fracasser, briser; fig be ~ ed être bouleversé; vi se fracasser

**shave** n acte m de raser; have a ~ se raser; (at barber's) se faire raser; coll have a close (narrow) ~ l'échapper belle; vt raser; (graze) friser, effleurer, frôler; (clip) rogner, tondre; vi se raser

**shaver** n rasoir m; (person) raseur m; coll gosse m; sl moutard m

**shaving** n action f de (se) raser; (wood) copeau m; (metal) rognure f

**shaving-brush** n blaireau m

**shaving-cream** n crème f à raser

**shaving-soap** n savon m à barbe

**shawl** n châle m

**she** n+adj femelle f; pron elle; there ~ is! la voilà!

**sheaf** n gerbe f; (papers) liasse f

**shear** vt tondre, couper

**shearing** n (sheep) tonte f; (hedge) taille f

**shear-legs** n grue f de chargement

**shears** npl cisailles fpl, grands ciseaux

**sheath** n (sword) fourreau m; (case) étui m; (knife) gaine f; anat enveloppe f; (contraceptive) condom m, coll capote anglaise

**sheathe** vt rengainer, (re)mettre au fourreau; (cover) recouvrir

**¹shed** n (store) hangar m; (lean-to) appentis m; (garden, tools) remise f; (cattle) étable f

**²shed** vt (tears, blood, etc) verser; (light, etc) répandre; (leaves) perdre; (skin) jeter; ~ light on sth éclairer une affaire

**shedding** n perte f, chute f; (skin) mue f; (blood) effusion f

**sheen** n éclat m, lustre m

**sheep** n mouton m; fig black ~ brebis galeuse; feel like a lost ~ se sentir dépaysé; lost ~ brebis égarée; make ~'s eyes at s/o regarder qn tendrement

**sheepdog** n chien m de berger

**sheepfold** n parc m à moutons; fig bercail m

**sheepish** adj penaud

**sheep-shearing** n tonte f

**sheepskin** n peau f de mouton

**¹sheer** adj pur, véritable; (cliff, etc) à pic; (transparent) transparent; a ~ impossibility une impossibilité absolue; a ~ waste of time une pure perte de temps; adv tout à fait, complètement

**²sheer** vi naut ~ off prendre le large; larguer les amarres; coll s'écarter

**¹sheet** n (bed) drap m; (paper) feuille f; coll (newspaper) journal m; (water) nappe f; (snow) couche f; have a clean ~ avoir une conduite impeccable

**²sheet** n naut écoute f

**³sheet** vt couvrir d'un drap

**sheet-anchor** n naut ancre f de veille; fig planche f de salut

**sheeting** n toile f pour draps de lit

**sheet-iron** n tôle f

**sheet-lightning** n éclairs mpl en nappe

**sheet-steel** n tôle f d'acier

**sheikh** n cheik m

**shelf** n rayon m, tablette f; (ledge) rebord m; (rock) corniche f; ~ space rayonnage m; coll be on the ~ être au rancart; (spinster) avoir coiffé Sainte-Catherine; continental ~ plateau continental

**shell** n coquille f; (crab, etc) carapace f; (oyster) écaille f; (ship) coque f; (peas, beans) cosse f, gousse f; (boat) canot m de course; (cannon) obus m; come out of one's ~ sortir de sa coquille; retire into one's ~ rentrer dans sa coquille; vt (peas) écosser; (nuts) écaler; mil bombarder; coll ~ out débourser; vi coll ~ out payer la note

**shellac** n laque f en plaques

**shellfish** n coquillage m, crustacé m

**shell-hole** n trou m d'obus

**shelling** n (prawns) épluchage m; (peas) égrenage m; mil bombardement m

**shell-shock** n psychose f traumatique

**shelter** n abri m, asile m, lieu m de refuge; take ~ se mettre à l'abri; under ~ à l'abri; vt abriter; (fugitive) donner asile à; vi s'abriter, se mettre à l'abri

**¹shelve** vt (defer) remettre, ajourner; (put aside) mettre au rancart

**²shelve** vi (slope) aller en pente, être en pente

**shelving** n (deferring) ajournement m; (putting aside) mise f au rancart; (shelves) rayonnage m, rayons mpl

**shepherd** n berger m; ~'s pie hachis aux pommes de terre cuit au four; vt garder; (guide) piloter

**shepherdess** n bergère f

**sherbet** n sorbet m

**sheriff** n shérif m; US chef m de la police; ~'s officer huissier m

**sherry** n xérès m, vin m de Xérès

**shew** vt see show vt

shibboleth *n* mot *m* d'ordre

shield *n* bouclier *m*; *her* écusson *m*; *mech* garde *f*; *fig* défense *f*; *vt* protéger, défendre

shift *n* changement *m* (de position); (means) expédient *m*, moyen *m*; (workmen) équipe *f*; (clothing) chemise *f*; ~ **work** travail *m* par équipes; **make ~ to do sth** trouver moyen de faire qch; **make ~ with** s'accommoder de; **make ~ without sth** se passer de qch; *vt* changer de place, déplacer; *vi* changer de place, se déplacer; (wind) tourner, virer; ~ **for oneself** se débrouiller

shiftiness *n* sournoiserie *f*

shifting *adj* qui se déplace; (scene) changeant; ~ **sands** sables mouvants

shift-key *n* (typewriter) touche *f* de majuscule

shiftless *adj* peu débrouillard; (lazy) paresseux -euse

shifty *adj* sournois, louche

shilling *n obs* shilling *m*

shilly-shally *n* vacillation *f*, hésitation *f*; *vi* barguigner, vaciller

shimmer *n* lueur *f*, chatoiement *m*; *vi* miroiter, chatoyer, luire

shin *n* devant *m* du tibia; (beef) jarret *m*; ~ **bone** tibia *m*; *vi* ~ **up** grimper à

shindy *n coll* chahut *m*, tapage *m*

shine *n* éclat *m*, brillant *m*; **give a ~ to** faire reluire; **rain or ~** par tous les temps; *vt* faire briller; (shoes) cirer, polir; *vi* briller, luire, reluire, rayonner; **his face is shining with joy** sa figure rayonne de joie; **the sun is shining** il fait du soleil

¹shingle *n bui* bardeau *m*

²shingle *n* (pebbles) galets *mpl*, cailloux *mpl*

shingles *n med* zona *m*

shiny *adj* luisant, brillant

ship *n* navire *m*, bateau *m*, vaisseau *m*; (war) bâtiment *m*; **on board ~** à bord; *vt* embarquer, mettre à bord; (send) expédier; (oars) armer, rentrer; *vi* s'embarquer

shipbuilder *n* constructeur *m* de navires

shipbuilding *n* construction navale

shipload *n* cargaison *f*, chargement *m*

shipmate *n* camarade *m* de bord

shipment *n* (load) chargement *m*; (shipping) expédition *f*

shipowner *n* armateur *m*

shipper *n* chargeur *m*, expéditeur *m*

shipping *n* (loading) embarquement *m*; (sending by ship) expédition *f*; (ships) navires *mpl*; (merchant) marine marchande

shipping-company *n* compagnie *f* maritime

shipshape *adj* en bon ordre

shipwreck *n* naufrage *m*; *vt* faire naufrager

shipwrecked *adj* naufragé; **be ~** faire naufrage

shipwright *n* charpentier *m* de navires

shipyard *n* chantier *m* de constructions navales

shire *n* comté *m*

shirk *vt* se dérober à, esquiver

shirker *n mil* embusqué *m*, tire-au-flanc *m invar*

shirt *n* chemise *f*; **in one's ~ sleeves** en bras de chemise; *coll* **keep your ~ on** ne vous fâchez pas

shirt-front *n* plastron *m*

shirt-maker *n* chemisier -ière

shirty *adj coll* irritable

shit *n vulg* merde *f*; (person) salaud *m*; *vi vulg* chier

¹shiver *n* éclat *m*, fragment *m*; *vt* fracasser; *vi* voler en éclats

²shiver *n* frisson *m*, frissonnement *m*; *vi* frissonner, trembler, grelotter

shivery *adj* tremblant, grelottant; **feel ~** avoir des frissons, grelotter de froid

¹shoal *n* haut-fond *m* (*pl* hauts-fonds)

²shoal *n* (fish) banc *m*; (large amount) tas *m*, grande quantité; *vi* se réunir (voyager) en bancs

¹shock *n* choc *m*, heurt *m*; (blow) coup *m*; (electric) secousse *f*; *med* commotion *f*; ~ **troops** troupes *fpl* d'assaut; **it gave me a terrible ~** cela m'a porté un coup terrible; *vt* choquer, scandaliser, bouleverser; ~ **the ear** blesser l'oreille

²shock *n* (hair) tignasse *f*

³shock *n agr* meulette *f*

shock-absorber *n* amortisseur *m*

shocker *n coll* (thing) chose affreuse; (person) personne affreuse

shock-headed *adj* à tignasse

shocking *adj* choquant, révoltant; (frightful) affreux -euse

shock-proof *adj* antichoc *invar*

shoddy *adj* de camelote, de pacotille

shoe *n* soulier *m*, chaussure *f*; (horse) fer *m*; (wood) sabot *m*; **court ~** escarpin *m*; *mot* Denvèr ~ sabot *m* de Denver; *fig* **step into s/o's ~s** prendre la place de qn; *vt* chausser; (horse) ferrer

shoeblack *n* cireur *m*

shoehorn *n* chausse-pied *m*

shoe-lace *n* lacet *m*

shoemaker *n* (mender) cordonnier *m*; (maker) bottier *m*; (manufacturer) fabricant *m* de chaussures

shoe-polish *n* cirage *m*

shoestring *n coll* **on a ~** à peu de frais, avec des moyens réduits

shoe-tree *n* forme *f*

shoot *n bot* rejeton *m*, pousse *f*; (rubbish) dépôt *m*; (hunt) partie *f* de chasse; (spout) gouttière f; (chute) glissière f; coll the whole ~ tout le bataclan; vt tirer; (kill) tuer; (hit) atteindre; (animal) abattre; (firing squad) fusiller; (throw) précipiter, lancer; (rays) darder; (gun, rubbish) décharger; (football) shooter; (arrow) décocher; (glance) lancer; coll ~ a line exagérer son importance, crâner; coll ~ one's mouth off bavarder indiscrètement; mot ~ the lights brûler les feux; ~ s/o (kill) tuer qn d'un coup de revolver (fusil); (hit) atteindre qn d'un coup de revolver (fusil); ~ up tirer des coups de feu sur, mitrailler; vi tirer; (rush) se précipiter, se lancer; (star) filer; (plant) pousser; (bud) bourgeonner; ~ ahead aller rapidement en avant; ~ at s/o tirer sur qn; ~ off filer, partir d'un trait; ~ out sortir précipitamment; ~ past passer comme un éclair; ~ straight bien viser; ~ up (flame) jaillir; (grow) grandir rapidement; go ~ing aller à la chasse

**shooter** n tireur -euse; US coll revolver m, arme f à feu

**shooting** n tir m; (hunting) chasse f; (firing) fusillade f; (wound) élancement m; (discharging) déchargement m; (rapids) franchissement m; (arrow) décochement m; cin tournage m; beginning of the ~ season ouverture f de la chasse; adj (pain) lancinant, jaillissant; (star) filant; ~ war guerre chaude

**shooting-box** n pavillon m de chasse

**shooting-brake** n mot break m

**shooting-range** n champ m de tir

**shooting-star** n étoile filante

**shooting-stick** n canne-siège f (pl cannes-sièges)

**shop** n magasin m, boutique f; coll be all over the ~ être en désordre; closed ~ atelier (usine) fermé(e) aux ouvriers non-syndiqués; go round the ~s courir les magasins; on the ~ floor dans l'atelier, dans l'usine; coll talk ~ parler métier; vi faire des achats; ~ around comparer les prix dans les magasins

**shop-assistant** n vendeur -euse, employé -e de magasin

**shop-front** n devanture f (de magasin)

**shop-girl** n vendeuse f

**shopkeeper** n commerçant -e, marchand -e

**shopkeeping** n commerce m

**shoplifter** n voleur -euse à l'étalage

**shoplifting** n vol m à l'étalage

**shopper** n acheteur -euse

**shopping** n achats mpl, emplettes fpl; go ~ faire ses (des) emplettes, faire ses courses

**shopsoiled** adj défraîchi

**shop-steward** n délégué -e syndical -e

**shop-walker** n inspecteur -trice (du magasin)

¹**shore** n rivage m, littoral m, bord m; in ~ près de la côte; keep close to the ~ côtoyer; off ~ au large; on ~ à terre

²**shore** n bui étai m; vi ~ up étayer

**short** n cin court métrage; elect abbr court-circuit m (pl courts-circuits); coll (drink) petit verre; ~s short m, culotte f; the long and the ~ of it le fin mot de l'affaire; adj court; (brief) bref (f brève); (insufficient) insuffisant; (person) de courte taille; (abrupt) brusque; (tone) cassant; ~ cut raccourci m; ~ pastry pâte brisée; ~ story conte m, nouvelle f; be ~ of sth manquer de qch; for a ~ time cours (pendant) peu de temps; for ~ pour abréger; get ~ er raccourcir; give ~ weight ne pas donner le poids; go ~ of sth se priver de qch; in a ~ time sous peu; in ~ bref; make ~ work of sth mener rondement les choses; nothing ~ of a bomb will move him seule une bombe le fera bouger; this is little ~ of madness cela tient de la folie; we are ~ of one person il nous manque une personne; adv ~ of going the whole way à moins d'aller jusqu'au bout; cut s/o ~ couper la parole à qn; fall ~ ne pas répondre à; stop ~ s'arrêter pile; vt elect court-circuiter

**shortage** n manque m, insuffisance f; (materials) crise f, pénurie f; (scarcity) disette f

**shortbread, shortcake** n sablé m

**shortchange** vt rendre une monnaie insuffisante à

**short-circuit** n court-circuit m (pl courts-circuits); vt court-circuiter

**shortcoming** n défaut m, imperfection f

**shorten** vt raccourcir; (abridge) abréger; naut ~ sail réduire la voilure; vi raccourcir

**shortfall** n déficit m

**shorthand** n sténographie f, coll sténo f; ~ typist sténodactylo f

**shorthanded** adj à court de personnel (de main d'œuvre)

**short-list** n liste choisie

**short-lived** adj (person) qui est mort jeune; (animal) qui vit peu de temps; (not lasting) éphémère, de courte durée, passager -ère

**shortly** adv (soon) bientôt; (briefly) brièvement; (abruptly) brusquement; ~ after(wards) peu (de temps) après

**shortness** n peu m de longueur; (stature) petitesse f; (brevity) brièveté f, courte durée; (abruptness) brusquerie *f*; (lack) manque *m*, insuffisance *f*

**short-sighted** *adj* myope

**short-spoken** *adj* brusque

**short-tempered** *adj* irascible

**short-winded** *adj* à l'haleine courte, poussif -ive

**shot** *n* coup *m* de feu; (bullet) balle *f*; (hunting) plomb *m*; (football) shoot *m*; (go) coup *m*; *cin* prise *f* de vue; *coll* (injection) piqûre *f*; *coll* (stimulant) coup *m* de fouet; *fig* ~ **in the arm** encouragement *m*; **at a** ~ d'un coup; **be a good** ~ être bon (*f* bonne) tireur -euse; **be off like a** ~ partir comme un trait; **big** ~ gros bonnet; *coll* **have a** ~ essayer; **like a** ~ très vite, avec empressement; *coll* **long** ~ coup *m* à tenter; *adj* (cloth) chatoyant; (colour) ~ **with** parsemé de; *coll* **be** ~ **of** être débarrassé de

**shotgun** *n* fusil *m* de chasse; ~ **wedding** mariage forcé

**shot-silk** *n* taffetas changeant

**shoulder** *n* épaule *f*; (mountain) contrefort *m*; (road) bas-côté *m*; *coll* **give the cold** ~ **to** battre froid à; **I let him have it straight from the** ~ je ne le lui ai pas envoyé dire; **over (across) the** ~ en bandoulière; **put one's** ~ **to the wheel** pousser à la roue; **stand head and** ~**s above** *s/o* dépasser qn de la tête; *vt* mettre (charger) sur l'épaule; (arms) porter; (responsibility) endosser; ~ **one's way through** se frayer un chemin à coups d'épaule

**shoulder-blade** *n* omoplate *f*

**shoulder-strap** *n* bretelle *f*, bandoulière *f*

**shout** *n* cri *m*, hurlement *m*; (laughter) éclat *m*; ~ **s of applause** acclamations *fpl*; *vt* crier; ~ **down** huer; *vi* crier, pousser des cris; ~ **out** s'écrier, crier

**shove** *n coll* coup *m* d'épaule; *vt coll* pousser; *coll* ~ **aside** écarter; *coll* ~ **back** repousser; *naut* ~ **off** pousser au large; *vi coll* se frayer un chemin; *coll* ~ **off** s'en aller

**shovel** *n* pelle *f*; *vt* peller, pelleter, prendre à la pelle; ~ **away** enlever à la pelle; ~ **up** ramasser à la pelle

**shovelful** *n* pelletée *f*

**show** *n* spectacle *m*; (exhibition) exposition *f*; (appearance) semblant *m*, apparence *f*; (display) étalage *m*; (competition) concours *m*; (motor) salon *m*; (ostentation) parade *f*; *cin* séance *f*; (fashion) collection *f*; *agr* comice *m*; ~ **flat (house)** appartement *m* (maison *f*) témoin; ~ **of friendship** démonstration *f* d'amitié; ~ **of hands** vote *m* à main levée; *coll* **give the** ~ **away** vendre la mèche; *coll* **good** ~! très

bien!, bravo!; **go to a** ~ aller au spectacle; **make a poor** ~ faire triste figure; **make a** ~ **of oneself** se donner en spectacle; *coll* **put up a good** ~ se comporter bien; *coll* **run the** ~ diriger l'affaire; *vt* montrer, faire voir; indiquer; (feeling) témoigner, faire preuve de; (prove) prouver; (exhibit) exposer; *cin* projeter; (passport) présenter; ~ **off** faire valoir, faire parade de; ~ **oneself** (put in appearance) faire acte de présence; ~ **one's face** se montrer; ~ **one's hand** jouer cartes sur table; (reveal intentions) dévoiler ses intentions; ~ *s/o* **into a room** faire entrer qn dans une pièce; ~ *s/o* **out** reconduire qn; ~ *s/o* **to his room** conduire qn à sa chambre; ~ *s/o* **up** (expose) démasquer qn; ~ *s/o* **up (upstairs)** faire monter qn; ~ *sth* **up** (schoolwork) donner; (relief) mettre en relief; ~ **the time** indiquer l'heure; **time will** ~ qui vivra verra; *vi* paraître, se montrer; (stick out) dépasser; ~ **off** poser; ~ **through** transparaître; ~ **to advantage** faire bonne figure; ~ **up** (turn up) arriver, se présenter; (stand out) ressortir, se détacher; *coll* ~ **willing** faire preuve de bonne volonté

**show-case** *n* vitrine *f*, montre *f*

**show-down** *n* confrontation *f*; **have a** ~ en venir au fait

**shower** *n* (rain) averse *f*, ondée *f*; (toilet) douche *f*; *fig* pluie *f*; *vt* faire pleuvoir, verser; ~ **blows on** *s/o* rouer qn de coups

**shower-bath** *n* douche *f*

**showery** *adj* pluvieux -ieuse

**showgirl** *n* girl *f*

**showily** *adv* d'une façon prétentieuse

**showiness** *n* prétention *f*, clinquant *m*

**showing** *n* exposition *f*; *cin* **first** ~ première exclusivité; **on your own** ~ à ce que vous dites vous-même

**show-jumping** *n* concours *m* de monte à l'obstacle

**showman** *n* animateur -trice; (circus) forain *m*; **be a great** ~ savoir attirer l'attention sur soi-même

**showmanship** *n* art *m* de la mise en scène; talent *m* d'animateur -trice

**show-off** *n* poseur -euse

**showpiece** *n* article *m* d'exposition; objet *m* de grand intérêt

**show-place** *n* endroit *m* d'intérêt touristique

**showroom** *n* magasin *m*, salon *m* (salle *f*) d'exposition

**showy** *adj* voyant; (person) prétentieux -ieuse; *coll* tape-à-l'œil *invar*

**shrapnel** *n* shrapnel *m*, éclats *mpl* d'obus

**shred** *n* brin *m*; (cloth) lambeau *m*; **there isn't a** ~ **of evidence** il n'y a pas l'ombre

692

d'une preuve (la moindre preuve); vt (paper) déchirer en lambeaux; (cloth) effilocher; (vegetables) couper en languettes

¹**shrew** n mégère f, femme f acariâtre

²**shrew** n zool musaraigne f

**shrewd** adj rusé, sagace; ~ **blow** coup bien placé; **I have a ~ idea** je suis porté à croire que

**shrewdness** n perspicacité f, finesse f

**shrewish** adj acariâtre

**shriek** n cri perçant; vi pousser des cris perçants; ~ **with laughter** éclater de rire

**shrill** adj aigu -uë, strident

**shrimp** n crevette f; coll fig gringalet m; vi faire la pêche aux crevettes

**shrine** n châsse f, reliquaire m; (tomb) tombeau m; chapelle f; lieu saint; fig sanctuaire m

**shrink** vt rétrécir; vi rétrécir; ~ **away** s'éloigner timidement; ~ **from doing sth** répugner à faire qch; ~ **from sth** reculer devant qch; ~ **in the wash** rétrécir au lavage

**shrinkage, shrinking** n (cloth) rétrécissement m; contraction f

**shrinking** n see shrinkage

**shrivel** vt ratatiner, rider; (plants) brûler; vi se ratatiner, se rider

**shroud** n linceul m, suaire m; vt ensevelir, envelopper d'un linceul; fig voiler; ~**ed in mystery** enveloppé de mystère

**Shrove Tuesday** n mardi gras

**shrub** n arbuste m, arbrisseau m

**shrubbery** n bosquet m, plantation f d'arbustes

**shrug** n haussement m d'épaules; vt ~ **one's shoulders** hausser les épaules; ~ **off** faire peu de cas de

**shucks** interj US allons donc!

**shudder** n frisson m, frémissement m; vi frissonner, frémir

**shuffle** n marche traînante; (cards) battement m; (evasion) détours mpl, tergiversation f; vt mêler; (cards) battre; vi traîner les pieds; tergiverser; ~ **off** s'en aller en traînant le pas

¹**shun** vt éviter, fuir

²**shun** interj abbr mil (= **attention!**) garde à vous!

**shunt** n manœuvre f; elect shunt m; ~ **line** voie f de garage; vt manœuvrer; elect shunter

**shut** vt fermer; ~ **down** fermer; ~ **in** enfermer; (enclosure) entourer; ~ **off** couper; séparer; ~ **out** exclure; ~ **up** enfermer; (silence) faire taire; sl ~ **your trap!** (ferme) ta gueule!; vi (se) fermer; coll ~ **up** se taire

**shut-down** n fermeture f

**shut-eye** n coll somme m

**shutter** n volet m; phot obturateur m

**shuttle** n navette f; ~ **service** navette f; vi faire la navette

**shuttlecock** n volant m

¹**shy** adj timide, sauvage; (animal) farouche; (horse) ombrageux -euse; **fight ~ of sth** se méfier de qch

²**shy** vi (horse) faire un écart; ~ **at sth** prendre ombrage de qch

³**shy** vt + vi coll lancer

**shyness** n timidité f, réserve f

**Siamese** n Siamois -e; adj siamois

**Siberia** n Sibérie f

**sibilant** n sifflante f; adj sifflant

**sibling** n frère m, sœur f

**Sicily** n Sicile f

**sick** adj malade; **be ~** vomir; (ill) être malade; coll **be ~ of sth** être dégoûté de qch; **feel ~** avoir mal au cœur; **I'm ~ of it!** j'en ai marre!; **report ~** se faire porter malade; **the ~** les malades

**sick-bay** n infirmerie f

**sick-bed** n lit m de douleur

**sicken** vt rendre malade; dégoûter; vi tomber malade; **be ~ing for an illness** couver une maladie

**sickening** adj coll écœurant

**sickle** n faucille f

**sick-leave** n congé m de maladie

**sickliness** n pâleur f; état maladif; (taste) fadeur f; (feeling) sentimentalité f

**sick-list** n rôle m des malades

**sickly** adj maladif -ive; (taste) doucereux -euse, fade; (smile) pâle; (light) faible; (unhealthy) insalubre

**sickness** n maladie f; (feeling) nausées fpl, mal m au cœur; **air ~** mal m de l'air; **car ~** mal m de voiture; **sea ~** mal m de mer; **sleeping ~** maladie f du sommeil

**sick-pay** n (benefit) allocation f de maladie; (salary) traitement m pendant la maladie

**side** n côté m; (flank) flanc m; (edge, ship) bord m; (river) rive f; (team) équipe f; (party) parti m; (slope) pente f; ~ **by** ~ côte à côte; **by my ~** à côté de moi; **hear both ~s of a question** entendre le pour et le contre d'une question; **on all ~s** de tous côtés; **on both ~s** des deux côtés; **on the other ~** de l'autre côté; coll **put on ~** faire de l'épate; **put sth on (to) one ~** mettre qch à l'écart; (cloth) **right ~** endroit m; **see the bright ~** voir le bon côté; **take ~s** prendre parti; **time is on our ~** le temps travaille pour nous; **wrong ~ up** sens dessus dessous; adj latéral, de côté; ~ **issue** question f d'intérêt secondaire; vi ~ **with s/o** se ranger du côté de qn

# sideboard

**sideboard** *n* buffet *m*
**sidecar** *n* sidecar *m*
**side-drum** *n* caisse *f*
**side-effect** *n* résultat *m* secondaire
**side-face** *n* profil *m*
**side-kick** *n* US coll subordonné -e
**sidelight** *n* mot feu *m* de position
**side-line** *n* (occupation) violon *m* d'Ingres, occupation *f* secondaire; *comm* article *m* à côté; (sport) ligne *f* de touche
**sidelong** *adj* oblique
**sidereal** *adj* sidéral
**side-saddle** *n* ride ~ monter en amazone
**sideshow** *n* spectacle forain; *coll fig* affaire *f* d'importance secondaire
**side-splitting** *adj* tordant; *sl* marrant
**side-step** *vt* éviter; *vi* faire un pas de côté
**sidestroke** *n* nage *f* sur le côté
**sidetrack** *vt fig* détourner l'attention de; (train) garer
**side-view** *n* vue *f* de côté, vue *f* de profil
**sidewalk** *n* US trottoir *m*
**sideward** *adj* latéral, de côté
**sidewards** *adv* de côté
**sideways** *adv* de côté, latéralement, en travers
**siding** *n* voie *f* de garage
**sidle** *vi* marcher de biais; ~ **along** s'avancer de côté; ~ **up to s/o** se couler auprès de qn
**siege** *n* siège *m*; **lay ~ to** assiéger
**siesta** *n* sieste *f*
**sieve** *n* crible *m*, tamis *m*; *vt* passer au crible, tamiser
**sift** *vt* passer au crible (au tamis), tamiser; *fig* examiner minutieusement; *vi* filtrer
**sifter** *n* cribleur *m*, tamiseur *m*; (thing) crible *m*, tamis *m*
**sigh** *n* soupir *m*; *vi* soupirer
**sight** *n* vue *f*; (spectacle) spectacle *m*; (gun) cran *m* de mire, guidon *m*; ~ **s** monuments *mpl* et curiosités *fpl*; **at first ~** au premier abord; **at (on) ~** à vue; **catch ~ of s/o** apercevoir qn; **come into ~** apparaître; *coll* **I can't bear the ~ of him** je ne peux pas le sentir; **keep s/o in ~** ne pas perdre qn de vue; **know s/o by ~** connaître qn de vue; **lose ~ of** perdre de vue; **love at first ~** coup *m* de foudre; **out of ~,** **out of mind** loin des yeux, loin du cœur; **short ~** myopie *f*; *vt* apercevoir; (gun) viser
**sightless** *adj* aveugle
**sightly** *adj* agréable à voir, avenant
**sight-reading** *n* lecture *f* à vue
**sightseeing** *n* visite *f* touristique; **go ~** visiter les curiosités (touristiques)
**sightseer** *n* touriste
**sign** *n* signe *m*; (advert) réclame *f*; (shop,

etc) enseigne *f*; (indication) indice *m*; (trace) trace *f*; (omen) présage *m*; symbole *m*; **road ~ s** signalisation routière; **show no ~ of life** ne donner aucun signe de vie; **there's no ~ of him** il reste invisible (introuvable); *vt* signer; (indicate) indiquer; ~ **away** céder par écrit; ~ **on (up)** embaucher, engager; *vi* ~ **off** (work) pointer au départ; (programme) terminer l'émission; ~ **on (up)** s'engager
**signal** *n* signal *m*; *rad* indicatif *m*; **traffic ~ s** feux *mpl* de circulation; *adj* insigne, remarquable; *vt* signaler; *vi* donner un signal; ~ **to s/o to do sth** faire signe à qn de faire qch
**signal-box** *n* poste *m* d'aiguillage
**signalize** *vt* signaler, marquer
**signaller** *n* signaleur *m*
**signally** *adv* remarquablement
**signalman** *n* aiguilleur *m*
**signatory** *n* + *adj* signataire
**signature** *n* signature *f*; ~ **tune** indicatif musical
**signboard** *n* (notice-board) écriteau *m*; (shop) enseigne *f*; (advert) réclame *f*
**signet** *n* sceau *m*, cachet *m*
**signet-ring** *n* chevalière *f*
**significance** *n* signification *f*, importance *f*
**significant** *adj* significatif -ive; (important) important
**signification** *n* signification *f*
**signify** *vt* signifier, vouloir dire; (declare) déclarer; *vi* importer
**signing** *n* signature *f*
**signpost** *n* poteau indicateur
**Sikh** *n* Sikh -e
**silage** *n* fourrage ensilé
**silence** *n* silence *m*; **dead ~** silence absolu; **pass over in ~** passer sous silence; *vt* faire taire, réduire au silence; (complaints) étouffer
**silencer** *n* mot pot *m* d'échappement; (gun) silencieux *m*; amortisseur *m* de son
**silent** *adj* silencieux -ieuse; **keep ~** garder le silence
**silhouette** *n* silhouette *f*; *vt* silhouetter
**silicon** *n* silicium *m*; ~ **chip** plaquette *f* de silicium
**silk** *n* soie *f*; (sewing) fil *m* de soie; ~ **handkerchief** foulard *m*; ~ **hat** (chapeau *m*) haut-de-forme *m* (*pl* hauts-de-forme); **oiled ~** taffetas *m* imperméable
**silken** *adj* soyeux -euse, de soie
**silkiness** *n* nature soyeuse
**silkworm** *n* ver *m* à soie
**silky** *adj* soyeux -euse, de soie
**sill** *n* (window) rebord *m*; (door) seuil *m*
**silliness** *n* sottise *f*

**silly** *n* (person) idiot -e; *adj* sot (*f* sotte), niais; **~ ass** imbécile *m*; **~ thing** bêtise *f*; **knock s/o ~** assommer qn

**silo** *n* silo *m*; **launching ~** puits *m* de lancement

**silt** *n geol* limon *m*; *vt* **~ up** ensabler; *vi* s'ensabler

**silver** *n* argent *m*; (plate) argenterie *f*; *adj* d'argent, en argent; **~ coin** pièce *f* d'argent; **~ fox** renard argenté; *fig* **~ lining** consolation *f*; **~ paper** papier *m* d'argent; *vt* argenter; (mirror) étamer

**silver-gilt** *n* vermeil *m*

**silver-haired** *adj* aux cheveux argentés

**silver-plated** *adj* argenté

**silverside** *n* gîte *m* à la noix

**silversmith** *n* orfèvre *m*

**silverware** *n* argenterie *f*

**silvery** *adj* argenté; (laugh) argentin

**simian** *adj* simiesque

**similar** *adj* semblable, pareil -eille

**similarity** *n* ressemblance *f*, similarité *f*

**simile** *n* comparaison *f*

**similitude** *n* similitude *f*

**simmer** *vt* faire mijoter; *vi* (liquid) frémir; (food) mijoter; *fig* **~ down** s'apaiser peu à peu, se calmer

**simony** *n eccles* simonie *f*

**simper** *n* sourire affecté; *vi* minauder

**simple** *n med* simple *m*; *adj* simple; (person) naturel -elle, sans affectation; *pej* naïf (*f* naïve), crédule

**simple-minded** *adj* naïf (*f* naïve)

**simpleness** *n see* simplicity

**simpleton** *n* nigaud -e

**simplicity** *n* simplicité *f*, candeur *f*; *pej* niaiserie *f*; **be ~ itself** être simple comme bonjour

**simplification** *n* simplification *f*

**simplify** *vt* simplifier

**simply** *adv* simplement; **~ marvellous** absolument (tout à fait) merveilleux -euse

**simulate** *vt* simuler, feindre

**simulation** *n* simulation *f*, feinte *f*

**simulator** *n* simulateur -trice; *aer* simulateur *m* de vol

**simultaneity** *n* simultanéité *f*

**simultaneous** *adj* simultané

**sin** *n* péché *m*; (offence) offense *f*; **original ~** péché originel; **ugly as ~** laid comme un singe; *vi* pécher

**since** *adv* depuis; **long ~** il y a longtemps; **many years ~** il y a bien des années; *prep* depuis; *conj* depuis que; (reason) puisque; **it's a year ~ he arrived** il y a un an qu'il est arrivé

**sincere** *adj* sincère

**sincerity** *n* sincérité *f*

**sine** *n math* sinus *m*

**sinecure** *n* sinécure *f*

**sinew** *n* tendon *m*; **~s** nerfs *mpl*; **the ~s**

**of war** le nerf de la guerre

**sinewy** *adj* (arm) musclé; (meat) tendineux -euse

**sinful** *adj* pécheur (*f* pécheresse); *coll fig* scandaleux -euse

**sing** *vt* + *vi* chanter; *vi* (ears) bourdonner, tinter; (wind) siffler; *US* (inform) moucharder

**singe** *n* légère brûlure; *vt* brûler légèrement, roussir; (poultry) passer à la flamme; **~ hair** brûler la pointe des cheveux

**singer** *n* chanteur -euse; (opera) cantatrice *f*

**Sing(h)alese, Cingalese** *adj* cingalais

**singing** *n* chant *m*

**single** *n* (ticket) aller *m* (simple), billet *m* simple; (record) 45 tours *m sing*; *sp* simple *m*, partie *f* simple; *adj* unique, seul; (not married) célibataire, pas marié; (character) simple, honnête; **~ bed** lit *m* pour une personne; **~ bedroom** chambre *f* à un lit; **~ ticket** billet *m* simple; *vt* **~ out** choisir; (for distinction) distinguer

**single-breasted** *adj* (jacket) droit

**single-handed** *adj* seul, sans aide

**single-minded** *adj* qui ne vise qu'un but

**singleness** *n* sincérité *f*; (one mind) unicité *f*; (celibacy) célibat *m*

**single-seater** *adj* à une place

**singlet** *n* gilet *m* de corps; (sport) maillot fin

**singly** *adv* séparément, un à un; (alone) seul

**singsong** *n* chant *m* monotone; *coll* chants *mpl* en chœur; *adj* **~ voice** voix *f* monotone

**singular** *n gramm* singulier *m*; *adj* singulier -ière, bizarre; (remarkable) remarquable

**singularity** *n* singularité *f*

**singularize** *vt* singulariser

**singularly** *adv* singulièrement, remarquablement

**sinister** *adj* sinistre; dangereux -euse, traître -esse

¹**sink** *n* évier *m*; *fig* cloaque *m*

²**sink** *vt* (ship) couler, faire sombrer; (lower) baisser; (push down) enfoncer; (dig) creuser; (money) placer, *pej* engloutir; (objection) supprimer; *vi* (ship) couler, sombrer; (in chair) se laisser tomber, s'affaisser; (into ground) s'enfoncer; (sun) baisser; **~ down** s'affaisser; **~ in** pénétrer; **~ to one's knees** tomber à genoux; **my heart sank** le cœur me manqua

**sinker** *n* plomb *m*; **hook, line and ~** à fond, totalement

**sinking** *n* enfoncement *m*; (ground, etc) affaissement *m*; (weakening) défaillance *f*, affaiblissement *m*; (well) creusage *m*

**sinless** *adj* innocent, sans péché

**sinner** *n* pécheur (*f* pécheresse)

**sinologist** *n* sinologue

**sinology** *n* sinologie *f*

**sinuosity** *n* sinuosité *f*

**sinuous** *adj* sinueux -euse; (supple) souple

**sinus** *n* sinus *m*

**sinusitis** *n* sinusite *f*

**sip** *n* petite gorgée, petit coup; *vt* boire à petits coups, siroter

**siphon** *n* siphon *m*; *vt* siphonner

**sir** *n* monsieur *m*; (letters) **dear Sir** Monsieur; *mil* yes, ~ oui, mon capitaine (général, etc); *naut* aye, aye, ~ oui, mon commandant (amiral, etc); *vt* ~ s/o donner du Monsieur à qn

**sire** *n* sire *m*; (father) père *m*; *vt* engendrer

**siren** *n* sirène *f*; (vamp) femme fatale

**sirloin** *n* aloyau *m*, faux-filet *m*

**sisal** *n* sisal *m*

**sissy** *n* coll garçon (homme) effeminé; (coward) poule mouillée

**sister** *n* sœur *f*; (nurse) infirmière *f* en chef

**sisterhood** *n* communauté religieuse; union fraternelle

**sister-in-law** *n* belle-sœur *f* (*pl* belles-sœurs)

**sisterly** *adj* de sœur

**sit** *vt* asseoir; ~ **out** ne pas prendre part à; (wait till end) rester assis jusqu'à la fin de; *vi* (sit down) s'asseoir; (be sitting) être assis; (assembly, M.P.) siéger; (committee, council) se réunir; (photo) poser; (hen) couver; (garment) aller, tomber; ~ **back in one's chair** se renverser dans sa chaise; *coll fig* se relaxer; ~ **down** s'asseoir; ~ **down to a meal** se mettre à table; *coll fig* ~ **on** s/o rabrouer qn; *coll fig* ~ **on sth** laisser dormir qch; ~ **tight** (resist) tenir ferme (bon); (stay put) ne pas bouger de sa place; ~ **up** se redresser, se tenir droit dans sa chaise; (stay up) veiller; ~ **up for** s/o attendre qn; ~ **with** s/o tenir compagnie à qn; (sick person) veiller qn

**sit-down** *adj* ~ **strike** grève *f* sur le tas

**site** *n* emplacement *m*; *archi* site *m*; **building** ~ chantier *m* de construction; **camping** ~ camping *m*, terrain *m* de camping; *vt* situer

**sit-in** *n* ~ **strike** grève *f* sur le tas

**siting** *n* (situation) emplacement *m*; choix *m* de l'emplacement

**sitter** *n* personne assise; (art) modèle *m*; **baby-**~ baby-sitter

**sitting** *n* posture assise; (session) séance *f*; (court) audience *f*; (hen) couvaison *f*; (lunch) service *m*; *adj* assis; (court) en séance; *coll fig* ~ **duck** cible *f* facile; **be** ~ **pretty** avoir trouvé le filon

**sitting-room** *n* salle *f* de séjour, living(-room) *m*

**situate** *vt* situer

**situated** *adj* situé; **awkwardly** ~ dans une position embarrassante

**situation** *n* situation *f*, position *f*; (post) place *f*, emploi *m*; ~ **s vacant** offres *fpl* d'emploi; ~ **s wanted** demandes *fpl* d'emploi

**six** *n* six *m invar*; **at** ~ **es and sevens** en désordre; **it is** ~ **of one and half a dozen of the other** c'est bonnet blanc et blanc bonnet; *adj* six

**sixteen** *n* seize *m invar*; *adj* seize *invar*

**sixteenth** *n* seizième; (date) seize *m*; *adj* seizième

**sixth** *n* sixième; (date) six *m*; *adj* sixième

**sixtieth** *n* + *adj* soixantième

**sixty** *n* soixante *m invar*; **he is in his sixties** il a passé soixante ans; **the sixties** les années soixante; *adj* soixante *invar*

**siz(e)able** *adj* assez grand

¹**size** *n* grandeur *f*; (person) taille *f*; (bulk) grosseur *f*; (volume) volume *m*; (books) format *m*; (shoes, gloves) pointure *f*; (collar, neck) encolure *f*; **full (life)** ~ grandeur naturelle; **small** ~ petit modèle; *vt* classer par grosseur; ~ **up** jauger; (person) juger

²**size** *n* (glue) colle *f*, apprêt *m*; (textiles) apprêt *m*; *vt* coller, apprêter

**sizzle** *n* grésillement *m*; *vi* grésiller

¹**skate** *n* patin *m*; *vi* patiner

²**skate** *n* (fish) raie *f*

**skateboard** *n* planche *f* à roulettes, skateboard *m*

**skater** *n* patineur -euse

**skating** *n* patinage *m*

**skating-rink** *n* patinoire *f*

**skedaddle** *vi* coll filer, se sauver à toutes jambes

**skein** *n* écheveau *m*

**skeletal** *adj* squelettique

**skeleton** *n* squelette *m*; (framework) charpente *f*, carcasse *f*; ~ **in the cupboard** secret honteux de la famille

**skeleton-key** *n* (master-key) passe-partout *m invar*; (locksmith's) crochet *m*

**sketch** *n* croquis *m*, esquisse *f*; (short play) sketch *m*, saynète *f*; (outline) exposé *m*; *vt* esquisser, croquer

**sketch-book** *n* cahier *m* de croquis, album *m*

**sketch-map** *n* carte-croquis *f* (*pl* cartes-croquis), coll topo *m*

**sketchy** *adj* imprécis, plutôt vague

**skew** *adj* biais, de biais; **on the** ~ de biais; *adv* en biais, de travers; *vi* obliquer, biaiser

**skewer** *n* brochette *f*; *vt* brocheter, embrocher

**ski** *n* ski *m*; **on ~ s** à skis; *vi* faire du ski, skier

**skid** *n* dérapage *m*; *vi* déraper, faire une embardée

**skidding** *n* dérapage *m*

**skid-lid** *n* *coll* casque *m* (de motocycliste)

**skid-pan** *n* *mot* piste savonnée

**skier** *n* skieur (*f* skieuse)

**skiff** *n* esquif *m*, skiff *m*

**skiffle** *n* jazz basé sur des chansons folkloriques

**skiing** *n* ski *m*; **water ~** ski *m* nautique

**ski-jump** *n* saut *m* à skis

**skilful** *adj* habile, adroit

**ski-lift** *n* téléski *m*, remonte-pente *m*

**skill** *n* habileté *f*, dextérité *f*; **lack of ~** maladresse *f*

**skilled** *adj* habile; (experienced) expérimenté; **~ worker** ouvrier spécialisé

**skillet** *n* poêlon *m* à long manche

**skim** *vt* écumer; (milk) écrémer; (soup) dégraisser; (surface) effleurer, raser; **~ over (through)** parcourir rapidement; *vi* **~ along** passer légèrement

**skimmer** *n* (soup) écumoire *f*; (milk) écrémeuse *f*

**skimp** *vt* (be sparing of) lésiner sur; *coll* bâcler, saboter

**skimpy** *adj* (insufficient) maigre; (garment) étriqué

**skin** *n* peau *f*; (hide) cuir *m*; *fig* **by the ~ of one's teeth** de justesse; *fig* **have a thin (thick) ~** être (peu) susceptible; *fig* **I've got her under my ~** je l'ai dans la peau; **next to one's ~** à même la peau; **wet to the ~** mouillé jusqu'aux os; *vt* écorcher, dépouiller; (fruit) peler, éplucher

**skin-deep** *adj* superficiel -ielle

**skin-disease** *n* maladie *f* de (la) peau

**skin-diving** *n* plongée *f* autonome

**skinflint** *n* grippe-sou *m*

**skinful** *n* pleine outre de vin; *sl* cuite *f*

**skin-graft** *n* greffe *f* de peau

**skin-grafting** *n* greffe cutanée

**skinny** *adj* maigre, décharné

**skint** *adj* *sl* sans argent, *sl* fauché

**skin-tight** *adj* collant

**¹skip** *n* benne *f*; panier *m*

**²skip** *n* petit saut, bond *m*, gambade *f*; *vt* sauter, passer; *sl* **~ it!** ça suffit!; *vi* sauter, gambader; (with rope) sauter à la corde

**¹skipper** *n* *naut* patron *m*; *sl* chef *m*

**²skipper** *n* sauteur -euse

**skipping-rope** *n* corde *f* à sauter

**skirmish** *n* *mil* escarmouche *f*; échauffourée *f*; *vi* escarmoucher

**¹skirt** *n* jupe *f*; *sl* femme *f*; **~ s** lisière *f*, bordure *f*

**²skirt** *vt* contourner; longer, serrer

**skirting-board** *n* plinthe *f*

**skit** *n* satire *f*; *theat* pièce *f* satirique

**skitter** *vi* raser l'eau

**skittish** *adj* (woman) volage, folâtre; (horse) ombrageux -euse

**skittle** *n* quille *f*

**skittle-alley** *n* jeu *m* de quilles

**skivvy** *n* *sl* bonne *f* à tout faire

**skulduggery** *n* *coll* manœuvres *fpl* louches

**skulk** *vi* (hide) se tenir caché; (creep about) rôder furtivement

**skull** *n* crâne *m*; **~ and crossbones** tête *f* de mort (et tibias)

**skull-cap** *n* calotte *f*

**skunk** *n* mouffette *f*; (fur) sconse *m*, skunks *m*; *coll* rosse *f*

**sky** *n* ciel *m*; (climate) climat *m*; **praise s/o to the skies** porter qn aux nues; *coll* **the ~ is the limit** il n'y a pas de limite; **under the open ~** au grand air; (at night) à la belle étoile; *vt* (ball) lancer en chandelle

**sky-blue** *adj* bleu ciel *invar*, azuré

**sky-high** *adv* jusqu'aux nues

**skylark** *n* alouette *f*; *vi* *coll* faire le fou (*f* la folle), rigoler, faire du chahut

**skylight** *n* lucarne *f*

**skyline** *n* horizon *m*, ligne *f* d'horizon

**skyscraper** *n* gratte-ciel *m* *invar*

**skyward(s)** *adv* vers le ciel

**slab** *n* (stone) dalle *f*; (metal) plaque *f*; (cake) grosse tranche; (chocolate) tablette *f*

**slack** *n* (rope) mou *m*; *mech* jeu *m*; **take up the ~ in a cable** mettre un câble au raide; *adj* (loose) lâche, mou (*f* molle), mal tendu; (screw) desserré; (careless) négligent; (not lively) peu vif (*f* vive); **~ period** accalmie *f*; (during day) heure(s) creuse(s); **~ season** morte-saison *f* (*pl* mortes-saisons); *naut* **~ water** mer *f* étale; **be ~ in doing sth** être lent à faire qch; **business is ~** les affaires vont mal; *vt* relâcher, détendre; *vi* (sail) prendre du lâche; *coll* se relâcher

**slacken** *vt* (loosen) relâcher, détendre; (screw) desserrer; (pace) ralentir; *vi* (speed) ralentir; (abate) diminuer; (wind) tomber; (person) devenir négligent, se relâcher

**slacker** *n* paresseux -euse, fainéant -e; *coll* flemmard -e

**slackness** *n* relâchement *m*, négligence *f*; (laziness) paresse *f*, manque *m* d'énergie; (slowness) lenteur *f*; (unpunctuality) inexactitude *f*; (looseness) détente *f*; (rope) mou *m*; *comm* stagnation f, marasme m

**slacks** npl pantalon m

**slag** n scories fpl

**slag-heap** n crassier m

**slake** vt ~ one's thirst étancher sa soif

**slalom** n slalom m

**¹slam** n (door) claquement m; vt + vi claquer; sl éreinter, blâmer

**²slam** n (cards) chelem (schelem) m

**slander** n calomnie f, médisance f, diffamation f; vt calomnier, médire de, diffamer

**slanderous** adj calomnieux -ieuse, diffamatoire

**slang** n argot m; vt coll injurier; sl engueuler

**slangy** adj argotique; (person) qui aime à employer des termes d'argot

**slant** n pente f, inclinaison f; biais m; (opinion) point m de vue; vt incliner; vi être en pente; être oblique

**slanting** adj (sloping) en pente, incliné; (direction) oblique

**slap** n claque f, tape f; (on face) gifle f; fig affront m; adv en plein; ~ in the middle en plein milieu; vt frapper avec la main; (child) donner une fessée à; (on face) gifler; coll ~ s/o down remettre qn à sa place; vi claquer

**slap-bang** adv see slap adv

**slapdash** adj sans soin; ~ work travail bâclé; adv sans soin

**slap-happy** adj coll fou-fou (f fofolle)

**slapstick** n farce bouffonne, burlesque m

**slap-up** adj coll fameux -euse

**slash** n entaille f; (face) balafre f; vt taillader; (face) balafrer; (strike wildly) frapper à droite et à gauche; coll (criticize) éreinter; coll (reduce) diminuer, réduire

**slashing** adj (criticism) mordant; (rain) cinglant

**slat** n lame f, planchette f

**¹slate** n ardoise f; US pol liste f provisoire de candidats; clean ~ passé m irréprochable; wipe the ~ (clean) passer l'éponge sur le passé; vt ardoiser

**²slate** vt coll réprimander, tancer; (book, play) éreinter

**slating** n coll (telling off) savon m; (criticism) éreintement m

**slatted** adj à planchettes; ~ shutters persiennes fpl

**slattern** n souillon f

**slatternly** adj mal soigné, malpropre

**slaughter** n massacre m; (cattle) abattage m; vt massacrer, tuer; (cattle) abattre

**slaughterer** n tueur m, égorgeur m

**slaughterhouse** n abattoir m

**Slav** n Slave; adj slave

**slave** n esclave; vi travailler dur, peiner;

~ away at sth s'éreinter à (faire) qch

**slave-driver** n fig patron dur (f patronne dure)

**slave-labour** n travail m d'esclave

**slavery** n esclavage m

**slave-trade, slave-traffic** n traite f des noirs, commerce m des esclaves; white ~ traite f des blanches

**Slavic** adj slave

**slavish** adj d'esclave, servile

**Slavonic** adj (language) slave

**slay** vt tuer

**sleazy** adj léger -ère; coll sordide

**sledge, sled** n traîneau m

**sledge-hammer** n marteau m à deux mains

**sleek** adj lisse, luisant; (manner) onctueux -euse

**sleep** n sommeil m; drop (go) off to ~ s'endormir; not have a wink of ~ ne pas fermer l'œil; put to ~ endormir; walk in one's ~ être somnambule; vi dormir; (at hotel) coucher; ~ in être logé dans l'établissement (la maison); (get up late) faire la grasse matinée; ~ lightly avoir le sommeil léger; ~ like a log (top) dormir sur les deux oreilles (à poings fermés); ~ out découcher; ~ with s/o coucher avec qn

**sleeper** n dormeur -euse; (rail track) traverse f; (sleeping-car) wagon-lit m (pl wagons-lits); be a light (heavy) ~ avoir le sommeil léger (profond)

**sleepily** adv d'un air endormi

**sleepiness** n somnolence f; léthargie f

**sleeping** n sommeil m; ~ accommodation logement m; adj dormant; (asleep) endormi; ~ partner (associé m) commanditaire m; ~ sickness maladie f du sommeil; let ~ dogs lie ne réveillez pas le chat qui dort

**sleeping-bag** n sac m de couchage

**sleeping-car** n wagon-lit m (pl wagons-lits), voiture-lit f (pl voitures-lits)

**sleeping-pill, sleeping-draught** n somnifère m

**sleeping-quarters** npl dortoir m

**sleepless** adj sans sommeil

**sleeplessness** n insomnie f

**sleepwalker** n somnambule

**sleepwalking** n somnambulisme m

**sleepy** adj somnolent, endormi; be (feel) ~ avoir sommeil

**sleepyhead** n coll endormi -e

**sleet** n grésil m, neige f à moitié fondue; US grêle f; vi grésiller

**sleeve** n manche f; mech manchon m; (record) pochette f

**sleeve-board** n jeannette f

**sleeveless** adj sans manches

**sleigh** n traîneau m

**sleight-of-hand** n prestidigitation f;

(trick) tour *m* de passe-passe

**slender** *adj* mince; (person) svelte; (hope) faible; (not much) modeste

**slenderize** *vt US* amincir

**sleuth** *n* (dog) limier *m*; *coll* (detective) détective *m*

**slew** *vi* pivoter, virer; *mot* faire un tête-à-queue

**slewed** *adj sl* ivre

**slice** *n* tranche *f*; (sausage, etc) rondelle *f*; ~ **of bread and butter** tartine *f*; ~ **of luck** coup *m* de veine; *vt* découper en tranches; (cut) couper, trancher

**slicer** *n* machine *f* à trancher

¹**slick** *n* escroc adroit, filou *m*

²**slick** *adj* lisse; *coll* habile, astucieux -ieuse; **look ~ about it** dépêchez-vous un peu; *vt US* (hair) lisser; mettre en ordre

**slicker** *n sl* escroc adroit, filou *m*

**slide** *n* glissade *f*, glissement *m*; (groove) coulisse *f*; (ice) glissoire *f*; (slipway) glissière *f*; *phot* diapositive *f*; (hair) barrette *f*; *vt* + *vi* glisser, couler; *vi* ~ **down** descendre en glissant; *coll* ~ **off** filer; *coll* **let a thing ~** se désintéresser de qch

**slide-rule** *n* règle *f* à calcul

**sliding** *adj* glissant, coulissant; ~ **door** porte coulissante; ~ **scale** échelle *f* mobile

¹**slight** *n* affront *m*, manque *m* de respect; *vt* manquer d'égards à; négliger

²**slight** *adj* mince, léger -ère; (figure) menu, frêle

**slightest** *adj* le (la) moindre; **not in the ~** pas le moins du monde

**slighting** *adj* exprimant le mépris; (air) de mépris

**slightly** *adv* légèrement, un peu, faiblement

**slightness** *n* minceur *f*; (figure) sveltesse *f*; légèreté *f*; peu *m* d'importance

**slim** *adj* svelte, élancé, mince; (hope, etc) léger -ère; *sl* rusé; *vt* amincir; *vi* se faire maigrir

**slime** *n* vase *f*, limon *m*; (snail) bave *f*

**sliminess** *n* viscosité *f*; *fig* servilité *f*

**slimming** *n* amaigrissement *m*; *adj* amaigrissant

**slimness** *n* sveltesse *f*, taille *f* mince

**slimy** *adj* limoneux -euse; (sticky) visqueux -euse; *fig* servile

¹**sling** *n* fronde *f*; (arm) écharpe *f*; *mech* élingue *f*, courroie *f*; *vt* lancer, jeter; (suspend) suspendre; *naut* élinguer; ~ **over one's shoulder** mettre en bandoulière

²**sling** *n* (drink) grog *m*

**slink** *vi* ~ **away** partir furtivement, s'éclipser

**slinking** *adj* furtif -ive

**slinky** *adj coll* svelte; (alluring) séduisant; (clothes) collant

**slip** *n* glissade *f*, glissement *m*; (mistake) erreur *f*; (underskirt) combinaison *f*, jupon *m*; (behaviour) écart *m* de conduite; (dog lead) laisse *f*; (briefs, bathing) slip *m*; *naut* cale *f*; (pathway) sentier *m*; *hort* bouture *f*; (paper) bande *f*, fiche *f*; (note) billet *m*; ~ **of the tongue** lapsus *m*; **detachable ~** volant *m*; **fine ~ of a girl** beau brin de fille; **give s/o the ~** faire faux bond à qn; **gym** ~ tunique *f*; **pillow ~** taie *f* d'oreiller; *vt* glisser, couler; (escape from) se dégager de; (cable) filer; ~ **off** ôter; ~ **on** mettre; **it has ~ped my memory** cela m'a échappé; *vi* (se) glisser, couler; ~ **away** **(off)** s'esquiver, s'échapper; (time) s'écouler; ~ **out** sortir; (escape) s'échapper; ~ **over (round) to the shops** faire un saut jusqu'aux magasins; ~ **up** tomber; *fig* se tromper; **let ~** laisser échapper

**slip-knot** *n* nœud coulant

**slipper** *n* pantoufle *f*

**slippered** *adj* en pantoufles

**slipperiness** *n* nature glissante; *fig* caractère rusé

**slippy** *adj coll* **look** ~ se dépêcher

**slip-road** *n* petite route de déviation

**slipshod** *adj* (work) négligé; (person) mal soigné, négligent

**slip-up** *n coll* erreur *f*, *coll* gaffe *f*

**slipway** *n* cale *f* de lancement

**slit** *n* fente *f*, fissure *f*; *surg* incision *f*; *vt* fendre; *surg* faire une incision dans; ~ **s/o's throat** égorger qn

**slither** *vi* glisser; (snake) ramper

**slithery** *adj* glissant

**sliver** *n* tranche *f*; (wood) éclat *m*

**slob** *n coll* goujat *m*, manant *m*

**slobber** *vi* baver; (sob) larmoyer

**sloe** *n bot* prunelle *f*

**slog** *n coll* (blow) coup violent; *coll* (hard work) corvée *f*; *vt coll* frapper violemment; *vi coll* (work hard) boulonner, turbiner

**slogan** *n* devise *f*; *pol* slogan *m*

**sloop** *n* sloop *m*

**slop** *n* boue *f*; liquide renversé; ~ **s** (for invalids) aliments *mpl* liquides; (dishwater) eaux ménagères; *vt* répandre; *vi* ~ **over** se répandre, déborder

**slop-basin** *n* petit bol pour recevoir les fonds de tasses de thé

¹**slope** *n* pente *f*, inclinaison *f*; (bank) talus *m*; (mountain) versant *m*; (railway) rampe *f*; (road) côte *f*; (rifle) **at the** ~ sur l'épaule; **on a (the)** ~ en pente; *vt* incliner; *mil* mettre (l'arme) sur l'épaule; *vi* incliner, être en pente; ~ **down** descendre; ~ **up(wards)** monter

²**slope** *vi sl* ~ **off** filer

**sloping** adj en pente, incliné; ~ shoulders épaules tombantes
**slop-pail** n seau m hygiénique
**sloppy** adj détrempé; (character) mou (f molle); (work) bâclé, négligé; (dress) mal ajusté, négligé; (feeling) larmoyant
**slosh** vt coll flanquer un coup à
**sloshed** adj sl soûl (saoul), paf invar
**slot** n entaille f, fente f, rainure f; vt tailler une fente dans, entailler; ~ in insérer par une fente; fig trouver une place pour
**sloth** n paresse f, indolence f; zool paresseux m
**slothful** adj paresseux -euse, indolent
**slot-machine** n distributeur m automatique
**slouch** n démarche lourde; épaules arrondies; vi traîner le pas, avoir une allure lourde
**¹slough** n bourbier m
**²slough** n (snake) dépouille f; vi se dépouiller, muer
**sloven** n personne mal soignée (malpropre)
**slovenliness** n manque m de tenue
**slovenly** adj mal soigné, mal peigné
**slow** adj lent; (dull) lourd; (clock) en retard; mech ~ running ralenti m; ~ train train omnibus m; be a ~ speaker avoir la parole lente; (clock) be ~ retarder; in a ~ oven à feu doux; not be ~ in doing sth ne pas tarder à faire qch; vt + vi ralentir; adv lentement
**slowcoach** n coll lambin -e
**slowly** adv lentement
**slow-motion** n in ~ au ralenti
**slowness** n lenteur f; (mind) lourdeur f; (clock) retard m
**slowpoke** n US coll lambin -e
**slow-worm** n orvet m
**sludge** n fange f; (sewage) vidanges fpl
**slug** n zool limace f; (air-gun) balle f; min + typ lingot m; vt coll assommer
**sluggard** n paresseux -euse, fainéant -e
**sluggish** adj léthargique, lourd; (river, pulse) lent; (engine) peu nerveux -euse; (digestion) paresseux -euse
**sluice** n écluse f; vt vanner; ~ out laver à grande eau; vi ~ out couler à flots
**sluice-gate** n vanne f
**slum** n bas quartier; (street) rue f sordide; (hovel) taudis m; the ~s les bas-fonds mpl; vi go ~ming coll pej fréquenter un milieu inférieur; ar faire des visites de charité dans les quartiers pauvres
**slumber** n sommeil m; vi dormir paisiblement
**slumber-wear** n vêtements mpl de nuit
**slum-clearance** n suppression f des taudis

**slummy** adj ~ district quartier m de taudis
**slump** n effondrement m; econ crise f; ~ in sales mévente f; vi tomber lourdement, s'écrouler; (prices, etc) baisser tout à coup, s'effondrer
**slur** n affront m, tache f; (speech) mauvaise articulation; cast a ~ on s/o's reputation porter atteinte à la réputation de qn; vt ne pas articuler clairement, bredouiller; mus lier; ~ over passer légèrement sur
**slush** n neige à demi fondue; (mud) fange f; coll sensiblerie f
**slushy** adj boueux -euse; détrempé par la neige; coll d'une sentimentalité exagérée
**slut** n souillon f; coll coureuse f
**sluttish** adj sale, malpropre
**sly** adj rusé, sournois, fin; (mischievous) malicieux -ieuse, espiègle; on the ~ à la dérobée
**slyness** n sournoiserie f; espièglerie f
**¹smack** n (flavour) petit goût; soupçon m; vi ~ of avoir un léger goût de
**²smack** n naut bateau m pêcheur
**³smack** n claquement m; (hand) claque f; ~ in the face gifle f; adv ~ in the middle en plein milieu; ~ into a tree en plein dans un arbre; vt faire claquer; (hit) frapper; coll ~ one's lips se lécher les babines; vi claquer
**smacker** n sl (smack) gifle retentissante; (kiss) gros baiser; (pound note) livre f, billet m d'une livre; US dollar m
**small** n ~ of the back creux m (chute f) des reins; ~s sous-vêtements mpl; adj petit, menu; (figure) de petite taille; (weak) faible; (in numbers) peu nombreux -euse; (unimportant) peu important; (petty) mesquin; ~ change petite (menue) monnaie; ~ letter minuscule f; ~ matter bagatelle f; in a ~ way en petit; fig look ~ avoir l'air penaud; make s/o look ~ humilier qn; adv menu, en morceaux
**small-arms** npl armes portatives
**small-holding** n petite ferme
**small-minded** adj à l'esprit mesquin
**smallpox** n petite vérole, variole f
**small-talk** n bavardage m, banalités fpl
**small-time** adj US de troisième ordre
**smarmy** adj coll doucereux -euse
**smart** n douleur aiguë; adj (alert) vif (f vive), alerte; (blow) fort, sec (f sèche); fig (sharp) éveillé, à l'esprit alerte; pej malin (f maligne), finaud; (dress) chic invar; ~ pace vive allure; look ~ se dépêcher; vi cuire, brûler; ~ under an injustice souffrir sous le coup d'une injustice; he will make us ~ for it il nous le fera payer cher

**smarten** vt (pace) accélérer; faire beau (f belle); ~ **oneself up** se faire beau (f belle); ~ **s/o up** dégourdir qn; vi ~ **up** s'animer, se dégourdir

**smartly** adv vivement, promptement; (cleverly) habilement; (dressed) élégamment

**smartness** n (liveliness) vivacité f; (cleverness) finesse f, habileté f; (dress) élégance f

**smash** n fracas m; (accident) accident m, collision f, sinistre m; (disaster) débâcle f; comm faillite f; (tennis) smash m; ~ **hit** succès fou; adv go ~ faire faillite; vt briser, écraser; (tennis) smasher; ~ **in** défoncer; ~ **open the door** enfoncer la porte; ~ **s/o's face in** casser la figure à qn; ~ **sth against sth** heurter qch contre qch; ~ **up** briser en morceaux; vi (break) éclater en morceaux, se briser; comm faire faillite; ~ **against sth** (se) heurter (contre) qch; ~ **into** rentrer dans, heurter

**smash-and-grab (raid)** n vol m après bris de vitrine

**smasher** n coup écrasant; coll **she's a ~!** elle est drôlement bien!

**smashing** adj écrasant; coll formidable

**smash-up** n (accident) collision f; (destruction) destruction totale; (bankruptcy) banqueroute f

**smattering** n légère connaissance

**smear** n tache f, souillure f; med frottis m; coll ~ **campaign** campagne f de diffamation; vt barbouiller, salir; fig diffamer

**smell** n odeur f, parfum m, senteur f; (sense) odorat m; vt sentir; (animal) flairer; ~ **out** flairer, dépister; vi sentir; ~ **nice (nasty)** sentir bon (mauvais); ~ **of sth** sentir qch

**smelliness** n puanteur f

**smelling-salts** npl sels mpl

**smelly** adj malodorant

¹**smelt** vt fondre

²**smelt** n éperlan m

**smelting** n fonte f

**smile** n sourire m; **be all ~s** être tout souriant; vi sourire

**smiling** adj souriant; fig serein, paisible

**smirch** n tache f; vt tacher, souiller

**smirk** n sourire satisfait; vi sourire d'un air satisfait

**smite** vt frapper; coll **be smitten with** être épris de

**smith** n forgeron m

**smithereens** npl **smash to ~** réduire en miettes, briser en éclats

**smithy** n forge f

**smock** n blouse f, sarrau m

**smog** n coll brouillard enfumé, brouillard industriel

**smoke** n fumée f; (something to smoke) qch à fumer, cigarette f, pipe f, cigare m; fig (plan) **go up in ~** n'aboutir à rien; **have a ~** fumer; vt + vi fumer; ~ **out** enfumer

**smoke-bomb** n bombe f fumigène

**smokeless** adj sans fumée

**smoker** n fumeur -euse; see **smoking-compartment**

**smokescreen** n rideau m de fumée

**smokestack** n cheminée f

**smokiness** n condition fumeuse, atmosphère enfumée

**smoking** n émission f de fumée; (curing) fumage m; action f de fumer; **no ~** défense f de fumer

**smoking-compartment, smoker** n compartiment m fumeurs

**smoking-jacket** n veston m d'intérieur

**smoky** adj fumeux -euse; (room) enfumé

**smooth** adj lisse; (level) uni; (soft) doux (f douce); (polished) poli; (calm) calme; (manner) doucereux -euse; (person) à l'air doucereux; vt lisser; (level) égaliser; (calm) calmer, apaiser; (brow) dérider; ~ **down** lisser; ~ **out** défroisser; ~ **over** aplanir; ~ **the way** aplanir le chemin

**smoothly** adv sans inégalités; (steadily) sans secousses; (softly) doucement

**smoothness** n (surface) égalité f; (softness) douceur f; (sea) calme m; (person) air doucereux

**smooth-spoken, smooth-tongued** adj aux paroles doucereuses

**smoothy** n coll personne trop polie

**smother** vt étouffer; (cover) recouvrir; vi étouffer, suffoquer

**smoulder** vi brûler lentement; fig couver

**smudge** n tache f; bavure f de plume; vt tacher, salir, barbouiller

**smudgy** adj taché, souillé, barbouillé

**smug** adj satisfait de soi-même; (air) suffisant

**smuggle** vt passer en fraude (en contrebande); vi faire de la contrebande

**smuggler** n contrebandier m, fraudeur m

**smuggling** n contrebande f, fraude f

**smugly** adv d'un air suffisant

**smugness** n suffisance f

**smut** n tache f de suie, flocon m de suie; coll grivoiseries fpl

**smutty** adj noirci de suie; fig grivois

**snack** n snack m, casse-croûte m invar; **have a ~** casser la croûte, manger sur le pouce

**snack-bar** n snack-bar m, snack m

**snaffle** vt chiper

**snag** n (hitch) accroc m, anicroche f; (tree-stump) chicot m; **strike a ~** se heurter à un obstacle; **that's the ~!** voilà le hic!

**snail** *n* escargot *m*, limaçon *m*

**snake** *n* serpent *m*; *fig* individu traître *m*; (game) ~s **and ladders** = le jeu de l'oie; *vi* serpenter

**snake-charmer** *n* charmeur *m* de serpent

**snaky** *adj* de serpent; (road) serpentant

**snap** *n* coup *m* de dents; (noise) bruit sec; (fingers) claquement *m*; (break) cassure *f*; (fastener) fermoir *m*, agrafe *f*, bouton-pression *m* (*pl* boutons-pression); *coll* (energy) vivacité *f*, énergie *f*; *coll phot* instantané *m*; *cul* petit biscuit croquant; **cold ~** période *f* de temps froid; *adj* imprévu, soudain; **make a ~ decision** prendre une décision sur le coup; *adv* crac; *vt* (bite) happer; (fingers) faire claquer; (break) casser, rompre; *phot* prendre un instantané de; **~ one's fingers at s/o** narguer qn; **~ up a bargain** saisir une occasion; *vi* (break) se casser (net); (fingers, whip) claquer; (dog, etc) chercher à mordre; **~ off** se détacher brusquement; **~ out of it** se grouiller

**snapdragon** *n bot* gueule *f* de loup

**snap-judgement** *n* décision soudaine, jugement *m* rapide

**snappish** *adj* hargneux -euse, irritable

**snappy** *adj* irritable; (lively) vif (*f* vive); *coll* (dress) chic *invar*; **make it ~!** grouillez-vous!

**snapshot** *n* instantané *m*

**snare** *n* piège *m*, collet *m*, lacet *m*; *fig* piège *m*; *fig* **be caught in a ~** être pris au piège; *vt* prendre au collet, attraper

**¹snarl** *n* grognement *m*, grondement *m*; *vi* grogner, gronder

**²snarl** *n* enchevêtrement *m*; (traffic) embouteillage *m*; *vt* enchevêtrer; **mot ~ed up** pris dans un embouteillage

**snatch** *n* mouvement vif pour saisir qch; (conversation) bribe *f*; (fragment) morceau *m*; (theft) vol exécuté rapidement; *vt* saisir, empoigner; *sl* kidnapper; **~ sth from s/o** arracher qch à qn

**snatchy** *adj* décousu, interrompu

**snazzy** *adj sl* voyant, *coll* tape-à-l'œil *invar*

**sneak** *n* (mean person) pleutre *m*; *coll* mouchard -e, rapporteur -euse; *vi coll* moucharder; **~ away** partir furtivement; **~ in (out)** entrer (sortir) furtivement

**sneakers** *npl US* chaussures *fpl* en toile à semelles de caoutchouc, souliers *mpl* de gymnastique

**sneaking** *adj* furtif -ive, sournois; **~ feeling** sentiment inavoué

**sneak-thief** *n* chapardeur -euse

**sneer** *n* ricanement *m*, sourire moqueur;

*vi* ricaner, sourire d'un air moqueur; **~ at sth** dénigrer qch

**sneeze** *n* éternuement *m*; *vi* éternuer; *coll* **not to be ~d at** pas à dédaigner

**snick** *n* encoche *f*, petite entaille; *vt* faire une entaille dans

**snicker** *n* + *vi see* **snigger**

**snide** *adj sl* (mocking) ricanant, narquois; **~ remark** remarque offensante

**sniff** *n* reniflement *m*; *vt* + *vi* renifler; **not to be ~ed at** pas à dédaigner

**sniffle** *n* léger reniflement; *vi* renifler légèrement; (cry) pleurnicher

**sniffy** *adj coll* dédaigneux -euse; (sniffing) morveux -euse

**snigger, snicker** *n* léger ricanement; *vi* rire sous cape, ricaner tout bas

**snip** *n* coup *m* de ciseaux; (bit) petit morceau, petit bout; *coll* certitude *f*; *coll* (racing) gagnant sûr; *vt* couper (avec des ciseaux)

**¹snipe** *n orni* bécassine *f*

**²snipe** *vi* + *at coll* canarder

**sniper** *n* tireur caché (embusqué)

**snippet** *n* petit bout, morceau coupé; (short extract) court extrait

**snitch** *vi sl* moucharder

**snivel** *vi* pleurnicher

**snob** *n* snob, poseur -euse

**snobbery** *n* snobisme *m*, morgue *f*

**snobbily** *adv* d'une manière snob

**snobbish** *adj* snob, poseur -euse

**snook** *n coll* pied de nez; **cock a ~ at s/o** faire un pied de nez à qn

**snooker** *n* sorte *f* de jeu de billard

**snoop** *vi* fouiner

**snooper** *n* fouineur -euse

**snooty** *adj sl* prétentieux -ieuse

**snooze** *n* petit somme, *sl* roupillon *m*; *vi* faire un petit somme, *sl* roupiller

**snore** *n* ronflement *m*; *vi* ronfler

**snorkel, schnorkel** *n* (submarine) schnorchel (schnorkel) *m*; (swimmer) masque sous-marin

**snort** *n* reniflement *m*; (horse) ébrouement *m*; *vi* renifler; (horse) s'ébrouer

**snorty** *adj coll* désapprobateur -trice

**snot** *n sl* morve *f*

**snotty** *adj sl* morveux -euse

**snout** *n* museau *m*; (pig) groin *m*

**snow** *n* neige *f*; *sl* (cocaine) cocaïne *f*; **~ flurry** rafale *f* de neige; *vi* neiger; *coll* **be ~ed under with work** être submergé de travail; **~ed up** bloqué par la neige

**snowball** *n* boule *f* de neige; *vt* lancer des boules de neige à; *vi* faire boule de neige

**snowblind** *adj* atteint de la cécité des neiges

**snowbound** *adj* bloqué par la neige; (person) retenu par la neige

**snowcapped** *adj* couronné de neige

**snowdrift** n amas m (amoncellement m) de neige, congère f

**snowdrop** n perce-neige f invar

**snowfall** n chute f de neige; quantité f de neige

**snow-field** n champ m de neige

**snowflake** n flocon m de neige

**snowline** n limite f des neiges perpétuelles

**snowman** n bonhomme m de neige

**snow-plough** n chasse-neige m invar

**snow-shoes** npl raquettes fpl

**snowstorm** n tempête f de neige

**snowy** adj neigeux -euse

**¹snub** n rebuffade f; vt infliger un affront à

**²snub** adj retroussé, camus

**snub-nosed** adj au nez retroussé

**¹snuff** n tabac m (à priser); **take** ~ priser

**²snuff** vt moucher, éteindre (avec des mouchettes)

**snuff-box** n tabatière f

**snuffle** n reniflement m; (speech) ton nasillard; vi renifler; (speech) nasiller

**snug** n see **snuggery**; adj (house, etc) confortable; (person) bien, bien au chaud

**snuggery** n coll petite pièce confortable et chaude

**snuggle** vi se pelotonner

**snugly** adv confortablement

**snugness** n confort m

**so** adv (thus) de cette façon (manière), ainsi; (to such degree) si, tellement; ~ **do I** moi aussi; ~ **long!** à bientôt!; ~ **long as** tant que; ~ **much** tant, tellement; ~ **nice a person** une personne si aimable; ~ **saying** ce disant; ~ **to say (speak)** pour ainsi dire; ~ **what?** et alors?, et puis quoi?; **and** ~ **on** et ainsi de suite; **fifty or** ~ environ cinquante; **how** ~? comment cela?; **if** ~ s'il en est ainsi; **not** ~ pas du tout; **not** ~ **bad** pas si mal, pas trop mal; **why** ~? pourquoi cela?; conj donc, ainsi; conj phr ~ **as to** afin de; ~ **that** de sorte que; (purpose) afin que

**soak** n trempe f; sl (drunkard) ivrogne m, soûlard m; sl beuverie f; vt tremper; coll (charge heavily) écorcher, faire payer; ~ **up** absorber; ~ **ed to the skin** trempé jusqu'aux os; vi tremper, baigner; sl (drink) boire comme un trou; ~ **into** s'infiltrer dans; ~ **through** s'infiltrer à travers

**soaking** adj trempé; ~ **wet** trempé jusqu'aux os

**so-and-so** n coll ceci et cela; **Mr (Mrs)** Monsieur (Madame) un tel (une telle); **old** ~ vieux salaud

**soap** n savon m; sl ~ **opera** feuilleton mélodramatique et sentimental; **cake**

**of** ~ savonnette f; **household** ~ savon m de Marseille; vt savonner

**soap-box** n caisse f à savon; fig estrade f

**soap-bubble** n bulle f de savon

**soap-flakes** npl savon m en paillettes

**soapiness** n caractère savonneux; goût m (odeur f) de savon; fig pej onction f

**soapsuds** npl eau f de savon, eau savonneuse

**soapy** adj savonneux -euse; (person) onctueux -euse

**soar** vi prendre son essor, s'élancer, s'élever; (prices) monter en flèche

**sob** n sanglot m; vi sangloter; ~ **one's heart out** pleurer à chaudes larmes

**sober** adj sobre, modéré, posé, calme; (not drunk) pas ivre; (colour) peu voyant; **in** ~ **fact** en réalité; vt dégriser; vi ~ **down** se dégriser

**sober-minded** adj sérieux -ieuse, pondéré

**soberness, sobriety** n sobriété f, tempérance f; (calm) tranquillité f

**sob-stuff** n coll sentimentalité exagérée

**so-called** adj soi-disant, prétendu

**soccer** n football m

**sociability** n sociabilité f

**sociable** adj sociable

**social** n réunion amicale; adj social; ~ **(gathering)** soirée f; ~ **insurance** assurances sociales; ~ **worker** assistant(e) social(e)

**socialism** n socialisme m

**socialist** n + adj socialiste

**socialistic** adj socialiste

**socialite** n coll habitué -e du beau monde

**socialize** vt socialiser; vi ~ **with** frayer avec

**socially** adv socialement

**society** n société f; compagnie f; (fashionable) monde m; (high) haute société, beau monde; **go into (move in)** ~ aller dans le monde

**sociological** adj sociologique

**sociologist** n sociologue

**sociology** n sociologie f

**¹sock** n chaussette f; (in shoe) semelle intérieure; **ankle** ~ s socquettes fpl; coll fig **pull up one's** ~ s se dégourdir

**²sock** n sl coup m; vt donner un coup de poing à

**socket** n (eye) orbite m; (tool) douille f; (lamp) bec m; (candle) bobèche f; (tooth) alvéole f; elect prise f de courant

**¹sod** n gazon m; (piece of turf) motte f

**²sod** n vulg sodomite m; coll salaud m

**soda** n soude f; US ~ **fountain** bar m pour rafraîchissements, milk bar m

**sodality** n eccles confrérie f

**soda-water** n soda m, eau f de seltz

**sodden** *adj* trempé, détrempé
**sodium** *n* sodium *m*
**sodomite** *n* pédéraste *m*, sodomite *m*
**sodomy** *n* pédérastie *f*, sodomie *f*
**sofa** *n* sofa *m*
**soft** *adj* doux (*f* douce); (to touch) mou (*f* molle); (tender) tendre; *coll* (simple) simple, niais; ~ **currency** devises *fpl* faibles; ~ **drink** boisson non alcoolisée; ~ **job** emploi *m* pépère; **become** ~ se ramollir; **have a** ~ **spot for** avoir un faible pour
**soften** *vt* amollir, ramollir; adoucir; (appease) apaiser; *vi* se ramollir; (feeling) s'attendrir
**softener** *n* substance amollissante; *coll* pot-de-vin *m* (*pl* pots-de-vin)
**softening** *n* amollissement *m*, ramollissement *m*; adoucissement *m*; (feeling) attendrissement *m*
**soft-hearted** *adj* au cœur tendre
**softly** *adv* doucement; tendrement; mollement
**softness** *n* douceur *f*; mollesse *f*; (stupidity) niaiserie *f*
**soft-pedal** *vt fig* atténuer, diminuer l'importance de; *vi fig* y aller doucement
**soft-sell** *n* promotion (de vente) discrète, publicité subtile
**soft-soap** *n* savon noir; *fig* flatterie *f*; *vt fig* flatter
**soft-spoken** *adj* doucereux -euse
**software** *n* (computer) software *m*, logiciel *m*
**softwood** *n* bois *m* tendre
**softy** *n coll* (simple-minded) niais -e; efféminé
**soggy** *adj* détrempé; (bread) pâteux -euse
¹**soil** *n* sol *m*, terre *f*
²**soil** *n* (mark) tache *f*; *vt* souiller, salir
**sojourn** *n lit* séjour *m*; lieu *m* de séjour; *vi lit* séjourner
**solace** *n* consolation *f*; *vt* consoler
**solar** *adj* solaire; ~ **plexus** plexus *m* solaire
**solder** *n* soudure *f*; *vt* souder
**soldering-iron** *n* fer *m* à souder
**soldier** *n* soldat *m*, militaire *m*; **foot** ~ fantassin *m*; **private** ~ simple soldat *m*; **tin (toy)** ~ soldat *m* de plomb; *vi* faire le métier de soldat; ~ **on** persévérer, aller de l'avant
**soldiering** *n* métier *m* de soldat
**soldierly** *adj* de soldat
¹**sole** *n* (foot) plante *f*; (shoe) semelle *f*; *vt* mettre une semelle à; ressemeler
²**sole** *n* (fish) sole *f*
³**sole** *adj* seul, unique; (legatee) universel -elle; ~ **agent** agent exclusif; ~ **right** droit exclusif
**solecism** *n* solécisme *m*

**solely** *adv* uniquement
**solemn** *adj* solennel -elle; (person) sérieux -ieuse
**solemnity** *n* solennité *f*; (bearing) gravité *f*; (ceremony) fête solennelle
**solemnize** *vt* solenniser; (celebrate) célébrer
**solemnly** *adv* solennellement; gravement
**solenoid** *n elect* solénoïde *m*
**sol-fa** *n mus* solfège *m*
**solicit** *vt* solliciter; (prostitute) racoler
**solicitation** *n* sollicitation *f*; (prostitute) racolage *m*
**soliciting** *n* (prostitute) racolage *m*
**solicitor** *n leg* = avoué *m*
**solicitous** *adj* (eager) désireux -euse; (anxious) inquiet -iète
**solicitude** *n* sollicitude *f*, préoccupation *f*, souci *m*
**solid** *n* solide *m*; *adj* solide; massif -ive; ~ **oak** chêne massif; ~ **state** état *m* solide; **become** ~ se solidifier; **six hours** ~ six heures d'affilée
**solidarity** *n* solidarité *f*
**solidify** *vt* solidifier; *vi* se solidifier, se figer
**solidity** *n* solidité *f*
**solidly** *adv* solidement
**soliloquize** *vi* monologuer
**soliloquy** *n* soliloque *m*, monologue *m*
**solitaire** *n* solitaire *m*
**solitary** *n* solitaire; *adj* solitaire; (place) retiré
**solitude** *n* solitude *f*, isolement *m*; (place) lieu *m* solitaire
**solo** *n mus* solo *m*; **violin** ~ solo *m* de violon; *adv* solo; *mus* **play** ~ jouer en solo
**soloist** *n* soliste
**solstice** *n* solstice *m*
**solubility** *n* solubilité *f*
**soluble** *adj* soluble
**solution** *n* solution *f*
**solve** *vt* résoudre
**solvency** *n* solvabilité *f*
**solvent** *n* dissolvant *m*; *adj* solvable
**somatic** *adj* somatique
**sombre** *adj* sombre, triste, morne
**sombrero** *n* sombrero *m*
**some** *adj* du, de la, de l', des; (unknown) quelque, quelconque; ~ **way or other** d'une manière ou d'une autre; *coll* **he's** ~ **teacher** c'est un professeur formidable; **I'll do it** ~ **day** je le ferai un de ces jours; *coll* **this is** ~ **place** c'est un endroit vraiment bien; **we'll be there for** ~ **time** nous y serons un certain temps; *pron pl* certains (*f* certaines), quelques-uns (*f* quelques-unes); en; ~ **of them** certains (quelques-uns) d'entre eux (*f* certaines (quelques-unes)

d'entre elles); ~ ... others (some) les uns (f les unes) ... les autres; pass me ~ of that cake passez-moi de ce gâteau; we have ~ nous en avons; adv environ, quelque; US this surprises me ~ cela m'étonne assez

somebody, someone pron quelqu'un, on; ~ or other je ne sais qui

somehow adv d'une manière ou d'une autre; ~, I can't find it je ne sais pas pourquoi, mais je ne le trouve pas

someone pron see somebody

somersault n culbute f; do a ~ (accidental) faire une culbute; (gym) faire une cabriole

something n + pron quelque chose m; ~ else autre chose; ~ good quelque chose de bon; ~ of a mystery plus ou moins (un peu) mystérieux; ~ or other une chose ou une autre, je ne sais quoi; that's ~, anyway en tout cas, c'est toujours quelque chose; there's ~ in that boy ce garçon a du bon; there's ~ in what she says il y a un fond de vérité dans ce qu'elle dit; there's ~ the matter with her elle a quelque peu, un peu; ~ like un peu semblable à

sometime adj my ~ friend autrefois mon ami; adv tôt ou tard; ~ last week au cours de la semaine passée; ~ soon bientôt

sometimes adv quelquefois, parfois; ~ good, ~ bad tantôt bon (f bonne), tantôt mauvais -e

somewhat adv un peu, quelque peu; do it ~ like he said faites-le à peu près comme il a dit

somewhere adv quelque part; ~ else ailleurs, autre part; ~ or other je ne sais où

somnambulism n somnambulisme m

somnambulist n somnambule

somnolence n somnolence f

somnolent adj somnolent

son n fils m

sonar n sonar m

sonata n sonate f

song n chant m, chanson f; eccles cantique m; buy sth for a ~ acheter qch pour un morceau de pain; make a (great) ~ and dance about sth faire un foin de tous les diables au sujet de qch

song-bird n oiseau chanteur

song-book n recueil m de chansons

songster n chanteur -euse; (bird) oiseau chanteur

sonic adj sonique; ~ barrier mur m du son; ~ boom bang m

son-in-law n beau-fils m (pl beaux-fils)

sonnet n sonnet m

sonny n coll mon petit, jeune homme m

sonority n sonorité f

sonorous adj sonore

soon adv bientôt; (early) tôt; (quickly) vite; ~er or later tôt ou tard; as ~ as aussitôt que; as ~ as possible le plus tôt possible; how ~? dans combien de temps?; en combien de temps?; none too ~ juste à temps; no ~er had they arrived than I left à peine furent-ils arrivés que je partis; see you (again) ~! à bientôt!; so ~ si tôt; the ~er the better le plus tôt sera le mieux; too ~ trop tôt; we would ~er die nous aimerions mieux mourir

soot n suie f; vt ~ up encrasser

soothe vt calmer, apaiser

soothing adj calmant, apaisant

sooty adj couvert de suie, noir de suie

sop n morceau (de pain) trempé; fig concession f; vt tremper; ~ up éponger

sophism n sophisme m

sophist n sophiste

sophistic(al) adj sophistique

sophisticated adj blasé; recherché, subtil; (device) compliqué

sophistication n sophistication f; (behaviour) usage m du monde

sophistry n sophistique f; sophismes mpl

sophomore n US étudiant -e de deuxième année

soporific n somnifère m; adj soporifique

sopping adj ~ wet tout trempé

soppy adj détrempé; coll (person) mou (f molle); coll (sloppily sentimental) larmoyant

soprano n soprano

sorbet n sorbet m

sorcerer n sorcier m

sorceress n sorcière f

sorcery n sorcellerie f

sordid adj sordide; (filthy) crasseux -euse; (base) vil, bas (f basse)

sore n plaie f, blessure f; (ulcer) ulcère m; fig souvenir m pénible; adj douloureux -euse, endolori; (sorry) chagriné; US (irritated) irrité, vexé; ~ point sujet m pénible; be in ~ need of sth avoir grandement besoin de qch; be like a bear with a ~ head être d'une humeur massacrante; have a ~ throat avoir mal à la gorge; that's a ~ point c'est une question délicate

sorely adv gravement, fortement; (wounded) grièvement

soreness n endolorissement m; (sorrow) chagrin m; (grudge) sentiment m de rancune

sorority n US cercle féminin

sorrel n bot oseille f

sorrow n chagrin m, peine f, douleur f, tristesse f; vi être affligé; ~ after s/o pleurer qn

sorrowful adj affligé, triste; (bringing

sorrow) attristant

**sorry** *adj* fâché, chagriné, désolé; (poor) misérable, pauvre; **be ~** regretter; **be ~ for s/o** plaindre qn; **look ~ for oneself** avoir l'air malheureux; **so ~!** pardon!

**sort** *n* sorte *f*, espèce *f*, genre *m*; *coll* **he's a good ~** c'est un brave type; **I shall do nothing of the ~** je n'en ferai rien; *coll* **I ~ of** told him to go away je lui ai plus ou moins dit de partir; **it was a meal of ~ s** c'était un soi-disant repas; **nothing of the ~** (not at all) pas du tout; (nothing like it) rien de semblable; **out of ~ s** peu bien, indisposé; **sth of the ~** qch comme cela; *vt* trier; classifier; (match) assortir

**sorter** *n* trieur (*f* trieuse); (machine) trieuse *f*

**sortie** *n* sortie *f*

**S.O.S.** *n* S.O.S. *m*

**so-so** *adj* médiocre; *adv* comme ci comme ça

**sot** *n* ivrogne *m*, alcoolique

**soufflé** *n* soufflé *m*

**sough** *n* murmure *m*; *vi* murmurer

**soul** *n* âme *f*; **not a ~** pas un chat; **poor ~!** le (la) pauvre!; **without meeting a living ~** sans rencontrer âme qui vive

**soulful** *adj* sentimental, expressif -ive

**soulless** *adj* sans âme; (job) abrutissant

**¹sound** *n* son *m*, bruit *m*; *rad* **~ engineer** ingénieur *m* du son; **I don't like the ~ of that** je n'aime pas du tout cela; **not a ~** pas le moindre bruit; *vt* sonner; (pronounce) prononcer; *med* ausculter; (praises) chanter; *naut* sonder; *vi* résonner, sonner, retentir; (seem) paraître, avoir l'air; *sl* **~ off** râler

**²sound** *n* (strait) détroit *m*

**³sound** *adj* (healthy) sain; (in good condition) en bon état; (construction) solide; (sleep) profond; (argument) valide, juste; (reliable) sérieux -ieuse; **safe and ~** sain et sauf (*f* saine et sauve); *adv* **sleep ~** dormir profondément

**sound-barrier** *n* mur *m* du son

**sound-effects** *npl* bruitage *m*

**sounding** *n* résonnement *m*, retentissement *m*; *med* auscultation *f*; *naut* + *fig* sondage *m*

**sounding-board** *n* abat-voix *m*; *mus* table *f* d'harmonie

**soundless** *adj* silencieux -ieuse

**soundly** *adv* sainement; (sleep) profondément; (reason) judicieusement

**soundness** *n* bon état; (mind) état sain; solidité *f*; (judgement) justesse *f*

**sound-proof** *adj* insonore; (material) isolant; *vt* insonoriser

**sound-track** *n* bande *f* sonore

**sound-wave** *n* onde *f* sonore

**¹soup** *n* potage *m*, soupe *f*; *coll* **be in the ~** être dans le pétrin; **clear ~** consommé *m*; **vegetable ~** potage *m* de légumes, julienne *f*

**²soup** *n*; *adj* **~ ed-up engine** moteur poussé

**soup-kitchen** *n* soupe *f* populaire

**soup-plate** *n* assiette creuse, assiette *f* à soupe

**soup-spoon** *n* cuiller *f* à potage (à soupe)

**soupy** *adj* qui ressemble à de la soupe; *coll* sentimental

**sour** *adj* aigre, acide; (person) revêche; (not ripe) vert; (wine) suret -ette; **that's ~ grapes** c'est pur dépit; **turn sth ~** aigrir qch; *vt* + *vi* aigrir

**source** *n* source *f*; *fig* origine *f*

**sourly** *adv* avec aigreur; d'un air revêche

**sourness** *n* aigreur *f*, acidité *f*

**souse** *n* *cul* marinade *f*; (drenching) saucée *f*; *vt* *cul* faire mariner; immerger, plonger; *vi* mariner

**south** *n* sud *m*; *adj* sud *invar*, du midi, du sud, méridional; *adv* au sud; vers le sud

**southbound** *adj* qui va vers le sud

**south-east** *n* sud-est *m*; *adj* du sud-est; *adv* vers le sud-est

**south-easterly** *adj* du sud-est

**south-eastern** *adj* du sud-est

**southerly** *adj* du sud; qui se dirige vers le sud

**southern** *adj* du midi, méridional; *astron* **the Southern Cross** la Croix du Sud

**southerner** *n* (in France) Méridional -e; habitant -e du sud; *US hist* sudiste

**southernmost** *adj* le plus au sud

**southward** *adj* au sud, du sud

**southwards** *adv* vers le sud

**south-west** *n* sud-ouest *m*; *adj* du sud-ouest; *adv* vers le sud-ouest

**south-westerly** *adj* du sud-ouest

**south-western** *adj* du sud-ouest

**south-westward** *n* sud-ouest *m*

**souvenir** *n* souvenir *m*

**sou'wester** *n* *naut* vent *m* du sud-ouest; (hat) chapeau *m* imperméable

**sovereign** *n* + *adj* souverain -e

**sovereignty** *n* souveraineté *f*

**Soviet** *n* soviet *m*; *adj* soviétique; **~ Union** Union *f* Soviétique

**¹sow** *vt* (seed, rumour) semer; (ground) ensemencer

**²sow** *n* truie *f*

**sower** *n* semeur -euse

**soya** *n* soja *m*, soya *m*

**sozzled** *adj* *coll* ivre

**spa** *n* ville *f* d'eau, station thermale

**space** *n* espace *m*; (room) place *f*; (extent) étendue *f*; (between two things) intervalle *m*, écartement *m*;

(empty) vide *m*; (on form) case *f*; *adj* spatial; *vt* ~ (out) espacer

**spacecraft** *n* astronef *m*, navire spatial

**space-flight** *n* vol spatial, voyage spatial

**spaceman** *n* cosmonaute *m*, astronaute *m*

**space-probe** *n* sonde *f* interplanétaire

**space-rocket** *n* fusée *f* interplanétaire

**space-saving** *adj* compact

**spaceship** *n* astronef *m*, vaisseau spatial

**space-shuttle** *n* navette spatiale

**space-suit** *n* scaphandre *m* (d'astronaute)

**space-travel** *n* navigation *f* interplanétaire

**spacing** *n* espacement *m*; (typing) **double** ~ double interligne *m*; **single** ~ interligne *m* simple

**spacious** *adj* spacieux -ieuse, vaste

¹**spade** *n* bêche *f*; (small) pelle *f*; *sl* nègre *m*, négresse *f*

²**spade** *n* (cards) pique *m*

**spadeful** *n* pelletée *f*

**spade-work** *n* *fig* travaux *mpl* préliminaires

**spaghetti** *n* spaghetti *mpl*

**Spain** *n* Espagne *f*

**span** *n* (hand) empan *m*; (wing) envergure *f*; (between supports) portée *f*; (arch) largeur *f*; (bridge) travée *f*; (short time) courte durée; *vt* (bridge) franchir, enjamber; mesurer à l'empan

**spangle** *n* paillette *f*; *vt* pailleter

**Spaniard** *n* Espagnol -e

**spaniel** *n* épagneul *m*

**Spanish** *n* (language) espagnol *m*; *adj* espagnol

**spank** *vt* fesser

¹**spanking** *n* fessée *f*

²**spanking** *adj coll* **go at a** ~ **pace** filer à toute allure

**spanner** *n* clef *f* (à écrous); **adjustable** ~ clef anglaise, clef à molette; *coll* **throw a** ~ **in the works** mettre le bâton dans les roues

¹**spar** *n naut* espar *m*

²**spar** *vi* (boxing) faire un assaut de boxe amical (d'entraînement)

**spare** *n mech* pièce *f* de rechange; *adj* (thin) maigre, sec (*f* sèche); (in reserve) de réserve; (left over) de reste; ~ **parts** (~s) pièces *f* de rechange; ~ **room** chambre *f* d'ami; ~ **time** loisir *m*, temps *m* disponible; *mot* ~ **tyre** pneu *m* de rechange; *mot* ~ **wheel** roue *f* de secours; *vt* épargner, ménager; (do without) se passer de; (lend, give) prêter, donner; (show mercy to) faire grâce à; (respect) respecter; ~ **no pains** ne pas ménager sa peine; ~ **s/o a few moments** accorder quelques moments (d'entretien) à qn; **have enough to** ~

avoir plus qu'il.n'en faut; **have nothing to** ~ n'avoir que le strict nécessaire; **have no time to** ~ n'avoir pas de temps libre; **I can** ~ **him** je n'ai pas besoin de lui

**spare-rib** *n* côte découverte de porc

**sparing** *adj* économe, ménager -ère

¹**spark** *n* étincelle *f*; *fig* (trace) trace *f*, trait *m*; *fig* (intelligence) intelligence *f*, vivacité *f*; *fig* ~ **s will fly** il y aura du grabuge; *vt* ~ **off** déclencher; *vi* émettre des étincelles

²**spark** *n* élégant *m*; **gay** ~ joyeux luron

**sparking-plug** *n* (*US* **spark plug**) mot bougie *f*

**sparkle** *n* étincellement *m*, pétillement *m*; *fig* éclat *m*; *vi* étinceler, scintiller; (wine) pétiller; *fig* briller

**sparkler** *n sl* diamant *m*

**sparklet** *n* petite étincelle; (soda) sparklet *m*

**sparkling** *n* étincellement *m*, pétillement *m*; *adj* étincelant; (wine) mousseux -euse; *fig* brillant; (drinks) gazeux -euse

**sparring** *n* boxe amicale

**sparrow** *n* moineau *m*

**sparrow-hawk** *n* épervier *m*

**sparse** *adj* épars, clairsemé

**spartan** *adj fig* spartiate; *fig* frugal

**spasm** *n* accès *m*, spasme *m*

**spasmodic** *adj* spasmodique, convulsif -ive

**spastic** *n med* handicapé -e moteur (*pl* handicapé(e)s moteur); *adj med* spasmodique; (person) handicapé -e moteur (*pl* handicapé(e)s moteur)

**spate** *n* crue *f*

**spatial** *adj* spatial

**spats** *npl* guêtres *fpl*

**spatter** *vt* éclabousser

**spatula** *n* spatule *f*

**spawn** *n* (fish) frai *m*; (mushroom) blanc *m* (de champignon); *coll pej* (offspring) progéniture *f*; *vi* (fish) frayer; (multiply) se multiplier

**spay** *vt vet* châtrer

**speak** *vt* (say) dire; (express) exprimer; (language) parler; *vi* parler; (at meeting) prendre la parole; (make speech) faire un discours; ~ **ill of** dire du mal de; ~**ing for myself** pour ma part; ~ **out** parler à haute voix; parler franchement; ~ **up** parler plus haut; ~ **up for** s/o prendre la défense de qn, parler en faveur de qn; ~ **well for** faire honneur à; **English spoken** (ici) on parle anglais; **nothing to** ~ **of** rien, peu de chose; **without** ~**ing** sans rien dire

**speak-easy** *n US hist* débit *m* de boisson clandestin

**speaker** *n* parleur -euse; (public) orateur *m*; (conversation) interlocuteur

707

-trice; (parliament) président *m*; (loudspeaker) haut-parleur *m*

**speaking** *adj* expressif -ive, parlant, vivant; **they are not on ~ terms** ils ne se parlent pas

**speaking-tube** *n* tuyau *m* acoustique

**spear** *n* lance *f*, javelot *m*; *vt* percer d'un coup de lance; (fish) prendre à la foëne

**spearhead** *n* fer *m* de lance; *vt mil* être le fer de lance de

**spearmint** *n* menthe verte

**special** *adj* spécial, particulier -ière; **~ case** cas *m* d'espèce; **~ correspondent** envoyé -e spécial -e; **~ friend** ami -e intime; **~ price** prix *m* de faveur; **take ~ care over sth** apporter des soins particuliers à qch

**specialist** *n* spécialiste

**speciality** *n* spécialité *f*

**specialization** *n* spécialisation *f*

**specialize** *vt* spécialiser; *vi* se spécialiser

**specially** *adv* spécialement, surtout, particulièrement

**specialty** *n see* **speciality**; *leg* contrat formel sous seing privé

**species** *n* espèce *f*, genre *m*

**specific** *adj* spécifique; (affirmation) précis, explicite

**specification** *n* spécification *f*; description *f*; devis descriptif

**specify** *vt* spécifier, préciser, déterminer

**specimen** *n* spécimen *m*, exemple *m*; (sample) échantillon *m*; *coll* **he's a queer ~** c'est un drôle de type

**specious** *adj* spécieux -ieuse, trompeur -euse

**speck** *n* petite tache, point *m*; (dust) grain *m*; *fig* brin *m*

**speckled** *adj* tacheté, moucheté

**specs** *npl coll* lunettes *fpl*

**spectacle** *n* spectacle *m*; **make a ~ of oneself** se donner en spectacle; **~s** lunettes *fpl*

**spectacle-case** *n* étui *m* à lunettes

**spectacled** *adj* à lunettes

**spectacular** *adj* spectaculaire, impressionnant

**spectator** *n* spectateur -trice, assistant -e

**spectral** *adj* spectral

**spectre** *n* spectre *m*, fantôme *m*

**spectrum** *n* spectre *m*

**speculate** *vi* spéculer; méditer

**speculation** *n* spéculation *f*; méditation *f*, conjecture *f*

**speculative** *adj* spéculatif -ive, contemplatif -ive

**speculator** *n* spéculateur -trice

**speech** *n* (faculty) parole *f*; (public) discours *m*; (language) langue *f*; **make a ~** prononcer (faire) un discours; **parts of ~** parties *fpl* du discours

**speech-day** *n* (school) distribution *f* des

prix

**speechify** *vi* pérorer, discourir

**speechless** *adj* (dumb) incapable de parler; (from surprise, etc) interdit, muet -ette

**speech-therapy** *n* orthophonie *f*

**speech-training** *n* cours *m* de diction

¹**speed** *n* vitesse *f*, rapidité *f*; (haste) hâte *f*; **at full ~** à toute vitesse; (running) à toutes jambes; **maximum ~** vitesse limite; *mot* plafond *m*; *vt* hâter, accélérer; (guest) souhaiter bon voyage à; *vi* se hâter; faire de la vitesse; **~ up** accélérer, aller plus vite

²**speed** *n ar* chance *f*; succès *m*; **wish s/o god (good) ~** souhaiter bonne chance à qn; *vt obs* **God ~ you** que Dieu vous fasse prospérer

**speedboat** *n* canot *m* automobile

**speeder** *n* contrôleur *m* de vitesse; *mot* (person) chauffard *m*

**speedily** *adv* rapidement, promptement

**speediness** *n* rapidité *f*, promptitude *f*

**speeding** *n mot* excès *m* de vitesse

**speed-limit** *n* limite *f* de vitesse, vitesse maximale

**speedometer** *n mot* compteur *m*, indicateur *m* de vitesse

**speedway** *n* autodrome *m*, piste *f* d'autodrome; (motorway) autoroute *f*

**speedy** *adj* rapide, prompt

**speleologist** *n* spéléologue

¹**spell** *n* (words) formule *f* magique; (magic power) charme *m*; **cast a ~ on (over)** s/o jeter un sort sur qn

²**spell** *n* période *f*; (work) tour *m*

³**spell** *vt* (orally) épeler; (writing) orthographier; (signify) signifier; **~ badly** faire des (beaucoup de) fautes d'orthographe; **~ out sth** déchiffrer qch; *fig* expliquer qch; **learn to ~** apprendre l'orthographe

**spellbound** *adj* ensorcelé, magnétisé

**speller** *n* **be a good (bad) ~** savoir (ne pas savoir) l'orthographe

**spelling** *n* (written) orthographe *f*; **~ mistake** faute *f* d'orthographe

**spelling-bee** *n* concours *m* d'orthographe

**spelling-book** *n* alphabet *m*

**spend** *vt* (money) dépenser; (time) passer; *coll* **~ a penny** aller au petit coin, aller faire pipi; **~ oneself** s'épuiser; **~ time on sth** consacrer du temps à qch

**spender** *n* **big ~** personne *f* qui dépense beaucoup

**spendthrift** *n* dépensier -ière, gaspilleur -euse; *adj* dépensier -ière, prodigue

**spent** *adj* (exhausted) épuisé; (storm) calmé; **~ bullet** balle morte

**sperm** *n* sperme *m*

**sperm-whale** *n* cachalot *m*

**spew** *vt* + *vi* vomir

**sphere** *n* sphère *f*; *fig* domaine *m*, champ *m*; **limited ~** cadre restreint

**spherical** *adj* sphérique

**sphincter** *n anat* sphincter *m*

**sphinx** *n* sphinx *m*

**spice** *n* épice *f*, aromate *m*; (tiny bit) soupçon *m*; *vt* épicer

**spicily** *adv* d'une manière piquante

**spiciness** *n* goût piquant; *fig* piquant *m*

**spick-and-span** *adj* propre comme un sou neuf; (person) tiré à quatre épingles

**spicy** *adj* épicé; (fragrant) parfumé; (story) piquant, salé

**spider** *n* araignée *f*; **~'s web** toile *f* d'araignée

**spider-crab** *n* araignée *f* de mer

**spidery** *adj* qui ressemble à une araignée; **~ handwriting** pattes *fpl* de mouches

**spiel** *n coll* boniment *m*

**spigot** *n* fausset *m*

**spike** *n* (sharp point) pointe *f*; (nail) clou *m* à large tête; *bot* épi *m*; *vt* clouer; armer de pointes; (gun) enclouer; *fig* **~ s/o's guns** déjouer les menées de qn

**spiked** *adj* garni de pointes

**spiky** *adj* à pointe(s) aiguë(s)

**¹spill** *n* culbute *f*, chute *f*; *vt* répandre; (overturn) renverser; *coll* **~ the beans** (betray secret) vendre la mèche; *vi* se répandre

**²spill** *n* allumette *f* de papier, allume-feu *m invar* en papier roulé

**spin** *n* tournoiement *m*, mouvement *m* de rotation; *aer* vrille *f*; (excursion) promenade *f*, randonnée *f*; *coll* **get into a flat ~** ne pas savoir où donner de la tête; *vt* (wool) filer; faire tourner; (top) faire aller; (tale) débiter; **~ a coin** jouer à pile ou face; **~ out** faire traîner en longueur; *vi* tourner; *aer* descendre en vrille; **~ along** filer, rouler; **~ round** pivoter; se retourner vivement; **my head is ~ning** la tête me tourne; **send s/o ~ning** envoyer rouler qn

**spinach** *n* épinards *mpl*

**spinal** *adj* spinal; **~ column** colonne vertébrale; **~ cord** cordon *m* médullaire

**spindle** *n* fuseau *m*; *mech* axe *m*, arbre *m*; **axle ~** fusée *f* d'essieu

**spindle-shanks** *npl* jambes *fpl* de fuseau

**spindly** *adj* très maigre

**spin-drier** *n* essoreuse *f*

**spine** *n anat* épine dorsale; (prickle) épine *f*, piquant *m*

**spineless** *adj fig pej* flasque, mou (*f* molle)

**spinner** *n* (person) fileur -euse; (machine) machine *f* à filer

**spinney, spinny** *n* bosquet *m*, petit bois

**spinning** *n* (thread) filage *m*; (movement) tournoiement *m*, mouvement *m* de rotation

**spinning-wheel** *n* rouet *m*

**spinster** *n* fille non mariée, célibataire *f*; *pej* vieille fille

**spiny** *adj* épineux -euse, couvert d'épines

**spiral** *n* spirale *f*; *aer* montée *f* en spirale; descente *f* en spirale; *adj* spiral

**spirally** *adv* en spirale

**spire** *n* flèche *f*

**spirit** *n* esprit *m*; (soul) âme *f*; (alcohol) alcool *m*, spiritueux *m*; (vivacity) entrain *m*, élan *m*, ardeur *f*; (courage) courage *m*; **~s** spiritueux *mpl*; **enter into the ~ of sth** entrer de bon cœur dans la partie; **in good ~s** de bonne humeur; **in high ~s** en train; **in low ~s** abattu; **man of ~** homme *m* de caractère; **recover one's ~s** reprendre courage; **surgical ~** alcool *m* à 90°; **take sth in the wrong ~** prendre qch en mauvaise part; *vt* **~ away** faire disparaître (comme par enchantement)

**spirited** *adj* vif (*f* vive), animé

**spirit-lamp** *n* lampe *f* à alcool; (for heating) réchaud *m* à alcool

**spiritless** *adj* sans vie; abattu; sans courage

**spirit-level** *n* niveau *m* à bulle d'air

**spiritual** *adj* spirituel -elle

**spiritualism** *n* spiritisme *m*; *philos* spiritualisme *m*

**spiritualist** *n* spirite; *philos* spiritualiste

**spirituality** *n* spiritualité *f*

**spiritualize** *vt* spiritualiser

**spiritually** *adv* spirituellement

**¹spit** *n* broche *f*; (modern) rôtissoire *f*; *geog* pointe *f*; *vt* embrocher

**²spit** *n* (spittle) salive *f*, crachat *m*; *coll* **he's the dead ~ of his father** c'est son père tout craché; *vt* + *vi* cracher; **it is ~ting (with rain)** il tombe quelques gouttes

**spite** *n* dépit *m*, rancune *f*; (nastiness) méchanceté *f*; **out of ~** par dépit; par méchanceté; *prep phr* **in ~ of** en dépit de, malgré; *vt* contrarier, vexer

**spiteful** *adj* rancunier -ière, vindicatif -ive; méchant

**spitfire** *n* coléreux -euse, rageur -euse

**spittle** *n* salive *f*, crachat *m*

**spittoon** *n* crachoir *m*

**splash** *n* éclaboussement *m*; (mud) éclaboussure *f*; (waves) clapotis *m*; (colour) tache *f*; **~ headline** grosse manchette; *fig* **make a ~** faire sensation; *vt* éclabousser; **~ money about** jeter son argent par les fenêtres; *vi* rejaillir en éclaboussures; (water) clapoter; (child) **~ about in the water**

barboter dans l'eau; ~ **up** gicler

**splash-down** *n* amerrissage *m*

**splay** *vt archi* ébraser, épanouir; *carp* couper en biseau; (dislocate) démettre

**spleen** *n anat* rate *f*; (bad temper) mauvaise humeur; *obs* (melancholy) spleen *m*

**splendid** *adj* splendide, magnifique; ~! à la bonne heure!

**splendour** *n* splendeur *f*, éclat *m*

**splenetic** *adj* coléreux -euse; *anat* splénique

**splice** *n* épissure *f*; *vt* épisser; *cin* réparer; *coll naut* ~ **the main-brace** donner une tournée de rhum supplémentaire; *coll* **get** ~ **d** se marier

**splint** *n* éclisse *f*; **put in** ~ **s** éclisser; *vt surg* éclisser

**splinter** *n* (wood, shell) éclat *m*; (bone) esquille *f*; (under skin) écharde *f*; ~ **group** groupe *m* fractionnaire; *vt* briser en éclats; *vi* éclater, voler en éclats

**splinter-proof** *adj* à l'épreuve des éclats

**splintery** *adj* plein d'éclats; qui vole en éclats facilement

**split** *n* fente *f*, fissure *f*; (division) division *f*; (secession) rupture *f*, scission *f*; (skin) gerçure *f*; *coll* demi-bouteille *f*; **do the** ~ **s** faire le grand écart; *vt* fendre; (divide) diviser; (share) partager; (cloth) déchirer; ~ **hairs** couper les cheveux en quatre; ~ **one's sides with laughter** se tordre de rire; ~ **the atom** désintégrer l'atome; *vi* se fendre; (skin) se gercer; *coll* moucharder; ~ **in two** se casser en deux; *coll* ~ **on** s/o dénoncer qn; ~ **up** se fractionner; **my head is** ~ **ting** j'ai un mal de tête terrible

**split-second** *adj* ultra-rapide; ultra-précis

**splodge, splotch** *n* tache *f*

**splurge** *n coll* épate *f*; *vi coll* faire de l'épate; (spend wildly) faire des dépenses extravagantes

**splutter** *n* bredouillement *m*; crachement *m*; *vt* + *vi* bredouiller, bafouiller; *vi* (emit saliva) lancer de la salive en parlant; *coll* envoyer des postillons

**spoil** *vt* gâter; (damage) abîmer, endommager; (despoil) dépouiller, piller; ~ **s/o's appetite** couper l'appétit à qn; *vi* se gâter; s'abîmer; (foodstuffs) s'avarier; *coll* **be** ~ **ing for a fight** avoir très envie de se battre

**spoils** *npl* butin *m*

**spoil-sport** *n* trouble-fête *invar*, rabat-joie *m invar*

**spoke** *n* rayon *m*; *fig* **put a** ~ **in s/o's wheel** mettre des bâtons dans les roues à qn

**spokesman** *n* porte-parole *m invar*

**spoliation** *n* spoliation *f*, dépouillement *m*

**sponge** *n* éponge *f*; *fig* **throw up the** ~ abandonner, s'avouer vaincu; *vt* éponger; nettoyer avec une éponge; ~ **down** éponger; ~ **out** enlever à l'éponge; *vi coll* ~ **on** (off) s/o vivre aux crochets de qn

**sponge-cake** *n* = biscuit *m* de Savoie

**sponger** *n coll* pique-assiette *m invar*, parasite *m*

**sponginess** *n* spongiosité *f*

**spongy** *adj* spongieux -ieuse

**sponsor** *n* garant -e, caution *f*; (baptism) parrain *m*, marraine *f*; *theat* + *rad* + *TV* commanditaire *m*; *vt* répondre pour, parrainer; (programme) offrir

**sponsorship** *n* parrainage *m*

**spontaneity** *n* spontanéité *f*

**spontaneous** *adj* spontané

**spoof** *n coll* mystification *f*, blague *f*; *adj coll* faux (*f* fausse); *vt coll* mystifier, duper

**spook** *n coll* fantôme *m*, revenant *m*

**spooky** *adj coll* hanté

**spool** *n* bobine *f*

**spoon** *n* cuiller *f*, cuillère *f*; **dessert-** ~ cuiller *f* à dessert; **table** ~ cuiller *f* à soupe; **tea** ~ petite cuiller; *vt* ~ **up** manger avec la cuiller; *vi sl* se faire des mamours

**spoon-feed** *vt* nourrir à la cuiller; *fig* mâcher la besogne à

**spoonful** *n* cuillerée *f*

**spoor** *n* piste *f*, trace *f*; foulées *fpl*

**sporadic** *adj* sporadique

**spore** *n* spore *f*

**sport** *n* sport *m*; (play) jeu *m*, divertissement *m*; (jesting) plaisanterie *f*, moquerie *f*; *biol* variété anormale; **be a** ~! sois chic! *invar*; *coll* **be a good** ~ (games) être beau joueur (*f* belle joueuse); (character) être un chic type (*f* une chic fille); **be the** ~ **of fortune** être le jouet de la fortune; **for** ~ par plaisanterie; **make** ~ **of** se moquer de; **mot** ~ **s model** modèle *m* grand sport; *vt coll* arborer, exhiber, étaler; *vi* jouer, se divertir; *biol* produire une variété anormale

**sportily** *adv* d'une façon sportive

**sportiness** *n* caractère sportif

**sporting** *adj* (of sport) (gun) de chasse; (attitude) sportif -ive, sport *invar*; **a** ~ **chance** une chance raisonnable

**sportive** *adj* badin, enjoué

**sports-car** *n* voiture *f* de sport

**sports-coat, sports-jacket** *n* veston *m* sport

**sports-day** *n* fête sportive

**sports-jacket** *n see* **sports-coat**

**sportsman** *n* amateur *m* de sport; *fig* beau joueur

**sportsmanship** *n* qualités sportives; (behaviour) conduite sportive, esprit sportif

**sportswoman** *n* (femme) sportive *f*

**sporty** *adj* sportif -ive; (decent) chic *invar*; (colours) voyant

**spot** *n* (stain) tache *f*; (place) endroit *m*, lieu *m*; (dress) pois *m*; (rain) goutte *f*; (on skin) bouton *m*; **a ~ of** un petit peu de; **a ~ of trouble** un petit ennui; **beauty ~** (on face) grain *m* de beauté; (place) site *m* remarquable; *coll* **be in a ~** être dans une situation dangereuse; **be on the ~** être là, être sur place; **have a soft ~ for s/o** avoir un faible pour qn; *coll* **knock ~s off s/o** battre qn à plate couture; **pay ~ cash** payer (argent) comptant; **put one's finger on a weak ~** mettre le doigt sur un point faible; *vt* tacher, tacheter; (notice) apercevoir, repérer; (recognize) reconnaître; **~ the winner** prédire le gagnant

**spot-check** *n* contrôle-surprise *m invar*

**spotless** *adj* sans tache

**spotlight** *n* projecteur *m*; *vt* diriger les projecteurs sur

**spotted** *adj* tacheté, moucheté

**spotter** *n* observateur *m*

**spotty** *adj* couvert de boutons; (spotted) tacheté

**spouse** *n* époux *m* (*f* épouse)

**spout** *n* (rain-water) tuyau *m* de décharge, gargouille *f*; (kettle, etc) bec *m*; *sl* **down the ~** perdu; *sl* **up the ~** (pawned) chez ma tante; (pregnant) enceinte; *vt* faire jaillir; *coll* (speech) dégoiser, déclamer; *vi* jaillir; *coll* (speech) pérorer

**sprain** *n* entorse *f*, foulure *f*; *vt* **~ one's ankle** se donner une entorse; **~ one's wrist** se fouler le poignet

**sprat** *n* sprat *m*

**sprawl** *vi* s'étendre, s'étaler

¹**spray** *n* poussière *f* d'eau, embrun *m*; (perfume, etc) jet pulvérisé; (device) vaporisateur; *vt* pulvériser, vaporiser; (garden) arroser; (sprinkle) asperger; (plant, etc) passer au vaporisateur

²**spray** *n* (branch) brin *m*, brindille *f*; (jewel) aigrette *f*

**sprayer** *n* vaporisateur *m*, pulvérisateur *m*

**spray-gun** *n* pistolet *m* (à peinture)

**spread** *n* étendue *f*; (wings) envergure *f*; (dissemination) diffusion *f*, propagation *f*; *coll* (feast) régal *m*, festin *m*; **cheese ~** fromage *m* à tartiner; **double-page ~** annonce *f* sur deux pages; **middle-aged ~** embonpoint *m* qui vient avec l'âge; *vt* étendre; (net) tendre; (news, etc) répandre, faire circuler; (sails) déployer; (tablecloth) mettre; **~ out** étaler; *vi* s'étendre, s'étaler; **~ over** (stagger) échelonner; *vi* s'étendre, s'étaler; (news) se répandre; (disease) se propager; **~ to** gagner

**spread-eagle** *vt* étaler; *vi* s'étaler, se vautrer

**spreader** *n* étendeur -euse; (news, ideas) propagateur -trice; (rumours) colporteur -euse

**spree** *n* **go on a ~** faire la noce, faire la bombe; **go on a spending ~** dépenser des sommes folles (à faire des achats)

**sprig** *n* brin *m*, brindille *f*

**sprightly** *adj* enjoué, éveillé

**spring** *n* (season) printemps *m*; (water) source *f*; (jump) saut *m*, bond *m*; (steel) ressort *m*; (elasticity) élasticité *f*; *mot* **~s** suspension *f*; *vt* (trap) faire jouer; (explosive) faire sauter; (oar) faire craquer; *US sl* faire relâcher, lâcher; *naut* **~ a leak** commencer à faire eau; **~ a question on s/o** poser une question à qn de façon inattendue; *vi* (jump) sauter, bondir; (water) jaillir; (grow) pousser; **~ from** provenir de; (be descended from) descendre de; **~ up** (storm) s'élever; (plant) pousser

**springboard** *n* tremplin *m*

**springbok** *n* springbok *m*

**spring-clean** *n* nettoyage *m* à fond au printemps; *vt* + *vi* nettoyer à fond au printemps

**spring-cleaning** *n* grand nettoyage fait au printemps

**springer** *n* sauteur -euse; (hunting) springer *m*

**springiness** *n* élasticité *f*

**spring-like** *adj* printanier -ière

**spring-tide** *n* grande marée

**springtime** *n* printemps *m*

**springy** *adj* élastique

**sprinkle** *vt* asperger, jeter; (with water) asperger, arroser; (powder) saupoudrer

**sprinkler** *n* arroseur automatique rotatif, arroseuse *f* à jet tournant; *eccles* goupillon *m*

**sprinkling** *n* arrosage *m*, saupoudrage *m*; (salt, etc) pincée *f*; (rain) quelques gouttes *fpl*

**sprint** *n* sprint *m*; *vi* sprinter, faire une course de vitesse

**sprinter** *n* sprinter *m*

**sprite** *n* lutin *m*, farfadet *m*

**sprocket** *n* dent *f*; **~ wheel** pignon *m* de chaîne

**sprout** *n* pousse *f*, rejeton *m*; **(Brussels) ~s** choux *mpl* de Bruxelles; *vt* pousser; *vi* pousser, bourgeonner

¹**spruce** *n* *bot* sapin *m*

²**spruce** *adj* pimpant, tiré à quatre

épingles; *vt* ~ **oneself up** se pomponner
**spud** *n* petite bêche; *coll* pomme *f* de terre, *coll* patate *f*
**spud-bashing** *n coll mil* corvée *f* de patates
**spunk** *n* (tinder) amadou *m*; *coll fig* courage *m*; *vulg* semence *f*
**spur** *n* éperon *m*; (cock) ergot *m*; (stimulus) stimulant *m*, aiguillon *m*; *geog* contrefort *m*, éperon *m*; **on the** ~ **of the moment** sous l'impulsion du moment; *vt* éperonner; *fig* ~ **on** aiguillonner, stimuler
**spurious** *adj* faux (*f* fausse), contrefait
**spurn** *vt* dédaigner, repousser, rejeter
**spur-road** *n* bretelle *f*
**spurt** *n* jaillissement *m*, jet *m*; effort soudain; (race) démarrage *m*; *vi* jaillir; ~ **out** gicler
**sputnik** *n* spoutnik *m*
**sputter** *vt* + *vi* bredouiller; *vi* (flame) grésiller
**sputum** *n med* crachat *m*
**spy** *n* espion -ionne *f*; *vt* apercevoir; détecter; ~ **out** explorer; *vi* espionner; ~ **on** s/o espionner qn
**spy-glass** *n* longue-vue *f* (*pl* longues-vues)
**spy-hole** *n* (door) judas *m*
**squabble** *n* querelle *f*, prise *f* de bec; *vi* se quereller, se chamailler
**squabbler** *n* chamailleur -euse
**squad** *n* escouade *f*; (team) équipe *f*, groupe *m*; **firing** ~ peloton *m* d'exécution; **flying** ~ brigade *f* mobile
**squadron** *n* escadron *m*; *aer* escadrille *f*; *naut* escadre *f*
**squadron-leader** *n mil* commandant *m* d'escadron; *aer* chef *m* d'escadrille
**squalid** *adj* misérable, sordide, minable
**squall** *n* (wind) bourrasque *f*, rafale *f*; (cry) cri *m* rauque; *fig* dispute *f*, *coll* grabuge *m*; *vi* crier, brailler
**squally** *adj* à rafales
**squalor** *n* misère *f*; aspect *m* sordide
**squander** *vt* gaspiller, dilapider
**square** *n* carré *m*; (town) place *f*, square *m*; (chessboard) case *f*; (instrument) équerre *f*; *coll* personne *f* vieux jeu; **set-** ~ équerre *f* à dessin; **silk** ~ foulard *m*; *adj* carré; (honest) honnête, *coll* vieux jeu; ~ **meal** repas copieux; **be** ~ **with** s/o être quitte envers qn; **get things** ~ mettre les choses en ordre; *adv* à angles droits; *vt* (stone, wood) équarrir; *math* carrer; (account) régler; *coll* (bribe) graisser la patte à, suborner; *vi* (agree) s'accorder, cadrer; ~ **up** se mettre en posture de combat
**square-bashing** *n coll mil* exercice *m*
**squarely** *adv* carrément; honnêtement
**squareness** *n* forme carrée; honnêteté *f*

**squash** *n* écrasement *m*; (crowd) cohue *f*, presse *f*; (game) squash *m*; **lemon** ~ citronnade *f*; **orange** ~ orangeade *f*; *vt* écraser; *coll* remettre à sa place
**squash-court** *n* terrain *m* de squash
**squash-rackets** *n* squash *m*
**squashy** *adj* mou (*f* molle) et humide
**squat** *adj* trapu; *vi* s'accroupir; (game) se tapir; (in premises) occuper une maison (un logement) sans autorisation, squatter
**squatter** *n* squatter *m*
**squaw** *n* femme *f* peau-rouge
**squawk** *n* cri *m* rauque; *vi* pousser des cris rauques
**squeak** *n* petit cri aigu; (machine) grincement *m*; *vi* pousser des petits cris aigus; (machine) grincer; *sl* moucharder
**squeaker** *n sl* mouchard -e
**squeaky** *adj* qui crie; (machine) qui grince
**squeal** *n* cri perçant; *vi* pousser des cris perçants; *coll* (protest) protester; *sl* (inform) trahir ses complices
**squealer** *n* criard -e; *sl* dénonciateur -trice
**squeamish** *adj* sujet -ette aux nausées; (sensitive) délicat, difficile
**squeeze** *n* étreinte *f*, compression *f*; (hand) serrement *m*; (crowd) cohue *f*; *coll econ* resserrement *m* du crédit; *vt* presser; (hand) serrer; (extort) extorquer; ~ **into** faire entrer dans; ~ **oneself into (through)** se faufiler dans (à travers); ~ **out** extorquer, arracher; (exclude) évincer; ~ **into** s'introduire dans; ~ **up** se serrer
**squelch** *n* giclement *m*, gargouillement *m*; *vt* écraser (en faisant gicler); *vi* (person) patauger; (thing) gargouiller
**squib** *n* pétard *m*; *fig* satire *f*
**squid** *n* calmar *m*, encornet *m*
**squiggle** *n* ligne ondulante; écriture *f* illisible; fioriture *f*; (after signature) parafe *m*
**squiggly** *adj* (writing) illisible; ondulant
**squint** *n* strabisme *m*, louchement *m*; *coll* coup *m* d'œil; *vi* loucher; ~ **at sth** regarder qch de côté
**squint-eyed** *adj* strabique
**squire** *n* (landowner) propriétaire terrien; *hist* hobereau *m*; (of knight) écuyer *m*
**squirm** *vi* se tordre, se tortiller
**squirrel** *n* écureuil *m*
**squirt** *n* (implement) seringue *f*; (of liquid) jet *m*; *coll* **little** ~ gringalet *m*; *vt* lancer en jet, faire jaillir; *vi* gicler, jaillir
**squit** *n sl* nabot *m*, avorton *m*
**stab** *n* coup *m* de poignard (de couteau); *fig* ~ **in the back** attaque déloyale; *coll*

have a ~ at sth tenter qch; vt donner un coup de couteau à, poignarder; vi (pain) lanciner

**stability** n stabilité f

**stabilization** n stabilisation f

**stabilize** vt stabiliser

**stabilizer** n stabilisateur m

¹**stable** n écurie f; vt loger

²**stable** adj stable, fixe, solide; (person) constant

**stable-boy** n valet m d'écurie, palefrenier m

**stably** adv d'une manière stable

**staccato** adj haché, saccadé

**stack** n pile f, tas m; (hay) meule f; (chimney) souche f, cheminée f d'usine; coll ~s of beaucoup de; vt empiler, entasser; (hay) mettre en meule; ~ the cards tricher aux cartes

**stadium** n stade m

**staff** n bâton m; mil état-major m (pl états-majors); (personnel) personnel m; fig soutien m; mus portée f; vt fournir de (pourvoir en) personnel, recruter du personnel pour

**staff-officer** n officier m d'état-major

**stag** n cerf m; ~ party réunion f entre hommes

**stag-beetle** n cerf-volant m (pl cerfs-volants)

**stage** n (platform) estrade f, échafaudage m; theat scène f, plateau m; (journey, etc) étape f; (step) phase f; (period) période f, stade m; (scene) scène f; **at this** ~ à ce point; **fare** ~ section f; **go on the** ~ se faire acteur -trice; vt (play) monter; (arrange) organiser

**stage-coach** n diligence f

**stagecraft** n technique f de la scène

**stage-door** n entrée f des artistes

**stage-effect** n effet m scénique

**stage-fright** n trac m

**stage-hand** n machiniste m

**stage-manage** vt theat faire la régie de; fig organiser

**stage-manager** n régisseur m

**stage-struck** adj entiché du théâtre

**stage-whisper** n aparté m

**stagger** n allure chancelante; vt consterner, bouleverser; (holidays) étaler, échelonner; (rivets) décaler; vi chanceler, tituber

**staggering** adj chancelant; fig renversant

**stagnant** adj stagnant

**stagnate** vi être stagnant; (water) croupir

**stagnation** n stagnation f

**stagy** adj théâtral; peu sincère

**staid** adj posé, sérieux -ieuse

**stain** n tache f; (colour) couleur f; ~ remover détachant m; vt tacher; fig souiller; (dye) teindre; (glass) peindre;

(wood) teinter; vi se tacher

**stained-glass** n ~ window vitrail m

**stainless** adj (steel) inoxydable; sans tache

**stair** n marche f, degré m

**staircase** n escalier m; **moving** ~ escalier roulant, escalator m

**stair-rod** n tringle f d'escalier

**stairway** n escalier m

**stake** n pieu m, poteau m; hort tuteur m; (gambling) mise f, enjeu m; (interest) intérêt m; **at** ~ en jeu; **be burnt at the** ~ mourir sur le bûcher; **his future is at** ~ il y va de son avenir; vt garnir de pieux; hort mettre un tuteur à; (gamble) jouer, mettre en jeu; (risk) hasarder; ~ **out** jalonner

**stake-holder** n celui qui tient les enjeux

**stalactite** n stalactite f

**stalagmite** n stalagmite f

**stale** adj (old) vieux (f vieille); (bread) rassis; (food) pas frais (f fraîche); (air) vicié; (tired) fatigué; vi (beer) s'éventer; fig perdre son intérêt

**stalemate** n impasse f; (chess) pat m

**staleness** n (age) vieillesse f; (joke) banalité f; (atmosphere) odeur f de renfermé; (bread) état rassis

¹**stalk** n tige f; (cabbage) trognon m

²**stalk** n (hunting) chasse f à l'approche; démarche fière; (striding) marche f à grandes enjambées; vt traquer, chasser; ~ s/o filer qn; vi ~ **along** marcher fièrement; marcher à grands pas

**stalker** n chasseur m à l'approche

¹**stall** n (stable) stalle f; (cattle) étable f; (goods) étalage m; (exhibition) stand m; eccles stalle f; (finger) doigtier m; theat ~s fauteuils mpl d'orchestre; **market** ~ boutique f en plein vent; **newspaper** ~ kiosque m (à journaux); vt mettre à l'écurie, établer

²**stall** vt + vi mot caler; vi (delay) chercher à gagner du temps

**stall-holder** n marchand -e, étalagiste

**stallion** n étalon m

**stalwart** n costaud m; **an old** ~ un vieux de la vieille; adj robuste, vigoureux -euse; loyal

**stamen** n bot étamine f

**stamina** n vigueur f, résistance f

**stammer** n bégaiement m, balbutiement m; vt + vi bégayer, balbutier

**stammerer** n bègue

**stammering** adj bègue

**stamp** n (with foot) battement m de pied, trépignement m; (instrument) poinçon m; (rubber) tampon m; (imprint) timbre m; (postage) timbre m, timbre-poste m (pl timbres-poste); (hall-mark) contrôle m; (trade-mark) estampille f; fig empreinte f; (character) trempe *f*; *vt* (documents, etc) timbrer; (letters) affranchir; (passport) viser; (metal, etc) estamper; (silver) poinçonner; (impress) imprimer; **~ one's foot** frapper du pied; **~ out** supprimer, étouffer; (fire) étouffer en piétinant; *vi* frapper du pied, piétiner; **~ on** piétiner

**stamp-album** *n* album *m* de timbres(-poste)

**stamp-collecting** *n* philatélie *f*

**stamp-collector** *n* philatéliste, collectionneur -euse *de* timbres(-poste)

**stamp-duty** *n* droit *m* de timbre

**stampede** *n* fuite précipitée, débandade *f*; (rush) ruée *f*; **~** *vt* jeter la panique parmi; *vi* fuir en désordre; (rush) se ruer

**stamper** *n* (machine) timbreuse *f*; (person) timbreur -euse

**stance** *n* position *f* des pieds; **take up one's ~** se mettre en posture

**stanch, staunch** *vt* étancher

**stanchion** *n* étançon *m*; *naut* épontille *f*

**stand** *n* position *f*, place *f*; (resistance) résistance *f*; (stopping) arrêt *m*, halte *f*; (vehicles) lieu *m* de stationnement, station *f*; (sportsground) tribune *f*; (platform) estrade *f*; (stall) étalage *m*; (exhibition) stand *m*; (base) pied *m*, dessous *m*, piédestal *m*; *US* **leg** barre *f* des témoins; **make a ~** résister; *theat* **one-night ~** représentation *f* unique; *sl* aventure passagère; **take one's ~** se placer; se baser; *vt* (endure) supporter, endurer; (put up with) tolérer; (undergo) subir; (place) mettre, poser; *coll* (pay) payer, offrir; **~ a chance** avoir une chance; *coll* **~ an employee off** mettre un employé (*f* une employée) à pied; *coll* **~ s/o up** faire faux bond à qn; **~ sth up** mettre qch debout; **~ the climate** résister au climat; *sl* **I can't ~ him** je ne peux pas le sentir; *vi* être debout, se tenir debout; (situation) se trouver, être situé; (building) se dresser; (vehicle) stationner; (remain) rester, demeurer, durer; (stop) s'arrêter; (be valid) être valable; (candidate) se porter; **~ against s/o** s'opposer à qn; **~ around** rester à regarder; **~ aside** se tenir à l'écart, se ranger; *mil* **~ at ease!** repos!; **~ back** (withdraw) reculer; se tenir en arrière; **~ by** (support) défendre, soutenir; (be near) être (au) près de; **~ down** se retirer; (election) retirer sa candidature; **~ fast** tenir bon; **~ for** signifier, vouloir dire; **~ for nothing** ne compter pour rien; **~ in for s/o** remplacer qn; **~ out** ressortir; (project) faire saillie; (resist) résister; (be outstanding) être exceptionnel -elle; **~ out for sth** s'obstiner à demander qch; **~ over** res-

ter en suspens; **~ to lose nothing** n'avoir rien à perdre; **~ to reason** aller de soi

**standard** *n* (flag) étendard *m*, pavillon *m*, bannière *f*; (measure) étalon *m*, unité *f*; (model) modèle *m*, type *m*; norme *f*; degré *m*; (level) niveau *m*, taux *m*; *obs* (school) classe *f*; (support) support *m*; *adj* standard *invar*; normal; **~ measurement** mesure-étalon *f* (*pl* mesures-étalons); **~ size** taille courante

**standard-bearer** *n* porte-drapeau *m* (*pl* porte-drapeau(x))

**standardization** *n* normalisation *f*, unification *f*, standardisation *f*

**standardize** *vt* normaliser, standardiser

**standard-lamp** *n* lampadaire *m*

**stand-by** *n* ressource *f*, expédient *m*; *adj* de réserve; **~ flight** vol *m* sans garantie d'embarquement au titulaire d'un billet à tarif réduit

**stand-in** *n* remplaçant -e; *theat* doublure *f*

**standing** *n* station *f* debout; (duration) durée *f*; (social) position *f*, standing *m*; **~ room** places *fpl* debout; *adj* debout *invar*; (army) permanent; (water) dormant; (crops) sur pied; **~ joke** plaisanterie courante; **~ rule** règle *f* fixe; **be left ~** être laissé sur place

**stand-offish** *adj* distant, réservé

**stand-offishness** *n* réserve *f*, raideur *f*

**standpoint** *n* point *m* de vue

**standstill** *n* arrêt *m*; **come to a ~** s'arrêter, s'immobiliser

**stanza** *n* stance *f*, strophe *f*

¹**staple** *n* (loop) crampon *m*; (for papers) agrafe *f*; *vt* agrafer; cramponner

²**staple** *n* produit principal; **~ diet** régime *m* de base; **~ industry** industrie principale

**stapler** *n* agrafeuse *f*

**star** *n* étoile *f*, astre *m*; *cin* + *theat* vedette *f*, étoile *f*, star *f*; **~ part** rôle *m* de vedette; **shooting ~** étoile filante; **the ~s and stripes** la bannière étoilée; *vt* marquer d'une étoile (d'un astérisque); *vi* jouer le rôle principal (l'un des rôles principaux)

**starboard** *n* *naut* tribord *m*; **on the ~ bow** par tribord devant; **on the ~ side** à tribord

**starch** *n* amidon *m*; (for linen) empois *m*; *cul* fécule *f*; *vt* empeser, amidonner

**starchy** *adj* (food) féculent; *coll* (person) guindé, empesé

**stardom** *n* célébrité *f*; **rise to ~** devenir une vedette

**stare** *n* regard *m* fixe; *vt* **~ s/o in the face** dévisager qn; **~ s/o out** faire baisser les yeux à qn; *coll* **it's staring you in the face** ça vous saute aux yeux; *vi* regarder fixement; **~ at s/o** regarder qn

fixement, dévisager qn
**starfish** n étoile f de mer
**star-gazer** n fig rêvasseur -euse
**star-gazing** n rêvasserie f
**staring** adj (eyes) fixe, grand ouvert; (look) ébahi, effaré
**stark** adj pur, absolu; adv tout, tout à fait
**stark-naked** adj nu comme un ver
**starless** adj sans étoiles
**starlet** n starlette f
**starlight** n lumière f des étoiles
**starling** n étourneau m
**starred** adj étoilé, parsemé d'étoiles; marqué d'une étoile
**starry** adj étoilé, parsemé d'étoiles
**starry-eyed** adj romanesque, idéaliste
**star-spangled** adj (par)semé d'étoiles; the ~ banner la bannière étoilée
**start** n (beginning) commencement m, début m; (departure) départ m; mot démarrage m; (fear) tressaillement m, sursaut m; (handicap) avance f; **flying ~** départ lancé; **for a ~** d'abord, pour commencer; **make a good ~** commencer bien; **make an early ~** commencer de bonne heure; (departure) partir de bonne heure; **wake with a ~** se réveiller en sursaut; vt (begin) commencer, (cake, conversation) entamer; (make depart) faire partir; (engine) faire marcher; mot mettre en marche; (game) lever; (business) lancer, fonder; (rumour) répandre; (cause) provoquer; vi (begin) commencer; (depart) partir, se mettre en route; (engine) démarrer; (fear) tressaillir, sursauter; **~ again from scratch** recommencer à zéro; **~ doing sth** se mettre (commencer) à faire qch; **~ up** se lever en sursaut; **to ~ with** en premier lieu, pour commencer
**starter** n (originator) auteur m; (race) starter m; mot démarreur m; (meal) hors-d'œuvre m invar, premier plat
**starting-handle** n mot manivelle f de mise en marche
**starting-point** n point m de départ
**starting-post** n poteau m de départ
**startle** vt effrayer, alarmer, faire tressaillir
**startling** adj (alarming) effrayant; (surprising) surprenant, sensationnel -elle
**starvation** n faim f, manque m de nourriture; **~ wages** salaire m de famine
**starve** vt faire mourir de faim, priver de nourriture; vi mourir de faim
**starveling** n + adj famélique
**starving** adj affamé
**stash** vt sl cacher
**state** n état m; (nation) État m; condition f, situation f; (rank) rang m, dignité

f; **~ apartments** salons mpl d'apparat; **~ coach** voiture f d'apparat; **~ control** étatisme m; US **State Department** = ministère m des Affaires étrangères; **~ school** école f d'état; **in ~** en grande pompe; **lie in ~** être exposé sur un lit de parade; **live in ~** mener grand train; **that's a fine ~ of affairs!** c'est du joli!; **the married ~** le mariage; hist **the States General** les États généraux; vt déclarer, affirmer; (problem) poser; (complaint) exposer; (fix) arrêter; **~ one's opinion** donner son opinion
**statecraft** n habileté f politique
**stated** adj **at ~ times** à (des) heures fixes; **on ~ days** à jours fixes
**stateless** adj apatride, sans patrie
**stately** adj majestueux -euse, imposant
**statement** n déclaration f; (explanation, account) exposé m, exposition f; (report) rapport m, compte rendu m; (accounts) relevé m de compte
**state-room** n naut cabine f de luxe; (palace) salle f de réception
**statesman** n homme m d'État
**statesmanship** n habileté f politique, science f du gouvernement
**static** adj stationnaire, statique
**station** n (position) position f, place f, poste m; (rank) rang m, condition f; (railway) gare f; (underground) station f; **action ~s** postes mpl de combat; **marry below one's ~** faire une mésalliance; mot **service ~** station-service f (pl stations-service); **the ~s of the Cross** le chemin de (la) Croix; vt placer, mettre; mil poster
**stationary** adj stationnaire, immobile; **~ engine** machine f fixe
**stationer** n papetier -ière; **~'s shop** papeterie f
**stationery** n papeterie f
**station-master** n chef m de gare
**station-wagon** n US mot familiale f, break m
**statistic(al)** adj statistique
**statistician** n statisticien -ienne
**statistics** npl (subject) statistique f; (alleged facts) statistiques fpl
**statuary** n statuaire f; adj statuaire
**statue** n statue f
**statuesque** adj sculptural
**statuette** n statuette f
**stature** n taille f
**status** n rang m, condition f; **~ quo** statu quo m invar; **civil ~** état civil
**statute** n loi f, ordonnance f; **~s** statuts mpl, règlements mpl
**statute-book** n code m
**statutory** adj établi, réglementaire, statutaire; (offence) prévu par la loi

**¹staunch** adj dévoué, ferme; (friend) à toute épreuve; (ship) étanche

**²staunch** vt see stanch

**stave** n bâton m; (barrel) douve f; mus portée f; vt ~ **in** défoncer, enfoncer; ~ **off** détourner, écarter; (danger) prévenir

**¹stay** n séjour m, visite f; ~ **of execution** sursis m; vt (stop) arrêter; leg remettre, ajourner; vi (remain) rester, demeurer; (visit) habiter, séjourner; (hotel) descendre; ~ **for** attendre; ~ **in** ne pas sortir; ~ **on** rester encore quelque temps; ~ **put** rester sur place; ~ **up** veiller, ne pas se coucher

**²stay** n support m, soutien m; ~**s** corset m; vt étayer

**³stay** n naut hauban m

**stay-at-home** n + adj casanier -ière

**stayer** n (sport) coureur m de fond; (horse) stayer m; coll personne f qui ne sait pas partir

**stead** n in s/o's ~ à la place de qn; **stand s/o in good** ~ être très utile à qn

**steadfast** adj ferme, inébranlable

**steadily** adv fermement, régulièrement; (diligently) assidûment

**steadiness** n fermeté f; assiduité f; stabilité f

**steady** adj (firm) ferme, solide; (constant) constant, soutenu; (person) sûr, rangé, sérieux -ieuse; (regular) régulier -ière; (rain) persistant; adv ~! ne bougez pas!; ~ **on!** doucement!; vt raffermir, affermir

**steak** n tranche f de viande, tranche f de poisson; (beef) bifteck m, entrecôte f; **fillet** ~ tournedos m; **rump** ~ romsteck m

**steal** vt voler, soustraire, dérober; ~ **a glance at s/o** jeter un regard furtif à qn; ~ **a march on s/o** devancer qn; vi ~ **away** partir furtivement; ~ **in** entrer à la dérobée; ~ **out** sortir furtivement

**stealth** n secret m; **by** ~ à la dérobée, furtivement

**stealthy** adj furtif -ive

**steam** n vapeur f; (on window, etc) buée f; **at full** ~ à toute vapeur; **get up** ~ chauffer; **keep up** ~ rester sous pression; **let off** ~ lâcher la vapeur; coll épancher sa bile; vt cul cuire à l'étuvée (à la vapeur); vi dégager de la vapeur, fumer; ~ **ahead** avancer rapidement; ~ **up** (window) s'embuer

**steamboat** n bateau m à vapeur, vapeur m

**steam-engine** n machine f à vapeur

**steamer** n navire m à vapeur; cul marmite f à vapeur

**steam-gauge** n manomètre m de pression

**steam-hammer** n marteau-pilon m (pl marteaux-pilons)

**steaminess** n atmosphère embuée; atmosphère f humide

**steam-roller** n rouleau m compresseur

**steamroller** vt écraser; ~ **one's way through sth** atteindre son but en forçant tous les obstacles

**steamship** n navire m à vapeur

**steamy** adj plein de vapeur; (atmosphere) humide

**steel** n acier m; (sharpening) fusil m; (sword) lame f; ~ **industry** industrie f sidérurgique; **heart of** ~ cœur m de fer; vt aciérer; ~ **oneself against sth** se raidir contre qch; ~ **oneself to do sth** s'armer de courage pour faire qch

**steel-plated** adj cuirassé

**steel-rimmed** adj (spectacles) à monture d'acier

**steelworks** n aciérie f

**steely** adj d'acier; fig dur, inflexible

**¹steep** adj raide, escarpé; coll **that's a bit** ~ ça, c'est un peu fort

**²steep** vt tremper, saturer; ~ **oneself in an atmosphere** se plonger dans une atmosphère; vi tremper

**steepen** vt augmenter; vi devenir plus raide

**steeple** n flèche f

**steeplechase** n course f d'obstacles; (racing) steeple-chase m

**steeplejack** n réparateur m de clochers, réparateur m de cheminées d'usine

**¹steer** n jeune bœuf m

**²steer** vt conduire, diriger; (ship) gouverner; ~ **a course for** mettre le cap sur; vi ~ **away from** (clear of) éviter

**steerable** adj gouvernable, dirigeable

**steerage** n **travel** ~ voyager dans l'entrepont (en troisième classe)

**steering** n direction f, conduite f; ~ **committee** comité m d'organisation; ~ **gear** appareil m à gouverner

**steering-column** n mot colonne f de direction

**steering-wheel** n mot volant m

**steersman** n timonier m

**stellar** adj stellaire

**¹stem** n bot tige f; (fruit) queue f; (glass) pied m; (pipe) tuyau m; naut avant m; vi ~ **from** être le résultat de, être issu de

**²stem** vt arrêter, contenir; (water) endiguer; (epidemic) enrayer; (brake) freiner; (attack) briser

**stench** n puanteur f

**stencil** n patron m; (typing) stencil m; (drawing) décoration f au poncif; vt imprimer au patron, marquer au patron; (typing) tirer au stencil, polycopier

**stenographer** n sténographe, coll sténo
**stenography** n sténographie f
**step** n pas m; (stair) marche f, degré m;
(ladder) échelon m; (vehicle) marchepied m; (measure) démarche f; (door)
seuil m, pas m de la porte; ~ by ~ pas à
pas; **flight of** ~ s escalier m; **follow in the**
~ **s of** marcher sur les traces de; **in** ~ au
pas; **pair of** ~ s échelle f double; **take a**
~ faire un pas; **take** ~ s faire des démar-
ches; **that's a good** ~ **forward** c'est déjà
un bon pas de fait; vt ~ **out** mesurer au
pas; ~ **up** augmenter; vi faire un pas;
(walk) marcher; ~ **across** traverser; ~
**aside** se ranger, s'écarter; ~ **back** reculer; ~ **down** descendre; fig démissionner; ~ **forward** s'avancer; ~ **in** entrer; ~
**off** (alight) descendre; mot ~ **on the**
**gas** écraser le champignon; ~ **out** sortir;
(hasten) allonger le pas; ~ **over** franchir; ~ **this way** venez par ici; ~ **up**
s'approcher
**stepbrother** n beau-frère m (pl beaux-
frères)
**stepchild** n enfant d'un autre lit
**stepdaughter** n belle-fille f (pl belles-
filles)
**stepfather** n beau-père m (pl beaux-
pères)
**step-ladder** n échelle f double
**stepmother** n belle-mère f (pl belles-
mères)
**stepping-stone** n marchepied m, tremplin
m
**stepsister** n demi-sœur f
**stepson** n beau-fils m (pl beaux-fils)
**stereo** n stéréo f; adj stéréo
**stereophonic** adj stéréophonique
**stereophony** n stéréophonie f
**stereotype** n cliché m; fig stéréotype m; vt
stéréotyper
**sterile** adj stérile
**sterility** n stérilité f
**sterilization** n stérilisation f
**sterilize** vt stériliser
**sterling** n econ sterling m; adj vrai, véritable, solide; econ sterling
**¹stern** n naut arrière m, poupe f; coll derrière m
**²stern** adj sévère, dur
**sternly** adv sévèrement, durement
**sternness** n sévérité f, dureté f
**steroids** npl stéroïdes mpl
**stet** vt (typing) maintenir
**stethoscope** n stéthoscope m
**stetson** n US chapeau m à très larges bords
**stevedore** n arrimeur m, déchargeur m
**stew** n ragoût m; (game) civet m; coll **be in**
**a** ~ être dans tous ses états; vt faire cuire
en ragoût; (fruit) mettre en compote; vi
cuire à la casserole; (simmer) mijoter;
coll (be hot) étouffer

**steward** n économe m, intendant m;
(household) maître m d'hôtel; naut +
aer steward m; **shop** ~ délégué syndical
**stewardess** n naut femme f de chambre;
**air** ~ hôtesse f de l'air
**stewardship** n économat m, intendance f
**stewed** adj cuit en ragoût; sl ivre; ~ **beef**
bœuf m en daube; ~ **fruit** compote f de
fruits; ~ **mutton** ragoût m de mouton;
~ **tea** thé trop infusé
**¹stick** n bâton m; (walking) canne f;
(wand) baguette f; (handle) manche m;
(hockey) crosse f; (wood) morceau m de
bois; (beans) rame f; (vine) échalas m;
~ **of bombs** chapelet m de bombes;
**bread** ~ gressin m; fig **get the wrong end**
**of the** ~ avoir mal compris; **queer** ~
drôle m de type; **the big** ~ le recours à la
force
**²stick** vt coller; (attach) attacher; (pierce)
percer; (pin) piquer; (fix) fixer; coll (put)
mettre, coll fourrer, coll ficher; coll
(bear) supporter, souffrir; ~ **down**
coller; (write) inscrire; ~ **'em up!** haut
les mains!; coll ~ **it** tenir le coup; ~ **on**
coller, fixer; ~ **one's chest out** bomber
le torse (la poitrine); ~ **out** faire dépasser, sortir; coll ~ **sth out** tenir qch jusqu'au bout; ~ **up** dresser; (notice)
afficher; vi s'enfoncer, se planter, se
piquer; (adhere) tenir, adhérer, rester
collé, coller; coll ~ **around** attendre; ~
**at** s'arrêter devant; (persist) persévérer
avec; ~ **at doing sth** se faire scrupule de
faire qch.; ~ **at nothing** ne reculer
devant rien; ~ **by s/o** ne pas abandonner qn, rester fidèle à qn; ~ **out** ressortir, faire saillie; ~ **out for** insister sur;
coll ~ **to one's guns** ne pas en démordre;
~ **to sth** persévérer avec qch; ~ **to the**
**facts** s'en tenir aux faits; ~ **up** se dresser; coll ~ **up for s/o** prendre la défense
de qn
**sticker** n (bills) colleur m (d'affiches);
(knife) couteau m de boucher; coll
(label) étiquette gommée; coll (stayer)
crampon m; coll (worker) travailleur m
**stickiness** n viscosité f
**sticking-plaster** n sparadrap m
**stick-insect** n phasme m
**stick-in-the-mud** n + adj routinier -ière
**stickleback** n épinoche f
**stickler** n rigoriste; **be a** ~ **for** être très à
cheval sur
**sticky** adj collant, gluant, visqueux -euse;
coll (person) difficile
**stiff** n sl (corpse) cadavre m; sl **big** ~ espèce
f d'idiot; adj raide, rigide, inflexible,
dur; (manner) guindé; (difficult) pénible, rude; (numb) engourdi; (muscles)
courbaturé; (resistance) opiniâtre; coll
(price) salé; ~ **as a poker** raide comme

**stiffen**

un pieu; ~ **neck** torticolis *m*; **become** ~ **neck** se raidir, s'ankyloser

**stiffen** *vt* raidir; (strengthen) renforcer, raffermir; *cul* lier; *vi* devenir raide, se raidir; (wind) fraîchir

**stiffener** *n* renfort *m*; *coll* verre *m* d'alcool, petit verre

**stiffening** *n* raidissement *m*; (strengthening) renforcement *m*, durcissement *m*

**stiffly** *adv* avec raideur; (manner) d'un air guindé; (resistance) opiniâtrement

**stiff-necked** *adj* entêté, obstiné

**stiffness** *n* raideur *f*, rigidité *f*; (manner) contrainte *f*; (obstinacy) opiniâtreté *f*; (difficulty) difficulté *f*

**stifle** *vt* étouffer; (repress) réprimer; *vi* étouffer, suffoquer

**stigma** *n* infamie *f*; *path* stigmate *m*

**stigmata** *npl eccles* stigmates *mpl*

**stigmatize** *vt* stigmatiser

**stile** *n* échalier *m*

**stiletto** *n* stylet *m*; ~ **heel** talon *m* aiguille

¹**still** *n phot* photographie (tirée d'un film); *adj* tranquille, calme; (stationary) immobile; ~ **waters run deep** il n'y a pire eau que l'eau qui dort; **keep** ~ ne pas bouger; **his heart stood** ~ son cœur cessa de battre; *vt* tranquilliser, calmer

²**still** *adv* encore, toujours; *conj* cependant, pourtant, toutefois

³**still** *n* alambic *m*

**still-born** *adj* mort-né (*f* mort-née)

**still-life** *n* nature morte

**stillness** *n* tranquillité *f*, calme *m*, silence *m*

**stilt** *n* échasse *f*; **on** ~**s** monté sur des échasses

**stilted** *adj* guindé

**stimulant** *n* stimulant *m*, remontant *m*

**stimulate** *vt* stimuler; exciter

**stimulation** *n* stimulation *f*

**stimulative** *adj* stimulateur -trice

**stimulus** *n* stimulant *m*

**sting** *n* (insect) aiguillon *m*, dard *m*; (wound) piqûre *f*; *fig* pointe *f*; (energy) vigueur *f*; *vt* piquer; *sl* **he stung me** il m'a fait payer le prix fort; *vi* cuire

**stinginess** *n* ladrerie *f*, pingrerie *f*

**stingy** *adj* ladre, pingre

**stink** *n* puanteur *f*; *sl* **raise a** ~ faire de l'esclandre; *vt* ~ **out** enfumer, chasser par la mauvaise odeur; *vi* puer

**stink-bomb** *n* boule puante

**stinker** *n sl fig* sale type *m*

**stinking** *adj* puant; *sl* dégoûtant; *sl* (drunk) ivre

**stint** *n* restriction *f*; (job) tâche *f*, besogne assignée; **without** ~ sans limite; *vt* réduire, limiter, restreindre; ~ **oneself** se priver du nécessaire

**stipend** *n* traitement *m*

**stipendiary** *adj* qui reçoit des appointements fixes; **magistrate** magistrat appointé

**stipulate** *vt* + *vi* stipuler

**stipulation** *n* stipulation *f*

**stir** *n* remuement *m*, mouvement *m*; (agitation) remue-ménage *m*, agitation *f*, émoi *m*; *vt* remuer; (move) bouger; *fig* agiter, exciter; ~ **up** fomenter, ameuter; *vi* bouger, remuer; **not** ~ **out of the house** ne pas sortir de la maison

**stirring** *adj* remuant; (rousing) entraînant, vibrant

**stirrup** *n* étrier *m*

**stirrup-cup** *n* coup *m* de l'étrier

**stirrup-pump** *n* pompe à main portative

**stitch** *n* point *m*; (knitting) maille *f*; *surg* (point *m* de) suture *f*; *med* point *m* de côté; **a** ~ **in time saves nine** un point à temps en épargne cent; **without a** ~ **on** tout nu, nu comme un ver; *vt* coudre; *surg* suturer; (book) brocher; ~ **up** recoudre

**stoat** *n* hermine *f*

**stock** *n* (goods) marchandises *fpl*, stock *m*; (quantity) quantité *f*; (stores) provision *f*; (race) famille *f*, lignée *f*; (cattle) bétail *m*; (tree) tronc *m*; *hort* porte-greffe *m* (*pl* porte-greffe(s)); *bot* giroflée *f*; *cul* bouillon *m*; (gun) fût *m*, bois *m*; *econ* valeurs *fpl*, actions *fpl*; ~ *m* pilori *m*; *naut* chantier *m*; ~ **s and shares** valeurs *fpl* de bourse; **in** ~ en magasin, en stock; **out of** ~ épuisé; **take** ~ **of** faire l'inventaire de; **take** ~ **of the situation** faire le point de la situation; *adj* (standard) courant; (goods) de série; ~**-car** stock-car *m*; ~ **phrase** phrase toute faite; *vt* approvisionner, stocker; (have in stock) tenir en magasin, stocker; (gun) monter; **well** ~**ed shop** magasin bien approvisionné

**stockade** *n* palissade *f*

**stock-breeder** *n* éleveur -euse

**stockbroker** *n* agent *m* de change, courtier *m* en bourse

**Stock Exchange** *n* Bourse *f*

**stockholder** *n* actionnaire

**stocking** *n* bas *m*

**stockinged** *adj* **in one's** ~ **feet** sans chaussures

**stock-in-trade** *n* stock *m*; *coll* répertoire *m*

**stockist** *n* stockiste *m*

**stock-market** *n* marché *m* des valeurs

**stockpile** *n* réserve *f*, stocks *mpl* de réserve; *vt* stocker

**stockpot** *n* pot-au-feu *m invar*

**stock-still** *adj* tout à fait immobile

**stock-taking** *n* inventaire *m*; *fig* examen *m* de la situation stocky *adj* trapu

stockyard *n* parc *m* à bestiaux

stodge *n coll* pudding *m*; aliment bourrant

stodginess *n* lourdeur *f*

stodgy *adj* lourd, indigeste; (person) rasoir *invar*

stoic *n* + *adj* stoïcien -ienne, stoïque

stoical *adj* stoïque

stoicism *n* stoïcisme *m*

stoke *vt* charger, chauffer; entretenir; *vi coll* ~ up bouffer

stokehold *n* chaufferie *f*

stoker *n* chauffeur *m*

stole *n* étole *f*

stolid *adj* lourd, flegmatique

stomach *n* estomac *m*; (belly) ventre *m*; (taste) goût *m*, envie *f*, inclination *f*; (courage) courage *m*; on an empty ~ à jeun; on one's ~ à plat ventre; turn s/o's ~ écœurer qn; *vt* supporter, tolérer; (insult) digérer

stomach-pump *n* pompe stomacale

stone *n* pierre *f*; (pebble) caillou *m*; (fruit) noyau *m*; *med* calcul *m*; (mill) meule *f*; (weight) = 6 kilos 38 grammes; a rolling ~ gathers no moss pierre qui roule n'amasse pas mousse; a ~'s throw away à quelques pas; leave no ~ unturned ne rien négliger; precious ~s pierres précieuses; *adj* de pierre; (earthenware) de grès; *vt* lapider; (fruit) dénoyauter

stone-blind *adj* complètement aveugle

stone-cold *adj* froid comme le marbre

stoned *adj sl* ivre; (drugs) chité

stone-deaf *adj* complètement sourd, *coll* sourd comme un pot

stonemason *n* maçon *m*

stonewall *vi* faire de l'obstruction

stoneware *n* poterie *f* de grès

stonework *n* maçonnerie *f*

stony *adj* pierreux -euse, rocailleux -euse; (hard) dur; (stare) glacé; *coll* (broke) à sec, fauché

stony-broke *adj* fauché, à sec

stony-hearted *adj* insensible, dur

stooge *n coll* dupe *f*; souffre-douleur *m invar*; subalterne *m; theat* faire-valoir *m invar*; *vi theat* servir de faire-valoir

stook *n agr* tas *m* de gerbes

stool *n* tabouret *m*; (three-legged) escabeau *m; med* ~ s selles *fpl*

stool-pigeon *n* appeau *m; coll fig* mouchard -e

¹stoop *n* dos voûté; walk with a ~ marcher le dos voûté; *vi* se pencher, se baisser; *fig* s'abaisser; (be round-shouldered) avoir le dos rond

²stoop *n see* stoup

stop *n* arrêt *m*, halte *f*; interruption *f*; (air travel) escale *f*; (punctuation) point *m;*

*mus* jeu *m*; (flute) trou *m*; (door) heurtoir *m*; (organ stop) trou *m* stop-per; *coll* pull out all the ~ s donner son maximum; put a ~ to mettre fin à; regular ~ arrêt *m* fixe; request ~ arrêt facultatif; *vt* arrêter; (cease) cesser; (prevent) empêcher; (suppress) supprimer; (hole) boucher; (shut) fermer; (road) barrer; (payment) suspendre; (cut off) couper; (tooth) plomber, obturer; ~ a blow parer un coup; ~ thief! au voleur!; get ~ ped up se boucher; *vi* s'arrêter; *mot* stopper; *naut* faire escale; (cease) cesser; ~ at nothing ne reculer devant rien; ~ away ne pas venir; ~ for s/o attendre qn; ~ off s'arrêter, faire étape; ~ short s'arrêter tout court; ~ there! restez là!; his knowledge ~ s there ses connaissances se bornent là; the matter will not ~ there l'affaire n'en demeurera pas là

stopcock *n* robinet *m*, robinet *m* de fermeture

stopgap *n* bouche-trou *m*

stop-off *n US* arrêt *m; aer* escale *f*

stop-light *n* feu *m* rouge; (on vehicle) stop *m*

stop-over *n US* arrêt *m*

stoppage *n* obstruction *f; sp* arrêt *m*; (work) suspension *f*; (pay) retenue *f*

stopper *n* bouchon *m*

stopping *n* arrêt *m*; (tooth) plombage *m*; (ceasing) cessation *f*, suspension *f*; (plug) tampon *m; adj* ~ train train *m* omnibus

stopping-place *n* arrêt *m*, halte *f; aer* escale *f*

stop-press *n* ~ news dernières informations

stop-watch *n* chronomètre *m*

storage *n* emmagasinage *m*, accumulation *f*; (place) entrepôts *mpl*, magasins *mpl*

store *n* provision *f*, approvisionnement *m*; abondance *f*; (place) entrepôt *m*; (furniture) garde-meuble *m* (*pl* garde-meuble(s)); (shop) magasin *m*; ~ s provisions *fpl*; keep sth in ~ tenir qch en réserve; have a surprise in ~ for s/o ménager une surprise à qn; set great ~ by faire grand cas de; *vt* emmagasiner; (put in store) mettre en dépôt; (store up) amasser, accumuler

storehouse *n* entrepôt *m*, magasin *m*

storekeeper *n* magasinier *m*

store-room *n* (pantry) office *m*; (warehouse) halle *f* de dépôt

storey *n* étage *m*; first ~ premier étage; *US* deuxième étage *m*

stork *n* cigogne *f*

storm *n* tempête *f*; (thunder) orage *m*; stir up a ~ soulever une tempête; take by

~ prendre d'assaut; *vt* livrer l'assaut à; (capture) prendre d'assaut; *vi* faire rage; (person) tempêter

**storm-bound** *adj* retenu par la tempête

**storm-centre** *n* centre *m* de dépression

**storm-cloud** *n* nuage menaçant

**storminess** *n* caractère orageux

**storm-troops** *npl* troupes *fpl* d'assaut

**stormy** *adj* orageux -euse; (sea) démonté; **it is** ~ le vent souffle en tempête

**story** *n* histoire *f*, récit *m*; (short) conte *m*; (plot) intrigue *f*; (lie) mensonge *m*; **it's a long** ~ c'est toute une histoire; **tall** ~ galéjade *f*; **to cut a long** ~ **short** en un mot

**storyteller** *n* conteur -euse

**stoup, stoop** *n eccles* bénitier *m*

¹**stout** *n* stout *m*, bière brune forte

²**stout** *adj* fort, vigoureux -euse; (resolute) résolu; (object) solide, résistant; (plump) gros (*f* grosse), corpulent; **get** ~ prendre de l'embonpoint

**stout-hearted** *adj* vaillant, courageux -euse

**stoutly** *adv* fortement, vigoureusement

**stoutness** *n* embonpoint *m*, corpulence *f*; courage *m*; vigueur *f*

**stove** *n* poêle *m*, fourneau *m*

**stovepipe** *n* tuyau *m* de poêle

**stow** *vt* ranger, mettre en place; *naut* arrimer

**stowage** *n naut* arrimage *m*

**stowaway** *n* passager clandestin

**straddle** *vt* chevaucher; (horse) enfourcher; ~ **one's legs** écarter les jambes

**strafe** *vt* bombarder; *coll* donner une bonne correction à

**straggle** *vi* rester en arrière; ~ **along** marcher sans ordre

**straggler** *n* traînard -e

**straggling** *adj* éparpillé, disséminé

**straight** *n* partie droite, bout droit; *adj* droit; (upright) d'aplomb; (in order) en ordre; (honest) intègre, honnête, loyal; (simple) sans complications; ~ **left** direct *m* de gauche; **put** ~ redresser; (order) arranger, mettre en ordre; *adv* droit; directement; ~ **ahead (on)** tout droit; ~ **away** immédiatement; ~ **off** tout de suite; ~ **out** franchement; **I'll be** ~ **back** je reviens tout de suite; **I'll tell you** ~ je vous le dis franchement; **keep a** ~ **face** ne pas sourciller; **walk** ~ **in** ne pas trop se frapper

**straighten** *vt* redresser; (order) arranger, mettre en ordre; *vi* se redresser

**straightforward** *adj* franc (*f* franche), honnête, loyal

**straightness** *n* rectitude *f*; (character) droiture *f*

¹**strain** *n* tension *f*, effort *m*; *med* entorse

*f*, foulure *f*; (tone) ton *m*; mélodie *f*; *mech* rapport *m* de la déformation; *vt* (stretch) tendre; (force) forcer; (filter) filtrer, passer au tamis; ~ **oneself** se forcer, faire un grand effort; ~ **one's eyes** s'abîmer les yeux; *vi* faire un grand effort; ~ **after sth** faire de grands efforts pour atteindre qch

²**strain** *n* race *f*, lignée *f*; qualité inhérente

**strained** *adj* tendu

**strainer** *n* passoire *f*, filtre *m*, tamis *m*

**strait** *n* détroit *m*; **be in dire** ~ **s** (money) être dans la gêne; (trouble) être aux abois; *adj obs* étroit

**strait-jacket** *n* camisole *f* de force

**strait-laced** *adj* collet monté *invar*

¹**strand** *n* (shore) plage *f*, rive *f*, grève *f*; *vt* (ship) échouer; abandonner

²**strand** *n* (rope) toron *m*; (thread) brin *m*; (hair) tresse *f*

**stranded** *adj* (ship) échoué; abandonné; *mot* + *coll* •**g be** ~ être en panne

**strange** *adj* étrange; (peculiar) singulier -ière, curieux -ieuse, bizarre; (unknown) inconnu; (new) nouveau (*f* nouvelle)

**stranger** *n* étranger -ère, inconnu -e; **I'm a** ~ **here** je ne suis pas d'ici; **you are quite a** ~ ! on ne vous voit plus!

**strangle** *vt* étrangler

**stranglehold** *n* prise *f* à la gorge; *fig* pouvoir *m* d'empêchement; **have a** ~ **on s/o** tenir qn par la gorge

**strangler** *n* étrangleur -euse

**strangulate** *vt* étrangler; ~ **d hernia** hernie étranglée

**strangulation** *n* étranglement *m*

**strap** *n* (leather) courroie *f*; (fabric) bande *f*, sangle *f*; (shoe) barrette *f*; (watch) bracelet *m*

**strap-hanger** *n coll* voyageur -euse debout (*pl* voyageurs -euses debout)

**strapping** *adj* solide, robuste, bien découplé; ~ **girl** beau brin de fille

**stratagem** *n* ruse *f*, stratagème *m*

**strategic** *adj* stratégique

**strategist** *n* stratège *m*

**strategy** *n* stratégie *f*

**stratification** *n* stratification *f*

**stratify** *vt* stratifier

**stratosphere** *n* stratosphère *f*

**stratum** *n* couche *f*

**straw** *n* paille *f*, chalumeau *m*; **it's not worth a** ~ cela ne vaut rien du tout; **it's the last** ~ ! c'est le comble!; **man of** ~ prête-nom *m*, homme *m* de paille

**strawberry** *n* fraise *f*; (plant) fraisier *m*; ~ **ice(-cream)** glace *f* à la fraise; **wild** ~ fraise *f* des bois

**stray** *n* bête perdue; (child) enfant perdu -e; (dog) chien perdu; *adj* égaré, errant;

*vi* s'égarer, errer

**streak** *n* raie *f*, bande *f*, strie *f*, trait *m*; (trace) trace *f*; ~ **of lightning** éclair *m*; *vt* rayer, strier; *vi* passer comme un éclair; *coll* courir tout nu (*f* toute nue) (dans un lieu public)

**streaky** *adj* rayé, strié; (bacon) entrelardé

**stream** *n* ruisseau *m*, cours *m* d'eau; (current) courant *m*; (flowing) ruissellement *m*; (lava) coulée *f*; (words, insults) torrent *m*; (vehicles) défilé *m*; (school) division *f*; **against the** ~ à contre-courant; **with the** ~ au fil de l'eau; *vi* sélectionner selon l'aptitude; *vi* couler, ruisseler; (flag, hair) flotter; ~ **forth** jaillir; ~ **in** pénétrer à flots; ~ **out** sortir à flots; ~ **with perspiration** être en nage

**streamer** *n* banderole *f*, serpentin *m*

**streaming** *n* sélectionnement *m* selon l'aptitude

**streamline** *vt* (car) caréner; (procedures) moderniser, rationaliser

**streamlined** *adj* caréné; *mot* aérodynamique

**street** *n* rue *f*; ~ **level** rez-de-chaussée *m invar*; **be** ~**s ahead of s/o** avoir devancé qn de beaucoup; **not in the same** ~ **as** pas à comparer avec; **the man in the** ~ l'homme moyen; *coll* **up one's** ~ de sa compétence; **walk the** ~**s** battre le pavé; (prostitute) faire le trottoir

**streetcar** *n US* tramway *m*

**street-door** *n* porte *f* d'entrée

**street-guide** *n* indicateur *m* des rues

**street-lamp** *n* réverbère *m*

**street-lighting** *n* éclairage *m* des rues

**street-urchin** *n* gamin -e des rues

**street-walker** *n* racoleuse *f*

**strength** *n* force *f*, forces *fpl*; (materials) solidité *f*, rigidité *f*; *mil* effectifs *mpl*; (intensity) intensité *f*; ~ **of mind** fermeté *f* d'esprit; ~ **of will** résolution *f*; **at full** ~ au grand complet; **in great** ~ en grand nombre; **on the** ~ **of** sur la foi de; **regain** ~ reprendre des forces; **with all one's** ~ de toutes ses forces

**strengthen** *vt* renforcer, consolider; (body) fortifier; (authority) raffermir

**strenuous** *adj* énergique, actif -ive; (work) ardu, pénible

**streptococcus** *n* (*pl* **streptococci**) streptocoque *m*

**streptomycin** *n* streptomycine *f*

**stress** *n* force *f*, contrainte *f*; (mental) tension *f*; *tech* effort *m*; (emphasis) insistance *f*; *gramm* accent *m* tonique; *med* stress *m*; *mech* **be in** ~ travailler; **lay** ~ **on** insister sur; *vt* souligner, appuyer sur, insister sur; *mech* faire

travailler; *gramm* accentuer

**stretch** *n* (extending) extension *f*, allongement *m*, étirage *m*; (strain) tension *f*; (extent) étendue *f*; ~ **stockings** bas *mpl* extensibles; **at a** ~ tout d'un(e) trait(e); **at full** ~ à toute allure; **by a** ~ **of the imagination** par un effort d'imagination; *coll* **do a** ~ faire de la prison; **for hours at a** ~ pendant des heures d'affilée; **have a** ~ s'étirer; *vt* tendre, tirer; (limbs) allonger, étirer; (widen) élargir; (wings) déployer; (prolong) prolonger; (sense) forcer; (exaggerate) exagérer; ~ **a point** faire une concession; ~ **oneself** s'étirer; ~ **one's legs** se dégourdir les jambes; ~ **out** allonger; *vi* s'étendre, s'élargir, s'allonger; (person) s'étirer

**stretcher** *n* brancard *m*, civière *f*

**stretcher-bearer** *n* brancardier *m*

**stretcher-party** *n* détachement *m* de brancardiers

**strew** *vt* répandre; ~ **with flowers** joncher de fleurs

**strewth** *interj sl* ça alors!

**striate** *vt* strier

**stricken** *adj* accablé, affligé, frappé

**strict** *adj* sévère, rigide; rigoureux -euse; (exact) précis

**strictness** *n* (precision) précision *f*, exactitude *f*; rigueur *f*, sévérité *f*

**stricture** *n* critique *f*; *med* rétrécissement *m*

**stride** *n* enjambée *f*, grand pas; **get into one's** ~ prendre son allure normale; **make great** ~**s** faire de grands progrès; **take sth in one's** ~ faire qch sans le moindre effort; **with giant** ~**s** à pas de géant; *vi* ~ **along** marcher à grandes enjambées; ~ **away** s'éloigner à grands pas; ~ **over** enjamber

**stridency** *n* stridence *f*

**strident** *adj* strident

**strife** *n* lutte *f*; **domestic** ~ querelles *fpl* de ménage

**strike** *n* grève *f*; (attack) raid *m*; **be on** ~ être en grève; **lightning** ~ grève surprise; **sympathy** ~ grève *f* de solidarité; **unofficial** ~ grève non autorisée par le syndicat; *vt* frapper; (match) frotter; (attitude) prendre; (find) trouver; (clock) sonner; ~ **a bargain** conclure un marché; ~ **a chord** plaquer un accord; ~ **against sth** heurter qch; ~ **an average** établir une moyenne; ~ **camp** lever le camp; ~ **down** abattre; ~ **in** enfoncer; ~ **off** abattre; (head) trancher; (name) rayer; ~ **oil** atteindre une nappe pétrolifère; *fig* trouver le filon; ~ **out** rayer, biffer; ~ **terror into s/o** frapper qn de terreur; ~ **the bottom** toucher le fond; ~

the eye attirer le regard; ~ the flag baisser le pavillon; ~ up an acquaintance with lier connaissance avec; ~ up a song entonner une chanson; be struck on s/o être entiché de qn; how does it ~ you? quelle impression cela vous fait-il?; it struck me that l'idée me vint que; you ~ me as being honest vous me paraissez honnête; vi frapper; (clock) sonner; (industry) se mettre en grève, faire grève; ~ across country prendre à travers les champs; ~ home frapper juste; ~ lucky avoir de la chance; ~ out at s/o allonger un coup à qn; ~ out for oneself voler de ses propres ailes; mus ~ up commencer à jouer; ~ while the iron is hot battre le fer pendant qu'il est chaud

**strikebound** adj paralysé par la grève

**strike-breaker** n jaune m, briseur m de grève

**strike-pay** n allocation f de grève

**striker** n gréviste; (device) marteau m; (arms) percuteur m

**striking** n frappement m; (coin) frappe f; (clock) sonnerie f; (rowing) rate of ~ cadence f de nage; adj frappant, remarquable; ~ force force f de frappe; within ~ distance à portée

**string** n ficelle f; (apron, purse) cordon m; (onions) chapelet m; (list) liste f; mus corde f; (beans) fil m; (people) procession f; mus ~s instruments mpl à cordes; ~ bag filet m (à provisions); ~ of beads collier m; eccles chapelet m; have s/o on a ~ tenir qn en lisières; pull ~s faire jouer ses relations; without ~s sans conditions; vt mettre une ficelle à; (parcel) ficeler; (beads) enfiler; (racket) corder; (bow) garnir d'une corde; (beans) effiler; highly strung nerveux -euse; vi coll ~ along with s/o suivre qn

**stringed** adj mus à cordes

**stringency** n rigueur f, sévérité f

**stringent** adj rigoureux -euse

**stringer** n (piano) monteur m de cordes; sl (journalism) pigiste m

**stringy** adj fibreux -euse, filandreux -euse; coll maigre

**strip** n bande f; vt (despoil) dépouiller; (undress) mettre tout nu (f toute nue); (take off) ôter, enlever; (bed) défaire; ~ down démonter; vi (person) se déshabiller, se dévêtir; (come off) se détacher; coll ~ naked se mettre à poil

**strip-cartoon** n bande illustrée

**stripe** n raie f, barre f; mil galon m, rayure f; vt rayer, barrer

**striped** adj à raies, rayé

**stripling** n adolescent m, jeune m

**stripper** n strip-teaseuse f

**strip-poker** n strip-poker m

**strip-tease** n strip-tease m

**strive** vi tâcher, s'efforcer; ~ against lutter contre; ~ for sth essayer d'obtenir qch

**stroboscope** n stroboscope m

¹**stroke** n coup m; (swimming) brassée f; med congestion cérébrale; (rowing) chef m de nage; (drawing) coup m de crayon; (painting) coup m de pinceau; ~ of luck coup m de chance; at one ~ d'un seul coup; breast-~ brasse f; not do a ~ of work ne rien faire de ses dix doigts; on the ~ of three sur le coup de trois heures; with a ~ of the pen d'un trait de plume; vt ~ a boat donner la nage

²**stroke** vt caresser, flatter

**stroll** n petit tour; go for a ~ (aller) faire un petit tour; vi flâner, coll se balader

**strolling** adj errant, vagabond; obs ~ player comédien ambulant

**strong** adj fort, robuste; (object) solide, résistant; (powerful) puissant; (measure) énergique; (drink) fort; (conviction) ferme; (solution) concentré; ~ language langage violent; ~ point fort m; army ten thousand ~ armée forte de dix mille hommes; be ~ enough to être de taille à; have a ~ smell sentir fort; adv be going ~ marcher très bien

**strong-arm** n coll homme fort, brute f; adj coll ~ tactics tactique brutale; vt coll tabasser

**strong-box** n coffre-fort m (pl coffres-forts)

**stronghold** n forteresse f, fig citadelle f

**strongly** adv fortement; solidement; vigoureusement, énergiquement; ~ marked accentué; feel ~ about sth attacher une grande importance à qch

**strong-minded** adj résolu, décidé

**strong-room** n cave f des coffres-forts

**strontium** n strontium m

**strop** n cuir m; vt affiler sur le cuir

**structural** adj structural

**structuralism** n structuralisme m

**structure** n structure f; bâtiment m, édifice m

**struggle** n lutte f; vi lutter; se débattre; ~ through surmonter tous les obstacles; se frayer un chemin à travers; ~ up gravir, escalader; ~ with adversity être aux prises avec l'adversité

**strum** vi ~ on the guitar gratter de la guitare; ~ on the piano tapoter un air au piano

**strumpet** n fille f des rues, prostituée f

¹**strut** n démarche fière; vi se pavaner

²**strut** n (support) support m, étai m

**struth** interj sl ça alors!

**strychnine** n strychnine f

**stub** *n* (tree, plant) souche *f*; (pencil) bout *m*; (cigarette) mégot *m*; (cheque) talon *m*; *vt* (roots) extirper; ~ **one's toe** se buter le pied; ~ **out a cigarette** écraser le bout d'une cigarette (pour l'éteindre)

**stubble** *n* chaume *m*; (beard) barbe *f* de plusieurs jours

**stubbly** *adj* couvert de chaume; ~ **beard** barbe *f* de plusieurs jours

**stubborn** *adj* obstiné, entêté, opiniâtre; (will) tenace; **as** ~ **as a mule** têtu comme un mulet

**stubbornness** *n* obstination *f*, opiniâtreté *f*, entêtement *m*

**stubby** *adj* trapu

**stucco** *n* stuc *m*; *vt* enduire de stuc

**stuck** *adj* (pig) égorgé; *coll* **be** ~ ne pas pouvoir avancer, être en panne; *sl* être amoureux -euse

**stuck-up** *adj coll* prétentieux -ieuse, snob *invar*

¹**stud** *n* clou *m* (à grosse tête); **collar** ~ bouton *m* de col; *vt* garnir de clous, clouter

²**stud** *n* (breeding) haras *m*; (racing) écurie *f* de course

**student** *n* étudiant -e

**studentship** *n* bourse *f* d'études

**stud-farm** *n* haras *m*

**studied** *adj* étudié, calculé; recherché

**studio** *n* studio *m*; (photographer, painter) atelier *m*

**studious** *adj* studieux -ieuse

**study** *n* étude *f*; (room) cabinet *m* de travail; (school) salle *f* d'étude; **brown** ~ rêverie *f*; *vt* étudier, faire des études de; (observe) observer; *vi* étudier, faire des études

**stuff** *n* (matter) matière *f*, substance *f*; (textiles) étoffe *f*, tissu *m*; **do one's** ~ faire ce qu'on attend de vous; **know one's** ~ s'y connaître; **that's the** ~ **to give him!** voilà comme il faut agir avec lui!; *vt* bourrer, remplir; (chair) rembourrer; *cul* farcir; (animal) empailler; *vulg* baiser; *sl* ~ **it!** va te faire fiche; *coll* ~ **oneself** bâfrer; *coll* ~ **sth in** fourrer qch dans; ~ **up** boucher; **be a** ~ **ed shirt** être très collet monté

**stuffiness** *n* manque *m* d'air; odeur *f* de renfermé; *fig* manière guindée; pruderie *f*

**stuffing** *n* bourrage *m*; empaillage *m*; (chair) bourre *f*; *cul* farce *f*

**stuffy** *adj* mal aéré; (person) collet monté *invar*; (dreary) ennuyeux -euse

**stultification** *n* abrutissement *m*

**stultify** *vt* rendre stupide, abrutir; (action) rendre inutile; ôter toute signification à

**stumble** *n* trébuchement *m*; *vi* trébucher, faire un faux pas; (horse) broncher; (speech) balbutier; ~ **across** rencontrer, tomber sur; ~ **over sth** buter contre qch; ~ **upon** tomber sur

**stumbling-block** *n* pierre *f* d'achoppement

**stump** *n* tronçon *m*; (limb) moignon *m*; (cabbage) trognon *m*; (tooth) chicot *m*; (pencil) bout *m*; (cigar) mégot *m*; (cricket) piquet *m*; (drawing) estompe *f*; *coll* **stir one's** ~ s se remuer, s'activer; *vt* (puzzle) coller; (drawing) estomper; *vi* ~ **along** clopiner; *coll* ~ **up** payer, *coll* casquer

**stumpy** *adj* (person) trapu; (thing) court dir

**stun** *vt* étourdir, assommer; *fig* abasourdir

**stunner** *n coll* **she's a** ~ elle est sensationnelle

**stunning** *adj* (blow) étourdissant; *coll fig* épatant, renversant, formidable

¹**stunt** *n* tour *m* de force; affaire *f* de publicité; *aer* acrobatie *f*; *vi aer* faire des acrobaties

²**stunt** *vt* arrêter dans sa croissance

**stunted** *adj* rabougri

**stunt-man** *n cin* cascadeur *m*

**stupefaction** *n* stupéfaction *f*

**stupefy** *vt* abrutir, hébéter; *med* stupéfier; **I'm stupefied by that** je n'en reviens pas

**stupendous** *adj* prodigieux -ieuse

**stupid** *adj* stupide, bête, idiot, sot (*f* sotte)

**stupidity** *n* stupidité *f*, sottise *f*, bêtise *f*

**stupidly** *adv* stupidement, sottement

**stupor** *n* stupeur *f*

**sturdy** *adj* vigoureux -euse, robuste

**sturgeon** *n* esturgeon *m*

**stutter** *n* bégaiement *m*; *vt* + *vi* bégayer, bredouiller

**stutterer** *n* bègue

**sty** *n* porcherie *f*; *coll fig* taudis *m*

**sty(e)** *n med* orgelet *m*, *med* compère-loriot *m* (*pl* compères-loriots)

**style** *n* style *m*, manière *f*; ton *m*, chic *m*, élégance *f*; (living) train *m* de maison; (type) type *m*, modèle *m*; (title) titre *m*, nom *m*; **live in fine** ~ mener grand train; **she has** ~ elle a du chic; **win in fine** ~ gagner haut la main; *vt* appeler, dénommer

**stylish** *adj* chic *invar*, élégant

**stylist** *n* styliste

**stylistic** *adj* du style

**stylistics** *npl* stylistique *f*

**stylization** *n* stylisation *f*

**stylize** *vt* styliser

**stylus** *n* style *m*, aiguille *f*

**stymie, stimy** *n* (golf) trou barré; *vt* (golf) barrer le trou; *coll* empêcher

**styptic** *n* styptique *m*; *adj* styptique

**suave** *adj* suave, doux (*f* douce)
**suavity** *n* suavité *f*
**subaltern** *n* mil sous-lieutenant *m*; *adj* subalterne
**subclass** *n* sous-classe *f*
**subcommission** *n* sous-commission *f*
**sub-committee** *n* sous-comité *m*
**subconscious** *n* subconscient *m*; *adj* subconscient
**subconsciousness** *n* subconscience *f*
**subcontinent** *n* sous-continent *m*
**subcontract** *n* contrat *m* en sous-traitance; *vt* sous-traiter
**subcontractor** *n* sous-traitant *m*
**subdivide** *vt* subdiviser; *vi* se subdiviser
**subdivision** *n* subdivision *f*
**subdue** *vt* subjuguer, soumettre; (tame) dompter; (fire) maîtriser; (light) adoucir, atténuer
**subdued** *adj* vaincu; (person) déprimé; ~ **light** demi-jour *m*; **in a ~ voice** à voix basse
**sub-edit** *vt* corriger, mettre au point
**sub-editor** *n* (newspaper) secrétaire de la rédaction
**subgroup** *n* groupement *m* secondaire, sous-groupe *m*
**subheading** *n* sous-titre *m*
**subhuman** *adj* pas tout à fait humain; stupide
**subject** *n* sujet -ette; (topic) sujet *m*, question *f*; *gramm* sujet *m*; (school) matière *f*; **change the ~** changer de sujet; **let us return to the ~** revenons à nos moutons; **on the ~ of** au sujet de; *adj* sujet -ette, exposé; (in subjection) assujetti, soumis; (condition) ~ **to** sous réserve de; *vt* assujettir, subjuguer, soumettre; exposer
**subject-heading** *n* (catalogue) titre *m* selon le sujet
**subjection** *n* sujétion *f*, soumission *f*
**subjective** *adj* subjectif -ive; *gramm* ~ **case** nominatif *m*
**subjectivism** *n* subjectivisme *m*
**subjectivist** *adj* subjectiviste *m*
**subjectivity** *n* subjectivité *f*
**subject-matter** *n* sujet *m*, contenu *m*
**subjugate** *vt* subjuguer, soumettre
**subjugation** *n* subjugation *f*, assujettissement *m*
**subjunctive** *n* subjonctif *m*; *adj* subjonctif -ive
**sub-lease** *n* sous-location *f*; *vt* sous-louer
**sub-let** *vt* sous-louer
**sub-lieutenant** *n* naut enseigne *m*
**sublimate** *vt* sublimer
**sublimation** *n* sublimation *f*
**sublime** *adj* sublime
**subliminal** *adj* subliminal
**sublimity** *n* sublimité *f*
**sub-machine-gun** *n* mitraillette *f*

**submarine** *n* sous-marin *m*; *adj* sous-marin
**submerge** *vt* submerger, immerger, inonder; *vi* plonger
**submission** *n* soumission *f*, résignation *f*
**submissive** *adj* soumis, résigné
**submit** *vt* soumettre, présenter; *vi* se soumettre; (allege) alléguer
**subnormal** *adj* au-dessous de la normale
**subordinate** *adj* subalterne, inférieur; secondaire; *gramm* subordonné; *vt* subordonner
**subordination** *n* subordination *f*, soumission *f*
**suborn** *vt* suborner, séduire
**sub-plot** *n* intrigue *f* secondaire
**subpoena** *n* leg assignation *f* (de témoins); *vt* leg ~ **s/o to appear** assigner qn à comparaître
**subscribe** *vt* souscrire; *vi* ~ **to** souscrire à; (take out subscription) s'abonner à
**subscriber** *n* signataire, souscripteur -trice; (magazine, etc) abonné -e; (payer) contractant -e; ~ **trunk dialling** téléphone *m* automatique
**subscription** *n* souscription *f*; signature *f*; (payment) cotisation *f*; (adherence) adhésion *f*; (magazine, etc) abonnement *m*; **pay a ~** verser une cotisation; **renew a ~** se réabonner; **take out a ~** prendre un abonnement
**subsection** *n* paragraphe *m*
**subsequence** *n* postériorité *f*, conséquence *f*
**subsequent** *adj* qui suit; (later) postérieur, ultérieur
**subservience** *n* servilité *f*, soumission *f*; (use) utilité *f*
**subservient** *adj* servile, obséquieux -ieuse; (useful) utile; (subordinate) subordonné
**subside** *vi* (ground) s'affaisser; (water) baisser; (precipitate) se précipiter; (anger, storm, etc) se calmer, s'apaiser; (stop talking) se taire
**subsidence** *n* (ground) affaissement *m*; (river) décrue *f*; (collapse) effondrement *m*; (anger) apaisement *m*
**subsidiary** *n comm* filiale *f*; *adj* subsidiaire
**subsidize** *vt* subventionner
**subsidy** *n* subvention *f*
**subsist** *vi* subsister; ~ **on sth** vivre de qch
**subsistence** *n* existence *f*, subsistance *f*
**subsoil** *n* sous-sol *m*
**subsonic** *adj* subsonique
**sub-species** *n* sous-espèce *f*
**substance** *n* substance *f*, matière *f*; (main meaning) fond *m*, essentiel *m*; (reality) réalité *f*; (possessions) avoir

*m*, biens *mpl*; **man of** ~ homme fortuné

**sub-standard** *adj* inférieur au niveau normal, inférieur

**substantial** *vt* substantiel -ielle, réel -elle; important; (considerable) appréciable; (big and robust) solide; (wealthy) cossu, aisé

**substantiality** *n* solidité *f*; réalité *f*; *leg* bien-fondé *m*

**substantially** *adv* substantiellement, réellement; solidement; (considerably) à un degré considérable

**substantiate** *vt* établir, prouver, justifier

**substantiation** *n* justification *f*

**substantive** *n gramm* substantif *m*; *adj* réel -elle; *gramm* substantif -ive

**sub-station** *n* sous-station *f*

**substitute** *n* remplaçant -e, suppléant -e; (agent) représentant -e; (food, etc) ersatz *m*, succédané *m*; *vt* substituer, remplacer

**substitution** *n* substitution *f*, remplacement *m*

**substratum** *n* couche inférieure

**subterfuge** *n* subterfuge *m*, faux-fuyant *m*

**subterranean** *adj* souterrain

**subtitle** *n* sous-titre *m*; *vt* sous-titrer

**subtle** *adj* subtil; (mind) fin, raffiné; (odour) délicat; (cunning) rusé

**subtlety** *n* subtilité *f*; finesse *f*; ruse *f*

**subtly** *adv* subtilement, avec finesse

**subtract** *vt* soustraire

**subtraction** *n* soustraction *f*

**subtropical** *adj* subtropical

**suburb** *n* faubourg *m*; **outer** ~ (s) banlieue *f*

**suburban** *adj* de banlieue, suburbain; (Paris) faubourien -ienne

**suburbanite** *n* banlieusard -e

**suburbia** *n* banlieue *f*

**subvention** *n* subvention *f*

**subversion** *n* subversion *f*, renversement *m*

**subversive** *adj* subversif -ive

**subvert** *vt* subvertir, renverser

**subway** *n* passage souterrain; *US* métro *m*

**succeed** *vt* (follow) succéder à, suivre; *vi* réussir, parvenir

**succeeding** *adj* (following) suivant; (future) à venir, successif -ive

**success** *n* réussite *f*, succès *m*; **her dress is a great** ~ sa robe est très réussie; **make a** ~ **of sth** réussir qch; **wish s/o** ~ souhaiter bonne chance à qn

**successful** *adj* (plan) couronné de succès; (event) heureux -euse; (attempt) réussi; **I am** ~ **in everything** tout me réussit

**succession** *n* succession *f*; (series) suite *f*; (inheritance) héritage *m*; **in rapid** ~

coup sur coup; **in** ~ de suite, successivement

**successive** *adj* successif -ive, consécutif -ive

**successor** *n* successeur *m*

**succinct** *adj* succinct

**succour** *n* secours *m*, aide *f*; *vt* secourir

**succulence** *n* succulence *f*

**succulent** *adj* succulent

**succumb** *vi* succomber

**such** *adj* tel (*f* telle); pareil -eille, semblable; (of that kind) de ce genre; ~ **a foolish man** un homme si stupide; ~ **a man** un tel homme; ~ **as do not like it** ceux qui ne l'aiment pas; ~ **is not the case** il n'en est pas ainsi; **he did no** ~ **thing** il n'a rien fait de la sorte; **her hate was** ~ **that** telle était sa haine que; **in** ~ **a way that** de telle sorte que; **in** ~ **cases** en pareils cas; **no** ~ **thing!** il n'en est rien!; **until** ~ **time as** jusqu'à ce que; **you have** ~ **methods!** vous avez de ces façons de procéder!

**such-and-such** tel et tel (*f* telle et telle)

**suchlike** *adj* semblable, de cette sorte, de ce genre, de cet acabit; **teachers, doctors and** ~ les professeurs, les médecins et autres gens de cette espèce

**suck** *n* action *f* de sucer; **have a** ~ (**at**) sucer; *vt* sucer; (baby) téter; ~ **down** engloutir; ~ **in** absorber, aspirer; *sl* duper, refaire; *fig* ~ **s/o dry** sucer qn jusqu'au dernier sou; ~ **up** sucer, aspirer, absorber; *vi* ~ **at** sucer; (pipe) tirer sur; *sl* ~ **up to s/o** lécher les bottes de qn

**sucker** *n* suceur -euse; *ent* suçoir *m*; *zool* ventouse *f*; *hort* rejeton *m*, surgeon *m*; *coll* blanc-bec *m* (*pl* blancs-becs), poire *f*

**sucking** *adj* qui tète

**sucking-pig** *n* cochon *m* de lait

**suckle** *vt* allaiter

**suckling** *n* allaitement *m*; (baby) nourrisson *m*; (animal) jeune animal *m* qui tète encore

**suction** *n* succion *f*, aspiration *f*

**suction-pump** *n* pompe aspirante

**suction-valve** *n* clapet *m* d'aspiration

**sudden** *adj* soudain, subit; (movement) brusque; **all of a** ~ soudain, tout à coup

**suddenly** *adv* tout à coup, soudain

**suddenness** *n* soudaineté *f*

**suds** *npl* eau *f* de savon; mousse *f* de savon

**sue** *vt leg* poursuivre, intenter un procès à; *vi* ~ **for** demander, solliciter, implorer

**suède** *n* (shoes) daim *m*; (gloves) suède *m*

**suet** *n* graisse *f* de rognon ·

**suffer** *vt* souffrir; (undergo) subir; (allow) permettre, tolérer; *vi* souffrir; (have losses, damage) subir des pertes (des dégâts); ~ **for one's mistakes** supporter les conséquences de ses erreurs

**sufferance** *n* tolérance *f*, souffrance *f*; **on** ~ par tolérance

**sufferer** *n* (disaster) victime *f*, sinistré -e; (accident) accidenté -e; (illness) malade

**suffering** *n* souffrance *f*

**suffice** *vt* suffire à; *vi* suffire; ~ **it to say that** qu'il suffise de dire que

**sufficiency** *n* suffisance *f*, quantité suffisante

**sufficient** *adj* suffisant, assez; **two are** ~ il suffit de deux

**suffix** *n* suffixe *m*

**suffocate** *vt* + *vi* étouffer, suffoquer

**suffocating** *adj* étouffant, suffocant

**suffocation** *n* suffocation *f*, étouffement *m*

**suffragan** *n eccles* suffragant *m*; *adj* suffragant

**suffrage** *n* suffrage *m*; vote *m*, voix *f*; (right) droit *m* de vote

**suffragette** *n hist* suffragette *f*

**suffuse** *vt* se répandre sur

**sugar** *n* sucre *m*; *fig* flatterie *f*; *sl* (money) fric *m*; **barley** ~ sucre *m* d'orge; **brown** ~ cassonade *f*; **caster** ~ sucre *m* en poudre; **granulated** ~ sucre crystallisé; **lump (loaf)** ~ sucre *m* en morceaux; *vt* sucrer; ~ **the pill** dorer la pilule

**sugar-basin** *n* sucrier *m*

**sugar-beet** *n* betterave *f* à sucre

**sugar-cane** *n* canne *f* à sucre

**sugar-coated** *adj* dragéifié

**sugar-daddy** *n sl* protecteur âgé

**sugariness** *n* goût sucré; *fig* douceur mielleuse

**sugar-plum** *n* bonbon *m* au sucre

**sugary** *adj* sucré; trop sucré; *coll fig* mielleux -euse, flatteur -euse

**suggest** *vt* suggérer, proposer; (idea) inspirer; (advise) conseiller; (hint) insinuer; (evoke) évoquer

**suggestibility** *n* suggestibilité *f*

**suggestible** *adj* que l'on peut suggérer; (person) influençable

**suggestion** *n* suggestion *f*; (tiny bit) pointe *f*, soupçon *m*

**suggestive** *adj* suggestif -ive, évocateur -trice

**suicidal** *adj* de suicide; ~ **attempt** tentative insensée; **it would be** ~ **to** ce serait un véritable suicide de

**suicide** *n* suicide *m*; (person) suicidé -e; **attempted** ~ tentative *f* de suicide; **commit** ~ se suicider

**suit** *n* (clothes) complet *m*, costume *m*; *leg* procès *m*; (request) demande *f*, prière *f*, requête *f*; (marriage) demande *f* en mariage; (cards) couleur *f*; ~ **of armour** armure complète; **bring a** ~ **against s/o** intenter un procès contre

qn; **follow** ~ (cards) jouer de la même couleur; (copy) en faire autant; **lounge** ~ complet-veston *m* (*pl* complets-veston); *vt* convenir à, aller à; (adapt) adapter; *coll* ~ **yourself!** faites comme vous voudrez; **that** ~ **s me fine** cela m'arrange tout à fait; **they are** ~ **ed to each other** ils sont faits l'un pour l'autre

**suitability** *n* convenance *f*; (relevance) à-propos *m*

**suitable** *adj* convenable; approprié; bon (*f* bonne), propre

**suitcase** *n* valise *f*, mallette *f*

**suite** *n* suite *f*, cortège *m*; *mus* suite *f*; (rooms) appartement *m*; ~ **of furniture** ameublement *m*, ensemble *m*; **drawing-room** ~ salon *m*

**suitor** *n leg* plaideur -euse; (marriage) prétendant *m*

**sulk** *vi* bouder, faire la mine

**sulkily** *adv* d'un air boudeur, en boudant

**sulkiness** *n* bouderie *f*

**sulky** *adj* boudeur -euse, maussade

**sullen** *adj* (person) maussade, morose

**sullenness** *n* air renfrogné

**sully** *vt* souiller, salir, flétrir

**sulphonamide** *n* sulfamide *m*

**sulphur** *n* soufre *m*

**sulphureous** *adj* sulfureux -euse; couleur de soufre *invar*

**sulphuric** *adj* sulfurique

**sulphurous** *adj* sulfureux

**sultan** *n* sultan *m*

**sultana** *n* sultane *f*; (dried grape) raisin *m* de Smyrne

**sultry** *adj* étouffant; (air) lourd, chaud; *coll* sexy

**sum** *n* somme *f*; total *m*, montant *m*; (arithmetic) problème *m*; *vt* ~ **up** résumer; (weigh up) juger, classer; ~ **up a situation** se rendre compte d'une situation; *leg* ~ **up the case** résumer les débats

**summarily** *adv* sommairement

**summarize** *vt* résumer

**summary** *n* sommaire *m*, résumé *m*; *adj* sommaire

**summer** *n* été *m*; ~ **holidays** grandes vacances; ~ **time** heure *f* d'été; ~ **visitor** estivant -e; **Indian** ~ été *m* de la Saint-Martin; **in** ~ en été; *vi* estiver

**summer-house** *n* pavillon *m*

**summer-school** *n* cours *m* d'été

**summer-time** *n* été *m*

**summing-up** *n leg* résumé *m* des débats; évaluation *f*

**summit** *n* sommet *m*, cime *f*; *fig* comble *m*; ~ **conference** conférence *f* au sommet

**summit-level** *n* niveau le plus élevé

**summit-meeting** *n* conférence *f* au sommet

**summon** *vt* appeler, faire venir; (meeting) convoquer; *leg* sommer de comparaître; (request) sommer; **~ a witness to attend** assigner un témoin; **~ up one's courage** faire appel à tout son courage

**summons** *n* appel *m*; *leg* assignation *f*; (meeting) convocation *f*; (from police) procès-verbal *m* (*pl* procès-verbaux); **take out a ~ against s/o** faire assigner qn; *vt leg* assigner, citer à comparaître

**sump** *n* mot fond *m* de carter; (pit) dépotoir *m*

**sumptuosity** *n* somptuosité *f*

**sumptuous** *adj* somptueux -euse

**sun** *n* soleil *m*; *coll* **get a touch of the ~** prendre un coup de soleil; **take the ~** prendre le soleil; **the ~ is shining** il fait du soleil; *vt* exposer au soleil; **~ oneself** se chauffer au soleil

**sunbathe** *vi* prendre des bains de soleil

**sunbathing** *n* bain *m* de soleil

**sunbeam** *n* rayon *m* de soleil

**sunburn** *n* (tan) hâle *m*; (burn) coup *m* de soleil

**sunburnt** *adj* hâlé, bronzé

**sundae** *n* glace *f* aux fruits, glace *f* au sirop

**Sunday** *n* dimanche *m*; *adj* du dimanche; **in one's ~ best** dans ses habits du dimanche, *pej* endimanché

**Sunday-school** *n* école *f* du dimanche

**sunder** *vt* séparer, fendre en deux

**sundial** *n* cadran *m* solaire

**sundown** *n* coucher *m* du soleil

**sundries** *npl* articles divers; (expenses) frais divers

**sundry** *adj* divers; **all and ~** tous sans exception

**sunflower** *n* tournesol *m*, soleil *m*

**sun-glasses** *npl* lunettes *fpl* de soleil (solaires)

**sun-god** *n* dieu *m* du soleil

**sun-hat** *n* chapeau *m* à larges bords

**sunk** *adj* sombré, coulé; *coll* perdu; *sl* foutu

**sunken** *adj* enfoncé, affaissé; (rock) submergé; (cheeks, road) creux (*f* creuse)

**sun-lamp** *n med* lampe *f* à rayons ultra-violets; *cin* sunlight *m*

**sunless** *adj* sans soleil

**sunlight** *n* lumière *f* du soleil; **in the ~** au soleil, au grand soleil

**sunlit** *adj* éclairé par le soleil

**sun-lounge** *n* solarium *m*

**sunny** *adj* ensoleillé, exposé au soleil; *fig* riant, radieux -ieuse; **it is ~** il fait du soleil

**sunrise** *n* lever *m* du soleil

**sun-roof** *n* mot toit ouvrant

**sunset** *n* coucher *m* du soleil, couchant *m*

**sunshade** *n* ombrelle *f*

**sunshine** *n* lumière *f* du soleil; *fig* gaieté *f*; **in the ~** au soleil

**sunspot** *n* tache *f* solaire

**sunstroke** *n* insolation *f*, coup *m* de soleil

**sun-tan** *n* hâle *m*

**sun-trap** *n* endroit très ensoleillé

**sun-up** *n US* lever *m* du soleil

**sup** *n* petite gorgée; *vi* souper

¹**super** *n theat* figurant -e

²**super** *adj coll* épatant, formidable

**superabundance** *n* surabondance *f*

**superabundant** *adj* surabondant

**superannuate** *vt* mettre à la retraite; *coll* mettre au rancart

**superannuated** *adj* (person) en (à la) retraite; (thing) suranné, démodé

**superannuation** *n* (action) mise *f* à la retraite; (pension) pension *f* de retraite *f*; **~ fund** caisse *f* des retraites

**superb** *adj* superbe, magnifique

**supercharge** *vt* suralimenter

**supercharger** *n mech* surcompresseur *m*

**supercilious** *adj* dédaigneux -euse; (haughty) hautain

**super-duper** *adj coll* formidable

**super-ego** *n* moi inconscient

**supererogation** *n* surérogation *f*

**supererogatory** *adj* surérogatoire

**superficial** *adj* superficiel -ielle

**superficiality** *n* nature superficielle; (shallowness) manque *m* de profondeur

**superficially** *adv* superficiellement

**superfluity** *n* superfluité *f*

**superfluous** *adj* superflu

**superhuman** *adj* surhumain

**superimpose** *vt* superposer, surimposer

**superintend** *vt* surveiller, diriger

**superintendent** *n* surintendant *m*; chef *m*; (police) commissaire *m*

**superior** *n* supérieur -ieure; *adj* supérieur -ieure; (person) sourcilleux -euse, arrogant; (condescending) condescendant

**superiority** *n* supériorité *f*

**superlative** *n* superlatif *m*; *adj* suprême, magnifique; *gramm* superlatif -ive

**superman** *n* surhomme *m*

**supermarket** *n* supermarché *m*

**supernational** *adj* supranational

**supernatural** *adj* surnaturel -elle

**supernaturalism** *n* croyance *f* au surnaturel

**supernaturally** *adv* surnaturellement

**supernumerary** *n* surnuméraire; *theat* +*cin* figurant -e; *adj* en surnombre, surnuméraire

**supersaturate** *vt* sursaturer

**superscribe** *vt* apposer une inscription sur

**superscription** *n* (heading) inscription *f*; (address) suscription *f*; (on document) en-tête *m*

**supersede** *vt* remplacer; (render invalid) annuler

**superseded** *adj* périmé; **~ by events** dépassé par les événements

**supersensitive** *adj* hypersensible

**supersonic** *adj* supersonique

**superstition** *n* superstition *f*

**superstitious** *adj* superstitieux -ieuse

**superstructure** *n* superstructure *f*

**supertax** *n* impôt *m* sur le revenu à taux très élevé

**supervene** *vi* survenir

**supervise** *vt* (watch over) surveiller; (control) diriger

**supervision** *n* surveillance *f*; direction *f*

**supervisor** *n* surveillant -e; directeur -trice

¹**supine** *n gramm* supin *m*

²**supine** *adj* couché, sur le dos; (indolent) indolent, inerte

**supper** *n* souper *m*; **have ~** souper; **the Last Supper** la Cène; **the Lord's Supper** la communion

**supplant** *vt* supplanter, évincer

**supple** *adj* souple, flexible; *fig* conciliant, complaisant; *vt* rendre souple

**supplement** *n* supplément *m*; (book) appendice *m*; *vt* compléter, augmenter, ajouter à

**supplementary** *adj* supplémentaire

**suppleness** *n* souplesse *f*; *fig* complaisance *f*

**suppliant** *n* suppliant -e; *adj* suppliant

**supplicate** *n* suppliant -e

**supplicate** *vt + vi* supplier

**supplication** *n* supplication *f*; (petition) supplique *f*

**supplier** *n* fournisseur -euse

¹**supply** *n* provision *f*; (supplying) approvisionnement *m*; *mil* (food) ravitaillement *m*; (person) suppléant -e; **supplies** (accessories) fournitures *fpl*; (stocks) stocks *mpl*; **~ and demand** l'offre *f* et la demande; **~ teacher** remplaçant -e (d'un professeur); **electricity ~** alimentation *f* en électricité; **take in a ~ of** s'approvisionner en; *vt* fournir, munir, approvisionner; (need) répondre à; **~ s/o's needs** pourvoir aux besoins de qn; *vi* **~ for s/o** remplacer qn

²**supply** *adv* avec souplesse, souplement

**support** *n* appui *m*, soutien *m*; (prop) support *m*; *bui* soutènement *m*; **be without means of ~** être sans ressources; **in ~ of** à l'appui de; *vt* soutenir, appuyer, supporter; (keep) maintenir; (life, family) entretenir; (theory) corroborer; (charity) patron-

ner; **~ oneself** gagner sa vie

**supportable** *adj* supportable, tolérable; (theory) soutenable

**supporter** *n* (adherent) adhérent -e, partisan -e; *sp* supporter *m*; (device) support *m*

**suppose** *vt + vi* supposer, s'imaginer; (believe) croire; **I ~ so** sans doute, bien probablement; **she is ~d to be ill** elle est censée être malade

**supposed** *adj* supposé, prétendu; (so-called) soi-disant

**supposing** *conj* si, supposé que

**supposition** *n* supposition *f*

**suppository** *n* suppositoire *m*

**suppress** *vt* supprimer, réprimer, étouffer; (hide) dissimuler; (information) taire, ne pas révéler

**suppressible** *adj* supprimable

**suppression** *n* suppression *f*, répression *f*; étouffement *m*; *rad + TV* antiparasitage *m*; (truth) dissimulation *f*

**suppressor** *n* étouffeur *m*; (information) dissimulateur *m*; *rad + TV* dispositif *m* antiparasite

**suppurate** *vi* suppurer

**supranational** *adj* supranational

**supremacy** *n* suprématie *f*

**supreme** *adj* suprême; **reign ~** régner en maître

**surcharge** *n* surtaxe *f*; (stamp) surcharge *f*; *vt* surtaxer; (letter) surcharger

**sure** *adj* sûr, certain; (infallible) infaillible; (success) assuré; *sl* **~ thing!** bien sûr!; **be ~ to do sth** ne pas manquer de faire qch; **for ~** sans faute; **I'm ~ of it** j'en suis convaincu; **it is ~ to be him** c'est sûrement lui; **make ~ of (obtaining) sth** s'assurer qch; **make ~ of sth** s'assurer de qch; **to be ~!** assurément!; *adv* vraiment, certainement; **~ enough!** bien sûr!

**sure-fire** *adj coll* infaillible

**sure-footed** *adj* au pied sûr

**surely** *adv* sûrement; (yes) assurément, bien sûr

**sureness** *n* (safety) sûreté *f*; (certainty) certitude *f*

**surety** *n* garantie *f*, caution *f*; (person) garant -e; **stand ~ for s/o** se porter garant pour qn

**surf** *n* ressac *m*; *vi* faire du surf

**surface** *n* surface *f*; extérieur *m*, dehors *m*; **break ~** revenir en surface; *fig* **on the ~** en apparence; **working ~** surface *f* d'appui; *vt* polir (apprêter) la surface de; (road) revêtir; *vi* revenir en surface

**surfboard** *n* planche *f* de surf

**surfeit** *n* excès *m*, surabondance *f*; satiété *f*; *vt* rassasier, gorger; *vi* se gorger

**surfing** *n* surf *m*

**surf-riding** n surf m
**surge** n houle f, vague f; ~ **of anger** vague f de colère; vi (water) se soulever, déferler; (crowd) déferler, se répandre; ~ **back** refluer
**surgeon** n chirurgien m
**surgery** n chirurgie f; (place) cabinet m de consultation; (hospital) dispensaire m; ~ **hours** heures fpl de consultation
**surgical** adj chirurgical, de chirurgie; ~ **spirit** alcool m (à 90°)
**surliness** n air bourru, caractère hargneux
**surly** adj bourru, hargneux -euse
**surmise** n conjecture f; vt + vi deviner
**surmount** vt surmonter
**surname** n nom m de famille
**surpass** vt surpasser; (exceed) dépasser
**surpassing** adj sans pareil -eille, incomparable
**surplice** n eccles surplis m
**surplus** n excédent m, surplus m; adj de surplus, en surplus
**surprise** n surprise f, étonnement m; **give s/o a ~** faire une surprise à qn; **take s/o by ~** prendre qn au dépourvu; **to my ~ he appeared** je fus étonné de le voir paraître; adj inattendu; vt étonner, surprendre; **I am ~d at you!** vous m'étonnez!
**surprising** adj étonnant, surprenant
**surrealism** n surréalisme m
**surrealist** n surréaliste
**surrealistic** adj surréaliste
**surrender** n mil reddition f; abandon m; leg cession f; (insurance) rachat m; vt mil rendre; leg céder; (renounce) renoncer à; ~ **oneself to** se livrer à; vi se rendre
**surreptitious** adj subreptice, clandestin
**surround** n bordure f; (frame) encadrement m; vt entourer; (encircle) cerner
**surrounding** adj environnant
**surroundings** npl (places) environs mpl, alentours mpl; (people) entourage m, milieu m
**surtax** n surtaxe f; vt surtaxer
**surveillance** n surveillance f
**survey** n aperçu m, vue générale; étude f, enquête f; (land) arpentage m; inspection f, visite f; **make a ~ of sth** examiner qch; **make a sample ~** faire une enquête par sondage; vt regarder, contempler; examiner, inspecter; (note down) faire le relevé de; (land) arpenter
**surveying** n arpentage m
**surveyor** n (land) arpenteur m; inspecteur m, surveillant m
**survival** n survivance f
**survive** vt survivre à; vi survivre
**survivor** n survivant -e; (disaster) rescapé -e

**susceptibility** n (subject to influence) susceptibilité f; sensibilité f; prédisposition f
**susceptible** adj (easily influenced) susceptible; (emotional) sensible; (to disease) prédisposé
**susceptive** adj susceptible
**suspect** n suspect -e; adj suspect; vt soupçonner; s'imaginer; (suppose) se douter de; ~ **danger** flairer le danger
**suspend** vt suspendre
**suspender-belt** n porte-jarretelles m invar
**suspenders** npl jarretelles fpl; US bretelles fpl
**suspense** n suspens m; (anxiety) suspense m; **keep s/o in ~** tenir qn en suspens
**suspension** n suspension f; ~ **bridge** pont suspendu; ~ **of driving licence** retrait m temporaire du permis de conduire
**suspicion** n soupçon m; leg suspicion f; (mistrust) méfiance f; **above ~** au-dessus de tout soupçon; **arouse ~** éveiller les soupçons; **have ~s about s/o** soupçonner qn; **lay oneself open to ~** s'exposer aux soupçons; **with ~** avec défiance
**suspicious** adj méfiant, soupçonneux -euse; (suspect) suspect, louche
**sustain** vt soutenir; (loss) éprouver, essuyer, subir; (life) entretenir; ~ **an injury** recevoir une blessure
**sustaining** adj ~ **food** nourriture fortifiante
**sustenance** n nourriture f
**suture** n suture f; vt suturer
**swab** n torchon m, serpillière f; naut faubert m; med tampon m; sl lourdaud m; vt essuyer avec un torchon; ~ **down** laver à grande eau
**swaddle** vt emmailloter
**swaddling-clothes** npl langes mpl
**swag** n sl butin m
**swagger** n air crâneur; (boasting) rodomontades fpl; vi se pavaner, crâner
**swagger-stick** n canne f de jonc, stick m
**swain** n poet + joc soupirant m
¹**swallow** n orni hirondelle f; **one ~ doesn't make a summer** une hirondelle ne fait pas le printemps
²**swallow** n gorgée f; (gullet) gosier m; vt avaler, gober; ~ **an affront** avaler un affront; ~ **a story** gober une histoire; ~ **one's pride** mettre son orgueil dans sa poche; ~ **one's words** se rétracter; ~ **the wrong way** avaler de travers; ~ **up** dévorer; (engulf) engloutir
**swallow-dive** n saut m de l'ange
**swallow-tail** n ent machaon m, coll grand porte-queue invar

**swamp** *n* marais *m*, marécage *m*; *vt* inonder; (boat) remplir d'eau; **be ~ ed with work** être débordé de travail

**swampy** *adj* marécageux -euse

**swan** *n* cygne *m*; *vi coll* **~ about (around)** se promener, errer à l'aventure

**swank** *n* coll prétention *f*; (person) crâneur -euse; *vi coll* crâner, se donner des airs

**swan-song** *n* chant *m* du cygne

**swap, swop** *n coll* troc *m*, échange *m*; *vt coll* troquer, échanger

**sward** *n* gazon *m*, pelouse *f*

**swarm** *n* essaim *m*; (people) foule *f*; *vi* (bees) essaimer; (people) se presser; *coll* grouiller; **~ up** grimper; **~ with** fourmiller de

**swarthy** *adj* basané

**swashbuckler** *n* fanfaron *m*, rodomont *m*

**swastika** *n* croix gammée

**swat** *vt coll* frapper; (fly) écraser

**swath** *n agr* andain *m*

**swathe** *n* bandage *m*; *agr* andain *m*; *vt* emmailloter, envelopper

**swatter** *n* (flies) tapette *f* (à mouches)

**sway** *n* balancement *m*; (rule) domination *f*, empire *m*; *vt* balancer, faire osciller; (rule) gouverner; (influence) influencer; **~ from** détourner; *vi* se balancer, osciller; (hesitate) balancer, rester indécis

**swear** *n coll* **have a good ~** lâcher une bordée de jurons; *vt* jurer; déclarer; **~ in** assermenter; **~ s/o to secrecy** faire jurer le secret à qn; *vi* jurer; prêter serment; **~ at** maudire, injurier; **~ by sth** jurer sur qch; (extol) vanter; **~ like a trooper** jurer comme un charretier; **~ to sth** affirmer qch sous serment

**swearer** *n* celui ( *f* celle) qui prête serment; jureur *m*

**swearing** *n* attestation *f* sous serment; (bad language) jurons *mpl*

**swear-word** *n* juron *m*, gros mot

**sweat** *n* transpiration *f*, sueur *f*; *coll* corvée *f*; *sl mil* **an old ~** un vieux troupier; **be in a ~** être trempé de sueur; **by the ~ of one's brow** à la sueur de son front; *vt* faire suer; *fig* exploiter; *vi* suer, transpirer; (work hard) peiner; (wall) suinter; **~ profusely** suer à grosses gouttes

**sweat-band** *n* (hat) cuir intérieur; *sp* bandeau *m*

**sweater** *n* chandail *m*

**sweating** *n* transpiration *f*; (labour) exploitation *f*

**sweaty** *adj* couvert de sueur

**swede** *n* rutabaga *m*

**Swede** *n* Suédois -e

**Sweden** *n* Suède *f*

**Swedish** *n* (language) suédois *m*; *adj* suédois

**sweep** *n* (with broom) coup *m* de balai; (arm) mouvement *m* circulaire; (bend) courbe *f*, boucle *f*; (chimneys) ramoneur *m*; (mines) drague *f*; (extent) étendue *f*; *coll* sweepstake *m*; **at one ~** d'un seul coup; **make a clean ~ of sth** faire table rase de qch; **make a wide ~** décrire une grande courbe; *vt* balayer; (chimney) ramoner; (mines) draguer; **~ along** entraîner; **~ aside** écarter; **~ away** balayer, emporter; (abolish) abolir; **~ off** emporter; **~ the board** tout rafler; **~ up** balayer, ramasser; *vi* **~ along (by, past)** passer rapidement; **~ down upon** fondre sur, s'abattre sur; **~ in** (person) entrer d'un air majestueux; **~ on** continuer d'avancer

**sweeper** *n* (machine) balayeuse *f*; (person) balayeur *m*

**sweeping** *n* balayage *m*; (chimney) ramonage *m*; *adj* rapide; (extensive) complet -ète, entier -ière, important; (exaggerated) un peu exagéré

**sweepings** *npl* balayures *fpl*

**sweepstake** *n* sweepstake *m*

**sweet** *n* bonbon *m*; (at meal) entremets *m*, dessert *m*; (person) chéri -e; *adj* doux ( *f* douce); (sugared) sucré; (person) gentil -ille, charmant; (smell) odorant; (sound) mélodieux -ieuse; **be ~ on s/o** avoir un (le) béguin pour qn; **have a ~ tooth** aimer les douceurs; **it's very ~ of her** c'est très aimable de sa part; *coll* **keep s/o ~** cultiver la bienveillance de qn; **smell ~** sentir bon

**sweetbread** *n cul* ris *m* de veau (d'agneau)

**sweet-corn** *n* maïs doux

**sweeten** *vt* sucrer; *sl* graisser la patte à; *vi* s'adoucir

**sweetener** *n* édulcorant *m*; *sl* pot-de-vin *m* ( *pl* pots-de-vin)

**sweetheart** *n* amoureux -euse

**sweetie** *n coll* bonbon *m*; (person) chérie *f*

**sweetmeat** *n obs* bonbon *m*

**sweetness** *n* douceur *f*; (person) gentillesse *f*

**sweet-pea** *n* pois *m* de senteur

**sweet-potato** *n* patate *f*

**sweet-scented** *adj* au parfum doux, odorant

**sweet-shop** *n* confiserie *f*

**sweet-william** *n bot* œillet *m* de poète

**swell** *n* gonflement *m*, bosse *f*; (sea) houle *f*; *coll* élégant *m*; *sl* gros personnage *m*; *adj coll* chic *invar*; épatant; *vt* gonfler, enfler; (increase) augmenter; *vi* s'enfler, se gonfler; (increase) augmenter; (sea) se soulever; *med* se tuméfier; **~ up** (rise) monter

**swelling** *n* enflement *m*, gonflement *m*; (river) crue *f*; (bump) bosse *f*; grosseur *f*, tumeur *f*

**swelter** *vi* étouffer de chaleur; **it's ~ing!** on étouffe ici!

**swerve** *n* déviation *f*, écart *m*; *vi* faire un écart; *mot* faire une embardée

**¹swift** *n orni* martinet *m*

**²swift** *adj* rapide; prompt

**swift-footed** *adj* au pied léger

**swiftness** *n* rapidité *f*; promptitude *f*

**swig** *n coll* grand trait; *vt coll* boire à grands traits

**swill** *n* lavage *m* à grande eau; (pigswill) pâtée *f* pour les cochons; *vt* laver à grande eau; *sl* boire avidement; **~ out** rincer

**swim** *n* action *f* de nager; *coll* **be in the ~** être dans le mouvement, être à la page; **go for a ~** aller nager; *vt* traverser à la nage; *vi* nager; (be flooded) être inondé; **~ across** traverser à la nage; **~ with the tide** nager dans le sens du courant; *fig* aller dans le sens de la foule; **my head is ~ming** la tête me tourne

**swimmer** *n* nageur -euse

**swimming** *n* natation *f*, nage *f*

**swimming-bath** *n* piscine *f*

**swimmingly** *adv coll* à merveille, comme sur des roulettes

**swimming-pool** *n* piscine *f*

**swim-suit** *n* costume *m* de bain

**swindle** *n* escroquerie *f*, filouterie *f*; *vt* escroquer, filouter

**swindler** *n* escroc *m*, filou *m*

**swine** *n* cochon *m*, porc *m*; *sl* salaud *m*

**swineherd** *n* porcher -ère

**swing** *n* balancement *m*, oscillation *f*; (child's) balançoire *f*, escarpolette *f*; (opinion) revirement *m*; (music, boxing) swing *m*; **be in full ~** battre son plein; **get into the ~ of things** se mettre au courant; **go with a ~** marcher très bien; (song) être entraînant; **walk with a ~** marcher d'un pas rythmé; *vt* balancer, faire osciller; (turn) faire tourner; (brandish) brandir; (hammock) accrocher; *coll* (fix) arranger; **~ one's arms** balancer les bras en marchant; **~ round** faire pivoter, faire tourner; influencer; *vi* se balancer, osciller, tournoyer; *sl* (hang) être pendu; (door) tourner; changer de direction; **~ along** marcher d'un pas rythmé; **~ back** se rabattre; (pendulum) revenir; *mot* **~ right round** faire un tête-à-queue; **~ round** se retourner; (change mind) faire volte-face; **~ to and fro** osciller, ballotter

**swing-boat** *n* bateau *m* balançoire, balançoire *f*

**swing-bridge** *n* pont tournant

**swing-door** *n* porte *f* va-et-vient

**swingeing** *adj* énorme; (measure) draconien -ienne

**swinging** *adj* oscillant; (arms) ballant; vigoureux -euse; *coll* dans le vent, à la mode; (daring) osé, avancé

**swinish** *adj* de cochon; *sl* grossier -ière, sale

**swipe** *n coll* taloche *f*; *vt coll* donner une taloche à; *sl* (steal) chiper, faucher

**swirl** *n* remous *m*, tourbillon *m*; *vi* tourbillonner

**swish** *n* sifflement *m*; (water, leaves) bruissement *m*; coup *m* de bâton; (dress) froufrou *m*; *adj coll* élégant; *vt* fouetter; (stick) faire siffler; *vi* (water, leaves) bruire; siffler

**Swiss** *n* Suisse -esse; *adj* suisse, helvétique

**switch** *n* (stick) badine *f*; *elect* interrupteur *m*, commutateur *m*; (radio) bouton *m*; (railway) aiguille *f*; **riding ~** cravache *f*; **two-way ~** interrupteur *m* va-et-vient; *vt* (change) changer; (train) aiguiller; (with stick) donner un coup de badine à; *elect* **~ off** couper, fermer; (light) éteindre; *elect* **~ on** ouvrir; (light) allumer; *mot* **~ on the ignition** mettre le contact; **~ round** changer; *vi* changer; **~ round** se retourner rapidement

**switchback** *n* montagnes *fpl* russes

**switchboard** *n elect* tableau *m* de distribution; (telephone) standard *m*

**Switzerland** *n* Suisse *f*; **French-speaking ~** la Suisse romande; **German-speaking ~** la Suisse allemande (alémanique)

**swivel** *n* émerillon *m*; *vt* faire pivoter, faire tourner; *vi* pivoter, tourner

**swiz(zle)** *n coll* déception *f*, duperie *f*

**swizzle-stick** *n* fouet *m* à champagne

**swollen** *adj* enflé, gonflé; (river) en crue; (face) bouffi

**swollen-headed** *adj* vaniteux -euse

**swoon** *n* évanouissement *m*; *vi obs* s'évanouir

**swoop** *n* descente *f*, attaque *f*; *aer* attaque *f* en piqué; **at one fell ~** d'un (seul) coup; *vi* fondre; **~ down on** s'abattre sur

**swop** *n* + *vt see* **swap**

**sword** *n* épée *f*, sabre *m*; *fig* **cross ~s with s/o** mesurer ses forces avec qn; **put s/o to the ~** passer qn au fil de l'épée

**sword-belt** *n* ceinturon *m*

**sword-dance** *n* danse *f* du sabre

**swordfish** *n* espadon *m*

**swordplay** *n* escrime *f*, maniement *m* de l'épée

**swordsman** *n* escrimeur *m*; **he's a good ~** c'est une fine lame

**swordsmanship** *n* escrime *f*

**sword-swallower** *n* avaleur *m* de sabres

**sword** *adj* (enemy) juré; (evidence) assermenté

**swot** *n coll* bûcheur -euse; *vt coll* ~ **up** piocher; *vi coll* bûcher, piocher
**sybarite** *n* sybarite
**sycamore** *n* sycomore *m*
**sycophant** *n* flagorneur -euse
**syllabic** *adj* syllabique
**syllable** *n* syllabe *f*
**syllabus** *n* programme *m*
**syllogism** *n* syllogisme *m*
**sylph** *n* sylphe *m*, sylphide *f*
**sylvan** *adj* sylvestre
**symbol** *n* symbole *m*
**symbolic(al)** *adj* symbolique
**symbolism** *n* symbolisme *m*
**symbolization** *n* symbolisation *f*
**symbolize** *vt* symboliser
**symmetric(al)** *adj* symétrique
**symmetry** *n* symétrie *f*
**sympathetic** *adj* compatissant; *anat* sympathique; *med* ~ **nerve** grand sympathique
**sympathize** *vi* compatir; sympathiser
**sympathizer** *n* sympathisant -e; (cause) partisan -e
**sympathy** *n* compassion *f*; sympathie *f*; **be in** ~ **with** s/o sympathiser avec qn; **deepest** ~ condoléances *fpl*
**symphonic** *adj* symphonique
**symphony** *n* symphonie *f*
**symposium** *n* symposium *m*, colloque *m*
**symptom** *n* symptome *m*, indice *m*
**symptomatic** *adj* symptomatique
**synagogue** *n* synagogue *f*
**synchromesh** *n* mot vitesse synchronisée
**synchronism** *n* synchronisme *m*
**synchronization** *n* synchronisation *f*
**synchronize** *vt* synchroniser; *vi* arriver simultanément; *elect* être en phase
**syncopate** *vt* syncoper
**syncopation** *n* syncope *f*

**syndic** *n* syndic *m*
**syndical** *adj* syndical
**syndicalism** *n* syndicalisme *m*
**syndicate** *n* syndicat *m*; *vt* syndiquer; (article) publier simultanément dans plusieurs journaux
**syndrome** *n* syndrome *m*
**synod** *n* concile *m*, synode *m*
**synonym** *n* synonyme *m*
**synonymity, synonymy** *n* synonymie *f*
**synonymous** *adj* synonyme
**synonymy** *n see* **synonymity**
**synopsis** *n.* (*pl* **synopses**) résumé *m*, abrégé *m*
**synoptic** *adj* synoptique
**synovitis** *n med* synovite *f*
**syntactic(al)** *adj* syntaxique, syntactique
**syntax** *n* syntaxe *f*
**synthesis** *n* synthèse *f*
**synthesize** *vt* synthétiser
**synthetic** *adj* synthétique, artificiel -ielle
**syphilis** *n med* syphilis *f*
**syphilitic** *adj med* syphilitique
**Syria** *n* Syrie *f*
**Syrian** *adj* syrien -ienne
**syringa** *n bot* seringa *m*
**syringe** *n* seringue *f*; *vt* seringuer, laver à l'aide d'une seringue
**syrup** *n* sirop *m*
**syrupy** *adj* sirupeux -euse
**system** *n* système *m*, méthode *f*; *anat* organisme *m*; **digestive** ~ appareil digestif; **feudal** ~ régime féodal; **railway** ~ réseau *m* ferroviaire; **road** ~ réseau routier
**systematic** *adj* systématique
**systematization** *n* systématisation *f*
**systematize** *vt* systématiser
**systole** *n med* systole *f*

# T

**t** *n fig* **cross one's** ~ **'s** mettre les points sur les i; **to a** ~ à la perfection, à merveille
**ta** *interj coll* merci
**tab** *n* (clothing) patte *f*; (shoe-lace) ferret *m*; (label) étiquette *f*; *coll* **keep** ~ **s on** s/o tenir qn à l'œil; *vt* étiqueter
**tabby** *n* chat tigré (*f* chatte tigrée)

**tabernacle** *n* tabernacle *m*
**table** *n* table *f*; (list) tableau *m*; **clear the** ~ desservir; **lay the** ~ mettre la table, dresser (mettre) le couvert; **nest of** ~ s table *f* gigogne; **occasional** ~ guéridon *m*; **turn the** ~ **s on** s/o renverser les rôles aux dépens de qn; *vt* (bill) déposer; *US* ajourner; cataloguer

**tableau** *n* tableau *m*

**tablecloth** *n* nappe *f*

**table-d'hôte** *n* table *f* d'hôte, repas *m* à prix fixe

**tableland** *n geog* plateau *m*

**table-mat** *n* dessous-de-plat *m invar*

**tablespoon** *n* cuiller *f* (cuillère *f*) à soupe

**tablespoonful** *n* cuillerée *f* à soupe

**tablet** *n* (writing) tablette *f*; (plaque) plaque commémorative; *med* comprimé *m*

**table-talk** *n* propos *mpl* de table, conversation familière

**table-tennis** *n* tennis *m* de table, ping-pong *m invar*

**table-turning** *n* phénomène *m* des tables tournantes

**tableware** *n* vaisselle *f*

**tabloid** *n med* comprimé *m*; (newspaper) journal *m* de petit format

**taboo, tabu** *n* tabou *m*; *adj* interdit, proscrit; *vt* déclarer tabou

**tabular** *adj* tabulaire

**tabulate** *vt* classifier, disposer en forme de table(s)

**tachometer** *n mot* compte-tours *m*; tachymètre *m*; contrôlographe *m*

**tacit** *adj* tacite

**taciturn** *adj* taciturne

**taciturnity** *n* taciturnité *f*

**tack** *n* petit clou, brocquette *f*; *naut* amure *f*; *naut* (manoeuvre) bordée *f*; *coll* **be on the right** ~ être sur la bonne voie; **get down to brass** ~ **s** en venir au fait; *vt* clouer; (needlework) bâtir; ~ **sth onto sth** attacher qch à qch; *vi naut* virer de bord, louvoyer

**tackle** *n* attirail *m*, engins *mpl*; (rugby) placage *m*; **fishing** ~ attirail *m* de pêche; (shop) articles *mpl* de pêche; *vt* (seize) empoigner, saisir à bras-le-corps; (task) s'attaquer à; (problem) aborder; (rugby) plaquer

**tackling** *n* (rugby) placage *m*

**tacky** *adj* collant, gluant

**tact** *n* tact *m*, savoir-faire *m*

**tactful** *adj* ~ **person** personne *f* de tact; **be** ~ avoir du tact

**tactical** *adj* tactique

**tactician** *n* tacticien *m*

**tactics** *npl* tactique *f*

**tactile** *adj* tactile; tangible

**tactless** *adj* maladroit, indiscret -ète, dépourvu de tact

**tadpole** *n* têtard *m*

**taffeta** *n* taffetas *m*

**taffy** *n US* berlingot *m*, caramel *m*

**tag** *n* (shoe-lace) ferret *m*; (end) bout *m* qui pend; (string) attache *f*; (label) étiquette *f*; (saying) cliché *m*, citation *f*; refrain *m*; (game) chat *m*; *vt* (shoe-lace) ferrer; (attach) attacher; *vi coll*

~ **along behind s/o** suivre qn, traîner derrière qn

**tail** *n* queue *f*; (coat) pan *m*; (coin) pile *f*; ~ **s** habit *m*; **be on s/o's** ~ suivre qn de près, filer qn; *coll* **keep one's** ~ **up** ne pas se laisser abattre; **turn** ~ s'enfuir; **wear** ~ **s** porter l'habit; *vt* suivre de près; enlever la queue (les queues) à; **attacher une queue à; *vi* ~ away (off)** diminuer; (voice) s'éteindre

**tail-board** *n* (vehicle) hayon *m*

**tail-coat** *n* habit *m*

**tailed** *adj* à queue

**tail-end** *n* extrémité *f*; queue *f*; fin *f*

**tail-light** *n mot* feu *m* arrière

**tailor** *n* tailleur *m*; *vt* façonner

**tailor-made** *adj* fait sur mesure

**tailpiece** *n* dernier paragraphe

**taint** *n* corruption *f*; (stain) souillure *f*; (hereditary) tare *f*; (infection) trace *f*; *vt* infecter, polluer; (spoil) gâter

**take** *n* prise *f*; *cin* prise *f* de vue; *rad* prise *f* de son; *vt* prendre; (person) emmener; (catch) attraper; (contain) contenir; (carry) porter; (bear) supporter; (house) louer; (opportunity) saisir; (understand) comprendre; (exam) se présenter à; (paper) s'abonner à; (money) gagner, se faire; (walk) faire; (require) demander; ~ **aback** déconcerter; ~ **a chair** s'asseoir; ~ **an hour to do sth** mettre une heure pour faire qch; ~ **apart** démonter; ~ **aside** prendre à part; ~ **away** emporter, enlever; (person) emmener; (withdraw) retirer; *math* soustraire; ~ **back** reporter; (person) reconduire; (accept again) reprendre; (words) retirer; ~ **down** descendre; (unhook) décrocher; (write) inscrire; (humiliate) humilier; (demolish) démolir; ~ **hold of** empoigner, saisir; ~ **in** rentrer; (receive) recevoir; (understand, include) comprendre; (lodger) prendre, loger; (cheat) tromper; (garment) reprendre; ~ **into account** tenir compte de; *naut* ~ **in water** faire eau; ~ **it easy** ne pas se faire de bile; *sl* se la couler douce; ~ **it from me!** croyez-moi!; ~ **it into one's head to do sth** s'aviser de faire qch; *coll fig* ~ **it out of** épuiser; *coll* ~ **it out on s/o** se venger de qn, s'en prendre à qn; ~ **it that** supposer que; ~ **off** ôter, enlever, retirer; (person) emmener; (mimic) imiter; ~ **on** (labour) embaucher; (undertake) entreprendre; (accept) accepter; (lead) mener; ~ **out** sortir; (person) emmener promener; (girl) sortir avec; (tooth) arracher; (insurance) contracter; ~ **over** reprendre, prendre la succession de; (show round) faire visiter; (company) racheter; ~ **pity on** avoir pitié de;

~ **place** avoir lieu; ~ **round** faire visiter; faire faire le tour de; ~ **s/o at his word** prendre qn au mot; ~ **s/o to be fifty** donner cinquante ans à qn; ~ **sth amiss** prendre qch en mauvaise part; ~ **sth from s/o** prendre qch à qn; ~ **that!** attrape ça!; ~ **the chair** présider; ~ **the trouble to do sth** se donner (prendre) la peine de faire qch; ~ **the wrong path** se tromper de chemin; ~ **up** prendre; (pick up) ramasser; (bring up) monter; (person) faire monter; (occupy) occuper, remplir; (remove) enlever; (adopt) adopter; (occupation) commencer, se mettre à; (stitch) relever; (subject) s'occuper de; (sleeve) raccourcir; (career) embrasser; (tell off) reprendre; **be ~n ill** tomber malade; **be ~n up with sth** être occupé à qch; **be ~n with** être attiré (séduit) par; **it ~s courage** il faut du courage; ~**n** (occupied) occupé; **taking all in all** à tout prendre; **what do you ~ me for?** pour qui me prenez-vous?; vi prendre; (succeed) réussir; ~ **after** ressembler à, tenir de; ~ **off** aer décoller; (go away) filer; ~ **on** (worry) s'inquiéter, s'affliger; (get excited) se monter; (succeed) réussir; ~ **over** prendre la succession; ~ **over from s/o** remplacer qn; ~ **to** (affection) s'attacher à; (things) prendre goût à; (get addicted) s'adonner à; (get used to) se faire à; (make for) se diriger vers, se réfugier dans; ~ **upon oneself to do sth** se charger de faire qch; (take liberty) se permettre de faire qch; ~ **up with s/o** se lier d'amitié avec qn; fréquenter qn; (live with) se mettre en ménage avec qn

**take-off** n aer décollage m; coll caricature f

**take-over** n prise f de possession; (business) reprise f; ~ **bid** offre publique d'achat

**taker** n preneur -euse; (bet) tenant m; **any ~s?** y a-t-il quelqu'un que ça intéresse?; y a-t-il preneur?

**taking** n prise f; adj attrayant, séduisant

**takings** npl recette f

**talc** n talc m

**talcum** n poudre f de talc

**tale** n conte m, récit m, histoire f; pej racontar m; **old wives' ~s** histoires fpl de bonne femme; **tell ~s** rapporter, coll moucharder

**talent** n talent m; aptitude f; don m

**talented** adj doué, de talent

**tale-teller** n rapporteur -euse

**talisman** n talisman m

**talk** n conversation f; (chat) causerie f; (rumour) bruit m; (gossip) bavardage m; **have a ~ with s/o** causer avec qn;

**have ~s** avoir des entretiens; **he's all ~** ce n'est qu'un bavard; **idle ~** paroles fpl en l'air; **there's some ~ of a visit** il est question d'une visite; **there is some ~ that** le bruit court que; vt parler; ~ **down** faire taire en parlant plus fort; ~ **English** parler anglais; ~ **s/o into doing sth** persuader qn de faire qch; ~ **s/o round** persuader qn, convaincre qn; vi parler; (chat) causer, bavarder; ~ **about** (gossip) jaser de; ~ **away** parler sans arrêt; ~ **big** se vanter; ~ **down to one's listeners** s'abaisser au niveau de son auditoire; ~ **on** continuer à parler; ~ **over** discuter; ~ **through one's hat** dire des bêtises; **now you're ~ing!** voilà qui s'appelle parler! ~**ing of that** à propos de cela

**talkative** adj bavard, loquace

**talker** n parleur -euse; coll **be a great ~** coll avoir la langue bien pendue

**talkie** n coll cin obs film parlant

**talking** n bavardage m, conversation f; adj parlant

**talking-point** n sujet m de discussion

**talking-to** n semonce f

**tall** adj grand, de haute taille; (building, etc) haut, élevé; coll invraisemblable, exagéré

**tallboy** n grande commode

**tallness** n (person) grande taille; (building, etc) hauteur f

**tallow** n suif m

**tally** n pointage m; (label) étiquette f; (stick) taille f; vt pointer; (goods) contrôler; vi correspondre, s'accorder

**tally-clerk** n pointeur -euse

**tally-ho** n + interj taïaut m

**Talmud** n Talmud m

**talon** n (bird) serre f; griffe f

**tamable** adj domptable

**tamarisk** n bot tamaris m

**tambour** n mus grosse caisse; (needlework) tambour m à broder

**tambourine** n tambourin m, tambour m de basque

**tame** adj (animal) apprivoisé; (person) docile; (poor) faible; (style) monotone; vt apprivoiser; (lion, etc) dompter; (passion) mater

**tamely** adv faiblement, avec soumission

**tameness** n docilité f; soumission f; caractère soumis; (insipidity) monotonie f, fadeur f

**tamp** vt tasser, damer

**tamper** vi ~ **with** toucher à; (document) falsifier; (witness) suborner, corrompre

**tampon** n tampon m

**tan** n tan m; (skin) hâle m; adj tanné; vt tanner; (sun) hâler, bronzer; coll

étriller; *vi* se hâler, se bronzer
**tandem** *n* tandem *m*
**tang** *n* saveur *f*, goût vif
**tangent** *n* tangente *f*; **fly off at a ~** prendre la tangente; *adj* tangent
**tangential** *adj* tangentiel -ielle
**tangerine** *n* mandarine *f*
**tangibility** *n* tangibilité *f*
**tangible** *adj* tangible
**tangle** *n* confusion *f*, embrouillement *m*, enchevêtrement *m*; (muddle) fouillis *m*; *coll* **be in a ~** ne plus savoir où on est; *coll* **get into a ~** s'embrouiller; *vt* embrouiller, emmêler; enchevêtrer; *vi* s'embrouiller, s'emmêler
**tangly** *adj* embrouillé, emmêlé
**tango** *n* tango *m*
**tank** *n* réservoir *m*; (water) citerne *f*; *mil* tank *m*, char *m* (de combat); *US* **~ truck (car)** camion-citerne *m* (*pl* camions-citernes); **petrol ~** réservoir *m* à essence; **septic ~** fosse *f* septique; *vi* **mot ~ up** faire le plein (d'essence)
**tankard** *n* chope *f*, grand pot
**tanker** *n* (ship) bateau-citerne *m* (*pl* bateaux-citernes); (vehicle) camion-citerne *n* (*pl* camions-citernes)
¹**tanner** *n* tanneur *m*
·²**tanner** *n* *coll* ar + *obs* pièce *f* de six pence
**tannery** *n* tannerie *f*
**tannin** *n* tan(n)in *m*
**tanning** *n* tannage *m*; *coll* raclée *f*
**Tannoy** *n* système *m* de diffusion par haut-parleur
**tantalization** *n* tentation *f*; provocation *f*
**tantalize** *vt* (tease) taquiner; mettre au supplice, infliger le supplice de Tantale à
**tantalizing** *adj* tentant; provocant
**tantamount** *adj* équivalent; **it is ~ to saying** c'est comme si on disait
**tantrum** *n* accès *m* de colère
¹**tap** *n* (water) robinet *m*; (barrel) fausset *m*, cannelle *f*; **be on ~** être toujours disponible; **on ~** en perce; (wine) au tonneau; **turn off (on) the ~** fermer (ouvrir) le robinet; *vt* (cask) percer, mettre en perce; (tree) gemmer; (wine) tirer; (main) brancher; (phone) écouter
²**tap** *n* tape *f*, petit coup; *vt* taper, tapoter, frapper légèrement; *vi* **~ at** frapper à
**tap-dance** *n* danse *f* à claquettes
**tape** *n* ruban *m*; (recording) bande *f* (magnétique); **adhesive ~** scotch *m*; *coll* **red ~** formalités *fpl* bureaucratiques, fonctionnarisme *m*; *vt* (garment) border; (measure) mesurer au cordeau; (record) enregistrer sur bande; **he's got it all ~d** il a la situation bien en main
**tape-machine** *n* téléimprimeur *m*

**tape-measure** *n* mètre *m* (à ruban)
**taper** *n* bougie filée; *eccles* cierge *m*; *vt* effiler; *vi* aller en diminuant; **~ off** s'effiler
**tape-recorder** *n* magnétophone *m*
**tape-recording** *n* enregistrement *m* sur bande (magnétique)
**tapering** *adj* effilé, en pointe
**tapestry** *n* tapisserie *f*
**tapeworm** *n* ver *m* solitaire, ténia *m*
**tapioca** *n* tapioca *m*
**tappet** *n* *mech* came *f* de distribution, taquet *m*
**tapping** *n* petits coups; (tree) incision *f*; (cask) mise *f* en perce; *elect* branchement *m*; (message) captation *f*
**tap-room** *n* bar *m*
**tap-root** *n* racine pivotante
**tap-water** *n* eau *f* du robinet, eau *f* de la ville
**tar** *n* goudron *m*; *coll* (sailor) loup *m* de mer; **spoil the ship for a ha'p'orth of ~** faire des économies de bouts de chandelle; *vt* goudronner; *coll* **be ~red with the same brush** avoir les mêmes défauts
**tarantella** *n* tarantelle *f*
**tarantula** *n* tarentule *f*
**tardy** *adj* lent; (lazy) paresseux -euse; (belated) tardif -ive
¹**tare** *n* *bot* ivraie *f*
²**tare** *n* *comm* tare *f*; poids *m* à vide
**target** *n* cible *f*; but *m*; objectif *m*; **be the (a) ~ for** être en butte à
**target-practice** *n* tir *m* à la cible
**tariff** *n* tarif *m*; (price-list) l'ste *f* des prix
**tarmac** *n* goudron *m*, bitume *m*; *aer* (runway) piste *f* d'envol; *aer* aire *f* de stationnement
**tarnish** *n* ternissure *f*; *vt* ternir; *vi* se ternir
**tarpaulin** *n* bâche *f*
¹**tarry** *adj* goudronneux -euse
²**tarry** *vi* s'attarder; (remain) rester, demeurer
¹**tart** *n* *cul* tarte *f*; (small) tartelette *f*, tourte *f*; *sl* (whore) poule *f*, grue *f*; *vt* **~ oneself up** s'attifer
²**tart** *adj* aigre, acide; (manner) acerbe; (wine) vert
**tartan** *n* tartan *m*
**tartar** *n* tartre *m*
**Tartar** *n* Tartare, Tatar -e; *coll* personne coléreuse
**tartness** *n* aigreur *f*, acidité *f*; (manner) acerbité *f*
**task** *n* tâche *f*, besogne *f*, ouvrage *m*; **take s/o to ~** prendre qn à partie
**task-force** *n* corps *m* expéditionnaire
**taskmaster** *n* *fig* tyran *m*
**tassel** *n* gland *m*, pompon *m*, houppe *f*; (book) signet *m*

**taste** n goût m, saveur f; (inclination) penchant m, prédilection f; ~ s differ à chacun son goût; **acquire a ~ for** prendre goût à; **have ~** avoir du goût; **in bad ~** de mauvais goût; **just a ~** un tout petit peu, un soupçon; vt goûter, goûter à; (eat a little) manger un petit peu de; (wine) déguster; (perceive a taste) sentir; (happiness, power, etc) connaître; vi ~ **of** avoir un (le) goût de
**taste-bud** n papille gustative
**tasteful** adj de bon goût; (dress) élégant
**tasteless** adj fade, insipide, sans saveur; (in bad taste) de mauvais goût
**taster** n dégustateur -trice
**tasty** adj succulent, savoureux -euse
**tat** vt (needlework) faire en frivolité; vi faire de la frivolité
**ta-ta** interj coll au revoir!
**tatter** n lambeau m; **in ~ s** en lambeaux
**tattered** adj en lambeaux, en loques
**tattiness** n (shabbiness) aspect défraîchi; (untidiness) aspect déguenillé
**tattle** n bavardage m, commérage m; vi cancaner
**tattler** n cancanier -ière
¹**tattoo** n mil retraite f; **beat a ~** tambouriner
²**tattoo** n (marking) tatouage m; vt tatouer
**tatty** adj (shabby) défraîchi; (untidy) déguenillé
**taunt** n reproche m; insulte f, injure f; vt railler, se moquer de; ~ **s/o with sth** reprocher qch à qn
**taut** adj tendu, raide
**tautological** adj tautologique
**tautology** n tautologie f
**tavern** n cabaret m, taverne f
**tawdry** adj clinquant, voyant, d'un mauvais goût criard
**tawny** adj fauve
**tax** n impôt m, taxe f, contribution f; (burden) charge f; **collect ~ es** percevoir des impôts; **direct (indirect) ~ es** contributions directes (indirectes); **value-added ~** taxe f à la valeur ajoutée; vt taxer, imposer; mettre un impôt sur; (accuse) accuser; (strain) mettre à l'épreuve
**taxable** adj imposable
**taxation** n imposition f, taxation f
**tax-collector** n percepteur -trice
**tax-free** adj exempt d'impôts
**taxi** n (also ~ **-cab**) taxi m; vi aer rouler au sol
**taxidermist** n empailleur -euse
**taxidermy** n taxidermie f, naturalisation f d'animaux
**taxi-driver, taximan** n chauffeur m de taxi
**taximeter** n taximètre m

**taxi-rank** n station f de taxis
**taxology, taxonomy** n taxonomie f
**tax-payer** n contribuable
**tea** n thé m; (herb) tisane f, infusion f; **afternoon ~** goûter m, five o'clock m; **beef ~** bouillon m; **China ~** thé m de Chine; **come to ~** venir prendre le thé; **Indian ~** thé m de Ceylan; coll **it's not my cup of ~** je n'aime pas ça
**tea-bag** n sachet m de thé
**tea-break** n = pause-café f (pl pauses-café)
**tea-caddy** n boîte f à thé
**teach** vt (subjects, pupils) enseigner, (pupils) instruire, apprendre à; ~ **s/o sth** enseigner (apprendre) qch à qn; **she ~ es** elle est dans l'enseignement
**tea-chest** n caisse f à thé
**teach-in** n débat public dans une université
**teaching** n enseignement m, instruction f; adj ~ **profession** corps enseignant; **the ~ staff** (secondary) les professeurs mpl; (primary) les instituteurs mpl
**tea-cloth** n (wiping) torchon m; (table) napperon m
**tea-cosy** n couvre-théière m
**teacup** n tasse f à thé; **storm in a ~** tempête f dans un verre d'eau
**tea-dance** n thé dansant
**tea-garden** n établissement m où l'on sert le thé en plein air; plantation f de thé
**teak** n teck m
**tea-leaf** n feuille f de thé
**team** n sp équipe f; (horses, etc) attelage m; ~ **spirit** esprit m d'équipe; **home ~** équipe f qui reçoit; vt atteler; vi ~ **up with** se joindre à
**teamwork** n travail m en équipe
**tea-party** n thé m
**teapot** n théière f
¹**tear** n larme f; **be in ~ s** être en larmes; **burst into ~ s** fondre en larmes; **shed ~ s** verser des larmes; **with ~ s in her eyes** les larmes aux yeux
²**tear** n (action) déchirement m; déchirure f; vt déchirer; ~ **away (down, off, from)** arracher; coll ~ **one's hair** s'arracher les cheveux; ~ **open** ouvrir en déchirant; ~ **up** déchirer (en morceaux); (tree) déraciner; (road) défoncer; **be torn between** hésiter entre; ~ **along** coll aller à toute vitesse; ~ **at** déchirer, arracher
**tear-drop** n larme f
**tear-duct** n conduit lacrymal
**tearful** adj en pleurs; pej pleurnichant, larmoyant
**tear-gas** n gaz m lacrymogène
**tear-jerker** n coll histoire f (film m, roman m, etc) très sentimental(e)

**tea-room** n salon m de thé
**tea-rose** n rose f thé
**tear-stained** adj barbouillé de larmes
**tease** n taquin -e; vt taquiner; (wool) démêler, carder
**teaser** n taquin -e; coll colle f, problème m difficile
**tea-service, tea-set** n service m à thé
**tea-shop** n salon m de thé
**teaspoon** n cuiller f à thé
**teaspoonful** n cuillerée f à thé; = cuillerée f à café
**tea-strainer** n passe-thé m invar
**teat** n mamelon m, tétin m, téton m; (bottle) tétine f
**tea-table** n table f à thé
**tea-things** npl service m à thé
**tea-towel** n torchon m
**tea-tray** n plateau m
**tea-urn** n = samovar m
**technical** adj technique
**technicality** n détail m technique
**technician** n technicien -ienne
**Technicolor** n Technicolor m
**technique** n technique f
**technocracy** n technocratie f
**technocrat** n technocrate
**technological** adj technologique
**technologist** n technologue
**technology** n technologie f
**techy** adj see tetchy
**teddy-bear** n ours m en peluche, coll nounours m
**Te Deum** n Te Deum m
**tedious** adj ennuyeux -euse, fatigant
**tedium, tediousness** n ennui m
**tee** n dé m, tee m; vt surélever
¹**teem** vi abonder, foisonner, fourmiller
²**teem** vt (discharge) déverser
**teenage** adj adolescent
**teenager** n adolescent -e
**teens** npl coll âge m entre douze et vingt ans
**teeny** adj coll tout petit, minuscule
**teeter** vi chanceler, basculer
**teething** n dentition f; adj fig ~ troubles difficultés initiales; be ~ faire ses dents
**teetotal** adj abstinent; antialcoolique
**teetotalism** n antialcoolisme m, abstention f de boissons alcooliques
**telecast** n émission f de télévision, programme télévisé
**telecommunications** npl télécommunications fpl
**telegram** n télégramme m, dépêche f
**telegraph** n télégraphe m; vt + vi télégraphier
**telegraphic** adj télégraphique
**telegraphist** n télégraphiste
**telegraph-pole** n poteau m télégraphique
**telegraphy** n télégraphie f; wireless ~ télégraphie f sans fils, T.S.F.

**telepathic** adj télépathique
**telepathy** n télépathie f
**telephone** n téléphone m; ~ call appel m téléphonique; ~ number numéro m de téléphone; be on the ~ avoir le téléphone; he's wanted on the ~ on le demande au téléphone; vt (person) téléphoner à; (message) téléphoner; vi téléphoner
**telephone-box (booth)** n cabine f téléphonique
**telephone-operator** n téléphoniste, standardiste
**telephonic** adj téléphonique
**telephonist** n téléphoniste, standardiste
**telephony** n téléphonie f
**telephotography** n photographie f au téléobjectif
**telephoto-lens** n téléobjectif m
**teleprint** vt transmettre par téléscripteur
**teleprinter** n téléscripteur m
**telerecord** vt enregistrer à la télévision
**telerecording** n émission de télévision enregistrée
**telescope** n télescope m; vt télescoper
**telescopic** adj télescopique; ~ lens téléobjectif m
**teletype** vt transmettre par téléscripteur
**teletypewriter** n téléscripteur m
**televiewer** n téléspectateur -trice
**televise** vt télévision
**television** n télévision f; ~ set poste m de télévision, téléviseur m
**telex** n télex m
**tell** vt dire; (relate) raconter; (inform) apprendre; (announce) proclamer, annoncer; (know) savoir; (distinguish) reconnaître, distinguer; (express) exprimer; (count) compter; ~ off (scold) laver la tête à, dire son fait à; (count) énumérer; ~ s/o sth dire qch à qn; ~ s/o to do sth ordonner (dire, commander) à qn de faire qch; (clock) ~ the time marquer l'heure; all told tout compris, en tout; I am told on me dit; I told you so! je vous l'avais bien dit!; you never can ~ on ne sait jamais; you're ~ing me! à qui le dites-vous!; vi produire son effet, porter; ~ on affecter, agir sur; coll moucharder
**tellable** adj que l'on peut dire; que l'on ose raconter
**teller** n narrateur -trice, conteur -euse; (bank) caissier -ière; (votes) scrutateur -trice
**telling** n récit m, narration f; (votes) énumération f; there's no ~ on ne sait jamais; adj efficace, frappant; ~ blow coup m qui porte
**telling-off** n coll semonce f, coll engueulade f
**telltale** n rapporteur -euse, coll cafard

-e; *adj* révélateur -trice

**telly** *n* télé *f*

**temerarious** *adj* téméraire

**temerity** *n* témérité *f*

**temp** *n coll* intérimaire

**temper** *n* (humour) humeur *f*; (anger) colère *f*; (disposition) caractère *m*; *metal* trempe *f*; **be in a ~** être en colère; **have a good ~** avoir bon caractère; **in a bad (good) ~** de mauvaise (bonne) humeur; **keep one's ~** rester calme; **lose one's ~** se mettre en colère, s'emporter; *vt* (moderate) tempérer, adoucir; (mix) délayer, broyer; *metal* tremper

**temperament** *n* tempérament *m*

**temperamental** *adj* capricieux -ieuse, fantasque

**temperance** *n* (drink) tempérance *f*; modération *f*; **~ society** ligue *f* antialcoolique

**temperate** *adj* (person) sobre; modéré; (climate) tempéré

**temperature** *n* température *f*

**tempered** *adj* (steel) trempé

**tempest** *n* tempête *f*

**tempestuous** *adj fig* orageux -euse; tempétueux -euse

¹**temple** *n* (church) temple *m*, église *f*

²**temple** *n anat* tempe *f*

**tempo** *n* rythme *m*; *mus* tempo *m*

¹**temporal** *adj anat* temporal

²**temporal** *adj* temporel -elle

**temporality** *n* pouvoir temporel

**temporarily** *adv* provisoirement, temporairement

**temporariness** *n* caractère *m* temporaire

**temporary** *n* intérimaire; *adj* temporaire, provisoire; (transient) passager -ère

**temporize** *vi* temporiser

**tempt** *vt* tenter; **be strongly ~ed to do sth** avoir bien envie de faire qch

**temptation** *n* tentation *f*; **yield to ~** se laisser tenter, succomber à la tentation

**tempter** *n* tentateur *m*

**tempting** *adj* tentant, attrayant, séduisant

**temptress** *n* tentatrice *f*

**ten** *n* dix *m invar*; **about ~** une dizaine; **they came in ~s** ils sont arrivés par dizaines; *adj* dix *invar*

**tenable** *adj* (argument) soutenable; (position) tenable

**tenacious** *adj* tenace

**tenaciously** *adv* avec ténacité

**tenacity** *n* ténacité *f*

**tenancy** *n* location *f*; (lease) bail *m* (*pl* baux)

**tenant** *n* locataire

**tenanted** *adj* occupé, habité (par un locataire)

**tench** *n* tanche *f*

¹**tend** *vt* soigner; (supervise) garder, surveiller; (garden) entretenir

²**tend** *vi* tendre; **~ to do sth** (be liable to) avoir une tendance à faire qch, être sujet -ette à faire qch; (have tendency to) tendre à faire qch

**tendency** *n* tendance *f*, inclination *f*

**tendentious, tendencious** *adj* tendancieux -ieuse

¹**tender** *n* offre *f*, soumission *f*; **be legal ~** avoir cours; **by ~** par voie d'adjudication; **invite ~s for work** mettre un travail en adjudication; *vt* offrir; *vi comm* faire une soumission

²**tender** *n* (guard) garde *m*, gardien *m*; (locomotive) tender *m*; *naut* bateau *m* annexe; **bar ~** barman *m*

³**tender** *adj* tendre; (to touch) sensible; (subject) délicat; (delicate) fragile; (person) affectueux -euse, tendre; **of ~ years** en bas âge

**tenderfoot** *n* novice

**tender-hearted** *adj* sensible, au cœur tendre

**tenderly** *adv* tendrement, avec tendresse

**tenderness** *n* (feelings) tendresse *f*, affection *f*; (skin, etc) sensibilité *f*; fragilité *f*; (steak, etc) tendreté *f*

**tendon** *n* tendon *m*

**tendril** *n* vrille *f*

**tenement** *n* appartement *m* dans une maison de rapport; **~ house** maison *f* de rapport

**tenet** *n* doctrine *f*, principe *m*

**tenfold** *adj* décuple; **increase ~** décupler

**tennis** *n* tennis *m*

**tennis-ball** *n* balle *f* de tennis

**tennis-court** *n* court *m* (terrain *m*) de tennis

**tenon** *n carp* tenon *m*

**tenor** *n* teneur *f*, sens général; (content) contenu *m*; *mus* ténor *m*; **~ of events** cours *m* des événements

¹**tense** *n gramm* temps *m*

²**tense** *adj* tendu, raide

**tenseness** *n* tension *f*, rigidité *f*

**tensile** *adj* extensible, élastique

**tension** *n* tension *f*; rigidité *f*; *elect* voltage *m*

**tent** *n* tente *f*; **pitch a ~** dresser une tente

**tentacle** *n* tentacule *m*

**tentative** *adj* d'essai, expérimental

**tenterhooks** *npl* **on ~** au supplice

**tenth** *n* dixième; (date) dix *m*; *adj* dixième

**tenthly** *adv* en dixième lieu, dixièmement

**tenuous** *adj* ténu, mince

**tenure** *n* possession *f*, occupation *f*; **during his ~ of office** pendant la période où il exerçait ses fonctions

**tepid** *adj* tiède

**tepidity** *n* tiédeur *f*

**tepidly** *adv* tièdement

**tercentenary** *n* tricentenaire *m*; *adj* tricentenaire

**term** *n* terme *m*, limite *f*; (period) temps *m*; (duration) durée *f*; (expression) terme *m*; (school) trimestre *m*; ~ s conditions *fpl*; (relations) rapports *mpl*, relations *fpl*; ~ s of reference attributions *fpl*; **beginning of** ~ rentrée *f* des classes; **be on good (bad)** ~ s **with** être bien (mal) avec; **by the** ~ s **of** aux termes de; **come to** ~ s **with** s'arranger avec; **contradiction in** ~ s contradiction *f* dans les termes; **inclusive** ~ s tout compris; **on easy** ~ s avec facilités de paiement; **on no** ~ s à aucun prix; **on these** ~ s à ces conditions; *vt* appeler, nommer

**termagant** *n* mégère *f*

**terminable** *adj* terminable; (contract) résiliable

**terminal** *n* (railway) gare *f* terminus; *aer* aérogare *f*; *elect* borne *f*; *adj* qui termine, terminal, dernier -ière; (school) de trimestre

**terminate** *vt* terminer, mettre fin à; (contract) résilier; *vi* se terminer, finir

**termination** *n* terminaison *f*, conclusion *f*; (stopping) cessation *f*

**terminological** *adj* terminologique

**terminology** *n* terminologie *f*

**terminus** *n* terminus *m*, tête *f* de ligne

**termite** *n* termite *m*

**tern** *n orni* sterne *f*, hirondelle *f* de mer

**terrace** *n* terrasse *f*; (houses) rangée *f* de maisons toutes pareilles; *vt* disposer en terrasses

**terracotta** *n* terre cuite

**terrain** *n* terrain *m*

**terrestrial** *adj* terrestre

**terrible** *adj* terrible, affreux -euse; *coll* excessif -ive

**terribly** *adv* terriblement, affreusement; *coll* très, extrêmement

**terrier** *n* terrier *m*

**terrific** *adj* épouvantable, terrible; *coll* formidable

**terrify** *vt* terrifier, épouvanter; ~ s/o **out of his (her) wits** rendre qn fou (*f* folle) de terreur

**terrine** *n* terrine *f*

**territorial** *adj* territorial; **the** ~ **army** = la réserve (composée de volontaires)

**territory** *n* territoire *m*

**terror** *n* terreur *f*, épouvante *f*; *coll* **be a** ~ **for driving fast** conduire à une vitesse terrifiante; *coll* **go in** ~ **of sth** avoir une peur bleue de qch; *coll* **he's a little** ~ c'est un enfant terrible

**terrorism** *n* terrorisme *m*

**terrorist** *n* terroriste

**terrorize** *vt* terroriser

**terror-struck** *adj* saisi de terreur

**terse** *adj* concis, net (*f* nette); (manner) brusque

**tertiary** *adj* tertiaire

**Terylene** *n* Térylène *m*

**test** *n* épreuve *f*; test *m*, examen *m*; ~ **case** précédent *m*; *leg* cas *m* faisant jurisprudence; *chem* réactif *m*; *fig* **acid** ~ épreuve concluante; **pass a** ~ être accepté; **put to the** ~ mettre à l'épreuve; *vt* éprouver; tester, examiner; mettre à l'épreuve; (try out) essayer; (check) contrôler

**testament** *n* testament *m*

**testator** *n leg* testateur *m*

**testatrix** *n leg* testatrice *f*

**tester** *n* (person) essayeur -euse; (device) appareil *m* de contrôle

**testicle** *n* testicule *m*

**testify** *vt* témoigner; (declare) affirmer; *vi* témoigner; ~ **against (in favour of)** s/o déposer contre (en faveur de) qn

**testily** *adv* d'un air irrité

**testimonial** *n* (presentation) témoignage *m* d'estime; (reference) certificat *m*, lettre *f* de recommandation

**testimony** *n* témoignage *m*; *leg* déposition *f*, attestation *f*; **in** ~ **of which** en foi de quoi

**testiness** *n* irritabilité *f*

**test-pilot** *n* pilote *m* d'essai

**test-tube** *n* éprouvette *f*

**testy** *adj* irritable, irascible

**tetanus** *n* tétanos *m*

**tetchy, techy** *adj* facilement irrité, susceptible

**tête-à-tête** *n* tête-à-tête *m invar*, entretien privé

**tether** *n* attache *f*, longe *f*; **be at the end of one's** ~ être à bout (à bout de forces, à bout de ressources); *vt* attacher

**Teutonic** *adj* teuton -onne, teutonique

**text** *n* texte *m*; **stick to one's** ~ s'en tenir au sujet

**text-book** *n* manuel *m*

**textile** *n* textile *m*, tissu *m*; *adj* textile

**textual** *adj* textuel -elle

**texture** *n* texture *f*; (skin) grain *m*

**thalidomide** *n* thalidomide *f*

**than** *conj* que; (with numbers) de; **more** ~ **seven** plus de sept; **more** ~ **you** plus que vous; **more** ~ **you think** plus que vous ne croyez

**thank** *vt* remercier, dire merci à; ~ **God!** Dieu merci!; ~ s/o **for sth** remercier qn de qch; **he has only himself to** ~ **for it** c'est uniquement de sa faute; **no** ~ **you** (non) merci

**thankful** adj reconnaissant

**thankfully** adv avec reconnaissance

**thankless** adj ingrat

**thank-offering** n sacrifice m d'actions de grâces

**thanks** npl remerciements mpl; ~! merci!; ~ **to** grâce à; **give her my** ~ remerciez-la de ma part; **give** ~ **to** remercier, rendre grâces à; **many** ~! merci bien!

**thanksgiving** n action f de grâces

**that** dem pron cela, ça; (the one, that one) celui(-là) (f celle(-là), mpl ceux(-là), fpl celles(-là)); ~ **is** (to say) c'est à dire; ~'s ~! et voilà!; ~'s the **house!** voilà la maison!; ~'s **why!** voilà pourquoi!; **at** ~ (moreover) ce qui plus est; **is** ~ **your father?** est-ce là votre père?; **it has come to** ~ les choses en sont venues là; **what is** ~? qu'est-ce que c'est que cela?; rel pron (subject) qui; (object) que; (after prepositions) lequel (f laquelle, mpl lesquels, fpl lesquelles); adj ce (cet before vowel or h mute) (f cette, mpl + fpl ces); ~ **house is bigger than this one** cette maison-là est plus grande que celle-ci; **those people who don't care** ceux qui ne s'en soucient pas; adv **he's not** ~ **rich** il n'est pas si riche que ça; **she's** ~ **pretty!** elle est si jolie!; conj que; (in order that) afin que, pour que; ~ **he should die so young!** dire qu'il est mort si jeune!

**thatch** n chaume m; vt couvrir de chaume; ~**ed cottage** chaumière f

**thaw** n dégel m; fonte f des neiges; fig dégel m; vt + vi dégeler, fondre; vi (person) perdre sa froideur

**the** def art le (f la) (both l' before vowel or h mute) (mpl + fpl les); **of** ~ du (f de la) (both de l' before vowel or h mute) (mpl + fpl des); **to** ~ au (f à la) (both à l' before vowel or h mute) (mpl + fpl aux); ~ **cheek!** quel culot!; **Henry Eighth** Henri huit; **it's** the **place for winter sports** c'est le meilleur endroit pour les sports d'hiver; adv ~ **less he works,** ~ **less he earns** moins il travaille, moins il gagne; ~ **more one has,** ~ **more one wants** plus on a, plus on en veut; ~ **sooner** ~ **better** le plus tôt sera le mieux; **all** ~ **better (more)** d'autant mieux (plus)

**theatre** n théâtre m; (drama) art m dramatique; (lecture) amphithéâtre m, coll amphi m; (operating) salle f d'opérations

**theatre-goer** n amateur m de théâtre

**theatrical** adj théâtral; ~ **company** troupe f d'acteurs (de comédiens)

**theatricals** npl amateur ~ spectacle m d'amateurs

**thee** pron ar + lit te; toi

**theft** n vol m; **petty** ~ larcin m

**their** adj leur

**theirs** pron le leur (f la leur), à eux (f à elles); **she is a cousin of** ~ c'est une de leurs cousines

**theism** n théisme m

**theist** n théiste

**them** pron les; eux (f elles); (to them) leur, y; **both of** ~ tous (f toutes) les deux; **I'll take half of** ~ j'en prendrai la moitié; **most of** ~ la plupart d'entre eux; **neither of** ~ ni l'un(e) ni l'autre; **of** ~ en

**thematic** adj thématique; par sujets

**theme** n thème m, sujet m

**themselves** pron pl se; eux-mêmes (f elles-mêmes)

**then** adj d'alors, de l'époque; adv alors, à cette époque, en ce temps-là; (next) puis, ensuite; ~ **and there** immédiatement, sur-le-champ; **before** ~ avant cela; **between now and** ~ d'ici là; **now and** ~ de temps en temps, de temps à autre; **since** ~ depuis ce temps-là; **till** ~ jusqu'alors, jusque-là; **what** ~? et puis après?; conj (therefore) donc, par conséquent, alors

**thence** adv de là; (therefore) par conséquent

**thenceforth** adv désormais

**thenceforward** adv à partir de ce temps-là

**theocracy** n théocratie f

**theodolite** n théodolite m

**theologian** n théologien -ienne

**theological** adj théologique

**theology** n théologie f

**theorem** n théorème m

**theoretical** adj théorique

**theorist** n théoricien -ienne

**theorize** vi faire de la théorie

**theory** n théorie f, hypothèse f; **in** ~ en principe, en théorie

**theosophy** n théosophie f

**therapeutic** adj thérapeutique

**therapeutics** npl thérapeutique f

**therapist** n praticien -ienne; **occupational** ~ spécialiste de thérapie rééducative

**therapy** n thérapie f

**there** impers pron ~ **is (are)** il y a; ~ **occurred sth terrible** il se passa qch de terrible; ~ **was once upon a time** il était une fois; adv là; y; (yonder) là-bas; ~ **and back** aller et retour; ~'s **the problem** c'est là le problème; ~, **take it!** tenez, prenez-le!; ~ **they are!** les voilà!; ~ **they come!** les voilà qui arrivent!; ~ **you are wrong** en cela (quant à cela) vous avez tort; coll **be all**

~ être avisé; **go** ~ **and back** aller et revenir; *coll* **he's not all** ~ il n'a pas toute sa tête; **he won't leave** ~ il refuse de partir de là; **in** ~ là-dedans; **out** ~ là-dehors; **over** ~ là-bas; **up** ~ là-haut

**thereabouts** *adv* près de là, par là; (approximately) à peu près, environ

**thereafter** *adv* ensuite, par la suite, après cela

**thereby** *adv* par ce moyen, de cette façon

**therefore** *adv* donc, par conséquent

**therein** *adv* en cela, à cet égard

**thereupon** *adv* là-dessus, sur ce

**therewith** *adv* avec cela

**therm** *n* unité *f* britannique de chaleur

**thermal** *adj* thermal; ~ **baths** thermes *mpl*

**thermodynamics** *npl* thermodynamique *f*

**thermometer** *n* thermomètre *m*

**thermonuclear** *adj* thermonucléaire

**Thermos** *n* Thermos *m or f*

**thermostat** *n* thermostat *m*

**thesaurus** *n* thesaurus *m*

**thesis** *n* thèse *f*

**they** *pron* ils (*f* elles); eux (*f* elles); ~ **are good pupils** ce sont de bons élèves; ~ **say** on dit; **here** ~ **are!** les voici!; **My parents? They don't know!** Mes parents? Eux, ils n'en savent rien!

**thick** *n* partie épaisse; **be in the** ~ **of the fight** être au plus fort du combat; **through** ~ **and thin** à travers toutes les épreuves; *adj* épais (*f* épaisse); (big) gros (*f* grosse); (dense) serré, touffu; (intimate) intime; *coll* stupide; (beard) fourni; (head) lourd; ~ **soup** crème *f*; **be as** ~ **as thieves** s'accorder comme larrons en foire; **be very** ~ **with s/o** être très lié avec qn; **have a** ~ **skin** être peu sensible; *adv* en couche épaisse; (slices) en tranches épaisses; **fall** ~ **and fast** tomber (pleuvoir) dru; **lay it on** ~ exagérer

**thicken** *vt* épaissir; (sauce) lier; *vi* (s') épaissir; (sauce) se lier; (plot) se compliquer

**thickening** *n* épaississement *m*

**thicket** *n* fourré *m*

**thick-headed** *adj* stupide, bête

**thickish** *adj* assez épais (*f* épaisse); *coll* assez stupide

**thickly** *adv* en couche épaisse; (snow, etc) dru

**thickness** *n* épaisseur *f*; (hair) abondance *f*; (liquid) consistance *f*; (layer) couche *f*

**thickset** *adj* épais (*f* épaisse); (person) trapu

**thick-skinned** *adj* à (la) peau épaisse; (person) peu sensible

**thief** *n* voleur -euse; **stop** ~ **!** au voleur!

**thieve** *vt* voler

**thieving** *n* vol *m*; **petty** ~ larcins *mpl*; *adj* voleur -euse

**thievish** *adj* voleur -euse

**thigh** *n* cuisse *f*

**thigh-bone** *n* fémur *m*

**thimble** *n* dé *m* (à coudre)

**thimbleful** *n fig* doigt *m*

**thin** *adj* mince, peu épais (*f* épaisse); (person) maigre; (slender) élancé; (tenuous) ténu; (clothing) léger -ère; (sparse) clairsemé, rare; (crowd) peu nombreux -euse; *coll* (argument) peu convaincant, pauvre; ~ **on top** déplumé; **get** ~ maigrir; **have a** ~ **time** passer un temps peu agréable; *vt* amincir, diminuer; (~ **out**) éclaircir; (sauce) allonger; (paint) délayer; *vi* maigrir; (crowd) s'éclaircir

**thine** *pron* le tien (*f* la tienne), à toi

**thing** *n* chose *f*, objet *m*; affaire *f*; ~ **s** (clothes) vêtements *mpl*; (belongings) effets *mpl*, affaires *fpl*; (luggage) bagages *mpl*; **as** ~ **s are** dans l'état actuel des choses; *coll* **be on to a good** ~ avoir trouvé le filon; **for one** ~ en premier lieu; **how are** ~ **s?** comment ça va?; **it's just one of those** ~ **s** qu'est-ce que vous voulez, c'est comme ça; **it's not the (done)** ~ ça ne se fait pas; **know a** ~ **or two** être malin (*f* maligne); **look here, old** ~ **!** écoute, mon vieux!; **money's the** ~ c'est l'argent qui compte; **poor little** ~ **!** pauvre petit!; **put on one's** ~ **s** s'habiller; **quite another** ~ tout autre chose; **take off one's** ~ **s** se déshabiller; *coll* **tell s/o a** ~ **or two** dire son fait à qn; **that's the** ~ **for me!** voilà mon affaire!; **that's the very** ~ c'est tout à fait ce qu'il faut

**thingummy**(**jig**) *coll* machin *m*, truc *m*, chose *m*

**think** *n* **have a** ~ réfléchir; *coll* **he's got another** ~ **coming** il se fait des illusions; il ferait bien de réfléchir; *vt* penser; (believe) croire; (deem) juger, estimer; ~ **nothing of** compter pour rien; ~ **out** méditer, imaginer; ~ **over** réfléchir à; **he** ~ **s a lot of himself** il se prend pour qn; *vi* penser; (believe) croire; (imagine) s'imaginer; (deem) considérer; ~ **about sth** penser à qch; (have opinion of) penser de qch; ~ **better of sth** se raviser de qch, changer d'avis; ~ **little of sth** faire peu de cas de qch; ~ **much of sth** faire grand cas de qch; ~ **nothing of sth** faire peu de cas de; ~ **of doing sth** penser à faire qch; ~ **too much of sth** attacher trop d'importance à qch; ~ **twice before doing sth** regarder à deux fois avant de faire

qch; ~ **up sth** inventer qch; ~ **well
(badly)** of s/o avoir bonne (mauvaise)
opinion de qn; **as you** ~ comme bon
vous semblera; **come to** ~ **of it** à la
réflexion; **I** ~ **it's very good** je le
trouve très bien; **I** ~ **so** je crois que
oui; **I thought as much** c'est bien ce que
je pensais, je m'en doutais bien; **just
~ !** pensez donc!; **one would** ~ **that**
on dirait que
**thinkable** adj concevable, imaginable
**thinker** n penseur -euse
**thinking** n pensée f, réflexion f; adj pensant
**thinly** adv clair, légèrement, à peine
**thinness** n minceur f, peu m d'épaisseur;
(leanness) maigreur f; (liquid) fluidité
f; (hair) rareté f
**thin-skinned** adj susceptible
**third** n troisième, tiers m; mot troisième
vitesse f; (dates, kings) trois m; adj
troisième
**third-degree** n passage m à tabac
**thirdly** adv troisièmement, en troisième
lieu
**third-party** n leg tiers m; adj ~ **insurance** assurance f au tiers
**third-rate** adj très inférieur; de troisième
qualité
**thirst** n soif f; vi avoir soif; ~ **after** avoir
soif de
**thirsty** adj altéré, assoiffé; **be** ~ avoir
soif; coll **that's** ~ **work** ça donne soif
**thirteen** n treize m invar; adj treize invar
**thirteenth** n treizième; (date) treize m;
adj treizième
**thirtieth** n trentième; (date) trente m; adj
trentième
**thirty** adj trente invar; **about** ~ une
trentaine
**this** adj ce (before vowel or h mute cet) (f
sing cette) (pl ces); ~ **way** par ici; **I
want** ~ **book, not that one** je veux ce
livre-ci, pas celui-là; pron ceci; ce; (this
one) celui-ci (pl ceux-ci, f sing celle-ci,
fpl celles-ci); ~ **is where** ~ **is** c'est ici que;
**after** ~ ensuite; **what's** ~ ? qu'est-ce
que c'est que ceci?; adv ~ **far** jusqu'ici; **he's** ~ **tall** il est grand comme
ça
**thistle** n chardon m
**thither** adv là; y
**thong** n lanière f, courroie f
**thorax** n thorax m
**thorn** n épine f; fig ~ **in the flesh** sujet m
d'irritation
**thorny** adj épineux -euse
**thorough** adj (work, person) consciencieux -ieuse; (search) minutieux -ieuse;
(profound) profond; (perfect) parfait;
(real) vrai; (very bad) achevé, fieffé
**thoroughbred** n animal m de race, pur-

sang m invar; adj pur-sang invar, de
race
**thoroughfare** n voie f de communication, rue f; **no** ~ passage interdit;
(temporary) route (rue) barrée
**thoroughgoing** adj (out and out) fieffé,
accompli; (thorough) consciencieux
-ieuse
**thoroughly** adv tout à fait; parfaitement; complètement, à fond
**thoroughness** n (work) perfection f;
(search) caractère approfondi
**thou** pron ar + lit tu; toi
**though** adv .(yet) pourtant, tout de
même; conj quoique, bien que; (even
if) quand (même); ~ **he is rich**
quoiqu'il soit riche; **as** ~ comme si; **as
~ nothing had happened** comme si de
rien n'était; **even** ~ **it were to cost me
my life** quand cela me coûterait la vie
**thought** n pensée f; idée f; réflexion f,
considération f; (care) souci m; (purpose) dessein m, intention f; **collect
one's** ~**s** rassembler ses idées; **on
second** ~**s** réflexion faite; **the mere** ~
**of it** rien que d'y penser
**thoughtful** adj pensif -ive, rêveur -euse;
(considered) réfléchi; (considerate)
prévenant; (book) profond
**thoughtless** adj étourdi; (careless)
irréfléchi; (inconsiderate) sans égards
**thought-reader** n liseur -euse de pensées
**thought-reading** n lecture f de la pensée
**thousand** n mille m invar; (dates) mil;
adj mille; **about a** ~ un millier, quelque mille; **a** ~ **thanks** mille fois merci;
~**s of soldiers** des milliers de soldats
**thousandth** n + adj millième
**thrash** vt battre; coll rosser; ~ **out**
débattre
**thrashing** n rossée f; (grain) battage m;
(defeat) défaite f
**thread** n fil m; (screw) pas m, filet m; vt
enfiler; (screw) fileter; ~ **one's way
through (into)** se faufiler à travers
(dans)
**threadbare** adj râpé, usé jusqu'à la
corde; (argument) usé jusqu'à la corde
**threat** n menace f
**threaten** vt menacer; ~ **to do sth**
menacer de faire qch
**threatening** adj menaçant, de menace
**three** n trois m; adj trois
**three-cornered** adj triangulaire; (hat)
tricorne
**three-dimensional** adj à trois dimensions
**threefold** adj triple
**three-legged** adj (stool) à trois pieds
**three-piece** adj en trois pièces; ~ **suit**
costume m trois-pièces
**three-quarter** n sp trois-quarts m invar;

*adj* (portrait) de trois-quarts; trois-quarts *invar*

**threesome** *n* partie *f* à trois

**three-speed** *adj* à trois vitesses

**thresh** *vt* battre

**thresher** *n* (person) batteur *m* en grange; (machine) batteuse *f*

**threshing** *n* battage *m*

**threshold** *n* seuil *m*, pas *m* de porte; (beginning) début *m*

**thrice** *adv* trois fois

**thrift** *n* économie *f*, frugalité *f*, épargne *f*

**thrifty** *adj* économe; *US* vigoureux -euse

**thrill** *n* tressaillement *m*, frisson *m*; *vt* faire tressaillir, faire frémir, émouvoir; **be ~ed at sth** être ravi de qch; *vi* frissonner, frémir

**thriller** *n* roman *m* (pièce *f*) à sensation; roman policier

**thrilling** *adj* émouvant, passionnant, saisissant

**thrive** *vi* prospérer, réussir; (plant) bien venir; **he ~s on it** il s'en trouve bien

**thriving** *adj* (plant) vigoureux -euse; (person, business) prospère

**throat** *n* gorge *f*, gosier *m*; *fig* **cut one's own ~** travailler à sa propre ruine; **have a sore ~** avoir mal à la gorge; *fig* **jump down s/o's ~** s'attaquer à qn; *fig* **thrust sth down s/o's ~** imposer qch à qn

**throaty** *adj* guttural

**throb** *n* battement *m*, pulsation *f*; (machine) vrombissement *m*; *vi* battre, palpiter; (machine) vrombir

**throes** *npl* douleurs *fpl*; **the ~ of death** les affres *fpl* de la mort, l'agonie *f*

**thrombosis** *n* thrombose *f*

**throne** *n* trône *m*

**throng** *n* foule *f*, cohue *f*; *vt* encombrer; *vi* affluer, se presser

**throttle** *n mech* pàpillon *m*; **open (out) the ~** mettre les gaz; *vt* étrangler; *vi* **mot ~ down** mettre le moteur au ralenti

**through** *adj* direct; *US* terminé, fini; (traffic) en transit; *adv* à travers, d'un bout à l'autre; **~ and ~** de part en part; (utterly) complètement; **be ~ with** (finish) avoir fini; (have done with) en avoir fini avec; **get ~** traverser; **get ~ to s/o** (telephone) avoir la communication avec qn; (be understood) réussir à se faire comprendre de qn; **let s/o ~** laisser passer qn; **she put me ~ to the manager** elle m'a passé le directeur; *prep* à travers, au travers de; par; (because of) à cause de, pour cause de; *US* jusqu'à; **get ~ an examination** être reçu à un examen; **get ~ sth** terminer qch; *coll fig* **go ~ it** en voir de dures; **sleep right ~ the night** dormir toute la nuit; *US* **Sunday ~ Saturday** de dimanche à samedi

**throughout** *adv* (time) tout le temps; (place) partout; *prep* d'un bout à l'autre de

**throughway** *n US* autoroute *f*

**throw** *n* jet *m*, lancement *m*; (dice) coup *m* de dés; (wrestling) mise *f* à terre; *vt* jeter, lancer; (hurl) projeter; (wrestling) terrasser; (rider) démonter, désarçonner; **~ about** éparpiller; *coll* **~ a fit** tomber en convulsions; *coll* **~ a party** faire une boum; **~ away** jeter; (waste) gaspiller; (lose) perdre; (chance) laisser passer; **~ back** rejeter; (ball) renvoyer; **~ down** jeter à terre; (person) renverser, terrasser; **~ in** jeter dedans; (add) ajouter; **~ in one's hand** abandonner (la partie); **~ in one's lot with s/o** partager le sort de qn; **~ light on sth** jeter de la lumière sur qch, éclaircir une question; **~ off** rejeter; (clothes) ôter; (illness) se débarrasser de; *fig* **~ oneself** se jeter à la tête de; **~ oneself into** se lancer dans; **~ open** ouvrir tout grand; **~ out** jeter dehors, chasser; (reject) rejeter; (hint) insinuer; **~ over** jeter pardessus; (upset) renverser; (abandon) abandonner; **~ s/o a kiss** envoyer un baiser à qn; **~ up** jeter en l'air; (abandon) renoncer à; (resign) se démettre de, démissionner de; (build) construire; *coll* (vomit) vomir

**throwaway** *n coll* prospectus *m*; *adj* énoncé avec une indifférence calculée

**throwback** *n* retour *m* atavique; (person) cas *m* d'atavisme

**thrower** *n* lanceur -euse

**throw-in** *n* (football) remise *f* en jeu

**throw-out** *n* rebut *m*

¹**thrush** *n* grive *f*

²**thrush** *n med* aphtes *mpl*

**thrust** *n* poussée *f*; (fencing) coup *m* d'estoc; *vt* pousser; **~ back** repousser; **~ forward** pousser en avant; **~ in(to)** enfoncer dans; **~ one's hands into one's pockets** fourrer les mains dans ses poches; **~ out** mettre dehors; *vi* **~ at s/o** porter une botte à qn

**thruster** *n coll* arriviste

**thrusting** *adj* agressif -ive

**thud** *n* bruit sourd; *vi* tomber avec un bruit sourd

**thug** *n* bandit *m*, apache *m*

**thuggery** *n* banditisme *m*

**thumb** *n* pouce *m*; *coll* **~s up!** chic alors!; *coll* **give s/o the ~s up** indiquer à qn que tout va (ira) bien; **rule of ~** méthode *f* empirique; **twiddle one's ~s** se tourner les pouces; **under s/o's ~** sous la domination de qn; *vt* manier; (books) feuilleter; (dirty) salir

**thumb-index** *n* **book bound with ~** livre relié avec encoches

**thumb-nail** n ongle m du pouce; ~ **sketch** croquis hâtif

**thumbscrew** n vis f à ailettes

**thumb-tack** n US punaise f

**thump** n coup sourd; (punch) coup m de poing; vt + vi cogner, frapper

**thumping** adj coll énorme

**thunder** n tonnerre m; **clap (peal) of** ~ coup m de tonnerre; coll **steal s/o's** ~ couper ses effets à qn; vi tonner; (person) tonitruer, fulminer

**thunderbolt** n foudre f, coup m de foudre

**thunderclap** n coup m de tonnerre

**thundercloud** n nuage orageux

**thundering** adj tonnant; coll formidable, à tout casser

**thunderous** adj tonnant, de tonnerre; fig retentissant

**thunderstorm** n orage m

**thunderstruck** adj sidéré, abasourdi

**thundery** adj orageux -euse

**Thursday** n jeudi m

**thus** adv ainsi, comme ça, de cette façon; donc; ~ **far** jusqu'ici; jusque-là

**thwack** n coup m; vt frapper vigoureusement

**¹thwart** n banc m de nage

**²thwart** vt déjouer, contrecarrer

**thy** adj ton (f sing ta, mpl + fpl tes)

**thyme** n thym m

**thyroid** n (glande f) thyroïde f

**thyself** pron toi-même; te

**tiara** n tiare f

**tic** n tic m

**tichy** adj coll tout petit (f toute petite)

**¹tick** n (clock, etc) tic-tac m invar; coll instant m; (mark) marque f; **do sth in two** ~ **s** faire qch en moins de rien; vt ~ **off** cocher, pointer; coll rembarrer; ~ **out** enregistrer; vi faire tic-tac; sl rouspéter; mech ~ **over** tourner au ralenti; coll **what makes him** ~? qu'est-ce qui le pousse?

**²tick** n (insect) tique f

**³tick** n (material) coutil m, toile f à matelas

**⁴tick** n coll **on** ~ à crédit

**ticker-tape** n bande f de téléimprimeur

**ticket** n billet m; (métro, bus) ticket m; (label) étiquette f; (traffic offence) papillon m; US pol liste électorale; **complimentary** ~ billet m de faveur; **get a** ~ attraper une contravention; **platform** ~ billet m de quai; **return** ~ billet m (d')aller et retour; **season** ~ abonnement m; **single** ~ billet m simple; coll **that's the** ~! c'est ça!, à la bonne heure!; vt étiqueter

**ticket-collector** n contrôleur m

**ticket-office** n US guichet m

**ticking-off** n coll semonce f

**tickle** n chatouillement m; vt chatouiller; coll (amuse) amuser; vi chatouiller; (itch) démanger

**tickler** n problème difficile, question délicate; mech poussoir m

**ticklish** adj chatouilleux -euse; fig susceptible; (task, problem) délicat

**tidal** adj qui a à faire avec la marée; (harbour, etc) à marée; ~ **wave** raz m de marée; fig vague f

**tiddler** n petit poisson; (stickleback) épinoche f; (child) mioche

**tiddley** adj coll ivre, pompette

**tiddley-winks** npl jeu m de puce

**tide** n marée f; (course) cours m; (time) temps m, saison f; **go (swim) with the** ~ suivre le courant; **the** ~ **is coming in** la marée monte; **the** ~ **is going out** la marée descend; vt ~ **over** aider à surmonter une difficulté, coll dépanner

**tidemark** n ligne f de marée; fig (dirt) ligne f de crasse

**tidily** adv proprement, de façon ordonnée

**tidiness** n bon ordre; (person) caractère ordonné

**tidings** npl ar nouvelles fpl

**tidy** adj (place) bien rangé, propre, bien tenu; (person) ordonné; coll (fairly good) passable, convenable; vt ranger, mettre en ordre; ~ **oneself up** faire un brin de toilette; vi ~ **up** mettre de l'ordre partout, tout remettre en place

**tie** n (bond) lien m, attache f; (string) cordon m; (garment) cravate f; (knot) nœud m; (burden) entrave f; (game) partie nulle, match nul; US (railway) traverse f; mus liaison f; vt lier, attacher; (parcel) ficeler; (knot) faire; med ligaturer; ~ **down** immobiliser; assujettir; astreindre; fig ~ **s/o's hands** enlever à qn toute liberté d'action; ~ **sth on** attacher qch avec de la (une) ficelle; ~ **up** ficeler, attacher; (person) ligoter; coll **be** ~**d up** être très pris (occupé); **be** ~**d up with another firm** avoir des accords avec une autre maison; coll **get** ~**d up** s'embrouiller; US **the traffic is** ~**d up** il y a un embouteillage; vi ~ **up (in) with** avoir rapport avec

**tie-pin** n épingle f de cravate

**tier** n rangée f; (cake) étage m

**tie-up** n coll rapport m; US (traffic) embouteillage m

**tiff** n petite dispute

**tiger** n tigre m

**tigerish** adj de tigre

**tiger-lily** n lis tigré

**tight** adj (stretched) tendu, raide; (clothes) collant, étriqué; (not leaking)

imperméable; (money) rare; *coll*
(drunk) gris, ivre; *adv* (firmly) fermement, étroitement; (stretched) fortement tendu; (sealed) hermétiquement;
**draw** ~ serrer bien; **hold** ~ tenir bien;
**hold** ~! tenez-vous bien!; **shut** ~ bien
fermer; **sit** ~ ne pas bouger

**tighten** *vt* serrer, resserrer; (tauten)
retendre; ~ **one's belt** se serrer la ceinture; ~ **up** renforcer; *vi* (screw) se resserrer; (rope) se tendre

**tight-fisted** *adj coll* ladre, pingre

**tight-lipped** *adj* aux lèvres serrées; à l'air
sévère; *fig* discret -ète, cachottier -ière

**tightly** *adv* fortement; étroitement

**tightness** *n* (tension) tension *f*, raideur *f*;
(clothing) étroitesse *f*; (leak-proof)
étanchéité *f*, imperméabilité *f*; (money)
rareté *f*

**tightrope** *n* corde *f* raide

**tights** *npl* collant *m*

**tigress** *n* tigresse *f*

**tike, tyke** *n coll* vilain chien; (dog) clebs
*m*; *fig* rustre *m*

**tilde** *n gramm* tilde *m*

**tile** *n* (roof) tuile *f*; (floor, wall) carreau
*m*; *coll* chapeau *m* haut de forme; *vt*
(roof) couvrir de tuiles; (floor) carreler

¹**till** *vt* labourer, cultiver

²**till** *n* caisse *f*

³**till** *prep* jusqu'à; ~ **now** jusqu'ici; ~
**then** jusque-là; **not** ~ pas avant; *conj*
jusqu'à ce que; **not** ~ pas avant que

¹**tiller** *n* laboureur *m*, cultivateur *m*

²**tiller** *n naut* barre *f*

¹**tilt** *n* (slope) inclinaison *f*, pente *f*; *hist*
joute *f*; **at full** ~ à fond de train; **have
a** ~ **at** s/o jouter contre qn; *vt* incliner,
pencher; *vi* s'incliner, pencher; ~ **at**
s/o critiquer qn; ~ **over** se renverser,
basculer

²**tilt** *n* (cover) bâche *f*

**timber** *n* bois *m* de construction; **piece of**
~ poutre *f*; **standing** ~ bois *m* sur
pied; *vt* boiser

**timbre** *n* timbre *m*

**time** *n* temps *m*; (occasion) fois *f*; (of
day) heure *f*; (period) époque *f*;
(moment) moment *m*; (season) saison
*f*; (term) terme *m*; *mus* mesure *f*; (pace)
pas *m*; ~ **after** ~ à maintes reprises;
~ **will show (tell)** qui vivra verra; *coll*
**about** ~ **too!** ce n'est pas trop tôt!;
**after a** ~ quelque temps après; **against**
~ contre la montre; **another** ~ une
autre fois; **at all** ~**s** toujours; **at any** ~
à tout moment; **at one** ~ autrefois; **at
one** ~ ... **at another** tantôt ... tantôt;
**at the right** ~ au bon moment, à
propos; **at the same** ~ en même temps;
(on the other hand) d'autre part; **beat**
~ battre la mesure; **before** ~ en

avance; **behind the** ~**s** arriéré; **by this**
~ à l'heure qu'il est; **for a long** ~
(now) depuis longtemps; (past) pendant longtemps; **for a** ~ pendant quelque temps; **four at a** ~ quatre à la fois;
(stairs) quatre à quatre; **from** ~ **to** ~
de temps en temps, de temps à autre;
**have a bad** ~ passer de mauvais moments; **have a good** ~ s'amuser bien;
*coll* **have no** ~ **for** s/o trouver qn peu
intéressant; **in good** ~ bien à l'heure,
bien à temps; **in my** ~ de mon temps;
**in no** ~ en un rien de temps, en un clin
d'œil; **serve one's** ~ faire son temps;
**spare** ~ loisir *m*; **take** ~ **to do sth**
mettre du temps à faire qch; **this** ~ **last
month** il y a un mois aujourd'hui;
**waste** ~ perdre du (son) temps; **what's
the** ~? quelle heure est-il?; *vt* calculer
la durée de, chronométrer; fixer l'heure
de; *mot* régler

**time-bomb** *n* bombe *f* à retardement

**time-exposure** *n phot* pose *f*

**time-fuse** *n* fusée *f* à retardement

**time-honoured** *adj* consacré par l'usage,
vénérable

**timekeeper** *n* chronométreur *m*; **good** ~
(watch) montre *f* qui est toujours à
l'heure; (person) personne *f* qui est
toujours à l'heure

**time-lag** *n* retard *m*

**timeless** *adj* éternel -elle, sans fin

**timely** *adj* opportun, à propos

**timepiece** *n* montre *f*; (clock) pendule *f*

**timer** *n* chronométreur *m*; (sand) sablier
*m*

**timesaving** *adj* qui économise le (du)
temps

**timeserver** *n* opportuniste

**timeserving** *n* opportunisme *m*; *adj*
opportuniste

**time-signal** *n* signal *m* horaire

**time-switch** *n* minuterie *f*

**timetable** *n* horaire *m*; (trains) indicateur *m*; (personal) emploi *m* du temps

**timeworn** *adj* usé par le temps

**timid** *adj* timide, peureux -euse

**timidity** *n* timidité *f*

**timing** *n* chronométrage *m*; *mech* réglage *m*; **show good** ~ bien calculer
son temps (son moment)

**timorous** *adj* peureux -euse, craintif
-ive

**tin** *n* étain *m*; (can) boîte *f* en fer blanc;
~ **hat** casque *m*; ~ **loaf** pain
moulé; *vt* étamer; (can) mettre en boîte

**tin-can** *n* boîte *f* en fer blanc

**tincture** *n* (colour) teinte *f*; *med* teinture
*f*; *vt* teinter

**tinder** *n* amadou *m*; *ar* mèche *f* de briquet

**tinder-box** *n ar* briquet *m*

745

**tinfoil** n feuille f d'étain; *coll* papier m d'argent
**ting** n tintement m; *vi* tinter
**tinge** n teinte f, nuance f; (tiny bit) soupçon m; *vt* teinter, nuancer
**tingle** n picotement m; (ears) tintement m; *vi* picoter; (ears) tinter; **my legs are tingling** j'ai des fourmis dans les jambes
**tininess** n petitesse f
**tinker** n rétameur m; *vt* (re-tin) rétamer; (try to repair) ~ **with** retaper, rafistoler; *vi* ~ **about** bricoler
**tinkle** n tintement m; *coll* coup m de fil; *vi* tinter
**tinned** adj étamé; (canned) en boîte, en conserve
**tinning** n mise f en boîte
**tinny** adj (sound) métallique; (taste) d'étain
**tin-opener** n ouvre-boîte(s) m invar
**tinpot** adj coll misérable, inférieur
**tinsel** n paillettes fpl; *fig* clinquant m; *adj* de clinquant; *vt* garnir de paillettes
**tint** n teinte f, nuance f; *vt* teinter, colorer
**tintack** n clou m de tapisserie
**tiny** adj tout petit (f toute petite), minuscule
**tip** n (end) bout m, extrémité f, pointe f; (stick) embout m; (money) pourboire m, gratification f; (touch) tape f; (advice) conseil m; (racing) tuyau m; (rubbish) dépotoir m; (heap) tas m; *vt* (shoe) mettre un bout à; (stick) mettre un embout à; (overturn) renverser, verser; (touch) effleurer, toucher légèrement; (money) donner un pourboire à; ~ **out** déverser; ~ **over** renverser; ~ **up** faire basculer; *vi* ~ (**over**) se renverser, basculer
**tip-off** n coll renseignement privé, avertissement privé
**tipple** n coll boisson f alcoolique; *vi* pinter, picoler
**tipsiness** n ivresse f
**tipstaff** n leg huissier m
**tipster** n donneur m de tuyaux
**tipsy** adj gris
**tiptoe** n on ~ sur la pointe des pieds; *vi* marcher sur la pointe des pieds
**tiptop** adj coll extra invar
**tirade** n tirade f
**¹tire** vt fatiguer, lasser; (exhaust) épuiser; (bore) ennuyer; *vi* se fatiguer, se lasser; ~ **of sth** se fatiguer de qch
**²tire** n US see **tyre**
**tired** adj fatigué; **be** ~ (sleepy) avoir sommeil; **get** ~ **of doing sth** se lasser de faire qch; *coll* **he makes me** ~ *sl* il me casse les pieds
**tiredness** n fatigue f, lassitude f

**tireless** adj infatigable, inlassable
**tiresome** adj fatigant; (boring) ennuyeux -euse; (irritating) exaspérant
**tiring** adj fatigant, lassant
**tissue** n tissu m, étoffe f; mouchoir m en papier
**tissue-paper** n papier m de soie
**¹tit** n mésange f
**²tit** n sl mamelle f
**Titan** n Titan m
**titanic** adj titanique
**titbit** n friandise f; (news) canard m
**tit-for-tat** adv à bon chat bon rat; **give s/o** ~ rendre à qn la pareille
**tithe** n hist dîme f; dixième m
**titillate** vt émoustiller, chatouiller
**titillation** n chatouillement m
**titivate** vt pomponner; *vi* se pomponner, se bichonner
**title** n titre m; (right) droit m; (nobility) titre m de noblesse; **have a** ~ **to sth** avoir droit à qch; *vt* intituler
**titled** adj noble, ayant un titre de noblesse
**title-deed** n leg titre m de propriété
**title-holder** n sp détenteur -trice du titre
**title-page** n titre m
**title-role** n theat rôle m qui donne le titre à la pièce
**titmouse** n mésange f
**titter** n (smothered laugh) rire étouffé; (giggle) rire m bête; *vi* avoir un rire étouffé; rire bêtement, ricaner
**tittle-tattle** n cancans mpl, commérages mpl
**titular** adj titulaire
**tizzy** n coll affolement m; **all of a** ~ complètement affolé
**T-junction** n carrefour m en forme de T
**to** prep à; (towards) vers; (till, as far as) jusqu'à; en; (in order to) pour, afin de; (against) contre; (feelings, obligations) envers; ~ **be sold** à vendre; ~ **Canada** au Canada; ~ **England** en Angleterre; ~ **the best of my knowledge** autant que je sache; ~ **the day** jour pour jour; ~ **the house (shop) of** chez; ~ **the trains** accès aux quais; **five** ~ **two** cinq contre deux; (time) deux heures moins cinq; **five trees** ~ **each street** cinq arbres par rue; **from town** ~ **town** de ville en ville; **go** ~ **and fro** aller et venir; **I'd like** ~ je voudrais bien; **I want you** ~ **come** je veux que vous veniez; **keep it** ~ **yourself** gardez ça pour vous; **push the door** ~ fermer la porte; **so** ~ **speak** pour ainsi dire; **there's no one** ~ **ask** il n'y a personne à qui on puisse demander; **there's nothing** ~ **it** c'est facile; (not worth it) ça ne vaut pas la peine; **the way** ~ **X** le chemin pour aller à X; **they died** ~ **a**

man ils sont morts jusqu'au dernier; **trains ~ Paris** les trains à destination de Paris; **walk ~ and fro** aller de long en large; **what's that ~ him?** qu'est-ce que ça peut lui faire?

**toad** n crapaud m

**toad-in-the-hole** n cul saucisses cuites au four dans une pâte à frire

**toadstool** n champignon vénéneux

**toady** n flagorneur -euse; vt + vi flagorner

**toast** n toast m, pain grillé; (drink) toast m; (person) personne f à qui on porte un toast; coll **have s/o on ~** tenir qn; vt griller, rôtir; (person) boire à la santé de, porter un toast à; vi rôtir, griller

**toaster** n grille-pain m invar

**toasting-fork** n fourchette f à toast

**toast-master** n annonceur m des toasts

**toast-rack** n porte-toasts m

**tobacco** n tabac m

**tobacconist** n marchand -e de tabac; (shop) bureau m de tabac

**tobacco-pouch** n blague f à tabac

**toboggan** n toboggan m, luge f; vi faire du toboggan

**toccata** n mus toccata f

**tocsin** n tocsin m

**today** adv aujourd'hui; **~ week** aujourd'hui en huit; **here ~ and gone tomorrow** ce que c'est de nous

**toddle** vi trottiner, marcher à petits pas

**toddler** n coll tout petit (f toute petite) (enfant); enfant qui commence à marcher

**toddy** n grog chaud

**to-do** n coll remue-ménage m invar; (scene) scène f; **what a ~!** quelle histoire!, quelle affaire!

**toe** n doigt m de pied, orteil m; (sock) bout m; (shoe) pointe f; **big ~** gros orteil; **from top to ~** de pied en cap; **on the tip of one's ~s** sur la pointe des pieds; fig **tread on s/o's ~s** offenser qn; vt toucher du bout de l'orteil; **~ the line** se conformer au mot d'ordre

**toe-cap** n bout rapporté

**toehold** n coll prise f précaire

**toenail** n ongle m de pied

**toff** n coll dandy m; personne huppée

**toffee** n caramel m (au beurre)

**toffee-nosed** adj coll bêcheur -euse

**tog** vt + vi **~ up** attifer

**toga** n toge f

**together** adv ensemble; (at the same time) en même temps; **~ with** avec; en même temps que; **all ~** tous (fpl toutes) ensemble; (united) réuni(e)s; (at the same time) tous (fpl toutes) à la fois; **for weeks ~** durant des semaines

**togetherness** n unité f, camaraderie f

**toggle** n barrette f; naut cabillot m (d'amarrage)

**togs** npl coll nippes fpl, frusques fpl

**toil** n peine f, labeur m, travail m pénible; vi peiner, travailler

**toiler** n travailleur -euse

**toilet** n toilette f; (W.C.) cabinets mpl, toilettes fpl, waters mpl

**toilet-paper** n papier m hygiénique

**toiletries** npl articles mpl de toilette

**toilet-roll** n rouleau m de papier hygiénique

**toilet-soap** n savon m de toilette

**toilet-table** n coiffeuse f

**toilet-water** n eau f de toilette

**toils** npl filet m, piège m

**toilsome** adj pénible

**token** n signe m, marque f; (coin) jeton m; (paper) bon m; **in ~ of** en signe de; **love ~** gage m d'amour; adj nominal, symbolique; **~ strike** grève f d'avertissement

**tolerable** adj tolérable, supportable; (fair) passable

**tolerance** n tolérance f

**tolerant** adj tolérant

**tolerate** vt tolérer, supporter

**toleration** n tolérance f

¹**toll** n péage m, droit m de passage; (losses) pertes fpl; US **~ call** communication interurbaine; fig **take ~ of** infliger des pertes à

²**toll** n son m de cloche; vt + vi sonner

**toll-bridge** n pont m à péage

**toll-gate** n barrière f à péage

**toll-road** n route f à péage

**tomahawk** n tomahawk m

**tomato** n tomate f

**tomb** n tombe f; fig mort f

**tombola** n tombola f

**tomboy** n garçon manqué

**tombstone** n pierre tombale

**tom-cat** n matou m

**tome** n tome m

**tomfoolery** n coll bêtises fpl

**tommy-gun** n mitraillette f

**tommy-rot** n coll bêtises fpl

**tomorrow** n lendemain m; adv demain; **~ week** demain en huit; **the day after ~** après-demain

**tomtom** n tam-tam m

**ton** n tonne f; naut tonneau m; coll **~s of** des tas de, des masses de, beaucoup de; coll **do the ~ (up)** faire du cent-soixante à l'heure; fig **weigh a ~** peser un poids énorme

**tonal** adj tonal

**tonality** n tonalité f

**tone** n ton m; (voice) voix f, accent m; mus son m; (pitch) timbre m; (muscles) tonicité f; **in a low ~** d'un ton bas; **in that ~ of voice** sur ce ton; vt phot virer; (skin) tonifier; ~ **down** atténuer, adoucir; (sound) baisser; *vi* (colours) s'harmoniser; ~ **down** se radoucir

**tone-control** *n* bouton *m* de tonalité

**tone-deaf** *adj* affligé de surdité musicale

**toneless** *adj* (sound) atone; (colour) sans éclat

**tongs** *npl* pincettes *fpl*, pinces *fpl*, tenailles *fpl*

**tongue** *n* langue *f*; (shoe) languette *f*; (bell) battant *m*; **hold one's** ~ se taire; **keep a civil** ~ **in one's head** rester poli; **put out one's** ~ tirer la langue; **with** ~ **in cheek** de façon ironique

**tongue-tied** *adj* muet -ette, interdit

**tongue-twister** *n* mot *m* (phrase *f*) difficile à prononcer

**tonic** *n* fortifiant *m*, reconstituant *m*; *mus* tonique *f*; *adj* tonique, réconfortant

**tonight** *n* ce soir; *adv* ce soir; cette nuit

**tonnage** *n* tonnage *m*

**tonne** *n* tonne *f*

**tonsil** *n* amygdale *f*

**tonsillitis** *n* angine *f*, amygdalite *f*

**tonsure** *n* tonsure *f*

**too** *adv* trop, par trop; (moreover) d'ailleurs, de plus; (also) aussi, également; ~ **bad!** dommage!; ~ **little** trop peu; ~ **much** trop; *coll* ~ **true!** et comment!; **a hundred francs** ~ **much** cent francs de trop; *coll* **have had one** ~ **many** être pompette; *coll* **he's** ~ **much for me** il est trop fort pour moi

**tool** *n* outil *m*, instrument *m*; (person) créature *f*; *vulg* membre viril, queue *f*; *vt* travailler, usiner; ~ **up** équiper

**tool-bag** *n* sac *m* à outils

**tool-box** *n* boîte *f* à outils

**tool-maker** *n* fabricant *m* d'outils

**tool-shed** *n* cabane *f* à outils

**toot** *n* mot coup *m* de klaxon; *vi* mot klaxonner, avertir

**tooth** *n* (*pl* **teeth**) dent *f*; ~ **and nail** de toutes ses forces, avec acharnement; *sl* **be fed up to the teeth** en avoir ras le bol; **be long in the** ~ n'être plus très jeune; **cast sth in s/o's teeth** reprocher qch à qn; **cut one's teeth** faire ses dents; **fight** ~ **and nail** se battre avec acharnement; **grind one's teeth** grincer des dents; **grit one's teeth** serrer les dents; **have a sweet** ~ aimer les sucreries; **have a** ~ **out** se faire arracher une dent; **have a** ~ **stopped** faire obturer (plomber) une dent; **in the teeth of** malgré, en dépit de; **set of teeth** (natural) denture *f*; (false) dentier *m*

**toothache** *n* mal *m* de dents; **have (a)** ~ avoir mal aux dents

**toothbrush** *n* brosse *f* à dents

**toothcomb** *n* peigne fin

**toothless** *adj* sans dents, édenté

**toothpaste** *n* pâte *f* dentifrice

**toothpick** *n* cure-dents *m invar*

**tootle** *vi* klaxonner doucement et de façon continue; *coll* mot ~ **along** rouler doucement

¹**top** *n* sommet *m*, cime *f*; (upper side) dessus *m*, surface *f*; (head, upper end) haut *m*; (lid) couvercle *m*; (tree) tête *f*; (roof) faîte *m*; (bottle) capsule *f*; *naut* hune *f*; **at the** ~ **of one's voice** à tue-tête; *coll* **blow one's** ~ s'emporter, se mettre en colère; **come out on** ~ avoir le dessus; **from** ~ **to bottom** de haut en bas, de fond en comble; **from** ~ **to toe** de la tête aux pieds; *mot* **hard** ~ berline *f*; *mot* **in** ~ en prise; **one on** ~ **of the other** l'un (*f* l'une) sur l'autre; (time) l'un (*f* l'une) après l'autre; **on** ~ dessus; **on** ~ **of it all** pour comble, par-dessus le marché; **on the** ~ **of one's form** en pleine forme; **sit at the** ~ **of the table** être assis au bout de la table; *coll* **the** ~ s ce qu'il y a de mieux; **work is getting on** ~ **of him** il est débordé par le travail; *adj* supérieur; principal, premier -ière; du haut, du dessus; ~ **floor** dernier étage; *coll* **be** ~ **dog** être vainqueur; *vt* (tree) étêter; surmonter, couronner, couvrir; (exceed) dépasser, surpasser; ~ **up** remplir (jusqu'au bord); *coll* **let me** ~ **you up!** encore un peu!

²**top** *n* (toy) toupie *f*

**topaz** *n* topaze *f*

**top-boot** *n* botte *f* à revers

**top-coat** *n* pardessus *m*; (paint) couche *f* de finition

**top-dressing** *n* fumure *f* en surface

**toper** *n* *coll* ivrogne *m*, buveur *m*

**top-hat** *n* (chapeau *m*) haut-de-forme *m* (*pl* hauts-de-forme)

**top-heavy** *adj* trop lourd du haut

**topic** *n* sujet *m*, thème *m*

**topical** *adj* courant, d'actualité; *med* topique

**topicality** *n* actualité *f*

**topknot** *n* (hair) chignon *m*; (bird) aigrette *f*

**top-level** *adj* au plus haut niveau, au sommet

**topmast** *n* mât *m* de hune

**topmost** *adj* le plus haut, le plus élevé

**topnotch** *adj* de premier ordre

**topographical** *adj* topographique

**topography** *n* topographie *f*

**topper** *n* *coll* (person) type épatant; (hat) (chapeau *m*) haut-de-forme *m* (*pl* hauts-de-forme)

**topple** *vt* faire tomber; ~ **over** faire

tomber, renverser; *vi* ~ **down (over)** tomber, s'écrouler, dégringoler

**topsail** *n naut* hunier *m*

**top-secret** *adj* très secret -ète

**topside** *n cul* tende *f* de tranche

**topsy-turvy** *adj + adv* sens dessus dessous

**torch** *n* torche *f*, flambeau *m*; (electric) lampe *f* électrique de poche

**torchlight** *n by* ~ à la lueur des flambeaux; ~ **procession** cortège *m* aux flambeaux

**toreador** *n* toréador *m*

**torment** *n* supplice *m*, torture *f*; tourment *m*; **be in** ~ être au supplice; *vt* torturer, tourmenter

**tormentor** *n* bourreau *m*, persécuteur -trice

**tornado** *n* tornade *f*, ouragan *m*

**torpedo** *n* torpille *f*; *vt* torpiller

**torpedo-boat** *n* (small) vedette *f* lance-torpilles, torpilleur *m*

**torpedo-tube** *n* lance-torpilles *m*

**torpid** *adj* engourdi, inerte

**torpidity** *n* engourdissement *m*, inertie *f*, torpeur *f*

**torpidly** *adv* de façon léthargique

**torpor** *n* torpeur *f*

**torque** *n mech* moment *m* de torsion, couple moteur

**torrefy** *vt* torréfier

**torrent** *n* torrent *m*

**torrential** *adj* torrentiel -ielle

**torrid** *adj* torride

**torso** *n* torse *m*

**tort** *n leg* dommage *m*, fait délictueux

**tortoise** *n* tortue *f*

**tortoiseshell** *n* écaille *f* (de tortue)

**tortuosity** *n* tortuosité *f*

**tortuous** *adj* tortueux -euse

**tortuousness** *n see* **tortuosity**

**torture** *n* torture *f*, question *f*, supplice *m*; *vt* torturer, mettre à la torture

**torturer** *n* bourreau *m*, tortionnaire *m*

**tosh** *n coll* bêtises *fpl*

**toss** *n* lancement *m*, jet *m*; (head) mouvement impatient; *sp* tirage *m* au sort; (coin) coup *m* de pile ou face; (fall) chute *f*; **argue the** ~ continuer à argumenter une fois la dispute réglée; *vt* lancer, jeter; (head) secouer; (horse) démonter; *cul* sauter; (salad) fatiguer; ~ **about** ballotter; ~ **a coin** jouer à pile ou face; ~ **aside** jeter de côté; ~ **off** (drink) avaler d'un trait; (work) expédier; *vi* ~ **about** s'agiter, se retourner; ~ **for sth** jouer qch à pile ou face; ~ **on the waves** être ballotté par les vagues; **pitch and** ~ tanguer

**toss-up** *n* (coin) coup *m* de pile ou face; **it's a** ~ c'est une affaire de chance

¹**tot** *n* (person) tout petit (toute petite),

marmot *m*; (drink) petit verre, goutte *f*

²**tot** *vt* ~ **up** additionner; *vi* s'élever

**total** *n* total *m*, montant *m*; *adj* total, entier -ière, complet -ète; *vt* additionner; *vi* totaliser; **it** ~ **s up to a big amount** cela s'élève à une somme considérable

**totalisator** *n see* **totalizator**

**totalitarian** *adj* totalitaire

**totalitarianism** *n* totalitarisme *m*

**totality** *n* totalité *f*

**totalizator, totalisator** *n* totalisateur *m*; *sp* = Pari Mutuel Urbain (P.M.U.)

**totally** *adv* totalement, complètement

**totem** *n* totem *m*

**totter** *vi* chanceler; (building) menacer ruine; ~ **in** entrer d'un pas chancelant

**tottery** *adj* chancelant

**toucan** *n* toucan *m*

**touch** *n* (sense) toucher *m*; (feel) contact *m*; communication *f*, rapport *m*, contact *m*; (painting) touche *f*, coup *m* de pinceau; *mus* toucher *m*; (bit) pointe *f*, soupçon *m*; (tiny blow) léger coup; **finishing** ~ dernière main; **get (keep) in** ~ **with** entrer (rester) en contact avec; *sp* **kick into** ~ envoyer en touche; **out of** ~ **with** pas au courant de; *vt* toucher; (feeling) émouvoir; (affect) affecter, produire de l'effet sur; (reach) atteindre; (meddle, be adjacent to) toucher à; (graze) effleurer; (equal) égaler; ~ **off** faire exploser; *coll* ~ **s/o for a hundred francs** taper qn de cent francs; ~ **up** faire des retouches à, retoucher; *sl* **peloter**; ~ **wood!** touche du bois!; **there's no one to** ~ **him** personne ne lui arrive à la cheville; **they can't** ~ **me** ils ne peuvent rien contre moi; *vi* se toucher, venir en contact; ~ **down** atterrir; *sp* marquer un essai; ~ **on** effleurer

**touch-and-go** *adj* risqué; **it was** ~! il était moins cinq!

**touchdown** *n* atterrissage *m*; (sea) amerrissage *m*

**touché** *interj* touché!

**touched** *adj* touché, ému; *coll* piqué, timbré

**touchiness** *n* susceptibilité *f*

**touching** *adj* touchant, émouvant; *prep* concernant, touchant

**touch-line** *n* ligne *f* de touche

**touchstone** *n* pierre *f* de touche

**touch-type** *vi* taper au toucher

**touch-typist** *n* dactylo *f* qui tape au toucher

**touchy** *adj* susceptible

**tough** *n* dur *m*; *adj* dur; (hard-wearing) résistant, solide; (work) difficile

**toughen** *vt* durcir; (person) endurcir

**toughly** *adv* avec ténacité, opiniâtrement

**toughness** n dureté f; résistance f, solidité f; (work) difficulté f
**toupee** n toupet m
**tour** n tour m, excursion f; mil + theat tournée f; vt voyager dans, faire le tour de; theat faire une tournée dans; vi voyager, faire du tourisme
**tour-de-force** n tour m de force
**tourer** n voiture f décapotable
**touring** n tourisme m; adj qui fait du tourisme; (troupe) en tournée
**tourism** n tourisme m
**tourist** n touriste f; ~ **office** syndicat m d'initiative
**tourmaline** n min tourmaline f
**tournament** n tournoi m
**tourniquet** n tourniquet m
**tour-operator** n organisateur m de voyages
**tousle** vt (hair) ébouriffer
**tout** n racoleur m; (racing) pronostiqueur m; **ticket** ~ revendeur m de billets; vi (racing) vendre des pronostics; ~ **for** racoler, courir après
¹**tow** n (hemp) étoupe f
²**tow** n remorque f; **take a boat in** ~ prendre un bateau à la remorque; vt remorquer; (from path) haler; ~ **away** (parked car) mettre en fourrière
**towards, toward** prep vers, du côté de; (feelings, etc) envers, à l'égard de; (purpose) pour; ~ **six o'clock** vers six heures
**towel** n serviette f; (small) essuie-mains m; **sanitary** ~ serviette f hygiénique; **Turkish** ~ serviette f éponge; vt essuyer avec une serviette
**towelling** n tissu-éponge m (pl tissus-éponges)
**towel-rail** n porte-serviettes m
**tower** n tour f; (church) clocher m; ~ **of strength** puissant appui; **water** ~ château m d'eau; vi s'élever, dominer; ~ **over** dominer
**towering** adj très haut; fig (rage) terrible, violent
**towline** n remorque f, corde f de halage
**town** n ville f; **country** ~ ville f de province; **county** ~ = ville f de préfecture; coll fig **go to** ~ bien s'amuser; coll fig **go to** ~ **on sth** ne pas regarder à la dépense; (make effort) mettre le paquet; **man about** ~ mondain m; adj de la ville, urbain, municipal
**town-clerk** n secrétaire m de mairie
**town-council** n conseil municipal
**town-councillor** n conseiller -ère municipal -e
**town-crier** n tambour m de ville
**town-hall** n mairie f, hôtel m de ville
**town-planner** n urbaniste m
**town-planning** n urbanisme m

**townsfolk** npl habitants mpl d'une ville
**township** n commune f
**townsman** n citadin m
**townspeople** npl habitants mpl d'une ville, citadins mpl
**towpath** n chemin m de halage
**tow-rope** n corde f de halage
**toxaemia** n toxémie f
**toxic** adj toxique
**toxicologist** n toxicologue m
**toxicology** n toxicologie f
**toxin** n toxine f
**toy** n jouet m, joujou m; ~ **soldier** soldat m de plomb; ~ **train** petit train; vi jouer; ~ **with an idea** caresser une idée; ~ **with one's food** manger du bout des dents
**toyshop** n magasin m de jouets
**trace** n trace f, vestige m; vt tracer; (follow) suivre, suivre la piste de; (recover) recouvrer; (on paper) calquer; ~ **out** esquisser; ~ **sth back to its source** remonter à l'origine de qch
**traceable** adj que l'on peut tracer
**tracer** n traceur m; ~ **bullet** balle traçante
**tracery** n archi réseau m, entrelacs m
**trachea** n anat trachée f
**tracheotomy** n trachéotomie f
**tracing** n tracé m; calque m
**tracing-paper** n papier-calque m invar
**track** n (path) chemin m, sentier m; (animal, footprints) piste f, trace f; (metal belt round wheel) chenille f; (rail) voie f; (bullet) trajectoire f; **be on s/o's** ~ (s) être sur la trace de qn; **be on the wrong** ~ faire fausse route; **keep** ~ **of s/o** ne pas perdre qn de vue; coll **make** ~**s** filer; **on the right** ~ sur la bonne voie; vt (animal) suivre à la piste; (criminal) traquer; ~ **down** dépister; vi cin faire un travel(l)ing
**tracked** adj (vehicle) à chenilles
**tracker** n traqueur m
**tracker-dog** n limier m, chien policier
**trackless** adj sans chemins; (vehicle) sans chenilles
¹**tract** n étendue f, région f; anat voie f
²**tract** n (document) brochure f, tract m
**tractability** n docilité f
**tractable** adj traitable, docile
**traction** n traction f
**traction-engine** n locomobile f
**tractor** n tracteur m; ~**-drawn** tracté
**trad** adj coll traditionnel -elle
**trade** n commerce m, affaires fpl, négoce m; (calling) métier (manuel), emploi m; (body) corps m de métier; ~**s** (winds) alizés mpl; ~ **secret** secret m de fabrication; **be in the** ~ être du métier; **be in** ~ être dans le commerce; **by** ~ de son (leur, etc) état; **each to his**

own ~ chacun son métier; **free** ~ libre-échange m; vt faire trafic de; ~ **in** donner en reprise; ~ **sth for sth** troquer qch contre qch; vi faire le commerce, faire des affaires, trafiquer

**trade-mark** n marque f de fabrique; **registered** ~ marque déposée

**trade-name** n nom m de marque, appellation f

**trade-price** n prix m à la production (fabrique)

**trader** n négociant -e, commerçant -e, marchand -e

**tradesman** n marchand m, commerçant m; ~ **'s entrance** entrée f de service

**trade-union** n syndicat (ouvrier)

**trade-unionism** n syndicalisme (ouvrier)

**trade-unionist** n syndiqué -e, syndicaliste, ouvrier -ière syndiqué -e

**trade-wind** n vent alizé, alizé m

**trading-stamp** n timbre-prime m (pl timbres-prime)

**tradition** n tradition f

**traditional** adj traditionnel -elle

**traditionalism** n traditionalisme m

**traditionalist** n traditionaliste

**traditionally** adv traditionnellement

**traduce** vt calomnier, diffamer

**traffic** n trafic m, commerce m, négoce m; (movement) mouvement m; (vehicles) circulation (routière); US ~ **circle** rond-point m (pl ronds-points); ~ **congestion** embouteillage m; **one-way** ~ sens m unique; **rail** ~ transport m (trafic m) ferroviaire; vi trafiquer

**trafficator** n mot flèche f de direction

**traffic-block** n embouteillage m

**traffic-controller** n aer contrôleur -euse de la navigation aérienne, coll aiguilleur m du ciel

**traffic-jam** n embouteillage m, encombrement m (de la circulation)

**trafficker** n trafiquant -e

**traffic-lights** npl feux mpl de circulation

**traffic-sign** n panneau m de signalisation

**traffic-warden** n contractuel -elle

**tragedian** n auteur m tragique; tragédien -ienne

**tragedy** n tragédie f; fig drame m

**tragic** adj tragique

**tragi-comedy** n tragi-comédie f

**tragi-comic** adj tragi-comique

**trail** n traînée f; (track) piste f, voie f; US sentier m; **on the** ~ **of** sur la piste de; **pick up the** ~ retrouver la piste; vt traquer, suivre à la piste; (drag) traîner; ~ **sth along** traîner qch après soi; vi traîner; (plants) grimper; ~ **along** se traîner; ~ **off** se perdre

**trailer** n (person) traqueur m; (vehicle) remorque f; US caravane f, roulotte f; cin extrait de film (projeté à des fins

publicitaires); US ~ **park** caravan(n)ing m; US ~ **truck** semi-remorque f

¹**train** n train m, convoi m; (retinue) suite f; (dress) traîne f, queue f; (succession) succession f, série f; (trail) traînée f; ~ **of thought** enchaînement m d'idées; **on the** ~ dans le train; **the** ~ **is in** le train est en gare

²**train** vt former, instruire; (animal) dresser; sp entraîner; (plant) diriger; (gun) braquer, pointer; vi s'exercer; sp s'entraîner

**train-bearer** n eccles caudataire m; (wedding) demoiselle f d'honneur, page m

**trainee** n stagiaire, élève

**trainer** n sp entraîneur m; (animals) dresseur -euse; aer avion-école m (pl avions-école)

**train-ferry** n ferry-boat m

**training** n sp entraînement m; éducation f, formation f, instruction f; (animals) dressage m; **physical** ~ éducation f physique

**training-college** n école normale

**training-ship** n navire-école m (pl navires-école)

**train-sickness** n mal m de train

**traipse, trapse** vi coll se balader, traîner çà et là; coll ~ **in** s'amener

**trait** n trait m de caractère

**traitor** n traître m

**traitorous** adj traître -esse, perfide

**traitress** n traîtresse f

**trajectory** n trajectoire f

**tram** n tramway m

**tram-car** n tram m, voiture f de tramway

**tramline** n voie f du tramway; ~ **s** (tennis) couloir m

**trammel** n entrave f; vt entraver

**tramp** n (noise) bruit m de pas; (walk) marche f, excursion f à pied; (person) vagabond -e, clochard -e, chemineau m; US prostituée f; naut cargo m; vt ~ **the streets** battre le pavé; vi marcher lourdement; (travel) aller à pied

**trample** vt ~ **down** piétiner, fouler; ~ **underfoot** fouler aux pieds; vi ~ **on** sth piétiner qch, marcher sur qch

**trampoline** n tremplin m de gymnastique

**tramway** n tramway m

**trance** n extase f; (hypnotic) transe f; **fall into a** ~ tomber en transe

**tranny** n coll abbr transistor m

**tranquil** adj tranquille, paisible, calme

**tranquillity** n tranquillité f, calme m

**tranquillize** vt tranquilliser

**tranquillizer** n tranquillisant m, calmant m

**transact** vt traiter; ~ **business with s/o** faire des affaires avec qn

**transaction** n transaction f, affaire f; (action) conduite f (d'une affaire), gestion f; **commercial** ~ opération commerciale

**transalpine** adj transalpin

**transatlantic** adj transatlantique

**transcend** vt surpasser, aller au delà de; philos transcender

**transcendence** n transcendance f

**transcendent** adj transcendant

**transcendental** adj transcendantal

**transcendentalism** n transcendantalisme m

**transcontinental** adj transcontinental

**transcribe** vt transcrire

**transcript** n copie f, transcription f

**transcription** n transcription f

**transept** n transept m

**transfer** n transport m; (official) déplacement m; (shares, rights) transfert m; (picture) décalcomanie f; (funds) virement m; vt transférer; (official) déplacer; leg céder; (funds) virer; (printing) décalquer

**transferability** n transmissibilité f

**transferable** adj transmissible

**transferee** n leg cessionnaire

**transference** n transfert m

**transfiguration** n transfiguration f

**transfigure** vt transfigurer

**transfix** vt transpercer; ~ **with fear** pétrifier de terreur

**transform** vt transformer; convertir

**transformation** n transformation f; conversion f

**transformer** n elect transformateur m

**transfuse** vt transfuser

**transfusion** n transfusion f

**transgress** vi transgresser

**transgression** n transgression f, violation f; (sin) péché m

**transgressor** n transgresseur m; (sinner) pécheur (f pécheresse)

**transience** n caractère m transitoire, nature passagère

**transient** adj transitoire, éphémère

**transistor** n transistor m

**transistorize** vt transistoriser, équiper de transistors

**transit** n (movement) passage m; transport m; (customs) transit m

**transition** n transition f; ~ **period** période f de transition

**transitional** adj de transition

**transitive** adj gramm transitif -ive

**transitory** adj transitoire, passager -ère

**translatable** adj traduisible

**translate** vt traduire; (bishop) transférer

**translation** n traduction f; (bishop) translation f

**translator** n traducteur -trice

**transliterate** vt transcrire

**translucence** n translucidité f

**translucent** adj translucide

**transmissible** adj transmissible

**transmission** n transmission f

**transmit** vt transmettre

**transmitter** n transmetteur m; rad émetteur m

**transmutable** adj transmuable

**transmutation** n transmutation f

**transmute** vt transformer

**transom** n traverse f; (lintel) linteau m

**transparence** n transparence f

**transparency** n transparence f; phot diapositive f

**transparent** adj transparent; (evident) clair, évident

**transpire** vt (liquid) exsuder; (smell) exhaler; vi transpirer; (occur) se passer

**transplant** n surg greffe f; vt transplanter; surg greffer

**transplantation** n transplantation f

**transport** n transport m; ~ **café** restaurant routier, restaurant m des routiers; ~ **plane** avion m de transport; vt transporter; leg hist déporter

**transportation** n US transport m; leg hist déportation f

**transporter** n transporteur m; **tank** ~ porte-chars m invar

**transporter-bridge** n pont transbordeur m

**transpose** vt transposer

**transposition** n transposition f

**transubstantiate** vt changer en une autre substance

**transubstantiation** n transsubstantiation f

**transversal** adj transversal

**transverse** adj transversal, en travers

**transvestism, transvestitism** n travestisme m

**transvestite** n travesti -e

**trap** n piège m, trappe f, traquenard m; (rabbits, etc) collet m; fig piège m, ruse f; (vehicle) carriole f; sl gueule f; **be caught in the** ~ se laisser prendre au piège; **set a** ~ tendre un piège; **walk into the** ~ donner dans le panneau; vt prendre au piège, attraper; (cut off) bloquer, coincer

**trap-door** n trappe f

**trapeze** n trapèze m; ~ **artist** trapéziste

**trapper** n trappeur m

**trappings** npl ornements mpl; (finery) atours mpl

**Trappist** n trappiste m; adj de la Trappe

**trapse** vi see traipse

**trash** n camelote f, choses fpl sans valeur; US détritus mpl, ordures fpl; US coll pej (people) racaille f; US coll pej **white** ~ blancs (f blanches) pauvres

**trash-can** n US poubelle f

**trashy** *adj* sans valeur

**trauma** *n* trauma *m*, traumatisme *m*

**traumatic** *adj* traumatique; (distressing) traumatisant

**travail** *n* peine *f*; (birth pains) douleurs *fpl* de l'enfantement; *vi* peiner; (childbirth) être en travail

**travel** *n* voyage *m*, voyages *mpl*; *vt* (distance) parcourir, faire; *vi* voyager; (light) se propager; (news) se répandre; (vehicle) marcher; *comm* être voyageur de commerce; *comm* ~ **in wine** être représentant en vins

**travel-agency** *n* agence *f* de voyages (tourisme)

**travel-bureau** *n* bureau *m* de tourisme

**travelled** *adj* **much** ~ qui a beaucoup voyagé

**traveller** *n* voyageur -euse; (commercial) représentant *m*, voyageur *m* de commerce; ~'**s cheque** chèque *m* de voyage; *bot* ~'**s joy** clématite *f* des haies

**travelling-bag** *n* sac *m* de voyage

**travelogue** *n* *coll* documentaire *m* de voyage

**traversable** *adj* traversable, franchissable

**traverse** *n* traversée *f*; *mech* traverse *f*; *vt* traverser, passer

**travesty** *n* travestissement *m*, parodie *f*

**trawl** *n* chalut *m*; *vi* pêcher au chalut

**trawler** *n* chalutier *m*

**tray** *n* plateau *m*

**treacherous** *adj* traître -esse, perfide

**treachery** *n* perfidie *f*, trahison *f*

**treacle** *n* mélasse *f*

**tread** *n* pas *m*; (sound) bruit *m* de(s) pas; (stairs) marche *f*; (tyre) chape *f*; *vt* fouler; ~ **underfoot** fouler aux pieds; ~ **water** battre debout; **well-trodden path** chemin battu; *vi* marcher; ~ **on** poser les pieds sur

**treadle, treddle** *n* pédale *f*

**treadmill** *n* *agr* trépigneuse *f*; *fig* besogne quotidienne, routine ingrate

**treason** *n* trahison *f*

**treasonable** *adj* de trahison, perfide

**treasure** *n* trésor *m*; ~ **hunt** chasse *f* au trésor; *vt* priser, tenir beaucoup à; (take care of) garder soigneusement

**treasure-house** *n* trésor *m*

**treasurer** *n* trésorier -ière

**treasure-trove** *n* trésor caché et découvert par hasard

**treasury** *n* trésorerie *f*, trésor public; **the Treasury** = le ministère des Finances

**treat** *n* régal *m*, plaisir *m*, fête *f*; (outing) sortie *f*; **a** ~ **in store** un plaisir à venir; **stand** ~ **all round** payer la tournée; *vt* traiter; (drink) payer à boire à; (regale) régaler; *med* soigner; ~ **oneself to sth**

se payer qch, s'offrir qch; *adv phr coll* **a** ~ très bien

**treatise** *n* traité *m*

**treatment** *n* traitement *m*; *med* traitement médical; ~ **of one's friends** manière *f* d'agir envers ses amis

**treaty** *n* traité *m*; contrat *m*, accord *m*

**treble** *n* triple *m*; *mus* soprano *m*; *adj* triple; *mus* de soprano; ~ **clef** clef *f* de sol; *vt* + *vi* tripler

**treddle** *n* *see* **treadle**

**tree** *n* arbre *m*; (beam) poutre *f*; *fig* **be at the top of the** ~ être au haut de l'échelle; *coll* **be up a** ~ être dans le pétrin; **climb a** ~ grimper sur un arbre; **family** ~ arbre *m* généalogique; **shoe** ~ tendeur *m*

**treeless** *adj* sans arbres

**trek** *n* voyage (long et pénible); *vi* *ar* voyager en chariot; faire un voyage long et pénible

**trellis(-work)** *n* treillis *m*, treillage *m*

**tremble** *n* frisson *m*, tremblement *m*; (voice) tremblotement *m*; **all of a** ~ tout tremblant; *vi* trembler, frissonner

**trembler** *n* trembleur -euse; *elect* trembleur *m*

**tremendous** *adj* énorme, immense; (marvellous) formidable

**tremolo** *n* *mus* trémolo *m*

**tremor** *n* tremblement *m*, frémissement *m*

**tremulous** *adj* tremblotant, tremblant

**trench** *n* tranchée *f*, fossé *m*; *vt* creuser un fossé dans; *vi* ~ **on** empiéter sur

**trenchant** *adj* tranchant, incisif -ive, mordant

**trench-coat** *n* trench-coat *m*

**trend** *n* tendance *f*, direction *f*

**trend-setting** *adj* à l'avant-garde de la mode

**trendy** *adj* dans le vent

**trepan** *vt* trépaner

**trepanning** *n* *surg* trépanation *f*

**trepidation** *n* trépidation *f*

**trespass** *n* *leg* violation *f* de propriété; (crime) délit *m*; (sin) péché *m*; *vi* (sin) pécher; ~ **against the law** enfreindre la loi; ~ **on** (domain) empiéter sur; (kindness) abuser de; ~ **on s/o's property** pénétrer sans autorité sur la propriété de qn

**trespasser** *n* (property) intrus -e; ~ **s will be prosecuted** défense d'entrer sous peine d'amende

**tress** *n* tresse *f*, boucle *f*

**trestle** *n* tréteau *m*, chevalet *m*

**triad** *n* triade *f*

**trial** *n* essai *m*, épreuve *f*; (law) procès *m*, jugement *m*, cause *f*; *leg* **go on** ~ passer en jugement; **on** ~ à l'essai; *adj* d'essai; ~ **balance** balance *f*

d'inventaire; ~ **run** essai *m*
**triangle** *n* triangle *m*
**triangular** *adj* triangulaire
**triangulate** *vt* trianguler
**triangulation** *n* triangulation *f*
**tribal** *adj* de tribu, de la tribu, tribal
**tribalism** *n* tribalisme *m*
**tribe** *n* tribu *f*
**tribesman** *n* membre *m* de la tribu
**tribulation** *n* tribulation *f*
**tribunal** *n* tribunal *m*, cour *f* de justice
**tributary** *n* tributaire *m*; (river) affluent *m*; *adj* tributaire
**tribute** *n* tribut *m*; *fig* hommage *m*
**trice** *n* in a ~ en un clin d'œil
**trick** *n* tour *m*; (dodge) ruse *f*; (practical joke) farce *f*, blague *f*; (habit) manie *f*, tic *m*, habitude *f*; ~ **of the trade** truc *m*; **conjuring** ~ tour de passe-passe; **dirty** ~ vilain tour; **know a** ~ **or two** avoir plus d'un tour dans son sac; **play a** ~ **on s/o** jouer un tour à qn; **that will do the** ~ ça fera l'affaire; *vt* duper, attraper; ~ **out** attifer
**trick-cyclist** *n* cycliste-acrobate (*pl* cyclistes-acrobates); *coll* psychiatre
**trickery** *n* tromperie *f*, fourberie *f*
**trickiness** *n* difficulté *f*
**trickle** *n* filet *m*; *vt* laisser dégoutter; *vi* couler (goutte à goutte); ~ **in** (liquid) s'infiltrer; (people) entrer par petits groupes
**trickling** *n* écoulement *m*
**trick-rider** *n* voltigeur *m*
**trickster** *n* escroc *m*, fourbe *m*
**tricky** *adj* rusé, astucieux -ieuse; (subtle) fin; compliqué; (difficult) difficile, délicat, épineux -euse
**tricycle** *n* tricycle *m*
**tricyclist** *n* tricycliste
**trident** *n* trident *m*
**tried** *adj* éprouvé
**triennial** *adj* qui a lieu une fois tous les trois ans, trisannuel -elle
**trier** *n* *coll* he's a ~ il fait toujours de son mieux
**trifle** *n* bagatelle *f*, rien *m*; *cul* = diplomate *m*; *adv phr* a ~ un peu; *vi* badiner; ~ **away one's time** perdre son temps; ~ **with one's health** jouer avec sa santé; ~ **with s/o** se jouer de qn
**trifler** *n* personne *f* frivole
**trifling** *adj* insignifiant, peu important
**trigger** *n* détente *f*, gâchette *f*; *vt* ~ **off** déclencher
**trigonometry** *n* trigonométrie *f*
**trike** *n* *coll* tricycle *m*
**trilateral** *adj* trilatéral
**trilby** *n* chapeau *m* en feutre, feutre *m*
**trilingual** *adj* trilingue

**trill** *n* *mus* trille *f*; *vt* *mus* triller; *vi* *mus* faire des trilles
**trilogy** *n* trilogie *f*
**trim** *n* bon ordre; (person) **in good** ~ en bonne forme; (things) **in perfect** ~ en parfait état; *adj* propre, soigné, en bon ordre, en bon état; *vt* arranger, mettre en ordre; (shape) tailler; (hair) rafraîchir; (dress) orner, garnir, parer; (sails) orienter; (boat) équilibrer, redresser; (lamp) émécher; (cargo) arrimer; ~ **up** (hat) garnir à neuf
**trimly** *adv* proprement, en bon ordre
**trimmer** *n* (hats) garnisseur -euse; *naut* arrimeur *m*; *coll* opportuniste
**trimming** *n* arrangement *m*; (hedge) taille *f*; (hats) garnissage *m*; (decoration) ornement *m*, garniture *f*; (cargo) arrimage *m*; (clothes) passementerie *f*; *cul* ~ **s** garniture *f*
**trimness** *n* élégance *f*, air bien tenu
**trinity** *n* groupe *m* de trois; *eccles* **Trinity** la Trinité
**trinket** *n* colifichet *m*, breloque *f*; (jewel) petit bijou
**trio** *n* trio *m*
**trip** *n* excursion *f*, voyage *m* d'agrément, tour *m*; (stumble) faux pas, faute *f*, croche-pied *m*; *sl* (drugs) trip *m*; **go for a** ~ faire une excursion; *vt* faire un croc-en-jambe à; (obstacle) faire trébucher; *fig* ~ **s/o up** prendre qn en défaut; *vi* trébucher, faire un faux pas; ~ **along** aller d'un pas léger; *fig* ~ **up** commettre une faute
**tripartite** *adj* tripartite
**tripe** *n* *cul* gras-double *m*; *coll* *fig* bêtises *fpl*; ~ **shop** triperie *f*
**triple** *adj* triple
**triplet** *n* *mus* triolet *m*; *pros* tercet *m*; ~ **s** triplés *mpl* (*fpl* triplées)
**triplicate** *n* triplicata *m*; **in** ~ en triple exemplaire; *adj* triple, triplé; *vt* tripler; rédiger en trois exemplaires
**tripod** *n* trépied *m*
**tripos** *n* = examen *m* de licence (à Cambridge)
**tripper** *n* excursionniste
**tripping** *adj* courant (marchant) d'un pas léger
**triptych** *n* triptyque *m*
**trip-wire** *n* fil *m* de détente, fil tendu
**trisect** *vt* triséquer
**trite** *adj* banal (*pl* banals), rebattu
**triteness** *n* banalité *f*
**triumph** *n* triomphe *m*; succès *m*; *vi* triompher
**triumphal** *adj* triomphal
**triumphant** *adj* triomphant
**triumvirate** *n* triumvirat *m*
**trivet** *n* trépied *m*
**trivia** *npl* riens *mpl*

**trivial** adj sans importance, insignifiant

**triviality** n insignifiance f; (remark) banalité f

**trochee** n pros trochée m

**troglodyte** n troglodyte m

**Trojan** n Troyen -enne; **work like a ~** travailler comme un nègre; adj troyen -enne; **~ horse** cheval m de Troie; **the ~ War** la guerre de Troie

¹**troll** n chanson f à reprises; vt chantonner; (fishing) pêcher à la cuiller

²**troll** n troll m

**trolley** n chariot m; (basket) poussette f; (porter) diable m; (dishes) table roulante; elect trolley m; (supermarket) caddie m

**trolley-bus** n trolleybus m

**trollop** n souillon f, putain f

**trombone** n trombone m

**troop** n troupe f, bande f; **~s** soldats mpl, troupes fpl; vt **~ the colours** présenter le drapeau; vi **~ in (out)** entrer (sortir) en bande

**trooper** n mil soldat m de cavalerie

**troop-ship** n transport m de troupes

**troop-train** n train m militaire

**trophy** n trophée m

**tropic** n tropique m

**tropical** adj tropical

**trot** n trot m; **at a ~** au trot; **at an easy (a slow) ~** au petit trot; **at full ~** au grand trot; vt faire trotter; coll **~ sth out** sortir qch; vi trotter, aller au trot; **~ away (off)** partir au trot

**trotter** n (horse, mare) trotteur -euse; (pig, sheep) pied m

**trouble** n (grief) chagrin m, peine f; (difficulty) difficulté f, problème m; (bother) dérangement m, peine f, ennui m; (worry) inquiétude f, souci m; mech panne f, avarie f; **ask for ~** se préparer des ennuis; **be in ~** avoir des ennuis; coll **get a girl into ~** rendre une fille enceinte; **get into ~** s'attirer des ennuis; **go to a great deal of ~** se donner beaucoup de mal; **have heart (etc) ~** souffrir du cœur (etc); **it's not worth the ~** cela ne vaut pas la peine; **make ~** semer la discorde; **money ~s** soucis mpl d'argent; **take the ~ to** se donner la peine de; **that's no ~** cela ne me dérange nullement; **what's the ~?** qu'est-ce qui ne va pas?; vt (grieve) affliger, chagriner; (worry) inquiéter, préoccuper; (bother) ennuyer; (disturb) déranger; **~ oneself about sth** se mettre en peine de qch; **~ oneself to do sth** se donner la peine de faire qch; **could I ~ you for the salt?** voudriez-vous s'il vous plaît me passer le sel?; vi (worry) s'inquiéter; (inconvenience) se déranger, se donner la peine

**troublemaker** n fauteur -trice, provocateur -trice, fomentateur -trice de troubles

**troubleshooter** n conciliateur m; mech dépanneur m

**troublesome** adj ennuyeux -euse, gênant, incommode

**troublespot** n point chaud

**trough** n auge f; (drinking) abreuvoir m; (kneading) pétrin m; (wave) creux m; meteor dépression f

**trounce** vt rosser, rouer de coups; (defeat) écraser; (scold) réprimander

**troupe** n troupe f

**trouper** n membre m d'une troupe, acteur -trice chevronné -e

**trouser-clip** n pince f à pantalon

**trousered** adj à pantalon, portant un pantalon

**trousers** npl pantalon m, pantalons mpl; coll **she's the one who wears the ~** c'est elle qui porte le pantalon; **short ~** culottes courtes

**trouser-suit** n tailleur-pantalon m (pl tailleurs-pantalons)

**trousseau** n trousseau m

**trout** n truite f

**trowel** n truelle f

**truancy** n absence f de l'école sans raison valable

**truant** n élève absent -e de l'école sans raison valable; **play ~** faire l'école buissonnière

**truce** n trêve f

¹**truck** n (barter) troc m, échange m; US produits maraîchers; US **~ farmer** maraîcher -ère; **have no ~ with** n'avoir rien à faire avec; vt troquer, échanger

²**truck** n chariot m; (railway) wagon m à marchandises; US camion m; min benne f; US **delivery ~** camionnette f

**truculence** n férocité f

**truculent** adj féroce, farouche, brutal

**trudge** n marche f pénible; vi marcher péniblement (lourdement)

**true** n **out of ~** (post, etc) hors d'aplomb; (axle) faussé; (wheel) décentré; adj vrai, véridique; (genuine) véritable, authentique, réel -elle; (faithful) fidèle, loyal; (accurate) juste, exact; leg **~ copy** copie f conforme; **come ~** se réaliser, se vérifier; **the same holds ~ in respect of** il en est de même pour; adv vraiment; (correctly) juste; vt ajuster, rectifier

**true-blue** adj coll loyal; à toute épreuve

**true-born** adj légitime

**true-bred** adj de race, (de) pur sang invar

**true-hearted** adj au cœur fidèle, loyal; sincère

**true-love** n bien aimé -e

**truffle** n truffe f

**truism** n truisme m, coll vérité f de la Palisse

**truly** adv vraiment; véritablement; justement; **(really and)** ~? vrai de vrai?; **(I am), (Sir), yours** ~ je vous prie de croire, Monsieur, à l'expression de mes sentiments respectueux; coll **yours** ~ votre humble serviteur m; sl bibi m

**trump** n atout m; coll bon type; **turn up** ~s (be helpful) être d'un grand secours; faire des merveilles; vt (cards) couper; ~ **up** inventer, fabriquer; vi jouer atout

**trump-card** n atout m; fig atout (majeur), carte maîtresse

**trumpery** adj (goods) sans valeur, de camelote; (argument) spécieux -ieuse

**trumpet** n trompette f; (person) trompettiste, trompette m; **blow one's own** ~ se vanter; fig **with a flourish of** ~s à cor et à cri; vt publier à son de trompe; ~ **abroad** proclamer; vi sonner de la trompette; (elephant) barrir

**trumpet-call** n sonnerie f de trompette

**trumpeter** n mil trompette m; mus trompettiste

**trumpeting** n (elephant) barrissement m

**truncate** vt tronquer

**truncheon** n bâton m, matraque f

**trundle** vt faire rouler; (barrow) pousser

**trunk** n (tree, body) tronc m; (luggage) malle f; med bandage m herniaire; vt (hay) mettre en bottes; bui renforcer; cul trousser; (tie) lier

**trunk-call** n (telephone) communication interurbaine

**trunk-line** n (railway) grande ligne; (telephone) ligne interurbaine

**trunk-road** n route nationale, grande route

**trunks** npl slip m

**truss** n bui armature f, ferme f; (hay) botte f; med bandage m herniaire; vt (hay) mettre en bottes; bui renforcer; cul trousser; (tie) lier

**trust** n confiance f; (hope) espoir m, espérance f; (office) charge f; (responsibility) responsabilité f; (care) garde f, dépôt m; (industry) trust m, cartel m; leg fidéicommis m; comm **on** ~ à crédit; vt avoir confiance en, se fier à; comm faire crédit à; (believe) croire; iron ~ **him!** ça, c'est bien lui!; ~ **oneself to do sth** se risquer à faire qch; ~ **one's own eyes (ears)** en croire ses yeux (oreilles); ~ **s/o with sth** confier qch à qn; vi ~ **in** mettre sa confiance en; (hope) mettre son espoir en; ~ **to luck** s'en remettre au hasard

**trusted** adj de confiance; (method) éprouvé

**trustee** n dépositaire, administrateur -trice; leg curateur -trice; **board of** ~s conseil m d'administration

**trusteeship** n administration f; leg fidéicommis m; pol tutelle f

**trustful** adj confiant

**trustiness** n fidélité f, loyauté f

**trustworthiness** n (person) loyauté f; (information) crédibilité f

**trustworthy** adj digne de confiance, honnête; (accurate) exact

**trusty** adj digne de confiance; fidèle

**truth** n vérité f; chose vraie; **not a word of** ~ pas un mot de vrai; **tell s/o some home** ~s dire son fait à qn; **there's some** ~ **in it** il y a du vrai là-dedans; **to tell the** ~ à vrai dire

**truthful** adj (person) qui dit la vérité; (statement) véridique, vrai; (likeness) fidèle

**try** n essai m, tentative f; **at the first** ~ du premier coup; **be worth a** ~ valoir la peine d'essayer; **have a** ~ **at doing sth** essayer de faire qch; (rugby) **score a** ~ marquer un essai; vt essayer, expérimenter; (test) éprouver, mettre à l'épreuve; (tire) fatiguer; (verify) vérifier; leg juger; (irritate) vexer; (taste) goûter, déguster; ~ **it on** (bluff) bluffer; ~ **on** essayer; ~ **one's best** faire tout son possible (de son mieux); ~ **one's strength against s/o** se mesurer avec qn; ~ **out** faire l'essai de; vi essayer; ~ **for sth** essayer d'obtenir qch

**trying** adj difficile, vexant

**try-on** n bluff m

**tryst** n lit rendez-vous m (d'amour)

**tsar** n tsar m

**tsetse-fly** n mouche f tsé-tsé

**T-shirt** n T-shirt m

**tub** n baquet m, cuve f; (bath) bain m, tub m; coll (boat) rafiot m; vt mettre dans un baquet; vi coll prendre un bain

**tuba** n tuba m

**tubby** adj coll rondelet -ette, pansu

**tube** n tube m, tuyau m; coll (underground) = métro m; US télé f; surg drain m; anat canal m; **inner** ~ chambre f à air

**tubeless** adj mot sans chambre à air

**tuber** n tubercule f

**tubercular** adj tuberculeux -euse

**tuberculosis** n tuberculose f

**tuberculous** adj tuberculeux -euse

**tube-station** n = station f de métro

**tube-train** n = métro m, rame f de métro

**tubing** n tubage m, tuyautage m, tubes mpl

**tub-thumper** n orateur m de carrefour

**tub-thumping** n discours bruyants et émotifs, discours mpl démagogiques;

*adj* porté à faire des discours bruyants et émotifs (démagogiques)

**tubular** *adj* tubulaire

**tuck** *n* pli *m*, rempli *m*; *coll* boustifaille *f*; *vt* (dressmaking) faire des plis à, remplier, plisser; (fold) replier, serrer; ~ **away** cacher; ~ **in** rentrer; (fold) replier; (person) border; ~ **in the bed-clothes** border le lit; ~ **up** (skirt) retrousser; *vi coll* ~ **in** s'en mettre jusque-là, bouffer

**tuck-box** *n coll* boîte *f* à provisions

**tuck-shop** *n coll* (school) pâtisserie *f*, boutique *f* de bonbons

**Tuesday** *n* mardi *m*

**tufa** *n geol* tuf *m*

**tuft** *n* touffe *f*; (bird) huppe *f*, aigrette *f*; (wool) flocon *m*

**tufted** *adj* en touffe; (bird) huppé

**tug** *n* traction *f*; (shake) secousse *f*; *naut* ~ (**boat**) remorqueur *m*; *vt* tirer (avec effort); ~ **along** traîner; *naut* remorquer; *vi* tirer (avec effort); ~ **at** tirer sur

**tug-of-war** *n* lutte *f* de traction à la corde

**tuition** *n* enseignement *m*, instruction *f*; **postal** ~ enseignement *m* par correspondance; **private** ~ leçons particulières, cours particuliers

**tulip** *n* tulipe *f*

**tumble** *n* chute *f*, culbute *f*; *vt* bouleverser, déranger; (knock over) faire tomber; (crease) chiffonner; ~ **down** (over) culbuter, renverser; *vi* tomber, culbuter; ~ **down** dégringoler; (building) s'écrouler; ~ **into** se jeter dans; *coll* ~ **on sth** tomber sur qch, trouver qch par hasard; *coll* ~ **to sth** comprendre qch; *sl* piger qch

**tumbledown** *adj coll* délabré, en ruine

**tumbler** *n* (circus) acrobate; verre *m*; *elect* culbuteur *m*

**tumbrel, tumbril** *n* tombereau *m*

**tumefaction** *n* tuméfaction *f*

**tumefy** *vt* tuméfier; *vi* se tuméfier

**tummy** *n coll* ventre *m*; (stomach) estomac *m*

**tumour** *n* tumeur *f*

**tumult** *n* tumulte *m*, agitation *f*

**tumultuous** *adj* tumultueux -euse

**tuna** *n* thon *m*

**tundra** *n* toundra *f*

**tune** *n* air *m*; *fig* **change one's** ~ changer de langage; **in** ~ d'accord; **sing out of** (**in**) ~ chanter faux (juste); *vt* accorder, mettre d'accord; *mot* mettre au point; ~ **in to a station** capter un poste; *vi* s'accorder

**tuneful** *adj* mélodieux -ieuse

**tuneless** *adj* inharmonieux -ieuse, discordant

**tuner** *n* (piano) accordeur *m*

**tungsten** *n* tungstène *m*

**tunic** *n* tunique *f*

**tuning** *n* accordage *m*; *mot* mise *f* au point

**tuning-fork** *n* diapason *m*

**Tunisia** *n* Tunisie *f*

**Tunisian** *n* Tunisien -ienne; *adj* tunisien -ienne

**tunnel** *n* tunnel *m*, passage souterrain; (mine) galerie *f*; *vt* percer un tunnel dans (à travers); *vi* percer un tunnel

**tunny(-fish)** *n* thon *m*

**turban** *n* turban *m*

**turbid** *adj* trouble

**turbine** *n* turbine *f*

**turbo-jet** *n* turboréacteur *m*

**turbo-prop** *n* turbopropulseur *m*

**turbot** *n* turbot *m*

**turbulence** *n* turbulence *f*

**turbulent** *adj* turbulent; (unruly) insubordonné

**turd** *n* étron *m*; *sl* (person) salaud *m*

**tureen** *n* soupière *f*

**turf** *n* (grass) gazon *m*; (lawn) pelouse *f*; (peat) tourbe *f*; (racing) turf *m*; *vt* gazonner; *coll* ~ **s/o out** flanquer qn dehors

**turf-accountant** *n* bookmaker *m*

**turgid** *adj* enflé; (style) ampoulé

**turgidity** *n* enflure *f*; (style) emphase *f*

**Turk** *n* Turc (*f* Turque)

**Turkey** *n* Turquie *f*

**turkey** *n* dindon *m*; (hen) dinde *f*; *coll* **talk** ~ parler sérieusement; **young** ~ dindonneau *m*

**Turkish** *n* (language) turc *m*; *adj* turc (*f* turque); ~ **bath** bain *m* de vapeur; ~ **delight** loukoum *m*; ~ **towel** serviette *f* éponge

**turmoil** *n* tumulte *m*, agitation *f*

**turn** *n* tour *m*; (wheel) révolution *f*; (road) tournant *m*; (bend) virage *m*; (change) changement *m*; (direction) changement *m* de direction; (walk) promenade *f*; (shock) coup *m*; (act) numéro *m*; (attack) crise *f*; ~ **of mind** tournure *f* d'esprit; **at every** ~ à tout propos, à tout bout de champ; **done to a** ~ cuit à point; **do s/o a bad** ~ jouer un mauvais tour à qn; **do s/o a good** ~ rendre service à qn; **give s/o a** ~ faire peur à qn; **in** ~ à tour de rôle; **play out of** ~ jouer avant son tour; **take a** ~ **for the better (worse)** s'améliorer (empirer); *vt* tourner; (change) transformer, changer; (make revolve) faire tourner; (direct) diriger; (soil) retourner; ~ **aside** détourner, écarter; ~ **away** (deflect) détourner; (dismiss) renvoyer; ~ **back** faire retourner; (send) renvoyer; ~ **down** rabattre; (fold) plier; (volume, gas, light) baisser; (offer, suggestion) repousser;

(candidate) refuser; ~ **in** (fold) replier; (hand over) livrer, rendre; ~ **off** fermer, couper; (light) éteindre; ~ **on** (water) ouvrir; (light) allumer; *sl* stimuler; ~ **one's attention** porter l'attention sur; ~ **one's stomach** soulever le cœur; ~ **out** (evict) mettre à la porte, expulser; (light) éteindre; (produce) produire; (clean) nettoyer à fond; (empty) vider; ~ **over** (overturn) renverser; (page) tourner; (pages) feuilleter; (hand over) remettre; (think about) réfléchir à; *comm* faire; ~ **round** retourner; ~ **tail** prendre la fuite; ~ **the scale** faire pencher la balance; ~ **up** retourner; (tuck up) retrousser; (collar) relever; (page) trouver; ~ **upside down** mettre sens dessus dessous; *fig* bouleverser; **be** ~ **ed fifty** avoir cinquante ans passés; **it is** ~ **ed five o'clock** il est cinq heures passées; **nicely** ~ **ed out** (person) soigné, élégant; **without** ~ **ing a hair** sans sourciller; *vi* se tourner; (revolve) tourner; (turn round) se retourner; (become) devenir; (wind, tide) changer; (milk) tourner; ~ **about** se retourner, se tourner; ~ **aside** se détourner, s'écarter; ~ **away** se détourner; ~ **back** rebrousser chemin, retourner; (look) regarder en arrière; ~ **down a street** prendre une rue; *coll* ~ **in** aller (se) coucher; ~ **into** se changer en; ~ **off** bifurquer, tourner; ~ **on s/o** se retourner contre qn, attaquer qn; ~ **out** (end) finir, se terminer; (go out) sortir; (become) devenir; (get up) se lever; (happen) arriver; ~ **out well** (badly) bien (mal) tourner; ~ **over** se retourner; (vehicle) verser, capoter; (boat) chavirer; ~ **round** se retourner; ~ **to** (change) se changer en; (refer) se reporter à; (for help) recourir à; *coll* se mettre au travail; ~ **towards** se diriger vers; ~ **up** se relever; *coll* (arrive) arriver (à l'improviste), se présenter; **as it** ~ **ed out** en l'occurrence; **not know which way to** ~ ne savoir où donner de la tête

**turncoat** *n* renégat -e

**turncock** *n* (instrument) clef *f*

**turner** *n* tourneur *m*

**turning** *n* (movement) rotation *f*; (road) tournant *m*; (change) changement *m*; *mot* virage *m*; (action) retournage *m*; (industry) tournage *m*

**turning-point** *n* moment *m* critique, point décisif

**turnip** *n* navet *m*

**turnkey** *n* geôlier -ière

**turn-out** *n* (concourse) assemblée *f*; (clothes) tenue *f*; (outfit) équipage *m*;

(production) rendement *m*, production *f*

**turnover** *n* chiffre *m* d'affaires; (personnel) mouvement *m*; (goods) écoulement *m*; *cul* chausson *m*

**turnpike** *n* *US* autoroute *f* à péage; *hist* barrière *f* de péage

**turn-round** *n* *comm* + *naut* rotation *f*

**turnstile** *n* tourniquet *m*

**turntable** *n* (record-player) platine *f*; (railway) plaque tournante

**turn-up** *n* (trousers) revers *m*; *coll* fracas *m*; *coll* surprise *f*

**turpentine** *n* térébenthine *f*

**turpitude** *n* turpitude *f*

**turquoise** *n* turquoise *f*; *adj* turquoise *invar*

**turret** *n* tourelle *f*

**turtle** *n* tortue *f* de mer; **turn** ~ chavirer

**turtle-dove** *n* tourterelle *f*

**Tuscany** *n* Toscane *f*

**tusk** *n* défense *f*

**tussle** *n* lutte *f*, mêlée *f*

**tussock** *n* touffe *f* d'herbe

**tut** *interj* allons donc!

**tutelage** *n* tutelle *f*

**tutelary** *adj* tutélaire

**tutor** *n* (teacher) professeur *m*; (individual) précepteur -trice; (university) directeur -trice d'études; *vt* instruire; donner des cours particuliers à

**tutorial** *n* cours particulier (donné à un étudiant); *adj* d'instruction, d'un précepteur

**tutorship** *n* préceptorat *m*

**tuxedo** *n* *US* smoking *m*

**twaddle** *n* fadaises *fpl*, futilités *fpl*

**twain** *n* *lit* **the** ~ les deux; *adj lit* **in** ~ en deux

**twang** *n* bruit sec (d'une corde); **nasal** ~ accent nasillard; *vt* faire résonner; *vi* vibrer, émettre un son vibrant

**tweak** *n* pincement *m*; *vt* pincer

**twee** *adj coll pej* (person) mignard, (object) un peu trop joli

**tweed** *n* tweed *m*

**tweet** *n* pépiement *m*; *vi* pépier

**tweezers** *npl* petite pince, brucelles *fpl*

**twelfth** *n* douzième *m*; (date) douze *m*; *adj* douzième; **Twelfth Night** la fête des Rois; **Twelfth Night cake** galette *f* des Rois

**twelve** *n* douze *m invar*; **about** ~ une douzaine; *adj* douze *invar*

**twentieth** *n* vingtième *m*; (date) vingt *m*; *adj* vingtième

**twenty** *n* vingt *m invar*; *adj* vingt *invar*

**twenty-first** *n* vingt-et-unième; (date) vingt-et-un *m*; *adj* vingt-et-unième

**twerp** *n* *coll* andouille *f*

**twice** *adv* deux fois, à deux reprises; **not have to be asked** ~ ne pas se faire prier

**twiddle** *vt* tourner; ~ **one's thumbs** se tourner les pouces

¹**twig** *n* brindille *f*

²**twig** *vt* + *vi coll* comprendre; *sl* piger

**twilight** *n* crépuscule *m*; **in the** ~ au crépuscule, entre chien et loup

**twin** *n* + *adj* jumeau -elle; ~ **beds** lits jumeaux; *vt* jumeler

**twine** *n* ficelle *f*; *vt* (twist) tordre; (entwine) entrelacer; (weave) tisser; *vi* se tordre; ~ **round** s'enrouler autour; (road) serpenter

**twin-engined** *adj* à deux moteurs

**twinge** *n* élancement *m*, tiraillement *m*; ~ **of conscience** remords *m*

**twinkle** *n* scintillement *m*; (eyes) pétillement *m*; *vi* scintiller; (eyes) pétiller

**twinkling** *n* scintillement *m*; (eyes) pétillement *m*; **in the** ~ **of an eye** en un clin d'œil

**twin-set** *n* twin-set *m*

**twirl** *n* pirouette *f*, tournoiement *m*; *vt* faire tournoyer, faire tourner; (twist) tortiller; *vi* tournoyer, pirouetter

**twist** *n* torsion *f*; (cotton, etc) cordon *m*, cordonnet *m*; (hair) torsade *f*; (road) coude *m*; (sheet of metal, etc) gondolage *m*; (sense) perversion *f*; (dance) twist *m*; ~ **s and turns** tours *mpl* et détours *mpl*; *vt* tordre, tortiller; (plait) tresser; (sense) altérer; ~ **one's ankle** se fouler la cheville; ~ **s/o round one's little finger** mener qn par le bout du nez; ~ **s/o's arm** tordre le bras à qn; *coll fig* exercer une pression sur qn; *vi* se tordre, se tortiller; (road) faire des détours (lacets); ~ **and turn** (struggle) se débattre; (wind) serpenter

**twister** *n* tordeur -euse; *coll* (person) fourbe; *coll* (problem) question *f* difficile

**twisty** *adj* qui serpente; *coll* malhonnête

¹**twit** *n coll* imbécile, idiot -e

²**twit** *vt* taquiner, railler

**twitch** *n* saccade *f*, secousse *f*; (pain) élancement *m*; (face) tic *m*; (limbs) mouvement convulsif; *vt* (snatch) tirer brusquement; (contort) crisper; *vi* se crisper, se contracter

**twitching** *n see* **twitch** *n*

**twitter** *n* gazouillement *m*; *vi* gazouiller

**twittering** *n see* **twitter** *n*

**two** *n* deux *m invar*; *adj* deux *invar*; **by** ~ deux à deux; **in a day or** ~ dans quelques jours, dans un ou deux jours; **put** ~ **and** ~ **together** tirer ses conclusions

**two-edged** *adj* à deux tranchants, à double tranchant

**two-faced** *adj coll* hypocrite

**twofold** *adj* double; *adv* doublement

**two-handed** *adj* à deux mains

**two-legged** *adj* bipède

**two-piece** *n* deux-pièces *m invar*

**two-ply** *adj* à deux brins

**two-seater** *n aer* avion *m* à deux places; *mot* voiture *f* à deux places

**twosome** *n* (couple) couple *m*; (game) jeu *m* pour deux personnes

**two-step** *n* pas *m* de deux

**two-stroke** *adj mech* à deux temps

**two-timing** *adj US coll* trompeur -euse

**two-way** *adj* (road) à deux sens

**tycoon** *n* grand manitou

**tyke** *n see* **tike**

**tympanum** *n* tympan *m*

**type** *n* type *m*, genre *m*; *typ* caractère *m*; *coll* type *m*, *sl* mec *m*; *vt* + *vi* taper à la machine

**typecast** *adj theat* à qui l'on donne toujours le même genre de rôle

**typescript** *n* manuscrit dactylographié

**type-setter** *n* compositeur -trice, typographe

**typewriter** *n* machine *f* à écrire

**typewriting** *n* dactylographie *f*

**typewritten** *adj* écrit à la machine

**typhoid** *n* (fièvre *f*) typhoïde *f*; *adj* typhoïde

**typhoon** *n* typhon *m*

**typhus** *n* typhus *m*

**typical** *adj* typique

**typify** *vt* représenter; être typique (caractéristique) de

**typing** *n* dactylographie *f*

**typing-paper** *n* papier *m* pour machine à écrire

**typist** *n* dactylographe, *coll* dactylo

**typographer** *n* typographe

**typographical** *adj* typographique

**typography** *n* typographie *f*

**typological** *adj* typologique

**typology** *n* typologie *f*

**tyrannical** *adj* tyrannique

**tyrannize** *vt* tyranniser; *vi* agir en tyran, faire le tyran

**tyrannous** *adj* tyrannique

**tyranny** *n* tyrannie *f*

**tyrant** *n* tyran *m*

**tyre**, *US* **tire** *n* (pneumatic) pneu *m*; (solid) bandage *m*

**tyre-gauge** *n* manomètre *m*

**tyro** *n* novice

**Tyrolean** *adj* tyrolien -ienne

# U

u *n* (snob behaviour, speech) **this is U**
c'est bien, c'est ce qu'il faut; (thought
to be vulgar) **non-U** peu recommandable

**ubiquitous** *adj* omniprésent, qui se
trouve partout, qu'on voit partout

**ubiquity** *n* ubiquité *f*, omniprésence *f*

**udder** *n* mamelle *f*; (cow) pis *m*

**Uganda** *n* Ouganda *m*, Uganda *m*

**ugh** *interj* pouah!

**ugliness** *n* laideur *f*

**ugly** *adj* laid, vilain, disgracieux -ieuse;
(wound) dangereux -euse; ~ **as sin**
laid comme un pou; ~ **customer** sale
type *m*; **grow** ~ enlaidir; **turn** ~ se fâcher

**ulcer** *n* ulcère *m*

**ulcerate** *vt* ulcérer; *vi* s'ulcérer

**ulceration** *n* ulcération *f*

**ulcerous** *adj* ulcéreux -euse

**ulna** *n anat* cubitus *m*

**Ulster** *n* Ulster *m*

**ult** *adv abbr see* **ultimo**

**ulterior** *adj* ultérieur; ~ **motive** but
secret; **without** ~ **motive** sans arrière-
pensée

**ultimate** *n* essentiel *m*; point final; **the**
~ **in refinement** ce qu'il y a de plus
raffiné; *adj* final, définitif -ive; (last) ultime

**ultimatum** *n* ultimatum *m*

**ultimo** *adv* **on the 10th** ~ le 10 du mois
dernier

**ultra** *n pol* ultra, extrémiste; *adj* extrême

**ultramarine** *adj* (country, etc) d'outre-
mer; (colour) bleu *m* outremer *invar*

**ultramodern** *adj* ultramoderne

**ultrasonic** *adj* ultrasonique

**ultra-violet** *adj* ultra-violet -ette

**ululate** *vi* (owl) ululer

**ululation** *n* (owl) ululement *m*

**umbilical** *adj* ombilical

**umbilicus** *n anat* ombilic *m*, nombril *m*

**umbrage** *n* ombrage *m*; **take** ~ **at**
s'offenser de

**umbrella** *n* parapluie *m*

**umbrella-stand** *n* porte-parapluies *m*

**umpire** *n* arbitre *m*, juge *m*; *vt* arbitrer;
*vi* servir d'arbitre

**umpteen** *adj sl* beaucoup de

**unabashed** *adj* aucunement ébranlé, aucunement décontenancé

**unabated** *adj* non diminué

**unable** *adj* incapable; (prevented) empêché

**unabridged** *adj* non abrégé; ~ **edition**
édition intégrale

**unaccented** *adj* non accentué

**unacceptable** *adj* inacceptable

**unaccommodating** *adj* peu accommodant

**unaccompanied** *adj* seul, non accompagné; *mus* sans accompagnement

**unaccountable** *adj* inexplicable; (odd)
étrange

**unaccounted** *adj* ~ **for** inexpliqué;
(missing) qui manque

**unaccustomed** *adj* (person) peu habitué;
(unusual) inaccoutumé

**unacknowledged** *adj* non reconnu;
(letter) resté sans réponse

**unacquainted** *adj* **be** ~ **with** ne pas connaître

**unadaptable** *adj* inadaptable

**unaddressed** *adj* sans adresse

**unadorned** *adj* sans ornement

**unadulterated** *adj* pur; sans mélange

**unadvised** *adj* imprudent, mal avisé

**unaffected** *adj* (natural) sans affectation,
naturel -elle, simple; non affecté; ~ **by
water** inaltérable à l'eau

**unafraid** *adj* sans peur

**unaided** *adj* sans aide, tout seul (*f* toute
seule); **by one's** ~ **efforts** par ses
propres efforts

**unalloyed** *adj* pur, parfait

**unalterable** *adj* immuable

**unambiguous** *adj* non équivoque, clair

**unambitious** *adj* sans ambition; (aim,
etc) modeste

**unamenable** *adj* réfractaire

**un-American** *adj* contraire à l'esprit
américain; indigne d'un Américain;
anti-américain

**unanimity** *n* unanimité *f*

**unanimous** *adj* unanime

**unanswerable** *adj* (question) qui
n'admet pas de réponse; (argument)
irréfutable

**unappetizing** *adj* peu appétissant

**unappreciated** *adj* peu estimé, inapprécié

**unappreciative** *adj* insensible, froid

**unapproachable** *adj* inabordable, inaccessible

**unarmed** *adj* non armé; (combat) sans
armes

**unashamed** *adj* sans honte, effronté;
(brazen) éhonté

**unasked** *adj* (guest) sans être invité -e

**unassailable** adj (reputation) inattaquable; (right) indiscutable

**unassisted** adj sans aide, tout seul (f toute seule)

**unassuming** adj modeste, sans prétention(s)

**unattached** adj indépendant; (single) seul, sans attaches

**unattainable** adj impossible à atteindre, inaccessible, hors de portée

**unattended** adj non accompagné; (neglected) négligé; (unmanned) non pourvu de personnel; (not controlled) sans surveillance

**unattractive** adj peu attrayant; (character) peu sympathique, déplaisant

**unauthorized** adj non autorisé; (illegal) illicite

**unavailable** adj introuvable, impossible à obtenir; (person) indisponible, pas libre

**unavailing** adj inutile, vain

**unavoidable** adj inévitable

**unaware** adj ignorant; **be ~ of** ignorer

**unawares** adv inconsciemment; **catch s/o ~** prendre qn au dépourvu

**unbalance** n déséquilibre m; vt déséquilibrer, déranger

**unbar** vt débarrer; fig ouvrir

**unbearable** adj insupportable

**unbeatable** adj imbattable

**unbeaten** adj invaincu, non battu

**unbecoming** adj déplacé, peu convenable; (dress) peu seyant

**unbefriended** adj sans ami(s)

**unbeknown** adj **~ to** à l'insu de

**unbelief** n incrédulité f

**unbelievable** adj incroyable

**unbeliever** n incrédule; (religion) incroyant -e

**unbelieving** adj incrédule

**unbend** vt détendre; (straighten) redresser; vi se détendre

**unbending** adj inflexible, intransigeant

**unbiased, unbiassed** adj impartial, objectif -ive, sans prévention

**unbidden** adj non invité; spontané

**unbind** vt délier; (wound) débander

**unblemished** adj sans défaut; fig sans tache

**unblock** vt dégager, déboucher

**unblushing** adj sans vergogne, éhonté

**unbolt** vt déverrouiller

**unborn** adj pas encore né; (future) à venir

**unbosom** vt **~ oneself to** s/o ouvrir son cœur à qn

**unbounded** adj sans bornes, illimité

**unbowed** adj fig insoumis

**unbreakable** adj incassable

**unbridled** adj débridé, effréné

**unbroken** adj non cassé, intact; (continuous) continu, ininterrompu; (unsubdued) indompté; (rule) toujours

observé; (record) non battu, pas encore battu

**unbuckle** vt dégrafer, déboucler

**unburden** vt alléger, soulager; **~ oneself of sth** se soulager de qch

**unbusinesslike** adj peu commerçant; (action) irrégulier -ière; (person) incompétent

**unbutton** vt déboutonner; vi fig se détendre

**uncalculated** adj indéfini; fig inattendu

**uncalled-for** adj (remark, action) déplacé; non justifié, non mérité

**uncanny** adj mystérieux -ieuse, inquiétant

**uncared-for** adj peu soigné, négligé; (abandoned) délaissé

**unceasing** adj incessant, continu; (effort) soutenu, assidu

**unceremonious** adj sans façon; brusque

**uncertain** adj incertain; (undecided) indéterminé, irrésolu; (step) mal assuré; (temper) inégal

**uncertainty** n incertitude f, doute m

**unchain** vt déchaîner

**unchallengeable** adj incontestable

**unchallenged** adj incontesté; (person) que personne ne vient contredire

**unchangeable** adj immuable

**unchanging** adj constant, invariable

**uncharitable** adj peu charitable

**uncharted** adj qui ne figure pas sur la carte; inexploré

**unchecked** adj (unrestrained) sans frein; (unhindered) qui ne rencontre pas d'obstacles; (bill, etc) non vérifié

**unchivalrous** adj peu courtois, peu galant

**unchristian** adj peu chrétien -ienne; coll impossible

**uncircumcised** adj incirconcis

**uncivil** adj impoli

**uncivilized** adj barbare, non civilisé

**uncivilly** adv impoliment

**unclaimed** adj non réclamé

**unclasp** vt dégrafer, défaire; (fist) desserrer

**unclassed** adj non classé

**unclassified** adj non classé

**uncle** n oncle m

**unclean** adj malpropre; impur

**unclench** vt desserrer

**uncloak** vt (plan) découvrir, dévoiler, démasquer

**unclothe** vt déshabiller, dévêtir

**unclouded** adj sans nuages, serein; (liquid) limpide; fig clair

**uncoil** vt dérouler; vi se dérouler

**uncoloured** adj non coloré; (colourless) incolore; fig impartial

**uncomfortable** adj (things) peu confortable, inconfortable; fig désagréable; (person) mal à son aise; (embarrassed) gêné; **feel ~** être mal à l'aise; **feel ~ about sth** être inquiet -iète au sujet de qch; **make things ~ for s/o** créer des ennuis pour qn

**uncommitted** *adj* non engagé, indépendant

**uncommon** *adj* rare, singulier -ière, peu commun

**uncommonly** *adv* singulièrement, particulièrement

**uncommunicative** *adj* peu communicatif -ive

**uncomplaining** *adj* qui ne se plaint pas, résigné

**uncomplimentary** *adj* peu flatteur -euse

**uncompromising** *adj* intransigeant, inflexible

**unconcealed** *adj* qui n'est pas caché; (feeling) non dissimulé

**unconcern** *n* indifférence *f*; insouciance *f*

**unconcerned** *adj* indifférent, insouciant

**unconditional** *adj* inconditionnel -elle, sans conditions, absolu

**unconfined** *adj* sans restrictions, illimité

**unconfirmed** *adj* non confirmé

**uncongenial** *adj* (person) peu sympathique, peu agréable; (task) ingrat

**unconnected** *adj* sans rapport; (thoughts) sans suite

**unconquerable** *adj* invincible

**unconquered** *adj* invaincu

**unconscionable** *adj* démesuré, déraisonnable

**unconscious** *n* inconscient *m*; *adj* inconscient; sans connaissance, inanimé; **be ~ of sth** ignorer qch

**unconsciously** *adv* inconsciemment

**unconsciousness** *n* inconscience *f*; (faint) évanouissement *m*

**unconsecrated** *adj* non béni

**unconsidered** *adj* (action) irréfléchi; (little valued) peu estimé

**unconstitutional** *adj* anticonstitutionnel -elle

**unconstrained** *adj* non contraint, libre

**uncontested** *adj* non contesté, incontesté

**uncontrollable** *adj* ingouvernable; (passion) irrésistible; **~ laughter** fou rire

**uncontrolled** *adj* incontrôlé, libre, indépendant

**unconventional** *adj* original, non-conformiste

**unconventionality** *n* originalité *f*; (manner) liberté *f* d'allures

**unconventionally** *adv* de façon non-conformiste

**unconverted** *adj* non converti

**unconvinced** *adj* sceptique, non convaincu

**unconvincing** *adj* peu convaincant

**uncooked** *adj* pas cuit; (raw) cru

**unco-operative** *adj* peu coopérateur -trice

**unco-ordinated** *adj* non coordonné

**uncork** *vt* déboucher

**uncorrected** *adj* non corrigé

**uncorroborated** *adj* non confirmé

**uncouple** *vt* découpler; (disengage) débrayer

**uncouth** *adj* grossier -ière, rude, fruste

**uncover** *vt* découvrir

**uncritical** *adj* (person) dépourvu de sens critique; (attitude) peu critique

**uncrowned** *adj* non couronné

**uncrushable** *adj* (material) infroissable; impossible à écraser

**unction** *n* onction *f*

**unctuous** *adj* onctueux -euse; *fig pej* mielleux -euse

**uncultivated** *adj* (land) inculte; (person) sans culture

**uncultured** *adj* sans culture; (land) inculte

**uncurl** *vt* défriser, dérouler; *vi* (hair) se défriser; (rope) se dérouler

**uncut** *adj* non coupé; (book) non abrégé; (hedge) non taillé; (diamond) brut; (text) intégral

**undamaged** *adj* intact, non endommagé

**undated** *adj* sans date

**undaunted** *adj* intrépide, non intimidé

**undeceive** *vt* détromper, désabuser

**undecided** *adj* indécis, incertain

**undecipherable** *adj* indéchiffrable

**undeclared** *adj* non déclaré; resté secret -ète, caché

**undefeated** *adj* invaincu

**undefended** *adj* sans défense, non défendu

**undefiled** *adj* pur, sans tache

**undefined** *adj* non défini, vague

**undemonstrative** *adj* peu expansif -ive, réservé

**undeniable** *adj* indéniable, incontestable

**undependable** *adj* sur lequel (*f* laquelle) on ne peut pas compter

**under** *adj* de dessous; (subordinate) subalterne; *prep* sous, au-dessous de; (less than) moins de; (according to) selon; **~ one's breath** à demi-voix; **~ repair** en réparation; **~ sentence of death** condamné à mort; **~ the circumstances** dans ces circonstances; **the necessity of** dans la nécessité de; **~ treatment** en traitement; **be ~ the doctor** être entre les mains du docteur; **in the phone-book ~ Smith** dans l'annuaire parmi les Smith; *adv* dessous, au-dessous, en-dessous; (too little) insuffisamment, trop peu; **keep s/o ~** tenir qn en soumission; **see ~** voir ci-dessous

**under-age** *adj* au-dessous de l'âge autorisé, trop jeune

**under-belly** *n* bas-ventre *m*; *fig* région mal protégée

**underbid** *vt* demander moins cher que

**undercarriage** *n* aer train *m* d'atterrissage

**undercharge** *vt* demander trop peu à

**underclothes** *npl*, **underclothing** *n* sous-vêtements *mpl*, linge *m* de corps; (women) lingerie *f*

**undercoat** *n* (paint) couche *f* de fond

**undercover** *adj* secret -ète, clandestin

**undercurrent** *n* courant *m* de fond; *fig* courant sous-jacent

**undercut** *vt* (charge less) faire payer moins cher que; faire des propositions plus avantageuses que

**underdevelop** *vt* phot développer insuffisamment

**underdeveloped** *adj* sous-développé; phot insuffisamment développé; (child) retardé dans sa croissance

**underdog** *n* celui (*f* celle) qui est opprimé -e; *collect* les opprimés *mpl*

**underdone** *adj* pas assez cuit; (meat) saignant

**underestimate** *n* sous-estimation *f*; *vt* sous-estimer

**under-exposure** *n* phot sous-exposition *f*

**underfelt** *n* assise *f* de feutre

**underfoot** *adv* sous les pieds; **trample ~** fouler aux pieds

**undergarment** *n* sous-vêtement *m*

**undergo** *vt* subir; (suffering) supporter

**undergraduate** *n* étudiant -e (n'ayant pas encore sa licence)

**underground** *n* = métro *m*; mouvement *m* de résistance clandestine; *adj* souterrain; (secret) clandestin; (mine) ~ **worker** ouvrier *m* du fond; *adv* sous (la) terre; secrètement

**undergrowth** *n* broussailles *fpl*, sous-bois *m*

**underhand** *adj* sournois, dissimulé; *adv* en-dessous, sournoisement

**underlay** *n* (carpet) assise *f* de feutre; *typ* hausse *f*

**underlie** *vt* être au-dessous de; *fig* être à la base de

**underline** *vt* souligner

**underling** *n* pej subalterne *m*

**underlying** *adj* sous-jacent; *fig* profond

**undermanned** *adj* ayant un personnel insuffisant

**undermentioned** *adj* ci-dessous

**undermine** *vt* miner, saper

**undermost** *adj* le plus bas (*f* la plus basse) inférieur

**underneath** *adj* de dessous, inférieur; *adv* au-dessous, dessous; *prep* au-dessous de, sous

**undernourished** *adj* sous-alimenté

**underpaid** *adj* mal rétribué, mal payé

**underpants** *npl* caleçon *m*, slip *m*

**underpass** *n* passage inférieur

**underpay** *vt* payer mal, rétribuer insuffisamment

**underpin** *vt* étayer; (foundations) reprendre en sous-œuvre

**underprivileged** *adj* déshérité

**underrate** *vt* sous-estimer, faire trop peu de cas de

**underscore** *vt* souligner

**under-sea** *adj* sous-marin, sous la mer

**under-secretary** *n* sous-secrétaire *m*

**undersell** *vt* vendre moins cher que

**undershirt** *n* US tricot *m* de corps

**undersigned** *n* + *adj* soussigné -e

**undersized** *adj* d'une taille au-dessous de la moyenne, de petite taille

**underskirt** *n* jupon *m*

**understaffed** *adj* à court de personnel

**understand** *vt* comprendre; (be judge of) se connaître en; **give s/o to ~** donner à entendre à qn; **make oneself understood** se faire comprendre; *vi* comprendre; (agree) convenir

**understandable** *adj* compréhensible

**understanding** *n* entendement *m*, intelligence *f*, jugement *m*, compréhension *f*; (agreement) accord *m*, entente *f*; **come to an ~ with s/o** s'entendre avec qn; **on the ~ that** à condition que; *adj* compréhensif -ive; (sympathetic) bienveillant

**understate** *vt* minimiser l'importance de

**understatement** *n* affirmation *f* qui ne dit pas assez, litote *f*

**understeer** *vi* car that ~s voiture sous-vireuse

**understood** *adj* compris; (agreed) convenu, entendu; *fig* + gramm sous-entendu; **that's ~** cela va sans dire

**understudy** *n* doublure *f*; *vt* doubler

**undertake** *vt* entreprendre; (take responsibility for) assumer; ~ **to do sth** se charger de faire qch

**undertaker** *n* entrepreneur *m* de pompes funèbres; *coll* croque-mort *m*

**undertaking** *n* entreprise *f*; (promise) engagement *m*, promesse *f*

**under-the-counter** *adj* coll louche, illégal

**undertone** *n* fond *m*; **in an ~** à voix basse

**undervalue** *vt* sous-évaluer, sous-estimer

**undervest** *n* tricot *m* de corps

**underwater** *adj* sous-marin

**underwear** *n* sous-vêtements *mpl*; (women) lingerie *f*

**underweight** *adj* trop léger -ère; au-dessous du poids voulu, d'un poids insuffisant

**underworld** n bas-fonds mpl de la société; coll pègre f; myth enfers mpl

**underwrite** vt garantir, souscrire à

**underwriter** n assureur m; (finance) membre m d'un syndicat de garantie, souscripteur m

**undeserved** adj immérité

**undeserving** adj (person) peu méritant; (cause) peu méritoire

**undesigned** adj involontaire; (unexpected) imprévu

**undesirable** n + adj indésirable

**undetected** adj inaperçu, qui a échappé à l'attention; non détecté

**undetermined** adj indéterminé; (person) indécis

**undeterred** adj aucunement découragé

**undeveloped** adj non développé, non exploité

**undeviating** adj direct, constant

**undigested** adj mal digéré

**undignified** adj manquant de dignité, peu digne

**undiluted** adj non dilué; concentré; pur

**undiminished** adj non diminué, toujours égal

**undimmed** adj non atténué; brillant, clair

**undisciplined** adj indiscipliné

**undisclosed** adj tenu secret -ète, non divulgué

**undiscovered** adj caché, non découvert

**undiscriminating** adj sans discernement

**undisguised** adj non déguisé; (open) franc (f franche), non dissimulé

**undismayed** adj sans peur, non découragé

**undisputed** adj incontesté

**undistinguished** adj médiocre, banal, quelconque

**undisturbed** adj (person) tranquille; (peaceful) paisible; (not moved) qui n'a pas été dérangé (remué); (peace, etc) ininterrompu

**undivided** adj entier -ière, sans partage, indivisé

**undo** vt défaire; (untie) délier, dénouer; (destroy) détruire; (repair) réparer

**undoing** n (act) action f de défaire; (ruin) ruine f, perte f

**undone** adj défait; (not done) pas fait, négligé, inaccompli; (ruined) ruiné, perdu

**undoubted** adj incontestable

**undramatic** adj peu dramatique; fig calme, ordinaire

**undreamed, undreamt** adj ~ of qu'on ne peut s'imaginer; (unsuspected) insoupçonné

**undress** n négligé m, petite tenue; vt déshabiller, dévêtir; vi se déshabiller

**undrinkable** adj (unpalatable) imbu-

vable; (unfit to drink) non potable

**undue** adj excessif -ive, exagéré

**undulate** vi + vi onduler, ondoyer

**undulating** adj onduleux -euse

**undulatory** adj ondulatoire; (surface) onduleux -euse

**unduly** adv sans raison; (excessively) à l'excès, outre mesure

**undutiful** adj désobéissant, qui ne remplit pas ses devoirs

**undying** adj immortel -elle; (lasting) impérissable, durable

**unearned** adj non gagné; (reward) immérité; ~ **income** rentes fpl

**unearth** vt déterrer; (discover) dénicher

**unearthly** adj surnaturel -elle, sinistre; coll (hour) indu; coll (terrific) de tous les diables

**uneasiness** n malaise m, gêne f; (worry) inquiétude f

**uneasy** adj mal à l'aise; (worried) inquiet -iète; (situation) gênant; ~ **feeling that** impression déconcertante que

**uneatable** adj immangeable

**uneconomic(al)** adj peu (non) économique; (work) peu (non) rentable

**unedifying** adj peu édifiant

**unedited** adj non édité; (not published) inédit; cin non monté

**uneducated** adj sans instruction; (speech, etc) vulgaire

**unemotional** adj peu émotif -ive

**unemployable** adj inemployable

**unemployed** n the ~ les chômeurs mpl; adj sans travail, sans emploi; (idle) désœuvré; (not used) inemployé

**unemployment** n chômage m, manque m de travail; ~ **benefit** allocation f de chômage

**unending** adj interminable, sans fin

**unendurable** adj insupportable

**un-English** adj contraire à l'esprit anglais (aux coutumes anglaises), peu anglais

**unenlightened** adj ignorant, peu éclairé

**unenterprising** adj peu entreprenant

**unenthusiastic** adj peu enthousiaste

**unenviable** adj peu enviable

**unequal** adj inégal; (irregular) irrégulier -ière; **be ~ to doing sth** ne pas avoir la force de faire qch; **be ~ to the task** ne pas être à la hauteur de la tâche

**unequalled** adj sans égal, inégalé

**unequivocal** adj clair, sans équivoque

**unerring** adj sûr, infaillible

**unessential** adj non essentiel -ielle

**unethical** adj immoral, malhonnête

**uneven** adj inégal; (rough) raboteux -euse; (ground) accidenté; (number) impair

**uneventful** adj sans incidents, calme

**unexampled** adj sans exemple; unique

**unexceptionable** *adj* irréprochable
**unexceptional** *adj* ordinaire
**unexciting** *adj* (life) peu passionnant; (boring) monotone, ennuyeux -euse
**unexpected** *adj* inattendu, imprévu
**unexpired** *adj* non expiré; (ticket, etc) encore valable
**unexplained** *adj* inexpliqué
**unexploded** *adj* non éclaté
**unexpressed** *adj* non exprimé, inexprimé
**unexpurgated** *adj* (text) intégral, non expurgé
**unfailing** *adj* (reliable) sûr, infaillible; (source) intarissable
**unfair** *adj* injuste; inéquitable
**unfairness** *n* injustice *f*
**unfaithful** *adj* infidèle
**unfaithfulness** *n* infidélité *f*
**unfaltering** *adj* ferme, assuré
**unfamiliar** *adj* peu familier -ière, inconnu; (little known) mal connu; (strange) étranger -ère
**unfamiliarity** *n* (ignorance) ignorance *f*; nouveauté *f*
**unfashionable** *adj* pas de mode; (out of fashion) démodé
**unfasten** *vt* détacher; (dress) défaire; (door) ouvrir
**unfathomable** *adj* insondable; (character, mystery, etc) impénétrable
**unfavourable** *adj* défavorable; (not propitious) inopportun
**unfeeling** *adj* insensible, impitoyable
**unfeigned** *adj* sincère
**unfettered** *adj* libre, sans liens
**unfinished** *adj* inachevé, incomplet -ète
**unfit** *adj* impropre, inapte; (health) en mauvaise santé; ~ **for traffic** impraticable
**unfitted** *adj* impropre, inapte
**unfitting** *adj* peu convenable, inconvenant, déplacé
**unfix** *vt* détacher, défaire
**unflagging** *adj* inlassable, infatigable; (sustained) soutenu
**unflappable** *adj* imperturbable
**unflattering** *adj* peu flatteur -euse
**unfledged** *adj* (bird) sans plumes; *fig* jeune, sans expérience
**unflinching** *adj* ferme, stoïque
**unfold** *vt* déplier; (unroll) dérouler; (wings) déployer; (reveal) révéler, exposer; *vi* se dérouler; (wings) se déployer; (flower) épanouir
**unforced** *adj* spontané, naturel -elle
**unforeseen** *adj* imprévu, inattendu
**unforgettable** *adj* inoubliable
**unforgivable** *adj* impardonnable
**unforgiving** *adj* implacable
**unforthcoming** *adj* peu aimable, peu avenant
**unfortified** *adj* sans fortifications

**unfortunate** *n* malheureux -euse; *adj* malheureux -euse, infortuné; regrettable
**unfounded** *adj* sans fondement, non fondé
**unfreeze** *vt* dégeler
**unfrequented** *adj* peu fréquenté; (place) isolé
**unfriendliness** *n* hostilité *f*, froideur *f*
**unfriendly** *adj* peu amical, hostile
**unfrock** *vt* eccles défroquer
**unfruitful** *adj* stérile; *fig* infructueux -euse
**unfulfilled** *adj* non accompli; non satisfait; (prophecy) irréalisé
**unfurl** *vt* (flag) déployer; (sail) déferler
**unfurnished** *adj* non meublé; (unprovided) dépourvu
**ungainly** *adj* gauche; (gait) dégingandé
**ungallant** *adj* peu galant
**ungenerous** *adj* peu généreux -euse
**ungentlemanly** *adj* mal élevé, impoli
**un-get-at-able** *adj coll* inaccessible
**ungifted** *adj* peu doué
**ungodliness** *n* impiété *f*
**ungodly** *adj* impie; *coll* terrible, affreux -euse
**ungovernable** *adj* ingouvernable; (rage, etc) effréné; (desire) irrépressible
**ungracious** *adj* peu aimable
**ungrammatical** *adj* incorrect, non grammatical
**ungrateful** *adj* ingrat, peu reconnaissant
**ungrounded** *adj* sans fondement
**ungrudging** *adj* libéral, généreux -euse; (given willingly) donné de bon cœur
**unguarded** *adj* (undefended) sans défense; irréfléchi, indiscret -ète; **in an ~ moment** dans un instant d'inattention (d'oubli)
**unguent** *n* onguent *m*
**unhallowed** *adj* non béni; (evil) impie
**unhampered** *adj* libre, non gêné
**unhand** *vt poet* lâcher
**unhandy** *adj* maladroit; (tool) peu maniable
**unhappily** *adv* malheureusement
**unhappiness** *n* malheur *m*, infélicité *f*; (expression) inopportunité *f*
**unhappy** *adj* malheureux -euse, infortuné, triste; (infelicitous) peu heureux -euse, regrettable
**unharmed** *adj* indemne, sain et sauf (*f* saine et sauve)
**unharness** *vt* dételer
**unhealthy** *adj* (person) maladif -ive; (place) insalubre, malsain
**unheard-of** *adj* inouï, extraordinaire
**unheeded** *adj* dédaigné, inaperçu
**unheeding** *adj* insouciant, inattentif -ive
**unhelpful** *adj* (person) peu secourable,

peu coopératif -ive; (no use) peu utile

**unhesitating** *adj* (person) ferme, résolu; (answer, etc) prompt

**unhindered** *adj* sans obstacle, sans empêchement

**unhinge** *vt* (door) enlever de ses gonds; (derange) détraquer

**unhitch** *vt* dételer, détacher

**unholy** *adj* profane; *coll* terrible, affreux -euse

**unhook** *vt* (take down) décrocher; (undo) dégrafer

**unhoped** *adj* ~ **for** inespéré

**unhorse** *vt* désarçonner

**unhurried** *adj* lent

**unhurt** *adj* (person) indemne; (unbroken) intact

**unhygienic** *adj* peu hygiénique

**unicellular** *adj* unicellulaire

**unicorn** *n* licorne *f*

**unidentified** *adj* non identifié; ~ **flying object (UFO)** objet volant non identifié (OVNI)

**unification** *n* unification *f*

**uniform** *n* uniforme *m*; *adj* uniforme, constant

**uniformed** *adj* en uniforme

**uniformity** *n* uniformité *f*

**uniformly** *adv* uniformément

**unify** *vt* unifier

**unilateral** *adj* unilatéral

**unimaginable** *adj* inimaginable, inconcevable

**unimaginative** *adj* dénué d'imagination

**unimpaired** *adj* non affaibli, intact, non diminué

**unimpassioned** *adj* sans passion

**unimpeachable** *adj* irréprochable; (testimony) irrécusable

**unimpeded** *adj* sans empêchement, libre

**unimportant** *adj* sans importance, peu important, insignifiant

**unimposing** *adj* peu imposant

**unimpressed** *adj* peu impressionné, peu convaincu

**unimpressive** *adj* peu frappant, peu impressionnant

**unimproved** *adj* non amélioré

**uninformed** *adj* ignorant, mal renseigné

**uninhabitable** *adj* inhabitable

**uninhabited** *adj* inhabité

**uninhibited** *adj* (person) sans inhibitions; (desire) non refréné

**uninitiated** *npl* profanes; *adj* non initié

**uninjured** *adj* indemne

**uninspired** *adj* sans inspiration; (style) banal (*pl* banals)

**uninsured** *adj* non assuré

**unintelligent** *adj* inintelligent

**unintelligible** *adj* inintelligible

**unintended** *adj* involontaire, inconscient

**unintentional** *adj* involontaire, inconscient

**uninterested** *adj* indifférent, non intéressé

**uninteresting** *adj* sans intérêt, inintéressant, ennuyeux -euse

**uninterrupted** *adj* ininterrompu, continu

**uninvited** *adj* qui n'a pas été invité; ~ **guest** hôte inattendu; **come** ~ venir sans être invité

**uninviting** *adj* peu attrayant; (food) peu appétissant

**union** *n* union *f*; harmonie *f*; mariage *m*; *med* raccord *m*; concorde *f*; (industry) syndicat (ouvrier); **Union Jack** pavillon *m* britannique; *US* **the Union** les États-Unis *mpl*

**unionism** *n* (industry) syndicalisme *m*

**unique** *adj* unique

**unisex** *adj* unisexe

**unison** *n* unisson *m*; **in** ~ à l'unisson

**unit** *n* unité *f*; (furniture) élément *m*; groupe *m*; ~ **trust** société *f* de gestion de portefeuille; **kitchen** ~ bloc *m* cuisine

**Unitarian** *n* + *adj* unitarien -ienne

**unitary** *adj* unitaire

**unite** *vt* unir; (unify) unifier; (in agreement) mettre d'accord; *vi* s'unir, se joindre; (companies) fusionner; *pol* ~ **against** faire bloc contre

**united** *adj* uni, réuni; **the United Kingdom** le Royaume-Uni; **the United Nations** les Nations Unies; **the United States** les États-Unis *mpl*

**unity** *n* unité *f*; concorde *f*, harmonie *f*

**universal** *n* proposition universelle; *adj* universel -elle

**universality** *n* universalité *f*

**universalize** *vt* universaliser

**universally** *adv* universellement

**universe** *n* univers *m*

**university** *n* université *f*; *adj* universitaire

**unjust** *adj* injuste

**unjustifiable** *adj* inexcusable, injustifiable

**unjustified** *adj* injustifié; non motivé

**unkempt** *adj* (hair) mal peigné; (appearance) mal soigné, débraillé

**unkind** *adj* peu aimable, pas gentil -ille; méchant, cruel -elle; **that's** ~ **of you** c'est peu aimable de votre part

**unkindly** *adv* d'une manière peu aimable; méchamment; **take sth** ~ prendre qch en mauvaise part

**unkindness** *n* manque *m* de bienveillance; méchanceté *f*

**unknowable** *adj* inconnaissable

**unknowing** *adj* inconscient

**unknowingly** *adv* sans le savoir, inconsciemment

**unknown** *n* inconnu *m*; *adj* inconnu; ~ **to me (him)** à mon (son) insu

**unlace** *vt* délacer

**unladen** *adj* sans charge, non chargé

**unladylike** *adj* peu distingué

**unlaid** *adj* (table) non mis; non posé; (ghost) non exorcisé; *sl* vierge

**unlatch** *vt* ouvrir

**unlawful** *adj* illégal; (means) illicite

**unlearn** *vt* oublier (ce qu'on a appris), désapprendre

**unlearned** *adj* ignorant; (inexpert) peu versé

**unleash** *vt* lâcher; *fig* déchaîner

**unleavened** *adj* sans levain, azyme

**unless** *conj* à moins que; ~ **he leaves straightaway** à moins qu'il ne parte tout de suite; ~ **I am mistaken** si je ne me trompe; ~ **I hear to the contrary** à moins (sauf) avis contraire

**unlettered** *adj* illettré

**unlicensed** *adj* non autorisé, illicite

**unlike** *adj* différent, dissemblable; *prep* à l'encontre de

**unlikelihood, unlikeliness** *n* improbabilité *f*; invraisemblance *f*

**unlikely** *adj* peu probable, improbable; (implausible) invraisemblable

**unlimited** *adj* illimité, sans bornes

**unload** *vt* décharger; *coll* (get rid of) se défaire de; (shares) vendre; *vi* mot décharger (la voiture)

**unlock** *vt* ouvrir; (wheel) débloquer

**unlooked-for** *adj* inattendu, inespéré

**unloose(n)** *vt* délier, détacher, desserrer

**unlovable** *adj* peu attachant

**unlovely** *adj* disgracieux -ieuse, laid, déplaisant

**unloving** *adj* peu affectueux -euse, froid

**unluckily** *adv* malheureusement

**unlucky** *adj* infortuné, malheureux -euse, malencontreux -euse; (star) maléfique; (day) néfaste; **be** ~ ne pas avoir de chance; **be** ~ **to** porter malchance de

**unmade** *adj* pas encore fait (créé); (road) non goudronné

**unmake** *vt* (destroy) détruire; (take to pieces) défaire; ruiner

**unman** *vt* *fig* émasculer, décourager; (castrate) émasculer

**unmanageable** *adj* ingouvernable; (unwieldy) difficile à manier

**unmanly** *adj* peu viril, efféminé; (cowardly) lâche

**unmanned** *adj* découragé, démoralisé; (crewless) sans équipage

**unmannerly** *adj* grossier -ière, malappris, impoli

**unmarked** *adj* ne portant aucune

marque; (unstained) sans tache; (schoolwork) non corrigé

**unmarketable** *adj* invendable

**unmarriageable** *adj* immariable, impossible à marier

**unmarried** *adj* célibataire, non marié; ~ **mother** fille-mère *f* (*pl* filles-mères)

**unmask** *vt* démasquer; *vi* se démasquer

**unmatched** *adj* (peerless) sans égal, incomparable

**unmeant** *adj* involontaire

**unmeasured** *adj* non mesuré; (boundless) infini; excessif -ive

**unmentionable** *adj* innommable, horrible

**unmerciful** *adj* sans pitié, impitoyable

**unmerited** *adj* immérité

**unmethodical** *adj* peu méthodique, sans méthode

**unminded** *adj* (neglected) non surveillé; n'ayant pas l'intention

**unmindful** *adj* oublieux -ieuse

**unmistakable** *adj* clair, évident; (likeness) facilement reconnaissable

**unmistakably** *adv* clairement; à ne pas s'y méprendre (tromper)

**unmitigated** *adj* non mitigé; dans toute la force du terme; *coll* parfait, pur; ~ **liar** fieffé menteur (*f* fieffée menteuse)

**unmixed** *adj* sans mélange

**unmolested** *adj* sans être inquiété, tranquille, en paix

**unmounted** *adj* non monté; (picture) non encadré; (jewel) non serti

**unmourned** *adj* non pleuré, non regretté

**unmoved** *adj* impassible, insensible

**unmusical** *adj* (sound) pas mélodieux -ieuse, inharmonieux -ieuse; (person) peu musicien -ienne

**unmuzzle** *vt* démuseler

**unnamable** *adj* innommable

**unnamed** *adj* sans nom; anonyme

**unnatural** *adj* anormal; monstrueux -euse, contre nature; (person) dénaturé

**unnavigable** *adj* (place) non navigable; (ship) que l'on ne peut gouverner (diriger)

**unnecessarily** *adv* inutilement

**unnecessary** *adj* non nécessaire, superflu

**unneighbourly** *adj* peu obligeant, indigne d'un bon voisin

**unnerve** *vt* déconcerter, faire perdre son courage à

**unnoticed** *adj* inaperçu, inobservé

**unnumbered** *adj* (countless) innombrable, sans nombre; non numéroté

**unobjectionable** *adj* irréprochable

**unobservant** *adj* peu observateur -trice

**unobserved** *adj* inaperçu

**unobstructed** *adj* non encombré, libre

**unobtainable** *adj* impossible à obtenir

**unobtrusive** *adj* discret -ète, effacé, modeste

**unoccupied** *adj* inoccupé; (seat) libre; (idle) sans occupation; (house) inhabité

**unoffending** *adj* innocent, inoffensif -ive

**unofficial** *adj* non officiel -ielle; (information) officieux -ieuse; ~ **strike** grève décidée sans l'appui du syndicat, grève *f* sauvage

**unopened** *adj* non ouvert; (letter) non décacheté; (bottle) non débouché

**unopposed** *adj* sans opposition

**unorganized** *adj* sans organisation, mal organisé

**unoriginal** *adj* (work, etc) banal (*pl* banals); (person) dépourvu d'originalité

**unorthodox** *adj* peu orthodoxe; *eccles* hétérodoxe

**unostentatious** *adj* (person) simple; (action) fait sans ostentation

**unpack** *vt* déballer; (luggage) défaire

**unpaid** *adj* non payé; (post) non rétribué; (person) qui ne reçoit pas de salaire; (bill) non acquitté

**unpalatable** *adj* peu agréable au goût; *fig* désagréable

**unparalleled** *adj* incomparable, sans pareil -eille •

**unpardonable** *adj* impardonnable

**unparliamentary** *adj* indigne d'un membre du parlement; (language) grossier -ière

**unpatriotic** *adj* (person) peu patriote; (action) peu patriotique

**unpaved** *adj* non pavé

**unpeg** *vt* dépendre; (prices) permettre l'augmentation de

**unperceived** *adj* inaperçu

**unperformed** *adj* inaccompli, inachevé; *theat* non joué

**unperturbed** *adj* impassible, calme

**unpick** *vt* (sewing) défaire

**unpicked** *adj* (sewing) défait; (flowers, etc) non cueilli; (not chosen) non choisi

**unpin** *vt* enlever les épingles de

**unplaced** *adj* (person) sans emploi; (candidate) non classé; (horse) non placé

**unplanned** *adj* qui n'a pas été organisé à l'avance; accidentel -elle, imprévu

**unplayable** *adj* injouable; *mus* inexécutable

**unpleasant** *adj* désagréable, déplaisant, fâcheux -euse

**unpleasantness** *n* désagrément *m*; (person) caractère déplaisant; (quarrel) brouille *f*

**unpleasing** *adj* peu agréable; (person) qui manque de grâce, déplaisant

**unplug** *vt elect* débrancher

**unpolished** *adj* non poli; (shoes) non ciré; (person) grossier -ière; (glass) dépoli

**unpolluted** *adj* non pollué, pur

**unpopular** *adj* impopulaire

**unpopularity** *n* impopularité *f*

**unpractical** *adj* peu pratique; (task) impraticable

**unprecedented** *adj* sans précédent, inouï

**unpredictable** *adj* imprévisible

**unprejudiced** *adj* sans préjugés, impartial

**unpremeditated** *adj* non prémédité

**unprepared** *adj* non préparé, improvisé; sans préparatifs; (food) inapprêté; **catch s/o ~** prendre qn au dépourvu

**unprepossessing** *adj* peu engageant, rébarbatif -ive

**unpresentable** *adj* peu présentable

**unpretentious, unpretending** *adj* modeste, sans prétentions

**unpriced** *adj* dont le prix n'est pas marqué

**unprincipled** *adj* sans principes, sans scrupules

**unprintable** *adj* que l'on n'ose pas imprimer; licencieux -ieuse

**unprivileged** *adj* sans privilèges

**unprized** *adj* peu estimé

**unprocurable** *adj* introuvable, impossible à obtenir

**unproductive** *adj* improductif -ive

**unprofessional** *adj* contraire aux usages de la profession (du métier), contraire au code professionnel

**unprofitable** *adj* peu lucratif -ive, peu rentable; (vain) inutile

**unpromising** *adj* peu prometteur -euse

**unprompted** *adj* spontané

**unpronounceable** *adj* imprononçable

**unprotected** *adj* sans protection, sans défense

**unprovable** *adj* impossible à prouver

**unproved** *adj* non prouvé; (not tested) inéprouvé

**unprovided** *adj* dépourvu, dénué; ~ **for** sans ressources

**unprovoked** *adj* non provoqué, gratuit

**unpublished** *adj* inédit

**unpunctual** *adj* inexact; (late) en retard; **always ~** jamais à l'heure

**unpunctuality** *n* inexactitude *f*, manque *m* de ponctualité

**unpunished** *adj* impuni

**unqualified** *adj* incompétent; n'ayant pas de diplôme(s); (not restricted) sans réserve, sans restriction; *coll* total, absolu

**unquenchable** *adj* (fire) inextinguible; insatiable

**unquenched** *adj* (fire) non éteint; (thirst) non étanché; (desire) inassouvi

**unquestionable** *adj* indiscutable, indubitable

**unquestioned** *adj* indisputé, incontesté

**unquestioning** *adj* inconditionnel -elle, aveugle

**unquestioningly** *adv* aveuglément

**unquiet** *adj* agité, inquiet -iète

**unquotable** *adj* que l'on ne peut citer (répéter)

**unquote** *vi* fermer les guillemets; **quote** ... ~ début *m* de citation ... fin *f* de citation

**unquoted** *adj* non cité; (share) non coté

**unravel** *vt* (thread) effiler, débrouiller; *fig* éclairer; *vi* (thread) s'effiler; *fig* se débrouiller

**unreachable** *adj* impossible à atteindre

**unread** *adj* non lu

**unreadable** *adj* illisible

**unreadiness** *n* manque *m* de préparation; manque *m* de promptitude

**unready** *adj* pas prêt; pas préparé; irrésolu

**unreal** *adj* irréel -elle, sans réalité

**unrealistic** *adj* peu réaliste

**unreality** *n* irréalité *f*

**unrealizable** *adj* irréalisable

**unrealized** *adj* non réalisé

**unreasonable** *adj* déraisonnable, peu raisonnable; (exaggerated) exagéré, exorbitant

**unrecognizable** *adj* méconnaissable

**unrecognized** *adj* méconnu; (government, etc) non reconnu

**unreconciled** *adj* irréconcilié

**unrecorded** *adj* dont on ne trouve aucune mention; (not on tape) non enregistré

**unredeemed** *adj* non racheté; (promise) non tenu; (pledge) non dégagé

**unreel** *vt* débobiner, dérouler

**unrefined** *adj* non raffiné, brut; (person) grossier -ière

**unreflecting** *adj* (light) non réfléchissant; (thoughtless) étourdi

**unreformed** *adj* non réformé

**unregarded** *adj* (not noticed) inaperçu; (of no value) non estimé

**unregistered** *adj* non enregistré, non inscrit; (letter) non recommandé; (birth) non déclaré; (car) non immatriculé

**unrehearsed** *adj* impromptu, non préparé; (play) non répété

**unrelated** *adj* sans rapport; (kinship) sans lien de parenté

**unrelenting** *adj* implacable, inexorable

**unreliability** *n* inexactitude *f*; (character) instabilité *f*

**unreliable** *adj* peu sûr, sur lequel (*f* laquelle) on ne peut pas compter; (information) sujet -ette à caution

**unrelieved** *adj* sans secours; (pain)

constant, non soulagé; (landscape) monotone; (continuous) continu, incessant

**unremarkable** *adj* peu remarquable, indigne d'attention, médiocre

**unremitting** *adj* incessant, inlassable

**unremittingly** *adv* inlassablement, sans cesse, sans relâche

**unremunerative** *adj* peu rémunérateur -trice, peu lucratif -ive

**unrepentant** *adj* impénitent

**unrepresentative** *adj* peu représentatif -ive, peu typique

**unrequited** *adj* non récompensé; (love) non partagé

**unreserved** *adj* sans réserve, franc (*f* franche); (seat, etc) non réservé

**unresolved** *adj* non résolu

**unresponsive** *adj* insensible, peu sensible, froid

**unrest** *n* inquiétude *f*, trouble *m*, agitation *f*

**unrestrained** *adj* libre, sans restriction; immodéré, outrancier -ière

**unrestricted** *adj* sans restriction, illimité

**unrewarded** *adj* non récompensé, sans récompense

**unrighteous** *adj* impie; (unjust) injuste, méchant

**unripe** *adj* pas mûr, vert; (corn) en herbe

**unrivalled** *adj* sans rival, incomparable

**unroll** *vt* dérouler; *vi* se dérouler

**unromantic** *adj* peu romantique; prosaïque, terre à terre *invar*

**unruffled** *adj* (person) placide, serein; (sea) calme; (hair) lisse

**unruly** *adj* indiscipliné, turbulent

**unsaddle** *vt* (person) désarçonner; (horse) desseller

**unsafe** *adj* dangereux -euse, peu sûr; hasardeux -euse; en danger

**unsaid** *adj* leave sth ~ passer qch sous silence

**unsal(e)able** *adj* invendable

**unsanctified** *adj* non béni

**unsanitary** *adj* peu hygiénique; (unhealthy) insalubre

**unsatisfactory** *adj* peu satisfaisant, qui laisse à désirer

**unsatisfied** *adj* insatisfait; (appetite) inassouvi

**unsatisfying** *adj* peu satisfaisant; insuffisant

**unsavoury** *adj* désagréable, mauvais; répugnant; (reputation) équivoque

**unsay** *vt* rétracter, se dédire de

**unscathed** *adj* (person) indemne, sain et sauf (*f* saine et sauve)

**unscholarly** *adj* indigne d'un savant; (person) peu savant

**unschooled** *adj* peu instruit

**unscientific** *adj* peu scientifique

**unscramble** vt (signals) décoder; coll
(plan) annuler

**unscratched** adj sans égratignure; fig
complètement indemne

**unscreened** adj (place) exposé; (without
screen) sans écran; cin qui n'a pas été
tourné en film; (not investigated) non
examiné

**unscrew** vt dévisser

**unscripted** adj sans script, improvisé

**unscrupulous** adj sans scrupules, peu
scrupuleux -euse

**unscrupulousness** n manque m de scrupules

**unseal** vt décacheter

**unsealed** adj non cacheté; (not stuck
down) ouvert

**unseasonable** adj hors de saison; fig
déplacé, inopportun

**unseat** vt (horseman) désarçonner; faire
perdre son siège (sa situation) à

**unseaworthy** adj hors d'état de prendre
la mer

**unsecured** adj (door) mal fermé; (loan)
non garanti

**unseeing** adj aveugle

**unseemliness** n inconvenance f, indécence f

**unseemly** adj inconvenant, peu convenable, indécent

**unseen** n version f; adj inaperçu; ~
translation version f

**unselfconscious** adj naturel -elle

**unselfish** adj sans égoïsme; généreux
-euse; (action) désintéressé

**unselfishness** n désintéressement m;
générosité f

**unserviceable** adj inutilisable, hors
d'état de servir

**unsettle** vt troubler le repos de, per-
turber; (disturb) déranger

**unsettled** adj (person) troublé, inquiet
-iète; (weather) variable, incertain;
(unpaid) non réglé; (question) indécis

**unsettling** adj troublant, inquiétant

**unshackled** adj libre, sans entraves

**unshaded** adj non ombragé; (lamp) sans
abat-jour; (drawing) non hachuré

**unshak(e)able** adj inébranlable

**unshaken** adj inébranlé

**unshapely** adj difforme, mal fait

**unshaven** adj non rasé; (bearded) barbu

**unsheathe** vt dégainer

**unsheltered** adj non abrité, exposé

**unship** vt décharger

**unshod** adj (person) sans chaussures,
nu-pieds invar; (horse) déferré

**unshrinkable** adj irrétrécissable

**unshriven** adj die ~ mourir sans confession ni absolution

**unsighted** adj inaperçu; (gun) sans
hausse

**unsightly** adj laid, vilain

**unsigned** adj sans signature

**unsinkable** adj insubmersible

**unskilful** adj inhabile, maladroit

**unskilled** adj inexpérimenté, inexpert;
~ labour main-d'œuvre (pl mains-
d'œuvre) non spécialisée; ~ labourer
(workman) manœuvre m

**unskimmed** adj (milk) non écrémé

**unsleeping** adj vigilant

**unsociable** adj insociable, farouche

**unsocial** adj contre les usages de la
société; insociable; ~ hours heures
anormales

**unsold** adj invendu

**unsoldierly** adj peu martial

**unsolicited** adj non sollicité; spontané

**unsolvable** adj insoluble

**unsolved** adj non résolu

**unsophisticated** adj (manner) naturel
-elle; (person) naïf (f naïve)

**unsound** adj (health) précaire; (mind)
dérangé; (opinion) erroné, mal fondé;
(weakened) affaibli, peu solide; (business) périclitant

**unsparing** adj prodigue; (merciless) impitoyable; be ~ of sth ne pas ménager
qch

**unspeakable** adj inexprimable, indicible; pej infect, détestable

**unspecialized** adj non spécialisé

**unspecified** adj non spécifié

**unspoilt** adj (child) non gâté;
(unaffected) inaltéré; (object, countryside, etc) qui n'est pas abîmé

**unspoken** adj tacite; (understood) sous-
entendu

**unsportsmanlike**, **unsporting** adj
déloyal, indigne d'un sportsman

**unspotted** adj sans tache, immaculé;
(not seen) inaperçu

**unstable** adj instable; (character) inconstant

**unstamped** adj (letter) sans timbre, non
affranchi

**unstatesmanlike** adj indigne d'un
homme d'état

**unsteadiness** n instabilité f; indécision f,
irrésolution f

**unsteady** adj peu solide, peu stable;
(character) irrésolu, inconstant; (step)
chancelant

**unstick** vt décoller

**unstinted** adj abondant, sans limite,
sans réserve

**unstinting** adj prodigue, libéral

**unstop** vt (bottle) déboucher; (unblock)
dégorger

**unstoppable** adj qu'on ne peut pas arrêter

**unstoppered** adj sans bouchon

**unstrap** *vt* ôter la courroie (les courroies) de

**unstressed** *adj* atone, sans accent

**unstuck** *adj* décollé; **come ~** se décoller; *coll* échouer

**unstudied** *adj* spontané, naturel -elle; **~ in** ignorant de

**unsubdued** *adj* indompté, non maîtrisé

**unsubmissive** *adj* insoumis

**unsubsidized** *adj* non subventionné

**unsubstantial** *adj* insubstantiel -ielle; (not firm) peu solide; (meal) léger -ère

**unsubstantiated** *adj* non prouvé; (rumour) non confirmé

**unsuccessful** *adj* non réussi, raté, infructueux -euse; (person) qui a échoué; (applicant) refusé; *pol* non élu; **be ~** échouer

**unsuccessfully** *adv* sans succès

**unsuitability** *n* impropreté *f*; inaptitude *f*; inopportunité *f*

**unsuitable** *adj* (thing) impropre; (person) inapte; (remark) déplacé, inopportun; (unbecoming) peu convenable

**unsuited** *adj* **~ for** (thing) impropre à; (person) peu fait pour; **they are ~ to each other** ils sont mal assortis

**unsullied** *adj* sans tache, sans souillure

**unsung** *adj fig* méconnu

**unsupported** *adj* (statement) non confirmé; (person, effort) sans soutien, non soutenu; (structure) sans support, non étayé

**unsure** *adj* incertain, peu sûr; **be ~ of oneself** manquer de confiance en soi-même

**unsurpassed** *adj* non surpassé

**unsuspected** *adj* insoupçonné

**unsuspecting** *adj* sans soupçons, sans méfiance

**unsuspicious** *adj* (feeling no suspicion) sans soupçons, peu méfiant; (arousing no suspicion) qui n'évoque aucun soupçon

**unsweetened** *adj* non sucré, sans sucre

**unswerving** *adj* inébranlable, constant

**unsymmetrical** *adj* asymétrique

**unsympathetic** *adj* indifférent, peu compatissant; (unlikeable) antipathique

**unsystematic** *adj* sans méthode, non systématique

**untack** *vt* (seam) défaire

**untainted** *adj* non corrompu; (food) frais (*f* fraîche)

**untamed** *adj* non apprivoisé, farouche; sauvage; (unsubdued) indompté

**untangle** *vt* (string, hair, etc) démêler; *fig* éclaircir, débrouiller

**untapped** *adj fig* inutilisé, inexploité

**untarnished** *adj* non terni; (reputation) sans tache

**untasted** *adj* auquel (*f* à laquelle) on n'a pas goûté

**untaught** *adj* ignorant, sans instruction; **do sth ~** faire qch sans avoir appris, faire qch naturellement

**untaxed** *adj* non imposé; (car) sans vignette; *fig* non surchargé

**unteachable** *adj* (thing) impossible à enseigner; (person) à qui l'on ne peut rien apprendre

**untempered** *adj* (steel) non revenu; non tempéré, non atténué

**untenable** *adj* (theory) insoutenable; (position) intenable

**untenanted** *adj* inoccupé, sans locataire

**untested** *adj* non éprouvé; (result) non vérifié

**untether** *vt* détacher

**unthankful** *adj* ingrat

**unthinkable** *adj* inimaginable, impensable, inconcevable

**unthinking** *adj* irréfléchi, étourdi

**unthought-of** *adj* inattendu

**untidily** *adv* sans ordre, sans soin

**untidiness** *n* désordre *m*; (dress) débraillé *m*

**untidy** *adj* (person) désordonné; (room) en désordre; (hair) mal peigné; (dress) débraillé

**untie** *vt* dénouer, défaire; (person) délier

**until** *prep* jusqu'à; **not do sth ~ after** ne faire qch qu'après; **not ~** pas avant; *conj* jusqu'à ce que; **~ he succeeds** jusqu'à ce qu'il réussisse; **not ~ he succeeds** pas avant qu'il (ne) réussisse

**untimely** *adj* (early) prématuré; (inopportune) inopportun

**untiring** *adj* infatigable; (activity) assidu

**unto** *prep lit see* to

**untold** *adj* passé sous silence; (unlimited) incalculable, immense, inouï, inimaginable

**untouchable** *adj* intouchable

**untouched** *adj* non touché; (unharmed) indemne

**untoward** *adj* malencontreux -euse, fâcheux -euse; *ar* (person) indocile

**untraceable** *adj* introuvable

**untrained** *adj* inexercé, inexpérimenté

**untrammelled** *adj* sans entraves, sans contrainte

**untransferable** *adj* non transmissible; *leg* incessible, inaliénable

**untranslatable** *adj* intraduisible

**untravelled** *adj* (person) qui n'a jamais voyagé; (country) inexploré

**untried** *adj* pas encore mis à l'épreuve; *leg* qui n'a pas encore été jugé

**untrodden** *adj* isolé, inexploré; (snow, forest) vierge

**untroubled** *adj* calme, paisible

**untrue** *adj* faux (*f* fausse), erroné; (person) déloyal

**untrustworthy** *adj* indigne de confiance; (memory) peu sûr; (information) douteux -euse

**untruth** *n* mensonge *m*

**untruthful** *adj* menteur -euse; (false) faux (*f* fausse); (statement) mensonger -ère

**untutored** *adj* ignorant, sans instruction, peu instruit

**untwist** *vt* détordre, démêler, défaire

¹**unused** *adj* inutilisé; (word) inusité; (new) neuf (*f* neuve)

²**unused** *adj* (unaccustomed) peu habitué, inaccoutumé

**unusual** *adj* extraordinaire, exceptionnel -elle, insolite, inhabituel -elle; (word) peu usité

**unusually** *adv* exceptionnellement

**unutterable** *adj* indicible

**unvalued** *adj* peu estimé; (not costed) non évalué

**unvaried** *adj* constant, uniforme; monotone

**unvarnished** *adj* non verni; *fig* simple, sans fard

**unvarying** *adj* invariable

**unveil** *vt* dévoiler

**unverifiable** *adj* invérifiable

**unverified** *adj* non vérifié

**unversed** *adj* peu versé, ignorant

**unvoiced** *adj* non exprimé; (consonant) sourd

**unwanted** *adj* non désiré; (surplus) superflu

**unwarily** *adv* imprudemment

**unwariness** *n* imprudence *f*

**unwarlike** *adj* peu guerrier -ière, paisible

**unwarrantable** *adj* inexcusable

**unwarranted** *adj* injustifié; (not guaranteed) sans garantie

**unwary** *adj* imprudent, sans méfiance

**unwashed** *adj* malpropre, non lavé; **the great** ~ le peuple, les prolétaires *mpl*

**unwavering** *adj* constant, ferme, inébranlable

**unweaned** *adj* non sevré

**unwearable** *adj* que l'on ne peut pas porter

**unwearied** *adj* non fatigué; infatigable

**unwearying** *adj* inlassable

**unwelcome** *adj* (person) mal venu, importun; (thing) désagréable, fâcheux -euse

**unwell** *adj* souffrant, peu bien

**unwholesome** *adj* malsain; (climate) insalubre

**unwieldy** *adj* (object) peu maniable; (person) gauche, lourd

**unwilling** *adj* peu serviable, pas d'accord; **be ~ to do sth** être peu disposé à faire qch, refuser de faire qch

**unwillingness** *n* mauvaise volonté, répugnance *f*

**unwind** *vt* dérouler; *vi* se dérouler; *sl* se détendre

**unwisdom** *n* imprudence *f*, stupidité *f*

**unwise** *adj* imprudent, malavisé

**unwitting** *adj* inconscient; (unintentional) involontaire

**unwittingly** *adv* sans le savoir, inconsciemment

**unwomanly** *adj* peu féminin

**unwonted** *adj* inaccoutumé, insolite

**unworkable** *adj* impraticable; (land, mine) inexploitable

**unworldly** *adj* détaché de ce monde, qui n'est pas de ce monde

**unworn** *adj* non usé; qui n'a pas été porté

**unworthiness** *n* peu *m* de mérite

**unworthy** *adj* indigne; (worthless) sans valeur, méprisable

**unwounded** *adj* sans blessure, non blessé, indemne

**unwrap** *vt* défaire

**unwritten** *adj* non écrit; **it's an ~ law that** il est accepté que

**unyielding** *adj* qui ne cède pas, ferme; (person) opiniâtre

**unzip** *vt* ouvrir en tirant la fermeture éclair

**up** *n* ~ **s and downs** les hauts *mpl* et les bas *mpl*, les vicissitudes *fpl*; *coll* **be on the ~ and** ~ être en train de faire son chemin, aller en progressant; *adj* montant, de montée; **the** ~ **train** le train qui va en direction de la ville (de la capitale); *vt coll* augmenter; *adv* en haut, vers le haut; (in the air) en l'air; (standing) debout; (out of bed) levé; (time) écoulé, expiré; (prices) en hausse; (tide) haut; (sun, moon) levé; (umbrella) ouvert; (shutters) fermé; à l'université; **above en haut;** ~ **there** là-haut; ~ **to now** jusqu'ici; **all the way** ~ jusqu'en haut; *coll* **be** ~ **against it** être aux prises avec des difficultés; **be** ~ **all night** ne pas se coucher de la nuit; **be** ~ **and doing** se mettre à la besogne; **be** ~ **to sth** (capable) être capable de faire qch; (scheme) mijoter qch, avoir qch en tête; **be well** ~ **in sth** connaître qch à fond; **business is looking** ~ les affaires reprennent; **further** ~ (higher) plus haut; (further away) plus loin; **go** ~ monter; (increase) augmenter; (to town) aller en ville; **go** ~ **to s/o** aborder qn, s'approcher de qn; **I don't feel** ~ **to it** je ne m'en sens pas la force; *coll* **it's all** ~ **with us** c'en est fait de nous; **it's** ~ **to him to do it** c'est à lui de le faire; **road** ~ route *f* en réparation, travaux *mpl*; *coll* **there's sth** ~ il y a qch; **two floors** ~ au deuxième étage; *US* au premier étage; **walk** ~ **and**

**down** aller (marcher) de long en large, faire les cent pas; *coll* what's ~ ? qu'y a-t-il?; *coll* what's ~ with you? qu'est-ce qui vous prend?, qu'est-ce que vous avez?; *prep* en haut de

**up-and-coming** *adj* d'avenir, qui avance bien

**upbraid** *vt* reprocher

**upbringing** *n* éducation *f*; formation *f*

**up-country** *adj* de l'intérieur; *fig* naïf (*f* naïve)

**up-date** *vt* moderniser; (report) mettre à jour

**up-end** *vt* mettre debout

**up-grade** *n* montée *f*, pente ascendante; **be on the ~** monter; (improving) reprendre, s'améliorer; *vt* donner un grade supérieur à; (job) revaloriser

**upheaval** *n* bouleversement *m*, agitation *f*; *geol* soulèvement *m*

**uphill** *adj* montant; *fig* dur, pénible, difficile; *adv* en montant

**uphold** *vt* supporter; (theory) soutenir; (confirm) confirmer; (verdict) maintenir; **~ the law** faire observer la loi

**upholster** *vt* tapisser; (chair) rembourrer, capitonner

**upholsterer** *n* tapissier *m*

**upholstery** *n* tapisserie *f* d'ameublement; (chair) rembourrage *m*

**upkeep** *n* entretien *m*; (cost) frais *mpl* d'entretien

**upland** *adj* des montagnes

**uplands** *npl* région montagneuse, hautes terres *fpl*

**uplift** *n* élévation *f*; *iron* élévation morale; *vt* soulever, hausser; *fig* élever, égayer; (morally) édifier

**upon** *prep see* **on**

**upper** *n* (shoe) empeigne *f*; **be down on one's ~ s** être dans la dèche; *adj* supérieur, plus élevé, de dessus, haut; *theat* **~ circle** deuxième balcon *m*; **gain the ~ hand** prendre le dessus; **the ~ part** le dessus; **the ~ Volga** la haute Volga

**upper-class** *adj* appartenant aux classes supérieures, typique des classes supérieures

**upper-cut** *n* (boxing) uppercut *m*

**uppermost** *adj* le plus haut (*f* la plus haute); *fig* premier -ière; *adv* au dessus, en dessus; **be ~** prédominer

**uppish** *adj coll* arrogant, présomptueux -euse

**upright** *n* montant *m*; (piano) piano droit; *adj* vertical, droit, perpendiculaire; *fig* honnête

**uprightness** *n* droiture *f*, intégrité *f*; verticalité *f*

**uprising** *n* soulèvement *m*, révolte *f*

**uproar** *n* vacarme *m*, *coll* chahut *m*

**uproarious** *adj* tumultueux -euse,

bruyant

**uproot** *vt* déraciner

**uprush** *n see* **upsurge**

**upset** *n* bouleversement *m*, chambardement *m*, remue-ménage *m invar*; (boat) chavirement *m*; (trouble) ennui *m*; (plans) renversement *m*; *adj* bouleversé, ému; (auction) ~ **price** mise *f* à prix; *vt* (knock over) renverser; (disturb) bouleverser; (boat) faire chavirer; (arrangements) désorganiser, déranger; (person) troubler, bouleverser; (stomach) déranger; *vi* se renverser

**upsetting** *adj* inquiétant, bouleversant, fâcheux -euse

**upshot** *n* résultat *m*, issue *f*

**upside-down** *adj* renversé; *adv* sens dessus dessous, la tête en bas, à l'envers; *coll fig* en désordre

**upstage** *vt* éclipser; *adj coll* hautain, snob *invar*; *adv theat* derrière les décors, dans les coulisses

**upstairs** *adj* d'en haut; *adv* en haut (de l'escalier); **go ~** monter (l'escalier)

**upstanding** *adj* debout *invar*; *fig* honnête, probe

**upstart** *n* parvenu -e

**upstream** *adv* en amont

**upsurge, uprush** *n* poussée *f*, accès *m*; recrudescence *f*

**uptake** *n* compréhension *f*; *coll* **be quick on the ~** avoir l'esprit éveillé; **be slow on the ~** avoir la compréhension lente

**uptight** *adj sl* tendu

**up-to-date** *adj* moderne, à la page; *coll* dans le vent; (fashion) à la mode, dernier cri *invar*

**up-to-the-minute** *adj* très récent, tout récent (*f* toute récente)

**upturn** *n* amélioration *f*; *vt* retourner, renverser

**upturned** *adj* (nose) retroussé; (edges) relevé

**upward** *adj* ascendant

**upwards** *adv* en montant, vers le haut; (facing) en dessus; **~ of** plus de; **look ~** regarder en l'air; **they cost from fifty francs ~** les prix vont à partir de cinquante francs

**uranium** *n* uranium *m*

**urban** *adj* urbain

**urbane** *adj* poli, courtois

**urbanity** *n* urbanité *f*, courtoisie *f*

**urbanization** *n* urbanisation *f*

**urbanize** *vt* urbaniser

**urchin** *n* gamin -e

**urethra** *n anat* urètre *m*

**urge** *n* impulsion *f*, poussée *f*; *vt* presser, encourager, exhorter, exciter; (advocate) alléguer, faire valoir; (entreat) prier instamment

**urgency** *n* urgence *f*

773

**urgent** *adj* urgent, pressant
**urinal** *n* urinoir *m*; (pot) urinal *m*
**urinary** *adj* urinaire
**urinate** *vi* uriner
**urination** *n* acte *m* d'uriner
**urine** *n* urine *f*
**urn** *n* urne *f*; (tea, etc) fontaine *f*
**Uruguay** *n* Uruguay *m*
**Uruguayan** *n* Uruguayen -enne; *adj* uruguayen -enne
**us** *pron* nous, nous autres
**usable** *adj* utilisable
**usage** *n* (use) traitement *m*; (custom) coutume *f*, usage *m*
**use** *n* usage *m*, emploi *m*; (utility) utilité *f*; (action) utilisation *f*; (need) besoin *m*; (habit) coutume *f*, habitude *f*; (right to use) jouissance *f*; **directions for ~** mode *m* d'emploi; **for the ~ of** à l'usage de; *coll* **have no ~ for s/o** être embêté par qn, détester qn; **have no ~ for sth** n'avoir aucun besoin de qch; **it was no ~ me (my) trying** j'avais beau essayer; **make ~ of sth** se servir de qch; **not in ~** pas en service; **out of ~** hors d'usage, hors de service; **that's no ~ at all** ça ne vaut rien du tout, ça ne sert à rien du tout; **what's the ~ of doing this?** à quoi bon faire cela?; *vt* employer, se servir de, utiliser; (treat) en user avec; (consume) consommer; **~ up** épuiser, finir; **I ~ this as a lever** cela me sert de levier; *vi* **I ~d to go** j'allais
**used** *adj* usagé; (stamp) oblitéré; **~ to** habitué à; **~ up** épuisé, fini; **get ~ to sth** s'habituer à qch
**useful** *adj* utile; pratique; profitable
**usefulness** *n* utilité *f*
**useless** *adj* inutile; (vain) vain; (person) bon (*f* bonne) à rien
**user** *n* usager -ère, utilisateur -trice
**usher** *n* huissier *m*; (doorkeeper) portier *m*; *theat* placeur *m*; *vt* **~ s/o in** faire entrer qn; **~ s/o out** reconduire qn (jusqu'à la porte)
**usherette** *n* ouvreuse *f*
**usual** *adj* habituel -elle, usuel -elle; (customary) d'usage; *adv* habituellement, d'habitude; **as ~** comme d'habitude
**usually** *adv* d'habitude, d'ordinaire, habituellement
**usurer** *n* usurier -ière
**usurious** *adj* usuraire
**usurp** *vt* usurper
**usurpation** *n* usurpation *f*
**usurper** *n* usurpateur -trice
**usury** *n* usure *f*
**utensil** *n* ustensile *m*
**uterus** *n* utérus *m*
**utilitarian** *adj* utilitaire
**utility** *n* utilité *f*; **public ~** entreprise *f* de service public; *adj* utilitaire
**utilizable** *adj* utilisable
**utilization** *n* utilisation *f*
**utilize** *vt* utiliser
**utmost, uttermost** *n* dernier degré; **at the ~** tout au plus; **do one's ~ to** faire tout son possible pour; *adj* dernier -ière, extrême; **of the ~ importance** de la dernière importance
**utopia** *n* utopie *f*
**utopian** *adj* utopique
¹**utter** *adj* complet -ète, absolu, entier -ière; **~ idiot** parfait imbécile
²**utter** *vt* (cry) pousser; (word) prononcer, dire; (circulate) mettre en circulation
**utterance** *n* déclaration *f*, expression *f*; articulation *f*
**utterly** *adv* complètement, tout à fait
**uttermost** *adj see* **utmost**
**U-turn** *n* demi-tour *m*, retour *m* en arrière
**uvula** *n* luette *f*
**uxorious** *adj* très attaché à sa femme

# V

**V VD** *abbr* maladie vénérienne; **V neck** décolleté *m* en V; **the V sign** le V de la victoire
**vac** *n abbr* vacances *fpl*
**vacancy** *n* (situation) vacance *f*; (emptiness) vide *m*; (stupidity) absence *f* d'idées
**vacant** *adj* (situation) vacant; (house, etc) inoccupé, vide; (look) distrait, niais, stupide; **~ possession** libre

possession f

**vacate** vt quitter, évacuer

**vacation** n vacances fpl; (university) **long ~** grandes vacances

**vacationist** n US vacancier -ière

**vaccinate** vt vacciner

**vaccination** n vaccination f

**vaccine** n vaccin m

**vacillate** vi vaciller, hésiter

**vacillating** adj irrésolu, indécis

**vacillation** n vacillation f, hésitation f

**vacuity** n vide m; fig manque m d'intelligence

**vacuous** adj niais, stupide; (face, eyes) sans expression; (remark) dénué de sens

**vacuum** n vide m; phys vacuum m; **~ brake** frein m à vide; **~ cleaner** aspirateur m; **~ flask** Thermos m; **~ packed** emballé sous vide; **~ pump** pompe f à vide

**vagabond** n + adj vagabond -e

**vagary** n caprice m, fantaisie f

**vagina** n vagin m

**vaginal** adj vaginal; **~ discharge** pertes blanches

**vagrancy** n vagabondage m

**vagrant** n + adj vagabond -e

**vague** adj vague; (outline) flou; (person) indécis; **not have the ~st idea** n'avoir pas la moindre idée

**vagueness** n vague m

**vain** adj vain; (useless) inutile; (person) vaniteux -euse; **in ~** en vain, inutilement; **it will be ~ for you to try** vous aurez beau essayer; **take God's name in ~** blasphémer le nom de Dieu

**vainglorious** adj orgueilleux -euse, vaniteux -euse

**vainglory** n gloriole f, prétention f

**vainly** adv vainement, inutilement

**valance** n (bed) tour m de lit, frange f

**vale** n poet val m, vallon m

**valediction** n adieu m, adieux mpl

**valedictory** adj d'adieu

**valency** n chem valence f

**valentine** n amoureux -euse; carte envoyée le jour de la Saint-Valentin

**valet** n valet m de chambre; vt nettoyer, remettre en état

**valetudinarian** n + adj valétudinaire

**valiant** adj valeureux -euse, vaillant

**valid** adj valable, valide; (ticket) **no longer ~** périmé

**validate** vt valider

**validity** n validité f

**valise** n sac m de voyage, mallette f

**valium** n valium m

**valley** n vallée f; bui noue f

**valorous** adj valeureux -euse

**valour** n vaillance f

**valuable** adj de valeur, précieux -ieuse

**valuables** npl objets mpl de valeur

**valuation** n évaluation f, estimation f; valeur estimée; leg expertise f

**value** n valeur f, prix m; fig mérite m; **~-added tax (V.A.T.)** taxe f à la valeur ajoutée (T.V.A.); **be of little ~** valoir peu de chose; **be of no ~** ne rien valoir; **be of ~** avoir de la valeur; **get good ~ for one's money** en avoir pour son argent; **increase in ~** plus-value f; vt évaluer, estimer

**valued** adj précieux -ieuse, estimé

**valueless** adj sans valeur

**valuer** n estimateur m, expert m; **official ~** commissaire-priseur m (pl commissaires-priseurs)

**valve** n soupape f; (tyre) valve f; anat valvule f; rad lampe f; **exhaust (outlet) ~** soupape f d'échappement; **inlet ~** soupape f d'admission; **safety ~** soupape f de sûreté

**valve-cap** n capuchon m

**valvular** adj valvulaire

**vamoose** vi US coll décamper, filer

**vamp** n coll vamp f, femme fatale; vt enjôler, envoûter; coll vamper

**vampire** n vampire m

**¹van** n (vehicle) fourgon m; (light) camionnette f; **delivery ~** camionnette f de livraison; **furniture (removal) ~** fourgon m de déménagement; **guard's ~** fourgon m (du chef de train); **luggage ~** fourgon m (à bagages)

**²van** n avant-garde f

**³van** n abbr (tennis) avantage m

**vandal** n vandale m

**vandalism** n vandalisme m

**vandalize** vt saccager

**vane** n (weather) girouette f; (windmill) bras m; (ventilator) pale f; (turbine) aube f

**vanguard** n avant-garde f

**vanilla** n vanille f; **~ ice-cream** glace f à la vanille

**vanish** vi disparaître

**vanishing** n disparition f; **~ point** point m de fuite; **do a ~ trick** disparaître; adj **~ cream** crème f de jour

**vanity** n vanité f; futilité f

**vanquish** vt vaincre

**vanquisher** n vainqueur m

**vantage** n **~ point** position avantageuse

**vapid** adj insipide, fade

**vapidity** n insipidité f, fadeur f

**vaporization** n vaporisation f

**vaporize** vt vaporiser; vi se vaporiser

**vaporizer** n vaporisateur m, pulvérisateur m, atomiseur m

**vaporous** adj vaporeux -euse

**vapour** n vapeur f; (on window) buée f, **~ trail** traînée f de condensation

**vapourings** npl fadaises fpl, bavardage m
inutile

**vapoury** adj vaporeux -euse; fig imaginaire, fantaisiste

**variability** n variabilité f

**variable** n math variable f; adj variable,
changeant

**variance** n désaccord m, discorde f; (temperature, etc) variation f; **at ~ with** en
désaccord avec

**variant** n variante f

**variation** n variation f, changement m

**varicoloured** adj de couleurs différentes,
bariolé, multicolore

**varicose** adj variqueux -euse; **~ veins**
varices fpl

**varied** adj varié, divers

**variegate** vt varier, diversifier; (colour)
barioler

**variegation** n diversité f de couleurs,
bigarrure f

**variety** n variété f, diversité f; **~ entertainment** numéros mpl de music-hall;
**~ theatre** théâtre m de variétés

**variform** adj diversiforme

**various** adj divers, varié, différent; (several) plusieurs

**varnish** n vernis m; vt vernir; (pottery)
vernisser; fig cacher, passer sous silence; (gloss over) farder

**vary** vt varier, faire varier; vi varier,
changer; être différent; (disagree) ne pas
être d'accord, différer

**vase** n vase m

**vasectomy** n vasectomie f

**vaseline** n vaseline f

**vassal** n vassal m

**vast** adj vaste, immense, énorme

**vastly** adv vastement; (very much) infiniment, immensément

**vat** n cuve f, bac m

**Vatican** n Vatican m; **~ City** Cité f du
Vatican

**vaudeville** n vaudeville m

¹**vault** n archi voûte f; (grave) caveau m;
(underground place) cave f; (bank)
chambre forte; **~ of heaven** voûte f céleste; vt voûter

²**vault** n (jump) saut m; vt sauter; vi **~
over** sauter, franchir d'un saut

**vaulted** adj voûté, en voûte

¹**vaulting** n construction f de voûtes

²**vaulting** n (jumping) exercice m du saut;
adj fig **~ ambition** ambition démesurée

**vaulting-horse** n cheval m d'arçons

**vaunt** vt vanter, se vanter de

**veal** n veau m

**vector** n vecteur m

**veer** n changement m de direction, virage
m; (opinion) revirement m; vt naut faire
virer; vi (ship) virer; (wind) tourner; fig
**~ round** changer d'opinion

**vegetable** n légume m; bot végétal m; **~
garden** (jardin m) potager m; **early ~ s**
primeurs fpl; adj végétal; (existence)
végétatif -ive

**vegetable-dish** n légumier m

**vegetarian** n + adj végétarien -ienne

**vegetarianism** n végétarisme m

**vegetative** adj végétatif -ive

**vehemence** n véhémence f

**vehement** adj véhément, impétueux
-euse

**vehicle** n véhicule m, voiture f; mil engin
m; med agent vecteur m

**vehicular** adj des voitures

**veil** n voile m; (hat) voilette f; vt voiler; fig
cacher, dissimuler

**veiled** adj voilé; fig caché

**vein** n veine f; bot + zool nervure f; geol
filon m; (humour) disposition f,
humeur f; vt veiner

**vellum** n vélin m

**velocity** n vélocité f, vitesse f

**velvet** n velours m; coll **on ~** sur du velours; adj de velours

**velveteen** n velours m de coton, velvet m

**velvety** adj velouté

**venal** adj vénal, corruptible

**vend** vt vendre

**vender, vendor** n vendeur -euse; leg vendeur -eresse

**vendetta** n vendetta f

**vending** n vente f; **~ machine** distributeur m automatique

**vendor** n see **vender**

**veneer** n revêtement m, placage m; fig
vernis m; vt plaquer

**veneering** n placage m

**venerable** adj vénérable

**venerate** vt vénérer

**veneration** n vénération f

**venereal** adj vénérien -ienne

**Venetian** n Vénitien -ienne; adj vénitien
-ienne; **~ blind** jalousie f

**Venezuela** n Venezuela m

**vengeance** n vengeance f; **take ~ on** s/o
se venger sur (de) qn; **with a ~** furieusement, pour de bon

**vengeful** adj vindicatif -ive

**venial** adj véniel -ielle, léger- ère

**veniality** n caractère véniel

**Venice** n Venise f

**venison** n venaison f

**venom** n venin m

**venomous** adj (snake, etc) venimeux
-euse; **~ tongue** langue f de vipère

**venous** adj veineux -euse

**vent** n trou m, orifice m, passage m;
(coat) fente f; geol cheminée f; **give ~
to** donner libre cours à, manifester, laisser éclater; (sigh, shout) laisser échapper; vt (anger) décharger, laisser éclater

**vent-hole** n (volcano) évent m; (barrel)

trou *m* de fausset

**ventilate** *vt* aérer, ventiler; (blood) oxy-géner; *coll* mettre en discussion, agiter

**ventilation** *n* aération *f*, ventilation *f*; (blood) oxygénation *f*

**ventilator** *n* ventilateur *m*

**ventricle** *n* ventricule *m*

**ventricular** *adj* ventriculaire

**ventriloquism** *n* ventriloquie *f*

**ventriloquist** *n* ventriloque

**venture** *n* risque *m*, aventure risquée; aventure *f*; *comm* spéculation *f*, opération *f*, entreprise risquée; **at a ~** à l'aventure, au hasard; *vt* risquer, hasarder; *vi* **~ into** s'aventurer dans; **~ to do sth** (risk) se risquer (hasarder) à faire qch; (dare) oser (se permettre de) faire qch; **~ (up)on sth** se risquer à faire qch

**venturesome** *adj* aventureux -euse; (action) risqué, hasardeux -euse

**venue** *n* lieu *m* de réunion, rendez-vous *m*; *leg* lieu *m* du jugement

**Venus** *n* Vénus *f*

**veracious** *adj* véridique

**veracity** *n* véracité *f*

**veranda** *n* véranda *f*

**verb** *n* verbe *m*

**verbal** *adj* verbal; (translation) littéral

**verbalism** *n* verbalisme *m*

**verbalization** *n* expression verbale

**verbalize** *vt* traduire (exprimer) en paroles

**verbally** *adv* verbalement; littéralement

**verbatim** *adj* textuel -elle; *adv* textuellement, mot pour mot

**verbena** *n* verveine *f*

**verbiage** *n* verbiage *m*

**verbose** *adj* verbeux -euse, diffus

**verbosity** *n* verbosité *f*

**verdancy** *n* verdure *f*; *fig* naïveté *f*

**verdant** *adj* vert, verdoyant

**verdict** *n* verdict *m*, jugement *m*; (opinion) avis *m*

**verdigris** *n* vert-de-gris *m*

**verdure** *n* verdure *f*, herbage *m*; *fig* verdeur *f*, jeunesse *f*

**verge** *n* bord *m*, bordure *f*; (road) accotement *m*; (wood) orée *f*; **on the ~ of disaster** à deux doigts de la catastrophe; **on the ~ of leaving** sur le point de partir; **on the ~ of tears** au bord des larmes; *vi* incliner, tendre; **~ on** toucher à; (age) friser; (colour) tirer sur

**verger** *n* bedeau *m*

**verifiable** *adj* vérifiable

**verification** *n* vérification *f*, contrôle *m*

**verify** *vt* vérifier

**verily** *adv* bibl + ar en vérité

**verisimilitude** *n* vraisemblance *f*

**veritable** *adj* véritable

**verity** *n* lit vérité *f*

**vermilion** *n* vermillon *m*; *adj* vermillon

*invar*, vermeil -eille

**vermin** *n* vermine *f*

**verminous** *adj* couvert de vermine

**vermouth** *n* vermout(h) *m*

**vernacular** *n* langue *f* du pays, langue *f* vulgaire; *adj* vernaculaire, du pays

**verruca** *n* verrue *f*

**versatile** *adj* aux talents variés; (mind) souple; *bot* + *zool* versatile

**versatility** *n* (person) faculté *f* d'adaptation; (mind) souplesse *f* d'esprit

**verse** *n* (line) vers *m*; (stanza) strophe *f*, couplet *m*; *bibl* verset *m*; (poetry) poésie *f*; *pej* poème *m* faible; **blank ~** vers blancs; **free ~** vers *mpl* libres

**versed** *adj* versé

**versification** *n* versification *f*

**versify** *vt* mettre en vers; *vi* faire des vers, versifier

**version** *n* version *f*, traduction *f*; interprétation *f*; **according to his ~** selon lui, d'après lui

**verso** *n* (page) verso *m*; (medal, coin) revers *m*

**versus** *prep* contre

**vertebra** *n* (*pl* **vertebrae**) vertèbre *f*

**vertebrate** *n* vertébré *m*; *adj* vertébré

**vertex** *n* (*pl* **vertices**) sommet *m*; *anat* vertex *m*

**vertical** *n* verticale *f*; *adj* vertical; **~ take-off aircraft** avion *m* à décollage vertical

**vertiginous** *adj* vertigineux -euse

**vertigo** *n* vertige *m*

**verve** *n* verve *f*

**very** *adj* vrai, véritable; (selfsame) même; complet -ète; **at the ~ beginning** tout au début; **do one's ~ best** faire tout son possible; **his ~ words** ses propres paroles; **in the ~ middle of** au beau milieu de; **in this ~ place** ici même; **the ~ idea!** ça, par exemple!; **the ~ thing I needed** justement ce qu'il me fallait; **the ~ thought** la seule pensée; **to the ~ day** jour pour jour; *adv* très, fort, bien; tout; **~ much** beaucoup, bien; **at the ~ latest** au plus tard; **at the ~ least** tout au moins; **at the ~ most** tout au plus; **not ~** pas tellement; **so ~ good** si bon (*f* bonne); **the ~ best** le meilleur de tous (*f* la meilleure de toutes); **the ~ first** le tout premier (*f* la toute première); **the ~ same day** le (ce) jour même

**vesicle** *n med* vésicule *f*

**vespers** *npl* vêpres *fpl*

**vessel** *n* (liquid) récipient *m*, vase *m*; (ship) vaisseau *m*, navire *m*; **blood ~** vaisseau sanguin

**¹vest** *n* gilet *m*; (underwear) tricot *m* (de corps); *vt* revêtir

**²vest** *vt* **~ s/o with authority** investir qn

de l'autorité; *vi leg* ~ **in** échoir à

**vested** *adj* dévolu; (invested) investi; ~ **interests** droits acquis

**vestibule** *n* vestibule *m*, entrée *f*

**vestige** *n* vestige *m*, trace *f*

**vestment** *n* vêtement *m*; *eccles* vêtement sacerdotal

**vestry** *n* sacristie *f*

**¹vet** *n coll* vétérinaire

**²vet** *vt* (person, statement) examiner (minutieusement); (text) corriger

**veteran** *n* vétéran *m*; *adj* vieux (*f* vieille), expérimenté, de vétéran

**veterinarian** *n* vétérinaire

**veterinary** *adj* vétérinaire

**veto** *n* veto *m*; *vt* interdire, mettre son veto à

**vex** *vt* vexer, contrarier, fâcher

**vexation** *n* vexation *f*, ennui *m*, tourment *m*

**vexatious** *adj* contrariant, ennuyeux -euse; *leg* vexatoire

**vexed** *adj* vexé, contrarié; ~ **question** question très débattue

**vexing** *adj* contrariant, vexant, ennuyeux -euse

**via** *prep* via, par

**viability** *n* viabilité *f*

**viable** *adj* viable

**viaduct** *n* viaduc *m*

**vial** *n* fiole *f*

**viands** *npl* aliments *mpl*

**viaticum** *n* viatique *m*

**vibrancy** *n* résonance *f*

**vibrant** *adj* vibrant

**vibraphone** *n* vibraphone *m*

**vibrate** *vt* faire vibrer; *vi* vibrer

**vibration** *n* vibration *f*, oscillation *f*

**vibrato** *n mus* vibrato *m*

**vibrator** *n* vibrateur *m*

**vicar** *n* pasteur *m*, vicaire *m*; (parish priest) = curé *m*; **the Vicar of Christ** le Pape

**vicarage** *n* (protestant) presbytère *m*; (Catholic) = cure *f*

**vicarious** *adj* (authority) délégué; (pleasure) ressenti par un autre; (punishment) souffert par un autre

**vicariously** *adv* à la place d'un autre

**¹vice** *n* vice *m*; (trait) défaut *m*

**²vice** *n* (tool) étau *m*

**³vice** *prep* à la place de; ~ **versa** vice versa, inversement

**vice-chairman** *n* vice-président *m*

**vice-chancellor** *n* vice-chancelier *m*; (university) recteur *m*

**vice-president** *n* vice-président -e

**vice-principal** *n* sous-directeur -trice

**viceroy** *n* vice-roi *m*

**vicinity** *n* voisinage *m*, proximité *f*

**vicious** *adj* dépravé, vicieux -ieuse; (spiteful) méchant; (ill-tempered) hai-

neux -euse; (horse) rétif -ive

**viciousness** *n* méchanceté *f*

**vicissitude** *n* vicissitude *f*, péripétie *f*

**victim** *n* victime *f*; **fall a** ~ **to** être victime de, succomber à

**victimization** *n* représailles *fpl*, oppression *f*

**victimize** *vt* exercer des représailles contre

**victor** *n* vainqueur *m*

**Victorian** *adj* victorien -ienne

**victorious** *adj* victorieux -ieuse

**victory** *n* victoire *f*; **gain a (the)** ~ remporter une (la) victoire

**victual** *vt* ravitailler, approvisionner

**victualler** *n* fournisseur *m* de vivres; **licensed** ~ débitant *m* de boissons

**victuals** *npl* vivres *mpl*, provisions *fpl*

**video** *n* télévision *f*; ~ **recorder** magnétoscope *m*; ~ **recording** enregistrement *m* sur magnétoscope

**vie** *vi* rivaliser, lutter; ~ **in politeness with s/o** faire assaut de politesse avec qn

**Vienna** *n* Vienne *f*

**Vietnam** *n* le Vietnam

**Vietnamese** *n* Vietnamien -ienne; *adj* vietnamien -ienne

**view** *n* vue *f*; coup d'œil *m*; opinion *f*, avis *m*; intention *f*; photo *f*; **get a good** ~ voir bien; **in my** ~ à mon avis; **in** ~ en vue; **in** ~ **of** en considération de, étant donné; **keep in** ~ ne pas perdre de vue; **on** ~ exposé au public; **point of** ~ point *m* de vue; **with a** ~ **to** dans le but de; *vt* regarder; examiner; (house) visiter; envisager

**viewer** *n* spectateur -trice; *TV* téléspectateur -trice

**view-finder** *n phot* viseur *m*

**viewpoint** *n* point *m* de vue; (panorama) belvédère *m*

**vigil** *n* veille *f*; *eccles* vigile *f*; **keep** ~ veiller

**vigilance** *n* vigilance *f*; *US* ~ **committee** comité *m* de surveillance des mœurs

**vigilante** *n* membre *m* d'un comité de vigilance

**vignette** *n* vignette *f*

**vigorous** *adj* vigoureux -euse, robuste

**vigour** *n* vigueur *f*, énergie *f*, vitalité *f*

**Viking** *n* Viking *m*

**vile** *adj* infâme, vil, bas (*f* basse); (worthless) sans valeur; (dreadful) abominable; (temper) exécrable, massacrant

**vileness** *n* bassesse *f*

**vilification** *n* dénigrement *m*, diffamation *f*

**vilify** *vt* dénigrer, diffamer

**villa** *n* villa *f*

**village** *n* village *m*; *adj* de village; de campagne

**villager** *n* villageois -e

**villain** *n* scélérat *m*, bandit *m*, coquin *m*

**villainess** *n* scélérate *f*, coquine *f*

**villainous** *adj* infâme, scélérat; *coll* exécrable, abominable

**villainy** *n* infamie *f*

**vindicate** *vt* défendre, justifier; prouver

**vindication** *n* défense *f*, justification *f*

**vindicative** *adj* justificatif -ive

**vindicator** *n* défenseur *m*

**vindictive** *adj* vindicatif -ive, rancunier -ière

**vine** *n* vigne *f*; (creeper) plante grimpante

**vine-dresser** *n* vigneron *m*

**vinegar** *n* vinaigre *m*; ~ **sauce** vinaigrette *f*; **wine** ~ vinaigre *m* de vin

**vinegary** *adj* vinaigré; *coll fig* aigre; (person) revêche

**vine-grower** *n* viticulteur *m*

**vineyard** *n* vigne *f*; (extensive) vignoble *m*

**vingt-et-un** *n* (card game) vingt-et-un *m*

**viniculture** *n* viniculture *f*

**vinous** *adj* vineux -euse

**vintage** *n* (harvest) vendanges *fpl*, récolte *f* du raisin; (crop) vendange *f*; (year) année *f*, cru *m*; *adj* ~ **car** voiture *f* du début du siècle; ~ **champagne** champagne *m* d'origine; ~ **wine** grand vin, grand cru; ~ **year** grande année

**vintner** *n* négociant *m* en vins

**vinyl** *n* vinyle *m*

**viol** *n mus* viole *f*

**viola** *n mus* alto *m*

**violable** *adj* qui peut être violé

**violate** *vt* violer; (peace) troubler; (sanctuary) profaner

**violation** *n* violation *f*; (sanctuary) profanation *f*; (order) infraction *f*; (woman) viol *m*

**violator** *n* violateur -trice

**violence** *n* violence *f*; **crime of** ~ voie *f* de fait; **do** ~ **to one's feelings** se faire violence; **resort to** ~ se livrer à des voies de fait, employer la violence; **robbery with** ~ vol *m* avec coups et blessures

**violent** *adj* intense, extrême; (colour) voyant, criard; (emotion) vif (*f* vive); *coll* (hell of a, rare old) carabiné; **in a** ~ **hurry** extrêmement pressé; **lay** ~ **hands on** s/o attaquer qn brutalement

**violet** *n* violette *f*; (colour) violet *m*; *adj* violet -ette

**violin** *n* violon *m*

**violinist** *n* violoniste

**violoncellist** *n* violoncelliste

**violoncello** *n* violoncelle *m*

**viper** *n* vipère *f*

**viperish** *adj* (tongue) de vipère

**virago** *n* mégère *f*

**virgin** *n* vierge *f*; *adj* de vierge, virginal; ~ **birth** parthénogenèse *f*

**virginal** *adj* virginal

**virginia** *n* ~ **creeper** vigne *f* vierge

**virginity** *n* virginité *f*

**viridescent** *adj* verdâtre

**virile** *adj* viril, mâle

**virility** *n* virilité *f*

**virology** *n* virologie *f*

**virtual** *adj* vrai, de fait, effectif -ive; (potential) virtuel -elle

**virtually** *adv* en pratique, effectivement; (almost) presque

**virtue** *n* vertu *f*; (property) qualité *f*, avantage *m*; (power) pouvoir *m*, efficacité *f*; **by** ~ **of** en vertu de, en raison de; **make a** ~ **of necessity** faire de nécessité vertu

**virtuosity** *n* virtuosité *f*

**virtuoso** *n mus* virtuose; amateur *m* d'art, connaisseur *m*; *adj* de virtuose

**virtuous** *adj* vertueux -euse

**virulence** *n* virulence *f*

**virulent** *adj* virulent

**virus** *n* virus *m*; *fig* poison *m*

**visa** *n* visa *m*; *vt* viser

**visage** *n* visage *m*

**vis-à-vis** *n* vis-à-vis *m*; *adv* vis-à-vis; *prep* vis-à-vis de, en face de

**viscera** *npl* viscères *mpl*

**visceral** *adj* viscéral

**viscose** *n* viscose *f*

**viscosity** *n* viscosité *f*

**viscount** *n* vicomte *m*

**viscountess** *n* vicomtesse *f*

**viscous** *adj* visqueux -euse, gluant

**visibility** *n* visibilité *f*

**visible** *adj* visible; manifeste

**vision** *n* vision *f*; (eyesight) vue *f*; imagination *f*; (ghost) fantôme *m*; **field of** ~ champ *m* de vue; **man of** ~ homme *m* qui voit loin; **within the range of** ~ à portée de vue

**visionary** *n* visionnaire; *adj* (person) visionnaire; (plan) chimérique

**visit** *n* visite *f*; (stay) séjour *m*; **be on a** ~ être en visite; **pay s/o a** ~ rendre visite à qn; *vt* rendre visite à, aller voir; (call on) passer chez; (sights, etc) visiter; (inspect) inspecter

**visitant** *n* visiteur *m*; (bird) oiseau migrateur; (ghost) fantôme *m*

**visitation** *n* visite *f* (d'inspection); *lit* (ghost) apparition *f*; *eccles* visite pastorale

**visiting** *n* visites *fpl*; **go** ~ faire des visites, aller en visite; *adj* en visite; ~ **card** carte *f* de visite; ~ **hours** heures *fpl* de visite; **not be on ~ terms** ne pas se voir

**visitor** *n* visiteur -euse; touriste, voyageur -euse; **~ s' book** livre *m* d'or, registre *m*; **have ~ s** avoir du monde; **summer ~ s** estivants *mpl*; **winter ~ s** hivernants *mpl*

**visor, vizor** *n* visière *f*

**vista** *n* (prospect) perspective *f*; (forest) éclaircie *f*, percée *f*

**visual** *adj* visuel -elle; **~ aid** support visuel; **~ distance** distance *f* de visibilité

**visualization** *n* visualisation *f*

**visualize** *vt* se représenter, se faire une image de, visualiser; (foresee) envisager, prévoir; *vi* s'imaginer; (foresee) prévoir, envisager

**visually** *adv* visuellement, de façon visuelle

**vital** *adj* vital, essentiel -ielle; (fatal) irrémédiable, mortel -elle; (lively) énergique; **matter of ~ importance** affaire *f* d'importance capitale

**vitality** *n* vitalité *f*, vigueur *f*

**vitalize** *vt* vitaliser, vivifier

**vitally** *adv* d'une manière vitale, vitalement

**vitals** *npl anat* organes vitaux

**vitamin** *n* vitamine *f*

**vitiate** *vt* vicier

**vitiation** *n* viciation *f*

**viticulture** *n* viticulture *f*

**vitreous** *adj* vitreux -euse

**vitrify** *vt* vitrifier

**vitriol** *n* vitriol *m*

**vitriolic** *adj chem* de vitriol; *fig* mordant; **~ pen** plume trempée dans du vitriol

**vituperate** *vt* injurier; *vi* vitupérer

**vituperation** *n* insultes *fpl*, injures *fpl*

**vituperative** *adj* injurieux -ieuse

**viva** *n coll* examen oral; **~ voce** de vive voix

**vivacious** *adj* vif (*f* vive), animé, enjoué

**vivacity** *n* vivacité *f*, animation *f*

**vivid** *adj* vif (*f* vive), éclatant, frappant

**vividness** *n* vivacité *f*, éclat *m*

**vivify** *vt* vivifier, ranimer

**vivisect** *vt* pratiquer des vivisections sur; *vi* faire de la vivisection

**vivisection** *n* vivisection *f*

**vixen** *n* renarde *f*; *coll fig* mégère *f*

**vixenish** *adj* (woman) méchant; (character) de mégère

**viz** *adv abbr* à savoir, c'est à dire

**vizier** *n* vizir *m*

**vizor** *n see* **visor**

**vocable** *n* vocable *m*

**vocabulary** *n* vocabulaire *m*

**vocal** *adj* vocal; (communication) verbal; (person) bruyant, qui aime se faire entendre

**vocalist** *n* chanteur -euse; (opera, classical music) cantatrice *f*

**vocalization** *n* vocalisation *f*

**vocalize** *vt* (air) chanter; *ling* vocaliser; *vi mus* faire des vocalises, vocaliser

**vocally** *adv* vocalement; (by speech) oralement

**vocation** *n* vocation *f*; profession *f*

**vocational** *adj* professionnel -elle

**vocative** *n gramm* vocatif *m*; *adj* vocatif -ive

**vociferate** *vt* + *vi* vociférer

**vociferation** *n* vociférations *fpl*, cris *mpl*

**vociferous** *adj* bruyant, criard

**vodka** *n* vodka *f*

**vogue** *n* vogue *f*, mode *f*; **in ~** en vogue, à la mode

**voice** *n* voix *f*; (tone of) ton *m*; **at the top of one's ~** à tue-tête; **have no ~ in the matter** n'avoir pas voix au chapitre; **in a low ~** à voix basse; **like the sound of one's own ~** aimer à s'entendre parler; **lose one's ~** avoir une extinction de voix; **with one ~** à l'unanimité; *vt* exprimer, énoncer

**voiced** *adj phon* sonore

**voiceless** *adj* sans voix, muet (*f* muette); *phon* sourd

**void** *n* vide *m*; *adj* vide; inoccupé; *leg* nul (*f* nulle); **~ of** dépourvu de; *vt* évacuer

**volatile** *adj* volatil; (person) léger -ère, inconstant

**volatility** *n* volatilité *f*

**volatilize** *vt* volatiliser

**vol-au-vent** *n cul* vol-au-vent *m invar*

**volcanic** *adj* volcanique

**volcano** *n* volcan *m*

**vole** *n* campagnol *m*

**volition** *n* volonté *f*, volition *f*; **do sth of one's own ~** faire qch de son propre gré

**volley** *n* (firing) décharge *f*, salve *f*; (abuse) bordée *f*; *sp* volée *f*; *vt sp* reprendre en volée

**volley-ball** *n* volley(-ball *m*) *m*

**volt** *n* volt *m*

**voltage** *n* voltage *m*

**volte-face** *n* volte-face *f invar*

**voltmeter** *n elect* voltmètre *m*

**volubility** *n* volubilité *f*

**voluble** *adj* (person) volubile, loquace; (speech) facile, aisé

**volume** *n* (book) volume *m*, tome *m*, livre *m*; *sci* volume *m*; (size) grosseur *f*, ampleur *f*; (smoke) nuages *mpl*

**volume-control** *n* bouton *m* de réglage du volume

**voluminous** *adj* volumineux -euse, abondant

**voluntarily** *adv* volontairement, de plein gré

**voluntary** *adj* volontaire; **~ organization** organisation *f* bénévole

**volunteer** n volontaire; vt offrir volontairement; ~ **an answer** hasarder une réponse; ~ **information** donner spontanément un renseignement; vi s'offrir comme volontaire; mil s'engager comme volontaire
**voluptuary** n + adj voluptueux -euse
**voluptuous** adj voluptueux -euse
**vomit** n vomi m; vt + vi vomir
**vomiting** n vomissement m
**voodoo** n vaudou m; adj vaudou invar
**voodooism** n pratique f du vaudou
**voracious** adj vorace
**voracity** n voracité f
**vortex** n tourbillon m
**votary** n fervent -e, adorateur -trice
**vote** n (practice, etc) vote m, scrutin m; (individual) voix f; ~ **of censure** motion f de censure; **have the** ~ avoir le droit de vote; **put a question to the** ~ mettre une question aux voix; **take the** ~ procéder au scrutin; vt voter, élire; ~ **down (out)** repousser; ~ **in** élire; vi voter, aller aux urnes; (suggest) proposer
**voter** n électeur -trice, votant m
**voting-paper** n bulletin m de vote
**votive** adj votif -ive; ~ **offering** ex-voto m invar
**vouch** vi ~ **for** garantir, répondre de
**voucher** n bon m, fiche f; (receipt) reçu m; (confirmatory document) pièce justificative
**vouchsafe** vt accorder; vi ~ **to do sth** daigner faire qch
**vow** n vœu m, serment m; **fulfil a** ~ accomplir un vœu; **take one's** ~ **s** entrer en religion; vt + vi jurer
**vowel** n voyelle f
**voyage** n voyage m; (sea) traversée f, voyage m par mer; vi naviguer
**voyager** n voyageur -euse (par mer), passager -ère
**voyeur** n voyeur m
**voyeurism** n voyeurisme m
**vulcanite** n caoutchouc vulcanisé, ébonite f
**vulcanize** vt vulcaniser
**vulgar** adj commun, vulgaire, grossier -ière; (general) très répandu; ~ **fraction** fraction f ordinaire
**vulgarism** n mot m vulgaire, expression f vulgaire
**vulgarity** n vulgarité f
**vulgarization** n vulgarisation f
**vulgarize** vt vulgariser
**vulgarly** adv vulgairement, grossièrement; (commonly) communément
**Vulgate** n Vulgate f
**vulnerability** n vulnérabilité f
**vulnerable** adj vulnérable
**vulture** n vautour m
**vulva** n anat vulve f
**vying** n rivalité f

# W

**wabble** n + vi see **wobble**
**wacky** adj coll fou-fou (f fofolle)
**wad** n (notes) liasse f; (material) bourre f; (cotton wool) tampon m; vt bourrer; ouater; (ears) bourrer de l'ouate dans
**wadding** n rembourrage m; (cotton wool) ouate f
**waddle** n dandinement m; vi marcher comme un canard, se dandiner
**wade** vt passer à gué; vi marcher dans l'eau (la boue, etc); ~ **across** traverser à gué; ~ **in** entrer dans l'eau; coll fig intervenir; ~ **through** traverser; coll fig achever péniblement
**wader** n orni échassier m; (person) personne f qui marche dans l'eau; (boots) ~ **s** bottes fpl cuissardes (de pêcheur)
**wafer** n cul gaufrette f; eccles hostie f; (sealing) pain m à cacheter
**wafer-thin** adj très mince
¹**waffle** n gaufre f
²**waffle** n coll laïus m, rabâchage m; vi raconter des bêtises; écrire (parler) autour du sujet (dans le vague)
**waft** n bouffée f; (wind) souffle m; vt porter (dans l'air)
¹**wag** n farceur -euse, badin -e
²**wag** n agitation f, mouvement m, frétillement m; vt agiter; (tail) remuer; (head) branler, secouer; vi se remuer,

s'agiter; **set tongues ~ging** faire jaser les gens

¹**wage** n salaire m, paie f; **~s** gages mpl; **minimum living ~** minimum vital; **minimum ~** salaire minimum interprofessionnel de croissance (S.M.I.C.)

²**wage** vt **~ war** faire la guerre

**wage-earner** n salarié -e

**wage-freeze** n blocage m des salaires

**wager** n gageure f, pari m; **lay a ~** faire un pari; vt gager, parier

**waggish** adj blagueur -euse, badin, plaisant

**waggle** vt remuer; secouer

**wagon, waggon** n (railway) wagon m; chariot m, charrette f

**wagtail** n bergeronnette f

**waif** n épave f; **~s and strays** enfants abandonnés

**wail** n gémissement m, plainte f; (baby) vagissement m; vi gémir; (baby) vagir

**wainscot(ing)** n boiserie f, lambris m; vt lambrisser

**waist** n taille f, ceinture f; **~ measurement** tour m de taille; **put one's arm round s/o's ~** prendre qn par la taille

**waistband** n ceinture f

**waistcoat** n gilet m

**waist-deep** adj jusqu'à la taille (la ceinture)

**waistline** n taille f

**wait** n attente f; (between two trains) battement m; **lie in ~** se tenir en embuscade; **lie in ~ for s/o** attendre qn au passage; vt (watch for) guetter; vi attendre; (at table) servir; **~ and see** voir venir; **~ for** attendre; **~ on** servir; **~ on s/o hand and foot** être l'esclave de qn; **~ up** veiller; **~ up for s/o** attendre (le soir) que qn rentre; **keep s/o ~ing** faire attendre qn

**waiter** n garçon m de restaurant (café); **head ~** maître m d'hôtel; **wine ~** sommelier m

**waiting** n attente f; **~ list** liste f d'attente; **lady in ~** dame f d'honneur; **lose nothing by ~** rien perdre pour attendre; **play a ~ game** attendre son heure

**waiting-room** n salle f d'attente

**waitress** n serveuse f; **~!** mademoiselle!

**waive** vt renoncer à, abandonner; (condition) ne pas insister sur

**waiver** n leg abandon m

¹**wake** n (ship) sillage m; **follow the ~ of s/o** marcher sur les traces de qn; **in the ~ of** à la suite de

²**wake** n veillée f mortuaire; hist fête f de la dédicace d'une église; vt réveiller; ranimer; exciter, provoquer; vi s'éveiller; (state) être éveillé, **~ (up)** se réveiller; **~ up to sth** se rendre enfin compte

de qch; **~ up with a start** se réveiller en sursaut

**wakeful** adj (vigilant) vigilant; éveillé, sans sommeil

**wakefulness** n insomnie f; vigilance f

**waken** vt réveiller; (feeling) éveiller; (suspicion) exciter; vi se réveiller

**wakening** n réveil m

**waking** n réveil m; **on ~** au réveil

**Wales** n le pays de Galles

**walk** n marche f, promenade f; (gait) démarche f; (place) allée f, avenue f, promenade f; **~ of life** position sociale; **at a ~** au pas; **go for a ~** aller se promener, faire une promenade; **take s/o for a ~** emmener qn en promenade; **take the dog for a ~** sortir le chien; vt faire marcher, promener; **~ a kilometre** faire un kilomètre à pied; **~ the streets** courir les rues; (prostitute) faire le trottoir; **I can ~ it in half an hour** j'en ai pour une demi-heure à pied; vi marcher; (stroll) se promener; (go on foot) aller à pied; **~ about** se promener; **~ away** s'en aller, partir; **~ back** retourner à pied; **~ home** rentrer à pied; **~ in** entrer; **~ in one's sleep** être somnambule; **~ off** s'en aller; **~ on** continuer (sa marche); **~ out** sortir; partir; abandonner; **~ round sth** faire le tour de qch (à pied); **~ up** monter à pied; (approach) s'approcher, s'avancer; **~ up and down** se promener de long en large; **go ~ing** aller en promenade

**walkabout** n promenade f parmi la foule, bain m de foule

**walker** n marcheur -euse, promeneur -euse; **be a good ~** être bon marcheur (f bonne marcheuse)

**walkie-talkie** n émetteur-récepteur m (pl émetteurs-récepteurs), talkie-walkie m (pl talkies-walkies), walkie-talkie m (pl walkies-talkies)

**walking** n marche f, promenade f à pied; adj ambulant; **the ~ wounded** les blessés qui peuvent marcher; **at a ~ pace** au pas; **the village is within ~ distance** on peut facilement se rendre au village à pied

**walking-stick** n canne f

**walk-on** n theat **~ part** rôle m de figurant -e

**walk-out** n coll grève f

**walk-over** n victoire f facile

**wall** n mur m, muraille f; (chest, rock) paroi f; (tyre) flanc m; **~-to-~ carpet** moquette f; **come up against a blank ~** se heurter contre un mur; **dry-stone ~** mur m en pierres sèches; coll **go to the ~** succomber; **tariff ~** barrière douanière; vt **~ in** murer; entourer de murs;

~ **off** séparer par un mur; ~ **up** murer
**wallaby** n wallaby m
**wallet** n portefeuille m
**wall-eye** n (squint) œil m à strabisme
divergent; œil m vairon
**wallflower** n giroflée f; coll fig be a ~
faire tapisserie
**wall-lamp** n applique f
**Walloon** n Wallon -onne
**wallop** n coll grand coup, sl gnon m,
torgnole f; **go down with a ~** tomber
lourdement; vt coll rosser
**walloping** n coll rossée f, volée f de
coups; adj coll énorme
**wallow** n trou bourbeux; vi se rouler,
se vautrer; ~ **in blood** se plonger dans le
sang; coll be ~ing in money rouler sur
l'or
**wallpaper** n papier peint
**walnut** n noix f
**walrus** n morse m
**waltz** n valse f
**wan** adj blême, pâle
**wand** n baguette f (de fée); verge f
**wander** vt parcourir; vi errer, se promener au hasard; (stray) s'égarer; ~
**about** errer à l'aventure; **his mind is
~ing** il divague, il a le délire; (vague) il
est distrait
**wanderer** n vagabond -e, rôdeur -euse
**wandering** n course vagabonde; (straying) égarement m; (mind) délire m; ~ s
voyages mpl; adj errant, vagabond;
(mind) distrait; (tribe) nomade
**wanderlust** n passion f des voyages
**wane** n déclin m; **be on the ~** (moon)
décroître; (person) être sur le déclin; vi
décroître, décliner
**wangle** n coll combine f; vt carotter, obtenir par le système D; (falsify) cuisiner; vi resquiller
**wangler** n combinard -e, carotteur -euse
**wangling** n carottage m
**wanly** adv smile ~ sourire d'un air triste
**wanness** n pâleur f
**want** n (lack) manque m, défaut m;
(need) besoin m; (poverty) pauvreté f,
misère f, indigence f; **attend to s/o's
~ s** pourvoir aux besoins de qn; **be in
~ of** avoir besoin de; **for ~ of** faute
de; **in ~** dans le besoin; vt désirer,
vouloir; (need) avoir besoin de; (lack)
manquer de; (require) exiger; **he's not
~ ed** on ne veut pas de lui; **he ~ s a
hundred francs for it** il en veut (demande) cent francs; **I have all I ~** j'ai
tout ce qu'il me faut; **that ~ s some
doing** ce n'est pas facile à faire; **they ~
us to go away** ils veulent que nous par-
tions; **you are ~ ed** on vous demande;
vi ~ **for nothing** ne manquer de rien
**wanted** adj désiré, voulu; demandé;

(sought) recherché; ~, **lady's bicycle**
on demande bicyclette de femme
**wanting** adj manquant, qui manque; ~
**in** dépourvu de; **be ~** faire défaut;
**there is sth ~** le compte n'y est pas
**wanton** n femme légère; adj (woman)
impudique; (action) gratuit; (playful)
folâtre; (undisciplined) déréglé
**war** n guerre f; ~ **memorial** monument
m aux morts; ~ **of words** dispute f de
mots; ~ **zone** zone f militaire; **on a ~
footing** sur un pied de guerre; **the
phoney ~** la drôle de guerre; vi lutter,
faire la guerre
**warble,** n gazouillement m; vi gazouiller; coll (person) chanter
**warbling** n see **warble** n
**war-cry** n cri m de guerre
**ward** n (person) pupille; (hospital) salle f
d'hôpital; pol circonscription f; (lock)
garde f; **emergency ~** salle f des urgences; **intensive-care ~** salle f de
réanimation; vt ~ **off** parer, détourner;
(illness) prévenir
**war-dance** n danse guerrière
**warden** n (guard) gardien -ienne, surveillant -e; (park) conservateur -trice;
(institution) directeur -trice; **air-raid
~** chef m d'îlot; **traffic ~** contractuel
-elle
**warder** n gardien m (de prison)
**wardress** n gardienne f (de prison)
**wardrobe** n garde-robe f, penderie f, armoire f
**wardrobe-keeper** n theat costumier -ière
**wardroom** n naut carré m des officiers
**ware** npl produits mpl, ustensiles mpl;
~ s marchandises fpl
**warehouse** n magasin m, entrepôt m;
**bonded ~** entrepôt m en douane
**warfare** n guerre f
**warhead** n tête f; (rocket) ogive f;
**nuclear ~** tête f nucléaire
**war-horse** n cheval m de bataille; coll fig
dur -e à cuire
**warily** adv prudemment, avec prudence
**wariness** n prudence f, circonspection f
**warlike** adj guerrier -ière; (air) martial;
(people) belliqueux -euse
**war-lord** n seigneur m de la guerre
**warm** adj chaud; (hearty) chaleureux
-euse; (generous) généreux -euse; coll
(rich) cossu; **be ~** (person) avoir
chaud; (thing) être chaud; **get ~** se
réchauffer; **it is ~** (weather) il fait
chaud; **keep ~** se tenir au chaud; vt
chauffer; ~ **the cockles of the heart**
réjouir le cœur; ~ **up** réchauffer; vi (se)
chauffer, se réchauffer; s'animer,
s'échauffer; ~ **to s/o** se prendre de
sympathie pour qn; ~ **up** (engine) se
réchauffer; fig s'animer

**warm-blooded** *adj* à sang chaud; *fig* ardent

**warm-hearted** *adj* généreux -euse, au cœur chaud

**warming-pan** *n* bassinoire *f*

**warmly** *adv* chaudement; (heartily) chaleureusement

**warmonger** *n* belliciste

**warmongering** *n* propagande *f* de guerre

**warmth** *n* chaleur *f*; cordialité *f*; (anger) emportement *m*; vivacité *f*

**warn** *vt* avertir, prévenir; ~ **off** détourner; ~ **s/o against** sth mettre qn en garde contre qch; ~ **s/o not to do sth** conseiller fortement à qn de ne pas faire qch

**warning** *n* avertissement *m*; (notice) avis *m*; (notification) préavis *m*; (air-raid) alerte *f*; **let this be a ~ to you** que cela vous serve de leçon; *adj* avertisseur -euse

**warp** *n* (textiles) chaîne *f*; *vt* (twist) tordre; (wood) déjeter; fausser; (mind) pervertir; *vi* se déformer; (wood) se déjeter; (wheel) se voiler

**war-paint** *n* peinture *f* de guerre; *coll* **be in one's ~** être sur son trente-et-un, être en grand tralala

**warpath** *n coll* **be on the ~** être parti en campagne, chercher noise à tout le monde

**warrant** *n* garantie *f*; autorisation *f*, justification *f*; (arrest) mandat *m* d'arrêt; (money) bon *m*, mandat *m*; *vt* garantir; justifier; **I ~ you he'll come** je vous assure qu'il viendra; il viendra, je vous en réponds

**warrant-officer** *n* adjudant *m*

**warranty** *n* autorisation *f*; garantie *f*

**warren** *n* garenne *f*; *fig* labyrinthe *m*, dédale *m*

**warrior** *n* guerrier *m*

**Warsaw** *n* Varsovie *f*

**warship** *n* bâtiment *m* de guerre

**wart** *n* verrue *f*

**wartime** *n* période *f* (temps *m*) de guerre

**wary** *adj* prudent, circonspect; **be ~ of** se méfier de; **keep a ~ eye on** surveiller attentivement

**wash** *n* lavage *m*; (laundry) lessive *f*, blanchissage *m*; (ship) sillage *m*; (propeller) souffle *m*; (painting) couche *f* (d'aquarelle); *US* ~ **cloth** gant *m* de toilette; **have a ~** faire sa toilette; *vt* laver; (clothes) blanchir, laver; (shore) baigner; ~ **away** enlever par le lavage; ~ **down** laver à grande eau; *coll* (drinking) faire descendre; ~ **off** enlever par le lavage; ~ **one's face** se débarbouiller; ~ **one's hands** se laver les mains; ~ **out** rincer, laver; ~ **sth ashore** rejeter qch sur le rivage; *coll* ~ **ed out** vanné; *coll* ~ **ed up** ruiné, fichu; *vi* se laver; ~ **over**

balayer; ~ **up** faire la vaisselle; (material) ~ **well** être très lavable, se laver bien; *coll* **that won't ~!** ça ne prendra pas!

**washable** *adj* lavable

**wash-basin** *n* lavabo *m*

**wash-board** *n* planche *f* à laver

**wash-bowl** *n US* lavabo *m*

**¹washer** *n* (person) laveur -euse; (machine) machine *f* à laver

**²washer** *n mech* rondelle *f*

**washer-up** *n* (restaurant) plongeur -euse

**washing** *n* lavage *m*; (laundry) blanchissage *m*, lessive *f*

**wash(ing)-day** *n* jour *m* de lessive

**washing-machine** *n* machine *f* à laver

**washing-soda** *n* cristaux *mpl* de soude

**washing-up** *n* vaisselle *f*; (restaurant) plonge *f*

**wash-leather** *n* peau *f* de chamois

**wash-out** *n coll* fiasco *m*; (play) four *m*; (person) raté -e

**wash-stand** *n* lavabo *m*

**washy** *adj* faible, fade, insipide; (colour) délavé

**wasp** *n* guêpe *f*; ~ **s' nest** guêpier *m*

**waspish** *adj* irascible, irritable

**wastage** *n* perte *f*; gaspillage *m*

**waste** *n* (loss) perte *f*; gaspillage *m*; (refuse) déchets *mpl*; désert *m*; terrain *m* vague, région *f* inculte; ~ **disposal unit** broyeur *m* à ordures; **go (run) to ~** se perdre; **sheer ~** pure perte; *adj* (land) désert, inculte; (useless) de rebut; ~ **ground** terrain *m* vague; ~ **paper** vieux papiers *m*; *vt* (squander) gaspiller; (time) perdre; (use up) consumer, user; ~ **one's words** prêcher dans le désert; **it's ~ d on him** c'est trop beau (bon) pour lui; ça ne lui sert à rien; *vi* ~ **away** dépérir; maigrir

**wasteful** *adj* gaspilleur -euse; ~ **habit** habitude *f* de gaspillage

**wastefulness** *n* prodigalité *f*, habitudes *fpl* de gaspillage

**waste-paper basket** *n* corbeille *f* à papier

**waste-pipe** *n* (tuyau *m* de) trop-plein *m*, tuyau *m* de dégagement

**waster, wastrel** *n* vaurien -ienne

**watch** *n* (guard) garde *f*; *naut* quart *m*; (timepiece) montre *f*; (staying up) veille *f*; **be on the ~** être sur ses gardes; **be on the ~ for** guetter, être à l'affût de; **keep a good ~** faire bonne garde; *vt* (look at) regarder, observer; (guard) veiller sur, garder; (game) assister à; ~ **closely** surveiller de près; ~ **one's opportunity** guetter l'occasion; ~ **your step!** prenez garde de tomber!; *fig* faites attention!; *vi* veiller; ~ **out** être sur ses gardes; ~ **out for s/o** attendre qn; ~ **over** surveiller

**watchdog** n chien m de garde; *fig* gardien -ienne

**watcher** n veilleur -euse

**watchful** *adj* vigilant, attentif -ive, alerte

**watchmaker** n horloger -ère

**watchman** n veilleur m, garde m; **night ~** veilleur m de nuit

**watch-tower** n tour f d'observation; (concentration camp) mirador m

**watchword** n mot m d'ordre

**water** n eau f; **~ on the knee** épanchement m de synovie; **be in low ~** (poor) être dans la dèche; (in a state) être bien bas; **by ~** par mer, par voie d'eau; **cold ~** eau froide; (cool) eau fraîche; **drinking ~** eau potable; *coll* **get into hot ~** se mettre dans le pétrin; **hard ~** eau dure; **have ~ laid on** faire mettre l'eau courante; **high (low) ~** marée haute (basse); **keep one's head above ~** se maintenir à la surface; *fig* faire face à ses obligations; **pour cold ~ on an idea** rejeter une idée; **soft ~** eau douce; **take the ~s** faire une cure, prendre les eaux; **turn on the ~** ouvrir l'eau; *vt* arroser; (animals) abreuver; (wine) couper; (silk) moirer; **~ down** atténuer; *vi* (eyes) pleurer; **it makes my mouth ~** ça me fait venir l'eau à la bouche

**water-bottle** n carafe f; gourde f; **hot ~** bouillotte f

**water-cannon** n lance f d'incendie

**water-closet** n cabinets mpl, waters mpl

**water-colour** n aquarelle f

**watercress** n cresson m de fontaine

**water-diviner** n sourcier -ière

**watered** *adj* arrosé; (wet) mouillé; **~ silk** soie moirée

**waterfall** n chute f d'eau, cascade f

**waterfront** n bord m de mer, quai m

**waterglass** n silicate m de potasse

**watering** n arrosage m; (animals) abreuvage m; (drink) dilution f; *comm* dilution f de capital

**watering-can** n arrosoir m

**watering-place** n (cattle) abreuvoir m; (spa) station f balnéaire, ville f d'eau

**water-level** n niveau m d'eau

**water-lily** n nénuphar m

**waterline** n *naut* ligne f de flottaison

**waterlogged** *adj* (ground) détrempé, imbibé d'eau; (ship) plein d'eau

**water-main** n conduite principale (d'eau)

**watermark** n (paper) filigrane m; *naut* laisse f de haute mer (de basse mer)

**water-melon** n pastèque f, melon m d'eau

**water-mill** n moulin m à eau

**water-pipe** n conduite f d'eau

**water-pistol** n pistolet m à eau

**water-polo** n water-polo m

**water-power** n énergie f hydraulique

**waterproof** n imperméable m; *adj* imperméable; *vt* imperméabiliser, rendre imperméable

**water-rat** n rat m d'eau

**water-rate** n impôt perçu par le service des eaux

**watershed** n ligne f de partage des eaux

**waterside** n bord m de l'eau

**water-ski** *vi* faire du ski nautique

**water-skiing** n ski m nautique

**water-softener** n adoucisseur m d'eau

**water-supply** n approvisionnement m en eau, service m des eaux

**watertight** *adj* étanche; *fig* irréfutable, où tout a été prévu

**water-tower** n château m d'eau

**water-wagon** n citerne f mobile; *coll* **on the ~** ne buvant que de l'eau

**water-wings** npl flotteur m de natation

**waterworks** npl usine f de distribution d'eau; *sl* **turn on the ~** (cry) chialer

**watery** *adj* aqueux -euse; (ground) noyé d'eau; (eyes) larmoyant; (clouds) chargé de pluie; (soup) clair

**watt** n watt m

**wattage** n *elect* puissance f

¹**wattle** n (hurdle) clayonnage m; *vt* clayonner

²**wattle** n (turkey) fanon m; (fish) barbe f

**wave** n vague f; *lit* flot m; *phys* onde f; (hand) signe m; (hair) ondulation f; (movement) ondoiement m; **heat ~** vague f de chaleur; **light ~** onde lumineuse; **long ~s** grandes ondes; **medium ~s** ondes moyennes; **permanent ~** permanente f, indéfrisable f; **short ~s** ondes courtes; **sound ~** onde f sonore; *vt* agiter; (stick, etc) brandir; (hair) onduler; **~ aside** écarter; **~ one's hand** faire signe de la main; **~ s/o down** faire signe d'arrêter à qn; *vi* flotter; (hair) onduler; **~ to s/o** faire signe à qn

**wave-length** n longueur f d'onde

**waver** *vi* hésiter, vaciller; (troops) fléchir

**waverer** n indécis -e

**wavering** n hésitation f; irrésolution f

**wavy** *adj* onduleux -euse

¹**wax** n cire f; (ear) cérumen m; (ski) fart m; **~ taper** rat m de cave; *eccles* cierge m; *vt* cirer; (furniture) encaustiquer; (skis) farter

²**wax** *vi* croître

**waxen** *adj* de cire; (complexion) cireux -euse

**waxwork** n modelage m en cire; **~s** figures fpl en cire; musée m de figures en cire

**way** n chemin m, route f, voie f;

(direction) sens *m*, direction *f*, côté *m*; (manner) manière *f*, méthode *f*, façon *f*; (means) moyen *m*; (progress) progrès *m*; (custom) habitude *f*; *naut* erre *f*; ~ **down** descente *f*; *fig* descente *f*; ~ **in** entrée *f*; ~ **out** sortie *f*; ~ **through** passage *m*; ~ **up** montée *f*; **all the** ~ tout au long du chemin; (to the end) jusqu'au bout; **a little** ~ **off** pas trop loin; **a long** ~ **off** très loin; **be (get) in the** ~ gêner; **by a long** ~ de beaucoup; **by the** ~ en passant, à propos; **down their** ~ du côté d'où ils habitent; **feel one's** ~ aller à tâtons; **find the** ~ **to do sth** trouver le moyen de faire qch; **get into the** ~ **of doing sth** prendre l'habitude de faire qch; **get one's own** ~ arriver à ses fins; **give** ~ céder; **go one's** ~ passer son chemin; **go the shortest** ~ prendre par le plus court; **go the wrong** ~ faire fausse route; **have one's own** ~ faire à sa guise; **if I had my** ~ si ce n'était que de moi; **in a** ~ en quelque sorte; **in a bad** ~ en mauvais état, mal en point; **in many** ~**s** à bien des égards; **in no** ~ nullement; **in the** ~ **of** en fait de; **in this** ~ de cette façon (manière); **keep out of the** ~ se tenir à l'écart; **lead the** ~ aller devant; **make a** ~ **through** se frayer un chemin à travers; **make one's** ~ **by hard work** arriver à force de travail; **make** ~ **for** faire place à; **not by a long** ~ il s'en faut de beaucoup; **on my** ~ chemin faisant; **on the** ~ en chemin, en allant, en cours de route; **out of the** ~ écarté, isolé; *fig* peu ordinaire; **out of the** ~**!** ôtez-vous de là!, rangez-vous!; **over the** ~ en face, vis à vis; **right of** ~ droit *m* de passage; **see one's** ~ *fig* voir comment on peut; **she has a** ~ **with her.** elle est insinuante; *fig* **stand in s/o's** ~ gêner qn; **that's the** ~**!** voilà qui est bien!, à la bonne heure!; **that** ~**!** par là!; **the other** ~ en sens contraire; **the right** ~ **up** dans le bon sens; **the wrong** ~ **up** à l'envers, sens dessus dessous; **things are in a bad** ~ les choses vont mal; **this** ~**!** par ici!; **this** ~ **and that** de-ci, de-là; **which** ~**?** par où?

**wayfarer** *n* voyageur *m*, passant *m*

**waylay** *vt* guetter au passage, tendre un guet-apens à

**wayside** *n* bord *m* de la route; **fall by the** ~ rester en chemin

**wayward** *adj* capricieux -ieuse, obstiné

**W.C.** *n* waters *mpl*, cabinets *mpl*

**we** *pron* nous; (one) on; **here** ~ **are!** nous voici!

**weak** *adj* faible; (drink) léger -ère; (solution) dilué; (body) chétif -ive

**weaken** *vt* affaiblir; amollir; *vi* s'affaiblir

**weak-kneed** *adj coll fig* sans caractère, mou (*f* molle)

**weakling** *n* être chétif; *coll* femmelette *f*

**weakly** *adj* chétif -ive; *adv* faiblement

**weak-minded** *adj* faible d'esprit

**weakness** *n* faiblesse *f*; **have a** ~ **for** avoir un faible pour

**weak-spirited** *adj* peu courageux -euse, irrésolu

**¹weal** *n* bien *m*; **the common** ~ le bien de tous

**²weal** *n* (mark) marque *f*, trace *f*

**wealth** *n* richesse *f*, fortune *f*

**wealthy** *adj* riche, opulent

**wean** *vt* sevrer

**weapon** *n* arme *f*

**weaponry** *n* armes *fpl*

**wear** *n* usage *m*; (clothes) vêtements *mpl*; ~ **and tear** usure *f*; **fair** ~ **and tear** usure normale; **for evening** ~ pour le soir; **the worse for** ~ usé; *fig* en piteux état; *vt* porter; (put on) mettre; ~ **away** user, ronger; ~ **down** user; ~ **off** faire disparaître; ~ **out** user, épuiser; (patience) lasser; *vi* s'user; (time) traîner; ~ **off** disparaître, s'effacer; ~ **on** s'écouler, s'avancer; ~ **out** s'user; ~ **through** se trouer (à force d'être usé); ~ **well** faire bon usage; (person) se conserver bien

**wearable** *adj* mettable

**wearily** *adv* d'un air fatigué; péniblement

**weariness** *n* fatigue *f*, lassitude *f*

**wearing** *n* (clothes) port *m*; (wear) usure *f*; *adj* fatigant, lassant

**wearisome** *adj* ennuyeux -euse

**weary** *adj* fatigué, las (*f* lasse)

**weasel** *n* belette *f*

**weather** *n* temps *m*; ~ **conditions** conditions *fpl* atmosphériques; **be under the** ~ être indisposé; **in this** ~ par un temps pareil; **it is fine** ~ il fait beau; **make heavy** ~ **of sth** compliquer les choses; **what's the** ~ **like?** quel temps fait-il?; *vt* (rocks) désagréger, altérer; (storm) résister à; (survive) survivre à; (wood) faire mûrir; *vi* (rocks) se désagréger; s'altérer

**weather-beaten** *adj* battu par la tempête; (complexion) basané, hâlé

**weather-bound** *adj* retenu par le mauvais temps

**weathercock** *n* girouette *f*

**weather-forecast** *n* prévisions *fpl* du temps, bulletin *m* météorologique, *coll* météo *f*

**weatherman** *n rad* + *TV* personne *f* qui lit le bulletin météorologique; météorologue *m*

**weatherproof** *adj* à l'épreuve du mauvais temps
**weather-vane** *n* girouette *f*
**weave** *n* tissage *m*; *vt* tisser; (plot) tramer; (plait) tresser; *vi* ~ **a way through** se faufiler à travers, se frayer un chemin à travers; *coll* **get weaving** s'y mettre
**weaver** *n* tisserand -e
**weaving** *n* tissage *m*
**weazen(ed)** *adj see* **wizen(ed)**
**web** *n* tissu *m*; *anat* membrane *f*, palmure *f*; (spider) toile *f*
**webbed** *adj* palmé
**webbing** *n* (chairs) sangles *fpl*; (bird) palmure *f*
**wed** *vt* épouser, se marier avec; (parson) marier; *vi* se marier
**wedded** *adj* marié; (of marriage) conjugal; (attached) attaché
**wedding** *n* noce *f*, noces *fpl*, mariage *m*; *adj* nuptial, de mariage; ~ **cake** gâteau *m* de mariage; ~ **day** jour *m* de noces; ~ **night** nuit *f* de noces
**wedding-breakfast** *n* repas *m* de noces
**wedding-dress** *n* robe *f* de mariée
**wedding-ring** *n* alliance *f*
**wedge** *n* coin *m*; **it's the thin end of the** ~ c'est un premier empiètement; *vt* coincer, caler, enfoncer
**wedlock** *n* mariage *m*; **born in (out of)** ~ légitime (illégitime)
**Wednesday** *n* mercredi *m*; **Ash** ~ le mercredi des Cendres
**¹wee** *adj coll* tout petit (*f* toute petite), minuscule
**²wee, wee-wee** *n* pipi *m*; *vi* faire pipi
**weed** *n* mauvaise herbe; *coll* personne chétive et maigre; *vt* désherber; ~ **out** extirper, éliminer
**weed-killer** *n* désherbant *m*, herbicide *m*
**weeds** *npl* vêtements *mpl* de deuil
**weedy** *adj* couvert de mauvaises herbes; *coll* malingre, peu robuste, chétif -ive
**week** *n* semaine *f*, huit jours *fpl*; **a** ~ **from now** (d')aujourd'hui en huit; **last** ~ la semaine dernière; **today (tomorrow)** ~ aujourd'hui (demain) en huit; **twice a** ~ deux fois par semaine; **yesterday** ~ il y a eu hier huit jours
**weekday** *n* jour *m* de semaine, jour *m* ouvrable; **on** ~ **s** en semaine
**week-end** *n* fin *f* de semaine, weekend *m*
**weekly** *n* revue *f* (journal *m*) hebdomadaire, hebdomadaire *m*; *adj* hebdomadaire; *adv* par semaine, tous les huit jours; **be paid** ~ être payé à la semaine
**weeny** *adj coll* minuscule
**weep** *vt* ~ **one's eyes out** pleurer à chaudes larmes; *vi* pleurer; (wall, etc) suinter
**weeper** *n* pleureur -euse

**weeping** *n* larmes *fpl*; (wall) suintement *m*; *adj* qui pleure; (wall) suintant; ~ **willow** saule pleureur
**weepy** *adj coll* larmoyant
**weevil** *n* charançon
**wee-wee** *n* + *vi see* **²wee**
**weigh** *vt* peser; (in hand) soupeser; (anchor) lever; ~ **down** (scales) faire pencher; (overload) surcharger; ~ **one's words** peser ses paroles, mesurer ses mots; ~ **out** peser en quantités déterminées; ~ **up** jauger; (consider) considérer, calculer; *vi* peser; (count) compter; ~ **a lot** (little) peser lourd (peu); ~ **in** *sp* se faire peser; (intervene) intervenir; ~ **on the mind** tracasser
**weigh-bridge** *n* pont-bascule *m* (*pl* ponts-bascules)
**weigh-in** *n* pesage *m*
**weight** *n* poids *m*; (weightiness) pesanteur *f*, lourdeur *f*; (power) force *f*; importance *f*; **carry** ~ avoir de l'autorité; **feel the** ~ **of** soupeser; **gain** ~ prendre du poids; **he's worth his** ~ **in gold** il vaut son pesant d'or; **of little** ~ peu important; *fig* **pull one's** ~ y mettre du sien; *sp* **put the** ~ lancer le poids; **set of** ~ **s** série f de poids; *vt* charger
**weight-lifter** *n* haltérophile *m*
**weighty** *adj* pesant, lourd; important, sérieux -ieuse
**weir** *n* déversoir *m*; barrage *m*
**weird** *adj* surnaturel -elle, mystérieux -ieuse; (strange) étrange
**weirdie** *n coll* excentrique
**Welch** *n* + *adj see* **Welsh**
**welch** *vi see* **welsh**
**welcome** *n* bienvenue *f*, accueil *m*; **give s/o a good** ~ faire bon accueil à qn; *adj* bienvenu; (pleasant) agréable; ~ **!** soyez le bienvenu (*f* la bienvenue)!; **you're** ~ à votre service, il n'y a pas de quoi; **you're** ~ **to have a go** libre à vous d'essayer; *vt* souhaiter la bienvenue à, accueillir; (event) se réjouir de
**weld** *n* soudure *f*; *vt* souder, unir à chaud; *fig* unir; *vi* se souder
**welder** *n* soudeur *m*
**welfare** *n* bien-être *m*; ~ **state** État-providence *m*; ~ **work** œuvres sociales; **child** ~ protection *f* de l'enfance
**¹well** *n* puits *m*; (hollow part) creux *m*; (ship) sentine *f*; **sink a** ~ forer un puits; *vi* ~ **up (out)** jaillir
**²well** *n* bien *m*; *adj* (good) bon (*f* bonne); (health) en bonne santé, bien, bien portant; (advisable) souhaitable; **all's** ~ **that ends** ~ tout est bien qui finit bien; **be** ~ **again** être rétabli; **look** ~ avoir bonne mine; **that's all very** ~ tout cela est bel et bon, c'est bien joli; *adv* bien;

~ ! eh bien!; ~ **and good!** à la bonne heure!; ~ **done!** bravo!; ~, **he doesn't know any better** que voulez-vous, il ne sait pas; ~ **I never!** ça alors!, pas possible!; **all being** ~ si tout va bien; **as** ~ aussi; **as** ~ **as** (in addition) ainsi que; **as** ~ **as I can** de mon mieux; **come off** ~ (be lucky) avoir de la chance; (happen) se passer bien; **do** ~ **by s/o** être généreux -euse envers qn; **he can't very** ~ **go away** il ne lui est guère possible de partir; **it's** ~ **past six** il est six heures bien sonnées; **it's** ~ **worth seeing** cela vaut bien la peine d'être vu; **one might as** ~ **do it** autant le faire; **pretty** ~ **finished** presque fini; **you are** ~ **out of it** vous avez bien de la chance d'en être quitte; **you might** ~ **ask** c'est une question qui s'impose

**well-advised** *adj* (person) bien avisé; (action) sage

**well-appointed** *adj* bien équipé, bien meublé

**well-balanced** *adj* bien équilibré

**well-behaved** *adj* (child) sage; (animal) bien dressé

**well-being** *n* bien-être *m*

**well-bred** *adj* bien élevé; (dog) de race

**well-disposed** *adj* bien disposé

**well-heeled** *adj coll* riche

**well-informed** *adj* bien renseigné; (learned) instruit; **keep (oneself)** ~ se tenir au courant

**Wellingtons** *npl* bottes *fpl* en caoutchouc

**well-intended** *adj* fait à bonne intention

**well-intentioned** *adj* plein de bonnes intentions

**well-kept** *adj* bien tenu, soigné

**well-known** *adj* connu, célèbre

**well-meaning** *adj* bien intentionné

**well-meant** *adj* fait avec une bonne intention

**well-nigh** *adv lit* presque

**well-off** *adj* aisé, riche, à l'aise; **be** ~ **for sth** être bien pourvu de qch; **you don't know when you are** ~ vous ne savez pas quand vous êtes bien

**well-read** *adj* (person) cultivé

**well-spoken** *adj* ayant un accent cultivé

**well-thought-of** *adj* bien considéré

**well-timed** *adj* bien calculé

**well-to-do** *adj* à l'aise, prospère

**well-wisher** *n* personne *f* qui vous veut du bien, ami -e

**well-worn** *adj* très usagé, usé jusqu'à la corde

**Welsh, Welch** *n* (language) gallois *m*; *adj* gallois

**welsh, welch** *vi* filer sans payer; ~ **on** trahir

**Welshman** *n* Gallois *m*

**Welshwoman** *n* Galloise *f*

**welt** *n* (shoe) trépointe *f*; (glove) bordure *f*; *vt* (shoe) mettre des trépointes à; (glove) border; *coll* rosser

**welter** *n* confusion *f*, désordre *m*

**welter-weight** *n* poids mi-moyen

**wen** *n* loupe *f*

**wend** *vt* ~ **one's way** diriger ses pas

**werewolf** *n* loup-garou *m* (*pl* loups-garous)

**west** *n* ouest *m*, occident *m*; *adj* ouest *invar*, occidental; (wind) d'ouest; **the West Indies** les Antilles *fpl*; *adv* à l'ouest; vers l'ouest; **go** ~ se diriger vers l'ouest; *coll* mourir

**westerly** *adj* d'ouest

**western** *n cin* western *m*; *adj* de l'ouest, occidental

**westernize** *vt* occidentaliser

**westernmost** *adj* situé le plus à l'occident

**westward** *n* direction *f* de l'ouest; *adj + adv* à l'ouest

**westwards** *adv* vers l'ouest; à l'ouest

**wet** *n* (rain) pluie *f*; humidité *f*; **go out in the** ~ sortir sous la pluie; *adj* humide, mouillé; *coll* ~ **blanket** rabat-joie *m invar*; (weather) **be** ~ pleuvoir; **be** ~ **through** être trempé jusqu'aux os; **get** ~ se mouiller; *vt* mouiller, tremper; *coll* ~ **one's whistle** boire un coup

**wetness** *n* humidité *f*

**wet-nurse** *n* nourrice *f*

**wetting** *n* mouillage *m*

**whack** *n* bon coup; action *f* de battre; *coll* part *f*; **have a** ~ **at sth** essayer de faire qch; *vt* rosser, donner des coups à; *coll* (defeat) battre

**whacked** *adj coll* éreinté, crevé

**whacking** *n coll* raclée *f*; *adj coll* énorme

**whale** *n* baleine *f*; *coll* as *m*, expert *m*; *coll* **a** ~ **of a storm** une tempête fantastique; *coll* **have a** ~ **of a time** s'amuser drôlement bien

**whalebone** *n* (in garment) fanon *m* de baleine

**whaler** *n* baleinier *m*

**whaling** *n* pêche *f* à la baleine

**wharf** *n* quai *m*, débarcadère *m*; *vt* déposer sur le quai; *vi* amarrer à quai

**what** *adj* (interrogative and exclamatory) quel (*f* quelle); ~ **a house!** quelle maison!; ~ (of) ~ **as m**, combien sommes-nous?; ~ **little I have** le peu que je possède; ~ **news?** quoi de nouveau?; ~ **right have you to do this?** de quel droit faites-vous cela?; ~ **silly boys they are!** que ces garçons sont stupides!; ~ **time is it?** quelle heure est-il?; *pron rel* ce qui, ce que; (interrogative) qu'est-ce qui, qu'est-ce que?, que?; quoi?; comment?; comment!; quel (*f* quelle); ~ **do you take**

me for? pour qui me prenez-vous?; ~ for? pourquoi?; ~! He's here already? Comment! Il est déjà arrivé?; ~ if he won't? et s'il ne veut pas?; ~ is the number of the house? quel est le numéro de la maison?; ~ is this for? à quoi sert ceci?; ~ is that? comment est-elle?; ~'s she like? qu'est-ce que c'est que cela?; ~'s that to you? qu'est-ce que cela peut vous faire?; ~'s the good of trying? à quoi bon essayer?; ~'s the matter? qu'est-ce qu'il y a?; ~'s the Spanish for 'table'? comment dit-on 'table' en espagnol?; ~'s to be done? que faire?; ~'s your name? comment vous appelez-vous?; easy, ~? c'est facile, hein?; eat ~ you like mangez ce que vous voulez; he knows ~'s ~ c'est un tout malin; I know ~ you're here for je sais pourquoi vous êtes ici; coll so ~? et puis après?

**what-do-you-call-him (her)** n monsieur (madame) machin

**what-do-you-call-it** n machin m

**whatever, whatsoever** adj quelque ... qui, que; aucun; quelconque; ~ shops you see quelques magasins que vous voyiez; in any way ~ d'une manière quelconque; I see no possibility ~ je ne vois absolument aucune possibilité; nothing ~ absolument rien; on no account ~ sous aucun prétexte; will she see any doctor ~? verra-t-elle un médecin quelconque?; pron quoi que, quel (f quelle) que; tout ce qui, tout ce que; ~ he wants tout ce qu'il voudra; ~ the answer may be quelle que soit la réponse; ~ they say quoi qu'ils disent

**what-for** n give s/o ~ dire à qn de quoi il retourne

**what-have-you** n all his belongings and ~ tous ses effets et tout ce qui s'ensuit

**whatnot** n (furniture) étagère f; coll machin m

**whatsoever** adj + pron see whatever

**wheat** n blé m, froment m

**wheedle** vt cajoler, enjôler

**wheedling** n cajolerie f; adj enjôleur -euse, câjoleur -euse

**wheel** n roue f; (steering) volant m; (ship) barre f; ~s (organization) rouages mpl; ~s within ~s complications fpl; vt tourner, faire tourner, faire pivoter; (cycle) pousser; ~ in apporter; vi tournoyer, tourner; mil faire une conversion

**wheelbarrow** n brouette f

**wheelbase** n empattement m

**wheelchair** n fauteuil roulant

**wheeled** adj à roues, sur roues

**wheeling** n ~ and dealing manigances fpl, combines fpl

**wheelwright** n charron m

**wheeze** n respiration sifflante; sl truc m; vi respirer difficilement; siffler en respirant

**wheezy** adj asthmatique; (horse) poussif -ive

**whelk** n buccin m

**whelp** n petit chien, chiot m; petit m d'un fauve; pej petit morveux

**when** adv quand; lorsque, quand; où; say ~! dites-moi quand ce sera assez!; conj quand, lorsque; après que; où, que; the day ~ le jour où; the week ~ he was here la semaine où il était ici

**whence** adv d'où

**whenever** adv + conj chaque fois que, toutes les fois que; ~ will you learn? quand donc apprendras-tu?; come ~ you like venez quand vous voudrez

**whensoever** adv à n'importe quel moment où

**where** adv où; là où; ~ does he come from? d'où vient-il?; I go ~ I am welcome je vais là où je suis le bienvenu (f la bienvenue); fig that's ~ he's got to voilà où il en est

**whereabouts** n lieu m où l'on se trouve; adv où; ~ can he be? où donc peut-il être?

**whereas** conj tandis que, alors que; (considering) vu que, attendu que

**whereat** adv sur quoi; à quoi

**whereby** adv par où, par lequel (f laquelle), par quoi

**whereof** adv de quoi, dont

**whereon** adv sur lequel (f laquelle), sur quoi

**wheresoever** adv see wherever

**whereupon** adv sur quoi, sur lequel (f laquelle); après quoi

**wherever, wheresoever** adv partout où; où que

**wherewith** adv avec quoi; avec lequel (f laquelle)

**wherewithal** n nécessaire m; find the ~ fournir les moyens

**whet** vt aiguiser, affiler; (appetite) stimuler; (curiosity, etc) exciter

**whether** conj si; que; ~ he's ill or not qu'il soit malade ou non; ~ ... or soit ...ou que ... soit que; I don't know ~ he's coming je ne sais pas s'il viendra

**whetstone** n pierre f à aiguiser

**whew** interj ouf!

**whey** n petit lait

**whey-faced** adj pâle, blême

**which** adj quel (f quelle); lequel (f laquelle, mpl lesquels, fpl lesquelles); ~ one lequel (f laquelle); he arrived at nine, at ~ time I was having breakfast il est arrivé à neuf heures, heure à laquelle je prenais mon petit déjeuner; *pron* (interrogative) lequel (*f* laquelle); *rel* qui, que, lequel (*f* laquelle); ce qui, ce que; quoi; ~ **are you voting for?** pour lequel (*f* laquelle) votez-vous?; **of** ~ dont; **the books** ~ **I need** les livres dont j'ai besoin; **the house** ~ **I can see** la maison que je vois; **the house** ~ **stands there** la maison qui se trouve là; **the house towards** ~ **I went** la maison vers laquelle je me dirigeai; **we are going out,** ~ **he hates** nous allons sortir, ce qu'il déteste; **they drink,** ~ **is bad** ils boivent, ce qui est mauvais; **they want to go out,** ~ **I object to** ils veulent sortir, ce à quoi je m'oppose

**whichever, whichsoever** *adj* n'importe quel (*f* quelle), le (*f* la) … que; quel (*f* quelle) que soit, quel que soit celui (*f* celle) qui (que); *pron* celui (*f* celle) qui, celui (*f* celle) que; n'importe lequel (*f* laquelle)

**whiff** *n* bouffée *f*; (wind) souffle *m*; *coll* petit cigare; *vi* souffler par bouffées; *coll* sentir mauvais, puer

**while** *n* temps *m*; **after a little** ~ au bout de quelque temps, quelque temps après; **a good** ~ assez longtemps, pas mal de temps; **a little** ~ **ago** il y a peu de temps; **be worth** ~ valoir la peine; **in a little** ~ sous peu; **once in a** ~ de temps à autre, une fois de temps en temps; **the** ~ pendant ce temps; *vt* ~ **away the time** faire passer le temps; *conj* pendant que, tandis que; en; (as long as) tant que; (concession) quoique, bien que, tout en; (whereas) tandis que; ~ **admitting he is wrong, he persists** tout en reconnaissant qu'il a tort, il persiste; ~ **eating** en mangeant

**whilst** *conj see* while; *conj*

**whim** *n* caprice *m*, fantaisie *f*

**whimper** *n* geignement *m*; *coll* pleurnicherie *f*; (pain) plainte *f*; *vi* pleurnicher; (dog) pousser des petits cris plaintifs

**whims(e)y** *n* fantaisie *f*, lubie *f*

**whimsical** *adj* capricieux -ieuse, fantasque; (queer) bizarre

**whimsicality** *n* caractère *m* fantasque; bizarrerie *f*

**whine** *n* plainte *f*, geignement *m*; *vi* se plaindre, geindre; ~ **about sth** se lamenter sur qch

**whinny** *n* hennissement *m*; *vi* hennir

**whip** *n* fouet *m*; coup *m* de fouet; *cul* mousse *f*; *pol* chef *m* de file; *vt* fouetter; (eggs) battre; ~ **off** enlever vivement; ~ **out** sortir vivement; ~ **through** parcourir rapidement; ~ **up** stimuler; *vi* fouetter; ~ **along** filer à bonne allure; ~ **down** descendre rapidement; ~ **round** se retourner vivement

**whipcord** *n* corde *f* à fouet; (fabric) whipcord *m*

**whiphand** *n* avantage *m*, dessus *m*

**whiplash** *n* mèche *f* (de fouet)

**whipper** *n* fouetteur -euse

**whipper-snapper** *n* (child) petit garnement; freluquet *m*

**whippet** *n* whippet *m*; *mil* char *m* (d'assaut) de type léger

**whipping** *n* fouettement *m*; **get a** ~ être fouetté

**whipping-boy** *n* bouc *m* émissaire

**whip-round** *n* collecte *f*

**whirl** *n* tournoiement *m*, mouvement *m* giratoire; *fig* tourbillon *m*; **my head is in a** ~ la tête me tourne; *vt* faire tournoyer, faire tourbillonner; ~ **s/o along** entraîner (emporter) qn à toute vitesse; *vi* tournoyer, tourbillonner; (on toes) pirouetter; ~ **along** filer à toute allure

**whirligig** *n* (toy) moulin *m* à vent; (merry-go-round) manège *m*; *fig* tourbillon *m*

**whirlpool** *n* tourbillon *m*

**whirlwind** *n* trombe *f*; **come in like a** ~ entrer en trombe

**whir(r)** *n* ronflement *m*, ronronnement *m*, sifflement *m*; *vi* ronfler, ronronner; (turn fast) tourner à toute vitesse

**whisk** *n* (movement) mouvement *m* en coup de fouet; (dusting) époussette *f*, plumeau *m*; *cul* fouet *m*, batteur *m*; *vt* (eggs) battre; (cream) fouetter; ~ **sth away** enlever qch rapidement; ~ **sth up** enlever qch rapidement

**whiskers** *npl* (man) favoris *mpl*; (cat) moustaches *fpl*

**whiskey** *n* whisky irlandais

**whisky** *n* whisky *m*, Scotch *m*

**whisper** *n* chuchotement *m*; *fig* murmure *m*, bruit *m*; **speak in a** ~ parler tout bas; *vt* chuchoter, souffler; *vi* chuchoter, parler tout bas

**whisperer** *n* chuchoteur -euse

**whispering** *n* chuchotement *m*

**whist** *n* whist *m*; ~ **drive** tournoi *m* de whist

**whistle** *n* sifflement *m*, coup *m* de sifflet; (object) sifflet *m*; **blow a** ~ donner un coup de sifflet; *coll* **wet one's** ~ boire un coup; *vt* siffler, siffloter; ~ **up** siffler; *fig* faire venir; *vi* siffler; *coll* **you can** ~ **for it** tu peux toujours courir après

**whistler** *n* siffleur *m*

**whistle-stop** *n* *US* (railway) halte *f*; *US pol* ~ **tour** tournée électorale faite par train spécial

**whit** *n* brin *m*; **every** ~ absolument; **not a** ~ pas le moins du monde

**Whit** *adj* ~ **Monday** le lundi de Pentecôte; ~ **Sunday** la Pentecôte

**white** *n* blanc *m*; (race) blanc (*f* blanche); (whiteness) blancheur *f*; ~ s linge *m*; (trousers) pantalon blanc; ~ **of the eye** cornée *f*; **dressed in** ~ habillé en blanc; *adj* blanc (*f* blanche); (reputation) sans tache; *fig* ~ **elephant** rossignol *m*; *US fig* ~ **man** homme loyal; **go** ~ blanchir; pâlir

**whitebait** *n* blanchaille *f*

**white-collar** *adj* ~ **worker** employé -e de bureau

**white-haired** *adj* aux cheveux blancs

**whiten** *vt* + *vi* blanchir

**whitener** *n* blanc *m*

**whiteness** *n* blancheur *f*; (face) pâleur *f*

**whitening** *n* blanchiment *m*; (hair, etc) blanchissement *m*; (powder) blanc *m* d'Espagne

**whitewash** *n* blanc *m* de chaux; *vt* blanchir à la chaux; *fig* blanchir, disculper

**whitewashing** *n* peinture *f* à la chaux; *fig* disculpation *f*

**whither** *adv* où; là où

¹**whiting** *n* (fish) merlan *m*

²**whiting** *n* (bleach) blanc *m* d'Espagne (de Meudon)

**whitish** *adj* blanchâtre

**whitlow** *n* panaris *m*

**Whitsun, Whitsuntide** *n* la Pentecôte; *adj* de Pentecôte

**whittle** *vt* tailler au couteau; ~ **away at** diminuer petit à petit; ~ **down** diminuer petit à petit, amenuiser

**whiz(z)** *n* sifflement *m*; *vi* siffler; ~ **past** passer en sifflant; (speed by) passer à toute allure

**whiz(z)-kid** *n* jeune prodige *m*

**who** *pron* qui?, qui-est-ce qui?; quel (*f* quelle)?; *rel* qui; lequel (*f* laquelle, *mpl* lesquels, *fpl* lesquelles); ~ **do you think you are?** pour qui vous prenez-vous?; ~ **is that man?** quel est cet homme?; **Who's Who** le Who's Who, l'annuaire *m* des notabilités; **I don't know** ~ **'s here** je ne connais personne ici; **my father's cousin,** ~ **is very rich** le cousin de mon père, lequel est très riche

**whoa** *interj* (to horse) ho!; (to person) holà!

**whodunit** *n* roman policier, roman *m* à suspense

**whoever, whosoever** *pron* (he who) celui qui (*f* celle qui); quiconque; (whoever it may be) qui que; (qui que ce soit qui; ~ **you may be** qui que vous soyez

**whole** *n* tout *m*, totalité *f*, ensemble *m*; **as a** ~ dans l'ensemble; **on the** ~ en

somme, à tout prendre; *adj* complet -ète, entier -ière, intégral; (unharmed) sain et sauf (*f* saine et sauve); (undamaged) intact; *coll* **go the** ~ **hog** aller jusqu'au bout; **the** ~ **truth** toute la vérité

**whole-hearted** *adj* (sincere) sincère; (single-minded) total

**wholemeal** *n* (bread) complet -ète

**wholesale** *n* vente *f* en gros; *adj* + *adv* en gros, en bloc; *fig* en masse

**wholesaler** *n* grossiste

**wholly** *adv* totalement, entièrement

**whoop** *n* grand cri; (cough) quinte *f* de toux; *vi* pousser de grands cris; tousser de façon prolongée

**whoopee** *n coll* **make** ~ faire la noce, faire la bombe; *interj* hourra!

**whooping-cough, hooping-cough** *n* coqueluche *f*

**whoosh** *vi* ~ **by** passer à toute allure

**whopper** *n coll* chose *f* énorme

**whopping** *adj coll* énorme, gros (*f* grosse), grand; *adv coll* **a** ~ **great chap** un type énorme

**whore** *n* putain *f*, prostituée *f*

**whorl** *n* (spiral) spire *f*; (shell) volute *f*; *bot* verticille *m*

**whose** *poss pron* de qui?, à qui?; ~ **are they?** à qui sont-ils?; ~ **book are you reading?** à qui est le livre que vous lisez?; ~ **pupil are you?** de qui êtes-vous l'élève?; *adj rel* dont; de qui, duquel (*f* de laquelle, *mpl* desquels, *fpl* desquelles); **the girl to** ~ **sister I sent it** la jeune fille à la sœur de qui (de laquelle) je l'ai envoyé

**whosoever** *pron see* **whoever**

**why** *n* pourquoi *m*; **the** ~ **s and wherefores** les pourquoi et les comment; *adv* pourquoi; ~ **not?** pourquoi pas?; **that's** ~ **he came** voilà pourquoi il est venu; **this is** ~ **he came** voilà pourquoi il est venu; *interj* tiens!; ~, **look here!** voyons!; ~, **of course!** mais bien sûr!; ~, **what do you want?** mais que voulez-vous donc?

**wick** *n* mèche *f*; *coll* **he gets on my** ~ il me tape sur les nerfs

**wicked** *adj* méchant, mauvais; (temper) dangereux -euse; (awful) affreux -euse; *coll* (mischievous) malicieux -ieuse; **it's** ~! c'est honteux!

**wickedness** *n* méchanceté *f*

**wicker** *n* rameau *m* d'osier; *adj* en osier

**wickerwork** *n* vannerie *f*; *adj* en osier, d'osier

**wicket** *n* (door) guichet *m*; *sp* (cricket) guichet *m*

**wide** *n* broke to the ~ complètement fauché -e; *adj* large; (extensive) étendu, vaste; (far) loin, éloigné; (great) grand, vaste; *sl* rusé, futé; **be ~ of the mark** être loin du compte; **how ~ is the garden?** de quelle largeur est le jardin?; **three metres ~** large de trois mètres; *adv* loin; à côté; **(extend) ~ open** grand ouvert

**wide-angle** *adj* **~ lens** objectif *m* grand angle *invar*

**wide-apart** *adj* espacé

**wide-awake** *n* chapeau *m* de feutre à larges bords; *adj* alerte

**wide-eyed** *adj* aux yeux grands ouverts, les yeux écarquillés

**widely** *adv* largement; très

**widen** *vt* élargir; (extend) étendre, étendre les limites de; *vi* s'élargir; s'étendre

**wide-ranging** *adj* de grande envergure; divers

**widespread** *adj* répandu, général; (extensive) étendu

**widow** *n* veuve *f*

**widowed** *adj* veuf (*f* veuve)

**widower** *n* veuf *m*

**widowhood** *n* veuvage *m*

**width** *n* largeur *f*; (dress) ampleur *f*

**wield** *vt* manier; **~ power** exercer le pouvoir

**wife** *n* femme *f*, épouse *f*; **take a ~** prendre femme, se marier; **the world and his ~** absolument tout le monde

**wifely** *adj* d'épouse; conjugal

**wig** *n* perruque *f*, postiche *m*

**wigging** *n coll* semonce *f*; **give s/o a good ~** laver la tête à qn

**wiggle** *vt* remuer, tortiller, agiter

**wig-maker** *n* perruquier -ière

**wigwam** *n* wigwam *m*

**wild** *n* état *m* sauvage; **~s** région *f* sauvage; *adj* sauvage; (mad) fou (*f* folle), insensé; (furious) furieux -ieuse; affolé, effaré; (wind) violent; (morals) dissolu, dissipé; (behaviour) déréglé, délirant, extravagant; **go on a ~ goose chase** courir après la lune; **make s/o ~** faire enrager qn; **run ~** courir en liberté

**wildcat** *n* chat *m* sauvage; **~ scheme** projet très risqué; **~ strike** grève *f* sauvage

**wildebeest** *n* gnou *m*

**wilderness** *n* désert *m*

**wild-eyed** *adj* aux yeux effarouchés

**wildfire** *n* **spread like ~** se répandre comme une traînée de poudre

**wildly** *adv* follement, exagérément; complètement

**wildness** *n* état *m* sauvage; férocité *f*; (wind) fureur *f*; (behaviour) dérèglement *m*, extravagance *f*

**wile** *n* ruse *f*; **~s** cajoleries *fpl*

**wilful** *adj* obstiné, entêté; (act) fait exprès, volontaire; *leg* prémédité

**wilfulness** *n* obstination *f*, entêtement *m*

**wilily** *adv* de façon rusée

**wiliness** *n* ruse *f*, astuce *f*

**will** *n* volonté *f*; (choice) gré *m*; testament *m*; **against one's ~** contre son gré; **at ~** à volonté; **bear s/o ill ~** en vouloir à qn; **mention s/o in one's ~** coucher qn sur son testament; **of one's own free ~** de son plein (propre) gré; **the last ~ and testament** les dernières volontés; **where there's a ~ there's a way** vouloir c'est pouvoir; **with a ~** de bon cœur; *vt* vouloir, ordonner; (bequeath) léguer; *vi+v aux* vouloir; translated as part of *fut* tense; **~ you come? – Yes, I ~** Viendrez-vous? – Oui (je viendrai); **as you ~** comme vous voulez; **do what you ~, it ~ be too late** quoi que vous fassiez, il sera trop tard; **he ~ play the fool at table** il insiste pour faire l'idiot à table; **my brother ~ always help you** mon frère vous aidera toujours; **she ~ have it that she tried** elle insiste qu'elle a essayé; **she would do that!** ça, c'est bien elle!; **she would not budge** elle ne voulait pas bouger; **they would do it if they could** ils le feraient s'ils le pouvaient; **this ~ be him** ce sera lui sans doute; **try to come, ~ you?** essayez de venir, hein?; **won't you come in?** veuillez entrer; **would that he could see you!** je voudrais bien qu'il vous voie (vît); **would to God that he were gone!** plût à Dieu qu'il fût parti!; **would you mind asking him?** voudriez-vous lui demander?; **you won't forget, ~ you?** vous n'oublierez pas, n'est-ce pas?; **you would never cry when you were little** tu ne pleurais jamais quand tu étais petit

**willies** *npl coll* **give s/o the ~** donner les chocottes à qn

**willing** *adj* bien disposé, de bonne volonté; **~ or no(t)** bon gré mal gré; **be ~ to do sth** être prêt à faire qch, vouloir bien faire qch; *coll* **show ~** faire preuve de bonne volonté

**will-o'-the-wisp** *n* feu follet

**willow** *n* saule *m*; **weeping ~** saule pleureur

**willowy** *adj* souple

**will-power** *n* volonté *f*

**willy-nilly** *adv* bon gré mal gré

**wilt** *vi* se flétrir, se faner; (person) dépérir

**wily** *adj* rusé, astucieux -ieuse

**win** *n* victoire *f*; *vt* gagner; (victory) remporter; (gain) acquérir, trouver; **~ back** regagner, reconquérir; **~ over** gagner, s'attirer; **~ round** persuader, convaincre; **~ s/o's love** se faire aimer de qn; *vi* gagner; **~ through** parvenir à son but

**wince** *n* tressaillement *m*; *vi* sourciller;

(pain) faire une grimace de douleur

**winch** n manivelle f; (hoist) treuil m; vt ~ **up (down)** monter (descendre) au treuil

¹**wind** n vent m; (breath) souffle m, haleine f, respiration f; med (belch) vents mpl; (bowels) gaz mpl; ~ **instrument** instrument m à vent; **get one's second** ~ reprendre haleine; coll **get the** ~ **up** avoir le trac (la frousse); **get** ~ **of** avoir vent de; **it's all** ~ ce n'est que du vent; **it's an ill** ~ **that blows no one any good** à qch malheur est bon; **north** ~ bise f; **put the** ~ **up** s/o donner le trac à qn; sl **raise the** ~ se procurer de l'argent; **sail close to the** ~ naut serrer le vent; fig friser l'indécence; **sow the** ~ **and reap the whirlwind** semer le vent et récolter la tempête; **take the** ~ **out of s/o's sails** couper l'herbe sous les pieds de qn; coll **there's sth in the** ~ il y a quelque anguille sous roche; vt (game) avoir vent de, flairer; (take breath away) couper le souffle à; ~ **the horn** sonner le cor

²**wind** vt tourner, rouler; (clock) remonter; (thread) dévider; (spool) bobiner; ~ **round** enrouler; ~ **up** (clock) remonter; comm liquider; (meeting) clore; vi tourner; (meander) serpenter; ~ **down (up)** descendre (monter) en serpentant; coll (finish) terminer, finir

**windbreak** n brise-vent m invar

**wind-cheater** n blouson m, anorak m

**windfall** n fruit tombé; fig aubaine f

**wind-gauge** n anémomètre m

**winding** n détour m, cours sinueux, méandre m; (clock) remontage m; (spooling) bobinage m; adj sinueux -euse; qui serpente

**winding-sheet** n linceul m

**wind-instrument** n instrument m à vent

**windmill** n moulin m à vent

**window** n fenêtre f; (vehicle) glace f; (shop) devanture f, vitrine f; (ticket) guichet m; French ~ porte-fenêtre f (pl portes-fenêtres); **look out of the** ~ regarder par la fenêtre; mot **rear** ~ lunette f arrière; **stained-glass** ~ vitrail m (pl vitraux)

**window-box** n caisse f à fleurs, jardinière f

**window-cleaner** n laveur m de vitres

**window-dresser** n étalagiste

**window-dressing** n art m de l'étalage; coll fig façade f, trompe-l'œil m invar

**window-frame** n chambranle m, châssis m de fenêtre

**window-ledge** n rebord m de fenêtre

**window-pane** n carreau m, vitre f

**window-shopping** n coll lèche-vitrines m

**window-sill** n appui m de fenêtre, rebord m de fenêtre

**windpipe** n trachée(-artère) f (pl trachées(-artères)), gosier m

**windproof** adj qui protège contre le vent

**windscreen** n mot pare-brise m invar; hort brise-vent m invar; ~ **washer** lave-glace m

**windscreen-wiper** n essuie-glace m

**windshield** n US mot pare-brise m invar

**wind-sock** n aer manche f à air

**windsurfer** n véliplanchiste; (craft) planche f à voile

**windswept** adj balayé par le vent

**wind-tunnel** n tunnel m aérodynamique

**wind-up** n coll liquidation f

**windward** n côté m du vent; adj + adv au vent

**windy** adj venteux -euse; (place) exposé au vent, balayé par le vent; coll (speech) verbeux -euse; **be** ~ faire du vent; coll (scared) avoir le trac

**wine** n vin m; ~ **and dine** s/o fêter qn

**wine-butler** n sommelier m

**wine-cellar** n cave f

**wineglass** n verre m à vin

**wine-list** n carte f des vins

**wine-press** n pressoir m

**wine-taster** n (person) dégustateur -trice; (cup) taste-vin (tâte-vin) m invar

**wine-waiter** n sommelier m

**wing** n aile f; mil escadre aérienne; theat ~ **s** coulisses fpl; (bird) **be on the** ~ voler; **take** s/o **under one's** ~ prendre qn sous sa protection; **take** ~ s'envoler; vt (wound) blesser; (arrow) empenner; ~ **one's way** voler

**winged** adj ailé; (wounded) blessé (à l'aile)

**winger** n (football) ailier m

**wing-nut** n écrou m à oreilles

**wing-span, wing-spread** n envergure f

**wink** n clin m d'œil, clignement m d'œil; **have forty** ~ **s** faire un petit somme; **not sleep a** ~ ne pas fermer l'œil; coll **tip** s/o **the** ~ faire signe de l'œil à qn, avertir qn; vi cligner de l'œil; (light) clignoter; coll fig ~ **at** sth fermer les yeux sur qch

**winker** n mot clignotant m

**winking** n clignement m de l'œil; coll **easy as** ~ simple comme bonjour; adj (light) clignotant

**winkle** n bigorneau m; vt ~ **out** extraire

**winner** n gagnant -e; coll **be a** ~ être un succès assuré

**winning** adj gagnant; (ways) séduisant, attrayant

**winning-post** n poteau m d'arrivée

**winnow** vt (grain) vanner; ~ **the good from the bad** séparer le bon du mauvais

**winsome** adj séduisant

**winter** n hiver m; ~ **sports** sports mpl d'hiver; **in** ~ en hiver; vt hiverner;

(plants) conserver pendant l'hiver; *vi* hiverner, passer l'hiver

**wintry** *adj* d'hiver, hivernal

**wipe** *n* coup *m* de torchon (d'éponge); *coll* taloche *f*; *vt* essuyer; effacer; *sl* frapper; ~ **away** essuyer; ~ **off** essuyer; (debt) acquitter; ~ **out** effacer; *coll* exterminer; *coll* ~ **the floor with** s/o battre qn à plate couture; ~ **up** nettoyer; *vi* ~ **up** essuyer la vaisselle

**wiper** *n* (cloth) torchon *m*; *mot* essuie-glace *m*

**wire** *n* fil *m* de fer, fil *m* métallique; télégramme *m*; ~ **brush** brosse *f* métallique; **he's a live** ~ il est énergique; *fig* **pull the** ~**s** tirer les ficelles; *vt* munir d'un fil métallique; attacher avec du fil de fer; (opening) grillager; *elect* faire l'installation électrique de; ~ **up** (batteries) accoupler; *vi* télégraphier

**wire-cutters** *npl* cisailles *fpl*

**wire-haired** *adj* (dog) à poil dur

**wireless** *n* télégraphie *f* sans fil, T.S.F. *f*, radio *f*; **on the** ~ à la T.S.F.

**wire-netting** *n* treillis *m* en fil de fer (métallique)

**wirepuller** *n coll* intrigant -e

**wire-tapping** *n* mise *f* sur écoute d'une ligne téléphonique

**wiriness** *n* vigueur *f*; (hair) raideur *f*

**wiring** *n elect* installation *f* électrique; *rad* montage *m*

**wiry** *adj* sec (*f* sèche) et vigoureux -euse; (hair) raide

**wisdom** *n* sagesse *f*

**wisdom-tooth** *n* dent *f* de sagesse

**¹wise** *n* façon *f*, manière *f*; **in no** ~ aucunement, nullement

**²wise** *adj* sage, prudent, avisé; (well-informed) avisé; (knowledgeable) savant; **be none the** ~**r** n'en être pas plus avancé; **no one will be any the** ~**r** personne n'en saura rien; *coll* **put s/o** ~ **to sth** expliquer qch à qn; **the (three) Wise Men** les Rois mages

**wiseacre** *n* prétendu sage *m*

**wisecrack** *n* bon mot

**wisely** *adv* sagement, prudemment

**wish** *n* désir *m*, vœu *m*, souhait *m*; **best** ~ **es** meilleurs vœux; **have no** ~ **to do sth** n'avoir aucune envie de faire qch; *vt* vouloir, désirer, souhaiter; ~ **s/o sth** souhaiter qch à qn; ~ **to do sth** désirer faire qch; *coll* **have sth** ~**ed on one** ne pas pouvoir refuser qch; **I** ~ **I had seen it** j'aurais voulu le voir

**wishbone** *n* fourchette *f*, bréchet *m*

**wishful** *adj* désireux -euse; **indulge in** ~ **thinking** prendre ses désirs pour des réalités

**wishy-washy** *adj coll* faible, fade

**wisp** *n* bouchon *m*, poignée *f*; (thin strand) brin *m*; (smoke) traînée *f*

**wistaria, wisteria** *n* glycine *f*

**wistful** *adj* pensif -ive; (look) d'envie, nostalgique

**wistfully** *adv* d'un air d'envie; d'un air de regret

**wistfulness** *n* envie *f*

**¹wit** *n* esprit *m*, intelligence *f*; (person) bel esprit; **be at one's** ~**'s end** ne plus savoir à quel saint se vouer; **collect one's** ~**s** se ressaisir; **flash of** ~ trait *m* d'esprit; **keep one's** ~**s about one** avoir toute sa présence d'esprit; **live by one's** ~**s** vivre d'expédients

**²wit** *vt obs* savoir; **to** ~ c'est-à-dire, à savoir

**witch** *n* sorcière *f*; *coll* ensorceleuse *f*

**witchcraft** *n* sorcellerie *f*

**witch-doctor** *n* sorcier guérisseur

**witchery** *n* sorcellerie *f*; fascination *f*

**witch-hunt** *n* chasse *f* aux sorcières

**witching** *adj* charmant, séduisant; magique

**with** *prep* avec; à, de; chez; (despite) malgré; ~ **all due respect** sauf votre respect; ~ **all his kindness** malgré toute sa bonté; ~ **all my heart** de tout mon cœur; ~ **black hair** aux cheveux noirs; ~ **both hands** à deux mains; ~ **child** enceinte; ~ **him you can never be right** à ses yeux, on n'a jamais raison; ~ **his money there's no problem** riche comme il est, il n'y a pas de problème; ~ **regret** à regret; ~ **tears in his eyes** les larmes aux yeux; ~ **the purpose of** dans le but de; ~ **these words** sur ces paroles, là-dessus; *coll* **be** ~ **it** être à la page, être dans le vent; **come** ~ **one's coat on** venir en pardessus; (illness) **go down** ~ attraper, succomber à; **he's** ~ **me there** là, il est d'accord avec moi; **stay** ~ **friends** séjourner chez des amis

**withal** *adv ar* aussi; d'ailleurs; (in spite of it all) en dépit de tout; *prep ar* avec

**withdraw** *vt* retirer, enlever; *vi* se retirer; (move away) s'éloigner; ~ **into oneself** se renfermer en soi-même

**withdrawal** *n* retraite *f*; (money) retrait *m*; (troops) repli *m*; ~ **symptoms** symptômes *mpl* d'abstinence

**withdrawn** *adj* timide, sauvage, renfermé; (absent-minded) distrait

**wither** *vt* flétrir, dessécher; *vi* se flétrir, se dessécher; ~ **away** (flowers) se faner; dépérir

**withered** *adj* (dried up) desséché; (limb) atrophié

**withering** *adj* qui flétrit, qui dessèche; (look) foudroyant

**withers** *npl* garrot *m*; *coll* **my** ~ **are unwrung** cela ne me touche pas

**withhold** *vt* retenir, refuser; (not reveal) cacher

**within** *adv* dedans, à l'intérieur; *prep* à l'intérieur de, en dedans de; ~ **an hour** avant une heure; ~ **an inch of death** à deux doigts de la mort; ~ **himself** en son fort intérieur; ~ **reason** dans des limites raisonnables; ~ **ten kilometres** à moins de dix kilomètres; ~ **these walls** entre ces murs; **come ~ the provisions of the law** tomber sous le coup de la loi; **live ~ one's means** vivre selon ses ressources

**without** *adv* dehors, à l'extérieur; *prep* (outside) en dehors de; sans; ~ **doing it** sans le faire; **be ~** être sans; (lack) manquer de; **do (go) ~** se passer de; **that goes ~ saying** cela va sans dire

**withstand** *vt* résister à

**witless** *adj* stupide, sans intelligence, imbécile, sot (*f* sotte)

**witness** *n* (person) témoin *m*; (testimony) témoignage *m*; ~ **for the defence (prosecution)** témoin *m* à décharge (charge); **bear ~ to** rendre témoignage de; **call s/o as ~** citer qn comme témoin; *leg* **in ~ thereof** en témoignage de quoi; *vt* être témoin de; (be present at) assister à, attester; ~ **...** voyez ..., regardez ...; *vi* ~ **to sth** témoigner de qch

**witness-box** *n* barre *f* des témoins

**witticism** *n* trait *m* d'esprit, bon mot

**wittily** *adv* spirituellement

**witting** *adj* fait de propos délibéré

**wittingly** *adv* sciemment, en toute connaissance de cause

**witty** *adj* spirituel -elle

**wizard** *n* sorcier *m*, magicien *m*; *adj coll* chic (*f invar*) épatant

**wizardry** *n* sorcellerie *f*, magie *f*

**wizen(ed), weazen(ed)** *adj* desséché, ratatiné

**woad** *n* guède *f*

**wobble, wabble** *n* branlement *m*, tremblement *m*; *mot* shimmy *m*; *vi* branler, ballotter, aller de travers; (stagger) tituber; *fig* hésiter, vaciller, tergiverser

**wobbly** *adj* branlant; vacillant; (furniture) bancal (*pl* bancals)

**wodge** *n coll* gros morceau

**woe** *n* malheur *m*, chagrin *m*; ~ **is me!** pauvre de moi!

**woebegone** *adj* triste, malheureux -euse; (expression) à l'air désolé, abattu

**woeful** *adj* triste, malheureux -euse

**wog** *n pej* Arabe, bicot *m*, moricaud -e; nègre (*f* négresse)

**wold** *n* plaine onduleuse; plateau *m*

**wolf** *n* loup (*f* louve); *coll* homme *m* à femmes; ~ **in sheep's clothing** loup déguisé en brebis; **cry ~** crier au loup;

**keep the ~ from the door** se mettre à l'abri du besoin; *vt* dévorer

**wolf-cub** *n* louveteau *m*

**wolf-dog, wolf-hound** *n* chien *m* de chasse au loup

**wolfish** *adj* de loup; vorace

**wolf-whistle** *n* sifflement admiratif

**woman** *n* (*pl* women) femme *f*; **run after women** courir les filles; **there's a ~ in it** cherchez la femme; *adj* femme; ~ **doctor** femme *f* médecin; ~ **friend** amie *f*

**woman-hater** *n* misogyne

**womanhood** *n* état *m* de femme

**womanish** *adj* efféminé

**womanize** *vi coll* être coureur, courir

**womankind, womenkind** *n collect* les femmes *fpl*

**womanly** *adj* de femme, féminin

**womb** *n* matrice *f*, utérus *m*; *fig* sein *m*

**wombat** *n zool* phascolome *m*

**womenfolk** *n* les femmes *fpl*

**womenkind** *n see* womankind

**wonder** *n* merveille *f*, prodige *m*; (surprise) étonnement *m*, surprise *f*; **a nine days' ~** la merveille d'un jour; **it's a ~ that he's still alive** c'est un miracle qu'il soit encore vivant; **no ~** ça n'a rien d'étonnant; **promise ~s** promettre monts et merveilles; *vi* s'étonner, s'émerveiller; (doubt) se demander; (reflect) penser, songer; **I don't ~ at it!** cela ne m'étonne nullement

**wonderful** *adj* merveilleux -euse, prodigieux -ieuse, étonnant

**wondering** *adj* émerveillé

**wonderland** *n* pays *m* des merveilles

**wonderment** *n* étonnement *m*

**wonder-struck** *adj* émerveillé

**wondrous** *adj* merveilleux -euse, étonnant, incroyable

**wonky** *adj coll* branlant

**won't** *abbr* will not

**wont** *n* coutume *f*, habitude *f*, usage *m*; *adj* **be ~ to do sth** avoir l'habitude de faire qch

**woo** *vt* (woman) courtiser; solliciter

**wood** *n* bois *m*; (bowls) boule *f*; (barrel) tonneau *m*; (beer) **drawn from the ~** tiré au fût; **they are not yet out of the ~** ils ne sont pas encore tirés d'affaire; **touch ~!** touchons du bois!

**woodbine** *n bot* chèvrefeuille *m*

**woodcock** *n* bécasse *f*

**woodcraft** *n* connaissance *f* de la forêt

**woodcut** *n* gravure *f* sur bois

**woodcutter** *n* bûcheron -onne

**wooded** *adj* boisé

**wooden** *adj* de bois, en bois; *coll* (stiff) raide; *coll* (stupid) bête, sans intelligence; ~ **shoes** sabots *mpl*

**wood-engraving** *n* gravure *f* sur bois

**wooden-headed** *adj* stupide

**woodland** *n* bois *m*, pays boisé; *adj* sylvestre, des bois

**woodlouse** *n* (*pl* **woodlice**) cloporte *m*

**woodman** *n* bûcheron *m*

**woodpecker** *n* pic *m*; **green** ~ pivert *m*

**wood-pigeon** *n* (pigeon *m*) ramier *m*

**wood-pulp** *n* pâte *f* de bois

**woodshed** *n* bûcher *m*

**woodwind** *n* collect *mus* les bois *mpl*

**woodwork** *n* boiserie *f*; (carpentry) menuiserie *f*, ébénisterie *f*

**woodworm** *n* ver *m* du bois

**woody** *adj* boisé; (vegetables) ligneux -euse

**wooer** *n ar* prétendant *m*

**woof** *n* trame *f*

**wooing** *n* cour *f*

**wool** *n* laine *f*; *fig* **dyed-in-the-** ~ intransigeant; **pull the** ~ **over s/o's eyes** donner le change à qn; **steel** ~ paille *f* de fer

**wool-gathering** *n* rêvasserie *f*

**woollen** *adj* de laine

**woolliness** *n* nature laineuse; *fig* manque *m* de netteté, verbosité *f*

**woolly** *n* vêtement *m* de laine; *adj* laineux -euse, de laine; (fruit) cotonneux -euse; (outline) flou; (style) mou (*f* molle)

**woolly-headed, woolly-minded** *adj* confus, nébuleux -euse

**woozy** *adj sl* un petit peu parti, un peu paf *invar*

**wop** *n sl pej* Italien -ienne, Espagnol -e, *sl* métèque *m*

**word** *n* mot *m*; (spoken) parole *f*; terme *m*; (promise) parole *f*; (information) avis *m*, nouvelle *f*; ~ **for** ~ textuellement; (translation) littéral; ~ **of command** ordre *m*; **a man of his** ~ un homme de parole; **a** ~ **to the wise** à bon entendeur salut; **break one's** ~ manquer à sa parole; **by** ~ **of mouth** de vive voix; **have a** ~ **with** s/o dire un mot à qn; **have** ~ **s with** s/o se disputer avec qn; **in a** ~ en un mot, bref; **in other** ~ s en d'autres termes; **in the** ~ **s of** selon l'expression de; **keep one's** ~ tenir parole; **put in a good** ~ **for** s/o glisser un mot en faveur de qn; **send** ~ envoyer dire; **sharp's the** ~! vite!, dépêchez-vous!; **take my** ~ **for it** croyez-m'en; *eccles* **the Word** le Verbe; **the** ~ **goes round** on se donne le mot; **too stupid for** ~ s stupide au possible; **upon my** ~! ça alors!; **we can't get a** ~ **out of him** nous ne pouvons pas tirer un mot de lui; **without a** ~ sans mot dire; *vt* exprimer, rédiger

**word-blind** *adj* dyslexique

**word-formation** *n* formation *f* des mots

**wordiness** *n* verbosité *f*

**wording** *n* rédaction *f*; mots *mpl*, langage *m*

**wordless** *adj* sans paroles; interdit

**word-perfect** *adj* qui connaît parfaitement son rôle

**word-processing** *n* traitement *m* de texte

**word-processor** *n* machine *f* de traitement de texte

**word-splitting** *n* ergotage *m*, ergoterie *f*

**wordy** *adj* verbeux -euse, diffus

**work** *n* travail *m*; (task) ouvrage *m*, besogne *f*, tâche *f*; (creative) œuvre *f*, ouvrage *m*; *collect* œuvre *m*; (business) affaire *f*; ~ s (factory) usine *f*, fabrique *f*, atelier *m*; (wheels) rouages *mpl*; (clockwork) mouvement *m*; (public) travaux *mpl*; ~ s **committee** comité *m* d'entreprise; *coll* **be all in the day's** ~ faire partie de la routine quotidienne; **be at** ~ être au travail; **be out of** ~ être sans travail; **day's** ~ journée *f*; (price) **ex** ~ s prix *m* à l'usine; *coll* **give** s/o **the** ~ s battre qn; (kill) tuer qn; **good** ~ s bonnes œuvres; **have lots of** ~ **to do** avoir du pain sur la planche; *coll* **have one's** ~ **cut out** avoir de quoi faire; **road** ~ s **ahead!** attention travaux!; **start** ~ se mettre au travail; *coll* **the whole** ~ s tout le bataclan; *vt* (make work) faire travailler; (machine, etc) faire fonctionner, faire marcher; (exploit) exploiter; (materials, etc) travailler; (shape) façonner; (embroider) broder; (cure) opérer; *coll* (fix) arranger; ~ **free** réussir à dégager; ~ **in** faire entrer petit à petit; ~ **into** introduire; ~ **off** se débarrasser de; ~ **oneself to death** se tuer au travail; ~ **one's passage** travailler pour payer son voyage; ~ **out** mener à bien; (idea) développer; (problem) résoudre; (calculation) calculer; (mine) épuiser; ~ s/o **hard** surmener qn; ~ **up** préparer; (person) exciter; *vi* travailler; (machine) fonctionner, marcher; (operate) opérer, agir; *sp* s'entraîner; ~ **in** pénétrer petit à petit; ~ **loose** se desserrer; ~ **off** se détacher; ~ **on** continuer à travailler; ~ **on** s/o agir sur qn; ~ **out** se terminer, aboutir; (cost) ~ **out** at s'élever à, se chiffrer à; ~ **out well** se terminer bien

**workable** *adj* (plan) réalisable, pratique; (mine) exploitable

**workaday** *adj* de tous les jours; (dull) prosaïque

**work-basket** *n* nécessaire *m* à ouvrage

**work-bench** *n* établi *m*

**workday** *n* jour *m* ouvrable

**worked-up** *adj* excité, emballé

**worker** *n* travailleur -euse; (workman)

**ouvrier** *m*; (working woman) ouvrière *f*; **heavy** ~ travailleur *m* de force; **he's a hard** ~ c'est un travailleur, il travaille dur

**work-force** *n* main-d'œuvre *f* (*pl* mains-d'œuvre)

**workhouse** *n* hospice *m*

**working** *n* travail *m*; (machine) fonctionnement *m*; *adj* qui travaille, ouvrier -ière; (machine) qui fonctionne; ~ **day** jour *m* ouvrable; ~ **hours** heures *fpl* de travail; ~ **man** travailleur *m*, ouvrier *m*; ~ **party** équipe *f*; **not** ~ (person) au repos; (machine) en panne; **the** ~ **class** la classe ouvrière

**working-out** *n* calcul *m*; développement *m*; (outcome) résultat *m*

**work-load** *n* quantité *f* de travail

**workman** *n* (*pl* **workmen**) ouvrier *m*

**workmanlike** *adj* bien fait

**workmanship** *n* exécution *f*, façon *f*

**workpeople** *npl* ouvriers *mpl*, ouvrières *fpl*

**workshop** *n* atelier *m*

**work-shy** *adj coll* flemmard, tire-au-flanc *invar*

**work-to-rule** *n* grève *f* du zèle

**world** *n* monde *m*; milieu *m*; ~ **war** guerre mondiale; *coll* **a** ~ **of** beaucoup de; **give the** ~ **to do sth** donner n'importe quoi pour faire qch; **go round the** ~ faire le tour du monde; **in this** ~ ici-bas; **it's a small** ~! que le monde est petit!; **not for (all) the** ~ pour rien au monde; *coll fig* **out of this** ~ sensationnel -elle, absolument extraordinaire; **such is the way of the** ~ ainsi va le monde; **the next** ~ l'autre monde; **the whole** ~ le monde entier; **the** ~ **of good** tout le bien du monde; **think the** ~ **of** s/o avoir une très bonne opinion de qn; **what in the** ~ **is wrong?** mais qu'est-ce qui ne va donc pas?

**world-famous** *adj* de renommée mondiale

**worldliness** *n* mondanité *f*

**worldly** *adj* du monde, mondain

**worldly-minded** *adj* attaché aux choses de ce monde (aux choses matérielles)

**worldly-wise** *adj* qui a l'expérience du monde (de la vie)

**world-shaking** *adj* stupéfiant

**world-wide** *adj* universel -elle, mondial

**worm** *n* ver *m*; (screw) filet *m*; *coll fig* pauvre type *m*; *vt* ~ **one's way into** se faufiler dans, se glisser dans; ~ **sth out of** s/o tirer qch de qn

**worm-eaten** *adj* vermoulu, piqué des vers; (fruit) véreux -euse

**worm-powder** *n* poudre *f* vermifuge

**wormwood** *n* absinthe *f*, armoise *f*

absinthe

**wormy** *adj* plein de vers; vermoulu

**worn** *adj* usé; (tired) fatigué, épuisé

**worn-out** *adj* usé; (person) épuisé, exténué

**worried** *adj* inquiet -iète, soucieux -ieuse

**worrier** *n* inquiet -iète, personne *f* qui s'inquiète facilement; *coll* bileux -euse

**worrisome** *adj* ennuyeux -euse, inquiétant

**worry** *n* inquiétude *f*, tracas *m*, tourment *m*; *vt* inquiéter, tourmenter, tracasser; (harry) harceler; *vi* s'inquiéter, se tourmenter, se tracasser; *coll* s'en faire, se faire du mauvais sang

**worrying** *adj* inquiétant

**worse** *n* pis *m*; **change for the** ~ altérer; s'altérer; **so much the** ~ tant pis; **they have been through** ~ **than that** ils en ont vu bien d'autres; *adj* pire; plus mauvais; (health) plus malade; **be none the** ~ **for sth** ne pas s'en porter plus mal; **from bad to** ~ de mal en pis; **grow** ~ empirer; **to make matters** ~ par surcroît de malheur; *adv* pis; plus mal

**worsen** *vt* + *vi* empirer

**worship** *n* culte *m*, adoration *f*; **hours of** ~ heures *fpl* des offices; **place of** ~ *RC* église *f*; (Protestant) temple *m*; **Your Worship** (mayor) Monsieur le Maire; (judge) Monsieur le Juge; *vt* adorer; rendre un culte à

**worshipful** *adj* honorable

**worshipper** *n* adorateur -trice; (church) **the** ~ **s** les fidèles *mpl*

**worst** *n* pire *m*; *lit* pis *m*; plus mauvais; **at (the)** ~ au pis aller; **do your** ~! vous pouvez toujours essayer!; **expect the** ~ s'attendre au pire; **get the** ~ **of it** avoir le dessous; **if the** ~ **comes to the** ~ en mettant les choses au pis; **that's the** ~ **of plastic furniture** c'est l'inconvénient des meubles en plastique; **the** ~ **of it is that ...** le pis c'est que ...; *adj* pire; plus mauvais; **he's the world's** ~ **driver** comme conducteur, il est zéro; *adv* le pis; le plus mal

**worsted** *n* laine peignée; laine filée

**worth** *n* valeur *f*; prix *m*, mérite *m*; **give me a hundred francs'** ~ donnez-m'en pour cent francs; **have one's money's** ~ en avoir pour son argent; *adj* **be a lot** avoir une grande valeur; **be** ~ **sth** valoir qch; **be** ~ **while (the trouble)** valoir la peine; *coll* **for all one's** ~ de toutes ses forces; **he's** ~ **millions** il est riche à millions; **it's as much as his life is** ~ ce serait risquer sa vie; **that's** ~ **knowing** c'est bon à savoir

**worthily** *adv* dignement

**worthiness** *n* mérite *m*

**worthless** *adj* sans valeur; ~ **person** vaurien -ienne

**worth-while** *adj* qui (en) vaut la peine, *coll* qui vaut le coup

**worthy** *adj* digne, estimable; (praise-worthy) brave

**would** *vi + v aux see* **will**

**would-be** *adj* prétendu, soi-disant *invar*

**wound** *n* blessure *f*, plaie *f*; *vt* blesser

**wow** *n coll* succès éclatant

**wraith** *n* revenant *m*, apparition *f*

**wrangle** *n* dispute *f*, querelle *f*; *vi* se disputer, se quereller

**wrangler** *n* querelleur -euse

**wrangling** *n* disputes *fpl*, querelles *fpl*

**wrap** *n* manteau *m*, pèlerine *f*; (blanket) couverture *f*; *vt* envelopper; ~ **oneself up** se couvrir bien; ~ **sth round sth** enrouler qch dans qch; *vi* ~ **up** s'emmitoufler

**wrapped** *adj* be ~ **in thought** être absorbé dans ses réflexions; **be** ~ **up in sth** être entièrement préoccupé de qch, être absorbé par qch

**wrapper** *n* enveloppe *f*; (book) couverture *f*, couvre-livre *m*; (newspaper) bande *f*; *US* (garment) robe *f* de chambre

**wrapping** *n* emballage *m*; enveloppe *f*, couverture *f*

**wrapping-paper** *n* papier *m* d'emballage

**wrath** *n* colère *f*

**wrathful** *adj* furieux -ieuse; *lit* courroucé

**wreak** *vt* ~ **havoc** semer la destruction; ~ **one's wrath on** passer sa colère sur; ~ **vengeance on** se venger de

**wreath** *n* couronne *f*, guirlande *f*; (funeral) couronne *f*

**wreathe** *vt* enguirlander, couronner de fleurs

**wreck** *n* (event) naufrage *m*; épave *f*, navire naufragé; (building) ruine *f*; *US* accident *m*; *coll* (person) be a ~ être une loque; *vt* (ship) faire faire naufrage à; (destroy) détruire; (demolish) démolir; (train) faire dérailler

**wreckage** *n* épaves *fpl*, débris *mpl*

**wrecker** *n* destructeur -trice; (vandal) casseur -euse

**wren** *n* roitelet *m*

**wrench** *n* (ankle) entorse, *f*, foulure, *f*; (twist) torsion *f*; (snatch) arrachement *m*; (tool) clef *f*; *coll* **it will be quite a** ~ **to leave** ça me fera de la peine de partir; *vt* arracher; (twist) tordrer; ~ **open** forcer; ~ **off** arracher; ~ **sth from s/o** arracher qch à qn

**wrest** *vt* arracher; (twist) tordre

**wrestle** *vi* lutter; ~ **with temptation** résister à la tentation

**wrestler** *n* lutteur *m*

**wretch** *n* malheureux -euse, misérable; **poor** ~ pauvre diable *m*

**wretched** *adj* malheureux -euse, misérable; (pitiful) pitoyable; ~ **weather** temps *m* de chien; **feel** ~ être mal en train; **where's that** ~ **book** où est ce diable de (sacré) livre?

**wriggle** *n* tortillement *m*; *vt* ~ **one's toes** remuer les doigts de pied; ~ **one's way into** se faufiler dans; *vi* se tortiller; (struggle) se débattre; ~ **out of a difficulty** se tirer d'une situation difficile; ~ **through** se faufiler à travers

**wring** *vt* tordre; ~ **one's hands** se tordre les mains; ~ **sth out of s/o** arracher qch à qn; ~ **the neck of an animal** tordre le cou à un animal

**wringer** *n* (washing) essoreuse *f*

**wringing** *adj* ~ **wet** (person) trempé jusqu'aux os; (things) détrempé

**wrinkle** *n* ride *f*; (cloth) faux pli; *coll* (tip) tuyau, *m*; *vt* rider; (cloth) plisser, chiffonner; *vi* se plisser

**wrist** *n* poignet *m*

**wristband** *n* poignet *m*, manchette *f*

**wristlet** *n* bracelet *m*

**wrist-watch** *n* ~ montre-bracelet *f* (*pl* montres-bracelets)

**writ** *n leg* ordonnance *f*, mandat *m*; **Holy Writ** les Saintes Écritures; **serve a** ~ **on s/o** assigner qn en justice

**write** *vt* écrire; (note down) noter, inscrire; (article) rédiger; ~ **a word in** insérer un mot; ~ **down** (note) inscrire; ~ **off** (capital) amortir; *comm* défalquer; ~ **out** écrire, transcrire; (prescription) rédiger; ~ **up** rédiger, écrire; (praise) prôner; *vi* écrire; ~ **back to s/o** répondre à la lettre de qn; ~ **off for sth** commander qch par écrit; **he can read and** ~ il sait lire et écrire

**write-off** *n* perte totale, perte sèche

**writer** *n* écrivain *m*, auteur *m*; **be a good** ~ (handwriting) avoir une bonne écriture

**write-up** *n* article *m*; **a good** ~ un article élogieux; *theat* une critique favorable

**writhe** *vi* se tordre, se tortiller

**writing** *n* écriture *f*; ~ **s** écrits *mpl*; ~ **is his life** écrire c'est sa vie; **at the time of** ~ au moment où j'écris; **in** ~ par écrit

**writing-case** *n* nécessaire *m* de correspondence

**writing-desk** *n* bureau *m*, secrétaire *m*

**writing-pad** *n* bloc *m* de papier à lettres

**writing-paper** *n* papier *m* à lettres

**writing-table** *n* bureau *m*

**wrong** *n mal m*; (injustice) injustice *f*; *leg* préjudice *m*; **be in the** ~ être dans son tort; *adj* mauvais, mal *invar*; (incorrect) faux (*f* fausse), pas juste; (inaccurate) inexact; ~ **side up** sens dessus dessous; **be on the ~ side of forty** avoir dépassé la quarantaine; **be ~** (person) avoir tort, se tromper; (watch) ne pas être à l'heure; **get on the ~ side of s/o** se faire mal voir de qn; (offend) prendre qn à rebrousse-poil; *coll* **get out of bed on the ~ side** se lever du pied gauche; **it's ~ to do that** c'est mal de faire cela; **say the ~ thing** commettre un impair; **set about things in the ~ way** s'y prendre mal; **sth is ~** il y a qch qui ne va pas; **take the ~ street** se tromper de rue; **what do you find ~ with him?** qu'avez-vous à lui reprocher?; **what's ~?** qu'est-ce qu'il y a qui ne va pas?; **what's ~ with you?** qu'avez-vous?; *adv* mal; (unjustly) à tort, injustement; inexactement, incorrectement;

*coll* **get s/o ~** mal comprendre qn; **go ~** (person) faire fausse route, tourner mal; (machine) se détraquer; (events) aller mal; *vt* faire du tort à; *leg* léser; (be unjust) être injuste envers

**wrongdoer** *n* méchant -e, délinquant -e
**wrongdoing** *n* mal *m*; injustice *f*
**wrongful** *adj* injuste
**wrong-headed** *adj* à l'esprit pervers
**wrongly** *adv* à tort; mal; **rightly or ~** à tort ou à raison
**wrought** *adj* travaillé, façonné; **~ iron** fer forgé
**wrought-up** *adj* agité
**wry** *adj* de travers, tordu; dégoûté; (smile) forcé; **pull a ~ face** faire la grimace
**wryness** *n* dégoût *m*

# X

**xenophobe** *n* xénophobe
**xenophobia** *n* xénophobie *f*
**xerography** *n* xérographie *f*

**Xmas** *n see* **Christmas**
**X-rays** *npl* rayons *mpl* X
**xylophone** *n* xylophone *m*

# Y

**yacht** *n* yacht *m*
**yacht-club** *n* cercle *m* nautique, yacht-club *m*
**yachting** *n* yachting *m*; **go ~** faire du yachting
**yachtsman** *n* yacht(s)man *m* (*pl* yacht(s)men)
**yachtsmanship** *n* qualités *fpl* de yachtman
**yachtswoman** *n* yacht(s)woman *f* (*pl* yacht(s)women)
**yak** *n* ya(c)k *m*
**yam** *n bot* igname *f*

**yammer** *vi coll* gémir, geindre
**yank** *n* secousse *f*; *vt coll* tirer; **~ off** emmener de force; **~ out** arracher
**Yank(ee)** *n coll* Amerloque, Yankee
**yap** *n* jappement *m*; *vi* japper
**¹yard** *n* (measure) yard *m*; *naut* vergue *f*; **by the ~** au mètre; *fig* à n'en plus finir
**²yard** *n* cour *f*; (works) chantier *m*; (materials) dépôt *m*; *US* jardin *m* de derrière; **the Yard** Scotland Yard *m* = le Quai des Orfèvres
**yardage** *n* métrage *m*
**yardstick** *n* yard *m*; **measure things by**

one's own ~ mesurer les autres à son aune

**yarn** *n* fil *m*; (story) histoire *f*, longue histoire; **spin a** ~ raconter une histoire; *vi* débiter des histoires

**yaw** *n naut* embardée *f*; *vi* faire des embardées

**yawl** *n* yole *f*

**yawn** *n* bâillement *m*; *vi* bâiller; (gape) être béant

**yawning** *n* bâillement *m*; *adj* bâillant; (gaping) béant

**year** *n* (age, dates) an *m*, année *f*; (age) ~ s âge *m*; ~ **by** ~ d'année en année; **Happy New Year** bonne (et heureuse) année; **be ten** ~ s **old** avoir dix ans; **by the** ~ à l'année; **five a** ~ cinq par an (année); **in the** ~ **X** en l'an X; **last** ~ l'année dernière; **leap** ~ année bissextile; **see the old** ~ **out** réveillonner

**year-book** *n* annuaire *m*

**yearling** *n* animal *m* d'un an; (horse) poulain *m* d'un an

**year-long** *adj* durant une année, durant toute une année

**yearly** *adj* annuel -elle; *adv* annuellement, chaque année, tous les ans

**yearn** *vi* ~ **for** languir après, soupirer après, avoir envie de; ~ **to do sth** avoir très envie de faire qch

**yearning** *n* envie *f*, désir ardent

**yeast** *n* levure *f*

**yell** *n* hurlement *m*; *vi* hurler, crier à tue-tête

**yellow** *n* jaune *m*; *adj* jaune; ~ **fever** fièvre *f* jaune; ~ **pages** = Bottin *m*; **go (make)** ~ jaunir

**yellow-hammer** *n* bruant *m* jaune

**yellowish, yellowy** *adj* jaunâtre

**yelp** *n* jappement *m*, glapissement *m*; *vi* japper, glapir

**¹yen** *n* yen *m*

**²yen** *n coll* désir ardent, grande envie

**yeoman** *n hist* franc tenancier; *mil* hallebardier *m*; **do** ~ **service** fournir un service précieux

**yeomanry** *n* fermiers propriétaires *mpl*; *mil hist* corps de volontaires formé de fermiers propriétaires

**yes** *adv* oui; (after *neg*) si; ~, **of course** mais oui; ~, **of course** mais bien sûr (que oui); **Didn't you see him?-Yes, I did** Ne l'avez-vous pas vu?-Si

**yes-man** *n coll* béni-oui-oui *m invar*

**yesterday** *n* hier *m*; *adv* hier; ~ **morning** hier (au) matin; ~ **week** hier il y a eu huit jours; **the day before** ~ avant-hier

**yet** *adv* encore; déjà; (notwithstanding) malgré tout; ~ **he won't yield** malgré tout il ne veut pas céder; **as** ~ jusqu'à présent; **not** ~ pas encore; **you're not going** ~ ! vous ne partez pas déjà!;

*conj* cependant, pourtant, néanmoins

**yeti** *n* homme *m* des neiges, yéti *m*

**yew** *n* if *m*

**yiddish** *n* (language) yiddish *m*; *adj* yiddish *invar*

**yield** *n* rendement *m*, produit *m*; (crop) récolte *f*; **give a good** ~ rapporter beaucoup; *vt* (produce) rendre, rapporter, produire; (give) donner, offrir; (give out) exhaler; (surrender) céder, livrer; *vi* céder, se rendre, se soumettre

**yielding** *n* rendement *m*; soumission *f*; (surrender) reddition *f*; (soil, etc) affaissement *m*; *adj* (person) complaisant, facile; (soft) mou (*f* molle); (supple) élastique, souple

**yob** *n sl pej* type *m*, mec *m*; butor *m*

**yodel** *n* tyrolienne *f*; *vi* jodler

**yoga** *n* yoga *m*

**yog(h)urt** *n* yog(h)ourt *m*, yaourt *m*

**yogi** *n* yogi *m*

**yoke** *n* joug *m*; (clothing) empiècement *m*; (pair) couple *m*; (oxen) attelage *m*; *vt* atteler; accoupler

**yokel** *n* rustre *m*

**yolk** *n* jaune *m* d'œuf

**yonder** *adj* cette ...-là (*f* cette ...-là, *pl* ces ...-là); *adv* là-bas

**yore** *adv ar* **in days of** ~ au temps jadis; **of** ~ d'autrefois

**you** *pron pl*, formal *sing* vous; *sing* +*familiar* tu, te, toi; *indef* on, vous; ~ **English** vous autres Anglais; ~ **fool!** idiot que tu es!; **away with** ~ ! allez-vous en!; *fig* **between** ~ **and me** entre nous; **if I were** ~ à votre place; **people seem strange to** ~ **when** ~ **are in a foreign country** les gens vous paraissent bizarres quand on est dans un pays étranger

**young** *npl* jeunesse *f*, jeunes *mpl*; (animals) petits *mpl*; *adj* jeune; (animals) petit; (night) peu avancé; (wine) vert; ~ **men** jeunes gens *mpl*; ~ **er son (daughter)** fils (fille) cadet(te); **grow** ~ **er** rajeunir

**youngish** *adj* assez jeune

**youngster** *n* jeune personne *f*, jeune homme *m*; garçon *m*; **he's just a** ~ c'est un gamin

**your** *adj* votre (*pl* vos); (familiar) ton (*f* ta, *pl* tes); *indef* son (*f* sa, *pl* ses); **it's** ~ **turn** c'est à vous; **please wash** ~ **hands** veuillez vous laver les mains

**yours** *pron* le vôtre, (*f* la vôtre); (familiar) le tien (*f* la tienne); **a friend of** ~ un de vos amis (*f* une de vos amies); **it's** ~ c'est à toi; **is this essay** ~ ? est-ce que cette dissertation est de vous?

**yourself** *pron* vous-même; (familiar) toi-même

**youth** *n* (age) jeunesse *f*, jeune âge *m*;

(person) jeune *m*, adolescent *m*, jeune homme *m*; **the fountain of Youth** la fontaine de Jouvence
**youthful** *adj* jeune, juvénile
**youth-hostel** *n* auberge *f* de (la) jeunesse
**youth-hosteller** *n coll* ajiste

**yowl** *n* hurlement *m*; *vi* hurler
**yo-yo** *n* yo-yo *m invar*
**Yugoslav** *n + adj see* Jugoslav
**Yugoslavia** *n see* Jugoslavia
**Yule** *n* Noël *m*
**Yule-log** *n* bûche *f* de Noël
**Yuletide** *n obs* époque *f* de Noël

# Z

**zany** *n* bouffon *m*; *adj* idiot, loufoque
**zeal** *n* zèle *m*, ardeur *f*
**zealot** *n* fanatique; *hist* zélote *m*
**zebra** *n* zèbre *m*; ~ **crossing** = passage clouté, passage *m* pour piétons
**Zeitgeist** *n* esprit *m* de l'époque
**Zen** *n* Zen *m*; *adj* zen *invar*
**zenith** *n* zénith *m*; *fig* apogée *f*, sommet *m*
**zephyr** *n* zéphyr *m*
**zeppelin** *n* zeppelin *m*
**zero** *n* zéro *m*
**zest** *n* entrain *m*, enthousiasme *m*; piquant *m*; **eat with** ~ manger avec appétit
**zigzag** *n* zigzag *m*; **in** ~s en zigzag; *vi* zigzaguer
**zinc** *n* zinc *m*
**zinc-ware** *n* zinguerie *f*
**Zionism** *n* sionisme *m*
**zip** *n* (whizz) sifflement *m*; *coll* (energy) vigueur *f*, énergie *f*; (fastener) fermeture *f* éclair; *vt* ~ **up** fermer la fermeture éclair de; *vi* filer; ~ **by (past)** passer comme un éclair
**zip-fastener** *n* fermeture *f* éclair
**zipper** *n US* fermeture *f* éclair
**zither** *n* cithare *f*
**zodiac** *n* zodiaque *m*
**zombie** *n* zombi *m*
**zonal** *adj* zonal
**zone** *n* zone *f*; *vt* diviser en zones; répartir en zones
**zoning** *n* répartition *f* en zones
**zoo** *n* zoo *m*, jardin *m* zoologique
**zoological** *adj* zoologique
**zoology** *n* zoologie *f*
**zoom** *n* bourdonnement *m*; *aer* montée *f* en chandelle; *vi* (rise fast) monter en flèche; *aer* monter en chandelle; bourdonner, vrombir
**Zulu** *n* Zoulou

# FOR THE BEST IN PAPERBACKS, LOOK FOR THE

In every corner of the world, on every subject under the sun, Penguin represents quality and variety – the very best in publishing today.

For complete information about books available from Penguin – including Pelicans, Puffins, Peregrines and Penguin Classics – and how to order them, write to us at the appropriate address below. Please note that for copyright reasons the selection of books varies from country to country.

**In the United Kingdom:** For a complete list of books available from Penguin in the U.K., please write to *Dept E.P. Penguin Books Ltd, Harmondsworth, Middlesex, UB7 0DA*

**In the United States:** For a complete list of books available from Penguin in the U.S., please write to *Dept BA, Penguin, 299 Murray Hill Parkway, East Rutherford, New Jersey 07073*

**In Canada:** For a complete list of books available from Penguin in Canada, please write to *Penguin Books Canada Ltd, 2801 John Street, Markham, Ontario L3R 1B4*

**In Australia:** For a complete list of books available from Penguin in Australia, please write to the *Marketing Department, Penguin Books Australia Ltd, P.O. Box 257, Ringwood, Victoria 3134*

**In New Zealand:** For a complete list of books available from Penguin in New Zealand, please write to the *Marketing Department, Penguin Books (NZ) Ltd, Private Bag, Takapuna, Auckland 9*

**In India:** For a complete list of books available from Penguin in India, please write to *Penguin Overseas Ltd, 706 Eros Apartments, 56 Nehru Place, New Delhi, 110019*

**In Holland:** For a complete list of books available from Penguin in Holland, please write to *Penguin Books Nederland B.V. Postbus 195, NL – 1380 AD WEESP Netherlands*

**In Germany:** For a complete list of books available from Penguin in Germany, please write to *Penguin Books Ltd, Friedrichstrasse, 10 – 12, D 6000, Frankfurt a m, Main 1, Federal Republic of Germany*

**In Spain:** For a complete list of books available from Penguin in Spain, please write to *Longman Penguin España, Calle San Nicolas 15, E – 28013 Madrid, Spain*

## FOR THE BEST IN PAPERBACKS, LOOK FOR THE

### PENGUIN DICTIONARIES

Archaeology

Architecture

Art and Artists

Biology

Botany

Building

Chemistry

Civil Engineering

Commerce

Computers

Decorative Arts

Design and Designers

Economics

English and European
   History

English Idioms

Geography

Geology

Historical Slang

Literary Terms

Mathematics

Microprocessors

Modern History 1789–1945

Modern Quotations

Physical Geography

Physics

Political Quotations

Politics

Proverbs

Psychology

Quotations

Religions

Saints

Science

Sociology

Surnames

Telecommunications

The Theatre

Troublesome Words

Twentieth Century History

Dictionaries of all these – and more – in Penguin

# FOR THE BEST IN PAPERBACKS, LOOK FOR THE

## PENGUIN REFERENCE BOOKS

### The Penguin Guide to the Law

This acclaimed reference book is designed for everyday use, and forms the most comprehensive handbook ever published on the law as it affects the individual.

### The Penguin Medical Encyclopedia

Covers the body and mind in sickness and in health, including drugs, surgery, history, institutions, medical vocabulary and many other aspects. 'Highly commendable' – *Journal of the Institute of Health Education*

### The Penguin French Dictionary

This invaluable French-English, English-French dictionary includes both the literary and dated vocabulary needed by students, and the up-to-date slang and specialized vocabulary (scientific, legal, sporting, etc) needed in everyday life. As a passport to the French language, it is second to none.

### A Dictionary of Literary Terms

Defines over 2,000 literary terms (including lesser known, foreign language and technical terms) explained with illustrations from literature past and present.

### The Penguin Map of Europe

Covers all land eastwards to the Urals, southwards to North Africa and up to Syria, Iraq and Iran. Scale – 1:5,500,000, 4-colour artwork. Features main roads, railways, oil and gas pipelines, plus extra information including national flags, currencies and populations.

### The Penguin Dictionary of Troublesome Words

A witty, straightforward guide to the pitfalls and hotly disputed issues in standard written English, illustrated with examples and including a glossary of grammatical terms and an appendix on punctuation.

**FOR THE BEST IN PAPERBACKS, LOOK FOR THE**

## A CHOICE OF PENGUINS AND PELICANS

### Asimov's New Guide to Science   Isaac Asimov

A fully updated edition of a classic work – far and away the best one-volume survey of all the physical and biological sciences.

### Relativity for the Layman   James A. Coleman

Of this book Albert Einstein said: 'Gives a really clear idea of the problem, especially the development of our knowledge concerning the propagation of light and the difficulties which arose from the apparently inevitable introduction of the ether.

### The Double Helix   James D. Watson

Watson's vivid and outspoken account of how he and Crick discovered the structure of DNA (and won themselves a Nobel Prize) – one of the greatest scientific achievements of the century.

### Ever Since Darwin   Stephen Jay Gould

'Stephen Gould's writing is elegant, erudite, witty, coherent and forceful' – Richard Dawkins, *Nature*

### Mathematical Magic Show   Martin Gardner

A further mind-bending collection of puzzles, games and diversions by the undisputed master of recreational mathematics.

### Silent Spring   Rachel Carson

The brilliant book which provided the impetus for the ecological movement – and has retained its supreme power to this day.

# FOR THE BEST IN PAPERBACKS, LOOK FOR THE

## A CHOICE OF PENGUINS AND PELICANS

**Metamagical Themas**   Douglas R. Hofstadter

A new mind-bending bestseller by the author of *Gödel, Escher, Bach*.

**The Body**   Anthony Smith

A completely updated edition of the well-known book by the author of *The Mind*. The clear and comprehensive text deals with everything from sex to the skeleton, sleep to the senses.

**Why Big Fierce Animals are Rare**   Paul Colinvaux

'A vivid picture of how the natural world works' – *Nature*

**How to Lie with Statistics**   Darrell Huff

A classic introduction to the ways statistics can be used to prove *anything*, the book is both informative and 'wildly funny' – *Evening News*

**The Penguin Dictionary of Computers**   Anthony Chandor and others

An invaluable glossary of over 300 words, from 'aberration' to 'zoom' by way of 'crippled lead-frog tests' and 'output bus drivers'.

**The Cosmic Code**   Heinz R. Pagels

Tracing the historical development of quantum physics, the author describes the baffling and seemingly lawless world of leptons, hadrons, gluons and quarks and provides a lucid and exciting guide for the layman to the world of infinitesimal particles.

## A CHOICE OF PENGUINS AND PELICANS

### Setting Genes to Work   Stephanie Yanchinski

Combining informativeness and accuracy with readability, Stephanie Yanchinski explores the hopes, fears and, more importantly, the realities of biotechnology – the science of using micro-organisms to manufacture chemicals, drugs, fuel and food.

### Brighter than a Thousand Suns   Robert Jungk

'By far the most interesting historical work on the atomic bomb I know of' – C. P. Snow

### Turing's Man   J. David Bolter

We live today in a computer age, which has meant some startling changes in the ways we understand freedom, creativity and language. This major book looks at the implications.

### Einstein's Universe   Nigel Calder

'A valuable contribution to the de-mystification of relativity' – *Nature*

### The Creative Computer   Donald R. Michie and Rory Johnston

Computers *can* create the new knowledge we need to solve some of our most pressing human problems; this path-breaking book shows how.

### Only One Earth   Barbara Ward and Rene Dubos

An extraordinary document which explains with eloquence and passion how we should go about 'the care and maintenance of a small planet'.